PRENTICE HALL'S
FEDERAL TAXATION

2007

Comprehensive

PRENTICE HALL'S
FEDERAL TAXATION
2007
Comprehensive

EDITORS

THOMAS R. POPE
University of Kentucky

KENNETH E. ANDERSON
University of Tennessee

JOHN L. KRAMER
University of Florida

CONTRIBUTING AUTHORS

D. DALE BANDY
University of Central Florida

N. ALLEN FORD
University of Kansas

ANNA C. FOWLER
University of Texas at Austin

ROBERT L. GARDNER
Brigham Young University

RICHARD J. JOSEPH
University of Texas at Austin

MICHAEL S. SCHADEWALD
University of Wisconsin—Milwaukee

PEARSON

Prentice
Hall

Upper Saddle River, NJ 07458

AVP/Executive Editor: Steve Sartori
VP/Editorial Director: Jeff Shelstad
Manager, Product Development: Pamela Hersperger
Project Manager: Joanna Doxey
Media Project Manager: Nancy Welcher
AVP/Executive Marketing Manager: John Wannemacher
Marketing Assistant: Patrick Barbera
Associate Director, Production Editorial: Judy Leale
Senior Managing Editor: Cynthia Regan
Permissions Coordinator: Charles Morris
Associate Director, Manufacturing: Vinnie Scelta
Manufacturing Manager: Arnold Vila
Design/Composition Manager: Christy Mahon
Cover Design: Kiwi Design
Composition: Publishing Solutions for Retail, Book, and Catalog; Schawk Inc.
Full-Service Project Management: Sandra Reinhard/Schawk Inc.
Printer/Binder: Courier–Kendalville
Typeface: 10/12 Sabon

Pearson Education LTD.
Pearson Education Singapore, Pte. Ltd
Pearson Education, Canada, Ltd
Pearson Education–Japan

Pearson Education Australia PTY, Limited
Pearson Education North Asia Ltd
Pearson Educación de Mexico, S.A. de C.V.
Pearson Education Malaysia, Pte. Ltd.

10 9 8 7 6 5 4 3 2 1
ISBN 0-13-238947-9

OVERVIEW

CONTENTS

CORPORATIONS

CHAPTER 1
▶ TAX RESEARCH 1-1

CHAPTER 2
▶ CORPORATE FORMATIONS AND CAPITAL STRUCTURE 2-1

CHAPTER 13
▶ THE ESTATE TAX 13-1

CHAPTER 14
▶ INCOME TAXATION OF TRUSTS AND ESTATES 14-1

CHAPTER 15
▶ ADMINISTRATIVE PROCEDURES 15-1

TABLES

APPENDICES

ABOUT THE EDITORS

THOMAS R. POPE

Thomas R. Pope is the Ernst & Young Professor of Accounting at the University of Kentucky. He received a B.S. from the University of Louisville and an M.S. and D.B.A. in business administration from the University of Kentucky. He teaches international taxation, partnership and S corporation taxation, tax research and policy, and introductory taxation and has won outstanding teaching awards at the University, College, and School of Accountancy levels. He has published articles in *The Accounting Review,* the *Tax Adviser, Taxes,* and a number of other journals. Professor Pope's extensive professional experience includes eight years with Big Four accounting firms. Five of those years were with Ernst & Whinney (now part of Ernst & Young), including two years with their National Tax Department in Washington, D.C. He subsequently held the position of Senior Manager in charge of the Tax Department in Lexington, Kentucky. Professor Pope also has been a leader and speaker at professional tax conferences all over the United States and is active as a tax consultant.

KENNETH E. ANDERSON

Kenneth E. Anderson is the Pugh & Company Professor of Accounting at the University of Tennessee. He earned a B.B.A. from the University of Wisconsin–Milwaukee and subsequently attained the level of tax manager with Arthur Young (now part of Ernst & Young). He then earned a Ph.D. from Indiana University. He teaches introductory taxation, corporate taxation, partnership taxation, tax research, and tax strategy, and has three times won the Beta Alpha Psi Outstanding Educator Award. Professor Anderson has published articles in *The Accounting Review, The Journal of the American Taxation Association,* the *Journal of Accountancy,* the *Journal of Financial Service Professionals,* and a number of other journals.

JOHN L. KRAMER

John L. Kramer is a Professor of Accounting and the Randall Parks Professor at the University of Florida. He is a recipient of a Teaching Improvement Program award given by the University of Florida in 1994. He holds a Ph.D. in Business Administration and an M.B.A. from the University of Michigan (Ann Arbor), and a B.B.A. from the University of Michigan (Dearborn). He is a past president of the American Taxation Association and the Florida Association of Accounting Educators, as well as a past editor of *The Journal of the American Taxation Association.* In 2001, Professor Kramer received the Ray M. Sommerfeld Outstanding Tax Education Award, co-sponsored by the American Taxation Association and Ernst & Young. Professor Kramer has taught for the American Institute of CPAs, American Tax Institute of Europe, and a number of national and regional accounting firms. He is a frequent speaker at academic and professional conferences, as well as having served as an expert witness in a number of court cases. He has published over 50 articles in *The Accounting Review, The Journal of the American Taxation Association,* the *Tax Adviser,* the *Journal of Taxation,* and other academic and professional journals. Professor Kramer has been an editor on *The Prentice Hall Federal Tax* series since 1989.

ABOUT THE AUTHORS

D. Dale Bandy is the C.G. Avery Professor of Accounting in the School of Accounting at the University of Central Florida. He received a B.S. from the University of Tulsa, an M.B.A. from the University of Arkansas, and a Ph.D. from the University of Texas at Austin. He helped to establish the Master of Science in Taxation programs at the University of Central Florida and California State University, Fullerton, where he previously taught. In 1985, he was selected by the California Society of Certified Public Accountants as the Accounting Educator of the year. Professor Bandy has published 8 books and more than 30 articles in accounting and taxation. His articles have appeared in the *Journal of Taxation,* the *Journal of Accountancy, Advances in Taxation,* the *Tax Adviser, The CPA Journal, Management Accounting* and a number of other journals.

N. Allen Ford is the Larry D. Homer/KPMG Peat Marwick Distinguished Teaching Professor of Professional Accounting at the University of Kansas. He received an undergraduate degree from Centenary College in Shreveport, Louisiana, and both the M.B.A. and Ph.D. in Business from the University of Arkansas. He has published over 30 articles related to taxation, financial accounting, and accounting education in journals such as *The Accounting Review, The Journal of the American Taxation Association,* and *The Journal of Taxation.* He served as president of the American Taxation Association in 1979–80. Professor Ford has received numerous teaching awards, at the college and university levels. In 1993, he received the Byron T. Shutz Award for Distinguished Teaching in Economics and Business. In 1996 he received the Ray M. Sommerfeld Outstanding Tax Educator Award, which is jointly sponsored by the American Taxation Association and Ernst & Young.

Anna C. Fowler is the John Arch White Professor Emeritus in the Department of Accounting at the University of Texas at Austin. She received her B.S. in accounting from the University of Alabama and her M.B.A. and Ph.D. from the University of Texas at Austin. Active in the American Taxation Association throughout her academic career, she has served on the editorial board of its journal and held many positions, including president. She is a former member of the American Institute of CPA's Tax Executive Committee and currently chairs the AICPA's Regulation/Tax Subcommittee for the CPA exam. She has published a number of articles, most of which have dealt with estate planning or real estate transaction issues. In 2002, she received the Ray M. Sommerfeld Outstanding Educator Award, co-sponsored by the American Taxation Association and Ernst & Young.

Robert L. Gardner is the Robert J. Smith Professor of Accounting and the Associate Director of the School of Accountancy and Information Systems at Brigham Young University. He received a B.S. and M.B.A. from the University of Utah and a Ph.D. from the University of Texas at Austin. He has authored or coauthored two books and over 25 articles, and has received several teaching awards. Professor Gardner has served on the Board of Trustees of the American Taxation Association and served as President of the ATA in 1999–2000. He actively consults with several national CPA firms in their continuing education programs.

Richard J. Joseph is a Senior Lecturer at the University of Texas at Austin. A graduate *magna cum laude* of Harvard College (B.A.), Oxford University (M.Litt.), and the University of Texas at Austin School of Law (J.D.), he has taught individual, corporate, international, state and local taxation, tax research methods, and the fundamentals of financial and managerial accounting. A former Adjunct Professor at The University of Texas at Arlington, he also has taught contract, corporate, securities, agency, and partnership law. Before embarking on his academic career, Mr. Joseph worked as an investment banker on Wall Street and as a mergers and acquisitions lawyer in Texas. His book, *The Origins of the American Income Tax*, discusses the original intent, rationale, and effect of the early income tax.

Michael S. Schadewald, Ph.D., CPA, is on the faculty of the University of Wisconsin–Milwaukee, where he teaches graduate courses in multistate and international taxation. A graduate of the University of Minnesota, Professor Schadewald is a co-author of several books on multistate and international taxation, and has published more than 30 articles in academic and professional journals, including *The Accounting Review, The Journal of Accounting Research, Contemporary Accounting Research, The Journal of the American Taxation Association, The CPA Journal*, the *Journal of Taxation*, and the *Tax Adviser*. Professor Schadewald has also served on the editorial boards of *The Journal of the American Taxation Association, The International Journal of Accounting*, the *International Tax Journal, Issues in Accounting Education*, and the *Journal of Accounting Education*.

Why is the Pope/Anderson/Kramer series the best choice for your students?

The Pope/Anderson/Kramer 2007 Series in Federal Taxation includes three volumes and is appropriate for use in any first course in federal taxation:

Federal Taxation 2007: Individuals

Federal Taxation 2007: Corporations, Partnerships, Estates, and Trusts
     (the companion book to *Individuals*)

Federal Taxation 2007: Comprehensive
     (includes 29 chapters; 14 chapters from *Individuals* and 15 chapters
     from *Corporations*)

For the 2007 Edition, the title has reverted to its original pre-2005 title of *Individuals* in response to user feedback. For 2005 and 2006, the title was *Principles*. We wanted to clarify to all users, through this name change, that topics applicable to individual taxpayers are covered in this volume because we specifically focus on corporations, partnerships, and other entities in the second volume (*Corporations*) of this series.

However, we want to stress that *all* entities are covered in this *Individuals* volume although the treatment is often briefer than in the *Corporations* and *Comprehensive* volumes. The *Individuals* volume, therefore, is appropriate for colleges and universities that require only one semester of taxation as well as those that require more than one semester of taxation. Further, this volume adapts the suggestions of the Model Tax Curriculum as promulgated by the American Institute of Certified Public Accountants.

The 2007 series represents the highest level of publisher service, author expertise, and unique learning resources for students, innovative technology, and supplements:

- **Blend of Technical Content and Readability**

  The Pope/Anderson/Kramer series is unsurpassed in blending the technical content of the tax law with a high level of readability for students. The authors continually refine this delicate balance to advance student learning.

- **Problem Materials**

  The problem materials in the series are continually praised for enabling students to apply the tax principles in the chapters to real-life situations. Learning is enhanced with challenging problem materials and the Pope/Anderson/Kramer series offer outstanding materials for classroom use.

- **Commitment to Early Publication Dates**

  Prentice Hall has made a long-term commitment to publishing the annual Pope/Anderson/Kramer series texts on or before April 15 of each year. The ancillaries for each book are published well in advance of fall classes.

- **JIT Custom Text**

  Now you can create your own tax book using content drawn from the Pope/Anderson/Kramer series. You can even include your own materials. Ask your Prentice Hall representative for specific information on custom text procedures and policies or log onto *www.prenhall.com/custombusiness* to learn more about your options.

- **NEW TaxACT 2005 Software Packaged with the Text for a Nominal Price**

  This user-friendly tax preparation program includes more than 80 tax forms, schedules, and worksheets. TaxACT calculates returns and alerts the user to possible errors or entries.

- **Commitment to Service**

  Faculty should log onto *www.prenhall.com/accounting* to locate their Prentice Hall representative using our unique "Rep Locator" search feature.

Expert Insights—Unique Student Learning Features

What Would You Do in This Situation? Boxes

Unique to the Pope/Anderson/Kramer series, these boxes place students in a decision-making role. The boxes include many *current controversies* that are as yet unresolved or are currently being considered by the courts.

These boxes make extensive use of **Ethical Material** as they represent choices that may put the practitioner at odds with the client.

WHAT WOULD YOU DO IN THIS SITUATION?

INVENTORY VALUATION

Jack is a new tax client. He says he and his previous accountant did not get along very well. Jack owns an automobile dealership with sales of $12 million. He has provided you with most of the information you need to prepare his tax return, but he has not yet given you the year-end inventory value. You have completed much of the work on his return, but cannot complete it without the inventory figure. You have called Jack three times about the inventory. Each time he has interrupted, and asked you what his tax liability will be at alternative inventory levels. What problem do you see?

Stop & Think Boxes

These "speed bumps" encourage students to pause and apply what they have just learned. Solutions for each issue are provided in the box.

 STOP & THINK

Question: When one company purchases the assets of another company, the purchasing company may acquire goodwill. Since purchased goodwill is a Sec. 197 intangible asset and may be amortized over 15 years, the determination of the cost of goodwill is important. How is the "cost" of goodwill determined when the purchasing company purchases many assets in the acquisition?

Solution: The IRS requires that taxpayers use the "residual method" as prescribed in Sec. 1060. Under this method, all of the assets except for goodwill are valued. The total value of these assets are then subtracted from the total purchase price and the residual value is the amount of the purchase price that is allocated to goodwill.

Unique Margin Notes

These provide an extensive series of learning tips for students and faculty. No other text can match the quantity, quality, or variety of these resources:
• Additional Comment
• Key Points
• Real-World Examples
• Typical Misconceptions
• Ethical Points
• Self-Study Questions and Answers
• Book-to-Tax Accounting Comparisons
• Historical Notes
• Tax Strategy Tips

ETHICAL POINT

An employer must have a reasonable basis for treating a worker as an independent contractor or meet the general common law rules for determining whether an employer-employee relationship exists. Otherwise, the employer is liable for federal and state income tax withholding, FICA and FUTA taxes, interest, and penalties associated with the misclassification.

TAX STRATEGY TIP

Rather than having the corporation borrow money, an S corporation shareholder might consider borrowing money directly from the bank and then lending the loan proceeds to the corporation with the corporation guaranteeing the bank loan. In this way, the shareholder will obtain debt basis.

ADDITIONAL COMMENT

Stock purchased on which a dividend has been declared has an increased value. This value will drop when the dividend is paid. If the dividend is eligible for a dividends-received deduction and the drop in value also creates a capital loss, corporate shareholders could use this event as a tax planning device. To avoid this result, no dividends-received deduction is available for stock held 45 days or less.

Innovative Technology and Supplements

FOR INSTRUCTORS

• *NEW TaxACT 2005 Software Packaged with the Text for a Nominal Price.* This user-friendly tax preparation program includes more than 80 tax forms, schedules, and worksheets. TaxACT calculates, returns, and alerts the user to possible errors or entries.

• *Instructor's Guide* contains sample syllabi, instructor outlines, and notes on the end-of-chapter problems. It also contains solutions to the tax form/tax return preparation problems. It is available as a password-protected download from the Instructor Resource Center on *www.prenhall.com/phtax*. Ask your Prentice Hall representative for your password.

• *Solutions Manual* contains solutions to discussion questions, problems, and comprehensive and tax strategy problems. It also contains all solutions to the case study problems, research problems, and "What Would You Do in This Situation?" boxes. It is available as a password-protected download from the Instructor Resource Center on *www.prenhall.com/phtax* and also in hard copy. Upon written request, Prentice Hall may grant permission for faculty to post solutions on a student-accessible site, provided that this is password-protected at the school.

• *Testing.* The **printed Test Item File** contains a wealth of true/false, multiple-choice, and calculative problems. A computerized program is available to adopters.

• *PowerPoint slides* include over 300 full-color electronic transparencies available for *Individuals* and *Corporations*. These are available for download on the Instructor's Resource Center where students and faculty have access to them.

Text Companion Web Site for Faculty and Students Available at *www.prenhall.com/phtax*

The Web site provides a wealth of FREE material to help students study and help faculty prepare for class.

1. Free Student Resources include

- True/False and Multiple-Choice Questions
- Current Events
- Internet Resources
- Tax Law Updates
- PowerPoint Slides
- Multistate Income Taxation chapter with accompanying questions

2. Free Instructor Resources include

Supplements and PowerPoint slides are available for download at *www.prenhall.com/phtax*.

Online Tax Cases for *Individuals* and *Corporations*

- Computational questions
- Case Study Problems

ACKNOWLEDGMENTS

Our policy is to provide annual editions and to prepare timely updated supplements when major tax revisions occur. We are most appreciative of the suggestions made by outside reviewers because these extensive review procedures have been valuable to the authors and editors during the revision process.

We are also grateful to the various graduate assistants, doctoral students, and colleagues who have reviewed the text and supplementary materials and checked solutions to maintain a high level of technical accuracy. In particular, we would like to acknowledge the following colleagues who assisted in the preparation of supplemental materials for this text:

Sally Baker	DeVry Institute of Technology—Kansas City
Arthur D. Cassill	Elon University
Ann Burstein Cohen	SUNY—Buffalo
Susan Crosson	Santa Fe Community College
Priscilla Kenney	
(Supplements Coordinator)	University of Florida
Craig J. Langstraat	University of Memphis
Pamela J. Legner	DeVry Institute of Technology—Addison
Richard Newmark	University of Northern Colorado
Thomas Omer	University of Illinois at Chicago
Michael Schadewald	University of Wisconsin—Milwaukee
Caroline D. Strobel	University of South Carolina
Don Trippeer	East Carolina University

Please send any comments to the editors:
Thomas R. Pope
Kenneth E. Anderson
John L. Kramer

PRENTICE HALL'S
FEDERAL TAXATION
2007

Comprehensive

1

CHAPTER

AN INTRODUCTION TO TAXATION

LEARNING OBJECTIVES

After studying this chapter, you should be able to

1. ▶ Discuss the history of taxation in the United States

2. ▶ Differentiate between the three types of tax rate structures

3. ▶ Describe the various types of taxes

4. ▶ Discuss what constitutes a "good" tax structure, the objectives of the federal income tax law, and recent tax reform proposals

5. ▶ Describe the tax entities in the federal income tax system

6. ▶ Identify the various tax law sources and understand their implications for tax practice

7. ▶ Describe the legislative process for the enactment of the tax law

8. ▶ Describe the administrative procedures under the tax law

9. ▶ Describe the components of a tax practice and understand the importance of computer applications in taxation

KEY POINT

In many situations, the use of the tax laws to influence human behavior is deliberate. As will be seen later in this chapter, tax laws are often used to achieve social and economic objectives.

Federal income taxes have a significant effect on business, investor, and personal decisions in the United States. Because tax rates can be as high as 35% on corporations and individuals, virtually every transaction is impacted by income taxes. The following examples illustrate the impact of the tax law on various decisions in our society:

▶ A corporation may get a larger tax deduction if it leases property rather than purchasing the property.

▶ An investor may decide to delay selling some stock because of the significant taxes that may result from the sale.

▶ Because of the deductibility of mortgage interest and real estate taxes, an individual may decide to purchase a home rather than to continue to rent an apartment.

The purpose of this text is to provide an introduction to the study of federal income taxation. However, before discussing the specifics of the U.S. federal income tax law, it is helpful to have a broad conceptual understanding of the taxation process. This chapter provides an overview of the following topics:

▶ Historical developments of the federal tax system

▶ Types of taxes levied and structural considerations

▶ Objectives of the tax law, including a discussion of recent tax reform proposals

▶ Taxpaying entities in the federal income tax system

▶ Tax law sources and the legislative process

▶ Internal Revenue Service (IRS) collection, examination, and appeals processes

▶ The nature of tax practice, including computer applications and tax research

HISTORY OF TAXATION IN THE UNITED STATES

OBJECTIVE 1

Discuss the history of taxation in the United States

EARLY PERIODS

The federal income tax is the dominant form of taxation in the United States. In addition, most states and some cities and counties also impose an income tax. Both corporations and individuals are subject to such taxes.

Before 1913 (the date of enactment of the modern-day federal income tax), the federal government relied predominantly on customs duties and excise taxes to finance its operations. The first federal income tax on individuals was enacted in 1861 to finance the Civil War but was repealed after the war. The federal income tax was reinstated in 1894, however, that tax was challenged in the courts because the U.S. Constitution required that an income tax be apportioned among the states in proportion to their populations. This type of tax system, which would be both impractical and difficult to administer, would mean that different tax rates would apply to individual taxpayers depending on their states of residence.

HISTORICAL NOTE

The reinstatement of the income tax in 1894 was the subject of heated political controversy. In general, the representatives in Congress from the agricultural South and West favored the income tax in lieu of customs duties. Representatives from the industrial eastern states were against the income tax and favored protective tariff legislation.

In 1895, the Supreme Court ruled that the tax was in violation of the U.S. Constitution.[1] Therefore, it was necessary to amend the U.S. Constitution to permit the passage of a federal income tax law. This was accomplished by the Sixteenth Amendment, which was ratified in 1913. The Sixteenth Amendment, while being an extraordinarily important amendment, consists of one sentence.

Sixteenth Amendment to the Constitution of the United States

The Congress shall have the power to lay and collect taxes on incomes, from whatever source derived, without apportionment among the several States, and without regard to any census or enumeration.

---

[1] *Pollock v. Farmers' Loan & Trust Co.*, 3 AFTR 2602 (USSC, 1895). Note, however, that a federal income tax on corporations that was enacted in 1909 was held to be constitutional because it was treated as an excise tax. See *Flint v. Stone Tracy Co.*, 3 AFTR 2834 (USSC, 1911).

REVENUE ACTS FROM 1913 TO THE PRESENT

HISTORICAL NOTE

The Revenue Act of 1913 contained sixteen pages.

The Revenue Act of 1913 imposed a flat 1% tax (with no exemptions) on a corporation's net income. The rate varied from 1% to 7% for individuals, depending on the individual's income level. However, very few individuals paid federal income taxes because a $3,000 personal exemption ($4,000 for married individuals) was permitted as an offset to taxable income. These amounts were greater than the incomes of most individuals in 1913.

HISTORICAL NOTE

Before 1939, the tax laws were contained in the current revenue act, a reenactment of a prior revenue act plus amendments. In 1939, a permanent tax code was established; it was revised in 1954 and 1986.

Various amendments to the original law were passed between 1913 and 1939 as separate revenue acts. For example, a deduction for dependency exemptions was provided in 1917. In 1939, the separate revenue acts were codified into the Internal Revenue Code of 1939. A similar codification was accomplished in 1954. The 1954 codification, which was known as the Internal Revenue Code of 1954, included the elimination of many "deadwood" provisions, a rearrangement and clarification of numerous code sections, and the addition of major tax law changes. Whenever changes to the Internal Revenue Code (IRC) are made, the old language is deleted and the new language added. Thus, the statutes are organized as a single document, and a tax advisor does not have to read through the applicable parts of all previous tax bills to find the most current law. In 1986, major changes were made to the tax law, and the basic tax law was redesignated as the Internal Revenue Code of 1986.

The federal income tax became a "mass tax" on individuals during the early 1940s. This change was deemed necessary to finance the revenue needs of the federal government during World War II. In 1939, less than 6% of the U.S. population was subject to the federal income tax; by 1945, 74% of the population was taxed.[2] To accommodate the broadened tax base and to avoid significant tax collection problems, Congress enacted pay-as-you-go withholding in 1943.

A major characteristic of the federal income tax since its inception to today is the manner in which the tax law is changed or modified. The federal income tax is changed on an **incremental** basis rather than a complete revision basis. Under so-called incrementalism, when a change in the tax law is deemed necessary by Congress, the entire law is not changed, but specific provisions of the tax law are added, changed, or deleted on an incremental basis. Thus, the federal income tax has been referred to as a "quiltwork" of tax laws, referring to the patchwork nature of the law. Without question, one of the principal reasons for the complexity of the federal income tax today is the incremental nature of the tax.

ADDITIONAL COMMENT

In 2003, over 130 million individual income tax returns were filed, and collections from individuals totaled $987 billion.

REVENUE SOURCES

As mentioned earlier, the largest source of federal revenues is individual income taxes. Other major revenue sources include Social Security (FICA) taxes and corporate income taxes (see Table I1-1). Two notable trends from Table I1-1 are (1) the gradual increase in social security taxes from 1965 to 2005 and (2) the gradual decrease in corporate income taxes for the same period. Individual income taxes have remained fairly stable during the past 40 years.

TYPICAL MISCONCEPTION

It is often assumed that the tax revenue from corporation income taxes is the largest source of tax revenue. However, the revenue generated from this tax represents approximately 13% of total federal revenues in 2005.

▼ **TABLE I1-1**

Breakdown of Federal Revenues

	1965	1975	1988	2005
Individual income taxes	43%	45%	44%	43%
Social insurance taxes and contribution	20	32	37	37
Corporation income taxes	23	15	10	13
Other	14	8	9	7
Total	100%	100%	100%	100%

Source: Council of Economic Advisers, *Economic Indicators* (Washington, DC: U.S. Government Printing Office, 1967, 1977, 2005).

[2] Richard Goode, *The Individual Income Tax* (Washington, DC: The Brookings Institution, 1964), pp. 2–4.

TYPES OF TAX RATE STRUCTURES

Differentiate between the three types of tax rate structures

THE STRUCTURE OF INDIVIDUAL INCOME TAX RATES

Virtually all tax structures are comprised of two basic parts: the **tax base** and the **tax rate**. The tax base is the amount to which the tax rate is applied to determine the tax due. For example, an individual's tax base for the federal income tax is *taxable income*, as defined and determined by the income tax law. Similarly, the tax base for the property tax is generally the fair market value of property subject to the tax. The tax rate is merely the percentage rate applied to the tax base.

Tax rates may be progressive, proportional, or regressive. A **progressive rate** structure is one where the rate of tax increases as the tax base increases. The most notable tax that incorporates a progressive rate structure is the federal income tax. Thus, as a taxpayer's taxable income increases, a progressively higher rate of tax is applied. For 2006, the federal income tax rates for individuals begin at 10% and increase to 15%, 25%, 28%, 33%, and 35% as a taxpayer's taxable income increases.[3] Examples I1-1 and I1-2 show how the progressive rate structure of the federal income tax operates.

ADDITIONAL COMMENT

In the 1950s, the top marginal tax rate for individual taxpayers reached 92%. This astonishingly high rate only applied to taxpayers with very high taxable incomes but still is an extremely confiscatory tax rate.

EXAMPLE I1-1 ▶

Alice, who is single, has $30,000 taxable income in 2006. Her federal income taxes for the year are $4,123 as the first $7,550 of taxable income is taxed at 10% and the remaining $22,450 at 15%. (For tax rates, see the inside front cover.)

Allen, who is also single, has taxable income of $60,000. A 10% rate applies to the first $7,550 of taxable income, 15% on the next $23,100, and a 25% rate applies to the taxable income over $30,650. Thus, Allen's total tax is $11,558 [(0.10 × $7,550) + (0.15 × $23,100) + (0.25 × $29,350)].

If Allen's taxable income is $120,000, a 28% rate applies to $45,800 of his taxable income ($120,000 − $74,200) because the 28% rate applies to taxable income above $74,200 for a single individual and his total tax for the year is $27,932. Thus, the tax rates are progressive because the rate of tax increases as a taxpayer's taxable income increases. ◀

Notice in Example I1-1 that taxable income has doubled in size in the three cases, but the income taxes have more than doubled (i.e., $4,123 to $11,558 to $27,932). This demonstrates how a progressive rate structure operates.

EXAMPLE I1-2 ▶

Assume the same facts as in Example I1-1 except that Alice has taxable income of $180,000. Of Alice's taxable income, $25,200 ($180,000 − $154,800) is subject to the 33% rate. Alternatively, if Allen has taxable income of $400,000, $63,450 ($400,000 − $336,550) is subject to the top marginal rate of 35%. ◀

A **proportional tax** rate, sometimes called a **flat tax**, is one where the rate of tax is the same for all taxpayers, regardless of the level of their tax base. This type of tax rate is generally used for real estate taxes, state and local sales taxes, personal property taxes, customs duties, and excise taxes. A flat tax has been the subject of considerable discussion in the last couple of years and promises to be a highly controversial topic as the debate on federal income tax reform continues into the future.

EXAMPLE I1-3 ▶

Assume the same facts as in Example I1-1, except that a 17% tax rate applies to all amounts of taxable income. Based on the assumed flat tax rate structure, Alice's federal income tax is $5,100 on $30,000 of taxable income; Allen's tax is $10,200 on $60,000 of taxable income and $20,400 on $120,000 of taxable income. The tax rate is proportional because the 17% rate applies to both taxpayers without regard to their income level. As you can see, a proportional tax rate results in substantially lower taxes for higher income taxpayers.[4] ◀

---

[3] See the inside front cover for the 2006 tax rates and Chapter I2 for a discussion of the computation procedures. 2005 rate schedules and tax tables are located immediately before Appendix A.

[4] This example assumes the same tax base (taxable income) for the flat tax as with the current federal tax. Most flat tax proposals allow only a few deductions and, therefore, would generate higher taxes than in the example.

A **regressive tax** rate decreases with an increase in the tax base (e.g., income). Regressive taxes, while not consistent with the fairness of the income tax,[5] are found in the United States. The Social Security (FICA) tax is regressive because a fixed rate of tax of 7.65% for both the employer and employee is levied up to a ceiling amount of $94,200 for 2006 ($90,000 in 2005). The employer and employee's FICA tax rate is only 1.45% for wages earned in excess of the ceiling amount. The sales tax, which is levied by many states, is also regressive when measured against the income base.

THE STRUCTURE OF CORPORATE TAX RATES

Corporations are separate entities and are subject to income tax. The federal corporate income tax reflects a stair-step pattern of progression that tends to benefit small corporations. The corporate rates, which have not changed for several years, are as follows:[6]

Taxable Income[7]	Tax
First $50,000	15% of taxable income
Over $50,000 but not over $75,000	$7,500 + 25% of taxable income over $50,000
Over $75,000 but not over $100,000	$13,750 + 34% of taxable income over $75,000
Over $100,000 but not over $335,000	$22,250 + 39% of taxable income over $100,000
Over $335,000	34% of taxable income
Over $10,000,000 but not over $15,000,000	$3,400,000 + 35% of taxable income over $10,000,000
Over $15,000,000 but not over $18,333,333	$5,150,000 + 38% over $15,000,000
Over $18,333,333	35% of taxable income

MARGINAL, AVERAGE, AND EFFECTIVE TAX RATES FOR TAXPAYERS

A taxpayer's **marginal tax rate** is the tax rate applied to an incremental amount of taxable income that is added to the tax base. The marginal tax rate concept is useful for planning because it measures the tax effect of a proposed transaction.

EXAMPLE I1-4 ►

Tania, who is single, is considering the purchase of a personal residence that will provide a $20,000 tax deduction for interest expense and real estate taxes in 2006. Tania's taxable income would be reduced from $120,000 to $100,000 if she purchases the residence. Because a 28% tax rate applies to taxable income from $100,000 to $120,000, Tania's marginal tax rate is 28%. Thus, Tania's tax savings from purchasing the personal residence would be $5,600 (0.28 × $20,000). ◄

While the marginal tax rate measures the tax rate applicable to the next $1 of income or deduction for a taxpayer, there are two other tax rates that are used primarily by tax policymakers: average tax rate and effective tax rate. The **average tax rate** is computed by dividing the total tax liability by the amount of taxable income. This represents the average rate of tax for each dollar of taxable income. For example, a single taxpayer with taxable income of $350,000 in 2006 would incur a total tax liability of $102,361. The taxpayer's marginal tax rate is 35%, but his average tax rate is 29.2% ($102,361/$350,000).

The **effective tax rate** is the total tax liability divided by total economic income. **Total economic income** includes all types of economic income that a taxpayer has for the year. Thus, economic income is much broader than taxable income and includes most types of

---

[5] See the discussion of equity and fairness later in this chapter.
[6] For C corporations with taxable income over $100,000, the lower rates of tax on the first $75,000 of income are gradually phased out by applying a 5-percentage-point surtax on taxable income from $100,000 to $335,000 so that benefits of the favorable rates are eliminated once a corporation's taxable income reaches $335,000. Once taxable income exceeds $335,000 the tax

equals 34% of taxable income. A 35% tax rate applies to taxable income in excess of $10 million. For corporations with taxable income in excess of $15 million, a 3 percentage-point-surtax applies to taxable income from $15 million to $18,333,333 to eliminate the lower 34% rate that applies to the first $10 million of taxable income.
[7] Also see the inside back cover for the 2006 corporation income tax rates.

excludible income, such as tax-exempt bond interest, and generally permits business deductions but not personal-type deductions. It should be pointed out that economic income is *not* statutorily defined and experts may disagree on a precise calculation. The basic purpose of calculating the effective tax rate is to provide a broad measure of taxpayers' ability to pay taxes. Accordingly, the effective tax rate mainly is used by tax policymakers to determine the fairness of the income tax system.

EXAMPLE I1-5 ▶

Amelia, who is single, has adjusted gross income of $140,000 and economic income of $175,000 in 2006. The difference is attributable to $35,000 of tax-exempt bond interest. If Amelia has deductions of $30,000, then her taxable income is $110,000, and her total tax is $25,132. Her average tax rate is 22.85% ($25,132 ÷ $110,000). Amelia's effective tax rate is 14.36% ($25,132 ÷ $175,000). Amelia's effective tax rate is considerably lower than her average tax rate because of her substantial amount of tax-exempt income. ◀

STOP & THINK

Question: Gwen, a single taxpayer, has seen her income climb to $200,000 in the current year. She wants a tax planner to help her reduce her tax liability. In planning for tax clients, tax professionals almost exclusively use the marginal tax rate in their analysis rather than the average tax rate. Why is the marginal tax rate much more important in the tax planning process than the average tax rate?

Solution: Because tax planning is done at the margin. A single taxpayer who has taxable income of $200,000 has a marginal tax rate of 33% (at 2006 rates), but an average tax rate of 26.30%, computed as follows:

Taxable income		$200,000
Tax on first $154,800 of taxable income		$37,676
Remaining taxable income	$45,200	
Times: Marginal tax rate	× 0.33	14,916
Total tax liability		$ 52,592

$$\text{Average tax rate} = \frac{\text{Total tax}}{\text{Taxable income}} = \frac{\$\ 52,592}{\$200,000} = 26.30\%$$

If a tax planner could reduce Gwen's taxable income by $10,000, Gwen's tax liability would decrease by $3,333 ($10,000 × 0.33). When the taxpayer wants to know how much she can save through tax planning, the appropriate marginal tax rate yields the answer.

Overall, effective federal income tax rates for individuals have decreased slightly during the period 1979–2002,[8] amounting to 9.7% in 2002 as compared with 11.1% in 1979. For the highest 20% of households, the effective individual income tax rate declined to 15.6% in 2002 from 16.0% in 1979.

DETERMINATION OF TAXABLE INCOME AND TAX DUE

As will be discussed in later chapters, the federal income taxes imposed on all taxpayers (individuals, corporations, estates, and trusts) are based on the determination of taxable income. In general, taxable income is computed as follows:

Total income (income from whatever source derived)	$xxx
Minus: Exclusions (specifically defined items, such as tax-exempt bond interest)	(xx)

ADDITIONAL COMMENT

In the determination of tax rates, one should consider the incidence of taxation that involves the issue of who really bears the burden of the tax. If a city raises the real property tax but landlords simply raise rents to pass on the higher taxes, the tax burden is shifted to their tenants. The concept has important implications in determining any kind of average or effective tax rate.

---

[8] Congressional Budget Office, *Historical Effective Federal Tax Rates: 1979 to 2002* (Washington, DC: U.S. Government Printing Office, March, 2005), p. 4.

Gross income	$xxx
Minus: Deductions (business expenses and itemized deductions)	(xx)
Exemptions (not applicable for corporations)	(xx)
Taxable income	$xxx
Times: Applicable tax rate	× .xx
Income tax before credits	$xxx
Minus: Tax credits	(xx)
Total tax liability	$xxx
Minus: Prepayments	(xx)
Balance due or refund	$xxx

Each different type of taxpayer (individuals, corporations, etc.) computes taxable income in a slightly different manner, but all use the general framework above. An introductory discussion of the various types of taxpayers is provided later in this chapter. More detailed discussions of individual taxpayers (Chapter I2) and corporation taxpayers (Chapter I16) are examined in this *Individuals* book. Corporations, estates, and trusts are further examined in *Prentice Hall's Federal Taxation: Corporations, Partnerships, Estates, and Trusts.*

OTHER TYPES OF TAXES

STATE AND LOCAL INCOME AND FRANCHISE TAXES

OBJECTIVE 3

Describe the various types of taxes

In addition to federal income taxes, many states and local jurisdictions impose income taxes on individuals and businesses. These state and local taxes have gradually increased over the years and currently represent a significant source of revenue for state and local governments but also represent a significant tax burden on taxpayers.

State and local income taxes vary greatly in both form and rates.[9] Only seven states do not impose an individual income tax.[10] In most instances, state income tax rates are mildly progressive and are based on an individual's federal adjusted gross income (AGI), with minor adjustments.[11] For example, a typical adjustment to a state income tax return is interest income on federal government bonds, which is subject to tax on the federal return but is generally not subject to state income taxes. Some states also allow a deduction for federal income taxes in the computation of taxable income for state income tax purposes.

ADDITIONAL COMMENT

State income tax rates for individuals have increased significantly in the past twenty years. Thirty-three states now have marginal tax rates of 6% or higher.

States imposing a state income tax generally require the withholding of state income taxes and have established mandatory estimated tax payment procedures. The due date for filing state income tax returns generally coincides with the due date for the federal income tax returns (e.g., the fifteenth day of the fourth month following the close of the tax year for individuals).

Most states impose a corporate income tax, although in some instances the tax is called a **franchise tax**. Franchise taxes usually are based on a weighted-average formula consisting of net worth, income, and sales.

WEALTH TRANSFER TAXES

U.S. citizens are subject to taxation on certain transfers of property to another person. The tax law provides a unified transfer tax system that imposes a single tax on transfers of property taking place during an individual's lifetime (gifts) and at death (estates). (See the inside back cover of the text for the transfer tax rate schedules.) Formerly, the gift and estate tax laws were separate and distinct. The federal estate tax was initially enacted in 1916. The original gift tax law dates back to 1932. The gift tax was originally imposed to prevent widespread avoidance of the estate tax (e.g., taxpayers could make tax-free gifts of property

---

[9] For a thorough discussion of state and local taxes, see the chapter entitled *Multistate Income Taxation* that accompanies this textbook in electronic form on the Prentice Hall Federal Taxation 2006 Web page at www.prenhall.com/phtax.
[10] These states are Alaska, Florida, Nevada, South Dakota, Texas, Washington, and Wyoming. New Hampshire has an income tax that is levied only on dividend and interest income and Tennessee's income tax applies only to income from stocks and bonds.
[11] See Chapter I2 for a discussion of the AGI computation.

before their death). Both the gift and estate taxes are wealth transfer taxes levied on the transfer of property and are based on the fair market value (FMV) of the transferred property on the date of the transfer. Following are brief descriptions of the gift tax and estate tax.

THE FEDERAL GIFT TAX. The **gift tax** is an excise tax that is imposed on the donor (not the donee) for transfers of property that are considered to be a taxable gift. A gift, generally speaking, is a transfer made gratuitously and with donative intent. However, the gift tax law has expanded the definition to include transfers that are not supported by full and adequate consideration.[12] To arrive at the amount of taxable gifts for the current year, a $12,000 annual exclusion is allowed per donee.[13] In addition, an unlimited marital deduction is allowed for transfers between spouses.[14] The formula for computing the gift tax is as follows:

KEY POINT

The $12,000 annual exclusion is an important tax-planning tool for wealthy parents who want to transfer assets to their children and thereby minimize their gift and estate taxes. A husband and wife who have three children could transfer a maximum of $72,000 [($12,000 × 2) × 3] to their children each year without incurring any gift tax.

FMV of all gifts made in the current year			$x,xxx
Minus: Annual donee exclusions ($12,000 per donee)	$xx		
Marital deduction for gifts to spouse	xx		
Charitable contribution deduction	xx	(xxx)	
Plus: Taxable gifts for all prior years		xxx	
Cumulative taxable gifts (tax base)		$x,xxx	
Times: Unified transfer tax rates		× .xx	
Tentative tax on gift tax base		$ xxx	
Minus: Unified transfer taxes paid in prior years		(xx)	
Unified credit		(xx)	
Unified transfer tax (gift tax) due in the current year		$ xx	

ADDITIONAL COMMENT

The gift tax was enacted to make the estate tax more effective. Without a gift tax, estate taxes could be easily avoided by large gifts made before death.

Note that the gift tax is cumulative over the taxpayer's lifetime (i.e., the tax calculation for the current year includes the taxable gifts made in prior years). The detailed tax rules relating to the gift tax are covered in Chapter C12 in both *Prentice Hall's Federal Taxation: Corporations, Partnerships, Estates, and Trusts* and the *Comprehensive* volume. The following general concepts and rules for the federal gift tax are presented as background material for other chapters of this text dealing with individual taxpayers:

▶ Gifts between spouses are exempted from the gift tax due to the operation of an unlimited marital deduction.

▶ The primary liability for payment of the gift tax is imposed on the **donor**. The donee is contingently liable for payment of the gift tax in the event of nonpayment by the donor.

▶ A donor is permitted a $12,000 annual exclusion for gifts of a present interest to each donee.[15]

▶ Charitable contributions are effectively exempted from the gift tax because an unlimited deduction is allowed.

▶ The tax basis of the property to the donee is generally the donor's cost. It is the lesser of the donor's cost and the property's FMV on the date of the gift if the property is sold by the donee at a loss. (See Chapter I5 for a discussion of the gift tax basis rules.)

▶ A unified tax credit equivalent to a $1,000,000 deduction is available to offset any gift tax on taxable gifts that exceed the $12,000 annual exclusion.[16]

EXAMPLE I1-6 ▶ Antonio makes the following gifts in the year 2006:

▶ $25,000 cash gift to his wife

▶ $15,000 contribution to the United Way

---

[12] Sec. 2512(b).

[13] Sec. 2503(b). The annual exclusion for gift tax purposes had been $10,000 for many years. However, for 2002–2005, the inflation adjustment increased the exclusion to $11,000. For 2006 and later years, the exclusion has been increasd to $12,000.

[14] Sec. 2523(a).

[15] A gift of a present interest is an interest that is already in existence and the donee is currently entitled to receive the income from the property. A gift of a

future interest comes into being at some future date (e.g., property is transferred by gift to a trust in which the donee is not entitled to the income from the property until the donor dies) and is not eligible for the $12,000 annual exclusion.

[16] The applicable exclusion amount was $675,000 in 2000 and 2001 and was increased to the current $1,000,000 in 2002 and later years. For further details, see *Prentice Hall's Federal Taxation: Corporations, Partnerships, Estates and Trusts*, 2007 Edition, Chapters 12 and 13.

► Gift of a personal automobile valued at $25,000 to his adult son

► Gift of a personal computer valued at $4,000 to a friend

The $25,000 gift to his wife is not taxed because of a $12,000 annual exclusion and a $14,000 tax exemption for transfers to spouses (i.e., the marital deduction). The $15,000 contribution to the United Way is also not taxed because of the $12,000 annual exclusion and the $3,000 deduction for charitable contributions. The $25,000 gift Antonio made to his son is reduced by the $12,000 annual exclusion to each donee, leaving a $13,000 taxable gift.[17] The $4,000 gift to the friend is not taxed because of the annual exclusion of up to $12,000 in gifts to a donee in a tax year. Thus, total taxable gifts for the current year subject to the unified transfer tax are $13,000. ◄

STOP & THINK

Question: An important but frequently overlooked aspect of gift taxes is the interaction of gift taxes and income taxes. In many cases, gifts are made *primarily* for income tax purposes. Why would a gift be made for income tax purposes?

Solution: Gifts are frequently made to shift income from one family member to another family member who is in a lower marginal tax bracket. For example, assume Fran and Jan are married, have one 15-year-old son, earn $400,000 per year from their business, and generate $100,000 per year in dividends and interest from a substantial portfolio of stocks and bonds. With such a high level of income, Fran and Jan are in the 35% marginal tax bracket. If they make a gift of some of the stocks and bonds to their son, the dividends and interest attributable to the gift are taxed to the son at his marginal tax rate (maybe 10% or 15%). If the son's marginal tax rate is lower than 35%, the family unit reduces its overall income taxes.

THE FEDERAL ESTATE TAX. The **federal estate tax** is part of the unified transfer tax system that is based on the total property transfers an individual makes both during his or her lifetime and at death.

EXAMPLE I1-7 ► Amy dies during the current year. The formula for computing the estate tax on Amy's estate is as follows:

TYPICAL MISCONCEPTION

It is sometimes thought that the federal estate tax raises significant amounts of revenue, but it has not been a significant revenue producer since World War II. Only 66,000 estate tax returns were filed in 2003.

Gross estate (FMV of all property owned by the decedent at the date of death)		$xxx,xxx
Minus: Deductions for funeral and administration expenses, debts of the decedent, charitable contributions, and the marital deduction for property transferred to a spouse		(x,xxx)
Taxable estate		$ x,xxx
Plus: Taxable gifts made after 1976		xx
Tax base		$ x,xxx
Times: Unified transfer tax rate(s)		× .xx
Tentative tax on estate tax base		$ xxx
Minus: Tax credits (e.g., the unified tax credit equivalent to a $2,000,000 deduction in 2006, 2007, and 2008 ($1,500,000 in 2004 and 2005)		(xx)
Gift taxes paid after 1976		(xx)
Unified transfer tax (estate tax) due		$ xx ◄

The estate tax rules are discussed in more detail in Chapter C13 in *Prentice Hall's Federal Taxation: Corporations, Partnerships, Estates, and Trusts* and in the *Comprehensive* volume. The following general rules are provided as background material for subsequent chapters of this text dealing with individual taxpayers:

► The decedent's property is valued at its FMV on the date of death unless the alternative valuation date (six months after the date of death) is elected. The alternative valuation date may be elected only if the aggregate value of the gross estate decreases during the

---

[17] This example assumes that the automobile is a gift rather than an obligation of support under state law and also assumes that Antonio's wife does not join with Antonio in electing to treat the gift to the son as having been made by both spouses (a gift-splitting election). In such event, donee exclusions of $24,000 (2 × $12,000) would be available, resulting in a taxable gift of only $3,000.

six-month period following the date of death and the election results in a lower estate tax liability.

▶ The basis of the property received by the estate and by the decedent's heirs is the property's FMV on the date of death (or the alternate valuation date if it is elected).

▶ Property transferred to the decedent's spouse is exempt from the estate tax because of the estate tax marital deduction provision.

EXAMPLE I1-8 ▶ Barry died in 2006, leaving a $2,500,000 gross estate. In years prior to 2004 (but after 1976), Barry had made taxable gifts of $250,000. Of the $2,500,000 gross estate, one-half of the estate was transferred to his wife, administrative and funeral expenses are $30,000, Barry had debts of $170,000, and the remainder of the estate was transferred to his children. The estate tax due is computed as follows:

Gross estate		$2,500,000
Minus:	Marital deduction	(1,250,000)
	Funeral and administrative expenses	(30,000)
	Decedent's debts	(170,000)
Taxable estate		$1,050,000
Plus:	Taxable gifts made after 1976	250,000
Tax base		$1,300,000
Tentative tax on estate tax base		$ 469,800[a]
Minus:	Tax credits (unified tax credit—see inside back cover for table)	(780,800)
Unified transfer tax due		$ —0— ◀

[a]$448,300 + (0.43 × $50,000)

Because of the generous credit and deduction provisions (e.g., the unified tax credit and the unlimited marital deduction), few estates are required to pay estate taxes. As can be seen above, the gross estate of the decedent was $2.5 million but no estate taxes were due primarily because of the large marital deduction and the unified credit. However, estate taxes rise quickly as is demonstrated below in Example I1-9.

EXAMPLE I1-9 ▶ Assume the same facts for Barry as in Example I1-8 except that Barry's gross estate is $5,000,000 rather than $2,500,000. The estate tax due is computed as follows:

Gross estate		$5,000,000
Minus:	Marital deduction	(2,500,000)
	Funeral and administrative expenses	(30,000)
	Decedent's debts	(170,000)
Taxable estate		$2,300,000
Plus:	Taxable gifts made after 1976	250,000
Tax base		$2,550,000
Tentative tax on estate tax base		$1,033,800
Minus:	Tax credits (unified tax credit)	(780,800)
Unified transfer tax due		$ 253,000 ◀

The estate tax (not the gift tax) is scheduled to be repealed in 2010. However, pursuant to so-called sunset provisions, the estate tax will be reinstated on January 1, 2011, unless Congress enacts specific legislation. The uncertainty of the estate tax is causing considerable anxiety to taxpayers in trying to plan their estates.

OTHER TYPES OF TAXES

ADDITIONAL COMMENT

Proposals to decrease reliance on the federal income tax have focused primarily on consumption taxes, such as a national sales tax or a value-added tax. A value-added tax basically is a sales tax levied at each stage of production on the "value added."

Although this text focuses primarily on the federal income tax, some mention should be made of the following other types of taxes levied by federal, state, and local governments.

▶ **Property taxes** are based on the value of a taxpayer's property, which may include both real estate and personal property. Real estate taxes are a major source of revenue for local governments. In addition, some state and local governments levy a personal property tax on intangibles such as securities and tangible personal property (e.g., the value of a personal automobile).

▶ **Federal excise taxes** and **customs duties** on imported goods have declined in relative importance over the years but remain significant sources of revenue. Federal excise taxes are imposed on alcohol, tobacco, gasoline, telephone usage, production of oil and gas, and many other types of goods. Many state and local governments impose similar excise taxes on goods and services.

▶ **Sales taxes** are a major source of revenue for state and local governments. Sales taxes are imposed on retail sales of tangible personal property (e.g., clothing and automobiles). Some states also impose a sales tax on personal services (e.g., accounting and legal fees). Certain items often are exempt from the sales tax levy (e.g., food items or medicines), and the rates vary widely between individual state and local governments. Sales taxes are not deductible for federal income tax purposes unless incurred in a trade or business.

▶ **Employment taxes** include Social Security (**FICA**) and federal and state unemployment compensation taxes. If an individual is classified as an employee, the FICA tax that is imposed on the employee is comprised of two parts, 6.2% for old-age, survivors, and disability insurance (OASDI) and 1.45% for hospital insurance (HI), for a total of 7.65%. The OASDI portion is imposed on the first $94,200 (2006) of wages, whereas the HI portion has no ceiling. Both of these taxes are imposed on both the employer and employee. If an individual is self-employed, a self-employment tax is imposed at a 15.3% rate (12.4% for OASDI and 2.9% for HI) on the individual's self-employment income, with a ceiling on the OASDI portion of $94,200 (in 2006).[18] Similar to employees, there is no ceiling on the HI portion for self-employed individuals.

▶ Employers are required to pay federal and state unemployment taxes to fund the payment of unemployment benefits to former employees. The federal rate is 6.2% on the first $7,000 of wages for each employee in 2005.[19] However, a credit is granted for up to 5.4% of wages for taxes paid to the state government so that the actual amount paid to the federal government may be as low as 0.8%.[20] The amount of tax paid to the state depends on the employer's prior experience with respect to the frequency and amount of unemployment claims. In Kentucky, for example, the highest rate of unemployment tax imposed is 3% and this rate is subsequently adjusted down if the employer has a small number of unemployment claims.

The types of taxes and structural considerations that were previously discussed are summarized in Topic Review I1-1.

CRITERIA FOR A TAX STRUCTURE

Establishing criteria for a "good" tax structure was first attempted in 1776 by economist Adam Smith.[21] Smith's four "canons of taxation"—equity, certainty, convenience, and economy—are still used today when tax policy issues are discussed. Many have added a fifth canon of simplicity. Below is a discussion of these criteria and how they relate to income taxes as well as other taxes.

EQUITY

A rather obvious criteria for a good tax is that the tax be equitable or fair to taxpayers. However, equity or fairness is elusive because of the subjectivity of the concept. What one person may conclude is fair in a particular situation may be considered totally unfair by another person. In other words, fairness is relative in nature and is extremely difficult to measure. For example, the deductibility of mortgage interest on a taxpayer's home

---

[18] Self-employed individuals receive an income tax deduction equal to 50% of taxes paid on their self-employment income and this deduction is also allowed to compute the amount of self-employment income (see Secs. 164(f) and 1402(a)(12) and Chapter I14).
[19] Sec. 3301.

[20] Sec. 3302. State unemployment taxes in some states are levied on tax bases above $7,000. For example, the wage base ceiling in North Carolina is $12,500 in 2005.
[21] Adam Smith, *The Wealth of Nations* (New York: Random House, Modern Library, 1937), pp. 777–779.

Topic Review I1-1

Types of Taxes and Tax Structure

TYPE OF TAX	TAX STRUCTURE	TAX BASE
Individuals:		
Federal income tax	Progressive	Gross income from all sources unless specifically excluded by law reduced by deductions and exemptions
State income tax	Progressive	Generally based on AGI for federal income tax purposes with adjustments
Federal gift tax	Progressive	FMV of all taxable gifts made during the tax year
Federal estate tax	Progressive	FMV of property owned at death plus taxable gifts made after 1976
Corporations:		
Federal corporate income tax	Progressive	Gross income from all sources unless specifically excluded by law reduced by deductions
State corporate income tax	Proportional or progressive	Federal corporate taxable income with adjustments
State franchise tax	Proportional	Usually based on a weighted-average formula consisting of net worth, income, and sales
Other Types of Taxes:		
Property taxes	Proportional	FMV of personal or real property
Excise taxes	Proportional	Customs and duties on imported and domestic goods from alcohol to telephone usage
Sales taxes	Proportional	Retail sales of tangible personal property or personal services
FICA and self-employment taxes	Regressive	Based on wages or self-employment income
Unemployment taxes	Regressive	Usually first $7,000 of an employee's wages

ADDITIONAL COMMENT

The Revenue Reconciliation Act of 1993 followed through on President Clinton's campaign promise to increase taxes on high-income taxpayers to correct perceived inequities resulting from the lowering of the top tax rates in the Tax Reform Act of 1986.

KEY POINT

Using retroactive dates for changes in the tax law does not help to accomplish the objective of certainty. For example, the effective date of the increase in the top tax rate was made retroactive to January 1, 1993, in tax legislation signed by President Clinton on August 19, 1993. This retroactive tax increase was unpopular with high-income taxpayers.

certainly seems to be a fair provision for taxpayers. However, for taxpayers who do not own a home but live in a rental apartment, the deductibility of mortgage interest may not be considered as fair because the renter cannot deduct any portion of the rent paid. In other types of situations, the federal tax law includes various measures to ensure that taxpayers are treated fairly. For example, a foreign tax credit is available to minimize the double taxation that would otherwise occur when U.S. taxpayers earn income in a foreign country that is taxed by both the United States and the country in which it is earned. (See the glossary at the end of this volume for a definition of tax credits and Chapter I14 for a discussion of the foreign tax credit.) Two aspects of equity are commonly discussed in the tax policy literature, **horizontal equity** and **vertical equity**. Horizontal equity refers to the notion that similarly situated taxpayers should be treated equally. Thus, two taxpayers who each have income of $50,000 should both pay the same amount of tax. Vertical equity, on the other hand, implies that taxpayers who are not similarly situated should be treated differently. Thus, if Taxpayer A has income of $50,000 and Taxpayer B has income of $20,000, Taxpayers A and B should not pay the same amount of income tax. Vertical equity provides that the incidence of taxation should be borne by those who have the **ability to pay** the tax, based on income or wealth. The progressive rate structure is founded on the vertical equity premise.

CERTAINTY

A certain tax (1) ensures a stable source of government operating revenues and (2) provides taxpayers with some degree of certainty concerning the amount of their annual tax liability. A tax that is simple to understand and administer provides certainty for taxpayers. For many years, our income tax laws have been criticized as being overly complex and difficult to administer. Consider the remarks of a noted tax authority at a conference on federal income tax simplification:

Tax advisers—at least some tax advisers—are saying that the income tax system is not working. They are saying that they don't know what the law provides, that the IRS does not know what the law provides, that taxpayers are not abiding by the law they don't know.[22]

While the above statement is over 20 years old, it is certainly still viable today. This uncertainty in the tax law causes frequent disputes between taxpayers and the IRS and has resulted in extensive litigation.

The federal tax system has made some attempts to provide certainty for taxpayers. For example, the IRS issues advance rulings to taxpayers, which provides some assurance concerning the tax consequences of a proposed transaction for the taxpayer who requests the ruling. The taxpayer may rely on the ruling if the transaction is completed in accordance with the terms of the ruling request. For example, if a merger of two corporations is being considered, the transaction can be structured so that the shareholders and the corporations do not recognize gain or loss. If a favorable ruling is received and the transaction is completed as planned, the IRS cannot later assert that the merger does not qualify for tax-free treatment.

CONVENIENCE

A tax law should be easily assessed, collected, and administered. Taxpayers should not be overly burdened with the maintenance of records and compliance considerations (preparation of their tax returns, payment of their taxes, and so on). One of the reasons that the sales tax is such a popular form of tax for state and local governments is that it is convenient for taxpayers to pay and for the government to collect. The consumer need not complete a tax return or keep detailed records.

ECONOMY

An economical tax structure should require only minimal compliance and administrative costs. The IRS collection costs, amounting to less than 0.5% of revenues, are minimal relative to the total collections of revenues from the federal income tax. Estimates of taxpayer compliance costs are less certain. One indicator of total compliance costs for taxpayers is the demand for tax professionals. Tax practice has been and continues to be one of the fastest growing areas in public accounting firms. Most large corporations also maintain sizable tax departments that engage in tax research, compliance, and planning activities. In addition, many commercial tax return preparer services are available to assist taxpayers who have relatively uncomplicated tax returns.

Complying with the tax laws is enormously expensive for both businesses and individuals in the United States. In 2002, businesses spent an estimated $102.5 billion to comply with the federal tax laws, while it cost individuals about $86.1 billion.[23] Compliance with state and local taxes costs another $80 billion. Clearly, the cost of complying with the nation's tax laws is significant, in terms of both money and time.

A more difficult question is whether the tax structure is economical in terms of taxpayer compliance. The issues of tax avoidance and tax evasion are becoming increasingly more important. The General Accounting Office (GAO) reported that two-thirds of tax returns are out of compliance, resulting in net income being underreported by 25 percent.[24]

SIMPLICITY

One of the important measures of any tax system is that of simplicity, or at least, not undue complexity. Taxpayers should be able to understand and comply with any tax system within reasonable boundaries. The sales tax is an example of a tax system that is relatively simple, although the sales tax as it applies to businesses can become fairly complex. The federal income tax system in the United States has become inordinately complex over the years and complexity is one of the major criticisms of the income tax. The following is a quote from the report from the President's Advisory Panel on Federal Tax Reform:[25]

---

[22] Sidney L. Roberts, "The Viewpoint of the Tax Adviser: An Overview of Simplification," *Tax Adviser*, January 1979, p. 32.
[23] Scott Moody, "The Cost of Tax Compliance," *Tax Foundation*, February, 2002, p. 1.
[24] News Report. "Compliance Said to Be Poor Among Sole Proprietorships," *Tax Notes*, December 12, 1994, p. 1328.

[25] Report of the President's Advisory Panel on Federal Tax Reform, *Simple, Fair, & Pro-Growth: Proposals to Fix America's Tax System*, November 2005, p. 2. See the discussion of tax reform in this chapter.

In short, our current tax code is a complicated mess. Instead of clarity, we have opacity. Instead of simplicity, we have complexity. Instead of fair principles, we have seemingly arbitrary rules. Instead of contributing to economic growth, it detracts from growth. Time and time again, witnesses told the Panel about these failings in the tax code.

While simplicity is an admirable goal of any tax system, achieving this goal in the federal income tax system is difficult and involves the trade-off of other important objectives. For example, simplicity and fairness are almost impossible to achieve together. If the income tax law is extremely simple, like a flat tax rate on all income, the possible result is that many taxpayers will not be treated fairly. Consider this case, two taxpayers, A and B both earn $100,000 per year and we have a flat rate tax of 20% so that each taxpayer will pay $20,000 in income taxes for the year. However, assume that taxpayer B has a severe illness that requires him to pay medical expenses of $60,000 per year. Should both A and B both pay the same income tax for the year? There is no absolute correct answer in this case, it depends on your definition of fairness. Thus, making the income tax law simple may not be the top priority in tax reform.

OBJECTIVES OF THE FEDERAL INCOME TAX LAW

The primary objective of the federal income tax law is to raise revenues for government operations. In recent years, the federal government has broadened its use of the tax laws to accomplish various economic and social policy objectives.

ECONOMIC OBJECTIVES

ADDITIONAL COMMENT

Among the provisions in the tax law that are designed to enhance the level of health care are the deductibility of medical expenses, deductibility of charitable contributions to hospitals, and exclusion of fringe benefits provided by employers for medical insurance premiums and medical care.

The federal income tax law is used as a fiscal policy tool to stimulate private investment, reduce unemployment, and mitigate the effects of inflation on the economy. Consider the following example: Tax credits for businesses operating in distressed urban and rural areas (empowerment zones) are allowed to provide economic revitalization of such areas. This is a clear example of using the federal income tax law to stimulate private investment in specific areas.

Many items in the tax law are adjusted for inflation by using the consumer price index, including the tax brackets, personal and dependency exemptions, and standard deduction amounts. These inflation adjustments provide relief for individual taxpayers who would otherwise be subject to increased taxes due to the effects of inflation. (See Chapter I2 for a discussion of the tax computation for individuals.)

ENCOURAGEMENT OF CERTAIN ACTIVITIES AND INDUSTRIES

The federal income tax law also attempts to stimulate and encourage certain activities, specialized industries, and small businesses. One such example is the encouragement of research activities by permitting an immediate write-off of expenses and a special tax credit for increasing research and experimental costs. Special incentives are also provided to the oil and gas industry through percentage depletion allowances and an election to deduct intangible drilling costs.

Certain favorable tax provisions are provided for small businesses, including reduced corporate tax rates of 15% on the first $50,000 of taxable income and 25% for the next $25,000 of taxable income. Favorable ordinary loss (instead of capital loss) deductions are granted to individual investors who sell their small business corporation stock at a loss, provided that certain requirements are met.[26] In addition, noncorporate investors may exclude up to 50% of the gain realized from the disposition of qualified small business stock issued after August 10, 1993, if the stock is held for more than five years.[27]

---

[26] Sec. 1244.

[27] Sec. 1202.

ADDITIONAL COMMENT

Deductible contributions made by self-employed individuals to their retirement plans (Keogh plans) totaled $17.8 billion in 2003. Charitable deductions totaled over $145 billion that same year.

SOCIAL OBJECTIVES

The tax law attempts to encourage or discourage certain socially desirable or undersirable activities. For example:

▶ Special tax-favored pension and profit-sharing plans have been created for employees and self-employed individuals to supplement the social security retirement system.

▶ Charitable contributions are deductible to encourage individuals to contribute to charitable organizations.

▶ The claiming of a deduction for illegal bribes, fines, and penalties has been prohibited to discourage activities that are contrary to public policy.

EXAMPLE I1-10 ▶ Able Corporation establishes a qualified pension plan for its employees whereby it makes all of the annual contributions to the plan. Able's contributions to the pension trust are currently deductible and not includible in the employees' gross income until the pension payments are distributed during their retirement years. Earnings on the contributed funds also are nontaxable until such amounts are distributed to the employees. ◀

EXAMPLE I1-11 ▶ Anita contributes $10,000 annually to her church, which is a qualified charitable organization. Anita's marginal tax rate is 25%. Her after-tax cost of contributing to the church is only $7,500 [$10,000 − (0.25 × $10,000)]. ◀

EXAMPLE I1-12 ▶ Ace Trucking Company incurs $10,000 in fines imposed by local and state governments for overloading its trucks during the current tax year. The fines are not deductible because the activity is contrary to public policy. ◀

The tax law objectives previously discussed are highlighted in Topic Review I1 2.

INCOME TAX REFORM PROPOSALS

Tax reform has been a much debated topic over the years but has taken center stage recently. There has been a flurry of books, articles, and newspaper editorials that range from installing a completely new tax system to a partial revision of the current income tax. Few people support keeping the income tax system as it currently stands. Some proponents of a new tax system advocate substituting a retail sales tax at the federal level for the income tax, others favor a value-added tax system (VAT tax) that is widely used in Europe. A partial revision of what we have now is also a popular option.

In early 2005, President George W. Bush appointed an advisory panel to completely study the current tax system and recommend options to the current tax system. The

Topic Review I1-2

Objectives of the Tax Law

OBJECTIVE	EXAMPLE
Stimulate investment	Provide a tax credit for the purchase of business equipment
Prevent taxpayers from paying a higher percentage of their income in personal income taxes due to inflation (bracket creep)	Index the tax rates, standard deduction, and personal and dependency exemptions for inflation
Encourage research activities that will in turn strengthen the competitiveness of U.S. companies	Allow research expenditures to be written off in the year incurred and offer a tax credit for increasing research and experimental costs
Encourage venture capital for small businesses	Reduce corporate income tax rates on the first $75,000 of taxable income. Allow businesses to immediately expense $108,000 (2006) of certain depreciable business assets acquired each year.
Encourage social objectives	Provide a tax deduction for charitable contributions; provide favorable tax treatment for contributions to qualified pension plans

President allowed the panel great latitude in making recommendations except that the new system must raise the same amount of tax revenues as the current tax system. In November, 2005, the Panel issued its report entitled *Simple, Fair, & Pro-Growth: Proposals to Fix America's Tax System.*[28] Below is a brief summary of the report:

▶ The Panel proposed two options, (1) The Simplified Income Tax Plan (SITP), and (2) The Growth and Investment Tax Plan (GITP). The SITP uses the current income tax system as a starting point for reform whereas the GITP would shift the current system toward a consumption tax.

▶ The SITP widens the tax base by eliminating most deductions that are currently in place, moderately reduces tax rates to four brackets of 15%, 25%, 30%, and 33%, replaces the personal exemptions and standard deduction with a new Family Credit, changes the mortgage interest deduction to a 15% credit, and allows charitable contributions that are in excess of 1% of income. A major thrust of the proposal is to simplify and streamline the computation and filing of annual income tax returns. Finally, the alternative minimum tax (AMT) is repealed.

▶ The SITP increases incentives to save and invest. Several new tax-favored savings plans are proposed, 100% of dividends from U.S. corporations are excluded from taxation, and 75% of capital gains from U.S. corporation stock are excluded.

▶ The SITP dramatically changes the taxation of U.S. taxpayers operating outside the United States. The proposal would move to a territorial system which essentially means that U.S. businesses are not taxed on earnings earned outside the country.

▶ The GITP would be very similar to the SITP for individual taxpayers except that there would only be three rate brackets of 15%, 25%, and 30%. And dividends and capital gains would continue to be taxed at 15% as under current law.

▶ The principal differences between the GITP and the SITP are related to business. Principally, businesses would be permitted to expense all business investments, such as machinery and equipment, but not land and buildings. Large businesses would not be taxed on interest income but would also not be allowed to deduct interest expense. Small businesses would be permitted to use a simplified method of accounting, very similar to a cash-basis of accounting.

At present, it is unclear as to the impact of the Panel's recommendations. While the recommendations are well thought-out, there are other pressing matters facing Congress that may postpone implementation of tax reform in a comprehensive manner. Piecemeal changes to the tax code certainly may continue and this only ensures continued complexity in the tax law.

ENTITIES IN THE FEDERAL INCOME TAX SYSTEM

OBJECTIVE 5

Describe the tax entities in the federal income tax system

The federal income tax law levies taxes on taxpayers. However, not all entities that file income tax returns pay income taxes. For example, a partnership is required to file a tax return but does not pay any income tax because the income (or loss) of the partnership is allocated to the partners who report the income or loss on their individual tax returns. Therefore, the various entities in the federal income tax system may be classified into two general categories, *taxpaying entities* and *flow-through entities.*[29] Taxpaying entities generally are required to pay income taxes on their taxable income. Flow-through entities, on the other hand, generally do not directly pay income taxes but merely pass the income on to a taxpaying entity. The major entities in each category are as follows:

---

[28] Supra, note 25.
[29] Some entities have characteristics of both categories of entities, including certain types of trusts and S corporations.

Taxpaying Entities	*Flow-through Entities*
Individuals	Sole proprietorship
C corporations (regular corporations)	Partnerships
	S corporations
	Limited Liability Company (LLC) or
	Limited Liability Partnership (LLP)
	Trusts

Each of these entities is discussed below. The purpose of this section is to provide an over-all picture of the various entities in the federal income tax system.

TAXPAYING ENTITIES

INDIVIDUALS. Individual taxpayers are the principal taxpaying entities in the federal income tax system. In 2005, income taxes paid by individual taxpayers comprised nearly 43% of total federal revenues. If Social Security taxes are included, individual taxpayers paid 80% of total federal revenues (see Table I1-1 for details). Thus, the study of taxation of indi-viduals is a very important topic and is discussed extensively in this *Principles* textbook.

Individuals pay income taxes on all gross income minus allowable deductions. Gross income minus allowable deductions is referred to as *taxable income*. Gross income subject to taxation may be broadly classified into three categories:

▶ Earned income from sources such as salaries and wages, business income, and retire-ment income.

▶ Investment income, including interest income, dividends, capital gains, and rents and royalties.

▶ Flow-through income from partnerships, limited liability companies (LLCs), Subchapter S corporations, estates, and trusts.

Allowable deductions include expenses attributable to the gross income above and certain personal deductions and exemptions specifically allowed under the tax law. Gross income and allowable deductions and exemptions are discussed in detail later in this textbook.

Individual taxpayers use the tax formula below to compute their taxable income:

Total income, from whatever source derived		$xxx
Minus:	Exclusions, as provided in the tax law	(xxx)
Gross income		xxx
Minus:	Deductions for adjusted gross income	(xxx)
Adjusted gross income (AGI)		xxx
Minus:	Deductions from AGI:	
	Greater of itemized deductions or standard deduction	(xxx)
	Personal and dependency exemptions	(xxx)
Taxable income		$xxx

Exclusions are items of income that the tax law specifically exempts from taxation. They include such items as gifts, inheritances, interest income from state and local bonds, loans, and life insurance proceeds. Exclusions are discussed in Chapter I4.

Once an individual determines that an expenditure is allowed as a deduction for tax purposes, he or she must classify the deduction as *for* AGI or *from* AGI. This classifica-tion is very important and is discussed in Chapter I6. Deductions *for* AGI basically are (1) expenses connected with a taxpayer's business or rental property, or (2) other specified deductions, such as moving expenses, contributions to an Individual Retirement Account (IRA), alimony, and a number of other specific items. Deductions *from* AGI are either itemized deductions or the standard deduction, whichever is greater, and personal and dependency exemptions. Itemized deductions primarily are personal-type deductions of the taxpayer, such as medical expenses, state and local taxes, mortgage interest, and char-itable contributions. Itemized deductions are discussed in Chapter I7. The standard deduction is a set amount that all taxpayers may deduct. For 2006, the standard deduc-tion is $5,150 ($10,300 for married couples filing a joint return) and is indexed annually for inflation. Thus, if a single taxpayer's itemized deductions for 2006 were $4,000, the taxpayer would deduct the standard deduction of $5,150 instead. On the other hand, if the taxpayer's itemized deductions were $6,000, the taxpayer would deduct $6,000 because that amount exceeds the standard deduction.

Personal and dependency exemptions also are specific deductions allowed to individuals. The personal exemption is for the taxpayer and spouse whereas dependency exemptions are for the taxpayer's children or other dependents. The personal and dependency exemption in 2006 is $3,300. So, a husband and wife who have two dependent children would be entitled to a deduction of $13,200 ($3,300 × 4). This exemption amount is phased-out for higher income taxpayers and is indexed annually for inflation. Personal and dependency exemptions are discussed further in Chapter I2.

Once taxable income is determined, tax rates are applied to this amount to arrive at the income tax liability for the year. Certain credits are allowed that reduce the income tax liability on a dollar-for-dollar basis. Individual income tax rates may be found inside the front cover of this textbook. Because individuals are subject to withholding and estimated tax payment rules, they may pay a balance due or receive a refund upon filing their tax return.

EXAMPLE I1-13 ▶ Jeff Payne, a single taxpayer, is employed by a large corporation and has the following information for the current year of 2006:

INCOME AND OTHER RECEIPTS	
Salary from corporation	$120,000
Interest income from savings account	13,000
Interest on New York City bond	600
Loan from bank	20,000
Share of income from a partnership in which Jeff is a partner	8,600
Gift from Jeff's grandmother	11,000
Total	$173,200
DEDUCTIONS, EXEMPTIONS, AND PAYMENTS	
Itemized deductions	17,000
Personal exemption (2006)	3,300
Federal income taxes withheld from salary	30,000

Jeff's taxable income and income tax liability for 2006 would be computed as follows:

Total income		$173,200
Minus: Exclusions:		
Interest on New York City bond	$ 600	
Loan from bank	20,000	
Gift from Jeff's grandmother	$11,000	31,600
Gross income		141,600
Minus: Deductions for AGI		0
Adjusted gross income (AGI)		141,600
Minus: Deductions from AGI:		
Itemized deductions	$17,000	
Personal exemption	3,300	(20,300)
Taxable income		$121,300

The itemized deductions of $17,000 exceed Jeff's allowable standard deduction for 2006 of $5,150 and, therefore, are used to reduce taxable income.

To compute Jeff's income tax liability for the year, the rate schedules inside the front cover of the textbook are used. Jeff's income tax liability (using single taxpayer rates) would be $28,295.50 [$15,107.50 + 0.28($121,300 − $74,200)]. Since Jeff had $30,000 of federal income taxes withheld from his salary, he would be entitled to a tax refund of $1,704.50 ($30,000.00 − $28,295.50). ◀

Individual taxpayers are required to file a tax return annually, Form 1040, which is due on or before April 15 of the year following the taxable year. As can be seen from the tax rate schedules located on the inside cover of this textbook, rates range from 10% to 35%. However, some types of income are taxed at lower rates. For example, dividends from most U.S. corporations are subject to a maximum rate of 15% through 2008. This 15%

rate also applies to long-term capital gains, such as gains on the sale of stocks and bonds. With these lower rates, a high-income taxpayer in the 35% marginal tax bracket would only pay a maximum of 15% on any qualified dividends received or long-term capital gains. The remainder of the taxpayer's income would be subject to the higher rates.

C CORPORATIONS. C corporations, many times referred to as regular corporations, also are taxpaying entities. These corporations, both publicly-held corporations traded on stock exchanges and privately-owned corporations, accounted for approximately 13% of total federal revenues in 2005. The percentage of federal revenues provided by C corporations has been steadily declining over the past 40 years, a concern of tax policymakers as more and more taxes are being shifted to individual taxpayers. A major disadvantage of C corporations is they are subject to so-called double taxation. Double taxation results from the corporation paying income tax on its taxable income and shareholders paying income tax on any dividends received from the corporation or on the gain from selling their stock in the corporation. Thus, the same corporate income is subjected to taxation twice—once at the corporate level and again at the shareholder level. For many years, much tax planning has been directed at trying to so arrange the tax affairs of a C corporation to avoid double taxation. This discussion of C corporations is divided into two parts, (1) taxation of C corporations and (2) the operation of double taxation.

Taxation of C corporations. C corporations are taxed on their taxable income in a manner similar to individuals. The major difference between corporations and individuals is that corporations are not allowed personal exemptions and personal deductions. Thus, the concept of AGI does not pertain to corporations. Taxable income for corporations is computed as follows:

Total income, from whatever source derived	$xxx
Minus: Exclusions, as provided in the tax law	(xxx)
Gross income	xxx
Minus: Deductions (ordinary and necessary expenses related to the corporation's trade or business)	(xxx)
Taxable income	$xxx

This taxable income is subject to tax rates that range from 15% to 35% (see rate schedule in the inside rear cover of the textbook). A more detailed discussion of corporation taxation is contained in Chapter I16 of this *Principles* textbook and Chapter C3 of the *Corporations, Partnerships, Estates, and Trusts* volume.

EXAMPLE I1-14 ▶ During the current taxable year, Crimson Corporation generated gross income of $1,500,000 and had ordinary and necessary deductions of $900,000, resulting in taxable income of $600,000. Based on the corporation rate schedules, Crimson would be subject to taxes of $204,000 [$113,900 + .34($600,000 − 335,000)]. ◀

C corporations are required to file tax returns annually using Form 1120, which is due on or after the 15th day of the third month after the close of the corporation's tax year (e.g., March 15 for calendar year taxpayers).

Double taxation of C corporation earnings. As mentioned previously, C corporations are subject to double taxation. The corporation pays income tax on its taxable income and then shareholders must pay income tax on any dividends paid by the corporation or on the sale of their stock. Recent tax legislation in 2003 substantially reduced the impact of double taxation by reducing to 15% the maximum tax rate on most corporate dividends received by individuals. This 15% rate is further reduced to 5% for lower-income taxpayers in the 10% or 15% tax brackets. Prior to this reduction in tax rates on qualified dividends, dividends were subject to tax at regular tax rates. Thus, under current tax law, a taxpayer in the 35% marginal tax bracket (see tax rate schedules inside the front cover of this textbook) pays only a 15% tax rate on any dividends received. The same reduced tax rates apply to long-term capital gains on the sale of their corporate stock. These tax rates apply through 2008 unless Congress acts to make them permanent.

EXAMPLE I1-15 ▶ Using the same facts for Crimson Corporation in Example I1-14, assume the corporation paid dividends to shareholders during 2006 of $400,000. Further assume that the marginal tax bracket of the shareholders is 28%. The shareholders collectively would have to pay individual income taxes of $60,000 ($400,000 × 15%) as the maximum tax rate on qualified dividends is 15%. The total tax on the corporation's taxable income of $600,000, therefore, would be $264,000 ($204,000 paid by Crimson Corporation plus $60,000 paid by the shareholders), or an effective tax rate of 44% ($264,000/$600,000). The 44% is only federal income taxes and does not include any state or local income taxes that the corporation may have to pay. Under prior law, the shareholders would have had to pay tax on the dividends at a 28% rate, or $112,000 ($400,000 × 28%). ◀

While the reduced rate of tax on qualified dividends is certainly favorable to shareholders, the double taxation of C corporation earnings is still an onerous tax. A common method to avoid this double taxation by C corporations with a small number of shareholders is to payout the corporate earnings in the form of salary and bonuses, thereby making the payout deductible by the corporation and eliminating double taxation. The Internal Revenue Service (IRS), however, may attack this plan by asserting that the salary and bonuses are unreasonably large and, in fact, a disguised dividend.

EXAMPLE I1-16 ▶ Assume in Example I1-14 that Crimson had only one shareholder, Joe Bank, who also is the president of the corporation. The corporation paid the entire $600,000 to Mr. Bank in the form of a bonus rather than as a dividend. The corporation could deduct the $600,000, thereby reducing its taxable income to zero. Mr. Bank would have to include the $600,000 in his personal income and would pay taxes on this amount. If his average tax rate on the $600,000 was 30%, he would owe $180,000 on the $600,000. The $180,000 would represent the total taxes of both the corporation and shareholder and would save $84,000 ($264,000 − $180,000) from the previous example. The IRS may attack this plan by alleging that Mr. Bank's salary and bonus are unreasonably high and recharacterize part of the $600,000 as a dividend. Because dividends are not deductible by the corporation, the corporation would be subject to additional income taxes. At the same time, if the IRS is successful, the portion of the salary and bonus of Mr. Bank that is recharacterized as a dividend would be subject to the maximum 15% tax rate. ◀

FLOW-THROUGH ENTITIES

The simplest form of a flow-through entity is the sole proprietorship as there are no formal requirements to form such an entity. The net income earned by the proprietor is reported on Schedule C of Form 1040. Thus, the income of the sole proprietorship merely flows to the proprietor's individual tax return. The net income of the sole proprietorship is subject to income tax only once (at the individual level) but is also subject to self-employment tax (Social Security and Medicare taxes).

Flow-through entities, such as partnership, limited liability companies (LLCs), limited liability partnerships (LLPs), and S corporations have the major advantage of being subject to only one level of taxation. All of these entities file tax returns, but, in general, the entities do not pay any income taxes. The income earned by the entity is allocated to the owners based on their proportionate ownership or some other allocation arrangement. Thus, the entity income tax return is really just an information return. The income allocated to the owners is then reported on their own tax returns. The income of the entity, therefore, is subject to a single level of taxation. This single level of tax is a major advantage of the flow-through form over C corporations.

To ensure a single level of taxation for flow-through entities, the tax law employs a unique method of basis adjustments. Every owner of the entity has an *adjusted basis* (basis) in his or her ownership interest. An owner's basis in a flow-through entity is determined as follows:

▶ Each owner obtains an original basis in his or her ownership interest upon the formation of the entity (investment in the entity) or purchase of the interest.

▶ The owner's basis increases for any additional capital contributions to the entity in subsequent years.

▶ The owner's basis increases for the owner's share of income reported for tax purposes (or decreases for losses reported by the owner).

▶ The owner's basis increases for the owner's share of entity liabilities. Differences exist between partnerships and S corporations as to which liabilities are added to an owner's basis. Details on this topic are covered in later chapters of this textbook.

▶ The owner's basis decreases for money or property distributed to the owner by the entity.

Without these basis adjustments, the owner could be subject to double taxation upon selling his or her interest or upon dissolution of the entity. Practitioners refer to this basis as "outside basis" as opposed to "inside basis," which is the entity's basis in its assets.

EXAMPLE I1-17 ▶ Wildcat Company is a flow-through entity with two owners, Rich and Teresa. Each owner has a $10,000 original basis in the entity. In its first year of operations, Wildcat Company earns $50,000, which is allocated $25,000 to each owner. Thus, each owner reports $25,000 in his individual income tax return even though the entity does not distribute any of the earnings to the owners. At the beginning of the second year, Rich sells his interest to Steve for $35,000. If Rich did not get an increased basis adjustment for his $25,000 of earnings, he would recognize a $25,000 gain ($35,000 selling price − $10,000 basis in the entity) on the sale of his interest, which taxes him twice on the $25,000. However, both Rich and Teresa do increase their bases to $35,000 ($10,000 original basis + $25,000 share of entity earnings) at the end of the first tax year. Therefore, when Rich sells his interest for $35,000, he incurs no additional taxable gain ($35,000 selling price − $35,000 basis in the entity = $0 gain). ◀

Below is a brief description of the four basic types of flow-through business entities.

PARTNERSHIPS. A partnership is the classic flow-through entity as it has been around the longest. The Internal Revenue Code (IRC) defines a partnership as "a syndicate, group, pool, joint venture, or other incorporated organization" that carries on any business, financial operation, or venture.[30] Thus, if two or more individuals, corporations, trusts, or estates decide to operate a business or financial venture, the business or venture can be classified as a partnership. Unlike a corporation, which must file incorporation documents with the state, partnerships require no legal documentation. However, tax advisors strongly advise partnerships to have written agreements as to the operation of the partnership and how income, deductions, losses, and credits will be allocated to the partners. Most states have laws that govern the rights and restrictions of partnerships and their partners.

Partnerships file an annual income tax return which is just an information return because the partnership entity is not subject to taxation. The return, Form 1065 (U.S. Partnership Return of Income), reports the results of the partnership's operations. An accompanying form, Schedule K-1, reports the separate income, deductions, losses, and credits that flow through to the partners. The partners, in turn, take the information from their Schedule K-1 and report the various items on their individual returns.

EXAMPLE I1-18 ▶ Donald and Minnie form a real estate company and decide to operate as a partnership, the DM Partnership. Donald is a 60% partner and Minnie is a 40% partner. Donald invests $60,000 into DM and Minnie contributes real estate with a basis and fair market value of $40,000. In its first year of operation, DM Partnership earns ordinary income of $150,000. The partnership files Form 1065 and reports the $150,000 but is not subject to any income taxation. Included in the partnership return are two Schedule K-1s that report $90,000 to Donald ($150,000 × 60%) and $60,000 ($150,000 × 40%) to Minnie. Donald reports $90,000 on his individual income tax return, Form 1040, and Minnie reports $60,000 on her individual return. If the partnership distributed $72,000 to Donald and $48,000 to Minnie during the year, the distributions are considered a return of capital and are not taxable to either partner. Donald's adjusted basis in his partnership interest would be $78,000 ($60,000 + $90,000 − $72,000) and Minnie's adjusted basis would be $52,000 ($40,000 + $60,000 − $48,000). ◀

S CORPORATIONS. S corporations are a special form of corporation treated by the tax laws as flow-through entities. They are incorporated under state law just as any other corporation but, if they so elect, are treated as flow-through entities for tax purposes. S corporations are so named because the rules pertaining to this type of entity are located in

---

[30] Sec. 761(a).

Subchapter S of the IRC. S corporations have been referred to as "corporations taxed like a partnership." Although this statement is partially true, important differences exist, such as a limitation on the number of shareholders, strict rules on allocation of income or losses, and several other differences. Similar to partnerships, S corporations art not taxed and income, deductions, losses, and credits flow through to its shareholders. Allocations of income, deductions, losses, and credits to shareholders are based on a per share-per day basis. Importantly, S corporation shareholders enjoy limited liability, as do C corporation shareholders.

To achieve S corporation status, the corporation must file an S election and all of its shareholders must consent to that election. S corporations annually file an information return, Form 1120S (U.S. Income Tax Return for an S Corporation), which reports the results of the corporation's operations and, like partnerships, also submits Schedule K-1 to each shareholder which reports the allocable share of income, deduction, loss, and credit that flow through to each shareholder.

Similar to partnerships, S corporations impose only a single level of taxation to its shareholders and the tax law uses basis adjustments to achieve this single level of taxation. The basis adjustments for S corporation shareholders are nearly identical to those for partnerships. The major difference is how liabilities affect the basis of S corporation shareholders. S corporation shareholders obtain basis only for *direct* loans to the corporation and they treat their debt basis separately from stock basis. Partners of a partnership increase their basis for all partnership liabilities.

EXAMPLE I1-19 ▶ Paul and Peter form a corporation in Ohio as equal shareholders. Upon advice from their tax advisor, they decide to elect S corporation status for federal and state tax purposes and file the necessary forms. Both Paul and Peter invest $25,000 in the corporation and each receives 100 shares of common stock of the corporation. During the first year, the corporation reports net ordinary income of $62,000 and a long-term capital gain of $10,000 of Form 1120S. Each shareholder receives a $20,000 distribution from the corporation during the year. In Year 1, the corporation pays no federal or state income taxes, but both Paul and Peter report $31,000 of ordinary income and $5,000 of long-term capital gain on their individual returns. Since the shareholders have sufficient basis, the $20,000 distribution to each shareholder is not subject to taxation. Paul and Peter would each have a basis in their S corporation stock of $41,000 ($25,000 + $31,000 + $5,000 − $20,000) at the end of Year 1. ◀

EXAMPLE I1-20 ▶ In Year 2, the corporation earns $74,000 of ordinary income and no capital gains. Also, on July 1 of Year 2, Peter sells one-half (50 shares) of his stock to Mary. So, from July 1 to December 31, Paul owns 50% of the corporate stock and Peter and Mary each own 25%. S corporation earnings must be allocated on a per share−per day basis, so the income of $74,000 is allocated to each shareholder as follows:

Paul	$74,000 × 365/365 × 50% = $37,000
Peter	($74,000 × 181/365 × 50%) + ($74,000 × 184/365 × 25%) = $27,674
Mary	$74,000 × 184/365 × 25% = $9,326)

◀

LIMITED LIABILITY COMPANIES. A limited liability company (LLC) is a legal entity under the laws of all 50 states and the District of Columbia and is a very popular organizational form. LLCs combine the best features of a partnership and a corporation by being treated as a partnership while providing the limited liability protection of a corporation. Thus, LLC owners, called members, are subject to a single level of taxation and are not liable for the liabilties of the LLC.

An LLC is formed under state law similar to a corporation. After formed, the LLC elects whether to be taxed either as a partnership or a corporation.[31] Under Treasury Regulations, an LLC with more than one member is treated as a partnership unless the LLC affirmatively elects to be classified as a corporation. In most cases, LLCs will prefer to be classified as a partnership because of the tax advantages of a single level of taxation.

[31] The LLC makes the election pursuant to the "check-the-box" Regulations, Reg. Secs. 301.7701-1 through -4.

If an LLC elects to be treated as a partnership, it files its tax return on Form 1065 (U.S. Partnership Return of Income). The LLC, however, is not legally a partnership; it is just treated as one for federal income tax purposes. A single member LLC is disregarded for tax purposes and the LLC income, deductions, etc. are reported directly on the member's Schedule C of Form 1040 as a sole proprietor. If an LLC elects to be taxed as a corporation under the Treasury Regulations, it would file Form 1120 (U.S. Corporation Income Tax Return). Further, S corporation status can be achieved by electing to be taxed as a corporation and then make an S election. Thus, the LLC would be considered an LLC for state law purposes but an S corporation for income tax purposes.

EXAMPLE I1-21 ▶ Karen and David start a wholesale business and decide to operate the business as an LLC. They first must legally form the organization under state law. After the LLC is legally formed, they must decide how the LLC will be treated for income tax purposes. Because they want a single level of taxation, Karen and David elect to be treated as a partnership. Since being treated as a partnership is the default classification under Treasury Regulations, no forms need to be filed with the IRS. At the end of the first year, the LLC will file a Form 1065 and check the box indicating that the entity is an LLC filing as a partnership. All partner allocations, basis adjustments, and all other tax rules for the LLC are identical with partnership rules. ◀

LIMITED LIABILITY PARTNERSHIPS. All 50 states and the District of Columbia have statutes that allow a business to operate as a limited liability partnership (LLP). Basically, an LLP is similar to an LLC except that a partner of an LLP *is* liable for any liability arising from his or her own acts of negligence or misconduct or similar acts of any person under his or her direct supervision. The partner, however, is not liable for liabilities arising from acts of negligence or negligence of other partners or employees in the LLP. Thus, an LLP is much more desirable than a general partnership where partners are liable for all partnership liabilities. Professional service organizations, such as many CPA firms, have adopted the LLP form, primarily to limit legal liability.

EXAMPLE I1-22 ▶ The accounting firm of Gartman & Kuhn, CPAs, is operating as a general partnership and has 20 partners in the firm. The firm is concerned about the unlimited liability that exists for the partnership, especially in today's litigious environment. The firm decides to convert from a partnership to an LLP. The conversion is simple and tax-free,[32] and protects the partners of the new LLP entity against liabilities of the LLP arising from acts of negligence or misconduct of other partners or employees. ◀

OTHER ENTITIES

TRUSTS. Trusts are somewhat of a hybrid entity in that they may either be a taxpaying entity or flow-through entity. Also, there are a number of different types of trusts, so the discussion here is very general in nature. Trusts typically are subject to income taxation on all of its net income that is *not* distributed to the beneficiaries. The portion of net income that is distributed to beneficiaries is taxed to the beneficiaries. One drawback to the use of trusts is that the income tax rates are extremely progressive, reaching the 35% bracket when the taxable income of the trust reaches $9,550 in 2004. Trusts use Form 1041 to file its tax information.

EXAMPLE I1-23 ▶ Ben establishes a trust for the benefit of his daughter. The principal amount of the trust is $500,000 and is projected to earn approximately 10% per year. In the current year, the trust earned $50,000 of investment income and had $5,000 of expenses. If the trust did not make any distributions during the year to the daughter, the entire $45,000 (less a small exemption) would be subject to income taxation to the trust. Much of the taxable income would be subject to taxation at the 35% rate. Alternatively, if the trust distributed the entire $45,000 to the daughter, she would report the $45,000 on her individual tax return. Assuming she does not have significant other income, she would most likely be in the 25% marginal tax bracket. The trust's taxable income would be zero and would have no income tax liability. ◀

---

[32] Rev. Rul. 95-37, 1995-1 C.B. 130.

TAX LAW SOURCES

The solution to any tax question may only be resolved by reference to tax law sources (also referred to as tax law authority). Tax law sources are generated from all three branches of the federal government, i.e., legislative, executive, and judicial. The principal sources of tax law are as follows:

Branch	Tax Law Source
Legislative	Internal Revenue Code
	Congressional Committee Reports
Executive (Administrative)	Income Tax Regulations
	Revenue Rulings
	Revenue Procedures
	Letter Rulings
Judicial	Court Decisions

A thorough knowledge of the various sources above as well as the relative weights attached to each source is vital to tax professionals. Because of the vast volume of tax law sources, the ability to "find the answer" to a tax question is of fundamental importance. In addition, the evaluation of the weight (or importance) of different sources of authority is also crucial in arriving at a proper conclusion. For example, a decision of the U.S. Supreme Court on a tax matter would certainly carry more weight than a Revenue Ruling issued by the Internal Revenue Service.

Clearly, the most authoritative source of tax law is the Internal Revenue Code, which is the tax law passed by Congress. However, Congress is not capable of anticipating every type of transaction that taxpayers might engage in, so most of the statutes in the Code contain very general language. Because of the general language contained in the Code, both administrative and judicial interpretations are necessary to apply the tax law to specific situations and transactions. Thus, the regulations and rulings of the IRS and the decisions of the courts are an integral part of the federal income tax law. For a detailed discussion of tax law sources, see Chapter I15 (Chapter C1 of the *Comprehensive* edition). Topic Review I1-3 provides an overview of the tax law sources.

ENACTMENT OF A TAX LAW

Under the U.S. Constitution, the House of Representatives is responsible for initiating new tax legislation. However, tax bills may also originate in the Senate as riders to nontax legislative proposals. Often, major tax proposals are initiated by the President and accompanied by a Treasury Department study or proposal, and then introduced into Congress by one or more representatives from the President's political party.

STEPS IN THE LEGISLATIVE PROCESS

The specific steps in the legislative process are discussed below and are summarized in Table I1-2. These steps typically include:

1. A tax bill is introduced in the House of Representatives and is referred to the House Ways and Means Committee.
2. The proposal is considered by the House Ways and Means Committee, and public hearings are held. Testimony may be given by members of professional groups such as the American Institute of CPAs and the American Bar Association and from various special-interest groups.
3. The tax bill is voted on by the House Ways and Means Committee and, if approved, is forwarded to the House of Representatives for a vote. Amendments to the bill from individual members of the House of Representatives are generally not allowed.

Topic Review I1-3

Tax Law Sources

SOURCE	KEY POINTS	WEIGHT OF AUTHORITY
LEGISLATIVE		
Internal Revenue Code	Contains provisions governing income, estate and gift, employment, alcohol, tobacco, and excise taxes.	Serves as the highest legislative authority for tax research, planning, and compliance activities.
ADMINISTRATIVE		
Treasury Regulations	Represents interpretations of the tax code by the Secretary of the Treasury. Regulations may be initially issued in proposed, temporary, and final form and are interpretative or legislative.	Legislative regulations have a higher degree of authority than interpretative regulations. Proposed regulations do not have authoritative weight.
IRS Rulings	The IRS issues Revenue Rulings (letter rulings or published rulings), Revenue Procedures, Information Releases, and Technical Advice Memoranda.	These pronouncements reflect the IRS's interpretation of the law and do not have the same level of scope and authority as Treasury Regulations.
JUDICIAL		
Judicial doctrines	Judicial doctrines are concepts that have evolved from Supreme Court cases that are used by the courts to decide tax issues. Examples include substance over form, tax benefit rule, and constructive receipt.	Judicial doctrines that evolve from Supreme Court cases have substantial weight of authority because a finding authority has the force and effect of law.
Judicial interpretations	Tax cases are initially considered by a trial court (i.e., the Tax Court, a Federal district court, or the U.S. Court of Federal Claims). Either the taxpayer or the IRS may appeal to an appeals court. A final appeal is to the U.S. Supreme Court.	A trial court must abide by the precedents set by the court of appeals of the same jurisdiction. An appeals court is not required to follow the decisions of another court of appeals. A Supreme Court decision must be followed by the IRS, taxpayers, and the lower courts.

ADDITIONAL COMMENT

The corridors near Congress's tax-writing rooms are called "Gucci Gulch," so named for the designer clothing worn by many of the lobbyists who congregate there when a tax bill is being considered.

HISTORICAL NOTE

The only practicing CPA ever elected to the U.S. Congress was Joe Dio Guardi. He was elected in 1984 from Westchester County, New York.

4. If passed by the House, the bill is forwarded to the Senate for consideration by the Senate Finance Committee, and public hearings are held.

5. The tax bill approved by the Senate Finance Committee may be substantially different from the House of Representatives' version.

6. The Senate Finance Committee reports the Senate bill to the Senate for consideration. The Senate generally permits amendments (e.g., new provisions) to be offered on the Senate floor.

7. If approved by the Senate, both the Senate and House bills are sent to a Joint Conference Committee consisting of an equal number of members from the Senate and the House of Representatives.

8. The Senate and House bills are reconciled in the Joint Conference Committee. This process of reconciliation generally involves substantial compromise if the provisions of both bills are different. A final bill is then resubmitted to the House and Senate for approval.

9. If the Joint Conference Committee bill is approved by the House and Senate, it is sent to the President for approval or veto.

10. A presidential veto may be overturned if a two-thirds majority vote is obtained in both the House and Senate.

11. Committee reports are prepared by the staffs of the House Ways and Means Committee, the Senate Finance Committee, and the Joint Conference Committee as the bill progresses through Congress. These reports help to explain the new law before the Treasury Department drafts regulations on the tax law changes as well as to explain the intent of Congress for passing the new law.

▼ **TABLE I1-2**
Steps in the Legislative Process

1. Treasury studies prepared on needed tax reform
2. President makes proposals to Congress
3. House Ways and Means Committee prepares House bill
4. Approval of House bill by the House of Representatives
5. Senate Finance Committee prepares Senate bill
6. Approval of Senate bill by the Senate
7. Compromise bill approved by a Joint Conference Committee
8. Approval of Joint Conference Committee bill by both the House and Senate
9. Approval or veto of legislation by the President
10. New tax law and amendments incorporated into the Code

ADMINISTRATION OF THE TAX LAW AND TAX PRACTICE ISSUES

OBJECTIVE 8

Describe the administrative procedures under the tax law

ORGANIZATION OF THE INTERNAL REVENUE SERVICE

The IRS is the branch of the Treasury Department that is responsible for administering the federal tax law. It is organized on a national, regional, district, and service center basis. The responsibilities and functions of the various administrative branches include the following:

▶ The Commissioner of Internal Revenue, appointed by the President, is the chief officer of the IRS. This individual is supported by the Chief Counsel's office, which is responsible for preparing the government's case for litigation of tax disputes.

▶ The National Office includes a deputy commissioner, a series of assistants to the commissioner, a chief inspector, and a chief counsel. A significant responsibility of the National Office is to process ruling requests and to prepare revenue procedures that assist taxpayers with compliance matters.

▶ Four divisions, organized functionally, including (1) Wage and Investment Income, (2) Small Business and Self-Employed, (3) Large and Mid-size Business, and (4) Tax Exempt.

ADDITIONAL COMMENT

A survey of members of the American Institute of CPAs found that more than half of the 1,036 members who responded had an unfavorable opinion of the IRS. However, the accountants gave the IRS good marks for courtesy and a willingness to solve problems.

▶ District directors supervise the performance of IRS audits and collection of delinquent taxes in 33 districts.

▶ Ten service centers perform tax return processing work. They also select tax returns for audit.

▶ For the 2004 fiscal year, the IRS had approximately 99,000 employees and a budget of $10.185 billion.

In 1998, the IRS Restructuring and Reform Act of 1998 (Act) was enacted with a major objective of reforming the manner in which the IRS administers the tax system. The taxpaying public has been increasingly crititcal of the IRS, especially in the allegedly insensitive and strong-arm tactics used against taxpayers. Therefore, the Act places a greater emphasis on serving the public and meeting taxpayer needs. While the Act mandates substantial organizational and operational changes to the IRS, only time will tell if this legislation will be successful. Details of the Act are outside the scope of this textbook.

ENFORCEMENT PROCEDURES

All tax returns are initially checked for mathematical accuracy and items that are clearly erroneous. The Form W-2 amounts (e.g., wages, and so on), Form 1099 information return amounts (e.g., relating to dividend and interest payments, and so on) and other forms filed with the IRS are checked against the amounts reported on the tax return. If differences are noted, the IRS Center merely sends the taxpayer a bill for the corrected amount of tax and a statement of the differences. In some instances, the difference is due to a classification error by the IRS, and the additional assessment can be resolved by written correspondence. A refund check may be sent to the taxpayer if an overpayment of tax has been made.

Bart is an author of books and properly reports royalties on Schedule C (Profit or Loss from Business). The IRS computer matching of the Form 1099 information returns from the publishing companies incorrectly assumes that the royalties should be reported on Schedule E (Supplemental Income and Loss). If the IRS sends the taxpayer a statement of the difference and an adjusted tax bill, this matter (including the abatement of added tax, interest, and penalties) should be resolved by correspondence with the IRS. ◀

SELECTION OF RETURNS FOR AUDIT

The U.S. tax system is based on self-assessment and voluntary compliance. However, enforcement by the IRS is essential to maintain the integrity of the tax system. The IRS uses both computers and experienced personnel to select returns for examination. With respect to the use of the computer, a **Discriminant Function System (DIF)** is used to classify returns to be selected for audit. The DIF system generates a "score" for a return based on the potential for the return to generate additional tax revenue. After returns are scored under the DIF system, the returns are manually screened by experienced IRS personnel who decide which returns warrant further examination. In the aggregate, less than 1% of all individual returns are selected for examination each year. Some examples of situations where individuals are more likely to be audited include the following:

▶ Investments and trade or business expenses that produce significant tax losses

▶ Itemized deductions exceeding an average amount for the person's income level

▶ Filing of a refund claim by a taxpayer who has been previously audited, where substantial tax deficiencies have been assessed

▶ Individuals who are self-employed with substantial business income or income from a profession (e.g., a medical doctor)

AUDIT PROCEDURES.   Audits of most individuals are handled through an **office audit procedure** in an office of the IRS. In most cases, an individual is asked to substantiate a particular deduction, credit, or income item (e.g., charitable contributions that appear to be excessive). The office audit procedure does not involve a complete audit of all items on the return.

Brad obtains a divorce during the current year and reports a $30,000 deduction for alimony. The IRS may conduct an office audit to ascertain whether the amount is properly deductible as alimony and does not represent a disguised property settlement to Brad's ex-wife. Brad may be asked to submit verification (e.g., a property settlement agreement between the spouses that designates the payments as alimony). ◀

A **field audit procedure** often is used for corporations and individuals engaged in a trade or business. A field audit generally is broader in scope than the office audit (e.g., several items on the tax return may be reviewed). A field audit usually is conducted at the taxpayer's place of business or the office of his or her tax advisor.

Most large corporations are subject to annual audits. The year under audit may be several years prior to the current year because the corporation often will waive the statute of limitations pending the resolution of disputed issues.

STATUTE OF LIMITATIONS

Most taxpayers feel a sense of relief after they have prepared their income tax return and have mailed it to the IRS. However, the filing of the tax return is not necessarily the end of the story for that particular taxable year. It is possible, of course, that the IRS may select their tax return for audit after the return has been initially processed or a taxpayer may have filed an amended return to correct an error or omission.

Both the IRS and taxpayers can make corrections to a return after it has been originally filed. Fortunately, both only have a limited time period in which to make such corrections. This time period is called the **statute of limitations** and prevents either the taxpayer or the IRS from changing a filed tax return after the time period has expired. The general rule for the statute of limitations is three years from the later of the date the tax return was actually filed or its due date.[33] However, a six-year statute of limitations applies if the taxpayer omits items of gross income that in total exceed 25% of the gross income reported on the return.[34] The statute of limitations remains open indefinitely if a fraudulent return is filed or if no return is filed.[35]

EXAMPLE I1-26 ▶

Betty, a calendar-year taxpayer, is audited by the IRS in February 2006 for the tax year 2003. During the course of the audit, the IRS proposes additional tax for 2003, because Betty failed to substantiate certain travel and entertainment expense deductions. During the course of the audit, the IRS discovers that Betty failed to file a tax return for 2001, and in 2002 an item of gross income amounting to $26,000 was not reported. Gross income reported on the 2002 return was $72,000. Assuming Betty's 2003 return was filed on or before its due date (April 15, 2004), the IRS may assess a deficiency for 2003 because the three-year statute of limitations will not expire until April 15, 2007. A deficiency also may be assessed for the 2002 return because a six-year statute of limitations applies since the omission is more than 25% of the gross income reported on the return. A deficiency also may be assessed for 2001 as there is no statute of limitations for fraud. ◀

INTEREST

ADDITIONAL COMMENT

More than 150 penalties can be imposed on taxpayers. In fact, applying the penalties has become so complicated that the IRS is currently considering ways to consolidate and simplify them.

Interest accrues on both assessments of additional tax due and on refunds that the taxpayer receives from the government.[36] No interest is paid on a tax refund if the amount is refunded by the IRS within 45 days of the day prescribed for filing the return (e.g., April 15) determined without regard to extensions.[37] If a return is filed after the filing date, no interest is paid if the refund is made within 45 days of the date the return was filed.

EXAMPLE I1-27 ▶

Beverly, a calendar-year taxpayer, files her 2005 tax return on February 1, 2006, and requests a $500 refund. No interest accrues on the refund amount if the IRS sends the refund check to Beverly within 45 days of the April 15, 2006, due date. ◀

ADDITIONAL COMMENT

In addition to the penalties listed on this page, the government also assesses penalties for civil fraud and criminal fraud. Criminal fraud carries a maximum penalty of $100,000, a prison sentence of up to five years, or both.

PENALTIES

Various nondeductible penalties are imposed on the net tax due for failure to comply, including

▶ A penalty of 5% per month (or fraction thereof) subject to a maximum of 25% for failure to file a tax return[38]

▶ A penalty of 0.5% per month (or fraction thereof) up to a maximum of 25% for failure to pay the tax that is due[39]

▶ An accuracy-related penalty of 20% of the underpayment for items such as negligence or disregard of rules or regulations, any substantial understatement of income tax, or any substantial misstatement of valuation[40]

▶ A 75% penalty for fraud[41]

▶ A penalty based on the current interest rate for underpayment of estimated taxes[42]

---

[33] Secs. 6501(a) and (b)(1). Similar rules apply to claims for a refund filed by the taxpayer. Section 6511(a) requires that a refund claim be filed within three years of the date the return was filed or within two years of the date the tax was paid, whichever is later.

[34] Sec. 6501(e). See also *Stephen G. Colestock*, 102 T.C. 380 (1994), where the Tax Court ruled that the extended six-year limitation period applied to a married couple's entire tax liability for the tax year at issue, not just to items that constituted substantial omissions of gross income. Thus, the IRS was able to assert an increased deficiency and additional penalties attributable to a disallowed depreciation deduction.

[35] Sec. 6501(c).

[36] Sec. 6621(a). The rate is adjusted four times a year by the Treasury Department based on the current interest rate for short-term federal obligations. The interest rate individual taxpayers must pay to the IRS on underpayments of tax is the federal short-term rate plus three percentage points. The interest rate paid to taxpayers on overpayments of tax is the federal short-term rate plus two percentage points. The annual interest rate on non-

corporate underpayments and overpayments for the period October 1, 2005, through December 31, 2005, was 7%.

[37] Sec. 6611(e).

[38] Sec. 6651(a)(1). The penalty assessed may be very small in some instances even though the taxpayer owes a large tax bill for the year because penalties are imposed on the net tax due. The percentages are increased to 15% per month (or fraction thereof) up to a maximum of 75% if the penalty is for fraudulent failure to file under Sec. 6651(f).

[39] Sec. 6651(a)(2). If the failure to file penalty (5%) and the failure to pay the tax penalty (0.5%) are both applicable, the failure to file penalty is reduced by the failure to pay penalty per Sec. 6651(c)(1). Further, the penalty is increased to 1% per month after the IRS notifies the taxpayer that it will levy on the taxpayer's assets.

[40] Sec. 6662.

[41] Sec. 6663.

[42] Sec. 6654.

ADMINISTRATIVE APPEAL PROCEDURES

If an IRS agent issues a deficiency assessment, the taxpayer may make an appeal to the IRS Appeals Division. Some disputes involve a gray area (e.g., a situation where some courts have held for the IRS whereas other courts have held for the taxpayer on facts that are similar to the disputed issue). In such a case, the taxpayer may be able to negotiate a compromise settlement (e.g., a percentage of the disputed tax amount plus interest and penalties) with the Appeals Division based on the "hazards of litigation" (i.e., the probability of winning or losing the case if it is litigated).

COMPONENTS OF A TAX PRACTICE

OBJECTIVE 9

Describe the components of a tax practice and understand the importance of computer applications in taxation

Tax practice is a rapidly growing field that provides substantial opportunities for tax specialists in public accounting, law, and industry. The tasks performed by a tax professional may range from the preparation of a simple Form 1040 for an individual to the conduct of tax research and planning for highly complex business situations. Tax practice consists of the following activities:

▶ Tax compliance and procedure (i.e., tax return preparation and representation of a client in administrative proceedings before the IRS)

▶ Tax research

▶ Tax planning and consulting

▶ Financial planning

TAX COMPLIANCE AND PROCEDURE

Preparation of tax returns is a significant component of tax practice. Tax practitioners often prepare federal, state, and local tax returns for individuals, corporations, estates, trusts, and so on. In larger corporations, the tax return preparation (i.e., compliance) function usually is performed by a company's internal tax department staff. In such a case, a CPA or other tax practitioner may assist the client with the tax research and planning aspects of their tax practice, and may even review their return before it is filed.

An important part of tax practice consists of assisting the client in negotiations with the IRS. If a client is audited, the practitioner acts as the client's representative in discussions with the IRS agent. If a tax deficiency is assessed, the practitioner assists the client if an administrative appeal is contemplated with the IRS's Appellate Division. In most instances, an attorney is retained if litigation is being considered.

TAX RESEARCH

Tax research is the search for the best possible defensibly correct solution to a problem involving either a completed transaction (e.g., a sale of property) or a proposed transaction (e.g., a proposed merger of two corporations). Research involves each of the following steps:

▶ Determine the facts.

▶ Identify the issue(s).

▶ Identify and analyze the tax law sources (i.e., code provisions, Treasury Regulations, administrative rulings, and court cases).

▶ Evaluate nontax (e.g., business) implications.

▶ Solve the problem.

▶ Communicate the findings to the client.

Tax research may be conducted in connection with tax return preparation, tax planning, or procedural activities. A more thorough discussion of tax research is presented in Chapter I15.

TAX PLANNING AND CONSULTING

Tax planning involves the process of structuring one's affairs so as to minimize the amount of taxes *and* maximize the after-tax return. Thus, optimal tax planning is *not* to just pay the least amount of tax but to maximize after-tax cash flows. A text on tax research and planning has delineated the following tax planning principles:[43]

► Keep sufficient records.

► Forecast the effect of future events.

► Support the plan with a sound business purpose.

► Base the plan on sound legal authorities.

► Do not carry a good plan too far.

► Make the plan flexible.

► Integrate the tax plan with other factors in decision making.

► Conduct research to learn whether a similar plan has previously proved unsuccessful (e.g., a court case involving similar facts may have upheld the IRS's position).

► Consider the "maximum" risk exposure of the client (e.g., if the plan is subsequently challenged by the IRS and the tax treatment is disallowed, what is the economic impact upon the taxpayer?).

► Consider the effect of timing (e.g., whether it is more beneficial to take a deduction in one year versus another).

► Shape the plan to the client's needs and desires.

ADDITIONAL COMMENT

Several national accounting firms have divided their tax departments into two basic groups, consulting and compliance. The tax consultants work with clients in tax planning and consulting matters and do not prepare tax returns. Tax returns are prepared by the compliance staff.

CPAs and attorneys frequently are engaged by their clients to perform consulting services to optimize the client's tax situation. For example, a major corporation client is considering the acquisition of a major international corporation and wants to make sure that the tax implications of such an acquisition are properly managed. The CPA will be engaged to perform a thorough review of the transaction to ensure that the client is fully aware of the tax results of the acquisition, and possibly may request an advance ruling from the IRS.

Because of the importance of planning in tax practice, subsequent chapters in this text include a separate section on tax planning to discuss issues that are related to the topical coverage. These tax planning principles should be kept in mind when attempting to use the tax planning recommendations. Also, a systematic approach to tax planning developed by two noted tax academicians, Myron Scholes and Mark Wolfson, is discussed in Chapter I18.

FINANCIAL PLANNING

A relatively new field for tax professionals is that of financial planning for individual clients. Since taxes are an integral part of any financial plan and since a tax specialist regularly meets with his or her clients (filing returns and other tax matters), the area of financial planning has become increasingly a part of tax practice. The typical steps in performing a financial planning engagement include the following steps:

► Determine the client's financial goals and objectives.

► Review the client's insurance coverage for adequacy and appropriateness.

► Recommend an investment strategy, including risk analysis and asset allocation.

► Review tax returns to ensure that, through proper tax planning, the client is maximizing his or her after-tax cash flow.

► Review the client's retirement plans to assure compliance with the law and possible new alternatives.

► Review all documents related to estate and gift planning and work with the client's attorney to minimize all transfer taxes and fulfill the client's objectives.

---

[43] Fred W. Norwood et al., *Federal Taxation: Research, Planning, and Procedures*, 2nd ed. (Englewood Cliffs, NJ: Prentice Hall, 1979), pp. 215–216.

COMPUTER APPLICATIONS IN TAX PRACTICE

TAX RETURN PREPARATION

To prepare tax returns, most tax practitioners purchase tax preparation software from companies such as Commerce Clearing House or Intuit. This software allows the preparation of accurate and professional-looking tax returns. A word of caution, however, is in order. As with any computer software, the preparation of tax returns using the computer requires as much knowledge and expertise from the preparer as doing the returns by hand. A recent trend in tax return preparation is the **electronic filing** of tax returns, i.e., a "paperless" tax return. Taxpayers send their returns electronically to the IRS for processing, thereby saving enormous amounts of paper and, perhaps, reducing human error. Computerized tax return software, *Tax Cut*, is available for use with this textbook.

TAX PLANNING APPLICATIONS

Performing tax planning for clients involves the evaluation of alternative courses of action. This evaluation process can be very time-consuming because of the tax calculations necessary to arrive at an optimal solution. The computer has become an essential tool in this process because of the speed with which the tax calculations can be made. Many tax professionals now use sophisticated software to perform tax planning for their clients. A prime example of the use of the computer in tax planning has been in deciding whether a taxpayer should invest in a Roth Individual Retirement Account (Roth IRA) or a regular IRA (see Chapter I9 for more details on IRAs). There are many factors to consider, including current and projected tax rates, current and projected level of income, etc. With the computer, a tax professional can vary the assumptions and create a number of alternatives within a relatively short period of time. To perform this task by hand would require an enormous commitment of time. As with most aspects of life, the impact of the computer on tax planning has been highly significant and will only increase in the future.

TAX RESEARCH APPLICATIONS

Computerized information-retrieval systems are used in tax research and are rapidly replacing books as the principal source of tax-related information. Most commercial research services are offered on the internet.[44] The principal Internet services are RIA's *Checkpoint* and CCH's *Tax Research Network*. These commercial Internet services contain a wide range of materials available to tax researchers who subscribe to the service. In addition, the IRS has a home page (www.irs.gov) that taxpayers can access for forms, publications, and other related materials. All of the major accounting firms and many other tax organizations have home pages that allow users to access a myriad of tax information.

PROBLEM MATERIALS

DISCUSSION QUESTIONS

I1-1 The Supreme Court in 1895 ruled that the income tax was unconstitutional because the tax needed to be apportioned among the states in proportion to their populations. Why would the requirement of proportionality be so difficult to administer?

I1-2 Why was pay-as-you-go withholding needed in 1943?

I1-3 Congressman Patrick indicates that he is opposed to new tax legislative proposals that call for a flat tax rate that are currently being considered by

---

[44] For a guide to tax information on the internet, link to the website of the American Taxation Association at www.atasection.org under Tax Directories.

Congress because the new taxing structure would not be in accord with our traditional practice of taxing those who have the ability to pay the tax. Discuss the position of the congressman, giving consideration to tax rate structures (e.g., progressive, proportional, and regressive) and the concept of equity.

I1-4 The governor of your state stated in a recent political speech that he has never supported any income tax increases as the tax rates have remained at the same level during his entire term of office. Yet, you believe that you are paying more tax this year than in previous years even though your income has not increased. How can both you and the governor be correct? In other words, is it possible for the government to raise taxes without raising tax rates?

I1-5 Carmen has computed that her average tax rate is 16% and her marginal tax rate is 25% for the current year. She is considering whether to make a charitable contribution to her church before the end of the tax year. Which tax rate is of greater significance in measuring the tax effect for her decision? Explain.

I1-6 Why are the gift and estate taxes called wealth transfer taxes? What is the tax base for computing each of these taxes?

I1-7 Cathy, who is single, makes gifts of $15,000 to each of her two children.
a. Who is primarily liable for the gift tax on the two gifts, Cathy or the two children?
b. If Cathy has never made a taxable gift in prior years, is a gift tax due on the two gifts?

I1-8 Carlos inherits 100 shares of Allied Corporation stock from his father. The stock cost his father $8,000 and had a $10,000 FMV on the date of his father's death. The alternate valuation date was not elected. What is Carlos's tax basis for the Allied stock when it is received from the estate?

I1-9 Most estates are not subject to the federal estate tax.
a. Why is this the case?
b. Do you believe most estates should be subject to the federal estate tax?

I1-10 Indicate which of the following taxes are generally progressive, proportional, or regressive:
a. State income taxes
b. Federal estate tax
c. Corporate state franchise tax
d. Property taxes
e. State sales taxes

I1-11 Carolyn operates a small business as a sole proprietor (unincorporated). Carolyn is considering operating the business as a corporation because of nontax advantages (e.g., limited liability and ability to raise outside capital). From the standpoint of paying Social Security taxes, would the total Social Security taxes increase or decrease if the business is incorporated? Why?

I1-12 The three different levels of government (federal, state, and local) must impose taxes to carry out their functions. For each of the types of taxes below, discuss which level of government primarily uses that type of tax.
a. Property taxes
b. Excise taxes
c. Sales taxes
d. Income taxes
e. Employment taxes

I1-13 A "good" tax structure has five characteristics.
a. Briefly discuss the five characteristics.
b. Using the five characteristics, evaluate the following tax structures:
1. Federal income tax
2. State sales tax
3. Local ad valorem property tax

I1-14 Two commonly-recognized measures of the fairness of an income tax structure are "horizontal equity" and "vertical equity."
a. Discuss what is meant by horizontal equity and vertical equity as it pertains to the income tax.
b. Why is it so difficult to design a "fair" tax structure?

I1-15 The primary objective of the federal income tax law is to raise revenue. What are its secondary objectives?

I1-16 If the objectives of the federal tax system are multifaceted and include raising revenues, providing investment incentives, encouraging certain industries, and meeting desired social objectives, is it possible to achieve a simplified tax system? Explain.

I1-17 Distinguish between *taxpaying entities* and *flow-through entities* from the standpoint of the federal income tax law.

I1-18 Sally and Tom are married, have three dependent children, and file a joint return in 2006. If they have adjusted gross income (AGI) of $70,000 and itemized deductions of $9,000, what is their taxable income for 2006?

I1-19 The Bruin Corporation, a C corporation, is owned 100% by John Bean and had taxable income in 2006 of $500,000. In December 2006, the corporation has decided to distribute $400,000 to John and has asked you whether it would be better to distribute the money as a dividend or salary. John is in the 35% marginal tax bracket. How would you respond to Bruin Corporation?

I1-20 Discuss what is meant by the term "double taxation" of corporations. Develop an example of double taxation using a corporation and shareholder.

I1-21 Limited liability companies (LLCs) are very popular today as a form of organization. Assume a client asks you to explain what this new type of organization is all about. Prepare a brief description of the federal income tax aspects of LLCs.

I1-22 For flow-through entities, such as partnerships, how does the tax law use partner basis adjustments to prevent double taxation of partnership income?

I1-23 Partnerships and S corporations are flow-through entities. In connection with filing annual tax returns, these entities must include Form K-1 in the returns. What is Form K-1, what is its purpose, and who receives the form?

I1-24 The PDQ Partnership earned ordinary income of $150,000 in 2006. The partnership has three equal partners, Pete, Donald, and Quint. Quint, who is single, uses the standard deduction, and has other income of $15,000 (not connected with the partnership) in 2006. He receives a $30,000 distribution from the partnership during the year. What are the total tax consequences for Quint in 2006?

I1-25 Why is a thorough knowledge of sources of tax law so important for a professional person who works in the tax area?

I1-26 The Internal Revenue Code is the most authoritative source of income tax law. In trying to resolve an income tax question, however, a tax researcher also consults administrative rulings (Income Tax Regulations, Revenue Rulings, etc.) and court decisions. Why wouldn't the tax researcher just consult the Code since it is the highest authority? Similarly, why is there a need for administrative rulings and court decisions?

I1-27 Congressional committee reports are an important source of information concerning the legislative enactment of tax law.
   a. Name the three Congressional committee reports that are issued in connection with a new tax bill.
   b. Of what importance are Congressional committee reports to tax practitioners?

I1-28 What is the primary service function provided by the National Office of the IRS?

I1-29 What types of taxpayers are more likely to be audited by the IRS?

I1-30 Anya is concerned that she will be audited by the IRS.
   a. Under what circumstances is it possible that the IRS will review each line item on her tax return?
   b. Is it likely that all items on Anya's return will be audited?

I1-31 a. What does the term "hazards of litigation" mean in the context of taxation?
   b. Why would the IRS or a taxpayer settle or compromise a case based on the "hazards of litigation"?

I1-32 If a taxpayer files his or her tax return and receives a tax refund from the IRS, does this mean that the IRS feels that the return is correct and will not be subject to audit?

I1-33 State the statute of limitations for transactions involving:
   a. Fraud (e.g., failure to file a tax return)
   b. Disallowance of tax deduction items
   c. The omission of rental income equal to greater than 25% of the taxpayer's reported gross income

I1-34 In reference to tax research, what is meant by *the best possible defensibly correct solution*?

I1-35 The profession of tax practice involves four principal areas of activity. Discuss these four areas.

I1-36 Many tax professionals have moved into the field of financial planning for their clients.
   a. How do taxes impact financial planning for a client?
   b. Why do tax professionals have a perfect opportunity to perform financial planning for their clients?

I1-37 Is the principal goal of tax planning to absolutely minimize the amount of taxes that a taxpayer must pay?

I1-38 Explain how a computer can assist a tax practitioner in tax planning activities and making complex tax calculations.

PROBLEMS

I1-39 *Tax Rates.* Latesha, a single taxpayer, had the following income and deductions for the tax year 2006:

INCOME:		
	Salary	$ 60,000
	Business Income	25,000
	Interest income from bonds	10,000
	Tax-exempt bond interest	5,000
	TOTAL INCOME	100,000
DEDUCTIONS:	Business expenses	$ 9,600
	Itemized deductions	20,000
	Personal exemption	3,300
	TOTAL DEDUCTIONS	32,900

   a. Compute Latesha's taxable income and federal tax liability for 2006.

b. Compute Latesha's marginal, average, and effective tax rates.

c. For tax planning purposes, which of the three rates in Part b is the most important?

I1-40   *Marginal Tax Rate.* Jill and George are married and file a joint return. They expect to have $350,000 of taxable income in the next year and are considering whether to purchase a personal residence that would provide additional tax deductions of $80,000 for mortgage interest and real estate taxes.

a. What is their marginal tax rate for purposes of making this decision? Ignore the effects of a phase-out of personal exemptions and itemized deductions (see Chapters I2 and I7, respectively).

b. What is the tax savings if the residence is acquired?

I1-41   *Gift Tax.* Chuck, a married taxpayer, makes the following gifts during the current year (2006): $20,000 to his church, $30,000 to his daughter, and $25,000 to his wife.

a. What is the amount of Chuck's taxable gifts for the current year (assuming that he does not elect to split the gifts with his spouse)?

b. How would your answer to Part a change if a gift-splitting election were made?

I1-42   *Estate Tax.* Clay dies in 2006 and has a gross estate valued at $3,800,000. Six months after his death, the gross assets are valued at $4,000,000. The estate incurs funeral and administration expenses of $125,000. Clay also had debts amounting to $75,000 and bequeathed $500,000 of the property to his wife. During his life, Clay made no taxable gifts.

a. What is the amount of Clay's taxable estate?

b. What is the tax base for computing Clay's estate tax?

c. What is the amount of estate tax owed if the tentative estate tax (before credits) is $1,286,800?

d. Alternatively, if, six months after his death, the gross assets in Clay's estate declined in value to $3,500,000, can the administrator of Clay's estate elect the alternate valuation date? What are the important factors that the administrator should consider as to whether the alternate valuation date should be elected?

I1-43   *Comparison of Tax Entities.*

a. Keith Thomas began a new consulting business on January 1, 2006. He organized the business as a C corporation, KT, Inc. During 2006, the corporation was reasonably successful and generated revenues of $1,050,000. KT had operating expenses of $800,000 before any payments to Keith. During 2006, KT paid dividends to Keith in the amount of $250,000. Assume that Keith had other taxable income of $120,000, itemized deductions of $40,000, is married (wife has no income), and has no children. Compute the total tax liability of KT and Keith for 2006. Ignore any phaseouts of itemized deductions or personal exemptions.

b. Instead of organizing the consulting business as a C corporation, assume Keith organized the business as a limited liability company, KT, LLC. KT made a distribution of $250,000 to Keith during 2006. Compute the total tax liability of KT and Keith for 2006. Ignore any phaseouts of itemized deductions or personal exemptions.

I1-44   *Partnership Income.* Howard Gartman is a 40% partner in the Horton & Gartman Partnership. During 2006, the partnership reported the total items below on its Form 1065:

Ordinary income	$180,000
Qualified dividends	10,000
Long-term capital loss	(12,000)
Long-term capital gain	28,000
Charitable contributions	4,000
Cash distributions to partners	150,000

Howard and his wife Dawn, who file a joint return, also had the following income and deductions from sources not connected with the partnership:

Income	
Dawn's salary	$40,000
Qualified dividends	1,000

Deductions	
Mortgage interest	6,000
Real estate taxes	1,800
Charitable contributions	1,000

Howard and Dawn have two dependent children. During 2006, Dawn had $6,000 in federal income taxes withheld from her salary and Howard made four estimated tax payments of $3,000 each ($12,000 total). Compute Howard and Dawn's Federal income tax liability for 2006 and whether they have a balance due or a tax refund.

I1-45 *Interest and Penalties.* In 2005, Paul, who is single, has a comfortable salary from his job as well as income from his investment portfolio. However, he is habitually late in filing his federal income tax return. He did not file his 2005 income tax return until November 30, 2006 (due date was April 15, 2006) and no extensions of time to file the return were filed. Below are amounts from his 2005 return:

Taxable income	$140,000
Total tax liability on taxable income	33,707
Total federal tax withheld from his salary	27,511

Paul sent a check with his return to the IRS for the balance due of $6,196. He is relieved that he has completed his filing requirement for 2005 *and* has met his financial obligation to the government for 2005.

Has Paul met *all* of his financial obligations to the IRS for 2005? If not, what additional amounts will Paul be liable to pay to the IRS?

I1-46 *IRS Audits.* Which of the following individuals is most likely to be audited?
a. Connie has a $20,000 net loss from her unincorporated business (a cattle ranch). She also received a $200,000 salary as an executive of a corporation.
b. Craig has AGI of $20,000 from wages and uses the standard deduction.
c. Dale fails to report $120 of dividends from a stock investment. His taxable income is $40,000 and he has no other unusually large itemized deductions or business expenses. A Form 1099 is reported to the IRS.

I1-47 *Statute of Limitations.* In April 2006, Dan is audited by the IRS for the year 2004. During the course of the audit, the agent discovers that Dan's deductions for business travel and entertainment are unsubstantiated and a $600 deficiency assessment is proposed for 2004. The agent also examined some prior year returns. The agent discovers that Dan failed to report $40,000 of gross business income on his 2002 return. Gross income of $60,000 was reported in 2002. The agent also discovers that Dan failed to file a tax return in 1996.

Will the statute of limitations prevent the IRS from issuing a deficiency assessment for 2004, 2002, or 1996? Explain.

TAX STRATEGY PROBLEM

I1-48 Pedro Bourbone is the founder and owner of a highly successful small business and, over the past several years, has accumulated a significant amount of personal wealth. His portfolio of stocks and bonds is worth nearly $5,000,000 and generates income from dividends and interest of nearly $250,000 per year. With his salary from the business and his dividends and interest, Pedro has taxable income of approximately $600,000 per year and is clearly in the top individual marginal tax bracket. Pedro is married and has three children, ages 16, 14, and 12. Neither his wife nor his children are employed and have no income. Pedro has come to you as his CPA to discuss ways to reduce his individual tax liability as well as to discuss the potential estate tax upon his death. You mention the possibility of making gifts each year to his children. Explain how annual gifts to his children will reduce both his income during lifetime and his estate tax at death.

CASE STUDY PROBLEM

I1-49 John Gemstone, a wealthy client, has recently been audited by the IRS. The agent has questioned the following deduction items on Mr. Gemstone's tax return for the year under review:

- A $10,000 loss deduction on the rental of his beach cottage.
- A $20,000 charitable contribution deduction for the donation of a painting to a local art museum. The agent has questioned whether the painting is overvalued.
- A $15,000 loss deduction from the operation of a cattle breeding ranch. The agent is concerned that the ranch is not a legitimate business (i.e., is a hobby).

Your supervisor has requested that you represent Mr. Gemstone in his discussions with the IRS.

a. What additional questions should you ask Mr. Gemstone in an attempt to substantiate the deductibility of the above items?

b. What tax research procedures might be applied to build the best possible case for your client?

RESEARCH PROBLEM

I1-50 Read the following two cases and explain why the Supreme Court reached different conclusions for cases involving similar facts and issues:

- *CIR v. Court Holding Co.*, 33 AFTR 593, 45-1 USTC ¶9215 (USSC, 1945)
- *U.S. v. Cumberland Public Service Co.*, 38 AFTR 978, 50-1 USTC ¶9129 (USSC, 1950)

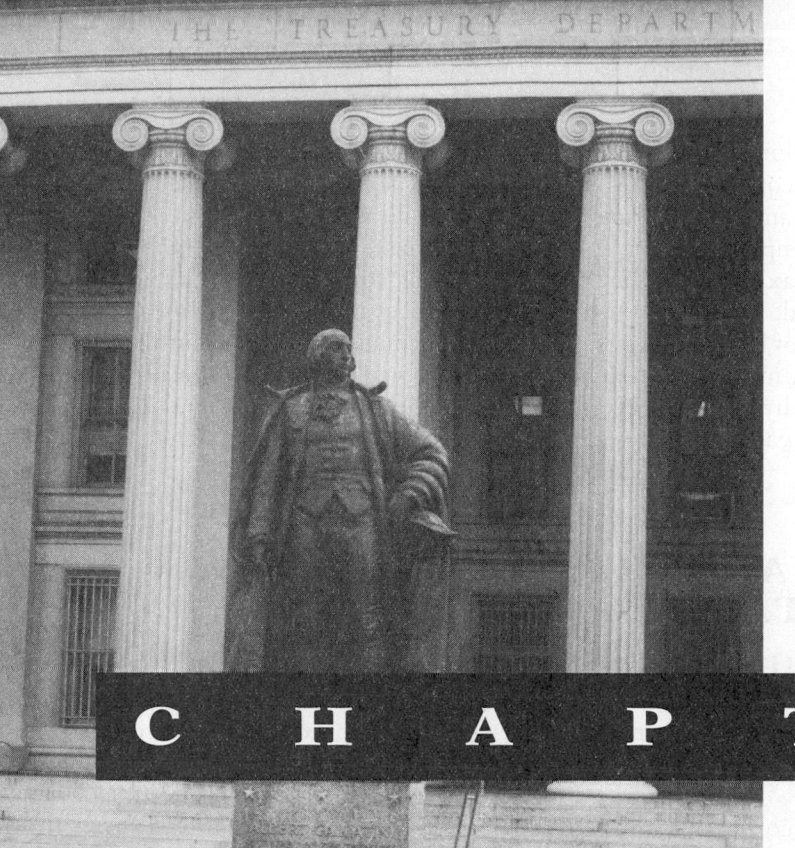

2

CHAPTER

DETERMINATION OF TAX

LEARNING OBJECTIVES

After studying this chapter, you should be able to

▶1 Use the tax formula to compute an individual's taxable income

▶2 Determine the amount allowable for the standard deduction

▶3 Determine the amount and the correct number of personal and dependency exemptions

▶4 Determine the amount of child credit

▶5 Determine the filing status of individuals

▶6 Explain the tax formula for corporations

▶7 Explain the basic concepts of property transactions

Each year, over 130 million individuals and married couples file tax forms on which they compute their federal income tax. The income tax is imposed "on the taxable income of every individual."[1] The amount of tax actually owed by an individual taxpayer is determined by applying a complex set of rules that together make up the income tax law. To understand the income tax, it is necessary to study the basic formula on which the income tax computation is based. Therefore, this chapter introduces the income tax formula and begins the development of its components. Because the income tax formula constitutes the basis of the income tax, most of the remainder of this book is an expansion of the formula. In addition to individual taxpayers, about 5 million corporations and 2 million partnerships file returns each year. These entities are also discussed in this chapter.

FORMULA FOR INDIVIDUAL INCOME TAX

OBJECTIVE 1

Use the tax formula to compute an individual's taxable income

BASIC FORMULA

Most individuals compute their income tax by using the formula illustrated in Table I2-1. The formula itself appears rather simple. However, the complexity of the income tax results from the intricate rules that must be applied in order to arrive at the amounts that enter into the formula.

The tax formula is incorporated into the income tax form. The tax formula illustrated in Table I2-1 can be compared with Form 1040, which is reproduced in Figure I2-1. Some differences exist between the tax formula below and the tax form itself. For example, taxpayers generally are not required to report exclusions (nontaxable income) on their tax returns. One exception does require taxpayers to disclose tax-exempt interest income. A number of separate schedules are used to report various types of income. For example, income from a sole proprietorship is reported on Schedule C, where gross income from the business is reduced by related expenses that are deductions for AGI. Only the net income from the business actually appears on Form 1040. Also, Form 1040 is used to collect other taxes such as the self-employment tax. Hence, a line is provided for that tax on Form 1040. The main reason for differences between the formula and the form is administrative convenience. That is, there is no reason to require taxpayers to disclose income if the income is not subject to tax, it is simpler to report business income on a separate schedule, and it is convenient to collect other taxes on the same tax form.

ADDITIONAL COMMENT

"There is one difference between a tax collector and a taxidermist—the taxidermist leaves the hide." This is a quote from Mortimer Caplan, former Director of the Bureau of Internal Revenue, *Time*, Feb. 1, 1963.

ADDITIONAL COMMENT

The IRS estimates that the average taxpayer will spend 3 hours and 59 minutes in preparing just a Form 1040. When the estimated time for recordkeeping, learning about the law, and sending the form is added to the preparation time, the total time estimate jumps to 9 hours and 54 minutes. Each additional form and schedule adds even more time.

ADDITIONAL COMMENT

Comedian Jay Leno's explanation as to why the IRS calls it Form 1040 was, "For every $50 you earn, you get $10 and they get $40."

▼ TABLE I2-1

Tax Formula for Individuals

Income from whatever source derived	$xxx,xxx
Minus: Exclusions	(xxx)
Gross income	$ xx,xxx
Minus: Deductions for adjusted gross income	(xxx)
Adjusted gross income	$ x,xxx
Minus: Deductions from adjusted gross income:	
Greater of itemized deductions or the standard deduction	(xx)
Personal and dependency exemptions	(xx)
Taxable income	$ x,xxx
Times: Tax rate or rates (from tax table or schedule)	× .xx
Gross tax	$ xx
Minus: Credits and prepayments	(x)
Net tax payable or refund due	$ xx

---

[1] Sec. 1.

Examination of the formula reveals terms such as *gross income, exclusions, adjusted gross income, exemptions, gross tax,* and *credits.* These terms and others that make up the formula are defined below.

DEFINITIONS

INCOME.   The term **income** includes both taxable and nontaxable income. Although the term is not specifically defined in the tax law, it does include income from any source.[2] Its meaning is close to that of the term **revenue**. However, it does not include a "return of capital." Thus, in the case of the sale of property, only the gain, not the entire sales proceeds, is viewed as income. This view extends to the sale of inventory, where gross profit is viewed as income, as opposed to the sale price.

EXCLUSION.   Not all income is taxable. An **exclusion** is any item of income that the tax law says is not taxable. Congress, over the years, has specifically excluded certain types of income from taxation for various social, economic, and political reasons. Chapter I4 discusses specific exclusions and the reasons for their existence. Table I2-2 contains a sample of the major exclusions from gross income.

GROSS INCOME.   **Gross income** is income reduced by exclusions. In other words, it is income from taxable sources and is reported on the return (excluded income need not be disclosed). Section 61(a) contains a partial list of items of gross income. The items listed in Sec. 61(a) are shown in Table I2-3. Note, however, that Sec. 61(a) states that unless otherwise provided, "gross income means all income from whatever source derived, including (but not limited to)" the listed items of income. Thus, even though an item is omitted from the list does not necessarily mean that the item is excluded. For example, illegal income, although omitted from the list, is taxable.[3]

TYPICAL MISCONCEPTION

It is easy to confuse an exclusion with a deduction. An exclusion is a source of income that is omitted from the tax base, whereas a deduction is an expense that is subtracted in arriving at taxable income. Both have the effect of reducing taxable income.

ADDITIONAL COMMENT

One common exclusion, interest on state and local government bonds, must be reported on the tax return in amount only. It is not added to the other income items. In 1996, this reported tax-exempt interest totaled $49 billion.

▼ **TABLE I2-2**
Major Exclusions

Gifts and inheritances
Life insurance proceeds
Welfare and certain other transfer payments
Certain scholarships and fellowships
Certain payments for injury and sickness
    Personal physical injury settlements
    Worker's compensation
    Medical expense reimbursements
Certain employee fringe benefits
    Health plan premiums
    Group term life insurance premiums (limited)
    Meals and lodging
    Employee discounts
    Dependent care
Certain foreign-earned income
Interest on state and local government bonds
Certain interest of Series EE bonds
Certain improvements by lessee to lessor's property
Child support payments
Property settlements pursuant to a divorce
Gain from the sale of a personal residence (limited)

---

[2] Sec. 61(a).

[3] *U.S. v. Manley S. Sullivan,* 6 AFTR 6753, 1 USTC ¶236 (USSC, 1927).

▼ **TABLE I2-3**
Gross Income Items Listed in Sec. 61(a)

Compensation for services, including fees, commissions, fringe benefits, and similar items
Gross income derived from business
Gains derived from dealings in property
Interest
Rents
Royalties
Dividends
Alimony and separate maintenance payments
Annuities
Income from life insurance and endowment contracts
Pensions
Income from the discharge of indebtedness
Distributive share of partnership gross income
Income in respect of a decedent
Income from an interest in an estate or trust

DEDUCTIONS FOR ADJUSTED GROSS INCOME. In general, taxpayers may deduct expenses that are specifically allowed by the tax law. Allowable deductions include business and investment expenses generally, along with personal expenses that are specifically provided for in the IRC, such as charitable contributions. Most purely personal expenses generally are not deductible.

Deductions fall into two categories for individual taxpayers: deductions *for* adjusted gross income and deductions *from* adjusted gross income. In general, **deductions for adjusted gross income** are expenses connected with a trade or business. For the most part, **deductions from adjusted gross income** are personal expenses that Congress has chosen to allow. This classification scheme, however, is not always followed. For example, alimony paid, which is not a business expense, is a deduction *for* adjusted gross income. Table I2-4 contains a partial list of deductions *for* adjusted gross income that is taken from Sec. 62. Deductions for adjusted gross income are discussed further in Chapter I6.

ADJUSTED GROSS INCOME. **Adjusted gross income (AGI)** is a measure of income that falls between gross income and taxable income. AGI is important because it is used in numerous other tax computations, especially to impose limitations. For example, AGI is used to establish floors for the medical deduction and casualty loss deduction and to establish a ceiling for the charitable contribution deduction.

DEDUCTIONS FROM ADJUSTED GROSS INCOME. Section 62 lists deductions *for* AGI (see Table I2-4). Thus, any allowable deduction not listed in Sec. 62 is a deduction *from* AGI. The two categories of deductions *from* adjusted gross income are (1) itemized deductions or the standard deduction and (2) personal and dependency exemptions.[4] Deductions from AGI are discussed further in Chapter I7 of this textbook.

ITEMIZED DEDUCTIONS AND THE STANDARD DEDUCTION. As mentioned above, taxpayers generally cannot deduct personal expenses.[5] Congress, however, allows taxpayers to deduct specified personal expenses such as charitable contributions and medical expenses. In addition, taxpayers are allowed to itemize expenses related to the pro-

ADDITIONAL COMMENT

In 2003, there were a total of 130.4 million individual income tax returns filed. 59.3 million of these returns had AGI under $25,000, and 2.5 million returns filed with AGI over $200,000.

ADDITIONAL COMMENT

In 2003, total AGI on all individual tax returns filed was just over $6.2 trillion, an increase of almost 3% from the previous year.

ADDITIONAL COMMENT

Itemized deductions were claimed on 33.7% of all returns filed in 2003.

---

[4] Sec. 63.   [5] Sec. 262.

▼ TABLE I2-4
Deductions for Adjusted Gross Income Listed in Sec. 62

Trade and business deductions
Reimbursed employee expenses and certain expenses of performing artists
Losses from the sale or exchange of property
Deductions attributable to rents and royalties
Certain deductions of life tenants and income beneficiaries of property
Contributions to retirement plans (Keoghs and IRAs) and certain distributions
Penalties forfeited because of premature withdrawal of funds from time savings accounts
*One-half of self-employment taxes paid
*Health insurance costs incurred by a self-employed person
Alimony
Moving expenses
Certain required repayments of supplemental unemployment compensation
Jury duty pay remitted to an individual's employer
Certain environmental expenditures (reforestation and clean fuel)
Interest on education loans
Contribution to medical savings account

*Though not actually mentioned in Sec. 62, self-employment taxes and health insurance costs of self-employed persons are defined by Secs. 164(f) and 162(l), respectively, as trade or business deductions thereby indirectly enabling taxpayers to deduct portions of these amounts for AGI.

HISTORICAL NOTE

In 1986, when parents were required merely to list the names of their children to claim them as a dependent, 77 million children were claimed. In 1987, when taxpayers were required to list children's Social Security numbers to prove that the exemptions were valid, the number of children claimed as dependents decreased to 70 million.

HISTORICAL NOTE

As recently as 1986, the highest marginal tax rate was 50%, and as recently as 1981, it was 70%.

duction or collection of income, the management of property held for the production of income, and the determination, collection, or refund of any tax.[6]

Taxpayers have the choice of claiming either itemized deductions or the standard deduction. The amount of the standard deduction varies depending on the taxpayer's filing status, age, and vision. As a practical matter, for most taxpayers the standard deduction is greater than the total itemized deductions. Taxpayers with small amounts of deductible expenses do not itemize and, in fact, do not have to keep records of medical expenses and other itemized deductions. The relationship between itemized deductions and the standard deduction is discussed later in this chapter.

PERSONAL AND DEPENDENCY EXEMPTIONS. A **personal exemption** generally is allowed for each taxpayer and his or her spouse and an additional dependency exemption is permitted for each dependent. Both personal and dependency exemptions are equal to $3,300 in 2006 and $3,200 in 2005. The amount of an exemption is adjusted annually for increases in the cost of living.

TAXABLE INCOME. **Taxable income** is adjusted gross income reduced by deductions *from* AGI. It is the amount of income that is taxed.

TAX RATES AND GROSS TAX. Tax rates are the percentage rates, set by Congress, at which income is taxed. Currently there are six tax rates that range from 10% to 35%.

2005 through 2010   10%, 15%, 25%, 28%, 33%, and 35%
2011 and later   15%, 28%, 31%, 36%, 39.6%

Taxpayers compute their tax by multiplying the percentage rates found in the tax rate schedules times taxable income. However, most taxpayers simply look in a tax table to find their gross tax. These two alternatives are discussed in more detail later in this chapter. The gross tax is the amount of tax determined by this process.

[6] Sec. 212.

▼ TABLE I2-5
Partial List of Tax Credits

Refundable

   Withholding from wages and back-up withholding
   Estimated tax payments
   Overpayment of prior year's tax
   Excess Social Security taxes paid
   Nonhighway-use gasoline tax
   Earned income credit
   Regulated investment company credit
   Payments made with extension request
   Child credit (in some cases)

Nonrefundable

   Adoption expense credit
   Credit for the elderly and disabled
   Foreign tax credit
   Child and dependent care credit
   Business energy credit
   Qualified electric vehicle credit
   Research and experimentation credit
   Low-income housing credit
   Building rehabilitation credit
   Hope and lifetime learning credits

SELF-STUDY QUESTION

If a taxpayer is in the 25% marginal tax bracket, would he or she prefer $100 of tax credits or $300 of tax deductions?

ANSWER

The taxpayer would prefer the $100 of tax credits. The $300 of deductions will result in a tax savings of $75 ($300 × 0.25), whereas the $100 of credits would result in a tax savings of $100.

CREDITS AND PREPAYMENTS. **Tax credits,** which include prepayments, are amounts that can be subtracted from the gross tax to arrive at the net tax due or refund due. Credits may be classified as either refundable or nonrefundable tax credits. **Refundable tax credits** are allowed to reduce a taxpayer's tax liability to zero and, if some credit still remains, are refundable (paid) by the government to the taxpayer. Prepayments of tax, which are amounts paid to the government during the year through means such as withholding from wages, and selected other items are classified as **refundable tax credits. Nonrefundable tax credits** are allowances that have been created by Congress for various social, economic, and political reasons such as the child and dependent care credits. Nonrefundable tax credits can be subtracted from the tax and may reduce the tax liability to zero. However, if the nonrefundable credits exceed the tax liability, none of the excess will be paid to the taxpayer. A partial list of refundable and nonrefundable tax credits can be found in Table I2-5 and are covered in detail in Chapter I14.

TAX FORMULA ILLUSTRATED

The following example illustrates the tax formula and Form 1040 for the tax year 2005.

EXAMPLE I2-1 ▶ The following facts relate to Larry S. and Jane V. Lane, who are married and file a joint return in 2005. Betty is their 9-year-old dependent daughter.

Salary	$75,000
Interest Income:	
Taxable	3,000
Exempt	500
Individual Retirement Account (IRA) contribution	4,000
Itemized deductions	12,300
Personal and dependency exemptions (3 × $3,200)	9,600
Federal income taxes withheld from salary	6,500

Their tax is computed as follows:

Income:			
	Salary		$75,000
	Taxable interest		3,000
	Tax-exempt interest		500
	Total		$78,500
Minus:	Exclusion:		
	Tax-exempt interest		(500)
Gross income			$78,000
Minus:	Deductions for AGI:		
	IRA contribution		(4,000)
Adjusted gross income			$74,000
Minus:	Deductions from AGI:		
	Itemized deductions		(12,300)
	Personal and dependency exemptions		(9,600)
Taxable income			$52,100
Gross tax (2005 tax table)			$ 7,089
Minus:	Credits and prepayments		
	Child credit	(1,000)	
	Federal income tax withheld	(6,500)	(7,500)
Tax refund			$ 411 ◄

This tax is also computed on Form 1040 (see Figure I2-1). Note that certain additional information, such as the taxpayers' address and Social Security numbers, also is included on the return.

DEDUCTIONS FROM ADJUSTED GROSS INCOME

ITEMIZED DEDUCTIONS

Itemized deductions are claimed only if the total of such expenses exceeds the standard deduction. Here, consideration is given to which expenses may be itemized and the relationship between itemized deductions and the standard deduction.

DEDUCTIBLE ITEMS. Congress allows taxpayers to itemize specified personal expenses. These specified expenses include medical expenses, taxes, investment and residential interest, charitable contributions, casualty and theft losses, and employee expenses. In addition, taxpayers are allowed to itemize expenses related to the production or collection of nonbusiness income, the management of property held for the production of income, and the determination, collection, or refund of any tax. A partial list of itemized deductions is found in Table I2-6.

ITEMIZED DEDUCTION FLOORS. There are four adjusted gross income floors associated with itemized deductions. AGI floors represent amounts subtracted from deductions in arriving at allowable amounts. Three of the floors apply to specific categories of itemized deductions; the remaining floor applies to total itemized deductions. The floors based on AGI are as follows:

▶ Medical expenses: only medical expenses over 7.5% of AGI of are deductible.

▶ Casualty losses: only casualty losses in excess of 10% of AGI are deductible.

▶ Miscellaneous itemized deductions: only miscellaneous itemized deductions in excess of 2% of AGI are deductible.

Department of the Treasury—Internal Revenue Service

U.S. Individual Income Tax Return 2005 (99) IRS Use Only—Do not write or staple in this space.

For the year Jan. 1–Dec. 31, 2005, or other tax year beginning , 2005, ending , 20

OMB No. 1545-0074

Label
(See instructions on page 16.)

Use the IRS label. Otherwise, please print or type.

Your first name and initial **Larry S.**   Last name **Lane**

Your social security number **123 45 6789**

If a joint return, spouse's first name and initial **Jane V.**   Last name **Lane**

Spouse's social security number **987 65 4321**

Home address (number and street). If you have a P.O. box, see page 16. **116 E. Edwards**   Apt. no.

▲ You **must** enter your SSN(s) above. ▲

City, town or post office, state, and ZIP code. If you have a foreign address, see page 16. **Lubbock, Texas**

Checking a box below will not change your tax or refund.

Presidential Election Campaign ▶ Check here if you, or your spouse if filing jointly, want $3 to go to this fund (see page 16) ▶ ☐ You ☐ Spouse

Filing Status

Check only one box.

1 ☐ Single
2 ☒ Married filing jointly (even if only one had income)
3 ☐ Married filing separately. Enter spouse's SSN above and full name here. ▶
4 ☐ Head of household (with qualifying person). (See page 17.) If the qualifying person is a child but not your dependent, enter this child's name here. ▶
5 ☐ Qualifying widow(er) with dependent child (see page 17)

Exemptions

6a ☒ **Yourself.** If someone can claim you as a dependent, **do not** check box 6a
b ☒ Spouse

Boxes checked on 6a and 6b **2**

c Dependents:

(1) First name Last name	(2) Dependent's social security number	(3) Dependent's relationship to you	(4) ✓ if qualifying child for child tax credit (see page 19)
Betty Lane	125 25 7774		☑
			☐
			☐
			☐

No. of children on 6c who:
• lived with you **1**
• did not live with you due to divorce or separation (see page 20)

Dependents on 6c not entered above

If more than four dependents, see page 19.

d Total number of exemptions claimed

Add numbers on lines above ▶ **3**

Income

Attach Form(s) W-2 here. Also attach Forms W-2G and 1099-R if tax was withheld.

If you did not get a W-2, see page 22.

Enclose, but do not attach, any payment. Also, please use **Form 1040-V.**

7	Wages, salaries, tips, etc. Attach Form(s) W-2	7	75,000
8a	**Taxable** interest. Attach Schedule B if required	8a	3,000
b	Tax-exempt interest. **Do not** include on line 8a	8b	500
9a	Ordinary dividends. Attach Schedule B if required	9a	
b	Qualified dividends (see page 23)	9b	
10	Taxable refunds, credits, or offsets of state and local income taxes (see page 23)	10	
11	Alimony received	11	
12	Business income or (loss). Attach Schedule C or C-EZ	12	
13	Capital gain or (loss). Attach Schedule D if required. If not required, check here ▶ ☐	13	
14	Other gains or (losses). Attach Form 4797	14	
15a	IRA distributions 15a	b Taxable amount (see page 25)	15b	
16a	Pensions and annuities 16a	b Taxable amount (see page 25)	16b	
17	Rental real estate, royalties, partnerships, S corporations, trusts, etc. Attach Schedule E	17	
18	Farm income or (loss). Attach Schedule F	18	
19	Unemployment compensation	19	
20a	Social security benefits 20a	b Taxable amount (see page 27)	20b	
21	Other income. List type and amount (see page 29)	21	
22	Add the amounts in the far right column for lines 7 through 21. This is your **total income** ▶	22	78,000

Adjusted Gross Income

23	Educator expenses (see page 29)	23	
24	Certain business expenses of reservists, performing artists, and fee-basis government officials. Attach Form 2106 or 2106-EZ	24	
25	Health savings account deduction. Attach Form 8889	25	
26	Moving expenses. Attach Form 3903	26	
27	One-half of self-employment tax. Attach Schedule SE	27	
28	Self-employed SEP, SIMPLE, and qualified plans	28	
29	Self-employed health insurance deduction (see page 30)	29	
30	Penalty on early withdrawal of savings	30	
31a	Alimony paid b Recipient's SSN ▶	31a	
32	IRA deduction (see page 31)	32	4,000
33	Student loan interest deduction (see page 33)	33	
34	Tuition and fees deduction (see page 34)	34	
35	Domestic production activities deduction. Attach Form 8903	35	
36	Add lines 23 through 31a and 32 through 35	36	4,000
37	Subtract line 36 from line 22. This is your **adjusted gross income** ▶	37	74,000

For Disclosure, Privacy Act, and Paperwork Reduction Act Notice, see page 78.   Cat. No. 11320B   Form **1040** (2005)

FIGURE 12-1 ▶ FORM 1040

Tax and Credits	38	Amount from line 37 (adjusted gross income)		38	74,000

39a	Check if: ☐ **You** were born before January 2, 1941, ☐ Blind. **Total boxes**	
	☐ **Spouse** was born before January 2, 1941, ☐ Blind. checked ▶ 39a	
b	If your spouse itemizes on a separate return or you were a dual-status alien, see page 35 and check here ▶39b ☐	

Standard Deduction for—

- People who checked any box on line 39a or 39b **or** who can be claimed as a dependent, see page 36.
- All others:

Single or Married filing separately, $5,000

Married filing jointly or Qualifying widow(er), $10,000

Head of household, $7,300

40	**Itemized deductions** (from Schedule A) **or** your **standard deduction** (see left margin)		40	12,300
41	Subtract line 40 from line 38		41	61,700
42	If line 38 is over $109,475, or you provided housing to a person displaced by Hurricane Katrina, see page 37. Otherwise, multiply $3,200 by the total number of exemptions claimed on line 6d		42	9,600
43	**Taxable income.** Subtract line 42 from line 41. If line 42 is more than line 41, enter -0-		43	52,100
44	**Tax** (see page 37). Check if any tax is from: **a** ☐ Form(s) 8814 **b** ☐ Form 4972		44	7,089
45	**Alternative minimum tax** (see page 39). Attach Form 6251		45	
46	Add lines 44 and 45 ▶		46	7,089
47	Foreign tax credit. Attach Form 1116 if required	47		
48	Credit for child and dependent care expenses. Attach Form 2441	48		
49	Credit for the elderly or the disabled. Attach Schedule R	49		
50	Education credits. Attach Form 8863	50		
51	Retirement savings contributions credit. Attach Form 8880	51		
52	Child tax credit (see page 41). Attach Form 8901 if required	52	1,000	
53	Adoption credit. Attach Form 8839	53		
54	Credits from: **a** ☐ Form 8396 **b** ☐ Form 8859	54		
55	Other credits. Check applicable box(es): **a** ☐ Form 3800 **b** ☐ Form 8801 **c** ☐ Form	55		
56	Add lines 47 through 55. These are your **total credits**		56	1,000
57	Subtract line 56 from line 46. If line 56 is more than line 46, enter -0- ▶		57	6,089

Other Taxes	58	Self-employment tax. Attach Schedule SE		58
	59	Social security and Medicare tax on tip income not reported to employer. Attach Form 4137		59
	60	Additional tax on IRAs, other qualified retirement plans, etc. Attach Form 5329 if required		60
	61	Advance earned income credit payments from Form(s) W-2		61
	62	Household employment taxes. Attach Schedule H		62
	63	Add lines 57 through 62. This is your **total tax** ▶		63	6,089

Payments	64	Federal income tax withheld from Forms W-2 and 1099	64	6,500

If you have a qualifying child, attach Schedule EIC.

65	2005 estimated tax payments and amount applied from 2004 return	65	
66a	**Earned income credit (EIC)**	66a	
b	Nontaxable combat pay election ▶ 66b		
67	Excess social security and tier 1 RRTA tax withheld (see page 59)	67	
68	Additional child tax credit. Attach Form 8812	68	
69	Amount paid with request for extension to file (see page 59)	69	
70	Payments from: **a** ☐ Form 2439 **b** ☐ Form 4136 **c** ☐ Form 8885	70	
71	Add lines 64, 65, 66a, and 67 through 70. These are your **total payments** ▶	71	6,500

Refund	72	If line 71 is more than line 63, subtract line 63 from line 71. This is the amount you **overpaid** ▶	72	411

Direct deposit? See page 59 and fill in 73b, 73c, and 73d.

73a	Amount of line 72 you want **refunded to you** ▶	73a 411
▶ b	Routing number [＿＿＿＿＿＿＿＿＿] ▶ **c** Type: ☐ Checking ☐ Savings	
▶ d	Account number [＿＿＿＿＿＿＿＿＿＿＿＿＿＿＿＿＿]	
74	Amount of line 72 you want **applied to your 2006 estimated tax** ▶	74

Amount You Owe	75	**Amount you owe.** Subtract line 71 from line 63. For details on how to pay, see page 60 ▶	75
	76	Estimated tax penalty (see page 60)	76

Third Party Designee	Do you want to allow another person to discuss this return with the IRS (see page 61)? ☐ **Yes.** Complete the following. ☐ **No**

Designee's name ▶	Phone no. ▶ ( )	Personal identification number (PIN) ▶ [＿＿＿＿＿]

Sign Here

Joint return? See page 17. Keep a copy for your records.

Under penalties of perjury, I declare that I have examined this return and accompanying schedules and statements, and to the best of my knowledge and belief, they are true, correct, and complete. Declaration of preparer (other than taxpayer) is based on all information of which preparer has any knowledge.

Your signature	Date	Your occupation	Daytime phone number
Larry S. Lane	4/15/06	Attorney	(555) 555-1212
Spouse's signature. If a joint return, **both** must sign.	Date	Spouse's occupation	
Jane V. Lane	4/15/06	Student	

Paid Preparer's Use Only

Preparer's signature ▶		Date	Check if self-employed ☐	Preparer's SSN or PTIN
Firm's name (or yours if self-employed), address, and ZIP code	▶		EIN Phone no. ( )	

Form **1040** (2005)

FIGURE 12-1   ▶   FORM 1040 (CONTINUED)

▼ **TABLE I2-6**
Partial List of Itemized Deductions

Medical expenses (over 7.5% of adjusted gross income)
Certain taxes
   State, local, and foreign income and real property taxes
   State and local personal property taxes
Residential interest and investment interest (limited)
Charitable contributions (limited)
Casualty and theft losses (over 10% of adjusted gross income)
Miscellaneous deductions (over 2% of adjusted gross income)
   Employee expenses (e.g., professional and union dues, professional publications, travel,
      transportation, education, job hunting, office-in-home, special clothing, and 50% of
      entertainment expenses)
   Expenses for producing investment income (e.g., accounting and legal fees, safe deposit
      rental, fees paid to an IRA custodian)
   Tax advice and tax return preparation and related costs
Other miscellaneous deductions
   Federal estate tax attributable to income in respect of a decedent
   Gambling losses to the extent of winnings
   Amortization of bond premium
   Amounts restored under claim of right

ADDITIONAL COMMENT

The phase-out of itemized deductions for taxpayers in the 35% tax bracket effectively raises their marginal tax rate by 1.05%, which could be considered a hidden tax rate.

▶ High income taxpayers: higher income taxpayers must reduce total itemized deductions by 2% (3% in 2005) of their AGI over $150,500 in 2006 ($145,950 in 2005).[7] The amount for married persons filing separate returns is $75,250 in 2006 ($72,975 in 2005). The reduction will be 2% again in 2007, 1% in 2008 and 2009, and will be eliminated in 2010.

These floors are discussed in more detail in Chapter I7.

EXAMPLE I2-2 ▶

John and Jane file a joint tax return in 2006 and report AGI of $170,000. Their itemized deductions include $15,500 of medical expenses and home mortgage interest of $10,000. The AGI floor reduces the medical expense deduction to $2,750 [$15,500 − (0.075 × $170,000)]. Total itemized deductions before the overall reduction is $12,750 ($2,750 + $10,000). This amount must be reduced by $390 [($170,000 − $150,500) × 0.02] as a result of the overall floor for itemized deductions. Thus, the total itemized deductions allowed is $12,360 ($12,750 − $390). ◀

OBJECTIVE 2

Determine the amount allowable for the standard deduction

STANDARD DEDUCTION

Itemized deductions are claimed only if the total amount of such deductions exceeds the standard deduction. The **standard deduction** is an amount set by Congress. It varies depending on the taxpayer's filing status, age, and vision.

KEY POINT

The dollar amount of the standard deduction generally increases each year because it is indexed to the rate of inflation.

Filing Status	Standard Deduction 2005	2006
Single individual other than heads of households	$ 5,000	$ 5,150
Married couples filing joint returns and surviving spouses	10,000	10,300
Married people filing separate returns	5,000	5,150
Heads of households	7,300	7,550

The differences between the 2005 and 2006 amounts represent adjustments for the increase in the cost of living.

---

[7] The reduction in the itemized deductions cannot exceed 80% of the total itemized deductions other than medical expenses, investment interest expenses, casualty losses, and wagering losses. (See Chapter I7 for a discussion of the 80% overall limitation.)

In 2006, a married taxpayer's standard deduction is increased by $1,000 (unchanged from 2005) if he or she is elderly or blind ($2,000 if the taxpayer is elderly *and* blind) or has a spouse who is elderly or blind (for a maximum possible increase of $4,000 for a married couple). If an unmarried taxpayer is elderly or blind, his or her standard deduction is increased by $1,250 (unchanged from 2005) and $2,500 (unchanged from 2005) if the taxpayer is elderly *and* blind. Thus, in 2006, a single taxpayer, age 65 and not blind, is entitled to a $6,400 ($5,150 + $1,250) standard deduction. Two special rules relating to age and blindness are noted below.

▶ The increase in the standard deduction for elderly taxpayers is available if the taxpayer turns 65 during the tax year. For purposes of this requirement, a taxpayer is considered to be age 65 on the day before his or her sixty-fifth birthday. Thus, a taxpayer who reaches age 65 on January 1 of a year is deemed to have reached age 65 on December 31 of the preceding year. The adjustment is allowed on the final return of a deceased taxpayer only if he or she reached age 65 before death.

▶ The IRC defines blindness as corrected vision in the better eye of no better than 20/200 or a field of no greater than 20 degrees. Vision is determined as of the last day of the tax year or, in the case of a deceased taxpayer, as of the date of death.

The standard deduction simplifies the computation of taxable income. As previously noted, for most taxpayers the standard deduction is greater than total itemized deductions. Those taxpayers do not itemize and, in fact, do not even have to keep records of medical expenses and other itemized deductions.

Who actually itemizes and who does not? High-income taxpayers are more likely to itemize than low-income taxpayers simply because they incur more expenses that can be itemized. This is true even though the AGI floors (previously discussed) affect high-income taxpayers more than low-income taxpayers. Another characteristic of taxpayers who generally itemize their deductions are individuals who own their homes and incur home mortgage expenses and property taxes. These two expenses are deductible and alone often exceed the standard deduction.

EXAMPLE I2-3 ▶ In 2006, Joan is single, and a homeowner who incurs property taxes on her home of $2,000, makes charitable contributions of $500, and pays mortgage interest of $4,000. Joan's adjusted gross income is $30,000. Her taxable income is computed as follows:

Adjusted gross income		$30,000
Minus: Itemized deductions:		
Charitable contributions	$ 500	
Property taxes	2,000	
Mortgage interest	4,000	(6,500)
Minus: Personal exemption		(3,300)
Taxable income		$20,200 ◀

Joan would itemize her deductions because they ($6,500) are greater than her standard deduction ($5,150).

EXAMPLE I2-4 ▶ Assume the same facts as in Example I2-3 except that Joan is not a homeowner. Thus, she has no property taxes or mortgage interest but does pay rent of $600 per month for an apartment. Her taxable income is computed as follows:

Adjusted gross income	$30,000
Minus: Standard deduction	(5,150)
Minus: Personal exemption	(3,300)
Taxable income	$21,550 ◀

Joan would use the standard deduction of $5,150 because it is greater than her itemized deductions of $500. Rent paid for a personal apartment is not deductible.

LOSS OF THE STANDARD DEDUCTION. Congress decided that some taxpayers should not be permitted to use the standard deduction as they possibly would receive an unintended tax benefit.[8] The standard deduction is unavailable to three categories of taxpayers:

▶ An individual filing a return for a period less than twelve months because of a change in accounting period.

▶ A married taxpayer filing a separate return in instances where the other spouse itemizes.

▶ Nonresident aliens.

To illustrate why Congress does not permit certain taxpayers to claim the standard deduction, consider what could happen if a married couple files separate returns but only one spouse itemizes. On a separate return in 2006 when the standard deduction is $5,150, one spouse could claim all itemized deductions while the other uses the standard deduction.

EXAMPLE I2-5 ▶ Clay and Joy, a married couple, have incomes of $35,000 and $34,000, respectively. Their itemized deductions total $9,000. They would claim a $10,300 standard deduction on a joint return. If Clay filed a separate return and claimed all of the deductions, his itemized deductions of $9,000 would be greater than the $5,150 standard deduction. If Joy could claim the standard deduction on her return, their total deductions would equal $14,150 ($9,000 + $5,150). The law, however, requires that either they both itemize or they both use the standard deduction. ◀

Limitation on the Standard Deduction. A special rule applies to any individual for whom the dependency exemption is allowable to another taxpayer. The standard deduction of the dependent is limited to the greater of (1) the dependent's earned income plus $300 ($250 in 2005) or (2) $850 ($800 in 2005). The purpose of this limitation is to prevent parents from shifting unearned income, such as interest and dividends, to their children and avoid paying tax on such income. Without this rule, children could use the standard deduction to offset interest and dividends.

EXAMPLE I2-6 ▶ Webb and Beth are married, in the 35% marginal tax rate bracket, and have one son, Vincent, age 15. Vincent has no income and is claimed as a dependent by his parents. Webb and Beth transfer stocks and bonds to Vincent that earn $3,000 in dividends and interest. Their goal is to shift the $3,000 of income to Vincent to utilize his standard deduction. However, since Vincent is claimed as a dependent by his parents on their return, Vincent's standard deduction is limited to $850, i.e., the *greater* of $850 or his earned income plus $300 ($0 + $300). ◀

EXAMPLE I2-7 ▶ Assume the same facts as in Example I2-6 except Vincent has a part-time job and earns $2,000 in wages. Vincent's standard deduction would be $2,300 ($2,000 + $300). Alternatively, if Vincent's wages were $6,000, his standard deduction would be $5,150 (the maximum for a single individual). ◀

OBJECTIVE 3

Determine the amount and the correct number of personal and dependency exemptions

PERSONAL EXEMPTIONS

Taxpayers cannot deduct personal expenses except for certain itemized deductions that are specifically authorized under the tax law. Congress has recognized the need to protect a small amount of income from tax in order to allow the taxpayer to meet personal expenses. Thus, almost every individual taxpayer is allowed a personal exemption of $3,300 ($3,200 in 2005). Because there are two taxpayers on a joint return filed by a married couple, they are allowed two personal exemptions. In addition, if a married person files a separate return, the taxpayer can claim a personal exemption for his or her spouse if the spouse has no gross income during the year and the spouse is not the dependent of another taxpayer.[9]

Only one personal exemption is allowed for each person. Therefore, if an individual can be claimed as a dependent by another person, that individual is not entitled to a personal exemption on his or her own return. Despite the loss of the personal exemption, most dependents owe little or no tax. Since a person who may be claimed as a dependent

[8] Sec. 63(c)(6).   [9] Sec. 151(b).

typically has a very low income, such a person can usually offset his or her income by the standard deduction.

ADDITIONAL COMMENT

One should forsake any preconceived notions as to what constitutes a dependent before examining the dependency tests.

DEPENDENCY EXEMPTIONS

Virtually all taxpayers can claim a *personal exemption* for themselves. In addition, taxpayers may also claim a *dependency exemption* for each dependent.[10] To qualify as a dependent, an individual must meet the definition of either a *qualifying child* or a *qualifying relative*. All dependents must meet several requirements. Four requirements are common to all dependents. All dependents must:

▶ Have a qualifying identification number.

▶ Meet a citizenship test.

▶ Meet a separate return test.

▶ Not themselves claim another person as a dependent.

Additional requirements also must be met depending on whether the dependent is a qualifying child or a qualifying relative.

REQUIREMENTS FOR ALL DEPENDENTS. The requirements applicable to all dependents are:

Identification number. Every dependent must have a Social Security number, and that number must be reported on the return.[11]

Citizenship. Dependents must be U.S. citizens[12] or nationals,[13] or residents[14] of the U.S., Canada, or Mexico for some part of the year.

Joint return. Married dependents cannot file joint returns. However, a taxpayer is entitled to the exemption if the dependent files a joint return solely to claim a refund of tax withheld (i.e., there is no tax on the joint return and there would have been no tax on two separate returns).[15] Married dependents should weigh the taxes that would be saved by the family from an exemption against the taxes that would be saved by filing a joint return. Depending on the circumstances, either alternative may be more beneficial.

No dependent. Dependents who file tax returns may not claim personal or dependency exemptions on their returns.

ADDITIONAL REQUIREMENTS FOR QUALIFYING CHILDREN. To claim a dependency exemption for an individual who is considered a *qualifying child*, the following additional requirements must be met:

▶ A relationship test.

▶ An age test.

▶ An abode test.

▶ A support test.

Relationship test. Eligible children include the taxpayer's children (including natural, adopted, foster, and stepchildren) and the taxpayer's siblings (including half-siblings and step-siblings) along with descendants of any of the above. A child is adopted if the child has been legally adopted or has been legally placed in a home for adoption.

[10] Sec. 152.
[11] Sec. 151(e). The IRS has the authority to disallow dependency exemptions for otherwise qualified dependents without Social Ssecurity numbers and with incorrectly reported Social Security numbers. A missing or incorrectly reported Social Security number may also bar an otherwise eligible individual from claiming head-of-household filing status.
[12] U.S. citizens living in foreign countries can claim dependency exemptions for adopted children even if the children are not U.S. citizens.

[13] A U.S. national is an individual born in an outlying possession such as American Samoa.
[14] A resident is a person who is not a U.S. citizen and who is legally residing in the United States with intent to stay here permanently (see Sec. 7701(b)).
[15] Rev. Rul. 54-567, 1954-2 C.B. 108 and Rev. Rul 65-34, 1965-1 C.B. 86. The theory is that the taxpayer is filing a claim for refund and not actually filing a tax return.

Age test. A qualifying child must be under age 19, a full-time student under age 24, or a permanently and totally disabled child.[16] A child is considered to be a student if he or she is in full-time attendance at a qualified educational institution during at least five months of the year. To be full-time, a student must carry the number of hours or courses the educational institution requires a student to take to be considered full-time.

Abode test. A qualifying child must have the same principal abode as the taxpayer for more than half of the year.

Support test. A qualifying child may not provide more than one-half of his or her own support during the year. Support is defined below in connection with the discussion of other dependents. Unlike other dependents, there is no requirement that the taxpayer provide more than one-half of the qualifying child's support, only that the dependent cannot provide more than one-half of his or her own support. This can be important in situations such as divorces where one spouse provides support, but the other has custody.

EXAMPLE 12-8 ▶ Keith and Barbara file a joint return and have one son, Jeff, age 28. Because of illness, Jeff had to quit his job in June and moved back home to live with his parents. Keith and Barbara provided 70% of Jeff's support. Jeff earned $18,000. Jeff is not a qualifying child for purposes of the dependency exemption. Although Jeff meets the relationship, abode, and support tests, he fails the age test. ◀

REQUIREMENTS FOR OTHER RELATIVES. A dependency exemption may also be claimed for a *qualifying relative*. To be eligible, dependents must meet the common requirements above and a:

▶ Relationship test.

▶ Gross income test.

▶ Support test.

Relationship test. Other relatives must either be related to the taxpayer or reside in the taxpayer's household for the entire year. Although this group is referred to as "other qualifying relatives," that term is misleading because individuals who live with the taxpayer do not actually have to be related to the taxpayer. The relationship between the taxpayer and the dependent cannot violate local law.[17] Relatives who can be claimed as dependents even if they do not live with the taxpayer include the taxpayer's parents and their ancestors and siblings, the taxpayer's stepparents, and specified in-laws (mother, father, brother, sister, son, and daughter) along with qualifying children discussed above. As a result, a qualifying child may be claimed as a dependent if the child meets the tests described here even if the child fails the requirements for qualifying children. Thus, a son who is age 24 can be claimed as a dependent if the son meets the support and gross income tests discussed below even though that son could not be claimed as a dependent under the requirements for a qualifying child.

EXAMPLE 12-9 ▶ Jesse supports three people: Tina, an unrelated child who lives with him; his cousin Judy, who lives in another state; and his daughter Vicki, who lives in her own home. Jesse can claim two dependency exemptions: one for Tina, who lives with him (a person who lives with the taxpayer need not be related) and one for his daughter. Jesse cannot claim a dependency exemption for Judy as cousins do not meet the relationship test. ◀

On a joint return the dependent needs to be related to only one spouse.[18] Once established, a relationship is not terminated by death or divorce.

---

[16] As noted, taxpayers attain the age 65, for purposes of the additional standard deduction, on the day before the anniversaries of their births. As a result, an individual whose birthday is January 1 is considered to be age 65 in the year prior to the individual's 65th birthday. A child whose 19th birthday falls on January 1 is considered to be under the age 19 in the previous year. The rule also is followed for purposes of determining whether the child is

under age 24, and is used in connection with age 17 threshold associated with the child credit. Rev. Rul. 2003-72, I.R.B. 2003-33.

[17] Sec. 152(f)(3). The exemption has been disallowed where the relationship constituted "cohabitation" and was illegal in the state (*Cassius L. Peacock, III,* PH T.C. Memo ¶78.030, 37 TCM 177).

[18] Reg. Sec. 1.152-2(d).

EXAMPLE I2-10 ▶ Ken and Lisa support Lisa's mother and claim her as a dependent on a joint return. Following Lisa's death, Ken continues to support Lisa's mother. Lisa's mother continues to be Ken's mother-in-law and can be claimed as a dependent. ◀

Gross income test. The dependent's gross income must be less than the exemption amount for the year ($3,300 in 2006). The statutory definition of gross income is used in applying this limitation. Therefore, nontaxable scholarships, tax-exempt bond interest, and nontaxable Social Security benefits are not considered, but salary, taxable interest, and rent are considered in deciding whether the person meets this test.

EXAMPLE I2-11 ▶ Jim, age 22, a full-time college student, lives with his cousin who provides more than one-half of Jim's support. Jim earned $8,000 from a summer job. Even though Jim's cousin provided over one-half of his support, Jim cannot be claimed as a dependent as Jim does not meet the gross income test. Alternatively, if Jim lived with and were supported by his brother, he could be claimed as a dependent because, as a brother, Jim is a qualifying child and is exempt from the gross income test. ◀

Support test. The taxpayer must normally provide more than one-half of a dependent's financial support during the year. Support includes amounts spent by the taxpayer, the dependent, and other individuals. Welfare[19] and Social Security benefits[20] spent on support count even if they are excluded from gross income.

EXAMPLE I2-12 ▶ Tarer provided $3,000 of support for his mother, Mary. Tarer's sister provided $1,000. Mary spent $4,500 of her savings for her own support. Because Mary provided over one-half of her own support, she cannot be claimed as a dependent. ◀

EXAMPLE I2-13

ADDITIONAL COMMENT

A TV set bought by a parent for his 12-year-old child and set up in her bedroom was considered support (Rev. Rul. 77-282, 1977-2 C.B. 52). A power lawn mower, however, bought by a parent of a 13-year-old child was not considered support. The parent had assigned the child the job of mowing the lawn, and the power mower was intended to make the job more palatable. The lawn mower was considered a family item that benefits all members of the household (Rev. Rul. 77-282, 1977-2 C.B. 52.)

▶ George's father received Social Security benefits of $6,600, of which $1,800 were deposited into a savings account. He spent the remaining $4,800 on food, clothing, and lodging. George spent $5,600 to support his father. George meets the support test because the amount saved is not counted in the support test. ◀

Support includes amounts spent for food, clothing, shelter, medical and dental care, education, and the like.[21] Support is not limited to these items.[22] Support does not include the value of services rendered by the taxpayer to the dependent.[23] Also, the IRS and the courts have excluded various other expenses from support.[24]

Generally, the amount of support equals the cost of the item, but in the case of support provided in a noncash form, such as lodging, the amount of support equals the fair market value or fair rental value. The cost of an item such as a television or an automobile is included in support if the item actually is support.[25]

EXAMPLE I2-14 ▶ Vicki's mother lives with her. Vicki purchased clothing for her mother costing $800 and provided her with a room that Vicki estimates she could have rented for $2,800. Vicki spent $2,500 for groceries she shared with her mother and $1,200 for utilities. In addition, Vicki purchased a television for $750 that she placed in the living room. Vicki and her mother both used the television. Vicki's support for her mother, at a minimum, includes:

Clothing	$ 800
Rental value of room	2,800
Food	1,250
Total	$4,850

[19] Rev. Rul. 71-468, 1971-2 C.B. 115.
[20] Rev. Ruls. 57-344, 1957-2 C.B. 112, and 58-419, 1958-2 C.B. 57.
[21] Reg. Sec. 1.152-1(a)(2)(i).
[22] Examples of other items that have been held to be support include church contributions (Rev. Rul. 58-67, 1958-1 C.B. 62), telephone (*William K. Price, III,* 1961 PH T.C. Memo ¶61,173, 20 TCM 886), medical insurance premiums (*James Edward Parker,* 1959 PH T.C. Memo ¶52,182, 18 TCM 800), child care (*Marvin D. Tucker,* 1957 PH T.C. Memo ¶57,118, 16 TCM 488), toys (*Loren S. Brumber,* 1952 PH T.C. Memo ¶52,087, 11 TCM 289), and vacations (*George R. Melat,* 1953 PH T.C. Memo ¶53,141, 12 TCM 443).

[23] *Frank Markarian v. CIR.,* 16 AFTR 2d 5785, 65-2 USTC ¶9699 (7th Cir., 1965).
[24] Examples of items that have been excluded are funeral expenses (Rev. Rul. 65-307, 1965-2 C.B. 40), taxes (Rev. Rul. 58-67, 1958-1 C.B. 62), a rifle, lawn mower, boat insurance (*Harriet C. Flower v. U.S.,* 52 AFTR 1383, 57-1 USTC ¶9655 (D.C. Pa., 1957)), and life insurance premiums (*John F. Miller,* 1959 PH T.C. Memo ¶59,155, 18 TCM 673).
[25] Rev. Rul. 77-282, 1977-2 C.B. 52.

Whether a portion of the utilities could be included in support would depend on whether the rental rate for the room included utilities. The fact that the mother used the television set probably would not be sufficient to cause its cost to be viewed as support. On the other hand, if the television set was a gift to the mother, was placed in her room, and was used exclusively by her, the cost probably would qualify as support. ◄

If a taxpayer contributes a lump sum for the support of two or more individuals, the amount is allocated between the individuals on a pro rata basis unless proof exists to the contrary.[26]

EXAMPLE I2-15 ► Jaime pays rent of $6,000 for an apartment occupied by his aunts Alice, Beth, and Cindy. Alice spends $3,000 toward her own support, Beth spends $1,000, and Cindy spends $1,000. Jaime is assumed to have provided $2,000 of support for each aunt. Thus, assuming the other tests are met, Jaime can claim exemptions for Beth and Cindy, but not for Alice. ◄

EXAMPLE I2-16 ► Paul and Mary have three children and are unclear whether they can claim their children as dependents in 2006. Information on the children is as follows:

► Peter, age 25, who served in the military immediately after high school, is a college senior. He worked part-time earning $2,200 and provided 20% of his support.

► Mark, age 22, graduated from college in May (he was a full-time student for five months of the year), and accepted a job in June. He lived with his parents for the entire year, earned $28,000, and provided 70% of his own support.

► Ruth, age 18, graduated from high school in May, and moved into an apartment immediately after graduation. She earned $5,500 from a job and provided 30% of her own support for the year.

The first step is to determine whether any of the children are considered qualifying children. None of the children are qualifying children. Peter is over age 23. Mark provided more than 50% of his own support. Ruth did not live with her parents for more than one-half of the year. The second step is to determine whether any of the children are considered qualifying relatives. Peter is considered as a qualifying relative as he meets the relationship, gross income, and support tests. Mark fails both the gross income and support tests, and Ruth fails the gross income test. Thus, only Peter can be claimed as a dependency exemption. ◄

TIE-BREAKER RULES FOR DEPENDENCY EXEMPTIONS. More than one person can meet the requirements to claim someone as a dependent. Tie-breakers decide who receives the exemption in such situations, as follows:

► First, taxpayers who meet the requirements to claim the dependent under the qualifying child rules have priority over individuals who meet the requirements for other dependents.

► The next priority provides that parents have priority over other individuals.

► Finally, if neither of the first two tie-breakers apply, the third tie-breaker specifies that if none of the taxpayers is the child's parent, the exemption is awarded to the taxpayer with the highest AGI.

Consider a niece who lives with three aunts who contribute equal amounts to her support. Assuming other requirements are met, all three aunts satisfy the requirements to claim the niece as a dependent under the qualifying child rule. Taxpayers who meet the requirements to claim a dependent under the qualifying child rules have priority over individuals who meet the requirements for other relatives. This first tie-breaker would not determine which aunt receives the exemption as each meets the qualifying child requirement. Moving to the second tie-breaker, parents have priority over other individuals. Again, the tie-breaker will not determine which aunt receives the exemption as they are not the child's parent. Thus, in this case, the aunt with the greatest AGI would receive the exemption. In cases involving two parents, the exemption is awarded to the parent with whom the child resided for the longer period of time during the year, and if the child spent equal amounts of time with each parent, the exemption is awarded to the parent with the higher AGI.

---

[26] Rev. Rul. 64-222, 1964-2 C.B. 47.

Two provisions can override the normal operation of dependency exemption rules:

▶ A Multiple Support Declaration (Form 2120) can enable a taxpayer to claim a dependency exemption in situations where the taxpayer does not provide over one-half of the dependent's support. This can be very important when several individuals contribute to the support of an individual who is not a qualifying child.

▶ A Release of Claim to Exemption for Child of Divorced or Separated Parents (Form 8332) can enable a noncustodial parent to claim an exemption.

MULTIPLE SUPPORT AGREEMENTS.   Often several people contribute to the support of a dependent. When a group provides over one-half of the support of an individual but no one member of the group provides over one-half of the support, eligible members of the group are allowed to designate one group member to claim the exemption. Each eligible member (other than the taxpayer receiving the exemption) must agree in writing. The taxpayer claiming the exemption must complete a Multiple Support Declaration (Form 2120, shown on page I2-18). An eligible member is one who contributes more than 10% of the dependent's support and meet all requirements for claiming a dependency exemption except the support requirement.[27]

EXAMPLE I2-17 ▶ John T. Abel lives alone. His support comes from the following sources:

Andy (son)	$ 400
Gabe (son)	2,800
Mable (daughter)	2,000
Betty (friend)	2,800
Total	$8,000

Either Gabe or Mable can claim a dependency exemption if the other agrees in writing. Andy cannot claim the exemption because he did not provide over 10% of John's support. Betty cannot claim a dependency exemption because she is not related and John does not live with her. For this reason, Andy and Betty need not agree in writing. Form 2120 is included in the return of the taxpayer claiming the exemption. A completed Form 2120 is illustrated in Figure I2-2. ◀

The Multiple Support Declaration can supercede the tie-breaker rules discussed above except that the agreement cannot be used to pass the exemption from a person who is entitled to claim the dependent under the qualifying child rules to a person who is entitled to claim the exemption under the other dependent's rule.[28]

ADDITIONAL COMMENT

Form 8332 may be completed each year by the custodial parent to relinquish the dependency exemption for only that year, or it may be completed once, relinquishing the exemption for all future years.

PARENTAL RELEASE.   In the case of divorced or separated parents, the dependency exemption of children generally is awarded to the custodial parent. However, the noncustodial parent may claim the dependency exemption if the divorce or separation instrument specifies so, or if the custodial parent agrees in writing. The signed statement must be attached to the noncustodial parent's return each year in which the exemption is claimed. Form 8332 may be used for this purpose. In the case of a divorce or separation, the custodial spouse probably would be reluctant to relinquish the dependency exemption for a child. A noncustodial parent, however, might be able to negotiate the exemption in exchange for increased child support payments.

EXAMPLE I2-18 ▶ Hal and Pam obtain a divorce under the terms of which Pam receives custody of their son. Hal is ordered to pay $600 per month of child support. In absence of a written agreement to the contrary, Pam will receive the dependency exemption for the child. ◀

EXAMPLE I2-19 ▶ Assume the same facts as in Example I2-18 except that Pam negotiates child support payments of $800 per month and agrees in writing to allow Hal to claim the dependency exemption for the child. The written agreement will enable Hal to claim the dependency exemption for the child. ◀

---

[27] Sec. 152(c).   [28] Reg. Sec. 152(d)(1)(D).

Form **2120** (Rev. October 2005) Department of the Treasury Internal Revenue Service	**Multiple Support Declaration** ▶ Attach to Form 1040 or Form 1040A.	OMB No. 1545-0074 Attachment Sequence No. **114**

Name(s) shown on return

Gabe I. Abel

Your social security number

123 45 6789

During the calendar year ...., the eligible persons listed below each paid over 10% of the support of:

....
John T. Abel
Name of your qualifying relative

I have a signed statement from each eligible person waiving his or her right to claim this person as a dependent for any tax year that began in the above calendar year.

Mable B. Abel
Eligible person's name

222 11 0001
Social security number

402 N. Lable Lane Lawrence, NJ 08649
Address (number, street, apt. no., city, state, and ZIP code)

Eligible person's name

Social security number

Address (number, street, apt. no., city, state, and ZIP code)

Eligible person's name

Social security number

Address (number, street, apt. no., city, state, and ZIP code)

Eligible person's name

Social security number

Address (number, street, apt. no., city, state, and ZIP code)

FIGURE I2-2 ▶ FORM 2120

EXAMPLE I2-20 ▶ Andy and Beth obtain a divorce under the terms of which they share custody of their daughter. Whoever has custody for the greater part of the year receives the dependency exemption for the daughter unless they agree otherwise in writing. If they share custody equally, the parent with the higher AGI receives the exemption. ◀

SELF-STUDY QUESTION

Beth's mother, who is a U.S. citizen, has moved to France to spend her retirement years. She has retained her U.S. citizenship, but she is now a resident of France. Is it possible for Beth to claim her mother as a dependent?

ANSWER

Yes, the mother need only be a U.S. citizen.

PHASE-OUT OF PERSONAL AND DEPENDENCY EXEMPTIONS. Personal and dependency exemptions currently are phased out for high-income taxpayers. However, this phaseout is reduced beginning in 2006 and is completely eliminated by 2010. The phaseout is reduced by one-third in 2006 and 2007, two-thirds in 2008 and 2009, and there is no phaseout in 2010 and future years.

Exemptions are phased out at a rate of 2% for each $2,500 ($1,250 for married persons filing separate returns), or fraction thereof, of adjusted gross income (AGI) above the thresholds shown below. Then, this amount is reduced by one-third in 2006. The resulting phaseout is then subtracted from the total amount of personal and dependency exemptions. Below are the phaseout amounts for 2006:[29]

	Phase-Out Begins	Phase-Out Ends (More Than)
Single	$150,500	$273,000
Joint return	225,750	348,250
Head of household	188,150	310,650
Married, filing separately	112,875	174,125

---

[29] Sec. 151(d). In 2005, the phase-out began at $145,950 for single taxpayers, $218,950 for a joint return, $182,450 for a head of household, and $109,475 for a married individual filing a separate return. The full amount of exemptions were phased-out using a rate of 2%.

EXAMPLE I2-21 ▶ In 2006, Lee, a single taxpayer with one dependent, reports AGI of $120,000. Her personal and dependency exemption amount is $6,600 ($3,300 × 2) and is not subject to any reduction as her AGI is less than $150,500. ◀

EXAMPLE I2-22 ▶ Use the same facts as in Example I2-21 except Lee's AGI is $175,000. Her exemption amount of $6,600 is reduced by $880 to $5,720, computed as follows:

Personal and dependency exemptions ($3,300 × 2)	$6,600
Phaseout: $175,000 − $150,500 = $24,500; $24,500/$2,500 = 9.8, which is rounded to 10.0; 10.0 × 2% = 20%; 20% × $6,600 = $1,320; $1,320 − ⅓ ($1,320) =	(880)
	$5,720 ◀

STOP & THINK

Question: Jack and Leslie, who have four dependent children, are in the process of obtaining a divorce. Leslie is a surgeon and earns a net income of $400,000 per year from her medical practice. Jack is a pilot and earns a salary of $140,000. The only other source of income is $20,000 of income from interest and dividends which is divided equally. One major stumbling block in structuring the divorce settlement is deciding who will be allowed to claim the children as dependents. The attorneys have come to you for advice. From an income tax standpoint, which parent would benefit the most from being able to claim the children in 2006, or should they each claim two of the children?

Solution: Since Leslie's income is well above the 2006 phase-out limit for personal and dependency exemptions ($310,650), she would receive only one-third of any tax benefit from claiming any or all of the children for income tax purposes. Jack, on the other hand, will benefit from the full amount of dependency exemptions because the phase-out amounts for a taxpayer filing as head of household begin at $188,150 and his AGI is only $150,000 ($140,000 + $10,000). Therefore, for income tax purposes only, Jack should claim the four children since he will receive more tax benefit from the dependency exemptions, whereas Leslie would receive limited tax benefit if she claimed the children because her AGI is so high that her deduction for personal and dependency exemptions would be reduced by two-thirds. Head of household filing status depends on whether the taxpayers have custody of one or more children for over one-half of the year.

The rules for deducting personal and dependency exemptions are summarized in Topic Review I2-1.

Topic Review I2-1

Personal and Dependency Exemptions

EXEMPTIONS IN GENERAL

▶ One exemption is available for each taxpayer (except when the taxpayer is the dependent of another) and for each dependent.
▶ The amount of each exemption, which is adjusted annually for inflation, is $3,300 in 2006 and $3,200 in 2005.
▶ Exemptions are partially phased out for high-income taxpayers. For example, on a joint return the phase-out begins when the couple's adjusted gross income exceeds $225,750 and is completed when AGI reaches $348,250.

DEPENDENCY EXEMPTIONS

▶ One exemption is allowed for each dependent. As noted above, the exemptions are phased out for higher-income taxpayers.
▶ Each dependent must meet multiple conditions. All dependents (1) must have Social Security numbers reported on the taxpayer's return, (2) must meet a citizenship test, (3) cannot normally file a joint return, and (4) cannot claim others as dependents. Qualifying children must (1) be the taxpayer's child or sibling, (2) be under 18, a full-time student under 24, or disabled, (3) live with the taxpayer, and (4) not be self-supporting. Other qualifying relatives must (1) be related to the taxpayer, (2) have gross income less than the amount of the personal exemption, and (3) receive over one-half of their support from the taxpayer.

CHILD CREDIT

Under Sec. 24 of the IRC, individual taxpayers may claim a "child credit" of $1,000 for each qualifying child. The credit is reduced by $50 for each $1,000 (or fraction thereof) by which the taxpayer's modified adjusted gross income exceeds a threshold amount ($110,000 on joint returns, $75,000 for single taxpayers, and $55,000 for married persons filing separate returns). Neither the amount of the credit or the phase-out thresholds is indexed for inflation. Modified adjusted gross income is AGI plus any amounts excluded from gross income under Secs. 911, 931, and 933 which relate to certain foreign earned income and possession's income. To qualify for the credit, a child must be under the age of 17 and be a "qualifying child" as defined in the above discussion of dependency exemptions. See Chapter I14 for more information regarding the child credit.

ADDITIONAL COMMENT

There are now two credits that have similar names: the child tax credit and the child and dependent care credit. They are quite different in how the credit amounts are computed and which dependents qualify.

EXAMPLE I2-22 ▶

Jane and Bill have two eligible dependent children and a modified AGI of $120,300. They have excess AGI of $10,300 ($120,300 − $110,000) and are entitled to a credit of $1,450 [(2 × $1,000) − (11 × $50)]. ◀

The child credit is refundable to the extent of 15% of the taxpayer's earned income in excess of $11,300 ($11,000 in 2004).

EXAMPLE I2-23 ▶

Georgia's four dependent children entitle her to a child credit of $4,000. Assume her salary is $25,000 and her gross tax is $1,000. Her child credit exceeds her tax by $3,000. A portion of the child credit is refundable, but her refund in this case is limited to $2,055 [15% × ($25,000 − $11,300)]. ◀

DETERMINING THE AMOUNT OF TAX

After taxable income is computed, the next step is to determine the gross tax. Most individuals determine the amount of gross tax by looking in the tax table. (See page T-2 after Chapter I18 in *Principles* volume or after Chapter C15 in the *Comprehensive* volume.) This method allows the taxpayer to arrive at the gross tax without the need for multiplication and, therefore, simplifies the computation and reduces the number of errors. Individuals are required to use the tax table unless taxable income exceeds the maximum income in the table (currently $100,000), or if the taxpayer files a short period return on account of a change in the annual accounting period.

Taxpayers who cannot use the tax table instead use the tax rate schedule (located after Chapter I18 and on the inside cover of the text). Taxpayers using the tax rate schedule must actually compute the tax.

EXAMPLE I2-24 ▶

Liz is single and has taxable income of $48,210 in 2005. Liz's tax is determined by reference to the tax table for single taxpayers. (At the time of this writing, the 2005 tax table was the most recent available.) The tax from the table is $8,721. ◀

EXAMPLE I2-25 ▶

Jack and Pam are married, file a joint tax return, and have taxable income of $105,000 in 2006. They will use the tax rate schedule to compute their tax. The tax is computed as follows:

Tax on $61,300	$ 8,440
Tax on remaining $43,700 at 25%	10,925
Gross tax	$19,365 ◀

FILING STATUS

For 2006, there are six tax brackets applicable to individual taxpayers: 10%, 15%, 25%, 28%, 33%, and 35%. These rates are progressive in that as a taxpayer's income increases, the taxpayer moves into higher tax brackets. The income level at which higher tax brackets begin depends on the taxpayer's filing status. There are five different filing statuses but only four rate schedules and/or tax tables because married couples filing jointly and certain surviving spouses use the same rate schedule or tax table. The five filing statuses are as follows:

▶ Married filing jointly

▶ Surviving spouse

▶ Head of household

▶ Single

▶ Married filing separately

Before 1948, one rate schedule was used by all taxpayers. If a husband and wife both had income, each filed a return. This treatment was deemed to be unfair because various states allocated income between spouses differently. Some states used a community property law system while other states used a common law system. Today, only a few states continue to use the community property law system.[30]

In general, community property law allocates community income equally between a husband and wife, regardless of which spouse actually earns the income. In other states, income belongs to the spouse who produces the income. With a progressive tax system, placing income on one return instead of two can result in a much greater tax. For this reason, couples residing in noncommunity property states often paid more tax than their counterparts who resided in community property states. In 1948, Congress developed the joint-rate schedule to rectify this problem. Unmarried taxpayers who headed families felt they also should receive tax relief because they shared their incomes with their families. So, in 1957, Congress created a rate schedule for heads of households. Below is a discussion of who is covered by each filing status.

JOINT RETURN

A *joint return* can be filed by a man and woman if they meet certain tests.

▶ They must be legally married as of the last day of the tax year.[31] Whether a couple is married depends on the laws of the state of residence.[32] Couples in the process of a divorce are considered married until the date the divorce becomes final. A couple need not be living together in order to file a joint return. A joint return can be filed if one spouse dies during the year as long as the survivor does not remarry before the year-end. The executor of the estate must agree to the filing of a joint return.

▶ They must have the same tax year-end (except in the case of death).

▶ Both the husband and wife must be U.S. citizens or residents. An exception allows a joint return if the nonresident alien spouse agrees to report all of his or her income on the return.[33]

STOP & THINK

Question: Some higher income couples who marry find that their tax liabilities increase even if their combined incomes remain unchanged. Others find that their tax liabilities decrease. Explain why taxes increase for some couples, but decrease for others.

Solution: Couples who marry ordinarily move from two individual returns where incomes are taxed using the rate schedule for single individuals to one return where the combined incomes are taxed using the joint rate schedule. The less progressive joint rate schedule results in a lower tax when one spouse has most of the income because more of that spouse's income is taxed at lower rates. However, when a higher income husband and wife have approximately equal incomes, their combined incomes are taxed at higher rates on one joint return. Even though the joint rate schedule is the least progressive, the combined tax for higher income couples is greater because the 25% and higher brackets in the

---

[30] Several states had either adopted or had begun to adopt community property laws in order to reduce the federal taxes paid by their residents. After the joint rate schedule was created, states without a tradition of community property law returned to common law. For a more detailed discussion of community property states, see page I3-6.

[31] Sec. 6013.

[32] Thus, common law marriages recognized by the state of residence are cov-

ered. On the other hand, an annulled marriage is viewed as never having been valid. Thus, such a couple cannot file a joint return.

[33] Nonresident aliens are taxed only on income earned in the United States. If a joint return is filed by a U.S. citizen and his or her foreign spouse, they would receive the benefit of the low rate schedule, even though only the U.S. citizen reported income on the return. Thus, to file a joint return, the couple must agree to report both incomes (Sec. 6013(g)).

ADDITIONAL COMMENT

Since marital status for the entire year is determined on the last day of the year, some couples actually plan for their wedding to occur on December 31 or January 1. In general, if only one person has income, the wedding should take place on December 31. If both have income, a January 1 wedding is better (for tax purposes).

joint rate schedule are less than twice as wide as the same brackets for single taxpayers. For example, two single individuals with $70,000 of taxable income each are in the 25% tax bracket, while a married couple with $70,000 of taxable income each is in the 28% bracket. This results because the 28% bracket begins at $74,200 for single taxpayers, but at $123,700 for married couples. Assuming the taxable income on the joint return is $140,000, the so-called marriage penalty is $489 because $16,300 of income is taxed at 28% instead of 25%. The additional tax is even greater for taxpayers with higher incomes. Nevertheless, because the lower tax brackets were widened in 2003, the additional tax for married couples is considerably less than it has been in the past.

SURVIVING SPOUSE

A widow or widower can file a joint return for the year his or her spouse dies if the widow or widower does not remarry. For the two years after the year of death, the widow or widower can file as a surviving spouse only if he or she meets specific conditions. The **surviving spouse** (sometimes called a qualifying widow or widower) must[34]

▶ Have not remarried as of the year end in which surviving spouse status is claimed.

▶ Be a U.S. citizen or resident.

▶ Have qualified to file a joint return in the year of death.

▶ Have at least one dependent child[35] living at home during the entire year and the taxpayer must pay over half of the expenses of the home.

KEY POINT

The surviving-spouse provision entitles the taxpayer to the lower joint return tax rate schedule and to the higher joint return standard deduction.

In the year of death, a joint return can be filed. On the joint return, the income of the deceased spouse (earned before death) and the survivor are both reported. Personal exemptions are allowed for both spouses. In the two years following death, surviving spouse status can be claimed only if the conditions outlined above are met. Only the surviving spouse's income is reported and, of course, no personal exemption is available for the deceased spouse. What the two situations have in common is that in both instances, the taxpayer can use the more favorable joint rate schedule and standard deduction amount.

EXAMPLE I2-26 ▶ Connie and Carl are married and have no dependent children. Carl dies in 2006. Connie can file a joint return, even though her husband died before the end of the year. Alternatively, Connie can file as a married individual filing a separate return. In 2007, however, Connie must file as a single taxpayer since she has no dependent children who would qualify her as a surviving spouse or a head of household. Alternatively, if Connie and Carl had dependent children, Connie could file as a surviving spouse for 2007 and 2008 and use the joint return rate schedules. ◀

 STOP & THINK

Question: Most recently-widowed individuals do not qualify for surviving spouse status. Why?

Solution: Most individuals are widowed late in life after their children are grown and have left home. As having a dependent child is a requirement for surviving spouse status, these individuals do not qualify for the special lower tax rate. Such individuals may ordinarily file a joint return in the year of the spouse's death.

ADDITIONAL COMMENT

Due in part to the high divorce rate in this country, the number of head-of-household returns has increased. In 1975, only 6% of all returns had the filing status of head-of-household. In 1996, that number was 11.6%, or 12.0 million returns.

HEAD OF HOUSEHOLD

A second rate schedule or tax table is available to a head of household. The head of household rates increase more rapidly than those applicable to married taxpayers filing jointly and surviving spouses, but more slowly than those applicable to other single taxpayers. To claim head-of-household status, a taxpayer must meet all of the following conditions:[36]

▶ Be unmarried as of the last day of the tax year. Exceptions apply to individuals married to nonresident aliens[37] and to abandoned spouses.[38] An individual cannot claim head-

---

[34] Sec. 2(a).
[35] Includes an adopted child, a stepchild, or a foster child.
[36] Sec. 2(b).
[37] Specifically, this refers to an individual married to a nonresident alien if he or she meets the remaining head-of-household requirements.

[38] Abandoned spouse rules are discussed under a separate heading later in this chapter.

of-household status in the year his or her spouse died. Such individuals must file a joint return or a separate return.

► Not be a surviving spouse.

► Be a U.S. citizen or resident.

► Pay over half of the costs of maintaining as his or her home a household in which a dependent relative lives for more than half of the tax year. The dependency exemption cannot be based on a multiple support agreement. A taxpayer with a dependent parent qualifies even if the parent does not live with the taxpayer. A taxpayer with a qualifying child[39] satisfies the requirement even if the taxpayer releases the exemption to the child's other parent.

The second exception often comes into play in cases of divorced parents. As noted earlier in the chapter, a written agreement can give the dependency exemption to the non-custodial parent. This exception may allow the custodial parent to still claim head-of-household status.

EXAMPLE I2-27 ►

Brad and Ellen divorce. Ellen receives custody of their child, and Brad is ordered by the court to pay child support of $6,000 per year. Ellen agrees in writing to allow Brad to claim the dependency exemption for the child. If Ellen maintains the home in which she and her child live, she can claim head-of-household status even though the child is Brad's dependent. ◄

ADDITIONAL COMMENT

In 2003, approximately 22 married couples filed joint returns for every married couple that filed separately.

As noted, the taxpayer must pay over half of the costs of maintaining the household. These expenses include property taxes, mortgage interest, rent, utility charges, upkeep and repairs, property insurance, and food consumed on the premises. Such costs do not include clothing, education, medical treatment, vacations, life insurance, transportation, or the value of services provided by the taxpayer.[40]

SINGLE TAXPAYER

An unmarried individual who does not qualify as a surviving spouse or a head of household must file as a single taxpayer. The tax rates progress more rapidly than those that apply to other unmarried taxpayers.

EXAMPLE I2-28 ►
KEY POINT

Several disadvantages are associated with the filing of separate returns by married individuals. For example, a taxpayer may lose all or part of the benefits of the deduction for individual retirement accounts, the child care credit, and the earned income credit.

Becky, a single taxpayer with no dependents, files her first tax return. She will file as a single taxpayer. ◄

MARRIED FILING A SEPARATE RETURN

Married individuals who choose to file separate returns must use the separate rate schedule. The rates on this schedule increase more rapidly than other individual rate schedules. The implications of joint returns versus separate returns are discussed later in this chapter.

EXAMPLE I2-29 ►

On December 31, Rose marries Joe. Because they were married before the year ended, they may elect to file jointly. Alternatively, they may file separate returns with each using the rate schedule applicable to separate returns. ◄

The filing requirements for individuals are summarized in Topic Review I2-2.

KEY POINT

When one thinks of a person who would qualify as an abandoned spouse, one thinks of a person in dire financial condition. If no relief were granted, this person would be required to use the married filing separately tax rate schedule, which contains the highest rates.

ABANDONED SPOUSE

The particular rate schedule a taxpayer uses can have a great impact on the amount of tax. Without any special rule, an abandoned spouse would be required to file using the rate schedules for a married person filing separately. Congress has provided relief for taxpayers in this situation if they can meet certain conditions. A married individual can claim head-of-household status if[41]

► The taxpayer lived apart from his or her spouse for the last six months of the year.

---

[39] Qualifying child has the same meaning as is associated with dependency exemptions except that the child cannot be married.

[40] Reg. Sec. 1.2-2(d).
[41] Sec. 2(c).

Topic Review I2-2

Filing Status and Requirements

FILING STATUS	MUST MAINTAIN HOUSEHOLD	MUST HAVE DEPENDENT	MARITAL STATUS	MUST BE CITIZEN	TAX RATES
Joint	No requirement	No	Married	Yes	Lowest rates, but two incomes are combined
Surviving spouse	Yes	Yes, son or daughter	Widowed in prior or second prior year	Yes	Uses same schedule as married couple filing joint return
Head of household	Yes	Generally, yes	Generally, single	Yes	Intermediate tax rates
Single	No requirement	No	Single	No	Highest tax rates for unmarried taxpayers
Separate	No requirement	No	Married	No	Highest tax rates

▶ The taxpayer pays over half of the cost of maintaining a household in which the taxpayer and a dependent son or daughter live for over half of the year.[42]

▶ The taxpayer is a U.S. citizen or resident.

The requirement that the taxpayer have a dependent child is met if a taxpayer who is otherwise qualified to claim the child as a dependent signs an agreement that allows the child's noncustodial parent to claim the dependency exemption for the child.[43]

EXAMPLE I2-30 ▶ In October, Bob and Gail decide to separate. Gail supports their children after the separation and pays the costs of maintaining their home. Gail cannot claim abandoned spouse status because Bob lived with her for over one-half of the year. If she had obtained a divorce before the end of the year, she could have filed as a head of household. In the absence of a divorce, Gail must file a separate return, unless both Bob and Gail agree to file a joint return. ◀

EXAMPLE I2-31 ▶ Assume the same facts as in Example I2-30 except that Gail continues to support her children and pay household expenses during the next year. She can file as a head of household even if she has not obtained a divorce. ◀

DEPENDENTS WITH UNEARNED INCOME

In the past, taxpayers in high tax brackets were able to reduce their tax liability by shifting income to children and other dependents. Under prior law, no tax was due if the income was less than the dependent's personal exemption and standard deduction. Even if the shifted income was greater than these amounts, there was a tax savings if the dependent was in a low tax bracket. Under current law, three rules curtail the advantages of shifting income to dependents:

▶ Dependents do not receive a personal exemption on their own returns.

▶ A dependent's standard deduction is reduced to the greater of $850 ($800 in 2005) or the dependent's earned income (such as salary) plus $300 ($250 in 2005).

KEY POINT

Children under the age of 14 will not have their net unearned income tax at their parents' tax rate until the children's unearned income exceeds $1,700.

▶ The tax on the net unearned income (such as dividends and interest) of a child under age 14 is figured by reference to the parents' tax rate if it is higher than the child's.

The first two rules have been discussed previously in this chapter. The third rule is discussed below.

---

[42] Includes adopted child, stepchild, and foster child.   [43] Sec. 152(e).

EXAMPLE I2-32 ▶ In 2006, Tim is a self-supporting 18-year-old who received $2,000 of interest income and $2,500 from a part-time job. He is entitled to the regular standard deduction and a personal exemption because his parents may not claim him as a dependent as he does not meet the support test. Tim owes no tax as these deductions exceed his income. ◀

EXAMPLE I2-33 ▶ Assume the same facts as in Example I2-32 except that Tim is a dependent of his parents, and they are in the 28% tax bracket. Because Tim is a dependent, he is not entitled to a personal exemption. Tim's standard deduction is limited to the greater of $850 or his earned income plus $300 (but not more than $5,150). Because his earned income is $2,500, the standard deduction is $2,800 ($2,500 + $300). Therefore, Tim's taxable income is $1,700 ($4,500 AGI − $2,800 standard deduction). Since Tim is over age 13, he is not subject to the kiddie tax on his unearned income and his regular tax rate (10%) applies. The tax is $170 (0.10 × $1,700). ◀

Under the third rule, often called the kiddie tax, part of the **net unearned income** of a dependent child under age 14 is taxed at the child's rate, and part at the parents' marginal tax rate if that rate is higher than the child's. This tax can be computed following a three-step process:

1. Compute the child's taxable income in the normal fashion for dependents as discussed earlier in this chapter.

2. Compute the child's net unearned income:

Unearned income (described below)	$xxx
Less: Statutory deduction of $850	(xxx)
Less: Greater of	
a. $850 of standard deduction, or	
b. Itemized deductions directly connected with	
the production of the unearned income.	(xxx)
Equals: Net unearned income	$xxx

3. Compute the child's tax:

Net unearned income times parents' marginal tax rate	$xxx
Plus: Difference between taxable income and net	
unearned income times child's tax rate	xxx
Equals: Child's total tax	$xxx

Unearned income is the child's investment income including dividends, taxable interest, capital gains, rents, royalties and other income that is not earned income (such as salary).[44]

EXAMPLE I2-34 ▶ Assume the same facts as in Example I2-33 except that Tim is age 13. His standard deduction is still $2,800 and his taxable income is also $1,700. Since Tim is under age 14, a portion of his unearned income may be subject to tax at his parents' 28% rate. The computation of Tim's tax is as follows:

1. Compute Tim's taxable income:

Wages		$2,500
Interest income		2,000
Adjusted gross income		$4,500
Standard deduction	$2,800	
Personal exemption	0	2,800
Taxable income		$1,700

2. Compute Tim's net unearned income:

Unearned income: Interest income	$2,000
Statutory deduction	(850)
Portion of standard deduction	(850)
Net unearned income	$ 300

---

[44] Sec. 1(g)(4).

3. Compute Tim's tax

Tax on net unearned income: $300 × 28%	$ 84
Tax on taxable income minus net unearned income: ($1,750 − $300) × 10%	145
Total income tax	$ 229 ◄

As discussed in more detail in Chapters I3 and I5, dividend income and capital gains are currently taxed at lower rates than other income. For example, the long-term capital gains and dividend income of individuals in the 25% and higher brackets are taxed 15% while individuals in the 10% and 15% brackets are taxed at 5%. These lower rates also apply to the kiddie tax calculation. In figuring the tax where the parents file separate returns, the tax rate of the parent with the greater taxable income is used. If the parents are divorced, the parent with custody is the relevant parent.

EXAMPLE I2-35 ▶ Celeste, age 12 and a dependent of her parents, received $2,000 of dividend income. This was her sole source of income during the year. Her parents are in the 25% income tax bracket. Her taxable income is $1,150 ($2,000 dividend − $850 standard deduction) and her net unearned income is $300 ($2,000 − $850 − $850). Her tax is $88 ($850 × 0.05 + $300 × 0.15). The first $850 of taxable income is taxed at Celeste's rate for dividends, which is 5%, while the balance of her income is taxed at her parents' rate for dividends of 15%. ◄

Parents of a child under age 14 may elect to include the child's dividend and interest income on their own return.[45] This rule eliminates the need to file a tax return for the child. To be eligible for the election, the child's gross income must come solely from dividends and interest, and such income must not exceed $8,500 ($8,000 in 2005). Furthermore, there can be no withholding or estimated payment using the child's Social Security number. Parents use Form 8814, Parents' Election to Report Child's Interest and Dividends.

BUSINESS INCOME AND BUSINESS ENTITIES

OBJECTIVE 6

Explain the tax formula for corporations

How business income is reported depends on the type of entity. Proprietors report their business income on Schedule C of Form 1040 (Schedule F in the case of farmers). The income is taxed on the proprietor's Form 1040 along with the taxpayer's other income. Approximately 17 million taxpayers report income on Schedule C each year.

Corporations are divided into two groups: C corporations and S corporations. **C corporations**, also called **regular corporations**, are treated as separate entities for tax purposes

WHAT WOULD YOU DO IN THIS SITUATION? °

CHOICE OF RATE SCHEDULES

Jane Brown married Jim four years ago. Two years ago Jim lost his job. After looking for work for several months, Jim left town to look for work, and Jane has not heard from him. Jim's brother told Jane that he had heard that Jim lived in Texas, but a friend said he heard that Jim had been killed in an automobile accident.

Jane went back to school and completed a program as an medical technician. She returned to work this year, and she earned $35,000. She has asked you to prepare her tax return this year. She has asked you whether she should file as a single taxpayer, married person filing separately, or as a married person filing jointly. Because she has had a low income until recently, she has taken no legal steps to resolve her status. What should she do?

---

[45] Sec. 1(g)(7).

ADDITIONAL COMMENT

In 2002, there were 5.3 million corporate tax returns filed.

KEY POINT

The tax formula for C corporations differs from the tax formula for individuals in several important respects. The corporate tax formula does not contain an adjusted gross income figure, personal and dependency exemptions, or the standard deduction.

and pay income taxes on the corporation's taxable income. Shareholders are taxed on dividends they receive from a C corporation but are not taxed on the corporation's undistributed income. Lower tax rates apply temporarily to dividends received by individual taxpayers. See Chapter I3. Approximately 2 million corporations file the regular corporate return, Form 1120, each year.

The tax formula for C corporations is presented in Table I2-7. The major difference between the formulas for individual and corporate taxpayers is the fact that there is only one category of deductions for corporations. Personal expenses do not come into consideration. Therefore, there are no itemized deductions, standard deductions, or personal exemptions. The tax rates applicable to C corporations are as follows:[46]

Taxable Income	Tax
First $50,000	15% of taxable income
Over $50,000, but not over $75,000	$7,500 + 25% of taxable income over $50,000
Over $75,000, but not over $100,000	$13,750 + 34% of taxable income over $75,000
Over $100,000, but not over $335,000	$22,250 + 39% of taxable income over $100,000
Over $335,000, but not over $10,000,000	$113,900 + 34% of taxable income over $335,000
Over $10,000,000, but not over $15,000,000	$3,400,000 + 35% of taxable income over $10,000,000
Over $15,000,000, but not over $18,333,333	$5,150,000 + 38% of taxable income over $15,000,000
Over $18,333,333	$6,416,667 + 35% of taxable income over $18,333,333

Note that the corporate tax rates reflect a stair-step pattern of progression, with the two highest rates of 39% and 38% in the middle of the progression. The benefits of the two lowest tax rates of 15% and 25% are completely eliminated by the application of the 39% tax rate to taxable income between $100,000 and $335,000. Likewise, the benefit of the 34% tax rate on taxable income between $335,000 and $10,000,000 is eliminated by the application of a 38% tax rate on taxable income between $15,000,000 and $18,333,333.

The second group of corporations, S corporations, generally are not treated as separate entities for tax purposes. They are referred to as flow-through entities. S corporation shareholders are required to report their respective shares of the S corporation's income on their individual tax returns even if the income is not distributed. All shareholders must

▼ **TABLE I2-7**
Tax Formula for C Corporations

Income from whatever source derived	$xxx
Minus: Exclusions	(xxx)
Gross income	$xxx
Minus: Deductions	(xxx)
Taxable income	$xxx
Times: Tax rates	× .xx
Gross tax	$xxx
Minus: Credits and prepayments	(xxx)
Net tax payable or refund due	$xxx

[46] Income of certain personal service corporations is taxed at a flat rate of 35%.

agree to the S corporation election when it is made. S corporations must also meet a series of conditions, such as having no foreign shareholders. S corporations report ordinary income and special items separately and shareholders in turn report their respective shares of the ordinary income and of each special item. Approximately 3 million corporations file S corporation returns, Form 1120S, each year.

In one sense, there is no formula to compute an S corporation's taxable income because the corporation normally does not pay a tax. S corporations do file returns, but the returns are more informational in nature, much like the returns of a partnership. A residual income total, known as ordinary income, is computed on the return. Special items, such as capital gains and losses and charitable contributions, are kept separate from the ordinary income amount. This is because every item that would receive special treatment on a shareholder's return is passed through to the shareholder with its status intact. Each shareholder reports his or her share of the ordinary income and his or her share of each special item. Losses pass through and generally can be deducted by shareholders up to their respective bases in the corporation's stock. Losses are also subject to other rules, such as the at-risk and passive activity loss rules, and are covered in Chapter I8.

Partnerships, like S corporations, are flow-through entities for tax purposes. Partners report their respective shares of the partnership's income on their tax returns even if the income is not distributed. Approximately 2 million partnerships file returns, Form 1065, each year. Like S corporations, partnerships report ordinary income and special items separately and the partners report their respective shares of the ordinary income and of each special item. Losses also pass through and generally can be deducted by partners on their returns.

EXAMPLE I2-36 ▶

Jane is starting Jane's Computer Services and is considering alternative organizational forms. She anticipates the business will earn $100,000 from operations before compensating her for her services and before charitable contributions. Jane, who is single, has $3,000 of income from other sources and other itemized deductions of $11,000. Her compensation for services will be $50,000. Charitable contributions to be made by the business are expected to be $4,000. Other distributions to her from the business are expected to be $15,000. Compare her current income tax for 2006 assuming she operates the business as a proprietorship, an S corporation, and a C corporation. Ignore payroll and other taxes.

	Proprietorship	S Corporation	C Corporation
Business Income			
Operating income	$100,000	$100,000	$100,000
Compensation paid to Jane		(50,000)	(50,000)
Contributions			(4,000)
Net	$100,000	$ 50,000	$ 46,000
Corporate income tax			$ 6,900
Jane's Income			
Business income (above)	$100,000	$ 50,000	
Compensation (above)		50,000	$ 50,000
Dividends			15,000
Other income	3,000	3,000	3,000
Adjusted Gross Income	$103,000	$103,000	$ 68,000
Contributions	$ 4,000	$ 4,000	
Other itemized deductions	11,000	11,000	11,000
Personal exemption	3,300	3,300	3,300
Taxable income	$ 84,700	$ 84,700	$ 53,700
Individual income tax	$ 18,048	$ 18,048	$ 8,483
Total tax	$ 18,048	$ 18,048	$ 15,383

In each of the alternatives, Jane reports other income of $3,000 and other itemized deductions of $11,000 on her personal return.

No separate return is filed for the proprietorship. Jane reports the $100,000 income from her business on Schedule C of her Form 1040 and she claims the $4,000 charitable contribution as an itemized deduction on Schedule A along with the other itemized deductions. In this case, whether Jane considers part of the income from the business to be compensation for her services is irrelevant.

With an S election, two returns are filed, a Form 1120S for the corporation and a Form 1040 on Jane's behalf. Because of the S election, the corporation pays no tax. Items reported on the Form 1120S "pass through" the corporation and are reported by Jane on her own return. The $50,000 of compensation paid to Jane by the corporation is deducted by the corporation in computing its income and is taxable to Jane. Jane also reports the remaining $50,000 of the corporation's income on her return and claims the $4,000 charitable contribution as an itemized deduction.

The C corporation is taxed as a separate entity. The corporation files a Form 1120 on which it would deduct the $50,000 of compensation paid to Jane along with the $4,000 charitable contribution and pay a $6,900 (15% × $46,000) tax on the remaining income. Jane reports the $50,000 salary along with the $15,000 dividend distributed by the corporation. Note that the dividend of $15,000 paid by the corporation is not deductible by the corporation. A temporary provision reduces the "double tax" on the dividends Jane receives from the corporation by subjecting the dividends to a 15% tax rate instead of the 25% rate that would otherwise apply. (See Chapter I3.) As a result, her tax on the dividends is $2,250 (15% × $15,000) and her tax on her remaining income of $38,700 ($53,700 − $15,000) is $6,233 (from the rate schedule). Her total tax is $8,483. The total tax for the corporation and Jane is $15,383.

As shown, Jane's total current income tax will be lower if she chooses to operate her business as a C corporation even though the $15,000 paid to her as a dividend is taxed twice—once inside the corporation when it is earned and again on Jane's return. The reason the total tax is lower is because the $31,000 of income retained by the corporation is taxed at the corporation's marginal tax rate of 15% instead of being taxed at Jane's marginal rates of 25% and 28%. The savings will be lost in the future if the corporation distributes the retained income as a dividend. Clearly, if the plans are to distribute the $31,000 in the near future, it is desirable to operate as a proprietorship or an S corporation so that the distribution can be made without any future tax.

Self-employment taxes and social security taxes would also be considered when an organizational form is selected for a new business. Although detailed consideration of these taxes is found in Chapter I14, it is noted here that the self-employment tax, which generally applies to the proprietorship and partnership forms of doing business, would be greater than the social security tax which would apply only to the wages paid to Jane by the S and C corporations. Given the facts in this case, Jane might judge the proprietorship organizational form less favorably when these taxes are taken into consideration. Jane should consider these taxes along with other taxes (e.g., state and local taxes) and other nontax factors such as liability protection before making a final decision. ◀

The detailed rules of C corporations are covered in Chapter I16 while S corporations and partnerships are covered in Chapter I17 of the *Individuals* volume. All three are covered more extensively in the *Corporations, Partnerships, Estates, and Trusts* volume and the *Comprehensive* volume.

TREATMENT OF CAPITAL GAINS AND LOSSES

OBJECTIVE 7

Explain the basic concepts of property transactions

Capital gains and losses have been accorded favored tax treatment since 1922. Favored tax treatment essentially means that capital gains are taxed at a lower rate than is ordinary income. A purpose of the special rules is to distinguish capital appreciation from gains attributable to ordinary business transactions and speculation. This goal is accomplished by defining capital assets to not include certain business property (e.g., inventory and trade receivables) and by requiring taxpayers to hold capital assets for minimum time periods in order to benefit from the lower rates that are available to capital gains.

The discussion below is intended as a brief introduction to capital gains and losses. A detailed discussion of this topic is contained in Chapter I5.

DEFINITION OF *CAPITAL ASSETS*

A **capital gain** or **loss** is the gain or loss from the sale or exchange of a capital asset. Unfortunately, the tax law merely states what is not a capital asset. In other words, **capital assets** are assets other than those listed in Sec. 1221. A detailed discussion is found in Chapter I5. Here we simply note the categories of properties included on the list, which are thereby excluded from capital asset status are inventory, trade receivables, certain properties created by the efforts of the taxpayer (such as works of art), depreciable business property and business land, and certain government publications. All other assets are considered capital assets and include investment property (such as stocks and bonds) and personal-use property (such as personal residence or automobile). As noted, a purpose of the rules applicable to capital gains and losses is to distinguish capital appreciation from gains derived from ordinary business operations. The profit from the sale of inventory and trade receivables is viewed as business profit as opposed to capital appreciation. Thus, a gain realized by an artist on the sale of one of his or her own works is ordinary income from personal services. However, gain from the sale of artwork held as an investment or for personal use would be treated as a capital gain.

TAX TREATMENT OF GAINS AND LOSSES

Capital gains and losses are divided into long-term (associated with property held over one year) and short-term (associated with property held one year or less). Individual taxpayers pay a maximum 15% tax on a net long-term capital gain (a 5% tax in the case of individuals who are in the 10% and 15% tax brackets). A net short-term capital gain is taxed at the same rate as other income.

On the other hand, individuals who suffer net capital losses can deduct only up to $3,000 of the losses from other income. A net capital loss in excess of $3,000 can be carried over and offset against future capital gains or, subject to the $3,000 limitation, deducted from other income.

TAX PLANNING CONSIDERATIONS

SHIFTING INCOME BETWEEN FAMILY MEMBERS

Because of the progressive tax system, families often can reduce their taxes by **shifting income** to family members who are in lower tax brackets.

EXAMPLE I2-37 ▶ Mary, who is in the 35% tax bracket, shifted $5,000 of income to her 22-year-old son, Steve, by making a gift of a 10%, $50,000 corporate bond. Steve had no income as he suffered a business loss. In absence of the shift, 35% of the income would have gone for taxes. There is no tax on Steve's return because the income is offset by his loss. ◀

EXAMPLE I2-38 ▶ Farouk, who is in the 35% tax bracket, shifted $2,000 of income to his 18-year-old daughter, Dana, who is in the 10% tax bracket. The tax savings from the shift is $500 [(0.35 × $2,000) − (0.10 × $2,000)]. ◀

As noted earlier in this chapter, the net unearned income of children under the age of 14 is taxed at their parents' tax rate. Hence, a shifting of income to young children is often an ineffective method of minimizing tax.

Shifting income must be distinguished from assigning income. Earned income is taxed to the person who produces it. Income from property is taxed to the person who owns the property. Ordering income to be paid to another is an assignment of income that does not change who is taxed on the income. Normally, in the case of income from property, ownership of the property must be transferred in order to shift the income.

EXAMPLE I2-39 ▶ John owns stock in Valley Corporation. John orders the corporation to pay this year's dividends to his daughter. John will be taxed on the income even though he has assigned it to another person. ◀

EXAMPLE I2-40 ▶ Kay owns stock in Valley Corporation. Kay gives the stock to her 17-year-old son. Future dividends on Valley stock will be taxed to the son instead of to Kay. ◀

Individuals often are unwilling to give property away completely. As a result, personal preference may limit the amount of tax planning that is possible.

SPLITTING INCOME

Splitting income consists of creating additional taxable entities, especially corporations, in order to reduce an individual's effective tax rate.

EXAMPLE I2-41 ▶ Tom is a taxpayer in the 35% tax bracket and is involved in a variety of businesses. One business has been producing $20,000 of income per year for several years. Tom incorporates the business. The first $50,000 of a corporation's income is taxed at a 15% rate. Thus, the tax on the income is reduced by $4,000 [(0.35 × $20,000) − (0.15 × $20,000)]. ◀

The creation of a new corporate entity to split income is not always desirable because the corporation's income will be taxed to the shareholder as a dividend if it is distributed. In addition, if income is allowed to accumulate in a corporation indefinitely, it may be subject to the accumulated earnings tax.[47]

MAXIMIZING ITEMIZED DEDUCTIONS

KEY POINT

The ability to maximize itemized deductions by the timing of expenditures is somewhat limited. The two most significant items that would lend themselves to such a strategy are property taxes and charitable contributions. Prepaid interest is not deductible until accrued.

Timing expenditures properly often can increase deductions. In general, cash-basis taxpayers deduct expenses in the year paid. If itemized deductions are less than the standard deduction, the taxpayer will receive no tax benefit from the deductions. A taxpayer in that situation could defer some payments or accelerate others to maximize expenses in one year, thereby creating a sufficient amount of deductions in that year.

EXAMPLE I2-42 ▶ Jean's property taxes are due on January 1 of each year. Jean is a single, cash-basis, calendar-year taxpayer. Itemized deductions other than property taxes total $3,000 in each year. Jean pays the 2006 property taxes of $1,600 on January 1, 2006, and the 2007 property taxes of $1,600 on December 31, 2006. In the absence of doubling up, Jean would not be able to itemize in either year. The itemized deductions of $4,600 ($3,000 + $1,600) would be less than the standard deduction of $5,150. By doubling up, Jean has itemized deductions of $6,200 ($3,000 + $1,600 + $1,600) in 2006. ◀

Medical expenses are deductible only to the extent they exceed 7.5% of a taxpayer's AGI. In situations where medical expenses are just under 7.5% of AGI, taxpayers may be able to create a deduction by doubling up.

EXAMPLE I2-43 ▶ Troy's AGI is $20,000. So far in 2006, Troy's medical expenses have totaled $1,300. Troy has received a bill from his dentist for $500 that is due January 15, 2007. By paying the bill in 2006, Troy will have a deduction for medical expenses of $300 [$1,300 + $500 − (0.075 × $20,000)]. This assumes that Troy's other itemized deductions exceed the standard deduction.[48] ◀

FILING JOINT OR SEPARATE RETURNS

FACTORS TO BE CONSIDERED. In general, married couples may file either joint or separate returns. As noted earlier, if one spouse has significantly more than half of their combined income, filing separately will increase the couple's total income tax. Because of the potential tax saving from a joint return and because it is simpler to prepare one return than two, most married couples file jointly.

It should be noted that the joint return is not always preferred. Separate returns may result in increased deductions. Because only one spouse's income is reported on a separate return, medical expenses are more likely to exceed the 7.5% of adjusted gross income

---

[47] Amounts accumulated in a corporation in excess of $250,000 may be subject to this tax. However, amounts accumulated for business purposes are exempt. This subject is discussed briefly in Chapter I16 and extensively in *Prentice Hall's Federal Taxation: Corporations, Partnerships, Estates and Trusts.*

[48] For a discussion of restrictions on the deductibility of prepaid medical expenses, see Chapter I7.

floor if one spouse incurs most of the medical expenses. Similarly, casualty losses involving personal-use assets, which are allowable only to the extent that they exceed 10% of AGI, may be deductible on separate returns.

One significant impact of the joint return is the joint income tax liability. Both the husband and wife may be liable for taxes owed on a joint return. This could be a major problem if a couple separates or divorces after filing a return.

EXAMPLE 12-44 ▶

Jim and Pat file a joint return. They are both informed as to the relevant information pertaining to the return. The next year they separate, and Jim moves out of town without leaving a forwarding address. The IRS audits their joint return and disallows $400 of charitable contributions deducted on the original return. Pat may be held responsible for the additional taxes owed. The IRS does not have to attempt to locate Jim in order to collect the tax. ◀

ETHICAL POINT

Because innocent spouse rules are strict, it may sometimes be safer to file a separate return than run the risk of being held responsible for the acts of another.

INNOCENT SPOUSE PROVISION. When married couples file a joint return, each spouse generally is liable for the entire tax and any penalties imposed.[49] This is the case even if all of the income was earned by one spouse. This rule could prove unfair in some instances, especially where one spouse concealed information from the other. For that reason, the Code contains an **innocent spouse** provision. An innocent spouse is relieved of the liability for tax on unreported income if:

▶ The amount is attributable to erroneous items of the other spouse.

▶ The innocent spouse did not know and had no reason to know that there was such an understatement of tax.

▶ Under the circumstances, it would be inequitable to hold the innocent spouse liable for the understatement.

▶ The innocent spouse elects relief within two years after the IRS begins collection activities.[50]

EXAMPLE 12-45 ▶

Dan and Joy file a joint return. Dan traveled much of the time and Joy had little information as to his whereabouts or income. Joy worked and her own salary was the sole source of her support. Their return was audited by the IRS. The audit disclosed that Dan had not reported income from a job he had held for several months during the year. In this situation, Joy may be able to use the innocent spouse provision in order to avoid being held liable for the tax on the unreported income. ◀

The election is permitted when the innocent spouse was aware of the understatement, but did not know or have reason to know the extent of the understatement. Relief is limited to the portion of the understatement attributable to the "unknown" amounts.

SEPARATE LIABILITY ELECTION. Couples who file joint returns and are subsequently divorced, widowed, or separated may make a separate liability election. An electing spouse is liable only for the portion of any understatement attributable to him or her.

EXAMPLE 12-46 ▶

Al and Ann divorce after filing a joint return. An IRS examination of the return reveals $20,000 of unreported income attributable to Al and $10,000 of unallowable deductions attributable to Ann. Together, these amounts result in an understatement of their tax by $9,000. If Ann can establish that she was unaware of Al's unreported income, she can make a separate liability election. She will be liable only for $3,000 of tax as she is responsible for only one third of the understatement. The allocation would not be different because only part of the deductions were disallowed because of an AGI floor. ◀

The election must be made within two years after the IRS begins collections efforts. The election may be made by both spouses. The election is invalid if the spouse responsible for the errors transfers assets to the "innocent" spouse in an effort to avoid payment.

[49] Sec. 6013(d)(3).   [50] Sec. 6015(b).

ELECTING TO CHANGE TO A JOINT RETURN.   In general, a husband and wife who file separate returns for a given year may elect to change to a joint return by filing an amended joint return. This change is permitted after the due date but must occur within three years of the due date including extensions. Taxpayers may not change from a joint return to separate returns after the due date.[51]

COMPLIANCE AND PROCEDURAL CONSIDERATIONS

WHO MUST FILE

Whether an individual must file a tax return is based on the amount of the individual's gross income.[52] The fact that the individual owes no tax does not mean that a return need not be filed. The gross income filing levels are as follows:[53]

	2005	2006
Single	$ 8,200	$ 8,450
Single (65 or over)	9,450	9,700
Married, filing jointly	16,400	16,900
Married, filing jointly (one spouse 65 or over)	17,400	17,900
Married, filing jointly (both 65 or over)	18,400	18,900
Surviving spouse	13,200	13,600
Surviving spouse (65 or over)	14,200	14,600
Married, filing separately	3,200	3,300
Married, living separately from spouse at year-end	3,200	3,300
Head of household	10,500	10,850
Head of household (65 or over)	11,750	11,850

There are three situations where taxpayers must file even if the gross income is less than the amounts shown above:

▶ Taxpayers who receive advance payments of the earned income credit (see Chapter I14) must file regardless of their income levels.

▶ Taxpayers with net self-employment income of $400 or more must file regardless of their total gross income.

▶ Taxpayers who can be claimed as a dependent by another must file if they have either unearned income over $850 or total gross income over the standard deduction.

In general, taxpayers must file if their gross income equals or exceeds the sum of the personal exemption and the standard deduction (including the additional standard deduction due to age but not blindness). The blindness allowance and dependency exemptions are not considered. If the disallowance of the standard deduction rules apply, the standard deduction is ignored in determining whether taxpayers must file.

EXAMPLE I2-47 ▶ In 2006, Carol is a single, self-supporting taxpayer with no dependents. Carol must file if her gross income is $8,450 or greater ($5,150 + $3,300). ◀

DUE DATES AND EXTENSIONS

Returns for individuals and partnerships are due on the fifteenth day of the fourth month following the close of the tax year, which for calendar-year taxpayers is April 15.[54] Returns for C corporations and S corporations are due on the fifteenth day of the third month following the close of the tax year, which for calendar-year corporations is

ADDITIONAL COMMENT
The IRS is encouraging nonfilers (i.e., individuals and businesses who should have filed previous tax returns but did not) to come forward. The IRS estimates that there were 6 million nonfilers in 1990 alone.

ADDITIONAL COMMENT
A file-by-telephone system has been tested in some states in the last few years. The filers dial a toll-free telephone number and enter tax return data with a touch-tone telephone. While the taxpayer is still on the line, the IRS calculates any refund or tax due. The taxpayers then mail a signed Form 1040-TEL.

ADDITIONAL COMMENT
The IRS is required to impound tax refunds to help other agencies collect overdue student loans, child support, etc. However, the IRS found that people whose refunds were offset in 1985 and 1986 were far more likely than others to file no returns in the next two years or to file returns without paying all they owed.

KEY POINT
It is possible that a taxpayer may be required to file an income tax return but still have no tax liability.

---

[51] Reg. Sec. 1.6013-1(a). However, a couple who filed a joint return whose marriage is later annulled must file amended returns as singles (Rev. Rul. 76-255, 1976-2 C.B. 40).
[52] *Gross income* has its usual meaning except that the gain excluded from the sale of a personal residence and excluded foreign earned income are included (Sec. 6012(c)).
[53] Sec. 6012(a)(1).
[54] Sec. 6072(a).

March 15.[55] A due date that falls on a Saturday, Sunday, or a holiday is automatically extended to the next day that is not a Saturday, Sunday, or holiday.[56] As noted, individuals are required to file only if their gross income exceeds prescribed thresholds. Partnerships and corporations, however, are required to file even if they have no gross income.

Individuals may obtain an automatic extension of six months by filing Form 4868 (Application for Automatic Extension of Time to File U.S. Individual Income Tax Return). C corporations, S corporations, and partnerships may obtain an automatic extension of six months by filing Form 7004.

An extension to file a return is not an extension to pay any tax that is owed. Taxpayers must project their tax liability to the best of their ability and remit with the extension any amount that has not been prepaid through withholding or estimated payments. Interest and penalty may apply to amounts paid after the regular due date. See Chapter C15 in the *Comprehensive* volume and the *Corporations, Partnerships, Estates, and Trusts* volume for more on payment requirements.

	Individuals	*Partnerships*	*Corporations*
Returns	Forms 1040, 1040A, 1040EZ	Form 1065	Forms 1120, 1120S
Return due date	15th day of 4th month	15th day of 4th month	15th day of 3rd month
Automatic extension	Form 4868 (6 months)	Form 7004 (6 months)	Form 7004 (6 months)

ADDITIONAL COMMENT

In 2003, of the 130 million returns filed, over 61 million returns were filed electronically.

USE OF FORMS 1040, 1040EZ, AND 1040A

The primary individual tax return is Form 1040. Complicated returns often involve many additional forms and schedules. Two shorter forms are available to taxpayers with less-complicated tax returns. Form 1040EZ is available to single taxpayers and married individuals who file a joint return. Such taxpayers must have taxable income of less than $50,000 and claim no dependents. To use Form 1040EZ, the taxpayer's income must consist of salary and wages plus no more than $1,500 of taxable interest income. No deductions (other than the standard deduction) or credits (other than withholding from salary and wages) can be taken on the return.

Form 1040A is available to taxpayers who have somewhat more involved returns. Form 1040A can be used by taxpayers claiming any number of exemptions or any filing status. Salary, wages, dividends, interest, pension and annuity income, and unemployment compensation can be reported on Form 1040A. Taxpayers may deduct IRA contributions. Taxpayers may also claim credits for withholding, child care, and earned income.

SELF-STUDY QUESTION

It is sometimes said that the hallmark of the U.S. federal income tax system is voluntary compliance. With so much information being reported to the IRS, how voluntary is the system?

ANSWER

The system is not very voluntary with respect to income subject to reporting. But some sources of income, such as income from self-employment, are not subject to reporting by a third party. Also, the IRS would have to audit a tax return to verify most of the deductions.

SYSTEM FOR REPORTING INCOME

There is a significant and expanding relationship between computers, tax returns, the taxpayer identification system, and information returns. The IRS keeps records based on taxpayer identification numbers. Individual taxpayers report information based on Social Security numbers, whereas employer identification numbers (EIN) are used by corporations, other taxpayers, and tax-exempt entities. Individuals who employ others have both a Social Security number and an employer identification number.

Employers, banks, stockbrokers, savings and loans, and so on report payments they make to others along with the payee's identification number. Today, the IRS computers match much of the reported information with tax returns, using the taxpayer identification number as the cross-reference. The need for accurate information returns is obvious. Some major information returns are listed below:

---

[55] Sec. 6072(b).
[56] Sec. 7503.

Basic Form	Type of Payment	Required if Amount Equals or Exceeds
1099-R	Pensions and annuities	$600
W-2	Salary, wages, etc.	600
1099-DIV	Dividends	10
1099-INT	Interest	600[57]
1099-B	Sale of a security	All
1099-G	Unemployment compensation, tax refunds, etc.	10
1099-MISC	Rent, royalties, etc.	600
1099-R	Total lump-sum distributions from retirement plans	600[58]

This information-reporting system makes it more difficult for taxpayers to avoid IRS detection if they omit income from their returns.

PROBLEM MATERIALS

DISCUSSION QUESTIONS

I2-1
a. The tax law refers to gross income, yet the term gross income is not found on Form 1040. Explain.
b. Why is it important to understand the concept of gross income even though the term is not found on Form 1040?

I2-2 Explain the distinction between income and gross income.

I2-3
a. Explain the distinction between a deduction and a credit.
b. Which is worth more, a $10 deduction or a $10 credit?
c. Explain the difference between refundable and nonrefundable credits.

I2-4 List the conditions that must be met in order to claim a dependency exemption for qualifying children and qualifying relatives. Briefly explain each one.

I2-5
a. Briefly explain the concept of support.
b. If a taxpayer provides 50% or less of another person's support, is it possible for the taxpayer to claim a dependency exemption? Explain.
c. Does support include the value of an automobile? Explain.

I2-6 Under what circumstances must a taxpayer use a rate schedule instead of a tax table?

I2-7
a. What determines who must file a tax return?
b. Is an individual required to file a tax return if he or she owes no tax?

I2-8 Many homeowners itemize deductions while many renters claim the standard deduction. Explain.

I2-9 Tax rules are often very precise. For example, a taxpayer must ordinarily provide "over 50%" of another person's support in order to claim a dependency exemption. Why is the threshold "over 50%" as opposed to "50% or more?"

I2-10 What is the normal due date for the tax return of calendar-year taxpayers? What happens to the due date if it falls on a Saturday, Sunday, or holiday?

I2-11 Sometimes taxpayers may not be able to file their tax returns by the normal due date. Are extensions available? How long are the extensions? Do extensions enable taxpayers to delay paying the tax they owe?

I2-12 Can tax-exempt income qualify as support? Explain.

I2-13 Can a scholarship qualify as support?

I2-14 Explain the purpose of the multiple support agreement.

I2-15 Summarize the rules that explain which parent receives the dependency exemption for children in cases of divorce.

I2-16 What conditions must be met by a married couple before they can file a joint return?

I2-17 Explain what is meant by the phrase *maintain a household*.

I2-18 Under what circumstances, if any, can a married person file as a head of household?

I2-19
a. Explain the principal difference in the tax treatment of an S corporation and a C corporation.
b. Why would a C corporation be used if an S corporation is generally exempt from tax?

---

[57] For banks and corporations the amount is $10.

[58] Except that all IRA distributions must be reported.

I2-20 Income earned by C corporations is taxed twice, once when the income is earned and again when it is distributed. If so, how is it possible that operating a business as a C corporation can reduce taxes.

I2-21 a. What assets are excluded from capital asset status?
b. Are capital gains given favorable tax treatment?
c. What is the significance of an asset being classified as a capital asset?
d. Are capital losses deductible?

I2-22 Is there any tax advantage for an individual who has held an appreciated capital asset for eleven months to delay the sale of the asset? Explain.

I2-23 a. Explain the difference between income splitting and income shifting.
b. Why are taxpayers interested in shifting income from one tax return to another within the same family or economic unit?
c. Is there a relationship between the tax on unearned income of a minor and taxpayers who attempt to shift income?

I2-24 a. Who is liable for additional taxes on a joint return?
b. Why is this so important?

I2-25 Can couples change from joint returns to separate returns? Separate to joint?

ISSUE IDENTIFICATION QUESTIONS

I2-26 This year, Yung Tseng, a U.S. citizen, supported his nephew who is attending school in the United States. Yung is a U.S. citizen, but his nephew is a citizen of Hong Kong. The nephew has a student visa, but he hopes to become a permanent U. S. resident. Other family members hope to come to the U.S. What issues must be considered by Yung?

I2-27 Carmen and Carlos, who have filed joint tax returns for several years, separated this year. Carlos works in construction and is often paid in cash. Carlos says he only worked a few weeks this year and made $11,000. In prior years he made approximately $35,000 per year, and Carmen is surprised that his income is so low this year. Carmen received a salary of $38,000 as a medical laboratory technician. They have no dependents and claim the standard deduction. What tax issues should Carmen and Carlos consider?

I2-28 Jane and Bill have lived in a home Bill inherited from his parents. Their son Jim lives with them. Bill and Jane obtain a divorce during the current year. Under the terms of the divorce, Jane receives possession of the home for a period of five years and custody of Jim. Bill is obligated to furnish over one-half of the cost of the maintenance, taxes, and insurance on the home and pay $6,000 of child support per year. Bill lives in an apartment. What tax issues should Jane and Bill consider?

PROBLEMS

I2-29 *Computation of Tax.* The following information relates to two married couples:

	Lanes	Waynes
Salary (earned by one spouse)	$26,000	$110,000
Interest income	1,000	7,000
Deductible IRA contribution	4,000	0
Itemized deductions	10,000	10,000
Exemptions	6,600	6,600
Withholding	700	18,700

Compute the 2006 tax due or refund due for each couple. Assume that the itemized deductions have been reduced by the applicable floors.

I2-30 *Computation of Taxable Income.* The following information for 2006 relates to Tom, a single taxpayer, age 18:

Salary	$1,800
Interest income	1,600
Itemized deductions	600

a. Compute Tom's taxable income assuming he is self-supporting.
b. Compute Tom's taxable income assuming he is a dependent of his parents.

I2-31 *Joint Versus Separate Returns.* Carl and Carol have salaries of $14,000 and $22,000, respectively. Their itemized deductions total $6,000. They are married and both are under age 65.

a. Compute their taxable income assuming they file jointly.

b. Compute their taxable incomes assuming they file separate returns and that Carol claims all of the itemized deductions.

I2-32 *Joint Versus Separate Returns.* Hal attended school much of 2006, during which time he was supported by his parents. Hal married Ruth in December 2006. Hal graduated and commenced work in 2007. Ruth worked during 2006 and earned $18,000. Hal's only income was $900 of interest. Hal's parents are in the 28% tax bracket. Thus, claiming Hal as a dependent would save them $924 (0.28 × $3,300) of taxes.

a. Compute Hal and Ruth's gross tax if they file a joint return.

b. Compute Ruth's gross tax if she files a separate return in order to allow Hal's parents to claim him as a dependent.

c. Which alternative would be better for the family? In other words, will filing a joint return save Hal and Ruth more than $924?

I2-33 *Dependency Exemptions.* Wes and Tina are a married couple and provide financial assistance to several persons during the current year. For the situations below, determine whether the individuals qualify as dependency exemptions for Wes and Tina. In all of the situations below, assume that any dependency tests not mentioned have been met.

a. Brian is age 24 and Wes and Tina's son. He is a full-time student and lives in an apartment near campus. Wes and Tina provide over 50% of his support. Brian works as a waiter and earned $3,800.

b. Same as Part a except that Brian is a part-time student.

c. Sherry is age 22 and Wes and Tina's daughter. She is a full-time student and lives in the college dormitory. Wes and Tina provide over 50% of her support. Sherry works part-time as a bookkeeper and earned $3,800.

d. Same as Part c except that Sherry is a part-time student.

e. Granny, age 82, is Tina's grandmother and lives with Wes and Tina. During the current year, Granny's only sources of income were her Social Security of $4,800 and interest on U.S. bonds of $3,800. Granny uses her income to pay for 40% of her total support, Wes and Tina provide the remainder of Granny's support.

I2-34 *Dependency Exemptions.* John and Carole file a joint return in 2006 and have three children: Jack, age 23; David, age 20; and Kristen, age 15. All three children live at home the entire year. Below is information about each of the children in 2006:

- Jack: graduated from college in December 2005 and is going to medical school beginning in July 2007. In 2006, Jack worked sparingly as he studied for the medical school entrance exam, but did earn $3,500. John and Carole provided 80% of Jack's support during the year.

- David: a full-time student at State U. in 2006, earned $6,400 from a part-time job, and provided 40% of his own support.

- Kristen: a full-time student in high school, had no gross income, and provided none of her own support.

a. Based on the above facts, which of the children can be claimed by John and Carole in 2006?

b. How would your answer to Part a change if Jack began medical school in July 2006?

c. How would your answer to Part a change if Jack earned $3,000 rather than $3,500 in 2006?

d. How would your answer to Part a change if David was a part-time student rather than a full-time student in 2006?

e. How would your answer to Part a change if David provided 60% of his own support rather than 40%?

I2-35 *Dependency Exemptions.* Robert provides much of the support for his daughter, Jane, and her two children. Jane earned $20,000. Robert, who earned $350,000, paid the rent of $11,000 on Jane's apartment and provided an additional $15,000 support. Jane is age 30, and her children are age 7 and age 4.

a. Can Robert claim a dependency exemption for Jane?

b. Can Jane claim her children as dependents?

c. Would you recommend that Robert try to claim the dependency exemption for his grandchildren?

I2-36 *Dependency Exemptions.* Juan helps support his mother Maria, his son Jose, and a niece Norma. How many dependency exemptions can Juan claim given these additional facts?

Maria lives with Juan. She receives $12,000 of Social Security benefits which she uses to pay for food, clothing, medical expenses, and other living expenses. Juan provides Maria's room which has a rental value of $5,000 and pays an additional $4,000 toward her support.

Jose, age 12, lives with his mother, Linda. Juan pays $12,000 per year child support, and Linda provides an additional $4,000 of support.

Norma, age 20, is a part-time college student who lives in an apartment. She earned $6,000 working part-time and received a scholarship of $2,000. Norma's father provided $4,000 toward her support, and Juan provided $7,000.

I2-37 *Dependency Exemptions.* Anna, age 65, who lives with her unmarried son, Mario, received $7,000, which was used for her support during the year. The sources of support were as follows:

Social Security benefits	$1,500
Mario	2,600
Caroline, an unrelated friend	800
Doug, Anna's son	500
Elaine, Anna's sister	1,600
Total	$7,000

a. Who is eligible to claim Anna as a dependent?
b. What must be done before Mario can claim the exemption?
c. Can anyone claim head-of-household status based on Anna's dependency exemption? Explain.
d. Can Mario claim an old age allowance for his mother? Explain.

I2-38 *Dependency Exemption and Child Credit: Divorced Parents.* Joe and Joan divorce during the current year. Joan receives custody of their three children. Joe agrees to pay $5,000 of child support for each child.
a. Assuming no written agreement, who will receive the dependency exemption and child credit for the children? Explain.
b. Would it make any difference if Joe could prove that he provided over one-half of the support for each child?

I2-39 *Filing Status, Dependency Exemptions, and Child Credit.* For the following taxpayers, indicate which tax form should be used, the applicable filing status, and the number of personal and dependency exemptions available, and the number of children who qualify for the child credit.
a. Arnie is a single college student who earned $7,700 working part-time. He had $200 of interest income and received $1,000 of support from his parents.
b. Buddy is a single college student who earned $7,700 working part-time. He had $1,600 of interest income and received $1,000 of support from his parents.
c. Cindy is divorced and received $6,000 of alimony from her former husband and earned $12,000 working as a secretary. She also received $1,800 of child support for her son who lives with her. According to a written agreement, her former husband is entitled to receive the dependency exemption.
d. Debbie is a widow, age 68, who receives a pension of $8,000, nontaxable social security benefits of $8,000, and interest of $4,000. She has no dependents.
e. Edith is married, but her husband left her two years ago and she has not seen him since. Edith supported herself and her daughter, age 6. She paid all household expenses. Her income of $16,000 consisted of a salary of $15,200 and interest of $800.

I2-40 *Dependency Exemptions and Child Credit.* How many dependency exemptions are the following taxpayers entitled to, assuming the people involved are U.S. citizens? Which dependents qualify for child credit?
a. Andrew supports his cousin Mary, who does not live with him. Mary has no income and is single.
b. Bob and Ann are filing a joint return. Bob provided over one-half of his father's support. The father received Social Security benefits of $6,000 and taxable interest income of $800. The father is single and does not live with them.
c. Clay provides 60% of his single daughter's support. She earned $3,000 while attending school during the year as a full-time student. She is 22 years old.
d. Dave provided 30% of his mother's support and she provided 55% of her own support. Dave's brother provided the remainder. The brother agreed to sign a multiple support agreement.

I2-41 *Amount of Personal Exemptions and Child Credit.* Juan and Maria are married and have two young children. Their adjusted gross income in 2006 is $290,000 and they have itemized deductions of $38,000.
   a. Assuming they can validly claim four personal and dependency exemptions, what is the amount of their personal and dependency exemptions that they will subtract in arriving at taxable income?
   b. What is the amount of their child credit?

I2-42 *Marriage and Taxes.* Bill and Mary plan to marry in December 2006. Bill's salary is $32,000 and he owns his own residence. His itemized deductions total $9,000. Mary's salary is $36,000. Her itemized deductions total only $1,600 as she does not own her own residence. For purposes of this problem, assume 2007 tax rates, exemptions, and standard deductions are the same as 2006.
   a. What will their tax be if they marry before year-end and file a joint return?
   b. What will their combined taxes be for the year if they delay the marriage until 2007?
   c. What factors contribute to the difference in taxes?

I2-43 *Filing Requirement.* Which of the following taxpayers must file a 2006 return?
   a. Amy, age 19 and single, has $7,050 of wages, $800 of interest, and $350 of self-employment income.
   b. Betty, age 67 and single, has a taxable pension of $4,100 and Social Security benefits of $6,200.
   c. Chris, age 15 and single, is a dependent of his parents. Chris has earned income of $1,600 and interest of $400.
   d. Dawn, age 15 and single, is a dependent of her parents. She has earned income of $400 and interest of $1,600.
   e. Doug, age 25, and his wife are separated. He earned $5,000 while attending school during the year.

I2-44 *Head of Household.* In the following situations, indicate whether the taxpayer qualifies as a head of household.
   a. Allen is divorced from his wife. He maintains a household for himself and his dependent mother.
   b. Beth is divorced from her husband. She maintains a home for herself and supports an elderly aunt who lives in a retirement home.
   c. Cindy was widowed last year. She maintains a household for herself and her dependent daughter, who lived with her during the year.
   d. Dick is not divorced, but lived apart from his wife for the entire year. He maintains a household for himself and his dependent daughter. He does not receive any financial support from his wife.

I2-45 *Filing Status.* For the following independent situations, determine the optimum filing status for the years in question.
   a. Wayne and Celia had been married for 24 years when Wayne died in an accident in October 2004. Celia and her son, Wally, age 21 in 2004, continued to live at home in 2004, 2005, 2006, and 2007. Wally worked part-time (earning $5,000 in each of the four years) and attended the university on a part-time basis. Celia provided more than 50% of Wally's support for all four years. What is Celia's filing status for 2004, 2005, 2006, and 2007?
   b. Juanita is a single parent who in 2006 maintained a household for her unmarried son Josh, age 19. Josh graduated from high school in 2005 and has not decided whether to attend college. Thus, in 2006, Josh worked full-time and earned $9,000. Juanita provided approximately 40% of Josh's support in 2006 but provided all the expenses of maintaining the household. What is Juanita's filing status for 2006?
   c. Gomer and Gertrude are married and have one dependent son in 2006. In April 2006, Gomer left Gertrude a note informing her that he needed his freedom and he was leaving her. As of December 31, 2006, Gertrude had not seen nor heard a word from Gomer since April. Gertrude fully supported her son and completely maintained the household. What is Gertrude's filing status in 2006 assuming she was still legally married at December 31, 2006?

I2-46 *Computation of Taxable Income.* Jim and Pat are married and file jointly. In 2006, Jim earned a salary of $46,000. Pat is self-employed. Her gross business income was $49,000 and her business expenses totaled $24,000. Each contributed $4,000 to a deductible IRA. Their itemized deductions total $13,000. Compute Parts a, b, and c without regard to self-employment tax.

a. Compute their gross income.
b. Compute their adjusted gross income.
c. Compute their taxable income assuming they have a dependent daughter.

I2-47 *Itemized or Standard Deduction.* Jan, a single taxpayer, has adjusted gross income of $250,000, home mortgage interest of $3,000, real estate taxes of $1,500, and charitable contributions of $3,000. Should she itemize her deductions or claim the standard deduction?

I2-48 *Kiddie Tax.* Debbie is 16 years old and a dependent of her parents. She earns $4,200 working part-time and receives $1,900 interest on savings. She saves both the salary and interest. What is her taxable income? Would her taxable income or tax be different if Debbie were 13 years old?

I2-49 *Computation of Tax, Standard Deduction, and Kiddie Tax.* Anthony and Latrisha are married and have two sons, James, age 16, and Jonas, age 13. Both sons are properly claimed as dependents. Anthony and Latrisha's taxable income is $130,000 in 2006 and they file a joint return. Both James and Jonas had part-time jobs as well as some unearned income. Below is a summary of their total income.

	James	Jonas
Wages	$2,800	$ 400
Taxable interest	1,800	2,000

Compute the taxable income and tax liability for James and Jonas.

I2-50 *Computation of Tax.* Georgia, a single taxpayer, operates a business that produces $100,000 of income before any amounts are paid to her. She has no dependents and no other income. She has itemized deductions of $18,000. Compute the *total* income tax that would be paid assuming the following additional facts. Ignore payroll taxes.
a. Georgia operates the business as an S corporation receiving a salary from the corporation of $60,000. The corporation distributes all of its remaining income to the shareholders.
b. She operates the business as a C corporation receiving a salary from the corporation of $60,000. The corporation distributes its *after* tax income to her as a dividend.
c. How would the total tax change in each of the first two requirements if the corporation made no payments to the owner other than the salary?

I2-51 *Child Credit.* In 2006, Lana, a single taxpayer with AGI of $85,400, claims exemptions for three dependent children, all under age 17. What is the amount of her child credit?

I2-52 *Capital Gains and Losses.* Bob and Anna are in the 35% tax bracket for ordinary income and the 15% bracket for capital gains. They have owned several blocks of stock for many years. They are considering the sale of two blocks of stock. The sale of one block would produce a gain of $10,000. The sale of the other would produce a loss of $15,000. For purposes of this problem, ignore personal exemptions, itemized deductions and other phase-outs. They have no other gains or losses this year.
a. How much tax will they save if they sell the block of stock that produces a loss?
b. How much additional tax will they pay if they sell the block of stock that produces a gain?
c. What will be the impact on their taxes if they sell both blocks of stock?

I2-53 *Timing of Deductions.* Virginia is a cash-basis, calendar-year taxpayer. Her salary is $20,000, and she is single. She plans to purchase a residence in 2007. She anticipates her property taxes and interest will total $7,200. Each year, Virginia contributes approximately $1,000 to charity. Her other itemized deductions total approximately $800. For purposes of this problem, assume 2007 tax rates, exemptions, and standard deductions are the same as 2006.
a. What will her gross tax be in 2006 and 2007 if she contributes $1,000 to charity in each year?
b. What will her gross tax be in 2006 and 2007 if she contributes $2,000 to charity in 2006 but makes no contribution in 2007?
c. What will her gross tax be in 2006 and 2007 if she makes no contribution in 2006 but contributes $2,000 in 2007?
d. Alternative c results in a lower tax than either a or b. Why?

I2-54 *Tax Forms and Filing Status.* Which tax form is used by the following individuals?
a. Anita is single, age 68, and has a salary of $22,000 and interest of $300.
b. Betty owns an apartment complex that produced rental income of $36,000. Expenses totaled $38,500.
c. Clay's wife died last year. He qualifies as a surviving spouse. His salary is $24,000.

d. Donna is a head of household. Her salary is $17,000 and she has $200 of interest income.

I2-55 *Computation of Tax.* Maria is a single taxpayer. Her salary is $51,000. Maria realized a short-term capital loss of $5,000. Her itemized deductions total $4,000.

a. Compute Maria's adjusted gross income.

b. Compute her taxable income.

c. Compute her tax liability.

I2-56 *Kiddie Tax.* Ralph and Tina (husband and wife) transferred taxable bonds worth $20,000 to Pam, their 12-year-old daughter. Pam received $1,800 of interest on the bonds in the current year. Ralph and Tina have a combined taxable income of $83,000.

a. Compute Ralph and Tina's gross tax. Assume they do not include Pam's income on their return.

b. Can Ralph and Tina claim a child credit for Pam?

c. Compute Pam's taxable income and gross tax.

d. What would be Pam's tax if she were age 16?

I2-57 *Filing Status.* Assume Gail is a wealthy widow whose husband died last year. Her dependent daughter lives with her for the entire year. Gail has interest income totaling $370,000 and she pays property taxes and home mortgage interest totaling $20,000.

a. What filing status applies to Gail?

b. Compute her taxable income and gross tax.

c. Assume that Gail does not have a daughter. What is Gail's filing status?

d. Compute Gail's taxable income and gross tax assuming she does not have a daughter.

TAX STRATEGY PROBLEMS

I2-58 Jack is starting a business that he expects to produce $60,000 of income this year before compensating Jack for his services. He has $1,000 of other income and itemized deductions totaling $10,000. He wants to know whether he should incorporate or operate the business as a proprietorship. If a corporation is formed, he wants to know whether he should make an S election. If he incorporates, the corporation will pay Jack a salary of $40,000. He expects to distribute an additional $5,000 of corporate profits to himself each year. Jack is single.

Required: Which organizational form, proprietorship, S corporation, or C corporation, will produce the lowest total current income tax liability for Jack and his business? Ignore payroll and other taxes.

I2-59 Andrea, who is in the 35% tax bracket, is interested in reducing her taxes. She is considering several alternatives. For each alternative listed below, indicate how much tax, if any, she would save?

a. Give $2,000 to a charity. Assume she itemizes.

b. Give $2,000 to a charity. Assume she does not itemize.

c. Make a gift of bonds valued at $8,000 yielding $600 of interest annually to her 15-year-old daughter who has no other income.

d. Sell the bonds from part c for $8,000 and buy tax exempt bonds yielding $300.

TAX FORM/RETURN PREPARATION PROBLEMS

I2-60 Aida Petosa (SSN 123-45-6789) is the 12-year-old daughter of Alfredo Petosa (SSN 987-65-4321). Her only income is $2,800 of interest on savings. Alfredo qualifies as a head of household, and his taxable income is $52,000. Compute her tax using Form 8615.

I2-61 James S. (SSN 123-45-6789) and Lulu B. Watson (SSN 987-65-4321) reside at 999 E. North Street, Richmond, Virginia 23174. They have one dependent child, Waldo, age 4 (SSN 123-45-4321) and they are both under 65 years old. They do not wish to take advantage of the presidential election campaign check-off. Other relevant information includes

James's salary as a mechanic	$19,000
Lulu's salary as a teacher	23,000
Interest (First National Bank)	2,100
Withholding	2,000

Complete their Form 1040A.

I2-62 John R. Lane (SSN 123-44-6666) lives at 1010 Ipsen Street, Yorba Linda, California 90102. John, a single taxpayer, age 66, provided 100% of his cousin's support. The cousin lives in Arizona. He wants to take advantage of the presidential election campaign check-off. John is an accountant. Other relevant information includes

Salary	$20,000
Taxable pension	31,000
Interest income	300
IRA deduction	3,000
Itemized deductions (from Schedule A)	6,000
Withholding	7,000

Assume that Schedule A, if necessary, has already been completed. Complete Form 1040.

CASE STUDY PROBLEMS

I2-63 Bala and Ann purchased as investments three identical parcels of land over a several-year period. Two years ago they gave one parcel to their daughter, Kim, who is now age 12. They have an offer from an investor who is interested in acquiring all three parcels. The buyer is able to purchase only two of the parcels now, but wants to purchase the third parcel two or three years from now, when he expects to have available funds to acquire the property. Because they paid different prices for the parcels, the sales will result in different amounts of gains and losses. The sale of one parcel owned by Bala and Ann will result in a $20,000 gain and the sale of the other parcel will result in a $28,000 loss. The sale of the parcel owned by Kim will result in a $19,000 gain. Kim has no other income and does not expect any significant income for several years. Bala and Ann, however, are in the 35% tax bracket. They do not have any other capital gains this year. Which two properties would you recommend that they sell this year? Why?

I2-64 Larry and Sue separated at the end of the year. Larry has asked Sue to sign a joint income tax return for the year because he feels that the tax will be lower on a joint return. Larry and Sue both work. Sue received a salary of $25,000 and Larry's salary was $20,000. Larry works as a waiter at a local restaurant and received tips. The restaurant asked Larry to indicate the amount of tips he received so that they could report the information to the IRS. Larry reported to the employer that the tips amounted to $3,000, but Sue believes that the amount was probably $6,000 to $10,000. They do not have enough expenses to itemize. Sue has asked you what are the advantages and risks of filing a joint return.

TAX RESEARCH PROBLEMS

I2-65 Ed has supported his stepdaughter, her husband, and their child since his wife's death three years ago. Ed promised his late wife that he would support her daughter from a former marriage and her daughter's husband until they both finished college. They live in another state, and meet gross income filing requirements. Is Ed entitled to dependency exemptions for the three individuals?

A partial list of research sources is

- Sec. 152
- Reg. Sec. 1.152-2
- *Desio Barbetti*, 9 T.C. 1097 (1947)

I2-66 Bob and Sue were expecting a baby in January, but Sue was rushed to the hospital in December. She delivered the baby but it died the first night. Are Bob and Sue entitled to a dependency exemption for the baby?

Research sources include Rev. Rul. 73-156, 1973-1 C.B. 58.

I2-67 Larry has severe vision problems and, in the past, he has claimed the additional standard deduction available to blind taxpayers. This year Larry's doctor prescribed a new type of contact lens that greatly improved his vision. Naturally, Larry was elated, but unfortunately new problems developed. He suffered severe pain, infection, and ulcers from wearing the new lens. The doctor recommended that he remove the lens and after several weeks his eyes healed. The doctor told him that he could wear the contacts again, but only for brief time periods, or the problems would recur. Can Larry claim the additional standard deduction available to blind taxpayers?

Research sources include *Emanuel Hollman*, 38 T.C. 251 (1963).

3

C H A P T E R

GROSS INCOME: INCLUSIONS

LEARNING OBJECTIVES

After studying this chapter, you should be able to

1 ▶ Explain the difference between the economic, accounting, and tax concepts of income

2 ▶ Explain the principles used to determine who is taxed on a particular item of income

3 ▶ Determine when a particular item of income is taxable under both the cash and accrual methods of reporting

4 ▶ Apply the rules of Sec. 61(a) to determine whether items such as compensation, dividends, alimony, and pensions are taxable

Computation of an individual's income tax liability begins with the determination of income. Although the meaning of the term *income* has long been debated by economists, accountants, tax specialists, and politicians, no universally operational definition has been accepted.

The Sixteenth Amendment to the Constitution gave Congress the power to tax "income from whatever source derived." To ensure the constitutionality of the income tax, this phrase is incorporated in Sec. 61(a), where **gross income** is defined as follows: "Except as otherwise provided . . . gross income means all income from whatever source derived."

This chapter examines the concept of income for the purpose of determining what items of income are taxable. Chapter I4 considers items of income that are excluded from gross income. As noted in Chapter I2, many provisions in the tax law are created by a process of political compromise. Thus, there is no single explanation of why certain items are taxable and others are not. For this reason, determining whether a particular item of income is taxable often proves difficult.

ECONOMIC AND ACCOUNTING CONCEPTS OF INCOME

OBJECTIVE 1

Explain the difference between the economic, accounting, and tax concepts of income

ECONOMIC CONCEPT

In economics, *income* is defined as the amount an individual could consume during a period and remain as well off at the end of the period as he or she was at the beginning of the period. To the economist, therefore, income includes both the wealth that flows to the individual and changes in the value of the individual's store of wealth. Or, more simply, income equals consumption plus the change in wealth.

EXAMPLE I3-1 ▶

Alice earned a salary of $40,000. She consumed $30,000 of food, clothing, housing, medical care, and other goods and services. Assets owned by Alice were worth $100,000 at the beginning of the year. Her assets, including $10,000 of salary that was saved, were worth $115,000 at the end of the year. Her liabilities did not change during the year. Alice's economic income is $45,000 [$30,000 + ($115,000 − $100,000)]. ◀

Under the economist's definition, unrealized gains, as well as gifts and inheritances, are income. Furthermore, the economist adjusts for inflation in measuring income. An individual has no income to the extent that an increase in the measured value of property is caused by a decrease in the value of the measuring unit. In other words, inflation does not increase wealth and, therefore, does not cause an individual to be better off.

ACCOUNTING CONCEPT

In accounting, income is measured by a transaction approach. Accountants usually measure income when it is *realized* in a transaction. Values measured by transactions are relatively objective as accountants recognize (i.e., report) income, expenses, gains, and losses that have been realized as a result of a completed transaction. Accountants believe that the economic concept of income is too subjective to be used as a basis for financial reporting and, therefore, have traditionally used historical costs in measuring income instead of using unconfirmed estimates of changes in market value. In accounting, the meaning of the term *realization* is critical to the income measurement process. *Realization* generally results upon the occurrence of two events: (1) a change in the form or substance of a taxpayer's property (or phrased another way, a severance of the economic interest in the property) and (2) a transaction with a second party. Thus, if a taxpayer sells some property for cash, a realization has clearly occurred, i.e., the property has been changed to cash and the transaction was with a second party. Conversely, the mere increase in value of property owned by a taxpayer will not result in the realization of income because there has been no change in the form of the property and no transaction with a second party.

EXAMPLE I3-2 ▶ Assume the same facts as in Example I3-1. The amount consumed by Alice, the increase in the value of the property owned by her, and inflation are all ignored by the accountant in measuring her income. Only when she sells or otherwise disposes of the assets that have increased in value will the accountant recognize the gain. Thus, Alice's accounting income is $40,000. ◀

TAX CONCEPT OF INCOME

The income tax law essentially has adopted the accountant's concept of income rather than the economist's. The reasons for this generally relate to matters of administrative convenience and the wherewithal-to-pay concept. However, as we will see later, there are many differences between income for tax purposes and accounting income.

In general, three conditions must be met for amounts to be taxable.

▶ There must be economic benefit. The economic benefit is not limited to cash payments. Employees who receive a company's stock, rather than cash, are receiving an economic benefit. Taxpayers benefit even if they direct that payments be made to other persons. As a result, employees cannot avoid being taxed on their earnings by ordering that their salaries be paid to creditors or family members.

▶ The income must be realized. In general, realization occurs when the earning process is complete and a transaction with another party takes place that permits an objective measure of the income. This objective measurement increases "administrative convenience" which is discussed below. Unlike financial accounting, there are many exceptions that result in income being reported when the taxpayer receives payment even if that is at a time other than when the earning process is complete. These exceptions result in taxes being owed when the taxpayer has the "wherewithal to pay" (see below). Taxpayers who use the "cash method" of reporting, discussed later in the chapter, are normally taxed when payment is received.

▶ The income must be recognized. Some items of income are not taxable because of special provisions in the tax law. For example, certain real estate exchanges and corporate reorganizations are not taxable because of statutory nonrecognition rules. In such cases, the taxpayer receives a lower basis in replacement property, and that often means the income is recognized when the replacement property is sold. The tax law also contains exclusions that exempt specific types of income such as scholarships, inheritances, and municipal bond interest. Within statutory limitations, taxpayers are never taxed on such items of income.

ADMINISTRATIVE CONVENIENCE

The economic concept of income is considered to be too subjective to be used in determining taxable income. The need for objectivity in taxation is evident. If taxpayers were required to report increases in value as income, some individuals would certainly understate values to reduce their tax liabilities. The IRS and even the most honest taxpayer often would disagree over values and, as a result, the tax system would be extremely difficult to administer. The disputes over valuation issues would be frequent and the courts would be burdened with added litigation. This problem is evidenced by the few situations where valuations are required in the determination of tax. For example, taxpayers who contribute property to charity usually can deduct the value of the property. The courts are continuously having to resolve disputes between taxpayers and the IRS over the value of such contributions. Furthermore, in the case of certain large contributions of property, taxpayers are required to attach to their returns appraisals of the contributed property. Penalties apply to taxpayers who substantially overvalue contributions.

In some instances, objectivity is achieved at the price of equity. For example, a taxpayer who owns land that has substantially declined in value generally cannot recognize the decline in value until it is realized through a disposition of the land. Similarly, an increase in value, no matter how large, is not taxed until a sale or exchange of the property has occurred. A taxpayer with a modest salary may feel that it is unfair that he or she is taxed on the salary while another person is not taxed on unrealized gains amounting to millions of dollars. As noted above, however, it would be practically impossible to fairly and consistantly administer an income tax law that was based on values.

WHEREWITHAL TO PAY

The wherewithal-to-pay concept holds that tax should be collected when the taxpayer is in the best position to pay the tax. A taxpayer who sells property and collects the cash is in a better position to pay the tax than a taxpayer who owns property that is merely increasing in value without a sale.

This concept is the rationale for several tax provisions. For example, the tax law allows a taxpayer who sells property on the installment basis to report the gain as the installment payments are collected, rather than at the time of the sale. Losses, on the other hand, cannot be reported on the installment basis, as the wherewithal-to-pay is not an issue. The concept is also used to justify differences between the tax law and financial accounting principles. Prepaid income is not income from an accounting standpoint until it is earned. The tax law, however, takes the position that prepaid income is subject to taxation at the time it is collected, rather than as it is earned. At the time of collection, the taxpayer clearly has the cash available to pay the tax. If the tax were deferred until the income is earned, the taxpayer may no longer have the cash.

GROSS INCOME DEFINED

Section 61(a) provides the following general definition and listing of income items:

> General Definition.—Except as otherwise provided in this subtitle, gross income means all income from whatever source derived, including (but not limited to) the following items:
>
> 1. Compensation for services, including fees, commissions, fringe benefits, and similar items
> 2. Gross income derived from business
> 3. Gains derived from dealings in property
> 4. Interest
> 5. Rents
> 6. Royalties
> 7. Dividends
> 8. Alimony and separate maintenance payments
> 9. Annuities
> 10. Income from life insurance and endowment contracts
> 11. Pensions
> 12. Income from discharge of indebtedness
> 13. Distributive share of partnership gross income
> 14. Income in respect of a decedent
> 15. Income from an interest in an estate or trust

This definition certainly is not all-inclusive. For example, it does not indicate whether specific items of income such as insurance settlements, gambling winnings, or illegal income are taxable. One point is apparent: The phrase *[e]xcept as otherwise provided* means that all sources of income are presumed to be taxable unless there is a specific exclusion in the income tax law. The IRS does not have to prove that an item of income is taxable. Rather, the taxpayer must prove that the item of income is excluded. Thus, gambling winnings and illegal income are taxable simply because no specific provisions in the tax law exclude such amounts from taxation. As we shall see, life insurance proceeds and certain other insurance proceeds are specifically excluded from gross income.

FORM OF RECEIPT. Gross income is not limited to amounts received in the form of cash. According to Reg. Sec. 1.61-1(a), income may be "realized in any form, whether in money, property, or services." The important question is whether the taxpayer receives an economic benefit. This rule covers barter transactions which are direct exchanges of property and services. Each party to the transaction is taxed on the value of the property or

KEY POINT

Section 446(a) states that taxable income shall be computed under the method of accounting on the basis of which the taxpayer regularly computes his or her income in keeping his or her books. This provision would seem to require that tax accounting rules would conform to financial accounting rules. However, as will be seen later in this and other chapters, there are many differences.

KEY POINT

Congress has not adopted any particular concept or theory of income for tax purposes. Except as specifically limited by statute, the definition of income is broad and general.

SELF-STUDY QUESTION

Why should taxpayers who are using the cash method of accounting be required to include in gross income the value of property or services received?

ANSWER

If taxpayers were not required to include the value of property or services received in gross income, many taxpayers would arrange their financial affairs so that they would receive property or services instead of cash.

services received in the exchange. In general, the cost basis of property given up in a barter transaction can be subtracted from the value of the property received in arriving at the taxable amount.

EXAMPLE I3-3 ▶ King Corporation transfers 1,000 shares of its stock to its president. The stock has no restrictions and is part of the president's compensation. The president must include the value of the stock in gross income. ◀

EXAMPLE I3-4 ▶ Ali, an attorney, performs legal services for Paul, a painter, in exchange for Paul's promise to paint Ali's residence. Each taxpayer realizes income equal to the value of services received. Thus, Ali must report income in an amount equal to the value of the painting services provided by Paul. Paul must report the value of Ali's legal services. These amounts, assuming an arm's-length transaction, should be the same. ◀

EXAMPLE I3-5 ▶ USA Corporation distributes an automobile to Vicki, a shareholder, in lieu of a cash dividend. Vicki must report the value of the automobile as dividend income. ◀

EXAMPLE I3-6 ▶ Len has fallen behind on loan payments due to a bank. The bank obtains a court order requiring Len's employer to pay part of Len's wages directly to the bank. Len will be taxed on the full wages even though a portion goes directly to the bank. ◀

EXAMPLE I3-7 ▶ Wayne borrowed $3,000 from his employer. The employer awarded year-end bonuses to other employees but told Wayne that the debt was being forgiven in lieu of a bonus. Wayne must include the $3,000 in income. ◀

STOP & THINK

Question: As noted, income is taxable even if it is paid in a form other than cash. What problem does this treatment produce for the IRS and taxpayers?

Solution: Two major problems are created: valuation and enforcement. First, it is necessary to determine the market value of property and services when income is received in a form other than cash. Determining values can be difficult. Second, enforcement by the IRS is made much more difficult because such income is not documented by canceled checks, credit card receipts, or other records. Thus, as demonstrated in Example I3-4 above, many of these so-called traded services are not reported as income. This evasion of income represents billions of lost tax revenues to the government.

INDIRECT ECONOMIC BENEFIT. As indicated earlier, the issue of taxability of income often depends on whether the taxpayer receives an economic benefit. In general, if a taxpayer benefits from an item, it is taxable. Frequently, however, an employer may make an expenditure in which its employees may incidentally or indirectly benefit. For example,

▶ Security guards patrol an employer's plant, protecting both the employer's property and the employees. The employees receive an indirect benefit for the protection provided by the security guards.

▶ An employer requires employees to undergo an annual checkup, the cost of which is paid by the employer.

▶ An employer provides protective clothing worn by employees while on the job.

▶ A shipping company provides sleeping accommodations to sailors while ships are at sea.

▶ A company requires certain employees to wear shoes manufactured by the company and provide regular reports on the quality of the shoes.

It is now well-established that taxpayers may exclude such indirect benefits from gross income. This judicially-developed rule holds that an expenditure is excludible if it is made in order to serve the business needs of the employer and any benefit to the employee is secondary and incidental.

Congress also has established rules dealing with situations where expenditures are made primarily to benefit employees. While expenditures made by employers that primarily benefit employees are generally taxable, there are instances whereby such expenditures are not taxable. These rules, which are discussed in Chapters I4 and I9, permit employees to exclude certain fringe benefits (such as employee discounts) from gross income.

TO WHOM IS INCOME TAXABLE?

Once it is established that income is taxable, it is necessary to determine to whom it is taxable. Although such determinations are usually easy, there are circumstances where income is not necessarily taxed to the person who receives it. If physical receipt of income was the only test, a family might reduce or eliminate its income tax by having income paid to children and other members who are in low tax brackets or have no tax liability.

ASSIGNMENT OF INCOME

In 1930, the Supreme Court held in a landmark case, *Lucas v. Earl,* that an individual is taxed on the earnings from his or her personal services.[1] Specifically, the Supreme Court held that a husband was taxed on the earnings from his law practice, even though he had signed a legally enforceable agreement with his wife that the earnings would be shared equally. An agreement to assign income does not permit a person to avoid being taxed on the income. The Court used the previously developed analogy that likens income to the fruit and capital to the tree.[2] Accordingly, the fruit (income) could not be attributed to a tree other than the one on which it grew.

In 1940, the Supreme Court, in *Helvering v. Horst,* extended the assignment of income doctrine to income from property.[3] In this case, the taxpayer detached interest coupons from bonds and gave the coupons to his son. The son collected the interest and reported it on his own return. The Supreme Court held that the taxpayer was taxed on the interest income because he owned the bonds. This holding leads to a basic rule that the income from property is taxed to the owner of the property. To transfer the income from property, the taxpayer must transfer ownership of the property itself.[4]

Although married couples may file joint returns today, this privilege did not become available until 1948. Assignment of income is an issue today when other individuals such as parents and children are involved, and it can still be an issue with married couples if they file separate returns.

ALLOCATING INCOME BETWEEN MARRIED PEOPLE

For federal income tax purposes, income is allocated between a husband and wife depending on the state of residence. Forty-two states follow a common law property system, whereas eight states[5] use a community property system. Under common law, income is generally taxed to the individual who earns the income, either through labor or capital. Thus, in the case of a married couple, if the wife owns stock in her separate name and receives dividends from such stock, the income is taxed entirely to the wife. Generally, the only **joint income** in a common law state is income from jointly owned property.[6]

In community property states, income may be either separate or community. **Community income** is considered to belong equally to the spouses. In all community property states, the income from the personal efforts of either spouse is considered to belong

---

[1] *Lucas v. Earl,* 8 AFTR 10287, 2 USTC ¶496 (USSC, 1930).
[2] The analogy had been used some ten years earlier in *Eisner v. Myrtle H. Macomber,* 3 AFTR 3020, 1 USTC ¶32 (USSC, 1920). The court originally used the analogy in efforts to distinguish income from capital.
[3] *Helvering v. Horst,* 24 AFTR 1058, 40-2 USTC ¶9787 (USSC, 1940).
[4] A series of rather specific rules allocates income between the former and current owner when income-producing property is transferred. For example, in the case of bonds transferred by gift, the IRS has ruled that interest must be allocated based on the number of days the bonds were held by each owner

during the interest period (Rev. Rul. 72-312, 1972-1 C.B. 22). A similar allocation must be made if bonds are sold (Rev. Rul. 72-224, 1972-1 C.B. 30).
[5] The states are Arizona, California, Idaho, Louisiana, Nevada, New Mexico, Texas, and Washington. Wisconsin's marital property law, though not providing for community property, is basically the same as community property.
[6] Historically, tenancy by the entirety, a form of joint ownership between spouses, allocated all income to the husband. Today, the laws of many states allocate income from property held in tenancy by the entirety equally between the spouses.

equally to the spouses. Furthermore, income from community property is considered to be community income. Thus, if a wife's salary is used to purchase stock, subsequent dividends are community income.

Couples can have separate property even in community property states. **Separate property** consists of all property owned before marriage and gifts and inheritances acquired after marriage. Whether income from separate property is community or separate depends on the state. In Idaho, Louisiana, and Texas, income from separate property is community income. In Arizona, California, Nevada, New Mexico, and Washington, such income is separate income.

EXAMPLE I3-8 ▶ A husband and wife file separate returns. The husband's salary is $40,000 and the wife's salary is $48,000. The wife received $1,000 of dividends on stock she had inherited from her parents. Interest of $1,200 was received on bonds that were purchased from the husband's salary. They received $2,600 in rent from farm land that they purchased jointly. The income would be allocated, depending on the state of residence, as follows:

California (Community Property State)	Husband	Wife
Salary	$44,000	$44,000
Dividends		1,000
Interest	600	600
Rent	1,300	1,300
Total	$45,900	$46,900
Texas (Community Property State)		
Salary	$44,000	$44,000
Dividends	500	500
Interest	600	600
Rent	1,300	1,300
Total	$46,400	$46,400
Pennsylvania (Common Law State)		
Salary	$40,000	$48,000
Dividends		1,000
Interest	1,200	
Rent	1,300	1,300
Total	$42,500	$50,300 ◀

These rules are important if couples file separate returns. The community income rules can prove to be a problem if one spouse conceals income from the other. Normally, each spouse is expected to report one-half of all community income. This treatment is inequitable if one spouse is not aware that the community income was earned. Special rules excuse an innocent spouse who fails to report community income on a separate return, provided that the spouse had no knowledge or reason to know of the item and, as a result, the inclusion of the community income would be inequitable.[7] A corresponding provision permits the IRS to include the entire amount in the income of the other spouse.[8]

 STOP & THINK

Question: The tax treatment of income earned in a common law state versus a community property state can be very inconsistent. As noted, the Supreme Court, in *Lucas v. Earl*, decided that a husband was taxed on all his income even though he agreed to share that income with his wife. Nevertheless, community income in a community property state is divided equally between husbands and wives even if one spouse earned all of the income. Why the tax distinction?

Solution: Lucas v. Earl dealt with a case in a common law state where the husband was legally entitled to the income, but decided to divide it with his wife. In community property states, couples are legally obligated to share their incomes. The federal income tax law respects the different property law systems of the states and taxes the income of

---

[7] Sec. 66(b). [8] Sec. 66(c).

persons based on state law. It would be unfairly burdensome to tax individuals on income to which they never had any legal right.

INCOME OF MINOR CHILDREN

As noted earlier, whether a husband or wife is taxed on income is determined by state law. However, earnings of a minor child are taxed to the child regardless of the state's property law system. Therefore, earnings of a child from either personal services (compensation) or from property (dividends, interest, rents, etc.) are taxed to the child, not the child's parents. As noted in Chapter I2, the unearned income of a child under age 14 may be taxed at the parents' tax rate if it is higher than the child's rate. Alternatively, the parents may elect to include the child's unearned income on their return. In the case of spouses, the spouse who has a legal right to such income determines who is taxed on it. In the case of children, however, the individual who earned the income determines who is taxed on it.

WHEN IS INCOME TAXABLE?

OBJECTIVE 3

Determine when a particular item of income is taxable under both the cash and accrual methods of reporting

The year in which income is taxed depends on the taxpayer's accounting method. The three primary overall accounting methods are the **cash receipts and disbursements method**, the **accrual method**, and the **hybrid method**. While taxpayers have the right to choose a method of accounting, the chosen method still must clearly reflect income as determined by the IRS. The IRS has the power to change the accounting method used by a taxpayer if, in the opinion of the IRS, the method being used does not clearly reflect income. Further, the Regulations require taxpayers to use the accrual method for determining purchases and sales when a taxpayer maintains an inventory.[9] However, the IRS recently ruled that taxpayers whose annual gross receipts for the three prior years do not exceed $1 million ($10 million if the taxpayer's principal business is not the sale of inventory) are exempt from the requirement and may use the cash method.[10] This exception for small taxpayers is discussed in more detail below.

KEY POINT

Neither the IRC nor the Regulations define the terms *accounting* and *accounting method.*

Section 448 requires C corporations (and partnerships with corporate partners), tax shelters, and certain trusts to use the accrual method of accounting. Qualified personal service corporations, certain types of farms, and entities with average gross receipts under $5 million are exempt from the requirement.

Once an accounting method has been adopted, it cannot be changed without permission of the IRS. See Chapter I11.

ADDITIONAL COMMENT

Taxpayers engaged in more than one trade or business may use a different method of accounting for each separate trade or business.

CASH METHOD

The **cash receipts and disbursements method** of accounting is used by most individual taxpayers and many small businesses. (See Chapter I11 for a more complete discussion of who is permitted to use the cash method.) Under this method, income is reported in the year the taxpayer actually or constructively receives the income rather than in the year the income is earned. The income can be received by the taxpayer or the taxpayer's agent and be in the form of cash, other property, or services.[11] In the case of property or services, the amount included in income is the value of the property or services. An accounts receivable or other unsupported promise to pay is considered to have no value under the cash method and, as a result, no income is recognized until the receivable is collected. Topic Review I3-1 summarizes when various types of income are reported.

ADDITIONAL COMMENT

The use of the cash receipts and disbursements method of accounting gives the taxpayer some control over the timing of the recognition of income and deductions. It also has the advantage of simplicity.

The fact that prepaid income is usually taxed when received, rather than when earned, often results in a mismatching of income and expenses.

EXAMPLE I3-9 ▶

In December of the current year, Troy, who owns an apartment building, collects the first and last months' rent from a new tenant. Troy must report two months' rent in the current year. The

---

[9] Reg. Sec. 1.446-1(c)(2)(i).
[10] Rev. Proc. 2000-22, 2000-01 C.B. 1008, Rev. Proc. 2001-1 C.B. 272, and Rev. Proc. 2002-28, 2002-1 C.B. 815.

[11] An agent can be an employee, relative, or other person authorized to receive the income.

Topic Review I3-1

When Income Is Taxable

Item	Cash Basis	Accrual Basis
Compensation	Year actually or constructively received.	Year earned or year received if prepaid.
Interest	Year actually or constructively received.	Year accrued or year received if prepaid.
Discount on Series E or EE Bonds	Choice of reporting interest as it accrues or at maturity.	Year accrued.
Dividends	Year actually or constructively received.	Year actually or constructively received.
Rent	Year actually or constructively received (does not apply to a deposit).	Year accrued or year received if prepaid (year accrued if services are associated, e.g., in a hotel or motel) (does not apply to a deposit).
Services (maintenance contracts, dance lessons, etc.)	Year actually or constructively received.	Year accrued or year received if prepaid except that a taxpayer may report the income as it accrues if all the services are to be performed by the end of the next tax year.
Sale of goods	Year actually or constructively received.	Year of sale or year cash is received if prepaid except may elect to report in year of sale if goods are not on hand, amount received is less than cost of item, and same accounting method is used for financial accounting.
Subscriptions (newspapers, magazines, etc.)	Year actually or constructively received.	Year earned or year cash is received, if prepaid, except may elect to report income as newspaper, etc., is published.
Memberships (automobile clubs, etc.)	Year actually or constructively received.	Year earned or year received if prepaid (certain nonstock corporations may elect to report prepaid amounts over the membership period, if the period covers three years or less).
Sale of property (other than stock)	Year actually or constructively received.	Year transaction is completed (e.g., the close of escrow in case of sale of real estate).
Sale of stock	Year transaction is executed.	Year transaction is executed.

actual expenses associated with the last month's rental are not incurred until the last month. However, Troy must report two months' income this year, but may only deduct one month's expenses. ◄

ADDITIONAL COMMENT

There is no recognized doctrine of constructive payment.

REAL-WORLD EXAMPLE

Paul Hornung, a former football player with the Green Bay Packers, was awarded an automobile in 1961 for being the outstanding player in the NFL championship game, but he did not actually receive it until 1962. He attempted to invoke the constructive receipt doctrine and report the income in 1961. The court held that he could not claim constructive receipt because the car was not set aside in the year of the award. *Paul V. Hornung,* 47 T.C. 428 (1967).

Reporting prepaid income can have harsh results because it is not offset by related deductions. If the income is taxed before the expenses are incurred, the taxpayer may not have enough cash to pay the expenses when they are incurred.[12] This burden is mitigated, in part, by Treasury Regulations and Revenue Procedures discussed in this chapter (e.g., the treatment of prepaid income, page I3-11).

CONSTRUCTIVE RECEIPT. As noted, a cash-basis taxpayer must report income in the year in which it is actually or constructively received. Constructive receipt means that the income is made available to the taxpayer so that he may draw upon it at any time. However, income is not constructively received if the taxpayer's control of its receipt is subject to substantial limitations or restrictions. This rule prevents taxpayers from deferring income that is otherwise available by merely "turning their backs" on it. A taxpayer cannot defer income recognition by refusing to accept payment until a later taxable year.

Examples of constructive receipt where taxpayers are required to report taxable income even though no cash is actually received include:

---

[12] This mismatching of income and expenses affects both cash and accrual basis taxpayers.

▶ A check received after banking hours[13]

▶ Interest credited to a bank savings account[14]

▶ Bond interest coupons that have matured but have not been redeemed[15]

▶ Salary available to an employee who does not accept payment[16]

An amount is not considered to be constructively received if:

▶ It is subject to substantial limitations or restrictions.

▶ The payor does not have the funds necessary to make payment.

▶ The amount is unavailable to the taxpayer.

EXAMPLE I3-10 ▶ Beth owns an ordinary life insurance policy with a cash surrender value. She need not report any income as the cash surrender value increases because the requirement that she cancel the policy in order to collect the cash surrender value constitutes a substantial restriction. If she cancels the policy, she reports as income the difference between the cash surrender value collected and net premiums paid. ◀

EXAMPLE I3-11 ▶ Cathy has received a paycheck from her employer but has been told to hold the check until the employer has sufficient funds to cover the payroll. Cathy need not report the amount of the check as income until funds are deposited to the employer's account. ◀

EXAMPLE I3-12 ▶ On December 2, 2006, Dan sold land for $100,000, payable on February 2, 2007. During the negotiations, the buyer offered to pay cash. Because the parties did not agree to a cash transaction, there was no constructive receipt in 2006. Under the terms of the sale, funds were not available at the time of sale. Thus, Dan is permitted to defer the recognition of income under the contract since the contract is made before the income is earned. ◀

HISTORICAL NOTE
Series EE bonds, officially known as United States Energy Savings Bonds, have been offered for sale since January 1, 1980.

EXCEPTIONS. There are exceptions to the basic rule that cash-basis taxpayers report income when it is actually or constructively received.

▶ The interest on Series E and Series EE U.S. savings bonds need not be reported until the final maturity date, which varies but may be as long as forty years after the date of issue, and can be deferred even longer if the bonds are exchanged within one year of the final maturity date for Series HH U.S. savings bonds.[17] Many taxpayers purchase bonds with a maturity date that occurs after retirement when the taxpayers expect to be in a lower tax bracket.

EXAMPLE I3-13 ▶ Tenisha purchased a Series EE U.S. savings bond in the current year for $2,500 that matures in 10 years. The bond will not pay any interest until the bond matures; at maturity, the bond will be worth $5,000. Tenisha is not required to report any interest income for tax purposes until the bond matures. At maturity, when Tenisha receives the $5,000, she will report $2,500 of interest income. If she desires to defer the interest further, she could exchange her Series EE bond for a Series HH bond within one year. ◀

▶ Special rules also apply to farmers and ranchers. Farmers may report crop insurance proceeds in the year following receipt if the crop would have ordinarily been sold in the following year. Ranchers who sell livestock on account of a drought, flood, or other weather related condition may delay reporting income until the following year if they can establish that the livestock sale would otherwise have taken place in a later tax year.[18] These rules help taxpayers avoid a bunching of income into one year.

▶ Small taxpayer exception for inventories. As noted above, taxpayers who have average annual gross receipts of $1 million or less for the prior three years ($10 million or less if the taxpayer's principal business is not the sale of inventory) are exempt from maintaining inventories and may use the cash method. The ruling was widely interpreted to

---

[13] *Charles F. Kahler,* 18 T.C. 31 (1952).
[14] Reg. Sec. 1.451-2(b).
[15] Ibid.
[16] *James J. Cooney,* 18 T.C. 883 (1952).
[17] Series E bonds were issued prior to 1980; Series EE bonds were issued after 1979. The interest on the Series HH bonds is taxable as received.

[18] Recognizing the volatile nature of farming and ranching, Congress established a special averaging technique for farmers and ranchers. Electing farmers and ranchers compute their tax on the average income for the current and three preceding years. Sec. 1301.

mean that small taxpayers did not need to account for inventories and could deduct the amount of their purchases in the year of payment. However, the IRS subsequently issued Rev. Proc. 2001-10, whereby it was clarified that the small taxpayer exception will only allow small taxpayers to deduct purchases of inventory in the year of purchase if (1) the inventory purchases are paid for by the end of the year and (2) the inventory is actually sold in such year. The effect of this new ruling basically is to eliminate the small taxpayer exception with respect to inventories.

EXAMPLE I3-14 ▶ The Cheryl Corporation began a new retail business in the current year and had sales of $400,000. The corporation had year-end accounts receivable of $15,000 and purchased $240,000 of merchandise during the year. At year-end, the corporation had not paid for $30,000 of the merchandise it had purchased and has $50,000 of inventory on hand at the end of the year. The corporation had paid operating expenses of $140,000 during the year. As the average gross receipts are less than $1 million, the corporation can use either the cash or accrual method. The corporation's income computed under both methods is as follows:

	Accrual		Cash	
Sales		$400,000		$385,000
Purchases	$240,000		$210,000	
Ending inventory	50,000		20,000*	
Cost of sales		190,000		190,000
Gross profit		210,000		195,000
Expenses		140,000		140,000
Net income		$ 70,000		$ 55,000

*$50,000 − $30,000 = $20,000

The difference between the accrual and cash methods is that the sales are not reported under the cash method until such sales are actually collected. Thus, the corporation does not include year-end receivables in this year's income. The year-end receivables will be reported when the receivables are collected in later taxable years.

As can be seen above, the cost of sales under both the accrual and cash methods are the same. This is because under Rev. Proc. 2001-10, taxpayers may not deduct inventory unless it is both paid for and sold. Since $30,000 was not paid for by year-end, it is not deductible and the purchases under the cash method are $30,000 less than under the accrual method. The ending inventory under the cash method is the physical inventory of $50,000 reduced by the $30,000 of inventory on hand that has not been paid for by year-end. ◀

ACCRUAL METHOD

REAL-WORLD EXAMPLE

The Ninth Circuit Court of Appeals has held that "markers" customers gave to a gambling casino to evidence their indebtedness to the casino required accrual even though the receivables were legally unenforceable under state law. The court found that there need only be a "reasonable expectancy" that payment would be made. *Flamingo Resort, Inc. v. U.S.*, 50 AFTR 2d 82-502, 82-1 USTC ¶9136 (9th Cir., 1982).

Taxpayers using the accrual method of accounting generally report income in the year it is earned. Income is considered to have been earned when all the events have occurred that fix the right to receive the income and when the amount of income can be determined with reasonable accuracy.[19] In the case of a sale of property, income normally accrues when title passes to the buyer.[20] Income from services accrues as the services are performed.

PREPAID INCOME. A major exception to the normal operation of the accrual method is the rules applicable to the receipt of prepaid income. Prepaid income is generally taxable in the year of receipt. For example, if a lender receives January interest in the preceding December, it is taxable in the year received, whether the lender uses the cash or accrual method. This treatment, of course, differs from financial accounting, where the interest would be reported as it accrues.

Two important exceptions to the general rule are worth noting. Accrual-basis taxpayers may defer recognizing income in the case of certain advance payments for *goods* and in the case of certain advance payments for *services* to be rendered. A taxpayer may defer advance payments for goods (inventory) if the taxpayer's method of accounting for the sale is the same for tax and financial accounting purposes.[21]

[19] Reg. Sec. 1.451-1(a).
[20] Regulation Sec. 1.446-1(c)(1)(ii), however, does permit taxpayers the right to accrue income from the sale of inventory when the goods are shipped, when the product is delivered or accepted, or when title passes, as long as the method is consistently used.
[21] Reg. Sec. 1.451-5.

Under Rev. Proc. 2004-34, taxpayers may defer payments for future services to the year following the year in which the payment is received.[22] Revenue relating to services provided in the year payment is received is reported currently. Revenue relating to future years is reported in the year following the year of receipt even if the payments relate to multiple future years. The rule can be applied to a variety of services such as Internet service, dance lessons, maintenance contracts (but not warranties included in the sales price of a product), membership fees, and rent (if services are associated with the rent, such as a hotel or motel). The procedure is available when service and products are provided together. The procedure does not apply to rent (if services are not associated with the rent), insurance premiums, interest, or warranty contracts included in the price of a product.

EXAMPLE I3-15 ▶

REAL-WORLD EXAMPLE

A dance studio using the accrual method was required to include in taxable income all advance payments for lessons in the form of cash and negotiable notes, plus contract installments due but remaining unpaid at year end. *Mark E. Schlude v. CIR*, 11 AFTR 2d 751, 63-1 USTC ¶9284 (USSC, 1963).

Bear Corporation, a publicly held, accrual-basis taxpayer that uses the calendar year as its tax year, sells computer courses under contracts ranging from three months to two years. When income is reported depends on the length of the contract and the month in which the contract is sold. Assume that Bear sells three contracts in July 2006. One is for three months costing $90, a second is for one year costing $300, and the third for two years costing $500. The $90 charged for the three month contract is reported currently as all services are provided currently. One-half of $300 charged for the one year contract is reported in 2006 and one-half is reported in 2007 as one-half of the services are provided currently and one-half will be provided in 2007. One-fourth of the $500 charged for the two year contract is reported in 2006 and the balance is reported in 2007. This is because Rev. Proc. 2004-34 does not permit income to be deferred beyond the end of the year following the year in which payment is received.

Length of Contract	Year Includible in Gross Income	
	2006	2007
3 months	$ 90	
12 months	150	$150
24 months	125	375

◀

HYBRID METHOD

The **hybrid method** of accounting is a combination of the cash and accrual methods. Under the hybrid method, some items of income or expense are reported under the cash basis and others are reported under the accrual method. The method is most often encountered in small businesses that maintain inventories and are required to use the accrual method of accounting for purchases and sales of goods. Such businesses often prefer to use the cash method of reporting for other items because the cash method is simpler and may provide greater flexibility for tax planning. A taxpayer using the hybrid method of accounting would use the accrual method with respect to purchases and sales of goods but would use the cash method in computing all other items of income and expenses.

 STOP & THINK

Question: Taxpayers who are eligible to use the cash method often choose the cash method of reporting income over the accrual method. Why is the cash method generally more favorable for income tax purposes?

Solution: Taxpayers who have the option frequently choose the cash method over the accrual method because it is simpler, offers greater tax planning opportunity, and results in taxes being owed when income is actually received. The cash method is simpler because taxpayers are not required to make the complex accruals associated with the accrual method. Planning opportunities are greater because cash basis taxpayers can deduct expenses when paid, thereby allowing taxpayers to control their tax liability. Under the accrual method, prepaid expenses are not deductible when paid, but must be deducted over the periods benefitted. Finally, cash basis taxpayers do not have to pay taxes until they receive the money. Under the accrual method, income is reported when it is earned even if it has not been received. As a result, accrual basis taxpayers sometimes have to pay the tax before they actually receive the income they have earned.

---

[22] I.R.B 2004-22.

ITEMS OF GROSS INCOME: SEC. 61(a)

Apply the rules of Sec. 61(a) to determine whether items such as compensation, dividends, alimony, and pensions are taxable

Section 61(a), quoted earlier in this chapter, states that gross income includes, but is not limited to, fifteen specifically listed types of income. Several of these items are discussed below.

COMPENSATION

Compensation is payment for personal services. It includes salaries, wages, fees, commissions, tips, bonuses, and specialized forms of compensation such as director's fees, jury fees, and marriage fees received by clergymen. What the compensation is called, how it is computed, the form and frequency of payment, and whether the compensation is subject to withholding is of little significance. Similarly, the fact that the services are part-time, one-time, seasonal, or temporary is immaterial.

ADDITIONAL COMMENT

Salaries and wages constituted 74.4% of total AGI reported in 1996.

There are exclusions, however, for a variety of employer-provided fringe benefits such as group term life insurance premiums, health and accident insurance premiums, employee discounts, contributions to retirement plans, and free parking. In addition, there is a limited exclusion applicable to foreign-earned income. Both fringe benefits and the foreign-earned income exclusion are discussed in Chapter I4.

BUSINESS INCOME

SELF-STUDY QUESTION

A retail company had sales of $1,000,000 and the following costs: goods sold, $400,000, salaries, $200,000, and rent and other expenses, $100,000. What is the company's gross income?

ANSWER

The gross income is $600,000. The sales figure is reduced by the cost of goods sold.

The term *gross income* usually refers to the total amount received from a particular source. In the case of businesses that provide services (e.g., accounting and law), the gross business income is the total amount received. In the case of manufacturing, merchandising, and mining, however, gross income is total sales less the cost of goods sold. Thus, gross income for tax purposes is comparable to gross profit for financial accounting purposes.

The cost of goods sold is, in effect, treated as a return of capital. Chapter I4 discusses a well-established tax concept that a return of capital is not income and, therefore, cannot be subject to the income tax. Chapter I11 discusses how inventories are valued.

GAINS FROM DEALINGS IN PROPERTY

Gains realized from property transactions are included in gross income unless a nonrecognition rule applies. As is true with business inventories, taxpayers may deduct the cost of property in order to arrive at the gain from a property transaction.[23] The tax law contains over 30 nonrecognition rules, which allow taxpayers to postpone the recognition of gains and losses from certain types of property transactions. In a few instances, these rules allow taxpayers to permanently exclude gains from gross income.[24]

Losses are not offset against gains in computing gross income. Rather, most losses are deductions *for* adjusted gross income. Furthermore, net capital losses for individuals are subject to provisions that limit the amount that can be deducted from other income to $3,000 per year. Losses from the sale or disposition of an asset held for personal use are not deductible.

INTEREST

TYPICAL MISCONCEPTION

It is sometimes mistakenly assumed that interest paid on federal obligations such as Treasury bonds, notes, and bills will also qualify for tax exemption.

Interest is compensation for the use of money. Taxable interest includes interest on bank deposits, corporate bonds, mortgages, life insurance policies, tax refunds, most U.S. government obligations,[25] and foreign government obligations.[26] Nontaxable interest is discussed below.

TAX-EXEMPT INTEREST. Since the inception of the federal income tax in 1913, interest on obligations of states, territories, and U.S. possessions and their political subdivisions

---

[23] Note that *business income* and *gains from dealings in property* are overlapping terms. The gross profit from the sale of inventory is actually both business income and a gain from a property transaction. Typically, however, the phrase *gains from dealings in property* may be assumed to mean gains from dealings in property other than inventory, so as to avoid confusion.

[24] For example, Sec. 121 allows taxpayers to exclude a limited amount of gain from a sale of a personal residence.
[25] The interest on many federal obligations issued before March 1, 1942 is tax exempt.
[26] Reg. Sec. 1.61-7.

ADDITIONAL COMMENT

Many tax advisers consider the exclusion of interest on municipal bonds to be one of the few remaining tax shelters. As a result, municipal bond funds have flourished in recent years.

ADDITIONAL COMMENT

The doctrine of intergovernmental immunity also results in most states exempting from taxation income received from U.S. obligations.

KEY POINT

The exclusion is available only to an individual who purchased the bond after reaching age 24. The exclusion is not available to an individual who owns a bond that was purchased by another individual, other than a spouse. Therefore, the exclusion is not allowable if bonds are purchased by a parent and put in the name of a child.

SELF-STUDY QUESTION

Young parents, whose annual income is currently $50,000, begin a regular program of purchasing Series EE savings bonds for their 8-year-old daughter's college education. Is there any risk that when the bonds are redeemed the interest income will not be excludable?

ANSWER

Yes, the parents' income may increase over the years to such an extent that the interest exclusion will not be available.

has been tax exempt.[27] Bonds issued by school districts, port authorities, toll road commissions, counties, and fire districts have been held to be tax exempt. In addition, Sec. 501(c)(3) organizations may issue up to $210 million of tax-exempt bonds. Such organizations include private universities, hospitals, churches, and similar nonprofit organizations.

As noted above, this exclusion does not extend to interest paid on most U.S. government obligations or foreign government obligations, nor does the exclusion exempt from taxation gains from the sale of state or local government bonds or interest on tax refunds paid by state and municipal governments.

There has always been some uncertainty as to whether the federal government could tax interest on state and local government obligations. The basic question is whether taxing these obligations would violate the doctrine of intergovernmental immunity in that the tax would reduce the ability of state and local governments to finance their operations because taxable bonds usually pay a higher rate of interest than tax-exempt bonds. The belief that taxing state and local government interest is unconstitutional is no longer widely held. While there have been efforts to tax interest on state and local bonds, the only changes have been to limit the use of bonds for private activities,[28] federally insured loans,[29] and arbitrage.[30]

SERIES EE SAVINGS BOND EXCLUSION. Taxpayers may purchase and eventually redeem Series EE bonds tax-free if they use the proceeds to pay certain college expenses for themselves, a spouse, or dependents.[31]

To qualify for the exclusion:

▶ The bonds must be purchased after 1989 by an individual who is age 24 or older at the time of the purchase.

▶ The bonds must be purchased by the owner and cannot be a gift to the owner.

▶ The receipts from the bond redemption must be used for tuition and fees, which are first reduced by tax-exempt scholarships, veterans benefits, Hope and Lifetime Learning credits, and other similar amounts.[32]

▶ Married couples living together must file a joint return to obtain the exclusion.

The full amount of interest is excluded only if the combined amount of principal and interest received during the year does not exceed the net qualified educational expenses (tuition and fees reduced by exempt scholarships, etc.), and the taxpayer's 2006 modified adjusted gross income is not over $63,100 ($94,700 for married individuals filing a joint return). The exclusion is fully phased-out for taxpayers whose 2006 modified AGI is more than $78,100 ($124,700 for married individuals filing a joint return).[33]

If the net qualified education expenses are less than the total principal and interest, a portion of the interest is excluded based on the ratio of the qualified educational expenses to the total principal and interest. The tentative exclusion is equal to

$$\text{Series EE interest} \times \frac{\text{Net qualified educational expenses}}{\text{Series EE interest} + \text{Principal}}$$

EXAMPLE I3-16 ▶ In 2006, Lois redeems Series EE bonds and receives $6,000, consisting of $1,875 of interest and $4,125 of principal. Assume that the net qualifying education expenses total $4,800. Lois's educational expenses equal 80% of the total amount received ($4,800 ÷ $6,000). Thus, her exclusion is limited to $1,500 (0.80 × $1,875). ◀

27 Sec. 103(a)(1).

28 Interest from state and local bonds issued for private activities such as the construction of sports facilities, convention centers, and industrial park sites is taxable. A limited amount of tax-exempt bonds can be issued each year by a state for "qualified" private activities such as airport construction, redevelopment, and student loans. The limit is the greater of $210 million or $50 per resident (Sec. 146(d)). The $210 million is scheduled to increase to $225 million in 2007. Though exempt from regular income tax, interest from these "qualified" private activity bonds is subject to the alternative minimum tax (see Chapter I14).

29 Sec. 149(b).

30 Sec. 148. Interest from state or local government bonds issued for the purpose of using the proceeds to buy higher-yield investments is taxable. Such bonds are called arbitrage bonds.

31 Sec. 135(c).

32 The exclusion is not permitted for amounts paid for sports, games, or hobbies unless they are part of a degree program (Sec. 135(c)(2)(B)).

33 Each of these amounts is adjusted annually for inflation. In 2004, the phase-out started at $61,200 ($91,850 on joint returns) and ended at $76,200 ($121,850 on joint returns).

ADDITIONAL COMMENT

A child born today will require about $100,000 for a four-year college education. If interest rates are around 6%, one would have to save about $245 a month until the child entered school to be able to pay this amount.

As noted, the amount of the exclusion is further reduced if modified adjusted gross income exceeds a $63,100 threshold ($94,700 for married individuals filing a joint return). Modified adjusted gross income includes the interest from education savings bonds and certain otherwise excludable foreign income.[34] The reduction is computed as follows:

$$\text{Otherwise excludable amount} \times \frac{\text{Excess modified AGI}}{\$15,000 \ (\$30,000 \text{ for joint filers})}$$

EXAMPLE I3-17 ▶ Assume the same facts as in Example I3-16 and that Lois is single and has other adjusted gross income of $66,225, making her total AGI $68,100 ($66,225 + $1,875). Lois's otherwise available exclusion of $1,500 is reduced by $500 to $1,000. This reduction is computed by dividing the excess modified AGI of $5,000 ($66,225 + $1,875 − $63,100) by $15,000 and multiplying the result by $1,500. ◀

One difficulty with the rules is that the phase-out of the exclusion is based on income in the year the bonds are redeemed, not the year they are purchased. As a result, some taxpayers who purchase bonds anticipating an exclusion find they are ineligible for the exclusion when the bonds are redeemed.

RENTS AND ROYALTIES

Amounts received as rents or royalties are included in gross income. As noted earlier, prepaid rent is taxable when received. Security deposits, which are refundable to tenants upon the expiration of a lease, are not included in gross income. The deposit is included in gross income only if it is not refunded upon the expiration of the lease.

EXAMPLE I3-18 ▶ In December 2006, Buddy rents an apartment to Gary. Buddy receives the first and last months' rent plus a security deposit of $500. Buddy must include in 2006 gross income both the first and last months' rent. Assume that Gary moves out of the apartment in 2008 and Buddy keeps $300 of the security deposit to cover repairs costing $200 and five days' unpaid rent, which amounts to $100. In 2008, Buddy would include the $300 in gross income and could deduct $200 for repairs. ◀

Royalties from copyrights, patents, and oil, gas, and mineral rights are all taxable as ordinary income. **Royalties** are proceeds paid to an owner by others who do business under some right belonging to the owner. Amounts received by a lessor to cancel, amend, or modify a lease also are taxable.

STOP & THINK

Question: Financial accounting contains extensive rules distinguishing "operating leases" from "capital leases." The IRC has no such rules. While the tax law does require the capitalization of leases that are in substance a purchase of the asset, most authority relating to the distinction comes from court cases. Why doesn't the tax law include specific rules relating to leased property?

Solution: The financial accounting rules that require businesses to capitalize some leases were established because of concern that long-term lease commitments represented unrecorded liabilities. The unrecorded liabilities distort a company's balance sheet, but may not distort reported income. Since the tax law is concerned with the reporting of income rather than the balance sheet, neither Congress nor the Treasury Department has seen the need to adopt leasing rules like those in financial accounting.

IMPROVEMENTS BY LESSEES. Improvements made by a lessee that increase the value of leased property are included in the lessor's income only if the improvements are made in lieu of paying rent or if rent is reduced because of the improvements. In such situations,

---

[34] Specifically, modified adjusted gross income includes amounts that qualify for the foreign earned income exclusion (Sec. 911), the exclusion for possession's income (Sec. 931), and the exclusion for income from Puerto Rico (Sec. 933). The limitation is determined after taking the partial exclusion for Social Security benefits and railroad retirement (Sec. 86), claiming the allowable deduction for retirement contributions (Sec. 219), and applying the passive loss limitation (Sec. 469).

the lessor must include the fair market value (FMV) of the improvement in gross income when it is made to the property.[35]

EXAMPLE I3-19 ▶ Rita rents an apartment to Anna. The apartment normally would rent for $1,000 per month, but Rita agrees to accept $400 per month for the first year if Anna builds a block wall around the property. Rita estimates that she would have to pay someone $6,000 to build the wall. Rita is accepting reduced rent and must report gross income of $6,000 when the wall is added to the property. The $6,000 could be added to Rita's basis in the property and should qualify as a depreciable asset. ◀

Improvements not made in lieu of rent are not income to the lessor. No adjustment is made to the lessor's basis in the property and, therefore, no depreciation is allowable. Gain or loss is recognized only when the property is disposed of.[36] Whether the improvements are in lieu of rent depends on the intent of the parties. This determination is based on the facts of the particular situation. The rental rate, the terms of the rental agreement, and whether the improvements have an estimated useful life exceeding the term of the lease may all be indications of intent.

DIVIDENDS

ADDITIONAL COMMENT

Shareholders of closely held corporations generally do not want to receive dividends from their corporations. The reason? They are taxed as ordinary income and the corporation does not receive a tax deduction for the payments.

Dividends are included in shareholder gross income. The result is a so-called double tax because corporations are taxed on income they earn, and shareholders are taxed when the income is distributed as dividends.

As noted in the previous chapter many corporations avoid the problem of "double taxation" by making S elections which result in the corporations and their shareholders being taxed much like partnerships. Two other important provisions reduce the tax burden on dividends:

▶ C Corporation receiving dividends from other C Corporations may claim a "dividends received deduction" that reduces, and in some cases eliminates, the second corporate tax on the income. The amount of the dividend received deduction is generally 70% of dividends received by a corporation owning less than 20% of the distributing corporation, 80% of dividends received by a corporation owning at least 20% but less than 80% of the distributing corporation, and 100% of the dividends received by a corporation owning 80% or more of the distributing corporation. This rule is discussed more in Chapter I16 and in-depth in *Prentice Hall's Federal Taxation: Corporations, Partnerships, Estates & Trusts* text and the *Comprehensive* volume.

▶ Lower tax rates temporarily apply to qualified dividends received by individuals. Between 2003 and 2007, dividends received by individuals in the 10% and 15% tax bracket are taxed at 5%. In 2008, there will be no tax on dividends received by individuals in the 10% and 15% brackets. Between 2003 and 2008, dividends received by individuals in higher tax brackets will be taxed at 15%. After 2008, dividends are scheduled to revert back and be taxed at the individual shareholder's regular tax rate. These lower tax rates on dividends only are available if the stock meets a special 60-day holding period.

In general, the above provisions apply to domestic corporations because foreign corporations are not automatically subject to the U.S. income tax. Only domestic corporations may make S elections. Dividends received from foreign corporations are generally ineligible for either the dividend received deduction or the lower tax rates discussed above.

EXAMPLE I3-20 ▶ Georgia is in the 25% tax bracket. She owns 10% of Orange Corporation, an S corporation with $20,000 of income. The corporation distributes $1,000 to Georgia. She receives a $500 dividend from Red Corporation, a U.S. corporation, and $300 from Blue Corporation, a foreign corporation. Georgia will include $2,800 in gross income. This includes her share of Orange Corporation's income or $2,000 (10% × $20,000) along with $500 she received from Red Corporation and $300 she received from Blue Corporation. As Orange Corporation made an S election, she must include in gross income her share of the corporation's income even though only part of it is distributed. The tax rate that applies to the $2,000 depends on the nature of the income earned by Orange Corporation. For example, part or all of the income could be treated as capital gains or dividend income if Orange earned those types of income while

---

[35] Reg. Sec. 1.109-1.   [36] Reg. Sec. 1.1019-1.

income from operations would be taxed at Georgia's higher tax rate of 25%. The dividend from Red Corporation qualifies for the favorable 15% tax rate applicable to dividends. The dividend from Blue Corporation will be taxed at Georgia's regular tax rate of 25% as it was paid by a foreign corporation. ◄

EXAMPLE I3-21 ▶ Celeste is a single taxpayer with a salary of $39,800, qualified divided income of $3,000, and itemized deductions of $8,000. Her taxable income is:

Adjusted gross income	$42,800
Itemized deductions	(8,000)
Personal exemption	(3,300)
Taxable income	$31,500

Her taxable income excluding dividends is $28,500 ($31,500 − $3,000), and is taxed at regular rates. The 15% tax bracket for single taxpayers ends at $30,650. As a result $2,150 ($30,650 − $28,500) of Celeste's dividends are taxed at the 5% rate available to taxpayers in the 10% and 15% brackets, and the balance of the dividends or $850 ($3,000 − $2,150) is taxed at 15%.

Tax on other income of $28,500 using rate schedule	$ 3,898
Tax on $2,150 of dividend income at 5%	108
Tax on $850 of dividend income at 15%	128
Taxable income	$ 4,134 ◄

DIVIDENDS DEFINED. Distributions to shareholders are taxable as dividends only to the extent they are made from either the corporation's current earnings and profits (a concept similar, although not identical, to current year's net income for financial accounting purposes) or accumulated earnings and profits (a concept similar, although not identical, to beginning of the year retained earnings).[37] Earnings and profits are discussed in Chapter I16 and in greater depth in *Prentice Hall's Federal Taxation: Corporations, Partnerships, Estates, and Trusts* text and the *Comprehensive* volume. Distributions in excess of current and accumulated earnings and profits are treated as a nontaxable recovery of capital. Such distributions reduce the shareholder's basis in the stock. Distributions in excess of the basis of the stock are classified as capital gains.

EXAMPLE I3-22 ▶ Liz is the sole shareholder in Atlantic Corporation and has owned the stock for five years. The basis of her stock is $50,000. Atlantic distributes $40,000 to Liz. Accumulated earnings and profits at the beginning of the year equal $25,000, and current earnings and profits equal $10,000. Liz will report $35,000 of taxable dividend income and a nontaxable return of capital equal to $5,000. In addition, Liz must reduce her basis in the stock by $5,000. Alternatively, if the distribution to Liz were $100,000, she would report $35,000 of taxable dividend income, $50,000 as a nontaxable return of capital, and a $15,000 long-term capital gain. ◄

STOCK DIVIDENDS. A **stock dividend** is a distribution by a corporation to its shareholders of the corporation's own stock. In 1920, the Supreme Court held that simple stock dividends could not be taxed because they were not income.[38] More precisely, income had not been realized because there was no real change in the taxpayer's interest or the risks faced by the taxpayer. Over the years, however, the exclusion for stock dividends has been narrowed. If a shareholder has the option of receiving either cash or stock, the shareholder is taxed even if he or she opts to receive stock. The option to receive cash constitutes constructive receipt of the cash. Today, many other features of a stock dividend may cause it to be taxed. For example, a distribution in which preferred stock is distributed to some common shareholders and common stock is distributed to others is taxable.[39] The recipient of a taxable stock dividend includes the value of the stock received in gross income, and that amount becomes the basis of the shares received.

A nontaxable stock dividend has no effect on a shareholder's income in the year received. The basis of the old shares is allocated between the old shares and the new

ADDITIONAL COMMENT

Many mutual funds do not want their shareholders to have a large tax bill on the undistributed capital gains allocated among the shareholders. Some mutual funds will sell stocks in the portfolio that can be sold at a loss to offset gains incurred earlier in the year.

---

[37] Sec. 316(a). The federal income tax became effective on March 1, 1913. Thus, income accumulated before that date can still be distributed on a tax-exempt basis.

[38] *Eisner v. Myrtle H. Macomber*, 3 AFTR 3020, 1 USTC ¶32 (USSC, 1920).
[39] Reg. Sec. 1.305-4.

shares. Furthermore, the holding period for the new shares starts on the same date as the holding period of the old.

EXAMPLE I3-23 ▶ Carol purchases 100 shares of Mesa Corporation stock for $1,100 (or $11 per share). Carol receives 10 shares of Mesa stock as a nontaxable stock dividend. After the dividend, Carol owns 110 shares of stock with a total basis of $1,100 (or $10 per share). All of the stock is assumed to have been acquired at the time of the original purchase. ◀

REAL-WORLD EXAMPLE

In the 1989 trial of Leona Helmsley, the billionaire hotel queen, it was disclosed that she had billed her companies for millions of dollars in personal items. The items ranged from a $12.99 girdle to a $1 million limestone-and-marble pool enclosure at her estate. She was sentenced to four years in prison and fined $7.1 million. The amounts paid to her by her companies represented constructive dividends.

CAPITAL GAIN DIVIDENDS. A **capital gain dividend** is a distribution by a regulated investment company (commonly called a *mutual fund*) of capital gains realized from the sale of investments in the fund. Such dividends also include any undistributed capital gains allocated to shareholders by such companies.[40] Capital gain dividends are long-term regardless of how long the shareholder has owned the stock of the regulated investment company.

CONSTRUCTIVE DIVIDENDS. In many corporations, the same individuals are both shareholders and employees. A corporation may not deduct dividends paid to shareholders but is permitted to deduct reasonable compensation. Questions are often raised as to whether amounts reported as compensation are really disguised dividends. If an amount called compensation is unreasonably high, it will be disallowed and reclassified as a dividend.[41] Often the reasonableness of compensation is determined by comparing the compensation paid to the employee-shareholders with amounts paid to others performing similar services.

EXAMPLE I3-24 ▶ Carmen owns 100% of the stock in Florida Corporation and receives a $400,000 salary for serving as president. The corporation reports no taxable income and pays no dividends. Presidents of similar companies received salaries ranging from $75,000 to $160,000. The IRS probably would disallow a portion of Carmen's salary as unreasonable. The disallowed portion would be treated as a dividend. ◀

ADDITIONAL COMMENT

In one case, the taxpayer, who was also the president and principal shareholder, diverted cash from vending and pinball machines at his truck stops/restaurants to his personal use. The IRS's position was that these diverted cash amounts were a constructive dividend. *Hagaman v. CIR.*, 69 AFTR 2d 92-906 (6th Cir., 1992).

Constructive dividends are not limited to shareholder-employee compensation payments but may include situations where the shareholder also is a landlord (e.g., property is rented to the corporation at an amount greater than its fair rental value). A shareholder also may receive a constructive dividend because of a creditor or vendor relationship. It is not necessary that a dividend be formally declared or that distributions be in proportion to stock holdings. **Constructive dividends** are often distributions that are intended to result in a deduction to the corporation and taxable income (such as compensation) to the shareholder.[42] Other constructive dividends are intended to produce a nonreportable benefit to the shareholder,[43] or even result in a deduction to the corporation without income to the shareholder.[44]

ALIMONY AND SEPARATE MAINTENANCE PAYMENTS

Any payment pursuant to a divorce or legal separation must be classified as one of the following for tax purposes:

(1) Alimony;

(2) Child support; or

(3) Property settlement.

The treatment of a payment depends on its classification. Alimony is deductible by the payor spouse and taxable to the payee spouse. Neither child support payments nor property settlements have any tax ramifications, that is, they are not subject to tax to the payee spouse nor deductible by the payor spouse.

Example I3-25 demonstrates the significant difference in taxation that can occur when a payment is classified as either alimony or a property settlement.

[40] Sec. 852(b).
[41] Sec. 162(a)(1).
[42] Other examples include excessive royalties (*Peterson & Pegau Baking Co.*, 2 B.T.A. 637 (1925)) and rent (*Limericks, Inc. v. CIR*, 36 AFTR 649, 48-1 USTC ¶9146 (5th Cir., 1948)).
[43] Examples include bargain sales of corporate assets to shareholders (*J. E. Timberlake v. CIR*, 30 AFTR 583, 42-2 USTC ¶9822 (4th Cir., 1942)),

redemptions of a shareholder's stock (Sec. 302), and loans to shareholders that are actually dividends (*George Blood Enterprises, Inc.*, 1976 PH T.C. Memo ¶76,102, 35 TCM 436).
[44] Examples include paying an employee's personal expenses (*The Lang Chevrolet Co.*, 1967 PH T.C. Memo ¶67,212, 26 TCM 1054) and purchasing assets for an employee's use (*Joseph Morgenstern*, 1955 PH T.C. Memo ¶55,086, 14 TCM 282).

EXAMPLE I3-25 ►

ADDITIONAL COMMENT

Child-support payments are not treated as alimony and are neither deductible by the payor spouse nor includible in income of the payee spouse.

ADDITIONAL COMMENT

If any amount specified in the divorce instrument will be reduced due to the happening of a contingency relating to a child or reduced at a time that can clearly be associated with such contingency, the amount of the reduction is treated as child support.

ETHICAL POINT

Tax consultants who advise divorcing couples may face an ethical dilemma because advice that benefits one spouse may be detrimental to the other, and because of the need to maintain confidential client relationships.

EXAMPLE I3-26 ►

Helen earns $500,000 and, as a result of her divorce, she is required to pay William $250,000. If the payment is a property settlement, Helen cannot deduct any of the $250,000 payment and William is not required to include the payment in his income. However, if the $250,000 is alimony, Helen can deduct the full amount in computing her adjusted gross income. William reports the $250,000 as alimony income. ◄

The tax law has rather specific rules that distinguish alimony, child support, and property settlements. Under current law, in order to be treated as **alimony**, payments must meet all of the following requirements:[45]

► Be made in cash (not property)

► Be made pursuant to a divorce, separation, or a written agreement between the spouses

► Terminate at the death of the payee

► Not be designated as being other than alimony (e.g., child support)

► Be made between people who are living in separate households

These rules are summarized in Topic Review I3-2. Certain aspects of these rules will be discussed further.

A **property settlement** is a division of property pursuant to a divorce. In general, each spouse is entitled to the property brought into the marriage and a share of the property accumulated during marriage.[46] A division of property does not result in any income to either spouse, nor does either spouse receive a tax deduction. The basis of property received by either spouse as a result of the divorce or separation remains unchanged.

As a result of a divorce, Dawn receives stock that she purchased with her former husband during their marriage for $12,000. At the time of the divorce, the stock was worth $14,000. Neither Dawn nor her former husband reports income from the transfer of the stock because the stock was acquired as a property settlement. If Dawn subsequently sold the stock for $15,000, she would report a $3,000 gain. ◄

Topic Review I3-2

Tax Rules for Alimony

TREATMENT OF RECIPIENT

The recipient of alimony must include the amounts received in gross income. Property settlements and child support payments are not taxable.

TREATMENT OF PAYOR

The payor of alimony may deduct amounts paid *for* adjusted gross income. Property settlements and child support payments are not deductible.

APPLICABLE TO

Payments must be pursuant to a divorce, separation, or a written agreement between spouses.

REQUIREMENTS

Spouses must be living in separate households. Payments must be in the form of cash paid to (or for the benefit of) a spouse or former spouse. Payments must terminate at the death of the payee. Payments may not be designated as being other than alimony (such as child support or a property settlement).

RECAPTURE

If the amount of payments declines in the second or third year, a portion of the early payments may have to be recaptured as income by the payor. The payee may deduct the same recaptured amount.

---

[45] Before 1942, alimony was not deductible (*Gould v. Gould*, 3 AFTR 2958, 1 USTC ¶13 (USSC, 1917)). The original rules were revised in 1984 and again in 1986. Prior rules apply to earlier divorces unless both spouses elect to apply current rules.

[46] How the property accumulated during marriage is divided may be determined by an agreement of the parties, or if they are unable to agree, on a basis of state law.

One unusual rule found in the current law that relates to alimony is the so-called **recapture provision**. This provision was established to prevent a large property settlement that might take place after a divorce from being treated as alimony so as to produce a deduction for the payor. In essence, the concept of recapture in connection with a divorce means that the payor of the alimony (who has taken a deduction for such amounts in prior years) must report the recapture amount in his or her income. The payee (who has reported the income in prior years) receives a deduction for the recaptured amount. This recapture occurs because the payments that originally were reported as alimony are being reclassified as property settlements.

Recapture occurs if payments decrease sharply in either the second or third year. Specifically, the amount of second-year alimony recaptured is equal to the second-year alimony reduced by the total of $15,000 plus the third-year alimony. The amount of first-year alimony recaptured is equal to the first-year alimony reduced by the total of $15,000 plus the average alimony paid in the second year (reduced by the recapture for that year) and the third year. The calculation of recapture for both the first and second years is shown below.

$$R_2 = A_2 - (\$15,000 + A_3)$$

$$R_1 = A_1 - [\$15,000 + (A_2 + A_3 - R_2)/2]$$

A_i = Alimony paid in first (A_1), second (A_2), and third year (A_3), respectively.

R_i = Recaptured alimony from the first (R_1) and second year (R_2), respectively.

Both first- and second-year amounts are recaptured by requiring the payor to report the excess as income (and allowing the payee to deduct the same amount) in the third year. Recapture is not required if payments cease because of the death of either spouse or remarriage of the recipient.

EXAMPLE I3-27 ▶ As a result of their divorce, Hal is ordered to pay to Rose $100,000 alimony in 2006 and $20,000 per year thereafter until her death or remarriage. Hal must recapture the amount of the decrease that exceeds $35,000, or $65,000 ($100,000 − $20,000 − $15,000). The $65,000 of alimony in 2006 must be reported by Hal as income during 2008. Also, Rose may deduct the $65,000 *for* AGI in 2008. ◀

EXAMPLE I3-28 ▶ As a result of their separation, Mary agrees to pay Tom $20,000 per year. The payments are to cease if Tom remarries. In the year after the agreement is reached, Tom remarries and Mary discontinues the payments. No recapture is required because the payments are contingent on the remarriage of the recipient and the payments have been discontinued because of the occurrence of this contingency. ◀

PENSIONS AND ANNUITIES

An **annuity** is a series of regular payments that will continue for a fixed period of time or until the death of the recipient. Taxpayers occasionally purchase annuities from insurance companies to provide a source of funds during retirement years. The insurance company may agree to make payments to the insured for the remainder of the insured's life. The retired individual is assured of a steady flow of funds for life. The price paid for the annuity represents its cost. The insured taxpayer is permitted to recover this cost tax-free.

Individuals receiving an annuity are permitted to exclude their cost, but are taxed on the remaining portion of the annuity. The following steps can be followed to determine the nontaxable portion of the annuity:

▶ Determine the **expected return multiple**. This multiple is the number of years that the annuity is expected to continue and may be a stated term, say ten years, or it may be for the remainder of the taxpayer's life. In the latter situation, the expected return multiple (life expectancy) is determined by referring to a table (see Table I3-1) developed by the IRS.

▶ Determine the **expected return**. This return is computed by multiplying the amount of the annual payment by the expected return multiple.

ADDITIONAL COMMENT

The three largest sources of non-wage income in 1996, in rank order, were net capital gains, pensions and annuities, and business and professional net income.

ADDITIONAL COMMENT

The expected return is limited to amounts receivable as an annuity. It does not include amounts that may be paid after death, nor does it include anticipated dividends.

▼ **TABLE I3-1**
Ordinary Life Annuities (One Life) Expected Return Multiple

Age	Multiple	Age	Multiple	Age	Multiple
5	76.6	42	40.6	79	10.0
6	75.6	43	39.6	80	9.5
7	74.7	44	38.7	81	8.9
8	73.7	45	37.7	82	8.4
9	72.7	46	36.8	83	7.9
10	71.7	47	35.9	84	7.4
11	70.7	48	34.9	85	6.9
12	69.7	49	34.0	86	6.5
13	68.8	50	33.1	87	6.1
14	67.8	51	32.2	88	5.7
15	66.8	52	31.3	89	5.3
16	65.8	53	30.4	90	5.0
17	64.8	54	29.5	91	4.7
18	63.9	55	28.6	92	4.4
19	62.9	56	27.7	93	4.1
20	61.9	57	26.8	94	3.9
21	60.9	58	25.9	95	3.7
22	59.9	59	25.0	96	3.4
23	59.0	60	24.2	97	3.2
24	58.0	61	23.3	98	3.0
25	57.0	62	22.5	99	2.8
26	56.0	63	21.6	100	2.7
27	55.1	64	20.8	101	2.5
28	54.1	65	20.0	102	2.3
29	53.1	66	19.2	103	2.1
30	52.2	67	18.4	104	1.9
31	51.2	68	17.6	105	1.8
32	50.2	69	16.8	106	1.6
33	49.3	70	16.0	107	1.4
34	48.3	71	15.3	108	1.3
35	47.3	72	14.6	109	1.1
36	46.4	73	13.9	110	1.0
37	45.4	74	13.2	111	.9
38	44.4	75	12.5	112	.8
39	43.5	76	11.9	113	.7
40	42.5	77	11.2	114	.6
41	41.5	78	10.6	115	.5

Source: Reg. Sec. 1.72-9, Table V.

Note: This table should be used if any or all investments were made on or after July 1, 1986. If all investments were made before July 1, 1986, use Reg. Sec. 1.72-9, Table I (not shown).

▶ Determine the **exclusion ratio.** This ratio is computed by dividing the investment in the contract (its cost) by the expected return (from above).

▶ Determine the **current year's exclusion.** This exclusion is computed by multiplying the exclusion ratio (from above) times the amount received during the year.

EXAMPLE I3-29 ▶ David, age 65, purchases an annuity for $30,000. Under the terms of the annuity, David is to receive $300 per month ($3,600 per year) for the rest of his life.

▶ The expected return multiple is 20.0. The multiple is obtained from Table I3-1.

▶ The expected return is $72,000 (20.0 × $3,600).

▶ The exclusion ratio is 0.417 ($30,000 ÷ $72,000).

▶ The exclusion is $1,500 (0.417 × $3,600). ◀

After the entire cost of an annuity has been recovered, the full amount of all future payments is taxable. On the other hand, if an individual dies before recovering the entire cost, the remaining unrecovered cost can be deducted as an itemized deduction on that individual's final return. Insurance companies and businesses with retirement plans compute the taxable portion of annuities and report the amounts to recipients on Form 1099.

KEY POINT

The simplified method is used only for annuity distributions from qualified retirement plans. All other annuity distributions are taxed in accordance with the general rules above.

SIMPLIFIED METHOD FOR QUALIFIED RETIREMENT PLAN ANNUITIES. Distributions from pensions and other qualified retirement plans are often paid in the form of an annuity. Both the employer and the employee often contribute funds to plans during the years of employment. When an employee retires, the amounts contributed and income accumulated thereon become available to the retired employee. In some cases, the retired employee has the option of receiving a lump-sum payment or an annuity. The employee's cost is limited to amounts contributed (usually through withholding) by the employee that were previously taxed to the employee. The employee may recover this cost tax-free. The employee's cost does not include employer contributions.

A simplified method is now used to determine the taxable portion of an annuity paid from a qualified retirement plan (such as a pension). Under the simplified method, the nontaxable portion of each annuity payment is equal to the employee's investment in the annuity divided by the number of anticipated payments as determined from the following table:

Age of Primary Annuitant on the Start Date	Number of Anticipated Payments
55 and under	360
56–60	310
61–65	260
66–70	210
71 and over	160

EXAMPLE I3-30 ▶

Jack, age 62, retires, and receives a $1,000 per month annuity from his employer's qualified pension plan. Jack contributed $65,000 to the plan prior to his retirement. Under the simplified method, Jack would exclude $250 per month as a return of capital. This is calculated by dividing $65,000 by 260 anticipated payments. ◀

If payments are paid other than monthly, the number of anticipated payments is adjusted accordingly. Thus, if payments are made quarterly, the number from the table is divided by four.

KEY POINT

Under current law, a taxpayer must generally pay tax on a portion of each withdrawal made before the normal starting date of the annuity.

ADVANCE PAYMENTS. Many pensions contain provisions that allow taxpayers to withdraw amounts before the normal starting date. Under current law, an amount withdrawn from a pension before the starting date is considered to be in part a recovery of the employee's contributions and in part a recovery of the employer's contributions.[47] After all contributions have been withdrawn, additional withdrawals are fully taxable. In addition to being subject to the regular income tax, any amount withdrawn may also be subject to a 10% nondeductible penalty. The penalty is not applicable to taxpayers who are age 59½ or older. Other exceptions to the early withdrawal penalty are discussed in Chapter I9.

EXAMPLE I3-31 ▶

Dick, age 45 and in good health, withdrew $2,000 from a pension plan during the current year. No exception exempts Dick from the 10% penalty. Dick had made $40,000 of after-tax contributions to the plan, and his employer had contributed $60,000. Dick must include $1,200 (0.60 × $2,000) in income. Because no exception applies, Dick must also pay an additional penalty of $120 (0.10 × $1,200). The penalty is not deductible by Dick. ◀

INCOME FROM LIFE INSURANCE AND ENDOWMENT CONTRACTS

The face amount of life insurance received because of the death of the insured is not taxable. If the proceeds are left with the insurance company and as a result earn interest, the interest payments are taxable. (See Chapter I4 for a detailed discussion of life insurance and endowment contracts.)

[47] Sec. 72(e).

INCOME FROM DISCHARGE OF INDEBTEDNESS

In general, the forgiveness of debt is a taxable event. The person who owed the money must report the amount forgiven as income unless one of several exceptions found in the tax law applies. These exceptions are discussed in Chapter I4.

INCOME PASSED THROUGH TO TAXPAYER

Generally, entities are subject to income tax based on the amount of taxable income. Corporations, as an example, are subject to income taxation. As noted, certain types of entities are not subject to income taxation as their income is taxed directly to the owners of the entity rather than to the entities. Such entities are referred to as "flow-through entities." Section 61 specifically lists three such instances: the distributive share of a partnership's income, income in respect of a decedent, and income from an interest in an estate or trust. Though not mentioned in Sec. 61, similar treatment is accorded S corporation income. In each case, the income that is produced by the entity merely flows through to the owner or beneficiary of such entity. The rules can be summarized as follows:

KEY POINT

The pass-through of income by a partnership can create a situation known as phantom income. In this situation, a partner is required to report income on his or her individual tax return, but the partner may not have received a cash distribution from the partnership.

▶ Each partner reports his or her share of the partnership's income. Each partner deducts his or her share of the partnership's expenses. The income and deductions are reported by the partners whether or not any amount is actually distributed by the partnership during the year.

▶ Income in respect of a decedent is income earned by an individual before death that is paid to another after the death. For example, salary earned by a husband before his death in an automobile accident may be paid to his widow after the accident. The recipient, in this case the widow, is taxed on the income if it has not been taxed to the decedent before his death.

▶ Income earned by estates and trusts is subject to taxation.[48] However, distributions to beneficiaries are deductible by estates and trusts and are taxable to the beneficiaries. Thus, if a trust with $20,000 of income distributes $15,000 to its beneficiary, the trust is taxed on $5,000, and $15,000 is taxed to the beneficiary. The income taxation of estates and trusts is covered more fully in *Prentice Hall's Federal Taxation: Corporations, Partnerships, Estates, and Trusts*.

▶ S corporations are taxed much like partnerships. Each shareholder in the corporation is taxed on his or her proportionate share of the corporation's income whether or not the income is actually distributed.

OTHER ITEMS OF GROSS INCOME

The preceding discussions considered items of gross income specifically listed in Sec. 61(a). However, the fact that an item of income is listed in Sec. 61(a) does not necessarily cause it to be taxable. Rather, the condition that causes an item of income to be taxable is that it is not specifically excluded. Some items of gross income not mentioned in Sec. 61(a) are discussed below.

PRIZES, AWARDS, GAMBLING WINNINGS, AND TREASURE FINDS

In general, prizes, awards, gambling winnings, and treasure finds are taxable.[49] Winnings in contests, competitions, and quiz shows as well as awards from an employer to an employee in recognition of some achievement in connection with his or her employment

---

[48] Note the distinction between income in respect of a decedent and the income of an estate. Income in respect of a decedent is the income earned before death that was never taxed to the decedent. An example would be interest that was accrued but unpaid at death. Income of an estate is income earned after death that is paid to the estate. An example would be interest that accrues after the decedent's death.

[49] Exclusions for scholarships and fellowships and a limited exclusion for prizes awarded for scientific, charitable, or similar meritorious achievements are discussed in Chapter I4.

are taxable.[50] The amount to be included in gross income is the fair market value of the goods or services received. Total gambling winnings must be included in gross income.[51] This includes proceeds from lotteries, raffles, sweepstakes, and the like. Gambling losses (up to the amount of the current year's winnings) are allowable as an itemized deduction.[52] The Regulations state that a treasure find constitutes gross income to the extent of its value in the year in which it is reduced to undisputed possession.[53]

EXAMPLE I3-32 ▶ Several years ago, Colleen purchased a used piano at an auction for $15. In the current year, she finds $4,500 of currency hidden in the piano. Colleen must report the $4,500 as income in the current year.[54] ◀

REAL-WORLD EXAMPLE

An accountant collected from a client money that was to be used to pay the client's taxes. Then the accountant appropriated the money for his own use. The accountant was held to have received unreported income. *Richard A. Reeves,* 1977 PH T.C. Memo ¶ 77,114, 36 TCM 500.

ILLEGAL INCOME

Income from illegal activities is taxable.[55] Some people find this part of the tax law surprising, but this fact serves as the basis for many criminal convictions given that few criminals report their illegal income. For example, Al Capone was convicted of income tax evasion, not bootlegging or other crimes. It is not necessary to prove that an individual had illegal income, but merely that the individual had income that was not reported.

Individuals have used varied defenses against this rule. One taxpayer was successful in convincing the Supreme Court that he should not be taxed on embezzlement gains because he had an unconditional obligation to repay the amount embezzled,[56] but the Supreme Court reversed this position in a later case.[57] The court concluded that although an obligation to repay existed, the taxpayer had no "consensual recognition" (intent) to repay. In addition to embezzlement of funds, the courts have held that a kidnapper's ransom was taxable,[58] along with profits from bookmaking,[59] card playing,[60] forgery,[61] stealing,[62] bank robbery,[63] sale of narcotics,[64] illegal sale of liquor,[65] and bribes.[66] (See Chapter I6 for a discussion of related deductions.)

UNEMPLOYMENT COMPENSATION

For many years, unemployment compensation was excluded from gross income. In 1978, Congress changed the law to tax unemployment compensation because these benefits are a substitute for taxable wages. Initially, unemployment compensation was taxable only if adjusted gross income exceeded certain base amounts. However, beginning in 1987, all unemployment compensation is now fully taxable for both government-financed programs and employer-financed benefits.

ADDITIONAL COMMENT

Welfare payments are not normally required to be included in gross income. However, if the welfare payments are fraudulently received under state or federal assistance programs, they must be included in the recipient's gross income.

SOCIAL SECURITY BENEFITS

Social Security benefits were excluded from gross income until 1984. Between 1984 and 1993, up to 50% of Social Security benefits were taxable. Beginning in 1994, up to 85% of Social Security benefits may be taxable. Under Sec. 86, the portion of Social Security benefits that are taxable depends on the taxpayer's provisional income and filing status. *Provisional income* is computed using the following formula:

Adjusted gross income (excluding Social Security benefits)		$xx,xxx
Plus:	Tax-exempt interest	x,xxx
	Excluded foreign income	x,xxx
	50% of Social Security benefits	x,xxx
Provisional income		$xx,xxx

[50] Sec. 74 and Reg. Sec. 1.74-1.
[51] *U.S. v. Manley S. Sullivan,* 6 AFTR 6753, 1 USTC ¶236 (USSC, 1927).
[52] Sec. 165(d).
[53] Reg. Sec. 1.61-14(a).
[54] *Ermenegildo Cesarini v. U.S.,* 26 AFTR 2d 5107, 70-2 USTC ¶9509 (6th Cir., 1970).
[55] Reg. 1.61-14(a).
[56] *CIR v. Laird Wilcox,* 34 AFTR 811, 46-1 USTC ¶9188 (USSC, 1946).
[57] *Eugene C. James v. U.S.,* 7 AFTR 2d 1361, 61-1 USTC ¶9449 (USSC, 1961).
[58] *Murray Humphreys v. CIR,* 28 AFTR 1030, 42-1 USTC ¶9237 (7th Cir., 1942).

[59] *James P. McKenna,* 1 B.T.A. 326 (1925).
[60] *L. Weiner,* 10 B.T.A. 905 (1928).
[61] *Cass Sunstein,* 1966 PH T.C. Memo ¶66,043, 25 TCM 247.
[62] *Mathias Schira v. CIR,* 50 AFTR 1404, 57-1 USTC ¶9413 (6th Cir., 1957).
[63] *Gary Ayers,* 1978 PH T.C. Memo ¶78,341, 37 TCM 1415.
[64] *Antonino Farina v. McMahon,* 2 AFTR 2d 5918, 58-2 USTC ¶9938 (D.C. N.Y., 1958).
[65] *U.S. v. Manley S. Sullivan,* 6 AFTR 6753, 1 USTC ¶236 (USSC, 1927).
[66] *U.S. v. Patrick Commerford,* 12 AFTR 364, 1933 CCH ¶9255 (2nd Cir., 1933).

MARRIED FILING SEPARATELY. In the case of married couples who live together but file separately, taxable Social Security benefits are equal to the lesser of

▶ 85% of Social Security benefits, or

▶ 85% of provisional income

MARRIED FILING JOINTLY. For married couples filing jointly, the computation of the taxable portion of Social Security benefits is as follows:

▶ If provisional income is $32,000 or less, no Social Security benefits are taxable.

▶ If provisional income is over $32,000 (but not over $44,000), taxable Social Security benefits equal the lesser of:
  50% of the Social Security benefits, or
  50% of the excess of provisional income over $32,000

▶ If provisional income is over $44,000, taxable Social Security benefits are equal to the lesser of:
  85% of the Social Security benefits, or
  85% of provisional income over $44,000, plus the lesser of (1) $6,000 or (2) 50% of Social Security benefits

SINGLE TAXPAYERS. For single taxpayers (and married persons living separately), the computation of the taxable portion of Social Security benefits is as follows:

▶ If provisional income is $25,000 or less, no Social Security benefits are taxable.

▶ If provisional income is over $25,000 (but not over $34,000), taxable Social Security benefits are equal to the lesser of:
  50% of the Social Security benefits, or
  50% of the excess of provisional income over $25,000

▶ If provisional income is over $34,000, taxable Social Security benefits are equal to the lesser of:
  85% of the Social Security benefits, or
  85% of provisional income over $34,000, plus the lesser of (1) $4,500 or (2) 50% of Social Security benefits

EXAMPLE I3-33 ▶

Holly is a single taxpayer with a taxable pension of $22,000, tax-exempt interest of $10,000, and Social Security benefits of $8,000. Her provisional income is $36,000, determined as follows:

Adjusted gross income	$22,000
Plus: Tax-exempt interest	10,000
50% of Social Security benefits	4,000
Provisional income	$36,000

The taxable Social Security benefits are equal to $5,700, which is the lesser of $6,800 (0.85 × $8,000) or $5,700 ($1,700* + the lesser of $4,500 or $4,000**).

*($36,000 provisional income − $34,000 threshold) × 0.85.
**50% of the Social Security benefits. ◀

The result of the computation excludes from gross income the Social Security benefits received by lower-income individuals but taxes a portion (up to 85%) of the benefits received by taxpayers with higher incomes. As the thresholds are not adjusted for inflation, an increasing number of retirees are finding that a portion of their Social Security benefits are taxable.

The term **Social Security benefits** refers to basic monthly retirement and disability benefits paid under Social Security and also to tier-one railroad retirement benefits. It does not include supplementary Medicare benefits that cover the cost of doctors' services and other medical benefits.

INSURANCE PROCEEDS AND COURT AWARDS

In general, insurance proceeds and court awards are taxable. Two exceptions are accident and health insurance benefits and the face amount of life insurance. (See Chapter I4 for a discussion of these benefits.)

Insurance proceeds or court awards received because of the destruction of property are included in gross income only to the extent that the proceeds exceed the adjusted basis of the property. Involuntary conversion provisions permit taxpayers to avoid being taxed if they reinvest the proceeds in a qualified replacement property.[67] If the proceeds are less than the property's adjusted basis, they reduce the amount of any deductible loss. Proceeds of insurance guarding against loss of profits because of a casualty are taxable.[68] Similarly, if a taxpayer had to sue a customer to collect income owed to the taxpayer, the amount collected is taxable just as it would have been had the taxpayer collected the income without going to court.

EXAMPLE I3-34 ▶ Gulf Corporation's factory was destroyed by fire. Gulf Corporation collected insurance of $400,000, which equaled the building's basis, and $250,000 for the profits lost during the time the company was rebuilding its factory. The $400,000 is not taxable because it constitutes a recovery of the basis of the factory. The $250,000 is taxable because it represents lost income. Recall that the income would have been taxable had it been earned by the company from regular operations. ◀

Although few exclusions are designed specifically for insurance proceeds or court awards, such amounts may be covered by other, more general exclusions. For example, Sec. 104(a)(2) excludes "damages (other than punitive damages) received . . . on account of personal physical injuries or sickness." Thus, amounts collected because of physical injury suffered in an automobile accident are excluded (see Chapter I4).

RECOVERY OF PREVIOUSLY DEDUCTED AMOUNTS

On occasion, a taxpayer may deduct an amount in one year but recover the amount in a subsequent year. In general, the amount recovered must be included in the gross income in the year it is recovered. Cash-basis taxpayers encounter this situation more often than accrual-basis taxpayers because their expenses are generally deductible in the year they are paid. If the amount was overpaid, the taxpayer can anticipate a refund.

EXAMPLE I3-35 ▶ During 2006, Cindy's employer withheld $1,000 from her wages for state income taxes. She claimed the $1,000 as an itemized deduction on her 2006 federal income tax return. Her itemized deductions totaled $12,000. On her 2006 state income tax return, her state income tax was only $800. As a result, Cindy received a $200 refund from the state in April 2007. Because Cindy deducted the full $1,000 in 2006, she must report the $200 refund as income on her 2007 federal income tax return. ◀

Any recovery of a previously deducted amount may lead to income recognition. Recovery, however, is often associated with expenses such as state income taxes or bad debts deducted in one year but recovered in a later year, medical expenses deducted in one year but reimbursed by insurance in a later year, casualty losses deducted in one year but reimbursed by court award or insurance in a later year, and deductions for amounts paid by check where the payee never cashed the check.

Several related rules should be noted:

▶ If the refund or other recovery occurs in the same year, the refund or recovery reduces the deduction and is not reported as income.

▶ Interest on the amount refunded is taxable and is not subject to the tax benefit rule (discussed below).

▶ The character of the income reported in the year of repayment is dependent on the type of deduction previously reported. For instance, if the taxpayer deducted a short-term capital loss in one year, the subsequent recovery would be a short-term capital gain.[69]

---

[67] The involuntary conversion provisions are discussed in Chapter I12.

[68] *Oppenheim's Inc. v. Kavanagh,* 39 AFTR 468, 50-1 USTC ¶9249 (D.C.-Mich., 1950).

[69] *F. Donald Arrowsmith Exr. v. CIR,* 42 AFTR 649, 52-2 USTC ¶9527 (USSC, 1952).

TAX BENEFIT RULE. As noted above, a taxpayer who recovers an amount deducted in a previous year must report as gross income the amount recovered. The amount recovered need not be included in income, however, if the taxpayer received no tax benefit. A tax benefit occurs only if the deduction reduced the tax for the year.[70]

EXAMPLE I3-36 ▶ In 2006, Jack's employer withheld $1,200 from his wages for state income tax. Jack claimed the $1,200 as an itemized deduction on his 2006 federal income tax return. Because of a variety of losses incurred by Jack, he reported a negative taxable income of $32,000 during 2006. The state refunded the $1,200 during 2007. Jack will not have to report the $1,200 as gross income on his federal return. He would have owed no federal income tax in 2006 even without the deduction for state income taxes. Therefore, Jack received no tax benefit from the deduction. ◀

Tax benefit may be absent in other situations. For example, a taxpayer's total itemized deductions may have been less than the standard deduction, or the expense may have been less than the applicable floor. To illustrate, medical expenses can be deducted only to the extent that they exceed 7.5% of adjusted gross income. If a taxpayer does not deduct medical expenses because they are less than the floor, the taxpayer does not have to report a subsequent reimbursement of the expense as income. If only a portion of an expense produces a tax benefit, only that portion has to be reported as income.

EXAMPLE I3-37 ▶

In 2006, Chris, an unmarried individual, had $1,350 withheld from her wages for state income tax. Her itemized deductions consisted of state income taxes of $1,500 and charitable contributions of $3,800. Her itemized deductions exceed the standard deduction ($5,150 in 2006) by $150 ($1,500 + $3,800 − $5,150). If Chris received a state income tax refund of $200 in 2007 she must report only $150 as gross income in 2007. She benefited only from $150 of the deduction and so that is all she has to report as income. ◀

CLAIM OF RIGHT

Sometimes taxpayers receive disputed amounts. For example, a contractor may receive payment on a job when the quality of the work is being questioned by the customer, a salesperson may receive commissions when there is a question as to whether the sales are final, or a litigant may receive a court award even though the case is on appeal. Under the claim of right doctrine, the recipient of a disputed amount must include the amount received in gross income as long as the use of the funds is unrestricted.

EXAMPLE I3-38 ▶ Jane wins a court case against a customer requiring the customer to pay her $10,000. The customer is unhappy with the result of the case and indicates that he plans to appeal, but pays the $10,000 to avoid interest on the amount in the event he loses the appeal. Jane must include the $10,000 in gross income even though she will have to repay the amount if she loses the appeal. ◀

EXAMPLE I3-39 ▶ Assume the same facts as in Example I3-38 except that the $10,000 is placed in escrow by the court awaiting the outcome of the appeal. Jane does not have to report the amount as she does not have use of the funds. ◀

Of course, taxpayers may be required to repay the disputed amount in a subsequent year. Such taxpayers may deduct the previously reported amount in the year of repayment. The taxes saved from such a deduction, however, may be considerably less than the original tax. If the repayment is over $3,000, taxpayers have the option of reducing the current tax by the tax paid in the prior year or years on the repaid amount.[71]

EXAMPLE I3-40 ▶ Assume the same facts as in Example I3-38, except that after reporting the disputed $10,000 Jane loses the appeal and must repay the $10,000 to her customer. If Jane was in the 25% tax bracket when she reported the disputed amount, she would have paid a $2,500 (0.25 × $10,000) tax on the disputed amount. If she were in the 15% bracket when she made the

---

[70] Sec. 111. [71] Sec. 1341.

repayment, she would recover only $1,500 by deducting the $10,000. Because the amount exceeds $3,000, Jane has the option of determining her current year's tax by deducting from the tax she would otherwise pay the $2,500 tax she paid in the earlier year. This credit is allowed in lieu of receiving a $10,000 deduction. ◄

TAX PLANNING CONSIDERATIONS

SHIFTING INCOME

A family can reduce its taxes by shifting income from family members who are in high tax brackets (e.g., parents) to family members who are in low tax brackets (e.g., children). Assignment of income rules prevent shifting from being done by merely redirecting the payment. Thus, a father cannot avoid a tax on his salary by ordering his employer to pay the salary to his daughter. Nevertheless, income can be shifted by transferring ownership of the property. For example, children may own stock in the family business. Dividends on the stock are taxed to the children. In the case of a child under age 14, however, the parents' (as opposed to the child's) tax rate applies to unearned income in excess of $1,600. Series EE bonds may prove useful to avoid the kiddie tax because the interest is deferred until the bond is redeemed or matures. The maturity date, of course, may be after the child reaches age 14. Another shifting technique is for the child to work for the family business and be paid a reasonable salary. Such income is taxed at the child's tax rate, even if the child is under 14 years old, and can be offset by the child's own standard deduction.

Shifting of income is constrained by several factors. As noted, the assignment of income doctrine limits transfers. Reasonableness limitations constrain compensation and other payments. Furthermore, outright gifts of property are subject to gift taxes. Also, individuals are reluctant to transfer wealth to children for a variety of personal reasons. However, the tax saving potential of shifting income is often so great as to prompt many well-to-do families to use available shifting techniques.

ALIMONY

Whether payments made in connection with a divorce or separation are classified as alimony is of major tax significance. Such classification results in a deduction for the payor and income to the payee. Alimony is actually one way to shift income.

EXAMPLE I3-41 ► Tony, who has a 35% marginal tax rate, makes payments of $40,000 to his former wife. If it is deductible as alimony, Tony will save $14,000 (0.35 × $40,000) a year in federal income taxes. The amount of tax that the former wife must pay depends on how much other income she has and whether she has deductions that reduce the tax. Her tax might be as high as her former husband's or as little as zero. ◄

ADDITIONAL COMMENT
In 1996, $5.4 billion of alimony paid was reported as a deduction, while only $4.6 billion was reported as taxable income.

Two points are clear. One is that both parties should understand the implication of having amounts treated as alimony. Second, the designation of the payments as alimony may be beneficial to both parties. The payor will, of course, benefit from a tax deduction. The payee may benefit because the payor may agree to make larger alimony payments since the payments are tax deductible.

PREPAID INCOME

As explained earlier in this chapter, prepaid income is generally taxable when received. This accelerated recognition of income may be a significant disadvantage to the taxpayer if the related expenses are incurred in a later tax year. Thus, tax planning for prepaid amounts is essential.

EXAMPLE I3-42 ► Phil owns an apartment complex and requires tenants to pay the first and last months' rent before they move in. Rita, on the other hand, owns an apartment complex and requires tenants to pay the first month's rent and a refundable deposit (which equals one month's rent).

Although the full amount received by Phil is taxable when it is received, only one-half of the amount received by Rita is taxable when it is received. Rita is required to refund the deposit, assuming the tenant vacates leaving the property in good condition and having paid all rent. Therefore, the deposit is not taxable. ◄

Taxpayers receiving advance payments in connection with services may be able to meet the requirements of Rev. Proc. 2004-34 (discussed earlier in the chapter); taxpayers receiving advance payments associated with the sale of merchandise may be able to meet the requirements of Reg. Sec. 1.451-5 (also discussed in this chapter). Also, special rules exist for subscription income, membership fees, crop insurance proceeds, and drought sales of livestock, all of which allow taxpayers to defer recognizing income.

TAXABLE, TAX-EXEMPT, OR TAX-DEFERRED BONDS

Which should a taxpayer choose: taxable bonds, tax-exempt bonds, or tax-deferred bonds? The answer depends on the relative interest rates and the taxpayer's current and future tax brackets. **Taxable bonds** yield the highest return, but the interest is taxable. **Tax-exempt bonds** yield a lower return. **Tax-deferred bonds** generally yield a return somewhere close to that of taxable bonds. Interest on U.S. Series EE savings bonds is tax exempt if it is used for educational purposes and if other requirements of Sec. 135 are met (see the discussion earlier in this chapter). If these conditions are not met, the tax is deferred until the bonds are redeemed. The taxpayer may be in a lower bracket when the tax is eventually paid, and in the meantime, the interest that will eventually go to pay taxes is earning additional income.

The decision between taxable and exempt bonds is a rather easy one if the risk of the investments is assumed to be approximately equal. A taxpayer should invest in exempt bonds instead of taxable bonds if the interest on the exempt bonds is greater than the interest on the taxable bonds multiplied by 1 minus the taxpayer's marginal tax bracket (expressed as a decimal). Stated in a formula, this means invest in tax-exempt bonds if

$$\text{Return on the tax-exempt bonds} \quad > \quad \text{Return on the taxable bonds} \quad \times \quad (1 - \text{Marginal tax bracket})$$

EXAMPLE I3-43 ▶ Robert's marginal tax bracket is 35% and he is trying to decide between tax-exempt bonds, which pay 6% interest, and taxable bonds paying 8% interest. Robert should invest in the exempt bonds because 6% is greater than 5.2% [0.08 × (1 − 0.35)]. ◄

Comparison of taxable bonds or exempt bonds to tax-deferred bonds is more complicated. As noted, the advantages of the tax-deferred bonds are twofold. First, the taxpayer may be in a lower tax bracket when the tax is paid (e.g., taxpayers who plan to redeem the bonds after retirement). Second, the amount that will eventually go to pay the tax earns income until the tax must be paid. Although the computation is not covered here, it is noted that taxpayers who anticipate that they will be in lower tax brackets and who plan to leave funds invested for several years may benefit from choosing Series EE U.S. savings bonds over taxable bonds. See Chapter I18 in the *Individuals* text for a further discussion of taxable, tax exempt, and tax deferred investments.

REPORTING SAVINGS BOND INTEREST

It may be desirable to purchase Series EE bonds in the child's name despite the fact that such interest is subject to the kiddie tax (see Chapter I2). This is because there is no income tax as long as the child's annual income is less than $800. However, even if a child is not otherwise required to file a return, it is necessary to report interest on Series EE bonds annually by filing a tax return.[72] Taxpayers who have not been reporting savings bond interest annually may change to annual reporting, but are required to report both current and previously accrued interest in the year of the change.[73]

---

[72] *Philip Apkin*, 86 T.C. 692 (1986).   [73] Reg. Sec. 1.454-1(a)(4), Ex. (1).

Taxpayers who report savings bond interest annually are allowed to change to the deferral method without IRS approval.[74] This is particularly useful where the decision to report interest currently was made before the imposition of the kiddie tax. Taxpayers who make this election are bound by it for five years.

DEFERRED COMPENSATION ARRANGEMENTS

Deferred compensation plans can be used as a means of avoiding the constructive receipt of income. Although income is normally taxable when the funds become available to the taxpayer, an advance contractual agreement can produce different results. Corporate executives, professional athletes, and others often sign agreements providing for compensation to be paid at future dates. Such agreements can produce tax savings because the recipients expect to be in a lower tax bracket. Because the arrangements are advance contractual agreements, the deferral of income does not constitute taxpayers "turning their backs" on the income.

EXAMPLE I3-44 ▶ Alonzo, a 35-year-old professional basketball player, signs a contract specifying that he will be paid $400,000 per year for ten years even if he does not play. Because of his age, both Alonzo and the team recognize that he will probably play for one or two more years. If the agreement had specified that he was to receive a salary of $1,300,000 per year for two years, most of the income would have been taxed at the highest rates. By spreading the amount over a longer period, Alonzo pays tax at lower rates on much of the income. Alonzo is compensated for the delayed payment by receiving a larger total amount [i.e., $4 million ($400,000 × 10 years) versus $2.6 million ($1.3 million × 2 years)]. ◀

COMPLIANCE AND PROCEDURAL CONSIDERATIONS

ADDITIONAL COMMENT

The dollar amount of tax-exempt interest income is recorded on Form 1040, line 8b, but is not included in the tax base. The IRS requires the reporting of this type of income probably because it may affect the taxability of Social Security benefits.

Form 1040 lists various types of income. Some items of income (wages, tax refunds, alimony, pensions and annuities, unemployment compensation, Social Security benefits, and other income) are listed directly on Form 1040. Most expenses related to these items of income are deducted as miscellaneous itemized deductions on Schedule A.

Most other types of income (and related deductions) are reported on special schedules.

Topic Review I3-3 summarizes the procedures for reporting income and related deductions.

EXAMPLE I3-45 ▶ John J. Alexander has several items of income and related deductions:

KEY POINT

The amount labeled "total income" on line 22 of Form 1040 is not gross income, adjusted gross income, or taxable income.

Salary	$40,000
Deductible alimony payments	6,000
Taxable interest	300
Dividends: Ford Motor Co.	1,150
Omaha Mutual Fund	430
Capital Gain Distribution: Omaha Mutual Fund	50
Rent income (depreciation, interest, repairs, and other related expenses total $9,000)	11,000

The reporting of these items of income is illustrated on page 1 of Form 1040 (Figure I3-1) and on Schedule B of Form 1040 (Figure I3-2). Salary and interest (because the interest is less than $1,500) are entered directly on Form 1040. Rental income would be entered on Schedule E (not illustrated), and the net income after deducting related expenses is transferred to Form 1040. Alimony received and alimony payments are reported on page 1 of Form 1040. ◀

---

[74] Rev. Proc. 89-46, 1989-2 C.B. 597.

Topic Review I3-3

Reporting of Income

TYPE OF INCOME	REPORTED ON	RELATED DEDUCTIONS ARE CLAIMED ON
Wages, salaries, tips, etc.	Form 1040	Schedule A and various other forms: moving, Form 3903; travel, transportation, etc., Form 2106
Interest	Form 1040 (if less than $1,500), otherwise Schedule B	Schedule A (miscellaneous deductions if any, e.g., safe deposit box fees)
Dividends	Form 1040 (if less than $1,500), otherwise Schedule B	Schedule A (miscellaneous deductions if any, e.g., safe deposit box fees)
Refund of state or local income taxes	Form 1040 (instructions contain a worksheet)	Schedule A (miscellaneous deductions if any, e.g., fee paid for tax advice)
Alimony	Form 1040	Schedule A (miscellaneous deduction, if any, e.g., legal fee associated with alimony)
Business income	Schedule C or C-EZ (net income or loss is transferred to Form 1040)	Schedule C or C-EZ (e.g., depreciation, advertising, repairs)
Capital gains	Schedule D	Schedule D (capital losses) or Schedule A (investment expenses)
Supplemental gains	Form 4797	Form 4797 (e.g., ordinary losses)
Pensions and annuities	Form 1040 (instructions contain a worksheet)	Generally no related deductions
Rents, royalties, partnerships, S corporations, estates, trusts, etc.	Schedule E	Schedule E
Farm income	Schedule F	Schedule F
Unemployment compensation	Form 1040	Generally no related deductions
Social Security benefits	Form 1040 (instructions contain a worksheet)	Generally no related deductions
Other income	Form 1040	Schedule A (miscellaneous deductions, if any)

PROBLEM MATERIALS

DISCUSSION QUESTIONS

I3-1 What phrase is found in both the Sixteenth Amendment to the Constitution and Sec. 61(a)? Why does the phrase appear in both locations?

I3-2 Contrast the accounting and economic concepts of income.

I3-3 Why does the tax concept of income more closely resemble the accounting concept of income than the economic concept?

I3-4 Explain the meaning of the term *wherewithal to pay* as it applies to taxation.

I3-5 If a loan is repaid, the lender does not have to include the repayment in gross income. There is no exclusion in the tax law that permits taxpayers to omit such amounts from gross income. How can this be explained?

I3-6 A landlord who receives prepaid rent is required to report that amount as gross income when the payment is received. Why would Congress choose to do this? What problem does this create for the taxpayer?

I3-7 Office space is often rented without carpet, wall covering, or window covering. Furthermore, many rental agreements specify that these improvements cannot be removed by a tenant if removal causes any damage to the property. What issue does this raise?

I3-8 Does the fact that an item of income is paid in a form other than cash mean it is nontaxable? Explain.

I3-9 Explain the significance of *Lucas v. Earl* and *Helvering v. Horst*.

I3-10 Under present-day tax law, community property rules are followed in allocating income between husband and wife. Is this consistent with *Lucas v. Earl*? Explain.

Form 1040
Department of the Treasury—Internal Revenue Service
U.S. Individual Income Tax Return 2005

(99)   IRS Use Only—Do not write or staple in this space.

For the year Jan. 1–Dec. 31, 2005, or other tax year beginning _____, 2005, ending _____, 20 ____   OMB No. 1545-0074

Label (See instructions on page 16.)

Use the IRS label. Otherwise, please print or type.

Your first name and initial: John J.	Last name: Alexander
If a joint return, spouse's first name and initial	Last name

Your social security number: 123 45 6789

Spouse's social security number:

Home address (number and street). If you have a P.O. box, see page 16.
41 Oak St.   Apt. no.

▲ You **must** enter your SSN(s) above. ▲

City, town or post office, state, and ZIP code. If you have a foreign address, see page 16.
Orlando, Fl 32816

Presidential Election Campaign ▶ Check here if you, or your spouse if filing jointly, want $3 to go to this fund (see page 16) ▶ ☐ You ☐ Spouse

Checking a box below will not change your tax or refund.

Filing Status
Check only one box.

1 ☒ Single
2 ☐ Married filing jointly (even if only one had income)
3 ☐ Married filing separately. Enter spouse's SSN above and full name here. ▶
4 ☐ Head of household (with qualifying person). (See page 17.) If the qualifying person is a child but not your dependent, enter this child's name here. ▶
5 ☐ Qualifying widow(er) with dependent child (see page 17)

Exemptions

6a ☒ Yourself. If someone can claim you as a dependent, **do not** check box 6a
b ☐ Spouse

c Dependents:

(1) First name Last name	(2) Dependent's social security number	(3) Dependent's relationship to you	(4) ✓ if qualifying child for child tax credit (see page 19)
			☐
			☐
			☐
			☐

If more than four dependents, see page 19.

Boxes checked on 6a and 6b: **1**

No. of children on 6c who:
• lived with you ____
• did not live with you due to divorce or separation (see page 20) ____
Dependents on 6c not entered above ____

Add numbers on lines above **1**

d Total number of exemptions claimed

Income

Attach Form(s) W-2 here. Also attach Forms W-2G and 1099-R if tax was withheld.

If you did not get a W-2, see page 22.

Enclose, but do not attach, any payment. Also, please use Form 1040-V.

7	Wages, salaries, tips, etc. Attach Form(s) W-2	7	40,000
8a	**Taxable** interest. Attach Schedule B if required	8a	300
b	**Tax-exempt** interest. **Do not** include on line 8a	8b	
9a	Ordinary dividends. Attach Schedule B if required	9a	1,580
b	Qualified dividends (see page 23)	9b	
10	Taxable refunds, credits, or offsets of state and local income taxes (see page 23)	10	
11	Alimony received	11	
12	Business income or (loss). Attach Schedule C or C-EZ	12	
13	Capital gain or (loss). Attach Schedule D if required. If not required, check here ▶ ☒	13	50
14	Other gains or (losses). Attach Form 4797	14	
15a	IRA distributions 15a ____ b Taxable amount (see page 25)	15b	
16a	Pensions and annuities 16a ____ b Taxable amount (see page 25)	16b	
17	Rental real estate, royalties, partnerships, S corporations, trusts, etc. Attach Schedule E	17	2,000
18	Farm income or (loss). Attach Schedule F	18	
19	Unemployment compensation	19	
20a	Social security benefits 20a ____ b Taxable amount (see page 27)	20b	
21	Other income. List type and amount (see page 29) ____	21	
22	Add the amounts in the far right column for lines 7 through 21. This is your **total income** ▶	22	43,930

Adjusted Gross Income

23	Educator expenses (see page 29)	23	
24	Certain business expenses of reservists, performing artists, and fee-basis government officials. Attach Form 2106 or 2106-EZ	24	
25	Health savings account deduction. Attach Form 8889	25	
26	Moving expenses. Attach Form 3903	26	
27	One-half of self-employment tax. Attach Schedule SE	27	
28	Self-employed SEP, SIMPLE, and qualified plans	28	
29	Self-employed health insurance deduction (see page 30)	29	
30	Penalty on early withdrawal of savings	30	
31a	Alimony paid b Recipient's SSN ▶ 987 65 4321	31a	6,000
32	IRA deduction (see page 31)	32	
33	Student loan interest deduction (see page 33)	33	
34	Tuition and fees deduction (see page 34)	34	
35	Domestic production activities deduction. Attach Form 8903	35	
36	Add lines 23 through 31a and 32 through 35	36	6,000
37	Subtract line 36 from line 22. This is your **adjusted gross income** ▶	37	37,930

For Disclosure, Privacy Act, and Paperwork Reduction Act Notice, see page 78.   Cat. No. 11320B   Form **1040** (2005)

FIGURE 13-1 ▶ FORM 1040 (PAGE 1)

3-32

Name(s) shown on Form 1040. Do not enter name and social security number if shown on other side.

John J. Alexander

Your social security number

123 : 45 : 6789

Schedule B—Interest and Ordinary Dividends

Attachment
Sequence No. **08**

			Amount
Part I **Interest** (See page B-1 and the instructions for Form 1040, line 8a.) **Note.** If you received a Form 1099-INT, Form 1099-OID, or substitute statement from a brokerage firm, list the firm's name as the payer and enter the total interest shown on that form.	**1**	List name of payer. If any interest is from a seller-financed mortgage and the buyer used the property as a personal residence, see page B-1 and list this interest first. Also, show that buyer's social security number and address ▶ --- --- --- --- --- --- --- --- --- --- --- ---	**1**
	2	Add the amounts on line 1	**2**
	3	Excludable interest on series EE and I U.S. savings bonds issued after 1989. Attach Form 8815	**3**
	4	Subtract line 3 from line 2. Enter the result here and on Form 1040, line 8a ▶	**4**

Note. If line 4 is over $1,500, you must complete Part III.

			Amount
Part II **Ordinary** **Dividends** (See page B-1 and the instructions for Form 1040, line 9a.) **Note.** If you received a Form 1099-DIV or substitute statement from a brokerage firm, list the firm's name as the payer and enter the ordinary dividends shown on that form.	**5**	List name of payer ▶ ------------------------- ----- *Ford Motor Company* ----------------- ----- *Omaha Mutual Fund* ----------------- --- --- --- --- --- --- --- --- --- --- --- --- --- --- ---	**5** *1,150* *430*
	6	Add the amounts on line 5. Enter the total here and on Form 1040, line 9a . ▶	**6** *1,580*

Note. If line 6 is over $1,500, you must complete Part III.

		Yes	No
Part III **Foreign** **Accounts** **and Trusts** (See page B-2.)	You must complete this part if you **(a)** had over $1,500 of taxable interest or ordinary dividends; or **(b)** had a foreign account; or **(c)** received a distribution from, or were a grantor of, or a transferor to, a foreign trust.		
	7a At any time during 2005, did you have an interest in or a signature or other authority over a financial account in a foreign country, such as a bank account, securities account, or other financial account? See page B-2 for exceptions and filing requirements for Form TD F 90-22.1.		X
	b If "Yes," enter the name of the foreign country ▶ -------------------------------------		
	8 During 2005, did you receive a distribution from, or were you the grantor of, or transferor to, a foreign trust? If "Yes," you may have to file Form 3520. See page B-2		X

For Paperwork Reduction Act Notice, see Form 1040 instructions.   Schedule B (Form 1040) 2005

FIGURE 13-2   ▶   SCHEDULES A & B (PAGE 2)

I3-11 Ricardo owns a small unincorporated business. His 15-year-old daughter Jane works in the business on a part-time basis and was paid wages of $3,000 during the current year. Who is taxed on the child's earnings: Jane or her father? Explain.

I3-12 Define the term *constructive receipt*. Explain its importance.

I3-13 Explain three restrictions on the concept of constructive receipt.

I3-14 When is income considered to be earned by an accrual-basis taxpayer?

I3-15
a. Explain the difference between the treatment of prepaid income under the tax law and under financial accounting.
b. Why are the two treatments so different?
c. What problem does this treatment create for taxpayers?

I3-16 Under what conditions is an accrual-basis taxpayer allowed to defer reporting amounts received in the advance of the delivery of goods?

I3-17 Under what conditions is an accrual-basis taxpayer allowed to defer reporting advance payments received for services?

I3-18
a. Is the interest received from government obligations taxable? Explain.
b. What impact does the fact that some bond interest is tax exempt have on interest rates?
c. Is an investor always better off buying tax-exempt bonds? Explain.

I3-19 Corporations are taxed on the income they earn, and shareholders are taxed on the dividends they receive. What provisions in the tax law reduce this "double tax" burden?

I3-20 Explain the relationship between dividends and earnings and profits.

I3-21 On what basis did the Supreme Court in *Eisner v. Macomber* decide that stock dividends are nontaxable?

I3-22 What is the significance of a constructive dividend?

I3-23 Explain the importance of the distinction between alimony and a property settlement.

I3-24
a. Are items of income not listed in Sec. 61 taxable? Explain.
b. Because there is no specific exclusion for unrealized income, why is it not taxable?
c. Can income be realized even when a cash-method taxpayer does not receive cash?
d. Does a cash basis taxpayer realize income upon the receipt of a note?

I3-25
a. Briefly explain the tax benefit rule.
b. Is a taxpayer required to report the reimbursement of a medical expense by insurance as income if the reimbursement is received in the year following the year of the expenditure?

I3-26 What opportunities are available for a taxpayer to defer the recognition of certain types of prepaid income? That is, what advice could you give someone who wishes to defer the reporting of prepaid income?

I3-27 Taxpayers who deduct an expense one year but recover it the next year are required to include the recovered amount in gross income. The tax benefit rule provides relief if the original deduction did not result in any tax savings. Does this rule provide relief to taxpayers who are in a higher tax bracket in the year they recover the previously deducted expense?

I3-28 George, a wealthy investor, is uncertain whether he should invest in taxable or tax-exempt bonds. What tax and nontax factors should he consider?

I3-29 Do you agree or disagree with the following statement: A taxpayer should not have to report income when debt is forgiven because the taxpayer receives nothing. Explain.

I3-30 Jack and June are retired and receive $10,000 of social security benefits and taxable pensions totaling $25,000. They have been offered $20,000 for a automobile that they restored after they retired. They did most of the restoration work themselves and the sale will result in a gain of $12,000. What tax issues should Jack and June consider?

ISSUE IDENTIFICATION QUESTIONS

I3-31 State Construction Company is owned equally by Andy, Bill, and Charlie. Andy works in the corporation full-time, and Bill and Charlie work elsewhere. When Andy left his previous job to work for State, he signed a contract specifying that he would receive a salary of $50,000 per year. This year, Andy felt that the company could expand if it purchased more equipment, and he offered to delay receiving $20,000 of his salary so the funds could be used to purchase the equipment. Bill and Charlie agreed, and the equipment was purchased. It is expected that State will have enough cash to pay Andy by early March of next year. What tax issues should Andy consider?

I3-32 Lisa and her daughter Jane are equal shareholders is Lisa's Flooring, Inc. Lisa founded the corporation and was the sole owner for over twenty years. The company is very successful and Lisa has accumulated a fairly large estate. When Jane turned age twenty-five last year, Lisa gave her half of the corporation's stock. The gift was properly reported on Lisa's gift tax return. Both Lisa and Jane now work full-time for the corporation. Lisa received a salary of $55,000 per year before Jane started working for the company. After Jane started working, Lisa reduced her salary to $15,000 and started paying Jane a salary of $50,000. Lisa indicates that she still makes most major decisions in the company, but she hopes that Jane will play a more important role as she becomes more familiar with the company. What tax issues should Lisa and the corporation consider?

I3-33   Larry's Art Gallery sells oil paintings, lithographs, and bronzes to collectors and corporations. Customers often come to Larry looking for special pieces. In order to meet customer needs, Larry often accepts orders and then travels looking for the desired item, which he purchases and delivers to the customer. The pieces are expensive, and Larry requires customers to demonstrate their sincerity by providing deposits. If it turns out that the item costs more than expected, Larry contacts the buyer and asks for additional funds. If the item costs less than expected, Larry refunds the excess amount. Also, Larry sometimes returns amounts he received in advance because he is unable to find what the customer wants. What tax issues should Larry's Art Gallery consider?

PROBLEMS

I3-34   *Noncash Compensation.* For each of the following items indicate, whether the individual taxpayer must include any amount in gross income.
a. Employees of Eastside Bookstore are given their birthdays off with pay.
b. Westside Hardware, Inc., gave each employee 10 shares of Westside stock worth $100 per share in lieu of a cash bonus.
c. Employees of Northside Manufacturing were allowed to take home the company's old computers when the company purchased new ones.

I3-35   *Constructive Receipt.* Which of the following constitutes constructive receipt in the current year ended December 31?
a. A salary check received at 6:00 p.m. on December 31, after all the banks have closed.
b. A rent check received on December 30 by the manager of an apartment complex. The manager normally collects the rent for the owner. The owner was out of town.
c. A paycheck received on December 29 that was not honored by the bank because the employer's account did not have sufficient funds.
d. A check received on December 30. The check was postdated January 2 of the following year.
e. A check received on January 2. The check had been mailed on December 30.

I3-36   *Cash and Accrual Methods.* Carmen opens a retail store. Her sales during the first year are $600,000, of which $30,000 has not been collected at year-end. Her purchases are $400,000. She still owes $20,000 to her suppliers, and at year-end she has $50,000 of inventory on hand. She incurred operating expenses of $160,000. At year-end she has not paid $15,000 of the expenses.
a. Compute her net income from the business assuming she elects the accrual method.
b. Compute her net income from the business assuming she elects the cash method.
c. Would paying the $15,000 she owes for operating expenses before year-end change her net income under accrual method of reporting? under the cash method?

I3-37   *Series EE Bond Interest.* In 2002, Harry and Mary purchased Series EE bonds, and in 2006 redeemed the bonds, receiving $500 of interest and $1,500 of principal. Their income from other sources totaled $30,000. They paid $2,200 in tuition and fees for their dependent daughter. Their daughter is a qualified student at State University.
a. How much of the Series EE bond interest is excludable?
b. Assuming that the daughter received a $1,000 scholarship, how much of the interest is excludable? Ignore any tax credits that might be available.
c. Assuming the daughter received the $1,000 scholarship and that the parents' income from other sources is $100,200, how much of the interest is excludable?

I3-38   *Alimony.* As a result of their divorce, Fred agrees to pay alimony to Tammy of $20,000 per year. The payments are to cease in the event of Fred's or Tammy's death or in the event of Tammy's remarriage. In addition, Tammy is to receive their residence, which cost them $100,000 but is worth $140,000.
a. Does the fact that Tammy receives the residence at the time of the divorce mean that there is a reduction in alimony, which will lead to Fred having to recapture an amount in the subsequent year?
b. How will the $20,000 payments be treated by Fred and Tammy?

c. Would recapture of the payments be necessary if payment ceased because of Tammy's remarriage?

d. What is Tammy's basis in the residence?

I3-39 *Constructive Dividend.* Brad owns a successful corporation that has substantial earnings and profits. During the year, the following payments were made by the corporation:

a. Salary of $250,000 to Brad. Officers in other corporations performing similar services receive between $50,000 and $85,000.

b. Rent of $25,000 to Brad. The rent is paid in connection with an office building owned by Brad and used by the corporation. Similar buildings rent for about the same amount.

c. Salary of $5,000 to Brad's daughter, who worked for the company full-time during the summer and part-time during the rest of the year while she attended high school.

d. Alimony of $40,000 to Brad's former wife. Although Brad was personally obligated to make the payments, he used corporation funds to make the payments.

Discuss the likelihood of these payments being treated as constructive dividends. If a payment is deemed to be a constructive dividend, indicate how such a payment will be treated.

I3-40 *Constructive Dividend.* Which of the following would likely be a constructive dividend?

a. An unreasonable salary paid to a shareholder.

b. An unreasonable salary paid to the daughter of a shareholder.

c. A sale of a corporation's asset to a shareholder at fair market value.

d. A payment by a corporation of a shareholder's debts.

e. A payment by a corporation of a shareholder's personal expenses.

I3-41 *Prepaid Rent.* Stan rented an office building to Clay for $3,000 per month. On December 29, 2005, Stan received a deposit of $4,000 in addition to the first and last months' rent. Occupancy began on January 2, 2006. On July 15, 2006, Clay closed his business and filed for bankruptcy. Stan had collected rent for February, March, and April on the first of each month. Stan had received May rent on May 10, but collected no payments afterwards. Stan withheld $800 from the deposit because of damage to the property and $1,500 for unpaid rent. He refunded the balance of the deposit to Clay. What amount would Stan report as gross income for 2005? for 2006?

I3-42 *Rental Income.* Ed owns Oak Knoll Apartments. During the year, Fred, a tenant, moved to another state. Fred paid Ed $1,000 to cancel the two-year lease he had signed. Ed subsequently rented the unit to Wayne. Wayne paid the first and last months' rents of $800 each and a security deposit of $500. Ed also owns a building that is used as a health club. The club has signed a fifteen-year lease at an annual rental of $17,000. The owner of the club requested that Ed install a swimming pool on the property. Ed declined to do so. The owner of the club finally constructed the pool himself at a cost of $15,000. What amount must Ed include in gross income?

I3-43 *Gross Income.* Susan's salary is $44,000 and she received dividends of $600. She received a statement from SJ partnership indicating that her share of the partnership's income was $4,000. The partnership distributed $1,000 to her during the year and $600 after year-end. She won $2,000 in the state lottery and spent $50 on lottery tickets. Which amounts are taxable?

I3-44 *Interest Income.* Holly inherited $10,000 of City of Atlanta bonds in February. In March, she received interest of $500, and in April she sold the bonds at a $200 gain. Holly redeemed Series E U.S. savings bonds that she had purchased several years ago. The accumulated interest totaled $800. Holly received $300 of interest on bonds issued by the City of Quebec, Canada. What amount, if any, of gross income must Holly report?

I3-45 *Annuity Income.* Tim retired during the current year at age 58. He purchased an annuity from American National Life Company for $40,000. The annuity pays Tim $500 per month for life.

a. Compute Tim's annual exclusion.

b. How much income will Tim report each year after reaching age 84?

I3-46 *Pension Income.* Beth turns 65 and retires from her position as a garment worker. She immediately began receiving a monthly pension for the remainder of her life of $300 from a qualified retirement plan. Over the years she worked, Beth made $13,104 of nondeductible contributions to the pension fund through withholding. How much must Beth report as income from the pension during the current year?

I3-47 *Social Security Benefits.* Dan and Diana file a joint return. Dan earned $30,000 during the year before losing his job. He subsequently received unemployment compensation of $1,000. Diana received Social Security benefits of $5,000.

a. Determine the taxable portion of the Social Security benefits.

b. What is the taxable portion of the Social Security benefits if Dan earned $45,000 before losing his job?

I3-48 *Social Security Benefits.* Lucia is a 69-year-old single individual who receives a taxable pension of $10,000 per year and Social Security benefits of $7,000. Lucia is considering the possibility of selling stock she has owned for years and using the funds to purchase a summer home. She will realize a gain of $20,000 when she sells the stock, which has been paying $1,000 of dividends each year. Lucia says her brother recommended that she sell half of the stock this year and half next year because selling all of the stock at once would affect the tax treatment of her Social Security benefits.

a. Compute her AGI under the assumption she sells all of the stock now after receiving $1,000 dividends from the stock.

b. Repeat the computation under the assumption she sells only half of the stock this year and also receives $1,000 dividends from the stock.

I3-49 *Social Security Benefits.* Bob received a salary of $27,000 before he retired in October of this year. After he retired, he received Social Security benefits of $3,000 during the year. What amount, if any, of the Social Security benefits are taxable for the year?

I3-50 *Adjusted Gross Income.* Amir, who is single, retired from his job this year. He received a salary of $25,000 for the portion of the year that he worked, tax-exempt interest of $3,000, and dividends from domestic corporations of $2,700. On September 1, he began receiving monthly pension payments of $1,000 and Social Security payments of $600. Assume an exclusion ratio of 40% for the pension. Amir owns a duplex that he rents to others. He received rent of $12,000 and incurred $17,000 of expenses related to the duplex. He continued to actively manage the property after he retired from his job. Compute Amir's adjusted gross income.

I3-51 *Recovery of Previously Deducted Expense.* In 2007, Fred received a $1,000 refund of state income taxes withheld from his salary during 2006. For each of the following cases, indicate whether Fred must include any portion of the refund in his 2007 gross income.

a. Fred did not itemize during 2006.

b. Fred does not itemize during 2007.

c. Fred uses the accrual method for determining his deduction for state income taxes.

d. Fred suffered a net loss during 2006 of $20,000.

e. Fred suffered a net loss during 2007 of $20,000.

f. Fred's itemized deductions during 2007 exceeded the standard deduction by $400.

I3-52 *Recovery of Previously Deducted Expense.* As the result of unexpected surgery, Jan incurred $14,000 of medical expenses in 2005. At the end of 2006, her medical insurance had paid only $5,000. Jan anticipates that the company will eventually pay an additional $7,000 of the bill. Because her AGI is $30,000 and there is a 7.5% floor for medical deductions, Jan can deduct medical expenses over $2,250. Her other itemized deductions exceed the standard deduction.

a. If Jan pays the balance of the $9,000 medical expenses before the end of the year, can she claim a deduction in 2006?

b. If she is reimbursed $7,000 in 2007, how will the reimbursement be treated?

I3-53 *Court Awards and Insurance Settlements.* What amount, if any, must be included in gross income by the following taxpayers?

a. Ann received $2,000 from her insurance company when her automobile which cost $3,000 was stolen.

b. Barry received $3,000 from his brother. Barry had initiated a lawsuit against his brother in an effort to recover $3,000 he had previously loaned to him. The brother paid Barry back before the case was tried, and Barry dropped the lawsuit.

c. Carry, an accountant, sued a client in order to collect her fee for doing tax work. Would Carry's accounting method make any difference?

d. Dave has incurred $6,000 of medical expenses so far this year. He paid $400 of the expenses himself. His insurance company paid $4,000 of the expenses. The hospital is suing Dave and the insurance company for the balance, $1,600.

I3-54 *Claim of Right.* USA Corporation hired Jesse to install a computer system for the company and paid him $8,000 for the work. USA soon realized that there were problems with the system and asked Jesse to refund the payment. At the end of the year the dispute had not been resolved. Jesse is in the 25% tax bracket in the year he did the original work. During the next year, when he is in the 15% tax bracket, Jesse refunds the $8,000 to USA.

a. Is the original payment taxable to Jesse when he receives it?
b. What options are available to Jesse when he repays the $8,000?
c. What option would have been available to Jesse if he had been asked to repay only $2,000?

I3-55   *Tax Planning.* Bart and Kesha are in the 35% tax bracket. They are interested in reducing the taxes they pay each year. They are currently considering several alternatives. For each of the following alternatives, indicate how much tax, if any, they would save.
a. Make a gift of bonds valued at $5,000 that yield $400 per year interest to their 14-year-old daughter, who has no other income.
b. Sell the bonds from Part a rather than give them to their daughter, and buy tax-exempt bonds that pay 6%. Assume the bonds can be sold for $5,000.
c. Give $1,000 cash to a charity. Assume they itemize deductions.
d. Pay their daughter a salary of $10,000 for services rendered in their unincorporated business.

I3-56   *Series EE Bond Interest and Kiddie Tax.* In 2006, Ken and Lynn paid $5,000 to purchase Series EE bonds in the name of their 11-year-old son. The son has no other income, and they are in the 28% tax bracket. The taxable interest during the first year will be $400 if an election is made to accrue the interest on an annual basis.
a. Will the child owe any tax on the bond interest?
b. Does the son need to file a tax return?
c. What are the tax consequences in 2006 and subsequent years if annual gifts are made to their son?

COMPREHENSIVE PROBLEMS

I3-57   Matt and Sandy reside in a community property state. Matt left home in April 2006 because of disputes with his wife, Sandy. Subsequently, Matt earned $15,000. Before leaving home in April, Matt earned $3,000. Sandy was unaware of Matt's whereabouts or his earnings after he left home. The $3,000 earned by Matt before he left home was spent on food, housing, and other items shared by Matt and Sandy. Matt and Sandy have one child, who lived with Sandy after the husband left home.
a. Is any portion of Matt's earnings after he left home taxable to Sandy?
b. What filing status is applicable to Sandy if she filed a return?
c. How much income would Sandy be required to report if she filed?
d. Is Sandy required to file?

I3-58   During 2006, Gary earned $57,000 as an executive. Gary, who is single, supported his half sister, who lives in a nursing home. Gary received the following interest: $400 on City of Los Angeles bonds, $200 on a money market account, and $2,100 on a loan made to his brother.

Gary spent one week serving on a jury and received $50.

Gary received a refund of federal income taxes withheld during the prior year of $1,200 and a state income tax refund of $140. Gary had itemized deductions last year of $8,000.

Gary received dividends on Ace Corporation of $1,000 and on Tray Corporation of $1,400. Gary's itemized deductions equal $9,000, and withholding for federal income taxes is $9,000. Compute Gary's tax due or refund due for 2006.

TAX STRATEGY PROBLEMS

I3-59   Kamal is starting a new business in 2006 which will operate as an S corporation. This means that income earned by the corporation will be reported by shareholders even if they do not receive distributions. Kamal has $110,000 of income from other sources, and itemized deductions totaling $15,000. He expects that the new business will produce $30,000 of income each year. He is considering giving his son Rashid 20% of the stock in the corporation. Rashid is age 16, and is Kamal's dependent. Rashid's only other income is $2,000 of interest. Neither Kamal nor Rashid will be employed by the corporation. Which alternative will produce a lower income tax liability—having all stock owned by Kamal or having Kamal own 80% of the stock and Rashid own 20%? Assume Kamal's filing status is head-of-household and Rashid is single. Ignore other taxes.

I3-60   Assume that it is December 31, and that Jake is considering making a $1,000 charitable contribution. Jake currently is in the 35% tax bracket, but expects that his tax bracket will be 28% next year. How much more will the deduction for the contribution be worth if it is made today compared to next year?

TAX FORM/RETURN PREPARATION PROBLEMS

I3-61   Sally W. Emanual had the following dividends and interest during the current year:

Acorn Corporation bond interest		$ 700
City of Boston bonds interest		1,000
Camp Bank interest		1,250
Jet Corporation dividend (qualified)		1,300
North Mutual fund		
Capital gain distribution	100	
Ordinary dividend (qualified)	150	
Nontaxable distribution	200	450
Blue Corporation foreign dividend		250

Additional information pertaining to Sally Emanual includes

Salary	$30,000
Rent income	12,000
Expenses related to rent income	14,000
Pension benefits	8,000
Alimony paid to Sally	4,000

The taxable portion of the pension is $7,000. Sally actively participates in the rental activity. Other relevant information includes

Address: 430 Rumsey Place, West Falls, California 92699
Occupation: Credit manager
Social Security number: 123-45-4321
Marital status: Single

Complete Sally's Schedule B and page 1 of her Form 1040. Assume Schedule E has already been prepared.

CASE STUDY PROBLEMS

I3-62   Jim and Linda are your tax clients. They were divorced two years ago, and the divorce decree stated that Jim was to make monthly payments to Linda. The court designated $300 per month as alimony and $200 per month as child support, or a total of $6,000 per year. Jim has been unemployed for much of the year and paid Linda $2,000 that he said was for child support. In addition, Jim transferred the title to a three-year-old automobile with a $4,000 FMV and basis of $7,000 in exchange for her promise not to pursue any claim she has against him for the unpaid child support and alimony. Does Linda have to report any alimony and is Jim entitled to an alimony deduction? Draft a memo for the file that discusses the tax consequences for both Jim and Linda.

I3-63   John and Mary (your clients) have two small children and are looking for ways to help fund the children's college education. They have heard that Series EE bonds are a tax-favored way of saving and have requested your opinion on the tax consequences. They have asked your opinion regarding the relative advantages of purchasing Series EE bonds in their names versus the children's names. John and Mary have indicated that they expect to have a high level of income in the future and that their children may receive other income sources from future inheritances. Prepare a client memo making recommendations about the tax consequences of Series EE bond investments for John and Mary.

I3-64   Lee and Jane have been your firm's clients for most of the twenty years they have been married. Recently Lee came to you and said that he and Jane are obtaining a divorce, and he wants you to help him with some of the tax and financial issues that may come up during the divorce. The next day, Jane called asking you for the same assistance. What ethical issues do you see in this case? What possible conflicts may arise if you represent both Lee and Jane?

TAX RESEARCH PROBLEM

I3-65   William owns a building that is leased to Lester's Machine Shop. Lester requests that William rewire the building for new equipment Lester plans to purchase. The wiring would cost about $4,000, but would not increase the value of the building because its only use is in connection with the specialized equipment. Rather than lose Lester as a lessee, William agrees to forgo one month's rent of $1,000 if Lester will pay for the wiring. Because Lester does not want to move, he agrees. What amount, if any, must William include in gross income?

A partial list of research sources is

- Sec. 109
- Reg. Sec. 1.109-1
- *CIR v. Grace H. Cunningham*, 2 AFTR 2d 5511, 58-2 USTC ¶9771 (9th Cir., 1958)

4

CHAPTER

GROSS INCOME: EXCLUSIONS

LEARNING OBJECTIVES

After studying this chapter, you should be able to

1. ► Explain the conditions that must exist for an item to be excluded from gross income

2. ► Determine whether an item is income

3. ► Decide whether specific exclusions are available

4. ► Understand employment-related fringe benefit exclusion items

Chapter 13 discussed specific items that must be included in gross income. This chapter considers items that are excluded from gross income. Under Sec. 61(a), all items of income are taxable unless specifically excluded. Taxpayers who wish to avoid being taxed have two basic alternatives. One approach is to establish that the item is not income. If an item is not income (e.g., if it is a return of capital), it is not subject to the income tax. The second approach is to establish that a specific exclusion applies to the item of income.

EXAMPLE 14-1
KEY POINT

Given the sweeping definition of *income,* it is generally difficult to establish that an item is not income.

▶ Matt borrowed $10,000 from the bank. Although Matt received $10,000, it is not income because he is obligated to repay the amount borrowed. No specific statutory authority states that borrowed funds are excluded from taxation. Presumably, the fact that borrowed funds are not income is considered to be both fundamental and obvious. ◀

EXAMPLE 14-2 ▶ Sheila enrolled in State University. The university awarded her a $1,000 tuition scholarship because of her high admission test scores and grades. Section 117 excludes such scholarships from gross income. As a result, Sheila need not report the scholarship as income. ◀

OBJECTIVE 1

Explain the conditions that must exist for an item to be excluded from gross income

The major source of exclusions are those specific items contained in the IRC. These exclusions have evolved over the years and were enacted by Congress for a variety of reasons, including social and economic objectives.

Another source of exclusions are referred to as *administrative exclusions.* Exclusions exist because specific provisions in the Internal Revenue Code allow them. While the IRS has no authority to create exclusions, the IRS does have the authority to interpret the meaning of the Code. A liberal interpretation of the statute by the IRS may result in a broad definition of what constitutes an exclusion, and such a broad definition may reasonably be termed an administrative exclusion. For example, Sec. 102 excludes gifts received from gross income. The IRS has followed the practice of excluding certain welfare benefits from gross income, presumably because such benefits may be viewed as gifts.[1] The IRS could take the position that welfare benefits are not gifts. That position would no doubt be challenged in the courts.

The term *judicial exclusions* should be considered in the same vein. Although the courts cannot create exclusions, they can interpret the statute and decide whether a particular item is covered by a statutory exclusion.

REAL-WORLD EXAMPLE

Grants made to Native Americans by the federal government under the Indian Financing Act of 1974 to expand Native American–owned economic enterprises are excludable from gross income. Rev. Rul. 77-77, 1977-1 C.B. 11.

ITEMS THAT ARE NOT INCOME

OBJECTIVE 2

Determine whether an item is income

As noted above, some items are not income and, therefore, are not subject to the income tax. In addition to amounts obtained by a loan (discussed above), four other items are not considered income:

▶ Unrealized income
▶ Self-help income
▶ Rental value of personal-use property
▶ Gross selling price of property (as opposed to the profit or gain earned on the sale)

UNREALIZED INCOME

Income that is not realized is not subject to income taxation. Thus, if a taxpayer owns stock in a company and the stock increases in value but the taxpayer does not sell the stock, no taxable income is realized.

This issue of the taxability of unrealized income was addressed over 80 years ago in *Eisner v. Macomber,* where the Supreme Court held that a stock dividend cannot be taxed

TYPICAL MISCONCEPTION

It is sometimes erroneously assumed that severance pay, embezzlement proceeds, gambling winnings, hobby income, prizes, rewards, and tips are not taxable.

---

[1] For example, see Rev. Rul. 57-102, 1957-1 C.B. 26, which excludes from gross income public assistance payments to blind persons.

because the taxpayer had "received nothing that answers the definition of income within the meaning of the Sixteenth Amendment."[2] An ordinary stock dividend does not alter the existing proportionate ownership interest of any stockholder, nor does it increase the value of the individual's holdings. In effect, the Court concluded that realization must occur before income is recognized. Although narrowed by subsequent legislation and litigation, ordinary stock dividends continue to be excluded from gross income even today. Perhaps more important, *Eisner v. Macomber* established realization as a criterion for the recognition of income.

SELF-HELP INCOME

Although self-help income is considered as income by economists, it is not recognized as income by the IRS or by the courts. Taxpayers commonly benefit from activities such as painting their own homes or repairing their own automobiles. If a taxpayer hires someone else to do the work, the taxpayer has to earn the income, pay tax on the income, and use the after-tax income to pay for the work. In either case, the taxpayer receives the same economic benefit, but the economic benefit derived from self-help is not included in the taxpayer's gross income.

This situation should be contrasted with taxable exchanges of services. A mechanic might agree to repair a painter's automobile in exchange for the painter's promise to paint the mechanic's home. In this instance, when the parties exchange services, each party realizes income equal to the value of the services received.

 STOP & THINK

Question: The discussion of self-help income refers to an exchange of services between two individuals, such as a painter and a mechanic. How can a taxable barter transaction be distinguished from an act of friendship which is repaid?

Solution: When one person helps another without any promise of repayment, the act of kindness does not represent an exchange and is not taxable. Friends help one another from time to time without contractual reciprocity. As a result, such acts are not taxable. The distinction between a taxable barter exchange and acts of friendship is not always easy to make.

RENTAL VALUE OF PERSONAL-USE PROPERTY

Taxpayers are not taxed on the rental value of personally owned property. For example, taxpayers who own their own home receive the economic benefit of occupancy without being taxed on the rental value of the property. It would be very difficult to keep records and value benefits obtained from self-help and the personal use of property. For that reason, no significant effort has ever been made to tax such benefits.[3]

SELLING PRICE OF PROPERTY

If property is sold at a gain, the gain and not the entire sales price is taxable. Because the basic principle is almost universally accepted, the Supreme Court has never had to rule directly on whether the entire sale proceeds could be taxed. The IRS and the courts seemed to accept the basic principle even before the rule became part of the statute.[4] The primary reason for this principle (often referred to as the "recovery of capital" principle) is that a portion of the selling price represents a return of capital to the seller.

---

[2] 3 AFTR 3020, 1 USTC ¶32 (USSC, 1920).

[3] In 1928, the government tried unsuccessfully to tax the value of produce grown and consumed by a farmer (*Homer P. Morris*, 9 B.T.A. 1273 (1928)). The court stated, "To include the value of such products [would be to] in effect include in income something which Congress did not intend should be so regarded." The court did not explain how or why it reached this conclusion. In 1957, the IRS successfully disallowed the deduction of expenses incurred in raising such produce (*Robert L. Nowland v. CIR*, 51 AFTR 423, 57-1 USTC ¶9684 (4th Cir., 1957)).

[4] Section 202(a) of the Revenue Act of 1924 is the predecessor of current Sec. 1001(a), which describes that only the gain portion of the sale proceeds is included in gross income. S. Rept. No. 398, 68th Cong., 1st Sess., p. 10 (1924) states that Sec. 202(a) sets forth general rules to be used in the computation of gain or loss. The Senate report further states that the provision "merely embodies in the law the present construction by the Department and the courts of the existing law."

MAJOR STATUTORY EXCLUSIONS

While Congress has created statutory exclusions for a variety of reasons, most exclusions have been enacted for reasons of social policy or reasons of incentive. The concept of social policy, that is, a concept of social generosity or benevolence, has prompted the government to exclude items such as:

▶ Gifts and inheritances (Sec. 102)

▶ Life insurance proceeds (Sec. 101)

▶ Public assistance payments

▶ Qualified adoption expenses (Sec. 137)

▶ Payments for personal physical sickness and injury (Sec. 104)

▶ Discharge of indebtedness during bankruptcy or insolvency (Sec. 108)

▶ Gain on sale of personal residence (Sec. 121)

▶ Partial exclusions for Social Security benefits (Sec. 86)

Other exclusions may be explained in terms of economic incentive, that is, the government's desire to encourage or reward a particular type of behavior.

▶ Awards for meritorious achievement (Sec. 74(b))

▶ Various employee fringe benefits (Secs. 79, 105, 106, 124, 125, 129, 132)

▶ Partial exclusion for scholarships (Sec. 117)

▶ Foreign-earned income (Sec. 911)

▶ Interest on state and local government obligations (Sec. 103)

Other reasons may exist for some of the exclusions listed above. For example, one reason income from the discharge of indebtedness during bankruptcy is excluded from gross income is the fact that such taxpayers would be unlikely to have the resources needed to pay the tax. (See Chapter I3 for a discussion of tax-exempt interest and Social Security benefits, and Chapter I12 for the treatment of gain on the sale of a personal residence.)

ADDITIONAL COMMENT

Tax expenditure estimates measure the decreases in individual and corporate income tax liabilities that result from provisions in income tax laws and regulations that provide economic incentives or tax relief to particular kinds of taxpayers.

GIFTS AND INHERITANCES

Congress has excluded the value of gifts and inheritances received from gross income since the inception of the income tax in 1913. Section 102 excludes the value of property received during the life of the donor (*inter vivos* gifts) and transfers at death (**testamentary transfers**—bequests, devises, and inheritances).[5] The recipient of such property is taxed on the income produced by the property after the transfer.[6] It should be noted that a donor, under the assignment of income doctrine, cannot avoid the income tax by making a gift of income. To avoid paying tax on income, a donor must make a gift of the underlying property to the donee.

TYPICAL MISCONCEPTION

Some people still believe that gifts above the gift exclusion amount of $11,000 are taxable to the donees. They are not since the Code specifically exempts all gifts, regardless of the amount. The donor may, however, depending on the circumstances, pay a gift tax.

EXAMPLE I4-3 ▶ Stan owns stock in a corporation and orders the corporation to pay dividends on the stock to his daughter. Even though his daughter received the dividends, Stan must include the dividends in his gross income. Stan could avoid being taxed on future dividends by giving the stock to his daughter before the dividend. ◀

It is often difficult to distinguish gifts, which are not included in the recipient's gross income, from other transfers, which are taxable. Gifts sometimes closely resemble prizes and awards.[7]

EXAMPLE I4-4 ▶ Tina received a free automobile for being the ten millionth paying guest at an amusement park. The automobile is not considered a gift but a prize and is taxable to Tina. ◀

---

[5] Although excluded from gross income, such transfers may be subject to the gift tax or the estate tax which are imposed on the transferor.
[6] Reg. Sec. 1.102-1.

[7] Recall that under Sec. 74 (discussed in Chapter I3) most prizes and awards are taxable.

Also, some payments made to employees by employers may resemble gifts.

EXAMPLE I4-5 ▶ At Christmas, Red Corporation paid $500 to each employee who had been with the company for more than five years. These payments are not considered gifts for tax purposes and are taxable to the employees. ◀

Whether a transfer is a gift depends on the intent of the donor. A donor is expected to be motivated by love, affection, kindness, sympathy, generosity, admiration, or similar emotions. In the two preceding examples, the transfers probably were made for business motives and not necessarily for donative reasons. Thus, the automobile is a taxable prize, and the amounts paid to employees represent taxable awards for services rendered, but see the discussion of Sec. 274 later in this chapter.

Transfers of money or property between family members frequently create problems of classification. For example, assume a father, who owns a business, hires his 10-year-old son to work in the business. Is the payment to the son a salary (and, therefore, deductible by the business) or is it really just a gift from the father to the son? The answer depends on the fair market value of the services performed by the son. If the son actually performs services that are commensurate with the salary paid, the payment may properly be classified as a salary. On the other hand, if the son is paid an amount that exceeds the value of the services, the excess amount will be treated as a gift.

LIFE INSURANCE PROCEEDS

Life insurance proceeds paid to a beneficiary because of the insured person's death are not taxable.[8] The exclusion applies whether the proceeds are paid in a lump sum or in installments. Amounts received in excess of the face amount of the policy usually are taxable as interest.

EXAMPLE I4-6 ▶ Buddy is the beneficiary of a $100,000 insurance policy on his mother's life. Upon her death, he elects to receive $13,000 per year for ten years instead of the lump sum. He receives $10,000 per year tax-free ($100,000 ÷ 10), but the remaining $3,000 per year is taxable as interest. ◀

EXAMPLE I4-7 ▶ Assume the same facts as in Example I4-6, except that Buddy elects to receive the full $100,000 face amount upon his mother's death. None of the $100,000 is taxable. ◀

The exclusion exists because life insurance benefits closely resemble inheritances, which are not taxable.

There is one exception that may result in a portion of the face amount of a life insurance policy being included in gross income.[9] The life insurance exclusion generally is not available if the insurance policy is obtained by the beneficiary in exchange for valuable consideration from a person other than the insurance company. For example, an individual may purchase an existing life insurance policy for cash from another individual. In this situation, the exclusion for death benefits is limited to the consideration paid plus the premiums or other sums subsequently paid by the buyer.

EXAMPLE I4-8 ▶ Kwame is the owner and beneficiary of a $100,000 policy on the life of his father. Kwame sells the policy to his brother Anwar for $10,000. Anwar subsequently pays premiums of $12,000. Upon his father's death, Anwar must include $78,000 [$100,000 − ($10,000 + $12,000)] in gross income. However, if Kwame gave the policy to his brother, all of the proceeds would be excluded from gross income because the gift of the policy does not constitute valuable consideration. ◀

The proceeds are excludable under the general exclusion for life insurance proceeds if the beneficiary's basis is found by reference to the transferor's basis (as would be true in the case of a gift), or if the policy is transferred to the insured, the insured's partner, a partnership that includes the insured, or a corporation in which the insured is a shareholder or officer.

---

[8] Sec. 101(a).   [9] Sec. 101(a)(2).

SURRENDER OR SALE OF POLICY.   The exclusion for life insurance is available for amounts payable by reason of the death of the insured. In general, if a life policy is sold or surrendered for a lump sum before the death of the insured, the amount received is taxable to the extent that it exceeds the net premiums paid.[10] On the other hand, no loss is recognized if a life insurance policy is surrendered before maturity and premiums paid exceed the cash surrender value.[11]

"Accelerated death benefits" may be excluded from gross income. Accelerated death benefits include payments made to a terminally ill person and periodic payments made to a chronically ill person. A person is terminally ill if a physician certifies that he is reasonably likely to die within 24 months. A person is chronically ill if he has a disability requiring long-term care (e.g., nursing home care). In general, the exclusion for periodic payments made to a chronically ill person is limited to the greater of $250 per day ($240 per day in 2005), or the actual cost of such care. The exclusion covers amounts received from the insurance provider or from a "viatical settlement provider" (i.e., person in the business of providing accelerated death benefits).

EXAMPLE I4-9 ▶ Harry has been diagnosed with AIDS and is expected to live less than a year. Harry is covered by a life insurance policy with a $100,000 face amount. The insurance company offers terminally ill individuals the option of receiving 75% of the policy face amount. If Harry accepts the settlement, the amount he receives is excludable from gross income because he is a terminally ill individual. ◀

EXAMPLE I4-10 ▶ Mary suffered a severe stroke and has been admitted to a nursing home where she is expected to remain for the rest of her life. She is certified by a licensed health care practitioner as being a "chronically ill individual." Her nursing home expenses amount to $200 per day. Mary has elected to receive $225 per day from a $1,000,000 face amount life insurance policy as accelerated death benefits. Because she is a chronically ill individual, Mary may exclude the full amount she receives as it is less than the daily limitation of $250 established by law. ◀

DIVIDENDS ON LIFE INSURANCE AND ENDOWMENT POLICIES.   Dividends on life insurance and endowment policies are normally not taxable because they are considered to be a partial return of premiums paid. The dividends are taxable to the extent that the total dividends received exceed the total premiums paid. Also, if dividends are left with the insurance company and earn interest, the interest is taxable.

ADOPTION EXPENSES

Congress provides tax benefits for qualified adoption expenses in the form of tax credits (see Chapter I14) or an exclusion for amounts paid pursuant to an adoption assistance plan created by an employer. An employee is allowed a $10,960 ($10,630 in 2005) per child exclusion from gross income for qualified adoption expenses paid by an employer under an adoption assistance program.[12] The exclusion is phased-out ratably for taxpayers with modified adjusted gross income of $164,410 to $204,410 ($159,450 to $199,450 in 2005).

Qualified adoption expenses include adoption fees, court costs, attorney fees, and other expenses related to an adoption. An adoption assistance program is a separate written plan of an employer, exclusively for the benefit of its employees, to provide adoption assistance.

EXAMPLE I4-11 ▶ Reggie and Rhonda are married, have AGI of $179,410, and adopt a child. Rhonda's employer maintains a written adoption assistance program. They spend $12,000 during the year in connection with the adoption, all of which is paid by Rhonda's employer pursuant to the plan. Reggie and Rhonda must include in their gross income an amount of $5,150, computed as follows:

---

[10] Sec. 72(e)(2). In some instances where distributions are made before the recipient reaches age 59½, a 10% penalty applies (see Sec. 72(q)).
[11] *London Shoe Co. v. CIR*, 16 AFTR 1398, 35-2 USTC ¶9664 (2nd Cir., 1935).

[12] Sec. 137.

Total adoption expenses paid from the plan	$12,000
Maximum exclusion	10,960
Phase-out percentage [($179,410 − $164,410)/($204,410 − $164,410)]	37.5%
Reduction in exclusion	4,110
Exclusion amount ($10,960 − $4,110)	6,850
Amount includible in gross income ($12,000 − $6,850)	5,150 ◄

In general, the exclusion cannot exceed the amount of qualified expenses. However, in the case of the adoption of a child with special needs, the exclusion is $10,960 (subject to the AGI phase-out). The exclusion is not limited to the actual expenses incurred.

EXAMPLE 14-12 ▶ Assume the same facts as in the previous example except that the amount of adoption expenses paid totaled $4,000. The exclusion would be limited to $4,000 except in the case of an adoption of a child with special needs in which case the exclusion would be $6,850. ◄

ADDITIONAL COMMENT

Notice that to exclude awards for meritorious achievement, the award must not come into the possession of the taxpayer.

AWARDS FOR MERITORIOUS ACHIEVEMENT

As noted in Chapter I3, prizes and awards generally are taxable. An exception is applicable to awards and prizes made for religious, charitable, scientific, educational, artistic, literary, or civic achievement if the recipient:

▶ Was selected without action on his or her part to enter the contest or the proceeding,

▶ Does not have to perform substantial future services as a condition to receiving the prize or award, and

▶ Designates that the payor is to pay the amount of the award to either a government unit or a charitable organization.[13]

The recipient of such an award normally would owe no tax if he or she collected the proceeds and then contributed the proceeds to a charity because the gift would qualify as a deductible charitable contribution. However, the exclusion changes AGI and thereby affects other computations. Also, this rule is beneficial in situations where the taxpayer could not deduct the full amount of the award because of the limitation on the charitable contribution deduction (generally 50% of AGI; see Chapter I7) or in the case of a small award to a taxpayer who does not itemize.

ADDITIONAL COMMENT

Athletic scholarships for fees, books, and supplies awarded by a university to students who are expected, but not required, to participate in a particular sport can be excludable.

KEY POINT

The exclusion for scholarships does not include amounts received for room, board, and laundry.

SCHOLARSHIPS AND FELLOWSHIPS

Subject to certain limitations, scholarships are excluded from gross income.[14] A scholarship is an amount paid or allowed to a student, whether an undergraduate or graduate, to aid degree-seeking individuals.

The exclusion for scholarships is limited to the amount of the scholarship used for *qualified tuition and related expenses*. Qualified tuition and related expenses typically include tuition and fees, books, supplies, and equipment required for courses of instruction at an educational organization. The value of services and accommodations supplied such as room, board, and laundry are not excluded. The exclusion for scholarships does not extend to salary paid for services even if all candidates for a particular degree are required to perform the services.[15]

EXAMPLE 14-13 ▶ Becky is awarded a $5,000 per year scholarship by State University. Becky spends $3,000 of the scholarship for tuition, books, and supplies, and $2,000 for room and board. In addition, Becky works part-time on campus and earns $4,000, which covers the rest of her room and board and other expenses. Becky is taxed on the $2,000 of the scholarship spent for room and board and $4,000 of salary earned from her part-time job. ◄

[13] Sec. 74.
[14] Sec. 117.
[15] Scholarships may need to be reviewed to determine whether the amount constitutes compensation. A "scholarship" awarded to the winner of a televised beauty pageant by a profit-making corporation was ruled to be compensation for performing subsequent services for the corporation (Rev. Rul. 68-20, 1968-1 C.B. 55). An employer-paid "scholarship" was held to be

compensation in a situation where the employee was on leave and was required to return to work after finishing the degree (*Richard E. Johnson v. Bingler*, 23 AFTR 2d 69-1212, 69-1 USTC ¶9348 (USSC, 1969)). However, in Ltr. Rul. 9526020 (September 10, 1995) the IRS ruled that grants to law students are not taxable even if they are conditioned upon the students agreeing to practice upon graduation in public, nonprofit, or other low paying sectors.

DISTRIBUTIONS FROM QUALIFIED TUITION PROGRAMS

To assist students (and/or their families) in meeting costs of higher education, Congress has expanded the income tax provisions dealing with *qualified tuition plans,* or so-called Section 529 plans. Basically, amounts are put into a qualified tuition plan (QTP) on behalf of a designated beneficiary and these amounts grow tax-free while in the QTP. The amounts may be withdrawn tax-free by the beneficiary if the amounts are used for qualified higher education expenses, including tuition, books, fees, supplies, equipment, and room and board. Room and board is a qualified higher education expense only if the beneficiary is at least a half-time student. The principal reason that these plans are so useful is that there is no income limitation for such plans. Therefore, taxpayers who have very high incomes can invest amounts into a QTP for their children and obtain tax benefits.

QTP plans, formerly called Qualified State Tuition Plans, may be maintained either by state governments or private universities.[16] These plans are classified into two basic types, (1) plans where tuition credits are purchased today for future use, and (2) plans where amounts are invested in mutual funds or similar investments and used to pay the beneficiary's future education expenses. Private universities may only offer the second type of plan. A QTP, while typically set up by parents or grandparents, may be set up and funded by anyone interested in the child's college education.

As mentioned above, for QTP distributions to be excluded, amounts must be used for qualified higher education expenses. Any portion of a QTP distribution not used for qualified expenses must be included in the beneficiary's gross income and is subject to a 10% penalty.

EXAMPLE I4-14 ▶   David, a high income taxpayer, lives in Kentucky and has two children, ages 10 and 8. Kentucky offers a Qualified Tuition Program and David establishes a separate QTP for each of his children, investing $5,000 in each account. The money is invested by the state of Kentucky in a mutual fund. The $5,000 is considered as a gift by David to each child but since the annual gift tax exclusion is $12,000, no gift tax is due. David plans to put $5,000 into each child's account for the next several years. The amounts in the QTP grow tax-free. When the children begin attending college, distributions may be made to the children to pay for their college education expenses and no taxes will be due as long as the distributions do not exceed the amount of qualified higher education expenses. Any distribution not used for qualified education expenses must be included in the child's income and is subject to a 10% penalty. ◀

There are several other important considerations in QTPs, including:

▶ A valuable feature of QTPs is the ability to change beneficiaries in the future without any tax consequences as long as the new beneficiary is a member of the original beneficiary's family. Members of the family are very broadly defined and include all of the relationships for determining a dependency exemption as well as first cousins.

▶ The exclusion permitted under Sec. 529 must be reduced by any amounts used to claim the HOPE credit or the lifetime learning credit.[17]

▶ The amounts transferred into a QTP are treated as a gift by the transferor to the designated beneficiary and, when combined with other gifts, are generally limited to $12,000 per year for each beneficiary.

PAYMENTS FOR INJURY AND SICKNESS

Sec. 104(a) excludes from gross income the "amount of any damages (other than punitive damages) . . . received . . . on account of personal physical injuries or physical sickness." Thus, for example, a taxpayer may exclude an insurance settlement for physical injury that resulted from an automobile accident. The exclusion does not cover amounts

---

[16] Under prior law, Section 529 plans could only be established and maintained by the states. For taxable years beginning after December 31, 2001, such plans can be established and maintained by eligible private institutions.

[17] Sec. 529(c)(3)(B)(v). These credits are discussed in Chapter I14 of this textbook.

awarded for nonphysical injuries (such as a damaged reputation or libel) except that taxpayers may exclude reimbursements for medical expenses related to nonphysical injuries.

EXAMPLE I4-15 ▶ After she was denied a promotion, Jane sued her employer claiming sex discrimination. She was awarded $5,000 to cover the medical bills she incurred because of the related emotional distress, $20,000 to punish her employer for discrimination, and $10,000 to compensate her for lost wages. The $5,000 awarded to cover medical bills is excluded from gross income, but not the amounts awarded as punitive damages or lost wages. ◀

The exclusion under Sec. 104(a) applies to damages received because of emotional distress in only two situations: (1) when the payments are for medical expenses related to the emotional distress, and (2) when the payments are for emotional distress *attributable* to a physical injury (including physical injury suffered by another person).

Sometimes, victims are awarded amounts that are intended to punish the guilty party. These so-called punitive damages are taxable even when they are awarded for physical injuries.

EXAMPLE I4-16 ▶ Mary was injured in an automobile accident caused by another driver. Mary's daughter, Sarah, was in the automobile, but she was not physically injured. The other driver's insurance company was required by a court to pay Mary $10,000 to cover medical bills relating to her injuries, $5,000 to compensate her for emotional distress caused by the injuries, and $15,000 of punitive damages. Sarah was paid $3,000 to compensate her for distress caused by her witnessing her mother's injuries. Only the $15,000 of punitive damages are taxable to Mary as the other amounts are compensatory damages related to her physical injuries. Sarah's damage award of $3,000 is also excludable. ◀

Sec. 104(a)(3) excludes from gross income amounts collected under an accident and health insurance policy purchased by the taxpayer, even if the benefits are a substitute for lost income. In addition, Sec. 101 specifies that benefits received under a qualified long-term care insurance contract may be excluded from gross income, but limits the exclusion to the greater of $250 per day ($240 per day in 2005) or the actual cost of such care.[18] Such policies pay for nursing home and other types of long-term care. If the benefits exceed the actual cost of such care but are less than $250 per day, no portion of the benefits is taxable.

EXAMPLE I4-17 ▶ Chuck purchased a disability income policy from an insurance company. Chuck subsequently suffered a heart attack. Under the terms of the policy, Chuck received $2,500 per month for the five months he was unable to work. The amounts received are not taxable, even though the payments are a substitute for the wages lost due to the illness. ◀

This exclusion is not applicable if the accident and health benefits are provided by the taxpayer's employer.[19]

EXAMPLE I4-18 ▶ Assume the same facts as in Example I4-17 except that Chuck's employer paid the premiums on the policy. The amounts received by Chuck are taxable. ◀

EXAMPLE I4-19 ▶ Ruth suffered a serious stroke and was admitted to a nursing home. During the year, she was in a nursing home for 140 days. Nursing home charges, physician fees, and other related expenses totaled $29,000.

Under Ruth's long-term care insurance contract, she received reimbursements of $31,000. The reimbursements are not includible in Ruth's gross income because the amounts are less than the allowed exclusion amount of $35,000 (140 days × $250). This exclusion applies even though she was reimbursed more than her actual costs. Alternatively, if the reimbursements had been $37,400, she would be required to report $2,400 ($37,400 − $35,000) as gross income. ◀

---

[18] Sec. 101.
[19] A limited credit is available to taxpayers who receive such benefits. See Chapter I14 for a discussion of the credit for the elderly and disabled.

If the cost of the coverage is shared by the employer and the taxpayer, a portion of the benefits is taxable. For example, if the employer paid one-half of the premiums, one-half of the benefits would be taxable. The principal reason for the different tax treatment is that employer-paid coverage represents a tax-free employee fringe benefit, whereas employee-paid premiums are from after-tax dollars.

In the case of an award intended to reimburse the taxpayer for medical expenses, it follows that the taxpayer cannot deduct the reimbursed medical expenses.[20] If the award exceeds the actual expense, it is not taxable except in the case of employer-financed accident and health insurance and in the case of excess long-term care discussed above.[21]

State worker's compensation laws establish fixed amounts to be paid to employees suffering specific job-related injuries. Section 104(a)(1) specifically excludes worker's compensation from gross income, even though the payments are intended, in part, to reimburse injured workers for loss of future income and even if the injuries are non-physical.

EMPLOYEE FRINGE BENEFITS

OBJECTIVE 4

Understand employment-related fringe benefit exclusion items

In general, employee compensation is taxable regardless of the form it takes. Nevertheless, the tax law encourages certain types of fringe benefits by allowing an employer to deduct the cost of the benefit, by permitting the employee to exclude the benefit from gross income, or by permitting both the employer deduction and an employee exclusion. Employee fringe benefits subject to special rules include employee insurance, Sec. 132 benefits, meals and lodging, dependent care, and cafeteria plans. These fringe benefits are discussed below.

EMPLOYER-PAID INSURANCE. Employers commonly provide group insurance coverage for employees. In general, employers may deduct the premiums paid for life, health, accident, and disability insurance. Normally an employee does not have to include in gross income premiums paid on his or her behalf for health, accident, and disability insurance. Special rules applicable to life insurance premiums are discussed below.

Benefits received from medical, health, and group term life insurance coverage generally are excluded from an employee's gross income. Benefits received from a disability policy are normally taxable, but may qualify for the credit for the elderly and disabled (see Chapter I14). The tax treatments of employer-financed and taxpayer-financed insurance coverage are compared in Topic Review I4-1.

The rules relating to accident and health insurance are more generous than those for some other types of benefits. Under Sec. 106, employers can deduct insurance premiums and employees need not report the premiums as income. This is true even if the insurance is offered only to officers and other highly compensated employees.

Some employers provide self-insured accident and health plans to employees. Under such plans the employer pays employee medical expenses directly rather than paying insurance premiums. Such plans are subject to nondiscrimination requirements. *Discrimination* is defined in terms of an eligibility test (whether a sufficient number of non-highly compensated employees are covered) and benefits (whether non-highly compensated employees receive benefits comparable to highly compensated employees). Highly compensated employees include the five highest-paid officers, greater-than-10% shareholders, and highest-paid 25% of other employees.[22] If a plan discriminates in favor of highly compensated employees, these employees must include in gross income any medical reimbursements they receive that are not available to other employees.

In general, life insurance premiums paid by an employer on an employee's behalf are deductible by the employer and are includable in the employee's gross income.[23] A limited exception is applicable to group term life insurance coverage. In general, premiums

ADDITIONAL COMMENT

Many companies provide health care benefits to retired employees. However, due to mounting medical insurance bills, a rising retiree population, and an FASB rule that requires firms to recognize the associated liability, a number of companies are requiring retired workers to pick up a larger portion of their medical costs.

ADDITIONAL COMMENT

The tax expenditure estimate associated with the exclusion of contributions by employers for medical insurance premiums and medical care for the period 1994–1998 is $213 billion.

KEY POINT

The nondiscrimination requirements for self-insured accident and health plans are designed to ensure that such plans do not discriminate against rank-and-file workers.

ADDITIONAL COMMENT

The Economic Strategy Institute estimates that domestic auto producers have to pay about $400 per car to cover their health care and pension costs.

---

[20] See Chapter I3 for a discussion of the reimbursement of an expense deducted in a preceding year.
[21] Sec. 105(a).
[22] Sec. 105(h)(5).

[23] If the employer is the beneficiary of the policy, the employee receives no economic benefit and, as a result, need not include the premiums in gross income. Such premium payments are not deductible by the employer. Subsequent benefits are not included in the employer's gross income.

Topic Review I4-1

Treatment of Insurance

	PREMIUMS PAID BY	
	EMPLOYER	*EMPLOYEE*
Medical and health		
Premiums	Premiums not included in employee's gross income. Premiums deductible by employer.	Premiums deductible as medical expense subject to 7.5% of AGI limitation.
Benefits	Excluded from employee's gross income except when benefits exceed actual expenses.	Excluded from gross income.
Disability		
Premiums	Premiums not included in employee's gross income. Premiums deductible by employer.	Not deductible.
Benefits	Included in employee's gross income. May qualify for credit for elderly and disabled.	Excluded from gross income.
Life insurance		
Premiums	Included in employee's gross income (except for limited exclusion applicable to group term life insurance). Premiums deductible by employer (assuming employer is not the beneficiary).	Not deductible.
Benefits	Excluded from gross income.	Excluded from gross income.

attributable to the first $50,000 of group term life insurance coverage may be excluded from an employee's gross income.[24] To qualify group term life insurance premiums for the exclusion, broad coverage of employees is required. Though somewhat different, the rules may be compared to those associated with self-insurance coverage.[25] The amount of coverage can vary between employees as long as the coverage bears a uniform relationship to each employee's compensation.

EXAMPLE I4-20 ▶ Data Corporation provides group term life insurance coverage for each full-time employee. The coverage is equal to one year's compensation. The arrangement constitutes a qualified group term life insurance plan. ◀

TYPICAL MISCONCEPTION

Many individuals erroneously believe that all life insurance coverage provided by employers is exempt from income.

In the case of coverage that exceeds $50,000, employees must include in gross income the amount established by the Regulations. (See Table I4-1.)

EXAMPLE I4-21 ▶ USA Corporation provides Joy, age 61, with $150,000 of group term life insurance coverage. Joy must include in gross income $792, an amount determined by reference to Table I4-1 [($100,000/$1,000 × $.66) × 12 = $792]. ◀

The amount that must otherwise be included in an employee's gross income is reduced by any premiums paid by the employee.

If group term life insurance coverage discriminates in favor of key employees, each key employee must include in gross income the greater of the premiums paid on his or her behalf or the amount determined based on Table I4-1 without any exclusion for the first $50,000 of coverage.

---

[24] Sec. 79(a).
[25] For example, the rules refer to "key employees" as opposed to highly compensated employees. The term *key employee* is somewhat narrower in scope.

▼ TABLE I4-1
Uniform One-Month Group Term Premiums for $1,000 of Life Insurance Coverage

Employee's age	Premiums
Under 25	$0.05
25 to 29	.06
30 to 34	.08
35 to 39	.09
40 to 44	.10
45 to 49	.15
50 to 54	.23
55 to 59	.43
60 to 64	.66
65 to 69	1.27
70 and above	2.06

Source: Reg. Sec. 1.79-3(d)(2).

 STOP & THINK

Question: Does the fact that employers can provide health insurance and group term life insurance to employees on a tax-favored basis mean that such benefits should be provided to all employees? Explain.

Solution: No. Providing such benefits to all employees may be inefficient. Some employees have other health coverage (e.g., coverage through a spouse's employer). Employees with no dependents may not want life insurance coverage. As a result, employers who provide all employees with such benefits may be spending money on coverage that some employees neither want nor need. A cafeteria plan, discussed later in this chapter, is often a more efficient option. Such plans permit employees to choose either cash or from a menu of tax-favored benefits.

HISTORICAL NOTE

A limited exclusion from income for unemployment compensation was repealed in the Tax Reform Act of 1986.

SECTION 132 FRINGE BENEFITS. It has become common for employers to provide employees with such diverse benefits as free parking, membership in professional organizations, and small discounts on products sold by the employer. Section 132 was added to the IRC in 1984 to clarify whether certain types of benefits are taxable. Section 132 lists six types of fringe benefits that may be excluded from an employee's gross income (see Topic Review I4-2). Any costs incurred by an employer to provide the specified benefits are deductible under Sec. 162 if they meet the "ordinary and necessary" test of that section.[26] Benefits covered by Sec. 132 include:

▶ No-additional-cost benefits (e.g., a hotel employee's use of a vacant hotel room)

▶ Qualified employee discounts (e.g., discounts on merchandise sold by the employer)

▶ Working condition benefits (e.g., membership fees in professional organizations paid by an employer)

▶ De minimis benefits (e.g., coffee provided by the employer)

ADDITIONAL COMMENT

The nondiscrimination rules do not apply to working condition fringe benefits. For example, if a corporation makes bodyguards available only to key officers, the working condition fringe benefit exclusion would still apply.

▶ Qualified transportation benefits such as transit passes, tokens, and vouchers are limited to $105 per month (unchanged from 2005) and qualified parking benefits are limited to $205 per month ($200 in 2005).

▶ Athletic facilities (e.g., employer-owned tennis courts used by employees)

[26] See Chapter I6 for a discussion of Sec. 162 and its requirements. Section 274 does provide one exception to the general rule. The costs of maintaining recreational facilities (such as swimming pools) are not deductible if the facilities are made available on a discriminatory basis (e.g., only officers may use the facilities).

Topic Review I4-2

Summary of Sec. 132 Fringe Benefits

Section	Benefit	May Be Made Available to	Comments
132(b)	No-additional-cost (e.g., telephone, unused hotel rooms for hotel employees, unused airline seats for airline employees)	Employees, spouses, dependents, and retirees	The services must be of the same types that are sold to customers and in the line of business in which the employee works. Discrimination is prohibited.
132(c)	Qualified employee discounts	Employees, spouses, dependents, and retirees	Discounts on services limited to 20%. Discounts on merchandise are limited to the employer's gross profit percentage. No discount is permitted on real estate, stock, or other investment type property. Discrimination is prohibited.
132(d)	Working condition (e.g., free magazines, out-placement, and memberships)	Employees	Discrimination is permitted. Special rules apply to tuition reductions for employees of educational institutions and to an auto salesperson's demonstrator.
132(e)	De minimis (e.g., free coffee, holiday turkeys, or use of company eating facilities)	Employees	Eating facilities must be made available on a nondiscriminatory basis.
132(f)	Qualified transportation fringes (e.g., transit passes, tokens, and parking)	Employees	Limited in 2006 to $205 per month for parking and $105 per month for other transportation fringes.
132(j)(4)	Recreation and athletic facilities (e.g., gyms, pools, saunas, and tennis courts)	Employees, spouses, dependents, and retirees	If discrimination is present, employer loses deduction.

No-additional-cost benefits are limited to services, as opposed to property. Common examples of no-additional-cost benefits include the use of vacant hotel rooms by hotel employees and standby air flights provided to airline employees. The employer may not incur substantial additional costs, including forgone revenue, in providing the services to the employee. Thus, a hotel may allow employees to stay in vacant hotel rooms even though the hotel incurs additional utility and laundry costs as a result of the stay. However, the hotel cannot allow the employees to stay in lieu of paying guests. No-additional-cost benefits are limited to services provided to employees, their spouses, dependent children, and to retired and disabled employees. The term employee includes partners who perform services for a partnership. In addition, the benefits may be extended, on a reciprocal basis, to employees of other companies in the same line of business.

Employers may permit employees to purchase goods and services at a discount from the price charged regular customers. In the case of services, the discount is limited to 20% of the price charged regular customers. In the case of property, the discount is limited to the company's gross profit percent. No discounts are permitted on real property or investment property (e.g., houses or stocks). Further, the discounts must be from the same line of business in which the employee works. The discounts may be provided to the same persons as no-additional-cost benefits except that the discounts may not be provided on a reciprocal basis to employees of companies in the same line of business.

Discrimination is prohibited with respect to certain benefits. The benefits must be made available to employees in general rather than to highly compensated employees only. (See Topic Review I4-2 for specific rules.)

EMPLOYEE AWARDS.   As noted earlier, it is often difficult to distinguish between gifts and awards. The de minimis rule mentioned above permits employers to make small gifts such as a holiday turkey or a watch at retirement without the employee having to include the value of the gift in gross income. The employer is entitled to a deduction for the cost of such gifts.

Section 74 provides a similar rule for **employee achievement awards** and **qualified plan awards**.[27] Such awards must be in the form of tangible personal property other than cash and must be based on safety records or length of service. Employee achievement awards are limited to $400 for any one employee during the year. Furthermore, the awards must be presented as part of a meaningful presentation and awarded under circumstances that do not create a significant likelihood of the payment being disguised compensation. Qualified plan awards must be granted under a written plan and may not discriminate in favor of highly compensated employees. The average cost of qualified plan awards is limited to $400, but individual awards can be as large as $1,600.

▶ An award for length of service cannot qualify under the IRC if it is received during the employee's first five years of employment or if the employee has received a length-of-service award during the year or any of the preceding four years.

▶ No more than 10% of an employer's eligible employees may receive an excludable safety achievement award during any year. Eligible employees are employees whose positions involve significant safety concerns.

EXAMPLE I4-22 ▶

Each year, USA Corporation presents length-of-service awards to employees who have been with the company five, ten, fifteen, or twenty years. The presentations are made at a luncheon sponsored by the company and include gifts such as desk clocks, briefcases, and watches, none of which cost more than $400. The awards, which qualify as employee achievement awards, are deductible by USA Corporation and are not taxable as income to USA's employees. ◀

Gifts to employees that do not qualify as employee achievement awards or qualified plan awards can be excluded by the employee only if the awards can be excluded as de minimis amounts under Sec. 132(e).

MEALS AND LODGING.   Section 119 provides a limited exclusion for the value of meals and lodging that are provided to employees at either no cost or a reduced cost.

▶ Meals provided by an employer may be excluded from an employee's gross income if they are furnished on the employer's premises and for the convenience of the employer.

▶ Lodging provided by an employer may be excluded from an employee's gross income if it is furnished on the employer's premises and for the convenience of the employer, and the employee is required to accept the lodging as a condition of employment.

The requirement that meals and lodging be furnished on the premises of the employer refers to the employee's place of employment.[28] In one case, the Tax Court held that the business premises requirement was met in a situation where a hotel manager lived in a residence across the street from the hotel he managed.[29]

The convenience of the employer test considers whether a substantial noncompensatory business reason exists for providing the meals or lodging. Thus, the test is met if the owner of an apartment complex furnishes a unit to the manager of the complex because it is necessary to have the manager present on the premises even when he or she is off duty.

The value of lodging cannot be excluded from gross income unless the employee is required to accept the lodging as a condition of employment. This requirement is not met

---

[27] Sec. 74(c). The definitions and requirements for employee achievement awards and qualified plan awards are contained in Sec. 274(j).

[28] Reg. Sec. 1.119-1(c)(1).
[29] *Jack B. Lindeman*, 60 T.C. 609 (1973).

if the employee has a choice of accepting the lodging or receiving a cash allowance. Furthermore, meal allowances do not qualify for the exclusion because the employer does not actually provide the meal.[30] Section 132 (discussed earlier in this chapter) provides a de minimis exception. Some employers provide supper money to employees who must work overtime. If such benefits are occasionally provided to employees, the amount is excludable from the employees' gross income.

EXAMPLE I4-23 ▶ A hospital maintains a cafeteria that is used by employees, patients, and visitors. Employees are provided free meals while on duty in order to be available for emergency calls. Since the meals are provided on the employer's premises and for the convenience of the employer, the value of the meals is excluded from the employees' gross income. ◀

EXAMPLE I4-24 ▶ A state highway patrol organization provides its officers with a daily meal allowance to compensate them for meals eaten while they are on duty. Officers typically eat their meals at the restaurant of their choice. Because the officers receive cash instead of meals, the amount provided must be included in the officers' gross income. ◀

EXAMPLE I4-25 ▶ A large corporation requires five of its employees to work overtime two evenings each year when the company takes inventory. The corporation gives each of the employees a small amount to cover the cost of the dinner for the two evenings. The amounts constitute supper money and are excluded from the employees' gross income. ◀

Section 119 provides that if employees can exclude the value of meals from gross income, the employer can deduct the full cost of the meal. Further, if more than half of the employees who receive meals meet the "convenience of the employer" test, then all employees who receive meals can exclude the value from gross income.

MEALS AND ENTERTAINMENT. One obvious question is whether employees who are reimbursed by their employers when they entertain customers must include the reimbursement in gross income. If they must include the reimbursement in gross income, can they deduct the cost of the entertainment and meals? Assuming conditions for deductibility are met, the tax law clearly allows 50% of the cost of entertaining customers to be deducted (discussed in Chapter I9). Can the employee deduct the meals and entertainment that he personally consumes?

EXAMPLE I4-26 ▶ Joe is a sales representative for Zero Corporation. As a part of his regular duties, Joe buys lunch for Wayne, a Zero Corporation customer. Fifty percent of the cost of Wayne's meal is deductible either by Joe if he pays for the luncheon without being reimbursed by his employer, or by the Zero Corporation if it reimburses Joe for the cost. Can Joe deduct 50% of the cost of his own meal if he pays for it and is not reimbursed? If Zero pays for the meal, must Joe include in his gross income the cost of his own lunch? ◀

In the above question, Joe apparently can deduct the portion of the luncheon that applies to himself. While this issue is not clear-cut, the IRS has indicated in Rev. Rul. 63-144 that it will not pursue the issue except where taxpayers claim deductions for substantial amounts of personal expenses.[31] In any case, it is an accepted practice today for taxpayers to deduct 50% of the total cost of a meal (taxpayer and customer) unless the practice is considered abusive.[32]

EMPLOYEE DEATH BENEFITS. Occasionally, an employer may make payments to the family or friends of an employee who dies. In some instances, the payments might be viewed as a gift made for reasons such as the financial need of the family, kindness, or charity. Alternatively, the amount might constitute a payment of compensation based on

[30] *CIR v. Robert J. Kowalski*, 40 AFTR 2d 77-6128, 77-2 USTC ¶9748 (USSC, 1977).
[31] Rev. Rul. 63-144, 1963-2 C.B. 129.
[32] See, however, *Richard A. Sutter*, 21 T.C. 170 (1953), where the Tax Court ruled that business meals, entertainment, etc. for one's own self are inherently personal and nondeductible. *Sutter* has been cited and upheld some 50 times.

WHAT WOULD YOU DO IN THIS SITUATION?

FRINGE BENEFIT

National Boats manufactures pleasure boats sold to consumers. The boats range in price from $40,000 to $1,500,000. Jake is the president of National Boats. The company provides Jake with one of its more expensive boats. The company pays for fuel, insurance, and other costs and deducts these expenses along with depreciation on the boat. The company states that Jake is responsible for testing and for demonstrating the boat to possible customers. Jake has had the same boat for two years, and the company plans to provide him with a new boat next month.

You asked Jake how often he uses the boat. He indicated that he uses it once or twice each month on weekends, except during the winter. You asked him who accompanies him, and what types of testing he conducts. He seemed reluctant to answer the question, but acknowledged that his family often accompanies him on the boat, and said that he tests it during ordinary operations to determine how it performs. He added that potential customers who have also accompanied him included neighbors and friends. What tax issues do you see?

the past services of the deceased employee. Gifts are, of course, excluded from gross income, whereas compensation is taxable. The treatment of payments made to the family or other beneficiaries of the employee's estate is determined by the following rules:

▶ Payments for past services (such as bonuses, accrued wages, and unused vacation pay) are taxable as income to the family and are deductible by the employer. The important issue is whether the employee would have received this amount had he or she lived. If the employer was legally obligated to make the payment at the time of the employee's death, the payments are taxable to the recipient.

▶ Other amounts may be either taxable compensation or excludable gifts depending on the facts and circumstances. If the amount is a gift, it is not deductible by the employer. If the amount is taxable income to the deceased employee's family, it is deductible by the employer.

In determining whether the amount is taxable, the courts have considered such factors as whether the employer derived benefit from the payment, whether the employee had been fully compensated, and whether the payment was made to the family and not to the estate. The Supreme Court stated, "The most critical consideration [in determining whether a transfer is a gift] is the transferor's 'intention.'"[33] Although the case did not deal with death benefits, it did establish the importance of motive in determining whether a payment is a gift. Thus, the transfer should be made for reasons such as kindness, sympathy, generosity, affection, or admiration.

It should be noted that it is more difficult to establish that a payment is a gift in situations where the payments are made to persons owning stock in the corporation making the payment. Such payments may be construed as constructive dividends, which are not deductible by the corporation but are taxable income to the recipients.[34]

ADDITIONAL COMMENT

The $5,000 limit was placed on the exclusion for dependent care assistance programs because it was thought to be inequitable to provide an unlimited dependent care exclusion but a limited child care credit for people who pay their own child care expenses.

DEPENDENT CARE. **Dependent care assistance programs** are employer-financed programs that provide care for an employee's children or other dependents. An employee may exclude up to $5,000 of assistance each year ($2,500 for a married individual filing a separate return). The care must be of a type that, if paid by the employee, would qualify for the dependent care credit. Furthermore, the credit is scaled down if the employee receives benefits under the employer's plan. (See Chapter I14 for a discussion of the child and dependent care rules.) The program cannot discriminate in favor of highly compensated employees or their dependents.[35]

---

[33] *CIR v. Mose Duberstein*, 5 AFTR 2d 1626, 60-2 USTC ¶9515 (USSC, 1960).

[34] *Ernest L. Poyner v. CIR*, 9 AFTR 2d 1151, 62-1 USTC ¶9387 (4th Cir., 1962).

[35] Sec. 129.

ADDITIONAL
COMMENT

The classification of an employee as highly compensated is made on the basis of the facts and circumstances of each case. Any officers and shareholders owning more than 5% of the stock are classified as highly compensated employees.

ADDITIONAL
COMMENT

About half of the large employers in the United States offer flexible spending accounts.

ADDITIONAL
COMMENT

While the main benefit of a cafeteria plan is to offer tax-free choices to employees, the plan must also offer at least one taxable benefit.

EDUCATIONAL ASSISTANCE. Under Sec. 127 educational assistance plans, employers pay employee educational costs. Employees may exclude from gross income annual payments of up to $5,250. The exclusion applies to payments for tuition and similar amounts, fees, books, supplies, and equipment.

CAFETERIA PLANS. **Cafeteria plans**, also called flexible spending accounts, are plans that offer employees the option of choosing cash or statutory nontaxable fringe benefits (such as group term life insurance, medical insurance, adoption expenses, child care, etc.). If the employee chooses cash, the cash is taxable. However, if the employee chooses a statutory nontaxable fringe benefit, the value of the benefit is excluded from gross income.[36] In other words, the fact that the employee could have chosen cash does not cause the fringe benefit to be taxed. The plan cannot discriminate in favor of highly compensated employees or their dependents or spouses.[37] Employer plans may specify what benefits are offered and may limit the amount of benefits individual employees may receive.

Some plans supplement wages; others are wage reduction plans. In supplemental wage plans, employer funds are used to pay fringe benefits. In the case of wage reduction plans, employees elect to receive reduced wages in exchange for the fringe benefits. In both cases, employees receive benefits without being taxed on them.

Employers often allow employees to use such funds to pay medical expenses. Typically, the plans supplement medical insurance, and funds are used to pay dental bills and other medical expenses not covered by regular insurance. In general, employees annually elect to set aside funds to pay medical expenses, and the employer pays the expenses using the set-aside funds. One problem with the agreements is that they are binding for one year. As a result, the employee loses the funds if the actual medical expenses are less than the amount set aside. Employers, on the other hand, are obligated to pay expenses up to the agreed amount even if the full amount has not yet been withheld from the employee's wages. Thus, the employer may lose money if an employee terminates employment after incurring the designated amount of medical expenses but before the full amount is withheld.

INTEREST-FREE LOANS. One benefit that was often used in the past was interest-free loans to employees. The advantage of this type of transaction was diminished by the Tax Reform Act of 1984. Under present law, interest must generally be imputed on interest-free loans (See Chapter I11 for a detailed discussion of rules applicable to interest-free loans.)

ADVANTAGE OF FRINGE BENEFITS. The major advantage of taking fringe benefits (such as those described above) in lieu of a cash payment is the fact that employees do not have to use after-tax income to obtain the product or service.

EXAMPLE I4-27 ▶ Dan, an employee of Central Corporation, has a $40,000 life insurance policy and pays the premiums out of his salary. Since his salary is taxable, the premiums are paid on an after-tax basis. Kay, an employee for Western Corporation, is covered by a $40,000 group term life insurance policy financed by Western Corporation. Western Corporation pays the premiums on the policy. Because the premiums are excludable, Kay does not have to report the premiums as income. ◀

EXAMPLE I4-28 ▶ John's employer establishes a cafeteria plan which allows each employee to set aside up to $5,000 for health insurance premiums and medical reimbursements. John, whose salary has been $30,000, agrees to a salary reduction of $4,000, of which $2,500 is to cover his health insurance premiums and $1,500 is available to reimburse his medical expenses. Under the arrangement, John's salary is reduced to $26,000 for tax purposes. Neither the health insurance coverage nor the medical expense reimbursement is taxable. During the year, John incurs $1,400 of medical expenses not covered by insurance. He receives a reimbursement for all of the expenses. His employer retains the remaining $100. Alternatively, if the medical expenses were $1,800, John would receive a reimbursement of $1,500 and he must pay the remaining $300 of expenses out of after-tax salary dollars. ◀

---

[36] Long-term care insurance (sometimes called nursing home insurance) can be offered to employees on a tax-favored basis, but that benefit cannot be offered as part of a flexible spending account.

[37] Sec. 125.

STOP & THINK

Question: Employers and employees both pay FICA taxes on salaries. Fringe benefits such as health insurance are exempt from both income taxes and FICA taxes. What is the tax effect of an employee's decision to elect health insurance coverage in exchange for a reduced salary?

Solution: The employee's income and FICA taxes are both lowered. The employer is permitted an income tax deduction for either the salary payment or the payment of the health insurance premium. The employer's FICA tax is reduced because the health insurance benefit also is exempt from that tax.

AVAILABILITY OF TAX-FAVORED FRINGE BENEFITS. The exclusion for many fringe benefits is only available to employees (and in some cases spouses, dependents, and retirees). Many tax-favored fringe benefits are unavailable to proprietors or partners. As a result, a partnership can provide $50,000 of group-term life insurance to employees on a tax-favored basis, but cannot provide the benefit on a tax-favored basis to its partners. Other fringe benefits that cannot be offered to proprietors or partners on a tax-favored basis include achievement awards, adoptions assistance, on-premises lodging, moving expense, and commuting and parking benefits (other than de minimis).[38]

Special rules apply to health insurance premiums and retirement plan contributions for proprietors and partners. The owners deduct these payments for AGI. This results in a self-employment tax on the amounts, but no income tax.

Shareholders, as such, are ineligible for tax-favored fringe benefits. In most cases employees of C corporations are eligible for tax-favored fringe benefits based on their wages even if they own stock. This is not true, however, for S corporation employees who own more than 2% of the corporation's stock. They are treated much like partners and proprietors with respect to fringe benefits. Health insurance premiums and retirement plan contributions made for these S corporation employee-shareholders are wages for income tax purposes. Like partners and proprietors, these S corporation employees-shareholders can deduct the amounts for AGI. Unlike partners and proprietors, the amounts are not subject to FICA or self-employment taxes.

The fact that fringe benefits provided to employee-shareholders of C corporations are treated more favorably than benefits provided to the owners of other businesses is an incentive for businesses to operate as C corporations.

ADDITIONAL COMMENT

Many U.S. embassies and consulates in foreign countries provide income tax assistance.

ADDITIONAL COMMENT

Foreign-earned income does not include amounts paid to an employee of the U.S. government or any U.S. government agency or instrumentality.

FOREIGN-EARNED INCOME EXCLUSION

In general, the income of U.S. citizens is subject to the U.S. income tax even if the income is derived from sources outside the United States. The foreign income of U.S. citizens also may be taxed by the host country possibly leading to a substantial double tax on the same income. The double tax is mitigated by a **foreign tax credit**. Subject to limitations, U.S. citizens may subtract from their U.S. income tax liability the income taxes they pay to foreign countries. (See Chapter I14 for a discussion of foreign tax credit.)

In the case of foreign-earned income, individuals have available the alternative option of excluding the first $80,000 of foreign-earned income from gross income.[39] The *exclusion* is available in lieu of the foreign tax credit. If both a husband and wife have foreign-earned income, each may claim an exclusion. Community property rules are ignored in determining the amount of the exclusion. Thus, if only one spouse has foreign-earned income, only one exclusion is available. The principal reasons for the exclusion are to encourage U.S. businesses to operate in foreign countries and to hire U.S. citizens and resident aliens to manage the businesses. The hope is that such operations will improve the balance of payments. Taxpayers who elect the exclusion in one year may switch to the foreign tax credit in any subsequent year. Taxpayers who change from the exclusion to the credit may not reelect the exclusion before the sixth tax year

---

[38] Benefits that can be offered to proprietors and partners on a tax-favored basis include athletic facilities, de minimis benefits, no additional cost fringe benefits, dependent care assistance, educational assistance, discounts, on-premises meals, and working condition fringes.

[39] Sec. 911(b)(2). The foreign earned income is scheduled to remain at $80,000 until 2008 when the exclusion will be indexed for inflation.

after the tax year in which the change was made.[40] The IRS can waive the six-year limitation in special situations (such as an individual employee changing the location of his or her foreign employment).

TYPICAL MISCONCEPTION

A taxpayer must be present in one or more foreign countries for 330 days during a period of twelve consecutive months, rather than 330 days during a calendar year.

Foreign-earned income includes an individual's earnings from personal services rendered in a foreign country. The place where the services are performed determines whether earned income is foreign or U.S. source income. If an individual is engaged in a trade or business in which both personal services and capital are material income-producing factors, no more than 30% of the net profits from the business may be excluded.[41] Furthermore, pensions, annuities, salary paid by the U.S. government, and deferred compensation do not qualify for the exclusion.[42]

To qualify for the foreign-earned income exclusion, the taxpayer must either be a bona fide resident of one or more foreign countries for an entire taxable year, or be present in one or more foreign countries for 330 days during a period of 12 consecutive months.[43] The exclusion limitation for a year must be prorated if the taxpayer is not present in, or a resident of, a foreign country or countries for the entire year.

EXAMPLE I4-29 ▶ Sondra is given a temporary assignment to work in foreign country T. She arrives in T on October 19, 2006, and leaves on October 1, 2007. Although Sondra does not establish a permanent residence in T, she is present in T for at least 330 days out of a twelve-month period beginning on October 20, 2006. Thus, 73 days fall in 2006 and the rest in 2007. Sondra's exclusion for 2006 is limited to $16,000 [(73 ÷ 365) × $80,000]. She may exclude $16,000 or the income she earns in foreign country T during 2006, whichever is less. ◀

Deductions directly attributable to the excluded foreign-earned income are disallowed. Expenses attributable to foreign-earned income must be allocated if foreign-earned income exceeds the exclusion. The disallowed portion is determined by multiplying the total amount of such expenses by the ratio of excluded earned income over total foreign-earned income.

EXAMPLE I4-30 ▶ Connie earned $120,000 while employed in a foreign country for the entire year. She is entitled to an exclusion of $80,000. Connie incurred $12,000 of travel, transportation, and other deductible expenses attributable to the foreign-earned income. She may deduct only $4,000 of such expenses because $8,000 [($80,000 ÷ $120,000) × $12,000] is allocated to the excluded income and, therefore, not deductible. The $4,000 is classified as a miscellaneous itemized deduction and subject to the 2% of AGI floor associated with such deductions. ◀

U.S. citizens working in foreign countries must often pay more for housing than they would pay in the United States. Therefore, an additional exclusion from gross income is available for housing costs that exceed 16% of the salary paid government employees in Step 1 of grade GS-14. This GS-14 grade is used to establish a standard for taxpayers in general.

EXAMPLE I4-31 ▶ Wayne is employed in Tokyo, Japan, and earns a salary of $120,000. His housing costs are $32,000 for the year and are reasonable considering the high cost of living in Tokyo. Assume that 16% of the GS-14 (Step 1) salary is $11,894. Wayne can exclude $100,106 from gross income [$80,000 + ($32,000 − $11,894)]. ◀

INCOME FROM THE DISCHARGE OF A DEBT

If debt of a taxpayer is cancelled or forgiven, the taxpayer may have to include the cancelled amount in gross income. It is important to distinguish a debt cancellation from a gift, a bequest, or a renegotiation of the purchase price.

EXAMPLE I4-32 ▶ Farouk loaned his daughter $4,000 to help her purchase an automobile. Several months after she purchased the automobile, but before she repaid the $4,000, Farouk's daughter married. Farouk told his daughter that he was "tearing up" the $4,000 note as a wedding present. In this instance, the amount forgiven would constitute an excludable gift and would not be taxable as income to the daughter. ◀

[40] Sec. 911(e)(2).
[41] Sec. 911(d)(2)(B).
[42] Sec. 911(b)(1)(B).
[43] Sec. 911(d).

EXAMPLE I4-33 ▶ Clay purchased a used automobile from a dealer for $6,000. He paid $2,000 down and agreed to pay the balance of $4,000 over three years. After Clay purchased the automobile, he determined that it was defective. Clay tried to return the automobile, but the automobile dealer refused. Clay threatened to sue the dealer. To resolve the problem, the dealer offered to reduce the balance due on the purchase-money debt from $4,000 to $2,500. Clay agreed. The transaction constitutes a reduction in the purchase price of the automobile. Clay will not recognize any income, but must reduce the basis in his automobile from $6,000 to $4,500. ◀

EXAMPLE I4-34 ▶ Blue Corporation issued bonds for $1,000 when interest rates were low. After a few years, interest rates increased and the bond price declined to $850. Blue Corporation purchased the bonds on the open market. Blue will recognize $150 of income from the discharge of indebtedness. ◀

EXAMPLE I4-35 ▶ Indy Coal Company has seen its business decline during the past two years. The Company has a significant amount of bank debt that was incurred over the years to fund its coal operations. In order to maintain its operations, Indy entered into an agreement with the bank whereby the bank agreed to cancel 50% of Indy's debt. Assuming Indy was solvent at the time of the cancellation, Indy must report the discharge of indebtedness as gross income. ◀

STOP & THINK

Question: In Example I4-35, the bank agreed to cancel 50% of Indy Coal Company's debt. Why would a lender agree to unilaterally cancel a borrower's debt?

Solution: A bank might cancel a portion of a borrower's debt in order to protect the remaining portion of the debt. If the debt forced the company into bankruptcy, the bank may be able to collect none or only a small percentage of the debt. If the cancellation would help stabilize Indy, the bank may be able to collect at least 50% of the debt. Further, if Indy becomes a viable company in the years ahead, the bank will have a good customer to earn profits in the future.

REAL-WORLD EXAMPLE

A taxpayer purchased and retired its own bonds. The purchase resulted in a gain because the bonds were payable in British pounds, which had been devalued. The gain was excludable. *Kentucky & Indiana Terminal Railroad Co. v. U.S.*, 13 AFTR 2d 1148, 64-1 USTC ¶9374 (6th Cir., 1964).

The enforceability of a debt under state law may also determine whether the forgiveness results in income. For example, one case held that the forgiveness of a gambling debt was not included in gross income where the debt was unenforceable under state law.[44]

DISCHARGE IN BANKRUPTCY AND INSOLVENCY. Section 61(a)(12) indicates that gross income includes income from the discharge of an indebtedness. Section 108, on the other hand, provides for the following exceptions where the discharge of an indebtedness is not taxable:

▶ The discharge occurs in bankruptcy.

▶ The discharge occurs when the taxpayer is insolvent.

KEY POINT

A discharge of debt in bankruptcy does not generate income.

These exceptions are intended to allow a "fresh start" for bankrupt and other financially troubled taxpayers. Since a taxpayer is not required to include the discharge in gross income, he is required to reduce certain tax attributes. For example, if the taxpayer has a net operating loss carryover, the NOL carryover must be reduced by the excluded discharge.

If a debt is reduced during bankruptcy proceedings, the taxpayer recognizes no income even if the reduction in debt exceeds the available tax attributes. In the case of an insolvent taxpayer, no income is recognized as long as the taxpayer is insolvent after the reduction in debt takes place. A taxpayer is insolvent if the debts owed by the taxpayer exceed the FMV of assets owned. Thus, an insolvent taxpayer reduces the tax attributes to the point of solvency. From that point on, any reduction in debt results in the recognition of income even if all tax attributes have not been offset.

ADDITIONAL COMMENT

Also excludable is the income from the cancellation of a student loan pursuant to a provision under which part of the debt is discharged due to working for a period of time in certain professions for a broad class of employers.

STUDENT LOAN FORGIVENESS. Under Sec. 108(f)(2), the discharge of certain student loans is excluded from gross income if the discharge is contingent on the individual's performing certain public services. The loans must have been made by governmental, educational, or charitable organizations, and the loan proceeds must have been used to pay

---

[44] *David Zarin v. CIR*, 66 AFTR 2d 90-5679, 90-2 USTC ¶50,530 (3rd Cir., 1990).

the cost of attending an educational institution or used to refinance outstanding student loans. Further, the loan forgiveness must be contingent upon the individual's working for a specified time period in certain professions, and the services must normally be performed for someone other than the lender.

EXAMPLE I4-36 ▶ Lee borrowed $60,000 from the federal government to attend medical school. Under the terms of the loan, $20,000 of debt is forgiven for each year she practices medicine in designated low-income neighborhoods. Lee does not have to include the debt forgiveness in gross income. ◀

EXCLUSION FOR GAIN FROM SMALL BUSINESS STOCK

Noncorporate taxpayers may exclude up to 50% of the gain realized on the disposition of qualified small business stock issued after August 10, 1993, if the stock is held for more than five years.[45] The remaining gain is taxed at a rate not greater than 28% resulting in a maximum effective rate of 14%. For each issuer of qualified small business stock, there is a limit on the amount of gain a taxpayer may exclude. The amount of gain eligible for the exclusion may not exceed the greater of $10 million, reduced by amounts previously excluded for gains on the company's stock, or ten times the taxpayer's aggregate adjusted basis of the stock disposed of during the year.[46] When measuring the taxpayer's aggregate basis for the stock to determine the maximum amount of gain to exclude, the fair market value of the assets contributed to the corporation is used.

EXAMPLE I4-37 ▶ Dennis contributed property with a basis of $1,000,000 and a FMV of $4,000,000 to a qualified small business corporation for all of its common stock. If he sells one-half of the stock after five years for $14,000,000, he may exclude $6,750,000 of the $13,500,000 ($14,000,000 − $500,000) realized gain. The maximum gain eligible for the exclusion is the greater of $10,000,000 or $20,000,000 [10 times the $2,000,000 basis ($4,000,000 FMV × 0.50) of the stock sold]. Thus, none of the $13,500,000 realized gain is subject to the limitation. ◀

Moreover, taxpayers do not have to recognize any gain if they reinvest the proceeds from the sale of small business stock in other small business stock within 60 days of the sale. Gain is recognized only to the extent that the amount realized from the sale exceeds the cost of the replacement stock. The basis of the replacement stock is reduced by the amount of gain not recognized. To qualify for the replacement provision the original stock must have been held for over 6 months.

EXAMPLE I4-38 ▶ Assume the same facts as in Example I4-37, except that Dennis purchases $13,000,000 of small business investment stock within 60 days. Dennis is taxed only on $1,000,000 ($14,000,000 − $13,000,000) of his $13,500,000 realized gain. Dennis' basis for the new stock, however, is $500,000 ($13,000,000 cost of the new stock − $12,500,000 portion of the gain that is not taxed). ◀

A corporation may issue qualified small business stock only if the corporation is a C corporation that is not an excluded corporation with an aggregate adjusted basis of not more than $50 million of gross assets, and at least 80% of the value of its assets must be used in the active conduct of one or more qualified trades or businesses.[47]

Currently the maximum tax rate applicable to long-term capital gains is 15%. As a result, the 14% maximum tax rate applicable to small business stock is only a small advantage. Nevertheless, taxpayers may still take advantage of the opportunity to reinvest the proceeds from the sale of such stock without any current tax.

OTHER EXCLUSIONS

The tax law contains other exclusions that are either covered elsewhere in the text or are of limited application. Table I4-2 lists several such exclusions.

---

[45] Sec. 1202(a). The exclusion is 60% in the case of empowerment zone stock acquired after December 21, 2000.
[46] Sec. 1202(b)(1).
[47] Secs. 1202(d) and (e). Excluded corporations are those engaged in providing professional services (e.g., law and health), financial services (e.g., banking and insurance), hospitality (e.g., hotels and restaurants), farming, and mining and oil and gas production.

▼ **TABLE I4-2**
Other Exclusions

Section	Applies to	Comments
121	Gain from sale of personal residence	Taxpayers may exclude up to $250,000 ($500,000 in the case of a married couple filing a joint return) of gain from the sale of a personal residence. (See Chapter I12 for a detailed discussion of this provision.)
101(h)	Annuities paid to survivors of public safety officers	Annuities paid to survivors of public safety officers, such as firefighters and police officers, killed in the line of duty are excluded.
104(a)	Military disability pay	Military personnel may exclude disability pay, combat pay
112	Combat pay	(noncommissioned personnel only), and housing allowances.
134	Military housing allowance	
107	Housing allowance for ministers	Ministers may exclude either the rental value of their homes or a rental allowance if provided in connection with their religious duties.
119	Campus housing	A limited exclusion is provided to employees of educational institutions when they are provided with on-campus housing.
131	Foster care payments	Certain allowances received by foster care providers are excluded from gross income.
162(o)	Rural letter carrier's allowance	Rural letter carriers may exclude the "equipment maintenance allowance" they receive for the use of their personal automobiles in delivering the mail. They receive no deduction for the use of their automobiles.
408A(d)	Roth IRA distributions	Qualified distributions from Roth IRAs are excluded from gross income (see Chapter I9 for a detailed discussion of the provisions).
530(d)	Education IRA distributions	Qualified distributions from Coverdell Education Savings Account IRAs are excluded from gross income (see Chapter I9 for a detailed discussion of this provision).
988(e)	Personal foreign currency gains	Individuals are excused from recognizing gain on the disposition of foreign currency in any personal transaction, provided that the gain does not exceed $200.

TAX PLANNING CONSIDERATIONS

EMPLOYEE FRINGE BENEFITS

The tax law encourages certain forms of fringe benefits by allowing an employer to deduct the cost of the benefit while permitting the employee to exclude the benefit from gross income. This deduction does not represent an income tax advantage to the employer because compensation, whether in the form of cash or nontaxable fringe benefits, is deductible if reasonable in amount. While employees receive the greatest income tax benefit from the exclusion of fringe benefits from gross income, employers receive a small benefit from the fact that fringe benefits are not subject to Social Security and Medicare taxes.

ADDITIONAL COMMENT

A case can be made for the desirability of encouraging employers to provide health insurance and other fringe benefits. However, these provisions may contribute to increases in the cost of insurance and medical care.

EXAMPLE I4-39 ▶

USA Company has decided to offer $20,000 of group term life insurance coverage for each of its employees at an average annual premium cost of $100 per employee. Tim, an employee of USA Corporation, is in the 15% tax bracket. Because USA is offering a nontaxable fringe benefit, Tim will owe no additional income tax. If Tim had received a salary increase of $100, he would have had to pay an additional income tax of $15 (0.15 × $100). The remaining $85 of after-tax income would probably not have been sufficient to obtain the same amount of life insurance coverage. ◀

Excluding fringe benefits from gross income favors employees who are subject to higher tax rates.

EXAMPLE I4-40 ▶ | Assume the same facts as in Example I4-39 except that Tim is in the 35% tax rate. Tim would save $35 (0.35 × $100) of taxes by receiving the group term life insurance coverage instead of the $100 salary increase. ◀

ADDITIONAL COMMENT

Fringe benefits offered by potential employers are important consideration factors when weighing total compensation packages.

It is not always desirable for employers to offer nontaxable fringe benefits. Some employees are not interested in certain benefits. For example, in the case of married couples where both spouses are employed, it is not necessary for both employers to provide medical insurance coverage for both spouses. Alternatively, single employees may not feel the need for group term life insurance and employees with no children are uninterested in employer-provided child care.

To avoid providing fringe benefits that are unneeded or unwanted, many employers have turned to cafeteria plans. Under cafeteria plans, employees may select from a list of nontaxable fringe benefits. On the other hand, employees who so choose may receive cash in lieu of some or all of the nontaxable benefits. Thus, each employee selects what he or she wants most. One common result is that high-tax-rate employees select the nontaxable fringe benefits, whereas other employees choose to receive cash.

SELF-HELP INCOME AND USE OF PERSONALLY OWNED PROPERTY

As noted earlier in this chapter, self-help income and income derived from the use of personal property are not taxable. Thus, self-help income and personal ownership of property are favored by the tax system. Taxpayers who rent their personal residences cannot deduct rental payments, but taxpayers who own their residences do not pay rent and may deduct interest and real estate taxes as itemized deductions. Thus, the tax law encourages ownership of personal residences.

Effective tax planning necessitates weighing the tax incentives with other nontax factors. Taxpayers with little accumulated funds may find it difficult to purchase a residence despite the availability of tax incentives. Taxpayers who move frequently may find that transaction costs such as real estate commissions and other closing costs are greater than the tax benefits obtained from home ownership. Other factors such as the personal preference of the taxpayer and anticipated inflation rates must also be considered.

Self-help income must be viewed in the same way. Taxpayers who are deciding whether to paint their own residences or hire someone else to do it must consider factors such as personal preference and the amount of income that could be produced if the time were spent working at an activity that produces taxable income.

COMPLIANCE AND PROCEDURAL CONSIDERATIONS

ADDITIONAL COMMENT

Taxpayers filing Form 1040 are asked to report any tax-exempt interest income on line 8b.

Taxpayers are usually not required to disclose excluded income on their tax returns. For example, a taxpayer who receives a tax-exempt scholarship need not disclose that income on his or her tax return. An exception is provided for tax-exempt interest and Social Security benefits, which must be disclosed on the tax return. If a taxpayer's only income is from tax-exempt sources, the taxpayer need not file a tax return. Whether an individual must file a return is based on the amount of the individual's gross income for the year (see Chapter I2).

This chapter considers the taxability of various fringe benefits. The rules regarding the need for an employer to withhold federal income taxes or to report a payment on an employee's Form W-2 (Statement of Income Tax Withheld on Wages) closely parallel the gross income rules. (See Chapter I14 for a discussion of these reporting requirements.) In general, if a fringe benefit is nontaxable, employers do not withhold from the benefit, nor do they report the benefit on the employee's W-2 at year-end. On the other hand, if the benefit is taxable, it is subject to withholding and is reported on the employee's W-2 at year-end. Thus, employers do not withhold for nontaxable meals and lodging provided to employees[48] or a moving expense reimbursement if the expenses are deductible.[49] Similarly, no withholding is required for the following fringe benefits if they are nontaxable: scholarships and fellowships covered by Sec. 117, dependent care covered by Sec. 129, and miscellaneous fringes covered by Sec. 132.

There are exceptions to this basic system. Certain fringe benefits are not subject to withholding even if the benefits are taxable. These include group term life insurance coverage and medical expense reimbursements.

In general, fringe benefits which are exempt from income tax are also exempt from Social Security and Medicare taxes. For example, medical insurance coverage and group term life coverage of up to $50,000 can be provided to employees without either the employer or the employee owing any Social Security or Medicare taxes on the premiums. This is true if the employee elects the benefits instead of cash salary under a cafeteria plan.

Employers who are obligated to withhold from employee wages are subject to penalty if they fail to withhold, fail to provide employees with correct W-2s, or fail to correctly report the compensation and withholding information to the IRS.[50] In general, the failure to report wages and withholding to either employees or the IRS is subject to penalty generally equal to $50 per failure. The failure to withhold can result in a penalty equal to 100% of the amount that should have been withheld. The penalty can be imposed on the employer and other people, such as officers or accountants, who are responsible for withholding.

Occasionally, employees do not want employers to withhold taxes from their wages. Officers or others who choose not to withhold from employee wages face an extremely burdensome penalty, particularly if a large number of employees are involved. Therefore, it is important that employers comply with withholding requirements. One closely related issue is whether an individual is an employee subject to withholding or an independent contractor, as only employee wages are subject to withholding (see Chapter I14).

PROBLEM MATERIALS

DISCUSSION QUESTIONS

I4-1 What is meant by the terms *administrative exclusion* and *judicial exclusion*?

I4-2 There is no specific statutory exclusion for welfare benefits. Nevertheless, the IRS has ruled that such benefits are not taxable. Is this within the authority of the IRS?

I4-3 What was the issue in the tax case *Eisner v. Macomber*? Why is the case important?

I4-4 Most exclusions exist for one of two reasons. What are those reasons? Give examples of exclusions that exist for each.

I4-5 a. If a gift of property is made, who is taxed on income produced by the property?
b. How can interfamily gifts reduce a family's total tax liability?

I4-6 a. What role does intent play in determining whether a transfer is a gift and therefore not subject to the income tax?
b. Are tips received by employees from customers excludable from gross income as gifts? Explain.

I4-7 What is the tax significance of the face amount of a life insurance policy?

I4-8 What conditions must be met for an award to qualify for an exclusion under Sec. 74?

I4-9 Which of the requirements for the Sec. 74 awards exclusion most severely limits its use? Does the exclusion benefit taxpayers more if they itemize their deductions or use the standard deduction?

I4-10 a. Define the term *scholarship* as it is used in Sec. 117.
b. If a scholarship covers room and board, is it excludable?
c. If an employer provides a scholarship to an employee who is on leave of absence, is that scholarship taxable?
d. Is the amount paid by a university to students for services excludable from the students' gross income?

I4-11 What special rules are applicable to non-degree candidates who receive scholarships?

---

[48] Reg. Sec. 31.3401(a)-1(b)(9).
[49] See Sec. 3401 for withholding requirements for numerous special situations.
[50] Secs. 6672, 6674, and 6721, respectively.

I4-12 Is the personal injury exclusion found in Sec. 104 limited to physical injury? Explain.

I4-13 Answer the following questions relative to employer-financed medical and health, disability, and life insurance plans.
   a. May employers deduct premiums paid on employee insurance?
   b. Do employees have to include such premiums in gross income?
   c. Are benefits paid to the employee included in the employee's gross income?

I4-14 Special rules are applicable in situations where group term life insurance coverage exceeds $50,000. How are key employees treated?

I4-15 a. What are the six major types of fringe benefits covered by Sec. 132?
   b. What tax advantage is offered relative to such benefits?
   c. Are such benefits available to employees only or may the benefits also be offered to spouses, dependents, and retirees?
   d. Is discrimination prohibited relative to Sec. 132 benefits?
   e. What is the tax impact on the employer and employees if an employer's plan is discriminatory?

I4-16 What conditions must be met if an employee is to exclude meals and lodging furnished by an employer?

I4-17 The president and vice president of USA Corporation receive benefits that are unavailable to other employees. These benefits include free parking, payment of monthly expenses in a local club, discounts on products sold by the corporation, and payment of premiums on a whole life insurance policy. Which of the benefits must be included in the gross income of the president and vice president?

I4-18 Are the same fringe benefits that are available to employees also available to self-employed individuals?

I4-19 If an employee takes a customer to lunch and discusses business, can the employee deduct 50% of the meal for both the customer and himself? Explain.

I4-20 Are distributions from a qualified state tuition program taxable?

I4-21 What types of income qualify for the foreign-earned income exclusion?

I4-22 Are taxpayers who claim the foreign-earned income exclusion entitled to deduct expenses incurred in producing that income? Explain.

I4-23 a. Why is it important to distinguish debt cancellation from a gift, bequest, or renegotiation of a purchase price?
   b. What happens to the basis of an asset if the taxpayer renegotiates its purchase price?

I4-24 a. Under what conditions is the discharge of indebtedness not taxable?
   b. If a father forgives a daughter's debt to him, is she required to include such amount in her gross income?

I4-25 Bankrupt and insolvent taxpayers do not recognize income if debt is discharged. They must, however, reduce specified tax attributes. What is involved?

I4-26 Are partners and proprietors at a disadvantage with respect to fringe benefits? Explain.

I4-27 Why are cafeteria plans helpful in the design of an employee benefit plan that provides nontaxable fringe benefits?

I4-28 Both high-income and low-income employees are covered by cafeteria plans. Under such plans, all employees may select from a list of nontaxable fringe benefits or they may elect to receive cash in lieu of these benefits.
   a. Which group of employees is more likely to choose nontaxable fringe benefits in lieu of cash? Explain.
   b. Is this result desirable from a social or economic point of view? Explain.

ISSUE IDENTIFICATION QUESTIONS

I4-29 Luke, who retired this year, lives in a four-plex owned by Julie. Luke's income decreased when he retired, and he now has difficulty paying his rent. Julie offered to reduce Luke's rent if he would agree to mow the lawn, wash windows, and provide other maintenance services. Luke accepted, and Julie reduced the monthly rental from $650 to $300. What are the tax issues that should be considered by Luke and Julie?

I4-30 Mildred worked as a maid for 27 years in the home of Larry and Kay. When she retired, they presented her with a check for $25,000, indicating that it was a way of showing their appreciation for her years of loyal service. What tax issues should Mildred and her employer consider?

I4-31 Troy Department Stores offers employees discounts on merchandise carried in the store. Newly hired employees receive a 10% discount. The discount rate increases 1% each year until employees have 20 years of service when the discount rate is capped at 30%. What tax issues should Troy and the employees consider?

I4-32 Jerry works in the human resources department of Ajax Corporation. One of his responsibilities is to interview prospective employees. Two or three days each week, Jerry takes a prospective employee to lunch, and Ajax reimburses him for the cost of the meals. What tax issues should Jerry and Ajax Corporation consider?

PROBLEMS

I4-33 *Self-Help Income.* In which of the following situations would the taxpayer realize taxable income?
a. A mechanic performs work on his own automobile. The mechanic would have charged a customer $400 for doing the same work.
b. A mechanic repairs his neighbor's personal automobile. In exchange, the neighbor, an accountant, agrees to prepare the mechanic's tax return. The services performed are each worth $200.
c. A mechanic repairs his daughter's automobile without any charge.

I4-34 *Excludable Gifts.* Which of the following would be includable in gross income?
a. Alice appeared on a TV quiz show and received a prize of $5,000.
b. Bart received $500 from his employer because he developed an idea that reduced the employer's production costs.
c. Chuck borrowed $500 from his mother in order to finance his last year in college. Upon his graduation, Chuck's mother told him he did not have to repay the $500. She intended the $500 to be a graduation present.

I4-35 *Life Insurance Proceeds.* Don is the beneficiary of a $50,000 insurance policy on the life of his mother, Anna. To date, Anna has paid premiums of $16,000. What amount of gross income must be reported in each of the following cases?
a. Anna elects to cancel the policy and receives $20,000, the cash surrender value of the policy.
b. Anna dies and Don receives the face amount of the policy, $50,000.
c. Anna dies and Don elects to receive $15,000 per year for four years.

I4-36 *Transfer of Life Insurance.* Ed is the beneficiary of a $20,000 insurance policy on the life of his mother. Because Ed needs funds, he sells the policy to his sister, Amy, for $6,000. Amy subsequently pays premiums of $9,000.
a. How much income must Amy report if she collects the face value of the policy upon the death of her mother?
b. Would Amy have to report any income if her brother had given her the policy? Assume the only payment she made was $9,000 for the premiums.

I4-37 *Settlement of Life Insurance Policy.* Sue is age 73 and has a great deal of difficulty living independently as she suffers from severe rheumatoid arthritis. She is covered by a $400,000 life insurance policy, and her children are named as her beneficiaries. Because of her health, Sue decides to live in a nursing home, but she does not have enough income to pay her nursing home bills which are expected to total $42,000 per year. The insurance company offers disabled individuals the option of either a reduced settlement on their policies or an annuity. Given Sue's age and health she has the option of receiving $3,200 per month or a lump sum payment of $225,000. To date, Sue has paid $80,000 in premiums on the policy.
a. How much income must Sue report if she chooses the lump sum settlement?
b. How much income must Sue report if she elects the annuity?
c. How much income would Sue have to report if her nursing home bills amounted to only $36,000 per year?

I4-38 *Insurance Policy Dividends.* Hank carries a $100,000 insurance policy on his life. Premiums paid over the years total $8,000. Dividends on the policy have totaled $6,000. Hank has left the dividends on the policy with the insurance company. During the current year, the insurance company credited $600 of interest on the accumulated dividends to Hank's account.
a. How much income is Hank obligated to report in connection with the policy?
b. Would it make any difference if the accumulated dividends equaled $9,000 instead of $6,000?

I4-39 *Prizes and Awards.* For each of the following, indicate whether the amount is taxable:
a. Peggy won $4,000 in the state lottery.
b. Jane won a $500 prize for her entry in a poetry contest.
c. Linda was awarded $2,000 when she was selected as "Teacher of the Year" by the local school district.

I4-40 *Scholarships.* For each of the following, indicate the amount that must be included in the taxpayer's gross income:

a. Larry was given a $1,500 tuition scholarship to attend Eastern Law School. In addition, Eastern paid Larry $4,000 per year to work part-time in the campus bookstore.

b. Marty received a $10,000 football scholarship for attending Northern University. The scholarship covered tuition, room and board, laundry, and books. Four thousand dollars of the scholarship was designated for room and board and laundry. It was understood that Marty would participate in the school's intercollegiate football program, but Marty was not required to do so.

c. Western School of Nursing requires all third-year students to work twenty hours per week at an affiliated hospital. Each student is paid $6 per hour. Nancy, a third-year student, earned $10,000 during the year.

I4-41 *Research Grant.* Otto is a biology professor at State University. The university gave Otto a sabbatical leave to study the surface of the flatworm. During the year he received a salary of $50,000, which is less than his regular salary of $56,000. Otto also received a grant to cover expenses associated with the study. The grant was $2,000, as were his related expenses. Otto also incurred memberships and other employment related expenses totaling $1,000. How much must Otto include in gross income?

I4-42 *Payments for Personal Injury.* Determine which of the following payments for sickness and injury must be included in the taxpayer's gross income.

a. Pat was injured in an automobile accident. The other driver's insurance company paid him $2,000 to cover medical expenses and a compensatory amount of $4,000 for pain and suffering.

b. A newspaper article stated that Quincy had been convicted of tax evasion. Quincy, in fact, had never been accused of tax evasion. He sued and won a compensatory settlement of $4,000 from the newspaper.

c. Rob, who pays the cost of a commercial disability income policy, fell and injured his back. He was unable to work for six months. The insurance company paid him $1,800 per month during the time he was unable to work.

d. Steve fell and injured his knee. He was unable to work for four months. His employer-financed disability income policy paid Steve $1,600 per month during the time he was unable to work.

e. Ted suffered a stroke. He was unable to work for five months. His employer continued to pay Ted his salary of $1,700 per month during the time he was unable to work.

I4-43 *Employee Benefits.* Ursula is employed by USA Corporation. USA Corporation provides medical and health, disability, and group term life insurance coverage for its employees. Premiums attributable to Ursula were as follows:

Medical and health	$3,600
Disability	300
Group term life (face amount is $40,000)	200

During the year, Ursula suffered a heart attack and subsequently died. Before her death, Ursula collected $14,000 as a reimbursement for medical expenses and $5,000 of disability income. Upon her death, Ursula's husband collected the $40,000 face value of the life insurance policy.

a. What amount can USA Corporation deduct for premiums attributable to Ursula?

b. How much must Ursula include in income relative to the premiums paid?

c. How much must Ursula include in income relative to the insurance benefits?

d. How much must Ursula's widower include in income?

I4-44 *Group Term Life Insurance.* Data Corporation has four employees and provides group term life insurance coverage for all four employees. Coverage is nondiscriminatory and is as follows:

Employee	Age	Key Employee	Coverage	Actual Premiums
Andy	62	yes	$200,000	$4,000
Bob	52	yes	40,000	700
Cindy	33	no	80,000	600
Damitria	33	no	40,000	300

a. How much may Data Corporation deduct for group term life insurance premiums?

b. How much income must be reported by each employee?

I4-45   *Life Insurance Proceeds.* Joe is the beneficiary of a life insurance policy taken out by his father several years ago. Joe's father died this year and Joe has the option of receiving $100,000 cash or electing to receive $14,000 per year for the remainder of his life. Joe is now 65. Joe's father paid $32,000 in premiums over the years.
   a. How much must Joe include in gross income this year if he elects to accept the $100,000 face amount?
   b. How much must be included in Joe's gross income this year if he elects to receive installment payments?

I4-46   *Employee Benefits.* Al flies for AAA Airlines. AAA provides its employees with several fringe benefits. Al and his family are allowed to fly on a space-available basis on AAA Airline. Tickets used by Al and his family during the year are worth $2,000. AAA paid for a subscription to two magazines published for pilots. The subscriptions totaled $80. The airline paid for Al's meals and lodging while he was away from home overnight in connection with his job. Such meals and lodging cost AAA $10,000. Although Al could not eat while flying, he was allowed to drink coffee provided by the airline. The coffee was worth about $50. AAA provided Al with free parking, which is valued at $100 per month. The airline treated Al and his family to a one-week all-expenses-paid vacation at a resort near his home. This benefit was awarded because of Al's outstanding safety record. The value of the vacation was $2,300. Which of these benefits are taxable to Al?

I4-47   *Employee Benefits.* Jet Corporation is involved in the purchase and rental of several large apartment complexes. Questions have been raised about the treatment of several items pertaining to Jet Corporation and its employees. Jet Corporation employs a manager for each complex. The manager is required to occupy a unit in the complex in order to be available at all hours. The average rental value of the units is $7,800 per year. The corporation's president finds that it is beneficial to the corporation if he entertains bankers and others with whom Jet does business. He does such entertaining about once each month and the corporation pays the cost. Business is discussed at the meals. The cost for the year of such entertaining was $1,500, and about one-third of the cost was attributable to meals consumed by the president.
   Each year as the company closes its books, the controller and certain other members of the accounting staff must work overtime. The company pays each employee supper money totaling $25 during this period.
   The corporation's vice president is expected to travel on business-related matters to visit various properties owned by the corporation. Because of the distances involved, the vice president must stay away from home several nights. Total meals and lodging incurred on the trips total $3,000, most of which is attributable to the vice president himself.
   Which amounts are deductible by the corporation? Which are taxable to the employee?

I4-48   *Death Benefits.* After a brief illness, Bill died. Bill's employer paid $20,000 to his widow. The corporation sent along a letter with the check indicating that $5,000 represented payment for Bill's accrued vacation days and back wages. The balance was being awarded in recognition of Bill's many years of loyal service. The company was obligated to pay the accrued vacation days and back wages, but the balance was discretionary.
   a. Is the employer entitled to deduct the $20,000 paid to Bill's widow?
   b. Is Bill's widow required to include the $20,000 in her gross income?

I4-49   *Foreign-Earned Income Exclusion.* For each of the following cases, indicate the amount of the foreign-earned income exclusion. (Disregard the effect of exemptions for certain allowances under Sec. 912.)
   a. Sam, a U.S. citizen, is an assistant to the ambassador to Spain. Sam lives and works in Spain. His salary of $90,000 is paid by the U.S. government.
   b. Jim, a U.S. citizen, owns an unincorporated oil drilling company that operates in Argentina, where he resides. The business is heavily dependent on equipment owned by Jim. His profit for the year totaled $100,000.
   c. Ken, a U.S. citizen, works for a large Japanese corporation. Ken is employed in the United States, but must travel to Japan several times each year. During the current year he spent sixty days in Japan. This is typical of most years. His salary is $95,000.

I4-50   *Foreign-Earned Income Exclusion.* On January 5, Rita left the United States for Germany, where she had accepted an appointment as vice president of foreign operations. Her employer, USA Corporation, told her the assignment would last about two years. Rita decided not to establish a permanent residence in Germany because her assignment was for only two years. Her salary for the year is $240,000. Rita incurred travel, transportation, and other related expenses totaling $6,000, none of which are reimbursed.

a. What is Rita's foreign-earned income exclusion?

b. How much may she deduct for travel and transportation?

I4-51 *Discharge of Debt.* During bankruptcy, USA Corporation debt was reduced from $780,000 to $400,000. USA Corporation's assets are valued at $500,000. USA's NOL carryover was $400,000.

a. Is USA Corporation required to report any income from the discharge of its debts?

b. Which tax attributes are reduced and by how much? Assume USA does not make any special elections when reducing its attributes.

I4-52 *Discharge of Debt.* Old Corporation has suffered losses for several years, and its debts total $500,000; Old's assets are valued at only $380,000. Old's creditors agree to reduce Old's debts by one-half in order to permit the corporation to continue to operate. Old's NOL carryover is $150,000.

a. What impact does the reduction in debt have on Old's NOL?

b. Is Old required to report any income?

I4-53 *Court and Insurance Awards.* Determine whether the following items represent taxable income.

a. As the result of an age discrimination suit, Pat received a cash settlement of $40,000. One-half of the settlement represented wages lost by Pat as a result of the discrimination and the balance represented an award based on personal injury.

b. Matt sued the local newspaper for a story that reported he was affiliated with organized crime. The court awarded him $50,000 of libel damages.

c. Pam was injured in an automobile accident and received $10,000 from an employer-sponsored disability policy. In addition, her employer-financed medical insurance policy reimbursed her for $15,000 of medical expenses.

I4-54 *Cafeteria Plan.* Jangyoun is a married taxpayer with a dependent 4-year-old daughter. His employer offers a flexible spending account under which he can choose to receive cash or, alternatively, choose from certain fringe benefits. These benefits include health insurance that costs $2,500 and child care that costs $2,600. Assume Jangyoun is in the 28% tax bracket.

a. How much income tax will Jangyoun save if he chooses to participate in the employer's health insurance plan? Assume that he does not have sufficient medical expenses to itemize his deductions.

b. Would you recommend that Jangyoun participate in the employer's health insurance plan if his wife's employer already provides comparable health insurance coverage for the family?

c. Would you recommend that Jangyoun participate in the employer-provided child care option if he has the alternative option of claiming a child care credit of $480?

I4-55 *Exclusion of Gain from Small Business Stock.* Jose acquired 1,000 shares of Acorn Corporation common stock by transferring property with an adjusted basis of $1,000,000 and fair market value of $4,000,000 for 100% of the stock. Acorn is a qualified small business corporation. After six years, Jose sells all of the Acorn Corporation common stock for $16,000,000.

a. What is the amount of gain that may be excluded from Jose's gross income?

b. What would your answer be if the fair market value of the Acorn stock were only $800,000 upon its issue?

c. What would your answer be if the stock were sold after two years?

d. Can Jose avoid recognizing gain by purchasing replacement stock?

COMPREHENSIVE PROBLEM

I4-56 Pat was divorced from her husband in 2001. During the current year she received alimony of $18,000 and child support of $4,000 for her 11-year-old son, who lives with her. Her former husband had asked her to sign an agreement giving him the dependency exemption for the child but she declined to do so. After the divorce she accepted a position as a teacher in the local school district. During the current year she received a salary of $32,000. The school district paid her medical insurance premiums of $1,900 and provided her with group term life insurance coverage of $40,000. The premiums attributable to her coverage equaled $160. During her marriage, Pat's parents loaned her $8,000 to help with the down payment on her home. Her parents told her this year that they understand her financial problems and that they were cancelling the balance on the loan, which was $5,000. They did so because they wanted to help their only daughter.

Pat received dividends from National Motor Company of $4,600 and interest on State of California bonds of $2,850.

Pat sold her personal automobile for $2,800 because she needed a larger car. The automobile had cost $8,000. She purchased a new auto for $11,000. Pat had itemized deductions of $8,600. Compute her taxable income for the current year.

TAX STRATEGY PROBLEMS

I4-57   Sally owns a small C corporation that has provided health insurance coverage for Sally and the company's three other employees. The insurance coverage for Sally and the three employees is individual coverage, not family coverage. Sally's own family coverage is through a separate private policy. She pays the premiums out of after-tax dollars. Sally's salary is $40,000 and the salary for the other three employees averages $30,000. The premiums on the health insurance policy average $2,000 per employee per year. The provider recently informed Sally that the premiums will increase to $2,500 per employee. The spouses of her two married employees have coverage through their employers. The third employee has announced that he will marry soon and would very much like to have family health insurance coverage. The insurance provider says that family coverage will approximately double the premiums. Sally is finding the cost of providing medical insurance coverage particularly burdensome for her small business. What planning suggestions can you offer?

I4-58   Maria was planning to paint the interior of her apartment over a three-day weekend. Her employer asked her to work all three days and will pay her $600 overtime. She called a professional painter who offered to do the job for $500. He is willing to use the paint she has already purchased. Maria is in the 28% tax bracket. Will she be better off financially to work the overtime and pay the painter or to turn down the overtime and do the work herself? What other factors should she consider?

TAX FORM/RETURN PREPARATION PROBLEMS

I4-59   A. J. Paige, Social Security number 111-22-3333, is the vice president of marketing (Japan) for International Industries, Inc. (III). III is headquartered at 123 Main Street, Los Angeles, California 92601. A. J., who is single, accepted the position and became a resident of Japan on July 8 of last year. Her business address is 86 Sano, Tokyo, Japan. A. J.'s visa permits her to stay in Japan indefinitely. Her only trips to the United States in the current year were for vacations (August 2 to 16 and December 21 to 28). A. J.'s contract specifies that her appointment is to last indefinitely, but states that III is to pay her $4,000 per year to cover the cost of two vacation trips to the United States. Her salary is $140,000, out of which she pays rent on an apartment of $28,000 per year. A. J. has no family or residence in the United States. She paid an income tax in Japan of $23,500. Complete a Form 2555 for the current year.

I4-60   Alice Johnson, Social Security number 222-23-3334, is a single taxpayer and is employed as a secretary by State University of Florida. She has the following items pertaining to her income tax return for the current year:

- Received a $20,000 salary from her employer, who withheld $3,000 federal income tax.
- Received a gift of 1,000 shares of Ace Corporation stock with a $100,000 FMV from her mother. She also received $4,000 of cash dividends from the Ace Corporation. The dividends are not qualified dividends.
- Received $1,000 of interest income on bonds issued by the City of Tampa.
- Received a regular stock dividend (nontaxable under Sec. 305) of 50 shares of Ace Corporation stock with a $5,000 FMV.
- Alice's employer paid $2,000 of medical and health insurance premiums on her behalf.
- Received $12,000 alimony from her ex-husband.
- State University provided $60,000 of group term life insurance. Alice is 42 years old and is not a key employee. The table in the text is applicable.

- Received a $1,000 cash award from her employer for being designated the Secretary of the Year.
- Total itemized deductions are $8,000.

Complete Form 1040 and accompanying schedules for Alice Johnson's federal income tax return for the current year.

CASE STUDY PROBLEMS

I4-61

Able Corporation is a closely held company engaged in the manufacture and retail sales of automotive parts. Able maintains a qualified pension plan for its employees but has not offered nontaxable fringe benefits.

You are a tax consultant for the company who has been asked to prepare suggestions for the adoption of an employee fringe benefit plan. Your discussions with the client's chief financial officer reveal the following:

- Employees currently pay their own premiums for medical and health insurance.
- No group term life insurance is provided.
- The company owns a vacant building that could easily be converted to a parking garage.
- Many of the employees purchase automobile parts from the company's retail outlets and pay retail price.
- The president of the corporation would like to provide a dependent care assistance program under Sec. 129 for its employees.

Required: Prepare a client memo that recommends the adoption of an employee fringe benefit program. Your recommendations should discuss the pros and cons of different types of nontaxable fringe benefits.

I4-62

Jay Corporation owns several automobile dealerships. This year, the corporation initiated a policy of giving the top salesperson at each dealership a free vacation trip to Florida. The president believes that this is an effective sales incentive. The cost of the vacations is deductible by the corporation as compensation paid to employees, and is taxable to the recipients. Nevertheless, the president objects to reporting the value of the vacations as income on the W-2s of the recipients and to withholding taxes from wages for the value of the trips. He feels that this undermines the effectiveness of the incentive. What are the implications of this behavior for the corporation and the president?

TAX RESEARCH PROBLEMS

I4-63

Ann is a graduate economics student at State University. State University awarded her a $1,000 scholarship. In addition, Ann works as a half-time teaching assistant in the Economics Department at State University. For her services she is paid $7,000 per year and her tuition is waived. Her tuition would be $8,000 were it not for the waiver. Ann paid $500 for her books and supplies and she incurred living expenses of $7,400. Determine how much gross income Ann must report.

A partial list of research sources is

- Sec. 117(d)
- Prop. Reg. 1.117-6(d)(5)

I4-64

Kim leased an office building to USA Corporation under a ten-year lease specifying that at the end of the lease USA had to return the building to its original condition if any modifications were made. USA changed the interior of the building, and at the end of the lease USA paid Kim $30,000 instead of making the required repairs. Does Kim have to include the payment in gross income?

A partial list of research sources is

- Sec. 109
- *Boston Fish Market Corp.*, 57 T.C. 884 (1972)
- *Sirbo Holdings Inc. v. CIR*, 31 AFTR 2d 73-1005, 73-1 USTC ¶9312 (2nd Cir., 1973)

I4-65

As a result of a fire damaging their residence, the Taylors must stay in a motel for three weeks while their home is being restored. They pay $2,000 for the room and $500 for meals. Their homeowner's policy pays $2,500 to reimburse them for the cost. They estimate that during the five-week period they would normally spend $300 for meals. Is the reimbursement taxable?

A partial list of research sources is

- Sec. 123
- Reg. Sec. 1.123-1

I4-66 Bold Corporation paid $25 to each full-time employee at year-end in recognition of the holidays. Bold Corporation is interested in whether the amounts are taxable income to its employees, and whether the company can deduct the amounts.

A partial list of research sources is

- Secs. 74(c), 102, 132(c), and 274(b)
- Reg. Sec. 1.132-6(e)(1)
- *Hallmark Cards, Inc. v. U.S.*, 9 AFTR 2d 391, 62-1 USTC ¶9162 (DC-Mo, 1961).
- Rev. Rul. 59-58, 1959-1 CB 17.

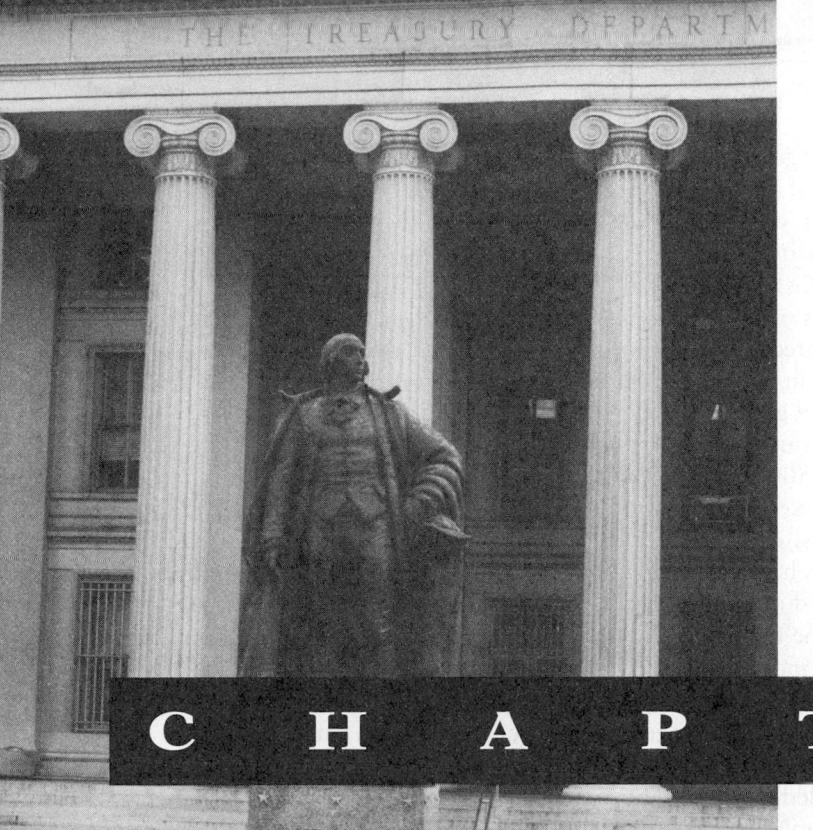

5

CHAPTER

PROPERTY TRANSACTIONS: CAPITAL GAINS AND LOSSES

LEARNING OBJECTIVES

After studying this chapter, you should be able to

▶1 Determine the realized gain or loss from the sale or other disposition of property

▶2 Determine the amount realized from the sale or other disposition of property

▶3 Determine the basis of property

▶4 Distinguish between capital assets and other assets

▶5 Understand how capital gains and losses affect taxable income

▶6 Recognize when a sale or exchange has occurred

▶7 Determine the holding period for an asset when a sale or disposition occurs

HISTORICAL NOTE

A preferential tax rate on capital gains was included in the tax law from 1921 until 1987. A modest preferential rate was reintroduced in 1991, with capital gains for noncorporate taxpayers being subject to a maximum 28% tax rate and ordinary income being subject to a maximum tax rate of 31%. The capital gains differential became more significant in 1993 when the highest marginal rate was increased to 39.6%.

ADDITIONAL COMMENT

For a discussion of the justification of preferential tax rates for long-term capital gains, see page I5-30.

Gross income includes "gains derived from dealings in property,"[1] and certain "losses from sale or exchange of property"[2] are allowed as deductions from gross income to determine adjusted gross income. All recognized gains and losses must eventually be classified either as *capital* or *ordinary*. Except for a brief time in the mid-to-late 1980s, long-term capital gains (LTCGs) of individual taxpayers have consistently been taxed at lower rates than ordinary gains or short-term capital gains (STCGs). This preferential treatment of capital gains, more precisely LTCGs, has been a much debated topic over the many years of the income tax in the United States. A discussion of the reasoning for imposing lower tax rates on capital gains is provided near the end of this chapter.

The preferential treatment of capital gains has fluctuated widely over the years. For example, in the early 1980s, taxpayers were allowed to deduct 60% of the gain. In 1991, net capital gains were taxed at a maximum rate of 28%, then reduced to 20% for most taxpayers in 1997. Thus, depending on the political persuasion of the government, tax rates on net capital gains have yo-yoed up and down. A significant change in the rates for net capital gains occurred in 2003 when the rates were reduced to 15% for most taxpayers (5% for lower income taxpayers). With the maximum ordinary tax rate for individuals being 35% in 2006, individuals can benefit by having a gain be classified as a LTCG rather than as ordinary gain or STCG. Thus, much planning is performed to attempt to arrange one's affairs to take advantage of the lower capital gain rates.

Capital losses must be offset against capital gains, and net capital losses are subjected to restrictions on their deductibility. Thus, most taxpayers prefer to have losses classified as ordinary instead of capital.

Most property transactions have tax consequences to the taxpayer. For example, when a sale, exchange, or abandonment occurs, the taxpayer must determine the realized gain or loss, the portion of the realized gain or loss that must be recognized (if any), and the character of the gain or loss. This chapter focuses on determining the realized gain or loss and the portion of the recognized gain or loss classified as capital or ordinary. When classifying a recognized gain or loss, (i.e., the gain or loss actually reported on the taxpayer's tax return) three important questions must be considered:

▶ What type of property has been sold or exchanged?

▶ When has a sale or exchange occurred?

▶ What is the holding period for the property?

In this chapter, these three questions are considered as well as difficulties associated with determining the basis of the property sold or exchanged and the amount of realized gains or losses.

DETERMINATION OF GAIN OR LOSS

Determine the realized gain or loss from the sale or other disposition of property

REALIZED GAIN OR LOSS

To determine the **realized gain** or **loss**, the amount realized from the sale or exchange of property is compared with the adjusted basis of that property. A gain is realized when the amount realized is greater than the basis, and a loss is realized when the amount realized is less than the basis of the property.[4]

EXAMPLE I5-1 ▶ Jack sells an asset with an adjusted basis of $10,000 to Judy for $14,000. Because the amount realized is greater than the basis, Jack has a realized gain of $4,000 ($14,000 − $10,000). ◀

Despite the fact that most transfers of property involve a sale, gains and losses may also be realized on certain other types of dispositions of property, such as exchanges, con-

---

[1] Sec. 61(a)(3).
[2] Sec. 62(a)(3).
[3] See page I5-28 and below for a discussion of the holding period for capital

assets. A capital gain or loss is long-term or short-term depending on the length of time the asset has been held by the taxpayer.
[4] Sec. 1001(a).

demnations, casualties, thefts, bond retirements, and corporate distributions. However, gains and losses are generally not realized when property is disposed of by gift or bequest.

EXAMPLE I5-2 ▶ Alice owns land held for investment with a basis of $20,000. The land is taken by the city by right of eminent domain, and she receives a payment of $30,000 for the land. This condemnation is treated as a sale or disposition for income tax purposes, and Alice's realized gain is $10,000 ($30,000 − $20,000). ◀

EXAMPLE I5-3 ▶ Two years ago, Bob purchased stock of a newly formed corporation for $10,000. During the current year, he receives a $12,000 distribution, constituting a return of capital, from the corporation. This distribution is treated as a sale. Therefore, Bob has a realized gain of $2,000 ($12,000 − $10,000). Bob's basis for the stock is now zero because his basis of $10,000 has been recovered. ◀

There must be an identifiable event for a sale or other disposition to occur. Mere changes in the value of property are not normally recognized as a disposition for purposes of determining a realized gain or loss.

Many reasons exist for not taxing unrealized gains and losses that arise due to a mere change in value. The Treasury Regulations state that "A loss is not ordinarily sustained prior to the sale or other disposition of the property, for the reason that until such sale or other disposition occurs there remains the possibility that the taxpayer may recover or recoup the adjusted basis of the property."[5] Because of administrative difficulties associated with determining fair market value (FMV), disputes with the Internal Revenue Service (IRS) would be greatly increased if unrealized gains were taxed and unrealized losses were allowed as deductions. In addition, payment of tax on income is generally required only when a taxpayer has the wherewithal to pay the tax (e.g., the taxpayer has received cash from the sale or other disposition of property and can therefore pay the tax on the gain).

AMOUNT REALIZED. The **amount realized** from a sale or other disposition of property is the sum of any money received, the FMV of all other property received, and any debt assumed by the buyer.

EXAMPLE I5-4 ▶ Tony sells land to Rita for $15,000 in cash and a machine having a $3,000 FMV. The amount realized by Tony is $18,000 ($15,000 + $3,000). ◀

The determination of FMV is a question of fact and often creates considerable controversy between taxpayers and the IRS. **Fair market value (FMV)** is "the price at which property would change hands between a willing buyer and a willing seller, neither being under any compulsion to buy or sell."[6] The FMV of the asset given in the exchange may be easier to determine than the FMV of the property received. In those cases, the FMV of the property given may be used to measure the amount realized. If a buyer assumes the seller's liability or takes the property subject to the debt, the courts have included the amount of the liability when determining the amount realized.[7]

EXAMPLE I5-5 ▶ Anna exchanges land subject to a liability of $20,000 for $35,000 of stock owned by Mario. Mario takes the property subject to the liability. The amount realized by Anna is $55,000 ($35,000 + $20,000 liability assumed by Mario). If Anna's adjusted basis for the land exchanged is $42,000, her realized gain is $13,000 ($55,000 − $42,000). ◀

In the above example, Anna receives stock with a $35,000 FMV and is relieved of a $20,000 debt. Mario's taking the property subject to the debt is equivalent to providing Anna with cash of $20,000. Thus, the amount realized by Anna is $55,000.

Generally, selling expenses such as sales commissions and advertising incurred in order to sell or dispose of the property reduce the amount realized.

---

[5] Reg. Sec. 1.1001-1(c)(1).
[6] CIR v. Homer H. Marshman, 5 AFTR 2d 1528, 60-2 USTC ¶9484 (6th Cir., 1960).
[7] Beulah B. Crane v. CIR, 35 AFTR 776, 47-1 USTC ¶9217 (USSC, 1947).

Doug sells stock of Briggs Corporation, which has a cost basis of $10,000, for $17,000. Doug pays a sales commission of $300. The amount realized by Doug is $16,700 ($17,000 − $300), and his realized gain is $6,700 ($16,700 − $10,000). ◀

TYPICAL MISCONCEPTION

The difference between the assumption of a liability and the taking of the property subject to the debt is sometimes confusing. The latter means that the lender can satisfy the debt only by repossessing the property. In the former case, where the buyer assumes the debt, the lender can satisfy the debt by repossessing the property and by going after other assets of the buyer.

ETHICAL POINT

The taxpayer may have lost records relating to the basis of the assets acquired many years earlier. In that case, the CPA can accept estimates of the missing data made by the taxpayer.

ADJUSTED BASIS.   The initial adjusted basis of property depends on how the property is acquired (e.g., by purchase, gift, or inheritance). Most property is acquired by purchase and therefore its initial basis is the cost of the property. However, if property is acquired from a decedent, its basis to the estate or heir is its FMV either at the date of death or, if the alternate valuation date is elected, six months from the date of death. The rules for determining the adjusted basis are discussed in subsequent sections of this chapter. Once the initial basis is determined, it may be adjusted upward or downward. Capital additions (also called capital expenditures) are expenditures that add to the value or prolong the life of property or adapt the property to a new or different use. Capital additions increase the basis. Capital recoveries, such as the deductions for casualty losses, cost recovery, and depreciation, reduce the basis. A property's adjusted basis can be determined by the following equation:

Initial basis
+ Capital additions (e.g., new porch for a building)
− Capital recoveries (e.g., depreciation deduction)
= Adjusted basis

Capital expenditures are distinguished from expenditures that are deductible as ordinary and necessary business expenses. For example, the cost of repairing a roof may be a deductible expense, whereas the cost of replacing a roof is a capital addition. It is sometimes difficult to determine whether an item is a capital expenditure or a business expense. Because of the preference for an immediate tax deduction, taxpayers normally prefer to classify expenditures as expenses rather than capital expenditures.

EXAMPLE I5-7 ▶ Ellen pays $2,500 for a major overhaul of an automobile used in her trade or business. The $2,500 is capitalized as part of the automobile's cost rather than deducted as a repair expense. ◀

Capital recoveries reduce the adjusted basis. The most common form of capital recovery is the deduction for depreciation or cost recovery. As discussed in Chapter I10, the modified accelerated cost recovery system (MACRS) is mandatory for most tangible depreciable property placed in service after 1986. The accelerated cost recovery system (ACRS) applies to most property placed in service after December 31, 1980, and before 1987.

EXAMPLE I5-8 ▶

ADDITIONAL COMMENT

In addition to depreciation, other capital recoveries that reduce the adjusted basis of property include depletion, amortization, corporate distributions that are a return of basis, compensation or awards for involuntary conversions, deductible casualty losses, insurance reimbursements, and cash rebates received by a purchaser.

Jeremy paid $100,000 for equipment two years ago and has claimed depreciation deductions of $37,000 for the two years. The cost of repairs during the same period was $6,000. At the end of the two-year period, the property's adjusted basis is $63,000 ($100,000 − $37,000). The amount spent for repairs does not affect the basis. ◀

RECOVERY OF BASIS DOCTRINE.   The **recovery of basis doctrine** states that taxpayers are allowed to recover the basis of an asset without being taxed because such amounts are a return of capital that the taxpayer has invested in the property. If a taxpayer receives a $12,000 return of capital distribution from a corporation when the taxpayer's basis for its investment in the corporation's stock is $10,000, the first $10,000 received represents a recovery of basis and only the $2,000 excess amount is treated as a gain realized on a sale or exchange of the stock investment. In many cases, basis is recovered in the form of a deduction for depreciation, cost recovery, or a casualty loss.

TYPICAL MISCONCEPTION

It is sometimes incorrectly believed that all realized gains and losses are recognized for tax purposes. Although most realized gains are recognized, some realized losses are not. For example, losses on the sale or exchange of property held for personal use cannot be recognized.

RECOGNIZED GAIN OR LOSS

Realized gain or loss represents the difference between the amount realized and the adjusted basis when a sale or exchange occurs. The amount of gain or loss that is actually reported on the tax return is the **recognized gain or loss.** In some instances, gain or loss is not recognized due to special provisions in the tax law (e.g., a gain or loss may be deferred or a loss may be disallowed).

Losses are generally deductible if they are incurred in carrying on a trade or business, incurred in an activity engaged in for profit, and casualty and theft losses. Realized losses on the sale or exchange of assets held for personal use are not recognized for tax purposes.

Therefore, a taxpayer who incurs a loss on the sale or exchange of a personal-use asset does not fully recover the basis. As explained in Chapter I8, realized losses on personal-use assets may be recognized to some extent if the property is disposed of by casualty or theft.

EXAMPLE I5-9 ▶ Ralph purchases a personal residence for $60,000. Deductions for depreciation are not allowed because the asset is not used in a trade or business or held for the production of income. If Ralph sells the house for $55,000, the realized loss of $5,000 is a capital loss but not deductible. He recovers only $55,000 of his original $60,000 basis. ◀

BASIS CONSIDERATIONS

OBJECTIVE 3

Determine the basis of property

COST OF ACQUIRED PROPERTY

In most cases, the basis of property is its cost. Cost is the amount paid for the property in cash or the FMV of other property given in the exchange. Any costs of acquiring the property and preparing the property for use are included in the cost of the property.

EXAMPLE I5-10 ▶ Penny purchases equipment for $15,000, pays delivery costs of $300, and installation costs of $250. The cost of the equipment is $15,550. ◀

Funds borrowed and used to pay for an asset are included in the cost. Obligations of the seller that are assumed by the buyer increase the asset's cost.

EXAMPLE I5-11 ▶ Peggy purchases an asset by paying cash of $40,000 and signs a note payable to the seller for $60,000. She also assumes a $2,000 lien against the property. Her basis for the asset is $102,000 and the amount realized by the seller is $102,000. ◀

UNIFORM CAPITALIZATION RULES. For financial accounting purposes, businesses must capitalize certain costs in connection with inventory, such as direct materials, direct labor, and overhead. For many years, businesses had a degree of flexibility with respect to capitalizing or expensing certain costs for tax purposes. However, the tax law now mandates one set of capitalization rules applicable to all taxpayers and all types of activities. These uniform capitalization rules, which apply principally to inventory, are provided in Sec. 263A and discussed in Chapter I11.

ADDITIONAL COMMENT

The sales tax is a good example of a tax that would be paid in connection with the acquisition of property.

The uniform capitalization rules also affect property other than inventory if the property is used in a taxpayer's trade or business or in an activity engaged in for profit. Taxes paid or accrued in connection with the acquisition of property are included as part of the cost of the acquired property. Taxes paid or accrued in connection with the disposition of property reduce the amount realized on the disposition.[8]

EXAMPLE I5-12 ▶ The Compact Corporation owns and operates a funeral home. The corporation purchases a hearse for $30,000 and pays sales taxes of $1,500. The cost basis for the hearse is $31,500. ◀

CAPITALIZATION OF INTEREST. Interest on debt paid or incurred during the production period to finance production expenditures incurred to construct, build, install, manufacture, develop, or improve real or tangible personal property must be capitalized.[9] The real or tangible personal property must have "a long useful life, an estimated production period exceeding two years, or an estimated production period exceeding one year and a cost exceeding $1,000,000."[10] Property has a long useful life if it is real property or property with a class life of at least 20 years. The production period starts when "production of the property begins and ends when the property is ready to be placed in service or is ready to be held for sale."[11]

EXAMPLE I5-13 ▶ The Indiana Corporation started construction of a $3 million motel on July 1, 2005, and borrowed an amount equal to the motel's construction costs. The motel is completed and ready for

---

[8] Sec. 164(a).
[9] Sec. 263A(f).

[10] Sec. 263A(f)(1)(B).
[11] Sec. 263A(f)(4)(B).

service on October 1, 2006. Interest incurred for the construction loan for the period from July 1, 2005, through October 1, 2006, is included in the motel's cost. The capitalized interest cost is depreciated over the motel's thirty-nine year recovery period (see Chapter I10). ◀

ADDITIONAL COMMENT

If a stockholder leaves his or her stock with a broker in street name, the stockholder can specifically identify the shares sold by simply informing the broker which shares he or she wishes to sell. The date basis of the shares sold should appear on the confirmation from the broker.

IDENTIFICATION PROBLEMS. In most cases, the adjusted basis of property sold is easily identified. However, problems arise when property is homogenous in nature such as when an investor owns several blocks of common stock of the same corporation purchased on different dates at different prices. The Regulations require the taxpayer to adequately identify the particular stock sold or exchanged.[12] Many investors allow brokers to hold their stock in street name (i.e., the brokerage firm holds title to the stock certificates) and thus do not make a physical transfer of securities. Such investors need to provide specific instructions to the broker as to which securities should be sold. If the stock sold or exchanged is not adequately identified, the first-in, first-out (FIFO) method must be used to identify the stock. With the FIFO method, the stock sold or exchanged is presumed to come from the first lot or lots acquired.

EXAMPLE I5-14 ▶

Judy purchased 300 shares of the Gustavel Corporation stock last year:

Month Acquired	Size of Block	Basis
January	100 shares	$4,000
May	100	5,000
October	100	6,000

In March of the current year, Judy sells 120 shares of the stock for $5,160. If Judy specifically identifies the stock sold as being all of the stock purchased in October and 20 shares purchased in May, her realized loss is $1,840 [$5,160 − ($6,000 + $1,000)]. ◀

If Judy does not specifically identify the stock sold, the FIFO method is used, and her realized gain is $160 [$5,160 − ($4,000 + $1,000)].

Owners of shares of mutual funds have more choices when determining the basis of shares sold. In addition to FIFO and specific identification, they may use an average cost method.[13]

EXAMPLE I5-15 ▶

Colin purchased 100 shares of Bluejay Mutual Fund on May 10, 2004, for $1,000, and has been reinvesting dividends. On December 20, 2006, he sells 115 shares.

ADDITIONAL COMMENT

Because of the difficulty and complexity of tracking basis of shares in a mutual fund, the average cost method is widely used by taxpayers.

	Amount	No. of Shares
Purchase May 10, 2004	$1,000	100
Reinvested Dividend Nov. 1, 2004	125	10
Reinvested Dividends Nov. 1, 2005	140	7
Reinvested Dividends Nov. 1, 2006	185	8
	1,450	125
	$11.60 Average Cost	

His basis for the 115 shares sold is $1,225 with FIFO, $1,334 (115 × $11.60) with average cost and could be as high as $1,350 with specific identification. Note that if he sells the shares obtained with the reinvested dividends in 2006, part of the gain or loss is short-term. ◀

PROPERTY RECEIVED AS A GIFT: GIFTS AFTER 1921

The basis of property received as a gift is generally the same as the donor's basis.[14] If the FMV of the property at time of the gift is less than the donor's basis, the donee may have to use one basis if the property is subsequently disposed of at a gain and another if the property is disposed of at a loss. As discussed later in this chapter, the basis may be increased by a portion or all of the gift tax paid because of the transfer.

---

[12] Reg. Sec. 1.1012-1(c)(1).
[13] For mutual fund investors, the IRS has authorized the use of FIFO, specific identification, or two average cost basis methods if only a portion of the fund shares is redeemed or sold. (See Reg. Sec. 1.1012-1(e) and Chapter I17.)

[14] Sec. 1015(a).

STOP & THINK

Question: Pete wants to make a gift of either ABC common stock (basis of $44,000 and FMV of $50,000) or XYZ common stock (basis of $73,000 and FMV of $50,000) to his nephew. Pete and his nephew have the same tax rate. Which stock should he give to his nephew?

Solution: Pete should give the ABC stock to his nephew because the nephew's basis for determining a gain or loss is $44,000 plus a portion of any gift tax Pete pays. The nephew's basis for XYZ common stock is $50,000 to determine a loss and $73,000 to determine a gain. If the nephew sells XYZ stock for less than $73,000, no loss is recognized and thus some of the basis is not used. Note that Pete would have a $23,000 loss if he sells the XYZ stock for $50,000. Furthermore, the nephew's basis for the XYZ stock is not increased if Pete has to pay a gift tax on the $40,000 taxable gift.

PROPERTY RECEIVED FROM A DECEDENT

The basis of property received from a decedent is generally the FMV of the property at the date of the decedent's death or an alternate valuation date (AVD).[17] This can result in either a step up (increase) or step down (decrease) in basis.

EXAMPLE I5-20 ▶

Patrick inherits property having an $80,000 FMV on the date of the decedent's death. The decedent's basis in the property is $47,000. The executor of the estate does not elect the AVD. Patrick's basis for the property is $80,000. ◀

EXAMPLE I5-21 ▶

Dianna inherits property having a $60,000 FMV at the date of the decedent's death. The decedent's basis in the property is $72,000. The AVD is not elected. Dianna's basis for the property is $60,000. ◀

REAL-WORLD EXAMPLE

The alternate valuation date was used in valuing the estates of many individuals owning large portfolios of common stocks who died shortly before the stock market crash in October 1987.

Instead of using the FMV on the date of death to determine the estate tax, the executor of the estate may elect to use the FMV on the AVD. The AVD is generally six months after the date of death. If the AVD is elected, the basis for all of the assets in the estate is their FMV on that date unless the property is distributed by the estate to the heirs or is sold before the AVD. If the AVD is used, property distributed or sold after the date of the decedent's death and before the AVD has a basis equal to its FMV on the date of distribution or the date of disposal.[18]

If the estate is small enough that an estate tax return is not required, the value of the property on the AVD may not be used.[19]

EXAMPLE I5-22 ▶

Marilyn inherits all of the property owned by an individual who dies in April, when the property has a $100,000 FMV. The value of the property six months later is $90,000. Because of the size of the estate, no estate tax is due. The AVD may not be used, and Marilyn's basis for the property is $100,000. Note that Marilyn does not want the AVD to be used because her basis would be $90,000 instead of $100,000. ◀

As noted above, the basis of the property to the estate and the heirs can be affected if the AVD is used to value the estate's assets. The AVD may be elected only if the value of the gross estate and the amount of estate tax after credits are reduced as a result of using the AVD.[20] This means that the aggregate value of the assets determined by using the AVD may be used only if the total value of the assets decreased during the six-month period.

EXAMPLE I5-23 ▶

Helmut inherits all of the property owned by an individual who dies in March when the FMV of the property is $900,000. Six months after the date of death, the property has a $950,000 FMV. The property is distributed to Helmut in December. Use of the AVD is not permitted because

---

[17] Sec. 1014(a).
[18] Sec. 2032(a).
[19] Rev. Rul. 56-60, 1956-1 C.B. 443. For a decedent dying in 2006–2008, Sec. 6018(a) requires an estate tax return to be filed if the gross estate exceeds $2,000,000 ($1,500,000 for decedents dying in 2004 or 2005).

[20] Credits available include the unified transfer tax credit and possibly credits for state death taxes, gift taxes, foreign death taxes, and the credit for taxes on prior transfers.

the value of the gross estate has increased. Therefore, his basis in the property is $900,000, the FMV on the date of death. ◀

An executor may elect to use the AVD to reduce the estate taxes owed by the estate. However, the income tax basis of the property included in the estate is also reduced for heirs who inherit the property.

EXAMPLE I5-24 ▶ Michelle inherits property with a $3,200,000 FMV at the date of the decedent's death. The FMV of the property on the AVD (six months after the date of the decedent's death) declines to $2,740,000. The executor of the estate elects to use $2,740,000 to value the property for estate tax purposes and Michelle's basis for the property is thus $2,740,000 instead of $3,200,000. ◀

COMMUNITY PROPERTY. If the decedent and the decedent's spouse own property under community property laws,[21] one-half of the property is included in the decedent's gross estate and its basis to the surviving spouse is its FMV.[22] The surviving spouse's one-half share of the community property is also adjusted to FMV.[23] In effect, the surviving spouse's share of the community property is considered to have passed from the decedent.

EXAMPLE I5-25 ▶ Matt and Jane, a married couple, live in Texas, a community property state, and jointly own land as community property that cost $110,000. The land has an $800,000 FMV when Jane dies, leaving all of her property to Matt. His basis for the entire property is $800,000. ◀

In a common law state, only one-half of the jointly owned property is included in the decedent's estate and is adjusted to its FMV. The survivor's share of the jointly held property is not adjusted.

EXAMPLE I5-26 ▶ Barry and Maria, a married couple, live in Iowa, a common law state, and jointly own land that cost $200,000. The property has a $700,000 FMV when Barry dies, leaving all of his property to Maria. Her basis for the land is $450,000 [$100,000 + (0.50 × $700,000)]. ◀

PROPERTY CONVERTED FROM PERSONAL USE TO BUSINESS USE

ADDITIONAL COMMENT

It is important to estimate the FMV of property at the time the property is converted from personal use to business use.

Often, taxpayers who own personal-use assets convert these assets to an income-producing use or for use in a trade or business. When this conversion occurs, the property's basis must be determined. The basis for computing depreciation is the lower of FMV or the adjusted basis of the property when the asset is transferred from personal use to an income-producing use or for use in a trade or business.[24] This rule prevents taxpayers from obtaining the benefits of depreciation to the extent that the property has declined in value during the period that it is held for personal use.

EXAMPLE I5-27 ▶

REAL-WORLD EXAMPLE

A taxpayer sold a personal residence to a purchaser, and the purchaser rented the property from the taxpayer until financing could be secured. The rental agreement was executed simultaneously with the sales agreement and was incidental to the sale. The taxpayer was not permitted to recognize any loss on the sale because the property was never converted to rental property. *Henry B. Dawson,* 1972 PH T.C. Memo 31 TCM 5.

Olga owns a boat that cost $2,000 and is used for personal enjoyment. At a time when the boat has a $1,400 FMV, Olga transfers the boat to her business of operating a marina. The basis for depreciation is $1,400 because the FMV is less than Olga's adjusted basis at the time of conversion to business use. The $600 decline ($2,000 − $1,400) that occurred while Olga used the boat for personal use may not be deducted as depreciation. ◀

If the boat's FMV in Example I5-27 is more than $2,000, the basis for depreciation is $2,000 because the FMV is higher than its adjusted basis at the time the asset is transferred to business use.

If a personal-use asset is transferred to business use when its FMV is less than its adjusted basis, the basis for determining a loss on a subsequent sale or disposition of the property is its FMV on the date of the conversion to business use less any depreciation taken before the disposition.[25]

---

[21] Community property states are Arizona, California, Idaho, Louisiana, New Mexico, Nevada, Texas, and Washington. Wisconsin has a marital property law that is basically the same as community property.
[22] Sec. 1014(a).

[23] Sec. 1014(b)(6).
[24] Reg. Sec. 1.167(g)-1.
[25] Reg. Sec. 1.165-9(b)(2).

EXAMPLE I5-28 ▶ Susanna purchased a personal residence in 1990 for $50,000 and converted the property to rental property in 1993 when its FMV was $46,000. Assume depreciation of $20,700 has been deducted, and the property is sold for $21,000. The basis of the property is $25,300 ($46,000 − $20,700), and her loss on the sale is $4,300 ($21,000 − $25,300). ◀

The rule for determining basis, that is, lower of adjusted basis or FMV, applies only to the sale of converted property at a loss. The basis for determining gain is its adjusted basis when converted less depreciation taken before the disposition.

EXAMPLE I5-29 ▶ Assume the same facts as in Example I5-28, except the property is sold for $31,000 instead of $21,000. The basis of the property is $29,300 ($50,000 − $20,700) and her gain is $1,700 ($31,000 − $29,300). ◀

Without the rule for determining basis of personal-use property converted to business property, taxpayers would have an incentive to convert nonbusiness assets that have declined in value to business use before selling the asset to convert nondeductible losses into deductible losses.

EXAMPLE I5-30 ▶ Craig owns a personal-use asset with a basis of $80,000 and a $50,000 FMV. If he sells the asset for its FMV, the $30,000 loss ($50,000 − $80,000) is not deductible because losses on the sale of personal-use assets are not deductible. If Craig converts the asset to business use and then immediately sells the asset for $50,000, no loss is realized because the basis of the asset for purposes of determining loss is $50,000, the FMV when property was converted. ◀

REAL-WORLD EXAMPLE

A taxpayer purchased a group of lots and allocated the total cost evenly among the lots. The court, however, held that more cost should be allocated to the waterfront lots than to the interior lots. *Biscayne Bay Islands Co.,* 23 B.T.A. 731 (1931).

ALLOCATION OF BASIS

When property is obtained in one transaction and portions of the property are subsequently disposed of at different times, the basis of the property is allocated to the different portions of the property. Gain or loss is computed at the time of disposal for each portion. If one purchases a 20-acre tract of land and later sells the entire tract, an allocation of basis is not needed. However, if the taxpayer divides the property into smaller tracts of land for resale, the cost of the 20-acre tract must be allocated among the smaller tracts of land.

BASKET PURCHASE. If more than one asset is acquired in a single purchase transaction (i.e., a basket purchase), the cost must be apportioned to the various assets acquired. The allocation is based on the relative FMVs of the assets.

EXAMPLE I5-31 ▶ Kelly purchases a duplex for $80,000 to use as a rental property. The land has a $15,000 FMV, and the building has a $65,000 FMV. Kelly's bases for the land and the building are $15,000 and $65,000, respectively. ◀

SELF-STUDY QUESTION

If Kelly in Example I5-31 paid $2,000 for the cost of a title search and other costs that must be capitalized, what is the basis of the land and building?

ANSWER

Land $15,375
Building $66,625

Because no depreciation deduction is allowed for land, taxpayers tend to favor a liberal allocation of the total purchase price to the building. Appraisals or other measures of FMV may be used to make the allocation.

COMMON COSTS. As in the case of financial accounting, common costs incurred to obtain or prepare an asset for service must be capitalized and allocated to the basis of the individual assets.

EXAMPLE I5-32 ▶ Priscilla acquires three machines for $60,000, which have FMVs of $30,000, $20,000, and $10,000, respectively. Costs of delivery amount to $2,000, and costs to install the three machines amount to $1,000. The total installation and delivery costs of $3,000 are allocated to the three machines based on their FMVs.

The allocation of the $3,000 of common costs occurs as follows:

$$\text{Machine No. 1:} \quad \frac{\$30,000 \text{ FMV}}{\$30,000 + \$20,000 + \$10,000} \times \$3,000 = \$1,500$$

$$\text{Machine No. 2:} \quad \frac{\$20,000 \text{ FMV}}{\$30,000 + \$20,000 + \$10,000} \times \$3,000 = \$1,000$$

$$\text{Machine No. 3:} \quad \frac{\$10,000 \text{ FMV}}{\$30,000 + \$20,000 + \$10,000} \times \$3,000 = \$500$$

The bases for each of the three machines are $31,500, $21,000, and $10,500, respectively. ◄

NONTAXABLE STOCK DIVIDENDS RECEIVED. If a nontaxable stock dividend is received, a portion of the basis of the stock on which the stock dividend is received is allocated to the new shares received from the stock dividend.[26] The cost basis of the previously acquired shares is reduced by the amount of basis allocated to the stock dividend shares. If the stock received as a stock dividend is the same type as the stock owned before the dividend, the total basis of the stock owned before the dividend is allocated equally to all shares now owned.

EXAMPLE I5-33 ▶ Wayne owns 1,000 shares of Bell Corporation common stock with a $44,000 basis. Wayne receives a nontaxable 10% common stock dividend and now owns 1,100 shares of common stock. The basis for each share of common stock is now $40 ($44,000 ÷ 1,100). ◄

If the stock received as a stock dividend is not the same type as the stock owned before the dividend, the allocation is based on relative FMVs.

EXAMPLE I5-34 ▶ Stacey owns 500 shares of Montana Corporation common stock with a $60,000 basis. She receives a nontaxable stock dividend payable in 50 shares of preferred stock. At time of the distribution, the common stock has a $40,000 FMV ($80 × 500 shares), and the preferred stock has a $10,000 FMV ($200 × 50 shares). After the distribution, Stacey owns 50 shares of preferred stock with a basis of $12,000 [($10,000 ÷ $50,000) × $60,000]. Thus, $12,000 of the basis of the common stock is allocated to the preferred stock and the basis of the common stock is reduced from $60,000 to $48,000. ◄

KEY POINT

Corporations issue stock rights to shareholders so that the shareholders will be able to maintain their same proportional ownership in the corporation. This is called the preemptive right.

NONTAXABLE STOCK RIGHTS RECEIVED. Stock rights represent rights to acquire shares of a specified corporation's stock at a specific exercise price when certain conditions are met. The exercise price is usually less than the market price when the stock rights are issued. Stock rights may be distributed to employees as compensation, and they are often issued to shareholders to encourage them to purchase more stock, thereby providing more capital for the corporation.

If the FMV of nontaxable stock rights received is less than 15% of the FMV of the stock, the basis of the stock rights is zero unless the taxpayer elects to allocate the basis between the stock rights and the stock owned before distribution of the stock rights.[27]

EXAMPLE I5-35 ▶ Tina owns 100 shares of Bear Corporation common stock with a $27,000 basis and a $50,000 FMV. She receives 100 nontaxable stock rights with a total FMV of $4,000. Because the FMV of the stock rights is less than 15% of the FMV of the stock (0.15 × $50,000 = $7,500), the basis of the stock rights is zero unless Tina elects to make an allocation. ◄

REAL-WORLD EXAMPLE

In 1993, United States Cellular Corporation issued one right for each common share held. Each whole right entitled the holder to buy one common share for $33.

If in Example I5-35, Tina elects to allocate the basis of $27,000 between the stock rights and the stock, the basis of the rights is $2,000 ([$4,000 ÷ $54,000] × $27,000) and the basis of the stock is $25,000 ([$50,000 ÷ $54,000] × $27,000).

The decision to allocate the basis affects the gain or loss realized on the sale or disposition of the stock rights because the basis of the rights is zero unless an allocation is made. Furthermore, the basis of any stock acquired by exercising the rights is affected by whether or not a portion of the basis is allocated to the rights. The basis of stock acquired by exercising the stock rights is the amount paid plus the basis of the stock rights exercised.

EXAMPLE I5-36 ▶ George receives 10 stock rights as a nontaxable distribution, and no basis is allocated to the stock rights. With each stock right, George may acquire one share of stock for $20. If he exercises all 10 stock rights, the new stock acquired has a basis of $200 ($20 × 10 shares). If George sells all 10 stock rights for $135, he has a realized gain of $135 ($135 − 0). ◄

---

[26] Sec. 307(a).

[27] Sec. 307(b)(1).

If the FMV of a nontaxable stock right received is equal to or greater than 15% of the FMV of the stock, the basis of the stock owned before the distribution must be allocated between the stock and the stock rights.

EXAMPLE I5-37 ▶ Helen owns 100 shares of NMO common stock with a $14,000 basis and a $30,000 FMV. She receives 100 stock rights with a total FMV of $5,000. Because the FMV of the stock rights is at least 15% of the FMV of the stock, the $14,000 basis must be allocated between the stock rights and the stock. The basis of the stock rights is $2,000 [($5,000 ÷ $35,000) × $14,000] and the basis of the stock is $12,000 [($30,000 ÷ $35,000) × $14,000]. ◀

A recipient of stock rights generally has three courses of action. The stock rights can be sold or exchanged, in which case the basis allocated to the stock rights, if any, is used to determine gain or loss. The stock rights may be exercised, and any basis allocated to the rights is added to the purchase price of the acquired stock. The stock rights may be allowed to expire, in which case no loss is recognized, and any basis allocated to the rights is reallocated back to the stock. If the stock rights received in Example I5-37 expire without being exercised, Helen does not recognize a loss and the basis of her 100 shares of common stock is $14,000.

Property basis rules are highlighted in Topic Review I5-1.

Topic Review I5-1

Property Basis Rules

METHOD ACQUIRED	BASIS OF THE ACQUIRED PROPERTY
1. Acquired by direct purchase	1. Basis includes the amount paid for the property, costs of preparing the property for use, obligations of the seller assumed by the buyer, and liabilities to which the property is subject.
2. Acquired as a gift. (a) FMV on the date of the gift is equal to or greater than the donor's basis (b) FMV on the date of the gift is less than the donor's basis	2. (a) The donee's basis is the same as the donor's basis plus a pro rata portion of the gift tax attributable to the property's unrealized appreciation at the time of the gift. (b) The donee's gain basis is the donor's basis and the loss basis is FMV. No increase for any gift tax paid.
3. Received from a decedent (a) AVD is not elected (b) AVD is elected	3. (a) The basis is its FMV on the date of death. (b) The basis of nondistributed property is its FMV on the AVD. If the property is distributed or sold before this date, its basis is FMV on the date of sale or distribution.
4. Converted from personal to business use	4. The basis for a loss (as well as for depreciation) is the lesser of its adjusted basis or FMV at date of conversion. The basis for a gain is its adjusted basis at date of conversion.
5. Nontaxable stock dividend	5. Basis of the stock dividend shares includes a pro rata portion of the adjusted basis of the underlying shares owned.
6. Nontaxable stock right	6. If the FMV of the rights is less than 15% of the stock's FMV, the basis of the rights is zero unless an election is made to allocate basis. Basis of the underlying stock is allocated to the rights based on the respective FMV's of the stock and rights.

DEFINITION OF A CAPITAL ASSET

TYPICAL MISCONCEPTION

It is common in financial accounting classes to include property used in a trade or business in the definition of a capital asset. For example, factory buildings, machinery, trucks, and office buildings would be defined as capital assets. However, such items are not capital assets for tax purposes.

Instead of defining capital assets, Sec. 1221 provides a list of properties that are **not** capital assets. Thus, a capital asset is any property owned by a taxpayer *other* than the types of property specified in Sec. 1221. Property that is not a capital asset includes the following:

1. Inventory or property held primarily for sale to customers in the ordinary course of a trade or business.
2. Property used in the trade or business and subject to the allowance for depreciation provided in Sec. 167 or real property used in a trade or business. (As explained in Chapter I13, these properties are referred to as *Sec. 1231 assets* if held by the taxpayer more than one year.)
3. Accounts or notes receivable acquired in the ordinary course of a trade or business for services rendered or from the sale of property described in item 1.
4. Other assets including
   a. A letter, memorandum, or similar property held by a taxpayer for whom such property was prepared or produced.
   b. A copyright; a literary, musical, or artistic composition; a letter or memorandum; or similar property held by a taxpayer whose personal efforts created such property or whose basis in the property for determining a gain is determined by reference to the basis of such property in the hands of one who created the property or one for whom such property was prepared or produced.
   c. A U.S. government publication held by a taxpayer who receives the publication by any means other than a purchase at the price the publication is offered for sale to the public.
   d. A U.S. government publication held by a taxpayer whose basis in the property for determining a gain is determined by reference to the basis of such property in the hands of a taxpayer in item 4c (e.g., certain property received by gift).

EXAMPLE I5-38 ▶ Maxine owns a building used in her business. Other business assets include equipment, inventory, and accounts receivable. None of the assets are classified as capital assets. ◀

Chapter I13 provides an in-depth discussion of business assets such as buildings, land, and equipment. Although these items are not capital assets, Sec. 1231 provides in many cases that the gain on the sale or exchange of such an asset is eventually taxed as LTCG.

EXAMPLE I5-39 ▶ Eric owns an automobile held for personal use and also owns a copyright for a book he has written. Because the copyright is held by the taxpayer whose personal efforts created the property, it is not a capital asset. The automobile held for personal use is a capital asset. ◀

SELF-STUDY QUESTION

Doug owns a personal residence, an automobile, 100 shares of Ford Motor Company, and a poem he wrote for his girlfriend. Which of these assets are capital assets?

ANSWER

All of the items are capital assets except the poem, which is a literary composition that Doug created.

By analyzing Examples I5-38 and I5-39, one can conclude that the classification of an asset is often determined by its use. An automobile used in a trade or business is not a capital asset but is a capital asset when held for personal use. Examples of assets that qualify as capital assets include a personal residence, land held for personal use, and investments in stocks and bonds. In addition, certain types of assets are specifically given capital asset status, such as patents, franchises, etc. These and other special assets are discussed later in this chapter.

INFLUENCE OF THE COURTS

In *Corn Products Refining Co.*, the Supreme Court rendered a landmark decision when it determined that the sale of futures contracts related to the purchase of raw materials resulted in ordinary rather than capital gains and losses.[28] The Corn Products Company, a

[28] *Corn Products Refining Co. v. CIR*, 47 AFTR 1789, 55-2 USTC ¶9746 (USSC, 1955).

manufacturer of products made from grain corn, purchased futures contracts for corn to ensure an adequate supply of raw materials. Delivery of the corn was accepted when needed for manufacturing operations, and unneeded contracts were later sold. Corn Products contended that any gains or losses on the sale of the unneeded contracts should be capital gains and losses because futures contracts are customarily viewed as security investments, which qualify as capital assets. The Supreme Court held that these transactions represented an integral part of the business for the purpose of protecting the company's manufacturing operations and the gains and losses should, therefore, be ordinary in nature.

Although the *Corn Products* doctrine has been interpreted as creating a nonstatutory exception to the definition of a capital asset when the asset is purchased for business purposes, the Supreme Court ruled in the 1988 *Arkansas Best Corporation* case that the motivation for acquiring assets is irrelevant to the question of whether assets are capital assets. Arkansas Best, a bank holding company, sold shares of a bank's stock that had been acquired for the purpose of protecting its business reputation. Relying on the *Corn Products* doctrine, the company deducted the loss as ordinary. The Supreme Court ruled that the loss was a capital loss because the stock is within the broad definition of the term *capital asset* in Sec. 1221 and is outside the classes of property that are excluded from capital-asset status.[29] *Arkansas Best* apparently limits the application of *Corn Products* to hedging transactions that are an integral part of a taxpayer's system of acquiring inventory.

OTHER IRC PROVISIONS RELEVANT TO CAPITAL GAINS AND LOSSES

A number of IRC sections provide special treatment for certain types of assets and transactions. For example, loss on the sale or exchange of certain small business stock that qualifies as Sec. 1244 stock is treated as an ordinary loss rather than a capital loss to the extent of $50,000 per year ($100,000 if the taxpayer is married and files a joint return).[30]

DEALERS IN SECURITIES. Normally, a security dealer's gain on the sale or exchange of securities is ordinary income. Section 1236 provides an exception for dealers in securities if the dealer clearly identifies that the property is held for investment. This act of identification must occur before the close of the day on which the security is acquired, and the security must not be held primarily for sale to customers in the ordinary course of the dealer's trade or business at any time after the close of the day of purchase.

EXAMPLE I5-40 ▶ Allyson, a dealer in securities, purchases Cook Corporation stock on April 8, and identifies the stock as being held for investment on that date. Four months later, Allyson sells the stock. Any gain or loss recognized due to the sale is capital gain or loss. ◀

Once a dealer clearly identifies a security as being held for investment, any loss on the sale or exchange of the security is treated as a capital loss.

EXAMPLE I5-41 ▶ Kris, a dealer in securities, purchases Boston Corporation stock and clearly identifies the stock as being held for investment on the date of purchase. Eight months later, the security is removed from the investment account and held as inventory. If the security is later sold at a gain, the gain is an ordinary gain. However, if the stock is sold at a loss, the loss is a capital loss. ◀

Securities dealers must use the mark-to-market method for their inventory of securities. This method requires that securities be valued at FMV at the end of each taxable year. Dealers in securities recognize gain or loss each year as if the security is sold on the last day of the tax year. Gains and losses are generally treated as ordinary rather than capital. Gains or losses due to adjustments in subsequent years or resulting from the sale of the security must be adjusted to reflect gains and losses already taken into account when determining taxable income.[31]

---

[29] *Arkansas Best Corporation v. CIR,* 61 AFTR 2d 88-655, 88-1 USTC ¶9210 (USSC, 1988).
[30] Secs. 1244(a) and (b). (See Chapter I8 for additional discussion on small business corporation stock losses.)

[31] Sec. 475. The mark-to-market rule also applies to some securities that are not inventory, but does not apply to any security that is held for investment and certain other transactions (see Sec. 475(b)).

EXAMPLE I5-42 ▶ Jim Spikes, a dealer in securities and calendar-year taxpayer, purchases a security for inventory on October 10, 2006, for $10,000 and sells the security for $18,000 on July 1, 2007. The security's FMV on December 31, 2006, is $15,000. Jim recognizes $5,000 of ordinary income in 2006 and $3,000 of ordinary income in 2007. ◀

REAL PROPERTY SUBDIVIDED FOR SALE. A taxpayer who engages in regular sales of real estate is considered to be a dealer, and any gain or loss recognized is ordinary gain or loss rather than capital gain or loss. A special relief provision is provided in Sec. 1237 for nondealer, noncorporate taxpayers who subdivide a tract of real property into lots (two or more pieces of real property are considered to be a tract if they are contiguous). Part or all of the gain on the sale of the lots may be treated as a capital gain if the following provisions of Sec. 1237 are satisfied:

▶ During the year of sale, the noncorporate taxpayer must not hold any other real property primarily for sale in the ordinary course of business.

▶ Unless the property is acquired by inheritance or devise, the lots sold must be held by the taxpayer for a period of at least five years.

▶ No substantial improvement may be made by the taxpayer while holding the lots if the improvement substantially enhances the value of the lot.[32]

▶ The tract or any lot may not have been previously held primarily for sale to customers in the ordinary course of the taxpayer's trade or business unless such tract at that time was covered by Sec. 1237.

The primary advantage of Sec. 1237 is that potential controversy with the IRS is avoided as to whether a taxpayer who subdivides investment property is a dealer. Section 1237 does not apply to losses. Such losses are capital losses if the property is held for investment purposes, or ordinary losses if the taxpayer is a dealer.

If the Sec. 1237 requirements are satisfied, all gain on the sale of the first five lots may be capital gain. Starting in the tax year during which the sixth lot is sold, 5% of the selling price for all lots sold in that year and succeeding years is ordinary income.

EXAMPLE I5-43 ▶ Jean subdivides a tract of land held as an investment into seven lots, and all requirements of Sec. 1237 are satisfied. The lots have a fair market value of $10,000 each and have a basis of $4,000. Jean incurs no selling expenses and sells four lots in 2006 and three lots in 2007. In 2006, all of the $24,000 [four lots × ($10,000 − $4,000)] gain is capital gain. In 2007, the year in which the sixth lot is sold, $1,500 of the gain is ordinary income [0.05 × ($10,000 × 3 lots)], and the remaining $16,500 {[three lots × ($10,000 − $4,000)] − $1,500} gain is capital gain. ◀

EXAMPLE I5-44 ▶ Assume the same facts as in Example I5-43, except that all seven lots are sold in 2006. The amount of ordinary income recognized is $3,500 [0.05 × ($10,000 × 7 lots)], and the remaining $38,500 {[seven lots × ($10,000 − $4,000)] − $3,500} gain is capital gain. ◀

Based on Examples I5-43 and I5-44, the advantage of selling no more than five lots in the first year should be apparent. Expenditures incurred to sell or exchange the lots are also treated favorably because they are first applied against the portion of the gain treated as ordinary income. Because selling expenses (e.g., commissions) are often equal to or greater than 5% of the selling price, this offset against ordinary income may result in the elimination of the ordinary income portion of the gain. Selling expenses in excess of the gain taxed as ordinary income reduce the amount realized on the sale or exchange.

NONBUSINESS BAD DEBT. Bad debt losses from nonbusiness debts are deductible only as short-term capital losses (STCLs),[33] regardless of when the debt occurred. A nonbusiness bad debt is deductible only in the year in which the debt becomes totally worthless.

---

[32] Certain improvements are not treated as substantial under Sec. 1237(b)(3) if the lot is held for at least ten years.

[33] Sec. 166(d)(1)(B). Also, see discussion of bad debts in Chapter I8.

EXAMPLE I5-45 ▶ Two years ago, Alice loaned $4,000 to a friend. During the current year, the friend declares bankruptcy and the debt is entirely worthless. Assuming that Alice has no other gains and losses from the sale or exchange of capital assets during the year, she deducts $3,000 in determining adjusted gross income (AGI) and has a STCL carry forward of $1,000. ◀

TAX TREATMENT FOR CAPITAL GAINS AND LOSSES OF NONCORPORATE TAXPAYERS

OBJECTIVE 5

Understand how capital gains and losses affect taxable income

To recognize capital gain or loss, it is necessary to have a sale or exchange of a capital asset. Once it is determined that a capital gain or loss has been realized and is to be recognized, it is necessary to classify the gains and losses as either short-term or long-term. If the asset is held for one year or less, the gain or loss is classified as a short-term capital gain (STCG) or a short-term capital loss (STCL). If the capital asset is held for more than one year, the gain or loss is classified as a long-term capital gain (LTCG) or long-term capital loss (LTCL).[34]

CAPITAL GAINS

ADDITIONAL COMMENT

The rates for long-term capital gains have been lower than rates for ordinary income for many years. However, preferential rates for qualified dividends were enacted in 2003. Qualified dividends are now taxed at a maximum 15% rate, the same as for long-term capital gains which are ANCG.

Net capital gain (NCG), which may receive favorable tax treatment, is defined as the excess of net long-term capital gain over net short-term capital loss.[35] NCG may be taxed at 5%, 15%, 25%, or 28%. Part or all of NCG may be classified as adjusted net capital gain (ANCG). ANCG, which is explained later, is subject to the lower rates of 5% and 15%.

To compute net capital gain, first determine all STCGs, STCLs, LTCGs, LTCLs, and then net gains and losses as described below.

NET SHORT-TERM CAPITAL GAIN. If total STCGs for the tax year exceed total STCLs for that year, the excess is defined as net short-term capital gain (NSTCG). As discussed later, NSTCG may be offset by net long-term capital loss (NLTCL).

EXAMPLE I5-46 ▶ Hal has two transactions involving the sale of capital assets during the year. As a result of those transactions, he has a STCG of $4,000 and a STCL of $3,000. Hal's NSTCG is $1,000 and his AGI increases by $1,000. His gross income increases by $4,000, and he is entitled to a $3,000 deduction for AGI. ◀

NET LONG-TERM CAPITAL GAIN. If the total LTCGs for the tax year exceed the total LTCLs for that year, the excess is defined as net long-term capital gain (NLTCG). As indicated earlier, a NCG exists when NLTCG exceeds net short-term capital loss (NSTCL).

EXAMPLE I5-47 ▶ Clay has two transactions involving the sale of capital assets during the year. As a result of the transactions, he has a LTCG of $5,000 and a LTCL of $3,000. Clay has a NLTCG and a net capital gain of $2,000. His AGI increases by $2,000. ◀

EXAMPLE I5-48 ▶ Linda has four transactions involving the sale of capital assets during the year. As a result of the transactions, she has a STCG of $5,000, a STCL of $7,000, a LTCG of $10,000, and a LTCL of $2,000. After the initial netting of short-term and long-term gains and losses, Linda has a NSTCL of $2,000 ($7,000 − $5,000) and a NLTCG of $8,000 ($10,000 − $2,000). Because the NLTCG exceeds the NSTCL by $6,000 ($8,000 − $2,000), her NCG is $6,000. ◀

LOWER RATES FOR ADJUSTED NET CAPITAL GAIN (ANCG). The new rates of 15% and 5% apply to ANCG recognized for sales after May 5, 2003, and the rate to use depends upon the taxpayer's tax bracket. The maximum rate for ANCG recognized by noncorporate

[34] While the Taxpayer Relief Act of 1997 reduced the rates for most LTCGs, it increased the required holding period to more than 18 months to be eligible for the lower rates of 10% and 20%. During the last few months of 1997, gain resulting from the sale of a capital asset might be taxed at many different rates depending on whether or not the holding period is one year or less, more than one year but not more than 18 months, or more than 18 months. These changes in the law dramatically increased the complexity associated with the taxation of capital gains. The 1998 Restructuring and Reform Act eliminated the more than 18-month holding period requirement for tax years ending after 1997 and returned to the more than one year requirement to be LTCG.

[35] Sec. 1222(11).

taxpayers (individuals, estates, and trusts) is 15% unless the taxpayer's regular tax rate is 15% or less. Taxpayers whose rate is 15% or less are subject to a maximum rate of only 5% on ANCG.[36]

EXAMPLE I5-49 ▶ Sandy is single with taxable income of $100,000 without considering the sale of Merck stock during 2006 for $15,000. The stock was purchased four years earlier for $3,000. Sandy has $12,000 of NLTCG which is ANCG taxed at 15%. To compute her total tax for 2006, ordinary rates would be applied to the $100,000 and then the tax on ANCG of 15% is added. ◀

EXAMPLE I5-50 ▶ Assume the same facts as in Example I5-49 except Sandy's taxable income without the capital gain is $11,400. The $12,000 ANCG is taxed at 5% because her taxable income is less than the $30,650 that is subject to the 15% rate.

SELF-STUDY QUESTION

Mary sells common stock for a gain of $10,000 on December 29, 2006. The settlement date, or date that Mary will receive the proceeds from the stockbroker, is January 2, 2007. Will Mary report the gain on her 2006 or 2007 tax return?

ANSWER

Mary is required to report the gain in the year of the sale (2006). Losses are also recognized in the year of sale.

Computation of the tax becomes more complicated if the ANCG causes taxable income to exceed the amount subject to the 15% tax rate, i.e., $30,650 for a single taxpayer. If a single taxpayer has taxable income of $33,000 that includes $8,000 of ANCG, the taxpayer's tax is determined as follows:

Tax on $25,000 (taxable income without the ANCG)	$3,372.50	($7,550 × 10%) + ($17,450 × 15%)
+ Tax on $7,700 ($30,650 − $25,000) of the ANCG at 5%	282.50	($5,650 × 5%)
+ Tax on $2,350 ($8,000 − $5,650) at 15% because the taxable income is greater than $30,650.	352.50	($2,350 × 15%)
Total tax	$4,007.50	◀

ADJUSTED NET CAPITAL GAINS (ANCG)

When computing ANCG, one has to consider that four different types of LTCGs may exist:

1. Collectibles gain
2. Part of the gain (generally 50%) resulting from the sale or exchange of qualified small business stock as defined in Sec. 1202
3. Unrecaptured Sec. 1250 gain[37]
4. All other LTCGs

It is the fourth group of LTCG that receives the preferential rates of 5% or 15%. The other three groups receive preferential treatment but not at the 5% or 15% rate. The first two gains above are referred to as 28% rate gain because the maximum rate for those gains is 28%; the maximum rate for unrecaptured Sec. 1250 gain is 25%. Collectibles gain, as explained below, is the net of LTCG and LTCL from the sale of collectibles. Sec. 1202 stock is qualified small business stock designed to encourage investment in small businesses. Unrecaptured Sec. 1250 gain, which is taxed at a maximum 25% rate, generally occurs when a building is sold. For the second and third types of LTCG, the special provisions only apply to gains. Losses from Sec. 1202 stock are treated as normal LTCLs, one cannot have a loss connected with an unrecaptured Sec. 1250 gain.

ANCG is defined as NCG less the first three gains listed above. However, the computation of ANCG is tricky because one has to consider the impact of net capital losses, both short-term and long-term. Taxpayers are permitted to offset capital losses against capital gains. But, as discussed above, there are four different types of LTCG. So, if a taxpayer has both LTCG and capital losses, the capital losses are first offset within the category (collectibles, Sec. 1202 stock, etc.), then any excess loss is offset against the highest rate LTCG category first and works down to the lowest rate category (i.e., 28% rate gain first, then 25%, then 15%). This topic is discussed in more detail on page I5-19 below.

When a taxpayer has no capital losses, ANCG is NCG reduced by the first three types of LTCG listed above. It should be noted that many taxpayers will not have the first three types of LTCG and therefore, NCG and ANCG will often be the same amount.

---

[36] Sec. 1(h).   [37] Sec. 1(h)(4).

EXAMPLE I5-51 ▶ During 2006, Charles sold two publicly-traded stocks. The first stock resulted in a LTCG of $10,000 while the second stock resulted in a LTCG of $15,000. These were the only capital gain transactions during the year, there were no loss transactions. Charles' NCG and ANCG would be $25,000 and this gain would be subject to a maximum tax rate of 15%. ◀

EXAMPLE I5-52 ▶ Assume in the example above that Charles also had a gain on the sale of a building that resulted in an unrecaptured Sec. 1250 gain of $50,000. Charles would have NCG of $75,000 and ANCG of $25,000. The $50,000 gain would be taxed at a maximum rate of 25% while the remaining $25,000 gain would be taxed at a maximum rate of 15%. ◀

COLLECTIBLES GAIN. Gains resulting from the sale of collectibles such as artwork, rugs, antiques, stamps and most coins are taxed at a maximum rate of 28%.

EXAMPLE I5-53 ▶ Danny, whose tax rate is 35%, purchased Bowling common stock and antique chairs for investment on March 10, 2004. He sells the assets in April 2006 and has a gain of $8,000 on the sale of the stock and $10,000 on the sale of the antique chairs. His NLTCG is $18,000, and his NCG is $18,000. His ANCG is $8,000 since $10,000 of the NCG is a collectibles gain. His tax on the capital gains is $4,000 [(15% × $8,000) + (28% × $10,000)]. ◀

SEC. 1202 GAIN. As explained in Chapter I4, Sec. 1202 provides that noncorporate taxpayers may exclude 50% of the gain resulting from the sale or exchange of qualified small business stock (QSBS) issued after August 10, 1993, if the stock is held for more than five years. A corporation may have QSBS only if the corporation is a C corporation and at least 80% of the value of its assets must be used in the active conduct of one or more qualified trades or businesses.[38]

Normally, the excluded gain is 50% of any gain resulting from the sale or exchange of QSBS held for more than five years and the remaining half of the gain is taxed at a maximum rate of 28%. However, the excluded gain may be less than 50% of the gain, because the amount of gain that may be excluded by a taxpayer for one corporation is 50% of the greater of $10,000,000 or ten times the aggregate basis of the qualified stock. If gain on the sale of QSBS is $11.4 million and $5 million of the gain is excluded, $5 million of the gain is taxed at 28% and the remaining $1.4 million gain is taxed at 15%.

EXAMPLE I5-54 ▶ Raef purchased $200,000 of newly issued Monona common stock on October 1, 2001. On December 15, 2006, he sells the stock for $4 million, resulting in a $3.8 million gain. He excludes $1.9 million of the gain, and the remaining $1.9 million of gain is Sec. 1202 gain taxed at 28%. ◀

EXAMPLE I5-55 ▶ Matthew, whose tax rate is 33%, has the following capital gains this year:

STCG	$10,000
LTCG (artwork)	12,000
LTCG (stock of AT&T)	17,000
LTCG (QSBS held more than five years)	45,000

Matthew may exclude $22,500 of the $45,000 Sec. 1202 gain. His NCG is $51,500 ($12,000 + $17,000 + $22,500). His ANCG is $17,000. The increase in his tax is $15,510. [33%($10,000) + 28%($12,000) + 15%($17,000) + 28%($22,500)]. ◀

CAPITAL LOSSES

To have a capital loss, one must sell or exchange the capital asset for an amount less than its adjusted basis. As in the case of capital gains, the one-year period is used to determine whether the capital loss is short-term or long-term.

NET SHORT-TERM CAPITAL LOSS. If total STCLs exceed total STCGs for the tax year, the excess is defined as a net short-term capital loss (NSTCL). As indicated above, the NSTCL is first offset against any NLTCG to determine net capital gain. If NSTCL

---

[38] Sec. 1202.

exceeds NLTCG, the capital loss may be offset, on a dollar-for-dollar basis, against a non-corporate taxpayer's ordinary income for amounts up to $3,000 in any one year.[39]

EXAMPLE I5-56 ▶

Bob has gross income of $60,000 before considering capital gains and losses. If Bob has a NLTCG of $10,000 and a NSTCL of $15,000, he has $5,000 of NSTCL in excess of NLTCG and may deduct $3,000 of the losses from gross income. Assuming no other deductions for AGI, Bob's AGI is $57,000 ($60,000 − $3,000). ◀

ADDITIONAL COMMENT

A husband and wife filing a joint return may use capital losses carried forward from years when they were single. Also, a divorced couple may use capital losses carried forward from a joint return year to their single returns.

In Example I5-56, $10,000 of the NSTCL is used to offset the $10,000 of NLTCG, and $3,000 of the NSTCL is used to reduce ordinary income. However, $2,000 of the loss is not used. This net capital loss is carried forward for an indefinite number of years.[40] The loss retains its original character and will be treated as a STCL occurring in the subsequent year. If a taxpayer dies with an unused capital loss carryover, it expires.

EXAMPLE I5-57 ▶

Last year, Milt had a NSTCL of $8,000 and a NLTCG of $2,600. The netting of short-term and long-term gains and losses resulted in a $5,400 excess of NSTCL over NLTCG, and $3,000 of this amount was offset against ordinary income. Milt's NSTCL carryforward is $2,400. During the current year he sells a capital asset and generates a STCG of $800. His NSTCL is $1,600 ($2,400 − $800), and the loss is offset against $1,600 of ordinary income. ◀

REAL-WORLD EXAMPLE

In 1975 an amendment was added to a tax bill in the House Ways and Means Committee that would have permitted individuals to take a three-year carryback for capital losses. When *The Wall Street Journal* disclosed that the provision would provide Ross Perot with a $15 million tax break, the amendment was defeated.

NET LONG-TERM CAPITAL LOSS. If total LTCLs for the tax year exceed total LTCGs for the year, the excess is defined as net long-term capital loss (NLTCL). If there is both a NSTCG and a NLTCL, the NLTCL is initially offset against the NSTCG on a dollar-for-dollar basis. If the NLTCL exceeds the NSTCG, the excess is offset against ordinary income on a dollar-for-dollar basis up to $3,000 per year.

EXAMPLE I5-58 ▶

In the current year, Gordon has a NLTCL of $9,000 and a NSTCG of $2,000. He must use $2,000 of the NLTCL to offset the $2,000 NSTCG, and then use $3,000 of the $7,000 ($9,000 − $2,000) NLTCL to offset $3,000 of ordinary income. Gordon's carryforward of NLTCL is $4,000 [$9,000 − ($2,000 + $3,000)]. This amount is treated as a LTCL in subsequent years. ◀

If an individual has both NSTCL and NLTCL, the NSTCL is offset against ordinary income first, regardless of when the transactions occur during the year.

EXAMPLE I5-59 ▶

In the current year, Beth has a NSTCL of $2,800 and a NLTCL of $2,000. The entire NSTCL is offset initially against $2,800 of ordinary income. Because capital losses may offset only $3,000 of ordinary income, $200 of NLTCL is used to offset $200 ($3,000 − $2,800) of ordinary income. The NLTCL carryover to the next year is $1,800 ($2,000 − $200). ◀

TAX STRATEGY TIP

Taxpayers who have realized capital gains during the tax year should consider selling securities with a loss during the same year. The losses can be offset against the gains and tax savings result.

CAPITAL LOSSES APPLIED TO CAPITAL GAINS BY GROUPS. Taxpayers separate their LTCGs and LTCLs into three tax rate groups: (1) 28% group, (2) 25% group, and (3) the 15% group. The 28% group includes capital gains and losses when the capital asset is a collectible held more than one year and part of the gain from the sale of QSBS held for more than five years. The 25% group consists of unrecaptured Sec. 1250 gain discussed in Chapter I13, and there are no losses for this group. The 15% or 5% group, depending upon the taxpayer's tax rate, includes capital gains and losses when the holding period is more than one year and the capital asset is not a collectible or Sec. 1202 small business stock.

When a taxpayer has NSTCL and NLTCG, the NSTCL is first offset against NLTCG from the 28% group, then the 25% group, and finally the 15% (or 5%) group. This treatment of NSTCL is favorable for taxpayers. Note that a taxpayer could have NLTCLs in one group, except the 25% group, and NLTCGs in another group. A net loss from the 28% group is first offset against gains in the 25% group then net gains in the 15% (or 5%) group. A net loss from the 15% group is first offset against net gains in the 28% group and then gains in the 25% group.[41]

---

[39] Sec. 1211(b). A $1,500 limitation applies to a married individual filing a separate return.

[40] Sec. 1212(b) and Reg. Sec. 1.1212-1(b).
[41] Notice 97-59, I.R.B. 1997-45.

EXAMPLE I5-60 ▶ Leroy, whose tax rate is 35%, has NSTCL of $20,000, a $25,000 LTCG from the sale of a rare stamp held 16 months and an $18,000 LTCG from the sale of stock held for three years. The $20,000 NSTCL is offset against $20,000 of the collectibles gain in the 28% group. Leroy's NCG is $23,000 and his ANCG is $18,000. Leroy's tax liability increases by $4,100 [($5,000 × 28%) + ($18,000 × 15%)]. ◀

EXAMPLE I5-61 ▶ Elizabeth, whose tax rate is 35%, has a $32,000 LTCL from the sale of stock held for four years and the following capital gains:

ADDITIONAL COMMENT

If Elizabeth in Example I5-61 also had a $9,000 LTCG from the sale of stock held for two years, she would only be able to offset $23,000 of the LTCG in the 28% group.

NSTCG	$40,000
LTCG from sale of collectible	$30,000
LTCG in the 25% group (unrecaptured Sec. 1250 gain)	$10,000

The $32,000 LTCL is offset first against $30,000 of the LTCG in the 28% group (collectibles) and then $2,000 against the unrecaptured Sec. 1250 gain. Her NLTCG is $8,000 taxed at 25% while her $40,000 NSTCG is taxed at her ordinary income rate of 35%. ◀

 STOP & THINK

Question: Srinija has a salary of $100,000. If she sells a non-personal use asset during the year and has a $40,000 loss, why is it important that the asset not be a capital asset?

Solution: Only $3,000 of a $40,000 capital loss is used as a deduction to reduce her gross income each year. Her AGI is $97,000 if the asset is a capital asset, and she has a $37,000 capital loss carryforward. All of the $40,000 loss is used to reduce her gross income if the asset is not a capital asset and her AGI is $60,000. It is possible that Srinija might not care whether or not the asset is a capital asset if she has capital gains that could be reduced by capital losses. If the asset is a personal-use asset, the loss is not deductible regardless of whether or not it is a capital asset.

TAX TREATMENT FOR NET CAPITAL GAIN. Congress eliminated preferential tax rates on NCG in 1986 by making the maximum ordinary income rate equal to the rate on net capital gains at 28%. However, this equality was short-lived as Congress, in 1991, increased the maximum ordinary income rate to 31% but left the NCG rate at 28%.[42] This newly-created preferential treatment for NCG's only applied to taxpayers whose tax rate exceeded 28%. The change in 1997 to rates as low as 10% benefited all noncorporate taxpayers if they held the capital asset for more than one year. The lower rates made taxpayers more interested in having capital gain income instead of ordinary income. Investors preferences for growth stocks as opposed to stocks with high dividends increased.

However, this preference was dramatically changed by the Jobs and Growth Tax Relief Reconciliation Act of 2003 which reduced the tax rate on qualified dividends to 5% and 15% as of January 1, 2003.[43] The rate on qualified dividends is 5% for a taxpayer with a regular tax rate of 15% or less, and 15% for a taxpayer with a regular tax rate greater than 15%. This significant reduction of tax rates for dividend income has resulted in an increased interest in stocks with high dividends.

Taxpayers who own mutual funds must recognize their share of capital gains even if no distributions are received. Many mutual fund shareholders reinvest their distributions instead of withdrawing assets from the mutual fund. Mutual funds must classify the gains as short-term or long-term, and long-term gains will need to be separated by rate groups. When shareholders of a mutual fund recognize their share of capital gains when no distribution is actually received, the basis for their shares is increased.

EXAMPLE I5-62 ▶ Eunice, whose tax rate is 35%, is a shareholder of Canyon Mutual Fund. The basis for her shares is $23,000. At the end of the current year, she received a statement from Canyon indicating her share of the following: qualified dividend income, $200; STCG, $300; 28-percent rate gain, $1,000; and ANCG of $1,500. The increase in her taxes as a result of her ownership of the mutual shares is $640 [($200 × 15%) + ($300 × 35%) + ($1,000 × 28%) + ($1,500 × 15%)]. The basis for her shares of Canyon Mutual Fund is $26,000. ◀

---

[42] For years prior to 1990, a myriad of rules have applied. Prior to 1987, noncorporate taxpayers received a deduction from gross income equal to 60% of the taxpayer's net capital gain. For years 1987–1990, net capital gains were subject to tax at ordinary income rates.

[43] Sec. 1(h)(11).

TAX TREATMENT OF CAPITAL GAINS AND LOSSES: CORPORATE TAXPAYERS

Most topics covered in this chapter concerning capital gains and losses, including the classification of an asset as a capital asset, rules for determining holding periods, and the procedure for offsetting capital losses against capital gains, apply to both corporate and noncorporate taxpayers. However, a major difference is that the lower tax rates of 5%, 15%, 25%, and 28% on net capital gain for noncorporate taxpayers do not apply to corporations. A second significant difference relates to the treatment of capital losses: Unlike the noncorporate taxpayer, who may offset capital losses against ordinary income up to $3,000, corporations may offset capital losses only against capital gains. Corporate taxpayers may carry capital losses back to each of the three preceding tax years (the earliest of the three tax years first and then to the next two years) and forward for five years to offset capital gains in such years. When a corporate taxpayer carries a loss back to a preceding year or forward to a following year, the loss is treated as a STCL.[44]

EXAMPLE I5-63 ▶

HISTORICAL NOTE

The House of Representatives proposed a reduction in corporate net capital gains in 1997, but the proposal was rejected.

The Peach Corporation has income from operations of $200,000, a NSTCG of $40,000, and a NLTCL of $56,000 during the current year. The $40,000 NSTCG is offset by $40,000 NLTCL. The remaining $16,000 of NSTCL may not be offset against the $200,000 of other income but may be carried back three years and then forward five years to offset capital gains arising in these years. If Peach has NLTCG and/or NSTCG in the previous three years, a refund of taxes paid during those years will be received during the current year. ◀

MAXIMUM RATE ON NET CAPITAL GAIN FOR CORPORATIONS. Unlike individual taxpayers, corporations do not receive any preferential rate reductions for net capital gains. Corporations apply a maximum rate of 35% to the corporation's net capital gain.[45] However, given the present tax rates for corporations, the existence of the 35% alternative rate for net capital gain has no benefit. A corporation subject to a rate of 39% because taxable income is greater than $100,000 but not more than $335,000 does not use the maximum 35% rate. In essence, therefore, corporations are taxed on capital gains at the same rates for ordinary income.

Topic Review I5-2 summarizes the principal differences in the tax treatment of capital gains and losses for corporate and noncorporate taxpayers.

STOP & THINK

Question: Most taxpayers believe that if they have a LTCG, their income taxes will be less on the LTCG than on their other ordinary income. Explain why all taxpayers do not have a tax savings from a net capital gain.

Solution: Noncorporate taxpayers whose marginal tax rate is 28% or less will not have a reduction in taxes if the LTCG is gain from the sale of a collectible, or the recognized half of the gain from the sale of qualified small business stock under Sec. 1202. Also, corporations are not eligible for the lower rates available to noncorporate taxpayers and pay taxes on NLTCG at the same rate as ordinary income.

Topic Review I5-2

Comparison of Corporate and Noncorporate Taxpayers: Capital Gains and Losses

	NONCORPORATE	CORPORATE
A statutory maximum tax rate applicable to net capital gain	Yes, 5%, 15%, 25%, and 28%	Yes, but rate is 35%
Offset of net capital losses against ordinary income	Yes, up to $3,000	No
Carryback of capital losses	No	Yes, three years as STCLs
Carryforward of capital losses	Yes, indefinitely	Yes, five years as STCLs

[44] Sec. 1212(a).   [45] Sec. 1201.

SALE OR EXCHANGE

As previously indicated, capital gains and losses result from the sale or exchange of capital assets. Although Sec. 1222 does not define a sale or an exchange, a **sale** is generally considered to be a transaction where one receives cash or the equivalent of cash, including the assumption of one's debt. An **exchange** is a transaction where one receives a reciprocal transfer of property, as distinguished from a transaction where one receives only cash or a cash equivalent.[46]

EXAMPLE I5-64 ▶

Two years ago, Bart acquired 100 shares of Alaska Corporation common stock for $12,000 to hold as an investment. Bart sells 50 shares of the stock to Sandy for $10,000 and transfers the other 50 shares to Gail in exchange for land that has a $10,000 FMV. In each transaction, Bart realizes a $4,000 ($10,000 − $6,000) LTCG due to the sale or exchange of a capital asset. The transfer to Sandy qualifies as a sale, and the transfer to Gail qualifies as an exchange. ◀

TYPICAL MISCONCEPTION

Because the carryover for net operating losses is 20 years, it is sometimes erroneously assumed that the carryover for corporate capital losses is also 20 years instead of five years.

To qualify as a sale or exchange, the transaction must be bona fide. Transactions between related parties such as family members are closely scrutinized. For example, a sale of property on credit to a relative may be a disguised gift if there is no intention of collecting the debt. If this is the case, a subsequent bad debt deduction due to the debt's worthlessness is disallowed. In some instances, the Code specifically states that a particular transaction or event either qualifies or does not qualify for sale or exchange treatment. For example, the holder of an option who fails to exercise such an option treats the lapse of the option as a sale or exchange.[47] However, abandonment of property is generally not deemed to be a sale or exchange.[48]

WORTHLESS SECURITIES

ADDITIONAL COMMENT

The worthlessness of a security is treated as a sale or exchange so that the taxpayer is not forced to arrange for someone to buy the security for a token amount.

If a security that is a capital asset becomes worthless during the year, Sec. 165(g)(1) specifies that any loss is treated as a loss from the sale or exchange of a capital asset on the last day of the tax year. The term includes stock, a stock option, and "a bond, debenture, note or certificate, or other evidence of indebtedness, issued by a corporation or by a government or political division thereof, with interest coupons or in registered form."[49] Whether a security has become worthless during the year is a question of fact, and the taxpayer has the burden of proof to show evidence of worthlessness.[50]

EXAMPLE I5-65 ▶

Charlotte purchased $40,000 of bonds issued by the Jet Corporation in March 2005. In February 2006, Jet is declared bankrupt, and its bonds are worthless. Charlotte has a LTCL of $40,000 because the bonds have become worthless and are deemed to have been sold on the last day of 2006. The more-than-one-year holding period requirement is satisfied by the last day of 2006. ◀

REAL-WORLD EXAMPLE

A corporation owned 76% of the stock of a Mexican company. The corporation later acquired the remaining 24% of the stock, allegedly for the purpose of avoiding interference by minority shareholders. Later the corporation claimed an ordinary loss on the worthless Mexican stock because it owned at least 80% of the stock. The Court treated the loss as a capital loss because the acquisition of the remaining stock was without a business purpose. *Hunter Mfg. Co.*, 21 T.C. 424 (1953).

SECURITIES IN AFFILIATED CORPORATIONS. If the security that becomes worthless is a security in a domestic affiliated corporation owned by a corporate taxpayer, the worthless security is not considered a capital asset. Thus, a corporate taxpayer's loss due to owning worthless securities in an affiliated corporation is treated as an ordinary loss. Because capital losses are of only limited benefit to corporate taxpayers, the classification of the loss as ordinary is preferable.

To qualify as an affiliated corporation, the parent corporation must own at least 80% of the voting power of all classes of stock and at least 80% of each class of nonvoting stock. The subsidiary corporation must be engaged in the active conduct of an operating business as opposed to being a passive investment company (i.e., more than 90% of its aggregate gross receipts must be from sources other than passive types of income such as royalties, dividends, and interest).[51]

---

[46] Reg. Sec. 1.1002-1(d).
[47] Sec. 1234(b) and Reg. Sec. 1.1234-1(b).
[48] Reg. Secs. 1.165-2 and 1.167(a)-8.

[49] Sec. 165(g)(2).
[50] *Minnie K. Young v. CIR*, 28 AFTR 365, 41-2 USTC ¶9744 (2nd Cir., 1941).
[51] Sec. 165(g)(3).

EXAMPLE I5-66 ▶ Ace Corporation owns 80% of all classes of stock issued by the same Jet Corporation described in Example I5-65. Jet Corporation is actively engaged in an operating business and has no income from passive investments before being declared bankrupt. Ace's loss from its worthless stock investment is an ordinary loss instead of a capital loss because Jet is an affiliated corporation. Ace owns at least 80% of all classes of Jet's stock and more than 90% of Jet's gross receipts are from sources other than passive types of income. ◀

RETIREMENT OF DEBT INSTRUMENTS

Generally, the collection of a debt is not a sale or an exchange. However, if a debt instrument is retired, amounts received by the holder are treated as being received in an exchange.[52] Debt instruments include bonds, debentures, notes, certificates, and other evidences of indebtedness.

EXAMPLE I5-67 ▶ In 2001 the Rocket Corporation issued $50,000 of five-year, interest-bearing bonds that were purchased by Elaine as an investment for $49,800. Elaine receives $50,000 at maturity in 2006. Retirement of the debt instrument is an exchange, and the $200 gain is a LTCG.[53] ◀

Although Congress has provided that retirements of debt instruments are treated as exchanges, Congress is not willing to allow taxpayers to convert large amounts of potential ordinary interest income into capital gain by purchasing debt instruments at a substantial discount. As illustrated in Example I5-67, a small amount of bond discount is sometimes converted to capital gain. However, if the discount is large enough to be classified as original issue discount, the discount must be amortized and included in gross income for each day the debt instrument is held. Original issue discount (OID) is defined as "the excess (if any) of the stated redemption price at maturity over the issue price."[54]

EXAMPLE I5-68 ▶ On January 1, 2006, Connie purchases $100,000 of the City Corporation's newly issued bonds for $85,000. The bonds mature in 20 years. In 2006 and in subsequent years Connie must annually recognize as interest income a portion of the $15,000 of OID. ◀

The OID is considered to be zero if the amount of discount "is less than ¼ of 1% of the stated redemption price at maturity, multiplied by the number of complete years to maturity."[55] In Example I5-63, the $200 discount is not OID because it is less than $625 (0.0025 × $50,000 × 5 years). If Connie pays more than $95,000 for the bonds in Example I5-68, the OID is zero.

ADDITIONAL COMMENT

Two different types of bonds are sold at a discount: original issue discount (OID) bonds and market discount bonds. OID bonds are issued at a discount, whereas market discount bonds have market discount resulting from a rise in interest rates after the issuance of the bonds.

ORIGINAL ISSUE DISCOUNT. Instead of spreading the OID ratably over the life of the bond, amortization of the discount is based on an interest amortization method called the **constant interest rate method**. The total amount of interest income is determined by multiplying the interest yield to maturity by the adjusted issue price. With this method of amortizing discount, the amount of OID amortized increases for each year the bond is held. In Example I5-68, Connie recognizes a larger amount of interest income in 2007 than in 2006 due to amortization of the OID.

The daily portion of the OID for any accrual period is "determined by allocating to each day in any accrual period its ratable portion to the increase during such accrual period in the adjusted issue price of the debt instrument."[56] The increase in the adjusted issue price for any accrual period is shown below.

$$\text{Increase in the adjusted issue price} = \left[\text{Adjusted issue price at the beginning of the accrual period} \times \text{Yield to maturity} \right] - \text{Interest payments during the accrual period}$$

[52] Sec. 1271(a).
[53] If Rocket Corporation issued the bonds with the intention of calling the bonds before maturity, Sec. 1271(a)(2) treats the gain as ordinary income.
[54] Sec. 1273(a)(1).
[55] Sec. 1273(a)(3).
[56] Sec. 1272(a)(3).

EXAMPLE I5-69 ▶

On June 30, 2006, Fred purchases a 10%, $10,000 corporate bond for $9,264. The bond is issued on June 30, 2006, and matures in five years. Interest is paid semiannually, and the effective yield to maturity is 12% compounded semiannually. In 2006, Fred recognizes interest income of $556, as illustrated in Table I5-1. The adjusted issue price as of January 1, 2007, is $9,320. This is the sum of the issue price plus any amounts of OID includible in the income of any holder since the date of issue. ◀

If a debt instrument is sold or exchanged before maturity, part of the OID is included in the seller's income. The amount to be included depends on the number of days the debt instrument is owned by the seller within the accrual period.

EXAMPLE I5-70 ▶

Assume the same facts as in Example I5-69, except that Fred sells the corporate bond to Carolyn on February 24, 2008 (the 55th day in the accrual period). Fred must include $20 [(55 days ÷ 181 days in the accrual period) × $67] of accrued interest for the period of January 1, 2008, to February 24, 2008, in income for 2008. Fred's basis for the bond increases by $20. Thus, his basis for determining a gain or loss is $9,462 ($9,442 + $20). ◀

MARKET DISCOUNT BONDS PURCHASED AFTER APRIL 30, 1993. The sale or exchange of a market discount bond may result in part or all of the gain being classified as ordinary income. The Revenue Reconciliation Act of 1993 substantially increased the number of bonds subject to the market discount provisions.[57] A market discount bond is a bond that is acquired in the bond market at a discount. Market discount is the excess of the stated redemption price of the bond at maturity over the taxpayer's basis for such bond immediately after it is acquired.

EXAMPLE I5-71 ▶

On January 1, Stephano purchased $100,000 of 8%, 20-year bonds for $82,000. The bonds were issued at par by the Solar Corporation two years ago on January 1. The bonds are market discount bonds. ◀

▼ TABLE I5-1

Computation for Interest Income in Examples I5-69 and I5-70

	Interest Received (1)	Amortization of Original Issue Discount (2)	Interest Income (3) = (1) + (2)	Taxpayer's Basis for the Bond
6-30-06				$ 9,264
12-31-06	$ 500	$ 56[a]	$ 556	9,320[b]
6-30-07	500	59	559	9,379
12-31-07	500	63	563	9,442
6-30-08	500	67	567	9,509
12-31-08	500	71	571	9,580
6-30-09	500	75	575	9,655
12-31-09	500	79	579	9,734
6-30-10	500	84	584	9,818
12-31-10	500	89	589	9,907
6-30-11	500	93[c]	593	10,000
	$5,000	$736	$5,736	

[a]6% × $9,264 − $500 = $56.
[b]$9,264 + $56 = $9,320.
[c]This figure is adjusted for rounding.

---

[57] Ordinary income treatment for accrued market discount does not apply to owners of taxable market discount bonds issued on or before July 18, 1984, if the bonds were acquired before May 1, 1993. Owners of tax-exempt bonds are not required to accrue market discount if the bonds were acquired before May 1, 1993 (regardless of the issue date).

Similar to OID, there is a de minimis rule for determining market discount. Market discount is zero if the discount is less than ¼ of 1% of the stated redemption price of the bond at maturity multiplied by the number of complete years to maturity.[58] If Stephano paid $95,500 or more for the Solar Corporation bonds in Example I5-71, the bonds would not be market discount bonds.[59]

Gain realized on disposition of the market discount bond is ordinary income to the extent of the accrued market discount.[60] The ratable accrual method (straight line method computed on a daily basis) is used to determine the amount of the accrued market discount recognized as ordinary income.[61] The market discount is allocated on the basis of the number of days the taxpayer held the bond relative to the number of days between the acquisition date and maturity date.

EXAMPLE I5-72 ▶ Assume the same facts as in Example I5-71 except that Stephano sells the bonds to Kimberly three years later for $86,400. $3,000 (³⁄₁₈ × $18,000) of the $4,400 ($86,400 − $82,000) gain is ordinary income and the remaining gain is LTCG. If Stephano sold the bond for more than $82,000 but less than $85,000, all of the gain is ordinary income. The entire $18,000 gain is ordinary income if the bond is held to maturity. ◀

ADDITIONAL COMMENT

An option is a contract in which the owner of property agrees with a potential buyer that the potential buyer has the right to buy the property at a fixed price within a certain period of time.

OPTIONS

The owner of an option to buy property may sell the option, exercise the option, or allow the option to expire. If the option is exercised, the amount paid for the option is added to the purchase price of the property acquired.[62]

EXAMPLE I5-73 ▶ On August 5, 2006, Len pays $600 for an option to acquire 100 shares of Hill Corporation common stock for $80 per share at any time before December 20, 2006. Len exercises the option on November 15, 2006, and pays $8,000 for the stock. Len's basis for the 100 shares of Hill is $8,600 ($8,000 + $600), and the stock's holding period begins on November 15, 2006. ◀

ADDITIONAL COMMENT

The Wall Street Journal publishes daily a list of all call and put options traded on the Chicago Board, the American Stock Exchange, and other exchanges where these options are traded.

When an option is sold or allowed to expire, a sale or exchange has occurred and gain or loss is therefore recognized.[63] The character of the underlying property determines whether the gain or loss from the sale or expiration of the option is capital or ordinary in nature. If the optioned property is a capital asset, the option is treated as a capital asset and capital gain or loss is recognized on the sale or exchange.

EXAMPLE I5-74 ▶ On March 2, 2006, Holly pays $270 for an option to acquire 100 shares of Arkansas Corporation stock for $30 per share at any time before December 10, 2006. As a result of an increase in the market value of the Arkansas stock, the market price of the option increases and Holly sells the option for $600 on August 2, 2006. Because the Arkansas stock is a capital asset in the hands of Holly, the option is a capital asset and she must recognize a STCG of $330 ($600 − $270). ◀

EXAMPLE I5-75 ▶ On October 12, 2005, Mary paid $400 for an option to acquire 100 shares of Portland Corporation stock for $50 per share at any time before February 19, 2006. The price never exceeds $50 before February 19, 2006, and Mary does not exercise the option. Because the option expires, Mary recognizes a STCL of $400 in 2006. ◀

SELF-STUDY QUESTION

Marc writes a call option on stock owned by him and receives $800 on November 1, 2005. The value of the stock declines and the option is allowed to expire on February 15, 2006. When does Marc recognize the $800 gain?

ANSWER

Marc recognizes the gain in 2006 when the transaction is completed.

Transactions in which taxpayers purchase or write options to buy (calls) are quite common today. An investor who anticipates that the market value of a stock or security (e.g., common stock) will increase during the next few months may purchase a call option instead of actually buying the stock. As indicated above, the tax treatment for the option depends on whether the call is exercised, sold, or expires. Someone, however, must be willing to write a call on the stock. Typically an owner of the same stock will write a call option. The writer of the call receives a payment for granting the right to purchase the stock at a fixed price within a given period of time.

---

[58] Sec. 1278(a)(2)(C).
[59] $100,000 × .25% × 18 years = $4,500.
[60] Sec. 1276(a)(1).
[61] Sec. 1276(b)(1). A taxpayer may elect to use the constant interest rate method (see Sec. 1276(b)(2)).

[62] Rev. Rul. 58-234, 1958-1 C.B. 279.
[63] Sec. 1234(a).

If the call is exercised, the writer of the call adds the amount received for the call to the sales price to determine the amount realized.[64] If the call is not exercised within the given time period and thus expires, the writer retains the amount received for the option and recognizes a STCG in the year the call expires. The gain is short-term even if the option is written and held for more than a year.

EXAMPLE I5-76 ▶ Sam owns 100 shares of Madison Corporation common stock, which he purchased on May 1, 1999, for $4,000. On November 8, 2006, Sam writes a call that gives Joan, an investor, the option to purchase Sam's 100 shares of Madison stock at $60 per share any time before April 19, 2007. The current market price of Madison stock is $56 per share, and Sam receives $520 for writing the call. If the call is exercised, Sam has a LTCG of $2,520 [($6,000 + $520) − $4,000] in the year the call is exercised. If the call is not exercised and expires on April 19, 2007, Sam must recognize a STCG of $520 in 2007. ◀

EXAMPLE I5-77 ▶ Assume the same facts as in Example I5-76, and consider the tax treatment for Joan, the holder of the call. If Joan exercises the call, the basis of the stock is $6,520 ($6,000 + $520). If she does not exercise the call, a STCL of $520 is recognized. If Joan sells the call, the amount received is compared with her basis in the call ($520) to compute Joan's gain or loss. ◀

PATENTS

To encourage technological progress and to clarify whether a transfer of rights to a patent is capital gain or ordinary income, Congress created Sec. 1235, which allows the holder of a patent to treat the gain resulting from the transfer of all substantial rights in a patent as LTCG. This tax treatment is more favorable than that accorded to producers of artistic, literary, and musical works, who receive ordinary rather than capital gain from the sale of their works.

KEY POINT

A copyright held by a taxpayer whose personal efforts created it is omitted from the definition of a capital asset. However, a patent can be considered a capital asset. In effect, the tax law could be said to favor individuals whose efforts lead to scientific or technological advancement.

REQUIREMENTS FOR CAPITAL GAIN TREATMENT. Section 1235 provides that the transfer of all substantial rights to a patent by the holder of the patent is treated as a sale or exchange of a capital asset that has been held long-term. Thus, long-term capital gain is recognized on the transfer of a patent regardless of its holding period or the character of the asset. Favorable long-term capital gain treatment applies even if the transferor of the patent receives periodic payments contingent on the productivity, use, or disposition of the property transferred.[65]

EXAMPLE I5-78 ▶ Clay invents a small utensil used to peel shrimp. He has a patent on the utensil and transfers all rights to the patent to a manufacturing company. Clay receives $100,000 plus 40 cents per utensil sold. Because Sec. 1235 applies, the total of the lump-sum payment and the royalty payments received less his cost basis for the patent is recognized as a LTCG. ◀

KEY POINT

Note that Sam in Example I5-76 did not have to recognize gross income when he received $520 on November 8.

SUBSTANTIAL RIGHTS. The principal requirement in Sec. 1235 is that the holder must transfer all substantial rights to the patent. The Regulations state that the circumstances of the whole transaction should be considered in determining whether all substantial rights to a patent have been transferred.[66] All substantial rights have not been transferred if the patent rights of the purchaser are limited geographically within the country of issuance or the rights are for a period less than a patent's remaining life.

EXAMPLE I5-79 ▶ Bruce, an inventor, transfers one of his U.S. patents on a manufacturing process to a manufacturer located in Utah. The manufacturer's rights to use the patent are limited to the state of Utah. Because the use of the patent is limited to a geographical area, all substantial rights have not been transferred, and Sec. 1235 does not apply. Payments received for the use of the patent are royalties and taxed as ordinary income. ◀

DEFINITION OF A HOLDER. Long-term capital gain treatment applies only to a holder of the patent rights. For purposes of Sec. 1235, a holder is an individual whose efforts created the property or an individual who acquires the patent rights from the cre-

---

[64] Rev. Rul. 58-234, 1958-1 C.B. 279.
[65] Sec. 1235(a).

[66] Reg. Sec. 1.1235-2(b).

ator for valuable consideration before the property covered by the patent is placed in service or used. Furthermore, the acquiring individual may not be related to the creator or be the creator's employer.

Section 1235 may not be used by corporate taxpayers because corporations are not permitted to be classified as holders. Although a partnership is not permitted to be a holder, individual partners may qualify as holders to the extent of the partner's interest in the patent owned by the partnership.

EXAMPLE 15-80 ▶ Joy purchases a patent from Martin, whose efforts created the patent. The purchase occurs before the property is placed in service or used. Joy and Martin are unrelated individuals, and Joy is not Martin's employer. For purposes of Sec. 1235, both Joy and Martin qualify as holders. ◀

FRANCHISES, TRADEMARKS, AND TRADE NAMES

ADDITIONAL COMMENT

The scope of Sec. 1253 is very broad. A franchise "includes an agreement which gives one of the parties to the agreement the right to distribute, sell, or provide goods, services, or facilities within a specified area."

Before the enactment of Sec. 1253, significant uncertainty existed as to whether the transfer of a franchise, trademark, or trade name should be treated as a sale or exchange or as a licensing agreement. If the transfer is tantamount to a sale of the property, payments received should be treated by the transferor as a return of capital and capital gain, and the transferee should be required to capitalize and amortize such payments. However, if the transfer represents a licensing agreement, the transferor should recognize ordinary income and the transferee should receive an ordinary deduction for such payments.

Section 1253, which applies to the granting of a franchise, trademark, or trade name, as well as renewals and transfers to third parties, attempts to resolve the uncertainty by stating, "A transfer of a franchise, trademark, or trade name shall not be treated as a sale or exchange of a capital asset if the transferor retains any significant power, right, or continuing interest with respect to the subject matter of the franchise, trademark, or trade name."[67]

REAL-WORLD EXAMPLE

Shaquille O'Neal, the NBA star of the Los Angeles Lakers, has obtained a trademark on his nickname, Shaq. The trademark covers nearly 200 products including athletic shoes, cake decorations, bathroom tissue, bathtub toys, and kites.

The IRC provides examples of some rights that are to be considered a "significant power, right, or continuing interest."[68] These rights include the right to

▶ Disapprove of any assignment.

▶ Terminate the agreement at will.

▶ Prescribe standards of quality for products, product services, and facilities.

▶ Require the exclusive selling or advertising of the transferor's products or services.

▶ Require the transferee to purchase substantially all of its supplies and equipment from the transferor.

If the transferor does not retain any significant power, right, or continuing interest in the property, the transferor treats the transfer as a sale of the franchise and has the benefits of capital gain treatment. However, any amounts received that are contingent on the productivity, use, or disposition of such property must be treated as ordinary income by the transferor.

EXAMPLE 15-81 ▶ Rose, who owns a franchise with a basis of $100,000, transfers the franchise to Ruth and retains no significant power, right, or continuing interest. Rose receives a $250,000 down payment when the agreement is signed and annual payments for five years equal to 10% of all sales in excess of $2,000,000. Rose has a capital gain of $150,000 with respect to the initial payment, but all of the payments received during the next five years will be ordinary income because they are contingent payments. ◀

Under Sec. 1253, the transferee may deduct payments that are contingent on the productivity, use, or disposition of such property as business expenses. Generally, other payments are capitalized and amortized over a period of 15 years.[69] In practice, payments received for the transfer of a franchise are generally treated as ordinary income to the transferor and are deductible by the transferee because in most franchise agreements the transferor desires to maintain significant powers, rights, or continuing interests in the franchise operation. Also, in many instances the payments are, in part, predicated on the success of the franchised business and are, therefore, established as contingent payments.

---

[67] Sec. 1253(a). Section 1253(e) prevents the basic Sec. 1253 rules from applying to the transfer of a professional sports franchise.

[68] Sec. 1253(b)(2).

[69] Sec. 197(a).

LEASE CANCELLATION PAYMENTS

A lease arrangement may be terminated before the lease period expires, and a lease cancellation payment may be made as consideration for the other party's agreement to terminate the lease. Either a lessor or a lessee may receive such a payment because the payment is normally made by the person who wants to cancel the lease. The tax treatment may differ significantly depending on which party is the recipient.

PAYMENTS RECEIVED BY LESSOR.   The Supreme Court has ruled that lease cancellation payments received by a lessor are treated as ordinary income on the basis that the payments represent a substitute for rent.[70] Lease cancellation payments are included in the lessor's income in the year received, even if the lessor uses an accrual method.[71]

PAYMENTS RECEIVED BY LESSEE.   Payments received by a lessee for canceling a lease are considered amounts received in exchange for the lease.[72] If the lease is a capital asset, any gain or loss is a capital gain or loss.

EXAMPLE I5-82 ▶ Jim has a three-year lease on a house used as his personal residence. The lessor has an opportunity to sell the house and has agreed to pay $1,000 to Jim to cancel the lease. Assuming that Jim has no basis in the lease, the gain of $1,000 is capital gain because the lease is a capital asset. ◀

HOLDING PERIOD

The length of time an asset is held before it is disposed of (i.e., the *holding period*) is an important factor in determining whether any gain or loss resulting from the disposition of a capital asset is treated as long-term or short-term. To be classified as a long-term capital gain or loss, the capital asset must be held more than one year.[73] To determine the holding period, the day of acquisition is excluded and the disposal date is included.[74]

If the date of disposition is the same date as the date of acquisition, but a year later, the asset is considered to have been held for only one year. If the property is held for an additional day, the holding period is more than one year.

EXAMPLE I5-83 ▶ Arnie purchased a capital asset on April 20, 2005, and sells the asset at a gain on April 21, 2006. The gain is classified as a LTCG. If the asset is sold on or before April 20, 2006, the gain is a STCG. ◀

The fact that all months do not have the same number of days is not a factor in determining the one-year period. Acquisitions made on the last day of any month must be held until the first day of the thirteenth subsequent month in order to have been held for more than one year.

EXAMPLE I5-84 ▶ Alford sells stock held as an investment and recognizes a gain. If the capital asset was purchased on May 31, 2005, the gain is LTCG subject to the 15% or 5% rate if the asset is sold on or after June 1, 2006. If sold on or before May 31, 2006, the 15% and 5% rates do not apply. ◀

PROPERTY RECEIVED AS A GIFT

If a person receives property as a gift and uses the donor's basis to determine the gain or loss from a sale or exchange, the donor's holding period is added to the donee's holding period.[75] In other words, the donee's holding period includes the donor's holding period. If, however, the donee's basis is the FMV of the property on the date of the gift, the donee's holding period starts on the day after the date of the gift. This situation occurs when the FMV is less than the donor's basis on the date of the gift and the property is subsequently sold at a loss.

---

[70] *Walter M. Hort v. CIR,* 25 AFTR 1207, 41-1 USTC ¶9354 (USSC, 1941).
[71] *Farrelly-Walsh, Inc.,* 13 B.T.A. 923 (1928).
[72] Sec. 1241.
[73] Sec. 1222. A six-month holding period was applied to property acquired after June 27, 1984 and before January 1, 1988.

[74] *H. M. Hooper,* 26 B.T.A. 758 (1932), and Rev. Rul. 70-598, 1970-2 C.B. 168.
[75] Sec. 1223(1) and Reg. Sec. 1.1223-1(b).

EXAMPLE I5-85 ▶ Cindy receives a capital asset as a gift from Marc on July 4, 2006, when the asset has a $4,000 FMV. Marc acquired the property on April 12, 2006, for $3,400. If Cindy sells the asset after April 12, 2007, any gain or loss is LTCG or LTCL. Cindy's basis is the donor's cost because the FMV of the property is higher than the donor's basis on the date of the gift. Because Cindy takes Marc's basis, Marc's holding period is included. ◀

EXAMPLE I5-86 ▶ Roy receives a capital asset as a gift from Diane on September 12, 2006, when the asset has a $6,000 FMV. Diane acquired the asset on July 1, 2005, for $6,500. If the asset is sold at a gain (i.e., for more than $6,500), Roy's holding period starts on July 1, 2005, the date when Diane acquired the property, because the donor's basis of $6,500 is used by Roy to compute the gain. If the asset is sold at a loss (i.e., for less than $6,000), Roy's holding period does not start until the day after the date of the gift, September 13, 2006, because Roy's basis is the $6,000 FMV. The FMV is used to compute the loss because it is less than the donor's basis on the date of the gift. ◀

ADDITIONAL COMMENT

The provision permitting the holding period of property received from a decedent to be deemed to be long-term is a rule of convenience. It is not necessary to try to determine when the decedent actually acquired the property.

PROPERTY RECEIVED FROM A DECEDENT

The holding period of property received from a decedent is always deemed to be long-term. If the person who receives the property from the decedent sells the property within one year after the decedent's death, the property is considered to be held for more than one year regardless of how long the property is actually held.[76]

EXAMPLE I5-87 ▶ The executor of Paul's estate sells certain securities for $41,000 on September 2, 2006, which are valued in the estate at their FMV of $40,000 on June 5, 2006, the date of Paul's death. The estate has a LTCG of $1,000 because the securities are considered to have been held long-term. The gain is taxed at 15% or 5%. ◀

NONTAXABLE EXCHANGES

ADDITIONAL COMMENT

The like-kind exchange rules under Sec. 1031 allow taxpayers to trade certain types of business and investment properties with no tax consequences arising from the exchange.

In a nontaxable exchange, the basis of the property received is determined by taking into account the basis of the property given in the exchange. If the properties are capital assets or Sec. 1231 assets, the holding period of the property received includes the holding period of the surrendered property.[77] In essence, the holding period of the property given up in a tax-free exchange is tacked on to the holding period of the property received in the exchange.

RECEIPT OF NONTAXABLE STOCK DIVIDENDS AND STOCK RIGHTS

If a shareholder receives nontaxable stock dividends or stock rights, the holding period of the stock received as a dividend or the stock rights received includes the holding period for the stock owned by the shareholder.[78] However, if the stock rights are exercised, the holding period for the stock purchased begins with the date of exercise.

EXAMPLE I5-88 ▶ As a result of owning Circle Corporation stock acquired three years ago, Paula receives nontaxable stock rights on June 5, 2006. Any gain or loss on the sale of the rights is long-term, regardless of whether any basis is allocated to the rights, because the holding period of the rights includes the holding period of the stock. ◀

EXAMPLE I5-89 ▶ Assume the same facts as in Example I5-88, except that the stock rights are exercised on August 20, 2006. The holding period for the newly acquired Circle stock begins on the date of exercise. ◀

 STOP & THINK

Question: Carter owns 500 shares of Okoboji, Inc. (current market price of $310) with a basis of $101,500 acquired three years ago. In May of the current year, she receives 500 stock rights and exercises those rights that entitle her to purchase 500 shares of Okoboji at $300 per share. The current market price of the stock right is $40 per right. She plans to sell the 500 shares obtained by exercising the stock rights in January when she expects the market price to be $400 per share. Why should she elect to allocate basis to the stock rights?

Solution: If she does not allocate basis, her STCG will be $50,000 ($200,000 − $150,000). If she allocates basis to the stock rights, the basis of the 500 shares obtained

---

[76] Sec. 1223(11).
[77] Sec. 1223(1).
[78] Sec. 1223(5) and Reg. Sec. 1.1223-1(e).

when she exercises the rights is $161,600 ($150,000 + $11,600), and her STCG will be $38,400 ($200,000 − $161,600). Note that Carter might benefit by waiting a few months before selling because the gain might then be LTCG. She could sell the original 500 shares and have a LTCG.

JUSTIFICATION FOR PREFERENTIAL TREATMENT OF NET CAPITAL GAINS

HISTORICAL NOTE

In part the preferential treatment of net capital gains was repealed in the Tax Reform Act of 1986 because Congress believed that the reduction of individual tax rates on such forms of capital income as business profits, interest, dividends, and short-term capital gains eliminated the need for a reduced rate for net capital gains.

Preferential treatment for capital gains was first created by the Revenue Act of 1921, which became effective on January 1, 1922. Despite almost continuous controversy concerning the need for preferential treatment, some form of preferential treatment for capital gains has existed since 1922. The range of controversy concerning the need for preferential tax treatment for capital gains is wide. Some maintain that capital gains do not represent income and should not be taxed, whereas others maintain that capital gains are no different from any other type of income and should be taxed accordingly.[79] A few of the most common arguments are discussed below.

MOBILITY OF CAPITAL

Without some form of preferential treatment, taxpayers who own appreciated capital assets may be unwilling to sell or exchange the asset if high tax rates exist, despite the presence of more attractive investment opportunities. In essence, the taxpayer may be "locked in" to holding an appreciated capital asset instead of shifting resources to more profitable investments.

EXAMPLE I5-90 ▶ Carmen owns Missouri Corporation stock with a $4,000 basis and a $20,000 FMV. She anticipates that the future after-tax annual return will be 10% on the Missouri stock and 12% on Kansas Corporation stock that has a similar level of risk. Assume her marginal tax rate is 35% (without consideration of favorable capital gain rates). Without preferential treatment of capital gains, Carmen will have to pay a tax of $5,600 ($16,000 × 0.35) on the sale of the Missouri stock and will have only $14,400 ($20,000 − $5,600) to invest in the Kansas stock. With a 12% return, she will receive an investment return of only $1,728 ($14,400 × 0.12), as compared with $2,000 ($20,000 × 0.10) if she maintains the investment in the Missouri stock. ◀

The "locked-in" effect is reduced when the difference between ordinary income tax rates and net capital gain rates is small. For a brief period in the 1990s, both the top ordinary income rate and the net capital gain rate were 28%. In this case, there is no "locked-in" effect. Today, with the top ordinary income rate being 35% and the maximum rate of 15% for ANCG, there is a "locked-in" effect in the tax law. The "locked-in" effect is even stronger for older taxpayers when one considers that the basis of inherited property is FMV at time of death.

MITIGATION OF THE EFFECTS OF INFLATION AND THE PROGRESSIVE TAX SYSTEM

Because the tax laws do not generally reflect the effect of changes in purchasing power due to inflation, the sale or exchange of a capital asset may produce inequitable results. In fact, taxes may have to be paid even where a transaction results in an inflation-adjusted loss.

EXAMPLE I5-91 ▶ Beverly purchased a capital asset nine years ago for $100,000. If the asset is sold today for $180,000 and the general price level has increased by 100% during the nine-year period, Beverly will have a taxable gain of $80,000, despite suffering an inflation-adjusted loss of $20,000 [$180,000 sale price − ($100,000 × 200%)]. ◀

---

[79] Walter J. Blum, "A Handy Summary of the Capital Gains Argument," *Taxes—The Tax Magazine*, 35 (April 1957), pp. 247–66.

With a progressive tax system, the failure to adjust for inflation creates an even greater distortion. However, it should be noted that this distortion applies to all assets, not just capital assets.

LOWERS THE COST OF CAPITAL

By reducing the tax rate on capital gains, investors are more willing to provide businesses with capital and the cost of capital is reduced. A lower cost of capital encourages capital formation to create more jobs and improve our competitive position in the global economy. Reducing the cost of capital is particularly important for the formation and growth of small business.

TAX PLANNING CONSIDERATIONS

SELECTION OF PROPERTY TO TRANSFER BY GIFT

Many tax reasons exist for making gifts of property, although the donor may incur a gift tax liability if the gift is a taxable gift. For example, taxpayers may give income-producing property to a taxpayer subject to a lower tax rate, or property expected to appreciate in the future may be given away to reduce estate taxes. Individuals may annually give property of $12,000[80] or less to a donee without making a taxable gift.[81]

EXAMPLE I5-92 ▶ Maya, who is single, owns marketable securities with a $6,200 basis and $10,400 FMV. She makes gifts of the marketable securities to Phil and cash of $12,000 to Roy. Because of the $12,000 annual exclusion per donee, Maya's gifts are not taxable gifts. ◀

EXAMPLE I5-93 ▶ Harry, who is single, makes a gift of land with a $312,000 basis and a $1,212,000 FMV to Rita. Harry's taxable gift is $1,200,000 ($1,212,000 − $12,000), and he incurs a gift tax liability. Rita's basis is $312,000 + 75% of the gift tax paid by Harry [($1,212,000 − $312,000)/$1,200,000 = 75%]. ◀

Individuals often reduce future estate taxes by making gifts. By using the annual exclusion, an individual may reduce future estate taxes and avoid the gift tax.

EXAMPLE I5-94 ▶ Christine owns only one asset—cash of $2,200,000—and has no liabilities. In December of the current year, she gives $12,000 to each of her five grandchildren. Because of the $12,000 annual exclusion per donee, Christine's gifts are not taxable gifts. By making the gifts, she reduces her potential gross estate by $60,000 (5 × $12,000). ◀

The selection of which property to give is important if one is attempting to reduce future estate taxes. It is generally preferable to make gifts of properties that are expected to significantly increase in value during the postgift period before the donor's death. Any increases in value after the date of the gift are not included in the donor's gross estate.

EXAMPLE I5-95 ▶ In 1994, Hal owned Sun Corporation stock with a $100,000 FMV and Union Corporation stock with a $100,000 FMV. Hal expected the Sun stock to increase in value at a moderate rate and the Union stock to increase at a substantial rate. In 1994, Hal made a gift of the Union stock to Dana. Hal's taxable gift in 1994 was $90,000 ($100,000 − $10,000). Hal dies in the current year when the FMVs of the Sun and Union stocks are $180,000 and $425,000, respectively. The postgift appreciation of $325,000 ($425,000 − $100,000) is not included in Hal's gross estate. By giving the Union stock instead of the Sun stock in 1994, Hal reduces his gross estate by $245,000. ◀

Gifts are often made for income tax purposes to shift income to other family members who are in a lower income tax bracket than the donor.

---

[80] Before 2005, the annual exclusion was $11,000.   [81] Sec. 2503(b).

EXAMPLE I5-96 ▶ In 2006, Anne has a marginal tax rate of 33% and owns Atlantic Corporation bonds, which have a $5,000 basis and $8,000 FMV. The bonds pay interest of $1,000 per year. If Anne gives the bonds to her dependent child, the interest income is shifted to the child. If the child has no other income, the child's taxable income is $150 ($1,000 − $850 standard deduction), and the child's marginal tax rate is 10%. The gift results in an annual income tax savings to the family unit of $315 [(0.33 × $1,000) − (0.10 × $150)]. The rate of tax that is imposed may be the parent's rate (see Chapter I2) if the child is less than 14 years old and has net unearned income in excess of $1,700.

In addition to shifting the interest income, Anne has also shifted a potential gain of $3,000. The child's basis for the bonds is $5,000 because the donee takes the donor's basis when the FMV of the property at the time of the gift is greater than the donor's basis. No gain is recognized by Anne when the gift is made, and a future sale of the property by the child may be taxed at a lower income tax rate. ◀

Although gifts of appreciated property may generate desirable income tax benefits, it is not usually advantageous to make a gift of property that has an FMV less than its basis because the donee's basis for determining a loss is the FMV. The excess of the donor's basis over the FMV at the time of the gift may never generate any tax benefit for the donor or the donee. Therefore, the donor should sell the asset and make a gift of the proceeds if the loss on the sale is deductible.

EXAMPLE I5-97 ▶ Bob owns Red Corporation stock with an $8,000 basis and $6,000 FMV, which is held as an investment. Bob wishes to make a graduation gift of the marketable securities to Angela, although he expects her to sell the stock and purchase a car. If Angela sells the stock for $6,000, no gain or loss is recognized because her loss basis for the stock is $6,000. In addition, no loss is recognized by Bob on the gift of the stock to Angela. Instead of giving the stock, Bob should sell it to recognize a $2,000 capital loss and then give the proceeds from the sale to Angela. ◀

SELF-STUDY QUESTION

Doug owns IBM Corporation shares, which have a $50,000 FMV and basis of $75,000. Doug makes a deathbed telephone call to his stockbroker and sells the IBM shares. Assuming that Doug is in the 35% bracket and had no other capital gains or losses, calculate the tax savings associated with the sale.

ANSWER

Doug saves $1,050 ($3,000 × 0.35). It should be noted that the loss is limited to $3,000; if Doug dies, the unused capital loss of $22,000 is lost.

The effect of gift taxes paid by the donor on the donee's basis for property received is another reason why it may be more advantageous to give appreciated property rather than property with an FMV less than its basis. A portion of the gift taxes paid as a result of giving appreciated property is added to the property's basis. However, payment of gift taxes due to the gift of property that has an FMV less than its basis does not result in an increase in the donee's basis.

SELECTION OF PROPERTY TO TRANSFER AT TIME OF DEATH

An integral part of gift and estate planning is the selection of property to be transferred to family members and others both during the taxpayer's lifetime and upon death. Usually, taxpayers find it advantageous to retain highly appreciated property in their estates and transfer such property at death to the taxpayer's heirs because the basis of the inherited property will be increased to its FMV at the date of death (or six months from the date of death if the alternate valuation date is elected). Of course, the impact of gift and estate taxes also play a major role in this planning process.

Investment and business assets that have declined in value (i.e., the FMV is less than the basis) should normally be sold before death to obtain an income tax deduction for the loss. If the property is not sold or otherwise disposed of before death, the basis of the inherited property is reduced to its FMV.

EXAMPLE I5-98 ▶ Paul owns two farms of similar size and quality. Each farm has a $500,000 FMV. Paul's basis for the first farm is $100,000, and his basis for the second farm is $430,000. Eventually, Paul plans for both farms to be owned by Amy. However, he would like to transfer ownership of one farm now and retain the other farm until his death. Paul should make a gift of the second farm and transfer the first farm to Amy upon his death because the second farm has appreciated less in value. When Paul dies and devises the first farm to Amy, she will have a basis for the property equal to its FMV at the date of death even though Paul's basis is only $100,000. ◀

COMPLIANCE AND PROCEDURAL CONSIDERATIONS

DOCUMENTATION OF BASIS

KEY POINT

Many taxpayers do not maintain adequate records that can be used to document the basis of their most important asset, their personal residence. For example, taxpayers can increase the basis of their residence if they have the driveway paved or add a new room or porch.

The importance of being able to determine and document the basis of assets acquired by a taxpayer cannot be overemphasized. Accurate records of asset acquisitions, dispositions, and adjustments to basis are essential. When more than one asset is acquired at the same time, the amount paid must be allocated among the assets acquired based on their relative FMVs. Subsequent adjustments to basis, such as those due to capital improvements and depreciation deductions, must be documented.

Because the basis of property can be determined by reference to another person's basis for that asset (e.g., gifts), taxpayers should be particularly aware of obtaining documentation for that basis at the time of the transfer. In the case of a gift, the taxpayer's basis may be affected by any gift tax paid by the donor. A copy of the donor's gift tax return is useful in documenting the upward adjustment to the donor's basis in determining the donee's basis.

KEY POINT

Schedule D refers to 28% gain which is NCG taxed at a maximum rate of 28% (collectible gain and Sec. 1202 gain).

Taxpayers who inherit property may use the decedent's federal Estate Tax Return (Form 706) to determine the FMV at the time of the decedent's death or FMV as of the alternate valuation date. However, the appraised value used for estate tax purposes is only presumptively correct for basis purposes. Although the FMVs used to determine the estate tax are typically used to determine basis, neither the taxpayer nor the IRS is barred from using an FMV for basis purposes that differs from the values used for the estate tax return.[82]

REPORTING OF CAPITAL GAINS AND LOSSES ON SCHEDULE D

Capital gains and losses are reported by individuals on Schedule D, which is then attached to Form 1040. Part I is used to report short-term capital gains and losses, and Part II is used to report long-term capital gains and losses. Part III is a summary of Parts I and II.

Capital gains due to installment sales are first reported on a separate form before being included on Schedule D. The taxpayer's share of capital gains and losses from partnerships, S corporations, and fiduciaries is reported in Parts I and II on lines 5 and 12. The carryover of capital losses is also included in Parts I and II on lines 6 and 14.

A filled-in copy of Schedule D and a Qualified Dividends and Capital Gains Tax Worksheet are shown in Figure I5-1. It includes computations relating to the information in Example I5-99.

EXAMPLE I5-99 ▶

Virgil Schmidt, a single taxpayer, uses the following information to prepare his Schedule D for 2005. Virgil received $8,000 of qualified dividends during the year. He sold 200 shares of Tennis Corporation stock for $13,000 on June 20, 2005. The shares were purchased on October 2, 2004, for $8,700. He has an STCL carryforward from 2004 of $8,200. He sold a piano for $4,000 on May 30, 2005. The piano was purchased on April 12, 1995, for $2,500 and used by his two sons. Virgil also sold 500 shares of Golf Corporation stock for $18,000 on November 30, 2005. He had purchased the stock on April 1, 1999, for $10,000.

Virgil has STCG of $4,300 that is offset by $8,200 of STCL carryforward on line 6. His NSTCL of $3,900 ($8,200 − $4,300) is shown on line 7. His $1,500 LTCG as a result of the sale of the piano (not a collectible) and his $8,000 LTCG from the sale of the Golf Corporation stock are on line 8. Thus, Virgil has a NLTCG of $9,500. He has ANCG of $5,600 ($9,500 − $3,900).

Because Virgil has ANCG of $5,600 and no 28% rate gains or unrecaptured Sec. 1250 gains, he computes his tax on the Qualified Dividends and Capital Gain Tax Worksheet. The preferential treatment for dividends and capital gains saves Virgil $1,768 of federal income taxes in 2005.

Virgil's taxable income including the above dividends and capital gains is $120,000. ◀

---

[82] Rev. Rul. 54-97, 1954-1 C.B. 113 and *Achille F. Ford v. U.S.*, 5 AFTR 2d 1157, 60-1 USTC ¶9375 (Ct. Cls., 1960).

Capital Gains and Losses

▶ Attach to Form 1040.   ▶ See Instructions for Schedule D (Form 1040).

▶ Use Schedule D-1 to list additional transactions for lines 1 and 8.

OMB No. 1545-0074

20**05**

Attachment
Sequence No. **12**

Name(s) shown on Form 1040

Virgil Schmidt

Your social security number

Part I — Short-Term Capital Gains and Losses—Assets Held One Year or Less

(a) Description of property (Example: 100 sh. XYZ Co.)	(b) Date acquired (Mo., day, yr.)	(c) Date sold (Mo., day, yr.)	(d) Sales price (see page D-6 of the instructions)	(e) Cost or other basis (see page D-6 of the instructions)	(f) Gain or (loss) Subtract (e) from (d)
1 *200 sh. Tennis Corp.*	*10-2-04*	*6-20-05*	*13,000*	*8,700*	*4,300*

2 Enter your short-term totals, if any, from Schedule D-1, line 2	**2**		
3 **Total short-term sales price amounts.** Add lines 1 and 2 in column (d)	**3**	*13,000*	

4 Short-term gain from Form 6252 and short-term gain or (loss) from Forms 4684, 6781, and 8824	**4**	
5 Net short-term gain or (loss) from partnerships, S corporations, estates, and trusts from Schedule(s) K-1	**5**	
6 Short-term capital loss carryover. Enter the amount, if any, from line 8 of your **Capital Loss Carryover Worksheet** on page D-6 of the instructions	**6**	(*8,200*)
7 **Net short-term capital gain or (loss).** Combine lines 1 through 6 in column (f)	**7**	*(3,900)*

Part II — Long-Term Capital Gains and Losses—Assets Held More Than One Year

(a) Description of property (Example: 100 sh. XYZ Co.)	(b) Date acquired (Mo., day, yr.)	(c) Date sold (Mo., day, yr.)	(d) Sales price (see page D-6 of the instructions)	(e) Cost or other basis (see page D-6 of the instructions)	(f) Gain or (loss) Subtract (e) from (d)
8 *Piano*	*4-12-95*	*5-3-05*	*4,000*	*2,500*	*1,500*
500 sh. Golf Corporation	*4-1-99*	*11-30-05*	*18,000*	*10,000*	*8,000*

9 Enter your long-term totals, if any, from Schedule D-1, line 9	**9**		
10 **Total long-term sales price amounts.** Add lines 8 and 9 in column (d)	**10**	*22,000*	

11 Gain from Form 4797, Part I; long-term gain from Forms 2439 and 6252; and long-term gain or (loss) from Forms 4684, 6781, and 8824	**11**	
12 Net long-term gain or (loss) from partnerships, S corporations, estates, and trusts from Schedule(s) K-1	**12**	
13 Capital gain distributions. See page D-1 of the instructions	**13**	
14 Long-term capital loss carryover. Enter the amount, if any, from line 13 of your **Capital Loss Carryover Worksheet** on page D-6 of the instructions	**14**	( )
15 **Net long-term capital gain or (loss).** Combine lines 8 through 14 in column (f). Then go to Part III on the back	**15**	*9,500*

For Paperwork Reduction Act Notice, see Form 1040 instructions.   Cat. No. 11338H   Schedule D (Form 1040) 2005

FIGURE 15-1   ▶   PARTS I–II OF SCHEDULE D FOR EXAMPLE 15-99

5-34

Part III   **Summary**

16	Combine lines 7 and 15 and enter the result. If line 16 is a loss, skip lines 17 through 20, and go to line 21. If a gain, enter the gain on Form 1040, line 13, and then go to line 17 below . .	**16**	**5,600**

17   Are lines 15 and 16 **both** gains?
     ☐ **Yes.** Go to line 18.
     ☑ **No.** Skip lines 18 through 21, and go to line 22.

18	Enter the amount, if any, from line 7 of the **28% Rate Gain Worksheet** on page D-7 of the instructions . . . . ▶	**18**	
19	Enter the amount, if any, from line 18 of the **Unrecaptured Section 1250 Gain Worksheet** on page D-8 of the instructions . . . . ▶	**19**	

20   Are lines 18 and 19 **both** zero or blank?
     ☑ **Yes.** Complete Form 1040 through line 43, and then complete the **Qualified Dividends and Capital Gain Tax Worksheet** on page 38 of the Instructions for Form 1040. **Do not** complete lines 21 and 22 below.

     ☐ **No.** Complete Form 1040 through line 43, and then complete the **Schedule D Tax Worksheet** on page D-9 of the instructions. **Do not** complete lines 21 and 22 below.

21   If line 16 is a loss, enter here and on Form 1040, line 13, the **smaller** of:

     • The loss on line 16 or
     • ($3,000), or if married filing separately, ($1,500)   }   . . . .   **21** (   )

     Note. When figuring which amount is smaller, treat both amounts as positive numbers.

22   Do you have qualified dividends on Form 1040, line 9b?
     ☐ **Yes.** Complete Form 1040 through line 43, and then complete the **Qualified Dividends and Capital Gain Tax Worksheet** on page 38 of the Instructions for Form 1040.
     ☑ **No.** Complete the rest of Form 1040.

                                                   Schedule D (Form 1040) 2005

FIGURE I5-1   ▶   PART III OF SCHEDULE D FOR EXAMPLE I5-99

Qualified Dividends and Capital Gain Tax Worksheet—Line 44

Keep for Your Records

Before you begin: ✓ See the instructions for line 44 on page 37 to see if you can use this worksheet to figure your tax.

✓ If you do not have to file Schedule D and you received capital gain distributions, be sure you checked the box on line 13 of Form 1040.

1. Enter the amount from Form 1040, line 43	1.	**120,000**
2. Enter the amount from Form 1040, line 9b 2. **8,000**		
3. Are you filing Schedule D?		
☑ **Yes.** Enter the **smaller** of line 15 or 16 of Schedule D, but do not enter less than -0- ⎫ ☐ **No.** Enter the amount from Form 1040, line 13 ⎭	3.	**5,600**
4. Add lines 2 and 3	4.	**13,600**
5. If you are claiming investment interest expense on Form 4952, enter the amount from line 4g of that form. Otherwise, enter -0-	5.	**-0-**
6. Subtract line 5 from line 4. If zero or less, enter -0-	6.	**13,600**
7. Subtract line 6 from line 1. If zero or less, enter -0-	7.	**106,400**
8. Enter the **smaller** of: • The amount on line 1, or • $29,700 if single or married filing separately, $59,400 if married filing jointly or qualifying widow(er), $39,800 if head of household. ⎫⎬⎭	8.	**29,700**
9. Is the amount on line 7 equal to or more than the amount on line 8? ☑ **Yes.** Skip lines 9 through 11; go to line 12 and check the "No" box. ☐ **No.** Enter the amount from line 7	9.	
10. Subtract line 9 from line 8	10.	
11. Multiply line 10 by 5% (.05)	11.	
12. Are the amounts on lines 6 and 10 the same? ☐ **Yes.** Skip lines 12 through 15; go to line 16. ☑ **No.** Enter the **smaller** of line 1 or line 6	12.	**13,600**
13. Enter the amount from line 10 (if line 10 is blank, enter -0-)	13.	**-0-**
14. Subtract line 13 from line 12.............................	14.	**13,600**
15. Multiply line 14 by 15% (.15)	15.	**2,040**
16. Figure the tax on the amount on line 7. Use the Tax Table or Tax Computation Worksheet, whichever applies	16.	**24,299**
17. Add lines 11, 15, and 16.............................	17.	**26,339**
18. Figure the tax on the amount on line 1. Use the Tax Table or Tax Computation Worksheet, whichever applies	18.	**28,107**
19. **Tax on all taxable income.** Enter the **smaller** of line 17 or line 18. Also include this amount on Form 1040, line 44	19.	**26,339**

FIGURE I5-1 ▶ QUALIFIED DIVIDENDS AND CAPITAL GAIN TAX WORKSHEET–LINE 43 FOR EXAMPLE I5-99

On the following pages are four worksheets that taxayers use to compute their tax if they have any 28% rate gains, unrecaptured Section 1250 gain or adjusted net capital gain (ANCG).

Taxpayers use the 28% Rate Gain Worksheet below if they have gains from collectibles or Sec. 1202 stock.

28% Rate Gain Worksheet—Line 18

Keep for Your Records

1. Enter the total of all collectibles gain or (loss) from items you reported on line 8, column (f), of Schedules D and D-1 . . . . **1.** _____

2. Enter as a positive number the amount of any section 1202 exclusion you reported on line 8, column (f), of Schedules D and D-1 . . . . **2.** _____

3. Enter the total of all collectibles gain or (loss) from Form 4684, line 4 (but only if Form 4684, line 15, is more than zero); Form 6252; Form 6781, Part II; and Form 8824 . . . . **3.** _____

4. Enter the total of any collectibles gain reported to you on:
   - Form 1099-DIV, box 2d;
   - Form 2439, box 1d; and
   - Schedule K-1 from a partnership, S corporation, estate, or trust. } . . . . **4.** _____

5. Enter your long-term capital loss carryovers from Schedule D, line 14, and Schedule K-1 (Form 1041), box 11, code C . . . . **5.** (_____)

6. If Schedule D, line 7, is a (loss), enter that (loss) here. Otherwise, enter -0- . . . . **6.** (_____)

7. Combine lines 1 through 6. If zero or less, enter -0-. If more than zero, also enter this amount on Schedule D, line 18 . . . . **7.** _____

Taxpayers use the Unrecaptured Section 1250 Gain Worksheet below if they have gains from depreciable real estate.

Unrecaptured Section 1250 Gain Worksheet—Line 19

Keep for Your Records

If you are not reporting a gain on Form 4797, line 7, skip lines 1 through 9 and go to line 10.

1. If you have a section 1250 property in Part III of Form 4797 for which you made an entry in Part I of Form 4797 (but not on Form 6252), enter the **smaller** of line 22 or line 24 of Form 4797 for that property. If you did not have any such property, go to line 4. If you had more than one such property, see instructions . . . . **1.** _____

2. Enter the amount from Form 4797, line 26g, for the property for which you made an entry on line 1 . . . . **2.** _____

3. Subtract line 2 from line 1 . . . . **3.** _____

4. Enter the total unrecaptured section 1250 gain included on line 26 or line 37 of Form(s) 6252 from installment sales of trade or business property held more than 1 year (see instructions) . . . . **4.** _____

5. Enter the total of any amounts reported to you on a Schedule K-1 from a partnership or an S corporation as "unrecaptured section 1250 gain" . . . . **5.** _____

6. Add lines 3 through 5 . . . . **6.** _____

7. Enter the **smaller** of line 6 or the gain from Form 4797, line 7 . . . . **7.** _____

8. Enter the amount, if any, from Form 4797, line 8 . . . . **8.** _____

9. Subtract line 8 from line 7. If zero or less, enter -0- . . . . **9.** _____

10. Enter the amount of any gain from the sale or exchange of an interest in a partnership attributable to unrecaptured section 1250 gain (see instructions) . . . . **10.** _____

11. Enter the total of any amounts reported to you on a Schedule K-1, Form 1099-DIV, or Form 2439 as "unrecaptured section 1250 gain" from an estate, trust, real estate investment trust, or mutual fund (or other regulated investment company) . . . . **11.** _____

12. Enter the total of any unrecaptured section 1250 gain from sales (including installment sales) or other dispositions of section 1250 property held more than 1 year for which you did not make an entry in Part I of Form 4797 for the year of sale (see instructions) . . . . **12.** _____

13. Add lines 9 through 12 . . . . **13.** _____

14. If you had any section 1202 gain or collectibles gain or (loss), enter the total of lines 1 through 4 of the **28% Rate Gain Worksheet** on page D-7. Otherwise, enter -0- . . . . . . **14.** _____

15. Enter the (loss), if any, from Schedule D, line 7. If Schedule D, line 7, is zero or a gain, enter -0- . . . . **15.** (_____)

16. Enter your long-term capital loss carryovers from Schedule D, line 14, and Schedule K-1 (Form 1041), box 11, code C . . . . **16.** (_____)

17. Combine lines 14 through 16. If the result is a (loss), enter it as a positive amount. If the result is zero or a gain, enter -0- . . . . **17.** _____

18. **Unrecaptured section 1250 gain.** Subtract line 17 from line 13. If zero or less, enter -0-. If more than zero, enter the result here and on Schedule D, line 19 . . . . **18.** _____

5-38 Individuals ▼ Chapter 5

Taxpayers such as Virgil in Example I5-99 use the Qualified Dividends Capital Gain Tax Worksheet below if they either have qualified dividends or ANCG *and* do not have any 28% rate gain property or unrecaptured Section 1250 gain. This worksheet applies the lower preferential tax rates of 5% or 15% for qualified dividends and ANCG.

Qualified Dividends and Capital Gain Tax Worksheet—Line 44

Keep for Your Records

Before you begin:
√ See the instructions for line 44 on page 37 to see if you can use this worksheet to figure your tax.
√ If you do not have to file Schedule D and you received capital gain distributions, be sure you checked the box on line 13 of Form 1040.

1. Enter the amount from Form 1040, line 43 . . . . **1.**

2. Enter the amount from Form 1040, line 9b . . . . **2.**

3. Are you filing Schedule D?
   ☑ **Yes.** Enter the **smaller** of line 15 or 16 of Schedule D, but do not enter less than -0-   **3.**
   ☐ **No.** Enter the amount from Form 1040, line 13

4. Add lines 2 and 3 . . . . **4.**

5. If you are claiming investment interest expense on Form 4952, enter the amount from line 4g of that form. Otherwise, enter -0- . . . . **5.**

6. Subtract line 5 from line 4. If zero or less, enter -0- . . . . **6.**

7. Subtract line 6 from line 1. If zero or less, enter -0- . . . . **7.**

8. Enter the **smaller** of:
   • The amount on line 1, or
   • $29,700 if single or married filing separately, ... **8.**
     $59,400 if married filing jointly or qualifying widow(er),
     $39,800 if head of household.

9. Is the amount on line 7 equal to or more than the amount on line 8?
   ☑ **Yes.** Skip lines 9 through 11; go to line 12 and check the ''No'' box.
   ☐ **No.** Enter the amount from line 7 . . . . **9.**

10. Subtract line 9 from line 8 . . . . **10.**

11. Multiply line 10 by 5% (.05) . . . . **11.**

12. Are the amounts on lines 6 and 10 the same?
    ☐ **Yes.** Skip lines 12 through 15; go to line 16.
    ☑ **No.** Enter the **smaller** of line 1 or line 6 . . . . **12.**

13. Enter the amount from line 10 (if line 10 is blank, enter -0-) . . . . **13.**

14. Subtract line 13 from line 12 . . . . **14.**

15. Multiply line 14 by 15% (.15) . . . . **15.**

16. Figure the tax on the amount on line 7. Use the Tax Table or Tax Computation Worksheet, whichever applies . . . . **16.**

17. Add lines 11, 15, and 16 . . . . **17.**

18. Figure the tax on the amount on line 1. Use the Tax Table or Tax Computation Worksheet, whichever applies . . . . **18.**

19. **Tax on all taxable income.** Enter the **smaller** of line 17 or line 18. Also include this amount on Form 1040, line 44 . . . . **19.**

Taxpayers use the Schedule D Tax Worksheet below if they either have qualified dividends or ANCG *and* they also have either a 28% rate gain or unrecaptured Sec. 1250 gain.

Schedule D Tax Worksheet

Keep for Your Records

Complete this worksheet only if line 18 or line 19 of Schedule D is more than zero. Otherwise, complete the Qualified Dividends and Capital Gain Tax Worksheet on page 38 of the Instructions for Form 1040 to figure your tax.

Exception: Do not use the Qualified Dividends and Capital Gain Tax Worksheet **or** this worksheet to figure your tax if:
- Line 15 or line 16 of Schedule D is zero or less **and** you have no qualified dividends on Form 1040, line 9b, **or**
- Form 1040, line 43, is zero or less.

Instead, see the instructions for Form 1040, line 44.

1. Enter your taxable income from Form 1040, line 43 . . . . **1.**
2. Enter your qualified dividends from Form 1040, line 9b . . . . . **2.**
3. Enter the amount from Form 4952, line 4g **3.**
4. Enter the amount from Form 4952, line 4e* **4.**
5. Subtract line 4 from line 3. If zero or less, enter -0- . . . . **5.**
6. Subtract line 5 from line 2. If zero or less, enter -0- . . . . **6.**
7. Enter the **smaller** of line 15 or line 16 of Schedule D . . . . . . **7.**
8. Enter the **smaller** of line 3 or line 4 . . . . **8.**
9. Subtract line 8 from line 7. If zero or less, enter -0- . . . . **9.**
10. Add lines 6 and 9 . . . . **10.**
11. Add lines 18 and 19 of Schedule D . . . . **11.**
12. Enter the **smaller** of line 9 or line 11 . . . . **12.**
13. Subtract line 12 from line 10 . . . . **13.**
14. Subtract line 13 from line 1. If zero or less, enter -0- . . . . **14.**
15. Enter the **smaller** of:
    - The amount on line 1 **or**
    - $29,700 if single or married filing separately;
      $59,400 if married filing jointly or qualifying widow(er); or . . . . **15.**
      $39,800 if head of household
16. Enter the **smaller** of line 14 or line 15 . . . . **16.**
17. Subtract line 10 from line 1. If zero or less, enter -0- . . . . **17.**
18. Enter the **larger** of line 16 or line 17 . . . . ▶ **18.**
    If lines 15 and 16 are the same, skip lines 19 and 20 and go to line 21. Otherwise, go to line 19.
19. Subtract line 16 from line 15 . . . . ▶ **19.**
20. Multiply line 19 by 5% (.05) . . . . **20.**
    If lines 1 and 15 are the same, skip lines 21 through 33 and go to line 34. Otherwise, go to line 21.
21. Enter the **smaller** of line 1 or line 13 . . . . **21.**
22. Enter the amount from line 19 (if line 19 is blank, enter -0-) . . . . **22.**
23. Subtract line 22 from line 21. If zero or less, enter -0- . . . . ▶ **23.**
24. Multiply line 23 by 15% (.15) . . . . **24.**
    If Schedule D, line 19, is zero or blank, skip lines 25 through 30 and go to line 31. Otherwise, go to line 25.
25. Enter the **smaller** of line 9 above or Schedule D, line 19 . . . . **25.**
26. Add lines 10 and 18 . . . . **26.**
27. Enter the amount from line 1 above . . . . **27.**
28. Subtract line 27 from line 26. If zero or less, enter -0- . . . . **28.**
29. Subtract line 28 from line 25. If zero or less, enter -0- . . . . ▶ **29.**
30. Multiply line 29 by 25% (.25) . . . . **30.**
    If Schedule D, line 18, is zero or blank, skip lines 31 through 33 and go to line 34. Otherwise, go to line 31.
31. Add lines 18, 19, 23, and 29 . . . . **31.**
32. Subtract line 31 from line 1 . . . . **32.**
33. Multiply line 32 by 28% (.28) . . . . **33.**
34. Figure the tax on the amount on **line 18**. Use the Tax Table or Tax Computation Worksheet, whichever applies . . . . **34.**
35. Add lines 20, 24, 30, 33, and 34 . . . . **35.**
36. Figure the tax on the amount on **line 1**. Use the Tax Table or Tax Computation Worksheet, whichever applies . . . . **36.**
37. **Tax on all taxable income (including capital gains and qualified dividends).** Enter the **smaller** of line 35 or line 36. Also include this amount on Form 1040, line 44 . . . . **37.**

*If applicable, enter instead the smaller amount you entered on the dotted line next to line 4e of Form 4952.

PROBLEM MATERIALS

DISCUSSION QUESTIONS

I5-1 What problem may exist in determining the amount realized for an investor who exchanges common stock of a publicly traded corporation for a used building? How is the problem likely to be resolved?

I5-2 In 1992 Ellen purchased a house for $60,000 to use as her personal residence. She paid $12,000 and borrowed $48,000 from the local savings and loan company. In 1995 she paid $10,000 to add a room to the house. In 1997 she paid $625 to have the house painted and $800 for built-in bookshelves. As of January 1 of the current year, she has reduced the $48,000 mortgage to $44,300. What is her basis for the house?

I5-3 Vincent pays $20,000 for equipment to use in his trade or business. He pays sales tax of $800 as a result of the purchase. Must the $800 sales tax be capitalized as part of the purchase price?

I5-4 Sergio owns 200 shares of Palm Corporation common stock, purchased during the prior year: 100 shares on July 5, for $9,000; and 100 shares on October 15, for $12,000. When Sergio sells 50 shares for $8,000 on July 18 of the current year, he does not identify the particular shares sold. Determine the amount and character of the gain.

I5-5 On October 21 of the current year, David receives stock of Western Corporation as a gift from his grandfather, who acquired the stock on January 20, 1995. Under what conditions would David's holding period start on
a. October 22 of the current year?
b. January 20, 1995?

I5-6 Jim inherits stock (a capital asset) from his brother, who dies in March of the current year, when the property has a $2,900,000 FMV. This property is the only property included in his brother's gross estate and there is a taxable estate. The FMV of the property as of the alternate valuation date is $2,700,000.
a. Why might the executor of the brother's estate elect to use the alternate valuation date to value the property?
b. Why might Jim prefer the executor to use FMV at time of the death to value the property?
c. If the marginal estate tax rate is 37% and Jim's marginal income tax rate is 25%, which value should the executor use?

I5-7 Martha owns 500 shares of Columbus Corporation common stock at the beginning of the year with a basis of $82,500. During the year, Columbus declares and pays a 10% nontaxable stock dividend. What is her basis for each of the 50 shares received?

I5-8 Mario owns 2,000 shares of Nevada Corporation common stock at the beginning of the year. His basis for the stock is $38,880. During the year, Nevada declares and pays a stock dividend. After the dividend, Mario's basis for each share of stock owned is $18. What is the percentage dividend paid by Nevada?

I5-9 A corporate taxpayer plans to build a $6 million office building during the next 18 months. How must the corporation treat the interest on debt paid or incurred during the production period?

I5-10 Andy owns an appliance store where he has merchandise such as refrigerators for sale. Roger, a bachelor, owns a refrigerator, which he uses in his apartment for personal use. For which individual is the refrigerator a capital asset?

I5-11 Why did the Supreme Court rule in the *Corn Products* case that a gain due to the sale of futures contracts is ordinary income instead of capital gain?

I5-12 When is the gain on the sale or exchange of securities by a dealer in securities classified as capital gain?

I5-13 In 1982, Florence purchased 30 acres of land. She has not used the land for business purposes or made any substantial improvements to the property. During the current year, she subdivides the land into 15 lots and advertises the lots for sale. She sells four lots at a gain.
a. What is the character of the gain on the sale of the four lots?
b. Explain how the basis of each lot would be determined.

I5-14 Amy has LTCGs that are taxed at different tax rates, 15%, 25% and 28%. She also has NSTCLs that amount to less than her NLTCG. The procedure for offsetting the NSTCL against the LTCGs is favorable to her. Explain.

I5-15 Four years ago, Susan loaned $7,000 to her friend Joe. During the current year, the $7,000 loan is considered worthless. Explain how Susan should treat the worthless debt for tax purposes.

I5-16 Why did the Supreme Court rule in *Arkansas Best* that the stock of a corporation purchased by the taxpayer to protect the taxpayer's business reputation was a capital asset?

I5-17 The effective tax rate on gain of $1,000,000 resulting from the sale of qualified small business stock held more than five years is 14%. Do you agree or disagree? Explain.

I5-18 Nancy and the Minor Corporation own bonds of the East Corporation. Minor Corporation owns 80% of the stock of East Corporation. East Corporation has declared bankruptcy this year, and bondholders will receive only 26% of the face value of the debt. Explain why the loss is a capital loss for Nancy but an ordinary loss for the Minor Corporation.

I5-19 On January 1 of the current year, the Orange Corporation issues $500,000 of 11%, 20-year bonds for $480,000. Determine the amount of original issue discount, if any.

I5-20 Today, Juanita purchases a 15-year, 7% bond of the Sunflower Corporation issued four years ago at par. She purchases the bond as an investment at a discount from the par value. If she sells the bonds two years from now, explain why some or all of the gain may be ordinary income.

I5-21 Judy just obtained a patent on a new product she has developed. Bell Corporation wishes to market the product and will pay 12% of all future sales of the product to Judy. How can she be sure that the payments received will be treated as a long-term capital gain?

I5-22 When is the transferor of a franchise unable to treat the transfer as a sale or an exchange of a capital asset?

I5-23 How does a lessor treat payments received for canceling a lease?

I5-24 What is the first day that an individual could sell a capital asset purchased on March 31, 2006 and have a holding period of more than one year?

I5-25 Phil, a cash-basis taxpayer, sells the following marketable securities, which are capital assets during 2006. Determine whether the gains or losses are long-term or short-term. Also determine the net capital gain and adjusted net capital gain for 2006.

Capital Asset	Basis	Date Acquired	Trade Date in 2006	Sales Price
A	$40,000	Feb. 10, 2005	Aug. 12	$52,000
B	20,000	Dec. 5, 2005	May 2	17,000
C	30,000	Apr. 9, 2004	Dec. 10	37,400

I5-26 How might the current treatment of capital losses discourage an individual investor from purchasing stock of a high-risk, start-up company?

I5-27 An individual taxpayer has realized a $40,000 loss on the sale of an asset that had a holding period of eight months. Explain why the taxpayer may be indifferent as to whether the asset is a capital asset.

I5-28 If Pam transfers an asset to Fred and the asset is subject to a liability that is assumed by Fred, how does Fred's assumption of the liability affect the amount realized by Pam? How does Fred's assumption of the liability affect his basis for the property?

ISSUE IDENTIFICATION QUESTIONS

I5-29 Acorn Corporation, a company that purchases malt barley from farmers and sells it to brewers, is interested in determining whether a new variety of barley will grow successfully in the Pacific Northwest. The corporation has acquired the seed from Europe and will conduct the experiments with the cooperation of farmers in the area. If the experiments prove successful, Acorn will sell the remaining seed to the farmers. What tax issues should Acorn Corporation consider?

I5-30 Lisa and John are in the business of breeding beavers to produce fur for sale. They recently purchased a pair of breeding beavers for $30,000 from XUN, Inc., and agreed to pay interest at 10% each year for five years. After the five-year period, they could pay the debt by delivering seven beavers to XUN, Inc., provided that each beaver was at least nine months old. Identify the tax issues involved in this situation.

I5-31 Mike, a real estate broker in California, recently inherited a farm from his deceased uncle and plans to sell the farm to the first available buyer. His uncle purchased the property 12 years ago for $600,000. The FMV of the farm on the date of the uncle's death was $500,000. Mike sells the farm for $520,000 seven months after his uncle's death. What tax issues should Mike consider?

I5-32 Sylvia, a dentist with excellent skills as a carpenter, started the construction of a house that she planned to give to her son as a surprise when he returned from Saudia Arabia, where he is serving in the military. She began construction on March 23, 2005, and finished the house on July 10, 2006, at a total cost of $70,000. Her son is expected to be home on September 1, 2006.

On July 30, 2006, Roscoe offered Sylvia $245,000 for the house and Sylvia considered the offer to be so attractive that she accepted it. She decided that she could purchase a suitable home for her son for about $200,000. What tax issues should Sylvia consider?

PROBLEMS

I5-33 *Amount Realized.* Tracy owns a nondepreciable capital asset held for investment. The asset was purchased for $250,000 six years earlier and is now subject to a $75,000 liability. During the current year, Tracy transfers the asset to Tim in exchange for $94,000 cash and a new automobile with a $50,000 FMV to be used by Tracy for personal use; Tim assumes the $75,000 liability. Determine the amount of Tracy's LTCG or LTCL.

I5-34 *Basis of Property Received as a Gift.* Doug receives a duplex as a gift from his uncle. The uncle's basis for the duplex and land is $90,000. At the time of the gift, the land and building have FMVs of $40,000 and $80,000, respectively. No gift tax is paid by Doug's uncle at the time of the gift.

a. To determine gain, what is Doug's basis for the land?

b. To determine gain, what is Doug's basis for the building?

c. Will the basis of the land and building be the same as in Parts a and b for purposes of determining a loss?

I5-35 *Sale of Property Received as a Gift.* During the current year, Stan sells a tract of land for $800,000. The property was received as a gift from Maxine on March 10, 1987, when the property had a $310,000 FMV. The taxable gift was $300,000. Maxine purchased the property on April 12, 1980, for $110,000. At the time of the gift, Maxine paid a gift tax of $12,000. In order to sell the property, Stan paid a sales commission of $16,000.

a. What is Stan's realized gain on the sale?

b. How would your answer to Part a change, if at all, if the FMV of the gift property was $85,000 as of the date of the gift?

I5-36 *Sale of Asset Received as a Gift.* Bud received 200 shares of Georgia Corporation stock from his uncle as a gift on July 20, 2005, when the stock had a $45,000 FMV. The uncle paid $30,000 for the stock on April 12, 1997. The taxable gift was $45,000, since his uncle made another gift to Bud for $20,000 in January. The uncle paid a gift tax of $1,500.

Without considering the transactions below, Bud's AGI is $45,000 in 2006. No other transactions involving capital assets occur during the year. Analyze each transaction below, independent of the others, and determine Bud's AGI in each case.

a. He sells the stock on October 12, 2006, for $48,000.

b. He sells the stock on October 12, 2006, for $28,000.

c. He sells the stock on December 16, 2006, for $42,000.

I5-37 *Basis of Property Converted from Personal Use.* Irene owns a truck costing $15,000 and used for personal activities. The truck has a $9,600 FMV when it is transferred to her business, which is operated as a sole proprietorship.

a. What is the basis of the truck for determining depreciation?

b. What is Irene's realized gain or loss if the truck is sold for $5,000 after claiming depreciation of $4,000?

I5-38 *Sale of Assets Received as a Gift and Inherited.* Daniel receives 400 shares of A&M Corporation stock from his aunt on May 20, 2006, as a gift when the stock has a $60,000 FMV. His aunt purchased the stock in 1999 for $42,000. The taxable gift is $60,000 because she made earlier gifts to Daniel during 2006 and used the annual exclusion. She paid a gift tax of $9,300 on the gift of A&M stock to Daniel.

Daniel also inherited 300 shares of Longhorn Corporation preferred stock when his uncle died on November 12, 2006, when the stock's FMV was $30,000. His uncle purchased the stock in 1990 for $27,600. Determine the gain or loss on the sale of A&M and Longhorn stock on December 15, 2006, under each alternative situation below.

a. A&M stock was sold for $62,600, and Longhorn stock was sold for $30,750.

b. A&M stock was sold for $58,200, and Longhorn stock was sold for $28,650.

c. Assume the same as in Part a except his aunt purchased A&M stock for $71,000 and his uncle purchased Longhorn stock for $31,200.

I5-39 *Personal-use Property Converted to Rental Property.* Tally owns a house that she has been living in for eight years. She purchased the house in 1990 for $245,000 and the FMV today is $200,000. She is moving into her friend's house and has decided to convert her residence to rental property. Assume 20% of the property's value is allocated to land.

a. What is the basis of the house for depreciation?

b. If she claims depreciation of $15,000 and sells the property six years later for $260,000 (20% allocated to land), determine the gain on the sale of the building and gain on the sale of the land.

c. How much of the gain is due to depreciation?

d. If the FMV is $290,000 when she converts the house to rental property instead of $200,000, what is the basis of the house for depreciation?

I5-40 *Stock Rights.* Kathleen owns 500 shares of Buda Corporation common stock which was purchased on March 20, 1999, for $48,000. On October 10 of the current year, she receives a distribution of 500 stock rights. Each stock right has a $20 FMV and the FMV of the Buda common stock is $100 per share. With each stock right, she may acquire one share of Buda common stock for $95.

a. How much gross income must Kathleen recognize?

b. What is the basis of each stock right received?

c. If she sells the 500 stock rights for $10,600, what is her gain?

d. If she exercises the 500 stock rights on November 10, what is the basis of the 500 shares she receives and when does the holding period for those shares start?

I5-41 *Stock Rights.* Martha Lou owns 100 shares of Blain Corporation common stock. She purchased the stock on July 25, 1986, for $4,000. On May 2 of the current year, she receives a nontaxable distribution of 100 stock rights. Each stock right has a $10 FMV, and the FMV of the Blain common stock is $70 per share. With each stock right, Martha Lou may acquire one share of Blain common for $68 per share. Assuming that she elects to allocate basis to the stock rights, answer the following:
a. What is the basis allocated to the stock rights?
b. If she sells the stock rights on June 10 for $1,080, determine the amount and character of the recognized gain?
c. If she exercises the stock rights on May 14, what is the basis of the 100 shares purchased and when does the holding period start?
d. If she does not elect to allocate basis to the stock rights, determine the amount and character of the gain if she sells the stock rights on June 10 for $1,080?

I5-42 *Real Property Subdivided for Sale.* Beth acquired only one tract of land seven years ago as an investment. In order to sell the land at a higher price, she decides to subdivide it into 20 lots. She pays for improvements such as clearing and leveling, but the improvements are not considered to be substantial. Each lot has a basis of $2,000, and a selling price of $6,000. Selling expenses of $480 were incurred to sell two lots last year. This year, ten lots are sold, and selling expenses amount to $1,900. How much ordinary income and capital gain must be recognized in the prior and current year?

I5-43 *Marginal Tax Rates.* Mr. and Mrs. Dunbar have taxable income of $190,000 without considering the following sales. Consider the following independent cases where capital gains are recognized and determine the marginal tax rate for the capital gain in each case. Ignore the effect of increasing AGI on deductions.
CASE A: $10,000 gain from sale of Storm Lake common stock held for seven months.
CASE B: $10,000 gain from sale of antique clock held for six years.
CASE C: $10,000 gain from sale of Ames preferred stock held for three years.

I5-44 *Netting Gains and Losses* Trisha, whose tax rate is 35%, sells the following capital assets in 2006 with gains and losses as shown:

Asset	Gain or (Loss)	Holding Period
A	$15,000	15 months
B	7,000	20 months
C	(3,000)	14 months

a. Determine Trisha's increase in tax liability as a result of the three sales. All assets are stock held for investment. Ignore the effect of increasing AGI on deductions and phase-out amounts.
b. Determine her increase in tax liability if the holding period for asset B is 8 months.
c. Determine her increase in tax liability if the holding periods are the same as in Part a but asset B is an antique clock.

I5-45 *Computing the Tax.* Donna files as a head of household in 2006 and has taxable income of $90,000, including the sale of a stock held as an investment for two years at a gain of $20,000. Only one asset was sold during the year and Donna does not have any capital loss carryovers.
a. What is the amount of Donna's tax liability?
b. What is the amount of Donna's tax liability if the stock is held for 11 months?

I5-46 *Computing the Tax.* Wayne is single and has no dependents. Without considering his $11,000 adjusted net capital gain (ANCG), his taxable income in 2006 is as follows:

AGI		$150,500
Home mortgage interest	$22,150	
State and local income taxes	8,000	
Charitable contributions	7,000	
Personal exemption	3,300	40,450
Taxable income		$110,050

a. What is Wayne's tax liability without the ANCG?
b. What is Wayne's tax liability with the ANCG?

I5-47 *Computing the Sales Price.* An investor in a 28% tax bracket owns land that is a capital asset with a $50,000 basis and a holding period of three years. The investor wishes to sell the asset at a price high enough so that he will have $120,000 in cash after paying the taxes. What is the minimum price which the investor could accept?

I5-48 *Capital Gains and Losses.* Consider the four independent situations below for an unmarried individual, and analyze the effects of the capital gains and losses on the individual's AGI. For each case, determine AGI after considering the capital gains and losses.

	Situation 1	Situation 2	Situation 3	Situation 4
AGI (excluding property transactions)	$40,000	$50,000	$60,000	$70,000
STCG	6,000	2,000	5,000	6,000
STCL	2,000	5,000	4,000	15,000
LTCG	3,500	15,000	10,000	9,000
LTCL	2,500	4,000	12,000	4,000

I5-49 *Capital Losses.* To better understand the rules for offsetting capital losses and how to treat capital losses carried forward, analyze the following data for an unmarried individual for the period 2003 through 2006. No capital loss carryforwards are included in the figures. For each year, determine AGI and the capital losses to be carried forward to a later tax year.

	2003	2004	2005	2006
AGI (excluding property transactions)	$40,000	$50,000	$60,000	$70,000
STCG	4,000	5,000	7,000	10,000
STCL	9,000	3,000	5,000	12,000
LTCG	6,000	10,000	2,200	6,000
LTCL	5,000	21,000	1,000	9,500
AGI (including property transactions)	_____	_____	_____	_____
STCL to be carried forward	_____	_____	_____	_____
LTCL to be carried forward	_____	_____	_____	_____

I5-50 *Character of Loss.* The Michigan Corporation owns 20% of the Wolverine Corporation. The Wolverine stock was acquired eight years ago to ensure a steady supply of raw materials. Michigan also owns 30% of Spartan Corporation and 85% of Huron Corporation. Stock in both corporations was acquired more than ten years ago for investment purposes. During the current year, Wolverine, Spartan, and Huron are deemed bankrupt, and the stocks are considered worthless. Describe how Michigan should treat its losses.

I5-51 *Original Issue Discount.* On December 31, 2005, Phil purchased $20,000 of newly issued bonds of Texas Corporation for $16,568. The bonds are dated December 31, 2005. The bonds are 9%, 10-year bonds paying interest semiannually on June 30 and December 31. The bonds are priced to yield 12% compounded semiannually.
a. What is the amount of the original issue discount?
b. For the first semiannual period, what is the amount of the original issue discount Phil must recognize as ordinary income?
c. What is the total amount of interest income Phil must recognize in 2006?
d. What is Phil's basis for the bonds as of December 31, 2006?

I5-52 On January 1, 2004, Swen paid $184,000 for $200,000 of the 8%, 20-year bonds of Penn Corporation, issued on January 1, 2000, at par. The bonds are held as an investment. Determine the gain and the character of the gain if the bonds are sold on January 1, 2006, for
a. $191,000
b. $185,750
c. $183,000

I5-53 *Capital Gains and Losses.* During 2006, Gary receives a $50,000 salary and has no deductions for AGI. In 2005, Gary had a $5,000 STCL and no other capital losses or capital gains. Consider the following sales and determine Gary's AGI for 2006.

• An automobile purchased in 2001 for $10,800 and held for personal use is sold for $7,000.

• On April 10, 2006, stock held for investment is sold for $21,000. The stock was acquired on November 20, 2005, for $9,300.

I5-54 *Call Options.* On February 10, 2006, Gail purchases 20 calls on Red Corporation for $250 per call. Each call represents an option to buy 100 shares of Red stock at $42 per share any time before November 25, 2006. Compute the gain or loss recognized, and determine whether the gain or loss is long-term or short-term for Gail in the following situations:
a. The 20 calls are sold on May 15, 2006, for $310 per call.
b. The calls are not exercised but allowed to expire.

c. The calls are exercised on July 15, 2006, and the 2,000 shares of Red Corporation stock are sold on July 20, 2007, for $50 per share.

I5-55 *Call Writing.* Dan owns 500 shares of Rocket Corporation common stock. The stock was acquired two years ago for $30 per share. On October 2, 2006, Dan writes five calls on the stock, which represent options to buy the 500 shares of Rocket at $75 per share. For each call, Dan receives $210. The calls expire on June 22, 2007. Consider the following transactions and describe the tax treatment for Dan:
a. The five calls are exercised on December 4, 2006.
b. The calls are not exercised and allowed to expire.

I5-56 *Corporate Capital Gains and Losses.* Determine the taxable income for the Columbia Corporation for the following independent cases:

Case	Income from Operations	STCG (NSTCL)	NLTCG (NLTCL)
A	$110,000	$30,000	$44,000
B	100,000	(50,000)	65,000
C	80,000	(37,000)	30,000
D	90,000	(15,000)	(9,000)

I5-57 *Original Issue Discount.* On January 1, 2005, Sean purchased an 8%, $100,000 corporate bond for $92,277. The bond was issued on January 1, 2005, and matures on January 1, 2010. Interest is paid semiannually, and the effective yield to maturity is 10% compounded semiannually. On July 1, 2006, Sean sells the bond for $95,949. A schedule of interest amortization for the bond is shown in Table I5-2.
a. How much interest income must Sean recognize in 2005?
b. How much interest income must Sean recognize in 2006?
c. How much gain must Sean recognize in 2006 on the sale of the bond?

I5-58 *Capital Gains and Losses.* Martha has $40,000 AGI without considering the following information. During the year, she incurs a LTCL of $10,000 and has a gain of $14,000 due to the sale of a capital asset held for more than a year.
a. If the $14,000 gain is not properly classified as a LTCG (i.e., is improperly treated as an ordinary gain), determine Martha's AGI.
b. If the $14,000 gain is properly classified as a LTCG, determine her AGI.
c. If Martha has a $2,500 STCL carryover from earlier years, how would the answers to Parts a and b be affected?

I5-59 *Capital Gains and Losses.* Without considering the following capital gains and losses, Charlene has taxable income of $140,000 and a marginal tax rate of 35%. During the year, she sold stock held for nine months at a gain of $10,000; stock held for three years at a gain of $15,000; and a collectible asset held for six years at a gain of $20,000. Ignore the effect of the gains on any threshold amounts and assume that her marginal tax rate of 35% does not change.
a. What is her taxable income after considering the three gains and the increase in her tax liability?

▼ **TABLE I5-2**
Interest Amortization for Problem I5-57

	Interest Received (1)	Amortization of Discount (2)	Interest Income (3) = (1) + (2)
6-30-05	$4,000	$614	$4,614
12-31-05	4,000	645	4,645
6-30-06	4,000	677	4,677
12-31-06	4,000	711	4,711
6-30-07	4,000	747	4,747
12-31-07	4,000	783	4,783
6-30-08	4,000	823	4,823
12-31-08	4,000	864	4,864
6-30-09	4,000	907	4,907
12-31-09	4,000	952	4,952

b. In addition to the above three sales, assume that she sells another asset and has a STCL of $14,000. What is her taxable income after considering the four transactions and the increase in her tax liability as a result of the four transactions?

c. In addition to the above three sales in Part a, assume that she sells another collectible asset held seven years as an investment and has a $27,000 capital loss. What is her taxable income after considering the four transactions and the increase in her tax liability?

I5-60 *Corporate Capital Gains and Losses.* In 2001, the Ryan Corporation sold a capital asset and incurred a $40,000 LTCL that was carried forward to subsequent years. That sale was the only sale of a capital asset that Ryan made until 2006, when Ryan sells a capital asset and recognizes a STCG of $53,000. Without considering the STCG from the sale, Ryan's taxable income is $250,000.
a. Determine the corporation's NSTCG for 2006.
b. Determine the corporation's 2006 taxable income.
c. If the sale of the asset in 2001 had occurred in 2000, determine the corporation's 2006 taxable income.

COMPREHENSIVE PROBLEM

I5-61 Betty incurs the following transactions during the current year. Without considering the transactions, her 2006 AGI is $40,000. Analyze the transactions and answer the following questions:

• On March 10, 2006, she sells a painting for $2,000. Betty is the artist, and she completed the painting in 2001. Her basis for the painting is $50.

• On June 18, 2006, she receives $28,500 from the sale of stock purchased by her uncle in 1996 for $10,000, which she inherits on February 20, 2006, as a result of her uncle's death. The stock's FMV on that date is $30,000.

• On July 30, 2006, she sells land for $25,000 that was received as a gift from her brother on April 8, 2006, when the land's FMV was $30,000. Her brother purchased the land for $43,000 on October 12, 1998. No gift tax was paid.

a. What is her NSTCL or NSTCG?
b. What is her NLTCL or NLTCG?
c. What is the effect of capital gains and losses on her AGI?
d. What is her capital loss carryforward to 2007?

TAX STRATEGY PROBLEMS

I5-62 Dale purchased Blue Corporation stock four years ago for $1,000 as an investment. He intended to hold the stock until funds were needed to help pay for his daughter's college education. Today the stock has a $6,500 FMV and Dale decides to sell the stock and give the proceeds, less any taxes paid on the sale, to Tammy, his 18-year-old daughter. Dale's marginal tax rate is 30%. Tammy has no other gross income and receives more than half of her support from Dale.
a. What advice would you give to Dale?
b. What is the cash savings if Dale follows your advice?

I5-63 Calvin, whose tax rate is 40% is considering two alternative investments on January 1, 20Y1. He can purchase $100,000 of 10% bonds due in five years or purchase $100,000 of Hobbes, Inc. common stock. The bonds are issued at par, pay interest annually on December 31, and mature at the end of five years. Interest received can be reinvested at 10%. Assume that he knows with relative certainty that the value of the stock will increase 8% each year (i.e., the value of the Hobbes stock will be $108,000 at the end of 20Y1) and the interest and principal for the bonds will be paid as scheduled. On December 31, 20Y5, he will sell the stock or receive the bond principal plus the last interest payment. Which alternative should Calvin select if he wants to have the greater amount of money as of January 1, 20Y6? Provide supporting information for your answer.

I5-64 On December 20 of the current year, Winneld has decided to sell all of the stock that she owns and reinvest the proceeds in state of Minnesota bonds. Without considering the sales, her taxable income is expected to exceed $400,000 this year and in future years. Information about the stocks are provided below:

Corporation	FMV	Basis	Holding Period
Viking, Inc.	$190,000	$140,000	7 months
Twins, Inc.	200,000	255,000	4 years
Timberwolves, Inc.	382,000	300,000	3 years

She is willing to sell some of the stock this year and the remaining stock next year if it is more advantageous to spread the sales over two years. Assume that the FMV of the stock will not change during the next 30 days, her regular tax rate is 35% and ignore the effect of a sale on threshold amounts.

Determine the increase in her tax for each of the following alternatives and advise Winneld.

a. Sell all stock this year.

b. Sell Twins and Timberwolves this year and Viking in March of next year.

c. Sell Viking and Twins this year and Timberwolves in March of next year.

TAX FORM/RETURN PREPARATION PROBLEMS

I5-65 Given the following information for Jane Cole, complete Schedule D of Form 1040 through Part III.

- Stock options, which she purchases on February 14 of the current year for $850, expire on October 1.

- On July 1, she sells for $1,500 her personal-use automobile acquired on March 31, 1990, for $8,000.

- On August 16, she sells for $3,100 her stock of York Corporation purchased as an investment on February 16, for $1,600.

- On March 15, she sells for $5,600 an antique ring, a gift from her grandmother on January 10, 1988, when its FMV was $1,600. The ring was purchased by her grandmother on April 2, 1979, for $1,800.

- She has a STCL carryover of $250 from last year.

I5-66 Spencer Duck (SSN 277-31-7264) is single and his eight-year-old son, Mitch, lives with him nine months of the year in a rented condominium at 321 Hickory Drive in Ames, Iowa. Mitch lives with his mother, Spencer's ex-wife, during the summer months. His mother provides more than half of Mitch's support and Spencer has agreed to allow her to claim Mitch as her dependent. Spencer has a salary of $39,000 and itemized deductions of $4,000. Taxes withheld during the year amount to $5,221. On July 14 of the current year, he sold the following assets:

- Spencer received a K-1 from a partnership indicating that his share of the partnership STCL is $200.

- Land was sold for $35,000. The land was received as a property settlement on January 10, 2001, when the land's FMV amounted to $30,000. His ex-wife's basis for the land, purchased on January 10, 1991, was $18,600.

- A personal-use computer acquired on March 2 last year for $4,000 was sold for $2,480.

- A membership card for a prestigious country club was sold for $8,500. The card was acquired on October 10, 1993, for $6,000.

- Marketable securities held as an investment were sold for $20,000. The securities were inherited from his uncle, who died on March 10 of the current year when FMV of the securities was $21,000. The uncle purchased the securities on May 10, 1990, for $10,700.

In addition to the above sales, Spencer received a $100 refund of state income taxes paid last year. Spencer used the standard deduction last year to compute his tax liability. Prepare Form 1040 and Schedule D for the current year.

CASE STUDY PROBLEMS

I5-67 As a political consultant for an aspiring politician, you have been hired to evaluate the following statements that pertain to capital gains and losses. Evaluate the statement and provide at least a one-paragraph explanation of each statement. As you prepare your answer, consider the fact that the aspiring politician does not have much knowledge about taxation.

a. The tax on capital gains is considered a voluntary tax.

b. On October 22, 1986, the Tax Reform Act of 1986 was passed, which eliminated the 60% of net capital gain deduction (i.e., an individual taxpayer with $10,000 of net capital gain was entitled to a $6,000 deduction when computing AGI) before January 1, 1987. Many state governments enjoyed a substantial increase in 1986 tax revenue.

c. High-income taxpayers receive the most benefit from preferential treatment for capital gains.

I5-68   Your client, Apex Corporation, entered into an agreement with an executive to purchase his personal residence at its current FMV in the event that his employment is terminated by the company during a five-year period. The executive's job was terminated before the end of the five-year period and Apex acquired the house for $500,000. Due to a downturn in the real estate market, a $200,000 loss was incurred by the company upon the resale of the house. The chief financial officer of Apex insists that the loss be characterized as ordinary, based on the *Corn Products* doctrine. Your research into this matter reveals that the weight of authority heavily favors capital loss treatment (i.e., case law based on facts identical to the above issue held that the loss was capital rather than ordinary). You therefore conclude that the client's position does not have a realistic possibility of being sustained administratively or judicially on its merits if challenged by the IRS. What responsibility do you have as a tax practitioner relative to preparing the client's tax return and rendering continuing tax consulting services to the client? (See the Section *Statements on Standards for Tax Services* in Chapter 11 for a discussion of these issues.)

TAX RESEARCH PROBLEMS

I5-69   Tom Williams is an equal partner in a partnership with the Kansas Corporation. Williams, an inventor, produced a new process while working for the partnership, which has been patented by the partnership. Before making any use of the patent, the partnership entered into a contract granting all rights to use the process for the life of the patent to the Mason Manufacturing Co.

    The time between receiving the patent and entering into the contract with Mason amounted to eight months. Mason agreed to pay 0.3% of all sales revenue generated by products produced as a result of the process. If Mason fails to make payments on a timely basis, Mason's right to use the process is forfeited and the agreement between the partnership and Mason is canceled. Will any of the proceeds collected qualify as LTCG under Sec. 1235?

    A partial list of research sources is

- Reg. Sec. 1.1235-2
- *George N. Soffron,* 35 T.C. 787 (1961)

I5-70   Lynette, a famous basketball player, is considering the possibility of transferring the sole right to use her name to promote basketball shoes produced and sold by the NIK Corporation. NIK will pay $2 million to obtain the right to use Lynette's name for the next 40 years. NIK may use the name on the shoes and as a part of any of the company's advertisements for basketball shoes. If Lynette signs the contract and receives the $2 million payment, will she have to recognize capital gain or ordinary income?

    A partial list of research sources is

- Sec. 1221
- Rev. Rul. 65-261, 1965-2 C.B. 281

I5-71   Jack, a tenured university professor, has been a malcontent for many years at Rockport University. The university has recently offered to pay $200,000 to Jack if he will relinquish his tenure position and resign. Jack is of the opinion that tenure is an intangible capital asset and the $200,000 received for release of the tenure should be a long-term capital gain. Explain why you agree or disagree.

    A partial list of research sources is

- *Harry M. Flower,* 61 T.C. 140 (1973)
- *Estelle Goldman,* 1975 PH T.C. Memo ¶75,138, 34 TCM 639

I5-72   Web Baker was hired three years ago by the Berry Corporation to serve as CEO for the company. As part of his employment contract, the corporation had agreed to purchase his residence at FMV in the event the company decided to fire him. Last year, Berry, unsatisfied with Web's performance, fired him and purchased the residence for $350,000. Berry immediately listed the house with a real estate agency. Soon after the purchase, the real estate market in the area experienced a serious decline, especially in higher-priced homes. Berry sold the house this year for $270,000 and paid selling expenses of $12,000. How should the Berry Corporation treat the $92,000 loss?

    A partial list of research sources is

- Sec. 1221
- Rev. Rul. 82-204, 1982-2 C.B. 192
- *Azar Nut Co. v. CIR,* 67 AFTR 2d 91-987, 91-1 USTC ¶50,257 (5th Cir., 1991)

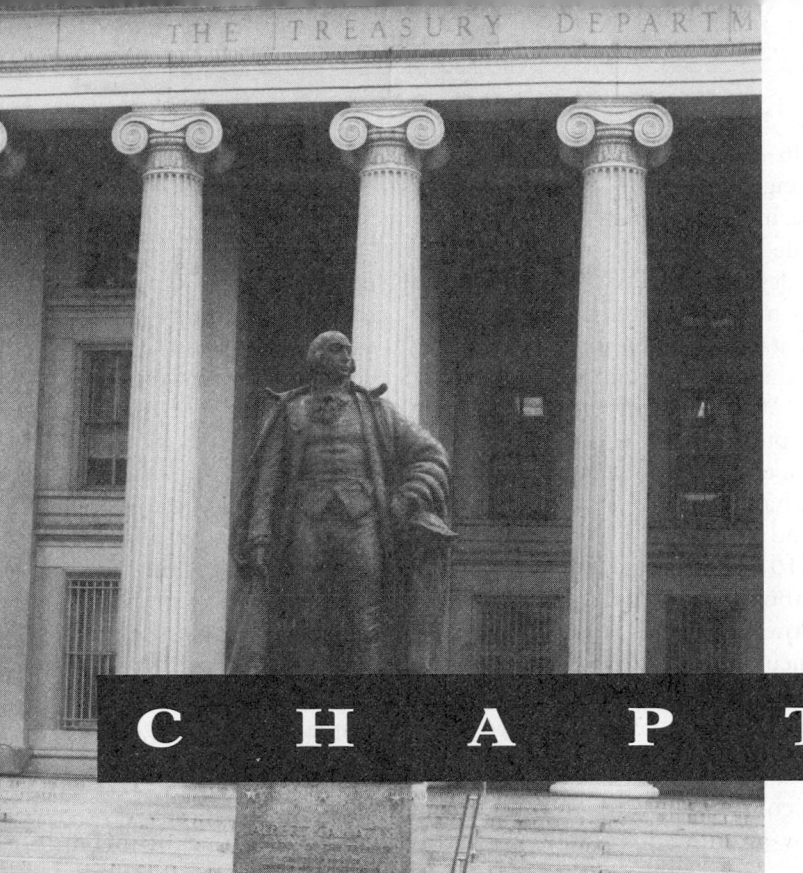

6

CHAPTER

DEDUCTIONS AND LOSSES

LEARNING OBJECTIVES

After studying this chapter, you should be able to

1 ▶ Distinguish between deductions *for* and *from* AGI

2 ▶ Discuss the criteria for deducting business and investment expenses

3 ▶ List the substantiation requirements for deducting travel and entertainment expenses

4 ▶ Explain the timing of deductions under both the cash and accrual methods of accounting

5 ▶ Explain the tax consequences of wash sales

6 ▶ Explain the tax consequences of transactions between related parties

7 ▶ Discuss the criteria for determining whether an activity is a hobby or a trade or business

8 ▶ Determine the tax consequences of vacation homes

CHAPTER OUTLINE

The next five chapters (I6–I10) deal with deductions. As you recall from Chapters I3 and I4, the principles governing the reporting of income are based on an "all inclusive" system of taxation; that is, gross income includes all items of income unless specifically excluded by statute. In contrast, deductions or losses are not allowed for tax purposes unless the statute specifically provides for them. For example, a taxpayer who makes a donation to a charity during the year may deduct the donation because the statute specifically allows for the deduction of charitable contributions under Sec. 170 of the IRC.

Chapter I6 discusses the general requirements for the deductibility of taxpayer expenditures and losses. Some of these requirements apply to all taxpayers while others apply only to individuals. Chapter I7 deals with itemized deductions of individual taxpayers, such as medical expenses, taxes, charitable contributions, interest expense, and other miscellaneous deductions. Chapter I8 covers two major areas that apply to all taxpayers, the deductibility of losses and bad debts. Chapter I9 discusses employee compensation and expenses, and Chapter I10 discusses tax depreciation, amortization, and depletion.

As was mentioned above, expenditures are deductible only if the IRC specifically allows the deduction. However, the IRC cannot possibly specify *every* deductible expense that a taxpayer might incur. Therefore, the IRC contains a framework for analyzing the nature of an expenditure. If the expenditure meets the criteria developed in the framework, the item is deductible. This framework provides for three general categories of deductions:

(1) Expenses incurred in connection with a **trade or business** (Sec. 162);
(2) Expenses incurred by an individual in connection with the **production of income** (Sec. 212);
(3) Other types of expenses that fall within specific provisions of the IRC, such as certain types of interest expense, taxes, bad debts, and other expenditures by individuals for personal items such as medical expenses, alimony, and moving.

The first two categories of deductions, trade or business (Sec. 162) and production of income expenses (Sec. 212), are those incurred in connection with profit-motivated activities. The IRC does not attempt to specify every conceivable type of deductible expense included in these two categories. Rather, the IRC sets forth general guidelines for deductibility. Any expense incurred in connection with a trade or business or for the production of income is deductible if (1) it falls within these general guidelines and (2) the IRC does not specifically exclude it from deductibility. For example, although the IRC does not specifically provide for the deductibility of utilities or maintenance and repairs, these expenditures are deductible if incurred in a profit-motivated activity. These general guidelines are discussed later in this chapter.

A trade or business is a business activity of the taxpayer and is discussed below. For individuals, deductible expenses related to the production of income include expenses incurred for the following:

▶ Production or collection of income

▶ Management, conservation, or maintenance of property held for the production of income

▶ Determination, collection, or refund of any tax

As will be discussed later, for individuals, the distinction between a trade or business and the production of income is important because it can affect both the amount and type of the deduction. Expenses incurred in both types of activities must meet additional standards of deductibility; that is, they must also be ordinary, necessary, and reasonable in the context of the activity in which they are incurred. Losses incurred in either type of activity are deductible.

Section 262 also provides, in general, that a deduction is not allowed for any personal, living, or family expenses. However, the tax law does specifically provide for the deductibility of certain personal expenditures or losses. For example, a taxpayer may deduct casualty losses (subject to certain limitations) for personal-use property. Taxpayers may also deduct personal expenditures for certain types of interest, taxes, medical expenses, alimony, and retirement savings if the expenditures meet strict requirements. Chapters I7, I8, and I9 discuss deductions and losses for personal expenditures.

CLASSIFYING DEDUCTIONS AS FOR VERSUS FROM ADJUSTED GROSS INCOME (AGI)

OBJECTIVE 1

Distinguish between deductions for and from AGI

As mentioned in Chapter I2, the tax formula for individuals divides all allowable business, investment, and personal deductions into the following two categories:

▶ Deductions subtracted from gross income in order to calculate adjusted gross income (*for* AGI deductions)

▶ Deductions subtracted from AGI to calculate taxable income (*from* AGI deductions)

The concept of AGI applies only to individuals.

Section 62 specifically identifies deductions *for* AGI. All other deductions for individuals are deductions *from* AGI. The more common *for* AGI deductions include the following, subject to certain limitations:

▶ All allowable expenses incurred in an individual's trade or business, but not including an employee's unreimbursed business expenses

▶ Reimbursed employee business expenses

▶ Certain unreimbursed business expenses incurred by performing artists and employees of a state or a political subdivision thereof

▶ Losses from the sale or exchange of trade, business, or investment property

▶ Expenses attributable to the production of rent or royalty income

▶ Moving expenses

▶ Contributions to certain pension, profit-sharing, or retirement plan arrangements

▶ Penalties paid to a bank or other savings institution because of the early withdrawal of funds from a certificate of deposit or time savings account

▶ Alimony

▶ Interest paid by certain individuals on qualified educational loans

▶ Contributions to qualified Archer medical savings accounts

▶ One-half of the self-employment tax imposed on self-employed individuals and 100% of health insurance costs paid by such individuals (see Chapter I14).[1]

KEY POINT

Many *for* AGI deductions are either expenses incurred in a trade or business or investment expenses or losses. Most of the deductible personal expenses are deductible *from* AGI.

For individuals, the distinction between deductions *for* AGI and *from* AGI is critical for two reasons. First, as explained in Chapter I2, the tax formula allows individuals to deduct the greater of the standard deduction or the total of the *from* AGI (itemized) deductions in arriving at taxable income. A taxpayer does not benefit from these deductions if the total for the year does not exceed the standard deduction. Deductions *for* AGI, on the other hand, reduce AGI (and consequently taxable income), even if the standard deduction is used in computing taxable income.

EXAMPLE I6-1 ▶ Brad, a single individual with no dependents, incurs $1,500 of deductible expenses and earns $30,000 in gross income during 2006. If the expenses are all deductions *from* AGI, Brad's taxable income is $21,550 (i.e., Brad receives a $3,300 deduction for his personal exemption and a $5,150 standard deduction). Brad receives no direct tax benefit from the expenses because they do not exceed the standard deduction. However, if the $1,500 of expenses are all deductions *for* AGI, Brad's taxable income is $20,050. In this latter case, Brad receives a full tax benefit from the expenses.

[1] Sections 62, 162(l) and 164(f). Other deductions *for* AGI include deductions for depreciation and depletion for life tenants and income beneficiaries of property, a portion of certain lump-sum distributions from qualified pension plans, reforestation expenses, required repayments of supplemental unemployment compensation benefits, certain expenses incurred for clean-fuel vehicles and refueling property, jury duty pay that is remitted to an employer, and attorney's fees paid out of awards in certain types of lawsuits, and certain trade or business expenses incurred by members of an Armed Forces unit when the individual is more than 100 miles away from home in connection with performing services as a member of that unit.

		Deductions from AGI	Deductions for AGI
Gross income		$30,000	$30,000
Minus:	*For* AGI deductions	0	(1,500)
AGI		$30,000	$28,500
Minus:	Standard deduction	(5,150)	(5,150)
	Personal exemption	(3,300)	(3,300)
Taxable income		$21,550	$20,050 ◀

The second important reason for the proper classification of deductions is that AGI acts as a limit on the amount of itemized deductions that can be taken. This limitation operates in three different ways:

▶ Certain itemized deductions such as medical expenses, casualty losses, and miscellaneous itemized deductions are only deductible to the extent they exceed a prescribed percentage of AGI. For example, an individual may deduct certain miscellaneous itemized deductions only to the extent that the sum of these deductions for the year exceeds 2% of the individual's AGI. These expenses include unreimbursed employee business expenses,[2] expenses incurred to produce investment income,[3] and the cost of tax advice and tax return preparation (see Chapter I7). A taxpayer may deduct medical expenses only to the extent their total exceeds 7.5% of the individual's AGI for the year. Individual taxpayers must first reduce casualty losses on personal-use property by $100 per casualty event. After this reduction, casualty losses are deductible only to the extent that the sum exceeds 10% of the individual's AGI.

▶ AGI also acts as a limit on the deductibility of certain itemized deductions by placing a limit on the total amount of the deduction. For example, the deduction for charitable contributions may not exceed 50% of the taxpayer's AGI.

▶ Finally, under Sec. 68(f), total itemized deductions are subject to a 2% reduction in 2006 (3% in 2005 and prior years) if the taxpayer's AGI exceeds certain threshold levels. However, this phase-out of itemized deductions for higher income individuals is being gradually eliminated and will be completely eliminated after 2009. (See Chapter I7 for a more detailed discussion of these deductions and their limits.) Also, remember that the concept of AGI has no application to corporations, estates, or trusts.

Deductions *for* AGI are generally located in two places on the tax return. First, some deductions *for* AGI appear on the front page of Form 1040. These deductions include such items as moving expenses, alimony paid, and student loan interest. Second, other deductions appear on separate schedules, including Schedule C (Profit or Loss from Business), Schedule E (Supplemental Income or Loss), or Schedule F (Profit or Loss from Farming). The profit or loss from these schedules carries over to the front page of Form 1040 as part of gross income. Thus, the deductions on these schedules are deductions *for* AGI. Figure P2-1 (Chapter I2) contains the front page of Form 1040.

CRITERIA FOR DEDUCTING BUSINESS AND INVESTMENT EXPENSES

Business and investment expenses are deductible only if certain requirements are met. Thus, deductible business or investment expenses must be:

▶ Related to a profit-motivated activity of the taxpayer (i.e., a business or investment activity rather than a personal expenditure)

---

[2] These expenses include unreimbursed expenditures for travel and transportation, supplies, special clothing or uniforms, union dues, and subscriptions to trade journals. Reimbursed employee expenses are deductible *for* AGI and thus, are deductible in full. See Chapter I9.

[3] These expenses include rental fees for safe deposit boxes used to hold investment property, subscriptions to investment journals, bank service charges on checking accounts used in an investment or income-producing activity, and fees paid for consulting advice. Expenses incurred in an investment or income-producing activity that generates either rental or royalty income are deductions *for* AGI.

OBJECTIVE 2

Discuss the criteria for deducting business and investment expenses

▶ Ordinary

▶ Necessary

▶ Reasonable in amount

▶ Properly documented (discussed later in the chapter under the heading Proper Substantiation Requirement), and

▶ An expense of the taxpayer (not someone else's expense)

Furthermore, as discussed later in this chapter under the heading General Restrictions on the Deductibility of Expenses, even if the expense meets the requirements for deductibility above, taxpayers may not deduct expenditures meeting certain other criteria. Thus, an expenditure is not deductible if it is

▶ A capital expenditure

▶ An expense related to tax-exempt income

▶ Illegal or in violation of public policy, or

▶ Specifically disallowed by the tax law.

Further discussion of these criteria and related matters follows.

BUSINESS OR INVESTMENT REQUIREMENT

Deductible expenditures generally originate from a profit-motivated activity. Business expenses for all taxpayers are deductible under Sec. 162. Additionally, under Sec. 212, an individual may deduct an expense incurred for the production of income or for the maintenance and conservation of income-producing property (an investment activity). Thus, the requirement of an activity being profit-motivated is really two-pronged: (1) a determination of whether an expenditure originates from an activity engaged in for profit and (2) for individuals, a distinction between a trade or business and an investment activity.

REAL-WORLD EXAMPLE

A taxpayer attempted to deduct treasure-hunting costs as a business expense, but the court concluded that there was no profit motive. The taxpayer kept no business records, the time spent was negligible and appeared to be recreational in nature, and no income was produced from the activity. *William J. Hezel*, 1985 PH T.C. Memo ¶85,010, 49 TCM 458.

ACTIVITY ENGAGED IN FOR PROFIT.   This first part of the test classifies the expense as resulting from either a profit-motivated activity or a personal activity. For individuals, classifying expenses as either profit-motivated or personal can be quite difficult. For example, is the activity of coin collecting a hobby that is personal in nature, a profit-motivated business, or an investment activity? No single objective test is available. Rather, a tax advisor must examine all the facts and circumstances surrounding the activity in which the taxpayer incurs expenses in order to make this distinction. The section in this chapter entitled Hobby Losses discusses these factors in more detail, as well as other issues dealing with the determination of whether or not a particular activity is profit-motivated.

TRADE OR BUSINESS VERSUS INVESTMENT CLASSIFICATION.   The second part of the profit-motive test is the determination of whether a particular activity is a trade or business of the taxpayer or only an investment. This distinction generally is important only to individuals since corporations are assumed to be engaged in a business. This distinction is important to individuals for several reasons. First, a loss on the sale of the assets used in the activity may be an ordinary loss if the activity is a trade or business.[4] If it is an investment activity, however, the loss is classified as a capital loss which, as explained in Chapter I5, receives different treatment. Second, this distinction may control whether an expense of the activity is a deduction *for* AGI or a deduction *from* AGI. In general, expenses incurred in a trade or business are deductions *for* AGI whereas investment expenses other than those incurred to produce rents and royalties are deductions *from* AGI. Finally, under Sec. 179, taxpayers may currently deduct up to $108,000 in 2006 ($105,000 in 2005) of tangible personal property purchased during the year and used in a trade or business. However, taxpayers must capitalize and depreciate the same expenditures over several years if they are incurred in an investment activity rather than in a trade or business. (See Chapter I10 for a discussion of the Sec. 179 current deduction for capital expenditures.)

---

[4] Under Sec. 1231, the exact treatment depends on the total gains and losses from such property for the year. See Chapter I13 for a discussion of Sec. 1231.

EXAMPLE I6-2 ▶ Robin is a self-employed financial consultant. She meets daily with a variety of clients to discuss their investments. Because she must keep abreast of the latest market quotes and strategies, Robin subscribes to several trade publications, newsletters, and quote services. During the year, Robin purchased a $4,000 computer to be used exclusively in her consulting business. Robin may deduct the expenses incurred for the publications and services as deductions for AGI because she incurred them in her consulting business. Furthermore, she can currently deduct the $4,000 paid for the computer under the special rules of Sec. 179 because it is a business asset, rather than an investment asset. ◀

Expenses incurred in an investment activity, other than those incurred to produce rents and royalties, are miscellaneous itemized deductions *from* AGI and are deductible only to the extent they exceed 2% of the taxpayer's AGI for the year (see Chapter I7).

EXAMPLE I6-3 ▶ Steve is a wealthy attorney who invests in the stock market and keeps abreast of the latest market quotes and strategies by subscribing to several trade publications and newsletters. He also purchased a computer to use exclusively for tracking his investments. Steve generally spends a few hours each day studying this information and analyzing his portfolio. The subscription expenses are deductions *from* AGI because they are incurred in an investment (rather than a business) activity and do not relate to the production of rents and royalties. Steve cannot currently deduct the entire cost of the computer but must depreciate the cost over a period of five years. Furthermore, the deductibility of all of the above items depends on whether Steve's total miscellaneous itemized deductions exceed 2% of his AGI and whether Steve itemizes his deductions instead of using the standard deduction. ◀

ADDITIONAL COMMENT

A trade or business is an activity with a profit motive and some type of economic activity. An investment activity requires a profit motive but does not require economic activity.

Despite these important differences in treatment, the distinction between an investment activity and a trade or business is not always clear. The IRC and the Treasury Regulations do not provide a precise definition of what constitutes a trade or business. Judicial law provides some guidelines. In one of the first cases dealing with the issue, the Supreme Court stated that the carrying on of a trade or business involves "holding one's self out to others as engaged in the selling of goods or services."[5]

Later, another Supreme Court case emphasized that one must examine all the surrounding facts and circumstances to determine the underlying nature of an activity.[6] In that case, the taxpayer owned a large portfolio of stocks, bonds, and real estate. The taxpayer's holdings were so large that he rented offices and hired employees to help him manage the properties. The Court, however, regarded these activities as investment activities despite the size of the holdings and the amount of work and effort involved because the taxpayer merely kept records and collected interest and dividends from his securities. Other cases, however, indicate that a taxpayer who invests in stocks and bonds may be considered to be in a business if he or she frequently buys and sells securities in order to make a short-term profit on the daily swings in the market.

LEGAL AND ACCOUNTING FEES. Taxpayers may generally deduct legal and accounting fees incurred in the regular conduct of a trade or business or for the production of income. Taxpayers may also deduct fees incurred for the determination, collection, or refund of any tax. As mentioned previously, trade or business expenses and expenses incurred in producing rents and royalties are deductible *for* AGI. Likewise, fees paid for the determination, collection, or refund of any tax are deductible *for* AGI if they are allocable to the taxpayer's trade or business or to the production of rents and royalties. These expenses include fees paid to prepare a taxpayer's Schedule C (Profit or Loss from Business), Part I of Schedule E (Supplemental Income and Loss, which is used to report rental and royalty income), and Schedule F (Farm Income and Expenses).[7] A filled-in Schedule C and copies of Schedule E and Schedule F are provided in Appendix B. Other tax related fees are deductible *from* AGI as miscellaneous itemized deductions, subject to the 2% of AGI limitation.

---

[5] *Deputy v. Pierre S. DuPont*, 23 AFTR 808, 40-1 USTC ¶9161 (USSC, 1940).
[6] *Eugene Higgins v. CIR*, 25 AFTR 1160, 41-1 USTC ¶9233 (USSC, 1941). See also *Chang H. Liang*, 23 T.C. 1040 (1955), and *Ralph E. Purvis v. CIR*,

37 AFTR 2d 76-968, 76-1 USTC ¶9270 (9th Cir., 1976); and *Samuel B. Levin v. U.S.*, 43 AFTR 2d 79-612, 79-1 USTC ¶9331 (Ct. Cls., 1979).
[7] Rev. Rul. 92-29, 1992-1 C.B. 20.

Taxpayers may not deduct legal fees incurred in the acquisition of property. Instead, taxpayers must capitalize these expenses and add them to the cost of the property. Likewise, taxpayers may not deduct legal expenses incurred for personal purposes.

EXAMPLE I6-4 ▶ During the current year, Lia pays legal and accounting fees for the following:

Services rendered with regard to a contract dispute in Lia's business	$ 8,000
Services rendered in resolving a federal tax deficiency relating to Lia's business	2,500
Tax return preparation fees:	
Allocable to preparation of Schedule C	1,600
Allocable to preparation of Schedules A and B and to the remainder of	
Form 1040	400
Legal fees incident to a divorce	1,200
Total	$13,700

Lia may deduct $12,100 ($8,000 + $2,500 + $1,600) *for* AGI. The remaining $400 of tax preparation fees are deductible *from* AGI as a miscellaneous itemized deduction subject to the 2% of AGI limitation. The legal fees incident to the divorce are personal expenses and generally are not deductible. However, Lia could take a partial deduction *from* AGI as a miscellaneous itemized deduction to the extent these legal fees relate to giving tax advice incident to the divorce. ◀

ORDINARY EXPENSE

Another requirement for deductibility is that a business or investment expense must be **ordinary**. Although the IRC does not provide either a definition or an application of this requirement, the Treasury Regulations under Sec. 212 indicate that for an expense to be ordinary it must be reasonable in amount and it must bear a reasonable and proximate relationship to the income-producing activity or property. This means that more than a remote connection must exist between the expense and the anticipated income. It does not mean that the property must be producing income currently.

EXAMPLE I6-5 ▶ Ahmed purchases a plot of land, on which there is an old vacant warehouse. Ahmed anticipates making a long-term profit from the investment because the value of the land is expected to appreciate eventually due to commercial development in the area. To help cover the costs of holding the property, Ahmed plans to rent storage space in the warehouse. During the current year, Ahmed incurs the following expenses, although he is unable to rent the warehouse:

Expenses	*Amount*
Property taxes	$1,000
Interest	4,000
Insurance	800
Utilities	200

All of these expenditures qualify as ordinary deductible expenses under Sec. 212 because they bear a reasonable and proximate relationship to the income Ahmed hopes to obtain, even though he generated no income from the property during the year. However, Ahmed might not be able to deduct them all in the current year because of the passive loss limitations explained in Chapter I8. ◀

The Supreme Court has ruled that for an expense to be ordinary it must be customary or usual in the context of a particular industry or business community.[8] Thus, an expenditure may be ordinary in the context of one type of business, but not in the context of another.

EXAMPLE I6-6 ▶ For many years, Hank has been an officer in Green Corporation, which is engaged in the grain business. Green Corporation purchases its grain from various suppliers. Last year, Green Corporation went bankrupt and was relieved from having to pay off its debts to its suppliers. In the current year, Hank enters into a contract to act as a commissioned agent to

---

[8] *Thomas H. Welch v. Helvering,* 12 AFTR 1456, 3 USTC ¶1164 (USSC, 1933) and *Deputy v. Pierre S. DuPont,* 23 AFTR 808, 40-1 USTC ¶9161 (USSC, 1940).

purchase grain for Green Corporation. To reestablish a relationship with suppliers whom Hank knew previously, Hank decides to pay off as many of Green Corporation's debts as he can. Hank is under no legal obligation to do so. Hank's payments are not ordinary. Rather, they are extraordinary expenditures made for goodwill to establish Hank in a new trade or business, and they must be capitalized. ◄

An expense may be ordinary with respect to a taxpayer even though that taxpayer encounters it only once.

EXAMPLE I6-7 ▶

For several years, Health for You, Inc., has been engaged in the business of making and selling dietary supplements. Most of the advertisements, orders, and deliveries of the supplements are done through the mail. During the current year, the post office judged that some of the advertisements were false. As a result, a fraud order is issued under which the post office stamps "Fraudulent" on all letters addressed to Health for You, Inc., and then returns them to the senders. In an unsuccessful suit to prevent the post office from continuing this practice, Health for You expends $50,000 in lawyer's fees. These fees are ordinary business expenses because they are incurred in an action that normally or ordinarily would be taken under the circumstances. ◄

The Supreme Court has also indicated that the term *ordinary* in this context refers to an expenditure that is currently deductible rather than an expenditure that must be capitalized.[9]

NECESSARY EXPENSE

In addition to being ordinary, a deductible investment or business expense must also be **necessary**. The Supreme Court has indicated that an expense is considered necessary if it is "appropriate and helpful" in the taxpayer's business.[10] To meet this appropriate or helpful standard, an expenditure need not be necessary in the sense that it is indispensable. Rather, the test is whether a reasonable or prudent businessperson would incur the same expenditure under similar circumstances.

EXAMPLE I6-8 ▶

The expenditures in Example I6-6 (the payment of debts from a former business) and Example I6-7 (the payment of legal fees) are both necessary because they are appropriate and helpful in each case. However, the expenditure in Example I6-6 is not ordinary and, therefore, is not deductible. The expenditure in Example I6-7 is deductible because it meets both tests. ◄

REASONABLE EXPENSE

Section 162 and Treasury Regulations under Sec. 212 provide that in order to be deductible the expense must be reasonable. Problems with meeting this standard generally arise when a closely-held company pays a salary to an individual who is both a shareholder and an employee. In this situation, a controlling shareholder of a corporation receives a payment, characterized as salary, that the IRS asserts is too large for the services rendered.

EXAMPLE I6-9 ▶

Brian, the controlling shareholder and an employee of Central Corporation, receives an annual salary of $650,000. Based on several factors, such as the size of Central Corporation's total operations and a comparison of salary received by officers of comparably sized corporations, the IRS contends that Brian's salary should be no higher than $300,000. If Central successfully defends the $650,000 salary, the corporation is able to deduct the full amount as salary expense. If the defense is not successful, the excess $350,000 is considered a dividend to the extent of earnings and profits, and no deduction is available to Central Corporation for this amount. In either event, Brian must take the full $650,000 into income. (See the Tax Planning Considerations section in this chapter for a discussion of the use of a payback agreement in these situations.) ◄

---

[9] *CIR v. S. B. Heininger*, 31 AFTR 783, 44-1 USTC ¶9109 (USSC, 1943). See also *CIR v. Walter F. Tellier*, 17 AFTR 2d 633, 66-1 USTC ¶9319 (USSC, 1966).

[10] *Thomas H. Welch v. Helvering*, 12 AFTR 1456, 3 USTC ¶1164 (USSC, 1933).

KEY POINT

Since the Sec. 162(m) compensation deduction limit applies only to publicly-held corporations, privately-held corporations are faced with the general reasonable standard which looks at the particular facts and circumstances.

In an attempt to link executive compensation to productivity and business performance and to discourage a common practice of increasing executive compensation despite declines in business performance, Congress enacted Sec. 162(m) that disallows a deduction for certain employee compensation that exceeds a yearly amount of $1 million. This limit applies to compensation payable by a publicly-held corporation to the corporation's chief executive officer and its four highest compensated officers for the taxable year. Compensation based on commissions or other performance goals is not subject to this limitation.

The tests for determining whether a business or investment expense is deductible are summarized in Topic Review I6-1.

EXPENSES AND LOSSES MUST BE INCURRED DIRECTLY BY THE TAXPAYER

Generally, taxpayers may not take a deduction for a loss or expense of another person. This requirement prevents taxpayers from engaging in manipulative schemes.

EXAMPLE I6-10 ▶ Juanita owns 60% of Hot Clothes, Inc. As CEO of Hot Clothes, Juanita is required to travel extensively. This year Hot Clothes purchases a business jet to facilitate Juanita's travel. In addition to her business travel, Juanita also uses the jet to take several vacations for her and her family. Hot Clothes may not take a deduction for Juanita's personal expenses. In order for the business to deduct these amounts, one of two procedures must be followed: (1) Juanita must report as additional compensation an amount that represents the use of the jet for her vacations, or (2) Juanita must reimburse Hot Clothes for the use of the jet for her vacations. ◀

This general rule applies to all types of expenditures, whether incurred in a trade or business, an investment activity, or a personal activity for which deductions are allowed. There is one exception: under Sec. 213 taxpayers may take a deduction for medical expenses paid on behalf of a dependent. Medical expenses are also deductible if paid for a person who would qualify as a dependent except for failing to meet the gross income and certain other tests (see Chapter I2).

Topic Review I6-1

Tests for Deductibility as a Business or Investment Expense

TEST	APPLICATION
Ordinary	▶ Based on the facts and circumstances. ▶ Reasonable and proximate relationship to the activity. ▶ Customary or usual in context of the industry. ▶ Need not be encountered by the taxpayer more than once.
Necessary	▶ Based on the facts and circumstances. ▶ Appropriate and helpful. ▶ Need not be indispensable. ▶ Would a reasonable or prudent businessperson incur the same expense?
Reasonable	▶ Based on the facts and circumstances. ▶ Applies to all business and investment expenses. ▶ Compensation paid to an owner-employee of a small corporation is the most commonly contested area. ▶ Compensation in excess of $1 million payable by a publicly-held corporation to its key executives may not be deductible.

EXAMPLE I6-11 ▶ During the current year, Dan incurs $3,400 in deductible medical expenses. Dan is not a full-time student and is not under age 19 but is otherwise supported by Tom, his father. Dan's gross income for the year is $15,000. If Tom pays Dan's medical expenses, Tom may deduct the expenses as an itemized deduction (subject to the 7.5% of AGI limitation) even though Tom may not take a dependency exemption for Dan. ◀

GENERAL RESTRICTIONS ON THE DEDUCTIBILITY OF EXPENSES

As mentioned earlier on page I6-5, certain types of expenditures are not deductible. These types of expenditures fall within certain categories discussed below.

CAPITALIZATION VERSUS EXPENSE DEDUCTION

GENERAL CAPITALIZATION REQUIREMENTS. Under Sec. 263, a taxpayer may not take a current deduction for capital expenditures. Generally, expenses that add to the value of, substantially prolong the useful life of, or change the use of the property are considered **capital expenditures**. Thus, capital expenditures include the cost of acquiring or constructing buildings, machinery, equipment, furniture, and any similar property that has a useful life that extends substantially beyond the end of the tax year. Taxpayers must also capitalize the cost of goodwill purchased in connection with the acquisition of the assets of a going concern.[11] (See Chapter I10 for a discussion of the amortization of goodwill.)

Some assets, such as buildings, machinery, equipment, furniture and fixtures, purchased goodwill, and customer lists are depreciable or amortizable and may provide deductions that spread over more than one tax year. Others, such as land, stock, and partnership interests, are neither depreciable nor amortizable and the taxpayer must wait until the taxpayer disposes of the asset to recover its cost. In some instances, it is difficult to ascertain whether an asset is eligible for depreciation or amortization. For example, the Tax Court has held that antique violin bows and an antique bass violin are depreciable property, overriding the IRS's arguments that they should not be depreciable because they were actually appreciating in value and it was impossible to determine their useful life.[12]

Maintenance and repair expenditures that only keep an asset in a normal operating condition are deductible if they do not increase the value or prolong the useful life of the asset. Distinguishing between a currently deductible expenditure and a capital expenditure can be difficult because expenditures for normal maintenance and repair can cost more than a capital improvement. Normal maintenance and repair may also increase the value of an asset. In one Tax Court case, the court held that expenditures incurred in replacing support beams and floor joists to shore up a sagging floor were deductible, whereas the court held that the cost of placing a new floor over an old one was a capital expenditure.[13] A tax advisor must examine all of the facts and circumstances to determine whether the expenditures constitute part of an overall plan of improvement or a change in use of the asset.

[11] Reg. Sec. 1.263(a)-2(h). See also *Indopco, Inc., v. CIR*, 69 AFTR 2d 92-694, 92-1 USTC ¶50,113 (USSC, 1992), where expenses incurred by a corporation that was the target of a "friendly" takeover were held to be nondeductible capital expenditures because they provided long-term benefits to the corporation. In this case, the Supreme Court held that these long-term benefits do not need to be associated with a specific identifiable asset.

[12] *Richard L. Simon*, 103 T.C. 247 (1994) and *Brian P. Liddle*, 76 AFTR 2d 95-6255, 95-2 USTC ¶50,488 (3rd Cir., 1959). The IRS has stated it will not follow these decisions. See AOD 96-9, 7/15/96.
[13] Reg. Sec. 1.162-4. See also *Standard Fruit Product* Co., 1949 PH T.C. Memo ¶49,207, 8 TCM 733.

ADDITIONAL COMMENT
Some provisions permit taxpayers to depreciate or amortize capital expenditures over a relatively short period of time. For example, there is a rapid write-off available for pollution control facilities under Sec. 169 and for organization costs of corporations under Sec. 248.

BOOK-TAX COMPARISON
Although for tax purposes a taxpayer may elect to deduct these capital expenditures, for book purposes capital expenditures must still be capitalized and depreciated or amortized. This difference in treatment gives rise to a book-tax adjustment on Schedule M-1 or M-3 of a corporation's Form 1120.

ELECTION TO DEDUCT CURRENTLY. Taxpayers sometimes may elect a current deduction for certain capital expenditures. Taxpayers often prefer a current deduction over capitalizing and depreciating an asset because of the time value of money. Some expenditures that taxpayers may elect to deduct currently[14] include

▶ Cost of fertilizers incurred by farmers

▶ Cost of soil and water conservation incurred by farmers

▶ Intangible drilling costs incurred in drilling oil and gas wells

▶ Costs for tertiary injectants

▶ Costs for certain mining development projects

▶ Costs incurred to remove architectural and transportation barriers to the handicapped and elderly

▶ Costs for certain qualified research and experimental expenditures

Taxpayers may also elect to deduct certain amounts each year for the purchase of qualified tangible personal property used in a trade or business instead of depreciating the property over its useful life. This deduction is limited to $105,000 (adjusted for inflation) per year for 2005 and $108,000 for 2006. Chapter I10 further examines the Sec. 179 election.

CAPITALIZATION OF DEDUCTION ITEMS. The exceptions mentioned above provide a current deduction for expenditures that are normally capital in nature. Conversely, Section 266 provides for the capitalization of certain expenses that are normally deductible. Section 266 is elective and applies to the following items:

▶ Annual property taxes, interest on a mortgage, and other carrying charges incurred on unimproved and unproductive real estate.

▶ Annual property taxes, interest, employment taxes, and other necessary expenses incurred for the development, improvement, or construction of real property, prior to the time construction is completed. For these expenses to be capitalized, the real property may be either improved or unimproved, productive or unproductive. After construction is completed, these types of expenses are fully deductible when incurred.

▶ Interest and employment taxes incurred in transporting and installing personalty (as opposed to realty) up to the time when the taxpayer first puts the property into use.

A taxpayer may make a new election to capitalize the expenses on unimproved and unproductive real estate each year.

EXAMPLE I6-12 ▶ During 2006 and 2007, Nancy pays property taxes of $5,000 on a piece of land. During 2006, the land is vacant and unproductive. In 2007, Nancy uses the land as a parking lot, generating $7,000 in income. Nancy can elect to capitalize the taxes in 2006 because the property is both unimproved and unproductive. In 2007, however, the land is productive, and Nancy cannot elect to capitalize the taxes. Because the expenses relate to the production of rental income, they are deductible *for* AGI. If the land remains unproductive during 2007, Nancy can elect to capitalize the taxes paid in 2007. However, the election is optional and need not be made for 2007 merely because it is made in 2006. ◀

For the development or construction of real property, an election to capitalize the other expenses incurred during the development or construction period remains in effect for that year and for all subsequent years until the end of the construction period. However, a taxpayer may make the election on each new project separately.

EXAMPLE I6-13 ▶ During the current year, Development, Inc. begins construction of an office building and a hotel. Development, Inc. incurs $20,000 in property taxes during the construction of the office building and $12,000 for the hotel. The election to capitalize the taxes on the office building does not bind Development, Inc. to make the same election with respect to the taxes on the hotel. ◀

[14] See Secs. 180, 175, 263(c), 193, 616, 190, and 174.

If a taxpayer elects to capitalize this type of expense under Sec. 266, the expense increases the basis of the property to which it pertains. If the property is depreciable, the taxpayer may deduct the expenses as depreciation deductions over a certain period. Taxpayers want to make this election if they have large net operating loss (NOL) carryovers, or if they expect to be in a significantly higher tax bracket in future years and thus feel that the benefit of the deduction is greater in the future.

Under Sec. 263A, certain taxpayers must capitalize certain costs into inventory instead of taking a current deduction. (See Chapter I11 for a discussion of inventories.)

EXPENSES RELATED TO EXEMPT INCOME

Under Sec. 265, taxpayers may not deduct any expense allocated or related to tax-exempt income. The purpose of this disallowance is to prevent the taxpayer from receiving a double tax benefit.

The IRC specifically disallows interest expense on debt the taxpayer incurs in order to purchase or hold tax-exempt securities. Thus, the disallowance depends on the taxpayer's intended use of the loan proceeds. Intent is generally determined by an examination of all the facts and circumstances surrounding the transaction. Intent to hold tax-exempt securities is shown if the tax-exempt securities are used as collateral in securing a loan.[15] If an individual who holds tax-exempt securities later incurs some debt, no disallowance will occur if the debt is incurred to finance personal items (e.g., a mortgage on a personal residence). However, if a taxpayer incurs the debt to finance an investment, deduction for a portion of the interest is generally disallowed. Even though the interest is not incurred to hold tax-exempt securities, it still may not be deductible. For example, if a taxpayer incurs interest on personal debt, it is not deductible. (See Chapter I7 for a discussion of limitations on the deductibility of personal interest.)

Asian, Inc. has invested $80,000 in Gold Corporation stock, $120,000 in real estate, and $50,000 in tax-exempt municipal bonds. During the current year, Asian borrows $70,000 for the purpose of investing in a limited partnership. For the year, the company pays $6,000 interest on the loan. Under these circumstances, the IRS will presume that Asian, Inc. has incurred a portion of the debt in order to hold the tax-exempt securities and will disallow a portion of the deduction. Asian may overcome that presumption if it can show that it could not have sold the tax-exempt securities. Merely showing that the sale of the bonds would result in a loss will not overcome this presumption. ◀

EXPENDITURES THAT ARE CONTRARY TO PUBLIC POLICY

Certain expenditures, even though incurred in a profit-motivated activity, may not be deductible if the payment itself is illegal or if the payment is a penalty or fine resulting from an illegal act. These nondeductible expenses generally fall within one of the following categories:

▶ Illegal payments to government officials or employees
▶ Other illegal payments
▶ Kickbacks, rebates, and bribes under Medicare and Medicaid
▶ Payments of fines and penalties
▶ Payment of treble damages under the federal antitrust laws

BRIBES AND KICKBACKS. Under Sec. 162(c)(1), any illegal bribe or kickback made to any official or employee of a government is not deductible. This applies to payments made to

▶ Federal officials and employees
▶ State, local, and foreign government officials and employees
▶ Officials and employees of an agency of a government

[15] Rev. Proc. 72-18, 1972-1 C.B. 740. See also *Wisconsin Cheeseman, Inc. v. U.S.*, 21 AFTR 2d 383, 68-1 USTC ¶9145 (7th Cir., 1968).

EXAMPLE I6-15 ▶ During February of the current year, Road Corporation enters into a contract with the State of Iowa to construct a five-mile stretch of a new highway. Under the terms of the contract, Road Corporation must complete the project by October 22 of the current year. If it is not completed and accepted by Iowa on or before that date, Iowa will fine Road Corporation $5,000 per day for every day after October 22 until the project is accepted. By October 20, the project foreman realizes that the company will not make the deadline if it complies with all the requirements imposed by the state inspector assigned to the project. To avoid the fine, the foreman arranges for the inspector to "look the other way" on several of the requirements in exchange for a payment of $8,000. Because this payment constitutes an illegal bribe to a government official, the payment is not deductible. ◀

Taxpayers may not deduct illegal payments to officials or employees of a foreign government if the payment is unlawful under the Foreign Corrupt Practices Act of 1977, unless such payments constitute a normal way of doing business in that country. In all cases, the burden rests on the government to prove the illegality of the payment.

Illegal bribes, kickbacks, and other illegal payments made to people other than a government official or employee are nondeductible if they are illegal under a federal law that subjects the payor to a criminal penalty or loss of the privilege of doing business. In addition, illegal payments under a state law imposing the same penalties are nondeductible, but only if the state generally enforces its law. Here, the definition of a kickback includes a payment for referring a client, patient, or customer.

The courts and the IRS have made a distinction between an illegal nondeductible kickback and a rebate on the purchase of an item. If the seller pays a rebate directly to the purchaser, it is an adjustment to the selling price and, as such, is an *exclusion* (rather than a deduction) from gross income.[16] The distinction between the two payments seems to be that the seller and purchaser negotiate the rebate as part of the selling price.

Section 162(c)(3) specifically disallows a deduction for any kickback, rebate, or bribe under Medicare and Medicaid. Disallowed amounts include payments made by physicians or by suppliers and providers of goods and services who receive payment under the Social Security Act or a federally funded state plan. Unlike payments to foreign government or nongovernment employees and officials, these payments need not be illegal under federal or state law.

ETHICAL POINT

A CPA discovers that a client included fines and penalties in a miscellaneous expense section of a previously filed tax return. The CPA should recommend the filing of an amended return. However, the CPA is not obligated to inform the IRS, and the CPA may not do so without the client's permission, except where required by law.

STOP & THINK

Question: Queen, Inc., is engaged in the ship and boat repair business. Since the competition is very tough, Queen generally kicks back approximately 10% of any repair bill to any ship captain who brings the ship to Queen for repairs. Queen's customers include individual owners of large ocean-going yachts and fishing boats, as well as government vessels owned by state, federal, and foreign governments. During the current year, Queen paid $80,000 in kickbacks to the captains of privately-owned yachts and boats, $40,000 to the owners of privately-owned vessels, and $100,000 to the captains of state, federal, and foreign government vessels. The crews of these government vessels are government employees. What is the proper tax treatment of these payments?

Solution: The $40,000 in kickbacks paid directly to the owners of the privately-owned vessels are treated as merely a rebate in the price of the services and reduces Queen's gross income, unless the payments could result in the imposition of a criminal penalty or loss of the privilege of doing business. The kickbacks paid to the captains of the state and federal vessels are not deductible because they are paid to employees of state and federal governments. The kickbacks paid to the captains of the privately-owned vessels are not deductible if they are illegal and subject the payor to a criminal penalty or loss of the privilege to do business. Likewise, the payments to the captains of the foreign vessels are not deductible if the payments are unlawful under the Foreign Corrupt Practices Act.

---

[16] Rev. Rul. 82-149, 1982-2 C.B. 56.

FINES AND PENALTIES. Section 162(f) of the IRC also disallows a deduction for the payment of any fine or penalty paid to a government because of the violation of a law.

Furthermore, it disallows a deduction for two-thirds of any payment for damages made as a result of a conviction (or a guilty or no-contest plea) in an action regarding a criminal violation of the federal antitrust laws.[17]

EXAMPLE I6-16 ▶ During the current year, the United States files criminal and civil actions against Allen, the president of Able Corporation, and Betty, the president of Bell Corporation, for conspiring to fix and maintain prices of electrical transformers. Both Allen and Betty enter pleas of no contest, and the appropriate judgments are entered. Subsequent to this action, Circle Corporation sues both Able and Bell Corporations for treble damages of $3,000,000. In settlement, Able and Bell Corporations each pay Circle Corporation $750,000. The maximum that Able and Bell Corporations may each deduct is $250,000 ($750,000 ÷ 3). ◀

EXPENSES RELATING TO AN ILLEGAL ACTIVITY. Interestingly, although the payment of an illegal bribe or kickback and the payment of a fine or penalty as the result of an illegal act are both nondeductible, expenses incurred in an illegal activity are generally deductible if they are ordinary, necessary, and reasonable and the taxpayer reports the income from the illegal activity.[18]

EXAMPLE I6-17 ▶ Acme, Inc., owns and operates a small financial services business involved in the sale of securities and the lending of money. Acme often sells securities to customers in other states. However, because it has not registered the business with the appropriate state or federal authorities, the operation of the business is illegal. During the current year, Acme incurs the following expenses:

Interest	$ 20,000
Salaries	140,000
Depreciation	7,000
Printing	5,000
Bribe to employee of state securities commission	12,000
Total	$184,000

If Acme reports the income from this activity, the deductible expenses for the year total $172,000. The illegal payment of $12,000 to the government employee is not deductible. ◀

One exception to this general rule exists. Section 280E disallows a deduction for expenses incurred in an illegal business of trafficking or dealing in drugs.

OTHER EXPENDITURES SPECIFICALLY DISALLOWED

The IRC also specifically disallows deductions for certain other expenses, even though they might meet all the requirements mentioned previously. These include political contributions and lobbying expenses and, in certain situations, business start-up expenses.

POLITICAL CONTRIBUTIONS AND LOBBYING EXPENSES. Political contributions and lobbying expenses constitute one general category of disallowed expenses. Taxpayers may not deduct expenditures made in connection with the following:

▶ Influencing legislation

▶ Participating or intervening in any political campaign of any candidate for public office

▶ Attempting to influence the general public with respect to elections, legislative matters, or referendums

▶ Communicating directly with the President, Vice President, and certain other federal employees and officials

---

[17] Sec. 162(g).
[18] CIR v. Neil Sullivan, et al., 1 AFTR 2d 1158, 58-1 USTC ¶9368 (USSC, 1958).

Sec. 162(e) also denies a deduction for contributions to tax-exempt organizations that carry on lobbying activities if a principal purpose of the contribution is to obtain a deduction for what otherwise would have been disallowed. Furthermore, the IRC disallows payments made for advertising in a convention or any other program if any part of the proceeds of the publication will directly or indirectly benefit a specific political party or candidate.[19]

Taxpayers may deduct lobbying expenses incurred to influence legislation on a local level if the legislation is of direct interest to the taxpayer's business. Local legislation includes actions by a legislative body of any political subdivision of a state (e.g., city or county council), but does not include any state or federal action. These deductible expenditures include expenses of communicating with or dues paid to an organization of which the taxpayer is a member. For administrative convenience, the deduction disallowance does not apply to any in-house expenditure attributable to such activities as long as the total of such expenditures for the taxable year does not exceed $2,000. In-house expenditures are expenses incurred directly by the taxpayer other than amounts paid to a professional lobbyist or dues that are allocable to lobbying. Additionally, the deduction disallowance does not apply to taxpayers engaged in the business of lobbying.

EXAMPLE I6-18 ▶ Kensey & Associates is a large New York law firm. It is not in the lobbying business. During the year, the firm sends people to Washington, D.C., to testify before a Congressional subcommittee with regard to proposed changes in the Social Security taxes imposed on employers. Such changes directly affect the firm's business because they affect the amount of taxes it must pay on behalf of its employees. The firm's ordinary and necessary expenses incurred with respect to the trip are not deductible because the expenses were incurred to influence federal rather than local legislation. ◀

If the legislation cannot reasonably be expected to directly affect the taxpayer's trade or business, the expenses are not deductible.

EXAMPLE I6-19 ▶ Realty, LLC, is a residential real estate company located in Chicago. The city of Chicago has proposed legislation to increase the hotel room tax. Realty spends time researching and traveling to speak to the Chicago City Council regarding this legislation, thus its lobbying expenses are not deductible. While they are used to influence legislation on the local level, they are not of direct interest to its business. ◀

BUSINESS INVESTIGATION AND PREOPENING EXPENSES. At the election of the taxpayer, Section 195 of the IRC allows a current deduction for business start-up expenditures for the lesser of the amount of the start-up expenditures or $5,000, with a dollar for dollar phase-out for amounts incurred over $50,000. The remaining portion of start-up expenditures must be capitalized and amortized over a period of 180 months starting with the month in which the new business begins. Start-up expenditures specifically include three types of expenditures:

▶ *Business investigation expenses.* These expenses are costs a taxpayer incurs in reviewing and analyzing a prospective business before deciding whether to acquire or create it. The key here is that the taxpayer incurs the expenses before making a decision. These expenses include such items as analyses and surveys of markets, traffic patterns, products, labor supplies, and distribution facilities.

ADDITIONAL COMMENT

Costs incurred in connection with the issuance of stock or securities do not qualify as start-up costs. These costs are charged to Paid in Capital.

▶ *Preopening or start-up costs.* Preopening or start-up costs are expenses incurred after a taxpayer decides to acquire or create a business but before the business activity itself has started. These costs include expenditures for training employees; advertising; securing supplies, distributors, and potential customers; and expenditures for professional services in setting up the business's books and records. A taxpayer not engaged in any existing business or engaged in a business unrelated to the business the taxpayer is acquiring or creating incurs these types of costs.

---

[19] Sec. 276(a). Nondeductible political contributions also include payments for admission to a dinner or program where the proceeds will benefit a party or candidate, or admission to an inaugural ball, party, or concert if the activity is identified with a political party or candidate.

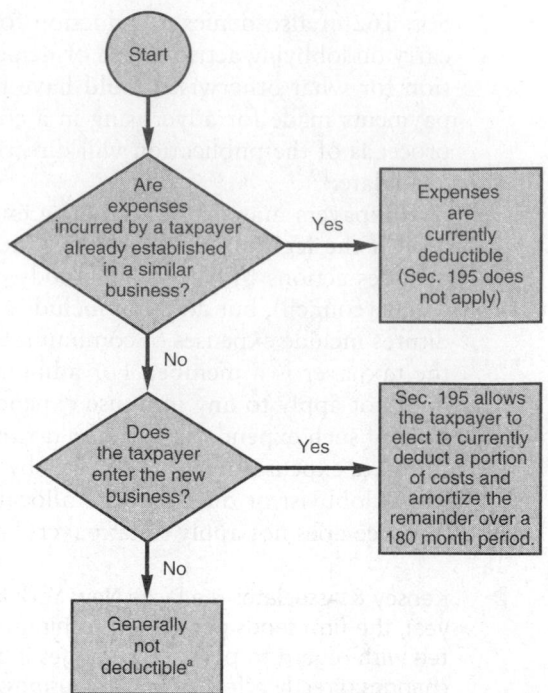

^a Rev. Rul. 57-418, 1957-2 C.B. 143 and Rev. Rul. 77-254, 1977-2 C.B. 63; *Morton Frank*, 20 T.C. 511 (1953).

FIGURE I6-1 ▶ DEDUCTIBILITY OF BUSINESS INVESTIGATION AND START-UP COSTS

▶ *Expenses incurred in connection with an investment activity.* These expenses are costs incurred in connection with an investment activity that the taxpayer anticipates will become an active trade or business.

As defined by Sec. 195, start-up expenditures do not include these same types of expenses when incurred by a taxpayer already engaged in a business similar to the new one being created or acquired. In such a case, the taxpayer may deduct these expenditures currently because they originate in the taxpayer's existing business. Figure I6-1 provides a flowchart to assist in properly classifying these types of expenditures.

STOP & THINK

Question: Shauna works in an automobile manufacturing plant in Detroit, Michigan. In January of the current year, she took a two-week vacation in order to fly to Orlando, Florida. While in Orlando, she spent some time investigating the possibility of opening a store in nearby Coco Beach. In total, she spent $800 on airfare, $1,500 on hotels and food, $300 on equipment rentals, and $300 on a car rental. In addition to spending time on the beach talking to people and checking out the rental equipment, she also spent some time talking to shop owners and real estate agents. After some analysis, however, Shauna has decided to keep her job in Detroit. What is the proper tax treatment for these expenditures?

Solution: In general, Sec. 162 of the IRC allows a deduction for expenses incurred in a business. Expenses incurred before the business starts are not incurred in a business and thus are not deductible under Sec. 162. However, under Sec. 195 a portion of certain expenditures such as business investigation expenses and start-up costs can be deducted currently while the remainder is capitalized and amortized over a 180-month period, beginning with the month in which the new business begins. Unfortunately Shauna did not open the new business. Thus, she may not deduct or amortize any of these expenses.

Topic Review I6-2 summarizes the restrictions on the deductibility of these items.

Topic Review I6-2

Restrictions on the Deductibility of Expense Items

ITEM	RESTRICTIONS IMPOSED
1. Capital expenditures	The general rule is that the expenditure is not currently deductible if its life extends beyond the end of the year. Special elections are available to currently deduct certain capital expenditures (e.g., research and experimental costs under Sec. 174; and limited amounts per year for acquisitions of tangible personal property used in a trade or business under Sec. 179).
2. Carrying charges	An election may be made under Sec. 266 to capitalize certain expenses that are normally deductible such as property and employment taxes, interest, and carrying charges on unimproved unproductive real estate.
3. Expenses related to tax exempt income	Expenses such as interest incurred on debt used to purchase or carry tax-exempt securities are disallowed under Sec. 265.
4. Expenditures contrary to public policy	Such expenditures are generally not deductible. Examples include bribes and kickbacks, fines and penalties, and expenses of an illegal activity involved with trafficking or dealing in drugs.
5. Legal and accounting fees	Legal and accounting fees can be either *for* AGI deductible business expenses, nondeductible personal use expenditures, or *from* AGI fees incurred in the determination of any tax (e.g., tax return preparation fees).
6. Political contributions and lobby expenses	The general rule is that such items are not deductible (e.g., costs of influencing public opinion), but there are certain exceptions (e.g., costs of appearing before local legislative bodies on topics directly related to the taxpayer's business).
7. Business investigation and preopening expenses	The following rules apply: a. Currently deductible if the taxpayer is already engaged in a similar business. b. Not deductible if the taxpayer is not currently engaged in a similar business and does not enter the new business. c. An amount equal to the lesser of the amount of the expenses or $5,000 reduced by amounts incurred over $50,000 is currently deductible with the remainder to be capitalized and amortized over a 180 month period if the taxpayer enters the new business and makes an election. d. Deductible if expenditures constitute specific items such as legal expenses incurred in drafting purchase documents in an unsuccessful attempt to acquire a specific business. However, general investigation expenditures in search of a new business are not deductible.

PROPER SUBSTANTIATION REQUIREMENT

OBJECTIVE 3

List the substantiation requirements for deducting travel and entertainment expenses

Generally, the burden of proving the existence of a deduction or loss falls on the taxpayer. Thus, a taxpayer must properly substantiate all deductible expenses. Because the IRS may audit a return and request proof, taxpayers should retain items such as receipts, cancelled checks, and paid bills. Occasionally, the courts will allow a deduction that is not properly substantiated by the taxpayer if an expenditure clearly has been made. In these cases, the court estimates the amount of the deduction based on all the facts and circumstances. This procedure is known as the *Cohan* rule and derives its name from a court case in which the judge allowed a deduction for an estimated amount of certain expenses.[20] The most prudent course of action, of course, is to retain proper documentation rather than to rely upon the *Cohan* rule.

EXAMPLE I6-20 ▶ In April of the current year, Terry took his tax records to a CPA to have his prior year's income tax return prepared. As part of the return, the CPA attached a supplemental schedule listing all of Terry's items of income and expense. After the return was prepared and filed, Terry's records

[20] *George M. Cohan v. CIR*, 8 AFTR 10552, 2 USTC ¶489 (2nd Cir., 1930). Interestingly, the *Cohan* case dealt with travel and entertainment expenses. Because of the subsequent enactment of Sec. 274(d), the *Cohan* rule may not be used to deduct entertainment expenses. It is still effective for other types of expenses.

were stolen. Upon audit two years later, the IRS disallowed Terry's deductions because he had no records to substantiate the expenses. When the case was litigated, the court allowed deductions for an estimated amount of expenses under the *Cohan* rule because of the list that was attached to Terry's return and because the court believed that Terry had testified honestly in his own behalf.[21]

HISTORICAL NOTE

Justice Learned Hand, in permitting a deduction for unsubstantiated amounts in *George M. Cohan v. CIR*, 8 AFTR 10552, 2 USTC ¶489 (2nd Cir, 1930), wrote "absolute certainty in such matters is usually impossible and it is not necessary; the Board should make as close an approximation as it can, bearing heavily if it chooses on the taxpayer whose inexactitude is of his own making."

Additionally, Sections 274 and 280F provide specific and more stringent recordkeeping requirements for travel, entertainment, business gifts, computers, and vehicles used for transportation. In these cases, the taxpayer may not take a deduction unless the taxpayer substantiates the expenditure by either an adequate record or sufficient evidence that corroborates the taxpayer's statement. This substantiation may take the form of account books, diaries, logs, receipts and paid bills, trip sheets, expense reports, and statements of witnesses. The information that requires substantiation includes the following:

▶ Amount of the expense

▶ Time and place of the travel or entertainment

▶ Date and description of the gift

▶ Business purpose of the expenditure

▶ Business relationship to the taxpayer of the person entertained or of the person who received the gift

The *Cohan* rule does not apply to these types of expenses. (See Chapter I9 for a more complete discussion regarding the deductibility of these types of expenses.)

WHEN AN EXPENSE IS DEDUCTIBLE

OBJECTIVE 4

Explain the timing of deductions under both the cash and accrual methods of accounting

Because the tax law generally requires calculating taxable income annually, the question of when a particular expense is deductible is especially important. The answer to this question largely depends on the taxpayer's method of accounting.[22] The most common methods include the following:

▶ Cash receipts and disbursements method (cash method)

▶ Accrual method

▶ Hybrid method (a combination of the cash and accrual methods where some items are accounted for on the cash method and other items are accounted for on the accrual method)

ADDITIONAL COMMENT

Section 446(b) provides that in cases where no method of accounting has been regularly used or if the method used does not clearly reflect income, then the computation of taxable income is to be made under a method that, in the opinion of the IRS, does clearly reflect income.

Taxpayers normally use the same method for computing taxable income that they use in keeping their financial accounting records. However, except for the use of the last-in, first-out (LIFO) method of accounting for inventory, the tax law does not generally require conformity. For example, many companies use the straight-line depreciation method for financial accounting purposes and the modified accelerated cost recovery system (MACRS) for tax purposes. This difference in depreciation methods, of course, results in a book-tax adjustment.

CASH METHOD

Under the **cash method of accounting**, expenses are deductible when actually paid. The cash method considers payment by check a cash payment as long as the bank subsequently honors the check. This is the case even if the payee receives the check so late on the last day of the year that the payee could not have cashed it.[23] If the taxpayer mails the check near the end of the year, the taxpayer must have evidence that the mailing took place in the year

---

[21] *Layard M. White*, 1980 PH T.C. Memo ¶80,582, 41 TCM 671.
[22] Methods of accounting as they relate to the reporting of income are discussed in Chapter I3. Methods of accounting as they relate to deductibility of expenses and losses are covered in this chapter. For an overall discussion of accounting methods, see Chapter I11.

[23] *CIR v. Estate of M. A. Bradley*, 10 AFTR 1405, 3 USTC ¶904 (6th Cir., 1932) and *Charles F. Kahler*, 18 T.C. 31 (1952).

for which the taxpayer claims a deduction. Furthermore, the cash method considers payment by credit card a cash payment at the time of the charge rather than at the time the taxpayer pays for the charge.

A mere promise to pay, or the issuance of a note payable, does not constitute a payment under the cash method. Thus, a charge on an open account with a creditor is not deductible until an actual payment of cash satisfies the charge.

EXAMPLE I6-21 ▶ Fox, Inc., a calendar-year taxpayer, is in the plumbing repair business. The business uses the cash method of accounting. Under an arrangement with one of its suppliers, Fox and its employees can pick up supplies at any time during the month by merely signing for them. At the end of the month, the supplier sends Fox a bill for the charges. Fox always pays the bill in full during the following month. In December of the current year, Fox charges $1,500 for supplies. During the same month Fox purchases a plumbing fixture for $250 from another supplier. Fox uses its charge card at the time of purchase. Fox may deduct the $250 during the current year. However, the $1,500 charged on the open account is deductible when paid in the following year. ◀

PREPAID EXPENSES. In general, a capital expenditure or the prepayment of expenses by a cash method taxpayer does not result in a current deduction if the expenditure creates an asset having a useful life that extends substantially beyond the close of the tax year. This can occur when a taxpayer makes expenditures for prepaid rent, services, or interest. However, in the case of prepaid rent, a circuit court of appeals decision has held that a taxpayer may take a current deduction for the entire amount of an expenditure if the period covered by the prepayment does not exceed one year and the rent agreement obligates the taxpayer to make the prepayment.[24]

EXAMPLE I6-22 ▶ On November 1 of the current year, Twyla Corporation enters into a lease arrangement with Rashad to rent Rashad's office space for the following 36 months. By prepaying the rent for the entire 36-month period, Twyla Inc. is able to obtain a favorable monthly lease payment of $1,800. This prepayment creates an asset (a leasehold) with a useful life that extends substantially beyond the end of the taxable year. Thus, only $3,600 ($1,800 × 2 months) of the total payment is deductible in the current year. The rest must be capitalized and amortized over the life of the lease. However, assume that under the terms of the lease, Twyla Inc. is obligated to make three annual payments of $21,600 each November 1 for the subsequent 12 months. On November 1 of the current year, Twyla Inc. pays Rashad $21,600 for the first 12-month period. Because Twyla Inc. is obligated to make the prepayment and the period covered by the prepayment does not exceed one year, the entire $21,600 is deductible in the current year using the reasoning of the previously cited circuit court decision. ◀

PREPAID INTEREST. The IRC requires that prepaid interest expense be deducted over the period of the loan to which the interest charge is allocated.[25] Receipt of a discounted loan does not represent prepaid interest expense. Instead, the IRC deems the interest paid when the taxpayer repays the loan.

EXAMPLE I6-23 ▶ During the current year, Richelle borrows $1,000 from the bank for use in her business. Richelle uses the cash method of accounting in her business. Under the terms of the loan, the bank discounts the loan by $80, paying Richelle $920. When the loan comes due in the following year, however, Richelle is to repay the full $1,000. Richelle cannot deduct the $80 of interest expense until she repays the loan in the following year. ◀

REAL-WORLD EXAMPLE

A taxpayer made an overpayment of the federal income tax in 1975. In 1979, the IRS offset the overpayment against interest the taxpayer owed to the IRS. The Tax Court held that the interest expense was deductible in 1979 rather than in 1975. *Saverio Eboli,* 93 T.C. 123 (1989).

Taxpayers often prepay interest in the form of points. A point is one percent of the loan amount. Thus, the payment of two points on a $100,000 loan amounts to $2,000. While tax law generally requires the amortization of points over the life of the loan, points paid in connection with the purchase or improvement of a principal residence may be deductible when paid. Points paid in connection with the purchase (but not the

---

[24] *Martin J. Zaninovich v. CIR*, 45 AFTR 2d 80-1442, 80-1 USTC ¶9342 (9th Cir., 1980) and *Bonaire Development Co. v. CIR*, 50 AFTR 2d 82-5167, 82-2 USTC ¶9428 (9th Cir., 1982). See also *Stephen A. Keller v. CIR*, 53 AFTR 2d 84-663, 84-1 USTC ¶9194 (8th Cir., 1984).

[25] Sec. 461(g).

improvement) of a principal residence are automatically deductible in the year paid if they satisfy the following four requirements:

▶ the closing agreement clearly designates the amounts as points

▶ the amount involves a computation as a percentage of the amount borrowed

▶ the charging of points is an established business practice in the geographic area, and

▶ the points are paid in connection with the purchase of the taxpayer's principal residence which is used to secure the loan.[26]

Although points paid on loans incurred to *improve* the taxpayer's principal residence do not fall under this safe harbor rule, they still are currently deductible if the residence is collateral for the loan, the payment of points is an established business practice in the geographic area in which it is incurred, and the amount of the prepayment does not exceed the amount generally charged.

A taxpayer may not currently deduct points paid to refinance a mortgage on a principal residence because the points are not paid in connection with the purchase or improvement of the taxpayer's residence.[27]

REAL-WORLD EXAMPLE
The mortgage company will, at the end of the year, mail to the taxpayer a Form 1098 which shows the amount of interest and points paid.

EXAMPLE I6-24 ▶ During the current year, Pam purchases a principal residence for $150,000, paying $50,000 down and financing the remainder with a 30-year mortgage secured by the property. Pam must make monthly payments on the mortgage. At the closing, Pam must pay three points as a loan origination fee. Because these points are paid in connection with the purchase of a principal residence, Pam may deduct $3,000 ($100,000 × 0.03) as interest expense during the current year. In addition, Pam may also deduct the interest portion of each monthly payment made during the year. On the other hand, assume that Pam takes out the $100,000 loan in order to refinance her home at a lower interest rate. The $3,000 prepaid interest is not currently deductible. Instead, Pam must deduct the interest ratably over the term of the loan. Thus, Pam may deduct an additional $8.33 ($3,000 ÷ 360 payments) interest expense for each payment that she makes during the year. ◀

If the taxpayer sells a home and pays off the refinanced mortgage, any unamortized portion of the points is deductible in the year of repayment. The tax law treats points paid by the seller as incurred by the purchaser, and therefore the points are currently deductible by the purchaser if they meet the other requirements and are subtracted from the purchase price of the residence.[28]

The cash method of accounting provides some degree of flexibility to taxpayers because, under this method, taxpayers can generally deduct expenses when paid rather than when accrued. Thus, subject to the limitations mentioned above with regard to prepaid expenses, taxpayers may to some degree accelerate or defer deductions from one year to another by merely accelerating or deferring payment. However, the IRC imposes limitations on the use of the cash method. For example, taxpayers must account for inventories under the accrual method.[29] Furthermore, under Sec. 448, most C corporations (corporations that have not elected Subchapter S status), partnerships that have a C corporation as a partner, and tax shelters may not use the cash method. However, the IRC makes exceptions to this general rule for personal service corporations, small businesses with average annual gross receipts of $5 million or less, and businesses involved in the farming and timber businesses. (See Chapter I11 for a complete discussion of the different accounting methods a taxpayer may use for computing taxable income.)

[26] Rev. Proc. 94-27, I.R.B. 94-15, 17. As explained in Chapter I7, acquisition indebtedness incurred to acquire a personal residence is limited to $1,000,000. Hence, points that are allocated to the loan principal in excess of this limit are not deductible either.
[27] Rev. Rul. 87-22, 1987-1 C.B. 146, and Rev. Proc. 87-15, 1987-1 C.B. 624. However, the Eighth Circuit has allowed a current deduction for points paid upon the refinancing of a mortgage loan because the original loan was merely a "bridge" or temporary loan until permanent financing could be arranged.

See *James R. Huntsman v. CIR*, 66 AFTR 2d 90-5020, 90-2 USTC ¶50,340 (8th Cir., 1990).
[28] Rev. Proc. 94-27, I.R.B. 94-15, 17.
[29] Reg. §1.446-1(c)(2). However, most taxpayers with less than $1,000,000 of average annual gross receipts may use the cash method. See Rev. Proc. 2001-10, 2001-1 CB 272. The cash method may also be used by select taxpayers whose annual gross receipts do not exceed $10,000,000. See Rev. Proc. 2002-28, I.R.B. 2002-18, 815.

ACCRUAL METHOD

An **accrual method** taxpayer deducts expenses in the period in which they accrue. Generally, items accrue when the transaction meets both an **all-events test** and an economic performance test.[30]

ALL-EVENTS TEST. The all-events test is met when both of the following occur:

▶ The existence of a liability is established.

▶ The amount of the liability is determined with reasonable accuracy.

EXAMPLE 16-25 ▶ During the current year, Phil provides services for Granite, Inc. Granite uses the accrual method of accounting. Phil claims that Granite owes $10,000 for the services. Granite admits owing Phil $6,000, but contests the remaining $4,000. Because the amount of the liability can be accurately established only with respect to $6,000, Granite can deduct only that amount. If Granite pays the full $10,000, it may deduct the full amount in the year of payment, even though the contested amount ($4,000) is not resolved until a subsequent taxable year.[31] If Phil loses the lawsuit and repays Granite the $4,000, Granite will include that amount in income in the year of repayment under the tax benefit rule (see Chapter I11). ◀

Because of the all-events test, taxpayers may not deduct additions to reserves for estimated expenses such as warranty expenses. Instead, the taxpayer deducts the expenses in the year in which such work is actually performed.

EXAMPLE 16-26 ▶ Best Corporation uses the accrual method of accounting and is engaged in the business of painting and rustproofing automobiles. Best Corporation provides a 5-year warranty for new vehicles and a 2-year warranty for used vehicles. Best Corp. extends the warranty only to the person who owns the car at the time the car is painted. Furthermore, in order to keep the warranty in force, the customer must present the vehicle to Best Corporation for inspection each year. The warranty is void if the vehicle is involved in an accident. Even though for financial accounting purposes Best Corporation may provide a reserve for estimated warranty expenses and deduct a reasonable addition to the reserve on an annual basis, no income tax deduction is allowed until the warranty work is actually done. ◀

ADDITIONAL COMMENT

Because of this difference between the tax treatment and the financial accounting treatment, an M-1 or M-3 adjustment must be made on a corporation's Form 1120.

ECONOMIC PERFORMANCE TEST. To be currently deductible under the accrual method, an expense must also meet an economic performance test. Exactly when economic performance occurs depends on the type of transaction. Table I6-1 contains a listing of various types of transactions that may arise and identifies when economic performance is deemed to have occurred under Sec. 461(h).

EXAMPLE 16-27 ▶ On December 20 of the current year, Pit Corporation, an accrual method taxpayer, enters into a binding contract with Pat to have Pat clean and paint the exterior of Pit's business building. Under the terms of the contract, Pat is to do the work in March of the following year. The total cost of the job is $4,000. Pit pays 10% down at the time the contract is signed. Because the job is not to be done until the following year, economic performance has not occurred in the current year and Pit may not deduct any portion of the expense in the current year. ◀

HISTORICAL NOTE

The economic performance test was added by Congress in the Tax Reform Act of 1984. Congress was concerned that in some situations taxpayers could deduct expenses currently, but the actual cash expenditure might not be made for several years. Taking a current deduction in such situations overstated the real cost because the time value of money was ignored.

An exception to the economic performance test provides that taxpayers may take a current deduction for recurring liabilities if all of the following occur:

▶ The item meets the all-events test during the year.

▶ Economic performance of the item occurs within the shorter of 8½ months after the close of the tax year, or a reasonable period after the close of the tax year.

▶ The expense is recurring and the taxpayer consistently treats the item as incurred in the tax year.

▶ Either the item is not material or the accrual of the item in the tax year results in a more proper matching against income than accruing the item in the tax year in which economic performance occurs.

---

[30] Reg. Sec. 1.461-1(a)(2) and Sec. 461(h).   [31] Reg. Sec. 1.461-2(a)(1).

▼ **TABLE I6-1**
When Economic Performance Is Deemed to Have Occurred

Event That Gives Rise to Liability	When Economic Performance Is Deemed to Have Occurred (i.e., when the accrual method taxpayer may take the deduction)
Another person provides the taxpayer with property or services	When the person actually provides the services[a]
Taxpayer uses property	As the taxpayer uses the property[a]
Taxpayer must provide property or services to another person	As the taxpayer provides property or services to the other person[b]
Taxpayer must make payments to another, including payments for rebates and refunds, awards or prizes, insurance or service contracts, and taxes.	As the taxpayer makes payments to the other person
Taxpayer must make payments to another person because of a tort, breach of contract, violation of law, or injury claim under a worker's compensation act	As the taxpayer makes payments to the other person

[a] Economic performance may be deemed to have occurred at the earlier date of payment if the taxpayer reasonably expects the property or services to be provided within 3½ months after the payment is made. Reg. Sec. 1.461-4(d)(6)(ii).
[b] Economic performance may also occur as the taxpayer incurs costs in connection with the obligation to provide the property or services. Reg. Sec. 1.461-4(d)(4)(i).

This exception for recurring liabilities is available for the first four types of transactions identified in Table I6-1, but it is not available for the last type of transaction in the table.

EXAMPLE I6-28 ▶ Dawn & Company, Inc. is a calendar-year, accrual method taxpayer. Every year at the end of October, Dawn, Inc., enters into a contract with Sam to provide snow removal services for the parking lots at Dawn, Inc.'s, corporate offices. This contract extends for five months through the end of March of the following year. Because the all-events test is met (the liability is fixed), the expense recurs every year, economic performance occurs within the requisite period of time, and the item is not material, Dawn, Inc. may deduct the entire expense in the year in which Dawn, Inc., and Sam enter into the contract. ◀

A special rule under Sec. 461(c) applies to real property taxes. Under this provision, a taxpayer may elect to accrue real property taxes ratably over the period to which the taxes relate. Once made, this election is irrevocable without permission from the IRS.

EXAMPLE I6-29 ▶ Under the law of State X, the lien date for real property taxes for calendar year 2006 is January 1, 2006. The tax is payable in full on November 30, 2006. Alpha Corp. is an accrual method taxpayer that has a January 31 fiscal year-end. On January 1, 2006, real property taxes of $100,000 are assessed against a building Alpha Corp. owns. Alpha pays the taxes on November 30, 2006. If Alpha does not make the election to use the ratable accrual method, none of the payment is deductible in Alpha's fiscal year ending January 31, 2006, because the payment date is more than 8½ months after the January 31, 2006, year-end.

On the other hand, if Alpha makes the election, it may deduct $8,333 ($100,000 × 1/12) in its fiscal year that ends January 31, 2006, and $91,667 ($100,000 × 11/12) in its fiscal year that ends January 31, 2007.

If the taxes are paid on September 30, 2006, Alpha would be better off not making the ratable accrual election. In this case, the recurring item exception applies because the payment is made within 8½ months of Alpha's 2006 fiscal year-end. Thus, if Alpha does not make the election, all of the $100,000 is deductible in the fiscal year ending on January 31, 2006. ◀

Topic Review I6-3 presents the rules for determining when an expense is deductible.

Topic Review I6-3

When an Expense Is Deductible

CASH METHOD: DEDUCTIBLE WHEN PAID

Payment Is Made When
► Cash or other property is transferred.
► A check is delivered or mailed.
► An item is charged on a credit card.
   Note: A mere promise to pay or delivery of a note payable is not deductible under the cash method.

Prepaid Expenses
► Generally are deductible over the period covered.
► Deductible when paid if the period covered does not exceed one year.
► Prepaid interest is generally deductible ratably over the period covered by the loan.
► Points are deductible when paid if:
   —The loan is used to purchase or improve the taxpayer's principal residence.
   —The loan is secured by the residence.
   —Points are established business practice in the geographical area.
   —The points do not exceed the amount generally charged.
   —For points paid to purchase a principal residence, the closing agreement clearly designates the amount as points and the amount must be computed as a percentage of the amount borrowed.

ACCRUAL METHOD: DEDUCTIBLE WHEN ACCRUED

In General
► Taxpayers maintaining inventories must use the accrual method of accounting (except for taxpayers with average annual gross receipts of $10 million or less).
► Accrual occurs when the item satisfies both the all-events test and economic performance.

All-Events Test
► The existence of a liability is established and
► The amount of the liability is determined.

Economic Performance
► When economic performance occurs depends on the transaction involved (see Table I6-1).
► Occurs in the year the item meets the all-events test and all of the following tests:
   —Actual economic performance occurs within the shorter of:
      8½ months after the taxable year or a reasonable period after the taxable year.
   —The expense is recurring and receives consistent treatment from year to year.
   —Either:
      The item is immaterial or
      Deducting the expense in the year it meets the all-events test results in a more proper matching of income and deductions.

SPECIAL DISALLOWANCE RULES

OBJECTIVE 5

Explain the tax consequences of wash sales

In addition to the general rules mentioned above, certain types of transactions are subject to further limitations and disallowances. These include wash sales, transactions between related persons, gambling losses, losses associated with an activity determined to be a hobby, expenses of renting a vacation home, and expenses of an office in the taxpayer's home. Further discussion of these special disallowance rules follows.

WASH SALES
Section 1091 disallows losses incurred on wash sales of stock or securities in the year of sale. For purposes of Sec. 1091, a **wash sale** occurs when

► A taxpayer realizes a loss on the sale of stock or securities, and

▶ The taxpayer acquires "substantially identical" stock or securities within a 61-day period of time that extends from 30 days before the date of sale to 30 days after the date of sale.[32]

Thus, the purpose of the wash sale rule is to prevent taxpayers from generating artificial tax losses in situations where taxpayers do not intend to reduce their holdings in the stock or securities sold.

EXAMPLE I6-30 ▶ Leslie realizes $10,000 in short-term capital gains (STCGs) through dealings in the stock market during the current year. Realizing that STCGs are fully includible in gross income unless they are offset against realized capital losses, Leslie analyzes her portfolio to determine whether she owns any stocks that have declined in value. She finds that the FMV of her Edison Corporation common stock is only $8,000, even though she originally purchased it for $16,000. Despite this paper loss on the stock, Leslie wants to retain the stock because she feels that Edison Corporation is still a good investment. If Leslie attempts to take advantage of the paper loss on the Edison stock by selling the stock she owns and repurchasing a similar number of shares of Edison common stock within the 61-day period, Sec. 1091 disallows the loss. ◀

SELF-STUDY QUESTION

During 2003, you bought 100 shares of X stock on each of three occasions. You paid $158 a share for the first block of 100 shares, $100 a share for the second block, and $95 a share for the third block. On December 23, 2006, you sold 300 shares of X stock for $125 a share. On January 6, 2007, you bought 250 shares of identical X stock. Can you deduct the loss realized on the first block of stock?

ANSWER

You cannot deduct the loss of $33 a share on the first block because within 30 days after the date of sale you bought 250 identical shares of X stock. In addition, you cannot reduce the gain realized on the sale of the second and third blocks of stock by this loss.

At times, taxpayers may attempt to circumvent the wash sale provisions through either a sham transaction or an indirect repurchase of the securities. If this is the case, the wash sale provisions still prevent the recognition of the loss. The Supreme Court has held that losses on sales of stock by a husband were disallowed when the stockbroker was instructed to purchase the same number of shares in his wife's name.[33]

In some instances a taxpayer may attempt to circumvent the wash sale provisions by merely delaying the repurchase of the substantially identical stock. This tactic should work as long as a written agreement to repurchase the stock does not exist at the time of the sale or at any time within the 61-day period mandated by the Sec. 1091 wash sale provisions. If such an agreement exists, the courts will disallow the loss, even though the actual purchase does not occur within the 61-day period.[34]

In certain cases, taxpayers may still recognize losses on transactions that literally fall within the wash sale requirements. For example, a taxpayer may purchase stock and then sell a portion of those shares within 30 days where the intent is merely to reduce the stock holdings. Taken together, these two transactions meet the tests of Sec. 1091. However, because the purpose of the sale is to reduce the taxpayer's holdings rather than to generate an artificial tax loss, Sec. 1091 does not disallow the loss.[35] Section 1091 also does not apply to losses that a dealer in stock or securities realizes in the ordinary course of business.

If the taxpayer acquires fewer shares of stock within the 61-day period than the number of shares disposed of, Sec. 1091 disallows only a proportionate amount of the total loss.

EXAMPLE I6-31 ▶ Several years ago, Henry purchased 100 shares of New Corporation common stock for $2,000 ($20 per share). On July 2 of the current year, Henry sells all 100 shares for $1,000. On July 30 of the current year, Henry purchases 75 shares (three-fourths of the original shares) of New Corporation common stock. As a result of the reacquisition, three-fourths of the total loss ($750) is disallowed. Henry recognizes the remaining $250 loss. ◀

SUBSTANTIALLY IDENTICAL STOCK OR SECURITIES. Only the acquisition of substantially identical stock or securities will cause a loss to be disallowed. The IRC and the Treasury Regulations do not define the term *substantially identical*. Judicial and administrative rulings have held that bonds issued by the same corporation generally are not substantially identical if they differ in terms (e.g., interest rate and term to maturity). However,

---

[32] Here the term *acquire* includes an acquisition of the stock either by purchase or in a taxable exchange. The term *stock or securities* includes contracts or options to acquire or sell stock or securities (see Sec. 1091(a)). The wash sale rules also apply to losses realized on the closing of a short sale of stock or securities if, within the 61-day period, substantially identical stock or securities were sold or another short sale of (or a securities futures contract to sell) substantially identical stock or securities was entered into.

[33] *John P. McWilliams v. CIR*, 35 AFTR 1184, 47-1 USTC ¶9289 (USSC, 1947).
[34] Rev. Rul. 72-225, 1972-1 C.B. 59, and *Frank Stein*, 1977 PH T.C. Memo ¶77,241, 36 TCM 992.
[35] Rev. Rul. 56-602, 1956-2 C.B. 527.

bonds of the same corporation that differ only in their maturity dates (e.g., the bonds do not come due for 16 years and mature within a few months of each other) have been held to be substantially identical. Generally, courts have not considered the preferred stock of a corporation to be substantially identical to the common stock of the same corporation.[36]

BASIS OF STOCK. If the wash sale provisions disallow a loss, then the disallowed loss increases the basis of the recently acquired stock. This increase in basis merely causes the disallowed loss to be deferred. The taxpayer will eventually recognize the loss upon the subsequent sale or disposition of the stock that causes the loss disallowance. If there has been more than one purchase of replacement stock and the amount of stock purchased within the 61-day period exceeds the stock that is sold, the stock that is deemed to have caused the loss to be disallowed is accounted for chronologically. The holding period of the replacement stock includes the period of time the taxpayer held the stock sold.

EXAMPLE I6-32 ▶ Ingrid enters into the following transactions with regard to Pacific Corporation common stock:

Date	Transaction	Amount
January 4, 2000	Purchases 600 shares	$30,000
October 2, 2006	Purchases 400 shares	10,000
October 12, 2006	Sells original 600 shares	12,000
October 20, 2006	Purchases 200 shares	5,000
October 25, 2006	Purchases 300 shares	8,400

Because Ingrid purchases more than 600 shares within the 61-day period before and after the date of sale (the purchases made on October 2, 20, and 25), the recognition of the entire loss of $18,000 ($30,000 − $12,000) is postponed. Four hundred shares (two-thirds of the number of shares sold) are purchased on October 2 and 200 shares (one-third) are purchased on October 20. Thus, the basis of the 400 shares of stock purchased on October 2 is $22,000 [$10,000 purchase price + ($18,000 disallowed loss × 0.667)]. The basis of the 200 shares of stock purchased on October 20 is $11,000 [$5,000 + ($18,000 disallowed loss × 0.333)]. Both of these blocks of stock have a holding period that starts on January 4, 2000.[37] The basis of the 300 shares of stock purchased on October 25 is its purchase price of $8,400. Its holding period begins on October 25. ◀

STOP & THINK *Question:* With regard to his investments in the stock market, the current year has been like a roller coaster ride for Doug. He now wants to do some year-end tax planning. For the year to date, he has realized a net gain of $12,000 on his stock investments. Although some of his current stock holdings have unrealized losses, he feels that they are excellent investments that will provide excellent returns in the next year or two. His stock broker has suggested that he sell enough of his holdings to realize a $12,000 loss (to offset the $12,000 capital gain) and then simply repurchase some of the stock. What advice would you give Doug as he discusses this strategy with his broker?

Solution: By realizing $12,000 in capital losses this year, Doug may be able to offset the capital gains he has already recognized. In order to recognize these losses, however, he must make sure that the wash sale provisions do not apply. Thus, he must either (1) purchase stock of different corporations or (2) delay the repurchase of the same issue of stock for at least 31 days after the date of sale. Since Doug is happy with his current investments, perhaps the second strategy is the best. Of course, other non-tax issues must also be considered. For example, does Doug think that the prices will go up quickly within the next 30 days? If so, he may lose out on some significant gains while he is waiting to repurchase the stock. Additionally, he must also consider the transaction costs (such as commissions).

---

[36] *Marie Hanlin, Executrix v. CIR*, 39-2 USTC ¶9783 (3d Cir., 1939). However, the IRS held in Rev. Rul. 77-201, 1977-1 C.B. 250, that the convertible preferred stock of a corporation is substantially identical to its common stock if the preferred stock has the same voting rights and is subject to the same dividend restrictions as the common stock, is unrestricted as to its convertibility, and sells at relatively the same price (taking into consideration the conversion ratio).

[37] An asset's holding period is important in determining whether subsequent gain or loss on the asset is long-term or short-term gain or loss. This is explained further in Chapter I5.

TRANSACTIONS BETWEEN RELATED PARTIES

Section 267 places transactions between certain related parties under special scrutiny because of the potential for tax abuse. For example, a taxpayer could sell a piece of property at a loss to a wholly owned corporation. Without any restrictions on the deductibility of the loss, the individual could recognize the loss while still retaining effective control of the property. Under Sec. 267, related taxpayers may not take current deductions on two specific types of transactions between them. These transactions are:

▶ Losses on sales of property

▶ Accrued expenses that remain unpaid to the related cash method taxpayer at the end of the tax year

ADDITIONAL COMMENT

Section 267 does not define the word property, but the IRS and the courts have given it a broad meaning.

RELATED PARTIES DEFINED. Section 267 defines the following relationships as related parties:

▶ Individuals and their families. The term family includes an individual's spouse, brothers and sisters (including half-brothers and half-sisters), ancestors, and lineal descendants.

▶ An individual and a corporation in which the individual owns more than 50% of the value of the outstanding stock.

▶ Various relationships between grantors, beneficiaries, and fiduciaries of a trust or trusts, or between the fiduciary of a trust and a corporation if they meet certain ownership requirements.

TAX STRATEGY TIP

The related party rules many times cause the tax consequences to be different than what was expected. Be sure that your clients provide all details to you ahead of time when related parties are involved in the transaction. You might be able to help structure the transaction in a way that meets your client's expectations.

▶ A corporation and a partnership if the same persons own more than 50% in value of the stock of the corporation and more than 50% of the partnership.

▶ Two corporations if the same persons own more than 50% in value of the outstanding stock of both corporations and at least one of the corporations is an S corporation.

▶ Other complex relationships involving trusts, corporations, and individuals.

Several of these relationships depend on an individual's ownership of a corporation. For example, if a taxpayer does not own more than 50% of a corporation's stock, the individual and the corporation are not related, and a loss on the sale of business or investment property between the two is deductible. Occasionally, individuals might attempt to circumvent the related party rules by dispersing the ownership of a corporation (e.g., among close family members) while retaining economic control. To prevent these tactics, Sec. 267 contains constructive ownership rules whereby a taxpayer is deemed to own stock owned by certain other persons. These constructive ownership rules are as follows:

▶ Stock owned by an individual's family is treated as owned by the individual. Here the definition of *family* is the same as that of *related parties* (i.e., spouse, brothers and sisters, ancestors, and lineal descendants).

▶ Stock owned by a corporation, partnership, estate, or trust is treated as owned proportionately by the shareholders, partners, or beneficiaries.

▶ If an individual partner in a partnership owns (or is treated as owning) stock in a corporation, the individual is treated as owning any stock of that corporation owned by any other partner in the partnership. This does not occur, however, if the only stock the individual owns (or is considered to own) is what his or her family owns.[38]

▶ Stock ownership that is attributed to a shareholder or partner from an entity can be reattributed to another taxpayer under any of the constructive ownership rules. In other words, the same stock can be constructively owned by more than one person. However, stock ownership attributed to a taxpayer under the family or partner rules cannot be reattributed.

---

[38] Reg. Sec. 1.267(c)-1(b), Exs. (2) and (3).

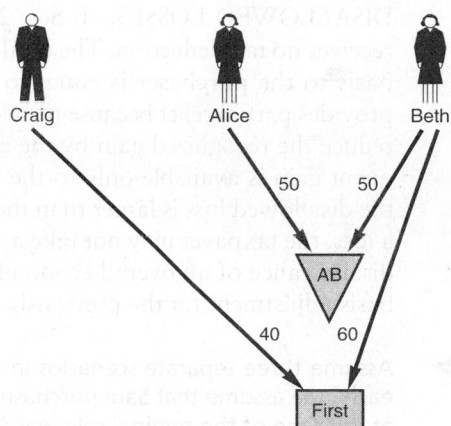

FIGURE I6-2 ▶ ILLUSTRATION FOR EXAMPLE I6-33

The following examples illustrate these rules:

EXAMPLE I6-33 ▶ Alice and Beth are equal partners in the AB Partnership. Beth owns 60% of First Corporation's stock, and Craig, Alice's husband, owns the other 40%. The ownership of the partnership and the corporation is demonstrated in Figure I6-2. Under the constructive ownership rules, Alice is considered to own Craig's 40% of the First Corporation stock. Alice is not considered to own the First Corporation stock owned by her partner, Beth, because the only First Corporation stock Alice owns (or is considered to own) is the stock owned by her husband. If Alice sells property at a loss to First Corporation, the loss is recognized because Alice does not directly or constructively own more than 50% of the First Corporation stock. ◀

EXAMPLE I6-34 ▶ Assume the same facts as in Example I6-33, except that the First Corporation stock is owned 50% by the AB Partnership and 25% each by Beth and Craig. The ownership of the partnership and the corporation is shown in Figure I6-3. In addition to Craig's 25%, Alice is considered to own 50% of the stock owned by the AB Partnership because of her 50% ownership in AB. The other half of AB's stock ownership is attributed to her partner, Beth. However, Alice is also treated as owning the First Corporation stock Beth owns both actually and constructively (50%). Thus, Alice is treated as owning 100% of the First Corporation stock. In this case, Alice will not be able to recognize a loss on the sale of property to First Corporation. ◀

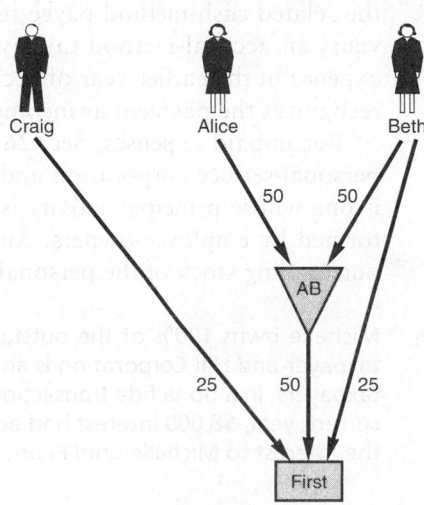

FIGURE I6-3 ▶ ILLUSTRATION FOR EXAMPLE I6-34

DISALLOWED LOSSES. If Sec. 267 disallows the loss, the original seller of the property receives no tax deduction. The disallowed loss has no effect on the purchaser's basis. The cost basis to the purchaser is equal to the amount paid for the property. However, Sec. 267 provides partial relief because on a subsequent sale of the property, the related purchaser may reduce the recognized gain by the amount of the disallowed loss. This offsetting of a subsequent gain is available only to the related person who originally purchased the property. If the disallowed loss is larger than the subsequent gain, or if the purchaser sells the property at a loss, the taxpayer may not take a deduction for the unused loss. This may result in a partial disallowance of an overall economic loss for the related parties because there is no upward basis adjustment for the previously disallowed loss (as is the case for a wash sale).

EXAMPLE I6-35 ▶ Assume three separate scenarios in which Sam sells a tract of land during the current year. In each case assume that Sam purchased the land from his father, Frank, for $10,000. Frank's basis at the time of the original sale was $15,000 in each case. Thus, Frank's $5,000 loss on each land sale was disallowed.

KEY POINT

The loss disallowance rule for related parties is more severe compared to the loss disallowance rule on wash sales. In a related party transaction, it is possible to lose the tax benefit of all or a portion of the economic loss.

	Scenario		
	1	2	3
Selling price	$17,000	$12,000	$ 8,000
Minus: Sam's basis	(10,000)	(10,000)	(10,000)
Sam's realized gain (loss)	$ 7,000	$ 2,000	$ (2,000)
Minus: Frank's disallowed loss (up to Sam's gain)	(5,000)	(2,000)	—0—
Sam's recognized gain (loss)	$2,000	—0—	($2,000)

In Scenario 1, Sam and Frank together have incurred an aggregate gain of $2,000 ($17,000 − $15,000). Thus, Frank's full disallowed loss reduces Sam's subsequent gain. In Scenario 2, the aggregate economic loss incurred by Sam and Frank is actually $3,000 ($12,000 − $15,000). However, the actual amount of the tax loss recognized by Sam and Frank is zero. In Scenario 3, the actual tax loss would have been $7,000 ($8,000 − $15,000) instead of $2,000 if Frank had held the land until its eventual sale. ◀

A similar rule found in Sec. 707(b)(1) disallows losses between a partner and a partnership in which the partner owns directly or indirectly over 50% of the partnership and between two partnerships in which the same people own directly or indirectly over 50% in each partnership. The constructive ownership rules of Sec. 267 apply here in determining ownership (see *Prentice Hall's Federal Taxation: Corporations, Partnerships, Estates, and Trusts* text or the *Comprehensive* volume).

KEY POINT

The effect of Sec. 267 with respect to unpaid expenses is to place an accrual method taxpayer on the cash method for amounts owed to a related cash method taxpayer.

UNPAID EXPENSES. Under Sec. 267, a related accrual-method obligor of any accrued but unpaid expenses must defer the deduction for those expenses until the year in which the related cash-method payee recognizes the amount as income. In effect, this rule prevents an accrual-method taxpayer (the payer) from taking a deduction for an unpaid expense in the earlier year of accrual while the related cash-method taxpayer (the payee) recognizes the payment as income in the subsequent year.

For unpaid expenses, Sec. 267 expands the definition of related parties to include a personal-service corporation and any employee-owner.[39] A personal-service corporation is one whose principal activity is the performance of personal services substantially performed by employee-owners. An employee-owner is an employee who owns any of the outstanding stock of the personal-service corporation.[40]

EXAMPLE I6-36 ▶ Michelle owns 100% of the outstanding stock of Hill Corporation. Michelle is a cash-method taxpayer and Hill Corporation is an accrual-method taxpayer. Both taxpayers are calendar-year taxpayers. In a bona fide transaction, Hill borrows some funds from Michelle. By the end of the current year, $8,000 interest had accrued on the loan. However, Hill Corporation does not pay the interest to Michelle until February of the following year. Because Michelle is a cash-method

---

[39] Sec. 267(a)(2).
[40] Secs. 269A(b) and 441(i)(2). In determining the ownership of an employee-owner, the constructive ownership rules of Sec. 318 as modified by Sec.

441(i)(2) are used. These rules differ substantially from the constructive ownership rules of Sec. 267.

taxpayer, she reports the interest income when she receives it in the following year. Although Hill is an accrual-method taxpayer, it must defer the deduction for the interest expense until it pays the interest in February of the following year. The results are the same if Hill Corporation is a personal service corporation and Michelle is an employee and owns any amount of the Hill stock. ◄

For purposes of these unpaid expenses, the definition of *related parties* also includes various relationships involving partnerships or S corporations and any person who owns (either actually or constructively) any interest in these entities.[41]

OBJECTIVE 7

Discuss the criteria for determining whether an activity is a hobby or a trade or business

HOBBY LOSSES

Certain activities have both profit-motivated and personal attributes. In these cases, a tax advisor must examine all the relevant factors to determine the tax status of the activity since, in general, expenses incurred in a profit-motivated activity such as a business or investment are deductible, whereas most expenses associated with personal activities such as hobbies are not. Reg. Sec. 1.183-2(b) lists the factors the IRS uses to determine whether an activity is profit-motivated. These factors include the following:

▶ Whether the taxpayer conducts the activity in a businesslike manner.

▶ The expertise of the taxpayer or the taxpayer's advisors.

▶ The time and effort expended by the taxpayer in carrying on the activity.

▶ Whether the assets used in the activity are expected to appreciate in value.

▶ The taxpayer's success in carrying on other similar activities.

▶ The taxpayer's history of income or losses with respect to the activity.

▶ The amount of occasional profits earned, if any.

ADDITIONAL COMMENT

Many of the court cases dealing with profit motive under Sec. 183 are ranch and farm cases. In fact, Sec. 183, now titled "Activities Not Engaged in for Profit" was originally titled "Farm Losses, etc." in the Tax Reform Act of 1969.

▶ The taxpayer's financial status.

▶ Any elements of personal pleasure or recreation the activity might involve.

No one of these factors is determinative. In fact, the IRS also may consider other factors not listed. Furthermore, the IRS does not make a determination by merely counting the number of factors that are present. Instead, the decision depends on an examination of all the factors together. The IRS can, therefore, make the decision on a more subjective basis than the taxpayer might like. If the IRS asserts that an activity is a personal one (i.e., a hobby) rather than a business or investment, the burden of proof rests on the taxpayer to prove otherwise.

EXAMPLE I6-37 ▶

Paula, a successful attorney with an annual income of $300,000, also enjoys raising and training quarter horses. She generally spends 5 to 6 hours each week training, showing, or racing the horses. Over the last 4 years her winnings from shows and races have amounted to $16,000. Over that same period, she has generated an additional $8,000 of income from stud fees and the sale of colts. Often the horses are used to take Paula's family or friends riding. In addition, Paula often participates in equestrian clinics and demonstrations for 4-H Clubs and other similar groups. Paula employs a high school student to feed the horses each day and clean the stalls weekly. Paula also hires a professional horse trainer for 4 hours each week to help her train the horses.

In this case, several factors such as the level of earnings, the hiring of professional help, and the amount of time spent in the activity might indicate that Paula is engaged in a business. Other factors, such as the time spent riding with family and friends, the voluntary clinics and demonstrations, and the small amount of revenue generated as compared with Paula's other income, support the position that Paula merely has a hobby of raising horses. ◄

In cases where a clear profit motive cannot be shown under the factors mentioned above, the Code provides a test whereby an activity may be presumed to be one engaged in for profit. The activity meets the test if it shows a profit for any three years during a consecutive five-year period. The five-year period consists of the year in question plus the previous four years.[42] This presumption is rebuttable (i.e., if the taxpayer meets the test,

---

[41] Sec. 267(e). A discussion of these modifications is beyond the scope of this book.
[42] Sec. 183(d). If the major part of the activity involves breeding, training,

showing, or racing horses, the five-year period is extended to a seven-year period, and a profit must be shown in only two, rather than three, of the years covered by that seven-year period.

the IRS has the burden of proof to show that the activity *is not* profit motivated). Otherwise, the taxpayer must prove that the activity *is* profit motivated.

If examination of the factors leads to the determination that the activity is a business, the taxpayer may deduct all qualified business expenses from the gross income, even if a net loss results.[43] However, if the factors lead to a determination that the activity is a hobby, the expenses are generally deductible as a miscellaneous itemized deduction but only to the extent of the gross income from the activity. A net loss may not be reported from the activity if it is a hobby.

EXAMPLE 16-38 ▶

Lorenzo, a stockbroker, enjoys raising pedigreed poodles. Although he mainly raises them for recreation and relaxation after work, Lorenzo periodically sells some of his poodles. Lorenzo reports $850 in income and $2,900 in expenses from the activity on his 2006 tax return. Upon auditing Lorenzo's 2006 return, the IRS disallowed the expenses in excess of the income, arguing that the activity is a hobby rather than a business or investment. If Lorenzo can prove that he realized a profit from the poodle-raising operation for any three years from 2002 through 2006 inclusive, the presumption will be made that the poodles are raised for a profit and not for recreation. The IRS then has the burden of proof to show that the activity is really a hobby. If Lorenzo cannot show a profit for three years out of the five-year period, he must rely on the factors mentioned in the Treasury Regulations to convince the IRS and/or the courts that the activity is a business.

If Lorenzo's poodle-raising activity is determined to be a business, Lorenzo will report a net loss of $2,050 ($2,900 expenses − $850 income), assuming the loss is not incurred in a passive activity (see Chapter 18). If the activity is determined to be a hobby, however, Lorenzo may deduct only $850 of the expenses (up to the amount of the gross income) as an itemized deduction. As explained later, these expenses must be deducted in a certain order. The remaining expenses are not allowed as tax deductions. ◀

DEDUCTIBLE EXPENSES. Some hobby activities generate gross income, even though profit is not a primary motive for the activity. In such situations, Sec. 183 allows the taxpayer to deduct the expenses related to the hobby, but only to the extent of the gross income from the hobby. Furthermore, a hobby-related expense is deductible only if it would have been deductible if incurred in a trade or business or an investment activity.

In essence, a taxpayer may deduct all the hobby-related expenses as long as there is enough gross income from the activity to cover the expenses. However, a taxpayer may not generate a tax loss from a hobby and then use it to offset the taxpayer's other types of income.

ORDER OF THE DEDUCTIONS. If the hobby expenses exceed the amount of gross income generated by the hobby, the expense deductions offset gross income in the following order:

▶ Tier 1: Expenses that are deductible even though not incurred in a trade or business (e.g., itemized deductions such as taxes, certain interest, and casualty losses)

▶ Tier 2: Other expenses of the hobby that could be deductible if incurred in a profit-motivated activity, but which do not reduce the tax basis of any of the assets used in the hobby (e.g., utilities and maintenance expenses)

▶ Tier 3: The expenses of the hobby that could be deductible if incurred in a profit-motivated activity and that reduce the basis of the hobby's assets (e.g., depreciation on fixed assets used in the hobby)[44]

To the extent that the expenses are deductible against the gross income of the activity, they are deductions *from* AGI and are deductible only if the taxpayer has itemized deductions in excess of the standard deduction. Form 1040 reports the tier 1 expenses in their respective sections on Schedule A. The tier 2 and tier 3 expenses allocated to the hobby are miscellaneous itemized deductions; therefore, these expenses are deductible only to the extent

---

[43] If the activity is a passive activity, however, the loss may be deferred or suspended. See Chapter 18 for a discussion of the passive loss rules.

[44] Reg. Sec. 1.183-1(b).

they exceed 2% of AGI (see Chapter I7). Form 1040 reports gross income from a hobby as other income. If gross income is not sufficient to cover all of the tier 1 expenses, the taxpayer may also deduct the excess tier 1 expenses as itemized deductions on Schedule A of Form 1040 because the tax law allows deductions for these expenses in any event. The tax law disallows deductions for any remaining expenses in the other two tiers, and the taxpayer may not carry them over to a subsequent year.

If depreciation expense is not deductible, then the taxpayer does not need to reduce the cost basis of the asset by the amount of the disallowed depreciation expense.

EXAMPLE I6-39 ▶

Lynn raises various plants and flowers in a small greenhouse constructed specifically for that purpose. During the current year, Lynn reports gross income from the greenhouse activities of $1,700. Lynn also incurs the following expenses:

Property taxes on the greenhouse	$1,150
Utilities	300
Depreciation (assuming the activity is considered a business)	800

If the greenhouse activity is considered to be a hobby rather than a business, the deductions Lynn may take are computed as follows:

Income From greenhouse		$1,700
Tier 1 Expenses:		
Property taxes	$1,150	
Tier 2 Expenses:		
Utilities	300	
Tier 3 Expenses:		
Depreciation[a]	250	$1,700
Total		$0

[a]Limited to greenhouse income remaining after accounting for the Tier 1 and Tier 2 expenses.   ◀

VACATION HOME

Because owning a second home or dwelling unit may have both personal and profit-motivated attributes, Sec. 280A may disallow or limit deductions for expenses related to the rental of a vacation home that is also used as a residence by the taxpayer.

RESIDENCE DEFINED. For the restrictive rules of Sec. 280A to apply, the property must be a dwelling unit that qualifies as the taxpayer's residence. As used in this context, the term *dwelling unit* is quite expansive. The term dwelling unit may even include property such as boats and mobile homes. The determining factor is whether the property provides shelter and accommodations for eating and sleeping.[45] Thus, a mini-motorhome that contains the appropriate accommodations has been held to be a dwelling unit subject to the rules and limitations of Sec. 280A. The determination disregards the fact that the unit is small and cramped.

A dwelling unit qualifies as a residence if the number of days during which the taxpayer uses the property for personal use throughout the year exceeds the greater of the following:

▶ 14 days, or

▶ 10% of the number of days during the year that the property is rented at a fair rental[46]

EXAMPLE I6-40 ▶

Sarah owns a houseboat on Lake Powell that she personally uses for 21 days out of the year. During the year she also rents out the boat for a total of 300 days. Even though Sarah's personal use exceeds 14 days during the year, the houseboat is not considered a residence under Sec. 280A because Sarah's personal use does not exceed 30 days during the year (10% of the 300 rental days for the year).   ◀

[45] *Ronald L. Haberkorn*, 75 T.C. 259 (1980), and *John O. Loughlin v. U.S.*, 50 AFTR 2d 82-5827, 82-2 USTC ¶9543 (D.C. Minn., 1982).
[46] Sec. 280A(d)(1). In certain cases, this residence test might be met when a taxpayer uses a property as his or her principal residence for part of the year and rents the property for the rest of the year. This could occur, for example, when a taxpayer moves from his or her home and turns the old residence into a rental unit. In such a case, special rules prevent the home from being classified as a residence under Sec. 280A, thus preventing the application of the limitations.

REAL-WORLD EXAMPLE

Good records are very important in establishing the existence of a business rather than a hobby. A taxpayer, who owned and operated an apple orchard, asserted that he maintained sufficient business records, consisting of bank deposit slips, check stubs, and tax forms. A separate bank account was also maintained. But the taxpayer did not present any production records for the apple orchard. In fact, at trial, the taxpayer was not even certain of the exact number of trees in the orchard. Thus, the court found that due to the limited records, the taxpayer's activity was considered to be a hobby rather than a business. *Zdun*, TC Memo 1998-296 (1998).

OBJECTIVE 8

Determine the tax consequences of vacation homes

SELF-STUDY QUESTION

What is the maximum number of days during a year that a taxpayer may use a property for personal use and not have it considered to be used as a residence?

ANSWER

If a property was rented for 332 days it could be used by the taxpayer for 33 days and not be considered a residence.

For purposes of the residence test, a day of personal use includes any of the following:

▶ Any day the taxpayer or the taxpayer's family uses the property for personal purposes. Family is defined here as including taxpayer's spouse, brothers and sisters, ancestors, and lineal descendants.[47]

▶ Any day any individual uses the property under a reciprocal-use arrangement.[48]

▶ Any day any individual used the property and does not pay a fair rental for its use.[49]

Despite the family-use rule, if a taxpayer rents property at a fair rental to a family member who uses the property as a principal residence, such use does not constitute personal use by the taxpayer.

EXAMPLE I6-41 ▶ During the current year, Peggy purchases a small house as an investment and rents the property to Stan, her married son, who uses the property as his principal residence. Peggy's son pays her a fair rental for the property. Because Stan uses the property as his principal residence and pays Peggy a fair rental for the property, Stan's personal use of the property does not constitute personal use by Peggy. Thus, the rules of Sec. 280A do not apply to limit the expenses that Peggy may deduct (although the passive loss rules may limit the deduction). ◀

KEY POINT

A second home is classified as either rental property, a residence, or some combination of the two. If it is classified as some combination of rental property and a residence, the expenses of the property must be allocated between the two categories.

ALLOCATION OF EXPENSES. The tax law requires allocation of the expenses related to the property between personal use and rental use. Generally, the tax law disallows a deduction for expenses allocable to personal use. However, qualified mortgage interest and real estate taxes are deductible even when allocated to personal use because such expenses are deductible on personal residences.[50] Expenses allocated to the rental use are deductible under Sec. 280A, but only to the extent of the gross income generated by the property. The property may not generate a loss used to reduce other income of the taxpayer. The taxpayer may carry over and deduct in a subsequent year expenses that are not currently deductible because they exceed the gross income from the property. However, the subsequent deduction may not exceed the gross income of the property for the subsequent year.[51] The order for deduction of the expenses allocated to the rental use of property is the same as the order for deduction of hobby losses under the rules of Sec. 183. Example I6-40 illustrates these rules.

Allocation Formula. Sec. 280A uses the following formula to allocate expenses between the personal use and the rental use of the property:[52]

$$\text{Rental use expenses} = \frac{\text{Number of rental days}}{\text{Total number of days used}} \times \frac{\text{Total expenses}}{\text{for the year}}$$

The denominator of the allocation fraction is the sum of the days the property is rented plus the days the taxpayer uses it for personal purposes. The formula does not include the days that no one uses the property.

Some courts have modified the allocation formula by allowing the use of the total number of days in the year as the denominator for qualified residential interest and taxes.[53] Use of this ratio allocates less interest and taxes to the rental use, allowing more of the other expenses to be deducted against the rental income. Subject to limitations, the interest and taxes not allocated to the rental use are still deductible as itemized deductions. Example I6-43 uses the allocation formula sanctioned by the courts.

---

[47] Under Sec. 280A(d)(2), a day during which the taxpayer spends substantially full time on repairs and maintenance does not count as a personal-use day.
[48] Sec. 280A(d)(2)(B). A reciprocal-use arrangement is one whereby another person uses the taxpayer's property in exchange for the taxpayer's use of the other person's property.
[49] Sec. 280A(d)(2)(C). Exactly what constitutes a fair rental must be determined by an examination of all the associated facts and circumstances.
[50] No deduction is allowed for interest incurred with respect to a personal residence if the debt on which the interest is paid is not secured by the property or the taxpayer has not chosen the property as a second residence for purposes of deducting the interest as qualified residential interest (see Chapter

I7). For purposes of the discussion and examples used here, the assumption is made that the interest qualifies as qualified residential interest.
[51] Sec. 280A(c)(5)(B). The expenses that are carried over to the subsequent year are deductible to the extent of the property's gross income of that year, even though the property is not used by the taxpayer as a residence during that year.
[52] Sec. 280A(e)(1).
[53] *Dorance D. Bolton v. CIR*, 51 AFTR 2d 83-305, 82-2 USTC ¶9699 (9th Cir., 1982). See also *Edith G. McKinney v. CIR*, 52 AFTR 2d 83-6281, 83-2 USTC ¶9655 (10th Cir., 1983).

EXAMPLE I6-42 ▶

Joan owns a cabin near the local ski resort. During the year, Joan and Joan's family use the cabin a total of 25 days. Joan also rents the cabin to out-of-state skiers for a total of 50 days during the year, generating rental income of $10,000. Joan incurs the following expenses:

Expense	Amount
Property taxes	$1,500
Interest on mortgage	3,000
Utilities	2,000
Insurance	1,500
Security and snow removal	2,500

Joan would have been entitled to $12,000 depreciation if the property had been entirely rental property held for investment. However, because the property is also used for personal purposes, the amount of deductions (for AGI) Joan may take with respect to the property during the year is as follows:

Item	Calculation	Amount
Rental income		$10,000
Interest and taxes	$4,500 \times \dfrac{50}{365}$	(616)[a]
All other expenses except depreciation	$6,000 \times \dfrac{50}{75}$	(4,000)
Depreciation	$12,000 \times \dfrac{50}{75}$	(5,384)[b]
Net income from property		$0

The income and these expenses are reported on Schedule E. Thus, the expenses allocated to the rental use are *for* AGI deductions. In addition to the deductions above, Joan may also deduct $3,884 ($4,500 − $616) interest and taxes as itemized deductions on Schedule A if the interest is qualified residence interest (see Chapter I7) and her total itemized deductions exceed her standard deduction.

[a] Under the approach favored by the IRS, $3,000 ($4,500 × 50/75) of interest and taxes would be used to offset the gross income and only $3,000 of depreciation would be deductible.
[b] $8,000 of the depreciation is allocated to the rental use (50/75 × $12,000). Since the deduction for depreciation is limited to $5,384, the additional $2,616 ($8,000 − $5,384) can be carried over and deducted in the next year if the gross income of that year is sufficient to cover all the expenses allocable to the rental use. If there had been sufficient gross income, Joan could have taken $8,000 depreciation. ◀

NOMINAL NUMBER OF RENTAL DAYS. If a property qualifies as a taxpayer's residence under Sec. 280A and the taxpayer rents the property for less than 15 days during the year, the law takes the approach that the property is completely personal in nature. As such, the taxpayer does not have to report the rental income and cannot deduct any of the related expenses. However, expenses such as qualified residential interest and taxes may still be deductible as itemized deductions. (See Chapter I7 for a discussion of the limitations on interest.)

EXAMPLE I6-43
KEY POINT ▶

Assume the same facts as in Example I6-42, except that during the year Joan rents the cabin out for only 12 days and the amount of rental income is $2,400. The cabin qualifies as Joan's residence because her personal use exceeds 14 days. Because the cabin is rented for less than 15 days during the year, Joan may only take itemized deductions of $4,500 for the qualified residential interest and taxes. She may not deduct the other expenses. In addition, she does not include the $2,400 in gross income. ◀

NOMINAL NUMBER OF PERSONAL USE DAYS. If a taxpayer does not have enough personal use days during the year to qualify the property as a residence (i.e., the personal use is not more than the greater of 14 days or 10% of the rental days), the Sec. 280A rules and limitations do not apply. In such a case the taxpayer must still allocate the expenses of the property between the personal use and the rental use days. The taxpayer may deduct the taxes allocated to the personal use as an itemized deduction. However, since the property does not qualify as the taxpayer's residence, the taxpayer may not deduct any of the interest allocated to the personal use because the interest is not "qualified residential interest" (see Chapter I7 for a discussion of the deductibility of personal interest and qualified residential

---

SELF-STUDY QUESTION

Assume that a taxpayer rents his cabin to an individual who occupies it on a Saturday afternoon. Two weeks later the tenant leaves the cabin on a Saturday morning. Has the cabin been rented for more than 14 days?

ANSWER

No. Although the tenant was on the premises for 15 calendar days, he is treated as having rented the property for only 14 days.

Assume that a taxpayer owns a beachfront condo. The taxpayer personally uses the condo for only 12 days during the year and rents the property for 35 days. Section 280A does not apply because the taxpayer has not used the property for over 14 days. However, if the taxpayer cannot demonstrate a profit motive, it may still be treated as a hobby. If so, the deductibility of the expenses allocated to the rental use is limited to the gross income generated by the property. Furthermore, the interest allocated to the personal use of the property is not deductible as qualified residential interest (see Chapter I7).

interest). The taxpayer may not deduct the tier 2 and 3 expenses allocated to the personal use. The income from the property and all of the expenses allocated to the rental use are reported on Schedule E of Form 1040. As such, the expenses are *for* AGI deductions. Any net income or loss from the property is subject to the passive loss rules, which may limit the deductibility of any losses from the property (see Chapter I8).

EXAMPLE I6-44 ▶ Assume the same facts as in Example I6-42 except that Joan and her family use the cabin only 10 days during the year and rent it out for 65 days of the year. Since Joan does not personally use the cabin for at least 14 days, the cabin is not considered her residence and the Sec. 280A rules do not apply. Instead, the interest allocated to the personal use is not deductible because it is not "qualified residential interest." Furthermore, the passive loss rules apply to the net income or loss from the property.

	Calculation	Amount
Rental income		$10,000
Interest	$ 3,000 \times \dfrac{65}{75}$	(2,600)[a]
Taxes	$ 1,500 \times \dfrac{65}{75}$	(1,300)[a]
Other expenses	$ 6,000 \times \dfrac{65}{75}$	(5,200)
Depreciation	$12,000 \times \dfrac{65}{75}$	(10,400)
	Total	$ (9,500)[b]

[a] Joan would treat the remaining $200 in taxes ($1,500 − $1,300) as an itemized deduction. However, Joan may not deduct the remaining $400 ($3,000 − $2,600) interest because it does not qualify as deductible residential interest.
[b] The deductibility of this $9,500 loss may be limited by the passive loss rules (see Chapter I8). ◀

The rule of Sec. 280A regarding the rental of property is summarized in Figure I6-4.

EXPENSES OF AN OFFICE IN THE HOME

Unless the taxpayer meets certain strictly imposed requirements, Sec. 280A disallows any deduction for home office expenses. In general, for a taxpayer to deduct office-in-home expenses, the office must have been used regularly and exclusively as either of the following:

▶ The principal place of business for a trade or business of the taxpayer; or

▶ A place where the taxpayer meets or deals with clients in the normal course of business

The term "principal place of business" includes a home office used by the taxpayer for administrative or management activities of the business if no other fixed location exists where the taxpayer conducts these administrative or managerial activities.

For employees to take a deduction for home office expenses, the use must also have been for the convenience of the employer. In addition, a separate structure not attached to the taxpayer's house may qualify if regularly and exclusively used in connection with the taxpayer's business. (See Chapter I9 for a comprehensive discussion of these rules.)

TAX PLANNING CONSIDERATIONS

HOBBY LOSSES

Deductions for expenses incurred in a hobby activity may not exceed the gross income generated by the hobby for the year. However, if the gross income exceeds the deductions from the activity in at least three out of five consecutive years (two out of seven for activities involving the breeding, training, showing, or racing of horses), tax law presumes the activity is a business, and the limits on the deductibility of expenses do not apply. Thus, if possible, taxpayers should use care in timing the realization of items of income and

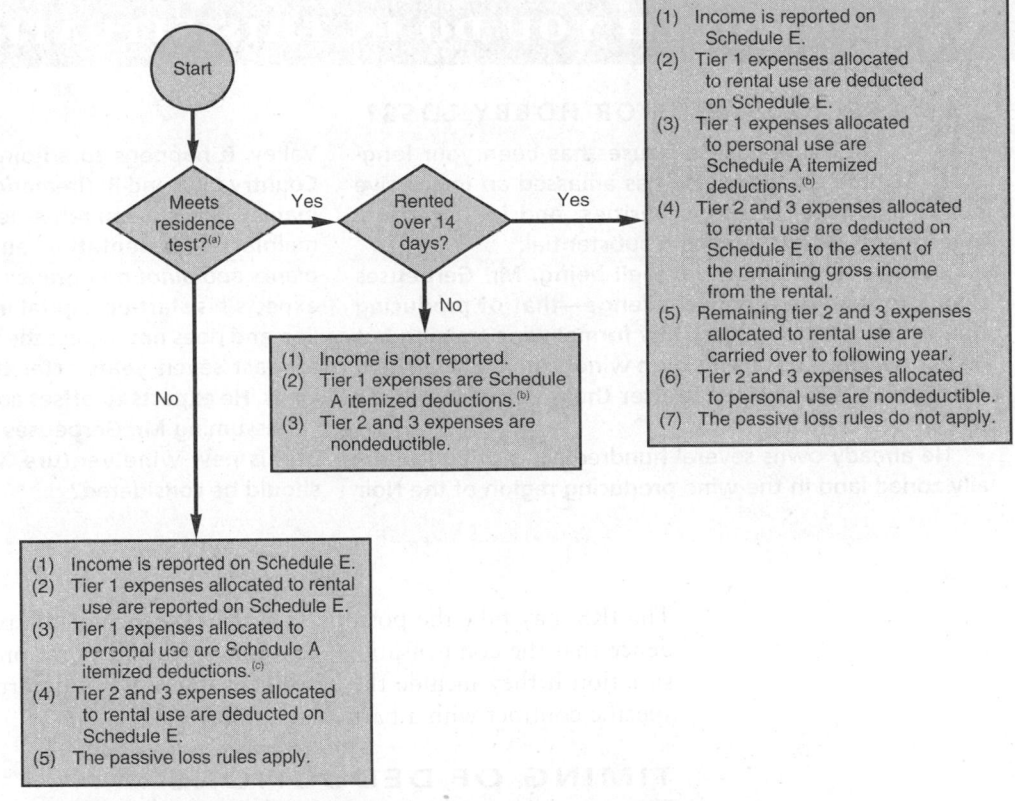

(1) Income is reported on Schedule E.
(2) Tier 1 expenses allocated to rental use are deducted on Schedule E.
(3) Tier 1 expenses allocated to personal use are Schedule A itemized deductions.(b)
(4) Tier 2 and 3 expenses allocated to rental use are deducted on Schedule E to the extent of the remaining gross income from the rental.
(5) Remaining tier 2 and 3 expenses allocated to rental use are carried over to following year.
(6) Tier 2 and 3 expenses allocated to personal use are nondeductible.
(7) The passive loss rules do not apply.

(1) Income is not reported.
(2) Tier 1 expenses are Schedule A itemized deductions.(b)
(3) Tier 2 and 3 expenses are nondeductible.

(1) Income is reported on Schedule E.
(2) Tier 1 expenses allocated to rental use are reported on Schedule E.
(3) Tier 1 expenses allocated to personal use are Schedule A itemized deductions.(c)
(4) Tier 2 and 3 expenses allocated to rental use are deducted on Schedule E.
(5) The passive loss rules apply.

(a) Personal use is more than the larger of (1) 14 days or (2) 10% of rental days.
(b) In order for the interest to be deductible, it must be "qualified residence interest" (see Chapter 7).
(c) In order for the interest to be deductible as qualified residence, the property must not have been rented at all during the year. If the property has been rented out, the interest allocated to personal use is not deductible (see Chapter 7).

FIGURE 16-4 ▶ SECTION 280A: LIMITATION OF DEDUCTIONS ON RENTAL OF RESIDENTIAL PROPERTY

expense. For example, if an activity has shown a profit in only two out of the previous four years, a taxpayer may consider accelerating some of the income into the fifth year or deferring some of the expenses of the activity into the following year. Under the cash method of accounting, this can be done by delaying payment for some of the expenses or accelerating income-generating transactions. Note that meeting the three-out-of-five-year test does not automatically ensure the activity will be treated as a business. It merely compels the IRS to prove the activity is *not* a business. Under these circumstances, the IRS is less likely to challenge the deductions.

UNREASONABLE COMPENSATION

If the IRS feels that a salary payment to an officer of a corporation is excessive, it will often recharacterize the excess portion as a dividend. If that happens, the corporation cannot deduct the full amount of the salary payment. To prevent a potential future disallowance, the parties may enter into a payback or hedge agreement, which provides that the employee must return to the corporation any payment held to be excessive. Under such an agreement, the employee receives a *for AGI* deduction for any amount he or she repays to the corporation. This deduction is available in the year of repayment. A payback agreement must meet the following requirements to be effective:

▶ The parties must enter into the agreement before actually making the payment.

▶ It must legally obligate the employee to repay the excess amount.[54]

---

[54] *Vincent E. Oswald,* 49 T.C. 645 (1968) and *J. G. Pahl,* 67 T.C. 286 (1976). See also *Ernest H. Berger,* 37 T.C. 1026 (1962).

WHAT WOULD YOU DO IN THIS SITUATION?

SERIOUS WINE OR HOBBY LOSS?

Mr. Bouteilles Gerbeuses has been your long-time tax client. He has amassed an impressive portfolio of real estate, securities, and joint venture investments. His net worth is substantial.

Despite all his material well-being, Mr. Gerbeuses wants to take on a new challenge—that of producing fine wines. He has not had any formal wine training but he has decided to start his own winery, named *Cuvée de Prestige.* He will pattern it after the great wine houses of Europe.

He already owns several hundred acres of agriculturally zoned land in the wine producing region of the Noir Valley. It happens to adjoin his home in the Wemadeit Country Club and Retirement Resort subdivision. He anticipates a life of semi-retirement by engaging in the art of malolactic fermentation and blending of his *blanc de blancs* and *pinot noir* grapes into his own estate wine. He expects his start-up capital investment to be over $5 million and does not expect the first harvest to take place for at least seven years after the initial planting of grape vines. He expects to offset any losses by his other income.

Assuming Mr. Gerbeuses comes to you for tax advice on his new wine venture, what tax and ethical issues should be considered?

The IRS may take the position that the existence of the payback agreement itself is evidence that the compensation is excessive. The corporation and employees can avoid this situation if they include the agreement in the general corporate bylaws rather than in a specific contract with a particular employee.[55]

TIMING OF DEDUCTIONS

Because of the time value of money, taxpayers generally prefer to deduct an expenditure as a current expense rather than capitalize it and spread the deductions over the next several years as depreciation or amortization. In addition, some capital expenditures (e.g., land) are not subject to depreciation or amortization. In some situations, however, the taxpayer may prefer to capitalize rather than expense a particular item. For example, if a taxpayer has net operating losses (NOLs) that are about to expire, a current deduction may prevent the use of these losses.[56]

In some cases it is difficult to determine whether an item should be treated as a capital expenditure or a deduction item (e.g., certain repairs may require capitalization). In addition, the taxpayer may elect to either capitalize or expense certain types of expenditures—such as those for research and experimentation. A tax practitioner should give consideration to the taxpayer's tax situation when making this decision. In making this decision, taxpayers and their advisors should consider NOL carryovers that might be expiring. They should also compare their current marginal tax rate with their anticipated future marginal tax rate.

COMPLIANCE AND PROCEDURAL CONSIDERATIONS

PROPER CLASSIFICATION OF DEDUCTIONS

Individuals report trade or business expenses on Schedule C (Profit or Loss from Business or Profession). It is similar to an income statement for business-related income and expenses. Income reported on Form 1040 includes the net income computed on Schedule

---

[55] *Charles Schneider and Co. v. CIR,* 34 AFTR 2d 74-5422, 74-2 USTC ¶9563 (8th Cir., 1974). See also *Plastics Universal Corp.,* 1979 PH T.C. Memo ¶79,355, 39 TCM 32. Additionally, some taxpayers have been successful in defending their current level of compensation where they proved that they had been undercompensated in prior years. See *Acme Construction Co., Inc.,* 1995 RIA T.C. Memo ¶95,600, 69 TCM 1596.

[56] A NOL arises when business expenses exceed business income for a year. This excess can be carried to another year (generally back two years and forward twenty years) and is deducted against the income of that year. If the years to which the NOL is carried do not have enough income, the NOL is lost when the carryover period expires. See Chapter I8 for a discussion of NOLs.

C, because the process of arriving at the taxable income from the business involves deducting business-related expenses. Thus, these expenses are deductions *for* AGI. Similar treatment is given to expenses attributable to the production of rental and royalty income reported on Schedule E, which is an income statement. The other deductions *for* AGI have specific lines on Form 1040 itself.[57] All of these deductions appear before line 37 (where AGI appears) of Form 1040.

Deductions *from* AGI are reported on Schedule A, where they are totaled and then transferred to Line 40 of Form 1040.

A filled-in Schedule C is provided in Appendix B.

PROPER SUBSTANTIATION

The burden of proving the deductibility of any expense generally rests on the taxpayer. This has always been the case. However, in recent years Congress and the IRS have become increasingly concerned about the propriety of many deductions. In the case of travel and entertainment expenses, the Code states that taxpayers may not take a deduction for an improperly documented expense. This documentation must include the amount of the expense, the time and place of the travel or entertainment activity, the business purpose, and the business relationship of the people entertained.

BUSINESS VERSUS HOBBY

Self-employed individuals who claim a home office deduction on Schedule C must attach a Form 8829, used to allocate direct and indirect expenses to the appropriate use. Form 8829 need not be filed by employees who claim home office expenses on Form 2106.

When an activity has both profit-making and personal attributes, the burden is normally on the taxpayer to prove that the activity is a business. However, if a taxpayer can show that the activity has generated a profit in at least three out of five consecutive years (two out of seven for activities involving the breeding, training, showing, and racing of horses), the burden of proof shifts to the IRS. Because the statute of limitations generally runs three years after a return is filed for any particular year (i.e., for audit purposes the year closes and the IRS cannot assess any tax deficiency for that year), a potential problem exists for taxpayers who want to rely on this presumption during the first year or two of an activity's life. In these cases, the taxpayer may elect to defer the determination of whether the presumption applies until the fifth (seventh) year of operation. The election keeps the year in question open with respect to that activity until sufficient years have passed to allow for application of the presumptive test. If the taxpayer subsequently does not meet the presumptive test, the IRS can still assess a deficiency for that activity for the prior year, because the year is still open. A taxpayer makes the election by filing Form 5213 (Election to Postpone Determination as to Whether the Presumption That an Activity Is Engaged In for Profit Applies) within three years after the due date for the year in which the taxpayer first engages in the activity.

PROBLEM MATERIALS

DISCUSSION QUESTIONS

I6-1 Why is the distinction between deductions *for* AGI and deductions *from* AGI important for individuals?

I6-2 Sam owns a small house that he rents out to students attending the local university. Are the expenses associated with the rental unit deductions *for* or *from* AGI?

I6-3 During the year, Sara sold a capital asset at a loss of $2,000. She had held the asset as an investment. This is the only capital asset she sold during the year. Is her deduction for this capital loss a deduction *for* or a deduction *from* AGI?

---

[57] Some of these expenses, such as employee business expenses (Form 2106) and moving expenses (Form 3903), are summarized on separate forms. These separate forms, however, are not net income statements in the same sense that Schedules C and E are.

I6-4 Discuss the difference in tax treatment between reimbursed employee business expenses and unreimbursed employee business expenses.

I6-5 For the current year, Mario, a single individual with no dependents, receives income of $55,000 and incurs deductible expenses of $9,000.
 a. What is Mario's taxable income assuming that the expenses are deductions *for* AGI?
 b. What is Mario's taxable income assuming that the expenses are miscellaneous itemized deductions *from* AGI?

I6-6 Deductible business or investment expenses must be related to a profit-motivated activity.
 a. What are the factors used in determining whether an activity is profit-motivated?
 b. Why are these factors so important in making this determination?

I6-7 If an activity does not generate a profit in three out of five consecutive years, is it automatically deemed to be a hobby? Why or why not?

I6-8 Because expenses incurred both in a business and for the production of investment income are deductible, why is it important to determine in which category a particular activity falls?

I6-9 In order for a business expense to be deductible it must be *ordinary, necessary,* and *reasonable.* Explain what these terms mean.

I6-10 What are the criteria for distinguishing between a deductible expense and a capital expenditure?

I6-11 Why are expenses related to tax-exempt income disallowed?

I6-12 Under what circumstances may a taxpayer deduct an illegal bribe or kickback?

I6-13 Michelle pays a CPA $400 for the preparation of her federal income tax return. Michelle's only sources of income are her salary from employment and interest and dividends from her investments.
 a. Is this a deductible expense? If so, is it a deduction *for* or *from* AGI?
 b. Assume the same facts as in Part a except that in addition to her salary and investment and dividend income, Michelle also owns a small business. Of the $400 fee paid to the CPA, $250 is for the preparation of her Schedule C (Profit or Loss from Business). How much, if any, of the $400 is a deductible expense? Identify it as either *for* or *from* AGI.

I6-14 Otter Corporation sends people to its state capital to lobby the legislature to build a proposed highway that is planned to run through the area where its business is located.
 a. If Otter Corp. incurs $3,200 of expenses, what part, if any, of its expenses are deductible?
 b. Would it make a difference if the proposed road were a city road rather than a state highway, and Otter lobbied its local government?
 c. Assume the same facts in Part a except that Otter's total expenses are $1,500. Are these expenses deductible?

I6-15 During November and December of last year, Tommy's, Inc., incurred the following expenses in investigating the feasibility of opening a new restaurant in town:

Expenses to do a market survey	$3,800
Expenses to identify potential suppliers of goods	$2,000
Expenses to identify a proper location	$1,000

Explain the proper treatment of these expenses under the following scenarios:
 a. Tommy's, Inc., already owns another restaurant in town and is wanting to expand. Tommy's, Inc. opens the new restaurant in February of the current year.
 b. Assume that Tommy's, Inc. is in the book selling business and feels that its bookstore business is not making a high enought return and it wants to move into the restaurant business. It opens the restaurant in February of the current year.
 c. Same as Part b except Tommy's decides against opening a restaurant after getting back the results of the investigation.

I6-16 What documentation is required in order for a travel or entertainment expense to be deductible?

I6-17 Under what circumstances can prepaid expenses be deducted in the year of payment by a taxpayer using the cash method of accounting?

I6-18 Under what circumstances would a taxpayer use both the cash method and the accrual method of accounting at the same time?

I6-19 Whether the economic performance test is satisfied depends on the type of transaction and whether the transaction is recurring.
 a. When does economic performance occur for a taxpayer who must provide property or services to another person?
 b. When does economic performance occur when another person provides the taxpayer with property or services?
 c. Explain the exception to the economic performance test for recurring liabilities.

I6-20 Why did Congress enact the wash sale provisions?

I6-21 The wash sale rules disallow a loss in the year of sale when substantially identical stock or securities are acquired by the taxpayer within a 61-day period. What types of stock or securities are considered substantially identical?

I6-22 Under Sec. 267, current deductions may not be taken for certain transactions between related parties.
 a. Who is considered a member of a taxpayer's family under the related party transaction rules of Sec. 267?
 b. Identify some of the other relationships that are considered related parties for purposes of

Sec. 267. Why are these other relationships included in the definition?

I6-23 Under the related party rules of Sec. 267, why has Congress imposed the concept of constructive ownership?

I6-24 If property is sold at a loss to a related taxpayer, under what circumstances can at least partial benefit be derived from the disallowed loss?

I6-25 Assume that Jill is engaged in painting as a hobby. During the year, she earns $1,000 from sales of her paintings and incurs $1,300 expenses for supplies and lessons. Jill's salary from her job is $70,000. What is the tax treatment of the hobby income and expenses?

I6-26 Under Sec. 280A, what constitutes personal use of a vacation home by the taxpayer?

I6-27 Under Sec. 280A, how are expenses allocated to the rental use of a vacation home? In what order must the expenses be deducted against the gross income of the property?

I6-28 Under Sec. 280A, how will a taxpayer report the income and expenses of a vacation home if it is rented out for only 12 days during the year?

ISSUE IDENTIFICATION QUESTIONS

I6-29 David, a CPA for a large accounting firm, works 10- to 12-hour days. As a requirement for his position, he must attend social events to recruit new clients. In addition to his job with the accounting firm, he also has private clients in his unincorporated professional practice. David purchased exercise equipment for $3,000. He works out on the equipment to maintain his stamina and good health that enable him to carry such a heavy workload. What tax issues should David consider?

I6-30 Gus, a football player who was renegotiating his contract with the Denver Broncos, paid his ex-girlfriend $25,000 to drop a sexual assault complaint against him and keep the matter confidential. The Broncos stated that if criminal charges were filed and made public, they would terminate his employment. What tax issues should Gus consider?

I6-31 Kathleen pays $3,000 mortgage interest on the home that she and her husband live in. Kathleen and her husband live with Molly, Kathleen's mother. The title to the home is in Kathleen's name. However, the mortgage is Molly's obligation. Kathleen claims Molly as her dependent on her current tax return. What tax issues should Kathleen consider?

I6-32 Katie and Alan are avid boaters and water skiers. They also enjoy parasailing. This year, they started a new parasailing venture to give rides to patrons. Katie and Alan are both employed full-time in other pursuits, but they take patrons out during the summer months, on weekends and holidays. Alan has attended classes on boat operation and parasailing instruction. Katie and Alan have owned a boat for four years, but because of the heavy usage this summer, they replaced their old boat in July. They plan on replacing their boat with a new one every two years now. They use their boat in the parasailing activity and for recreational purposes. This year, Katie and Alan earned $5,400 from chartering activities and incurred $11,600 of expenses associated with their boating and parasailing. What tax issues should Katie and Alan consider?

PROBLEMS

I6-33 *For or from AGI Deductions.* Roberta is an accountant employed by a local firm. During the year, Roberta incurs the following unreimbursed expenses:

Item	Amount
Travel to client locations	$750
Subscriptions to professional journals	215
Taking potential clients to lunch	400
Photocopying	60

a. Identify which of these expenses are deductible and the amount that is deductible. Indicate whether they are deductible *for* or *from* AGI.

b. Would the answers to Part a change if the accounting firm reimburses Roberta for these expenses?

c. Assume all of the same facts as in Part a, except that Roberta is self-employed. Identify which of the expenses are deductible, and indicate whether they are deductions *for* or *from* AGI.

I6-34 *For vs. from AGI.* During the current year, Kent, a single taxpayer, reports the following items of income and expense:

Income:	
Salary	$170,000
Dividends from Alta Corporation	800
Interest income from a savings account	1,500
Rental income from a small apartment he owns	8,000
Expenses:	
Medical	6,000
Interest on a principal residence	7,000
Real property taxes on the principal residence	4,300
Charitable contributions	4,000
Casualty loss—personal	6,100
Miscellaneous itemized deductions	1,200
Loss from the sale of Delta Corporation stock (held for two years)	2,000
Expenses incurred on the rental apartment:	
Maintenance	500
Property taxes	1,000
Utilities	2,400
Depreciation	1,700
Insurance	800
Alimony payments to former wife	10,000

Assuming all of these items are deductible and that the amounts are before any limitations, what is Kent's taxable income for the year?

I6-35 *Capitalization Versus Expense.* Rentals R Us incurs the following expenditures on an apartment building it owns:

Item	Amount
Replace the roof	$25,000
Repaint the exterior	7,000
Install new locks	1,500
Replace broken windows	1,200
Replace crumbling sidewalks and stairs	7,000

Discuss the proper tax treatment for these expenditures.

I6-36 *Political Contributions and Lobbying Expenses.* Eljay LLP owns several apartment complexes and office buildings. The leasing and managing of these buildings constitutes Eljay's only business activity. During the current year Eljay incurred the following:

- $900 in airfare and lodging incurred on a trip to Washington, D.C. The purpose of the trip was to protest proposed tax rate increases for individuals and corporations.

- $700 for renting space on billboards along the highway. The billboards express its concern regarding pending legislation that would significantly increase property taxes.

- $500 in airfare and hotel bills incurred on a trip to the state capital. The purpose of the trip was to meet with the legislative subcommittee on property taxation.

- $50 for a subscription to a political newsletter published by a national political party.

- $150 in making a presentation to the county council protesting a proposed increase in the property tax levy.

a. What is the total amount Eljay may deduct because of these expenditures?
b. Assume all the same facts as in Part a except that the expenses for the trip to the state capital are only $300 instead of $500. What amount may Eljay deduct because of these expenditures?

I6-37 *Legal and Accounting Expenses.* Sam is a sole proprietor who owns, leases, and manages several apartment complexes and office buildings. During the current year, Sam incurs the following expenses. Which of these expenditures are deductible? Are they *for* or *from* AGI deductions?
a. $200 in attorney's fees for title searches on a new property Sam has acquired.
b. $450 in legal fees in an action brought to collect back rents.

c. $500 to his CPA for the preparation of his federal income tax return. $400 is for the preparation of Schedule C (Profit or Loss from Business).

d. $300 in attorney's fees for drafting a will.

e. $250 in attorney's fees in an unsuccessful attempt to prevent the city from rezoning the area of the city where several of his office buildings are located.

I6-38 *Illegal Payments.* Damian Corporation is engaged in the business of purchasing and importing carpets from Iran. Importing these carpets from Iran is illegal. Following is a list of income and expense items for the year:

Item	Amount
Sales	$750,000
Cost of goods sold	270,000
Salaries	75,000
Freight	22,500
Bribes to customs officials	30,000
Lease payments on warehouses	15,000
Interest expense	12,000

a. What is the taxable income of Damian Corporation from the illegal business activity?

b. Assume the same facts as in Part a except that Damian's business consists of buying and selling marijuana and cocaine. What is Damian's taxable income from this illegal business activity?

I6-39 *Illegal Payments.* Indicate whether Glenda can deduct the $5,000 payment in each of the following independent situations.

a. Glenda is a supplier of medical supplies. In order to secure a large sales contract to the regional Veterans Administration Hospital, Glenda makes a gift of $5,000 to the hospital's purchasing agent. The payment is illegal under state law.

b. Assume the same facts as in Part a, except that the payment is made to the purchasing agent of a government-owned hospital in Brazil.

c. Assume the same facts in Part a, except that the payment is made to the purchasing agent of a privately owned hospital in Idaho.

I6-40 *Business Investigation Expenditures.* During January and February of the current year, Big Bang LLC incurs $3,000 in travel, feasibility studies, and legal expenses to investigate the feasibility of opening a new entertainment gallery in one of the new suburban malls in town. Big Bang already owns two other entertainment galleries in other malls in town.

a. What is the proper tax treatment of these expenses if Big Bang decides not to open the new gallery?

b. What is the proper tax treatment of these expenses if Big Bang decides to open the new gallery?

I6-41 *Business Investigation Expenditures.* Assume the same facts as in Problem I6-40, except that Big Bang LLC incurs $41,000 in expenses, it does *not* already own the other entertainment galleries and it does not own anything similar.

a. What is the proper tax treatment of these expenses if Big Bang does not open the new gallery?

b. What is the proper tax treatment of these expenses if Big Bang decides to open the new gallery on May 1 of the current year?

I6-42 *Timing of Expense Recognition.* Solutions Corporation, a computer vendor and consulting company, uses the accrual method of accounting. Its tax year is the calendar year. The following are three of the corporation's transactions during the current year:

1. Solutions Corporation hired a contractor to remodel its sales floor. The contractor completed the remodeling on November 30. On December 15, Solutions received a $21,000 bill from the contractor. Solutions immediately contacted the contractor to contest the $8,000 labor charge included in the total bill, which Solutions claims should only be $7,000. Solutions made no payment on the bill.

2. Solutions offers a 2-year warranty on all of its computer systems. For sales of computers in the current year, it paid $11,500 to service warranties during the current tax year, and it expects to pay $12,000 to fulfill the remaining warranty obligations next year.

3. Every year, Solutions offers a series of six trade seminars from November 1 through March 31. It receives all registration fees from participants by October 1, before the

seminars begin. As of December 31, two of the six seminars are completed, and the next seminar is scheduled for January 14–15. The expenses incurred in performing the seminars are routine each year. On the first of each month from November through March, Solutions pays the $625 monthly rent for the seminar location. On September 16, Solutions signs a contract with the seminar teacher, a computers expert and excellent public speaker. The contract requires Solutions to pay the teacher $900 after each seminar, a total of $5,400. On October 3, Solutions signs a contract with a local printing company, which will provide text materials for the seminars. Solutions pays the printer $350 after each seminar's materials are delivered the day before the seminar.

Required:

a. How should Solutions Corporation treat these transactions? What rules apply?

b. How would your answer change if Solutions Corporation were a cash-method taxpayer?

I6-43 *Prepaid Expenses.* Pamello, Inc., an engineering consulting firm, uses the cash method of accounting. Compute the amount of Pamello's current year deductions for the following transactions:

a. On November 1 of the current year, it entered into a lease to rent some office space for five years. The lease agreement states that the lease payments are $12,000 per year, payable in advance each November 1 for the following 12-month period. Under the terms of the lease, Pamello is required to pay a $5,000 deposit, refundable upon the termination of the lease.

b. On December 1 of the current year, Pamello also renewed its malpractice insurance, paying $18,000 for the three-year contract.

c. On December 31 of the current year, Pamello mailed out a check for $5,000 for drafting services performed for it by an individual who lives in another city.

d. On December 31, the firm received a shipment of $700 worth of stationery and other office supplies. Pamello has an open charge account with the office supply company, which bills the firm monthly for charges made during the year.

e. Finally, on December 31, Pamello picked up some work that a local printing company had done for it, which amounted to $1,000. The firm charged the $1,000 with its corporate credit card.

I6-44 *Prepaid Interest.* During the current year, Richard and Alisha, a married couple who use the cash method of accounting, purchased a principal residence for $320,000. They paid $40,000 down and financed the remaining $280,000 of the purchase price with a 30-year mortgage. At the closing, they also paid $500 for an appraisal, $500 for a title search, and 1.5 points representing additional interest over the term of the loan. At the end of the year, Richard and Alisha received a statement from the mortgage company indicating that $12,000 of their total monthly payments made during the year represents interest and $1,000 is a reduction of the principal balance.

a. What is the total amount Richard and Alisha may deduct in the current year arising from the purchase and ownership of their home?

b. What is the treatment of the other items that are not deductible?

I6-45 *Wash Sales.* Broward Corp. owns 1,500 shares of Silver Fox Corporation common stock. Broward Corp. purchased the 1,500 shares on April 17, 2001, for $20,000. On December 8, 2005, Broward sells 750 shares for $5,000. On January 2, 2006, Broward Corp. buys 250 shares of Silver Fox Corporation common stock for $1,750 and 50 shares of Silver Fox Corporation preferred stock for $1,000. The preferred stock is nonvoting, nonconvertible.

a. What is Broward's realized and recognized loss on the December 8 sale of stock?

b. What is Broward's basis and the holding periods of the stock?

I6-46 *Wash Sales.* Cougar Corporation owns 1,000 shares of Western Corporation common stock, which it purchased on March 8, 2001, for $12,000. On October 3, 2006, Cougar purchases an additional 300 shares for $3,000. On October 12, 2006, it sells the original 1,000 shares for $8,500. On November 1, 2006, it purchases an additional 500 shares for $4,000.

a. What is Cougar's recognized gain or loss as a result of the sale on October 12, 2006?

b. What are the basis and the holding period of the stock Cougar continues to hold?

c. How would your answers to Parts a and b change if the stock Cougar purchases during 2006 is Western nonvoting, nonconvertible, preferred stock instead of Western common stock?

I6-47   *Constructive Ownership.* During the current year, Troy sells land to Berry Corporation for $165,000. Troy purchased the land in 1998 for $170,000. The Berry Corporation is owned as follows:

Owner	Percentage Ownership
Tom (Troy's son)	20%
Jimmy (Troy's cousin)	15%
Jimmy's father (Troy's uncle)	30%
Angie (Troy's wife)	10%
Nicole (Angie's Sister)	25%

Troy and Jimmy are equal partners in a separate entity, TJ Partnership.
a. What is Troy's constructive ownership in Berry Corporation?
b. What is the amount of loss Troy may recognize?
c. How would your answers to Parts a and b change if TJ Partnership owned 25%, instead of Nicole?

I6-48   *Constructive Ownership.* PIB Partnership is owned 20% by Shore, 40% by Steve, and 40% by Thann. Burnham, Inc. is owned 70% by PIB Partnership, 10% by Ralph, 10% by Thann, and 10% by Shore. Ralph and Thann are brothers. All other individuals are unrelated. During the current year, Ralph sold a piece of land to Burnham, Inc., for $90,000. Ralph originally purchased the land as an investment a few years ago for $100,000.
a. How much of the loss may Ralph recognize?
b. Now assume all the same facts except that the sale occurred between Thann and Burnham, Inc. How much of the loss may Thann recognize?
c. Now assume the same facts as in b except that Burnham, Inc., is owned 60% by Shore and 40% by Ralph. Thann sells the land to Burnham, Inc. How much of the loss may Thann recognize?

I6-49   *Related Party Transactions.* Sally is an attorney who computes her taxable income using the cash method of accounting. Sage Corporation, owned 40% by Sally's brother, 40% by her cousin, and 20% by her grandmother, uses the accrual method of accounting. Sally is a calendar-year taxpayer, whereas Sage Corporation's fiscal year ends on January 31. During 2006, Sally does some consulting work for Sage Corporation for a fee of $10,000. The work is completed on December 15 and Sage receives Sally's invoice on that date. For each of the following assumptions, answer the following questions: During which tax year must Sally report the income? During which tax year must Sage Corporation deduct the expense?
a. The payment to Sally is made on December 27, 2006.
b. The payment to Sally is made on January 12, 2007.
c. The payment to Sally is made on February 3, 2007.

I6-50   *Related Party Transactions.* During the current year, CVI Corporation sells a tract of land for $75,000. The sale is made to Sandi, CVI Corporation's sole shareholder. CVI Corporation originally purchased the land five years earlier for $98,000.
a. What is the amount of gain or loss that CVI Corporation will recognize on the sale during the current year?
b. Assume that in the following year, Sandi sells the land for $85,000. What is the amount of gain or loss Sandi will recognize? What are the tax consequences to CVI Corporation upon the subsequent sale by Sandi?
c. Assume that in the following year, Sandi sells the land for $70,000. What is the amount of gain or loss Sandi will recognize?
d. Assume that in the following year, Sandi sells the land for $105,000. What is the amount of gain or loss Sandi will recognize?

I6-51   *Hobby Loss Presumptive Rule.* Rachel Schutz is a high school English teacher. In her spare time, she likes to make her own body lotion, lip-gloss, and bath and shower gel. She uses the bath products herself and gives them to her friends and relatives as gifts. In 2005, Rachel started attending arts and crafts festivals to sell her products three or four times a year, and she hands out her business card so her customers can buy directly from her by phone or email. In 2005, Rachel reported a net loss of $375 from the activity. In 2006, she reported a loss of $460. Rachel is audited for the year 2006, and the agent disallows the $460 loss. Rachel is pretty sure she will make a profit on her sales in 2007, and she assumes she will continue to make a profit after 2007. Rachel is not sure that she can prove that her activity is not a hobby right now. What can she do to avoid proving that her loss is not a hobby loss?

I6-52   *Hobby Loss Presumptive Rule.* Emily is an interior decorator who does consulting work for several furniture stores. Additionally, she has been designing and creating rubber stamps for the past several years. She sells the stamps to local stationary and novelty shops. Emily has reported the following net income or loss from the rubber stamp activity:

Year	Net Income (Loss)
2001	$ 300
2002	(900)
2003	(400)
2004	600
2005	(550)
2006	(800)

Emily is audited for the year 2006, and the agent disallows the $800 loss. Can Emily make an election for 2006 to keep the year open in anticipation of meeting the presumptive rule for the year? Why or why not?

I6-53   *Hobby Losses.* Chuck, a dentist, raises prize rabbits for breeding and showing purposes. Assume that the activity is determined to be a hobby. During the year the activity generates the following items of income and expense:

Item	Amount
Sale of rabbits for breeding stock	$800
Prizes and awards	300
Property taxes on rabbit hutches	300
Feed	600
Veterinary fees	500
Depreciation on rabbit hutches	300

a. What is the total amount of deductions Chuck may take during the year with respect to the rabbit raising activities?
b. Identify which expenses may be deducted and indicate whether they are deductions *for* or *from* AGI.
c. By what amount is the cost basis of the rabbit hutches to be reduced for the year?

I6-54   *Hobby Losses.* Assume the same facts as in Problem I6-53, except that the income from the sale of rabbits is $1,200.
a. What is the total amount of deductions Chuck may take during the year with respect to the rabbit raising activities?
b. Identify which expenses may be deducted and indicate whether they are deductions *for* or *from* AGI.
c. By what amount is the cost basis of the rabbit hutches to be reduced for the year?

I6-55   *Rental of Vacation Home.* During the current year, Kim incurs the following expenses with respect to her beachfront condominium in Hawaii:

Item	Amount
Insurance	$ 500
Repairs and maintenance	700
Interest on mortgage	3,000
Property taxes	1,000
Utilities	800

In addition to the expenses listed above, Kim could have deducted a total of $8,000 depreciation if the property had been acquired only for investment purposes. During the year, Kim uses the condominium 20 days for vacation. She also rented it out for a total of 60 days during the year, generating a total gross income of $9,000.
a. What is the total amount of deductions for and from AGI that Kim may take during the current year with respect to the condominium?
b. What is the effect on the basis of the condominium?

I6-56   *Rental of Vacation Home.* Assume all of the same facts as in Problem I6-55, except that during the year Kim rents the condominium a total of 14 days. How does Kim report the income and deductions from the property?

COMPREHENSIVE PROBLEMS

I6-57   Bryce, a bank official, is married and files a joint return. During 2006 he engages in the following activities and transactions:

a. Being an avid fisherman, Bryce develops an expertise in tying flies. At times during the year, he is asked to conduct fly-tying demonstrations, for which he is paid a small fee. He also periodically sells flies that he makes. Income generated from these activities during the year is $2,500. The expenses for the year associated with Bryce's fly-tying activity include $125 personal property taxes on a small trailer that he uses exclusively for this purpose, $2,900 in supplies, $270 in repairs on the trailer, and $200 in gasoline for traveling to the demonstrations.

b. Bryce sells a small building lot to his brother for $40,000. Bryce purchased the lot four years ago for $47,000, hoping to make a profit.

c. Bryce enters into the following stock transactions: (None of the stock qualifies as small business stock.)

Date	Transaction
March 22	Purchases 100 shares of Silver Corporation common stock for $2,800.
April 5	Sells 200 shares of Gold Corporation common stock for $8,000. The stock was originally purchased two years ago for $5,000.
April 15	Sells 200 shares of Silver Corporation common stock for $5,400. The stock was originally purchased three years ago for $9,400.
May 20	Sells 100 shares of United Corporation common stock for $12,000. The stock was originally purchased five years ago for $10,000.

d. Bryce's salary for the year is $115,000. In addition to the items above, he also incurs $5,000 in other miscellaneous deductible itemized expenses.

Answer the following questions regarding Bryce's activities for the year.
1. Compute Bryce's taxable income for the year.
2. What is Bryce's basis in the Silver stock he continues to own?

I6-58   Using the following facts, answer the questions below concerning Jaron's 2006 tax liability.

1. Two years ago when his wife died, Jaron left the CPA firm he was working for and started his own practice so he could have more time to spend with his four children. Jaron's children are 14, 16, 19, and 24 years old, respectively. The three youngest live at home with their father. Danny, Jaron's 19-year-old son, graduated from high school a year ago and is currently working at a local golf course. Danny earned $17,000 in the current year. Jaron's oldest daughter, Laura, is married and lives in town with her husband, Chad. Laura graduated from college two years ago and now works for a local advertising agency. What are Jaron's filing status and personal and dependency exemptions for 2006?

2. Jaron rents a small office downtown where he meets with clients and conducts business while his children are at school. He keeps all his client files and business records in this office. After school, he uses a converted bedroom in their home as his office. The following expenses are allocated to his home office (by square feet):
    a. Depreciation $2,150
    b. Taxes $1,500
    c. Utilities $75
    Can Jaron claim a deduction for his home office?

3. Jaron owns a condominium downtown. He rented it out 270 days during the year. He also allowed Laura and her husband to stay in the home rent-free for 24 days while they were looking for a place to stay. Fortunately, the condominium wasn't rented during the time they needed it. The following items of annual income and expense relate to the condominium:
    a. Rental income $18,000
    b. Interest $3,150
    c. Taxes $1,700
    d. Other expenses $6,000
    e. Depreciation $7,090
    What is the tax treatment of the condominium for Jaron in 2006?

4. On April 6, Jaron sold a parcel of land he had held for investment to a real estate development firm for $75,000. He purchased the land 3 years earlier from his brother for $70,000. His brother had originally purchased the land for $74,000. What is the amount and character of Jaron's gain or loss on the sale of the land?

5. On May 1, Jaron purchased 1,000 shares in Genomics Ltd. for $10 per share. In December he was forced to sell all 1,000 shares at $8 per share to avoid a conflict of interest. What is the amount and character of Jaron's gain or loss on the sale of the stock?

6. Jaron reported the following items of income and expense from his consulting practice:
   a. Consulting fees received $185,000
   b. Wages expense $47,400
   c. Rent expense $20,000
   d. Depreciation $2,100
   e. Other expenses $17,000
   What is Jaron's net income from his consulting practice?

7. When asked about potential itemized deductions, Jaron mentions that his house is fully paid-off and he paid off his student loans decades ago. He did pay, however, $2,100 in property taxes in the current year. Can Jaron deduct the property taxes paid in 2006?

8. Calculate Jaron's 2006 income tax liability. Be sure to take advantage of all available credits and deductions.

TAX STRATEGY PROBLEMS

I6-59 Danielle Anderson, your client and a cash method taxpayer, works full-time at a music store located in a mall. She assists the manager in buying decisions, serves customers on the sales floor, and plays music to draw in customers. On the weekends, she plays in various orchestras, working as an independent contractor. She does not work under a business name, maintain an office, or maintain a separate bank account for her performing activities. She always pays her bills as soon as possible, well before the bill due date. In prior years, she has taken every allowable deduction related to the performing activities. Prior year returns show the following taxable income on her Schedule C:

2002	$(5,000)
2003	2,100
2004	3,000
2005	(1,800)

Danielle has come to you on December 12, 2006. She understands that the IRS can deny losses generated by her performing business if it determines the business is actually a hobby. Because of the uncertainty of the entertainment industry, she will likely continue to generate profits in some years and losses in others. Still, she continues the activities with the intent to earn a profit.

Danielle routinely sends bills to orchestra clients at the end of the month for work she performed during the month. Most of her clients, including the Springville Orchestra, send payment within ten days of when they receive her bill.

The following is a summary of the business' financial position for 2006 as of 12/20/2006:

Income received to date:	$9,000
General expenses paid to date:	9,200
Other items:	
Bill for refurbishing work on cello, due 1/2/2007	$ 300
Newspaper bill for monthly advertisement, due 1/14/2007	200
Printer bill for business cards, due 1/5/2007	500
Meals eaten while in transit to performance locations	150
Income for 12/3/2006 performance with the Springville Orchestra	1,000

What will you recommend to your client? What issues must you address? What actions will you take to ensure the most favorable tax outcome possible? What advice, if any, will you give your client for the future?

I6-60 Peter Baumann, your client, wants to sell a printing press to Chamberlain Corporation for $50,000. Pete has used the press in his business for two years and its adjusted basis is

$90,000. The Coxmann Partnership, Chloe International, Inc., Watts, Inc., and Raleigh Corporation own Chamberlain Corporation equally. Pete and Emily Cox each own 50% of the Coxmann Partnership. Emily owns 70% of Chloe International, Inc., and Pete's sister Susan owns the other 30%. Pete's brother, Brian, owns 100% of Watts, Inc. And, Wade and Catherine Chamberlain, friends of Pete, own Raleigh Corporation equally. Peter wants to know what the tax consequences will be if he sells the printing press to Chamberlain Corporation. In a memo to Pete, explain any tax consequences of the proposed sale and any alternatives that would provide a better result.

TAX FORM/RETURN PREPARATION PROBLEMS

I6-61 Dave Stevens, age 34, is a self-employed physical therapist. His wife Sarah, age 31, teaches English as a Second Language at a local language school. Dave's Social Security number is 417-46-9403. Sarah's Social Security number is 528-95-6271. Sarah and Dave have three children—Andrew, age 8; Isaac, age 6; and Mira, age 3. The children's Social Security numbers are, respectively, 377-83-2836, 377-64-7283, and 377-17-1415. They live at 12637 Pheasant Run, West Bend, Oregon 74658. They paid $8,900 in qualified residence interest and $2,400 in property taxes on their home. They had cash charitable contributions of $14,000. They also paid $180 to a CPA for preparing their federal and state income tax returns for the prior year, $100 of which was for the preparation of Dave's Schedule C. Sarah and Dave earned interest on CDs of $3,200. Sarah's salary for the year is $32,000, from which $9,600 in federal income tax and $1,400 in state income tax were withheld. Dave's office is located at Suite 402, 942 Woodview Drive, Portland, Oregon 74624, and his employer ID number is 22-7584904. Dave has been practicing for 4 years, and he uses the cash method of accounting. During the current year, Dave recorded the following items of income:

Revenue from patient visits	$300,000
Interest earned on the office checking balance	225

The following expenses were recorded on the office books:

Property taxes on the office	$ 4,500
Mortgage interest on the office	12,000
Depreciation on the office	4,500
Malpractice insurance	37,500
Utilities	3,750
Office staff salaries	51,000
Rent payments on equipment	15,000
Office magazine subscriptions	150
Office supplies	24,000
Medical journals	330

Dave pays $50 annually for use of a safety deposit box to store certain confidential documents related to his business. In addition to his medical practice, Dave spends 15 hours every week managing his real estate investments. To make sure he is aware of all current investment strategies and best practices, he subscribes to the following journals:

Wall Street Journal	$150
U.S. News & World Report	55
Money Magazine	45

Dave also paid $30,000 in estimated federal income taxes. Prepare Dave and Sarah's tax return (Form 1040, Schedules A, B, C, and SE) for the current year. Disregard any tax credits they may be eligible for.

I6-62 Lyle and Kaye James are married, have two minor children, Jessica age 8 and Jerron age 4, and are filing a joint tax return in the current year. They are both employed. Lyle and Kaye, ages 38 and 37, respectively, have combined salaries of $240,000, from which $42,000 of federal income tax and $10,000 of state income tax are withheld. Lyle and Kaye own two homes. Their primary residence is located at 11620 N. Mount Ave., New Haven, Connecticut 22222, and their vacation home is on the beach in Fort Lauderdale, Florida. They often rent their vacation home to supplement their income. The following items are related to the James' ownership of the two homes:

Item	New Haven	Fort Lauderdale
Rental income	$ —	$15,000
Qualified residence interest	7,200	5,000
Property taxes	1,400	1,000
Utilities	1,000	1,300
Repairs	200	300
Depreciation	0	3,500
Advertising	0	200
Insurance	1,500	1,500

The James family used their Fort Lauderdale home 20 days during the year. They rented the vacation home 60 days during the year. Lyle and Kaye jointly purchase stock in various corporations and make the following transactions in the current year. (None of the stock qualifies as small business stock.)

Date	Transaction	Price Paid/Sold
2/15	Bought 50 shares of Lake common stock (they own no other Lake stock)	$1,000
5/14	Bought 100 shares of Bass common stock (they own no other Bass stock)	3,000
5/24	Sold 25 shares of Lake common stock	250
5/27	Bought 50 shares of Lake common stock	900
	Sold 50 shares of Bass common stock	1,750
7/12	Bought 100 shares of Bass common stock	2,800

The James' have no other income or expense items. Lyle and Kaye's Social Security numbers are 111-22-3333 and 444-55-6666, respectively. Jessica and Jerron's Social Security numbers are 123-45-6789 and 888-99-1010. The James' use the IRS method of allocating all expenses between personal and rental use.

File the James' income tax return Form 1040, Schedules A, D, and E using the currently available forms and rates. Disregard any tax credits for which they may be eligible.

I6-63 Scarlet Furniture Corporation, an accrual-method taxpayer, retails custom office furniture. On January 1 of the current year, Peter Marlin and John Tanner incorporated Scarlet Furniture Corporation. Peter transferred $350,000 cash for 70% of Scarlet's outstanding stock, and John transferred $150,000 cash for 30% of the outstanding stock. Scarlet generated the following financial statements at the end of its first year of operations:

Scarlet Corporation's Balance Sheet

Assets

Cash	$ 91,400
Inventory	48,000
Other Current Assets	50,000
Office Equipment	170,000
Building	250,000
Accumulated Depreciation	(20,000)
Land	550,000
Total Assets	$1,139,400

Liabilities and Owner's Equity

Accrued Expenses	$ 100,000
Long Term Debt	400,000
Common Stock	500,000
Retained Earnings	139,400
Total Liabilities and Owners' Equity	$1,139,400

Scarlet Corporation's Income Statement

Revenues	$650,000
Costs of Goods Sold	100,000
Gross Income	$550,000

Advertising Expense	40,000
Depreciation Expense	20,000*
Miscellaneous Expense	10,600**
Office Supplies	5,000
Property Tax Expense	60,000
Wages & Salaries Expense	135,000***
Warranty Expense	10,000****
Operating Income	$269,400
Interest Expense	30,000
Federal Income Tax Expense	100,000
Net Income	$139,400

*Depreciation expense for tax purposes was $120,441 because Scarlet made a Sec. 179 election to expense $105,000 of the cost of the equipment purchased this year.
**Miscellaneous expense relates to a $600 penalty fee as a result of a breached customer contract and a $10,000 fine assessed by OSHA for hazardous conditions in its storage facility.
***Wages and salary expense includes Peter's salary of $40,000 and the accrual of $15,000 of bonuses payable to Peter which Scarlet actually paid on February 10 of the following year.
****The actual expenditure paid for warranty repairs during the year is $2,000.

Scarlet does not make any sales or purchases on account. Scarlet's employer identification number is 12 34567. Its address is 789 Presidential Way, Seattle, Washington 54789. Peter Marlin's Social Security number is 555-66-8888. During the current year, the Corporation made federal estimated income tax payments of $50,000.

Prepare a Form 1120 for the initial return for Scarlet.

CASE STUDY PROBLEM

I6-64

John and Kathy Brown have just been audited and the IRS agent disallowed the business loss they claimed in 2004. The agent asserted that the activity was a hobby, not a business.

John and Kathy live in Rochester, New York, near Lake Ontario. Kathy is a CPA, and John was formerly employed by an insurance firm. John's firm moved in 1999 and John resolved not to move to the firm's new location. Instead of seeking other employment John felt he could supplement his income by using his fishing expertise. He had been an avid fisherman for 15 years, and he owned a large Chris-Craft fly-bridge that he chartered to paying parties.

In 2000, Kathy and John developed a business plan, established a bank account for the charter activities, developed a bookkeeping system, and acquired insurance to cover the boat and the passengers. John fulfilled all the requirements to receive a U.S. Coast Guard operating license, a New York sport trolling license, and a seller's permit. These licenses and permits were necessary to legally operate a charter boat. 2000 was the first year of their activity.

John advertised in local papers and regional sport fishing magazines. He usually had three or four half-day paying parties each week. John spent at least one day maintaining and repairing his boat. Kathy usually accompanied John on charters three or four times each year.

John's charter activity was unprofitable the first two years. In 2002, John and Kathy restructured the activity to improve profitability. The restructuring included increasing advertising, participating in outdoor shows, and negotiating small contracts with local businesses. After the restructuring, the activity provided a small profit in 2002 and 2003.

In 2004, John started working with another insurance company in the area on a full-time basis. Even though he returned to the insurance business, John normally took two paying parties and one nonpaying, promotional party each week throughout the fishing season. John's costs unexpectedly increased and he lost $8,000 in the activity during 2004. John and Kathy deducted the entire loss on Schedule C of their 2004 tax return.

Required: Prepare a memo to the Browns recommending what position they should take and why. Show the logic used in arriving at your recommendation.

TAX RESEARCH PROBLEM

I6-65

Richard Penn lives in Harrisburg, Pennsylvania. Richard is the president of an architectural firm. Richard has become known throughout the community for excellent work and honesty in his business dealings. Richard believes his reputation is an integral part of the success of the firm.

Oil was found recently in the area around Harrisburg and some geologists believed the reserves were large. A few well-respected businesspeople organized Oil Company to develop a few wells. Although some oil was being extracted, the oil corporation lacked capital to develop the oil fields to their expected potential. After reading the geologists' report, Richard felt that Oil Company was a good investment; therefore, he acquired 25% of the company. A short time after Richard's acquisition, the price of foreign oil decreased sharply. The drop in foreign oil prices caused Oil Company to be unprofitable due to its high production costs. Three months later Oil Company filed bankruptcy.

The bankruptcy proceedings were reported in the local newspaper. Many of Oil Company's creditors were real estate developers that engaged Richard's architectural firm to provide designs. After Oil Company declared bankruptcy the architectural firm's business noticeably decreased.

Richard felt the decline in business was related to the bankruptcy of Oil Company. Richard convinced his partner to use the accumulated earnings of the firm to repay all the creditors of Oil Company.

Richard has asked you whether his firm can deduct the expenses of repaying Oil Company's creditors. After completing your research explain to Richard why the expenses are or are not deductible.

A partial list of research sources is as follows:

- Sec. 162

- *Thomas H. Welch v. Helvering*, 12 AFTR 1456, 3 USTC ¶1164 (USSC, 1933)

- *William A. Thompson, Jr.*, 1983 PH T.C. Memo ¶83,487, 46 TCM 1109

TAX RESEARCH CASE

I6-66   Three years ago, Paul Wilde exercised all his stock options in the start up company he helped establish, and walked away with over $100 million. Since that time, he has spent all his energy, time, and effort in managing his portfolio. His investment philosophy is one of steady, careful investment in a well-balanced portfolio. Thus, although each year he engages in several sales and purchases, he generally buys and holds the securities for both the dividends and the growth potential. Consequently, most of the stock sales he makes are of securities he has held for over one year. Because his investment activities have grown so large, this year he rented a suite of offices and hired two investment advisors and five secretaries to help him. He also purchased several new computers and some new office furniture for the office.

Paul has now come to you for some tax help. Specifically, he would like to know if his activities are considered a business or whether they are an investment activity. In your explanation to him, please include whether the expenses incurred in the activity are deductions *for* or *from* AGI.

A partial list of research sources is as follows:

- *Higgins v. CIR*, 25 AFTR 1160, 41-1 USTC §9233 (USSC, 1941)

- *Estate of Louis Yaeger, Deceased, Judith Winters, Ralph Meisels, Abraham J. Weber and the Bank of New York*, 889 F2d 29, 89-2 USTC ¶9633 (CA-2)

- *Frederick Mayer and Jan Perry Mayer*, 67 TCM 2949 (1994)

- *Rudolph W. and Abbie A. Steffler*, 69 TCM 2940 (1995)

- Sec. 179

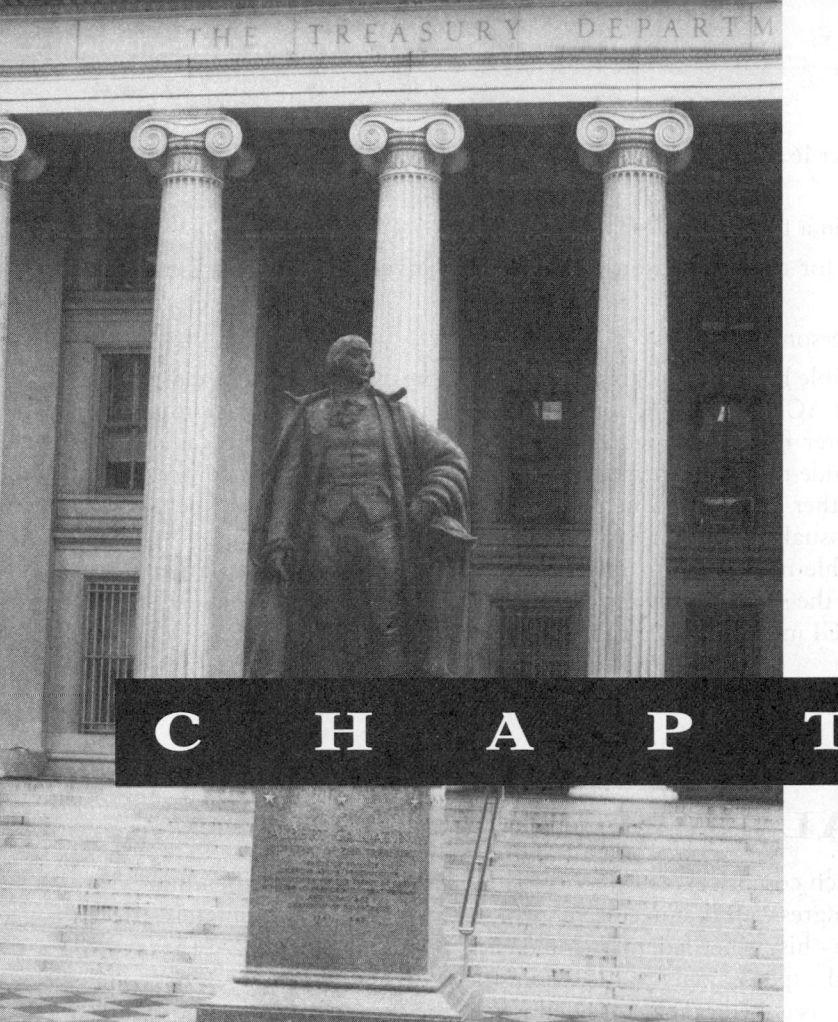

7

CHAPTER

ITEMIZED DEDUCTIONS

LEARNING OBJECTIVES

After studying this chapter, you should be able to

1 ▶ Identify qualified medical expenses and compute the medical expense deduction

2 ▶ Determine the timing of a medical expense deduction and the effect of a reimbursement

3 ▶ Identify taxes that are deductible as itemized deductions

4 ▶ Identify different types of interest deductions

5 ▶ Compute the amount of investment interest deduction

6 ▶ Compute the deduction for qualified residence interest

7 ▶ Compute the amount of a charitable contribution deduction and identify limitations

8 ▶ Identify certain miscellaneous itemized deductions subject to the 2% of AGI limit

9 ▶ Compute total itemized deductions for a taxpayer who is subject to the itemized deduction phase-out.

As explained in Chapter I6, most deductible expenses for individuals fit into three general categories:

▶ Expenses incurred in a trade or business

▶ Expenses incurred for the production of income (an investment activity) or for tax advice

▶ Certain specified personal expenses

If an expense is deductible based on the above categories, the expense must be classified as either *for* AGI or *from* AGI. The distinction between *for* and *from* AGI was discussed in Chapter I6. This chapter focuses on deductions *from* AGI, also referred to as **itemized deductions**, which include medical expenses, taxes, interest, and charitable contributions. Chapter I9 discusses other itemized deductions, such as employee business expenses, and Chapter I8 discusses casualty losses on personal-use property.

In arriving at taxable income, individuals may subtract from AGI the larger of the standard deduction or the sum of all itemized deductions. However, as explained later in this chapter, having AGI in excess of certain limits causes certain itemized deductions to be reduced.

MEDICAL EXPENSES

Medical expenses, which comprise one category of deductible personal expenditures, are deductible because Congress felt that excessive medical expenses might ultimately affect a taxpayer's ability to pay his or her federal income tax. However, under Sec. 213, taxpayers may deduct medical expenses only to the extent the expenses exceed 7.5% of the taxpayer's AGI. To qualify as a medical expense deduction, the expenditure must be incurred for the medical care of a qualified individual. Taxpayers may not take a deduction for medical expenses to the extent the expenses are reimbursed (i.e., compensated for by insurance or otherwise).

QUALIFIED INDIVIDUALS

To deduct medical expenses, taxpayers must pay the expenses on behalf of themselves, their spouses, or their dependents.

TAXPAYER'S DEPENDENT. Deductible medical expenses include those paid on behalf of a taxpayer's dependent as well as on behalf of a person for whom the taxpayer could take a dependency exemption except for the failure to meet the gross income or joint return tests.[1]

EXAMPLE I7-1 ▶

KEY POINT

Medical expenses are deductible for a person who satisfies only the support, relationship, and citizenship dependency tests.

In March of the current year, Jean's son, Steve, is involved in an automobile accident. Steve is 25 years old at the time of the accident and has worked full-time for part of the year, earning a total of $15,000. Because Steve has no medical insurance and cannot pay the medical bills or support himself as a result of the accident, Jean pays Steve's medical expenses and supports him for the rest of the year. Because Jean provides over one-half of Steve's support for the year and Steve, except for the gross income test, otherwise qualifies as Jean's dependent, Jean may deduct the medical expenses she pays on his behalf. Jean may not claim a dependency exemption for Steve because the gross income test is not satisfied. ◀

CHILDREN OF DIVORCED PARENTS. As long as one divorced parent qualifies to claim the dependency exemption under Sec. 152(e), the parent who pays medical expenses on behalf of the children may deduct the expenses. The parent taking the medical expense deduction need not be the parent who may claim the dependency exemption.

---

[1] Sec. 152. See Chapter I2 for the tests that must be met to claim a qualifying child or qualifying relative as a dependent.

Identify qualified medical expenses and compute the medical expense deduction

QUALIFIED MEDICAL EXPENSES

The **medical expense deduction** is available only for expenditures paid for medical care. Section 213 defines *medical care* as amounts paid for

▶ The diagnosis, cure, mitigation, treatment, or prevention of disease

▶ The purpose of affecting any structure or function of the body

▶ Transportation primarily for and essential to the first two items listed above

▶ Qualified long-term care services

▶ Insurance covering all of the items listed above

ADDITIONAL COMMENT

In 2003, the deduction for medical expenses totaled over $55 billion, representing 6.1% of the total dollar amount of itemized deductions, making it the fifth largest itemized deduction.

DIAGNOSIS, CURE, MITIGATION, TREATMENT, OR PREVENTION OF DISEASE. Although the tax law does not precisely define the term *medical expense*, it is clear that medical expenses are deductible only if paid for procedures or treatments that are legal in the locality in which they are performed. For example, taxpayers may not deduct expenditures for controlled substances.[2] The definition of medical care includes preventive measures such as routine physical and dental examinations. However, other expenses should be "confined strictly to expenses incurred primarily for the prevention or alleviation of a physical or mental defect or illness." Thus, unless they are for routine physical or dental examinations, the expenditures must be for the purpose of curing a specific ailment rather than related to the general health of an individual. This determination is especially critical when the expenditures in question are for items such as vacations, weight loss programs, or stop smoking programs. The taxpayer may or may not incur such expenses for a specific ailment.

EXAMPLE I7-2 ▶ Helmut is nervous and irritable because of pressures at work and begins to suffer angina symptoms. In order to relax and get away from it all, he takes an ocean cruise around the world. Helmut's angina symptoms ease while he is on the cruise. However, the Tax Court held that a cruise is not a proven medical necessity because Helmut's physician did not specifically prescribe it. Although the cruise was beneficial to Helmut's general health, it was not deductible.[3] ◀

EXAMPLE I7-3 ▶ Dave enrolls in a weight reduction program on the advice of two doctors who prescribe the program as a means of relieving his obesity, hypertension, and certain hearing problems. These expenses qualify as deductible medical expenditures because they are incurred for specific medical conditions.[4] ◀

Although receipt of a doctor's recommendation for incurring the cost appears to lend a great deal of weight to deductibility, it is not always sufficient. For example, a taxpayer could not deduct the cost of dancing lessons for an emotionally disturbed child, even though the lessons proved to be beneficial and were recommended by a physician. Likewise, a taxpayer suffering from arthritis could not deduct the cost of ballroom dance lessons, even though a doctor recommended the lessons. On the other hand, the IRS has ruled that the cost of a clarinet and clarinet lessons was deductible when recommended by an orthodontist to correct a malocclusion of a child's teeth.[5] In short, determining the deductibility of certain expenditures can be difficult.

ADDITIONAL COMMENT

One cannot deduct the cost of nonprescription medicine (except insulin), toothpaste, toiletries, maternity clothes, diaper service, or funeral expenses.

Range of Deductible Medical Services. According to the Treasury Regulations, typical medical expenses include payments for a wide range of medical, dental, and other diagnostic and healing services. Thus, taxpayers may deduct payments to licensed or certified medical professionals such as general practitioners, obstetricians, surgeons, ophthalmologists, opticians, dentists, and orthodontists. Furthermore, deductible medical expenditures

[2] Reg. Sec. 1.213-1(e)(1)(ii). See also Rev. Rul. 97-9, I.R.B. 1997-9 and IRS Publication 502 (2004) which contains the IRS's recommended treatment for a number of medical expenses.
[3] *Daniel E. Mizl,* 1980 PH T.C. Memo ¶80,227, 40 TCM 552. Even if the taxpayer's physician had prescribed the trip, it still may not have been deductible. See Reg. Sec. 1.213-1(e)(1)(ii).
[4] Rev. Rul. 2002-19, 2002-1 C.B. 778. However, the cost of diet foods or weight loss programs directed at general health or appearance is not deductible. Furthermore, costs incurred for prescription drugs and programs to stop smoking are deductible but over-the-counter stop smoking aids are not. See Rev. Rul. 99-28, 1999-1 C.B. 1269.
[5] *John J. Thoene,* 33 T.C. 62 (1959), *Rose C. France v. CIR,* 50 AFTR 2d 82-5504, 1982-1 USTC ¶9225 (6th Cir., 1982), and Rev. Rul. 62-210, 1962-2 C.B. 89.

include payments for medical services rendered by individuals such as chiropractors, osteopaths, and psychotherapists who may or may not be required to be licensed or certified.[6] Taxpayers may deduct payments to Christian Science practitioners as well as acupuncture treatment if the taxpayer receives the treatment for a specific medical purpose.[7] Qualified medical expenses also include payment for hospital services, nursing services, laboratory fees, X-rays, artificial teeth or limbs, ambulance hire, eyeglasses, and prescribed medicines and insulin. Nondeductible expenses include expenditures for nonprescription medicines, drugs, vitamins, and other types of health foods that improve the individual's general health.

To deduct costs incurred for schools and camps, the taxpayer must show that the facility has the appropriate medical equipment and regularly engages in providing medical services. For example, a court held that expenses a taxpayer incurred to send his mentally handicapped son to a school with a special curriculum for such children was deductible. Similarly, another court allowed a taxpayer to deduct the cost of sending a child with psychiatric problems to a school specializing in learning disorders. However, taxpayers generally may not deduct the cost of sending children with special medical problems to schools or camps that do not have the proper equipment, facilities, or curriculum for such problems.

TYPICAL MISCONCEPTION

Taxpayers tend to define qualifying medical expenses too narrowly. This may be caused, in part, by comparison with expense reimbursement limitation policies of health insurance companies.

MEDICAL PROCEDURES AFFECTING ANY FUNCTION OR STRUCTURE OF THE BODY. Deductible medical expenditures also include payments for services affecting any function or structure of the body, even though no specific illness or disease exists. Thus, qualifying medical expenses include expenditures for such items as physical therapy, obstetrical services, eyeglasses, dental examinations and cleaning, and hearing aids. Under Sec. 213, cosmetic surgery or any other similar procedure does not qualify as a medical expense unless such surgery is necessary to correct a deformity arising from a congenital abnormality, a personal injury resulting from an accident or trauma, or a disfiguring disease. Cosmetic surgery is defined as any procedure undertaken to improve a person's appearance that does not meaningfully promote the proper function of the body or prevent or treat an illness or disease.

TRANSPORTATION ESSENTIAL TO MEDICAL CARE. Taxpayers may deduct transportation expenses that are essential to and incurred primarily for qualified medical care. Thus, taxpayers may deduct actual out-of-pocket automobile expenditures, taxis, airfare, ambulance fees, and other forms of transportation if the travel is for medical reasons. However, the tax law disallows a deduction if the travel is undertaken for recreational purposes or for the general improvement of the taxpayer's health.

In lieu of the actual cost of the use of an automobile, in 2006 the IRS allows a deduction of 18 cents for each mile that the automobile is driven for medical reasons. In addition to this standard mileage rate, taxpayers may also deduct the cost of tolls and parking.

Certain courts have held that the cost of meals and lodging while en route to a medical facility is part of deductible travel costs incurred for medical purposes. However, taxpayers may not deduct the cost of meals eaten on trips that are too short to warrant a stop for meals. Additionally, taxpayers may deduct only 50% of the cost of meals. (See Chapter I9 for a discussion of the 50% disallowance rule for meals and entertainment.) The IRC limits the potential deduction for the cost of lodging to $50 per night. Furthermore, lodging expenses qualify as medical expenditures only if the travel is primarily for and essential to medical care, the medical care is provided in a licensed hospital (or a facility related or equivalent to a licensed hospital), and there is no significant element of personal pleasure or recreation in the travel. The tax law imposes the $50 limitation on lodging on a per-individual basis. Thus, if the patient is unable to travel alone, the taxpayer may deduct an additional $50 per night for the lodging costs of a nurse, parent, or spouse.

---

[6] Reg. Sec. 1.213-1(e)(1) and Rev. Rul. 63-91, 1963-1 C.B. 54. See also Ltr. Rul. 8919009 (February 6, 1989) where a pregnant woman was entitled to a deduction for the cost of childbirth classes to the extent that they prepared her for the childbirth. However, the cost of the classes where she received instructions on the care of the unborn child represented a flat fee that allowed a coach

to attend the class with the taxpayer. Thus, one-half of the fee was deemed attributable to the coach and was not allowed as a qualified medical expense.
[7] Rev. Rul. 72-593, 1972-2 C.B. 180 and IRS Special Ruling, February 2, 1943.

Qualified Long-Term Care. Taxpayers may also deduct expenditures for qualified long-term care as medical expenses subject to the 7.5% of AGI limitation. Long-term care is defined as medical services required by a chronically ill individual which are provided under a prescribed plan of care. Under Sec. 7702B, such items include expenditures for diagnostic, preventive, therapeutic, curing, treating, mitigating, rehabilitative, and personal care services. A chronically ill individual generally is someone who, for a period of at least 90 days, cannot perform at least two daily living tasks such as eating, toileting (including continence), bathing, or dressing.

Expenditures for long-term care insurance premiums also qualify as medical deductions, subject to an annual limit based upon the age of an individual.[8]

CAPITAL EXPENDITURES FOR MEDICAL CARE. Generally, taxpayers may not currently deduct capital expenditures for federal income tax purposes. For assets used in a trade or business or held for the production of income, taxpayers must recover such costs through depreciation, cost recovery, or amortization. Capital expenditures incurred for personal medical purposes are not depreciable or amortizable. However, a current deduction is available when the capital expenditure is made to acquire an asset primarily for the medical care of the taxpayer, the taxpayer's spouse, or the taxpayer's dependents. To qualify as a deduction, the taxpayer must incur the expenditure as a medical necessity for primary use by the individual in need of medical treatment, and the expenditure must be reasonable in amount. The following are the three categories of deductible capital expenditures for medical care:[9]

▶ Expenditures that relate only to the sick or handicapped person, not to the permanent improvement or betterment of the taxpayer's property (e.g., eyeglasses, dogs or other animals that assist the blind or the deaf, artificial teeth and limbs, wheelchairs, crutches, and portable air conditioners purchased for the sole use of a sick person)

▶ Expenditures that permanently improve or better the taxpayer's property as well as provide medical care (e.g., a swimming pool installed in the home of an individual suffering from arthritis)

▶ Expenditures to remove structural barriers in the home of a physically handicapped individual such as costs of constructing entrance ramps, widening doorways and halls, lowering kitchen cabinets, adding railings, etc.

Capital expenditures that relate only to the sick person (the first category) are fully deductible in the year paid. Expenditures that improve the residence (the second category) are deductible only to the extent that the amount of the expenditure exceeds the increase in the fair market value (FMV) of the residence brought about by the capital expenditure. Expenditures to remove physical barriers in the home of a physically handicapped individual (the third category) are deductible in full (i.e., the increase in the home's value is deemed to be zero). In addition, any costs of operating or maintaining the assets in all three categories are deductible as long as the medical reason for the capital expenditure continues to exist.[10] All of the above expenditures are subject to the 7.5% floor.

EXAMPLE I7-4 ▶ During the current year, Rita is injured in an industrial accident. As a result, she sustains a chronic disabling leg injury, which requires her to spend much time in a wheelchair. Rita's physician recommends that a swimming pool be installed in her backyard and that she devote several hours each day to physical exercise. During the year, Rita makes the following expenditures:

Wheelchair	$ 2,500
Swimming pool	27,000
Operation and maintenance of the pool	1,800
Entrance ramp and door modification	5,000

---

[8] For 2006, if the individual is 40 years of age or less, the annual deductible limit for the premiums is $280. For individuals over 40 but less than 50 the limit is $530. For those over 50 but less than 60 the limit is $1,060; over 60 but less than 70 the limit is $2,830; and over 70 the limit is $3,530.

[9] Reg. Sec. 1.213-1(e)(1)(iii) and H. Rept. No. 99-841, 99th Cong., 2d Sess., p. II-22 (1986).
[10] Rev. Rul. 87-106, 1987-2 C.B. 67.

REAL-WORLD EXAMPLE

Taxpayers made nonrefundable advance payments required as a condition for an institution's future acceptance of their handicapped child for lifetime care in the event that taxpayers could not care for the child. The amounts paid were deductible as expenses for medical care in the year paid. Rev. Rul. 75-303, 1975-2 C.B. 87. This current deduction for prepaid amounts is only available for certain lifetime care expenditures incurred in situations described in this ruling. Rev. Rul. 93-72, I.R.B. 1993-34,7.

A qualified appraiser estimates that the swimming pool increases the value of Rita's home by only $20,000. Rita's medical expenses for the year include $2,500 for the wheelchair, $7,000 for the swimming pool (the excess of the cost of the pool over the increase in the FMV of the home), $1,800 for the operation and maintenance of the pool, and $5,000 for the ramp and door modification. ◄

COSTS OF LIVING IN INSTITUTIONS. The entire cost of in-patient hospital care, including meals and lodging, qualifies as a medical expense. However, if an individual is in an institution other than a hospital (e.g., a nursing home or a special school for the handicapped), the deductibility of the costs involved depends on the facts of the particular case. If the principal reason for the taxpayer's presence in an institution is the need for and availability of the medical care furnished by that institution, the qualified medical expenditures include the entire costs of meals, lodging, and other services necessary for furnishing the medical care.

ADDITIONAL COMMENT

A taxpayer cannot deduct the 1.45% Medicare (hospital insurance benefits) tax that is withheld from wages as part of the Social Security tax.

MEDICAL INSURANCE PREMIUMS. Qualified medical expenses also include all premiums paid for medical insurance, including premiums paid for supplementary medical insurance for the aged under the Social Security Act and premiums paid for qualified long-term care insurance contracts. In many cases, taxpayers pay premiums for insurance coverage that extends beyond mere medical care. For example, in addition to the standard medical care coverage, an insurance policy may provide coverage for loss of income or loss of life, limb, or sight. In such cases, the tax law allows a deduction for the medical care portion of the premium only if the cost of each type of insurance is either separately stated in the contract or furnished to the policyholder by the insurance company in a separate statement.[11]

EXAMPLE I7-5 ▶ Each month Malazia pays $300 for an insurance policy under which she is reimbursed for any doctor or hospital charges she incurs. In addition, the policy will pay two-thirds of her regular salary each month if she becomes disabled. Finally, the policy will pay her $10,000 for the loss of any limb. At the end of the year, her insurance company issues a statement that allocates two-thirds of the premiums to the medical insurance coverage. Malazia's medical care expenditure is $2,400 ($300 × 12 × 0.667). ◄

If a taxpayer pays the premiums attributable to an individual or group medical insurance plan, the payments are deductible as medical expenses which in most cases are itemized deductions. Self-employed individuals may deduct 100% of these amounts as deductions *for* AGI. Any amounts paid by the taxpayer's employer are excluded from the employee's gross income and are not includible in the taxpayer's medical expenses.[12]

Chapter I9 discusses the deduction for medical savings accounts established for employees.

AMOUNT AND TIMING OF DEDUCTION

OBJECTIVE 2

Determine the timing of a medical expense deduction and the effect of a reimbursement

The amount and timing of the allowable medical expense deduction depend on when the taxpayer actually pays the medical expenses, the taxpayer's AGI, and whether the taxpayer receives any reimbursement for the medical expenses.

TIMING OF THE PAYMENT. In general, taxpayers may deduct medical expenses only in the year they actually pay the expenses. This rule applies regardless of the taxpayer's method of accounting or when the event that caused the expenditure occurs.[13] Thus, if taxpayers receive medical care during the year but have not paid for it as of the end of the year, taxpayers must defer the deduction for that care until the year they pay for the medical care. If the obligation is charged on a credit card, payment is deemed to have been

---

[11] Sec. 213(d). See also Rev. Ruls. 66-216, 1966-2 C.B. 100, and 79-175, 1979-1 C.B. 117.
[12] Sections 162 and 106.

[13] Reg. Sec. 1.213-1(a)(1). However, medical expenses paid within one year from the day following the taxpayer's death are treated as paid at the time they are incurred (see Sec. 213(c)).

made on the date of the charge, not on the later date when the taxpayer pays the credit card balance. Conversely, if medical care is prepaid, the deduction is deferred until the year the taxpayer receives the care unless there is a legal obligation to prepay or unless the prepayment is a requirement for the receipt of the medical care.[14]

LIMITATION ON AMOUNT DEDUCTIBLE.   As previously noted, the tax law allows a medical expense deduction only for the years in which the taxpayer itemizes his or her deductions and the taxpayer's expenditures for medical care exceed 7.5% of AGI.

EXAMPLE 17-6 ▶ During the current year, Kelly incurs qualified medical expenditures of $3,000. Her AGI for the year is $30,000. After subtracting the floor, she has $750 ($3,000 − [0.075 × $30,000]) of deductible medical expenses. These medical expenses are added to Kelly's other itemized deductions to determine whether they exceed the standard deduction. ◀

SELF-STUDY QUESTION

Why does the IRS not require that the taxpayer file an amended return when a reimbursement is received in a later year?

ANSWER

The administrative burden on the IRS of processing additional returns would be too great.

MEDICAL INSURANCE REIMBURSEMENTS.   Taxpayers may only deduct unreimbursed medical expenditures. It does not matter whether the reimbursement is from an insurance plan purchased from an insurance company, a medical reimbursement plan of an employer, or a payment resulting from litigation.

If the taxpayer receives reimbursement in the same year he or she pays for the medical expenses, the amount of the reimbursement reduces the allowed deduction. If a taxpayer receives a reimbursement in a year subsequent to the year of payment, the taxpayer must include the reimbursement in gross income in the year of receipt to the extent that the taxpayer derived a tax benefit from the deduction in the previous year. If the taxpayer did not take a deduction in the prior year, the taxpayer doesn't need to report the reimbursement as income. This may occur because the taxpayer's total itemized deductions do not exceed the standard deduction or because the taxpayer's total medical expenses do not exceed 7.5% of AGI. If the taxpayer took a deduction in the prior year, however, the taxpayer must report as income the lesser of the amount of the reimbursement or the amount that medical expenses reduced the taxable income in the prior year.

EXAMPLE 17-7 ▶ During 2006, Diane, a single taxpayer under age 65, reports the following items of income and expense:

AGI	$60,000
Total qualified medical expenses	6,500
Itemized deductions other than medical	3,900

Diane's taxable income for 2006 is calculated as follows:

AGI			$60,000
Reduction: Larger of itemized deductions or standard deduction			
Medical expenses	$6,500		
Minus: 7.5% of AGI	(4,500)	2,000	
Other itemized deductions		3,900	
Total itemized deductions		$5,900	
Standard deduction		$5,150	(5,900)
Personal exemption			(3,300)
Taxable income			$50,800

If during 2007 Diane receives a reimbursement of $1,500 for medical expenses incurred the prior year, she must include $750 ($5,900 − $5,150) in gross income for 2007, which is the amount of the tax benefit from the medical expense deduction for the prior year. This amount can be calculated by comparing the actual taxable income for 2006 with what would have been the 2006 taxable income if the reimbursement had been received that year.

[14] Rev. Rul. 78-39, 1978-1 C.B. 73 and *Robert M. Rose v. CIR*, 26 AFTR 2d 70-5653, 70-2 USTC ¶9646 (5th Cir., 1970). See also Rev. Rul. 93-72, Rev. Rul. 1993-2 C.B. 77, Rev. Rul. 75-302, 1975-2 C.B. 86, and Rev. Rul. 75-303, 1975-2 C.B. 87.

AGI		$60,000
Reduction: Larger of itemized		
deductions or standard deduction		
Medical expenses	$6,500	
Minus: Reimbursement	(1,500)	
7.5% of AGI	(4,500)	
Excess medical expenses	500	
Plus: Other itemized deductions	3,900	
Total itemized deductions	$4,400	
Standard deduction	$5,150	(5,150)
Personal exemption		(3,300)
Taxable income (assuming reimbursement		
was received in 2006)		$51,550
Minus: Actual 2006 taxable income		(50,800)
Tax benefit		$ 750 ◄

Topic Review I7-1 highlights the principal requirements for the medical expense deduction previously discussed.

STOP & THINK

Question: Vince and Diane are married and file a joint tax return. For the current year they estimate their AGI at $100,000. They also estimate their itemized deductions for taxes, interest, and charitable contributions total $9,000. Up to the current date they have incurred $7,000 in deductible medical expenses. For several months they have been considering laser surgery on Diane's eyes. The total expenditure for the operations will be $4,000 and is not covered by their medical insurance. Since they already have spent so much this year on medical expenses and they do not anticipate such large expenses next year, they are considering delaying the eye operation until next year. They estimate next year's AGI to be approximately $110,000. Does this decision make sense from a tax point of view?

Solution: From a tax point of view, Diane should consider having and paying for the operation this year. If so, $4,000 is added to the prior $7,000 medical expenditures for a total of $11,000 for the year. After applying the 7.5% of AGI limitation, $3,500 [$11,000 − ($100,000 × 0.075)] of the medical expenses is deductible. If they wait until next year and if their estimates are correct, none of the medical expenses in either year are deductible because of the 7.5% of AGI limitation.

Topic Review I7-1

Medical Expense Deductions

ITEMS	DEDUCTION RULES AND LIMITATIONS
Qualifying expenditures	(a) Expenditures for the diagnosis, cure, mitigation, treatment, or prevention of disease and qualified long-term care.
	(b) Transportation at $0.18 per mile and lodging limited to $50 per night, per person, and 50% of meals.
	(c) Medical and qualified long-term care insurance premiums.
	(d) Capital expenditures (subject to specific limitations).
Qualifying individuals	Taxpayer, spouse, dependents, and children of divorced parents even if not dependent.
Amount and timing of the deduction	Deduct in the year paid unless prepayment is required or there is a legal obligation to pay. Medical expenses are subject to a 7.5% of AGI nondeductible limitation.
Treatment of insurance reimbursements	The deduction is reduced if the reimbursement is received in the year of payment. Reimbursements received in a subsequent year are included in gross income of the year received to the extent that a tax benefit was received in the earlier year.

TAXES

Section 164 provides taxpayers with a deduction for specifically listed taxes paid or accrued during the taxable year. Generally, cash-method taxpayers deduct the taxes when they pay for them, whereas taxpayers using the accrual method deduct taxes in the year the taxes accrue. The tax law specifically lists other taxes as nondeductible. To be deductible as a tax, the assessment in question must be a tax rather than a fee or charge imposed by a government for providing specific goods or services.

DEFINITION OF A TAX

A **tax** is a mandatory assessment levied under the authority of a political entity for the purpose of raising revenue to use for public or governmental purposes. Thus, fees, assessments, or fines imposed for specific privileges or services are not deductible as taxes under Sec. 164. These nontax items include

▶ Vehicle registration and inspection fees

▶ Registration tags for pets

▶ Toll charges for highways and bridges

▶ Parking meter charges

▶ Charges for sewer, water, and other services

▶ Special assessments against real estate for items such as sidewalks, lighting, and streets

However, if taxpayers incur these nontax fees and charges in a business or income-producing activity, the taxpayers may either capitalize or deduct these items as ordinary and necessary business expenses or ordinary and necessary expenses incurred for the production of income.

DEDUCTIBLE TAXES

The following taxes are specifically deductible under Sec. 164:

▶ State, local, and foreign real property taxes

▶ State and local personal property taxes if based on value

▶ State, local, and foreign income, war profits, and excess profits taxes

▶ State and local sales taxes if an election is made to deduct these taxes instead of deducting state and local income taxes

▶ Other state, local, and foreign taxes that are paid or incurred in either a trade or business or an income-producing activity

A government body other than the federal government imposes all of these taxes. Federal taxes other than the generation-skipping transfer tax are not deductible for federal income tax purposes.[15] However, federal customs and excise taxes incurred in the taxpayer's business or income-producing activity are deductible as ordinary and necessary expenses under Secs. 162 or 212. Likewise, the *employer's* portion of federal Social Security taxes and federal and state unemployment taxes are deductible by the employer as ordinary and necessary business expenses if the employee works in the employer's business or income-producing activity.

NONDEDUCTIBLE TAXES

The following taxes are not deductible under Sec. 164:

▶ Federal income taxes

▶ Federal estate, inheritance, legacy, succession, and gift taxes

▶ Federal import or tariff duties and excise taxes unless incurred in the taxpayer's business or for the production of income

[15] The generation-skipping transfer tax is imposed by the United States on certain distributions from a trust (see Sec. 2601). Furthermore, under Sec. 691(c) a taxpayer who includes income in respect of a decedent in taxable income may deduct estate tax attributable to that amount.

▶ Employee's portion of Social Security and other payroll taxes

▶ State and local sales taxes and state inheritance, legacy, succession, and gift taxes

▶ Foreign income taxes if the taxpayer elects to take the taxes as a credit against his or her federal income tax liability

▶ Property taxes on real estate to the extent treated as imposed on another taxpayer

STATE AND LOCAL INCOME TAXES

For individuals, state and local income taxes are normally an itemized (*from* AGI) deduction. Thus, a taxpayer does not receive any federal income tax benefit if these taxes, in addition to the other itemized deductions, do not exceed the standard deduction. Cash-method taxpayers deduct all state and local income taxes paid or withheld during the year even if the taxes are attributable to another tax year.

> During 2006, Rita had $1,500 in state income taxes withheld from her salary. On April 15, 2007, Rita pays an additional $400 when she files her 2006 state income tax return. On her 2006 federal income tax return, Rita may deduct the $1,500 in state income taxes withheld from her salary during 2006 as an itemized deduction. The $400 that Rita pays on April 15, 2007, is deductible on her 2007 federal income tax return, even though the liability relates to her 2006 state income tax return. ◀

If a taxpayer receives a refund of state income taxes deducted in a prior year, the taxpayer must include the refund as income in the year of the refund to the extent the taxpayer received a tax benefit from the prior deduction. This calculation is similar to the calculation of the tax benefit from a medical expense reimbursement in Example I7-7.

STATE AND LOCAL SALES TAXES

Taxpayers are allowed to deduct state and local sales taxes in lieu of state and local income taxes. This election is available for tax years beginning after December 31, 2003, and before January 1, 2007.[16] Taxpayers electing to deduct state and local sales taxes have two options for determining the deductible amount. Taxpayers may deduct the actual amount of taxes paid by accumulating receipts showing the actual amount of taxes paid, or they may deduct the appropriate amount from tables provided by the Treasury Department.

PERSONAL PROPERTY TAXES

Many state and local governments impose personal property taxes. For individuals, the key issue is whether the levy is a deductible tax under Sec. 164 or a nondeductible fee. To qualify as a deductible personal property tax, the levy must meet two basic tests:

▶ The tax must be an ad valorem tax on personal property. In other words, the property's value determines the amount of the tax rather than some other measure such as a vehicle's weight or model year.

▶ The tax must be imposed on an annual basis, even if not collected annually.[17]

If a personal property tax is based partly on value and partly on some other basis, only the ad valorem portion is deductible.

> Banner County imposes on all passenger automobiles a property tax of 1% of value plus 20 cents per hundredweight. Clay's automobile has a value of $20,000 and weighs 1,500 pounds. Clay may deduct $200 ($20,000 × 0.01) under Sec. 164. Clay may not deduct the remaining $300 (1,500 × 0.20) under Sec. 164; however, he may deduct it as an ordinary business expense if the automobile is used in his business. ◀

For individuals, personal property taxes are *from* AGI (itemized) deductions unless incurred in an individual's trade or business or for the production of rental income.

BOOK-TAX DIFFERENCE

For financial accounting purposes, all taxes are deducted in arriving at net income after taxes. However, for tax purposes, only certain taxes are deductible. This gives rise to an M-1 or M-3 adjustment.

EXAMPLE I7-8 ▶

ADDITIONAL COMMENT

Every state except Alaska, Florida, Nevada, New Hampshire, South Dakota, Tennessee, Texas, Washington, and Wyoming impose a personal income tax. Although New Hampshire and Tennessee do not impose a personal income tax, they do tax interest and dividends at the individual level.

EXAMPLE I7-9 ▶

ADDITIONAL COMMENT

Several states impose a tax on the value of a taxpayer's investment portfolio. This is an example of a deductible intangible personal property tax.

---

[16] The deduction of sales taxes was scheduled to expire after December 31, 2005. At the date of printing of this textbook, both the House and Senate have approved the extension of this deduction through 2006.

[17] Reg. Sec. 1.164-3(c).

REAL ESTATE TAXES

Apportionment of Taxes. When real estate is sold during the year, the federal income tax deduction for property taxes imposed on that real estate is allocated between the seller and the purchaser based on the amount of time each taxpayer owns the property during the real property tax year. The real property tax year may or may not coincide with the taxpayer's tax year. The apportionment, based on the number of days each party holds the property during the real property tax year of sale, assumes that the purchaser owns the property on the date of the sale. This apportionment is mandatory for all taxpayers even though one of the parties (i.e., the purchaser or seller) may have actually paid the entire property tax bill. The party who actually pays the taxes (either the buyer or the seller) deducts his or her share of the taxes in the year he or she pays the taxes unless the tax-payer makes an election under Sec. 461(c) to accrue the taxes. The tax consequences do not depend on whether the agreement requires proration of the real estate taxes. Both the purchaser and the seller may deduct their apportioned share of the taxes, regardless of who actually pays it. If the seller does not actually pay his or her share of the taxes, the selling price of the property will increase by the amount of the tax and the buyer's basis will increase by the same amount. If the buyer does not actually pay his or her share of the taxes, the selling price will be decreased by the amount of the tax and the buyer's basis will decrease by the same amount.

EXAMPLE I7-10 ▶ The real property tax year for Bannock County is the calendar year. Property taxes for a particular real property tax year become a lien against the property as of June 30 of that year, and the owner of the property on that date becomes liable for the tax. However, the taxes are not payable until February 28 of the subsequent year. On May 30 of the current (non-leap) year, Sandy, a cash-method taxpayer, sells a building to Roger, who is also a cash-method taxpayer. The real estate taxes on the property for the current year are $1,095. Although Roger is liable for the payment of the tax, Sandy is treated as having paid $447 ($1,095 × 149/365 [the numerator of 149 is the number of days from January 1 through May 29 and the denominator is the entire real property tax year]) on the date of the sale. Roger may deduct his share of the taxes, equaling $648 ($1,095 × 216/365), in the subsequent year (i.e., the year during which Roger actually pays the full amount of property tax due of $1,095). On the other hand, if the taxes become a lien against the property on April 1, Sandy is the owner of the building on that date and, since she is liable for the tax, she will be the one who actually pays the tax. Under these circumstances, the result is the same (i.e., Sandy deducts $447 and Roger deducts $648) except that Roger may take the $648 deduction in the year of sale rather than in the year of payment. ◀

ADDITIONAL COMMENT

Delinquent taxes of the seller that are paid by the buyer as part of the contract price are not deductible.

TYPICAL MISCONCEPTION

Taxpayers often fail to differentiate between assessments for new construction and for repairs. For example, an assessment for street repairs is deductible, but an assessment for the construction of a new street is not deductible.

Generally, the sales agreement provides for the proper apportionment of property taxes between the buyer and seller. Thus, in the closing statement, the agreement generally states the amount of the taxes apportioned to each party separately from the selling price of the property.[18]

REAL PROPERTY ASSESSMENTS FOR LOCAL BENEFITS. Local governments often make assessments against real estate for the purpose of funding local improvements. These assessments may be for such items as street improvements, sidewalks, lighting, drainage, and sewer improvements. If the tax assessment is only against the property that benefits from the improvement, it is not deductible, even though the general public may also incidentally benefit.[19] The tax law requires capitalization of such assessments as part of the property's adjusted basis.

Real property taxes incurred on personal-use assets, such as a personal residence, are deductible *from* AGI. Real property taxes incurred on business property or property held for the production of rental income are deductions *for* AGI.

---

[18] However, if the agreement does not provide for an apportionment of taxes, the seller's gain or loss on the sale (and the purchaser's basis in the property) must be adjusted either upward or downward, depending on which party actually pays the taxes.

[19] Reg. Sec. 1.164-4. However, if the assessment against the local benefits is made for maintenance, repair, or interest charges on the benefits, the assessment is deductible. The burden of proof to show how much of the assessment is deductible falls on the taxpayer (see Sec. 164(c)(1)).

SELF-EMPLOYMENT TAX

Self-employed individuals pay a tax on their self-employment income in lieu of the payment of a Social Security payroll tax on salary. The self-employment tax rate and total amount of tax are equal to the combined employee and employer Social Security tax (i.e., 12.4% with a ceiling of $94,200 in 2006 ($90,000 in 2005); and no ceiling for the 2.9% additional Medicare hospital insurance premium for self-employed individuals). However, self-employed individuals may deduct one-half of the self-employment taxes paid as a *for* AGI deduction.[20]

INTEREST

OBJECTIVE 4

Identify different types of interest deductions

In years past, taxpayers could deduct virtually all interest paid or accrued in the taxable year. Gradually, however, Congress has enacted numerous exceptions into the tax law rendering several types of interest nondeductible. For example, individuals may not deduct personal interest expense, such as interest paid on personal credit cards, automobile loans, etc. Interest incurred in connection with a trade or business is always deductible. Thus, to determine the amount of interest expense deduction, taxpayers must properly classify their interest expense for the year. The interest expense categories include the following:

▶ Active trade or business
▶ Passive activity
▶ Investment
▶ Personal
▶ Qualified residence
▶ Student loan

ADDITIONAL COMMENT

In 2003, the deduction for interest paid totaled $332 billion representing 36.5% of the total dollar amount of itemized deductions, making it the largest itemized deduction.

DEFINITION OF INTEREST

Interest is defined as "compensation for the use or forbearance of money."[21] Thus, finance charges, carrying charges, loan discounts, premiums, loan origination fees, and points are all considered interest if they represent a cost for the use of money.

CHARGE FOR SERVICES. In addition to interest, borrowers may incur other charges in connection with borrowing money. These service charges include fees for appraisals, title searches, bank service charges, and the annual service charge on credit cards. Unless incurred in a trade or business, these expenses are not deductible because they all represent nondeductible personal expenses. As explained in the section in this chapter entitled Personal Interest, although finance charges on credit cards represent interest rather than service costs, they likewise are not deductible unless incurred in a trade or business.

BANK SERVICE CHARGES AND FINANCE CHARGES. Bank service charges on checking accounts are nondeductible expenses for services rendered rather than interest. The annual service charge on credit cards is also a charge for services rather than interest. However, finance charges on credit cards are interest. Late payments charged by public utilities are interest expense because they do not relate to any specific service.[22] Of course, if taxpayers incur these expenses in a trade or business, they are deductible.

KEY POINT

In general, the classification of interest expense depends on the use to which the borrowed money is put, not on the nature of the property used to secure the loan.

CLASSIFICATION OF INTEREST EXPENSE

The deductibility of interest generally depends on the purpose for which the taxpayer incurs the indebtedness because interest incurred in certain activities is subject to limitation and disallowance. For example, interest expense incurred in the taxpayer's active business is deductible in full against the business income (a deduction *for* AGI, taken on Schedule

---

[20] Sec. 164(f). (See Chapter I14 for a discussion of the self-employment tax.)
[21] *Deputy v. Pierre S. DuPont*, 23 AFTR 808, 40-1 USTC ¶9161 (USSC, 1940).
[22] Rev. Rul. 73-136, 1973-1 C.B. 68 and Rev. Rul. 74-187, 1974-1 C.B. 48.

However, interest on a credit card or interest charged by a public utility is not deductible if it is personal interest.

C), whereas interest expense allocated to the purchase of the taxpayer's residence is subject to the limitations applicable to that type of interest and is an itemized deduction (a deduction *from* AGI). Except for certain student loan interest and certain interest on a personal residence, taxpayers may not deduct interest allocated to personal-use expenditures.

Pursuant to the Treasury Regulations, taxpayers must allocate interest expense to the different interest expense categories by identifying the use of the borrowed money. Property used as collateral in securing the debt normally has no bearing on the allocation of the interest expense.[23]

EXAMPLE I7-11 ▶ Cathy pledges some stock and securities as collateral for a $30,000 loan. She then purchases an automobile with the proceeds of the loan. The automobile is used 100% of the time for personal use. Even though the collateral for the loan is investment property, the interest expense is allocated to a personal-use asset and is not deductible. ◀

If the taxpayer deposits borrowed funds in a bank rather than spending them immediately, the deposit is treated as an investment, and the interest on the loan is investment interest until the taxpayer withdraws or expends the funds. Then the taxpayer allocates the interest expense to a category based on the reason for making the expenditure, regardless of when the taxpayer actually pays the interest expense for the debt. This reallocation occurs as of the date the taxpayer writes the check on the account, as long as the delivery or mailing of the check occurs within a reasonable period of time.[24]

EXAMPLE I7-12 ▶ On March 1 of the current year, José borrows $100,000 and immediately deposits the funds into an account that contains no other funds. José makes no additional deposits or payments. On May 1 of the current year, he withdraws $40,000 from the account and purchases a sailboat to be used for personal purposes. On July 1, José withdraws an additional $50,000 and purchases a passive activity. For the current year, the interest expense on the loan is categorized as follows: from March 1 through April 30, all of the expense is investment interest expense. 40% ($40,000/$100,000) of the interest expense attributable to the period May 1 through June 30 is classified as personal interest and the remainder is investment interest. The interest expense attributable to the period from July 1 to the end of the year is classified as 40% personal interest, 50% passive activity interest, and 10% investment interest. ◀

If both borrowed and personal funds are mingled in the same account, expenditures from that account are treated as coming first from the borrowed funds.[25]

EXAMPLE I7-13 ▶ On April 1 of the current year, Diane borrows $30,000 and deposits it into a checking account that contains $10,000 of personal funds. On May 1 of the current year, Diane purchases a passive activity for $15,000, and on June 1 she purchases a personal automobile for $20,000. The $15,000 expended for the passive activity on May 1 is treated as coming from the borrowed funds. Thus, as of that date, one-half of the interest expense on the debt is reallocated from investment interest to passive activity interest. $15,000 of the funds expended for the personal automobile on June 1 is treated as coming from the borrowed funds, and the remaining $5,000 is treated as coming from the personal funds. Thus, as of June 1, the remaining interest expense on the debt is reallocated to personal interest. ◀

When the taxpayer repays the debt, the allocation of the repayment to the expenditures made with the borrowed funds occurs in the following order: (1) personal expenditures, (2) investment expenditures and passive activity expenditures other than rental real estate, (3) passive activity expenditures in rental real estate, and (4) trade or business expenditures.

---

[23] Temp. Reg. Sec. 1.163-8T. The major exception to this rule deals with home equity loans where the funds borrowed may be used for any purpose. Home equity loans are discussed later in this chapter.

[24] Temp. Reg. Sec. 1.163-8T(c). If during any one month several expenditures are made from an account, the taxpayer may elect to treat all the expenditures as if made on the first day of the month. However, this election is made on each account separately and is available only for accounts where the borrowed funds are already in the account as of the first day of the month. If the funds are not in the account as of the first day of the month, the expenditures may be treated as made on the date that the borrowed funds are deposited in the account. See Temp. Reg. Sec. 1.163-8T(c)(4)(iv).

[25] Temp. Reg. Sec. 1.163-8T(c)(4)(ii). However, if an expenditure is made out of the mingled funds within 15 days of the deposit of the borrowed funds into the account, the taxpayer may designate the expenditure to which the borrowed funds are allocated.

ACTIVE TRADE OR BUSINESS. Generally, a taxpayer may deduct without limit any interest expense incurred in the taxpayer's active trade or business. As explained in Chapter I6, the determination of whether a particular activity constitutes a trade or business or an investment depends on an examination of all the relevant facts and circumstances. For individuals, estates, trusts, and certain corporations, however, it is not sufficient that the taxpayer incur the interest in a trade or business. In addition, the taxpayer must *materially participate* in the business. If not, the activity is considered a passive activity, and losses from the activity (including the interest expense) are subject to the passive loss limitation rules (see Chapter I8 for a discussion of these rules). Interest incurred in an active trade or business is a deduction *for* AGI.

PASSIVE ACTIVITY. Individuals, estates, trusts, and certain corporations that incur losses from passive activities are subject to the passive loss limitation rules explained in Chapter I8. These rules prevent taxpayers from offsetting passive activity losses against other types of income such as salary, interest, dividends, and income from an active business. Taxpayers must include interest expense attributable to the passive activity in computing the net income or loss generated from the activity, and thus may not be able to deduct the interest under these limitation rules (see Chapter I8 for a discussion of these rules).

OBJECTIVE 5

Compute the amount of investment interest deduction

INVESTMENT INTEREST. Individuals and other noncorporate taxpayers are limited on the deductibility of interest expense attributable to investments. Without any limitation, high-income taxpayers could realize significant tax savings by borrowing money to invest in assets that are appreciating in value but produce little or no current income. This would enable the taxpayer to offset current highly taxed income with a current interest deduction, while deferring the taxable income from the investment until it is sold at a later date. This technique also would enable taxpayers to increase their future capital gain income and reduce their current ordinary income. This procedure is favorable to individual and noncorporate taxpayers because the tax on capital gains is less than the tax on ordinary income.

Because of these concerns, Sec. 163(d) limits the current deduction for investment interest expense to the noncorporate taxpayer's net investment income for the taxable year. Any investment interest expense disallowed as a current deduction is carried over and treated as investment interest expense incurred in the following year.

EXAMPLE I7-14 ▶

In the current year, Rita earns $27,000 in net investment income and incurs $40,000 of investment interest expense. Rita's interest expense deduction for the year is limited to $27,000, the amount of her net investment income.

The remaining investment interest expense of $13,000 ($40,000 − $27,000) may be carried over and deducted in a subsequent year. This carryover amount is treated as paid or accrued in the subsequent year and is subject to the disallowance rules that pertain to the subsequent year. ◀

Investment Interest. **Investment interest** is interest expense on indebtedness properly allocable to property held for investment. This includes property that generates portfolio types of income such as interest, dividends, annuities, and royalties. It does not include business interest, personal interest, qualified residence interest, or interest incurred in connection with any passive activity. Under Sec. 469, all rental activities are passive (see Chapter I8 for a discussion of the passive loss limitation rules). Thus, interest incurred in owning and renting property is subject to the passive loss limitation rather than the investment interest limitation.

Investment interest also does not include interest expense incurred to purchase or hold tax-exempt securities. This interest is not deductible at all. Without this disallowance, a taxpayer could, in certain circumstances, actually borrow funds at a higher rate of interest than the rate at which they were reinvested, while still generating a positive net cash flow because the government would be subsidizing the transaction through the interest deduction on the borrowings.

Net Investment Income. For purposes of the investment interest limitation, the term **net investment income** means the excess of the taxpayer's investment income over investment expenses. Investment income is gross income from property held for investment, including items such as dividends, interest, annuities, net short-term capital gains, and royalties (if not earned in a trade or business), but excluding qualified dividends and net long-term capital gains taxed at the preferential 15% or lower rate.

As explained in earlier chapters, generally, the maximum tax rate on net capital gain and qualified dividends is 15%. Including either of these two items in the definition of investment income would increase the amount of deductible investment interest expense, which might offset other income that is taxed at higher rates. Thus, the definition of investment income generally excludes net capital gain attributable to the disposition of property held for investment and qualified dividends. However, at the election of the taxpayer, net capital gain from the disposition of investment property and qualified dividends can be included in investment income. To the extent the taxpayer elects to include gains from the disposition of investment property and qualified dividends in investment income, these items are taxed at the regular tax rates rather than at the preferential long-term capital gain rates.[26] The calculation of investment income does not include gains on business and personal-use property.

EXAMPLE I7-15 ▶ During the current year, Michael incurs $15,000 investment interest expense, earns $7,000 of qualified dividends and $3,000 interest income. He also reports the following gains and losses from the sale of stocks and bonds during the year:

Short-term capital gains	$4,000
Short-term capital losses	(3,000)
Long-term capital gains	5,000
Long-term capital losses	(2,000)

Considering all of Michael's other income and deductions for the year, assume that he is subject to a 35% marginal tax rate. Michael's net capital gain is $3,000 (net long-term capital gain of $3,000 in excess of net short-term capital losses of $0). He also has a $1,000 ($4,000 − $3,000) net short-term capital gain. Thus, of his total capital gain of $4,000 ($9,000 of total gains − $5,000 of total losses), only $1,000 ($4,000 net gain − $3,000 net capital gain) is included in investment income. In addition, the $7,000 of qualified dividends also are not included in investment income. If Michael does not make an election, his investment income is $4,000 ($3,000 of interest plus $1,000 net short-term capital gain). He may deduct $4,000 of the investment interest expense in the current year. The excess investment interest for the current year of $11,000 ($15,000 − $4,000) is carried over to the next year. The $3,000 net capital gain and the qualified dividends are subject to the 15% ceiling tax rate on net capital gain. If Michael makes the election, his investment income is $14,000 (the $3,000 net capital gain and $7,000 of qualified dividends are included), and he may deduct $14,000 of the investment interest expense. Thus, only $1,000 ($15,000 − $14,000) of investment interest expense is not currently deductible and is carried over to the next year. However, his $3,000 net capital gain and $7,000 of qualified dividends are subject to the 35% ordinary income tax rate. ◀

ADDITIONAL COMMENT

Investment expenses are those which are deductible on the tax return, after the 2% limitation.

Investment expenses include all deductions (except interest) that are directly connected with the production of investment income. These expenses include rental fees for safe-deposit boxes, fees for investment counsel,[27] and subscriptions to investment and financial planning journals. As explained later in this chapter (see the section of this chapter titled Miscellaneous Itemized Deductions), these investment expenses are deductible only to the extent they exceed 2% of the taxpayer's AGI for the year. Only the investment expenses remaining after application of this limitation are used in computing the net investment income. Furthermore, in computing the amount of the disallowed investment expenses, the 2% of AGI limitation applies to the noninvestment expenses first.[28] Any remaining 2% of AGI limitation then reduces the noninterest investment expenses.

EXAMPLE I7-16 ▶ Kevin's AGI for the current year is $200,000. Included in his AGI is $175,000 salary and $25,000 of investment income. In earning the investment income, Kevin paid investment interest expense of $33,000. He also incurred the following expenditures subject to the 2% of AGI limitation:

---

[26] Secs. 1(h)(3) and 163(d)(4)(B).

[27] Sec. 163(d)(4)(C). Commissions for the sale or purchase of investment property are not included here. A commission paid on the purchase of property is added to the purchase price (and the basis) of the property. A commission paid on the sale of property reduces the amount realized.

[28] H. Rept. No. 99-841, 99th Cong., 2d Sess., pp. II-153 and 154 (1986). The noninvestment expenses subject to the 2% of AGI limitation include unreimbursed employee business expenses, hobby expenses up to the income from the hobby, and tax return preparation fees.

Investment expenses:		
Subscriptions to investment journals		$ 700
Investment counseling		2,000
Safe-deposit box rental		300
Noninvestment expenses:		
Unreimbursed employee business expenses		1,500
Tax return preparation fees (non–business-related)		500

Kevin's investment interest expense deduction for the year is computed by first determining the deductible investment expenses (other than interest) and the net investment income.

Investment expenses:		
Subscriptions	$ 700	
Investment counseling	2,000	
Safe-deposit box rental	300	$3,000
Disallowed by the 2% limitation:		
2% of AGI ($200,000 × 0.02)	$4,000	
Unreimbursed employee expenses	(1,500)	
Tax return preparation fees	(500)	
Investment expenses (remainder of 2% limit allocated to investment expenses)		(2,000)
Deductible investment expenses		$1,000
Net investment income ($25,000 − $1,000)		$24,000

The investment interest expense deduction is limited to $24,000. The remaining investment interest of $9,000 ($33,000 − $24,000) is carried over and deducted in a subsequent year (subject to the disallowance rules that pertain to the subsequent year). ◄

OBJECTIVE 6

Compute the deduction for qualified residence interest

PERSONAL INTEREST. In general, the tax law does not allow a deduction for interest expense on debt incurred for personal purposes. Thus, taxpayers may not deduct interest on credit cards, car loans, and consumer debt. However, taxpayers generally may deduct interest on debt to acquire a personal residence as well as interest on certain student loans.

QUALIFIED RESIDENCE INTEREST. Subject to certain limitations discussed below, individuals may deduct **qualified residence interest**. To be qualified residence interest, the interest payment must be either acquisition indebtedness or home equity indebtedness with respect to a qualified residence of the taxpayer. In all cases the residence must secure the debt.[29] A qualified residence (discussed below) may consist of the taxpayer's principal residence and a second residence.

Acquisition Indebtedness. Acquisition indebtedness is any debt secured by the residence and incurred in acquiring, constructing, or substantially improving the qualified residence. Debt may be treated as qualified acquisition indebtedness if the taxpayer acquires the residence within 90 days before or after the date that the debt is incurred. In the case of the construction or substantial improvement of a residence, debt incurred before the completion of the construction or improvement can qualify as acquisition debt to the extent of construction expenditures that are made no more than 24 months before the date the debt is incurred. Furthermore, debt incurred after construction is complete and within 90 days of the completion date may qualify as acquisition indebtedness to the extent of any construction expenditures made within the 24-month period ending on the date the debt is incurred.[30] Making payments of principal on the loan reduces the amount of acquisition debt. The only way to increase the amount of acquisition debt is to make substantial improvements to the property.

ADDITIONAL COMMENT

Banks and other financial institutions that receive mortgage interest from homeowners are required to report interest of $600 or more to the IRS and to the homeowners on Form 1098.

---

[29] Sec. 163(h). If the loan is not secured by the residence, it does not qualify. In one instance the taxpayer agreed to purchase her ex-husband's interest in their residence. The terms of the sale were $10,000 down plus an unsecured $25,000 note. In a private ruling, the IRS ruled that because the note was not secured by the residence, the interest on the note was not qualified residence interest. (See Ltr. Rul. 8752010 September 18, 1987.) However, if under any state or local homestead law the security interest is ineffective or unenforce-

able, the interest expense still qualifies as qualified residence interest. See Sec. 163(h)(4)(C). In another letter ruling the taxpayer borrowed money to purchase a residence securing the debt by pledging stock and bonds. Here also, the IRS denied the deduction because the loan was not secured by the residence. (See Ltr. Rul. 8906031 November 10, 1988.)
[30] Notice 88-74, 1988-2 C.B. 385.

The taxpayer may refinance acquisition indebtedness (and therefore treat it as acquisition indebtedness) to the extent that the principal amount of the refinancing does not exceed the principal amount of the acquisition debt immediately before the refinancing.

EXAMPLE 17-17 ▶ Kay acquired a personal residence in 1997 for $220,000 and borrowed $140,000 on a mortgage that was secured by the property. In the current year the principal balance of the mortgage has been reduced to $100,000. Kay's acquisition indebtedness in the current year is only $100,000 and cannot be increased above $100,000 (except by indebtedness incurred to substantially improve the residence). If she refinances the existing mortgage in the current year and the refinanced debt is $110,000, only $100,000 (the principal balance of the existing acquisition indebtedness) qualifies as acquisition indebtedness. ◀

The limitation for qualified acquisition indebtedness is $1,000,000 ($500,000 for a married individual filing a separate return). Qualified acquisition indebtedness incurred before October 13, 1987 (pre-October 13, 1987 indebtedness) is not subject to any limitation. However, the aggregate amount of pre-October 13, 1987 indebtedness reduces the $1,000,000 limitation on the indebtedness incurred after October 13, 1987.

ADDITIONAL COMMENT

Many banks, in attempting to generate new loan business, have heavily advertised the tax advantages of home equity indebtedness.

Home Equity Indebtedness. Taxpayers may also deduct interest incurred on home equity indebtedness (so-called home equity loans). Subject to certain limits, home equity indebtedness is any indebtedness (other than acquisition indebtedness) secured by a qualified residence of the taxpayer. The taxpayer may use the proceeds of the loan for any purpose (including purchasing or improving a qualified residence), as long as the taxpayer's qualified residence secures the loan. However, the tax law limits home equity indebtedness to the lesser of:

▶ The FMV of the qualified residence in excess of the acquisition indebtedness with respect to the residence, or

▶ $100,000 ($50,000 for a married individual filing a separate return)

The $1,000,000 limit on acquisition indebtedness and the $100,000 limit on home equity indebtedness are two separate limits. The maximum amount of indebtedness on which a taxpayer may deduct qualified residence interest is $1,100,000 if an individual has $100,000 or more equity in the property.

EXAMPLE 17-18 ▶ On April 23 of the current year, Kesha borrows $125,000 to purchase a new sailboat. The loan is secured by her personal residence. On that date, the outstanding balance on the original debt Kesha incurred to purchase the residence is $400,000 and the FMV of the residence is $900,000. The original debt is also secured by Kesha's residence. Kesha may deduct the interest paid on the $400,000 of acquisition indebtedness, plus the interest paid on $100,000 of the home equity loan. The interest on $25,000 ($125,000 − $100,000) is treated as personal interest and is, therefore, not deductible. The home equity loan is limited to the lesser of $100,000 or the FMV of the residence in excess of the outstanding acquisition indebtedness (the lesser of $100,000 or ($900,000 − $400,000)). ◀

Points Paid as Qualified Residence Interest. Often taxpayers must pay **points** on real estate debt. A point is equal to 1% of the loan amount. Thus, two points paid on a $120,000 mortgage equal $2,400 (120,000 × .02). Points often represent prepaid interest because the stated rate of interest for the loan is lower than the current rate of interest. Generally, prepaid interest paid in the form of points must be capitalized and amortized over the life of the loan. However, points paid on a loan incurred to purchase the taxpayer's principal residence (acquisition indebtedness) are automatically deductible when paid if certain requirements are met. The IRS has also indicated that points paid on Veteran Administration (VA) and Federal Home Administration (FHA) loans are also currently deductible as interest if clearly designated as points incurred in connection with the indebtedness.[31]

---

[31] These requirements, mentioned in Chapter 16, are as follows: The points must be paid in connection with the purchase (not the improvement) of the taxpayer's principal residence, the closing agreement must clearly designate the amounts as points paid in connection with the acquisition debt, the amount must be computed as a percentage of the amount borrowed, the points must conform with established business practices, and the loan must be secured by the residence. Rev. Proc. 94-27, I.R.B. 94-15, 17. See also Rev. Proc. 92-12A, 1992-1 C.B. 664.

EXAMPLE I7-19 ▶ During the current year, Kevin and Donna purchase a new home for $300,000, putting $100,000 down and borrowing $200,000. At the closing, they are required to pay one and one-half points as a loan discount in connection with the loan, which is secured by a mortgage against the home. The practice of charging points is an established business practice where they live.

These points represent prepaid interest on the purchase of a principal residence. Thus, in addition to the interest portion of every payment they make during the year, Kevin and Donna may also deduct $3,000 ($200,000 × 0.015) as interest paid during the year of purchase. ◀

Taxpayers must capitalize points paid on a loan to purchase property other than a principal residence or for refinancing a mortgage on a principal residence. If the property is business, investment, or a qualified residence (the taxpayer's principal residence and one other that the taxpayer chooses) the taxpayers may amortize the points over the life of the loan.[32]

In order for the points to be currently deductible, the purchaser of the principal residence (borrower) must have paid for them with unborrowed funds. However, amounts provided by the borrower as down payments, escrow deposits, earnest money, or other funds are treated as paid for the points. Furthermore, as long as the borrower provides sufficient funds in these other categories, he or she is treated as having paid the points even if the seller has paid for them on behalf of the borrower.[33]

Qualified Residence. For any tax year, a taxpayer may have two qualified residences:

▶ Taxpayer's principal residence

▶ One other residence selected by the taxpayer, with regard to which the taxpayer meets the residence test of Sec. 280A(d)(1).

In order to meet this residence test, the taxpayer must have personally used the property more than the greater of 14 days or 10% of any rental days during the year.[34]

EXAMPLE I7-20 ▶
ADDITIONAL COMMENT

Whether property is a residence for tax purposes is determined based on all the facts and circumstances, including the good faith of the taxpayer. A residence generally includes a house, condominium, mobile home, boat, or house trailer, that contains sleeping space and toilet and cooking facilities. Treas. Reg. § 1.163-10T(p)(3)(ii).

Fred owns a lakeside cabin that he uses for vacations. He also rents the cabin out to others when he is not using it. During the year Fred rents the cabin out at a fair rental for 90 days. Fred personally uses the cabin for a total of 22 days. Because Fred's personal use for the year (22 days) exceeds 14 days [the greater of 14 days or 9 days (10% of the rental days)], the cabin qualifies as his residence for purposes of deducting qualified residence interest for the year. ◀

Despite the residence test, the taxpayer may select a property that has not been rented by the taxpayer at any time during the year as the second residence on which the taxpayer may deduct qualified residence interest.

 STOP & THINK

Question: Jana is about to purchase a new sport utility vehicle for $35,000. If she pays $5,000 down, the dealer is prepared to offer her a loan for the remaining $30,000 at 8% interest. In investigating other possible sources of funds, she found out that her brokerage firm would lend her the $30,000 at 9% interest if she pledged her stock as collateral. At her local credit union, she found that she could borrow the $30,000 at 10% interest if she took out a home equity loan by using her home as security. Jana is confused about which loan she should take.

Solution: The best way to analyze this problem is to compare the after-tax interest rates of the loans. Jana may not deduct the interest paid to the car dealer because it is personal interest. Thus, its after-tax interest rate remains at 8%. Furthermore, even though Jana

---

[32] Rev. Rul. 87-22, 1987-1 C.B. 146, and Rev. Proc. 87-15, 1987-1 C.B. 624. The 8th Circuit Court of Appeals has held in one case that points paid on refinancing a "bridge" or temporary loan are currently deductible. *James R. Huntsman v. CIR*, 66 AFTR 2d 90-5020, 90-2 USTC ¶ 50,340 (8th Cir., 1990), rev'g 91 TC 57 (1988). However, the IRS has announced that it will not follow *Huntsman* in circuits other than the circuit in which the case was decided (IRS Action on Decision CC-1991-02, Feb. 11, 1991).

[33] Reg. Sec. 1.6050H-1(f)(3). See also Rev. Proc. 94-27, I.R.B. 94-15, 17.
[34] Sec. 280A(d)(1). Use by the taxpayer's family, as defined in Sec. 267(c)(4), other individuals under a reciprocal-use arrangement, and anyone when a fair rental is not charged is counted as a day of personal use by the taxpayer (see Sec. 280A(d)(2) and Chapter I6).

uses her stock holdings as collateral, the interest on the loan from the brokerage firm is non-deductible personal interest because she uses the proceeds of the loan to purchase personal property rather than investment property. Its after-tax interest rate remains at 9%. Only the interest on the home equity loan from the credit union is potentially deductible. This depends, of course, on the amount of Jana's total itemized deductions. Assuming Jana's total itemized deductions exceed the standard deduction and Jana is in the 30.0% marginal tax bracket, the after-tax interest rate of the home equity loan drops from 10% to 7.0% [10% × (1 − 0.30)].

STUDENT LOAN INTEREST. If the loan meets certain requirements, individuals may take a *for* AGI deduction for interest paid on qualified education loans. The maximum annual interest deduction for qualified student loans is $2,500. Furthermore, the deduction is phased out ratably for individuals with modified AGI of $50,000 to $65,000 ($105,000 to $135,000 for individuals filing joint returns).[35]

EXAMPLE I7-21 ▶ During 2006, Ryan paid a total of $2,800 in interest on a loan incurred for qualified education expenses. Ryan is single and reports modified AGI of $59,000 for the year. Since his modified AGI of $59,000 is $9,000 greater than $50,000, the maximum deduction of $2,500 is reduced by 60% ($9,000/$15,000). Ryan may take a *for* AGI deduction of $1,000. If Ryan paid only $1,800 of interest (rather than $2,800), the potential deduction of $1,800 would be reduced by 60% to $720 [$1,800 − (60% × $1,800)]. ◀

To qualify for this deduction, the interest must be payable on a loan incurred solely to pay qualified higher education expenses. If a taxpayer takes out a loan to pay for higher education expenses and for other purposes, none of the interest on the loan qualifies. Higher education expenses include tuition, fees, books and equipment, and room and board incurred during a time the taxpayer, the taxpayer's spouse, or the taxpayer's dependent is a student at a qualified higher education institution on at least a half-time basis. However, these qualified expenditures do not include amounts excluded from income under an employer educational assistance program or from United States savings bonds, as well as any scholarship or allowance that is excluded from income. Furthermore, to prevent a double deduction, the tax law allows no deduction to an individual for whom a dependency exemption may be taken on another's tax return or for any amount that is deductible under any other provision of the Code.

TIMING OF THE INTEREST DEDUCTION
Under Sec. 163, deductible interest becomes deductible in the year the interest is paid or accrued. This generally means that cash method taxpayers deduct interest in the year paid, whereas accrual method taxpayers deduct interest as it accrues. However, the IRC makes exceptions to this general rule.

ADDITIONAL COMMENT

Points paid on the refinancing of an existing mortgage must be written off over the life of the new mortgage.

PREPAID INTEREST. If a cash method taxpayer prepays interest and the prepayment relates to a loan that extends beyond the end of the tax year, generally the taxpayer must capitalize the prepayment and amortize it over the periods to which the interest relates (i.e., the accrual method applies to cash method taxpayers in regards to prepaid interest). As previously discussed, the law makes one exception to this rule involving interest paid in the form of points charged in connection with the purchase or improvement of the taxpayer's principal residence. If these points represent prepaid interest, the taxpayer may deduct them in the year paid.[36]

INTEREST PAID WITH LOAN PROCEEDS. Assuming the interest is otherwise deductible, if an individual borrows money from a third party rather than from the original lending institution and uses the funds to make a payment on a previously outstanding

---

[35] The phase-out range is $15,000 ($30,000 for married filing jointly). Modified AGI includes certain excluded income from Guam, American Samoa, or Puerto Rico, as well as any income excluded under the foreign earned income provisions. Furthermore, the deduction for qualified tuition and related expenses is not allowed.

[36] Sec. 461(g). In order for the exception to apply, the home must be used to secure the loan, and the charging of points must be an established business practice in the area where the loan is granted. (See the discussion of the deductibility of points in this chapter under the heading Definition of *Interest* as well as the discussion in Chapter I6.)

loan, the individual generally may deduct the interest portion of the payment. However, if the taxpayer borrows the funds used to pay the interest on the first loan from the same lender to whom the interest is due, and either (1) the purpose of the second loan is to pay the interest on the first or (2) the borrower does not have unrestricted control of the funds, then the borrower may not deduct the interest.[37]

DISCOUNTED NOTES. Lending institutions often discount notes. In effect, the borrower pays the interest by repaying more money than is received when the note is signed. A cash method taxpayer can deduct this interest at the time of repayment, whereas an accrual method taxpayer must deduct the interest as it accrues over the term of the loan.

EXAMPLE I7-22 ▶

On December 1, 2006, Stan borrows $1,000 from his credit union to use in his business. Under the terms of the contract, Stan actually receives $970 but is required to repay $1,000 on February 28, 2007 (three months later). Because Stan is a cash method taxpayer, he may deduct the full $30 interest in 2007 when the note is repaid. If he were an accrual method taxpayer, he could deduct $10 ($30 × 0.333) in 2006, and $20 ($30 × 0.667) in 2007. ◀

INTEREST OWED TO A RELATED PARTY BY AN ACCRUAL METHOD TAXPAYER. One of the purposes of Sec. 267 is to require related cash method lenders and accrual method borrowers to report the results of their joint transaction in the same year. Thus, an accrual method taxpayer who is related to a cash method creditor must defer the deduction for any accrued expense (including interest) until the year in which the taxpayer actually pays the expense and the creditor reports the income. Section 267 also disallows losses on the sale of property between related parties. Chapter I6 discusses the disallowance of such losses.

The relationships covered by this rule are quite extensive. Some of the more common relationships include the following:

▶ Members of a family (defined as an individual's brothers, sisters, spouse, ancestors, and lineal descendants)

▶ An individual and a C corporation in which the individual owns directly or indirectly more than 50% of the outstanding stock

▶ A corporation and a partnership which are both over 50% owned directly or indirectly by the same people

▶ A partnership and any partner of the partnership

▶ An S Corporation and any shareholder of the S Corporation[38]

EXAMPLE I7-23 ▶

During the current year, Lisa, a cash method taxpayer, loans some money to her 100%-owned corporation, which uses the accrual method of accounting. As of December 31 of the current year, the corporation owes Lisa $3,000 in interest. However, because of a shortage of funds, the corporation does not actually pay the interest until February 15 of the following year. Despite the fact that the corporation uses the accrual method of accounting, the corporation cannot deduct the $3,000 until the corporation actually pays the interest to Lisa in the subsequent year. The result would be the same if the corporation were an S Corporation even if Lisa owned 50% or less of the outstanding stock. ◀

IMPUTED INTEREST. Under certain circumstances, if a taxpayer charges less than an adequate rate of interest, the IRS is authorized to impute an interest charge. This may cause the lender to have additional interest income and the borrower to have additional interest expense. The deductibility of this imputed interest expense depends on the classification of the expense (i.e. personal, investment, etc.). (See Chapter I11 for a discussion of imputed interest.)

Topic Review I7-2 summarizes the rules for deducting various types of interest.

---

[37] *H. C. Franklin v. CIR*, 50 AFTR 2d 82-5551, 82-2 USTC ¶9532 (5th Cir., 1982) and *Newton A. Burgess*, 8 T.C. 47 (1947). See also *Norman W. Menz*, 80 T.C. 1174 (1983). The IRS has also announced that it will disallow a deduction for interest paid with funds obtained through a second loan from the same lender (see IRS News Release 83-93, July 6, 1983).
[38] Secs. 267(b) and (e). The list of relationships is much more extensive than those mentioned. An S corporation is one that meets certain requirements and has made an election to have its income taxed directly to its shareholders. A C corporation is one that has not made an S election. (See Chapter C11 of the *Prentice Hall's Federal Taxation: Corporations, Partnerships, Estates, and Trusts* text or Chapter C11 of the *Prentice Hall's Federal Taxation: Comprehensive* text.)

Topic Review I7-2

Deductibility of Interest Expense

TYPE OF INTEREST	RULES
Business	Deductible in full as a *for* AGI deduction.
Passive	Subject to the passive loss limits (see Chapter I8).
Investment	Deductible as an itemized deduction to the extent of the taxpayer's net investment income for the year. Any amount not deductible is carried over to subsequent years.
Personal	Not deductible.
Qualified residence	(a) Must be attributable to debt secured by the taxpayer's principal residence and one other residence selected by the taxpayer.
	(b) Interest on up to $1,000,000 of home acquisition indebtedness is deductible as an itemized deduction.
	(c) Interest on home equity debt is deductible as an itemized deduction. Home equity debt is limited to the lesser of $100,000 or the excess of the FMV of the residence over the home acquisition indebtedness.
Student Loan Interest	(a) Payable on loan incurred to pay qualified higher education expenses.
	(b) Taken as a *for* AGI deduction.
	(c) Maximum deductible amount is $2,500. Deduction is phased out ratably for AGI between $50,000 to $65,000 ($105,000 to $135,000 for married filing jointly).

CHARITABLE CONTRIBUTIONS

Compute the amount of a charitable contribution deduction and identify limitations

Under Sec. 170, corporations and individuals who itemize their deductions can deduct **charitable contributions** to qualified organizations. With the exception of certain contributions made by corporations (explained later in this chapter), a taxpayer takes the deduction in the year the contribution is made, regardless of the taxpayer's method of accounting. The amount of the deduction depends on the type of charity receiving the contribution, the type of property contributed, and the applicable limitations.

QUALIFYING ORGANIZATION

ADDITIONAL COMMENT

In 2003, the deduction for charitable contributions totaled $139.7 billion representing 15.4% of the total dollar amount of itemized deductions, making it the third largest itemized deduction.

To deduct a contribution for federal income tax purposes, a taxpayer must make the contribution to or for the use of a qualified organization.[39] Contributions made directly to individuals, even though the individuals may be needy, are generally not deductible.[40] Under Sec. 170, qualified organizations include the following:

▶ The United States, the District of Columbia, a state or possession of the United States, or a political subdivision of a state or possession

▶ A corporation, trust, community chest, fund or foundation created or organized under the laws of the United States, a state, possession, or the District of Columbia[41]

▶ A post or organization of war veterans

▶ A domestic fraternal society, order, or association[42]

▶ Certain cemetery companies

Because of the restrictions and limitations examined later in this chapter, these qualifying organizations are further classified into public charities and private nonoperating foundations. Different restrictions and limitations apply to each type of organization.

---

[39] The Supreme Court has ruled that in order for a contribution to be for the use of a qualifying organization, the gift must be held either in a legally enforceable trust or in a similar legal arrangement. (See *U.S. v. Harold Davis*, 65 AFTR 2d 90-1051, 90-1 USTC ¶50,270 (USSC, 1990).)

[40] Under certain circumstances, a taxpayer may take a deduction (limited to $50 per month) for maintaining a student as a member of his or her household. The student may not be a dependent or relative of the taxpayer and must be placed in the taxpayer's home under an arrangement with a qualifying organization (see Sec. 170(g)).

[41] These organizations must be organized and operated exclusively for religious, charitable, scientific, literary, or educational purposes; to foster national or international amateur sports competition; or for the prevention of cruelty to children or animals.

[42] Furthermore, gifts to these organizations must be made by individuals and must be used exclusively for religious, charitable, scientific, literary, or educational purposes, or for the prevention of cruelty to children or animals.

Public charities include:

▶ Churches or a convention or association of churches

▶ Educational institutions that normally maintain a regular faculty, curriculum, and regularly enrolled students

▶ Organizations such as hospitals and medical schools whose principal function is medical care or medical education and research

▶ Government-supported organizations that exist to receive, hold, invest, and administer property for the benefit of a college or university

▶ Any qualified governmental unit

▶ Organizations that normally receive a substantial part of their support from either a governmental unit or the general public

▶ Certain private operating foundations[43]

Because several thousand organizations meet these requirements, the IRS publishes a list of many of the organizations that have applied for and received tax-exempt status.[44] Although the IRS updates this publication regularly, an organization need not be listed in order to qualify.

TYPE OF PROPERTY CONTRIBUTED

If a taxpayer makes a contribution in cash, the amount of the deduction is easily determinable. However, if noncash property is donated, the amount of the contribution is not as easy to identify. In the case of noncash property, the amount of the donation depends on two factors: (1) the type of property donated and (2) the type of qualifying organization (public charity or private nonoperating foundation) to whom the property is given. Furthermore, a gift of property that consists of less than the donor's entire interest in the property is not usually considered a contribution of property. Thus, for example, no charitable contribution is allowed when an individual donates the use of a vacation home for a charitable fund-raising auction.[45]

CONTRIBUTION OF CAPITAL GAIN PROPERTY. In general, the amount of a donation of capital gain property is its FMV. Regulation Sec. 1.170A-1(c)(2) defines a property's FMV as the price at which the property would change hands between a willing buyer and a willing seller, neither being under any compulsion to buy or sell and both having reasonable knowledge of relevant facts. For purposes of charitable contributions, **capital gain property** is property held over one year on which the taxpayer would recognize a long-term capital gain if the taxpayer sold it at its FMV on the date of the contribution. If a capital loss or a short-term capital gain would be recognized on the sale of the capital asset, the property is considered to be ordinary income property for purposes of the charitable contribution deduction.

Contribution to a Private Nonoperating Foundation. The tax law provides an exception to this general rule for contributions of capital gain property to private nonoperating foundations. In general, a private nonoperating foundation is an organization that does not receive funding from the general public (e.g., the Carnegie Foundation). Private nonoperating foundations distribute funds to various charitable organizations that actually perform the charitable services. The amount of the contribution to a private nonoperating foundation is the property's FMV, reduced by the capital gain that would be recognized if the property were sold at its FMV on the date of the contribution. This means that generally the deductible amount of the contribution is the property's adjusted basis.[46]

---

[43] Sec. 170(b)(1)(E). The distinction between a private operating foundation and a private nonoperating foundation generally depends on the way the foundation spends or distributes its income and contributions. The details of this distinction are beyond the scope of this text.

[44] IRS, Pub. No. 78, Cumulative List of Organizations, 2005.

[45] Sec. 170(f)(3), Reg. Sec. 1.170A-7(a)(1) and Rev. Rul. 89-51, 1989-1 C.B. 89. Note, however, that certain transfers of partial interests in property do

qualify (e.g., the contribution of certain remainder interests to a trust, the transfer of a remainder interest in a personal residence or a farm, or a contribution of an undivided interest in property). These exceptions are beyond the scope of this text.

[46] The amount of a contribution of appreciated stock made to a private nonoperating foundation remains at its FMV.

EXAMPLE I7-24 ▶ Betty purchases land in 1991 for $10,000. In the current year, she contributes the land to the United Way. At the time of the contribution, the FMV of the property is $25,000. Because the land is long-term capital gain property donated to a public charity, the amount of the contribution is $25,000 (its FMV).

On the other hand, if Betty donates the land to Cherry Foundation, a private nonoperating foundation, the amount of the contribution is $10,000 ($25,000 − $15,000 capital gain that would be recognized if the land were sold). ◀

<table>
<tr>
<td valign="top" width="28%">

TYPICAL MISCONCEPTION

Many people do not understand that the unrelated use restriction applies only to tangible personal property. A gift of shares of stock (intangible property) would not be a gift of unrelated use property where the stock is sold by the donee.

</td>
<td valign="top">

Unrelated Use Property. A second exception applies to capital gain property (that is also tangible personal property) contributed to a public charity and used by the organization for purposes unrelated to the charity's function. In such cases, the amount of the contribution deduction is equal to the property's FMV minus the capital gain that would be recognized if the property were sold at its FMV. This amount generally is the property's adjusted basis. Tangible property is all property that is not intangible property (e.g., property other than stock, securities, copyrights, patents, and so on). Personal property is all property other than real estate. The taxpayer is responsible for proving that the property was not put to unrelated use. However, a taxpayer meets this burden of proof if, at the time of the contribution, the taxpayer reasonably anticipates that the property will not be put to unrelated use. The immediate sale of the property by the charitable organization is a use unrelated to its tax-exempt purpose.

</td>
</tr>
</table>

EXAMPLE I7-25 ▶ Laura purchases a painting for $3,000. Several years later she contributes the painting to a local college. The FMV of the painting is $5,000 at the time the property is contributed. The painting is both tangible personal property and capital gain property. The college places the painting in the library for display and study by art students. Because the college uses the painting for purposes related to its function as an educational institution, the amount of Laura's contribution is equal to its FMV ($5,000). On the other hand, if the college had sold the painting immediately after receiving it, the presumption is that the property's use was unrelated to the college's tax-exempt purpose. In this case, Laura's contribution is only $3,000. ◀

Certain Intangibles. Under Sec. 170(e)(1)(B), a third exception applies to the contribution of certain intangibles to a charitable organization. In this case, the amount of the charitable contribution is the FMV of the property, reduced by the amount of long-term capital gain that would have been recognized if the taxpayer had sold the property. These intangibles include patents, trademarks, a trade name or secret, know-how, a purchased copyright, and certain software.

CONTRIBUTION OF ORDINARY INCOME PROPERTY

General Rule. If a taxpayer contributes ordinary income property to a charitable organization, the deduction is equal to the property's FMV minus the amount of gain that would be recognized if the taxpayer had sold the property at its FMV on the date of the contribution. In most cases, this deduction is equal to the property's adjusted basis. This rule applies regardless of the type of charitable organization to which the property is donated.

<table>
<tr>
<td valign="top" width="28%">

REAL-WORLD EXAMPLE

A retired congressman was not entitled to a charitable contribution of his papers because the papers were ordinary income property and had no basis. *James H. Morrison*, 71 T.C. 683 (1979).

</td>
<td valign="top">

For this purpose, **ordinary income property** includes any property that would result in the recognition of income taxed at ordinary income rates if the taxpayer sold the property. Thus, ordinary income property includes inventory, works of art or manuscripts created by the taxpayer, capital assets that have been held for one year or less, and Sec. 1231 property to the extent a sale would result in the recognition of ordinary income due to depreciation recapture.[47]

</td>
</tr>
</table>

EXAMPLE I7-26 ▶ During the current year Bart purchases land as an investment for $10,000. Five months later he contributes the land to the United Way. At the time of the contribution the property's FMV is $15,000. The amount of Bart's contribution is $10,000 ($15,000 − [$15,000 − $10,000]) because he held the land for less than one year. ◀

---

[47] Reg. Secs. 1.170A-4(b)(1) and 1.170A-4(d). Sec. 1231 property includes property used in a trade or business that is subject to depreciation. If it is sold at a gain, part or all of the gain is treated as ordinary income. Any remaining gain is subject to the Sec. 1231 rules. (See Chapter I13 for an explanation of the depreciation recapture and Sec. 1231 rules.)

EXAMPLE I7-27 ▶ Paul purchased a machine a few years ago for $20,000. During the current year, Paul donates the machine, which he used in his business, to a local community college. At the time of the contribution, the machine's adjusted basis is $5,000 and its FMV is $8,000. Because Paul would have recognized a $3,000 gain (all ordinary income under Sec. 1245) if the machine were sold at its FMV, the amount of the contribution is $5,000 ($8,000 − $3,000), which is equal to the machine's adjusted basis. ◀

Donation of Inventory by a Corporation. Under certain circumstances, a corporation's donation of inventory to certain public charities gives rise to a contribution that is valued at more than the adjusted basis of the inventory. One exception is available if the charity uses the inventory solely for the care of the ill, needy, or infants.[48] Another exception involves the donation of scientific equipment constructed by the taxpayer and donated to a college, university, or qualified research organization for use in research, experimentation, or research training in the physical or biological sciences. A third exception is available for contributions of computer technology and equipment donated to public libraries and elementary and secondary schools.[49] In all three cases, the amount of the charitable contribution is the property's FMV, reduced by 50% of the ordinary income that the taxpayer would recognize if he or she sold the property at its FMV. However, the amount of the contribution may not exceed twice the basis of the property.

EXAMPLE I7-28 ▶ During the current year, Able Corporation, a manufacturer of medical supplies, donates some of its inventory to the American Red Cross. The Red Cross intends to use the inventory for the care of the needy and ill. At the time of the contribution, the FMV of the inventory is $10,000. Able's basis in the inventory is $3,000. Because this transaction qualifies under the exception, the amount of Able's contribution (before any limitations are applied) is $6,500 [$10,000 − (0.50 × $7,000)] but the actual amount of the contribution is limited to $6,000 (2 × the $3,000 basis in the property). ◀

ADDITIONAL COMMENT

The standard charitable mileage rate for use of a car to provide relief related to Hurricane Katrina is increased to approximately 70% of the business rate for the period beginning on August 25, 2005, and ending on December 31, 2006. Thus, in 2006, this increased charitable mileage rate would be 32 cents per mile.

CONTRIBUTION OF SERVICES. When a taxpayer renders services to a qualified charitable organization, the taxpayer may only deduct the unreimbursed expenses incurred incident to rendering the services. These items include out-of-pocket, transportation expenses, the cost of lodging and 50% of the cost of meals while away from home, and the cost of a uniform that is required to be worn in performing the donated services but is not suitable for general wear. The out-of-pocket expenses are deductible only if incurred by the taxpayer who actually renders the services to the charity. Taxpayers cannot take a deduction for expenses while away from home unless they experience no significant element of personal pleasure, recreation, or vacation in such travel. Instead of the actual costs of operating an automobile while performing the donated services, the law permits a deduction of 14 cents per mile.[50]

EXAMPLE I7-29 ▶

REAL-WORLD EXAMPLE

The cost of newspaper advertising, paper, pencils, and other supplies purchased by volunteers in connection with their involvement in the Volunteer Income Tax Assistance Program (VITA) is deductible. Rev. Rul. 80-45, 1980-1 C.B. 54.

During the current year, Tony spends a total of 100 hours developing an accounting system for the local council of the Boy Scouts of America. As an accountant, Tony earns $200 per hour. During the year, Tony also drives his car a total of 500 miles in performing the services for the Boy Scouts of America. If he uses the automatic mileage method to compute the amount of the charitable contribution, he can deduct $70 (0.14 × 500). No deduction is available for the value of 100 hours of Tony's contributed services. ◀

DEDUCTION LIMITATIONS

OVERALL 50% LIMITATION. The charitable contribution deduction available for any tax year is subject to certain limitations. For individuals, the general overall limitation applicable to public charities is 50% of the taxpayer's AGI for the year. Any contributions in excess of the overall limitation may be carried forward and deducted in the subsequent five tax years. In addition, the tax law imposes further limitations on contributions of

---

[48] Sec. 170(e). These charitable organizations are known as Sec. 501(c)(3) charities.

[49] Sec. 170(e)(6). This provision expires for contributions made after December 31, 2005. At the date of printing of this textbook, both the House and Senate have approved the extension of this deduction through 2006.

[50] Rev. Proc. 2004-64 I.R.B. 2004-49.

capital gain property to either a public charity or a private nonoperating foundation and all types of property contributions to private nonoperating foundations.

KEY POINT

The generosity of Congress in permitting individuals to use FMV is tempered by the 30% of AGI limitation.

30% LIMITATION. Under certain circumstances, a special 30% of AGI limitation applies. Contributions of capital gain property (capital assets held over one year on which a gain would be realized if sold) to public charities are generally valued at the property's FMV, but the deduction may not exceed an overall limit of 30% of AGI instead of a 50% limit. This special 30% limit does not apply, however, in the following situations:

▶ Capital gain property (which is tangible personal property) donated to a public charity that does not put the property to its related use. In such cases, the amount of the contribution is reduced by the capital gain that would be recognized if the property were sold.

▶ The taxpayer elects to reduce the amount of the charitable contribution deduction by the capital gain that the taxpayer would recognize if he or she sold the property.

EXAMPLE I7-30 ▶ Joy donates a painting to the local university during a year in which she has AGI of $50,000. The painting, which cost $10,000 several years before, is valued at $30,000 at the time of the contribution. The university exhibits the painting in its art gallery. Because the painting is put to a use related to the university's purpose, the amount of Joy's contribution is $30,000. The amount of Joy's charitable deduction for the year, however, is limited to $15,000 (0.30 × $50,000 AGI) unless she elects to reduce the amount of the contribution by the long-term capital gain. ◀

ADDITIONAL COMMENT

The Katrina Emergency Tax Relief Act of 2005 suspends the percentage limitations at the election of the taxpayer for all qualified charitable contributions given between August 28, 2005, and December 31, 2005. This special rule applied to all qualified contributions, not just those related to the hurricane.

The overall deduction limitation of 30% of AGI also applies to the contribution of all types of property other than capital gain property (e.g., cash and ordinary income property) to a private nonoperating foundation. However, further restrictions may apply to the deductibility of certain contributions to this type of charity.

20% LIMITATION ON CAPITAL GAIN PROPERTY CONTRIBUTED TO PRIVATE NONOPERATING FOUNDATIONS. Contributions of capital gain property to private nonoperating foundations may not exceed the lesser of (1) 20% of the taxpayer's AGI or (2) 30% of the taxpayer's AGI, reduced by any contributions of capital gain property donated to a public charity.

CONTRIBUTIONS FOR ATHLETIC EVENTS. If a taxpayer makes a contribution to a college or university and in return receives the right to purchase tickets to athletic events, the taxpayer may deduct only 80% of the payment.

APPLYING THE DEDUCTION LIMITATIONS. Contributions subject only to the 50% of AGI limitation are accounted for before the contributions subject to the 30% of AGI limitation.

EXAMPLE I7-31 ▶ During a year when Ted's AGI is $70,000, he donates $22,000 to his church and $18,000 to a private nonoperating charity. The church contribution is initially subject to the 50% limitation and is fully deductible because the $22,000 contribution is less than the limitation amount of $35,000 (0.50 × $70,000). Ted's deduction for the contribution to the private nonoperating charity (a 30% charity) is limited to $13,000 (the lesser of the following three amounts):

The actual contribution	$18,000
The remaining 50% limitation after the contribution to Ted's church [(0.50 × $70,000) − $22,000]	$13,000
30% of AGI (0.30 × $70,000)	$21,000 ◀

APPLICATION OF CARRYOVERS

As noted earlier, any contributions that exceed the 50% limitation may be carried over and deducted in the subsequent five years. These carryovers are subject to the limitations that apply in subsequent years. Thus, taxpayers may deduct carryovers only to the extent that the limitation of the subsequent year exceeds the contributions made during that year.

TAX PLANNING

If a taxpayer has contribution carryovers that are about to expire, the taxpayer should consider reducing the current year's contribution so that the carryovers can be deducted.

EXAMPLE I7-32 ▶

These general rules also apply with regard to the special limitations. For example, if the taxpayer donates property subject to the 30% limitation during the current year and the amount of the contribution exceeds the limitation, the excess may carry over to the five subsequent years subject to the 30% limitation in the carryover years. In the carryover year, a deduction may be taken for the excess contribution to the extent that the 30% limitation of the subsequent year exceeds the amount of the property donated during the subsequent year subject to the 30% limitation. Excess contributions of property subject to the 20% limitation may also carry over to the subsequent five years. This carryover is also subject to the special restrictions noted above for the 30% limitation. The carryovers are used in chronological order.

Assume that for the years 2004 through 2006, Joan reports AGI and makes charitable contributions in the following amounts:

	2004	2005	2006
AGI	$40,000	$40,000	$60,000
Cash contributions subject to the 50% of AGI limitation	25,000	23,000	24,000
50% of AGI limitation	20,000	20,000	30,000

The amount of the charitable contribution deduction for each year and the order in which the deduction and carryovers are used are as follows:

	2004	2005	2006
Amount of deduction	$20,000	$20,000	$30,000
Amount of carryover			
From 2004	5,000	5,000	0
From 2005		3,000	2,000	◀

SPECIAL RULES FOR CHARITABLE CONTRIBUTIONS MADE BY CORPORATIONS

The rules governing charitable contributions made by corporations are generally the same as those pertaining to contributions made by individuals. However, certain differences do exist.

ETHICAL POINT

A tax practitioner should not be a party to the backdating of a Board of Director's authorization of a charitable contribution pledge so that the corporation may improperly deduct the contribution in the earlier year.

PLEDGES MADE BY AN ACCRUAL METHOD CORPORATION. Generally, taxpayers may only deduct actual contributions (not pledges) made during the tax year. This rule applies to both cash and accrual method taxpayers. A major exception to this general rule exists for accrual method corporations. Such corporations may elect to claim a charitable deduction for the year in which the corporation makes a pledge as long as the actual contribution is made by the fifteenth day of the third month following the close of the year in which the pledge is made.

LIMITATION APPLICABLE TO CORPORATIONS. Corporate charitable deductions may not exceed 10% of the corporation's taxable income for the year. This amount is computed without regard to the dividends-received deduction, net operating loss or capital loss carrybacks, or any deduction for the charitable contribution itself. Excess contributions may be carried forward for five years and are deductible only if the current-year contributions are less than the current year's 10% limitation. The corporation uses the carryovers in chronological order.

SUMMARY OF DEDUCTION LIMITATIONS

Topic Review I7-3 summarizes the rules governing the deduction for charitable contributions.

STOP & THINK

Question: During the current year, Kim pledges to contribute $10,000 to both the Boy Scouts of America (BSA) and to a private nonoperating foundation. She wants to satisfy those pledges before the end of the year in order to take a deduction this year. She has enough cash to satisfy one of the pledges, but must either sell or donate some land in order to satisfy the other. The land she has in mind has a fair market value of $10,000

Topic Review I7-3

Deduction Rules for Charitable Contributions

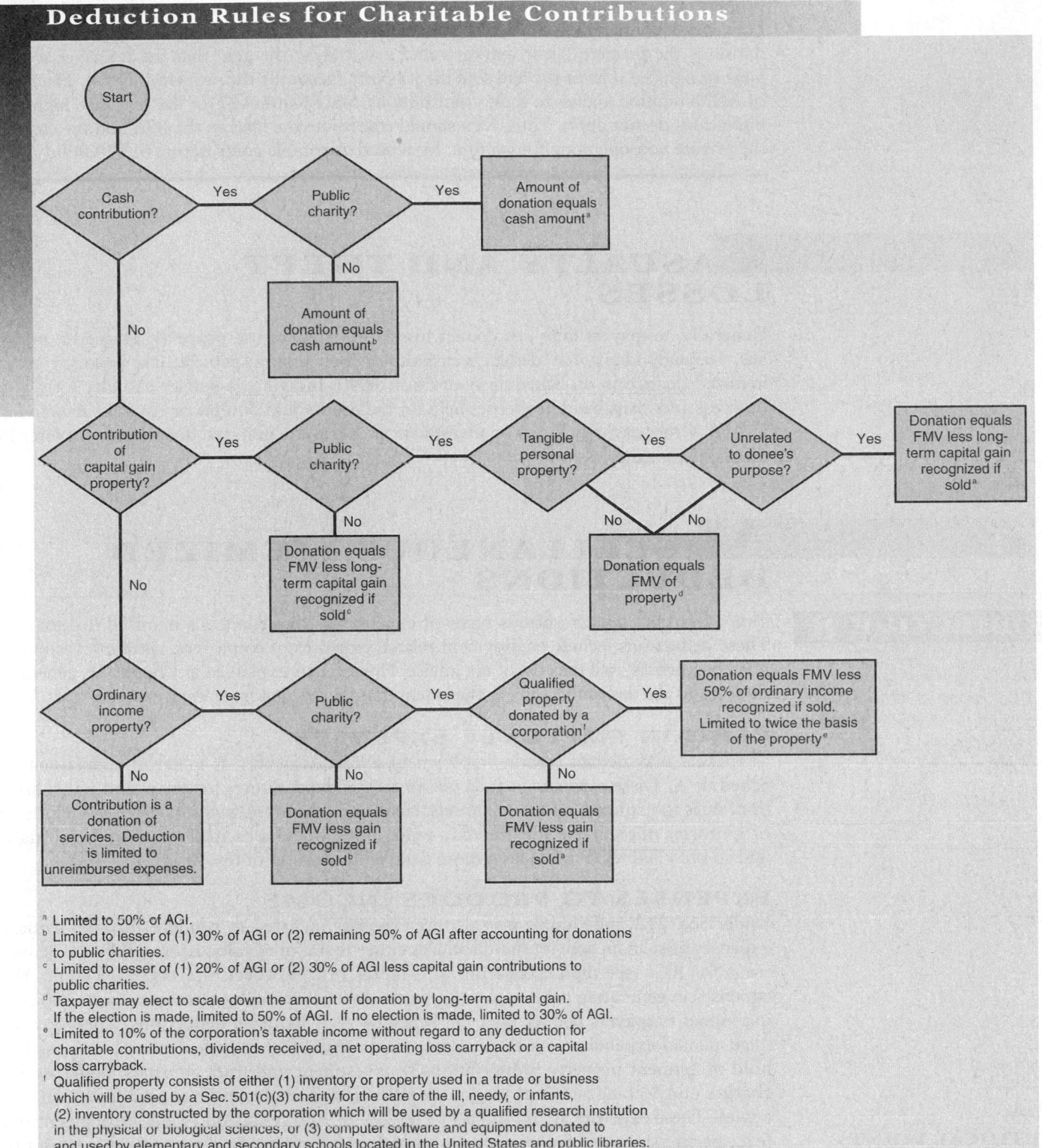

ᵃ Limited to 50% of AGI.

ᵇ Limited to lesser of (1) 30% of AGI or (2) remaining 50% of AGI after accounting for donations
  to public charities.

ᶜ Limited to lesser of (1) 20% of AGI or (2) 30% of AGI less capital gain contributions to
  public charities.

ᵈ Taxpayer may elect to scale down the amount of donation by long-term capital gain.
  If the election is made, limited to 50% of AGI. If no election is made, limited to 30% of AGI.

ᵉ Limited to 10% of the corporation's taxable income without regard to any deduction for
  charitable contributions, dividends received, a net operating loss carryback or a capital
  loss carryback.

ᶠ Qualified property consists of either (1) inventory or property used in a trade or business
  which will be used by a Sec. 501(c)(3) charity for the care of the ill, needy, or infants,
  (2) inventory constructed by the corporation which will be used by a qualified research institution
  in the physical or biological sciences, or (3) computer software and equipment donated to
  and used by elementary and secondary schools located in the United States and public libraries.

and a cost basis of $2,000. She purchased the land four years ago. Kim estimates that she
will have AGI of $300,000 and will be in the 35% marginal tax bracket. Assuming that
both charities would gladly accept either contribution, how should Kim satisfy these
pledges?

Solution: The amount of contribution of capital gain property to a public charity is the property's fair market value. The 30% of AGI limitation applies to such contributions. However, a contribution of capital gain property to a private non-operating private foundation is the property's fair market value, reduced by the gain that the taxpayer would have recognized if he or she had sold the property (generally the property's basis). The 50% of AGI limitation applies to these contributions. Since Kim's AGI for the year is so high, the limitations do not apply. Thus, Kim should contribute the land to the BSA and the cash to the private non-operating foundation, for a total charitable contribution of $20,000.

CASUALTY AND THEFT LOSSES

Generally, taxpayers may not deduct losses on personal-use property. However, under Sec. 165 individuals may deduct a casualty or theft loss on personal-use property as an itemized deduction on Schedule A of Form 1040. Individuals deduct casualty losses on business and investment properties held for the production of rents or royalties in arriving at AGI. Other casualty losses on investment property are itemized deductions. Chapter I8 discusses casualty losses in greater depth.

MISCELLANEOUS ITEMIZED DEDUCTIONS

OBJECTIVE 8

Identify certain miscellaneous itemized deductions subject to the 2% of AGI limit

Taxpayers may deduct various types of expenses as miscellaneous itemized deductions. These deductions include employment-related expenses of employees, certain investment-related expenses, and the cost of tax advice. However, as explained in Chapter I9, generally these items are deductible only to the extent that, in the aggregate, they exceed 2% of AGI.

CERTAIN EMPLOYEE EXPENSES

Taxpayers may deduct certain employment-related expenses as itemized deductions on Schedule A. These expenses include *unreimbursed* expenditures for travel and transportation, dues to professional organizations, costs of job hunting, items of protective clothing or uniforms not suitable for everyday wear, union dues, subscriptions to trade journals, and so on. Chapter I9 provides a more detailed discussion of this topic.

EXPENSES TO PRODUCE INCOME

Under Sec. 212, individuals may deduct expenses incurred to produce income. If these expenses arise in an activity that produces either rental or royalty income, they are deductions *for* AGI (see the explanation in Chapter I6). However, if a taxpayer incurs the expenses in generating other types of investment income, such as interest, dividends, etc., individual taxpayers deduct them on Schedule A as itemized deductions. These investment-related expenditures include items such as rental fees for safe-deposit boxes used to hold investment property, subscriptions to investment and trade journals, bank service charges on checking accounts used in an investment activity, and fees paid for consulting advice. These expenses are all subject to the 2% of AGI reduction. Flow-through entities (e.g., partnerships and S corporations) must report these types of investment expenses to their owners as separately stated items so that the 2% of AGI reduction may be applied.

COST OF TAX ADVICE

Section 212 provides individuals with a deduction for expenses incurred in connection with the determination, collection, or refund of any tax, including federal, state, local, and foreign income taxes as well as estate, gift, and inheritance taxes. These items include (1) tax return preparation fees, (2) appraisal fees incurred in determining the amount of a casualty loss, certain capital improvements for a medical deduction, or the FMV of property donated to a qualified charity, (3) fees paid to an accountant for representation in a

ETHICAL POINT

If a client furnishes a handwritten list of his or her miscellaneous itemized deductions to a CPA, the CPA may in good faith rely on the information without verification. However, the CPA should not ignore the implications of information that is provided and should make reasonable inquiries if the information furnished appears to be incorrect, incomplete, or inconsistent.

tax audit, (4) long-distance telephone calls responding to IRS questions, (5) costs of tax return preparation materials and books, and (6) legal fees incurred in planning the tax consequences dealing with estate planning. If an individual incurs these items in connection with the taxpayer's (1) trade or business (reported on Schedule C), (2) farm income (reported on Schedule F), or (3) an activity which produces rents or royalties (reported on Part I of Schedule E), they are *for* AGI deductions.[51] All other expenses incurred for tax advice are miscellaneous itemized deductions subject to the 2% of AGI limitation.

Fees not directly connected with the determination, collection, or refund of a tax or with the taxpayer's trade or business are personal expenses and are not deductible. Thus, legal fees incurred for drafting wills generally are not deductible. However, legal expenses incurred in tax fraud cases in connection with the filing of a fraudulent return generally are deductible.[52] Legal fees relating to a divorce generally are not deductible, unless they deal with tax-related items such as determining who will receive the exemption for dependent children. Chapter I3 discusses these fees in greater detail.

REDUCTION OF CERTAIN ITEMIZED DEDUCTIONS

Because of concerns with the budget deficit, Congress enacted Sec. 68 which provides for a reduction in the total amount of certain itemized deductions for high-income taxpayers.[53] This reduction applies only to individuals with AGI in excess of a certain threshold amount. This AGI threshold amount for 2006 is $150,500 ($75,250 for married people filing separate returns), and will be adjusted by an inflation factor for subsequent years. Starting in 2006, these phaseouts will gradually be reduced and will be completely eliminated by the year 2009. In 2006, taxpayers will lose only 2/3 of the amount that would normally be lost under the regular computation. The reduction of the itemized deductions is normally 3% of the amount that the individual's AGI for the year exceeds the threshold amount. Thus, the reduction percentage for 2006 is 2% (2/3 × 3%). However, two other limitations apply. First, the reduction in the itemized deductions cannot exceed 80% of the total itemized deductions other than medical expenses, investment interest, casualty losses, and wagering losses. Second, the reduction is applied after taking into account the other limitations on itemized deductions (e.g., the 2% of AGI limitation on miscellaneous itemized deductions).

EXAMPLE I7-33 ▶

During 2006, John and Sue (a married couple filing a joint return) report AGI of $250,000. In addition, their itemized deductions consist of $10,000 charitable contributions, $4,000 real property taxes, $8,000 state income taxes, and deductible investment interest expense of $5,000. Because their AGI exceeds $150,500, their itemized deductions for the year are limited to $25,010 ($27,000 − $1,990), computed as follows:

AGI	$250,000
Threshold	(150,500)
Excess	$ 99,500
Times: Reduction percentage	× 0.02
Potential reduction	$1,990
Limit to reduction (not including investment interest):	
Charitable contributions	$ 10,000
Property taxes	4,000
State income taxes	8,000
Total	$ 22,000
Times: Limitation percentage	× 0.80
Overall limit on reduction	$ 17,600

The 80% limitation does not apply because the $1,990 reduction is less than $17,600. ◀

[51] Rev. Rul. 92-29, 1992-1 C.B. 20.
[52] Rev. Rul. 68-662, 1968-2 C.B. 69.

[53] In 2001, Congress authorized the elimination of these phase-outs, which will begin in 2006 and be complete in 2009.

EXAMPLE I7-34 ▶ Assume the same facts as Example I7-33 except that John and Sue's AGI is $1,100,000. Now John and Sue's allowable itemized deductions for the year are $9,400 ($27,000 − 17,600), computed as follows:

AGI	$1,100,000
Threshold	(150,500)
Excess	$ 949,500
Times: Reduction percentage	× 0.02
Potential reduction	$ 18,990
Limit to reduction (not including investment expense):	
Charitable contributions	$ 10,000
Property taxes	4,000
State income taxes	8,000
Total	$ 22,000
Times: Limitation percentage	× 0.80
Overall limit on reduction	$ 17,600

The 80% limitation applies in this case. Since the potential reduction of $18,990 is greater than 80% of the itemized deductions, other than investment interest expense, the total reduction is limited to $17,600. As can be seen from this example, the 80% limitation applies only to high income taxpayers with relatively small itemized deductions. ◀

STOP & THINK

Question: Joe is a general contractor who uses the cash method of accounting. He has been hired to do a job that will pay him $30,000. Under the terms of the agreement, Joe is to receive the full $30,000 when the job is complete. By December 15 of the current year, Joe estimates that the job can be completed with approximately seven more days of work. The person who hired Joe doesn't care if the job is completed in December of the current year or January of the subsequent year. Joe's AGI for the current year, excluding this job, will be $150,000. Joe and his wife, Kim, estimate that their state income taxes, residential interest, and charitable contributions for the current year total approximately $10,000. Because of a general economic slowdown, Joe estimates that his AGI for the subsequent year will be $90,000. What advice can you give Joe regarding when he should complete this job and collect the income?

Solution: For tax purposes, Joe should complete the job in January of the subsequent year for a couple of reasons. First, if their estimates are correct, Joe and Kim likely will be in the 28% marginal tax bracket for the current year and the 25% marginal tax bracket for the subsequent year. Second, if Joe is paid for the job in the current year, Joe and Kim's AGI will exceed the threshold amount, thus causing a reduction in their itemized deductions. This reduction increases their effective tax rate. On the other hand, if Joe and Kim report the $30,000 in income in the subsequent year, they will not have to reduce their itemized deductions of that year. Finally, since there is only a delay of a few days between collecting the income in the current year and delaying the collection into the subsequent year, present value issues regarding the receipt of the income don't need to be addressed.

TAX PLANNING CONSIDERATIONS

MEDICAL EXPENSE DEDUCTION

WORKING WITH THE 7.5% OF AGI FLOOR. As explained previously, a deduction for medical expenses is available to individuals only to the extent that those expenditures exceed 7.5% of the taxpayer's AGI for the year. Thus, many individuals find that no deduction is available, even though their medical expenses are relatively high. In these cases, taxpayers may obtain some benefit if they can bunch the medical expenses into one year. Orthodontic work, certain orthopedic treatment, noncosmetic elective surgery, and new eyeglasses are all examples of medical expenditures that may be either accelerated or delayed into a year in which other medical expenses are high or AGI is lower.

Generally, a taxpayer may take a deduction for medical expenses only in the year in which the expense is actually paid. The mere prepayment of future expenses usually does not accelerate the deduction. However, taxpayers may take a deduction in the earlier year of payment if there is a legal obligation to pay or if the prepayment is a requirement for the receipt of the medical care.[54] If the taxpayer has already received the medical treatment, but the taxpayer does not have sufficient cash to pay the bill, the taxpayer may preserve a deduction for the current year by either borrowing the cash to satisfy the bill or by using a credit card.

EXAMPLE I7-35 ▶

During the current year, Marty's estimated AGI is $50,000. Marty has already incurred $2,000 in medical expenses for himself and his family during the year. Because 7.5% of AGI for the year is $3,750, he receives no medical expense deduction. Marty plans to incur $4,000 in medical expenses for orthodontic work for his son next year. No other major medical expenses are anticipated, and Marty expects his AGI in the following year to remain the same. If these estimates are accurate, he will receive no medical deduction in either year. However, if the orthodontic work is started in the current year and Marty pays for the work, he will incur a total of $6,000 in medical expenses in the current year. Thus, $2,250 ($6,000 − $3,750) of the medical expenses may be deducted.

KEY POINT

Even if the medical expenses exceed 7.5% of AGI the taxpayer may not benefit from the deduction if the medical expenses in addition to the other itemized deductions do not exceed the standard deduction.

Mere prepayment in this case is not sufficient. Marty must have a portion of the orthodontic services performed in the earlier year. If he does not have sufficient cash to pay the bill in the current year, he could borrow the money or use a bank credit card. ◀

MULTIPLE SUPPORT AGREEMENTS. An individual may deduct medical expenses incurred for himself or herself, his or her spouse, and any dependents. In cases where a multiple support agreement has been filed, the tax law treats the individual who is the subject of the agreement as the dependent of the taxpayer entitled to the dependency exemption. Thus, to preserve the medical expense deduction, the taxpayer entitled to the dependency exemption should pay all medical expenditures for the dependent individual.

EXAMPLE I7-36 ▶

Amy, Bart, Clay, and Donna each provide 25% of the support of their father, Eric. Under the terms of a multiple support agreement, Bart, Clay, and Donna all agree to allow Amy to claim the dependency exemption with respect to Eric. During the year, $3,000 in medical expenses are incurred on Eric's behalf. If Amy pays these expenses, she may deduct them (subject to limitations). However, if Bart, Clay, or Donna pays these expenses, no one may claim the medical expenses as a deduction. ◀

INTEREST EXPENSE DEDUCTION

A taxpayer may deduct qualified residence interest incurred on a principal residence and one other qualified residence that the taxpayer selects. The taxpayer makes this choice annually. The taxpayer may choose any residence that is not a rental property. Otherwise, in order for the second residence to qualify, the taxpayer must use it personally for more than the greater of 14 days or 10% of the rental days during the year. If this test is met, however, the Sec. 280A limitations on the rental of vacation homes also apply. As explained in Chapter I6, under these rules, taxpayers must allocate expenses between the rental use and the personal use of the property. Taxpayers may deduct the expenses allocated to the rental use only to the extent of the rental income. Of the expenses allocated to the personal use, only the taxes and interest (if the residence is selected and if the loan is secured by the residence) are deductible as itemized deductions.

If the personal use by the taxpayer does not meet the test mentioned above, the interest allocated to the personal use cannot qualify as residence interest and it becomes nondeductible personal interest. Furthermore, the passive loss rules apply to the rental income and expenses allocated to the rental use of the property (see Chapter I8). Under these rules, individuals generally can deduct losses generated from a passive activity only to the extent of the individual's passive income. Certain individuals, however, may deduct up to $25,000 of losses from the rental of real estate. Thus, the two alternatives and their consequences are as follows:

---

[54] *Robert M. Rose v. CIR*, 26 AFTR 2d 70-5653, 70-2 USTC ¶9646 (5th Cir., 1970). See also Rev. Ruls. 75-302, 1975-2 C.B. 86, and 75-303, 1975-2 C.B. 87, both clarified by Rev. Rul. 93-72, 1993-2 C.B. 77.

▶ Meet the test. No loss from the rental portion of the property is deductible. However, the interest allocated to the personal use portion may be fully deductible as qualified residence interest.

▶ Do not meet the test. The interest allocated to the personal use portion is nondeductible personal interest. However, all of the passive loss from the rental portion is deductible against passive income. Furthermore, certain individuals may deduct up to $25,000 additional passive loss.

The alternative a taxpayer chooses depends on several factors, including the amount of the taxpayer's passive income, the total amount of itemized deductions, and whether the loan is secured by the vacation home, etc.

DEDUCTION FOR CHARITABLE CONTRIBUTIONS

ELECTION TO REDUCE THE AMOUNT OF A CHARITABLE CONTRIBUTION. The election to reduce the contribution of capital gain property to public charities by the long-term capital gain that the taxpayer would recognize if he or she sold the property is an annual election that applies to all capital gain property donated to public charities during the year. Because the election increases the ceiling limitation from 30% to 50%, under certain circumstances a taxpayer may actually receive a larger deduction for the year than would normally be available if the taxpayer did not make the election.

EXAMPLE I7-37 ▶

During the current year, Jane has AGI of $50,000. She donates a painting to the local university during the same year. The painting, valued at $30,000 at the time of contribution, cost her $25,000 several years before. The university displays the painting in its art museum. If Jane does not make the election, the amount of the contribution is equal to its FMV ($30,000). However, Jane's charitable contribution deduction for the year is limited to $15,000 ($50,000 × 0.30). If Jane makes the election to scale down the contribution amount, the deduction is reduced to $25,000 ($30,000 − $5,000 LTCG). The deduction limitation, however, increases to $25,000 for the year because the limitation is now based on 50% of AGI instead of 30%. In this case, Jane will receive a larger deduction for the year by making the election. However, the cost associated with this election is the loss of $5,000 of deduction because the total deduction is reduced from $30,000 to $25,000 if she makes the election. ◀

Many tax practitioners make this election only when preparing the taxpayer's final tax return. The taxpayer makes the election at this time because charitable contribution carryovers to the decedent's estate are not permitted.

DONATION OF APPRECIATED CAPITAL GAIN PROPERTY. Instead of selling substantially appreciated capital gain property and donating the cash proceeds, the taxpayer should donate the property directly to charity. If property is donated in this way, the donor receives a deduction equal to the FMV of the property and does not recognize any taxable gain on the disposition.

EXAMPLE I7-38 ▶

Colleen wishes to satisfy a pledge of $100,000 made to a local university. She owns $100,000 worth of marketable securities purchased ten years ago for $30,000. Because the securities are marketable, the university is indifferent as to whether Colleen donates cash or the securities. Although her marginal tax rate is 35%, Colleen would be subject to a tax rate of 15% on the sale of the securities. She has enough AGI to be able to deduct the full contribution in the current year. The following chart summarizes the cash flows to Colleen under two different alternatives:

	Donate Securities	Sell Securities and Donate Cash
Proceeds of sale	0	$100,000
Tax on gain	0	(10,500)[a]
Cash payment to charity		(100,000)
Tax savings from the contribution deduction	$35,000[b]	35,000
Net cash flow	$35,000	$ 24,500

[a]($100,000 − $30,000) × 0.15 = $10,500.
[b]$100,000 × 0.35 = $35,000.

◀

In order to take a tax loss on business or investment property, a taxpayer should not donate property that has decreased in value. Rather, the taxpayer should sell the property and donate the cash proceeds.

COMPLIANCE AND PROCEDURAL CONSIDERATIONS

MEDICAL EXPENSES

In certain cases, expenditures qualify as both a medical care expense and a dependent care expense (i.e., expenses for household and dependent care services that the taxpayer must pay to be gainfully employed). A taxpayer who incurs an expense that qualifies under both provisions may choose to take either a medical expense deduction or a tax credit under Sec. 21.[55] However, if a taxpayer takes a credit for these expenses, they are not deductible as medical expenses.

EXAMPLE I7-39 ▶ Joel's daughter, Debbie, is physically handicapped. As a result, Joel hires a nurse who provides daily care while he is at work. During the year, Joel pays the nurse a total of $3,000. This amount qualifies for both the dependent care credit and the medical expense deduction. If Joel takes the dependent care credit, the $3,000 may not be deducted as a medical expense. Because of the limitations imposed on each, the determination of which treatment is more advantageous depends on items such as the taxpayer's AGI, other medical expenses, and total itemized deductions. ◀

CHARITABLE CONTRIBUTIONS

Over the past several years, the IRS has at times challenged taxpayers' charitable contribution deductions. Part of the IRS's motivation is to make sure the contribution has actually occurred. In addition, when a taxpayer donates property other than cash to a qualifying charity, proper determination of the property's FMV is a critical issue. Because of actual and perceived abuses in this area, the IRS often scrutinizes and, if necessary, challenges the valuation of contributed property. This is especially true for contributions of property for which no published market quotes exist. Thus, the taxpayer must (1) properly substantiate the fact that the contribution has actually been made, and (2) in the case of the contribution of property, the taxpayer may be required to acquire and retain or provide to the IRS information documenting the property's FMV. As noted below, special detailed substantiation and documentation requirements apply to the contribution of used motor vehicles, boats, and airplanes.

ADDITIONAL COMMENT

On Form 8283, the charitable organization is required to acknowledge receipt of the gift and to file an information return if the property is sold or disposed of within two years.

REAL-LIFE EXAMPLE

In one case the taxpayer, a CPA, failed to support a contribution with a qualified appraisal. As a result, his charitable deduction for art and printing supplies donated to a high school was denied. To substantiate the claimed $40,000 charitable deduction, the taxpayer submitted with Form 8283 an appraisal of the donated items made by the high school's principal. The principal, however, wasn't a "qualified appraiser." *D'Arcangelo,* TC Memo 1994-572 (1994).

PROPER SUBSTANTIATION. If the contribution is made in cash, the taxpayer must retain evidence of the donation by keeping a cancelled check or a receipt from the charitable organization. In the absence of a cancelled check or receipt, other reliable written records showing the charity's name and the date and amount of the contribution is acceptable to the IRS. If the contribution is in the form of noncash property, the taxpayer must maintain records containing the following:

▶ Name and address of the charity to which the contribution was made

▶ Date and location of the contribution

▶ Description of the property

▶ FMV of the property

---

[55] A credit of 35% of expenses for child and dependent care services is allowed if the dependent is under age 13 or a spouse or dependent who is mentally or physically incapable of caring for himself or herself. The credit is reduced 1% for every $2,000 (or portion thereof) of AGI over $15,000.

However, the credit may not be reduced below 20%. (See the discussion on Personal Tax Credits in Chapter I14 for a more detailed explanation of the child and dependent care credit.)

ADDITIONAL COMMENT

If the taxpayer's total deduction for art is $20,000 or more, he or she must include an 8 × 10 inch color photograph or a color transparency no smaller than 4 × 5 inches.

▶ Method of determining the property's FMV

▶ Signed copy of the appraisal report if an appraiser was used[56]

For charitable contributions of $250 or more, no deduction is allowed unless the contribution is substantiated by a contemporaneous, written acknowledgment (receipt) by the donee organization. This acknowledgment must contain the following information:

▶ The amount of cash and a description of any property contributed

▶ Whether or not the organization provided any goods or services in consideration for the cash or property received, including a description and good faith estimate of the value of any goods or services provided by the organization.

The acknowledgment is contemporaneous if obtained by the earlier of the date the taxpayer files a return for the year in question or the extended due date for filing such a return. This substantiation requirement is waived if the donee organization files a return that contains the required information.[57]

DOCUMENTATION OF PROPERTY'S FMV. In addition to the substantiation requirement, in certain cases the taxpayer must also properly document the property's FMV. The specific documentation requirements depend upon the amount of the claimed deduction for the contributed property. If a claimed deduction for a contribution of property exceeds $500, noncorporate taxpayers (and closely held C corporations and personal service corporations) must include with their tax return a description of the property and any other information the IRS requires, including the type, location, holding period, basis, and FMV of the property. This information is reported on Form 8283 (see Appendix B). If the claimed deduction exceeds $5,000, in addition to the above requirements, all taxpayers must obtain a qualified appraisal of the property and must include with their tax return any additional information that the IRS requires. Finally, if the claimed deduction exceeds $500,000, all taxpayers are additionally required to obtain a qualified appraisal and actually attach the appraisal to their tax return. Because these documentation requirements are based on the amount of a claimed contribution, the donation of similar items of property donated to all charities will be treated as the donation of one property. This requirement prevents taxpayers from avoiding these documentation requirements by spreading out their contributions. If a partnership or an S corporation donates property, these documentation requirements are applied at the entity level. However, if the documentation requirements are not met, the deduction is denied at the partner or shareholder level. In general, these documentation rules to not apply to contributions of cash, certain intangibles, inventory, or publicly traded securities.

CONTRIBUTION OF USED MOTOR VEHICLES, BOATS, AND AIRPLANES. Special documentation rules apply to contributions of motor vehicles, boats, and airplanes if the claimed value of the property exceeds $500. However, these rules do not apply if the contributed vehicle, boat, or airplane is inventory in the hands of the donor. If these special rules apply, the substantiation rules for a donation of property exceeding $250 are no longer applicable. Instead, the charity must give the taxpayer and the IRS a contemporaneous written acknowledgment of the contribution. This acknowledgment must be included with the taxpayer's tax return. The information included in the acknowledgment and the date by which the charity must give the acknowledgment to the taxpayer depend upon whether or not the charity sells the vehicle without any significant use or any material improvement of the vehicle. In either case, the acknowledgment must include the name and taxpayer identification number of the taxpayer who donated the vehicle, as well as the vehicle identification number. If the vehicle is sold by the charity before any significant use or material improvement, the acknowledgment must also include (1) a certification that the vehicle was sold in an arm's length transaction to an unrelated party, (2) the gross proceeds from the sale, and (3) a statement that the deductible amount may not exceed the

---

[56] Reg. Sec. 1.170A-13.
[57] Sec. 170(f)(8) and Reg. Sec. 1.170A-13(f).

amount of the gross proceeds. This acknowledgment must be given to the taxpayer within 30 days of the contribution of the vehicle to the charity, and, as mentioned earlier, the amount of the deduction for the vehicle is limited to the gross proceeds received from the sale. On the other hand, if the charity uses or improves the vehicle, the acknowledgment must also state: (1) the intended use or improvement and the intended duration of the use and (2) a certification that the vehicle will not be transferred or sold before completion of the intended use or improvement. This acknowledgment must be given to the taxpayer within 30 days of the sale of the vehicle.[58]

EXAMPLE I7-40 ▶ During the current year, Peter Smith (SSN. 276-31-7242) reports AGI of $250,000. Smith also makes the following charitable contributions during the year:

▶ Smith performs voluntary dental work three days each month in rural areas of the state. Smith drives a total of 4,000 miles on these trips during the year.

▶ Smith makes the following contributions by cash or check: $750 to the city library, $2,000 to the United Way, $500 to a local community college, and $4,000 to his church.

▶ Smith contributes a tract of land to a small rural town. The town plans to erect a public library on the site. Smith purchased the land in 1997 for $5,000. Its appraised value at the time of the contribution is $8,000.

Smith's contributions are reported on the partially completed Schedule A shown in Figure I7-1. The out-of-pocket expenses of $560 (4,000 miles × $0.14) and the contributions by cash or check of $7,250 (library, United Way, church, and community college) are totaled and reported on line 15. The property contribution of $8,000 is separately stated on line 16. Because Smith contributes property with a value exceeding $500, Form 8283, an appraisal summary, and signed statements by the qualified appraiser and an authorized official of the organization that received the property must be attached to the return. In addition, for the donations that separately exceed $250, Peter must obtain and retain written acknowledgments from the donee organizations in order for the contributions to be deductible. ◀

TAXES

Individuals generally report their deduction for property taxes on Schedule A of Form 1040. However, if the taxpayer incurs the taxes in his or her business, they are reported on Schedule C. Taxes incurred for the production of rents and royalties are reported on Schedule E. Taxes incurred in the taxpayer's farming business are reported on Schedule F. State and local income taxes imposed on individuals are always reported on Schedule A, even if the individual is self-employed.

Real estate brokers must report any real estate tax allocable to the purchaser of a residence. (See the discussion in this chapter regarding the allocation of real estate taxes between the seller and buyer of a residence.)[59] The broker reports this information on Form 1099-S (Proceeds from Real Estate Transactions).

EXAMPLE I7-41 ▶ During the year, Andrea incurs $1,500 in property taxes on a two-family house. Andrea lives in one unit and rents out the other. She also pays $100 in registration fees and $600 in personal property taxes on her automobile, based on its value. Andrea uses the automobile 80% of the time in an unincorporated business. During the current year, she also pays $2,000 in state income taxes, all of which is attributable to her income of the prior year from the unincorporated business.

Because one-half of the real estate taxes are attributable to property used to produce rental income, $750 (0.50 × $1,500) is reported on Schedule E, and the remaining personal-use portion ($750) is reported on Schedule A. Because 80% of the use of the automobile is in Andrea's business, $80 (0.80 × $100) of the registration fee is deductible as a business expense on Schedule C. The remaining $20 is not deductible because the registration fee is not a tax. However, $480 (0.80 × $600) of the personal property tax on the automobile is deductible as a business expense on Schedule C. The remaining $120 is deductible as a tax on Schedule A. Finally, even though the tax is related to Andrea's business income, all $2,000 of the state income tax is reported on Schedule A. Because the state income tax is paid in the current year, it is deductible in the current year. ◀

---

[58] Sec. 170(f)(11) and (f)(12).

[59] Sec. 6045(e)(4) and NOTICE 93-4, 1993-1 C.B. 295.

Schedule A—Itemized Deductions
(Schedule B is on back)

▶ **Attach to Form 1040.**   ▶ **See Instructions for Schedules A&B (Form 1040).**

OMB No. 1545-0074

2005

Attachment
Sequence No. **07**

Name(s) shown on Form 1040

Peter Smith

Your social security number

276 | 31 | 7242

Medical and Dental Expenses		**Caution.** Do not include expenses reimbursed or paid by others.		
	1	Medical and dental expenses (see page A-2) . . .	1	
	2	Enter amount from Form 1040, line 38 ⌐2⌐		
	3	Multiply line 2 by 7.5% (.075)	3	
	4	Subtract line 3 from line 1. If line 3 is more than line 1, enter -0-		4
Taxes You Paid (See page A-2.)	5	State and local (**check only one box**):		
		a ☐ Income taxes, **or**	5	
		b ☐ General sales taxes (see page A-3)		
	6	Real estate taxes (see page A-5)	6	
	7	Personal property taxes	7	
	8	Other taxes. List type and amount ▶.............		
			8	
	9	Add lines 5 through 8		9
Interest You Paid (See page A-5.)	10	Home mortgage interest and points reported to you on Form 1098	10	
	11	Home mortgage interest not reported to you on Form 1098. If paid to the person from whom you bought the home, see page A-6 and show that person's name, identifying no., and address ▶		
Note. Personal interest is not deductible.		....	11	
	12	Points not reported to you on Form 1098. See page A-6 for special rules	12	
	13	Investment interest. Attach Form 4952 if required. (See page A-6.)	13	
	14	Add lines 10 through 13		14
Gifts to Charity If you made a gift and got a benefit for it, see page A-7.	15a	Total gifts by cash or check. If you made any gift of $250 or more, see page A-7	15a	7,810
	b	Gifts by cash or check after August 27, 2005, that you elect to treat as qualified contributions (see page A-7) ⌐15b⌐		
	16	Other than by cash or check. If any gift of $250 or more, see page A-7. You **must** attach Form 8283 if over $500	16	8,000
	17	Carryover from prior year	17	
	18	Add lines 15a, 16, and 17		18	15,810
Casualty and Theft Losses	19	Casualty or theft loss(es). Attach Form 4684. (See page A-8.)		19
Job Expenses and Certain Miscellaneous Deductions (See page A-8.)	20	Unreimbursed employee expenses—job travel, union dues, job education, etc. Attach Form 2106 or 2106-EZ if required. (See page A-8.) ▶.............	20	
	21	Tax preparation fees.	21	
	22	Other expenses—investment, safe deposit box, etc. List type and amount ▶.............		
			22	
	23	Add lines 20 through 22	23	
	24	Enter amount from Form 1040, line 38 ⌐24⌐		
	25	Multiply line 24 by 2% (.02)	25	
	26	Subtract line 25 from line 23. If line 25 is more than line 23, enter -0-		26
Other Miscellaneous Deductions	27	Other—from list on page A-9. List type and amount ▶.............		
		....		27
Total Itemized Deductions	28	Is Form 1040, line 38, over $145,950 (over $72,975 if married filing separately)?		
		☐ **No.** Your deduction is not limited. Add the amounts in the far right column for lines 4 through 27. Also, enter this amount on Form 1040, line 40. ▶		28
		☐ **Yes.** Your deduction may be limited. See page A-9 for the amount to enter.		
	29	If you elect to itemize deductions even though they are less than your standard deduction, check here ▶ ☐		

For Paperwork Reduction Act Notice, see Form 1040 instructions.   Cat. No. 11330X   Schedule A (Form 1040) 2005

FIGURE 17-1   ▶   PARTIALLY COMPLETED SCHEDULE A

WHAT WOULD YOU DO IN THIS SITUATION?

GIVING TO BOTH: GOODWILL AND THE IRS

Much has been written about abusive practices concerning the valuation of noncash property donated to qualified charities. Under Sec. 170, both corporations and individuals may deduct the FMV of property contributed to charitable organizations. Of course, a number of valuation and percentage limitations and carryover rules are applicable to both individual and corporate taxpayers.

Assume your clients, Mr. and Mrs. Nicholas Nice, come into your office on December 27 for some year-end

tax planning. Your review of their tax situation indicates that they have made substantial donations of clothing and household goods to Goodwill Industries. They have obtained proper documentation for donations made during the year but do not know how to qualify for taking a charitable deduction vis-à-vis valuation, forms, and the like. They do know that their original cost basis in the donated goods was $15,000 and that the goods were in usable condition at the time of the donation. What tax and ethical issues should be considered?

PROBLEM MATERIALS

DISCUSSION QUESTIONS

I7-1 a. A taxpayer may deduct medical expenses incurred on behalf of which people?

b. In the case of children of divorced parents, must the parent who is entitled to the dependency exemption pay the medical expenses of the child to ensure that the expenses are deductible? Explain.

c. Who should pay the medical expenses of an individual who is the subject of a multiple support agreement?

I7-2 What is the definition of medical care for purposes of the medical care deduction?

I7-3 a. What is the definition of cosmetic surgery under the Internal Revenue Code?

b. Is the cost of cosmetic surgery deductible as a medical expense? Explain.

I7-4 a. If a taxpayer must travel away from his or her home in order to obtain medical care, which en route costs, if any, are deductible as medical expenses?

b. Are there any limits imposed on the deductibility of these expenses?

I7-5 What are the rules dealing with the deductibility of the cost of meals and lodging incurred while away from home in order to receive medical treatment as an outpatient?

I7-6 a. Which types of capital expenditures incurred specifically for medical purposes are deductible?

b. What limitations, if any, are imposed on the deductibility of these expenditures?

I7-7 Bill, a plant manager, is suffering from a serious ulcer. Bill's doctor recommends that he spend three weeks fishing and hunting in the Colorado

Rockies. Can Bill deduct the costs of the trip as a medical expense?

I7-8 In what cases are medical insurance premiums paid by an individual not deductible as qualified medical expenses?

I7-9 What is the limit placed on medical expense deductions? When can a deduction be taken for medical care? What if the medical care is prepaid?

I7-10 a. Which taxes are specifically deductible for federal income tax purposes under Sec. 164?

b. If a tax is not specifically listed in Sec. 164, under what circumstances may it still be deductible?

I7-11 If Susan overpays her state income tax due to excess withholdings, can she deduct the entire amount in the year withheld? When Susan receives a refund from the state how must she treat that refund for tax purposes?

I7-12 What is an ad valorem tax? If a tax that is levied on personal property is not an ad valorem tax, under what circumstances may it still be deductible?

I7-13 When real estate is sold during a year, why is it necessary that the real estate taxes on the property be apportioned between the buyer and seller?

I7-14 a. Identify the different categories of interest expense an individual may incur. How is the classification of the interest determined?

b. Are these different categories of interest deductible? If so, how?

I7-15 At times, the term *points* is used to refer to different types of charges. Define the term and describe when points are deductible.

I7-16 In which year or years are points (representing prepaid interest on a loan) deductible?

I7-17 Why does Sec. 267 impose a restriction on the deductibility of expenses accrued and payable by an accrual method taxpayer to a related cash method taxpayer?

I7-18 a. What is the amount of the annual limitation placed on the deductibility of investment interest expense?
b. Explain how net investment income is calculated.
c. Is any disallowed interest expense for the year allowable as a deduction in another year? If so, when?

I7-19 Explain what acquisition indebtedness and home equity indebtedness are with respect to a qualified residence of a taxpayer, and identify any limitations on the deductibility of interest expense on this indebtedness.

I7-20 Explain what a qualified residence is for purposes of qualified residence interest.

I7-21 Why is interest expense disallowed if it is incurred to purchase or hold tax-exempt obligations?

I7-22 When is interest generally deductible for cash-method taxpayers? Explain if the general rule applies to prepaid interest, interest paid with loan proceeds, discounted notes, and personal interest. If the general rule does not apply, explain when these interest expenses are deductible.

I7-23 a. For purposes of the charitable contribution deduction, what is capital gain property? Ordinary income property?
b. What is the significance of classifying property as either capital gain property or ordinary income property?

I7-24 How is the *amount* of a charitable contribution of capital gain property determined if it is donated to a private nonoperating foundation? How does this determination differ if capital gain property is donated to a public charity?

I7-25 May an individual who is married and files a joint return deduct any charitable contributions if the itemized deductions total $7,000 (of which $3,000 are qualified charitable contributions)?

I7-26 For individuals, what is the overall deduction limitation on charitable contributions? What is the limitation for corporations?

I7-27 If a taxpayer's charitable contributions for any tax year exceed the deduction limitations, may the excess contributions be deducted in another year? If so, in which years may they be deducted?

I7-28 How are charitable contribution deductions reported on the tax return for individuals? What reporting requirements must be met for the contribution of property?

I7-29 List some of the more common miscellaneous itemized deductions and identify any limitations that are imposed on the deductibility of these items.

I7-30 Certain itemized deductions of high-income taxpayers must be reduced. Which itemized deductions are subject to this reduction and when does the reduction apply?

ISSUE IDENTIFICATION QUESTIONS

I7-31 Wayne and Maria file a joint tax return on which they itemize their deductions and report AGI of $50,000. During the year they incurred $1,500 of medical expenses when Maria broke her leg. Furthermore, their dentist informed them that their daughter, Alicia, needs $3,000 of orthodontic work to correct her overbite. Wayne also needs a new pair of eyeglasses that will cost $300. What tax issues should Wayne and Maria consider?

I7-32 This year, Chuck took out a loan to purchase some raw land for investment. He paid $40,000 for the land, and he expects that within 5 years the land will be worth at least $75,000. Chuck is married, and his AGI for the year is $325,000. Chuck paid $4,300 in interest on the loan this year. Chuck has $2,600 in interest income and $1,300 in dividend income for the year. He plans to itemize his deductions, so he can use the interest expense to offset his investment income. What tax issues should Chuck consider?

I7-33 During the current year, George made contributions totaling $40,000 to an organization called the National Endowment for the Preservation of Liberty (NEPL). Later during the year, the NEPL started giving money to a political candidate to help with his campaign expenses. What tax issues should George consider?

I7-34 During the current year, Bob has AGI of $100,000. He donates stock to his church that was purchased two years ago for $55,000. The FMV of the stock is $60,000. Bob has $5,000 of unused excess contributions from a prior year. What tax issues should Bob consider?

PROBLEMS

I7-35 *Medical Expense Deduction.* During 2006, Angela sustains serious injuries from a snow-skiing accident. She incurs the following expenses:

Item	Amount
Doctor bills	$11,700
Hospital bills	9,400
Legal fees in suit against ski resort	3,000

Angela is single and has no dependents. During 2006, her salary is $58,000. She pays $600 in medical and dental insurance premiums, $2,750 in mortgage interest on her home, and $1,200 in interest on her car loan. Her health insurance provider reimburses her for $10,000 of the medical expenses. What is her 2006 taxable income?

I7-36 *Reimbursement of Previously Deducted Medical Expenses.* Assume the same facts as in Problem I7-35. In addition, assume that in 2007, Angela receives an additional $7,000 in a settlement of a lawsuit arising because of the snow-skiing accident. $4,000 of the settlement is to pay Angela's medical bills, and $3,000 is to reimburse her legal expenses. What is the proper tax treatment of this $7,000 settlement?

I7-37 *Medical Expense Deduction.* Dan lives in Duncan, a small town in Arizona. Because of a rare blood disease, Dan is required to take special medical treatments once a month. The closest place these treatments are available to Dan is in Phoenix, 200 miles away. The treatments are provided on an outpatient basis but require him to stay overnight in Phoenix. During the year, Dan makes 12 trips to Phoenix by automobile to receive the treatments. The motel he always stays in charges $85 per night. For the year, Dan also spends a total of $250 for meals on these trips. $100 of this $250 is spent while en route to Phoenix. What is the amount of Dan's qualified medical expenses for 2006?

I7-38 *Medical Expense Deduction.* Chad is divorced and has custody of Brett, his 14-year-old son. Chad's ex-wife has custody of their daughter, Sara. During the year, Chad incurs $3,000 for orthodontic work for Sara to correct a severe overbite and $2,000 in unreimbursed medical expenses associated with Brett's broken leg. Chad also pays $900 in health insurance premiums. Both Brett and Sara are covered under Chad's medical insurance plan. In addition, Chad incurs $400 for prescription drugs and $1,000 in doctor bills for himself. Chad's AGI is $40,000. What is Chad's medical expense deduction for the year assuming that his other itemized deductions exceed the standard deduction?

I7-39 *Medical Expense Deduction.* In 2006, Charla, a single taxpayer with no dependents, was severely hurt in a farm accident. The accident left Charla's legs 85% paralyzed. After incurring $14,000 of medical expenses at the hospital, the doctor recommended that Charla install a pool at her home for therapy. The pool cost $25,000 to install and increased the value of her home by $22,000. She spent $930 maintaining the pool in 2006 and $1,060 in 2007. Charla also purchased a wheelchair on December 28, 2006, for $2,300, which she charged to her credit card. She paid her credit card bill on January 6, 2007. She also purchased a hospital bed for $3,800 but did not pay for the bed until 2007. Charla paid her physical therapist $4,000 for services to be performed in 2007. Charla paid $1,200 in medical insurance premiums in both 2006 and 2007. In 2007, the insurance company reimbursed Charla $9,000 for her hospital stay in 2006. Her AGI for 2006 and 2007 is $38,000 and $43,000, respectively, not considering any of the above items. Charla has no other itemized deductions in either year.
a. What is Charla's taxable income for 2006?
b. What is Charla's medical expense deduction for 2007? How does she treat the reimbursement?

I7-40 *Deduction of Taxes.* Joyce is a single, cash-method taxpayer. On April 11, 2005, Joyce paid $120 with her 2004 state income tax return. During 2005, Joyce had $1,600 in state income taxes withheld. On April 13, 2006, Joyce paid $200 with her 2005 state tax return. During 2006, she had $2,100 in state income taxes withheld from her paycheck. Upon filing her 2006 tax return on April 15, 2007, she received a refund of $450 for excess state income taxes withheld. Joyce had total AGI in 2006 and 2007 of $51,000 and $53,500, respectively. In 2006, Joyce also paid $2,900 in qualified residence interest.
a. What is the amount of state income taxes Joyce may include as an itemized deduction for 2005?
b. What is the allowed itemized deduction for state income taxes for 2006?

c. What is her taxable income for 2006?

d. What is her AGI for 2007?

I7-41 Assume the same facts as Problem I7-40, but change the amount of Joyce's mortgage interest to $3,300 and assume her state sales taxes were $3,000.

a. What is her taxable income for 2006?

b. What is her AGI for 2007?

I7-42 *Deduction of Taxes.* Dawn, a single, cash method taxpayer, paid the following taxes in 2006: Dawn's employer withheld $5,400 for federal income taxes, $2,000 for state income taxes, and $3,800 for FICA from her 2006 paychecks. Dawn purchased a new car and paid $600 in sales tax and $70 for the license. The car's FMV was $20,000 and it weighed 3,000 pounds. The county also assessed a property tax on the car. The tax was 2% of its value and $10 per hundredweight. The car is used 100% of the time for personal purposes. Dawn sold her house on April 15, 2006. The county's property tax on the home for 2006 is $1,850, payable on February 1, 2007. The county's real property tax year is the calendar year. Dawn's AGI for the year is $50,000 and her other itemized deductions exclusive of taxes are $4,000.

a. What is Dawn's deduction for taxes in 2006 assuming she did not elect to deduct sales taxes instead of income taxes?

b. Where on Dawn's tax return should she report her deduction for taxes?

I7-43 *Apportionment of Real Estate Taxes.* On May 1 of the current year, Tara sells a building to Janet for $500,000. Tara's basis in the building is $300,000. The county in which the building is located has a real property tax year that ends on June 30. The taxes are payable by September 1 of that year. On September 1, Janet pays the annual property taxes of $6,000. Both Tara and Janet are calendar-year, cash method taxpayers. The closing agreement does not separately account for the property taxes. Disregard any leap year.

a. What amount of real property taxes may Janet deduct in the current year?

b. What amount of real property taxes may Tara deduct in the current year?

c. If no apportionment on the real property taxes is made in the sales agreement, what is Tara's total selling price of the building? Janet's basis for the building?

I7-44 *Classification of Interest Expense.* On January 1 of the current year, Scott borrowed $80,000, pledging the assets of his business as collateral. He immediately deposited the money in an interest-bearing checking account. Scott already had $20,000 in this account. On April 1, Scott invests $75,000 in a limited real estate partnership. On July 1, he buys a new ski boat for $12,000. On August 1, he makes a $10,000 capital contribution to his unincorporated business. Scott repays $50,000 of the loan on November 30 of the current year. Classify Scott's interest expense for the year.

I7-45 *Investment Income and Deductions.* During 2006, Travis takes out a $40,000 loan, using stock he owns as collateral. He uses $10,000 to purchase a car, which he uses 100% for personal use. He uses the remaining funds to purchase stocks and bonds. He pays $3,200 interest on the loan. Travis also reports the following for the year:

AGI without any investment income	$150,000
State income taxes paid	8,400
Dividend income	10,000
Interest income	2,100
Investment expenses (exclusive of interest)	8,000
Net short term capital gains	7,300
Net long term capital gain	8,800

Travis is married and files a joint tax return. What is his net taxable income?

I7-46 *Qualified Residence Interest.* During the current year, Tina purchases a beachfront condominium for $600,000, paying $150,000 down and taking out a $450,000 mortgage, secured by the property. At the time of the purchase, the outstanding mortgage on her principal residence is $700,000. This debt is secured by the residence and the FMV of the principal residence is $1,400,000. She purchased the principal residence in 1997. What is the amount of qualified indebtedness on which Tina may deduct the interest payments?

I7-47 *Qualified Residence Interest.* Several years ago, Magdelena purchased a new residence for $300,000. Currently, the outstanding mortgage on the residence is $260,000. The current fair market value of the home is $330,000. Magdelena wants to borrow a sizable sum of money to pay for the college education costs of her two children and believes the interest would be deductible if she takes out a home equity loan. For each of the independent situations below, determine the amount of the loan on which Magdelena may deduct the interest as qualified residence interest.

a. Magdelena borrows $50,000 as a home equity loan.
b. Magdelena borrows $80,000 as a home equity loan.
c. Alternatively, assume the current fair market value of her residence is $375,000 and she borrows $110,000 as a home equity loan.
d. Alternatively, assume the current outstanding balance of the mortgage Magdelena incurred to purchase the home is $1,200,000, the home's fair market value is $1,400,000, and she borrows $80,000 as a home equity loan.

I7-48 *Interest Between Related Parties.* Crown Corporation is an accrual method taxpayer owned 55% by Brett and 45% by Susie. Brett and Susie are good friends and have been business associates for several years. BJ Partnership is a cash method taxpayer, owned 40% by Brett and 60% by Jeremy, Brett's uncle. Both Crown Corporation and BJ Partnership are calendar year entities. On January 5 of the current year, Crown borrows $50,000 from BJ Partnership, and pays 8% interest on the loan. Crown must pay the interest on January first of next year.

a. What amount of interest expense can Crown Corporation deduct in the current year?
b. How would your answer change if Jeremy were Brett's brother, instead of his uncle?

I7-49 *Timing of Interest Deduction.* On April 1 of the current year, Henry borrows $12,000 from the bank for a year. Because the note is discounted for the interest charge and Henry receives proceeds of $10,200, he is required to repay the face amount of the loan ($12,000) in four equal quarterly payments beginning on July 1 of the current year. Henry is a cash method individual.

a. What is the amount of Henry's interest expense deduction in the current year with respect to this loan?
b. Assume the same facts except that the initial starting date when the repayments begin is April 1 of the following year. What is the amount of Henry's interest expense deduction in the current year?
c. Assume the same facts as in Part b, except that Henry is an accrual method taxpayer. What is the amount of his interest expense deduction in the current year?

I7-50 *Itemized Deductions.* During 2006, Doug incurs the following deductible expenses: $2,100 in state income taxes, $2,000 in local property taxes, $800 in medical expenses, and $1,500 in charitable contributions. He is single, has no dependents, and has $35,000 AGI for the year. What is the amount of Doug's taxable income?

I7-51 *Computation of Taxable Income.* During 2006, James, a single, cash method taxpayer incurred the following expenditures:

Qualified medical expenses	$ 8,000
Investment interest expense	16,000
Other investment activity expenses	15,000
Qualified residence interest	12,000
Interest on loan on personal auto	2,000
Charitable contributions	3,000
State income tax paid	7,000
State sales tax paid	4,500
Property taxes	4,000
Tax return preparation and consulting fees	5,000

James's income consisted of the following items:

Salary	$70,000
Interest and dividend income	20,000
Long-term capital gains	23,000
Long-term capital losses	(15,000)

a. Compute James's taxable income for the year (assuming that he makes an election to have the net capital gain taxed at the regular tax rates).
b. What is James' investment interest carryover (if any)?

I7-52 *Computation of Taxable Income.* Assume all the same facts as in Problem I7-51 except that James's salary income is $150,000 instead of $70,000 and that he does not make the election. Compute James's taxable income for the year.

I7-53 *Charitable Contributions: Services.* Donna is an attorney who renders volunteer legal services to a Legal Aid Society, which provides legal advice to low-income individuals. The Legal Aid Society is a qualified charitable organization. During the current year she spends a total of 200 hours in this volunteer work. Her regular billing rate is $150 per hour. In addition, she spends a total of $800 in out-of-pocket costs in providing these services. She receives no compensation and is not reimbursed for her out-of-pocket costs. What is Donna's charitable contribution for the year because of these activities?

I7-54 *Charitable Contribution Limitations.* In each of the following independent cases, determine the amount of the charitable contribution and the limitation that would apply. In each case, assume that the donee is a qualified public charity.
a. Sharon donates a tract of land to a charitable organization. She has held the land for seven years. Her basis in the land is $10,000 and its FMV is $40,000.
b. Assume the same facts in Part a, except that Sharon has held the land for only 11 months and that its FMV is $23,000.
c. Jack purchases a historical document for $50,000. He donates the historical document to a charitable organization two years later. The organization plans to use it for research and study. Its FMV at the time of the donation is $100,000.
d. Assume the same facts in Part c, except that the organization plans to sell the document and put the money into an endowment fund.
e. Valerie donates some inventory to a charitable organization. The inventory is purchased for $500 and its FMV is $1,200 at the time of the donation. She held the inventory for seven months.

I7-55 *Charitable Contributions to Private Nonoperating Foundations.* Assume the same facts as Problem I7-54, except that the qualified organization is a private nonoperating foundation. Determine the amount of the charitable contribution for Parts a through e.

I7-56 *Charitable Contribution Limitations.* During the current year, Helen donates stock worth $50,000 to her local community college. Two years ago the stock cost Helen $40,000. Her AGI for the current year is $100,000. Beginning next year, the bulk of her income will be from tax-exempt municipal securities. Thus, she is not interested in any carryover of excess charitable contribution. What is the maximum charitable contribution deduction Helen may take this year?

I7-57 *Charitable Contribution Limitations.* During the current year, Melissa reports AGI of $200,000. As part of some estate planning, she donates $30,000 to her alma mater, Middle State University, and $65,000 to a private nonoperating foundation.
a. What is the amount of Melissa's charitable deduction for the current year?
b. Assume the same facts in Part a except that she donates $45,000 to Middle State University.

I7-58 *Corporate Charitable Contributions.* Circle Corporation, an accrual method taxpayer, manufactures and sells mainframe computers. In January of the current year, Circle Corporation donates a mainframe that was part of its inventory to City College. City College will use the computer for physical science research. Circle's basis in the mainframe is $300,000. The computer's FMV is $650,000. On December 15 of the current year, Circle also pledged stock to the Red Cross and promised delivery of the stock by March 1 of the following year. The stock's FMV is $100,000 and Circle's adjusted basis in the stock is $50,000. Circle has held the stock for over one year. Circle's taxable income (before deducting any charitable contributions) for the current year is $4,000,000.
a. What is the amount of Circle's charitable contribution for the current year?
b. How much of the contribution can Circle deduct in the current year and how much may be carried over, if any?

I7-59 *Charitable Contribution Carryovers.* Bonnie's charitable contributions and AGI for the past four years were as follows:

	2003	2004	2005	2006
AGI	$50,000	$55,000	$58,000	$60,000
Contributions subject to the 50% limitation	40,000	29,000	25,000	10,000

What is the amount of the charitable deduction for each year and the order in which the deduction and carryovers are used?

COMPREHENSIVE PROBLEM

I7-60 Tim and Monica Nelson are your newest tax clients. They provide you with the following information relating to their 2006 tax return:

1. Tim works as a pediatrician for the county hospital. The W-2 form he received from the hospital shows wages of $150,000 and state income tax withheld of $8,500.

2. Monica spends much of her time volunteering, but also works as a substitute teacher for the local schools. During the year, she spent 900 hours volunteering. When she doesn't volunteer, she earns $8.00 per hour working as a substitute. The W-2 form she received from the school district shows total wages of $3,888 and state income tax withheld of $85.

3. On April 13, the couple paid $250 in state taxes with their 2005 state income tax return. The Nelson's state and local sales taxes in 2006 were $5,500.

4. On December 18, the Nelsons donated a small building to the Boy Scouts of America. They purchased the building three years ago for $80,000. A professional appraiser determined the fair market value of the home was $96,000 on December 12.

5. Tim and Monica both received corrective eye surgery, at a total cost of $3,000. They also paid $1,900 in health insurance premiums.

6. On June 1, the couple bought a car for $16,000, paying $4,000 down and borrowing $12,000. They paid $750 total interest on the loan in 2006.

7. On June 10, the Nelsons took out a home equity loan of $20,000 to expand their home. They paid a total of $850 interest with their monthly payments on the loan.

8. The Nelsons paid a total of $2,300 interest on their original home loan.

9. They sold stock in Cabinets, Inc., for $5,200, which they purchased for $7,900 in March of the current year. They also sold stock in The Outdoor Corporation for $12,500, which they purchased several years ago for $8,600.

10. Tim incurred the following expenses related to his profession, none of which were reimbursed by his employer:

Item	Amount
Subscriptions to medical journals	$400
American Medical Association (AMA) annual membership fee	250

11. During the year, the couple paid their former tax advisor $700 to prepare their prior year tax return.

12. The Nelsons do not have children, and they do not provide significant financial support to any family members.

Required: Compute the Nelson's taxable income for 2006.

TAX STRATEGY PROBLEMS

I7-61 Dean makes a pledge of $30,000 to a local college. The college is willing to accept either cash or marketable securities in fulfillment of the pledge. Dean owns stock in Ajax Corporation worth $30,000. The stock was purchased five years ago for $10,000, Dean's marginal tax rate is 35%. Should Dean sell the stock and then donate the cash, or should he donate the stock directly? Compute the net tax benefit from each alternative and explain the difference.

I7-62 On December 5, 2006, Rebecca Ward, a single taxpayer, comes to you for tax advice. At the end of every year, she donates $3,800 to charity. She has no other itemized deductions. This year, she plans to make her charitable donation with stock. She presents you with the following information relating to her stock investments:

Corporation	FMV on Dec. 1	Adjusted Basis	Date Purchased
Sycamore	9,600	7,800	5/22/02
Oak	2,900	3,800	9/10/03
Redwood	5,400	4,900	6/15/05

Which stock should Rebecca donate to charity? What other tax advice would you give her?

TAX FORM/RETURN PREPARATION PROBLEMS

I7-63 Following is a list of information for Peter and Amy Jones for the current tax year. Peter and Amy are married and have three children, Aubrynne, Bryson, and Caden. They live at 1846 Joplin Way, Lakeville, MN 55022. Peter is a lawyer working for a Native American law firm. Amy works part-time in a genetic research lab. The Jones' Social Security numbers and ages are as follows:

Name	S.S. No.	Age
Peter	215-60-1989	32
Amy	301-60-2828	28
Aubrynne	713-84-5555	5
Bryson	714-87-2222	3
Caden	714-89-1684	1

Receipts

Peter's salary	$70,000
Amy's salary	32,000
Interest income on municipal bonds	2,400
Interest income on certificate of deposit (Universal Savings)	3,100
Dividends on GM stock	1,600

Disbursements

Eyeglasses and exam for Aubrynne	$ 600
Orthodontic work for Bryson to correct a congenital defect	2,500
Medical insurance premiums	1,800
Withholding for state income taxes	7,200
Withholding for federal income taxes	16,000
State income taxes paid with last year's tax return (paid when the return was filed in the current year)	500
Property taxes on home	1,100
Property taxes on automobile	300
Interest on home	9,700
Interest on credit cards	200
Cash contribution to church	3,900

In addition to the above, on September 17, Peter and Amy donate some Beta Trader, Inc. stock to Lakeville Community College. Beta Trader, Inc. is publicly traded. The FMV of the stock on the date of the contribution is $700. Peter and Amy had purchased the stock on November 7, 2001 for $300.

Compute Peter and Amy's income tax liability for the current year using Form 1040, Schedules A and B, and Form 8283, if necessary.

I7-64 Kelly and Chanelle Chambers, ages 47 and 45, are married and live at 584 Thoreau Drive, Boston, MA 59483. Kelly's Social Security number is 254-93-9483 and Chanelle's is 374-48-2938. The Chambers have two children; Emma, age 23, and Chet, age 19. Their Social Security numbers are 385-64-8496 and 385-68-9462, respectively. Emma is a single college student and earned $8,000 during the summer. Kelly and Chanelle help Emma through school by paying for her room, board, and tuition. Emma lives at home during the summer. Chet has a physical handicap and lives at home. He attends a local university and earned $4,000 working for a marketing firm. In sum, Kelly and Chanelle provide more than 50% of both Emma's and Chet's total support for the year.

Kelly is a commercial pilot for a small airline. His salary is $95,000, from which $19,000 of federal income tax and $8,000 of state income tax were withheld. Kelly also pays premiums for health, disability, and life insurance. $2,000 of the premium was for health insurance, $250 for disability, and $400 for life insurance.

Chanelle owns Alliance Networks, a proprietorship that does network consulting. During the year, Chanelle's gross revenues were $23,000. She incurred the following expenses in her business:

Liability insurance	$ 700
Software rental	5,400
Journals and magazines	150

Training seminars	1,200
Supplies	1,300
Donations to a political campaign fund	800

Kelly enjoys playing guitar and plays in a band. Kelly's band has developed a local following. This year, his gross revenues were $1,200 for playing shows and $700 on CD sales. He incurred the following expenses:

Studio rent expense	$1,300
Sound system repairs	200
CD production	500
New guitar and amplifier	800

Kelly's father passed away during the year. Kelly and Chanelle received $100,000 from the life insurance policy. Neither Kelly nor Chanelle paid any of the premiums.

Chanelle purchased 100 shares of Thurston Co. stock on May 1, 1991, for $1,000. Thurston Co. was declared bankrupt during the current year.

Chet's physician recommended that he see a physical therapist to help with his disability. Kelly paid the therapist $7,000 during the year because his insurance would not cover the bills.

Kelly and Chanelle went to Las Vegas and won $5,000 at the blackjack table. The next night, they lost $6,000.

Kelly and Chanelle gave $900 to their church and, during the year, they had the following other income and expenses:

Real estate taxes	$1,400
Property taxes on car (determined by value)	500
Home mortgage interest	9,000
Credit card finance charges	2,600
Tax return preparation fees ($600 is allocable to Corinne's business)	1,000
Sales tax on purchases during the year	6,200
Interest from a savings account	800
Interest from City of Boston Bonds	700
Dividend from 3M stock	400

Prepare Kelly and Chanelle's tax return Form 1040 and Schedules A, B, C, and SE for the current year.

CASE STUDY PROBLEMS

I7-65 Brian Brown, an executive at a manufacturing enterprise, comes to you on December 1 of the current year for tax advice. He has agreed to donate a small tract of land to the Rosepark Community College. The value of the land has been appraised at $58,000. Mr. Brown purchased the land 14 months ago for $50,000. Mr. Brown's estimated AGI for the current year is $100,000. He plans to retire next year and anticipates that his AGI will fall to $35,000 for all subsequent years. He does not anticipate making any additional large charitable contributions. He understands that there are special rules dealing with charitable contributions, and wants your advice in order to get the maximum overall tax benefit from his contribution. Because the college plans to use the property, selling the land is not an alternative. You are to prepare a letter to Mr. Brown explaining the tax consequences of the different alternatives. His address is 100 East Rosebrook, Mesa, Arizona 85203. For purposes of your analysis, assume that Mr. Brown is married and files a joint return. Also assume that Mr. Brown feels that an appropriate discount rate is 10%. In your analysis, use the tax rate schedules for the current year.

I7-66 For several years, you have prepared the tax return for Alpha Corporation, a closely held corporation engaged in manufacturing garden tools. On February 20 of the current year, Bill Johnson, the president of Alpha Corporation, delivered to your office the files and information necessary for you to prepare Alpha's tax return for the immediately preceding tax year. Included in this information were the minutes of all meetings held by Alpha's Board of Directors during the year in question.

Then on February 27, Bill stops by your office and hands you an "addendum" to the minutes of the director's meeting held December 15 of the tax year for which you are preparing the tax return. The addendum is dated the same day as the director's meeting, and authorizes a charitable contribution pledge of $20,000 to the local community college. With a wink and a big smile, Bill explains that the addendum had been misplaced. In reviewing the original minutes, you find no mention of a charitable contribution pledge.

What should you do? (See Appendix E and the *Statements on Standards for Tax Services* section in Chapter I15 (or C1 of the *Comprehensive* volume) for a discussion of these issues.)

TAX RESEARCH PROBLEMS

I7-67   Mark Hancock is a self-employed attorney who operates his law practice as an unincorporated sole proprietorship. In 2005, the IRS disallowed several business deductions he took in 2002 and 2003. In addition to paying the deficiency and assessed penalties, he also pays $18,000 in interest on the tax owed. Can he deduct that interest in the current year?

- Sec. 162, Sec. 163
- Reg. Sec. 1.163-9T
- *Kikalos v. Comm.*, 84 AFTR 2d 99-5933

I7-68   Last year Mr. Smith was involved in an automobile accident, severely injuring his legs. As part of a long-term rehabilitation process, his physician prescribes a daily routine of swimming. Because there is no readily available public facility nearby, Smith investigates the possibility of either building a pool in his own back yard or purchasing another home with a pool. In the current year he finds a new home with a pool and purchases it for $175,000. He then obtains some estimates and finds that it would cost approximately $20,000 to replace the pool in the home he has just purchased. He also obtains some real estate appraisals, which indicate that the existing pool increases the value of the home by only $8,000. During the current year, Smith also expends $500 in maintaining the pool and $1,800 in other medical expenses. What is the total amount of medical expenses he may claim in the current year? Smith's AGI for the year is $60,000.

A partial list of research sources is

- Sec. 213
- Reg. Sec. 1.213-1(e)(1)(iii)
- *Richard A. Polacsek*, 1981 PH T.C. Memo ¶81,569, 42 TCM 1289
- *Paul A. Lerew*, 1982 PH T.C. Memo ¶82,483, 44 TCM 918
- *Jacob H. Robbins*, 1982 PH T.C. Memo ¶82,565, 44 TCM 1254

8

CHAPTER

LOSSES AND BAD DEBTS

LEARNING OBJECTIVES

After studying this chapter, you should be able to

▶1 Identify transactions that may result in losses

▶2 Determine the proper classification for losses

▶3 Calculate the suspended loss from passive activities

▶4 Identify what constitutes a passive activity loss

▶5 Determine when a taxpayer has materially participated in a passive activity

▶6 Identify and calculate the deduction for a casualty or theft loss

▶7 Compute the deduction for a bad debt

▶8 Compute a net operating loss deduction

Taxpayers often sustain losses on property sold, exchanged, or otherwise disposed of. If the taxpayer uses the property in a trade or business or holds the property for investment, the tax law generally provides a deduction for these losses. The tax law also provides noncorporate taxpayers a limited deduction for losses on personal-use property that is either stolen or damaged in a casualty. Other losses on personal-use property (e.g., a sale of a personal residence at a loss) are not deductible. The tax law also provides a deduction for losses that taxpayers may incur because of uncollectible business or nonbusiness debts.

This chapter discusses the rules concerning the deductibility of these types of losses.

TRANSACTIONS THAT MAY RESULT IN LOSSES

OBJECTIVE 1

Identify transactions that may result in losses

For taxpayers to deduct a loss on property, the loss must be both realized and recognized for tax purposes. Generally, *realization* occurs in a completed (closed) transaction evidenced by an identifiable event. This is referred to as the closed transaction doctrine. As a general rule, taxpayers recognize realized losses on business or investment property unless a specific provision holds otherwise (see pages I8-6 and I8-7).

EXAMPLE I8-1 ▶

Capital Corporation purchased 500 shares of Data Corporation stock for $10,000 on February 22 of the current year. By October 31 of the same year, the price of the stock declines to $8,000. Even though Capital has suffered an economic loss on the stock, no realization event has occurred, and the corporation may not deduct the $2,000 loss. However, if Capital sells the stock for $8,000 on October 31, it realizes the loss for tax purposes in the current year. ◀

ADDITIONAL COMMENT

If property is used partly for business and partly for personal use, the loss attributable to the business portion is deductible but the loss on the personal-use portion is not unless the loss was sustained in a casualty.

KEY POINT

Anticipated losses, including those for which reserves have been established, are not deductible.

Losses on property may arise in a variety of transactions, including

▶ Sale or exchange of the property

▶ Expropriation, seizure, confiscation, or condemnation of the property by a government

▶ Abandonment of the property

▶ Worthlessness of stock or securities

▶ Planned demolition of the property in order to construct other property in its place

▶ Destruction of the property by fire, storm, or other casualty

▶ Theft

▶ Deductible business expenses exceeding business income, giving rise to a net operating loss (NOL)

SALE OR EXCHANGE OF PROPERTY

The amount of the loss a taxpayer incurs in a sale or exchange of property equals the excess of the property's adjusted basis over the amount realized for the property.[1] The amount realized for the property equals the sum of the money received plus the fair market value (FMV) of any other property received in the transaction. If the property sold or exchanged is subject to a mortgage or other liability, the amount realized also includes the amount of the liability transferred to the buyer.[2] The treatment of any selling costs depends on the type of property sold or exchanged. If the property is inventory (i.e., property normally held for sale in the taxpayer's business), the selling costs are generally deductible expenses in the year in which they are paid or incurred. However, if the sale involves property not normally held for sale by the taxpayer, the selling costs reduce the amount realized from the sale or exchange.

---

[1] Sec. 1001.

[2] *Beulah B. Crane v. CIR*, 35 AFTR 776, 47-1 USTC ¶9217 (USSC, 1947); and Reg. Sec. 1.1001-2.

EXAMPLE I8-2 ▶ Four years ago, Boyer Corporation purchased a plot of land as an investment for $50,000. Unfortunately, local economic conditions worsened after the land was purchased, and its value declined to $35,000. Boyer sells the property in the current year. At the time of the sale, the land is subject to a $10,000 mortgage. The terms of the sale are $25,000 paid in cash with the purchaser assuming the mortgage. Boyer also incurs $2,000 in sales commissions. The amount realized is $33,000 ($25,000 cash + $10,000 mortgage assumed by the buyer − $2,000 commissions). The loss on the sale is $17,000 ($50,000 basis − $33,000 amount realized). ◀

Taxpayers can only deduct losses they incur in the sale or exchange of property used in a trade or business or held for investment. Taxpayers cannot deduct losses they incur in the sale or exchange of personal-use property. Furthermore, the type of deduction a taxpayer may take for a loss realized on the sale or exchange of business or investment property depends on the type of property sold. For example, if the sale is of inventory, the loss is an ordinary loss. If the asset is a capital asset, the loss is a capital loss (see Chapter I5). If the sale is of property used in a trade or business (a Sec. 1231 asset), the type of loss depends on the total net gain or loss realized on all the taxpayer's Sec. 1231 transactions during the year (see Chapter I13).

EXPROPRIATED, SEIZED, OR CONFISCATED PROPERTY

A taxpayer may own property that the government expropriates, seizes, confiscates, or condemns. In these cases, the taxpayer incurs a deductible loss if the taxpayer used the property in a trade or business or held it for investment. However, the Tax Court has held that the confiscation, seizure, condemnation, or expropriation of property does not constitute a theft or a casualty. Rather, it is treated as a sale or exchange. Thus, no deductible loss arises if the seized property is personal-use property.[3] If the seized or condemned property is business or investment property, the classification of the loss depends on the type of property. (See the section in this chapter titled Classifying the Loss on the Taxpayer's Return.) A taxpayer may take the deduction only in the year in which the property is actually seized. Whether formal expropriation or nationalization occurs in a later year is irrelevant.[4] A taxpayer realizes gain if he or she receives compensation for the property in excess of its basis. Under certain circumstances, the taxpayer may defer this gain. (See Chapter I12 for a discussion of the nonrecognition of gain in an involuntary conversion.)

ABANDONED PROPERTY

If a taxpayer's property becomes worthless or if it is not worth placing into a serviceable condition, the taxpayer may simply abandon the property. If the property still has basis, the taxpayer realizes a loss. The taxpayer may not deduct such losses if the property is personal-use property. However, the taxpayer may deduct losses on business or investment property. Furthermore, because the abandonment of property is not a sale or exchange, the loss is an ordinary loss. The amount of the loss is the property's adjusted basis on the date of abandonment. The taxpayer bears the burden of proof to show that the property was actually abandoned. If the property is depreciable (e.g., machinery and buildings), the taxpayer must actually physically abandon it to take the full amount of the loss.[5]

WORTHLESS SECURITIES

A taxpayer may take a deduction for securities that become completely worthless during the tax year.[6] Because the deduction is only available in the year the security actually becomes worthless, both the taxpayer and the IRS may have problems determining the year in which the security becomes worthless. A mere decline in value is not sufficient to create a deductible loss if the stock has any recognizable value. Furthermore, the sale of the stock for a nominal amount such as $1 does not necessarily establish that the stock became

[3] *William J. Powers*, 36 T.C. 1191 (1961).
[4] Rev. Rul. 62-197, 1962-2 C.B. 66 as modified by Rev. Rul. 69-498, 1969-2 C.B. 31. See also *Estate of Frank Fuchs v. CIR*, 24 AFTR 2d 69-5077, 69-2 USTC ¶9505 (2nd Cir., 1969).
[5] Reg. Sec. 1.167(a)-8(a)(4).

[6] For this purpose, a *security* is defined in Sec. 165(g)(2) as stock in a corporation, the right to subscribe for or receive a share of stock in a corporation, or a bond, debenture, note, or certificate of indebtedness issued by a corporation or a government either in registered form or with interest coupons. Promissory notes issued by a corporation are generally not securities.

worthless in the year of the sale. The taxpayer must show that the security is completely worthless and that the security became worthless during the year.

Under Sec. 165, once the taxpayer determines the year of worthlessness, the taxpayer treats the loss as a loss from the sale of a capital asset on the last day of the tax year. Although this provision does not help in determining the year of worthlessness, it does establish a definite date for purposes of measuring whether the loss is short- or long-term. In some cases, this provision causes the loss to be long-term because it extends the time when the worthlessness occurs to the end of the year.

EXAMPLE I8-3 ▶ On February 20 of the current year, Control Corporation enters into bankruptcy with no possibility for the shareholders to receive anything of value. Because the amount of Control Corporation's outstanding liabilities exceeds the FMV of its assets on that date, the stock of the corporation becomes worthless. Janet, a calendar-year taxpayer, owns 500 shares of Control's common stock, which she had purchased for $10,000 through her broker on June 17 of the prior year. Under Sec. 165(g), she treats the loss as having arisen from the sale of a capital asset on the last day of the current year. Thus, Janet incurs a $10,000 long-term capital loss because the holding period for the stock is more than one year. On the other hand, if Janet had received the stock directly from Control Corporation in exchange for either money or other property, and if certain other requirements are met, the stock may qualify as Sec. 1244 stock. Individuals who sustain losses on Sec. 1244 stock receive a limited amount of ordinary loss treatment rather than capital loss treatment. (See the discussion in this chapter under the heading "Losses on Sec. 1244 Stock.") ◀

Under certain circumstances, if a domestic corporation owns worthless securities of an affiliated corporation, the domestic corporation treats the loss as having arisen from the sale of a noncapital asset. This allows the corporation to treat the loss as an ordinary loss rather than as a capital loss.[7] For this exception to apply, the corporation must meet the following requirements:

▶ The domestic corporation that is deducting the loss must own at least 80% of the voting power of all classes of the affiliated corporation's stock (and 80% of all classes of nonvoting stock).

▶ More than 90% of the affiliated corporation's gross receipts for all its taxable years must be from nonpassive income.[8]

DEMOLITION OF PROPERTY
At times, taxpayers, intent on building their own facilities, purchase land with an existing structure that must first be removed. Taxpayers may also demolish a structure they currently use to construct new facilities. In both cases, taxpayers may not deduct any demolition costs or any loss sustained on account of the demolition. Instead, under Sec. 280B, taxpayers must add these amounts to the basis of the land on which the demolished structure previously stood.

OBJECTIVE 2

Determine the proper classification for losses

CLASSIFYING THE LOSS ON THE TAXPAYER'S TAX RETURN

If a loss is deductible, the taxpayer must determine whether the loss is an ordinary loss or a capital loss. In addition, individual taxpayers must also identify the amount as either a deduction *for* or *from* AGI.

---

[7] As explained in Chapter I5, the deductibility of capital losses is limited. For corporate taxpayers, capital losses must initially be offset against capital gains of the current year, and any excess loss is not deductible but must be carried back 3 years and forward for 5 years. Individuals may offset capital losses against capital gains and any excess loss is deductible up to $3,000 per year as an offset to ordinary income. Capital losses in excess of this amount

for an individual are carried forward for an indefinite period. Thus, taxpayers generally prefer ordinary losses rather than capital losses.
[8] Sec. 165(g)(3). *Nonpassive income* includes all income other than royalties, rents, dividends, interest, annuities, and gains from the sale or exchange of stocks and securities.

ORDINARY VERSUS CAPITAL LOSS

Whether a deductible loss is ordinary or capital depends on the type of property involved and the transaction in which the taxpayer sustains the loss. To incur a capital loss, a sale or exchange of a capital asset must occur. If both elements (i.e., a sale or exchange and a capital asset) are not present, the deduction is an ordinary loss. In general, all assets except inventory, notes and accounts receivable, and depreciable property and land used in a trade or business (i.e., property, plant, and machinery) are classified as **capital assets**.[9]

Because a casualty is not a sale or exchange, the destruction of a capital asset in a casualty creates an ordinary rather than a capital loss. Likewise, a deductible loss realized on the abandonment of property is an ordinary loss because an abandonment is not a sale or exchange.

EXAMPLE I8-4 ▶

BOOK-TAX DIFFERENCE

For book purposes, it makes no difference if a gain or loss is ordinary or capital. The full amount of the loss is deductible. However, because corporations may not deduct a capital loss in excess of its capital gains for the year, a book-tax timing (temporary) difference may arise, making an M-1 or M-3 adjustment necessary.

On July 24 of the current year, Jermaine & Associates, LLP sells some investment property for $75,000. The property's adjusted basis is $85,000. The investment property is a capital asset. Jermaine realizes a $10,000 ($75,000 − $85,000) capital loss. If, instead, the property had been destroyed by fire and the partnership had received $75,000 in insurance proceeds, the $10,000 loss would have been an ordinary loss since a casualty is not a sale or exchange. ◀

Certain transactions, though not actually constituting a sale or exchange, receive sale or exchange treatment. For example, if a security owned by an individual investor becomes worthless during the year, the individual treats the loss as a loss from the sale of a capital asset on the last day of the tax year, even though no sale actually occurs. Thus, the loss is a capital loss. Likewise, the seizure or condemnation of property is treated as a sale or exchange.

SECTION 1231 PROPERTY. Whether a loss on a particular transaction is treated as a capital loss may also depend on the gains and losses reported from other property transactions for the tax year. For instance, under Sec. 1231, taxpayers must net certain gains and losses together. If the Sec. 1231 gains exceed the Sec. 1231 losses for the year, the taxpayer treats the net gain as a long-term capital gain. However, if the losses equal or exceed the gains, both the gains and the losses are treated as ordinary. **Section 1231 property** includes real property or depreciable property used in a trade or business and held for more than one year. (See Chapter I13 for a discussion of the netting procedure under Sec. 1231.)

LOSSES ON SEC. 1244 STOCK. Taxpayers generally recognize capital gain or loss on the sale of stock or securities. For individuals, the tax law provides an exception for losses from the sale or worthlessness of small business corporation (Sec. 1244) stock. Individuals may deduct these losses as ordinary losses up to a maximum of $50,000 per tax year ($100,000 for married taxpayers filing a joint return). Any remaining loss for the year is a capital loss.

To qualify the loss as ordinary under Sec. 1244, the following requirements must be met:

▶ The stock must be owned by an individual or a partnership.

▶ The stock must have been originally issued by the corporation to the individual or to a partnership in which an individual is a partner.[10]

▶ The stock must be stock in a domestic (U.S.) corporation.

▶ The stock must have been issued for cash or property other than stock or securities. Stock issued for services rendered is not eligible for Sec. 1244 treatment.

[9] Sec. 1221. Certain other exceptions also exist. The definition of a capital asset is more fully examined in Chapter I5.
[10] Stock received in certain reorganizations of corporations in exchange for Sec. 1244 stock is also considered Sec. 1244 stock. Section 1244 does not apply to stock that the individual has received through other means such as purchase in a secondary market, exchange, gift, or inheritance.

▶ The corporation must not have derived over 50% of its gross receipts from passive income sources during the five tax years immediately preceding the year of sale or worthlessness.[11]

▶ The amount of money and property contributed to both capital and paid-in surplus may not exceed $1 million at the time the corporation issues the stock.

Note that the last test listed above occurs when the corporation *actually issues the stock*. As long as the corporation's capital and paid-in surplus does not exceed $1 million at the time the stock was issued, the individual taxpayer may still report an ordinary loss on the stock even if at the time the loss is realized, the corporation has capital and paid-in surplus in excess of the $1 million limit.

STOP & THINK

Question: Tony, a single taxpayer, incorporated Waffle, Inc., three years ago by contributing $70,000 in exchange for the stock. Waffle owns and operates a small restaurant. Unfortunately, Waffle's business never really became profitable. Tony has been trying to sell the Waffle stock since July of last year, but because the corporation had become insolvent, he couldn't find any buyers. In February of the current year Waffle was judged to be bankrupt. Tony didn't receive anything for his stock. What issues should Tony's tax advisor address with regard to the Waffle, Inc., stock?

Solution: Tony's tax advisor must determine (1) the amount of any realized loss, (2) the year in which the loss is recognized, and (3) the character of the realized loss. The Waffle, Inc., stock is considered a security under Sec. 165. Whenever a security becomes completely worthless and it is determined that the owner will receive nothing for it, the owner realizes a loss to the extent of the security's basis ($70,000). The loss is deemed to be realized in the year in which the security becomes worthless. While the bankruptcy court ruled the stock to be worthless in February of the current year, the fact that Tony could not find any buyers last year because the corporation was insolvent may indicate that the stock really became worthless last year. This determination is important because Tony must recognize the loss in the year in which the stock becomes worthless. Furthermore, the stock is deemed to become worthless on the last day of that year. Since Tony received the stock directly from the corporation in exchange for contributed cash, Waffle, Inc.'s, gross receipts are from business operations, and the capitalization at the time the stock is issued is less than $1 million, the stock qualifies as Sec. 1244 stock. Thus, $50,000 of the loss is characterized as ordinary loss. The remaining $20,000 is a long-term capital loss.

DISALLOWANCE POSSIBILITIES

The tax law may disallow or defer losses incurred in certain transactions and activities. Some of these transactions are the following:

▶ Transfers of property to a controlled corporation in exchange for stock of the corporation (see the discussion in Chapter C2 of *Prentice Hall's Federal Taxation: Corporations, Partnerships, Estates, and Trusts* text and Chapter C2 of the *Comprehensive* volume)

▶ Exchanges of property for other property considered to be like-kind to the property given up (see the discussion in Chapter I12)

▶ Property sold to certain related parties (see the discussion in Chapter I6)

▶ Wash sale transactions (see the discussion in Chapter I6)

▶ Losses limited because the losses exceed the amount for which the taxpayer is at risk (see the discussion in Chapter C9 of *Prentice Hall's Federal Taxation: Corporations, Partnerships, Estates, and Trusts* text and Chapter C9 of the *Comprehensive* volume)

In addition, the passive loss rules discussed below may limit the amount of losses that individuals and certain corporations may deduct.

Topic Review I8-1 contains a summary of loss transactions.

---

[11] For this purpose, passive income sources include royalties, rents, dividends, interest, annuities, and sales or exchanges of stocks and securities. If the corporation has not been in existence for a full five years, the gross receipts test is applied to the shorter period. If the corporation has not been in existence for an entire taxable year, the test is applied to the time period up to the date of the loss (see Sec. 1244(c)(2)).

Topic Review I8-1

Transactions That May Result in Losses

TYPE OF TRANSACTION	RESULT
Sale or exchange	Taxpayers may not deduct a loss on personal-use property. The tax treatment of a loss on business or investment property depends on the type of property. Losses on capital assets result in capital losses. Losses on Sec. 1231 assets are subject to the Sec. 1231 netting rules discussed in Chapter I13.
Seizure, expropriation, confiscation, or condemnation	Treated as a sale or exchange.
Abandonment	Not treated as a sale or exchange. No deduction is allowed for a loss on personal-use property. Business or investment property is given ordinary loss treatment.
Worthless securities	Treated as a loss from the sale of the securities on the last day of the year in which the securities become worthless. This generally will result in a capital loss. However, if the requirements of Sec. 1244 are met, at least part of the loss may be treated as an ordinary loss. (See Sec. 1244 stock below.) A loss realized by a corporation on worthless securities of an affiliated corporation results in an ordinary loss.
Demolition	No deductible loss is allowed. Instead, losses and costs of demolition are added to the basis of the land where the demolished structure was located.
Sec. 1244 stock	An ordinary loss is allowed for individuals up to $50,000 per year ($100,000 for married filing jointly). The remaining loss is capital. The stock must have been originally issued to the individual for property or cash, and the corporation must meet the requirements to be a small business corporation.

PASSIVE LOSSES

HISTORICAL NOTE

Before the passive activity loss limits became effective in 1987, most tax shelters were concentrated in the areas of real estate, oil and gas, equipment leasing, farming, motion pictures, timber, and research and development. Many tax shelters took advantage of liberal depreciation rules during the early 1980s such as the rapid depreciation of real estate over a 15-year period.

Before 1987, taxpayers were able to reduce their income tax liability on income from one business or investment activity with deductions, losses, and credits arising in another activity. Thus, taxpayers often invested in activities, called **tax shelters**, that would spin off tax deductions and credits. Many of these tax shelters were simply *passive investments* because they did not require the taxpayer's involvement or participation. In some situations, tax shelters had real economic substance, i.e., a taxpayer's economic return in this type of shelter was not based solely on the tax benefits that the activity generated. In many cases, however, tax shelters had no real economic substance other than the creation of deductions and credits that enabled taxpayers to reduce and sometimes eliminate the income tax liability from their other business activities. To prevent these perceived and real abuses, Congress enacted Sec. 469, which restricts the current use of losses and credits that arise in rental activities and in other activities in which the taxpayer does not materially participate. These activities constitute passive activities. (See the "Definition of a Passive Activity" section in this chapter for an extended discussion of what constitutes a passive activity.)

COMPUTATION OF PASSIVE LOSSES AND CREDITS

OBJECTIVE 3

Calculate the suspended loss from passive activities

In enacting the passive loss rules, Congress did not want to prevent taxpayers from currently deducting or using losses and credits generated in active business endeavors of the taxpayer. At the same time, Congress realized that certain investments (such as investments that generate interest or dividend income) normally give rise to taxable income, which could itself be sheltered by losses and credits that arise in other passive activities. Thus, Sec. 469 requires certain taxpayers to classify their income into three categories: *active income* (such as wages, salaries, and active business income), *portfolio (or investment) income*, and *passive income*. **Portfolio income** includes dividends, interest, annuities, and royalties (and allocable expenses and interest expense) not derived in the ordinary course of a trade or business. Portfolio income also includes gains and losses on property that produces these types of income if the disposition of the property does not occur in the ordinary course of business.[12] Portfolio income becomes part of net investment income, which is used in computing the deduction limit for investment interest expense. (See Chapter I7 for a discussion of the investment interest expense limitation.)

PASSIVE INCOME AND LOSSES. Taxpayers compute income and loss in the passive category separately for each passive activity in which they have invested. In general, for any tax year, a taxpayer may use losses generated in one passive activity to offset income from other passive activities, but may not use them to offset either active or portfolio income.

EXAMPLE I8-5 ▶ During the year, Kasi, a CPA, reports $100,000 of active business income from his CPA practice. He also owns two passive activities. From activity A, he earns $10,000 of income, and from activity B, he incurs a $15,000 loss. Kasi may use $10,000 of the loss from activity B to offset the $10,000 of income from activity A. However, Kasi may not deduct the $5,000 excess loss from activity B in the current year, even though he has $100,000 of active business income. ◀

CARRYOVERS

KEY POINT

Excess passive activity losses are not "lost" because they can be carried over to future years.

A taxpayer carries over disallowed passive activity losses indefinitely and treats them as losses allocable to that specific passive activity in the following tax years. The taxpayer may use these losses, known as **suspended losses,** to offset passive activity income of the subsequent year, but generally may not offset other types of income. If a taxpayer has invested in several passive activities, and for the year some of the activities generate income while others generate losses, the loss carried over for each loss activity is a pro rata portion of the total passive loss for the year.

EXAMPLE I8-6 ▶ Tammy reports the following income and loss for the year:

Salary	$200,000
Loss from activity X	(40,000)
Loss from activity Y	(10,000)
Income from activity Z	30,000

X, Y, and Z are all passive activities. The losses generated in activities X and Y offset the income from activity Z, but none of the salary income is offset. Thus, Tammy has a net passive loss for the year of $20,000 ($40,000 + $10,000 − $30,000), which must be carried over to subsequent years. The amount of the carryover attributable to each activity is as follows:

Activity X: $20,000 \times \dfrac{\$40,000}{\$50,000} = \$16,000$

Activity Y: $20,000 \times \dfrac{\$10,000}{\$50,000} = \$ 4,000$ ◀

TAXABLE DISPOSITION OF INTEREST IN A PASSIVE ACTIVITY. When a taxpayer disposes of a passive activity in a taxable transaction, the taxpayer can compute the economic gain or loss generated by the activity and can deduct the suspended losses of the activity against other income. However, the amount of the total net economic loss from the asset disposed of must first offset any passive income for the year from other passive activities.[13]

EXAMPLE I8-7 ▶ During the current year, Pam realizes $6,000 of taxable income from activity A, $1,000 of loss from activity B, and $8,000 of taxable income from activity C. All three activities are passive activities with regard to Pam. In addition, $30,000 of passive losses from activity C are carried over from prior years. During the current year, Pam sells activity C for a $15,000 taxable gain. Pam reports salary income of $90,000 for the year. Because Pam sells activity C in a fully taxable transaction, Pam may deduct $2,000 of loss against the salary income:

---

[12] Sec. 469(e)(1). Gain or loss on property dispositions occurring in the ordinary course of business is either passive or active business income, depending on the taxpayer's level of involvement (i.e., material participation) in the activity.

[13] Sec. 469(g). Income from the activity for prior years may also be taken into account in arriving at the net income from all passive activities for the year if it is necessary to prevent avoidance of the passive loss rules.

Income for the year from C	$ 8,000
Gain from the sale of C	15,000
Suspended losses from C	(30,000)
Total loss from C	($7,000)
Income for the year from A	$ 6,000
Loss for the year from B	(1,000) 5,000
Pam's deduction against salary income	($2,000) ◄

BOOK-TAX DIFFERENCE

Since passive losses are not limited under financial accounting rules, the limitation and carryover of passive losses for tax purposes will create a timing (temporary) difference between book and tax. However, most taxpayers subject to the passive loss rules do not use financial accounting rules.

If the taxpayer sells the passive activity to a related party, he or she may not deduct the suspended loss until the related party sells the activity to a nonrelated person. The definition of *related persons* includes spouse, brothers and sisters, ancestors, lineal descendants, and corporations or partnerships in which the individual has a greater than 50% ownership.[14]

Although the death of a taxpayer is not a taxable disposition of the asset, some of the suspended losses may be deductible when a taxpayer dies. The amount of the deduction allowed is the amount by which the suspended losses exceed the increase in basis of the property. The decedent's final income tax return generally includes the deduction for these losses. Any suspended losses up to the amount of the increase in basis will never be deductible.[15]

EXAMPLE I8-8 ► At the time that John died, he owned passive activity property with an adjusted basis of $20,000 and a FMV of $35,000. Suspended losses attributable to the property totalled $25,000. Because the increase in the basis of the property is $15,000 ($35,000 − $20,000), $15,000 of the suspended losses are lost. However, $10,000 ($25,000 suspended losses − $15,000 increase in basis) of the suspended losses are deductible on John's final income tax return. ◄

In general, the suspended losses of a passive activity become deductible only when the taxpayer completely disposes of his or her interest in the activity. However, in Treasury Reg. 1.469-4(g) the government has stated that taxpayers may treat the disposition of a substantial part of an activity as the disposition of a separate activity. This treatment is only available, however, if the taxpayer can establish with reasonable certainty the amount of income, deductions, credits, and suspended losses and credits that are allocable to that part of the activity.

CARRYOVERS FROM A FORMER PASSIVE ACTIVITY. The determination of whether an activity is passive with respect to a taxpayer must be made annually. Thus, an activity that was previously passive may not be passive with respect to the taxpayer for the current year. This is called a **former passive activity**. A taxpayer may deduct any loss carryover from a former passive activity against the current year's income of that activity even though the activity is not a passive activity in the current year. However, any suspended loss in excess of the activity's income for the year is still subject to the carryover limitations. Because the activity is no longer passive for the year, the current year's loss is deductible against active business income.

EXAMPLE I8-9 ► Kris owns activity A, which, for the immediately preceding tax year, was considered a passive activity with regard to Kris. $10,000 in losses from activity A were disallowed and carried over to the current year. Because of Kris' increased involvement in activity A in the current year, it is not considered passive with regard to Kris for the current year. During the current year, activity A generates a $5,000 loss. During the current year, Kris also has an investment in activity B, a passive activity. Her share of activity B's income is $7,000. Kris reports $60,000 in salary. Because for the current year activity A is not a passive activity, the $5,000 current year loss is fully deductible against her salary. However, the $10,000 loss carryover from the prior year is deductible only against the $7,000 of income from passive activity B. The $3,000 ($10,000 − $7,000) excess is carried over to the subsequent year. ◄

---

[14] Other relationships described in Secs. 267(b) and 707(b) are also considered related parties for this purpose.

[15] Sec. 469(g)(2). Generally, the basis of inherited property is its FMV on the date of death (see Chapter I5).

Credits. A taxpayer may only use tax credits generated in a passive activity against the portion of the tax liability that is attributable to passive income. The taxpayer determines this amount by comparing the tax liability on all income for the year with the tax liability on all income excluding the passive income.

EXAMPLE I8-10 ▶ Dale invests in a passive activity. For the year, he must report $10,000 of taxable income from the passive activity. Dale's share of tax credits generated by the passive activity is $5,000. Assume Dale's precredit tax liability on all income (including the $10,000 from the passive activity) is $25,000, and his precredit tax liability on all income excluding the passive activity income is $22,000. He may use only $3,000 ($25,000 − $22,000) of the tax credits generated by the passive activity. The remaining $2,000 of tax credits is carried forward and may be used in a subsequent year against the portion of the tax liability attributable to passive activity income in that year. However, these credits may never offset any portion of the tax liability attributable to nonpassive activities. (See Chapter I14 for a discussion of credits and their carryovers.) ◀

DEFINITION OF A PASSIVE ACTIVITY

OBJECTIVE 4

Identify what constitutes a passive activity loss

The term *passive activity* includes any rental activity or any trade or business in which the taxpayer does not materially participate.[16] The definition of a passive activity is based on two critical elements: an identification of exactly what constitutes an activity and a determination of whether the taxpayer has materially participated in that activity.

IDENTIFICATION OF AN ACTIVITY. Identification of the activity becomes critical for several reasons. The determination of whether a taxpayer materially participates in an activity is determined separately for each activity. A taxpayer may deduct suspended losses of a passive activity when the taxpayer completely terminates his or her ownership of the activity. As explained in a subsequent section of this chapter, taxpayers may deduct currently up to $25,000 of passive losses from rental real estate activities. Thus, taxpayers must not combine losses from passive business and rental real estate activities into one activity.

The way taxpayers combine or separate operations into activities can significantly impact the deductibility of losses generated by the activities. Taxpayers may treat one or more activities as a single activity only if they constitute an "appropriate economic unit."[17] Although the taxpayer makes this determination by examining all the relevant facts and circumstances, the following factors receive the greatest weight:

▶ Similarities and differences in the types of business
▶ The extent of common control
▶ The extent of common ownership
▶ The geographical location, and
▶ Any interdependencies between the operations (i.e., the extent to which they purchase or sell goods between the activities, have the same customers, are accounted for with a single set of books, etc.).

A taxpayer may treat more than one operation as a single activity, even if all of these factors do not apply. Furthermore, a taxpayer may use any reasonable method of applying the relevant facts and circumstances in grouping the activities.

EXAMPLE I8-11 ▶ Carla owns a bakery and a movie theater in each of two different shopping malls, one located in Baltimore and the other in Philadelphia. Depending on other relevant facts and circumstances, a reasonable grouping of the operations may result in any of the following:

ADDITIONAL COMMENT

Tax year 1991 gave a clearer review of the impact of the passive loss provisions that were enacted in 1986. Net losses of limited partnerships, the types that are used as tax shelters, declined to $16.7 billion in 1991 from $35.5 billion in 1986.

---

[16] Secs. 469(c)(1) and (c)(2). Sec. 469(c)(6) also includes investment (production of income) activities under Sec. 212 as a passive activity. Section 469(j)(8) defines the term *rental activity* as any activity where payments are principally for the use of tangible property. Pursuant to the Regulations, there are six exceptions to this general rule. These exceptions include (1) providing the use of tangible property where the average period of customer use is seven days or less, (2) the average period of customer use is 30 days or less and significant personal services are provided by the owner in conjunction with the use of the property, (3) extraordinary personal services are provided by the

owner in conjunction with the use of the property, (4) the rental of the property is incidental to a nonrental activity of the taxpayer, (5) the property is customarily made available during defined business hours for nonexclusive use by various customers, or (6) the property is provided for use in a nonrental activity conducted by a partnership, S corporation, or joint venture in which the taxpayer owns an interest. The details of these exceptions are beyond the scope of this text. See Reg. Sec. 1.469-1(e)(3)(iii).
[17] Reg. Sec. 1.469-4.

▶ One activity involving all four operations

▶ Two activities: a bakery activity and a theater activity

▶ Two activities: a Baltimore activity and a Philadelphia activity

▶ Four activities ◀

Under the Treasury Regulations, taxpayers apparently have some degree of flexibility in determining the grouping into activities of different business operations. However, once taxpayers establish the activities, they must be consistent in grouping these activities in subsequent years unless material changes in the facts and circumstances clearly make the groupings inappropriate.

In identifying separate activities, taxpayers generally may not group rental operations with trade or business operations. However, a combination is allowed if either the rental operation is insubstantial in relation to the business operation or vice versa. Unfortunately, the Treasury Regulations do not give any guidance with regard to what is insubstantial. Furthermore, because of the special rules dealing with real estate rental activities (explained later in this chapter), the taxpayer may not combine rental activities involving real estate with rental activities involving personal property.

EXAMPLE 18-12 ▶ Sandy owns a building in which she (1) operates a restaurant and (2) leases out apartments to tenants. Generally the tenants sign apartment leases of one year or longer. Of the total gross income derived from the building, 15% comes from the apartment rentals and 85% comes from the restaurant operation. If the apartment rental operation is insubstantial in relation to the restaurant operation, the taxpayer may combine the two into one activity. If it is not insubstantial, the two operations are considered two separate activities: a business activity and a rental real estate activity. ◀

Partnerships and S corporations (pass-through entities) must identify their business and rental activities by applying these rules at the partnership or S corporation level and then must report the results of their operations by activity to the partners or shareholders. Each partner or shareholder must then take the results from these activities and, using these same rules, combine them where appropriate with operations conducted either directly or through other pass-through entities. In fact, taxpayers hold many real estate passive activities as either partnerships or S corporations.

OBJECTIVE 5

Determine when a taxpayer has materially participated in a passive activity

MATERIAL PARTICIPATION. Once each activity is identified, taxpayers must determine whether the activity is passive or active. If the taxpayer does not **materially participate** in the activity, it is deemed to be a passive activity with respect to that taxpayer. Pursuant to the Treasury Regulations,[18] taxpayers materially participate in an activity if they meet at least one of the following tests:

▶ The individual participates in the activity for more than 500 hours during the year.

▶ The individual's participation in the activity for the year constitutes substantially all of the participation in the activity by all individuals, including individuals who do not own any interest in the activity.

▶ The individual participates in the activity for more than 100 hours during the year, and that participation is more than any other individual's participation for the year (including participation by individuals who do not own any interest in the activity).

▶ The individual participates in "significant participation activities" for an aggregate of more than 500 hours during the year.[19] Thus, an individual who spends over 100 hours each in several separate significant participation activities may aggregate the time spent in these activities in order to meet the 500-hour test.

▶ The individual materially participated in the activity in any five years during the immediately preceding ten taxable years. These five years need not be consecutive.

---

[18] Temp. Reg. Sec. 1.469-5T(a).

[19] A significant participation activity is a trade or business in which the individual participates for more than 100 hours during the year but for which the individual does not meet the material participation test alone (i.e., with respect to that activity, the individual does not meet one of the other material participation tests). See Temp. Reg. Sec. 1.469-5T(c).

▶ The individual materially participated in the activity for any three years preceding the year in question, and the activity is a personal service activity.[20]

▶ The individual participates in the activity on a regular, continuous, and substantial basis during the year, taking into account all the relevant facts and circumstances.

<table>
<tr><td>

ADDITIONAL COMMENT

A taxpayer may be a material participant in an activity one year and a passive investor the next year. A taxpayer must satisfy one of the material participation tests each year to be treated as a material participant for that year.

</td><td>

Note that the first four tests are based on the number of hours the taxpayer spent in the activity during the current year. The fifth and sixth tests are based on the material participation of the taxpayer in prior years and are designed to prevent taxpayers from asserting that retirement income is passive and offsetting it with passive losses from tax shelters. To determine whether a taxpayer materially participates in an activity, the participation of the taxpayer's spouse is taken into account.

LIMITED PARTNERSHIPS. A limited partner has limited liability for his or her investment in the partnership and normally is not actively involved in the business of the partnership. As a consequence, a limited partner generally does not meet the material participation test and the limited partner's investment is treated as passive. Thus, most income and deductions passed through to a limited partner from a limited partnership are passive. However, a limited partner can meet the material participation test if the individual meets either the 500 hour test or the fifth and sixth tests above (prior year tests).

WORKING INTEREST IN AN OIL AND GAS PROPERTY. A working interest is an interest that is responsible for the cost of development or operation of the oil and gas property. This type of interest in an oil and gas property is not a passive activity as long as the taxpayer's liability in the interest is not a limited interest. Thus, even though a taxpayer may not materially participate in the activity, the passive loss rules do not apply. This is so even if the taxpayer holds the interest through an entity such as a partnership.

TAXPAYERS SUBJECT TO PASSIVE LOSS RULES

The passive loss limitation rules apply to:

▶ Individuals, estates, trusts

▶ Any closely held C corporation

▶ Any personal service corporation

▶ Certain publicly traded partnerships

Because the income and losses of partnerships and S corporations are taxed directly to the partners and shareholders, the passive loss rules do not apply to these entities.[21] Rather, the passive loss limitations apply directly at the partner or shareholder level. Thus, the situation may arise where one partner or shareholder is subject to the passive loss rules with regard to an activity conducted by the partnership or S corporation while other partners or shareholders are not.

Generally, regular corporations (i.e., C corporations) are not subject to the passive loss limitation rules. However, to prevent certain individuals from avoiding the passive loss rules through the use of a regular corporation, the rules do apply to closely held C corporations and personal service corporations.

</td></tr>
<tr><td>

ADDITIONAL COMMENT

Because a closely held C corporation's passive losses may offset its income from active business operations, some tax professionals advise their clients to transfer their investments that generate passive losses to their profitable corporations.

</td><td>

CLOSELY HELD C CORPORATIONS. The passive loss rules apply to closely held C corporations but only on a limited basis. A **closely held C corporation** is a C corporation where more than 50% of the stock is owned by five or fewer individuals at any time during the last half of the corporation's taxable year.[22] Without this special rule involving

</td></tr>
</table>

---

[20] A personal service activity involves rendering personal services in the fields of health, law, engineering, architecture, accounting, actuarial science, performing arts, or consulting. It also includes any other trade or business in which capital is not a material income-producing factor. See Temp. Reg. Sec. 1.469-5T(d).

[21] An S corporation is a corporation that has elected for federal income tax purposes to be treated basically like a partnership. Thus, the income or losses and separately stated items of an S corporation flow through to the shareholders and are reported on their individual tax returns.

[22] Secs. 469(j)(1), 465(a)(1)(B), and 542(a)(2).

closely held C corporations, taxpayers would be motivated to transfer their investments (both portfolio investments and passive activities) to a C corporation where the portfolio income could be offset by the corporation's passive losses. Thus, as applied to a closely held C corporation, the passive loss rules prevent passive activity losses from offsetting portfolio income. However, a closely held C corporation's passive losses may offset its income from active business operations.

EXAMPLE 18-13 ▶ All of the outstanding stock of Delta Corporation is owned equally by individuals Allen and Beth. During the current year, Delta generates $15,000 taxable income from its active business operations. It also earns $10,000 of interest and dividends from investments and reports a $30,000 loss from a passive activity. Because Delta is a closely held C corporation, the $15,000 of taxable income from the active business is offset by $15,000 of the passive loss. However, the $10,000 of portfolio income may not be offset. Thus, for the current year, Delta reports $10,000 of taxable income from its portfolio income and has a $15,000 passive loss carryover. ◀

PERSONAL SERVICE CORPORATION. A **personal service corporation (PSC)** is a regular C corporation whose principal activity is the performance of personal services that are substantially performed by owner-employees.[23] However, a corporation is not a PSC unless owner-employees own more than 10% of the value of the stock. In contrast with a non-PSC closely held C corporation, the passive loss limitation rules apply in their entirety to a PSC. If a corporation is both a PSC and a closely held C corporation, the more restrictive rules for PSCs apply. Thus, passive losses of a PSC may not offset the PSC's active business income or portfolio income.

MATERIAL PARTICIPATION BY PSCs AND CLOSELY HELD C CORPORATIONS. Special rules apply for determining whether closely held C corporations or PSCs materially participate in an activity. These corporations materially participate in an activity only if one or more shareholders who own more than 50% in value of the outstanding stock materially participate in the activity. In addition, a closely held C corporation (other than a PSC) materially participates in an activity if it meets *all* of the following tests with regard to an activity:

1. A substantial portion of the services of at least one full-time employee is in the active management of the activity.
2. A substantial portion of the services of at least three full-time nonowner employees is directly related to the activity.
3. The Sec. 162 business deductions of the activity exceed 15% of the activity's gross income for the period.[24]

PUBLICLY TRADED PARTNERSHIPS

In many cases, the tax law provisions for corporations apply to publicly traded partnerships (PTP). For purposes of the passive loss rules, a PTP is defined as any partnership if interests in the partnership are either traded on an established securities market or readily tradable on a secondary market.[25] If the corporate tax provisions apply to a PTP, the passive loss rules generally do not apply. However, if a PTP meets certain gross income requirements, the partnership tax provisions may still apply, causing its items of income, loss, and credit to flow through to the partners.[26] If this is the case, the passive loss rules apply at the partner level separately to the flow through items from each PTP. Thus, partners treat losses from a PTP as separate from any other type of income (passive, active

---

[23] Secs. 469(j)(2) and 269A(b)(1). For this purpose any employee who owns any stock of the corporation is an owner-employee. This stock ownership is determined by using the Sec. 318 constructive ownership rules as modified by Sec. 469(j)(2).

[24] Secs. 469(h)(4) and 465(c)(7). Tests 1 and 2 must be met for the 12-month period ending on the last day of the tax year. Test 3 must be met for the tax year. Furthermore, the Sec. 404 deductions are also included in the 15% of gross income test.

[25] Sec. 469(k)(2). See Chapter C10 of *Prentice Hall's Federal Taxation:*

Corporations, Partnerships, Estates, and Trusts and Chapter C10 of the *Comprehensive* volume for a definition and discussion of publicly traded partnerships.

[26] Sec. 7704(c). For the taxable year and all preceding years beginning after Dec. 31, 1987, at least 90% of the PTP's gross income consists of dividends, interest, real property rents, income from certain gas, oil, mineral or timber activities, and gains from the sale of real estate or certain capital assets. Furthermore, certain other PTPs may also elect to continue to be treated as a partnership rather than as a corporation.

business, or portfolio), and separate from any income from other PTPs. Partners can only carry these losses forward and offset them against income generated by that particular PTP in a subsequent year. Furthermore, a PTP loss may not offset any portfolio income that the PTP might generate. Any net income from PTPs is portfolio income.

EXAMPLE I8-14 ▶ Mark owns interests in partnerships A and B, both of which are PTPs that are treated as partnerships. During the current year, Mark's share of the income from A is $2,000. Mark's share of B's loss is $1,200. B also generates some portfolio income. Mark's share of B's portfolio income is $800. The $1,200 loss from B may not offset any of B's $800 portfolio income. Furthermore, it may not offset any of the $2,000 income from A. The $2,000 income from A is treated as portfolio income. Thus, Mark reports $2,800 portfolio income and has a $1,200 suspended loss from B. In a subsequent year, Mark's share of any income from B can be offset by the $1,200 of suspended loss that is carried forward. ◀

Partners may deduct suspended losses from a PTP only in the year the partner disposes of his or her interest in the PTP. Partners do not recognize a loss in the year that the PTP itself sells a passive activity.

RENTAL REAL ESTATE TRADE OR BUSINESS

In general, rental activities are considered passive activities. However, the passive activity loss rules do not apply to certain taxpayers who are involved in real property trades or businesses. Instead, these activities are treated as active businesses. A real property trade or business involves the development, redevelopment, construction, reconstruction, acquisition, conversion, rental, operation, management, leasing, or brokering of real property.

This exception only applies to a taxpayer if he or she meets both of the following requirements:

▶ More than one-half of the personal services the taxpayer performs in all trades or businesses during the year are in real property trades or businesses in which the taxpayer materially participates.

▶ The taxpayer performs more than 750 hours of work during the taxable year in real property trades or businesses in which the taxpayer materially participates.

In meeting these tests, personal services a taxpayer renders in his or her capacity as an employee are not treated as performed in real property trades or businesses unless the employee owns at least 5% of the employer. Furthermore, for married taxpayers filing a joint return, the exception applies only if one of the spouses separately meets both requirements. The time spent in the activity by both spouses counts toward the determination of whether or not the taxpayer meets the material participation test.

EXAMPLE I8-15 ▶ Anwar and Anya are married and file a joint return. They own four large apartment complexes which they manage themselves. Neither is employed elsewhere. During the current year, Anya spent 500 hours keeping records and corresponding with tenants. Anwar spent 700 hours during the year maintaining and repairing the apartments. Even though all of Anya and Anwar's personal services are connected with a real property trade or business in which they materially participate, this rental activity is considered passive because neither Anwar nor Anya alone spends more than 750 hours doing services related to the rental activity. ◀

For a closely held C corporation to meet this rental real estate business exception, the corporation must derive more than one-half of its gross receipts from real property businesses in which it materially participates.

Any deduction allowed under the previously discussed exception for taxpayers involved in real property trades or businesses is not considered in determining the taxpayer's AGI for purposes of the phase-out of the $25,000 deduction available for taxpayers who actively participate in a rental real estate activity. (See the following section in this chapter for a discussion of the $25,000 active participation exception.)

OTHER RENTAL REAL ESTATE ACTIVITIES

Many rental real estate activities are not considered rental real estate businesses and are, therefore, subject to the passive loss rules. However, if an individual taxpayer meets certain requirements, the taxpayer still may deduct against other income up to $25,000 of annual losses from these passive rental real estate activities. To meet this exception, an individual must do both of the following:

▶ *Actively* participate in the activity

▶ Own at least 10% of the value of the activity for the entire tax year

Additionally, in order to take a deduction in the current year for a loss sustained in a prior year, Section 469(i) requires the taxpayer to actively participate in the activity during both years.

KEY POINT

Active participation is different from *material participation,* and is a lesser standard of involvement.

ACTIVE PARTICIPATION. A taxpayer can achieve *active participation,* as opposed to material participation, without regular, continuous, and material involvement in the activity and without meeting any of the material participation tests. However, the taxpayer still must participate in making management decisions or arranging for others to provide services in a significant and bona fide sense. This includes approving new tenants, deciding on rental terms, approving expenditures, and other similar decisions. Taxpayers may achieve active participation even if they hire a rental agent and others provide the services. However, a lessor under a net lease arrangement generally does not achieve active participation. Additionally, a limited partner generally cannot actively participate in any activity of a limited partnership.

ADDITIONAL COMMENT

In calculating AGI to determine the amount of the $25,000 that is phased out, married taxpayers filing joint returns must include the income of both spouses. This provision results in a marriage penalty where both spouses have income.

LIMITATION ON DEDUCTION OF RENTAL REAL ESTATE LOSS. Taxpayers must first apply rental real estate losses against other net passive income for the year. Taxpayers may then reduce their portfolio or active business income by up to $25,000. However, the tax law requires reduction of the $25,000 amount by 50% of the taxpayer's AGI in excess of $100,000.[27] For this purpose, AGI does not include any passive activity loss or any loss allowable to taxpayers who materially participate in real property trades or businesses (e.g., a real estate developer). Thus, if a taxpayer has AGI of $150,000 or more, the rental real estate losses are not eligible for the $25,000 deduction and are aggregated with the taxpayer's other passive losses.

EXAMPLE I8-16 ▶

During the current year, Penny, a married individual who files a joint return, reports the following items of income and loss:

Salary income	$120,000
Activity A (passive)	15,000
Activity B (nonbusiness rental real estate)	(50,000)

Penny owns over 10% and actively participates in activity B. Her AGI for the year is as follows:

Salary		$120,000
Passive income from activity A	$15,000	
Minus: Passive loss from activity B ($50,000, but limited to $15,000)	(15,000)	–0–
Minus: Maximum rental real estate loss (from activity B)	$25,000	
Reduced by phase-out: [($120,000 − $100,000)× 0.50]	(10,000)	
Deductible amount (but not to exceed actual loss)		(15,000)
AGI		$105,000

Penny may deduct $30,000 of the loss from activity B during the year ($15,000 as an offset to the passive income from activity A + $15,000 deductible against portfolio or active business income). Penny has $20,000 ($50,000 − $30,000) of suspended passive losses from activity B that are carried over to the following year. ◀

---

[27] This reduction does not apply to any portion of a passive activity loss attributable to the commercial revitalization deduction under Sec. 1400I. The commercial revitalization deduction is beyond the scope of this discussion. Additionally, AGI is modified by certain items that are beyond this discussion.

The $25,000 limit applies to the sum of both deductions and credits. Thus, in order to properly apply the limit, taxpayers must convert the credits into deduction equivalents. A *deduction equivalent* is an amount that, if taken as a deduction, would reduce the tax liability by an amount equal to the credits. The amount of deduction equivalents can be computed by dividing the amount of the credit by the taxpayer's marginal tax rate. If the sum of the deductions and the deduction equivalents exceeds the $25,000 limit, the taxpayer must first use the deductions.

EXAMPLE I8-17 ▶ Hal owns over 10% of activity A, in which he actively participates. Activity A is a passive real estate rental activity. Hal's marginal tax rate is 25% and he has AGI of less than $100,000. For the year, activity A generates a $20,000 net loss and $10,000 in tax credits, which amounts to $40,000 in deduction equivalent {$10,000/25%}. After deducting the $20,000 net loss against his active business and portfolio income, Hal has a remaining real estate deduction under the limit of $5,000 ($25,000 − $20,000). Thus, Hal may use $1,250 ($5,000 × 0.25) of the credits. The remaining $8,750 ($10,000 − $1,250) of tax credits must be carried over to subsequent years. ◀

If deductions and credits exceeding the $25,000 limit arise from more than one passive activity, the taxpayer must allocate the deductions and credits between the activities.[28]

EXAMPLE I8-18 ▶ Mary has AGI of less than $100,000 and a 25% marginal tax rate. During the year she reports a $30,000 loss from activity A and a $10,000 loss from activity B, neither one of which involves a commercial revitalization deduction. Additionally, activity A generates $5,000 of tax credits. Both activities A and B are passive real estate rental activities in which Mary actively participates and owns over 10% of each activity. The $25,000 deduction is first allocated to the losses. Because the sum of the losses ($40,000) exceeds the limit, the deductible loss must be allocated ratably between the activities as follows:

Activity A: $25,000 × $30,000 ÷ $40,000 = $18,750
Activity B: $25,000 × $10,000 ÷ $40,000 = $6,250

Activity A has an $11,250 ($30,000 − $18,750) suspended loss, and activity B has a $3,750 ($10,000 − $6,250) suspended loss. In addition, activity A has $5,000 of suspended tax credits. ◀

Topic Review I8-2 summarizes the passive activity loss rules.

? STOP & THINK

Question: Jana is a businesswoman who has successfully invested in various stock and bond funds. Now she is considering diversifying her holdings by investing in real estate. One of the alternatives she is considering is purchasing an interest in a limited partnership that invests in real estate. A friend is also urging Jana to go into a partnership with him in order to purchase a small office building they would rent out. Assume that the size of Jana's investment in the two alternatives would be exactly the same and that Jana estimates the economic results to be equivalent (e.g., she expects both to spin off equivalent losses for the first few years and then begin turning a profit). What tax issues should Jana consider when making her investment decision?

Solution: In comparing alternatives such as these, of course, the most important considerations should be the non-tax factors such as cash flow from the investment, the capital appreciation of the assets, the marketability of the investment, and the risk. For example, as a limited partner, Jana will not personally be liable for debts of the partnership or lawsuits filed against the partnership. Purchase of the office building as a general partner with her friend will cause her to be personally liable unless it is done through an LLC or LLP. Additionally, in comparing these two alternatives, certain tax issues may come into play. Both alternatives are investments in rental real estate. However, Jana is not eligible to deduct up to $25,000 of the passive losses from the limited partnership because she will

---

[28] A taxpayer may earn different types of credits, based upon the different types of investments. Furthermore, the phase-out of the $25,000 limit is treated differently for different types of credits. For example, the phase-out for the rehabilitation credit only begins when the taxpayer's AGI exceeds $200,000. Additionally, there is no phase-out applied to the credit for low income hous-ing. See Sec. 469(e)(3) and Chapter I14 for a discussion of these credits. Thus, taxpayers are required to allocate the deductions and credits among the activities and account for them in a specific order. A complete analysis of these rules is beyond the scope of this discussion. Example I8-18 assumes both activities earn the same type of credit and are subject to the $25,000 limit.

Topic Review I8-2

Passive Losses

TOPIC	SUMMARY
Taxpayers covered	Individuals, estates, trusts, closely held C corporations, personal service corporations, certain publicly traded partnerships.
Passive activity	Any trade or business activity in which the taxpayer does not materially participate. Includes all rental activities except for certain rental real estate activities and exceptions contained in regulations. Does not include working interests in oil and gas property.
Limitation	Passive losses are deductible against passive income, but not against active or portfolio income. Disallowed losses are carried over to subsequent years (suspended losses). Losses must be accounted for separately by activity. Activities are identified by examining the taxpayer's undertakings.
Suspended losses	Must be allocated and attributed among the passive activities that generated the losses.
Disposition of interest	Suspended losses may be deducted in the year of a taxable disposition. For inherited property, suspended losses in excess of the increase in basis may be deducted on the final return of a decedent. Losses up to the amount of the basis increase are lost.
Material participation	Must be regular, continuous, and substantial. The regulations contain seven separate tests; four based on current-year participation; two based on participation in prior years; and one based on facts and circumstances.
Real property trades or businesses	Passive activity loss rules do not apply to taxpayers who materially participate in real property trade or business activities constituting more than 750 hours. Additionally, more than one-half of the taxpayer's personal services must be performed in real property trades or businesses in which the taxpayer materially participates.
Rental of real estate	Individuals may deduct losses up to $25,000 against active and portfolio income if they actively participate in the activity and own at least 10% of the value of the activity. Additionally they may take certain credits generated in passive rental activities in which they actively participate. Active participation is a lesser standard than material participation, but the taxpayer must still participate in management decisions or arranging for others to provide services. The deduction and credits phase out at a 50% rate for AGI in excess of $100,000.

not actively participate in the partnership. On the other hand, if she is involved in management decisions regarding the office building, she will be actively participating and will be eligible for the $25,000 passive loss deduction exception. Of course, the benefit of this exception is phased out if her AGI exceeds $100,000.

CASUALTY AND THEFT LOSSES

OBJECTIVE 6

Identify and calculate the deduction for a casualty or theft loss

Taxpayers may deduct losses incurred in connection with business or investment property, but taxpayers generally are not allowed a deduction for losses on personal-use property. However, under Sec. 165, taxpayers may take a limited deduction if the loss on personal-use property arises from a fire, storm, shipwreck, other casualty, or theft. In other words, losses on personal-use property are deductible only if the loss results from a casualty. In order for an event to qualify as a casualty, the event must meet certain requirements.

CASUALTY DEFINED
According to the IRS, a deductible **casualty loss** is one that occurs in an identifiable event that is sudden, unexpected, or unusual.[29]

---

[29] IRS *Publication No. 547* (Nonbusiness Disasters, Casualties, and Thefts), 2004, p. 4.

IDENTIFIABLE EVENT. Because the event that causes the loss must be *identifiable*, the act of losing or misplacing property is generally not considered a casualty.

However, in some cases, taxpayers have proven that the loss of property was the result of an identifiable event.

EXAMPLE I8-19 ▶

> One evening Troy and his wife, Lynn, go to the theater. Troy accidentally slams the car door on Lynn's hand. The impact breaks the flanges holding the diamond in her ring. As a result, the diamond falls from the ring and is lost. In this case, a deductible casualty loss has occurred.[30]◀

KEY POINT

The taxpayer has the burden of proof to establish that a loss was caused by a casualty. The taxpayer should gather as much evidence as possible. Newspaper clippings, police reports, photographs, and insurance reports can be helpful in establishing the cause of the loss.

SUDDEN, UNEXPECTED, OR UNUSUAL EVENTS. According to the IRS, a *sudden event* is one that is swift, not gradual or progressive. An *unexpected event* is one that is ordinarily unanticipated and not intended. An *unusual event* is one that is not a day-to-day occurrence and that is not typical of the activity.

Thus, the IRS has ruled that a deductible casualty loss occurred when a taxpayer went ice fishing and his automobile fell through the ice.[31] A taxpayer whose automobile was damaged as the result of an accident also sustained a deductible casualty loss. However, a taxpayer may not deduct losses incurred in an accident caused by the taxpayer's willful negligence or willful act.[32] Damage sustained as the result of an accident in an automobile race was held to be nondeductible because accidents occur often and are not unusual events in automobile races.[33]

The following are a few examples of events that the courts have held to constitute a deductible casualty loss:

ADDITIONAL COMMENT

Sudden, unexpected, or unusual events must also be accompanied by an external force. For example, a blown engine in an automobile is a sudden event but because no external force caused the event, the loss is not a casualty loss.

▶ Rust and water damage to furniture and carpets caused by the bursting of a water heater

▶ Damage to the exterior paint of a residence caused by a severe, sudden, and unexpected concentration of chemical fumes in the air

▶ Loss caused by fire (unless the taxpayer sets the fire, in which case no deduction is available)

▶ Damage to a building caused by an unusually large blast at a nearby quarry or a jet sonic boom[34]

▶ Death of trees just a few days after a sudden infestation of pine beetles[35]

The following are examples of events that the courts have held *not* to be a casualty:

▶ Water damage to the walls and ceiling of a taxpayer's personal residence as the result of the gradual deterioration of the roof[36]

▶ Trees dying because of gradual suffocation of the root systems

ETHICAL POINT

A client loses his diamond ring while fishing and wants to deduct the loss as a casualty. The CPA should not sign the tax return unless he or she believes that the client's position has a realistic possibility of being sustained on its merits if challenged, which is doubtful in this situation.

▶ The loss of trees and shrubs because of disease[37]

▶ Damage to carpet and clothing caused by moths and carpet beetles[38]

▶ Damage to a road due to freezing, thawing, and gradual deterioration[39]

▶ Damage to a residence caused by the gradual sinking of the land underneath the home[40]

▶ Damage caused by drought because it occurs through progressive deterioration

▶ The steady weakening of a building caused by normal wind and weather conditions

▶ The rusting and deterioration of a water heater[41]

---

[30] *John P. White*, 48 T.C. 430 (1967), *acq.* 1969-2 C.B. xxv. In another case, the taxpayer convinced the Tax Court to allow a deduction for a lost diamond, even though the taxpayer could not remember a specific blow to the ring. In this instance, the taxpayer obtained an expert witness to testify that the flanges of the ring were strong enough and in good enough repair that the loss of the diamond had to have been caused by a sudden, unexpected blow rather than by progressive deterioration.
[31] Rev. Rul. 69-88, 1969-1 C.B. 58.
[32] *Willie C. Robinson*, 1984 PH T.C. Memo ¶84,188, 47 TCM 1510 and Reg. Sec. 1.165-7(a)(3).
[33] Ltr. Rul. 8227010 (March 30, 1982) contains the above examples.
[34] *Ray Durden*, 3 T.C. 1 (1944), *acq.* 1944 C.B. 8 and Rev. Rul. 60-329, 1960-2 C.B. 67.
[35] Rev. Rul. 79-174, 1979-1 C.B. 99. See also *Charles A. Smithgall v. U.S.*, 47 AFTR 2d 81-695, 81-1 USTC ¶9121 (D.C.-Ga., 1980). However, the IRS has ruled in Ltr. Rul. 8544001 (July 12, 1985) that no casualty loss results when the time interval between the infestation and the death of the trees was too long.

[36] *Lauren Whiting*, 1975 PH T.C. Memo ¶75,038, 34 TCM 241.
[37] *William R. Miller*, 1970 PH T.C. Memo ¶70,167, 29 TCM 741 and Rev. Rul. 57-599, 1957-2 C.B. 142. See also *Howard F. Burns v. U.S.*, 6 AFTR 2d 6036, 61-1 USTC ¶9127 (6th Cir., 1960).
[38] Rev. Rul. 55-327, 1955-1 C.B. 25. See also *J. P. Meersman v. U.S.*, 18 AFTR 2d 6152, 67-1 USTC ¶9125 (6th Cir., 1966).
[39] *Howard Stacy*, 1970 PH T.C. Memo ¶70,127, 29 TCM 542. However, the breaking up of a road over a 4-month period because of extreme weather conditions was held to be a casualty. See *Emmett J. O'Connell v. U.S.*, 29 AFTR 2d 72-596, 72-1 USTC ¶9312, (D.C. Cal., 1972). See also *Stephen L. Shaffer*, 1983 PH T.C. Memo ¶83,677, 47 TCM 285.
[40] *Henry W. Berry*, 1969 PH T.C. Memo ¶69,162, 28 TCM 802. See also *David McDaniel*, 1980 PH T.C. Memo ¶80,557, 41 TCM 563.
[41] IRS *Publication No. 547* (Nonbusiness Disasters, Casualties, and Thefts), 2004, contains the above examples.

At times it is very difficult to determine under the particular facts whether the necessary incidents of suddenness, unexpectedness, or unusualness exist. For example, damage caused by the sudden infestation of pine beetles in some instances has been held to be a casualty, but in other instances it has not constituted a casualty.[42]

THEFT DEFINED

Under Sec. 165, a taxpayer may also deduct a loss sustained as the result of a theft. This includes theft of business, investment, or personal-use property. The Treasury Regulations state that "the term theft shall be deemed to include, but shall not necessarily be limited to, larceny, embezzlement, and robbery."[43] A determination whether other actions also constitute theft often depends on whether the action involves criminal intent and the action is illegal under the state law where the action has occurred. Thus, the IRS has stated that blackmail, extortion, and kidnapping for ransom may also constitute theft.[44]

DEDUCTIBLE AMOUNT OF CASUALTY LOSS

The amount of a casualty loss deduction depends on the amount of the loss sustained, any insurance or other reimbursement received, and, in the case of personal-use property, the limitations imposed under the tax law.

MEASURING THE LOSS. In general, the amount of loss sustained in a casualty is the amount by which the casualty reduces the property's FMV. This is measured by comparing the property's FMV immediately before and immediately after the casualty.[45] The amount of the loss may not include any reduction in the FMV of the taxpayer's surrounding but undamaged property.

EXAMPLE 18-20 ▶

ADDITIONAL COMMENT

Taxpayers cannot deduct a loss unless they own the damaged property. Therefore, a taxpayer cannot deduct amounts he or she paid to another individual for damage he or she caused to the other individual's property.

Gail purchased a vacation home for $310,000. Shortly after she purchased the property, a mudslide completely destroyed several neighboring cabins. Gail's cabin sustained no damage. After the slide, an appraisal reveals that the FMV of the cabin has declined to $250,000 because of fears that other mudslides might occur. The $60,000 reduction in the FMV of the cabin does not constitute a deductible casualty loss. ◀

The taxpayer must use actual market value, not sentimental value, to compute the reduction in the FMV. Additionally, the cost of protecting property to prevent damage from a casualty is not a deductible loss.

If the property involved in the casualty is only partially destroyed, the amount of the loss is the lesser of the reduction in the property's FMV or the taxpayer's adjusted basis in the property.

EXAMPLE 18-21 ▶
TYPICAL MISCONCEPTION

Taxpayers sometimes think their loss should be based on the total economic loss rather than just the property's basis. Taxpayers should remember that they have not paid a tax on the appreciation in value and, therefore, should not be entitled to a deduction for a loss on the unrealized gain.

Troy purchased a home for $225,000 several years ago. Through the years, the value of the home appreciated until it was appraised at $325,000 in the current year. Shortly after the appraisal, a flood swept through the area and severely damaged Troy's home. After the flood, the value of the home declined to $90,000. Troy does not have any flood insurance. His loss is limited to the $225,000 basis in the home even though the economic loss is $235,000 ($325,000 − $90,000). ◀

If business or investment property is totally destroyed in a casualty, the amount of the loss is the taxpayer's adjusted basis in the property, even if it is greater than the property's FMV. However, if personal-use property is totally destroyed, the amount of the loss is limited to the lesser of the reduction in the property's FMV or the property's adjusted basis.

[42] Rev. Rul. 79-174, 1979-1 C.B. 99 and *George K. Notter*, 1985 PH T.C. Memo ¶85,391, 50 TCM 614. A graphic illustration of the controversy that may arise when determining whether an event is a casualty can be made by comparing the following two cases. In one case the taxpayer was washing dishes. Seeing a glass of water on the windowsill, he quickly dumped the contents down the drain and turned on the garbage disposal, not realizing that his wife's rings were in the glass. Damage to the rings in this case was deemed to be a casualty (*William H. Carpenter*, 1966 PH T.C. Memo ¶66,228, 25 TCM 1186). In the second case, the taxpayer gathered up some tissues

from the night stand and flushed them down the toilet, not knowing that his wife's rings were wrapped in one of them. This event was held not to be a casualty (*W.J. Keenan, Jr. v. Bowers*, 39 AFTR 849, 50-2 USTC ¶9444 (D.C.-S.C., 1950)).
[43] Reg. Sec. 1.165-8(d).
[44] Rev. Rul. 72-112, 1972-1 C.B. 60 and IRS *Publication No. 547* (Nonbusiness Disasters, Casualties, and Thefts), 2004, p. 1.
[45] Reg. Sec. 1.165-7(a)(2).

EXAMPLE I8-22 ▶ A machine Beth uses in her business is completely destroyed by fire. At the time of the fire, the adjusted basis of the machine is $5,000 and its FMV is $3,000. Because the machine is business property, Beth's loss is $5,000. If the machine were a personal-use asset, the amount of the loss would be $3,000. ◀

ADDITIONAL COMMENT

In 2005, Congress passed emergency tax relief for persons affected by Hurricane Katrina. Casualty losses on personal use property which arise in the Hurricane Katrina disaster area on or after August 25, 2005 that are attributable to Hurricane Katrina will not be subject to the $100 limitation or the 10% of AGI limitation. However, the 10% of AGI limitation for other losses shall be applied without regard to these losses.

Generally, taxpayers must establish the reduction in the FMV of the property by an appraisal. If an appraisal is difficult or impossible to obtain, the taxpayer may use the cost of the repairs instead. The repairs must meet all of the following requirements before the taxpayer may use this alternative:

▶ The repairs will bring the property back to its condition immediately before the casualty.

▶ The cost of the repairs is not excessive.

▶ The repairs do no more than repair the damage incurred in the casualty.

▶ The repairs do not increase the value of the property over its value immediately before the casualty.

If the same casualty destroys more than one property, the taxpayer calculates the loss on each property separately.[46] Thus, the taxpayer compares each property's basis with the reduction in the FMV of that property, rather than aggregating the basis and FMV amounts for all the properties destroyed in the casualty.

If the taxpayer receives insurance or any other type of recovery, the taxpayer must reduce the amount of the loss by these amounts. In some cases these payments may actually exceed the taxpayer's basis in the property, causing the realization of a gain. If certain requirements are met, taxpayers may defer or exclude the recognition of these gains. (See the detailed discussion of involuntary conversions in Chapter I12.)

LIMITATIONS ON PERSONAL-USE PROPERTY

The amount an individual may deduct for a casualty loss on personal-use property is subject to two limitations: (1) losses sustained in each separate casualty must be reduced by $100, and (2) the total amount of all net casualty losses for personal-use property is reduced by 10% of the taxpayer's AGI for the year. For property destroyed in the same casualty, only $100 is deducted from all the properties. (The taxpayer does not reduce the loss from each separate property by $100.)

EXAMPLE I8-23 ▶ A windstorm blows over a large tree in front of Cathy's house, damaging the house and totally destroying her automobile. After the insurance reimbursement, the loss on the house amounts to $3,000, and the loss on the automobile is $2,500. Because the losses occur in the same casualty, the total amount of the loss is reduced to $5,400 ($3,000 + $2,500 − $100). If the damage to the car was sustained in a separate event such as an automobile accident, the total amount of the casualty losses incurred by Cathy during the year would have been $5,300 ($3,000 + $2,500 − $200). This $5,300 or $5,400 loss is then further reduced by 10% of Cathy's AGI for the year. ◀

EXAMPLE I8-24 ▶ As the result of a storm, Liz incurs a $4,500 casualty loss on personal-use property during the current year. She also sustains a $600 theft loss. Liz's AGI for the year is $50,000. She receives no tax deduction for the casualty and theft losses because they do not exceed the following limitations:

KEY POINT

Many taxpayers cannot deduct their casualty losses because of the $100 floor and 10% of AGI limitation.

	Storm	Theft	Total
Loss before limitations	$4,500	$600	$5,100
Minus: $100 floor	(100)	(100)	(200)
	$4,400	$500	$4,900
Minus: 10% of AGI (0.10 × $50,000)			(5,000)
Deductible loss			0 ◀

---

[46] Reg. Sec. 1.165-7(b)(2). For personal-use property, losses on real property and improvements to the property are computed in the aggregate. Thus, no separate basis need be apportioned to the improvements. See Reg. Secs. 1.165-7(b)(2)(ii) and 1.165-7(b)(3) Example (3).

Because of these limitations, many taxpayers who sustain casualty and theft losses on personal-use property do not receive a tax deduction. Furthermore, if the taxpayer's insurance covers the property, the taxpayer cannot take a casualty loss deduction unless he or she timely files an insurance claim for the loss. This disallowance relates only to the portion of the loss covered by the insurance.

Below is a summary of the rules concerning deductibility of casualty losses:

Result of Casualty		Business	Investment	Personal Use
Total Destruction	Amount of Casualty[a]	Basis	Basis	Lesser of: basis or decline in FMV, reduced by $100 and 10% of AGI
	Type	For AGI	From AGI (For AGI if Rental)	From AGI
Partial Destruction	Amount of Casualty[a]	Lesser of: basis or decline in FMV	Lesser of: basis or decline in FMV	Lesser of: basis or decline in FMV, reduced by $100 and 10% of AGI
	Type	For AGI	From AGI (For AGI if Rental)	From AGI

[a]All amounts are first reduced by any insurance reimbursement.

NETTING CASUALTY GAINS AND LOSSES ON PERSONAL-USE PROPERTY

Taxpayers must net casualty gains and losses incurred during the year on personal-use assets. They are not combined with casualty gains and losses on business and investment property. For purposes of the netting process, the losses should be reduced by any insurance reimbursements and the $100 limitation, but not the 10% of AGI floor. If the gains exceed the losses for the year, all the gains and losses are treated as capital gains and losses.

EXAMPLE I8-25 ▶

During the current year, Pat incurs the following casualty gains and losses on personal-use assets. Assets W and X are destroyed in one casualty, and asset Y is destroyed in another. Pat acquired assets X and Y in the current year, whereas she acquired asset W several years ago.

Asset	Reduction in FMV	Adjusted Basis	Insurance	Holding Period
W	$10,000	$3,000	$10,000	More than 12 months
X	4,000	5,000	2,000	Less than one year
Y	2,000	3,000	0	Less than one year

Pat realizes a $7,000 ($10,000 − $3,000) gain on asset W because the insurance proceeds received for the asset exceed its basis. She realizes a $2,000 ($4,000 reduction in FMV − $2,000 insurance) loss on asset X. This loss is reduced to $1,900 because of the $100 reduction for personal casualty losses. She realizes a $2,000 loss on asset Y. Because this loss of $2,000 is realized as a result of the second casualty, the $100 limitation is deducted, resulting in a $1,900 loss from that casualty. Pat realizes a $3,200 [$7,000 − ($1,900 + $1,900)] net casualty gain for the year. Thus, the gain or loss on each asset is treated as a capital gain or loss. Pat must report a $7,000 long-term capital gain on asset W, a $1,900 short-term capital loss on asset X, and a $1,900 short-term capital loss on asset Y. ◀

If the casualty losses on personal-use property exceed the casualty gains for the year, the taxpayer must further reduce the net loss by 10% of AGI. The taxpayer performs all of these calculations (the netting process and reductions) on Form 4684. If any loss remains after the netting and reductions, the taxpayer reports the loss as an itemized deduction on Schedule A of Form 1040.

CASUALTY GAINS AND LOSSES ATTRIBUTABLE TO BUSINESS AND INVESTMENT PROPERTY

Taxpayers must net casualty gains and losses on business and investment property. (See Chapter I13 for a discussion of the netting procedure under Sec. 1231.) If the losses exceed the gains, the business losses and losses on investment property that generate rents or royalties are *for* AGI deductions. Losses on other investment property (e.g., the theft of a security) are itemized deductions but are not subject to the 2% of AGI floor or the overall reduction of itemized deductions imposed if AGI exceeds certain limitation amounts. The $100 or 10% of AGI limitations do not apply to losses on business and investment property.

WHEN LOSSES ARE DEDUCTIBLE

In general, taxpayers must deduct casualty losses in the tax year in which the taxpayer sustains the loss. In the following instances, however, taxpayers may deduct the loss in another year:

▶ Theft losses

▶ Insurance or other reimbursements that the taxpayer can reasonably expect to receive in a subsequent year

▶ Certain disaster losses (discussed later in this chapter)

THEFT. Taxpayers must deduct a theft loss in the tax year in which the taxpayer discovers the theft. This rule is equitable and practical because a taxpayer may not discover a theft until a subsequent year.

EXAMPLE I8-26 ▶

Dale owns a hunting lodge in upstate New York. Sometime after his last trip to the lodge in November 2006, someone breaks into the lodge and steals several guns and paintings. Dale discovers the theft when he returns to the lodge on May 19, 2007. Dale's insurance does not cover the entire cost of the items. The loss is deductible in 2007, even though the theft may have occurred in 2006. ◀

INSURANCE AND OTHER REIMBURSEMENTS. Taxpayers must subtract any reimbursement received as compensation for a loss in arriving at the amount of the loss. This is necessary even when the taxpayer has not yet received the reimbursement, as long as there is a reasonable prospect that the taxpayer will receive it in the future. Thus, the taxpayer may not take a deduction in the year of loss if in that year a reasonable expectation of full recovery exists.[47] If no anticipation of full recovery exists, the taxpayer may deduct a loss in the year the casualty occurs for the estimated unrecovered amount. As previously mentioned, the taxpayer may not take a deduction to the extent the taxpayer has insured the personal-use property and the taxpayer does not file a timely insurance claim.

EXAMPLE I8-27 ▶

In December of the current year, Andrea suffers a $10,000 casualty loss when her personal automobile is struck by a city bus. Although she does not receive any reimbursement from the insurance company by December 31, she reasonably expects to recover the full amount. Andrea may not deduct a casualty loss in the current year. ◀

EXAMPLE I8-28 ▶

Assume the same facts as in Example I8-27, except that Andrea reasonably anticipates her reimbursement from the insurance company will be only $7,000. In this case, her casualty loss in the current year is $3,000 (before reduction by the limitations). ◀

If the taxpayer does not receive the full amount of the anticipated recovery in the subsequent year, he or she may deduct the unrecovered portion. However, rather than filing an amended return for the year of loss, the taxpayer deducts the loss in the subsequent year. Thus in some cases, the taxpayer may spread the income tax consequences for a single casualty loss over two years.

EXAMPLE I8-29 ▶

During the current year, Javier's home is damaged by an exceptionally severe blast at a nearby stone quarry owned by Acme Corporation. Although the amount of the damage is properly appraised at $20,000, Javier can reasonably anticipate a recovery of only $15,000 from Acme

---

[47] Reg. Sec. 1.165-1(d)(2)(i).

Corporation at the end of the current year. He does not receive any recovery from Acme during the current year. Unfortunately, in the subsequent year Acme Corporation is declared bankrupt, and Javier does not receive any reimbursement. Javier's AGI is $40,000 in the current year and $45,000 in the subsequent year. During the current year, Javier may deduct $900 {$5,000 loss reasonably anticipated in the current year − [$100 limitation + (0.10 × $40,000)]}. In the subsequent year, Javier may deduct an additional casualty loss of $10,500 [$15,000 additional loss − (0.10 × $45,000)]. ◄

If a taxpayer receives a subsequent recovery for a previously deducted loss, the taxpayer includes the reimbursement in income in the year of recovery. The taxpayer does not file an amended return. However, the amount that the taxpayer must include in income is limited to the amount of tax benefit the taxpayer received for the previous deduction.

EXAMPLE I8-30 ▶ During the current year, Becky's automobile sustains $5,000 in damages when it is struck by another automobile. The driver of the other automobile is at fault and is uninsured, and Becky does not reasonably expect to recover any of the loss. Becky's AGI for the current year is $35,000. Becky deducts $1,400 ($5,000 loss − [$100 + $3,500]). During the subsequent year, the other driver reimburses Becky for the full amount of the damage. Because Becky received a tax benefit of only $1,400 for the loss in the year of the accident, she must only include $1,400 in gross income in the subsequent year, even though she receives a $5,000 reimbursement. Becky does not file an amended return for the year of the accident. ◄

REAL-WORLD EXAMPLE

In 2005, certain parts of Louisiana, Mississippi and surrounding areas were declared disaster areas due to Hurricane Katrina.

DISASTER LOSSES. Under certain circumstances, a taxpayer may elect to deduct a casualty loss in the year preceding the year in which the loss actually occurs. This election is available to taxpayers who suffer losses attributable to a disaster that occurs in an area subsequently declared by the President of the United States as a disaster area.[48] Thus, an individual can elect to deduct a disaster loss occurring in 2006 on his or her 2005 tax return or report it in the regular way on his or her 2006 return. The taxpayer must file an amended return (Form 1040X) unless he or she has not filed the prior year's return when the disaster occurs. This election allows taxpayers the possibility of receiving financial help sooner from potential tax refunds by filing an amendment to the prior year's return.

Topic Review I8-3 summarizes the casualty loss deduction rules.

STOP & THINK

Question: Due to a series of hurricanes that hit Louisiana during the current year, many homes, roads, and other property are destroyed. Because of the tremendous destruction, the President of the United States declares the area a disaster area. One of the properties totally destroyed is Jack's vacation home in New Orleans. Jack uses the home exclusively for vacationing. The value of the home is $190,000. Unfortunately, Jack had not insured the home against a hurricane. What issues must Jack consider in determining the year in which to take the casualty loss?

Solution: Since the property was destroyed in a disaster and is located in an area which the President subsequently declared as a disaster area, Jack may take the casualty deduction either in the year of the casualty or in the previous year. The year which is most beneficial is based on several factors. The destroyed property was personal use property, so the deduction is an itemized deduction that would normally be subject to the 10% of AGI limitation. Thus, Jack should compare his estimated AGI for the current year with his AGI in the last year. However, if Jack's casualty loss is a result of Hurricane Katrina, it is not subject to this limitation or the $100 reduction. He also should consider his other itemized deductions, including any other casualty losses that might be subject to the $100 or 10% of AGI limitation. In addition, he should compare his marginal tax rates in the two years. Jack should also consider the time value of money, since by taking the deduction on his prior year return, he will receive the tax benefit earlier than if he takes the deduction on the current year return.

[48] Sec. 165(i). Additionally, the same treatment may apply under Sec. 165 to taxpayers who live in a disaster area and who are ordered by a state or local government to move from or relocate their residence because the disaster caused the residence to be unsafe. In order to qualify for this treatment, the order to move must come from the state or local government within 120 days of the date that the President determines the area to be a disaster area. If the property destroyed in a presidentially declared disaster area is the taxpayer's principal residence and the casualty results in a gain, the taxpayer may exclude a portion of the gain if certain conditions are met (see Chapter I12).

Topic Review I8-3

Casualty Losses

Type of Property	Limitation and Treatment
Personal use	The amount of the loss is the lesser of the property's adjusted basis or the reduction of the asset's FMV. This amount is reduced by any insurance reimbursement. If the insurance reimbursement exceeds the property's basis, a gain is realized. To the extent the property is insured, a claim must be filed or the loss is disallowed.
	The amount of loss incurred in each separate casualty event during the year is reduced by $100.
	All casualty gains and losses for the year are netted. If the gains exceed the losses, all gains and losses are treated as capital gains and losses. If the losses exceed the gains, the net loss is reduced by 10% of AGI. Any remaining loss is an itemized deduction.
Business or investment	If the property is totally destroyed, the amount of the loss is the adjusted basis of the property. If only partially destroyed, the amount of the loss is the lesser of the property's adjusted basis or the reduction of the asset's FMV. This amount is reduced by any insurance reimbursement. A gain is realized if the insurance reimbursement exceeds the property's basis.
	For property held one year or less, the losses and gains are ordinary losses and gains. For property held over one year, the casualty gains and losses for the year are netted. The treatment depends on the total of the taxpayer's other Sec. 1231 transactions (see Chapter I13). Business casualty losses and losses on investment property that generate rents or royalties are not subject to the $100 or 10% of AGI limitations.

BAD DEBTS

In addition to losses on property, taxpayers may also sustain losses generated by uncollectible debts. In dealing with a deduction for **bad debts**, taxpayers must address the following requirements and issues:

▶ A bona fide debtor-creditor relationship must exist between the taxpayer and some other person or entity.

▶ The taxpayer must have basis in the debt.

▶ The debt must actually have become worthless during the year.

▶ The type and timing of a bad debt deduction depend on whether the debt is a business or nonbusiness bad debt.

▶ Generally, taxpayers may use only the specific write-off method of accounting in deducting the bad debt.

▶ A partial or complete recovery of a debt that was previously deducted may occur. In many cases a recovery of this type causes income recognition in the year of the recovery.

BONA FIDE DEBTOR-CREDITOR RELATIONSHIP

Only items constituting bona fide debt are eligible to be deducted as a bad debt. A **bona fide debt** is one that arises from a valid and enforceable obligation to pay a fixed or determinable sum of money and results in a debtor-creditor relationship.[49]

RELATED-PARTY TRANSACTIONS. Determining whether a bona fide loan transaction has actually taken place is especially critical when the transaction is between the taxpayer and a family member or other related party (e.g., a controlled corporation). The taxpayer must carefully examine all the facts and circumstances surrounding the transaction because a gift does not constitute a debt. The taxpayer's intent is critical here. For example, if the taxpayer's intent is to provide property, cash, or services to someone else

KEY POINT

The tax provisions that deal with deductions for losses and the tax provisions that deal with the deductions for bad debts are mutually exclusive, and an amount properly deductible as a loss cannot be deducted as a bad debt or vice versa.

KEY POINT

The fact that the debtor is a related party does not preclude deduction of a bad debt, but the taxpayer should be able to document the debt as being bona fide.

---

[49] Reg. Sec. 1.166-1(c).

without receiving any consideration in return, a gift—not a loan—has been made. Some tests used to determine the taxpayer's intent include the following:

▶ Does a note or other written instrument exist which evidences an obligation to repay?[50]
▶ Have the parties established a definite schedule of repayment?
▶ Is a reasonable rate of interest stated?
▶ Would a person unrelated to the debtor make the loan?[51]

EXAMPLE I8-31 ▶

REAL-WORLD EXAMPLE

A taxpayer advanced $8,500 to his son-in-law who operated a live-stock auction barn. The taxpayer was entitled to a bad debt deduction upon default because notations on the checks indicated that they were loans and undisputed testimony indicated that repayment was to be made within 90 days. *Giffin A. Andrew,* 54 T.C. 239 (1970).

During the current year Maria loaned $20,000 to her son Sam, who used the money in his business. Although they signed no written note or contract, Sam orally promised to repay Maria as soon as his business became profitable. No rate of interest was stated. Unfortunately, the business failed and Sam went out of business in the subsequent year. He never repaid the loan principal or interest.

In this case, no valid debt exists because the taxpayer did not establish an interest rate or a repayment schedule. An unrelated person would not have made a loan to Sam under these conditions. In addition, Maria does not receive any consideration in return for the "loan." Since the facts indicate that the transaction is actually a gift, Maria may not claim a bad debt deduction because of Sam's failure to repay. ◀

Tax advisors should also closely examine other related party transactions. For example, a loan from a shareholder to a controlled corporation may actually be an additional contribution to capital disguised as a loan. Thus, a transfer of cash by a shareholder who owns a controlling (i.e., more than 50%) interest in the stock of a corporation may indicate a capital contribution rather than a loan. Likewise, a "loan" from a corporation to a controlling shareholder may actually be a disguised dividend or a salary payment.

THIRD PARTY DEBT. Generally, a taxpayer may deduct a bad debt only when a debtor-creditor relationship exists. However, in some cases a taxpayer will guarantee or endorse someone else's obligation. If the terms of the guarantee force the taxpayer to pay the third party's debt, the guarantor may actually be the creditor. If the original debtor does not repay the taxpayer who guarantees and pays the debt, the guarantor may deduct the loss. Any accrued interest that the guarantor pays may also be deductible as a bad debt. However, the interest is not deductible as interest when paid by the guarantor because it accrued on someone else's debt. Here, too, the taxpayer's intent determines whether the guarantee and payment constitute a gift.

EXAMPLE I8-32 ▶

Ron is the sole shareholder and a full-time employee of Zip Corporation. For Zip Corporation to obtain a bank loan, Ron personally signs a guarantee that the loan will be repaid. Unfortunately, Zip Corporation defaults on the loan and Ron must repay the loan. In this case, Ron signed the guarantee to preserve his job and enhance his investment in Zip Corporation. Although Ron receives no direct consideration for having signed the note, he does receive indirect consideration in the form of continued job security and protection of his investment. Because a business or investment purpose motivated Ron to sign the loan guarantee, Ron may deduct the bad debt. ◀

TYPICAL MISCONCEPTION

Taxpayers sometimes mistakenly assume that a cash method taxpayer can take a bad debt deduction on a debt that arose from services rendered by the taxpayer.

TAXPAYER'S BASIS IN THE DEBT

For a bad debt to be deductible, the creditor must have basis in the debt. The taxpayer may acquire this basis in different ways. If a taxpayer loans money, the taxpayer's basis in the debt is the amount loaned. If the debt arises because the taxpayer provides property or

---

[50] A written note or other instrument is an evidence of a bona fide debtor-creditor relationship. However, if the note or other instrument is registered or has interest coupons and is issued by a corporation or a government, the bad debt provisions of Sec. 166 do not apply. Instead, the worthless security provisions of Sec. 165 (previously discussed) apply.

[51] *Jean C. Tyler v. Tomlinson,* 24 AFTR 2d 69-5426, 69-2 USTC ¶9559 (5th Cir., 1969). See also, *C. L. Hunt,* 1989 PH T.C. Memo ¶89,335, 57 TCM 919, where certain loans that the taxpayer made to his children were treated as bona fide loans, whereas others were treated as gifts. In that case, the chil-

dren had been trading in silver futures and were required to make margin calls. Because they could not make the calls, the children's positions were involuntarily liquidated. Up to the date of the liquidation, the taxpayer had made loans to the children that were payable on demand and were subject to the prime rate of interest. These loans were evidenced by promissory notes. After the liquidation, the taxpayer continued to make loans to the children. However, these loans were not evidenced by notes. The loans up to the time of the liquidation were treated as bona fide loans and the subsequent loans were treated as gifts.

services for the other party, basis is established only if the taxpayer has previously included the FMV of the property or services in income. This often depends on the taxpayer's method of accounting. An accrual method taxpayer generally reports income in the year the services are performed or the property is provided. (See the discussion in Chapter I11.) Thus, an accrual method taxpayer has a basis in either a note receivable or an open account receivable equal to the amount included in gross income (i.e., the FMV of the services). A cash method taxpayer, however, reports income only in the year in which payment in the form of cash or property is received. Because a note constitutes the receipt of property, a cash method taxpayer reports income (and establishes basis) in the year the note is received. However, if the cash method taxpayer does not receive a note and the receivable is an open account item, the taxpayer reports no income until the receivable is collected. Thus, the taxpayer has no basis in the receivable and does not receive a bad debt deduction if the receivable is not collected.

EXAMPLE I8-33 ▶

In October of the current year, Jim performs some legal services for Joy. Jim bills Joy for $10,000. Joy does not sign a note for the debt. As a cash method taxpayer, Jim does not include the $10,000 in his current year's income. After repeated efforts to collect the fee, Jim discovers in June of the subsequent year that Joy has left the city and cannot be found. Jim may not deduct a bad debt for the uncollected amount in the subsequent year because he has not taken the amount into income and he has no basis in the debt. If Joy had signed a note for the debt, Jim would have reported income in the current year in an amount equal to the note's FMV and could have deducted the loss when the note became uncollectible in the subsequent year. ◀

DEBT MUST BE WORTHLESS

To deduct a bad debt, the taxpayer must show that the debt is worthless. This determination is made by reference to all the pertinent evidence, including the general financial condition of the debtor and whether the debt is secured by collateral.

In proving the worthlessness of a debt, a taxpayer does not need to take legal action if the surrounding circumstances indicate that legal action probably would not result in the collection of the debt. By simply showing that legal action is not warranted, the taxpayer provides sufficient proof that the debt is worthless.[52] Indications that an unsecured debt is worthless include bankruptcy of the debtor, disappearance or death of a debtor, and repeated unsuccessful attempts at collection. Furthermore, if the surrounding circumstances warrant it, a taxpayer may deduct a worthless debt even before the debt comes due. As will be explained later in this chapter, a nonbusiness debt must be totally worthless before a deduction is allowed. However, a current deduction is allowed for a partially worthless business bad debt.

NONBUSINESS BAD DEBTS

The distinction between a business bad debt and a nonbusiness bad debt is important because the character of the debt determines its tax treatment. A business bad debt gives rise to an ordinary deduction, whereas a taxpayer must treat a nonbusiness bad debt as a short-term capital loss. All loans made by a corporation are assumed to be associated with the corporation's business; therefore, the provisions for nonbusiness bad debts do not apply to corporations.

DEFINITION OF A NONBUSINESS BAD DEBT. A *nonbusiness debt* is defined as any debt other than (1) a debt created or acquired in connection with a trade or business of the taxpayer or (2) a debt the loss from the worthlessness of which is incurred in the taxpayer's trade or business. This determination depends on an examination of the facts and circumstances surrounding the debt in question.

A debt incurred in a taxpayer's business continues to be a business debt for that taxpayer even if, at the time the debt goes bad, the taxpayer has ceased conducting that particular business. This is situation (1) above. If another taxpayer acquires a business, any outstanding debt at the time the business is acquired continues to be business debt as long as the pur-

---

[52] Reg. Sec. 1.166-2.

chaser continues the business. This is situation (2) above. The debt is a nonbusiness debt if the person who owns the debt when it becomes worthless is not engaged in the business in which the debt is incurred either at the time the debt arose or when it becomes worthless.

EXAMPLE I8-34 ▶ Matt, an individual who uses the accrual method of accounting, is engaged in the grocery business. During 2006, he extends credit to Jeff on an open account. In 2007, Matt sells his business to Joan, but retains Jeff's account. Jeff's account becomes worthless in 2007. Even though Matt is no longer engaged in the grocery business at the time the debt becomes worthless, he may deduct the loss as a business bad debt in 2007. If Joan purchases Jeff's account upon acquiring the grocery business, Joan is entitled to a business bad debt deduction in 2007 because the debt was incurred in the trade or business in which Joan is currently engaged. ◀

In addition, classification as a business debt requires a proximate relationship between the loan and the taxpayer's business.[53] According to the Supreme Court, this relationship exists if a business motive is the taxpayer's dominant motivation in making the loan. This determination must be made on a case-by-case basis. For example, when an individual stockholder who is also an employee of the corporation loans money to the corporation, is the loan a business or nonbusiness debt? Because an employee is considered to be engaged in the business of working for a corporation, a loan made to the corporation in an attempt to protect the employment relationship may be held to be a business debt. However, if the individual's dominant motive is to protect his or her stock investment, the loan is a nonbusiness debt.[54]

EXAMPLE I8-35 ▶ Lisa is an individual engaged in the advertising business. If clients occasionally need additional funds to meet their cash-flow obligations, Lisa sometimes lends them money. Lisa's dominant motive for making the loans is to retain the clients. She has no ownership interests in these clients. Under these facts, if any of these loans becomes worthless, it would be considered a business bad debt.[55] ◀

TAX TREATMENT. Individuals deduct nonbusiness debts that become wholly worthless during the year as short-term capital losses. The length of time the debt is outstanding has no bearing on this treatment.

Individuals generally prefer an ordinary deduction over a short-term capital loss because the tax deduction attributable to net capital losses is limited to $3,000 each year. Any loss in excess of this limit is carried over to subsequent years to be included in the capital gain and loss netting process in those years (see Chapter I5).

EXAMPLE I8-36 ▶

TYPICAL MISCONCEPTION

Partial worthlessness means that a debt is still partially recoverable. The term is sometimes erroneously applied to debt where there has been a partial recovery even though there is no prospect for further recovery.

During 2005, Kim loaned her friend $10,000. The friend used the funds to invest in commodities futures. The transaction had all the characteristics of a bona fide debt rather than a mere gift to a friend. Unfortunately, the commodities market prices declined, and Kim's friend incurred substantial losses. In 2006, Kim's friend declared personal bankruptcy and Kim was unable to collect any of the loan. Kim did not recognize any other capital gains or losses during 2006. The $10,000 bad debt loss recognized in 2006 is treated as a short-term capital loss. Thus, Kim may deduct only $3,000 in 2006. The remaining $7,000 is carried over indefinitely to 2007 and subsequent years. ◀

PARTIAL WORTHLESSNESS. As previously noted, taxpayers may not deduct a partially worthless nonbusiness debt. Thus, a taxpayer cannot deduct a loss for a nonbusiness debt that is still partially recoverable during the year.

EXAMPLE I8-37 ▶ Gordon, an individual, made a $5,000, five-year interest-bearing loan to a small company in 2004. Gordon was not in the trade or business of making commercial loans. In 2006, Gordon received word from the attorney who was appointed trustee of the company that bankruptcy proceedings had been filed. The trustee indicated that, although final disposition of the case will not occur until 2007, Gordon can reasonably expect to receive only 20 cents for every $1

[53] Reg. Sec. 1.166-5(b)(2).
[54] *John M. Trent v. CIR,* 7 AFTR 2d 1599, 61-2 USTC ¶9506 (2nd Cir., 1961). See also *Charles L. Hutchinson,* 1982 PH T.C. Memo ¶82,045, 43

TCM 440 and *U.S. v. Edna Generes,* 29 AFTR 2d 72-609, 72-1 USTC ¶9259 (USSC, 1972).
[55] *Stuart Bart,* 21 T.C. 880 (1954), *acq.* 1954-1 C.B. 3.

invested. Because this is a nonbusiness bad debt that is still partly recoverable in 2006, Gordon may not deduct the partial loss as a short-term capital loss in 2006. ◄

BUSINESS BAD DEBTS

The tax treatment of losses from business bad debts differs substantially from the treatment of nonbusiness bad debts. As previously discussed, a business bad debt provides an ordinary loss deduction. Furthermore, taxpayers may also deduct a business debt that has become only partially worthless during the year.

EXAMPLE I8-38 ▶ Assume the same facts as in Example I8-37 except that Gordon's loan is made for business reasons (e.g., to provide assistance to a customer in financial difficulty). Because 80% of the loan is reasonably expected to be unrecoverable during 2006, Gordon may deduct $4,000 (0.80 × $5,000) as an ordinary loss in 2006. If Gordon receives only $600 in 2007 as a settlement, he may deduct an additional $400 of ordinary loss for the year. ◄

ACCOUNTING FOR THE BUSINESS BAD DEBT

BOOK-TAX DIFFERENCES

In general, for tax purposes, taxpayers can use only the specific write-off method of accounting for bad debts. However, a corporation or other taxpayer would probably be required to use the reserve method for financial reporting purposes. This book-tax difference is one of the most common M-1 or M-3 adjustments in filing a Form 1120 for corporate taxpayers.

In general, two basic methods are available to account for business bad debts: the specific write-off method and the reserve method. Except for certain specialized industries, however, taxpayers can use only the specific write-off method for tax purposes. Under the **specific write-off method,** the taxpayer deducts each bad debt individually as it becomes worthless and writes it off as an expense. Taxpayers use this method for (1) business bad debts that are either totally or partially worthless and (2) nonbusiness bad debts that are totally worthless. However, as previously noted, taxpayers take no deduction for partially worthless nonbusiness bad debts.

In the case of a partially worthless business bad debt, taxpayers may only deduct the worthless part of the debt. The taxpayer must prove to the satisfaction of the IRS the amount of the debt that has become worthless.

RECOVERY OF BAD DEBTS

A taxpayer may collect a debt that was previously written off for tax purposes. Since the taxpayer previously deducted the uncollectible debt, the taxpayer must report the recovery as income in the year it is collected. The amount of the income that must be reported depends on the tax benefit rule discussed in Chapter I4.

DEPOSITS IN INSOLVENT FINANCIAL INSTITUTIONS

KEY POINT

If a loss is treated as a casualty loss, it is subject to a $100 floor, and total net casualty losses for the year are deductible only to the extent that they exceed 10% of AGI.

At their election, qualified individuals may treat a loss on deposits in qualified bankrupt or insolvent financial institutions as a personal casualty loss in the year in which the individual can reasonably estimate the loss. The recognized loss is the difference between the taxpayer's basis in the deposit and a reasonable estimate of the amount that the taxpayer will receive. This treatment allows the individual an ordinary loss deduction, but subjects the loss to the personal casualty loss limitations. In lieu of this election, qualified individuals may elect to treat these losses as if they were incurred in a transaction entered into for profit (but not connected with a trade or business). This election is available only with respect to deposits that are not insured under federal law, and is limited to $20,000 ($10,000 if married and filing separately) per institution per year. This limitation is reduced by any insurance proceeds expected to be received under state law. This election also allows the individual an ordinary loss deduction but subjects the loss to the $20,000 limitation as well as the 2% of AGI floor on miscellaneous itemized deductions. If the taxpayer makes neither of these elections, the taxpayer may claim the loss as a nonbusiness bad debt (a short-term capital loss) in the year of worthlessness or partial recovery, whichever comes last.

A qualified individual is any individual *except* one who

▶ Owns at least 1% of the outstanding stock of the financial institution

▶ Is an officer of the financial institution

▶ Is a relative of an officer or a 1% owner of the financial institution[56]

---

[56] Sec. 165(l). A *relative* is defined as a sibling, spouse, aunt, uncle, nephew, niece, ancestor, or lineal descendant.

Qualified financial institutions include banks, federal or state chartered savings and loans and thrift institutions, and federal or state insured credit unions.

This election applies to all losses sustained by the individual in the same institution and cannot be revoked unless the taxpayer receives IRS permission.[57]

The treatment of business and nonbusiness bad debts is summarized in Topic Review I8-4.

NET OPERATING LOSSES

OBJECTIVE 8

Compute a net operating loss deduction

KEY POINT

If taxpayers were not entitled to a deduction for net operating losses, taxpayers would actually pay a tax on an amount that exceeded their economic income over a period of time. The NOL deduction permits taxpayers to offset taxable income with losses incurred in other years.

A **net operating loss** (NOL) under Sec. 172 generally involves only business income and expenses. An NOL occurs when taxable income for any year is negative because business expenses exceed business income. A deduction for the NOL arises when a taxpayer carries the NOL to a year in which the taxpayer has taxable income. Thus, an NOL for one year becomes a deduction against taxable income of another year. This is accomplished in one of two ways:

▶ The year's NOL is carried back and deducted from the income of a previous year. This procedure provides for a refund of some of the taxes previously paid for the prior year.

▶ The year's NOL is carried forward and deducted from the income of a subsequent year. This procedure provides a reduction in the taxable income of the subsequent year, thus reducing the tax liability associated with that year.

The NOL deduction is intended to mitigate the inequity caused by the interaction of the progressive rate structure and the requirement to report income on an annual basis. This inequity arises between taxpayers whose business income fluctuates widely from year to year and those whose business income remains relatively constant.

EXAMPLE I8-39 ▶ Julie and Ken are both married (not to each other) and both file a joint return with their respective spouses. Over a two-year period they both report a total of $140,000 in taxable income. However, Julie and her husband report $70,000 of taxable income each year; Ken and his wife report $200,000 of taxable income in the first year and a $60,000 loss in the second year. Without the NOL provisions, Julie would report a $21,230 ($10,615 + $10,615) total tax liability for the two years, whereas Ken would report a total tax liability of $45,982 (taxable income of $200,000).[58] However, Ken can carry back the $60,000 loss to recover a portion of the taxes paid on the $200,000 in the prior year. Based on 2006 rates, Ken would recover $17,378 of the $45,982 paid, resulting in a net tax liability for both years of $28,604 ($45,982 − $17,378). Although the total tax liability over the two years for the two couples is still unequal, the ability to carryover NOL's provides some degree of fairness. ◀

Topic Review I8-4

Bad Debts

TYPE OF DEBT	RESULTS
Nonbusiness	Deductible as a short-term capital loss. Deductible only when the debt is totally worthless. The taxpayer must have basis in the debt.
Business	Deductible as an ordinary loss. Except for certain specialized exceptions, the specific write-off method must be used. The reserve method is not available. May deduct partial worthlessness. Must have basis in the debt.

[57] The rules dealing with this special election are found in Notice 89-28, (1989-1 C.B. 667).

[58] Using the 2006 tax rate schedules.

COMPUTING THE NET OPERATING LOSS FOR INDIVIDUALS

ADDITIONAL COMMENT

In computing the NOL for corporations, only minor adjustments are necessary.

ADDITIONAL COMMENT

If taxpayers were permitted to calculate the NOL for the current year by including NOL carryovers from earlier years, they could possibly extend the carryover period beyond the statutorily established 20-year carryforward period.

The starting point in calculating an individual's NOL is generally taxable income. As mentioned earlier in this chapter, individuals may deduct three basic types of expenses to arrive at the amount of taxable income: business-related expenses, investment-related expenses, and certain personal expenses. The NOL, however, generally attempts to measure only the economic loss that occurs when business expenses exceed business income. Thus, individual taxpayers must make several adjustments to taxable income to arrive at the amount of the NOL for any particular year. These include adjustments for an NOL deduction, a capital loss deduction, the deduction for personal exemptions, and the excess of nonbusiness deductions over nonbusiness income.

ADD BACK ANY NOL DEDUCTION. Under certain circumstances, a taxpayer might have taken a deduction for an NOL arising from another tax year in computing the taxable loss for the current loss year. To allow this deduction to create or increase the NOL of the current loss year would provide an unwarranted benefit. Thus, taxable income for the current loss year must be increased for this deduction.

ADD BACK ANY CAPITAL LOSS DEDUCTION. To compute taxable income, individuals may deduct up to a maximum of $3,000 capital losses in excess of capital gains in any year. Any capital loss in excess of this limit can be carried over and deducted in a subsequent tax year, subject to the same limitation. Because capital losses have their separate carryover provisions, taxpayers must add back any deduction associated with these losses to taxable income to arrive at the NOL for the current loss year. To make this adjustment, the taxpayer must follow several steps:

Step 1: A taxpayer must separate nonbusiness capital gains and losses from business capital gains and losses. The nonbusiness gains and losses are then netted, while the business gains and losses are netted separately.

Step 2: If the nonbusiness capital gains exceed the nonbusiness capital losses, the excess, along with other types of nonbusiness income, is first used to offset any nonbusiness ordinary deductions. Any nonbusiness capital gain remaining is then used to offset any business capital loss in excess of the business capital gain for the year.[59]

Step 3: If both groups of transactions result in net losses, the capital loss deduction provided by these transactions must be added back. For purposes of the NOL, no deduction is allowed for either business or nonbusiness net capital losses.

Step 4: If the taxpayer's nonbusiness capital losses exceed the nonbusiness capital gains, the losses may not be offset against the taxpayer's excess business capital gains. Allowing this offset would provide an indirect deduction for a nonbusiness economic loss.[60]

EXAMPLE I8-40 ▶ During the current year, Nils recognizes a short-term capital loss of $10,000 on the sale of an investment capital asset. He also recognizes a $5,000 long-term capital gain on the sale of a business capital asset. For taxable income purposes, the loss is netted against the gain, leaving a $5,000 net short-term capital loss. This loss provides a $3,000 deduction from taxable income, with the remaining $2,000 being carried forward to the following year. To compute the NOL, however, none of the $10,000 nonbusiness capital loss is deductible. Thus, the $3,000 deduction as well as the $5,000 loss that offset the business capital gain must be added back because in computing taxable income the taxpayer, in essence, has received a total $8,000 reduction from the nonbusiness capital loss. ◀

ADD BACK THE DEDUCTION FOR PERSONAL EXEMPTIONS. Because the deduction for personal and dependency exemptions is strictly a personal deduction, it must be added back to arrive at the year's NOL.

---

[59] Reg. Sec. 1.172-3. If the nonbusiness deductions exceed the nonbusiness income, the excess is added back. This adjustment is discussed later in the chapter.
[60] Sec. 172(d)(2). Note that all deductible nonbusiness capital losses involve investment property because capital losses on personal-use assets are not deductible in arriving at taxable income. To make the adjustment for any capital loss, the exclusion under Sec. 1202 for gains from small business stock is not allowed (see Chapter I5).

ADD BACK EXCESS OF NONBUSINESS DEDUCTIONS OVER NONBUSINESS INCOME. Because nonbusiness deductions do not reflect an economic loss from business, they are not deductible in arriving at the NOL. However, these deductions do offset any nonbusiness income reported during the year. Nonbusiness income includes sources of income such as dividends and interest, as well as nonbusiness capital gains in excess of nonbusiness capital losses. Wages and salary, even if they are earned in part-time employment, are considered business income. Nonbusiness deductions include itemized deductions such as charitable contributions, medical expenses, and nonbusiness interest and taxes. Casualty losses on personal-use assets, however, are treated as business losses and are excluded from this adjustment.[61] If a taxpayer does not have itemized deductions in excess of the standard deduction, the standard deduction is used as the amount of the nonbusiness deductions.

Following are several independent examples demonstrating these required adjustments. In each case, assume that Nancy is a single taxpayer.

EXAMPLE 18-41 ▶ During 2006, Nancy, who is single, reports the following taxable income:

Gross income from business			$123,000	
Minus:	Business expenses		(147,000)	($24,000)
Plus:	Interest income			700
	Dividend income			400
AGI				($22,900)
Minus:	Greater of itemized deductions or standard deduction:			
	Interest expense	$ 6,000		
	Taxes	4,000		
	Casualty loss (reduced by the $100 floor)	1,000		
	Total itemized deductions		$ 11,000	
			or	
	Standard deduction		5,150	(11,000)
Minus:	Personal exemption			(3,300)
Taxable income				($37,200)

Nancy's NOL for the year is computed as follows:

Taxable income				($37,200)
Nonbusiness deductions:				
Itemized deductions		$11,000		
Minus:	Casualty loss	(1,000)	$ 10,000	
Minus:	Nonbusiness income:			
	Interest	$700		
	Dividends	400	(1,100)	
Plus:	Excess of nonbusiness deductions over nonbusiness income			8,900
Plus:	Personal exemption			3,300
Net operating loss				($25,000)[a] ◀

[a]Note that the NOL equals the total of the $24,000 net business loss and the $1,000 casualty loss.

EXAMPLE 18-42 ▶ During 2006, Nancy, who is single, reports the following taxable income:

Gross income from business			$123,000	
Minus:	Business expenses		(147,000)	($24,000)
Plus:	Interest income			700
	Dividend income			400
AGI				($22,900)
Minus:	Greater of itemized deductions or standard deduction:			
	Interest expense		$ 2,000	
			or	
	Standard deduction		5,150	(5,150)
Minus:	Personal exemption			(3,300)
Taxable income				($31,350)

[61] Sec. 172(d)(4)(C).

Nancy's NOL for the year is computed as follows:

Taxable income		($31,350)
Nonbusiness deductions:		
Standard deduction	$ 5,150	
Minus: Nonbusiness income:		
Interest	$700	
Dividends	400	(1,100)
Plus: Excess of nonbusiness deductions over nonbusiness income		4,050
Plus: Personal exemption		3,300
Net operating loss		($24,000)ᵃ ◄

ᵃNote that the NOL equals the net business loss for the year.

EXAMPLE I8-43 ▶ During 2006, Nancy, who is single, reports the following taxable income:

Gross income from business		$123,000	
Minus Business expenses		(147,000)	($24,000)
Plus:	Interest income		700
	Dividend income		400
	Salary		6,000
	Nonbusiness LTCG		10,000
AGI			($6,900)
Minus:	Greater of itemized deductions or standard deduction:		
	Interest expense	$ 6,000	
	Taxes	4,000	
	Casualty (reduced by the $100 floor)	1,000	
Total itemized deductions		$ 11,000	
		or	
Standard deduction		5,150	(11,000)
Minus: Personal exemption			(3,300)
Taxable income			($21,200)

Nancy's NOL for the year is computed as follows:

Taxable income			($21,200)
Plus:	Nonbusiness deductions:		
	Itemized deductions	$11,000	
Minus: Casualty loss		(1,000)	$ 10,000
Minus:	Nonbusiness income:		
	Interest	$700	
	Dividends	400	
	LTCG	10,000	(11,100)
Excess of nonbusiness deductions over nonbusiness income			0
Plus:	Personal exemption		3,300
Net operating loss			($17,900)ᵃ ◄

ᵃNote that the NOL can also be calculated as follows:

Loss from business	($24,000)
Salary	6,000
Casualty loss	(1,000)
Excess of nonbusiness income ($11,100) over nonbusiness deductions ($10,000)	1,100
NOL	($17,900)

CARRYBACK AND CARRYOVER PERIODS

Under Sec. 172, an NOL is initially carried back for two years and is deductible as an offset to the taxable income of the carryback years. Except as noted below, taxpayers must carry the loss back first. If any loss remains, taxpayers may then carry it forward for a period of 20 years.[62] Furthermore, in both the carryback and carryforward periods, the loss must be deducted from the years in chronological order. Thus, if an NOL is sustained

---

[62] For NOLs arising in a farming business, in a qualified small business attributable to a Presidentially declared disaster, or in a casualty or theft sustained by an individual, the carryback period is extended to three years. These NOLs are taken after the regular NOL. Certain "specified liability losses" are entitled to a 10-year carryback. Sec. 172(b)(1)(C) and (f).

in 2006, it first must be carried back to 2004, then to 2005, followed by 2007, 2008, and so on until the loss is completely used. Any NOL that is not used during the carryover period expires and is of no further tax benefit.

If the NOL is carried back to a prior year, the taxpayer must file for a refund of taxes previously paid. If the NOL deduction is carried forward, it reduces the taxable income and the tax liability for the carryover year.

ELECTION TO FORGO CARRYBACK PERIOD. A taxpayer may elect not to carry back the NOL, but to carry the loss forward. This election, which is made with respect to the entire carryback period, does not extend the carryforward period beyond 20 years. This allows a taxpayer some degree of flexibility in using the NOL deduction to the greatest advantage. (See the Tax Planning Considerations section in this chapter for a discussion of this topic.)

LOSS CARRYOVERS FROM TWO OR MORE YEARS. At times, a taxpayer might have NOL carryovers that are incurred in two or more taxable years. Often these losses are carried to the same years in the carryover period. If such is the case, the loss of the earliest year is always completely used first before deducting any of the loss incurred in a subsequent year. Because of the limited carryover period, this rule is beneficial to the taxpayer.

RECOMPUTATION OF TAXABLE INCOME IN THE CARRYOVER YEAR

When the taxpayer carries back the NOL deduction to a prior year, the taxpayer must recompute that year's taxable income. Because the NOL is attributable to a taxpayer's trade or business, it is deductible *for* AGI. As a result, the recomputation of taxable income for the carryback year may affect the deductible amount of certain itemized deductions because some of the deductions (e.g., the deductions for medical expenses, charitable contributions, and casualty losses) are limited or measured by reference to the taxpayer's AGI. All of these deductions except the deduction for charitable contributions must be recomputed using the reduced AGI amount.[63]

Once the taxpayer determines the tax refund for the carryback year, the taxpayer must calculate the amount of the NOL available to be deducted in subsequent carryover years. This is done by adjusting the recomputed income of the prior carryover year. Although certain differences exist, these adjustments are similar to those mentioned above.

The rules for computing and deducting NOLs are presented in Topic Review I8-5.

ADDITIONAL COMMENT
An election to forgo the carryback period for the NOL of any year is irrevocable.

Topic Review I8-5

Net Operating Losses

ITEM	RULES
Computation of NOL (adjustments to taxable income)	Add back any NOL deduction carried to the current year. Add back any capital loss deduction. Add back the deduction for personal and dependency exemptions. Add back the excess of nonbusiness deductions over nonbusiness income. For this purpose, casualty losses on personal-use property are treated as business losses.
Carryover period	May be carried back two years and forward twenty years (certain exceptions apply). Must be carried to the carryover years in chronological order: first carried back to the second prior year, then to the first prior year, then to the first succeeding year, etc. An election may be made to forgo the carryback. This does not extend the carryforward period. If losses from two or more years are carried to the same year, the losses from the earliest year are completely used first.

[63] Reg. Sec. 1.172-5(a)(3)(ii).

TAX PLANNING CONSIDERATIONS

BAD DEBTS

To deduct a bad debt, a taxpayer must show that the debt is worthless. At times the IRS might assert that the debt being written off is either not yet worthless or that it became worthless in a previous year. If the taxpayer is unable to overcome the IRS's assertion concerning the year of worthlessness, the taxpayer might be barred from filing an amended return for the prior year because of the statute of limitations.[64] Thus, taxpayers should carefully document all efforts at collection and other facts that show the debt is worthless.

As previously mentioned, a third-party guarantor of a loan who is required to repay the debt may, under certain circumstances, be entitled to a bad debt deduction. The guarantor must demonstrate that he or she received reasonable consideration in the form of cash or property in exchange for guaranteeing the debt. If the taxpayer does not receive proper consideration, the guarantee and subsequent payment of the loan by the guarantor is considered to be a gift rather than a loan. Reasonable consideration is also deemed to be received if the taxpayer enters into the agreement for a good faith business purpose or in accordance with normal business practice. However, if the taxpayer guarantees the debt of a spouse or a relative, the taxpayer must receive the consideration in the form of cash or property.

In the case of an outright loan between related taxpayers, the lender should always make sure to retain proper documentation to substantiate the fact that the transaction is a loan. If the taxpayer does not keep such documentation, the IRS may assert that the transaction is a gift.

CASUALTIES

A deduction is allowed for stolen property, but no deduction is allowed for lost property. Thus, taxpayers should always carefully document losses of property through theft (e.g., the filing of police reports or claims with the taxpayer's insurance company). In addition, pictures and written appraisals may be helpful to prove the amount of the loss.

NET OPERATING LOSSES

If a taxpayer incurs a net operating loss, the taxpayer should carefully analyze whether to elect to forgo the carryback period. Situations under which a taxpayer might elect to only carry the loss deduction forward include the following:

▶ A taxpayer might anticipate being in a higher marginal tax rate in future years than in the carryback years. If such is the case, the value of the deduction is higher in the carryforward years than in the carryback years. Taxpayers should consider, however, cash flows and the time value of money (e.g., the tax benefits from a refund of taxes are immediately available only if the NOL is carried back).

▶ General business and other tax credits that are nonrefundable (i.e., the credits are limited to the tax liability or some percentage thereof) may be reduced or eliminated for the carryback years because these credits must be recomputed based on the adjusted tax liability after applying the NOL carryback. (See Chapter I14 for a discussion of tax credits.)

COMPLIANCE AND PROCEDURAL CONSIDERATIONS

CASUALTY LOSSES

If a taxpayer sustains a casualty loss in a location that the President of the United States declares a disaster area, he or she may make an election to deduct the loss in the year preceeding the year in which the loss occurred. A taxpayer makes this election by either filing

---

[64] However, the statute of limitations for claims for a refund or credit because of a bad debt is extended from three years to seven years under Sec. 6511(d)(1), thus giving the taxpayer additional time if this is the case.

ADDITIONAL COMMENT

Instant access for downloading federal income tax forms, instructions, publications, etc. is available on the Internet (http://www.irs.gov).

the return for the previous year and including the loss in that year (if the return has not already been filed) or filing an amended return or claim for refund for that year.[65] The return should clearly include all the following information:

▶ That the election is being made

▶ The date of the disaster giving rise to the loss

▶ The city, county, and state in which the damaged property is located

The taxpayer must make the election before the due date of the return for the year in which the disaster actually occurs. Although the Regulations state that the election may not be revoked more than 90 days after it is made, the Tax Court has held that this part of the Regulation is invalid.[66]

NET OPERATING LOSSES

When a taxpayer carries an NOL deduction back to a prior year, the taxpayer claims a refund of taxes by either filing an amended return on Form 1040X or filing for a quick refund on Form 1045. Corporations use Form 1139. If the taxpayer uses Form 1045, the IRS must act on the application for refund within 90 days of the later of the date of the application and the last day of the month in which the return of the loss year must be filed.[67] A taxpayer must file Form 1045 within one year after the end of the year in which the NOL arose. The taxpayer must attach additional information such as pages 1 and 2 of Form 1040 for the year of loss, a copy of the application for an extension of time to file the return for the year of loss, and copies of forms or schedules for items refigured in the carryback years.

WORTHLESS SECURITIES

As explained earlier in this chapter, securities that become worthless during the taxable year are deemed to have become worthless on the last day of the year. In many cases, this treatment causes the loss to be treated as a long-term capital loss. If the loss from the worthless security is long term, the taxpayer reports it in Part II of Schedule D (Form 1040) along with the other long-term gains and losses for the year. The taxpayer reports short-term capital losses in Part I of Schedule D.

WHAT WOULD YOU DO IN THIS SITUATION?

A client comes to you with an idea to treat a loan that he made to one of his children two years ago as a bad debt. The loan is evidenced by a properly executed note with stated interest and payment dates. However, the client has not collected any loan payments or interest during the two-year period.

The child is insolvent and has declared bankruptcy. Before leaving your office, the client also mentions in passing that the child is in London on vacation with other members of the family and will stay in Europe for six weeks. What would you do about classifying this loan as a bad debt?

PROBLEM MATERIALS

DISCUSSION QUESTIONS

I8-1 What is the closed transaction doctrine, and why does it exist for purposes of recognizing a loss realized on holding property?

I8-2 When property is disposed of, what factors influence the amount of the deductible loss?

I8-3 Describe the usual tax consequences that apply to a worthless security.

I8-4 Under what circumstances will a loss that is realized on a worthless security not be treated as a capital loss?

---

[65] Reg. Sec. 1.165-11(e).
[66] *Chester Matheson*, 74 T.C. 836 (1980), *acq.* 1981-2 C.B. 2.

[67] IRS, 2005 *Instructions for Filing Form 1045*.

I8-5 What two general requirements must be met for a transaction to result in a capital loss?

I8-6 What requirements must be met for stock to be considered Sec. 1244 stock?

I8-7 What tax treatment applies to gains and losses on Sec. 1244 stock?

I8-8 Describe a situation where a loss on the sale of business or investment property is not currently deductible, and explain why.

I8-9 a. What is a passive activity?
b. Who is subject to the passive loss limitation rules?

I8-10 a. For purposes of the passive loss rules, what is a closely held C corporation?
b. In what way do the passive loss rules differ from the regular passive loss rules when applied to closely held C corporations?

I8-11 Why is it important to identify exactly what constitutes an activity for purposes of the passive activity rules?

I8-12 a. If a taxpayer is involved in several different business operations during the year, how is the determination made as to how many activities these operations constitute for purposes of the passive activity loss rules?
b. Can a business operation and a rental operation ever be combined into one activity? Explain.

I8-13 Which of the following activities are considered passive for the year? Explain. Consider each situation independently.
a. Laura owns a rental unit that she rents out to students. The rental unit is Laura's only business and she spends approximately 875 hours per year managing, collecting the rent, advertising, and performing minor repairs. At times she must hire professionals such as plumbers to do the maintenance. Is the rental unit a passive activity with respect to Laura?
b. Kami is a medical doctor who works four days a week in a medical practice that she and five other doctors formed. Last year she and her partners formed another partnership that owns and operates a medical lab. The lab employs ten technicians, one of whom also acts as manager. During the year Kami spent 120 hours in meetings, reviewing records, etc., for the lab. Is the lab a passive activity with respect to Kami?
c. Assume the same facts in part b. In addition, assume that the same group of doctors have formed two other partnerships. One is a medical supply partnership. Kami spent 150 hours working for this partnership. The medical supply partnership has five full-time employees. Kami also spent 250 hours during the year working for the other partnership. This partnership specializes in providing medical services to individuals from out of town who are staying at local hotels and motels. This part-

nership hires two full-time and six part-time nurses. Are the lab and the two other partnerships passive activities with respect to Kami?

I8-14 Explain the difference between materially participating and actively participating in an activity. When is the active participation test used?

I8-15 a. What requirements must be met in order for a taxpayer to deduct up to $25,000 of passive losses from rental real estate activities against active and portfolio income?
b. What requirements must be met in order for a real estate rental activity to be considered a real estate business that is not subject to the passive loss rules?

I8-16 Are the losses suspended under the passive loss rules lost forever? Explain.

I8-17 What tests must be met to qualify a loss as deductible under the casualty loss provisions? Discuss the application of each of these tests.

I8-18 Explain how a taxable gain on property can be realized because of a casualty event such as a fire or theft. How are these gains treated?

I8-19 During the current year, Rulon's toilet overflowed because of a mechanical problem. Rulon was outside playing croquet, and by the time he returned inside, the water had flooded the basement, causing damage to the carpet, walls, and ceiling. The cost of repairing the damage was $9,000. Rulon has homeowners insurance that will cover half of the damage. However, because he has already had claims this year, Rulon does not want to report the incident to his insurance company for fear of a large increase in insurance rates. Instead, Rulon wants to deduct the loss as a casualty loss on his tax return. His AGI for this year is $50,000, and he has other itemized deductions of $6,000. Rulon is single. What amount of the casualty loss may he deduct?

I8-20 Compare and contrast the computational rules for deducting casualty losses on personal-use property with casualty losses incurred on business or investment property.

I8-21 Under what circumstances may a loss arising from a casualty or theft be deducted in a year other than the year in which the loss occurs?

I8-22 For individuals, how are casualty losses on personal-use property reported on the tax return? How are casualty losses on business property reported?

I8-23 Is the $100 floor on personal-use casualty losses imposed on each individual loss item if more than one item of property is destroyed in a single casualty? Is the floor imposed before or after the casualty gains are netted against the casualty losses?

I8-24 Sarah loans $50,000 to her best friend, John. John uses the money to open a pizza parlor next to the local high school. Three years later, when John still owed Sarah $15,000, John closed the pizza parlor and declared bankruptcy. Discuss the appropriate tax treatment for Sarah.

I8-25 Dana is an attorney who specializes in family law. She uses the cash method of accounting and is a calendar-year taxpayer. Last year, she represented a client in a lawsuit and billed the client $5,000 for her services. Although she made repeated attempts, Dana was unable to collect the outstanding receivable. Finally, in November of the current year, she finds out that the individual has moved without leaving any forwarding address. Dana's attempts to locate the individual are futile. What is the amount of deduction that Dana may take with respect to this bad debt?

I8-26 Under what circumstances may a taxpayer deduct a bad debt even though another party to the transaction is the creditor?

I8-27 What is the definition of a nonbusiness debt? What is the character of the deduction for a nonbusiness bad debt?

I8-28 a. What alternatives do individuals have in deducting a loss on a deposit in a qualified financial institution?
b. Explain when it might be better to elect one over the other.

I8-29 A taxpayer collects a debt that was previously written off as a bad debt. What tax consequences arise if the recovery is received in a subsequent tax year?

I8-30 What is an NOL deduction, and why is it allowed?

I8-31 List the adjustments to an individual taxpayer's negative taxable income amount that must be made in computing an NOL for the year. What is the underlying rationale for requiring these adjustments for individuals?

I8-32 a. What is the NOL carryback and carryover period?
b. Does a taxpayer have any choice in deciding the years to which the NOL should be carried?
c. Explain the circumstances under which a taxpayer might elect not to use the regular carryback or carryover period.

I8-33 Can a casualty loss on a personal-use asset create or increase an NOL? Explain.

I8-34 If an NOL is carried back to a prior year, what adjustments must be made to the prior year's taxable income? What are the possible results of the adjustments?

ISSUE IDENTIFICATION QUESTIONS

I8-35 On January 12 of the current year, Barney Corporation, a publicly-held corporation, files for bankruptcy. During the bankruptcy proceedings it is determined that creditors will only receive 10% of what they are owed and that the shareholders will receive nothing. Sheryl, a calendar-year taxpayer, purchased 1,000 shares of Barney Corporation common stock for $7,000 on February 22 of the prior year. What tax issues should Sheryl consider?

I8-36 Five years ago, Cora incorporated Gold, Inc., by contributing $80,000 and receiving 100% of the Gold common stock. Cora is single. Gold experienced financial difficulties. On December 22 of the current year, Cora sold all of her Gold stock for $5,000. What tax issues should Cora consider?

I8-37 In a rage because of personal difficulties, Evan drove recklessly and crashed his automobile, doing $8,000 worth of damage. Fortunately, no one was injured. Since Evan received two speeding tickets during the past year, he is concerned about losing his insurance if he files an insurance claim. What tax issues should Evan consider?

I8-38 Dan, a full-time employee of Beta, Inc., also owns 10% of its outstanding stock. The other 90% is owned by his three brothers. During the year, the president of Beta came to Dan, expressing grave concern about whether the company had the financial resources to remain in business. He mentioned specifically that a bank was threatening to force Beta to file bankruptcy if it didn't repay its $100,000 loan in full. After some negotiation, Dan agreed to loan Beta the $100,000 for one year until permanent financing could be obtained. A reasonable interest rate was set and a payment schedule was documented. Unfortunately, business did not improve, and Beta discontinued its business and did not repay the loan. What tax issues should Dan consider?

PROBLEMS

I8-39 *Section 1244 Losses.* During the current year, Karen sells her entire interest in Central Corporation common stock for $22,000. She is the sole shareholder, and originally organized the corporation several years ago by contributing $89,000 in exchange for her stock, which qualifies as Sec. 1244 stock. Since its incorporation, Central has been involved in the manufacture of items that protect personal computers from static electricity. Unfortunately, this market is extremely competitive, and Central Corporation incurs substantial losses throughout its existence.
a. Assuming Karen is single, what are the amount and the character of the loss recognized on the sale of the Central Corporation stock?

b. Assuming Karen is married and files a joint return, what are the amount and the character of the loss recognized on the sale of the Central Corporation stock?

c. How would your answer to Part a change if Karen had originally purchased the stock from another shareholder rather than organizing the corporation?

d. How might Karen have structured the transaction in Part a to receive a greater tax advantage?

I8-40 *Amount and Character of Loss Transactions.* On September 30 of the current year Silver Fox Corporation files for bankruptcy. At the time, it estimates that the total FMV of its assets is $725,000, whereas the total amount of its outstanding debt amounts to $950,000. Silver Fox Corporation has been engaged in the resale of tax preparation and tax research-related books and software for several years.

a. At the time of the bankruptcy, Silver Fox is owned by Randall, who purchased the stock from an investor for $250,000 several years ago. Randall is single. What are the amount and character of the loss sustained by Randall upon Silver Fox's bankruptcy?

b. How would your answer to part a change if Randall originally organized Silver Fox Corporation, capitalizing it with $250,000 of cash and assuming Silver Fox qualifies as a small business corporation?

c. How would your answer to Part a change if Randall were a corporation instead of an individual?

d. How would your answer to Part b change if Randall were a corporation instead of an individual?

I8-41 *Character of Losses.* Five years ago, Brian and his brother Boyd formed Stewart Corp., a golf apparel manufacturing corporation. At that time, Brian contributed $300,000 to the corporation in exchange for 50% of its stock. During the current year, Brian needed some cash to purchase a golf course so he sold a third of his interest in Stewart Corp. for $85,000. He also sold stock in the following companies for the amounts indicated:

Corporation	Sales Proceeds	Adjusted Basis	When Acquired
IBM	$15,000	$10,000	52 months ago
Microsoft	25,000	45,000	18 months ago
Tidal Radio	32,000	12,000	7 months ago
Wavetable	20,000	26,000	4 months ago

During the year Brian hired a collection agency to collect a $14,000 loan he made to an old friend, which was due in full on January 1 of the current year. The agency found no trace of his friend. Also during the year, BTR Corporation, in which he owns stock, went bankrupt. His investment was worth $94,000 on January 1, he purchased it six years ago for $100,000, and he expects to receive only $8,000 in redemption of his stock. Finally, Brian's salary for the year was $114,000 for his work as an associate professor.

a. What are the net gains and losses from the above items and their character?

b. What is Brian's AGI for the year assuming he has no other items of income or deduction?

I8-42 *Passive Losses.* In the current year Alice reports $150,000 of salary income, $20,000 of income from activity X, and $35,000 and $15,000 losses from activities Y and Z, respectively. All three activities are passive with respect to Alice and are purchased during the current year. What is the amount of loss that may be deducted with respect to each of these activities? Also compute the amount of loss that must be carried over for each activity.

I8-43 *Passive Losses.* In the current year Clay reports income and losses from the following activities:

Activity X	$ 28,000
Activity Y	(10,000)
Activity Z	(20,000)
Salary	100,000

Activities X, Y, and Z are all passive with respect to Clay. Activity Z has $40,000 in passive losses which are carried over from the prior year. In the current year Clay sells activity Z for a taxable gain of $30,000.

a. What is the amount of loss that Clay may deduct and what is the amount that must be carried over in the current year?

b. Based solely on the amounts above, compute Clay's AGI for the current year.

I8-44 *Passive Losses: Rental Real Estate.* During the current year, Irene, a married individual who files a joint return, reports the following items of income and loss:

Salary	$130,000
Activity X (passive)	10,000
Activity Y (rental real estate, nontrade or business)	(30,000)
Activity Z (rental real estate, nontrade or business)	(20,000)

Irene actively participates in activities Y and Z and owns 100% of both Y and Z.

a. What is Irene's AGI for the year?

b. What is the amount of suspended losses (if any) that may be carried over with respect to each activity?

I8-45 *Passive Losses.* In 2004, Mark purchased two separate activities. Information regarding these activities for 2004 and 2005 is as follows:

	2004			2005	
Activity	Status	Income (Loss)	Activity	Status	Income (Loss)
A	Passive	($24,000)	A	Active	$10,000
B	Passive	(8,000)	B	Passive	20,000

The 2004 losses were suspended losses for that year. During 2005, Mark also reports salary income of $120,000 and interest and dividend income of $20,000. Compute the amount (if any) of losses attributable to activities A and B that are deductible in 2005 and any suspended losses carried to 2006.

I8-46 *Passive Losses.* During the current year, Juan, a single individual, has AGI of $125,000 before taking into account any passive activity losses. He also actively participates and owns 100% of activity A, which is a real estate rental activity. For the year, activity A generates a net loss of $6,000 and $3,000 in tax credits. Juan is in the 28% tax bracket. What is the amount of suspended loss and credit from activity A that must be carried to subsequent years?

I8-47 *Passive Losses.* In 2006, Julie, a single individual, reported the following items of income and deduction:

Salary	$146,000
Dividend income	14,000
Long-term capital gain from sales of stock	22,000
Short-term capital losses from sales of stock	(17,000)
Loss from a passive rental real estate activity	(20,000)
Interest expense on loan to purchase stock	(21,000)
Qualified residence interest on residence	(12,000)
Charitable contributions	(8,000)
Property taxes on residence	(5,000)
Tax return preparation fees	(2,500)
Unreimbursed employee business expenses	(2,000)

Julie owns 100% and is an active participant in the rental real estate activity. What is Julie's taxable income in 2006?

I8-48 *Casualty Losses.* Tony is a carpenter who owns his own furniture manufacturing business. During the current year, vandals broke into the workshop, damaged several pieces of equipment, stole his delivery truck, and also stole his personal automobile, which he often kept in the workshop garage. The asset descriptions and related values are as follows:

Asset	FMV Before Casualty	FMV After Casualty	Cost to Repair/Replace	Adjusted Basis	Insurance Proceeds
Equipment A	$12,300	$4,000	$ 8,700	$ 9,000	$ 3,700
Equipment B	8,100	0	9,000	3,000	7,800
Equipment C	Not Available	Not Available	13,800	15,300	11,400
Delivery Truck	18,000	0	32,000	17,500	16,000
Automobile	15,000	0	12,000	28,000	12,000

Although he could not obtain its fair market value after the casualties, Troy decided to repair rather than replace Equipment C.

Before considering any deductions because of these casualties, Troy's AGI is $80,000. What deductions may Tony take relating to the vandalism?

I8-49 *Theft Losses.* On December 17 of the current year, Kelly's business office safe is burglarized. The theft is discovered a few days after the burglary. $3,000 cash for the cash registers is stolen. A diamond necklace and a ring that Kelly frequently wore are also stolen. The necklace cost Kelly $2,300 many years ago and is insured for its $6,000 FMV. Kelly purchased the ring for $3,000 just two weeks before the burglary. Unfortunately, the ring and the cash are not insured. Kelly's AGI for the year, not including the items noted above, is $70,000.

a. What is Kelly's deductible theft loss in the current year?

b. What is Kelly's deductible theft loss in the current year if the theft is not discovered until January of the following year?

I8-50 *Casualty Losses: Year of Deduction.* Jerry sprayed all of the landscaping around his house with a pesticide in June 2006. Shortly thereafter, all of the trees and shrubs unaccountably died. The FMV and the adjusted basis of the plants were $15,000. Later that year, the pesticide manufacturer announced a recall of the particular batch of pesticide that Jerry used. It also announced a program whereby consumers would be repaid for any damage caused by the improper mixture. Jerry is single and reports $38,000 AGI in 2006 and $42,000 in 2007.

a. Assume that in 2006 Jerry files a claim for his losses and receives notification that payment of $15,000 will be received in 2006. Jerry receives full payment for the damage in 2006. How should the loss and the reimbursement be reported?

b. How will your answer to Part a change if in 2007 the manufacturer files bankruptcy and Jerry receives $1,500 in total and final payment for his claim?

c. How will your answer to Part a change if the announcement and the reimbursement do not occur until late in 2007, after Jerry has already filed his tax return for 2006?

I8-51 *Personal-Use Casualty Losses.* In the current year Ned completely destroys his personal automobile (purchased two years earlier for $28,000) in a traffic accident. Fortunately none of the occupants are injured. The FMV of the car before the accident is $18,000; after the accident it is worthless. Ned receives a $14,000 settlement from the insurance company. Later in the same year his house is burglarized and several antiques are stolen. The antiques were purchased a number of years earlier for $8,000. Their value at the time of the theft is estimated at $12,000. They are not insured. Ned's AGI for the current year is $60,000. What is the amount of Ned's deductible casualty loss in the current year, assuming the thefts are discovered in the same year?

I8-52 *Casualty Losses.* During 2006, Pam incurred the following casualty losses:

Asset	FMV Before	FMV After	Basis	Insurance
Business 1	$18,000	$ 0	$15,000	$ 4,000
Business 2	25,000	10,000	8,000	3,000
Business 3	20,000	0	18,000	19,000
Personal 1	12,000	0	20,000	2,000
Personal 2	8,000	5,000	10,000	0
Personal 3	9,000	0	6,000	8,000

All of the items were destroyed in the same casualty. Before considering the casualty items, Pam reports business income of $80,000, qualified residential interest of $6,000 property taxes on her personal residence of $2,000, and charitable contributions of $4,000. Compute Pam's taxable income for 2006. Pam is single.

I8-53 *Business Bad Debt.* Elaine is a physician who uses the cash method of accounting for tax purposes. During the current year, Elaine bills Ralph $1,200 for office visits and outpatient surgery. Unfortunately, unknown to Elaine, Ralph moves away leaving no payment and no forwarding address. What is the amount of Elaine's bad debt deduction with respect to Ralph's debt?

I8-54 *Nonbusiness Bad Debt.* During 2005, Becky loans her brother Ken $5,000, which he intends to use to establish a small business. Because Ken has no other assets and needs cash to expand the business, the agreement provides that Ken will repay the debt if (and when) sufficient funds are generated from the business. No interest rate is agreed upon. The business is unsuccessful, and Ken is forced to file for bankruptcy in 2006. By the end of 2006, it is estimated that the creditors will receive only 20% of the amount owed. In 2007 the bankruptcy proceedings are closed, and the creditors receive 10% of the amount due on the debt. What is Becky's bad debt deduction for 2006? For 2007?

I8-55 *Bad Debt Deduction.* Assume the same facts as in Problem I8-54, except that Becky and Ken are not related and that under the terms of the loan Ken agrees to repay Becky the $5,000 plus interest (at a reasonable stated rate) over a five-year period. What is Becky's bad debt deduction for 2006? For 2007?

I8-56 *Net Operating Loss Deduction.* Michelle and Mark are married and file a joint return. Michelle owns an unincorporated dental practice. Mark works part-time as a high school math teacher, and spends the remainder of his time caring for their daughter. During the current year, they report the following items:

Mark's salary	$18,000
Interest earned on savings account	1,200
Interest paid on personal residence	7,100
Itemized deductions for state and local taxes	3,400
Items relating to Michelle's dental practice	
Revenues	65,000
Payroll and salary expense	49,000
Supplies	17,000
Rent	16,400
Advertising	4,600
Depreciation	8,100

a. What is Michelle and Mark's taxable income or loss for the year?
b. What is Michelle and Mark's NOL for the year?

I8-57 *Net Operating Loss Deduction.* Assume the same facts as in Problem I8-56, except in addition to the other itemized deductions Michelle and Mark suffer a $4,500 deductible personal casualty loss (after limitations).
a. What is Michelle and Mark's taxable income or loss for the year?
b. What is Michelle and Mark's NOL for the year?

I8-58 *Net Operating Loss Deduction.* Assume the same facts as in Problem I8-56, except instead of a $3,400 itemized deduction for state and local taxes, Michelle and Mark have a $3,400 deductible casualty loss (after limitations).
a. What is Michelle and Mark's taxable income or loss for the year?
b. What is Michelle and Mark's NOL for the year?

I8-59 *Net Operating Loss.* During the year, Karen, a single taxpayer, reports the following income and expense items relating to her interior design business:

Revenues	$52,000
Cost of goods sold	41,000
Advertising	3,300
Office supplies	1,700
Rent	13,800
Contract labor	28,000

Karen also worked part-time during the year, earning $13,500. She reports a long-term capital gain of $4,200, and a short-term capital loss of $3,800. Her itemized deductions total $5,200.
a. What is Karen's taxable income or loss for the year?
b. What is Karen's NOL for the year?

TAX STRATEGY PROBLEMS

I8-60 In 2003, Annie Cook and several family members formed Treehouse Rentals, Inc., in Denver, Colorado. Treehouse is a closely-held C corporation engaged in the rental real estate business. Treehouse properly classifies its activities as passive. In 2003, 2004, and 2005, the corporation generated net passive losses of $380,000, $145,000, and $194,000, respectively, all of which were properly suspended.

Effective January 2006, Treehouse elected to be taxed as an S Corporation. Also during 2006, Treehouse sold two pieces of rental real estate property. The suspended losses related to these properties were $63,000 and $112,000.

How should Treehouse treat the disposition of the rental properties in 2006?

- Sec. 469, Sec. 1371
- TAM 9628002
- *St. Charles Investment Co. v. Comm.,* 86 AFTR 2d 2000-6882

I8-61 Jace Seaton is a single taxpayer living in Eugene, Oregon. From 2000 to 2005, he worked as the CEO of Wengren & Jeffers, a local architectural firm. In 2006, he left the firm to start his own company. On October 25, 2006, he formed Seaton & Associates, a Limited Liability Company (LLC) under Oregon law.

Upon forming the LLC, Jace received an 80% interest in the company. Two other architects, Maria Juarez and Jaman Turhoon, each received a 10% interest in the company. Jace provided all necessary capital, whereas Maria and Jamal provided experience and a commitment to work for the company. Seaton & Associates chose to be taxed as a partnership for federal income tax purposes.

During 2006, Jace worked approximately 215 hours for Seaton & Associates, and received compensation of $7,200. Maria and Jamal each worked approximately 600 hours each, and each received compensation of $16,000. In 2006, the company generated a net loss of $530,000.

How should the LLC members, particularly Jace, treat the loss generated in 2006?

- Reg. 1.469-5T
- *Gregg v. U.S.*, 87 AFTR 2d 2001-337

I8-62 On November 15, Alex and Deanna Kent come to you for tax advice. The Kents, a married couple that files a joint tax return, own a rental home in Southern California. From January to November 1 of the current year, they rented out the home for 210 days. Since they live in Minnesota, they are considering staying in their rental home from December 10 to 31. If they do not stay in the home during that period, it will sit vacant. They ask you if this decision would have any tax consequences. They also provide you with the following information for the year:

Rental home income and expenses:

Rental income	$12,000
Mortgage interest	12,400
Management fees	1,200
Utilities	2,300
Property taxes	4,300

Other income and expenses:

Deanna's salary	75,000
Alex's salary	65,000
Passive income	
(from an investment in a limited partnership)	1,000
Mortgage interest	7,800
Charitable contributions	14,200
Medical expenses	8,100
Property taxes	2,900
State income taxes	9,700

What do you recommend to the Kents?

I8-63 Jim had $100,000 in deposits in a savings account at a bank in Page, Arizona. The bank collapsed and Jim did not receive anything for his deposits. The bank was chartered by the state of Arizona and was not insured by federal law. Jim is not sure what his options are in deducting this loss on his tax return. What can Jim do to take advantage of this loss on his tax return? He has an AGI of $110,000 and no capital gains for the current year.

TAX FORM/RETURN PREPARATION PROBLEMS

I8-64 Heather and Nikolay Laubert are married and file a joint income tax return. Their address is 3847 Jackdaw Path, Madison, WI 58493. Nikolay's Social Security number is 968-84-8532, and Heather's is 498-65-5432. Nikolay is a mechanical engineer, and Heather is a highly renowned speech therapist. She is self-employed. They report all their income and expenses on the cash method. For 2005, they report the following items of income and expense:

Gross receipts from Heather's business	$110,000
Rent on Heather's office	12,000
Receivables written off during the year (received in Heather's business)	1,300
Subscriptions to linguistic journals for Heather	250
Salary for Heather's secretary-receptionist	22,000
Nikolay's salary	78,000
Qualified medical expenses	12,000
Property taxes on their personal residence	4,200
State income tax refund received this year (the tax benefit was received in the prior year from the state income tax deduction)	400
State income taxes withheld on Nikolay's salary	4,600
Federal income taxes withheld on Nikolay's salary	12,000
Heather's estimated tax payments	20,000
Interest paid on residence	11,000

Income tax preparation fee for the prior year's return paid this
year ($500 is allocated to preparation of Schedule C) $940

Heather and Nikolay sold the following assets:

Asset	Acquired	Sold	Sales Price	Cost
KNA stock	2/15/02	3/13/05	$14,000	$ 8,000
AEN stock	3/2/05	7/7/05	20,000	22,000
KLN stock	6/8/02	4/10/05	13,000	17,000
Motorcycle	5/3/00	9/12/05	2,500	6,000

Heather owned the KLN stock and sold it to her brother, Jacob. Heather and Nikolay used the motorcycle for personal recreation.

In addition to the items above, they donate Miner Corporation stock to their community church. The FMV of the stock on the date it is donated (8/18/05) is $6,200. It cost $2,700 when purchased on 3/12/91. Heather and Nikolay's home is burglarized during the year. The burglar stole an entertainment system (FMV $3,500; cost $5,000), an antique diamond ring and pendant (FMV $12,000; cost $10,000), and a painting (FMV $1,500; cost $1,300). The insurance company pays $1,500 for the entertainment system, $4,000 for the jewelry, and $500 for the painting. Complete Heather and Nikolay's Form 1040, Schedules A, C, D, and SE, Form 4684, and Form 8283.

I8-65   Kara and Brandon Arnold are married and file a joint return. Their Social Security numbers are 587-64-5235 and 588-54-8623, respectively. Kara and Brandon have one son, Henry, age 3. His Social Security number is 587-45-3197. They live at 356 Welcome Lane, Woodbury, WA 84653. They report their income on the cash method. During 2005, they report the following items:

Salary	$103,000
Interest income from money market accounts	600
Dividend income from Davis Corp. stock	700
Cash contributions to church	6,000
Rental of a condominium in Lutsen:	
Rental income (30 days)	12,000
Interest expense	7,000
Property taxes	3,200
Maintenance	1,700
Depreciation (entire year)	7,500
Insurance	2,000
Days of personal use	16

During the year the following events also occur:
a. In 2002, Brandon had loaned a friend $3,000 to help pay medical bills. During 2005, he discovers that his "friend" has skipped town.
b. On June 20, 2005, Brandon sells Kim Corporation stock for $16,000. He purchased the stock on December 12, 2001 for $22,000.
c. On September 19, 2005, Kara discovers that the penny stock of Roberts, Inc. she purchased on January 2 of the prior year is completely worthless. She paid $5,000 for the stock.
d. Instead of accepting the $60 the repairperson offers for their old dishwasher, they donate it to Goodwill on November 21, 2005. They purchased the dishwasher for $750 on March 30, 1999. The new dishwasher cost $900.
e. Kara and Brandon purchased a new residence for $250,000. As part of the closing costs, they pay two points, or $3,800, on the mortgage, which is interest rather than loan processing fees. This payment enables them to obtain a more favorable interest rate for the term of the loan. They also paid $8,400 in interest on their mortgage on their personal residence.
f. They paid $4,100 in property taxes on their residence and $7,500 in state income taxes.
g. On July 20, 2005, Kara and Brandon donated 1,000 shares of Anton, Inc. stock to the local community college. The value of the stock on that date was $10,200. Anton, Inc. is a listed stock. They had purchased the stock on November 10, 2001 for $1,000.
h. $16,450 in federal income tax was withheld during the year.
Complete Kara and Brandon's Form 1040, Schedules A, B, D, and E, and Form 8283. For purposes of this problem, disregard the alternative minimum tax.

CASE STUDY PROBLEMS

I8-66 Dr. John Brown is a physician who expects to make $150,000 this year from his medical practice. In addition, Dr. Brown expects to receive $10,000 dividends and interest income.

Last year, on the advice of a friend, Dr. Brown invested $100,000 in Limited, a limited partnership. He spends no time working for Limited. Limited's operations did not turn out exactly as planned, and Dr. Brown's share of Limited's losses last year amounted to $15,000. Dr. Brown has already been informed that his share of Limited's losses this year will be $10,000.

In January of the current year, Dr. Brown set up his own laboratory. Originally he intended to have the lab only do the work for his own practice, but other physicians in the area were impressed with the quick turnaround and convenience that the lab provided and began sending their work. This year Dr. Brown estimates that the lab will generate $30,000 of taxable income. The work in the lab is done by 2 full-time qualified laboratory technicians. A part-time bookkeeper is hired to keep the books. Dr. Brown has spent 320 hours to date establishing and managing the lab. He plans to hire another technician, who will also manage the lab so that it can operate on its own.

In November, Dr. Brown calls you requesting some tax advice. Specifically, he would like to know what actions he should take before the end of the year in order to reduce his tax liability for the current year.

Write a memo to Dr. Brown, detailing your suggestions. His address is: Dr. John Brown, 444 Physicians Drive, Suite 100, Anytown, USA 88888.

I8-67 In preparing the tax return for one of your clients, Jack Johnson, you notice that he has listed a deduction for a large business bad debt. Jack explains that the loan was made to his corporate employer when the corporation was experiencing extreme cash flow difficulties. In fact, Jack was very concerned at the time he made the loan that the corporation would go bankrupt. This would have been extremely bad, because not only would he have lost his job, but he also would have lost the $80,000 he had invested in the common stock of the corporation.

You know that if the loan is a business loan Jack will receive an ordinary deduction. However, if the loan is a nonbusiness debt, it becomes a short-term capital loss (and Jack can only currently deduct $3,000).

After thoroughly reviewing all of the facts, you do a complete search of the relevant judicial and administrative authority. There you find that the courts are split as to whether under these circumstances the loan should be treated as a business or nonbusiness bad debt.

What position should you take on Jack's federal income tax return? (See the *Statements on Standards for Tax Services* section in Chapter I15 and Appendix E for a discussion of this issue.)

TAX RESEARCH PROBLEM

I8-68 Early in 2006, Kay meets Dan through a business associate. Dan tells Kay that he is directing a business venture that purchases poorly managed restaurants in order to turn them around and make them profitable. Dan mentions that he is currently involved in acquiring a real "gold mine" but needs to raise additional cash in order to purchase it. On the strength of Dan's representations, Kay loans Dan $30,000 for the venture. An agreement is written up between Kay and Dan, wherein Dan agrees to repay Kay the entire amount over a 5-year period plus 14% interest per annum on the unpaid balance. Later in the year, however, Kay discovers that Dan had never intended to purchase the restaurant and, in fact, had used most of the money for his own benefit. Upon making this discovery, Kay sues Dan for recovery of the money, alleging that Dan falsely, fraudulently, and deceitfully represented that the money would be invested and repaid, in order to cheat and defraud Kay out of her money. Unfortunately for Kay, she is never able to recover any amount of the loan. Discuss the tax treatment that Kay may claim with regard to the loss.

A partial list of research sources is

- *Robert S. Gerstell*, 46 T.C. 161 (1966)
- *Michele Monteleone*, 34 T.C. 688 (1960)

9

CHAPTER

EMPLOYEE EXPENSES AND DEFERRED COMPENSATION

LEARNING OBJECTIVES

After studying this chapter, you should be able to

▶ **1** Determine the proper classification and deductibility of travel and transportation expenses

▶ **2** Determine the proper deductible amount for entertainment expenses under the 50% disallowance rule

▶ **3** Identify deductible moving expenses and determine the amount and year of deductibility

▶ **4** Describe the requirements for deducting education expenses

▶ **5** Determine whether the expenses of an office in home meet the requirements for deductibility and apply the gross income limitations

▶ **6** Discuss the tax treatment and requirements for various deferred compensation arrangements

This chapter discusses the tax consequences that arise from two types of expenditures:

▶ Expenditures incurred by an employee in connection with his or her job

▶ Deferred compensation payments made to employees

Employees routinely incur expenses in connection with their jobs, such as travel, entertainment, professional journals, etc. The tax law considers **employee expenses** to be incurred in connection with a trade or business and, therefore are deductible under Sec. 162. However, employee expenses are subject to a myriad of special rules and limitations. Because of the large number of taxpayers who are employees and the importance of the topic, this chapter discusses the rules as well as tax planning opportunities.

Deferred compensation refers to methods of compensating employees that are based on their current service, but the actual payments are deferred until future periods. Deferred compensation arrangements are very popular and widely used in business. The two principal types of deferred compensation methods are qualified plans and nonqualified plans. Qualified plans, such as pension and profit-sharing plans, have very favorable tax benefits but also impose strict eligibility and coverage requirements. Nonqualified plans, while not as tax advantageous as qualified plans, are very useful for highly compensated employees. Both of these types of deferred compensation arrangements are discussed later in this chapter.

CLASSIFICATION AND LIMITATIONS OF EMPLOYEE EXPENSES

Employee expenses, for purposes of the tax law, are divided into two classifications: *reimbursed* employee expenses and *unreimbursed* employee expenses. Reimbursed employee expenses are expenses incurred by the employee that are reimbursed by the employer. IRC Section 62(a)(2) provides that an employee may deduct reimbursed employee expenses *for* AGI. This presumes, of course, that the employee has included the reimbursement in his gross income. Unreimbursed employee expenses are generally deductible by employees, but are deductible *from* AGI. A more detailed discussion of the proper treatment of employee expenses under accountable and nonaccountable plans is presented later in this chapter.

Some of the more frequently encountered employee expenses discussed in this chapter include

▶ Travel

▶ Transportation

▶ Moving

▶ Entertainment

▶ Education

▶ Office in home

Each of these types of employee expenses are discussed later in this chapter.

NATURE OF THE EMPLOYMENT RELATIONSHIP

KEY POINT

The business expenses of a self-employed individual and the reimbursed business expenses of an employee are deductible *for* AGI. The unreimbursed business expenses of an employee are deductible *from* AGI.

An individual who provides services for another person or entity may be classified either as an employee or as a self-employed individual (also referred to as an independent contractor). If the individual is classified as self-employed, expenses are deductible *for* AGI under Sec. 162, and are reported on Schedule C of Form 1040. Conversely, expenses of employees are deductible either *for* or *from* AGI depending on whether such expenses are reimbursed or unreimbursed (see discussion above). In addition to the deductibility of expenses, the proper classification is also important due to employment taxes, such as Social Security taxes. As is discussed below, self-employed taxpayers must pay both the employee's and employer's shares of social security taxes.

EMPLOYER-EMPLOYEE RELATIONSHIP DEFINED. The Treasury Regulations provide that an employer-employee relationship generally exists where the employer has the

4enop

right to control and direct the individual who provides services with regard to the end result and the means by which the result is accomplished.[1]

EXAMPLE I9-1 ▶ Carmen is a nurse who assists a group of doctors in a clinic. Carmen is under the direct supervision of the doctors and is told what procedures to perform and when to perform them. Therefore, Carmen is classified as an employee. ◀

EXAMPLE I9-2 ▶ Carol is a live-in nurse who is paid by the patient and receives instructions from the patient's doctor regarding such items as medications and diet. Carol is directly responsible for the delivery of nursing care and is in control of the end result. Thus, Carol is self-employed. ◀

ADDITIONAL COMMENT

Anyone in a trade or business making payments of $600 or more to an independent contractor during a year must file Form 1099-MISC.

IMPORTANCE OF PROPER CLASSIFICATION. As mentioned above, proper classification is important both to employers and employees. If an individual is classified as an employee, the employer must match the Social Security and Medicare taxes that are paid by the employee. In addition, employers are generally liable for unemployment taxes for their employees. Thus, an employer must pay these employment taxes to the federal and/or state governments in addition to the wages, which means that the cost of an employee generally is higher than for a non-employee. If an individual is determined to *not* be an employee, the individual is considered to be self-employed (also called an independent contractor). Amounts paid to a self-employed individual are not considered to be wages and the payor is not responsible for any employment taxes. However, the self-employed individual must pay both the employee and employer portions of Social Security and Medicare taxes. This tax is referred to as the self-employment tax. As can be seen from the above discussion, employment taxes are shifted from the employer to the self-employed individual if the individual is not considered to be an employee.

Individuals may prefer to be classified as employees because the employee portion of the Social Security and Medicare taxes (7.65% in 2006) is only one-half of the self-employment tax rate (15.3% in 2006). Of the 7.65%, 6.2% (12.4% for self-employed individuals) is for the old age, survivors and disability insurance (OASDI) portion of the FICA tax and is assessed on a maximum income amount of $94,200 (2006). The remaining 1.45% (2.9% for self-employed individuals) portion of the FICA tax is for hospital insurance and has no ceiling limitation.[2]

LITIGATION ISSUES AND ADMINISTRATIVE ENFORCEMENT. The determination as to whether an individual who performs services is either an employee or an independent contractor has been a major area of contention between the IRS and taxpayers. In Rev. Rul. 87-41, 1987-1 CB 296, the IRS enumerated 20 factors as guides for determining whether an individual is an employee or an independent contractor. These factors are designed to help determine whether the person or persons for whom the services are performed exercises sufficient **control** over the individual for such an individual to be classified as an employee. Some of the factors include instructions, set hours of work, work on employer's premises, and method of payment (hourly versus commission, for example).

Substantial litigation has occurred in the interpretation of these factors. For example, truck drivers who were owner-operators and were engaged under contract by an interstate trucking company were considered independent contractors because they selected their own routes and were paid a percentage of the company's receipts for shipment.[3] However, drivers for a moving van company were considered employees because the company exercised control over their assignments.[4]

KEY POINT

Even if the employee expenses exceed 2% of AGI, the employee may not derive a tax benefit if the deductible employee expenses, when added to the other itemized deductions, do not exceed the standard deduction.

LIMITATIONS ON UNREIMBURSED EMPLOYEE EXPENSES

2% NONDEDUCTIBLE FLOOR. Section 67 imposes a nondeductible floor of 2% of AGI to the following types of itemized deductions:

---

[1] Reg. Sec. 31.3401(c)-1(b).
[2] For a more detailed discussion of the self-employment tax, see Chapter I14.
[3] Rev. Rul. 76-226, 1976-1 CB 332
[4] *R. N. Smith v. U.S.*, 78-1 USTC ¶9263 (CA-5, 1978).

ADDITIONAL COMMENT

Unreimbursed employee business expenses are reported by the tax-payer first on Form 2106, then carried to Schedule A as a miscel-laneous itemized deduction.

1) Unreimbursed employee business expenses,
2) Investment expenses, and
3) Other miscellaneous itemized deductions (i.e., tax return preparation fees)

All of these types of expenses are referred to as **miscellaneous itemized deductions** in Sec. 67.[5] Unreimbursed employee expenses that are classified as miscellaneous itemized deductions include

TAX STRATEGY TIP

For taxpayers who typically do not have enough miscellaneous itemized deductions to get over the 2% floor, "bunching" of expenses in a particular tax year may allow some of the expenses to be deducted.

▶ The cost and maintenance of special clothing (e.g., uniforms for an airline pilot)

▶ Job-hunting expenses for seeking employment in the same trade or business (e.g., employment agency fees)

▶ Professional journals, professional dues, union dues, small tools and supplies

Investment expenses include expenses connected with the earning of investment income, such as publications and safe deposit box rentals. Other miscellaneous itemized deductions include items such as fees for tax return preparation and appraisal fees for charitable contributions.

EXAMPLE I9-3 ▶

SELF-STUDY QUESTION

Before the Tax Reform Act of 1986, unreimbursed employee business expenses were not sub-ject to the 2% nondeductible floor. Why did Congress decide to subject these expenses to this floor?

In 2006, Charles incurs and pays $3,000 of unreimbursed employee expenses, $1,000 of invest-ment counseling fees, and $500 for the preparation of his 2005 tax return. Charles's AGI is $100,000. The total miscellaneous itemized deductions are $4,500 ($3,000 + $1,000 + $500). Charles is limited to a $2,500 deduction ($4,500 − $2,000) because of the application of the 2% nondeductible floor (0.02 × $100,000 AGI = $2,000).   ◀

EXCEPTIONS TO THE 2% FLOOR. The 2% floor only applies to certain miscella-neous itemized deductions. Some miscellaneous itemized deductions, such as gambling losses (see footnote 5 below), are not subject to the 2% floor. Further, most itemized deductions, such as charitable contributions, mortgage interest and real estate taxes on a principal residence, are not subject to the 2% nondeductible floor.

EXAMPLE I9-4 ▶

ANSWER

Prior law required extensive recordkeeping with regard to items that were commonly small expenditures. These small amounts presented significant administrative and enforcement problems for the IRS. The use of a nondeductible floor also takes into account the fact that some expenses are sufficiently personal in nature that they might be incurred apart from any business activities.

In the current year Carmelia, who is single, incurs $1,500 of unreimbursed employee expenses, $3,000 of charitable contributions, and $4,000 of mortgage interest and real estate taxes on her principal residence. She has no other miscellaneous itemized deductions or investment expenses, and her AGI is $100,000. The $1,500 of employee expenses are not deductible because the 2% nondeductible floor ($2,000 in this case) is higher than the $1,500 of expenses. The $3,000 of charitable contributions and $4,000 of mortgage interest and real estate taxes are fully deductible as itemized deductions because Carmelia's total itemized deductions of $7,000 exceed the standard deduction amount ($5,150 for a single taxpayer in 2006). The char-itable contributions, mortgage interest, and real estate taxes are not subject to the 2% nonde-ductible floor.   ◀

TRAVEL EXPENSES

OBJECTIVE 1

Determine the proper classification and deductibility of travel and transportation expenses

DEDUCTIBILITY OF TRAVEL EXPENSES

The deductibility of travel expenses depends on the nature of the expenditure and whether the employee receives a reimbursement from the employer. The following rules apply to the deductibility of travel expenses.

▶ If the taxpayer is engaged in a trade or business as a self-employed individual or is engaged in an activity for the production of rental and royalty income, the travel-related expenditures are deductible *for* AGI and the 2% nondeductible floor is not applicable.

---

[5] The 2% disallowance applies before considering the 2% (2006) scale down of total itemized deductions under Sec. 68 for upper-income individuals with AGI in excess of $150,500 (2006). See Chapter I7 for a discussion of these rules. The 2% floor does not apply to certain other miscellaneous itemized deductions, including impairment-related work expenses for handicapped employees, amortizable bond premiums, certain short sale expenses, termi-nated annuity payments, and gambling losses to the extent of winnings.

▶ If the taxpayer is an employee and incurs travel expenses in connection with his job, the expenses are deductible either *for* AGI or *from* AGI depending on whether the expenses are reimbursed by the employer.

▶ Personal travel expenses are not deductible.

REIMBURSED EXPENSES. If business travel expenses are reimbursed and the reimbursement is included in the employee's gross income, the expenses are deductible *for* AGI.

UNREIMBURSED EXPENSES. Generally, if business travel expenses are not reimbursed by the taxpayer's employer, the expenses are a deduction *from* AGI subject to the 2% floor.

The tax rules for reporting reimbursed and unreimbursed employee business expenses are discussed in more detail later in this chapter. Table I9-1 illustrates these tax consequences.

DEFINITION OF TRAVEL EXPENSES

Travel expenses include transportation, meals, lodging, and other reasonable and necessary expenses incurred by a taxpayer while "away from home" in the pursuit of a trade or business or an employment-related activity. The term *travel expense* is more broadly defined in the IRC than is the term **transportation expense**. If an individual is not away from home, expenses related to local transportation are classified as transportation expenses rather than travel expenses. Transportation expenses for employees are deductible under certain conditions and are discussed later in this chapter.

EXAMPLE I9-5 ▶ Ahmed is away from home overnight on a job-related business trip and incurs airfare, hotel, and taxi fares amounting to $800. Because Ahmed is away from home, the $800 is deductible as travel expenses. ◀

EXAMPLE I9-6 ▶ Charlotte uses her personal automobile to make deliveries of company products to customers in the same local area of her employer's place of business. Charlotte's automobile expenses are classified as transportation expenses (rather than travel expenses) because she was not away from home when they were incurred. As is discussed later in this chapter, transportation expenses are deductible but are subject to strict recordkeeping rules. If Charlotte stopped to eat lunch alone during her delivery activities, the meals are not deductible as they are neither travel nor transportation expenses. ◀

▼ TABLE I9-1
Classification of Travel Expenses

Situation Facts	TAX TREATMENT		
	Deductible *for* AGI	Deductible *from* AGI	Not Deductible
1. Cindy is a self-employed attorney who incurs travel expenses related to her business.	X[a]		
2. Jose, who lives in Dallas, is the owner of several apartment buildings in Denver. Periodically he travels to Denver to inspect and manage the properties.	X[a]		
3. Clay is an employee who is required to travel to company facilities throughout the U.S. in the conduct of his management responsibilities. Clay is not reimbursed by his employer.		X[b]	
4. Same as Situation 3, except that Clay is fully reimbursed by his employer and includes the reimbursement in his gross income.	X[a]		
5. Colleen is a student who travels to her parents' home during the holidays.			X

[a] The 2% nondeductible floor is not applicable.
[b] The 2% nondeductible floor is applicable and the expenses are only deductible in excess of the floor.

GENERAL QUALIFICATION REQUIREMENTS

To qualify as a travel expense deduction, the following requirements must be met:

▶ The purpose of the trip must be connected with a trade or business or be employment-related (e.g., personal vacation trips or commuting to and from a job location are nondeductible personal expenses).[6]

▶ The taxpayer must be away from his tax home overnight or for a sufficient duration to require sleep or rest before returning home.

AWAY-FROM-TAX-HOME REQUIREMENT.   Travel expenses are deductible if the taxpayer is temporarily away from his tax home overnight. While this seems simple enough, there has been considerable debate as to what the words actually mean. There are three important aspects of this requirement: (1) where is the taxpayer's home, (2) how is *temporarily* distinguished from *indefinite* or *permanent,* and (3) how the term *overnight* is interpreted.

Taxpayer's home: The IRS's position is that a person's tax home is the location of his principal place of employment regardless of where the family residence is maintained. Thus, a taxpayer who works permanently or for an indefinite period of time away from his or her family residence is *not* considered to be away from home and, therefore, travel expenses are not deductible. In this situation, the taxpayer's *tax home* is considered to be his work location.

Temporary vs. Indefinite: To meet the away from home requirement, a taxpayer must be away from home on a temporary basis. Thus, an employee who travels out of town on a three-day business trip clearly meets this requirement. However, an employee whose primary residence is in one location but works on a permanent basis during the week at another location, and possibly has an apartment in the work location, is not considered away from home at the *work location.* In this case, the work location is considered his tax home for income tax purposes, and he is not considered to be away from home.

The determination of whether a taxpayer is away from home temporarily or indefinitely is based upon the length of time the taxpayer is at such location. Work assignments of more than one year are treated as indefinite.[7] Work assignments for one year or less are classified as either temporary or indefinite depending on the facts and circumstances of each case. If an employee is reassigned only for a temporary period, then his tax home does not change and the travel expenses are deductible. However, if the assignment is for an indefinite period, the individual's tax home shifts to the new location. The following bulleted items and examples are taken from Rev. Rul. 93-86[8] and are used to illustrate the IRS's position concerning whether a taxpayer is away from home temporarily for purposes of deducting travel expenses:

▶ A taxpayer accepts away from home employment where it is realistically expected that the work will be completed in six months. The actual employment period lasts ten months. Because the employment period is realistically expected to last (and does in fact last) for one year or less, the IRS's position is that the employment is temporary and the taxpayer's travel expenses are deductible.

▶ A taxpayer accepts away from home employment where it is realistically expected that the work will be completed in 18 months but the work is actually completed in ten months. In such case the IRS's position is that the employment is treated as indefinite, regardless of whether it actually exceeds one year or not.

▶ A taxpayer accepts away from home employment where it is realistically expected that the work will be completed in nine months. After eight months the taxpayer is asked to remain for seven more months or a total period of more than one year. Based on these facts, the IRS's position is that the employment is temporary for eight months and the travel expenses are deductible for the eight-month period. The job is consid-

---

[6] Travel expenses incurred in the production or collection of income are also deductible from AGI under Sec. 212(1), even though the travel is not connected with employment or with the conduct of a trade or business. See Rev. Rul. 84-113, 1984-2 C.B. 60.

[7] Sec. 162(a). See also Rev. Rul. 99-7, 1999-1 C.B. 361.

[8] Rev. Rul. 93-86, 1993-2 C.B. 71.

ered indefinite for the remaining seven months and no travel expense deduction is allowed for the travel expenses during this period.

Overnight test: To satisfy the overnight test, a taxpayer must show that it was reasonable for him to need to obtain sleep or rest during release time on such trips in order to meet the demands of his job.[9] Generally, costs of meals on one-day business trips are not deductible since the taxpayer was not away from home overnight. The Supreme Court held that a taxpayer who took short rest stops on long one-day business trips was not allowed to deduct his meals.[10] However, whether it is reasonable to need sleep or rest depends on the specific circumstances. A railroad conductor was allowed to deduct lodging, meals, and tips incurred during a six-hour layover on a total trip of 16 hours.[11]

EXAMPLE I9-7 ▶ Roberto lives and works in Baltimore. He occasionally travels to New York City on business and stays overnight for two or three days at a time. Roberto clearly meets the away from home test and all of his travel expenses, including airfare, lodging, tips, taxi, and food (subject to the 50% disallowance) are deductible as travel expenses. ◀

EXAMPLE I9-8 ▶ Tom lives with his family in Baltimore. In 2006, Tom loses his job in Baltimore and accepts a new full-time position in New York City. However, he decides not to move his family to New York but to rent an apartment and stay there during the week and return home on weekends. Tom's work assignment would be considered indefinite and the cost of his apartment, food, and other incidental expenses would not be deductible travel expenses because his tax home is New York and he is not considered to be away from home. ◀

EXAMPLE I9-9 ▶ Gunther lives and works in Baltimore. Gunther's employer asks him to accept a temporary assignment in New York City for approximately seven months to work on a special project. Gunther rents an apartment in New York for the seven months, then returns to his regular office in Baltimore. Gunther's work assignment in New York is considered temporary because it is less than one year, and therefore, all of his apartment rent, food, laundry, and other incidental costs are deductible as travel expenses. Because apartments and food are expensive in New York, his travel expense deduction will be substantial. Good records to substantiate the work assignment and the expenses are very important in this case. ◀

SELF-STUDY QUESTION

A student accepts employment in another state during his summer vacation. Would the cost of his meals and lodging at the job location be deductible?

ANSWER

No, the student did not travel to the job because of the employer's business needs. *Peter F. Janiss v. CIR*, 2 AFTR 2d 5927, 58-2 USTC ¶9873 (8th Cir., 1958).

BUSINESS VERSUS PLEASURE

Travel expenses are deductible only if they are incurred in the pursuit of a trade or business activity or are related to the taxpayer's employment. Thus, if a taxpayer takes a trip that is primarily personal in nature but some business is transacted, the only deductions allowed are those that are directly related to the business activity.[12] In such event, all of the traveling expenses to and from the destination are treated as nondeductible personal expenditures. However, if the trip is *primarily related* to business or employment, all of the traveling expenses to and from the destination are deductible, and meals and lodging, local transportation, and incidental expenses are allocated to the business and personal activities, respectively. In effect, an all-or-nothing approach is applied to the deductibility of traveling expenses to and from the destination depending upon the primary purpose for making the trip.

In determining the primary purpose for a trip, the amount of time spent on personal activities compared to the time spent on business activities is an important factor. However, the fact that a taxpayer may spend slightly more time on personal activities than business activities will not automatically prohibit the deductibility of the transportation expenses to and from the destination. The taxpayer must clearly show that the purpose of the trip was *primarily business*.

EXAMPLE I9-10 ▶ Dana travels to New York on a business trip for her employer. She is not reimbursed for the travel expenses. Dana spends three days in business meetings and vacations for two days. Because the trip is primarily business, the traveling expenses to and from the destination (e.g., airfare) are fully deductible by Dana. If Dana's meals, lodging, and incidental expenses amount to $100 per day, only $300 ($100 × 3 business days) of such travel expenses is also deductible. The deductible business meal expenses are reduced by 50%, and the total amount of deductible travel expenses are subject to the nondeductible 2% floor on miscellaneous

---

[9] Rev. Rul. 75-168, 1975-1 C.B. 58.
[10] *Correll v. U.S.*, 389 U.S. 299 (1968).
[11] *Williams v. Patterson*, 286 F2d 333 (5th Cir. 1961) and Rev. Rul. 75-170,

1975-1 C.B. 60.
[12] Reg. Sec. 1.162-2(b)(1).

itemized deductions. A proration of the meals, lodging, and incidental expenses based on the number of days may not be appropriate if the expenses are uneven or are directly related to either business or personal activities. ◄

EXAMPLE I9-11 ►

Assume that the facts in Example I9-10 are reversed (i.e., that two days are employment-related and three days are personal). Because more time was spent on personal activities, the general rule would hold that the trip is primarily personal and the traveling expenses to and from the destination are not deductible. Thus, only $200 ($100 × two business days) of travel expenses related to meals, lodging, and incidental expenses are deductible (subject to the limitations previously discussed). None of the traveling expenses to and from the destination (i.e., the airfare) are deductible. ◄

EXAMPLE I9-12 ►

Carroll, who lives and works in St. Louis, is required by his employer to attend a sales meeting in San Francisco. The meeting lasts two days. Carroll decides to take three days of vacation and sightsee in the San Francisco area. Even though Carroll spent more days on personal activities than business activities, Carroll's airfare would be deductible if he can clearly show that the primary purpose of the trip was business. ◄

REAL-WORLD EXAMPLE

It is very difficult to deduct expenses of a spouse who accompanies his or her spouse to a business meeting or convention. The accompanying spouse not only must be an employee of the corporation but the reason for accompanying his or her spouse must be for must be for bona fide business purpose.

The IRS has ruled that the incremental expenses of an additional night's lodging and an additional day's meals that are incurred to obtain "excursion" airfare rates with respect to employees whose business travel extends over Saturday night are deductible business expenses.[13] The reimbursement for these expenses is deductible by the employer (subject to the 50% disallowance for meals). The employer is not required to report the reimbursement on the employee's Form W-2 as gross income or withhold employment taxes.

Stringent rules are applied if the taxpayer is accompanied by family members because of the likelihood that the trip is primarily for personal reasons. No deduction is permitted for travel expenses of a spouse or dependent (or other person accompanying the taxpayer) unless the person is an employee, the travel is for a bona fide business purpose, and the expenses would be otherwise deductible.[14]

FOREIGN TRAVEL

Due to the potential for abuse, special rules apply to foreign travel and foreign convention expenses.[15] Travel expenses related to foreign conventions, seminars, or similar types of meetings are disallowed unless it can be shown that the meeting is directly related to the taxpayer's trade or business (including employment) activity and that it is reasonable for the meeting to be held outside North America. In addition, complex expense allocation rules are applied to business trips made outside the United States.[16]

SELF-STUDY QUESTION

Would the cost of going on a safari in Africa be deductible if the taxpayer were in the business of selling guns?

ANSWER

In an actual case, the Court held that the safari expenses were not sufficiently connected to the taxpayer's gun-selling business. Therefore, the safari costs were not deductible. *Vincent W. Eckel,* 1974 PH T.C. Memo ¶74,033, 33 TCM 147.

ADDITIONAL LIMITATIONS ON TRAVEL EXPENSES

IRC Section 274 also provides several limitations on the deductibility of certain types of travel expenses, including the following:

▶ Travel deductions are disallowed if the expenses are deductible only as a form of education. For example, a French language professor cannot deduct travel expenses to France if the purpose of the trip is to maintain a general familiarity with the French language and customs.

▶ Deductions allowed for luxury water travel (i.e., ocean liners, cruise ships, or other forms of water transportation) are limited to twice the highest per diem amount allowable for a day of domestic travel by employees in the executive branch of the federal government.

▶ Travel deductions to attend a convention, seminar, or meeting are not allowed if they are related to income-producing activities coming under Sec. 212. Expenses to attend a convention, seminar, or meeting are deductible if directly connected with a taxpayer's trade or business. However, expenses to attend such meetings on a U.S. cruise ship are deductible but only to a maximum amount of $2,000.

---

[13] Ltr. Rul. 9237014 (June 10, 1992).
[14] Sec. 274(m)(3).
[15] Secs. 274(c) and (h).
[16] Reg. Sec. 1.274-4. No allocation of total expenses is made to the personal-use (nondeductible) element if an individual is away from home for seven

days or less or if less than 25% of the time is devoted to personal purposes. In all other cases, all of the foreign travel expenses (including transportation costs) must be apportioned between business and personal activities based on the relative percentage of time devoted to each activity.

EXAMPLE I9-13 ▶ Dawn travels on a cruise ship to attend a business meeting in Bermuda. The round-trip cost of the cruise is $4,000, and the travel is for a period of four days. If the daily per diem amount is $150 for a government employee, the travel expenses related to the cruise ship are limited to $1,200 ($300 per day × 4 days travel). ◀

EXAMPLE I9-14 ▶ Danielle is an investor in the stock market who attends investment counseling seminars. During the current year, she incurs $4,000 in travel expenses to attend the seminars. None of the travel expenses are deductible because the expenses are related to income-producing activities coming under Sec. 212. If Danielle was employed as a stockbroker (rather than an investor) and attended investment seminars, her travel expenses would be deductible. ◀

Transportation expenses

The deductibility and classification of transportation expenses also depends on the nature of the expenditure, as follows:

▶ Trade or business-related transportation expenses are deductible *for* AGI and are not subject to specific limitations.

▶ Transportation expenses related to the production of rental and royalty income (e.g., an owner-investor in rental properties) are deductible *for* AGI and are not subject to specific limitations.

▶ Reimbursed employee transportation expenses are deductible *for* AGI (assuming that an adequate accounting is made to the employer; see discussion of reimbursed employee business expenses on page I9-16).

▶ Unreimbursed employee transportation expenses are deductible *from* AGI as itemized deductions subject to the 2% nondeductible floor for miscellaneous itemized deductions.

▶ Commuting expenses are nondeductible personal expenses.

DEFINITION AND CLASSIFICATION

KEY POINT

The primary difference between travel expenses and transportation expenses for tax purposes is that travel expenses are broad in nature and include transportation, lodging, meals, and other necessary expenses, whereas transportation expenses include only the cost of transportation.

Transportation expenses include such items as taxi fares, automobile expenses, airfares, tolls, and parking fees incurred in a trade or business or employment-related activity. Generally speaking, transportation expenses are those incurred for "local transportation" and are not treated as travel expenses because the away from home requirements have not been met. The cost of commuting to and from an employee's job location are nondeductible personal expenditures regardless of the length of the trip. Both unreimbursed employment-related travel and transportation expenses for employees are subject to the 2% floor on miscellaneous itemized deductions. If a reimbursement is received, such expenses would be deductible *for* AGI.

EXAMPLE I9-15 ▶ Eurie's employer requires her to call on several customers at different locations in the metropolitan area during the course of the workday. Her transportation expenses (e.g., auto expenses, tolls, and parking) are deductible as transportation expenses because they are related to providing services as an employee. If Eurie is required to travel away from home overnight, the transportation costs are included with meals and lodging and deducted as a travel expense. In either situation, the unreimbursed employment-related expenses are treated as miscellaneous itemized deductions and are subject to the 2% nondeductible floor limitation. If the expenses were reimbursed by Eurie's employer and an adequate accounting is made to the employer, the expenses would be deductible *for* AGI. ◀

EXAMPLE I9-16 ▶ David accepts a permanent job with a company located 80 miles from his principal residence. He decides not to move to the new location and drives the 160-mile roundtrip each day. None of David's transportation expenses are deductible because they are personal commuting expenses. (Note: Because the job is a permanent assignment, it is for an indefinite period rather than a temporary period and the transportation expenses are not deductible as travel expenses.) ◀

ADDITIONAL COMMENT

The IRS takes the position that the hauling of equipment, tools, etc., in an automobile for business purposes does not make the commuting expenses deductible. This position is based on the Supreme Court's decision in *Donald W. Fausner v. CIR*, 32 AFTR 2d 73-5202, 73-2 USTC ¶9515 (USSC, 1973). The Court held that it was not possible to allocate the automobile expenses between nondeductible commuting expenses and deductible business expenses. However, if the taxpayer incurs additional costs, such as in renting a trailer, these additional costs are deductible.

The following exceptions or unusual circumstances should be noted:

▶ Transportation expenses incurred to go from one job to another are deductible if an employee has more than one job. If the employee goes home between jobs, the deduction is only the amount it would have cost him to go directly from the first location to the second.[17]

▶ Certain transportation expenses related to income-producing activities are deductible under Sec. 212. Expenses are deductible *for* AGI if they are related to the production of rental or royalty income; expenses connected with other investment-related activities are deductible as miscellaneous itemized deductions subject to the 2% floor.

▶ Transportation expenses related to medical treatment may be deductible from AGI as a medical expense (subject to the limitations on the deductibility of medical expenses discussed in Chapter I7).

▶ Transportation expenses related to charitable activities may be deductible as a charitable contribution (subject to the limitations on the deductibility of charitable contributions discussed in Chapter I7).

▶ Transportation expenses incurred in going between the taxpayer's residence and a temporary work location outside the metropolitan area are deductible.[18] Further, assuming a taxpayer has at least one regular work location (such as his primary office location), transportation expenses are deductible in going between the taxpayer's residence and a temporary work location, regardless of the distance.[19] Thus, a CPA who is employed by a CPA firm and who maintains a regular work location (e.g., an office is provided at the CPA firm's work location) may deduct transportation expenses for trips from home to clients in the metropolitan area. Unreimbursed transportation costs for an employee are deductible *from* AGI as unreimbursed employee expenses that are subject to the 2% nondeductible floor. Transportation expenses for a self-employed individual are deductible *for* AGI.

EXAMPLE I9-17 ▶ As shown in Figure I9-1 below, Dick has two jobs that are 10 miles apart. Dick lives 5 miles from the first job site and 8 miles from the second job site. If Dick drives directly from Job 1 to Job 2, he may deduct the automobile costs associated with the 10-mile trip. If he goes home from the first job before driving to the second job, the deduction is still limited to 10 miles, even though he actually travels 13 miles. ◀

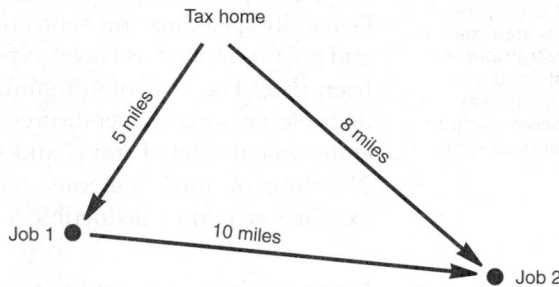

FIGURE I9-1 ▶ ILLUSTRATION FOR EXAMPLE I9-17

EXAMPLE I9-18 ▶ Diana owns a duplex, which she rents to tenants. She periodically drives from her place of business to this income-producing property to collect the rents and to inspect the property. The transportation expenses are deductible *for* AGI as an expense related to the production of rental income under Sec. 212. ◀

EXAMPLE I9-19 ▶ Donna, an accountant who is employed by a CPA firm, travels from her home to an audit client located in the local metropolitan area. The firm maintains an office for Donna at their business location. She is not reimbursed for her transportation costs. The transportation costs are

---

[17] IRS, *Publication No. 463* (Travel, Entertainment, Gift, and Car Expenses), 2003.

[18] Rev. Rul. 99-7, 1999-1 C.B. 361.
[19] Ibid.

deductible *from* AGI as unreimbursed employee expenses that are subject to the 2% nondeductible floor. If Donna were instead a self-employed CPA operating a business from her home, her transportation expenses would be deductible *for* AGI. ◀

TREATMENT OF AUTOMOBILE EXPENSES

An employee or self-employed person may use either of two methods to deduct allowable automobile expenses. First, actual automobile expenses, including gas, oil, repairs, depreciation, interest, property taxes, license fees, and insurance are deductible based on the percentage of business miles to total miles. Detailed records to support the expenses are necessary in order to properly claim the deduction. To help reduce the burden of detailed recordkeeping, a second method, the standard mileage rate method, is available to taxpayers.

The standard mileage rate method permits a deduction based on a mileage rate of 44.5 cents per mile for the year 2006.[20] Parking and tolls for business purposes are allowed as an addition to this deduction as well as interest expense on an automobile loan and personal property taxes on the automobile. The following restrictions apply when the standard mileage rate is used:

▶ The standard mileage rate method cannot be used if two or more automobiles are used simultaneously for business purposes.

ADDITIONAL COMMENT

It should be remembered that in many cases the taxpayer can choose between the automatic mileage method and calculating the actual costs of operating the car. Although the automatic mileage method has the advantage of convenience, a calculation of the actual costs might produce a larger deduction.

▶ If a taxpayer changes from the standard mileage rate method rate in one year to the actual expense method in a later year, the basis of the used automobile must be reduced by 17 cents per mile for 2005 and 2006, and 16 cents per mile for 2003 and 2004, for any year or years in which the standard mileage rate method was used. The modified accelerated cost-recovery system (MACRS) rules (discussed in Chapter I10) cannot be used for computing depreciation in the year of the change and for the remaining useful life of the automobile. In such case, only the straight-line method under the alternative depreciation system (ADS) may be used (see Chapter I10).

▶ A change to the standard mileage rate method is not allowed for an automobile that was previously depreciated under the MACRS rules or where an election was made under Sec. 179 to expense part or all of the automobile's cost in the year of acquisition. (See Chapter I10 for a discussion of the Sec. 179 election.)

▶ The actual expense method is based on the ratio of business or employment-related miles to total miles. (See Chapter I10 for a discussion of specific restrictions on the computation of depreciation where mixed business- and personal-use automobiles are acquired.)

STOP & THINK

Question: Assume a taxpayer uses his car (original cost, $20,000) in his business, drives a total of 25,000 miles per year, and can substantiate 80% of the mileage as business use. In general, will the taxpayer benefit more from the standard mileage method of deducting automobile expenses or from the actual expenses method?

Solution: In general, the actual expenses method will yield a higher deduction. The AAA (American Automobile Association) estimates that it costs approximately $0.60 per mile or more (depending on the size of the car) to operate a car in the United States in 2006. Therefore, the actual cost of operating the automobile would be approximately $15,000 (25,000 miles × $0.60). The deductible amount for tax purposes would be 80% of $15,000, or $12,000 for the actual expense method. Compare this amount with the standard mileage amount of $8,900 (25,000 miles × 80% business usage × $0.445/mile) and the actual expenses method yields a higher deduction. Of course, each individual situation is different and the actual results can vary based on circumstances, such as the amount of repairs, depreciation, and so on.

EXAMPLE I9-20 ▶

Danielle owns two automobiles that are used at the same time in her small unincorporated business. One automobile is driven by an employee of the business, and Danielle drives the other vehicle for business use. Danielle cannot use the standard mileage rate method for either automobile because both cars are used in the business simultaneously. ◀

---

[20] Rev. Proc. 2004-64 as modified by Announcement 2005-71. For the taxable year 2005, the standard mileage rate was 40.5 cents per mile from January 1 through August 31 and 48.5 cents per mile from September 1 through December 31, 2005.

EXAMPLE I9-21 ▶ Doug acquired an automobile for use in his unincorporated business in 2004 and used the standard mileage rate method in 2004 and 2005. If the actual expense method is used for 2006 and later years, the automobile's adjusted basis (for depreciation purposes) must be reduced by 17 cents per mile for its 2005 business usage and 16 cents per mile for 2004. Thus, if the automobile originally cost $20,000 in 2004 and was used 10,000 miles for business purposes during the initial year and 15,000 miles in 2005, the adjusted basis for computing depreciation in 2006 is reduced to $15,850 {$20,000 − [(0.16 × 10,000) + (0.17 × 15,000)]}. The remaining $15,850 basis must be depreciated using straight-line depreciation over the automobile's estimated useful life if the actual expense method is used. ◀

EXAMPLE I9-22 ▶ Edith uses her automobile 50% of the time for business and employment-related use and 50% for personal use. These percentages are substantiated by records that document the total usage for the automobile. During 2006, Edith drives 3,000 miles per month or a total of 36,000 miles for the year. If the standard mileage rate method is used, she can deduct $8,010 [(0.445 × 36,000 miles) × 50%] for the business and employment-related use. Additionally, Edith may deduct any business-related parking fees and tolls. ◀

HISTORICAL NOTE

Congress enacted a "contemporaneous" records test in 1984 for substantiating expenses for automobiles and certain other activities. Public outcry caused Congress to repeal this requirement in 1985. Now the business use of an automobile can be substantiated either by keeping adequate records or by sufficient corroborating evidence, oral or written.

REIMBURSEMENT OF AUTOMOBILE EXPENSES

An employee is entitled to deduct actual automobile expenses (or amounts derived under the standard mileage rate method if applicable) in excess of reimbursed amounts received from the employer. The computation is made on Form 2106 (Employee Business Expenses) and is reported on Schedule A of Form 1040.

EXAMPLE I9-23 ▶ Elizabeth, who makes an adequate accounting to her employer, receives a $4,000 (20,000 miles at 20 cents per mile) reimbursement in 2006 for employment-related business miles. She incurs the following expenses related to both business and personal use:

ADDITIONAL COMMENT

The kind of written record that could corroborate the business use of an automobile would include account books, diaries, logs, trip sheets, expense reports, or written statements from witnesses.

Gas and oil	$ 5,000
Repairs and maintenance	2,700
Depreciation	3,000
Insurance	1,900
Total	$12,600

Elizabeth also spent $100 on parking fees and tolls that were all related to business. Elizabeth drives a total of 32,000 miles during the year. Thus, she uses her car 62.5% (20,000 miles ÷ 32,000 miles) for business use. After subtracting the employer's $4,000 reimbursement and adding the parking fees and tolls, Elizabeth may deduct $3,975 [($12,600 × 0.625) + $100 − $4,000] as a miscellaneous itemized deduction (subject to the 2% nondeductible floor) in 2006. Alternatively, if 2006 is the first year she used the car in her business, she could have claimed a deduction using the standard mileage rate method. In this case, before the reimbursement, the $7,975 ($7,875 + $100) of actual expenses is less than the $9,000 ($8,900 + $100) permitted under the standard mileage rate method [(32,000 miles × 62.5% × $0.445) + $100 business-related fees and tolls]. ◀

ENTERTAINMENT EXPENSES

OBJECTIVE 2

Determine the proper deductible amount for entertainment expenses under the 50% disallowance rule

Entertainment of business customers and clients is a routine and, in many cases, an essential practice in business. Because entertainment expenses are considered ordinary and necessary practices of a business, they are deductible under either Sec. 162 or Sec. 212. However, the nature of entertainment expenses lend themselves to abuse by taxpayers. There certainly is an element of personal pleasure in taking a client or customer to a hockey game or a Philharmonic orchestra performance and allowing taxpayers to deduct such expenses creates serious enforcement problems for the IRS.

For the reasons above, Congress enacted Sec. 274, which is strictly a disallowance section and contains classification rules, restrictive tests, and specific recordkeeping requirements. To deduct entertainment expenses, taxpayers must first show that the expenditure qualifies for a deduction under Sec. 162 (trade or business expense) or Sec. 212 (investment-type expense). Then the various requirements of Sec. 274 must be adhered to in order for an entertainment expense to be deductible. Over the years, Congress has continued to tighten the rules for the deductibility of entertainment expenses.

50% DISALLOWANCE FOR MEAL AND ENTERTAINMENT EXPENSES

Section 274(n) provides that any expense incurred for either business meals or entertainment must be reduced by 50%.[21] Business meals may be deductible either as travel expenses or as entertainment, depending on the nature of the expenditure. In either case, the 50% limit applies to the cost of food and beverages including tips and taxes but is not applicable to transportation expenses incurred going to and from a business meal. Further, any portion of a business meal that is considered lavish or extravagant is disallowed.[22] In such a situation, the 50% reduction rule is applied to the allowable portion of the business meal.

EXAMPLE I9-24 ▶ Krishna, a self-employed individual, pays $80 for a business meal plus $4 sales tax and a $16 tip. The total cost of the meal is $100. If $40 of the meal is considered lavish or extravagant, Krishna could deduct $30 ($60 × 0.50). ◀

If an employee incurs entertainment or business meal expenses that are fully reimbursed by the employer, it is the employer rather than the employee who is limited to a deduction for 50% of the expenses. Assuming the reimbursement is made pursuant to an accountable plan (see discussion later in this chapter), the employee would not include the reimbursement in income and would not be allowed a deduction.

EXAMPLE I9-25 ▶ Gordon incurs employment-related entertainment expenses of $1,000 and is fully reimbursed by his employer pursuant to an accountable plan. The employer may deduct $500 [$1,000 − ($1,000 × 0.50)] of entertainment expenses. Gordon would not include the $1,000 reimbursement in gross income and would not be allowed to deduct the $1,000 as a deduction. Thus, there is no overall tax effect to Gordon. ◀

ADDITIONAL COMMENT

Entertainment expenses are not considered "directly related" if there are substantial distractions. Therefore, if a meeting takes place at a sporting event, theater, or night club, the entertainment cannot be "directly related." This type of entertainment could qualify as an "associated with" expense. An example of a "directly related" expense would be the costs related to a hospitality room at a convention.

Certain meals are not subject to the 50% disallowance, including meals that are treated as compensation to employees, employee picnics or other social gatherings primarily for the benefit of employees, or infrequent meals that would qualify as a de minimus fringe benefit.

CLASSIFICATION OF EXPENSES

If an individual is engaged in a trade or business (but not as an employee), allowable entertainment expenses are deductible *for* AGI. Employees, however, may deduct entertainment expenses only as a miscellaneous itemized deduction (subject to the 2% nondeductible floor) unless the expenses are reimbursed. The tax rules for reimbursements of employee business expenses are discussed more fully later in this chapter.

EXAMPLE I9-26 ▶ Helen is a self-employed attorney who entertains clients and prospective clients. To the extent that these expenditures meet the Sec. 274 requirements, they are deductible by Helen as a *for AGI* expense on Schedule C of Form 1040 because Helen is engaged in a trade or business activity. The entertainment expenses are subject to the 50% limit but are not subject to the 2% nondeductible floor because the entertainment is deductible when determining AGI as a trade or business expense. ◀

CRITERIA FOR DEDUCTION. To be deductible as an entertainment expense, an expenditure must be either **directly related** to the active conduct of a trade or business or **associated with** the active conduct of a trade or business. Different restrictions apply to each of these categories. The Regulations under Sec. 274 provide the substantive rules for the two types of entertainment expenses.

ADDITIONAL COMMENT

With respect to the "associated with" type of expense, there is *no* requirement that the business discussion last for any specified period, or that more time be devoted to business than to entertainment.

"Directly Related" Expenses. To meet the requirements for a "directly related" **entertainment expense**, some business benefit must be expected from the business conducted other than goodwill and the expense must be incurred in a clear business setting (i.e., where there are no substantial distractions). In other words, business in anticipation of a business benefit must actually be conducted during the entertainment period.

"Associated With" Expenses. To qualify an expense as an "associated with" entertainment expenditure, the taxpayer must show a clear business purpose, such as obtaining

---

[21] For pre-1994 tax years, the disallowance was 20%.   [22] Sec. 274(k).

new business or encouraging the continuation of an existing business relationship. An added restriction is placed on "associated with" entertainment in that the entertainment must directly precede or follow a bona fide business discussion. This means that the entertainment generally must occur on the same day that business is discussed.

EXAMPLE I9-27 ▶ Holly is a lawyer who hosts a birthday party in her home. Most of the guests are law partners or clients. No formal business discussions are conducted either before or immediately following the party. The expenditures for the birthday party are not deductible because they do not meet either the "directly related" or "associated with" tests. ◀

Substantiation Requirements. In addition to both the directly related and associated with requirements, Sec. 274 imposes stringent substantiation requirements for entertainment expenses. In order to deduct entertainment expenses, taxpayers are required to substantiate each expenditure for which a deduction is claimed. Lack of documentation alone will cause the disallowance of a deduction.

BUSINESS MEALS

Business meals related to travel or entertainment activities are subject to the same business-connection requirements as other types of entertainment expenses. Thus, an entertainment deduction is allowed only if the meal meets the "directly related" or "associated with" tests previously discussed. In addition, the expense must not be lavish or extravagant under the circumstances, and the taxpayer (or an employee of the taxpayer) must generally be present when the food or beverages are furnished. These requirements do not apply to a business meal associated with travel where the taxpayer claims a deduction only for his or her own expenses.

EXAMPLE I9-28 ▶ Hank is a salesman for a manufacturing supply company. Hank meets Harold, a purchasing agent who is a substantial customer, for lunch during a normal business day. Business is actually conducted during the lunch, and the lunch expenses are not lavish or extravagant under the circumstances. Hank is fully reimbursed by his employer for the $30 lunch expenses after an adequate accounting of the expenses is submitted. The business meal qualifies as "directly related" entertainment because the entertainment involved the actual conduct of business where some business benefit is reasonably expected and a business discussion was conducted during the meal. Hank's employer may deduct $15 ($30 × 0.50) of entertainment expenses. ◀

EXAMPLE I9-29 ▶ Assume the same facts as in Example I9-28, except that the purchasing agent is a prospective customer and no business is actually discussed either during, directly preceding, or immediately following the meal. Thus, no deduction is allowed because no business is discussed either before, during, or after the meal. ◀

WHAT WOULD YOU DO IN THIS SITUATION?

You have recently acquired a new individual tax client, Joe Windsack, who is a manufacturer's representative for a local tool and die company. You have been engaged by Windsack to prepare his individual income tax return for the current year. Before the current tax year is over, you are at a party where Windsack is also a guest. You overhear Windsack bragging to a group of people that he substantially reduces his income tax liability by overstating meal and entertainment expenses. He indicated that he overstates the deductions in several ways: (1) when he goes out to lunch or dinner that is personal in nature, such as with his family, he always uses a credit card and fictitiously writes the name

of a client or prospective client on the charge card receipt, (2) when he goes out to lunch with several colleagues from his office (not business related), he charges the entire amount on his credit card (for everyone at the table), collects the cash from his colleagues for the cost of their meals, and then writes the entire amount off as a business-related meal, and (3) whenever he goes to any entertainment event, such as a ballgame, he always says that he took a client to the game with him and deducts the cost of the ticket as a business expense. When Windsack brings his tax information to you a couple of months later and you see a substantial amount of meal and entertainment expenses, what should you do?

The Regulations provide that the surroundings in which food or beverages are furnished must be in an atmosphere where there are no substantial distractions to the discussion (e.g., a floor show).[23]

EXAMPLE I9-30 ▶

Harry is a salesman who takes a customer to a local nightclub to watch a floor show and to have a few drinks. No business is discussed either before, during, or after the entertainment. The expenses for the beverages and floor show are not deductible because neither of the business meal requirements are met (i.e., the floor show produced substantial distractions, and no business was discussed). Even if business was actually discussed, no deduction would be allowed because there were substantial distractions. ◀

ENTERTAINMENT FACILITIES AND CLUB DUES

KEY POINT

Subject to a very few exceptions, no deduction is permitted for costs related to yachts, swimming pools, fishing camps, tennis courts, bowling alleys, vacation resorts, etc. This highly visible type of entertainment contributed to the public perception that the tax system was unfair.

No deduction is permitted for costs (e.g., depreciation, maintenance, repairs, and so on) related to the maintenance of facilities that are used for entertainment, amusement, or recreation. Facilities include yachts, hunting lodges, beach cottages, and so on.

No deduction is permitted for any type of club dues (including business, social, athletic, luncheon, and sporting clubs, as well as airline and hotel clubs).[24] Professional, civic and public service organizations (e.g., business leagues, trade associations, chambers of commerce, boards of trade, and real estate boards) are generally not subject to the dues disallowance rules. Initiation fees that are paid only upon joining a club are treated as nondeductible capital expenditures. While club dues are not deductible, other business expenses (e.g., business meals) are deductible if the general requirements for entertainment deductions are met.

EXAMPLE I9-31 ▶

Heidi is a self-employed CPA who entertains clients at her country club. Her club expenses include the following:

Annual dues	$ 4,000
Meal and entertainment charges related to business use	3,000
Personal-use meal charges	2,500
Initiation fee	10,000
Total expenses	$19,500

The only expense that is deductible is 50% of the specific business charges relating to the meals and entertainment. Thus, Heidi may deduct $1,500 ($3,000 × 0.50) *for* AGI as a business expense because she is a self-employed CPA. ◀

BUSINESS GIFTS

Business gifts are subject to an annual ceiling amount of $25 per donee.[25] Amounts in excess of the $25 limit per donee are disallowed. The following rules and exceptions apply to determine the business gift deduction:

▶ Multiple gifts to each donee are aggregated for purposes of applying the $25 per donee annual limitation. Husbands and wives and other family members are treated as a single donee.

▶ Husbands and wives who make gifts to a particular donee are treated as a single taxpayer and are subject to a single $25 limit.

▶ Incidental costs such as gift wrapping, mailing, and delivery of gifts and certain imprinted gift items costing $4 or less are excluded.

▶ Employee achievement awards made for length of service or safety that are under $400 per individual are excluded.[26]

▶ A gift from an employee to his or her supervisor does not qualify as a business gift because such gifts are personal rather than business related and are, therefore, not deductible.

---

[23] Reg. Sec. 1.274-2(f)(2)(i)(b).
[24] Sec. 274(a)(3).
[25] Sec. 274(b)(1).

[26] Sec. 274(j). The total limit including both qualified and nonqualified plan awards is $1,600 per individual (see Chapter I4).

REAL-WORLD EXAMPLE

A taxpayer who had deducted the full cost of two wedding gifts, both of which were in excess of $25 apiece, was able to deduct only $25 for each gift. *Jack R. Howard,* 1981 PH T.C. Memo ¶81,250, 41 TCM 1554.

Jack, an employee, makes the following gifts during the year, none of which are reimbursed by his employer:

Jack's immediate supervisor	$20
Jack's secretary	15
Jeff (a customer of Jack's)	24
Jeff's wife (a noncustomer)	26
Gift-wrapping for the gift to Jeff	6
Total	$91

Jack's total deduction for business gifts is $46 ($15 + $25 + $6) and is classified as a miscellaneous itemized deduction subject to the 2% nondeductible floor as an employee business expense. The $20 gift to Jack's immediate supervisor is not deductible. The gifts of $24 and $26 to Jeff and Jeff's wife must be aggregated and are limited to $25. The gift-wrapping charge is fully deductible because it is an incidental cost. ◀

LIMITATIONS ON ENTERTAINMENT TICKETS

In addition to the general 50% meals and entertainment limitation, the cost of a ticket for any entertainment activity or facility is limited to the ticket's face value. Thus, the 50% limit applies to the face value of the ticket. Further restrictions are placed on the rental of skyboxes that are leased for more than one event.[27]

EXAMPLE I9-33 ▶

Able Corporation acquires four tickets to a football game for $500 that are used for entertaining customers. The face amount of the four tickets is only $100 in total. Able's deduction for entertainment is initially limited to the $100 face value of the tickets. The deductible amount is $50 ($100 × 0.50) after applying the 50% limit on entertainment expenses. ◀

REIMBURSED EMPLOYEE BUSINESS EXPENSES

The tax treatment of reimbursements received by an employee from his employer for employment-related expenses depends upon whether the reimbursement is made pursuant to an **accountable** or **nonaccountable** plan. An accountable plan is a reimbursement arrangement that meets both of the following two tests.[28]

ADDITIONAL COMMENT

While reimbursed business expenses under an accountable plan are technically deductions for AGI, they do not actually appear on the employee's tax return as a deduction. This is because the reimbursement itself is not included on the Form W-2.

1. Substantiation—the employee must make an adequate accounting of expenses to his employer, which means that each business expense must be substantiated (an expense report, for example); and
2. Return of excess reimbursement—within a reasonable period of time, the employee is required to return to the employer any portion of the reimbursement in excess of the substantiated expenses.

If both of these tests are not met, amounts paid to an employee generally are treated as paid under a nonaccountable plan. However, a special rule in Reg. Sec. 1.62-2(c) provides that if an employee does not return the excess reimbursement within a reasonable time period, only the portion of the reimbursement in excess of substantiated expenses is considered as being paid under a nonaccountable plan. The portion of the reimbursement for substantiated expenses is considered as being paid under an accountable plan.

ACCOUNTABLE PLAN. Under an accountable plan, reimbursements are included in gross income and expenses are deductible *for* AGI. Therefore, a taxpayer's AGI will not increase if employee business expenses are reimbursed under an accountable plan. Because reimbursements and expenses offset each other, when expenses are reimbursed

---

[27] Sec. 274(l)(2). The cost of a skybox is disallowed to the extent that it exceeds the cost of the highest-priced nonluxury box seat tickets multiplied by the number of seats in the skybox (e.g., if a skybox contains 30 seats and the cost of the highest-priced nonluxury box seat for a particular event is $40,

the deduction for the skybox is limited to $1,200 ($40 × 30). The deduction would be also reduced by the 50% limitation applicable to entertainment expenses.
[28] Reg. Sec. 1.62-2(c).

under an accountable plan, taxpayers do not report the reimbursement or the expenses on their tax return. However, if an excess reimbursement is not returned to the employer, the excess reimbursement is included in the employee's gross income.

EXAMPLE I9-34 ▶ Antoine is an employee of the Bluechip Corporation, which maintains an accountable plan for purposes of reimbursing employee expenses. During the current year, Antoine went on a business trip and incurred $1,500 of expenses as follows: airfare, $800; lodging, $450; meals, $200; and tips, $50. Bluechip reimbursed him $1,500. Antoine does have gross income of $1,500 and a deduction for AGI of $1,500. Because the reimbursement is pursuant to an accountable plan, Antoine will not report the $1,500 reimbursement in his gross income and will not report any of the business expenses on his tax return. ◀

EXAMPLE I9-35 ▶ Assume the same facts as in Example I9-34 except that Bluechip advanced Antoine $1,800, rather than $1,500, for his business trip and his expenses were the same as above. If Antoine returned the excess $300 to Bluechip within a reasonable period of time, the result would be the same as in Example I9-34. However, if Antoine did not return the excess reimbursement (even though he is required to under the terms of the plan), Antoine must include the $300 in his gross income. The portion of the $1,800 reimbursement that pertains to the substantiated expenses, $1,500, is treated as being paid under an accountable plan. Thus, $1,500 of the reimbursement and the $1,500 of substantiated expenses are netted together and not reported. However, the excess $300 reimbursement is treated as being paid under a nonaccountable plan and, therefore, includible in Antoine's gross income. ◀

If an employee receives a reimbursement that is not as much as his expenses, a proration is required.

EXAMPLE I9-36 ▶ Fred, an employee, incurs employment-related expenses of $4,500 consisting of $1,200 business meals, $1,800 local transportation, and $1,500 entertainment of customers. He is only reimbursed $3,000 from his employer. Since the reimbursement is less than the amount of expenses, Fred must prorate the expenses as follows:

Expense	Total Amount	Reimbursed Expense[a]	Unreimbursed Expense
Business meals	$1,200	$ 800	$ 400
Local transportation	1,800	1,200	600
Entertainment	1,500	1,000	500
Total	$4,500	$3,000	$1,500

The reimbursed expenses of $3,000 are not reported by Fred and the $3,000 reimbursement is not reportable as income. The $1,500 of unreimbursed expenses are deductible *from* AGI (subject to 2% of AGI) as follows:

Business meals ($400 × 50%)	$ 200
Local transportation	600
Entertainment ($500 × 50%)	250
	$1,050

[a]Reimbursements are allocated to each expense category on a prorata basis. For example, the $800 for business meals is computed, $\frac{\$1,200}{\$4,500} \times \$3,000$. ◀

KEY POINT

Why does the government require reimbursements from nonaccountable plans to be included in the employee's gross income? Because these types of plans are often referred to as "expense accounts paid to employees as additional compensation."

NONACCOUNTABLE PLAN. Under a nonaccountable plan, reimbursements are included in the employee's gross income and the expenses are deductible by the employee as miscellaneous itemized deductions, subject to the 2% of AGI floor and the 50% disallowance for meals and entertainment expenses.

EXAMPLE I9-37 ▶ Use the same facts as in Example I9-34 except that Bluechip does not require its employees to submit an accounting of expenses incurred. Bluechip's plan is a nonaccountable plan. Antoine must include the $1,500 in his gross income and may deduct the expenses as miscellaneous itemized deductions, subject to the 2% of AGI floor, in the amount of $1,400 [$800 + 450 + (200 × 50%) + 50]. ◀

PER DIEM ALLOWANCES FOR MEALS AND LODGING. The IRS permits employers and employees to use optional "per diem allowances" for meals and lodging expenses in lieu of actual expenses. The use of per diem allowances is intended to simplify the burden of keeping detailed records for taxpayers who incur significant travel expenses. Special tables have been issued by the IRS that provide fixed per diem amounts for lodging as well as meals and incidental expenses (M&IE). The per diem allowances vary in amount depending on the city in which the travel took place. The tables list many cities in the United States as well as many cities in foreign countries. Thus, a taxpayer must only substantiate the time, place, and business purpose of the trip and then is permitted to use the per diem allowances. The per diem system is permitted only for payments under an accountable plan, the expenses must be reasonably expected to be incurred, and the amount of expenses should be in reasonable proximity to the expected actual expense amount.[29] A full discussion of this topic is outside the scope of this textbook.

EXAMPLE I9-38 ▶ Peyton Boying is an employee of UT, Inc. UT maintains an accountable plan for reimbursing employees for their business expenses. Peyton travels extensively in the United States for business purposes. Instead of requiring Peyton to keep actual records of his travel expenses, UT reimburses Peyton the per diem amounts as allowed by the IRS. Assuming Peyton traveled exclusively in low-cost localities (see footnote below) and was away from home for 100 days, UT could reimburse Peyton in the amount of $12,900 (100 days × $129) without the necessity of Peyton keeping detailed records of his actual travel expenses. The amount that Peyton actually spent is irrelevant as the IRS will accept the per diem amounts. ◀

Table I9-2 summarizes the concepts relating to employee business expenses and reimbursements.

▼ **TABLE I9-2**
Treatment of Employee Reimbursements

TYPE OF PLAN	TAX EFFECT
ACCOUNTABLE PLAN	
Reimbursement = Expense	No effect, amounts are netted and not reported on employee's return.
Reimbursement > Expense	Not permissible under plan, but should it occur, excess reimbursement is included in employee's gross income.
Reimbursement < Expense	Expenses are prorated to amount of reimbursement. Reimbursed expenses—no effect; unreimbursed expenses are deductible as miscellaneous itemized deductions subject to 2% of AGI "floor" or nondeductible amount.
NONACCOUNTABLE PLAN	
Reimbursements	Always included in employee's gross income.
Expenses	Deductible as miscellaneous itemized deductions subject to 2% of AGI "floor" or nondeductible amount.

MOVING EXPENSES

ADDITIONAL COMMENT

In 1999, moving expenses deducted on tax returns totaled $2.2 billion.

Moving expenses are generally nondeductible personal expenditures. However, Sec. 217 allows a limited deduction for moving expenses for employees and self-employed people. The underlying rationale for this deduction is that such moves are similar to business expenditures because they are either employment-related or connected with a trade or business.

[29] The IRS tables for per diem allowances paid on or after January 1, 2005, may be found in Rev. Proc. 2005-10 I.R.B. 2005-3 (December 22, 2004) or IRS Publication 1542, which is periodically updated. In 2005, for example, 19 locations had their per diem rates changed. The rate for high-cost localities (specifically identified by the IRS) is $204 per day (including $46 for M&IE); low-cost localities are $129 per day (including $36 for M&IE). Further, self-employed individuals who are not reimbursed for their travel expenses may use the M&IE rate, but must substantiate lodging with actual receipts.

EXAMPLE I9-39 ▶ Ken retires from his job and moves from Tennessee to Arizona. His moving expenses are non-deductible personal expenditures because the move is not employment-related and he is not moving to look for a new job. ◀

OBJECTIVE 3

Identify deductible moving expenses and determine the amount and year of deductibility

Two conditions must be met for a moving expense to be deductible:[30]

▶ *Distance requirement.* The new job location must be at least 50 miles farther from the taxpayer's old residence than the old residence was from the former place of employment. If an individual has no former place of employment, the new job must be at least 50 miles from the old residence.

▶ *Time requirement.* A new or transferred employee must be employed on a full-time basis at the new location for at least 39 weeks during the 12-month period immediately following the move. More stringent requirements must be met by self-employed people who either work as an employee at the new location or continue to be self-employed. Such individuals are subject to a 78-week minimum work period during the first two years following the move. At least 39 of the 78 weeks must be in the first 12-month period. A waiver of the time requirements is permitted for both employees and self-employed individuals if the taxpayer becomes disabled, dies, or is involuntarily terminated (other than for willful misconduct). Unemployed or retired individuals are generally not able to deduct moving expenses because they do not meet the 39- or 78-week test.

ADDITIONAL COMMENT

The time requirement test ensures that taxpayers cannot use temporary jobs as a pretext for deducting the cost of moving for personal reasons.

EXAMPLE I9-40 ▶ Ellen is employed by the Able Company in Dallas, Texas. She lives 30 miles from her place of employment in Dallas. If Ellen accepts a new job in Houston, the new job location is 270 miles from her former residence in Dallas. The 50-mile distance requirement is satisfied because the distance from her old residence to her new job in Houston exceeds the distance from her old residence to her old job by 240 miles (270 − 30). In addition, to meet the time requirement, Ellen must be employed on a full-time basis in Houston for at least 39 weeks during the 12-month period immediately following the move. ◀

EXAMPLE I9-41 ▶ Assume the same facts as in Example I9-40, except that Ellen accepts a new job and moves to a new residence in a small town outside of Dallas. Her new job location is 55 miles from her former residence. The 50-mile distance requirement is not met because the distance from her old residence to her new job is 55 miles and the distance from her old residence to her old job is 30 miles; thus, the excess distance is only 25 miles. ◀

ADDITIONAL COMMENT

The individual need not be employed at the location that he or she is leaving. For example, a graduating college student who has not been employed for the most recent four years could deduct moving costs if the distance requirement is satisfied and if he or she has been employed at the *new* location for the minimum time period.

EXPENSE CLASSIFICATION

Moving expenses of an employee or a self-employed individual are deductible *for* AGI.[31] Thus, a taxpayer may receive a tax benefit from the deduction of moving expenses even if the standard deduction is used in lieu of itemizing deductions.

DEFINITION OF MOVING EXPENSES

DIRECT MOVING EXPENSES. Only direct moving expenses are deductible. These expenses are deductible without limit as long as they are reasonable in amount and include:

▶ The cost of moving household goods and personal effects from the former residence to the new residence (e.g., moving van).

KEY POINT

The standard mileage rate for purposes of the moving expense deduction is only 18 cents per mile, compared to the 2006 standard business mileage rate of 44.5 cents per mile.

▶ The cost of traveling (including lodging but excluding meals) from the former residence to the new residence. If the trip is by personal automobile, a deduction of 18 cents per mile (or actual expenses) is allowed for each automobile that is driven in 2006 (15 cents per mile in 2005).

The expenses of moving household goods and personal effects do not include storage charges in excess of 30 days, penalties for breaking leases, mortgage penalties, expenses of refitting drapes, or losses on deposits and club memberships.[32]

---

[30] The requirements for deducting moving expenses are contained in Sec. 217 and the Treasury Regulations thereunder.

[31] Sec. 62(a)(15). For years before 1994 moving expenses were deductible *from* AGI as an itemized deduction (not subject to the 2% nondeductible floor).

[32] Reg. Sec. 1.217-2(b)(3). In-transit storage charges for up to 30 consecutive days are allowable moving expenses.

EXAMPLE I9-42 ▶ Gail, a resident of California and a college student in that state, graduates from college and accepts a new position with an accounting firm in Atlanta. Thus, Gail is an employee of the Atlanta firm. Because the move meets the distance requirement (i.e., more than 50 miles), Gail qualifies for the deduction if she also meets the 39-week time requirement. Gail incurs the following expenses pursuant to the move: moving van, $1,200; lodging en route, $400; automobile expenses, $450 (2,500 miles × $0.18 cents per mile); and tolls and parking, $25. Assuming these expenses are reasonable, they qualify as direct moving expenses and are deductible without limitation. The cost of any meals incurred by Gail en route is not deductible. ◀

Otherwise allowable expenses of any individual other than the taxpayer are taken into account only if the individual has both the former residence and the new residence as his principal place of abode and is a member of the taxpayer's household.

EXAMPLE I9-43 ▶ Assume the same facts as in Example I9-42 except that Gail's son Paul is a member of her household. Additional automobile expenses (including tolls and parking) of $275 are incurred during the move because Paul owns an automobile which is driven to the new location. The $275 of additional automobile expenses are deductible as moving expenses because Paul is a member of Gail's household and his principal place of abode includes both the former and the new residences. ◀

HISTORICAL NOTE

Indirect moving expenses are not deductible after December 31, 1993. In the Revenue Reconciliation Act of 1993, Congress eliminated the deduction for costs associated with pre-move househunting trips, temporary quarters, and selling the old residence. Congress felt that a deduction was not justified for expenses that were not directly related to the move.

NONDEDUCTIBLE INDIRECT MOVING EXPENSES. In addition to the disallowed moving expenses previously discussed (e.g., meals en route, storage charges, etc.), the following indirect or moving-related expense items are not deductible:[33]

▶ Househunting trips including meals, lodging, and transportation

▶ Temporary living expenses at the new job location

▶ Qualified expenses related to a sale, purchase, or lease of a residence (e.g., attorney's fees, points, or payments to a lessor to cancel a lease)

TREATMENT OF EMPLOYER REIMBURSEMENTS

Moving expense reimbursements made by an employer, either paid directly or through reimbursement, are excluded from the employee's gross income as a qualified fringe benefit under Sec. 132 to the extent that the expenses meet the requirements for deductibility (i.e., the reimbursement is for moving expenses that are otherwise deductible under Sec. 217). Moving expense reimbursements must be included in gross income if the employee actually deducted the expenses in a prior tax year or if the expenses are otherwise not deductible under Sec. 217.[34]

EXAMPLE I9-44 ▶ In 2006, Ralph incurs $2,400 of moving expenses related to moving household effects and traveling to his new residence. He also incurs $2,600 of nondeductible moving-related expenses (e.g., househunting trips and temporary living expenses). Ralph receives a $5,000 reimbursement from his employer. Of the total reimbursement, $2,400 is excluded from gross income as a Sec. 132 fringe benefit. However, the $2,600 reimbursement for nondeductible moving-related expenses is included in Ralph's gross income under Sec. 82. None of the $2,400 of moving expenses may be deducted by Ralph because they were reimbursed by his employer and were not included in Ralph's gross income. ◀

EDUCATION EXPENSES

OBJECTIVE 4

Describe the requirements for deducting education expenses

Generally, education expenses are considered personal expenses and, therefore, are not deductible despite the obvious benefits that accrue to society from the pursuit of such activities. However, education expenses that are necessary in the pursuit of an employment-related or trade or business activity are deductible. It would be inequitable if such educational expenditures were not deductible because they are incurred to produce income from employment or business activities. The education expenses discussed in this chapter pertain

---

[33] Before 1994, indirect moving expenses were deductible subject to a $1,500 limit for househunting trips and temporary living expenses with a $3,000 overall limitation being applied to all indirect moving expenses.

[34] Sec. 82 and Sec. 132(g).

to expenses that are related to an individual's trade or business, such as a job in the case of an employee or the business of a self-employed individual. However, there are a number of other provisions in the tax law that provide favorable tax advantages for education expenses. Most of these rules are covered elsewhere in this textbook; however, the major tax provisions dealing with education are summarized below.

▶ Tax credits—two important provisions benefiting education are the HOPE scholarship credit and the lifetime learning credit. Both of these items are credits and are available for the taxpayer and his dependents and are discussed in Chapter I14.

▶ Exclusion for scholarships—scholarships received by students are generally excludable from gross income under Sec. 117. See the discussion of scholarships in Chapter I4.

▶ Educational assistance for employees—if an employer maintains an educational assistance plan, amounts received by the employee for tuition and other expenses are excludable from the employee's gross income under Sec. 127. This exclusion is also discussed in Chapter I4.

▶ Student loan interest—a *for* AGI deduction is permitted for certain student loan interest under Sec. 221. See Chapter I6 for a further discussion of this topic.

▶ Deduction for higher education expenses—for tax years 2004–2006, taxpayers may deduct up to $4,000 *for* AGI for tuition and related expenses under Sec. 222.[35] This deduction, as is the case for the tax credits and the student loan interest, is subject to a phase-out based on AGI. If a taxpayer's AGI does not exceed $65,000 ($130,000 on a joint return) in 2004–2006, the taxpayer may deduct up to $4,000. However, taxpayer's with AGI exceeding $65,000 but not exceeding $80,000 may deduct up to $2,000 in qualified expenses. No deduction is permitted for taxpayers with AGI in excess of $80,000. Further, taxpayers are not permitted to claim this deduction and also claim one of the tax credits above using the same expenses.

▶ Qualified state tuition programs—a very popular program for higher income taxpayers is the use of so-called Section 529 plans. These plans allow taxpayers to invest funds to be used for education and the income earned on such funds is not subject to tax. When amounts are withdrawn from the plan, the amounts are also not taxable if used for qualified education expenses. These plans are discussed in Chapter I4.

▶ Coverdell Education IRA—these special IRAs are discussed later in this chapter and enable a taxpayer to invest up to $2,000 per year in a tax-deferred IRA.

CLASSIFICATION OF EDUCATION EXPENSES

Depending on the nature of the education-related activity, educational expenses may be either personal and nondeductible, deductible *for* AGI, deductible *from* AGI (as a miscellaneous itemized deduction), or reimbursed by an employer and excluded from gross income. Table I9-3 illustrates the tax consequences that are accorded to various types of education expenses depending on the facts and circumstances and the type of expenditure for each case.

The discussion below focuses on the deductibility of education expenses that are related to a taxpayer's trade or business.

GENERAL REQUIREMENTS FOR A DEDUCTION

An employee generally may deduct education expenses if either of the following two requirements are met:[36]

▶ The expenditure is incurred to maintain or improve skills required by the individual in his or her employment, trade, or business; or

▶ The expenditure is incurred to meet requirements imposed by law or by the employer for retention of employment, rank, or compensation rate.

Even if one of the two requirements above are met, education expenses are not deductible if:

ADDITIONAL COMMENT

Attendance at a convention or professional meeting is one of the most common deductible education expenses. Almost every profession or occupation has its own society or association. Often these organizations sponsor local, regional, or national meetings. Training sessions or other types of educational activities are normally included on the program.

TYPICAL MISCONCEPTION

Education costs include more than the cost of books, tuition, registration fees, and supplies. Transportation costs and travel costs are also included.

[35] This deduction was scheduled to expire after 2005. However, both the House and Senate propose to extend this provision through 2006. For years 2002 and 2003, the maximum deduction was $3,000 and no deduction if AGI exceeded $65,000 ($130,000 on a joint return).

[36] Reg. Sec. 1.162-5.

▼ TABLE I9-3

Classification and Tax Treatment of Educational Expenses

Situation Facts	Classification and Tax Treatment
▶ Jeremy is a college student who is not classified as an employee and is pursuing a general course of study.	▶ The expenses are nondeductible personal expenditures regardless of whether Jeremy or his parents pay them.
▶ Irene is an employee who incurs certain employment-related educational expenses including travel, transportation, tuition, and books. Her expenses are not reimbursed by her employer.	▶ If the expenses meet the two general deduction requirements, the education expenses are deductible *from* AGI as a miscellaneous itemized deduction (subject to the 2% nondeductible floor).
▶ Jesse is an employee who receives educational assistance payments from his employer to reimburse him for certain educational expenses incurred in attending college at the undergraduate level.	▶ Educational assistance payments up to $5,250 per year are excluded from Jesse's gross income and are deductible by the employer as trade or business expenses if the requirements of Sec. 127 are met.[37]
▶ Jackie is a self-employed CPA who incurs education expenses including travel, transportation, books, registration fees, and so on to attend a continuing education conference.	▶ All of the education expenses are deductible *for* AGI as trade or business expenses.
▶ Jim is an employee who incurs education expenses for a continuing education course related to his employment, and the expenses are reimbursed by the employer.	▶ The reimbursement is deductible by the employer as a trade or business expense. There is no tax effect to the employee because the education expenses are offset by the reimbursement.

ETHICAL POINT

A client asks advice from his CPA as to whether certain educational expenses are deductible. The CPA should inform the client that the advice reflects professional judgment based on an existing situation. The CPA should use cautionary language to the effect that the advice is based on facts as stated and authorities that are subject to change.

▶ The education is required to meet minimum educational requirements for qualification in the taxpayer's employment; or

▶ The education qualifies the taxpayer for a new trade or business (or employment activity).

The deductibility of education expenses has been a frequent source of controversy and litigation because of the uncertainty in interpreting the above Regulations. The principal area of disagreement has been the interpretation of the term "qualifies the taxpayer for a new trade or business." If a taxpayer undertakes education and that education will *qualify* her for a new trade or business, then her expenses will not be deductible. For example, several courts have disallowed deductions to IRS agents and accountants for educational expenses incurred in obtaining a law degree, even though such training would be helpful in the taxpayer's employment.[38] The courts reasoned that the taxpayers were qualifying for a new profession (i.e., the practice of law). However, the IRS has ruled that a practicing dentist may deduct educational expenses in becoming an orthodontist under the theory that a dentist becoming an orthodontist is not entering a new trade or business.[39]

STOP & THINK

Question: The Regulations clearly provide that if the education "qualifies" a taxpayer for a new trade or business, the cost of such education is not deductible. If taken to the extreme, could the IRS argue that *any* course would qualify an individual for a new trade or business? For example, if a person took a basket weaving course, could not the IRS argue that the person is now qualified for the new trade or business of basket weaving? How can a taxpayer support his position that the education does not qualify him for a new trade or business in order to meet the deductibility requirements?

---

[37] The Sec. 127 exclusion is applicable for expenses paid by an employer for courses taken by employees. Qualified expenses include tuition, fees, and related expenses. Both undergraduate and graduate-level courses qualify for the exclusion.

[38] *Jeffry L. Weiler*, 54 T.C. 398 (1970).
[39] Rev. Rul. 74-78, 1974-1 C.B. 44.

ADDITIONAL COMMENT

The same course could be deductible as a qualified educational expense or not depending on the particular situation of the student. For example, a CPA enrolled in a taxation course to update his or her tax knowledge could deduct the expense. On the other hand, a non-CPA taking the course as part of a series of courses meeting the requirements to sit for the CPA exam could not deduct the expense. The CPA has already met the minimum education requirements for the profession and the non-CPA has not.

Solution: This is a difficult question and many commentators have written that the Regulations are unfairly harsh toward taxpayers. The courts have required that the IRS be "reasonable" in its interpretations of qualification of a new trade or business. The best way for a taxpayer to support his position is to find a case where the facts are approximately the same as the taxpayer's and where the court has upheld the taxpayer's position in that case.

Generally, a taxpayer must be employed or self-employed to be eligible for an education expense deduction. However, some courts have permitted individuals to qualify if they are unemployed for a temporary period.[40] School teachers have generally qualified for an education expense deduction in situations where the public school system requires advanced education courses as a condition for retention of employment or renewal of a teaching certificate or where state law imposes similar requirements. However, college instructors who are working on a doctorate in a college where the Ph.D. is the minimum degree for holding a permanent position generally have not been permitted to deduct the expenditures made to obtain the degree.[41] The Tax Court recently allowed a taxpayer to deduct the cost of earning an M.B.A. because the education merely enhanced and maintained the skills he already had and did not qualify him for a new trade or business.[42]

EXAMPLE I9-45 ▶ Jane is a self-employed dentist who incurs education expenses attending a continuing education conference on new techniques in her field. Such expenditures are incurred to maintain or improve her skills as a practicing dentist (a trade or business activity). All of her educational expenses are deductible *for* AGI because Jane is currently engaged in a trade or business activity. ◀

EXAMPLE I9-46 ▶ Juan is a business executive who incurs education expenses in the pursuit of an MBA degree in management. None of the expenses are reimbursed by Juan's employer. The expenses are deductible because they are incurred to maintain or improve Juan's skills as a manager and do not qualify Juan for a new trade or business. All of Juan's education expenses (e.g., travel, transportation, tuition, books, and word processing) are deductible *from* AGI as a miscellaneous itemized deduction (subject to the 2% nondeductible floor). ◀

EXAMPLE I9-47 ▶ Janet is a high school teacher who is required by state law to complete a specified number of additional graduate courses to renew her provisional teaching certificate. None of the expenses are reimbursed by Janet's employer. The educational expenses are deductible *from* AGI as a miscellaneous itemized deduction (subject to the 2% nondeductible floor) because the expenditures are incurred to meet the requirements imposed by law to retain her job and do not qualify her for a new trade or business. ◀

EXAMPLE I9-48 ▶ Jean is an accountant with a public accounting firm who incurs expenses in connection with taking the CPA examination (e.g., CPA review course fees, travel, and transportation). None of the expenses are reimbursed by Jean's employer. Even though the expenditures may improve her employment-related skills, they are not deductible because they are incurred to meet the minimum educational standards for qualification in Jean's accounting position.[43] ◀

EXAMPLE I9-49 ▶

KEY POINT

The deduction for travel expenses is not permitted if the travel itself is the educational activity. Therefore, a high school teacher who teaches Spanish cannot deduct expenses incurred in living in Madrid during the summer.

Joy is a tax accountant who incurs expenses to obtain a law degree. Despite the fact that the law school courses may be helpful to Joy to maintain or improve her skills as a tax practitioner, such expenses are not deductible because the taxpayer is qualifying for a new trade or business. If Joy were not a degree candidate at the law school and merely took a few tax law courses for continuing education, the educational expenses would be deductible because they are incurred to maintain or improve Joy's skills as a tax specialist and do not qualify her for a new trade or business. In such a case, the expenses are deductible *for* AGI if Joy is self-employed and *from* AGI as a miscellaneous itemized deduction (subject to the 2% nondeductible floor) if Joy is an employee. ◀

---

[40] *Robert J. Picknally,* 1977 PH T.C. Memo ¶77,321, 36 TCM 1292. The IRS has conceded that a deduction may be warranted in periods where the cessation of business activity was for periods of a year or less (Rev. Rul. 68-591, 1968-2 C.B. 73).

[41] *Kenneth C. Davis,* 65 T.C. 1014 (1976).

[42] *Daniel R. Allmeier, Jr.,* 90 TCM 197 (2005).

[43] Rev. Rul. 69-292, 1969-1 C.B. 84.

OFFICE IN HOME EXPENSES

Employees or self-employed individuals who use a portion of their home for trade or business or employment-related activities should be entitled to a deduction because the property is used for trade or business or employment-related activities. However, it is often difficult to determine whether a taxpayer is using a portion of the home for business or personal use.

For over twenty years, there has been an ongoing controversy in the tax law as to the deductibility of office in home expenses. Because of the possibility of abuse by taxpayers, the IRC, Treasury Regulations, and the courts[44] have been extremely strict as to who qualifies to deduct office in home expenses. In order to promote fairness and consistency in the tax law, Congress, effective for tax years beginning after December 31, 1998, liberalized the definition of an office in home that qualifies for a tax deduction.

GENERAL REQUIREMENTS FOR A DEDUCTION

ADDITIONAL COMMENT

Approximately 24 million individuals, or 23% of the work force, work at least part-time at home.

Employees and self-employed individuals are permitted to deduct office in home expenses only if the office is exclusively used on a regular basis under any of the following conditions:

▶ The office is used as the principal place of business for *any* trade or business of the taxpayer;

▶ The office is used as a place for meeting or dealing with patients, clients, or customers in the normal course of business; or

REAL-WORLD EXAMPLE

Most teachers have been denied a home office deduction because the home office is not the principal place of business. Also, most teachers cannot demonstrate that their office in the home is for the convenience of the employer because the employer typically provides an office at the school.

▶ If the office in home is located in a separate structure which is not attached to the dwelling unit, the office is used partially or totally in connection with the taxpayer's trade or business.[45]

In addition to meeting any of these tests, an employee further must prove that the exclusive use is for the convenience of the *employer*. It is not enough that it is merely appropriate or helpful to the employee.

The first condition above has caused the major controversy in this area. Taxpayers are required to prove that the office is used exclusively as the "principal place of business." Under prior law, the principal place of business was interpreted to mean the "most important or significant place for the business," or more precisely, where the primary services were performed. Thus, a physician who performed medical services at a hospital but maintained an office in home to perform administrative duties was not allowed a deduction for the office because the principal place of business was interpreted to be the hospital.

EXAMPLE I9-50 ▶

In the *Soliman* case, Dr. Soliman was a self-employed anesthesiologist who performed medical services at three hospitals, none of which provided him with an office. He spent approximately two hours per day in his office in home where he maintained patient records and correspondence and he performed billing procedures. The office was not used as a place for meeting with or dealing with patients, clients, or customers in the normal course of his business. The U.S. Supreme Court denied a deduction for Dr. Soliman's office in home because it concluded that the essence of professional service rendered by the doctor was the actual medical treatment in the hospitals. A second factor considered by the court was the amount of time spent at the office relative to the total work effort. The effect of this case was to deny a deduction for an office in home for any type of taxpayer in a trade or business where the primary services were performed outside of the office (such as plumbers, electricians). This case was highly criticized. ◀

To combat the perceived unfairness of the *Soliman* case, Congress expanded the definition of "principal place of business" for tax years beginning after December 31, 1998. An office in home now qualifies as a taxpayer's principal place of business if:

1. the office is used by the taxpayer for *administrative or management* activities of the taxpayer's trade or business, and

---

[44] See, for example, *CIR v. Nader E. Soliman*, 71 AFTR 2d 93-463, 93-1 USTC 50,014 (USSC, 1993).

[45] Sec. 280A(c)(1).

KEY POINT

The office-in-home deduction is available only where the office is being used for trade or business purposes. No deduction is permitted if the office is used to carry on investment activities.

2. there is no other fixed location of the trade or business where the taxpayer conducts substantial administrative or management activities of the trade or business.[46]

Thus, the law essentially allows a deduction for an office in home even though the taxpayer provides his primary service away from the office. The above tests are clearly intended for self-employed taxpayers. However, they also apply to employees except that the additional "convenience of the employer" test will still apply.

EXAMPLE I9-51 ▶ David is a self-employed electrician who performs his electrical services at the location of his customers. He also maintains an office where he does his administrative and management duties. David is permitted a deduction for an office in home even though his primary duties of providing electrical services are performed away from his office. ◀

EXAMPLE I9-52 ▶ Barbara is an employee of DRK, Inc., and is provided with an office on DRK's premises. However, Barbara's job requires significant administrative work after normal working hours and she prefers to perform these duties in her office at home. Barbara may not deduct the costs of her office in home because she uses her office at home for *her* convenience, not her employer's convenience. ◀

As can be seen from the discussion above, the deduction for an office in home is generally restricted to self-employed taxpayers and employees who are not provided with an office by their employer. If a self-employed taxpayer maintains an office in home, the expenses are deductible *for* AGI. Employees must deduct the office in home expenses as miscellaneous itemized deductions, subject to the 2% nondeductible floor.

DEDUCTION AND LIMITATIONS

The deduction for home office expenses is computed using the following two categories of expenses:

1. Expenses directly related to the office, and
2. Expenses indirectly related to the office.

Direct expenses include operating expenses (supplies, etc.) that are used in the business as well as other expenses that relate solely to the office, such as painting and decorating just the office. Indirect expenses are the pro rata share of expenses that benefit the entire house or apartment, such as mortgage interest (or rent), real estate taxes, insurance, utilities, and maintenance. The office in the home expense is the sum of the direct expenses plus the pro rata share (generally based on square footage) of indirect expenses.

To compute the office in home deduction, taxpayers first subtract all expenses not connected with the office from the income generated by the business. Then, 100% of the direct expenses of the office and the percentage of indirect expenses based on the pro rata share of the house are deducted. The total of the office in home expenses cannot create a loss.

EXAMPLE I9-53 ▶ Julie works as a full-time employee for a local company. She also operates a mail order business out of her home and maintains an office in her home that is used exclusively for business. The size of her home in total is 2,400 square feet and her office is 300 square feet. During the current year, she generated gross income of $18,000 and had $6,000 of business expenses, such as supplies and shipping charges. She also had the following expenses in connection with the office in her home:

TAX STRATEGY TIP

When a taxpayer depreciates his office in the home, the office becomes business property. Upon the sale of the residence, the portion of the sale price attributable to the office will not be eligible for the sale of principal residence exclusion. Therefore, taxpayers might consider only deducting direct expenses of an in-home office to preserve the exclusion.

Painting of office	$ 600
Decorations in office	900
Mortgage interest (total)	3,200
Real estate taxes (total)	1,800
Insurance (total)	600
Utilities (total)	2,400
Depreciation (total)	800

[46] Ibid. For years before 1999, this new definition of principal place of business does not apply. Thus, the restrictive rules promulgated by *Soliman* apply to these years.

Julie's home office expense for the current year would be computed as follows:

Direct expenses:		
Painting	$ 600	
Decorations	900	$1,500
Indirect expenses:		
Mortgage interest	3,200	
Real estate taxes	1,800	
Insurance	600	
Utilities	2,400	
Depreciation	800	
	8,800	
Business percentage (300/2,400)	×12.5%	1,100
Total expense for office in home		$2,600

Julie would be allowed to deduct all of the $2,600 of office in home expenses as they do not exceed the $12,000 ($18,000 − $6,000) of income from the business. If Julie only had $8,000 of gross income and $6,000 of business expenses, her office in home expenses of $2,600 would be limited to $2,000. ◄

As mentioned above, the total allowable office in home expenses may not exceed the taxpayer's gross income from the business (or rental) activity.[47] This ceiling limitation on office in home deductions is intended to prevent taxpayers from recognizing tax losses if the business (or rental) activity does not produce sufficient amounts of gross income. Expenses disallowed because of the gross income limitation can be carried forward but are subject to the gross income limitation in the later year and are subject to specific ordering rules.[48]

Employee expense classifications and deduction limitations are summarized in Topic Review I9-1.

DEFERRED COMPENSATION

Various types of benefit plans providing favorable tax treatment are available to employees and self-employed individuals. These tax benefits are provided to stimulate savings accumulations for retirement as a supplement to the Social Security system. Favorable tax consequences generally include the following benefits:

▶ Deferral of taxes on amounts contributed to retirement plans until the individual retires or receives a distribution from the plan

▶ An immediate deduction for contributions to qualified retirement plans for the employer or self-employed individual

▶ Deferral of taxation on income earned on retirement plan assets

The following types of *deferred compensation arrangements* are discussed here:

▶ Qualified pension and profit-sharing plans

▶ Nonqualified deferred compensation arrangements, including restricted property and employee stock option plans

▶ Self-employed (H.R. 10) retirement plans and individual retirement accounts (IRAs)

QUALIFIED PENSION AND PROFIT-SHARING PLANS

The federal tax law provides favorable tax benefits for *qualified* pension and profit-sharing plans. A **qualified plan** is one that must meet strict requirements, such as not discriminating in favor of highly compensated individuals, be formed and operated for the exclusive

---

[47] Sec. 280A(c)(5).
[48] See Prop. Reg. Sec. 1.280A-2 for the ordering rules. These rules are similar, but not identical to the ordering rules for hobby losses under Sec. 183.

Topic Review I9-1

Classification and Deductibility of Employee Expenses

TYPE OF EXPENDITURE	50% DISALLOWANCE	FOR OR FROM AGI	OTHER LIMITATIONS
Miscellaneous itemized deductions	Applies to unreimbursed meals and entertainment	*From* AGI	Subject to 2% of AGI nondeductible floor.
Reimbursed travel expenses (adequate accounting is made)	Applies to the employer for meals portion of the travel only	*For* AGI	2% of AGI nondeductible floor applies only to employee expenses that exceed the reimbursement.
Unreimbursed travel expenses	Applies to meals portion of travel only	*From* AGI	Subject to the 2% of AGI nondeductible floor. Employee must be away from his or her tax home overnight.
Automobile expenses	Not applicable	*From* AGI	Subject to the 2% of AGI nondeductible floor. Actual costs or the standard mileage rate method may be used.
Moving expenses	Not applicable because meals are not deductible	*For* AGI	Indirect moving-related expenses are not deductible.
Entertainment expenses	Applies to all entertainment expenses	*From* AGI	Subject to the 2% of AGI nondeductible floor. Club dues and initiation fees are not deductible.
Education expenses deductible per Reg. Sec. 1.162-5	Applies to meal portion of education expenses	*From* AGI	Qualifying expenses are subject to the 2% of AGI nondeductible floor.
Office-in-home	Not applicable	*From* AGI; If trade- or business-related, the expenses are for AGI	Employment-related expenses (other than real estate taxes and interest) are subject to the 2% of AGI nondeductible floor. Gross income limitations apply to allowable expenses.

benefit of employees, and meet specified vesting and funding requirements. In a qualified plan, both the employer and employee receive significant tax benefits, as follows:

EMPLOYER: receives an immediate tax deduction for pension and profit-sharing contributions made on behalf of employees.

EMPLOYEE: is not taxed on either employer or employee contributions or earnings of the plan assets until funds are withdrawn from the plan at retirement.[49] Thus, funds invested in a qualified plan grow tax-free during an employee's working years.

TYPES OF PLANS. Qualified plans[50] include

► Pension plans

► Profit-sharing plans (including Sec. 401(k) plans)

► Stock bonus plans, including employee stock ownership plans (ESOPs)

Pension Plans. The features that distinguish a *qualified pension plan* include the following:

► Systematic and definite payments are made to a pension trust (without regard to profits) based on formulas or actuarial methods.

---

[49] An employee may not be liable for federal income taxes but may be subject to Social Security taxes and possibly local or city income taxes.

[50] Qualified plans are generally covered in Secs. 401-416 of the IRC.

▶ A pension plan may provide for incidental benefits such as disability, death, or medical insurance benefits.

A pension plan may be either contributory or noncontributory. Under a **noncontributory pension plan**, the contributions are made solely by the employer. Under a **contributory pension plan**, the employee makes voluntary contributions into the plan that supplement any contributions made by the employer.

Pension plans also may be either defined contribution plans or defined benefit plans. In a **defined contribution pension plan**, a separate account is established for each participant and certain amounts are contributed based on a specific formula (e.g., a specified percentage of compensation). The benefits payable to the participant at retirement are based on the value of the participant's account (including the amount of earnings that accrue to the account) at the time of retirement.

EXAMPLE I9-54 ▶

Alabama Corporation establishes a qualified pension plan for its employees that provides for employer contributions equal to 8% of each participant's salary. Retirement payments to each participant are based on the amount of accumulated benefits in the employee's account at the retirement date. The pension plan is a defined contribution plan, because the contribution rate is based on a specific and fixed percentage of compensation. ◀

KEY POINT

All qualified plans can be classified into two broad categories. They are either defined contribution plans or defined benefit plans. An understanding of the distinction between these two broad categories is important because some rules will apply to one type of plan but not the other.

Defined benefit plans establish a contribution formula based on actuarial techniques that are sufficient to fund a fixed benefit amount to be paid upon retirement. For example, a defined benefit plan might provide fixed retirement benefits equal to 40% of an employee's average salary for the five years before retirement.

A distinguishing feature of a defined benefit plan is that forfeitures of unvested amounts (e.g., due to employee resignations) must be used to reduce the employer contributions that would otherwise be made under the plan. In a defined contribution plan, however, the forfeitures related to unvested amounts may either be reallocated to the other participants in a nondiscriminatory manner or used to reduce future employer contributions.

Profit-Sharing Plans. A qualified **profit-sharing plan** also may be established by an employer in addition to, or in lieu of, a qualified pension plan arrangement. Profit-sharing plans include the following distinguishing features:

▶ A definite, predetermined formula must be used to allocate employer contributions to individual employees and to establish benefit payments.

▶ Annual employer contributions are not required, but substantial and recurring contributions must be made to satisfy the requirement that the plan be permanent.

▶ Employees may be given the option to receive cash that is fully taxable as current compensation or to defer taxation on employer contributions by having such amounts contributed to the profit-sharing trust. Plans of this type are called Sec. 401(k) plans.[51]

▶ Forfeitures arising under the plan may be reallocated to the remaining participants to increase their profit-sharing benefits, provided that certain nondiscrimination requirements are met.

▶ Lump-sum payments made to an employee before retirement may be provided following a prescribed period for the vesting of such amounts.

▶ Incidental benefits such as disability, death, or medical insurance may also be provided in a profit-sharing arrangement.

Stock Bonus Plan. A **stock bonus plan** is a special type of defined contribution plan whereby the investments of the plan are in the employer-company's own stock. The employer makes its contribution to the trust either in cash or in stock. If in cash, the amounts are invested in the company's stock. The stock is allocated and subsequently distributed to the participants. Stock bonus plan requirements are similar to profit-sharing plans. An **employee stock ownership plan (ESOP)** is a type of qualified stock bonus plan.[52] An ESOP, funded by a combination of employer and employee contributions and plan loans, invest primarily in employer stock. The stock is held for the benefit of the employees. ESOPs are attractive

---

[51] Sec. 401(k).   [52] Secs. 409(a) and 4975(e)(7).

because the employer is allowed to reduce taxable income by deducting any dividends that are paid to the participants (or their beneficiaries) in the year such amounts are paid and are taxable to the participant. For employer securities acquired by the ESOP, the dividends-paid deduction is limited to dividends paid on employer stock acquired with an ESOP loan.

QUALIFICATION REQUIREMENTS FOR A QUALIFIED PLAN

Qualified pension, profit-sharing, and stock bonus plans must meet complex qualification rules and requirements to achieve and maintain their favored qualifying status. A summary of the important requirements are discussed below.

▶ Section 401(a) requires that the plan must be for the employee's exclusive benefit. For example, the trust must follow prudent investment rules to ensure that the pension benefits will accrue for the employees' benefit.

▶ The plan may not discriminate in favor of highly compensated employees. Highly compensated employees are employees who meet either of two tests: (1) own more than 5% of the corporation's stock in either the current or prior year or (2) receive compensation of greater than $100,000 ($95,000 in 2005) in the prior year.[53]

▶ Contributions and plan benefits must bear a uniform relationship to the compensation payments made to covered employees. For example, if contributions for the benefit of the participants are based on a fixed percentage of the employee's compensation (e.g., 4%), the plan should not be disqualified despite the fact that the contributions for highly-compensated employees are greater on an actual dollar basis than those for lower paid individuals.

▶ Certain coverage requirements that are expressed in terms of a portion of the employees covered by the plan must be met.

▶ An employee's right to receive benefits from the employer's contributions must vest (i.e., become nonforfeitable) after a certain period or number of years of employment. The vesting requirement is intended to ensure that a significant percentage of employees will eventually receive retirement benefits. Employer-provided benefits must be 100% vested after 5 years of service.[54] In all cases, any employee contributions to the plan must vest immediately.

EXAMPLE I9-55 ▶ Ken is a participant in a noncontributory qualified pension plan that provides for no vesting until an employee completes three years of service. Ken terminates his employment with the company after two years of service. Because Ken has not met the minimum vesting requirements, he is not entitled to receive any of the employer contributions that are made on his behalf. ◀

TAX TREATMENT TO EMPLOYEES AND EMPLOYERS

Employer contributions to a qualified plan are immediately deductible (subject to specific limitations on contribution amounts), and earnings on pension fund investments are tax-exempt to the plan. Amounts paid into a plan by or for an employee are not taxable until the pension payments are received, normally at retirement. At the election of the employee, amounts may be treated as having been made from either pre-tax or after-tax earnings. If amounts contributed to a qualified plan by an employee are made on a pre-tax basis, the taxable portion of the employee's earnings is reduced by the contribution amount. This has the effect of permitting a deduction for the contribution amount. When amounts are withdrawn at retirement, the entire distribution is subject to taxation.

EXAMPLE I9-56 ▶ Larry is an employee of Cisco Corporation, which maintains a Sec. 401(k) plan. Larry contributes 5% of his gross salary into the plan on a pre-tax basis. During the current year, Larry's gross salary is $80,000 so his Sec. 401(k) contribution is $4,000. Since Larry's contribution is made on a pre-tax

---

[53] Sec. 414(q). The $100,000 amount is subject to annual indexing for inflation. Alternatively, an employer may elect to define a highly-compensated group as employees earning more than $100,000 *and* the top 20% group of employees based on compensation.

[54] Sec. 411(a)(2)(A). An alternative vesting schedule may also be used that provides for 20% vesting each year beginning in the third year of service, Sec. 411(a)(2)(B). Thus, after a total of seven years of service, an employee would be 100% vested. In addition, a faster vesting schedule is provided in Sec. 411(a)(12) whereby the vesting begins after two years of service and increases at a rate of 20% per year to 100% after six years.

basis, his taxable salary for the current year will be $76,000. In effect, Larry is able to deduct the $4,000 from his salary in the current year. When Larry retires and begins withdrawing amounts from the plan, the entire amount withdrawn will be subject to income taxation. ◄

Conversely, an employee may elect to contribute to a qualified plan on an after-tax basis. If, in Example I9-56, Larry contributed to the Sec. 401(k) plan on an after-tax basis, his taxable salary would have been $80,000. The $4,000 contributed to the plan is treated as an investment in the plan and is considered a tax-free return of capital when this amount is withdrawn at retirement.[55]

EMPLOYEE RETIREMENT PAYMENTS. An employee's retirement benefits are generally taxed under the Sec. 72 annuity rules (see Chapter I3). If the plan is noncontributory (i.e., no employee contributions are made to the plan), all of the pension benefits when received by the employee are fully taxable. If the plan is contributory, the taxability depends on whether the employee's contributions were made on a pre-tax or after-tax basis. If the contributions were made on a pre-tax basis, *all* retirement payments received by the employee are taxable. Alternatively, if the contributions were made on an after-tax basis, each payment is treated, in part, as a tax-free return of the employee's contributions and the remainder is taxable. The excluded portion is based on the ratio of the employee's investment in the contract to the expected return under the contract. However, the total amount that may be excluded is limited to the amount of the employee's contributions to the plan. If the employee dies before the entire investment in the contract is recovered, the unrecovered amount is allowed as an itemized deduction in the year of death.

EXAMPLE I9-57 ►

Kevin retires in 2006 at age 64 and will receive monthly annuity payments of $2,000 for life from his employer's qualified pension plan beginning in 2007. Kevin's investment in the contract (represented by his contributions made on an after-tax basis) is $100,000. Kevin's life expectancy per Sec. 72 is 260 months from the annuity starting date. So, for the next 260 months, Kevin can exclude $384.62 ($100,000/260 months). In 2007, Kevin would exclude $4,615.44 ($384.62 × 12 months) and $19,384.56 ($24,000.00 − $4,615.44) would be taxable. After Kevin receives payments for 260 months and his $100,000 investment in the contract is recovered, all subsequent payments are fully taxable. (See Chapter I3 for a discussion of the annuity formula and related rules.) ◄

EXAMPLE I9-58 ►

ADDITIONAL COMMENT

Many individuals have the option of taking their retirement savings from traditional pensions, profit-sharing plans, and 401(k)s as a lump sum or an annuity. Those who want to take a lump-sum distribution can delay taxes by transferring the money directly into a tax-deferred IRA.

Assume the same facts as in Example I9-57 except that Kevin made all of his contributions to the plan on a pre-tax basis. In other words, the amount that he contributed to the plan was subtracted from his salary each year. When Kevin starts receiving payments from the plan, all amounts received will be taxable. Therefore, in 2007, Kevin will include $24,000 in his gross income. Most employees elect to "tax defer" their contributions into retirement plans in order to reduce their current year taxable income and take advantage of the time value of money principle. ◄

If an employee age 59½ or older receives a lump-sum distribution from a qualified plan, a five-year forward income-averaging technique was generally available through 1999 to mitigate the effects of receiving a large amount of income in the year of the distribution.[56] Special tax treatment for lump-sum distributions is now available only for employees born before 1936. However, all taxpayers are eligible to make nontaxable rollovers of distributions from one qualified plan to another. Special rules apply to such rollovers.

LIMITATION ON EMPLOYER CONTRIBUTIONS. The Code places limitations on (1) amounts an employer may contribute to qualified pension, profit-sharing, and stock bonus plans and (2) amounts that the employer may deduct:

---

[55] Amounts contributed to a qualified plan on an after-tax basis are treated as an investment in the contract under the annuity rules of Sec. 72. Amounts withdrawn during retirement are taxed under the general rules of Sec. 72. See Chapter I3 for a discussion of taxation of annuities.

[56] Sec. 402(e). The five-year forward averaging provision was repealed for tax years beginning after December 31, 1999.

KEY POINT

For purposes of the limitation on employer contributions, all defined contribution plans maintained by one employer are treated as a single defined contribution plan. Furthermore, under some circumstances a group of employers can be treated as a single employer.

▶ Defined contribution plan contributions in 2006 are limited to the lesser of $44,000 or 100% of the employee's compensation.[57]

▶ Defined benefit plans are restricted to an annual benefit to an employee equal to the lesser of $175,000 for 2006 or 100% of the participant's average compensation for the highest three years.[58]

▶ An overall maximum annual employer deduction of 25% of compensation paid or accrued to plan participants is placed on defined contribution, profit-sharing, and stock bonus plans.[59] If an employer has more than one type of qualified plan (e.g., a defined benefit pension plan and a profit-sharing plan), a maximum deduction of 25% of compensation is allowed.

The distinguishing features and major requirements for qualified pension and profit-sharing plans are summarized in Topic Review I9-2.

NONQUALIFIED PLANS

KEY POINT

Although nonqualified plans are not subject to the same restrictions as imposed upon qualified plans, they do not receive the same tax benefits that are available under qualified plans. For example, the employer may not be able to deduct amounts that are set aside for employees.

Nonqualified deferred compensation plans are often used by employers to provide incentives or supplementary retirement benefits for executives. Common forms of nonqualified plans include the following:

▶ An unfunded, nonforfeitable promise to pay fixed amounts of compensation in future periods.[60]

▶ Restricted property plans involving property transfers (usually in the form of the employer-company stock), where the property transferred is subject to a substantial risk of forfeiture and is nontransferable.[61]

DISTINGUISHING CHARACTERISTICS OF NONQUALIFIED PLANS. Nonqualified plans are not subject to the same restrictions imposed on qualified plans (such as the nondiscrimination and vesting rules), although nonqualified plans may have some vesting rules. Thus, such plans are particularly suitable for use in executive compensation

Topic Review I9-2

Qualified Pension and Profit-Sharing Plans

DISTINGUISHING FEATURES AND MAJOR REQUIREMENTS

▶ Employer contributions and earnings on contributed amounts are not taxed to employees until distributed or made available. The contributions are immediately deductible by the employer.
▶ Pension plans can be established as either defined contribution or defined benefit plans in which systematic and definite payments are made to a pension trust. Incidental benefits (e.g., death and disability payments) can be provided under the plan.
▶ Profit-sharing plans require the use of a predetermined allocation formula and substantial and recurring contributions must be made although annual employer contributions are not required and the contributions need not be based on profits. Section 401(k) plans can be established where employees have the option to receive cash or to have such amounts contributed to the profit-sharing trust. The employer may also establish an ESOP where the plan is funded by a contribution of the employer's stock.
▶ Qualified plans must be created for the employees' exclusive benefit.
▶ The plans may not discriminate in favor of highly compensated employees.
▶ Contributions and plan benefits must bear a uniform relationship to the compensation of covered employees.
▶ Minimum vesting requirements must be met (e.g., 100% vesting after five years).
▶ Employee benefits are taxed under the Sec. 72 annuity rules.
▶ Total employer contributions to the plan are subject to specific ceiling limitations.

---

[57] Sec. 415(c). The deduction limit for 2005 was $42,000. In addition, individuals over 50 years of age are now eligible to contribute extra amounts into their plans. The amount of the so-called catch-up contributions depend on the type of plan.
[58] Sec. 415(b)(1). The benefit amount for 2005 was $170,000. These amounts are subject to indexing each year.

[59] Sec. 404(a)(3)(A).
[60] Rev. Rul. 60-31, 1960-1 C.B. 174.
[61] Sec. 83.

planning. In general, nonqualified plans impose certain restrictions on the outright transfer of the plan's benefits to the employee. This avoids immediate taxation under the constructive receipt doctrine, which does not apply if the benefits are not yet credited, set apart, or made available so that the employee may draw on them. The amount is taxed to the employee upon the lapse of such restrictions, and the employer receives a corresponding deduction in the same year.

UNFUNDED DEFERRED COMPENSATION PLANS. **Unfunded deferred compensation plans** are often used to compensate highly compensated employees who desire to defer the recognition of income until future periods (e.g., a professional athlete or a business executive who receives a signing bonus may prefer to defer the recognition of income from the bonus). In general, if the promise to make the compensation payment in a future period is nonforfeitable, the agreement must not be funded (e.g., the transfer of assets to a trust for the employee's benefit) or evidenced by a negotiable note. The employer, however, may establish an *escrow account* on behalf of the employee. Such an account is used to accumulate and invest the deferred compensation amounts. If the requirements for deferral are met, the employee is taxed when the amounts are actually paid or made available, and the employer receives a corresponding deduction in the same year.[62]

EXAMPLE I9-59 ▶

In 2006, Kelly signs an employment contract to play professional football for the Chicago Skyhawks. The contract includes a $500,000 signing bonus that is payable in five annual installments beginning in 2012. The bonus agreement is nonforfeitable and is unfunded. The Skyhawks have agreed to place sufficient amounts of money into an escrow account to fund the future payments to Kelly. None of the $500,000 bonus is deductible by the employer or taxable to Kelly when the agreement is signed in 2006. The Skyhawks do not receive a deduction for any amounts that are deposited into the escrow account during the 2006–2011 period. In 2012, Kelly receives $100,000 taxable compensation (interest, if any, that accrued and was paid to Kelly is also taxable) upon receipt of the initial payment, and the Skyhawks receive a corresponding tax deduction. ◀

The 2005 Jobs Act enacted significant new requirements for nonqualified deferred compensation plans effective for amounts deferred in tax years beginning after December 31, 2004.[63] While a detailed examination of these new rules is outside the scope of this textbook, some major features of the new law are as follows:

▶ The new rules apply to any plan by which executive employees are permitted to defer the receipt and taxability of compensation from the current year to a future year. In prior years, the tax laws in this area were a wide range of cases and rulings.

▶ If deferred amounts under a plan fail to satisfy the new requirements at any time during the tax year, the recipient must pay the tax on the deferred compensation plus interest and an additional 20% excise tax.

▶ Distributions from the plan to recipients are subject to strict rules. Deferrals may be distributed to participants no earlier than the time of separation of service, pursuant to a fixed schedule in the plan, death, disability, an unforeseeable emergency, or upon a change in control of the company. Thus, early distributions are not generally permitted. In addition, acceleration of payment amounts are severely curtailed.

▶ Funding rules essentially have remained the same except that employers generally may no longer use offshore trusts.

Because of the complexity of the new rules in this area, taxpayers are strongly urged to look closely at their nonqualified deferred compensation plans to ensure that they comply with the new rules for 2005 and later years.

RESTRICTED PROPERTY PLANS. **Restricted property plans** are used to attract and retain key executives. Under such arrangements, the executive generally obtains an ownership interest (i.e., stock) in the corporation. Restricted property plans are governed by

---

[62] Reg. Sec. 1.451-2(a).   [63] Sec. 409A.

the income recognition rules contained in Sec. 83. Under these rules, the receipt of restricted property in exchange for services rendered is not taxable if the property is non-transferable and subject to a substantial risk of forfeiture.

The employee is treated as receiving taxable compensation based on the amount of the property's fair market value (FMV) (less any amount paid for the property) at the earlier of the time the property is no longer subject to a substantial risk of forfeiture or is transferable. The employer receives a corresponding compensation deduction at the same time the income is taxed to the employee.

EXAMPLE I9-60 ▶

In 2006, Allied Corporation transfers 1,000 shares of its common stock to employee Karen as compensation pursuant to a restricted property plan. The FMV of the Allied stock is $10 per share on the transfer date. The restricted property agreement provides that the stock is nontransferable by Karen until the year 2008 (i.e., Karen cannot sell the stock to outsiders until year 2008). The stock is also subject to the restriction that if Karen voluntarily leaves the company before the year 2008, she must transfer the shares back to the company and will receive no benefit from the stock other than from the receipt of dividends. The FMV of the stock is $100 per share in year 2008 when the forfeiture and nontransferability restrictions lapse. Because the stock is both nontransferable and subject to a substantial risk of forfeiture from the issue date to year 2008, the tax consequences from the stock transfer are deferred for both Karen and Allied Corporation until the lapse of the nontransferability or forfeiture restrictions in year 2008. Thus, no tax consequences result in 2006. In year 2008, Karen must report ordinary (compensation) income of $100,000 ($100 × 1,000 shares), and Allied Corporation is entitled to a corresponding compensation deduction of the same amount. Karen is taxed currently on the dividends she receives because they are not subject to any restrictions. ◀

KEY POINT

If an employee makes the election to be taxed immediately, he or she should be aware of the adverse consequences of leaving the company before the forfeiture restrictions lapse. The employee will not receive the property, and no deduction is allowed on the forfeiture.

Election to Be Taxed Immediately. An exception which permits an employee to elect (within 30 days after the receipt of restricted property) to recognize income immediately upon receipt of the restricted property is provided in Sec. 83(b). If the election is made, the employer is entitled to a corresponding deduction at the time the income is taxed to the employee. This election is frequently made when the fair market value of the restricted property is expected to increase significantly in the future and the future gain would be taxed as long-term capital gain. Because the current rate of tax on long-term capital gains has been reduced to 15%, one would expect that more taxpayers will now make the Sec. 83(b) election.

EXAMPLE I9-61 ▶

Assume the same facts as Example I9-60, except that Karen elects to recognize income in 2006 (i.e., the transfer date). Karen must include $10,000 ($10 × 1,000 shares) in gross income as compensation in the current year and Allied Corporation is entitled to a corresponding deduction in the same year. Karen will report no income in 2008 when the restrictions lapse and her basis in the Allied Corporation stock remains at $10,000. If Karen sells the stock for $100,000 in the year 2008 after the restrictions lapse, Karen reports a $90,000 ($100,000 − $10,000) long-term capital gain on the sale.[64] If Karen voluntarily leaves the company before the forfeiture restrictions lapse, no deduction is allowed when the forfeiture occurs, despite the fact that Karen is previously taxed on the stock's value on the transfer date (i.e., $10,000 of income is recognized by Karen in the current year). In such event, Allied Corporation must include $10,000 in gross income in the year of the forfeiture (i.e., the amount of the deduction that is taken in the year of the transfer to the extent of any previous tax benefit). ◀

Nonqualified plan features and requirements are summarized in Topic Review I9-3.

EMPLOYEE STOCK OPTIONS

Stock option plans are used by corporate employers to attract and retain key management employees. Both stock option and restricted property arrangements using the employer's stock permit the executive to receive a proprietary interest in the corporation. Thus, an executive may identify more closely with shareholder interests and the firm's long-run profit-maximization goals. The tax law currently includes two types of stock-option

---

[64] Sec. 1223. The holding period originates on the day following the transfer date because Karen made the election to be taxed immediately under Sec. 83(b).

Topic Review I9-3

Nonqualified Plans

DISTINGUISHING FEATURES AND MAJOR REQUIREMENTS

1. The employee is taxed upon the lapse of restrictions imposed on the availability or withdrawal of funds and the employer receives a corresponding deduction in the same year.
2. Nonqualified plans may discriminate in favor of highly compensated employees and no minimum vesting rules are required.
3. Restricted property (usually employer stock) may be offered to executives where the incidents of taxation are deferred if the property is nontransferable and subject to a substantial risk of forfeiture. An election may be made under Sec. 83(b) to recognize income immediately upon the receipt of the restricted property.
4. Restrictions must be imposed to avoid immediate taxation to the employee under the constructive receipt doctrine.
5. To avoid immediate taxation, restricted property plans must be both nonforfeitable and subject to a substantial risk of forfeiture.

REAL-WORLD EXAMPLE

The use of employee stock options has come under criticism recently in the financial press. The pressure to increase earnings has been a major issue in recent corporate scandals. Further, the Financial Accounting Standards Board has issued a statement requiring the current expensing of stock options in certain circumstances.

KEY POINT

Incentive stock options have the disadvantage of not providing a compensation deduction for the employer.

KEY POINT

Incentive stock options can be a valuable tax planning tool because the earliest that they are generally taxed is when they are exercised. Also, when an employee realizes profits from stock options, those profits in certain cases may qualify as capital gains.

arrangements: the incentive stock option and the nonqualified stock option.[65] Each type is treated differently for tax purposes.

As will be seen in the discussions below, both types of plans have their respective advantages and disadvantages. Incentive stock option arrangements generally are preferred when long-term capital gain rates are low as compared to ordinary income rates. Thus, because long-term capital gain rates are 15% and marginal tax rates for ordinary income are rather high (35%), interest should continue in incentive stock option arrangements. However, an employer is more favorably treated under the nonqualified stock-option rules (i.e., the employer receives a tax deduction for the compensation related to a nonqualified stock option but does not receive a corresponding deduction if an incentive stock-option plan is adopted) and may therefore still prefer to continue to use nonqualified stock options.

INCENTIVE STOCK OPTION PLANS.

Employer Requirements. An **incentive stock option (ISO)** must meet the following plan or employer requirements:[66]

▶ The option price must be equal to or greater than the stock's FMV on the option's grant date.

▶ The option must be granted within ten years of the date the plan is adopted, and the employee must exercise the option within ten years of the grant date.

▶ The option must be both exercisable only by the employee and nontransferable except in the event of death.

▶ The employee cannot own more than 10% of the voting power of the employer corporation's stock immediately before the option's grant date.

▶ The total FMV of the stock options that become exercisable to an employee in any given year may not exceed $100,000 (e.g., an employee can be granted ISOs to acquire $200,000 of stock in one year, provided that no more than $100,000 is exercisable in any given year).

▶ Other procedural requirements must be met (e.g., shareholder approval of the plan).

Employee Requirements. In addition to the above plan requirements, the employee must meet the following requirements:

▶ The employee must not dispose of the stock within two years of the option's grant date nor within one year after the option's exercise date.

---

[65] The incentive stock option rules are provided in Sec. 422, whereas the rules governing nonqualified stock options are contained in Reg. Sec. 1.83-7.

[66] Sec. 422.

▶ The employee must be employed by the issuing company on the grant date and continue such employment until within three months before the exercise date.

If an employee meets the requirements listed above, no tax consequences occur on the grant date or the exercise date. However, the excess of the FMV over the option price on the exercise date is an adjustment for purposes of the alternative minimum tax (see Chapter I14). When the employee sells the optioned stock, a long-term capital gain or loss is recognized. If the employee meets the two requirements, the employer does not receive a corresponding compensation deduction. If the requirements are not met, the option is treated as a nonqualified stock option.

EXAMPLE I9-62 ▶ American Corporation grants an incentive stock option to Kay, an employee, on January 1, 2006. The option price is $100, and the FMV of the American stock is also $100 on the grant date. The option permits Kay to purchase 100 shares of American stock. Kay exercises the option on June 30, 2008, when the stock's FMV is $400. Kay sells the 100 shares of American stock on January 1, 2010, for $500 per share. Because Kay holds the stock for the required period (at least two years from the grant date and one year from the exercise date) and because Kay is employed by American Corporation on the grant date and within three months before the exercise date, all of the requirements for an ISO have been met. No income is recognized on the grant date or the exercise date, although $30,000 [($400 − $100) × 100 shares] is a tax preference item for the alternative minimum tax in 2008. Kay recognizes a $40,000 [($500 − $100) × 100 shares] long-term capital gain on the sale date in 2010. American Corporation is not entitled to a compensation deduction in any year. ◀

EXAMPLE I9-63 ▶ Assume the same facts as Example I9-62, except that Kay disposes of the stock on August 1, 2008, thus violating the one-year minimum holding period requirement after the exercise date. Kay must recognize ordinary income on the sale date equal to the spread between the option price and the exercise price, or $30,000 [($400 − $100) × 100 shares]. The $30,000 spread between the FMV and the option price is no longer a tax preference item because the option ceases to qualify as an ISO. American Corporation can claim a $30,000 compensation deduction in 2008. Kay also recognizes a $10,000 [($500 − $400 adjusted basis) × 100 shares] short-term capital gain on the sale date, which represents the appreciation of the stock from the exercise date to the sale date. The gain is short-term because the holding period from the exercise date to the sale date does not exceed one year. ◀

KEY POINT

With ISOs the employee does not recognize income when the option is exercised; income is recognized only when the stock is sold. With nonqualified stock options, income is recognized when the option is exercised or on the grant date and when the stock is sold at a gain.

NONQUALIFIED STOCK OPTION PLANS. Stock options that do not meet the plan requirements for incentive stock options are referred to as **nonqualified stock options**. The tax treatment of nonqualified stock options depends on whether the option has a **readily ascertainable fair market value** (e.g., whether the option is traded on an established options exchange).

Readily Ascertainable Fair Market Value. If a nonqualified stock option has a readily ascertainable FMV (e.g., the option is traded on an established options exchange), the employee recognizes ordinary income on the grant date equal to the difference between the stock's FMV and the option's exercise price. The employer receives a compensation deduction on the grant date equal to the same amount of income that is recognized by the employee. In such case, no tax consequences occur on the date the option is exercised, and the employee recognizes capital gain or loss upon the sale or disposition of the stock.

No Readily Ascertainable Fair Market Value. If a nonqualified stock option has no readily ascertainable FMV, no tax consequences occur on the grant date. On the exercise date the employee recognizes ordinary income equal to the spread between the FMV of the stock and the option price, and the employer receives a corresponding compensation deduction. When the stock option is exercised, the employee's basis in the stock is equal to the option price plus the amount reported as ordinary income on the exercise date. Capital gain or loss is recognized upon the subsequent sale of the stock by the employee.

The alternative minimum tax does not apply to nonqualified stock options regardless of whether the option has a readily ascertainable FMV. Table I9-4 illustrates the tax consequences to employees and employers for such options.

As illustrated in Table I9-4, Kim reports a total gain of $11,000 from the nonqualified stock option transaction under both circumstances. However, the character of her profit

▼ TABLE I9-4
Taxation of Nonqualified Stock Options

Situation Facts	Readily Ascertainable FMV	No Readily Ascertainable FMV
Grant date: On January 1, 2005, Kim is granted a nonqualified stock option to purchase 100 shares of stock from Apple Corporation (Kim's employer) at $90 per share. The stock's FMV is $100 on the grant date.	Ordinary income of $1,000 is recognized [($100 − $90) × 100 shares] by Kim in 2005. Apple Corporation receives a corresponding $1,000 compensation deduction in 2005.	No tax consequences to Kim or Apple Corporation.
Exercise date: On January 31, 2007, Kim exercises the option and acquires the 100 shares of Apple Corporation stock for the $90 option price when the FMV is $190.	No tax consequences to Kim or Apple Corporation.	Kim recognizes ordinary income in 2006 of $10,000 [($190 − $90) × 100 shares], and Apple Corporation receives a $10,000 compensation deduction.
Sale date: On February 1, 2008, Kim sells the stock for $200 per share and realizes $20,000 ($200 × 100 shares).	Kim recognizes a $10,000 ($20,000 − $10,000 basis) long-term capital gain.[a]	Kim recognizes a $1,000 ($20,000 − $19,000 basis) long-term capital gain on the sale.[b]

[a] Kim's basis includes the amount paid for the optioned stock of $9,000 plus ordinary income of $1,000 recognized on the grant date. Kim's holding period commences on the January 1, 2005, grant date for determining whether the gain is long-term.

[b] Kim's basis includes the $9,000 paid for the option stock plus the $10,000 ordinary income recognized on the exercise date. Kim's holding period commences on the January 31, 2007, exercise date for determining whether the gain is long-term.

(i.e., ordinary income or capital gain) and the timing of the profit recognition (i.e., grant date or exercise date) depends on whether the option's FMV is readily ascertainable.

The distinguishing features and major requirements for employee stock options are summarized in Topic Review I9-4.

ADDITIONAL COMMENT

If you are self-employed and establish a Keogh plan, you must include any employees in the plan.

PLANS FOR SELF-EMPLOYED INDIVIDUALS

Self-employed individuals, such as sole proprietors and partners who practice a trade or business, are not classified as employees and are subject to special retirement plan rules known as **H.R. 10 plans** (also called **Keogh plans**). Retirement plans of self-employed people are generally subject to the same contribution and benefit limitations as other

Topic Review I9-4

Employee Stock Options

DISTINGUISHING FEATURES AND MAJOR REQUIREMENTS

▶ For an incentive stock option (ISO) plan no tax consequences occur on the grant or the exercise date (except for the recognition of a tax preference item under the AMT provisions on the exercise date). Capital gain or loss is recognized by the employee upon the sale or exchange of the stock. No deduction is allowed to the employer.

▶ ISOs and nonqualified stock options may be issued to highly-compensated employees without regard to nondiscrimination rules.

▶ If a nonqualified stock option has a readily ascertainable FMV, the employee recognizes ordinary income equal to the spread between the FMV of the stock and the option price on the grant date and the employer receives a corresponding deduction. If the option has no readily ascertainable FMV, income is recognized on the exercise date equal to the spread between the FMV of the stock and the option price and a corresponding deduction is available to the employer.

▶ For an ISO, the option price must be equal to or greater than the FMV of the stock on the grant date, employees cannot own more than 10% of the voting power of the employer's stock, and restrictions are placed on the total FMV of stock options that may be issued.

▶ To qualify under the ISO rules, a two-year holding period from the grant date is required (and at least one year after the exercise date) and the employee must continue to be employed by the company until within three months of the exercise date.

qualified corporate plans. An employee who is covered under a qualified pension or profit-sharing plan for wages earned as an employee and who is also self-employed may establish an H.R. 10 plan for earned income derived from self-employment activities.

For a **defined contribution H.R. 10 plan**, a self-employed individual in 2006 may contribute the smaller of $44,000 or 25% of earned income from the self-employment activity.[67] *Earned income* refers to net earnings from self-employment. However, for purposes of computing the maximum amount that may be contributed to a Keogh plan by a self-employed individual, earned income must be reduced by two amounts: (1) the 50% deduction for self-employment taxes and (2) the Keogh contribution itself. Since the contribution is based on earned income *after* the contribution, the 25% contribution percentage must be reduced to 20%.[68] To compute the limitations for 2006, a maximum of $220,000 of earned income may be taken into account for any one individual.[69]

EXAMPLE I9-64 ▶ Larry is a self-employed CPA whose 2006 net earnings from his trade or business (before the H.R. 10 plan contribution but after the deduction for one-half of the self-employment taxes paid under Sec. 164(f) [see Chapter I14]) is $100,000. Larry may contribute $20,000 to the plan for 2006. Larry must also provide coverage for all of his eligible full-time employees under the general rules provided in the law for qualified plans (e.g., nondiscrimination, vesting, and so on).[70] ◀

EXAMPLE I9-65 ▶ Assume the same facts as in Example I9-64 except that Larry's earnings from his trade or business (before the H.R. 10 plan contribution but after the deduction for one-half of the self-employment (taxes) is $250,000. The maximum contribution that Larry can make on his behalf in 2006 is $44,000 ($220,000 × 0.20). Even though his earnings were $250,000, the maximum compensation that can be used to calculate the H.R. 10 plan contribution in 2006 is $220,000. ◀

An H.R. 10 plan must be established before the end of the tax year, but contributions may be made up to the due date for the tax return (including extensions). All H.R. 10 pension contributions made by a self-employed individual for *employees* are deductible for AGI on Schedule C. The H.R. 10 contribution for the self-employed individual is deductible *for* AGI on page 1 of Form 1040.

INDIVIDUAL RETIREMENT ACCOUNTS (IRAs)

Under current law, there are three types of IRAs that are available to taxpayers:

▶ Traditional IRA
▶ Roth IRA
▶ Coverdell Education Savings Account IRA[71]

Each of these three types of IRAs is discussed below.

TRADITIONAL IRA

Traditional IRAs have been in the law for about 25 years and taxpayers may make either deductible or nondeductible contributions to the IRA. A contribution to a traditional IRA that is deductible has two principal benefits: (1) the amount contributed to the IRA (maximum $4,000 per year) is deductible on the taxpayer's return[72] and (2) the income earned on the investments in the IRA is not subject to current taxation. However, when amounts are withdrawn from the IRA at retirement, such amounts are fully subject to taxation. Nondeductible contributions to a traditional IRA may not be deducted on the taxpayer's return, but such contributions are not subject to taxation when withdrawn from the IRA.

[67] Sec. 415(c)(1). Prior to 2002, the limitations were considerably lower. In 2001, for example, a self-employed individual could only contribute 25% of earned income to a maximum of $35,000.
[68] This reduction in contribution percentage is computed as follows: 0.25/1.00 + 0.25 = 0.20. If the Keogh contribution rate is 15% rather than 25%, the deductible percentage would be 13.0435%, computed as above, 0.15/1.00 + 0.15 = 0.130435. Other percentages can be calculated accordingly.
[69] Secs. 401(a)(17) and 404(l). The ceiling in 2005 was $210,000.
[70] Sec. 401(d).

[71] The Coverdell Education Savings Account was named after the late Senator Paul Coverdell of Georgia.
[72] The deductible amount to an IRA was increased from $2,000 prior to 2002 to $3,000 for 2002–2004, $4,000 for 2005–2007, and $5,000 in 2008 and future years. See Sec. 219 (b)(5). After 2008, the deductible amount will be indexed for inflation. Prior to 2002, the deductible amount was $2,000. In addition, individuals over 50 years of age are now eligible to contribute an extra $500 into their IRA in years 2002–2005 (increasing to $1,000 in 2006 and future years). These extra amounts are referred to as "catch-up contributions."

While contributions are not subject to taxation, any earnings are subject to taxation when withdrawn.

Individuals may make deductible contributions equal to the lesser of $4,000 or 100% of compensation only if either of the following conditions exists:

▶ The individual is *not* an active participant in an employer-sponsored retirement plan, including tax-sheltered annuities, government plans, simplified employee pension plans, and H.R. 10 plans; or

▶ Individuals who are active participants in an employer-sponsored retirement plan must have an AGI equal to or below the following applicable dollar limits for 2006:[73] $50,000 for an unmarried taxpayer; $75,000 for a married couple filing a joint return; zero for a married individual filing separately. If an individual has AGI above these amounts, the deductible IRA contribution amounts are phased out on a pro rata basis as AGI increases from $50,000 to $60,000 for unmarried taxpayers and from $75,000 to $85,000 for married taxpayers filing a joint return.

EXAMPLE I9-66 ▶ Laura is an unmarried taxpayer who is not an active participant in an employer-sponsored retirement plan or other qualified plan. In 2006, Laura's AGI is $60,000, consisting of earned income from wages. Laura is not subject to the dollar limitation because she is not an active participant in a qualified plan and may, therefore, contribute and deduct up to $4,000 to a traditional IRA. Laura's AGI is reduced to $56,000 ($60,000 − $4,000) because the amount is deductible *for* AGI. ◀

EXAMPLE I9-67 ▶ Judy is an unmarried taxpayer who is an active participant in her employer's qualified retirement plan. In 2006, Judy's AGI is $56,000, consisting of earned income from wages of $53,000 and interest and dividends of $3,000. Since she is an active participant in a qualified plan and her AGI is over $50,000, her deductible contribution to a traditional IRA is subject to the phaseout. Since the ceiling amount is exceeded by $6,000 ($56,000 − $50,000), the maximum IRA contribution is reduced by 60% ($6,000/$10,000). Thus, the maximum that Judy can contribute and deduct to her IRA in 2006 is $1,600 ($4,000 − $2,400). ◀

ADDITIONAL COMMENT

Banks, savings and loan associations, insurance companies, and stock brokerage firms make IRAs available to taxpayers. Usually, the amounts are invested in long-term savings accounts. However, self-directed plans are offered by some stock brokerage firms. In this type of IRA, the taxpayer can specify how the contributions will be invested.

If a taxpayer's AGI exceeds the above limits, the taxpayer may make a nondeductible contribution of up to $4,000 to a traditional IRA. The benefit of making a nondeductible contribution to an IRA is that the earnings of the IRA investments grow tax-free. Thus, even though the *earnings* of the nondeductible IRA will be taxed when distributed, the ability to allow investments to compound before-tax is a major advantage for taxpayers. However, as will be seen in the discussion of Roth IRAs below, if a taxpayer can qualify for a Roth IRA rather than a traditional nondeductible IRA, the choice clearly favors a Roth IRA. The maximum amount of a nondeductible contribution that may be made to a traditional IRA is $4,000 minus the amount that is allowed as a deduction. Also, a taxpayer may elect for all of his contributions to be nondeductible even though the contributions are otherwise eligible to be deducted.

EXAMPLE I9-68 ▶ Using the same facts as in Example I9-67, Judy is permitted to make a nondeductible contribution to her IRA of $2,400 ($4,000 − $1,600). She also could elect to designate all $4,000 as a nondeductible contribution even though she is eligible to deduct the $1,600. ◀

Two special rules apply to married couples relative to traditional IRAs. First, if only one spouse is employed and this working spouse is otherwise eligible to make IRA contributions, the nonworking spouse may contribute up to $4,000 per year to an IRA (a so-called spousal IRA). Thus, a total of $8,000 may be deductible by a married couple ($4,000 to each spouse's IRA) even though only one spouse has earned income. It should be noted that even though only the working spouse must have earned income, such working spouse must have at least $8,000 of earned income in order to contribute $8,000 to the two IRAs. Second, if one spouse is covered under a qualified retirement plan but the

---

[73] Sec. 219(g). The phaseout limits for unmarried individuals increased from $45,000 in 2004 to $50,000 in 2005 and thereafter. For married taxpayers filing a joint return, the $75,000 limit in 2006 increases to $80,000 in 2007.

other spouse is not covered, the non-covered spouse may contribute to a traditional deductible IRA. However, the contribution to a traditional deductible IRA is phased out at adjusted gross incomes between $150,000 and $160,000.

EXAMPLE I9-69 ▶ Gary and Babs are a married couple. Gary is covered under a qualified retirement plan at his job and earned $170,000 in 2006. Babs is employed as a secretary and earned $10,000 but is not covered under a qualified retirement plan. They file a joint return, have interest and dividend income of $20,000, and their AGI, therefore, is $200,000. Neither Gary nor Babs is entitled to deduct contributions to a traditional IRA because their AGI exceeds $160,000. However, both Gary and Babs are allowed to make nondeductible contributions of $4,000 each to the IRA. ◀

EXAMPLE I9-70 ▶ Assume the same facts as in Example I9-69 but that Gary's income is $100,000 and their AGI is $130,000. Babs may contribute and deduct $4,000 to a traditional IRA because their AGI is less than $150,000. However, Gary may not make a deductible contribution because he is covered under a qualified plan and their AGI exceeds $80,000. Gary is permitted to make a $4,000 contribution to a nondeductible IRA. ◀

The following significant tax rules apply to traditional IRAs:

ADDITIONAL COMMENT

A contribution to an IRA for the year 2005 can be made as late as the due date for filing the 2006 return.

▶ An IRA plan may be established between the end of the tax year and the due date for the tax return (not including any extensions that are permitted). Any deductible contributions made during this time are treated as a deduction for the prior year. Contributions are deductible if made by the due date for the tax return (i.e., contributions for 2006 must be made no later than April 16, 2007, as April 15, 2007, falls on a Sunday). Contributions to nondeductible IRAs also must be made by April 15 of the following year.

▶ Distributions from a traditional IRA are taxed under the annuity rules in Sec. 72. Normally distributions from an IRA are fully subject to taxation. However, if nondeductible contributions are made to an IRA, these amounts would represent the investment in the contract in calculating the exclusion ratio.

▶ Withdrawals by a participant before age 59½ are both includible in income and subject to a nondeductible 10% penalty tax.[74]

▶ Withdrawals must begin no later than April 1 of the year following the end of the tax year in which the individual reaches age 70½. IRA contributions that were deducted over the years on the taxpayer's returns are fully taxable as ordinary income when the amounts are distributed.

▶ A nondeductible 6% penalty is levied on excess contributions to an IRA.[75]

ROTH IRA

The Roth IRA[76] is a relatively new type of IRA that is a so-called "backloaded IRA" because the tax benefits come at the end, not at the beginning, of the IRA. Contributions to a Roth IRA are nondeductible but all distributions from the IRA, including earnings, are nontaxable. The maximum amount that may be contributed to a Roth IRA is $4,000. However, taxpayers who are eligible for both a Roth IRA and a traditional IRA may only contribute a total of $4,000 to both types of IRAs. As with traditional IRAs, Roth IRAs are also subject to AGI phaseout limitations, although the limitation amounts are higher than with traditional IRAs.

ADDITIONAL COMMENT

Some financial advisors recommend the following approach when someone can only afford to have limited amounts set aside for retirement. Have pre-tax dollars withheld from salary up to the employer-matching amount in 401(k) plans, then place $4,000 in a Roth IRA. This maximizes employer contributions and places the maximum amount allowable into the much favored Roth IRA.

All taxpayers may contribute up to $4,000 to a Roth IRA; however, this amount is phased-out for single taxpayers if their AGI is between $95,000 and $110,000 ($150,000 and $160,000 for married couples filing a joint return and $0 and $10,000 for married individuals filing separate returns). The principal advantage of the Roth IRA is the nontaxability of qualified distributions. One requirement of a qualified distribution is that the distribution must meet a five-year holding period. More specifically, the distribution may not be made before the end of the five-tax-year period beginning with the first tax year for

---

[74] Sec. 72(t). The amount subject to the 10% penalty is the portion of the amount that must be included in gross income. Exceptions to the 10% penalty are provided in the event of death, disability, and certain non-lump-sum distributions. Two additional exceptions also apply: (1) withdrawals used to pay qualified higher education costs for taxpayer, spouse, children or

grandchildren and (2) up to $10,000 to buy or build the principal residence for a "first time homebuyer."
[75] Sec. 4973(b).
[76] Sec. 408A.

which a contribution was made to the Roth IRA. The first tax year begins on the first day of the tax year (i.e., January 1 in most cases) in which a contribution was made even though such contribution may have been made later in such tax year. In addition to satisfying the five-year test, a qualifying distribution must also meet one of the following:

▶ made on or after the date on which the individual attains age 59½,

▶ made to a beneficiary (or the individual's estate) on or after the individual's death,

▶ attributable to the individual being disabled, or

▶ a distribution for first-time homebuyer expenses (maximum of $10,000).

An important aspect of distributions from a Roth IRA is a special ordering rule for determining the taxability of nonqualifying withdrawals. Under this rule, distributions are treated as being made from contributions first and, thus, are nontaxable. After all contributions have been withdrawn, any remaining amounts are considered taxable and subject to the 10% penalty.

EXAMPLE I9-71 ▶ Ray and Sandy are married and Ray is covered under his employer's qualified retirement plan. Their AGI on a joint return is $130,000. Ray can contribute $4,000 to a Roth IRA. Alternatively, however, if their AGI was $156,000, Ray would be limited to a maximum contribution of $1,600. Since their AGI exceeds the threshold of $150,000 by $6,000, the $4,000 contribution is reduced by 60% ($6000/$10,000), or $2,400. ◀

EXAMPLE I9-72 ▶ Bob, age 60 in 2005, contributes $4,000 each year to a Roth IRA in 2006, 2007, and 2008. On November 30, 2010, the value of the Roth IRA is $15,000. Bob has experienced some financial setbacks and needs to withdraw the money from the Roth IRA. If Bob withdraws $12,000 in 2010 and waits until January 2011 to withdraw the remaining $3,000, none of the distributions are taxable. This result occurs because the first $12,000 is treated as coming from contributions. The remaining $3,000 is nontaxable because Bob has met the five-year test and is over age 59½. Conversely, if Bob withdraws the entire $15,000 in 2010, $3,000 must be included in his income because the five-year test was not met. ◀

A final aspect of Roth IRAs is the ability to "rollover" funds from an existing deductible IRA into a Roth IRA. However, since the taxpayer received a deduction for the contribution into the deductible IRA, any rollover amount must be included in gross income in the year the rollover occurred. More specifically, if a taxpayer's AGI does not exceed $100,000 and he or she does not file as married filing separately, the taxpayer is eligible to rollover any amount of funds from a deductible IRA into a Roth IRA. Such rollover amount is includible in the taxpayer's income, but is not subject to the 10% penalty for early withdrawals.

EXAMPLE I9-73 ▶ Mikael has a traditional IRA that has a balance of $60,000 on June 30, 2006. He is single and has AGI of $80,000. Mikael is eligible to rollover the $60,000 to a Roth IRA. If he completes the rollover in 2006, he will be required to include the $60,000 in his gross income for 2006. He is not subject to the 10% early withdrawal penalty on the rollover. ◀

Below is a discussion of some of the important tax rules for Roth IRAs:

TAX STRATEGY TIP

Because of the tax-deferral of income within a Roth IRA and the ability to withdraw amounts at retirement tax-free, the Roth IRA generally is superior to a traditional IRA for younger taxpayers. Once a taxpayer reaches 50 years of age, the two types of IRAs become more equal.

▶ Like traditional IRAs, Roth IRAs must be established by the due date of the tax return (not including extensions). Similarly, contributions to a Roth IRA also must be made by the due date of the return (i.e., April 16, 2007, for 2006 contributions as April 15, 2007, falls on a Sunday).

▶ Contributions to a Roth IRA are never deductible.

▶ Contributions to a Roth IRA are subject to special modified AGI limitations.

▶ Contributions to a Roth IRA can be made after the owner has reached age 70½. Similarly, no distributions are required at any age from a Roth IRA. (Remember: owners of traditional IRAs must begin taking distributions in the year after the taxpayer has reached age 70½).

▶ Withdrawals from a Roth IRA are not taxable if such withdrawals are "qualified distributions." If a withdrawal is not a qualified distribution, the amount is taxed under special ordering rules and subject to the 10% penalty.

▶ A taxpayer whose AGI is $100,000 or less may rollover his traditional IRA to a Roth IRA. However, the total amount rolled over from a traditional deductible IRA must be included in the taxpayer's gross income.

STOP & THINK

Question: Both nondeductible contributions to a traditional IRA and contributions to a Roth IRA are similar in the sense that neither provides a tax deduction at the date of contribution. Which of the two types would be most advantageous to taxpayers?

Solution: Clearly, if a taxpayer qualifies for a Roth IRA, that type of IRA is superior to a nondeductible contribution to a traditional IRA. The reason is that distributions from a Roth IRA are totally excluded from gross income while only the principal portion of nondeductible contributions to a traditional IRA are excludable. In other words, the earnings generated in a Roth IRA are excluded from gross income whereas earnings associated with nondeductible contributions to a traditional IRA are subject to taxation. Generally, a nondeductible contribution to a traditional IRA will not be advantageous unless the taxpayer's AGI exceeds $160,000.

For a discussion of the decision whether to invest in a traditional deductible IRA or a Roth IRA, see the Tax Planning Considerations later in this chapter. Also, for a more detailed analysis including computations, see Chapter I18 of the *Individuals* textbook.

Topic Review I9-5 contains a table which summarizes the eligibility rules for traditional and Roth IRAs.

COVERDELL EDUCATION SAVINGS ACCOUNT

A special type of IRA, referred to as an Education IRA, was established in 1997 to specifically assist low- and middle-income taxpayers with higher education expenses. The Education IRA was renamed the Coverdell Education Savings Account (CESA) in 2001. CESAs have a number of attractive features:

ADDITIONAL COMMENT

Any number of people may contribute funds to a Coverdell Education Savings Account for one child, but all of the contributions may not total more than $2,000 for that child.

▶ The maximum annual contribution into such plan is $2,000.

▶ CESAs may be used for elementary and secondary education expenses as well as for higher education expenses, and

▶ Taxpayers can claim either the HOPE scholarship credit or lifetime learning credit as well as excluding distributions from a CESA in the same year.

A contributor can make a *nondeductible* contribution of up to $2,000 per year into a CESA for a designated beneficiary until the beneficiary reaches age 18.[77] The contributor

Topic Review I9-5

If 2006 AGI Is	Eligible for **IRA** (Joint Returns)				
	Traditional IRA (Deductible)			Roth	Traditional IRA
	A	B	C	**IRA**	(Nondeductible)*
Up to $75,000	Yes	Yes	Yes	Yes	Yes
$75,000–$85,000	Yes	Partially	Yes	Yes	Yes
$85,000–$150,000	Yes	No	Yes	Yes	Yes
$150,000–$160,000	Yes	No	Partially	Partially	Yes
Over $160,000	Yes	No	No	No	Yes

A   If neither spouse is an active participant in an employer-sponsored plan
B   For the IRA of a spouse who is an active participant in an employer-sponsored plan
C   For the IRA of a spouse who is not an active participant in an employer-sponsored plan

* If AGI is not above $160,000, a nondeductible IRA will not be advantageous.

---

[77] Sec. 530. Contributions are allowed to continue past age 18 for a special-needs beneficiary, Sec. 530(b)(1).

need not be related to the beneficiary and there is no limit on the number of CESAs that can be set up by a contributor. Distributions to the beneficiary are excluded from gross income provided the distribution does not exceed the *qualified education expenses* of the designated beneficiary during the taxable year. Qualified education expenses include tuition, fees, books, supplies, equipment, and room and board. In the case of elementary and secondary education expenses, qualified education expenses include academic tutoring and Internet access fees. Distributions in any tax year in excess of qualified education expenses are includible in the gross income of the beneficiary and subject to a 10% penalty.

Similar to other IRA-type accounts, there are phaseout limits based on the contributor's AGI. The $2,000 annual contribution is phased out for married taxpayers filing joint returns with AGI from $190,000 to $220,000 ($95,000 to $110,000 for other taxpayers). In addition, if the taxpayer claims either the HOPE scholarship credit or the lifetime learning credit, the education expenses used for these credits must reduce the qualified expenses for exclusion from a CESA.

EXAMPLE I9-74 ▶ Lee and Patsy are married and have two young grandchildren. To assist the grandchildren with their future education expenses, they set up a CESA for each child in 2006 and plan to deposit $2,000 in both accounts. Their AGI for 2006 is $202,000. Because their AGI exceeds $190,000, they are limited to putting $1,200 [$2,000 − $2,000($202,000 − $190,000)/$30,000)] into the accounts in 2006. In the future, the children can withdraw amounts tax-free from their CESA to pay for qualified education expenses for elementary, secondary, or higher education. ◀

EXAMPLE I9-75 ▶ Craig Shaw is about to enter State University as a freshman and plans to withdraw amounts from his CESA to help pay his expenses. His expenses for the Fall Semester 2006 are as follows:

Tuition and fees	$2,200
Books	500
Supplies	300
Room and board	2,400
Total	$5,400

Craig's parents plan on paying Craig's tuition and fees, and Craig will pay the remaining $3,200 from his CESA. Craig qualifies as a dependent of his parents for the tax year. Craig's parents plan on claiming the HOPE scholarship credit. Craig is not required to include the $3,200 in his gross income in 2006 as his qualified education expenses are at least $3,200. Craig's parents will use $2,200 to claim the HOPE credit. ◀

HEALTH SAVINGS ACCOUNTS

The Medicare Act of 2003 established Health Savings Accounts (HSAs) for eligible individuals for taxable years beginning after December 31, 2003.[78] The purpose of HSAs is to enable individuals to accumulate funds on a tax-free basis to pay qualified medical expenses currently or in the future. In summary, HSAs operate as follows:

▶ Taxpayer contributes money into an HSA with a qualified trustee or custodian (much like an IRA). The taxpayer must be an eligible individual and the contributions are subject to limitations. These detailed issues are discussed below.

▶ The taxpayer is allowed a *for* AGI deduction in the year the contributions are made.

▶ Distributions from the HSA that are used exclusively to pay for qualified medical expenses (medical expenses as defined in Sec. 213(d), but not health insurance premiums) are excludable from gross income. However, any amount of the distribution that is not used to pay for qualified medical expenses is includable in the gross income of the taxpayer and subject to an additional 10% penalty. The 10% penalty is waived if the beneficiary/taxpayer is age 65 or older.

HSAs are only available to eligible individuals. An eligible individual is any individual who (1) is covered under a high-deductible health plan (HDHP), (2) is not also covered by any other health plan that is not an HDHP, (3) is not entitled to benefits under Medicare (i.e.,

---

[78] Sec. 223. Archer Medical Savings Accounts are similar to HSAs but cannot be established after 12/31/05. MSAs have a more restrictive definition of HDHP so there is little incentive to use them.

generally, has not reached age 65), and (4) may not be claimed as a dependent on another person's tax return. An HDHP is a plan with an annual deductible in 2006 of at least $1,050 and annual out-of-pocket expenses (other than premiums) required to be paid not exceeding $5,250. For family coverage, these amounts are $2,100 and $10,500, respectively.

Annual contributions to an HSA are determined separately for each month the plan is in effect and is $1/12$ of the *lesser* of (1) 100% of the annual deductible under the HDHP ($1,050) or (2) $2,700. For individuals with family coverage under an HDHP, the amounts are (1) 100% of the annual deductible under the HDHP (minimum of $2,100) or (2) $5,450. Catch-up contributions are permitted for individuals age 55 to 64.

EXAMPLE I9-76 ▶ Roy, age 45, established an HDHP for his family with a $2,400 annual deductible on May 1, 2006. Roy is eligible to put $1,600 (8 months × $200) into an HSA for the calendar year 2006. The purpose of the fund is to pay for medical expenses for himself and his family. In 2006, Roy is allowed to deduct the $1,600 as a deduction for AGI. Any earnings of the fund investments are not subject to tax if the distribution is used to pay qualified medical expenses. ◀

EXAMPLE I9-77 ▶ In 2010, Roy takes a $5,000 distribution from the HSA to make a down payment on a new automobile. Since the distribution was not used to pay qualified medical expenses, Roy must include the $5,000 in his income and pay a $500 ($5,000 × 10%) penalty in 2010. ◀

SIMPLIFIED EMPLOYEE PENSIONS

Due to the administrative complexity associated with qualified pension and profit-sharing plans, small businesses often establish simplified employee pension (SEP) plans for their employees. In a SEP, the employer makes contributions to the IRAs of its employees.[79] The following is a summary of the tax rules that apply to a SEP:

▶ The employer receives an immediate tax deduction for contributions made under the plan. The annual deductible contributions for each participant are limited to the lesser of 25% of the participant's compensation (up to a ceiling of $220,000 for 2006) and the dollar limitations for defined contribution plans.[80]

▶ Contributions are treated as being made on the last day of the tax year if they are made by the due date of the tax return (including extensions).

▶ Employer contributions must be nondiscriminatory.

▶ Distributions from a SEP are subject to taxation based on the IRA rules (previously discussed) including the penalty tax for premature distributions.

▶ A self-employed person (i.e., a partner or sole proprietor) may establish a SEP rather than using an H.R. 10 plan arrangement because of reduced administrative complexity associated with a SEP.

SIMPLE RETIREMENT PLANS

Another more recent type of retirement savings plan for small businesses is called the savings incentive match plan for employees (SIMPLE).[81] This type of plan can be adopted by employers who have 100 or fewer employees who received at least $5,000 in compensation from the employer in the preceding year. A SIMPLE plan may be set up either as an IRA for each employee or part of a qualified cash or deferred arrangement (401(k) plan). Essentially, employees are allowed to make elective contributions in 2006 of up to $10,000 per year and employers are required to make matching contributions.

The unique features of the SIMPLE plans are (1) that elective contributions by employees must be matched by the employer or the employer has the option of making nonelective contributions, (2) that all contributions to an employee's SIMPLE account must be fully vested, and (3) the SIMPLE plans are not subject to the special nondiscrimination rules generally applicable to qualified plans. This last feature is important in that there is no requirement that a set number of employees *participate* in the plan, the only requirement is that all employees who had $5,000 in compensation in the previous year and are reasonably expected to have $5,000 in compensation in the current year must be eligible to participate.

---

[79] Sec. 408(k).
[80] Sec. 404(h)(1).

[81] Sec. 408(p).

TAX PLANNING CONSIDERATIONS

MOVING EXPENSES

To be eligible for the moving expense deduction, the moving expenses must be paid in connection with the commencement of work by the taxpayer as a full-time employee or self-employed individual. Therefore, it is important to secure full-time employment or to carry on a trade or business as a self-employed individual at the new location. Taxpayers who are approaching retirement are eligible for a moving expense deduction only if they continue to work in the new location before their actual retirement (e.g., 39 weeks in the 12-month period following the move).

EXAMPLE I9-78 ▶ Louis decides to quit his job and return to school as a full-time graduate student. Louis incurs substantial long-distance moving expenses that would otherwise be deductible to relocate to the university where the education is to be taken. No deduction is allowed unless Louis is employed on a full-time basis or is engaged in a self-employment activity at the new location. ◀

REIMBURSED AMOUNTS. Moving expense reimbursements are often greater than the amounts allowable as a deduction. This is caused by the common practice of reimbursing nondeductible items (e.g., an employer may reimburse an employee for the cost of certain indirect moving expenses such as househunting trips, which do not qualify as deductible moving expenses). This results in an increase in the employee's gross income to the extent of the excess reimbursement. From a tax planning standpoint, the employer may provide an additional payment to compensate the employee for the additional tax cost associated with the move (commonly referred to as a "gross-up").

EXAMPLE I9-79 ▶ Austin Corporation has a policy of reimbursing transferred employees for 30% of their moving reimbursement that exceeds their deductible expenses to cover the federal and state tax costs associated with the excess reimbursement. Kathy, an employee, is transferred by the company to a new job location and incurs $6,000 of deductible moving expenses and receives an $8,000 reimbursement. Austin also will make an additional payment to Kathy of $600 (0.30 × $2,000) to cover the additional federal and state income tax costs. Kathy must include $2,600 ($2,000 + $600) of the reimbursement in gross income. ◀

PROVIDING NONTAXABLE COMPENSATION TO EMPLOYEES

Employers should consider the tax consequences to employees when changes in fringe benefit and deferred compensation arrangements are evaluated. For example, it is preferable for an employer to pay for fringe benefit items such as group term life insurance (up to $50,000 in coverage), health and accident insurance, employee parking, and so on rather than to give cash raises of a comparable amount. Such payments are nontaxable to the employee up to certain limits, whereas a comparable salary increase is fully taxable. Both types of payments are deductible by the employer.

Consideration should also be given to increased deferred compensation benefit programs for employees, particularly highly-compensated individuals. The use of nonqualified deferred compensation plans, restricted property, and stock options result in tax deferrals and may result in the eventual recognition of capital gains that may be used to offset capital losses or that are taxed at a maximum 15% marginal tax rate.

All eligible employees should consider establishing an individual retirement account (IRA) because of the available tax deferral benefits. Even if a premature withdrawal (i.e., before age 59½ occurs), the time value of the deferred benefits for the plan contributions and the earnings may be greater than the penalty tax imposed.

ROLLOVER OF TRADITIONAL IRA TO ROTH IRA

Taxpayers have the ability to rollover amounts from a traditional IRA to a Roth IRA. However, if such a rollover is made, the taxpayer must include the rollover amount in gross income in the year of the rollover. The principal benefit of the rollover is that once the

REAL-WORLD EXAMPLE

Banks and other financial institutions in their ads sometimes compare the accumulated wealth in an IRA to the accumulated wealth in a fully taxable investment. Although the IRA is generally advantageous, the ads sometimes overstate the advantages because they fail to deduct the tax that will be paid when amounts are withdrawn from the IRA.

amounts are in the Roth IRA, no further taxes are due on these amounts upon distribution (assuming the five-year test is met). The essential question, therefore, is whether it is advantageous to rollover amounts from a traditional IRA to a Roth IRA and pay the tax now or keep the traditional IRA intact and pay the tax when regular distributions are made.

The decision rests on several factors, including (1) the marginal tax rate at retirement, (2) age of taxpayer, and (3) payment of tax from rollover from post-tax funds. First, if a taxpayer's marginal tax rate at retirement is expected to be lower than the current tax rate, a rollover may not be advantageous. Second, younger taxpayers are more likely to benefit from a rollover because they have more years to accumulate earnings tax-free and may be in a lower tax bracket today than at retirement. Finally, if the taxes that accrue from the rollover must be paid from the rollover funds, a rollover will probably not be in the taxpayer's favor. In other words, taxpayers should have sufficient funds from other sources to pay the tax, then the entire amount of rollover into the Roth IRA will have maximum ability to grow on a tax-free basis.

Each case must be analyzed based on the unique factors of that particular situation. However, for most taxpayers, it is generally advantageous to rollover funds from a traditional IRA to a Roth IRA. Of course, as is pointed out earlier in this chapter, the individual must have AGI of $100,000 or less (before the rollover distribution) to qualify for the rollover.

COMPLIANCE AND PROCEDURAL CONSIDERATIONS

SUBSTANTIATING TRAVEL AND ENTERTAINMENT EXPENSES

Travel and entertainment expenses are disallowed if the taxpayer does not maintain adequate records or documentary proof of the expenditures.[82] Normally, documentation includes expense statements (diary or account book) and proof of the amount, time, place, and business purpose. Strict substantiation rules are enacted in the law to curb widespread abuses in the so-called expense account living practices engaged in by some taxpayers.

To make compliance easier, the IRS formulated the following administrative procedural rules:

▶ If an employee makes an adequate accounting of the expenditures to the employer, it is not necessary to submit a detailed statement on the employee's tax return unless the expenses exceed the reimbursements.

▶ The standard mileage rate may be used to compute automobile expenses in lieu of actual expenses and is reported on Form 2106 (Employee Business Expenses).

▶ Taxpayers may elect an optional method for computing deductions for business travel and meal expenses in lieu of using actual costs. If a per diem allowance is paid by an employer in lieu of reimbursing actual expenses, the reimbursement is deemed to be substantiated if it does not exceed a federal per diem rate for the travel locality. In lieu of using actual expenses an employee or self-employed individual may use the applicable federal per diem rate. The taxpayer must still provide documentation of time, place, and business purpose for the expenditures.

REPORTING EMPLOYEE BUSINESS EXPENSES

Form 2106 (Employee Business Expenses) is used to report employee business expenses (see Appendix B). Part I of Form 2106 is a recap of travel and transportation expenses. Part II includes a computation of automobile expenses using either actual expenses or the standard rate mileage method. Employer reimbursements must be included in the employee's wages on Form W-2 if an adequate accounting of the expenses is not made.

Employer withholding of federal income tax is also required for nonaccountable plan reimbursements. Form 2106-EZ may be used by employees who do not receive an employer reimbursement, and where the standard mileage rate is used for the current year and for the year the taxpayer's automobile was first placed in service.

Moving expenses are reported on Form 3903 (Moving Expenses) instead of Form 2106 because they are treated differently from other employee expenses (e.g., unreimbursed moving expenses are deductible *for* AGI). Expenses such as entertainment, union dues, business gifts, and education expenses are reported on Schedule A of Form 1040 as itemized deductions (see Appendix B).

A filled-in copy of Form 2106 is shown in Figure I9-2. It includes the computations relating to the information in Example I9-80.

EXAMPLE I9-80 ▶

ADDITIONAL COMMENT

Many of the provisions related to employee business expenses are very complex. It has been said of the general complexity of the tax law that "If Patrick Henry thought taxation without representation was bad, he should have seen taxation with representation."

Eric Graber, SSN 231-54-9876, is single and employed as a salesman by the Houston Corporation. Eric is required to use his personal automobile for employment-related business. He uses only one automobile for business purposes. During 2005, Eric drives his automobile 80% of the time for business use and incurs the following total expenses:

Gas and oil	$5,000
Repairs	600
Depreciation	2,960
Insurance	1,400
Parking and tolls (all business related)	250
Total	$10,210

During the year, Eric drives a total of 30,000 miles evenly throughout the year, of which 24,000 are business miles. Of the 6,000 personal miles, 2,000 miles are commuting to and from work. Eric receives a reimbursement of 20 cents per business mile from his employer. Eric also incurred $4,000 of unreimbursed employment-related travel and entertainment expenses. These expenses include the following:

KEY POINT

If a taxpayer who is an employee moves in early December, the earliest that the 39-week test could be met would be early September of the following year. This is well after the April 15 due date for the individual return. The taxpayer may nevertheless deduct the moving expenses in the earlier year.

Airfare	$ 2,500
Car rental	250
Business meals at which business was discussed	150
Laundry	100
Lodging	200
Entertainment of customers	800
Total	$ 4,000

Step 1, line 1: Vehicle expense [(16,000 × $0.405) + (8,000 × $0.485)]	$10,360
Step 2, line 7: (24,000 miles × $0.20)	$4,800
Section C, line 23: Actual expenses:	
Gas and oil	$5,000
Repairs	600
Insurance	1,400
Total	$ 7,000
Section C, line 28: Depreciation ($2,960 × .80)	$ 2,368

As can be seen from the completed Form 2106, Eric receives a larger deduction from the mileage method. This method is selected. ◀

REPORTING MOVING EXPENSES

Employer reimbursements for qualifying moving expenses reduce the otherwise deductible amount for the employee. Reimbursements for nondeductible moving expenses are included in gross income and should be included in total wages on the employee's Form W-2 and reported on page 1 (line 7) of Form 1040. Employers should complete Form 4782 (Employee Moving Expense Information) which summarizes the moving expense payments made to the employee and to third parties. The form is provided to an employee to properly report his moving expenses and reimbursements. Form 3903 (Moving Expenses) is used to compute the allowable moving expenses and is attached to the employee's tax return (see Appendix B). Moving expenses are

Form **2106**		**Employee Business Expenses**		OMB No. 1545-0074

Department of the Treasury
Internal Revenue Service (99)

▶ See separate instructions.

▶ Attach to Form 1040.

2005

Attachment
Sequence No. **54**

Your name Eric Grabar	Occupation in which you incurred expenses Salesman	Social security number 231 : 54 : 9876

Part I   Employee Business Expenses and Reimbursements

Step 1   Enter Your Expenses

		Column A Other Than Meals and Entertainment		Column B Meals and Entertainment	
1	Vehicle expense from line 22c or line 29. (Rural mail carriers: See instructions.)	1	10,360		
2	Parking fees, tolls, and transportation, including train, bus, etc., that **did not** involve overnight travel or commuting to and from work . .	2	250		
3	Travel expense while away from home overnight, including lodging, airplane, car rental, etc. **Do not** include meals and entertainment	3	3,050		
4	Business expenses not included on lines 1 through 3. **Do not** include meals and entertainment.	4			
5	Meals and entertainment expenses (see instructions)	5			950
6	**Total expenses.** In Column A, add lines 1 through 4 and enter the result. In Column B, enter the amount from line 5	6	13,660		950

Note: *If you were not reimbursed for any expenses in Step 1, skip line 7 and enter the amount from line 6 on line 8.*

Step 2   Enter Reimbursements Received From Your Employer for Expenses Listed in Step 1

7	Enter reimbursements received from your employer that were **not** reported to you in box 1 of Form W-2. Include any reimbursements reported under code "L" in box 12 of your Form W-2 (see instructions)	7	4,800		– 0 –

Step 3   Figure Expenses To Deduct on Schedule A (Form 1040)

8	Subtract line 7 from line 6. If zero or less, enter -0-. However, if line 7 is greater than line 6 in Column A, report the excess as income on Form 1040, line 7	8	8,860		950
	Note: *If **both columns** of line 8 are zero, you cannot deduct employee business expenses. Stop here and attach Form 2106 to your return.*				
9	In Column A, enter the amount from line 8. In Column B, multiply line 8 by 50% (.50). (Employees subject to Department of Transportation (DOT) hours of service limits: Multiply meal expenses incurred while away from home on business by 70% (.70) instead of 50%. For details, see instructions.)	9	8,860		475
10	Add the amounts on line 9 of both columns and enter the total here. **Also, enter the total on Schedule A (Form 1040), line 20.** (Reservists, qualified performing artists, fee-basis state or local government officials, and individuals with disabilities: See the instructions for special rules on where to enter the total.) . . . . ▶	10	9,335		

For Paperwork Reduction Act Notice, see instructions.   Cat. No. 11700N   Form **2106** (2005)

FIGURE 19-2   ▶   PAGE 1 OF FORM 2106 FOR EXAMPLE 19-80

Part II	**Vehicle Expenses**		

Section A– General Information (You must complete this section if you are claiming vehicle expenses.)

			(a) Vehicle 1	**(b)** Vehicle 2
11	Enter the date the vehicle was placed in service	11	7 / 1 / 03	/ /
12	Total miles the vehicle was driven during 2005	12	30,000 miles	miles
13	Business miles included on line 12	13	24,000 miles	miles
14	Percent of business use. Divide line 13 by line 12	14	80 %	%
15	Average daily roundtrip commuting distance	15	8 miles	miles
16	Commuting miles included on line 12	16	2,000 miles	miles
17	Other miles. Add lines 13 and 16 and subtract the total from line 12	17	4,000 miles	miles
18	Do you (or your spouse) have another vehicle available for personal use?			☒ Yes ☐ No
19	Was your vehicle available for personal use during off-duty hours?			☒ Yes ☐ No
20	Do you have evidence to support your deduction?			☒ Yes ☐ No
21	If "Yes," is the evidence written?			☒ Yes ☐ No

Section B–Standard Mileage Rate (See the instructions for Part II to find out whether to complete this section or Section C.)

22a	Multiply business miles driven **before** September 1, 2005 by 40.5¢ (.405)	22a	6,480
b	Multiply business miles driven **after** August 31, 2005 by 48.5¢ (.485)	22b	3,880
c	Add lines 22a and 22b. Enter the result here and on line 1	22c	10,360

Section C– Actual Expenses

			(a) Vehicle 1	**(b)** Vehicle 2
23	Gasoline, oil, repairs, vehicle insurance, etc.	23	7,000	
24a	Vehicle rentals	24a		
b	Inclusion amount (see instructions)	24b		
c	Subtract line 24b from line 24a	24c		
25	Value of employer-provided vehicle (applies only if 100% of annual lease value was included on Form W-2–see instructions)	25		
26	Add lines 23, 24c, and 25	26	7,000	
27	Multiply line 26 by the percentage on line 14	27	5,600	
28	Depreciation (see instructions)	28	2,368	
29	Add lines 27 and 28. Enter total here and on line 1	29	8,968	

Section D–Depreciation of Vehicles (Use this section only if you owned the vehicle and are completing Section C for the vehicle.)

			(a) Vehicle 1	**(b)** Vehicle 2
30	Enter cost or other basis (see instructions)	30		
31	Enter section 179 deduction (see instructions)	31		
32	Multiply line 30 by line 14 (see instructions if you claimed the section 179 deduction or special allowance)	32		
33	Enter depreciation method and percentage (see instructions)	33		
34	Multiply line 32 by the percentage on line 33 (see instructions)	34		
35	Add lines 31 and 34	35		
36	Enter the applicable limit explained in the line 36 instructions	36	2,960	
37	Multiply line 36 by the percentage on line 14	37	2,368	
38	Enter the **smaller** of line 35 or line 37. If you skipped lines 36 and 37, enter the amount from line 35. Also enter this amount on line 28 above	38	2,368	

Form **2106** (2005)

FIGURE 19-2 ▶ PAGE 2 OF FORM 2106 FOR EXAMPLE 19-80

deductible *for* AGI on line 26 of page 1 of the 2005 Form 1040. Moving expenses are not subject to federal income tax withholding if it is reasonable to believe that an employee will be entitled to a deduction for such amounts. Reimbursements in excess of the deductible amounts, however, are subject to the withholding of income and social security taxes.

A taxpayer may deduct moving expenses, even though the tests for qualification have not been met (e.g., the 39-week test). If the individual subsequently fails to satisfy the requirements, gross income for the subsequent year must be increased by the previous tax benefit.[83] Another alternative is to wait until the tests have been met and then file an amended return (Form 1040X–see Appendix B) for the prior year.

REPORTING OFFICE IN HOME EXPENSES

Form 8829 (Expenses for Business Use of Your Home) must be used to figure the allowable expenses for business use that are reported on Schedule C (Profit or Loss from Business) and the carryover of any nondeductible amounts from prior years. Form 4562 (Depreciation and Amortization) must also be used to compute depreciation on the office portion of the residence. These tax forms are reproduced in Appendix B.

QUALIFICATION OF PENSION AND PROFIT-SHARING PLANS

The reporting requirements to establish and maintain a qualified pension or profit-sharing plan are too complex for this text. However, it should be noted that it is generally advisable for a taxpayer to obtain advance approval of the plan from the district director of the IRS by requesting a determination letter that all requirements for qualification have been met. A new determination letter should generally be requested when any material (e.g., substantial) modification is made to a plan. Material changes are frequently required when major tax legislation is enacted. In addition, several reports must be filed with the IRS and the U.S. Department of Labor.

PROBLEM MATERIALS

DISCUSSION QUESTIONS

I9-1 Why is it important to distinguish whether an individual is an employee or an independent contractor (self-employed)?

I9-2 Matt, a CPA, is employed full-time as a tax accountant for a major company. He also operates a small tax practice in his spare time. Matt incurs local transportation and unreimbursed travel expenses for both his employment and business activities. How does Matt report these expenses on his tax return?

I9-3 Determine whether the following expenses are either deductible *for* AGI or *from* AGI or nondeductible on an employee's return. Indicate whether the expenses are subject to the 2% nondeductible floor for miscellaneous itemized deductions and whether the 50% meals and entertainment deduction limit applies.

a. Business meals that were reimbursed by the employer (an adequate accounting is made to the employer and any excess reimbursement must be repaid)
b. Automobile expenses associated with commuting to and from work
c. Legal expenses incurred to prepare the taxpayer's income tax return
d. Unreimbursed travel and transportation expenses (including meals)
e. Unreimbursed entertainment expenses
f. Qualified moving expenses of an employee
g. Education-related expenses involving tuition and books

I9-4 Which of the following deduction items are subject to the 2% nondeductible floor applicable to miscellaneous itemized deductions?

---

[83] Secs. 217(d)(2) and (3).

a. Investment counseling fees
b. Fees for tax return preparation
c. Unreimbursed professional dues for an employee
d. Gambling losses
e. Interest on a personal residence
f. Unreimbursed employee travel expenses
g. Reimbursed employee travel expenses (an adequate accounting is made to the employer and any excess reimbursement must be repaid)
h. Safe deposit box rental expenses for an investor

I9-5   In each of the following cases involving travel expenses, indicate how each item is reported on the taxpayer's tax return. Include any limitations that might affect its deductibility.
a. Marilyn, who lives in Houston, owns several apartments in Denver. To supervise the management of these properties, Marilyn incurs travel expenses including airfare, lodging, and meals while traveling to and from the apartment site.
b. Marc is an employee who incurs travel expenses as a salesperson. The expenses are fully reimbursed by his employer after an adequate accounting has been made.
c. Assume the same facts as in Part b, except that the expenses are not reimbursed.
d. Kay is a self-employed attorney who incurs travel expenses (including meals) to prepare a court case in a nearby city where she spends the night.

I9-6   Kelly is an employee who incurs $2,000 of business meal expenses in connection with business entertainment and travel, none of which are reimbursed by her employer. $500 of the business meal costs are considered to be lavish or extravagant. How much can Kelly deduct before applying the 2% nondeductible floor on miscellaneous itemized deductions?

I9-7   Latoya is a college professor who takes a nine-month leave of absence from her employment at a college in Ohio and accepts a visiting professorship (temporary assignment) at a college in Texas. Latoya leaves her husband and children in Ohio and incurs the following expenses in connection with the temporary assignment:

Airfare to and from the temporary assignment	$ 1,000
Living expenses in the new location (including meals of $1,000)	8,000
Personal clothing	1,500
Total	$10,500

a. Which (if any) of these items can Latoya deduct?
b. Would your answer to Part a change if Latoya, after completing the nine month assignment, resigned her position in Ohio and accepted a full-time assignment with the college in Texas?

I9-8   Louie is a full-time employee for a retail company and also an investor in real estate in his spare time. In the current year, Louie incurs $2,500 of travel expenses and $1,000 in registration fees related to attending real estate investment seminars. He deducts the expenses on his income tax return as a *for* AGI expense related to the production of income. Are the travel expenses and registration fees deductible? Should they be classified as *for* AGI or *from* AGI?

I9-9   If an employee receives a specific monthly amount from his or her employer as a reimbursement for employment-related entertainment, travel, and transportation expenses, why is it necessary to allocate a portion of the total reimbursement to each expense category?

I9-10   If an employee receives a reimbursement of 20 cents a mile from her employer for employment-related transportation expenses, is the employee permitted to deduct the difference between the standard mileage rate and the reimbursement rate as an unreimbursed employee expense? What other alternative is available for claiming the transportation deduction?

I9-11   If an employee (or self-employed individual) uses the standard mileage rate method for the year in which an automobile is acquired, may the actual expense method be used in a subsequent year? If so, what restrictions are imposed (if any) on depreciation methods? What adjustments to basis are required?

I9-12   What reporting procedures should be followed by an employee who deducts unreimbursed employee expenses on his or her tax return?

I9-13   Discuss the reporting procedures that should be followed by an employee to report employment-related expenses on his or her tax return under the following conditions:
a. Expenses are less than reimbursements, and no accounting is made to the employer.
b. Expenses equal reimbursements, and an adequate accounting is made to the employer.
c. Expenses exceed reimbursements, and an adequate accounting is made to the employer.
d. Expenses are less than reimbursements. An adequate accounting is made to the employer and the employee is required to repay any excess amount.

I9-14   Why were distance and time requirements legislated as conditions for eligibility for a moving expense deduction?

I9-15   Does it matter whether a moving expense is incurred by an employee, a self-employed individual, or an unemployed person?

I9-16   Len incurs $2,000 of deductible moving expenses in the current year and is fully reimbursed by his employer in the same year.
a. How are the expense deduction and the reimbursement reported on Len's tax return if he uses the standard deduction?

b. What tax consequences occur if the reimbursement is $2,000 but only $1,200 of the $2,000 of moving expenses are tax deductible?

I9-17 Why are strict recordkeeping requirements required for the deduction of entertainment expenses?

I9-18 Louis incurs "directly related" entertainment expenses of $4,000, but he is reimbursed by his employer for only $3,000 after an adequate accounting is made.
a. How are these amounts reported on Louis's tax return?
b. What are the tax consequences if Louis is unable to provide adequate documentation of the expenditures during the course of an IRS audit of his tax return?

I9-19 Latasha is a self-employed attorney who entertains clients and potential clients in her home.
a. What requirements must be met to qualify the outlays as deductible entertainment expenses?
b. What is the difference between "directly related" and "associated with" entertainment?

I9-20 Liz is an employee who regularly entertains customers in connection with her job. In the current year, Liz incurs $6,000 in business meal expenses that are connected with entertainment. Liz's expenses are not lavish or extravagant. She itemizes her deductions in the current year.
a. If none of these expenses are reimbursed by Liz's employer, what amounts are deductible and how are they classified?
b. How are these amounts reported by Liz and her employer if all of her expenses are reimbursed and an adequate accounting is made by Liz?

I9-21 Atlantic Corporation provides a cafeteria for its employees. The meal charges are set at a sufficiently high level that the employees are not taxed on the subsidized eating facilities. Are Atlantic's cafeteria-related costs subject to the 50% disallowance for business meals?

I9-22 Lynn is a salesperson who entertains clients at business luncheons. A business relationship exists for the entertainment, and there is a reasonable expectation of business benefit. However, no business discussions are generally conducted before, during, or immediately following the meals. Do the business meal expenditures qualify as entertainment expenses?

I9-23 If an individual belongs to a country club and uses the facility primarily for business entertainment of customers, what portion of the club dues is deductible?

I9-24 Bass Corporation purchases 10 tickets to the Super Bowl in January 2006 for entertaining its customers. Due to unusually high demand, the tickets have to be purchased from scalpers for $6,000 (10 × $600). The face value of the tickets is only $900 (10 × $90). What amount is deductible by Bass in 2006?

I9-25 **a.** Discuss the two requirements for an employee expense reimbursement plan to be treated as an accountable plan.
b. How are expenses and reimbursements treated under an accountable plan?
c. How are expenses and reimbursements treated under a nonaccountable plan?

I9-26 Martin is a tax accountant employed by a public accounting firm. He incurs the following expenses:

CPA review course	$ 400
Law school tuition and books	4,000
Accounting continuing education course (travel, fees, and transportation (including meals of $200)	600
Total	$5,000

Martin is a degree candidate at the law school. Which (if any) of these expenditures qualify as deductible education expenses? How are they reported?

I9-27 Why are public school teachers generally allowed a deduction for education expenses related to graduate school or advanced courses?

I9-28 Discuss whether any of the following individuals are entitled to an office-in-home deduction:
a. Maggie is a self-employed management consultant who maintains an office in her home exclusively used for client meetings and other business-related activities. Maggie has no other place of business and her office is the most significant place for her business. She has substantial income from the consulting practice.
b. Marty is a college professor who writes research papers for academic journals in his office at home which is used exclusively for this purpose. Although Marty has an office at his place of employment, he finds it very convenient to maintain an office at home to avoid distractions from students and colleagues. Marty receives no income from the publication of the research articles for the year in question.
c. Bobby operates his own sole proprietorship as an electrician. He maintains an office at home where he keeps his books, takes phone calls from customers, and does the payroll for his five employees. All of his electrical work is done at the location of his customers.

I9-29 Compare and contrast the tax advantages accruing to employers and employees from the establishment of a qualified pension or profit-sharing plan versus a nonqualified deferred compensation arrangement (e.g., a restricted property plan).

I9-30 What is the difference between a defined benefit pension plan and a defined contribution pension plan?

I9-31 Austin Corporation is proposing the establishment of a pension plan that will cover only employees with salaries in excess of $100,000. No other employees are covered under comparable qualified plans. What problems (if any) do you envision regarding the plan's qualification with the IRS?

I9-32 Babson Corporation is proposing the creation of a qualified profit-sharing plan for its employees. The proposed plan provides for vesting of employer contributions after 20 years because the company wants to discourage employee turnover and does not feel that short-term employees should qualify for benefits. Will this plan qualify? Why or why not?

I9-33 Explain how distributions from a qualified pension plan, which are made in the form of annuity payments, are reported by an employee under the following circumstances:
a. No employee contributions are made to the plan.
b. The pension plan provides for matching employee contributions.

I9-34 Discuss the limitations and restrictions that the Internal Revenue Code places on employer contributions to qualified pension and profit-sharing plans.

I9-35 Why are nonqualified deferred compensation plans particularly well-suited for use in executive compensation arrangements?

I9-36 If a newly-formed corporation is considering going public and anticipates substantial future appreciation in its stock, would it be advisable for an executive receiving restricted property to elect to recognize income immediately under Sec. 83(b)? Contrast the tax consequences of a restricted property arrangement for both the employer and employee when this election is made versus when it is not made. Consider the effect of the subsequent lapsing of the restrictions and the employee's sale of the stock.

I9-37 List and discuss the qualification requirements for an incentive stock option plan (ISO). Describe the advantages and disadvantages of ISOs compared to nonqualified stock option plans.

I9-38 What difference does it make if a nonqualified stock option has a readily ascertainable FMV on the grant date?

I9-39 Is a self-employed individual, who is also employed and covered by an employer's qualified pension plan, eligible to establish an H.R. 10 or an SEP plan on his or her self-employment income?

I9-40 What limitations are placed on self-employed individuals for contributions made to defined contribution H.R. 10 plans? Must self-employed individuals cover their full-time employees if an H.R. 10 plan is established?

I9-41 Would you be more favorably inclined to advise a 50-year-old individual or a 30-year-old individual to establish a traditional deductible IRA? Why? A traditional nondeductible IRA? Why? Consider any tax problems involved if the IRA funds are needed before age 59½.

I9-42 Discuss the essential differences between a traditional IRA and a Roth IRA.

I9-43 Would it generally be advisable for a 30-year-old individual to invest in a traditional deductible IRA or a Roth IRA?

I9-44 Your client, Charley Long, age 40, has requested your advice with respect to his IRA. He has a traditional IRA with a balance of $80,000 and his current AGI is $50,000. He expects his income to increase slightly when he retires at age 65. Charley has been reading about Roth IRAs and wants your advice as to whether he should rollover the $80,000 from his traditional IRA into a Roth IRA. He has sufficient outside money to pay any taxes due on the rollover. What advice would you give Charley?

I9-45 Sally, who is single and age 40, made deductible IRA contributions in several early years, but has not been eligible to make deductible IRA contributions for the last 5 years because she is covered under her employer's plan. Her AGI is $60,000. She is interested in making IRA contributions in the current year. What advice would you give her?

I9-46 Discuss the major features of a Coverdell Education Savings Account (CESA).

I9-47 The owner of an unincorporated small business is considering whether to establish a simplified employee pension (SEP) plan for its employees.
a. What nontax factors might make an SEP attractive as an alternative to establishing a qualified pension or profit-sharing plan?
b. Is the owner of the small business eligible to make contributions on his or her behalf to the SEP?

ISSUE IDENTIFICATION QUESTIONS

I9-48 Georgia is an executive who recently completed an assignment with her employer at an away-from-home location. It was realistically expected that the assignment would be completed in 15 months but the actual time period was only 11 months. Georgia incurred $15,000 of away-from-home expenses during the 11-month period, none of which were reimbursed by her employer. What tax issues should Georgia consider?

I9-49 Jeremy is an executive for Columbia Corporation, which is going through a restructuring of its corporate headquarters operations. Columbia has offered to relocate Jeremy from its New York headquarters to its divisional operation in South Carolina and will reimburse him for both direct and indirect moving expenses. What tax issues should Jeremy consider?

I9-50 Juan, a self-employed medical doctor, maintains an office in his home where he maintains patient records and performs billing procedures. Most of his time is spent visiting patients and performing surgical procedures in the operating room at several local hospitals. Juan intends to deduct his expenses of his office in his home. What tax issues should Juan consider?

I9-51 David is on the audit staff of a national accounting firm. He has been with the firm for three years and is a CPA. David has applied and been accepted into a prestigious MBA program. The program is two years in duration. David has decided to resign from the accounting firm even though the firm has indicated that it would very much like David to return to work for the firm after he receives his MBA degree. David is somewhat interested in returning to public accounting but will certainly look at all of his options when he completes the program. David wants to deduct his education expenses. What are the relevant tax issues in this case?

PROBLEMS

I9-52 *Employment-Related Expenses.* Mike incurs the following employment-related expenses in the current year:

Actual automobile expenses	$ 2,500
Moving expenses (deductible under Sec. 217)	4,000
Entertainment expenses	1,500
Travel expenses (including $500 of business meals)	2,500
Professional dues and subscriptions	500
Total	$11,000

Mike's AGI is $120,000 before the above expenses are deducted. None of the expenses listed above are reimbursed by Mike's employer. He has no other miscellaneous itemized deductions and does not use the standard deduction.
a. What is the amount of Mike's deduction for employment-related expenses?
b. How are these items reported in Mike's tax return?

I9-53 *Travel and Entertainment.* Monique is a self-employed manufacturer's representative who solicits business for clients and receives a commission based on sales. She incurs the following expenditures during the current year:

Airfare and lodging while away from home overnight	$ 4,000
Business meals while traveling at which business is discussed	1,000
Local transportation costs for automobile, parking, tolls, etc. (business-related)	2,000
Commuting expenses	1,000
Local entertainment of customers	2,000
Total	$10,000

a. Which of the expenditures listed above (if any) are deductible by Monique?
b. Are each of these items classified as *for* AGI or *from* AGI deductions?
c. How would your answers to Parts a and b change if Monique were an employee rather than self-employed and none of the expenses were reimbursed by her employer?

I9-54 *Unreimbursed Employee Expenses.* In the current year Mary incurs $3,600 of unreimbursed employment-related travel and entertainment expenses. These expenses include the following:

Airfare	$1,500
Taxi fare	100
Meals eaten alone while away from home on business	300

Laundry	50
Lodging	650
Business meals with customers at which business is discussed	500
Entertainment of customers	500
Total	$3,600

Mary also pays $1,000 of investment counseling fees and $500 of tax return preparation fees in the current year. Mary's AGI is $70,000.
a. What is the total amount of Mary's deductible expenses?
b. Are the deductible expenses classified as *for* AGI or *from* AGI?

I9-55 *Travel Expenses.* Marilyn, a business executive who lives and works in Cleveland, accepts a temporary out-of-town assignment in Atlanta for a period of ten months. Marilyn leaves her husband and children in Cleveland and rents an apartment in Atlanta during the ten-month period. Marilyn incurs the following expenses, none of which are reimbursed by her employer:

Airfare to and from Atlanta	$ 800
Airfare for weekend trips to visit her family	8,000
Apartment rent	10,000
Meals in Atlanta	8,500
Entertainment of customers	2,000
Total	$29,300

a. Which of the expenditures listed above (if any) are deductible by Marilyn (before any limitations are applied)?
b. Are each of these expenditures classified as *for* AGI or *from* AGI deductions?
c. If Marilyn's AGI is $120,000, what is the amount of the deduction for the expenditures?
d. Do the tax consequences change if Marilyn's assignment is for a period of more than one year and is for an indefinite period rather than a temporary period?
e. Do the tax consequences in Parts a through c change if it was realistically expected that the work would be completed in ten months but after the ten-month period Marilyn is asked to continue for seven more months and if an additional $10,000 of travel expenses are incurred during the extended period?

I9-56 *Business/Personal Travel Expenses.* In the current year Mike's AGI is $50,000. Mike has no miscellaneous itemized deductions other than the employment-related expenses listed below. Mike attends a professional trade association convention in Los Angeles. He spends three days at the meeting and two days vacationing before the meeting. Mike was unable to obtain excursion airfare rates (i.e., staying over a Saturday night) despite the fact that he was on vacation immediately before the meeting. Mike's total expenses include the following:

Airfare	$ 450
Meals ($50 per day)	250
Hotel ($100 per day)	500
Entertainment of customers (business is discussed)	500
Total	$1,700

Mike's employer reimburses him for the business-related expenses and, accordingly, Mike receives a reimbursement of $1,400 ($450 + 150 + 300 + 500).
a. How much can Mike deduct for employment-related expenses?
b. How is the reimbursement reported on Mike's tax return?
c. Is the reimbursement fully deductible by Mike's employer?

I9-57 *Employment-Related Expenses and Reimbursements.* Maxine incurs the following employment-related business expenses in the current year:

Professional dues and subscriptions	$1,000
Airfare and lodging	2,000
Local transportation for employment-related business activities	1,000

Customer entertainment (business lunches where business is discussed)	1,000
Total	$5,000

After making an adequate accounting of the expenses, Maxine receives a reimbursement of $3,000 from her employer. Assume that Maxine's AGI is $60,000, she has other miscellaneous itemized deductions of $1,000, and she does not use the standard deduction.

a. What amount of the expenses are deductible by Maxine?

b. Are each of these expenditures classified as *for* AGI or *from* AGI deductions?

c. How would your answers to Parts a and b change if Maxine instead received a $6,000 reimbursement?

I9-58 *Miscellaneous Itemized Deductions.* In the current year, Melissa, a single employee whose AGI is $100,000 before any of the items below, incurs the following expenses:

Safe deposit box rental for investments	$ 100
Tax return preparation fees	500
Moving expenses (deductible under Sec. 217)	2,000
Mortgage interest on Melissa's principal residence	12,000
Real estate taxes on Melissa's principal residence	1,800
Unreimbursed employment-related expenses (other than business meals and entertainment)	6,000
Unreimbursed employment-related expenses for business meals and entertainment (business is discussed)	1,200
Total	$23,600

a. What is the amount of Melissa's total miscellaneous itemized deductions (after deducting the 2% floor)?

b. What is the amount of Melissa's total itemized deductions?

c. What is the amount of Melissa's total itemized deductions if her AGI, after all adjustments above, is $160,000?

I9-59 *Transportation Expenses.* Cassady, an employee of a law firm, maintains an office at the principal business location of her firm. She frequently travels directly from her home to client locations within and outside the metropolitan area. Cassady is not reimbursed for her transportation expenses and has incurred the following:

Transportation expenses associated with trips to clients within the metropolitan area	$2,000
Transportation expenses associated with trips to clients located outside the metropolitan area	3,000
Total	$5,000

a. What is the amount of Cassady's deduction for transportation expenses?

b. How is the deduction reported on Cassady's tax return?

c. What is the amount of Cassady's deduction for transportation expenses and its classification if she is self-employed and operates her office from her home? Assume that the requirements of Sec. 280A are satisfied.

I9-60 *Auto Expenses.* Michelle is an employee who must use her personal automobile for employment-related business trips. During 2006, Michelle drives her car 60% for business use and incurs the following total expenses (100% use of car):

Gas and oil	$ 5,000
Repairs	1,400
Depreciation	4,700
Insurance and license fees	1,300
Parking and tolls (business related)	100
Total	$12,500

Michelle drives 24,000 business miles during 2006 and receives a reimbursement of 25 cents per mile from her employer. Assume that the 2% nondeductible floor on miscellaneous itemized deductions is not applicable and that an adequate accounting is made to Michelle's employer.

a. What amount is deductible if Michelle elects to use the standard mileage method?
b. What amount is deductible if Michelle uses the actual cost method?
c. Can taxpayers switch back and forth between the mileage and actual methods each year?

I9-61 *Entertainment Expenses.* Milt, a self-employed attorney, incurs the following expenses in the current year:

Dues paid to the local chamber of commerce	$ 1,000
Business lunches for clients and prospective clients (Milt does not believe in conducting business discussions during lunch)	4,000
Entertainment of professional associates in his home (immediately following business meetings)	2,000
Country club dues (the club is used exclusively for business)	2,500
Entertainment of clients and prospective clients at the country club (meals and drinks)	1,500
Total	$11,000

a. Which of the expenditures listed above (if any) are deductible by Milt?
b. Are each of these items classified as *for* AGI or *from* AGI deductions?

I9-62 *Entertainment Expenses.* Beach Corporation purchases tickets to sporting events and uses them to entertain customers. In the current year Beach Corporation purchases the following tickets:

100 tickets to football games (face value of the tickets is $3,600)	$ 6,000
A skybox rented for six NFL football games (seating capacity of the skybox is 20, and the highest price of a nonluxury box seat is $60)	18,000 .

What amount of the entertainment expenses is deductible in the current year?

I9-63 *Reimbursed Employee Expenses.* Latrisha is an employee of the Cooper Company and incurs significant employment-related expenses. During the current year, she incurred the following expenses in connection with her job:

Travel: Airfare	$ 5,850
Lodging	1,800
Meals	1,200
Entertainment of customers	2,400
Total	$11,250

a. Determine the amount of deductible expenses for both Latrisha and the Cooper Company and, for Latrisha, whether they are deductible *for* AGI or *from* AGI assuming Cooper Company maintains an accountable plan for employee expense reimbursements, if the reimbursements are alternatively:

1. $11,250
2. $9,000
3. $14,000

b. What would be the result in Part a for each of the three situations if the plan was a nonaccountable plan?

I9-64 *Moving Expenses.* Michael graduates from New York University and on February 1, 2006, accepts a position with a public accounting firm in Chicago. Michael is a resident of New York. In March, Michael travels to Chicago to locate a house and starts to work in June. He incurs the following expenses, none of which are reimbursed by the public accounting firm:

Automobile expense enroute (1,000 miles at 18 cents per mile—standard mileage rate)	$	180
Cost of meals en route		100
Househunting trip travel expenses		1,400
Moving van expenses		3,970
Commission on the sale of Michael's New York condominium		3,500

Points paid to acquire a mortgage on Michael's new residence in Chicago	1,000
Temporary living expenses for one week in Chicago (hotel and $100 in meals)	400
Expenses incurred in decorating the new residence	500
Total expenses	$11,050

a. What is Michael's moving expense deduction?

b. How are the deductible expenses classified on Michael's tax return?

c. How would your answer to Part a change if all of Michael's expenses were reimbursed by his employer and he received a check for $11,050?

I9-65 *Education Expenses.* For each of the following independent situations, determine whether any of the expenditures qualify as deductible education expenses in connection with a trade or business (Reg. Sec. 1.162-5). Are the expenditures classified as *for* AGI or *from* AGI deductions?

a. Law school tuition and books for an IRS agent who is pursuing a law degree: $2,000.

b. Continuing professional accounting education expenses of $1,900 for a self-employed CPA: travel, $1,000 (including $200 meals); registration fees, $800; books, $100.

c. MBA education expenses totaling $5,000 for a business executive of a major corporation: tuition, $4,000; transportation, $800; and books, $200.

d. Tuition and books acquired for graduate education courses required under state law for a schoolteacher in order to renew a provisional certificate: $1,000.

e. Bar review courses for a recent law school graduate: $1,000.

I9-66 *Education Expenses.* Anne works for a CPA firm as a secretary/receptionist and earns approximately $27,000 per year. About five years earlier, she had completed 70 credit hours at State U. To increase her career potential, she decided to enroll at the local university to continue her college education and get an undergraduate degree in accounting with the ultimate goal of obtaining her CPA certificate. During 2006, she incurred the following education expenses:

Tuition and fees	$3,500
Books and supplies	800

What are Anne's options as to the deductibility of the above expenses?

I9-67 *Office in Home.* Nancy is a self-employed artist who uses 10% of her residence as a studio. The studio portion is used exclusively for business and is frequented by customers on a regular basis. Nancy also uses her den as an office (10% of the total floor space of her home) to prepare bills and keep records. However, the den is also used by her children as a TV room. Nancy's income from the sale of the artwork amounts to $40,000 in the current year. She also incurs $2,000 of expenses directly related to the business other than home office expenses (e.g., art supplies and selling expenses). Nancy incurs the following expenses in the current year related to her residence:

Real estate taxes	$ 2,000
Mortgage interest	5,000
Insurance	500
Depreciation	3,500
Repairs and utilities	1,000
Total	$12,000

a. Which of the expenditures above (if any) are deductible? Are they *for* AGI or *from* AGI deductions?

b. Would your answer to Part a change if Nancy's income from painting were only $2,500 for the year? What is the amount of the office-in-home deduction and the amount of the carryover (if any) of the unused deductions? (Assume that Nancy is not subject to the hobby loss restrictions.)

I9-68 Darrell is a self-employed consultant who uses 15% of his home exclusively as an office. Darrell operates completely out of his home office and makes all of his appointments from the office as well as keeping his books and records in the office. Darrell's gross income from his consulting business is $60,000 in 2006. He incurs $6,000 of expenses that are directly related to his business, such as computer and office supplies. Below are expenses that relate to Darrell's residence for 2006:

Real estate taxes	$ 4,000
Mortgage interest	6,000
Insurance	1,000
Depreciation	4,000
Repairs and utilities	1,000
Total	$16,000

a. Which of the above expenditures (if any) are deductible? Are they *for* AGI or *from* AGI deductions?

b. How would your answer change if Darrell was an employee of a consulting company and maintained an office at home in order to take work home with him so he did not have to spend so many hours at his consulting company office?

I9-69 *Deferred Compensation Plan Requirements.* Identify whether each of the following plan features is associated with a qualified pension plan, a qualified profit-sharing plan, an employee stock ownership plan, a nonqualifed plan, or none of these plans.

a. Annual employer contributions are not required, but substantial and recurring contributions must be made based on a predetermined formula.

b. Annual, systematic, and definite employer contributions are required without regard to profits but based on actuarial methods.

c. Forfeitures must be used to reduce contributions that would otherwise be made under the plan.

d. The plan may discriminate in favor of highly compensated individuals.

e. The trust is funded with the contribution of employer stock, which is subsequently distributed to employees.

I9-70 *Taxability of Pension Payments.* Pat is a participant in a qualified pension plan. She retires on January 1, 2006, at age 63, and receives pension payments beginning in January 2006. Her pension payments, which will be received monthly for life, amount to $1,000 per month. Pat contributed $30,000 to the pension plan on a pre-tax (or tax-deferred) basis, and the number of anticipated payments based on Pat's age of 63 years is 260 months (see IRS table in Chapter I3) from the date she starts receiving payments.

a. What gross income will Pat recognize in 2006 and each year thereafter?

b. How would your answer to Part a change if Pat made contributions to the plan on an after-tax basis?

c. If, in Part b, Pat dies in December 2007 after receiving pension payments for two full years, what tax consequences occur in the year of death?

I9-71 *Restricted Property.* In 2006, Bear Corporation transfers 100 shares of its stock to its employee Patrick. The stock is valued at $10 per share on the issue date. The stock is subject to the following restrictions:

• Patrick cannot transfer the stock by sale or other disposition (except in the event of death) for a five-year period.

• The stock must be forfeited to Bear Corporation if Patrick voluntarily terminates his employment with the company within a five-year period.

In the year 2011, the Bear stock is worth $100 per share when the restrictions expire.

a. Assuming that no Sec. 83(b) election is made, what are the tax consequences to Patrick and Bear Corporation in 2006?

b. What are the tax consequences to Patrick and Bear Corporation if Patrick makes a valid Sec. 83(b) election in 2006?

c. What are the tax consequences to Patrick and Bear Corporation if Patrick forfeits the stock back to the company in 2007 when the stock is worth $20 per share if an election was made under Sec. 83(b)? What would happen if no Sec. 83(b) election were made?

d. What are the tax consequences to Patrick and Bear Corporation upon the lapse of the restrictions in the year 2011 if an election has been made under Sec. 83(b)? What would the results be if no Sec. 83(b) election were made?

e. What are the tax consequences to Patrick and Bear Corporation if Patrick sells the Bear stock in the year 2012 for $120 per share if a Sec. 83(b) election is made? if no Sec. 83(b) election is made?

I9-72 *IRAs.* On February 15, 2007, Jamal, who is single and age 30, establishes an IRA and contributes $4,000 to the account. Jamal's adjusted gross income is $56,000 in 2006 and $51,000 in 2007. Jamal is an active participant in an employer-sponsored retirement plan.

a. What amount of the contribution is deductible? In what year is it deductible?

b. How is the deduction (if any) reported (i.e., *for* AGI or *from* AGI)?

c. How would your answer to Part a change, if at all, if Jamal were not an active participant in an employer-sponsored retirement plan?

d. How would your answer to Part a change if Jamal were married and files a joint return with his spouse, who has no earned income? (Assume their combined AGI is $60,000.)

I9-73 *IRAs.* Phil, age 30, is married and files a joint return with his spouse. On February 15, 2007, Phil establishes an IRA for himself and a spousal IRA for his spouse with an $8,000 contribution, $4,000 for himself and $4,000 for his wife. Phil's spouse earned $1,000 in 2006 from a part-time job, and their combined AGI is $55,000. Neither Phil nor his spouse is an active participant in an employer-sponsored retirement plan.

a. What amount of the contribution is deductible?

b. To what year does the contribution apply? (Assume that an election is made to treat Phil's spouse as having no compensation.)

c. Is the deduction reported as *for* AGI or *from* AGI?

d. How would your answer to Part a change, if at all, if Phil and his spouse were active participants in an employer-sponsored retirement plan?

e. If a portion of the contribution is nondeductible in Part d, is it possible for Phil to make a deductible and a nondeductible contribution in the same year? Explain.

f. How would your answer to Part a change if Phil and his spouse's combined AGI were $92,000 in 2006 and Phil was an active participant in an employer-sponsored retirement plan?

I9-74 *Roth IRA.* Chatham Mae is single, age 35, and wants to make a contribution to an IRA for the year ended December 31, 2006. She is an active participant in a qualified retirement plan sponsored by her employer. Her AGI for 2006 is $100,000 before considering any IRA contribution.

a. What type of IRA, if any, is Chatham Mae eligible to make a contribution to for 2006? If she is eligible to contribute to an IRA, what is the maximum amount that she can contribute to the IRA?

b. Assume Chatham Mae makes contributions of $2,000 per year for six years to a Roth IRA. In 2012, she withdraws $15,000 to pay off her car loan. Her financial advisor suggested she withdraw the money from the IRA for two major reasons: (1) to eliminate her debt and (2) no tax would be due on distributions from a Roth IRA after five years. Chatham Mae wants to verify the accuracy of her advisor's advice. What would be the tax consequences of this withdrawal? Alternatively, what if Chatham Mae withdrew the $15,000 to purchase a house (she is a first-time homebuyer)?

c. Alternatively to Part b above, assume Chatham Mae has a traditional deductible IRA that has a balance of $50,000. She has been able to deduct all of her contributions to the IRA in prior years. Her financial advisor has recommended that she rollover the funds from her traditional IRA to a Roth IRA in 2006. What are the tax consequences of this rollover in 2006?

I9-75 *Coverdell Education Savings Accounts.* Jack and Katie have five grandchildren, ages 19, 16, 15, 12, and 10. They have established Coverdell Education Savings Accounts (CESA) for each of the grandchildren and would like to contribute the maximum amount allowable to each CESA for the 2006 taxable year. Jack and Katie's AGI for 2006 is $196,000.

a. How much can Jack and Katie contribute to each grandchild's CESA in 2006?

b. Assume that the 19-year-old granddaughter is a freshman in college and makes a withdrawal of $7,000 from her CESA during the year 2006. Her college expenses for 2006 were as follows:

Tuition	$1,500
Room and board	2,500
Books and supplies	500

The extra amount withdrawn was used a down payment on a car that the granddaughter purchased during the year. She needed the car in order to drive to school rather than having to either ride the bus or ride with a friend. What are the tax consequences of the $7,000 distribution to the granddaughter?

I9-76 *H.R. 10 Plans.* Paula is a self-employed doctor who is considering whether to establish a defined contribution H.R. 10 plan. Paula's only employee is a full-time nurse who has been employed by Paula for seven years. Paula's net earnings from self-employment (before the H.R. 10 plan contribution but after the deduction for one-half of self-employment taxes paid) is expected to be $100,000 during the current year and in future years.

a. If the H.R. 10 plan is established, what is the maximum amount Paula can contribute for the nurse's benefit?

b. What is the maximum amount Paula can contribute for herself? Is the amount reported as a *for* AGI or *from* AGI deduction?

c. Is Paula's nurse required to be included in the plan?

d. What are the tax consequences if Paula makes a premature withdrawal from the plan before reaching age 59½?

I9-77 *Stock Options.* Bell Corporation grants an incentive stock option to Peggy, an employee, on January 1, 2006, when the option price and FMV of the Bell stock is $80. The option entitles Peggy to buy 10 shares of Bell stock. Peggy exercises the option and acquires the stock on April 1, 2008, when the stock's FMV is $100. Peggy, while still employed by the Bell Corporation, sells the stock on May 1, 2010, for $120 per share.

a. What are the tax consequences to Peggy and Bell Corporation on the following dates: January 1, 2006; April 1, 2008; and May 1, 2010? (Assume all incentive stock option qualification requirements are met.)

b. How would your answer to Part a change if Peggy instead sold the Bell stock for $130 per share on May 1, 2008?

I9-78 *Stock Options.* Bender Corporation grants a nonqualified stock option to Penny, an employee, on January 1, 2006, that entitled Penny to acquire 1,000 shares of Bender stock at $80 per share. On this date, the stock has a $100 FMV and the option has a readily ascertainable FMV. Penny exercises the option on January 1, 2007 (when the FMV of the stock is $150), and acquires 1,000 shares of the stock for $80 per share. Penny later sells the Bender stock on January 1, 2009, for $200 per share.

a. What are the tax consequences to Penny and Bender Corporation on the following dates: January 1, 2006; January 1, 2007; and January 1, 2009?

b. How would your answer to Part a change if the Bender stock were instead closely-held and the option had no readily ascertainable FMV?

COMPREHENSIVE PROBLEM

I9-79 Dan and Cheryl are married, file a joint return, and have no children. Dan is a pharmaceutical salesman and Cheryl is a nurse at a local hospital. Dan's SSN is 400-20-1000 and Cheryl's SSN is 200-40-8000 and they reside at 2033 Palmetto Drive, Nashville, TN 28034. Dan is paid according to commissions from sales; however, his compensation is subject to withholding of income and payroll taxes. He also maintains an office in his home as the pharmaceutical company does not have an office in Nashville and when he is not traveling, Dan operates his business from his home office. During 2006, Dan earned total compensation from his job of $125,000, on which $20,000 of federal income taxes were withheld, $5,840 of OASDI, and $1,813 of Medicare taxes. No state income taxes were withheld. Cheryl earned a salary during 2006 of $45,400, on which federal taxes withheld were $5,000, OASDI of $2,815, and Medicare taxes of $658.

During 2006, Dan and Cheryl had interest income from corporate bonds and bank accounts of $1,450 and dividends from stocks of $5,950. Dan also actively trades stocks and had the following results for 2006:

LTCG	$4,900
LTCL	(3,200)
STCG	0
STCL	(7,800)

He had no capital loss carryovers from previous years.

Dan does a considerable amount of travel in connection with his job. He uses his own car and is reimbursed $0.20 per business mile. During 2006, Dan drove his car a total of 38,000 miles, of which 32,000 were business related. He also had parking fees and tolls during the year of $280. Dan uses the mileage method for deducting auto expenses. Dan also had the following travel expenses while away from home during the year:

Hotel	$4,200
Meals	820
Entertainment of customers	1,080
Tips	100
Laundry and cleaning	150
Total	$6,350

Dan was reimbursed for the travel expenses by his employer, pursuant to an accountable plan, in the amount of $5,080.

Dan's expenses in connection with his office in the home were as follows:

Office supplies	$ 290
Telephone (separate line)	1,100
Utilities (entire house)	3,400
Homeowners insurance	600
Interest and property taxes (see below for totals)	
Repairs and maintenance (entire house)	800

Dan's office is 300 square feet and the total square footage of the house is 3,000 square feet. Dan and Cheryl purchased the house on June 12, 1996, for $280,000, of which $40,000 is attributable to the land.

Cheryl incurred several expenses in connection with her nursing job. She paid $450 in professional dues, $200 in professional journals, and $350 for uniforms.

Dan and Cheryl had the following other expenditures during the year:

Health insurance premiums		$ 4,400
Doctor bills		470
Real estate taxes on home		2,200
Personal property taxes		400
Mortgage interest		15,600
Charitable contributions—cash		9,000
Charitable contributions—GE stock		
FMV	$12,000	
Adjusted basis	2,000	
Tax preparation fees		750

Compute Dan and Cheryl's income tax liability for 2006.

TAX STRATEGY PROBLEM

I9-80   Paul Price is the president and majority stockholder of Lightmore Communications, Inc. Lightmore is a C corporation and has been extremely successful over the past 20 years. Paul travels extensively in connection with the business to meet with existing and prospective clients. Paul's wife, Laura, would be helpful to Paul in his business entertaining if she could accompany him on many of his business trips and, furthermore, she was unable to go on these trips in the past because of their children at home. Their youngest child is now in college, and Laura's duties at home have diminished. During the current year, Laura has made a number of trips with Paul, but after conferring with the company's tax advisor, had been informed that Laura's expenses would not be deductible for tax purposes. The tax advisor suggested the possibility of putting Laura on the Lightmore payroll as an employee.

a. Would Laura's travel expenses be deductible if she was an employee of the corporation?

b. What other benefits would be available to Laura if she was an employee of the corporation?

c. Are there any detriments to putting Laura on the payroll?

TAX FORM/RETURN PREPARATION PROBLEMS

I9-81   In 2005, Micah Johnson (SSN 277-33-7263) incurs the following unreimbursed employee business expenses:

Airplane and taxi fares	$ 4,000
Lodging away from home	5,000
Meals while away from home	1,000
Automobile expenses (related to 100% of	
the use of his personal automobile):	
Gasoline and oil	5,500
Repairs	1,000
Insurance	900
Depreciation	1,775
Parking and tolls (includes only	
business use)	100
Total	$19,275

Johnson receives a $7,800 reimbursement for the travel expenses. He did not receive any reimbursement for the auto expenses. He uses his personal automobile 80% for business use and placed his current automobile in service on October 1, 2001. Total business miles evenly driven during the year amount to 26,400, his commuting miles in 2005 amount to 2,000, and other personal miles amount to 4,600 miles. Johnson's AGI is $60,000, and he has no other miscellaneous itemized deductions.

a. Calculate Johnson's expense deduction using the 2005 Form 2106 (Employee Business Expenses) based on actual automobile expenses and other employee business expenses.

b. Calculate Johnson's expense deduction for 2005 using the standard mileage rate method and other employee business expenses. (Assume that none of the restrictions on the use of the standard mileage rate method are applicable.)

I9-82   George Large (SSN 414-33-5688) and his wife Marge Large (SSN 555-81-9495), who live at 2000 Lakeview Drive, Cleveland, OH 49001, want you to prepare their 2005 income tax return based on the information below:

George Large worked as a salesman for Toyboat, Inc. He received a salary of $80,000 ($8,500 of income taxes withheld) plus an expense reimbursement from Toyboat of $5,000 to cover his employee business expenses. George must make an adequate accounting to his employer and return any excess reimbursement. Additionally, Toyboat provides George with medical insurance worth $7,200 per year. George drove his car 24,000 miles during the year. His log indicates that 18,000 miles, evenly driven during the year, were for sales calls to customers at the customers' offices and the remainder was personal mileage. George uses the standard mileage rate method. George is a professional basketball fan. He purchased two season tickets for a total of $4,000. He takes a customer to every game, and they discuss a little business at the games. George also takes clients to business lunches. His log indicates that he spent $1,500 on these business meals. George also took a five-day trip to the Toyboat head-quarters in Musty, Ohio. He was so well prepared that he finished his business in three days, so he spent the other two days sightseeing. He had the following expenses during each day of his trip:

Airfare	$200
Lodging	$85/day
Meals	$50/day
Taxicabs	$20/day

Marge Large is self-employed. She repairs rubber toy boats in the basement of their home, which is 25% of the house's square footage. She had the following income and expenses:

Income from rubber toy boat repairs	$12,000
Cost of materials	5,000
Contract labor	3,500
Long-distance phone calls (business)	500

The Large's home cost a total of $150,000, of which the cost of the land was $20,000. The FMV of the house is $225,000. The house is depreciable over a 39-year recovery period. The Larges incurred other expenses:

Utility bills for the house	$2,000
Real estate taxes	2,500
Mortgage interest	4,500
Cash charitable contributions	3,500

Prepare Form 1040, Schedules A and C for Form 1040, and Forms 2106 and 8829 for the 2005 year. (Assume no depreciation for this problem and that no estimated taxes were paid by the Larges.)

CASE STUDY PROBLEMS

I9-83   Ajax Corporation is a young high-growth company engaged in the manufacture and distribution of automotive parts. Its common stock has doubled in value since the company was listed on the NASDAQ exchange about two years ago. Ajax currently has a high debt/equity ratio due to the issuance of debt to finance its capital expansion needs. Despite rapid growth in assets and profitability, Ajax has severe cash flow problems and a poor working capital ratio. The company urgently needs to attract new executives to the organization and to provide financial incentives to existing top management because of recent turnover and high growth. Approximately 55% of the common stock is owned by Andrew Ajax, who is the CEO, and his immediate family. None of the other officers own stock in the company.

You are a tax consultant for the company who has been asked to prepare suggestions after reviewing the compensation system. Your discussions with several top management individuals reveal the following aspects of corporate strategy and philosophy:

- The company needs to expand the equity capital base because of its concern for the high risk caused by large amounts of debt.

- Improvement in cash flow and liquidity would enhance its stock price and enable the company to continue its high growth rate.

- Top management feels that employee loyalty and productivity would be improved if all employees owned some stock in the company. The company currently offers a qualified pension plan to its employees and executives that provides only minimal pension benefits. No other deferred compensation or bonus arrangements are currently being offered.

- Andrew Ajax feels that the top management group should own a substantial amount of Ajax stock to ensure that the interests of management correspond with the shareholder interests (i.e., the maximization of shareholder wealth).

The following four types of executive compensation arrangements have been discussed:

- Sec. 401(k) and ESOP plans for employees.

- Encourage all employees and executives to independently fund their retirement needs beyond any Social Security benefits by establishing IRA plans.

- Provide restricted property arrangements (using Ajax stock) to attract new top level executives and to retain existing executives.

- Offer nonqualified or incentive stock options to existing and new executives.

Required: Prepare a client memo that recommends revisions to Ajax Corporation's existing compensation system for both its employee and executive groups. Your recommendations should discuss the pros and cons of different deferred compensation arrangements and should consider both tax and nontax factors.

I9-84 Steve is part owner and manager of a small manufacturing company that makes keypads for alarm systems. The keypads are sold to several different alarm companies throughout the country. Steve must travel to several cities each year to meet with current customers and to attract new business. When you meet with Steve to obtain information to prepare his current year tax return, he tells you that he has spent about $5,000 during the current year on airfare and taking his customers out to dinner to discuss business. Because he took most of his trips in the summer and fall, and it is now April of the following year, Steve cannot remember the exact time and places of the business dinners and did not retain any receipts for the cash used to pay the bills. However, he remembers the names of the customers he went to see, the business topics that were discussed, and the restaurants where he had his meals. As Steve's tax consultant, what is your responsibility regarding the treatment of the travel and entertainment expenses under the mandates of the AICPA's *Statements on Standards for Tax Services*? Prepare a client letter explaining to Steve the requirements under Sec. 274(d) for sufficient substantiation of travel and entertainment expenses. (See the *Statements on Standards for Tax Services* section in Chapter I15 for a discussion of these issues and Appendix E.)

TAX RESEARCH PROBLEM

I9-85 Charley Long is a truck driver, the 18-wheeler variety. He works for Fishy Co., a seafood company in Mobile, Alabama, and drives a company truck. Charley's job entails leaving Mobile at 4:00 PM each day (five days per week) and delivering fresh fish to restaurants and wholesale fish distributors in Mississippi and Louisiana. His last stop, in Lafayette, Louisiana, is generally around 12:00 midnight. It normally takes Charley about five hours to get back to Mobile.

Charley's routine is varied. Sometimes, he drives straight back to Mobile from Lafayette. On other occasions, he will pull off at a truck stop and sleep in his cab before returning to Mobile. His cab is equipped with sleeping facilities, although small and sparse. Finally, on other occasions, Charley will spend the night in a motel along the road. The Fishy Co. has no preference as to what Charley does and has given him permission to either drive back or stay overnight. However, the company does not reimburse him for his food and lodging expenses.

When Charley drives straight back to Mobile, Charley will eat one meal. When he sleeps overnight (either in his cab or in a motel), he will eat two meals, a late dinner and breakfast. He spends an average of $6.00 for dinner and $4.00 for breakfast. The cost of his motel averages $50.00 per night. When Charley sleeps in the cab, he generally sleeps about 4–5 hours and then drives on to Mobile.

During the current year, Charley incurred the following expenses:

Meals incurred on nonstop trips		$1,000
Meals incurred when: slept in cab		600
	slept in motel	400
Lodging		2,300
Total		$4,300

The IRS has disallowed all of the above expenses on the grounds that they are not bona fide travel expenses but personal expenses. Would you advise Charley to contest this issue?

A partial list of research sources is:

- Sec. 162(a)(2) and Reg. Sec. 1.162-2(a)
- *U.S. v. Correll*, 389 U.S. 299 (1967)
- *Williams v. Patterson*, 286 F.2d 333 (5th Cir. 1961)
- Rev. Rul. 75-168, 1975-1 C.B. 58 and Rev. Rul. 75-432, 1975-2 C.B. 60

10

C H A P T E R

DEPRECIATION, COST RECOVERY, AMORTIZATION, AND DEPLETION

LEARNING OBJECTIVES

After studying this chapter, you should be able to

1 ▶ Understand the general concepts of tax depreciation

2 ▶ Classify property and calculate depreciation under the MACRS rules

3 ▶ Calculate amortization for intangible assets and understand the difference between amortizable and non-amortizable assets

4 ▶ Apply cost and percentage depletion methods and understand the treatment for intangible drilling costs

The tax law allows taxpayers to deduct a reasonable allowance for the exhaustion, wear and tear, and obsolescence of property used in a trade or business or held for the production of income.[1] The purpose of allowing a depreciation deduction is to enable taxpayers to recover the cost of an asset under the return of capital doctrine. Depreciation, therefore, is the systematic allocation of the cost of an asset over its estimated economic life. *Depreciation* relates to deductions for most tangible property, *amortization* relates to deductions for intangible property, and *depletion* relates to deductions for natural resources (oil and gas, coal, etc.). While the concepts of depreciation, amortization, and depletion are similar to those in financial accounting, the income tax rules are unique. This chapter discusses the income tax rules relating to depreciation, amortization, and depletion.

DEPRECIATION AND COST RECOVERY

GENERAL CONSIDERATIONS

Taxpayers must use specific depreciation methods depending on *when* an asset is placed into service. Three separate depreciation and cost recovery systems are currently in place. These three distinct systems are the result of tax law changes in 1981 and 1986. The systems that taxpayers must use are as follows:

▶ Property placed into service after December 31, 1986. Taxpayers must use the Modified Accelerated Cost Recovery System (MACRS) as provided in Sec. 168.

▶ Property placed into service after December 31, 1980 and before January 1, 1987. Taxpayers must use the Accelerated Cost Recovery System (ACRS) as provided in Sec. 168.

▶ Property placed into service prior to 1981. Taxpayers must use the rules contained in Sec. 167 and these rules basically follow financial accounting principles.

The primary emphasis in this chapter is placed upon the MACRS rules because most assets placed into service before 1987 are now fully depreciated.

The terms *depreciation* and *cost recovery* are used interchangeably in this text. The rules in Sec. 167 (or pre-ACRS) and the MACRS rules under Sec. 168 both refer to depreciation. However, the deduction under ACRS is referred to as cost recovery. In 1981, Congress initiated the original ACRS system to achieve a number of objectives, including a stimulus for private investment, improving business productivity, simplifying taxpayer compliance, and facilitating IRS administration of the tax law. Therefore, less importance was placed on the financial accounting concept of matching costs and revenues, which is the primary theory that governed the Sec. 167 depreciation rules. The primary objective of Congress in 1981 was to allow businesses and investors to recover the cost of capitalized expenditures over a period of time that is substantially shorter than the property's economic useful life. Thus, the term *cost recovery* rather than *depreciation* was used under the ACRS system. The post-1986 MACRS rules more closely follow the concept of economic useful life and, therefore, the MACRS rules refer to depreciation rather than cost recovery.

COMMON RULES OF ALL SYSTEMS. Regardless of the particular system of depreciation that is required to be used (i.e., MACRS, ACRS, etc.), there are certain rules that are common to all systems of depreciation. These common rules are discussed below.

▶ As discussed above, depreciation may only be claimed on property used in a trade or business or for the production of income. Thus, personal-use assets, such as a personal-use automobile or the taxpayer's personal residence, are not depreciable.

---

[1] Sec. 167(a).

▶ No depreciation is permitted for land or other assets that have an indefinite life. Assets such as works of art are generally not depreciable.

▶ Depreciation for the first year is permitted only in the year the asset is placed in service. For example, a taxpayer may purchase a depreciable asset in December 2006, but not place it in service until January 2007. In this case, depreciation is not allowed until 2007.

▶ Regardless of the depreciation system, consistency is required. Taxpayers must consistently use the method selected in the year the asset was placed in service unless a change of accounting method is requested from the IRS.

▶ The basis of the property being depreciated must be reduced by the amount of depreciation that is allowable for each taxable year. An important aspect of depreciation is determining the amount of depreciation that is *allowed* and *allowable*. The depreciation allowed is the actual depreciation that is claimed by the taxpayer for a particular taxable year. Allowable depreciation is the amount of depreciation to be claimed under the tax law by using the slowest possible method (i.e., straight-line using the longest permissible recovery period). If a taxpayer does not take any depreciation during a particular year, the basis of the property must be reduced by the amount of depreciation that should have been taken during the year (i.e., the allowable depreciation).

EXAMPLE I10-1 ▶ Maria acquires a machine in the current year for $50,000 to be used in her business and elects straight-line depreciation under MACRS. The machine is classified as 7-year property for tax purposes. Maria properly takes depreciation in the first two years the asset is used in her business in the amount of $10,714 ($3,571 in Year 1 assuming the half-year convention and $7,143 in Year 2). However, because of a net operating loss in Year 3, Maria did not take any depreciation on the tax return. The allowable depreciation in Year 3 was $7,143. Even though Maria did not claim the $7,143 of depreciation in Year 3, the basis of the machine must still be reduced by that amount. Thus, at the end of Year 3, the basis of the machine would be $32,143 ($50,000 minus the allowable accumulated depreciation of $17,857). This is the case even though she did not actually claim any depreciation in Year 3. Obviously, Maria should amend her tax return for Year 3 and claim the allowable depreciation. This would increase her net operating loss for Year 3 which either can be carried back two years or forward 20 years. ◀

TYPES OF PROPERTY. Before examining the specific depreciation rules, it is necessary to define certain terms relating to the various types of property. For both property law and income tax purposes, there are two basic types of property, tangible and intangible. **Tangible property** refers to property that has physical substance, such as land, buildings, natural resources, equipment, etc. **Intangible property** refers to property that does not have physical substance, such as goodwill, patents, and stocks and bonds. The cost of tangible property (other than land, of course) is systematically written off through depreciation or depletion. Natural resources, such as oil and gas reserves, are recovered through depletion. Intangible property is written off through amortization.

Tangible property is further classified as either real property or personal property. **Real property** (often referred to as real estate or realty) is defined as land or any structure permanently attached to the land, such as buildings. **Personal property** is any tangible property that is not real property, and includes items such as equipment, vehicles, furniture, etc. It is important to distinguish between personal property and personal-use property. **Personal-use property** is any property, tangible or intangible, real or personal, that is used by the taxpayer for his own personal use rather than in a trade or business or for the production of income.

CAPITALIZATION VERSUS EXPENSE. A frequent dilemma for taxpayers is whether an expenditure either should be capitalized (and depreciated) or expensed entirely in the current year. As is discussed in Chapter I6, if an expenditure either improves the efficiency of an asset or extends the life of an asset beyond the end of the year, the expenditure should generally be capitalized. However, most taxpayers have established materiality limits in order to justify the expensing of small expenditures that technically should be considered a capital expenditure. Since the capitalization-expense decisions many times are subjective in nature, disputes between the IRS and taxpayers are common.

CONVERSION OF PERSONAL-USE PROPERTY. If personal-use property is either converted to business use or held for the production of income (e.g., a rental house), the property's basis for depreciation purposes is the lesser of its adjusted basis or its fair market value (FMV) determined as of the conversion date.[2] This lower of cost or market rule is intended to prevent taxpayers from depreciating the portion of the cost that represents a nondeductible loss on a personal-use asset.

EXAMPLE I10-2 ▶ Marty acquires a personal residence for $115,000 in 2002. In 2006, he converts the property to rental use because he is unable to sell the house due to a depressed local real estate market. The property's FMV is only $100,000 when it is converted to rental status in 2006. The $15,000 ($115,000 − $100,000) decline in value represents a nondeductible personal loss and is not depreciable. The depreciable basis is $100,000 (minus the portion of the property's FMV that represents land which is not depreciable). ◀

OBJECTIVE 1

Classify property and calculate depreciation under the MACRS rules

DEPRECIATION METHODS

As mentioned previously, the method of depreciation required for income tax purposes depends on the date the asset was placed in service. Assets placed in service prior to 1987 must use the old depreciation methods that were in place during those years.[3] Under current law, for assets placed in service after 1986, the MACRS system of depreciation is required for most assets. There are several unique features of the MACRS system that are different from depreciation methods used for financial accounting purposes. These features include the following:

▶ Salvage value is not considered in the computation of the depreciation amount.

▶ Specific asset classes are used. Both tangible personal property and real property must be placed into specific asset classes, based on the type of property. Asset classes merely refer to the number of years over which the asset must be depreciated, such as 5-year property, 7-year property, etc.

▶ Fewer depreciation methods are used and the methods are built into the MACRS tables. Both accelerated and straight-line methods are used in MACRS, however, accelerated methods are not permissible for real property. The MACRS tables are summarized in Appendix C.

▶ The term *convention* in the tax law refers to the assumption as to when an asset is either placed into service or disposed of and is used extensively in the MACRS system. The **half-year convention** generally is required for all tangible personal property and assumes that all asset acquisitions or dispositions are made at the midpoint of the tax year, regardless of when the actual acquisition or disposition is made. A special convention that may apply to tangible personal property is the **mid-quarter convention**. This special convention is discussed later in this chapter. For real estate, the **mid-month convention** is used and assumes that all asset acquisitions or dispositions are made at the midpoint of the month in which the transaction occurs.

EXAMPLE I10-3 ▶ Golden Corporation, a calendar-year taxpayer, purchases a machine for its business on March 10, 2006. For depreciation purposes, under the half-year convention, the machine is treated as if it were placed in service on July 1, 2006, and one-half year's depreciation is allowable in 2006. The half-year convention assumes all asset acquisitions and dispositions occur at the midpoint of the tax year. ◀

EXAMPLE I10-4 ▶ Assume that Golden Corporation, in Example I10-3 above, uses the machine for four years and decides to sell the machine on October 30, 2009. To compute the depreciation deduction for

[2] Reg. Sec. 1.168(i)-4(b)(1).
[3] For assets placed into service between 1981 and 1986, taxpayers were required to use the ACRS method; for assets placed into service before 1981, a pre-ACRS method was required. The pre-ACRS methods more closely resemble depreciation methods used for financial statement purposes.

the year 2009, under the half-year convention, Golden is permitted one-half year's depreciation. This one-half year's depreciation is required even though the actual sale occurred on October 30. ◄

EXAMPLE I10-5 ▶   Silver, Inc., a calendar-year taxpayer, purchases a building for its business on March 5, 2006. For depreciation purposes, under the mid-month convention, the building is treated as if it were placed in service on March 15, 2006, and 9½ months of depreciation is allowable in 2006 (one-half of a month for March plus nine full months). ◄

CALCULATION OF DEPRECIATION

The calculation of the annual depreciation deduction involves a number of variables that each taxpayer must consider. Below is a discussion of these variables in connection with the two principal types of depreciable property: tangible personal property and real property.

TANGIBLE PERSONAL PROPERTY: CLASSIFICATION AND RECOVERY RATES. Tangible personal property, such as equipment, furniture, computers, etc., are depreciable under MACRS if used in a trade or business or held for the production of income. For property depreciated under MACRS, each property acquired must be classified into one of six categories and depreciation computed using the percentages contained in Table I10-1. The classification of assets is based upon the determination of a class life from a listing of assets published by the IRS.[4]

The following classifications apply to personal property placed in service after December 31, 1986, under the MACRS system.[5]

ADDITIONAL COMMENT

Most depreciable personal property is classified as 7-year property under MACRS.

KEY POINT

Notice that the recovery period for tax purposes is not necessarily dependent upon the asset's actual economic life. A property's class life and its actual economic life may be different.

▶ 3-Year   Property with a class life of 4 years or less. This category includes property such as tractor units, race horses over 12 years old, and special tools.

▶ 5-Year   Property with a a class life of more than 4 years but less than 10 years. This category includes property such as automobiles, light and heavy-duty general purpose trucks, computers, and research and experimental (R&E) equipment.

▶ 7-Year   Property with a class life of 10 years or more but less than 16 years. This category includes property such as office furniture and equipment, horses, single-purpose agricultural or horticultural structures, and property with no class life and not classified elsewhere. Most types of machinery are included in this class.

▶ 10-Year   Property with a class life of more than 16 years, but less than 20 years. This category includes property such as barges, vessels, and petroleum and food processing equipment.

▶ 15-Year   Property with a class life of more than 20 years, but less than 25 years. This category includes property such as billboards, service station buildings, and land improvements.

▶ 20-Year   Property with a class life of 25 or more years, including property such as utilities and sewers.

KEY POINT

Remember that salvage value is not taken into consideration under the MACRS system.

The depreciation rates for the 3-year, 5-year, and 7-year recovery classes are provided in Table I10-1. (See Table 1 in Appendix C for depreciation rates for all classes of property.) The rates in Table I10-1 are based on the 200% DB method switching to straight-line when it yields a larger amount. A half-year convention is used in the year of acquisition and zero salvage value is assumed. In the year of disposition, the amount calculated from the table must be reduced by one-half in order to properly apply the half-year convention.

---

[4] To determine the class life of assets, see Rev. Proc. 87-56, modified by Rev. Proc. 88-22, which sets forth the class life of property for depreciation purposes.

[5] Sec. 168(e)(1).

▼ TABLE I10-1

MACRS Rates for Tangible Personal Property (using half-year convention)

Recovery Year	Recovery Classes		
	3-Year	5-Year	7-Year
1	0.3333	0.2000	0.1429
2	0.4445	0.3200	0.2449
3	0.1481	0.1920	0.1749
4	0.0741	0.1152	0.1249
5	—	0.1152	0.0893
6	—	0.0576	0.0892
7	—	—	0.0893
8	—	—	0.0446

Source: Table 1 of Rev. Proc. 87-57, 1987-2 C.B. 674.

EXAMPLE I10-6 ▶ In March 2006, Mary acquires and places in service a business machine which costs $20,000. The machinery has a 7-year recovery period under the MACRS rules. The depreciation deduction for 2006 is $2,858 (0.1429 × $20,000). The rate is applied from Table I10-1 (0.1429) and is based on the 200% DB method, a half-year convention, and zero salvage value. The MACRS depreciation deduction for the year of acquisition can also be computed by applying the accelerated depreciation rate (using the half-year convention) to the basis of the assets. Thus the depreciation deduction for 2006 is $2,857 ($20,000 ÷ 7 years × 200% DB × 0.50 year). Minor differences between the two calculations are due to rounding. ◀

Certain types of property are *excluded* from being depreciated under MACRS, including:[6]

▶ Property depreciated under a method not expressed in terms of years, such as the units of production method, and the taxpayer elects to not depreciate the property under MACRS;

▶ Intangible assets, such as goodwill or copyrights;

▶ Films, videotapes, or sound recordings.

Section 179 Expensing Election. In lieu of depreciating the cost of new or used tangible personal business property under the regular MACRS methods discussed above, taxpayers in years 2003–2007 may elect to expense up to $100,000 (adjusted for inflation) of the acquisition cost as an ordinary deduction in the year of acquisition.[7] For 2006, the $100,000 has been increased to $108,000 ($105,000 in 2005). To qualify for the deduction, the property must actually be placed into service during the year. The immediate expensing election is not applicable to real estate. The election is made on an annual basis, and the taxpayer must select the assets to which the $108,000 write-off applies. The MACRS rules apply to any residual amount of an asset's cost that is not expensed under Sec. 179.

The amount that may be expensed under Sec. 179 has been increasing over the past several years as follows:

---

[6] Sec. 168(f).
[7] Sec. 179. The Sec. 179 deduction for 2003 was scheduled to be $25,000. However, the 2003 Jobs Act increased this amount to $100,000 (adjusted for inflation) for property placed in service in 2003, 2004, and 2005. The 2004 Jobs Act extended the $100,000 amount to 2006 and 2007. Congress is currently considering whether to extend the increased Sec. 179 deduction to 2008 and future years.

▼ TABLE I10-2
Section 179 Expense Amounts

Tax Year Beginning In	Maximum Sec. 179 Expense
2006	$108,000
2005	105,000
2004	102,000
2003	100,000
2002	24,000
2001	24,000
2000	20,000
1999	19,000
1998	18,500
1997	18,000
1996	17,500

HISTORICAL NOTE

Section 179 originally allowed a $10,000 deduction. This amount was increased to $17,500 for property placed in service after December 31, 1992, and before January 1, 1997.

EXAMPLE I10-7 ▶ Tanya acquires and places into service business equipment (tangible personal property qualifying under Sec. 179) for $150,000 in July 2006. The equipment has a 7-year MACRS recovery period. Tanya elects to immediately expense $108,000 of the asset's cost under Sec. 179. Tanya's remaining basis for calculating the MACRS depreciation deduction is $42,000 ($150,000 − $108,000). Tanya's 2006 regular depreciation allowance is $6,002 ($42,000 × 0.1429). Tanya's total depreciation deduction for 2006 is $114,002 ($108,000 expensed under Sec. 179 + $6,002 MACRS depreciation). Clearly, small businesses are allowed substantial first year depreciation deductions under current law. ◀

The following limitations and special rules apply to the Sec. 179 election:

▶ The property must be purchased for use in an active trade or business as distinguished from property that is acquired for the production of income (e.g., personal property used in a rental activity held by an investor does not qualify).

▶ While qualified property is generally tangible personal property, off-the-shelf computer software that is placed in service after 2002 and before 2008 may be expensed under Sec. 179. This is software that is readily available for purchase by the general public, is subject to a nonexclusive license, and has not been substantially modified.

▶ The property cannot be acquired from a related party under Sec. 267 or by gift or inheritance.

ADDITIONAL COMMENT

Married taxpayers who file separate tax returns are each entitled to a maximum $54,000 ($108,000 ÷ 2) limitation under Sec. 179.

▶ The Sec. 179 tax benefits are recaptured if the property is no longer predominantly used in a trade or business (e.g., the property is converted to personal use) at any time.[8] In the year of recapture, the taxpayer must include in gross income the amount previously expensed reduced by the amount of depreciation that would have been allowed for the period the property was held for business use.[9]

SELF-STUDY QUESTION

Are corporations entitled to the election to expense up to $108,000 under Sec. 179?

ANSWER

Yes, but larger corporations will not receive the benefit from it because the Sec. 179 deduction is reduced when the cost of qualified property exceeds $430,000.

▶ If the total cost of qualified property placed into service during the year is more than $430,000 ($420,000 in 2005 and $410,000 in 2004), the $108,000 ceiling is reduced on a dollar-for-dollar basis by the excess amount. Thus, no deduction is permitted for the 2006 tax year in which $538,000 ($430,000 + $108,000) or more of Sec. 179 property is placed into service. No carryovers of Sec. 179 depreciation under this provision are permitted.

▶ A second limitation on the total Sec. 179 deduction is that it cannot exceed the taxpayer's taxable income (before deducting the Sec. 179 expense) from the trade or busi-

---

[8] Sec. 179(d)(10).   [9] Reg. Sec. 1.179-1(e).

ness.[10] Any acquisition cost that is unable to be deducted because of the limitation based on taxable income is carried forward for an unlimited number of years and is added to the other amounts eligible for the Sec. 179 deduction in the future year. The carryover amount is subject to the taxable income limitation in the carryover year.

EXAMPLE I10-8 ▶ Pam owns an unincorporated manufacturing business. In 2006, she purchases and places in service $460,000 of qualifying equipment for use in her business. Pam's taxable income from the business (before deducting any Sec. 179 amount) is $28,000. The $108,000 ceiling amount is initially reduced by $30,000 ($460,000 − $430,000) to reflect the fact that the qualified property placed in service during the year exceeded $430,000. The remaining $78,000 Sec. 179 deduction is further reduced by the taxable income limitation. Pam's Sec. 179 deduction is $28,000; $50,000 ($78,000 − $28,000) is available for use as a carryover to 2007. The cost basis of the equipment for MACRS purposes is reduced by $78,000 in 2006 despite the fact that only $28,000 was immediately deductible under Sec. 179. ◀

KEY POINT

Bonus depreciation is not permitted for any property placed in service after December 31, 2004.

ADDITIONAL COMMENT

As a result of the hurricanes in the Gulf of Mexico region, 50% bonus depreciation may still be available for certain Gulf Opportunity Zone property.

Bonus Depreciation. In response to the terrorist attacks on September 11, 2001, Congress enacted special bonus depreciation for new qualified property placed in service after September 10, 2001 and before January 1, 2005. These special depreciation provisions were very effective in encouraging taxpayers to continue to invest in tangible personal property during this trying period of time. However, these provisions have now expired and were not extended by Congress, so bonus depreciation is not available after December 31, 2004. Bonus depreciation is still important in determining current year depreciation for property in which bonus depreciation was claimed (i.e., for example, depreciation for 2006 for property placed in service in 2003).

The original bonus depreciation rate was an additional 30% first-year depreciation for qualified property. This rate was in effect from September 11, 2001 to May 5, 2003. In 2003, the 30% first-year bonus depreciation was increased to 50% for qualified property placed in service after May 5, 2003 and before January 1, 2005. The specific rules discussed below are the same for both 30% and 50% bonus depreciation property.

Qualified property (generally non-real estate) includes: (1) MACRS property with a recovery period of 20 years or less; (2) computer software (other than computer software that must be amortized under Sec. 197); or (3) qualified leasehold improvement property (see discussion of qualified leasehold improvement property later in this chapter in connection with real property). In order to qualify, the property must be new property and the original use of the property must begin with the taxpayer. Used property does not qualify for bonus depreciation.

The bonus depreciation deduction was equal to 50% (or 30%) of the adjusted basis of the qualified property and is allowed for both the regular tax and the AMT. The remaining basis of the qualified property will be depreciated under the usual rules for depreciating such property. If the taxpayer elects to expense property under Sec. 179, the Sec. 179 expense is deducted first, then the additional first-year bonus depreciation and, third, regular MACRS depreciation.[11] In years after the first year, regular MACRS depreciation is allowable under the normal rules.

EXAMPLE I10-9 ▶ On March 25, 2004, the Wildcat Corporation, a calendar-year taxpayer, purchases and places into service machinery that cost $252,000. The machinery is 7-year MACRS property and the mid-quarter convention does not apply. Wildcat was eligible to expense $102,000 of the cost of the machinery placed in service during the year under Sec. 179. Wildcat also would have claimed bonus depreciation for 2004 of $75,000 [($252,000 − $102,000) × 0.50]. In addition to the Sec. 179 depreciation and the bonus depreciation, Wildcat also was eligible to claim regular depreciation on the machinery of $10,718 [($252,000 − $102,000 − $75,000) × 0.1429]. For

---

[10] Sec. 179(b)(3). Under Reg. Sec. 1.179-2(c)(5)(iv), employees are considered to be engaged in the active conduct of the trade or business from their employment. Thus, a small business person who is also an employee may include wages and salary derived from employment in determining taxable income for purposes of this limitation. Such amounts are considered derived

from the conduct of a trade or business. For an individual, taxable income is also computed without regard to the deduction for one-half of self-employment taxes paid under Sec. 164(f) (see Chapter I14).
[11]Temp. Reg. 1.168(k)-1T(d)(3) Example 2.

2006, Wildcat's allowable depreciation would be $1,312 ($75,000 × 0.1749). The $75,000 is the remaining basis after the Sec. 179 and bonus depreciation claimed in 2004.   ◄

EXAMPLE I10-10 ► Assume the same facts as in Example I10-9 *except* the machinery was placed into service on March 25, 2006, rather than in 2004. No bonus depreciation is permitted as these provisions expire after December 31, 2004. Wildcat Corporation may claim $108,000 of Sec. 179 depreciation and then also claim regular depreciation on the machinery of $20,578 [($252,000 − $108,000) × 0.1429]. Wildcat's total depreciation for 2006 would be $128,578 ($108,000 + $20,578). Obviously, without bonus depreciation, depreciation deductions will be significantly less for property placed into service in 2006 and later years compared with 2001–2004.   ◄

KEY POINT

Remember, the mid-quarter convention does *not* apply to real property.

Use of the Mid-Quarter Convention. As mentioned previously, the MACRS system generally requires the use of the half-year convention. However, the MACRS system requires the use of the **mid-quarter convention** if the aggregate basis of all *personal property* placed in service during the last three months of the year exceeds 40% of the cost of all personal property placed in service during the tax year.[12] Therefore, if the test is met, the mid-quarter convention must be used instead of the half-year convention and special mid-quarter tables must be used to compute depreciation under this convention. (See Tables 2 through 5 in Appendix C.) Property placed in service and disposed of during the same tax year is not taken into account for purposes of the mid-quarter test.[13] Also, property expensed under Sec. 179 is excluded in computing the 40% test for the applicability of the mid-quarter convention.[14]

The 40% rule prevents taxpayers from using the half-year convention and thereby obtaining one-half year's depreciation in the year of acquisition when a substantial portion of the assets are acquired during the last quarter of the tax year.

EXAMPLE I10-11 ► Michael, a calendar-year taxpayer, acquires 5-year tangible personal property in 2006, does not elect Sec. 179, and places the properties in service on the following schedule:

Date Placed in Service	Acquisition Cost
January 20	$100,000
April 18	200,000
November 5	252,000
Total	$552,000

Because more than 40% of the property acquired during the year is placed in service in the last three months ($252,000/$552,000 = 46%), the mid-quarter convention will apply for all property placed in service during the year. The depreciation for 2006 is computed as follows. (See Tables 2 through 5 in Appendix C for the percentages that are used to make this calculation.)

Property Placed in Service	Year 1 MACRS Depreciation	Appendix C Table
January 20	$100,000 × 35% = $35,000	Table 2
April 18	200,000 × 25% = 50,000	Table 3
November 5	252,000 × 5% = 12,600	Table 5
Total	$97,600	

◄

EXAMPLE I10-12 ► Assume the same facts as in Example I10-11 except that Michael elects to expense $108,000 under Sec. 179 and selects the property placed in service on November 5. In this case, the mid-quarter convention would not apply because less than 40% of property (after the Sec. 179 deduction) was placed in service in the last quarter of the year ($144,000/$444,000 = 32.4%). Therefore, Michael would use the half-year convention and his depreciation for 2006 would be computed as follows:

---

[12] Sec. 168(d)(3).
[13] Sec. 168(d)(3)(B) and Reg. Sec. 1.168(d)-1(b)(3).

[14] PLR 9126014 (March 29, 1991).

Property Placed in Service	Year 1 MACRS Depreciation	Sec. 179 Depreciation	Total 2006 Depreciation
January 20	$100,000 × 0.20 = $20,000	–0–	$ 20,000
April 18	200,000 × 0.20 = 40,000	–0–	40,000
November 5	144,000* × 0.20 = 28,800	$108,000	136,800
Total			$196,800

* After Sec. 179 depreciation

In this case, the half-year convention yielded larger depreciation. In some cases, the mid-quarter convention can yield a larger depreciation deduction. This occurs only when a large amount of property is placed in service in the first quarter of the year but enough property is placed in service in the fourth quarter to require the mid-quarter convention. ◄

Year of Disposition. The MACRS system allows depreciation to be taken in the year of disposition using the same convention that applied on acquisition (e.g., half-year, mid-month, or mid-quarter convention). Therefore, if property is disposed of during the year in which the half-year convention is applicable, the depreciation for the year of disposition will be one-half of the amount computed by using the table percentages.

EXAMPLE I10-13 ▶ Michelle acquires machinery in March 2004 that qualifies as 7-year MACRS property and has a $100,000 basis for depreciation. The half-year convention is applied in the year of acquisition and no Sec. 179 or bonus depreciation was taken on the machinery. In December 2006, the machinery is sold. Michelle's depreciation deduction in 2006 is $8,745 [$100,000 × (0.1749 × 0.50)] for the equipment (see Table I10-1). ◄

For property disposed of which was subject to the mid-quarter convention, the property is treated as being disposed of at the midpoint of the quarter.

EXAMPLE I10-14 ▶ Jason acquires $200,000 of 5-year property in May 2004 that is required to be depreciated using the mid-quarter convention. If Jason sells the property on July 14, 2006 (third quarter), the property will be treated as if it were sold on August 15, 2006, which is the midpoint of the third quarter. Thus, $22,500 of depreciation is claimed in 2006 [($200,000 × 0.18) × (2.5 ÷ 4)]. (See Table 3 in Appendix C.) ◄

REAL PROPERTY: CLASSIFICATION AND RECOVERY RATES. The MACRS recovery periods that apply to real property placed in service in years after 1986 are as follows:

▶ Residential rental property: 27.5 years
▶ Nonresidential real property: 39 years[15]

Straight-line depreciation must be used and is so reflected in the tables. A mid-month convention is used in the year of acquisition and in the year of disposition. The tables for computing depreciation for real property are located in Tables 7, 8 and 9 in Appendix C.

EXAMPLE I10-15 ▶

On October 4, 2006, Husker, Inc., acquired an office building to relocate its rapidly-growing staff. The property was purchased for $1,500,000, of which $200,000 was allocated to the underlying land. Since the property is nonresidential real property, it is classified as 39-year property. Using Table 9 in Appendix C, the depreciation percentage is 0.535%, and the depreciation deduction for the year 2006, using the mid-month convention, is $6,955 ($1,300,000 × .00535). In 2007, the depreciation on the building would be $33,332 ($1,300,000 × .02564). ◄

A common transaction for taxpayers owning buildings is the depreciation of subsequent capital improvements. Capital improvements are depreciated over the full life of the improvement, not over the remaining life of the building. Thus, the cost of a new roof on an office building must be depreciated over 39 years even though the building may have been placed into service several years ago.

---

[15] Sec. 168(c)(1). A 31.5-year recovery period applied to nonresidential real property placed in service on or after January 1, 1987, and before May 13, 1993.

KEY POINT

Depreciable real property placed in service after 1986 must be depreciated using the straight-line method.

ADDITIONAL COMMENT

For purposes of determining whether at least 80% of the gross rental income is rental income from dwelling units, a taxpayer living in any part of the building includes the fair rental value of his unit in the gross rental income.

Real properties are divided into two categories: residential rental property and nonresidential real property. **Residential rental property** is defined as property from which at least 80% of the gross rental income is rental income from dwelling units.[16] Dwelling units include houses, apartments, and manufactured homes that are used for residential purposes but not hotels, motels, or other establishments for transient use. Nonresidential real property is any real property other than residential rental property.

As mentioned previously, bonus depreciation (50% or 30%) was allowed for *qualified leasehold improvement property* if the leasehold improvements are made and placed in service after September 10, 2001, and before January 1, 2006.[17] The calculation is made in the same manner as for tangible personal property. Qualified leasehold improvement property is any improvement to an interior portion of nonresidential real property made under or pursuant to a lease by the lessee, sublessee, or lessor, and must be placed in service more than three years after the date the building was first placed in service. Expenditures that enlarge a building, any elevator or escalator, any structural component that benefits a common area or the internal structural framework are not considered qualified leasehold improvement property.

EXAMPLE I10-16 ▶

The Shaheen Corporation leases office space to operate its business in a 20-year-old building. In early 2004, the corporation made some major leasehold improvements that qualify as capital improvements, such as changing the size of offices by rearranging the walls, new ductwork, and other similar capital improvements to the office. The overall size of the office did not change. The leasehold improvements were completed and placed into service on July 15, 2004, at a total cost of $120,000 and are considered qualified leasehold improvement property. For regular depreciation purposes, the leasehold improvements must be depreciated over 39 years. For 2004, Shaheen Corporation was permitted to take the 50% bonus depreciation and the regular depreciation on the leasehold improvements. The depreciation deduction for 2006 is computed as follows:

Cost of qualified leasehold improvements	$120,000
Less bonus depreciation	60,000
Depreciable basis	60,000
Depreciation rate	0.02564
Depreciation for 2006	$ 1,538

◀

While bonus depreciation is no longer available after December 31, 2004, the 2004 Jobs Act now allows qualified leasehold improvement property to be depreciated over 15 years (rather than 39 years). The straight-line method must be used. This shorter recovery period for qualified leasehold improvement property is effective for property placed in service after October 22, 2004, and before January 1, 2006.

EXAMPLE I10-17 ▶

Assume the same facts as in Example I10-16 except that the leasehold improvements were placed into service in January 2005 rather than in early 2004. In this case, no bonus depreciation is available as the bonus depreciation provisions expire after December 31, 2004. However, the leasehold improvements may be depreciated over 15 years rather than 39 years under the 2004 Jobs Act. Thus, Shaheen's depreciation deduction for 2006, using mandatory straight-line depreciation, is $8,000 ($120,000/15 years). ◀

STRAIGHT-LINE (METHOD) ELECTION UNDER MACRS. Instead of using the accelerated methods previously described under the MACRS rules, taxpayers may elect to use the straight-line method for tangible personal property. If the straight-line election is made, the taxpayer must use either the same depreciation period or an extended period based on the alternative depreciation system, as discussed below.[18]

ALTERNATIVE DEPRECIATION SYSTEM. The MACRS system provides an alternative depreciation system (ADS) that is required for certain property and is also available

---

[16] Secs. 168(e)(2)(A).
[17] This provision is expected to be extended through 2006 by Congress although final approval has not passed at print time.
[18] Sec. 168(g)(7).

for all other depreciable assets if the taxpayer so elects.[19] The principal type of property for which the ADS is *required* is any tangible property which is used predominantly outside the United States. The recovery periods are specified under the ADS and, many times, are longer than the recovery periods under MACRS. Under the ADS, assets must be depreciated using the class life as set forth in Rev. Proc. 87-56. Personal property with no specific class life is assigned a 12-year life and real property is assigned a 40-year life. Further, the ADS requires the use of the straight-line method with a half-year, mid-quarter, or mid-month convention, whichever is applicable. The *election* of the ADS is generally made by taxpayers who want to use the straight-line method over a longer recovery period. These taxpayers frequently have net operating losses or are subject to the alternative minimum tax (see Chapter I14 for a discussion of the alternative minimum tax).

The ADS generally is an elective provision made on a year-by-year basis. Once the election is made for specified property, it is irrevocable. Also, for personal property, the ADS election applies to all property within a class (all five-year property, for example); for real property, the ADS election may be made on an individual property basis.

EXAMPLE I10-18 ▶ In May 2006, Bob Roaster purchased an office building for $300,000 ($50,000 allocated to the land) as rental property. Because he has substantial net operating losses from other business ventures, Roaster elects to depreciate the building using the ADS. Depreciation expense for 2006, using the mid-month convention and a 40-year life is $3,906 ($250,000 ÷ 40 years × 7.5/12). If Roaster had not elected the ADS, his depreciation would have been $4,013 [$250,000 × .01605 (from Table 9, Appendix C)]. The difference is small because the recovery period is 39 years under regular MACRS and 40 years under the ADS. ◀

The 30% and 50% bonus depreciation was allowed under the ADS if the taxpayer elected to use the ADS. For property *required* to be depreciated under the ADS, bonus depreciation was not permitted.

The alternative depreciation system is also used to compute earnings and profits (E&P) for a corporation and to compute the alternative minimum tax for both individuals and corporations (see Chapter I14).

A comparison of the ACRS and MACRS rules is presented in Topic Review I10-1.

Topic Review I10-1

Comparison of MACRS and ADS

	MACRS	ADS
Recovery Periods:		
Automobiles	5 years	5 years
Computers	5 years	5 years
Office furniture and equipment	7 years	10 years
Residential rental property	27.5 years	40 years
Nonresidential real property	39 years[b]	40 years
Conventions:		
Personal property	Half-year or mid-quarter[a]	Half-year or mid-quarter[a]
Real property	Mid-month	Mid-month
Depreciation in year of sale:		
Personal property	Yes	Yes
Real property	Yes	Yes

[a] If more than 40% of personal property is placed in service during the last quarter of year.
[b] For property placed in service prior to May 13, 1993, the recovery period is 31.5 years.

[19] Sec. 168(g). See Tables 10–12 in Appendix C.

MACRS RESTRICTIONS

ETHICAL POINT

The personal use of a corporate automobile by a shareholder-employee may be a constructive dividend. Personal use by a non-shareholder-employee results in additional taxable compensation to the employee and may present an ethical dilemma for the tax consultant.

PERSONAL-USE ASSETS. The personal use portion of an asset's cost is not depreciable. For example, if a taxpayer owns a duplex and uses one unit as a personal residence, only the portion of the unit that is rented to tenants qualifies for depreciation.

LISTED PROPERTY RULES. Because Congress was concerned about taxpayers claiming large depreciation deductions (using accelerated methods) on certain types of assets that are conducive to mixed business/personal use, restrictions are placed on assets that are classified as *listed property*. Listed property includes automobiles, computers and peripheral equipment, cellular telephones, and property generally used for purposes of entertainment, recreation, or amusement (for example, a video recorder). If a listed property's business usage is greater than 50% of its total usage, the taxpayer may use the regular MACRS tables for the business-use portion of the asset's cost, including the 50% or 30% bonus depreciation. However, if the business use is 50% or less, the taxpayer must use the alternative depreciation system (e.g., five-year straight-line cost recovery period for automobiles and computers).

EXAMPLE I10-19 ▶ Patrick acquires an automobile for $10,000 in June 2006. It is used 60% for business. The depreciation deduction on the business-use portion of the automobile's cost is based on the MACRS system and five-year recovery class because the automobile is predominantly used in business (i.e., more than 50%). The MACRS depreciation allowance in 2006 is $1,200 [($10,000 × 20%) × 60% business use percentage]. See Table I10-1 for the MACRS rate. ◀

EXAMPLE I10-20 ▶ Paula acquires an automobile for $10,000 in 2006. It is used only 40% for business. Paula must use the alternative depreciation system (ADS) to claim depreciation allowances on the business portion of the automobile. The business portion is $4,000 ($10,000 × 0.40). Paula's depreciation allowance in 2006 using the straight-line method is $400 [($4,000 ÷ 5 years) × 0.50] and the half-year convention. ◀

ADDITIONAL COMMENT

The restrictions on automobiles were enacted in 1984 because of a concern that the tax system was underwriting the acquisition of automobiles whose cost and luxury far exceeded what was required for business needs.

Additional restrictions apply to employees who acquire listed property (e.g., an automobile, personal computer, etc.) for use in employment-related activities. In addition to the "more than 50% test," the use must be for the convenience of the *employer* and be required as a condition of employment.[20] This rule is strictly interpreted by the IRS.

EXAMPLE I10-21 ▶ Raul, a college professor, acquired a personal computer for use at home. He used the computer 60% of the time on teaching- and research-related activities associated with his job. The remaining usage was for personal activities. Raul's employer finds that it is helpful for employees to own a personal computer but does not require them to purchase a computer as a condition of employment. Raul meets the first requirement (i.e., the 60% business usage is greater than the 50% threshold). However, the second requirement for employees (that the use must be for the convenience of the employer and required as a condition of employment) is not met. Thus, no depreciation may be taken because the employment-related use is not deemed to be business use. ◀

RECAPTURE OF EXCESS COST-RECOVERY DEDUCTIONS. For listed property, if the MACRS rules were used and the business-use percentage decreases to 50% or less in a subsequent year, the property is subject to depreciation recapture. The depreciation deductions for all years are recomputed using the alternative depreciation system. The excess depreciation that has been taken is recaptured as ordinary income by including the excess amount in the taxpayer's gross income in the year the business-use percentage first falls to 50% or below.[21] Once the business use falls to 50% or below, the alternative depreciation system must be used for the current year and for all subsequent years, even if the business-use percentage increases to more than 50% in a subsequent year. This excess depreciation also includes any bonus depreciation taken by the taxpayer.

---

[20] Sec. 280F(d)(3). Any other property used for transportation (e.g., a pickup truck) qualifies as listed property if the nature of the property lends itself to personal use. See Sec. 280F(b)(4).

[21] Sec. 280F(b)(3).

EXAMPLE I10-22 ▶

Paul, a self-employed attorney, acquires an automobile in June 2004 for $12,000. Paul's business-use percentage is 60% in 2004 and 2005, but declines to 40% in 2006. Paul's depreciation under MACRS in 2004 and 2005 is as follows:

2004: Bonus depreciation assuming 100% business use ($12,000 × 50%)	$6,000
Regular MACRS depreciation assuming 100% business use	1,200
Total depreciation assuming 100% business use	$7,200
Business-use percentage	× 60%
Total depreciation at 60% business use	$4,320
2005: Regular MACRS depreciation assuming 100% business use ($6,000 × 32%)	$1,920
Business-use percentage	× 60%
Total depreciation at 60% business use	$1,152

In 2006, Paul's business-use percentage declines to 40%. Therefore, he must use ADS for 2006 and also recapture the excess depreciation taken in 2004 and 2005. The recapture is computed as follows:

MACRS depreciation taken in 2004 and 2005 ($4,320 + $1,152)		$5,472
2004: Recomputed ADS depreciation ($12,000 × 60% × 10%)	$ 720	
2005: Recomputed ADS depreciation ($12,000 × 60% × 20%)	1,440	(2,160)
Recapture of excess depreciation in 2006		$3,312

Notice that the 50% bonus depreciation is not allowed when ADS is required in the recomputed amounts for 2004 and 2005. Paul's depreciation deduction in 2006 is computed under ADS, using the straight-line method, and amounts to $960 ($12,000 × 40% × 20%). ◀

LIMITATIONS ON LUXURY AUTOMOBILES. Because Congress believed that the depreciation deduction for automobiles used for business was too large, additional limitations to MACRS deductions are placed on the purchase of luxury passenger automobiles.[22] A passenger automobile is defined as a 4-wheeled vehicle which is manufactured primarily for use on public streets, roads, and highways and which is *rated* at 6,000 pounds unloaded gross vehicle weight rating (GVWR) or less.[23] These passenger automobiles are subject to so-called ceiling limitations for MACRS depreciation. In essence, taxpayers are still allowed to fully depreciate luxury cars, but must depreciate them over a longer period of time than the normal five-year recovery period.

EXAMPLE I10-23 ▶

Joe Q. purchases a $60,000 automobile in 2006 that he uses 100% for business purposes. Under normal MACRS rules and without considering Sec. 179, Joe could take depreciation of $12,000 in the first year ($60,000 × 20%) and $19,000 ($60,000 × 32%) in the second year. Thus, Joe could deduct 52% ($31,200/$60,000) of the cost of his automobile in the first two years and considerable tax savings would result. ◀

To prevent such perceived abuse, Congress has implemented ceiling limitations. The ceiling limitations for MACRS depreciation for passenger automobiles placed in service in 2006 (based on 100% business-use) are as follows:

ADDITIONAL COMMENT

The limitations on luxury automobiles mean that the depreciation deductions are limited during the normal five-year recovery period on business automobiles costing more than $15,300 (for 2006).

Year 1 (2006)	$2,960
Year 2 (2007)	4,800
Year 3 (2008)	2,850
Year 4 (2009) and succeeding years	1,775

For prior year amounts, see Table 6 in Appendix C. The bonus depreciation rules also applied to automobiles placed in service during the applicable years.[24]

To compute the maximum MACRS depreciation deduction for a passenger automobile for any year, taxpayers must first compute their depreciation under the normal MACRS

---

[22] Sec. 280F. The term *luxury automobile* may be an overstatement, as the limitations apply to automobiles acquired in 2006 which cost in excess of $14,800 ($2,960/0.20).

[23] Sec. 280F(d)(5)(A).

[24] Sec. 280F(a)(2). Taxpayers were allowed an additional $7,650 of depreciation on luxury automobiles placed in service after May 5, 2003, and before

December 31, 2004, under the 50% bonus depreciation rules. For automobiles placed in service prior to May 6, 2003, and after September 10, 2001, the additional amount is $4,600 pursuant to the 30% bonus depreciation rules. Also, the above ceiling amounts include any Sec. 179 first-year depreciation expense. The ceiling amounts are indexed each year, ceiling amounts for the past several years are contained in Table 6 of Appendix C.

rules, then compare this amount to the ceiling limitation for that year. The maximum depreciation deduction allowed for any year cannot exceed the ceiling limitation amount. This maximum depreciation deduction also includes Sec. 179 depreciation. Because of the ceiling limitation, Sec. 179 routinely is not elected by taxpayers on passenger automobiles.

EXAMPLE I10-24 ▶

Amy purchased a $60,000 automobile in 2006 that she uses 100% for business purposes. She would be limited to $2,960 of depreciation as this is the maximum luxury car amount and is less than regular MACRS depreciation ($60,000 × 0.20 = $12,000). If Amy purchased the automobile in 2004 and elected 50% bonus depreciation, her maximum depreciation for 2004 would be $10,610 (See Table 6). Her depreciation deductions in 2005 and 2006 would be $4,800 and $2,850 respectively. ◀

After the first year, the procedure to compute the depreciation is the same as above. The regular MACRS deduction is computed and compared with the appropriate year of the ceiling limitation and the deduction allowed cannot exceed the ceiling amount. After the regular recovery period ends for passenger automobiles placed in service in 2006, the taxpayer would be entitled to depreciation of $1,775 per year until the automobile is fully depreciated.

If a taxpayer uses the passenger automobile less than 100% for business, both the regular MACRS deduction and the ceiling limitation are limited to the business-use percentage. For example, if a taxpayer only uses his car 80% for business, his regular MACRS deduction would only be 80% and his ceiling amount in 2006 would be $2,368 ($2,960 × 0.80). Example I10-25 provides a comprehensive illustration of computing depreciation for a passenger automobile used 80% for business.

EXAMPLE I10-25 ▶

Phil acquires an automobile for $50,000 in 2006. The automobile is used 80% for business and 20% for personal activities during 2006 and all succeeding years. Table I10-3 lists the depreciation amounts for a six-year period, assuming that the 80% business use continues for the life of the automobile and that no amount is expensed under Sec. 179. At the end of the regular six-year depreciation period, the unrecovered cost in the business use portion of the automobile may be recovered in year 2012 and succeeding years at an annual rate not to exceed $1,420 ($1,775 × 0.80). ◀

TRUCKS, VANS, AND SUVs. As mentioned previously, limitations are placed on "passenger automobiles" that have a gross vehicle weight rating (GVWR) of 6,000 pounds or less. A major tax planning tool utilized by many taxpayers during the past several years has been to purchase vehicles that are rated at more than 6,000 GVWR to avoid the ceiling limitation. As a result, many SUVs rated at a GVWR exceeding 6,000 pounds were not subject to the ceiling limitations and taxpayers could expense up to $100,000 (adjusted for inflation) under Sec. 179. Persuant to the 2004 Jobs Act, this controversial provision has been curtailed. For SUVs placed into service after October 22, 2004, the maximum Sec. 179 expense amount is $25,000,[25] rather than $108,000 in 2006 ($105,000 in 2005). However, SUVs with a GVWR of greater than 6,000 pounds will continue to have significant depreciation advantages over other vehicles as the ceiling limitations do not apply. Example I10-26 illustrates the depreciation after the 2004 Jobs Act.

EXAMPLE I10-26 ▶

Assume two taxpayers purchase $60,000 vehicles that are used 100% for business in July 2006. One taxpayer purchases a BMW sedan that is considered a passenger automobile for tax purposes. The other taxpayer purchases a Ford Expedition which is rated at over 6,000 GVWR and, therefore, is not considered a passenger automobile and not subject to the ceiling limitations. The first-year depreciation for each vehicle for 2006 is computed below.

BMW: Regular MACRS depreciation from table ($60,000 × 0.20)	$12,000
Ceiling limitation	2,960

In this case, the maximum depreciation deduction on the vehicle for 2006 is $2,960

---

[25] Sec. 179(b)(6). Vehicles with a GVWR of more than 14,000 pounds are not considered SUVs and are not subject to the $25,000 limitation.

▼ TABLE I10-3

Depreciation Amounts for Example I10-25

	MACRS Deduction 100% Business Use	Ceiling Limit 100% Business Use	Deduction Allowed 80% of Lesser	Unrecovered Basis
2006				
Regular MACRS calculation ($50,000 × 0.20)	$10,000	$ 2,960	$ 2,368	$47,040
2007				
Regular MACRS calculation ($50,000 × 0.32)	$16,000	$ 4,800	$ 3,840	$42,240
2008				
Regular MACRS calculation ($50,000 × 0.192)	$ 9,600	$ 2,850	$ 2,280	$39,390
2009				
Regular MACRS calculation ($50,000 × 0.1152)	$ 5,760	$ 1,775	$ 1,420	$37,615
2010				
Regular MACRS calculation ($50,000 × 0.1152)	$ 5,760	$ 1,775	$ 1,420	$35,840
2011				
Regular MACRS calculation ($50,000 × 0.0576)	$ 2,880	$ 1,775	$ 1,420	$34,065
Total through 2011	$50,000	$16,235	$12,988	
2012 and later years until fully depreciated				
Ceiling limit		$ 1,775	$ 1,420	

Note: Based on the unrecovered basis of $34,065 at December 31, 2011, it would take Phil another 20 years to fully depreciate the automobile ($34,065/$1,775 = 19 years).

Ford Expedition: Section 179 depreciation (maximum)	$25,000
Regular MACRS depreciation from table [($60,000 − $25,000) × .020]	7,000
Total depreciation for 2006	$32,000

The ceiling limitations do not apply as the vehicle has a GVWR of greater than 6,000 pounds.

This example shows the significant tax savings from buying a vehicle that has greater than a 6,000 GVWR and is not subject to the ceiling limitations. It should be noted that any vehicle that avoids the ceiling limitations must be used for greater than 50% business use, under the general listed property rules. ◄

While some taxpayers avoid the ceiling limitations by purchasing heavy vehicles, other taxpayers who use light trucks and vans (6,000 GVWR or less) in their businesses are hurt by the ceiling limitations. In response to small business concerns, two recent exceptions to the ceiling limitations have been issued to address these inequities: (1) exemption from the ceiling limitations for vehicles that clearly are not for personal-use and (2) higher ceiling limitation amounts for other light trucks and vans.

▶ Exemption from ceiling limitations: Certain "nonpersonal use" vehicles are completely exempted from the ceiling limitations.[26] These vehicles must be specifically modified so that it is not likely to be used more than a de minimis amount for personal purposes. This somewhat vague definition is explained further in the regulations as a van that only has a front bench for seating, permanent shelving that fills most of the cargo area, or has been painted with advertising or the company's logo.

---

[26] Temp. Reg. Sec. 1.274-5T(k), T.D. 9064 (6-30-2003) amending T.D. 8061.

► Higher ceiling limitations: Even if a light truck or van does not meet the nonpersonal use criteria above, higher ceiling limitations have been issued for vehicles on a truck chassis.[27] For trucks and vans on a truck chassis that have a GVWR of 6,000 pounds or less, the ceiling amounts for 2006 are as follows:

	Annual Ceiling Limitations
Year 1 (2006)	$3,260
Year 2 (2007)	5,200
Year 3 (2008)	3,150
Year 4 (2009) and succeeding years	1,875

ADDITIONAL COMMENT

The amount that can be deducted for leased automobiles is also limited.

ADDITIONAL COMPUTATIONS FOR LEASED VEHICLES. If a taxpayer leases an automobile or light truck or van for business purposes, the deduction for rental payments is reduced to reflect the limitations on depreciation deductions that are imposed on owners of automobiles under Sec. 280F. If these restrictions were not applied to leased automobiles, the ceiling limitations could be avoided by leasing instead of purchasing an automobile. The leasing restriction is accomplished by requiring taxpayers to include in their gross income an "inclusion amount" obtained from an IRS table.[28] This amount is based on the automobile's FMV and the tax year in which the lease commences, and is prorated for the percentage of business use and number of days used during the year. Partial lease inclusion tables are provided in Tables 13 and 14 in Appendix C.

EXAMPLE I10-27 ► On April 1, 2005, Jim leases and places into service an automobile with a FMV of $40,000. Business use is 60%. The "inclusion amount" for the initial year of the lease (2005) from the IRS lease inclusion table is $113 (see Table 13 in Appendix C). This amount is prorated for the number of days the automobile is leased ($275/365$) and is then multiplied by the percentage of business use (60%). Jim is entitled to deduct 60% of the lease payments but must include $51 [($113 × $275/365$) × 60%] in his gross income for the current year. In 2006, the second year of the lease, the inclusion amount from the table is $249. Thus, Jim must include $149 ($249 × 60%) in his gross income for the second year. Subsequent years follow the same procedures. ◄

Special elections and restrictions are summarized in Topic Review I10-2.

AMORTIZATION

OBJECTIVE 2

Calculate amortization for intangible assets and understand the difference between amortizable and non-amortizable assets

An amortization deduction is allowed for a variety of intangible assets. While the amortization period varies greatly depending on the type of asset, a characteristic of all intangible assets is that they are amortized on a *straight-line basis*. The major intangible assets that may be amortized are as follows:

► Goodwill and Other Purchased Intangibles, Sec. 197
► Research and Experimental Expenditures, Sec. 174
► Computer software
► Start-up Expenditures, Sec. 195
► Organizational Expenditures, Sec. 248
► Pollution Control Facilities, Sec. 169

Several of the above intangibles are discussed below.

HISTORICAL NOTE

Prior to the tax change in 1993, no amortization for goodwill was allowed. So, in business acquisitions, the purchaser typically tried to allocate as little of the purchase price as possible to goodwill. These allocations frequently caused disputes with the IRS. Under current law, these disputes have lessened for purchased goodwill.

SEC. 197 INTANGIBLES

Sec. 197 was enacted in 1993 to provide greater certainty as to the amortization of many acquired intangible assets and to specifically allow the amortization of *purchased goodwill*. An amortization deduction is permitted for certain acquired Sec. 197 intangible

---

[27] Rev. Proc. 2003-75, 2003-2 C.B. 1018.
[28] The latest lease inclusion table at the date of printing of this textbook is contained in Rev. Proc. 2005-13, I.R.B. 2005-12, 759. The luxury deprecia-tion amounts for 2005 are based on changes to the Consumer Price Index. Tables for passenger automobiles are presented in Table 17 of Appendix C and for trucks and vans, see Table 18 of Appendix C.

Topic Review I10-2

Special Elections and Restrictions

SECTION 179 EXPENSING ELECTION

Deduction: $108,000 on the purchase of new or used tangible personal business property used in the conduct of a trade or business and placed in service in 2006 ($105,000 for 2005).

Limitations:

Asset purchases: The $108,000 limit is reduced by the excess of qualified purchases over $430,000 in 2006 ($420,000 in 2005).

Taxable income limitation: Limited to taxable income before the Sec. 179 deduction.

Basis reduction: The depreciable basis is reduced by the amount of the Sec. 179 deduction.

Recapture: Occurs when the asset is no longer predominantly used in a trade or business. The recapture amount equals the excess of the Sec. 179 expense amount minus the amount that would have been claimed as depreciation if no Sec. 179 election were made.

BUSINESS USE RESTRICTION

Listed property: Business use must be more than 50% to use the regular MACRS rules. If business use is less than 50%, the alternative depreciation system's straight-line method must be used.

Recapture: If business use falls below 50%, the taxpayer must recompute depreciation using the alternative depreciation system's straight-line method and recapture the difference between the prior depreciation taken and straight-line depreciation. The straight-line method is continued for the remaining useful life even if business use subsequently exceeds 50%.

LUXURY AUTOMOBILE LIMITATIONS

Sum of depreciation and Sec. 179 expense limits:

	2003[a]	2003[b]	2004[c]	2004[d]	2005	2006
1st year	7,660	10,710	10,610	2,960	2,960	2,960
2nd year	4,900	4,900	4,800	4,800	4,700	4,800
3rd year	2,950	2,950	2,850	2,850	2,850	2,850
4th and later years	1,775	1,775	1,675	1,675	1,675	1,775

LEASED LUXURY AUTOMOBILE LIMITATIONS

An "inclusion amount" is added to gross income based on the automobile's FMV on the date placed in service to approximate the depreciation restrictions. Special tables that are revised annually are used to calculate the inclusion amount. A partial lease inclusion table is provided in Appendix C.

[a] If 30% bonus depreciation is elected
[b] If 50% bonus depreciation is elected
[c] If 30% or 50% bonus depreciation is elected
[d] If bonus depreciation is not elected

assets. The amortization is deducted on a ratable basis over a 15-year period beginning with the month of acquisition.[29] In general, Sec. 197 applies only to intangible assets that are *acquired* in connection with the conduct of a trade or business or an activity engaged in for the production of income. For example, Sec. 197 does not apply to an intangible asset that is internally created by the taxpayer, such as a patent resulting from the taxpayer's research and development lab. Internally-created patents and copyrights both have definite and limited lives and are therefore amortizable over the defined period.[30] Internally created patents are generally amortized over 17 years; internally created copyrights over 28 years.

EXAMPLE I10-28 ▶

ADDITIONAL COMMENT

The only way goodwill will appear on a balance sheet is if the business was purchased.

On January 1, 2006, Central Corporation receives patent approval on an internally created process improvement. Legal costs associated with the patent are $100,000 and the patent has a legal life of 17 years. The patent does not qualify as a Sec. 197 intangible. The patent has a definite and limited life and is amortizable ratably over its legal life of 17 years beginning with the month of its creation. ◀

---

[29] Sec. 197(a).

[30] Reg. Sec. 1.167(a)-3.

DEFINITION OF A SEC. 197 INTANGIBLE ASSET.   Sec. 197 intangibles (i.e., intangible assets that are subject to 15-year ratable amortization) include the following:

▶ Goodwill and going concern value. Conceptually, goodwill is an intangible asset that is neither separately identified or valued but possesses characteristics that allow a business to earn greater returns than would be possible without such characteristics. The characteristics that make up goodwill include many items, such as valued employees, superior management team, loyal customer base, strategic location, etc. For income tax purposes, however, goodwill is determined in a much more practical manner. **Goodwill** is defined as the value of a trade or business that is attributable to the expectancy of continued customer patronage, whether due to the name or reputation of the trade or business or to any other factor.[31] Going concern value is the added value that attaches to acquired property because it is an integral part of a going concern.

▶ Intangible assets relating to the workforce, information base, know-how, customers, suppliers, or similar items, (e.g., the portion of the purchase price of an acquired business that is attributable to an existing employment contract for a key employee) may be amortized over a 15-year period. An example of an information base intangible would be a customer list. Know-how related intangibles include patents, copyrights, formulas, and processes.

▶ Licenses, permits, or other rights granted by a governmental unit or agency (e.g., the capitalized cost of acquiring a radio broadcasting license).

▶ Covenants not to compete. A covenant not to compete represents an agreement between a buyer and seller of a business that the seller (i.e., the selling corporation and/or its shareholders) will not compete with the buyer for a limited period. The covenant may also be limited to a geographic area. A covenant not to compete must be amortized over 15 years even though the agreement was only for five years.[32]

▶ Franchises, trademarks, and trade names. A franchise includes any agreement that gives one of the parties the right to distribute, sell, or provide goods, services, or facilities, within a specified area.

EXAMPLE I10-29 ▶ During the current year, Chicago Corporation acquires all of the net assets of Coastal Corporation for $1,000,000. The following intangible assets are included in the purchase agreement:

Assets	Acquisition Cost
Goodwill and going concern value	$100,000
Licenses	55,000
Patents	45,000
Covenant not to compete for five years	100,000

All of the intangible assets above qualify as Sec. 197 intangible assets and are amortizable on a ratable basis over 15 years beginning with the month of the acquisition. This 15-year amortization period applies to the convenant not to compete even though the convenant is only for five years. ◀

STOP & THINK

Question: When one company purchases the assets of another company, the purchasing company may acquire goodwill. Since purchased goodwill is a Sec. 197 intangible asset and may be amortized over 15 years, the determination of the cost of goodwill is important. How is the "cost" of goodwill determined when the purchasing company purchases many assets in the acquisition?

Solution: The IRS requires that taxpayers use the "residual method" as prescribed in Sec. 1060. Under this method, all of the assets except for goodwill are valued. The total value of these assets are then subtracted from the total purchase price and the residual value is the amount of the purchase price that is allocated to goodwill.

---

[31] Reg. Sec. 1.197-2(b)(1).
[32] Frontier Chevrolet Co., 2003-1 USTC ¶50,490 (9th Cir., 2003) aff'g 116 T.C. 289 (2001).

ADDITIONAL COMMENT

Sec. 1231 generally allows gains to be treated as long-term capital gains and losses to be deducted as ordinary losses. Sec. 1245 requires gains to be classified as ordinary income to the extent depreciation, amortization or depletion was claimed as an ordinary deduction in prior periods (see Chapter I13).

CLASSIFICATION AND DISPOSITION OF INTANGIBLE ASSETS. A Sec. 197 intangible asset is treated as depreciable property so that Sec. 1231 treatment is accorded the disposition if the intangible asset is held for more than one year.[33] Gain from the disposition of a Sec. 197 intangible is subject to depreciation recapture under Sec. 1245 (see Chapter I13).[34] A loss on the disposition of a Sec. 197 intangible asset, however, is not deductible if other intangibles acquired in the same asset acquisition of a trade or business are retained. In such case, the bases of the retained Sec. 197 intangibles are increased by the unrecognized loss.[35]

EXAMPLE I10-30 ▶ Assume the same facts as in Example I10-29 except that after five years the covenant not to compete expires when its adjusted basis is $66,667 [$100,000 − (0.333 × $100,000)]. The loss is not deductible and the $66,667 disallowed loss is allocated to the retained Sec. 197 assets based on their respective FMVs. ◀

EXAMPLE I10-31 ▶ Assume the same facts as in Example I10-30 except that after one year the patent is sold for $50,000. In the initial year, $3,000 of amortization was deducted. The recognized gain is $8,000 ($50,000 − $42,000) and $3,000 of the gain is recaptured as ordinary income under Sec. 1245. The remaining $5,000 of gain is classified as Sec. 1231 gain. ◀

RESEARCH AND EXPERIMENTAL EXPENDITURES

TYPICAL MISCONCEPTION

It is sometimes mistakenly believed that if a company constructs a new building to be used entirely as a research facility, the entire cost of the building can be expensed. However, the expensing election applies only to the depreciation allowances on the building.

In general, research and experimental (R&E) expenditures, as defined in Sec. 174, include experimental and laboratory costs incidental to the development of a product.[36] Sec. 174 was enacted to clarify the income tax treatment of research and experimental expenditures. Without statutory guidance, the decision to either capitalize or currently expense such expenditures would be in doubt. The Regulations define items that do and do not qualify as research and experimental expenditures. These items are summarized in Table I10-4. For income tax purposes, the following alternatives are available for R&E expenditures:

▶ Expense in the year paid or incurred

▶ Defer and amortize the costs as a ratable deduction over a period of 60 months or more

▶ Capitalize and write off the costs only when the research project is abandoned or is worthless[37]

▼ **TABLE I10-4**
Research and Experimental Expenditures

Items That Qualify	Items That Do Not Qualify[a]
▶ Costs incident to the development of an experimental or pilot model, a plant process, a product, a formula, an invention	▶ Expenditures for ordinary testing or inspection of materials or products for quality control purposes
▶ Costs associated with product improvements	▶ Efficiency surveys and management studies
▶ Costs of obtaining a patent, such as attorney fees	▶ Marketing research, advertising, and so on
▶ Research contracted to others	▶ Cost of acquiring another person's patent, model, production, or process
▶ Depreciation or cost-recovery amounts attributable to capitalized R&E items (e.g., research laboratory and equipment)	▶ Research incurred in connection with literary, historical, or similar projects

[a] Certain of these expenses may be deductible as trade or business expenses under Sec. 162, subject to amortization under Sec. 197, or treated as start-up expenditures under Sec. 195.

[33] Sec. 197(f)(7).
[34] Sec. 1245(a)(2)(C).
[35] Sec. 197(f)(1).

[36] Reg. Sec. 1.174-2(a)(2). The Regulations define the term *product* to include any pilot model, formula, invention, technique, patent, or similar product.
[37] Sec. 174.

A taxpayer must make an election to expense or defer and amortize the costs in the initial year the R&E expenditures are incurred. If no election is made, the costs must be capitalized. The taxpayer must continue to use the same accounting method for the R&E expenditures unless IRS approval to change methods is obtained.

The following points are significant regarding the computation of the deduction for R&E expenditures:

► Most taxpayers elect to expense the R&E expenditures because they prefer the immediate tax benefit.

► The deferral and amortization method is desirable if the taxpayer is currently in a low tax rate situation or expects initial NOLs during a start-up period.

► If the deferral and amortization method is used, the amortization period of 60 or more months commences with the month in which the benefits from the expenditures are first realized.

► R&E expenses include depreciation allowances related to capitalized expenditures. Thus, if the deferral and amortization method is used, depreciation allowances are deferred as part of the R&E expenditures that are amortized over a period of at least 60 months. Capital expenditures made in connection with R&E activities cannot be expensed when they are incurred merely because an election to expense R&E costs are made.

► There is a 20% tax credit that applies to certain incremental research expenditures and a 20% credit for basic research activities. (See Chapter I14 for a discussion of the research activities credit.) If either of the credits are claimed by a taxpayer, any R&E expenses must be reduced by the amount of the credit.

EXAMPLE I10-32 ►

In 2006, Control Corporation leases a research laboratory to develop new products and to improve existing products. Control Corporation, a calendar-year taxpayer that uses the accrual method of accounting, incurs the following expenditures during 2006:

Laboratory supplies and materials	$ 40,000
Laboratory equipment	60,000[a]
Utilities and rent	50,000
Salaries	50,000
Total expenditures	$200,000

[a] The MACRS recovery period is 5 years at a 20% rate for the initial year.

REAL-WORLD EXAMPLE

An airline company made payments to an aircraft manufacturer to help defray the cost of designing, developing, producing, and testing a supersonic transport prototype aircraft. These payments were considered R&E expenditures. Rev. Rul. 69-484, 1969-2 C.B. 38.

Assume the benefits from the R&E expenditures are first realized in January 2007. If Control Corporation elects to expense the R&E expenditures, the deduction in 2006 is $152,000 ($40,000 laboratory supplies and materials + $12,000 depreciation on the equipment + $50,000 utilities and rent + $50,000 salaries). If the deferral and amortization method is elected, none of the expenditures above are deductible in 2006 because the benefits of the R&E activities are not first realized until January 2007. If the 60-month minimum amortization period is elected, the monthly amortization commencing in January, 2007 is $2,533 ($152,000 ÷ 60 months). The $48,000 ($60,000 − $12,000) of laboratory equipment cost is depreciated over the remaining MACRS recovery period beginning in 2007. ◄

COMPUTER SOFTWARE

The amortization or depreciation of computer software depends on the nature of the software and how it is acquired. Basically, computer software is either developed by the taxpayer or purchased or leased from an outside party.

DEVELOPED COMPUTER SOFTWARE. The cost of developing computer software that is considered research and development is treated under Sec. 174 of the IRC. Thus, such software costs may either be expensed in the year the costs are incurred or, if the taxpayer so elects, amortize the costs over 60 months beginning with the month in which the taxpayer first realizes benefits from such expenditures. If the costs incurred to develop the software are not considered research and development costs (e.g., the software is not in the experimental stage), such costs should be depreciated on a straight line basis over 36 months beginning with the date the software is placed in service.[38]

ACQUIRED COMPUTER SOFTWARE.   Computer software that is purchased generally may be depreciated in two alternative ways: (1) if the software is included in the cost of the computer hardware, the software does not have to be separately stated as long as the taxpayer consistently follows this treatment and, therefore, the computer and software would be depreciated together under MACRS over five years; or (2) if the software is purchased separately, the software must be depreciated on a straight-line basis over 36 months. An exception to these rules occurs if computer software is purchased in connection with the acquisition of a number of assets of an existing trade or business. In this case, the computer software is considered to be a Sec. 197 intangible and must be amortized over a period of 15 years.[39]

EXAMPLE I10-33 ▶   Morris Corporation purchased all these assets of an existing trade or business on April 1, 2006 for $1,000,000. Included in the assets that Morris Corporation purchased was some computer software that the corporation intends to use in its business. The software is specialized for use by Morris Corporation. Based on relative fair market values, the computer software is allocated a cost of $63,000. The software is considered a Sec. 197 intangible and would be amortized over 15 years beginning in the month of acquisition. For the eight month period in calendar year 2006, Morris Corporation's amortization deduction would be $2,800 ($63,000/15 years × 8/12).   ◀

EXAMPLE I10-34 ▶   Using the same facts as in Example I10-33, if Morris Corporation alternatively purchased computer software on April 1, 2006 (not in connection with an asset acquisition) for $63,000, the software would not be considered a Sec. 197 intangible and would be depreciable under Sec. 167(f) on a straight-line basis over a period of 36 months. Therefore, in 2007, Morris Corporation's depreciation deduction would be $14,000 ($63,000/36 × 8 months).   ◀

Certain computer software is now eligible for first-year expensing under Sec. 179. Off-the-shelf computer software is defined as software that is readily available for purchase by the general public, is subject to a nonexclusive license, and has not been substantially modified.

LEASED OR LICENSED COMPUTER SOFTWARE.   Computer software that is leased or licensed for use in the taxpayer's trade or business generally is deductible in full in the year paid.[40]

DEPLETION, INTANGIBLE DRILLING AND DEVELOPMENT COSTS

OBJECTIVE 3

Apply cost and percentage depletion methods and understand the treatment for intangible drilling costs

The taxation of natural resources, such as oil and gas, iron ore, etc. is an area that has many of its own specific rules. This section of the text discusses some of the concepts that apply to the oil and gas industry. While other natural resources may have slightly different rules, the oil and gas industry is used here to demonstrate the taxation of natural resources.

The exploration, development, and operation of oil and gas properties require an outlay of various types of expenditures. These expenditures must be properly classified to determine the correct income tax treatment of such expenditures. Below are the four major types of expenditures of an oil and gas property and their income tax treatment.

---

[38] Sec. 167(f)(1) and Rev. Proc. 2000-50, 2000-2 C.B. 601.
[39] Sec. 197(e)(3)(A). If the computer software acquired in an asset acquisition is software that is readily available for purchase by the general public, such software would not be considered a Sec. 197 intangible. See Sec. 197(e)(3)(A)(i).

[40] Reg. Sec. 1.162-11 and Rev. Proc. 2000-50, 2000-2 C.B. 601.

▶ Payments for the mineral interest. These costs are capitalized and recovered through depletion.

▶ Intangible drilling and development costs (e.g., labor and other operating costs to clear land, erect a derrick, and drill the well). Taxpayers elect to either capitalize or immediately write off these expenditures.

▶ Tangible asset costs (e.g., machinery, pipe). These expenditures must be capitalized and depreciated under the MACRS rules.

▶ Operating costs after the well is producing. These expenditures are deductible under Sec. 162 as ordinary and necessary business expenses.

DEPLETION METHODS

KEY POINT

A depletion deduction is available in the case of mines, oil and gas wells, other natural resources, and timber. However, the percentage depletion method is not available in the case of timber.

Depletion is similar to depreciation but refers to natural resources, such as oil and gas, timber, and coal. Depletion is the using up of natural resources by the process of mining (coal, for example) or drilling (oil and gas) and is calculated under the **cost depletion method** or the **percentage depletion method** for each period. The method that is used in any year is the one that results in the largest deduction. Thus, percentage depletion may be used in one year and cost depletion may be used in the following year.

Depletion is allowed to the taxpayer who has an **economic interest** in the property. The person who typically has an economic interest in the property is the owner of the natural resource (i.e., the oil, gas, coal, etc.). Thus, depletion may be claimed by the persons who either own the natural resource property or retain a royalty interest. A mining company that only mines coal from a property and does not own (or lease) the underlying coal is not considered to hold an economic interest and, therefore, is not allowed a depletion deduction. The landowner who owns the coal would be entitled to the depletion deduction.

ADDITIONAL COMMENT

Note that a taxpayer must use the greater of cost depletion or percentage depletion. If percentage depletion is used, the adjusted basis of the property is reduced by the percentage depletion amount.

COST DEPLETION METHOD. The cost depletion method is similar to the units-of-production method of depreciation. The adjusted basis of the asset is divided by the estimated recoverable units to arrive at a per-unit depletion cost. This per-unit cost is then multiplied by the number of units sold to determine the cost depletion deduction.[41] If percentage depletion is used in any one year because it is greater than the cost depletion amount, the property's adjusted basis for purposes of determining cost depletion in the following year and the gain or loss on disposition of the property is reduced by the amount of percentage depletion claimed. If the original estimate of recoverable units is subsequently determined to be incorrect, the per-unit cost depletion rate must be revised and used on a prospective basis to determine cost depletion in future years.[42] It is not proper to file an amended return for the years in which the incorrect estimated unit cost was used.

EXAMPLE I10-35 ▶

Ralph acquires an oil and gas property interest for $100,000 in 2006. The estimate of recoverable units is 10,000 barrels of oil. The per-unit cost depletion amount is $10 ($100,000 ÷ 10,000). If 3,000 units are produced and 2,000 units are sold in 2006, the cost depletion amount is $20,000 (2,000 units × $10 per unit). If cost depletion is used because it exceeds the percentage depletion amount, the cost basis of the property is reduced to $80,000 ($100,000 − $20,000) at the beginning of 2007. If the estimate of remaining recoverable units is revised downward from 8,000 units in 2007 (10,000 − 2,000 units sold in 2006) to 5,000 units (including the 1,000 barrels produced but not sold in 2006), the property's $80,000 adjusted basis is divided by 5,000 units to arrive at a new per-unit cost depletion amount of $16 for 2007. This process is continued each year until the cost of the oil and gas property interest is fully depleted. ◀

REAL-WORLD EXAMPLE

Taxpayers are entitled to a depletion deduction if they have an economic interest in the property. This economic interest may be in the form of a royalty interest where a landowner receives a certain amount per unit extracted from her land, such as $10 for each barrel of oil. The landowner would be entitled to a depletion deduction based on the royalty income received.

PERCENTAGE DEPLETION METHOD. Percentage depletion generally offers substantial tax benefits for taxpayers in the natural resources industry. The purpose of allowing percentage depletion is to encourage persons to invest and/or operate in an industry that is both capital intensive and high risk but is also vital to our national interests. Percentage depletion may be used by taxpayers for a wide variety of natural resources, such as oil and gas, coal, gold, etc. However, the percentage depletion method has not been available to *large* oil and gas producers since 1974, but is still available to *small* oil and gas producers

---

[41] Sec. 612.

[42] Sec. 611(a).

and royalty owners under a specific exemption in the law.[43] Percentage depletion is computed by multiplying the percentage depletion rate times the gross income from the property. However, the depletion amount may not exceed 50% of the taxable income from the property before depletion is deducted (100% for oil and gas properties).[44] Percentage depletion may not be calculated on any lease bonus, advance royalty, or other amount payable without regard to production from the property.

When using either cost depletion or percentage depletion, the amount of the depletion deduction reduces the basis of the natural resource property. Once the basis of depletable property has been reduced to zero, a taxpayer may no longer claim depreciation using the cost depletion method. However, the taxpayer may continue to claim percentage depletion, even though subsequent percentage depletion will not reduce the basis of the property below zero. It should be apparent that percentage depletion is a very advantageous method because the amount of depletion that is allowed over the life of the property may exceed the property's cost.[45]

Percentage depletion rates vary by the type of mineral. Depletion rates for selected minerals are as follows:

Mineral	Depletion Rate
Oil and gas	15%[46]
Coal, asbestos	10%
Gold, silver, copper, iron ore	15%
Sulphur and uranium	22%
Gravel, stone	5%

EXAMPLE I10-36 ▶

Carmen acquires an oil and gas property interest for $400,000 in the current year with 200,000 barrels of estimated recoverable oil. During the year, 10,000 barrels of oil are sold for $250,000. Intangible drilling and development costs amount to $100,000 and are expensed in the current year. Other expenses are $50,000. Cost depletion is $20,000 (10,000 × $2) in the current year. The computation of percentage depletion is as follows:

(1) Percentage depletion before taxable income limitation	
$250,000 × 0.15	$ 37,500
(2) Taxable income ceiling:	
Gross income	$250,000
Minus: Intangible drilling costs	(100,000)
Other expenses	(50,000)
Taxable income before depletion	$100,000
(3) Percentage depletion (lesser of (1) or (2))	$ 37,500

Carmen's depletion deduction is $37,500 because the percentage depletion amount is greater than the $20,000 of cost depletion. The adjusted basis of the property is reduced by $37,500, the amount of depletion actually claimed. ◀

TREATMENT OF INTANGIBLE DRILLING AND DEVELOPMENT COSTS

Intangible drilling and development costs (IDCs) may either be deducted as an expense or capitalized.[47] IDCs apply only to oil, gas, and geothermal wells and basically include all expenditures, other than the acquisition costs of the underlying property, that are incurred for the drilling and preparation of wells. If the IDCs are capitalized, the amounts are added to the property's basis for determining cost depletion, and the costs are written off through cost depletion. For a well that is nonproductive (i.e., a dry hole), an ordinary

---

[43] Sec. 613A(c). To be classified as a small oil and gas producer or royalty owner, the maximum depletable quantity is based on average daily production of not more than 1,000 barrels of oil or 6 million cubic feet of natural gas.
[44] Sec. 613(a).
[45] Depletion in excess of the adjusted basis of the property is a tax preference item under Sec. 57(a)(1).

[46] For small producers and royalty owners of oil and gas properties, there is a further limitation: the percentage depletion deduction may not exceed 65% of taxable income from all sources before the depletion deduction. Sec. 631A(d)(1).
[47] Sec. 263(c).

loss is allowed for any IDC costs that have been capitalized and not recovered through depletion. The amount of depletion claimed in a tax year equals the greater of the percentage depletion and cost depletion amounts. If IDCs are capitalized and cost depletion is thereby increased, little or no tax benefit may result because the percentage depletion may still produce a greater deduction than cost depletion. Therefore, it is generally preferable to expense the IDCs if the percentage depletion is expected to be more than the cost depletion and is used to compute the depletion allowance.

EXAMPLE I10-37 ▶ Penny acquires certain rights to oil and gas property in the current year for $1,000,000. In the current year Penny incurs $300,000 of IDCs. If the IDCs are capitalized, the basis for cost depletion purposes is $1,300,000. Assume that the cost depletion amounts are $100,000 in the current year if the IDCs are expensed and $130,000 if IDCs are capitalized. If the percentage depletion amount is $150,000, percentage depletion will be used because it is greater than either of the cost depletion amounts. Thus, the expensing of the IDCs permits the taxpayer to deduct the entire $300,000 of IDCs in the current year plus $150,000 of percentage depletion. ◀

TAX PLANNING CONSIDERATIONS

ALTERNATIVE DEPRECIATION SYSTEM UNDER MACRS

ADDITIONAL COMMENT

A taxpayer who is attempting to report a profit in three out of five years in an attempt to avoid the hobby loss rules might want to use the alternative depreciation system.

In some instances, it may be preferable to elect to use the alternative depreciation system rather than the regular MACRS rules. For example, a taxpayer who anticipates losses during the next few years or who currently has NOL carryovers may elect to use the alternative depreciation system, which employs the straight-line method of depreciation over a longer recovery period.

EXAMPLE I10-38 ▶ Delta Corporation has substantial NOL carryovers that will expire if not used during the next few years. Delta Corporation anticipates it will not have taxable income for each of the next seven years if the regular MACRS rules are used to depreciate its fixed asset additions. In the current year, Delta Corporation acquires new machinery and equipment at a cost of $100,000. Depreciation deductions using the MACRS rules and a seven-year recovery period are $14,290 (0.1429 × $100,000). Depreciation deductions under the straight-line method using the alternative depreciation system (a 12-year life) and the half-year convention are only $4,167 [($100,000 ÷ 12 years) × 0.50 year]. The alternative depreciation system election increases taxable income in the current year by $10,123 and allows Delta Corporation to offset additional loss carryovers (which might otherwise expire) against this income amount. ◀

USE OF UNITS OF PRODUCTION DEPRECIATION

Many times, the MACRS depreciation system requires taxpayers to use a recovery period that is much longer than the actual useful life of the asset. For example, assume a taxpayer uses a machine in his or her business that is required to be classified as 7-year property under MACRS. However, the machine is operated 24 hours a day, seven days a week and will completely wear out in two years. The use of the 7-year recovery period substantially understates the depreciation for the machine. Under Sec. 168(f), taxpayers may exclude property from the MACRS system if the property is depreciated under the unit-of-production method or any other method not expressed in terms of years. Therefore, if a taxpayer can express the useful life of the machine in terms of some other base than years (such as machine hours, units produced, etc.), it may be possible for the taxpayer to depreciate the machine over a much shorter period than the seven years required under MACRS.

STRUCTURING A BUSINESS COMBINATION

Tax planning is necessary to ensure favorable tax consequences for the acquiring company if the assets of the acquired company are purchased as part of a business combination. The sales agreement must specify the amounts that have been paid for the tangible

WHAT WOULD YOU DO IN THIS SITUATION?

Your CPA firm has a long-standing tax client named Widgets R Us, Incorporated (WRU). WRU has been a worldwide leader in widget technology for years and continues to expand its global market share of Class A Crystal Widgets through a substantial program of basic research and development of widget crystallization processes. You have always advised WRU as to which of these expenditures qualify as research and experimental (R&E) expenditures. In addition, you have always given timely advice as to when to expense rather than capitalize these expenditures.

You are having your monthly tax conference with Ms. Ima Worthmore, president of WRU, and Mr. Stan Cunning, tax counsel of WMU, and Ms. Worthmore relates to you a conversation she had with the local manager of a competitor CPA firm, Ms. Ruth Less. Ms. Less told Ms. Worthmore that she had discovered that

WRU was one of the top spenders on research and development in the area and that her firm was "certified" to practice before the IRS and had experienced great success in gaining better R&E write-offs for comparable firms. Ms. Less went on to say that, "For you, for this one year only, we offer to prepare your tax returns on a contingent basis. We promise to save you at least $1 million from what you are now paying the IRS through our better use of R&E write-offs and our fee will only be 30% of the tax savings!"

Ms. Worthmore was excited that WRU might pay considerably less taxes under the plan of Ruth Less and is somewhat perturbed at you because you had not brought this tax opportunity to her attention. She wants your firm to provide her with a counteroffer. How do you ethically respond to your client's request to match or better Ms. Ruth Less' proposal?

REAL-WORLD EXAMPLE

A taxpayer purchased a business that owned retail franchises. It was the opinion of the IRS that the amounts paid in excess of the value of the net assets represented a nondepreciable "indivisible asset." However, the taxpayer was able to show that retail franchises have limited useful lives, and was able to amortize the excess costs. *Super Food Services, Inc. v. U.S.,* 24 AFTR 2d 69-5309, 69-2 USTC ¶9558 (7th Cir., 1969).

depreciable and nondepreciable assets and the intangible assets and the reporting requirements of Sec. 1060 must be complied with. Under the requirements of Sec. 1060, both the transferor and the transferee are bound by their written agreement as to the allocation of the purchase price to individual assets unless the IRS determines that such allocation is not appropriate. The amounts paid for the tangible assets should be documented by appraisals and evidence of negotiations between the buyer and seller. Within reason, the purchaser should attempt to allocate as much of the total price to the tangible depreciable assets, such as machinery and equipment. The purchaser should also consider allocating part of the purchase price to amortizable Sec. 197 intangible assets such as goodwill, a covenant not to compete, patents, copyrights, licenses, and customer lists because such asset costs are recovered over a 15-year period. This is preferable to allocating to depreciable real estate because such property must be depreciated over 39 years.

COMPLIANCE AND PROCEDURAL CONSIDERATIONS

REPORTING COST RECOVERY, DEPRECIATION, DEPLETION, AND AMORTIZATION DEDUCTIONS

If an individual is engaged in a trade or business as a sole proprietor, depreciation, cost recovery, depletion, and amortization deductions are initially computed and reported on Form 4562 (Depreciation and Amortization) and the totals are then carried to Schedule C. Depletion and depreciation on rental properties are reported on Schedule E instead of Schedule C if the taxpayer is an investor. Depreciation on employee business property is reported on Form 2106. Separate Form 4562s are required for each different activity.

The election to expense property under Sec. 179 is made by claiming the deduction on Part I of Form 4562. The taxpayer must specify the items of property and the portion of the cost for each asset being expensed. Form 4562 is not required of individuals and noncorporate taxpayers (including S corporations) when filing their 2005 tax returns if the depreciation deduction is for assets, other than listed property, placed in service before

2005. In such cases, the depreciation deduction is entered directly on Form 1040 or other equivalent tax forms. However, even though a Form 4562 may not be required to be filed with the return, detailed depreciation records must still be maintained by the taxpayers to support the deduction.

EXAMPLE I10-39 ▶ George Jones, SSN 277-32-6542, is a building contractor who owns the following properties:

- ▶ Specialized utility repair truck (5-year property that is not listed property under Sec. 280F(d)(4)), costing $40,000, acquired on February 15, 2005.
- ▶ Machinery and equipment (7-year property), costing $140,000, acquired on June 10, 2005. The election to expense under Sec. 179 is made for $105,000.
- ▶ Patent, costing $20,000, that was developed and placed in service on June 1, 2005, when it had a remaining legal life of 17 years.
- ▶ MACRS deduction for assets placed into service before 2005 is $66,000.

Jones has taxable income (before the Sec. 179 deduction and the deduction for one-half of self-employment taxes paid under Sec. 164(f)) of $460,000. The depreciation and amortization amounts are reported on Form 4562 and are shown in Figures I10-1 and I10-2. This example assumes that Jones takes the maximum Sec. 179 deduction. ◀

PROBLEM MATERIALS

DISCUSSION QUESTIONS

I10-1 Which of the following assets are subject to either amortization, depreciation, or cost recovery? Explain.
 a. An automobile held for personal use.
 b. Excess amounts paid in a business combination that are attributable to goodwill.
 c. Excess amounts paid in a business combination that are attributable to customer lists that have a limited useful life.
 d. A patent that has been created internally and has a legal life of 17 years.
 e. Land that is being held for investment purposes.
 f. A covenant not to compete which is entered into by the buyer and seller of a business.

I10-2 Rick is a sole proprietor who has a small business that is currently operating at a loss. He would like to discontinue depreciating the fixed assets of the business for the next few years in order to carry the deductions over to a future period. What tax consequences would result if Rick implements the plan to discontinue depreciation and then sells some of the depreciable assets several years later?

I10-3 Rita acquired a personal residence two years ago for $120,000. In the current year, she purchases another residence and attempts to sell her former residence. Due to depressed housing conditions in the town where she used to live, Rita is unable to sell the house. Her former residence is now being offered for sale at $100,000 (its current FMV according to real estate appraisal experts). Rita has decided to rent the house rather than "give it away." She states that renting the house on a permanent basis will permit her to write off the orig-

inal $120,000 investment over its useful life and to, therefore, recoup her investment. What restrictions in the tax law may prevent her from accomplishing this objective? Explain.

I10-4 Daytona Corporation, a manufacturing corporation, acquires the following business assets in the current year:
- Furniture
- Plumbing fixtures
- Land
- Goodwill and a trademark acquired in the acquisition of a business
- Automobile
- Heavy truck
- Machinery
- Building used in manufacturing activities
 a. Which of the assets above are eligible for depreciation under the MACRS rules or amortization under Sec. 197?
 b. What recovery period should be used for each of the assets above that come under the MACRS rules or under Sec. 197?

I10-5 Robert, a sole proprietor who uses the calendar year as his tax year, acquired a business machine during 2004. Machine A, a seven-year asset, was acquired on July 20, 2004, for $50,000. No other property was acquired in 2004.
 a. What is the amount of depreciation that Robert is allowed in 2004 and 2006 if neither bonus depreciation nor Sec. 179 depreciation (first-year expense election) was elected?

Form **4562**	**Depreciation and Amortization**	OMB No. 1545-0172
(Rev. January 2006)	**(Including Information on Listed Property)**	**2005**
Department of the Treasury Internal Revenue Service	▶ See separate instructions. ▶ Attach to your tax return.	Attachment Sequence No. **67**

Name(s) shown on return	Business or activity to which this form relates	Identifying number
George Jones	Building Contractor	277-32-6542

Part I   Election To Expense Certain Property Under Section 179

Note: If you have any listed property, complete Part V before you complete Part I.

1	Maximum amount. See the instructions for a higher limit for certain businesses	1	$105,000
2	Total cost of section 179 property placed in service (see instructions)	2	180,000
3	Threshold cost of section 179 property before reduction in limitation	3	$420,000
4	Reduction in limitation. Subtract line 3 from line 2. If zero or less, enter -0-	4	-0-
5	Dollar limitation for tax year. Subtract line 4 from line 1. If zero or less, enter -0-. If married filing separately, see instructions	5	105,000

(a) Description of property	(b) Cost (business use only)	(c) Elected cost	
6 Truck	40,000	-0-	
Machinery and Equipment	140,000	105,000	

7	Listed property. Enter the amount from line 29	7	-0-
8	Total elected cost of section 179 property. Add amounts in column (c), lines 6 and 7	8	105,000
9	Tentative deduction. Enter the **smaller** of line 5 or line 8.	9	105,000
10	Carryover of disallowed deduction from line 13 of your 2004 Form 4562	10	
11	Business income limitation. Enter the smaller of business income (not less than zero) or line 5 (see instructions)	11	105,000
12	Section 179 expense deduction. Add lines 9 and 10, but do not enter more than line 11 . . .	12	105,000
13	Carryover of disallowed deduction to 2006. Add lines 9 and 10, less line 12 ▶	13	-0-

Note: Do not use Part II or Part III below for listed property. Instead, use Part V.

Part II   Special Depreciation Allowance and Other Depreciation (Do not include listed property.) (See instructions.)

14	Special allowance for certain aircraft, certain property with a long production period, and qualified NYL or GO Zone property (other than listed property) placed in service during the tax year (see instructions)	14	
15	Property subject to section 168(f)(1) election	15	
16	Other depreciation (including ACRS)	16	

Part III   MACRS Depreciation (Do not include listed property.) (See instructions.)

Section A

17	MACRS deductions for assets placed in service in tax years beginning before 2005	17	66,000
18	If you are electing to group any assets placed in service during the tax year into one or more general asset accounts, check here . . . . ▶ ☐		

Section B—Assets Placed in Service During 2005 Tax Year Using the General Depreciation System

(a) Classification of property	(b) Month and year placed in service	(c) Basis for depreciation (business/investment use only—see instructions)	(d) Recovery period	(e) Convention	(f) Method	(g) Depreciation deduction
19a 3-year property						
b 5-year property		40,000	5 yr.	HY	MACRS	8,000
c 7-year property		35,000	7 yr.	HY	MACRS	5,002
d 10-year property						
e 15-year property						
f 20-year property						
g 25-year property			25 yrs.		S/L	
h Residential rental property			27.5 yrs.	MM	S/L	
			27.5 yrs.	MM	S/L	
i Nonresidential real property			39 yrs.	MM	S/L	
				MM	S/L	

Section C—Assets Placed in Service During 2005 Tax Year Using the Alternative Depreciation System

20a Class life					S/L	
b 12-year			12 yrs.		S/L	
c 40-year			40 yrs.	MM	S/L	

Part IV   Summary (see instructions)

21	Listed property. Enter amount from line 28	21	
22	**Total.** Add amounts from line 12, lines 14 through 17, lines 19 and 20 in column (g), and line 21. Enter here and on the appropriate lines of your return. Partnerships and S corporations—see instr.	22	184,002
23	For assets shown above and placed in service during the current year, enter the portion of the basis attributable to section 263A costs . .	23	

For Paperwork Reduction Act Notice, see separate instructions.   Cat. No. 12906N   Form **4562** (2005) (Rev. 1-2006)

Line 19c: $140,000 − $105,000 = $35,000.

FIGURE I10-1   ▶   FORM 4562

10-28

Part V **Listed Property** (Include automobiles, certain other vehicles, cellular telephones, certain computers, and property used for entertainment, recreation, or amusement.)

Note: *For any vehicle for which you are using the standard mileage rate or deducting lease expense, complete **only** 24a, 24b, columns (a) through (c) of Section A, all of Section B, and Section C if applicable.*

Section A—Depreciation and Other Information (Caution: *See the instructions for limits for passenger automobiles.***)**

24a Do you have evidence to support the business/investment use claimed? ☐ **Yes** ☐ **No**   **24b** If "Yes," is the evidence written? ☐ **Yes** ☐ **No**

(a) Type of property (list vehicles first)	(b) Date placed in service	(c) Business/ investment use percentage	(d) Cost or other basis	(e) Basis for depreciation (business/investment use only)	(f) Recovery period	(g) Method/ Convention	(h) Depreciation deduction	(i) Elected section 179 cost
25 Special allowance for certain aircraft, certain property with a long production period, and qualified NYL or GO Zone property placed in service during the tax year and used more than 50% in a qualified business use (see instructions)				**25**				
26 Property used more than 50% in a qualified business use:								
		%						
		%						
		%						
27 Property used 50% or less in a qualified business use:								
		%				S/L –		
		%				S/L –		
		%				S/L –		

28 Add amounts in column (h), lines 25 through 27. Enter here and on line 21, page 1. . . | **28** |
29 Add amounts in column (i), line 26. Enter here and on line 7, page 1. . . . . | **29** |

Section B—Information on Use of Vehicles

Complete this section for vehicles used by a sole proprietor, partner, or other "more than 5% owner," or related person.

If you provided vehicles to your employees, first answer the questions in Section C to see if you meet an exception to completing this section for those vehicles.

		(a) Vehicle 1		(b) Vehicle 2		(c) Vehicle 3		(d) Vehicle 4		(e) Vehicle 5		(f) Vehicle 6	
30	Total business/investment miles driven during the year (**do not** include commuting miles)												
31	Total commuting miles driven during the year												
32	Total other personal (noncommuting) miles driven												
33	Total miles driven during the year. Add lines 30 through 32												
34	Was the vehicle available for personal use during off-duty hours?	**Yes**	**No**	**Yes**	**No**	**Yes**	**No**	**Yes**	**No**	**Yes**	**No**	**Yes**	**No**
35	Was the vehicle used primarily by a more than 5% owner or related person?												
36	Is another vehicle available for personal use?												

Section C—Questions for Employers Who Provide Vehicles for Use by Their Employees

Answer these questions to determine if you meet an exception to completing Section B for vehicles used by employees who **are not** more than 5% owners or related persons (see instructions).

		Yes	No
37	Do you maintain a written policy statement that prohibits all personal use of vehicles, including commuting, by your employees?		
38	Do you maintain a written policy statement that prohibits personal use of vehicles, except commuting, by your employees? See the instructions for vehicles used by corporate officers, directors, or 1% or more owners		
39	Do you treat all use of vehicles by employees as personal use?		
40	Do you provide more than five vehicles to your employees, obtain information from your employees about the use of the vehicles, and retain the information received?		
41	Do you meet the requirements concerning qualified automobile demonstration use? (See instructions.)		

Note: *If your answer to 37, 38, 39, 40, or 41 is "Yes," do not complete Section B for the covered vehicles.*

Part VI **Amortization**

(a) Description of costs	(b) Date amortization begins	(c) Amortizable amount	(d) Code section	(e) Amortization period or percentage	(f) Amortization for this year
42 Amortization of costs that begins during your 2005 tax year (see instructions):					
Patent	6-1-05	20,000	167	17	686*
43 Amortization of costs that began before your 2005 tax year.			**43**		
44 **Total.** Add amounts in column (f). See the instructions for where to report.			**44**		686

* $20,000/17 yrs. = $1,176 x 7/12 = $686.

FIGURE 110-2   ▶   FORM 4562 (CONTINUED)

b. What is the amount of depreciation that Robert is allowed in 2004 and 2006 if bonus depreciation was taken but not Sec. 179?

c. What is the amount of depreciation that Robert is allowed in 2004 and 2006 if Sec. 179 was elected?

I10-6 Roberta, a sole proprietor who uses the calendar year as her tax year, acquires two business machines during 2006. Machine C, a seven-year asset, was acquired on January 20, 2006, for $80,000 and Machine D, a five-year asset, was acquired on August 1, 2006, for $40,000. No other property was acquired in 2006.

a. What is the amount of depreciation that Roberta is allowed in 2006 if Sec. 179 (first-year expense election) is not elected?

b. What is the amount of depreciation that Roberta is allowed in 2006 if Sec. 179 is elected?

I10-7 Is a depreciation deduction allowed under the MACRS rules for depreciable real estate (used in a business or held for investment) in the year the property is sold? If so, explain how it is calculated.

I10-8 Jose is considering acquiring a new luxury automobile costing $45,000 that will be used 100% in his business. The salesperson at the automobile dealership states that Jose will be entitled to substantial tax benefits in the initial year (2006) including:

If Sec. 179 is elected:

• A deduction for $45,000 of the acquisition cost under Sec. 179.

If Sec. 179 is not elected:

• A $9,000 ($45,000 × 0.20) MACRS depreciation deduction.

a. Are the salesperson's assertions relative to the tax benefits accurate? Explain.

b. How would your answer to Part a differ (if any) if the automobile were used only 60% for business purposes?

c. How would your answer to Part a differ (if any) if Jose instead was to lease the automobile?

d. How would your answers to Part a differ if the vehicle was a large SUV (gross vehicle weight rating (GVWR) greater than 6,000 pounds) rather than an automobile?

I10-9 Explain why the straight-line MACRS method (using the ADS) might be preferable over the regular MACRS method under the following circumstances:

a. Ray incurs NOLs in his business for a number of years and has NOL carryovers he would like to use.

b. Rhonda's marginal tax rate is 15% but is expected to increase to 35% in three years.

I10-10 Rudy is considering whether to make the election under Sec. 179 to expense $108,000 (2006) of the acquisition cost related to certain fixed asset additions. What advantages are associated with the Sec. 179 election?

I10-11 Luby Corporation has maintained an office in a leased building for several years. The corporation has decided to make some significant leasehold improvements to enhance the property. How should Luby Corporation depreciate the leasehold improvements?

I10-12 Your client is a self-employed attorney who is considering the purchase of a $32,000 automobile that will be used 80% of the time for business and a $4,000 personal computer that will be used 100% of the time for business, but is located in his home.

a. What depreciation methods and recovery periods may be used under MACRS for the automobile and the personal computer?

b. How would your answer to Part a change if your client were an employee and the computer and automobile were not required as a condition of employment?

c. What tax consequences occur in Part a if the business use of the personal computer or the automobile decreases to 50% or less in a succeeding year? Explain.

I10-13 Congress enacted a provision in the tax law in 2001 that permitted an additional 30% bonus depreciation for certain assets. Later the 30% was increased to 50%.

a. What types of assets qualified for the 50% or 30% bonus depreciation and when must the assets be placed in service?

b. How does the 50% or 30% bonus depreciation interface with Sec. 179 first-year depreciation?

c. When do the bonus depreciations provisions expire?

I10-14 Sarah enters into a three-year lease of an automobile on March 1, 2005 that is used exclusively in her business. The automobile's FMV was $59,000 at the inception of the lease. Sarah made ten monthly lease payments of $600 each during the current year. Is Sarah able to avoid the luxury automobile restrictions on depreciation by leasing instead of purchasing the automobile? Explain. (The inclusion amount for 2005 for Sarah's automobile under the current Rev. Proc. is $200.)

I10-15 What difference does it make for income tax purposes whether an intangible asset (1) is acquired in connection with a business acquisition, (2) is acquired by the purchase of an individual asset (e.g., a patent), or (3) is created internally? Explain.

I10-16 In January of the current year, Park Corporation incurs $34,000 of legal costs associated with the obtaining of a patent that was developed internally and has a legal life of 17 years. Park also acquired for cash the net assets of Central Corporation on January 1, for $1,000,000. The following assets are specified in the purchase agreement:

Land	$ 200,000
Goodwill and going concern value	100,000
Covenant not to compete	50,000
Licenses	125,000

Customer lists	25,000
Inventory	100,000
Equipment and other tangible depreciable business assets	400,000
Total	$1,000,000

a. What tax treatment should be accorded the intangible assets?

b. Assuming that you were advising Park Corporation during the negotiations before the drafting of the purchase agreement, what suggestions would you make regarding the allocation of the total purchase price to the individual assets? How could the purchase price of individual assets be substantiated?

I10-17 Why do most taxpayers prefer to currently expense research and experimental expenditures?

I10-18 In a business combination, why does the buyer generally prefer to allocate as much of the purchase price to short-lived depreciable assets, ordinary assets such as inventory, and Sec. 197 intangible assets?

I10-19 Explain the difference between cost depletion and percentage depletion. Which of these two methods will generally provide the largest deduction?

I10-20 Simon acquires an interest in an oil property for $50,000. Intangible drilling costs (IDCs) in the initial year are $10,000. Cost depletion is $5,000 if the IDCs are expensed and $6,000 if the costs are capitalized. Percentage depletion is $15,000 if the IDCs are expensed and $20,000 if the costs are capitalized. The difference in the percentage depletion amounts is due to the 100% taxable income limitation.

a. What method (i.e., immediate write-off or capitalization and amortization) should be elected for the treatment of the IDCs in the initial year if Simon wants to maximize his deductions?

b. Why are intangible drilling costs expensed by most taxpayers?

ISSUE IDENTIFICATION QUESTIONS

I10-21 Georgia Corporation acquires a business automobile for $30,000 on December 31 of the current year but does not actually place the automobile into service until January 1 of the following year. What tax issues should Georgia Corporation consider?

I10-22 Paula is planning to acquire by purchase or by lease a $50,000 luxury automobile. She anticipates that the business use will be 60% for the first two years but will decline to 40% in years three through five. Currently, Paula's marginal tax rate is 15% but she anticipates that her marginal tax rate will be 35% after a few years. What tax issues should Paula consider relative to the decision to purchase or lease the automobile?

I10-23 In the current year, Coastal Corporation acquires all of the net assets of Acorn Corporation for $2,000,000. The purchase agreement allocated the following amounts to the individual assets and liabilities:

Land and building	$1,400,000
Accounts receivable	200,000
Inventory	300,000
Goodwill	400,000
Patents (remaining legal life of ten years)	100,000
Covenant not to compete	200,000
Liabilities	(600,000)
Total	$2,000,000

What tax issues should Coastal Corporation consider relative to the asset acquisitions?

I10-24 Weiskopf, a sole proprietor and a calendar-year taxpayer, purchased $400,000 of equipment during 2006, as follows:

	Cost	Recovery Period
March 1	$100,000	7 years
September 18	$160,000	7 years
October 2	$140,000	5 years

Weiskopf's CPA, to maximize the depreciation deduction, elected to take Sec. 179 depreciation on the March 1 property of $100,000 and $5,000 on the September 18 property. What tax issue should be considered with respect to the total depreciation deduction for the current year?

PROBLEMS

I10-25 *Allowed Versus Allowable Depreciation.* Sandy acquires business machinery (which qualifies as 7-year MACRS property) on July 15, 2004, for $10,000. In 2004, Sandy claims a $1,429 regular MACRS depreciation deduction and she elected not to claim any bonus depreciation or Sec. 179 depreciation. Because of net operating losses in 2005 and 2006, Sandy did not claim any depreciation deduction on her tax returns in 2005 or 2006. The machine is sold on July 1, 2006, for $6,000.
a. What is the adjusted basis of the machine on the sale date?
b. How much gain or loss is recognized on the sale of the machine?

I10-26 *Conversion of Personal Asset to Business Use.* Sid purchased an automobile for personal use on January 18, 2004 for $10,000. On January 1, 2006, Sid starts a small business and begins to use the automobile exclusively in the business. The automobile's FMV on this date is $6,000. MACRS depreciation deductions are taken in 2006 based on a 5-year recovery period.
a. What is the automobile's basis for depreciation purposes when converted to business use in 2006?
b. What is Sid's depreciation deduction in 2006?

I10-27 *MACRS and Bonus Depreciation.* Small Corporation acquired and placed in service the following business assets in 2004 (no other assets were placed in service during the year) and the corporation elected the 50% bonus depreciation for all eligible property:
• Light-duty truck costing $20,000 (on February 15) with a 5-year MACRS recovery period
• Machinery costing $50,000 (on May 1) with a 7-year MACRS recovery period
• Land costing $60,000 (on July 1)
• Building costing $100,000 (on December 1) with a 39-year MACRS recovery period
• Equipment costing $40,000 (acquired on December 24, but not placed in service until January of the following year) with a 5-year MACRS recovery period
a. What is the MACRS depreciation deduction for each asset in 2006 (assume Sec. 179 was not elected for any asset)?
b. What is the MACRS deduction for each asset in 2006 if the machinery was instead acquired on November 1, 2004?
c. Assume the facts in Part a. If Small Corporation sells the machinery on June 15, 2006 and sells the building on October 20, 2006, compute the depreciation deductions for 2004, 2005, and 2006 and the adjusted basis for these two assets at the respective dates of sale.

I10-28 *MACRS Depreciation for 2006.* Large Corporation acquires and places into service the following business assets in 2006 (no other assets were placed in service during the year):
• Light-duty truck costing $20,000 (on February 15) with a 5-year recovery period.
• Machinery costing $50,000 (on May 1) with a 7-year MACRS recovery period.
• Land costing $60,000 (on July 1).
• Building costing $100,000 (on December 1) with a 39-year MACRS recovery period.
• Equipment costing $40,000 (acquired on December 24 but not placed into service until January, 2006) with a 5-year MACRS recovery period.
a. What is the MACRS depreciation deduction for each asset in 2006 assuming Sec. 179 was not elected for any asset?
b. What is the MACRS deduction for each asset in 2006 if the machinery is instead acquired on November 1 and Sec. 179 is not elected for any asset?
c. Assume the facts in Part a. If Large Corporation sells the machinery on June 15, 2008, and sells the building on October 20, 2008, compute the depreciation deductions for 2006, 2007, and 2008 and the adjusted basis for these two assets at the respective dates of sale.

I10-29 *Sec. 179 Expensing Election and MACRS Depreciation.* Ted is in the real estate business and owns rental property. On May 12, 2006, Ted purchased a small apartment building for $200,000 ($180,000 for the building and $20,000 for the land). In addition, Ted purchased 5-year recovery period personal property costing $60,000 on April 10, 2006, and 7-year recovery period personal property costing $80,000 on November 1, 2006.

a. What is the amount of the MACRS depreciation deduction for each asset in 2006 and 2007 assuming Ted does not elect the Sec. 179 expensing election?

b. Compute the MACRS depreciation deduction on the 5-year and 7-year property for 2006 and 2007 if Ted elects the maximum Sec. 179 deduction in 2006 by expensing $28,000 of the 5-year property and $80,000 of the 7-year property.

I10-30 *Sec. 179 Expensing Election and MACRS Depreciation.* Tish acquires and places in service a business machine with a 7-year MACRS recovery period in July 2006. The machine costs $130,000, and Tish elects to expense the maximum amount allowable under Sec. 179. The total cost of qualifying property placed in service during the year amounts to $440,000. Tish's taxable income (before deducting the Sec. 179 amount and one-half of self-employment taxes paid) is $27,000.

a. What is the amount of total depreciation that Tish can deduct in 2006?

b. What is the amount of MACRS depreciation deduction for the machine in 2007 assuming the total cost of qualifying property placed in service in 2007 was less than $430,000?

I10-31 *MACRS Dispositions.* Tampa Corporation sold the following assets in 2006:

	Date Acquired	Date Sold	Original Cost Basis	Depreciation/ Cost-Recovery Method	Recovery Period (Years)	Sales Price
Auto	1/1/03	12/1/06ᵃ	9,000	MACRS	5	1,200
Equipment	1/6/03	9/1/06ᵃ	20,000	MACRS	7	9,500
Building	4/1/97	12/10/06	100,000	MACRS	39	240,000

ᵃ Assume that the half-year convention was used in the year of acquisition and Sec. 179 expense election was not made.

a. What is the amount of depreciation deduction for each asset in 2006?

b. Compute the gain or loss on each asset that was sold in 2006.

I10-32 *Sec. 179 Expensing Election and MACRS Depreciation.* Thad acquires a machine for use in his business on April 1, 2006, for $235,000. The machinery is depreciated under MACRS, with a 7-year recovery period. Thad elects to expense $108,000 of the acquisition cost under Sec. 179 and to take 50% bonus depreciation.

a. What is the depreciation deduction for the machine in 2006?

b. Assume Thad depreciates the machine in 2006 and 2007 and then sells the machine on October 5, 2008, for $80,000. Compute Thad's depreciation deductions for 2006 through 2008, the adjusted basis of the machine on October 5, 2008, and the gain or loss on the sale.

I10-33 *Sec. 179 Expensing Election and Mid-Quarter Convention.* Todd acquired two pieces of equipment for use in his business during the year as follows:

Item	Date Acquired	Recovery Period	Cost
Equipment A	April 2006	5-year	$208,000
Equipment B	November 2006	7-year	$208,000

Todd elects to expense $108,000 of the acquisition cost under Sec. 179. Assuming he wants to maximize the amount of depreciation for the year, compute Todd's depreciation in order to yield the highest depreciation possible. (Hint: The mid-quarter convention is calculated after taking Sec. 179 on any asset or assets.)

I10-34 *Straight-Line Depreciation.* Long Corporation has been unprofitable for several years and has substantial NOL carryovers. Therefore, the company policy has been to use the straight-line MACRS rules for property acquisitions. The following assets are acquired, held, or sold in 2006:

	Date Acquired	Date Sold	Original Cost Basis	Selling Price	Depreciation Method	Recovery Period (Years)
Equipment	6/1/06	—	$40,000	—	SL	7
Light duty truck	7/1/03	12/1/06	30,000	$12,000	SL	5
Furniture	3/1/04	—	10,000	—	SL	7
Automobile	7/1/04	12/1/06	12,000	10,000	SL	5

Assume the expensing election under Sec. 179 was not made in any year and no bonus depreciation was taken in 2003 and 2004.

a. What is the depreciation deduction for each asset in 2006?

b. What amount of gain or loss is recognized on the properties sold in 2006?

I10-35 *Mixed Personal/Business Use.* Trish, a self-employed CPA and calendar-year taxpayer, acquires an automobile and a personal computer in 2006. Pertinent data include the following:

Asset	Date Acquired	Total Original Cost Basis	Portion of Business Usage	Sec. 179 Election
Automobile	1/2/06	$21,000	60%	No
Personal computer	7/1/06	4,000	40%	No

For each asset, calculate the MACRS current year depreciation deduction.

I10-36 *Employee Listed Property.* Assume the same facts as in Problem I10-35, except that Trish is an employee and uses the automobile and personal computer on employment-related activities. While both assets are helpful to Trish in performing her job duties, her employer does not require employees to purchase a car or a personal computer as a condition of employment. What is the amount of depreciation for each asset?

I10-37 *Recapture of Depreciation Deductions Due to Personal Use.* Tammy acquires an automobile for $20,000 on July 1, 2004. She uses the automobile partially for business purposes during the 2004–2006 period. The percentage of business use is as follows: 2004, 70%, 2005, 70%; 2006, 40%. The automobile is 5-year recovery property and no Sec. 179 was elected. Tammy did elect 50% bonus depreciation in 2004.

a. What is the amount of the MACRS depreciation deduction for 2004? 2005? 2006?

b. What is the amount of recapture of previously claimed depreciation deductions (if any) that must take place in 2006?

I10-38 *Luxury Auto Limitations—2004 Acquistion.* Lutz Corporation acquires a luxury automobile on July 1, 2004 for $36,000 that is used 100% for business use. The Sec. 179 expensing election is not made but the company chooses to claim the maximum amount of MACRS depreciation deductions available, including the 50% bonus depreciation. What is the depreciation deduction amount for 2004, 2005, 2006, and any subsequent years?

I10-39 *Luxury Auto Limitations—2006 Acquistion.* Luby Corporation acquires a luxury automobile on July 1, 2006 for $36,000 that is used 100% for business use. The Sec. 179 expensing election is not made but the company otherwise desires to claim the maximum amount of MACRS depreciation. What is the depreciation deduction amount for 2006, 2007, and 2008?

I10-40 *Luxury Auto Limitations.* Tracy acquires a luxury automobile on March 1, 2006, that is used 80% of the time in his business and 20% of the time for personal use. The automobile cost $36,000, and no amounts are expensed under Sec. 179.

a. What is the depreciation amount for 2006–2008 and any subsequent years?

b. How would your answer change in a if the vehicle was a SUV with a gross vehicle weight rated (GVWR) of over 6,000 pounds and Tracy elected to expense the SUV under Sec. 179?

I10-41 *Luxury Auto Limitations—Leasing.* Troy enters into a 3-year lease of a luxury automobile on January 1, 2005, for use 80% in business and 20% for personal use. The FMV of the automobile at the inception of the lease is $40,500 and twelve monthly lease payments of $600 were made in 2005 and 2006.

a. What is the amount of lease payments that are deductible in 2005 and 2006?

b. What portion, if any, of the "inclusion amount" must be included in gross income in 2005 and 2006?

c. How would your answers to Parts a and b change if the FMV of the auto were instead $15,000 and the monthly lease payments were $200?

I10-42 *Goodwill.* On January 1 of the current year, Palm Corporation acquires the net assets of Vicki's unincorporated business for $600,000. The tangible net assets have a $300,000 book value and $400,000 FMV. The purchase agreement states that Vicki will not compete with Palm Corporation by starting a new business in the same area for a period of five years. The stated consideration received by Vicki for the covenant not to compete is $50,000. Other intangible assets included in the purchase agreement are as follows:

- Goodwill: $70,000

- Patents (12-year remaining legal life): $30,000
- Customer list: $50,000

a. How would Vicki's assets be recorded for tax purposes by Palm Corporation?
b. What is the amortization amount for each intangible asset in the current year?

I10-43 *R&E Expenditures.* Park Corporation incurs the following costs in the initial year of doing business:

Materials and supplies for research laboratory	$ 80,000
Utilities and depreciation on research laboratory and equipment	40,000
Costs of acquiring another person's patent for a new product	20,000
Market research salaries for surveys relative to proposed new products	60,000
Labor and supplies for quality control tests	50,000
Research costs subcontracted to a local university	35,000
Total	$285,000

Park's controller states that all of these costs are qualifying R&E expenditures and that the company policy is to expense such amounts for tax purposes in the year they are incurred. Which of these expenditures are deductible as R&E costs under Sec. 174?

I10-44 *R&E Expenditures.* In 2006, Phoenix Corporation acquires a new research facility and hires several scientists to develop new products. No new products are developed until 2007, although the following expenditures were incurred in 2006:

Laboratory materials	$ 40,000
Research salaries	80,000
Overhead attributable to the research facility	30,000
R&E equipment placed into service (5-year MACRS recovery period)	100,000
Total	$250,000

a. What is Phoenix Corporation's deduction for R&E expenditures in 2006 and 2007 if the expensing method is elected?
b. How would your answer to Part a change if the deferral and amortization method were elected and the amortization period were 60 months?

I10-45 *Computer Software.* The Phillips Corporation, a construction company that specializes in home construction, uses special computer software to schedule its jobs and keep track of job costs and uses generic software for bookkeeping and spreadsheet analysis. During 2006, Phillips Corporation had the following transactions relating to computer software:

- The corporation purchased a new computer system on May 12, 2006, for $15,000. The system included computer hardware and built-in computer software valued at $3,000. The corporation has never separated computer software from the hardware in prior years when a computer system was purchased.

- The corporation separately purchased new bookkeeping software on September 1, 2006, for $5,760.

- On June 1, 2006, Phillips Corporation acquired another home building company to strengthen its position in higher-priced homes. The total purchase price was $700,000 and the allocation to specific assets was as follows:

Equipment	$500,000
Goodwill	150,000
Computer software	50,000

What amount can the Phillips Corporation deduct in 2006 with respect to computer software?

I10-46 *Cost Depletion.* Tina acquires an oil and gas property interest for $200,000 in the current year. The following information about current year operations is supplied for purposes of computing the amount of Tina's depletion and IDC deductions:

Estimated recoverable units	20,000
Units produced	6,000
Units sold	4,000
IDCs	$20,000
Percentage depletion (after limitations)	$25,000

a. What is the cost depletion amount if the IDCs are expensed?
b. What is the cost depletion amount if the IDCs are capitalized?
c. How much depletion is deducted on the tax return?
d. Should the IDCs be capitalized or expensed? Explain.

I10-47 *Percentage Depletion.* Tony has owned an oil and gas property for a number of years. The following information is provided about the property's operations in the current year:

Gross income	$500,000
Minus: Expenses (including IDCs of $100,000)	(300,000)
Taxable income (before depletion)	$200,000
Cost depletion (if IDCs are expensed)	$ 20,000
Cost depletion (if IDCs are capitalized)	$ 30,000

a. What is the percentage depletion amount if the IDCs are expensed?
b. What is the percentage depletion amount if the IDCs are capitalized?
c. What is the depletion deduction amount assuming that the IDCs are expensed?
d. Based on the information above, which method should be used for the IDCs? Explain.

COMPREHENSIVE PROBLEM

I10-48 John and Ellen Brite (SSN 265-32-1497 and 571-07-7345, respectively) are married and file a joint return. John owns an unincorporated specialty electrical lighting retail store, Brite-On. Brite-On had the following assets on January 1, 2005:

Assets	*Cost*
Building purchased April 1, 1996	$100,000
7-year recovery period equipment purchased January 10, 2001	30,000
Inventory valued using FIFO method:	
Inventory: 4,000 light bulbs	$5/bulb

Brite-On purchased a competitor's store on March 1, 2005, for $107,000. The purchase price included the following:

	FMV
Store building	$60,000
Land	18,000
5-year recovery period equipment	11,000
Inventory: 3,000 light bulbs	$ 6/bulb

On June 30, 2005, Brite-On sold the 7-year recovery period equipment for $12,000. Brite-On leased a $30,000 car for $500/month beginning on January 1, 2005. The car is used 100% for business and the car was driven 14,000 miles during the year. Brite-On sold 8,000 light bulbs at $15/bulb during the year. Also, Brite-On made additional purchases of 4,000 light bulbs in August 2005 at $7/bulb. Brite-On had the following revenues (in addition to the sales of light bulbs) and additional expenses:

Service revenues	$64,000
Interest expense on business loans	4,000
Auto expenses (gas, oil, etc.)	3,800
Taxes and licenses	3,300
Utilities	2,800
Salaries	24,000

John and Ellen also had some personal expenses:

Medical bills	$4,500
Real property taxes	3,800
Home mortgage interest	9,000
Charitable contributions (cash)	600

They had interest income on a bank savings account of $275. John and Ellen made four $5,000 quarterly estimated tax payments. For self-employment tax purposes, assume John spent 100% of his time at the store while Ellen spends no time at the store.

Additional Facts:

- Assume that an election is made under Sec. 179 to expense the cost of the 5-year equipment that was acquired in 2005.
- The latest IRS lease inclusion table requires the Brites to include $67 in their gross income due to the leased automobile restrictions.

Compute the Brite's taxable income for 2005.

TAX STRATEGY PROBLEM

I10-49 Stan Bushart works as a customer representative for a large corporation. Stan's job entails traveling to meet with customers, and he uses his personal car 100% for business use. In 2005, Stan has decided to acquire a new car and is trying to decide whether to buy or lease the car. After bargaining with several car dealers, Stan has agreed to a price of $30,000 for the car. If he buys the car, he will borrow the entire $30,000 at an annual interest rate of 8% and pay monthly payments over 60 months. If he leases the car, his lease payment will be $450 per month for 60 months with a residual amount of $10,000 at the end of the lease. Therefore, Stan will pay the $450 each month for 60 months. At the end of the lease, he has the option of purchasing the car for $10,000. For income tax purposes, assume a lease inclusion amount of $350 per year and Stan's marginal income tax rate is 28%. From a financial standpoint, is Stan better off leasing or buying the car?

For purposes of your analysis, if Stan purchases the car, assume he sells the car for $10,000 at the end of five years. If he leases the car, assume he merely turns the car in at the end of the lease.

TAX FORM/RETURN PREPARATION PROBLEMS

I10-50 Thom Jones (SSN 277-31-7253) is an unincorporated manufacturer of widgets. He uses the LCM method to value his inventory and has the following transactions during the year 2005:

Sales (less returns and allowances)	$900,000
Cost of goods sold	500,000
Office expenses	10,000
Depreciation (including the Sec. 179 deduction (see the schedule below)	*Compute*
Legal services	4,000
Salary expenses	36,000
Travel expenses	30,000
Repairs	20,000

Mr. Jones's depreciation schedule is as follows:

Office furniture held for business use is purchased on April 15, 2005, and an election is made to expense the maximum amount possible under Sec. 179.	$130,000
Depreciation on other recovery property acquired and placed into service on August 1, 2005:	
5-year recovery period property (computers-not listed property)	6,000
7-year recovery period property (equipment)	14,000
Depreciation on assets purchased prior to 2005	28,000

Complete Form 4562 and Schedule C of Form 1040 for 2005 for Mr. Jones.

I10-51 Using the facts in Problem I10-48 for John and Ellen Brite, complete 2005 Form 1040, Schedules A, C, and SE, and Forms 4562 and 4797.

CASE STUDY PROBLEMS

I10-52 Able Corporation is a manufacturer of electrical lighting fixtures. Able is currently negotiating with Ralph Johnson, the owner of an unincorporated business, to acquire his retail electrical lighting sales business. Johnson's assets that are to be acquired include the following:

Assets	Adjusted Basis	FMV
Inventory of electrical fixtures	$ 30,000	$ 50,000
Store buildings	80,000	100,000
Land	40,000	100,000
Equipment: 7-year recovery period	30,000	50,000
Equipment: 5-year recovery period	60,000	100,000
Total	$240,000	$400,000

Mr. Johnson indicates that a total purchase price of $1,000,000 in cash is warranted for the business because of its high profitability and strategic locations and Able has agreed that the business is worth $1,000,000. Despite the fact that both parties attribute the excess payment to be for goodwill, Able would prefer that the $600,000 excess amount be designated as a 5-year covenant not to compete so that he can amortize the excess over a 5-year period.

You are a tax consultant for Able who has been asked to make recommendations as to the structuring of the purchase agreement and the amounts to be assigned to individual assets. Prepare a client memo to reflect your recommendations.

I10-53 The Margate Corporation acquired an automobile with an acquisition cost of $30,000 for use in its business in 2004. During this time, Margate Corporation was experiencing a seasonal decline in sales. Several employees were laid off and the automobile was not immediately needed for any of the sales personnel. Instead of letting the new automobile sit in the corporate lot, the president decided to permit a corporate officer to use the automobile for personal use. The officer used the automobile in 2004 and 2005 only. In 2006, Margate Corporation has hired you as their new CPA (tax consultant). You learn about the officer's personal use of the corporate automobile that took place for the two prior years without proper accounting of the automobile to the IRS. As Margate Corporation's tax consultant, what actions (if any) should you take regarding the proper treatment of the automobile? What are your responsibilities as a CPA regarding this matter under the rules of the AICPA's *SSTS* No. 6? (See the *Statements on Standards for Tax Services (SSTS)* section in Chapter I15 and Appendix E for a discussion of *SSTS* No. 6.)

TAX RESEARCH PROBLEM

I10-54 The Morriss Corporation is a very successful and profitable manufacturing corporation. The corporation just completed the construction of new corporate offices, primarily for its top executives. The president and founder of the corporation, Mr. Timothy Couch, is an avid collector of artwork and has instructed that the lobby and selected offices be decorated with rare collections of art. These expensive works of art were purchased by the corporation in accordance with Couch's directives. Couch justified the purchase of these artworks on the premise that (1) they are excellent investments and should increase in value in the future, (2) they provide an appropriate and impressive office atmosphere when current and prospective customers visit the corporation's offices, and (3) the artwork is depreciable property and the corporation will be able to take sizable writeoffs against its income. The Financial Vice-President of the corporation has requested your advice as to whether the works of art are, in fact, depreciable property. Prepare a research memorandum for the Financial Vice-President on this issue.

A partial list of research sources is provided below.

- *Rev. Rul. 68-232, 1968-1 C.B. 70*
- *Shauna C. Clinger, 60 T.C.M. 598 (1990).*
- *Simon v. Comr.,* 103 T.C. 247 (1994), *aff'd,* 95-2 USTC ¶50,552 (2d Cir. 1995) *nonacq.* 1996-2 C.B.I.
- *Liddle v. Comr.,* 103 T.C. 285 (1994), *aff'd,* 95-2 USTC ¶50,488 (3rd Cir. 1995)

11

CHAPTER

ACCOUNTING PERIODS AND METHODS

LEARNING OBJECTIVES

After studying this chapter, you should be able to

▶1 Explain the rules for adopting and changing an accounting period

▶2 Explain the differences among cash, accrual, and hybrid accounting

▶3 Determine whether specific costs must be included in inventory

▶4 Determine the amount of income to be reported from a long-term contract

▶5 Compute the gain to be reported from an installment sale

▶6 Compute the amount of imputed interest in a transaction

▶7 Determine the tax treatment of duplications and omissions that result from changes of accounting methods

An **accounting method** is a system of rules and procedures used to determine the year in which income and expenses are reported for tax purposes. The accounting methods used in computing income for tax purposes generally must be the same as those used in keeping the taxpayer's books and records and determine *when* income and expenses are reported, not whether they are reported. Although the accounting methods used by a taxpayer do not necessarily affect the amount of income reported over the life of a business, they do affect the tax burden in two ways. First, selecting the appropriate accounting method can accelerate deductions or defer income recognition in order to postpone tax payments, and second, because of the progressive tax rate structure, taxpayers can save taxes by spreading income over several accounting periods rather than having income bunched into one period.

EXAMPLE I11-1 ▶ Jane, a taxpayer using the cash method of accounting, has a 28% marginal tax rate for 2006 and expects to have a 15% marginal tax rate in 2007. Jane plans to make a charitable contribution of $1,000 in January 2007. A contribution in 2007 will reduce Jane's tax by $150 (0.15 × $1,000), whereas a contribution in 2006 will reduce Jane's tax by $280 (0.28 × $1,000). Obviously Jane may wish to accelerate the contribution in order to reduce her tax liability. ◀

ACCOUNTING PERIODS

OBJECTIVE 1

Explain the rules for adopting and changing an accounting period

Taxable income is computed on the basis of the taxpayer's annual **accounting period**, which is ordinarily 12 months (either a calendar year or a fiscal year). A **fiscal year** is a 12-month period that ends on the last day of any month other than December. The tax year must coincide with the year used to keep the taxpayer's books and records. Taxpayers who do not have books (e.g., an individual with wage income) must use the calendar year.[1] A taxpayer with a seasonal business may find a fiscal year to be advantageous. During the slow season, inventories may be lower and employees are available to take inventory and perform other accounting duties associated with the year-end. The tax year is elected on the first tax return that is filed by a taxpayer and cannot be changed without consent from the IRS.[2]

A partnership generally must use the same tax year of the partners who own the majority (greater than 50%) of partnership income and capital. If a majority of partners do not have the same year, the partnership must use the tax year of its principal partners (those with more than a 5% interest in the partnership). If the principal partners do not have the same tax year, the partnership must use the taxable year that results in the least aggregate deferral of income to the partners.[3] An exception is made for partnerships that can establish to the satisfaction of the IRS a business purpose for having a different year.

The purpose of the strict rules for selecting accounting periods is to prevent partners from deferring partnership income by choosing a different tax year for the partnership. For example, calendar-year partners might select a partnership year that ends on January 31. Because partnership income is considered to be earned by the partners on the last day of the partnership's tax year, reporting the profits would thus be deferred 11 months because the partnership year ends after the partner's year. (See the section entitled Required Payments and Fiscal Years in this chapter for further discussion of the calendar-year requirement.)

A similar rule generally requires S corporations and personal service corporations to adopt a calendar year unless the corporation has a business purpose for electing a fiscal year.[4] Taxpayers willing to make required payments or distributions may choose a fiscal year. (See the Required Payments and Fiscal Years section in this chapter.)

 STOP & THINK *Question:* The tax rules related to accounting periods essentially require most partnerships, S corporations, and personal service corporations to report on the calendar

---

[1] Sec. 441(g).
[2] Reg. Sec. 1.441-1(b)(4).

[3] Reg. Sec. 1.706-1(a)(3).
[4] Sec. 1378(a).

year basis. Of course, almost all individual taxpayers also report on the calendar year basis. What impact does this have on accountants?

Solution: The principal impact is a compression of tax compliance work into the "accounting busy season." A substantial portion of auditing and other accounting work also takes place shortly after the year-end. As a result, these services are also compressed into the accounting busy season. The accounting profession has sought to have these tax rules changed, but has, at least so far, been unsuccessful.

An improper election to use a fiscal year automatically places the taxpayer on the calendar year.[5] Thus, if the first return is filed late because of oversight, the option to choose a fiscal year is lost.

EXAMPLE I11-2 ▶ City Corporation receives its charter in 2004 but does not begin operations until 2006. Tax returns are required for 2004 and 2005 as well as for 2006. Timely returns are not filed because the City's officers are unaware that returns must be filed for inactive corporations. Thus, City Corporation must use the calendar year. City Corporation may petition the IRS for approval to use a fiscal year. ◀

ADDITIONAL COMMENT

The use of a 52–53-week year aids in budgetary matters and statistical comparisons because a four-week period, unlike a calendar month, is a uniform, fixed period.

REAL-WORLD EXAMPLE

Merrill Lynch & Company uses a 52–53-week year ending on the last Friday in December.

TYPICAL MISCONCEPTION

It is sometimes mistakenly believed that a tax year can end on a day in the middle of the month.

While most tax years end on the last day of a month, the tax law allows taxpayers to use a tax year that always ends on the same day of the week, such as the last Friday in October. This means that the tax years will vary in length between 52 and 53 weeks. Taxpayers who regularly keep their books over a period that varies from 52 to 53 weeks may elect the same period for tax purposes. A 52–53-week taxable year must end either the last time a particular day occurs during a calendar month (e.g., the last Friday in October) or the occurrence of the particular day that is closest to the end of a calendar month (e.g., the Saturday closest to the end of November).[6] Under the first alternative, the year may end as many as six days before the end of the month, but must end within the month. Under the second alternative, the year may end as many as three days before or after the end of the month.

The 52–53-week year is especially useful to businesses with inventories. For example, a manufacturer might choose a 52–53-week year that ends on the last Friday in December to permit inventory to be taken over the weekend without interfering with the company's manufacturing activity. Similarly, wage accruals would be eliminated for a company with a weekly payroll if the payroll period always ends on Friday.

Although the 52–53-week year may actually end on a day other than the last day of the month, it is treated as ending on the last day of the calendar month for "effective date" changes in the tax law that would otherwise coincide with the year-end.

EXAMPLE I11-3 ▶ Eagle Corporation has adopted a 52–53-week year. Eagle's tax year begins on December 29, 2006. Assume that a new tax rate schedule applies to tax years beginning after December 31, 2006. The new tax rate schedule is applicable to Eagle because, in the absence of the 52–53-week year, its tax period would have started on January 1, 2007. ◀

REQUIRED PAYMENTS AND FISCAL YEARS

Virtually all C corporations (other than personal service corporations) have flexibility in choosing an accounting period. Other taxpayers, such as partnerships and S corporations, may use a fiscal year if they have an acceptable business purpose. However, most of these businesses are unable to meet the rather rigid business purpose requirements outlined by the IRS. As a result, these businesses report using the calendar year concentrating most tax work during the early months of the year. Concern over this problem led Congress to enact Sec. 444 which allows partnerships, S corporations, and personal service corporations (such as incorporated medical practices) to elect a taxable year that results in a tax deferral of three months or less (e.g., a partnership with calendar-year partners may elect a September 30 year-end). This is called the **Sec. 444 election**. Furthermore, partnerships,

---

[5] *Q.A. Calhoun v. U.S.*, 33 AFTR 2d 74-305, 74-1 USTC ¶9104 (D.C. Va., 1973).   [6] Sec. 441(f).

S corporations, and personal service corporations may continue using the fiscal year they were using when the current law was passed in 1986 even if that fiscal year results in a deferral beyond three months.

Partnerships and S corporations making the Sec. 444 election, however, must make annual required payments by April 15 of the following year. The purpose of the required payment is to offset the tax deferral advantage obtained when fiscal years are used.

The amount of the required payment is determined by multiplying the maximum tax rate for individuals plus 1% (i.e., 36% in 2006) times the previous year's taxable income times a deferral ratio.[7] The deferral ratio is equal to the number of months in the deferral period divided by the number of months in the taxable year. An adjustment is made for deductible amounts distributed to the owners during the year. If the amount due is $500 or less, no payment is required.

ADDITIONAL COMMENT

The American Institute of Certified Public Accountants and accounting firms lobbied extensively for the provision that permits partnerships, S corporations, and personal service corporations to continue to use a fiscal year if annual required payments are made.

EXAMPLE I11-4 ▶

ABC Partnership begins operations on October 1, 2006, and elects a September 30 year-end under Sec. 444. The partnership's net income for the fiscal year ended September 30, 2007, is $100,000. ABC must make a required payment of $9,000 ($100,000 × 36% × 3/12) on or before April 15, 2008. ◀

The owners of businesses making such payments do not claim a credit for the amount paid. Instead, the partnership or S Corporation subtracts the previous year's required payment from the current year's required payment. If the result is negative, then the entity is entitled to a refund.

EXAMPLE I11-5 ▶

Assume the same facts as in Example I11-14 except that ABC Partnership's required payment for the year ended September 30, 2008 is $6,000. ABC is entitled to a refund of the difference of $3,000 ($9,000 − $6,000). ◀

Personal service corporations also may elect a fiscal year. However, deductions to shareholder/employees may be limited if distributions to such shareholder/employees during the deferral period do not exceed a minimum amount.[8] Personal service corporations are incorporated medical practices and other similar businesses owned by individuals who provide their services through the corporation. In general, the rules prevent a distribution pattern that creates a tax deferral. This is achieved by requiring that the deductible payments made to owners during the deferral period be at a rate no lower than during the previous fiscal year.

EXAMPLE I11-6 ▶

Austin, Inc., is a personal service corporation of attorneys with a fiscal year ending September 30. For the year ended September 30, 2006 the company earned a profit of $480,000 before any salary payments to the owners. The entire profit, however, was paid out as wages to the owners, resulting in a taxable income of zero. To avoid any deduction limitation, Austin must pay salaries to its owners of no less than $120,000 ($480,000 × 3/12) during the period October 1, 2006, to December 31, 2006. If less than $120,000 is paid during this deferral period, deductions are limited for the year ended September 30, 2007. ◀

An option allows personal service corporations to compute the amount of the minimum distribution by using a three-year average of income and distributions.

CHANGES IN THE ACCOUNTING PERIOD

KEY POINT

The use of a natural business year helps in the matching of revenue and expense because the business is normally in a maximum state of liquidity and the problems associated with making estimates involving uncompleted transactions are reduced to a minimum.

Once adopted, an accounting period cannot normally be changed without approval of the IRS.[9] The IRS will usually approve a change only if the taxpayer can establish a substantial business purpose for the change (e.g., changing to a natural business year).[10] A natural business year ends at or soon after the peak income earning period (e.g., the natural business year for a department store that has a seasonal holiday business may be on January 31). A business without a peak income period may not be able to establish a natural business year and may, therefore, be precluded from changing its tax year. In general,

---

[7] Sec. 7519(b).
[8] Sec. 280H(a).

[9] Sec. 442.
[10] Rev. Proc. 74-33, 1974-2 C.B. 489 and Rev. Proc. 87-32, 1989-2 C.B. 32.

at least 25% of revenues must occur during the last two months of the year in order to qualify as a natural business year.

EXAMPLE I11-7 ▶ USA Department Store's sales reach their peak during the holiday season in December. During January the department store further reduces its inventory through storewide clearance sales. USA elects a "natural" business year-end of January 31 because its inventory levels are lowest at the end of January. Also, USA meets the prescribed test because at least 25% of its revenues for the year occur in December and January. ◀

In a few instances IRS approval is not required to change to another accounting period.

REAL-WORLD EXAMPLE

J.C. Penney, Kmart, and Wal-Mart all use an accounting period ending January 31.

▶ A newly married person may change tax years to conform to that of his or her spouse so that a joint return may be filed. The election must be made in either the first or second year after the marriage date.[11]

▶ A change to a 52–53-week year that ends with reference to the same calendar month in which the former tax year ended.[12]

▶ A taxpayer who erroneously files tax returns using an accounting period other than that on which his or her books are kept is not required to obtain permission to file returns for later years based on the way the books are kept.[13]

▶ A corporation meeting the following specified conditions may change without IRS approval: (1) There has been no change in its accounting period within the past ten calendar years, (2) the resulting year does not have a net operating loss (NOL), (3) the taxable income for the resulting short tax year when annualized is at least 90% of the taxable income for the preceding full tax year, and (4) there is no change in status of the corporation (such as an S corporation election).[14]

▶ An existing partnership can change its tax year without prior approval if the partners with a majority interest have the same tax year to which the partnership changes or if all principal partners who do not have such a tax year concurrently change to such a tax year.[15]

There is one instance, however, when a change in tax years is required: A subsidiary corporation filing a consolidated return with its parent corporation must change its accounting period to conform with its parent's tax year.

Application for permission to change accounting periods is made on Form 1128, Application for Change in Accounting Period, on or before the due date of the return including extensions. The application must be sent to the Commissioner of the IRS, Washington, D.C.

The IRS may establish certain conditions for the taxpayer to meet before it approves the change to a new tax year. For example, the IRS has ruled that if the short period that results from a change involves a NOL greater than $50,000, the taxpayer may have to forgo a carryback of the loss.[16]

RETURNS FOR PERIODS OF LESS THAN 12 MONTHS

Most income tax returns cover an accounting period of 12 months. On two occasions, however, a taxpayer's accounting period may be less than 12 months: when the taxpayer's first or final return is filed and when the taxpayer changes accounting periods.

Taxpayers filing an initial tax return and executors filing a taxpayer's final return or corporations filing their last return are not required to annualize the year's income, nor are personal exemptions or tax credits prorated. These returns are prepared and filed, and taxes are paid as though they are returns for a 12-month period ending on the last day of

[11] Reg. Sec. 1.442-1(e). A statement should be attached to the resulting short period return indicating that the change is being made.
[12] Reg. Sec. 1.441-2(c)(2). A statement should be attached to the first return filed under the election indicating that the change is being made.
[13] Rev. Rul. 58-256, 1959-1 C.B. 215.

[14] Reg. Sec. 1.442-1(c). A statement should be attached to the return indicating that each condition is met.
[15] Reg. Sec. 1.442-1(b)(2).
[16] Rev. Proc. 2000-11, 2000-1 C.B. 309.

the short period. An exception permits the final return of a decedent to be filed as though the decedent lived throughout the entire tax year.[17]

EXAMPLE I11-8 ▶ ABC Partnership, which has filed its returns on a calendar-year basis, terminates on June 30, 2006. ABC's final return is due on October 15, 2006. ◀

EXAMPLE I11-9 ▶ Joy, a single individual who has filed her returns on a calendar-year basis, dies on June 30, 2006. Joy's final return is due on April 15, 2007. ◀

Taxpayers who change from one accounting period to another must annualize their income for the resulting short period. This prevents income earned during the resulting short period from being taxed at lower rates. Income is annualized as follows:

1. Determine modified taxable income. Individuals must compute their taxable income for the short period by itemizing their deductions (i.e., the standard deduction is not allowed) and personal and dependency exemptions must be prorated.[18]
2. Multiply modified taxable income by the following fraction:

$$\frac{12}{\text{Number of months in short period}}$$

3. Compute the tax on the resulting taxable income using the appropriate tax rate schedule.
4. Multiply the resulting tax by the following fraction:

$$\frac{\text{Number of months in short period}}{12}$$

EXAMPLE I11-10 ▶ Pat, a single taxpayer, obtains permission to change from a calendar year to a fiscal year ending on June 30, 2006. During the six months ending June 30, 2006, Pat earns $25,000 and has $5,000 in itemized deductions.[19]

Gross Income	$25,000
Minus: Itemized deductions	(5,000)
Personal exemption [(6 ÷ 12) × $3,300]	(1,650)
Modified taxable income	$18,350
Annualized income [(12 ÷ 6) × $18,350]	$36,700
Tax on annualized income	$ 5,733
Current tax [(6 ÷ 12) × $5,733]	$ 2,866 ◀

Topic Review I11-1 summarizes the available accounting periods and the rules for changing accounting periods.

 STOP & THINK *Question:* Why are taxpayers required to annualize when they change tax years? What provision of the tax law creates this need?

Solution: A change of tax years results in a shortened filing period during the period the change takes place. For example, a taxpayer who changes from a calendar year to a June 30 year-end reports income for only a 6-month period on the first return following the change. Less income is reported, and that income would be taxed at lower rates without annualization. Annualization is necessary because of the progressive tax rate structure.

---

[17] Reg. Sec. 1.443-1(a)(2).
[18] The exemptions are prorated as follows: exemptions × (number of months in the short period ÷ 12).
[19] An alternative method to compute the tax is provided in Sec. 443(b)(2) and

Reg. Sec. 1.443-1(b)(2) whereby the taxpayer can elect to compute the tax for a 12-month period beginning on the first day of the short period and then convert the tax to a short-period tax.

Topic Review I11-1

Accounting Periods and Changes

AVAILABLE YEARS

▶ Available tax years include the calendar year, a fiscal year (a year that ends on the last day of any month other than December), and a 52–53-week year (a year that always ends on the same day of the week).

▶ A partnership must use the tax year of its partners unless the partnership can establish a satisfactory business purpose for having a different year or if the partnership makes required payments.

▶ Similar rules generally require S corporations and personal service corporations to adopt a calendar year unless the corporation has a business purpose for electing a fiscal year. Taxpayers willing to make required payments or distributions may choose a fiscal year ending on September 30, October 31, or November 30.

CHANGE IN ACCOUNTING PERIODS

▶ Once adopted, an accounting period normally cannot be changed without approval by the IRS. The IRS is more likely to approve a change to a natural business year. In general, at least 25% of revenues must occur during the last two months of the year in order to qualify as a natural business year.

▶ Taxpayers who change from one accounting period to another must annualize their income for the resulting short period. This prevents income earned during the resulting short period from being taxed at lower rates.

OVERALL ACCOUNTING METHODS

OBJECTIVE 2

Explain the differences among cash, accrual, and hybrid accounting

A taxpayer's method of accounting determines the year in which income is reported and expenses are deducted. Taxable income must be computed using the method of accounting regularly used by the taxpayer in keeping his or her books if that method clearly reflects income.[20] Permissible overall accounting methods are

▶ Cash receipts and disbursements method (often called the cash method of accounting)

▶ Accrual method

▶ A combination of the first two methods, often called the hybrid method

KEY POINT

The Code provides the IRS with broad powers in ascertaining whether the taxpayer's accounting method clearly reflects income. It entitles the IRS to more than the usual presumption of correctness.

New taxpayers may generally choose any of the accounting methods listed above. However, the accrual method must be used for sales and cost of goods sold if inventories are an income-producing factor to the business. Exceptions permit businesses with inventories to use the cash method if their average annual gross receipts for the three preceding years do not exceed $1 million ($10 million if the taxpayer's principal business is not the sale of inventory).[21] The fact that an overall accounting method is used in one trade or business does not mean that the same method must be used in a second trade or business or for nonbusiness income and deductions.

EXAMPLE I11-11 ▶

Troy, a practicing CPA, also owns an appliance store. The fact that Troy uses the accrual method of reporting income from the appliance store, where inventories are an income-producing factor, does not preclude Troy from using the cash method to report income from his service-based accounting practice. Troy could also use the cash method for reporting nonbusiness income (such as dividends) and nonbusiness expenses (such as itemized deductions). ◀

REAL-WORLD EXAMPLE

It has been held that the cash method of accounting can be used where inventories are inconsequential. *Michael Drazen,* 34 T.C. 1070 (1960).

The term *method of accounting* is used to include not only overall methods of accounting listed above but also the accounting treatment of any item.[22]

CASH RECEIPTS AND DISBURSEMENTS METHOD

Most individuals and service businesses use the cash receipts and disbursements method of accounting. Taxpayers cannot use the cash method in a business for sales and cost of goods

---

[20] Sec. 446.
[21] Rev. Proc. 2000-22, 2000-1 C.B. 1008. This Revenue Procedure has been modified and superseded by Rev. Proc. 2001-10, 2001-1 C.B. 272 and Rev. Proc. 2002-28, 2002-1 C.B. 815.

[22] Reg. Sec. 1.446-1(a)(1). Examples of accounting methods for specific items include Sec. 174, relating to research and experimentation expenses; Sec. 451, relating to reporting income from long-term contracts; and Sec. 453, relating to reporting income from installment sales.

sold if inventories are an income-producing factor.[23] However, as noted above, businesses with inventories are permitted to use the cash method if their average annual gross receipts for the three preceding tax years do not exceed $1 million ($10 million if the taxpayer's principal business is not the sale of inventory). However, C corporations and partnerships with a corporate partner may use the cash method only if their average annual gross receipts for the three preceding tax years do not exceed $5 million or if the business meets the requirements associated with providing personal services (i.e., if it is owned by professionals who are using the business to provide professional services).[24] Thus, a law or accounting firm can use the cash method even if its average receipts exceed $5 million. However, other C corporations with greater than $5 million average gross receipts must use the accrual method even if they have no inventory.

Under the cash receipts and disbursements method of accounting, a taxpayer is required to report income for the tax year in which payments are actually or constructively received. While it might seem that receipts under the cash method of accounting should only be recognized if the taxpayer receives cash, this is not the case. The Regulations clearly provide that gross income under the cash method includes cash, property, or services.[25] Thus, if a CPA accepts a set of golf clubs as payment from a client for services rendered, the CPA must include the fair market value of the golf clubs in his gross income. However, an accounts receivable or other unsupported promise to pay is considered to have no value and, as a result, no income is recognized until the receivable is collected. Expenses are deducted in the year paid. Because the recognition of expense is measured by the flow of cash, a taxpayer can determine the year in which an expense is deductible by choosing when to make the payment. Individual taxpayers do not have the same opportunity to determine the year in which income is recognized, because the constructive receipt rule requires taxpayers to recognize income if a payment is available, even if actual payment has not been received. (See Chapter I3 for a discussion of constructive receipt.)

KEY POINT

A taxpayer using the cash method is entitled to certain deductions that do not involve current year cash disbursements, such as depreciation, depletion, and losses.

CAPITALIZATION REQUIREMENTS FOR CASH-METHOD TAXPAYERS. Taxpayers who use the cash receipts and disbursements method are required to capitalize fixed assets and to recover the cost through depreciation or amortization. The Regulations state that prepaid expenses must be capitalized and deducted over the life of the asset if the life of the asset extends substantially beyond the end of the tax year.[26] Typically, capitalization is required only if the life of the asset extends beyond the close of the tax year following the year of payment.[27]

EXAMPLE I11-12 ▶

On July 1, 2006, Acme Corporation, a cash basis, calendar-year taxpayer, pays an insurance premium of $3,000 for a policy that is effective July 1, 2006, to June 30, 2007. The full $3,000 is deductible in 2006. ◀

EXAMPLE I11-13 ▶

Assume the same facts as in Example I11-12, except that the premium covers a three-year period beginning July 1, 2006, and ending June 30, 2009. Acme Corporation may deduct $500 in 2006, $1,000 in 2007 and 2008, and $500 in 2009. ◀

One notable exception to the one-year rule denies a deduction for prepaid interest. Cash-method taxpayers must capitalize such amounts and allocate interest over the prepayment period. A special rule allows homeowners to deduct points paid on a mortgage used to buy or improve a personal residence. The payment must be an established business practice in the area and not exceed amounts generally charged for such home loans. (See Chapter I7 for a discussion of the deductibility of points.)

To be deductible, a payment must be more than just a refundable deposit. A taxpayer who has an option of cancelling delivery and receiving a refund of amounts prepaid is not normally entitled to deduct the amount of the deposit.

---

[23] Reg. Sec. 1.471-1. However, Sec. 448(b) permits farmers to use the cash method even though they have inventories. Sec. 448(a) denies tax shelters the right to use the cash method even if they do not have inventories.
[24] Secs. 448(b) and (c).

[25] Reg. Sec. 1.446-1(c)(1)(i).
[26] Reg. Sec. 1.461-1(a)(1).
[27] *Bonaire Development Co.*, 76 T.C. 789 (1981), and *Martin J. Zaninovich v. CIR*, 45 AFTR 2d 80-1442, 80-1 USTC ¶9342 (9th Cir., 1980).

Payments can be made either by a check that is honored in due course or by the use of a credit card.[28] Payment by credit card is considered to be the equivalent of borrowing funds to pay the expense. However, a taxpayer's note is not the equivalent of cash, so if a cash method taxpayer gives a note in payment, he or she cannot take the deduction until the note is paid, even if the note is secured by collateral.[29]

ACCRUAL METHOD

There are two tests used to determine when an item of income must be reported or an expense deducted: the **all-events test** and the **economic performance test**.

ADDITIONAL COMMENT

The phrase *reasonable accuracy* means that approximate amounts are ascertainable. Although the word *accuracy* means exactness or precision, when it is used with the word *reasonable* it implies something less than an exact amount.

ALL-EVENTS TEST. An accrual-method taxpayer reports an item of income when "all events" have occurred that fix the taxpayer's right to receive the item of income and the amount can be determined with reasonable accuracy.[30] Similarly, an expense is deductible when all events have occurred that establish the fact of the liability and the amount of the expense can be determined with reasonable accuracy. For deductions, the all-events test is not satisfied until economic performance has taken place.

ECONOMIC PERFORMANCE TEST. Economic performance (of services or property to be provided to a taxpayer) occurs when the property or services are actually provided by the other party.

EXAMPLE I11-14 ▶ The owner of a professional football team provides medical benefits for injured players through insurance coverage. Economic performance occurs over the term of the policy rather than when the team enters into a binding contract with the insurance company or during the season when the player earns the right to medical benefits. Thus, a one-year premium is deductible over the year of the insurance coverage rather than over the term of the player's contract under which the benefit is earned. But see below for a possible waiver. ◀

Similarly, if a taxpayer is obligated to provide property or services, economic performance occurs in the year the taxpayer provides the property or service.

EXAMPLE I11-15 ▶ Assume the same facts as in Example I11-14 except that medical benefits are required under the terms of a player's contract. Also, the team decides to pay medical costs directly. Economic performance occurs as the team actually provides the benefits. Thus, the deduction is permitted only as medical care is provided. ◀

REAL-WORLD EXAMPLE

Before the economic performance test was added to the tax law, a company engaged in strip mining coal was able to deduct the future land reclamation costs as the coal was mined because the liability was certain and the cost could be estimated. *Ohio River Collieries*, 77 T.C. 1369 (1981).

The requirement that economic performance take place before a deduction is allowed is waived if all of the following five conditions are met:

▶ The all-events test, without regard to economic performance, is satisfied.

▶ Economic performance occurs within a reasonable period (but in no event more than 8½ months) after the close of the tax year.

▶ The item is recurring in nature, and the taxpayer consistently treats items of the same type as incurred in the tax year in which the all-events test is met.

▶ The taxpayer is not a tax shelter.

▶ Either the amount is not material or the earlier accrual of the item results in a better matching of income and expense.[31]

EXAMPLE I11-16 ▶ Bass Corporation, a calendar year taxpayer, pays its annual insurance premium each year on April 30, the anniversary of the policy. The premium paid this year is $6,000 while last year's premium was $5,400. Accrual accounting indicates that Bass deduct $4,000 ($8/12 \times$ $6,000) of the premium paid this year along with $1,800 ($4/12 \times$ $5,400) of the premium paid last year, or a total of $5,800. As all of the conditions for the exception to the economic performance requirements are met, Bass Corporation can deduct $6,000 this year. This assumes that Bass has been consistently following the practice and deducted $5,400 last year. ◀

[28] Rev. Rul. 78-39, 1978-1 C.B. 73.
[29] *Frank D. Quinn Exec. v. CIR*, 24 AFTR 927, 40-1 USTC ¶9403 (5th Cir., 1940).
[30] Reg. Sec. 1.451-1(a). See Chapter I3 for a discussion of the all-events test as it applies to gross income.
[31] Sec. 461(h).

TYPICAL MISCONCEPTION

It is sometimes mistakenly believed that taxpayers can deduct warranty expenses and bad debts using the allowance method instead of the direct write-off method.

Reserves for items such as product warranty expense and uncollectible accounts are commonly encountered in financial accounting. The all-events and economic performance tests prevent the use of such reserves for tax purposes. This is because the amount of such expense is not usually determinable with sufficient accuracy.

HYBRID METHOD

Taxpayers may use a combination of accounting methods as long as income is clearly reflected. Taxpayers with inventories are required to use the accrual method to report sales and purchases if their average gross receipts for the three preceding years exceeds $1 million ($10 million if the taxpayer's principal business is not the sale of inventory). These taxpayers may use the cash method to report other items of income and expense. To ensure that income is clearly reflected, certain restrictions have been placed on combining accounting methods.

KEY POINT

A taxpayer who uses the cash method in computing gross income from his or her business must use the cash method in computing expenses of such business.

Taxpayers who use the cash method of accounting in determining gross income from a trade or business must use the cash method for determining expenses of the same trade or business. Similarly, taxpayers who use the accrual method of accounting for expenses must use the accrual method in computing gross income from the trade or business.

The basic rules relating to accounting methods, the all-events test, and economic performance are summarized in Topic Review I11-2.

STOP & THINK

Question: If an accountant does tax work for an automobile dealer, in exchange for free use of an automobile, does the accountant have to report any income? Does it make a difference whether the accountant uses the automobile in her business? When is any taxable income reported?

Solution: The rental value of the automobile must be included in gross income. If the automobile is used in the accountant's business, a portion of the rental value is deductible as a business expense. Although it is not entirely clear, it seems that an accrual basis accountant would report income as tax services are provided to the dealer. A cash basis taxpayer would report income over the time the automobile is used.

Topic Review I11-2

Accounting Methods

AVAILABLE METHODS

▶ Permissible overall accounting methods are the cash receipts and disbursements method, the accrual method, and the hybrid method.

▶ The cash method is available to taxpayers without inventories and to taxpayers with inventories whose average gross receipts during the three preceding years was $1 million or less ($10 million if the taxpayer's principal business is not the sale of inventory). C corporations whose average gross receipts fall between $1 and $5 million thresholds may use the cash method if they do not have inventories. C corporations (other than personal service corporations) may not use the cash method if their average gross receipts in the three preceding tax years exceed $5 million.

ALL-EVENTS TEST AND ECONOMIC PERFORMANCE TEST

▶ An accrual-method taxpayer reports an item of income when all events have occurred that fix the taxpayer's right to receive the item of income and when the amount of the item can be determined with reasonable accuracy.

▶ An expense is deductible when all events have occurred that establish that there is a liability and when the amount of the expense can be determined with reasonable accuracy. The all-events test is not satisfied until economic performance has taken place.

▶ Economic performance takes place when property or services are actually provided.

INVENTORIES

Determine whether specific costs must be included in inventory

KEY POINT

Taxpayers cannot always use inventory methods for tax purposes that conform with generally accepted accounting principles.

In general, manufacturing and merchandising companies are required to use the accrual method of accounting for purchases and sales of merchandise. The inventory method used by a taxpayer must conform to the best accounting practice in the trade or business, and it must clearly reflect income. However, best accounting practices (synonymous with generally accepted accounting principles) and clear reflection of income (which is determined by the IRS) occasionally conflict. The Supreme Court has held that the standard of clear reflection of income prevails in a case where the two standards conflict. In the *Thor Power Tool Co.* case, the company wrote off the cost of obsolete parts for both tax and financial accounting purposes even though the parts were kept on hand and their selling price was not reduced.[32] Regulation Sec. 1.471-4(b) states that obsolete or other slow-moving inventory cannot be written down unless the selling price is also reduced.

Although the company's practice conformed with generally accepted accounting principles, it did not, according to the Supreme Court, clearly reflect income. Hence, generally accepted accounting principles are used only when the Regulations do not specify the treatment of an item or, alternatively, when the Regulations provide more than one alternative accounting method.

Taxpayers who value inventory at cost may write down goods that are not salable at their normal price (e.g., damaged, obsolete, or shopworn goods) only after the selling price has been reduced. Items may be valued at a bona fide selling price reduced by the direct cost of disposal.[33] The option to write down this type of merchandise is available even if the taxpayers use the LIFO inventory method.

EXAMPLE I11-17 ▶

KEY POINT

The uniform capitalization rules, included in the Tax Reform Act of 1986, require the capitalization of significant overhead costs that previously were expensed.

Stone Corporation publishes books for small academic audiences in Sanskrit and other ancient languages. There is typically one printing of a few hundred or perhaps a thousand copies of each book. Stone may sell a few copies a year of each book. Only after several years can the Corporation determine whether they will ever sell all copies of a given work. Based upon the *Thor Power Tool Co.* case, Stone Corporation cannot write off unsold copies unless they are destroyed or otherwise disposed of, and they cannot write down unsold copies unless the selling price is reduced below cost. ◀

DETERMINATION OF INVENTORY COST

Inventories may be valued at either cost or at the lower of cost or market value. Taxpayers who use the LIFO inventory valuation method (discussed later in this chapter) may not use the lower of cost or market method. In the case of merchandise purchased, cost is the invoice price less trade discounts, plus freight and other handling charges.

ETHICAL POINT

The UNICAP rules must be followed by taxpayers. To bring a business into compliance with these rules, the taxpayer may need to make certain estimates. SRTP No. 4 provides that a CPA may use a client's estimates if such use is generally acceptable or if it is impractical to obtain exact data. If a change in the overhead application rate is contemplated, it may be desirable to request IRS approval.

Unlike financial accounting, purchasing costs (e.g., salaries of purchasing agents), warehousing costs, packaging, and administrative costs related to these functions must be allocated between cost of goods sold and inventory. The costs that must be included in inventory are found in Sec. 263A and are referred to as the Uniform Capitalization rules (UNICAP). This requirement is applicable only to taxpayers whose average gross receipts for the three preceding years exceed $10 million.[34]

In the case of goods manufactured by the taxpayer, cost is determined by using the UNICAP rules, which may be thought of as an expanded version of the full absorption costing method. Thus, direct costing and prime costing are not acceptable inventory methods. Direct labor and materials along with manufacturing overhead must be included in inventory. Under UNICAP, the following overhead items are included in inventory:

▶ Factory repairs and maintenance, utilities, rent, insurance, small tools, and depreciation (including the excess of tax depreciation over accounting depreciation)

▶ Factory administration and officers' salaries related to production

▶ Taxes (other than the income tax)

---

[32] *Thor Power Tool Co. v. CIR*, 43 AFTR 2d 79-362, 79-1 USTC ¶9139 (USSC, 1979).

[33] Reg. Sec. 1.471-2(c).
[34] Sec. 263A(b)(2)(B).

▶ Quality control and inspection

▶ Rework, scrap, and spoilage

▶ Current and past service costs of pension and profit-sharing plans

▶ Service support such as purchasing, payroll, and warehousing costs

Nonmanufacturing costs (e.g., advertising, selling, and research and experimental costs) are not required to be included in inventory. Interest must be inventoried if the property is real property, long-lived property, or property requiring more than two years (one year in the case of property costing more than $1 million) to produce.

KEY POINT

Identifying the appropriate additional overhead costs to capitalize can be confusing and extremely time consuming.

The main difference between full absorption costing traditionally used for financial reporting purposes and UNICAP costing required for tax purposes is that UNICAP expands the list of overhead costs to include certain indirect costs that have not always been included in overhead for financial reporting purposes. For example, for financial reporting purposes, the costs of operating payroll and personnel departments have sometimes been considered sufficiently indirect or remote to justify omitting them from manufacturing overhead. This is true even though much of the effort of the payroll and personnel departments may be directed toward manufacturing operations. For simplicity and other reasons, overhead costs included in inventory for financial purposes are often limited to those incurred in the factory. UNICAP requires that costs associated with these departments be allocated between manufacturing and nonmanufacturing functions (e.g., sales, advertising, research and experimentation).

EXAMPLE I11-18 ▶

Best Corporation manufactures traditional style rocking chairs in a small factory with 34 employees. The office staff consists of four employees who handle payroll, receivables, hiring, and other office responsibilities. The sales staff includes three employees who travel the region selling to furniture and craft stores. The remaining 27 employees all work in the factory. Under UNICAP, factory costs including the wages of the 27 factory workers are generally all manufacturing costs. The costs associated with the sales staff are not manufacturing costs. This would include their compensation along with related costs such as travel. Office expenses including the wages paid to the four office workers can be allocated between manufacturing overhead and sales. Reasonable allocation methods are acceptable. One possibility might be to allocate office overhead between sales and manufacturing on a basis as simple as the number of employees in sales (3) and the number in manufacturing (27). Thus, 90% of the cost of the office operation could be treated as manufacturing-related and 10% sales-related. In such case, 90% of the office expenses would be allocated to manufacturing and 10% deducted as a period cost (i.e., selling expenses). The office expenses allocated to manufacturing would in turn be allocated between cost of sales and ending inventory. This allocation could be done on a basis as simple as multiplying the allocated office expenses by the number of chairs in ending inventory and dividing by the total number of chairs made during the year. ◀

A manufacturer may use standard costs to value inventory if any significant variance is reallocated pro rata to ending inventory and cost of goods sold.[35] Taxpayers may determine inventory costs by the following methods: specific identification method; first-in, first-out method (FIFO); last-in, first-out method (LIFO); or average cost method. A few taxpayers, such as an automobile or large appliance dealer, may find it practical to determine the specific cost of items in inventory. Most taxpayers, however, must rely on a flow of goods assumption (e.g., FIFO or LIFO). A discussion of the LIFO method is presented below.

LIFO METHOD. Many taxpayers use the LIFO cost flow assumption because, during inflationary periods, LIFO normally results in the lowest inventory value and hence the lowest taxable income. Once LIFO has been elected for tax purposes, the taxpayer's financial reports must also be prepared using LIFO.[36] This requirement to conform financial reporting often discourages companies from electing LIFO because lower earnings must be reported to shareholders. However, taxpayers may make footnote disclosure of the amount

---

[35] Reg. Sec. 1.471-11(d)(3).   [36] Sec. 472(c).

of net income that would have been reported under FIFO or other inventory methods.[37] Taxpayers may adopt LIFO by attaching a completed Form 970 (or by a statement acceptable to the IRS) to the return for the tax year in which the method is first used.

STOP & THINK

Question: As noted, many publicly held companies do not use LIFO inventory valuation. This is, in part, attributed to the fact that LIFO ordinarily results in lower reported income for accounting purposes than FIFO, and management prefers to report higher profits. Many small, closely-held companies also use FIFO even though their earnings are not reported to the public. Why wouldn't closely-held companies use LIFO?

Solution: There are a variety of reasons. Some businesses are very interested in how their financial statements look to banks and other lenders and to potential investors. In some industries, such as electronics, FIFO may actually provide lower inventory values. Also, LIFO cannot be used with lower of cost or market. As a result, some businesses may elect FIFO to be eligible to use lower of cost or market.

Perhaps, however, the main reason is that LIFO is more complex, and small businesses prefer to simplify their accounting. The advent of computers, accounting software, and bar codes may be having some impact on inventory valuation choices. Nevertheless, many accounting packages only track units on hand and sales revenue. They do not track inventory value (cost). Thus, the company must assign a value to inventory at year-end, and the complexity of LIFO remains a deterrent.

REAL-WORLD EXAMPLE

An automobile dealer, using the dollar-value LIFO method in maintaining its inventory, was required to use one pool for new automobiles and a separate pool for new trucks. *Fox Chevrolet, Inc.,* 76 T.C. 708 (1981).

Recordkeeping under LIFO can be cumbersome. For this reason, taxpayers are permitted to determine inventories using "dollar-value" pools and government price indexes rather than by maintaining a record of actual costs.[38] Retailers use appropriate categories in the Consumer Price Index; other taxpayers use categories in the Producer Price Index. Taxpayers using the index method must divide their inventories into one or more pools (groups of similar items). Thus, a department store might create separate pools for automobile parts, appliances, clothing, furniture, and other products. Dividing inventory into pools can be critical because of the different inflation rates associated with various goods and because, if a particular pool is depleted, the taxpayer loses the right to use the lower prices associated with past layers. An important exception permits taxpayers with average annual gross receipts of $5 million or less for the current and two preceding tax years to use the **simplified LIFO method**.[39] The simplified LIFO method uses a single LIFO pool, thereby avoiding problems with multiple pools.

EXAMPLE I11-19 ▶ In 2006, King Department Store changes its inventory method from FIFO to LIFO. Because King's gross receipts have never exceeded $5 million, the simplified LIFO method is available. King's year-end inventories under FIFO are as follows:

2005	$100,000
2006	$130,000

Assume the 2005 price index is 120% and the 2006 index is 125%. King must convert its 2006 inventory to 2005 prices.

$$\frac{120\%}{125\%} \times \$130,000 = \$124,800$$

A base period inventory of $100,000 is established. The increase in inventory (the 2006 layer) is valued at 2006 prices.

Base inventory (2005)	$100,000
Plus: 2006 layer [(125% ÷ 120%) × ($124,800 − $100,000)]	25,833
2006 ending inventory	$125,833

Assume the 2007 inventory valued under FIFO is $136,000 and the 2007 price index is 130%. The 2007 inventory is converted to 2005 prices.

---

[37] Reg. Sec. 1.472-2(e).
[38] Sec. 472(f).

[39] Sec. 474(c).

$$\frac{120\%}{130\%} \times \$136,000 = \$125,538$$

The 2007 increase in inventory (the 2007 layer) is valued at 2007 prices.

Base inventory (2005)	$100,000
2006 layer	25,833
2007 layer	800[a]
2007 ending inventory	$126,633

[a] [(130% ÷ 120%) × ($125,538 − $124,800)].

ADDITIONAL COMMENT

For tax purposes the lower of cost or market method must ordinarily be applied to each separate inventory item, but for financial accounting purposes it can be applied using an aggregate approach.

LOWER OF COST OR MARKET METHOD. Inventory may be valued at the **lower of cost or market.** This option is available to all taxpayers other than those who determine cost using the LIFO method.[40] The term *market* refers to replacement cost. On the date an inventory is valued, the replacement cost of each item in the inventory is compared with its cost. The lower figure is used as the inventory value. The lower of cost or market method must ordinarily be applied to each separate item in the inventory.

Recall the *Thor Power Tool* case (discussed earlier in this chapter) in which the Supreme Court distinguished market value from expected selling price. **Market value** is the price at which the taxpayer can replace the goods in question. Replacement cost is used in the lower of cost or market determination. Obsolete or other slow-moving inventory can be written down below replacement cost only if the selling price has been reduced.

CYCLE INVENTORY VALUATION. Computer technology, including bar codes and software developments, enables businesses to maintain real-time perpetual inventory records. Many businesses, especially those with multiple locations, do not attempt to count all inventory items on the last day of the taxable period. Instead they count inventory following a scheduled cycle. At year-end, businesses adjust quantities shown in perpetual records for shrinkage since the most recent physical count utilizing estimates based on past experiences. The IRS challenged this practice unsuccessfully arguing that the adjustments failed the "all events" test which requires that amounts must be determined with reasonable accuracy.[41] In midst of the litigation, Congress specifically permitted the method in instances where "the taxpayer makes proper adjustment to such inventories and its estimation method [for] actual shrinkage."[42]

WHAT WOULD YOU DO IN THIS SITUATION?

INVENTORY VALUATION

Jack is a new tax client. He says he and his previous accountant did not get along very well. Jack owns an automobile dealership with sales of $12 million. He has provided you with most of the information you need to prepare his tax return, but he has not yet given you the year-end inventory value. You have completed much of the work on his return, but cannot complete it without the inventory figure. You have called Jack three times about the inventory. Each time he has interrupted, and asked you what his tax liability will be at alternative inventory levels. What problem do you see?

[40] Reg. Secs. 1.471-2(b) and (c).
[41] *Wal-Mart Stores Inc. v. CIR*, 82 AFTR 2d 5601, 98-2 USTC ¶50,645 (8th Cir., 1998), *Dayton Hudson Corp. v. CIR*, 82 AFTR 2d 5610, 98-2 USTC ¶50,644 (8th Cir., 1998), and *Kroger Co.*, 1997 RIA T.C. Memo ¶97,002, 73 TCM 1637.
[42] Sec. 471(b).

SPECIAL ACCOUNTING METHODS

The term *method of accounting* is used to include not only overall methods of accounting (i.e., cash, accrual, and hybrid) but also the accounting treatment of specific items. Special rules have been established for two types of transactions that cover long periods of time. One rule applies to installment sales (a sale in which final payment is not received until a subsequent tax year) and a separate set of rules applies to long-term contracts (construction and similar contracts that are not completed in the same year they are started). These special rules permit taxpayers to report income from this type of transaction when they have the wherewithal to pay the tax (i.e., the year in which payment is received).

OBJECTIVE 4

Determine the amount of income to be reported from a long-term contract

LONG-TERM CONTRACTS

Long-term contracts include building, installation, construction, or manufacturing contracts that are not completed in the same tax year in which they began.[43] A manufacturing contract is long-term only if the contract involves the manufacture of either a unique item not normally carried in finished goods inventory or items that normally require more than 12 calendar months to complete. Contracts for services (architectural, accounting, legal, and so on) do not qualify for long-term contract treatment.[44]

EXAMPLE I11-20 ▶

Diamond Corporation manufactures two types of airplanes: small, general aviation planes that require approximately six months to complete and large jet aircrafts sold to airlines that require two years to complete. Diamond maintains an inventory of the small planes but manufactures the large planes to contract specification. Diamond can use long-term contract accounting only for the large planes. Assume Diamond also offers aircraft design assistance to the government and others who seek such services. The long-term contract method of accounting is not available for such services. ◀

HISTORICAL NOTE

The use of the completed contract method was severely restricted in the Tax Reform Act of 1986 because Congress found that several large corporations, particularly those with large defense contracts, had significant deferred taxes attributable to this method. Many of these companies had extremely low or negative tax rates for several years.

The accounting method selected by a taxpayer must be used for all long-term contracts in the same trade or business.[45] In general, the income and expenses associated with long-term contracts may be accounted for by using either the **percentage of completion method** or the **modified percentage of completion method**. In limited instances (explained below), taxpayers may use the **completed contract method**. Under the percentage of completion method, income from a project is reported in installments as the work progresses. Under the completed contract method, income from a project is recognized upon completion of the contract. The modified percentage of completion method is a hybrid that combines two methods (discussed below). Alternatively, taxpayers may use any other accounting method (e.g., the accrual method) that clearly reflects income.

ADDITIONAL COMMENT

In general, a construction contract must involve what has historically been thought of as construction which includes erecting buildings, building dams, roads, and power plants.

COSTS SUBJECT TO LONG-TERM CONTRACT RULES. Direct contract costs are subject to the long-term contract rules. Labor, materials, and overhead costs must be allocated to the contract and accounted for accordingly. Thus, under the completed contract method, such costs are capitalized and deducted from revenue in the year the contract is completed. Selling, marketing and advertising expenses, expenses for unsuccessful bids and proposals, and research and development costs not associated with a specific contract may be deducted currently.

In general, administrative overhead must be allocated to long-term contracts. (See the earlier list of overhead items that must be included in inventory.) This is not required of taxpayers (other than homebuilders) using the completed contract method, but as noted below, the use of the completed contract method is limited.

As previously mentioned, interest must be capitalized if the property being produced is real property, long-lived property, or property requiring more than two years (one year in

---

[43] Reg. Sec. 1.451-3(b).
[44] Rev. Proc. 71-21, 1971-2 C.B. 549, does establish rules for service contracts that extend into the year following the receipt of payment. These rules are discussed in Chapter I3.

[45] Reg. Sec. 1.451-3(a)(1).

the case of property costing more than $1 million) to produce. Interest costs directly attributable to a contract and those that could have been avoided if contract costs had not been incurred must be allocated to long-term contracts.

COMPLETED CONTRACT METHOD. Under the completed contract method of accounting, income from a contract is reported in the taxable year in which the contract is completed. This is true without regard to whether the contract price is collected in advance, upon completion of the contract, or in installments. Costs associated with the contract are accumulated in a work-in-progress account and deducted upon completion. Several courts are in conflict with regard to determining when a contract is completed. Some courts have required total completion and acceptance of the contract.[46] Other courts have held the contract to have been completed when the only work remaining consists of correcting minor defects or furnishing incidental parts.[47]

The use of the completed contract method may only be used in two limited circumstances. First, the method can be used by smaller companies (those whose average gross receipts for the three preceding tax years is $10 million or less) for construction contracts that are expected to take two years or less to complete and second, for home construction contracts.[48] It cannot be used by larger companies for manufacturing, or for other long-term contracts other than construction or for construction contracts expected to last longer than two years.

PERCENTAGE OF COMPLETION METHOD. Under the percentage of completion method of reporting income, the taxpayer reports a percentage of the gross income from a long-term contract based on the portion of work that has been completed. The portion of the total contract price reported in a given year is determined by multiplying the total contract price by the percentage of work completed in the year. The percentage is determined by dividing current year costs by the expected total costs.

MODIFIED PERCENTAGE OF COMPLETION METHOD. At the beginning of a contract, it is difficult to estimate total costs. For this reason, taxpayers may elect to defer reporting any income from a contract until they have incurred at least 10% of the estimated total cost.[49] This is called the modified percentage of completion method. Under this method, if a contract has just been started as of the end of the year, the taxpayer does not have to estimate the profit on the contract during that year. The next year the taxpayer will report profit on all work that has been completed, including work done during the first year. Of course, this assumes that at least 10% of the work has been completed as of the end of the taxable year. If more than 10% of the costs are incurred during the first year, the modified percentage of completion method is identical to the regular percentage of completion method.

The completed contract method, the percentage of completion method, and the modified percentage of completion method are compared in Example I11-21.

EXAMPLE I11-21 ▶

In 2006, a contractor enters into a contract to construct a bridge for $1,400,000. At the outset, the contractor estimates that it will cost $1,200,000 to build the bridge. Actual costs in 2006 are $540,000 (45% of the $1,200,000 total estimated costs). Actual costs in 2007 are less than expected and amount to $600,000. The profits reported in both years of the contract are illustrated below.

	2006	2007
Completed contract		
Revenue	0	$1,400,000
Costs incurred	0	(1,140,000)
Gross profit	0	$ 260,000

[46] E. E. Black Limited v. Alsup, 45 AFTR 1345, 54-1 USTC ¶9340 (9th Cir., 1954), and Thompson-King-Tate, Inc. v. U.S., 8 AFTR 2d 5920, 62-1 USTC ¶9116 (6th Cir., 1961).
[47] Ehret-Day Co., 2 T.C. 25 (1943), and Nathan Wohlfeld, 1958 PH T.C. Memo ¶58,128, 17 TCM 677.
[48] Sec. 460(e).
[49] Sec. 460(a).

Percentage of completion

Revenue	$630,000[a]	$770,000[b]
Costs incurred	(540,000)	(600,000)
Gross profit	$ 90,000	$170,000

[a] 540,000/1,200,000 × $1,400,000 = $630,000.
[b] $1,400,000 − $630,000 = $770,000.

◄

In Example I11-21, the modified percentage of completion method results in the same income being reported each year as the percentage of completion method because more than 10% of the estimated costs were incurred during the first year. Note that the completed contract method defers reporting income until the contract is completed, causing all income from the project to be reported in a single year. Thus, the tax is deferred but the taxpayer may end up being taxed at higher rates. As noted, the completed contract is available only for home construction contracts and to certain smaller contractors for projects of two years or less.

LOOK-BACK INTEREST. Certain contracts (or portions of a contract) accounted for under either the regular or modified percentage of completion method are subject to a **look-back interest** adjustment. When a contract is completed, a computation is made to determine whether the tax paid each year during the contract is more or less than the tax that would have been paid if the actual total cost of the contract had been used rather than the estimated cost.[50] Interest is paid on any additional tax that would have been paid. The taxpayer receives interest on any additional tax that was paid.

Look-back interest is applicable only to contracts completed more than two years after the commencement date. Furthermore, look-back interest is applicable only if the contract price equals or exceeds either 1% of the taxpayer's average gross receipts for the three taxable years preceding the taxable year the contract was entered into or $1 million.[51]

Taxpayers may elect a "de minimis" exception to the "look-back" interest computation. If elected, the exception is applicable to all contracts completed within a year, and the election to use the exception can be revoked only with IRS approval. Under the exception, if income reported each year on a contract is within 10% of the recomputed "look-back income," no interest computation is made for the contract. Whether reported income is within 10% of recomputed income is determined separately for each completed contract.

EXAMPLE I11-22 ▶

The contractor in Example I11-21 is exempt from the look-back rule because the contract is completed within two years after the commencement date. On the other hand, if the contract took more than two years to complete, interest would be owed on the underpaid taxes for the first and subsequent contract years. The underreported income for the first year would be $33,158 [($260,000 profit × $540,000 first year's costs ÷ $1,140,000 total costs) − $90,000 first year reported income]. Assuming a 35% tax bracket, the underpaid tax for the first year is $11,605. Upon completion of the contract, interest would be paid on this amount and underpaid taxes for other years. Even if elected, the "de-minimis" exception would be inapplicable as the reported income in the first year of the contract ($90,000) is not within 10% of the income that would have been reported if actual costs had been used in the computation ($123,158 = $33,158 + $90,000). ◄

OBJECTIVE 5

Compute the gain to be reported from an installment sale

INSTALLMENT SALES METHOD

In general, the gain or loss from the sale of property is reported in the year the property is sold. If the sales proceeds are collected in years after the sale, the taxpayer may find it difficult to pay the tax on the entire amount of the gain in the year of sale. To reduce the burden, the tax law permits taxpayers to spread the gain from installment sales over the collection period. The installment method is applicable only to gains and is used to report income from an installment transaction unless the taxpayer elects not to use the

---

[50] Sec. 460(b)(3).   [51] Sec. 460(b)(3).

installment method. An **installment sale** is any disposition of property where at least one payment is received after the close of the taxable year in which the disposition occurs. The installment method is *not* applicable to sales of:

▶ inventory, or

▶ marketable securities[52]

COMPUTATIONS UNDER SEC. 453. Income under the installment sales method is computed as follows:

STEP 1: Compute the gross profit from the sale.

Selling price	$xx,xxx
Minus: Adjusted basis	(x,xxx)
Selling expenses	(x,xxx)
Depreciation recapture[53]	(x,xxx)
Gross profit	$ x,xxx

STEP 2: Determine the contract price.

Contract price (greater of the gross profit from above or the selling price reduced by any existing mortgage assumed or acquired by the purchaser) $xx,xxx

STEP 3: Compute the gross profit percentage.

$$\frac{\text{Gross profit}}{\text{percentage}} = \frac{\text{Gross profit}}{\text{Contract price}} = xx\%$$

STEP 4: Compute the gain to be reported in the year of sale.

Collections of principal received during year (exclusive of interest)	$xx,xxx
Plus: Excess mortgage (if any)[a]	x,xxx
Total	$xx,xxx
Times: Gross profit percentage	× xx%
Net gain recognized in year of sale	$ x,xxx
Plus: Depreciation recapture	x,xxx
Gain reported in year of sale	$ x,xxx

STEP 5: Compute the gain to be reported in subsequent years.

Collections of principal received	$ x,xxx
Times: Gross profit percent	× xx%
Gain reported in each of the subsequent years	$ x,xxx

[a] Mortgage − Basis − Selling expense − Depreciation recapture = Excess mortgage

Note that depreciation recapture (see Chapter I13) must be reported in the year of the sale even if no payment is received.

EXAMPLE I11-23 ▶ Gina, a cash basis taxpayer, sells equipment for $200,000. The equipment originally cost $70,000, and $10,000 of MACRS depreciation has been deducted before the sale. The $10,000 of depreciation must be recaptured as ordinary income under Sec. 1245. The buyer assumes the existing mortgage of $50,000, pays $10,000 down, and agrees to pay $10,000 per year for 14 years plus interest at a rate acceptable to the IRS. Selling expenses are $13,000. The selling price is $200,000 [($50,000 + $10,000) + (14 × $10,000)]. The gain to be reported is $127,000 [$200,000 − $13,000 − ($70,000 − $10,000)]. Using the steps listed above, calculations are made as follows:

---

[52] Sec. 453(b)(2) and (k).

[53] For a discussion of depreciation recapture, see Chapter I13.

STEP 1:   Compute the gross profit from the sale.

Selling price	$200,000
Minus: Adjusted basis	(60,000)
Selling expenses	(13,000)
Depreciation recapture	(10,000)
Gross profit	$117,000

STEP 2:   Determine the contract price.

Greater of gross profit of $117,000 or selling price minus mortgage assumed by purchaser ($150,000 = $200,000 − $50,000)	$150,000

STEP 3:   Compute the gross profit percentage.

$$\frac{\text{Gross profit}}{\text{percentage}} = \frac{\text{Gross profit (\$117,000)}}{\text{Contract price (\$150,000)}} = 78\%$$

STEP 4:   Compute the gain to be reported in the year of sale.

Principal received during year	$ 10,000
Plus: Excess mortgage	0
Total amount realized	$ 10,000
Times: Gross profit percentage	
Gross profit	$ 7,800
Plus: Depreciation recapture	10,000
Gain reported in year of sale	$ 17,800

STEP 5:   Compute the gain to be reported in subsequent years.

Principal received	$ 10,000
Times: Gross profit percentage	× 78%
Gain reported in each subsequent year	$ 7,800

Thus, the total gain reported is $127,000 [$17,800 + ($7,800 × 14)]. This is equal to the gross profit of $117,000 (which is the amount of Sec. 1231 gain reported on the sale) plus the $10,000 of depreciation recapture. As a cash basis taxpayer Gina will report the interest income as it is collected. See Figure I11-1 at the end of this chapter which illustrates this computation on Form 6252, Installment Sale Income. ◀

REAL-WORLD EXAMPLE

When an installment obligation is assigned as collateral for a loan, the transaction is treated as a disposition of the obligation. Rev. Rul. 65-185, 1965-2 C.B. 153.

DISPOSITION OF INSTALLMENT OBLIGATIONS.   A taxpayer who sells property on the installment basis may decide not to hold the obligation until maturity. For example, the holder may sell the obligation to a financial institution for the purpose of raising cash. Alternatively, the holder may not be able to collect the full amount of the installments because of the inability of the buyer to make payments. Thus, the holder must determine the adjusted basis of the obligation in order to compute the gain or loss realized on the disposition. The adjusted basis of an installment obligation is equal to the face amount of the obligation reduced by the gross profit that would be realized if the holder collects the face amount of the obligation. In general, this means the adjusted basis of an obligation is equal to

$$\text{Face amount} \times (100\% - \text{Gross profit percentage})$$

EXAMPLE I11-24 ▶   Assume the same facts as in Example I11-23 except that Gina immediately sells a single $10,000 installment to a bank for $9,700. Gina reports a gain of $7,500 computed as follows:

Selling price	$9,700
Minus: Adjusted basis of installment	(2,200)[a]
Recognized gain	$7,500

[a] $10,000 face amount × (100% − 78% gross profit percentage) = $2,200

Gina would have reported a gain of $7,800 had she decided not to sell the installment but to collect the face amount. Because the obligation is discounted by $300 ($10,000 − $9,700), the reported gain is reduced by $300. If the installment had not been sold immediately, the bank would probably also pay to Gina an amount for the accrued interest. In such a situation Gina would report the gain from the sale and the accrued interest as income. ◄

EXAMPLE I11-25 ▶ Assume that Gina in Example I11-24 is unable to collect the final $10,000 installment because the individual who purchases the property declares bankruptcy. Gina would be entitled to a bad debt deduction of $2,200, the basis of the installment. Gina does not receive a bad debt deduction for the accrued interest because the interest has not been included in her gross income. ◄

KEY POINT

A donor of property does not normally recognize gain, but a gift of certain installment obligations causes the recognition of gain.

Certain dispositions of installment obligations, such as gifts, are taxable events.[54] The main objective of this rule is to prevent income from being shifted from one taxpayer to another. Thus, if a corporation distributes an installment obligation as a dividend or if a father gives his daughter an installment obligation, gain or loss is recognized. In general, the gain or loss recognized is equal to the difference between the FMV of the obligation and its adjusted basis. In the case of a gift, the gain recognized is equal to the difference between the face of the obligation and its adjusted basis. However, certain exceptions to this rule exist. Transfers to controlled corporations under Sec. 351, certain corporate reorganizations and liquidations, transfers on the taxpayer's death, transfers incident to divorce, distributions by partnerships, and contributions of capital to a partnership are exceptions to this rule. In these cases, the recipients of the obligations report income when the installments are collected.

REPOSSESSIONS OF PROPERTY SOLD ON THE INSTALLMENT BASIS. In general, the repossession of property sold on the installment basis is a taxable event. The gain or loss recognized is generally equal to the difference between the value of the repossessed property (reduced by any costs incurred as a result of the repossession) and the adjusted basis of any remaining installment obligations.

EXAMPLE I11-26 ▶ Yuji sells stock of a non–publicly traded corporation with a $7,000 adjusted basis for $10,000. Yuji receives a $1,000 down payment, and the balance of $9,000 is due the following year. In the year of the sale Yuji reports a capital gain of $300 (0.30 × $1,000) under the installment method of accounting. Yuji is unable to collect the $9,000 note, and after incurring legal fees of $500, he repossesses the stock. When Yuji repossesses the stock it is worth $8,700. The adjusted basis of the note is $6,300 (0.70 × $9,000). Yuji must report a capital gain of $1,900 ($8,700 − $500 − $6,300). The basis of the stock to Yuji is its FMV at the time it is repossessed ($8,700). ◄

The amount of gain recognized from the repossession of real property is limited to the lesser of (1) the gross profit in the remaining installments reduced by the costs incurred as a result of the repossession or (2) the cash and FMV of other property received from the buyer in excess of the gain previously recognized.[55] In the case of the repossession of either real or personal property, the gain or loss retains the same character as the gain or loss on the original sale.

EXAMPLE I11-27 ▶ Assume the same facts as in Example I11-26, except that the property sold is land. Yuji reports a capital gain of $700, which is the lesser of $2,200 [(0.30 × $9,000) − $500] or $700 ($1,000 − $300). The basis of the land is $7,500 [$9,000 − (0.30 × $9,000) unrealized profit + $700 gain previously recognized + $500 legal fees]. ◄

INSTALLMENT SALES FOR MORE THAN $150,000. Special rules apply to nondealers who sell property for more than $150,000. The special rules do not apply to sales of personal use property, to sales of property used or produced in the trade or business of farming, or to sales of timeshares or residential lots.

First, if the taxpayer borrows funds using the installment obligations as security, the amount borrowed is treated as a payment received on the installment obligation.[56] This

---

[54] Sec. 453B(a).
[55] Sec. 1038.

[56] Sec. 453A(d).

prevents the taxpayer from using the installment method to defer tax and yet obtain cash by borrowing against the installment obligation. Second, if the installment method is used, interest must be paid to the government on the deferred tax.[57] This rule, however, applies only to deferred principal payments over $5 million.[58]

INSTALLMENT SALES BETWEEN RELATED PERSONS. Installment sales between related persons are subject to the same rules as other installment sales except when the property is resold by the related purchaser. The primary purpose of the resale rule is to prevent the original owner from deferring gain recognition by selling the property to a related person who, in turn, resells the property.

Sec. 453(e) requires the first seller to treat amounts received by the related person (second seller) as having been personally received. Thus, the first seller would be required to report the gain in the year (or years) in which proceeds are received by the second seller. This acceleration provision is applicable only if the resale takes place within two years of the initial sale. For purposes of Sec. 453(e), the term *related person* includes a spouse, children, grandchildren, and parents. Controlled corporations, partnerships, estates, and trusts are also covered.

DEFERRED PAYMENT SALES

The installment sale rules are not applicable to all sales involving future payments. The installment method cannot be used when the sale of property produces a loss. Also, a taxpayer can elect out of the installment method when a sale results in a gain. The manner in which these transactions are reported depends on the taxpayer's accounting method. For accrual method taxpayers, the total *amount receivable* from the buyer (exclusive of interest) is treated as part of the amount realized. Thus, the entire gain or loss is reported in the year of sale. For cash method taxpayers, the FMV of the installment obligation is treated as part of the amount realized in the year of sale. The amount realized, however, cannot be considered to be less than the FMV of the property sold minus any other consideration received (e.g., cash).[59]

EXAMPLE I11-28 ▶

USA Corporation, an accrual method taxpayer, sells land for $100,000. USA receives $50,000 down and a $50,000 note payable in 12 months plus 14% interest. Assume the basis of the land is $80,000 and that it is a capital asset. Because of the buyer's poor credit, the value of the note is only $45,000. USA affirmatively elects not to report the installment sale on the installment method. USA reports a capital gain of $20,000 ($100,000 − $80,000). If USA collects the face of the note at maturity, no additional gain or loss is recognized. If USA sells the note for $45,000, a $5,000 capital loss is recognized. ◀

EXAMPLE I11-29 ▶

Assume the same facts as in Example I11-28, except that USA is a cash method taxpayer. If the FMV of the land is $100,000 (the stated selling price), the treatment of the transaction is exactly the same as it is using the accrual method. If the FMV of the land is assumed to be $95,000 (cash received plus FMV of the note received), USA recognizes a $15,000 ($95,000 − $80,000) capital gain in the year of the sale. If USA collects the face of the note at maturity, $5,000 of ordinary income is recognized. If USA sells the note for $45,000, no gain or loss is recognized. ◀

INDETERMINATE MARKET VALUE. In certain transactions, the value of obligations received cannot be determined (e.g., a mineral interest is sold for an amount equal to 10% of the value of future production). Under the Regulations, the value of obligations with an **indeterminate market value** is assumed to be no lower than the value of the property sold less the value of other property received.[60] Hence, if the value of property sold is determinable, the recognized gain equals the excess of the value of the property sold over its basis. On occasion, however, neither the value of the obligation received nor the value of property sold can be determined.

Temporary regulations specify how these types of transactions are to be treated.[61] The basic rules relating to special accounting methods are summarized in Topic Review I11-3.

---

[57] The interest computation is described in Sec. 453A(c).
[58] Sec. 453A(b)(2)(B).
[59] Temp. Reg. Sec. 15A.453-1(d)(2)(ii)(A).

[60] Reg. Sec. 1.453-1(d)(3)(iii).
[61] Temp. Reg. Sec. 15A.453-1(c).

Topic Review I11-3

Special Accounting Methods

LONG-TERM CONTRACTS

▶ Long-term contracts include building, installation, construction, or manufacturing contracts that are not completed in the same tax year in which they are entered into. A manufacturing contract is long-term only if the contract involves the manufacture of either a unique item not normally carried in inventory or an item that normally requires more than 12 calendar months to complete.

▶ Long-term contracts may be reported under the regular or the modified percentage of completion method. Under both methods income is reported as work is completed, except that under the modified percentage of completion method no income is reported until at least 10% of the work is completed.

▶ The completed contract method is available only for home construction contracts, for construction contracts expected to take two years or less to complete, and for use by smaller companies (those whose average gross receipts for the three preceding tax years are $10 million or less).

INSTALLMENT METHOD

▶ Under the installment method gain is reported as the sales proceeds are collected. The installment method is generally not available for sales of inventory or publicly traded property. Furthermore, the method is available only for gains.

▶ Gain is reported as sales proceeds are collected. However, both depreciation recapture and any mortgage in excess of basis must be reported in the year of sale. Gain recognition is also accelerated in certain situations if the seller borrows against the installment obligation or if a related buyer resells the property within two years.

IMPUTED INTEREST

OBJECTIVE 6

Compute the amount of imputed interest in a transaction

KEY POINT

Imputed interest is important because it alters the amount of gain on the sale and causes an interest expense deduction for the buyer and interest income for the seller.

TYPICAL MISCONCEPTION

Some people mistakenly assumed that the imputed interest rules do not apply if the property is sold for a loss.

Before the enactment of Sec. 1274 and the amendment of Sec. 483, property could be sold on an installment basis in a contract providing for little or no interest. Instead of charging interest, the seller charged a higher price for the property. If the property sold was a capital asset, the result of the arrangement was to reduce the interest income reported by the seller and to increase the amount of favorably taxed capital gain. Sections 483 and 1274 now *impute* interest in a deferred payment contract where no interest or a low rate of interest is provided. Another impact of the **imputed interest rules** on sellers is to reallocate payments received between interest (which is fully taxable) and principal (only the gain portion of which is taxable). The result is often an increase in the income reported in early years and a decrease in later years. The rules are generally applicable to both buyers and sellers. In certain instances, the buyer may want interest to be imputed in order to increase his interest deduction in early years.

The following transactions are exempt from the imputed interest rules:

▶ Debt subject to original issue discount provisions (basically bonds issued for less than face where amortization of the discount is required under Sec. 1274; see Chapter I5)

▶ Sales of property for $3,000 or less

▶ Any sales where all of the payments are due within six months

▶ Sales of patents to the extent the payment is contingent on the use or disposition of the patent

▶ Certain carrying charges for personal property or educational services covered by Sec. 163(b) when the interest charge cannot be ascertained

▶ Charges for the purchase of personal-use property (purchaser only)[62]

---

[62] Sec. 483(d). The rule lowers the basis of a personal-use asset in order to increase any gain on the future sale of the property.

EXAMPLE I11-30 ▶ Joan is involved in several transactions during the current year. No interest is stated on any of the transactions. The terms of the transactions and the applicability of the imputed interest rules are summarized below:

Transaction	*Imputation of Interest*
Purchases furniture costing $8,000 for her residence. Full price is payable within four months.	Not applicable because property is for personal use. Also, all payments are due within six months.
Sells a boat for $2,000. Payment is due in a year.	Not applicable because sales price is not more than $3,000.
Sells land for $100,000. Payment is due in five years.	Interest must be imputed because no exception is applicable.
Purchases a newly issued bond for $650 (face of $1,000).	Not applicable because transaction is subject to the original issue discount rules in Sec. 1274. Also, the price is not more than $3,000. ◀

IMPUTED INTEREST COMPUTATION

In order to avoid the imputation of interest, the stated interest rate must be at least equal to 100% of the applicable federal rate (110% of the applicable federal rate in the case of sale–lease back arrangements). Lower rates are specified for two types of transactions: (1) If the stated principal amount for qualified debt obligations that are issued in exchange for property under Sec. 1274A does not exceed $2,800,000, the interest rate is limited to 9% compounded semiannually; and (2) the interest rate is limited to 6% compounded semiannually in the case of sales of land between related individuals (unless the sales price exceeds $500,000).

The **applicable federal rate** is determined monthly and is based on the rate paid by the federal government on borrowed funds. The rate varies with the terms of the loan. Loans are divided into short-term (not over three years), mid-term (over three years but not over nine years), and long-term (over nine years).

EXAMPLE I11-31 ▶ Kasi sells land for $100,000 to Bill, an unrelated person. The sales price is to be paid to Kasi at the end of five years in a single installment with no stated interest. Kasi paid $60,000 for the land. Assume the current federal rate is 10%. Because the amount of the stated principal is less than $2,800,000, interest is imputed at a rate not to exceed 9% compounded semiannually. As a result, the effective rate is 9.2025% (9% compounded semiannually), and the present value factor is .64393 ($1 \div 1.092025^5$). Thus, the present value of the final payment is $64,393 ($0.64393 \times $100,000$). Kasi reports a $4,393 ($64,393 − $60,000) gain on the sale of the land and $35,607 ($100,000 − $64,393) interest income instead of a $40,000 gain and no interest income. The buyer is treated as incurring $35,607 in interest and has a $64,393 basis in the land. Whether the interest is deductible depends on a variety of other factors (see Chapter I7). ◀

ACCRUAL OF INTEREST

Is imputed interest reported under the cash or the accrual method? In other words, is imputed interest reported when it accrues or when it is paid? In general, imputed interest is reported as it accrues. However, there are some major exceptions, as follows:

ADDITIONAL COMMENT

The $2,000,000 limit on the stated principal is subject to inflation adjustments for calendar years beginning after 1989.

▶ Sales of personal residences

▶ Most sales of farms for $1 million or less

▶ Sales involving aggregate payments of $250,000 or less

▶ Sales of land between related persons unless the sales price exceeds $500,000[63]

In addition, if the borrower and lender jointly elect, and if the stated principal does not exceed $2,000,000, accrual of interest is not required. This election is not available if the lender is an accrual method taxpayer or a dealer with respect to the property sold or exchanged.[64]

---

[63] Sec. 1274(c)(4).   [64] Sec. 1274A(c).

EXAMPLE I11-32 ▶   Assume the same facts as in Example I11-31. Because the aggregate payments do not exceed $250,000, the transaction is exempt from the requirement that interest be accrued. As a result, Kasi reports interest income and Bill reports interest expense in the fifth year when the final payment is made on the transaction. Under the installment method, $4,393 gain on the sale is recognized in the fifth year.   ◀

GIFT, SHAREHOLDER, AND OTHER LOANS

Imputed interest rules are not limited to installment transactions. Sec. 7872 applies to transactions involving related parties whose taxes are lowered as a result of low interest or interest-free loans. These situations include

▶ *Gift loans.* For example, parents in higher tax brackets loan money to their children without charging interest. If the children invest the borrowed money and are taxed on the income at a lower rate, the family has reduced its total tax liability in the absence of imputed interest rules.

▶ *Corporation shareholder loans.* In the absence of imputed interest rules, taxes may be saved by a corporation that makes an interest-free loan to a shareholder. If the corporation had invested the money and paid out the resulting income as a dividend, it would have first been taxed on the profit. By making the interest-free loan, the corporation could, in the absence of imputed interest rules, reduce its taxes by avoiding the otherwise taxable income.

▶ *Compensation-related loans.* Employers may loan money to employees without charging interest. Without the requirement to impute interest, this could produce tax savings if the employer was unable to deduct additional compensation because of the reasonable compensation limitation or if the employee was unable to deduct the interest, say, because the borrowed funds were used to purchase personal use property.

▶ *Other tax avoidance loans.* Any other low-interest or interest-free loan that produces tax savings may be subject to the imputed interest rules. For example, a club may offer its members a choice of either paying dues or making a large refundable deposit. The club can invest the money and earn interest perhaps equal to the dues. In the absence of imputed interest rules, the member avoids taxes by not having to report the income that would have been earned if the member personally invested the funds. The club is indifferent between the alternatives because both the dues and the interest income are taxable.

In general, interest is imputed on the above loans by applying the applicable federal rates discussed earlier. The resulting interest income is taxable to the lender. Whether the interest expense is deductible by the borrower is determined by applying the usual interest deduction rules (see Chapter I7).

The imputation process involves a second step. The lender is treated as returning the imputed interest to the borrower. This is necessary because the interest was not actually paid. For example, in the case of a gift loan, the lender is treated as giving the imputed interest back to the borrower. This would not normally have income tax implications, but if the imputed interest were large enough, it could result in a gift tax. In the case of the corporation-shareholder loan, the corporation is treated as paying the imputed interest back to the shareholder as a dividend. Typically, this does not increase the corporation's tax, but it results in the recognition of dividend income to the shareholder. For compensation-related loans, the second step is to impute compensation paid by the employer and received by the employee. The compensation is taxable to the employee and, if reasonable in amount, is deductible by the employer.

There are several important exceptions intended to limit the application of imputed interest in situations where tax avoidance may be immaterial:

▶ Interest is not imputed on gift loans between two individuals totaling $10,000 or less, except when the borrowed funds are used to purchase income-producing property.

▶ If the gift loans between two individuals total $100,000 or less, the imputed interest is limited to the borrower's "net investment income" as defined by Sec. 163(d)(4). (See Chapter I7 for a discussion of net investment income.) If the net investment income is $1,000 or less, it is not necessary to impute interest.

▶ Interest is not imputed on compensation-related and corporate shareholder loans totaling $10,000 or less.

These exceptions do not apply when tax avoidance is one of the principal purposes of the loans.

EXAMPLE I11-33 ▶ Linda made interest-free gift loans to each of her four children: Andy, Bob, Cathy, and Donna. Andy borrowed $9,000 to purchase an automobile. Bob borrowed $25,000 to buy stock. Bob's net investment income is $800. Cathy also borrowed $25,000 to buy stock, but her net investment income is $1,100. Donna borrowed $120,000 to purchase a residence, and her net investment income is $500. Tax avoidance is not a motive for any of the loans. Imputation of interest is not required for the loans to Andy or Bob. The loan to Andy is exempt because the amount is less than $10,000, and the loan to Bob is exempt because his net investment income is under $1,000. Imputation of interest is required for the loans to Cathy and Donna. In the case of Cathy, the amount of imputed interest is limited to her net investment income of $1,100. The imputed interest for Donna, however, is not limited to her net investment income because the amount of the loan is over $100,000. ◀

The imputed interest rules are summarized in Topic Review I11-4.

CHANGE IN ACCOUNTING METHODS

In general, a new taxpayer elects an accounting method by simply applying the selected method when computing income for the initial tax return.[65] If a particular item does not occur in the first year, the accounting method is elected the first year in which the item occurs.

EXAMPLE I11-34 ▶ Gordon opened a beauty shop several years ago. Because he had no inventory, no inventory method was selected. In the current year, Gordon expanded his business to offer beauty supplies to his customers. Gordon can delay electing the FIFO inventory method until the current year, the first year in which he has an inventory. ◀

Topic Review I11-4

Imputed Interest

PURPOSE

The imputed interest rules are intended to prevent taxpayers from reducing their taxes by charging little or no interest on installment payment transactions and loans.

APPLIES TO

In most cases applies to both parties, the debtor and the creditor. The result is to impute interest income to the lender and interest expense to the borrower. Several exceptions exempt small transactions from imputed interest. For example, sales involving payments of $3,000 or less are generally exempt as are loans of less than $10,000.

RATE

Interest is imputed at the applicable federal rate if the stated interest rate is lower. The applicable federal rate is the rate the federal government pays on borrowed funds and is determined monthly. In general, the current rate at the time of the transaction is used throughout the term of the loan. The rate varies with the term of the loan. Loans are divided into short-term (not over three years), mid-term (over three years but not over nine years), and long-term (over nine years).

---

[65] Reg. Sec. 1.446-1(e)(1).

In general, once an accounting method is chosen, it cannot be changed without IRS approval. There are a few exceptions. For example, taxpayers may adopt the LIFO inventory method without prior IRS approval.[66] Once such methods are adopted, however, they cannot be changed without IRS approval.

As previously noted, the term *accounting method* indicates not only the overall accounting method used by the taxpayer, but also the treatment of any item of income or deduction.[67] A change of accounting methods should not be confused with the correction of an error. Errors include mathematical mistakes, posting errors, deductions of the wrong amount for an expense, omission of an item of taxable income, or incorrect computation of a credit. An error is normally corrected by filing an amended return for the tax year or years in which the error occurs. In general, there is a three-year statute of limitations on the correction of errors. After three years, the tax year is closed and changes cannot be made.[68]

Taxpayers wishing to change accounting methods must file Form 3115 with the IRS in Washington, D.C., on or before the due date of the tax return including extensions. A duplicate copy of Form 3115 must be filed with the tax return for the year. A taxpayer who amends the original income tax return within six months of its due date may request a change of accounting methods with the amended return.[69]

In general, taxpayers initiate a change in accounting methods from an incorrect to a correct method are exempt from penalty and from retroactive application of the new reporting method. Although changes in accounting methods require IRS approval, the IRS states that approval will automatically be granted for a wide variety of changes if the taxpayer meets specific requirements that include proper filing of both Form 3115 and the current year's tax return, agreeing to take into account the Sec. 481(a) adjustment (as described below), not being under examination, and not having changed the same method of accounting within the last four years.[70] Although the IRS retains the right to again change any method of accounting adopted under these procedures it states that such changes will not be retroactive except in rare or unusual circumstances. Examples of situations where retroactive application may occur include misstatement or omission of material facts, change in material facts, and changes in applicable authority.

AMOUNT OF CHANGE

A change in accounting methods usually results in duplications or omissions of items of income or expense.

EXAMPLE I11-35 ▶

Bonnie, a practicing CPA, has been reporting income using the cash method. In the current year, Bonnie obtains permission to change to the accrual method. At the beginning of the current year, Bonnie has $80,000 of receivables that have not been reported in prior years. The receivables were not reported in prior years because they were not collected. Although the receivables are collected in the current year, they are not taxable because, under the accrual method, Bonnie now reports income as it is earned and the income is not earned in the current year. In this case, the income was earned in prior years.

Also, assume Bonnie has accounts payable of $15,000 at the beginning of the current year. The accounts payable were not deducted in prior years because the expenses had not been paid. Furthermore, the accounts payable are not deductible in the current year even if they are paid. This is because the expenses were incurred in prior years. Obviously, the IRS expects to collect the tax on the $80,000 of receivables, and Bonnie is entitled to deduct the $15,000 of payables. In the absence of any special provision, both amounts would be omitted from the computation of taxable income. On the other hand, if the change were from the accrual

---

[66] A taxpayer may adopt LIFO by merely determining year-end inventory by that method and attaching Form 970 to the tax return for the year (Reg. Sec. 1.472-3(a)).

[67] Reg. Sec. 1.446-1(e)(2)(ii)(b).

[68] Exceptions are applicable when the taxpayer omits from the return an amount of income that is over 25% of the gross income stated on the return (6 years) or where fraud occurs (no limitation).

[69] The extension will be granted if the taxpayer (a) files the original income

tax return on time, (b) uses the new method of accounting on the amended return, (c) attaches the application to change methods to the amended return, (d) files a copy of the application with the national office no later than when the original is filed with the amended return, and (e) writes at the top of the application "FILED PURSUANT TO §301.9100-2." Rev. Proc. 99-49, 1999-2, C.B. 725.

[70] 1997-2 C.B. 455.

method to the cash method, both amounts would be reported twice (in the year prior to the change because they had accrued and in the year of the change because they are collected or paid). Thus, a special provision is also needed for duplications. ◄

REPORTING THE AMOUNT OF THE CHANGE

The net amount of the change must be taken into account.[71] A positive adjustment is added to income, whereas a negative adjustment is subtracted from income. This adjustment can, of course, be made in the year of the change. If the amount is small, recognizing the full amount of the net adjustment in the year of the change is both simple and equitable. Reporting a large positive adjustment in one year could push the taxpayer into a higher marginal tax bracket and result in a significant tax increase. Because the extra income is due to changing accounting methods, not increasing cash flows, the taxpayer may not have the wherewithal to pay the additional tax.

As a result, there are alternative methods that may be used to report the amount of the change. The methods that are available depend on whether the change is voluntary (a change that is initiated by the taxpayer) or involuntary (a change from an unacceptable to an acceptable method that is required by the IRS).

In the case of an involuntary change, several alternative methods are available to the IRS.[72]

In the case of voluntary changes, taxpayers must agree to report the adjustment over a period not to exceed four years. When the amount of the adjustment is $25,000 or less, taxpayers may elect to include the full amount in the current year.[73] In the case of a change spread over four years, equal portions of the change are reported in each of the four years beginning with the year of the change.

EXAMPLE I11-36 ▶

In 2006, Diana obtains permission to change from the accrual to the cash method of reporting income. The change results in a $30,000 negative adjustment to income. The IRS requires Diana to spread the adjustment over four years. As a result, she may deduct $7,500 in 2006 and $7,500 per year through year 2009. Note that because the amount of the adjustment is spread over the current and future years, the tax savings associated with the deduction are deferred. ◄

In general, the amount of the adjustment cannot be spread over a period longer than the method being changed has been used.

OBTAINING IRS CONSENT

REAL-WORLD EXAMPLE

A pipeline company was required to capitalize reconditioning costs on its natural gas pipelines instead of expensing these costs. *Mountain Fuel Supply Co. v. U.S.,* 28 AFTR 2d 71-5833, 71-2 USTC ¶9681 (10th Cir., 1971).

Most changes in accounting method require IRS approval. Sec. 446(e) states that a taxpayer changing the method of accounting "on the basis of which he regularly computes his income in keeping his books" must obtain consent before computing taxable income under the new method. This implies that a taxpayer who has been computing taxable income on a method other than that used in computing book income does not need approval to conform the computation of taxable income to the method regularly used on the taxpayer's books. This conclusion is supported by Sec. 441(a), which requires that the same method of accounting be used in computing taxable income as is used in keeping the books. The alternative might be to require the taxpayer to conform his or her book accounting method with the tax accounting method. The answer may well be in how one defines "books." The IRS has ruled that a reconciliation of taxable income with accounting income was a part of the taxpayer's auxiliary records.[74] Hence, the taxpayer was using the same accounting method for book and tax reporting. As a result, a taxpayer who changes the method of accounting used for financial reporting may not be required to change the method of accounting used for tax reporting as long as financial income and book income are reconciled.

---

[71] Sec. 481.
[72] Secs. 481(a), (b)(1), (b)(2), and (c).

[73] Rev. Rul. 97-37, 1997-2 C.B. 455.
[74] Rev. Rul. 58-601, 1958-2 C.B. 81.

TAX PLANNING CONSIDERATIONS

ACCOUNTING PERIODS

New corporations often routinely adopt a calendar year. Consideration should be given, however, to adopting a tax year for the initial reporting period that ends before the amount of taxable income exceeds the amount that is taxed at the lowest tax rates (e.g., when taxable income is $50,000 or less). This is less critical for a corporation suffering losses because the NOLs may be carried forward for a 20-year period.

In the past, taxpayers were able to defer income by selecting different tax years for partners and partnerships or S corporations and shareholders. Current law limits this opportunity. Nevertheless, partnerships and S corporations may adopt a tax year that differs from that of their owners if that year qualifies as a natural business year (i.e., at least 25% of revenues occur during the last two months of the year). Furthermore, deferral is possible in the case of estates, because they are not subject to similar restrictions on the choice of tax years.

ACCOUNTING METHODS

New businesses should consider the tax implications of electing an accounting method. For example, taxpayers may benefit from the LIFO inventory method because LIFO typically reduces gross profit and defers the payment of taxes during inflationary periods. Similarly, service companies usually choose the cash method of reporting income because it permits receivables to be reported when collected rather than when the income is earned. Choosing an accounting method requires an understanding not only of the available accounting methods, but also the nature of the taxpayer's business. Will a specific election be to the tax advantage of the taxpayer? LIFO inventory is often recommended because, during inflationary periods, it tends to reduce inventory values and increase the cost of goods sold. In certain industries, such as the computer industry, however, costs are declining, and LIFO actually may result in a higher inventory value.

In other industries, inventories may fluctuate widely from one year to the next because of changing demand, shortages of materials, strikes, or other causes. LIFO layers may have to be depleted simply to continue business operations. This can cause one of two things to happen: (1) incurring extra recordkeeping costs of LIFO for little or no benefit because the inventories are depleted before they produce significant tax deferrals or (2) depleting low-cost layers from years past, resulting in a substantial increase in taxable income in the year of occurrence.

INSTALLMENT SALES

Taxpayers normally choose the installment method of reporting income from casual sales of property. By spreading the gain from a sale over more than one tax year, the taxpayer normally remains in lower tax brackets and defers the tax. A taxpayer with low current taxable income may elect not to use the installment sale method in order to take advantage of the lower current tax rates.

COMPLIANCE AND PROCEDURAL CONSIDERATIONS

REPORTING INSTALLMENT SALES ON FORM 6252

Form 6252 (Installment Sale Income) is used to report income under the installment method from sales of real property and casual sales of personal property other than inventory. Figure I11-1 illustrates how an installment sale transaction is reported. The illustration is based on Example I11-23. A separate Form 6252 is normally used for each installment sale. Form 6252 is used in the year of the sale and any year in which the taxpayer receives a payment from the sale. Taxpayers who do not wish to use the installment method may report the transaction on either Schedule D or on Form 4797.

Form **6252**	**Installment Sale Income**	OMB No. 1545-0228

Form **6252**

Department of the Treasury
Internal Revenue Service

Installment Sale Income

► **Attach to your tax return.**
► **Use a separate form for each sale or other disposition of property on the installment method.**

OMB No. 1545-0228

2005

Attachment
Sequence No. **79**

Name(s) shown on return	Identifying number
Gina Green	123 - 45 - 6789

1 Description of property ► ....

2a Date acquired (month, day, year) ► 7 / 01 / 02   **b** Date sold (month, day, year) ► 8 / 31 / 05

3 Was the property sold to a related party (see instructions) after May 14, 1980? If "No," skip line 4. . . . ☐ Yes ☒ No

4 Was the property you sold to a related party a marketable security? If "Yes," complete Part III. If "No," complete Part III for the year of sale and the 2 years after the year of sale . . . . ☐ Yes ☒ No

Part I Gross Profit and Contract Price. Complete this part for the year of sale only.

5	Selling price including mortgages and other debts. **Do not** include interest whether stated or unstated		**5**	200,000
6	Mortgages, debts, and other liabilities the buyer assumed or took the property subject to (see instructions)	**6**	50,000	
7	Subtract line 6 from line 5	**7**	150,000	
8	Cost or other basis of property sold	**8**	70,000	
9	Depreciation allowed or allowable	**9**	10,000	
10	Adjusted basis. Subtract line 9 from line 8	**10**	60,000	
11	Commissions and other expenses of sale	**11**	13,000	
12	Income recapture from Form 4797, Part III (see instructions) . .	**12**	10,000	
13	Add lines 10, 11, and 12		**13**	83,000
14	Subtract line 13 from line 5. If zero or less, **do not** complete the rest of this form (see instructions)		**14**	117,000
15	If the property described on line 1 above was your main home, enter the amount of your excluded gain (see instructions). Otherwise, enter -0-		**15**	
16	**Gross profit.** Subtract line 15 from line 14		**16**	117,000
17	Subtract line 13 from line 6. If zero or less, enter -0-		**17**	
18	**Contract price.** Add line 7 and line 17		**18**	150,000

Part II Installment Sale Income. Complete this part for the year of sale and any year you receive a payment or have certain debts you must treat as a payment on installment obligations.

19	Gross profit percentage. Divide line 16 by line 18. For years after the year of sale, see instructions	**19**	78%
20	If this is the year of sale, enter the amount from line 17. Otherwise, enter -0-	**20**	—
21	Payments received during year (see instructions). **Do not** include interest, whether stated or unstated	**21**	10,000
22	Add lines 20 and 21	**22**	10,000
23	Payments received in prior years (see instructions). **Do not** include interest, whether stated or unstated	**23**	
24	**Installment sale income.** Multiply line 22 by line 19	**24**	7,800
25	Enter the part of line 24 that is ordinary income under the recapture rules (see instructions) . .	**25**	
26	Subtract line 25 from line 24. Enter here and on Schedule D or Form 4797 (see instructions)	**26**	7,800

Part III Related Party Installment Sale Income. Do not complete if you received the final payment this tax year.

27 Name, address, and taxpayer identifying number of related party ....

28 Did the related party resell or dispose of the property ("second disposition") during this tax year? . . . . ☐ Yes ☐ No

29 If the answer to question 28 is "Yes," complete lines 30 through 37 below unless one of the following conditions is met. Check the box that applies.

a ☐ The second disposition was more than 2 years after the first disposition (other than dispositions of marketable securities). If this box is checked, enter the date of disposition (month, day, year) ► ___ / ___ / ___

b ☐ The first disposition was a sale or exchange of stock to the issuing corporation.

c ☐ The second disposition was an involuntary conversion and the threat of conversion occurred after the first disposition.

d ☐ The second disposition occurred after the death of the original seller or buyer.

e ☐ It can be established to the satisfaction of the Internal Revenue Service that tax avoidance was not a principal purpose for either of the dispositions. If this box is checked, attach an explanation (see instructions).

30	Selling price of property sold by related party (see instructions)	**30**	
31	Enter contract price from line 18 for year of first sale	**31**	
32	Enter the **smaller** of line 30 or line 31	**32**	
33	Total payments received by the end of your 2005 tax year (see instructions)	**33**	
34	Subtract line 33 from line 32. If zero or less, enter -0-	**34**	
35	Multiply line 34 by the gross profit percentage on line 19 for year of first sale	**35**	
36	Enter the part of line 35 that is ordinary income under the recapture rules (see instructions) . .	**36**	
37	Subtract line 36 from line 35. Enter here and on Schedule D or Form 4797 (see instructions) .	**37**	

For Paperwork Reduction Act Notice, see page 4.   Cat. No. 13601R   Form **6252** (2005)

FIGURE I11-1 ► REPORTING INSTALLMENT SALE INCOME ON FORM 6252 (BASED ON EXAMPLE I11-23) **11-29**

PROCEDURES FOR CHANGING TO LIFO

The LIFO method may be adopted in the initial year that inventories are maintained by merely using the method in that year. In addition, advance approval (e.g., within 180 days following the start of the year) from the IRS is not required for an adoption of the LIFO method in the initial year that inventories are maintained on the LIFO method. However, Form 970 should be filed along with the taxpayer's tax return for the year of the change.[75] The application must include an analysis of the beginning and ending inventories. Further, if a taxpayer is changing to the LIFO method from another method (e.g., FIFO), advance approval from the IRS is also not required. Form 970 must be filed with the return and the beginning inventory for LIFO purposes is the same as under the former inventory method.[76]

If the former inventory is valued based on the lower of cost or market (LCM) method, an adjustment is required to restate the beginning inventory to cost because the LCM method cannot be used under LIFO. Generally, the beginning LIFO inventory is the same as the closing inventory for the prior year, except for the required restatement of previous writedowns to market. This adjustment to the beginning inventory can be spread ratably over the year of the change and the next two years.[77]

EXAMPLE I11-37 ▶ Delaware Corporation elects to change to the LIFO inventory method for 2006. In 2005 Delaware's inventories are valued using the LCM method based on the FIFO cost-flow assumption. The FIFO cost for the ending inventory in 2005 is $50,000, and its LCM amount is $35,000. The initial inventory for 2006 under LIFO must be restated to its cost, or $50,000. The $15,000 ($50,000 cost − $35,000 LCM value) difference can be included in taxable income over the current year and next two years. $5,000 is added to taxable income in 2006, 2007, and 2008. ◀

PROBLEM MATERIALS

DISCUSSION QUESTIONS

I11-1 Do accounting rules determine the amount of income to be reported by a taxpayer?

I11-2 How does a taxpayer's tax accounting method affect the amount of tax paid?

I11-3 Most individuals use the calendar year as their tax year. What requirement, if any, in the tax law causes this?

I11-4 Why is it desirable for a new taxpayer to select an appropriate tax year?

I11-5 What restrictions apply to partnerships selecting a tax year?

I11-6 Does a similar restriction apply to S corporations? Explain.

I11-7 How could the 52–53-week year prove to be beneficial to taxpayers? Explain.

I11-8 Under what circumstances can an individual taxpayer change tax years without IRS approval?

I11-9 Is there any instance in which a change in tax years is required? Explain.

I11-10 a. In what situations will a tax year cover a period of less than 12 months?
b. Under what conditions is a taxpayer required to annualize income?

c. Does annualizing income increase or decrease the taxpayer's tax liability? Explain.

I11-11 When is a final tax return due for an individual who uses a calendar year and who dies during the year?

I11-12 a. Is it correct to say that businesses with inventories must use the accrual method?
b. What other restrictions apply to taxpayers who are choosing an overall tax accounting method?
c. Why is the cash method usually preferred to the accrual method?

I11-13 a. Does the term *method of accounting* refer only to overall methods of accounting? Explain.
b. Does a taxpayer's accounting method affect the total amount of income reported over an extended time period?
c. How can the use of an accounting method affect the total amount of tax paid over time?

I11-14 a. When are expenses deductible by a cash method taxpayer?
b. Are the rules that determine when interest is deductible by a cash method taxpayer the same as for other expenses?

---

[75] An acceptable election is considered to have been made even if Form 970 is not filed as long as all of the information required by Reg. Sec. 1.472-3(a) is provided by the taxpayer.

[76] Reg. Sec. 1.472-2(c).
[77] Sec. 472(d).

c. Is a cash method taxpayer subject to the same rules for depreciable assets as accrual method taxpayers?

I11-15 Who may use the completed contract method of reporting income from long-term contracts?

I11-16 When is a cash method taxpayer allowed to deduct deposits?

I11-17 What constitutes a payment in determining when a cash-basis taxpayer is entitled to deduct an expense?

I11-18 What is meant by economic performance?

I11-19 What conditions must be met if the economic performance test is to be waived for an accrual-method taxpayer?

I11-20 Is an accrual method taxpayer permitted to deduct estimated expenses? What about prepaid expenses? Explain.

I11-21 What is the significance of the *Thor Power Tool Co.* decision?

I11-22 a. How are overhead costs treated in determining a manufacturing company's inventory?
b. Do retailers have a similar rule?
c. Are these rules the same as for financial accounting? If not, explain.

I11-23 What transactions are subject to the long-term contract method of reporting?

I11-24 a. What conditions must be met in order to use the installment method?
b. Why would a taxpayer elect not to use the installment method?

I11-25 What is the impact of having the entire gain on an installment sale consist of ordinary income from depreciation recapture?

I11-26 What impact does the gifting of an installment obligation have on the donor?

I11-27 What treatment is given to an installment sale involving related people?

I11-28 What is the primary impact of the imputed interest rules on installment sales?

I11-29 What changes in accounting method can be made without IRS approval?

I11-30 Can the IRS require a taxpayer to change accounting methods?

I11-31 Explain the purpose of the four-year method used in computing the tax resulting from a net adjustment due to a change in accounting methods.

I11-32 If a taxpayer changes the method of accounting used for financial reporting purposes, must the taxpayer also change his or her method of accounting for tax purposes?

ISSUE IDENTIFICATION QUESTIONS

I11-33 Judy's Cars, Inc., sells collectible automobiles to consumers. She employs the specific identification inventory valuation method. Prices are negotiated by Judy and individual customers. Judy accepts trade-ins when she sells an automobile. Judy negotiates the allowance for trade with the customer. Occasionally, Judy finds that it can take two or three years to sell a given automobile. Judy now has four automobiles that she has held for over two years. She expects to eventually sell those automobiles, but expects that they will sell for less than their original cost. What tax issues should Judy consider?

I11-34 Lana operates a real estate appraisal service business in a small town serving local lenders. After noting that lenders must pay to bring in a surveyor from out of town, she completes a course and obtains a surveyor's license that enables her to provide this service also. She now provides both services as a proprietor. What tax issues should Lana consider?

I11-35 John owns a small farm on a lake. A local developer offers John $400,000 cash for his farm. The developer believes John's farm will be very attractive to home buyers because it is on a lake. After John turns down the initial offer, the developer offers to pay John $250,000 plus an amount equal to 10% of the selling price for the homes that are developed and sold. Identify the tax issues John should consider if he accepts the offer.

I11-36 Lee is starting a small lawn service. On the advice of his accountant, Lee has formed a corporation and made an S corporation election. The accountant has asked Lee to consider electing a fiscal year ending on the last day in February. The accountant pointed out that Lee's business is likely to slow down in the winter. Also, the accountant indicated that the February year end would permit the accountant to do Lee's accounting work after the busy season in accounting is over. What tax issues should Lee consider?

PROBLEMS

I11-37 *Allowable Taxable Year.* For each of the following cases, indicate whether the taxpayer has selected an allowable tax year in an initial year. If the year selected is not acceptable, indicate what an acceptable year would be.
a. A corporation selects a January 15 year-end.
b. A corporation selects a March 31 year-end.

c. A corporation selects a year that ends on the last Friday in March.

d. A partnership selects a year that ends on December 31 and has three equal partners whose years end on March 31, April 30, and June 30.

e. An S corporation selects a December 31 year-end.

I11-38 *Change in Accounting Period.* In which of the following instances is a taxpayer permitted to change accounting periods without IRS approval?

a. A calendar-year taxpayer who wishes to change to a year that ends on the last Friday in December.

b. ABC Partnership has filed its tax return using a fiscal-year ending on March 31 for over 40 years. The partnership wishes to change to a calendar year-end that coincides with its partners' year-end.

c. Iowa Corporation, a newly acquired subsidiary, wishes to change its year-end to coincide with its parent.

I11-39 *Annualization.* Each of the following cases involves a taxable year of less than 12 months. In which situations is annualization required?

a. A new corporation formed in September elects a calendar year.

b. A calendar-year individual dies on June 15.

c. Jean, who has been using a calendar year, marries Hank, a fiscal-year taxpayer. Soon after the marriage, Jean changes her tax year to coincide with her husband's tax year.

d. A calendar-year corporation liquidates on April 20.

I11-40 *Short Period Return.* Lavanya, a single taxpayer, is a practicing accountant. She obtains permission to change her tax year from the calendar year to a year ending July 31. Her practice income for the seven months ending July 31 is $40,000. In addition, Lavanya has $3,000 of interest income and $6,250 of itemized deductions. She is entitled to one exemption. What is her tax for the short period?

I11-41 *Cash Basis Expenses.* How much of the following expenses are currently deductible by a cash basis taxpayer?

a. Medical prescriptions costing $20 paid by credit card (medical expenses already exceed the 7.5% of AGI floor).

b. Prepaid interest (not related to points) of $200 on a residential loan.

c. Taxpayer borrows $300 from the bank to make a charitable contribution. The $300 is paid to the charitable organization before the end of the tax year.

d. Taxpayer gives a note to his church indicating an intent to contribute $300.

e. A calendar-year individual mails a check for $200 to his church on December 31. The check is postmarked December 31 and clears the bank on January 4.

I11-42 *Economic Performance.* In light of the economic performance requirement, how much is deductible by the following accrual-basis corporate taxpayers in 2006?

a. Camp Corporation sells products with a one-year warranty. In 2006 Camp estimates that the warranty costs on products sold during the year will amount to $80,000. In 2006 Camp performs $38,000 of warranty work on products sold during 2005 and $36,000 of warranty work on products sold in 2006.

b. Data Corporation agrees to pay $10,000 per year for two years to a software developer. The developer has completed all work on the software and delivers the product to Data before the end of 2006.

c. In 2006 Palm Corporation pays $5,000 to a supplier to guarantee delivery of raw materials. The $5,000 is refundable if Palm decides not to acquire the materials.

d. In 2006 North Corporation pays a $1,000 security deposit on space it rents for a new office. In addition, North pays 2006 rent of $18,000. The security deposit is refundable if the property is returned in good condition.

I11-43 *Manufacturing Inventory.* Which of the following costs must be included in inventory by a manufacturing company?

a. Raw materials

b. Advertising

c. Payroll taxes for factory employees

d. Research and experimental costs

e. Factory insurance

f. Repairs to factory equipment

g. Factory utility costs

h. Factory rent

I11-44 *Single Pool LIFO.* Prime Corporation begins operations in late 2006. Prime decides to use the single pool LIFO method. Year-end inventories under FIFO are as follows:

2006	$110,000
2007	134,000
2008	125,000

The price index for 2006 is 130%; for 2007, 134%; and 2008, 140%. What are 2007 and 2008 inventories?

I11-45 *Installment Sale.* In 2006, Ace Construction Company sells a used crane to Go Construction Company. The crane, which cost $87,000 in 1998, sells for $80,000. Ace has deducted the entire cost of the crane under MACRS depreciation. Ace receives $20,000 down and is to receive $20,000 per year plus 10% interest for four years. Under the Sec. 1245 depreciation recapture rules, the entire gain is taxable as ordinary income. There is no applicable installment obligation. How much of the gain is taxable in 2006? 2007?

I11-46 *Inventory Method.* Zap Company manufactures computer hard drives. The cost of hard drives has been declining for years. Sales totaled $4,000,000 last year. Zap's ending inventory was valued at $300,000 under FIFO. The company's new president is trying to cut taxes and asks you whether the company should switch to LIFO. What do you recommend?

I11-47 *Installment Sales.* First Company sold the following assets during the year. Indicate whether First Company can use the installment method to report each transaction. If not, how is the transaction reported? Assume First Company is an accrual basis taxpayer.
a. First Company sold stock in a publicly held company costing $35,000. First Company received a $20,000 down payment and is to receive $20,000 per year for two years plus interest.
b. First Company sold land costing $150,000. First Company received a $20,000 down payment and is to receive $20,000 per year for five years plus interest.
c. First Company initiated credit sales of merchandise. The company previously sold merchandise only to cash customers. Cash sales this year totaled $4,000,000. Credit sales totaled $500,000. At year end, First Company has receivables of $100,000. The company expects to collect only $85,000 of the current receivables.

I11-48 *Installment Sale.* On December 31, 2006, Dan sells unlisted stock with a cost of $14,000 for $20,000. Dan collects $5,000 down and is scheduled to receive $5,000 per year for three years plus interest at a rate acceptable to the IRS.
a. How much gain must Dan recognize in 2006? Assume Dan uses the installment method to report the gain.
b. In early January 2007, Dan sells the three installments for a total of $13,800. How much gain or loss must Dan recognize from the sale?

I11-49 *Repossession.* Lina, an attorney, sold an antique rug for $45,000 that had been in her home. The rug cost Lina $12,000 several years ago. Lina collected $15,000 down and received a one-year interest bearing note for the balance. She is unable to collect the balance, and after incurring court costs of $500, she repossesses the rug. The rug is damaged when she recovers it and is now worth only $30,000.
a. How much gain must Lina report in the year of the sale?
b. How much gain, in any, must Lina report in the year she repossesses the rug?
c. What is the basis of the rug after the repossession?

I11-50 *Deferred Payment Sale.* Joe sells land with a $60,000 adjusted basis for $42,000. He incurs selling expenses of $2,000. The land is subject to a $10,000 mortgage. The buyer, who assumes the mortgage, pays $8,000 down and agrees to pay Joe $8,000 per year for three years plus interest. The installment obligations are worth $24,000.
a. How much gain or loss does Joe report in the year of the sale?
b. When does Joe report the interest income from the sale?
c. Does Joe report gain or loss when he collects the installment payments

I11-51 *Imputed Interest.* On January 30, 2006, Amy sells land to Bob for a stated price of $200,000. The full $200,000 is payable on January 30, 2008. No interest is stated. Amy, a cash-method taxpayer, purchased the land in 2002 for $130,000.
a. How much interest income must be reported by Amy on the sale? Assume a 9% rate compounded semiannually. The present value factor is 0.83856.
b. In what year is the interest reported?
c. How much gain is reported by Amy on the sale?

d. In what year is the gain reported?

e. What is Bob's basis in the land?

I11-52   *Change of Accounting Method.* Dana manages real estate and is a cash method taxpayer. She changes to the accrual method in 2007. Dana's business income for 2007 is $30,000 computed on the accrual method. Her books show the following:

	December 31, 2006	December 31, 2007
Accounts receivable	$16,000	$25,300
Accounts payable	15,200	11,800

a. What adjustment is necessary to Dana's income?

b. How should Dana report the adjustment?

I11-53   *Required Payment.* BCD Partnership has, for many years, had a March 31 year-end. The partnership's net income for the fiscal year ended March 31, 2007 is $400,000. Because of its fiscal year, BCD has $100,000 on deposit with the IRS from 2006.

a. How much must BCD add to the deposit?

b. When must BCD make the addition?

c. Will the partners receive any credit for the deposit? That is, are they permitted to treat the amount as estimated payments?

I11-54   *Change to LIFO.* Lance Corporation's management has asked whether they may change their inventory valuation method to LIFO. They now report their inventory using FIFO. If they can change, how would they go about it? How is the related adjustment handled?

I11-55   *Imputed Interest.* Jane loans $80,000 to John, her son, to permit him to purchase a principal residence. The loan principal is secured by John's residence, but the agreement does not specify any interest. The applicable federal rate for the year is 8%. John's net investment income is $800.

a. How much interest is imputed on the loan each year?

b. Assume that the amount of the loan is $125,000. How much interest is imputed on the loan?

c. Is John allowed to deduct the imputed interest?

d. What other tax implications are there for the loan?

I11-56   *Long-Term Contract.* King Construction Company is engaged in a road construction contract to build a highway over a three-year period. King will receive $11,200,000 for building five miles of highway. King estimates that it will incur $10,000,000 of costs before the contract is completed. As of the end of the first year King incurred $3,000,000 of costs allocated to the contract.

a. How much income from the contract must King report during the first year?

b. Assume King incurs an additional $5,000,000 of costs during the second year. How much income is reported during that year?

c. Assume that King incurs an additional $2,500,000 of costs in the third and final year of the contract. How much does King report during the third year?

d. Will King receive or pay look-back interest? Explain.

COMPREHENSIVE PROBLEM

I11-57   Dan turned age 65 and retired this year. He owned and operated a tugboat in the local harbor before his retirement. The boat cost $100,000 when he purchased it two years ago. A tugboat is 10-year property. Dan deducted $10,000 of depreciation on the boat the year he purchased it and he deducted $18,000 of depreciation last year. He sold the tugboat in November of this year for $90,000 collecting an $18,000 down payment. The buyer agreed to pay 8% interest annually on the unpaid balance and to pay $18,000 annually for four years toward the principal. The four $18,000 principal payments and related interest payments begin next year. Dan received $72,000 of business income and incurred other business expenses of $30,000 this year before he retired. He received Social Security benefits of $2,000 and withdrew $10,000 from a regular IRA account. He contributed $4,000 to his church, paid real property taxes of $2,000, and home mortgage interest of $6,500. Dan paid $200 of state income taxes when he filed last year's return earlier this year and he made estimated state income tax payments of $800 during the this year and $220 after year end. In addition, Dan made federal estimated payments of $8,000. Dan is a single, cash basis taxpayer. Ignore self-employment taxes.

a. Compute the depreciation for the current year on the tugboat.
b. Compute the amount of gain to be reported currently on the sale of the tugboat. Assume that Dan wants to use the installment method if it can be used. The accumulated depreciation on the tugboat is subject to Sec. 1245 depreciation recapture and must be reported currently.
c. How much interest, if any, must Dan report this year?
d. What is the income from the business, excluding the gain on the sale of the tugboat?
e. What is Dan's AGI?
f. What is the amount of Dan's itemized deductions?
g. What is Dan's taxable income?

TAX STRATEGY PROBLEMS

I11-58 Leon has a substantial portfolio of stocks and bonds as well as cash from some bonds that have recently matured. He has been looking at investing $200,000 in corporate bonds that pay 7% interest. The $14,000 of annual interest would be used to pay his 18-year-old son's tuition at State University. A friend suggested that Leon loan the money "interest free" to his son, a student who has no other income. The son would then invest the $200,000 in the corporate bonds and use the $14,000 interest to pay his tuition. Leon is in the 28% tax bracket. Would such a strategy reduce his family's tax? Assume the applicable federal rate is 6.5%.

I11-59 Linda is selling land she has owned for many years. The land cost $80,000 and will sell for $200,000. The buyer has offered to pay $100,000 down and pay the balance next year plus interest at 8%. Assume that Linda's after tax rate of return on investments is 10%. Would she be better off receiving the installment payments or receiving cash? Assume her ordinary income is taxed at 28% and that long-term capital gains are taxed at 15%.

TAX FORM/RETURN PREPARATION PROBLEM

I11-60 Barbara B. Kuhn (SSN 987-65-4321) purchases a fourplex on January 8, 2002, for $175,000. She allocates $25,000 of the cost to the land, and she deducts MACRS depreciation totaling $16,364. Barbara sells the fourplex on January 6, 2005, for $225,000. The buyer assumes the existing mortgage of $180,000, pays $15,000 down, and agrees to pay $15,000 per year for two years plus 12% interest. Barbara incurs selling expenses of $18,000. Complete Form 6252.

CASE STUDY PROBLEMS

I11-61 Lavonne just completed medical school and residency. She plans to open her medical practice soon. She is not familiar with the intricacies of accounting methods and periods. On advice of her attorney, she plans to form a professional corporation (a form of organization permitted under the laws of most states that does not have the usual limited liability found with business corporations, but is taxed as a corporation). She has asked you whether she should elect a fiscal year and whether she should use the cash or accrual method of reporting income. Discuss whether the options are available to her and the implications of available choices.

I11-62 Don owns equipment that he purchased several years ago for $400,000. Over the years he properly deducted $110,000 of depreciation. The depreciation will have to be recaptured as ordinary income on the sale. There is a $90,000 mortgage on the property. Don has an offer for the equipment from an individual who says he will pay $100,000 down and $100,000 per year for five years. There is no mention of interest. As the mortgage is nonassumable, Don will pay off the mortgage using most of the down payment. Don is age 61, and proceeds from the sale along with a pension from his employer will provide for his retirement. Don plans to retire next year. He currently has a 25% marginal tax rate. Discuss the tax implications of the sale. Is there anything Don can do to improve his situation?

I11-63 Troy Tools manufactures over one hundred different hand tools used by mechanics, carpenters, and plumbers. Troy's cost accounting system has always been very simple. The costs allocated to inventory have included only materials, direct labor, and factory overhead. Other overhead costs such as costs of the personnel department, purchasing, payroll, and computer services have never been treated as manufacturing overhead even though many of the activities of the departments relate to the manufacturing operations.

You are preparing Troy's tax return for the first time and determine that the company is not following the uniform capitalization rules prescribed in the tax law. You have explained to the company's president that there is a problem, and she is reluctant to change accounting methods. She says allocating these costs to the many products the company makes will be a time-consuming and expensive process. She feels that the cost of determining the additional amounts to include in inventory under the uniform capitalization rules will probably be more than the additional tax that the company will pay. What is the appropriate way to handle this situation? (See the *Statements on Standards for Tax Services* section in Chapter I15 for a discussion of these issues.)

TAX RESEARCH PROBLEMS

I11-64 Eagle and Hill Corporations discuss the terms of a land sale in December 2006, and they agree to a price of $230,000. Eagle wants to use the installment sale method, but is not sure Hill is a reliable borrower. As a result, Eagle requires Hill to place the entire purchase price in escrow to be released in five yearly installments by the escrow agent. Is the installment method available to Eagle?

A partial list of research sources is

- Rev. Rul. 77-294, 1977-2 C.B. 173
- Rev. Rul. 79-91, 1979-1 C.B. 179
- *H. O. Williams v. U.S.*, 46 AFTR 1725, 55-1 USTC ¶9220 (5th Cir., 1955)

I11-65 Texas Corporation disassembles old automobiles for the purpose of reselling their components (i.e., different types of metals, plastics, rubber, and other materials). Texas sells some of the items for scrap, but must pay to dispose of environmentally hazardous plastics and rubber. At year-end, Texas Corporation has a difficult time determining the cost of the individual parts that are stacked in piles. In fact, it would be very expensive to even weigh some of the materials on hand. Texas has followed the practice of having two experienced employees estimate the weight of different stacks and then pricing them based on quotes found in trade journals. If Texas must pay to dispose of an item, it is assigned a value of zero. In other words, Texas does not value its inventory using standard FIFO or LIFO methods. Is such a practice acceptable?

A partial list of research sources is

- Reg. Secs. 1.471-2(a) and 1.471-3(d)
- *Morrie Chaitlen*, 1978 PH T.C. Memo ¶78,006, 37 TCM 17
- *Justus & Parker Co.*, 13 BTA 127 (1928)

I11-66 Apple Corporation has never been audited before the current year. An audit is now needed from a CPA because the company is expanding rapidly and plans to issue stock to the public in a secondary offering. A CPA firm has been doing preliminary evaluations of the Apple Corporation's accounts and records. One major problem involves the valuation of inventory under GAAP. Apple Corporation has been valuing its inventory under the cost method and no write-downs have been made for obsolescence. A review of the inventory indicates that obsolescence and excess spare parts in the inventory are two major problems. The CPA states that for GAAP the company will be required to write down its inventory by 25% of its stated amount, or $100,000, and charge this amount against net income from operations for the current period. Otherwise, a "clean opinion" will not be rendered. The company controller asks your advice regarding the tax consequences from the obsolescence and spare parts inventory write-downs for the current year and the procedures for changing to the LCM method for tax purposes. Apple Corporation is on a calendar year, and the date of your contact with the company is December 1 of the current year.

A partial list of research sources is

- Secs. 446 and 471
- Reg. Secs. 1.446-1(e)(3), 1.471-2 and 1.471-4
- *American Liberty Pipe Line Co. v. CIR*, 32 AFTR 1099, 44-2 USTC ¶9408 (5th Cir., 1944)
- *Thor Power Tool Co. v. CIR*, 43 AFTR 2d 79-362, 79-1 USTC ¶9139 (USSC, 1979)

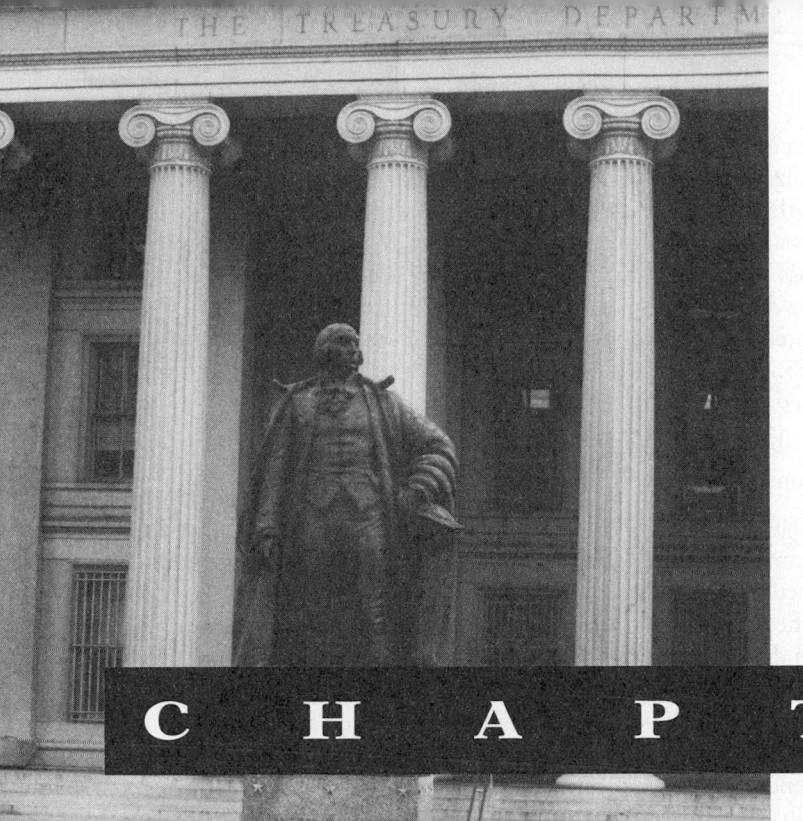

12

CHAPTER

PROPERTY TRANSACTIONS: NONTAXABLE EXCHANGES

LEARNING OBJECTIVES

After studying this chapter, you should be able to

1. ▶ Understand the tax consequences arising from a like-kind exchange

2. ▶ Determine the basis of property received in a like-kind exchange

3. ▶ Determine whether gain from an involuntary conversion may be deferred

4. ▶ Determine the basis of replacement property in an involuntary conversion

5. ▶ Determine when a gain resulting from the sale of a principal residence is excluded

KEY POINT

The transactions examined in this chapter override the normal rule that provides for the recognition of realized gains and realized losses on property used in a business or held for investment.

Taxpayers who sell or exchange property for an amount greater or less than their basis in that property have a realized gain or loss on the sale or exchange. Almost any transfer of property is treated as a sale or other disposition (see Chapter I5). The realized gain or loss must be recognized unless a specific Code section provides for nonrecognition treatment. If the realized gain or loss is not recognized at the time of the transaction, the nonrecognized gain or loss may be deferred in some cases and excluded in others.

The general rules related to the computation of realized and recognized gains or losses are covered in Chapter I5. This chapter discusses three of the most common transactions that may result in *nonrecognition* of a realized gain or loss:

► Like-kind exchanges under Sec. 1031 (deferred gain or loss)

► Involuntary conversions under Sec. 1033 (deferred gain)

► Sales of a personal residence under Sec. 121 (excluded gain)

Nonrecognition of gain treatment for like-kind exchanges, involuntary conversions, and the sale of a residence may be partially justified by the fact that taxpayers may lack the wherewithal to pay the tax despite the existence of a realized gain. For example, a taxpayer who realizes a gain due to an involuntary conversion of property (damage from fire, storm, etc.) may have to use the amount received to replace the converted property.

A typical requirement in a nontaxable exchange is that the taxpayer is required to maintain a continuing investment in comparable property (e.g., a building is exchanged for another building). In essence, a change in form rather than a change in substance occurs.

A transaction generally considered to be nontaxable may be taxable in part. In a like-kind exchange, for example, the taxpayer may also receive money or property that is not like-kind property. If non–like-kind property or money is received, the realized gain is taxable to the extent of the sum of the money and the fair market value (FMV) of the non–like-kind property received.[1]

LIKE-KIND EXCHANGES

OBJECTIVE 1

Understand the tax consequences arising from a like-kind exchange

Section 1031(a) provides that "No gain or loss shall be recognized on the exchange of property held for productive use in a trade or business or for investment if such property is exchanged solely for property of like-kind which is to be held either for productive use in a trade or business or for investment."[2]

In a **like-kind exchange**, both the property transferred and the property received must be held either for productive use in the trade or business or for investment.

EXAMPLE I12-1 ►

Tom owns land used in his trade or business. He exchanges the land for other land, which is to be held for investment. No gain or loss is recognized by Tom because he has exchanged property used in a trade or business for like-kind property to be held for investment. ◄

EXAMPLE I12-2 ►

REAL-WORLD EXAMPLE

An exchange or trade of professional football player contracts qualifies as a like-kind exchange. Rev. Rul. 71-137, 1971-1 C.B. 104.

Dawn's automobile is held for personal use. She exchanges the automobile, with a $10,000 basis, for stock of AT&T with a $12,000 FMV. The stock is held for investment. A $2,000 gain is recognized because the automobile is not used in Dawn's trade or business or held for investment. The exchange is not a like-kind exchange because neither personal-use assets nor stock qualify as like-kind property. ◄

ADDITIONAL COMMENT

The mandatory nonrecognition of loss under Sec. 1031 can be avoided by selling the old property in one transaction and buying the new property in a separate, unrelated transaction.

Section 1031 is not an elective provision. If the exchange qualifies as a like-kind exchange, nonrecognition of gain or loss is mandatory. To qualify for like-kind exchange treatment, a direct exchange must occur and the property exchanged must be like-kind. A taxpayer who prefers to recognize a loss on an exchange must structure the transaction to avoid having the exchange qualify as a like-kind exchange.

LIKE-KIND PROPERTY DEFINED

CHARACTER OF THE PROPERTY. To be a nontaxable exchange under Sec. 1031, the property exchanged must be like-kind. The Treasury Regulations specify that "the words

---

[1] Sec. 1031(b).

[2] Sec. 1031(a).

'like-kind' have reference to the nature or character of the property and not to its grade or quality."[3] Thus, exchanges of real property qualify even if the properties are dissimiliar.

EXAMPLE I12-3 ▶ Eric owns an apartment building held for investment. Eric exchanges the building for farmland to be used in his trade or business. The exchange is a like-kind exchange because both the building and the farmland are classified as real property and both properties are used either in business or held for investment. ◀

EXAMPLE I12-4 ▶ Trail Corporation exchanges improved real estate for unimproved real estate, both of which are held for investment. The exchange is a like-kind exchange.[4] ◀

ADDITIONAL COMMENT
Real property is often referred to as real estate.

LOCATION OF THE PROPERTY. Transfers of real property located in the U.S. and real property located outside the U.S. after July 9, 1989, are not like-kind exchanges. Exchanges of personal property predominantly used in the United States and personal property used outside of the United States that occur after June 8, 1997, are not like-kind exchanges. To determine where the property is predominantly used, the two-year period ending on the date the property is exchanged is analyzed. For property received, the location of predominant use is determined by analyzing the use during the two-year property after the property is received.

PROPERTY MUST BE THE SAME CLASS. An exchange is not a like-kind exchange when property of one class is exchanged for property of a different kind or class.[5] For example, if real property is exchanged for personal property (or vice versa), no like-kind exchange occurs.[6]

EXAMPLE I12-5 ▶ Gail exchanges an office building with a $400,000 adjusted basis for an airplane with a $580,000 FMV to be used in business. This is not a like-kind exchange because the office building is real property and the airplane is personal property. Gail must recognize a $180,000 ($580,000 − $400,000) gain. ◀

EXAMPLE I12-6 ▶ Gary exchanges a business truck for another truck to use in his business. This is an exchange of like-kind property. ◀

ADDITIONAL COMMENT
The rules in the Regulations dealing with exchanges of personal property are not interpreted as liberally as the rules relating to real property.

PROPERTY OF A LIKE CLASS. The Treasury Regulations provide that personal property of a **like class** meets the definition of *like-kind*.[7] Like class property is defined as depreciable tangible personal properties within the same General Asset Class or within the same Product Class.[8] Property within a General Asset Class consists of depreciable tangible personal property described in one of the asset classes provided in Rev. Proc. 87-56 for depreciation.[9] Some of the General Asset Classes are as follows:

▶ Office furniture, fixtures, and equipment (Asset Class 00.11)

▶ Information systems such as computers and peripheral equipment (Asset Class 00.12)

▶ Automobiles and taxis (Asset Class 00.22)

▶ Buses (Asset Class 00.23)

▶ Light general purpose trucks (Asset Class 00.241)

▶ Heavy general purpose trucks (Asset Class 00.242)

▶ Vessels, barges, tugs, and similar water-transportation equipment except those used in marine construction (Asset Class 00.28)

For purposes of the like-kind exchange provisions, a single property may not be classified in more than one General Asset Class or more than one Product Class. Furthermore, property in any General Asset Class may not be classified in a Product Class. A property's General Asset Class or Product Class is determined as of the exchange date.

---

[3] Reg. Sec. 1.1031(a)-1(b).
[4] *Ibid.*
[5] *Ibid.*
[6] Real property includes land and property attached to land in a relatively permanent manner. Personal property that is affixed to real property in a rel-

atively permanent manner is a fixture and is considered part of the real property. Personal property is all property that is not real property or a fixture.
[7] Reg. Sec. 1.1031(a)-2.
[8] Reg. Sec. 1.1031(a)-2(b).
[9] 1987-2 C.B. 674.

EXAMPLE I12-7 ▶ Wint transfers a personal computer used in his trade or business for a printer to be used in his trade or business. The exchange is a like-kind exchange because both properties are in the same General Asset Class (00.12). ◀

EXAMPLE I12-8 ▶ Renee transfers an airplane (Asset Class 00.21) that she uses in her trade or business for a heavy general purpose truck to use in her trade or business. The properties are not of a like class because they are in different General Asset Classes. The heavy general purpose truck is in Asset Class 00.242. ◀

Example I12-8 is taken from the Treasury Regulations, which further state: "Because each of the properties is within a General Asset Class, the properties may not be classified within a Product Class. The airplane and heavy general purpose truck are also not of a like kind. Therefore, the exchange does not qualify for nonrecognition of gain or loss under Sec. 1031."[10]

If two properties are not within a General Asset Class, it still may be possible to be considered like-kind if the properties are within the same Product Class. Property in a Product Class consists of depreciable tangible personal property listed in the North American Classification System prepared by the Office of Management and Budget.[11] The Regulations state that an exchange of a grader for a scrapper is an exchange of properties of like class because neither property is in a General Asset Class and both properties are listed in the same Product Class.[12]

There are no like classes for intangible personal property, nondepreciable personal property, or personal property held for investment. To have a like-kind exchange of property held for investment, the property must be exchanged for like-kind property. To determine whether an exchange of intangible personal property is a like-kind exchange, one must consider the type of right involved as well as the underlying property to which the intangible property relates. An exchange of a copyright for a novel for a copyright on a different novel is a like-kind exchange, but the exchange of a copyright on a novel for a copyright on a song is not a like-kind exchange.[13]

ADDITIONAL COMMENT

An exchange can be a like-kind exchange for one party to the transaction but not qualify as a like-kind exchange for the other party.

NON–LIKE-KIND PROPERTY EXCHANGES. An exchange of inventory or securities does not qualify as a like-kind exchange.[14]

EXAMPLE I12-9 ▶ Antonio, a dealer in farm equipment, exchanges a new combine for other property in the same General Asset Class to be used in Antonio's trade or business. Because Antonio is a dealer, the new combine is inventory and the exchange does not qualify as a like-kind exchange. ◀

EXAMPLE I12-10 ▶ Nancy owns Able Corporation stock as an investment. Nancy exchanges the stock for antiques to be held as investments. This exchange is taxable because stock does not qualify as like-kind property. ◀

In most cases, to qualify as a like-kind exchange of personal property, the property must be nearly identical. For example, livestock of different sexes are not like-kind property.[15] An exchange of gold bullion held for investment for silver bullion held for investment is not a like-kind exchange. Silver and gold are intrinsically different metals and primarily are used in different ways.[16] Currency exchanges are not like-kind exchanges,[17] and the exchange of a partnership interest for an interest in another partnership is not a like-kind exchange.[18]

---

[10] Reg. Sec. 1.1031(a)-2(b)(7) Ex. 2.
[11] Reg. Sec. 1.1031(a)-2(b)(3).
[12] Reg. Sec. 1.1031(a)-2(b)(7) Ex. 3.
[13] Reg. Sec. 1.1031(a)-2(c)(1).
[14] Sec. 1031(a)(2). An exchange of stock is not a like-kind exchange. However, an exchange of stock is a nontaxable exchange if the exchange is related to a tax-free reorganization.

[15] Sec. 1031(e).
[16] Rev. Rul. 82-166, 1982-2 C.B. 190.
[17] Rev. Rul. 74-7, 1974-1 C.B. 198.
[18] Sec. 1031(a)(2).

EXCHANGE OF SECURITIES. The like-kind exchange rules do not apply to stocks, bonds, or notes.[19] However, Sec. 1036 provides that no gain or loss is recognized on the exchange of common stock for common stock or preferred stock for preferred stock in the same corporation. Sec. 1036 applies even if voting common stock is exchanged for nonvoting common stock of the same corporation. The nontaxable exchange of stock of the same corporation may be between two stockholders or a stockholder and the corporation.[20]

Section 1036 does not apply to exchanges of common stock for preferred stock; stock for bonds of same corporation, or any kind of stock in different corporations.

EXAMPLE I12-11 ▶ Kelly owns common stock of Best Corporation. Best issues class B common stock to Kelly in exchange for her common stock. No gain or loss is recognized because this is an exchange of common stock for common stock in the same corporation. If Best issues its preferred stock for Kelly's common stock, Kelly will have a recognized gain or loss unless there is a tax-free reorganization. ◀

EXAMPLE I12-12 ▶ Shirley owns 100 shares of Top Corporation common stock. The stock has a $40,000 adjusted basis and a $50,000 FMV. Bob owns 100 shares of Star Corporation common stock with a $50,000 FMV. If Shirley and Bob exchange their stock, the exchange is taxable, and Shirley has a $10,000 ($50,000 − $40,000) recognized gain. The exchange is neither a like-kind exchange nor an exchange of stock for stock of the same corporation. ◀

A DIRECT EXCHANGE MUST OCCUR

To qualify as a like-kind exchange, a direct exchange of property must occur.[21] Thus, the sale of property and the subsequent purchase of like-kind property does not qualify as a like-kind exchange unless the two transactions are interdependent.

EXAMPLE I12-13 ▶ Karen sells a lathe used in her business to Rashad for an amount greater than the lathe's adjusted basis. After the sale, Karen purchases another lathe from David. The gain is recognized because these two transactions do not qualify as an exchange of like-kind property. ◀

A sale and a subsequent purchase may be treated as an exchange if the two transactions are interdependent. The IRS indicates that a nontaxable exchange may exist when the taxpayer sells property to a dealer and then purchases like-kind property from the same dealer.[22]

THREE-PARTY EXCHANGES

The typical two-party exchange is not always practical. If both parties do not own like-kind property that meets each other's needs, a three-party exchange might be necessary. A three-party exchange is also useful when the taxpayer is willing to exchange property for like-kind property but is not willing to sell the property to a prospective buyer. The taxpayer's unwillingness to sell the property may be motivated by the desire to avoid an immediate tax on a gain resulting from the sale of the property. Therefore, the taxpayer may arrange to have the prospective buyer purchase property from a third party that fulfills the taxpayer's needs. The three-party exchange can be an effective way of allowing the taxpayer to consummate a like-kind exchange.

EXAMPLE I12-14 ▶

KEY POINT

Transfers of property in a three-party exchange must be part of a single, integrated plan. It is important that the taxpayers can show their intent to enter into a like-kind exchange even though contractual interdependence is not necessary to the finding of an exchange.

Kathy owns a farm in Nebraska, which Dick offers to purchase. Kathy is not willing to sell the farm but is willing to exchange the farm for an apartment complex in Arizona. The complex is available for sale. Dick purchases the apartment complex in Arizona from Allyson and transfers it to Kathy in exchange for Kathy's farm. The farm and the apartment complex each have a $900,000 FMV. For Kathy, the transaction qualifies as a like-kind exchange because it is a direct exchange of business real property (the farm) for investment real estate (the apartment complex). For Dick, the exchange is not a like-kind exchange. ◀

In the example above, the exchange is convenient for all the parties. However, it is not always this convenient to execute a three-party exchange. For example, Kathy may want

---

[19] Reg. Sec. 1.1031(a)-1(a)(1)(ii).
[20] Reg. Sec. 1.1036-1(a).

[21] Sec. 1031(a).
[22] Rev. Rul. 61-119, 1961-1 C.B. 395.

to own an apartment complex in Arizona, but the property she prefers may not be currently available. In this case, a nonsimultaneous exchange may occur.

NONSIMULTANEOUS EXCHANGE. A nonsimultaneous exchange is treated as a like-kind exchange if the exchange is completed within a specified time period. The property to be received in the exchange must be identified within 45 days after the date of the transfer of the property relinquished in the exchange. The replacement property must be received within the earlier of 180 days after the date the taxpayer transfers the property relinquished in the exchange or the due date for filing a return (including extensions) for the year in which the transfer of the relinquished property occurs.[23]

EXAMPLE I12-15 ▶

On May 5, 2006, Joal transfers property to Lauren, who transfers cash to an escrow agent. The escrow agent is to purchase suitable like-kind property for Joal. Joal does not have actual or constructive receipt of the cash during the delayed period. To be a like-kind exchange for Joal, the suitable like-kind property must be identified by June 19, 2006 (45 days after the transfer), and Joal must receive the property by November 1, 2006 (180 days after the transfer). ◀

EXAMPLE I12-16 ▶

Assume the same facts as Example I12-15 except that the transfer by Joal occurs on November 10, 2006. To be a like-kind exchange for Joal, the suitable like-kind property must be identified by December 25, 2006, and Joal must receive the property by April 15, 2007, unless Joal files an automatic four-month extension for the filing of his return (i.e., the due date is extended until August 15, 2007). In such a case, the property must be received no later than 180 days following the transfer of the property relinquished in the exchange, or by May 8, 2007 (i.e., 180 days after November 10, 2006). ◀

RECEIPT OF BOOT

Taxpayers who want to exchange property do not always own property of equal value. To complete the exchange, non–like-kind property or money may be given or received. Cash and non–like-kind property constitute **boot**.

Gain is recognized to the extent of the boot received. However, the amount of recognized gain is limited to the amount of the taxpayer's realized gain.[24] In effect, the realized gain serves as a ceiling for the amount of the recognized gain. The receipt of boot as part of a nontaxable exchange does not cause a realized loss to be recognized.[25]

EXAMPLE I12-17 ▶

Mario exchanges business equipment with a $50,000 adjusted basis for $10,000 cash and business equipment with a $65,000 FMV. The realized gain is $25,000 ($75,000 − $50,000). Because the $10,000 of boot received is less than the $25,000 realized gain, the recognized gain is $10,000. ◀

EXAMPLE I12-18 ▶

Mary exchanges business equipment with a $70,000 adjusted basis for $20,000 cash and business equipment with a $65,000 FMV. Her realized gain is $15,000 ($85,000 − $70,000). Because the $20,000 of boot received is more than the $15,000 realized gain, $15,000 of gain is recognized. ◀

Taxing part or all of the gain when cash is received in like-kind exchanges is consistent with the wherewithal-to-pay concept. However, boot may not always be in the form of a liquid asset. If non–like-kind property other than cash is received as boot, the amount of the boot is the property's FMV.

EXAMPLE I12-19 ▶

Jane exchanges land held as an investment with a $70,000 basis for other land with a $100,000 FMV and a motorcycle with a $2,000 FMV. The acquired land is to be held for investment, and the motorcycle is for personal use. Personal-use property is non–like-kind property and constitutes boot. The realized gain is $32,000 [($100,000 + $2,000) − $70,000]. The amount of boot received is equal to the FMV of the motorcycle. The recognized gain is $2,000, the lesser of the amount of boot received ($2,000) or the realized gain ($32,000). ◀

---

[23] Secs. 1031(a)(3)(A) and (B).
[24] Sec. 1031(b).

[25] Sec. 1031(c).

EXAMPLE I12-20 ▶

SELF-STUDY QUESTION

Why is the relief of a liability treated as if one has received cash?

ANSWER

If it were not treated as such, a taxpayer could receive cash shortly before the exchange by borrowing from a bank, using the property as collateral. Then, if the taxpayer is relieved of the debt in the like-kind exchange, he or she would still have cash without having paid a tax on the gain.

Assume the same facts in Example I12-19 except that Jane uses the motorcycle in a business. The motorcycle is boot, and a $2,000 gain is still recognized because the exchange of real property for personal property is not a like-kind exchange. ◀

PROPERTY TRANSFERS INVOLVING LIABILITIES. If a liability is assumed (or the property is taken subject to a liability), the amount of the liability is considered money received by the taxpayer on the exchange.[26] One who assumes the debt or takes the property subject to a liability is treated as having paid cash, while the party that is relieved of the debt is treated as having received cash. If each party assumes a liability of the other party, only the net liability given or received is treated as boot.[27]

EXAMPLE I12-21 ▶

Mary exchanges land with a $550,000 FMV that is used in her business for Doug's building, which has a $450,000 FMV. Mary's basis in the land is $400,000, and the land is subject to a liability of $100,000, which Doug assumes. Mary's realized gain is $150,000 [($450,000 + $100,000) − $400,000]. Because assumption of the $100,000 liability is treated as boot, Mary recognizes a $100,000 gain. ◀

EXAMPLE I12-22 ▶

Matt owns an office building with a $700,000 basis, which is subject to a liability of $200,000. Susan owns an apartment complex with a $900,000 FMV, which is subject to a $150,000 liability. Matt and Susan exchange buildings and assume the related liabilities. Matt's realized gain is $250,000 [($900,000 + $200,000) − ($700,000 + $150,000)]. Matt receives boot of $50,000 ($200,000 − $150,000) and recognizes a $50,000 gain. ◀

BASIS OF PROPERTY RECEIVED

OBJECTIVE 2

Determine the basis of property received in a like-kind exchange

LIKE-KIND PROPERTY RECEIVED. The basis of property received in a nontaxable exchange is equal to the adjusted basis of the property exchanged increased by gain recognized and reduced by any boot received or loss recognized on the exchange.[28]

$$\begin{matrix} \text{Basis of property} \\ \text{received in a non-} \\ \text{taxable exchange} \end{matrix} = \begin{matrix} \text{Basis of} \\ \text{property} \\ \text{exchanged} \end{matrix} - \begin{matrix} \text{Boot} \\ \text{received} \end{matrix} + \begin{matrix} \text{Gain} \\ \text{recognized} \end{matrix} - \begin{matrix} \text{Loss} \\ \text{recognized}^{29} \end{matrix}$$

EXAMPLE I12-23 ▶

ADDITIONAL COMMENT

In effect the formula used to calculate the basis of the new property involves nothing more than journalizing the transaction and adjusting the basis of the new property by an amount needed to make the entry balance.

Chuck, who is in the business of racing horses, exchanges a racehorse with a $30,000 basis for $10,000 cash and a trotter with an $80,000 FMV. Chuck's realized gain is $60,000 [($80,000 + $10,000) − $30,000], and $10,000 of the gain is recognized because the boot received is less than the realized gain. Chuck's basis for the replacement property (i.e., the trotter) is $30,000 ($30,000 basis of property exchanged − $10,000 of boot received + $10,000 of gain recognized). ◀

The basis of the like-kind property received can also be computed by subtracting the unrecognized gain from its FMV or by adding the unrecognized loss to its FMV. Chuck's $30,000 basis for the trotter in Example I12-23 may be computed by subtracting the $50,000 of unrecognized gain from the $80,000 FMV.

EXAMPLE I12-24 ▶

KEY POINT

The basis adjustment is the mechanism that ensures that gain or loss is temporarily postponed rather than permanently excluded.

Pam, who operates a circus, exchanges an elephant with a $15,000 basis for $3,000 cash and a tiger with a $10,000 FMV. The $2,000 realized loss [($10,000 + $3,000) − $15,000] is not recognized. The receipt of boot does not cause a realized loss to be recognized. Pam's basis for the replacement property (i.e., the tiger) is $12,000 ($15,000 basis of property exchanged − $3,000 boot received). ◀

As indicated earlier, realized gains and losses resulting from nontaxable exchanges are deferred. This deferral is reflected in the basis of property received and is illustrated in the

[26] Sec. 1031(d). If a liability is assumed, the taxpayer agrees to pay the debt. If property is taken subject to the liability, the taxpayer is responsible for the debt only to the extent that the property could be used to pay the debt.
[27] Reg. Sec. 1.1031(b)-1(c).

[28] Sec. 1031(d).
[29] A loss is recognized only when the taxpayer transfers boot with a basis greater than its FMV. Transfers of non–like-kind property (i.e., boot) are discussed in a separate section of this chapter.

two preceding examples. In Example I12-23, the $50,000 ($60,000 − $10,000) unrecognized gain may be recognized when the trotter is sold or exchanged in a taxable transaction, because the basis of the replacement property is less than its FMV by the amount of the deferred gain. For example, if the trotter is sold in a taxable transaction for its $80,000 FMV, the $50,000 ($80,000 − $30,000 basis) of previously unrecognized gain would be recognized. In Example I12-24, the $2,000 unrecognized loss is reflected in the basis of the tiger. If Pam sells the tiger for its $10,000 FMV, a $2,000 loss ($10,000 − $12,000 basis) is recognized.

If more than one item of like-kind property is received, the basis is allocated among the properties in proportion to their relative FMVs on the date of the exchange.

EXAMPLE I12-25 ▶

Saul, who operates a zoo, exchanges a boa constrictor with a $300 basis for a python with a $400 FMV and an anaconda with a $600 FMV. The $700 realized gain [($400 + $600) − $300] is not recognized. The total bases of the properties received is $300. This amount is allocated to the properties (i.e., the python and the anaconda) based on their relative FMVs. Saul's basis for the python is $120 [($400 ÷ $1,000) × $300], and the basis for the anaconda is $180 [($600 ÷ $1,000) × $300]. ◀

NON–LIKE-KIND PROPERTY RECEIVED. The basis of non–like-kind property received is "an amount equivalent to its FMV at the date of the exchange."[30]

EXAMPLE I12-26
KEY POINT

Steve had basis of $20,000 before the exchange. Since he recognized gain of $5,000, the total basis of the two assets should be $25,000.

▶

Steve exchanges a punch press with a $20,000 adjusted basis for a press brake with a $50,000 FMV and $5,000 of marketable securities. Steve's realized gain is $35,000 [($50,000 + $5,000) − $20,000], and $5,000 of the realized gain is recognized due to the receipt of boot. Steve's basis for the marketable securities is $5,000, and the basis for the press brake is $20,000 ($20,000 basis of property exchanged − $5,000 boot received + $5,000 gain recognized). ◀

 STOP & THINK

Question: Chris Reedy owns 40 houses that he uses as rental property. All houses have a FMV greater than their adjusted basis. Chris wishes to diversify his investments and is considering selling ten of his houses and using the proceeds to purchase other types of investment assets such as stocks, bonds, commercial parking lots and land near town that he expects to increase in value. He asks you for advice.

Solution: If he sells the ten houses, he will have a gain and must pay taxes on the gain. He could defer the gain by exchanging the houses for like-kind property. Stocks and bonds are not like-kind property, but the commercial parking lots and the land should qualify as like-kind property, therefore the tax law encourages him to exchange the houses for the commercial parking lot and/or the land.

ADDITIONAL COMMENT

The running of the two-year holding period is suspended during any period in which the property holder's risk of loss is substantially diminished.

EXCHANGES BETWEEN RELATED PARTIES

Prior to 1990, related taxpayers could often use the like-kind exchange provisions to lower taxes because the tax basis for the property received is determined by the basis of the property exchanged. Related taxpayers could take advantage of the shift in tax basis to transfer a gain on a subsequent sale to a related party.[31] However, exchanges of property between related parties are not like-kind exchanges under current law if either party disposes of the property within two years of the exchange. Any gain resulting from the original exchange is recognized in the year of the subsequent disposition.[32] Dispositions due to death or involuntary conversion, or for non–tax avoidance purposes are disregarded.[33]

EXAMPLE I12-27 ▶

Melon Corporation, which is 100% owned by Linda, owned land with a basis of $200,000 that was held for investment. Rick wanted to purchase the land for $900,000. Linda owned an office building with a basis of $750,000 and a FMV of $900,000. Instead of selling the land to Rick, Melon Corporation exchanged the land for Linda's office building in December 2005.

---

[30] Reg. Sec. 1.1031(d)-1(c).
[31] The definition of *related parties* is the same as those for Sec. 267(a) which is discussed in Chapter I6, and includes brothers, sisters, parents, children, and corporations where the taxpayer owns at least 50% in value. See Sec. 1031(f)(3).

[32] Sec. 1031(f)(1)(C).
[33] Sec. 1031(f)(2).

Two months later, Linda sells the land to Rick for $900,000. The exchange of the land for the office building is not a like-kind exchange because one of the related parties disposes of the property within two years of the exchange. In 2006, Melon's recognized gain on the exchange of the land is $700,000 ($900,000 − $200,000) and Linda's recognized gain on the exchange of the office building is $150,000 ($900,000 − $750,000). Because Linda's basis for the land is now $900,000, no gain is recognized on the sale of the land to Rick. ◀

If the parties in Example I12-27 were not related, a like-kind exchange occurred in 2005 and Linda's gain on the sale of the land to Rick is $150,000 ($900,000 − $750,000). Of course, the exchange is not a like-kind exchange if Linda does not hold the land for investment or for use in her trade or business after receiving it from Melon.

TRANSFER OF NON–LIKE-KIND PROPERTY

In all of the preceding examples that include a transfer of boot, the transferor (i.e., the taxpayer) received boot. If the taxpayer transfers non–like-kind property, gain or loss equal to the difference between the FMV and the adjusted basis of the non–like-kind property surrendered must be recognized. However, if the non–like-kind property is a personal use asset, the loss is not recognized.

EXAMPLE I12-28 ▶ Shirley exchanges land with a $30,000 basis and marketable securities with a $10,000 basis to David for land with a $60,000 FMV in a transaction that otherwise qualifies as a like-kind exchange. The FMV of the marketable securities and the land surrendered by Shirley is $14,000 and $46,000, respectively. Because the non–like-kind property that Shirley transfers has a FMV greater than its basis, she recognizes $4,000 ($14,000 − $10,000) of gain. Shirley's basis for the land received is $44,000 ($30,000 + $10,000 + $4,000), which is the basis of both assets exchanged plus the gain recognized on the exchange. ◀

EXAMPLE I12-29 ▶ Paul exchanges timberland held as an investment for undeveloped land with a $200,000 FMV. Paul's basis for the timberland is $125,000. His tractor with a $6,000 basis and a $4,000 FMV is also transferred. Because the non–like-kind property (i.e., the tractor) that Paul transfers has a FMV less than its basis, he recognizes a $2,000 ($4,000 − $6,000) loss. Paul's basis for the undeveloped land is $129,000 ($125,000 + $6,000 − $2,000). ◀

In Example I12-29, Paul recognizes a loss on the non–like-kind property he surrenders, despite receiving property in the aggregate with a FMV greater than the total adjusted basis of the transferred assets. Paul is actually making two exchanges. His exchange of timberland with a basis of $125,000 for undeveloped land with a $196,000 FMV is a like-kind exchange, but his exchange of the tractor with a basis of $6,000 for undeveloped land with a $4,000 FMV is a taxable exchange. In Example I12-30, Ed also makes two exchanges. He has a realized and recognized gain as well as a realized but unrecognized loss.

EXAMPLE I12-30 ▶

Ed owns equipment used in business with a $20,000 adjusted basis and a $15,000 FMV and marketable securities with a $10,000 basis and an $18,000 FMV. Ed exchanges the marketable securities and the equipment for business equipment in the same General Asset Class with a $33,000 FMV. Although the net realized gain is $3,000 [$33,000 − ($20,000 + $10,000)], Ed recognizes an $8,000 gain because he has transferred non–like-kind property with a $10,000 basis and an $18,000 FMV. The $5,000 realized loss on the transfer of equipment is not recognized due to the nonrecognition of gain or loss rules of Sec. 1031. Ed's basis for the equipment received is $38,000 ($20,000 + $10,000 + $8,000). ◀

HOLDING PERIOD FOR PROPERTY RECEIVED

LIKE-KIND PROPERTY. The holding period of like-kind property received in a nontaxable exchange includes the holding period of the property exchanged if the like-kind property surrendered is a capital asset or an asset that is Sec. 1231 property. In essence, the holding period of the property exchanged carries over to the holding period of the like-kind property received.[34] The rule regarding the holding period carryover is consistent with the notion of a continuing investment in the underlying property that has been transferred.

---

[34] Sec. 1223(1) and Reg. Sec. 1.1223-1(a).

BOOT. The holding period for the boot property received begins the day after the date of the exchange.[35]

EXAMPLE I12-31 ▶ Mario owns a Van Gogh painting acquired on May 1, 1992, as an investment. He exchanges the painting on April 10, 2006, for a Picasso sculpture and marketable securities to be held as investments. The holding period for the sculpture begins on May 1, 1992, and the holding period for the marketable securities starts on April 11, 2006. ◀

The like-kind exchange provisions are summarized in Topic Review I12-1.

Topic Review I12-1

Section 1031—Like-Kind Exchanges

▶ Gains and losses are not recognized for like-kind exchanges.

▶ Nonrecognition of gains and losses is mandatory if the exchange is a like-kind exchange.

▶ Section 1031 applies to exchanges of property used in a trade or business or held for investment.

▶ Property exchanged and received must be like-kind.

▶ Subject to certain time constraints, a nonsimultaneous exchange may qualify as a like-kind exchange.

▶ Some gain may be recognized if the taxpayer receives or gives non–like-kind property (boot) in an otherwise like-kind exchange.

▶ A loss may be recognized if the taxpayer transfers non–like-kind property (boot) in an otherwise like-kind exchange.

▶ The basis of property received in an exchange is the basis of the property exchanged less the boot received plus the gain recognized and less any loss recognized.

▶ The nonrecognized gain or loss is deferred.

▶ The holding period of like-kind property received includes the holding period of the property exchanged.

INVOLUNTARY CONVERSIONS

OBJECTIVE 3

Determine whether gain from an involuntary conversion may be deferred

Taxpayers who realize a gain due to the involuntary conversion of property may elect to defer recognition of the entire gain if qualifying replacement property is acquired within a specified time period at a cost equal to or greater than the amount realized from the involuntary conversion. No gain is recognized if the property is converted "into property similar or related in service or use to the property so converted."[36]

The opportunity provided in Sec. 1033 to defer recognition of the gain reflects the fact that the taxpayer maintains a continuing investment and may lack the wherewithal to pay the tax on the gain that would otherwise be recognized. Furthermore, the involuntary conversion is beyond the taxpayer's control.

Note that the gain is deferred, not excluded. The basis of the replacement property is the property's cost reduced by the amount of gain deferred. The tax treatment for an involuntary conversion is similar to the tax treatment of a like-kind exchange.

KEY POINT

Unlike the like-kind exchange provisions which are mandatory, the involuntary conversion provisions are elective. Further, the involuntary conversion rules apply only to gains, not losses.

EXAMPLE I12-32 ▶

ADDITIONAL COMMENT

Property involved in an involuntary conversion need not be used in a trade or business or held for investment to qualify for the deferral of gain.

Lenea's warehouse with a $500,000 basis is destroyed by a hurricane. She collects $650,000 from the insurance company and purchases a new warehouse for $720,000. Lenea may elect to defer recognition of the $150,000 gain ($650,000 − $500,000). If the election is made, the basis of the new warehouse is $570,000 ($720,000 − $150,000). The $150,000 gain is merely deferred rather than excluded, because an immediate sale of the replacement property at its $720,000 FMV results in a recognized gain equal to the deferred gain on the involuntarily converted property. For example, if the new warehouse is sold for $720,000, the recognized gain is $150,000 ($720,000 − $570,000). ◀

---

[35] Sec. 1223 and Reg. Sec. 1.1223-1(a).   [36] Sec. 1033(a)(1).

TYPICAL MISCONCEPTION

Occasionally, taxpayers fail to realize that Sec. 1033 applies only to gains, not losses.

Section 1033 does not apply to losses realized from an involuntary conversion. A taxpayer may not elect to defer recognition of a loss resulting from an involuntary conversion.

EXAMPLE I12-33 ▶

Barry's offshore drilling rig with an $800,000 adjusted basis is destroyed by a typhoon. He collects $700,000 from the insurance company and purchases a new drilling rig for $760,000. The $100,000 loss ($700,000 − $800,000) is recognized as a casualty loss, and the basis of the new drilling rig is its purchase price of $760,000. ◀

INVOLUNTARY CONVERSION DEFINED

ADDITIONAL COMMENT

Typically, an involuntary conversion consists of either a casualty or a condemnation.

For Sec. 1033 to apply, property must be compulsorily or involuntarily converted into money or other property. An **involuntary conversion** may be due to theft, seizure, requisition, condemnation, or destruction of the property. The destruction of the property may be complete or partial.[37] For purposes of Sec. 1033, destruction of property does not have to meet the "suddenness" test if the cause of destruction otherwise falls within the general concept of a casualty.[38]

An involuntary conversion occurs when a governmental unit exercises its power of eminent domain to acquire the taxpayer's property without the taxpayer's consent. Furthermore, the threat or imminence of requisition or condemnation of property may permit a taxpayer to defer recognition of gain from the sale or exchange of property under the involuntary conversion rules. Taxpayers who transfer property due to such a threat must be careful to confirm that a decision to acquire their property for public use has been made.[39] Written confirmation of potential condemnation is particularly helpful.[40]

EXAMPLE I12-34 ▶

Bruce owns an automobile dealership near a state university campus. On a number of occasions, the president of the university expressed an interest in acquiring Bruce's property for additional parking space. The president is not certain about the availability of funds for the purchase, and the university is reluctant to have the property condemned for its use. Based on the university's interest in the property, Bruce sells the property to the Jet Corporation. The threat or imminence of conversion does not exist merely because the property is being considered for acquisition. The sale does not constitute an involuntary conversion.[41] ◀

THREAT OF CONDEMNATION.   If a threat of condemnation exists and the taxpayer has reasonable grounds to believe that the property will be condemned, Sec. 1033 applies even if the taxpayer sells the property to an entity other than the governmental unit that is threatening to condemn the property.[42]

EXAMPLE I12-35 ▶

ADDITIONAL COMMENT

If the property in Example I12-35 is later condemned, Marty may be able to defer part or all of the gain.

At its regular meeting on Tuesday night, the city commission authorized the city attorney to start the process of condemning two lots owned by Beth for use as a public park. On Wednesday afternoon, Beth sells the two lots to Marty at a gain. The sale of property to Marty is an involuntary conversion, and Beth may elect to defer recognition of the gain if she satisfies the Sec. 1033 requirements. ◀

CONVERSION MUST BE INVOLUNTARY.   The conversion must be involuntary. For example, an involuntary conversion does not occur when a taxpayer pays someone to set fire to his or her building.[43] An involuntary conversion also does not occur when a taxpayer who is developing a subdivision reserves certain property for a school site and later sells the property to the school district under condemnation proceedings. In this situation, the taxpayer was required to reserve property for a school site in order to receive zoning approval for development of the subdivision.[44]

---

[37] Reg. Sec. 1.1033(a)-1.
[38] Rev. Rul. 59-102, 1959-1 C.B. 200.
[39] Rev. Rul. 63-221, 1963-2 C.B. 332, and *Joseph P. Balistrieri*, 1979 PH T.C. Memo ¶79,115, 38 TCM 526.
[40] Rev. Rul. 63-221, 1963-2 C.B. 332.

[41] *Forest City Chevrolet*, 1977 PH T.C. Memo ¶77,187, 36 TCM 768.
[42] Rev. Rul. 81-180, 1981-2 C.B. 161, and *Creative Solutions, Inc. v. U.S.*, 12 AFTR 2d 5229, 1963-2 USTC ¶9615 (5th Cir., 1963).
[43] Rev. Rul. 82-74, 1982-1 C.B. 110.
[44] Rev. Rul. 69-654, 1969-2 C.B. 162.

Although the typical involuntary conversion generally results from a casualty or condemnation, Sec. 1033 provides that certain transactions involving livestock are to be treated as involuntary conversions.[45] For example, the destruction or sale of livestock because of disease is an involuntary conversion.

TAX TREATMENT OF GAIN DUE TO INVOLUNTARY CONVERSION INTO BOOT

Gain may be deferred if the property is involuntarily converted into money or property that is not similar or related in service or use to the converted property.[46] The taxpayer must make a proper replacement of the converted property within a specific time period and elect to defer the gain.

REALIZED GAIN. The taxpayer's realized gain is the excess of the amount received due to the involuntary conversion over the adjusted basis of the property converted. The total award or proceeds received are reduced by expenses incurred to determine the amount realized (e.g., attorney's fees incurred in connection with determining the settlement to be received from a condemnation). If the payment of the award or proceeds is delayed, any amounts paid as interest are not included in determining the amount realized.[47] Amounts received as interest on an award for property condemned are taxed as ordinary income even if the interest is paid by a state or political subdivision.[48]

EXAMPLE I12-36 ▶ Richard's property with a $100,000 basis is condemned by the city of Phoenix. Richard receives a $190,000 award and pays $1,000 in legal expenses for representation at the condemnation proceedings and $800 for an appraisal of the property. The amount realized is $188,200 [$190,000 − ($1,000 + $800)]. The gain realized is $88,200 ($188,200 − $100,000). Part or all of the realized gain may be deferred if the requirements of Sec. 1033 are satisfied and an election is made to defer the gain. ◀

GAIN RECOGNIZED. To defer the entire gain, the taxpayer must purchase replacement property with a cost equal to or greater than the amount realized from the involuntary conversion. If the replacement property is purchased for an amount less than the amount realized, that portion of the realized gain that is equal to the excess of the amount realized from the conversion over the cost of the replacement property must be recognized.[49] Stated differently, the recognized gain is the lesser of the realized gain or the excess of the amount realized over the cost of the replacement property.

EXAMPLE I12-37 ▶ Bob owns a restaurant with a $200,000 basis. The restaurant is destroyed by fire, and he receives $300,000 from the insurance company. Bob's realized gain is $100,000 ($300,000 − $200,000). He purchases another restaurant for $275,000. Bob may elect to defer $75,000 of the gain under Sec. 1033, and $25,000 ($300,000 − $275,000) of Bob's gain must be recognized because he failed to reinvest all of the $300,000 insurance proceeds in a suitable replacement property. ◀

EXAMPLE I12-38 ▶ Stacey owns a racehorse with a $450,000 basis used for breeding purposes. The racehorse is killed by lightning, and she collects $800,000 from the insurance company. Stacey's realized gain is $350,000 ($800,000 − $450,000). She purchases another racehorse for $430,000. The entire $350,000 of gain is recognized, because the amount realized from the involuntary conversion exceeds the cost of the replacement property by $370,000 ($800,000 − $430,000) which is more than the realized gain. ◀

OBJECTIVE 4

Determine the basis of replacement property in an involuntary conversion

BASIS OF REPLACEMENT PROPERTY. If replacement property is purchased, the basis of the replacement property is its cost less any deferred gain. If the taxpayer elects to defer the gain, the holding period of the replacement property includes the holding period of the converted property.[50]

---

[45] Secs. 1033(d) and (e). If a taxpayer sells or exchanges more livestock than normal because of a drought, the sale or exchange of the excess amount is treated as an involuntary conversion. The livestock must be other than poultry and be held by the taxpayer for draft, breeding, or dairy purposes.

[46] Sec. 1033(a)(2).

[47] *Flushingside Realty & Construction Co.*, 1943 PH T.C. Memo ¶43,286, 2 TCM 259.

[48] *Spencer D. Stewart v. CIR*, 52 AFTR 2d 83-5885, 83-2 USTC ¶9573 (9th Cir., 1983).

[49] Sec. 1033(a)(2)(A).

[50] Sec. 1223(1)(A).

EXAMPLE I12-39 ▶ Tracy owns a yacht that is held for personal use and has a $20,000 basis. The yacht is destroyed by a storm, and Tracy collects $24,000 from the insurance company. She purchases a new $35,000 yacht for personal use and elects to defer the $4,000 ($24,000 − $20,000) gain. The basis of the new yacht is $31,000 ($35,000 − $4,000). The holding period for the new yacht includes the holding period of the destroyed yacht. ◀

SEVERANCE DAMAGES. If a portion of the taxpayer's property is condemned, the taxpayer may receive **severance damages** as compensation for a decline in the value of the retained property. For example, if access to the retained property becomes difficult or if the property is exposed to greater damage from flooding or erosion, its value may decline.

The IRS considers severance damages to be "analogous to the proceeds of property insurance; they represent compensation for damages to the property."[51] Amounts received as severance damages reduce the basis of the retained property, and any amount received in excess of the property's basis is treated as gain.[52]

EXAMPLE I12-40 ▶ Cindy owns a 500-acre farm with a $200 basis per acre ($100,000 basis). The state condemns ten acres across the northwest corner of her farm to build a major highway. Cindy receives a condemnation award of $500 per acre for the ten acres. The highway separates the farm into a 25-acre tract and a 465-acre tract. Because her ability to efficiently use the 25-acre tract for farming is reduced, the state pays additional severance damages of $90 per acre for the 25 acres. Cindy's gain realized from condemnation of the ten acres is $3,000 [$5,000 − ($200 × 10 acres)]. The $2,250 ($90 × 25 acres) of severance damages reduce the basis of the 25-acre tract from $5,000 to $2,750 [($200 × 25 acres) − $2,250]. The reduction in basis is applied solely to the 25 acres because of its decline in value as farmland. ◀

REAL-WORLD EXAMPLE

Seven of the 18 holes of a golf course were condemned. Although 11 holes remained, it was anticipated that the course would have to be reduced to 9 holes. Therefore, $21,000 of the condemnation award was allocated to severance damages to reflect the decline in value of the two lost holes. *Marco S. Marinello Associates, Inc.,* 1975 PH T.C. Memo ¶75,078, 34 TCM 392.

The Sec. 1033 provisions concerning nonrecognition of gain may apply to severance damages. For instance, if severance damages are used to restore the retained property, only that portion of severance damages not spent for restoration reduces the basis of the retained property. A taxpayer who uses severance damages to purchase adjacent farmland to replace the portion of the farm condemned may use Sec. 1033 to defer a gain due to the receipt of the severance damages.[53]

REPLACEMENT PROPERTY

To qualify for nonrecognition of gain due to an involuntary conversion, the taxpayer must acquire qualified replacement property. With some exceptions, the **replacement property** must be "similar or related in service or use to the property so converted."[54] Taxpayers who own and use the property must use the functional use test although replacement may be made with like-kind property in certain cases. A taxpayer who owns and leases the property that is involuntarily converted may use the taxpayer-use test.

REAL-WORLD EXAMPLE

The replacement of bowling alleys destroyed in a fire with a recreational billiards center did not pass the functional-use test. Rev. Rul. 76-319, 1976-2 C.B. 242.

FUNCTIONAL-USE TEST. The **functional-use test** is more restrictive than the like-kind test. To be considered similar or related in service or use, the replacement property must be functionally the same as the converted property. For example, the exchange of a business building for land used in business qualifies as a like-kind exchange. Replacing a building with land does not qualify as replacement property under the involuntary conversion rules. The building must be replaced with a building that is functionally the same as the converted building.

EXAMPLE I12-41 ▶ Julie's movie theater is destroyed by fire, and she uses the insurance proceeds to purchase a skating rink. The converted property has not been replaced with property that is similar or related in service or use under the functional-use test. The election to defer gain under Sec. 1033 is not available. ◀

---

[51] Rev. Rul. 53-271, 1953-2 C.B. 36.
[52] Rev. Rul. 68-37, 1968-1 C.B. 359.
[53] Rev. Ruls. 69-240, 1969-1 C.B. 199, 73-35, 1973-1 C.B. 367, and 83-49, 1983-1 C.B. 191.
[54] Secs. 1033(a)(2)(A) and 1033(f). The replacement of property requirement is modified when proceeds from the involuntary conversion of livestock may

not be reinvested in property similar or related in use to the converted livestock because of soil contamination or other environmental contamination. Sec. 1033(f) permits the livestock to be replaced with other property, including real property, used for farming purposes.

REPLACEMENT WITH LIKE-KIND PROPERTY. If real property held for productive use in a trade or business or for investment is **condemned**, a proper replacement may be made by acquiring like-kind property.[55] This exception to the functional use test applies only to real property used in a trade or business or held for investment.

EXAMPLE I12-42 ▶ Ken owns a building used in his business that is condemned by the state to widen a highway. He uses the proceeds to purchase land to be held for investment. The land is a qualified replacement property because the condemned building is real property used in a trade or business, and the like-kind exchange rule may be applied to the condemnation. ◀

EXAMPLE I12-43 ▶ Assume the same facts as in Example I12-42 except that the building is destroyed by a violent windstorm. Ken's purchase of the investment land is not qualified replacement property because the more flexible like-kind exchange rules apply only to condemnations. He must purchase property with the same functional use as the business building. ◀

REAL-WORLD EXAMPLE

A nursery with its trees and shrubs was condemned, and the taxpayer replaced the condemned property with land and greenhouses. The replacement was considered to have been made with like-kind property. *Evert Asjes, Jr., 74 T.C. 1005 (1980).*

If business or investment property is involuntarily converted as a result of a Presidentially declared disaster after 1994, the taxpayer may replace the property with any tangible property that is held for productive use in a trade or business.

TAXPAYER-USE TEST. The **taxpayer-use test** applies to the involuntary conversion of rental property owned by an investor. This test permits greater flexibility than the functional-use test. The principal requirement is that the owner-investor must lease out the replacement property that is acquired. However, the lessee is not required to use the leased property for the same functional use.[56]

EXAMPLE I12-44 ▶ Sally owns an apartment complex that is rented to college students. The apartment complex is destroyed by fire. She uses the insurance proceeds to purchase a medical building that is leased to physicians. This is a qualified replacement property by Sally under the taxpayer-use test, and the gain, if any, may be deferred if an election is made under Sec. 1033. ◀

STOP & THINK

Question: Greg Stacey's motel is destroyed by fire on March 10 of the current year. The basis of the property is $400,000 and he receives $2,000,000 from the insurance company. Greg is concerned about the possibility of having to pay income tax on the $1,600,000 gain and is aware of the tax rules relating to involuntary conversions. Greg is considering replacing the destroyed motel by building either a new motel or an ice skating rink on the vacant lot. The cost of a new motel or an ice skating rink is expected to be $2,500,000, and he expects to borrow 60% of the cost. What tax advice would you give him?

REAL-WORLD EXAMPLE

Taxpayer owned land and a warehouse held for rental purposes. Upon condemnation of this property, taxpayer invested the proceeds in a gas station on land already owned by the taxpayer which was also held for rental purposes. The taxpayer-use test applied, and taxpayer was able to defer the gain. Rev. Rul. 71-41, 1971-1 C.B. 223.

Solution: Greg may defer the $1,600,000 gain if the involuntary conversion requirements are met and he makes a proper election. The principal issue in this case is whether the replacement property is considered to be "similar in service or use" to the converted property. Because the functional-use test is applicable in this case, an ice skating rink is not similar property and the gain of $1,600,000 must be recognized. Conversely, the new motel is similar property and, since Greg is reinvesting an amount greater than $2,000,000, none of the gain is recognized. His basis in the new motel is $900,000 ($2,500,000 − deferred gain of $1,600,000). The fact that he borrows money and does not spend the $2,000,000 insurance proceeds does not prevent him from electing to defer the gain. The tax requirement is only that he must reinvest an amount equal to or greater than the $2,000,000 insurance proceeds. In this case, the tax law clearly encourages the taxpayer to build a new motel rather than an ice skating rink.

OBTAINING REPLACEMENT PROPERTY

The general rule is that the taxpayer must purchase the replacement property.[57] Taxpayers may purchase replacement property indirectly by purchasing control (i.e., 80% or more of the stock) of a corporation that owns the replacement property.[58] However,

---

[55] Sec. 1033(g)(1).
[56] Rev. Rul. 64-237, 1964-2 C.B. 319.
[57] To qualify as a purchase of property or stock under Sec. 1033(a)(2)(A)(ii), the unadjusted basis of the property or stock must be its cost within the mean-

ing of Sec. 1012 without considering the basis adjustment for the deferred gain. Property acquired by inheritance, gift, or a nontaxable exchange does not qualify as replacement property (see Reg. Sec. 1.1033(a)-2(c)(4)).
[58] Sec. 1033(a)(2)(A) and Reg. Sec. 1.1033(a)-2(c).

this exception is not applicable to the purchase of like-kind property to replace condemned real property used in a trade or business or held for investment.[59]

EXAMPLE I12-45 ▶ Hank's airplane, used in business, is hijacked and taken to a foreign country. He uses the insurance proceeds to purchase 80% of Fast Corporation stock. Fast Corporation owns an airplane which is qualified replacement property. The involuntary conversion requirements are satisfied if Hank elects to defer any gain realized. ◀

EXAMPLE I12-46 ▶ Lynn's farm is condemned by the state for public use. She uses the proceeds to purchase 80% of Vermont Corporation stock. Vermont Corporation owns eight parking lots. A qualified replacement property has not been obtained through the stock purchase because the parking lots are not functionally the same as the farm. A qualified replacement does occur if she buys the parking lots from the Vermont Corporation. ◀

TIME REQUIREMENTS FOR REPLACEMENT

TYPICAL MISCONCEPTION

The first taxable year in which any part of the gain on the conversion is realized is the year in which the insurance proceeds are received, not the year in which the involuntary conversion took place.

To qualify for nonrecognition of gain treatment, the converted property must be replaced within a specified time period. The general rule is that the period begins with the date of disposition of the converted property and ends "two years after the close of the first taxable year in which any part of the gain upon the conversion is realized."[60] If the involuntary conversion is due to condemnation or requisition, or the threat of such, the replacement period begins on the date of the threat or imminence of the requisition or condemnation. The replacement period may be extended by obtaining permission from the IRS.[61]

EXAMPLE I12-47 ▶ On December 8, 2006, Craig's business property was destroyed by fire. Craig receives insurance proceeds in 2007 and elects to defer recognition of the gain. He must replace the property between December 8, 2006, and December 31, 2009. The two-year time period includes 2009 because the gain is realized when the insurance proceeds are received in 2007. ◀

KEY POINT

The replacement period is three years instead of two years on the condemnation of real property used in a business or held for investment.

The replacement period is longer if the involuntary conversion is due to the condemnation of real property (excluding inventory) held for productive use in a trade or business or for investment. The replacement period ends three years after the close of the first tax year in which any part of the gain is realized.[62] This provision for a longer replacement period applies to the same type of real property that may be replaced with like-kind property.

EXAMPLE I12-48 ▶ Beth owns a building used in her dry cleaning business. In 2006, the state condemns the building and awards Beth an amount greater than the adjusted basis of the building. Beth may replace the property with like-kind property, and the replacement period ends on December 31, 2009. ◀

The involuntary conversion rules are summarized in Topic Review I12-2.

Topic Review I12-2

Section 1033: Involuntary Conversions

1. Section 1033 applies only to gains, not losses.
2. Nonrecognition of gain under Section 1033 is elective. (Nonrecognition of gain is mandatory in a direct conversion, but direct conversions seldom occur.)
3. Section 1033 applies to involuntary conversions of all types of properties.
4. Some gain may be recognized if the taxpayer replaces the involuntarily converted property with property that costs less than the amount realized in the involuntary conversion.
5. The nonrecognized gain is deferred.
6. The basis of property acquired to replace the involuntarily converted property is the cost of the property less the deferred gain.
7. Property acquired to replace the involuntarily converted property generally must be functionally related property.
8. The required replacement period generally begins with the date of disposition of the converted property and ends two years after the close of the first taxable year in which any part of the gain on the conversion is realized. (A three-year period applies to condemnations of real property used in a trade or business or held for the production of income.)

---

[59] Sec. 1033(g)(2).
[60] Sec. 1033(a)(2)(B).
[61] Sec. 1033(a)(2)(B)(ii).
[62] Sec. 1033(g)(4).

SALE OF PRINCIPAL RESIDENCE

Congress uses the tax law to encourage home ownership in many ways: (1) Real estate taxes and interest on a mortgage used to acquire a principal or second residence are deductible (see Chapter I7), (2) part or all of the interest on home equity debt may be deductible, and (3) taxpayers may elect to exclude up to $250,000 ($500,000 on a joint return) of gain from the sale of a principal residence.

Individuals who sell or exchange their personal residence after May 6, 1997, may exclude up to $250,000 of gain if it was owned and occupied as a principal residence for at least two years of the five-year period before the sale or exchange. A married couple may exclude up to $500,000 when filing jointly if both meet the use test, at least one meets the ownership test and neither spouse is ineligible for the exclusion because he or she sold or exchanged a residence within the last two years.[63]

The Sec. 121 exclusion is available regardless of age, and taxpayers do not have to purchase a replacement residence. Any gain not excluded is capital gain because a personal residence is a capital asset. A loss on the sale or exchange of a personal residence is not deductible because the residence is personal-use property.[64]

EXAMPLE I12-49 ▶ Maki, who is single and 35 years old, sells her principal residence that she purchased four years ago and realizes a $230,000 gain. Maki may exclude the entire gain regardless of her age or whether she purchases a new principal residence. ◀

EXAMPLE I12-50 ▶ Assume the same facts as in Example I12-49 except the realized gain is $320,000. Maki may exclude $250,000 and recognize a $70,000 LTCG. ◀

EXAMPLE I12-51 ▶ Assume the same facts as in Example I12-50 except Maki is married to Yixin, and they have owned and occupied the residence for the last four years. They may exclude the entire $320,000 gain. ◀

Prior to the Taxpayer Relief Act of 1997, taxpayers could defer gain resulting from sale of a personal residence if they purchased another principal residence within two years at a cost greater than the adjusted sales price. Taxpayers who were at least 55 years old could exclude up to $125,000 of gain resulting from the sale of a personal residence. The deferral provision of Sec. 1034 has been repealed; the exclusion has been increased to $250,000 or $500,000; and taxpayers may exclude gain regardless of age and use the exclusion more than once.

Today, the rules for excluding gain resulting from the sale of a personal residence are more favorable for most taxpayers than the old rules because Congress wanted to eliminate the need for homeowners to maintain records for long periods of time. However, taxpayers who expect to sell their homes for more than $250,000, or $500,000 if a joint return is filed, still need to maintain records. Also, taxpayers who convert their personal residence to business property or rental property will need to know the property's correct adjusted basis to compute depreciation.

DETERMINING THE REALIZED GAIN. Gain realized is the excess of the amount realized over the property's adjusted basis.[65] The amount realized on the sale of the property is equal to the selling price less selling expenses.[66] Selling expenses include commissions, advertising, deed preparation costs, and legal expenses incurred in connection with the sale.[67]

EXAMPLE I12-52 ▶ Kirby sells his personal residence, which has a $100,000 basis, to Maxine. To make the sale, Kirby pays a $7,000 sales commission and incurs $800 of legal costs. Maxine pays $30,000 cash and assumes Kirby's $90,000 mortgage. The amount realized is $112,200 [($30,000 + $90,000) − ($7,000 + $800)]. The realized gain is $12,200 ($112,200 − $100,000). ◀

---

[63] Sec. 121(a) and (b).
[64] Reg. Secs. 1.165-9(a) and 1.262-1b)(4).
[65] Reg. Sec. 1.1034-1(b)(5).
[66] Reg. Sec. 1.1034-1(b)(4).
[67] Reg. Sec. 1.1034-1(b)(4)(i).

ADJUSTED BASIS OF RESIDENCE. The original basis of a principal residence is a function of how the residence is obtained. It could be purchased, received as a gift, or inherited. The cost of a residence includes all amounts attributable to the acquisition including commissions and other purchasing expenses paid to acquire the residence.[68] Capital improvements, but not repairs, increase the adjusted basis of the residence. The costs of adding a room, installing an air conditioning system, finishing a basement, and landscaping are capital improvements. Expenses incurred to protect the taxpayer's title in the residence are also capitalized. Under Sec. 1034, which was repealed in 1997, a taxpayer who deferred gain on the sale of a principal residence was required to reduce the basis of the replacement residence by the amount of the deferred gain.[69]

EXAMPLE I12-53 ▶

REAL-WORLD EXAMPLE

An unmarried taxpayer plans to make good use of the multiple exclusion allowance. He has purchased two houses; one to live in and one to use as rental property. After a certain number of years he will sell his personal residence and move into the rental house. After at least two more years he will then sell the second house. Except for the gain due to depreciation on the rental house, the gain from both houses will be tax-free up to $250,000 each.

In 1996, Susan paid $200,000 to purchase a new residence. She paid a realtor $4,000 to help locate the house and paid legal fees of $1,200 to make certain that the seller had legal title to the property. As a result of the purchase, she deferred a gain of $50,000 from the sale a former residence in 1995. In 1997, she added a new porch to the house at a cost of $6,000 and installed central air conditioning at a cost of $5,200. Since purchasing the house, she has paid $1,500 for repairs. The adjusted basis of her house is $166,400 [$200,000 + $4,000 + $1,200 − $50,000 + $6,000 + $5,200]. ◀

MULTIPLE USE OF THE EXCLUSION. Previously under Sec. 121, a taxpayer was limited to the exclusion once in their lifetime, and a married taxpayer whose spouse had taken the exclusion could not use the exclusion even if the taxpayer filed as married filing separately. The exclusion is now determined on an individual basis. An individual may claim the exclusion even if the individual's spouse used the exclusion within the past two years. Also, for a married couple filing a joint return when each spouse maintains a separate principal residence, the $250,000 exclusion is available for the sale or exchange of each spouse's principal residence.

EXAMPLE I12-54 ▶

Krista, who has owned and used a house as her principal residence for the last seven years, marries Josh in January 2005. Josh sold his residence in October 2005 and excluded a $145,000 gain. Krista sells her residence in December 2006 and realizes a gain of $378,000. She may exclude $250,000 of the gain.

Assuming that Krista and Josh use her residence in the above example for a two-year period starting in January 2006, they could exclude up to $500,000 if she waits to sell the house until January 2008. ◀

PRINCIPAL RESIDENCE DEFINED

For Sec. 121 to apply, taxpayers must sell property that qualifies as their principal residence. Whether property is used as the taxpayer's principal residence depends upon all the facts and circumstances. If a taxpayer uses more than one property as a residence during the year, the property used a majority of the time will normally be the principal residence.[70]

EXAMPLE I12-55 ▶

KEY POINT

A taxpayer may own two or more residences, but only one of them qualifies as the principal residence.

Lanny, a 40-year-old college professor, owns and occupies a house in Oklahoma. During the summer, he lives in a cabin in Idaho. After owning the cabin for eight years, Lanny sells it for $50,000 and realizes a gain. Gain on the sale of the cabin in Idaho must be recognized because Lanny's principal residence is in Oklahoma. ◀

Factors other than use of the property that are relevant when determining a taxpayer's principal residence include place of employment, mailing address for bills and correspondence, address for tax returns and voter registration, and location of religious organizations and recreational clubs with which the taxpayer is affiliated. The principal place of abode for the taxpayer's family members is also relevant.[71]

The property does not have to be one's principal residence at time of the sale to qualify for the exclusion. The exclusion applies if the property has been used as a principal residence for at least two of the five years before the sale or exchange and the exclusion has not been used within the past two years.

---

[68] Reg. Sec. 1.1034-1(c)(4).
[69] Sec. 1034(e).

[70] Reg. Sec. 1.121-1(b)(2).
[71] Reg. Sec. 1.121-1(b)(2).

EXAMPLE I12-56 ▶ Canan owns and uses a house in Buffalo as her principal residence from March 10, 2002, until November 21, 2004, when she purchases a new house in Kansas on December 1, 2004. Her brother lives in the house in Buffalo until Canan sells it on July 10, 2006, and realizes a gain of $288,000. She may exclude $250,000 and recognize a $38,000 LTCG. ◀

Condominium apartments, houseboats, and housetrailers may qualify as principal residences.[72] Stock held by a tenant-stockholder in a cooperative housing corporation is a principal residence if the dwelling that the taxpayer is entitled to occupy as a stockholder is used as his or her principal residence.[73]

ADDITIONAL COMMENT

The taxpayer does not have to be occupying the old residence at the date of sale. The taxpayer may have already moved to a new residence and be renting the old residence temporarily before its sale.

SALE OF MORE THAN ONE PRINCIPAL RESIDENCE WITHIN A TWO-YEAR PERIOD

The new exclusion provided by Sec. 121 applies to only one sale or exchange every two years. However, a portion of the gain may be excluded in certain circumstances even if the two-year requirement is not satisfied.

If a principal residence is sold within two years of a previous sale or exchange of a residence, part of the gain may be excluded if the sale or exchange is due to a change in employment, health or unforseen circumstances. The portion of the gain excluded is based on a ratio with a numerator in days or months and a denominator of 730 days or 24 months.[74] The numerator is the shorter of:

(1) the period during which the ownership and use tests were met during the five-year period ending on the date of sale, or

(2) the period of time after the date of the most recent prior sale or exchange for which the exclusion applied until the date of the current sale or exchange.[75]

The amount excluded is $250,000 or $500,000 times the above ratio.

EXAMPLE I12-57 ▶ Winnie, who is single, sold her principal residence in Detroit on November 1, 2006, and excluded the $127,000 gain because she owned and used the residence for two of the last five years. Winnie had purchased another residence in Cleveland on October 1, 2006. She occupies the residence in Cleveland until June 12, 2007, when she moves to Dallas to accept a new job. She sells the residence in Cleveland on November 15, 2007, and realizes a gain of $40,000. Winnie may exclude all of the gain because the sale of her Cleveland residence was due to a change in employment and 254/730 of $250,000 is more than the $40,000 realized gain. She owns and uses the residence in Cleveland for 254 days, and the period between the sale of the residence in Detroit and the sale in Cleveland is 378 days. ◀

ADDITIONAL COMMENT

If Winnie's gain in Example I12-57 is $100,000, she may exclude $86,986 (254/730 × $250,000).

OWNERSHIP AND USE TESTS If a principal residence is sold before satisfying the ownership and use tests, part of the gain may be excluded if the sale is due to a change in employment, health, or unforeseen circumstances. The portion of the gain excluded is determined by multiplying the amount of the exclusion (i.e., $250,000 or $500,000) by a fraction whose numerator is the number of days the use and ownership tests were met and whose denominator is 730 days (or 24 months).

EXAMPLE I12-58 ▶ Tim, a single taxpayer who purchased his home on January 1, 2006, for $500,000, recently became ill and sells his home in order to move closer to a relative who can care for him. Tim sells his principal residence on June 14, 2006, for $620,000, realizing a gain of $120,000. Because he owned and occupied the residence for 165 days and the sale was due to a change in his health, he may exclude $56,164 ($250,000 × 164/730). ◀

For purposes of the two-year ownership rule, a taxpayer's period of ownership includes the period during which the taxpayer's deceased spouse owned the residence. When a taxpayer receives a residence from a spouse or an ex-spouse incident to a divorce, the taxpayer's period of owning the property includes the time the residence was owned by the spouse or ex-spouse.[76] When attempting to determine if the taxpayer has occupied

---

[72] Rev. Rul. 64-31, 1964-1 C.B. 300.
[73] Reg. Sec. 1.1034-1(c)(3).
[74] Reg. Sec. 1.121-3(g).

[75] Sec. 121(c).
[76] Sec. 121(d)(2) and (3).

the residence for two years, short temporary absences such as for vacation or other seasonal absence are counted as use by the taxpayer.[77]

EXAMPLE I12-59 ▶ Sachie receives an $800,000 residence owned for six years by Richard, her former spouse, as part of a divorce settlement. Richard's basis for the residence is $430,000. They lived in the house for five years prior to the divorce. Three months after transfer of the residence to Sachie, she sells it for $825,000, and $250,000 of her $395,000 realized gain is excluded. Sachie must recognize a $145,000 LTCG. Sachie's period of ownership includes the six years Richard owned the residence. ◀

CHANGE DUE TO EMPLOYMENT, HEALTH, OR UNFORESEEN CIRCUMSTANCES. The Treasury has issued Regulations to provide guidance as to how a homeowner may qualify for partial exclusion if the sale was before the two-year use and ownership test is satisfied or if the sale occurs within two years of a previous sale where the exclusion was used. The exceptions may apply even if a person other than the taxpayer has a change in employment or health.

A taxpayer is viewed as being eligible for partial exclusion if she sells her residence because a qualified individual has a change in employment that satisfies the test under Sec. 217 for the moving expense deduction. A qualified individual includes the taxpayer, the taxpayer's spouse, co-owner of the residence, or a person who uses the residence as a principal place of abode. Taxpayers may qualify for the exclusion and the moving expense deduction if moving to take a new job, continue with present employer or accept a job if the 50-mile distance test is satisfied. The change in employment must occur when the taxpayer is satisfying the ownership and use test for the residence except for the two-year requirement.[78]

EXAMPLE I12-60 ▶ Mark has lived in his first house for one year in Omaha when he marries Karen. Six months later, Karen receives a job offer and they move to Florida. Mark may exclude a realized gain equal to $18/24$ of $250,000, because the move is due to a change in employment of a qualified individual. ◀

When determining if the sale or exchange of the residence is due to a change in health, the definition of a "qualified individual" is expanded to include relatives who satisfy the relationship test used to determine if one is a dependent of the taxpayer. The relative must satisfy the relationship test but does not have to be a dependent to be a qualified individual. A sale or exchange is because of health if the primary reason is "to obtain, provide, or facilitate the diagnosis, cure, mitigation, or treatment of a disease, illness, or injury of a qualified individual."[79]

EXAMPLE I12-61 ▶ Daniel has lived in his first house in Virginia for eight months when he sells the house and moves to Texas to take care of his 60-year-old father who recently suffered a stroke. Daniel may exclude a realized gain equal to $8/24$ of $250,000 because the primary reason for the sale is due to the health of a qualified individual. ◀

A sale or exchange is due to unforeseen circumstances if the primary reason for the sale or exchange is an event that the taxpayer could not reasonably have anticipated before purchasing and occupying the residence. For the unforeseen circumstances exception, a qualified individual is the same as a qualified individual for the change in employment test.

The following are specific events considered to qualify as unforeseen circumstances:

1. Involuntary conversion of residence;
2. Natural or man-made disasters or acts of war or terrorism resulting in a casualty to the residence;
3. Death of a qualified individual;
4. Loss of employment by a qualified individual if the individual is eligible for unemployment compensation;
5. Change of employment that results in the taxpayer's inability to pay housing costs and reasonable basic living expenses;

[77] Reg. Sec. 1.121-1(c)(2)(i).
[78] Reg. Sec. 1.121-3T(c).
[79] Reg. Sec. 1.121-3T(d).

6. Divorce or legal separation;
7. Multiple births from the same pregnancy.[80]

Note that marriage and adoption are not included in the above safe-harbor list of unforeseen circumstances. One who sells her residence before meeting the two-year test because she has adopted a child will not be assured of qualifying for possible exclusion under the unforeseen circumstances exception. She will have to argue that the facts and circumstances justify her use of the partial exclusion.

EXAMPLE I12-62 ▶ Benjamin purchases a house near the airport and sells it four months later because of noise caused by planes. He may not exclude any of the gain, because the airport noise is not an unforeseen circumstance. ◀

 STOP & THINK *Question:* Rebecca's uncle told her that she could purchase his house for $150,000 in five years provided that she could pay at least $30,000 of the purchase price in cash. Rebecca has $15,000 and is considering two alternative methods to obtain the remaining $15,000 in five years. The first alternative is to purchase $15,000 of non-dividend paying stock that she expects to increase in value to $30,000 within five years. The second alternative is to purchase an $80,000 residence by paying $15,000 and borrowing $65,000. Payments on the mortgage will be interest only for five years and amount to $450 per month. Insurance, property taxes, and other home ownership expenses average $90 per month. She expects the house to be worth $95,000 at the end of five years. She will rent an apartment for $540 per month, including utilities, if she buys the stock. Ignoring transaction costs and assuming that she does not itemize deductions, should Rebecca purchase the stock or the house?

Solution: The $15,000 gain resulting from sale of the stock is LTCG and probably taxed at 15%. If the rate is 15%, she must pay taxes of $2,250 and has only $27,750 available to purchase her uncle's house. She will have a gain of $15,000 if she sells the house but the gain is excluded. She has $30,000 of cash and is able to buy her uncle's house. The tax law encourages Rebecca to buy a principal residence.

INVOLUNTARY CONVERSION OF A PRINCIPAL RESIDENCE

Ordinarily, the involuntary conversion of a principal residence is governed by Sec. 1033, discussed earlier in this chapter. A gain due to an involuntary conversion of a personal residence may be deferred if the requirements of Sec. 1033 are satisfied. The functional-use test must be satisfied regardless of the type of involuntary conversion.

For purposes of Sec. 121, the destruction, theft, seizure, requisition, or condemnation of property is treated as a sale.[81] Thus, taxpayers may exclude a gain of up to $250,000 or $500,000 due to the involuntary conversion of a principal residence if the use and ownership test is satisfied. Taxpayers normally prefer to exclude gain if the use and ownership tests are satisfied rather than defer gain under the involuntary conversion provisions.

If taxpayers make a proper and timely replacement of the residence subject to the involuntary conversion, gain may be excluded up to $250,000, or $500,000, and the remaining gain may be deferred. For purposes of applying the involuntary conversion provisions, the amount realized due to the involuntary conversion is reduced by any gain excluded under Sec. 121.[82]

EXAMPLE I12-63 ▶ The Kochs' principal residence, with an adjusted basis of $200,000, has been used and owned by them for nine years. The house is destroyed by a hurricane, and the Kochs receive insurance proceeds of $820,000. Four months later, they purchase another residence for $900,000. The Kochs have a realized gain of $620,000 and may exclude $500,000 under Sec. 121. The remaining $120,000 gain may be deferred and the basis of their replacement residence is $780,000 ($900,000 − $120,000). ◀

---

[80] Reg. Sec. 1.121-3T(e).
[81] Sec. 121(d)(5)(A).

[82] Sec. 121(d)(5)(B).

Because the amount realized is reduced by the gain excluded, the Kochs could have deferred the $120,000 gain in the above example by investing only $320,000 in a replacement residence.

If gain due to the involuntary conversion of a principal residence is deferred under Sec. 1033, the holding period of the replacement residence includes the holding period of the converted property for purposes of satisfying the use and ownership tests of Sec. 121.[83] The Kochs satisfy the use and ownership requirements for Sec. 121 with respect to their new residence in Example I12-63 because gain is deferred under Sec. 1033.

A loss due to a condemnation of a personal residence is not recognized. If the loss is due to a casualty, the loss is deductible and is treated like other casualty losses of non-business property (see Chapter I8).

TAX PLANNING CONSIDERATIONS

AVOIDING THE LIKE-KIND EXCHANGE PROVISIONS

In some cases, a taxpayer may prefer a taxable exchange to a nontaxable like-kind exchange. For instance, if the gain is taxed as a capital gain and the taxpayer has capital losses to offset the gain, the taxpayer may prefer to recognize the gain during the current year. If gain on the exchange is recognized instead of deferred, the basis of the property received in the exchange is higher.

EXAMPLE I12-64 ▶ Connie owns land with a $20,000 basis. The land is held as an investment. Connie exchanges the land for a duplex with a $100,000 FMV. Because the exchange qualifies as a like-kind exchange, no gain is recognized and Connie's basis for the duplex is $20,000. If the exchange does not qualify as a like-kind exchange (e.g., the land is a personal-use asset), Connie recognizes an $80,000 capital gain. Connie's basis for the duplex is $100,000. The basis of the duplex, except for the portion allocable to land, is eligible for depreciation. ◀

If an exchange qualifies as a like-kind exchange, no loss on the exchange is recognized. A taxpayer who prefers to recognize a loss should avoid making a like-kind exchange. It may be advantageous to sell the property to recognize the loss and then purchase the replacement asset in two independent transactions. If the sale and purchase transactions are with the same party, the IRS may maintain that the like-kind exchange rules apply because the two transactions are in substance a like-kind exchange (i.e., the judicial doctrine of substance over form might be applied).

SALE OF A PRINCIPAL RESIDENCE

ELECTION PROVISION. When the requirements of Sec. 121 are satisfied, gain is excluded unless the taxpayer elects not to have Sec. 121 apply.[84]

EXAMPLE I12-65 ▶ Paula has owned a house in Wyoming for eight years and occupied it until 18 months ago when she moved to Idaho and purchased a new house. She sells the house in Wyoming on May 23, 2006, and the realized gain is $25,000. Paula anticipates that she will move next year and have to sell the house in Idaho which has appreciated more than $100,000 since purchased. Paula may want to elect not to have Sec. 121 apply and recognize the $25,000 gain and then use the exclusion when she sells the house in Idaho next year. ◀

PROPERTY USED AS RESIDENCE AND FOR BUSINESS. If a house is used for both residential use and business use, the tax treatment depends on whether or not the business portion of the house is conducted in a separate structure. If the business portion of the house is conducted in a separate structure, the sale should be treated as a sale of two assets, the residence and the portion of the property used as a business. The Sec. 121 exclusion only applies to the residence portion of the property.

---

[83] Sec. 121(d)(8). [84] Sec. 121(f).

EXAMPLE I12-66 ▶

ADDITIONAL COMMENT

As explained in Chapter I13, Mormor's $24,000 gain in Example 66 is a Sec. 1231 gain and $6,000 is taxed at a maximum rate of 25% because it is unrecaptured Sec. 1250 gain.

Mormor owns a one-acre lot with a house she uses as her residence and a barn that she uses to display and sell antiques. She purchased the property in 1990 for $100,000 and $10,000 of the purchase price was allocated to the barn. Depreciation of $4,000 has been allowed for the barn. She sells the property during the current year for $300,000 and estimates that 10% of the price received is for the barn. She may exclude the $180,000 ($270,000 − $90,000) gain on the sale of the residence. Her $24,000 ($30,000 − $6,000) gain on the sale of the barn is recognized.[85] ◀

If the business activity is conducted within the house and not in a separate structure, the sale does not have to be treated as a sale of two different assets. However, gain attributable to depreciation after May 6, 1997, is not eligible for the exclusion. The remaining gain is eligible for the exclusion.

EXAMPLE I12-67 ▶

Kate purchased a house in 2000 for $200,000 and uses 15% of the house as an office. The office is used on a regular and exclusive basis and is her principal place of business. Depreciation of $3,400 has been deducted when she sells the house for $430,000. Her gain is $233,400 ($430,000 − $196,600), and she may exclude $230,000 but must recognize $3,400 of the gain. ◀

The government's decision to allow Kate to treat the property in the above example as one property instead of two is beneficial for her. If the property was viewed as two properties or if the office was in a separate structure, only $195,500 ($365,500 − $170,000) of the gain would qualify for the exclusion.

EXAMPLE I12-68 ▶

Bobbi purchased a house in 1988 and used it as her principal residence until March 1, 1999, when she rented the house to the Allens while she lived with her mother. On November 1, 2005, the Allens' lease expired and she moved back into the house. She sells the house on July 12, 2006, and realizes a gain of $210,000. She may not exclude any of the gain because she has not used the property as her principal residence for two of the last five years. ◀

EXAMPLE I12-69 ▶

Assume the same facts as in I12-68 except that Bobbi sells the house on December 12, 2007. Because she has used the property as her principal residence for two of the last five years, she may exclude the excess of the $210,000 gain over depreciation allowed after May 6, 1997. ◀

COMPLIANCE AND PROCEDURAL CONSIDERATIONS

REPORTING OF INVOLUNTARY CONVERSIONS

ADDITIONAL COMMENT

The failure to include gain from an involuntary conversion in gross income is deemed to be an election even though the details are not reported.

The election to defer recognition of the gain from an involuntary conversion is made by not reporting the gain as income for the first year in which gain is realized. All details pertaining to the involuntary conversion (including those relating to the replacement of the converted property) should be reported for the taxable year or years in which any of the gain is realized.[86]

A taxpayer who elects to defer recognition of the gain but does not make a proper replacement of the property within the required period of time must file an amended return for the year or years for which the election was made. An amended return may be needed if the cost of the replacement property is less than expected at the time of the election. All details pertaining to the replacement of converted property must be reported in the year in which replacement occurs.[87]

EXAMPLE I12-70 ▶

Bob's property, with a $40,000 adjusted basis, was destroyed by a storm in 2004. Bob received $45,000 insurance proceeds in 2004 and planned to purchase property similar to the converted property in 2005 at a cost of $47,000. Bob elected to defer recognition of the gain in 2004. In 2005 the replacement property is purchased for $44,500. Bob must file an amended return for 2004 and recognize a $500 ($45,000 − $44,500) gain. ◀

---

[85] As explained in Chapter I13, the gain is Sec. 1231 gain and $4,000 is unrecaptured Sec. 1250 gain.

[86] Reg. Sec. 1.1033(a)-2(c)(2).
[87] Ibid.

A taxpayer who either is ineligible or does not want to defer the gain must report the gain in the usual manner. If a taxpayer does not elect to defer the gain in the year the gain is realized and the replacement period has not expired, a subsequent election may be made. In such an event, a refund claim should be filed for the tax year in which the gain was realized and previously recognized.[88]

Taxpayers who do not initially elect to defer the gain from an involuntary conversion may later make the election, but the election may not subsequently be revoked. The Tax Court has ruled that the Treasury Regulations allow the filing of an amended return for a year in which the election is made only if proper replacement is not made within the specified time period or the replacement is made at a cost lower than anticipated at the time of the election.[89] The IRS takes the position that taxpayers who designate qualifying property as replacement property may not later designate other qualifying property as the replacement property.[90]

EXAMPLE I12-71 ▶

In 2004 Troy collected $200,000 from an insurance company as the result of the destruction of rental property with a $140,000 basis. He made the election to defer the gain realized in 2004 and attached a supporting schedule of details regarding the involuntary conversion including a designation of replacement property to be acquired in 2005. In 2005 Troy purchased the designated replacement rental property for $225,000. In 2006 Troy purchases other rental property for $400,000 and now wants to designate that property as the replacement property for the property destroyed in 2004. Troy may not designate the property acquired in 2006 as the replacement property because the rental property purchased in 2005 was already designated as such. ◀

REPORTING OF SALE OR EXCHANGE OF A PRINCIPAL RESIDENCE

Taxpayers only have to report the sale if any of the gain is not excluded. If the taxpayer does not qualify to exclude all of the gain or elects not to exclude the gain, the entire gain realized is reported on Schedule D either on line 1, if residence is held for one year or less, or on line 8. On the line below where the entire gain is shown, the taxpayer should indicate on the following line the amount of the gain that is being excluded as a loss (i.e., show in parentheses).

Publication 523, Selling Your Home, provides the following worksheet that may be used to determine if any gain is recognized. If the taxpayer has to utilize the exceptions to the two-year ownership and use tests, a different worksheet is provided.

Worksheet 2. Gain (or Loss), Exclusion, and Taxable Gain

Part 1–Gain (or Loss) on Sale

1. Selling price of home . . . . _____
2. Selling expenses. . . . . _____
3. Subtract line 2 from line 1 . . . . _____
4. Adjusted basis of home sold. (From Worksheet 1, line 15.) . . . . _____
5. Subtract line 4 from line 3. This is the **gain (or loss)** on the sale. If this is a loss, stop here . . _____

Part 2–Exclusion and Taxable Gain

6. Maximum exclusion. (See *Amount of Exclusion* in this chapter.) . . . . _____
7. Enter any depreciation claimed on the property for periods after May 6, 1997. If none, enter zero _____
8. Subtract line 7 from line 5. (If the result is less than zero, enter zero.) . . . . _____
9. Subtract line 7 from line 6 . . . . _____
10. Enter the smaller of line 8 or 9. This is your exclusion. If you are reporting the sale on the installment method, enter this amount on line 15 of Form 6252 . . . . _____
11. Subtract line 10 from line 5. This is your taxable gain. Report it on Schedule D (Form 1040) as described under *Reporting the Gain* in this chapter. If the amount on this line is zero, do not report the sale or exclusion on your tax return . . . . _____

---

[88] *Ibid.*
[89] *John McShain,* 65 T.C. 686 (1976).

[90] Rev. Rul. 83-39, 1983-1 C.B. 190.

PROBLEM MATERIALS

DISCUSSION QUESTIONS

I12-1 Evaluate the following statement: The underlying rationale for the nonrecognition of a gain or loss resulting from a like-kind exchange is that the exchange constitutes a liquidation of the taxpayer's investment.

I12-2 Why might a taxpayer want to avoid having an exchange qualify as a like-kind exchange?

I12-3 Debbie owns office equipment with a basis of $300,000 acquired on May 10, 1999. Debbie exchanges the equipment for other office equipment owned by Doug on July 23, 2006. Doug's equipment has an FMV of $500,000. Both Debbie and Doug use the equipment in their businesses.

    a. What is Debbie's basis for the office equipment received in the exchange and when does the holding period start for that equipment?

    b. If Debbie and Doug are related taxpayers, explain what action could occur that would cause the exchange not to qualify as a like-kind exchange.

I12-4 Kay owns equipment used in her business and exchanges the equipment for other like-kind equipment and marketable securities.

    a. Will Kay's recognized gain ever exceed the realized gain?

    b. Will Kay's recognized gain ever exceed the FMV of the marketable securities?

    c. What is the basis of the marketable securities received?

    d. When does the holding period of the marketable securities begin?

I12-5 Demetrius sells word processing equipment used in his business to Edith. He then purchases new word processing equipment from Zip Corporation.

    a. Do the sale and purchase qualify as a like-kind exchange?

    b. When may a sale and a subsequent purchase be treated as a like-kind exchange?

I12-6 When determining whether property qualifies as like-kind property, is the quality or grade of the property considered?

I12-7 What is personal property of a like class that meets the definition of like-kind?

I12-8 When does a nonsimultaneous exchange qualify as a like-kind exchange?

I12-9 Burke is anxious to purchase land owned by Kim for use in his trade or business. Kim's basis for the land is $150,000, and Burke has offered to pay $800,000 if she will sell within the next 10 days. Kim is interested in selling but wants to avoid recognizing gain. What advice would you give?

I12-10 Lanny wants to purchase a farm owned by Jane, but Jane does not want to recognize a gain on the transfer of the appreciated property. Explain how a three-party exchange might be used to allow Lanny to obtain the farm without Jane having to recognize a gain.

I12-11 Does the receipt of boot in a transaction that otherwise qualifies as a like-kind exchange always cause the exchange to be at least partially taxable?

I12-12 When must a taxpayer who gives boot recognize a gain or loss?

I12-13 What is the justification for Sec. 1033, which allows a taxpayer to elect to defer a gain resulting from an involuntary conversion? May a taxpayer elect under Sec. 1033 to defer recognition of a loss resulting from an involuntary conversion?

I12-14 Must property be actually condemned for the conversion of property to be classified as an involuntary conversion? Explain.

I12-15 What are severance damages? What is the tax treatment for severance damages received if the taxpayer does not use the severance damages to restore the retained property?

I12-16 The functional use test is often used to determine whether the replacement property is similar or related in service or use to the property converted. Explain the functional use test.

I12-17 In what situations may a gain due to an involuntary conversion of real property be deferred if like-kind property is purchased to replace the converted property?

I12-18 Prior to the Taxpayer Relief Act of 1997, taxpayers could defer a gain on the sale of a principal residence sold before May 7, 1997, if they purchased and occupied a new principal residence within two years before or after the sale and the cost of the new residence was at least equal to the adjusted sales price of the old residence. Some taxpayers who were at least 55 years old had a once-in-a-lifetime exclusion up to $125,000 if they owned and used the property as a principal residence for at least three years of the five-year-period ending on the date of sale. Discuss why current law with respect to the sale of a personal residence is more favorable than the law prior to the Taxpayer Relief Act of 1997.

I12-19 One reason Congress expanded the exclusion of gain on the sale of a principal residence and eliminated the deferral provision was to eliminate the need for many taxpayers to keep records of capital improvements that increase the basis of their residence. Why might taxpayers still need to maintain such records to substantiate the adjusted basis of their principal residence?

I12-20 Steve maintains that the cost of wallpapering his three-bedroom house is a capital expenditure while Martha maintains that the cost of wallpapering her three-bedroom house is an expense. Steve uses his house as his personal residence while Martha's house is rental property. Explain why Steve and Martha view the cost of wallpapering differently.

I12-21 The Nelsons purchased a new residence in 1992 for $300,000 from David who owned and used the residence as rental property. When the Nelsons wanted to purchase the property, it was being rented to tenants who had four months remaining on their lease. The Nelsons paid the tenants $1,000 to relinquish the lease and vacate the property. In 1996, they added a family room to the house at a cost of $79,200. In 1998, they suffered hail damage to the roof and received $7,000 from the insurance company. They did not repair the damaged roof, and no casualty loss deduction was allowed. What is their adjusted basis for the house today?

I12-22 What requirements must be satisfied by an unmarried taxpayer under Sec. 121 to be eligible for the election to exclude a gain up to $250,000 on the sale or exchange of a principal residence?

ISSUE IDENTIFICATION QUESTIONS

I12-23 John owns 25% of the ABC Partnership and Jane owns 25% of the XYZ Partnership. The ABC Partnership owns a farm and produces corn and the XYZ Partnership owns a farm and produces soybeans. John and Jane agree to exchange their partnership interests. What tax issues should John and Jane consider?

I12-24 Chauvin Oil Corporation operates primarily in the United States and owns an offshore drilling rig with an adjusted basis of $400,000 that it uses near Louisiana. Chauvin exchanges the rig for a new rig with a FMV of $1,000,000, and Chauvin also pays $250,000. Chauvin plans to expand its drilling operations to offshore sites near Finland. What tax issues should the Chauvin Oil Corporation consider?

I12-25 Jaharta, Inc., owns land used for truck farming and cattle raising. The California Division of Highways condemned 36 acres of Jaharta's land to build a new highway. Jaharta owned a 50% interest in property being used for apricot, prune, and walnut orchards. Jaharta used the proceeds received as a result of the condemnation to purchase the remaining interest in the property being used for orchards. What tax issues should Jaharta consider?

PROBLEMS

I12-26 *Like-Kind Property.* Which of the following exchanges qualify as like-kind exchanges under Sec. 1031?
  a. Acme Corporation stock held for investment purposes for Mesa Corporation stock also held for investment purposes
  b. A motel used in a trade or business for an apartment complex held for investment
  c. A pecan orchard in Texas used in a trade or business for an orange grove in Florida used in a trade or business
  d. A one-third interest in a general partnership for a one-fourth interest in a limited partnership
  e. Inventory for equipment used in a trade or business
  f. Unimproved land held as an investment for a warehouse used in a trade or business
  g. An automobile used as a personal-use asset for marketable securities held for investment

I12-27 *Like-Kind Property.* Which of the following exchanges qualify as like-kind exchanges under Sec. 1031?
  a. A motel in Texas for a motel in Italy
  b. An office building held for investment for an airplane to be used in the taxpayer's business
  c. Land held for investment for marketable securities held for investment
  d. Land held for investment for a farm to be used in the taxpayer's business

I12-28 *Like-Kind Exchange: Boot.* Determine the realized gain or loss, the recognized gain or loss, and the basis of the equipment received for the following like-kind exchanges:

Basis of Equipment Exchanged	FMV of Boot Received	FMV of Equipment Received
$20,000	$-0-	$85,000
45,000	14,000	70,000
60,000	25,000	65,000
70,000	38,000	60,000
90,000	22,000	55,000

I12-29 *Like-Kind Exchange: Personal Property.* Beach Corporation owns a computer with a $34,000 adjusted basis. The computer is used in the company's trade or business. What is the realized and recognized gain or loss for each of the following independent transactions where the computer is exchanged for?
a. A used computer with a $70,000 FMV plus $16,000 cash.
b. A used computer with a $18,000 FMV plus $7,000 cash.
c. Marketable securities with a $61,000 FMV.

I12-30 *Like-Kind Exchange: Personal Property.* Boise Corporation exchanges a machine with a $14,000 basis for a new machine with an $18,000 FMV and $3,000 cash. The machines are used in Boise's business and are in the same General Asset Class.
a. Determine Boise Corporation's recognized gain and the basis for the new machine.
b. How would your answer to Part a change if the corporation's machine is also subject to a $6,000 liability, and the liability is assumed by the other party?

I12-31 *Exchange of Personal Property.* Lithuania Corporation operates a ferry service and owns four barges. Lithuania exchanges one of the barges with an adjusted basis of $350,000 for a used smaller barge with a FMV of $444,000 and a $26,000 computer. Without considering the exchange, Lithuania Corporation's taxable income is $700,000. Determine Lithuania's
a. realized gain on the exchange.
b. recognized gain.
c. basis of the new barge.
d. basis of the computer.
e. Assume that the recognized gain is $26,000 and the gain is not capital gain. What is the increase in Lithuania's tax liability as a result of the exchange?

I12-32 *Like-Kind Exchange: Liabilities.* Paul owns a building used in his business with an adjusted basis of $340,000 and a $750,000 FMV. He exchanges the building for a building owned by David. David's building has a $950,000 FMV but is subject to a $200,000 liability. Paul assumes David's liability and uses the building in his business. What is Paul's
a. realized gain?
b. recognized gain?
c. basis for the building received?

I12-33 *Like-Kind Exchange: Liabilities.* Helmut exchanges his apartment complex for Heidi's farm, and the exchange qualifies as a like-kind exchange. Helmut's adjusted basis for the apartment complex is $600,000 and the complex is subject to a $180,000 liability. The FMV of Heidi's farm is $770,000 and the farm is subject to a $100,000 liability. Each asset is transferred subject to the liability. What is Helmut's recognized gain and the basis of the new farm?

I12-34 *Like-Kind Exchange: Liabilities.* Sheila owns land with a basis of $100,000 and FMV of $230,000. The land is subject to an $80,000 liability. Sheila plans to exchange the land for land owned by Tony that has a $250,000 FMV but is subject to a liability of $150,000. Sheila plans to assume Tony's debt and Tony will assume her $80,000 debt. Because the exchange is not of equal value, how much cash must Tony transfer to equalize the exchange?

I12-35 *Like-Kind Exchange: Transfer of Boot.* Wayne exchanges unimproved land with a $50,000 basis and marketable securities with a $10,000 basis for an eight-unit apartment building having a $150,000 FMV. The land and marketable securities are held by Wayne as investments, and the apartment building is held as an investment. The marketable securities have a $25,000 FMV. What is his realized gain, recognized gain, and the basis for the apartment building?

I12-36 *Like-Kind Exchange: Related Parties.* Bob owns a duplex used as rental property. The duplex has a basis of $86,000 and $300,000 FMV. He transfers the duplex to Cindy, his sister, in exchange for a triplex that she owns. The triplex has a basis of $279,000 and a

$300,000 FMV. Two months after the exchange, Cindy sells the duplex to a business associate for $312,000. Determine:

a. Bob's realized and recognized gain on the exchange.

b. Cindy's realized and recognized gain on the exchange.

I12-37 *Like-Kind Exchange: Related Parties.* Assume the same facts as in I12-36 except Cindy sells the duplex to a nonrelated individual more than two years after the exchange with Bob. Ignore any changes in adjusted basis due to depreciation that would have occurred after the exchange. Determine:

a. Bob's realized and recognized gain on the exchange.

b. Cindy's realized and recognized gain on the exchange.

c. Cindy's realized and recognized gain on the sale.

I12-38 *Involuntary Conversion.* Duke Corporation owns an office building with a $400,000 adjusted basis. The building is destroyed by a tornado. The insurance company paid $750,000 as compensation for the loss. Eight months after the loss, Duke uses the insurance proceeds and other funds to acquire a new office building for $682,000 and machinery for one of the company's plants at a $90,000 cost. Assuming that Duke elects to defer as much of the gain as possible, what is the recognized gain, the basis for the new office building, and the basis for the machinery acquired?

I12-39 *Involuntary Conversion: Replacement Period.* The Madison Corporation paid $3,000 for several acres of land in 1993 to use in its business. The land is condemned and taken by the state in March 2006. The company receives $25,000 from the state. Whenever possible, the corporation elects to minimize taxable income. For each of the following independent cases, what is the recognized gain or loss in 2006 on the conversion and the tax basis of the replacement property (replacement land will be purchased in July)?

a. 2007 for $22,500.

b. 2008 for $28,500.

c. 2009 for $23,600.

I12-40 *Involuntary Conversion of Real Property.* On April 27, 2006, an office building owned by Newark Corporation, an offshore drilling company that is a calendar-year taxpayer, is destroyed by a hurricane. The basis of the office building is $600,000, and the corporation receives $840,000 from the insurance company.

a. To defer the entire gain due to the involuntary conversion, what amount must the corporation pay for replacement property?

b. To defer the gain due to the involuntary conversion, by what date must the corporation replace the converted property?

c. If Newark replaces the office building by purchasing a 900,000 gallon storage tank for $810,000, may it defer any of the gain due to the involuntary conversion?

d. Will answers to Parts b and c change if the office building had been condemned by the state? Explain.

I12-41 *Involuntary Conversion: Different Methods of Replacement.* On September 3, 2006, Federal Corporation's warehouse is totally destroyed by fire. $800,000 of insurance proceeds are received, and the realized gain is $300,000. Whenever possible, Federal elects to defer gains. For each of the following independent situations, what is the amount of gain recognized? Explain why the gain is not deferred, if applicable.

a. On October 23, 2006, Federal purchases a warehouse for $770,000.

b. On February 4, 2007, Federal purchases 100% of the Park Corporation, which owns a warehouse. Federal pays $895,000 for the stock.

c. On March 10, 2007, Federal receives a capital contribution from its majority shareholder. The shareholder transfers a warehouse to the corporation. The warehouse's FMV is $975,000. The shareholder's basis in the warehouse is $635,000.

d. On November 20, 2008, Federal purchases an apartment complex for $900,000.

e. On March 26, 2009, Federal purchases a warehouse for $888,000.

I12-42 *Severance Damages.* Twelve years ago, Marilyn purchased two lots in an undeveloped subdivision as an investment. Each lot has a $10,000 basis and a $40,000 FMV when the city condemns one lot for use as a municipal sewage treatment plant. As a result of the condemnation, Marilyn receives $40,000 from the city. Because the value of the other lot is reduced, the city pays $7,500 severance damages. She does not plan to replace the condemned lot. What is her:

a. recognized gain due to the condemnation?

b. recognized gain from the receipt of the severance damages?

c. basis for the lot she continues to own?

I12-43 *Sale of a Principal Residence.* Marc, age 45, sells his personal residence on May 15, 2006, for $180,000. He pays $8,000 in selling expenses and $900 in repair expenses to help sell the residence. He has lived in the residence since 1980, when he purchased it for $55,000. In 1994, he paid $6,000 to install central air conditioning. If Marc purchases a new principal residence in December of the current year for $162,000, what is the realized gain, recognized gain, and the basis for the new residence?

I12-44 *Sale of a Principal Residence.* Mr. and Mrs. Rusbarsky purchased a residence on June 12, 2003, for $200,000. On March 12, 2006, they sell the residence for $300,000, and selling expenses amount to $11,000. They purchase another house in a new subdivision for $275,000. Determine the gain realized and recognized.

I12-45 *Sale of a Principal Residence.* On January 10, 2006, Kirsten married Joe. Joe sold his personal residence on October 25, 2005, and excluded the entire gain of $175,000. Although they had originally planned to live in the house that Kirsten had received as a gift from her parents in 1997, they decided to purchase a larger house, and Kirsten sold her house and realized a $370,000 gain.

a. If they file a joint return, how much of the $370,000 gain may be excluded?

b. If Kirsten files as married filing separately, how much of the $370,000 gain may be excluded?

I12-46 *Involuntary Conversion of Principal Residence.* Mr. and Mrs. Mahan own and live in a house, with an adjusted basis of $300,000, that was purchased in 1994. The house is destroyed by a tornado on March 10 of the current year, and the Mahans receive insurance proceeds of $410,000. They purchase another residence for $480,000 four months later.

a. May they exclude the $110,000 gain, and if so, what is the basis of the residence purchased in July?

b. May they defer the $110,000 gain, and if so, what is the basis of the residence purchased in July?

I12-47 *Sale of a Principal Residence.* Mr. and Mrs. Kitchens purchased their first home in Ohio for $135,000 on October 1, 2005. Because Mr. Kitchens' employer transferred him to Utah, they sold the house for $160,000 on January 10, 2006. How much of the gain is recognized?

I12-48 *Sale of a Principal Residence.* Prior to the Taxpayer Relief Act of 1997, taxpayers could defer a gain on the sale of a principal residence sold before May 7, 1997. To defer all of the gain, the taxpayer had to make a timely purchase of a replacement residence that cost more than the adjusted sales price of the residence sold. The basis of the replacement residence was reduced by the gain deferred.

Answer the following questions to demonstrate why Beverley and George might prefer the law prior to the Taxpayer Relief Act if they sell their principal residence for $900,000, with an adjusted basis of $200,000. Selling expenses of $20,000 were paid. They owned and occupied the home for 20 years and file a joint return. The amount realized is equal to the adjusted sales price, and they purchase a new residence for $1,000,000 two weeks after the sale.

a. Under current law, what is the gain recognized and the basis of their new residence?

b. If the sale had occurred prior to May 7, 1997, what is the gain recognized and the basis of their new residence?

c. Which law might they prefer?

I12-49 *Definition of a Principal Residence.* Ken's parents lived with him in a house on 23rd Street purchased by Ken in March 2003 for $30,000. In October 2004, Ken married Beth and moved to a rented apartment. In 2006 they purchase a house on 42nd Street for $90,000 and Ken sells the house on 23rd Street for $60,000 in 2006 when his parents move to a nursing home. Ken pays $4,000 selling expenses and $1,000 repair expenses. How much of the realized gain on the sale of the house on 23rd Street is recognized?

I12-50 *Sale of a Principal Residence: Rental Property.* For the last five years, Mr. and Mrs. Cockrell rented their furnished basement to local college students. When determining their taxable income each year, they deducted a portion of the utilities, property taxes, interest, and depreciation based on the fact that 15% of the house is used for rental purposes. The original basis of the property is $100,000, and depreciation of $4,000 has been allowed on the rental portion of the property. During the current year, Mr. and Mrs. Cockrell sell the house for $300,000. No selling expenses or fixing-up expenses are incurred. Determine:

a. realized gain on the sale.
b. recognized gain on the sale.

I12-51 *Multiple Sales of a Principal Residence.* Consider the following information for Mr. and Mrs. Di Palma:

- On June 10, 2005, they sold their principal residence for $80,000 and incur $6,000 of selling expenses. The basis of the residence, acquired in 1998, is $50,000.
- On June 25, 2005, they purchased a new principal residence for $90,000 and occupied it immediately.
- On May 10, 2006, they purchase their neighbor's residence for $115,000 and occupy the residence immediately.
- On August 29, 2006, they sell the residence purchased on June 25, 2005, for $148,000. They pay $7,000 of selling expenses. Determine:

a. realized gain on the sale of the residence in 2005.
b. recognized gain on the sale of the residence in 2005.
c. realized gain on the sale of the residence in 2006.
d. recognized gain on the sale of the residence in 2006.

I12-52 *Multiple Sales of a Principal Residence.* Consider the following information for Mr. and Mrs. Gomez:

- On May 26, 2005, they sold their principal residence, acquired in 1996, for $200,000. They paid $8,000 of selling expenses. Their basis in the residence was $70,000.
- On July 25, 2005, they purchased a new principal residence for $250,000.
- On June 2, 2006, Mr. Gomez, a bank officer, is transferred to another bank in the northern part of the state and they vacate their house.
- On July 1, 2006, they purchase a new principal residence for $420,000.
- On October 6, 2006, they sell the residence that was purchased on July 25, 2005, for $520,000. They pay $30,000 of selling expenses. Determine:

a. realized gain on the sale of the residence in 2005.
b. recognized gain on the sale of the residence in 2005.
c. realized gain on the sale of the residence in 2006.
d. recognized gain on the sale of the residence in 2006.

COMPREHENSIVE PROBLEM

I12-53 Paden, who is single and has been employed as an accountant for 27 years with Harper, Inc., lost his job due to company downsizing. His last day of employment is July 31, 2006, and Harper provides a $9,000 severance payment. The severance payments are based on an employee's time of employment. During the year, Paden received a salary from Harper of $36,000. Harper also paid $1,500 of Paden's medical insurance premiums.

In May 2006, Paden, who had always wanted to be associated with a football team, applied for the head coaching job at Hawk University in Iowa and, much to his surprise, received the job beginning on August 1. In June and July, Paden paid $4,500 to take courses in sports management at the local university. Hawk University is substantially short of funding and Paden paid $2,000 for entertainment expenses related to his job and $500 for supplies. No reimbursement was received.

His salary from Hawk is $4,000 per month payable at the end of each month. His salary for December was not received until January 6, 2007.

On August 1, he sold his house for $329,000 and paid a sales commission of $14,000. He inherited the house 20 years ago when his mother died. Her basis for the house was $37,000 and the FMV when she died was $50,000. Property taxes for the 2006 calendar year amount to $3,600, and property taxes were apportioned at the closing. Property taxes are payable on October 1. He paid $12,000 of interest on home equity debt of $150,000.

To move to Iowa, he drove 700 miles and spent $45 for meals during the trip. Movers charged $4,150 to move his household items. He purchased a new house in Iowa for $150,000 on August 15 and borrowed $110,000. He also agreed to pay all property taxes for 2006. Real property taxes for the home in Iowa will be paid on January 30, 2007, and amount to $1,500. Interest on the $110,000 debt during the current year is $1,475. To obtain the loan, Paden paid points of $1,000.

He contributed common stock (basis of $1,000 and FMV of $6,000) held as an investment for three years to Hawk University and cash of $1,765 to the First United Methodist Church. He paid personal property taxes of $435 for his car.

Paden sold 200 shares of Dell Corporation stock on April 10 for $100 per share. His basis was $145 per share. On May 1, he purchased 300 shares of Dell at $89 per share.

Determine:

1. gross income without considering the sale of his house or the Dell Corporation stock.
2. recognized gain due to the sale of his house.
3. net capital gain.
4. adjusted gross income.
5. total amount of itemized deductions.
6. taxable income.
7. basis of his house in Iowa.
8. if the sales price for his home was $470,000 instead of $370,000, would his taxable income increase by more than $100,000. If yes, explain.

TAX STRATEGY PROBLEM

I12-54 *Sale of a Principal Residence.* Ray and Ellie have each owned a principal residence for more than five years. Ray's residence has an adjusted basis of $100,000 and a FMV of $325,000, while Ellie's residence has an adjusted basis of $300,000 and a FMV of $490,000. They plan to marry and will purchase another house.
a. Should they sell their houses before the marriage in order to minimize their taxes?
b. Will your answer to Part a change if the FMV of Ellie's house is $690,000?
c. In Part b, what tax strategy should Ray and Ellie consider?

TAX FORM/RETURN PREPARATION PROBLEMS

I12-55 On October 29, 2005, Miss Joan Seely (SSN 123-45-6789) sells her principal residence for $150,000 cash. She purchased the residence on May 12, 1998, for $85,000. She spent $12,000 for capital improvements in 1998. To help sell the house, she pays $300 on October 2, 2005, for minor repairs made on that date. The realtor's commission amounts to $7,500. On February 3, 2006, she purchases a new principal residence for $130,000. Her old residence is never rented out or used for business. Complete the worksheet on page 12-23 for Miss Seely for 2005.

I12-56 At the beginning of the current year, Donna Harp was employed as a cinematographer by Farah Movie, Inc., a motion picture company in Los Angeles, California. In June, she accepted a new job with Ocala Production in Orlando, Florida. Donna is single and her social security number is 223-77-6793. She sold her house in California on August 10 for $500,000. She paid a $14,000 sales commission. The house was acquired on March 23, 1987, for $140,000.

The cost of transporting her household goods and personal effects from California to Orlando amounted to $2,350. To travel from California to Florida, she paid travel and lodging costs of $370 and $100 for meals.

On July 15, she purchased a house for $270,000 on 1225 Minnie Lane in Orlando. To purchase the house, she incurred a 20-year mortgage for $170,000. To obtain the loan, she paid points of $3,400. The $3,600 of property taxes for the house in Orlando were prorated with $1,950 being apportioned to the seller and $1,650 being apportioned to the buyer. In December of the current year she paid $3,600 for property taxes.

Other information related to her return:

Salary from Farah Movie, Inc.	$30,000
Salary from Ocala Production, Inc.	70,000
Federal income taxes withheld by Farah	6,000
Federal income taxes withheld by Ocala	22,000

FICA taxes withheld by Farah	2,295
FICA taxes withheld by Ocala	5,355
Dividend income	10,000
Interest paid for mortgage:	
Home in California	6,780
Home in Orlando	3,800
Property taxes paid in California	4,100
Sales taxes paid in California and Florida	3,125
State income taxes paid in California	2,900
Interest income from Sun National Bank	1,800

Prepare Form 1040 including Schedules A, B, and D and Form 3903. Use the worksheet on page 12-23 to determine the amount of recognized gain on the sale of the residence.

I12-57   Jim Sarowski (SSN 344-77-9255) is 70 years old and single. He received social security benefits of $16,000. He works part-time as a greeter at a local discount store and received wages of $7,300. Federal income taxes of $250 were withheld from his salary. Jim lives at Rt. 7 in Daingerfield, Texas.

In March of the current year, he purchased a duplex at 2006 Tennessee Street to use as rental property for $100,000, with 20% of the price allocated to land. During the current year, he had the following receipts and expenditures with respect to the duplex:

Rent receipts	$8,800
Interest paid	5,900
Property taxes	1,400
Insurance	800
Maintenance	300

Other expenditures during the current year:

Contributions to the church	$2,600
Personal property taxes	225
Sales tax	345

On July 24 of the current year, he exchanged ten acres of land for a car with a $16,500 FMV to be held for personal use. The land was purchased on November 22, 1991, for $18,000 as an investment. Because of pollution problems in the area, the value of the land declined.

On December 1 of the current year, he sold his residence, which had been his home for 30 years, for $475,000. Sales commissions of $16,000 were paid, and the adjusted basis for his home is $110,000. He plans to rent an apartment and does not plan to purchase another home. His only other sale of a principal residence occurred 32 years ago.

Prepare Forms 1040 and 4562 and Schedules D and E. Use the worksheet on page 12-23 to determine the amount of recognized gain on the sale of the residence.

CASE STUDY PROBLEMS

I12-58   The Electric Corporation, a publicly held corporation, owns land with a $1,600,000 basis that is being held for investment. The company is considering exchanging the land for two assets owned by the Quail Corporation: land with a FMV of $3,000,000 and marketable securities with a $1,000,000 FMV. Both assets will be held by the Electric Corporation for investment, although the corporation is considering the possibility of developing the land and building residential houses. The president of the corporation has hired you to prepare a report explaining how the exchange will affect the corporation's reported net income and its tax liability. The corporation has a tax rate of 34%.

TAX RESEARCH PROBLEMS

I12-59   For the last nine years, Mr. and Mrs. Orchard live in a residence located on eight acres. In January of the current year they sell the home and two acres of land. The purchaser of the residence does not wish to own the entire eight acres of land. In December they sell the remaining 6 acres of land to another individual for $60,000. The house and the land have never been used by the Orchards in a trade or business or held for investment. The realized gains resulting from the two sales are computed as follows:

	House and Two Acres _January Sales_	Eight Acres _December Sale_
Selling price	$140,000	$60,000
Minus: Selling expenses	(8,000)	(3,000)
Amount realized	$132,000	$57,000
Minus: Basis	(80,000)	(18,000)
Realized gain	$ 52,000	$39,000

As a result of the sales described above, what is the amount of realized gain that must be recognized during the current year?

A partial list of research sources is

- Reg. Sec. 1.121-1(b)

I12-60 George, age 68, decides to retire from farming and is considering selling his farm. The farm has a $100,000 basis and a $400,000 FMV. George's two sons are not interested in farming. Both sons have large families and would like to own houses suitable for their needs. The Iowa Corporation is willing to purchase George's farm. George's tax advisor suggests that Iowa Corporation should buy the two houses the sons want to own for $400,000 and then exchange the houses for George's farm. After the exchange, George could make a gift of the houses to the sons.

a. If the transactions are executed as suggested by the tax advisor, George's recognized gain will be $300,000. Explain why the transaction does not qualify as a like-kind exchange.

b. George wants the exchange to qualify as a like-kind exchange and still help his sons obtain the houses. What advice do you have for him?

A partial list of research sources is

- _Dollie H. Click,_ 78 T.C. 225 (1982)

- _Fred S. Wagensen,_ 74 T.C. 653 (1980)

I12-61 On March 10, 19Y1, Elizabeth, a college professor, purchased a house for $300,000. She did not move into the house until August 8, 19Y1. On August 1, 19Y2, she accepted a position as a visiting professor at Hogwatts University for one year and moved to Liverpool where she rented an apartment. While away at Hogwatts, two of her former students lived in the house but did not pay rent. She returned to the house on August 1, 19Y3, and lived in the house until July 15, 19Y4, when she sold the house for $500,000. The realtor's commission was $35,000. Determine her recognized gain.

A partial list of research sources is

- Reg. Sec. 1.121-1(c)

I12-62 Mr. and Mrs. Hattan have lived in their residence for 20 years and purchased the house for $100,000 as joint tenants with right of survivorship. Mr. Hattan died in May of the current year when the house's FMV was $800,000. Mrs. Hattan wants to sell the house. What is the tax effect of selling the house this year for $825,000 or next year for $830,000?

A partial list of research sources is

- Sections 121 and 1014

I12-63 Joseph Allen, who is single, purchased his first house in Orono, ME. one year ago for $200,000. Katahdin wants to purchase the house for $360,000. Refer to the regulations to determine if he may exclude part of the gain in the following independent cases:

a. He has been unemployed for 16 months and has a chance to start work for Penobscot Manufacturing whose plant is located 62 miles from Joseph's home in Orono.

b. His dependent son, Ryan, has chronic asthma, and the son's doctor has advised Joseph that Ryan should live in a warm, dry climate to mitigate the chronic asthma. Joeseph and Ryan move to Nevada.

c. Joseph has become increasingly annoyed at the amount of traffic in his neighborhood although the amount of traffic has not increased much compared to the traffic when he purchased the house.

A partial list of research sources is:

- Reg. Sec. 1.121-3(c), (d) and (e)

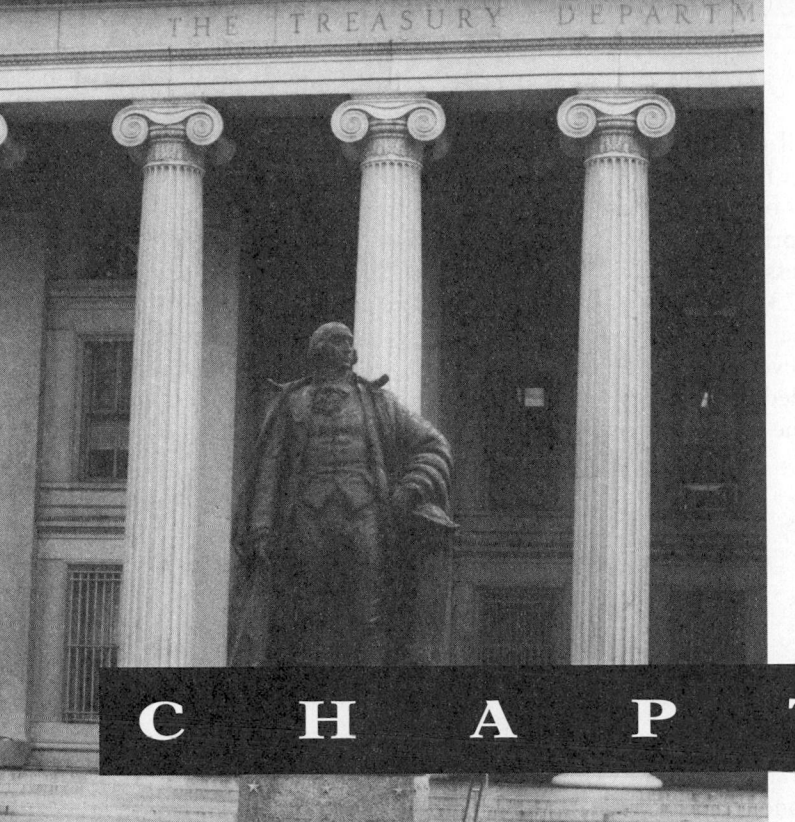

13

CHAPTER

PROPERTY
TRANSACTIONS:
SECTION 1231
AND RECAPTURE

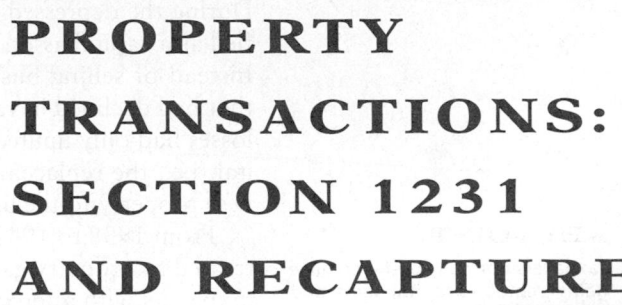

LEARNING OBJECTIVES

After studying this chapter, you should be able to

1. ▶ Identify Sec. 1231 property

2. ▶ Understand the tax treatment for Sec. 1231 transactions

3. ▶ Apply the recapture provisions of Sec. 1245

4. ▶ Apply the recapture provisions of Sec. 1250

5. ▶ Describe other recapture applications

Chapter 15 states that all recognized gains and losses must eventually be designated as either capital or ordinary. However, gains or losses on certain types of property are designated as Sec. 1231 gains or losses, which are given preferential treatment under the tax law. Sec. 1231 property primarily is business property, either real or depreciable property used in a trade or business.[1] A net Sec. 1231 loss, which is defined as the excess of Sec. 1231 losses over Sec. 1231 gains, is treated as an ordinary loss.[2] Net Sec. 1231 gain, which is the excess of Sec. 1231 gains over Sec. 1231 losses, is generally treated as long-term capital gain.[3] However, the preferential treatment of Sec. 1231 gains is diminished, principally by the so-called depreciation recapture rules and the five-year lookback rule. This chapter discusses the important rules dealing with Sec. 1231 gains and losses and depreciation recapture.

HISTORY OF SEC. 1231

KEY POINT

Taxpayers normally prefer to have gains treated as capital gains, and losses treated as ordinary losses. Because Sec. 1231 property receives the preferable treatment for both net gains and losses, it has been said that this property enjoys the best of both worlds.

During the depressed economy of the early and mid-1930s, business property was classified as a capital asset. Many business properties were worth less than their adjusted basis. Instead of selling business properties, taxpayers found it advantageous to retain assets that had declined in value because they could recover the full cost as depreciation. Capital losses had only limited deductibility during this period. To encourage the mobility of capital (i.e., the replacement of business fixed assets), the Revenue Act of 1938 added business property to the list of properties not considered to be capital assets.

From 1938 to 1942, gains and losses on the sale or exchange of business property were treated as ordinary gains and losses. Favorable capital gain treatment was eliminated and taxpayers with appreciated business properties were reluctant to sell the assets because of the high tax cost. This restriction on the mobility of capital was more significant than usual because business assets had to be shifted into industries that were more heavily involved in the production of military goods. Furthermore, taxpayers were often forced to recognize ordinary gains because the government used the condemnation process to obtain business property for the war effort. In 1942, Congress created the predecessor of Sec. 1231, which allowed taxpayers to treat net gains from the sale of business property as capital gains and net losses as ordinary losses. Before 1987, only 40% of an individual's net capital gain might be subject to tax because of the 60% long-term capital gain deduction.

The Tax Reform Act of 1986 eliminated the 60% long-term capital gain deduction for net long-term capital gains. Favorable long-term capital gain treatment was reinstated into the tax law in 1991 in the form of a 28% maximum tax rate applying to net capital gains for noncorporate taxpayers. The Taxpayer Relief Act of 1997 significantly increased the preferential tax treatment by reducing the maximum rate to 20% for net capital gain that is adjusted net capital gain. The maximum rate was reduced by the Jobs and Growth Tax Relief Reconciliation Act of 2003 (2003 Tax Act) to 15%, for sales after May 5, 2003.

It may also be advantageous to have gains classified as capital or Sec. 1231 if taxpayers have capital losses or capital loss carryovers because of the limitations imposed on the deductibility of capital losses. Furthermore, there are other situations where it may be important for the property to be Sec. 1231 property (e.g., a contribution of appreciated property to a charitable organization).

---

[1] See page I13-5 for a more complete definition of Sec. 1231 property.
[2] Secs. 1231(c)(4) and (a)(2).

[3] Secs. 1231(c)(3) and (a)(1). There are several exceptions to this rule that are covered later in this chapter.

OVERVIEW OF BASIC TAX TREATMENT FOR SEC. 1231

NET GAINS

At the end of the tax year, Sec. 1231 gains are netted against Sec. 1231 losses. If the overall result is a net Sec. 1231 gain, the gains and losses are treated as long-term capital gains (LTCGs) and long-term capital losses (LTCLs), respectively.[4] For the sake of expediency, it is often stated that a net Sec. 1231 gain is treated as a LTCG. For tax years beginning after 1984, however, a portion or all of the net Sec. 1231 gain may be treated as ordinary income because of a special five-year lookback rule (see discussion below).

EXAMPLE I13-1 ▶ Dawn owns a business that has $20,000 of Sec. 1231 gains and $12,000 of Sec. 1231 losses during the current year. Because the Sec. 1231 gains exceed the Sec. 1231 losses, the gains and losses are treated as LTCGs and LTCLs. After the gains and losses are offset, there is an $8,000 net long-term capital gain (NLTCG). ◀

EXAMPLE I13-2 ▶ Assume the same facts as in Example I13-1 except that Dawn also recognizes a $7,000 LTCG from the sale of a capital asset. After considering the $8,000 net Sec. 1231 gain, which is treated as a LTCG, Dawn has a $15,000 NLTCG ($8,000 + $7,000). ◀

NET LOSSES

If the netting of Sec. 1231 gains and losses at the end of the year results in a net Sec. 1231 loss, the Sec. 1231 gains and losses are treated as ordinary gains and losses.[5] For expediency, it is often stated that the net Sec. 1231 loss is treated as an ordinary loss.

EXAMPLE I13-3 ▶ David owns an unincorporated business and has $30,000 of Sec. 1231 gains and $40,000 of Sec. 1231 losses in the current year. Because the losses exceed the gains, they are treated as ordinary losses and gains. ◀

EXAMPLE I13-4 ▶ Assume the same facts as in Example I13-3 except that David receives a $37,000 salary as a corporate employee. David has no other income, losses, or deductions affecting his adjusted gross income (AGI). The Sec. 1231 gains and losses are treated as ordinary gains and losses, and David's AGI is $27,000 ($37,000 salary − $10,000 of ordinary loss). The $40,000 of ordinary losses offsets the $30,000 of ordinary gains and $10,000 of David's salary. ◀

TYPICAL MISCONCEPTION

It is sometimes erroneously thought that each Sec. 1231 gain should be treated as a LTCG and each Sec. 1231 loss as an ordinary loss. However all Sec. 1231 gains and losses must be combined to determine whether the Sec. 1231 gains and losses are LTCGs and LTCLs or ordinary gains and losses.

ADDITIONAL COMMENT

A taxpayer's share of a Sec. 1231 loss from a partnership or S Corporation may be subject to the passive activity loss rules.

One important advantage of Sec. 1231 is illustrated in Example I13-4. Because the Sec. 1231 gains and losses are treated as ordinary, the $10,000 net Sec. 1231 loss is fully deductible in the current year. If the gains and losses were classified as long-term capital gains and losses, David would have a $10,000 NLTCL. Only $3,000 of the $10,000 NLTCL would have been deductible against David's other income. As explained in Chapter I5, only $3,000 of net capital losses may be deducted from noncapital gain income per year.

FIVE-YEAR LOOKBACK RULE Beginning in 1985, the benefits of Sec. 1231 were reduced. For tax years beginning after 1984, any net Sec. 1231 gain is ordinary gain to the extent of any nonrecaptured net Sec. 1231 losses from the previous five years.[6] This provision is referred to as the *five-year lookback rule*. In essence, net Sec. 1231 losses previously deducted as ordinary losses are recaptured by changing what would otherwise be a LTCG into ordinary income.

EXAMPLE I13-5 ▶ In 2006, Craig recognizes $25,000 of Sec. 1231 gains and $15,000 of Sec. 1231 losses. In 2002, Craig reported $14,000 of Sec. 1231 losses and no Sec. 1231 gains. No other Sec. 1231 gains or

---

[4] Sec. 1231(a)(1).
[5] Sec. 1231(a)(2).
[6] Sec. 1231(c)(1).

losses were recognized by Craig during the prior five-year period, 2001–2005. The $10,000 ($25,000 − $15,000) of net Sec. 1231 gain in 2006 is treated as ordinary income due to the $14,000 of nonrecaptured net Sec. 1231 losses. ◀

To determine the amount of nonrecaptured net Sec. 1231 losses, compare the aggregate amount of net Sec. 1231 losses for the most recent preceding five tax years with the amount of such losses recaptured as ordinary income for those preceding tax years. The excess of the aggregate amount of net Sec. 1231 losses over the previously recaptured loss is the nonrecaptured net Sec. 1231 loss. In Example I13-5, $4,000 of nonrecaptured net Sec. 1231 losses remain that can be recaptured in 2007. In 2007, the preceding five-year period includes 2002 through 2006.

TAX RATE FOR NET SEC. 1231 GAIN

In general, Sec. 1231 gains are taxed similarly to the taxation of net long-term capital gains. Thus, a Sec. 1231 gain may be taxed at a rate of 15% (or 5% if the taxpayer's regular tax rate is 15% or less). Sec. 1231 property must have a holding period of more than one year. Recall from Chapter I5 that adjusted net capital gain (ANCG) is net capital gain (NCG) determined *without* regard to:

(1) the 28% rate gain, and
(2) unrecaptured Sec. 1250 gain, which is taxed at no more than 25% as explained later.

ANCG might be taxed at 15% or 5%. If Sec. 1231 property is sold at a gain, the Sec. 1231 gain is LTCG if there are no Sec. 1231 losses or nonrecaptured net Sec. 1231 losses. However, all or part of this gain is unrecaptured Section 1250 gain if the asset is a building. Thus, net Sec. 1231 gain might be taxed today at 5%, 15%, or 25% depending on the taxpayer's tax rate and whether or not the gain is unrecaptured section 1250 gain.

EXAMPLE I13-6 ▶ Savannah, whose tax rate is 28%, sells land at a gain of $10,000 and other land at a gain of $15,000. Both tracts of land qualify as Sec. 1231 property. She has no other transactions involving capital assets or 1231 property and no nonrecaptured net Sec. 1231 losses. Savannah has net Sec. 1231 gain of $25,000 that is NLTCG and her NCG is $25,000. Her ANCG is $25,000 taxed at a rate of 15%. ◀

EXAMPLE I13-7 ▶ Assume the same facts as in Example I13-6 except Savannah also has a $7,000 loss from the sale of a third tract of land that is Sec. 1231 property. Her net Sec. 1231 gain is $18,000. Her NCG is $18,000 and her ANCG is $18,000 taxed at a rate of 15%. ◀

EXAMPLE I13-8 ▶ Grace, whose tax rate is 10% or 15%, sells land that is Sec. 1231 property at a gain of $2,000. She has no other transactions involving capital assets or 1231 property and no nonrecaptured net Sec. 1231 losses. The $2,000 gain is taxed at 5%. ◀

APPLYING THE FIVE-YEAR LOOKBACK RULE. As explained earlier, net Sec. 1231 gain is ordinary income to the extent of nonrecaptured net Sec. 1231 losses. Net Sec. 1231 gain is recharacterized as ordinary income under the five-year lookback rule in the following order:

(1) Net Sec. 1231 gain in the 25% group (unrecaptured Sec. 1250 gain)
(2) Net Sec. 1231 gain in the 15% group

EXAMPLE I13-9 ▶ Chris, whose tax rate is 33%, has nonrecaptured net Sec. 1231 losses of $20,000 at the beginning of the current year when he recognizes gains from the sale of two assets used in his trade or business and held more than one year. Asset #1 is a building and the entire $14,000 Sec. 1231 gain is unrecaptured Sec. 1250 gain. Asset #2 is land and the Sec. 1231 gain is $15,000. All gain resulting from the sale of asset #1 is ordinary income and $6,000 of the gain from the sale of asset #2 is ordinary income because of the five-year lookback rule. The remaining $9,000 gain from the sale of asset #2 (land) is taxed at 15%. ◀

SECTION 1231 PROPERTY

OBJECTIVE 1

Identify Sec. 1231 property

SECTION 1231 PROPERTY DEFINED

Section 1231 property includes the following types of property:

▶ Real property or depreciable property used in a trade or business with a holding period of more than one year

▶ Timber, coal, or domestic iron ore

▶ Livestock

▶ Unharvested crops

Each of these types of Sec. 1231 assets are discussed below.

REAL OR DEPRECIABLE PROPERTY USED IN TRADE OR BUSINESS

KEY POINT

Inventory, free publications of the U.S. government, and copyrights, literary, musical, or artistic compositions are not capital assets.

As noted in Chapter I5, the Code does not provide a definition of a capital asset. Instead, Sec. 1221 provides a list of noncapital assets. This list includes both depreciable property and real property used in a trade or business.[7] These properties are treated as Sec. 1231 properties if held for more than one year. Depreciable property and real property used in a trade or business and held for **one year or less** are neither capital assets nor Sec. 1231 property. Any gain or loss resulting from the disposition of such assets is ordinary.

EXAMPLE I13-10 ▶

The Prime Corporation owns land held as an investment and land used as an employee parking lot. The land held as an investment is a capital asset. The land used as a parking lot is real property used in a trade or business and is not a capital asset. The land used as a parking lot is a Sec. 1231 asset if held for more than one year. ◀

EXAMPLE I13-11 ▶

KEY POINT

Only property used in a trade or business is included in the definition of Sec. 1231 property. Gains and losses on property held for investment may be included only if the result of a condemnation or casualty.

Dale, a self-employed plumber, owns an automobile held for personal use and a truck used in his trade. The automobile is a capital asset because it is held for personal use, but the truck is a Sec. 1231 asset if held for more than one year. As described later, a portion or all of any gain realized on the sale of the truck may be taxed as ordinary income due to the Sec. 1245 depreciation recapture provisions. ◀

Certain types of property do not qualify as Sec. 1231 property, even if used in a trade or business. For example, inventory is not Sec. 1231 property. Thus, a sale of inventory results in ordinary gain or loss. Publications of the U.S. Government received other than by purchase at its regular sale price; a copyright; literary, musical, or artistic compositions; letters or memorandums; or similar properties held by certain taxpayers are not classified as Sec. 1231 property.[8]

EXAMPLE I13-12 ▶

Carl, who owns a recording studio, writes a musical composition to be sold to a record company. Because the musical composition is created by the personal efforts of the taxpayer, the musical composition is not Sec. 1231 property, and the sale results in ordinary gain from the sale of an ordinary asset. ◀

TIMBER. Section 631 allows taxpayers to elect to treat the cutting of timber as a sale or exchange of such timber. To be eligible to make this election, the taxpayer must own the timber or hold the contract right on the first day of the year and for more than one year. Furthermore, the timber must be cut for sale or for use in the taxpayer's trade or business.[9]

REAL-WORLD EXAMPLE

Christmas trees can be included in the definition of Sec. 1231 property.

The gain or loss is determined by comparing the timber's adjusted basis for depletion with its fair market value (FMV) on the first day of the tax year in which it is cut. If the timber is eventually sold for more or less than its FMV (determined on the first day of the year the timber is cut), the difference is ordinary gain or loss.

---

[7] Sec. 1221(2).
[8] Sec. 1231(b)(1).

[9] Sec. 631(a) and Reg. Sec. 1.631-1.

EXAMPLE I13-13 ▶ Vermont Corporation owns timber with a $60,000 basis for depletion. The timber, acquired four years ago, is cut during the current year for use in the corporation's business. The FMV of the timber on the first day of the current year is $200,000. Vermont Corporation may elect to treat the cutting of the timber as a sale or exchange and recognize a $140,000 ($200,000 − $60,000) gain. ◀

SELF-STUDY QUESTION

Is the possible inclusion of timber and coal or domestic iron ore in the definition of Sec. 1231 property favorable to the taxpayers who produce these items?

ANSWER

Yes, it can result in income being taxed at rates applicable for LTCG instead of ordinary income from the sale of inventory.

ADDITIONAL COMMENT

Livestock includes cattle, hogs, horses, mules, donkeys, sheep, goats, fur-bearing animals, and other mammals but excludes poultry, fish, frogs, and reptiles.

ADDITIONAL COMMENT

The treatment of unharvested crops as a Sec. 1231 asset is largely a rule of convenience. If the taxpayer were not permitted to treat the crops in this fashion, it would be necessary to allocate the selling price between the land and crops.

If the election is made to treat the cutting of timber as a sale or exchange, the timber is considered Sec. 1231 property.[10] Thus, the $140,000 gain in Example I13-13 is Sec. 1231 gain. If the taxpayer does not make the election, the character of any gain or loss depends on whether the timber is held for sale in the ordinary course of the taxpayer's trade or business, held for investment, or held for use in a trade or business.

COAL OR DOMESTIC IRON ORE. An owner who disposes of coal (including lignite) or domestic iron ore while retaining an economic interest in it must treat the disposal as a sale.[11] The coal or iron ore is considered Sec. 1231 property.[12] The owner must own and retain an economic interest in the coal or iron ore in place.[13] An economic interest is owned when one acquires by investment any interest in mineral in place and seeks a return of capital from income derived from the extraction of the mineral.

LIVESTOCK. Livestock held by the taxpayer for draft, breeding, dairy, or sporting purposes is considered Sec. 1231 property if held for 12 months or more from the date of acquisition. However, cattle and horses must be held for 24 months or more from the date of acquisition to qualify as Sec. 1231 property.[14]

UNHARVESTED CROPS AND LAND. An unharvested crop growing on land used in a trade or business is considered Sec. 1231 property if the crop and the land are both sold at the same time to the same person and the land is held more than one year.[15] Section 1231 does not apply to the sale or exchange of an unharvested crop if the taxpayer retains any right or option to reacquire the land.[16]

If Sec. 1231 applies to the sale or exchange of an unharvested crop sold with the land, no deductions are allowed for expenses attributable to the production of the unharvested crop.[17] Instead, costs of producing the crop must be capitalized.

INVOLUNTARY CONVERSIONS

Gains and losses from involuntary conversions of property used in a trade or business generally are classified as Sec. 1231 gains and losses. Involuntary conversions of capital assets that are held in connection with a trade or business or in a transaction entered into for profit also generally qualify for Sec. 1231 treatment. The property that is involuntarily converted must be held for more than one year. Certain involuntary conversions are treated differently for income tax purposes. For example, the tax rules are different for condemnations and casualties, even though both are involuntary conversions of property.

CONDEMNATIONS

Gains and losses resulting from condemnations of Sec. 1231 property and capital assets held more than one year are classified as Sec. 1231 gains and losses. As indicated above, the capital assets must be held in connection with a trade or business or with a transaction entered into for profit.[18]

EXAMPLE I13-14 ▶ Kathryn owns land with a $20,000 basis and a $30,000 FMV as well as a building with a $40,000 adjusted basis and a $26,000 FMV. Both assets are used in her trade or business and have been held for more than one year. As a result of the state exercising its powers of requisition or con-

---

[10] Sec. 1231(b)(2) and Reg. Sec. 1.631-1(d)(4).
[11] Sec. 631(c) and Reg. Sec. 1.631-3(a)(1).
[12] Sec. 1231(b)(2) and Reg. Sec. 1.631-3(a)(2).
[13] Reg. Sec. 1.631-3(b)(4).
[14] Sec. 1231(b)(3).

[15] Sec. 1231(b)(4) and Reg. Secs. 1.1231-1(c)(5) and 1(f).
[16] Reg. Sec. 1.1231-1(f).
[17] Sec. 268 and Reg. Sec. 1.268-1.
[18] Secs. 1231(a)(3)(A) and (4)(B).

demnation, Kathryn is required to transfer both properties to the state for cash equal to their FMVs. No other transfers of assets occur during the current year. The $10,000 gain due to condemnation of the land is a Sec. 1231 gain and the $14,000 loss due to condemnation of the building is a Sec. 1231 loss. ◄

OTHER INVOLUNTARY CONVERSIONS

TYPICAL MISCONCEPTION

The inclusion of gains and losses from condemnations in the netting of the other involuntary conversions is a common error.

Gains or losses resulting from an involuntary conversion arising from fire, storm, shipwreck, other casualty, or theft are not classified as Sec. 1231 gains or losses if the recognized losses from such conversions exceed the recognized gains.[19] In such a case, the involuntary conversions are treated as ordinary gains and losses. However, if the gains from such involuntary conversions exceed the losses, both are classified as Sec. 1231 gains and losses.

EXAMPLE I13-15 ►

Jose owns equipment having a $50,000 adjusted basis and a $42,000 FMV and a building having a $30,000 adjusted basis and a $35,000 FMV which are used in Jose's trade or business. The straight-line method of depreciation is used for the building. Both assets are held for more than a year. As a result of a fire, both assets are destroyed, and Jose collects insurance proceeds equal to the assets' FMV. No other transfers of assets occur during the current year. Because the $8,000 ($42,000 − $50,000) recognized loss exceeds the $5,000 ($35,000 − $30,000) recognized gain, the recognized loss and gain are both treated as ordinary. ◄

PROCEDURE FOR SEC. 1231 TREATMENT

OBJECTIVE 2

Understand the tax treatment for Sec. 1231 transactions

After determining the recognized gains and losses from transfers of property qualifying for Sec. 1231 treatment, it is necessary to determine whether any gain must be recaptured as ordinary income under Secs. 1245 and 1250. The recaptured gain, discussed later in this chapter, is not eligible for Sec. 1231 treatment. After eliminating the gain recaptured as ordinary income due to the recapture of depreciation, the procedure for analyzing Sec. 1231 transactions is as follows:

STEP 1. Determine all gains and losses resulting from casualties or thefts of Sec. 1231 property and non–personal-use capital assets held for more than one year. Gains and losses are netted and treated as Sec. 1231 gains and losses if the gains exceed the losses.

If the losses exceed the gains, both are treated as ordinary losses and gains and do not, therefore, enter into the Sec. 1231 netting procedure. Recall from Chapter I7 that business casualty losses are deductible *for* AGI and other casualty losses are deductible *from* AGI.

KEY POINT

Gains that are recaptured under Secs. 1245 and 1250 are not eligible for Sec. 1231 treatment.

STEP 2. Combine the following gains and losses to determine whether Sec. 1231 gains exceed Sec. 1231 losses or vice versa:

► Net casualty and theft *gains* resulting from Step 1, if any

► Gains and losses resulting from the sale or exchange of Sec. 1231 property

► Gains and losses resulting from the condemnation of Sec. 1231 property and non–personal-use capital assets held more than one year.

If a net Sec. 1231 loss is the result, the losses and gains are treated as ordinary losses and gains. If a net Sec. 1231 gain is the result, the gains and losses are treated as LTCGs and LTCLs, although a portion or all of the capital gain may be recaptured as ordinary income as outlined in Step 3 (five-year lookback rule) below.

STEP 3. If a net Sec. 1231 gain is the result of Step 2, determine if the taxpayer has any nonrecaptured net Sec. 1231 losses. Nonrecaptured net Sec. 1231 losses are the excess of aggregate net Sec. 1231 losses for the preceding five years over losses previously recaptured as ordinary income due to the recapture provision of Sec. 1231. Net Sec. 1231 gains to the extent of any nonrecaptured net Sec. 1231 losses are treated as ordinary income. Sec. 1231 gain that is unrecaptured Sec. 1250 gain is first treated as ordinary income to the extent of nonrecaptured net Sec. 1231 losses. Any net Sec. 1231 gain in excess of nonrecaptured net Sec. 1231 loss is treated as a LTCG.

---

[19] Sec. 1231(a)(4)(C).

EXAMPLE I13-16 ▶ The following gains and losses pertain to Danielle's business assets that qualify as Sec. 1231 property. Danielle does not have any nonrecaptured net Sec. 1231 losses from previous years, and the portion of gain recaptured as ordinary income due to the depreciation recapture provisions has been considered.

Gain due to an insurance reimbursement for fire damage	$10,000
Loss due to condemnation	(19,000)
Gain due to the sale of Sec. 1231 property	22,000

The $10,000 casualty gain is classified as a Sec. 1231 gain because gains resulting from casualties or thefts of Sec. 1231 property exceed losses. Danielle has $32,000 ($10,000 + $22,000) of Sec. 1231 gains and a $19,000 Sec. 1231 loss. Danielle's $13,000 net Sec. 1231 gain is treated as a LTCG. No portion of the $13,000 LTCG is recaptured as ordinary income because Danielle does not have any nonrecaptured net Sec. 1231 losses during the preceding five-year period. ◀

EXAMPLE I13-17 ▶ Assume the same facts as in Example I13-16 except that Danielle has a $10,000 loss because of the fire instead of a $10,000 gain. The $10,000 casualty loss is an ordinary loss, not a Sec. 1231 loss because losses resulting from casualties or thefts of Sec. 1231 property exceed gains. Because the loss is a business loss, it is deductible *for* AGI. Due to the $19,000 condemnation loss and the $22,000 of Sec. 1231 gain, she has a $3,000 net Sec. 1231 gain that is treated as a LTCG. ◀

EXAMPLE I13-18 ▶ The following gains and losses recognized in 2006 pertain to Fred's business assets that were held for more than one year. The assets qualify as Sec. 1231 property.

Gain due to an insurance reimbursement for a casualty	$15,000
Gain due to a condemnation	25,000
Loss due to the sale of Sec. 1231 property	(12,000)

A summary of Fred's net Sec. 1231 gains and losses for the previous five-year period is as follows:

Year	Sec. 1231 Gain	Sec. 1231 Loss	Cumulative Nonrecaptured Net Sec. 1231 Losses (from five prior years)
2001	$ 5,000		–0–
2002		$2,000	$2,000
2003		6,000	8,000
2004	13,000		–0–
2005		9,000	9,000

The $15,000 gain due to the insurance reimbursement for a casualty is treated as a Sec. 1231 gain. The $25,000 gain from the condemnation is also a Sec. 1231 gain. Fred's net Sec. 1231 gain in 2006 is $28,000 [($15,000 + $25,000) − $12,000]. However, $9,000 of the Sec. 1231 gain is recaptured as ordinary income due to the $9,000 of nonrecaptured net Sec. 1231 loss from 2005. The remaining $19,000 of net Sec. 1231 gain is a LTCG. ◀

RECAPTURE PROVISIONS OF SEC. 1245

OBJECTIVE 3

Apply the recapture provisions of Sec. 1245

In 1962, Congress enacted Sec. 1245, which substantially reduced the advantages of Sec. 1231. A gain from the disposition of Sec. 1245 property is treated as ordinary income to the extent of the total amount of depreciation (or cost-recovery) deductions allowed since January 1, 1962. The gain recaptured as ordinary income cannot exceed the amount of the realized gain.

EXAMPLE I13-19 ▶ Adobe Corporation sells equipment used in its trade or business for $95,000. The equipment was acquired several years ago for $110,000 and is Sec. 1245 property.[20] The equipment's adjusted basis is $60,000 because $50,000 of depreciation was deducted. The entire $35,000 ($95,000 − $60,000) gain is treated as ordinary income because the total amount of depreciation taken ($50,000) is greater than the $35,000 realized gain. ◀

---

[20] Throughout this chapter, property is considered to be placed in service when it is purchased or acquired. The term *Sec. 1245 property* is used here to refer to either recovery property under the ACRS or MACRS rules or nonrecovery property that falls outside of the ACRS or MACRS rules.

The recapture provisions of Sec. 1245 apply to the total amount of depreciation (or cost recovery) allowed or allowable for Sec. 1245 property. It makes no difference which method of depreciation is used.[21]

Generally, the entire gain from the disposition of Sec. 1245 property is recaptured as ordinary income because the total amount of depreciation (or cost recovery) is greater than the gain realized. A portion of the gain will receive Sec. 1231 treatment if the realized gain exceeds total depreciation or cost recovery.

EXAMPLE I13-20 ▶

Assume the same facts as in Example I13-19 except that the asset is sold for $117,000. Because the $57,000 ($117,000 − $60,000) realized gain is greater than the $50,000 of total depreciation, $50,000 of the gain is ordinary income and the remaining $7,000 is a Sec. 1231 gain. ◀

PURPOSE OF SEC. 1245

The purpose of Sec. 1245 is to eliminate any advantage taxpayers would have if they were able to reduce ordinary income by deducting depreciation and subsequently receive Sec. 1231 treatment when the asset was sold. For individuals, Sec. 1245 recapture prevents net Sec. 1231 gain from being treated as LTCG. The conversion of Sec. 1231 gain to Sec. 1245 ordinary income also prevents taxpayers from possibly using capital losses.

EXAMPLE I13-21 ▶

During the current year, Coastal Corporation has capital losses of $50,000 and no capital gains for the current year or the preceding three years. The corporation owns equipment purchased several years ago for $90,000, and depreciation deductions of $48,000 have been allowed. If Coastal sells the equipment for $72,000, the entire $30,000 ($72,000 − $42,000) gain, which is due to the depreciation deductions, is Sec. 1245 ordinary income. Without Sec. 1245, the $30,000 gain is a Sec. 1231 gain that could be offset by $30,000 of the corporation's capital loss. ◀

Note that Sec. 1245 does not apply to losses. If Coastal Corporation sells the equipment in Example I13-21 for $40,000, a $2,000 ($40,000 − $42,000 basis) Sec. 1231 loss is recognized.

SECTION 1245 PROPERTY. **Section 1245 property** is certain property subject to depreciation and, in some cases, amortization. The most common example of Sec. 1245 property is depreciable personal property such as equipment. Automobiles, livestock, railroad grading, and single-purpose agricultural or horticultural structures are Sec. 1245 properties as well as intangible assets subject to amortization under Sec. 197 (see Chapter I10).[22] Except for certain buildings placed in service after 1980 and before 1987, buildings and structural components generally are not Sec. 1245 property.[23]

EXAMPLE I13-22 ▶

Buckeye Corporation owns the following assets acquired in 1999: equipment, a patent, an office building (including structural components), and land. The equipment and patent are Sec. 1245 property. The office building and the land are not Sec. 1245 property. ◀

In many cases, taxpayers are allowed preferential treatment with respect to amortizing certain costs. For example, taxpayers may elect to expense up to $15,000 of the cost of making any business facility more accessible to handicapped and elderly people,[24] or to amortize pollution control facilities over 60 months[25] and reforestation expenditures over 84 months.[26] If taxpayers have amortized the costs of any real property under the special provisions, Sec. 1245 applies to the gain resulting from the disposition of such property.[27]

If taxpayers elect to expense certain depreciable property under Sec. 179, the amount deducted is treated as a depreciation deduction for purposes of the Sec. 1245 recapture provisions.[28]

[21] As explained later in this chapter, the method of cost recovery used determines whether certain real property is treated as Sec. 1245 recovery property.
[22] Sec. 1245(a)(3).
[23] Sec. 1245(a)(3)(B)(i). Tangible real property "used as an integral part of the manufacturing, production, extraction, or furnishing of transportation, communication, electrical energy, gas, water, or sewage disposal services" is Sec. 1245 property.

[24] Sec. 190.
[25] Sec. 169(a).
[26] Sec. 194(a).
[27] Sec. 1245(a)(3)(C). The Sec. 1245 rules recapture amortization deductions claimed on real property under Secs. 169, 179, 185, 188, 190, 193, and 194.
[28] Sec. 1245(a)(2)(C). The maximum amount deductible under Sec. 179 is $108,000 in 2006 and $105,000 in 2005.

EXAMPLE I13-23 ▶ Compact Corporation purchased $90,000 of five-year equipment on March 10, 2005, and elected to expense $20,000 of the cost under Sec. 179. Compact sells the equipment on July 30, 2006, for $95,000. Regular depreciation allowed under MACRS for 2005 and 2006 is $14,000 and $11,200 (½ year), respectively. The adjusted basis of the equipment on the date of sale is $44,800 ($90,000 − $20,000 − $25,200 depreciation). The realized gain is $50,200 ($95,000 − $44,800), and $45,200 ($20,000 + $25,200) of the gain is Sec. 1245 ordinary income. The remaining $5,000 is Sec. 1231 gain. ◀

TYPICAL MISCONCEPTION

The categorization of nonresidential real estate acquired between 1981 and 1986 on which an accelerated depreciation method was used as Sec. 1250 property rather than as Sec. 1245 property is a common error.

APPLICATION OF SEC. 1245 TO NONRESIDENTIAL REAL ESTATE. Most real property is not affected by Sec. 1245. However, Sec. 1245 does apply to nonresidential real estate that qualified as recovery property under the ACRS rules (i.e., placed in service after 1980 and before 1987) unless the taxpayer elected to use the straight-line method of cost recovery.[29] Section 1245 does not apply to nonresidential real estate acquired after 1986, because only straight-line depreciation may be used for nonresidential real estate acquired after 1986 (see Chapter I10).

EXAMPLE I13-24 ▶ Brad sells two warehouses during the current year that are totally depreciated because their recovery period is 19 years.

KEY POINT

Taxpayers acquiring nonresidential real property between 1981 and 1986 were confronted with choosing between straight-line ACRS and ACRS using the statutory rates. In making the decision, these taxpayers should have considered the number of years the property would be held, the estimated selling price, the present value of the additional depreciation deductions, and any preferential treatment for net capital gains.

	Warehouse 1	Warehouse 2
Year of purchase	1985	1985
Cost*	$720,000	$900,000
Cost recovery—straight line ACRS	720,000	
Cost recovery—ACRS statutory rates (accelerated)		900,000
Adjusted basis	0	0
Selling price	700,000	800,000

*does not consider the cost of land

Both warehouses were placed in service after 1980 and before 1987 and qualify as recovery property under ACRS. The $700,000 ($700,000 − $0) gain on the sale of Warehouse 1 is a Sec. 1231 gain. Section 1245 does not apply because the straight-line method of cost recovery was used. Section 1245 applies to the sale of Warehouse 2 because ACRS was used and the property is nonresidential real estate placed in service after 1980 and before 1987. Therefore, the $800,000 ($800,000 − $0) gain is Sec. 1245 ordinary income because the $800,000 gain is less than the $900,000 total ACRS cost-recovery allowance. ◀

As illustrated in the example above, nonresidential buildings placed in service after 1980 and before 1987 are Sec. 1245 property if an accelerated method of cost recovery was used.

If the properties in Example I13-24 were acquired before 1981 or after 1986, they would not be subject to the Sec. 1245 recapture rules regardless of the method of depreciation used. However, nonresidential real estate (e.g., a warehouse) acquired after 1970 and before 1981 is subject to the Sec. 1250 recapture rules, and a portion of the gain from its disposition may be treated as ordinary income if accelerated depreciation was used.[30]

The Sec. 1245 recapture rules are summarized in Topic Review I13-1.

RECAPTURE PROVISIONS OF SEC. 1250

OBJECTIVE 4

Apply the recapture provisions of Sec. 1250

In 1964, Sec. 1250 was enacted to extend the recapture concept to include most depreciable real property. Unlike Sec. 1245, where the recapture is based upon the total amount of depreciation (or cost recovery) allowed, Sec. 1250 applies solely to additional depreciation. **Additional depreciation,** also referred to as **excess depreciation,** is the excess of the actual amount of accelerated depreciation (or cost-recovery deductions under ACRS) over

---

[29] Sec. 1245(a)(5).

[30] Gain due to the sale or exchange of Sec. 1250 property placed in service before 1981 is ordinary income to the extent of additional depreciation.

Topic Review I13-1

Section 1245 Recapture

► Section 1245 affects the character of the gain, not the amount of gain.

► Section 1245 does not apply to assets sold or exchanged at a loss.

► Section 1245 ordinary income is never more than the realized gain.

► Section 1245 recapture applies to the total depreciation or amortization allowed or allowable but not more than the realized gain.

► Section 1245 property includes depreciable personal property and amortizable intangible assets (e.g., a patent).

► Section 1245 property includes nonresidential real estate placed in service after 1980 and before 1987 under the ACRS rules *unless* the taxpayer elected to use the straight-line method of cost recovery.

► Section 1245 does not apply to any buildings placed in service after 1986.

the amount of depreciation that would be deductible under the straight-line method. Any gain due to excess depreciation is Sec. 1250 ordinary income.

EXAMPLE I13-25 ► Wyatt sells a building that was placed in service before 1981 and the gain is $50,000. Accelerated depreciation was used and excess depreciation amounts to $74,000. All $50,000 of the gain is Sec. 1250 ordinary income. If the gain is $90,000, $74,000 is Sec. 1250 ordinary income and $16,000 is Sec. 1231 gain. ◄

PURPOSE OF SEC. 1250

Section 1250 has the effect of converting a portion of the Sec. 1231 gain into ordinary income when real property is sold or exchanged. The incremental benefits from using accelerated depreciation or ACRS cost recovery may be recaptured when the property is sold. Noncorporate taxpayers can avoid Sec. 1250 recapture by either using the straight-line method of depreciation or cost recovery or holding the Sec. 1250 property for its entire useful life or recovery period.

The Sec. 1250 recapture rules are applied solely to the additional depreciation amount instead of total depreciation claimed as is the case for Sec. 1245 property. Sec. 1250 provides for less depreciation recapture than Sec. 1245.

ADDITIONAL COMMENT

Elevators and escalators are Sec. 1245 property if placed in service before 1987, but Sec. 1250 property if placed in service after 1986.

KEY POINT

An apartment building is the most common type of property classified as residential real estate.

SECTION 1250 PROPERTY DEFINED

Section 1250 property is any depreciable real property other than Sec. 1245 property.[31] As stated on page I13-10, nonresidential real estate placed in service after 1980 and before 1987 is Sec. 1245 property unless the straight-line method of cost recovery is elected. The property is Sec. 1250 property if straight-line cost recovery is elected.

Depreciation recapture is not required on real property placed in service after 1986 because such property must be depreciated under the straight-line MACRS rules.[32]

EXAMPLE I13-26 ►

ADDITIONAL COMMENT

If the building in Example I13-26 was placed in service after 1980 and before 1987, the building is Sec. 1245 property if Frances uses accelerated cost recovery and not the straight-line method.

Frances sells an office building during the current year for $800,000. The office building was purchased in 1980 for $700,000* and depreciation of $500,000 has been allowed using an accelerated method of depreciation. If the straight-line method was used, depreciation would be $420,000. The office building is Sec. 1250 property. Her recognized gain is $600,000 and $80,000 is Sec. 1250 ordinary income due to excess depreciation ($500,000−$420,000). The remaining $520,000 gain is Sec. 1231 gain.

If Frances purchased the building after 1986, she was required to use the straight-line method. Thus her recognized gain is $520,000 ($800,000 − $280,000) with straight-line depreciation being $420,000. None of the gain is Sec. 1250 ordinary income. The gain is Sec. 1231 gain. ◄

*does not consider the cost of land

---

[31] Sec. 1250(c).

[32] As explained in the Additional Recapture for Corporations section in this chapter, corporations may have depreciation recapture under Sec. 291(a) despite the use of straight-line depreciation.

SELF-STUDY QUESTION

In Example I13-24, how much of the $700,000 Sec. 1231 gain resulting from the sale of warehouse #1 is unrecaptured Sec. 1250 gain?

ANSWER

All $700,000

HISTORICAL NOTE

Prior to the Taxpayer Relief Act of 1997, all LTCGs were taxed at a maximum rate of 28%. When the maximum rate was reduced to 20% (now 15%), Congress did not extend this favorable treatment to depreciable real estate. The maximum rate on this type of property was reduced from 28% to 25%. Even though Congress recently reduced the maximum LTCG rate to 15%, this lower rate still does not apply to depreciable real estate for unrecaptured Sec. 1250 gain.

As explained below, $420,000 of the Sec. 1231 gain in Example 13-26 is taxed at a maximum rate of 25% and $100,000 is taxed at 15% if there are no Sec. 1231 losses, nonrecaptured net Sec. 1231 losses, and no capital gains and losses from other transactions. Recall from Chapter I5 that the tax rate on LTCG may be 15% or 5%.

UNRECAPTURED SECTION 1250 GAIN

For sales of real property, some or all of the Sec. 1231 gain may be LTCG that is unrecaptured Sec. 1250 gain taxed at a rate of 25%. Unrecaptured Sec. 1250 gain is the amount of LTCG which would be taxed as ordinary if Sec. 1250 provided for the recapture of all depreciation and not just additional depreciation. When a taxpayer sells Sec. 1250 property (e.g., an office building) at a gain, any gain due to excess depreciation is ordinary income. Any remaining gain is Sec. 1231 gain and may be LTCG; however, any of the LTCG due to depreciation other than excess depreciation is unrecaptured Sec. 1250 gain taxed at a maximum rate of 25%.

An individual taxpayer who uses straight-line depreciation for Sec. 1250 property does not have any additional depreciation that would be recaptured as ordinary gain under Sec. 1250. Therefore, for buildings placed in service after 1986, all of the Sec. 1231 gain to the extent of the depreciation is unrecaptured Sec. 1250 gain subject to a maximum tax rate of 25% because only straight-line depreciation may be used. In Example I13-26, $420,000 of the gain is unrecaptured Sec. 1250 gain because $420,000 of the gain would be taxed as ordinary income if all depreciation had been recaptured.

EXAMPLE I13-27 ▶ Linnie owns a building used in her trade or business that was placed in service in 1999. She has no Sec. 1231 losses, nonrecaptured net Sec. 1231, losses or capital gains and losses. The building cost $400,000* and depreciation-to-date amounts to $172,000. If she sells the building for $350,000, her $122,000 gain ($350,000−$228,000) is Sec. 1231 gain and there is no depreciation recapture under Sec. 1250 because straight-line depreciation was allowed. The $122,000 Sec. 1231 gain is LTCG taxed at a maximum rate of 25% because it is unrecaptured Sec. 1250 gain. ◀

*does not consider the cost of land

 STOP & THINK

Question: What is the difference between *Sec. 1250 depreciation recapture* and *unrecaptured Sec. 1250 gain*?

Solution: Section 1250 depreciation recapture is the recharacterization of some or all of the Sec. 1231 gain on a building to ordinary income. Section 1250 depreciation recapture only applies to a noncorporate taxpayer if accelerated depreciation was used. Because accelerated depreciation is not allowed after 1986, this provision does not apply to noncorporate taxpayers for buildings placed in service after 1986. Unrecaptured Sec. 1250 gain is taxed at a maximum rate of 25% and occurs when there is a sale or an exchange of a building that is not Sec. 1245 property. If straight-line depreciation is used for a building, the gain is Sec. 1231 gain and the portion of the gain due to depreciation is unrecaptured Sec. 1250 gain. Part or all of the Sec. 1231 gain is taxed at a maximum rate of 25% with any excess taxed at 15%.

EXAMPLE I13-28 ▶ Assume the same facts as in Example I13-27 except Linnie sells the building for $500,000. Her Sec. 1231 gain is $272,000 ($500,000−$228,000), and $172,000 of the gain is taxed at 25% because it is unrecaptured Sec. 1250 gain. The remaining $100,000 of gain is taxed at 15%. ◀

ADDITIONAL COMMENT

When a building is sold at a gain, different tax rates might apply to portions of the gain: rate for ordinary income, 25% for unrecaptured Sec. 1250 gain, and 15% (or 5%) for ANCG.

RECAPTURE RULES FOR RESIDENTIAL RENTAL PROPERTY

All residential rental property is Sec. 1250 property. For a building or structure to qualify as residential rental property, 80% or more of the gross rental income from the building or structure must be rental income from dwelling units. Residential rental property does not include any unit in a hotel, motel, inn, or other establishment if more than one-half of the units are used on a transient basis.[33]

---

[33] Reg. Sec. 1.167(j)-3(b)(1)(i).

For depreciable residential rental property, Sec. 1250 recapture as ordinary income applies only to **additional depreciation** allowed after 1975.

EXAMPLE I13-29 ▶

Buddy sells an apartment complex used as residential rental property and placed in service on January 1, 1977. The cost of the apartment complex is $900,000,* and the complex is sold on January 1, 2006, for $700,000. Depreciation claimed by Buddy on the property is as follows:

Time Period	Depreciation Allowed	Straight-Line Depreciation	Additional Depreciation
Jan. 1, 1977–Jan. 1, 2006	$800,000	$710,000	$90,000

On the date of sale, the adjusted basis of the apartment is $100,000 ($900,000 − $800,000) and the realized gain is $600,000 ($700,000 − $100,000). All $90,000 of additional depreciation allowed is recaptured as ordinary income because the additional depreciation is less than the realized gain. The remaining $510,000 ($600,000 − $90,000) of gain is a Sec. 1231 gain, which is taxed at 25% because it is unrecaptured Sec. 1250 gain. ◀

*does not consider the cost of land

RESIDENTIAL RENTAL PROPERTY THAT IS RECOVERY PROPERTY

For residential rental property that is placed in service after 1980 and before 1987, all of the **additional depreciation** is recaptured as ordinary income to the extent of gain. Additional depreciation is the excess of the ACRS deduction using the percentages provided in the ACRS tables over a hypothetical cost recovery amount based upon the straight-line ACRS method using the length of the recovery period (i.e., 15, 18, or 19 years).

EXAMPLE I13-30 ▶

Joal purchased depreciable residential rental property for $800,000 ($100,000 is for land) on January 1, 1986. The property is 19-year recovery property and accelerated cost recovery was used. Joal sells the property on March 1, 2006, for $980,000 ($150,000 for land).

Cost Recovery Deductions Allowed	Cost Recovery with Straight-Line	Additional Depreciation
$700,000	$700,000	0

Joal's realized gain on the sale of the building is $830,000 [$830,000 − 0] and none of the gain is Sec. 1250 ordinary income. The $830,000 gain is Sec. 1231 gain and $700,000 is taxed at 25% because it is unrecaptured Sec. 1250 gain. $130,000 of the gain on sale of the building is taxed at 15%. The $50,000 gain on sale of land is Sec. 1231 gain taxed at 15%. ◀

There is a difference between Sec. 1250 ordinary income and unrecaptured Sec. 1250 gain. Sec. 1250 ordinary income could be taxed at 35% for noncorporate taxpayers while unrecaptured Sec. 1250 gain is taxed at a maximum rate of 25%. To have unrecaptured Sec. 1250 gain, the property must have a holding period greater than one year.

EXAMPLE I13-31 ▶

Erin, whose tax rate is 35%, owns an office building purchased for $1,000,000* on April 10 of last year. The building is sold on March 28 of the current year for $990,000 when its adjusted basis is $966,850. The $23,150 gain is not Sec. 1231 gain and none of the gain is unrecaptured Sec. 1250 gain because the holding period is not more than one year. The $23,150 gain is ordinary taxed at 35%. If the holding period was more than one year, the Sec. 1231 gain of $23,150 is LTCG that is unrecaptured Sec. 1250 gain taxed at 25%. ◀

*does not consider the cost of land

RECAPTURE RULES FOR NONRESIDENTIAL REAL ESTATE

Depreciable nonresidential real property (office building, manufacturing plant) is Sec. 1250 property except when the property is placed in service after 1980 and before 1987 and accelerated cost recovery was allowed. If the property is placed in service after 1980 and before 1987, the property is Sec. 1245 property if accelerated cost recovery is used.[34]

---

[34] Sec. 1245(a)(5), before amendment by the Tax Reform Act of 1986.

There is no depreciation recapture if the noncorporate taxpayer elected to use the straight-line method of cost recovery[35] for nonresidential ACRS property.[36]

EXAMPLE I13-32 ▶ The AB partnership purchased an office building in 1981 and a warehouse in 1982. The statutory percentages provided in the ACRS table are used to determine cost-recovery deductions for the office building. The straight-line method is used to determine cost-recovery deductions for the warehouse. The office building is subject to the Sec. 1245 recapture rules, and the warehouse is Sec. 1250 property. Even though the warehouse is Sec. 1250 property, the gain realized on the sale is Sec. 1231 gain because the straight-line ACRS method was used. However, the Sec. 1231 gain realized on the sale at the warehouse is unrecaptured Sec. 1250 gain to the extent of depreciation allowed. ◀

NONRESIDENTIAL REAL ESTATE PLACED IN SERVICE BEFORE 1981 (PRE-ACRS). All additional depreciation allowed after December 31, 1969, is subject to recapture as ordinary income under Sec. 1250.[37] The recaptured amount is limited to the realized gain.

EXAMPLE I13-33 ▶ Wayne sells his manufacturing plant during the current year. The plant was purchased in 1972 for use in his business. Additional depreciation (excess of accelerated depreciation under ACRS over straight-line) of $375,000 has been taken on the building. Information pertaining to the sale is as follows:

	Original Cost	Total Depreciation	Adjusted Basis	Selling Price
Plant	$3,000,000	$2,400,000	$600,000	$1,100,000
Land	300,000		300,000	900,000

The realized gain from the sale of the plant is $500,000 ($1,100,000 − $600,000) and $375,000 of the gain is recaptured as ordinary income under Sec. 1250. The remaining $125,000 of gain is Sec. 1231 gain taxed at 25% because it is unrecaptured Sec. 1250 gain. The $600,000 of realized gain from the sale of the land is a Sec. 1231 gain. ◀

EXAMPLE I13-34 ▶ Assume the same facts as in Example I13-33 except the selling price of the plant is $850,000. All of the $250,000 realized gain ($850,000 − $600,000) is recaptured as ordinary income because the $375,000 of additional depreciation is greater than the $250,000 of realized gain. ◀

ADDITIONAL COMMENT

The amount recaptured as ordinary income under either Sec. 1245 or Sec. 1250 can never exceed the realized gain.

NONRESIDENTIAL REAL ESTATE PLACED IN SERVICE AFTER 1980 AND BEFORE 1987. Section 1245 applies to nonresidential real property (1) if ACRS statutory rates were used to determine the cost-recovery deductions (as opposed to straight-line rates) and (2) if the property was placed in service after December 31, 1980, and before January 1, 1987. For Sec. 1245 recovery property, all gain to the extent of the lesser of the gain realized or the cost recovery deductions claimed is ordinary income. If the straight-line method of cost recovery is elected, the property is Sec. 1250, and none of the cost-recovery deductions are recaptured under Sec. 1250.[38]

EXAMPLE I13-35 ▶

SELF-STUDY QUESTION

If the asset in Example I13-30 is an office building, how much ordinary income must Joal recognize?

ANSWER

$700,000.
The office building is Sec. 1245 property. Joal must recognize ordinary income of $700,000 and a $130,000 Sec. 1231 gain.

Larry owns the following two buildings used in his business. Both buildings were purchased in 1985 and qualify as recovery property under the ACRS rules. Larry uses the ACRS statutory rates to determine cost-recovery deductions for Building 1 and the straight-line method for Building 2.

	Original Cost	Cost-Recovery Deductions	Adjusted Basis
Building 1 (accelerated)	$1,000,000	$1,000,000	0
Building 2 (SL)	1,000,000	1,000,000	0

If Building 1 is sold for $1,200,000, the realized gain is $1,200,000. Section 1245 applies, and $1,000,000 is ordinary income. The remaining $200,000 is Sec. 1231 gain. If Building 2 is sold for

---

[35] The cost of 18-year recovery property may be recovered under Sec. 168(b)(3)(A) over a period of 18, 35, or 45 years.

[36] Sec. 1245(a)(5)(C), before being repealed by the Tax Reform Act of 1986.

[37] Secs. 1250(a)(1)(B)(v) and (a)(2)(B)(v).

[38] An exception is provided for corporate taxpayers under Sec. 291. (See the Additional Recapture for Corporations section in this chapter.)

$1,200,000, the realized gain is $1,200,000. None of the gain is Sec. 1245 ordinary income because the straight-line cost recovery method is used, and Sec. 1245 does not apply unless the ACRS statutory rates are used. $1,000,000 of the Sec. 1231 gain realized on the sale of Building 2 is unrecaptured Sec. 1250 gain, thus $1,000,000 may be taxed at 25%, and $200,000 at 15%. ◀

Real property placed in service during ACRS (after 1980 and before 1987) is fully depreciated today, thus there is no additional depreciation. There is a major difference in the tax treatment for residential real property used for rental and nonresidential real property placed in service during ACRS if accelerated cost recovery was used. The nonresidential real property is Sec. 1245 property and the residential rental property is Sec. 1250. Refer to Table I13-1 and note that the tax treatment of the gain is the same when the properties are placed in service before 1981 or after 1986.

EXAMPLE I13-36 ▶ In 1983, Kathy purchased an office building and Ashlyn purchased an apartment complex. Each paid $800,000, with $100,000 for land, and each used accelerated cost recovery. The buildings are sold today for $600,000 and the properties are fully depreciated. Kathy's $600,000 gain is Sec. 1245 gain and Ashlyn's gain is Sec. 1231 gain taxed at 25% because it is unrecaptured Sec. 1250 gain. ◀

LOW-INCOME HOUSING

Congress has provided incentives for the construction and rehabilitation of low-income housing. For tax years after 1986, a low-income housing credit is available to owners of qualified low-income housing projects.[39]

▼ **TABLE I13-1**

CHARACTER OF GAIN ON SALE OR EXCHANGE OF DEPRECIABLE REAL PROPERTY FOR NONCORPORATE TAXPAYERS

	Sec. 1245 Ordinary	Sec. 1250 Ordinary	Sec. 1231	Unrecaptured Sec. 1250 (Maximum rate of 25%)
RESIDENTIAL RENTAL				
Placed in Service Before 1981				
Use straight-line depreciation	No	No	Yes	Yes
Use accelerated depreciation	No	Yes	Yes	Yes
Placed in Service After 1980 & Before 1987				
Use straight-line depreciation	No	No	Yes	Yes
Use accelerated depreciation	No	Yes	Yes	Yes
Placed in Service After 1986				
Use straight-line depreciation	No	No	Yes	Yes
NONRESIDENTIAL				
Placed in Service Before 1981				
Use straight-line depreciation	No	No	Yes	Yes
Use accelerated depreciation	No	Yes	Yes	Yes
Placed in Service After 1980 and Before 1987				
Use straight-line depreciation	No	No	Yes	Yes
Use accelerated depreciation	Yes	No	Yes	No
Placed in Service After 1986				
Use straight-line depreciation	No	No	Yes	Yes

---

[39] Sec. 42.

If the low-income housing unit is held for 16 years and 8 months, none of the additional depreciation is subject to recapture as ordinary income.[40] Thus noncorporate taxpayers will not have any Sec. 1250 ordinary income if the low-income housing is sold after 2002.

The Sec. 1250 recapture rules for noncorporate taxpayers are summarized in Topic Review I13-2.

Topic Review I13-2

Section 1250 Recapture for Noncorporate Taxpayers

► Section 1250 affects the character of the gain, not the amount of gain.

► Section 1250 does not apply to assets sold or exchanged at a loss.

► Section 1250 ordinary income is never more than the realized gain.

► Section 1250 ordinary income is never more than the *additional* depreciation allowed. (Note, that this statement is not true for corporate taxpayers.)

► Section 1250 property includes depreciable real property unless the real property is nonresidential real estate placed in service in 1980 and before 1987 under the ACRS rules and the straight-line method is not elected.

► Section 1250 ordinary income does not exist if the straight-line method of depreciation is used. (This statement is not true for corporate taxpayers because of the additional recapture requirements under Sec. 291.)

ADDITIONAL RECAPTURE FOR CORPORATIONS

KEY POINT

Section 291 has no effect on Sec. 1245 property because gain is already recaptured to the extent of all depreciation.

ADDITIONAL COMMENT

Corporations are subject to an additional 20% depreciation recapture rule under Sec. 291 on sales of Sec. 1250 property.

Corporations are subject to additional recapture rules under Sec. 291 if depreciable real estate is sold or otherwise disposed of. This recapture is in addition to the normal recapture rules under Sec. 1250. The additional ordinary income that is recaptured effectively reduces the amount of the Sec. 1231 gain.

The additional recapture amount under Sec. 291 is equal to 20% of the difference between the amount that would be recaptured if the property was Sec. 1245 property and actual recapture amount under Sec. 1250.[41]

EXAMPLE I13-37 ►

SELF-STUDY QUESTION

If the taxpayer in Example I13-37 is a noncorporate taxpayer, how much of the gain is Sec. 1250 ordinary income?

ANSWER

$85,000

In 1980, Orlando Corporation purchased an office building for $500,000* for use in its business. The building is sold during the current year for $480,000. Below are pertinent details relating to depreciation of the building and realized gain on the sale:

► Total depreciation allowed for the building is $345,000.

► If straight-line depreciation had been used, the depreciation allowed would have been $260,000.

► Building's adjusted basis is $155,000 ($500,000 − $345,000).

► Realized and recognized gain is $325,000 ($480,000 − $155,000).

To determine the character of the $325,000 gain, the following analysis must be made:

► Additional depreciation is $85,000 ($345,000 − $260,000). Gain to the extent of additional depreciation is recaptured as Sec. 1250 ordinary income.

► Section 291 depreciation recapture applies because the taxpayer is a corporation. If the property was Sec. 1245 property, $325,000 of the gain would be ordinary income.

► Because of Sec. 291, Orlando has more Sec. 1250 ordinary income: $48,000 [0.20 × ($325,000 − $85,000)].

In summary, of the total recognized gain of $325,000, $133,000 is recaptured as ordinary income ($85,000 + $48,000) and the remaining $192,000 ($325,000 − $133,000) is Sec. 1231 gain. ◄

*does not consider the cost of land

---

[40] Secs. 1250(a)(1)(B)(i), (ii), (iii), and (iv).　　　　　　[41] Sec. 291(a)(1).

EXAMPLE I13-38 ▶

Pacific Corporation purchased an office building in 1981 for $800,000* for use in its trade or business. The building is sold during the current year for $850,000. Pacific elected to use the straight-line method of cost recovery and $800,000 cost-recovery deductions have been allowed. The realized gain is $850,000 ($850,000 − 0). There is no excess depreciation, so none of the gain is ordinary income under Sec. 1250 if Sec. 291 is not considered. If the building were instead Sec. 1245 recovery property, $800,000 of the gain would be treated as ordinary income. The amount of Sec. 1250 ordinary income under Sec. 291 is $160,000 [0.20 × ($800,000 − $0)]. The remaining $690,000 ($850,000 − $160,000) gain is Sec. 1231 gain. ◀

*does not consider the cost of land

For corporations, none of the Sec. 1231 gain is unrecaptured Sec. 1250 gain.

SUMMARY OF SECS. 1231, 1245, AND 1250 GAINS

Section 1231 property is depreciable property and nondepreciable real property used in one's trade or business and held for more than one year. Net Sec. 1231 gain, the excess of Sec. 1231 gain over Sec. 1231 loss, is LTCG unless the five-year lookback rule applies in which case the gain is ordinary to the extent of the nonrecaptured net Sec. 1231 loss. Net Sec. 1231 loss, the excess of Sec. 1231 loss over Sec. 1231 gain, is ordinary.

Section 1245 applies to depreciable personal property and amortizable intangible assets. It also applies to certain nonresidential real property placed in service during ACRS (after 1980 and before 1987) if accelerated cost recovery is used. Gain to the extent of depreciation is ordinary income. All of the gain resulting from the sale of Sec. 1245 property is ordinary income unless the asset is sold for more than its original basis.

Section 1250 property is depreciable real property, and gain is ordinary income to the extent of additional depreciation, the excess of accelerated depreciation over straight-line. After 1986, the straight-line method must be used for real property and thus noncorporate taxpayers will not have any Sec. 1250 ordinary income on the sale of depreciable real property placed in service after 1986. Unfortunately, Congress made the sale and exchange of buildings more complicated in 1997 when it created the concept of unrecaptured Sec. 1250 gain that is taxed at 25%. When a noncorporate taxpayer sells depreciated buildings at a gain, any gain to the extent of straight-line depreciation is Sec. 1231 gain but is taxed at a rate no higher than 25% because it is unrecaptured Sec. 1250 gain.

To further illustrate Sec. 1231, 1245, and 1250, refer to Topic Review I13-3 where a noncorporate taxpayer with a 35% tax rate sells various assets during the current year. Each asset was purchased in 1997 and the selling price is $450,000 for each of the first three assets. All assets are used in a trade or business. There are no other gains and losses and no nonrecaptured net Sec. 1231 losses.

OBJECTIVE 5

Describe other recapture applications

RECAPTURE PROVISIONS— OTHER APPLICATIONS

Secs. 1245 and 1250 recapture provisions take precedence over other provisions of the tax law.[42] Unless an exception or limitation is specifically stated in Secs. 1245 or 1250, gain is recognized under Secs. 1245 or 1250 despite the existence of provisions elsewhere in the Code that allow nonrecognition of gain.[43]

GIFTS OF PROPERTY SUBJECT TO RECAPTURE

A gift of appreciated depreciable property does not result in the recapture of depreciation or cost-recovery deductions under Secs. 1245 or 1250.[44] The donee must consider the recapture potential when disposing of the property. The recapture amount for the donee is computed by including the recaptured amount attributable to the donor.[45]

---

[42] Secs. 1245(d) and 1250(i).
[43] Reg. Secs. 1.1245-6(a) and 1.1250-1(c)(1).

[44] Secs. 1245(b)(1) and 1250(d)(1).
[45] Reg. Secs. 1.1245-2(a)(4) and 1.1250-2(d).

Topic Review I13-3

Sections 1231, 1245, and 1250—Comparison of Various Assets

The taxpayer is a noncorporate taxpayer with a 35% tax rate who sells each of the first three assets for $450,000. Each asset was purchased in 1997 and is used in a trade or business. The difference between the original basis and the adjusted basis of the equipment and building is attributable to depreciation. There are no other gains and losses and no nonrecaptured net Sec. 1231 losses.

	ORIGINAL BASIS	ADJUSTED BASIS	TAX TREATMENT
1. Land	$400,000	$400,000	$50,000 Sec. 1231 gain taxed at 15%.
2. Equipment	600,000	400,000	$50,000 Sec. 1245 ordinary income taxed at 35%. All gain is due to depreciation.
3. Building	500,000	400,000	$50,000 Sec. 1231 gain which is unrecaptured Sec. 1250 gain taxed at 25%.

For assets 4, 5, & 6, assume the selling price is $700,000.

	ORIGINAL BASIS	ADJUSTED BASIS	TAX TREATMENT
4. Land	$400,000	$400,000	$300,000 Sec. 1231 gain taxed at 15%.
5. Equipment	600,000	400,000	$200,000 Sec. 1245 ordinary income taxed at 35% and $100,000 Sec. 1231 gain taxed at 15%.
6. Building	500,000	400,000	$300,000 Sec. 1231 gain with $100,000 of unrecaptured Sec. 1250 gain taxed at 25% and $200,000 taxed at 15%.

EXAMPLE I13-39 ▶ Ashley makes a gift of equipment with an $8,200 FMV to Helmut. Ashley paid $10,000 for the equipment and deducted $4,000 of depreciation before making the gift. Ashley does not have to recapture any depreciation when making the gift. Helmut's basis for the equipment is $6,000 and the potential depreciation recapture carries over to Helmut. ◀

EXAMPLE I13-40 ▶

ADDITIONAL COMMENT

If the taxpayer in Topic Review I13-3 is a corporation, the character of the gain is the same for assets 1, 2, 4, and 5. For asset 3, $10,000 of the gain is Sec. 1250 ordinary income under Sec. 291 and $40,000 is Sec. 1231 gain. For asset 6, $20,000 is Sec. 1250 ordinary income under Sec. 291 and $280,000 is Sec. 1231 gain.

Assume the same facts as in Example I13-39 except that Helmut uses the equipment in a trade or business, deducts $1,500 of depreciation, and sells the equipment for $7,100. When determining the amount of depreciation subject to recapture, Helmut must also consider the depreciation allowed to Ashley. The entire $2,600 [$7,100 − ($6,000 − $1,500)] of gain is recaptured as ordinary income because it is less than the $5,500 ($4,000 + $1,500) of depreciation claimed. ◀

TRANSFER OF PROPERTY SUBJECT TO RECAPTURE AT DEATH

The transfer of appreciated property at death does not cause a recapture of depreciation deductions to the decedent's estate under Secs. 1245 and 1250.[46] In addition, recapture potential does not carry over to the person who receives the property from the decedent.

EXAMPLE I13-41 ▶

KEY POINT

Death is one of the few ways to avoid the recapture provisions.

Jackie dies while owning a building with a $900,000 FMV. The building is Sec. 1245 property acquired in 1985 for $800,000* on which cost-recovery deductions of $800,000 have been claimed. Pam inherits the building from Jackie. Pam's basis for the building is $900,000, and the $800,000 of cost-recovery deductions are not recaptured. If Pam immediately sells the building, there is no depreciation recapture attributable to the $800,000 of cost-recovery deductions taken by the decedent. ◀

*does not include cost of land

CHARITABLE CONTRIBUTIONS

As discussed in Chapter I7, the deduction for a charitable contribution of ordinary income property is generally limited to its adjusted basis (i.e., the amount of the contribution deduction is equal to the FMV of the property less the amount of gain that would not have been LTCG [or Sec. 1231 gain] if the contributed property had been sold by the tax-

---

[46] Secs. 1245(b)(2) and 1250(d)(2).

payer at its FMV).[47] Thus, the contribution deduction for recapture property is reduced to reflect the ordinary income that would be recognized if the property were sold rather than contributed to the charity.

EXAMPLE I13-42 ▶

Ralph makes a gift of an organ to a church. The organ is used in Ralph's trade or business and has a $6,300 FMV. Ralph paid $10,000 for the organ, and $8,000 depreciation has been claimed. If the organ were sold for its $6,300 FMV, the realized and recognized gain would be $4,300 ($6,300 − $2,000) and all of the gain would be ordinary income due to the recapture of depreciation under Sec. 1245. The charitable contribution deduction is limited to $2,000 ($6,300 − $4,300), because none of the $4,300 gain would be taxed as a LTCG if the organ were sold. ◀

ADDITIONAL COMMENT

If the FMV of the organ in Example I13-42 is $11,000, the charitable contribution deduction is limited to $3,000, the $11,000 FMV less $8,000. If the organ is sold for $11,000, $8,000 of the gain is ordinary income.

LIKE-KIND EXCHANGES

A taxpayer who receives boot (i.e., non–like-kind property) in a transaction that otherwise qualifies as a like-kind exchange recognizes gain equal to the lesser of the realized gain and the amount of boot received. If the property is Sec. 1245 or 1250 property, the gain is first considered to be ordinary income up to the maximum amount of the gain that is subject to the recapture provisions.

EXAMPLE I13-43 ▶

REAL-WORLD EXAMPLE

A taxpayer's exchange of yachts used for business was a nontaxable transaction under Sec. 1031. Because no gain was recognized on the transaction, no gain could be subject to the recapture rules. *J. Wade Harris,* 1975 PH T.C. Memo ¶75,276, 34 TCM 1192.

Virginia owns a duplex that is residential rental property. The duplex cost $300,000* in 1979 and has a $140,000 adjusted basis. Additional depreciation of $22,000 has been deducted. Virginia exchanges the duplex for a four-unit apartment building with a $250,000 FMV and $25,000 in cash. Gain realized on the exchange is $135,000 [($250,000 + $25,000) − $140,000], and the recognized gain is $25,000. Gain recognized is the lesser of the $25,000 boot received or the $135,000 gain realized. Because additional depreciation is recaptured as ordinary income under Sec. 1250, $22,000 of the gain is ordinary income and $3,000 of the gain is Sec. 1231 gain which may be taxed at 25% because it is unrecaptured Sec. 1250 gain. ◀

*does not include cost of land

If gain is not recognized in a like-kind exchange, the recapture potential carries over to the replacement property (i.e., any recapture potential associated with the property exchanged attaches to the property received in the exchange).[48]

EXAMPLE I13-44 ▶

Melissa owns a Chevrolet pickup truck used in her trade or business that cost $10,000 and has a $6,000 adjusted basis due to $4,000 in depreciation deductions she has claimed. The truck is exchanged for a Ford pickup truck with a $9,000 FMV. The Ford truck is used in Melissa's business. Melissa does not recognize any portion of the $3,000 realized gain because the exchange qualifies as a like-kind exchange and no boot is received. Her basis for the Ford truck is $6,000 (i.e., a substituted basis).

After deducting $2,000 of depreciation, Melissa sells the Ford truck for $7,300. All of the recognized gain of $3,300 ($7,300 − $4,000) is ordinary income. The depreciation recapture amount under Sec. 1245 is equal to the total $6,000 in depreciation (including $4,000 on the Chevrolet pickup truck) but the recognized gain is only $3,300.[49] ◀

INVOLUNTARY CONVERSIONS

If an involuntary conversion of Sec. 1245 property occurs and all or a portion of the gain is not recognized,[50] the amount of gain that is considered to be Sec. 1245 ordinary income is limited and cannot be more than the recognized gain.[51] A similar provision exists for the involuntary conversion of Sec. 1250 property.[52]

EXAMPLE I13-45 ▶

The Ryan Corporation's printing equipment with original cost of $600,000 and adjusted basis of $200,000 is destroyed by fire. Ryan, Inc. receives $550,000 of insurance proceeds and purchases $510,000 of printing equipment. If the corporation elects to defer gain, it must recognize a $40,000 gain which is Sec. 1245 ordinary income. The basis of the printing equipment acquired is $200,000. ◀

---

[47] Sec. 170(e)(1)(A).
[48] Reg. Sec. 1.1245-2(c)(4).
[49] Reg. Sec. 1.1245-2(a)(4).
[50] As discussed in Chapter I12, one may elect to defer recognition of the gain if the Sec. 1033 requirements are satisfied.

[51] Sec. 1245(b)(4) and Reg. Sec. 1.1245-4(d)(1).
[52] Sec. 1250(d)(4) and Reg. Sec. 1.1250-3(d).

INSTALLMENT SALES

As discussed in Chapter I11, gain resulting from an installment sale is generally recognized as payments are received. Thus, the gain may be spread over more than one accounting period. An installment sale of depreciable property may result in all of the recaptured gain being taxed in the year of the sale.[53] Recapture income is "the aggregate amount which would be treated as ordinary income under Sec. 1245 or 1250 for the taxable year of the disposition if all payments to be received were received in the taxable year of disposition."[54] Recapture income must be recognized in the year of sale, even if no payments are received.

REAL-WORLD EXAMPLE

Taxpayer received insurance proceeds in excess of the adjusted basis of a business automobile upon the destruction of the auto in an accident. The taxpayer did not use Sec. 1033 to defer the gain and the court held that the gain was subject to recapture under Sec. 1245. *Anthony Astone*, 1983 PH T.C. Memo ¶83,747, 47 TCM 632.

EXAMPLE I13-46 ▶

KEY POINT

In the case of an installment sale of Sec. 1245 or 1250 property, it is possible to report a large taxable gain even though the taxpayer has not yet received the cash to pay the tax on such gain.

Pat owns equipment with a $100,000 acquisition cost and a $42,000 adjusted basis. Depreciation of $58,000 has been allowed. During the current year, Pat sells the property for $30,000 cash and a $60,000 ten-year interest-bearing note. The realized gain is $48,000 ($90,000 − $42,000), and the recapture income amount is $48,000 (the lesser of total depreciation deductions of $58,000 or the $48,000 of realized gain). The $48,000 of gain is all recognized as ordinary income in the current year, despite the fact that the transaction qualifies as an installment sale and only $30,000 of cash is received in the year of sale. ◀

If gain realized from the installment sale exceeds the recapture income, the excess gain is reported under the installment method.[55] The amount of recapture income recognized is added to the adjusted basis to determine the gross profit ratio.

EXAMPLE I13-47 ▶

SELF-STUDY QUESTION

What method of cost recovery is Bob using in Example I13-47?

ANSWER

Accelerated cost recovery. The office building is subject to Sec. 1245 recapture.

Bob owns an office building acquired for $700,000* in 1986 and subject to the Sec. 1245 recapture rules. After claiming $700,000 of cost recovery deductions, Bob sells the building to Janet in 2005 for $1,000,000. Bob receives $200,000 in cash and an $800,000 interest-bearing note. The note is to be paid with annual principal payments of $100,000 beginning in 2007. The total amount of realized gain is $1,000,000 ($1,000,000 − 0). In 2006, Bob recognizes $700,000 of Sec. 1245 ordinary income. The gross profit ratio is determined by adding $700,000 recapture income to the $0 basis. The gross profit ratio is 30% [($1,000,000 − $700,000) ÷ $1,000,000]. In addition to recognizing $700,000 of ordinary income, Bob recognizes $60,000 (0.30 × $200,000) Sec. 1231 gain in 2006 because a $200,000 cash down payment was received in the year of the sale. In 2007 and in each subsequent year, $30,000 (0.30 × $100,000) of Sec. 1231 gain is recognized as the cash payments on the principal are received. ◀

*does not include cost of land

SECTION 179 EXPENSING ELECTION

In lieu of capitalizing the cost of new or used tangible personal business property, taxpayers may elect to expense up to $108,000 of the acquisition cost in 2006[56] (see Chapter I10). If the property is subsequently converted to nonbusiness use, previous tax benefits derived from the immediate expensing election must be recaptured and added to the taxpayer's gross income in the year of the conversion.[57] The recaptured amount equals the difference between the amount expensed under Sec. 179 and the total depreciation that would otherwise have been claimed for the period of business use.

EXAMPLE I13-48 ▶

SELF-STUDY QUESTION

If Behren in Example I13-48 sells the equipment for $15,000 instead of converting it to a non-business use, what is the character of the gain?

ANSWER

$15,000 of Sec. 1245 ordinary income

Behren purchased business equipment (a five-year recovery period) in 2005 for $18,100 and elected to expense the entire amount under Sec. 179. In 2006, he converts the equipment to nonbusiness use. Depreciation of $3,620 (0.20 × $18,100) under the MACRS rules would have been allowed during the period the equipment was held for business use if Behren had not elected to expense the $18,100 cost. Behren must recognize $14,480 ($18,100 − $3,620) of Sec. 1245 ordinary income the current year. ◀

CONSERVATION AND LAND CLEARING EXPENDITURES

Taxpayers engaged in the business of farming may deduct expenditures paid or incurred during the taxable year for soil and water conservation or the prevention of erosion. The

[53] Sec. 453(i)(1).
[54] Sec. 453(i)(2).
[55] Sec. 453(i)(1)(B).0.
[56] Secs. 179(a) and (b)(1).
[57] Sec. 179(d)(10) and Reg. Sec. 1.179-1(e).

WHAT WOULD YOU DO IN THIS SITUATION?

You recently graduated with an advanced degree in taxation and have accepted a job with a CPA firm in the tax department. One of the firm's clients, a wealthy individual, was in need of cash and decided to sell some assets to raise the cash. The client asked the firm to advise him, from a tax standpoint, which assets he should sell. The client is in the 35% tax bracket. You suggested in a written memo that the client sell one of the client's jet airplanes. The plane you recommended to be sold had originally cost $16 million and now had an adjusted basis of $5 million. A buyer had offered to buy the plane for $12 million on the installment basis, paying $4 million per year for three years plus interest at 9%. The principal reason for selling that particular plane is that it would raise $12 million over three years, but the tax could be spread over three years by using the installment sale method. The client took your advice and sold the plane in the current year.

Later, when preparing the client's tax return, you realize that gain due to depreciation of the airplane must be recognized in the year of sale, even if the property is sold under the installment sale method. Thus, *all* of the gain on the sale of the plane must be recognized in the year of sale, not spread over three years. You go to your manager and tell him about your major mistake. Your manager, who reviewed your original memo, indicates that he thinks that the two of you should not tell anyone about the mistake as it will negatively impact both of your careers. The manager thinks that because the client has such a large amount of income, reporting the entire gain on the sale of the plane on the client's return might not be detected by the client. Thus, the manager instructs you to prepare the current year return with the entire $7 million of gain and not tell anyone about the mistake. What should you do in this situation?

expenditures must be made with respect to land used in farming and would be capital expenditures except for this provision.[58]

The deductions for conservation expenditures may be partially or fully recaptured as ordinary income if the farmland is disposed of before the land is held for more than nine years.[59] The amount of deductions recaptured as ordinary income under Sec. 1252 is a percentage of the aggregate deductions allowed for conservation expenditures. The amount of ordinary income recognized under Sec. 1252 is limited to the lesser of the taxpayer's realized gain or the applicable recapture percentage times the total conservation expenditures.

The recapture percentage is 100% if the farmland is disposed of within five years after the date it is acquired. The percentage declines by 20 percentage points for each additional year the property is held. If the land is disposed of after being held for more than nine years, none of the expenses are recaptured.[60]

KEY POINT

There is no recapture of conservation costs if the farmland is held for at least 10 years.

EXAMPLE I13-49 ▶ Paula owns farmland with a $400,000 basis. She has deducted $50,000 for soil and water conservation expenditures. After farming the land for six years and five months, Paula sells the land for $520,000. The realized gain is $120,000 ($520,000 − $400,000) and the recapture percentage is 60%, because the farmland is disposed of within the seventh year after it was acquired. The amount of ordinary income due to recapture under Sec. 1252 is $30,000, the lesser of the $120,000 realized gain or the $30,000 (0.60 × $50,000) recapture amount. ◀

ADDITIONAL COMMENT

Intangible drilling and development costs represent the major cost of operations and can provide investors with working interests in oil and gas properties with a first-year write-off of substantially all of their investment.

INTANGIBLE DRILLING COSTS AND DEPLETION

Taxpayers may elect to either expense or capitalize intangible drilling and development costs (IDC).[61] If the election to expense is not made, the costs are capitalized and recovered through additional depletion deductions. Intangible drilling and development costs include "all expenditures made by an operator for wages, fuel, repairs, hauling, supplies, etc., incident to and necessary for the drilling of wells and the preparation of wells for the production of oil or gas."[62]

---

[58] Sec. 175(a).
[59] Sec. 1252(a)(1).
[60] Sec. 1252(a)(3).

[61] Sec. 263(c).
[62] Reg. Sec. 1.612-4(a).

Part or all of the gain from the sale of oil and gas properties may be recaptured as ordinary income due to the recapture of the IDC deduction and the deduction for depletion. However, the amount of ordinary income recognized from the recapture of IDC and depletion is limited to the gain realized from the disposition of the property.[65]

EXAMPLE I13-50 ▶

In 1999, Marty purchased undeveloped property for the purpose of drilling for oil and gas. Intangible drilling and development costs of $400,000 were paid in 1999. Marty elected to expense the IDC. During the current year, Marty sells the property and realizes a $900,000 gain. $300,000 of cost depletion was allowed. Marty must recognize $700,000 of ordinary income because of the recapture of IDC ($400,000) and the recapture of depletion ($300,000). The remaining $200,000 ($900,000 − $700,000) gain is Sec. 1231 gain. ◀

EXAMPLE I13-51 ▶

In 2000, Tina acquired oil and gas properties for $700,000 and paid $200,000 for intangible drilling costs. During 2000, she elected to expense the $200,000 of IDC. Total depletion allowed was $80,000. During the current year, Tina sells the property for $840,000 and realizes a $220,000 [($840,000 − ($700,000 − $80,000)] gain. The amount of ordinary income due to recapture is $220,000, because both IDC and depletion must be recaptured only to the extent of the gain. ◀

GAIN ON SALE OF DEPRECIABLE PROPERTY BETWEEN RELATED PARTIES

All gain recognized on the sale or exchange of property between related parties is ordinary income if the property is subject to depreciation in the hands of the transferee (i.e., the person who purchases the property). The sale or exchange may be direct or indirect.[64]

EXAMPLE I13-52 ▶

Phil owns a building with a $500,000 adjusted basis and $800,000 FMV. The building, which cost $700,000, is used in his business, and the straight-line method of depreciation is used. $200,000 of depreciation deductions were allowed. If the building is sold to Phil's 100%-owned corporation for $800,000, the $300,000 realized gain ($800,000 − $500,000) is treated as ordinary income under Sec. 1239, because the property is subject to depreciation in the hands of the transferee and the corporation and Phil are related parties. ◀

A sale or exchange of property could be subject to depreciation recapture under Sec. 1245 or 1250 as well as the Sec. 1239 related party rules. If so, recapture under Sec. 1245 or 1250 is considered before recapture under Sec. 1239.[65]

EXAMPLE I13-53 ▶

Assume the same facts as in Example I13-52 except that Phil sells equipment to the corporation instead of a building. All of the $300,000 realized gain is treated as ordinary income. The recapture amount under Sec. 1245 is $200,000, and Sec. 1239 applies to the remaining $100,000 gain. ◀

PURPOSE OF SEC. 1239. Without Sec. 1239, a taxpayer could transfer appreciated depreciable property to a related party and recognize a Sec. 1231 gain on the sale. Net Sec. 1231 gain is treated as LTCG. The related purchaser of the property would receive a step up in the depreciable basis of the property to its FMV and be able to claim a larger amount of depreciation. In Example I13-52, Phil might prefer to recognize a $300,000 Sec. 1231 gain if the 100%-owned corporation was able to obtain a step-up in the property's basis to $800,000. Because Sec. 1239 applies, Phil must recognize $300,000 of ordinary income rather than Sec. 1231 gain. This rule prevents an individual taxpayer from receiving favorable Sec. 1231 gain treatment and prevents all taxpayers having large capital loss carryovers from using a related party to recognize a Sec. 1231 or capital gain which can be offset against their capital losses.

RELATED PARTIES. A person is related (1) to any corporation if the individual owns (directly or indirectly) more than 50% of the value of the outstanding stock and (2) to any partnership in which the person has a capital or profits interest of more than 50%.[66]

---

[63] Sec. 1254(a)(1).
[64] Sec. 1239(a).

[65] Reg. Sec. 1.1245-6(f).
[66] Sec. 1239(c).

Constructive ownership rules apply when determining whether the person owns more than 50% of the corporation or has more than a 50% interest in the partnership. Thus, an individual is considered to own stock that is owned by other family members and related entities (e.g., corporations, partnerships, estates, and trusts).

EXAMPLE I13-54 ▶ Tony sells a truck used for nonbusiness purposes to the Able Corporation for $15,000 when its adjusted basis is $12,000. Tony owns 30% of Able and his spouse owns 40% of Able. Tony and Able are related parties because Tony is deemed to own 70% of Able under the constructive ownership rules and $3,000 of ordinary income must be recognized under Sec. 1239. ◀

A person is related to any trust in which such a person or the person's spouse is a beneficiary.[67] Section 1239 also applies to a sale or exchange of depreciable property between two corporations if the same individual owns more than 50% of each corporation.[68]

TAX PLANNING CONSIDERATIONS

For noncorporate taxpayers, net Sec. 1231 gains are generally preferable to ordinary gains because of the possible lower tax rate applicable to net capital gains. The tax rate could be 5%, 15%, or 25%. For corporate taxpayers, however, after 1986 it usually does not make any difference whether a gain is classified as Sec. 1231 or ordinary unless the corporation has capital losses. Corporations do not have preferential tax rates on net capital gains.

EXAMPLE I13-55 ▶ Western Corporation has taxable income of $550,000 without considering the sale of equipment for $400,000 during the current year. The equipment originally cost $500,000 and has a $350,000 adjusted basis after deducting depreciation. The corporation has no other gains and losses during the year or any capital loss carryovers from previous years. For Western Corporation, it does not make any difference whether the gain is Sec. 1245 ordinary income or Sec. 1231 gain. The effect on the corporation's taxable income and tax liability is the same regardless of how the gain is classified. ◀

The avoidance of the recapture provisions is important to both corporate and noncorporate taxpayers if capital loss carryovers exist. For example, if Western Corporation has a capital loss carryforward of $40,000 in Example I13-55, the corporation's taxable income is increased by $10,000 ($50,000 − $40,000) if the $50,000 gain is Sec. 1231 gain. However, because the gain is Sec. 1245 ordinary income, the corporation's taxable income is increased by $50,000. The $40,000 capital loss carryforward is deductible only if Western has capital gain or net Sec. 1231 gain.

AVOIDING THE RECAPTURE PROVISIONS

In view of the pervasiveness of the recapture provisions discussed in this chapter, recapture is difficult to avoid. In some cases, recapture can be avoided by holding the property a specific length of time before disposing of it (e.g., the recapture of conservation and land clearing expenses can be avoided by holding the farmland for more than nine years).[69] Contributing appreciated property to a qualified charitable organization cannot be used to circumvent the recapture provisions because in such case the amount of the charitable contribution is reduced by the amount of the gain that would not be a LTCG if the property were sold by the taxpayer.[70]

Although it is often difficult to avoid the recapture provisions, taxpayers may dispose of the property and defer recapture if the disposition is a nontaxable exchange. In a like-kind exchange where no boot is received, the recapture potential is carried over to the property received in the exchange.

---

[67] Sec. 1239(b)(2).
[68] Rev. Rul. 79-157, 1979-1 C.B. 281.

[69] Sec. 1252(a)(1).
[70] Sec. 170(e)(1)(A).

Proper timing of the asset's disposition may be advantageous. Disposition may be delayed until the taxpayer's tax rate is low or the property can be sold in the same year that the taxpayer has an NOL that is about to expire.

Taxpayers can shift the recapture potential to other taxpayers by making a gift of property subject to recapture. The recapture potential remains with the property and must be considered when the donee disposes of the property.

RESIDENTIAL RENTAL PROPERTY. Noncorporate taxpayers can avoid the recapture provisions for residential rental property by using the straight-line method of depreciation.[71] The recapture provisions do not apply to residential rental property acquired after 1986 because only the straight-line depreciation method may be used. Recapture can also be avoided if the asset is fully depreciated at the date of disposal because no additional depreciation or cost recovery exists.

EXAMPLE I13-56 ▶ Vincent owns a building used as residential rental property. The building was purchased before 1981 and is not ACRS recovery property. If Vincent uses the straight-line method of depreciation, he could avoid Sec. 1250 depreciation recapture. If Vincent uses an accelerated method of depreciation, recapture is avoided if the disposition does not occur until the asset is fully depreciated. ◀

EXAMPLE I13-57 ▶ Assume the same facts as in Example I13-56 except that Vincent purchased the building after 1980 and before 1987 and the building is ACRS recovery property. Vincent could avoid recapturing cost recovery deductions when he disposes of the asset by using the straight-line method of cost recovery. If Vincent uses the accelerated method of cost recovery and disposes of the residential rental property at a gain, the amount of gain due to additional cost recovery is recaptured as ordinary income. He cannot avoid recapture unless the asset's cost is fully recovered (i.e., no additional cost recovery exists). ◀

KEY POINT

For noncorporate taxpayers, there is no recapture on either residential or nonresidential real property placed in service after 1986 because the property can be depreciated only by using the straight-line method.

NONRESIDENTIAL REAL PROPERTY. For noncorporate taxpayers, the Sec. 1250 recapture provisions do not apply to nonresidential real property acquired after 1986 because only the straight-line method may be used. However, to avoid recapture on the disposition of appreciated nonresidential real property acquired after 1980 and before 1987, noncorporate taxpayers must use the straight-line method of depreciation. Nonresidential real property acquired before 1987, which is recovery property subject to ACRS, is subject to the Sec. 1245 recapture rules unless the straight-line method is used. If the accelerated method of cost recovery is used, recapture cannot be avoided by waiting until the asset's cost is fully recovered before disposing of the asset.

EXAMPLE I13-58 ▶ Christine purchased an office building in 1982 for $225,000* for use in her trade or business. The property is ACRS recovery property, and she uses the accelerated method to compute the cost-recovery deductions. Cost-recovery deductions taken before the sale of the building amount to $225,000. If she sells the building for $250,000, $225,000 of the $250,000 ($250,000 − 0) realized gain is recaptured as ordinary income under Sec. 1245. The remaining gain of $25,000 is Sec. 1231 gain. Recapture could have been avoided if Christine had instead used the straight-line method of cost recovery. If the straight-line method were used instead, she would still report a $250,000 realized gain, but all would be Sec. 1231 gain. ◀

SELF-STUDY QUESTION

If the building in Example I13-57 is nonresidential real property, is the building Sec. 1245 property?

ANSWER

Yes

*does not include cost of land

TRANSFER PROPERTY AT DEATH. One of the most effective ways to avoid the recapture provisions is to transfer the property at death. No recapture occurs at the time of the transfer, and the basis of property received from a decedent is generally the FMV of the property at the date of the decedent's death.[72] The property's recapture potential does not carry over to the beneficiary as in the case of a gift made to a donee.

---

[71] Corporate taxpayers must consider Sec. 291(a). (See the Additional Recapture for Corporations section in this chapter.)

[72] Sec. 1014(a).

COMPLIANCE AND PROCEDURAL CONSIDERATIONS

ADDITIONAL COMMENT

Form 4797 has four major parts. In completing this form one should normally begin with Part III on page 2, where the recapture is calculated. Note that the total amount recaptured from line 31 is carried forward to Part II, where it is combined with other ordinary gains and losses. Any unrecaptured gain from line 32 is carried forward to Part I, where it is netted with other Sec. 1231 gains and losses.

Form 4797, Supplemental Schedule of Gains and Losses, is used to report gains and losses from sales or exchanges of assets used in a trade or business (see Figures I13-1 through I13-3). The form is also used to report gains or losses resulting from involuntary conversions, other than casualties or thefts, of property used in the trade or business and capital assets held more than a year. If gains or losses due to casualties or thefts of property used in a trade or business or property held to produce income are recognized, they are reported on Form 4684, Casualties and Thefts (see Figure I13-3). If such casualties or thefts occur, Form 4684 is prepared either before or at the same time as Form 4797.

REPORTING SEC. 1231 GAINS AND LOSSES ON FORM 4797

Part I of Form 4797, which is reproduced in Figure I13-1, is used to report gains and losses resulting from

▶ The sale or exchange of Sec. 1231 property

▶ An involuntary conversion, other than a casualty or theft, of Sec. 1231 property

▶ An involuntary conversion, other than a casualty or theft, of capital assets held more than one year and used to produce income.

As indicated on lines 3 through 6 in Part I of Form 4797, gains and losses recorded on other forms and in Part III of Form 4797 are reported in Part I. The netting of Sec. 1231 gains and losses occurs in Part I of Form 4797. All gains and losses are recorded in column (g). If line 7(g) has a loss, Sec. 1231 losses exceed Sec. 1231 gains and the net loss is reported on line 11 as ordinary loss. If there is no nonrecaptured net section 1231 losses, all gain reported on line 7(g) is transferred to Schedule D. If the taxpayer does have nonrecaptured net Sec. 1231 losses, that amount is reported on line 8. Gains reported on line 7(g) will be recharacterized as ordinary income to the extent of the nonrecaptured net Sec. 1231 losses and reported as ordinary income on line 12.

Ordinary gains and losses recognized including those recorded on other forms and in Parts I and III of Form 4797 are reported on lines 11 through 17 in Part II of Form 4797.

REPORTING GAINS RECAPTURED AS ORDINARY INCOME ON FORM 4797

Part III of Form 4797, reproduced in Figure I13-2, is completed before Parts I and II to determine and report ordinary income due to the recapture provisions of Secs. 1245, 1250, 1252, 1254, and 1255. To illustrate the use of Part III, assume an individual sells equipment (7-year recovery) used in a trade or business for $60,000 on April 30, 2005. The equipment cost $58,000 on March 10, 2003, and depreciation deductions through the date of sale of $27,565 were allowed. The $29,565 ($60,000 − $30,435) total gain is reported on line 24. On line 30, total gains resulting from the sale of all properties ($29,565 in this illustration) reported in Part III are combined. The total amount of ordinary income due to the recapture provisions ($27,565 in this illustration) is reported on line 31 and then reported as ordinary income on line 13 in Part II. The excess of the gain over the amount of ordinary income is reported on line 32. The portion of this gain not due to casualty or theft ($2,000 in this illustration) is a Sec. 1231 gain and is reported on line 6 of Part I of Form 4797. If any of the gain is due to casualty or theft, that portion of the gain is reported on Section B of Form 4684.

REPORTING CASUALTY OR THEFT GAIN OR LOSS ON FORM 4684

Section A of Form 4684 is used to report gains and losses resulting from a casualty or theft of personal-use property. These gains and losses are not Sec. 1231 transactions, and Sec. A of Form 4684 is not discussed in this chapter.

Section B of Form 4684, reproduced in Figure I13-3, is used to report gains and losses resulting from a casualty or theft of property used in a trade or business or held for the

Form **4797**	**Sales of Business Property**	OMB No. 1545-0184
Department of the Treasury Internal Revenue Service (99)	(Also Involuntary Conversions and Recapture Amounts Under Sections 179 and 280F(b)(2)) ▶Attach to your tax return. ▶See separate instructions.	20**05** Attachment Sequence No. **27**

Name(s) shown on return	Identifying number

1 Enter the gross proceeds from sales or exchanges reported to you for 2005 on Form(s) 1099-B or 1099-S (or substitute statement) that you are including on line 2, 10, or 20 (see instructions). . . . . | **1** | |

Part I Sales or Exchanges of Property Used in a Trade or Business and Involuntary Conversions From Other Than Casualty or Theft—Most Property Held More Than 1 Year (see instructions)

(a) Description of property	**(b)** Date acquired (mo., day, yr.)	**(c)** Date sold (mo., day, yr.)	**(d)** Gross sales price	**(e)** Depreciation allowed or allowable since acquisition	**(f)** Cost or other basis, plus improvements and expense of sale	**(g)** Gain or (loss) Subtract (f) from the sum of (d) and (e)
2						

3	Gain, if any, from Form 4684, line 42	**3**	
4	Section 1231 gain from installment sales from Form 6252, line 26 or 37	**4**	
5	Section 1231 gain or (loss) from like-kind exchanges from Form 8824 .	**5**	
6	Gain, if any, from line 32, from other than casualty or theft	**6**	**2,000**
7	Combine lines 2 through 6. Enter the gain or (loss) here and on the appropriate line as follows:	**7**	**2,000**

Partnerships (except electing large partnerships) and S corporations. Report the gain or (loss) following the instructions for Form 1065, Schedule K, line 10, or Form 1120S, Schedule K, line 9. Skip lines 8, 9, 11, and 12 below.

Individuals, partners, S corporation shareholders, and all others. If line 7 is zero or a loss, enter the amount from line 7 on line 11 below and skip lines 8 and 9. If line 7 is a gain and you did not have any prior year section 1231 losses, or they were recaptured in an earlier year, enter the gain from line 7 as a long-term capital gain on the Schedule D filed with your return and skip lines 8, 9, 11, and 12 below.

8	Nonrecaptured net section 1231 losses from prior years (see instructions)	**8**	
9	Subtract line 8 from line 7. If zero or less, enter -0-. If line 9 is zero, enter the gain from line 7 on line 12 below. If line 9 is more than zero, enter the amount from line 8 on line 12 below and enter the gain from line 9 as a long-term capital gain on the Schedule D filed with your return (see instructions).	**9**	

Part II Ordinary Gains and Losses (see instructions)

10 Ordinary gains and losses not included on lines 11 through 16 (include property held 1 year or less):

11	Loss, if any, from line 7	**11** (	)
12	Gain, if any, from line 7 or amount from line 8, if applicable	**12**	
13	Gain, if any, from line 31	**13**	**27,565**
14	Net gain or (loss) from Form 4684, lines 34 and 41a	**14**	
15	Ordinary gain from installment sales from Form 6252, line 25 or 36	**15**	
16	Ordinary gain or (loss) from like-kind exchanges from Form 8824	**16**	
17	Combine lines 10 through 16	**17**	**27,565**

18 For all except individual returns, enter the amount from line 17 on the appropriate line of your return and skip lines a and b below. For individual returns, complete lines a and b below:

a If the loss on line 11 includes a loss from Form 4684, line 38, column (b)(ii), enter that part of the loss here. Enter the part of the loss from income-producing property on Schedule A (Form 1040), line 27, and the part of the loss from property used as an employee on Schedule A (Form 1040), line 22. Identify as from "Form 4797, line 18a." See instructions . . . . | **18a** | |

b Redetermine the gain or (loss) on line 17 excluding the loss, if any, on line 18a. Enter here and on Form 1040, line 14 . . . . | **18b** | **27,565** |

For Paperwork Reduction Act Notice, see separate instructions.   Cat. No. 13086I   Form **4797** (2005)

FIGURE I13-1 ▶ PART I AND PART II OF FORM 4797

Part III Gain From Disposition of Property Under Sections 1245, 1250, 1252, 1254, and 1255
(see instructions)

19	(a) Description of section 1245, 1250, 1252, 1254, or 1255 property:	(b) Date acquired (mo., day, yr.)	(c) Date sold (mo., day, yr.)
A	Equipment	3-10-03	4-30-05
B			
C			
D			

	These columns relate to the properties on lines 19A through 19D. ▶		Property A	Property B	Property C	Property D
20	Gross sales price (**Note:** *See line 1 before completing.*) . .	20	60,000			
21	Cost or other basis plus expense of sale	21	58,000			
22	Depreciation (or depletion) allowed or allowable	22	27,565			
23	Adjusted basis. Subtract line 22 from line 21	23	30,435			
24	Total gain. Subtract line 23 from line 20	24	29,565			
25	**If section 1245 property:**					
a	Depreciation allowed or allowable from line 22	25a	27,565			
b	Enter the **smaller** of line 24 or 25a	25b	27,565			
26	**If section 1250 property:** If straight line depreciation was used, enter -0- on line 26g, except for a corporation subject to section 291.					
a	Additional depreciation after 1975 (see instructions) . . .	26a				
b	Applicable percentage multiplied by the **smaller** of line 24 or line 26a (see instructions)	26b				
c	Subtract line 26a from line 24. If residential rental property **or** line 24 is not more than line 26a, skip lines 26d and 26e	26c				
d	Additional depreciation after 1969 and before 1976 . . .	26d				
e	Enter the **smaller** of line 26c or 26d	26e				
f	Section 291 amount (corporations only)	26f				
g	Add lines 26b, 26e, and 26f	26g				
27	**If section 1252 property:** Skip this section if you did not dispose of farmland or if this form is being completed for a partnership (other than an electing large partnership).					
a	Soil, water, and land clearing expenses	27a				
b	Line 27a multiplied by applicable percentage (see instructions)	27b				
c	Enter the **smaller** of line 24 or 27b	27c				
28	**If section 1254 property:**					
a	Intangible drilling and development costs, expenditures for development of mines and other natural deposits, and mining exploration costs (see instructions)	28a				
b	Enter the **smaller** of line 24 or 28a	28b				
29	**If section 1255 property:**					
a	Applicable percentage of payments excluded from income under section 126 (see instructions)	29a				
b	Enter the **smaller** of line 24 or 29a (see instructions) . .	29b				

Summary of Part III Gains. Complete property columns A through D through line 29b before going to line 30.

30	Total gains for all properties. Add property columns A through D, line 24	30	29,565
31	Add property columns A through D, lines 25b, 26g, 27c, 28b, and 29b. Enter here and on line 13	31	27,565
32	Subtract line 31 from line 30. Enter the portion from casualty or theft on Form 4684, line 36. Enter the portion from other than casualty or theft on Form 4797, line 6	32	2,000

Part IV Recapture Amounts Under Sections 179 and 280F(b)(2) When Business Use Drops to 50% or Less
(see instructions)

			(a) Section 179	(b) Section 280F(b)(2)
33	Section 179 expense deduction or depreciation allowable in prior years	33		
34	Recomputed depreciation (see instructions).	34		
35	Recapture amount. Subtract line 34 from line 33. See the instructions for where to report . . .	35		

Form **4797** (2005)

FIGURE I13-2 ▶ PART III OF FORM 4797

Name(s) shown on tax return. Do not enter name and identifying number if shown on other side.

Identifying number

SECTION B—Business and Income-Producing Property

Part I — Casualty or Theft Gain or Loss (Use a separate Part I for each casualty or theft.)

22 Description of properties (show type, location, and date acquired for each property). Use a separate line for each property lost or damaged from the same casualty or theft.

Property **A** _____

Property **B** _____

Property **C** _____

Property **D** _____

			Properties			
			A	**B**	**C**	**D**
23	Cost or adjusted basis of each property. . . .	23				
24	Insurance or other reimbursement (whether or not you filed a claim). See the instructions for line 3 . **Note:** *If line 23 is **more** than line 24, skip line 25* .	24				
25	Gain from casualty or theft. If line 24 is **more** than line 23, enter the difference here and on line 32 or line 37, column (c), except as provided in the instructions for line 36. Also, skip lines 26 through 30 for that column. See the instructions for line 4 if line 24 includes insurance or other reimbursement you did not claim, or you received payment for your loss in a later tax year.	25				
26	Fair market value **before** casualty or theft . . .	26				
27	Fair market value **after** casualty or theft. . . .	27				
28	Subtract line 27 from line 26	28				
29	Enter the **smaller** of line 23 or line 28 . . . . **Note:** *If the property was totally destroyed by casualty or lost from theft, enter on line 29 the amount from line 23.*	29				
30	Subtract line 24 from line 29. If zero or less, enter -0-	30				
31	Casualty or theft loss. Add the amounts on line 30. Enter the total here and on line 32 **or** line 37 (see instructions).				31	

Part II — Summary of Gains and Losses (from separate Parts I)

(a) Identify casualty or theft	(b) Losses from casualties or thefts		(c) Gains from casualties or thefts includible in income
	(i) Trade, business, rental or royalty property	(ii) Income-producing and employee property	

Casualty or Theft of Property Held One Year or Less

32	_____	( )	( )	
	_____	( )	( )	
33	Totals. Add the amounts on line 32 33	( )	( )	
34	Combine line 33, columns (b)(i) and (c). Enter the net gain or (loss) here and on Form 4797, line 14. If Form 4797 is not otherwise required, see instructions			34
35	Enter the amount from line 33, column (b)(ii) here. Individuals, enter the amount from income-producing property on Schedule A (Form 1040), line 27, and enter the amount from property used as an employee on Schedule A (Form 1040), line 22. Estates and trusts, partnerships, and S corporations, see instructions			35

Casualty or Theft of Property Held More Than One Year

36	Casualty or theft gains from Form 4797, line 32			36
37	_____	( )	( )	
	_____	( )	( )	
38	Total losses. Add amounts on line 37, columns (b)(i) and (b)(ii) . . . 38	( )	( )	
39	Total gains. Add lines 36 and 37, column (c)			39
40	Add amounts on line 38, columns (b)(i) and (b)(ii)			40
41	If the loss on line 40 is **more** than the gain on line 39:			
a	Combine line 38, column (b)(i) and line 39, and enter the net gain or (loss) here. Partnerships (except electing large partnerships) and S corporations, see the note below. All others, enter this amount on Form 4797, line 14. If Form 4797 is not otherwise required, see instructions			41a
b	Enter the amount from line 38, column (b)(ii) here. Individuals, enter the amount from income-producing property on Schedule A (Form 1040), line 27, and enter the amount from property used as an employee on Schedule A (Form 1040), line 22. Estates and trusts, enter on the "Other deductions" line of your tax return. Partnerships (except electing large partnerships) and S corporations, see the note below. Electing large partnerships, enter on Form 1065-B, Part II, line 11.			41b
42	If the loss on line 40 is **less** than or **equal** to the gain on line 39, combine lines 39 and 40 and enter here. Partnerships (except electing large partnerships), see the note below. All others, enter this amount on Form 4797, line 3 . . .			42

Note: *Partnerships, enter the amount from line 41a, 41b, or line 42 on Form 1065, Schedule K, line 11.*
S corporations, enter the amount from line 41a or 41b on Form 1120S, Schedule K, line 10.

FIGURE I13-3 ▶ SECTION B OF FORM 4684

Form **4684** (2005) (Rev. 1-2006)

production of income. Note that a separate Part I is used for each different casualty or theft. Gains are reported on line 25, and losses are reported on line 30. For properties held a year or less, the gains and losses are reported on lines 32 through 35 of Part II. These gains and losses are either recorded as ordinary gains and losses on line 14 of Part II of Form 4797 or as itemized deductions on Schedule A of Form 1040.

For properties held more than a year, the gains and losses are reported on lines 36 and 37. If gains exceed losses, the net gain is reported on line 42 and then on line 3 of Part I of Form 4797 (i.e., the gains and losses are treated as Sec. 1231 gains and losses). If the losses exceed the gains, all or part of the gains and losses are reported as ordinary in Part II of Form 4797 and/or on Schedule A of Form 1040.

PROBLEM MATERIALS

DISCUSSION QUESTIONS

I13-1 Explain how the gain on the sale or exchange of land could be classified as either ordinary income, a Sec. 1231 gain, or a LTCG, depending on the facts and circumstances.

I13-2 Why were taxpayers reluctant to sell appreciated business property between 1938 and 1942? What effect did this reluctance have on the tax law?

I13-3 Alice owns timber, purchased six years ago, with an adjusted basis of $50,000. The timber is cut for use in her furniture business on October 1, when the FMV of the timber is $200,000. The FMV of the timber on January 1 is $190,000. May Alice treat any of the gain as Sec. 1231 gain? If so, how much?

I13-4 Explain how the gain from an involuntary conversion of business property held more than one year is taxed if the involuntary conversion is the result of a condemnation. Explain the tax treatment if the involuntary conversion is due to a casualty.

I13-5 When is livestock considered Sec. 1231 property?

I13-6 When is a net Sec. 1231 gain treated as ordinary income?

I13-7 Carlie has a Sec. 1231 gain of $10,000 and no Sec. 1231 losses during the current year. Explain why the gain might be taxed at (a) 15%, (b) 35%, (c) 25%, or (d) 5%.

I13-8 Why is it unlikely that gains due to the sale of equipment will be treated as Sec. 1231 gains?

I13-9 Hank sells equipment used in a trade or business for $25,000. The equipment costs $30,000 and has an adjusted basis of $25,500. Why is it important to know the holding period?

I13-10 Jackie purchases equipment during the current year for $800,000 that has a seven-year MACRS recovery period. She expects to sell the property after three years. Jackie anticipates that her marginal tax rate in the year of sale will be significantly higher than her current marginal tax rate. Why might it be advantageous for her to use the straight-line method of depreciation?

I13-11 Karen purchased a computer three years ago for $15,300 to use exclusively in her business. She expensed the entire cost of the computer under Sec. 179. If she sells the computer during the current year for $3,721, what is the amount and character of her recognized gain?

I13-12 Sheila owns a motel that is used in a trade or business. If she sells the motel, the gain will be Sec. 1245 ordinary income. During what period of time was the motel placed into service?

I13-13 How may a taxpayer avoid having additional depreciation?

I13-14 Marty sells his fully depreciated building at a gain to an unrelated party. The building is purchased before 1981. Is any of the gain taxed as ordinary income?

I13-15 Which of the following assets (assume all assets have a holding period of more than one year) do not qualify as Sec. 1231 property: inventory, a pig held for breeding, land used as a parking lot for customers, and marketable securities?

I13-16 When is an office building subject to the depreciation recapture rules of Sec. 1245?

I13-17 Does a building that is 60% rented for residential use and 40% for commercial use qualify as residential rental property?

I13-18 Roger owns an apartment complex with a FMV of $2 million. If he sells the apartment complex, $700,000 of the gain is Sec. 1231 gain with $600,000 taxed at 25% because it is unrecaptured Sec. 1250 gain. If he dies before selling the apartment complex and his estate sells the property for $2 million, how much ordinary income must the estate recognize?

I13-19 Rashad owns a duplex used 100% as residential rental property. Under what conditions, if any, will any gain that he recognizes be Sec. 1245 ordinary income?

I13-20 John and Karen are unrelated individuals. John sold land that is Sec. 1231 property held for three years and recognized a $50,000 gain. Karen sold a building that is Sec. 1231 property held for three years and recognized a $50,000 gain. Straight-line depreciation was used. John and Karen both have a 30% tax rate, no other transactions involving capital assets or 1231 assets, and no nonrecaptured Sec. 1231 losses. Except for the sales of different assets, their tax situation is exactly the same. As a result of selling his Sec. 1231 property, will John pay more, less or the same amount of taxes than Karen as a result of selling her Sec. 1231 property? Explain.

I13-21 Why may a corporation recognize a greater amount of ordinary income due to the sale of Sec. 1250 property than a noncorporate taxpayer?

I13-22 Assume a taxpayer sells equipment used in a trade or business for a gain that is less than the depreciation allowed. If the taxpayer is a corporation, will a greater amount of Sec. 1245 income be recognized than if the taxpayer is an individual? Explain.

I13-23 Dale owns business equipment with a $100,000 FMV and an adjusted basis of $60,000. The property was originally acquired for $150,000. Which one of the following transactions would result in recognition of $40,000 ordinary income by Dale due to the depreciation recapture rules of Sec. 1245?
a. He makes a gift of the property to a daughter.
b. He contributes the property to a qualified charitable organization.

c. He disposes of the equipment in an installment sale and receives $10,000 cash in the year of sale.

I13-24 Carlos owns an office building with a $800,000 acquisition cost, a $270,000 adjusted basis, and a $500,000 FMV. The office building was acquired before 1981, and additional depreciation amounts to $175,000. Carlos makes a gift of the building to a charitable organization. What is the amount of his charitable contribution deduction?

I13-25 Ted owns a warehouse that cost $850,000 in 1984 and is subject to depreciation recapture under Sec. 1245. The warehouse, which has an adjusted basis of zero, is destroyed by a tornado and Ted receives $580,000 from the insurance company. Within nine months, he pays $500,000 for a new warehouse and an election is made to defer the gain under Sec. 1033. What is the amount and character of Ted's recognized gain?

I13-26 When a taxpayer disposes of oil, gas, or geothermal property, part or all of the gain may be recaptured as ordinary income. Explain how the recapture amount is determined for oil and gas and geothermal properties.

I13-27 William owns two appreciated assets, land and a building, which have been used in his trade or business for several years. The straight-line method of depreciation is used for the building. If he sells the two assets to his 100%-owned corporation, will William have to recognize any ordinary income? Explain.

ISSUE IDENTIFICATION QUESTIONS

I13-28 Six years ago Joelle started raising chinchillas. She separates her chinchillas into two groups, a breeding group and a market group. During the year, she had the following sales of chinchillas from her market group: 400 to producers of fur products; 100 to pet stores; and 25 to individuals to use as pets. From her breeding stock, she sold six chinchillas to Rebecca, an individual who is starting a chinchilla ranch, and five to Fur Pelts, a producer of fur products. All 11 chinchillas from the breeding group have been held for at least 22 months, and the five sold to Fur Pelts were poor performers.

I13-29 Green Acres, Inc., owns 1,400 acres adjacent to land owned by the U.S. government. The government, wanting to sell timber from its land, had to assure prospective bidders of access to the timber. The government entered into an agreement with Green Acres for a logging road easement across land owned by Green Acres. The government agreed to pay $2 per thousand board feet of timber removed up to a maximum of $130,000. Bidders for the rights to obtain the government's timber had to agree to pay the fee to Green Acres as part of their bids for the timber. Stanley Lumberyard, Inc. provided the highest bid and paid $80,000 to Green Acres during the first year of cutting and removing the timber and $50,000 during the second year. What tax issues should Green Acres and Stanley Lumberyard consider?

I13-30 Sarah, who has been in the business of erecting, maintaining, and renting outdoor advertising displays for 18 years, has an offer to purchase her business. Two basic types of advertising displays are used in her business: structure X and structure Y. Structure X consists of a single sign face nailed to a wooden support frame and attached to wooden poles 30 feet long. Its structure is rather easy to dismantle and move from one location to another. In contrast, structure Y is a permanent sign that is designed to withstand winds of up to 100 miles per hour. None of the Structure Y signs have ever been moved. What tax issues should Sarah consider?

I13-31 Sylvester owns and operates an unincorporated pizza business that delivers pizza to customers. Three years ago, he acquired an automobile for $10,000 to provide delivery service. Recently, Sylvester hired an employee who prefers to use his personal automobile to make the deliveries. Thus, Sylvester decided to permit his 18-year old daughter to use the automobile for her personal use. The automobile's adjusted basis is $3,080 and its FMV is $4,700. What tax issues should Sylvester consider?

PROBLEMS

I13-32 *Secs. 1231, 1245, and 1250 Transactions.* All assets listed below have been held for more than one year. Which assets might be classified as Sec. 1231, Sec. 1245, or Sec. 1250 property? An asset may be classified as more than one type of property.
a. Land on which a factory is located
b. Equipment used in the factory
c. Raw materials inventory
d. Patent purchased to allow use of a manufacturing process
e. Land held primarily for sale
f. Factory building acquired in 1986 (the straight-line ACRS recovery method is used)

I13-33 *Sec. 1231 Gains and Losses.* Vivian's AGI is $40,000 without considering the gains and losses below. Determine her revised AGI after the inclusion of any applicable gains or losses for the following independent cases. Assume she has no nonrecaptured net Sec. 1231 losses at the beginning of the year.

	Case A	Case B	Case C	Case D
Sec. 1231 gain	$19,000	$10,000	$30,000	$ 5,000
Sec. 1231 loss	5,000	22,000	39,000	12,000
LTCG	–0–	–0–	6,300	–0–
LTCL	–0–	–0–	–0–	4,200

I13-34 *Sec. 1231 Gains and Losses.* Edith, who has no other sales or exchanges and no nonrecaptured Sec. 1231 losses, sells three tracts of land that are used in her trade or business. Her regular income tax rate is 35%.
Asset #1—$15,000 gain and holding period of 20 months
Asset #2—$17,000 loss and holding period of 25 months
Asset #3— $ 5,000 gain and holding period of 13 months
a. What is the increase in her taxes as a result of the three sales?
b. If the holding period for Asset #2 is nine months, what is the decrease in her taxes as a result of the three sales?

I13-35 *Sec. 1231 Transactions.* Which of the following transactions or events is treated as a Sec. 1231 gain or loss? All assets are held for more than one year.
a. Theft of uninsured diamond ring, with an $800 basis and a $1,000 FMV.
b. Gain due to condemnation of land used in business.
c. Loss on the sale of a warehouse.
d. Gain of $4,000 on the sale of equipment. Depreciation deductions allowed amount to $10,000.

I13-36 *Capital Loss Versus Sec. 1231 Loss.* Vicki has an AGI of $70,000 without considering the sale of a nondepreciable asset for $23,000. The asset was acquired six years ago and has an adjusted basis of $35,000. She has no other sales or exchanges. Determine her AGI for the following independent situations when the asset is:
a. A capital asset.
b. Sec. 1231 property.

I13-37 *Ordinary Income Versus Sec. 1231 Gain.* At the beginning of 2006, Silver Corporation has a $95,000 capital loss carryforward from 2005. During 2006, the corporation sells land, held for four years, and realizes an $80,000 gain. Silver has no unrecaptured net Sec. 1231 losses, and it made no other sales during the current year. Determine the amount of capital loss carryforward that Silver can use in 2006 if the land is
a. Sec. 1231 property.
b. Not a capital asset or Sec. 1231 property.

I13-38 *Sec. 1231 Transactions.* During the current year, Sean's office building is destroyed by fire. After collecting the insurance proceeds, Sean has a $50,000 recognized gain. The building was acquired in 1978, and the straight-line method of depreciation has been used. He does not plan to acquire a replacement building. Consider the following independent cases and determine his net capital gain. For each case, include the $50,000 casualty gain described above.

a. Land used in his trade or business and held more than a year is condemned by the state. The recognized gain is $60,000.

b. Assume the same facts as in Part a, except the condemnation results in a $60,000 loss.

c. An apartment building used as residential rental property and held more than one year is destroyed by a sudden, unexpected mudslide. The building is not insured, and the loss amounts to $200,000.

I13-39 *Nonrecaptured Net Sec. 1231 Losses.* Consider the following summary of Sec. 1231 gains and losses recognized by Janet during the period 2001–2006. If Janet has no capital gains and losses during the six-year period, determine her net capital gain for each year.

	Sec. 1231 Gains	Sec. 1231 Losses
2001	$ 9,000	$ 7,000
2002	20,000	24,000
2003	12,000	19,000
2004	9,000	4,000
2005	25,000	13,200
2006	10,000	17,000

I13-40 *Nonrecaptured Net Sec. 1231 Losses.* Dillion has a tax rate of 30% on his ordinary income and $40,000 of net nonrecaptured Sec. 1231 losses at the start of the year. During the year, he recognizes a Sec. 1231 gain of $53,000 from the sale of land. As a result of the sale, how much does Dillion's tax liability increase?

I13-41 *Sec. 1245.* The Pear Corporation owns equipment with a $300,000 adjusted basis. The equipment was purchased six years ago for $650,000. If Pear sells the equipment for the selling prices given in the three independent cases below, what are the amount and character of Pear's recognized gain or loss?

Case	Selling Price
A	$407,000
B	752,000
C	245,000

I13-42 *Sec. 1245.* Elizabeth owns equipment that cost $500,000 and has an adjusted basis of $230,000. If the straight-line method of depreciation had been used, the adjusted basis would be $300,000.

a. What is the maximum selling price that she could sell the equipment for without having to recognize Sec. 1245 ordinary income?

b. If she sold the equipment and had to recognize $61,000 of Sec. 1245 ordinary income, what was the selling price?

I13-43 *Sale of Business and Personal-Use Property.* Arnie, a college student, purchased a new truck in 2004 for $6,000. He used the truck 70% of the time as a distributor for the local newspaper and 30% of the time for personal use. The truck has a five-year recovery period, and he claimed depreciation deductions of $840 in 2004 and $1,344 in 2005. Arnie sells the truck on June 20, 2006, for $3,000.

a. What is the amount of allowable depreciation in 2006?

b. Determine Arnie's realized and recognized gain or loss and its character.

I13-44 *Like-Kind Exchange of Sec. 1245 Property.* General Corporation owns equipment which cost $70,000 and has a $44,000 adjusted basis. General exchanges the equipment for other equipment ($42,000 FMV) and marketable securities ($30,000 FMV). Determine the following:

a. Realized gain

b. Recognized gain

c. Gain treated as ordinary income

d. Gain treated as Sec. 1231 gain

e. Basis of marketable securities received

f. Basis of equipment received

I13-45 *Like-Kind Exchange of Sec. 1245 Property.* Leroy owns a truck used in his trade or business that cost $50,000 and has an adjusted basis of $34,000. The truck is exchanged for a

new truck that is like-kind property with a FMV of $40,000. Prior to selling the new truck two years later, Leroy is allowed depreciation of $13,000 for the new truck. Determine:
a. Gain realized on the exchange
b. Gain recognized on the exchange
c. Basis of truck received
d. Gain recognized, and the character of the gain, if the sales price of the truck is $41,000
e. Gain recognized, and the character of the gain, if the sale price of the truck is $52,000

I13-46 *Purpose of Sec. 1245.* Martin owns equipment used in his trade or business that was purchased four years ago for $200,000. Martin sells the equipment in the current year for $110,000 when its adjusted basis is $52,000. No other sales or exchanges are made this year or the preceding five years. His tax rate is 35% for all years since the year of purchase.
a. Determine the increase in Martin's AGI for the current year as a result of the sale if Sec. 1245 did not exist.
b. Determine the increase in Martin's AGI for the current year as a result of the sale if Sec. 1245 does exist.
c. Given that Sec. 1245 does exist, what is the increase in his tax as a result of the sale?

I13-47 *Secs. 1231 and 1250.* Charles owns an office building and land that are used in his trade or business. The office building and land were acquired in 1978 for $800,000 and $100,000, respectively. During the current year, the properties are sold for $900,000 with 20% of the selling price being allocated to the land. The assets as shown on the taxpayer's books before their sale are as follows:

Building	$800,000	
Accumulated depreciation	590,000ª	$210,000
Land		100,000

ªIf the straight-line method of depreciation had been used, the accumulated depreciation would be $440,000.

a. What is the recognized gain due to the sale of the building?
b. What is the character of the recognized gain due to the sale of the building?
c. What is the recognized gain and character of the gain due to the sale of the land?

I13-48 Assume the same facts as in Problem I13-47 except the taxpayer is a corporation. How will the answers change?

I13-49 *Secs. 1231, 1245, and Unrecaptured Sec. 1250.* Brigham is single, in the 30% marginal income tax bracket, and has the sales or exchanges below. At the beginning of the year, he has nonrecaptured net Sec. 1231 losses of $10,000. Determine the increase or decrease in Brigham's tax liability as a result of the following independent sales or exchanges.
a. Sells equipment used in his trade or business for $40,000. The equipment was purchased for $100,000 and depreciation allowed amounts to $72,000.
b. Sells land used in his trade or business for $80,000. The land was purchased four years ago for $61,000.
c. He sells a building used in his trade or business for $163,000. The building was purchased in 1988 for $250,000 and depreciation allowed amounts to $110,000.
d. Same as Part c except he sells the building for $127,000.

I13-50 *Secs. 1245 and 1231.* The LaPoint Corporation placed in service $550,000 of equipment (7-year recovery property) on June 3 of last year and sold the equipment for $377,000 on November 22 of the current year. Determine the following:
a. Amount of Sec. 179 expense allowed last year
b. Depreciation allowed last year if the corporation wants to maximize depreciation
c. Depreciation allowed during the current year
d. Amount of gain and character of gain

I13-51 *Secs. 1250 and 1231.* Mr. Briggs purchased an apartment complex on January 10, 2004, for $2,000,000 with 10% of the price allocated to land. He sells the complex on October 22, 2006, for $2,500,000.
a. How much depreciation was allowed for 2004?
b. How much depreciation is allowed for 2006?
c. Will any of the gain be ordinary income?
d. What is the amount of gain and the character of the gain on the sale of the building?
e. What is the amount of gain and the character of the gain on the sale of the land?
f. Will any of the gain be taxed at 25%?

I13-52   *Sec. 1250 Residential Rental Property.* Jesse owns a duplex that he uses as residential rental property. The duplex cost $100,000 in 1986, and 10% of the cost was allocated to the land. Total cost-recovery deductions allowed amount to $81,000. The statutory percentages were used to compute cost-recovery deductions. If the straight-line method of cost recovery were used instead, $76,000 of cost-recovery deductions would have been allowed.

a. What is the amount of recognized gain and the character of the gain if Jesse sells the duplex for $125,000 with 10% of the price allocated to land?

b. What is the amount of recognized gain in the year of sale and the character of the gain if Jesse sells the property under the installment sale method? Terms of the installment sale are as follows: $25,000 in the year of sale and a $100,000 note to be paid in four annual payments. The note is an interest-bearing note at the market rate of interest.

I13-53   *Sec. 1250.* Rosemary owns an office building placed in service before 1981 that cost $625,000 and has an adjusted basis of $227,000. If the straight-line method of depreciation were used, the adjusted basis would be $300,000.

a. What is the maximum selling price that she could sell the building for without having to recognize Sec. 1250 ordinary income?

b. If she sold the building and had to recognize $51,000 of Sec. 1250 ordinary income, what was the selling price?

I13-54   *Nonresidential Real Property-Noncorporate Taxpayer.* Consider three office buildings placed in service as shown below and answer the following true-false questions. Assume all assets are sold by a noncorporate taxpayer at a gain and there are no other sales or exchanges or nonrecaptured Sec. 1231 loss unless told otherwise. None of the buildings are fully depreciated when sold.

	Placed in Service
Building #1	Before 1981
Building #2	After 1980 and before 1987
Building #3	After 1986

1. Some or all of the gain on sale of #1 is ordinary if accelerated depreciation was used.
2. If the straight-line method of depreciation was used for #1, some or all of the gain may be taxed at 25%.
3. Gain on the sale of #2 could be Sec. 1245 ordinary income.
4. Gain on the sale of #2 could be Sec. 1231 gain.
5. Part of the gain on the sale of #2 could be Sec. 1245 ordinary income and part could be Sec. 1231 gain.
6. If the straight-line method of depreciation was used for #2, some or all of the gain may be taxed at 25%.
7. Some or all of the gain on the sale of #3 could be Sec. 1245 ordinary income.
8. Some or all of the gain on the sale of #3 could be taxed at 25%.
9. Some of the gain on the sale of #3 could be Sec. 1250 ordinary income.
10. If the taxpayer has a nonrecaptured Sec. 1231 loss of $30,000 and the gain on the sale of #3 is $40,000, all $40,000 of the gain is taxed as ordinary income.

I13-55   *Nonresidential Real Property-Corporate Taxpayer.* Assume the same facts as in Problem I13-54 except the taxpayer is a corporate taxpayer and answer the ten true-false questions.

I13-56   *Secs. 1231 and 1250.* Molly sells an apartment complex for $4,500,000 with 10% of the price allocated to land. The apartment complex was purchased in 1991. She has no other sales or exchanges during the year and no nonrecaptured net Sec. 1231 losses. Information about the assets at the time of sale is:

	Building	*Land*
Original Cost	$2,700,000	$300,000
Accumulated Depreciation	1,000,000	0

a. What is the recognized gain on the sale of the building and the character of the gain?
b. What is the recognized gain on the sale of the land and the character of the gain?
c. How much of the Sec. 1231 gain is taxed at 25%?
d. If Molly has NSTCL of $50,000, will the capital loss reduce the Sec. 1231 gain taxed at 25% or 15%?

I13-57   *Secs. 1231 and 1250 for Corporate Taxpayer.* Assume the same facts as in Problem I13-56 except the taxpayer is a corporation instead of an individual.

a. What is the recognized gain on the sale of the building and the character of the gain?

b. What is the recognized gain on the sale of the land and the character of the gain?

c. How much of the Sec. 1231 gain is taxed at 25%?

I13-58 *Charitable Contribution of Sec. 1231 Property.* Raquel owns land used in her trade or business for more than one year. The basis is $10,000 and its FMV is $40,000. Her tax rate is 33% and her AGI is $150,000. She makes no other charitable contributions except for the ones considered below.

a. If she gives the land to a university, determine her tax savings.

b. If she sells the land for $40,000, pays the tax and then contributes the remainder of the cash to the charity, determine her net tax savings and the amount that the university receives. Assume that she has no other sales or exchanges during the year.

I13-59 *Secs. 1231, 1245 and 1250.* Glen, whose tax rate is 33%, sells each of the following assets for $200,000. Each case is an independent case.

	Sec. 1231 Gain (Loss)	Ordinary Income	Taxed at 33%	Taxed at 25%	Taxed at 15%
Building purchased in 1995 for $220,000 with adjusted basis of $165,000.	_____	_____	_____	_____	_____
Equipment purchased in 2002 for $300,000 with adjusted basis of $144,000	_____	_____	_____	_____	_____
Land purchased in 1990 for $30,000 to use as a building site	_____	_____	_____	_____	_____
Building purchased in 1994 for $150,000 with adjusted basis of $112,000	_____	_____	_____	_____	_____
Equipment purchased in 2003 for $180,000 with adjusted basis of $140,000	_____	_____	_____	_____	_____

I13-60 *Recapture of Soil and Water Conservation Expenditures.* Bob owns farmland with a $600,000 basis, and he elects to expense $100,000 of expenditures incurred for soil and water conservation purposes. Bob sells the farmland after farming for seven years and four months. What is the amount of the recognized gain and the character of the gain if the selling price is

a. $825,000

b. $615,000

I13-61 *Recapture of Intangible Drilling Costs.* Jeremy purchased undeveloped oil and gas property five years ago. He paid $300,000 for intangible drilling and development costs and elected to expense the $300,000. During the current year, Jeremy sells the property, which has an $800,000 adjusted basis, for $900,000. What is the amount of gain treated as ordinary income under Sec. 1254 because of the election to expense intangible drilling and development costs?

I13-62 *Recapture of Intangible Drilling Costs and Depletion.* In 1997, Jack purchased undeveloped oil and gas property for $900,000 and paid $170,000 for intangible drilling and development costs. He elected to expense the intangible drilling and development costs. During the current year he sells the property for $950,000 when the property's adjusted basis is $700,000. Depletion of $200,000 was allowed on the property.

a. What is the realized gain and how much of the gain is ordinary income?

b. For Jack to have a Sec. 1231 gain, the selling price must exceed what amount?

I13-63 *Related Party Transactions.* Ed operates a storage business as a sole proprietorship and owns the following assets acquired in 1977:

Warehouse	$400,000
Minus: Accumulated depreciation (straight-line method)	(230,000)
Adjusted basis	$170,000
Land	65,000

The FMV of the warehouse and the land are $500,000 and $200,000, respectively. Ed owns 75% of the stock of the Crane Corporation. If he sells the two assets to Crane at a price equal to the FMV of the assets, determine the recognized gain and its character due to the sale of the

a. Building

b. Land

COMPREHENSIVE PROBLEM

I13-64
Betty is in the business of breeding and racing horses. Except for the transactions below, she has no other sales or exchanges and she has no unrecaptured net Sec. 1231 losses. Consider the following transactions that occur during the year:

- A building with an adjusted basis of $300,000 is destroyed by fire. Insurance proceeds of $500,000 are received, but Betty does not plan to replace the building. The building was built 12 years ago at a cost of $430,000 and used to provide lodging for her employees. Straight-line depreciation has been used.

- Four acres of the farm are condemned by the state to widen the highway and Betty receives $50,000. The land was inherited from her mother 15 years ago when its FMV was $15,000. Her mother purchased the land for $10,300. Betty does not plan to purchase additional land.

- A racehorse purchased four years ago for $200,000 was sold for $550,000. Total depreciation allowed using the straight-line method amounts to $160,000.

- Equipment purchased three years ago for $200,000 is exchanged for $100,000 of IBM common stock. The adjusted basis of the equipment is $120,000. If straight-line depreciation had been used, the adjusted basis would be $152,000.

- A pony, with an adjusted basis of $20,000 and FMV of $35,000, that her daughter uses only for personal use is injured while attempting a jump. Because of the injury, the uninsured pony has to be destroyed by a veterinarian.

a. What amount of Sec. 1245 ordinary income must be recognized?

b. What amount of Sec. 1250 ordinary income must be recognized?

c. Will the loss resulting from the destruction of her daughter's pony be used to determine net Sec. 1231 gains or losses?

d. What is the amount of the net Sec. 1231 gain or loss?

e. After all of the netting of gains or losses is completed, will the gain resulting from the involuntary conversion of the building be treated as LTCG?

f. What is the amount of her unrecaptured Sec. 1250 gain?

TAX STRATEGY PROBLEMS

I13-65
Russ has never recognized any Sec. 1231 gains or losses. In December 2006, Russ is considering the sale of two Sec. 1231 assets. The sale of one asset will result in a $20,000 Sec. 1231 gain while the sale of the other asset will result in a $20,000 Sec. 1231 loss. Russ has no other capital or Sec. 1231 gains and losses in 2006 and does not expect to have any other capital or Sec. 1231 gains and losses in 2006. He is aware that it might be advantageous to recognize the Sec. 1231 gain and the Sec. 1231 loss in different tax years. However, he does not know whether he should recognize the Sec. 1231 gain in 2006 and the Sec. 1231 loss in 2007 or vice versa. His marginal tax rate for each year is expected to be 33%. Advise the taxpayer with respect to these two alternatives:

a. Recognize the $20,000 Sec. 1231 loss in 2006 and the $20,000 Sec. 1231 gain in 2007.

b. Recognize the $20,000 Sec. 1231 gain in 2006 and the $20,000 Sec. 1231 loss in 2007.

I13-66
Holly has recognized a $9,000 STCL. She has no other recognized capital gains and losses in 2006. She is considering the sale of a Sec. 1231 asset held for four years at a $5,000 gain in 2006. She had not recognized any Sec. 1231 losses during the previous five years and does not expect to have any other Sec. 1231 transactions in 2006. Her marginal tax rate for 2006 is 31%. What is the amount of increase in her 2006 taxes if Holly recognizes the $5,000 Sec. 1231 gain in 2006?

TAX FORM/RETURN PREPARATION PROBLEMS

I13-67
George Buckner sells an apartment building on October 10th of the current year for $1,750,000. The building was purchased on January 1, 1995, for $2,000,000. Depreciation of $420,000 has been taken. The figures given above do not include the pur-

chase price or the selling price of the land. Mr. Buckner's adjusted basis for the land is $200,000, and the sales price is $350,000. Mr. Buckner, who owns and operates a taxi business, sells one of the automobiles for $1,800 on November 14th. The automobile's adjusted basis is zero, and the original cost is $15,000. The automobile was purchased on April 25, 2000. Mr. Buckner has no other gains and losses during the year, and nonrecaptured net Sec. 1231 losses amount to $32,000. Prepare Form 4797 for the current year.

I13-68 Julie Hernandez is single and has no dependents. She operates a dairy farm and her Social Security number is 510-88-6387. She lives at 1325 Vermont Street in Costa, Florida. Consider the following information for the current year:

- Schedule C was prepared by her accountant and the net profit from the dairy operations is $48,000.
- Itemized deductions amount to $4,185.
- Dividend income (qualified dividend) amounts to $280.
- State income tax refund received during the year is $125. She did not itemize her deductions last year.
- In June, a burglar broke into her house and stole the following two assets, which were acquired in 1987:

	Basis	FMV	Insurance Proceeds Received
Painting	$2,000	$10,000	$9,000
Sculpture	1,700	1,500	0

The following assets used in her business were sold during the year:

	Acquisition Date	Original Cost	Depreciation to Date of Sale	Date of Sale	Selling Price
Tractor	June 10, 1994	$25,000	$25,000	Oct. 20	$ 8,300
Barn	May 23, 1989	90,000	61,000	May 13	87,000
Land	May 23, 1989	15,000	–0–	May 13	27,000
Cows	Sept. 7, 2001	20,000	13,000	Nov. 8	21,300

In August, three acres of the farm were taken by the state under the right of eminent domain for the purpose of building a highway. The basis of the three acres is $1,500, and the state paid the FMV, $22,000, on February 10. The farm was purchased on August 12, 1971.

Nonrecaptured net Section 1231 losses from the five most recent tax years preceding the current year amount to $7,000. Estimated taxes paid during the year amount to $32,000.

Prepare Forms 1040, 4684 Section A, 4797, and Schedule D for the current year. (Do not consider self-employment taxes discussed in Chapter I14.)

CASE STUDY PROBLEMS

I13-69 Your client, Kent Earl, whose tax rate is 35%, owns a bowling alley and has indicated that he wants to sell the business for $1,000,000 and purchase a minor league baseball franchise. His business consists of the following tangible assets:

	Acquisition Date	Original Cost	Adjusted Basis
Equipment	1998	$600,000	$150,000
Building	1988	900,000	494,000
Land	1978	100,000	100,000
Inventory	Current year	50,000	50,000

Because you have another client, Tom Quick, who is interested in purchasing a business, you informed Tom of Kent's interest in selling. Tom wants to purchase the bowling alley, and the price sounds right to him. The bowling alley business has been very profitable in the last few years because Kent has developed a loyal group of customers by promoting bowling leagues during the week days and a special Saturday afternoon session for children in the elementary school grades. Kent and Tom have come to you and want to know how the transaction should be handled for the best tax results. You know that the $1,000,000 purchase price will have to be allocated among the assets and it will be necessary to estimate the FMV of all assets. Because FMV is often subjective, Kent and Tom recognize that some flexibility might exist in allocating the purchase price. For example, it might be just as easy to justify a FMV of $300,000 or $325,000 for the equipment.

a. What advice do you have for Kent with respect to the allocation (i.e., should he be interested in allocating more to some assets than others)? Explain the reasoning for your advice.

b. Would your advice to Kent be different if he had a large amount of capital losses and no nonrecaptured net Sec. 1231 losses?

c. What advice do you have for Tom with respect to the allocation (i.e., should he be interested in allocating more of the purchase price to some assets than to others)? Explain the reasoning for your advice.

d. What advantages might result from having Kent sign an agreement not to compete (i.e., operate a bowling alley)?

e. Should you have a concern about the ethical implications of advising both Kent and Tom?

I13-70   Assume the same facts as in Case Study Problem I13-69 except you have the following market values as a result of an appraisal:

Equipment	$ 250,000
Building	500,000
Land	140,000
Inventory	110,000
Total	$1,000,000

Tom insists that $150,000 of the purchase price should be allocated to inventory and $100,000 should be allocated to land. He refuses to complete the purchase unless the allocation is made as he requests. What action should you take with respect to Tom's request? (See Chapter I10 for a discussion of valuation issues in the purchase and sale of a business.)

TAX RESEARCH PROBLEM

I13-71   Berkeley Corporation has a policy of furnishing new automobiles to the athletic department of the local university. The automobiles are used for short periods of time by the extremely popular head basketball coach. When the automobiles are returned to Berkeley Corporation, they are sold to regular customers. The owner of Berkeley Corporation maintains that any such cars held for more than one year should qualify as Sec. 1231 property. Do you agree?

Research sources include

• Rev. Rul. 75-538, 1975-2 C.B. 34

14

CHAPTER

SPECIAL TAX COMPUTATION METHODS, TAX CREDITS, AND PAYMENT OF TAX

LEARNING OBJECTIVES

After studying this chapter, you should be able to

▶1 Calculate the alternative minimum tax

▶2 Describe what constitutes self-employment income and compute the self-employment tax

▶3 Describe the various business and personal tax credits

▶4 Understand the mechanics of the federal withholding tax system and the requirements for making estimated tax payments

Chapter I2 discussed the basic tax computation for individuals using the tax table and tax rate schedules. This chapter completes the discussion of the tax computation by examining three principal topics:

1. Two special methods of tax computation: the alternative minimum tax and self-employment tax;
2. Various tax credits that are available to reduce a taxpayer's tax liability; and
3. Methods for payment of an individual's tax liability, including the pay-as-you-go withholding rules and estimated tax payment requirements.

ALTERNATIVE MINIMUM TAX

OBJECTIVE 1

Calculate the alternative minimum tax

HISTORICAL NOTE

The original add-on minimum tax, enacted in 1969, was 10% times the taxpayer's tax preferences in excess of a $30,000 statutory exemption.

Over the years, Congress has used the income tax law for a variety of purposes other than just raising revenue to fund government operations, such as enacting provisions to promote economic and social goals. As the number of special tax provisions increased, many taxpayers were able to carefully plan their financial affairs so as to use these special tax provisions to substantially reduce or eliminate their entire income tax liability. As a result, a new set of rules was implemented in 1969 to ensure that all taxpayers would pay at least a minimum amount of income tax. Thus was born what is known today as the **alternative minimum tax (AMT)**.

The original minimum tax was referred to as an add-on minimum tax because it was added to the taxpayer's regular income tax liability. The present AMT system was created in 1978 and is no longer an add-on tax but actually is a separate and parallel tax system. Taxpayers are first required to compute their regular income tax liability and then compute their tax under the AMT system. The AMT system requires taxpayers to adjust their regular taxable income by a number of adjustments and preferences, then subtract an exemption amount to arrive at the AMT base. The AMT base is then multiplied by the special AMT rates to compute the tax under the AMT system which is called the Tentative Minimum Tax (TMT), and taxpayers are required to pay the *greater* of (1) the regular income tax, or (2) the TMT.

The present AMT system applies to individuals, corporations, estates, and trusts.[1] Most individual taxpayers are not subject to the AMT because their regular income tax is greater than the TMT. This is caused primarily because many taxpayers do not have substantial adjustments and preferences and the AMT exemption is liberal in amount (i.e., $58,000 for married individuals filing a joint return and $40,250 for single individuals). However, more and more individuals in recent years are being subjected to the AMT. Many of these individuals are not the high-income individuals for which the AMT was intended. The primary reason for this unusual phenomena is the structure of the AMT system and the fact that the AMT is not indexed for inflation.

EXAMPLE I14-1 ▶ Ricardo and Sue are married and file a joint return for the current year with taxable income of $30,000 and tax preferences and adjustments of $12,000 for AMT purposes. Their alternative minimum taxable income (AMTI) is $42,000 ($30,000 + $12,000), but the alternative minimum tax base is zero because of the $58,000 exemption. Thus, their tax liability is based on the regular tax computation and no AMT liability is owed. ◀

EXAMPLE I14-2 ▶ Assume the same facts for Ricardo and Sue above except that they have tax preferences and adjustments of $50,000. Their alternative minimum taxable income (AMTI) is $80,000 ($30,000 + $50,000). Their regular tax for 2006 based on taxable income of $30,000 would be $3,745. The total tax computed under the AMT system (TMT) would be $5,720 ($80,000 minus the AMT exemption of $58,000 yields the AMT base of $22,000; $22,000 × AMT tax rate of 26% equals

---

[1] The AMT applicable to corporations is discussed in *Prentice Hall's Federal Taxation: Corporations, Partnerships, Estates, and Trusts* text and in the *Comprehensive* volume.

$5,720). Thus, Ricardo and Sue must pay $5,720 in tax since it is greater than their regular tax of $3,745. ◄

COMPUTATIONAL ASPECTS

The formula for computing the alternative minimum tax for individuals for the tax year is to apply a two-tiered graduated rate schedule to the AMT tax base. The tax base consists of the following items:[2]

<table>
<tr><td colspan="2">TAXABLE INCOME</td></tr>
<tr><td>Plus:</td><td>Tax preference items[3]</td></tr>
<tr><td>Plus:</td><td>Personal and dependency exemptions
The standard deduction if the taxpayer does not itemize</td></tr>
<tr><td>Plus or minus:</td><td>Adjustments required because different rules are used for calculating the alternative minimum taxable income as compared with taxable income (e.g., special AMT limitations on certain itemized deductions)</td></tr>
<tr><td>EQUALS:</td><td>ALTERNATIVE MINIMUM TAXABLE INCOME (AMTI)</td></tr>
<tr><td>Minus:</td><td>Exemption amount ($58,000 for a married couple filing a joint return and surviving spouses, $40,250 for single individuals, and $29,000 for a married individual filing separately—see note 4 below). The exemption amount is reduced by 25% of AMTI in excess of $150,000 for a married couple filing a joint return and surviving spouses, $112,500 for single individuals, and $75,000 for a married individual filing separately.[4]</td></tr>
<tr><td>EQUALS:</td><td>ALTERNATIVE MINIMUM TAX BASE</td></tr>
<tr><td>Times:</td><td>Tax rate (26% of first $175,000; 28% of amounts in excess of $175,000)[5]</td></tr>
<tr><td>EQUALS:</td><td>TENTATIVE MINIMUM TAX</td></tr>
<tr><td>Minus:</td><td>Nonrefundable personal credits
Regular tax</td></tr>
<tr><td>EQUALS:</td><td><u>ALTERNATIVE MINIMUM TAX</u></td></tr>
</table>

EXAMPLE I14-3 ▶

Rita, a single taxpayer, has taxable income of $158,200, a regular tax liability after credits of $37,605, a positive AMT adjustment due to limitations on itemized deductions of $25,000, and tax preferences of $10,000 in 2006. Rita has an adoption credit of $1,000 and a child and dependent care credit of $600. Rita's alternative minimum tax for 2005 is calculated as follows:

Taxable income		$158,200
Plus:	Tax preferences	10,000
Plus:	Adjustments related to itemized deductions	25,000
Plus:	Personal exemption	3,200
Alternative minimum taxable income		$196,400
Minus:	Exemption	(19,300)[a]
Alternative minimum tax base		$177,100
Tax on first $175,000: $175,000 × 0.26 =		$ 45,500
Tax on excess over $175,000: $2,100 × 0.28 =		588
Tentative minimum tax		$ 46,088
Minus:	Nonrefundable tax credits	$ (1,600)
	Regular tax	(37,605)
Alternative minimum tax		$ 6,883

Rita will pay a total federal income tax liability of $44,488 ($37,605 regular tax + $6,883 AMT).

[a]$40,250 − [0.25 × ($196,300 − $112,500)] = $19,300 ◄

---

[2] Sec. 55(b)(1).
[3] Sec. 57.
[4] Sec. 55(d)(3). Beginning in 2007, the exemption amounts are scheduled to revert back to the pre-2003 amounts of $45,000, $33,750, and $22,500 respectively. However, both the House and Senate have authorized higher

exemption amounts. At the date of printing of this textbook, these extensions have not been finalized.
[5] The AMT rate on net capital gains has been reduced from the 26%/28% rates to 15%/5% to correspond with the reduction in rates on net capital gains for regular tax purposes.

ADDITIONAL COMMENT

Most taxpayers will not have tax preference items. Over the years, tax preference items have diminished in importance while adjustments create most AMT.

TAX PREFERENCE ITEMS

Tax preferences are certain provisions in the Internal Revenue Code (IRC) that grant favorable treatment to taxpayers. However, Congress is concerned that some taxpayers may take over-advantage of these favorable provisions and therefore classify them as tax preferences. For example, accelerated depreciation allowed for real property placed in service before 1987 is a tax preference item. (See Chapter I10 for a discussion of ACRS depreciation.) To compute the tax base for the AMT, the tax preferences designated in Sec. 57 must be added to taxable income. Some of the most common tax preference items include the following:

▶ Excess of accelerated depreciation (or ACRS cost recovery) claimed over a hypothetical straight-line depreciation amount for real property placed in service before 1987 computed on an item-by-item basis.

▶ Tax-exempt interest on certain private activity bonds. In general, private activity bonds are state or local bonds that are issued to help finance a private business.

▶ Excess of percentage depletion over the adjusted basis of the property. This item of tax preference does not apply to the percentage depletion deduction claimed by independent oil and gas producers and royalty owners.

▶ Exclusion of gain on the sale of certain small business stock. The exclusion is 7% of the gain on the disposition of qualified small business stock under Sec. 1202[6] (see Chapter I5).

It should be noted, however, that not all items receiving preferential treatment are tax preference items. For example, most municipal bond interest income is exempt from the federal income tax but is not a tax preference item. Only tax-exempt interest on private activity bonds (e.g., bonds issued by a municipality to fund certain nongovernmental activities such as industrial parks) issued after August 7, 1986, are subject to the AMT.

EXAMPLE I14-4 ▶

Richard, a single taxpayer, has the following tax preference items for the current year:

▶ $15,000 ACRS cost-recovery deduction on real property placed in service before 1987 and held for investment. The straight-line ACRS deduction would have been $10,000.

▶ $10,000 of tax-exempt interest on private activity bonds.

Richard's total tax preferences are $15,000, consisting of $5,000 excess cost recovery deductions and $10,000 tax-exempt interest on the private activity bonds. ◀

As one can see from the discussion above, most taxpayers will have little, if any, tax preferences.

AMT ADJUSTMENTS

ADDITIONAL COMMENT

Some tax advisors recommend that cash basis taxpayers prepay their local property taxes or state income taxes before the end of the year in order to reduce the current year's tax liability. However, if the taxpayer is subject to the AMT, this may not be a valid strategy.

As previously discussed, AMTI equals taxable income as modified by certain adjustments and increased by tax preference items. For most individual taxpayers AMT adjustments represent itemized deductions that are not allowed in computing AMTI or timing differences relating to the deferral of income or the acceleration of deductions under the regular tax rules. These adjustments generally increase the AMT tax base, although the AMT tax base may be reduced when the timing differences reverse. Some of the more important adjustments are discussed below.

LIMITATION ON ITEMIZED DEDUCTIONS. Only certain itemized deductions are allowed in computing AMTI. Additionally, the standard deduction is not allowed if an individual does not itemize deductions. The following items **are** deductible for AMT purposes:

▶ Casualty and theft losses in excess of 10% of AGI

▶ Charitable contributions (but not in excess of the 20%, 30%, and 50% of AGI limitation amounts)

▶ Medical expenses in excess of 10% of AGI (a 7.5% ceiling applies to the regular tax computation)

---

[6] Sec. 57(a)(7). The 7% rate was formerly 28%. Before 2001, the 28% rate was 42%.

▶ Qualified housing interest and certain other interest up to the amount of qualified net investment income included in the AMT base

▶ Estate tax deduction on income in respect of a decedent

▶ Gambling losses

Some of the more significant itemized deductions that **are not** deductible for the AMT include miscellaneous itemized deductions (e.g., unreimbursed employee expenses), state, local, and foreign income taxes, and real and personal property taxes. The 3% reduction of itemized deductions of high-income taxpayers does not apply to the AMT.

EXAMPLE I14-5 ▶ Robin, a single taxpayer, has AGI of $100,000 and the following itemized deductions in 2006:

Charitable contributions	4,000
Medical expenses not reimbursed by insurance	10,500
Mortgage interest on Robin's personal residence	18,500
Real estate taxes	4,000
State income taxes	6,000
Personal casualty loss, net of insurance, before any limitations	$15,000

From the information above, Robin's taxable income would be as follows:

AGI			$100,000
Itemized deductions:			
Charitable contributions		$ 4,000	
Medical expenses	$10,500		
Less 7.5% of AGI	(7,500)	3,000	
Mortgage interest		18,400	
Real estate taxes		4,000	
State income taxes		6,000	
Personal casualty loss	$15,000		
Less $100 floor	(100)		
Less 10% of AGI	(10,000)	4,900	(40,300)
Personal exemption			(3,300)
Taxable income			$56,400

To obtain her AMTI, Robin must make adjustments to her taxable income. Assume that Robin also has $20,000 of tax preferences. Her AMTI would be computed as follows:

Taxable income	$56,400
Tax preferences	20,000
AMT adjustments:	
Medical expenses (only $500 allowed for AMTI [$10,500 − .10($100,000)]	2,500
Real estate and state income taxes (not allowed for AMTI)	10,000
Personal exemption (not allowed for AMTI)	3,300
AMTI	$92,200 ◀

AMT ADJUSTMENTS DUE TO TIMING DIFFERENCES. Other adjustments are required when the rules for calculating taxable income permit the taxpayer to temporarily defer the recognition of income or to accelerate deductions. This temporary benefit is caused by applying different accounting methods that result in timing differences when income or expenses are recognized. The most common AMT adjustments for individuals that represent timing differences include:

▶ For personal property placed in service after 1998, the difference between the MACRS deduction and the amount determined by using the 150% declining balance method (switching to the straight-line method) over the recovery period used for regular tax purposes.[7] Bonus depreciation (50% or 30%) is allowed in full for purposes of the AMT.

▶ For real property placed in service after 1986 and before January 1, 1999, the difference between the MACRS depreciation claimed using the property's actual recovery

---

[7] For personal property placed in service after 1986 and prior to 1999, the 150% declining balance method (switching to the straight-line method) was used for AMT purposes, but the ADS recovery period was required rather than the recovery period for regular tax purposes.

period and a hypothetical straight-line depreciation amount calculated using a 40-year life (see Chapter I10 for a discussion of the alternative depreciation system).[8]

▶ For research and experimental (R&E) expenditures, the difference between the amount expensed and the deduction that would have been allowed if the expenditures were capitalized and amortized over a ten-year period.[9]

EXAMPLE I14-6 ▶

Rob has the following AMT adjustments caused by timing differences in 2006:

▶ Depreciation in 2006 on residential rental property costing $100,000 and placed in service in January 1998 is $3,636 using the straight-line method, a 27½-year recovery period, and based on MACRS rules. The depreciation in 2006 for AMT purposes is $2,500 based on the straight-line method and a 40-year recovery period under the alternative depreciation system. Thus, the positive AMT adjustment is $1,136 ($3,636 − $2,500). (See footnote 8 for real property placed in service after December 31, 1998.)

▶ Depreciation on a computer used in business costing $10,000 and placed in service in 2006 is $2,000 based on the MACRS rules (i.e., 200% DB method, a half-year convention, and a five-year recovery period). The depreciation for AMT purposes is $1,500 based on the alternative depreciation system (i.e., 150% DB method, half-year convention, and a five-year recovery period). Thus, the positive AMT adjustment is $500 ($2,000 − $1,500).

ADDITIONAL COMMENT

For corporate taxpayers only, there is a 0.12% environmental tax imposed on the excess of the corporation's modified alternative minimum taxable income over $2 million. This additional tax levy is primarily imposed on corporations larger than mom and pop entities.

▶ R&E expenditures amounting to $50,000 are expensed in the current year. For AMT purposes, the R&E deduction would be $5,000 ($50,000 ÷ 10 years) since the expenditures are capitalized and amortized over a 10-year period. Thus, the positive AMT adjustment is $45,000 ($50,000 − $5,000).

Rob's total positive AMT adjustment to his taxable income in 2006 to arrive at AMTI is $46,636 ($1,136 + $500 + $45,000). ◀

CREDITS THAT REDUCE THE AMT. As we will discuss later in this chapter, there are a number of credits that are allowed to reduce a taxpayer's regular tax liability. However, for purposes of the AMT, only the foreign tax credit and nonrefundable personal credits are allowed to reduce the tentative minimum tax. The foreign tax credit that may be deducted from the AMT is a specially computed credit, called the "alternative minimum tax foreign tax credit" and basically is computed using the various amounts used in computing alternative minimum taxable income instead of taxable income. Nonrefundable personal credits include the following:

▶ Child and dependent care credit
▶ Credit for the elderly and totally disabled
▶ Adoption expense credit
▶ Child tax credit
▶ HOPE and lifetime learning credits

Thus, the AMT is likely to apply to a taxpayer who uses credits (other than foreign tax credits and nonrefundable personal credits) to reduce his regular tax liability.

STOP & THINK

Question: What are the most common characteristics of taxpayers who are subject to the AMT?

Solution: While each situation is certainly unique, there are certain taxpayers who are more likely to be subject to the AMT. First, taxpayers who have materially invested in real estate before January 1, 1999, are likely candidates for the AMT because they will have a large positive adjustment caused from the differences in depreciation. Second, as discussed above, taxpayers who use credits to reduce their regular tax liability may well be subject to the AMT because only certain credits can reduce the AMT. Third, taxpayers who have very large itemized deductions, primarily from large state and local tax liabilities, may be subject to the AMT because state and local taxes are not deductible for AMT purposes.

---

[8] For real property being depreciated under the straight-line method and placed in service after 1998, the Taxpayer Relief Act of 1997 eliminates this adjustment.

[9] Sec. 56(b)(2). However, this adjustment does not apply if the taxpayer materially participates in the activity, Sec. 56(b)(2)(D).

AMT CREDIT.   Under Sec. 53, taxpayers are allowed an AMT credit which can be used against their *regular tax liability*. Basically, if a taxpayer pays AMT in a taxable year, that amount of AMT is eligible to be used as a credit against the taxpayer's regular tax liability in a future year. While this may seem unusual at first glance, the underlying reasoning for the AMT credit is as follows: since the AMT is caused primarily by adjustments that will reverse in the future and the taxpayer will actually pay a higher regular tax in those future years, the imposition of a prior year AMT and the current year regular tax essentially would constitute double taxation. Thus, a taxpayer who has paid AMT in prior years, but is not subject to the AMT in the current year, may be entitled to an AMT credit against his regular tax liability in the current year.[10]

SUMMARY ILLUSTRATION OF THE AMT COMPUTATION

The AMT formula is illustrated in the following example:

EXAMPLE I14-7 ▶ Roger and Kate are married, file a joint return, and have four dependent children. All the children are under age 17. They have the following items that are used to compute taxable income in 2006:

<table>
<tr><td>Gross income:</td><td></td><td></td></tr>
<tr><td>Salary</td><td></td><td>$ 70,000</td></tr>
<tr><td>Interest income</td><td></td><td>10,000</td></tr>
<tr><td>Business income</td><td></td><td>30,000[a]</td></tr>
<tr><td>AGI</td><td></td><td>$110,000</td></tr>
<tr><td>Minus: Itemized deductions:</td><td></td><td></td></tr>
<tr><td>State and local taxes</td><td>$9,400</td><td></td></tr>
<tr><td>Mortgage interest on their personal residence</td><td>12,000</td><td></td></tr>
<tr><td>Charitable contributions</td><td>3,000</td><td>(24,400)</td></tr>
<tr><td>Minus: Personal and dependency exemptions ($3,300 × 6)</td><td></td><td>(19,800)</td></tr>
<tr><td>Taxable income</td><td></td><td>$ 65,800</td></tr>
</table>

[a]MACRS depreciation deductions of $70,000 on personal property placed in service after 1986 were claimed in arriving at business income. Only $50,000 of depreciation would be claimed under the alternative depreciation system using the 150% declining balance method.

<table>
<tr><td>Roger's AMT is computed as follows:</td><td></td><td></td></tr>
<tr><td>Taxable income</td><td></td><td>$ 65,800</td></tr>
<tr><td>Plus: Personal and dependency exemptions</td><td></td><td>19,800</td></tr>
<tr><td>AMT adjustments:</td><td></td><td></td></tr>
<tr><td>Excess depreciation ($70,000 − $50,000)</td><td>$20,000</td><td></td></tr>
<tr><td>State and local taxes</td><td>9,400</td><td>29,400</td></tr>
<tr><td>AMTI</td><td></td><td>$115,000</td></tr>
<tr><td>Minus: AMT exemption</td><td></td><td>(58,000)</td></tr>
<tr><td>Tax base</td><td></td><td>$ 57,000</td></tr>
<tr><td>Times: Tax rate</td><td></td><td>× 0.26</td></tr>
<tr><td></td><td></td><td>$ 14,820</td></tr>
<tr><td>Minus: Child tax credit (4 × $1,000)</td><td></td><td>(4,000)</td></tr>
<tr><td>Tentative minimum tax</td><td></td><td>10,820</td></tr>
<tr><td>Minus: Regular tax (based on taxable income of $65,800)</td><td>9,565</td><td></td></tr>
<tr><td>Child tax credit (4 × $1,000)</td><td>(4,000)</td><td>(5,565)</td></tr>
<tr><td>Alternative minimum tax</td><td></td><td>$ 5,255[a]</td></tr>
</table>

[a]An AMT credit may be available in future years to offset any regular tax that is owed. However, the AMT credit applies only to the AMT that results from timing differences such as depreciation adjustments and not from exclusions (e.g., personal exemptions and taxes).

The total tax liability for Roger and Kate for 2006 is $10,820 ($5,565 + $5,255). ◀

ADDITIONAL COMMENT

In some circumstances, the AMT applies to unsuspecting taxpayers. In a recent case, *D.R. Klaussen*, T.C. Memo 1998-241 (affd, CA-10), the taxpayers had 12 personal exemptions and were subject to the AMT even though they had no tax preferences or adjustments.

---

[10] A detailed discussion of the rules for computing the AMT credit is beyond the scope of this book. See Sec. 53 for additional information.

SELF-EMPLOYMENT TAX

Most individuals are classified as employees and are not subject to the self-employment tax. Employees are covered under the Federal Insurance Contributions Act (FICA) through the payment of payroll taxes. The employer must withhold the employee's share of the FICA tax and provide a matching amount. Employees are not subject to an additional employment tax upon the filing of their federal income tax return.

The self-employment tax is imposed to finance Social Security coverage for self-employed individuals. Thus, the distinction between a self-employed individual (often referred to as an independent contractor) and an employee is important because no employer FICA contribution is required if the payee is deemed to have independent contractor status. Independent contractors are subject to self-employment tax on the amount of net earnings from the self-employment activity. Employees who have a small business in addition to their regular employment (e.g., an accountant, who is an employee for a large corporation, also prepares tax returns in a sideline consulting practice) may be subject to the self-employment tax on the consulting income in addition to the FICA tax on wages.

ETHICAL POINT

An employer must have a reasonable basis for treating a worker as an independent contractor or meet the general common law rules for determining whether an employer-employee relationship exists. Otherwise, the employer is liable for federal and state income tax withholding, FICA and FUTA taxes, interest, and penalties associated with the misclassification.

HISTORICAL NOTE

The ceiling amount on income from self-employment was $7,800 in 1971.

COMPUTING THE TAX

Self-employed individuals are subject to the self-employment (SE) tax if their net earnings are $400 or more.[11] The SE tax rate is a total of 15.3%, comprised of 12.4% for old-age, survivors, and disability insurance (OASDI) up to a ceiling amount of $94,200 in 2006 ($90,000 in 2005), and 2.9% for hospital insurance (HI), commonly referred to as Medicare taxes. No ceiling amount applies to the HI portion. Note that the SE tax rates are exactly twice the rates for employees under FICA (e.g., 6.2% for OASDI up to a ceiling amount of $94,200 in 2006, and 1.45% for HI). For employee wages, the 6.2% and 1.45% (total of 7.65%) must be matched by the employer. This matching requirement for employers effectively equalizes Social Security taxes for employees and self-employed individuals.

One-half of the self-employment tax imposed is allowed as a *for* AGI deduction and is reported on page 1 of Form 1040.[12] Net earnings from self-employment are determined by multiplying self-employment income by 0.9235 (which is equivalent to 100% of self-employment income minus one-half of self-employment taxes, or 7.65%, resulting in net earnings from self-employment of 92.35%) to compute the amount that is subject to self-employment tax.

HISTORICAL NOTE

The Revenue Reconciliation Act of 1993 eliminated the wage cap on the hospital insurance component of wages. Though presented as a tax increase for high-income individuals, it also increases the tax burden for employers of high-income individuals.

EXAMPLE I14-8 ▶

Rose is a CPA and operates her practice as a sole proprietorship. She has $120,000 of earnings from self-employment in 2006. Her net earnings from self-employment is $110,820 ($120,000 × 0.9235). The OASDI portion of the tax is $11,681 ($94,200 × 0.124). The amount of self-employment income that is subject to the hospital insurance portion of the tax is $110,820 and the HI tax is $3,214 ($110,820 × 0.029). Thus, the total self-employment tax reported on Schedule SE is $14,895. Rose also receives a *for* AGI tax deduction of $7,448 ($14,895 × 0.50), which is reported on page 1 of Form 1040. ◀

If an individual is an employee and also has income from self-employment, the tax base for computing the self-employment tax is reduced by the wages that are subject to the FICA tax. The self-employment tax base for the OASDI component is equal to the lesser of the primary ceiling ($94,200 in 2006) reduced by the FICA wages or the self-employment income multiplied by 0.9235.

EXAMPLE I14-9 ▶

Sandy receives wages as an employee of $75,000 in 2006 that are subject to FICA tax. In addition, Sandy has a small consulting practice that generates $10,000 of income from self-employment. The tentative tax base for computing the self-employment tax is $9,235 ($10,000 × 0.9235) net earnings from self-employment. Thus, the tax base for computing the OASDI portion of the tax is the lesser of $9,235 net earnings from self-employment or $19,200 ($94,200 ceiling − $75,000 FICA wages). Sandy's self-employment tax for the OASDI portion is

---

[11] Sec. 6017.

[12] Sec. 164(f).

$1,145 ($9,235 × 0.124) and the HI component is $268 ($9,235 × 0.029) The total amount of self-employment tax is therefore $1,413 ($1,145 + $268) and Sandy also receives a *for* AGI deduction of $707 ($1,413 × 0.50), which is reported on page 1 of Form 1040. ◀

EXAMPLE I14-10 ▶ Assume the same facts as in Example I14-9 except that Sandy's wages are $100,000. Sandy's taxable self-employment income for the OASDI portion of the tax is zero because her FICA wages exceed the $94,200 primary ceiling amount. However, she is subject to self-employment tax with respect to the HI portion. The tax base for the HI portion is the $9,235 net earnings from self-employment because no ceiling amount is applicable. The HI portion of the self-employment tax is $268 ($9,235 × 0.029) and Sandy also receives a *for* AGI deduction for $134 ($268 × 0.50). ◀

KEY POINT

In the case of married taxpayers filing joint returns, it is important on Schedule SE of Form 1040 to fill in the name and Social Security number of the spouse with the self-employment income. This information is used to establish benefit eligibility.

WHAT CONSTITUTES SELF-EMPLOYMENT INCOME

Individuals who carry on a trade or business as a proprietor or partnership are considered to render services as independent contractors and are, therefore, subject to the self-employment tax. If an individual has two separate self-employment activities, the *net* earnings from each activity are aggregated. However, where a husband and wife file a joint return and both have self-employment income, the self-employment tax must be computed separately.

EXAMPLE I14-11 ▶ Russ and Ruth are married and file a joint return. Russ has $13,000 net earnings from a consulting business and a $4,000 net loss from a retail store that is operated as a sole proprietorship. Ruth has wages of $50,000 from her employer that are subject to FICA taxes. Russ's net earnings from self-employment are $8,312 ($9,000 × 0.9235). No reduction in the self-employment tax base is allowed for Ruth's wages as an employee because Ruth is not self-employed and the tax is computed separately for Russ and Ruth. ◀

ADDITIONAL COMMENT

For some self-employed taxpayers, the amount of self-employment tax exceeds the amount of income tax for the year. For example, a married couple with two children and $17,000 of self-employment income would not owe any income tax, but would have a $2,402 (17,000 × .9235 × 15.3%) self-employment tax liability.

Among the items that constitute earnings that are subject to the self-employment tax are:

▶ Net earnings from a sole proprietorship

▶ Director's fees[13]

▶ Taxable research grants

▶ Distributive share of partnership income plus guaranteed payments from the partnership

The self-employment tax is computed on Schedule SE of Form 1040 (see Appendix B). The rules for computing the self-employment tax are summarized in Topic Review I14-1.

Topic Review I14-1

Self-Employment Tax Summary

▶ The self-employment tax is imposed on net earnings from self-employment over $400.

▶ The tax base for computing the self-employment tax is generally the amount of self-employment income multiplied by 0.9235.

▶ A $94,200 (2006) ceiling applies to the old age, survivors, and disability (OASDI) portion. However, no ceiling applies to the hospital insurance (HI) portion of the tax.

▶ Self-employment tax is computed separately for married individuals filing joint returns.

▶ One-half of the self-employment tax that is imposed is allowed as a business deduction *for* AGI.

▶ The self-employment tax rate is 15.3% which includes 12.4% for the OASDI portion and 2.9% for the hospital insurance (HI) portion.

---

[13] Rev. Rul. 57-246, 1957-1 C.B. 338. It is a factual question whether an officer who also serves as a director is performing services as an employee or as an independent contractor. The courts have recognized that an individual can perform services as a director and also perform employment-related services but the director fees may be recharacterized by the courts if the fees are in reality compensation for services rendered as an employee. See *Peter H. Jacobs*, 1993 RIA T.C. Memo ¶ 93, 570, 66 TCM 1470.

OVERVIEW OF TAX CREDITS

OBJECTIVE 3

Describe the various business and personal tax credits

USE AND IMPORTANCE OF TAX CREDITS

Tax credits are often used by the federal government to implement tax policy objectives. For example, tax credits may help to increase employment, encourage energy conservation and research and experimental activities, encourage certain socially desired activities, and provide tax relief for low-income taxpayers. Tax credits are also used to mitigate the effects of double taxation on income from foreign countries. Thus, tax credits are an important part of the income tax law.

Credits may be classified into two broad categories, **nonrefundable** and **refundable**. Nonrefundable credits may only be used to offset a taxpayer's tax liability. Refundable credits, on the other hand, not only offset a taxpayer's tax liability but if the credits exceed the tax liability, the excess will be paid (refunded) directly to the taxpayer. Topic Review I14-2, on page 14–29, provides a summary of selected tax credits and the rationale for their inclusion in the tax law. Note that most tax credits are nonrefundable. The principal refundable credits include taxes withheld on wages and the earned income credit.

VALUE OF A CREDIT VERSUS A DEDUCTION

Tax credits are extremely valuable for taxpayers as they reduce the tax liability on a dollar-for-dollar basis. This is in contrast to a tax deduction which reduces taxable income and the value of a tax deduction is limited by the taxpayer's marginal tax rate. Thus, tax deductions are more valuable to high-income taxpayers than lower-income taxpayers because their marginal tax rate is higher. Tax credits, however, benefit all taxpayers in the same amount regardless of their marginal tax rate.

EXAMPLE I14-12 ▶

Tasha and Sean are both single taxpayers and each have an $800 expenditure that qualifies for either a tax deduction or a 20% credit. Tasha is in the 15% marginal tax bracket while Sean is in the 33% marginal tax bracket. If the $800 is claimed as a tax deduction, Tasha would receive a tax benefit of $120 ($800 × 15%) whereas Sean would receive a tax benefit of $264 ($800 × 33%). Thus, higher income taxpayers realize greater benefits from the same amount of deduction because of the progressive nature of the federal income tax system. Conversely, if the credit is claimed, both Tasha and Sean would benefit equally as the $160 credit ($800 × 20%) would reduce each taxpayer's tax liability on a dollar-for-dollar basis. Thus, tax credits provide the same benefit to taxpayers regardless of the applicable marginal tax bracket. In this case, Tasha would benefit more from the credit while Sean would prefer the tax deduction. ◀

CLASSIFICATION OF CREDITS

ADDITIONAL COMMENT

The total amount of tax credits claimed by individual taxpayers has increased significantly over the past few years. Much of this increase can be attributed to the recently adopted child tax credit.

As mentioned earlier, credits may be classified into two general categories, refundable and nonrefundable credits. Table I14-1 lists and further classifies the various types of major credits available under the tax law. The reason why it is important to properly classify the credits is that limitations are imposed on credits depending on the classification.

PERSONAL TAX CREDITS

As a result of tax legislation in the last few years, the number of personal tax credits for individual taxpayers has increased significantly. Nonrefundable personal credits are allowed as an offset against both an individual's regular tax liability and AMT.[14] Most of the personal tax credits have been enacted for social welfare rather than economic reasons. The more important personal tax credits are discussed below.

---

[14] Sec. 26. See detailed discussion below on limitation on nonrefundable personal credits.

▼ **TABLE I14-1**
CLASSIFICATION OF MAJOR TAX CREDITS

NONREFUNDABLE CREDITS

Personal Credits
▶ Child and dependent care credit—Sec. 21
▶ Credit for the elderly and disabled—Sec. 22
▶ Adoption credit—Sec. 23
▶ Child tax credit—Sec. 24
▶ Residential mortgage credit—Sec. 25
▶ HOPE scholarship credit—Sec. 25A
▶ Lifetime learning credit—Sec. 25A
▶ Qualified retirement savings contributions credit—Sec. 25B
▶ Residential energy property credit—Sec. 25C
▶ Residential energy efficient property credit—Sec. 25D

Miscellaneous Credits
▶ Foreign tax credit—Sec. 27
▶ Nonconventional source fuel credit—Sec. 29
▶ Credit for qualified electric vehicles—Sec. 30
▶ Qualified hybrid and lean burn motor vehicle credit—Sec. 30B

General Business Credits
▶ Manufacturer's credit for energy efficient appliances—Sec. 38
▶ Research credit—Sec. 41
▶ Low income housing credit—Sec. 42
▶ Disabled access credit—Sec. 44
▶ Rehabilitation credit—Sec. 47
▶ Business energy credit—Sec. 48
▶ Solar and geothermal tax credit—Sec. 48
▶ Work opportunity credit—Sec. 51
▶ Welfare-to-work credit—Sec. 51A
▶ Empowerment zone employment credit—Sec. 1396

REFUNDABLE CREDITS

▶ Tax withheld on wages—Sec. 31
▶ Earned income credit—Sec. 32

CHILD TAX CREDIT

Taxpayers are allowed a nonrefundable credit of $1,000 for each qualifying child under the age of 17.[15] The child tax credit was increased from $600 to $1,000 for 2003 and later years. The credit begins to phaseout when married taxpayers who file a joint return have their modified AGI[16] reach $110,000 ($75,000 for single taxpayers and $55,000 for married taxpayers filing separately) at a rate of $50 for each $1,000, or fraction thereof, that modified AGI exceeds the above thresholds.

---

[15] Sec. 24(a).
[16] Modified AGI means AGI increased by any amount excluded from gross income under Secs. 911, 931, or 933. Sec. 911, 931, and 933 are special exclusions in the international tax area.

A qualifying child must be a dependent of the taxpayer and must be the taxpayer's son or daughter (or a descendent of either), a stepchild, an eligible foster child or the taxpayer's sibling or their descendants. A qualifying child must share the same principal place of abode as the taxpayer. The child must not have attained the age of 17 by the end of the taxable year. Further, the child must also be a U.S. citizen, a U.S. national, or a resident of the U.S.[17]

In general, the child tax credit is limited to the taxpayer's income tax liability. However, the child tax credit is now refundable to the extent of the greater of: (1) 15% of the taxpayer's earned income in excess of $11,300 (2006), or (2) if the taxpayer has three or more qualifying children, the excess of his social security taxes for the tax year over his earned income credit for the year.

CHILD AND DEPENDENT CARE CREDIT

ADDITIONAL COMMENT

The dollar amount of the child and dependent care credit amounted to $2.5 billion in 1996.

The child and dependent care credit provides relief for taxpayers who incur child and dependent care expenses because of employment activities.[18] To qualify for the credit, which ranges from 20% to 35% of eligible expenses, an individual must meet two requirements: (1) eligible child or dependent care expenses must be incurred to enable the taxpayer to be gainfully employed, and (2) the dependent must be under age 13 or an incapacitated dependent or spouse and must live with the taxpayer for more than one-half of the year.[19]

EXAMPLE I14-13 ▶

Tim and Tina are married and have two children under age 13. They incur child care expenses (e.g., a housekeeper and nurse) to enable both Tim and Tina to work on a full-time basis. The child care expenditures are eligible for the child and dependent care credit because Tim and Tina incurred the child care expenses to enable the taxpayers to be gainfully employed. Alternatively, if Tina was not employed but incurred the child care expenses to play tennis and other social activities, the expenditures would not be eligible for the child and dependent care credit. ◀

ADDITIONAL COMMENT

Qualifying child care expenses include amounts spent to send a child to nursery school or kindergarten, but not first grade.

QUALIFYING EMPLOYMENT-RELATED EXPENSES. Eligible expenses include amounts spent for housekeeping, nursing, cooking, baby-sitting, etc. in the taxpayer's home, but do not include expenses for a chauffeur or gardener. If the child or dependent care is provided outside the home by a dependent care facility (e.g., a day care facility), the amounts generally will qualify only if the dependent care facility provides care for more than six individuals. Employment-related expenses do not include amounts paid for services outside of the taxpayer's household at a camp where the qualifying individual stays overnight. In addition, amounts paid for services outside of the taxpayer's household (e.g., adult day care) that are spent for the care of an incapacitated dependent or spouse qualify only if the individual lives in the taxpayer's home for at least eight hours a day.

EXAMPLE I14-14 ▶

Tony is divorced and has two children under age 13. He is employed and incurs child care expenses at a preschool nursery for one of the children. He also has a live-in nanny who provides housekeeping services and a gardener to care for his yard. The expenditures for the preschool nursery and the live-in nanny qualify because these services constitute eligible household services and care of a qualifying individual. However, the payments to the gardener do not constitute qualifying household services. ◀

The following special rules also apply:

▶ The maximum amount of child and dependent care expenses that qualify for the credit is $3,000 for one qualifying individual and $6,000 for two or more individuals.[20] These ceilings are reduced by the aggregate amount excludable from gross income due to the exclusion under Sec. 129 relating to dependent care assistance programs. No carryover is permitted for expenses that exceed these maximum amounts.

---

[17] Sec. 24(c).
[18] Sec. 21. The complete title of this credit is *Expenses for Household and Dependent Care Services Necessary for Gainful Employment.*
[19] Secs. 21(b)(1) and (e)(1). The old rule that the taxpayer must maintain the household in which the qualifying child lives was replaced by the simpler rule

that the child must live with the taxpayer for more than half the year in the Working Families Tax Relief Act of 2004. Married individuals must generally file a joint return to obtain the credit.
[20] Prior to 2003, the maximum amounts were $2,400 and $4,800, respectively.

► Payments to a relative qualify unless the relative is a dependent or a child (under age 19) of the taxpayer.[21]

► The credit is only allowed if the child care expense permits the taxpayer to be gainfully employed. Gratuitous services performed by the taxpayer for charitable organizations were held to not be considered gainful employment.[22]

► The maximum child and dependent care expenses cannot exceed the individual's earned income. For married individuals, the limitation is applied to the earned income of the spouse with the smaller amount of earned income.

► The credit will not be allowed unless the qualifying individual's Social Security number is reported on the return on which the credit is claimed.

► A spouse who either is a full-time student or is incapacitated is deemed to have earned income of $250 per month.[23] The amount is increased to $500 per month if there are two or more qualifying individuals (e.g., children under age 13) in the household.

EXAMPLE I14-15 ►

KEY POINT

The percentage used to calculate the credit varies from 20% to 35% depending on the taxpayer's AGI.

Troy and Tracy are married and in 2006 incur qualifying child care expenses of $4,000 to take care of their two children, ages 1 and 3. Tracy's earned income is $20,000, and Troy's earned income from a part-time job is $3,000. The limitation on qualifying child care expenses is $3,000. Although the overall limitation of $6,000 is not exceeded, the earned income limitation applies because Troy's earned income ($3,000) is less than the child care expenses ($4,000). Therefore, the amount of eligible child care expenses is limited to $3,000. ◄

COMPUTATION OF THE CREDIT RATE AND AMOUNT. The credit is 35% of the qualifying expenses (not to exceed the ceiling limitations of $3,000 or $6,000).[24] However, the credit rate is reduced by one percentage point for each $2,000 (or fraction thereof) of adjusted gross income (AGI) in excess of $15,000 but goes no lower than 20%. The minimum credit (20%) is applied once a taxpayer's AGI exceeds $43,000.

EXAMPLE I14-16 ►

Vincent and Vicki are married, file a joint return in 2006, and have three children under age 13. Vincent and Vicki's employment-related earnings are $25,000 and $10,000, respectively. Including all sources of income, their AGI is $36,000. They incur $8,000 of child care expenses during the current year. The eligible child care expenses are limited to $6,000, because Vincent and Vicki have more than one child who is qualified and this limitation is less than Vicki's earned income or the actual expenses incurred. Because their AGI is greater than $15,000, the credit rate is subject to the reduction. For 2006, the credit rate would be reduced from 35% to 24%, computed as follows:

Adjusted gross income (AGI)	$36,000
Base amount	(15,000)
Excess	21,000
Divided by $2,000 ($21,000/$2,000)	10.5
Rounded up to	11
Applicable credit (35% − 11%)	24%

Therefore, Vincent and Vicki's child and dependent care credit for the year is $1,440 ($6,000 × 24%). ◄

DEPENDENT CARE ASSISTANCE. An employee may exclude amounts up to $5,000 from gross income for dependent care assistance payments made by the individual's employer and provided to the employee.[25] The exclusion amount is limited to the earned income of the employee (or in the case of a married taxpayer, the lesser of the employee's earned income or the earned income of the spouse). To avoid a double benefit, the otherwise eligible expenses for purposes of computing the child and dependent care credit are reduced by the amount of assistance that is excluded from gross income.[26]

[21] Sec. 21(e)(6).
[22] Rev. Rul. 73-597, 1973-2 CB 69.
[23] Sec. 21(d)(2). To qualify as a full-time student, the individual must enroll in an educational institution on a full-time basis for at least five calendar months of the year (Reg. Sec. 1.44A-2(b)(3)(B)(ii)).
[24] This percentage was 30% for tax years beginning on or before December 31, 2002.
[25] Sec. 129. (See Chapter I4 for a discussion of the requirements for exclusion.)
[26] Sec. 21(c).

EXAMPLE I14-17 ▶ Assume the same facts as in Example I14-16 except that Vincent was reimbursed $4,000 by his employer under a qualified dependent care assistance program and this amount was excluded from his gross income. Since $4,000 was excluded under a Sec. 129 qualified dependent care assistance program, expenses eligible for the child and dependent care credit must be reduced. Thus, the eligible child care expenses are reduced to $2,000 ($6,000 − $4,000) and the child care credit is $480 (0.24 × $2,000). ◀

TAX CREDIT FOR THE ELDERLY AND DISABLED

ADDITIONAL COMMENT

The tax credit for the elderly or disabled has been declining in recent years and amounted to only $32 million in 2000, down 32% from 1995.

A limited, personal, nonrefundable credit is provided for certain low-income elderly individuals who have attained age 65 before the end of the tax year and individuals who retired because of a permanent and total disability and who receive insubstantial Social Security benefits. Most elderly taxpayers are ineligible for the credit because they receive Social Security benefits in excess of the ceiling limitations that apply to the credit (e.g., an initial amount of $5,000 per year for a single taxpayer) or they have AGI amounts in excess of the limitations, which effectively reduces or eliminates the allowable credit.

The maximum credit is 15% times an initial amount of $5,000 ($7,500 for married individuals filing jointly if both spouses are 65 or older).[27] This initial amount is reduced by:

▶ Social Security, railroad retirement, or Veterans Administration pension or annuity benefits that are excluded from gross income

▶ One-half of AGI in excess of $7,500 for a single individual ($10,000 for married taxpayers filing a joint return).[28] All types of taxable income items are included in AGI (e.g., salaries, taxable pension and taxable Social Security benefits, and investment income).

EXAMPLE I14-18 ▶ Wayne and Tammy are both 67 years old and file a joint return. They have AGI of $11,000 and receive nontaxable Social Security payments of $3,000 during the current year. Their tax credit for the elderly is computed as follows:

Initial ceiling amount		$7,500
Minus: Nontaxable social security	$3,000	
One-half of AGI in excess of $10,000		
(0.50 × [$11,000 − $10,000])	500	(3,500)
Total credit base		$4,000
Times: Credit percentage		× 0.15
Tax credit		$ 600

The $600 credit is allowed only to the extent that Wayne and Tammy's total personal tax credits do not exceed the actual tax due before credits. ◀

ADOPTION CREDIT

ADDITIONAL COMMENT

The adoption credit is also available for unsuccessful efforts to adopt an eligible child. Qualified adoption expenses are amounts expended for the *principal purpose* of adopting a child. For foreign adoptions, only expenses connected with successful adoptions qualify for the credit.

A nonrefundable credit is allowed for qualified adoption expenses. The amount of the credit in 2006 is limited to a maximum of $10,960 (including a child with special needs) and generally is allowable in the year the adoption is finalized.[29] If adoption expenses are paid *prior* to the year the adoption is finalized, such expenses are not eligible until the year the adoption is finalized. If the adoption expenses are paid during or after the year the adoption is finalized, the credit is allowable in the year the expenses are paid or incurred. Further, there is a phase-out of the credit based on AGI. For taxpayers with AGI in 2006 between $164,410 and $204,410, the credit is ratably phased out and is fully phased out when a taxpayer's AGI reaches $204,410.[30] In the case of the adoption of a child with special needs, $10,960 is allowed as an adoption credit regardless of whether the taxpayer has qualified adoption expenses.

Qualified adoption expenses include reasonable and necessary adoption fees, court costs, attorney fees, and other expenses that are directly related to the legal adoption by the

---

[27] Sec. 22(c)(2). The initial ceiling amount is $5,000 if one spouse filing a joint return is less than age 65 and the limitation is $3,750 for a married individual filing a separate return. Unless married individuals are living apart for the entire year, they must file a joint return in order to obtain the credit.

[28] The AGI ceiling is $5,000 for married individuals filing a separate return. To obtain the credit, however, a separate return can be filed only if both spouses live apart for the entire tax year.

[29] The credit as well as the AGI phaseout amounts are adjusted for inflation each year. In 2005, the credit was $10,630.

[30] For purposes of the phase-out of the credit, AGI must be modified. AGI for this purpose is determined without regard to the exclusions from gross income for foreign earned income under Sec. 911 and after the application of the rules relating to the taxation of Social Security, as well as selected other items. See Sec. 23. In addition, these limits were $159,450 and $199,450 for 2005.

taxpayer of an eligible child. An eligible child is defined as a child who has not reached 18 years old when the adoption takes place or is physically or mentally incapable of self-care.

EXAMPLE I14-19 ▶

Oscar and Betty began adoption proceedings in June 2005 to adopt an infant child. They incurred attorney fees and adoption agency fees in 2005 of $5,000. In 2006, they incurred an additional $7,000 of qualified adoption expenses when the adoption became final. Oscar and Betty's AGI in 2006 is $180,000. The adoption credit is allowable in 2006 in the amount of $6,688, computed as follows:

Total qualified adoption expenses in 2005 and 2006	$12,000
Maximum credit	10,960
Phase-out percentage based on AGI ($15,590*/$40,000)	38.975%
Amount of credit disallowed	4,272
Amount of credit allowed ($10,960 − $4,272)	6,688

Oscar and Betty only can use $10,960 of expenses (maximum) and must claim the expenses in 2006, the year the adoption becomes final. Finally, the adoption is limited based upon the level of their AGI.

*$180,000 − $164,410 ◀

HOPE SCHOLARSHIP CREDIT

Two credits are available to assist taxpayers who incur higher education expenses for themselves, their spouses, and dependents. The two credits are the "HOPE scholarship credit" and the "lifetime learning credit."[31] The Hope scholarship credit (HOPE credit) is discussed first, then the lifetime learning credit is discussed.

Taxpayers are allowed up to a $1,650 credit for tuition and related expenses paid during the taxable year for each qualified student. Qualified tuition and related expenses include only tuition and fees required for enrollment and do not include books, room and board, student activity fees, and other expenses unrelated to an individual's academic course of instruction. Below are a number of requirements and limitations that exist for the HOPE credit:

ADDITIONAL COMMENT

In addition to the Hope and Lifetime Learning credits, there have been a plethora of new tax laws that encourage education, including:
(1) a *for* AGI deduction of up to $3,000;
(2) Sec. 529 plans;
(3) Improved student loan interest deduction rules;
(4) Increased limits for Coverdell Education IRAs.

▶ The $1,650 credit is allowed only for a maximum of two years per student and is computed by taking 100% of the first $1,100 ($1,000 in 2005) of tuition and fees *plus* 50% of the second $1,100 ($1,000 in 2005) of tuition and fees. In addition, the HOPE credit may not be claimed in more than two taxable years for any eligible student.

▶ Qualified tuition and related expenses eligible for the HOPE credit are limited to the first two years of postsecondary education. The first two years of postsecondary education is measured at the *beginning* of the taxable year. If a student has not completed the first two years of postsecondary education by the beginning of the taxable year, qualified tuition and related fees are eligible for the HOPE credit. The first two years is determined based on whether the educational institution awards the student two years of academic credit at that institution.

▶ If a taxpayer pays qualified education expenses in one year but the expenses relate to an academic period that begins during January, February, or March of the next taxable year, the academic period is treated as beginning during the taxable year in which the payment is made. Thus, a payment of tuition in December 2005 for the Spring Semester, 2006 (which begins in January 2006) would be eligible for the HOPE credit in 2005.

▶ An eligible student must carry at least one-half of the normal full-time load for the course of study the student is pursuing.

▶ The HOPE credit is not available to any student who has been convicted of a federal or state felony offense for possession or distribution of a controlled substance as of the end of the taxable year for which the credit is claimed.

▶ Qualified tuition and related expenses eligible for the credit must be reduced by amounts received under other sections of the tax law, such as scholarships (Sec. 117),

---

[31] Sec. 25A. Both credits are contained in Sec. 25A, the HOPE credit is specifically described in Sec. 25A(b) while the lifetime learning credit is described in Sec. 25A(c). The various definitions contained in Sec. 25A apply to both credits.

employer-sponsored educational reimbursement plans (Sec. 127), Education IRAs (Sec. 530), or other provisions of the tax law.

▶ The allowable credit (including both the HOPE credit and the lifetime learning credit) is reduced for taxpayers who have modified AGI above certain amounts. The phase-out for taxpayers filing joint returns for 2006 is $90,000 to $110,000 ($45,000 to $55,000 for other taxpayers). The HOPE credit and lifetime learning credit are ratably phased-out for joint filers using the formula below:

$$\text{Sum of HOPE credit and lifetime learning credit} \times \frac{\text{Modified AGI} - \$90,000}{\$20,000}$$

For taxpayers other than joint filers, the $90,000 is replaced with $45,000 and the $20,000 is replaced with $10,000.

It is important to understand that the HOPE credit applies to each student. Thus, parents who have two children in their first two years of college may claim up to a $1,650 credit for each child.

<table>
<tr><td>

ADDITIONAL COMMENT

The education expenses for the HOPE and lifetime learning credits must be incurred at an educational institution that is eligible to participate in Department of Education student aid programs.

</td><td>

LIFETIME LEARNING CREDIT

The lifetime learning credit is computed differently than the HOPE credit and is less restrictive; however, most of the definitions regarding eligible students and qualified expenses are identical with the HOPE credit. The credit is 20% of a maximum of $10,000 per year of qualified tuition and fees paid by the taxpayer for one or more eligible students. However, unlike the HOPE credit, the $10,000 limitation is imposed at the taxpayer level, not on a per student basis. Below are some important requirements for the lifetime learning credit.

▶ The definition of qualified tuition and related expenses are the same as for the HOPE credit above.

▶ The lifetime learning credit is available for an unlimited number of years and may be used for undergraduate, graduate, and professional degree expenses.

▶ The lifetime learning credit and HOPE credit may not be taken in the same tax year with respect to the same student's tuition and related expenses, i.e., no doubling-up is permitted. For example, if Son A's tuition for the academic year is $10,000 and is used to claim $1,650 HOPE credit, none of the $10,000 may be used for the lifetime learning credit with respect to Son A. However, if Son B also has tuition expenses in the same tax year, either the lifetime learning credit or the HOPE credit is allowed for Son B.

▶ The lifetime learning credit may be claimed for any course (degree or nondegree) at a college or university that helps an individual acquire or improve their job skills, such as credit or noncredit courses that qualify as continuing professional education (CPE). Also, the requirement that a student take at least one-half of a full load does not apply to the lifetime learning credit.

</td></tr>
</table>

EXAMPLE I14-20 ▶

Mark and Jane are married, file a joint return, and have three dependent children in college, Ron, Rhonda, and Ray. All three children attend State U. Mark and Jane's modified AGI is $95,000 in 2006, and the classification of each of the three children for each semester is as follows: Ron was a junior during the Spring Semester 2006 and a senior in Fall Semester 2006; Rhonda was a sophomore during the Spring Semester 2006 and a junior in Fall Semester 2006; Ray was in high school until the Fall Semester 2006. Below are the expenses incurred in calendar year 2006 for the three children's college expenses:

		Spring Semester 2006 (Paid in January 2006)	**Fall Semester 2006** (Paid in August 2006)
Ron:	Tuition and fees	$1,500	$1,550
	Books	300	300
	Room and board	3,500	3,700
Rhonda:	Tuition and fees	1,500	1,550
	Books	275	325
	Room and board	4,000	4,200

Ray:	Tuition and fees	1,550
	Books	325
	Room and board	3,700

Mark and Jane are allowed to claim the HOPE credit and the lifetime learning credit for 2006 as follows:

HOPE credit: Only Ray qualifies for the credit because the HOPE credit is limited to the first two years of postsecondary education and can only be claimed in two taxable years for each eligible student. Rhonda does not qualify for the HOPE credit in 2006 because Mark and Jane presumably claimed the HOPE credit for Rhonda in 2004 and 2005. Thus, the tentative HOPE credit is $1,325 for Ray [100%($1,100) + 50%($1,550 − $1,100)]. Only tuition and fees qualify for the HOPE credit; the books and room and board are not qualified education expenses.

Lifetime learning credit: Both Rhonda and Ron qualify for the credit. Rhonda and Ron's tuition and fees total $3,050 each, for a total of $6,100. The tentative lifetime learning credit is $1,220 ($6,100 × 20%). Only tuition and fees qualify for the credit; the books and room and board are not qualified education expenses.

Since Mark and Jane have modified AGI above $90,000, the above credits of $2,545 ($1,325 + $1,220) are partially phased-out as follows:

$$\$2,545 \times \frac{\$95,000 - \$90,000}{\$20,000} = \$636$$

Thus, the total HOPE and lifetime learning credits for 2006 are $1,909 ($2,545 − $636). ◀

RESIDENTIAL ENERGY CREDITS

The Energy Tax Incentives Act of 2005 (2005 Energy Act) enacted into law a wide range of incentives for both individuals and businesses to promote domestic energy production and conservation. Most of these incentives are in the form of tax credits. Two major credits enacted in the 2005 Energy Act for individual taxpayers are (1) the residential energy property credit, and (2) the residential energy efficient property credit. Both of these credits are discussed below.

RESIDENTIAL ENERGY PROPERTY CREDIT. Individuals are allowed a $500 tax credit for nonbusiness energy property, such as residential windows and exterior doors, insulation, heat pumps, furnaces, central air conditioners, and water heaters.[32] The credit is limited to $500 for a lifetime and also contains limitations for specific types of property, such as no more than $200 for windows, and applies to property placed into service after December 31, 2005, and before January 1, 2008.

The credit is the sum of (1) 10% of the cost of *qualified energy efficiency improvements* plus (2) the *residential energy property expenditures* installed during the year at the taxpayer's principal residence. Qualified energy efficiency improvements include insulation materials, exterior windows (including skylights), exterior doors, and metal roofs with special pigmented coatings. These improvements must meet specific energy efficiency requirements, the original use must begin with the taxpayer, and the improvement must be reasonably expected to remain in use for at least five years. Residential energy property includes electric and geothermal heat pumps, central air conditioners, water heaters, and advanced main air circulating fans. This property must also meet minimum energy standards to qualify.

Below are other selected features of the credit:

▶ The taxpayer's basis in the property is reduced by the amount of the credit.

▶ The credit has several additional limitations, including no more than $200 for windows, $50 for an advanced main air circulating fan, and $300 for energy property such as heat pumps, central air conditioners, and water heaters.

▶ If a dwelling unit is owned and occupied by more than one owner, the $500 maximum credit must be allocated between the owners.

---

[32] Sec. 25C.

▶ The cost of labor for installation of residential energy property expenditures is specifically eligible for the credit. However, the new law is silent with respect to labor for qualified energy efficiency improvements. While it seems reasonable to assume that labor costs would qualify, the fact that it is specific for energy property and silent for energy improvements would lead one to assume that labor is not includible for energy improvements. Additional guidance in this area should be forthcoming.

▶ Rental property and vacation homes do not qualify for the credit as they are not the principal residence of the owner.

▶ If less than 80% of the use of the dwelling is for nonbusiness use, then only the percentage of nonbusiness use can be taken into account.

▶ The credit is a nonrefundable personal credit and is limited to the excess of the taxpayer's regular tax liability over the alternative minimum tax liability.

EXAMPLE I14-21 ▶ Tom and Sandra Mireaut are married, file a joint return, and own and live in a home that is their personal residence. In 2006, they install new energy efficient windows in their home at a cost of $3,500 and purchase and install a new replacement energy efficient heat pump at a cost of $2,500. Their residential energy property credit for 2006 is $500 and is computed as follows:

Windows — 10% × $3,500 = $350 but limited to $300	$300
Heat pump — $2,800 but cannot exceed $300	300
Total potential credit	$600

However, the credit is limited to a maximum of $500. No carryforwards are permitted. ◀

RESIDENTIAL ENERGY EFFICIENT PROPERTY CREDIT. For tax years 2006 and 2007 only, a tax credit is allowed for three types of energy efficient property installed on a taxpayer's principal residence:[33]

▶ Solar hot water heaters

▶ Photovoltaic property (property that generates electricity from solar power)

▶ Fuel cell property

The credit is 30% of the cost of eligible property. For the first two types of property above, taxpayers are permitted a maximum credit of $2,000 for each type of property for the taxable year. A taxpayer would have to install $6,667 of qualifying property to earn the maximum credit ($6,667 × 30% = $2,000). For qualified fuel cell property, the credit is 30% of the cost of the property to a maximum of $500 for each 0.5 kilowatt of capacity. There is no limit to the credit for fuel cell property. For example, if a taxpayer installed a 3.0 kW fuel cell system in her home, she would be entitled to a $3,000 ($500 × 3kW/0.5) credit. Other selected features of the credit for credit are:

▶ Labor costs to install the property are included in the qualified cost of the property.

▶ Second homes or vacation homes do not qualify for the credit.

▶ If less than 80% of the use of the dwelling is for nonbusiness use, then only the percentage of nonbusiness use can be taken into account.

▶ The taxpayer's basis in the property is reduced by the amount of the credit.

▶ The credit is not available for use with swimming pools or hot tubs.

▶ The credit is a nonrefundable personal credit and is limited to the excess of the taxpayer's regular tax liability over the alternative minimum tax liability. Credits earned but not used in 2006 can be carried forward to 2007.

QUALIFIED RETIREMENT SAVINGS CONTRIBUTIONS CREDIT

To encourage low and middle income taxpayers to save for retirement, a *temporary* nonrefundable credit for contributions or deferrals to retirement savings plans has been established for tax years beginning after December 31, 2001.[34] This credit is in addition to the

[33] Sec. 25D.

[34] Sec. 25B.

exclusion or deduction from gross income for contributions or deferrals that are otherwise allowable. The credit is scheduled to terminate after December 31, 2006.

The credit is computed by multiplying the amount contributed to a qualified retirement plan by an applicable percentage. The maximum amount to compute the credit for each eligible individual is $2,000 per year. The applicable percentage depends on the amount of the taxpayer's adjusted gross income as shown in the following table:

Adjusted Gross Income						Applicable
Joint Return		Head of Household		All Other		Percentage
Over	Not Over	Over	Not Over	Over	Not Over	
$ 0	$30,000	$ 0	$22,500	$ 0	$15,000	50
30,000	32,500	22,500	24,375	15,000	16,250	20
32,500	50,000	24,375	37,500	16,250	25,000	10
50,000	—	37,500	—	25,000	—	0

The qualified retirement savings contribution amounts for any tax year equals the sum of contributions or deferrals by the taxpayer to specified types of retirement plans, including IRAs (Roth and Traditional), 401(k) plans, 403(b) plans, and certain other plans. These amounts must be reduced for any distributions from such plans.

EXAMPLE I14-22 ▶

Steve is single and has AGI of $16,000 in 2006. During the year, he contributes $2,000 to his Roth IRA. Steve is eligible for the Qualified Retirement Savings Contributions Credit in the amount of $400 ($2,000 × 20%). The credit would be the same if he contributed $2,000 to a traditional IRA. In addition to the $400 credit, Steve also would be permitted to deduct the $2,000 contribution to the traditional IRA on his individual return. ◀

To be eligible for the credit, a taxpayer must be at least 18 years of age as of the close of the tax year, must not be claimed as a dependent on someone else's tax return, and must not be a full-time student as defined in Sec. 152(f)(2) for purposes of the dependency exemption (full-time student for at least 5 calendar months).

LIMITATION ON NONREFUNDABLE PERSONAL CREDITS

Sec. 26 imposes limitations of the amount of nonrefundable personal credits for individual taxpayers (see Table I14-1 for a listing of such credits). For tax years beginning in 2000–2006, nonrefundable personal credits may not exceed (1) the taxpayer's regular tax liability for the taxable year plus (2) the tentative minimum tax for the taxable year.[35] Thus, individual taxpayers may offset both their regular tax liability and AMT liability with nonrefundable personal credits.

MISCELLANEOUS CREDITS

The miscellaneous credits, with the exception of the foreign tax credit, are highly-specialized types of tax credits. For this reason, only the foreign tax credit is discussed in this textbook.

FOREIGN TAX CREDIT

KEY POINT

The foreign tax credit is available only on income, war profits, and excess profits taxes or taxes paid in lieu of such taxes. It is sometimes difficult to determine whether a particular foreign tax falls into the qualifying category.

U.S. citizens, resident aliens, and U.S. corporations are subject to U.S. taxation on their worldwide income.[36] To reduce double taxation, the tax law provides a foreign tax credit for income taxes paid or accrued to a foreign country or a U.S. possession.[37]

---

[35] Allowing taxpayers to reduce AMT with nonrefundable personal credits was extended to 2006.

[36] Certain exceptions are provided by treaty agreements between the United States and foreign countries whereby certain types of foreign-source income may be exempt from taxation in the foreign country or taxed at a reduced tax rate.

[37] Under Sec. 911, U.S. citizens and resident aliens may elect to exclude from gross income up to $80,000 (2002 and thereafter) of foreign-earned income and certain housing cost amounts. The foreign taxes that are attributable to the excluded income cannot be taken as a credit. (See Chapter I4 for a discussion of these exclusions.)

Taxpayers may elect to take a deduction for the taxes paid or accrued in lieu of a foreign tax credit.[38] In general, the foreign tax credit results in a greater tax benefit because (as previously discussed) a credit is fully offset against the tax liability, while a deduction merely reduces taxable income.

ADDITIONAL COMMENT

In 2000, 3.9 million tax returns of individual taxpayers claimed $5.0 billion in foreign tax credits.

Computation of Allowable Credit. The **foreign tax credit** amount equals the lesser of the foreign taxes paid or accrued in the tax year or the portion of the U.S. income tax liability attributable to the income earned in all foreign countries.[39] This limitation, which restricts the claiming of foreign tax credit if the effective foreign tax rate on the foreign earnings exceeds the effective U.S. tax rate on these earnings, may result in double taxation if the unused credit cannot be used as a carryback or carryover (see discussion under the next heading). The foreign tax credit limitation is based on the following formula:

$$\frac{\text{Foreign source taxable income}}{\text{Worldwide taxable income}} \times \frac{\text{U.S. income tax}}{\text{before credits}} = \frac{\text{Foreign tax credit}}{\text{limitation}}$$

EXAMPLE I14-23 ▶ Edison Corporation has $200,000 of U.S. source taxable income and $100,000 of foreign source taxable income from country A. Total worldwide taxable income is $300,000 ($200,000 + $100,000). Country A levies a total of $40,000 in foreign income taxes upon the foreign source taxable income (i.e., a 40% effective tax rate). The U.S. tax before credits is $100,250 on the $300,000 of taxable income. Using the formula given above, the overall foreign tax credit limitation is computed as follows:[40]

$$\frac{\$100,000}{\$300,000} \times \$100,250 = \$33,417$$

Because the foreign tax payments ($40,000) exceed the U.S. tax attributable to the foreign source income ($33,417), the limitation applies. Thus, $6,583 ($40,000 − $33,417) of foreign tax credit cannot be used in the current year. ◀

STOP & THINK *Question:* Since a credit is generally much more valuable than a deduction, under what circumstances would it be more beneficial for a taxpayer to take a deduction for foreign taxes in lieu of the foreign tax credit?

Solution: If a taxpayer has foreign source taxable income from one country and an equal loss from another foreign country, the foreign tax credit limitation is zero because the net foreign source taxable income is zero. Because none of the taxes paid in the foreign country in which taxable income was produced can be claimed as a credit, the taxpayer may choose to deduct them unless the credits are carried back or forward.

Treatment of Unused Credits. Unused foreign tax credits are carried back one year and then forward for ten years to tax years where the limitation is not exceeded (i.e., the foreign tax payment is lower than the U.S. taxes attributable to the foreign source income in the carryback or carryover years). The unused credits are lost if they are not used by the end of the ten-year carryover period.

---

[38] Sec. 164(a)(3).
[39] Sec. 904.
[40] There are two types of income that have a separate foreign tax credit limitation. These types of income are passive income and all other income. See Chapter C16 of *Prentice Hall's Federal Taxation: Corporations, Partnerships, Estates, and Trusts* for a more detailed discussion of these separate limitations.

GENERAL BUSINESS CREDITS

The tax credits commonly available to businesses are grouped into a special credit category called the **general business credit** and are summarized in Table I14-1 on page I14-11. The general business credits are combined for the purpose of computing an overall dollar limitation on their use because these credits are nonrefundable. The general business credit is subject to a limitation based upon the taxpayer's tax liability. This limitation is discussed in more detail later in this chapter. If the general business credits exceed the limitation they may be carried back one year and carried forward 20 years.[41]

During the carryover years, the unused credits from prior years are first applied (commencing with the earliest carryover year) before the current year credits that are earned are used (i.e., a first-in, first-out [FIFO] method is applied). This method permits the use of credits from the earliest of the carryover years and may prevent such carryovers from expiring.

EXAMPLE I14-24 ▶ Eastern Corporation has unused general business tax credits of $10,000 in 2005 that are carried forward to 2006. Eastern earns $5,000 of additional credits in 2006 and has a $12,000 limitation. The $12,000 of credits that are used consist of the $10,000 carryover from 2005 and $2,000 from 2006. The remaining $3,000 ($5,000 − $2,000) of 2006 credits are carried forward to 2007. ◀

The more important general business credits are discussed below.

TAX CREDIT FOR REHABILITATION EXPENDITURES

Congress provides incentives for the rehabilitation of older industrial and commercial buildings and certified historic structures. A credit for rehabilitation expenditures is available subject to the following special rules and qualification requirements:[42]

▶ The credit is 10% for structures that were originally placed in service before 1936 and 20% for certified historic structures.[43]

▶ The credit applies only to trade or business property and property held for investment that is depreciable. Residential rental property does not qualify unless the building is a certified historic structure.

▶ Rehabilitation includes renovation, restoration, or construction of a building, but not an enlargement or new construction. For buildings other than certified historic structures, a rehabilitation project must meet certain structural tests. At least 75% of the external walls, including at least 50% utilization of external walls, and at least 75% of the building's internal structural framework must remain in place.[44]

▶ For certified historic structures, the total rehabilitation must be certified by the Department of the Interior as being consistant with the historic character of the building.

▶ Straight-line depreciation generally must be used with the applicable Sec. 168 recovery periods with respect to rehabilitation expenditures. The regular MACRS depreciation rules apply to the portion of the property's basis that is not eligible for the credit.

▶ The basis of the property for depreciation is reduced by the full amount of the credit taken.[45]

▶ The rehabilitation expenditures must exceed the greater of the property's adjusted basis or $5,000.

▶ The rehabilitation credit is recaptured at a rate of 20% per year if there is an early disposition of the property.

REAL-WORLD EXAMPLE

Taxpayers incurred substantial rehabilitation expenditures on an old factory building, but the tax credit was not allowed because the taxpayers did not use the straight-line depreciation method. *Frank DeMarco,* 87 T.C. 518 (1986).

---

[41] For tax years prior to 1998, the carryback period was three years and the carryforward period was 15 years.

[42] Sec. 47.

[43] Secs. 47(a)(1) and (2). A certified historic structure must be certified by the Department of the Interior and must be located in a registered historic district or listed in the *National Register.*

[44] Sec. 47(c)(1)(A).

[45] Sec. 50(c)(1).

EXAMPLE I14-25 ▶ During the current year, Ted incurs $40,000 of rehabilitation expenditures in connection with a certified historic structure used in his business. The adjusted basis of the certified historic structure was $38,000 at the time the rehabilitation began. The property qualifies for the rehabilitation credit because

▶ It is used in Ted's trade or business and is depreciable.

▶ The property is a certified historic structure.

▶ The amount of the expenditure exceeds the greater of the property's $38,000 adjusted basis or the $5,000 statutory minimum.

The credit is $8,000 (0.20 × $40,000). The basis of the rehabilitation expenditures for depreciation purposes is reduced by the full amount of the credit to $32,000 ($40,000 − $8,000). If the property is disposed of after one year, $1,600 of the credit (0.20 × $8,000) is earned and $6,400 ($8,000 − $1,600) is recaptured. ◀

BUSINESS ENERGY CREDITS

To encourage energy conservation measures, additional credits are available to businesses that invest in energy-conserving properties (e.g., solar and geothermal property).[46] The business energy credit is 10%. However, the 2005 Energy Act has increased the credit to 30% for solar property, and qualified fuel cell property beginning in tax years ending after December 31, 2005. The construction, reconstruction, or erection of the property must be completed by the taxpayer and its original use must commence with the taxpayer. This credit is part of the general business credit and is subject to the same limitations on deductibility and carryback and carryover rules as other general business credits.

WORK OPPORTUNITY CREDIT

ADDITIONAL COMMENT

The employer must receive or request the certification in writing no later than the employee's first day of work.

A work opportunity tax credit (WOTC) is available on an elective basis and is intended to reduce unemployment for individuals who are considered economically disadvantaged. The WOTC has been allowed to expire several times but has been repeatedly restored by Congress. The current WOTC is scheduled to expire for individuals beginning work after December 31, 2005.[47] This constant reshuffling of effective dates creates considerable uncertainty and complexity for taxpayers. However, Congress presumably wants to allow the credit on a year-by-year basis in order to evaluate its effectiveness in creating employment opportunities for economically disadvantaged individuals.

The WOTC includes the following targeted groups:[48]

(1) Qualified IV-A (Aid to Families with Dependent Children) recipient,
(2) Qualified veteran,
(3) Qualified ex-felon,
(4) High-risk youth,
(5) Vocational rehabilitation referral,
(6) Qualified summer youth employee,
(7) Qualified food stamp recipient, or
(8) Qualified SSI recipient.

The credit is 40% of the first $6,000 of qualified wages paid to employees hired from one or more of the eight targeted groups. The credit imposes a minimum employment period for qualified employees: employment for at least 180 days (20 days for qualified summer youth employee) or completes at least 400 hours of service for the employer (120 hours for a qualified summer youth employee). For employees working fewer than 400 hours, but at least 120 hours, the credit is reduced to 25%. No credit is available for an employee who works less than 120 hours. To qualify for the credit, the employer must obtain a certification from a local jobs service office of a state employment security agency stating that the unemployed individual is a qualified member of a targeted group. Further, an employee is not eligible for the credit if such employee was formerly employed by the employer at any time (i.e., a rehire). A disadvantage associated with the WOTC is that the employer's deduction for wages must be reduced by the amount of the credit.

---

[46] Sec. 48(a)(2).
[47] The Work Opportunity Credit was most recently extended by the *2004 Families Act*.
[48] Sec. 51.

EXAMPLE I14-26 ▶ Jet Corporation hires two individuals in the current year, one a qualified ex-felon and the other a qualified food stamp recipient. Both individuals are properly certified by the state agency. One of the individuals is paid $8,000 of wages during the year, and the second individual is paid $4,000. The amount of wages eligible for the work opportunity credit is $10,000 ($6,000 ceiling limit for the first employee plus $4,000 actual wages paid to the second employee). The credit is $4,000 (40% × $10,000). Jet must reduce its $12,000 deduction for wages paid to the two individuals by the $4,000 amount of the credit in the current year. ◀

The WOTC is one of the items included in the general business credit. Thus, the limitation is based on the taxpayer's tax liability, and the carryback and carryover of excess credits are governed by the Sec. 38 rules.

WELFARE-TO-WORK CREDIT

The welfare-to-work credit was enacted in 1997 to encourage employers to hire individuals who are on welfare.[49] The credit is 35% of the qualified first-year wages plus 50% second-year wages for "long-term family assistance recipients" up to a maximum of $10,000 of wages during the applicable tax years. Thus, the maximum credits are $3,500 for the first year and $5,000 for the second year. First- and second-year wages refer to the periods beginning with the date employment begins. This credit is scheduled to expire for employees who begin work for the employer after December 31, 2006.[50]

Long-term family assistance recipients generally include members of a family that has been receiving family assistance for at least the 18-month period ending on the hiring date or no more than two years after a family is no longer eligible for assistance because they have reached the maximum duration for such assistance. If an employer takes the welfare-to-work credit for a recipient, the employer is not permitted to claim the work opportunity credit under Sec. 51 for such recipient.

CREDIT FOR EMPLOYER-PROVIDED CHILD CARE

Adequate and affordable child care for working parents is a major problem in the United States. To create an incentive for small and medium-sized businesses to provide child care for their employees, the employer-provided child care credit was enacted effective for taxable years beginning after December 31, 2001.[51] The credit is the *sum* of the following two amounts:

▶ 25% of qualified child care expenses. These expenses basically are amounts paid to acquire, construct, rehabilitate, expand, and operate a qualified child care facility.

▶ 10% of qualified child care resources and referral expenditures. These are expenses paid or incurred by a taxpayer under a contract to provide child care resource and referral services to employees.

These are several special rules with regard to the credit, including

▶ The total credit amount allowed for any given year cannot exceed $150,000.

▶ Employers claiming this credit are not permitted a double benefit, that is, they cannot claim a deduction for child care expenses and also claim the credit. Therefore, the law requires that any associated expenses that would be otherwise deductible must be reduced by the amount of the credit claimed.

▶ If an employer ceases child care operations or otherwise terminates the child care services, all or part of the credits claimed must be recaptured as an increase in tax. The recapture amount depends on how long the child care services have been provided. For example, if the recapture event occurs within the first three years, 100% of the credits are recaptured. No recapture results if the child care services are provided for more than ten years.

▶ The credit is part of, and subject to the limitations of, the general business credit.

---

[49] Sec. 51A.
[50] The welfare-to-work credit expired on December 31, 2005 but was restored and extended through December 31, 2006.

[51] Sec. 45F.

EXAMPLE I14-27 ▶ Gamechicken, Inc., began a child care facility for its employees during the year. The corporation incurred the following expenses:

Rent on facility	$ 25,000
Leasehold improvements	60,000
Equipment, toys, etc.	18,000
Salaries of child care employees	30,000
Other operating expenses of facility	12,000
Qualified child care referral fees*	8,000
Total expenses	$153,000

*Fees paid to a firm to place children in other facilities.

Gamechicken's credit for the year would be $37,050 [($145,000 × 25%) + ($8,000 × 10%)]. All of the above amounts are also deductible, but would need to be reduced by the amount of the credit. So, the rent, salaries, and operating expenses of $67,000 ($25,000 + $30,000 + $12,000) must be reduced by a total of $16,750 ($67,000 × 25%), the referral fees must be reduced by $800, and the basis of the leasehold improvements and equipment must be reduced by $19,500 ($78,000 × 25%). ◀

DISABLED ACCESS CREDIT

A nonrefundable tax credit is available to eligible small businesses for expenditures incurred to make existing business facilities accessible to disabled individuals. Eligible access expenditures include payments for the purpose of removing architectural, communication, physical, or transportation barriers that prevent a business from being accessible or usable by disabled individuals. Expenditures made in connection with new construction are not eligible for the credit. The disabled access credit is equal to 50% of eligible expenditures that exceed $250 but do not exceed $10,250.[52] Thus, the annual credit limitation is $5,000. The basis of the property is reduced by the allowable credit. An eligible small business is any business that either (1) had gross receipts of $1 million or less in the preceding year or, (2) in the case of a business failing the first test, had no more than 30 full-time employees in the preceding year and makes a timely election to claim the credit.

EXAMPLE I14-28 ▶ Crane Corporation had 14 employees during the preceding tax year and $2 million of gross receipts. During the current year, Crane installed concrete access ramps at a total cost of $14,000. Crane is an eligible small business because the company had 30 or fewer full-time employees during the preceding year even though its gross receipts exceed the threshold amount (i.e., $1 million). Only $10,000 of eligible expenditures qualify for the credit, thereby limiting the credit to $5,000 ($10,000 × 0.50). The depreciable basis of the property is reduced by the credit amount to $9,000 ($14,000 − $5,000). ◀

The disabled access credit is also one of the items included in the general business credit. Thus, the limitation is based on the taxpayer's tax liability, and the carryback and carryover of excess credits are governed by the Sec. 38 rules.

CREDIT FOR INCREASING RESEARCH ACTIVITIES

To encourage businesses to conduct research and experimentation, a credit is allowed under Sec. 41. As the name of the credit denotes, the credit is allowed for *increasing* research activities. In essence, taxpayers compare their qualified research activities to a base amount and the excess is eligible for the credit. The research credit is comprised of two types, an *incremental research credit* and a *basic research credit*.

The research credit is equal to the sum of:

(1) 20% of the excess of qualified research expenses for the taxable year over a base amount, and
(2) 20% of basic research payments made to qualified organizations, such as universities and scientific research organizations, over a qualified organization base period amount.

---

[52] Sec. 44.

INCREMENTAL RESEARCH CREDIT. The first type of credit involves identifying qualified research expenses and computing the base amount. Qualified research expenses are defined in the Treasury Regulations[53] and essentially are internal and external research expenses that are incident to the development or improvement of a product or component. Research conducted after commercial production commences does not qualify for the credit nor do marketing, advertising, or production expenses.

The base amount is computed by multiplying (1) the taxpayer's fixed-base percentage times (2) the average annual gross receipts for the four tax years preceding the credit year. The base amount may not be less than 50% of the qualified research expenses for the year of the credit. The fixed-base percentage for start-up companies generally begins and remains at 3% for five years and then is adjusted annually through a complicated formula that is beyond the scope of this textbook.

EXAMPLE I14-29 ▶ Northern Inc. began operations in 2002 and had the following gross receipts for the period 2002–2005:

2002	$4,500,000
2003	7,000,000
2004	8,000,000
2005	8,500,000

Northern's average annual gross receipts for the four-year period is $7,000,000. Assuming Northern Inc. uses a fixed-base percentage of 3%, the corporation's base amount for 2006 would be $210,000 ($7,000,000 × 3%). ◀

EXAMPLE I14-30 ▶ Using the information in the previous example, if Northern Inc. incurred qualified research expenses of $500,000 in 2006, the corporation's incremental research credit would be $58,000 [($500,000 − $210,000) × 20%]. ◀

ADDITIONAL COMMENT

The basic research credit is clearly focused on scientific and technological research in the United States.

BASIC RESEARCH CREDIT. The second type of research credit is the basic research credit, which is allowed only to certain corporations for basic research payments made in cash to a qualified organization,[54] such as a university. Basic research is defined as any original investigation for the advancement of scientific knowledge *not* having a specific commercial objective.[55] Basic research does not include research conducted outside the United States nor basic research in the social sciences, arts, or humanities. The base amount is a complex calculation that is different than that of the incremental research credit and is referred to as the *qualified organization base period amount*. Any basic research payments that do not exceed this base amount may be treated as qualified research expenses for purposes of the incremental research credit.

EXAMPLE I14-31 ▶ Medical Inc. makes payments of $100,000 to State University for purposes of basic scientific research. If Medical Inc.'s base amount is $60,000, the corporation's basic research credit would be $8,000 [($100,000 − $60,000) × 20%]. The $60,000 not used for the basic research credit would be qualified research expenses for the incremental research credit. ◀

INTERACTION WITH THE RESEARCH DEDUCTION. A business deduction is allowed for research and experimentation expenditures under Sec. 174. This deduction must be reduced by the amount of the research credit.[56]

EXPIRATION OF THE RESEARCH CREDIT. The research tax credit has been extended for 18 months for qualified research expenditures (as defined in Code Section 41(h)(1)(B)) on or before December 31, 2006. The research credit is subject to the limitations of the general business credit and may be carried forward or carried back under the rules for the general business credit.

---

[53] Reg. Sec. 1.41-2.
[54] Sec. 41(e)(2)(A)

[55] Sec. 41(e)(7)(A)
[56] Sec. 280(c)(2)

LIMITATION BASED UPON TAX LIABILITY

As mentioned previously on page I14-19, there is an overall dollar limitation of the general business credit based on the tax liability of the taxpayer. The general business credit may not exceed the *net income tax* minus the greater of the tentative minimum tax or 25% of the *net regular tax liability* above $25,000.[57] Net income tax means the sum of the regular tax liability and the AMT, reduced by the nonrefundable personal credits and the foreign tax credit. The term *net regular tax liability* means the regular tax liability reduced by nonrefundable personal credits and the foreign tax credit. This complicated limitation is demonstrated in the example below.

EXAMPLE I14-32 ▶ Steve's general business tax credit includes a $40,000 research credit and a $10,000 work opportunity credit. Steve's regular tax liability (before credits) is $45,000, and his tentative minimum tax is $10,000 (thus, Steve is not subject to the AMT). Nonrefundable tax credits also include a $1,200 child and dependent care credit (a nonrefundable personal tax credit) and a $1,800 foreign tax credit. Steve's dollar limitation on the general business tax credit is initially limited by the amount of net income tax of $42,000 ($45,000 regular tax minus $3,000 other nonrefundable credits). This amount is reduced by the $10,000 tentative minimum tax because this amount is greater than the net regular tax ceiling of $4,250 [0.25 × ($45,000 regular tax − $3,000 nonrefundable credits − $25,000)]. Thus, the limitation upon the $50,000 of general business tax credits ($40,000 + $10,000) is $32,000 ($42,000 − $10,000). ◀

REFUNDABLE CREDITS

As mentioned earlier, refundable credits not only may offset a taxpayer's income tax liability but, if the refundable credits exceed the taxpayer's tax liability, such excess will be refunded by government to the taxpayer. The principal type of refundable credit is the earned income credit, which is discussed below.

HISTORICAL NOTE

The earned income credit was claimed on 19.4 million tax returns in 2000 and amounted to $32.5 billion. This compares with 19.7 million returns and $29.4 billion in 1996.

EARNED INCOME CREDIT

The earned income credit is refundable and, as such, the earned income credit is a special type of "negative income tax" or welfare benefit for certain low-income families. The credit is based on earned income that includes wages, salaries, tips, and other employee compensation plus net earnings from self-employment and is designed to encourage low-income individuals to become gainfully employed.[58] Earned income does not include any form of employee compensation that is not includible in the taxpayer's income for the year.

ADDITIONAL COMMENT

Under tax law enacted in 2002, kidnapped children will now meet the principal place of abode test. Such children must be presumed by law enforcement authorities to have been kidnapped by someone other than a family member.

ELIGIBILITY RULES. The credit is available to individuals with qualifying children and to certain individuals without children if the earned income and AGI thresholds are met.[59] A qualifying child must be the taxpayer's child, stepchild, foster child, a descendant of the taxpayer's child or stepchild, sibling of the taxpayer, or descendant of the sibling. The child must share the same principal place of abode with the taxpayer for more than one-half of the tax year and the child must be less than age 19 or be a full-time student under age 24 or be permanently and totally disabled. The earned income credit applies to married individuals only if a joint return is filed. Individuals without children are eligible only if the following requirements are met:

▶ The individual's principal place of abode is in the United States for more than one-half of the tax year.

▶ The individual (or spouse if married) is at least age 25 and not more than age 64 at the end of the tax year.

▶ The individual is not a dependent of another taxpayer for the tax year.[60]

---

[57] The limitation discussed above actually must be separated into two parts: (1) all general business credits other than the empowerment zone and New York Liberty Zone employment credits and (2) the empowerment zone and New York Liberty Zone employment credits. Only the first part is covered here. The second part allows these credits to reduce, in whole or part, the AMT. See Sec. 38(c) for details.

[58] See Chapter I2 for a discussion of the relationship between the child tax credit and the earned income credit.
[59] Sec. 32(c).
[60] Sec. 32(c)(1)(A).

A taxpayer will become ineligible for the earned income credit if the taxpayer has excessive investment income. Excessive investment income is defined as disqualified income that exceeds $2,800 for the taxable year 2006 ($2,700 for 2005). Disqualified income includes:

(1) Dividends,
(2) Interest (both taxable and tax-free),
(3) Net rental income, and
(4) Capital gain net income.

COMPUTATION OF THE CREDIT AMOUNT. The earned income credit percentages and the maximum amount of earned income used to compute the credit for 2006 are summarized in Table I14-2. The basic percentage rate and the maximum amount of earned income used to compute the credit depend on the number of qualifying children (from none to two or more) and filing status. The maximum allowable credit is then reduced by a phase-out percentage if the taxpayer's AGI or earned income (whichever is greater) exceeds a specified amount (see Table I14-3).[61]

EXAMPLE I14-33 ▶

Vivian is not married, has one qualifying child, and is eligible for the earned income credit in 2006. In the current year, she has $15,400 of earned income from wages and $3,600 of alimony. The wages are considered earned income; the alimony is not earned income but is included in AGI. Vivian's AGI is $19,000. Using Table I14-2, the tentative credit is $2,747 (0.34 × the first $8,080 of earned income). This amount is reduced by $670 [0.1598 × ($19,000 − $14,810)]. The allowable credit is therefore $2,077 ($2,747 − $670), and this amount is refundable to Vivian.[62] ◀

▼ **TABLE I14-2**
2006 Earned Income Credit Table

Number of Qualifying Children	Basic Percentage	Maximum Amount of Earned Income to Compute Credit	Maximum Tentative Credit
All taxpayers			
No children	7.65%	$ 5,380	$ 412
One child	34.0%	8,080	2,747
Two or more children	40.0%	11,340	4,536

▼ **TABLE I14-3**
2006 Earned Income Credit Phase-Out Table

Number of Qualifying Children	Phase-Out Begins at[a]	Phase-Out Percentage	Phase-Out Ends at
Married filing joint return			
No children	$ 8,740	7.65%	$14,120
One child	16,810	15.98%	34,001
Two or more children	16,810	21.06%	38,348
Other taxpayers			
No children	$ 6,740	7.65%	$12,120
One child	14,810	15.98%	32,001
Two or more children	14,810	21.06%	36,348

[a]Larger of AGI or earned income.

[61] The percentages are adjusted annually for inflation.
[62] Sec. 32(b)(1). $19,000 is used in the formula because AGI of $19,000 is greater than $14,810 of earned income. In years prior to 2002, the phase-out computation used modified AGI. AGI is now used to simplify the earned income credit calculation.

PAYMENT OF TAXES

The IRS collects federal income taxes during the year either through withholding on wages or quarterly estimated tax payments. If the withholdings and estimated taxes are less than the amount of tax computed on the tax return, the taxpayer must pay the balance of the tax due when the tax return is filed. If there has been an overpayment of tax, the taxpayer may either request a refund or choose to apply the overpayment to the following year's quarterly estimated taxes.

Substantial penalties are imposed if an employer fails to withhold federal income tax and pay such amounts to the IRS.[63] In addition, a taxpayer may be subject to a nondeductible penalty upon an underpayment of estimated tax.[64]

WITHHOLDING OF TAXES

An employer must withhold federal income taxes and FICA taxes from an employee's wages. No withholdings are required if an employer-employee relationship does not exist (e.g., an individual who performs services as an independent contractor). Generally, unless a specific exemption is provided under the IRC, withholding is required on all forms of remuneration paid to an employee. Thus, salaries, fees, bonuses, dismissal payments, commissions, vacation pay, and taxable fringe benefits are subject to withholding.[65] Below are some special rules relating to withholding of federal taxes:

▶ *More than one employer during the same year.* Each employer must withhold FICA and federal income taxes without regard to the fact that the employee has more than one employer. This requirement may result in an overwithholding of FICA taxes if the ceiling amount on the OASDI portion of the tax is exceeded. In the event of an overwithholding of FICA taxes, the employee may credit the excess amount as an additional payment of tax on line 66 on page 2 of Form 1040. However, the excess FICA contributions related to the matching employer contributions are not refundable or creditable against the tax liabilities of either employer.

▶ *Exemptions for certain employment activities.* Certain employees such as agricultural laborers, ministers, household employees, newspaper carriers under age 18, and tips of less than $20 per month from an employer are exempt from income tax withholding. Note, however, that the earnings of such individuals are fully taxable and that an employer may be liable for FICA tax payments on these earnings.[66]

▶ *Special rules for supplemental wage payments.* If an employee receives supplemental wage payments (in addition to regular wage payments), the withholding amount is determined under either of two methods:[67]
- Concurrent payments—if the supplemental wages are included in the payment of regular wages, the tax is withheld as if the total was a single wage payment for the payroll period.
- Separate payments—if the supplementary wages are paid separately, the tax withheld is either a flat 25% or by aggregating the supplemental wage payment with wages paid within the same calendar year for the last preceding payroll period or the current payroll period.

Supplemental wages payments include items such as bonuses, commissions, overtime, accumulated sick pay, severance pay, awards, prizes, back pay, and retroactive pay increases.

▶ *Backup withholding.* Backup withholding rules were enacted to prevent abusive noncompliance situations, such as not providing a payor of a dividend with the payee's Social Security number. A 28% withholding rate is required on most types of pay-

---

[63] Sec. 3403. Employers are liable for payment of the full amount of withholdings that must be withheld and paid to the IRS. In addition, responsible individuals (e.g., corporate officers, directors, and consultants) may be held personally liable for payment of the tax. (See *Renate Schiff v. U.S.*, 69 AFTR 2d 92-804, 92-1 USTC ¶50,248 (D.C. NV, 1992), *Ted E. Tsouprake v. U.S.*, 69

AFTR 2d 92-821, 92-1 USTC ¶50,249 (D.C. FL, 1992), and *Ralph M. Guito, Jr. v. U.S.*, 67 AFTR 2d 91-1066, 92-1 USTC ¶ 50,231 (D.C. FL, 1991).
[64] Sec. 6654.
[65] Reg. Sec. 31.3401(a)-1(a)(2).

Topic Review I14-2

Summary of Selected Tax Credits

TAX CREDIT ITEM	RATIONALE
PERSONAL CREDITS	
Child and dependent care credit	To provide equitable relief for parents and other individuals who are employed and who must incur expenses for household and dependent care services
Tax credit for the elderly	To provide tax relief for elderly taxpayers who are not substantially covered by the Social Security system
Adoption credit	To provide relief for taxpayers who incur expenses in the adoption of children
Child tax credit	To reduce the tax burden on families with dependent children.
Residential mortgage interest credit	To encourage qualified first-time home buyers to purchase a principal residence (this credit is not discussed in the text due to its limited applicability)
HOPE scholarship credit and lifetime learning credit	To assist students and families of students with the cost of postsecondary education.
Qualified retirement savings contributions credit	To encourage low- and middle-income taxpayers to save for retirement.
MISCELLANEOUS CREDITS	
Foreign tax credit	To mitigate the effects of double taxation on foreign source income
Qualified electrical vehicles credit[a]	To encourage energy conservation (this credit is not discussed in the text due to its limited applicability)
GENERAL BUSINESS CREDITS	
Rehabilitation expenditure credit[a]	To encourage the rehabilitation of older buildings including certified historic structures
Business energy credits[a]	To encourage energy conservation measures and the use of fuel other than petroleum
Work opportunity credit[a]	To encourage employers to hire unemployed people from disadvantaged groups
Welfare-to-work credit[a]	To encourage employees to hire persons who are on welfare
Credit for employer provided child care	To provide an incentive for small and medium-sized businesses to provide adequate and affordable child care for their employees.
Empowerment zone employment credit[a]	To reduce the level of unemployment in distressed urban and rural areas.
Disabled access credit[a]	To encourage small businesses to provide access for disabled
Credit for increasing research activities[a]	To encourage research and development activities to enhance our technological base
Low-income housing credit[a]	To encourage construction, rehabilitation, and ownership of qualified low-income housing projects (this credit is not discussed in the text due to its limited applicability)
REFUNDABLE CREDITS	
Earned income credit	To provide an incentive for low-income individuals to work.

[a]Part of the general business credit.

ments that are reported on Form 1099 (e.g., interest, dividends, royalties, etc.) where a proper taxpayer identification number is not provided.

▶ *Other special rules.* There are many other special rules on withholding in certain circumstances, such as for fringe benefits, pension and annuity payments, etc.

WITHHOLDING ALLOWANCES AND METHODS. Every employee must file an employee's withholding allowance certificate (Form W-4), which lists the employee's marital status and number of withholding allowances and becomes the basic source of input for the computation of the amount to be withheld. If an employee's circumstances change (e.g., a married taxpayer is divorced or the amount of allowances claimed is reduced), an amended Form W-4 must be filed within 10 days. In general, the employee's Form W-4 is not sent to the IRS unless the number of withholding allowances exceeds 10 or an employee claims an exemption from withholding when his earnings are more than $200 per week.[68] This procedure is intended to prevent employees from avoiding the withholding of income tax on amounts that are otherwise due.

Withholding allowances on Form W-4 may be claimed for the same number of personal and dependency exemptions that will be taken on the employee's tax return for the year. An additional special withholding allowance that reflects the standard deduction may be claimed by a taxpayer who has one job or, if married, has a spouse who is unemployed.[69] Additional withholding allowances may be claimed if an individual who has deductions, losses, or credits from a wide variety of sources, including itemized deductions, alimony payments, moving expenses, and losses from a trade or business, rental property, or a farm. Tables and a worksheet are provided to compute the amount of the additional withholding allowances.[70]

EXAMPLE I14-34 ▶ Sam and Sally are married and have three dependent children. They file a joint return. Sally is not employed, and Sam does not claim additional withholding allowances for unusually large deductions or tax credits. Sam may claim six allowances (two personal exemptions [for Sam and Sally] plus three dependency exemptions plus one special withholding allowance to reflect the standard deduction). The special allowance is available because Sally is not employed and Sam has only one job. ◀

STOP & THINK

Question: Many taxpayers believe that they must claim the same number of withholding allowances for withholding purposes as the number of personal exemptions on their income tax return. Why is this not correct?

Solution: While the starting point for determining withholding allowances is the taxpayer's marital status and number of personal exemptions, taxpayers are allowed to claim more or less withholding allowances based on their individual situations. According to the IRS, taxpayers may claim additional withholding allowances for two principal reasons: (1) a taxpayer has high deductions, losses, or credits; or (2) an unmarried taxpayer qualifies for head of household filing status. The withholding tables are constructed by assuming that the taxpayer's qualifying deductions will be equal to the standard deduction. Therefore, if a taxpayer has much higher itemized deductions than the standard deduction, the withholding tables may prescribe too much tax to be withheld and the taxpayer would have a large refund at the end of the year. To alleviate this situation, taxpayers are allowed to claim additional withholding allowances so as to prevent a large overpayment. Similarly, the withholding tables only have two categories of marital status, single or married. Thus, if an unmarried taxpayer qualifies for the head of household status, the "single" withholding tables may cause over-withholding of tax.

COMPUTATION OF FEDERAL INCOME TAX WITHHELD. The computation of the amount to be withheld is made by using wage bracket tables or by an optional percentage method of withholding. Both methods produce approximately the same results. Wage bracket tables are available for daily, weekly, biweekly, and monthly payroll periods. Separate tables are used for single (including heads-of-household) and married individuals. Partial wage bracket tables for married and single persons using a monthly payroll period for wages are located in the 2006 Tax Tables and Rate Schedules on page T-16.

---

[66] Reg. Sec. 31.3401(a)(10)-1(a). An employer is liable for FICA tax payments for domestic servants if $1,400 or more is paid to an individual in any calendar year.
[67] Reg. Sec. 31.3402(g)-1(a).
[68] Reg. Sec. 31.3402(f)(2)-1.

[69] Sec. 3402(f)(1)(E).
[70] Married taxpayers who are both employed may allocate withholding allowances as they see fit as long as the same allowance is not claimed more than once.

EXAMPLE I14-35 ▶ Henry is married and claims four withholding allowances. His monthly salary is $3,000. The federal income tax withheld per month for 2006 using the wage bracket table on page T-16 is $126. ◀

ESTIMATED TAX PAYMENTS

ADDITIONAL COMMENT

The IRS does not mail reminder statements for the required quarterly estimated payments.

Certain types of income are not subject to withholding (e.g., investment income, rents, income from self-employment, and capital gains). Taxpayers who earn this type of income must make quarterly estimated tax payments.

The purpose of the estimated tax system is to ensure that all taxpayers have paid enough tax by the end of the tax year to cover most of their tax liability. Thus, estimated tax payments may also be required if insufficient tax is being withheld from an individual's salary, pension, or other income (although many taxpayers prefer to file an amended Form W-4 instead and request additional withholding amounts or reduce the number of withholding allowances). The amount of estimated tax is the taxpayer's tax liability (including self-employment tax and alternative minimum tax) reduced by withholdings, tax credits, and any excess FICA amounts.[71]

ADDITIONAL COMMENT

The comedian, Red Skelton, on the IRS: "I get even with them. I send in an estimated tax form, but I don't sign it. If I've got to guess what I'm making, let them guess who's making it."

REQUIRED ESTIMATED TAX PAYMENTS. For calendar-year individuals, required quarterly payments are due by April 15, June 15, September 15 of the current year, and January 15 of the following year. The estimated tax payments must be the lesser of the following amounts to avoid the imposition of a penalty[72] on the underpaid amount:

▶ 90% of the tax liability shown on the return for the current year;

▶ 100% of the tax liability shown on the return for the prior year if the taxpayer's AGI for such prior year was $150,000 or less. If the taxpayer AGI is greater than $150,000, no penalty will be imposed if the taxpayer pays estimated tax payments in the current year equal to 110% of the preceding year's income tax liability.

▶ 90% of the tax liability shown on the return for the current year computed on an annualized basis.

Further, no penalty is imposed if (1) the estimated tax for the current year is less than $1,000 or (2) the individual had no tax liability for the prior year.

WHAT WOULD YOU DO IN THIS SITUATION?

THE NANNY TAX: DON'T PAY NOW, WORRY LATER

You are a CPA engaged in tax practice, and one of your clients is Mr. Throckmorton D. Princeton IV, J.D. He is a senior partner in the prestigious employment litigation firm of Huey, Dewey and Fooey. Mr. Princeton is known for his ruthless style of litigation services.

Things were really rosy for Mr. Princeton until last week, when there was some speculation in the press about his being appointed to a cabinet-level position by the President. A TV news magazine show looked into Mr. Princeton's domestic worker situation. It appears that Mr. Princeton has long engaged in the practice of hiring part-time workers in his household to clean his house, tend to his gardens, walk his dogs, cook his meals, service his car, and nurse him when he is ill. All told, he used over twenty-five people at one time or another over the past year. These workers were all paid as little as possible, and all were asked to sign a contract with Mr. Princeton that declared that they were to be classified as independent contractors. The total amount paid out to these workers added up to $50,000. No payroll taxes of any kind were paid by Mr. Princeton, although he did file Forms 1099 with the IRS. What tax and ethical issues should be considered?

---

[71] Excess FICA payments will likely occur if an employee has more than one employer during the year and the total FICA payments from all employers exceed in the aggregate the ceiling on FICA taxes.

[72] Sec. 6654.

It should be noted that no penalty is imposed for failure to file quarterly estimated tax payments, even though the IRC includes specific filing requirements. A penalty is imposed only if the taxpayer fails to meet the minimum payment requirements or one of the previously mentioned exceptions does not apply.

EXAMPLE I14-36 ▶ Sarah does not make quarterly estimated tax payments for 2006, even though she has a substantial amount of income not subject to withholding. Her taxable income in 2006 is $140,000. Her actual tax liability (including self-employment taxes and the alternative minimum tax) for 2006 is $40,000. Withholdings from her salary are $30,000. She pays the $10,000 balance due to the IRS with the filing of the 2006 return on April 3, 2007. Sarah's tax liability for 2005 was $28,000. There is no penalty for failure to make the quarterly estimated tax payments because she meets one or more of the exceptions relating to the minimum payment requirement. Although the first exception is not met because her $30,000 of withholdings (plus zero estimated tax payments) is less than 90% of her $40,000 tax liability for 2006 ($30,000 ÷ $40,000 = 75%), she meets the second exception because the $30,000 of withholdings is more than 100% of her $28,000 tax liability for 2005.

EXAMPLE I14-37 ▶ Assume the same facts in Example I14-37 except Sarah's AGI in 2005 was $180,000. Since her AGI exceeded $150,000 in 2005, the second safe harbor amount would be $110% (instead of 100%) of the prior year's tax or $30,800 ($28,000 × 1.10). Because the $30,000 of withholding is less than 110% of her $28,000 tax liability, Sarah would not meet the second exception and would be subject to the underpayment penalty. ◀

Form 2210 (see Appendix B) should be completed and submitted with the tax return if a possible underpayment of tax is indicated. This form is used to determine whether one of the exceptions is applicable and, if not, to compute the amount of the underpayment penalty. The actual computation of the underpayment penalty is not shown here because of the length and complexity of the rules. Topic Review I14-3 summarizes the withholding tax and estimated payment requirements.

Topic Review I14-3

Withholding Taxes and Estimated Payments

WITHHOLDING OF TAXES

	FICA	INCOME TAX
When to withhold	All employee earnings up to $94,200 (in 2006) per employer. No ceiling applies to the 1.45% hospital insurance portion of the tax.	All employee wages, salaries, fees, bonuses, commissions, taxable fringe benefits, and so on.[a]
Amount to withhold	7.65% of FICA wages including 1.45% for the hospital insurance portion of the tax. 1.45% for amounts in excess of $94,200 is withheld from the employee's earnings.	Determined by using withholding tables or the percentage method based on an individual's filing status and number of exemptions.

[a]Exceptions are provided for certain nontaxable fringe benefits.

ESTIMATED TAX PAYMENTS

▶ To avoid an underpayment penalty, the estimated tax payments and withholdings for the year must be equal to or exceed any one of the following:
90% of the tax liability shown on the return for the current year, or 100% of the tax liability shown on the return for the prior year (110% if AGI for the prior year exceeds $150,000), or 90% of the tax liability shown on the return for the current year computed on an annualized basis.

▶ The underpayment penalty is not deductible for income tax purposes.

▶ Form 2210 should be completed and submitted with the tax return if an underpayment is indicated.

Tax Planning Considerations

AVOIDING THE ALTERNATIVE MINIMUM TAX

KEY POINT

The alternative minimum tax can be avoided or its impact lessened by various tax strategies.

Taxpayers with substantial amounts of tax preference items and a corresponding low regular tax liability may be subject to the AMT. These taxpayers need to engage in tax planning in order to minimize or avoid the AMT. Because a liberal exemption is provided for most individuals (i.e., $58,000 for married individuals filing a joint return and $40,250 for single taxpayers and heads-of-households), the timing of certain income and deduction items may result in the full use of the exemption in each year. For example, planning to avoid the AMT may be accomplished by delaying the payment of certain itemized deductions (e.g., state and local taxes) that reduce the regular income tax but do not reduce the AMT. A cash method of accounting taxpayer who defers the payment of state income taxes into the following year triggers an increase in the regular tax for the current year. This increase can eliminate the AMT liability. However, it is necessary to consider the tax effects for both the current and following years because state income taxes are deductible for purposes of the regular tax calculation when the payment is made in the following year. This reduction may affect the AMT calculation in such a year and increase the amount of tax that is owed.

Certain tax-exempt investments generate additional tax preferences for the investor such as interest on private activity bonds. Before such investments are acquired, an investor should determine the impact on his or her AMT.

AVOIDING THE UNDERPAYMENT PENALTY FOR ESTIMATED TAX

Many taxpayers find it difficult to estimate their taxes for the purposes of making quarterly estimated payments and are uncertain whether their withholdings and estimated tax will equal or exceed 90% or more of their actual tax liability for the year. A common planning technique to avoid a possible underpayment tax penalty is to make estimated tax payments and withholdings in an amount that is at least 100% (or 110%[73] if AGI was in excess of $150,000 for the prior year) of the actual tax liability for the prior year, thereby meeting one of the exceptions that prevents the underpayment penalty from being imposed. This technique is commonly referred to as a "safe estimate."

EXAMPLE I14-38 ▶ Yong expects his federal income tax withholdings to be $14,000 for 2006 and estimates that his income tax liability will be $24,000. Yong's actual federal income taxes in 2005 were $20,000. If estimated taxes of at least $6,000 are paid during the year, Yong's estimated taxes plus withholding will be at least 100% of his prior year's tax liability ($14,000 + $6,000 = $20,000) and no underpayment penalty is due despite the fact that there is a $4,000 ($24,000 − $20,000) balance due of the actual tax liability. If Yong's AGI was in excess of $150,000 for 2005, his estimated taxes plus withholding must be at least 110% of his 2005 tax liability or $22,000 (1.10 × $20,000) to avoid the underpayment penalty. Thus, his estimated tax payments must be at least $8,000. ◀

CASH-FLOW CONSIDERATIONS

KEY POINT

A taxpayer should avoid making estimated payments that exceed the actual tax liability because the taxpayer is making an interest-free loan to the IRS. Nevertheless, many taxpayers deliberately have excess amounts withheld from their wages or make excessive estimated payments in order to receive a refund. These taxpayers view this strategy as a forced saving plan.

Assuming that the underpayment penalty can be avoided, it is generally preferable to have an underpayment of tax to the government at the time for filing the return rather than to receive a refund resulting from an overpayment of tax. No interest is paid on a refund if the IRS pays the refund within 45 days from the later of the due date of the return or its filing date.[74] In addition, the IRS has, in effect, received an interest-free loan from the taxpayer during the period such overpayment is made. To avoid an overpayment, a taxpayer may file an amended W-4 form and claim additional withholding allowances if the requirements are met (e.g., the taxpayer has unusually large itemized deductions, tax credits, alimony payments, etc.).

[73] The 110% is applicable for tax years 2003 and thereafter. The percentages were different in earlier years. [74] Sec. 6611(e).

If an individual anticipates that her estimated tax payments and withholdings are insufficient to avoid the underpayment penalty, it may be preferable to increase amounts withheld before the end of the tax year (e.g., amounts withheld in the fourth quarter) to avoid the penalty rather than to increase the estimated tax payments.[75] This technique may be advantageous because the penalty is calculated on a quarterly basis, and the withholdings are spread evenly over the year, despite the fact that such increased withholding amounts are paid near the end of the year. The end result is cash-flow savings to the taxpayer. Another way to avoid the underpayment penalty is to accelerate certain deductions (e.g., real estate taxes on a personal residence) by paying such amounts before the end of the current tax year. Additionally, otherwise deductible contributions to an IRA made between the end of the tax year and the due date for the tax return may be treated as a deduction for the prior year, thereby avoiding the underpayment penalty (see Chapter I9).

USE OF GENERAL BUSINESS TAX CREDITS

Business tax credits (e.g., the disabled access credit and the work opportunity credit) are combined for the purpose of computing an overall limitation based on the taxpayer's tax liability. Also, an individual's personal tax credits (e.g., the child and dependent care credit) and the foreign tax credit are deducted from the tax liability before the limitations are applied to the general business tax credit. Similarly, the nonrefundable personal tax credits reduce the tax liability before the foreign tax credit limitation is applied. Therefore, it is necessary to consider the priority and interrelated aspects of these credits to ensure that a particular credit is fully used.

FOREIGN TAX CREDITS AND THE FOREIGN EARNED INCOME EXCLUSION

Individuals who accept foreign job assignments should consider the federal income tax implications because U.S. citizens are subject to U.S. tax on their worldwide income. Assuming that certain requirements and limitations are met, an individual may elect to take either a foreign tax credit or a foreign-earned income exclusion of $80,000 (2004 and future years) with respect to salaries, allowances, and other forms of earned income that are earned while on extended non-U.S. assignments.[76] Any taxes that are paid or accrued with respect to the excluded income are not available as a foreign tax credit. In general, the exclusion is preferable if the effective foreign tax rate is less than the effective U.S. tax rate because the foreign tax credit that can be claimed does not equal the gross U.S. tax owed on the income. If the effective foreign tax rate on the earned income exceeds the effective U.S. tax rate, U.S. taxpayers ordinarily elect not to use the exclusion. Instead, the excess tax credits on earned income are used to offset the U.S. taxes owed on other types of foreign income. Detailed coverage of foreign tax credits and the exclusion is contained in Chapter C16 of the *Prentice Hall's Federal Taxation: Corporations, Partnerships, Estates, and Trusts* text.

COMPLIANCE AND PROCEDURAL CONSIDERATIONS

ALTERNATIVE MINIMUM TAX FILING PROCEDURES

Form 6251 is used by individuals to compute the AMT, and corporations must use Form 4626 (see Appendix B for both forms). Form 6251 must be completed and attached to an individual's income tax return in any of the following situations:

▶ An AMT tax liability actually exists.

▶ The taxpayer has tax credits that are limited by the tentative minimum tax.

---

[75] To completely avoid the underpayment penalty, the tax law generally requires the estimated payments to be made equally on the four installment dates.

[76] Sec. 911(a). The foreign income exclusion requirements are discussed in Chapter I4.

► The AMT base exceeds the exemption amounts and an individual has AMT adjustment or tax preference items.

WITHHOLDING AND ESTIMATED TAX

Taxpayers who have income taxes withheld from wages, pensions, and so on should receive a Form W-2 (or Form 1099-R for pensions) by January 31. These forms should be attached to the tax return to substantiate the amount of the withholdings. If the form is incorrect, the taxpayer should request a corrected form from the payor.

If an individual makes quarterly estimated tax payments, Form 1040A or Form 1040EZ may not be used. Married individuals may make either joint estimated tax payments or separate estimated tax payments. If joint estimated tax payments are made and the married individuals subsequently file separate returns (e.g., in the case of a divorce that is pending or a divorce completed before the end of the year), the joint estimated tax payments are divided in proportion to each spouse's individual tax if no agreement is reached concerning an appropriate division.

EXAMPLE I14-39 ► Allen and Alice are married and make joint estimated tax payments during 2006 of $10,000. Allen and Alice are separated in February 2007 and Alice refuses to file a joint return with Allen for tax year 2006. Allen's tax liability for 2006 on his separate return is $20,000 and Alice's tax liability on her separate return is $5,000. If no agreement is reached concerning the allocation of the joint estimated payments of $10,000, Alice is entitled to claim $2,000 of the estimated tax payments on her return [($5,000 ÷ $25,000) × $10,000]. The remaining $8,000 is apportioned to Allen. ◄

GENERAL BUSINESS TAX CREDITS

The computation of the business energy credit is made on Form 3468. Individuals must transfer the totals to page 2 of Form 1040. Form 3800 must be filed if any other general business credits are claimed.

PERSONAL TAX CREDITS

KEY POINT
The earned income credit is available even in cases where the taxpayer has no tax liability. The refund of taxes not even paid or incurred is often called a negative income tax.

Personal tax credits are reported on page 2 of Form 1040. These credits are deducted from the taxpayer's tax liability before other credits. The credits section on page 2 of Form 1040 limits the deduction for personal tax credits to the amount of the tax due. Form 2441 (see Appendix B) must be filed to claim the child and dependent care credit. Taxpayers who claim the child and dependent care credit must also include the care provider's name, address, and taxpayer identification number on their tax return. If the caregiver will not provide the required information, the taxpayer has the option to supply the name and address of the caregiver on Form 2441 and attach a statement explaining that the caregiver has refused to provide his or her taxpayer identification number (TIN). Schedule R of Form 1040 (see Appendix B) is filed to claim the credit for the elderly. An elderly individual may elect to have the IRS compute the tax and the amount of the tax credit.[77]

The earned income credit is refundable to an individual even if no tax is owed. The IRS will automatically compute the credit amount.[78] However, tax tables to assist in the process are included in the IRS instructions to Forms 1040 and 1040A. Schedule EIC of Form 1040 (see Appendix B) is used to compute the credit if Form 1040 is used. If an individual expects to be eligible for the earned income credit, he or she can obtain advance payments of the credit amount by filing Form W-5 (Earned Income Credit Advance Payment Certificate) with his or her employer, who will increase the employee's pay by the amount of the credit. Individuals who receive advance payments must file Form 1040 or Form 1040A to obtain the credit even if they are not required to file a tax return. Taxpayers who are eligible for the earned income credit cannot use Form 1040EZ.

The foreign tax credit for individuals is computed on Form 1116 (see Appendix B). The foreign tax credit amount so determined is entered on page 2 of Form 1040.

[77] Sec. 6014. See Form 1040 instructions for more reporting details.
[78] Sec. 6695(g) requires preparers to meet due diligence requirements with respect to the earned income credit (EIC). If the EIC is incorrectly computed or overlooked, the *preparer* could be subject to a $100 penalty.

PROBLEM MATERIALS

DISCUSSION QUESTIONS

I14-1 Why are most taxpayers not subject to the alternative minimum tax (AMT)?

I14-2 Does the AMT apply if an individual's tax liability as computed under the AMT rules is less than his or her regular tax amount?

I14-3 Which of the following are tax preference items for purposes of computing the individual AMT?
a. Net long-term capital gain
b. Excess depreciation for real property placed in service before 1987
c. Straight-line depreciation on residential real estate acquired in 1992
d. Appreciated element for charitable contributions of capital gain real property

I14-4 Which of the following are individual AMT adjustments (more than one answer may be correct)?
a. Itemized deductions that are allowed for regular tax purposes but not allowed in computing AMTI.
b. Excess of MACRS depreciation over depreciation computed under the alternative depreciation system for real property placed in service after 1986 and before 1999.
c. Excess of MACRS depreciation over depreciation computed under the alternative depreciation system for personal property placed in service after 1986
d. Tax-exempt interest earned on State of Michigan general revenue bonds.

I14-5 Which of the following itemized deductions are deductible when computing the alternative minimum tax for individuals (more than one answer may be correct)?
a. Charitable contributions
b. Mortgage interest on a personal residence
c. State and local income taxes
d. Interest related to an investment in undeveloped land where the individual has no investment income
e. Medical expenses amounting to 9% of AGI

I14-6 Why are most individuals not subject to the self-employment tax?

I14-7 Tony, who is single and 58 years old, is considering early retirement from his salaried job. He currently has $70,000 salary and also earns $50,000 of profits from a consulting business. What advice would you give Tony relative to the need to make Social Security tax payments if he retires and continues to be actively engaged as a consultant during his retirement?

I14-8 Theresa is a college professor who wants to work for a consulting firm during the summer. She will be working on special projects relating to professional development programs. What advantages might accrue to the consulting firm if the engagement is set up as a consulting arrangement rather than an employment contract?

I14-9 Ted and Tina, a married couple, both have self-employment income and file a joint return in 2006. Ted has self-employment income of $20,000 and receives a $30,000 salary from his employer. Tina has no salary and self-employment income from a sole proprietorship of $10,000.
a. How much self-employment tax is due for Ted and Tina on a joint return?
b. How much, if any, of the self-employment tax payments may be deducted on Ted and Tina's income tax return?

I14-10 Discuss the underlying rationale for the following tax credit items:
a. Foreign tax credit
b. Research credit
c. Business energy credit
d. Work opportunity credit
e. Child and dependent care credit
f. Earned income credit
g. HOPE scholarship credit
h. Disabled access credit
i. Empowerment Zone employment credit
j. Adoption credit

I14-11 If Congress is considering a tax credit or deduction as an incentive to encourage certain activities, is a $40 tax credit more valuable than a $200 tax deduction for a taxpayer with a 15% marginal rate? a 25% marginal rate?

I14-12 What are the more significant tax credit items included in the computation of the general business tax credit?

I14-13 Discuss the limitations that have been imposed on the claiming of the general business tax credit including the following:
a. Overall ceiling limitation based on the tax liability
b. Priority of general business and personal credits
c. Carryback and carryover of unused credits (including the application of the FIFO method)

I14-14 Wayne, a married taxpayer who files a joint return, is considering a foreign assignment for two years. He will earn approximately $90,000 in the foreign country and will be eligible for either the foreign tax credit or the earned income exclusion. The average tax rate on Wayne's earnings if fully taxable under U.S. law would be 30%. The average tax rate for the foreign salary is 20% under the foreign country's laws.

a. Discuss in general terms the computation of the foreign tax credit and its limitation.

b. Would Wayne be better off electing the foreign tax credit or the earned income exclusion? Explain.

I14-15 King Corporation is expanding its business and is planning to hire four additional employees at an annual labor cost of $12,000 each. What will the tax consequences be if King hires employees who are eligible for the work opportunity tax credit?

I14-16 Queen Corporation has been in business since 1989. During the preceding year the company had 25 full-time employees and gross receipts of $8,000,000. During the current year Queen spent $20,000 to install access ramps for disabled individuals. Is Queen Corporation eligible for the disabled access credit? If so, what is the credit amount and the basis reduction (if any) for the depreciable property?

I14-17 Discuss the special tax rules that apply to the tax credit for rehabilitation expenditures including the following:
a. Types of eligible expenditures
b. Applicable tax credit rates
c. Restrictions on depreciation methods
d. Calculation of basis for expenditures
e. Potential recapture of the credit

I14-18 What types of business property qualify for the business energy credit?

I14-19 What is the underlying reason for enactment of most of the personal tax credits?

I14-20 Discuss the difference between a refundable tax credit and a nonrefundable tax credit. Give at least one example of each type of credit.

I14-21 If an individual is not employed and has no earned income, is it possible to receive a child and dependent care credit for otherwise qualifying child and dependent care expenses? Explain.

I14-22 Discuss the major differences between the HOPE scholarship credit and the lifetime learning credit. Include in your discussion the type of taxpayers that would likely qualify for each of the credits.

I14-23 What is the maximum child and dependent care credit available to an individual who has $8,000 of qualifying child care expenses and two or more qualifying children or incapacitated dependents?

I14-24 Vivian is a single taxpayer with two children who qualify for the child and dependent care credit. She incurred $7,000 of qualifying child care expenses during the current year. She also received $4,000 in reimbursements from her employer from a qualified employee dependent care assistance program. What is the maximum child and dependent care credit available to Vivian if her AGI is $24,500?

I14-25 The adoption credit is intended to assist taxpayers with the financial burden of adopting children.

a. Discuss how the credit is computed.

b. Why did Congress impose a phase-out of the credit for taxpayers based on AGI?

I14-26 Alice is a single mother, 37 years old, and has two qualifying children, ages 3 and 6. She receives $3,600 alimony and earns $18,000 in wages resulting in $21,600 of AGI in 2006. Is Alice eligible for the earned income credit? If so, is it possible for her to receive advance payments of the credit amounts rather than receiving a tax refund when the tax return is filed?

I14-27 Why are most elderly people unable to qualify for the tax credit for the elderly?

I14-28 If an employer fails to withhold federal income taxes and FICA taxes on wages or fails to make payment to the IRS, what adverse tax consequences may result? May corporate officers or other corporate officials be held responsible for the underpayment?

I14-29 Taxpayers are permitted to contribute money into qualified retirement plans and receive very favorable tax benefits. Now Congress has provided further incentives to contribute money into such plans by enacting the Qualified Retirement Savings Contributions Credit.
a. Why did Congress enact this credit when such contributions already receive favorable tax treatment?
b. Briefly describe how the credit is computed.

I14-30 The credit for employer-provided child care is comprised of two major components, a credit for qualified child care expenses and a credit for qualified child care resources and referral expenditures.
a. Discuss each of the two components. What type of expenses are included in each component?
b. The two components are added together to compute the credit for employer-provided child care. Discuss the rates for each component, the limitation for the credit, and the tax result if the employer ceases to offer child care operations within the first three years after claiming the credit.

I14-31 A credit is allowed to encourage businesses to conduct research and experimentation. One component of the research credit is the so-called *incremental research credit*. Explain the concept that the credit is allowed for *increasing* research activities.

I14-32 Although Virginia is entitled to five personal and dependency exemptions, she claims only one withholding allowance on Form W-4.
a. Is it permissible to claim fewer allowances than an individual is entitled to?
b. Why would an individual claim fewer allowances?
c. Is it possible for Virginia to claim more than five withholding allowances?

I14-33 Mario is a college student who had no income tax liability in the prior year and expects to have no tax liability for the current year.
  a. What steps should Mario take to avoid having amounts being withheld from his summer employment wages?
  b. What are the cash-flow implications to Mario if the employer withholds federal income taxes?

I14-34 What is backup withholding? What is its purpose?

I14-35 In March 2006, Vincent anticipates that his actual tax liability for the 2006 tax year will be $12,000 and that the federal income taxes withheld from his salary will be $9,000. Thus, when he files his 2006 income tax return in 2007, he will have a $3,000 balance due. His actual federal income tax liability for 2005 was $8,000 and his AGI in 2005 was less than $150,000.
  a. Is Vincent required to make estimated tax payments in 2006?
  b. If no estimated tax payments are made, will Vincent be subject to an underpayment penalty if the actual tax liability for the 2006 tax year is $12,000? Why or why not?
  c. Will Vincent be subject to an underpayment penalty if his actual tax liability for 2006 is instead $25,000? Why?

I14-36 What tax planning strategy can you suggest to avoid the penalty for underpayment of estimated tax for an individual who has increasing levels of income each year and is uncertain regarding the amount of his or her estimated taxable income for any given year?

I14-37 From a cash-flow perspective, why is it generally preferable to have an underpayment of tax (assuming there is no underpayment penalty imposed) rather than an overpayment of tax?

I14-38 Why do many taxpayers intentionally overpay their tax through withholdings so as to obtain a tax refund?

ISSUE IDENTIFICATION QUESTIONS

I14-39 Daryl is an executive who has an annual salary of $120,000. He is considering early retirement so that he can pursue a career as a management consultant. Daryl estimates that he could earn approximately $80,000 annually from his consulting business. What tax issues should Daryl consider?

I14-40 Jennifer recently received a check for $30,000 and securities with an FMV of $200,000 from her former husband pursuant to a divorce. The $30,000 represents alimony and the securities were transferred pursuant to the property settlement. The property settlement is nontaxable to Jennifer. Assuming the alimony is taxable and no income taxes are being withheld, what tax issues should Jennifer consider?

I14-41 Coastal Corporation is planning an expansion of its production facilities and is considering whether to hire additional employees from economically disadvantaged groups so as to be able to avail itself of the targeted jobs credit. The company plant is not located in an empowerment zone. New employees are paid approximately $18,000 per year. If economically disadvantaged employees are hired, additional job training expenses of $5,000 per employee will be required. What tax issues should Coastal consider with regard to the hiring and training of its new employees?

PROBLEMS

I14-42 *AMT Computation.* William and Maria are a married couple, have no children, and report the following items in 2006:

Taxable income	$70,000
Tax preferences	20,000
AMT adjustments related to itemized deductions	15,000
Regular tax liability	10,615

  a. What is William's AMT liability in the current year?
  b. What is William's AMT liability in the current year if he is instead a single taxpayer and his regular tax liability is $14,058 rather than $10,615?

I14-43 *AMT Computation.* Jose, a single taxpayer with no dependents, has AGI of $200,000 and reports the following items in 2006:

Taxable income	$160,000
Tax preferences	10,000
AMT adjustments related to itemized deductions	30,000
Regular tax liability	39,392

What is Jose's AMT liability in the current year?

I14-44   *AMT Computation.* Harry and Mary Prodigious are married and have 12 children. With the large number of children, they live in a very austere manner. Harry, in his spare time, works a large garden that provides most of their food. Mary makes all the children's clothes. Harry works for a local engineering firm and earns a salary of $100,000 in 2006. Mary does not work outside the home. The only other income is interest and dividends in the amount of $3,000. They claim the standard deduction in filing their 2006 return and have no tax preferences or adjustments for purposes of the AMT.
a. Compute Harry and Mary's regular tax and AMT under the facts above.
b. Comment on the tax policy implications of your answer in Part a above.

I14-45   *AMT Adjustments and Computation of Tax.* Allen, a single taxpayer, reports the following items on his 2006 federal income tax return:

Adjusted gross income	$75,000
Taxable income	48,000
Regular tax liability	8,558
Tax preferences	20,000
Itemized deductions including:	
Charitable contributions	7,500
Medical expenses (before AGI floor)	10,000
Mortgage interest on personal residence	10,000
State income taxes	5,000
Real estate taxes	8,000

a. What is the amount of Allen's AMT adjustments related to the itemized deductions?
b. What is Allen's AMT liability for the current year?

I14-46   *Self-Employment Tax.* In the current year, Amelia has wages of $40,000 and net earnings from a small unincorporated business of $60,000.
a. What is the amount of Amelia's self-employment tax and *for* AGI deduction relative to her self-employment tax?
b. How would your answer to Part a change if Amelia's wages were $100,000 rather than $40,000?

I14-47   *Self-Employment Tax.* Arnie and Angela are married and file a joint return in the current year. Arnie is a partner in a public accounting firm. His share of the partnership's income in the current year is $40,000, and he receives guaranteed payments of $30,000. Angela receives wages of $50,000 from a large corporation. What is each taxpayer's self-employment tax amount? (Hint: Guaranteed payments received from a partnership are considered self-employment income.)

I14-48   *Self-Employment Tax.* Anita, a single taxpayer, reports the following items for the current year:

Salary (subject to withholding)	$20,000
Income for serving on the Board of Directors for XYZ Corporation	11,000
Consulting gross income	9,000
Expenses related to consulting practice	(15,000)

a. What is the amount of Anita's self-employment tax?
b. How would your answer to Part a change if Anita's salary were $100,000?

I14-49   *Computation of Tax Credits.* During the current year, Becky has personal credits as well as business credits related to her sole proprietorship. Her tentative tax credits for the current year include the following:

Work opportunity credit	$ 1,000
Child and dependent care credit	1,200
Research credit	14,000
Business energy credit	600
Total	$16,800

Becky's regular tax liability before credits is $14,000. Assume that there is no alternative minimum tax liability.
a. What is the amount of allowable personal tax credits?
b. What is the amount of allowable business tax credits?
c. What treatment is accorded to the unused tax credits for the current year?

I14-50 *Child and Dependent Care Credit.* In each of the following independent situations, determine the amount of the child and dependent care tax credit. (Assume that both taxpayers are employed.)

a. Brad and Bonnie are married and file a joint return. Brad and Bonnie have earned income of $40,000 and $14,000, respectively. Their combined AGI is $52,000. They have two children ages 10 and 12 and employ a live-in nanny at an annual cost of $9,000.

b. Assume the same facts as in Part a, except that Brad and Bonnie employ Bonnie's mother, who is not their dependent, as the live-in nanny.

c. Bruce is divorced and has two children ages 10 and 16. He has AGI and earned income of $27,000. Bruce incurs qualifying child care expenses of $8,000 during the year which were incurred equally for both children. Bruce's employer maintains an employee dependent care assistance program. $1,000 was paid to Bruce from this program and excluded from Bruce's gross income.

d. Buddy and Candice are married and file a joint return. Their combined AGI is $50,000. Buddy earns $46,000, and Candice's salary from a part-time job is $4,000. They incur $5,000 of qualifying child care expenses for a day-care facility for their two children, ages 2 and 4.

e. Ben and Bunny are married and file a joint return. Their AGI is $75,000, all earned by Bunny. Ben was a full-time student for two semesters (10 months) at State U. during the year. They incur $7,000 of qualifying child care expenses for their two children, ages 6 and 4.

I14-51 *Adoption Credit.* Brad and Valerie decided to adopt a child and contacted an adoption agency in August 2005. After extensive interviews and other requirements (such as financial status, etc.), Brad and Valerie were approved as eligible parents to adopt a child. The agency indicated that it might take up to two years to find a proper match. In November 2006, the adoption became final and Brad and Valerie adopted an infant daughter (not a special needs child). Below is a list of expenses that they incurred:

2005:		
Agency fees (first installment)	$5,000
Travel expenses for interviews, etc.	1,500
Publications for prospective adoptive parents	300
Legal fees connected with the adoption	1,000
Kennel fees for dog while on adoption trips	250

2006:		
Agency fees (final installment)	$3,000
Travel expenses	400
Court costs for adoption	200
Kennel fees	100
Nursery furniture (baby's room) and supplies	2,000

Brad and Valerie's AGI for 2005 was $70,000 and in 2006 was $90,000.

a. Compute Brad and Valerie's qualified adoption expenses for 2005 and 2006.

b. Compute Brad and Valerie's adoption credit. What year(s) may the credit be taken?

c. Would your answer to Part b change if the adopted child was a special needs child?

I14-52 *HOPE Scholarship Credit and Lifetime Learning Credit.* John and Mary, a married couple who file a joint return, have two dependent children in college, Jeff and Brooke. Jeff attends Pepper College, a private, liberal arts college, and Brooke attends State U. During the calendar year 2006, Jeff was a sophomore during the Spring Semester 2006 and a junior during the Fall Semester 2006. Brooke was a freshman during the Fall Semester 2006 and was in high school during the Spring Semester 2006. Below are the college expenses paid by John and Mary for Jeff and Brooke during 2006:

	Spring Semester 2006 (Paid in January 2006)		Fall Semester 2006 (Paid in August 2006)	
	Jeff	*Brooke*	*Jeff*	*Brooke*
Tuition	$7,500		$8,000	$1,200
Laboratory fees	500		500	0
Student activity fees	100		100	100
Books	400		350	400
Room and board	3,000		3,200	3,500

a. Compute any education credits that John and Mary may claim in 2006 assuming that neither Jeff nor Brooke receive any type of financial assistance and John and Mary's modified AGI is less than $90,000.

b. Would your answer in Part a change if Jeff received an academic scholarship of $2,500 for each semester in 2006?

c. How would your answer in Part a change if John and Mary's modified AGI for 2006 was $98,000?

d. How would your answer in Part a change if Jeff was a junior during the Spring Semester, 2006 and a senior during the Fall Semester 2006?

I14-53 *Tax Credit for the Elderly.* Caroline, age 66 and single, receives the following income items for the current year:

Social Security payments	$ 3,000
Fully taxable pension	6,450
Interest income	2,050
Total	$11,500

Caroline's tax liability (before credits) is $300 in the current year.

a. What is Caroline's tentative tax credit for the elderly (before the tax liability limitation is applied) in the current year? The Social Security payments are nontaxable.

b. What is the amount of Caroline's allowable tax credit for the elderly in the current year?

I14-54 *Business Tax Credit Carrybacks and Carryovers.* In 2006, Large Corporation, which was incorporated in 2000, has an unused general business tax credit of $40,000 in 2003. The following schedule shows the amount of business tax credits earned and used for the period 2000–2006:

	Credits Earned During the Year	Credit Limitation for the Carryback or Carryover Year
2000	$40,000	$40,000
2001	30,000	40,000
2002	25,000	25,000
2003	60,000	20,000
2004	20,000	22,000
2005	15,000	20,000
2006	15,000	15,000

a. How much of the unused 2003 credit may be carried back to prior years?

b. What is the amount of the unused credit that is carried forward to 2004, 2005, 2006, and 2007? In what years are the credits used? Identify the tax years in which the credit carryovers are earned.

I14-55 *Foreign Tax Credit.* Laser Corporation, a U.S. corporation, has a foreign office that conducts business in France. Laser pays foreign taxes of $40,000 on foreign-source taxable income of $100,000. Its U.S.-source taxable income is $200,000, total U.S. taxable income (worldwide) of $300,000, and the total U.S. tax liability (before reductions for the foreign tax credit) is $100,250. What is Laser's foreign tax credit? What is Laser's foreign tax credit carryback or carryover?

I14-56 *Work Opportunity Credit.* Last Corporation hires two economically disadvantaged youths (qualified for the work opportunity credit) in August of the current year. Each employee receives $8,000 of wages in the current year. Salaries and wages paid to other employees in the current year are $50,000. Last Corporation has a regular income tax liability of $50,000 in the current year before deducting its tax credits assuming the appropriate deduction is claimed for the youths' salaries. Its tentative minimum tax is $10,000. Business tax credits other than the work opportunity credit amount to $50,000 in the current year.

a. What is Last Corporation's tentative work opportunity credit (before limitations) in the current year?

b. What is Last Corporation's total general business credit that is used in the current year? What amount is available for carryover or carryback?

c. What is Last Corporation's deduction for salaries and wages paid to the two youths?

I14-57 *Empowerment Zone Employment Credit.* Acorn Corporation operates its business in an Empowerment Zone and John, one of its employees, lives in the zone. In the current year

John received $12,000 in wages. In addition, Acorn incurred $4,000 of training expenses related to John's employment.
a. What is Acorn Corporation's tentative Empowerment Zone credit (before any limitations on the general business credit are considered)?
b. What is Acorn Corporation's deduction for wages paid to John?

I14-58 *Rehabilitation Tax Credit.* Bob acquires a certified historic structure on August 4 of the current year to be used as an office for his business. He pays $20,000 for the building (exclusive of the land) and spends $40,000 for renovation costs.
a. What is the rehabilitation tax credit (before limitations)?
b. Compute the depreciation that Bob would be entitled to on the building for the current year.
c. What is the basis of the building for MACRS depreciation purposes?

I14-59 *Research Credit.* Pharm Inc. is a small pharmaceutical company that is heavily involved in drug research. During 2006, Pharm Inc. incurred the following expenditures that are related to the company's research efforts:

Salaries of research scientists and technicians	$180,000
Supplies and materials	42,000
Depreciation on research equipment	30,000

For the years 2002-2005, Pharm Inc. had average gross receipts of $5,000,000 and the company's fixed-base percentage is 3%. Also, during 2006 the company paid $200,000 to State University for the express purpose of doing basic research in the scientific field. Pharm Inc.'s qualified organization base period amount is $120,000. Compute Pharm Inc.'s credit for increasing research activities for 2006. Is Pharm Inc. entitled to claim any deduction for research and experimentation expenses for the year?

I14-60 *Earned Income Credit.* Carolyn is single and has one dependent child, age 6, who lived with her for the entire year. She has earned income of $12,000 of wages and $4,000 of alimony in 2006. Her AGI is $16,000.
a. What is Carolyn's tentative earned income credit (before the phase-out reduction is applied)?
b. What is Carolyn's allowable earned income credit?
c. If Carolyn has no income tax liability (before the earned income credit is subtracted), is she entitled to a tax refund in the current year?

I14-61 *Earned Income Credit.* Jose is single with no qualifying children. He has $7,800 of wages during the current year and is otherwise eligible for the earned income credit. Jose has $200 of interest income and no *for* AGI deductions. His AGI is $8,000.
a. What is Jose's tentative earned income credit before the phase-out reduction is applied?
b. What is Jose's allowable earned income credit?
c. If Jose has no income tax liability (before the earned income credit is subtracted), is he entitled to a refund for the current year?
d. Would your answer to Part b change if Jose had dividend and interest income of $3,000 during the taxable year?

I14-62 *Penalties for Nonpayment of Withholding and FICA Taxes.* Lake Corporation has some severe cash-flow problems. You are the company's financial and tax consultant. The treasurer of the company has informed you that the company has failed to make FICA and federal income tax withholding payments for both the employer and employee contributions to the IRS for a period of approximately six months.
a. What advice can you give to the company treasurer regarding the nonpayment of taxes?
b. Can the liability for payment of the taxes extend to parties other than the corporation? Explain.

I14-63 *Exemptions from Withholding.* Which of the following categories of individuals or income are exempt from the federal withholding tax requirements?
a. Domestic servants
b. Independent contractors
c. Newspaper carriers over age 18
d. Bonuses
e. Commissions
f. Vacation pay
g. Tips under $20 per month from a single employer

I14-64 *Withholding Exemptions.* Barry is a college student who is employed as a waiter during the summer. He earns approximately $1,500 during the summer and estimates that he will not be required to file a tax return and will have no federal income tax liability. Last year, however, he made $6,000 and was required to file a return and pay $400 in taxes. Barry is single and is supported by his parents. He has no dependents and does not have any other sources of income or deductions.
a. Can Barry claim an exempt status on Form W-4 for withholding purposes?
b. Can Barry claim more than one exemption on Form W-4 (e.g., additional withholding allowances or the standard deduction allowance) to minimize the amount withheld? Explain.

I14-65 *Withholding Allowances.* Bart's spouse is not employed. They plan to file a joint return. Bart obtains a new job and is asked to fill out a Form W-4. His monthly gross earnings will be $3,000. Bart, who has two dependent children, can claim three additional withholding allowances because he is obligated to pay substantial alimony to his ex-wife.
a. What is the correct number of withholding allowances that he may claim on Form W-4?
b. What is the amount of federal income tax to be withheld using the wage bracket tables (see withholding table on page T-15)?
c. What disclosure procedures must Bart's employer follow if Bart claims more than ten allowances?

I14-66 *Estimated Tax Requirements.* Anna does not make quarterly estimated tax payments even though she has substantial amounts of income that are not subject to withholding. In 2005, Anna's tax liability was $18,000. This year, in 2006, Anna's actual tax liability is $30,000, although only $18,200 was withheld from her salary. Anna's AGI for 2005 was $135,000.
a. Is Anna subject to the underpayment penalty? Why?
b. If Anna's withholdings were only $15,000, would she be subject to the underpayment penalty? Why?
c. If Anna is subject to an underpayment penalty, can she deduct this amount as interest? Explain.

I14-67 *Estimated Tax Underpayment Penalty.* Anne's estimated tax payments for 2006 are $14,000 and federal income taxes withheld from her salary amount to $12,000. Anne's actual tax liability for 2006 is $30,000. Her income was earned evenly throughout the current year. Anne's AGI for 2005 was $160,000 and her tax liability in 2005 was $25,000. Is Anne subject to the underpayment penalty? Explain.

COMPREHENSIVE PROBLEM

I14-68 Mike Webb, married to Nancy Webb, is employed by a large pharmaceutical company and earns a salary. In addition, Mike is an entrepreneur at heart and has two small businesses on the side. One business is a consulting business where Mike provides financial and retirement assistance to pharmacists. The consulting business is doing very well. The other business involves the manufacture of Christmas novelties in China and reselling the products in gift shops in the U.S. This business, operated as a sole proprietorship, is struggling. However, Mike feels the Christmas novelty business has great potential. In 2006, Mike had the following information for tax purposes:

Salary			$150,000
Consulting practice:	Revenues	$65,000	
	Ordinary expenses	12,000	53,000
Sole proprietorship:	Revenues	$22,000	
	Ordinary Expenses	40,000	(18,000)
Interest (none tax-exempt)			3,000
Dividends, qualified			9,000
LTCG		$24,000	
STCL		(4,000)	20,000
Itemized deductions:			
State and local taxes		$14,000	
Real estate taxes		5,000	
Mortgage interest on personal residence		10,000	
Charitable contributions		8,000	37,000

Child care expenses:

Mike and his wife, Nancy, have two children, ages 13 and 11 and pay child care expenses of $4,000 per year for each child, for a total of $8,000. Nancy is not employed, but is a full-time student at University of South Carolina. She has gone back to school to get her degree in Accounting. Both children are dependents of Mike and Nancy.

Federal income tax withheld from salary	$28,000
Estimated taxes paid for 2006 during the year	12,000

Mike and Nancy's AGI in 2005 was $175,000 and actual federal income tax liability for 2005 was $35,000.

Compute Mike and Nancy's federal income tax liability for 2006, including self-employment taxes and AMT, if applicable. Also, are Mike and Nancy subject to any underpayment penalties for 2006?

TAX STRATEGY PROBLEM

I14-69 Mike and Linda Foley are married and file a joint income tax return. Mike is a lawyer and a partner in the firm of Foley & Looby, Attorneys at Law. Mike is a 50% partner in the firm along with his partner, John Looby who is the other 50% partner. Foley & Looby (F&L) currently rent office space in a prestigious building and pay rent of $6,000 per month or $72,000 per year for their 4,000 square foot office. Thus, the firm pays $18 per square foot per year. As no equity is being generated by paying rent, Mike and John are considering buying an office building. They have two buildings under consideration, as follows:

Building #1

Building #1 is a relatively new building and has 10,000 square feet of space. The new building can be purchased for a total price of $1,000,000. F&L would only use 4,000 square feet of the space and have other businesses that would rent the 6,000 from F&L for $15 per square foot per year. Maintenance costs would amount to approximately $10 per square foot per year. The building is in excellent condition and is ready to be moved into immediately and would require very little other outlays by F&L.

Building #2

Building #2 is located in the downtown area in a certified historic district and would qualify as a certified historic structure. This building, nearly 80 years old, also has 10,000 square feet and, like Building #1, the other 6,000 square feet can be rented to other tenants at $15 per square foot per year. However, Building #2 is not in as good a condition as the above building. The purchase price of the building would be $400,000 and Mike and John estimated that approximately $600,000 would have to be invested in capital expenditures to make the building suitable for their business. After the significant capital expenditures, F&L estimate the maintenance costs to be similar to Building #1, or $10 per square foot per year.

Both buildings can be 100% financed at 8% annual interest rate for 15 years. The annual payment on the $1,000,000 mortgage would be $117,000. Also, assume both buildings will appreciate at a rate of 8% per year.

Mike Foley and John Looby have come to you as their financial and tax advisor to help them make the decision as to which building to purchase. If the buildings are equally desirable from a non-financial and non-tax standpoint, what is the best decision for Mike and John? That is, should they stay where they are and rent or purchase one of the two buildings? Assume both Mike and John are in the top 35% marginal tax bracket.

TAX FORM/RETURN PREPARATION PROBLEMS

I14-70 Warren (SSN 123-45-6789) and Alice (SSN 987-65-4321) Williams have the following tax credits for 2005:

General business credits:		
Disabled Access credit	6,000	
Nonconventional source fuel credit	3,000	$ 9,000
Child and dependent care credit		1,200
Total		$10,200

Warren and Alice Williams have two children and incur $5,000 of qualifying child care expenses ($5,000 for day care and $2,000 for a nurse). The oldest child is Vanessa, age 7, SSN 000-00-0000 and the younger child is Brian, age 5, SSN 999-99-9999. The expenses, equally spent for the two children were paid to the Alphine Daycare, 100 Pine St., Boone, NC 29001, EIN 66-666666, and the nurse is Bonnie Jones, SSN 555-55-5555 and her address is 400 Maple Lane, Boone, NC 29004. Warren had earned income of $90,000; Alice's earned income was $25,000 and their AGI was $116,988. Their itemized deductions are $14,200, taxable income was $89,988, regular tax liability (before credits) was $15,827 and federal taxes withheld during 2005 of $7,200. Disregard any limitations that might be imposed by the tentative minimum tax. Complete Form 2441, Form 3800 and the Tax Credits section on page 2 of Form 1040 for 2005.

I14-71 Harold J. Milton (SSN 574-45-5477) is single and had the following income and deductions for 2005:

Salary	$177,000	State income taxes	$18,000
Interest income from bank	12,000	Mortgage interest expense	
Dividend income (qualified)	18,000	on residence	19,000
Deductible IRA contribution	4,000	Interest expense on car loan	3,000
Tax-exempt interest		Real estate taxes	
from private activity		on residence	2,000
bonds issued in 1990	24,000	Miscellaneous deductions	
Charitable contributions	27,000	(before the 2% AGI floor)	7,000
		Income taxes withheld	20,000
		Estimated tax payments	
		($2,500 per quarter)	10,000

Complete Milton's 2005 Form 1040, Schedule A, B, D, Form 6251, and Form 2210. Milton had AGI in 2004 of $200,000 and his 2004 income tax liability was $46,000. (Note: Milton is eligible to use the Short Method on Form 2210.)

CASE STUDY PROBLEMS

I14-72 Barbara was divorced in 2003. However, the final property settlement and determination of alimony payments was not made until February 2006 because of extended litigation. Barbara received a $20,000 payment of back alimony in March 2006 and will receive monthly alimony payments of $2,000 for the period April through December 2006. Last year, in 2005, Barbara's income consisted of $15,000 salary and $2,000 of taxable interest income. She used the standard deduction and had no dependents. In 2005, Barbara's tax liability was $1,900. In 2006, she expects to continue working at an annual salary of $15,000 and will have $2,000 of interest income in 2006. Her federal income taxes withheld from her salary in 2006 will be $1,500. Her monthly alimony payments of $2,000 are also expected to continue for an indefinite period.

In early April 2006 Barbara requests your advice regarding the payment of quarterly estimated taxes for 2006. Prepare a memo to your client that discusses these requirements, including any possible penalties for not making quarterly payments and nontax issues such as cash-flow and investment income decisions.

I14-73 Chips-R-Us is a computer technology corporation that designs hardware and software for use in large businesses. The corporation regularly pays individuals to install programs and give advice to different companies that buy their software. In the current year, Simone, a computer expert, was sent to a customer of Chips-R-Us by the corporation to perform computer services. Simone is not a regular employee of the corporation and the corporation did not train Simone for the task. Simone keeps track of the time spent on the job at the customer and reports to the corporation, which pays Simone for her services. The corporation specifies the work to be done for their client. The corporation can also replace Simone with another individual if her work is not satisfactory. Chips-R-Us treats Simone as an independent contractor for employment tax purposes. In the current year the IRS challenges the corporation that it has failed to remit FICA taxes and income taxes that should have been withheld with respect to Simone's employment. Chips-R-Us refuses to pay the amount, stating that it is not required to do so because Simone is not an employee of the corporation. What will be the likely outcome of the IRS's decision concerning the status of Simone as an employee or independent contractor? Who may be liable for payment of the employment taxes, interest, and penalties to the government? What ethical responsibilities should be followed in the remittance of taxes on behalf of an employee?

TAX RESEARCH PROBLEM

I14-74 Lean Corporation was incorporated in 1981 by Bruce Smith, who has served as an officer and member of the Board of Directors. Carl Jones has served as the secretary-treasurer of the company as a convenience to his friend Bruce Smith. He acted as a part-time book-keeper but did not run the everyday business affairs and paid only the bills he was instructed to pay. Carl was an authorized signatory for the corporate bank accounts but had no final control over expenditures.

Beginning in the last quarter of 2005, the company failed to pay all of the taxes with-held from employees and the employer's share of FICA taxes to the IRS. Despite this delinquency, the corporation continued to pay other creditors, including its employees, in preference to the IRS.

In January, 2006 Lean Corporation entered into an installment agreement with the IRS to keep current on its withholding taxes and to make payments on the past due balance until paid in full. The company subsequently defaulted on the agreement in April 2006. During this period, Bruce Smith was serving as chief financial officer and was a member of the board of directors. He had the authority to make policy decisions. He was responsible for negotiating the installment agreement with the IRS and the decision to default on the agreement.

Who is liable for the penalty for the nonpayment of the payroll tax withholdings?

A partial list of research sources is

- Sec. 6672
- *Ernest W. Carlson v. U.S.*, 67 AFTR 2d 91-1104, 91-1 USTC ¶50,262 (D.C. UT, 1991)

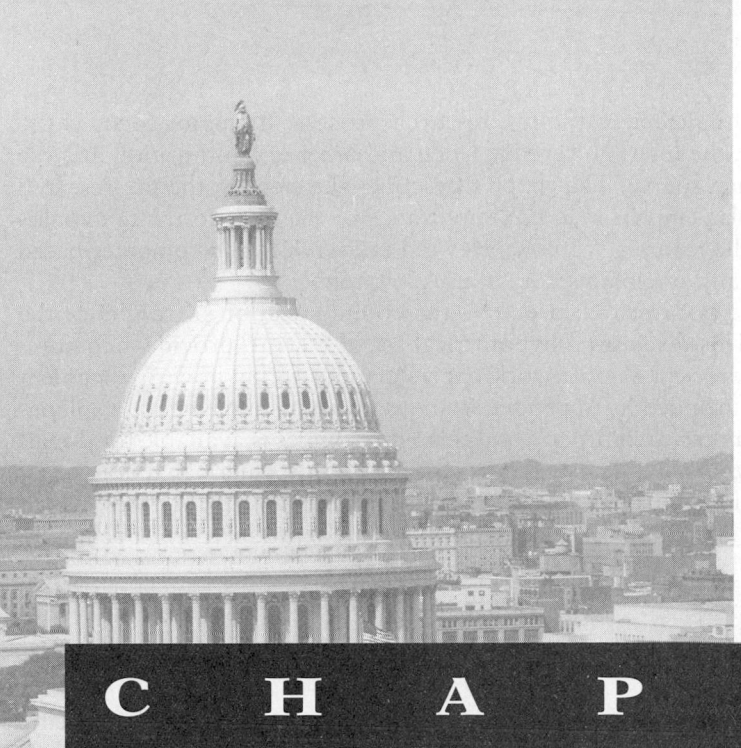

1

CHAPTER

TAX RESEARCH

LEARNING OBJECTIVES

After studying this chapter, you should be able to

1 ▶ Describe the steps in the tax research process

2 ▶ Explain how the facts influence the tax consequences

3 ▶ Identify the sources of tax law and understand the authoritative value of each

4 ▶ Consult tax services to research an issue

5 ▶ Use a citator to assess tax authorities

6 ▶ Grasp the basics of computerized tax research

7 ▶ Understand guidelines that CPAs in tax practice should follow

8 ▶ Prepare work papers and communicate to clients

This chapter introduces the reader to the tax research process. Its major focus is the sources of the tax law (i.e., the Internal Revenue Code and other tax authorities) and the relative weight given to each source. The chapter describes the steps in the tax research process and places particular emphasis on the importance of the facts to the tax consequences. It also describes the features of frequently used tax services and computer-based tax research resources. Finally, it explains how to use a citator.

The end product of the tax research process—the communication of results to the client—also is discussed. This text uses a hypothetical set of facts to provide a comprehensive illustration of the process. Sample work papers demonstrating how to document the results of research are included in Appendix A. In addition, a supplemental explanation of the computerized tax research process and related resources is available for download at *www.prenhall.com/phtax*. The text also discusses the American Institute of Certified Public Accountants' (AICPA's) *Statements on Standards for Tax Services*, which provide guidance for CPAs in tax practice. These statements are reproduced in Appendix E.

OVERVIEW OF TAX RESEARCH

Tax research is the process of solving tax-related problems by applying tax law to specific sets of facts. Sometimes it involves researching several issues and often is conducted to formulate tax policy. For example, policy-oriented research would determine how far the level of charitable contributions might decline if such contributions were no longer deductible. Economists usually conduct this type of tax research to assess the effects of government action.

Tax research also is conducted to determine the tax consequences of transactions to specific taxpayers. For example, client-oriented research would determine whether Smith Corporation could deduct a particular expenditure as a trade or business expense. Accounting and law firms generally engage in this type of research on behalf of their clients.

This chapter deals only with client-oriented tax research, which occurs in two contexts:

1. **Closed-fact or tax compliance situations:** The client contacts the tax advisor after completing a transaction or while preparing a tax return. In such situations, the tax consequences are fairly straightforward because the facts cannot be modified to obtain different results. Consequently, tax savings opportunities may be lost.

ADDITIONAL COMMENT

Closed-fact situations afford the tax advisor the least amount of flexibility. Because the facts are already established, the tax advisor must develop the best solution possible within certain predetermined constraints.

EXAMPLE C1-1 ▶

Tom informs Carol, his tax advisor, that on November 4 of the current year, he sold land held as an investment for $500,000 cash. His basis in the land was $50,000. On November 9, Tom reinvested the sales proceeds in another plot of investment property costing $500,000. This is a closed fact situation. Tom wants to know the amount and the character of the gain (if any) he must recognize. Because Tom solicits the tax advisor's advice after the sale and reinvestment, the opportunity for tax planning is limited. For example, the possibility of deferring taxes by using a like-kind exchange or an installment sale is lost. ◀

ADDITIONAL COMMENT

Open-fact or tax-planning situations give a tax advisor flexibility to structure transactions to accomplish the client's objectives. In this type of situation, a creative tax advisor can save taxpayers dollars through effective tax planning.

2. **Open-fact or tax-planning situations:** Before structuring or concluding a transaction, the client contacts the tax advisor to discuss tax planning opportunities. Tax-planning situations generally are more difficult and challenging because the tax advisor must consider the client's tax and nontax objectives. Most clients will not engage in a transaction if it is inconsistent with their nontax objectives, even though it produces tax savings.

EXAMPLE C1-2 ▶

Diane is a widow with three children and five grandchildren and at present owns property valued at $10 million. She seeks advice from Carol, her tax advisor, about how to minimize her estate taxes while passing the greatest value of property to her descendants. This is an open-fact situation. Carol could advise Diane to leave all but a few hundred thousand dollars of her property to a charitable organization so that her estate would owe no estate taxes. Although this recommendation would minimize Diane's estate taxes, Diane is likely to reject it because she wants her children or grandchildren to be her primary beneficiaries. Thus, reducing estate taxes to zero is inconsistent with her objective of allowing her descendants to receive as much after-tax wealth as possible. ◄

When conducting research in a tax-planning context, the tax professional should keep a number of points in mind. First, the objective is not to minimize taxes per se but rather to maximize the after-tax return. For example, if the federal income tax rate is a constant 30%, an investor should not buy a tax-exempt bond yielding 5% when he or she could buy a corporate bond of equal risk that yields 9% before tax and 6.3% after tax. This is the case even though his or her explicit taxes (actual tax liability) would be minimized by investing in the tax-exempt bond.[1] Second, taxpayers typically do not engage in unilateral or self-dealing transactions; thus, the tax ramifications for all parties to the transaction should be considered. For example, in the executive compensation context, employees may prefer to receive incentive stock options (because they will not recognize income until they sell the stock), but the employer may prefer to grant a different type of option (because the employer cannot deduct the value of incentive stock options upon issuance). Thus, the employer might grant a different number of options if it uses one type of stock option as compensation versus another type. Third, taxes are but one cost of doing business. In deciding where to locate a manufacturing plant, for example, factors more important to some businesses than the amount of state and local taxes paid might be the proximity to raw materials, good transportation systems, the cost of labor, the quantity of available skilled labor, and the quality of life in the area. Fourth, the time for tax planning is not restricted to the beginning date of an investment, contract, or other arrangement. Instead, the time extends throughout the duration of the activity. As tax rules change or as business and economic environments change, the tax advisor must reevaluate whether the taxpayer should keep an investment and must consider the transaction costs of any alternatives.

One final note: the tax advisor should always bear in mind the financial accounting implications of proposed transactions. An answer that may be desirable from a tax perspective may not always be desirable from a financial accounting perspective. Though interrelated, the two fields of accounting have different orientations and different objectives. Tax accounting is oriented primarily to the Internal Revenue Service (IRS). Its objectives include calculating, reporting, and predicting one's tax liability according to legal principles. Financial accounting is oriented primarily to shareholders, creditors, managers, and employees. Its objectives include determining, reporting, and predicting a business's financial position and operating results according to Generally Accepted Accounting Principles. Success in any tax practice, especially at the managerial level, requires consideration of both sets of objectives and orientations.

STEPS IN THE TAX RESEARCH PROCESS

In both open- and closed-fact situations, the tax research process involves six basic steps:

1. Determine the facts.
2. Identify the issues (questions).
3. Locate the applicable authorities.
4. Evaluate the authorities and choose those to follow where the authorities conflict.
5. Analyze the facts in terms of the applicable authorities.
6. Communicate conclusions and recommendations to the client.

---

[1] For an excellent discussion of explicit and implicit taxes and tax planning see M. S. Scholes, M. A. Wolfson, M. Erickson, L. Maydew, and T. Shevlin, *Taxes and Business Strategy: A Planning Approach*, third edition (Upper Saddle River, NJ: Pearson Prentice Hall, 2005). See also Chapter 18 of the *Individuals* volume. An example of an implicit tax is the excess of the before-tax earnings on a taxable bond over the risk-adjusted before-tax earnings on a tax-favored investment (e.g., a municipal bond).

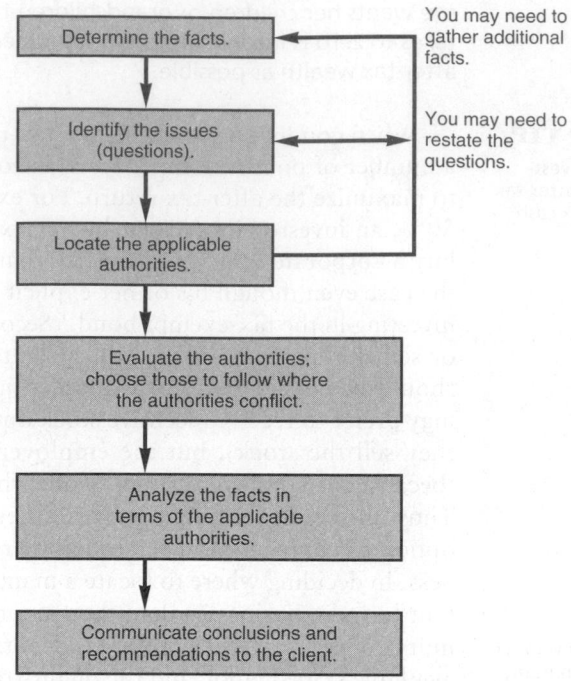

You may need to gather additional facts.

You may need to restate the questions.

FIGURE C1-1 ▶ STEPS IN THE TAX RESEARCH PROCESS

ADDITIONAL COMMENT

The steps of tax research provide an excellent format for a written tax communication. For example, a good format for a client memo includes (1) statement of facts, (2) list of issues, (3) discussion of relevant authority, (4) analysis, and (5) recommendations to the client of appropriate actions based on the research results.

TYPICAL MISCONCEPTION

Many taxpayers think the tax law is all black and white. However, most tax research deals with gray areas. Ultimately, when confronted with tough issues, the ability to develop strategies that favor the taxpayer and then to find relevant authority to support those strategies will make a successful tax advisor.

Although the above outline suggests a lock-step approach, the tax research process often is circular. That is, it does not always proceed step-by-step. Figure C1-1 illustrates a more accurate process, and Appendix A provides a comprehensive example of this process.

In a closed-fact situation, the facts have already occurred, and the tax advisor's task is to analyze them to determine the appropriate tax treatment. In an open-fact situation, by contrast, the facts have not yet occurred, and the tax advisor's task is to plan for them or shape them so as to produce a favorable tax result. The tax advisor performs the latter task by reviewing the relevant legal authorities, particularly court cases and IRS rulings, all the while bearing in mind the facts of those cases or rulings that produced favorable results compared with those that produced unfavorable results. For example, if a client wants to realize an ordinary loss (as opposed to a capital gain) on the sale of several plots of land, the tax advisor might consult cases involving similar land sales. The advisor might attempt to distinguish the facts of those cases in which the taxpayer realized an ordinary loss from the facts of those cases in which the taxpayer realized a capital gain. The advisor then might recommend that the client structure the transaction based on the fact pattern in the ordinary loss cases.

Often, the research pertains to a gray area (i.e., it involves a question for which no clearcut, unequivocally correct answer exists). In such situations, probing a related issue might lead to a solution pertinent to the central question. For example, in researching whether the taxpayer may deduct a loss as ordinary instead of capital, the tax advisor might research the related issue of whether the presence of an investment motive precludes classifying a loss as ordinary. The solution to the latter issue might be relevant to the central question of whether the taxpayer may deduct the loss as ordinary.

Identifying the issue(s) to be researched often is the most difficult step in the tax research process. In some instances, the client defines the issue(s) for the tax advisor, such as where the client asks, "May I deduct the costs of a winter trip to Florida recommended by my physician?" In other instances, the tax advisor, after reviewing the documents submitted to him or her by the client, defines the issue(s) himself or herself. Doing so presupposes a firm grounding in tax law.[2]

---

[2] Often, in an employment context, supervisors define the questions to be researched and the authorities that might be relevant to the tax consequences.

Once the tax advisor locates the applicable legal authorities, he or she might have to obtain additional information from the client. Example C1-3 illustrates the point. The example assumes that all relevant tax authorities are in agreement.

EXAMPLE C1-3 ▶ Mark calls his tax advisor, Al, and states that he (1) incurred a loss on renting his beach cottage during the current year and (2) wonders whether he may deduct the loss. He also states that he, his wife, and their minor child occupied the cottage only eight days during the current year.

This is the first time Al has dealt with the Sec. 280A vacation home rules. On reading Sec. 280A, Al learns that a loss is *not* deductible if the taxpayer used the residence for personal purposes for longer than the greater of (1) 14 days or (2) 10% of the number of days the unit was rented at a fair rental value. He also learns that the property is *deemed* to be used by the taxpayer for personal purposes on any days on which it is used by any member of his or her family (as defined in Sec. 267(c)(4)). The Sec. 267(c)(4) definition of family members includes brothers, sisters, spouse, ancestors, or lineal descendants (i.e., children and grandchildren).

Mark's eight-day use is not long enough to make the rental loss nondeductible. However, Al must inquire about the number of days, if any, Mark's brothers, sisters, or parents used the property. (He already knows about use by Mark, his spouse, and his lineal descendants.) In addition, Al must find out how many days the cottage was rented to other persons at a fair rental value. Upon obtaining the additional information, Al proceeds to determine how to calculate the deductible expenses. Al then derives his conclusion concerning the deductible loss, if any, and communicates it to Mark. (This example assumes the passive activity and at-risk rules restricting a taxpayer's ability to deduct losses from real estate activities will not pose a problem for Mark. See Chapter I8 of *Prentice Hall's Federal Taxation: Individuals* for a comprehensive discussion of these topics.) ◀

Many firms require that a researcher's conclusions be communicated to the client in writing. Members or employees of such firms may answer questions orally, but their oral conclusions should be followed by a written communication. According to the AICPA's *Statements on Standards for Tax Services* (reproduced in Appendix E),

> Although oral advice may serve a client's needs appropriately in routine matters or in well-defined areas, written communications are recommended in important, unusual, or complicated transactions. The member may use judgment about whether, subsequently, to document oral advice in writing.[3]

IMPORTANCE OF THE FACTS TO THE TAX CONSEQUENCES

OBJECTIVE 2

Explain how the facts influence the tax consequences

Many terms and phrases used in the Internal Revenue Code (IRC) and other tax authorities are vague or ambiguous. Some provisions conflict with others or are difficult to reconcile, creating for the researcher the dilemma of deciding which rules are applicable and which tax results are proper. For example, as a condition to claiming another person as a dependent, the taxpayer must provide more than half of such person's support.[4] Neither the IRC nor the Treasury Regulations define "support." The lack of definition could be problematic. For example, if the taxpayer purchased a used automobile costing $5,000 for an elderly parent whose only source of income is $4,800 in Social Security benefits, the question of whether the expenditure constitutes support would arise. The tax advisor would have to consult court opinions, revenue rulings, and other IRS pronouncements to ascertain the legal meaning of the term "support." Only after thorough research would the meaning of the term become clear.

In other instances, the legal language is quite clear, but a question arises as to whether the taxpayer's transaction conforms to the specific pattern of facts necessary to obtain a particular tax result. Ultimately, the peculiar facts of a transaction or event determine its tax consequences. A change in the facts can significantly change the consequences. Consider the following illustrations:

---

[3] AICPA, *Statement on Standards for Tax Services*, No. 8, "Form and Content of Advice to Clients," 2000, Para. 6.   [4] Sec. 152(a).

Illustration One

Facts: A holds stock, a capital asset, that he purchased two years ago at a cost of $1,000. He sells the stock to B for $920. What are the tax consequences to A?

Result: Under Sec. 1001, A realizes an $80 capital loss. He recognizes this loss in the current year. A must offset the loss against any capital gains recognized during the year. Any excess loss is deductible from ordinary income up to a $3,000 limit.

Change of Facts: A is B's son.

New Result: Under Sec. 267, A and B are related parties. Therefore, A may not recognize the realized loss. However, B may use the loss if she subsequently sells the stock at a gain.

Illustration Two

Facts: C donates to State University ten acres of land that she purchased two years ago for $10,000. The fair market value (FMV) of the land on the date of the donation is $25,000. C's adjusted gross income is $100,000. What is C's charitable contribution deduction?

Result: Under Sec. 170, C is entitled to a $25,000 charitable contribution deduction (i.e., the FMV of the property unreduced by the unrealized long-term gain).

Change of Facts: C purchased the land 11 months ago.

New Result: Under the same IRC provision, C is entitled to only a $10,000 charitable contribution deduction (i.e., the FMV of the property reduced by the unrealized short-term gain).

Illustration Three

Facts: Acquiring Corporation pays Target Corporation's shareholders one million shares of Acquiring voting stock. In return, Target's shareholders tender 98% of their Target voting stock. The acquisition is for a bona fide business purpose. Acquiring continues Target's business. What are the tax consequences of the exchange to Target's shareholders?

Result: Under Sec. 368(a)(1)(B), Target's shareholders are not taxed on the exchange, which is solely for Acquiring voting stock.

Change of Facts: In the transaction, Acquiring purchases the remaining 2% of Target's shares with cash.

New Result: Under the same IRC provision, Target's shareholders are now taxed on the exchange, which is not solely for Acquiring voting stock.

ABILITY TO CREATE A FACTUAL SITUATION FAVORING THE TAXPAYER

TYPICAL MISCONCEPTION

Many taxpayers believe tax practitioners spend most of their time preparing tax returns. In reality, providing tax advice that accomplishes the taxpayer's objectives is one of the most important responsibilities of a tax advisor. This latter activity is tax consulting as compared to tax compliance.

Based on his or her research, a tax advisor might recommend to a taxpayer how to structure a transaction or plan an event so as to increase the likelihood that related expenses will be deductible. For example, suppose a taxpayer is assigned a temporary task in a location (City Y) different from the location (City X) of his or her permanent employment. Suppose also that the taxpayer wants to deduct the meal and lodging expenses incurred in City Y as well as the cost of transportation thereto. To do so, the taxpayer must establish that City X is his or her tax home and that he or she temporarily works in City Y. (Section 162 provides that a taxpayer may deduct travel expenses while "away from home" on business. A taxpayer is deemed to be "away from home" if his or her employment at the new location does not exceed one year, i.e., it is "temporary.") Suppose the taxpayer wants to know the tax consequences of his or her working in City Y for ten months and then, within that ten-month period, finding permanent employment in City Y. What is tax research likely to reveal?

Tax research is likely to reveal an IRS ruling that states that, in such circumstances, the employment will be deemed to be temporary until the date on which the realistic expectation about the temporary nature of the assignment changes.[5] After this date, the employment will be deemed to be permanent, and travel expenses relating to it will be nondeductible. Based on this finding, the tax advisor might advise the taxpayer to postpone his or her permanent job search in City Y until the end of the ten-month period and simply treat his or her assignment as temporary. So doing would lengthen the time he or she is deemed to be "away from home" on business and thus increase the amount of meal, lodging, and transportation costs deductible as travel expenses.

---

[5] Rev. Rul. 93-86, 1993-2 C.B. 71.

THE SOURCES OF TAX LAW

The language of the IRC is general; that is, it prescribes the tax treatment of broad categories of transactions and events. The reason for the generality is that Congress can neither foresee nor provide for every detailed transaction or event. Even if it could, doing so would render the statute narrow in scope and inflexible in application. Accordingly, interpretations of the IRC—both administrative and judicial—are necessary. Administrative interpretations are provided in Treasury Regulations, revenue rulings, and revenue procedures. Judicial interpretations are presented in court opinions. The term *tax law* as used by most tax advisors encompasses administrative and judicial interpretations in addition to the IRC. It also includes the meaning conveyed in reports issued by Congressional committees involved in the legislative process.

THE LEGISLATIVE PROCESS

Tax legislation begins in the House of Representatives. Initially, a tax proposal is incorporated in a bill. The bill is referred to the House Ways and Means Committee, which is charged with reviewing all tax legislation. The Ways and Means Committee holds hearings in which interested parties, such as the Treasury Secretary and IRS Commissioner, testify. At the conclusion of the hearings, the Ways and Means Committee votes to approve or reject the measure. If approved, the bill goes to the House floor where it is debated by the full membership. If the House approves the measure, the bill moves to the Senate where it is taken up by the Senate Finance Committee. Like Ways and Means, the Finance Committee holds hearings in which Treasury officials, tax experts, and other interested parties testify. If the committee approves the measure, the bill goes to the Senate floor where it is debated by the full membership. Upon approval by the Senate, it is submitted to the President for his or her signature. If the President signs the measure, the bill becomes public law. If the President vetoes it, Congress can override the veto by at least a two-thirds majority vote in each chamber.

Generally, at each stage of the legislative process, the bill is subject to amendment. If amended, and if the House version differs from the Senate version, the bill is referred to a House-Senate conference committee.[6] This committee attempts to resolve the differences between the House and Senate versions. Ultimately, it submits a compromise version of the measure to each chamber for its approval. Such referrals are common. For example, in 1998 the House and Senate disagreed over what the taxpayer must do to shift the burden of proof to the IRS. The House proposed that the taxpayer assert a "reasonable dispute" regarding a taxable item. The Senate proposed that the taxpayer introduce "credible evidence" regarding the item. A conference committee was appointed to resolve the differences. This committee ultimately adopted the Senate proposal, which was later approved by both chambers.

After approving major legislation, the Ways and Means Committee and Senate Finance Committee usually issue official reports. These reports, published by the U.S. Government Printing Office (GPO) as part of the *Cumulative Bulletin* and as separate documents, explain the committees' reasoning for approving (and/or amending) the legislation.[7] In addition, the GPO publishes both records of the committee hearings and transcripts of the floor debates. The records are published as separate House or Senate documents. The transcripts are incorporated in the *Congressional Record* for the day of the debate. In tax research, these records, reports, and transcripts are useful in deciphering the meaning of the statutory language. Where this language is ambiguous or vague, and the courts have not interpreted it, the documents can shed light on **Congressional intent**, i.e., what Congress *intended* by a particular term, phrase, or provision.

EXAMPLE C1-4 ▶ As mentioned earlier, in 1998 Congress passed legislation concerning shifting the burden of proof to the IRS. This legislation was codified in Sec. 7491. The question arises as to what constitutes "credible evidence." (Remember, the taxpayer must introduce "credible evidence" to

---

[6] The size of a conference committee can vary. It is made up of an equal number of members from the House and the Senate.

[7] The *Cumulative Bulletin* is described in the discussion of revenue rulings on pages C1-11 and C1-12.

shift the burden of proof to the IRS). Section 7491 does not define the term. Because the provision was relatively new, few courts had an opportunity to interpret what "credible evidence" means. In the absence of relevant statutory or judicial authority, the researcher might have looked to the committee reports to ascertain what Congress intended by the term. Senate Report No. 105-174 states that "credible evidence" means evidence of a quality, which, "after critical analysis, the court would find sufficient upon which to base a decision on the issue if no contrary evidence were submitted."[8] This language suggests that Congress intended the term to mean evidence of a kind sufficient to withstand judicial scrutiny. Such a meaning should be regarded as conclusive in the absence of other authority.　◀

THE INTERNAL REVENUE CODE

ADDITIONAL COMMENT

According to Sheldon S. Cohen, in *The Wall Street Journal's* weekly tax column, a bound volume of the Internal Revenue Code in 1952 measured three-fourths of an inch thick. Treasury Regulations could fit in one bound volume measuring one-half of an inch thick. Now, a bound volume of the Internal Revenue Code measures over four inches thick, and Treasury Regulations fit into five or six bound volumes measuring around ten inches thick.

The IRC, which comprises Title 26 of the United States Code, is the foundation of all tax law. First codified (i.e., organized into a single compilation of revenue statutes) in 1939, the tax law was recodified in 1954. The IRC was known as the Internal Revenue Code of 1954 until 1986, when its name was changed to the Internal Revenue Code of 1986. Whenever changes to the IRC are approved, the old language is deleted and new language added. Thus, the IRC is organized as an integrated document, and a researcher need not read through the relevant parts of all previous tax bills to find the current version of the law.

The IRC contains provisions dealing with income taxes, estate and gift taxes, employment taxes, alcohol and tobacco taxes, and other excise taxes. Organizationally, the IRC is divided into subtitles, chapters, subchapters, parts, subparts, sections, subsections, paragraphs, subparagraphs, and clauses. Subtitle A contains rules relating to income taxes, and Subtitle B deals with estate and gift taxes. A set of provisions concerned with one general area constitutes a subchapter. For example, the topics of corporate distributions and adjustments appear in Subchapter C, and topics concerning partners and partnerships appear in Subchapter K. Figure C1-2 presents the organizational scheme of the IRC.

An IRC section contains the operative provisions to which tax advisors most often refer. For example, they speak of "Sec. 351 transactions," "Sec. 306 stock," and "Sec. 1231 gains and losses." Although a tax advisor need not know all the IRC sections, paragraphs, and parts, he or she must be familiar with the IRC's organizational scheme to read and interpret it correctly. The language of the IRC is replete with cross-references to titles, paragraphs, subparagraphs, and so on.

EXAMPLE C1-5 ▶ Section 7701, a definitional section, begins, "When used in this title . . ." and then provides a series of definitions. Because of this broad reference, a Sec. 7701 definition applies for all of Title 26; that is, it applies for purposes of the income tax, estate and gift tax, excise tax, and so on.　◀

EXAMPLE C1-6 ▶ Section 302(b)(3) allows taxpayers whose stock holdings are completely terminated in a redemption (a corporation's purchase of its stock from one or more of its shareholders) to receive capital gain treatment on the excess of the redemption proceeds over the stock's basis instead of ordinary income treatment on the entire proceeds. Section 302(c)(2)(A) states, "In the case of a distribution described in subsection (b)(3), section 318(a)(1) shall not apply if. . . ." Further, Sec. 302(c)(2)(C)(i) indicates "Subparagraph (A) shall not apply to a distribution to any entity unless. . . ." Thus, in determining whether a taxpayer will receive capital gain treatment for a stock redemption, a tax advisor must be able to locate and interpret various cross-referenced IRC sections, subsections, paragraphs, subparagraphs, and clauses.　◀

TREASURY REGULATIONS

The Treasury Department issues regulations that expound upon the IRC. Treasury Regulations often provide examples with computations that assist the reader in understanding the IRC's statutory language.[9]

---

[8] S. Rept. No. 105-174, 105th Cong., 1st Sess. (unpaginated) (1998).

[9] Treasury Regulations are formulated on the basis of Treasury Decisions (T.D.s). The numbers of the Treasury Decisions that form the basis of a Treasury Regulation usually are found in the notes at the end of the regulation.

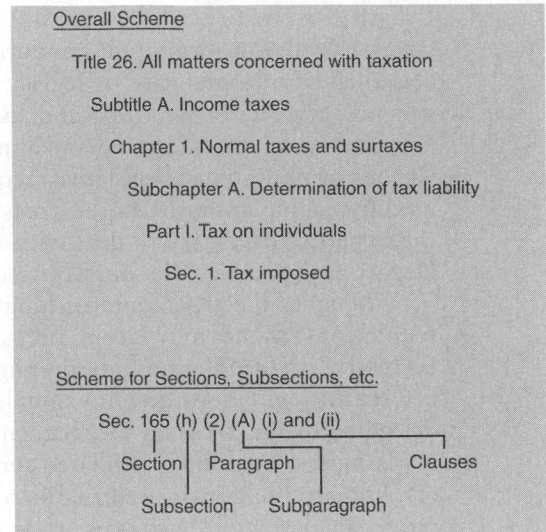

FIGURE C1-2 ▶ ORGANIZATIONAL SCHEME OF THE INTERNAL REVENUE CODE

Because of frequent IRC changes, the Treasury Department does not always update the regulations in a timely manner. Consequently, when consulting a regulation, a tax advisor should check its introductory or end note to determine when the regulation was adopted. If the regulation was adopted before the most recent revision of the applicable IRC section, the regulation should be treated as authoritative to the extent consistent with the revision. Thus, for example, if a regulation issued before the passage of an IRC amendment specifies a dollar amount, and the amendment changed the dollar amount, the regulation should be regarded as authoritative in all respects except for the dollar amount.

PROPOSED, TEMPORARY, AND FINAL REGULATIONS. A Treasury Regulation is first issued in proposed form to the public, which is given an opportunity to comment on it. Parties most likely to comment are individual tax practitioners and representatives of organizations such as the American Bar Association, the Tax Division of the AICPA, and the American Taxation Association. The comments may suggest that the proposed rules could affect taxpayers more adversely than Congress had anticipated. In drafting a final regulation, the Treasury Department generally considers the comments and may modify the rules accordingly. If the comments are favorable, the Treasury Department usually finalizes the regulation with minor revisions. If the comments are unfavorable, it finalizes the regulation with major revisions or allows the proposed regulation to expire.

Proposed regulations are just that—proposed. Consequently, they carry no more authoritative weight than do the arguments of the IRS in a court brief. Nevertheless, they represent the Treasury Department's official interpretation of the IRC. By contrast, **temporary regulations** are binding on the taxpayer. Effective as of the date of their publication, they often are issued immediately after passage of a major tax act to guide taxpayers and their advisors on procedural or computational matters. Regulations issued as temporary are concurrently issued as proposed. Because their issuance is not preceded by a public comment period, they are regarded as somewhat less authoritative than final regulations.

Once finalized, regulations can be effective as of the date they were proposed or the date temporary regulations preceding them were first published in the *Federal Register*, a daily publication that contains federal government pronouncements. For changes to the IRC enacted after July 29, 1996, the Treasury Department generally cannot issue regulations with retroactive effect.

INTERPRETATIVE AND LEGISLATIVE REGULATIONS. In addition to being officially classified as proposed, temporary, or final, Treasury Regulations are unofficially classified as interpretative or legislative. **Interpretative regulations** are issued under the general authority of Sec. 7805 and, as the name implies, merely make the IRC's statutory language easier to understand and apply. In addition, they often provide illustrations as to various computations. **Legislative regulations**, by contrast, arise where Congress delegates its rule-making authority to the Treasury Department. Because Congress believes it lacks the expertise necessary to deal with a highly technical matter, it instructs the Treasury Department to articulate substantive tax principles relating to the matter.

Whenever the IRC contains language such as "The Secretary shall prescribe such regulations as he may deem necessary" or "under regulations prescribed by the Secretary," the regulations interpreting the IRC provision are legislative. The consolidated tax return regulations are an example of legislative regulations. In Sec. 1502, Congress delegated to the Treasury Department authority to issue regulations that determine the tax liability of a group of affiliated corporations filing a consolidated tax return. As a precondition to filing such a return, the corporations must consent to follow the consolidated return regulations.[10] Such consent generally precludes the corporations from later arguing in court that the regulatory provisions are invalid.

AUTHORITATIVE WEIGHT. Final regulations are presumed to be valid and have almost the same authoritative weight as the IRC. Despite this presumption, taxpayers occasionally argue that a regulation is invalid and, consequently, should not be followed. A court will not strike down an interpretative regulation unless, in its opinion, the regulation is "unreasonable and plainly inconsistent with the revenue statutes."[11] In other words, a court is unlikely to invalidate a legislative regulation because it recognizes that Congress has delegated to the Treasury Department authority to issue a specific set of rules. Nevertheless, courts have invalidated legislative regulations where, in their opinion, the regulations exceeded the scope of power delegated to the Treasury Department,[12] were contrary to the IRC,[13] or were unreasonable.[14]

In assessing the validity of Treasury Regulations, some courts apply the **legislative reenactment doctrine**. Under this doctrine, a regulation is deemed to receive Congressional approval whenever the IRC provision under which the regulation was issued is reenacted without amendment.[15] Underlying this doctrine is the rationale that, if Congress believed that the regulation offered an erroneous interpretation of the IRC, it would have amended the IRC to conform to its belief. Congress's failure to amend the IRC signifies approval of the regulation.[16] This doctrine is predicated upon the power of Congress under the Constitution to lay taxes. The power implies that, if Congress is dissatisfied with the manner in which either the executive or the judiciary have interpreted the IRC, it can invalidate these interpretations through new legislation.

KEY POINT

The older a Treasury Regulation becomes, the less likely a court is to invalidate the regulation. The legislative reenactment doctrine holds that if a regulation did not reflect the intent of Congress, lawmakers would have changed the statute in subsequent legislation to obtain their desired objectives.

STOP & THINK

Question: You are researching the manner in which a deduction is calculated. You consult Treasury Regulations for guidance because the IRC states that the calculation is to be done "in a manner prescribed by the Secretary." After reviewing these authorities, you conclude that another way of doing the calculation arguably is correct under an intuitive approach. This approach would result in a lower tax liability for the client. Should you follow the Treasury Regulations or use the intuitive approach and argue that the regulations are invalid?

---

10 Sec. 1501.
11 *CIR v. South Texas Lumber Co.*, 36 AFTR 604, 48-1 USTC ¶5922 (USSC, 1948). In *U.S. v. Douglas B. Cartwright, Executor*, 31 AFTR 2d 73-1461, 73-1 USTC ¶12,926 (USSC, 1973), the Supreme Court concluded that a regulation dealing with the valuation of mutual fund shares for estate and gift tax purposes was invalid.
12 *McDonald v. CIR*, 56 AFTR 2d 5318, 85-2 USTC ¶9494 (5th Cir., 1985).
13 *Jeanese, Inc. v. U.S.*, 15 AFTR 2d 429, 65-1 USTC ¶9259 (9th Cir., 1965).

14 *United States v. Vogel Fertilizer Co.*, 49 AFTR 2d 82-491, 82-1 USTC ¶9134 (USSC, 1982).
15 *United States v. Homer O. Correll*, 20 AFTR 2d 5845, 68 USTC ¶9101 (USSC, 1967).
16 One can rebut the presumption that Congress approved of the regulation by showing that Congress was unaware of the regulation when it reenacted the statute.

Solution: Because of the language "in a manner prescribed by the Secretary," the Treasury Regulations dealing with the calculation are legislative. Whenever Congress calls for legislative regulations, it explicitly authorizes the Treasury Department to write the "rules." As a consequence, such regulations are more difficult than interpretative regulations to be overturned by the courts. Thus, unless you intend to challenge the Treasury Regulations and believe you will prevail in court, you should follow them.

CITATIONS. Citations to Treasury Regulations are relatively easy to understand. One or more numbers appear before a decimal place, and several numbers follow the decimal place. The numbers immediately following the decimal place indicate the IRC section being interpreted. The numbers preceding the decimal place indicate the general subject of the regulation. Numbers that often appear before the decimal place and their general subjects are as follows:

Number	General Subject Matter
1	Income tax
20	Estate tax
25	Gift tax
301	Administrative and procedural matters
601	Procedural rules

The number following the IRC section number indicates the numerical sequence of the regulation, such as the fifth regulation. No relationship exists between this number and the subsection of the IRC being interpreted. An example of a citation to a final regulation is as follows:

Reg. Sec.   1.165 – 5

Income tax   IRC section   Fifth regulation

Citations to proposed or temporary regulations follow the same format. They are referenced as Prop. Reg. Sec. or Temp. Reg. Sec. For temporary regulations the numbering system following the IRC section number always begins with the number of the regulation and an upper case T (e.g., -1T).

Section 165 addresses the broad topic of losses and is interpreted by several regulations. According to its caption, the topic of Reg. Sec. 1.165-5 is worthless securities, which also is addressed in subsection (g) of IRC Sec. 165. Parenthetical information following the text of the Treasury Regulation indicates that the regulation was last revised on December 5, 1972, by Treasury Decision (T.D.) 7224. Section 165(g) was last amended on December 21, 2000. Thus, a researcher must be aware that some regulations may be outdated by subsequent IRC amendments.

When referencing a regulation, the researcher should fine-tune the citation to indicate the precise passage that supports his or her conclusion. An example of such a detailed citation is Reg. Sec. 1.165-5(i), Ex. 2(i), which refers to paragraph (i) of Example 2, found in paragraph (i) of the fifth regulation interpreting Sec. 165.

ADMINISTRATIVE PRONOUNCEMENTS

The IRS interprets the IRC through **administrative pronouncements,** the most important of which are discussed below. After consulting the IRC and Treasury Regulations, tax advisors are likely next to consult these pronouncements.

REVENUE RULINGS. In **revenue rulings,** the IRS indicates the tax consequences of specific transactions encountered in practice. For example, in a revenue ruling, the IRS might indicate whether the exchange of stock for stock derivatives in a corporate acquisition is tax-free.

The IRS issues more than 50 revenue rulings a year. These rulings do not rank as high in the hierarchy of authorities as do Treasury Regulations or federal court cases. They simply represent the IRS's view of the tax law. Taxpayers who do not follow a revenue ruling will not incur a substantial understatement penalty if they have substantial authority for different treatment.[17] Nonetheless, the IRS presumes that the tax treatment specified in a revenue ruling is correct. Consequently, if an examining agent discovers in an audit that a taxpayer did not adopt the position prescribed in a revenue ruling, the agent will contend that the taxpayer's tax liability should be adjusted to reflect that position.

Soon after it is issued, a revenue ruling appears in the weekly *Internal Revenue Bulletin* (cited as I.R.B.), published by the U.S. Government Printing Office (GPO). Revenue rulings later appear in the *Cumulative Bulletin* (cited as C.B.), a bound volume issued semiannually by the GPO. An example of a citation to a revenue ruling appearing in the *Cumulative Bulletin* is as follows:

Rev. Rul. 97-4, 1997-1 C.B. 5.

This is the fourth ruling issued in 1997, and it appears on page 5 of Volume 1 of the 1997 *Cumulative Bulletin*. Before the GPO publishes the pertinent volume of the *Cumulative Bulletin*, researchers should use citations to the *Internal Revenue Bulletin*. An example of such a citation follows:

Rev. Rul. 2004-21, 2004-10 I.R.B. 544.

For revenue rulings (and other IRS pronouncements) issued after 1999, the full four digits of the year of issuance are set forth in the title. For revenue rulings (and other IRS pronouncements) issued before 2000, only the last two digits of the year of issuance are set forth in the title. The above citation represents the twenty-first ruling for 2004. This ruling is located on page 544 of the *Internal Revenue Bulletin* for the tenth week of 2004. Once a revenue ruling is published in the *Cumulative Bulletin*, only the citation to the *Cumulative Bulletin* should be used. Thus, a citation to the I.R.B. is temporary.

REVENUE PROCEDURES. As the name suggests, **revenue procedures** are IRS pronouncements that usually deal with the procedural aspects of tax practice. For example, one revenue procedure deals with the manner in which tip income should be reported. Another revenue procedure describes the requirements for reproducing paper substitutes for informational returns such as Form 1099.

As with revenue rulings, revenue procedures are published first in the *Internal Revenue Bulletin*, then in the *Cumulative Bulletin*. An example of a citation to a revenue procedure appearing in the *Cumulative Bulletin* is as follows:

Rev. Proc. 97-19, 1997-1 C.B. 644.

This pronouncement is found in Volume 1 of the 1997 *Cumulative Bulletin* on page 644. It is the nineteenth revenue procedure issued in 1997.

In addition to revenue rulings and revenue procedures, the *Cumulative Bulletin* contains IRS notices, as well as the texts of proposed regulations, treaties and tax conventions, committee reports, and U.S. Supreme Court decisions.

LETTER RULINGS. **Letter rulings** are initiated by taxpayers who ask the IRS to explain the tax consequences of a particular transaction.[18] The IRS provides its explanation in the form of a letter ruling, that is, a personal response to the taxpayer requesting an answer. Only the taxpayer to whom the ruling is addressed may rely on it as authority. Nevertheless, letter rulings are significant to other taxpayers and to tax advisors because they offer insight into the IRS's position on the tax treatment of particular transactions.

SELF-STUDY QUESTION

Are letter rulings of precedential value for third parties?

ANSWER

No. A letter ruling is binding only on the taxpayer to whom the ruling was issued. Nevertheless, letter rulings can be very useful to third parties because they provide insight as to the IRS's opinion about the tax consequences of various transactions.

[17] Chapter C15 discusses the authoritative support taxpayers and tax advisors should have for positions they adopt on a tax return.

[18] Chapter C15 further discusses letter rulings.

Originally the public did not have access to letter rulings issued to other taxpayers. As a result of Sec. 6110, enacted in 1976, letter rulings (with confidential information deleted) are accessible to the general public and have been reproduced by major tax services. An example of a citation to a letter ruling appears below:

Ltr. Rul. 200130006 (August 6, 2001).

The first four digits (two if issued before 2000) indicate the year in which the ruling was made public, in this case, 2001.[19] The next two digits denote the week in which the ruling was made public, here the thirtieth. The last three numbers indicate the numerical sequence of the ruling for the week, here the sixth. The date in parentheses denotes the date of the ruling.

OTHER INTERPRETATIONS

Technical Advice Memoranda. When the IRS audits a taxpayer's return, the IRS agent might ask the IRS national office for advice on a complicated, technical matter. The national office will provide its advice in a **technical advice memorandum**, released to the public in the form of a letter ruling.[20] Researchers can identify which letter rulings are technical advice memoranda by introductory language such as, "In response to a request for technical advice. . . ." An example of a citation to a technical advice memorandum is as follows:

T.A.M. 9801001 (January 1, 1998).

This citation refers to the first technical advice memorandum issued in the first week of 1998. The memorandum is dated January 1, 1998.

Information Releases. If the IRS wants to disseminate information to the general public, it will issue an **information release**. Information releases are written in lay terms and are dispatched to thousands of newspapers throughout the country. The IRS, for example, may issue an information release to announce the standard mileage rate for business travel. An example of a citation to an information release is as follows:

I.R. 86-70 (June 12, 1986).

This citation is to the seventieth information release issued in 1986. The release is dated June 12, 1986.

Announcements and Notices. The IRS also disseminates information to tax practitioners in the form of **announcements** and **notices**. These pronouncements generally are more technical than information releases and frequently address current tax developments. After passage of a major tax act, and before the Treasury Department has had an opportunity to issue proposed or temporary regulations, the IRS may issue an announcement or notice to clarify the legislation. The IRS is bound to follow the announcement or notice just as it is bound to follow a revenue procedure or revenue ruling. Examples of citations to announcements and notices are as follows:

Announcement 2004-1, 2004-1 I.R.B. 254.
Notice 2004-3, 2004-5 I.R.B. 391.

The first citation is to the first announcement issued in 2004. It can be found on page 254 of the first *Internal Revenue Bulletin* for 2004. The second citation is to the third notice issued in 2004. It can be found on page 391 of the fifth *Internal Revenue Bulletin* for 2004. Notices and announcements appear in both the *Internal Revenue Bulletin* and the *Cumulative Bulletin*.

---

[19] Sometimes a letter ruling is cited as PLR (private letter ruling) instead of Ltr. Rul.

[20] Technical advice memoranda are discussed further in Chapter C15.

JUDICIAL DECISIONS

Judicial decisions are an important source of tax law. Judges are reputed to be unbiased individuals who decide questions of fact (the existence of a fact or the occurrence of an event) or questions of law (the applicability of a legal principle or the proper interpretation of a legal term or provision). Judges do not always agree on the tax consequences of a particular transaction or event. Therefore, tax advisors often must derive conclusions against the background of conflicting judicial authorities. For example, a U.S. district court might disagree with the Tax Court on the deductibility of an expense. Likewise, one circuit court might disagree with another circuit court on the same issue.

OVERVIEW OF THE COURT SYSTEM.   A taxpayer may begin tax litigation in any of three courts: the U.S. Tax Court, the U.S. Court of Federal Claims (formerly the U.S. Claims Court), or U.S. district courts. Court precedents are important in deciding where to begin such litigation (see page C1-21 for a discussion of precedent). Also important is when the taxpayer must pay the deficiency the IRS contends is due. A taxpayer who wants to litigate either in a U.S. district court or in the U.S. Court of Federal Claims must first pay the deficiency. The taxpayer then files a claim for refund, which the IRS is likely to deny. Following this denial, the taxpayer must petition the court for a refund. If the taxpayer wins the refund lawsuit, he or she receives a refund of the taxes in question plus interest. If the taxpayer begins litigation in the Tax Court, on the other hand, he or she need not pay the deficiency unless and until the court decides the case against him or her. In that event, the taxpayer also must pay interest and penalties.[21] A taxpayer who believes that a jury would be sympathetic to his or her case should litigate in a U.S. district court, the only forum where a jury trial is possible.

If a party loses at the trial court level, it can appeal the decision to a higher court. Appeals of Tax Court and U.S. district court decisions are made to the court of appeals for the taxpayer's circuit. There are eleven geographical circuits designated by numbers, the District of Columbia Circuit, and the Federal Circuit. The map in Figure C1-3 shows the states that lie in the various circuits. California, for example, lies in the Ninth Circuit. When referring to these appellate courts, instead of saying, for example, "the Court of Appeals for the Ninth Circuit," one generally says "the Ninth Circuit." All decisions of the U.S. Court of Federal Claims are appealable to one court—the Court of Appeals for the Federal Circuit—irrespective of where the taxpayer resides or does business.[22] The only cases the Federal Circuit hears are those that originate in the U.S. Court of Federal Claims.

The party losing at the appellate level can petition the U.S. Supreme Court to review the case under a **writ of certiorari**. If the Supreme Court agrees to hear the case, it grants certiorari.[23] If it refuses to hear the case, it denies certiorari. In recent years, the Court has granted certiorari in only about six to ten tax cases per year. Figure C1-4 and Table C1-1 provide an overview and summary of the court system with respect to tax matters.

THE U.S. TAX COURT.   The U.S. Tax Court was created in 1942 as a successor to the Board of Tax Appeals. It is a court of national jurisdiction that hears only tax-related cases. All taxpayers, regardless of their state of residence or place of business, may litigate in the Tax Court. It has 19 judges, including one chief judge.[24] The President, with the consent of the Senate, appoints the judges for a 15-year term and may reappoint them for an additional term. The judges, specialists in tax-related matters, periodically travel to roughly 100 cities throughout the country to hear cases. In most instances, only one judge hears a case.

The Tax Court issues both regular and memorandum (memo) decisions. Generally, the first time the Tax Court decides a legal issue, its decision appears as a **regular decision**.

SELF-STUDY QUESTION

What are some of the factors that a taxpayer should consider when deciding in which court to file a tax-related claim?

ANSWER

(1) Each court's published precedent pertaining to the issue, (2) desirability of a jury trial, (3) tax expertise of each court, and (4) when the deficiency must be paid.

ADDITIONAL COMMENT

Because the Tax Court deals only with tax cases, it presumably has a higher level of tax expertise than do other courts. Tax Court judges are appointed by the President, in part, due to their considerable tax experience. In August 2005, the Tax Court judges faced a backlog of about 22,457 cases.

---

[21] Revenue Procedure 84-58, 1984-2, C.B. 501, provides procedures for taxpayers to make remittances or apply overpayments to stop the accrual of interest on deficiencies.
[22] The Court of Claims was reconstituted as the United States Court of Claims in 1982. In 1992, this court was renamed the U.S. Court of Federal Claims.
[23] The granting of certiorari signifies that the Supreme Court is granting an appellate review. The denial of certiorari does not necessarily mean that the

Supreme Court endorses the lower court's decision. It simply means the court has decided not to hear the case.
[24] The Tax Court also periodically appoints, depending on budgetary constraints, a number of trial judges and senior judges who hear cases and render decisions with the same authority as the regular Tax Court judges.

FIGURE C1-3 ▶ MAP OF THE GEOGRAPHICAL BOUNDARIES OF THE CIRCUIT COURTS OF APPEALS

Source: Reprinted from *West's Federal Reporter,* with permission. © West, a Thomson business.

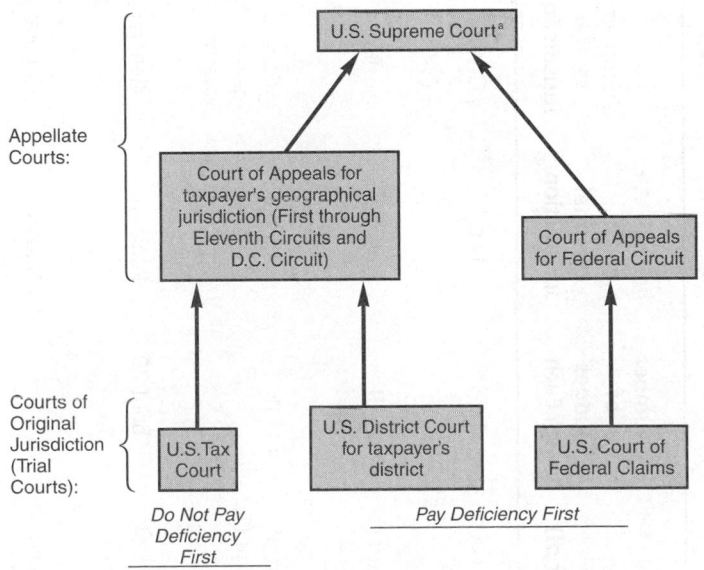

FIGURE C1-4 ▶ OVERVIEW OF COURT SYSTEM—TAX MATTERS

▼ TABLE C1-1
Summary of Court System—Tax Matters

Court(s) (Number of)	Number of Judges on Each	Personal Jurisdiction	Subject Matter Jurisdiction	Determines Questions of Fact	Trial by Jury	Precedents Followed	Where Opinions Published
U.S. district courts (over 95)	1-28*	Local	General	Yes	Yes	Same court Court for circuit where situated U.S. Supreme Court	Federal Supplement American Federal Tax Reports United States Tax Cases
U.S. Tax Court (1)	19	National	Tax	Yes	No	Same court Court for taxpayer's circuit U.S. Supreme Court	Tax Court of the U.S. Reports CCH Tax Court Memorandum Decisions RIA Tax Court Memorandum Decisions
U.S. Court of Federal Claims (1)	16	National	Claims against U.S. Government	Yes	No	Same court Federal Circuit Court U.S. Supreme Court	Federal Reporter (pre-1982) U.S. Court of Federal Claims American Federal Tax Reports United States Tax Cases
U.S. Courts of Appeals (13)	About 20	Regional	General	No	No	Same court U.S. Supreme Court	Federal Reporter American Federal Tax Reports United States Tax Cases
U.S. Supreme Court (1)	9	National	General	No	No	Same court	U.S. Supreme Court Reports Supreme Court Reporter United States Reports, Lawyers' Edition American Federal Tax Reports United States Tax Cases

*Although the number of judges assigned to each court varies, only one judge decides a case.

Memo decisions, on the other hand, usually deal with factual variations of previously decided cases. Nevertheless, regular and memo decisions carry the same authoritative weight.

At times, the chief judge determines that a particular case concerns an important issue that the entire Tax Court should consider. In such a situation, the words *reviewed by the court* appear at the end of the majority opinion. Any concurring or dissenting opinions follow the majority opinion.[25]

Another phrase sometimes appearing at the end of a Tax Court opinion is *Entered under Rule 155*. This phrase signifies that the court has reached a decision concerning the tax treatment of an item but has left computation of the deficiency to the two litigating parties.

Small Cases Procedure. Taxpayers have the option of having their cases heard under the **small cases procedure** of the Tax Court if the amount in controversy on an annual basis does not exceed $50,000.[26] This procedure is less formal than the regular Tax Court procedure, and taxpayers can appear without an attorney.[27] The cases are heard by special commissioners instead of by one of the 19 Tax Court judges. A disadvantage of the small cases procedure for the losing party is that the decision cannot be appealed. The opinions of the commissioners generally are not published and have no precedential value.

Acquiescence Policy. The IRS has adopted a policy of announcing whether, in future cases involving similar facts and similar issues, it will follow federal court decisions that are adverse to it. This policy is known as the IRS **acquiescence policy**. If the IRS wants taxpayers to know that it will follow an adverse decision in future cases involving similar facts and issues, it will announce its "acquiescence" in the decision. Conversely, if it wants taxpayers to know that it will not follow the decision in such future cases, it will announce its "nonacquiescence." The IRS does not announce its acquiescence or nonacquiescence in every decision it loses.

The IRS publishes its acquiescences and nonacquiescences as "Actions on Decision" first in the *Internal Revenue Bulletin,* then in the *Cumulative Bulletin.* Before 1991, the IRS acquiesced or nonacquiesced in regular Tax Court decisions only. In 1991, it broadened the scope of its policy to include adverse U.S. Claims Court, U.S. district court, and U.S. circuit court decisions.

In cases involving multiple issues, the IRS may acquiesce in some issues but not others. In decisions supported by extensive reasoning, it may acquiesce in the result but not the rationale (*acq. in result*). Furthermore, it may retroactively revoke an acquiescence or nonacquiescence. The footnotes to the relevant announcement in the *Internal Revenue Bulletin* and *Cumulative Bulletin* indicate the nature and extent of IRS acquiescences and nonacquiescences.

These acquiescences and nonacquiescences have important implications for taxpayers. If a taxpayer bases his or her position on a decision in which the IRS has nonacquiesced, he or she can expect an IRS challenge in the event of an audit. In such circumstances, the taxpayer's only recourse may be litigation. On the other hand, if the taxpayer bases his or her position on a decision in which the IRS has acquiesced, he or she can expect little or no challenge. In either case, the examining agent will be bound by the IRS position.

Published Opinions and Citations. Regular Tax Court decisions are published by the U.S. Government Printing Office in a bound volume known as the *Tax Court of the United States Reports*. Soon after a decision is made public, Research Institute of America

---

[25] A judge who issues a concurring opinion agrees with the basic outcome of the majority's decision but not with its rationale. A judge who issues a dissenting opinion believes the majority reached an erroneous conclusion.
[26] Sec. 7463. The $50,000 amount includes penalties and additional taxes but excludes interest.

[27] Taxpayers can represent themselves in regular Tax Court proceedings also, even though they are not attorneys. Where taxpayers represent themselves, the words *pro se* appear in the opinion after the taxpayer's name. The Tax Court is the only federal court before which non-attorneys, including CPAs, may practice.

(RIA) and CCH Incorporated (CCH) each publish the decision in its reporter of Tax Court decisions. An official citation to a Tax Court decision is as follows:[28]

MedChem Products, Inc., 116 T.C. 308 (2001).

The citation indicates that this case appears on page 308 in Volume 116 of *Tax Court of the United States Reports* and that the case was decided in 2001.

From 1924 to 1942, regular decisions of the Board of Tax Appeals (predecessor of the Tax Court) were published by the U.S. Government Printing Office in the *United States Board of Tax Appeals Reports.* An example of a citation to a Board of Tax Appeals case is as follows:

J.W. Wells Lumber Co. Trust A., 44 B.T.A. 551 (1941).

This case is found in Volume 44 of the *United States Board of Tax Appeals Reports* on page 551. It is a 1941 decision.

If the IRS has acquiesced or nonacquiesced in a federal court decision, the IRS's action should be denoted in the citation. At times, the IRS will not announce its acquiescence or nonacquiescence until several years after the date of the decision. An example of a citation to a decision in which the IRS has acquiesced is as follows:

Security State Bank, 111 T.C. 210 (1998), *acq.* 2001-1 C.B. xix.

The case appears on page 210 of Volume 111 of the *Tax Court of the United States Reports* and the acquiescence is reported on page xix of Volume 1 of the 2001 *Cumulative Bulletin.* In 2001, the IRS acquiesced in this 1998 decision. A citation to a decision in which the IRS has nonacquiesced is as follows:

Estate of Algerine Allen Smith, 108 T.C. 412 (1997), *nonacq.* 2000-1 C.B. xvi.

The case appears on page 412 of Volume 108 of the *Tax Court of the United States Reports.* The nonacquiescence is reported on page xvi of Volume 1 of the 2000 *Cumulative Bulletin.* In 2000, the IRS nonacquiesced in this 1997 decision.

Tax Court memo decisions are not published by the U.S. Government Printing Office. They are, however, published by RIA in *RIA T.C. Memorandum Decisions* and by CCH in *CCH Tax Court Memorandum Decisions.* In addition, shortly after its issuance, an opinion is made available electronically and in loose-leaf form by RIA and CCH in their respective tax services. The following citation is to a Tax Court memo decision:

Edith G. McKinney, 1981 PH T.C. Memo ¶81,181, 41 TCM 1272.

McKinney is found at Paragraph 81,181 of Prentice Hall's (now RIA's)[29] 1981 *PH T.C. Memorandum Decisions* reporter, and in Volume 41, page 1272, of CCH's *Tax Court Memorandum Decisions.* The 181 in the PH citation indicates that the case is the Tax Court's 181st memo decision of the year. A more recent citation is formatted in the same way but refers to RIA memo decisions.

Paul F. Belloff, 1992 RIA T.C. Memo ¶92,346, 63 TCM 3150.

ADDITIONAL COMMENT

Once the IRS has acquiesced in a federal court decision, other taxpayers generally will not need to litigate the same issue. However, the IRS can change its mind and revoke a previous acquiescence or nonacquiescence. References to acquiescences or nonacquiescences in federal court decisions can be found in the citators.

KEY POINT

To access all Tax Court cases, a tax advisor must refer to two different publications. The regular opinions are found in the *Tax Court of the United States Reports,* published by the U.S. Government Printing Office, and the memo decisions are published by both RIA (formerly PH) and CCH in their own court reporters.

---

[28] In a citation to a case decided by the Tax Court, only the name of the plaintiff (taxpayer) is listed. The defendant is understood to be the Commissioner of Internal Revenue whose name usually is not shown in the citation. In cases decided by other courts, the name of the plaintiff is listed first and the name of the defendant second. For non-Tax Court cases, the Commissioner of Internal Revenue is referred to as *CIR* in our footnotes and text.

[29] For several years the Prentice Hall Information Services division published its *Federal Taxes 2nd* tax service and a number of related publications, such as the *PH T.C. Memorandum Decisions.* Changes in ownership occurred, and in late 1991 Thomson Professional Publishing added the former Prentice Hall tax materials to the product line of its RIA tax publishing division. Some print products such as the *PH T.C. Memorandum Decisions* still have the Prentice Hall name on the spine of older editions.

U.S. DISTRICT COURTS.   Each state has at least one U.S. district court, and more populous states have more than one. Each district court is independent of the others and is thus free to issue its own decisions, subject to the precedential constraints discussed later in this chapter. Different types of cases—not just tax cases—are heard in this forum. A district court is the only forum in which the taxpayer may have a jury decide questions of fact. Depending on the circumstances, a jury trial might be advantageous for the taxpayer.[30]

District court decisions are officially reported in the *Federal Supplement* (cited as F. Supp.) published by West Publishing Co. (West). Some decisions are not officially reported and are referred to as **unreported decisions**. Decisions by U.S. district courts on the topic of taxation also are published by RIA and CCH in secondary reporters that contain only tax-related opinions. RIA's reporter is *American Federal Tax Reports* (cited as AFTR).[31] CCH's reporter is *U.S. Tax Cases* (cited as USTC). A case not offically reported nevertheless might be published in the AFTR and USTC. An example of a complete citation to a U.S. district court decision is as follows:

Alfred Abdo, Jr. v. IRS, 234 F. Supp. 2d 553, 90 AFTR 2d 2002-7484, 2003-1 USTC ¶50,107 (DC North Carolina, 2002).

ADDITIONAL COMMENT

A citation, at a minimum, should contain the following information: (1) the name of the case, (2) the reporter that publishes the case along with both a volume and page (or paragraph) number, (3) the year the case was decided, and (4) the court that decided the case.

In the example above, the **primary citation** is to the *Federal Supplement*. The case appears on page 553 of Volume 234 of the second series of this reporter. **Secondary citations** are to *American Federal Tax Reports* and *U.S. Tax Cases*. The same case is found in Volume 90 of the second series of the AFTR, page 2002-7484 (meaning page 7484 in the volume containing 2002 cases) and in Volume 1 of the 2003 USTC at Paragraph 50,107. The parenthetical information indicates that the case was decided in 2002 by the U.S. District Court for North Carolina. Because some judicial decisions have greater precedential weight than others (e.g., a Supreme Court decision versus a district court decision), information relating to the identity of the adjudicating court is useful in evaluating the authoritative value of the decision.

ADDITIONAL COMMENT

The U.S. Court of Federal Claims adjudicates claims (including suits to recover federal income taxes) against the U.S. Government. This court usually hears cases in Washington, D.C., but will hold sessions in other locations as the court deems necessary.

U.S. COURT OF FEDERAL CLAIMS.   The U.S. Court of Federal Claims, another court of first instance that addresses tax matters, has nationwide jurisdiction. Originally, this court was called the U.S. Court of Claims (cited as Ct. Cl.), and its decisions were appealable to the U.S. Supreme Court only. In a reorganization, effective October 1, 1982, the reconstituted court was named the U.S. Claims Court (cited as Cl. Ct.), and its decisions became appealable to the Circuit Court of Appeals for the Federal Circuit. In October 1992, the court's name was again changed to the U.S. Court of Federal Claims (cited as Fed. Cl.).

Beginning in 1982, U.S. Claims Court decisions were reported officially in the *Claims Court Reporter*, published by West from 1982 to 1992.[32] An example of a citation to a U.S. Claims Court decision appears below:

Benjamin Raphan v. U.S., 3 Cl. Ct. 457, 52 AFTR 2d 83-5987, 83-2 USTC ¶9613 (1983).

The *Raphan* case appears on page 457 of Volume 3 of the *Claims Court Reporter*. Secondary citations are to Volume 52, page 83-5987 of the AFTR, Second Series, and to Volume 2 of the 1983 USTC at Paragraph 9613.

---

[30] Taxpayers might prefer to have a jury trial if they believe a jury will be sympathetic to their case.
[31] The *American Federal Tax Reports* (AFTR) is published in two series. The first series, which includes opinions issued up to 1957, is cited as AFTR. The second series, which includes opinions issued after 1957, is cited as AFTR 2d. The *Alfred Abdo, Jr.* decision cited as an illustration of a U.S. district court decision appears in the second *American Federal Tax Reports* series.

[32] Before the creation in 1982 of the U.S. Claims Court (and the *Claims Court Reporter*), the opinions of the U.S. Court of Claims were reported in either the *Federal Supplement* (F. Supp.) or the *Federal Reporter, Second Series* (F.2d). The *Federal Supplement* is the primary source of U.S. Court of Claims opinions from 1932 through January 19, 1960. Opinions issued from January 20, 1960, to October 1982 are reported in the *Federal Reporter, Second Series*.

Effective with the 1992 reorganization, decisions of the U.S. Court of Federal Claims are now reported in the *Federal Claims Reporter.* An example of a citation to an opinion published in this reporter is presented below:

> *Jeffrey G. Sharp v. U.S.*, 27 Fed. Cl. 52, 70 AFTR 2d 92-6040, 92-2 USTC ¶50,561 (1992).

The *Sharp* case appears on page 52 of Volume 27 of the *Federal Claims Reporter,* on page 6040 of the 70th volume of the AFTR, Second Series, and at Paragraph 50,561 of Volume 2 of the 1992 USTC reporter. Note that, even though the name of the reporter published by West has changed, the volume numbers continue in sequence as if no name change had occurred.

CIRCUIT COURTS OF APPEALS. Lower court decisions are appealable by the losing party to the court of appeals for the circuit in which the litigation originated. Generally, if the case began in the Tax Court or a U.S. district court, the case is appealable to the circuit for the individual's residence as of the appeal date. For a corporation, the case is appealable to the circuit for the corporation's principal place of business. The Federal Circuit hears all appeals of cases originating in the U.S. Court of Federal Claims.

As mentioned earlier, there are 11 geographical circuits designated by numbers, the District of Columbia Circuit, and the Federal Circuit. In October 1981, the Eleventh Circuit was created by moving Alabama, Georgia, and Florida from the Fifth to a new geographical circuit. The Eleventh Circuit has adopted the policy of following as precedent all decisions made by the Fifth Circuit during the time the states currently constituting the Eleventh Circuit were part of the Fifth Circuit.[33]

EXAMPLE C1-7 ▶ In the current year, the Eleventh Circuit first considered an issue in a case involving a Florida taxpayer. In 1980, the Fifth Circuit had ruled on the same issue in a case involving a Louisiana taxpayer. Because Florida was part of the Fifth Circuit in 1980, under the policy adopted by the Eleventh Circuit, it will follow the Fifth Circuit's earlier decision. Had the Fifth Circuit's decision been rendered in 1982—after the creation of the Eleventh Circuit—the Eleventh Circuit would not have been bound by the Fifth Circuit's decision. ◀

As the later discussion of precedent points out, different circuits may reach different conclusions concerning similar facts and issues.

Circuit court decisions—regardless of topic (e.g., civil rights, securities law, and taxation)—are now reported officially in the *Federal Reporter, Third Series* (cited as F.3d), published by West. The third series was created in October 1993 after the volume number for the second series reached 999. The primary citation to a circuit court opinion should be to the *Federal Reporter.* Tax decisions of the circuit courts also appear in the *American Federal Tax Reports* and *U.S. Tax Cases.* Below is an example of a citation to a 1994 circuit court decision:

> *Leonard Greene v. U.S.*, 13 F.3d 577, 73 AFTR 2d 94-746, 94-1 USTC ¶50,022 (2nd Cir., 1994).

The *Greene* case appears on page 577 of Volume 13 of the *Federal Reporter, Third Series.* It also is published in Volume 73, page 94-746 of the AFTR, Second Series, and in Volume 1, Paragraph 50,022, of the 1994 USTC. The parenthetical information indicates that the Second Circuit decided the case in 1994. (A *Federal Reporter, Second Series* reference is found in footnote 33 of this chapter.)

---

[33] *Bonner v. City of Prichard*, 661 F.2d 1206 (11th Cir., 1981).

ADDITIONAL COMMENT

A judge is not required to follow judicial precedent beyond his or her jurisdiction. Thus, the Tax Court, the U.S. district courts, and the U.S. Court of Federal Claims are not required to follow the others' decisions, nor is a circuit court required to follow the decision of a different circuit court.

U.S. SUPREME COURT. Whichever party loses at the appellate court level can request that the U.S. Supreme Court hear the case. The Supreme Court, however, hears very few tax cases. Unless the circuits are divided on the proper treatment of a tax item, or the issue is deemed to be of great significance, the Supreme Court probably will not hear the case.[34] Supreme Court decisions are the law of the land and take precedence over all other court decisions, including the Supreme Court's earlier decisions. As a practical matter, a Supreme Court interpretation of the IRC is almost as authoritative as an act of Congress. If Congress does not agree with the Court's interpretation, it can amend the IRC to achieve a different result and has in fact done so on a number of occasions. If the Supreme Court declares a tax statute to be unconstitutional, the statute is invalid.

All Supreme Court decisions, regardless of subject, are published in the *United States Supreme Court Reports* (cited as U.S.) by the U.S. Government Printing Office, the *Supreme Court Reporter* (cited as S. Ct.) by West, and the *United States Reports, Lawyers' Edition* (cited as L. Ed.) by Lawyer's Co-Operative Publishing Co. In addition, the AFTR and USTC reporters published by RIA and CCH, respectively, contain Supreme Court decisions concerned with taxation. An example of a citation to a Supreme Court opinion appears below:

> *Boeing Company v. U.S.,* 537 U.S. 437, 91 AFTR 2d 2003-1088, 2003-1 USTC ¶50,273 (USSC, 2003).

According to the primary citation, this case appears in Volume 537, page 437, of the *United States Supreme Court Reports.* According to the secondary citation, it also appears in Volume 91, page 2003-1088, of the AFTR, Second Series, and in Volume 1, Paragraph 50,273, of the 2003 USTC.

Table C1-2 provides a summary of how the IRC, court decisions, revenue rulings, revenue procedures, and other administrative pronouncements should be cited. Primary citations are to the reporters published by West or the U.S. Government Printing Office, and secondary citations are to the AFTR and USTC.

SELF-STUDY QUESTION

Is it possible for the Tax Court to intentionally issue conflicting decisions?

ANSWER

Yes. If the Tax Court issues two decisions that are appealable to different circuit courts and these courts have previously reached different conclusions on the issue, the Tax Court follows the respective precedent in each circuit and issues conflicting decisions. This is a result of the *Golsen* Rule.

PRECEDENTIAL VALUE OF VARIOUS DECISIONS.
Tax Court. The Tax Court is a court of national jurisdiction. Consequently, it generally rules uniformly for all taxpayers, regardless of their residence or place of business. It follows U.S. Supreme Court decisions and its own earlier decisions. It is not bound by cases decided by the U.S. Court of Federal Claims or a U.S. district court, even if the district court has jurisdiction over the taxpayer.

In 1970, the Tax Court adopted what has become known as the *Golsen* Rule.[35] Under this rule, the Tax Court departs from its general policy of adjudicating uniformly for all taxpayers and instead follows the decisions of the court of appeals to which the case in question is appealable. Stated differently, the *Golsen* Rule holds that the Tax Court should rule consistently with decisions of the court for the circuit where the taxpayer resides or does business.

EXAMPLE C1-8 ▶ In the year in which an issue was first litigated, the Tax Court decided that an expenditure was deductible. The government appealed the decision to the Tenth Circuit Court of Appeals and won a reversal. This is the only appellate decision regarding the issue. If and when the Tax Court addresses this issue again, it will hold, with one exception, that the expenditure is deductible. The exception applies to taxpayers in the Tenth Circuit. Under the *Golsen* Rule, these taxpayers will be denied the deduction. ◀

---

[34] *Vogel Fertilizer Co. v. U.S.,* 49 AFTR 2d 82-491, 82-1 USTC ¶9134 (USSC, 1982), is an example of a case the Supreme Court heard to settle a split in judicial authority. The Fifth Circuit, the Tax Court, and the Court of Claims had reached one conclusion on an issue, while the Second, Fourth, and Eighth Circuits had reached another.

[35] The *Golsen* Rule is based on the decision in *Jack E. Golsen,* 54 T.C. 742 (1970).

▼ TABLE C1-2
Summary of Tax-related Primary Sources—Statutory and Administrative

Source Name	Publisher	Materials Provided	Citation Example
U.S. Code, Title 26	Government Printing Office	Internal Revenue Code	Sec. 441(b)
Code of Federal Regulations, Title 26	Government Printing Office	Treasury Regulations (final)	Reg. Sec. 1.461-1(c)
		Treasury Regulations (temporary)	Temp. Reg. Sec. 1.62-1T(e)
Internal Revenue Bulletin	Government Printing Office	Treasury Regulations (proposed)	Prop. Reg. Sec. 1.671-1(h)
		Treasury decisions	T.D. 8756 (January 12, 1998)
		Revenue rulings	Rev. Rul. 2004-18, 2004-8 I.R.B. 509
		Revenue procedures	Rev. Proc. 2004-23, 2003-16 I.R.B. 785
		Committee reports	S.Rept. No. 105-33, 105th Cong., 1st Sess., p. 308 (1997)
		Public laws	P.L. 105-34, Sec. 224(a), enacted August 6, 1997
		Announcements	Announcement 2004-5, 2004-4 I.R.B. 362
		Notices	Notice 2004-14, 2004-10 I.R.B. 582
Cumulative Bulletin	Government Printing Office	Treasury Regulations (proposed)	Prop. Reg. Sec. 1.671-1(h)
		Treasury decisions	T.D. 8756 (January 12, 1998)
		Revenue rulings	Rev. Rul. 84-111, 1984-2 C.B. 88
		Revenue procedures	Rev. Proc. 77-28, 1977-2 C.B. 537
		Committee reports	S.Rept. No. 105-33, 105th Cong., 1st Sess., p. 308 (1997)
		Public laws	P.L. 105-34, Sec. 224(a), enacted August 6, 1997
		Announcements	Announcement 98-1, 1998-1 C.B. 282
		Notices	Notice 88-74, 1988-2 C.B. 385

Summary of Tax-related Primary and Secondary Sources—Judicial

Reporter Name	Publisher	Decisions Published	Citation Example
U.S. Supreme Court Reports	Government Printing Office	U.S. Supreme Court	Boeing Company v. U.S., 537 U.S. 437 (2003)
Supreme Court Reports	West Publishing Company	U.S. Supreme Court	Boeing Company v. U.S., 123 S. Ct. 1099 (2003)
Federal Reporter (1st-3d Series)	West Publishing Company	U.S. Court of Appeal Pre-1982 Court of Claims	Leonard Green v. U.S., 13 F.3d 577 (2nd Cir., 1994)
Federal Supplement Series	West Publishing Company	U.S. District Court	Alfred Abdo, Jr. v. IRS, 234 F. Supp. 2d 553 (DC North Carolina, 2002)
U.S. Court of Federal Claims	West Publishing Company	Court of Federal Claims	Jeffery G. Sharp v. U.S., 27 Fed. Cl. 52 (1992)
Tax Court of the U.S. Reports	Government Printing Office	U.S. Tax Court regular	Security State Bank, 111 T.C. 210 (1998), acq. 2001-1 C.B. xix
Tax Court Memorandum Decisions	CCH Incorporated	U.S. Tax Court memo	Paul F. Belloff, 63 TCM 3150 (1992)
RIA Tax Court Memorandum Decisions	Research Institute of America	U.S. Tax Court memo	Paul F. Belloff, 1992 RIA T.C. Memo ¶92,346
American Federal Tax Reports	Research Institute of America	Tax: all federal courts except Tax Court	Boeing Company v. U.S., 91 AFTR 2d 2003-1 (USSC, 2003)
U.S. Tax Cases	CCH Incorporated	Tax: all federal courts except Tax Court	Ruddick Corp. v. U.S., 81-1 USTC ¶9343 (Ct. Cls., 1981)

U.S. District Court. Because each U.S. district court is independent of the other district courts, the decisions of each have precedential value only within its own jurisdiction (i.e., only with respect to subsequent cases brought before that court). District courts must follow decisions of the U.S. Supreme Court, the circuit court to which the case is appealable, and the district court's own earlier decisions regarding similar facts and issues.

EXAMPLE C1-9 ▶ The U.S. District Court for Rhode Island, the Tax Court, and the Eleventh Circuit have decided cases involving similar facts and issues. Any U.S. district court within the Eleventh Circuit must follow that circuit's decision in future cases involving similar facts and issues. Likewise, the U.S. District Court for Rhode Island must decide such cases consistently with its previous decision. Tax Court decisions are not binding on the district courts. Thus, all district courts other than the one for Rhode Island and those within the Eleventh Circuit are free to decide such cases independently. ◀

U.S. Court of Federal Claims. In adjudicating a dispute, the U.S. Court of Federal Claims must rule consistently with U.S. Supreme Court decisions, decisions of the Circuit Court of Appeals for the Federal Circuit, and its own earlier decisions, including those rendered when the court had a different name. It need not follow decisions of other circuit courts, the Tax Court, or U.S. district courts.

EXAMPLE C1-10 ▶ Assume the same facts as in Example C1-9. In a later year, a case involving similar facts and issues is heard by the U.S. Court of Federal Claims. This court is not bound by precedents set by any of the other courts. Thus, it may reach a conclusion independently of the other courts. ◀

Circuit Courts of Appeals. A circuit court is bound by U.S. Supreme Court decisions and its own earlier decisions. If neither the Supreme Court nor the circuit in question has already decided an issue, the circuit court has no precedent that it must follow, regardless of whether other circuits have ruled on the issue. In such circumstances, the circuit court is said to be writing on a clean slate. In rendering a decision, the judges of that court may adopt another circuit's view, which they are likely to regard as relevant.

EXAMPLE C1-11 ▶ Assume the same facts as in Example C1-9. Any circuit other than the Eleventh would be writing on a clean slate if it adjudicated a case involving similar facts and issues. After reviewing the Eleventh Circuit's decision, another circuit might find it relevant and rule in the same way. ◀

In such a case of "first impression," when the court has had no precedent on which to base a decision, a tax practitioner might look at past opinions of the court to see which other judicial authority the court has found to be "persuasive."

Forum Shopping. Not surprisingly, courts often disagree as to the appropriate tax treatment of the same item. This disagreement gives rise to differing precedents within the various jurisdictions (what is called a "split in judicial authority"). Because taxpayers have the flexibility of choosing where to file a lawsuit, these circumstances afford them the opportunity to **forum shop**. Forum-shopping involves choosing where among the courts to file a lawsuit based on differing precedents.

An example of a split in judicial authority concerned the issue of when it became too late for the IRS to question the proper tax treatment of items that "flowed through" an S corporation's return to a shareholder's return. The key question was this: if the time for assessing a deficiency (limitations period) with respect to the corporation's, but not the shareholder's, return had expired, was the IRS precluded from collecting additional taxes from the shareholder? In *Kelley,*[36] the Ninth Circuit Court of Appeals ruled that the IRS would be barred from collecting additional taxes from the shareholder if the limitations period for the S corporation's return had expired. In *Bufferd,*[37] *Fehlhaber,*[38] and *Green,*[39]

[36] *Daniel M. Kelley v. CIR,* 64 AFTR 2d 89-5025, 89-1 USTC ¶9360 (9th Cir., 1989).
[37] *Sheldon B. Bufferd v. CIR,* 69 AFTR 2d 92-465, 92-1 USTC ¶50,031 (2nd Cir., 1992).
[38] *Robert Fehlhaber v. CIR,* 69 AFTR 2d 92-850, 92-1 USTC ¶50,131 (11th Cir., 1992).
[39] *Charles T. Green v. CIR,* 70 AFTR 2d 92-5077, 92-2 USTC ¶50,340 (5th Cir., 1992).

three other circuit courts ruled that the IRS would be barred from collecting additional taxes from the shareholder if the limitations period for the *shareholder's* return had expired. The Supreme Court affirmed the *Bufferd* decision,[40] establishing that the statute of limitations for the shareholder's return governed. This action brought about certainty and uniformity within the judicial system.

Dictum. At times, a court may comment on an issue or a set of facts not central to the case under review. A court's remark not essential to the determination of a disputed issue, and therefore not binding authority, is called *dictum*. An example of dictum is found in *Central Illinois Public Service Co.*[41] In this case, the U.S. Supreme Court addressed whether lunch reimbursements received by employees constitute wages subject to withholding. Justice Blackman remarked in passing that earnings in the form of interest, rents, and dividends are not wages. This remark is dictum because it is not essential to the determination of whether lunch reimbursements are wages subject to withholding. Although not authoritative, dictum may be cited by taxpayers to bolster an argument in favor of a particular tax result.

 STOP & THINK

Question: You have been researching whether an amount received by your new client can be excluded from her gross income. The IRS is auditing the client's prior year tax return, which another firm prepared. In a similar case decided a few years ago, the Tax Court allowed an exclusion, but the IRS nonacquiesced in the decision. The case involved a taxpayer in the Fourth Circuit. Your client is a resident of Maine, which is in the First Circuit. Twelve years ago, in a case involving another taxpayer, the federal court for the client's district ruled that this type of receipt is not excludable. No other precedent exists. To sustain an exclusion, must your client litigate? Explain. If your client litigates, in which court of first instance should she begin her litigation?

Solution: Because of its nonacquiescence, the IRS is likely to challenge your client's tax treatment. Thus, she may be compelled to litigate. She would not want to litigate in her U.S. district court because it would be bound by its earlier decision, which is unfavorable to taxpayers generally. A good place to begin would be the Tax Court because it is bound by appellate court, but not district court, decisions and because of its earlier pro-taxpayer position. No one can predict how the U.S. Court of Federal Claims would rule because no precedent that it must follow exists.

TAX TREATIES

The United States has concluded **tax treaties** with numerous foreign countries. These treaties address the avoidance of double taxation and other matters. A tax advisor exploring the U.S. tax consequences of a U.S. corporation's business operations in another country should determine whether a treaty between that country and the United States exists. If one does, the tax advisor should ascertain the applicable provisions of the treaty. (See Chapter C16 of this text for a more extensive discussion of treaties.)

TAX PERIODICALS

Tax periodicals assist the researcher in tracing the development of, and analyzing tax law. These periodicals are especially useful when they discuss the legislative history of a recently enacted IRC statute that has little or no administrative or judicial authority on point.

Tax experts write articles on landmark court decisions, proposed regulations, new tax legislation, and other matters. Frequently, those who write articles of a highly technical nature are attorneys, accountants, or professors. Among the periodicals that provide in-depth coverage of tax-related matters are the following:

---

[40] *Sheldon B. Bufferd v. CIR,* 71 AFTR 2d 93-573, 93-1 USTC ¶50,038 (USSC, 1993).

[41] *Central Illinois Public Service Co. v. CIR,* 41 AFTR 2d 78-718, 78-1 USTC ¶9254 (USSC, 1978).

The Journal of Taxation
The Tax Adviser
Practical Tax Strategies
Taxes—the Tax Magazine
Tax Law Review
Tax Notes
Corporate Taxation
Business Entities
Real Estate Taxation
The Review of Taxation of Individuals
Estate Planning

The first six journals are generalized; that is, they deal with a variety of topics. As their titles suggest, the next five are specialized; they deal with specific subjects. All these publications (other than *Tax Notes,* which is published weekly) are published either monthly or quarterly. Daily newsletters, such as the *Daily Tax Report,* published by the Bureau of National Affairs (BNA), are used by tax professionals when they need updates more timely than can be provided by monthly or quarterly publications.

Tax periodicals and tax services are secondary authorities. The IRC, Treasury Regulations, IRS pronouncements, and court opinions are primary authorities. In presenting research results, the tax advisor should always cite primary authorities.

TAX SERVICES

Various publishers provide multivolume commentaries on the tax law in what are familiarly referred to as **tax services**. These commentaries are available in print form and in electronic form via the Internet. While the organizational scheme of the print and Internet versions of each tax service is substantially the same (see "Computers as a Research Tool" below for a description of their salient differences), the organizational schemes of the various tax services differ significantly. Some are updated more frequently than others. Each has its own special features and unique way of presenting material. The best way to acquaint oneself with the various tax services is to use them in researching hypothetical or actual problems.

Organizationally, there are two types of tax services: "annotated" and "topical" (although this distinction has become somewhat blurred in the Internet version of these services). An **annotated tax service** is organized by IRC section. The IRC-arranged subdivisions of this service are likely to encompass several topics. A **topical tax service** is organized by broad topic. The topically-arranged subdivisions of this service are likely to encompass several IRC sections. The principal annotated tax services are the *United States Tax Reporter* and *Standard Federal Tax Reporter.* The main topical services are the *Federal Tax Coordinator 2d, Law of Federal Income Taxation* (Mertens), *Tax Management Portfolios,* and *CCH Federal Tax Service.* Each of these services is discussed below.

ADDITIONAL COMMENT

Tax services often are consulted at the beginning of the research process. A tax service helps identify the tax authorities pertaining to a particular tax issue. The actual tax authorities, and not the tax service, are generally cited as support for a particular tax position.

KEY POINT

Both the *United States Tax Reporter* and the *Standard Federal Tax Reporter* services are organized by IRC section. Many tax advisors find both of these services easy to use. The other major tax services are organized by topic.

UNITED STATES TAX REPORTER

The *United States Tax Reporter* is a multivolume series published by RIA. It is devoted to income, estate, gift, and excise taxes and is organized by IRC section number. Accordingly, its commentary begins with Sec. 1 of the IRC and proceeds in numerical order through the last section of the IRC. Researchers who know the number of the IRC section applicable to their problem can turn directly to the paragraphs that discuss that section. Each organizational part presents an editorial commentary (with access to the text of the relevant IRC section), committee reports, Treasury Regulations, and IRS pronouncements, all indexed according to IRC section number. Separate volumes in the print version contain an index and finding lists that reference explanatory paragraphs respectively by topic and by case name or IRS pronouncement. These resources enable the researcher to access this service in one of three ways: first, by IRC section number; second, by topic; and third, by citation.

One of the more salient features of this service (as well as the CCH service discussed below) are the annotations accompanying the editorial commentaries. These annotations consist of digests or summaries of IRS pronouncements and court opinions that interpret a particular IRC section. They are classified by subtopic and cite pertinent primary authorities.

The print version of *United States Tax Reporter* is updated weekly. Information on recent developments is referenced in a table in Volume 16 and periodically moved into the main body of the text. To determine whether any recent developments impact a particular issue, the researcher should look in the table for references to the numbers of paragraphs that discuss the issue. The print service includes, in addition to the recent developments volume, several volumes on the IRC and Treasury Regulations, a compilation of newly issued *American Federal Tax Reports* decisions, and practical aids such as tax rate, interest rate, and per diem rate tables. The Internet version of the *United States Tax Reporter* is available on RIA CHECKPOINT™.

REAL-WORLD EXAMPLE

The 1913 CCH explanation of the federal tax law was a single 400-page volume. The current *Standard Federal Tax Reporter* is 25 volumes and over 100,000 pages in length.

STANDARD FEDERAL TAX REPORTER

CCH publishes the *Standard Federal Tax Reporter*, also organized by IRC section number. Separate services devoted to income taxes, estate and gift taxes, and excise taxes are available. Like RIA's *United States Tax Reporter*, the CCH service compiles in its main volumes editorial commentaries (with access to the text of the IRC), Treasury Regulations, and annotations. Also like the RIA service, the print version of the CCH service includes a topical index and finding lists that reference explanatory paragraphs respectively by topic and by authority. Thus, like the *United States Tax Reporter*, the CCH service can be accessed by IRC section number, topic, and citation.[42]

The IRC volumes of the CCH print version contain tables that cross-reference sections of the current IRC with other sections of the current IRC and with predecessor provisions of the 1954 IRC. The first of these tables enables the researcher to identify other sections of the current IRC that potentially impact a transaction or taxable event. The second table enables the researcher to trace the statutory history of particular IRC provisions. The IRC volumes of the CCH print version also contain a comprehensive listing of committee reports organized by IRC section number. This listing enables the researcher to locate sources that suggest the legislative intent behind a particular IRC provision.

The CCH service provides articles on current developments. Until the end of the calendar year, when CCH publishes a new reporter series, it supplies periodic updates of court opinions and revenue rulings. Throughout the year, information on major developments, such as new tax legislation and Supreme Court decisions, is incorporated in the main body of the text. The Internet version of the CCH service is available on the CCH Internet Tax Research NetWork™.

ADDITIONAL COMMENT

The RIA *Federal Tax Coordinator 2d* service is a more voluminous service than either the *United States Tax Reporter* or *Standard Federal Tax Reporter* services because it has more editorial commentary. The *Federal Tax Coordinator 2d* updates are integrated into the main body of the text. The service is not replaced each year. By contrast, both the *United States Tax Reporter* and *Standard Federal Tax Reporter* services compile their updates in one volume. CCH issues a new *Standard Federal Tax Reporter* service each year. The other services integrate the updates into the body of existing text at the beginning of each year.

FEDERAL TAX COORDINATOR 2d

The *Federal Tax Coordinator 2d* (FTC service), also published by RIA, is a multivolume publication organized by broad topic. It covers three major areas: income taxes, estate and gift taxes, and excise taxes. Unlike the print version of the annotated services, the print version of the FTC service presents its editorial commentary before excerpts of relevant IRC and Treasury Regulation sections. The latter excerpts are placed behind a tab titled Code & Regs within the same topical volume. The editorial commentary is heavily footnoted with references to court cases, revenue rulings, and other primary authorities that pertain to the topical discussion. An index volume references the numbers of paragraphs that discuss various topics. Cross-reference tables reference the numbers of paragraphs that discuss particular IRC sections, Treasury Regulations, IRS pronouncements, and court cases. Instead of providing a separate volume for new developments, the FTC service incorporates new developments information in the main body of the service.

A peculiar feature of the FTC service is its editorial notations, which suggest the practical implications of the tax principle under discussion. Among the notations are *illustration*, which offers examples of how the principle is applied; *caution*, which points to the

---

[42] Examples of citations to these tax services are as follows: (2005) 6 *United States Tax Reporter* (RIA) ¶3025 and (2005) 8 *Std. Fed. Tax Rep.* (CCH) ¶21,966.02, where 6 and 8 represent the volume numbers, and the paragraph numbers refer to the cited passages in the volume. Because citations should be to primary authorities, citations to secondary authorities are rarely used.

risks associated with application; *recommendation*, which suggests ways to minimize the risk; and *observation*, which offers an editorial analysis of the principle.

One part of the FTC service titled Practice Aids provides tools useful in tax practice. Other tax services provide similar tools. Such tools include Tax Savings Opportunity Checklists, designed to assist taxpayers in proceeding with business and personal transactions; a Current Legislation Table, which indicates the status of pending tax legislation; and an IRS Forms Table, which cross-references the numbers of IRS forms to those of paragraphs in the topical discussion; and tax calendars, tax schedules, sample client letters, and daily compound interest tables. Other segments of the FTC service present the text of tax treaties, revenue rulings, revenue procedures, and proposed Treasury Regulations. A separate part compiles issues of *Weekly Alert*, RIA's tax newsletter. The Internet version of the FTC service is available on RIA CHECKPOINT™.

LAW OF FEDERAL INCOME TAXATION (MERTENS)

The *Law of Federal Income Taxation*, published by West, originally was edited by Merten's and is called "Mertens" by tax practitioners and in this text. Legalistic in orientation, Mertens deals only with federal income taxation. Its commentary is narrative in form and reads like a treatise. Mertens is highly regarded by tax accountants and tax lawyers. It is the only tax service cited by the U.S. judiciary with any regularity. The text of Mertens is heavily footnoted. The footnotes contain a wealth of information relating to the IRC, Treasury Regulations, IRS pronouncements, and court opinions.

Mertens includes several parts devoted exclusively to Treasury Regulations and IRS pronouncements. These segments contain the full text of *current* Treasury Regulations and IRS pronouncements (this text does not appear in the main commentary volumes), as well as the full text of *old* Treasury Regulations and IRS pronouncements. The old versions enable the researcher to reconstruct the state of the tax law in any given year. Such reconstruction is useful in three contexts: first, where the IRS audits a taxpayer's return for a previous year; second, where the researcher evaluates the effects of a transaction beginning in a previous year; and third, where the researcher analyzes a court opinion issued in a previous year.

Like the annotated services, the print version of Mertens contains a topical index and finding lists cross-referenced to the IRC, Treasury Regulations, IRS pronouncements, and court opinions. Its *Current Rulings Materials* volume includes a Code-Rulings Table that lists by IRC section the numbers of all post-1954 revenue rulings that interpret a particular section. The same volume also includes a Rulings Status Table that indicates the status of every post-1954 revenue ruling (i.e., whether the ruling has been revoked, modified, amplified, or otherwise impacted by an IRS decision).[43] Its *Current Materials* volume compiles issues of *Development and Highlights*, Mertens' monthly periodical. The Internet version of Mertens is available on WESTLAW™.

TAX MANAGEMENT PORTFOLIOS

BNA publishes over 200 booklets of specialized tax materials called *Tax Management Portfolios* (referred to as BNA portfolios by many practitioners and in this text). BNA portfolios are issued in three series: U.S. income; foreign income; and estates, gifts, and trusts. Each portfolio is prepared by a specialized tax practitioner. Thus, the particular slant of BNA portfolios is practical application, as opposed to the theoretical. In each portfolio, the author's discussion of a particular topic is found in the Detailed Analysis section. Here, provisions of the IRC and Treasury Regulations are explained, court opinions are analyzed, and transactional structures are proposed. The text of the Detailed Analysis is heavily footnoted. The footnotes cite and summarize relevant primary and secondary sources.

A noteworthy feature of each BNA portfolio is its Working Papers, which are tools designed to aid the practitioner in tax planning and compliance. Among such tools are tax-related checklists, IRS forms and instructions, computational worksheets, and draft legal documents. The Bibliography and References section at the back of each print version

---

[43] RIA and CCH services provide essentially the same information in different formats.

volume lists primary and secondary sources used by the author to prepare the portfolio. In this section, the researcher will find a listing of IRC sections, Treasury Regulations, IRS pronouncements, and court opinions that support the Detailed Analysis, as well as references to pertinent law review articles and tax treatises.

Unlike the print version of the other services, the print version of BNA portfolios does not contain finding lists indexed to court opinions or IRS pronouncements. On the other hand, it does contain a topical index, an IRC reference table, and an IRS forms index that cross-references the numbers of IRS forms to pertinent pages in the portfolios. Like CCH and RIA, BNA publishes a weekly newsletter as part of its tax service. The Internet version of BNA portfolios is available in the BNA Tax Management Library and WESTLAW™.

CCH FEDERAL TAX SERVICE

The newest of the major tax services is the *CCH Federal Tax Service,* currently published by CCH and formerly published by Matthew Bender & Company. The print version of this service is a multivolume looseleaf publication that, like RIA's FTC service and Mertens, is organized by broad topic. Just like portfolios in the BNA service, chapters of the *CCH Federal Tax Service* are authored by tax practitioners and thus are practical in orientation.

The *CCH Federal Tax Service* does not compile sections of the IRC and Treasury Regulations in the same volumes in which the topical analysis appears. Rather, it publishes them in separate volumes devoted exclusively to the IRC and proposed, temporary, and final Treasury Regulations. A particular IRC section and its related Treasury Regulations are found in the same volume.

CCH periodically updates the *Federal Tax Service* to reflect current developments. As with its annotated tax service, CCH issues a weekly newsletter as part of this topical tax service. The Internet version of the *CCH Federal Tax Service* is available on the CCH Internet Tax Research NetWork™.

Figure C1-5 provides an overview of one approach for using the tax services to research a tax question.

CITATORS

OBJECTIVE 5

Use a citator to assess tax authorities

Citators serve two functions: first, they trace the judicial history of a particular case (e.g., if the case under analysis is an appeals court decision, the citator indicates the lower court that heard the case and whether the Supreme Court reviewed the case); and second, they list other authorities (e.g., cases and IRS pronouncements) that cite the case in question. Two principal tax-related citators are the CCH citator and the *Research Institute of America Citator 2nd Series* (RIA citator).

CCH CITATOR

The print verison of the CCH citator consists of two loose-leaf volumes, one for cases with names beginning with the letters A through M and the other for cases with names starting with the letters N through Z. In the CCH Internet Tax Research NetWork™, this information is integrated into one citator service. The CCH citator analyzes every decision reported in CCH's *Standard Federal Tax Reporter,* its *Excise Tax Reporter,* and its *Federal Estate and Gift Tax Reporter* and selectively lists cases that cite the decision under analysis. (CCH editors decide which of these other cases influence the precedential weight of the decision under analysis.)

Although the CCH citator does not analyze IRS pronouncements, "status lists" found in the second citator volume of the CCH service does. (Comparable lists are found in the *United States Tax Reporter,* the FTC service, and Mertens.) These lists indicate the current status of revenue rulings, revenue procedures, private letter rulings, and other IRS pronouncements. They reveal whether these authorities have been cited in court cases, their impact on other IRS pronouncements, and whether they have been modified, superceded, or obsoleted. In the CCH Internet Tax Research NetWork™ and in RIA CHECKPOINT™, the status lists have been integrated in the main citator service. An excerpt from the CCH citator appears in Figure C1-6.

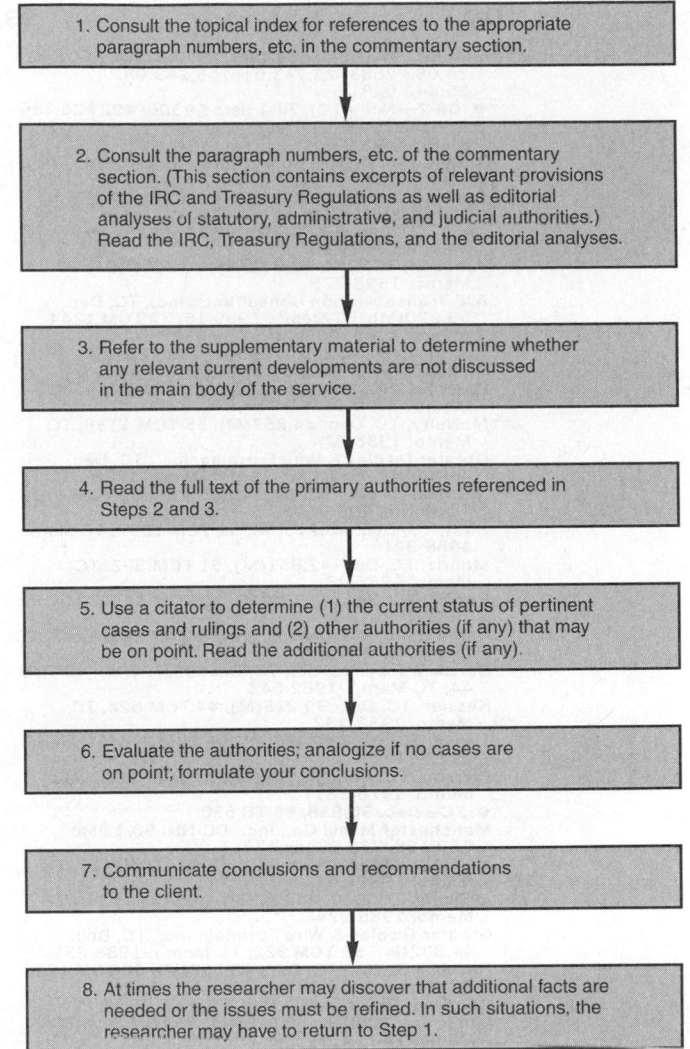

1. Consult the topical index for references to the appropriate paragraph numbers, etc. in the commentary section.

2. Consult the paragraph numbers, etc. of the commentary section. (This section contains excerpts of relevant provisions of the IRC and Treasury Regulations as well as editorial analyses of statutory, administrative, and judicial authorities.) Read the IRC, Treasury Regulations, and the editorial analyses.

3. Refer to the supplementary material to determine whether any relevant current developments are not discussed in the main body of the service.

4. Read the full text of the primary authorities referenced in Steps 2 and 3.

5. Use a citator to determine (1) the current status of pertinent cases and rulings and (2) other authorities (if any) that may be on point. Read the additional authorities (if any).

6. Evaluate the authorities; analogize if no cases are on point; formulate your conclusions.

7. Communicate conclusions and recommendations to the client.

8. At times the researcher may discover that additional facts are needed or the issues must be refined. In such situations, the researcher may have to return to Step 1.

FIGURE C1-5 ▶ USE OF TAX SERVICES TO RESEARCH A TAX QUESTION

Refer to Figure C1-6 and find the *Leonarda C. Diaz* case. The information in bold print with bullets to the left denotes that *Diaz* was first decided by the Tax Court and then by the Second Circuit Court. It shows that the Second Circuit affirmed (upheld) the Tax Court's decision. The two cases listed beneath the Second Circuit decision (i.e., *Kuh* and *Damm*) cite the *Diaz* decision. The six cases listed beneath the Tax Court decision (i.e., *German, Jr., Orr, Zeidler, Schwerm, Wassenaar,* and *Toner*) cite the Tax Court's opinion in *Diaz*. The abbreviation *Dec.* appearing in some of the citations stands for *decision*. The CCH citator lists the decision numbers of the Tax Court cases.

The main CCH citator volumes are published once a year. The first of these volumes contains a "Current Citator Table," which lists court decisions recently cited, as well as additional citing cases for court decisions previously cited. Citator updates are issued quarterly. The *Diaz* decision has not been cited in any opinion issued since 2005, the year in which the CCH citator was last published. The applicable page from the main citator table for the *Diaz* decision is reproduced here.

The entry "¶5504.20" appearing to the right of *Alfonso Diaz* denotes the number of the *Standard Federal Tax Reporter* paragraph that discusses the case. Usually, before consulting the citator, a researcher already would have read about this case in the referenced paragraph and would have decided that it was relevant to his or her research. In such circumstances, the reference would not be particularly useful. In other circumstances, the reference would be useful. For example, if the researcher had heard about the case from a colleague and wanted to read more about it, he or she could readily locate the passage that discusses it.

DIA   93,302   ————CCH————

Diamond, Sol . . . ¶5508.085, 8520.517, 21,005.123,
25,083.2683, 25,243.016, 25,243.08,
25,442.023
● **CA-7**—(aff'g TC), 74-1 USTC ¶9306; 492 F2d 286
Campbell, CA-8, 91-2 USTC ¶50,420
Rev. Proc. 93-27
Anderson, TC, Dec. 50,410(M), 69 TCM 1609, TC
Memo. 1995-8
Banks, TC, Dec. 47,832(M), 62 TCM 1611, TC
Memo. 1991-641
Arcia, TC, Dec. 52,701(M), 75 TCM 2287, TC
Memo. 1998-178
Johnson, TC, Dec. 52,812(M), 76 TCM 194, TC
Memo. 1998-275
AJF Transportation Consultants, Inc., TC, Dec.
53,220(M), TC Memo. 1999-16, 77 TCM 1244
Pacheco, CA-9, 90-2 USTC ¶50,458
Vestal, CA-8, 74-2 USTC ¶9501, 498 F2d 487
St. John, DC-III, 84-1 USTC ¶9158
Campbell, TC, Dec. 46,493(M), 59 TCM 236, TC
Memo. 1990-162
McNulty, TC, Dec. 44,857(M), 55 TCM 1138, TC
Memo. 1988-274
Greater Display & Wire Forming, Inc., TC, Dec.
44,802(M), 55 TCM 922, TC Memo. 1988-231
National Oil Co., TC, Dec. 43,557(M), 52 TCM 1223,
TC Memo. 1986-596
Hirst, TC, Dec. 43,215(M), 51 TCM 1597, TC Memo.
1986-321
Mouriz, TC, Dec. 42,851(M), 51 TCM 392, TC
Memo. 1986-43
Parker, TC, Dec. 42,129(M), 50 TCM 14, TC Memo.
1985-263
Kenroy, Inc., TC, Dec. 41,186(M), 47 TCM 1749, TC
Memo. 1984-232
Bertolini Trucking Co., TC, Dec. 39,474(M), 45 TCM
44, TC Memo. 1982-643
Kessler, TC, Dec. 39,226(M), 44 TCM 624, TC
Memo. 1982-432
Tooke, TC, Dec. 34,336(M), 36 TCM 396, TC Memo.
1977-91
Pierson, TC, Dec. 34,009(M), 35 TCM 1256, TC
Memo. 1976-281
● **TC**—Dec. 30,838; 56 TC 530
Manchester Music Co., Inc., DC-NH, 90-1 USTC
¶50,168, 733 FSupp 473
Miller, Jr., TC, Dec. 45,977(M), 57 TCM 1419, TC
Memo. 1989-461
McNulty, TC, Dec. 44,857(M), 55 TCM 1138, TC
Memo. 1988-274
Greater Display & Wire Forming, Inc., TC, Dec.
44,802(M), 55 TCM 922, TC Memo. 1988-231
National Oil Co., TC, Dec. 43,557(M), 52 TCM 1223,
TC Memo. 1986-596
Goodwin, David C., TC, Dec. 36,413, 73 TC 215
Schaevitz, TC, Dec. 30,925(M), 30 TCM 823, TC
Memo. 1971-197
Diamond, Solomon . . . . ¶8632.68
● **TC**—Dec. 25,981(M); 22 TCM 229; TC Memo.
1963-57
Diamond T Motor Car Co.: Allen v. . . . . . ¶38,160.82
● **CA-10**—(rev'g DC), 61-1 USTC ¶9484; 291 F2d
115
Randall, CA-5, 76-2 USTC ¶9770, 542 F2d 270
Jefferson Bank and Trust, DC-Colo, 89-1 USTC
¶9221
Rodkey, DC-Okla, 87-1 USTC ¶9218
Nevada Rock & Sand Co., DC-Nev, 74-2 USTC ¶9617,
376 FSupp 161
Nomellini Construction Co., DC-Calif, 71-2 USTC
¶9510, 328 FSupp 1281
● **DC-Colo**—60-2 USTC ¶9557
Diamondhead Corp. v. Fort Hope Development, Inc.
. . . . ¶40,720.1945
● **DC-Ga**—78-2 USTC ¶9718
Diamondstone, I. A. (See Kann, William L.)
DiAndre, Anthony F. . . . . . . ¶36,894.7255, 41,758.30
● **SCt**—Cert. denied, 3/19/93
● **CA-10**—(rev'g and rem'g unreported DC), 92-2
USTC ¶50,373; 968 F2d 1049
Stewart, DC-Ohio, 95-1 USTC ¶50,249
Russell, DC-Mich, 95-1 USTC ¶50,029
Jones, DC-Neb, 94-2 USTC ¶50,562, 869 FSupp 747
Schachter, DC-Calif, 94-1 USTC ¶50,242
Fostvedt, DC-Colo, 93-1 USTC ¶50,299, 824 FSupp
978
Jones, DC-Neb, 95-2 USTC ¶50,567, 898 FSupp
1360
May, DC-Mo, 95-2 USTC ¶50,605
Spence, DC-NM, 96-2 USTC ¶50,615
Spence, CA-10, 97-1 USTC ¶50,485
Roebuck, DC-NC, 99-2 USTC ¶50,627

DiAndrea, Inc. . . . ¶16,233.25, 21,817.108, 44,507.09
● **TC**—Dec. 40,697(M); 47 TCM 731; TC Memo.
1983-768
Johnson, TC, Dec. 47,836(M), 62 TCM 1629, TC
Memo. 1991-645
Diaz, Alfonso . . . . ¶5504.195
● **TC**—Dec. 31,442; 58 TC 560; A. 1972-2 CB 2
Marrone, TC, Dec. 50,424(M), 69 TCM 1684, TC
Memo. 1995-22
Sloan, TC, Dec. 50,305(M), 68 TCM 1489, TC
Memo. 1994-628
Muniz, TC, Dec. 49,775(M), 67 TCM 2625, TC
Memo. 1994-151
Drabiuk, TC, Dec. 50,692(M), 69 TCM 2890, TC
Memo. 1995-260
Jackson, TC, Dec. 50,736(M), TC Memo. 1995-300,
70 TCM 12
Levin, TC, Dec. 51,326(M), 71 TCM 2938, TC
Memo. 1996-211
American Underwriters, Inc., TC, Dec. 51,694(M),
TC Memo. 1996-548, 72 TCM 1511
Solaas, TC, Dec. 52,529(M), 75 TCM 1613, TC
Memo. 1998-25
Arcia, TC, Dec. 52,701(M), 75 TCM 2287, TC
Memo. 1998-178
Maslow, TC, Dec. 52,302(M), TC Memo. 1997-466,
74 TCM 910
Neff Est., TC, Dec. 51,999(M), TC Memo. 1997-186,
73 TCM 2606
Swiatek, TC, Dec. 53,485(M), 78 TCM 223, TC
Memo. 1999-257
Schirle, TC, Dec. 52,398(M), TC Memo. 1997-552,
74 TCM 1379
Kong, TC, Dec. 46,090(M), 58 TCM 378, TC Memo.
1989-560
Caglia, E. Bonnie, TC, Dec. 45,585(M), 57 TCM 1,
TC Memo. 1989-143
Ettig, TC, Dec. 44,736(M), 55 TCM 720, TC Memo.
1988-182
Heller, TC, Dec. 44,083(M), 53 TCM 1486, TC
Memo. 1987-376
Anastasato, TC, Dec. 43,309(M), 52 TCM 293, TC
Memo. 1986-400
Stevenson, TC, Dec. 43,068(M), 51 TCM 1050, TC
Memo. 1986-207
Wilhelm, TC, Dec. 42,813(M), 51 TCM 261, TC
Memo. 1986-12
Branson, TC, Dec. 38,026(M), 42 TCM 281, TC
Memo. 1981-338
Calloway, TC, Dec. 37,019(M), 40 TCM 495, TC
Memo. 1980-211
Greenfield, TC, Dec. 35,253(M), 37 TCM 1082, TC
Memo. 1978-251
Leong, TC, Dec. 34,232(M), 36 TCM 89, TC Memo.
1977-19
Dougherty, TC, Dec. 32,138, 60 TC 917
Hernandez, TC, Dec. 52,552(M), TC Memo.
1998-46, 75 TCM 1714
Diaz, Antonio A. v. Southern Drilling Corp. . . . . .
. . . . ¶41,699.45
● **CA-5**—(aff'g unreported DC), 71-1 USTC ¶9236
Diaz, Enrique . . ¶33,538.43, 39,475.65, 39,585.63,
41,688.377
● **DC-Calif**—90-1 USTC ¶50,209
Van Camp & Bennion, P.S., DC-Wash, 96-2 USTC
¶50,438
Diaz, Frank . . . . ¶29,412.9911
● **TC**—Dec. 42,922(M); 51 TCM 594; TC Memo.
1986-98
**Diaz, Greg, Acting County Recorder for the City and
County of San Francisco** (See Chase Manhattan
Bank, N.A. v. City & County of San Francisco)
Diaz, Humberto (See Flicker, Marvin)
Diaz, Juan (See Setal, Manuel G.)
Diaz, Leonarda C. . . . . ¶8632.3876
● **CA-2**—(aff'g TC), 79-2 USTC ¶9473; 607 F2d 995
Kuh, TC, Dec. 40,461(M), 46 TCM 1405, TC Memo.
1983-572
Damm, TC, Dec. 37,861(M), 41 TCM 1359, TC
Memo. 1981-203
● **TC**—Dec. 35,436; 70 TC 1067
German, Jr., TC, Dec. 48,867(M), 65 TCM 1931, TC
Memo. 1993-59
Orr, TC, Dec. 48,532(M), 64 TCM 882, TC Memo.
1992-566
Zeidler, TC, Dec. 51,264(M), 71 TCM 2603, TC
Memo. 1996-157
Schwerm, TC, Dec. 42,817(M), 51 TCM 270, TC
Memo. 1986-16
Wassenaar, TC, Dec. 36,359, 72 TC 1195
Toner, TC, Dec. 35,877, 71 TC 772
Diaz, Miguel A. (See Powers (Belcher), Sandra L.)
Dibble, Leon N., Exr. . . . . ¶29,225.442
● **BTA**—Dec. 2320; 6 BTA 732; A. VI-2 CB 2

FIGURE C1-6 ▶ EXCERPT FROM THE CCH CITATOR

The CCH citator lists cases even where they have not been cited in other cases. For example, refer to the entry for *Frank Diaz*. This Tax Court memo decision is listed among the cases analyzed, even though no other published decision has referred to it. Moreover, the citator indicates whether the IRS Commissioner has acquiesced or nonacquiesced in a Tax Court decision. For example, refer to the entry for *Alfonso Diaz*. Note that the first Tax Court citation is followed by a capital "A," then another citation. The "A" indicates that the IRS Commissioner acquiesced in the Tax Court decision. The second citation indicates that the Commissioner's acquiescence is found on page 2 of Volume 2 of the 1972 *Cumulative Bulletin*.

RESEARCH INSTITUTE OF AMERICA CITATOR 2nd SERIES

Like the CCH citator, the RIA citator[44] provides the history of each authority and lists the cases and pronouncements that have cited that authority. The RIA citator, however, conveys more information than does the CCH citator. This information includes the following:

▶ Whether the citing authorities comment favorably or unfavorably on the cited case, or whether they can be distinguished from the cited case[45]

▶ The specific issue(s) in the cited case that is (are) referenced by the citing authorities

ADDITIONAL COMMENT

The history of a case may be easier to find in CCH because each of the courts that tried the case is listed in a single volume in boldface print.

In print form, the RIA citator (formerly, the Prentice Hall citator) consists of seven hardbound volumes and several cumulative supplements. The first hardbound volume lists cases decided from 1919 through 1941; the second, cases decided from 1942 through September 30, 1948; the third, cases decided from October 1, 1948, through July 29, 1954; the fourth, cases decided from July 30, 1954, through December 15, 1977; the fifth, cases cited from December 15, 1977, through December 20, 1989; the sixth, cases decided from January 4, 1990, to December 26, 1996; and the seventh, cases decided from January 2, 1997, to December 19, 2002. A softback cumulative supplement lists cases decided from December 27, 2002, to January 8, 2004. Each year, a revised annual supplement is published. Each month, a revised monthly supplement is published. In analyzing a 1945 case, a researcher should consult every cumulative supplement and every main volume except the first. In analyzing a 1980 case, the researcher should consult every cumulative supplement and the last three bound volumes. The Internet version of the RIA citator (i.e., in RIA CHECKPOINT™) integrates this information, thus allowing the researcher to consult only one citator source.

As mentioned earlier, the RIA citator reveals the manner in which the citing authorities comment on the case under analysis. The nature of the comment is indicated by symbols that appear to the left of the citing authority. The RIA citator also reveals the history of the case under analysis (e.g., whether it was affirmed, reversed, etc.).[46] This history is indicated by symbols that appear to the left of citations to the same case heard at different appellate levels (parallel citations). Figure C1-7 explains the meaning of the various symbols, which are spelled out in the Internet version.

The RIA citator is especially useful if the cited case deals with more than one issue. As previously pointed out, the citator reports the issue(s) addressed in the cited case that is (are) referenced in the citing authority. The numbers to the left of this authority denote the specific issue(s) referenced. These numbers correspond to headnotes published in *American Federal Tax Reports*. A **headnote** is an editorial summary of a particular point of case law. Headnotes appear in case reporters immediately before the text of the opinions authored by the judges.

An excerpt from the 1978–1989 citator volume appears in the first column of Figure C1-8. Refer to it and locate the Tax Court decision for *Leonarda C. Diaz*. All the cases that cite the decision after 1977 and through 1989 are listed. (*Diaz* was decided by the

---

[44] The *Research Institute of America Citator 2nd Series* is published currently by RIA. It originally was published by Prentice Hall's Information Services Division, which was acquired in 1990 by Maxwell Macmillan. *Prentice Hall* and/or *Maxwell Macmillan* appears on the spines and title pages of the older citators and will remain there because, unlike the CCH citator, the RIA citator is not republished each year.

[45] When a court distinguishes the facts of one case from those of an earlier

case, it suggests that its departure from the earlier decision is justified because the facts of the two cases are different.

[46] If a case is *affirmed*, the decision of the lower court is upheld. *Reversed* means the higher court invalidated the decision of the lower court because it reached a conclusion different from that derived by the lower court. *Remanded* signifies that the higher court sent the case back to the lower court with instructions to address matters not earlier addressed.

SYMBOLS USED IN CITATOR COURT DECISIONS
Judicial History

a   affirmed by a higher court (Note: When available, the official cite to the affirmance is provided; if the affirmance is by unpublished order or opinion, the date of the decision and the court deciding the case are provided.)

App auth   appeal authorized by the Treasury

adptd   magistrate judge's decision is accepted by district court

adptg   district court accepts magistrate judge's decision

App   appeal pending (Note: Later volumes may have to be consulted to determine if appeal was decided or dismissed.)

cert gr   petition for certiorari was granted by the U.S. Supreme Court

d   appeal dismissed by the court or withdrawn by the party filing the appeal

ep   citing case is an earlier proceeding of the cited case

(G)   following an appeal notation, this symbol indicates that it was the government filing the appeal

lp   citing case is a later proceeding of the cited case

m   the earlier decision has been modified by the higher court, or by a later decision.

o   decision has been overruled by legislation

r   the decision of the lower court has been reversed on appeal

rc   related case arising out of the same taxable event or concerning the same taxpayer

reh dend   rehearing of cited case has been denied by the citing case

reh deng   cited case has denied rehearing of citing case

reinst   a dismissed appeal has been reinstated by the appellate court and is under consideration again

remd   the case has been remanded for proceedings consistent with the higher court decision

remg   the cited case is remanding the earlier case

revg & remg   the decision of the lower court has been reversed and remanded by a higher court on appeal

revd & remd   a higher court has reversed and remanded to the lower court a decision of that lower court

s   same case or ruling

sa   the cited case is affirming the earlier case

sm   the cited case is modifying the earlier case

sr   the cited case is reversing the earlier case

sx   the cited case is an earlier proceeding in a case for which a petition for certiorari was denied

(T)   an appeal was filed from the lower court decision by the taxpayer

vacd   the lower court decision was vacated on appeal or by the original court on remand

vacg   a higher court or the original court on remand has vacated the lower court decision

widm   the original opinion was withdrawn by the court

x   petition for certiorari was denied by the U.S. Supreme Court

•   Supreme Court cases are designated by a bold-faced bullet (•) before the case line for easy location

Certain notations appear at the end of the cited case line. These notations include:

(A) or acq   the government has acquiesced in the reasoning or the result of the cited case

(NA) or nonacq   the government has refused to acquiesce or to adopt the reasoning or the result of the cited case, and will challenge the position adopted if future proceedings arise on the same issue

on rem   the case has been remanded by a higher court and the case cited is the resulting decision

Evaluation of Cited Cases

c   the citing case court has adversely commented on the reasoning of the cited case, and has criticized the earlier decision

e   the cited case is used favorably by the citing case court

f   the reasoning of the court in the cited case is followed by the later decision

g   the cited and citing cases are distinguished from each other on either facts or law

inap   the citing case court has specifically indicated that the cited case does not apply to the situation stated in the citing case.

iv   on all fours (both the cited and citing cases are virtually identical)

k   the cited and citing case principles are reconciled

l   the rationale of the cited case is limited to the facts or circumstances surrounding that case (this can occur frequently in situations in which there has been an intervening higher court decision or law change)

n   the cited case was noted in a dissenting opinion

o   the later case directly overrules the cited case (use of the evaluation is generally limited to situations in which the court notes that it is specifically overturning the cited case, and that the case will no longer be of any value)

q   the decision of the cited case is questioned and its validity debated in relation to the citing case at issue

The evaluations used for the court decisions generally are followed by a number. That number refers to the headnoted issue in the American Federal Tax Reports (AFTR) or Tax Court decision to which the citing case relates. If the case is not directly on point with any headnote, a bracketed notation at the end of the citing case line directs the researcher to the page in the cited case on which the issue appears.

A blank may appear in the evaluation space. Generally, this means that the citing court didn't comment on any of the legal issues raised in the cited case.

vi

v

FIGURE C1-7   ▶   ABBREVIATIONS USED IN RIA CITATOR 2ND SERIES

Source: Reprinted from Citator 2nd Series 2003–2005, ©2006 by RIA, 395 Hudson Street, New York, NY 10014

ADDITIONAL COMMENT

The RIA citator has the advantage of providing the most references for a cited case. This point is apparent when one compares RIA's six volumes plus supplements with CCH's two volumes. Also, RIA numbers each tax issue litigated in a court case. This coding allows the tax advisor to identify cases dealing with the specific issue being researched. For example, if the advisor is interested in the first issue in the *Leonarda C. Diaz* Tax Court decision, the citator reproduced in Figure C1-8 denotes five cases that deal specifically with issue 1 of which three follow the *Diaz* reasoning.

1978–1989
Citator Volume

DiANDREA, YOLANDA, TRANSFEREE, 1983 PH TC Memo ¶ 83,768 See DiAndrea, Inc.)
DIAZ, ALFONSO & MARIA de JESUS, 58 TC 560, ¶ 58.57 PH TC
  Reilly, Peter W., Est. of, 76 TC 374, 76 PH TC 201 [See 58 TC 565, n. 2]
  e—Greenfield, Stuart & Eileen, 1978 PH TC Memo 78-1070 [See 58 TC 564]
  e—Calloway, Johnny T., 1980 PH TC Memo 80-952 [See 58 TC 564]
  e—Branson, David L., 1981 PH TC Memo 81-1199 [See 58 TC 564, 565]
  e—Cohen, Robert B. & Marilyn W., 1983 PH TC Memo 83-1042 [See 58 TC 564]
  e—Patton, Luther R., 1985 PH TC Memo 85-629 [See 58 TC 564]
  e—Malek, Theresa M. & Edward J., Sr., 1985 PH TC Memo 85-1905 [See 58 TC 574]
  e—Wilhelm, Mary R., 1986 PH TC Memo 86-39 [See 58 TC 564]
  e—Stevenson, Wayne E. & Marilyn J., 1986 PH TC Memo 86-866, 86-873 [See 58 TC 564]
  e—Anastasato, Pano & Janice, 1986 PH TC Memo 86-1811 [See 58 TC 564]
  e—Shih-Hsieh, Marilan, 1986 PH TC Memo 86-2429 [See 58 TC 562]
  e—Heller, Jacob W. & Esther R., 1987 PH TC Memo 87-1881 [See 58 TC 562]
  e—Ettig, Tobin R., 1988 PH TC Memo 88-953 [See 58 TC 564]
  e—Belli, Melia, 1989 PH TC Memo 89-1950 [See 58 TC 564]
  f—Kong, Young E. & Jeen K., 1989 PH TC Memo 89-2781 [See 58 TC 564-565]
  e-1—Caglia, E. Bonnie, 1989 PH TC Memo 89-689
DIAZ, FRANK & AMPARO R., 1986 PH TC Memo ¶ 86,098
DIAZ, LEONARDA C., 70 TC 1067, ¶ 70.95 PH TC
  a—Diaz, Leonarda C. v Comm., 44 AFTR2d 79-6027 (USCA 2)
  e—Stazer, Alan K. & Katalin V., 1981 PH TC Memo 81-505 [See 70 TC 1076]
  e—Damm, Marvin V. & Nina M., 1981 PH TC Memo 81-673 [See 70 TC 1074-1075]
  e—Stuart, Ian & Maria, 1981 PH TC Memo 81-1311, 81-1312 [See 70 TC 1076]
  e—Olsen, Randy B. & Deborah R., 1981 PH TC Memo 81-2409 [See 70 TC 1076]
  f—Kuh, Johannes L. & Adriana, 1983 PH TC Memo 83-2311 [See 70 TC 1075, 1076]
  f-1—Wassenaar, Paul R., 72 TC 1200, 72 PH TC 659
  f-1—Browne, Alice Pauline, 73 TC 726, 73 PH TC 402 [See 70 TC 1074]
  f-1—Rehe, William G. & Suzanne M., 1980 PH TC Memo 80-1426
  g-1—Schwerm, Gerald & Joyce J., 1986 PH TC Memo 86-54, 86-55
  e-1—Baist, George A. & Janice, 1988 PH TC Memo 88-2859
  f-2—Toner, Linda M. Liberi, 71 TC 778, 779, 781, 71 PH TC 435, 436, 437 [See 70 TC 1075]
  2—Toner, Linda M. Liberi, 71 TC 782, 783, 71 PH TC 437, 438
  n-2—Toner, Linda M. Liberi, 71 TC 790, 71 PH TC 441
  f-2—Robinson, Charles A. & Elaine M., 78 TC 552, 78 PH TC 290 [See 70 TC 1074]
  2—Gruman, David T., 1982 PH TC Memo 82-1700 [See 70 TC 1074]
DIAZ, LEONARDA C. v COMM., 44 AFTR2d 79-6027 (USCA 2, 6-25-79)
  sa—Diaz, Leonarda C., 70 TC 1067, ¶ 70.95 PH TC
  e—Stazer, Alan K. & Katalin V., 1981 PH TC Memo 81-505
  e—Damm, Marvin V. & Nina M., 1981 PH TC Memo 81-673
  e—Olsen, Randy B. & Deborah R., 1981 PH TC Memo 81-2409
  f—Kuh, Johannes L. & Adriana, 1983 PH TC Memo 83-2311
  e—Malek, Theresa M. & Edward J., Sr., 1985 PH TC Memo 85-1905
  f-1—Rehe, William G. & Suzanne M., 1980 PH TC Memo 80-1426
  g-1—Schwerm, Gerald & Joyce J., 1986 PH TC Memo 86-54, 86-55
  e-1—Baist, George A. & Janice, 1988 PH TC Memo 88-2859
DIAZ, MIGUEL A. & FELICIA N., 1981 PH TC Memo ¶ 81,069 (See Powers, Sandra L.)

1990–1996
Citator Volume

DiANDRE, ANTHONY F. v U.S., 70 AFTR 2d 92-5190, 968 F2d 1049, 92-2 USTC ¶ 50,373, (CA10, 7-7-92)
  x—Metro Denver Maintenance Cleaning, Inc. v. U.S., 507 US 1029, 113 S Ct 1843, 123 L Ed 2d 468, (US, 4-19-93), (T)
  e-1—Barnes, William R. v U.S., 73 AFTR 2d 94-1161, (CA3)
  e-1—Fostvedt, Robert J. v U.S., 71 AFTR 2d 93-1573, 824 F Supp 983, (DC CO)
  e-1—Jones, Terry L., et al v. U.S., et al. 74 AFTR 2d 94-6706, 869 F Supp 753, (DC NE), [Cited at 71 AFTR2d 93-1573, 824 F Supp 983]
  g-1—Russell, Orval D. v. U.S., 75 AFTR 2d 95-496, (DC MI)
  e-1—Stewart, Daniel v. U.S., 75 AFTR 2d 95-2250, 95-2251, (DC OH)
  e-1—Jones, Terry L., et al v. U.S., et al. 76 AFTR 2d 95-6607, 95-6615, 898 F Supp 1373, 1380, (DC NE), [Cited at 71 AFTR2d 93-1573, 824 F Supp 983]
  e-1—May, Joseph A. v. U.S., 76 AFTR 2d 95-7228, (DC MO)
  e-1—Cassity, James v. Great Western Bank, 76 AFTR 2d 95-8035, (DC CA)
  e-1—Spence, Raymond v. U.S., 78 AFTR 2d 96-5777, (DC NM)

DiANDREA, INC., 1983 PH TC Memo ¶ 83,768
  e-1—Johnson, Peter A., 1991 TC Memo 91-3185
DIAZ, ALFONSO & MARIA de JESUS, 58 TC 560, ¶ 58.57 PH TC, (A), 1972-2 CB 2
  Sanai, Farhin, 1990 PH TC Memo 90-2459, [See 58 TC 564-565]
  e—Hawkins, Robert Lavon & Pamela, 1993 RIA TC Memo 93-2734, [See 58 TC 564]
  e—Muniz, Rolando, 1994 RIA TC Memo 94-760, [See 58 TC 564]
  e—Sloan, Lorin G., 1994 RIA TC Memo 94-3427, [See 58 TC 564]
  e—Marrone, Anthony & Carol, 1995 RIA TC Memo 95-145, [See 58 TC 564]
  e—Wada, Takeshi & Young Sook, 1995 RIA TC Memo 95-1532, [See 58 TC 564]
  e—Drabiuk, Stanislaw & Jeanette, 1995 RIA TC Memo 95-1649, [See 58 TC 565]
  e—Jackson, Sammy Lee, 1995 RIA TC Memo 95-1875, [See 58 TC 564]
  e—Levin, Harris & Gayle, 1996 RIA TC Memo 96-1557, [See 58 TC 564]
  e—American Underwriters Inc. 1996 RIA TC Memo 96-3980, [See 58 TC 564]
DIAZ, BARBARA E., 1990 PH TC Memo ¶ 90,559, (See Taylor, Barbara E.)
DIAZ, ENRIQUE v. U.S., 71A AFTR 2d 93-3563, 90-1 USTC ¶ 50209, (DC CA, 3/19/90)
  g-1—Van Camp & Bennion, P.S. v. U.S., 78 AFTR 2d 96-5847, (DC WA)
DIAZ, LEONARDA C., 70 TC 1067, ¶ 70.95 PH TC
  a—Diaz, Leonarda C. v Comm., 44 AFTR 2d 79-6027, 607 F2d 995, (CA2)
  f—Wiertzema, Vance v U.S., 66 AFTR 2d 90-5371, 747 F Supp 1365, (DC ND), [See 70 TC 1074-1075]
  e—Barboza, David, 1991 TC Memo 91-1905, [See 70 TC 1074]
  e—Orr, J. Thomas, 1992 RIA TC Memo 92-2912, [See 70 TC 1073]
  e—German, Harry, Jr. & Carol, 1993 RIA TC Memo 93-261—93-262, [See 70 TC 1074-1075]
  e—Meredith, Judith R., 1993 RIA TC Memo 93-1247, [See 70 TC 1074, cited at 73 TC 726]
  e—Holmes, Lynn J., 1993 RIA TC Memo 93-1978, [See 70 TC 1072-1073]
  e—Kersey, Robert C., 1993 RIA TC Memo 93-3396, [See 70 TC 1072-1073]
  e—Zeidler, Gerald L. & Joy M., 1996 RIA TC Memo 96-1151, [See 70 TC 1074, cited at 73 TC 726]
DIAZ, LEONARDA C. v COMM., 44 AFTR 2d 79-6027, 607 F2d 995, (CA2, 6-25-79)
  e—Wiertzema, Vance v U.S., 66 AFTR 2d 90-5371, 747 F Supp 1363, (DC ND)
  e—Zeidler, Gerald L. & Joy M., 1996 RIA TC Memo 96-1151
DiBENEDETTO, FRANK R. v U.S., 35 AFTR 2d 75-1502, 75-1 USTC ¶ 9503, (DC RI, 11-7-74)
  e-1—Seachrist, Craig v Riggs, C.W., 67 AFTR 2d 91-453, (DC VA)
  e-1—Cook, Dean A. v U.S., 68 AFTR 2d 91-5053—91-5056, 765 F Supp 219, 221, (DC PA)
  e-1—Carlucci, Joseph P. v U.S., 70 AFTR 2d 92-6002, 793 F Supp 484, (DC NY)
  e-1—Padalino, Vincent v. U.S., 71A AFTR 2d 93-3016, (DC NJ)

FIGURE C1-8 ▶ EXCERPTS FROM THE RIA CITATOR

Reprinted from Citator 2nd Series 1990–1196, ©1997 by RIA, 395 Hudson Street, New York, NY 10014

Tax Court in 1978, so no earlier references will be found.) *Diaz* has been cited with respect to its first and second AFTR headnotes. If there are other AFTR headnotes, the case has not been cited with respect to them.

The "a" on the first line beneath the name of the case indicates that the Tax Court's decision was affirmed by the Second Circuit. The Tax Court's opinion has been explained and followed in various cases, but it has not been cited in an unfavorable manner. Thus, its authoritative weight is substantial.

The Second Circuit's decision appears as a separate entry. The letters "sa" signify that the circuit court affirmed the Tax Court decision in the *Diaz* case. The cases that have cited the circuit court's opinion are listed under the entry for such opinion. The appellate decision has not been questioned or criticized; thus, its authority is relatively strong.

More recent references to *Leonarda C. Diaz* are reported in the 1990–96 citator volume (see Figure C1-8, Column 2). Nine additional cases cite the Tax Court decision[47]; two additional cases cite the Second Circuit Court decision. Recall that the CCH citator indicates that in 1972 the IRS Commissioner acquiesced in the Tax Court decision in *Alphonso Diaz*. This acquiescence is denoted by the capital "A," which appears after the citation to the same decision in the 1990–1996 citator volume.

One additional case citing the Leonarda C. Diaz Tax Court decision is listed in the 2003–2004 cumulative supplement.

COMPUTERS AS A RESEARCH TOOL

OBJECTIVE 6

Grasp the basics of computerized tax research

Tax professionals are increasingly using computers to conduct their tax-related research. Tax services have shifted most of their resources to media accessible by computer. With the technological advances in computer hardware and software, large databases are becoming more accessible and less costly. In the coming years, computer-assisted tax research will become an even more important tool for the tax advisor. A supplement to this chapter, which discusses this development, is available for download at *www.prenhall.com/phtax*. It also presents an overview of tax resources on the Internet.

In the major computerized tax services, most of the primary authorities discussed in this chapter appear as databases. Typically, each authority constitutes a separate database. Thus, the Internal Revenue Code comprises a separate database, as do Treasury Regulations, revenue rulings, revenue procedures, and other IRS pronouncements. Supreme Court opinions constitute a separate database, as do opinions of the Tax Court, the U.S. district courts, the Court of Federal Claims, and the circuit courts. Likewise, most of the secondary authorities discussed in this chapter appear as databases. Some authorities, however, are found exclusively in one service, while others are found in another. For example, the *Standard Federal Tax Reporter, Federal Tax Service,* and CCH citator are found exclusively in the CCH Internet Tax Research NetWork™. The *U.S. Tax Reporter, Federal Tax Coordinator 2d,* and RIA citator are found in RIA CHECKPOINT™. The basic features of the computerized and print sources generally are the same, with the following notable exceptions:

▶ Computerized sources have no finding lists. Cross referencing is facilitated through hyperlinks.

▶ Computerized sources have no cumulative supplements. New developments information is integrated into the main text.

▶ On computer, primary sources pertinent to explanatory paragraphs are accessible through hyperlink.

▶ On computer, citator symbols are explicitly spelled out.

---

[47] The first listing under the citation to the Tax Court decision in *Leonarda C. Diaz* refers to the same case decided at the Second Circuit Court level.

STATEMENTS ON STANDARDS FOR TAX SERVICES

OBJECTIVE 7

*Understand guidelines
that CPAs in tax practice
should follow*

Tax advisors confronted with ethical issues frequently turn to a professional organization for guidance. Although the guidelines set forth by such organizations are not *legally* enforceable, they carry significant moral weight, and may be cited in a negligence lawsuit as the proper "standard of care" for tax practitioners. They also may provide grounds for the termination or suspension of one's professional license. One such set of guidelines is the *Statements on Standards for Tax Services* (SSTSs),[48] issued by the American Institute of Certified Public Accountants (AICPA) and reproduced in Appendix E. Inspired by the principles of honesty and integrity, these guidelines define standards of ethical conduct for CPAs engaged in tax practice. In the words of the AICPA:

> In our view, practice standards are the hallmark of calling one's self a professional. Members should fulfill their responsibilities as professionals by instituting and maintaining standards against which their professional performance can be measured. The promulgation of practice standards also reinforces one of the core values of the AICPA Vision—that CPAs conduct themselves with honesty and integrity.[49]

The SSTSs differ in one important way from the AICPA's predecessor standards, *Statements on Responsibilites in Tax Practice,* in that the SSTSs are *professionally* enforceable; that is, they may be enforced through a disciplinary proceeding conducted by the AICPA, which may terminate or suspend a practitioner from AICPA membership.

Statement No. 1 defines the circumstances under which a CPA should (or should not) recommend a tax return position to a taxpayer. It also prescribes a course of conduct that the CPA should follow when making such a recommendation. Specifically,

▶ A member should not recommend that a tax return position be taken with respect to any item unless the member has a good-faith belief that the position has a realistic possibility of being sustained administratively or judicially on its merits if challenged . . .

▶ [A] member may recommend a tax return position that the member concludes is not frivolous so long as the member advises the taxpayer to appropriately disclose . . .

▶ When recommending tax return positions and when preparing or signing a return on which a tax return position is taken, a member should, when relevant, advise the taxpayer regarding potential penalty consequences of such tax return position and the opportunity, if any, to avoid such penalties through disclosure.

The "realistic possibility standard" set forth in Statement No. 1 parallels that of Sec. 6694. (For a discussion of the latter IRC section, see Chapter C15.) However, it differs from the IRC standard in that it allows as support for a tax return position well-reasoned articles or treatises, in addition to primary tax authorities. The IRC standard allows as support for a tax return position only primary tax authorities.

Statement No. 3 addresses (1) whether tax practitioners can reasonably rely on information supplied to them by the taxpayer, (2) when they have a duty to examine or verify such information, (3) when they have a duty to make inquiries of the taxpayer, and (4) what information they should consider in preparing a tax return. Specifically,

▶ In preparing or signing a return, a member may in good faith rely, without verification, on information furnished by the taxpayer or by third parties. However, a member should make reasonable inquiries if the information furnished appears to be incorrect, incomplete, or inconsistent either on its face or on the basis of other facts known to a member . . .

---

[48] AICPA, *Statements on Standards for Tax Services*, 2000, effective October 31, 2000. The SSTSs supercede the AICPA's *Statements on Responsibilities in Tax Practice*, 1991 Revision.

[49] Letter to AICPA members by David A. Lifson, Chair, AICPA Tax Executive Committee, and Gerald W. Padwe, Vice President, AICPA Taxation Section (April 18, 2000).

WHAT WOULD YOU DO IN THIS SITUATION?

Regal Enterprises and Macon Industries, unaffiliated corporations, have hired you to prepare their respective income tax returns. In preparing Regal's return, you notice that Regal has claimed a depreciation deduction for equipment purchased from Macon on February 22 at a cost of $2 million. In preparing Macon's return, you notice that Macon has reported sales proceeds of $1.5 million from the sale of equipment to Regal on February 22. One of the two figures must be incorrect. How do you proceed to correct it?

▶ If the tax law or regulations impose a condition with respect to the deductibility or other tax treatment of an item . . . a member should make appropriate inquiries to determine to the member's satisfaction whether such condition has been met.

▶ When preparing a tax return, a member should consider information actually known to that member from the tax return of another taxpayer if the information is relevant to that tax return and its consideration is necessary to properly prepare that tax return . . .

Note that the duty to verify arises only when taxpayer-provided information appears "strange" on its face. Otherwise, the tax practitioner has no duty to investigate taxpayer facts and circumstances.

Statement No. 4 defines the circumstances in which a tax practitioner may use estimates in preparing a tax return. In addition, it cautions the practitioner as to the manner in which he or she may use estimates. Specifically,

▶ A member may advise on estimates used in the preparation of a tax return, but the taxpayer has the responsibility to provide the estimated data. Appraisals or valuations are not considered estimates . . .

▶ [A] member may use the taxpayer's estimates in the preparation of a tax return if it is not practical to obtain exact data and if the member determines that the estimates are reasonable based on the facts and circumstances known to the member. If the taxpayer's estimates are used, they should be presented in a manner that does not imply greater accuracy than exists.

Notwithstanding this statement, the tax practitioner may not use estimates when such use is implicitly prohibited by the IRC. For example, Sec. 274(d) disallows deductions for certain expenses (e.g., meals and entertainment) unless the taxpayer can substantiate the expenses with adequate records or sufficient corroborating information. The documentation requirement effectively precludes the taxpayer from estimating such expenses and the practitioner from using such estimates.

Statement No. 6 defines a tax practitioner's duty when he or she becomes aware of (1) an error in the taxpayer's return, (2) the taxpayer's failure to file a required return, or (3) the taxpayer's failure to correct an error in a prior year's return. Specifically,

▶ A member should inform the taxpayer promptly upon becoming aware of an error in a previously filed return or upon becoming aware of a taxpayer's failure to file a required return. A member should recommend the corrective measures to be taken . . . The member is not obligated to inform the taxing authority, and a member may not do so without the taxpayer's permission, except when required by law.

▶ If a member is requested to prepare the current year's return and the taxpayer has not taken appropriate action to correct an error in a prior year's return, the member should consider whether to withdraw from preparing the return and whether to continue a professional or employment relationship with the taxpayer . . .

This statement implies that the tax practitioner's primary duty is to the taxpayer, not the taxing authority. Furthermore, upon the taxpayer's failure to correct a tax-related error, the practitioner may exercise discretion in deciding whether or not to terminate the professional relationship.

Occasionally, the tax practitioner discovers a taxpayer error in the course of an administrative proceeding (e.g., an IRS audit or appeals conference). The practitioner may advise the client to disclose the error, and the taxpayer may refuse. Statement No. 7 provides guidance as to what to do in these situations. Specifically,

► If a member is representing a taxpayer in an administrative proceeding with respect to a return that contains an error of which the member is aware, the member should inform the taxpayer promptly upon becoming aware of the error. The member should recommend the corrective measures to be taken. . . . A member is neither obligated to inform the taxing authority nor allowed to do so without the taxpayer's permission, except where required by law.

► A member should request the taxpayer's agreement to disclose the error to the taxing authority. Lacking such agreement, the member should consider whether to withdraw from representing the taxpayer in the administrative proceeding and whether to continue a professional or employment relationship with the taxpayer.

Finally, Statement No. 8 addresses the quality of advice provided by the tax practitioner, what consequences presumably ensue from such advice, and whether the practitioner has a duty to update advice to reflect subsequent developments. Specifically,

► A member should use judgment to ensure that tax advice provided to a taxpayer reflect professional competence and appropriately serves the taxpayer's needs . . .

► A member should assume that tax advice provided to a taxpayer will affect the manner in which the matters or transactions considered would be reported on the taxpayer's tax returns . . .

► A member has no obligation to communicate with a taxpayer when subsequent developments affect advice previously provided with respect to significant matters except while assisting a taxpayer in implementing procedures or plans associated with the advice provided or when a member undertakes an obligation by specific agreement.

The statement implies that practitioner-taxpayer dealings should be neither casual nor nonconsensual nor open-ended; rather, they should be professional, contractual, and definite.

From the foregoing emerges the following picture of the normative relationship between the tax advisor and his or her client: unlike an auditor, a tax advisor is an advocate. His or her primary duty is to the client, not the IRS. In fullfilling this duty, the advisor is bound by the highest standards of care. These standards include a good-faith belief that a tax return position has a realistic possibility of being sustained on its merits and on quality advice based on professional competence and client needs. Encompassed under the advisor's duty is the obligation to inform the client of the potential adverse consequences of a tax return position, how the client can avoid a penalty through disclosure, errors in a previously filed tax return, and corrective measures to be taken. Also encompassed is the obligation to determine by inquiry that the client satisfies conditions for taking a deduction, and to obtain information when material provided by the client appears incorrect, incomplete, or inconsistent. Excluded from the advisor's duty is the obligation to verify client-provided information when, based on the advisor's own knowledge, such information is not suspicious on its face. Also excluded is the obligation to update professional advice based on developments following its original conveyance. In preparing a tax return, the advisor may use estimates if obtaining concrete data is impractical and if the advisor determines that the estimates are reasonable. Although responsibility for providing the estimates resides with the client, responsibility for presenting them in a manner that does not imply undue accuracy resides with the advisor. Finally, the advisor may terminate a professional relationship if the client refuses to correct a tax-related error. On the other hand, unless legally bound, the advisor may not disclose the error to the IRS without the client's consent.

In addition to these obligations, the tax advisor has a strict duty of confidentiality to the client. Though not encompassed under the SSTSs, this duty is implied in the accountant-client privilege. (For a discussion of this privilege, see Chapter C15.)

STOP & THINK

❓

Question: As described in the Stop & Think box on page C1-10, you are researching the manner in which a deduction is calculated. The IRC states that the calculation is to be made "in a manner prescribed by the Secretary." After studying the IRC, Treasury Regulations, and committee reports, you conclude that another way of doing the calculation is arguably correct under an intuitive approach. This approach would result in a lower tax liability for the client. According to the *Statements on Standards for Tax Services*, may you take a position contrary to final Treasury Regulations based on the argument that the regulations are not valid?

Solution: You should not take a position contrary to the Treasury Regulations unless you have a "good-faith belief that the position has a realistic possibility of being sustained administratively or judicially on its merits." However, you can take a position that does not meet the above standard, provided you adequately disclose the position, and the position is not frivolous. Whether or not you have met the standard depends on all the facts and circumstances. Chapter C15 discusses tax return preparer positions contrary to Treasury Regulations.

SAMPLE WORK PAPERS AND CLIENT LETTER

OBJECTIVE 8

Prepare work papers and communicate to clients

Appendix A presents a set of sample work papers, including a draft of a client letter and a memo to the file. The work papers indicate the issues to be researched, the authorities addressing the issues, and the researcher's conclusions concerning the appropriate tax treatment, with rationale therefor.

    The format and other details of work papers differ from firm to firm. The sample in this text offers general guidance concerning the content of work papers. In practice, work papers may include less detail.

PROBLEM MATERIALS

DISCUSSION QUESTIONS

C1-1 Explain the difference between closed-fact and open-fact situations.

C1-2 According to the AICPA's *Statements on Standards for Tax Services,* what duties does the tax practitioner owe the client?

C1-3 Explain what is encompassed by the term *tax law* as used by tax advisors.

C1-4 The U.S. Government Printing Office publishes both hearings on proposed legislation and committee reports. Distinguish between the two.

C1-5 Explain how committee reports can be used in tax research. What do they indicate?

C1-6 A friend notices that you are reading the Internal Revenue Code of 1986. Your friend inquires why you are consulting a 1986 publication, especially when tax laws change so frequently. What is your response?

C1-7 Does Title 26 contain statutory provisions dealing only with income taxation? Explain.

C1-8 Refer to IRC Sec. 301.
a. Which subsection discusses the general rule for the tax treatment of a property distribution?
b. Where should one look for exceptions to the general rule?
c. What type of Treasury Regulations would relate to subsection (e)?

C1-9 Why should tax researchers note the date on which a Treasury Regulation was adopted?

C1-10 a. Distinguish between proposed, temporary, and final Treasury Regulations.

b. Distinguish between interpretative and legislative Treasury Regulations.

C1-11 Which type of regulation is more difficult for a taxpayer to successfully challenge, and why?

C1-12 Explain the legislative reenactment doctrine.

C1-13 **a.** Discuss the authoritative weight of revenue rulings.
b. As a practical matter, what consequences are likely to ensue if a taxpayer does not follow a revenue ruling and the IRS audits his or her return?

C1-14 **a.** In which courts may litigation dealing with tax matters begin?
b. Discuss the factors that might be considered in deciding where to litigate.
c. Describe the appeals process in tax litigation.

C1-15 May a taxpayer appeal a case litigated under the Small Cases Procedure of the Tax Court?

C1-16 Explain whether the following decisions are of the same precedential value: (1) Tax Court regular decisions, (2) Tax Court memo decisions, (3) decisions under the Small Cases Procedures of the Tax Court.

C1-17 Does the IRS acquiesce in decisions of U.S. district courts?

C1-18 The decisions of which courts are reported in the AFTR? In the USTC?

C1-19 Who publishes regular decisions of the Tax Court? Memo decisions?

C1-20 Explain the *Golsen* Rule. Give an example of its application.

C1-21 Assume that the only precedents relating to a particular issue are as follows:
Tax Court—decided for the taxpayer
Eighth Circuit Court of Appeals—decided for the taxpayer (affirming the Tax Court)
U.S. District Court for Eastern Louisiana—decided for the taxpayer
Fifth Circuit Court of Appeals—decided for the government (reversing the U.S. District Court of Eastern Louisiana)
a. Discuss the precedential value of the foregoing decisions for your client, who is a California resident.
b. If your client, a Texas resident, litigates in the Tax Court, how will the court rule? Explain.

C1-22 Which official publication(s) contain(s) the following:
a. Transcripts of Senate floor debates
b. IRS announcements
c. Tax Court regular opinions
d. Treasury decisions
e. U.S. district court opinions
f. Technical advice memoranda

C1-23 Under what circumstances might a tax advisor find the provisions of a tax treaty useful?

C1-24 Compare the print version of the tax services listed below (if they are found in your tax library) with respect to (a) how they are organized and (b) where current developments are reported.
a. *United States Tax Reporter*
b. *Standard Federal Tax Reporter*
c. *Federal Tax Coordinator 2d*
d. *Law of Federal Income Taxation* (Mertens)
e. BNA's *Tax Management Portfolios*
f. CCH's *Federal Tax Service*

C1-25 Indicate (1) which Internet tax service provides each of the following secondary sources and (2) whether the source is annotated or topical.
a. *Federal Tax Coordinator 2d*
b. Mertens
c. *BNA Tax Management Portfolios*
d. *Standard Federal Tax Reporter*
e. *United States Tax Reporter*

C1-26 What two functions does a citator serve?

C1-27 Describe two types of information that can be gleaned from citing cases in the RIA citator but not those in the CCH citator.

C1-28 Explain how your research approach might differ if you use the computerized version of a tax service instead of the print version (e.g., RIA or CCH).

C1-29 Access the CCH Internet Tax Research NetWork™ at *http://tax.cch.com/network* and RIA CHECKPOINT™ at *http://checkpoint.riag.com*. Then answer the following questions:
a. What are the principal primary sources found in both Internet tax services?
b. What are the principal secondary sources found in each Internet tax service?
c. What citator is found in each Internet tax service?
(In answering these questions, consult the supplement to this chapter available for download at *www.prenhall.com/phtax*.)

C1-30 Compare the features of the computerized tax services with those of Internet sites maintained by noncommercial institutions. What are the relative advantages and disadvantages of each? Could the latter sites serve as a substitute for a commercial tax service? (In answering these questions, consult the supplement to this chapter available for download at *www.prenhall.com/phtax*.)

C1-31 According to the *Statements on Standards for Tax Services*, what belief should a CPA have before taking a pro-taxpayer position on a tax return?

C1-32 Under the AICPA's *Statements on Standards for Tax Services*, what is the tax practitioner's professional duty in each of the following situations?
a. Client erroneously deducts $5,000 (instead of $500) on a previous year's tax return.
b. Client refuses to file an amended return to correct the deduction error.
c. Client informs tax practitioner that client incurred $200 in out-of-pocket office supplies expenses.

d. Client informs tax practitioner that client incurred $700 in business-related entertainment expenses.

e. Tax practitioner learns that the exemption amount for single taxpayers has been increased by $1,000. Client is a single taxpayer.

PROBLEMS

C1-33 *Interpreting the IRC.* Under a divorce agreement executed in the current year, an ex-wife receives from her former husband cash of $25,000 per year for eight years. The agreement does not explicitly state that the payments are excludible from gross income.
a. Does the ex-wife have gross income? If so, how much?
b. Is the former husband entitled to a deduction? If so, is it for or from AGI? Refer only to the IRC in answering this question. Start with Sec. 71.

C1-34 *Interpreting the IRC.* Refer to Sec. 385 and answer the questions below.
a. Whenever Treasury Regulations are issued under this section, what type are they likely to be: legislative or interpretative? Explain.
b. Assume Treasury Regulations under Sec. 385 have been finalized. Will they be relevant to estate tax matters? Explain.

C1-35 *Using the Cumulative Bulletin.* Consult any volume of the *Cumulative Bulletin*. In what order are revenue rulings arranged?

C1-36 *Using the Cumulative Bulletin.* Which IRC section(s) does Rev. Rul. 2001-29 interpret? (Hint: consult the official publication of the IRS.)

C1-37 *Using the Cumulative Bulletin.* Refer to the 1989-1 *Cumulative Bulletin*.
a. What time period does this bulletin cover?
b. What appears on page 1?
c. What items are found in Part I?
d. In what order are the items presented in Part I?
e. What items are found in Part II?
f. What items are found in Part III?

C1-38 *Using the Cumulative Bulletin.* Refer to the 1990-1 *Cumulative Bulletin*.
a. For the time period covered by the bulletin, in which cases did the IRS nonacquiesce?
b. What is the topic of Rev. Rul. 90-10?
c. Does this bulletin contain a revenue ruling that interprets Sec. 162? If so, specify.

C1-39 *Determining Acquiescence.*
a. What official action (acquiescence or nonacquiescence) did the IRS Commissioner take regarding the 1986 Tax Court decision in *John McIntosh*? (Hint: Consult the 1986-1 *Cumulative Bulletin*.)
b. Did this action concern *all* issues in the case? If not, explain. (Before answering this question, consult the headnote to the court opinion.)

C1-40 *Determining Acquiescence.*
a. What original action (acquiescence or nonacquiescence) did the IRS Commissioner take regarding the 1952 Tax Court decision in *Streckfus Steamers, Inc.*?
b. Was the action complete or partial?
c. Did the IRS Commissioner subsequently change his mind? If so, when?

C1-41 *Determining Acquiescence.*
a. What original action (acquiescence or nonacquiescence) did the IRS Commissioner take regarding the 1956 Tax Court decision in *Pittsburgh Milk Co.*?
b. Did the IRS Commissioner subsequently change his mind? If so, when?

C1-42 *Evaluating a Case.* Look up *James E. Threlkeld*, 87 T.C. 1294 (1988) either in print or in an Internet tax service, and answer the questions below.
a. Was the case reviewed by the court? If so, was the decision unanimous? Explain.
b. Was the decision entered under Rule 155?
c. Consult a citator. Was the case reviewed by an appellate court? If so, which one?

C1-43 *Evaluating a Case.* Look up *Bush Brothers & Co.*, 73 T.C. 424 (1979) either in print or in an Internet tax service, and answer the questions below.
a. Was the case reviewed by the court? If so, was the decision unanimous? Explain.
b. Was the decision entered under Rule 155?
c. Consult a citator. Was the case reviewed by an appellate court? If so, which one?

C1-44   *Writing Citations.* Provide the proper citations (including both primary and secondary citations where applicable) for the authorities listed below. (For secondary citations, reference both the AFTR and USTC.)
a. *National Cash Register Co.*, a 6th Circuit Court decision
b. *Thomas M. Dragoun v. CIR*, a Tax Court memo decision
c. *John M. Grabinski v. U.S.*, a U.S. district court decision
d. *John M. Grabinski v. U.S.*, an Eighth Circuit Court decision
e. *Rebekah Harkness*, a 1972 Court of Claims decision
f. *Hillsboro National Bank v. CIR*, a Supreme Court decision
g. Rev. Rul. 78-129.

C1-45   *Writing Citations.* Provide the proper citations (including both primary and secondary citations where applicable) for the authorities listed below. (For secondary citations, reference both the AFTR and USTC.)
a. Rev. Rul. 99-7
b. *Frank H. Sullivan*, a Board of Tax Appeals decision
c. *Tate & Lyle, Inc.*, a 1994 Tax Court decision
d. *Ralph L. Rogers v. U.S.*, a U.S. district court decision
e. *Norman Rodman v. CIR*, a Second Circuit Court decision

C1-46   *Interpreting Citations.* Indicate which courts decided the cases cited below. Also indicate on which pages and in which publications the authority is reported.
a. *Lloyd M. Shumaker v. CIR*, 648 F.2d 1198, 48 AFTR 2d 81-5353 (9th Cir., 1981)
b. *Xerox Corp. v. U.S.*, 14 Cl. Ct. 455, 88-1 USTC ¶9231 (1988)
c. *Real Estate Land Title & Trust Co. v. U.S.*, 309 U.S. 13, 23 AFTR 816 (USSC, 1940)
d. *J. B. Morris v. U.S.*, 441 F. Supp. 76, 41 AFTR 2d 78-335 (DC TX, 1977)
e. Rev. Rul. 83-3, 1983-1 C.B. 72
f. *Malone & Hyde, Inc. v. U.S.*, 568 F.2d 474, 78-1 USTC ¶9199 (6th Cir., 1978)

C1-47   *Using a Tax Service.* Use the topical index of the *United States Tax Reporter*, either in print or in RIA CHECKPOINT™, to locate authorities dealing with the deductibility of the cost of a facelift.
a. In which paragraph(s) does the *United States Tax Reporter* summarize and cite these authorities?
b. List the authorities.
c. May a taxpayer deduct the cost of a facelift paid in the current year? Explain.

C1-48   *Using a Tax Service.* Refer to Reg. Sec. 1.302-1 at ¶3022 of the *United States Tax Reporter*, either in print or in RIA CHECKPOINT™. Does this Treasury Regulation reflect recent amendments to the IRC? Explain.

C1-49   *Using a Tax Service.* Use the topical index of the *Standard Federal Tax Reporter*, either in print or in the CCH Internet Tax Research NetWork™, to locate authorities addressing whether termite damage constitutes a casualty loss.
a. In which paragraph(s) does the *Standard Federal Tax Reporter* summarize and cite these authorities?
b. List the authorities.
c. Have there been any recent developments concerning the tax consequences of termite damage? (*Recent* suggests authorities appearing in the cumulative index section of the print version or the current developments section of the Internet version.)

C1-50   *Using a Tax Service.*
a. Locate in the *Standard Federal Tax Reporter*, either in print or in the CCH Internet Tax Research NetWork™, where Sec. 303(b)(2)(A) appears. This provision states that Sec. 303(a) applies only if the stock in question meets a certain percentage test. What is the applicable percentage?
b. Locate Reg. Sec. 1.303-2(a) in the same service. Does this Treasury Regulation reflect recent amendments to the IRC with respect to the percentage test addressed in Part a? Explain.

C1-51   *Using a Tax Service.* The questions below deal with BNA's *Tax Management Portfolios*.
a. What is the number of the main portfolio that deals with tax-free exchanges under Sec. 1031?
b. On which page does a discussion of "boot" begin?
c. What are the purposes of Worksheets 1 and 5 of this portfolio?
d. Refer to the bibliography and references at the end of the portfolio. Indicate the numbers of the IRC sections listed as "secondarily" relevant.

C1-52   *Using a Tax Service.* This problem deals with Mertens' *Law of Federal Income Taxation.*

a. Refer to Volume 5. What general topics does it discuss?

b. Which section of Volume 5 discusses the principal methods for determining depreciation amounts?

c. In Volume 5, what is the purpose of the yellow and white sheets appearing before the tab labeled "Text"?

d. Refer to the Ruling Status Table in the Current Rulings Materials volume. What is the current status of Rev. Ruls. 79-433 and 75-335?

e. Refer to the Code-Rulings Tables in the same volume. List the numbers (e.g., Rev. Rul. 83-88) of all 1983 revenue rulings and revenue procedures that interpret Sec. 121.

C1-53   *Using a Tax Service.* This problem deals with RIA's *Federal Tax Coordinator 2d.*

a. Use the topical index, either in print or in RIA CHECKPOINT™, to locate authorities dealing with the deductibility of the cost of work clothing by ministers (clergymen). List the authorities.

b. Where does this tax service report new developments?

C1-54   *Using a Tax Service.* Refer to the print versions of the *United States Tax Reporter* and *Standard Federal Tax Reporter.* Then, for each tax reporter, answer the following questions.

a. In which volume is the index located?

b. Is the index arranged by topic or IRC section?

c. If you know an IRC section number, how do you locate additional authorities?

d. If you know the name of a court decision, how do you locate additional authorities?

C1-55   *Using a Citator.* Trace *Biltmore Homes, Inc.,* a 1960 Tax Court memo decision, in both the CCH and RIA citators (either print or Internet form).

a. According to the RIA citator, how many times has the Tax Court decision been cited by other courts on Headnote Number 5?

b. How many issues did the lower court address in its opinion? (Hint: Refer to the case headnote numbers.)

c. Did an appellate court review the case? If so, which one?

d. According to the CCH citator, how many times has the Tax Court decision been cited by other courts?

e. According to the CCH citator, how many times has the circuit court decision been cited by other courts on Headnote Number 5?

C1-56   *Using a Citator.* Trace *Stephen Bolaris,* 776 F.2d 1428, in both the CCH and RIA citators (either print or Internet form).

a. According to the RIA citator, how many times has the Ninth Circuit's decision been cited?

b. Did the decision address more than one issue? Explain.

c. Was the decision ever cited unfavorably? Explain.

d. According to the CCH citator, how many times has the Ninth Circuit's decision been cited?

e. According to the CCH citator, how many times has the Tax Court's decision been cited on Headnote Number 1?

C1-57   *Interpreting a Case.* Refer to the *Holden Fuel Oil Company* case (31 TCM 184).

a. In which year was the case decided?

b. What controversy was litigated?

c. Who won the case?

d. Was the decision reviewed at the lower court level?

e. Was the decision appealed?

f. Has the decision been cited in other cases?

C1-58   *Internet Research.* Access the IRS Internet site at *http://www.irs.gov* and answer the following questions: (In answering them, consult the supplement to this chapter available for download at *www.prenhall.com/phtax.*)

a. How does one file a tax return electronically?

b. How can the taxpayer transmit funds electronically?

c. What are the advantages of electronic filing?

C1-59   *Internet Research.* Access the IRS Internet site at *http://www.irs.gov* and indicate the titles of the following IRS forms: (In so doing, consult the supplement to this chapter available for download at *www.prenhall.com/phtax.*)

a. Form 4506

b. Form 973

c. Form 8725

C1-60 *Internet Research.* Access the Federation of Tax Administrators Internet site at *http://www.taxadmin.org/fta/link/forms.html* and indicate the titles of the following state tax forms and publications: (In so doing, consult the supplement to this chapter available for download at *www.prenhall.com/phtax.*)

a. Minnesota Form M-3

b. Illinois Schedule CR

c. New York State Form CT-3-C

C1-61 *Internet Research.* Access Emory's *Federal Courts Finder* at *http://www.law.emory.edu/FEDCTS/* and answer the following questions: (In answering them, consult the supplement to this chapter available for download at *www.prenhall.com/phtax.*)

a. What is the historical timespan of the underlying databases?

b. In what ways can they be accessed?

c. What 1995 Eleventh Circuit Court decisions address the issue of the charitable deduction for estates?

COMPREHENSIVE PROBLEM

C1-62 Your client, a physician, recently purchased a yacht on which he flies a pennant with a medical emblem on it. He recently informed you that he purchased the yacht and flies the pennant to advertise his occupation and thus attract new patients. He has asked you if he may deduct as ordinary and necessary business expenses the costs of insuring and maintaining the yacht. In search of an answer, consult either CCH's *Standard Federal Tax Reporter* or RIA's *United States Tax Reporter* first in print, and then on the Internet (i.e., the CCH Internet Tax Research NetWork or RIA CHECKPOINT). Then compare the steps taken on each to find your answer.

TAX STRATEGY PROBLEM

C1-63 Your client, Home Products Universal (HPU), distributes home improvement products to independent retailers throughout the country. Its management wants to explore the possibility of opening its own home improvement centers. Accordingly, it commissions a consulting firm to conduct a feasibility study, which ultimately persuades HPU to expand into retail sales. The consulting firm bills HPU $150,000, which HPU deducts on its current year tax return. The IRS disputes the deduction, contending that, because the cost relates to entering a new business, it should be capitalized. HPU's management, on the other hand, firmly believes that, because the cost relates to expanding HPU's existing business, it should be deducted. In contemplating legal action against the IRS, HPU's management considers the state of judicial precedent: The federal court for HPU's district has ruled that the cost of expanding from distribution into retail sales should be capitalized. The appellate court for HPU's circuit has stated in *dictum* that, although in some circumstances switching from product distribution to product sales entails entering a new trade or business, improving customer access to one's existing products generally does not. The Federal Circuit Court has ruled that wholesale distribution and retail sales, even of the same product, constitute distinct businesses. In a case involving a taxpayer from another circuit, the Tax Court has ruled that such costs invariably should be capitalized. HPU's Chief Financial Officer approaches you with the question, "In which judicial forum should HPU file a lawsuit against the IRS: (1) U.S. district court, (2) the Tax Court, or (3) the U.S. Court of Federal Claims?" What do you tell her?

CASE STUDY PROBLEM

C1-64 A client, Mal Manley, fills out his client questionnaire for the previous year and on it provides information for the preparation of his individual income tax return. The IRS has never audited Mal's returns. Mal reports that he made over 100 relatively small cash contributions totaling $24,785 to charitable organizations. In the last few years, Mal's charitable contributions have averaged about $15,000 per year. For the previous year, Mal's adjusted gross income was roughly $350,000, about a 10% increase from the year before.

Required: According to the *Statements on Standards for Tax Services*, may you accept at face value Mal's information concerning his charitable contributions? Now assume that the IRS recently audited Mal's tax return for two years ago and denied 75% of that year's charitable contribution deduction because the deduction was not substantiated. Assume also that Mal indicates that, in the previous year, he contributed $25,000 (instead of $24,785). How do these changes of fact affect your earlier decision?

TAX RESEARCH PROBLEMS

C1-65 The purpose of this problem is to enhance your skills in interpreting the authorities that you locate in your research. In answering the questions that follow, refer only to *Thomas A. Curtis, M.D., Inc.*, 1994 RIA TC Memo ¶94,015.
  a. What general controversy was litigated in this case?
  b. Which party—the taxpayer or the IRS—won?
  c. Why is the corporation instead of Dr. and/or Ms. Curtis listed as the plaintiff?
  d. What is the relationship between Ellen Barnert Curtis and Dr. Thomas A. Curtis?
  e. Approximately how many hours a week did Ms. Curtis work, and what were her credentials?
  f. For the fiscal year ending in 1989, what salary did the corporation pay Ms. Curtis? What amount did the court decide was reasonable?
  g. What dividends did the corporation pay for its fiscal years ending in 1988 and 1989?
  h. To which circuit would this decision be appealable?
  i. According to *Curtis*, what five factors did the Ninth Circuit mention in *Elliotts, Inc.* as relevant in determining reasonable compensation?

C1-66 Josh contributes $5,000 toward the support of his widowed mother, aged 69, a U.S. citizen and resident. She earns gross income of $2,000 and spends it all for her own support. In addition, Medicare pays $3,200 of her medical expenses. She does not receive financial support from sources other than those described above. Must the Medicare payments be included in the support that Josh's mother is deemed to provide for herself?
  Prepare work papers and a client letter (to Josh) dealing with the issue.

C1-67 Amy owns a vacation cottage in Maine. She predicts that the time during which the cottage will be used in the current year is as follows:

By Amy, solely for vacation	12 days
By Amy, making repairs ten hours per day and vacationing the rest of the day	2 days
By her sister, who paid fair rental value	8 days
By her cousin, who paid fair rental value	4 days
By her friend, who paid a token amount of rent	2 days
By three families from the Northeast, who paid fair rental value for 40 days each	120 days
Not used	217 days

Calculate the ratio for allocating the following expenses to the rental income expected to be received from the cottage: interest, taxes, repairs, insurance, and depreciation. The ratio will be used to determine the amount of expenses that are deductible and, thus, Amy's taxable income for the year.
  For the tax manager to whom you report, prepare work papers in which you address the calculation method. Also, draft a memo to the file dealing with the results of your research.

C1-68 Look up *Summit Publishing Company*, 1990 PH T.C. Memo ¶90,288, 59 TCM 833, and *J.B.S. Enterprises*, 1991 PH T.C. Memo ¶91,254, 61 TCM 2829, and answer the following questions:
  a. What was the principal issue in these cases?
  b. What factors did the Tax Court consider in resolving the central issue?
  c. How are the facts of these cases similar? How are they dissimilar?

C1-69 Your supervisor would like to set up a single Sec. 401(k) plan exclusively for the managers of your organization. Concerned that this arrangement might not meet the requirements for a qualified plan, he has asked you to request a determination letter from the IRS. In a brief memorandum, address the following issues:
  a. What IRS pronouncements govern requests for determination letters?
  b. What IRS forms must be filed with the request?
  c. What information must be provided in the request?
  d. What actions must accompany the filing?
  e. Where must the request be filed?

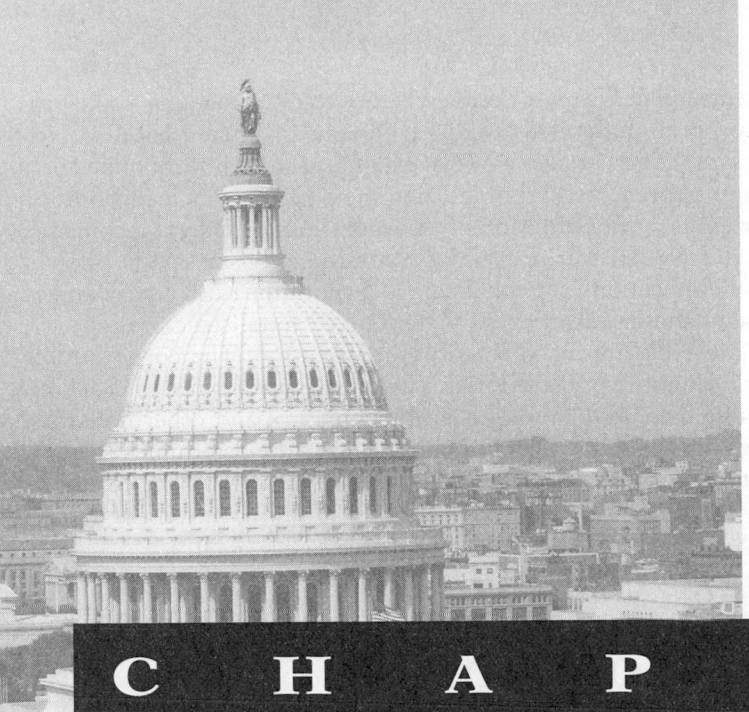

2

CHAPTER

CORPORATE FORMATIONS AND CAPITAL STRUCTURE

LEARNING OBJECTIVES

After studying this chapter, you should be able to

1. ▶ Explain the tax advantages and disadvantages of alternative business forms

2. ▶ Apply the check-the-box regulations to partnerships, corporations, and trusts

3. ▶ Determine the legal requirements for forming a corporation

4. ▶ Explain the requirements for deferring gain or loss upon incorporation

5. ▶ Understand the tax implications of alternative capital structures

6. ▶ Determine the tax consequences of worthless stock or debt obligations

When starting a business, entrepreneurs must decide whether to organize it as a sole proprietorship, partnership, corporation, limited liability company, or limited liability partnership. This chapter discusses the advantages and disadvantages of each form of business association. Because many entrepreneurs find organizing their business as a corporation advantageous, this chapter looks at the definition of a corporation for federal income tax purposes. It also discusses the tax consequences of incorporating a business. The chapter closes by examining the tax implications of capitalizing a corporation with equity and/or debt as well as the advantages and disadvantages of alternative capital structures.

This textbook takes a life-cycle approach to corporate taxation. The corporate life cycle starts with corporate formation, discussed in this chapter. Once formed and operating, the corporation's taxable income (or loss), federal income tax and other liabilities, and the tax consequences of distributions to its shareholders must be determined. Finally, at some point the corporation may outlive its usefulness and be dissolved. The corporate life cycle is too complex to discuss in one chapter. Therefore, additional coverage follows in Chapters C3 through C8.

ORGANIZATION FORMS AVAILABLE

OBJECTIVE 1

Explain the tax advantages and disadvantages of alternative business forms

Businesses can be organized in several forms including

▶ Sole proprietorships

▶ Partnerships

▶ Corporations

▶ Limited liability companies

▶ Limited liability partnerships

A discussion of the tax implications of each form is presented below.

SOLE PROPRIETORSHIPS

ADDITIONAL COMMENT

The income/loss of a sole proprietorship reported on Schedule C carries to page 1 of Form 1040 and is included in the computation of the individual's taxable income. Net income, if any, also carries to Schedule SE of Form 1040 for computation of the sole proprietor's self-employment tax.

A **sole proprietorship** is a business owned by one individual. It often is selected by entrepreneurs with a modest amount of capital who are beginning a new business. From a tax and legal perspective, a sole propriertorship is not a separate entity. Rather, it is considered to be a legal extension of its individual owner. Thus, the individual owns all the business assets and reports income or loss from the sole proprietorship directly on his or her individual tax return. Specifically, the individual owner (proprietor) reports all the business's income and expenses for the year on Schedule C (Profit or Loss from Business) or Schedule C-EZ (Net Profit from Business) of Form 1040. A completed Schedule C is included in Appendix B, where a common set of facts (with minor modifications) illustrates the similarities and differences in tax reporting for a sole proprietorship, C corporation, partnership, and S corporation.

If the business is profitable, the profit is added to the proprietor's other income.

EXAMPLE C2-1 ▶ John, a single taxpayer, starts a new computer store, which he operates as a sole proprietorship. John reports a $15,000 profit from the store in his first year of operation. Assuming he has enough income from other sources to be taxed at a 35% marginal tax rate, John's tax on the $15,000 of profit from the store is $5,250 (0.35 × $15,000).[1] ◀

If the business is unprofitable, the loss reduces the proprietor's taxable income, thereby providing tax savings.

EXAMPLE C2-2 ▶ Assume the same facts as in Example C2-1 except John reports a $15,000 loss instead of a $15,000 profit in his first year of operation. Assuming he still is taxed at a 35% marginal tax rate, the $15,000 loss on the new venture produces tax savings of $5,250 (0.35 × $15,000). ◀

---

[1] The $15,000 Schedule C profit in Example C2-1 will increase adjusted gross income (AGI). The AGI level affects certain deduction calculations (e.g., medical, charitable contributions, and miscellaneous itemized) and may result in a taxable income increase different from the $15,000 AGI increase.

ADDITIONAL COMMENT

Although this chapter emphasizes the tax consequences of selecting the entity in which a business will be conducted, other issues also are important in making such a decision. For example, the amount of legal liability assumed by an owner is important and can vary substantially among the different business entities.

TAX ADVANTAGES.   The tax advantages of conducting business as a sole proprietorship are as follows:

▶ The sole proprietorship, as a business, is not subject to taxation. Rather, the sole proprietor, as an individual, is taxed at his or her marginal tax rate on income earned by the business.

▶ The proprietor's marginal tax rate may be lower than the marginal tax rate that would have applied had the business been organized as a corporation.

▶ The owner may contribute cash to, or withdraw profits from, the business without tax consequences. Although the owner usually maintains separate books, records, and bank accounts for the business, the money in these accounts belongs to the owner personally.

▶ The owner may contribute property to, or withdraw property from, the business without recognizing gain or loss.

▶ Business losses may offset nonbusiness income, such as interest, dividends, and any salary earned by the sole proprietor or his or her spouse, subject to the passive activity loss rules.

TAX DISADVANTAGES.   The tax disadvantages of conducting business as a sole proprietorship are as follows:

▶ The profits of a sole proprietorship business are currently taxed to the individual owner, whether or not the profits are retained in the business or withdrawn for personal consumption. By contrast, the profits of a corporate business are taxed to its shareholders only when the corporation distributes the earnings as dividends.

▶ At times, corporate tax rates have been lower than individual tax rates. In such times, businesses conducted as sole proprietorships have been taxed more heavily than businesses organized as corporations.

▶ A sole proprietor must pay the full amount of Social Security taxes because he or she is not considered to be an employee of the business. By contrast, shareholder-employees must pay only half their Social Security taxes; the corporate employer pays the other half. (The employer, however, might pass this half onto employees in the form of lower wages.)

▶ Sole proprietorships may not deduct compensation paid to owner employees. By contrast, corporations may deduct compensation paid to shareholder-employees.

▶ Certain tax-exempt benefits (e.g., premiums for group term life insurance) available to shareholder-employees are not available to owner-employees.[2]

▶ A sole proprietor must use the same accounting period for business and personal purposes. Thus, he or she cannot defer income by choosing a business fiscal year that differs from the individual's calendar year. By contrast, a corporation may choose a fiscal year that differs from the shareholder's calendar years.

PARTNERSHIPS

REAL-WORLD EXAMPLE

The IRS estimates the following business entity returns to be filed for 2005:

Entity	Number
Partnership	2.52 million
C corporation	2.26 million
S corporation	3.62 million

A **partnership** is an unincorporated business carried on by two or more individuals or other entities. The partnership form often is used by friends or relatives who decide to go into business together and by groups of investors who want to share the profits, losses, and expenses of some type of business or investment such as a real estate project.

A partnership is a tax reporting, but not taxpaying, entity. The partnership acts as a conduit for its owners. Its income, expenses, losses, credits, and other tax-related items flow through to the partners who report these items in their separate tax returns.

Each year a partnership must file a tax return (Form 1065—U.S. Partnership Return of Income) to report the results of its operations. When the partnership return is filed, the preparer must send each partner a statement (Schedule K-1, Form 1065) that reports the partner's allocable share of partnership income, expenses, losses, credits, and other tax-related

---

[2] Section 162(1) permits self-employed individuals to deduct all of the health insurance costs incurred on behalf of themselves, their spouses, and their dependents as a trade or business expense.

items. The partners then must report these items on their individual tax returns. A completed Form 1065 is included in Appendix B.

Just as with a sole proprietorship, if the business is profitable, the partners' allocable shares of business profits are added to the partners' other income and taxed at each partner's respective marginal tax rate.

EXAMPLE C2-3 ▶ Bob is single and owns a 50% interest in the BT Partnership, a calendar year entity. The BT Partnership reports $30,000 of profits in its first year of operation. Bob's $15,000 share flows through from the partnership to Bob's individual tax return. Assuming Bob is taxed at a 35% marginal tax rate on the additional income, his tax on his $15,000 share of partnership profits is $5,250 (0.35 × $15,000). Bob must pay the $5,250 in taxes whether or not the BT Partnership distributes any of its profits to him. ◀

If a partnership reports a loss, the partners' allocable shares of the loss reduce the partners' other income and provide tax savings based on the partners' marginal tax rates. The passive activity loss rules, however, may limit the amount of any loss deduction available to the partners. (See Chapter C9 of this book.)

EXAMPLE C2-4 ▶ Assume the same facts as in Example C2-3 except that, instead of a profit, the BT Partnership reports a $30,000 loss for its first year of operation. Assuming Bob is taxed at a 35% marginal tax rate, his $15,000 share of the first year loss produces a $5,250 (0.35 × $15,000) tax savings. ◀

A partnership can be either general or limited. In a general partnership, each partner has unlimited liability for partnership debts. Thus, these partners are at risk for more than the amount of their capital investment in the partnership. In a limited partnership, at least one partner must be a general partner, and at least one partner must be a limited partner. As in a general partnership, the general partners are liable for all partnership debts, but the limited partners are liable only to the extent of their capital investment in the partnership plus any amount they are obligated to contribute to the partnership if called upon. Moreover, limited partners generally may not participate in the management of the partnership.

The tax advantages and disadvantages of doing business as a partnership are similar to those relative to a sole proprietorship.

TAX ADVANTAGES. The tax advantages of doing business as a partnership are as follows:

▶ The partnership as an entity is exempt from taxation. The income of the partnership flows through to the individual tax returns of the partners and is taxed directly to them. Their individual tax rates may be lower than the corporate marginal tax rate on the same amount of taxable income.

▶ Partnership income is not subject to double taxation. Although partnership profits are accounted for at the partnership level, they are taxed only at the partner level. Additional taxes generally are not imposed on distributions to the partners. With limited exceptions, partners can contribute money or property to, or withdraw money or property from, the partnership without gain or loss recognition.

▶ Subject to limitations, partners can use losses to offset income from other sources.

▶ A partner's basis in a partnership interest is increased by his or her share of partnership income. This basis adjustment reduces the amount of gain recognized when the partner sells his or her partnership interest, thereby preventing double taxation.

ADDITIONAL COMMENT

If two or more owners exist, a business cannot be conducted as a sole proprietorship. From a tax compliance and recordkeeping perspective, conducting a business as a partnership is more complicated than conducting the business as a sole proprietorship.

TAX DISADVANTAGES. The tax disadvantages of doing business as a partnership are as follows:

▶ All the partnership's profits are taxed to the partners when earned, even if reinvested in the business. The partners' tax rates may be higher than the marginal tax rate that applies to a corporation.

▶ A partner is not considered to be an employee of the partnership. Therefore, partners must pay the full amount of self-employment taxes on their share of partnership income. Some tax-exempt fringe benefits (e.g., premiums for group term life insurance) are not available to partners.[3]

▶ Partners generally cannot defer income by choosing a fiscal year for the partnership that differs from the tax year of the principal partner(s). However, if the partnership can establish a business purpose, or if it makes a special election, the partnership can use a fiscal year.

Chapters C9 and C10 of this volume provide a detailed discussion of partnerships.

CORPORATIONS

Corporations can be divided into two categories: C corporations and S corporations. A C corporation is subject to double taxation. Its earnings are taxed first at the corporate level when earned, then again at the shareholder level when distributed as dividends. An S corporation, by contrast, is subject to single-level taxation, much like a partnership. Its earnings are accounted for at the corporate level but are taxed only at the shareholder level.

C CORPORATIONS. A **C corporation** is a separate entity taxed on its income at rates ranging from 15% to 35%.[4] A corporation must report all its income and expenses and compute its tax liability on Form 1120 (U.S. Corporation Income Tax Return). A completed Form 1120 appears in Appendix B. Shareholders are not taxed on the corporation's earnings unless these earnings are distributed as dividends. For years 2003 through 2008, the dividends received by a noncorporate shareholder are taxed at the same rate that applies to net capital gains. This special dividend rate is 15% for taxpayers whose tax bracket exceeds 15%. (See Chapter I5 of the *Individuals* volume for details of this 2003 Act provision.)

EXAMPLE C2-5 ▶

Jane owns 100% of York Corporation's stock. York reports taxable income of $50,000 for the current year. The first $50,000 of taxable income is taxed at a 15% rate, so York pays a corporate income tax of $7,500 (0.15 × $50,000). If the corporation distributes none of its earnings to Jane during the year, she pays no taxes on York's earnings. However, if York distributes its current after-tax earnings to Jane, she must pay tax on $42,500 ($50,000 − $7,500) of dividend income. Assuming she is in the 35% marginal tax bracket, the tax Jane pays on the dividend income is $6,375 (0.15 × $42,500). The total tax on York's $50,000 of profits is $13,875 ($7,500 paid by York + $6,375 paid by Jane). ◀

Even when a corporation does not distribute its profits, double taxation may result. The profits are taxed to the corporation when they are earned. Then they may be taxed a second time (as capital gains) when the shareholder sells his or her stock or when the corporation liquidates.

EXAMPLE C2-6 ▶

On January 2 of the current year, Carl purchases 100% of York Corporation stock for $60,000. In the same year, York reports taxable income of $50,000, on which it pays tax of $7,500. The corporation distributes none of the remaining $42,500 to Carl. On January 3 of the next year, Carl sells his stock to Mary for $102,500 (his initial investment plus the current year's accumulated earnings). Carl must report a capital gain of $42,500 ($102,500 − $60,000). Thus, York's profit is taxed twice—first at the corporate level when earned and again at the shareholder level when Carl sells the stock. ◀

Tax Advantages. The tax advantages of doing business as a C corporation are as follows:

▶ Because a corporation is an entity independent of its shareholders, its marginal tax rate may be lower than its shareholders' marginal tax rates. Tax savings may result as long as the earnings are not distributed and taxed to both the shareholders and the corporation. If the earnings are not distributed, they may be used for reinvestment and the retirement of debt. This advantage, however, may be limited by the accumulated earnings tax and the personal holding company tax. (See Chapter C5 for a discussion of these two penalty taxes.)

---

[3] Partners are eligible to deduct their health insurance costs in the same manner as a sole proprietor. See footnote 2 for details.

[4] As discussed in Chapter C3, the corporate tax rate is 39% and 38% in certain ranges of taxable income.

▶ Shareholders employed by the corporation are treated as employees for tax purposes. Consequently, they are liable for only half of their Social Security taxes, while their corporate employer is liable for the other half. In addition, shareholder-employees are entitled to tax-free fringe benefits (e.g., premiums paid on group term life insurance and accident and health insurance). The corporation can provide these benefits with before-tax dollars (instead of after-tax dollars). Because sole proprietors and partners are not considered to be employees, they are ineligible for some tax-free benefits, although they are permitted to deduct their health insurance premiums.

▶ A corporation may deduct compensation paid to shareholder-employees. Within reasonable limits, it may adjust this compensation upward to shelter corporate taxable income.

▶ A C corporation can use a fiscal year instead of a calendar year as its reporting period. A fiscal year could permit a corporation to defer income to a later reporting period. A personal service corporation, however, generally must use a calendar year as its tax year.[5]

▶ Special rules allow a 50% exclusion of gain recognized on the sale or exchange of stock held more than five years if the C corporation meets certain requirements.

Tax Disadvantages. The tax disadvantages of doing business as a C corporation are as follows:

▶ Double taxation of income results when the corporation distributes its earnings as dividends to shareholders or when shareholders sell or exchange their stock.

▶ Shareholders generally cannot withdraw money or property from the corporation without income recognition. A distribution of profits to a shareholder is taxable as a dividend if the corporation has sufficient earnings and profits (E&P). (See Chapter C4 for a discussion of E&P.)

▶ Net operating losses provide no tax benefit in the year they are incurred. They can be carried back or carried forward to offset the corporation's income in other years. For start-up corporations, these losses cannot provide tax benefits until the corporation earns a profit in a subsequent year. Shareholders cannot use these losses to offset their income from other sources.

▶ Capital losses provide no tax benefit in the year they are incurred. They cannot offset ordinary income of either the corporation or its shareholders. These losses must be carried back or carried forward to offset corporate capital gains realized in other years.

S CORPORATIONS. An **S corporation** is so designated because rules governing its tax treatment are found in Subchapter S of the IRC. Like a partnership, an S corporation is a flow-through entity. Income, deductions, losses, and credits are accounted for by the S corporation, which generally is not subject to taxation. They flow through to the returns of the individual shareholders, who generally are subject to taxation. These entities, however, still are corporations so that corporate tax rules apply to them unless overridden by the Subchapter S provisions. Like C corporation shareholders, S corporation shareholders enjoy limited liability. On the other hand, S corporations offer their owners less flexibility than do partnerships. For example, the number and type of S corporation shareholders are limited, and the shareholders cannot agree to allocate income, deductions, losses, and credits in a way that differs from their proportionate ownership.

To obtain S corporation status, a corporation must make a special election, and its shareholders must consent to that election. The corporation then files this election with the IRS. Each year, an S corporation files an information return, Form 1120S (U.S. Income Tax Return for an S Corporation), which reports the results of its operations and indicates the items of income, deduction, loss, and credit that flow through to the individual returns of its shareholders.

---

[5] Sec. 441. See Chapter C3 for the special tax year restrictions applying to personal service corporations.

EXAMPLE C2-7 ▶ Chuck owns 50% of the stock in Maine, an S corporation that uses the calendar year. For its first year of operation, Maine reports $30,000 of taxable income, all ordinary in character. Maine pays no corporate income taxes. Chuck must pay taxes on his share of Maine's income, $15,000 (0.50 × $30,000), whether or not the corporation distributes this income to him. If his marginal tax rate is 35%, Chuck pays $5,250 (0.35 × $15,000) of tax on his share of Maine's income. If Maine instead reports a $30,000 loss, Chuck's $15,000 share of the loss reduces his tax liability by $5,250 (0.35 × $15,000). ◀

TAX STRATEGY TIP

If a corporation anticipates losses in its early years, it might consider operating as an S corporation (see Chapter C11) so that the losses pass through to the shareholders. When the corporation becomes profitable, it can revoke the S election if it wishes to accumulate earnings for growth.

Tax Advantages. The tax advantages of doing business as an S corporation are as follows:

▶ S corporations generally are not subject to taxation. Corporate income flows through and is taxed to the shareholders. The shareholders' marginal tax rates may be lower than a C corporation's marginal tax rate.

▶ Corporate losses flow through to the individual returns of the shareholders and may be used to offset income earned from other sources. (Passive loss and basis rules, however, may limit loss deductions to shareholders. See Chapter C11.) This tax treatment can be beneficial to owners of start-up corporations that generate losses in their early years of operation.

▶ Because income, loss, and other tax-related items retain their character when they flow through to the individual returns of shareholders, shareholders are taxed on capital gains as though they directly realized these gains. Consequently, they can offset such gains with capital losses from other sources. Furthermore, they may be taxed on these flow through gains at the appropriate capital gains rates for individuals.

▶ Shareholders generally can contribute money to or withdraw money from an S corporation without gain recognition.

▶ Corporate profits are taxed only at the shareholder level in the year earned. Generally, the shareholders incur no additional tax liability when the corporation distributes the profits.

▶ A shareholder's basis in S corporation stock is increased by his or her share of corporate income. This basis adjustment reduces the shareholder's gain when he or she sells the S corporation stock, thereby avoiding double taxation.

TAX STRATEGY TIP

The reduced individual tax rates under the 2003 Act may increase the attractiveness of an S corporation relative to the C corporation form of doing business.

Tax Disadvantages. The tax disadvantages of doing business as an S corporation are as follows:

▶ Shareholders are taxed on all of an S corporation's current year profits whether or not these profits are distributed. If the shareholders' marginal tax rates exceed those for a C corporation, the after-tax earnings available for reinvestment and debt retirement may be reduced.

▶ Nontaxable fringe benefits generally are not available to S corporation shareholder-employees.[6] Ordinarily, fringe benefits provided by an S corporation are deductible by the corporation and taxable to the shareholder. On the other hand, S corporation shareholder-employees pay half of Social Security taxes while the S corporation employer pays the other half.

▶ S corporations generally cannot defer income by choosing a fiscal year other than a calendar year unless the S corporation can establish a legitimate business purpose for a fiscal year or unless it makes a special election.

Chapter C11 of this volume discusses S corporations in greater detail. In addition, Appendix F presents a comparison of the tax rules for partnerships, C corporations, and S corporations.

ADDITIONAL COMMENT

All 50 states have adopted statutes allowing LLCs.

LIMITED LIABILITY COMPANIES

A **limited liability company** (LLC) combines the best features of a partnership with those of a corporation even though, from a legal perspective, it is neither. An LLC generally is treated like a partnership while offering its owners the limited liability of a corporation.

---

[6] S corporation shareholders are eligible to deduct their health insurance costs in the same manner as sole proprietors and partners. See footnote 2 for details.

This limited liability extends to all the LLC's owners. In this respect, the LLC is similar to a limited partnership with no general partners. Unlike an S corporation, however, an LLC may have an unlimited number of owners who can be individuals, corporations, estates, and trusts. As discussed below, the LLC may elect to be taxed as a corporation or treated as a partnership under the check-the-box regulations. Assuming the LLC elects partnership treatment, it files Form 1065 (U.S. Partnership Return of Income) with the IRS.

LIMITED LIABILITY PARTNERSHIPS

REAL-WORLD EXAMPLE

All the Big 4 accounting firms have converted general partnerships into LLPs.

Many states allow a business to operate as a **limited liability partnership** (LLP). This partnership form is attractive to professional service organizations, such as public accounting firms, that have adopted LLP status primarily to limit their legal liability. Under state LLP laws, partners are liable for their own acts and omissions as well as the acts and omissions of individuals under their direction. However, LLP partners are not liable for the negligence or misconduct of the other partners. Thus, from a liability perspective, an LLP partner is like a limited partner with respect to other partners' acts but like a general partner with respect to his or her own acts as well as the acts of his or her agents. Like a general partnership or an LLC, an LLP can elect to be treated as a corporation or a partnership under the check-the-box regulations. If it elects partnership treatment, it files Form 1065 (U.S. Partnership Return of Income) with the IRS.

CHECK-THE-BOX REGULATIONS

OBJECTIVE 2

Apply the check-the-box regulations to partnerships, corporations, and trusts

Most unincorporated businesses may choose whether to be taxed as a partnership or a corporation under rules commonly referred to as the **check-the-box regulations**. According to these regulations, an unincorporated business with two or more owners is treated as a partnership, for tax purposes, unless it elects to be taxed as a corporation. An unincorporated business with one owner is disregarded as a separate entity for tax purposes. Thus, like a sole proprietorship, its income is taxed directly to the owner and reported on the owner's return unless the entity elects to be taxed as a corporation.[7]

TAX STRATEGY TIP

When applying the federal check-the-box regulations, taxpayers also must check to see whether or not their state will treat the entity in a consistent manner.

An eligible entity (i.e., an unincorporated business entity) may elect its classification by filing Form 8832 (Entity Classification Election) with the IRS. The form must be signed by each owner of the entity, or any officer, manager, or owner of the entity authorized to make the election. The signatures must specify the date on which the election will be effective. The effective date cannot be more than 75 days before or 12 months after the date the entity files Form 8832. A copy of the form must be attached to the entity's tax return for the election year.

EXAMPLE C2-8 ▶ On January 10 of the current year, a group of ten individuals organizes an LLC to conduct a bookbinding business in Texas. In the current year, the LLC is an eligible entity under the check-the-box regulations. Therefore, it may elect (with the owners' consent) to be taxed as a corporation. If the LLC does not make the election, it will be treated as a partnership for tax purposes by default. ◀

EXAMPLE C2-9 ▶ Assume the same facts as in Example C2-8 except only one individual organized the LLC. Unless the LLC elects to be taxed as a corporation, it will be disregarded for tax purposes by default. Consequently, its income will be taxed directly to the owner as if it were a sole proprietorship. ◀

If an entity elects to change its tax classification, it cannot make another election until 60 months following the effective date of the initial election.

Following the election, certain tax consequences ensue. For example, following a partnership's election to be taxed as a corporation, the partnership is deemed to distribute its

---

[7] This rule does not apply to corporations, trusts, or certain special entities such as real estate investment trusts, real estate mortgage investment conduits, or publicly traded partnerships. Reg. Sec. 301.7701-2(b)(8). Publicly traded partnerships are discussed in Chapter C10. Special check-the-box rules apply to foreign corporations. These rules are beyond the scope of this text.

assets to the partners, who are then deemed to contribute the assets to a new corporation in a tax-free exchange for stock. If an eligible entity that previously elected to be taxed as a corporation subsequently elects to be treated as a partnership or disregarded entity, it is deemed to have distributed its assets and liabilities to its owners or owner in a liquidation as described in Chapter C6. If a partnership, the deemed distribution is followed by a deemed contribution of its assets and liabilities to a newly formed partnership.[8]

LEGAL REQUIREMENTS FOR FORMING A CORPORATION

OBJECTIVE 3

Determine the legal requirements for forming a corporation

The legal requirements for forming a corporation depend on state law. These requirements may include

▶ A minimum amount of capital

▶ The filing of articles of incorporation

▶ The issuance of stock

▶ The payment of state incorporation fees

ADDITIONAL COMMENT

States are not consistent in how they tax corporations. Certain states have no state income taxes. Other states do not recognize an S election, thereby taxing an S corporation as a C corporation.

One of the first decisions an entrepreneur must make when organizing a corporation is the state of incorporation. Although most entrepreneurs incorporate in the state where they conduct business, many incorporate in other states with favorable corporation laws. Such laws might provide for little or no income, sales, or use taxes; low minimum capital requirements; and modest incorporation fees. Regardless of the state of incorporation, the entrepreneur must follow the incorporation procedure set forth in the relevant state statute. Typically, under this procedure, the entrepreneur must file articles of incorporation with the appropriate state agency. The articles must specify certain information, such as the formal name of the corporation; its purpose; the par value, number of shares, and classes of stock it is authorized to issue; and the names of the individuals who will initially serve on the corporation's board of directors. The state usually charges a fee for incorporation or filing. In addition, it periodically may assess a franchise tax for the privilege of doing business in the state.

TAX CONSIDERATIONS IN FORMING A CORPORATION

Once the entrepreneur decides on the corporate form, he or she must transfer money, property (e.g., equipment, furniture, inventory, and receivables), or services (e.g., accounting, legal, or architectural services) to the corporation in exchange for its debt or equity. These transfers may have tax consequences for both the transferor investor and the transferee corporation. For instance, an exchange of property for stock usually is taxable to the transferor.[9] However, if Sec. 351(a) (which treats an investor's interest in certain transferred business assets to be "changed in form" rather than "disposed of") applies, any gain or loss realized on the exchange may be deferred. In determining the tax consequences of incorporation, one must answer the following questions:

▶ What property should be transferred to the corporation?

▶ What services should the transferors or third parties provide for the corporation?

▶ What liabilities, in addition to property, should be transferred?

▶ How should the property be transferred (e.g., sale, contribution to capital, or loan)?

Table C2-1 and Example C2-10 compare the tax consequences of taxable and tax-free property transfers.

---

[8] Reg. Sec. 301.7701-3(g). An alternative way for a corporation to be taxed as a flow-through entity is to make an election to be taxed as an S corporation. See Chapter C11.

[9] Sec. 1001.

▼ **TABLE C2-1**

Overview of Corporate Formation Rules

Tax Treatment for:	Taxable Property Transfer	Tax-Free Property Transfer
Transferors:		
1. Gain realized	FMV of stock received Money received FMV of nonmoney boot property (including securities) received Amount of liabilities assumed by transferee corporation Minus: Adjusted basis of property transferred Realized gain (Sec. 1001(a))	Same as taxable transaction
2. Gain recognized	Transferors recognize the entire amount of realized gain (Sec. 1001(c)) Losses may be disallowed under related party rules (Sec. 267(a)(1)) Installment sale rules may apply to the realized gain (Sec. 453)	Transferors recognize none of the realized gain unless one of the following exceptions applies (Sec. 351(a)): a. Boot property is received (Sec. 351(b)) b. Liabilities are transferred to the corporation for a nonbusiness or tax avoidance purpose (Sec. 357(b)) c. Liabilities exceeding basis are transferred to the corporation (Sec. 357(c)) d. Services, certain corporate indebtednesses, and interest claims are transferred to the corporation (Sec. 351(d)) The installment method may defer recognition of gain when a shareholder receives a corporate note as boot (Sec. 453)
3. Basis of property received	FMV (Cost) (Sec. 1012)	Basis of property transferred to the corporation Plus: Gain recognized Minus: Money received (including liabilities treated as money) FMV of nonmoney boot property Total basis of stock received (Sec. 358(a)) Allocation of total stock basis is based on relative FMVs Basis of nonmoney boot property is its FMV
4. Holding period of property received	Day after the exchange date	Holding period of stock received includes holding period of Sec. 1231 property or capital assets transferred; otherwise it begins the day after the exchange date
Transferee Corporation:		
1. Gain recognized	The corporation recognizes no gain or loss on the receipt of money or other property in exchange for its stock (including treasury stock) (Sec. 1032)	Same as taxable transaction except the corporation may recognize gain under Sec. 311 if it transfers appreciated nonmoney boot property (Sec. 351(f))
2. Basis	FMV (Cost) (Sec. 1012)	Generally, same as in transferor's hands plus any gain recognized by transferor (Sec. 362) If the total adjusted basis for all transferred property exceeds the total FMV of the property, the total basis to the transferor is limited to the property's total FMV
3. Holding period	Day after the exchange date	Transferor's carryover holding period for the property transferred regardless of the property's character (Sec. 1223(2)) Day after the exchange date if basis is reduced to FMV

EXAMPLE C2-10 ▶ For several years Brad has operated a successful manufacturing business as a sole proprietorship. To limit his liability, he decides to incorporate his business as Block Corporation. Immediately preceding the incorporation, his sole proprietorship, which uses the accrual method of accounting, reports the following balance sheet:

BOOK-TO-TAX ACCOUNTING COMPARISON

The IRC treats most corporate formations as nontaxable transactions. Property received in a corporate formation transaction generally is recorded on the tax books using the carryover basis rules. Services are recorded at their FMV. The financial accounting rules, however, record services and noncash property received for stock at either the FMV of the stock issued or the FMV of the noncash consideration received, whichever is more readily determinable.

		Adjusted Basis	Fair Market Value
Assets:			
Cash		$ 10,000	$ 10,000
Accounts receivable		15,000	15,000
Inventory		20,000	25,000
Equipment	$120,000		
Minus: Depreciation	(35,000)	85,000	100,000
Total		$130,000	$150,000
Liabilities and owner's equity:			
Accounts payable		$ 30,000	$ 30,000
Note payable on equipment		50,000	50,000
Owner's equity		50,000	70,000
Total		$130,000	$150,000

When Brad transfers the assets to Block in exchange for its stock, he realizes a gain because the value of the stock received exceeds his basis in the assets. If the exchange is taxable, Brad recognizes $5,000 of ordinary income on the transfer of the inventory ($25,000 FMV − $20,000 basis) and, because of depreciation recapture, $15,000 of ordinary income on the transfer of the equipment ($100,000 FMV − $85,000 basis). However, if the exchange meets the requirements of Sec. 351(a), it is tax-free. In other words, Brad recognizes none of the income or gain realized on the transfer of assets and liabilities to Block. ◀

STOP & THINK *Question:* Joyce has conducted a business as a sole proprietorship for several years. She needs additional capital and wants to incorporate her business. The assets of her business (building, land, inventory, and so on) have a $400,000 adjusted basis and a $1.5 million FMV. Joyce is willing to exchange the assets for 1,500 shares of Ace Corporation stock each having a $1,000 fair market value. Bill and John are willing to invest $500,000 each in Joyce's business for 500 shares of stock. Why is Sec. 351 important to Joyce? Does it matter to Bill and John?

Solution: If not for Sec. 351, Joyce would recognize gain on the incorporation of her business. She realizes a gain of $1.1 million ($1,500,000 − $400,000) on her contribution of proprietorship assets to a new corporation in exchange for 60% of its outstanding shares (1,500 ÷ [1,500 + 500 + 500] = 0.60). However, she recognizes none of this gain because she meets the requirements of Sec. 351 for tax-free treatment. Section 351 does not affect Bill or John because each is simply purchasing 20% of the new corporation's stock (i.e., a noncontrolling interest) for $500,000 cash. They will not realize or recognize any gain or loss unless they sell their stock at a price above or below the $500,000 cost.

If all exchanges of property for corporate stock were taxable, many entrepreneurs would find the tax cost of incorporating their business prohibitively high. In Example C2-10, for example, Brad would recognize a $20,000 gain on the exchange of his assets for the corporate stock. Moreover, because losses also are realized in an exchange, without special rules, taxpayers could exchange loss property for stock and recognize the loss while maintaining an equity interest in the property transferred.

To allow taxpayers to incorporate without incurring a high tax cost and to prevent taxpayers from recognizing losses while maintaining an equity claim to the loss assets, Congress enacted Sec. 351.

SECTION 351: DEFERRING GAIN OR LOSS UPON INCORPORATION

OBJECTIVE 4

Explain the requirements for deferring gain or loss upon incorporation

TAX STRATEGY TIP

A transferor who wishes to recognize gain or loss must take steps to avoid Sec. 351 by failing at least one of its requirements or by engaging in sales transactions. See Tax Planning Considerations later in this chapter for details.

Section 351(a) provides that transferors recognize no gain or loss when they transfer property to a corporation solely in exchange for the corporation's stock provided that, immediately after the exchange, the transferors are in control of the corporation. Section 351 does not apply to a transfer of property to an investment company, nor does it apply in certain bankruptcy cases.

This rule is based on the premise that, when property is transferred to a controlled corporation, the transferors merely exchange direct ownership for indirect ownership through a stock interest in the transferee corporation. In other words, the transferors maintain a continuity of interest in the transferred property. Furthermore, if the only consideration the shareholders receive is stock, they have not generated cash with which to pay their taxes. Therefore, they may not have the "wherewithal-to-pay." If the transferors of property receive other consideration in addition to stock, such as cash or debt instruments, they do have the wherewithal-to-pay and under Sec. 351(b) may have to recognize some or all of their realized gain.

A transferor's realized gain or loss that is unrecognized for tax purposes is not permanently exempt from taxation, however. It is only *deferred* until the shareholder sells or exchanges the stock received in the Sec. 351 exchange. Shareholders who receive stock in such an exchange take a stock basis that reflects the deferred gain or loss. For example, if a shareholder receives stock in exchange for property and recognizes no gain or loss, the stock basis equals the basis of property transferred less liabilities assumed by the corporation (see Table C2-1). Further discussion of this tax treatment appears later in this chapter. Under an alternative approach, the stock basis can be calculated as follows: FMV of qualified stock received minus any deferred gain (or plus any deferred loss). This latter approach highlights the deferral aspect of this type of transaction. If the shareholder later sells the stock, he or she will recognize the deferred gain or loss inherent in the basis adjustment.

EXAMPLE C2-11 ▶ Assume the same facts as in Example C2-10. If Brad satisfies the conditions of Sec. 351, he will not recognize the $20,000 realized gain ($15,000 gain on equipment + $5,000 gain on inventory) when he transfers the assets and liabilities of his sole proprietorship to Block Corporation. Under the alternative approach, Brad's basis for the Block stock is decreased to reflect the deferred gain. Thus, Brad's basis in the Block stock is $50,000 ($70,000 FMV of Block stock − $20,000 deferred gain). If Brad later sells his stock for its $70,000 FMV, he will recognize the $20,000 gain at that time. ◀

The specific requirements for complete deferral of gain and loss under Sec. 351(a) are

▶ The transferors must transfer property to the corporation.

▶ The transferors must receive stock of the transferee corporation in exchange for their property.

▶ The transferors of the property must be in control of the corporation immediately after the exchange.

Each of these requirements is explained below.

THE PROPERTY REQUIREMENT

Nonrecognition of gain or loss applies only to transfers of property to a corporation in exchange for the corporation's stock. Section 351 does not define the term *property*. However, the courts and the IRS have defined *property* to include money and almost any other asset, including installment obligations, accounts receivable, inventory, equipment, patents and other intangibles representing know-how, trademarks, trade names, and computer software.[10]

---

[10] For an excellent discussion of the definition of *property*, see footnote 6 of *D.N. Stafford v. U.S.*, 45 AFTR 2d 80-785, 80-1 USTC ¶9218 (5th Cir., 1980).

Excluded from the statutory definition of property are[11]

▶ Services (such as legal or accounting services) rendered to the corporation in exchange for its stock

▶ Indebtedness of the transferee corporation not evidenced by a security

▶ Interest on transferee corporation debt that accrued on or after the beginning of the transferor's holding period for the debt

The first of these exclusions is perhaps the most important. A person receiving stock as compensation for services must recognize the stock's FMV as compensation (ordinary income) for tax purposes. In other words, an exchange of services for stock is a taxable transaction even if Sec. 351 applies to other property transfers.[12] A shareholder's basis in the stock received as compensation for services is the stock's FMV.

EXAMPLE C2-12 ▶ Amy and Bill form West Corporation. Amy exchanges cash and other property for 90 shares (90% of the outstanding shares) of West stock. The exchange is tax-free because Sec. 351(a) applies. Bill performs accounting services in exchange for ten shares of West stock worth $10,000. Bill's exchange is *not* tax-free under Sec. 351. Thus, Bill must recognize $10,000 of ordinary income—the FMV of the West stock received—as compensation for his services. Bill's basis in the West stock received is its $10,000 FMV. ◀

THE CONTROL REQUIREMENT

Section 351 requires the transferors, as a group, to be in control of the transferee corporation immediately after the exchange. A transferor may be an individual or any type of tax entity (such as a partnership, another corporation, or a trust). Section 368(c) defines *control* as ownership of at least 80% of the total combined voting power of all classes of stock entitled to vote and at least 80% of the total number of shares of all other classes of stock (e.g., nonvoting preferred stock).[13] The minimum ownership levels for nonvoting stock apply to each class of stock rather than to the nonvoting stock in total.[14]

EXAMPLE C2-13 ▶ Dan exchanges property having a $22,000 adjusted basis and a $30,000 FMV for 60% of newly created Sun Corporation's single class of stock. Ed exchanges $20,000 cash for the remaining 40% of Sun stock. The transaction qualifies as a tax-free exchange under Sec. 351 because the transferors, Dan and Ed, together own at least 80% of the Sun stock immediately after the exchange. Therefore, Dan defers recognition of his $8,000 ($30,000 − $22,000) realized gain. ◀

Because services do not qualify as property, stock received by a transferor exclusively in exchange for services does not count in determining whether the 80% control test has been met. Unless 80% of the corporation's stock is owned by the transferors who exchanged property for stock, the control requirement is not met, and the entire transaction is taxable.

EXAMPLE C2-14 ▶ Dana exchanges property having an $18,000 adjusted basis and a $35,000 FMV for 70 shares of newly created York Corporation stock. Ellen provides legal services worth $15,000 for the remaining 30 shares of York stock. Because Ellen does not transfer property to York, her stock is not counted toward the 80% stock ownership threshold. On the other hand, because Dana transfers property to York, his stock is counted toward this threshold. However, Dana is not in control of York immediately after the exchange because he owns only 70% of York stock. Therefore, Dana must recognize all $17,000 ($35,000 − $18,000) of his realized gain on the exchange. Dana's basis in his York stock is $35,000, its FMV. Ellen must recognize $15,000 of ordinary income, the FMV of stock received for her services. The tax consequences to Ellen are the same whether or not Dana meets the control requirement. Ellen's basis in her York stock is $15,000. ◀

If the property transferors own at least 80% of the stock after the exchange, they, but not the provider of services, will be in control of the transferee corporation.

11 Sec. 351(d).
12 Secs. 61 and 83.
13 In determining whether the 80% requirements are satisfied, the construc-

tive ownership rules of Sec. 318 do not apply (see Rev. Rul. 56-613, 1956-2 C.B. 212). See Chapter C4 for an explanation of Sec. 318.
14 Rev. Rul. 59-259, 1959-2 C.B. 115.

EXAMPLE C2-15 ▶ Assume the same facts as in Example C2-14, except a third individual, Fred, contributes $35,000 in cash for 70 shares of York stock. Now Dana and Fred together own more than 80% of the York stock (140 ÷ 170 = 0.82). Therefore, the Sec. 351 control requirement is met, and neither Dana nor Fred recognizes gain on the exchange. Ellen still must recognize $15,000 of ordinary income, the FMV of the stock she receives for her services. ◀

TRANSFERORS OF BOTH PROPERTY AND SERVICES. If a person transfers both services *and* property to a corporation in exchange for the corporation's stock, all the stock received by that person, including stock received in exchange for services, is counted in determining whether the property transferors have acquired control.[15]

EXAMPLE C2-16 ▶ Assume the same facts as in Example C2-14 except that, in addition to providing legal services worth $15,000, Ellen contributes property worth at least $1,500. In this case, all of Ellen's stock counts toward the 80% minimum stock ownership threshold. Because Dana and Ellen together own 100% of the York stock, the exchange meets the Sec. 351 control requirement. Therefore, Dana recognizes no gain on the property exchange. However, Ellen still must recognize $15,000 of ordinary income, the FMV of the stock received as compensation for services. ◀

When a person transfers both property and services in exchange for a corporation's stock, the property must have more than nominal value for that person's stock to count toward the 80% control requirement.[16] The IRS generally requires that the FMV of the stock received for transferred property be at least 10% of the value of the stock received for services provided. If the value of the stock received for the property is less than 10% of the value of the stock received for the services, the IRS will not issue an advance ruling stating that the transaction meets the requirements of Sec. 351.[17]

EXAMPLE C2-17 ▶ Assume the same facts as in Example C2-16 except that Ellen contributes only $1,000 worth of property in addition to $15,000 of legal services. In this case, the IRS will not issue an advance ruling that the transaction meets the Sec. 351 requirements because the FMV of stock received for the property transferred ($1,000) is less than 10% of the value of the stock received for services provided ($1,500 = 0.10 × $15,000). Consequently, if the IRS audits her tax return for the year of transfer, it probably will challenge Dana's and Ellen's tax treatment if they report the transfer as tax-free under Sec. 351. ◀

TRANSFERS TO EXISTING CORPORATIONS. Section 351 applies to transfers to an existing corporation as well as transfers to a newly created corporation. The same requirements must be met in both cases. Property must be transferred in exchange for stock, and the property transferors must be in control of the corporation immediately after the exchange.

EXAMPLE C2-18 ▶ Jack and Karen own 75 shares and 25 shares of Texas Corporation stock, respectively. Jack transfers property with a $15,000 adjusted basis and a $25,000 FMV to Texas in exchange for an additional 25 shares of Texas stock. The Sec. 351 control requirement is met because, after the transfer, Jack owns 80% (100 ÷ 125 = 0.80) of the Texas stock. Therefore, Jack recognizes no gain on the exchange. ◀

If a shareholder transfers property to an existing corporation for additional stock but does not own at least 80% of the stock after the exchange, the control requirement is not met. Thus, Sec. 351 denies tax-free treatment for many transfers of property to an existing corporation by a new shareholder. A new shareholder's transfer of property to an existing corporation is tax-free only if that shareholder acquires at least 80% of the corporation's stock, or enough existing shareholders also transfer additional property so that the transferors as a group, including the new shareholder, control the corporation immediately after the exchange.

[15] Reg. Sec. 1.351-1(a)(2), Ex. (3).
[16] Reg. Sec. 1.351-1(a)(1)(ii).

[17] Rev. Proc. 77-37, 1977-2 C.B. 568, Sec. 3.07.

EXAMPLE C2-19 ▶ Alice owns all 100 shares of Local Corporation stock, valued at $100,000. Beth owns property with a $15,000 adjusted basis and a $100,000 FMV. Beth contributes the property to Local in exchange for 100 shares of newly issued Local stock. The Sec. 351 control requirement is not met because Beth owns only 50% of the Local stock after the exchange. Therefore, Beth must recognize an $85,000 ($100,000 − $15,000) gain. ◀

If an existing shareholder exchanges property for additional stock to enable another shareholder to qualify for tax-free treatment under Sec. 351, the stock received must be of more than nominal value.[18] For advance ruling purposes, the IRS requires that this value be at least 10% of the value of the stock already owned.[19]

EXAMPLE C2-20 ▶ Assume the same facts as in Example C2-19 except that Alice transfers additional property worth $10,000 for an additional ten shares of Local stock. Now both Alice and Beth are considered to be transferors, and the Sec. 351 control requirement is met. Consequently, neither Alice nor Beth recognizes gain on the exchange. If Alice receives fewer than ten shares, the IRS will not issue an advance ruling that the exchange is tax-free under Sec. 351. ◀

? STOP & THINK

Question: Matthew and Michael each own 50 shares of Main Corporation stock having a $250,000 FMV. Matthew wants to transfer property with a $40,000 adjusted basis and a $100,000 FMV to Main for an additional 20 shares. Can Matthew avoid recognizing $60,000 ($100,000 − $40,000) of the gain realized on the transfer?

Solution: If Matthew simply exchanges the property for additional stock, he must recognize the gain. The Sec. 351 control requirement will not have been met because Matthew owns only 70 of the 120 outstanding shares (or 58.33%) immediately after the exchange.

Matthew can avoid gain recognition in two ways:
1. Matthew can transfer sufficient property to Main to receive 150 additional shares (i.e., $750,000 worth of property) so that, after the exchange, he owns 80% (200 out of 250 shares) of the Main stock.
2. Alternatively, Michael can contribute sufficient property to be counted in the control group since, together, the two shareholders will own 100% of the Main stock. Specifically, Michael can contribute cash or other property worth at least $25,000, 10% of the $250,000 value of the Main stock that Michael already owns.

DISPROPORTIONATE EXCHANGES OF PROPERTY AND STOCK. Section 351 does not require that the value of the stock received by the transferors be proportional to the value of the property transferred. However, if the value of the stock received is *not* proportional to the value of the property transferred, the exchange may be treated in accordance with its economic effect, that is, a proportional exchange followed by a gift, payment of compensation, or payment of a liability owed by one shareholder to another.[20] If the deemed effect of the transaction is a gift from one transferor to another transferor, for example, the "donor" is treated as though he or she received stock equal in value to that of the property contributed and then gave some of the stock to the "donee."

EXAMPLE C2-21 ▶ Don and his son John transfer property worth $75,000 (adjusted basis to Don of $42,000) and $25,000 (adjusted basis to John of $20,000), respectively, to newly formed Star Corporation in exchange for all 100 shares of Star stock. Don and John receive 25 and 75 shares of Star stock, respectively. Because Don and John are in control of Star Corporation immediately after the transaction, they recognize no gain or loss on the exchange. However, because the stock was not received by Don and John in proportion to the FMV of their property contributions, Don might be deemed to have received 75 shares of Star stock (worth $75,000), then to have given 50 shares of Star stock (worth $50,000) to John, thereby leaving Don with $25,000 of Star stock. If a gift is deemed to have been made, Don may be required to pay gift taxes. Don's basis in the 25 shares of Star stock is $14,000 [(25 ÷ 75) × $42,000 basis in the property transferred]. John's

---

[18] Reg. Sec. 1.351-1(a)(1)(ii).
[19] Rev. Proc. 77-37, 1977-2 C.B. 568, Sec. 3.07.

[20] Reg. Sec. 1.351-1(b)(1).

basis in the 75 shares is $48,000 [$20,000 basis in the property transferred by John + ($42,000 − $14,000) basis in the shares deemed to have been received from Don]. ◄

IMMEDIATELY AFTER THE EXCHANGE. Section 351 requires that the transferors be in control of the transferee corporation "immediately after the exchange." This requirement does not mean that all transferors must simultaneously exchange their property for stock. All the exchanges must be agreed to beforehand, and the agreement must be executed in an expeditious and orderly manner.[21]

EXAMPLE C2-22 ►

Art, Beth, and Carlos agree to form New Corporation. Art and Beth each transfer noncash property worth $25,000 for one-third of the New stock. Carlos contributes $25,000 cash for another one-third of the New stock. Art and Carlos exchange their property and cash, respectively, for stock on January 10. Beth exchanges her property for stock on March 3. Because all three transfers are part of the same prearranged transaction, the transferors are deemed to be in control of the corporation immediately after the exchange. ◄

Section 351 does not require the transferors to retain control of the transferee corporation for any specific length of time after the exchange. Control is required only "immediately after the exchange." However, the transferors must not have a prearranged plan to dispose of their stock outside the control group. If they do have such a plan, they are not considered to be in control immediately after the exchange.[22]

EXAMPLE C2-23 ►

Amir, Bill, and Carl form White Corporation. Each contributes appreciated property worth $25,000 in exchange for one-third of White stock. Before the exchange, Amir arranges to sell his stock to Dana as soon as he receives it. This prearranged plan implies that Amir, Bill, and Carl do *not* have control immediately after the exchange. Therefore, each must recognize gain in the exchange. ◄

THE STOCK REQUIREMENT

Under Sec. 351, transferors who exchange property solely for transferee corporation stock recognize no gain or loss if they control the corporation immediately after the exchange. Stock for this purpose includes voting or nonvoting stock. However, nonqualified preferred stock is treated as boot. Preferred stock is stock with a preferred claim to dividends and liquidating distributions. Such preferred stock is nonqualified if

► The shareholder can require the corporation to redeem the stock,

► The corporation is either required to redeem the stock or is likely to exercise a right to redeem the stock, or

► The dividend rate on the stock varies with interest rates, commodity prices, or other similar indices.

These characteristics make the preferred stock function more like cash or debt than stock and, hence, like boot. In addition, stock rights or stock warrants are not considered stock for purposes of Sec. 351.[23]

Topic Review C2-1 summarizes the major requirements for a tax-free exchange under Sec. 351.

EFFECT OF SEC. 351 ON THE TRANSFERORS

If all Sec. 351 requirements are met, the transferors recognize no gain or loss on the exchange of their property for stock in the transferee corporation. The receipt of property other than stock does not necessarily disqualify the entire transaction from tax-free treatment. However, the receipt of such property could result in the recognition of all or part of the transferors' realized gain.

[21] Reg. Sec. 1.351-1(a)(1).
[22] Rev. Rul. 79-70, 1979-1 C.B. 144.
[23] Reg. Sec. 1.351-1(a)(1)(ii).

Topic Review C2-1

Major Requirements of Sec. 351

1. Nonrecognition of gain or loss applies only to transfers of property in exchange for a corporation's stock. It does not apply to an exchange of services for stock.
2. The property transferors must be in control of the transferee corporation immediately after the exchange. Control means ownership of at least 80% of the voting power and 80% of the total number of shares of all other classes of stock. Stock disposed of after the exchange pursuant to a prearranged plan does not count toward control.
3. Nonrecognition applies only to the gain realized in an exchange of property for stock. If the transferor receives property other than stock, the property is considered to be boot. The transferor recognizes gain to the extent of the lesser of the FMV of any boot received or the realized gain.

RECEIPT OF BOOT. If a transferor receives any money or property other than stock in the transferee corporation, the additional property is considered to be **boot.** Boot may include cash, notes, securities, or stock in another corporation. Upon receipt of boot, the transferor recognizes gain to the extent of the lesser of the transferor's realized gain or the FMV of the boot property received.[24] A transferor never recognizes a loss in an exchange qualifying under Sec. 351 whether or not he or she receives boot.

The character of the gain recognized upon the receipt of boot depends on the type of property transferred. For example, if the shareholder transfers a capital asset such as stock in another corporation, the recognized gain is capital in character. If the shareholder transfers Sec. 1231 property, such as equipment or a building, the recognized gain is ordinary in character to the extent of any depreciation recaptured under Sec. 1245 or 1250.[25] If the shareholder transfers inventory, the recognized gain is entirely ordinary in character. Note that depreciation recapture is *not* required unless the transferor receives boot and recognizes a gain on the depreciated property transferred.[26]

EXAMPLE C2-24 ▶ Pam, Rob, and Sam form East Corporation and transfer the following property:

Transferor	Asset	Transferor's Adj. Basis	FMV	Consideration Received
Pam	Machinery	$10,000	$12,500	25 shares East stock
Rob	Land	18,000	25,000	40 shares East stock and $5,000 East note
Sam	Cash	17,500	17,500	35 shares East stock

The machinery and land are Sec. 1231 property and a capital asset, respectively. The exchange meets the requirements of Sec. 351 except that, in addition to East stock, Rob receives boot of $5,000 (the FMV of the note). Rob realizes a $7,000 ($25,000 − $18,000) gain on the exchange. Rob must recognize $5,000 of gain—the lesser of the $7,000 realized gain or the $5,000 boot received. The gain is capital in character because the property transferred was a capital asset in Rob's hands. Pam realizes a $2,500 gain on her exchange of machinery for East stock. However, even though Pam would have been required to recapture depreciation on the machinery had she sold or exchanged it, Pam recognizes no gain on the exchange because she received no boot. Sam neither realizes nor recognizes gain on his cash purchase of the East stock. ◀

ADDITIONAL COMMENT

If multiple assets were aggregated into one computation, any built-in losses would be netted against the gains. Such a result is inappropriate because losses cannot be recognized in a Sec. 351 transaction.

COMPUTING GAIN WHEN SEVERAL ASSETS ARE TRANSFERRED. Revenue Ruling 68-55 adopts a "separate properties approach" for computing gain or loss when a shareholder transfers more than one asset to a corporation.[27] Under this approach, the gain or loss realized and recognized is computed separately for each property transferred. The transferor is deemed to have received a proportionate share of the stock, securities, and boot in exchange for each property transferred, based on the assets' relative FMVs.

---

[24] Sec. 351(b).
[25] Section 1239 also may require some gain to be characterized as ordinary income. Section 1250 ordinary depreciation recapture will not apply to real property placed in service after 1986 because MACRS mandates straight-line depreciation.

[26] Secs. 1245(b)(3) and 1250(c)(3).
[27] 1968-1 C.B. 140.

EXAMPLE C2-25 ▶ Joan transfers two properties to newly created North Corporation in a transaction qualifying in part for tax-free treatment under Sec. 351. The total FMV of the assets transferred is $100,000. The consideration received by Joan consists of $90,000 of North stock and $10,000 of North notes. The following data illustrate how Joan determines her realized and recognized gain under the procedure set forth in Rev. Rul. 68-55.

	Asset 1	Asset 2	Total
Asset's FMV	$40,000	$60,000	$100,000
Percent of total FMV	40%	60%	100%
Consideration received in exchange for asset:			
Stock (Stock × percent of total FMV)	$36,000	$54,000	$ 90,000
Notes (Notes × percent of total FMV)	4,000	6,000	10,000
Total proceeds	$40,000	$60,000	$100,000
Minus: Adjusted basis	(65,000)	(25,000)	(90,000)
Realized gain (loss)	($25,000)	$35,000	$10,000
Boot received	$ 4,000	$ 6,000	$ 10,000
Recognized gain (loss)	None	$ 6,000	$ 6,000

Under the separate properties approach, the loss realized on the transfer of Asset 1 does not offset the gain realized on the transfer of Asset 2. Therefore, Joan recognizes only $6,000 of the total $10,000 realized gain, even though she receives $10,000 of boot. A sale of Asset 1 to North so as to recognize the loss might be advisable. See, however, the Sec. 267 loss limitation rules that may apply to Joan if she is a controlling shareholder (see page C2-35). ◀

COMPUTING A SHAREHOLDER'S BASIS.
Boot Property. A transferor's basis for any boot property received is the property's FMV.[28]

Stock. A shareholder computes his or her adjusted basis in stock received in a Sec. 351 exchange as follows:[29]

Adjusted basis of property transferred to the corporation
Plus: Any gain recognized by the transferor
Minus: FMV of boot received from the corporation
Money received from the corporation
Amount of any liabilities assumed by the corporation
Adjusted basis of stock received

EXAMPLE C2-26 ▶

ADDITIONAL COMMENT

Because Sec. 351 is a deferral provision, any unrecognized gain must be reflected in the basis of the stock received by the transferor shareholder and is accomplished by substituting the transferor's basis in the property given up for the basis of the stock received. This substituted basis may be further adjusted by gain recognized and boot received.

Bob transfers Sec. 1231 property having a $50,000 adjusted basis and an $80,000 FMV to South Corporation. He acquired the property two years earlier. Bob receives all 100 shares of South stock, having a $70,000 FMV, and a $10,000 90-day South note (boot property). Bob realizes a $30,000 gain on the exchange, computed as follows:

FMV of stock received	$70,000
Plus: FMV of 90-day note	10,000
Amount realized	$80,000
Minus: Adjusted basis of property transferred	(50,000)
Realized gain	$30,000

Bob's recognized gain is $10,000, i.e., the lesser of the $30,000 realized gain or the $10,000 FMV of the boot property. This gain is a Sec. 1231 gain. The Sec. 351 rules effectively require Bob to defer $20,000 ($30,000 − $10,000) of his realized gain. Bob's basis for the South stock is $50,000, computed as follows:

[28] Sec. 358(a)(2).   [29] Sec. 358(a)(1).

Adjusted basis of property transferred	$50,000
Plus: Gain recognized by Bob	10,000
Minus: FMV of boot received	(10,000)
Adjusted basis of Bob's stock	$50,000 ◄

SELF-STUDY QUESTION

What is an alternative method for determining the basis of the assets received by the transferor shareholder? How is this method applied to Bob in Example C2-26?

If a transferor receives more than one class of qualified stock, his or her basis must be allocated among the classes of stock according to their relative FMVs.[30]

EXAMPLE C2-27 ▶

ANSWER

The basis of all boot property is its FMV, and the basis of stock received is the stock's FMV minus any deferred gain or plus any deferred loss. Bob's stock basis under the alternative method is $50,000 ($70,000 FMV of stock − $20,000 deferred gain).

Assume the same facts as in Example C2-26 except Bob receives 100 shares of South common stock with a $45,000 FMV, 50 shares of South qualified preferred stock with a $25,000 FMV, and a 90-day South note with a $10,000 FMV. The total adjusted basis of the stock is $50,000 ($50,000 basis of property transferred + $10,000 gain recognized − $10,000 FMV of boot received). This basis must be allocated between the common and qualified preferred stock according to their relative FMVs, as follows:

$$\text{Basis of common stock} = \frac{\$45,000}{\$45,000 + \$25,000} \times \$50,000 = \$32,143$$

$$\text{Basis of preferred stock} = \frac{\$25,000}{\$45,000 + \$25,000} \times \$50,000 = \$17,857$$

Bob's basis for the note is its $10,000 FMV.　◄

TRANSFEROR'S HOLDING PERIOD. The transferor's holding period for any stock received in exchange for a capital asset or Sec. 1231 property includes the holding period of the property transferred.[31] If any other kind of property (e.g., inventory) is exchanged for the stock, the transferor's holding period for the stock received begins on the day after the exchange. The holding period for boot property begins on the day after the exchange.

EXAMPLE C2-28 ▶

Assume the same facts as in Example C2-26. Bob's holding period for the stock includes the holding period for the Sec. 1231 property. His holding period for the note starts on the day after the exchange.　◄

 STOP & THINK

Question: The holding period for stock received in exchange for a capital asset or Sec. 1231 asset includes the holding period of the transferred asset. The holding period for inventory or other assets begins on the day after the exchange. Why the difference?

Solution: Because stock received in a Sec. 351 exchange represents a "continuity of interest" in the property transferred, the stock should not only be valued and characterized in the same manner as the asset exchanged for the equity claim, but also accorded the same tax attributes. Because the holding period of a capital asset is relevant in determining the character of gain or loss realized (i.e., long-term or short-term) on the asset's subsequent sale, stock received in a tax-free exchange of the asset should be accorded the same holding period for the purpose of determining the character of gain or loss realized on the stock's subsequent sale. By the same token, because the holding period of a noncapital asset is less relevant in determining the character of gain or loss realized on the asset's subsequent sale, stock received in a tax-free exchange of the asset need not be accorded the same holding period for the purpose of determining the character of gain or loss realized on the stock's subsequent sale. Given the very nature of a noncapital asset, this gain or loss generally is ordinary in character, in any event. Moreover, if stock received in exchange for a noncapital asset were accorded a holding period that includes that of the transferred property, a transferor could sell the stock in a short time for a long-term capital gain, thereby converting ordinary income (potentially from the noncapital asset) to capital gain from the sale of stock.

[30] Sec. 358(b)(1) and Reg. Sec. 1.358-2(b)(2).
[31] Sec. 1223(1). Revenue Ruling 85-164 (1985-2 C.B. 117) holds that a single share of stock may have two holding periods: a carryover holding period for the portion of such share received in exchange for a capital asset or Sec. 1231 property and a holding period that begins on the day after the exchange for the portion of such share received for inventory or other property. The split holding period is relevant only if the transferor sells the stock received within one year of the transfer date.

Topic Review C2-2 summarizes the tax consequences of a Sec. 351 transaction to the transferor and the transferee corporation.

ADDITIONAL COMMENT

The nonrecognition rule for corporations that issue stock for property applies whether or not the transaction qualifies the transferor shareholder for Sec. 351 treatment.

TAX CONSEQUENCES TO TRANSFEREE CORPORATION

A corporation that issues stock or debt for property or services is subject to various IRC rules for determining the tax consequences of that exchange.

GAIN OR LOSS RECOGNIZED BY THE TRANSFEREE CORPORATION.   Corporations recognize no gain or loss when they issue their own stock for property or services.[32] This rule applies whether or not Sec. 351 governs the exchange and also applies whether the corporation issues new stock or treasury stock.

EXAMPLE C2-29 ▶ West Corporation pays $10,000 to acquire 100 shares of its own stock from existing shareholders. The next year, West reissues these 100 shares of treasury stock for land having a $15,000 FMV. West realizes a $5,000 ($15,000 − $10,000) gain on the exchange. The corporation, however, recognizes none of this gain. ◀

Corporations also recognize no gain or loss when they exchange their own debt instruments for property or services.

A corporation, however, must recognize gain (but not loss) if it transfers appreciated property to a transferor as part of a Sec. 351 exchange. The amount and character of the gain are determined as though the property had been sold by the corporation immediately before the transfer.

EXAMPLE C2-30 ▶ Alice, who owns 100% of Ace Corporation stock, transfers to Ace land having a $100,000 FMV and a $60,000 adjusted basis. In return, Alice receives 75 additional shares of Ace common stock having a $75,000 FMV, and Zero Corporation common stock having a $25,000 FMV. Ace's basis in the Zero stock, a capital asset, is $10,000. Alice realizes a $40,000 gain [($75,000 + $25,000) − $60,000] on the land transfer, of which $25,000 must be recognized. In addition, Ace recognizes a $15,000 capital gain ($25,000 − $10,000) upon transferring the Zero stock to Alice. ◀

Topic Review C2-2

Tax Consequences of a Sec. 351 Transaction

To Shareholders:

1. Transferors recognize no gain or loss when they exchange property for stock. Exception: A transferor recognizes gain equal to the lesser of the realized gain or the sum of any money received plus the FMV of any other boot property received. The character of the gain depends on the type of property transferred.
2. The basis of the stock received equals the adjusted basis of the property transferred plus any gain recognized minus the FMV of any boot property received minus any money received (including liabilities assumed or acquired by the transferee corporation).
3. The holding period of stock received in exchange for capital assets or Sec. 1231 property includes the holding period of the transferred property. The holding period of stock received in exchange for other property begins on the day after the exchange.

To Transferee Corporation:

1. A corporation recognizes no gain or loss when it exchanges its own stock for property or services.
2. The corporation's basis in property received in a Sec. 351 exchange is the transferor's basis plus any gain recognized by the transferor. However, if the total adjusted basis of all transferred property exceeds the total FMV of the property, the total basis to the transferee is limited to the property's total FMV.
3. The corporation's holding period for property received in a Sec. 351 exchange includes the transferor's holding period.

---

[32] Sec. 1032.

ADDITIONAL
COMMENT

If a shareholder transfers built-in gain property in a Sec. 351 transaction, the built-in gain actually is duplicated. This duplication occurs because the transferee corporation assumes the potential gain through its carryover basis in the assets it receives, and the transferor shareholder assumes the potential gain through its substituted basis in the transferee corporation stock. A similar duplication occurs for built-in loss property. This result reflects the double taxation characteristic of C corporations.

TRANSFEREE CORPORATION'S BASIS FOR PROPERTY RECEIVED. A corporation that acquires property in exhange for its stock in a transaction that is taxable to the transferor takes a cost (i.e., its FMV) basis in the property. On the other hand, if the exchange qualifies for nonrecognition treatment under Sec. 351 and is wholly or partially tax-free to the transferor, the corporation's basis for the property is computed as follows:[33]

> Transferor's adjusted basis in property transferred to the corporation
> Plus: Gain recognized by transferor (if any)
> Minus: Reduction for loss property (if applicable)
> _____
> Transferee corporation's basis in property

The transferee corporation's holding period for property acquired in a transaction satisfying the Sec. 351 requirements includes the period the property was held by the transferor.[34] This general rule applies to all properties without regard to their character in the transferor's hands or the amount of gain recognized by the transferor. However, if the corporation reduces a property's basis to its FMV under the loss property limitation rule discussed below, the holding period will begin the day after the exchange date because no part of the basis refers to the transferor's basis.

EXAMPLE C2-31 ▶ Top Corporation issues 100 shares of its stock for land having a $15,000 FMV. Tina, who transferred the land, had a $12,000 basis in the property. If the exchange satisfies the Sec. 351 requirements, Tina recognizes no gain on the exchange. Top's basis in the land is $12,000, the same as Tina's basis. Top's holding period includes Tina's holding period. However, if the exchange does *not* satisfy the Sec. 351 requirements, Tina must recognize $3,000 of gain. Top's basis in the land is its $15,000 acquisition cost, and its holding period begins on the day after the exchange date. ◀

REDUCTION FOR LOSS PROPERTY. The 2004 Jobs Act added Sec. 362(e)(2), which prevents shareholders from creating double losses by transferring loss property to a corporation. The double loss potential exists because the corporation would hold property with a built-in loss, and the shareholders would hold stock with a built-in loss.

A special rule applies if a corporation's total adjusted basis for all property transferred by a shareholder would exceed the total FMV of that property without the special rule. In such case, the basis to the corporation of the properties transferred is limited to the total FMV of those properties. The reduction in basis must be allocated among the properties transferred in proportion to their respective built-in losses. The limitation applies on a shareholder-by-shareholder basis. In other words, the property values and the built-in losses of all shareholders are not aggregated.

EXAMPLE C2-32 ▶ John transfers the following assets to Pecan Corporation in exchange for all of Pecan's stock worth $26,000.

Assets	Adjusted Basis to John	FMV
Inventory	$ 5,000	$ 8,000
Equipment	15,000	11,000
Furniture	9,000	7,000
Total	$29,000	$26,000

The transaction meets the requirements of Sec. 351. Because the total basis of the assets transferred ($29,000) exceeds the total FMV of those assets, the total basis of the assets to Pecan is limited to their FMV ($26,000). The $3,000 ($29,000 − $26,000) reduction in basis must be allocated among the properties transferred in proportion to their respective built-in losses as follows:

_____

[33] Sec. 362.   [34] Sec. 1223(2).

Assets	Built-in Losses	Allocated Reduction
Equipment	$4,000	$2,000
Furniture	2,000	1,000
Total	$6,000	$3,000

Thus, Pecan's bases for the assets transferred by John are:

Inventory	$ 5,000
Equipment ($15,000 − $2,000)	13,000
Furniture ($9,000 − $1,000)	8,000
Total	$26,000

Because each property's basis was not reduced to the property's FMV, the holding period of each property includes the tranferor's holding period. ◄

A corporation subject to the basis limitation described above can avoid this result if the corporation and all its shareholders so elect. Under the election, the corporation does not have to reduce the bases of the assets received, but the affected shareholders' bases in stock received for the property are limited to the stock's FMV.

EXAMPLE C2-33 ► Assume the same facts as in Example C2-32 except John and Pecan elect not to reduce the bases of the assets that Pecan received. Instead, John's basis in his Pecan stock is limited to its $26,000 FMV. Absent this election, John's basis would be $29,000. ◄

A corporation and its shareholders can avoid the basis limitation altogether if each shareholder transfers enough appreciated property to offset any losses built into the value of his or her property. This avoidance opportunity exists because in making the comparison, each shareholder aggregates the adjusted bases and FMVs of property transferred.

EXAMPLE C2-34 ► Assume the same facts as in Example C2-32 except the inventory's FMV is $12,000. In this case, total basis equals $29,000 and total FMV equals $30,000. Because total basis does not exceed total FMV, the limitation does not apply. Consequently, the corporation takes a carryover basis in each asset even though some specific assets have built-in losses. ◄

ASSUMPTION OF THE TRANSFEROR'S LIABILITIES

When a shareholder transfers property to a controlled corporation, the corporation often assumes the transferor's liabilities. The question arises as to whether the transferee corporation's assumption of liabilities is equivalent to a cash payment to the transferor and, therefore, is boot. In many other kinds of transactions, the transferee's assumption of a transferor's liability is treated as a payment of cash to the transferor. For example, in a like-kind exchange, if a transferee assumes a transferor's liability, the transferor is treated as though he or she received a cash payment equal to the amount of the liability assumed. In contrast, if a transaction satisfies the Sec. 351 requirements, the special rules of Sec. 357 apply, and the liability transfer is not treated as a cash payment.

GENERAL RULE—SEC. 357(a). The transferee corporation's assumption of liabilities in a property transfer qualifying under Sec. 351 is *not* considered equivalent to the receipt of money by the transferor. Therefore, the transferee corporation's assumption of liabilities does not cause the transferor to recognize part or all of his or her realized gain. For purposes of the transferor's stock basis calculation, however, the liabilities are treated as money received.[35]

---

[35] Sec. 358(d)(1).

EXAMPLE C2-35 ▶ Roy and Eduardo transfer the following assets and liabilities to newly formed Palm Corporation:

Transferor	Asset/ Liability	Transferor's Adj. Basis	FMV	Consideration Received
Roy	Machinery	$15,000	$32,000	50 shares Palm stock
	Mortgage	8,000	—	Assumed by Palm
Eduardo	Cash	24,000	24,000	50 shares Palm stock

The transaction meets the requirements of Sec. 351. Roy's recognized gain is determined as follows:

FMV of stock received	$24,000
Plus: Release from mortgage assumed by Palm	8,000
Amount realized	$32,000
Minus: Basis of machinery	(15,000)
Realized gain	$17,000
Boot received	$ –0–
Recognized gain	$ –0–

Roy recognizes none of this gain because Sec. 351 applies, and the mortgage assumption is not considered to be money paid to Roy. Eduardo recognizes no gain because he transferred only cash. Roy's stock basis is $7,000 ($15,000 basis of property transferred − $8,000 liability assumed by the corporation). Eduardo's stock basis is $24,000. ◀

The general rule of Sec. 357(a), however, has two exceptions. These exceptions, discussed below, are (1) transfers made for the purpose of tax avoidance or that have no bona fide business purpose and (2) transfers where the liabilities assumed by the corporation exceed the total basis of the property transferred.

TAX AVOIDANCE OR NO BONA FIDE BUSINESS PURPOSE—SEC. 357(b). All liabilities assumed by a controlled corporation *are* considered money received by the transferor (and, therefore, boot) if the principal purpose of the transfer of any portion of such liabilities is tax avoidance or if the liability transfer has no bona fide business purpose.

Liabilities whose transfer might be considered to have tax avoidance as the principal purpose are those the transferor incurred shortly before transferring the property and liabilities to the corporation. Perhaps the most important factor in determining whether a tax avoidance purpose exists is the length of time between the incurrence of the liability and the transfer of the liability to the corporation.

The assumption of liabilities normally is considered to have a business purpose if the transferor incurred the liabilities in the normal course of business or in the course of acquiring business property. Examples of liabilities that have no business purpose and whose transfer would cause *all* liabilities transferred to be considered boot are personal obligations of the transferor, including a home mortgage or any other loans of a personal nature.

EXAMPLE C2-36 ▶ David owns land having a $100,000 FMV and a $60,000 adjusted basis. The land is not encumbered by any liabilities. To obtain cash for his personal use, David transfers the land to his wholly owned corporation in exchange for additional stock and $25,000 cash. Because the cash received is considered boot, David must recognize $25,000 of gain. Assume instead that David mortgages the land for $25,000 to obtain the needed cash. If shortly after obtaining the mortgage, David transfers the land and the mortgage to his corporation for additional stock, the transfer of the mortgage appears to have no business purpose. Therefore, the $25,000 mortgage assumed by the corporation is considered boot. David's recognized gain is $25,000, i.e., the lesser of the boot received ($25,000) or his realized gain ($40,000). The special liability rule prevents David from obtaining cash without boot recognition. ◀

LIABILITIES IN EXCESS OF BASIS—SEC. 357(c). Under Sec. 357(c), if the total amount of liabilities transferred to a controlled corporation exceeds the total adjusted basis of all property transferred, the excess liability is a gain taxable to the transferor. This rule applies regardless of whether the transferor realizes any gain or loss. The rule recognizes that the transferor has received a benefit (in the form of a release from liabilities) that exceeds his or her original investment in the transferred property. Therefore, the excess amount should be taxable. The character of the recognized gain depends on the type of property transferred to the corporation. The transferor's basis in any stock received is zero.

EXAMPLE C2-37 ▶ Judy transfers $10,000 cash and land, a capital asset, to Duke Corporation in exchange for all its stock. The land has a $70,000 adjusted basis and a $125,000 FMV immediately before the exchange. Duke assumes a $100,000 mortgage on the land for a bona fide business purpose. Although Judy receives no boot, Judy must recognize a $20,000 ($100,000 − $80,000) capital gain, the amount by which the liabilities assumed by Duke exceed the basis of the land and the cash transferred by Judy. Judy's basis in the Duke stock is zero, computed as follows:

Judy's basis in the land transferred		$ 70,000
Plus:	Cash transferred	10,000
	Gain recognized	20,000
Minus:	Boot received (i.e., liabilities assumed by Duke)	(100,000)
Judy's basis in the Duke stock		$ −0−

Note that, without the recogniton of a $20,000 gain under Sec. 357(c), Judy's basis in the Duke stock would be a negative $20,000 ($80,000 − $100,000). ◀

STOP & THINK

Question: What are the fundamental differences between the liability exceptions of Sec. 357(b) and Sec. 357(c)?

Solution: Section 357(b) treats all "tainted" liabilities as boot so that gain recognition is the lesser of gain realized or the amount of boot. Excess liabilities under Sec. 357(c) are not treated as boot; they require gain recognition whether or not the transferor realizes any gain. Section 357(b) tends to be punitive in that the tax avoidance liabilities cause all the "offending" shareholder's transferred liabilities to be treated as boot even if some liabilities do not have a tax avoidance purpose. Section 357(c) is not intended to be punitive. Rather, it recognizes that the shareholder has received an economic benefit to the extent of excess liabilities, and it prevents a negative stock basis. In short, Section 357(b) deters or punishes tax avoidance while Sec. 357(c) taxes an economic gain.

KEY POINT

Because of the "liabilities in excess of basis" exception, many cash basis transferor shareholders might inadvertently create recognized gain in a Sec. 351 transaction. However, a special exception exists that protects cash basis taxpayers. This exception provides that liabilities that would give rise to a deduction when paid are not treated as liabilities for purposes of Sec. 357(c).

LIABILITIES OF A CASH METHOD TAXPAYER—SEC. 357(c)(3). Special problems arise when a taxpayer using the cash or hybrid method of accounting transfers property and liabilities of an ongoing business to a corporation in a Sec. 351 tax-free exchange.[36] Occasionally, the main assets transferred are accounts receivable having a zero basis. Liabilities usually are transferred as well. Consequently, the amount of liabilities transferred may exceed the total basis (but not the FMV) of the property transferred.

Under Sec. 357(c), gain equal to the amount by which the liabilities assumed exceed the total basis of the property transferred ordinarily must be recognized. However, a special exception to Sec. 357(c) provides that the term *liabilities* does *not* include any amount that (1) would give rise to a deduction when paid or (2) any amount payable under Sec. 736(a) (i.e., amounts payable to a retiring partner or to liquidate a deceased partner's interest). These amounts also are not considered liabilities when determining the shareholder's basis in stock received.[37] Therefore, they generally do not reduce this basis. However, if after application of all other basis adjustments the stock's basis exceeds its FMV, these liabilities under some circumstances will reduce stock basis, but not below the stock's FMV.[38]

---

[36] Sec. 357(c)(3).
[37] Sec. 358(d)(2).

[38] Sec. 358(h)(1).

EXAMPLE C2-38 ▶ Tracy operates an accounting practice as a sole proprietorship. She transfers the assets of her cash basis accounting practice to Prime Corporation in exchange for all the Prime stock. The items transferred are

Assets and Liabilities	Adjusted Basis	FMV
Cash	$ 5,000	$ 5,000
Furniture	5,000	8,000
Accounts receivable	–0–	50,000
Total	$10,000	$63,000
Accounts payable (expenses)	$ –0–	$25,000
Note payable (on office furniture)	2,000	2,000
Owner's equity	8,000	36,000
Total	$10,000	$63,000

If, for purposes of Sec. 357(c), the accounts payable were considered liabilities, the $27,000 of liabilities transferred (i.e., the $25,000 of accounts payable and the $2,000 note payable) would exceed the $10,000 total basis of property transferred. However, because paying the $25,000 of accounts payable gives rise to a deduction, they are not considered liabilities for purposes of Sec. 357(c). The $2,000 note payable *is* considered a liability because paying it would *not* give rise to a deduction. Thus, for purposes of Sec. 357(c), the total liabilities transferred to Prime amount to $2,000. Because that amount does not exceed the $10,000 total basis of the property transferred, Tracy recognizes no gain, and her basis for her stock is $8,000 ($10,000 − $2,000). The accounts payable are not considered liabilities for purposes of computing Tracy's basis in her stock because the stock's basis ($8,000) does not exceed its FMV ($36,000). ◀

Topic Review C2-3 summarizes the liability assumption and acquisition rules of Sec. 357.

OTHER CONSIDERATIONS IN A SEC. 351 EXCHANGE

RECAPTURE OF DEPRECIATION. If a Sec. 351 exchange is completely nontaxable (i.e., the transferor receives no boot), no depreciation is recaptured. Instead, the corporation inherits the entire amount of the transferor's recapture potential. Where the transferor recognizes some depreciation recapture as ordinary income (e.g., because of boot recognition), the transferee inherits remaining recapture potential. If the transferee corporation subsequently disposes of the depreciated property, the corporation is subject to recapture rules on all depreciation it has claimed plus the recapture potential it inherited from the transferor.

Topic Review C2-3

Liability Assumption and Acquisition Rules of Sec. 357

1. *General Rule (Sec. 357(a)):* A transferee corporation's assumption of liabilities in a Sec. 351 exchange is not treated as the receipt of money/boot by the shareholder for gain recognition purposes. The liabilities assumed, however, are treated as money for purposes of determining the basis of the stock received.
2. *Exception 1 (Sec. 357(b)):* All liabilities assumed by a transferee corporation *are* considered money/boot received by the transferor if the principal purpose of the transfer of any of the liabilities is tax avoidance or if no bona fide business purpose exists for the transfer.
3. *Exception 2 (Sec. 357(c)):* If the total amount of liabilities assumed by a transferee corporation exceeds the total basis of property transferred, the transferor recognizes the excess liability amount as gain.
4. *Special Rule (Sec. 357(c)(3)):* For purposes of Exception 2, the term *liabilities* for a transferor using a cash or hybrid method of accounting does not include any amount that (a) would give rise to a deduction when paid or (b) is payable to a retiring partner or to liquidate a deceased partner's interest.

EXAMPLE C2-39 ▶ Azeem transfers machinery having a $25,000 original cost, an $18,000 adjusted basis, and a $35,000 FMV for all 100 shares of Wheel Corporation's stock. Before the transfer, Azeem used the machinery in his business and claimed $7,000 of depreciation. In the transfer, Azeem recaptures no depreciation. Instead, Wheel inherits the $7,000 recapture potential. After claiming an additional $2,000 of depreciation, Wheel has a $16,000 adjusted basis in the machinery. If Wheel now sells the machinery for $33,000, it must recognize a $17,000 ($33,000 − $16,000) gain. Of this gain, $9,000 is ordinary income recaptured under Sec. 1245. The remaining $8,000 is Sec. 1231 gain. ◀

COMPUTING DEPRECIATION. When a shareholder transfers depreciable property to a corporation in a nontaxable Sec. 351 exchange and the shareholder has not fully depreciated the property, the corporation must use the same depreciation method and recovery period as the transferor used.[39] For the year of the transfer, the depreciation must be allocated between the transferor and the transferee corporation according to the number of months the property was held by each. The transferee corporation is assumed to have held the property for the entire month in which the property was transferred.[40]

EXAMPLE C2-40 ▶ On June 10, 2005, Carla paid $6,000 for a computer (five-year property for MACRS purposes), which she used in her sole proprietorship. In 2005, she claimed $1,200 (0.20 × $6,000) of depreciation and did not elect Sec. 179 expensing. On February 10, 2006, she transfers the computer and other assets of her sole proprietorship to King Corporation in exchange for King stock. Because under Sec. 351 the exchange is tax-free, she recognizes no gain or loss. King must use the same MACRS recovery period and method that Carla used. Depreciation for 2006 is $1,920 (0.32 × $6,000). That amount must be allocated between Carla and King. The computer is considered to have been held by Carla for one month and by King for 11 months (including the month of transfer). The 2006 depreciation amounts claimed by Carla and King are calculated as follows:

Carla	$6,000 × 0.32 × 1/12 = $ 160
King Corporation	$6,000 × 0.32 × 11/12 = $1,760

King's basis in the computer is calculated as follows:

Original cost	$6,000
Minus: 2005 depreciation claimed by Carla	(1,200)
2006 depreciation claimed by Carla	(160)
Adjusted basis on transfer date	$4,640

King's depreciation for 2006 and subsequent years is as follows:

2006 (as computed above)	$1,760
2007 ($6,000 × 0.1920)	1,152
2008 ($6,000 × 0.1152)	691
2009 ($6,000 × 0.1152)	691
2010 ($6,000 × 0.0576)	346
Total	$4,640 ◀

If the transferee corporation's basis in the depreciable property exceeds the transferor's basis, the corporation treats the excess amount as newly purchased MACRS property and uses the recovery period and method applicable to the class of property transferred.[41]

EXAMPLE C2-41 ▶ Assume the same facts as in Example C2-40 except that, in addition to King stock, Carla receives a King note. Consequently, she must recognize $1,000 of gain on the transfer of the computer. King's basis in the computer is calculated as follows:

Original cost	$6,000
Depreciation claimed by Carla	(1,360)
Adjusted basis on transfer date	$4,640
Plus: Gain recognized by Carla	1,000
Basis to King on transfer date	$5,640

---

[39] Sec. 168(i)(7).
[40] Prop. Reg. Secs. 1.168-5(b)(2)(i)(B), 1.168-5(b)(4)(i), and 1.168-5(b)(8).
[41] Prop. Reg. Sec. 1.168-5(b)(7).

ADDITIONAL COMMENT

Currently, we have no clear guidance on how the corporation depreciates transferred property that has a reduced basis under the loss property limitation rule discussed on page C2-21. For now, taxpayers probably should rely on Prop. Reg. 1.168-2(d)(3), which provides a method for calculating depreciation when the transferee's basis is less than the transferor's basis.

The additional $1,000 of basis is depreciated as though it were separate, newly purchased MACRS property. Thus, King claims depreciation of $200 (0.20 × $1,000) on this portion of the basis in addition to the $1,760 of depreciation on the $4,640 carryover basis. Alternatively, King could elect to expense the $1,000 "new" basis under Sec. 179. ◀

ASSIGNMENT OF INCOME DOCTRINE. The **assignment of income doctrine** holds that income be taxed to the person who earns it and that it may not be assigned to another taxpayer.[42] The question arises as to whether the assignment of income doctrine applies where a cash method taxpayer transfers uncollected accounts receivable to a corporation in a Sec. 351 exchange. The question is: who must recognize the income when it is collected—the taxpayer who transferred the receivable to the corporation or the corporation that now owns and collects on the receivable? The IRS has ruled that the doctrine does *not* apply in a Sec. 351 exchange if the transferor transfers substantially all the business assets and liabilities, and a bona fide business purpose exists for the transfer. Instead, the accounts receivable take a zero basis in the corporation's hands and are included in the corporation's income when the corporation collects on the receivables.[43]

EXAMPLE C2-42 ▶ For a legitimate business reason, Ruth, a lawyer who uses the cash method of accounting, transfers all the assets and liabilities of her legal practice to Legal Services Corporation in exchange for all of Legal Services' stock. The assets include $30,000 of accounts receivable that will generate earnings that Ruth has not included in her gross income. The assignment of income doctrine does not apply to the transfer of the accounts receivable. Legal Services Corporation's basis in the receivables is zero, and the corporation includes the receivables in income as the corporation collects on the receivables. ◀

The question of whether a transferee corporation can deduct the accounts payable transferred to it in a nontaxable transfer has frequently been litigated.[44] Most courts have held that ordinarily expenses are deductible only by the party that incurred those liabilities in the course of its trade or business. However, the IRS has ruled that in a nontaxable exchange the transferee corporation may deduct the payments it makes to satisfy the transferred accounts payable even though they arose in the transferor's business.[45]

CHOICE OF CAPITAL STRUCTURE

OBJECTIVE 5

Understand the tax implications of alternative capital structures

When a corporation is formed, decisions must be made as to its capital structure. The corporation may obtain capital from shareholders, nonshareholders, and creditors. In exchange for their capital, shareholders may receive common stock or preferred stock; nonshareholders may receive benefits such as employment or special rates on products produced by the corporation; and creditors may receive long-term or short-term debt obligations. Each of these alternatives has tax advantages and disadvantages for the shareholders, creditors, and corporation.

CHARACTERIZATION OF OBLIGATIONS AS DEBT OR EQUITY CAPITAL

The deductibility of interest payments provides an incentive for corporations to incur as much debt as possible. Because debt financing often resembles equity financing (e.g., preferred stock), the IRS and the courts have refused to accept the form of the obligation as controlling.[46] In some cases, debt obligations that possess equity characteristics have been

[42] See, for example, *Lucas v. Guy C. Earl*, 8 AFTR 10287, 2 USTC ¶496 (USSC, 1930).

[43] Rev. Rul. 80-198, 1980-2 C.B. 113.

[44] See, for example, *Wilford E. Thatcher v. CIR*, 37 AFTR 2d 76-1068, 76-1 USTC ¶9324 (9th Cir., 1976), and *John P. Bongiovanni v. CIR*, 31 AFTR 2d 73-409, 73-1 USTC ¶9133 (2nd Cir., 1972).

[45] Rev. Rul. 80-198, 1980-2 C.B. 113.

[46] See, for example, *Aqualane Shores, Inc. v. CIR*, 4 AFTR 2d 5346, 59-2 USTC ¶9632 (5th Cir., 1959) and *Sun Properties, Inc. v. U.S.*, 47 AFTR 273, 55-1 USTC ¶9261 (5th Cir., 1955).

treated as common or preferred stock for tax purposes. The courts have relied on no single factor in determining the appropriate tax treatment.

In 1969, Congress enacted Sec. 385 to establish a workable standard for determining whether an obligation is debt or equity. Section 385 provides that the following factors be taken into account in the determination:

▶ Whether there is a written unconditional promise to pay on demand or on a specified date a certain sum of money in return for adequate consideration in the form of money or money's worth, in addition to an unconditional promise to pay a fixed rate of interest

▶ Whether the debt is subordinate to, or preferred over, other indebtedness of the corporation

▶ The ratio of debt to equity of the corporation

▶ Whether the debt is convertible into stock of the corporation

▶ The relationship between holdings of stock in the corporation and holdings of the interest in question[47]

DEBT CAPITAL

Tax laws govern (1) the issuance of debt; (2) the payment of interest on debt; and (3) the extinguishment, retirement, or worthlessness of debt. The tax implications of each of these three occurrences are examined below.

ISSUANCE OF DEBT. Under Sec. 351, appreciated assets may be exchanged tax-free for stock, provided the transferors control the transferee corporation immediately after the exchange. On the other hand, if the transferor transfers assets for corporate debt instruments as part of a Sec. 351 exchange or independently of such an exchange, the FMV of the debt received is treated as boot, which may result in gain recognition.

PAYMENT OF INTEREST. Interest paid on indebtedness is deductible by the corporation in deriving taxable income.[48] Moreover, a corporation is not subject to the limitations on interest deductions that apply to individual taxpayers (e.g., investment interest or personal interest). Dividends paid on equity securities are not deductible.

If the corporation issues a debt instrument at a discount, Sec. 1272 requires the holder to amortize the original issue discount over the term of the obligation and treat the accrual as interest income. The debtor corporation amortizes the original issue discount over the term of the obligation and treats the accrual as an additional cost of borrowing.[49] If the corporation repurchases the debt instrument for more than the issue price (plus any original issue discount deducted as interest), the corporation deducts the excess of the purchase price over the issue price (adjusted for any amortization of original issue discount) as interest expense.[50]

If the corporation issues the debt instrument at a premium, Sec. 171 permits the holder to elect to amortize the premium over the term of the obligation and treat the accrual as a reduction in interest income earned on the obligation. The debtor corporation must amortize the premium over the term of the obligation and treat the accrual as additional interest income.[51] If the corporation repurchases the debt instrument at a price greater than the issue price (minus any premium reported as income), the corporation deducts the excess of the purchase price over the issue price (adjusted for any amortization of premium) as interest expense.[52]

EXTINGUISHMENT OF DEBT. Generally, the retirement of debt is not a taxable event. Thus, a debtor corporation's extinguishing an obligation at face value does not result in the creditor's recognizing gain or loss. However, Sec. 1271(a) treats amounts received by

HISTORICAL NOTE
The Treasury Department at one time issued proposed and final regulations covering Sec. 385. These regulations were the subject of so much criticism that the Treasury Department eventually withdrew them. The 1989 amendment to Sec. 385 makes it clear that Congress wants the Treasury Department to make another attempt at clarifying the debt-equity issue. So far, the Treasury Department has issued no "new" proposed or final regulations.

SELF-STUDY QUESTION
From a tax perspective, why is the distinction between debt and equity important?

ANSWER
Interest paid with respect to a debt instrument is deductible by the payor corporation. Dividends paid with respect to an equity instrument are not deductible by the payor corporation. Thus, the determination of whether an instrument is debt or equity can provide different results to the payor corporation. Different results apply to the payee as well. Qualified dividends are subject to the 15% maximum tax rate (through 2008) while interest is ordinary income.

[47] See also *O.H. Kruse Grain & Milling v. CIR*, 5 AFTR 2d 1544, 60-2 USTC ¶9490 (9th Cir., 1960), which lists additional factors that the courts might consider.
[48] Sec. 163(a).
[49] Sec. 163(e).
[50] Reg. Sec. 1.163-7(c).
[51] Reg. Sec. 1.61-12(c)(2).
[52] Reg. Sec. 1.163-7(c).

the holder of a debt instrument (e.g., note, bond, or debenture) at the time of its retirement as received "in exchange for" the obligation. Thus, if the obligation is a capital asset in the holder's hands, the holder will recognize a capital gain or loss if the amount received differs from its face value or adjusted basis, unless the difference is due to original issue or market discount.

EXAMPLE C2-43 ▶

ADDITIONAL COMMENT

Even though debt often is thought of as a preferred instrument because of the deductibility of the interest paid, the debt must be repaid at its maturity, whereas stock has no specified maturity date. Also, interest usually must be paid at regular intervals, whereas dividends do not have to be declared if sufficient funds are not available.

Titan Corporation issues a ten-year note for its $1,000 face amount. Rick purchases the note for $1,000 on the issue date. Because of a decline in interest rates, Titan calls the note at a price of $1,050 paid to each note holder. Rick will treat the premium as a $50 capital gain. Titan will deduct total premiums as interest expense. ◀

Table C2-2 presents a comparison of the tax advantages and disadvantages of using debt in the capital structure.

EQUITY CAPITAL

Corporations can raise equity capital through the issuance of various types of securities. Some corporations issue only a single class of stock, whereas others issue numerous classes of stock. Reasons for the use of multiple classes of stock include

▶ Permitting nonfamily employees of family owned corporations to obtain an equity interest in the business while keeping voting control in the hands of family members

▶ Financing a **closely held corporation** through the issuance of preferred stock to an outside investor or wealthy individual, while leaving voting control in the hands of existing common stockholders.

Table C2-3 lists some of the major tax advantages and disadvantages of using common and preferred stock in a corporation's capital structure.

CAPITAL CONTRIBUTIONS BY SHAREHOLDERS

SELF-STUDY QUESTION

Does the transferee corporation recognize gain on the receipt of appreciated property from a shareholder?

ANSWER

No. A corporation does not recognize gain when it receives property from its shareholders, whether or not it exchanges its own stock. However, the transfer must qualify as a Sec. 351 exchange or the transaction will be taxable to the shareholders.

A corporation recognizes no income when it receives money or property as a capital contribution from a shareholder.[53] If the shareholders make voluntary pro rata payments to a corporation but do not receive any additional stock, the payments are treated as an additional price paid for the stock already owned.[54] The shareholders' bases in their stock are increased by the amount of money contributed, plus the basis of any nonmoney property contributed, and plus any gain recognized by the shareholders. The corporation's basis in any property received as a capital contribution from a shareholder equals

▼ **TABLE C2-2**

Tax Advantages and Disadvantages of Using Debt in a Corporation's Capital Structure

Advantages:
1. A corporation can deduct interest paid on debt instruments.
2. Shareholders do not recognize income when they receive an amount in repayment of debt as they would in the case of a stock redemption.

Disadvantages:
1. If at the time the corporation is formed or later when a shareholder makes a capital contribution, the shareholder receives a debt instrument in exchange for property, the debt is treated as boot, and the shareholder recognizes gain to the extent of the lesser of the boot received or the realized gain.
2. If debt becomes worthless or is sold at less than face value, the loss generally is a nonbusiness bad debt (short-term capital loss) or a capital loss. Section 1244 ordinary loss treatment applies only to stock (see pages C2-32 and C2-33).

[53] Sec. 118(a).　　　　[54] Reg. Sec. 1.118-1.

▼ TABLE C2-3

Tax Advantages and Disadvantages of Using Equity in a Corporation's Capital Structure

Advantages:

1. A 70%, 80%, or 100% dividends-received deduction is available to a corporate shareholder receiving dividends. A similar deduction is not available for the receipt of interest (see Chapter C3).
2. A shareholder can receive common and preferred stock in a tax-free corporate formation under Sec. 351 or a tax-free reorganization under Sec. 368 without recognizing gain (see Chapters C2 and C7, respectively). Receipt of debt obligations in each of these two types of transactions generally results in the shareholder's recognizing gain.
3. Common and preferred stock can be distributed tax-free to the corporation's shareholders as a stock dividend. Some common and preferred stock distributions, however, may be taxable as dividends under Sec. 305(b). Distributions of debt obligations generally are taxable as a dividend (see Chapter C4).
4. Common or preferred stock that the shareholder sells or exchanges or that becomes worthless is eligible for limited ordinary loss treatment under Sec. 1244 (see pages C2-32 and C2-33). The loss recognized on similar transactions involving debt obligations generally is treated as capital in character.
5. Section 1202 permits a 50% capital gains exclusion on the sale or exchange of qualified small business (C) corporation stock that has been held for more than five years.
6. For years 2003 through 2008, qualified dividends are taxed at a maximum 15% tax rate.

Disadvantages:

1. Dividends are not deductible in determining a corporation's taxable income.
2. Redemption of common or preferred stock generally is taxable to the shareholders as a dividend. Under the general rule, none of the redemption distribution offsets the shareholder's basis for the stock investment. Redemption of common and preferred stock by the issuing corporation is eligible for exchange treatment only in certain situations specified in Secs. 302 and 303 (see Chapter C4).
3. Preferred stock received by a shareholder as a tax-free stock dividend may be treated as Sec. 306 stock. Sale, exchange, or redemption of such stock can result in the recognition of ordinary income instead of capital gain (see Chapter C4).

TYPICAL MISCONCEPTION

The characteristics of preferred stock can be similar to those of a debt security. Often, a regular dividend is required at a stated rate, much like what would be required with respect to a debt obligation. The holder of preferred stock, like a debt holder, may have preferred liquidation rights over holders of common stock. Also, preferred stock is not required to possess voting rights. However, differences remain. A corporation can deduct its interest expense but not dividends. Interest income is ordinary income to shareholders, but qualified dividends are subject to the 15% maximum tax rate (through 2008).

the shareholder's basis plus any gain recognized by the shareholder.[55] Normally, the shareholders recognize no gain when they contribute property to a controlled corporation as a capital contribution.

EXAMPLE C2-44 ▶ Dot and Fred own equally all of Trail Corporation's stock, and each has a $50,000 basis in that stock. Later, as a voluntary contribution to Trail's capital, Dot contributes $40,000 in cash and Fred contributes property having a $25,000 basis and a $40,000 FMV. Trail recognizes no income because of the contributions. However, Dot's basis in her stock is increased to $90,000 ($50,000 + $40,000), and Fred's basis in his stock is increased to $75,000 ($50,000 + $25,000). Trail's basis in the property contributed by Fred is $25,000—the same as Fred's basis in the property. ◀

If a shareholder-lender gratuitously forgives corporate debt, the debt forgiveness might be treated as a capital contribution equal to the principal amount of the forgiven debt. A determination of whether debt forgiveness is a capital contribution is based on the facts and circumstances of the transaction.

---

[55] Sec. 362(a).

WHAT WOULD YOU DO IN THIS SITUATION?

You are a CPA who has a corporate client that wants to issue 100-year bonds. The corporation's CEO reads *The Wall Street Journal* regularly and has seen that similar bonds have been issued by a number of companies, including Coca-Cola and Disney. He touts the fact that the interest rate on these bonds is little more than 30-year U.S. Treasury bonds. In addition, interest on the bonds would be deductible, whereas dividends paid on preferred or common stock would be nondeductible. You are concerned that the IRS may treat the bonds as equity because of their extraordinarily long term. If they are treated as equity, the "interest" paid would be characterized as dividends and therefore not deductible.

Your CPA firm is advising your client on the prospective bond issue. What advice would you give your client now and when preparing its tax return after the new bonds have been issued?

CAPITAL CONTRIBUTIONS BY NONSHAREHOLDERS

BOOK-TO-TAX ACCOUNTING COMPARISON

The IRC requires capital contributions of property other than money made by a nonshareholder to be reported at a zero basis. Financial accounting rules, however, require donated capital to be reported at the FMV of the asset on the financial accounting books. Neither set of rules requires the property's value to be included in income.

Nonshareholders sometimes contribute capital in the form of money or property. For example, a city government might contribute land to a corporation to induce the corporation to locate within the city and provide jobs for its citizens. Such contributions are excluded from the corporation's gross income if the money or property contributed is neither a payment for goods or services rendered nor a subsidy to induce the corporation to limit production.[56]

If a nonshareholder contributes property other than money to a corporation, the corporation's basis in such property is zero.[57] The zero basis precludes the transferee corporation from claiming either a depreciation deduction or capital recovery offset with respect to the contributed property.

If a nonshareholder contributes money, the basis of any property acquired with the money during a 12-month period beginning on the day the corporation received the contribution is reduced by the amount of the contribution. This rule limits the corporation's deduction to the amount of funds it invested in the property. The amount of any money received from nonshareholders that the corporation did not spend to purchase property during the 12-month period reduces the basis of any other property held by the corporation on the last day of the 12-month period.[58]

The basis reduction applies to the corporation's property in the following order:

1. Depreciable property
2. Amortizable property
3. Depletable property
4. All other property

A property's basis may not be reduced below zero as a result of these downward adjustments.

EXAMPLE C2-45 ▶ The City of San Antonio contributes $100,000 in cash and a tract of land having a $500,000 FMV to Circle Corporation to induce the company to locate there. Because of a downturn in Circle's business, the company spends only $70,000 of the contributed funds over the next 12 months. Circle recognizes no income as a result of the contribution. Circle's bases in the land and the property purchased with the contributed funds are zero. Starting with its depreciable property, the basis of Circle's remaining property must be reduced by the $30,000 ($100,000 − $70,000) contributed but not spent. ◀

---

[56] Reg. Sec. 1.118-1.
[57] Sec. 362(c)(1).
[58] Sec. 362(c)(2).

WORTHLESSNESS OF STOCK OR DEBT OBLIGATIONS

Investors who purchase stock in or lend money to a corporation usually intend to earn a profit and recover their investment. Unfortunately, some investments do not provide a good return on capital, and an investor may lose part or all of the investment. This section examines the tax consequences of stock or debt becoming worthless.

SECURITIES

A debt or equity investment that is evidenced by a **security** and that becomes worthless results in a capital loss for the investor as of the last day of the tax year in which the security becomes worthlessness. For purposes of this rule, the term *security* includes (1) a share of stock in the corporation; (2) a right to subscribe for, or the right to receive, a share of stock in the corporation; or (3) a bond, debenture, note, or other evidence of indebtedness issued by a corporation with interest coupons or in registered form.[59]

In some situations, investors recognize an ordinary loss when a security becomes worthless. Investors who contribute capital, either in the form of equity or debt to a corporation that later fails, generally will prefer ordinary losses because they are deductible against ordinary income reported on the investor's tax return. Ordinary losses that generate an NOL can be carried back or forward under the general NOL rules. Ordinary loss treatment generally is available in the following circumstances:

▶ *Securities that are noncapital assets.* Ordinary loss treatment results when a security that is a noncapital asset is sold or exchanged or becomes totally worthless. Securities in this category include those held as inventory by a securities dealer.

▶ *Affiliated corporations.* A domestic corporation can claim an ordinary loss for any security of an affiliated corporation that becomes worthless during the tax year. The domestic corporation must own at least 80% of the total voting power of all classes of stock entitled to vote, and at least 80% of each class of nonvoting stock (other than stock limited and preferred as to dividends). At least 90% of the aggregate gross receipts of the loss corporation for all tax years must have been derived from sources other than passive income.

▶ *Section 1244 stock.* Section 1244 permits a shareholder to claim an ordinary loss if qualifying stock issued by a small business corporation is sold or exchanged or becomes worthless. This treatment is available only to an individual who was issued the qualifying stock or who was a partner in a partnership at the time the partnership acquired the qualifiying stock. In the latter case, the partner's distributive share of partnership losses includes the loss sustained by the partnership on such stock. Ordinary loss treatment is not available for stock inherited, received as a gift, or purchased from another shareholder. The ordinary loss is limited to $50,000 per year (or $100,000 if the taxpayer is married and files a joint return). Losses exceeding the dollar ceiling in any given year are considered capital in character.

EXAMPLE C2-46 ▶

Tammy and her husband purchased 25% of the initial offering of Minor Corporation's single class of stock for $175,000. Minor is a small business corporation, and the Minor stock satisfies all the Sec. 1244 requirements. On September 1 of the current year Minor filed for bankruptcy. After substantial litigation, the shareholders are notified two years later that the Minor stock is worthless. In that year, Tammy and her husband can deduct $100,000 of their initial investment as an ordinary loss. The remaining $75,000 loss is capital in character. ◀

If Sec. 1244 stock is issued for property whose adjusted basis exceeds its FMV immediately before the exchange, the basis of the stock is reduced to the property's FMV for purposes of determining the ordinary loss amount.

---

[59] Sec. 165(g).

EXAMPLE C2-47 ▶ In a Sec. 351 tax-free exchange, Penny transfers property having a $40,000 adjusted basis and a $32,000 FMV for 100 shares of Sec. 1244 stock. Ordinarily, Penny's basis in the stock would be $40,000. However, for Sec. 1244 purposes only, her stock basis is the property's FMV, or $32,000. If Penny sells the stock for $10,000, her recognized loss is $30,000 ($10,000 − $40,000). Her ordinary loss under Sec. 1244 is $22,000 ($10,000 − $32,000 Sec. 1244 basis). The remaining $8,000 loss is capital in character. ◀

No special election is required for Sec. 1244 loss treatment. Investors, however, should be aware that, if they fail to satisfy certain requirements, ordinary loss treatment will be unavailable, and their loss will be capital in character. The requirements are as follows:

▶ The issuing corporation must be a small business corporation at the time it issues the stock. A small business corporation is a corporation whose aggregate money and other property received for stock is $1 million or less.[60]

▶ The stock must be issued for money or property other than stock and securities.

▶ The issuing corporation must have derived more than 50% of its aggregate gross receipts from "active" sources (i.e., other than royalties, rents, dividends, interest, annuities, and gains on sales of stock and securities) during the five most recent tax years ending before the date on which the shareholder sells or exchanges the stock or the stock becomes worthless.

TAX STRATEGY TIP

If a shareholder contributes additional money or property to an existing corporation, he or she should be sure to receive additional stock in the exchange so that it will qualify for Sec. 1244 treatment if all requirements are met. If the shareholder does not receive additional stock, the increased basis of existing stock resulting from the capital contribution will not qualify for Sec. 1244 treatment.

If a shareholder contributes additional money or property to a corporation after acquiring Sec. 1244 stock, the amount of ordinary loss recognized on the sale, exchange, or worthlessness of the Sec. 1244 stock is limited to the shareholder's capital contribution at the time the shares were issued.

UNSECURED DEBT OBLIGATIONS

In addition to holding an equity interest, shareholders may lend money to the corporation. The type of loss allowed if the corporation does not repay the borrowed funds depends on the nature of the loan or advance. If the advance is treated as additional paid-in capital, the worthless security loss claimed by the shareholder for his or her stock investment is increased.

If the unpaid loan was not evidenced by a security (i.e., an unsecured debt obligation), it is considered to be either a business or nonbusiness bad debt. Nonbusiness bad debts are treated less favorably than business bad debts. Under Sec. 166, nonbusiness bad debts are deductible as short-term capital losses (up to the $3,000 annual limit for net capital losses) when they are determined to be totally worthless. Business bad debts are deductible as ordinary losses without limit when they are either partially or totally worthless. The IRS generally treats a loan made by a shareholder to a corporation in connection with his or her stock investment as a nonbusiness activity.[61] It is understandable why a shareholder might attempt to rebut this presumption with the argument that a business purpose exists for the loan.

An advance in connection with the shareholder's trade or business, such as a loan to protect the shareholder's employment at the corporation, may be treated as an ordinary loss under the business bad debt rules. Regulation Sec. 1.166-5(b) states that whether a bad debt is business or nonbusiness related depends on the taxpayer's motive for making the advance. The debt is business related if the necessary relationship between the loss and the conduct of the taxpayer's trade or business exists at the time the debt was incurred, acquired, or became worthless.

In *U.S. v. Edna Generes,* the U.S. Supreme Court held that where multiple motives exist for advancing funds to a corporation, such as where a shareholder-employee advances funds to protect his or her employment interest, determining whether the advance is business or nonbusiness related must be based on the "dominant motivation"

---

[60] Regulation Sec. 1.1244(c)-2 provides special rules for designating which shares of stock are eligible for Sec. 1244 treatment when the corporation has issued more than $1 million of stock.

[61] The assumption is made here that the loan is not considered to be an additional capital contribution. In such a case, the Sec. 165 worthless security rules apply instead of the Sec. 166 bad debt rules.

KEY POINT

In many closely held corporations, the shareholders are also employees. Thus, when a shareholder-employee makes a loan to the corporation, a question arises whether the loan is being made in the individual's capacity as an employee or a shareholder. The distinction is important because an employee loan that is worthless is entitled to ordinary loss treatment, whereas a shareholder loan that is worthless is treated as a nonbusiness bad debt (short-term capital loss).

for the advance.[62] If the advance is only "significantly motivated" by considerations relating to the taxpayer's trade or business, such motivation will not establish a proximate relationship between the bad debt and the taxpayer's trade or business. Therefore, it may result in a nonbusiness bad debt characterization. On the other hand, if the advance is dominantly motivated by considerations relating to the taxpayer's trade or business, such motivation usually is sufficient to establish such a proximate relationship. Therefore, it may result in a business bad debt characterization.

Factors deemed important in determining the character of bad debt include the taxpayer's equity in the corporation relative to compensation paid by the corporation. For example, a modest salary paid by the corporation relative to substantial stockholdings in the corporation suggests an investment motive for the advance. Conversely, a substantial salary paid by the corporation relative to modest stockholdings in the corporation suggests a business motive for the advance. The business motive suggested here is the protection of the employee-lender's employment because the advance may help save the business from failing. Reasonable minds may differ on what is substantial and what is modest, and monetary stakes often are quite high in these cases. Consequently, the determination frequently requires litigation.

EXAMPLE C2-48 ▶

ADDITIONAL COMMENT

For the act of lending money to a corporation to be considered the taxpayer's trade or business, the taxpayer must show that he or she was individually in the business of seeking out, promoting, organizing, and financing business ventures. *Ronald L. Farrington v. CIR*, 65 AFTR 2d 90-617, 90-1 USTC ¶50,125 (DC, OK, 1990).

Top Corporation employs Mary as its legal counsel. It pays Mary an annual salary of $100,000. In March of the current year, Mary advances the corporation $50,000 to assist it financially. In October of the current year, Top declares bankruptcy and liquidates. In the liquidation, Mary and other investors receive 10 cents on every dollar advanced. If Mary can show that her advance was dominantly motivated by her employment interest, her $45,000 ($50,000 × 0.90) loss will be treated as business bad debt, ordinary in character, and fully deductible in the current year. On the other hand, if Mary shows only that the advance was significantly motivated by her employment interest, her $45,000 loss will be treated as nonbusiness bad debt, capital in character, and deductible in this year and in subsequent years only to the extent of $3,000 in excess of any capital gains she recognizes. ◀

A loss sustained by a shareholder who guarantees a loan made by a third party to the corporation generally is treated as a nonbusiness bad debt. The loss can be claimed only to the extent the shareholder actually pays the third party and is unable to recover the payment from the debtor corporation.[63]

TAX PLANNING CONSIDERATIONS

SELF-STUDY QUESTION

Which tax provisions may potentially limit a transferor shareholder from recognizing a loss on the transfer of property to a corporation?

ANSWER

Such transfer cannot be to a controlled corporation, or Sec. 351 will defer the loss. Even if Sec. 351 can be avoided, losses on sales between a corporation and a more than 50% shareholder are disallowed under Sec. 267. Thus, to recognize a loss on the sale of property, such shareholder must, directly or indirectly, own 50% or less of the transferee corporation's stock.

AVOIDING SEC. 351

Section 351 is not an elective provision. If its requirements are met, a corporate formation is tax-free, even if the taxpayer does not want it to be. Most often, taxpayers desire Sec. 351 treatment because it allows them to defer gains when transferring appreciated property to a corporation. In some cases, however, shareholders find such treatment disadvantageous because they would like to recognize gain or loss on the property transferred.

AVOIDING NONRECOGNITION OF LOSSES UNDER SEC. 351. If a shareholder transfers to a corporation property that has declined in value, the shareholder may want to recognize the loss so it can offset income from other sources. The shareholder can recognize the loss only if the Sec. 351 nonrecognition rules and the Sec. 267 related party rules do not apply to the exchange.

Avoiding Sec. 351 treatment requires that one or more of its requirements not be met. The simplest way to accomplish this objective is to ensure that the transferors of property do not receive 80% of the voting stock.

[62] 29 AFTR 2d 72-609, 72-1 USTC ¶9259 (USSC, 1972). [63] Reg. Sec. 1.166-8(a).

Even if a shareholder avoids Sec. 351 treatment, he or she still may not be able to recognize the losses because of the Sec. 267 related party transaction rules. Under Sec. 267(a)(1), if the shareholder owns more than 50% of the corporation's stock, directly or indirectly, he or she is a related party and therefore cannot recognize loss on an exchange of property for the corporation's stock or other property. If the transferors of property receive less than 80% of the corporation's voting stock and if the transferor of loss property does not own more than 50% of the stock, the transferor of loss property may recognize the loss.

EXAMPLE C2-49 ▶

Lynn owns property having a $100,000 basis and a $60,000 FMV. If Lynn transfers the property to White Corporation in a tax-free exchange under Sec. 351, she will not recognize the loss, which will be deferred until she sells her White stock. If the Sec. 351 requirements are not met, she will recognize a $40,000 loss in the year she transfers the property. If Lynn receives 50% of the White stock in exchange for her property, Cathy, an unrelated individual, receives 25% of the stock in exchange for $30,000 cash, and John, another unrelated individual, receives the remaining 25% for services performed, the Sec. 351 control requirement will not be met because the transferors of property receive less than 80% of the stock. Moreover, Lynn will not be a related party under Sec. 267 because she will not own more than 50% of the stock either directly or indirectly. Therefore, Lynn will recognize a $40,000 loss on the exchange. ◀

ADDITIONAL COMMENT

Any potential built-in gain on property transferred to the transferee corporation is duplicated because such gain may be recognized at the corporate level and at the shareholder level. This double taxation may be another reason for avoiding the nonrecognition of gain under Sec. 351.

AVOIDING NONRECOGNITION OF GAIN UNDER SEC. 351. Sometimes a transferor would like to recognize gain when he or she transfers appreciated property to a corporation so the transferee corporation can obtain a higher basis in the transferred property. Some other possible reasons for recognizing gain are as follows:

▶ If the transferor's gain is capital in character, he or she can offset this gain with capital losses from other transactions.

▶ Individual long-term capital gains are taxed at a maximum 15% rate (for years 2003 through 2008). This rate is below the 35% top marginal tax rate applicable to corporate-level capital gains.

▶ The corporation's marginal tax rate may be higher than a noncorporate transferor's marginal tax rate. In such case, it might be beneficial for the transferor to recognize gain so the corporation can obtain a higher basis in the property. A higher basis would either reduce the corporation's gain when it later sells the property or allow the corporation to claim higher depreciation deductions when it uses the property.

A transferor who does not wish to recognize gain on a transfer of appreciated property to a corporation can avoid Sec. 351 treatment through one of the following planning techniques:

▶ The transferor can sell the property to the controlled corporation for cash.

▶ The transferor can sell the property to the controlled corporation for cash and debt. This transaction involves relatively less cash than the previous transaction. However, the sale may be treated as a tax-free exchange if the debt instruments received are recharacterized as equity.[64]

▶ The transferor can sell the property to a third party for cash and have the third party contribute the property to the corporation for stock.

▶ The transferor can have the corporation distribute sufficient boot property so that, even if Sec. 351 applies to the transaction, he or she will recognize gain.

▶ The transferors can fail one or more of the Sec. 351 tests. For example, if the transferors do not own 80% of the voting stock immediately after the exchange, the Sec. 351 control requirement will not have been met, and they will recognize gain.

---

[64] See, for example, *Aqualane Shores, Inc. v. CIR*, 4 AFTR 2d 5346, 59-2 USTC ¶9632 (5th Cir., 1959) and *Sun Properties, Inc. v. U.S.*, 47 AFTR 273, 55-1 USTC ¶9261 (5th Cir., 1955).

▶ To trigger gain recognition under Sec. 357(b) or (c), the transferors may transfer to the corporation either debt that exceeds the basis of all property transferred or debt that lacks a business purpose.

EXAMPLE C2-50 ▶ Ten years ago, Jaime purchased land as an investment for $100,000. The land is now worth $500,000. Jaime plans to transfer the land to Bell Corporation in exchange for all its stock. Bell will subdivide the land and sell individual tracts. Its gain on the land sales will be ordinary income. Jaime has realized a large capital loss in the current year and would like to recognize capital gain on the transfer of the land to Bell. One way for Jaime to accomplish this objective is to transfer the land to Bell in exchange for all the Bell stock plus a note for $400,000. Because the note is boot, Jaime will recognize $400,000 of gain even though Sec. 351 applies to the exchange. However, if the note is due in a subsequent year, Jaime's gain will be deferred until collection unless she elects out of the installment method. ◀

COMPLIANCE AND PROCEDURAL CONSIDERATIONS

REPORTING REQUIREMENTS UNDER SEC. 351

A taxpayer who receives stock or other property in a Sec. 351 exchange must attach a statement to his or her tax return for the period encompassing the date of the exchange.[65] The statement must include all facts pertinent to the exchange, including:

ADDITIONAL COMMENT

The required information provided to the IRS by both the transferor-shareholders and the transferee corporation should be consistent. For example, the FMVs assigned to the stock and other properties included in the exchange should be the same for both sides of the transaction.

▶ A description of the property transferred and its adjusted basis to the transferor

▶ A description of the stock received in the exchange, including its kind, number of shares, and FMV

▶ A description of the securities received in the exchange, including principal amount, terms, and FMV

▶ The amount of money received

▶ A description of any other property received, including its FMV

▶ A statement of the liabilities transferred to the corporation, including the nature of the liabilities, when and why they were incurred, and the business reason for their transfer

The transferee corporation must attach a statement to its tax return for the year in which the exchange took place. The statement must include

▶ A complete description of all property received from the transferors

▶ The transferors' adjusted bases in the property

▶ A description of the stock issued to the transferors

▶ A description of the securities issued to the transferors

▶ The amount of money distributed to the transferors

▶ A description of any other property distributed to the transferors

▶ Information regarding the transferor's liabilities assumed by the corporation

---

[65] Reg. Sec. 1.351-3.

PROBLEM MATERIALS

DISCUSSION QUESTIONS

C2-1 What entities or business forms are available for a new business? Explain the advantages and disadvantages of each.

C2-2 Alice and Bill plan to go into business together. They anticipate losses for the first two or three years, which they would like to use to offset income from other sources. They also are concerned about exposing their personal assets to the business liabilities. Advise Alice and Bill as to what business form would best satisfy their concern.

C2-3 Bruce and Bob organize Black LLC on May 10 of the current year. What is the default rule for the entity's tax classification? Are any alternative classification(s) available? If so, (1) how do Bruce and Bob elect the alternative classification(s) and (2) what are the tax consequences of electing an alternative classification?

C2-4 John and Wilbur form White Corporation on May 3 of the current year. What is the default rule for the entity's tax classification? Are any alternative classification(s) available? If so, (1) how do John and Wilbur elect the alternative classification(s) and (2) what are the tax consequences of electing an alternative classification?

C2-5 Barbara organizes Blue LLC on May 17 of the current year. What is the default rule for the entity's tax classification? Are any alternative classification(s) available? If so, (1) how does Barbara elect the alternative classification(s) and (2) what are the tax consequences of electing an alternative classification?

C2-6 Debate the following proposition: All corporate formation transactions should be treated as taxable events.

C2-7 What are the tax consequences of Sec. 351 for the transferor and transferee when property is transferred to a newly created corporation?

C2-8 What items are included in the property definition for purposes of Sec. 351(a)? What items are excluded from the property definition?

C2-9 How is control defined for purposes of Sec. 351(a)?

C2-10 Explain how the IRS has interpreted the phrase "in control immediately after the exchange" for purposes of a Sec. 351 exchange.

C2-11 John and Mary each exchange property worth $50,000 for 100 shares of New Corporation stock. Peter exchanges services for 98 shares of stock and $1,000 in money for two shares of stock. Are the Sec. 351 requirements met? Explain why or why not. What advice would you give the shareholders?

C2-12 Does Sec. 351 require shareholders to receive stock equal in value to the property transferred? Suppose Fred and Susan each transfer property worth $50,000 to Spade Corporation. Fred receives 25 shares of Spade stock and Susan receives 75 shares. Are the Sec. 351 requirements met? Explain the tax consequences of the transaction.

C2-13 Does Sec. 351 apply to property transfers to an existing corporation? Suppose Ken and Lynn each own 50 shares of North Corporation stock. Ken transfers property worth $50,000 to North for an additional 25 shares of stock. Does Sec. 351 apply? Explain why or why not. If not, what can be done to make the transaction qualify?

C2-14 How are a transferor's basis and holding period determined for stocks and other property (boot) received in a Sec. 351 exchange? How does the transferee corporation's assumption of liabilities affect the transferor's basis in the stock?

C2-15 How are the transferee corporation's basis and holding period determined for property received in a Sec. 351 exchange?

C2-16 Under what circumstances is a corporation's assumption of liabilities considered boot in a Sec. 351 exchange?

C2-17 What factor(s) would the IRS likely consider to determine whether the transfer of a liability to a corporation in a Sec. 351 exchange was motivated by a business purpose?

C2-18 Mark transfers all the property of his sole proprietorship to newly formed Utah Corporation in exchange for all the Utah stock. Mark has claimed depreciation on some of the property. Under what circumstances is Mark required to recapture previously claimed depreciation deductions? How is the depreciation deduction calculated for the year of transfer? What are the tax consequences if Utah sells the depreciable property?

C2-19 How does the assignment of income doctrine apply to a Sec. 351 exchange?

C2-20 What factors did Congress mandate should be considered in determining whether indebtedness is classified as debt or equity for tax purposes?

C2-21 What are the advantages and disadvantages of using debt in a firm's capital structure?

C2-22 How are capital contributions by shareholders and nonshareholders treated by the recipient corporation?

C2-23 What are the advantages of qualifying for Sec. 1244 loss treatment when a stock investment becomes worthless? What requirements must be satisfied to obtain Sec. 1244 benefits?

C2-24 What are the advantages of business bad debt treatment when a shareholder's loan or advance to a corporation cannot be repaid? How can one avoid having such a loss treated as a nonbusiness bad debt?

C2-25 Why might shareholders want to avoid Sec. 351 treatment? Explain three ways they can accomplish this.

C2-26 What are the reporting requirements under Sec. 351?

ISSUE IDENTIFICATION QUESTIONS

C2-27 Peter Jones has owned all 100 shares of Trenton Corporation's stock for the past five years. This year, Mary Smith contributes property with a $50,000 basis and an $80,000 FMV for 80 newly issued Trenton shares. At the same time, Peter contributes $15,000 in cash for 15 newly issued Trenton shares. What tax issues should Mary and Peter consider with respect to the stock acquisitions?

C2-28 Carl contributes equipment with a $50,000 adjusted basis and an $80,000 FMV to Cook Corporation for 50 of its 100 shares of stock. His son, Carl Jr., contributes $20,000 cash for the remaining 50 Cook shares. What tax issues should Carl and his son consider with respect to the stock acquisitions?

C2-29 Several years ago, Bill acquired 100 shares of Bold Corporation stock directly from the corporation for $100,000 in cash. This year, he sold the stock to Sam for $35,000. What tax issues should Bill consider with respect to the stock sale?

PROBLEMS

C2-30 *Transfer of Property and Services to a Controlled Corporation.* In 2006, Dick, Evan, and Fran form Triton Corporation. Dick contributes land (a capital asset) purchased in 2004 for $60,000 that has a $50,000 FMV in exchange for 50 shares of Triton stock. Evan contributes machinery (Sec. 1231 property) purchased in 2003 that has a $45,000 adjusted basis and a $30,000 FMV in exchange for 30 shares of Triton stock. Fran contributes services worth $20,000 in exchange for 20 shares of Triton stock.
a. What is the amount of Dick's recognized gain or loss?
b. What is Dick's basis in his Triton shares? When does his holding period begin?
c. What is the amount of Evan's recognized gain or loss?
d. What is Evan's basis in his Triton shares? When does his holding period begin?
e. How much income, if any, must Fran recognize?
f. What is Fran's basis in her Triton shares? When does her holding period begin?
g. What is Triton's basis in the land and the machinery? When does its holding period begin? How does Triton treat the amount paid to Fran for her services?

C2-31 *Transfer of Property and Services to a Controlled Corporation.* In 2006, Ed, Fran, and George form Jet Corporation. Ed contributes land purchased as an investment in 2002 for $15,000 that has a $35,000 FMV in exchange for 35 shares of Jet stock. Fran contributes machinery (Sec. 1231 property) purchased in 2002 and used in her business in exchange for 35 shares of Jet stock. Immediately before the exchange, the property had a $45,000 adjusted basis and a $35,000 FMV. George contributes services worth $30,000 in exchange for 30 shares of Jet stock.
a. What is the amount of Ed's recognized gain or loss?
b. What is Ed's basis in his Jet shares? When does his holding period begin?
c. What is the amount of Fran's recognized gain or loss?
d. What is Fran's basis in her Jet shares? When does her holding period begin?
e. How much income, if any, must George recognize?
f. What is George's basis in his Jet shares? When does his holding period begin?
g. What is Jet's basis in the land and the machinery? When does its holding period begin? How does Jet treat the amount paid to George for his services?
h. How would your answers to Parts a through g change if George instead contributed $5,000 cash and services worth $25,000 for his 30 shares of Jet stock?

C2-32 *Control Requirement.* In which of the following independent situations is the Sec. 351 control requirement met?
a. Olive transfers property to Quick Corporation for 75% of Quick stock, and Mary provides services to Quick for the remaining 25% of Quick stock.
b. Pete transfers property to Target Corporation for 60% of Target stock, and Robert transfers property worth $15,000 and performs services worth $25,000 for the remaining 40% of Target stock.
c. Herb and his wife, Wilma, each have owned 50 of the 100 outstanding shares of Vast Corporation stock since it was formed three years ago. In the current year, their son, Sam, transfers property to Vast for 50 newly issued shares of Vast stock.
d. Charles and Ruth develop a plan to form Tiny Corporation. On June 3 of this year, Charles transfers property worth $50,000 for 50 shares of Tiny stock. On August 1, Ruth transfers $50,000 cash for 50 shares of Tiny stock.
e. Assume the same facts as in Part d except that Charles has a prearranged plan to sell 30 of his shares to Sam on October 1.

C2-33 *Control Requirement.* In which of the following exchanges is the Sec. 351 control requirement met?
a. Fred exchanges property worth $50,000 and services worth $50,000 for 100 shares of New Corporation stock. Greta exchanges $100,000 cash for the remaining 100 shares of New stock.
b. Maureen exchanges property worth $2,000 and services worth $48,000 for 100 shares of Gemini Corporation stock. Norman exchanges property worth $50,000 for the remaining 100 shares of Gemini stock.
If the transaction does not meet the Sec. 351 requirements, suggest ways in which the transaction can be structured so as to meet these requirements.

C2-34 *Sec. 351 Requirements.* Al, Bob, and Carl form West Corporation and transfer the following assets:

		Property Transferred		
Transferor	Asset	Transferor's Basis	FMV	Shares Received by Transferor
Al	Patent	–0–	$25,000	1,000 common
Bob	Cash	$25,000	25,000	250 preferred
Carl	Services	–0–	7,500	300 common

The common stock has voting rights. The preferred stock does not.
a. Does the transaction qualify as tax-free under Sec. 351? Explain the tax consequences of the transaction to Al, Bob, Carl, and West Corporation.
b. How would your answer to Part a change if Bob instead had received 200 shares of common stock and 200 shares of preferred stock?
c. How would your answer to Part a change if Carl instead had contributed $800 cash as well as services worth $6,700?

C2-35 *Incorporating a Sole Proprietorship.* Tom incorporates his sole proprietorship as Total Corporation and transfers all assets to Total in exchange for all 100 shares of Total stock, with a $125,000 FMV, and four $10,000 interest-bearing notes that mature consecutively on the first four anniversaries of the incorporation date. The assets transferred are:

Assets		Adjusted Basis	FMV
Cash		$ 5,000	$ 5,000
Equipment	$130,000		
Minus: Accumulated depreciation	(70,000)	60,000	90,000
Building	$100,000		
Minus: Accumulated depreciation	(49,000)	51,000	40,000
Land		24,000	30,000
Total		$140,000	$165,000

a. What are the amounts and character of Tom's recognized gains or losses?
b. What is Tom's basis in his Total stock and notes?
c. What is Total's basis in the property received from Tom?

C2-36 *Transfer to an Existing Corporation.* For the last five years, Ann and Fred each have owned 50 of the 100 outstanding shares of Zero Corporation stock. Ann transfers land having a $10,000 basis and a $25,000 FMV to Zero for an additional 25 shares of Zero stock. Fred transfers $1,000 to Zero for one additional share of Zero stock. What amount of the gain or loss must Ann recognize on the exchange? If the transaction does not meet the Sec. 351 requirements, suggest ways in which the transaction can be structured so as to meet these requirements.

C2-37 *Transfer to an Existing Corporation.* For the last three years, Lucy and Marvin each have owned 50 of the 100 outstanding shares of Lucky Corporation stock. Lucy transfers property that has an $8,000 basis and a $12,000 FMV to Lucky for an additional ten shares of Lucky stock. How much gain or loss must Lucy recognize on the exchange? If the transaction does not meet the Sec. 351 requirements, suggest ways in which the transaction can be structured so as to meet these requirements.

C2-38 *Disproportionate Receipt of Stock.* Jerry transfers property with a $28,000 adjusted basis and a $50,000 FMV to Texas Corporation for 75 shares of Texas stock. Frank, Jerry's father, transfers property with a $32,000 adjusted basis and a $50,000 FMV to Texas for the remaining 25 shares of Texas stock.
a. What is the amount of each transferor's recognized gain or loss?
b. What is Jerry's basis for his Texas stock?
c. What is Frank's basis for his Texas stock?

C2-39 *Sec. 351: Boot Property Received.* Sara transfers land (a capital asset) having a $30,000 adjusted basis to Temple Corporation in a transaction qualifying as a tax-free exchange under Sec. 351. In return, Sara receives the following consideration:

Consideration	FMV
100 shares of Temple common stock	$100,000
50 shares of Temple qualified preferred stock	50,000
Temple note due in three years	20,000
Total	$170,000

a. What are the amount and character of Sara's recognized gain or loss?
b. What is Sara's basis for her common stock, preferred stock, and note?
c. What is Temple's basis for the land?

C2-40 *Receipt of Bonds for Property.* Joe, Karen, and Larry form Gray Corporation. Joe contributes land (a capital asset) having an $8,000 adjusted basis and a $15,000 FMV to Gray in exchange for a similar dollar amount of its ten-year bonds. Karen contributes equipment (a Sec. 1231 asset), which has an $18,000 adjusted basis and a $25,000 FMV on which $10,000 of depreciation had previously been claimed, for 50 shares of Gray stock. Larry contributes $25,000 cash for 50 shares of Gray stock.
a. What are the amount and character of Joe's, Karen's, and Larry's recognized gains or losses on the transactions?
b. What basis do Joe, Karen, and Larry take in the stock or bonds they receive?
c. What basis does Gray take in the land and equipment? What happens to the $10,000 of depreciation recapture potential on the equipment?

C2-41 *Transfer of Depreciable Property.* Nora transfers depreciable machinery that originally cost $18,000 and has a $15,000 adjusted basis to Needle Corporation in exchange for all 100 shares of Needle stock, having an $18,000 FMV, and a three-year Needle note having a $4,000 FMV.
a. What are the amount and character of Nora's recognized gain or loss?
b. What are Nora's bases for the stock and note she received?
c. What is Needle's basis for the depreciable machinery received from Nora?

C2-42 *Transfer of Personal Liabilities.* Jim owns 80% of Gold Corporation's stock. He transfers a business automobile to Gold in exchange for additional Gold stock worth $5,000 and its assumption of his $1,000 debt on the automobile and his $2,000 education loan. The automobile originally cost Jim $12,000 and has a $4,500 adjusted basis and an $8,000 FMV on the transfer date.
a. What are the amount and character of Jim's recognized gain or loss?
b. What is Jim's basis for his additional Gold shares?

c. When does Jim's holding period begin for the additional shares?

d. What basis does Gold take in the automobile?

C2-43 *Liabilities in Excess of Basis.* Barbara transfers machinery having a $15,000 basis and a $35,000 FMV along with $10,000 cash to Moore Corporation in exchange for 50 shares of Moore stock. The machinery was used in Barbara's business, originally cost Barbara $50,000, and is subject to a $28,000 liability, which Moore assumes. Sam exchanges $17,000 cash for the remaining 50 shares of Moore stock.

a. What are the amount and character of Barbara's recognized gain or loss?

b. What is her basis in the Moore stock?

c. What is Moore's basis in the machinery?

d. What are the amount and character of Sam's recognized gain or loss?

e. What is Sam's basis in the Moore stock?

f. When do Barbara and Sam's holding periods for their stock begin?

g. How would your answers to Parts a through f change if Sam received $17,000 of Moore stock for legal services (instead of for money)?

C2-44 *Transfer of Business Properties.* Jerry transfers property having a $32,000 adjusted basis and a $50,000 FMV to Emerald Corporation in exchange for all its stock worth $15,000, and for Emerald's assumption of a $35,000 mortgage on the property.

a. What is the amount of Jerry's recognized gain or loss?

b. What is Jerry's basis in his Emerald stock?

c. What is Emerald's basis in the property?

d. How would your answers to Parts a through c change if the mortgage assumed by Emerald were $15,000 and the Emerald stock were worth $35,000?

C2-45 *Incorporating a Cash Basis Proprietorship.* Ted decides to incorporate his medical practice. He uses the cash method of accounting. On the date of incorporation, the practice reports the following balance sheet:

	Basis	FMV
Assets:		
Cash	$ 5,000	$ 5,000
Accounts receivable	-0-	65,000
Equipment (net of $15,000 depreciation)	35,000	40,000
Total	$40,000	$110,000
Liabilities and Owner's Equity:		
Current liabilities	$ -0-	$ 35,000
Note payable on equipment	15,000	15,000
Owner's equity	25,000	60,000
Total	$40,000	$110,000

All the current liabilities would be deductible by Ted if he paid them. Ted transfers all the assets and liabilities to a professional corporation in exchange for all of its stock.

a. What are the amount and character of Ted's recognized gain or loss?

b. What is Ted's basis in the shares he receives?

c. What is the corporation's basis in the property it receives?

d. Who must recognize the income from the receivables when they are collected? Can the corporation obtain a deduction for the liabilities when they are paid?

C2-46 *Transfer of Depreciable Property.* On January 10, 2006, Mary transfers to Green Corporation a machine purchased on March 3, 2003, for $100,000. The machine has a $60,000 adjusted basis and a $110,000 FMV on the transfer date. Mary receives all 100 shares of Green stock, worth $100,000, and a two-year Green note worth $10,000.

a. What are the amount and character of Mary's recognized gain or loss?

b. What is Mary's basis in the stock and note? When does her holding period begin?

c. What are the amount and character of Green's gain or loss?

d. What is Green's basis for the machine? When does Green's holding period begin?

C2-47 *Contribution to Capital by a Nonshareholder.* The City of San Antonio donates land worth $500,000 to Ace Corporation to induce it to locate in San Antonio and provide 2,000 jobs for its citizens.

a. How much income, if any, must Ace report because of the land contribution?

b. What basis does the land have to Ace?

c. Assume the same facts except that the City of San Antonio also donated $100,000 cash to Ace, which the corporation used to pay a portion of the $250,000 cost of equipment that it purchased six months later. How much income, if any, must Ace report because of the cash contribution? What basis does the equipment that was purchased have to Ace?

C2-48   *Choice of Capital Structure.* Reggie transfers $500,000 in cash to newly formed Jackson Corporation for 100% of Jackson's stock. In the first year of operations, Jackson's taxable income before any payments to Reggie is $120,000. What total amount of taxable income must Reggie and Jackson each report in the following two scenarios?
a. Jackson distributes a $70,000 dividend to Reggie.
b. Assume that when Jackson was formed, Reggie transferred his $500,000 to the corporation for $250,000 of Jackson stock and $250,000 in Jackson notes payable in five annual installments of $50,000 plus 8% annual interest on the unpaid balance. During the current year, Jackson pays Reggie $50,000 in repayment of the first note plus $20,000 interest.

C2-49   *Worthless Stock or Securities.* Tom and Vicki, who are husband and wife and who file a joint tax return, each purchase one-half of the stock in Guest Corporation from Al, for which they each pay $75,000. Tom is employed full-time by Guest and is paid $100,000 in salary annually. Because of Guest's financial difficulties, Tom and Vicki each lend Guest an additional $25,000. The $25,000 is secured by registered bonds and is to be repaid in five years, with interest being charged at a rate acceptable to the IRS. Guest's financial difficulties continue, and it declares bankruptcy. Tom and Vicki receive nothing for their Guest stock or for their Guest bonds.
a. What are the amount and character of each shareholder's loss on the worthless stock and bonds?
b. How would your answer to Part a change if the liability were not secured by a bond?
c. How would your answer to Part a change if Tom and Vicki had each purchased their stock for $75,000 at the time Guest was formed?

C2-50   *Worthless Stock.* Duck Corporation is owned equally by Harry, Susan, and Big Corporation. Harry and Susan are both single. Harry, Tom, and Big, the original investors in Duck, each paid $125,000 for their Duck stock in 1998. Susan purchased her stock from Tom in 2001 for $175,000. No adjustments to basis occur after the stock acquisition date. Duck suffers some financial difficulties as the result of losing a large judgment in a lawsuit brought by a person who purchased a defective product, resulting in a serious personal injury. Duck files for bankruptcy, and all its assets ultimately are used to pay its creditors in 2006. What are the amount and character of each shareholder's loss?

C2-51   *Sale of Sec. 1244 Stock.* Lois, who is single, transfers property with an $80,000 basis and a $120,000 FMV to Water Corporation in exchange for all of Water's 100 shares of stock. The shares qualify as Sec. 1244 stock. Two years later, Lois sells the stock for $28,000.
a. What are the amount and character of Lois's recognized gain or loss?
b. How would your answer to Part a change if the FMV of the property transferred were $70,000?

C2-52   *Transfer of Sec. 1244 Stock.* Assume the same facts as in Problem C2-51 except that Lois gave the Water stock to her daughter, Sue, six months after she received it. The stock had a $120,000 FMV when Lois received it and when she made the gift. Sue sold the stock two years later for $28,000. How is the loss treated for tax purposes?

C2-53   *Avoiding Sec. 351 Treatment.* Donna purchased land six years ago as an investment. The land cost her $150,000 and is now worth $480,000. Donna plans to transfer the land to Development Corporation, which will subdivide the land and sell individual parcels. Development's profit on the land sales will be ordinary income.
a. What are the tax consequences of the asset transfer and land sales if Donna contributes the land to Development in exchange for all its stock?
b. In what alternative ways can the transaction be structured to achieve more favorable tax results? Assume Donna's marginal tax rate is 35%. Development's marginal tax rate is 34%.

COMPREHENSIVE PROBLEMS

C2-54   On March 1 of the current year, Alice, Bob, Carla, and Dick form Bear Corporation and transfer the following items:

Property Transferred

Transferor	Asset	Basis to Transferor	FMV	Number of Common Shares Issued
Alice	Land	$12,000	$30,000	
	Building	38,000	70,000	400
	Mortgage on the land and building	60,000	60,000	
Bob	Equipment	25,000	40,000	300
Carla	Van	15,000	10,000	50
Dick	Accounting services	–0–	10,000	100

Alice purchased the land and building several years ago for $12,000 and $50,000, respectively. Alice has claimed straight-line depreciation on the building. Bob also receives a Bear note for $10,000 due in three years. The note bears interest at a market rate. Bob purchased the equipment three years ago for $50,000. Carla also receives $5,000 cash. Carla purchased the van two years ago for $20,000.
a. Does the transaction satisfy the requirements of Sec. 351?
b. What are the amount and character of the recognized gains or losses for Alice, Bob, Carla, Dick, and Bear?
c. What is each shareholder's basis for his or her Bear stock? When does the holding period for the stock begin?
d. What is Bear's basis for its property and services? When does the holding period for each property begin?

C2-55 On June 3 of the current year, Eric, Florence, and George form Wildcat Corporation and transfer the following items:

Property Transferred

Transferor	Asset	Basis to Transferor	FMV	Number of Common Shares Issued
Eric	Land	$200,000	$50,000	500
Florence	Equipment	–0–	25,000	250
George	Legal services	–0–	25,000	250

Eric purchased the land (a capital asset) five years ago for $200,000. Florence purchased the equipment three years ago for $48,000. The equipment is fully depreciated.
a. Does the transaction meet the requirements of Sec. 351?
b. What are the amount and character of the recognized gains or losses for Eric, Florence, George, and Wildcat?
c. What is each shareholder's basis in his or her Wildcat stock? When does the holding period for the stock begin?
d. What is Wildcat's basis in the land, equipment, and services? When does the holding period for each property begin?

TAX STRATEGY PROBLEMS

C2-56 Assume the same facts as in Problem C2-55.
a. Under what circumstances is the tax result in Problem C2-55 a good one, and for which shareholders?
b. Can you suggest ways to improve the result?

C2-57 Paula Green owns and operates the Green Thumb Nursery as a sole proprietorship. The business has assets with a $260,000 adjusted basis and a $500,000 FMV. Paula wants to expand into the landscaping business. She views this expansion as risky and therefore wants to incorporate so as not to put her personal assets at risk. Her friend, Mary Brown, is willing to invest $250,000 in the enterprise, so together they will have sufficient capital.

Although Green Thumb has earned approximately $55,000 per year, Paula and Mary anticipate that, when the new landscaping business is launched, the new corporation will incur losses of $50,000 per year for the next two years. After that, they expect profits of at least $80,000 per year. Paula and Mary have approximately $50,000 of income from other sources.

They are considering the following alternative capital structures and elections:

a. Green Thumb issues 50 shares of common stock to Paula and 25 shares of common stock to Mary.

b. Green Thumb issues 50 shares of common stock to Paula and a $250,000 ten-year bond bearing interest at 8% to Mary.

c. Green Thumb issues 40 shares of common stock to Paula plus a $100,000 ten-year bond bearing interest at 6% and 15 shares of common stock to Mary, plus a $100,000 ten-year bond bearing interest at 6%.

d. Green Thumb issues 50 shares of common stock to Paula and 25 shares of preferred stock to Mary. The preferred stock is nonparticipating but pays a cumulative preferred dividend of 8% of its $250,000 stated value.

What are the advantages and disadvantages of each of these alternatives? What are the main considerations in determining the best alternative?

CASE STUDY PROBLEMS

C2-58 Bob Jones has approached you for advice. He has a small repair shop that he has run for several years as a sole proprietorship. The proprietorship has used the cash method of accounting and the calendar year as its tax year. He needs additional capital for expansion and knows two people who might be interested in investing in the business. One would like to work in the business. The other would be an investor only.

Bob wants to know the tax consequences of incorporating his business. His business assets include a small building, equipment, accounts receivable, and cash. Liabilities include a mortgage on the building and a few accounts payable, which represent deductible expenses.

Required: Write a memorandum to Bob explaining the tax consequences of the incorporation. As part of your memorandum examine the possibility of having the corporation issue common and preferred stock and debt for the shareholders' property and money.

C2-59 Eric Wright conducts a dry cleaning business as a sole proprietorship. The business operates in a building that Eric owns. Last year, he mortgaged the building and the land on which the building sits for $150,000. He used the money for a down payment on his personal residence and college expenses for his two children. He now wants to incorporate his business and transfer the building and the mortgage to his new corporation, along with other assets and some accounts payable. The amount of the unpaid mortgage balance will not exceed Eric's adjusted basis in the land and building at the time he transfers them to the corporation. Eric is aware that Sec. 357(b) is likely to affect this transaction because no bona fide business purpose exists for the transfer of the mortgage, and the IRS probably will consider it to have been transferred for tax avoidance purposes. However, Eric refuses to acknowledge this problem when you confront him about the situation. He maintains that many taxpayers play the audit lottery and that, in the event of an audit, this issue can be used as a bargaining ploy.

Required: What information about the transaction must accompany the transferor and transferee's tax returns for the year in which the transfer takes place? Discuss the ethical issues defined by the AICPA's *Statements on Standards for Tax Services No. 1, Tax Return Positions* (which can be found in Appendix E) as it relates to this situation. Should the tax practitioner act as an advocate for the client's position? Should the practitioner sign the return?

TAX RESEARCH PROBLEMS

C2-60 Anne and Michael own and operate a mattress business. It has been quite successful, and they now have decided to take the business public. They contribute all the assets of the business to newly formed Spring Corporation each in exchange for 20% of the stock. The remaining 60% is issued to an underwriting company that will sell the stock to the public and keep 10% of the sales proceeds as a commission. Prepare a memorandum for your tax manager explaining whether or not this transaction meets the tax-free requirements of Sec. 351.

C2-61 Bob and Carl transfer property to Stone Corporation for 90% and 10% of Stone stock, respectively. Pursuant to a binding agreement entered into before the transfer, Bob sells half of his stock to Carl. Prepare a memorandum for your tax manager explaining why the exchange does or does not meet the Sec. 351 control requirement. Your manager has suggested that, at a minimum, you consult the following authorities:

- IRC Sec. 351
- Reg. Sec. 1.351-1

C2-62 In an exchange qualifying for Sec. 351 tax-free treatment, Greta receives 100 shares of White Corporation stock plus a contingent right to receive another 25 shares. The shares are contingent on the valuation of a patent contributed by Greta. Because the patent license is pending, the patent cannot be valued for several months. Prepare a memorandum for your tax manager explaining whether the contingent shares are considered "stock" for purposes of Sec. 351 and what tax consequences ensue from Greta's receipt of the actual and contingent shares of stock.

C2-63 Your clients, Lisa and Matthew, are planning to form Lima Corporation. Lisa will contribute $50,000 cash to Lima for 50 shares of its stock. Matthew will contribute land having a $35,000 adjusted basis and a $50,000 FMV for 50 shares of its stock. Lima will borrow additional capital from a bank and then will subdivide and sell the land. Prepare a draft memorandum for your tax manager outlining the tax treatment of the corporate formation. In your memorandum, compare tax and financial accounting reporting of this transaction. References:

- IRC Sec. 351
- APB, *Opinions of the Accounting Principles Board No. 29* [Accounting for Nonmonetary Transactions]

C2-64 John plans to transfer the assets and liabilities of his business to Newco, a new corporation, in exchange for all of Newco's stock. The assets have a $250,000 basis and an $800,000 FMV. John also plans to transfer $475,000 of liabilities (all business related). Can John avoid recognizing a $175,000 gain (the excess of liabilities over the basis of assets tranferred) under Sec. 357(c) by contributing a personal promissory note for $175,000 to the corporation along with the assets and liabilities?

C2-65 Six years ago, Leticia, Monica, and Nathaniel organized Lemona Corporation to develop and sell computer software. Each individual contributed $10,000 to Lemona in exchange for 1,000 shares of Lemona stock (for a total of 3,000 shares issued and outstanding). The corporation also borrowed $250,000 from Venture Capital Associates to finance operating costs and capital expenditures.

Because of intense competition, Lemona struggled in its early years of operation and sustained chronic losses. This year, Leticia, who serves as Lemona's president, decided to seek additional funds to finance Lemona's working capital.

Venture Capital Associates declined Leticia's request for additional capital because of the firm's already high credit exposure to the software corporation. Hi-Tech Bank proposed to lend Limona $100,000, but at a 10% premium over the prime rate. (Other software manufacturers in the same market can borrow at a 3% premium.) Investment Managers LLC proposed to inject $50,000 of equity capital into Lemona, but on condition that the investment firm be granted the right to elect five members to Lemona's board of directors. Discouraged by the "high cost" of external borrowing, Leticia turned to Monica and Nathaniel.

She proposed to Monica and Nathaniel that each of the three original investors contribute an additional $25,000 to Lemona, each in exchange for five 20-year debentures. The debentures would be unsecured and subordinated to Venture Capital Associates debt. Annual interest on the debentures would accrue at a floating 5% premium over the prime rate. The right to receive interest payments would be cumulative; that is, each debenture holder would be entitled to past and current interest payents before Lemona's board could declare a common stock dividend. The debentures would be both nontransferable and noncallable.

Leticia, Monica, and Nathaniel ask you, their tax accountant, to advise them on the tax implications of the proposed financing arrangement. After researching the issue, set forth your advice in a client letter. At a minimum, you should consult the following authorities:

- IRC Sec. 385
- *Rudolph A. Hardman*, 60 AFTR 2d 87-5651, 82-7 USTC ¶9523 (9th Cir., 1987)
- *Tomlinson v. The 1661 Corporation*, 19 AFTR 2d 1413, 67-1 USTC ¶9438 (5th Cir., 1967)

CHAPTER

THE CORPORATE INCOME TAX

LEARNING OBJECTIVES

After studying this chapter, you should be able to

1. ▶ Apply the requirements for selecting tax years and accounting methods to various types of C corporations

2. ▶ Compute a corporation's taxable income

3. ▶ Compute a corporation's income tax liability

4. ▶ Understand what a controlled group is and the tax consequences of being a controlled group

5. ▶ Understand how compensation planning can reduce taxes for corporations and their shareholders

6. ▶ Determine the requirements for paying corporate income taxes and filing a corporate tax return

A **corporation** is a separate taxpaying entity that must file a tax return every year even if it has no income or loss for the year. This chapter covers the tax rules for **domestic corporations** (i.e., corporations incorporated in one of the 50 states or under federal law) and other entities taxed as domestic corporations under the check-the-box rules.[1] It explains the rules for determining a corporation's taxable income, loss, and tax liability and for filing corporate tax returns. See Table C3-1 for the general formula for determining the corporate tax liability.

The corporations discussed in this chapter are sometimes referred to as regular or C corporations because Subchapter C of the Internal Revenue Code (IRC) dictates much of the tax treatment of these corporations. Corporations that have a special tax status include S corporations and affiliated groups of corporations that file consolidated returns. A comparison of the tax treatments of C corporations, S corporations, and partnerships appears in Appendix F.

CORPORATE ELECTIONS

OBJECTIVE 1

Apply the requirements for selecting tax years and accounting methods to various types of C corporations

Once formed, a corporation must make certain elections, such as selecting its **tax year** and its basic accounting method. The corporation makes these elections on its first tax return. They are important and should be considered carefully because, once made, they generally can be changed only with permission from the Internal Revenue Service (IRS).

CHOOSING A CALENDAR OR FISCAL YEAR

A new corporation may elect to use either a calendar year or a fiscal year as its accounting period. The corporation's tax year must be the same as the annual accounting period used for financial accounting purposes. The corporation makes the election by filing its first tax return for the selected period. A calendar year is a 12-month period ending on December 31. A fiscal year is a 12-month period ending on the last day of any month other than December. Examples of acceptable fiscal years are February 1, 2006, through January 31, 2007, and October 1, 2006, through September 30, 2007. A fiscal year that runs from September 16, 2006, through September 15, 2007 is not an acceptable tax year because it does not end on the last day of the month. The IRS will require a corporation using an unacceptable tax year to change to a calendar year.[2]

KEY POINT

Whereas partnerships and S corporations generally must adopt a calendar year, C corporations (other than personal service corporations) have the flexibility of adopting a fiscal year. The fiscal year must end on the last day of the month.

SHORT TAX PERIOD. A corporation's first tax year might not cover a full 12-month period. If, for example, a corporation begins business on March 10, 2006, and elects a fiscal year ending on September 30, its first tax year covers the period from March 10, 2006, through September 30, 2006. Its second tax year covers the period from October 1, 2006, through September 30, 2007. The corporation must file a **short-period tax return** for its first tax year.[3] From then on, its tax returns will cover a full 12-month period. The last year of a corporation's life, however, also may be a short period covering the period from the beginning of the last tax year through the date the corporation goes out of existence.

RESTRICTIONS ON ADOPTING A TAX YEAR. A corporation may be subject to restrictions in its choice of a tax year. An S corporation generally must use a calendar year (see Chapter C11). All members of an affiliated group filing a consolidated return must use the same tax year as the group's parent corporation (see Chapter C8).

A personal service corporation generally must use a calendar year as its tax year. This restriction prevents a personal service corporation with, for example, a January 31 year-end from distributing a large portion of its income earned during the February through December portion of 2006 to its calendar year shareholder-employees in January 2007, thereby deferring income largely earned in 2006 to 2007. For this purpose, the IRC

---

[1] Sec. 7701(a)(4). Corporations that are not classified as domestic are **foreign corporations**. Foreign corporations are taxed like domestic corporations if they conduct a trade or business in the United States.

[2] Sec. 441. Accounting periods of either 52 or 53 weeks that always end on the same day of the week (such as Friday) are also permitted under Sec. 441.

[3] Sec. 443(a)(2).

▼ **TABLE C3-1**

General Rules for Determining the Corporate Tax Liability

Income Tax	Alternative Minimum Tax (AMT)
Gross income Minus: Deductions and losses	
Taxable income before special deductions Minus: Special deductions	
Taxable income Times: Corporate tax rates	Taxable income before NOL deduction Plus or minus: Adjustments to taxable income Plus: Tax preference items Minus: Alternative tax NOL deduction
Regular tax liability Minus: Foreign tax credit and possessions tax credit	Alternative minimum taxable income Minus: Statutory exemption
Regular tax Minus: Other tax credits Plus: Recapture of previously claimed tax credits	Tax base Times: 20% tax rate
Income tax liability	Tentative minimum tax before credits Minus: AMT foreign tax credit
	Tentative minimum tax Minus: Regular (income) tax
	Alternative minimum tax liability (if greater than zero) (See Table C5-1)

Income (regular) tax liability
Plus: Alternative minimum tax liability
             Special taxes (if applicable):
                  Accumulated earnings tax
                  Personal holding company tax
Minus: Estimated tax payments

Net tax liability (or refund due)

defines a **personal service corporation** (PSC) as one whose principal activity is the performance of personal services by its employee-owners who own more than 10% of the stock (by value) on any day of the year.[4]

A PSC, however, may adopt a fiscal tax year if it can establish a business purpose for such a year. For example, it may be able to establish a natural business year and use that year as its tax year.[5] Deferral of income by shareholders is not an acceptable business purpose.

A PSC may elect to use certain fiscal years even when no business purpose exists.[6] Under this rule, a new PSC may elect to use a September 30, October 31, or November 30 year-end if it meets minimum distribution requirements to employee-owners during the deferral period. If it fails to meet these distribution requirements, the PSC's deduction for amounts paid to employee-owners may have to be deferred to the corporation's next fiscal year.[7]

---

[4] Sec. 441(i).
[5] The natural business year rule requires that the year-end used for tax purposes coincide with the end of the taxpayer's peak business period. (See the partnership and S corporation chapters and Rev. Proc. 2002-38, 2002-1 C.B. 1038, for a further explanation of this exception.)

[6] Sec. 444.
[7] Sec. 280H.

EXAMPLE C3-1 ▶ Alice and Bob form Cole Corporation with each shareholder owning 50% of its stock. Alice and Bob use the calendar year as their tax year. Alice and Bob are both active in the business and are the corporation's primary employees. The new corporation performs engineering services for the automotive industry. Cole Corporation must use a calendar year as its tax year unless it qualifies for a fiscal year based on a business purpose exception. Alternatively, it may adopt a fiscal year ending on September 30, October 31, or November 30, provided it complies with certain minimum distribution requirements. ◀

CHANGING THE ANNUAL ACCOUNTING PERIOD. A corporation that desires to change its annual accounting period must obtain the prior approval of the IRS unless Treasury Regulations specifically authorized the change or IRS procedures allow an automatic change. A change in accounting period usually results in a short period running from the end of the old annual accounting period to the beginning of the new accounting period. A request for approval of an accounting period change must be filed on Form 1128 (Application for Change in Annual Accounting Period) on or before the fifteenth day of the third calendar month following the close of the short period. The IRS usually will approve a request for change if a substantial business purpose exists for the change, and the taxpayer agrees to the IRS's prescribed terms, conditions, and adjustments necessary to prevent any substantial distortion of income. A substantial distortion of income includes, for example, a change that causes the "deferral of a substantial portion of the taxpayer's income, or shifting of a substantial portion of deductions, from one taxable year to another."[8]

Under IRS administrative procedures, a corporation may change its annual accounting period without prior IRS approval if it meets the following conditions:

▶ The corporation files a short-period tax return for the year of change and annualizes its income when computing its tax for the short period.

▶ The corporation files full 12-month returns for subsequent years ending on the new year-end.

▶ The corporation closes its books as of the last day of the short-period and subsequently computes its income and keeps its books using the new tax year.

▶ If the corporation generates an NOL or capital loss in the short period, it may not carry back the losses but must carry them over to future years.

▶ The corporation must not have changed its accounting period within the previous 48 months (with some exceptions).

▶ The corporation must not have an interest in a flow-through entity as of the end of the short period (with some exceptions).

▶ The corporation is not an S corporation, personal service corporation, tax-exempt organization, or other specialized corporation (however, see footnote 9 below).[9]

ACCOUNTING METHODS

BOOK-TO-TAX ACCOUNTING COMPARISON

Treasury Regulations literally require taxpayers to use the same overall accounting method for book and tax purposes. However, the courts have allowed different methods if the taxpayer maintains adequate reconciling workpapers. The IRS has adopted the courts' position on this issue.

A new corporation must select the overall **accounting method** it will use to keep its books and records for tax purposes. The method chosen must be indicated on the corporation's initial return. The three possible accounting methods are: accrual, cash, and hybrid.[10]

ACCRUAL METHOD. Under the accrual method, a corporation reports income when it has been earned and reports expenses when they have been incurred. A corporation must use this method unless it qualifies under one of the following exceptions:

▶ A qualified family farming corporation.[11]

[8] Reg. Sec. 1.442-1(b)(3). Also see Rev. Proc. 2002-39, 2002-1 C.B. 1046.
[9] Rev. Proc. 2002-37, 2002-1 C.B. 1030. For automatic change procedures for S corporations and personal service corporations, see Rev. Proc. 2002-38, 2002-1 C.B. 1037.
[10] Sec. 446.

[11] Sec. 448. Certain family farming corporations having gross receipts of less than $25 million may use the cash method of accounting. Section 447 requires farming corporations with gross receipts over $25 million to use the accrual method of accounting.

► A qualified personal service corporation, which is a corporation substantially all of whose activities involve the performance of services in the fields of health, law, engineering, architecture, accounting, actuarial science, performing arts, or consulting; and substantially all of whose stock is held by current (or retired) employees performing the services listed above, their estates, or (for two years only) persons who inherited their stock from such employees.[12]

► Corporations that meet a $5 million gross receipts test for all prior tax years beginning after December 31, 1985. A corporation meets this test for any prior tax year if its average gross receipts for the three-year period ending with that prior tax year do not exceed $5 million. If the corporation was not in existence for the entire three-year period, the period during which the corporation *was* in existence may be used.

► S corporations.

If a corporation meets one of the exceptions listed above, it may use either the accrual method or one of the following two methods.

ADDITIONAL COMMENT

Whereas partnerships and S corporations are generally allowed to be cash method taxpayers, most C corporations must use the accrual method of accounting. This restriction can prove inconvenient for many small corporations (with more than $5 million of gross receipts) that would rather use the less complicated cash method of accounting.

CASH METHOD. Under the cash method, a corporation reports income when it is actually or constructively received and reports expenses when they are paid. Corporations in service industries such as engineering, medicine, law, and accounting generally use this method because they do not want to report their income until they actually receive payment. This method may not be used if inventories are a material income-producing factor. In such case, the corporation must use either the *accrual* method or the *hybrid* method of accounting.

HYBRID METHOD. Under the hybrid method, a corporation uses the accrual method of accounting for sales, cost of goods sold, inventories, accounts receivable, and accounts payable, and the cash method of accounting for all other income and expense items. Small businesses with inventories (e.g., retail stores) often use this method. Although they must use the accrual method of accounting for sales-related income and expense items, they often find the cash method less burdensome to use for other income and expense items, such as utilities, rents, salaries, and taxes.

GENERAL FORMULA FOR DETERMINING THE CORPORATE TAX LIABILITY

Each year, C corporations must determine their corporate income (or regular) tax liability. In addition to the income tax, a C corporation may owe the corporate alternative minimum tax and possibly either the accumulated earnings tax or the personal holding company tax. A corporation's total tax liability equals the sum of its regular income tax liability plus the amount of any additional tax levy that it owes.

This chapter explains how to compute a corporation's income (or regular) tax liability. Chapter C5 explains the computation of the corporate alternative minimum tax, personal holding company tax, and accumulated earnings tax.

---

[12] The personal service corporation definition for the tax year election [Sec. 441(i)] is different from the personal service corporation definition for the cash accounting method election [Sec. 448].

COMPUTING A CORPORATION'S TAXABLE INCOME

OBJECTIVE 2

Compute a corporation's taxable income

Like an individual, a corporation is a taxpaying entity with gross income and deductions. However, a number of differences arise between individual and corporate taxation as summarized in Figure C3-1. This section of the text expands on some of these items and discusses other tax aspects particular to corporations.

SALES AND EXCHANGES OF PROPERTY

Sales and exchanges of property generally are treated the same way for corporations as they are for an individual. However, special rules apply to capital gains and losses, and corporations are subject to an additional 20% depreciation recapture rule under Sec. 291 on sales of Sec. 1250 property.

Common Book - Tax Differences
O = more difficult

1. **Gross income:** Generally, the same gross income definition applies to individuals and corporations. Certain exclusions are available to individuals but not to corporations (e.g, fringe benefits); other exclusions are available to corporations but not to individuals (e.g., capital contributions).
2. **Deductions:** Individuals have above-the-line deductions (*for* AGI), itemized deductions (*from* AGI), and personal exemptions. Corporations do not compute AGI, and their deductions are presumed to be ordinary and necessary business expenses.
3. **Charitable contributions:** (a) Individuals are limited to 50% of AGI (30% for capital gain property). Corporations are limited to 10% of taxable income computed without regard to the dividends-received deductions, the U.S. production activities deduction, NOL and capital loss carrybacks, and the contribution deduction itself. (b) Individuals deduct a contribution only in the year they pay it. Accrual basis corporations may deduct contributions in the year of accrual if the board of directors authorizes the contribution by the end of the tax year, and the corporation pays it by the fifteenth day of the third month of the next year.
4. **Depreciation on Sec. 1250 property:** Individuals generally do not recapture depreciation under the MACRS rules because straight-line depreciation applies to real property. Corporations must recapture 20% of the excess of the amount that would be recaptured under Sec. 1245. Individuals are subject to a 25% tax rate on Sec. 1250 gains. Corporations are not subject to this rate.
5. **Net capital gains:** Individuals usually are taxed at a maximum rate of 15% (however, 5%, 25%, and 28% apply in special cases). Corporate capital gains are taxed at the regular corporate tax rates without any special rate ceiling.
6. **Capital losses:** Individuals can deduct $3,000 of net capital losses to offset ordinary income. Individual capital losses carry over indefinitely. Corporations cannot offset any ordinary income with capital losses. However, capital losses carry back three years and forward five years and offset capital gains in those years.
7. **Dividends-received deduction:** Not available for individuals. Corporations receive a 70%, 80%, or 100% special deduction depending on the percentage of stock ownership.
8. **NOLs:** Individuals must make many adjustments to arrive at the NOL they are allowed to carry back or forward. A corporation's NOL is simply the excess of its deductions over its income for the year. The NOL carries back two years and forward 20 years, or the corporation can elect to forgo the carryback and only carry the NOL forward.
9. For individuals, the U.S. production activities deduction is based on the lesser of qualified production activities income or AGI. For corporations, the deduction is based on the lesser of qualified production activities income or taxable income.
10. **Tax rates:** Individual's tax rates range from 10% to 35% (in 2006). Corporate tax rates range from 15% to 39%.
11. **AMT:** Individual AMT rates are 26% or 28%. The corporate AMT rate is 20%. Corporations are subject to a special AMTI adjustment called the adjusted current earnings (ACE) adjustment that does not apply to individuals.
12. **Passive Losses:** Passive loss rules apply to individuals, partners, S corporation shareholders, closely held C corporations, and PSCs. They do not apply to widely held C corporations.
13. **Casualty losses:** Casualty losses are deductible in full by a corporation because all corporate casualty losses are considered to be business related. Moreover, they are not reduced by a $100 offset, nor are they restricted to losses exceeding 10% of AGI, as are an individual's nonbusiness casualty losses.

FIGURE C3-1 ▶ DIFFERENCES BETWEEN INDIVIDUAL AND CORPORATE TAXATION

CAPITAL GAINS AND LOSSES. A corporation has a capital gain or loss if it sells or exchanges a capital asset. As with individuals, a corporation must net all of its capital gains and losses to obtain its net capital gain or loss position.

Net Capital Gain. A corporation includes all its net capital gains (net long-term capital gains in excess of net short-term capital losses) for the tax year in gross income. Unlike with individuals, a corporation's capital gains receive no special tax treatment and are taxed in the same manner as any other ordinary income item.

EXAMPLE C3-2 ▶ Beta Corporation has a net capital gain of $40,000, gross profits on sales of $110,000, and deductible expenses of $28,000. Beta's gross income is $150,000 ($40,000 + $110,000). Its taxable income is $122,000 ($150,000 − $28,000). The $40,000 of net capital gain receives no special treatment and is taxed using the regular corporate tax rates described below. ◀

Net Capital Losses. If a corporation incurs a net capital loss, it cannot deduct the loss in the current year. A corporation's capital losses can offset only capital gains. They never can offset the corporation's ordinary income.

A corporation must carry back a net capital loss as a short-term capital loss to the three previous tax years and offset capital gains in the earliest year possible (i.e., the losses carry back to the third previous year first). If the loss is not totally absorbed as a carryback, the remainder carries over as a short-term capital loss for five years. Any unused losses remaining at the end of the carryover period expire.

EXAMPLE C3-3 ▶

SELF-STUDY QUESTION

How does the use of a net capital loss differ for individual and corporate taxpayers?

ANSWER

Individuals and corporations treat net capital losses differently. Individuals may use up to $3,000 per year of net capital losses to offset ordinary income. They cannot carry back net capital losses but can carry over net capital losses indefinitely. In contrast, corporations may not use any net capital losses to offset ordinary income, can carry net capital losses back three years, and can carry over net capital losses for only five years.

In 2006, East Corporation reports gross profits of $150,000, deductible expenses of $28,000, and a net capital loss of $10,000. East reported the following capital gain net income (excess of gains from sales or exchanges of capital assets over losses from such sales or exchanges) during 2003 through 2005:

Year	Capital Gain Net Income
2003	$6,000
2004	–0–
2005	3,000

East has gross income of $150,000 and taxable income of $122,000 ($150,000 − $28,000) for 2006. East also has a $10,000 net capital loss that carries back to 2003 first and offsets the $6,000 capital gain net income reported in that year. East receives a refund for the taxes paid on the $6,000 of capital gains in 2003. The $4,000 ($10,000 − $6,000) remainder of the loss carryback carries to 2005 and offsets East's $3,000 capital gain net income reported in that year. East still has a $1,000 net capital loss to carry over to 2007. ◀

SEC. 291: TAX BENEFIT RECAPTURE RULE. If a taxpayer sells Sec. 1250 property at a gain, Sec. 1250 requires that the taxpayer report the recognized gain as ordinary income to the extent the depreciation taken exceeds the depreciation that would have been allowed if the straight-line method had been used. This ordinary income is known as Sec. 1250 depreciation recapture. For individuals, any remaining gain is characterized as a combination of Sec. 1250 gain and Sec. 1231 gain. However, corporations must recapture as ordinary income an additional amount equal to 20% of the additional ordinary income that would have been recognized had the property been Sec. 1245 property instead of Sec. 1250 property.

EXAMPLE C3-4 ▶ Texas Corporation purchased residential real estate in January 2004 for $125,000, of which $25,000 was allocated to the land and $100,000 to the building. Texas took straight-line MACRS depreciation deductions of $10,606 on the building in the years 2004 through 2006. In December 2006, Texas sells the property for $155,000, of which $45,000 is allocated to the land and $110,000 to the building. Texas has a $20,000 ($45,000 − $25,000) gain on the land sale, all of which is Sec. 1231 gain. This gain is not affected by Sec. 291 because land is not Sec. 1250 property. Texas has a $20,606 [$110,000 sales price − ($100,000 original cost − $10,606 depreciation)] gain on the sale of the building. If Texas were an individual taxpayer, $10,606 would be a Sec. 1250 gain subject to a 25% tax rate, and the remaining $10,000 would be a Sec. 1231 gain. However, a corporate taxpayer reports $2,121 of gain as ordinary income. These amounts are summarized below:

	Land	Building	Total
Amount of gain:			
Sales price	$45,000	$110,000	$155,000
Minus: adjusted basis	(25,000)	(89,394)	(114,394)
Recognized gain	$20,000	$ 20,606	$ 40,606
Character of gain:			
Ordinary income	$ -0-	$ 2,121[a]	$ 2,121
Sec. 1231 gain	20,000	18,485	38,485
Recognized gain	$20,000	$ 20,606	$ 40,606

[a]0.20 × lesser of $10,606 depreciation claimed or $20,606 recognized gain.   ◀

BUSINESS EXPENSES

Corporations may deduct most of the same type of business expenses that a sole proprietor may deduct on Schedule C (or Schedule C-EZ) of an individual return. Deductions are allowed for ordinary and necessary business expenses, including salaries paid to officers and other employees of the corporation, rent, repairs, insurance premiums, advertising, interest, taxes, losses on sales of inventory or other property, bad debts, and depreciation.[13]

No deductions are allowed for interest on amounts borrowed to purchase tax-exempt securities, illegal bribes or kickbacks, fines or penalties imposed by a government, or insurance premiums incurred to insure the lives of officers and employees when the corporation is the beneficiary.

ORGANIZATIONAL EXPENDITURES. When formed, a corporation may incur some organizational expenditures such as legal fees and accounting fees incident to the incorporation process. These expenditures must be capitalized. Unless the corporation makes an election under Sec. 248, however, it cannot amortize these expenditures because they have an unlimited life. A Sec. 248 election allows a corporation to deduct the first $5,000 of organizational expenditures. However, the corporation must reduce the $5,000 by the amount by which cumulative organizational expenditures exceed $50,000 although the $5,000 cannot be reduced below zero. The corporation can amortize the remaining organizational expenditures over a 180-month period beginning in the month it begins business.

EXAMPLE C3-5 ▶   Sigma Corporation incorporates on January 10 of the current year, and begins business on March 3. Sigma elects a September 30 year-end. Thus, it conducts business for seven months during its first tax year. During the period January 10 through September 30, Sigma incurs

WHAT WOULD YOU DO IN THIS SITUATION?

You are a CPA with a medium-size accounting firm. One of your corporate clients is an electrical contractor in New York City. The client is successful and had $10 million of sales last year. The contracts involve private and government electrical work. Among the corporation's expenses are $400,000 of kickbacks paid to people working for general contractors who award electrical subcontracts to the corporation, and $100,000 of payments made to individuals in the electricians' union. Technically, these payments are illegal. However, your client says that everyone in this business needs to pay kickbacks to obtain contracts and to have enough electricians to finish the projects in a timely manner. He maintains that it is impossible to stay in business without making these payments. In preparing its tax return, your client wants you to deduct these expenses. What is your option concerning the client's request?

---

[13] Sec. 162.

$52,000 of organizational expenditures. Because these expenditures exceed $50,000, Sigma must reduce the first $5,000 by $2,000 ($52,000 − $50,000), leaving $3,000. Sigma amortizes the remaining $49,000 ($52,000 − $3,000) over 180 months beginning in March of its first year. This portion of the deduction equals $1,906 ($49,000/180 × 7 months). Accordingly, its total first-year deduction is $4,906 ($3,000 + $1,906). ◀

This rule applies to organizational expenditures incurred after October 22, 2004. Prior to October 23, 2004, a corporation was not allowed an initial deduction but had to amortize its organizational expenditures over a period of at least 60 months beginning in the month it began business.

The corporation makes the Sec. 248 amortization election in a statement attached to its first tax return filed no later than the due date of the tax return (including permitted extensions). If the corporation does not make an amortization election, it cannot deduct organizational expenditures until the corporation liquidates.

The election applies only to expenditures incurred before the end of the tax year in which the corporation begins business regardless of whether the corporation uses the cash or accrual method of accounting. A corporation begins business when it starts the business operations for which it was organized. Expenditures incurred after the first tax year has ended (e.g., legal expenses incurred to modify the corporate charter) must be capitalized and cannot be deducted until the corporation liquidates.[14]

Organizational expenditures include expenditures incident to the corporation's creation; chargeable to the corporation's capital account; and of a character that, if expended incident to the creation of a corporation having a limited life, would be amortizable over that life.

Specific organizational expenditures include

▶ Legal services incident to the corporation's organization (e.g., drafting the corporate charter and bylaws, minutes of organizational meetings, and terms of original stock certificates)

▶ Accounting services necessary to create the corporation

▶ Expenses of temporary directors and of organizational meetings of directors and stockholders

▶ Fees paid to the state of incorporation.[15]

Organizational expenditures do not include expenditures connected with issuing or selling the corporation's stock or other securities (e.g., commissions, professional fees, and printing costs) and expenditures related to the transfer of assets to the corporation.

EXAMPLE C3-6 ▶ Omega Corporation incorporates on July 12 of the current year, starts business operations on August 10, and elects a tax year ending on September 30. Omega incurs the following expenditures during the current year while organizing the corporation:

Date	Type of Expenditure	Amount
June 10	Legal expenses to draft charter	$ 2,000
July 17	Commission to stockbroker for issuing and selling stock	40,000
July 18	Accounting fees to set up corporate books	2,400
July 20	Temporary directors' fees	1,000
August 25	Directors' fees	1,500
October 9	Legal fees to modify corporate charter	1,000

Omega's first tax year begins July 12 and ends on September 30. Omega has organizational expenditures of $5,400. The legal expenses to modify the corporate charter do not qualify because Omega did not incur them during the tax year in which it began its business operations. The commission for selling the Omega stock is treated as a reduction in the amount of Omega's paid-in capital. Omega deducts the directors' fees incurred in August as a trade or business expense under Sec. 162 because Omega had begun business operations by that date. If Omega elects to amortize its organizational expenditures, it can deduct $5,000 in its first tax

---

[14] Reg. Sec. 1.248-1(a).

[15] Reg. Sec. 1.248-1(b)(2).

year and amortize the remaining $400 over 180 months. Thus, its first year deduction is $5,004 [$5,000 + ($400/180) × 2 months].

The following table summarizes the classification of expenditures:

| | | | | Type of Expenditure | |
Date	Expenditure	Amount	Organizational	Capital	Business
6/10	Legal	$ 2,000	$2,000		
7/17	Commission	40,000		$40,000	
7/18	Accounting	2,400	2,400		
7/20	Directors' fees	1,000	1,000		
8/25	Directors' fees	1,500			$1,500
10/9	Legal	1,000		1,000	
	Total	$47,900	$5,400	$41,000	$1,500 ◄

If a corporation discontinues or disposes of its business before the end of the amortization period, it may deduct any remaining organizational expenditures as a loss.

START-UP EXPENDITURES. A distinction must be made between a corporation's organizational expenditures and its start-up expenditures. Start-up expenditures are ordinary and necessary business expenses paid or incurred by an individual or corporate taxpayer

▶ To investigate the creation or acquisition of an active trade or business

▶ To create an active trade or business

▶ To conduct an activity engaged in for profit or the production of income before the time the activity becomes an active trade or business

Examples of start-up expenditures include the costs for a survey of potential markets; an analysis of available facilities; advertisements relating to opening the business; the training of employees; travel and other expenses for securing prospective distributors, suppliers, or customers; and the hiring of management personnel and outside consultants.

The expenditures must be such that, if incurred in connection with the operation of an existing active trade or business, they would be allowable as a deduction for the year in which they are paid or incurred. However, under Sec. 195, they must be capitalized.

Under Sec. 195, a corporation may elect to deduct the first $5,000 of start-up expenditures. However, this amount is reduced (but not below zero) by the amount by which the cumulative start-up expenditures exceed $50,000. The corporation can amortize the remaining start-up expenditures over a 180-month period beginning in the month it begins business. This rule applies to start-up expenditures incurred after October 22, 2004.

Prior to October 23, 2004, a corporation could not deduct start-up expenditures currently but had to amortize them over a period of at least 60 months starting with the month in which its business began.

If the corporation makes no election, it must capitalize start-up expenditures and cannot deduct them until the corporation liquidates. If the corporation discontinues or disposes of the business before the end of the amortization period, it may deduct any remaining start-up expenditures as a loss.

STOP & THINK

Question: What is the difference between an organizational expenditure and a start-up expenditure?

Solution: Organizational expenditures are outlays made in forming a corporation, such as fees paid to the state of incorporation for the corporate chapter and fees paid to an attorney to draft the documents needed to form the corporation. Start-up expenditures are outlays that otherwise would be deductible as ordinary and necessary business expenses but that are capitalized because they were incurred prior to the start of the corporation's business activities.

A corporation may elect to deduct the first $5,000 of organizational expenditures and the first $5,000 of start-up expenditures. The corporation can amortize the remainder of each set of expenditures over 180 months. Like a corporation, a partnership can deduct and amortize its organizational and start-up expenditures. A sole proprietorship may incur start-up expenditures, but sole proprietorships do not incur organizational expenditures.

LIMITATION ON DEDUCTIONS FOR ACCRUED COMPENSATION. If a corporation accrues an obligation to pay compensation, the corporation must make the payment within 2½ months after the close of its tax year. Otherwise, the deduction cannot be taken until the year of payment.[16] The reason is that, if a payment is delayed beyond 2½ months, the IRS treats it as a deferred compensation plan. Deferred compensation cannot be deducted until the year the corporation pays it and the recipient includes the payment in income.[17]

EXAMPLE C3-7 ▶ On December 10, 2006, Bell Corporation (a calendar year taxpayer) accrues an obligation for a $100,000 bonus to Marge, a sales representative who has had an outstanding year. Marge owns no Bell stock. Bell must make the payment by March 15, 2006. Otherwise, Bell Corporation cannot deduct the $100,000 in its 2006 tax return but must wait until the year it pays the bonus. ◀

CHARITABLE CONTRIBUTIONS. The treatment of charitable contributions by individual and corporate taxpayers differs in three ways: the timing of the deduction, the amount of the deduction permitted for the contribution of certain nonmoney property, and the maximum deduction permitted in any given year.

Timing of the Deduction. Corporations may deduct contributions to qualified charitable organizations. Generally, the contribution must have been *paid* during the year (not just pledged) for a deduction to be allowed for a given year. A special rule, however, applies to corporations using the accrual method of accounting (corporations using the cash or hybrid methods of accounting are not eligible).[18] These corporations may elect to treat part or all of a charitable contribution as having been made in the year it accrued (instead of the year paid) if

▶ The board of directors authorizes the contribution in the year it accrued

▶ The corporation pays the contribution on or before the fifteenth day of the third month following the end of the accrual year.

The corporation makes the election by deducting the contribution in its tax return for the accrual year and by attaching a copy of the board of director's resolution to the return. Any portion of the contribution for which the corporation does not make the election is deducted in the year paid.

EXAMPLE C3-8 ▶ Echo Corporation is a calendar year taxpayer using the accrual method of accounting. In 2006, its board of directors authorizes a $10,000 contribution to the Girl Scouts. Echo pays the contribution on March 10, 2007. Echo may elect to treat part or all of the contribution as having been paid in 2006. If the corporation pays the contribution after March 15, 2007, it may not deduct the contribution in 2006 but may deduct it in 2007. ◀

Deducting Contributions of Nonmonetary Property. If a taxpayer donates money to a qualified charitable organization, the amount of the charitable contribution deduction equals the amount of money donated. If the taxpayer donates property, the amount of the charitable contribution deduction generally equals the property's fair market value (FMV). However, special rules apply to donations of appreciated nonmonetary property known as ordinary income property and capital gain property.[19]

In this context, **ordinary income property** is property whose sale would have resulted in a gain other than a long-term capital gain (i.e., ordinary income or short-term capital gain). Examples of ordinary income property include investment property held for one

---

[16] Temp. Reg. Sec. 1.404(b)-1T.
[17] Sec. 404(b).

[18] Sec. 170(a).
[19] Sec. 170(e).

year or less, inventory property, and property subject to depreciation recapture under Secs. 1245 and 1250. The deduction allowed for a donation of such property is limited to the property's FMV minus the amount of ordinary income or short-term capital gain the corporation would have recognized had it sold the property.

In three special cases, a corporation may deduct the donated property's adjusted basis plus one-half of the excess of the property's FMV over its adjusted basis (not to exceed twice the property's adjusted basis). This special rule applies to inventory if

1. The use of the property is related to the donee's exempt function, and it is used solely for the care of the ill, the needy, or infants;
2. The property is not transferred to the donee in exchange for money, other property, or services; and
3. The donor receives a statement from the charitable organization stating that conditions (1) and (2) will be complied with.

A similar rule applies to contributions of scientific research property if the corporation created the property and contributed it to a college, university, or tax-exempt scientific research organization for its use within two years of creating the property.

EXAMPLE C3-9 ▶ King Corporation donates inventory having a $26,000 adjusted basis and a $40,000 FMV to a qualified public charity. A $33,000 [$26,000 + (0.50 × $14,000)] deduction is allowed for the contribution of the inventory if the charitable organization will use the inventory for the care of the ill, needy, or infants, or if the donee is an educational institution or research organization that will use the scientific research property for research or experimentation. Otherwise, the deduction is limited to the property's $26,000 adjusted basis. If instead the inventory's FMV is $100,000 and the donation meets either of the two sets of requirements outlined above, the charitable contribution deduction is limited to $52,000, the lesser of the property's adjusted basis plus one-half of the appreciation [$63,000 = $26,000 + (0.50 × $74,000)] or twice the property's adjusted basis ($52,000 = $26,000 × 2). ◀

When a corporation donates appreciated property whose sale would result in long-term capital gain (also known as **capital gain property**) to a charitable organization, the amount of the contribution deduction generally equals the property's FMV. However, special restrictions apply if

▶ The corporation donates a patent, copyright, trademark, trade name, trade secret, know-how, certain software, or other similar property;

▶ A corporation donates tangible personal property to a charitable organization and the organization's use of the property is unrelated to its tax-exempt purpose; or

▶ A corporation donates appreciated property to certain private nonoperating foundations.[20]

In these cases, the amount of the corporation's contribution is limited to the property's FMV minus the long-term capital gain that would have resulted from the property's sale.

EXAMPLE C3-10 ▶ Fox Corporation donates artwork to the MacNay Museum. The artwork, purchased two years earlier for $15,000, is worth $38,000 on the date of the donation. At the time of the donation, the museum's directors intend to sell the work to raise funds to conduct museum activities. Fox's deduction for the gift is limited to $15,000. If the museum plans to display the artwork to the public, the entire $38,000 deduction is permitted. Fox Corporation can avoid the loss of a portion of its charitable contribution deduction by placing restrictions on the sale or use of the property at the time it is donated. ◀

Substantiation Requirements. The 2004 Jobs Act added Sec. 170(f)(11), which imposes substantiation requirements for non-cash charitable contributions. If the corporation does not comply, it will lose the charitable contribution deduction. The requirements are as follows:

---

[20] Sec. 170(e)(5). The restriction on contributions of appreciated property to private nonoperating foundations does not apply to contributions of stock for which market quotations are readily available.

▶ If the contribution deduction exceeds $500, the corporation must include with its tax return a description of the property and any other information required by Treasury Regulations.

▶ If the contribution deduction exceeds $5,000, the corporation must obtain a qualified appraisal and include with its tax return any information and appraisal required by Treasury Regulations. (Current regulations require an appraisal summary.)

▶ If the contribution deduction exceeds $500,000, the corporation must attach a qualified appraisal to the tax return.

The second and third requirements, however, do not apply to contributions of cash; publicly traded securities; inventory; or certain motor vehicles, boats, or aircraft the donee organization sells without any intervening use or material improvement. With regard to these vehicles, the donor corporation's deduction is limited to the amount of gross proceeds the donee organization receives on the sale.

BOOK-TO-TAX ACCOUNTING COMPARISON

For financial accounting purposes, all charitable contributions can be claimed as an expense without regard to the amount of profits reported. Only the tax deduction for charitable contributions is limited.

Maximum Deduction Permitted. A limit applies to the amount of charitable contributions a corporation can deduct in a given year. The limit is calculated differently for corporations than for individuals. Contribution deductions by corporations are limited to 10% of adjusted taxable income. Adjusted taxable income is the corporation's taxable income computed without regard to any of the following amounts:

▶ The charitable contribution deduction

▶ An NOL carryback

▶ A capital loss carryback

▶ The dividends-received deduction[21]

▶ The U.S. production activities deduction

Contributions that exceed the 10% limit are not deductible in the current year. Instead, they carry forward to the next five tax years. Any excess contributions not deducted within those five years expire. The corporation may deduct excess contributions in the carryover year only after it deducts any contributions made in that year. The total charitable contribution deduction (including any deduction for contribution carryovers) is limited to 10% of the corporation's adjusted taxable income in the carryover year.[22]

EXAMPLE C3-11 ▶ Golf Corporation reports the following results in 2006 and 2007:

	2006	*2007*
Adjusted taxable income	$200,000	$300,000
Charitable contributions	35,000	25,000

Golf's 2006 contribution deduction is limited to $20,000 (0.10 × $200,000). Golf has a $15,000 ($35,000 − $20,000) contribution carryover to 2007. The 2007 contribution deduction is limited to $30,000 (0.10 × $300,000). Golf's deduction for 2007 is composed of the $25,000 donated in 2007 and $5,000 of the 2006 carryover. The remaining $10,000 carryover from 2006 carries over to 2008, 2009, 2010, and 2011. ◀

Topic Review C3-1 summarizes the basic corporate charitable contribution deduction rules.

SPECIAL DEDUCTIONS

C corporations are allowed three special deductions: the U.S. production activities deduction, the dividends-received deduction, and the NOL deduction.

U.S. PRODUCTION ACTIVITIES DEDUCTION. The 2004 Jobs Acts added Sec. 199, effective for tax years beginning after 2004. This IRC section allows a **U.S. production activities deduction** equal to a percentage times the lesser of (1) qualified production

---

[21] Sec. 170(b)(2).   [22] Sec. 170(d)(2).

Topic Review C3-1

Corporate Charitable Contribution Rules

1. Timing of the contribution deduction
   a. General rule: A deduction is allowed for contributions paid during the year.
   b. Accrual method of accounting corporations can accrue contributions approved by their board of directors prior to the end of the accrual year and paid within 2½ months of the end of the accrual year.
2. Amount of the contribution deduction
   a. General rule: A deduction is allowed for the amount of money and the FMV of other property donated.
   b. Exceptions for ordinary income property:
      1. If donated property would result in ordinary income or short-term capital gain being recognized if sold, the deduction is limited to the property's FMV minus this potential ordinary income or short-term capital gain. Thus, for gain property the deduction equals the property's cost or adjusted basis.
      2. Special rule: For donations of (1) inventory used for the care of the ill, needy, or infants or (2) scientific research property or computer technology and equipment to certain educational institutions, a corporate donor may deduct the property's basis plus one-half of the excess of the property's FMV over its adjusted basis. The deduction may not exceed twice the property's adjusted basis.
   c. Exceptions for capital gain property: If the corporation donates tangible personal property to a charitable organization for a use unrelated to its tax-exempt purpose, or the corporation donates appreciated property to a private nonoperating foundation, the corporation's contribution is limited to the property's FMV minus the long-term capital gain that would result if the property were sold.
3. Limitation on contribution deduction
   a. The contribution deduction is limited to 10% of the corporation's taxable income computed without regard to the charitable contribution deduction, any NOL or capital loss carryback, the dividends-received deduction, and the U.S production activities deduction.
   b. Excess contributions carry forward for a five-year period.

ADDITIONAL COMMENT

The IRS has issued detailed interim guidance on the U.S. production activities deduction in Notice 2005-14 I.R.B. 2005-7 and in Proposed Regulations under Sec. 199. Also, while discussed in this text under special deductions, the U.S. production activities deduction actually appears before Line 28 on Form 1120.

activities income for the year or (2) taxable income before the U.S. production activities deduction. The phased-in percentages are as follows:

2005, 2006	3%
2007, 2008, 2009	6%
2010 and thereafter	9%

The deduction, however, cannot exceed 50% of the corporation's W-2 wages for the year.

Qualified production activities income is the taxpayer's domestic production gross receipts less the following amounts:

▶ Cost of goods sold allocable to these receipts;

▶ Other deductions, expenses, and losses directly allocable to these receipts; and

▶ A ratable portion of other deductions, expenses, and losses not directly allocable to these receipts or to other classes of income.

Domestic production gross receipts include receipts from the following taxpayer activities:

▶ The lease, rental, license, sale, exchange, or other disposition of (1) qualified production property (tangible property, computer software, and sound recordings) manufactured, produced, grown, or extracted in whole or significant part within the United States; (2) qualified film production; or (3) electricity, natural gas, or potable water produced within the United States

▶ Construction performed in the United States

▶ Engineering or architectural services performed in the United States for construction projects in the United States

ADDITIONAL COMMENT

In addition to providing a benefit, the U.S. production activities deduction will increase a corporation's compliance costs because of the time necessary to determine what income and deductions pertain to U.S. production activities.

Domestic production gross receipts, however, do not include receipts from the sale of food and beverages the taxpayer prepares at a retail establishment and do not apply to the transmission of electricity, natural gas, or potable water.

The U.S. production activities deduction has the effect of reducing a corporation's marginal tax rate on qualifying taxable income. For example, a 3% deduction (in 2005–2006) for a corporation in the 35% tax bracket produces about a 1% decrease in the corporation's marginal tax rate ($0.03 \times 35\% = 1.05\%$). Similarly, a 6% deduction (in 2007–2009) will decrease the marginal tax rate by about 2% ($0.06 \times 35\% = 2.1\%$), and a 9% deduction (after 2009) will decrease the marginal tax rate by about 3% ($0.09 \times 35\% = 3.15\%$).

EXAMPLE C3-12 ▶ In 2006, Gamma Corporation earns domestic production gross receipts of $1 million and incurs allocable expenses of $400,000. Thus, its qualified production activities income is $600,000. In addition, Gamma has $200,000 of income from other sources, resulting in taxable income of $800,000 before the U.S. production activities deduction. Its U.S. production activities deduction, therefore, is $18,000 ($600,000 × 0.03), and its taxable income is $782,000 ($800,000 − $18,000). ◀

EXAMPLE C3-13 ▶ Assume the same facts as in Example C3-12 except Gamma has $100,000 of losses from other sources rather than $200,000 of other income, resulting in taxable income of $500,000 before the U.S. production activities deduction. In this case, its U.S. production activities deduction is $15,000 ($500,000 × 0.03), and its taxable income is $485,000 ($500,000 − $15,000). ◀

BOOK-TO-TAX ACCOUNTING COMPARISON

A corporation includes dividends in its financial accounting income but does not subtract a dividends-received deduction in determining its net income. The dividends-received deduction is available only when calculating taxable income.

DIVIDENDS-RECEIVED DEDUCTION. A corporation must include in its gross income any dividends received on stock it owns in another corporation. As described in Chapter C2, the taxation of dividend payments to a shareholder generally results in double taxation. When a distributing corporation pays a dividend to a corporate shareholder and the recipient corporation subsequently distributes these earnings to its shareholders, triple taxation of the earnings potentially can result.

EXAMPLE C3-14 ▶ Adobe Corporation owns stock in Bell Corporation. Bell Corporation reports taxable income of $100,000 and pays federal income taxes on its income. Bell distributes its after-tax income to its shareholders. The dividend Adobe Corporation receives from Bell must be included in its gross income and, to the extent that it reports a profit for the year, Adobe will pay taxes on the dividend. Adobe Corporation distributes its remaining after-tax income to its shareholders. The shareholders must include Adobe's dividends in their gross income and pay federal income taxes on the distribution. Thus, Bell's income in this example is potentially taxed three times. ◀

To partially mitigate the effects of multiple taxation, corporations are allowed a **dividends-received deduction** for dividends received from other domestic corporations and from certain foreign corporations.

General Rule for Dividends-Received Deduction. Corporations that own less than 20% of the distributing corporation's stock may deduct 70% of the dividends received. If the shareholder corporation owns 20% or more of the distributing corporation's stock (both voting power and value) but less than 80% of such stock, it may deduct 80% of the dividends received.[23]

EXAMPLE C3-15 ▶ Hale Corporation reports the following results in the current year:

Gross income from operations	$300,000
Dividends from 15%-owned domestic corporation	100,000
Operating expenses	280,000

Gross income from operations and expenses both pertain to qualified production activities, so Hale's qualified production activities income is $20,000 ($300,000 − $280,000). Hale's dividends-received deduction is $70,000 (0.70 × $100,000). Thus, Hale's taxable income is computed as follows:

Gross income	$400,000
Minus: Operating expenses	(280,000)
Taxable income before special deductions	$120,000
Minus: Dividends-received deduction	(70,000)
Taxable income before the U.S. production activites deduction	$ 50,000
Minus: U.S. production activities deduction ($20,000 × 0.03)	(600)
Taxable income	$49,400 ◀

---

[23] Secs. 243(a) and (c).

Limitation on Dividends-Received Deduction. In the case of dividends received from corporations that are less than 20% owned, the deduction is limited to the lesser of 70% of dividends received or 70% of taxable income computed without regard to any NOL deduction, any capital loss carryback, the dividends-received deduction itself, or the U.S. production activities deduction.[24] In the case of dividends received from a 20% or more owned corporation, the dividends-received deduction is limited to the lesser of 80% of dividends received or 80% of taxable income computed without regard to the same deductions.

EXAMPLE C3-16 ▶ Assume the same facts as in Example C3-15 except Hale Corporation's operating expenses for the year are $310,000 and that qualified production activities income is zero (or negative). Thus, the corporation cannot claim the U.S. production activities deduction. Hale's taxable income before the dividends-received deduction is $90,000 ($300,000 + $100,000 − $310,000). The dividends-received deduction is limited to the lesser of 70% of dividends received ($70,000) or 70% of taxable income before the dividends-received deduction ($63,000 = $90,000 × 0.70). Thus, the dividends-received deduction is $63,000. Hale's taxable income is $27,000 ($90,000 − $63,000). ◀

A corporation that receives dividends eligible for both the 80% dividends-received deduction and the 70% dividends-received deduction must compute the 80% dividends-received deduction first and then reduce taxable income by the aggregate amount of dividends eligible for the 80% deduction before computing the 70% deduction.

EXAMPLE C3-17 ▶ Assume the same facts as in Example C3-16 except Hale Corporation receives $70,000 of the dividends from a 25%-owned corporation and the remaining $30,000 from a 15%-owned corporation. The tentative dividends-received deduction from the 25%-owned corporation is $56,000 ($70,000 × 0.80), which is less than the $72,000 ($90,000 × 0.80) limitation. Thus, Hale can deduct the entire $56,000. The tentative dividends-received deduction from the 15%-owned corporation is $21,000 ($30,000 × .70). The limitation, however, is $14,000 [($90,000 − $70,000) × 0.70]. Note that, in computing this limitation, Hale reduces its taxable income by the entire $70,000 dividend received from the 25%-owned corporation. Thus, Hale can deduct only $14,000 of the $21,000 amount. Hale's taxable income is $20,000 ($90,000 − $56,000 − $14,000). ◀

Exception to the Limitation. The taxable income limitation on the dividends-received deduction does not apply if, after taking into account the full dividends-received deduction, the corporation has an NOL for the year.

EXAMPLE C3-18 ▶ Assume the same facts as in Example C3-16 except Hale Corporation's operating expenses for the year are $331,000. Hale's taxable income before the dividends-received deduction is $69,000 ($300,000 + $100,000 − $331,000). The tentative dividends-received deduction is $70,000 (0.70 × $100,000). Hale's dividends-received deduction is not restricted by the limitation of 70% of taxable income before the dividends-received deduction because, after taking into account the tentative $70,000 dividends-received deduction, the corporation has a $1,000 ($69,000 − $70,000) NOL for the year. ◀

The following table compares the results of Examples C3-15, C3-16, and C3-18:

ADDITIONAL COMMENT

When the dividends-received deduction creates (or increases) an NOL, the corporation gets the full benefit of the deduction because it can carry back or carry forward the NOL.

	Example C3-15	Example C3-16	Example C3-18
Gross income	$400,000	$400,000	$400,000
Minus: Operating expenses	(280,000)	(310,000)	(331,000)
Taxable income before special deductions	$120,000	$ 90,000	$ 69,000
Minus: Dividends-received deduction	(70,000)	(63,000)	(70,000)
U.S. production activities deduction	(600)	–0–	–0–
Taxable income (NOL)	$ 49,400	$ 27,000	$ (1,000)

---
[24] Sec. 246(b).

Of these three examples, the only case where the dividends-received deduction does not equal the full 70% of the $100,000 dividend is Example C3-16. In that case, the deduction is limited to $63,000 because taxable income before special deductions is less than the $100,000 dividend *and* because the full $70,000 deduction would not create an NOL. The special exception to the dividends-received deduction can create interesting situations. For example, the additional $21,000 of deductions incurred in Example C3-18 (as compared to Example C3-16) resulted in a $28,000 reduction in taxable income. Corporate taxpayers should be aware of these rules and consider deferring income or recognizing expenses to ensure being able to deduct the full 70% or 80% dividends-received deduction. If the taxable income limitation applies, the corporation loses the unused dividends-received deduction.

Members of an Affilliated Group. Members of an affiliated group of corporations can claim a 100% dividends-received deduction with respect to dividends received from other group members.[25] A group of corporations is affiliated if a parent corporation owns at least 80% of the stock (both voting power and value) of at least one subsidiary corporation, and at least 80% of the stock (both voting power and value) of each other corporation is owned by other group members. The 100% dividends-received deduction is not subject to a taxable income limitation and is taken before the 80% or 70% dividends-received deduction.[26]

EXAMPLE C3-19 ▶

Hardy Corporation reports the following results for the current year:

Gross income from operations	$520,000
Dividend received from an 80%-owned affiliated corporation	100,000
Dividend received from a 20%-owned corporation	250,000
Operating expenses	550,000

Because Hardy's qualified production activities income is negative, it cannot claim the U.S. production activities deduction. Hardy's taxable income before any dividends-received deduction is $320,000 ($520,000 + $100,000 + $250,000 − $550,000). Hardy can deduct the entire dividend received from the 80%-owned affiliate without limitation. The tentative dividends-received deduction from the 20%-owned corporation is $200,000 ($250,000 × 0.80). The limitation, however, is $176,000 [($320,000 − $100,000) × 0.80]. Note that, in computing this limitation, Hardy first reduces its taxable income by the $100,000 dividend received from the 80%-owned affiliate. Thus, Hardy can deduct only $176,000 of the $200,000 amount. Hardy's taxable income is $44,000 ($320,000 − $100,000 − $176,000). ◀

Dividends Received from Foreign Corporations. The dividends-received deduction applies primarily to dividends received from domestic corporations. The dividends-received deduction does not apply to dividends received from a foreign corporation because the U.S. Government does not tax its income. Thus, that income is not subject to the multiple taxation illustrated above.[27]

Stock Held 45 Days or Less. A corporation may not claim a dividends-received deduction if it holds the dividend paying stock for less than 46 days during the 91-day period that begins 45 days before the stock becomes ex-dividend with respect to the dividend.[28] This rule prevents a corporation from claiming a dividends-received deduction if it purchases stock shortly before an ex-dividend date and sells the stock shortly thereafter. (The ex-dividend date is the first day on which a purchaser of stock is not entitled to a previously declared dividend.) Absent this rule, such a purchase and sale would allow the corporation to receive dividends at a low tax rate—a maximum of a 10.5% [(100% − 70%) × 0.35] effective tax rate—and to recognize a capital loss on the sale of stock that could offset capital gains taxed at a 35% tax rate.

EXAMPLE C3-20 ▶

Theta Corporation purchases 100 shares of Maine Corporation's stock for $100,000 one day before Maine's ex-dividend date. Theta receives a $5,000 dividend on the stock and then sells

[25] Sec. 243(a)(3).
[26] Secs. 243(b)(5) and 1504.
[27] Sec. 245. A limited dividends-received deduction is allowed on dividends received from a foreign corporation that earns income by conducting a trade or business in the United States and, therefore, is subject to U.S. taxes.
[28] Sec. 246(c)(1).

the stock for $95,000 on the forty-fifth day after the dividend payment date. Because the stock is worth $100,000 immediately before the $5,000 dividend payment, its value drops to $95,000 ($100,000 − $5,000) immediately after the dividend. The sale results in a $5,000 ($100,000 − $95,000) capital loss that may offset a $5,000 capital gain. The following table summarizes the profit (loss) to Theta with and without the 45-day rule.

	If Deduction Is Allowed	If Deduction Is Not Allowed
Dividends	$5,000	$5,000
Minus: 35% tax on dividend	(525)[a]	(1,750)
Dividend (after taxes)	$4,475	$3,250
Capital loss	$5,000	$5,000
Minus: 35% tax savings on loss	(1,750)	(1,750)
Net loss on stock	$3,250	$3,250
Dividend (after taxes)	$4,475	$3,250
Minus: Net loss on stock	(3,250)	(3,250)
Net profit (loss)	$1,225	$ −0−

[a][$5,000 − (0.70 × $5,000)] × 0.35 = $525

ADDITIONAL COMMENT

Borrowing money with deductible interest to purchase a tax-advantaged asset, such as stock eligible for the dividends-received deduction, is an example of "tax arbitrage." Many provisions in the IRC, such as the limits on debt-financial stock, are aimed at curtailing tax arbitrage transactions.

The profit is not available if Theta sells the stock shortly after receiving the dividend because Theta must hold the Maine stock for at least 46 days to obtain the dividends-received deduction. ◄

Debt-Financed Stock. The dividends-received deduction is not allowed to the extent the corporation borrows money to acquire the dividend paying stock.[29] This rule prevents a corporation from deducting interest paid on money borrowed to purchase the stock, while paying little or no tax on the dividends received on the stock.

EXAMPLE C3-21 ►

Palmer Corporation, whose marginal tax rate is 35%, borrows $100,000 at a 10% interest rate to purchase 30% of Sun Corporation's stock. The Sun stock pays an $8,000 annual dividend. If a dividends-received deduction were allowed for this investment, Palmer would have a net profit of $940 annually on owning the Sun stock even though the dividend received is less than the interest paid. The following table summarizes the profit (loss) to Palmer with and without the debt-financing rule.

REAL-WORLD EXAMPLE

Although sound in theory, the debt-financed stock limitation may be difficult to apply in practice. This difficulty became particularly apparent in a recent district court case, *OBH, Inc. v. U.S.*, 96 AFTR 2d, 2005-6801, 2005-2 USTC ¶50,627 (DC NB, 2005), where the IRS failed to establish that a corporation's debt proceeds were directly traceable to the acquisition of dividend paying stock.

	If Deduction Is Allowed	If Deduction Is Not Allowed
Dividends	$ 8,000	$ 8,000
Minus: 35% tax on dividend	(560)[a]	(2,800)
Dividend (after taxes)	$ 7,440	$5,200
Interest paid	$10,000	$10,000
Minus: 35% tax savings on deduction	(3,500)	(3,500)
Net cost of borrowing	$ 6,500	$6,500
Dividend (after taxes)	$ 7,440	$ 5,200
Minus: net cost of borrowing	(6,500)	(6,500)
Net profit (loss)	$ 940	$(1,300)

[a][$8,000 − (0.80 × $8,000)] × 0.35 = $560

This example illustrates how the rule disallowing the dividends-received deduction on debt-financed stock prevents corporations from making an after-tax profit by borrowing funds to purchase stocks paying dividends that are less than the cost of the borrowing. ◄

---

[29] Sec. 246A.

NET OPERATING LOSSES (NOLs). If a corporation's deductions exceed its gross income for the year, the corporation has a **net operating loss (NOL)**. The NOL is the amount by which the corporation's deductions (including any dividends-received deduction) exceed its gross income.[30] In computing an NOL for a given year, no deduction is permitted for a carryover or carryback of an NOL from a preceding or succeeding year. However, unlike an individual's NOL, no other adjustments are required to compute a corporation's NOL. If the corporation has an NOL, it also would not be allowed a U.S. production activities deduction because it has no positive taxable income.

A corporation's NOL carries back two years and carries over 20 years. It carries to the earliest of the two preceding years first and offsets taxable income reported in that year. If the loss cannot be used in that year, it carries to the immediately preceding year, and then to the next 20 years in chronological order. The corporation may elect to forgo the carryback period entirely and instead carry over the entire loss to the next 20 years.[31]

EXAMPLE C3-22 ▶

In 2006, Gray Corporation has gross income of $150,000 (including $100,000 from operations and $50,000 in dividends from a 30%-owned domestic corporation) and $180,000 of expenses. Gray has a $70,000 [$150,000 − $180,000 − (0.80 × $50,000)] NOL. The NOL carries back to 2004 unless Gray elects to forego the carryback period. If Gray had $20,000 of taxable income in 2004, $20,000 of Gray's 2006 NOL offsets that income. Gray receives a refund of all taxes paid in 2004. Gray carries the remaining $50,000 of the 2006 NOL to 2005. Any of the NOL not used in 2005 carries over to 2007. ◀

A corporation might elect not to carry an NOL back because its income was taxed at a low marginal tax rate in the carryback period and the corporation anticipates income being taxed at a higher marginal tax rate in later years or because it used tax credit carryovers in the earlier year that were about to expire. The corporation must make this election for the entire carryback by the due date (including extensions) for filing the return for the year in which the corporation incurred the NOL. The corporation makes the election by checking a box on Form 1120 when it files the return. Once made for a tax year, the election is irrevocable.[32] However, if the corporation incurs an NOL in another year, the decision as to whether that NOL should be carried back is a separate decision. In other words, each year's NOL is treated separately and is subject to a separate election.

To obtain a refund due to carrying an NOL back to a preceding year, a corporation must file either Form 1120X (Amended U.S. Corporation Income Tax Return) or Form 1139 (Corporation Application for a Tentative Refund).

THE SEQUENCING OF THE DEDUCTION CALCULATIONS. The rules for charitable contributions, dividends-received, NOL, and U.S. production activities deductions require that these deductions be taken in the correct sequence. Otherwise, the computation of these deductions may be incorrect. The correct order for taking deductions is

1. All deductions other than the charitable contributions deduction, the dividends-received deduction, and the NOL deduction
2. The charitable contributions deduction
3. The dividends-received deduction
4. The NOL deduction
5. The U.S. production activities deduction

As stated previously, the charitable contributions deduction is limited to 10% of taxable income before the charitable contributions deduction, any NOL or capital loss carryback, the dividends-received deduction, or the U.S. production activities deduction, but *after* any NOL carryover deduction. Once the corporation determines its charitable contributions deduction, it adds back any NOL carryover deduction and subtracts the charitable

---

[30] Sec. 172(c).
[31] The two year carryback and 20-year carryforward applies to NOLs incurred in tax years beginning after August 5, 1997. The change does not apply to NOLs carried forward from earlier years. These NOLs are, in general, carried back three years and carried forward 15 years. NOLs incurred in 2001 and 2002 were allowed a five-year carryback period.
[32] Sec. 172(b)(3)(C).

contributions deduction before computing the dividends-received deduction. The corporation then subtracts the NOL deduction, if any, before determining its U.S. production activities deduction.

EXAMPLE C3-23 ▶ East Corporation reports the following results:

Gross income from operations	$150,000
Dividends from 30%-owned domestic corporation	100,000
Operating expenses	100,000
Charitable contributions	30,000

In addition, East has $50,000 of qualified production activities income in the current year and a $40,000 NOL carryover from the previous year. East's charitable contributions deduction is computed as follows:

Gross income from operations	$150,000
Plus: Dividends	100,000
Gross income	$250,000
Minus: Operating expenses	(100,000)
NOL carryover	(40,000)
Base for calculation of the charitable contributions limitation	$110,000

East's charitable contributions deduction is limited to $11,000 (0.10 × $110,000). The $11,000 limitation means that East has a $19,000 ($30,000 − $11,000) excess contribution that carries forward for five years. East Corporation computes its taxable income as follows:

Gross income	$250,000
Minus: Operating expenses	(100,000)
Charitable contributions deduction	(11,000)
Taxable income before special deductions	$139,000
Minus: Dividends-received deduction ($100,000 × 0.80)	(80,000)
NOL carryover deduction	(40,000)
Taxable income before the U.S. production activities deduction	$ 19,000
Minus: U.S. production activities deduction ($19,000 × 0.03)	(570)
Taxable income	$ 18,430 ◀

ADDITIONAL COMMENT

The U.S. production activities deduction is last in the ordering of deductions because it is limited to taxable income after all other deductions. However, on the corporate tax return, it appears after the charitable contributions deduction but before the dividends-received and NOL deductions. Specifically, it appears on Form 1120, Line 25, before Line 28.

Note that, if an NOL is carried *back* from a later year, it is *not* taken into account in computing a corporation's charitable contributions limitation. In other words, the contribution deduction remains the same as in the year of the original return.

EXAMPLE C3-24 ▶ Assume the same facts as in Example C3-23, except the facts pertain to a prior year, and East carries back a $40,000 NOL to that year. East's base for calculation of the charitable contributions limitation was computed as follows when it filed the original return:

ADDITIONAL COMMENT

These computations in the carryback year are done on an amended return or an application for refund.

Gross income from operations	$150,000
Plus: Dividends	100,000
Gross income	$250,000
Minus: Operating expenses	(100,000)
Base for calculation of the charitable contributions limitation	$150,000

East's charitable contributions deduction was limited to $15,000 (0.10 × $150,000). The $15,000 limitation means that East had a $15,000 ($30,000 − $15,000) contribution carryover from the prior year. East Corporation computes its taxable income after the NOL carryback as follows:

Gross income ($150,000 + $100,000)	$250,000
Minus: Operating expenses	(100,000)
Charitable contributions deduction	(15,000)
Taxable income before special deductions	$135,000
Minus: Dividends-received deduction ($100,000 × 0.80)	(80,000)
NOL carryback deduction	(40,000)
Taxable income before the U.S. production activities deduction	$ 15,000
Minus: U.S. production activities deduction ($15,000 × 0.03)	(450)
Taxable income as recomputed	$ 14,550

Thus, East's prior-year charitable contributions deduction remains the same as originally claimed. ◄

STOP & THINK

Question: Why does a corporation's NOL or capital loss carryback not affect its charitable contributions deduction, but yet an NOL or capital loss carryover must be taken into account when calculating its charitable contribution limitation?

Solution: Remember that a carryback affects a tax return already filed in a prior year. If a carryback had to be taken into account when calculating the charitable contribution deduction limitation in the prior year, it might change the amount of the allowable charitable contribution. This change in turn might affect other items such as the carryback year's dividends-received deduction and some later years' deductions as well. For example, assume Alpha Corporation has a $10,000 NOL in 2006 that it carries back to 2004. If the NOL were permitted to reduce Alpha's allowable charitable contribution for 2004 by $1,000, Alpha's dividends-received deduction for 2004 and its charitable contribution deductions for 2005 as well might change.

To avoid these complications, which might force Alpha to amend its tax returns from the carryback year (2004) to the current year (2006), the law states that carrybacks are not taken into account in calculating the charitable contribution deduction limitation. Also, in the prior year, management made its charitable contribution decisions without knowledge of future NOLs. Altering the result of those prior decisions with future events might be unfair.

EXCEPTIONS FOR CLOSELY HELD CORPORATIONS

Congress has placed limits on certain transactions to prevent abuse in situations where a corporation is closely held. Some of these restrictions are explained below.

TRANSACTIONS BETWEEN A CORPORATION AND ITS SHAREHOLDERS. Special rules apply to transactions between a corporation and a controlling shareholder. Section 1239 may convert a capital gain realized on the sale of depreciable property between a corporation and a controlling shareholder into ordinary income. Section 267(a)(1) denies a deduction for losses realized on property sales between a corporation and a controlling shareholder. Section 267(a)(2) defers a deduction for accrued expenses and interest on certain transactions involving a corporation and a controlling shareholder.

In all three of the preceding situations, a controlling shareholder is one who owns more than 50% (in value) of the corporation's stock.[33] In determining whether a shareholder owns more than 50% of a corporation's stock, certain constructive stock ownership rules apply.[34] Under these rules, a shareholder is considered to own not only his or her own stock, but stock owned by family members (e.g., brothers, sisters, spouse, ancestors, and lineal descendants) and entities in which the shareholder has an ownership or beneficial interest (e.g., corporations, partnerships, trusts, and estates).

Gains on Sale or Exchange Transactions. If a controlling shareholder sells depreciable property to a controlled corporation (or vice versa) and the property is depreciable in the purchaser's hands, any gain on the sale is treated as ordinary income under Sec. 1239(a).

EXAMPLE C3-25 ► Ann owns all of Cape Corporation's stock. Ann sells a building to Cape and recognizes a $25,000 gain, which usually would be Sec. 1231 gain or Sec. 1250 gain (taxed at a maximum 15% or 25% capital gains tax rate, respectively). However, because Ann owns more than 50% of the Cape stock and the building is a depreciable property in Cape's hands, Sec. 1239 causes Ann to recognize the entire $25,000 gain as ordinary income. ◄

---

[33] Sec. 267(b)(2).   [34] Sec. 267(e)(3).

BOOK-TO-TAX ACCOUNTING COMPARISON

The denial of deductions for losses involving related party transactions is unique to the tax area. Financial accounting rules contain no such disallowance provision.

Losses on Sale or Exchange Transactions. Section 267(a)(1) denies a deduction for losses realized on a sale of property by a corporation to a controlling shareholder or on a sale of property by the controlling shareholder to the corporation. If the purchaser later sells the property to another party at a gain, that seller recognizes gain only to the extent it exceeds the previously disallowed loss.[35] Should the purchaser instead sell the property at a loss, the previously disallowed loss is never recognized.

EXAMPLE C3-26 ▶

Quattros Corporation sells an automobile to Juan, its sole shareholder, for $6,500. The corporation's adjusted basis for the automobile is $8,000. Quattros realizes a $1,500 ($6,500 − $8,000) loss on the sale. Section 267(a)(1), however, disallows the loss to the corporation. If Juan later sells the auto for $8,500, he realizes a $2,000 ($8,500 − $6,500) gain. He recognizes only $500 of that gain, the amount by which his $2,000 gain exceeds the $1,500 loss previously disallowed to Quattros. If Juan instead sells the auto for $7,500, he realizes a $1,000 ($7,500-$6,500) gain but recognizes no gain or loss. The previously disallowed loss reduces the gain to zero but may not create a loss. Finally, if Juan instead sells the auto for $4,000, he realizes and may be able to recognize a $2,500 ($4,000 − $6,500) loss. However, the $1,500 loss previously disallowed to Quattros is permanently lost. ◀

KEY POINT

Section 267(a)(2) is primarily aimed at the situation involving an accrual method corporation that accrues compensation to a cash method shareholder-employee. This provision forces a matching of the income and expense recognition by deferring the deduction to the year the shareholder recognizes the income.

Corporation and Controlling Shareholder Using Different Accounting Methods. Section 267(a)(2) defers a deduction for accrued expenses or interest owed by a corporation to a controlling shareholder or by a controlling shareholder to a corporation when the two parties use different accounting methods and the payee will include the accrued expense as part of gross income at a date later than when the payer accrues the deduction. Under this rule, accrued expenses or interest owed by a corporation to a controlling shareholder may not be deducted until the shareholder includes the payment in gross income.

EXAMPLE C3-27 ▶

Hill Corporation uses the accrual method of accounting. Hill's sole shareholder, Ruth, uses the cash method of accounting. Both taxpayers use the calendar year as their tax year. The corporation accrues a $25,000 interest payment to Ruth on December 20 of the current year. Hill makes the payment on March 20 of next year. Hill, however, cannot deduct the interest in the current year but must wait until Ruth reports the income next year. Thus, the expense and income are matched. ◀

LOSS LIMITATION RULES

At-Risk Rules If five or fewer shareholders own more than 50% (in value) of a C corporation's outstanding stock at any time during the last half of the corporation's tax year, the corporation is subject to the at-risk rules.[36] In such case, the corporation can deduct losses pertaining to an activity only to the extent the corporation is at risk for that activity at year-end. Any losses not deductible because of the at-risk rules must be carried over and deducted in a succeeding year when the corporation's risk with respect to the activity increases. (See Chapter C9 for additional discussion of the at-risk rules.)

Passive Activity Limitation Rules. Personal service corporations (PSCs) and **closely held C corporations** (those subject to the at-risk rules described above) also may be subject to the **passive activity limitations**.[37] If a PSC does not meet the material participation requirements, its net **passive losses** and credits must be carried over to a year when it has **passive income**. In the case of closely held C corporations that do not meet material participation requirements, passive losses and credits are allowed to offset the corporation's net active income but not its portfolio income (i.e., interest, dividends, annuities, royalties, and capital gains on the sale of investment property).[38]

---

[35] Sec. 267(d).
[36] Sec. 465(a).

[37] Secs. 469(a)(2)(B) and (C).
[38] Sec. 469(e)(2).

COMPUTING A CORPORATION'S INCOME TAX LIABILITY

OBJECTIVE 3

Compute a corporation's income tax liability

Once a corporation determines its taxable income, it then must compute its tax liability for the year. Table C3-2 outlines the steps for computing a corporation's regular (income) tax liability. This section explains the steps involved in arriving at a corporation's income tax liability in detail.

GENERAL RULES

REAL-WORLD EXAMPLE

In 2004, the IRS collected $231 billion from corporations, which was 11.5% of the $2 trillion collected by the IRS. This percentage is up from 9.9% in 2003.

All C corporations (other than members of controlled groups of corporations and personal service corporations) use the same tax rate schedule to compute their **regular tax** liability. The following table shows these rates, which also are reproduced on the inside back cover.

Taxable Income Over	But Not Over	The Tax Is	Of the Amount Over
$ –0–	$50,000	15%	$ –0–
50,000	75,000	$7,500 + 25%	50,000
75,000	100,000	13,750 + 34%	75,000
100,000	335,000	22,250 + 39%	100,000
335,000	10,000,000	113,900 + 34%	335,000
10,000,000	15,000,000	3,400,000 + 35%	10,000,000
15,000,000	18,333,333	5,150,000 + 38%	15,000,000
18,333,333	—	6,416,667 + 35%	18,333,333

EXAMPLE C3-28 ▶ Copper Corporation reports taxable income of $100,000. Copper's regular tax liability is computed as follows:

Tax on first $50,000:	0.15 × $50,000 =	$7,500
Tax on second $25,000:	0.25 × 25,000 =	6,250
Tax on remaining $25,000:	0.34 × 25,000 =	8,500
Regular tax liability		$22,250

This tax liability also can be determined from the above tax rate schedule. ◀

If taxable income exceeds $100,000, a 5% surcharge applies to the corporation's taxable income exceeding $100,000. The surcharge phases out the lower graduated tax rates that apply to the first $75,000 of taxable income for corporations earning between $100,000 and $335,000 of taxable income. The maximum surcharge is $11,750 [($335,000 − $100,000) × 0.05]. The above tax rate schedule incorporates the 5%

▼ **TABLE C3-2**
Computation of the Corporate Regular (Income) Tax Liability

Taxable income
Times: Income tax rates
Regular tax liability
Minus: Foreign tax credit (Sec. 27)
Regular tax
Minus: General business credit (Sec. 38)
       Minimum tax credit (Sec. 53)
       Other allowed credits
Plus: Recapture of previously claimed tax credits
Income tax liability

surcharge by imposing a 39% (34% + 5%) rate on taxable income from $100,000 to $335,000.

EXAMPLE C3-29 ▶ Delta Corporation reports taxable income of $200,000. Delta's regular tax liability is computed as follows:

Tax on first $50,000:	0.15 × $ 50,000 =	$ 7,500
Tax on next $25,000:	0.25 × 25,000 =	6,250
Tax on remaining $125,000:	0.34 × 125,000 =	42,500
Surcharge (income over $100,000):	0.05 × 100,000 =	5,000
Regular tax liability		$61,250

Alternatively, from the above tax rate schedule, the tax is $22,250 + [0.39 × ($200,000 − $100,000)] = $61,250. ◀

If taxable income is at least $335,000 but less than $10 million, the corporation pays a flat 34% tax rate on all of its taxable income. A corporation whose income is at least $10 million but less than $15 million pays $3.4 million plus 35% of the income above $10 million.

EXAMPLE C3-30 ▶ Elgin Corporation reports taxable income of $350,000. Elgin's regular tax liability is $119,000 (0.34 × $350,000). If Elgin's taxable income is instead $12 million, its tax liability is $4.1 million [$3,400,000 + (0.35 × $2,000,000)]. ◀

If a corporation's taxable income exceeds $15 million, a 3% surcharge applies to the corporation's taxable income exceeding $15 million (but not exceeding $18,333,333). The surcharge phases out the one percentage point lower rate (34% vs. 35%) that applies to the first $10 million of taxable income. The maximum surcharge is $100,000 [($18,333,333 − $15,000,000) × 0.03]. A corporation whose taxable income exceeds $18,333,333 pays a flat 35% tax rate on all its taxable income.

STOP & THINK

Question: Planner Corporation has an opportunity to realize $50,000 of additional income in either the current year or next year. Planner has some discretion as to the timing of this additional income. Not counting the additional income, Planner's current year taxable income is $200,000, and it expects next year's taxable income to be $500,000. In what year should Planner recognize the additional $50,000?

Solution: Even though Planner's current year taxable income is lower than next year's expected taxable income, Planner will have a lower marginal tax rate next year. The current year's marginal tax rate is 39% because Planner's taxable income is in the 5% surtax range (or 39% "bubble"). Next year's taxable income is beyond the 39% bubble and is in the flat 34% range. Thus, Planner can save $2,500 (0.05 × $50,000) in taxes by deferring the $50,000 until next year.

PERSONAL SERVICE CORPORATIONS

Personal service corporations are denied the benefit of the graduated corporate tax rates. Thus, all the income of personal service corporations is taxed at a flat 35% rate.

Section 448(d) defines a personal service corporation as a corporation that meets the following two tests:

▶ Substantially all its activities involve the performance of services in the fields of health, law, engineering, architecture, accounting, actuarial science, performing arts, and consulting.

▶ Substantially all its stock (by value) is held directly or indirectly by employees performing the services or retired employees who performed the services in the past, their estates, or persons who hold stock in the corporation by reason of the death of an employee or retired employee within the past two years.

This rule encourages employee-owners of personal service corporations either to withdraw earnings from the corporation as deductible salary (rather than have the corporation retain them) or make an S election.

CONTROLLED GROUPS OF CORPORATIONS

OBJECTIVE 4

Understand what a controlled group is and the tax consequences of being a controlled group

Special tax rules apply to corporations under common control to prevent them from avoiding taxes that otherwise would be due. The rules apply to corporations that meet the definition of a controlled group. This section explains why special rules apply to controlled groups, how the IRC defines controlled groups, and what special rules apply to controlled groups.

WHY SPECIAL RULES ARE NEEDED

Special controlled group rules prevent shareholders from using multiple corporations to avoid having corporate income taxed at a 35% rate. If these rules were not in effect, the owners of a corporation could allocate the corporation's income among two or more corporations and take advantage of the lower 15%, 25%, and 34% rates on the first $10 million of corporate income for each corporation.

The following example demonstrates how a group of shareholders could obtain a significant tax advantage by dividing a business enterprise among several corporate entities. Each corporation then could take advantage of the graduated corporate tax rates. To prevent a group of shareholders from using multiple corporations to gain such tax advantages, Congress enacted laws that limit the tax benefits of multiple corporations.[39]

EXAMPLE C3-31 ▶ Axle Corporation reports taxable income of $450,000. Axle's regular tax liability on that income is $153,000 (0.34 × $450,000). If Axle could divide its taxable income equally among six corporations ($75,000 apiece), each corporation's federal income tax liability would be $13,750 [(0.15 × $50,000) + (0.25 × $25,000)], or an $82,500 total regular tax liability for all the corporations. Thus, Axle could save $70,500 ($153,000 − $82,500) in federal income taxes. ◀

The law governing controlled corporations requires special treatment for two or more corporations controlled by the same shareholder or group of shareholders. The most important restrictions on a controlled group of corporations are that the group must share the benefits of the progressive corporate tax rate schedule and pay a 5% surcharge on the group's taxable income exceeding $100,000, up to a maximum surcharge of $11,750, and also pay a 3% surcharge on the group's taxable income exceeding $15 million, up to a maximum surcharge of $100,000.

EXAMPLE C3-32 ▶ White, Blue, Yellow, and Green Corporations belong to a controlled group. Each corporation reports $100,000 of taxable income (a total of $400,000). Only one $50,000 amount is taxed at 15% and only one $25,000 amount is taxed at 25%. Furthermore, the group is subject to the maximum $11,750 surcharge because its total taxable income exceeds $335,000. This surcharge is levied on the group member(s) that received the benefit of the 15 and 25% rates. Therefore, the group's total regular tax liability is $136,000 (0.34 × $400,000), as though one corporation earned the entire $400,000. Each corporation would be allocated $34,000 of this tax liability. ◀

WHAT IS A CONTROLLED GROUP?

A **controlled group** is comprised of two or more corporations owned directly or indirectly by the same shareholder or group of shareholders. Controlled groups fall into three categories: a parent-subsidiary controlled group, a brother-sister controlled group, and a combined controlled group. Each of these groups is subject to the limitations described above.

PARENT-SUBSIDIARY CONTROLLED GROUPS. In a **parent-subsidiary controlled group**, one corporation (the parent corporation) must directly own at least 80% of the voting power of all classes of voting stock, or 80% of the total value of all classes of stock, of a second corporation (the subsidiary corporation).[40] The group can contain more than one

---

[39] Secs. 1561 and 1563.
[40] Sec. 1563(a)(1). Section 1563(d)(1) requires that certain attribution rules apply to determine stock ownership for parent-subsidiary controlled groups.

If any person has an option to acquire stock, such stock is considered owned by the person having the option. Section 1563(c) excludes certain types of stock from the controlled group definition of stock.

subsidiary corporation. If the parent corporation, the subsidiary corporation, or any other members of the controlled group in total own at least 80% of the voting power of all classes of voting stock, or 80% of the total value of all classes of stock, of another corporation, that other corporation also is included in the parent-subsidiary controlled group.

EXAMPLE C3-33 ▶ Parent Corporation owns 80% of Axle Corporation's single class of stock and 40% of Wheel Corporation's single class of stock. Axle also owns 40% of Wheel's stock. (See Figure C3-2.) Parent, Axle, and Wheel are members of the same parent-subsidiary controlled group because Parent directly owns 80% of Axle's stock and therefore is its parent corporation, and Wheel's stock is 80% owned by Parent (40%) and Axle (40%).

If Parent and Axle together owned only 70% of Wheel's stock and an unrelated shareholder owned the remaining 30%, Wheel would not be included in the parent-subsidiary group. The controlled group then would consist only of Parent and Axle. ◀

EXAMPLE C3-34 ▶ Beta Corporation owns 70% of Spectrum Corporation's single class of stock and 60% of Red Corporation's single class of stock. Blue Corporation owns the remaining stock of Spectrum (30%) and Red (40%). No combination of these corporations forms a parent-subsidiary group because no corporation has direct stock ownership of at least 80% of any other corporation's stock. ◀

BROTHER-SISTER CONTROLLED GROUPS. After the 2004 Jobs Act, the IRC contains two definitions of a **brother-sister controlled group**. This textbook will refer to them as the 80%-50% definition and the 50%-only definition. Under the 80%-50% definition, a group of two or more corporations is a brother-sister controlled group if five or fewer individuals, trusts, or estates own

▶ At least 80% of the voting power of all classes of voting stock (or at least 80% of the total value of the outstanding stock) of each corporation, and

▶ More than 50% of the voting power of all classes of stock (or more than 50% of the total value of the outstanding stock) of each corporation, taking into account only the stock ownership that is common with respect to each corporation.[41] A common ownership is the percentage of stock a shareholder owns that is common or identical in each of the corporations. For example, if a shareholder owns 30% of New Corporation and 70% of Old Corporation, his or her common ownership is 30%.

Thus, under the 50%-80% definition, the five or fewer shareholders not only must have more than 50% common ownership in the corporations, they also must own at least 80% of the stock of each corporation in the brother-sister group. This definition is narrow because the shareholders must meet two tests.

FIGURE C3-2 ▶ PARENT-SUBSIDIARY CONTROLLED GROUP (EXAMPLE C3-33)

[41] Sec. 1563(a)(2). Section 1563(d)(2) requires that certain attribution rules apply to determine stock ownership for brother-sister controlled groups. If any person has an option to acquire stock, such stock is considered to be owned by the person having the option. A proportionate amount of stock owned by a partnership, estate, or trust is attributed to partners having an interest of 5% or more in the capital or profits of the partnership or beneficiaries having a 5% or more actuarial interest in the estate or trust. A proportionate amount of stock owned by a corporation is attributed to shareholders owning 5% or more in value of the corporate stock. Family attribution rules also can cause an individual to be considered to own the stock of a spouse, child, grandchild, parent, or grandparent.

The 50%-only definition, on the other hand, is broader than the 50%-80% definition in that the five or fewer shareholders must satisfy only the 50% common ownership test described above. Consequently, in situations where the 50%-only definition applies, more corporations may be pulled into the controlled group than under the 50%-80% definition. The list on page C3-29 indicates which definition applies to specific situations.

EXAMPLE C3-35 ▶ North and South Corporations have only one class of stock outstanding, owned by the following individuals:

	Stock Ownership Percentages		
Shareholder	North Corp.	South Corp.	Common Ownership
Walt	30%	70%	30%
Gail	70%	30%	30%
Total	100%	100%	60%

Five or fewer individuals (Walt and Gail) together own at least 80% (actually 100%) of each corporation's stock, and the same individuals own more than 50% (actually 60%) of the corporations' stock taking into account only their common ownership in each corporation. Because their ownership satisfies both tests, North and South are a brother-sister controlled group under the 50%-80% definition and under the 50%-only definition. (See Figure C3-3.) ◀

EXAMPLE C3-36 ▶ East and West Corporations have only one class of stock outstanding, owned by the following individuals:

	Stock Ownership Percentages		
Shareholder	East Corp.	West Corp.	Common Ownership
Javier	80%	25%	25%
Sara	20%	75%	20%
Total	100%	100%	45%

Five or fewer individuals (Javier and Sara) together own at least 80% (actually 100%) of each corporation's stock. However, those same individuals own only 45% of the corporations' stock taking into account only their common ownership. Because their ownership does not satisfy the more-than-50% test, East and West are not a brother-sister controlled group under either the 50%-80% or the 50%-only definition. Consequently, each corporation is taxed on its own income without regard to the earnings of the other. ◀

An individual's stock ownership can be counted for the 80% test only if that individual owns stock in each and every corporation in the controlled group.[42]

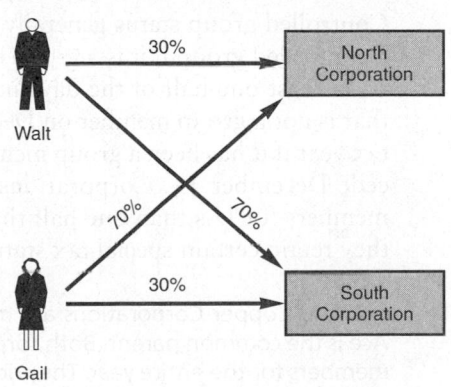

[42] Reg. Sec. 1.1563-1(a)(3).

FIGURE C3-3 ▶ BROTHER-SISTER CONTROLLED GROUP (EXAMPLE C3-35)

EXAMPLE C3-37 ▶

Long and Short Corporations each have only a single class of stock outstanding, owned by the following individuals:

| | Stock Ownership Percentages | | |
Shareholder	Long Corp.	Short Corp.	Common Ownership
Al	50%	40%	40%
Beth	20%	60%	20%
Carol	30%	—	—
Total	100%	100%	60%

Carol's stock does not count for purposes of Long's 80% stock ownership requirement because she owns no stock in Short. Only Al's and Beth's stock holdings count, and together they own only 70% of Long's stock. Thus, the 80% test fails. Consequently, Long and Short are not a brother-sister controlled group under the 50%-80% defintion, but they are a brother-sister controlled group under the 50%-only definition. ◀

COMBINED CONTROLLED GROUPS. A **combined controlled group** is comprised of three or more corporations meeting the following criteria:

▶ Each corporation is a member of a parent-subsidiary controlled group or a brother-sister controlled group

▶ At least one of the corporations is both the parent corporation of a parent-subsidiary controlled group and a member of a brother-sister controlled group.[43]

EXAMPLE C3-38 ▶

Able, Best, and Coast Corporations each have a single class of stock outstanding, owned by the following shareholders:

| | Stock Ownership Percentages | | |
Shareholder	Able Corp.	Coast Corp.	Best Corp.
Art	50%	50%	—
Barbara	50%	50%	—
Able Corp.	—	—	100%

Able and Coast are a brother-sister controlled group under the 50%-80% *and* 50%-only definitions because Art's and Barbara's ownership satisfy both the 80% and 50% tests. Able and Best are a parent-subsidiary controlled group because Able owns all of Best's stock. Each of the three corporations is a member of either the parent-subsidiary controlled group (Able and Best) or the brother-sister controlled group (Able and Coast), and the parent corporation (Able) of the parent-subsidiary controlled group also is a member of the brother-sister controlled group. Therefore, Able, Best, and Coast Corporations are members of a combined controlled group. (See Figure C3-4.) ◀

APPLICATION OF THE CONTROLLED GROUP TEST

Controlled group status generally is tested on December 31. A corporation is included in a controlled group if it is a group member on December 31 and has been a group member on at least one-half of the days in its tax year that precede December 31. A corporation that is not a group member on December 31, nevertheless, is considered a member for the tax year if it has been a group member on at least one-half the days in its tax year that precede December 31. Corporations are excluded from the controlled group if they were members for less than one-half the days in their tax year that precede December 31 or if they retain certain special tax statuses such as being a tax-exempt corporation.

EXAMPLE C3-39 ▶

Ace and Copper Corporations are members of a parent-subsidiary controlled group of which Ace is the common parent. Both corporations are calendar year taxpayers and have been group members for the entire year. They do not file a consolidated return. Bell Corporation, which has a fiscal year ending on August 31, becomes a group member on December 1 of the current year. Although Bell is a group member on December 31 of the current year, it has been a group

---

[43] Sec. 1563(a)(3).

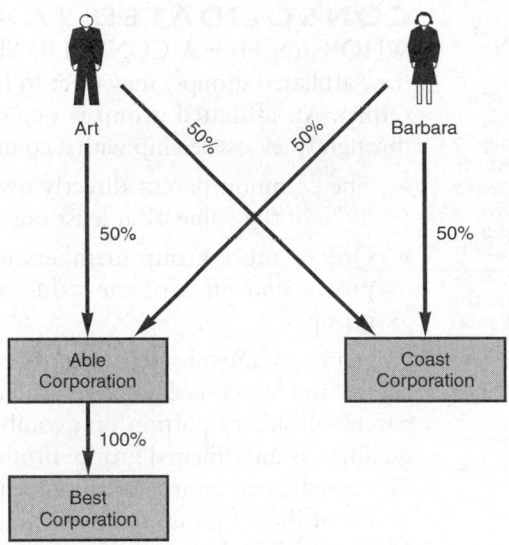

FIGURE C3-4 ▶ COMBINED CONTROLLED GROUP (EXAMPLE C3-38)

member for less than half the days in its tax year that precede December 31—only 30 of 121 days starting on September 1. Therefore, Bell is not a member of the Ace-Copper *controlled* group for its tax year beginning on September 1 of the current year. ◀

SPECIAL RULES APPLYING TO CONTROLLED GROUPS

As discussed earlier, if two or more corporations are members of a controlled group, the member corporations are limited to a total of $50,000 taxed at 15%, $25,000 being taxed at 25%, and $9,925,000 million being taxed at 34%. For brother-sister corporations, the broader 50%-only definition applies for limiting the reduced tax rates.

In addition, a controlled group must apportion certain other items among its group members, some of which are listed below. Notations in parentheses indicate which definition applies in the case of a brother-sister controlled group.

▶ The 5% and 3% surcharges (50%-only)

▶ The $40,000 exemption for the alternative minimum tax (50%-only)

▶ The $250,000 minimum accumulated earnings tax credit (50%-only)

▶ The $108,000 (in 2006) of depreciable assets that can be expensed annually (50%-80%)

▶ The $25,000 general business tax credit limitation (50%-80%)

Furthermore, Sec. 267(a)(1) allows no deduction for any loss on the sale or exchange of property between two members of the same controlled group. However, in contrast to losses between a corporation and controlling shareholder described earlier in this chapter, a loss realized on a transaction between members of a controlled group is deferred (instead of being disallowed). The original selling member recognizes the deferred loss when the property sold or exchanged in the intragroup transaction is sold outside the controlled group.

Section 267(a)(2) allows no deduction for certain accrued expenses or interest owed by one member of a controlled group to another member of the same controlled group when the two corporations use different accounting methods so that the payments would be reported in different tax years. (See page C3-21 for a detailed discussion of Sec. 267.) The Sec. 1239 rules that convert capital gain into ordinary income on depreciable property sales between related parties also apply to sales or exchanges involving two members of the same controlled group. Sections 267 and 1239, however, provide special definitions of controlled groups that differ somewhat from those described above. These details are beyond the scope of this textbook.

TAX STRATEGY TIP

A controlled group of corporations should elect to apportion the tax benefits in a manner that maximizes the tax savings from the tax benefits. See Tax Planning Considerations later in this chapter for details.

stop

CONSOLIDATED TAX RETURNS

WHO CAN FILE A CONSOLIDATED RETURN. Some groups of related corporations (i.e., affiliated groups) may elect to file a single income tax return called a **consolidated tax return.** An **affiliated group** is one or more chains of includible corporations connected through stock ownership with a common parent,[44] but only if the following criteria are met:

▶ The common parent directly owns stock with at least 80% of the voting power *and* 80% of the value of at least one includible corporation.

▶ One or more group members directly owns stock with at least 80% of the voting power *and* 80% of the value of each other corporation included in the affiliated group.[45]

Many parent-subsidiary controlled groups also qualify as affiliated groups and thus are eligible to file a consolidated return in place of separate tax returns for each corporation. The parent-subsidiary portion of a combined group also can file a consolidated tax return if it qualifies as an affiliated group. Brother-sister controlled groups, however, are not eligible to file consolidated returns because the requisite parent-subsidiary relationship does not exist.

An affiliated group makes the election to file a consolidated tax return by filing Form 1120, which includes all the income and expenses of each of its members. Each corporate member of the affiliated group must consent to the original election. Thereafter, any new member of the affiliated group must join in the consolidated return.

ADVANTAGES OF FILING A CONSOLIDATED RETURN. A consolidated return, in effect, is one tax return for the entire affiliated group of corporations. The main advantages of filing a consolidated return are

▶ Losses of one member of the group can offset profits of another member of the group.

▶ Capital losses of one member of the group can offset capital gains of another member of the group.

▶ Profits or gains realized on intercompany transactions are deferred until a sale outside the group occurs (i.e., if one member sells property to another member, the gain is postponed until the member sells the property to someone outside the affiliated group).

In contrast, if the group members file separate returns, members with NOLs or capital losses must either carry back these losses to earlier years or carry them over to future years rather than offset another member's profits or gains.

Although the losses of one group member can offset the profits of another group member when the group files a consolidated return, some important limitations apply to the use of a member corporation's NOL. These limitations prevent one corporation from purchasing another corporation's NOL carryovers to offset its own taxable income or purchasing a profitable corporation to facilitate the use of its own NOL carryovers. (See Chapters C7 and C8.)

The following example illustrates the advantage of a consolidated return election.

EXAMPLE C3-40 ▶ Parent Corporation owns 100% of Subsidiary Corporation's stock. Parent reports $110,000 of taxable income, including a $10,000 capital gain. Subsidiary incurs a $100,000 NOL and a $10,000 capital loss. If Parent and Subsidiary file separate returns, Parent has a $26,150 [$22,250 + 0.39 × ($110,000 − $100,000)] tax liability. Subsidiary has no tax liability but may be able to use its $100,000 NOL and $10,000 capital loss to offset taxable income in other years. On the other hand, if Parent and Subsidiary file a consolidated return, the group's consolidated taxable income is zero and the group has no tax liability. By filing a consolidated return, the group saves $26,150 in taxes for the year. ◀

DISADVANTAGES OF FILING A CONSOLIDATED RETURN. The main disadvantages of a consolidated return election are

▶ The election is binding on all subsequent tax years unless the IRS grants permission to discontinue filing consolidated returns or the affiliated group terminates.

[44] Includible corporations are those eligible to join in the consolidated tax return election under Sec. 1504(b).　　[45] Sec. 1504(a).

▶ Losses on intercompany transactions are deferred until a sale outside the group takes place.

▶ One member's Sec. 1231 losses offset another member's Sec. 1231 gains instead of being reported as an ordinary loss.

▶ Losses of an unprofitable member of the group may reduce the deduction or credit limitations of the group below what would be available had the members filed separate tax returns.

▶ The group may incur additional administrative costs in maintaining the records needed to file a consolidated return.

Determining whether to make a consolidated tax return election is a complex decision because of the various advantages and disadvantages and because the election is so difficult to revoke once made. Chapter C8 provides detailed coverage of the consolidated return rules.

TAX PLANNING CONSIDERATIONS

OBJECTIVE 5

Understand how compensation planning can reduce taxes for corporations and their shareholders

COMPENSATION PLANNING FOR SHAREHOLDER-EMPLOYEES

Compensation paid to a shareholder-employee in the form of salary has the advantage of single taxation because, while taxable to the employee, salary is deductible by the corporation. Dividend payments, on the other hand, are taxed twice. The corporation is taxed on its income when earned, and the shareholder is taxed on profits distributed as dividends. Double taxation occurs because the corporation may not deduct dividend payments. The reduced tax rate on dividends after the 2003 Act, however, makes the difference between salary and dividends much less substantial than under pre-2003 Act law.

EXAMPLE C3-41 ▶

Delta Corporation earns $500,000 and wishes to distribute $100,000 or as much of the $100,000 as possible to Mary, its sole sharholder and CEO. Mary's ordinary tax rate is 35%, and the corporation's marginal tax rate is 34%. Ignoring payroll taxes, the following table compares salary and dividend payments to Mary with respect to the $100,000 of partial earnings:

	Salary	Dividend Pre-2003 Act	Dividend Post-2003 Act
1. Corporate earnings (partial)	$100,000	$100,000	$100,000
2. Minus: Salary deduction	(100,000)	-0-	-0-
3. Corporate taxable income (partial)	$ -0-	$100,000	$100,000
4. Times: Corporate tax rate	0.34	0.34	0.34
5. Corporate income tax (on partial income)	$ -0-	$ 34,000	$ 34,000
6. Payment to Mary (Line 1 − Line 5)	$100,000	$ 66,000	$ 66,000
7. Times: Mary's tax rate	0.35	0.35	0.15
8. Mary's tax	$ 35,000	$ 23,100	$ 9,900
9. Total tax (Line 5 + Line 8)	$ 35,000	$ 57,100	$ 43,900
10. Effective tax rate (Line 9 ÷ Line 1)	35%	57.1%	43.9%

Thus, the preferential dividend rate reduces the effective tax rate on the corporate earnings from 57.1% to 43.9% and lessens the difference between salary and dividends from 22.1% (57.1% − 35%) to 8.9% (43.9% − 35%). This example demonstrates Congress's intent of reducing the double taxation of corporate earnings when the corporation pays dividends. ◀

To avoid double taxation, some owners of closely held corporations prefer to be taxed under the rules of Subchapter S (see Chapter C11). Other owners of closely held corporations retain C corporation status to use the 15% and 25% marginal corporate tax rates and to benefit from tax-free fringe benefits such as health and accident insurance. These fringe benefits are nontaxable to the employee and deductible by the corporation. For both tax and nontax reasons, closely held corporations must determine the appropriate level of earnings to be withdrawn from the business in the form of salary and fringe benefits and the amount of earnings to be retained in the business.

ADVANTAGE OF SALARY PAYMENTS. If a corporation distributes all its profits as deductible salary and fringe benefit payments, it will eliminate double taxation. However, the following considerations limit such tax planning opportunities:

▶ Regulation Sec. 1.162-7(a) requires salary or fringe benefit payments to be reasonable in amount and to be paid for services rendered by the employee. If the IRS deems compensation to be unreasonable, it may disallow the portion of the salary it deems unreasonable while still requiring the employee to include all compensation in gross income (see Chapter C4). This disallowance will result in double taxation. The reasonable compensation restriction primarily affects closely held corporations.

▶ A corporation may not deduct compensation paid to an executive of a publicly traded corporation that exceeds $1 million. However, this limitation does not apply to compensation paid to an executive other than the corporation's top five officers, or to performance-based compensation.[46]

▶ A corporation is a tax-paying entity independent of its owners. The first $75,000 of a corporation's earnings is taxed at 15% and 25% corporate tax rates. These rates are lower than the marginal tax rate that may apply to an individual taxpayer and provides an incentive to retain some earnings in the corporation instead of paying them out as salaries.

▶ A combined employee–employer social security tax rate of 15.3% applies in 2006. Employers and employees are each liable for 6.2% of old age security and disability insurance tax, or a total of 12.4% of the first $94,200 of wages in 2006. Employers and employees also are each liable for a 1.45% Medicare hospital insurance tax, for a total of 2.9% of all wages. In addition to these taxes, state and federal unemployment taxes may be imposed on a portion of wages paid.

ADVANTAGE OF FRINGE BENEFITS. Fringe benefits provide two types of tax advantages: a tax deferral or an exclusion. Qualified pension, profit-sharing, and stock bonus plans provide a tax deferral; that is, the corporation's contribution to such a plan is not taxable to the employees when the corporation makes the contribution. Instead, employees are taxed on the benefits when they receive them. Other common fringe benefits, such as group term life insurance, accident and health insurance, and disability insurance, are exempt from tax altogether; that is, the employee never is taxed on the value of these fringe benefits.

Because the employee excludes the value of fringe benefits from gross income, the marginal individual tax rate applicable to these benefits is zero. Thus, conversion of salary into a fringe benefit provides tax savings for the shareholder-employee equal to the amount of the converted salary times the employee's marginal tax rate, assuming the shareholder-employee could not purchase the same fringe benefit and deduct its cost on his or her individual tax return.

SPECIAL ELECTION TO ALLOCATE REDUCED TAX RATE BENEFITS

A controlled group may elect to apportion the tax benefits of the 15%, 25%, and 34% tax rates to the member corporations in any manner it chooses. If the corporations elect no special apportionment plan, the $50,000, $25,000, and $9,925,000 amounts allocated to the three reduced tax rate brackets are divided equally among all the corporations in the group.[47] If a controlled group has one or more group members that report little or no taxable income, the group should elect special apportionment of the reduced tax benefits to obtain the full tax savings resulting from the reduced rates.

---

[46] Sec. 162(m).

[47] Sec. 1561(a).

EXAMPLE C3-42 ▶ North and South Corporations are members of the North-South controlled group. The corporations file separate tax returns for the current year and report the following results:

Corporation	Taxable Income (NOL)
North	$(25,000)
South	100,000

If they elect no special apportionment plan, North and South are limited to $25,000 each taxed at a 15% rate and to $12,500 each taxed at a 25% rate. The tax liability for each corporation is determined as follows:

Corporation	Calculation	Tax
North		$ –0–
South	15% tax bracket: 0.15 × $25,000	$ 3,750
	25% tax bracket: 0.25 × $12,500	3,125
	34% tax bracket: 0.34 × $62,500	21,250
	Subtotal for South Corporation	$28,125
Total for North-South controlled group		$28,125

If the corporations elect a special apportionment plan, the group may apportion the full $50,000 and $25,000 amounts for each of the reduced tax rate brackets to South. The tax liability for each corporation is determined as follows:

Corporation	Calculation	Tax
North		$ –0–
South	15% tax bracket: 0.15 × $50,000	$ 7,500
	25% tax bracket: 0.25 × $25,000	6,250
	34% tax bracket: 0.34 × $25,000	8,500
	Subtotal for South Corporation	$22,250
Total for North-South controlled group		$22,250

By shifting the benefit of low tax brackets away from a corporation that cannot use it (North) to a corporation that can (South), the special apportionment election reduces the total tax liability for the North-South group by $5,875 ($28,125 − $22,250). ◀

If a controlled group's total taxable income exceeds $100,000 ($15 million), a 5% (3%) surcharge recaptures the benefits of the reduced tax rates. The component member (or members) that took advantage of the lower tax rates pays this additional tax.

EXAMPLE C3-43 ▶ Hill, Jet, and King Corporations are members of the Hill-Jet-King controlled group. The corporations file separate tax returns and report the following results:

Corporation	Taxable Income
Hill	$200,000
Jet	100,000
King	100,000
Total	$400,000

All the reduced tax rate benefits are allocated to Hill Corporation under a special apportionment plan. Hill's income tax is calculated as follows:

15% tax bracket: 0.15 × $50,000	$ 7,500
25% tax bracket: 0.25 × $25,000	6,250
34% tax bracket: 0.34 × $125,000	42,500
Surcharge	11,750
Hill's total tax liability	$68,000

Jet and King each have a regular tax liability of $34,000 (0.34 × $100,000). Thus, the group's total regular tax liability is $136,000 ($68,000 + $34,000 + $34,000). Because Hill, Jet, and King each report taxable income exceeding $75,000, the group would have the same total regular tax liability if the special apportionment plan apportioned all the tax benefit to Jet or King Corporation or divided them equally among the three corporations.[48]   ◀

USING NOL CARRYOVERS AND CARRYBACKS

When a corporation incurs an NOL for the year, it has two choices:

▶ Carry the NOL back to the second and first preceding years in that order, and then forward to the succeeding 20 years in chronological order until the NOL is exhausted.

▶ Forgo any carryback and just carry the NOL forward to the 20 succeeding years.

A corporation might elect to forgo an NOL carryback if it would offset income at a low tax rate, resulting in a small tax refund compared to a greater anticipated benefit if the NOL instead were carried over to a high tax rate year.

EXAMPLE C3-44 ▶

Boyd Corporation incurs a $30,000 NOL in 2006. Boyd's 2004 taxable income was $50,000. If Boyd carries the NOL back to 2004, Boyd's tax refund is computed as follows:

Original tax on $50,000 (using 2004 rates)	$7,500
Minus: Recomputed tax on $20,000 [($50,000 − $30,000) × 0.15]	(3,000)
Tax refund	$4,500

If Boyd anticipates taxable income (after reduction for any NOL carryovers) of $75,000 or more in 2007, carrying over the NOL will result in the entire loss offsetting taxable income that otherwise would be taxed at a 34% or higher marginal tax rate. The tax savings is computed as follows:

Tax on $105,000 of expected taxable income	$24,200
Minus: Tax on $75,000 ($105,000 − $30,000)	(13,750)
Tax savings in 2007	$10,450

Thus, if Boyd expects taxable income to be $105,000 in 2007, it might elect to forgo the NOL carryback and obtain the additional $5,950 ($10,450 − $4,500) tax benefit. Of course, by carrying the NOL over to 2007, Boyd loses the value of having the funds immediately available. However, Boyd may use the NOL to reduce its estimated tax payments for 2007. If the corporation expects the NOL carryover benefit to occur at an appreciably distant point in the future, the corporation would have to determine the benefit's present value to make it comparable to a refund from an NOL carryback. This example ignores the effect the NOL carryover has on the U.S. production activities deduction in the carryover year.   ◀

COMPLIANCE AND PROCEDURAL CONSIDERATIONS

ESTIMATED TAXES

Every corporation that expects to owe more than $500 in tax for the current year must pay four installments of estimated tax, each equal to 25% of its required annual payment.[49] For corporations that are not large corporations (defined below), the required annual payment is the lesser of 100% of the tax shown on the return for the current year or 100% of the tax shown on the return for the preceding year. A corporation may not base its required estimated tax amount on the tax shown on the return for the preceding tax year if the preceding year tax return showed a zero tax liability.[50] The estimated tax amount is the sum of the corporation's income tax and alternative minimum tax liabilities that exceeds its tax credits. The amount of estimated tax due may be computed on Schedule 1120-W (Corporation Estimated Tax).

[48] A 3% surcharge applies if the controlled group's total taxable income exceeds $15 million. The recapture rule applies in a fashion similar to Example C3-42.

[49] Sec. 6655.
[50] Rev. Rul. 92-54, 1992-2 C.B. 320.

ESTIMATED TAX PAYMENT DATES. A calendar year corporation must deposit estimated tax payments in a Federal Reserve bank or authorized commercial bank on or before April 15, June 15, September 15, and December 15.[51] This schedule differs from that of an individual taxpayer. The final estimated tax installment for a calendar year corporation is due in December of the tax year rather than in January of the following tax year, as is the case for individual taxpayers. For a fiscal year corporation, the due dates are the fifteenth day of the fourth, sixth, ninth, and twelfth months of the tax year.

EXAMPLE C3-45 ▶

Garden Corporation, a calendar year taxpayer, expects to report the following results for 2006:

Regular tax	$119,000
Alternative minimum tax	25,000

Garden's 2006 estimated tax liability is $144,000 ($119,000 regular tax liability + $25,000 AMT liability). Garden's 2005 tax liability was $120,000. Assuming Garden is not a large corporation, its required annual payment for 2006 is $120,000, the lesser of its 2005 liability ($120,000) or its 2006 tax return liability ($144,000). Garden will not incur a penalty if it deposits four equal installments of $30,000 ($120,000 ÷ 4) on or before April 15, June 15, September 15, and December 15, 2006. ◀

TYPICAL MISCONCEPTION

The easiest method of determining a corporation's estimated tax payments is to pay 100% of last year's tax liability. Unfortunately, for "large corporations," other than for its first quarterly payment, last year's tax liability is not an acceptable method of determining the required estimated tax payments. Also, last year's tax liability cannot be used if no tax liability existed in the prior year or if the corporation filed a short-year return for the prior year.

Different estimated tax payment rules apply to large corporations. A large corporation's required annual payment is 100% of the tax shown on the return for the current tax year. The estimated tax payments for a large corporation cannot be based on the prior year's tax liability, although a large corporation may base its first installment payment for the year on last year's tax liability. If a large corporation elects to base its first estimated tax payment on the prior year's liability, any shortfall between the required payment based on the current year's tax liability and the actual payment must be made up with the second payment.[52] A large corporation is one whose taxable income was $1 million or more in any of its three immediately preceding tax years. Controlled groups of corporations must allocate the $1 million amount among its group members.

EXAMPLE C3-46 ▶

SELF-STUDY QUESTION

What is the consequence of underpaying a corporation's estimated taxes?

ANSWER

The IRS assesses a nondeductible penalty if a corporation does not pay its estimated taxes on time. The amount of penalty depends on three factors: the applicable underpayment rate, the amount of the underpayment, and the amount of time that lapses until the corporation makes the payment.

Assume the same facts as in Example C3-45 except Garden is a large corporation (i.e., it had more than $1 million of taxable income in one of its prior three years). Garden can base its first estimated tax payment on either 25% of its 2006 tax liability or 25% of its 2005 tax liability. Garden should elect to use its 2005 tax liability as the basis for its first installment because it can reduce the needed payment from $36,000 (0.25 × $144,000) to $30,000 (0.25 × $120,000). However, it must recapture the $6,000 ($36,000 − $30,000) shortfall when it pays its second installment. Therefore, the total second installment is $42,000 ($36,000 second installment + $6,000 recapture from first installment). ◀

PENALTIES FOR UNDERPAYMENT OF ESTIMATED TAX. The IRS will assess a nondeductible penalty if a corporation does not deposit its required estimated tax installment on or before the due date for that installment. The penalty is the underpayment rate found in Sec. 6621 times the amount by which the installment(s) due by a payment date exceed the payment(s) actually made.[53] The penalty accrues from the payment due date for the installment until the earlier of the actual date of the payment or the due date for the tax return (excluding extensions).

EXAMPLE C3-47 ▶

Globe Corporation is a calendar year taxpayer that reported a $100,000 tax liability for 2005. Globe's tax liability for 2004 was $125,000. It should have made estimated tax payments of $25,000 ($100,000 ÷ 4) on or before April 15, June 15, September 15, and December 15, 2005. No penalty is assessed if Globe deposited the requisite amounts on or before each of the those dates. However, if Globe deposited only $16,000 ($9,000 less than the required $25,000) on

---

[51] Sec. 6655(c)(2). Fiscal year corporations must deposit their taxes on or before the fifteenth day of the fourth, sixth, ninth, and twelfth month of their tax year. If the fifteenth falls on a weekend or holiday, the payment is due on the next business day.

[52] Sec. 6655(d)(2)(B). A revision to the required estimated tax payment amount also may be needed if the corporation is basing its quarterly payments on the current year's tax liability. Installments paid after the estimate of the current year's liability has been revised must take into account any short-

age or excess in previous installment payments resulting from the change in the original estimate.

[53] Sec. 6621. This interest rate is the short-term federal rate as determined by the Secretary of the Treasury plus three percentage points. It is subject to change every three months. The interest rate for large corporations is the short-term federal rate plus five percentage points. This higher interest rate begins 30 days after the issuance of either a 30-day or 90-day deficiency notice.

April 15, 2005, and did not deposit the remaining $9,000 before the due date for the 2005 return, the corporation must pay a penalty on the $9,000 underpayment for the period of time from April 15, 2005, through March 15, 2006. The completed Form 2220 in Appendix B calculates the penalty assuming Globe pays in $16,000 on each installment date. If Globe deposits $34,000 on the second installment date (June 15, 2005), so that a total of $50,000 has been paid by the due date for the second installment, the penalty runs only from April 15, 2005, through June 15, 2005. ◀

SPECIAL COMPUTATION METHODS. In lieu of the current year and prior year methods, corporations can use either of two special methods for calculating estimated tax installments:

▶ The annualized income method
▶ The adjusted seasonal income method

The Annualized Income Method. This method is useful if a corporation's income is likely to increase a great deal toward the end of the year. It allows a corporation to base its first and second quarterly estimated tax payments on its annualized taxable income for the first three months of the year. The corporation then must base its third payment on its annualized taxable income for the first six months of the year and its fourth payment on annualized taxable income for the first nine months of the year. (Two other options for the number of months used for each installment also are available.)

EXAMPLE C3-48 ▶

Erratic Corporation, a calendar year taxpayer, reports taxable income of: $10,000 in each of January, February, and March; $20,000 in each of April, May, and June; and $50,000 in each of the last six months of the current year. Erratic's annualized taxable income and annualized tax are calculated as follows:

TAX STRATEGY TIP

Both the "annualized income exception" and the "adjusted seasonal income exception" are complicated computations. However, due to the large amounts of money involved in making corporate estimated tax payments along with the possible underpayment penalties, the time and effort spent in determining the least amount necessary for a required estimated tax payment are often worthwhile.

Through	Cumulative Taxable Income	Annualization Factor	Annualized Taxable Income	Tax on Annualized Taxable Income
Third month	$ 30,000	12/3	$120,000	$ 30,050
Sixth month	90,000	12/6	180,000	53,450
Ninth month	240,000	12/9	320,000	108,050

Assuming Erratic uses the annualized method for all four estimated tax payments, its installments will be as follows:

Installment Number	Annualized Tax	Applicable Percentage	Installment Amount	Cumulative Installment
One	$ 30,050	25%	$ 7,513[a]	$ 7,513
Two	30,050	50	7,512[b]	15,025
Three	53,450	75	25,063[c]	40,088
Four	108,050	100	67,962[d]	108,050

[a]$30,050 × 0.25
[b]($30,050 × 0.50) − $7,513
[c]$53,450 × 0.75) − $15,025
[d]($108,050 × 1.00) − $40,088

◀

A corporation may use the annualized income method for an installment payment only if it is less than the regular required installment. It must recapture any reduction in an earlier required installment resulting from use of the annualized income method by increasing the amount of the next installment that does not qualify for the annualized income method.

For small corporations, the sure way to avoid a penalty for the underpayment of estimated tax is to base the current year's estimated tax payments on 100% of last year's tax. This approach is not possible, however, for large corporations or for corporations that did not owe any tax in the prior year or that filed a short period tax return for the prior year. This approach also is not advisable if the corporation had a high tax liability in the prior year and expects a low tax liability in the current year.

Adjusted Seasonal Income Method. A corporation may base its installments on its adjusted seasonal income. This method permits corporations that earn seasonal income to annualize their income by assuming income earned in the current year is earned in the same pattern as in preceding years. As in the case of the annualized income exception, a corporation can use the seasonal income exception only if the resulting installment payment is less than the regular required installment. Once the exception no longer applies, any savings resulting from its use for prior installments must be recaptured.

REPORTING THE UNDERPAYMENT. A corporation reports its underpayment of estimated taxes and the amount of any penalty on Form 2220 (Underpayment of Estimated Tax by Corporations). A copy of a completed Form 2220 using the facts from Example C3-47 appears in Appendix B.

PAYING THE REMAINING TAX LIABILITY. A corporation must pay all of its remaining tax liability for the year when it files its corporate tax return. An extension of time to file the tax return does *not* extend the time to pay the tax liability. If any amount of tax remains unpaid after the original due date for the tax return, the corporation must pay interest at the underpayment rate prescribed by Sec. 6621 from the due date until the corporation pays the tax. In addition to interest, the IRS assesses a penalty if the corporation does not pay the tax on time and cannot show reasonable cause for the failure to pay. The IRS presumes that reasonable cause exists if the corporation requests an extension of time to file its tax return and the amount of tax shown on the request for extension (Form 7004) or the amount of tax paid by the original due date of the return is at least 90% of the corporation's tax shown on its Form 1120.[54] A discussion of the failure-to-pay penalty and the interest calculation can be found in Chapter C15.

STOP & THINK

Question: Why does the tax law permit a corporation to use special methods such as the annualized income method to calculate its required estimated tax installments?

Solution: A large corporation whose income varies widely may not be able to estimate its taxable income for the year until late in the year, and it is not allowed to base its estimates on last year's income. If, for example, a calendar year corporation earns income of $100,000 per month during the first six months of its year, it might estimate its first two installments on the assumption that it will earn a total taxable income of $1.2 million for the year. But if its income unexpectedly increases to $500,000 per month in the seventh month, it would need an annualized method to avoid an underpayment penalty for the first two installments. Were it not for the ability to use the annualized method, the corporation would have no way to avoid an underpayment penalty even though it could not predict its taxable income for the year when it made the first two installment payments.

OBJECTIVE 6

Determine the requirements for paying corporate incomes taxes and filing a corporate tax return

REQUIREMENTS FOR FILING AND PAYING TAXES

A corporation must file a tax return even if it has no taxable income for the year.[55] If the corporation did not exist for its entire annual accounting period (either calendar year or fiscal year), it must file a short period return for the part of the year during which it did exist. For tax purposes, a corporation's existence ends when it ceases business and dissolves, retaining no assets, even if state law treats the corporation as continuing for purposes of winding up its affairs.[56]

Corporations use Form 1120 (U.S. Corporation Income Tax Return) or Form 1120-A (U.S. Corporation Short-Form Income Tax Return) to file their tax returns. A corporation is eligible to use Form 1120-A if it satisfies the following requirements:[57]

---

[54] Reg. Sec. 301.6651-1(c)(4).
[55] Sec. 6012(a)(2).
[56] Reg. Sec. 1.6012-2(a)(2).

[57] See the instructions to Form 1120-A for a series of additional requirements (e.g., the corporation is not filing its final return).

▶ Its gross receipts are under $500,000.

▶ Its total income is under $500,000.

▶ Its total assets is under $500,000.

A completed Form 1120 corporate income tax return appears in Appendix B. A spreadsheet that converts book income into taxable income for the Johns and Lawrence business enterprise (introduced in Chapter C2) is presented with the C corporation tax return.

WHEN THE RETURN MUST BE FILED

Corporations must file their tax returns by the fifteenth day of the third month following the close of their tax year.[58] A corporation can obtain an automatic six-month extension to file its tax return by filing Form 7004 (Application for Automatic Extension of Time to File Corporation Income Tax Return) by the original due date for the return. Corporations that fail to file a timely tax return are subject to the failure-to-file penalty. Chapter C15 discusses this penalty in some detail.

EXAMPLE C3-49 ▶ Palmer Corporation's fiscal tax year ends on September 30. Its corporate tax return for the year ending September 30, 2006, is due on or before December 15, 2006. If Palmer files Form 7004 by December 15, 2006, it can obtain an automatic extension of time to file until June 15, 2007. Assuming Palmer expects its 2006 tax liability to be $72,000 and it has paid $68,000 in estimated tax during the year, it must pay an additional $4,000 to the IRS by December 15, 2006. A completed Form 7004 appears in Appendix B. ◀

Additional extensions beyond the automatic six-month period are not available. The IRS can rescind the extension period by mailing a ten-day notice to the corporation before the end of the six-month period.[59]

TAX RETURN SCHEDULES

SCHEDULE L (OF FORM 1120): THE BALANCE SHEET. Schedule L of Form 1120 requires a balance sheet showing the financial accounting results at the beginning and end of the tax year.

RECONCILIATION SCHEDULES. The IRS also requires the reconciliation of the corporation's financial accounting income (also known as book income) and its taxable income (before special deductions). Book income is calculated according to generally accepted accounting principles (GAAP) including rules promulgated by the Financial Accounting Standards Board (FASB). On the other hand, taxable income must be calculated using tax rules. Therefore, book income and taxable income usually differ.

Some small corporations that do not require audited statements keep their books on a tax basis. For example, they may calculate depreciation for book purposes the same way they do for tax purposes. Income tax expense for book purposes may simply reflect amounts paid as estimated taxes. Most corporations, however, must use GAAP to calculate net income per books. For such corporations, taxable income and book income may differ significantly. The reconciliation of book income and taxable income provides the IRS with information that helps it audit a corporation's tax return.

For many corporations, the reconciliation must be provided on Schedule M-1 of Form 1120. For tax years ending on or after December 31, 2004, however, corporations with total assets of $10 million or more on the last day of the tax year must complete Schedule M-3 instead of Schedule M-1. This schedule provides the IRS with much more detailed information on differences between book income and taxable income than does Schedule M-1. This additional transparency of corporate transactions will increase the IRS's ability to audit corporate tax returns. Form 1120 also requires an analysis of unappropriated retained earnings on Schedule M-2.

---

[58] Sec. 6072(b).　　　　　　　　　　　　　[59] Reg. Sec. 1.6081-3.

BOOK-TAX DIFFERENCES. A corporation's book income usually differs from its taxable income for a large number of transactions. Some of these differences are permanent. **Permanent differences** arise because:

▶ Some book income is never taxed. Examples include:
1. Tax-exempt interest received on state and municipal obligations
2. Proceeds of life insurance carried by the corporation on the lives of key officers or employees

▶ Some book expenses are never deductible for tax purposes. Examples include:
1. Expenses incurred in earning tax-exempt interest
2. Premiums paid for life insurance carried by the corporation on the lives of key officers or employees
3. Fines and expenses resulting from a violation of law
4. Disallowed travel and entertainment costs
5. Political contributions
6. Federal income taxes per books, which is based on GAAP (FAS 109)

▶ Some tax deductions are never taken for book purposes. Examples include:
1. The dividends-received deduction
2. The U.S. production activities deduction
3. Percentage depletion of natural resources in excess of their cost

Some of the differences are temporary. **Temporary differences** arise because:

▶ Some revenues or gains are recognized for book purposes in the current year but not reported for tax purposes until later years. Examples include:
1. Installment sales reported in full for book purposes in the year of sale but reported over a period of years using the installment method for tax purposes
2. Gains on involuntary conversions that are recognized for book purposes but deferred for tax purposes

▶ Some revenues or gains are taxable before they are reported for book purposes. These items are included in taxable income when received but are included in book income as they accrue. Examples include:
1. Prepaid rent or interest income
2. Advance subscription revenue

▶ Some expenses or losses are deductible for tax purposes after they are recognized for book purposes. Examples include:
1. Excess of capital losses over capital gains, which are expensed for book purposes but carry back or forward for tax purposes
2. Book depreciation in excess of tax depreciation
3. Charitable contributions exceeding the 10% of taxable income limitation, which are currently expensed for book purpose but carry over for tax purposes
4. Bad debt accruals using the allowance method for book purposes and the direct write-off method for tax purposes
5. Organizational and start-up expenditures, which are expensed currently for book purposes but partially deducted and amortized for tax purposes
6. Product warranty liabilities expensed for book purposes when estimated but deducted for tax purposes when the liability becomes fixed

▶ Some expenses or losses are deductible for tax purposes before they are recognized for book purposes. Examples include:
1. Tax depreciation in excess of book depreciation
2. Prepaid expenses deducted on the tax return in the period paid but accrued over a period of years for book purposes

SCHEDULE M-1. The Schedule M-1 reconciliation of book to taxable income begins with net income per books and ends with taxable income before special deductions, which corresponds with Line 28 of Form 1120. Thus, some book-tax differences enumerated above do not appear in the reconciliation, for example, the dividends-received deduction and the net operating loss deduction.

The left side of Schedule M-1 contains items the corporation must add back to book income. These items include the following categories:

▶ Federal income tax expense

▶ Excess of capital losses over capital gains

▶ Income subject to tax but not recorded on the books in the current year

▶ Expenses recorded on the books but not deductible for tax purposes in the current year

The right side of the schedule contains items the corporation must deduct from book income and include the following categories:

▶ Income recorded on the books in the current year that is not taxable in the current year

▶ Deductions or losses claimed in the tax return that do not reduce book income in the current year

These categorizations, however, do not distinguish between permanent and temporary differences as does Schedule M-3 discussed below. The following example illustrates a Schedule M-1 reconciliation.

EXAMPLE C3-50 ▶ Valley Corporation reports the following items for book purposes (with some tax numbers in parentheses):

Gross profit from operations	$201,000
Minus: Operations expenses	(62,000)
Net income from operations	$139,000
Plus: Proceeds of insurance on life of key employee	50,000
Tax-exempt interest income	12,500
Minus: Depreciation ($28,000 for tax)	(26,000)
Interest on loan to buy tax-exempt bonds	(15,000)
Net capital loss	(10,750)
Insurance premiums on key employee where Valley is the beneficiary	(800)
Prepaid expenses ($10,000 for tax)	(0)
U.S. production activities deduction ($3,000 for tax)	(0)
Federal income tax expense per books	(27,250)
Net income per books	$121,700

Valley's Schedule M-1 reconciliation appears in Figure C3-5.[60] ◀

SCHEDULE M-3. Schedule M-3 requires extensive detail in its reconciliation. Moreover, the schedule has the corporation distinguish between its permanent and temporary differ-

1	Net income (loss) per books	121,700	7	Income recorded on books this year not included on this return (itemize):			
2	Federal income tax	27,250					
3	Excess of capital losses over capital gains .	10,750		Tax-exempt interest $ 12,500			
4	Income subject to tax not recorded on books this year (itemize): Prepaid rent	10,000		Insurance proceeds 50,000			62,500
5	Expenses recorded on books this year not deducted on this return (itemize):		8	Deductions on this return not charged against book income this year (itemize):			
a	Depreciation . . . . $		a	Depreciation . . . . $ 2,000			
b	Contributions carryover $		b	Contributions carryover $			
c	Travel and entertainment $ Premiums on life insurance 800 Interest on loan 15,000	15,800		U.S. prod. act. ded. 3,000			5,000
6	Add lines 1 through 5	185,500	9	Add lines 7 and 8			67,500
			10	Income (line 28, page 1)—line 6 less line 9			118,000

FIGURE C3-5 ▶ VALLEY CORPORATION'S FORM 1120 SCHEDULE M-1 (EXAMPLE C3-50)

---

[60] A worksheet for converting book income to taxable income for a sample Form 1120 return is provided in Appendix B with that return.

BOOK-TO-TAX COMPARISON

Schedule M-1 and M-3 adjustments highlight the fact that financial accounting and tax accounting differ in many ways. A review of Schedule M-1 or M-3 is an excellent way to compare the financial accounting and tax accounting differences in a corporation.

ences. The schedule contains three parts. Part I adjusts worldwide income per books to worldwide book income for only includible corporations. As described in Chapter C8, some corporation may be included in the financial statement consolidation that might be excluded from the tax consolidated tax return. This resulting figure is then reconciled to taxable income before special deductions (again Line 28 of Form 1120). Part II enumerates the corporation's income and loss items, and Part III enumerates the expense and deduction items. The total items from Part III carry over to Part II for the final reconciliation. Both Parts II and III contain the following four columns: (a) book items, (b) temporary differences, (c) permanent differences, and (d) tax items.

Appendix B provides an example of Schedule M-3 using the data from Example C3-50. Valley Corporation in that example is too small to be required to use Schedule M-3 although it may elect to do so. Nevertheless, that data is used to allow for comparison between Schedules M-1 and M-3.

SCHEDULE M-2 (OF FORM 1120). Schedule M-2 of Form 1120 requires an analysis of changes in unappropriated retained earnings from the beginning of the year to the end of the year. The schedule supplies the IRS with information regarding dividends paid during the year and any special transactions that caused a change in retained earnings for the year.

Schedule M-2 starts with the balance in the unappropriated retained earnings account at the beginning of the year. The following items, which must be added to the beginning balance amount, are listed on the left side of the schedule:

▶ Net income per books
▶ Other increases (e.g., refund of federal income taxes paid in a prior year taken directly to the retained earnings account instead of used to reduce federal income tax expense)

The following items, which must be deducted from the beginning balance amount, are listed on the right side of the schedule:

▶ Dividends (e.g., cash or property)
▶ Other decreases (e.g., appropriation of retained earnings made during the tax year)

The result is the amount of unappropriated retained earnings at the end of the year.

ADDITIONAL COMMENT

Schedule M-2 requires an analysis of a corporation's retained earnings. Retained earnings is a financial accounting number that has little relevance to tax accounting. It would seem much more worthwhile for the IRS to require an analysis of a corporation's earnings and profits, which is an extremely important number in determining the taxation of a corporation and its shareholders.

EXAMPLE C3-51 ▶

In the current year, Beta Corporation reports net income and other capital account items as follows:

Unappropriated retained earnings, January 1, current year	$400,000
Net income	350,000
Federal income tax refund for capital loss carryback	15,000
Cash dividends paid in the current year	250,000
Unappropriated retained earnings, December 31, current year	515,000

Beta Corporation's Schedule M-2 appears in Figure C3-6. ◀

Topic Review C3-2 summarizes the requirements for paying the taxes due and filing the corporate tax return.

	Analysis of Unappropriated Retained Earnings per Books (Line 25, Schedule L)

1	Balance at beginning of year	400,000	5	Distributions: a Cash		250,000
2	Net income (loss) per books	350,000		b Stock		
3	Other increases (itemize):			c Property		
			6	Other decreases (itemize):		
	Federal tax refund	15,000	7	Add lines 5 and 6		250,000
4	Add lines 1, 2, and 3	765,000	8	Balance at end of year (line 4 less line 7)		515,000

FIGURE C3-6 ▶ BETA CORPORATION'S FORM 1120 SCHEDULE M-2 (EXAMPLE C3-51)

Topic Review C3-2

Requirements for Paying Taxes Due and Filing Tax Returns

1. Estimated Tax Requirement
   a. Corporations that expect to owe more than $500 in tax for the current year must pay four installments of estimated tax, each equal to 25% of its required annual payment.
   b. Taxes for which estimated payments are required of a C corporation include regular tax and alternative minimum tax, minus any tax credits.
   c. If a corporation is not a large corporation, its required annual payment is the lesser of 100% of the tax shown on the current year's return or 100% of the tax shown on the preceding year's return.
   d. If a corporation is a large corporation, its required annual payment is 100% of the tax shown on the current year's return. Its first estimated tax payment may be based on the preceding year's tax liability, but any shortfall must be made up when the second installment is due.
   e. Special rules apply if the corporation bases its estimated tax payments on the annualized income or adjusted seasonal income method.
2. Filing Requirements
   a. The corporate tax return is due by the fifteenth day of the third month after the end of the tax year.
   b. A corporate taxpayer may request an automatic six-month extension to file its tax return (but not to pay its tax due).

PROBLEM MATERIALS

DISCUSSION QUESTIONS

C3-1 High Corporation incorporates on May 1 and begins business on May 10 of the current year. What alternative tax years can High elect to report its initial year's income?

C3-2 Port Corporation wants to change its tax year from a calendar year to a fiscal year ending June 30. Port is a C corporation owned by 100 shareholders, none of whom own more than 5% of the stock. Can Port change its tax year? If so, how can it accomplish the change?

C3-3 Stan and Susan, two calendar year taxpayers, are starting a new business to manufacture and sell digital circuits. They intend to incorporate the business with $600,000 of their own capital and $2 million of equity capital obtained from other investors. The company expects to incur organizational and start-up expenditures of $100,000 in the first year. Inventories are a material income-producing factor. The company also expects to incur losses of $500,000 in the first two years of operations and substantial research and development expenses during the first three years. The company expects to break even in the third year and be profitable at the end of the fourth year, even though the nature of the digital circuit business will require continual research and development activities. What accounting methods and tax elections must Stan and Susan consider in their first year of operation? For each method/election, explain the possible alternatives and the advantages and disadvantages of each alternative.

C3-4 Compare the tax treatment of capital gains and losses by a corporation and by an individual.

C3-5 Explain the effect of the Sec. 291 recapture rule when a corporation sells depreciable real estate.

C3-6 What are organizational expenditures? How are they treated for tax purposes?

C3-7 What are start-up expenditures? How are they treated for tax purposes?

C3-8 Describe three ways in which the treatment of charitable contributions by individual and corporate taxpayers differ.

C3-9 Carver Corporation uses the accrual method of accounting and the calendar year as its tax year. Its board of directors authorizes a cash contribution on November 3, 2006 that the corporation pays on March 10, 2007. In what year(s) is it deductible? What happens if the corporation does not pay the contribution until April 20, 2007?

C3-10 Zero Corporation contributes inventory (computers) to State University for use in its mathematics program. The computers have a $1,225 cost basis and an $2,800 FMV. How much is Zero's charitable contribution deduction for the computers? (Ignore the 10% limit.)

C3-11 Why are corporations allowed a dividends-received deduction? What dividends qualify for this special deduction?

C3-12 Why is a dividends-received deduction disallowed if the stock on which the corporation pays the dividend is debt-financed?

C3-13 Crane Corporation incurs a $75,000 NOL in the current year. In which years can Crane use this NOL if it makes no special elections? When might a special election to forgo the carryback of the NOL be beneficial for Crane?

C3-14 What special restrictions apply to the deduction of a loss realized on the sale of property between a corporation and a shareholder who owns 60% of the corporation's stock? What restrictions apply to the deduction of expenses accrued by a corporation at year-end and owed to a cash method shareholder who owns 60% of the corporation's stock?

C3-15 Deer Corporation is a C corporation. Its taxable income for the current year is $200,000. What is Deer Corporation's income tax liability for the year?

C3-16 Budget Corporation is a personal service corporation. Its taxable income for the current year is $75,000. What is Budget Corporation's income tax liability for the year?

C3-17 Why do special restrictions on using the progressive corporate tax rates apply to controlled groups of corporations?

C3-18 Describe the three types of controlled groups.

C3-19 List five restrictions on claiming multiple tax benefits that apply to controlled groups of corporations.

C3-20 What are the major advantages and disadvantages of filing a consolidated tax return?

C3-21 What are the tax advantages of substituting fringe benefits for salary paid to a shareholder-employee?

C3-22 Explain the tax consequences to both the corporation and a shareholder-employee if an IRS agent determines that a portion of the compensation paid in a prior tax year exceeds a reasonable compensation level.

C3-23 What is the advantage of a special apportionment plan for the benefits of the 15%, 25%, and 34% tax rates to members of a controlled group?

C3-24 What corporations must pay estimated taxes? When are the estimated tax payments due?

C3-25 What is a "large" corporation for purposes of the estimated tax rules? What special rules apply to such large corporations?

C3-26 What penalties apply to the underpayment of estimated taxes? The late payment of the remaining tax liability?

C3-27 Describe the situations in which a corporation must file a tax return.

C3-28 When is a corporate tax return due for a calendar-year taxpayer? What extension(s) of time in which to file the return are available?

C3-29 List four types of differences that can cause a corporation's book income to differ from its taxable income.

ISSUE IDENTIFICATION QUESTIONS

C3-30 X-Ray Corporation received a $100,000 dividend from Yancey Corporation this year. X-Ray owns 10% of the Yancey's single class of stock. What tax issues should X-Ray consider with respect to its dividend income?

C3-31 Williams Corporation sold a truck with an adjusted basis of $100,000 to Barbara for $80,000. Barbara owns 25% of the Williams stock. What tax issues should Williams and Barbara consider with respect to the sale/purchase?

C3-32 You are the CPA who prepares the tax returns for Don, his wife, Mary, and their two corporations. Don owns 100% of Pencil Corporation's stock. Pencil's current year taxable income is $100,000. Mary owns 100% of Eraser Corporation's stock. Eraser's current year taxable income is $150,000. Don and Mary file a joint federal income tax return. What issues should Don and Mary consider with respect to the calculation of the three tax return liabilities?

C3-33 Rugby Corporation has a $50,000 NOL in the current year. Rugby's taxable income in each of the previous two years was $25,000. Rugby expects its taxable income for next year to exceed $400,000. What issues should Rugby consider with respect to the use of the NOL?

PROBLEMS

C3-34 *Depreciation Recapture.* Young Corporation purchased residential real estate in 2002 for $225,000, of which $25,000 was allocated to the land and $200,000 was allocated to the building. Young took straight-line MACRS deductions of $30,000 during the years 2002–2006. In 2006, Young sells the property for $285,000, of which $60,000 is allocated to the land and $225,000 is allocated to the building. What are the amount and character of Young's recognized gain or loss on the sale?

C3-35 *Organizational and Start-up Expenditures.* Delta Corporation incorporates on January 7, begins business on July 10, and elects to have its initial tax year end on October 31. Delta incurs the following expenses between January and October related to its organization during the current year:

Date	Expenditure	Amount
January 30	Travel to investigate potential business site	$2,000
May 15	Legal expenses to draft corporate charter	2,500
May 30	Commissions to stockbroker for issuing and selling stock	4,000
May 30	Temporary directors' fees	2,500
June 1	Expense of transferring building to Delta	3,000
June 5	Accounting fees to set up corporate books	1,500
June 10	Training expenses for employees	5,000
June 15	Rent expense for June	1,000
July 15	Rent expense for July	1,000

a. What alternative treatments are available for Delta's expenditures?
b. What amount of organizational expenditures can Delta Corporation deduct on its first tax return for the fiscal year ending October 31?
c. What amount of start-up costs can Delta Corporation deduct on its first tax return?

C3-36 *Charitable Contribution of Property.* Yellow Corporation donates the following property to the State University:

• ABC Corporation stock purchased two years ago for $18,000. The stock, which trades on a regional stock exchange, has a $25,000 FMV on the contribution date.

• Inventory with a $17,000 adjusted basis and a $22,000 FMV. State will use the inventory for scientific research that qualifies under the special Sec. 170(e)(4) rules.

• An antique vase purchased two years ago for $10,000 and having an $18,000 FMV. State University plans to sell the vase to obtain funds for educational purposes.

Yellow Corporation's taxable income before any charitable contributions deduction, NOL or capital loss carryback, or dividends-received deduction is $250,000.
a. What is Yellow Corporation's charitable contributions deduction for the current year?
b. What is the amount of its charitable contributions carryover (if any)?

C3-37 *Charitable Contributions of Property.* Blue Corporation donates the following property to Johnson Elementary School:

• XYZ Corporation stock purchased two years ago for $25,000. The stock has a $16,000 FMV on the contribution date.

• Computer equipment built one year ago at a cost of $16,000. The equipment has a $50,000 FMV on the contribution date. Blue is not in the business of manufacturing computer equipment.

• PQR Corporation stock purchased six months ago for $12,000. The stock has an $18,000 FMV on the contribution date.

The school will sell the stock and use the proceeds to renovate a classroom to be used as a computer laboratory. Blue's taxable income before any charitable contribution deduction, dividends-received deduction, or NOL or capital loss carryback is $400,000.
a. What is Blue's charitable contributions deduction for the current year?
b. What is the amount of Blue's charitable contribution carryback or carryover (if any)? In what years can it be used?
c. What would have been a better tax plan concerning the XYZ stock donation?

C3-38 *Charitable Contribution Deduction Limitation.* Zeta Corporation reports the following results for 2006 and 2007:

	2006	2007
Adjusted taxable income	$180,000	$125,000
Charitable contributions (cash)	20,000	12,000

The adjusted taxable income is before Zeta claims any charitable contributions deduction, NOL or capital loss carryback, dividends-received deduction, or U.S. production activities deduction.

a. How much is Zeta's charitable contributions deduction in 2006? In 2007?

b. What is Zeta's contribution carryover to 2008, if any?

C3-39 *Taxable Income Computation.* Omega Corporation reports the following results for the current year:

Gross profits on sales	$120,000
Dividends from less-than-20%-owned domestic corporations	40,000
Opcrating expenses	100,000
Charitable contributions (cash)	11,000

a. What is Omega's charitable contributions deduction for the current year and its charitable contributions carryover to next year, if any?

b. What is Omega's taxable income for the current year, assuming qualified production activities income is $20,000?

C3-40 *Dividends-Received Deduction.* Theta Corporation reports the following results for the current year:

Gross profits on sales	$220,000
Dividends from less-than-20%-owned domestic corporations	100,000
Operating expenses	218,000

a. What is Theta's taxable income for the current year, assuming qualified production activities income is $2,000?

b. How would your answer to Part a change if Theta's operating expenses are instead $234,000, assuming qualified production activities income is zero or negative?

c. How would your answer to Part a change if Theta's operating expenses are instead $252,000, assuming qualified production activities income is zero or negative?

d. How would your answers to Parts a, b, and c change if Theta received $75,000 of the dividends from a 20%-owned corporation and the remaining $25,000 from a less-than-20%-owned corporation?

C3-41 *Stock Held 45 Days or Less.* Beta Corporation purchased 100 shares of Gamma Corporation common stock (less than 5% of the outstanding stock) two days before the ex-dividend date for $200,000. Beta receives a $10,000 cash dividend from Gamma. Beta sells the Gamma stock one week after purchasing it for $190,000. What are the tax consequences of these three events?

C3-42 *Debt-financed Stock.* Cheers Corporation borrowed $400,000 and used $100,000 of its cash to purchase 5,000 shares of Beer Corporation common stock (less than 5% of the outstanding Beer stock) at the beginning of the current year. Cheers paid $50,000 of interest on the debt this year. Cheers received a $40,000 cash dividend on the Beer stock on September 1 of the current year.

a. What amount can Cheers deduct for the interest paid on the loan?

b. What dividends-received deduction can Cheers claim with respect to the dividend?

C3-43 *Net Operating Loss Carrybacks and Carryovers.* In 2006, Ace Corporation reports gross income of $200,000 (including $150,000 of profit from its operations and $50,000 in dividends from less-than-20%-owncd domestic corporations) and $220,000 of operating expenses. Ace's 2004 taxable income (all ordinary income) was $75,000, on which it paid taxes of $13,750.

a. What is Ace's NOL for 2006?

b. What is the amount of Ace's tax refund if Ace carries back the 2006 NOL to 2004?

c. Assume that Ace expects 2007's taxable income to be $400,000. Assume further that qualified production activities income is sufficiently less than taxable income so that the carryover will not affect the U.S. production activities deduction. What election could Ace make to increase the tax benefit from its NOL? What is the dollar amount of the expected benefit (if any)?

C3-44 *Ordering of Deductions.* Beta Corporation reports the following results for the current year:

Gross income from operations	$180,000
Dividends from less-than-20%-owned domestic corporations	100,000
Operating expenses	150,000
Charitable contributions	20,000

In addition, Beta has a $50,000 NOL carryover from the preceding tax year, and its qualified production activities income is $30,000.
a. What is Beta's taxable income for the current year?
b. What carrybacks or carryovers are available to other tax years?

C3-45   *Sale to a Related Party.* Union Corporation sells a truck for $18,000 to Jane, who owns 70% of its stock. The truck has a $24,000 adjusted basis on the sale date. Jane sells the truck to an unrelated party, Mike, for $28,000 two years later after claiming $5,000 in depreciation.
a. What is Union's realized and recognized gain or loss on selling the truck?
b. What is Jane's realized and recognized gain or loss on selling the truck to Mike?
c. How would your answers to Part b change if Jane instead sold the truck for $10,000?

C3-46   *Payment to a Cash Basis Employee/Shareholder.* Value Corporation is a calendar year taxpayer that uses the accrual method of accounting. On December 10, 2006, Value accrues a bonus payment of $100,000 to Brett, its president and sole shareholder. Brett is a calendar year taxpayer who uses the cash method of accounting.
a. When can Value deduct the bonus if it pays it to Brett on March 11, 2007? On March 18, 2007?
b. How would your answers to Part a change if Brett were an employee of Value who owns no stock in the corporation?

C3-47   *Capital Gains and Losses.* Western Corporation reports the following results for the current year:

Gross profits on sales	$150,000
Long-term capital gain	8,000
Long-term capital loss	15,000
Short-term capital gain	10,000
Short-term capital loss	2,000
Operating expenses	61,000

a. What are Western's taxable income and income tax liability for the current year, assuming qualified production activities income is $89,000?
b. How would your answers to Part a change if Western's short-term capital loss is $5,000 instead of $2,000?

C3-48   *Computing the Corporate Income Tax Liability.* What is Beta Corporation's income tax liability assuming its taxable income is (a) $94,000, (b) $300,000, and (c) $600,000. How would your answers change if Beta were characterized as a personal service corporation?

C3-49   *Computing the Corporate Income Tax Liability.* Fawn Corporation, a C corporation, paid no dividends and recognized no capital gains or losses in the current year. What is its income tax liability assuming its taxable income for the year is
a. $50,000
b. $14,000,000
c. $18,000,000
d. $34,000,000

C3-50   *Computing Taxable Income and Income Tax Liability.* Pace Corporation reports the following results for the current year:

Gross profit on sales	$120,000
Long-term capital loss	10,000
Short-term capital loss	5,000
Dividends from 40%-owned domestic corporation	30,000
Operating expenses	65,000
Charitable contributions	10,000

a. What are Pace's taxable income and income tax liability, assuming qualified production activities income is $55,000?
b. What carrybacks and carryovers (if any) are available and to what years must they be carried?

C3-51   *Computing Taxable Income and Income Tax Liability.* Roper Corporation reports the following results for the current year:

Gross profits on sales	$80,000
Short-term capital gain	40,000
Long-term capital gain	25,000
Dividends from 25%-owned domestic corporation	15,000
NOL carryover from the preceding tax year	9,000
Operating expenses	45,000

What are Roper's taxable income and income tax liability, assuming qualified production activities income is $35,000?

C3-52 ***Controlled Groups.*** Which of the following groups constitute controlled groups? (Any stock not listed below is held by unrelated individuals each owning less than 1% of the outstanding stock.) For brother-sister corporations, which definition applies?

a. Judy owns 90% of the single classes of stock of Hot and Ice Corporations.

b. Jones and Kane Corporations each have only a single class of stock outstanding. The two controlling individual shareholders own the stock as follows:

	Stock Ownership Percentages	
Shareholder	*Jones Corp.*	*Kane Corp.*
Tom	60%	80%
Mary	30%	0%

c. Link, Model, and Name Corporations each have a single class of stock outstanding. The stock is owned as follows:

	Stock Ownership Percentages	
Shareholder	*Model Corp.*	*Name Corp.*
Link Corp.	80%	50%
Model Corp.		40%

Link Corporation's stock is widely held by over 1,000 shareholders, none of whom owns directly or indirectly more than 1% of Link's stock.

d. Oat, Peach, Rye, and Seed Corporations each have a single class of stock outstanding. The stock is owned as follows:

	Stock Ownership Percentages			
Shareholder	*Oat Corp.*	*Peach Corp.*	*Rye Corp.*	*Seed Corp.*
Bob	100%	90%		
Oat Corp.			80%	30%
Rye Corp.				60%

C3-53 ***Controlled Groups of Corporations.*** Sally owns 100% of the outstanding stock of Eta, Theta, Phi, and Gamma Corporations, each of which files a separate return for the current year. During the current year, the corporations report taxable income as follows:

Corporation	*Taxable Income*
Eta	$40,000
Theta	(25,000)
Phi	50,000
Gamma	10,000

a. What is each corporation's separate tax liability, assuming the corporations do not elect a special apportionment plan for allocating the corporate tax rates?

b. What is each corporation's separate tax liability, assuming the corporations make a special election to apportion the reduced corporate tax rates in such a way that minimizes the group's total tax liability? Note: More than one plan can satisfy this goal.

C3-54 ***Compensation Planning.*** Marilyn owns all of Bell Corporation's stock. Bell is a C corporation and employs 40 people. Marilyn is married, has two dependent children, and files a joint tax return with her husband. In the past, Marilyn has not itemized her deductions. She projects that Bell will report $400,000 of pretax profits for 2006. Marilyn is considering five salary levels as shown below. Ignore the U.S. production activities deduction for this problem.

Total Income	Salary Paid to Marilyn	Earnings Retained by Bell Corporation	Tax Liability Marilyn	Tax Liability Bell Corporation	Tax Liability Total
$400,000	$ -0-	$400,000			
400,000	$100,000	300,000			
400,000	200,000	200,000			
400,000	300,000	100,000			
400,000	400,000	-0-			

a. Determine the total tax liability for Marilyn and Bell for each of the five proposed salary levels. Assume no other income for Marilyn's family, and assume that Marilyn and her husband claim the standard deduction. Also, ignore employment taxes.

b. What recommendations can you make about a salary level for Marilyn that will minimize the total tax liability? Assume salaries paid up to $400,000 are considered reasonable compensation.

c. What is the possible disadvantage to Marilyn if Bell retains funds in the business and distributes some of the accumulated earnings as a dividend in a later tax year?

C3-55 *Fringe Benefits.* Refer to the facts in Problem C3-54. Marilyn has read an article explaining the advantages of paying tax-free fringe benefits (premiums on group term life insurance, accident and health insurance, etc.) and having deferred compensation plans (e.g., qualified pension and profit-sharing plans). Provide Marilyn with information on the tax savings associated with converting $3,000 of her salary into tax-free fringe benefits. What additional costs might Bell Corporation incur if it adopts a fringe benefit plan?

C3-56 *Estimated Tax Requirement.* Zeta Corporation's taxable income for 2005 was $1.5 million, on which Zeta paid federal income taxes of $510,000. Zeta estimates calendar year 2006's taxable income to be $2 million, on which it will owe $680,000 in federal income taxes.

a. What are Zeta's minimum quarterly estimated tax payments for 2006 to avoid an underpayment penalty?

b. When is Zeta's 2006 tax return due?

c. When are any remaining taxes due? What amount of taxes are due when Zeta files its return assuming Zeta timely pays estimated tax payments equal to the amount determined in Part a?

d. If Zeta obtains an extension to file, when is its tax return due? Will the extension permit Zeta to delay making its final tax payments?

C3-57 *Filing the Tax Return and Paying the Tax Liability.* Wright Corporation's taxable income for calendar years 2003, 2004, and 2005 was $120,000, $150,000, and $100,000, respectively. Its total tax liability for 2005 was $22,250. Wright estimates that its 2006 taxable income will be $500,000, on which it will owe federal income taxes of $170,000. Assume Wright earns its 2006 taxable income evenly throughout the year.

a. What are Wright's minimum quarterly estimated tax payments for 2006 to avoid an underpayment penalty?

b. When is Wright's 2006 tax return due?

c. When are any remaining taxes due? What amount of taxes are due when Wright files its return assuming it timely paid estimated tax payments equal to the amount determined in Part a?

d. How would your answer to Part a change if Wright's tax liability for 2005 had been $200,000?

C3-58 *Converting Book Income to Taxable Income.* The following income and expense accounts appeared in the accounting records of Rocket Corporation, an accrual basis taxpayer, for the current calendar year.

Account Title	Book Income Debit	Book Income Credit
Net sales		$ 3,000,000
Dividends		8,000 (1)
Interest		18,000 (2)
Gain on sale of stock		5,000 (3)
Key-person life insurance proceeds		100,000
Cost of goods sold	$2,000,000	
Salaries and wages	500,000	
Bad debts	13,000 (4)	

Payroll taxes	62,000	
Interest expense	12,000 (5)	
Charitable contributions	50,000 (6)	
Depreciation	60,000 (7)	
Other expenses	40,000 (8)	
Federal income taxes	96,000	
Net income	298,000	
Total	$3,131,000	$3,131,000

The following additional information applies.
1. Dividends were from Star Corporation, a 30%-owned domestic corporation.
2. Interest revenue consists of interest on corporate bonds, $15,000; and municipal bonds, $3,000.
3. The stock is a capital asset held for three years prior to sale.
4. Rocket uses the specific writeoff method of accounting for bad debts.
5. Interest expense consists of $11,000 interest incurred on funds borrowed for working capital and $1,000 interest on funds borrowed to purchase municipal bonds.
6. Rocket paid all contributions in cash during the current year to State University.
7. Rocket calculated depreciation per books using the straight-line method. For income tax purposes, depreciation amounted to $85,000.
8. Other expenses include premiums of $5,000 on the key-person life insurance policy covering Rocket's president, who died in December.
9. Qualified production activities income is $250,000.

Required: Prepare a worksheet reconciling Rocket's book income with its taxable income (before special deductions). Six columns should be used—two (one debit and one credit) for each of the following three major headings: book income, Schedule M-1 adjustments, and taxable income. (See the sample worksheet with Form 1120 in Appendix B if you need assistance).

C3-59 *Reconciling Book Income and Taxable Income.* Zero Corporation reports the following results for the current year:

Net income per books (after taxes)	$33,000
Federal income tax per books	12,000
Tax-exempt interest income	6,000
Interest on loan to purchase tax-exempt bonds	8,000
MACRS depreciation exceeding book depreciation	3,000
Net capital loss	5,000
Insurance premium on life of corporate officer where Zero is the beneficiary	10,000
Excess charitable contributions carried over to next year	2,500
U.S. production activities deduction	1,000

Prepare a reconciliation of Zero's taxable income before special deductions with its book income.

C3-60 *Reconciling Unappropriated Retained Earnings.* White Corporation's financial accounting records disclose the following results for the period ending December 31 of the current year:

Retained earnings balance on January 1	$246,500
Net income for year	259,574
Contingency reserve established on December 31	60,000
Cash dividend paid on July 23	23,000

What is White's unappropriated retained earnings balance on December 31 of the current year?

COMPREHENSIVE PROBLEM

C3-61 Jackson Corporation prepared the following *book* income statement for its year ended December 31, 2006:

Sales	$765,000
Minus: Cost of goods sold	(400,000)
Gross profit	$365,000

Plus:	Dividends received on Invest Corporation stock	$ 3,000	
	Gain on sale of Invest Corporation stock	30,000	
	Total dividends and gain		33,000
Minus:	Depreciation ($7,500 + $8,000)	$ 15,500	
	Charitable contributions	20,000	
	Other operating expenses	105,500	
	Loss on sale of Equipment 1	70,000	
	Federal income taxes per books	60,000	
	Total expenses and loss		(271,000)
Net income per books			$127,000

Information on equipment depreciation and sale:

Equipment 1:

- Acquired March 3, 2004 for $180,000
- For books: 12-year life; straight-line depreciation
- Sold February 17, 2006 for $80,000

Sales price			$ 80,000
Cost		$180,000	
Minus:	Depreciation for 2004 (½ year)	$ 7,500	
	Depreciation for 2005 ($180,000/12)	15,000	
	Depreciation for 2006 (½ year)	7,500	
	Total depreciation	(30,000)	
Book value at time of sale			(150,000)
Book loss on sale of Equipment 1			($70,000)

- For tax: 7-year MACRS property for which the corporation made no Sec. 179 election in the acquisition year and did not claim additional first-year depreciation.

Equipment 2:

- Acquired February 16, 2006 for $192,000
- For books: 12-year life; straight-line depreciation
- Book depreciation in 2006: $192,000/12 × 0.5 = $8,000
- For tax: 7-year MACRS property for which the corporation makes the Sec. 179 election.

Other information:

- Jackson has a $40,000 NOL carryover and a $6,000 capital loss carryover from last year.
- Jackson purchased the Invest Corporation stock (less than 20% owned) on June 21, 2004 for $25,000 and sold the stock on December 22, 2006 for $55,000.
- Jackson Corporation has qualified production activities income of $123,000. Its W-2 payroll wages equal $120,000.

Required:
a. For 2006, calculate Jackson's tax depreciation deduction for Equipment 1 and Equipment 2, and determine the tax loss on the sale of Equipment 1.
b. For 2006, calculate Jackson's taxable income and tax liability.
c. Prepare a schedule reconciling net income per books to taxable income before special deductions.

TAX STRATEGY PROBLEM

C3-62　Mike Barton owns Barton Products, Inc. The corporation has 30 employees. Barton Corporation expects $500,000 of net income before taxes in 2006. Mike is married and files a joint return with his wife, Elaine, who has no earnings of her own. They have one dependent son, Robert, who is 16 years old. Mike and Elaine have no other income and do not itemize. Mike's salary is $230,000 per year (already deducted in computing Barton Corporation's $500,000 net income). Assume that variations in salaries will not affect the U.S. production activities deduction already reflected in taxable income.

a. Should Mike increase his salary from Barton to reduce the overall tax burden to himself and Barton Products? If so, by how much?

b. Should Barton employ Mike's wife for $50,000 rather than increase Mike's salary? Take into consideration employment taxes as well as federal income taxes.

c. How much would be saved in overall taxes if Barton employs Robert part-time for $20,000 per year? Assume the corporation and Robert each would incur a 7.65% payroll tax with the corporate portion being deductible.

TAX FORM/RETURN PREPARATION PROBLEM

C3-63 Knoxville Musical Sales, Inc. is located at 5500 Kingston Pike, Knoxville, TN 37919. The corporation uses the calendar year and accrual basis for both book and tax purposes. It is engaged in the sale of musical instruments with an employer identification number (EIN) of 75-2007005. The company incorporated on December 31, 2001 and began business on January 2, 2002. Table C3-3 contains balance sheet information at January 1, 2005, and December 31, 2005. Table C3-4 presents an income statement for 2005. These schedules are presented on a book basis. Other information follows.

Estimated Tax Payments (Form 2220):
The corporation deposited estimated tax payments as follows:

April 15, 2005	$ 130,000
June 15, 2005	270,000
September 15, 2005	316,000
December 15, 2005	316,000
Total	$1,032,000

Taxable income in 2004 was $2,400,000, and the 2004 tax was $816,000. The corporation earned its 2005 taxable income evenly throughout the year. Therefore, it does not use the annualization or seasonal methods.

▼ TABLE C3-3
Knoxville Musical Sales, Inc.—Book Balance Sheet Information

Account	January 1, 2005 Debit	January 1, 2005 Credit	December 31, 2005 Debit	December 31, 2005 Credit
Cash	$ 229,741		$ 259,841	
Accounts receivable	464,400		540,000	
Allowance for doubtful accounts		$ 39,474		$ 45,900
Inventory	2,500,000		3,500,000	
Investment in corporate stock	160,000		36,000	
Investment in municipal bonds	20,000		20,000	
Cash surrender value of insurance policy	20,000		34,000	
Land	200,000		200,000	
Buildings	2,000,000		2,000,000	
Accumulated depreciation—Buildings		100,000		140,000
Equipment	520,000		780,000	
Accumulated depreciation—Equipment		86,667		103,167
Trucks	250,000		160,000	
Accumulated depreciation—Trucks		75,000		16,000
Accounts payable		1,400,000		550,000
Notes payable (short-term)		500,000		600,000
Accrued payroll taxes		25,000		28,000
Accrued state income taxes		8,000		11,000
Accrued federal income taxes				140,000
Bonds payable (long-term)		1,600,000		1,200,000
Deferred tax liability		80,000		85,000
Capital stock—Common		1,200,000		1,200,000
Retain earnings—Unappropriated		1,250,000		3,410,774
Totals	$6,364,141	$6,364,141	$7,529,841	$7,529,841

▼ **TABLE C3-4**

Knoxville Musical Sales, Inc.—Book Income Statement 2005

Sales		$10,000,000
Returns		(250,000)
Net sales		$ 9,750,000
Beginning inventory	$2,500,000	
Purchases	5,500,000	
Ending inventory	(3,500,000)	
Cost of goods sold		(4,500,000)
Gross profit		$ 5,250,000
Expenses:		
Amortization	$ –0–	
Depreciation	131,500	
Repairs	20,800	
General insurance	55,000	
Premium–Officers' life insurance (net of cash buildup)	45,000	
Officer's compensation	650,000	
Other salaries	400,000	
Utilities	72,000	
Advertising	48,000	
Legal and accounting fees	50,000	
Charitable contributions	30,000	
Employment tax	62,500	
State tax	75,000	
Interest	210,000	
Bad debts	46,426	
Total expenses		(1,896,226)
Loss on exchange of trucks		(20,000)
Gain on sale of equipment		64,000
Interest on municipal bonds		5,000
Net gain on stock sales		13,000
Dividend income		12,000
Net income before FIT expense		$ 3,427,774
Federal income tax (FIT) expense		(1,177,000)
Net income per books		$ 2,250,774

Inventory and Cost of Goods Sold (Schedule A):
The corporation uses the periodic inventory method and prices its inventory using the lower of FIFO cost or market. Only beginning inventory, ending inventory, and purchases should be reflected in Schedule A. No other costs or expenses are allocated to cost of goods sold. Note: the corporation is exempt from the uniform capitalization (UNICAP) rules because average gross income for the previous three years was less than $10 million.

Line 9 (a)	Check (ii)
(b), (c) & (d)	Not applicable
(e) & (f)	No

Compensation of Officers (Schedule E):

(a)	(b)	(c)	(d)	(f)
Mary Travis	345-82-7091	100%	50%	$295,000
John Willis	783-97-9105	100%	25%	180,000
Chris Parker	465-34-2245	100%	25%	175,000
Total				$650,000

Bad Debts:
For tax purposes, the corporation uses the direct writeoff method of deducting bad debts. For book purposes, the corporation uses an allowance for doubtful accounts. During 2005,

the corporation charged $40,000 to the allowance account, such amount representing actual writeoffs for 2005.

Additional Information (Schedule K):

1 b	Accrual	6-7	No
2 a	451140	8	Do not check box
b	Retail sales	9	Fill in the correct amount
c	Musical instruments	10	3
3-4	No	11	Do not check box
5	Yes, 50%	12	Not applicable
		13	No

Organizational Expenditures:
The corporation incurred $5,100 of organizational expenditures on January 2, 2002. For book purposes, the corporation expensed the entire expenditure pursuant to Statement of Position 98-5. For tax purposes, the corporation elected under Sec. 248 to amortize this amount over 60 months (the rule then in effect), with a full month's amortization taken for January 2002. The corporation reports this amortization in Part VI of Form 4562 and includes it in "Other Deductions" on Form 1120, Line 26.

Capital Gains and Losses:
The corporation sold 100 shares of PDQ Corp. common stock on March 7, 2005 for $85,000. The corporation acquired the stock on December 15, 2004 for $60,000. The corporation also sold 75 shares of JSB Corp. common stock on September 17, 2005 for $52,000. The corporation acquired this stock on September 18, 2002 for $64,000. The corporation has a $5,000 capital loss carryover from 2004.

Fixed Assets and Depreciation:
For book purposes: The corporation uses straight-line depreciation over the useful lives of assets as follows: Store building, 50 years; Equipment, 15 years (old) and ten years (new); and Trucks, five years (old and new). The corporation takes a half-year's depreciation in the year of acquisition and the year of disposition and assumes no salvage value. The book financial statements in Tables C3-3 and C3-4 reflect these calculations. The designation "old" refers to property placed in service before 2005, and the designation "new" refers to property placed in service in 2005.

For tax purposes: All assets are MACRS property as follows: Store building, 39-year non-residential real property; Equipment, seven-year property; and Trucks, five-year property. The corporation acquired the store building for $2 million and placed it in service on January 2, 2002. The corporation acquired two pieces of equipment for $170,000 (Equipment 1) and $350,000 (Equipment 2) and placed them in service on January 2, 2002. The corporation acquired the old trucks for $250,000 and placed them in service on July 18, 2003. The corporation did not make the expensing election under Sec. 179 on any property acquired before 2005 and elected not to claim bonus depreciation. Also, the corporation did not elect the straight-line option or the alternative depreciation system (ADS) under MACRS. Accumulated tax depreciation through December 31, 2004 on these properties is as follows:

Store building	$151,780
Equipment 1	95,659
Equipment 2	196,945
Trucks	130,000

On November 16, 2005, the corporation sold for $200,000 Equipment 1 that originally cost $170,000 on January 2, 2002. The corporation had no Sec. 1231 losses from prior years. In a separate transaction on November 17, 2005, the corporation acquired and placed in service a piece of equipment costing $430,000. These two transactions do *not* qualify as a like-kind exchange under Reg. Sec. 1.1031(k)-1(a). The new equipment is seven-year property. The corporation made the Sec. 179 expensing election with regard to the new equipment. The corporation relies on Sec. 179(d)(3) and Reg. Sec. 1.179-4(d) to determine the cost of its Sec. 179 property.

On May 15, 2005, the corporation exchanged its entire fleet of delivery trucks, which cost $250,000 on July 18, 2003 for similar trucks. On the date of exchange, the old trucks had a $130,000 FMV, and the new trucks had a $160,000 FMV. As part of the exchange, the corporation paid $30,000 cash in addition to the old trucks. For tax purposes, the exchange qualifies as a like-kind exchange. The new trucks are five-year property. Assume that neither the old nor new trucks are listed property according to Reg. Sec. 1.280F-6(c)(3)(iii) and Temp. Reg. Sec. 1.274-5T(k). The corporation relies on Temp. Reg. Sec. 1.168(i)-6T to compute depreciation on the new trucks.

Where applicable, use published IRS depreciation tables to compute 2005 depreciation (reproduced in Appendix C of this text).

Other Information:

- The corporation's activities do not qualify for the U.S. production activities deduction.
- Ignore the AMT and accumulated earnings tax.
- The corporation received the $12,000 in dividends from taxable, domestic corporations, the stock of which Knoxville Musical Sales, Inc. owns less than 20%.
- The corporation paid $90,000 in cash dividends to its shareholders during 2005 and charged the payment directly to retained earnings.
- The corporation issued the bonds payable at par. Thus, no premium or discount need be amortized.
- The corporation is not entitled any credits.

Required: Prepare the 2005 corporate tax return for Knoxville Musical Sales, Inc. along with any necessary supporting schedules.

C3-64 Permtemp Corporation formed in 2004 and, for that year, reported the following book income statement and balance sheet, excluding the federal income tax expense, deferred tax assets, and deferred tax liabilities:

Sales		$20,000,000
Cost of goods sold		(15,000,000)
Gross profit		$ 5,000,000
Dividend income		50,000
Tax-exempt interest income		15,000
Total income		$ 5,065,000
Expenses:		
Depreciation	$ 800,000	
Bad debts	400,000	
Charitable contributions	100,000	
Interest	475,000	
Meals and entertainment	45,000	
Other	3,855,000	
Total expenses		(5,675,000)
Net loss before federal income taxes		$ (610,000)
Cash		$ 500,000
Accounts receivable	$ 2,000,000	
Allowance for doubtful accounts	(250,000)	1,750,000
Inventory		4,000,000
Fixed assets	$10,000,000	
Accumulated depreciation	(800,000)	9,200,000
Investment in corporate stock		1,000,000
Investment in tax-exempt bonds		50,000
Total assets		$16,500,000
Accounts payable		$2,610,000
Long-term debt		8,500,000
Common stock		6,000,000
Retained earnings		(610,000)
Total liabilities and equity		$16,500,000

Additional information for 2004:

- The investment in corporate stock is comprised of less-than-20%-owned corporations.
- Depreciation for tax purposes is $1.4 million under MACRS.
- Bad debt expense for tax purposes is $150,000 under the direct writeoff method.

- Limitations to charitable contribution deductions and meals and entertainment expenses must be tested and applied if necessary.

Required for 2004:
a. Prepare page 1 of the 2004 Form 1120, computing the corporation's NOL.
b. Determine the corporation's deferred tax asset and deferred tax liability situation, and then complete the income statement and balance sheet to reflect proper SFAS 109 accounting. Use the balance sheet information to prepare Schedule L of the 2004 Form 1120.
c. Prepare the 2004 Schedule M-3 for Form 1120. Fill out all columns even though some are designated as optional.

Note: For 2004 forms, go to previous year forms at the IRS website, *www.irs.gov.*

For 2005, Permtemp reported the following book income statement and balance sheet, excluding the federal income tax expense, deferred tax assets, and deferred tax liabilities:

Sales		$33,000,000
Cost of goods sold		(22,000,000)
Gross profit		$11,000,000
Dividend income		55,000
Tax-exempt interest income		15,000
Total income		$11,070,000
Expenses:		
Depreciation	$ 800,000	
Bad debts	625,000	
Charitable contributions	40,000	
Interest	455,000	
Meals and entertainment	60,000	
Other	4,675,000	
Total expenses		(6,655,000)
Net income before federal income taxes		$ 4,415,000
Cash		$ 2,125,000
Accounts receivable	$ 3,300,000	
Allowance for doubtful accounts	(450,000)	2,850,000
Inventory		6,000,000
Fixed assets	$10,000,000	
Accumulated depreciation	(1,600,000)	8,400,000
Investment in corporate stock		1,000,000
Investment in tax-exempt bonds		50,000
Total assets		$20,425,000
Accounts payable		$ 2,120,000
Long-term debt		8,500,000
Common stock		6,000,000
Retained earnings		3,805,000
		$20,425,000

Additional information for 2005:
- Depreciation for tax purposes is $2.45 million under MACRS.
- Bad debt expense for tax purposes is $425,000 under the direct writeoff method.
- Qualified production activities income is $3 million.

Required for 2005:
a. Prepare page 1 of the 2005 Form 1120, computing the corporation's taxable income and tax liability.
b. Determine the corporation's deferred tax asset and deferred tax liability situation, and then complete the income statement and balance sheet to reflect proper SFAS 109 accounting. Use the balance sheet information to prepare Schedule L of the 2005 Form 1120.
c. Prepare the 2005 Schedule M-3 for Form 1120.

CASE STUDY PROBLEMS

C3-65 Marquette Corporation, a tax client since its creation three years ago, has requested that you prepare a memorandum explaining its estimated tax requirements for 2007. The corporation is in the fabricated steel business. Its earnings have been growing each year. Marquette's taxable income for the last three tax years has been $500,000, $1.5 million, and $2.5 million, respectively. The Chief Financial Officer expects its taxable income in 2007 to be approximately $3 million.

Required: Prepare a one-page client memorandum explaining Marquette's estimated tax requirements for 2007, providing the necessary supporting authorities.

C3-66 Susan Smith accepted a new corporate client, Winter Park Corporation. One of Susan's tax managers conducted a review of Winter Park's prior year tax returns. The review revealed that an NOL for a prior tax year was incorrectly computed, resulting in an overstatement of NOL carrybacks and carryovers to prior tax years.

a. Assume the incorrect NOL calculation does not affect the current year's tax liability. What recommendations (if any) should Susan make to the new client?

b. Assume the IRS is currently auditing a prior year. What are Susan's responsibilities in this situation?

c. Assume the NOL carryover is being carried to the current year, and Winter Park does not want to file amended tax returns to correct the error. What should Susan do in this situation?

C3-67 The Chief Executive Officer of a client of your public accounting firm saw the following advertisement in *The Wall Street Journal:*

DONATIONS WANTED
The Center for Restoration of Waters
A Nonprofit Research and Educational Organization
Needs Donations—Autos, Boats, Real Estate, Etc.
ALL DONATIONS ARE TAX-DEDUCTIBLE

Prepare a memorandum to your client Phil Nickelson explaining how the federal income tax laws regarding donations of cash, automobiles, boats, and real estate apply to corporate taxpayers.

TAX RESEARCH PROBLEMS

C3-68 Wicker Corporation makes estimated tax payments of $6,000 in 2005. On March 15, 2006, it files its 2005 tax return showing a $20,000 tax liability, and it pays the $14,000 balance at that time. On April 15, 2006, it discovers an error and files an amended return for 2005 showing a reduced tax liability of $8,000. Prepare a memorandum for your tax manager explaining whether Wicker can base its estimated tax payments for 2006 on the $8,000 tax liability for 2005, or must it use the $20,000 tax liability reported on its original return. Your manager has suggested that, at a minimum, you consult the following resources:

- IRC Sec. 6655(d)(1)
- Rev. Rul. 86-58, 1986-1 C.B. 365

C3-69 Alice, Bill, and Charles each received an equal number of shares when they formed King Corporation a number of years ago. King has used the cash method of accounting since its inception. Alice, Bill, and Charles, the shareholder-employees, operate King as an environmental engineering firm with 57 additional employees. King had gross receipts of $4.3 million in 2005. Gross receipts have grown by about 15% in each of the last three years and were just under $5 million in 2006. The owners expect the 15% growth rate to continue for at least five years. Outstanding accounts receivable average about $600,000 at the end of each month. Forty-four employees (including Alice, Bill, and Charles) actively engage in providing engineering services on a full-time basis. The remaining 16 employees serve in a clerical and support capacity (secretarial staff, accountants, etc.). Bill has read about special restrictions on the use of the cash method of accounting and requests information from you about the impact these rules might have on King's continued use of that method. Prepare a memorandum for your tax manager addressing the following issues: (1) If the corporation changes to the accrual method of accounting, what adjustments must it make? (2) Would an S election relieve King from having to make a change? (3) If the S election relieves King from having to make a change, what factors should enter into the decision about whether King should make an S election?

Your manager has suggested that, at a minimum, you should consult the following resources:

- IRC Secs. 446 and 448
- Temp. Reg. Secs. 1.448-1T and -2T
- H. Rept. No. 99-841, 99th Cong., 2d Sess., pp. 285–289 (1986)

C3-70 James Bowen owns 100% of Bowen Corporation stock. Bowen is a calendar year, accrual method taxpayer. During 2006, Bowen made three charitable contributions:

Donee	Property Donated	FMV of Property
State University	Bates Corporation stock	$110,000
Red Cross	Cash	5,000
Girl Scouts	Pledge to pay cash	25,000

Bowen purchased the Bates stock three years ago for $30,000. Bowen holds a 28% interest, which it accounts for under GAAP using the equity method of accounting. The current carrying value for the Bates stock for book purposes is $47,300. Bowen will pay the pledge to the Girl Scouts by check on March 1, 2007. Bowen's taxable income for the current year before the charitable contributions deduction, dividends-received deduction, NOL deduction, and U.S. production activities deduction is $600,000. Your tax manager has asked you to prepare a memorandum explaining how these transactions are to be treated for tax purposes and for accounting purposes. Your manager has suggested that, at a minimum, you should consult the following resources:

- IRC Sec. 170
- FASB, *Statement of Financial Accounting Standards No. 116*

C3-71 Production Corporation owns 70% of Manufacturing Corporation's common stock and Rita Howard owns the remaining 30%. Each corporation operates and sells its product within the United States, and the corporations engaged in no intercompany transactions. Production's Chief Financial Officer (CFO) presents you with the following information pertaining to 2006 operations:

	Production Corporation	Manufacturing Corporation
Gross profit on sales	$500,000	$225,000
Minus: Operating expenses	(200,000)	(100,000)
Qualified production activities income	$300,000	$125,000
Plus: Dividends received from 20%-owned corporations	20,000	-0-
Minus: Dividends-received deduction	(16,000)	-0-
NOL carryover deduction	-0-	(15,000)
Taxable income before the U.S. production activities deduction	$304,000	$110,000

Operating expenses include W-2 wages of $75,000 and $35,000 for Production and Manufacturing, respectively. Given this information, the CFO asks you to determine each corporation's qualified production activities deduction. At a minimum, you should consult the following resources:

- IRC Sec. 199
- Prop. Reg. Sec. 1.199-7

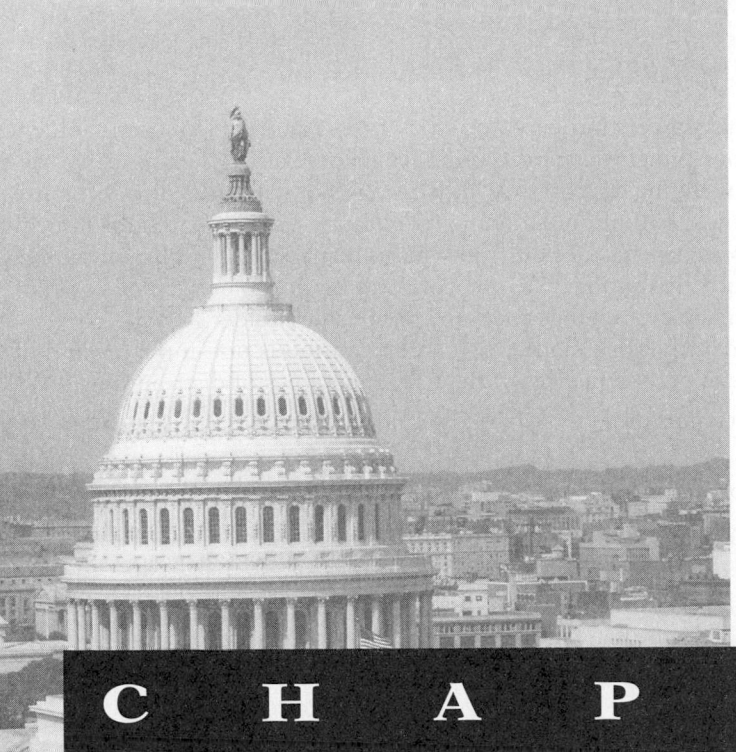

4

CHAPTER

CORPORATE NONLIQUIDATING DISTRIBUTIONS

LEARNING OBJECTIVES

After studying this chapter, you should be able to

1. ► Calculate corporate current earnings and profits (E&P)

2. ► Distinguish between current and accumulated E&P

3. ► Determine the tax consequences of nonliquidating distributions

4. ► Determine the tax consequences of stock dividends and distributions of stock rights

5. ► Discern when a stock redemption is treated as a sale and when it is treated as a dividend

6. ► Explain the tax treatment of preferred stock bailouts

7. ► Determine the applicability and tax consequences of Sec. 304 to stock sales

A corporation may distribute money, property, or stock to its shareholders. Shareholders who receive such distributions might recognize ordinary income, capital gain, or no taxable income at all. The distributing corporation may or may not be required to recognize gain or loss when making the distribution. How the corporation and its shareholders treat distributions for tax purposes depends not only on what is distributed but also on the circumstances surrounding the distribution. Was the corporation in the process of liquidating? Was the distribution made in exchange for some of the shareholder's stock?

This chapter discusses distributions made when a corporation is not in the process of liquidating. It discusses the tax consequences of the following types of distributions:

▶ Distributions of cash or other property where the shareholder does not surrender any stock

▶ Distributions of stock or rights to acquire stock of the distributing corporation

▶ Distributions of property in exchange for the corporation's own stock (i.e., stock redemptions)

Chapter C6 discusses **liquidating distributions**. Chapter C7 discusses a parent corporation's distribution of stock it owns in a controlled subsidiary corporation.

NONLIQUIDATING DISTRIBUTIONS IN GENERAL

SELF-STUDY QUESTION

How does a shareholder classify a distribution for tax purposes?

ANSWER

Distributions are treated as follows: (1) dividends to the extent of corporate E&P, (2) return of capital to the extent of the shareholder's stock basis, and (3) gain from the sale of stock.

When a corporation makes a nonliquidating distribution to a shareholder, the shareholder must answer the following three questions:

▶ What is the amount of the distribution?

▶ To what extent is the amount distributed a dividend?

▶ What is the basis of the distributed property, and when does its holding period begin?

In addition, the distributing corporation must answer the following two questions:

▶ What are the amount and character of the gain or loss that the corporation must recognize on the distribution?

▶ What effect does the distribution have on the distributing corporation's earnings and profits (E&P) account?

A brief summary of the rules for determining the taxability of a distribution follows, along with a simple example.

Section 301 requires a shareholder to include in gross income the amount of any corporate distribution to the extent it is a dividend. Qualified dividends received by a noncorporate schareholder in 2003 through 2008 are subject to a maximum 15% tax rate. Section 316(a) defines a **dividend** as a distribution of property made by a corporation out of its E&P. Earnings and profits are discussed in the next section of this chapter. Section 317(a) defines **property** broadly to include money, securities, and any other property except stock or stock rights of the distributing corporation. Distributed amounts that exceed a corporation's E&P are treated as a return of capital that reduces the shareholder's basis in his or her stock (but not below zero). Distributions exceeding the shareholder's basis are treated as gain from the sale of the stock. If the stock is a capital asset in the shareholder's hands, the gain is capital in character.

EXAMPLE C4-1 ▶ On March 1, Gamma Corporation distributes $60,000 in cash to each of its two equal shareholders, Ellen and Bob. At the time of the distribution, Gamma's E&P is $80,000. Ellen's basis in her stock is $25,000, and Bob's basis in his stock is $10,000. Ellen and Bob each recognize $40,000 (0.50 × $80,000) of dividend income. This portion of the distribution reduces Gamma's E&P to zero. The additional $20,000 that each shareholder receives is a return of capital or capital gain as calculated in the table below.

	Ellen	Bob	Total
Distribution	$60,000	$60,000	$120,000
Dividend income[a]	(40,000)	(40,000)	(80,000)
Remaining distribution	$20,000	$20,000	$ 40,000
Return of capital[b]	(20,000)	(10,000)	(30,000)
Capital gain[c]	$ –0–	$10,000	$ 10,000

[a]Smaller of E&P allocable to the distribution or the amount of the distribution.
[b]Smaller of remaining distribution to shareholder or his or her stock basis.
[c]Any amount received that exceeds the shareholder's basis in his or her stock.

◀

EARNINGS AND PROFITS (E&P)

TYPICAL MISCONCEPTION

Because E&P is such an important concept in many corporate transactions, one would assume that corporations know exactly what their E&P is. However, many corporations do not compute their E&P on a regular basis.

The term E&P is not specifically defined in the IRC. Its meaning must be inferred from judicial opinions, Treasury Regulations, and IRC rules regarding how certain transactions affect E&P.

To some extent, E&P measures a corporation's economic ability to pay dividends to its shareholders. Distributions are presumed to be made out of the corporation's E&P unless the corporation reports no E&P.

CURRENT EARNINGS AND PROFITS

A corporation maintains E&P in two accounts: current E&P and accumulated E&P. **Current E&P** is calculated annually as explained below. **Accumulated E&P** is the sum of undistributed current E&P balances for all previous years reduced by the sum of all previous current E&P deficits and any distributions the corporation has made out of accumulated E&P. Distributions are deemed to have been made first out of current E&P and then out of accumulated E&P to the extent that current E&P is insufficient.

EXAMPLE C4-2 ▶

Zeta Corporation formed in 2003. Its current E&P (or current E&P deficit) and distributions for each year through 2006 are as follows:

Year	Current E&P (Deficit)	Distributions
2003	$(10,000)	–0–
2004	15,000	–0–
2005	18,000	$9,000
2006	8,000	–0–

The corporation makes the $9,000 distribution from its 2005 current E&P account. At the beginning of 2006, Zeta's accumulated E&P balance is $14,000 ($10,000 + $15,000 + $18,000 − $9,000). At the beginning of 2007, Zeta's accumulated E&P balance is $22,000 ($14,000 + $8,000). ◀

OBJECTIVE 1

Calculate corporate current earnings and profits (E&P)

COMPUTING CURRENT E&P. A corporation computes its current E&P on an annual basis at the end of each year. The starting point for computing current E&P is the corporation's taxable income or net operating loss (NOL) for the year. Taxable income or the NOL must be adjusted to derive the corporation's economic income or loss (current E&P) for the year. For example, federal income taxes must be deducted from taxable income when determining E&P. Because the corporation must pay these taxes to the U.S. government, they reduce the amount available to pay dividends to shareholders. On the other hand, tax-exempt income must be added to taxable income (or the NOL) because, even though not taxable, it increases the corporation's ability to pay dividends.

Table C4-1 presents a partial listing of the adjustments the corporation must make to taxable income (NOL) to derive current E&P. Some of these adjustments are explained below.[1]

---

[1] The adjustments are based on rules set forth in Sec. 312 and related Treasury Regulations.

▼ **TABLE C4-1**
Computation of Current E&P

Taxable income

Plus: *Income excluded from taxable income but included in E&P*
    Tax-exempt interest income
    Life insurance proceeds where the corporation is the beneficiary
    Recoveries of bad debts and other deductions from which the corporation received no tax benefit
    Federal income tax refunds from prior years

Plus: *Income deferred to a later year when computing taxable income but included in E&P in the current year*
    Deferred gain on installment sales is included in E&P in the year of sale

Plus or
minus: *Income and deduction items that must be recomputed when computing E&P*
    Income on long-term contracts must be based on percentage of completion method rather than completed
      contract method
    Depreciation on personal and real property must be based on:
      The straight-line method for property other than MACRS or ACRS property
      A straight-line ACRS calculation with an extended recovery period for ACRS property
      The alternative depreciation system for MACRS property
    Excess of percentage depletion over cost depletion

Plus: *Deductions that reduce taxable income but are not allowed in computing E&P*
    Dividends-received deduction
    NOL carryovers, charitable contribution carryovers, and capital loss carryovers used in the current year
    U.S. production activities deduction

Minus: *Expenses and losses that are not deductible in computing taxable income but that reduce E&P*
    Federal income taxes
    Life insurance premiums where the corporation is the beneficiary
    Excess capital losses that are not currently deductible
    Excess charitable contributions that are not currently deductible
    Expenses related to the production of tax-exempt income
    Nondeductible losses on sales to related parties
    Nondeductible penalties and fines
    Nondeductible political contributions and lobbying expenses

Current E&P balance (or deficit)

INCOME EXCLUDED FROM TAXABLE INCOME BUT INCLUDED IN E&P. Although certain income is specifically excluded from taxable income, any income received by the corporation must be included in its E&P if it increases the corporation's ability to pay a dividend and is not a contribution to capital. Thus, a corporation's current E&P includes both tax-exempt interest income and life insurance proceeds. Current E&P also includes any recovery of an item deducted in a previous year if the deduction did not result in a tax benefit to the corporation and therefore was excluded from taxable income.

EXAMPLE C4-3 ▶ Ace Corporation deducted $10,000 of bad debts in 2005. Because Ace Corporation had an NOL in 2005 that it was unable to carry back or forward, it received no tax benefit from the deduction. Ace Corporation recovers $8,000 of the amount due in 2006. Ace excludes the $8,000 from its gross income for 2006 because it received no tax benefit from the bad debt deduction in 2005. However, Ace must add the $8,000 to its taxable income when determining current E&P for 2006 because the NOL reduced current E&P in 2005. ◀

INCOME DEFERRED TO A LATER YEAR WHEN COMPUTING TAXABLE INCOME BUT INCLUDED IN E&P IN THE CURRENT YEAR. Gains and losses on property transactions generally are included in E&P in the same year they are recognized for tax purposes. For example, gain deferred in a like-kind exchange is deferred for E&P purposes as well.

EXAMPLE C4-4 ▶ Stone Corporation exchanges investment property that has a $12,000 basis and an $18,000 fair market value (FMV) for investment property worth $17,000 and $1,000 cash. Stone recognizes a $1,000 gain on the like-kind exchange—the amount of boot received—and defers $5,000 of gain. Stone includes the recognized gain in both taxable income and current E&P. It does not include the deferred gain in either taxable income or current E&P. ◀

In the case of an installment sale, the entire gain must be included in current E&P in the year of the sale. This rule applies to sales made by dealers and nondealers.

EXAMPLE C4-5 ▶ In the current year, Tally Corporation sells land that has a $12,000 basis and a $20,000 FMV to Rick, an unrelated individual. Rick makes a $5,000 down payment this year and will pay Tally an additional $5,000 in each of the next three years, plus interest on the unpaid balance at a rate acceptable to the IRS. Tally's realized gain is $8,000 ($20,000 − $12,000). Tally recognizes gain on the sale under the installment method for nondealers. In computing taxable income, Tally recognizes $2,000 of gain [($8,000 ÷ $20,000) × $5,000] this year. All $8,000 of Tally's realized gain must be included in current E&P. In computing current E&P, Tally's taxable income for this year must be increased by $6,000. As it collects the installments, Tally will recognize the remaining $6,000 of gain over the next three years ($2,000 per year). Accordingly, E&P will have to be reduced by $2,000 in each of those years because all $8,000 was included in E&P in the current year. ◀

SELF-STUDY QUESTION

In computing taxable income and E&P, different depreciation methods are often used. What happens when the taxpayer sells such assets?

ANSWER

The taxpayer must calculate a gain/loss for taxable income and E&P purposes separately. This difference is an added complexity in making E&P calculations.

INCOME AND DEDUCTION ITEMS THAT MUST BE RECOMPUTED WHEN COMPUTING E&P. Some deductions must be computed differently for E&P purposes than for taxable income purposes. Therefore, an adjustment must be made for the difference between the two computations.

▶ E&P must be computed under the percentage of completion method even if the corporation uses the completed contract method of accounting for tax purposes.

▶ Depreciation must be recomputed under the alternative depreciation system of Sec. 168(g). The cost of property expensed under Sec. 179 must be recovered ratably over a five-year period starting with the month in which it is deductible for Sec. 179 purposes. Other personal property must be depreciated over the property's class life under the half-year convention. Real property must be depreciated over a 40-year period for E&P purposes under the straight-line method and mid-month convention.

EXAMPLE C4-6 ▶ In January 2003, Radon Corporation paid $5,000 for equipment with a ten-year class life. Radon expensed the entire cost of the equipment in 2003 under Sec. 179. Radon's depreciation deduction for E&P purposes is $1,000 ($5,000 ÷ 5) in each year from 2003 through 2007. ◀

▶ Cost depletion must be used for E&P purposes even if percentage depletion is used when computing taxable income.

▶ Intangible drilling costs must be capitalized and amortized over 60 months for E&P purposes.

BOOK-TO-TAX ACCOUNTING COMPARISION

Many corporations use retained earnings to measure the taxability of their dividend payments. However, because retained earnings are based on financial accounting concepts, E&P may represent a different amount and may provide a different measure of the corporation's economic ability to pay dividends.

DEDUCTIONS THAT REDUCE TAXABLE INCOME BUT ARE NOT ALLOWED IN COMPUTING E&P. Some deductions claimed when computing taxable income are not allowed when computing current E&P.

▶ The dividends-received deduction is not permitted for E&P purposes because it does not reduce the corporation's ability to pay dividends. Therefore, it must be added back to taxable income to compute E&P.

▶ NOL carryovers, charitable contribution carryovers, and capital loss carryovers that reduce taxable income for the current year cannot be deducted when determining E&P. These losses or excess deductions reduce E&P in the year they are incurred.

▶ The U.S. production activities deduction is not permitted for E&P purposes because it does not reduce the corporation's ability to pay dividends. Therefore, it must be added back to taxable income to compute E&P. See Chapter C3 for a description of this deduction.

▶ Amortization of organizational expenses is not permitted as a deduction for E&P purposes.

EXAMPLE C4-7 ▶ Thames Corporation's taxable income is $500,000 after deductions for the following items: a $10,000 NOL carryover from two years ago, a $20,000 dividends-received deduction, and an $8,000 U.S. production activities deduction. Thames must add $38,000 to its taxable income to compute current E&P. The full $10,000 NOL reduced E&P in the year it was incurred, Thus, current E&P is $538,000. ◀

EXPENSES AND LOSSES THAT ARE NOT DEDUCTIBLE IN COMPUTING TAXABLE INCOME BUT THAT REDUCE E&P. Some expenses and losses that are not deductible in computing taxable income are deductible in computing current E&P.

▶ Federal income taxes are not deductible when computing taxable income. For E&P purposes, federal income taxes are deductible in the year they accrue if the corporation uses the accrual method of accounting and in the year they are paid if the corporation uses the cash method of accounting.

EXAMPLE C4-8 ▶ Perch Corporation, which uses the accrual method of accounting, earns taxable income of $100,000 on which it owes $22,250 of federal income taxes. In computing its current E&P, Perch must reduce taxable income by $22,250. ◀

▶ Charitable contributions are deductible in full for current E&P purposes without regard to the 10% limitation on such deductions. Thus, when current E&P is computed, taxable income must be reduced by any charitable contributions disallowed because of the 10% limitation.

EXAMPLE C4-9 ▶ Dot Corporation has $25,000 of taxable income before any charitable contribution deduction. Dot contributed $10,000 to the Red Cross. Although Dot's contribution deduction is limited to $2,500 in computing taxable income because of the 10% limitation on charitable contribution deductions, Dot deducts the entire $10,000 in computing current E&P. Therefore, it must subtract the remaining $7,500 from taxable income of $22,500 ($25,000 − $2,500) to compute current E&P. In a later year, when the corporation deducts the $7,500 carryover in determining taxable income, it must add that amount to taxable income in deriving that year's current E&P. ◀

▶ Life insurance premiums paid on policies to insure the lives of key corporate personnel (net of any increase in the cash surrender value of the policy) are not deductible when computing taxable income but are deductible when computing E&P.

▶ Capital losses exceeding capital gains cannot be deducted when computing taxable income but can be deducted when computing current E&P.

▶ Nondeductible expenses related to the production of tax-exempt income (e.g., interest charges to borrow money to purchase tax-exempt securities) are deductible when computing E&P.

▶ Losses on related party sales that are disallowed under Sec. 267 are deductible when computing E&P.

▶ Nondeductible fines, penalties, and political contributions are deductible for E&P purposes.

The adjustments listed in Table C4-1 and described above are only a partial list of the adjustments that must be made to taxable income to compute current E&P. The basic rule is that adjustments are made to taxable income so that current E&P represents the corporation's economic ability to pay dividends out of its current earnings.

OBJECTIVE 2

Distinguish between current and accumulated E&P

DISTINCTION BETWEEN CURRENT AND ACCUMULATED E&P

A distinction must be made between current and accumulated E&P. A nonliquidating distribution is taxed as a dividend if it is deemed to have been made out of either current or accumulated E&P. Corporate distributions are deemed to be made first out of current E&P and then out of accumulated E&P to the extent that current E&P is insufficient.[2] If current E&P is sufficient to cover all distributions made during the year, each distribution

---

[2] The distinction between current and accumulated E&P is explained in Reg. Sec. 1.316-2.

is treated as a taxable dividend. This rule applies even if the corporation reports a deficit in its beginning accumulated E&P account. Current E&P is computed as of the last day of the tax year with no reduction for distributions made during the year.

EXAMPLE C4-10 ▶

TAX STRATEGY TIP

A corporation with an accumulated deficit and current E&P may want to postpone distributions to a later year to avoid dividend treatment in the current year. See Example C4-53 later in this chapter.

At the beginning of the current year, Water Corporation has a $30,000 accumulated E&P deficit. For the entire year, Water generates current E&P of $15,000. Water distributes $10,000 to its shareholders during the current year. The $10,000 distribution is a taxable dividend to the shareholders because it is made out of current E&P. At the beginning of the next tax year, Water records an accumulated E&P deficit of $25,000 (− $30,000 E&P deficit + $5,000 undistributed current E&P). ◀

If distributions made during the year exceed current E&P, current E&P is allocated to those distributions on a pro rata basis regardless of when during the year the distributions were made. Distributions exceeding current E&P are deemed to be made out of accumulated E&P (if any) in chronological order. Distributions exceeding current and accumulated E&P are treated as a return of capital and reduce the shareholder's basis on a dollar-for-dollar basis. However, these distributions cannot create an E&P deficit. Deficits arise only as a result of losses. These rules are important if stock changes hands during the year and total E&P is insufficient to cover all distributions.

EXAMPLE C4-11 ▶

At the beginning of the current year, Cole Corporation has $20,000 of accumulated E&P. For the entire year, Cole's current E&P is $30,000. On April 10, Cole distributes $20,000 cash to Bob, its sole shareholder. On July 15, Cole distributes an additional $24,000 cash to Bob. On August 1, Bob sells all of his Cole stock to Lynn. On September 15, Cole distributes $36,000 cash to Lynn. Cole's current and accumulated E&P must be allocated to the three distributions as follows:

Date	Distribution Amount	Current E&P	Accumulated E&P	Dividend Income	Return of Capital
April 10	$20,000	$ 7,500	$12,500	$20,000	$ –0–
July 15	24,000	9,000	7,500	16,500	7,500
September 15	36,000	13,500	–0–	13,500	22,500
Total	$80,000	$30,000	$20,000	$50,000	$30,000

Current = %
accumulated = FIFO

The current E&P allocated to the April 10 distribution is calculated as follows:

$$\$30,000 \text{ (Current E\&P)} \times \frac{\$20,000 \text{ (April 10 distribution)}}{\$80,000 \text{ (Total distributions)}}$$

Note that the total amount of dividends paid by Cole equals $50,000, the sum of $30,000 of current E&P and $20,000 of accumulated E&P. Current E&P is allocated to all three distributions on a pro rata basis, whereas accumulated E&P is allocated first to the April 10 distribution ($12,500), then to the July 15 distribution, so that no accumulated E&P is available to allocate to the September 15 distribution. Thus, Bob's dividend income from Cole is $36,500 ($20,000 + $16,500). He also receives a $7,500 return of capital that reduces his stock basis. Lynn's dividend income from Cole is $13,500. She also receives a $22,500 return of capital that reduces her stock basis. Note that Bob cannot determine his gain on the stock sale until after the end of the year. He must wait until he knows the extent to which the April 10 and July 15 distributions reduce his stock basis. ◀

If the corporation generates a current E&P deficit and has an accumulated E&P deficit, none of the distributions is treated as a dividend. Instead, all distributions are treated as a return of capital to the extent of the shareholder's stock basis. Distributions exceeding basis are taxed as a capital gain.

EXAMPLE C4-12 ▶

At the beginning of the current year, Rose Corporation has a $15,000 accumulated E&P deficit. Rose's current E&P deficit is $20,000. Rose distributes $10,000 on July 1. The distribution is not treated as a dividend but rather as a return of capital to the extent of the shareholder's stock basis. Any amounts exceeding stock basis are taxed as a capital gain. Rose's accumulated E&P deficit on January 1 of next year is $35,000 because the distribution was not made out of E&P and because the negative balance in the current E&P account is transferred to the accumulated E&P account at the end of the current year. ◀

If the corporation has a current E&P deficit and a positive accumulated E&P balance, it must net the two accounts at the time of the distribution to determine the amount of any distribution made out of E&P.[3] The deficit in current E&P that has accrued up through the day before the distribution reduces the accumulated E&P balance on that date. If the balance remaining after the reduction is positive, the distribution is a dividend to the extent of the lesser of the distribution amount or the E&P balance. If the E&P balance is zero or negative, the distribution is a return of capital. If the actual deficit in current E&P to the date of distribution cannot be determined, the current E&P deficit is prorated on a daily basis to the day before the distribution date.

EXAMPLE C4-13 ▶ Assume the same facts as in Example C4-12 except that Rose Corporation has a $15,000 accumulated E&P balance. The current E&P deficit of $20,000 accrues on a daily basis unless information indicates otherwise. The amount of the July 1 distribution that is a dividend is calculated as follows:

Date	Distribution Amount	Accumulated E&P	Dividend Income	Return of Capital
Jan. 1	$ –0–	$15,000		
July 1	10,000	(9,918)[a]	$5,082	$4,918
Total	$10,000	$ 5,082[b]	$5,082	$4,918

[a]181/365 × ($20,000) = ($9,918)—the current E&P deficit accrued up to the distribution date. (The 181/365 fraction assumes a nonleap year.)

[b]$15,000 − $9,918 = $5,082—accumulated E&P at beginning of year minus the current E&P deficit accrued up to the distribution date. ◀

STOP & THINK *Question:* Why is it necessary to keep separate balances for current and accumulated E&P?

Solution: If the total current and accumulated E&P is less than the total distributions made to the shareholders, E&P must be allocated to all distributions made during the year to determine the amount of each distribution that is a dividend. When no change in the shareholder's stock ownership occurs during the year and all distributions are proportional to stock ownership, an E&P allocation is needed only to track each shareholder's stock basis. Tracking E&P to individual distributions is necessary to determine the taxability of a particular distribution when a change in a shareholder's stock ownership occurs because current E&P is allocated on a pro rata basis and accumulated E&P is allocated chronologically. As a result of the chronological allocation, a greater portion of distributions made early in a tax year may be taxed as a dividend relative to distributions made later in the year. On the other hand, because accrued current E&P deficits offset accumulated E&P balances, a smaller portion of distributions made later in a tax year may be taxed as a dividend relative to distributions made earlier in the year.

NONLIQUIDATING PROPERTY DISTRIBUTIONS

CONSEQUENCES OF NONLIQUIDATING PROPERTY DISTRIBUTIONS TO THE SHAREHOLDERS

Property includes money, securities, and any other property except stock in the corporation making the distribution (or rights to acquire such stock).[4] When a corporation makes a property distribution to its shareholders, the following three questions must be answered:

▶ What is the amount of the distribution?

▶ To what extent is the amount distributed a dividend to the shareholder?

---

[3] Reg. Sec. 1.316-2(b).   [4] Sec. 317(a).

▶ What is the basis of the property to the shareholder, and when does its holding period begin?

For cash distributions, these questions are easy to answer. The distribution amount is the amount of cash distributed. This distribution is a dividend to the extent it is made out of the corporation's current and accumulated E&P, and the E&P account is reduced by the cash dividend amount. The shareholder's basis in the cash received is its face amount. The distributing corporation recognizes no gain or loss on the distribution of cash.

When the corporation distributes property such as land or inventory to a shareholder, these questions are more difficult to answer. Neither the amount of the distribution nor the basis of the property to the shareholder is immediately apparent. The corporation must recognize gain (but not loss) on the distribution, and the impact of the distribution on the corporation's E&P, as well as the taxability of the distribution, must be determined. The following sections set forth rules that address these questions.

When the corporation distributes property to a shareholder, the amount of the distribution is the FMV of the property distributed.[5] The value is determined as of the date of the distribution. The amount of any liability assumed by the shareholder in connection with the distribution, or to which the distributed property is subject, reduces the distribution amount. However, the distribution amount cannot be reduced below zero. The distribution amount is a dividend to the shareholder to the extent of the distributing corporation's E&P.

The shareholder's basis in any property received is the property's FMV. The basis is not reduced by any liabilities assumed by the shareholder or to which the property is subject.[6] The holding period of the property begins on the day after the distribution date. It does not include the holding period of the distributing corporation.

EXAMPLE C4-14 ▶ Post Corporation has $100,000 of current and accumulated E&P. On March 1, Post distributes to Meg, its sole shareholder, land with a $60,000 FMV and a $35,000 adjusted basis. The land is subject to a $10,000 liability, which Meg assumes. The distribution amount is $50,000 ($60,000 − $10,000), all of which is a dividend to Meg because it does not exceed Post's E&P balance. Meg's basis in the property is its $60,000 FMV, and her holding period for the property begins on March 2. ◀

STOP & THINK

Question: Why do liabilities reduce the amount of income reported when a corporation makes a distribution to a shareholder, but do not reduce the shareholder's adjusted basis for the property?

Solution: The amount of a distribution to a shareholder is the property's FMV on the distribution date. In Example C4-14, Meg receives land worth $60,000 and also acquires the $10,000 debt, which she is obligated to pay. Therefore, the value of the distribution to Meg is the net amount that she receives, or $50,000 ($60,000 − $10,000). The adjusted basis of the land to Meg is its $60,000 FMV. This result is the same as Meg's purchasing the land for $60,000 but her financing the purchase by borrowing $10,000. The basis of the land to Meg still would be its $60,000 FMV.

Topic Review C4-1 summarizes the tax consequences of a nonliquidating distribution to the shareholders.

CONSEQUENCES OF PROPERTY DISTRIBUTIONS TO THE DISTRIBUTING CORPORATION

Two questions must be answered with respect to a corporation that distributes property:

▶ What amount and character of gain or loss must the distributing corporation recognize on the distribution?

▶ What effect does the distribution have on the corporation's E&P?

---

[5] Sec. 301(b).

[6] Sec. 301(d).

Topic Review C4-1

Tax Consequences of a Nonliquidating Distribution to the Shareholders

1. The amount of a distribution is the amount of money received plus the FMV of any nonmoney property received reduced by any liabilities assumed or acquired by the shareholder.
2. The distribution is a dividend to the extent of the distributing corporation's current and accumulated E&P. Any excess distribution is a return of capital that reduces the shareholder's stock basis (but not below zero). Any further excess distribution is a capital gain.
3. The shareholder's basis in the property received is its FMV.
4. The shareholder's holding period begins on the day after the distribution date.

CORPORATE GAIN OR LOSS ON PROPERTY DISTRIBUTIONS. When a corporation distributes property that has appreciated in value, the corporation must recognize gain as though the corporation had sold the property for its FMV. On the other hand, a corporation does not recognize loss when it distributes property that has depreciated in value even though the corporation would have recognized a loss upon selling the property.[7]

EXAMPLE C4-15 ▶

TAX STRATEGY TIP

Rather than distribute loss property, the corporation should consider selling it and distributing the proceeds. The sale will allow the corporation to deduct the loss.

Silver Corporation distributes to Mark, a shareholder, land (a capital asset) worth $60,000. Silver's adjusted basis in the land is $20,000. Upon distributing the land, Silver recognizes a $40,000 ($60,000 − $20,000) capital gain, as if Silver had sold the property. If the land instead had a $12,000 FMV, Silver would have recognized no loss. ◀

If the distributed property is subject to a liability or the shareholder assumes a liability in the distribution, for the purpose of calculating gain, the property's FMV is deemed to be no less than the amount of the liability.[8]

EXAMPLE C4-16 ▶

TAX STRATEGY TIP

If possible, a corporation should avoid distributing property subject to a liability exceeding the property's FMV because of the potential gain recognition caused by the excess liability.

Assume the same facts as in Example C4-15 except the land's FMV is instead $25,000, and the land is subject to a $35,000 mortgage. For the purpose of calculating gain, the land's FMV is deemed to be $35,000 because this value cannot be less than the liability amount. Thus, Silver Corporation's gain is $15,000 ($35,000 − $20,000), the amount by which the land's deemed FMV exceeds its adjusted basis.[9] ◀

stop

EFFECT OF PROPERTY DISTRIBUTIONS ON THE DISTRIBUTING CORPORATION'S E&P. Distributions have two effects on E&P:[10]

▶ When a corporation distributes appreciated property to its shareholders, it must increase E&P by the **E&P gain,** which is the excess of the property's FMV over its adjusted basis for E&P purposes. Because a property's **E&P adjusted basis** may differ from its tax basis (as discussed earlier in this chapter), this E&P gain may differ from the corporation's recognized gain for tax reporting purposes.

▶ If the E&P adjusted basis of the noncash asset distributed equals or exceeds its FMV, E&P is reduced by the asset's E&P adjusted basis. If the FMV of the asset distributed exceeds its E&P adjusted basis, E&P is reduced by the asset's FMV. In either case, the E&P reduction is net of any liability to which the asset is subject or that the shareholder assumes in the distribution. E&P also is reduced by the income taxes incurred on any gain recognized.[11]

---

[7] Sec. 311(a).
[8] Sec. 311(b)(2).
[9] The tax treatment of the shareholder is not entirely clear. Section 336(b), which Sec. 311(b)(2) makes applicable to nonliquidating distributions, specifically states that this liability rule applies only for determining the corporation's gain or loss. Thus, its applicability does not seem to extend to Sec. 301(d), which gives the shareholder a FMV basis in the distributed property. Some commentators have suggested that a strict interpretation of the statutory provision that gives the shareholder an actual FMV basis, rather than the greater

liability basis, produces an illogical result. (See B.C. Randall and D.N. Stewart, "Corporate Distributions: Handling Liabilities in Excess of the Fair Market Value of Property Remains Unresolved," *The Journal of Corporate Taxation,* 1992, pp. 55-64.) Also, given that the liability exceeds the distributed property's FMV, the shareholder's amount distributed should be zero, resulting in no dividend.
[10] Secs. 312(a) and (b).
[11] Secs. 312(a) and (c).

EXAMPLE C4-17 ▶ Brass Corporation distributes to its shareholder, Joan, property with a $25,000 adjusted basis for tax reporting purposes, a $22,000 adjusted basis for E&P calculation purposes, and a $40,000 FMV. The property is subject to a $12,000 mortgage, which Joan assumes. In the distribution, Brass recognizes a $15,000 ($40,000 FMV − $25,000 tax adjusted basis) gain for tax reporting purposes. For E&P calcuation purposes, Brass's E&P is increased by $18,000 ($40,000 FMV − $22,000 E&P adjusted basis) and is reduced by $28,000 ($40,000 FMV − $12,000 liability). E&P also is reduced by the amount of income taxes paid or accrued by Brass on the $15,000 gain. ◀

A special rule applies when a corporation distributes its own obligation (e.g., its notes, bonds, or debentures) to a shareholder. In such case, the distributing corporation's E&P is reduced by the principal amount, not the fair market value, of the obligation distributed.[12]

Topic Review C4-2 summarizes the tax consequences of a nonliquidating distribution to the distributing corporation.

BOOK-TO-TAX ACCOUNTING COMPARISON *start*

The distributing corporation reports divdends-in-kind at their FMV for financial accounting (book) purposes. For book purposes, the distributing corporation recognizes the difference between the property's FMV and its carrying value as a gain or loss. For tax purposes, however, the corporation recognizes gains but not losses.

CONSTRUCTIVE DIVIDENDS

A **constructive dividend** (or deemed distribution) is the manner in which the IRS or the courts might recharacterize an excessive corporate payment to a shareholder to reflect the true economic benefit conferred upon the shareholder. As a result of the recharacterization, the IRS or courts usually recast a corporate-shareholder transaction as an E&P distribution, deny the corporation an offsetting deduction, and treat all or a portion of the income recognized by the shareholder as a dividend. Ordinarily, a corporate dividend involves a direct, pro rata distribution to all shareholders, which generally is declared by the board of directors. By contrast, a constructive dividend need not be direct or pro rata, nor be declared by the board of directors.

Constructive dividends are generally deemed to be paid in the context of a closely held corporation where the shareholders (or relatives of shareholders) and management groups overlap. In such situations, the dealings between the corporation and its shareholders are likely to be less structured and subject to closer review than dealings between a publicly held corporation and its shareholders. Nevertheless, constructive dividends also may occur in the context of a publicly held corporation.

ADDITIONAL COMMENT

The incentive to disguise dividends as salary, however, is somewhat diminished with the reduced tax rate on dividends. (See Example C3-36 in Chapter C3).

INTENTIONAL EFFORTS TO AVOID DIVIDEND TREATMENT. The recharacterization of a payment as a constructive dividend often stems from an attempt to bail out a corporation's E&P without subjecting it to taxation at the shareholder level or to obtain a deduction at the corporate level for distributions to shareholders that otherwise would not be deductible. If a corporation generates sufficient E&P, dividend distributions are fully taxable to the shareholder but are not deductible by the distributing corporation.

Topic Review C4-2

Tax Consequences of a Nonliquidating Distribution to the Distributing Corporation

1. When a corporation distributes appreciated property, it must recognize gain as if it sold the property for its FMV immediately before the distribution.
2. For gain recognition purposes, a property's FMV is deemed to be at least equal to any liability to which the property is subject or that the shareholder assumes in connection with the distribution.
3. A corporation recognizes no loss when it distributes to its shareholders property that has depreciated in value.
4. A corporation's E&P is increased by any E&P gain resulting from a distribution of appreciated property.
5. A corporation's E&P is reduced by (a) the amount of money distributed plus (b) the greater of the FMV or E&P adjusted basis of any nonmoney property distributed, minus (c) any liabilities to which the property is subject or that the shareholder assumes in connection with the distribution. E&P also is reduced by taxes paid or incurred on the corporation's recognized gain, if any.

[12] Sec. 312(a)(2).

Shareholders may try to disguise a dividend as a salary payment. If the attempt is successful, the payment is taxable to the shareholder-employee and is deductible by the distributing corporation as long as the payment is reasonable in amount. Shareholders also may try to disguise a dividend as a loan to the shareholder. If this attempt is successful, the payment is neither deductible by the corporation nor taxable to the shareholder. If the IRS reclassifies either payment as a dividend, the payment is taxable to the shareholder and nondeductible by the corporation.

UNINTENTIONAL CONSTRUCTIVE DIVIDENDS. Some constructive dividends are unintentional. Shareholders may not realize that the benefits they receive from the corporation in which they own stock are actually taxable dividends until a tax consultant or the IRS examines the transactions. If a payment in the form of a salary, loan, lease, etc. is recast as a dividend, appropriate adjustments must be made at the corporate and shareholder levels. These adjustments may increase the shareholder's taxable income (e.g., because the distribution has been recharacterized as a dividend rather than a loan) or increase the distributing corporation's taxable income (i.e., because of lower deductions). Transactions most likely to be recast and treated as dividends are described below.

LOANS TO SHAREHOLDERS. Loans to shareholders may be considered disguised dividends unless the shareholders can prove that the loans are bona fide. Whether a loan is bona fide ordinarily depends on the shareholder's intent when he or she makes the loan. To prove that the loan is bona fide (and thus to avoid recharacterization of the loan as a dividend), the shareholder must show that he or she intends to repay the loan. Evidence of an intent to repay includes

▶ Recording the loan on the corporate books

▶ Evidencing the loan by a written note

▶ Charging a reasonable rate of interest

▶ Scheduling regular payments of principal and interest

Factors that suggest the loan is *not* bona fide include

▶ Borrowing on "open account" (i.e., the shareholder is borrowing from the corporation, with no fixed schedule for repayment, whenever he or she needs cash)

▶ Failing to charge a market rate of interest on the loan

▶ Failing to enforce the payment of interest and principal

▶ Paying advances in proportion to stockholdings

▶ Paying advances to a controlling shareholder

If the corporation lends money to a shareholder and then, after a period of time, cancels the loan, the amount cancelled is treated as a dividend distribution to the extent of E&P. If the corporation charges a below market interest rate, the IRS will inpute interest on the loan. The corporation will be deemed to have earned interest income on the loan, and the shareholder may be allowed a deduction for interest deemed paid. The imputed interest will be treated as a dividend paid to the shareholder, thereby resulting in no offsetting corporate level deduction.

EXCESSIVE COMPENSATION PAID TO SHAREHOLDER-EMPLOYEES. Shareholders may be compensated for services with salary, bonus, or fringe benefits. The corporate employer may deduct such compensation as long as it represents an ordinary and necessary business expense and is reasonable in amount. However, if the IRS finds the payments to be excessive, the excess amounts will not be deductible by the corporation, but they still will be taxable to the shareholder. Depending upon the circumstances, excess amounts may be treated as dividends or simply be included in the gross income of the recipient. No hard and fast rules offer guidance in determining when compensation is excessive. As a result, the issue frequently is litigated.

Prior to 2003, the IRS's main focus was the corporation's deducting the excess amount. The shareholder-employee recognized ordinary income whether the excess amount was classified as compensation or a dividend. With the tax rate on dividends reduced to a maximum of 15% for 2003 through 2008, the corporation still will lose the deduction for excess compensation, but the IRS is unlikely to classify the excess as a dividend. Instead, the IRS probably will treat the excess as ordinary compensation income to the shareholder-employee even though the corporation is not allowed to deduct it.[13]

EXCESSIVE COMPENSATION PAID TO SHAREHOLDERS FOR THE USE OF SHAREHOLDER PROPERTY. As with compensation, corporate payments to shareholders for the use of property (i.e., rents, interest, and royalties) are deductible under Sec. 162(a) if they are ordinary, necessary, and reasonable in amount. The corporation may not deduct any amount exceeding what it would have paid to an unrelated party.

CORPORATE PAYMENTS FOR THE SHAREHOLDER'S BENEFIT. If a corporation extinguishes a personal obligation of a shareholder, the corporate payment may be treated as gross income to the shareholder. Such payments may cover the shareholder's personal debt obligations, expenses in connection with the shareholder's personal residence, expenses incurred for the improvement of the shareholder's land and property, and debt obligations personally guaranteed by the shareholder.

In addition, if the IRS denies a corporate deduction, the disallowed deduction may result in gross income to the shareholder, if the expenditure associated with the deduction provided the shareholder with an economic benefit. Examples of such expenditures are unsubstantiated travel and entertainment expenses; club dues; and automobile, airplane, and yacht expenses related to the shareholder-employee's personal use of the property.

BARGAIN PURCHASE OF CORPORATE PROPERTY. If a shareholder purchases corporate property at a price less than the property's FMV, the discount may be treated as a constructive dividend to the shareholder.

SHAREHOLDER USE OF CORPORATE PROPERTY. If a shareholder uses corporate property (such as a hunting lodge, yacht, or airplane) without paying adequate consideration to the corporation, the FMV of such use (minus any amounts paid) may be treated as a constructive dividend to the shareholder.

Stock Dividends and Stock Rights

OBJECTIVE 4

Determine the tax consequences of stock dividends and distributions of stock rights

TYPICAL MISCONCEPTION

Stock dividends generally are nontaxable as long as a shareholder's proportionate interests in the corporation do not increase. If a shareholder's stock interest increases, Sec. 305(b) causes the dividend to be taxable.

In 1919, the Supreme Court held in *Eisner v. Macomber* that a stock dividend is not income to the shareholder because it takes no property from the corporation and adds no property to the shareholder.[14] Subsequently, Congress enacted the Revenue Act of 1921, which provides that stock dividends are nontaxable. Although this general rule still applies today, Congress has carved out exceptions to prevent perceived abuses.

Section 305(a) states, "Except as otherwise provided in this section, gross income does not include the amount of any distribution of the stock of a corporation made by such corporation to its shareholders with respect to its stock." Thus, a distribution of additional common stock made with respect to a shareholder's common stock represents a tax-free stock dividend. However, whenever a stock dividend changes or has the potential to change the shareholders' proportionate interests in the distributing corporation, the distribution will be taxable. Taxable stock distributions include those where

▶ Any shareholder can elect to receive either stock of the distributing corporation or other property (e.g., money).

▶ Some shareholders receive property and other shareholders receive an increase in their proportionate interests in the distributing corporation's assets or E&P.

---

[13] *Sterno Sales Corp. v. U.S.*, 15 AFTR 2d 979, 65-1 USTC ¶9419 (Ct. Cl., 1965).

[14] *Eisner v. Myrtle H. Macomber*, 3 AFTR 3020, 1 USTC ¶32 (USSC, 1919).

> ► Some holders of common stock receive preferred stock and others receive additional common stock.

> ► The underlying stock is preferred, unless the distribution involves a change in the conversion ratio of convertible preferred stock to take into account a common stock dividend or a common stock split.

> ► The distributed stock is convertible preferred, unless it can be established that the distribution will have no disproportionate effect.

> The following example illustrates how these exceptions work.

EXAMPLE C4-18 ►

Two shareholders, Al and Beth, each own 100 of the 200 outstanding shares of Peach Corporation stock. Because Al's marginal tax rate is high, he does not want to realize any additional income in the current year. Beth has a low marginal tax rate and needs additional cash. Peach, whose current E&P is $100,000, declares a dividend payable in stock or money. Each taxpayer can receive one share of Peach stock (valued at $100) or $100 in cash for each share of Peach stock already owned. Al, who elects to receive stock, receives 100 additional shares of Peach stock. Beth, who elects to receive cash, receives $10,000. Beth's distribution is taxable as a dividend. Absent any exceptions to Sec. 305, Al would receive a nontaxable stock dividend because he chose to receive Peach stock. After the distribution, however, he owns two-thirds of the outstanding shares of Peach stock, whereas before the distribution he owned only one-half of Peach's outstanding shares. Therefore, an exception to the general rule of Sec. 305(a) applies here, so Al is deemed to have received a taxable stock dividend equal to the value of the additional shares he received. Even if both shareholders were to elect a stock dividend, they each would be deemed to have received a taxable dividend because they each had the option to receive cash. In this example, Al and Beth each have a $10,000 dividend. Al's basis in his new shares is their $10,000 FMV. His basis in his original shares is unchanged. Peach reduces its E&P by $20,000, the amount of the taxable dividend to Al and Beth. ◄

TAX-FREE STOCK DIVIDENDS

If a **stock dividend** is nontaxable, the basis of the stock with respect to which the distribution was made must be allocated between the old and new shares.[15] The holding period of the new shares includes the holding period of the old shares.[16]

If the old and new shares are identical, the basis of each share is determined by dividing the basis of the old shares by the total number of shares held by the shareholder after the distribution.

EXAMPLE C4-19 ►

Barbara owns 1,000 shares of Axle Corporation common stock with a $66,000 basis, or $66 per share. Barbara receives a nontaxable 10% common stock dividend and now owns 1,100 shares of Axle common stock. Her basis in each share of common stock is now $60 ($66,000 ÷ 1,100). ◄

If the old and new shares are not identical, the allocation of the old shares' basis is based on the relative FMVs of the old and new shares on the distribution date.

EXAMPLE C4-20 ►

REAL-WORLD EXAMPLE

Tracking the effects of nontaxable dividends, stock splits, stock dividends, and stock rights distributions on the basis of a stock investment can be difficult and time consuming. A number of publishers offer capital change reporters that provide a complete history of these four types of events for publicly traded companies. These reporters greatly simplify the making of stock basis calculations.

Mark owns 1,000 shares of Axle Corporation common stock with a $60,000 basis. Mark receives a nontaxable preferred stock dividend. At the time of the distribution, the FMV of the common stock is $90,000 ($90 × 1,000 shares), and the FMV of the preferred stock is $10,000 ($200 × 50 shares). After the distribution, Mark owns 50 shares of preferred stock with a basis of $6,000 [($10,000 ÷ $100,000) × $60,000]. Thus, $6,000 of the basis of the common stock is allocated to the preferred stock, and the basis of the common stock is reduced from $60,000 to $54,000. ◄

TAX-FREE STOCK RIGHTS

Under Sec. 305, a distribution of **stock rights** is tax-free unless it changes, or has the potential to change, the shareholders' proportionate interests in the distributing corporation. The same exceptions to the tax-free treatment of stock dividends set forth in Sec. 305(b) also apply to distributions of stock rights.

If the value of the stock rights is less than 15% of the value of the stock with respect to which the rights were distributed (i.e., the underlying stock), the basis of the rights is zero

---

[15] Sec. 307(a) and Reg. Secs. 1.307-1 and -2.   [16] Sec. 1223(5).

unless the shareholder elects to allocate stock basis to those rights.[17] If the taxpayer plans to sell the rights, it might be desirable to allocate stock basis to the rights so as to minimize the amount of gain recognized on the sale. The election to allocate stock basis to the rights must be made in the form of a statement attached to the shareholder's return for the year in which the rights are received. The allocation is based on the relative FMVs of the stock and the stock rights. The holding period for the rights includes the holding period for the underlying stock.[18]

EXAMPLE C4-21 ▶ Linda owns 100 shares of Yale Corporation common stock with a $27,000 basis and a $50,000 FMV. Linda receives 100 nontaxable stock rights with a $4,000 FMV. Because the FMV of the stock rights is less than 15% of the FMV of the underlying stock (0.15 × $50,000 = $7,500), the basis of the stock rights is zero unless Linda elects to allocate the $27,000 stock basis between the stock and the stock rights. If Linda makes the election, the basis of the rights is $2,000 [($4,000 ÷ $54,000) × $27,000], and the basis of the stock is $25,000 ($27,000 − $2,000). ◀

If the value of the stock rights is 15% or more of the value of the underlying stock, the shareholder must allocate the basis of the underlying stock between the stock and the stock rights.

EXAMPLE C4-22 ▶ Kay owns 100 shares of Minor common stock with a $14,000 basis and a $30,000 FMV. Kay receives 100 stock rights with a total FMV of $5,000. Because the FMV of the stock rights is at least 15% of the stock's FMV (0.15 × $30,000 = $4,500), the $14,000 basis must be allocated between the stock rights and the underlying stock. The basis of the stock rights is $2,000 [($5,000 ÷ $35,000) × $14,000], and the basis of the underlying stock is $12,000 ($14,000 − $2,000). ◀

TYPICAL MISCONCEPTION

Taxpayers often get confused about what happens to a stock right. A stock right may be sold or exercised, which means the actual stock is acquired. If the rights are not sold or exercised, they eventually will lapse.

If the taxpayer sells the stock rights, gain or loss is calculated by subtracting the allocated basis of the rights (if any) from the sale price. A shareholder cannot claim a loss if the stock rights expire. If the stock rights do expire, the allocated rights basis is added back to the underlying stock basis. If the taxpayer exercises the rights before they expire, the allocated rights basis is added to the basis of the stock purchased through the exercise of those rights.[19] The holding period for the stock acquired with the rights begins on the exercise date.[20]

EXAMPLE C4-23 ▶ In a nontaxable distribution, Jeff receives ten stock rights to which no stock basis is allocated. Each stock right entitles Jeff to acquire one share of Jackson stock for $20. If Jeff exercises all ten rights, the Jackson stock acquired will have a $200 (10 rights × $20) basis. If instead Jeff sells the ten rights for $30 each, he will recognize a gain of $300 [($30 × 10 rights) − 0 basis]. If the rights expire, Jeff can claim no loss. ◀

EFFECT OF NONTAXABLE STOCK DIVIDENDS ON THE DISTRIBUTING CORPORATION

From a tax perspective, nontaxable distributions of stock and stock rights have no effect on the distributing corporation. The corporation neither recognizes gain or loss, nor does it reduce its E&P balance.[21]

TAXABLE STOCK DIVIDENDS AND STOCK RIGHTS

BOOK-TO-TAX ACCOUNTING COMPARISON

For financial accounting purposes, stock dividends reduce retained earnings. However, for tax purposes, nontaxable stock dividends have no effect on a corporation's E&P.

If a distribution of stock or stock rights is taxable, the distribution amount equals the FMV of the stock or stock rights on the distribution date. The distribution is treated in the same way as any other property distribution. It is a dividend to the extent of the distributing corporation's E&P, and the recipient takes a FMV basis in the stock or stock rights.[22] The holding period of the stock or stock rights begins on the day after the distribution date. No adjustment is made to the basis of the underlying stock. The distributing corporation recognizes no gain or loss on the distribution,[23] and the corporation reduces its E&P by the FMV of the stock or stock rights on the distribution date.

---

[17] Sec. 307(b)(1).
[18] Sec. 1223(5).
[19] Reg. Sec. 1.307-1(b).
[20] Sec. 1223(6).
[21] Secs. 311(a) and 312(d).

[22] Reg. Sec. 1.301-1(h)(2)(i).
[23] Sec. 311(a). Gain may be recognized when the shareholder can elect to receive either appreciated property or stock or stock rights of the distributing corporation.

STOCK REDEMPTIONS

A **stock redemption** is a corporation's acquisition of its own stock in exchange for property. The property exchanged may be cash, securities of other corporations, or any other consideration the corporation wants to use to acquire its own stock.[24] The corporation may cancel the acquired stock, retire it, or retain it as treasury stock.

A stock redemption may be desirable for the following reasons:

▶ A shareholder may want to withdraw from the corporate business and sell his or her stock. In such a case, the shareholder may prefer that the corporation, rather than an outsider, purchase the stock so the remaining shareholders (who may be family members) retain complete control and ownership of the corporation after his or her withdrawal.

▶ A shareholder may be required to sell stock to the corporation under the terms of a stock purchase agreement that he or she has with the issuing corporation.

▶ A shareholder may want to reduce his or her equity interest in a corporation but may be unwilling or unable to sell stock to outsiders. For example, no market may exist for the shares, or sales to outsiders may be restricted.

▶ A shareholder may want to withdraw assets from a corporation before a sale of the corporation's business. A potential purchaser of the business may not be interested in acquiring all the assets of the corporation or be able to pay the full value for all shares issued and outstanding. A withdrawal of some assets by the seller in exchange for some of his or her shares allows the purchaser to acquire the remaining shares and business assets for a lower total price.

▶ After the death of a major shareholder, a corporation may agree to purchase the decedent's stock from either the estate or a beneficiary to provide sufficient funds to pay estate and inheritance taxes as well as funeral and administrative expenses.

▶ Management may believe that the corporation's stock is selling at a low price and that, to increase share value, it should acquire some of this stock on the open market.

Whatever the reason for the redemption, the shareholder must answer the following questions:

▶ What are the amount and character of the income, gain, or loss recognized as a result of the stock redemption?

▶ What basis does the shareholder take in any property received in exchange for the redeemed stock?

▶ When does the holding period for the property begin?

▶ What basis does the shareholder take for any distributing corporation stock held after the redemption?

The distributing corporation must answer the following questions:

▶ What amount and character of gain or loss, if any, must the distributing corporation recognize when it redeems stock with property?

▶ What effect does the redemption have on the corporation's E&P?[25]

TAX CONSEQUENCES OF THE REDEMPTION TO THE SHAREHOLDER

As a general rule, when a shareholder sells or exchanges corporate stock, any gain or loss in the transaction is capital in character. In some cases, a redemption is treated in the same way as any other stock sale. In other cases, a redemption is treated differently. Specifically, in some redemptions, the entire amount received by a shareholder in exchange for stock is

---

[24] Sec. 317.
[25] The stock redemption discussion is for C corporation stock. Different rules apply if an S corporation redeems its stock.

taxed as a dividend. The reason for this difference is that some redemptions more closely resemble a stock sale to a third party, whereas others are essentially equivalent to a dividend. The following two examples illustrate the difference between a redemption resembling a dividend and a redemption resembling a sale. (The IRC refers to a "sale or exchange," but for simplicity in this chapter, we will use just the term "sale.")

EXAMPLE C4-24 ▶ John owns all 100 outstanding shares of Tango Corporation stock. John's basis for his shares is $50,000. Tango has E&P of $100,000. If Tango redeems 25 of John's shares for $85,000, John still owns 100% of Tango stock. Because John's proportionate ownership of Tango is not affected by the redemption, the redemption resembles a dividend. Accordingly, John is deemed to have received an $85,000 dividend. ◀

EXAMPLE C4-25 ▶ Carol has owned three of the 1,000 outstanding shares of Water Corporation's stock for two years. Her basis in the shares is $1,000. Water has E&P of $100,000. If Water redeems all three of Carol's shares for $5,000, Carol is in essentially the same position as though she had sold the stock to a third party. She has received $5,000 for her stock and has no further ownership interest in Water. This redemption resembles a sale because it terminates Carol's interest in the corporation. It is not essentially equivalent to a dividend. Accordingly, Carol reports a $4,000 ($5,000 − $1,000) capital gain. ◀

Example C4-24 is an extreme case involving a redemption that clearly should be treated as a dividend to the shareholder. Example C4-25 is an extreme case involving a redemption that clearly should be treated as a sale of stock by the shareholder. Many cases, however, fall between the two extremes, and how the redemption should be treated is not immediately apparent. The problem for Congress and the courts has been distinguishing redemptions that should be treated as sales from those that should be treated as dividends. Under current law, a redemption qualifies for sale treatment only if it satisfies at least one of the following conditions:

▶ The redemption is substantially disproportionate.

▶ The redemption is a complete termination of the shareholder's interest.

▶ The redemption is not essentially equivalent to a dividend.

▶ The redemption involves a partial liquidation of the distributing corporation and a distribution to a noncorporate shareholder.

▶ The redemption provides funds for an estate to pay death taxes.

If a redemption qualifies as a sale, the shareholder is treated as though he or she sold the stock to an outside party. The shareholder recognizes gain or loss equal to the FMV of the property received less the shareholder's adjusted basis for the stock surrendered. The gain or loss is capital in character if the stock is a capital asset in the hands of the shareholder. The shareholder's basis for any property received is its FMV. The holding period for the property begins on the day following the exchange date.

A redemption that does not satisfy any of the five conditions necessary for sale treatment is regarded as a property distribution under Sec. 301. Accordingly, the entire amount of the distribution is treated as a dividend to the extent of the distributing corporation's E&P.[26] The shareholder's surrender of stock is ignored in determining the dividend amount. The basis of the surrendered stock is added to the basis of any remaining shares owned by the shareholder. If all the shareholder's stock has been redeemed, the basis of the redeemed shares is added to the basis of shares owned by those individuals whose ownership is attributed to the shareholder under the constructive stock ownership rules described below.[27]

ADDITIONAL COMMENT

Proposed Reg. Sec. 1.302-5, when finalized, would treat the surrendered stock basis as a deferred loss.

EXAMPLE C4-26 ▶ Amy and Rose each own 50 of the 100 outstanding shares of stock in York Corporation, which reports $100,000 of E&P. On May 10, York redeems 20 of Amy's shares with property worth $25,000. Amy's adjusted basis for those shares is $20,000. If the redemption satisfies one of the

---

[26] Sec. 302(d).

[27] Reg. Sec. 1.302-2(c).

ADDITIONAL COMMENT

Prior to 2003, sale or exchange treatment provided a third advantage, specifically, the capital gain received preferential tax treatment as compared to ordinary income treatment for dividends. As a result of the 2003 Act, however, dividends received by a noncorporate shareholder in 2003 through 2008 also obtain preferential treatment, thereby removing this advantage. Thus, because capital gains and qualified dividends are now taxed at the same rate, the difference in tax between exchange treatment and dividend treatment is solely a function of the taxpayer's basis in the redeemed stock.

conditions necessary for sale treatment, Amy recognizes a capital gain of $5,000 ($25,000 − $20,000). Her basis in the property received is its $25,000 FMV, and its holding period begins on May 11. If the redemption does not satisfy any of the conditions necessary for sale treatment, Amy reports a $25,000 dividend. Her $20,000 basis in the surrendered stock is added to the basis of her remaining 30 shares of York stock. ◀

Structuring a stock redemption as a sale offers two advantages. First, capital gains may be offset by capital losses. Second, in a sale, the basis of the shares redeemed reduces the amount of gain recognized. If a redemption is treated as a dividend, the basis of the shares redeemed does not reduce the amount of the dividend. However, because the basis shifts to the shareholder's remaining stock, this increment reduces the gain (or increases the loss) recognized on a later sale of the distributing corporation stock held by the shareholder.

Topic Review C4-3 summarizes the tax consequences of stock redemptions to both the shareholder and the distributing corporation.

ATTRIBUTION RULES

Three of the five tests that determine whether a redemption distribution should be treated as a nonliquidating distribution (e.g., a dividend) are based on stock ownership before and after the redemption. The tests measure the extent to which the shareholder's ownership interest in the corporation has been substantially reduced. In general, if the shareholder's ownership interest has been substantially reduced, the redemption is treated as a sale. On the other hand, if the shareholder's ownership interest remains substantially the same or increases, the redemption is treated as a nonliquidating distribution.

Stock ownership for this purpose is determined under the constructive ownership or attribution rules of Sec. 318.[28] According to these rules, a shareholder owns not only the shares he or she directly owns but also shares owned by his or her spouse, other immediate family members, and related entities. Entities such as corporations, partnerships, trusts, and estates are considered to own shares owned by their shareholders, partners, and beneficiaries.

The attribution rules prevent shareholders from either taking advantage of favorable tax rules or avoiding unfavorable rules by transferring to family members or related entities stock that the shareholder previously owned. All stock ownership tests would be subject to abuse if only direct ownership were considered.

Topic Review C4-3

Tax Consequences of Stock Redemptions

Shareholders:

General Rule: The amount received by the shareholder in exchange for his or her stock is treated as a dividend to the extent of the distributing corporation's E&P. The basis of the surrendered stock increases the basis of the shareholder's remaining stock.

Sale Exception: The amount received by the shareholder is offset by the adjusted basis of the shares surrendered. The difference generally is a capital gain or loss. No basis adjustment occurs.

Distributing Corporation:

Gain/Loss Recognition: The corporation recognizes gain (but not loss) as though it had sold the distributed property for its FMV immediately before the redemption.

Earnings and Profits Adjustment: E&P is reduced for redemptions treated as a dividend in the same manner as for an ordinary distribution (e.g., the amount of money distributed). E&P is reduced for redemptions treated as an exchange by the portion of the current and accumulated E&P attributable to the redeemed stock. The remainder of the distribution reduces the corporation's paid-in capital.

[28] Sec. 302(c).

Section 318(a) prescribes four types of attribution rules: family attribution, attribution from entities, attribution to entities, and option attribution. These rules are discussed below.

ADDITIONAL COMMENT

The family attribution rules of Sec. 318 are not as inclusive as the family attribution rules of Sec. 267 (covered in Chapter C3). For example, siblings and grandparents are not considered family members by Sec. 318 but are included under Sec. 267.

FAMILY ATTRIBUTION.   An individual is considered to own all stock owned by or for a spouse, children, grandchildren, and parents. The individual is not considered to own stock owned by brothers, sisters, or grandparents.

Stock ownership once attributed to an individual is not further reattributed from that individual to another individual under the same rules. Thus, stock ownership attributed to one family member under the family attribution rules cannot be reattributed from that family member to a second family member. However, stock ownership once attributed to an individual under an attribution rule may be reattributed from that individual to another individual under a different attribution rule. For example, stock ownership attributed by the corporate attribution rule from a corporation to its shareholder may be reattributed from the shareholder to the shareholder's spouse under the family attribution rules.

EXAMPLE C4-27 ▶

Harry; his wife, Wilma; their son, Steve; and Harry's father, Frank, each own 25 of the 100 outstanding shares of Strong Corporation stock. Harry is considered to own all 100 Strong shares (25 directly plus constructively the shares owned by Wilma, Steve, and Frank). Wilma is considered to own 75 shares (25 directly plus constructively the 50 shares owned by Harry and Steve). Ownership of Frank's shares is not attributed to Wilma, nor is ownership of his shares that are attributed to Harry reattributed to Wilma. Steve is considered to own 75 shares (25 directly plus constructively the 50 shares owned by his parents Harry and Wilma). Steve is not considered to own the shares owned by his grandfather (Frank), nor is Frank's stock ownership attributed to Harry and then reattributed to Steve. Frank is considered to own 75 shares (25 directly plus constructively the shares owned by Harry and Steve (his grandson)). Wilma's stock ownership attributed to Harry is not reattributed to Frank.

The diagram below illustrates the stock ownership of the four shareholders. Constructive ownership is shown by the lines. The arrows indicate the direction(s) in which stock ownership attribution occurs.

The table below shows each shareholder's direct and constructive stock ownership.

Shareholder	Direct Ownership	Shares Owned via Constructive Ownership From:				
		Spouse	Child	Grandchild	Parent(s)	Total
Frank	25		25	25		75
Harry	25	25	25		25	100
Wilma	25	25	25			75
Steve	25				50	75
	100					

◀

ATTRIBUTION FROM ENTITIES.   Stock owned by or for a partnership is considered to be owned proportionately by the partners, and stock owned by or for an estate is considered to be owned proportionately by the beneficiaries. Stock owned by or for a trust is considered to be owned by the beneficiaries in proportion to their actuarial interests. Stock owned by or for a C corporation is considered to be owned proportionately only by shareholders owning (directly or indirectly) 50% or more in value of the corporation's stock.[29]

EXAMPLE C4-28 ▶

Bill, who is married, has a 50% ownership interest in a partnership. The partnership owns 40 of the 100 outstanding shares of Yellow Corporation stock, and Bill owns the remaining 60 shares. Under the attribution rules Bill is considered to own 80 shares, 60 directly and 20 (0.50 × 40 shares) constructively. In addition, the stock ownership attributed to Bill under the partnership attribution rules is reattributed to Bill's spouse under the family attribution rules. ◀

ATTRIBUTION TO ENTITIES. All stock owned by or for a partner is considered to be owned by the partnership. All stock owned by or for a beneficiary of an estate or a trust is considered to be owned by the estate or trust. All stock owned by or for a shareholder who owns (directly or indirectly) 50% or more in value of a C corporation's stock is considered to be owned by the corporation.

Stock ownership attributed to a partnership, estate, trust, or corporation from a partner, beneficiary, or shareholder is not reattributed to another partner, beneficiary, or shareholder.

EXAMPLE C4-29 ▶

Assume the same facts as in Example C4-28. The partnership in which Bill is a partner is considered to own all 100 shares of Yellow stock (40 directly and 60 owned by Bill). Bill's stock ownership attributed to the partnership cannot be reattributed from the partnership to Bill's partners. ◀

OPTION ATTRIBUTION. A person who has an option to purchase stock is considered to own the underlying stock.

EXAMPLE C4-30 ▶

John owns 25 of the 100 outstanding shares of Yard Corporation stock. He has an option to acquire an additional 50 shares. John is considered to own 75 Yard shares (25 directly plus constructively the 50 shares he has an option to buy). ◀

SUBSTANTIALLY DISPROPORTIONATE REDEMPTIONS

If a stock redemption qualifies as substantially disproportionate under Sec. 302(b)(2), the redemption is treated as a sale. This IRC provision provides a safe haven for capital gain as opposed to dividend treatment. A redemption is substantially disproportionate with respect to a shareholder if all the following conditions are met:

▶ After the redemption, the shareholder owns less than 50% of the total combined voting power of all classes of voting stock.

▶ After the redemption, the shareholder owns less than 80% of his or her percentage ownership of voting stock before the redemption.

▶ After the redemption, the shareholder owns less than 80% of his or her percentage ownership of common stock (whether voting or nonvoting) before the redemption.

TAX STRATEGY TIP

If possible, taxpayers should structure a redemption to meet the substantially disproportionate test rather than the subjective "not equivalent to a dividend" test (discussed on page C4-23), thereby obtaining certainty of results rather than uncertainty.

These tests apply mechanically to each shareholder's ownership interest. The 50% test prevents shareholders from qualifying for capital gain treatment if they own a controlling interest in the distributing corporation after the redemption. The 80% tests indicate a degree of change in the shareholder's proportionate interest that makes the redemption substantially disproportionate. A redemption may be substantially disproportionate with respect to one shareholder but not with respect to another. If only one class of stock is outstanding, the second and third requirements are the same.

---

[29] For purposes of the attribution rules, S corporations are treated as partnerships, not as corporations. Thus, attribution occurs to and from shareholders owning less than 50% of the S corporation stock. All corporations in the examples are C corporations unless otherwise stated.

EXAMPLE C4-31 ▶ Long Corporation has 400 shares of common stock issued and outstanding. Before the redemption, Ann, Bob, Carl, and Dana (all unrelated) each own 100 shares. Long redeems 55 shares from Ann, 25 shares from Bob, and 20 shares from Carl.

ADDITIONAL COMMENT

In calculating the percentage of stock owned *after* a redemption note that the denominator used is the number of shares outstanding *after* the redemption.

	Before Redemption			After Redemption	
Shareholder	No. of Shares Owned	Percentage of Ownership	Shares Redeemed	No. of Shares Owned	Percentage of Ownership
	(1)	(1) ÷ 400	(2)	(1) − (2)	[(1) − (2)] ÷ 300
Ann	100	25%	55	45	15.00%
Bob	100	25%	25	75	25.00%
Carl	100	25%	20	80	26.67%
Dana	100	25%	—	100	33.33%
Total	400	100%	100	300	100.00%

The redemption is substantially disproportionate with respect to Ann because, after the redemption, she owns less than 50% of Long's stock, and her stock ownership percentage (15%) is less than 80% of her stock ownership percentage before the redemption (0.80 × 25% = 20%). The redemption is not substantially disproportionate with respect to Bob because the percentage reduction in his stock ownership is less than 80%. In fact, Bob owns the same percentage of stock (25%) after the redemption as he did before the redemption (25%). The redemption also is not substantially disproportionate for Carl, because his stock ownership percentage increases from 25% to 26.67%. ◀

The constructive ownership rules of Sec. 318(a) apply in determining whether the shareholder has met the three requirements for a substantially disproportionate redemption.[30]

EXAMPLE C4-32 ▶ Assume the same facts as in Example C4-31 except that Ann is Bob's mother. In this case, the redemption is not substantially disproportionate for either Ann or Bob because each is considered to own 200 shares, or 50%, of the Long stock before the redemption, and each is considered to own 120 shares, or 40%, after the redemption. Although the 50% test is met, neither Ann nor Bob satisfies the 80% test. After the redemption each owns *exactly* 80% of the percentage owned before the redemption (0.80 × 50% = 40%). ◀

COMPLETE TERMINATION OF THE SHAREHOLDER'S INTEREST

Under Sec. 302(b)(3), if a stock redemption qualifies as a complete termination of a shareholder's interest in a corporation, the redemption also is treated as a sale. At first glance, this rule does not offer a route to sale treatment that is not already provided by the other Sec. 302 rules. If a corporation redeems all of a shareholder's stock, the requirements for a substantially disproportionate redemption under Sec. 302(b)(2) would seem to have been satisfied. However, the complete termination rule extends sale treatment to two redemptions not covered by the substantially disproportionate redemption rules:

▶ If a shareholder's interest in a corporation consists exclusively of nonvoting stock, a redemption of all the stock could not qualify as substantially disproportionate under Sec. 302(b)(2) because no reduction of voting power occurs. However, it does qualify for sale treatment as a complete termination of the shareholder's interest under Sec. 302(b)(3) because, in this situation, the interest does not have to consist of voting stock.

▶ If a shareholder owns some voting stock and his or her entire interest in the corporation is completely terminated through a redemption, the family attribution rules of Sec. 318(a)(1) may be waived, and the redemption can qualify for sale treatment even if other family members continue to own some or all of the corporation's stock.[31]

---

[30] Reg. Sec. 1.302-3(a).

[31] Section 302(c)(2) provides for the waiver of family attribution rules.

To have the family attribution rules waived, the shareholder must meet all of the following requirements:

▶ The shareholder must not retain any interest in the corporation after the redemption except as a creditor. This restriction includes any interest as an officer, director, or employee.

▶ The shareholder must not acquire any such interest (other than by bequest or inheritance) for at least ten years from the date of the redemption.

▶ The shareholder must file a written agreement with the IRS that he or she will notify the IRS upon acquiring any prohibited interest.

The written agreement allows the IRS to assess additional taxes for the year of the redemption if the prohibited interest is acquired, even if the basic three-year limitations period has expired.

EXAMPLE C4-33 ▶ Father and Son each own 50 of the 100 outstanding shares of Short Corporation stock. Short redeems all of Father's shares. Under the family attribution rules, Father is considered to own 100% of the Short stock both before and after the redemption. Thus, the redemption is not substantially disproportionate. However, if Father files the necessary agreement not to retain or acquire any interest in Short for ten years (except as a creditor or an interest acquired by bequest or inheritance), the family attribution rules may be waived. Consequently, the redemption qualifies as a complete termination of Father's interest and is treated as a stock sale. ◀

Waiver of the family attribution rules is not permitted in the following two situations involving related parties:

▶ Within the ten-year period ending on the distribution date, the distributee acquired, directly or indirectly, part or all of the redeemed stock from a person whose stock ownership would be attributable (at the time of the distribution) to the distributee under Sec. 318.

▶ Any person owns (at the time of the distribution) stock of the redeeming corporation the ownership of which is attributable to the distributee under Sec. 318, and such person acquired any stock in the redeeming corporation, directly or indirectly, from the distributee within the ten-year period ending on the distribution date.

The first restriction deters an individual from transferring stock to a related party (e.g., family member or controlled entity) so that the related party might use the complete termination provision to recognize a capital gain when the transferred stock is redeemed. The second restriction deters an individual from transferring a portion of his or her stock to a related party and then using the complete termination provision to recognize a capital gain when the remaining stock is redeemed. These prohibitions against waiving the family attribution rules do not apply if the shareholder transferred the stock more than ten years before the redemption or if the distributee can show that the acquisition or disposition of the stock did not have as one of its purposes the avoidance of federal income taxes. The family attribution rules also can be waived in the second situation above if the stock acquired by the related party from the distributee is redeemed in the same transaction.

Note that only the family attribution rules can be waived. However, entities are permitted to have the family attribution rules waived if both the entity and the individual whose stock is attributed to the entity agree not to have any prohibited interest in the corporation for at least ten years.

EXAMPLE C4-34 ▶ Andrew created the A Trust, which owns 30% of Willow Corporation stock. Andrew's wife, Wanda, is the sole beneficiary of the trust. Their son, Steve, owns the remaining 70% of Willow stock. Willow redeems all of its stock owned by the A Trust. The redemption does not qualify for sale treatment because the trust is deemed to own all the stock owned by Wanda, and Wanda is deemed to own all the stock owned by Steve. However, the family attribution rules can be waived if A Trust and Wanda both agree not to acquire any interest in the corporation for ten years. The redemption then will be treated as a complete termination of the trust's interest in Willow and will be eligible for sale treatment. ◀

REDEMPTIONS NOT ESSENTIALLY EQUIVALENT TO A DIVIDEND

Section 302(b)(1) provides that a redemption will be treated as a sale if it is not essentially equivalent to a dividend. The tax law sets forth no mechanical test to determine when a redemption is not essentially equivalent to a dividend. Instead, it implies that a determination should be based on the facts and circumstances of each case.[32] Therefore, Sec. 302(b)(1) does not provide a safe harbor afforded by the rules for substantially disproportionate redemptions or redemptions that are a complete termination of a shareholder's interest. On the other hand, the provision keeps the rules on redemptions from being too restrictive, especially in the case of transactions involving preferred stock.

The Supreme Court's decision in *Maclin P. Davis* defined criteria for determining when a redemption is not essentially equivalent to a dividend.[33] The Supreme Court held that (1) in this determination, a business purpose is irrelevant; (2) the Sec. 318 attribution rules must be applied to establish dividend equivalency; and (3) a redemption of part of a sole shareholder's stock is always essentially equivalent to a dividend. The Court further held that for Sec. 302(b)(1) to apply, there must be a "meaningful reduction" in the shareholder's proportionate interest in the corporation after taking into account the constructive ownership rules of Sec. 318(a). Despite this holding, the definition of "a meaningful reduction in interest" remains unclear.

Because of this lack of clarity, Sec. 302(b)(1) generally applies to a redemption of nonvoting preferred stock only when the shareholder does not own any common stock,[34] or to redemptions resulting in a substantial reduction in the shareholder's right to vote and exercise control over the corporation, right to participate in earnings, and right to share in net assets upon liquidation. Generally, the IRS allows sale treatment if a controlling shareholder reduces his or her interest to a noncontrolling position,[35] or a noncontrolling shareholder further reduces his or her minority interest.[36] A shareholder does not qualify for sale treatment if he or she retains control both before and after the redemption,[37] or if he or she assumes a controlling position.

EXAMPLE C4-35 ▶ Four unrelated individuals own all of Thyme Corporation's single class of stock in the following proportions: Alan, 27%; Betty, 24.33%; Clem, 24.33%, and David, 24.33%. Thyme redeems some of Alan's stock holdings, resulting in a reduction of Alan's interest to 22.27%. Betty, Clem, and David own equally the remaining 77.73% of Thyme stock. The redemption of Alan's stock does not qualify as substantially disproportionate because Alan's interest is not reduced below 21.6% (0.80 × 27% = 21.6%). Nor does the redemption qualify as a complete termination of Alan's interest because Alan retains shares of Thyme stock. However, the redemption might be treated as a sale under Sec. 302(b)(1) because the transaction results in a meaningful reduction of Alan's noncontrolling interest in Thyme. ◀

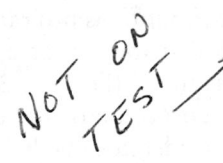

NOT ON TEST

PARTIAL LIQUIDATIONS

Under Sec. 302(b)(4), a redemption involving a noncorporate shareholder qualifies for sale treatment if the redemption qualifies as a **partial liquidation**. A partial liquidation occurs when a corporation discontinues one line of business, distributes the assets related to that business to its shareholders, and continues at least one other line of business.[38] A distribution qualifies as a partial liquidation if it is not essentially equivalent to a dividend. In either case, the distribution must be made within the tax year in which a plan of partial liquidation has been adopted or within the succeeding tax year.

---

[32] Reg. Sec. 1.302-2(b).

[33] *U.S. v. Maclin P. Davis,* 25 AFTR 2d 70-827, 70-1 USTC ¶9289 (USSC, 1970).

[34] Reg. Sec. 1.302-2(a).

[35] A reduction in stock ownership from 57% to 50% where the shareholder no longer had control was considered a meaningful reduction in interest in Rev. Rul. 75-502, 1975-2 C.B. 111.

[36] A reduction in stock ownership from 27% to 22% was considered a meaningful reduction in interest in Rev. Rul. 76-364, 1976-2 C.B. 91.

[37] See *Jack Paparo,* 71 T.C. 692 (1979), where reductions in stock ownership from 100% to 81.17% and from 100% to 74.15% were not considered meaningful reductions in interest.

[38] A partial liquidation also can occur when a corporation sells one line of business, distributes the sales proceeds (after paying corporate income taxes on the sale), and continues at least one other line of business. See Rev. Rul. 79-275, 1979-2 C.B. 137.

DETERMINATION MADE AT THE CORPORATE LEVEL. For purposes of Sec. 302(b)(4), whether a distribution is not essentially equivalent to a dividend is determined at the corporate level.[39] The distribution must be the result of a bona fide contraction of the corporate business. The government provides guidance as to what constitutes a corporate contraction in relevant Treasury Regulations and revenue rulings. Some examples of bona fide corporate contractions include

▶ The distribution of insurance proceeds received as a result of a fire that destroys part of a business.[40]

▶ Termination of a contract representing 95% of a domestic corporation's gross income.[41]

▶ Change in a corporation's business from a full-line department store to a discount apparel store, which resulted in the elimination of certain units; elimination of most forms of credit; and a reduction in inventory, floor space, and employees.[42]

SAFE HARBOR RULE. Under Sec. 302(e)(2), a distribution satisfies the not essentially equivalent to a dividend requirement and qualifies as a partial liquidation if

▶ The distribution is attributable to the distributing corporation's ceasing to conduct a qualified trade or business, or consists of the assets of a qualified trade or business; and

▶ Immediately after the distribution, the distributing corporation is engaged in the active conduct of at least one qualified trade or business.

A qualified trade or business is any trade or business that

▶ Has been actively conducted throughout the five-year period ending on the date of the redemption; and

▶ Was not acquired by the corporation within such five-year period in a partially or wholly taxable transaction.

The definition of an active trade or business is the same as that used for Sec. 355 (corporate division) purposes as set forth in Chapter C7.

EXAMPLE C4-36 ▶ Sage Corporation has manufactured hats and gloves for the past five years. In the current year, Sage discontinues hat manufacturing, sells all of its hat-making machinery, and distributes the proceeds to its shareholders in redemption of part of their stock. The corporation continues glove manufacturing. The distribution constitutes a partial liquidation and qualifies for sale treatment. ◀

TAX CONSEQUENCES OF A PARTIAL LIQUIDATION TO THE SHAREHOLDERS. If a distribution qualifies as a partial liquidation, a noncorporate shareholder treats the redemption of his or her stock as a sale, whether or not the distribution is pro rata. On the other hand, a corporate shareholder treats the redemption distribution as a dividend unless the corporation meets one of the other tests for sale treatment (i.e., Sec. 302(b)(1)-(3) or Sec. 303). In determining whether stock is held by a corporate or noncorporate shareholder, stock held by a partnership, trust, or estate is considered to be held proportionately by its partners or beneficiaries. Dividend treatment may be more advantageous than sale treatment for a corporate shareholder because a corporation receives no preferential tax rate on capital gains, but it is eligible for a 70%, 80%, or 100% dividends-received deduction.

EXAMPLE C4-37 ▶ Assume the same facts as in Example C4-36 except Sage Corporation is owned by Ted and Jolly Corporation. Each shareholder owns 50 shares of Sage stock with a $20,000 basis. Sage reports $100,000 of current and accumulated E&P. Sage distributes $18,000 to each shareholder in redemption of ten shares of stock worth $18,000. Because the redemption qualifies as a partial liquidation, Ted treats the transaction as a sale and recognizes a capital gain of $14,000 ($18,000 − $4,000). Jolly, however, cannot treat the transaction as a sale because it is a corpo-

---

[39] Sec. 302(e)(1)(A).
[40] Reg. Sec. 1.346-1.
[41] Rev. Rul. 75-3, 1975-1 C.B. 108.
[42] Rev. Rul. 74-296, 1974-1 C.B. 80.

rate shareholder. Therefore, Jolly must report $18,000 of dividend income. Jolly is eligible for a $14,400 (0.80 × $18,000) dividends-received deduction. Jolly's $4,000 basis in the redeemed stock is added to the basis of its remaining stock, resulting in $20,000 basis in its 40 remaining Sage shares. (If Jolly owned the Sage stock since Sage's inception, Jolly makes no further basis adjustments. However, if Jolly did not own the Sage stock since inception, Sec 1059(e) applies to reduce Jolly's basis in the Sage stock to $5,600 ($20,000 − $14,400) because the dividend is considered extraordinary.) ◄

STOP & THINK

Question: Why is a distribution in partial liquidation of a corporation treated as a sale by its noncorporate shareholders and as a dividend by its corporate shareholders?

Solution: The different tax treatment reflects different tax advantages. Noncorporate shareholders benefit most from sale treatment because they can offset their stock basis against any amount realized in the distribution. Corporate shareholders benefit most from dividend treatment because they can deduct the distribution as a dividend received from the distributing corporation. These disparate advantages stem from the different tax status of corporations, other entities, and individuals.

TAX STRATEGY TIP

An estate with liquidity problems owing to large holdings of a closely held business also may want to consider installment payment of the estate tax under Sec. 6166. See Chapter C13 for further details.

REDEMPTIONS TO PAY DEATH TAXES

If corporate stock represents a substantial portion of a decedent's gross estate, a redemption of the stock from the estate or its beneficiaries may be eligible for sale treatment under Sec. 303. This IRC section helps shareholders who inherit stock in a closely held corporation and who must sell some of their stock to pay estate taxes, inheritance taxes, and funeral and administrative expenses. If the stock is not readily marketable, a stock redemption may be the only way to provide the estate and beneficiaries with sufficient liquidity to meet their cash needs. In most cases, attribution rules would prevent such a redemption from qualifying as substantially disproportionate or as a complete termination of the shareholder's interest. The redemption then would be treated as a dividend. However, attribution rules do not apply to the portion of a stock redemption that qualifies under Sec. 303.

Section 303 provides that a redemption of stock that was included in a decedent's gross estate is treated as a sale of stock by the shareholder (i.e., either the estate or the beneficiary of the estate) if the following conditions are met:

1. The value of the redeeming corporation's stock included in the decedent's gross estate is more than 35% of the adjusted gross estate. The adjusted gross estate is the total gross estate (i.e., the FMV of all property owned by the decedent on the date of death) less allowable deductions for funeral and administrative expenses, claims against the estate, debts, and casualty and other losses.

EXAMPLE C4-38 ▶

A decedent's gross estate, valued at $5.8 million, includes Pepper Corporation stock worth $2.4 million and $3.4 million in cash. Funeral expenses, debts, and other administrative expenses allowable as estate tax deductions amount to $1.8 million. Thus, the decedent's adjusted gross estate is $4 million ($5,800,000 − $1,800,000). Because the $2.4 million value of the Pepper stock included in the gross estate exceeds 35% of the adjusted gross estate ($1.4 million = 0.35 × $4,000,000), a redemption of some of Pepper's stock qualifies as a stock sale under Sec. 303. ◄

2. The maximum amount of the redemption distribution that can qualify for sale treatment under Sec. 303 is the sum of all federal and state estate and inheritance taxes, plus any interest due on those taxes, and all funeral and administrative expenses allowable as deductions in computing the federal estate tax. The redemption must be of stock held by the estate or by the decedent's heirs who are liable for the estate taxes and other administrative expenses.

3. Section 303 applies to a redemption distribution only to the extent the recipient shareholder's interest in the estate is reduced by the payment of death taxes and funeral and administration expenses. The maximum distribution to any shareholder that is eligible for sale treatment under Sec. 303 is the amount of estate taxes and expenses the shareholder is obligated to bear.

EXAMPLE C4-39 ▶ Assume the same facts as in Example C4-38 except that all the stock is bequeathed to the decedent's son, Sam. The remainder of the estate is bequeathed to the decedent's wife, Wilma, and she is liable for all estate taxes and administrative expenses. In such case, Sec. 303 could not be used by Sam. He is not liable for any of the estate taxes or administrative expenses. If instead $1.6 million is bequeathed to Wilma and the remainder of the estate to Sam, Sam would be liable for all estate taxes and administrative expenses. He could use Sec. 303 to obtain sale treatment on a redemption of enough of his stock to pay the estate taxes and administrative expenses. ◀

4. Section 303 applies only to distributions made within certain time limits.

a. In general, the redemption must occur not later than 90 days after the expiration of the period for assessment of the federal estate tax. Because the limitations period for the federal estate tax expires three years after the estate tax return is due and because the return is due nine months after the date of death, the redemption generally must occur within four years after the date of death.

b. If a petition for redetermination of an estate tax deficiency is filed with the Tax Court, the distribution period is extended to 60 days after the Tax Court's decision becomes final.

c. If the taxpayer made a valid election under Sec. 6166 to defer payment of federal estate taxes under an installment plan, the distribution period is extended to the time the installment payments are due.

5. The stock of two or more corporations may be aggregated to satisfy the 35% requirement provided that 20% or more of the value of each corporation's outstanding stock is included in the gross estate.

EXAMPLE C4-40 ▶ A decedent's gross estate, valued at $5.8 million, includes 80% of the stock of Curry Corporation, valued at $800,000, and 90% of the stock of Brodie Corporation, valued at $900,000. Allowable estate tax deductions for administrative expenses and debts amount to $1.8 million. Thus, the decedent's adjusted gross estate is $4 million. Although the value of neither the Curry stock nor the Brodie stock exceeds 35% of the $4 million adjusted gross estate, the total value of both corporations' stock ($1.7 million = $800,000 + $900,000) exceeds 35% of the adjusted gross estate ($1.4 million = 0.35 × $4,000,000). Therefore, a redemption of sufficient Curry stock and/or Brodie stock to pay estate taxes and funeral and administrative expenses qualifies for sale treatment under Sec. 303. ◀

Although the legislative intent behind Sec. 303 is to provide liquidity for the payment of estate taxes and administrative expenses when a significant portion of the estate consists of stock in a closely held corporation, a redemption can qualify for sale treatment under Sec. 303 even when the estate includes sufficient liquid assets to pay estate taxes and other expenses. The redemption proceeds need not be used for this purpose.

The advantage of a Sec. 303 redemption is that the redeeming shareholder usually has little or no capital gain to report because his or her basis in the redeemed stock is the stock's FMV on the decedent's date of death (or an alternate valuation date, if applicable). If the redemption does *not* qualify as a sale, the redeeming shareholder will recognize dividend income equal to the entire distribution amount in redemption of his or her stock.

EXAMPLE C4-41 ▶ Chili Corporation redeems 100 shares of stock for $105,000 from Art, who inherited the stock from his father, Fred. The stock's FMV on Fred's date of death was $100,000. Chili reports an E&P balance of $500,000. If the redemption qualifies as a sale under Sec. 303, Art recognizes a $5,000 ($105,000 − $100,000) capital gain. On the other hand, if the redemption does not qualify as a sale under Sec. 303 or one of the other redemption provisions, Art recognizes $105,000 of dividend income. Both the capital gain and the dividend are subject to a maximum 15% tax rate. However, the dividend amount significantly exceeds the capital gain amount. ◀

SELF-STUDY QUESTION

How much gain is the redeeming shareholder likely to recognize in a qualifying Sec. 303 redemption?

ANSWER

Probably little or none. The basis in the redeemed stock equals its FMV at the decedent's date of death (or an alternate valuation date). The recognized gain generally is only the post-death appreciation.

Thus, Sec. 303 can make a difference in the amount of income a redeeming shareholder must report.

EFFECT OF REDEMPTIONS ON THE DISTRIBUTING CORPORATION

As in the case of property distributions that are not in redemption of a shareholder's stock, two questions must be answered with respect to distributions in redemption of stock:

▶ What amount and character of gain or loss must the distributing corporation recognize upon the distribution?

▶ What effect does the distribution have on the corporation's E&P?

Each of these questions is addressed below.

CORPORATE GAIN OR LOSS ON PROPERTY DISTRIBUTIONS. The rules for gain or loss recognition for a corporation that distributes property in redemption of its stock are the same as the rules under Sec. 311 for gain or loss recognition on property distributions not in redemption of corporate stock.

▶ The corporation recognizes gain when it distributes appreciated property in redemption of its stock. The character of the gain depends on the character of the property in the corporation's hands before the distribution.

▶ The corporation recognizes no loss when it distributes property that has declined in value.

EFFECT OF REDEMPTIONS ON E&P. A stock redemption affects a corporation's E&P accounts in two ways. First, if the corporation distributes appreciated property, the excess of FMV over the property's E&P adjusted basis increases the balance in the corporation's E&P account. Next, the corporation's E&P balance is reduced to reflect the distribution of property. The amount of the reduction depends on whether the redemption is treated as a sale or as a dividend by the shareholder whose stock is redeemed.

If the shareholder treats the redemption as a dividend, the corporation reduces its E&P by the amount of money, the principal amount of any obligations, and the greater of the adjusted basis or FMV of any other property distributed, in the same way as it does for a property distribution that is not in redemption of stock.

If the redemption qualifies for sale treatment, E&P is reduced by the portion of the current and accumulated E&P attributable to the redeemed stock. In other words, E&P is reduced by a percentage equal to the percentage of the total outstanding shares redeemed, but not by more than the actual redemption distribution amount. The remainder of the distribution reduces the corporation's paid-in capital.[43] An ordinary dividend distribution has first claim to current E&P ahead of any stock redemptions. No such priority exists for accumulated E&P. Both ordinary dividend distributions and redemption distributions reduce accumulated E&P in chronological order.

EXAMPLE C4-42 ▶ Apex Corporation has 100 shares of stock outstanding, 30 of which are owned by Mona. On December 31, Apex redeems all 30 of Mona's shares for $36,000 in a redemption qualifying as a sale under Sec. 302(b)(3). At the time of the redemption, Apex has $60,000 in paid-in capital and $40,000 of E&P. Because Apex redeemed 30% of its outstanding stock, the distribution reduces Apex's E&P by $12,000 (0.30 × $40,000). The remaining $24,000 ($36,000 − $12,000) of the distribution reduces Apex's paid-in capital to $36,000 ($60,000 − $24,000).[44] ◀

PREFERRED STOCK BAILOUTS

The stock redemption rules permit sale treatment for stock redemptions under certain circumstances and require dividend treatment in all other situations. Generally, taxpayers prefer sale treatment. First, sale treatment allows taxpayers to offset their stock basis against distribution proceeds. Second, gain on the stock sale generally is long-term and capital in character. It may be offset by the taxpayer's capital losses and thus not taxed at all. With these results in mind, taxpayers have devised methods to obtain sale rather than dividend treatment.

---

[43] Sec. 312(n)(7).
[44] Distributions made during the year require a different calculation, which is beyond the scope of this text.

ADDITIONAL COMMENT

When the term *bailout* is used in the corporate context, it generally refers to a scheme that allows a corporation to make a dividend distribution that for tax purposes is treated as a sale of a capital asset.

One such method is known as the **preferred stock bailout.** Prior to Congress' enacting anti-tax avoidance measures, a preferred stock bailout proceeded as follows:

1. A corporation issued a nontaxable dividend of nonvoting preferred stock with respect to its common stock. Under the rules relating to nontaxable stock dividends, a portion of the common stock's basis is allocated to the preferred stock. Its holding period includes the holding period for the common stock.

2. The recipient shareholder then sold the preferred stock to an unrelated third party at its FMV. As a result of the sale, the shareholder recognized a capital gain equal to the difference between the preferred stock's sale price and its allocated basis.

3. Next, the corporation redeemed the preferred stock from the third-party purchaser (usually at a small premium to reward the third party for his or her cooperation in the scheme).

4. As an alternative to steps 2 and 3, the corporation redeemed the preferred stock directly from the shareholder.

As a result of the preferred stock bailout, the shareholder received the corporation's earnings in the form of a long-term capital gain without changing his or her equity position in the company.

To deter this tax-avoidance scheme, Congress enacted Sec. 306, which "taints" certain stock (usually preferred stock) when distributed to the shareholder in a nontaxable stock dividend. Prior to 2003, Sec. 306 treated the distribution proceeds as a dividend if the corporation redeemed the tainted stock directly from the shareholder or treated the amount realized as ordinary income if the shareholder sold the stock to a third party. In this way, Sec. 306 prevented shareholders from using a preferred stock bailout to convert ordinary income into capital gain.

The 2003 Act, however, took the "sting" out of Sec. 306 by reducing the tax rate on dividends to a maximum of 15%. Thus, for 2003 through 2008, the dividend recognized on a direct redemption of Sec. 306 stock is taxed at 15%, and the amount realized on a third party sale of the stock is treated as a "deemed" dividend, also taxed at 15%. Nevertheless, the Sec. 306 taint is still disadvantageous because dividends, even though subject to the preferential capital gains tax rate, cannot offset capital losses as can "real" capital gains. Also, if Sec. 306 recasts the redemption as a dividend, the shareholder is taxed on the entire amount of distribution proceeds rather than just the gain.

SEC. 306 STOCK DEFINED

Section 306 stock is defined as follows:[45]

1. Stock (other than common stock issued with respect to common stock) received in a nontaxable stock dividend
2. Stock (other than common stock) received in a tax-free corporate reorganization or corporate division if the effect of the transaction was substantially the same as the receipt of a stock dividend, or if the stock was received in exchange for Sec. 306 stock
3. Stock that has a basis determined by reference to the basis of Sec. 306 stock (i.e., a substituted or transferred basis)
4. Stock (other than common stock) acquired in an exchange to which Sec. 351 applies if the receipt of money (in lieu of the stock) would have been treated as a dividend

Preferred stock issued by a corporation with no current or accumulated E&P in the year the stock is issued is not Sec. 306 stock. Also, inherited stock is not Sec. 306 stock because the basis of such stock is its FMV on the date of the decedent's death (or alternate valuation date) and, therefore, is not determined by reference to the decedent's basis.[46]

DISPOSITIONS OF SEC. 306 STOCK

If a shareholder sells or otherwise disposes of Sec. 306 stock (except in a redemption), the amount realized is treated as a deemed dividend to the extent the shareholder would have recognized a dividend at the time of the distribution had money equal to the stock's FMV

TYPICAL MISCONCEPTION

Although the amount of deemed dividend income recognized on a sale of Sec. 306 stock is measured by the E&P existing in the year the Sec. 306 stock was distributed, the E&P of the distributing corporation is not reduced by the amount of the deemed dividend.

[45] Sec. 306(c).

[46] Reg. Sec. 1.306-3(e).

of the stock been distributed instead of the stock itself. The shareholder's deemed dividend is measured by reference to the corporation's E&P in the year the Sec. 306 stock was distributed, although the corporation does not reduce its E&P upon the sale. Any additional amount received for the Sec. 306 stock generally constitutes a return of capital. If the additional amount exceeds the shareholder's basis in the Sec. 306 stock, the excess receives a capital gain treatment. If the additional amount is less than the shareholder's basis, the unrecovered basis is added back to the shareholder's basis in his or her common stock and is not recognized as a loss.

EXAMPLE C4-43 ▶ Carlos owns all 100 outstanding shares of Adobe Corporation common stock. His basis in those shares is $100,000. Adobe, which has $150,000 of E&P, distributes 50 shares of nonvoting preferred stock to Carlos in a nontaxable stock dividend. The FMV of the preferred stock on the distribution date is $50,000 and the FMV of the common stock on the distribution date is $200,000. Carlos must allocate his $100,000 common stock basis to the common and preferred stock according to their relative FMVs as follows:

	FMV	Basis
Common stock	$200,000	$ 80,000[a]
Preferred stock	50,000	20,000[b]
Total	$250,000	$100,000

[a] $\dfrac{\$200,000}{\$250,000} \times \$100,000$ [b] $\dfrac{\$ 50,000}{\$250,000} \times \$100,000$

Carlos subsequently sells the preferred stock to Dillon for $50,000. The $50,000 sales proceeds is deemed a dividend because Adobe's E&P in the year the corporation paid the preferred stock dividend exceeded the FMV of the preferred stock. Carlos's $20,000 basis in the preferred stock is added back to his basis in his common stock so that his common stock basis is restored to $100,000. If instead Carlos sells the preferred stock for $100,000, he recognizes $50,000 of deemed dividend income, a $20,000 return of capital, and $30,000 of capital gain computed as follows:

Sales price	$100,000
Minus: Deemed dividend income[a]	(50,000)
Remaining sales proceeds	$ 50,000
Minus: Return of capital[b]	(20,000)
Capital gain[c]	$ 30,000

[a]Smaller of E&P in year stock was issued or stock's FMV on the distribution date.
[b]Smaller of remaining sales proceeds or stock adjusted basis.
[c]Sales proceeds received in excess of stock adjusted basis.   ◀

REDEMPTIONS OF SEC. 306 STOCK

KEY POINT

The amount realized in a redemption of Sec. 306 stock is a dividend to the extent of E&P existing in the year of redemption. Unlike a sale of Sec. 306 stock, E&P is reduced as a result of a redemption.

If the issuing corporation redeems Sec. 306 stock, the shareholder's total amount realized is treated as a distribution to which the Sec. 301 distribution rules apply. It is, therefore, a dividend to the extent of the redeeming corporation's E&P *in the year of the redemption* and reduces corporate E&P accordingly. Amounts received in excess of the corporation's E&P are treated as a recovery of the shareholder's basis in his or her Sec. 306 stock, and then as a capital gain to the extent such amounts exceed basis. If all or portion of the shareholder's basis in the redeemed stock is not recovered, the unrecovered amount increases the basis of the shareholder's common stock.

EXAMPLE C4-44 ▶ Don owns all 100 shares of Brigham Corporation's common stock with a $300,000 adjusted basis. On January 1, 2002, Brigham issued 50 shares of preferred stock to Don. On the distribution date, the FMVs of the preferred stock and common stock were $100,000 and $400,000, respectively. Brigham's current and accumulated E&P for 2002 was $200,000. Don's allocated basis in the preferred stock was $60,000 {[$100,000 ÷ ($100,000 + $400,000)] × $300,000}. The basis of Don's common stock was reduced to $240,000 ($300,000 − $60,000) as a result of the basis allocation. On January 2, 2006, Brigham redeems the preferred shares for $250,000. In the year of the redemption, Brigham's current and accumulated E&P is $400,000. Don recognizes dividend income of $250,000 (because Brigham's E&P was at least $250,000 in the year of the redemption). If Brigham's E&P instead had been $200,000 in the year of the redemption, Don would have recognized $200,000 of dividend income and a $50,000 tax-free return of capital. Because Don's basis in his preferred stock is $60,000, the $10,000 unrecovered basis increases his basis in the common stock to $250,000 ($240,000 + $10,000). ◄

EXCEPTIONS TO SEC. 306 TREATMENT
Section 306 does not apply in the following situations.

► A shareholder sells all of his or her common and preferred stock, thereby completely terminating his or her interest in the issuing corporation. Section 306 does not apply even if some of the stock sold is Sec. 306 stock.

► The corporation redeems all the shareholder's common and preferred stock, completely terminating the shareholder's interest in the corporation.

► The corporation redeems an individual shareholder's stock in a partial liquidation qualifying as a sale under Sec. 302(b)(4).

► A shareholder disposes of Sec. 306 stock in a way that triggers no gain or loss recognition (e.g., a gift). Although the donor recognizes no income when he or she disposes of Sec. 306 stock by gift, the stock retains its taint and remains Sec. 306 stock in the donee's hands. The taint disappears, however, where stock is inherited.

► Section 306 does not apply if the taxpayer demonstrates to the IRS's satisfaction that the distribution and subsequent disposition of Sec. 306 stock did not have tax avoidance as one of its principal purposes.

TAX STRATEGY TIP

A taxpayer owning a portfolio of stock that includes Sec. 306 stock may want to retain the Sec. 306 stock and pass it on to his or her heirs, thereby eliminating the Sec. 306 taint, which again will have onerous effects after 2008. Market conditions, however, will dictate whether retaining the stock is a good investment strategy.

STOCK REDEMPTIONS BY RELATED CORPORATIONS

OBJECTIVE 7

Determine the applicability and tax consequences Sec. 304 to stock sales

If a shareholder sells stock in one corporation (the issuing corporation) to a second corporation (the acquiring corporation), the shareholder usually recognizes a capital gain or loss. However, if the shareholder controls both corporations, he or she may have to recognize dividend income because the net result may be more similar to a dividend than to a sale.

To prevent shareholders from using two corporations they commonly control to realize a capital gain rather than a dividend, Sec. 304 requires that a sale of stock of one controlled corporation to a second controlled corporation be treated as a stock redemption. If the redemption meets the requirements for sale treatment (e.g., if the redemption is substantially disproportionate), the transaction will be treated as a sale. Otherwise, the redemption will be treated as a dividend, assuming sufficient E&P. As in the case of Sec. 306 preferred stock bailouts, now that individuals pay a maximum tax rate of 15% on dividends and capital gains, Sec. 304 no longer delivers the "sting" it had before 2003. Nevertheless, Sec. 304 still is in effect. When it does apply, shareholders may have to recognize dividend income rather than long-term capital gain.

Section 304 applies to two types of sales. The first is a sale of stock involving two brother-sister corporations. The second is a sale of a parent corporation's stock to one of its subsidiary corporations. The following sections define brother-sister groups and parent-subsidiary groups and explain how Sec. 304 applies to each group.

ADDITIONAL COMMENT

The definition of brother-sister corporations for Sec. 304 differs from the definition for controlled groups discussed in Chapter C3.

BROTHER-SISTER CORPORATIONS
Two corporations are called brother-sister corporations when one or more shareholders control each of the corporations and a parent-subsidiary relationship does not exist. Control means ownership of at least 50% of the voting power or 50% of the total value of all the corporation's stock. The shareholder(s) who have acquired such ownership are called controlling shareholders. If a controlling shareholder (or shareholders) transfers stock in one corporation to the other corporation in exchange for property, the exchange is recast as a redemption.

To determine whether the redemption is a sale or a dividend, reference is made to the shareholder's stock ownership in the issuing corporation. For purposes of making this determination, the attribution rules of Sec. 318(a) apply.[47]

REDEMPTION TREATED AS A DISTRIBUTION. If the redemption does not qualify as a sale, it is treated as a dividend paid first by the acquiring corporation to the extent of its E&P, and then by the issuing corporation to the extent of its E&P. The shareholder's basis in the issuing corporation's stock sold is added to his or her basis in the acquiring corporation's stock. The acquiring corporation takes the same basis in the issuing corporation's shares as the shareholder's.

EXAMPLE C4-45 ▶ Bert owns 60 of the 100 outstanding shares of Frog Corporation stock and 60 of the 100 outstanding shares of Tree Corporation stock. Frog and Tree have $50,000 and $20,000 of E&P, respectively. Bert sells 20 shares of Frog stock with an adjusted basis of $10,000 to Tree for $20,000. Because Bert owns at least 50% of each corporation's stock, Bert is deemed to control both Frog and Tree, and Sec. 304 governs the tax consequences of the transaction. Thus, the transaction is recast as a redemption. To determine whether the transaction qualifies for sale treatment, reference is made to Bert's ownership of Frog stock. Before the redemption, Bert owned 60% of Frog stock. After the redemption, Bert owns 52% of Frog stock (40 shares directly and 12 [0.60 × 20] shares constructively through Tree). The redemption is treated as a Sec. 301 distribution because it satisfies none of the tests set forth in Sec. 302 for sale treatment. In this case, the entire distribution is treated as a dividend because it does not exceed Frog and Tree's total E&P of $70,000. All $20,000 of the distribution is deemed to be from Tree's E&P. Tree's basis in the Frog stock is $10,000, the same as Bert's basis in the Frog stock. Bert's basis in his Tree stock is increased by $10,000, his basis in the Frog stock that he is deemed to have contributed to Tree. ◀

Bert's Ownership of Frog Corporation Stock:

Before: 60 shares (60%) directly
After: 52 shares [40 shares directly + 12 shares (60% × 20 shares) constructively]

FIGURE C4-1 ▶ ILLUSTRATION OF A BROTHER-SISTER REDEMPTION (EXAMPLE C4-45)

REDEMPTION TREATED AS A SALE. If the redemption qualifies as a sale, the shareholder's recognized gain or loss equals the difference between the amount received from the acquiring corporation and the shareholder's basis in the surrendered shares. The acquiring corporation is treated as having purchased the issuing corporation's shares and takes a cost basis for such shares.

EXAMPLE C4-46 ▶ Assume the same facts as in Example C4-45 except Bert sells 40 shares of Frog stock with an adjusted basis of $20,000 to Tree Corporation for $40,000. After the redemption, Bert owns 44 shares of Frog stock (20 shares directly and 24 [0.60 × 40] shares constructively through Tree).

---

[47] For Sec. 304 purposes, the attribution rules of Sec. 318(a) are modified so that a shareholder is considered to own an amount of stock proportionate to that owned by any corporation of which he or she owns 5% or more (instead of 50% or more) of the value of the stock.

Therefore, he meets both the 50% and the 80% tests for a substantially disproportionate redemption, treats the redemption as a sale, and recognizes a capital gain of $20,000 ($40,000 received from Tree − $20,000 adjusted basis in the Frog shares). Tree's basis in the Frog shares acquired from Bert equals its $40,000 purchase price. ◀

ADDITIONAL COMMENT

The definition of a parent-subsidiary relationship for Sec. 304 differs from the definition for controlled groups or affiliated corporations discussed in Chapter C3.

PARENT-SUBSIDIARY CORPORATIONS

If a shareholder sells stock in a parent corporation to a subsidiary of the parent corporation, the sale is treated as a distribution in redemption of part or all of the shareholder's stock in the parent corporation. For this purpose, a parent-subsidiary relationship exists if one corporation owns at least 50% of the voting power or 50% of the total value of all stock in the subsidiary.

To determine whether the redemption is treated as a sale or a dividend, reference is made to the shareholder's ownership of the parent corporation stock before and after the redemption. The constructive ownership rules of Sec. 318 apply in this determination.

REDEMPTION TREATED AS A DIVIDEND. If the redemption does not qualify as a sale, the distribution is treated as a dividend, first from the subsidiary to the extent of its E&P and then from the parent to the extent of its E&P. The effect of this prescribed treatment is to make the E&P of both corporations available in determining the portion of the distribution that constitutes a dividend. The shareholder's basis in his or her remaining parent stock is increased by his or her basis in the stock transferred to the subsidiary. The subsidiary's basis in the parent stock is the amount the subsidiary paid for the stock.[48]

EXAMPLE C4-47 ▶ Of the 100 shares of Parent Corporation stock, Brian owns 60 with a $15,000 basis. Parent owns 60 of the 100 shares of Subsidiary stock. Parent and Subsidiary have $10,000 and $30,000 of E&P, respectively. Brian sells ten of his Parent shares to Subsidiary for $12,000. (See Figure C4-2.) Parent is deemed to have redeemed its stock from Brian, who owned 60% of Parent stock before the redemption and 53 shares (50 shares directly and 3 [0.60 × 0.50 × 10] shares constructively) after the redemption. Because the 50% and 80% tests are not met, the redemption is not substantially disproportionate and does not qualify for sale treatment. Therefore, Brian

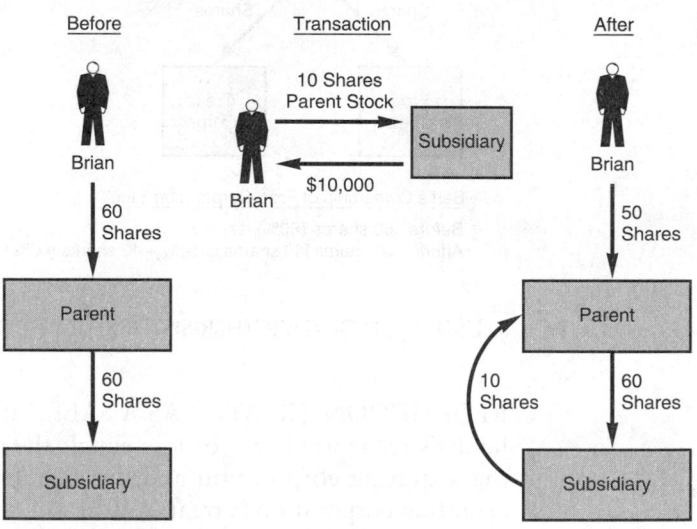

Brian's Ownership of Parent Corporation Stock:

Before: 60 shares (60%) directly
After: 53 shares [50 shares directly + 3 shares (50% × 60% × 10 shares) constructively]

FIGURE C4-2 ▶ ILLUSTRATION OF A PARENT-SUBSIDIARY REDEMPTION (EXAMPLE C4-47)

---

[48] Rev. Rul. 80-189, 1980-2 C.B. 106.

recognizes a dividend. The $12,000 distribution is deemed to have been made out of Subsidiary's E&P. Brian's $2,500 basis in the redeemed shares increases his $12,500 basis in his remaining Parent shares, so that his total basis in those shares remains $15,000. Subsidiary's basis in the ten Parent shares acquired from Brian is $12,000, the amount that Subsidiary paid for the shares.   ◀

REDEMPTION TREATED AS A SALE. If the redemption of the parent corporation's stock qualifies as a sale, the basis of the stock transferred to the subsidiary is subtracted from the amount received in the distribution to derive the shareholder's recognized gain or loss.

EXAMPLE C4-48 ▶ Assume the same facts as in Example C4-47 except Brian sells 40 shares of Parent stock to Subsidiary for $48,000. Because Brian owns 60% of Parent stock before the redemption and 24.8% (20 shares directly and 4.8 [0.60 × 0.20 × 40] shares constructively) after the redemption, the redemption meets the 50% and 80% tests for a substantially disproportionate redemption. In this case, Brian recognizes a capital gain of $38,000 ($48,000 − $10,000 adjusted basis in the 40 shares sold). Brian's adjusted basis for his remaining 20 shares of Parent stock is $5,000. Subsidiary's basis in the 40 Parent shares purchased from Brian is $48,000, the amount that Subsidiary paid for the shares.   ◀

Topic Review C4-4 summarizes the conditions under which a redemption may be characterized as a sale, as well as the special stock redemption rules.

Topic Review C4-4

Alternative Treatments of Stock Redemptions

General Rule: A distribution in redemption of stock is a dividend (Secs. 302(d) and 301).
Exception: Redemptions Treated as Sales

1. Redemptions that are not essentially equivalent to a dividend (Sec. 302(b)(1))
2. Substantially disproportionate redemptions (Sec. 302(b)(2))
3. Complete terminations of a shareholder's interest (Sec. 302(b)(3))
4. Partial liquidation of a corporation in redemption of a noncorporate shareholder's stock (Sec. 302(b)(4))
5. Redemption to pay death taxes (Sec. 303)

Special Redemption Rules

1. Redemptions of Sec. 306 stock generally are treated as dividends to the shareholder (Sec. 306).
2. A sale of stock in one controlled corporation to another controlled corporation is treated as a redemption (Sec. 304).

TAX PLANNING CONSIDERATIONS

AVOIDING UNREASONABLE COMPENSATION

The advantage of using salary payments and fringe benefits to permit a shareholder of a closely held corporation to withdraw funds from the corporation and still be subject to single level taxation was discussed in Chapter C3. If a corporation pays too large a salary to a shareholder-employee, some of the salary may be disallowed as a deduction to the corporation while still being taxed to the shareholder-employee. In such case, double taxation results.

Corporations can avoid the double taxation associated with excess compensation by entering into a **hedge agreement** with a shareholder-employee. The agreement obligates the shareholder-employee to repay any portion of salary the IRS disallows as a deduction. The shareholder-employee may deduct the amount of any repayment under Sec. 162 in the year he or she makes the repayment, provided a legal obligation exists under state law to make the payment.[49] If a hedge agreement is not in effect, voluntary repayment of the salary is not deductible by the shareholder-employee.[50]

EXAMPLE C4-49 ▶ Theresa owns one-half the stock of Marine Corporation and serves as its president. The remaining Marine stock is owned by eight investors, none of whom owns more than 10% of the outstanding shares. In 2001, Theresa and Marine conclude a hedge agreement requiring Theresa to repay all compensation the IRS declares unreasonable. In 2003, Marine pays Theresa a salary and bonus of $750,000. The IRS subsequently alleges that $300,000 of the salary is unreasonable and thus is not deductible by Marine. After negotiation, Marine Corporation and the IRS settle for $180,000. Theresa repays the $180,000 in 2006. The entire $750,000 is taxable to Theresa in 2003. However, she can deduct the $180,000 as a trade or business expense in 2006. ◀

Hedge agreements also have been used in connection with other payments involving a corporation and its shareholders (e.g., travel and entertainment expenses). Some employers shy away from hedge agreements because the IRS is likely to consider the existence of such an agreement as evidence of unreasonable compensation.

BOOTSTRAP ACQUISITIONS

A prospective purchaser who wants to acquire the stock of a corporation may not have sufficient cash to make the purchase. To facilitate the purchase in this situation, corporate funds may be used in the following way: the corporation's shareholder could sell part of his or her stock to the purchaser and then cause the corporation to redeem the remainder of the selling shareholder's stock. Such an arrangement is called a **bootstrap acquisition.**

EXAMPLE C4-50 ▶ Ted owns all 100 shares of Dragon Corporation stock having a $100,000 FMV. Vickie wants to purchase the stock from Ted but has only $60,000. Dragon has a large cash balance, which it does not need for its operations. Ted sells Vickie 60 shares of Dragon stock for $60,000 and then causes Dragon to redeem his remaining shares for $40,000. The redemption qualifies as a complete termination of Ted's interest under Sec. 302(b)(3) and, therefore, is eligible for capital gain treatment. ◀

Court cases have held that such redemptions qualify for sale treatment as long as the third-party sale and redemption are part of an integrated plan to terminate the seller's entire interest in the corporation. It does not matter whether the redemption precedes the sale.[51] In such situations, however, the purchaser must be careful to avoid generating dividend income. For example, a purchaser who contracts to acquire all the stock in a corporation on an installment plan and then uses corporate funds to pay the installment obligations will recognize dividend income. The use of corporate funds constitutes a constructive dividend to the purchaser when the corporation discharges a purchaser's legal obligation. Even if the corporation uses its own funds to redeem the seller's shares, a purchaser who was legally obligated to purchase the shares is considered to have received a constructive dividend.[52]

EXAMPLE C4-51 ▶ Assume the same facts as in Example C4-50 except that, after Vickie purchases the 60 shares from Ted, she becomes legally obligated to purchase the remaining 40 shares from Ted. After entering into the contract, Vickie causes Dragon Corporation to redeem Ted's 40 shares. Because Dragon has extinguished Vickie's legal obligation, the corporation is deemed to have paid Vickie a $40,000 constructive dividend. No constructive dividend would result from the redemption if Vickie were legally obligated to purchase only 60 shares from Ted. ◀

Rev. Rul. 69-608 provides guidelines for the buyer in a bootstrap redemption transaction to avoid constructive dividend treatment.[53] A key guideline is that the buyer does not have a constructive dividend when the corporation redeems some of the seller's shares, as

[49] Rev. Rul. 69-115, 1969-1 C.B. 50, and *Vincent E. Oswald*, 49 T.C. 645 (1968), *acq.* 1968-2 C.B. 2.
[50] *Ernest H. Berger*, 37 T.C. 1026 (1962), and *John G. Pahl*, 67 T.C. 286 (1976).
[51] See, for example, *U.S. v. Gerald Carey*, 7 AFTR 2d 1301, 61-1 USTC ¶9428 (8th Cir., 1961).
[52] *H. F. Wall v. U.S.*, 36 AFTR 423, 47-2 USTC ¶9395 (4th Cir., 1947).
[53] Rev. Rul. 69-608, 1969-2 C.B. 42.

WHAT WOULD YOU DO IN THIS SITUATION?

One of the most cherished traditions followed by many professional firms involves the year-end bonus. Professionals engaged in the healing arts, law, business services, and accounting often have used bonus compensation to clear the books at the end of the year. In partnerships, bonuses have been characterized as distributive shares or a form of compensation. As such, they are taxed only once as income paid to the professional for services rendered, net of appropriate accounting adjustments.

With the advent of the professional corporation, an entity designed to limit personal liability, many professionals have opted to do business as shareholders. The continued use of the year-end bonus in the professional corporation has come under greater IRS scrutiny. The position taken by the IRS is clear. If the payments made to the shareholder-professional are in exchange for his or her services rendered to the firm, the corporation may deduct them as salaries (assuming they are reasonable). However, if they are a disguised payout of owners' profits, the corporation cannot deduct them. As a result, the corporation's taxable income is increased by the amount of the disallowed deductions. The shareholder who received the bonus, must treat the payment as dividend income rather than salary. However, treating the bonus payments as dividends rather than salary

generally results in less tax paid by the shareholder because dividends are taxed at a maximum rate of 15%. The negative consequences are only to the corporation, which may not deduct the dividend payments.

This principle is illustrated in a case decided by the Second Circuit Court of Appeals, *Rapco, Inc. v. CIR*, 77 AFTR 2d 2405, 96-1 USTC ¶50,297 (CA-2, 1996). In *Rapco*, the Second Circuit denied a deduction for bonus payments to the president of the company, even though he played a significant role in the company's rapid growth and had guaranteed large loans to Rapco. Reasons cited by the court were that Rapco's compensation scheme was "bonus-heavy and salary light," suggesting dividend avoidance; Rapco had ignored its own bonus policy set forth in its preincorporation minutes; it had a history of never paying dividends; the shareholder who determined his own salary owned 95% of the corporation's stock; and Rapco's own expert testified that $400,000 to $500,000 was fair compensation for the president's services (the IRS allowed a salary of $405,000).

Assuming your CPA firm is acting as a tax advisor to several similarly situated professional corporations, what advice that complies with the Internal Revenue Code, Treasury Regulations, and the AICPA's *Statements on Standards for Tax Services* would you give?

long as the buyer does not have a primary and unconditional obligation to purchase the stock, and as long as the corporation pays no more than the FMV for the redeemed stock. A stock purchaser who has an option—not a legal obligation—to purchase the seller's remaining stock, and who assigns the option to the redeeming corporation, is unlikely to generate a constructive dividend.[54]

TIMING OF DISTRIBUTIONS

Dividends can be paid only out of a corporation's E&P. Therefore, if distributions can be timed to be made when the corporation has little or no E&P, the distributions are treated as a return of capital rather than as a dividend.

If a corporation generates a current E&P deficit, the deficit reduces accumulated E&P evenly throughout the year unless the corporation can demonstrate that the deficits arose on particular dates. Thus, if a corporation with a current E&P deficit, but a positive accumulated E&P balance, makes a distribution in the current year, the timing of the distribution may determine whether the distribution will be treated as a dividend or a return of capital.

EXAMPLE C4-52 ▶ Major Corporation has a $30,000 accumulated E&P balance at the beginning of the year and incurs a $50,000 deficit during the year. Because of its poor operating performance, Major pays only two of its four usual $5,000 quarterly dividend payments to its sole shareholder, the two being those ordinarily paid on March 31 and June 30. The tax treatment of the two distributions is determined as follows:

---

[54] *Joseph R. Holsey v. CIR*, 2 AFTR 2d 5660, 58-2 USTC ¶9816 (3rd Cir., 1958).

E&P balance, January 1	$30,000
Minus: Reduction for first quarter loss	(12,500)
Reduction for March 31 distribution	(5,000)
E&P balance, April 1	$12,500
Minus: Reduction for second quarter loss	(12,500)
E&P balance, June 30	$ –0–

The first and second quarter losses each are $12,500 [($50,000) × 0.25 = ($12,500)].

The operating loss reduces the accumulated E&P balance evenly throughout the year. All of the March 31 distribution is taxable because the corporation has not incurred sufficient losses to offset the positive accumulated E&P balance at the beginning of the year. The second quarter loss causes the June 30 distribution and any other distributions made before year-end to be tax-free returns of capital (assuming that the shareholder's basis in his or her stock exceeds the distribution amount). Delaying all the distributions until late in the year could result in the tax-free return of capital. ◀

The timing of a distribution also can be critical if the distributing corporation has an accumulated E&P deficit and a positive current E&P balance.

EXAMPLE C4-53 ▶ Yankee Corporation has an accumulated E&P deficit of $250,000 at the beginning of 2005. During 2005 and 2006, Yankee reports the following current E&P balances and makes the following distributions to Joe, its sole shareholder:

Year	Current E&P	Distributions	Distribution Date
2005	$100,000	$75,000	December 31
2006	–0–	–0–	None

The $75,000 distribution in 2005 is taxable as a dividend. The $25,000 of current E&P that is not distributed reduces Yankee's accumulated E&P deficit to $225,000. Had Yankee delayed making the $75,000 distribution until January 1, 2006, or later in 2006, the distribution would have been a tax-free return of Joe's investment. ◀

COMPLIANCE AND PROCEDURAL CONSIDERATIONS

CORPORATE REPORTING OF NONDIVIDEND DISTRIBUTIONS

ADDITIONAL COMMENT

Information on basis adjustments for tax-free dividends, stock splits, stock dividends, etc. for individual firms can be found in special tax services.

A corporation that makes a nondividend distribution to its shareholders must file Form 5452 (Corporate Report of Nondividend Distributions) and supporting computations with its income tax return. Form 5452 reports the E&P of the distributing corporation so that the IRS can verify that the distributions are indeed nontaxable to shareholders. Specifically, the form requires the following information: the corporation's current and accumulated E&P, amounts paid to shareholders during the tax year, the percentage of each payment that is taxable and nontaxable, and a detailed computation of the corporation's E&P from the date of its incorporation.

AGREEMENT TO TERMINATE INTEREST UNDER SEC. 302(b)(3)

KEY POINT

The statute of limitation extends to one year beyond the date a shareholder notifies the IRS that a forbidden interest has been acquired. Otherwise, it would be almost impossible for the IRS to administer this provision.

If a redemption completely terminates a shareholder's interest in a corporation, the family attribution rules of Sec. 318(a)(1) may be waived. To have the rules waived, the shareholder must file a written agreement with the Treasury Department that he or she will notify the IRS upon acquiring any prohibited interest within the ten-year period following the redemption. A copy of this agreement (which should be in the form of a statement in duplicate signed by the distributee shareholder) must be attached to the first return filed by the shareholder for the tax year in which the redemption occurs. If the agreement is not filed on time, the IRS may grant an extension. Regulation Sec. 1.302-4(a) provides that an extension will be granted only if reasonable cause exists for failure to file the agreement on time and if the request for such an extension is filed within such time as the appropriate IRS official considers reasonable in the circumstances.

Treasury Regulations do not indicate what constitutes reasonable cause for failure to file or what constitutes a reasonable extension of time. In *Edward J. Fehrs* the U.S. Court of Claims held that late filing of a ten-year agreement is permissible where a taxpayer could not reasonably have expected that a filing would be necessary, where the taxpayer files the agreement promptly after he or she has received notice that it is required, and where the agreement is filed before the issues in question are presented for trial.[55] However, in *Robin Haft Trust*, an agreement was filed *after* an adverse court ruling. In an appeal for a rehearing, the judge ruled that the filing of the agreement after the case came to trial was too late. Consequently, the judge denied the appeal for a rehearing.[56]

If the shareholder *does* acquire a prohibited interest in the corporation within the ten-year period following the redemption, the IRS may assess additional taxes. Such an acquisition ordinarily results in recasting the redemption as a dividend rather than a sale. The limitations period for assessing additional taxes extends to one year following the date the shareholder files with the IRS notice of the acquisition of the prohibited interest.[57]

PROBLEM MATERIALS

DISCUSSION QUESTIONS

C4-1 Explain how a corporation computes its current E&P and its accumulated E&P.

C4-2 Why is it necessary to distinguish between current and accumulated E&P?

C4-3 Describe the effect of a $100,000 cash distribution paid on January 1 to the sole shareholder of a calendar year corporation whose stock basis is $25,000 when the corporation has
a. $100,000 of current E&P and $100,000 of accumulated E&P
b. $50,000 of accumulated E&P deficit and $60,000 of current E&P
c. $60,000 of accumulated E&P deficit and $60,000 of current E&P deficit
d. $80,000 of current E&P deficit and $100,000 of accumulated E&P
Answer Parts a through d again, assuming instead that the corporation makes the distribution on October 1 in a nonleap year.

C4-4 Pecan Corporation distributes land to a noncorporate shareholder. Explain how the following items are computed:
a. The amount of the distribution
b. The amount of the dividend
c. The basis of the land to the shareholder
d. When the holding period for the land begins
How would your answers change if the distribution were made to a corporate shareholder?

C4-5 What effect do the following transactions have on the calculation of Young Corporation's current E&P? Assume that the starting point for the calculation is Young's taxable income for the current year.
a. The corporation earns tax-exempt interest income of $10,000.
b. Taxable income includes a $10,000 dividend received and is reduced by a $7,000 dividends-received deduction.
c. A $5,000 capital loss carryover from the preceding tax year offsets $5,000 of capital gains.
d. The corporation accrued federal income taxes of $25,280.
e. The corporation took a U.S. production activities deduction of $3,000.

C4-6 Badger Corporation was incorporated in the current year. It reports an $8,000 NOL on its initial tax return. Badger distributed $2,500 to its shareholders. Is it possible for this distribution to be taxed as a dividend to Badger's shareholders? Explain.

C4-7 Does it matter when during the tax year a corporation makes a distribution as to whether it is taxed as a dividend or as a return of capital? Explain.

C4-8 Hickory Corporation owns a building with a $160,000 adjusted basis and a $120,000 FMV. Hickory's E&P is $200,000. Should the

---

[55] *Edward J. Fehrs v. U.S.*, 40 AFTR 2d 77-5040, 77-1 USTC ¶9423 (Ct. Cl., 1977).

[56] *Robin Haft Trust*, 62 T.C. 145 (1974).

[57] Sec. 302(c)(2)(A).

C4-9 Walnut Corporation owns a building with a $120,000 adjusted basis and a $160,000 FMV. Walnut's E&P is $200,000. Should the corporation sell the property and distribute the sale proceeds to its shareholders or distribute the property to its shareholders and let them sell the property? Why?

C4-10 What is a constructive dividend? Under what circumstances is the IRS likely to argue that a constructive dividend has been paid?

C4-11 Why are stock dividends generally nontaxable? Under what circumstances are stock dividends taxable?

C4-12 For tax purposes, how is a distribution of stock rights treated by a shareholder? By the distributing corporation?

C4-13 What is a stock redemption? What are some reasons for making a stock redemption? Why are some redemptions treated as sales and others as dividends?

C4-14 Field Corporation redeems 100 shares of its stock from Andrew for $10,000. Andrew's basis in those shares is $8,000. Explain the possible tax treatments of the $10,000 received by Andrew.

C4-15 What conditions must be met for a redemption to be treated as a sale by the redeeming shareholder?

C4-16 Explain the purpose of the attribution rules in determining stock ownership in a redemption. Describe the four types of attribution rules that apply to redemptions.

C4-17 Abel, the sole shareholder of Ace Corporation, has an opporunity to purchase the assets of a sole proprietorship for $50,000 in cash. Ace has a substantial E&P balance. Abel does not have sufficient cash to personally make the purchase. If Abel obtains the needed $50,000 from Ace via a nonliquidating distribution, Abel will have to recognize dividend income. Alternatively, would Ace's purchase of the assets of the sole proprietorship followed by their distribution to Abel in redemption of part of his stock holdings constitute a partial liquidation? Explain.

C4-18 Why does a redemption that qualifies for sale treatment under Sec. 303 usually result in the shareholder's recognizing little or no gain or loss?

C4-19 Under what circumstances does a corporation recognize gain or loss when it distributes noncash property in redemption of its stock? What effect does a redemption distribution have on the distributing corporation's E&P?

C4-20 What is a preferred stock bailout? How does Sec. 306 operate to prevent a shareholder from realizing the expected benefits of a preferred stock bailout?

C4-21 Bill owns all 100 of the outstanding shares of Plum Corporation stock and 80 of the 100 outstanding shares of Cherry Corporation stock. He sells 20 Plum shares to Cherry for $80,000. Explain why this transaction is treated as a stock redemption and how the tax consequences of the transaction are determined.

C4-22 Explain the tax consequences to both the corporation and a shareholder-employee of an IRS determination that a portion of the compensation paid in a prior tax year is unreasonable. What steps can the corporation and the shareholder-employee take to avoid the double taxation usually associated with such a determination?

C4-23 What is a bootstrap acquisition? What are the tax consequences of such a transaction?

ISSUE IDENTIFICATION QUESTIONS

C4-24 Marsha receives a $10,000 cash distribution from Dye Corporation in April of the current year. Dye has $4,000 of accumulated E&P at the beginning of the year and $8,000 of current E&P. Dye also distributed $10,000 in cash to Barbara, who purchased all 200 shares of Dye stock from Marsha in June of the current year. What tax issues should be considered with respect to the distributions paid to Marsha and Barbara?

C4-25 Neil purchased land from Spring Harbor, his 100%-owned corporation, for $275,000. The corporation purchased the land three years ago for $300,000. Similar tracts of land located nearby have sold for $400,000 in recent months. What tax issues should be considered with respect to the corporation's sale of the land?

C4-26 Price Corporation has 100 shares of common stock outstanding. Price repurchased all of Penny's 30 shares for $35,000 cash during the current year. Penny received the shares as a gift from her mother three years ago. They have a basis to her of $16,000. Price has $100,000 in current and accumulated E&P. Penny's mother owns 40 of the remaining shares; unrelated individuals own the other 30 shares. What tax issues should be considered with respect to the corporation's purchase of Penny's shares?

C4-27 George owns all 100 shares of Gumby's Pizza Corporation. The shares are worth $200,000, but George's basis is only $70,000. Mary and George have reached a tentative agreement for George to sell all his shares to Mary. However, Mary is unwilling to pay more than

$150,000 for the stock because the corporation currently has excess cash balances. They have agreed that George can withdraw $50,000 in cash from Gumby's before the stock sale. What tax issues should be considered with respect to George and Mary's agreement?

PROBLEMS

C4-28   *Current E&P Calculation.* Beach Corporation reports the following results in the current year based on the accrual method of accounting:

Income:	
Gross profit from manufacturing operations	$250,000
Dividends received from 25%-owned domestic corporation	20,000
Interest income: Corporate bonds	10,000
Municipal bonds	12,000
Proceeds from life insurance policy on key employee	100,000
Section 1231 gain on sale of land	8,000
Expenses:	
Administrative expenses	110,000
Bad debt expense	5,000
Depreciation:	
Financial accounting	68,000
Taxable income	86,000
Alternative depreciation system (Sec. 168(g))	42,000
NOL carryover	40,000
Charitable contributions: Current year	8,000
Carryover from last year	3,500
Capital loss on sale of stock	1,200
U.S. production activities deduction	1,500
Penalty on late payment of federal taxes	450

a. What is Beach's taxable income?
b. What is Beach's current E&P?

C4-29   *Current E&P Computation.* Water Corporation reports $500,000 of taxable income for the current year. The following additional information is available:

- Water reported an $80,000 long-term capital loss for the current year. It reported no capital gains this year.

- Taxable income included $80,000 of dividends from a 10%-owned domestic corporation.

- Water paid fines and penalties of $6,000 that were not deducted in computing taxable income.

- Water deducted a $20,000 NOL carryover from a prior tax year in computing this year's taxable income.

- Water claimed a $10,000 U.S. production activities deduction.

- Taxable income includes a deduction for $40,000 of depreciation that exceeds the depreciation allowed for E&P purposes.

Assume a 34% corporate tax rate. What is Water's current E&P for this year?

C4-30   *Calculating Accumulated E&P.* Peach Corporation formed in 2003. Its current E&P (or current E&P deficit) and distributions for the period 2003–2006 are as follows:

Year	Current E&P (Deficit)	Distributions
2003	$ (8,000)	$ 2,000
2004	(12,000)	–0–
2005	10,000	5,000
2006	14,000	17,000

What is Peach's accumulated E&P at the beginning of 2004, 2005, 2006, and 2007?

C4-31   *Consequences of a Single Cash Distribution.* Clover Corporation is a calendar year taxpayer. Connie owns all of its stock. Her basis for the stock is $10,000. On April 1 of the current year (not a leap year) Clover Corporation distributes $52,000 to Connie. Determine the tax consequences of the cash distribution in each of the following independent situations:
a. Current E&P $15,000; accumulated E&P $25,000.
b. Current E&P $30,000; accumulated E&P ($20,000).

c. Current E&P ($73,000); accumulated E&P $50,000.

d. Current E&P ($20,000); accumulated E&P ($15,000).

C4-32 *Consequences of a Single Cash Distribution.* Pink Corporation is a calendar year taxpayer. Pete owns one third of the stock (100 shares). His basis for his stock is $25,000. Cheryl owns two-thirds of the stock (200 shares). Her basis for her stock is $40,000. On June 10 of the current year, Pink distributes $120,000, $40,000 to Pete and $80,000 to Cheryl. Determine the tax consequences of the cash distributions to Pete and Cheryl in each of the following independent situations:

a. Current E&P $60,000; accumulated E&P $100,000.

b. Current E&P $36,000; accumulated E&P $30,000.

C4-33 *Consequences of Multiple Cash Distributions.* At the beginning of the current year (not a leap year), Charles owns all of Pearl Corporation's outstanding stock. His basis in the stock is $80,000. On July 1, he sells all his stock to Donald for $125,000. During the current year, Pearl, a calendar year taxpayer, makes two cash distributions: $60,000 on March 1 to Charles and $90,000 on September 1 to Donald. How are these distributions treated in the following independent situations? What are the amount and character of Charles' gain on his sale of stock to Donald? What is Donald's basis in his Pearl stock at the end of the year?

a. Current E&P $40,000; accumulated E&P $30,000.

b. Current E&P $100,000; accumulated E&P ($50,000).

c. Current E&P ($36,500); accumulated E&P $120,000.

C4-34 *Distribution of Appreciated Property.* In the current year, Sedgwick Corporation has $100,000 of current and accumulated E&P. On March 3, Sedgwick distributes to Dina, a shareholder, a parcel of land (a capital asset) having a $56,000 FMV. The land has a $40,000 adjusted basis (for both tax and E&P purposes) to Sedgwick and is subject to an $8,000 mortgage, which Dina assumes. Assume a 34% marginal corporate tax rate.

a. What are the amount and character of the income Dina recognizes as a result of the distribution?

b. What is Dina's basis in the land?

c. What are the amount and character of Sedgwick's gain or loss as a result of the distribution?

d. What effect does the distribution have on Sedgwick's E&P?

C4-35 *Distribution of Property Subject to a Liability.* On May 10 of the current year, Stowe Corporation distributes to Arlene, a shareholder, $20,000 in cash and land (a capital asset) having a $50,000 FMV. The land has a $15,000 adjusted basis (for both tax and E&P purposes) and is subject to a $60,000 mortgage, which Arlene assumes. Stowe has an E&P balance exceeding the amount distributed and is subject to a 34% marginal corporate tax rate.

a. What are the amount and character of the income Arlene recognizes as a result of the distribution?

b. What is Arlene's basis in the land?

c. What are the amount and character of Stowe's gain or loss as a result of the distribution?

C4-36 *Distribution of Depreciable Property.* On May 15 of the current year, Quick Corporation distributes to Calvin, a shareholder, a building having a $250,000 FMV used in its business. The building originally cost $180,000. Quick claimed $30,000 of straight-line depreciation, so that the adjusted basis of the building on the date of distribution for taxable income purposes is $150,000. The adjusted basis of the building for E&P purposes is $160,000. The building is subject to an $80,000 mortgage, which Calvin assumes. Quick has an E&P balance exceeding the amount distributed and is subject to a 34% marginal corporate tax rate.

a. What are the amount and character of the income Calvin recognizes as a result of the distribution?

b. What is Calvin's basis in the building?

c. What are the amount and character of Quick's gain or loss as a result of the distribution?

d. What effect does the distribution have on Quick's E&P?

C4-37 *Distribution of Various Types of Property.* During the current year, Zeta Corporation distributes the assets listed below to its sole shareholder, Susan. For each asset listed, determine the gross income recognized by Susan, her basis in the asset, the amount of gain or loss recognized by Zeta, and the effect of the distribution on Zeta's E&P. Assume that

Zeta has an E&P balance exceeding the amount distributed and is subject to a 34% marginal corporate tax rate. Unless stated otherwise, tax and E&P adjusted bases are the same.

a. A parcel of land used in Zeta's business that has a $200,000 FMV and a $125,000 adjusted basis.

b. Assume the same facts as Part a except that the land is subject to a $140,000 mortgage.

c. FIFO inventory having a $25,000 FMV and an $18,000 adjusted basis.

d. A building used in Zeta's business having an original cost of $225,000, a $450,000 FMV, and a $150,000 adjusted basis for taxable income purposes. Zeta has claimed $75,000 of depreciation for taxable income purposes under the straight-line method. Depreciation for E&P purposes is $60,000.

e. An automobile used in Zeta's business having an original cost of $12,000, an $8,000 FMV, and a $5,760 adjusted basis, on which Zeta has claimed $6,240 of MACRS depreciation for taxable income purposes. For E&P purposes, depreciation was $5,200.

f. Installment obligations having a $35,000 face amount (and FMV) and a $24,500 adjusted basis. The obligations were created when Zeta sold a Sec. 1231 asset.

C4-38   *Disguised Dividends.* King Corporation is a profitable manufacturing corporation with $800,000 of E&P. It is owned in equal shares by Harry and Wilma, who are husband and wife. Both individuals are actively involved in the business. Determine the tax consequences of the following independent events:

a. In reviewing a prior year tax return for King, the IRS determines that the $500,000 of salary and bonuses paid to Wilma is unreasonable. Reasonable compensation would be $280,000.

b. King has loaned Harry $400,000 over the past three years. None of the money has been repaid. Harry does not pay interest on the loans.

c. King sells a building to Wilma for $150,000 in cash. The property has an adjusted basis of $90,000 and is subject to a $60,000 mortgage, which Wilma assumes. The FMV of the building is $350,000.

d. Harry leases a warehouse to King for $50,000 per year. According to an IRS auditor, similar warehouses can be leased for $35,000 per year.

e. Wilma sells land to King for $250,000 on which King intends to build a factory. According to a recent appraisal, the FMV of the land is $185,000.

f. The corporation owns an airplane that it uses to fly executives to business meetings. When the airplane is not being used for business, Harry and Wilma use it to fly to their ranch in Idaho for short vacations. The approximate cost of their trips to the ranch in the current year is $8,000.

C4-39   *Unreasonable Compensation.* Forward Corporation is owned by a group of 15 shareholders. During the current year, Forward pays $550,000 in salary and bonuses to Alvin, its president and controlling shareholder. The corporation's marginal tax rate is 34%, and Alvin's marginal tax rate is 35%. The IRS audits Forward's tax return and determines that reasonable compensation for Alvin would be $350,000. Forward Corporation agrees to the adjustment. What effect does the disallowance of part of the deduction for Alvin's salary and bonuses have on Forward and Alvin? Ignore payroll taxes, such as FICA.

C4-40   *Stock Dividend Distribution.* Wilton Corporation has a single class of common stock outstanding. Robert owns 100 shares, which he purchased in 2000 for $100,000. In 2006, when the stock is worth $1,200 per share, Wilton declares a 10% dividend payable in common stock. Robert receives ten additional shares on December 10, 2006. On January 30, 2007, he sells five of the new shares for $7,000.

a. How much income must Robert recognize when he receives the stock dividend?

b. How much gain or loss must Robert recognize when he sells the common stock?

c. What is Robert's basis in his remaining common stock? When does his holding period in the new common stock begin?

C4-41   *Stock Dividend Distribution.* Moss Corporation has a single class of common stock outstanding. Tillie owns 1,000 shares, which she purchased in 2002 for $100,000. Moss declares a stock dividend payable in 8% preferred stock having a $100 par value. Each shareholder receives one share of preferred stock for ten shares of common stock held. On the distribution date—December 10, 2006—the common stock was worth $180 per share, and the preferred stock was worth $100 per share. On April 1, 2006, Tillie sells half of her preferred stock for $5,000.

a. How much income must Tillie recognize when she receives the stock dividend?

   b. How much gain or loss must Tillie recognize when she sells the preferred stock? (Ignore the implications of Sec. 306.)

   c. What is Tillie's basis in her remaining common and preferred stock? When does her holding period for the preferred stock begin?

C4-42 *Stock Rights Distribution.* Trusty Corporation has a single class of common stock outstanding. Jim owns 200 shares, which he purchased for $50 per share two years ago. On April 10 of the current year, Trusty distributes to its shareholders one right to purchase a share of common stock at $60 per share for each share of common stock held. At the time of the distribution, the common stock is worth $75 per share, and the rights are worth $15 per right. On September 10, Jim sells 100 rights for $2,000 and exercises the remaining 100 rights. He sells 60 of the shares acquired through exercise of the rights for $80 each on November 10.

   a. What are the amount and character of income Jim recognizes upon receiving the rights?

   b. What are the amount and character of gain or loss Jim recognizes upon selling the rights?

   c. What are the amount and character of gain or loss Jim recognizes upon exercising the rights?

   d. What are the amount and character of gain or loss Jim recognizes upon selling the newly acquired common stock?

   e. What basis does Jim have in his remaining shares?

C4-43 *Attribution Rules.* George owns 100 shares of Polar Corporation's 1,000 outstanding shares of common stock. Under the family attribution rules of Sec. 318, to which of the following individuals will George's stock be attributed?

   a. George's wife
   b. George's father
   c. George's brother
   d. George's mother-in-law
   e. George's daughter
   f. George's son-in law
   g. George's grandfather
   h. George's grandson
   i. George's mother's brother (his uncle)

C4-44 *Attribution Rules.* Moose Corporation has 400 shares of stock outstanding owned as follows:

Name	Shares
Lara (an individual)	60
LMN Partnership (Lara is a 20% partner)	50
LST Partnership (Lara is a 70% partner)	100
Lemon Corporation (Lara is a 30% shareholder)	100
Lime Corporation (Lara is a 60% shareholder)	90
Total	400

How many shares is Lara deemed to own under the Sec. 318 attribution rules?

C4-45 *Redemption from a Sole Shareholder.* Paul owns all 100 shares of Presto Corporation's stock. His basis in the stock is $10,000. Presto has $100,000 of E&P. Presto redeems 25 of Paul's shares for $30,000. What are the tax consequences of the redemption to Paul and to Presto?

C4-46 *Multiple Redemptions.* Benton Corporation has 400 shares of stock outstanding owned by four unrelated shareholders. Benton redeems 100 shares from the shareholders as shown below for $500 per share. Each shareholder has a $230 per share basis for his or her stock. Benton's current and accumulated E&P at the end of the tax year is $150,000.

Shareholder	Shares Held Before the Redemption	Shares Redeemed
Ethel	200	40
Fran	100	30
Georgia	50	30
Henry	50	–0–
Total	400	100

a. What are the tax consequences (e.g., amount and character of income, gain, or loss recognized and basis of remaining shares) of the redemptions to Ethel, Fran, and Georgia?

b. How would your answer to Part a change if Ethel is Georgia's mother?

C4-47 *Partial Liquidation.* Unrelated individuals Amy, Beth, and Carla, and Delta Corporation each own 25 of the 100 outstanding shares of Axle Corporation's stock. Axle distributes $20,000 to each shareholder in exchange for five shares of Axle stock in a transaction that qualifies as a partial liquidation. Each share redeemed has a $1,000 basis to the shareholder and a $4,000 FMV. How does each shareholder treat the distribution?

C4-48 *Redemption to Pay Death Taxes.* John died on March 3. His gross estate of $2.5 million includes First Corporation stock (400 of the 1,000 outstanding shares) worth $1.5 million. John's wife, Myra, owns the remaining 600 shares. Funeral and administrative expenses deductible under Secs. 2053 and 2054 amount to $250,000. John, Jr. is the sole beneficiary of John's estate. Estate taxes amount to $350,000.

a. Does a redemption of First stock from John's estate, John. Jr., or John's wife qualify for sale treatment under Sec. 303?

b. On September 10, First Corporation redeems 200 shares of its stock from John's estate for $800,000. How does the estate treat this redemption?

C4-49 *Effect of Redemption on E&P.* White Corporation has 100 shares of stock outstanding. Ann owns 40 of these shares, and unrelated shareholders own the remaining 60 shares. White redeems 30 of Ann's shares for $30,000. In the year of the redemption, White has $30,000 of paid-in capital and $80,000 of E&P.

a. How does the redemption affect White's E&P balance if the redemption qualifies for sale treatment?

b. How does the redemption affect White's E&P balance if the redemption does *not* qualify for sale treatment?

C4-50 *Various Redemption Issues.* Alan, Barbara, and Dave are unrelated. Each has owned 100 shares of Time Corporation stock for five years and each has a $60,000 basis in those 100 shares. Time's E&P is $240,000. Time redeems all 100 of Alan's shares for $100,000, their FMV.

a. What are the amount and character of Alan's recognized gain or loss? What basis do Barbara and Dave have in their remaining shares? What effect does the redemption have on Time's E&P?

b. Assuming that Alan is Barbara's son, answer the questions in Part a again.

c. Assume the same facts as in Part b except that Alan signs an agreement under Sec. 302(c)(2)(A) to waive the family attribution rules. Answer the questions in Part a again.

C4-51 *Various Redemption Issues.* Andrew, Bea, Carl, and Carl, Jr. (Carl's son), and Tetra Corporation own all of the single class of Excel Corporation stock as follows:

Shareholder	Shares Held	Adjusted Basis
Andrew	20	$3,000
Bea	30	6,000
Carl	25	4,000
Carl, Jr.	15	3,000
Tetra Corporation	10	2,000
Total	100	

Andrew, Bea, and Carl are unrelated. Bea owns 75% of the Tetra stock, and Andrew owns the remaining 25%. Excel's E&P is $100,000. Determine the tax consequences of the following independent redemptions to the shareholders and Excel:

a. Excel redeems 25 of Bea's shares for $30,000.

b. Excel redeems 10 of Bea's shares for $12,000.

c. Excel redeems all of Carl's shares for $30,000.

d. Assume the same facts as in Part c except the stock is redeemed from Carl's estate to pay death taxes. The entire redemption qualifies for sale treatment under Sec. 303. The stock has a $28,000 FMV on Carl's date of death. The alternate valuation date is not elected.

e. Excel redeems all of Andrew's shares for land having a $6,000 basis for taxable income and E&P purposes to Excel and a $24,000 FMV. Assume a 34% marginal corporate tax rate.

f. Assume that Carl owns 25 shares of Excel stock and that Carl, Jr. owns the remaining 75 shares. Determine the tax consequences to Carl and Excel if Excel redeems all 25 of Carl's shares for $30,000.

C4-52 *Comparison of Dividends and Redemptions.* Bailey is one of four equal unrelated shareholders of Checker Corporation. Bailey has held the stock for four years and has a basis in her stock of $40,000. Checker has $280,000 of current and accumulated E&P and distributes $100,000 to Bailey.

a. What are the tax consequences to Checker and to Bailey assuming Bailey is an individual and the distribution is a dividend?

b. What are the tax consequences in Part a if Bailey is a corporation?

c. What are the tax consequences to Checker and to Bailey (an individual) assuming Bailey surrenders all her stock in a redemption qualifying for sale treatment?

d. What are the tax consequences in Part c if Bailey is a corporation?

e. Which treatment would Bailey prefer if Bailey is an individual? Which treatment would Bailey Corporation prefer?

C4-53 *Preferred Stock Bailout.* In each of the following situations, does Sec. 306 apply? If so, what is its effect?

a. Beth sells her Sec. 306 stock to Marvin in a year when the issuing corporation has no E&P.

b. Zero Corporation redeems Sec. 306 stock from Jim in a year in which it has no E&P.

c. Zero Corporation redeems Sec. 306 stock from Ruth in a year in which it has a large E&P balance.

d. Joan gives 100 shares of Sec. 306 stock to her nephew, Barry.

e. Ed completely terminates his interest in Zero Corporation by having Zero redeem all his common and preferred stock (the Sec. 306 stock in question).

f. Carl inherits 100 shares of Sec. 306 stock from his uncle Ted.

C4-54 *Preferred Stock Bailout.* Fran owns all 100 shares of Star Corporation stock in which her adjusted basis is $60,000. On December 1, 2005, Star distributes 50 shares of preferred stock to Fran in a nontaxable stock dividend. In the year of the distribution, Star's total E&P is $100,000, the preferred shares are worth $150,000, and the common shares are worth $300,000.

a. What are the tax consequences to Fran and to Star if Fran sells her preferred stock to Ken for $200,000 on January 10, 2006? In 2006, Star's current E&P is $75,000 (in addition to the $100,000 from the prior year).

b. How would your answer to Part a change if Fran sells her preferred stock to Ken for $110,000 instead of $200,000?

c. How would your answer to Part a change if Star redeems Fran's preferred stock for $200,000 on January 10, 2006?

C4-55 *Brother-Sister Redemptions.* Bob owns 60 of the 100 outstanding shares of Dazzle Corporation's stock and 80 of the 100 outstanding shares of Razzle Corporation's stock. Bob's basis in his Dazzle shares is $12,000, and his basis in his Razzle shares is $8,000. Bob sells 30 of his Dazzle shares to Razzle for $50,000. At the end of the year of the sale, Dazzle and Razzle have E&P of $25,000 and $40,000, respectively.

a. What are the amount and character of Bob's gain or loss on the sale?

b. What is Bob's basis in his remaining shares of the Dazzle and Razzle stock?

c. How does the sale affect the E&P of Dazzle and Razzle?

d. What basis does Razzle take in the Dazzle shares it purchases?

e. How would your answer to Part a change if Bob owns only 50 of the 100 outstanding shares of Razzle stock?

C4-56 *Parent-Subsidiary Redemptions.* Jane owns 150 of the 200 outstanding shares of Parent Corporation's stock. Parent owns 160 of the 200 outstanding shares of Subsidiary Corporation's stock. Jane sells 50 shares of her Parent stock to Subsidiary for $40,000. Jane's basis in her Parent shares is $15,000 ($100 per share). Subsidiary and Parent have E&P of $60,000 and $25,000, respectively, at the end of the year in which the redemption occurs.

a. What are the amount and character of Jane's gain or loss on the sale?

b. What is Jane's basis in her remaining shares of Parent stock?

c. How does the sale affect the E&P of Parent and Subsidiary?

d. What basis does Subsidiary take in the Parent shares it purchases?

e. How would your answer to Part a change if Jane instead sells 100 of her Parent shares to Subsidiary for $80,000?

C4-57 *Bootstrap Acquisition.* Jana owns all 100 shares of Stone Corporation stock having a $1 million FMV. Her basis in the stock is $400,000. Stone's E&P balance is $600,000. Michael would like to purchase the stock but wants only the corporation's non-cash assets valued at $750,000. Michael is willing to pay $750,000 for these assets.

a. What are the tax consequences to Jana, Michael, and Stone if Michael purchases 75 shares of Stone stock for $750,000 and Stone redeems Jana's remaining 25 shares for $250,000 cash?

b. How would your answer to Part a change (if at all) if Stone first redeems 25 shares of Jana's stock for $250,000 and then Michael purchases the remaining 75 shares from Jana for $750,000?

COMPREHENSIVE PROBLEM

C4-58 Several years ago, Brian formed Sigma Corporation, a retail company that does not qualify for the U.S. production activities deduction. Sigma uses the accrual method of accounting. In 2006, the corporation reported the following items:

Gross profit	$290,000
Long-term capital gain	20,000
Tax-exempt interest received	7,000
Salary paid to Brian	80,000
Payroll tax on Brian's salary (Sigma's share)	6,000
Depreciation	25,000 ($21,000 for E&P purposes)
Other operation expenses	89,000
Dividend distribution to Brian	60,000

In addition to owning 100% of Sigma's stock, Brian manages Sigma's business and receives the $80,000 salary listed above. This salary is an ordinary and necessary business expense of the corporation and is reasonable in amount. The payroll tax on Brian's $80,000 salary is $12,000, $6,000 of which Sigma pays and deducts, and the other $6,000 of which Brian pays through wage withholding. Brian is single with no dependents and claims the standard deduction.

a. Compute Sigma's and Brian's taxable income and total tax liability for 2006 as well as their combined tax liability. Also, calculate the corporation's current E&P after the dividend distribution.

b. Assume instead that Brian operates Sigma as a sole proprietorship. In the current year, the business reports the same operating results as above, and Brian withdraws $140,000 in lieu of the salary and dividend. Assume Brian's self-employment tax is $15,000. Compute Brian's total tax liability for 2006.

c. Assume a C corporation such as in Part a distributes all of its after-tax earnings. Compare the tax treatment of long-term capital gains, tax-exempt interest, and operating profits if earned by a C corporation with the tax treatment of these items if earned by a sole proprietorship.

TAX STRATEGY PROBLEM

C4-59 John owns all 100 shares of stock in Jamaica Corporation, which has $100,000 of current E&P. John would like a $50,000 distribution from the corporation. Jamaica owns the following assets that it could distribute to John. What are the tax consequences of distributing each of the following assets? Assume Jamaica has a 34% marginal tax rate and that its basis for E&P and for tax purposes are the same, unless stated otherwise.

a. $50,000 cash.

b. 100 shares of XYZ stock purchased two years ago for $10,000 and now worth $50,000.

c. 100 shares of ABC stock purchased one year ago for $72,000 and now worth $50,000.

d. Equipment purchased four years ago for $120,000 that now has a tax adjusted basis of $22,000 and an E&P adjusted basis of $40,000. John would assume a liability on the equipment of $31,000. The equipment is now worth $81,000.

e. An installment obligation with a face value of $50,000 and a basis of $32,000. Jamaica acquired this obligation when it sold land held as an investment three years ago.

f. Would it make any difference in Parts a-e if Jamaica redeems 50 of John's shares for each of the properties listed?

g. Which distribution would you recommend? Which distribution(s) should be avoided?

CASE STUDY PROBLEMS

C4-60 Amy, Beth, and Meg each own 100 of the 300 outstanding shares of Theta Corporation stock. Amy wants to sell her shares, which have a $40,000 basis and a $100,000 FMV. Either Beth and/or Meg can purchase her shares (50 shares each) or Theta can redeem all of Amy's shares. Theta has a $150,000 E&P balance.

Required: Write a memorandum comparing the tax consequences of the two options to the three sisters, who are active in managing Theta.

C4-61 Maria Garcia is a CPA whose firm has for many years prepared the tax returns of Stanley Corporation. A review of Stanley's last three tax returns by a new staff accountant, who has been assigned to the client for the first time, reveals that the corporation may be paying to one of its key officers excessive compensation that the IRS might deem to be a constructive dividend. The staff accountant feels that the firm should inform the IRS and/or report the excess amount as a nondeductible dividend. The facts are sufficiently gray, i.e., reasonable support exists for the assertion that the amount of compensation paid in the current year and prior years is reasonable.

Required: Discuss Maria's role as an advocate for Stanley, and discuss the possible consequences of a subsequent audit.

TAX RESEARCH PROBLEMS

C4-62 Fifteen years ago, husband and wife Stuart and Marsha Widell organized Widell Engineering Associates (WEA), a Delaware corporation that builds, repairs, and manages waste treatment plants throughout the Southwest. The Widells capitalized WEA with cash of $500,000 and industrial equipment having an adjusted basis of $4.5 million, each in exchange for 2,500 shares of WEA common stock. Three years later, Stuart and Marsha each gifted 500 shares of their WEA stock to their son Weymouth.

As a result of a sharp upswing in the economy, WEA's profits swelled under the joint management of Stuart and Weymouth. After ten years of joint control, however, and because of irreconcilable differences with his father, Weymouth decided to leave WEA and organize his own engineering firm, Fortunelle.

To keep WEA's business in the family and to give Stuart complete WEA management control, Stuart, Marsha, and Weymouth agreed that WEA would redeem all of Weymouth's 1,000 shares with waste treatment property worth $8.5 million. To ensure capital gains treatment, Weymouth obtained a waiver of the family attribution rules in return for an agreement with the IRS not to acquire an equity interest in WEA for ten years and to notify the IRS if he does so. Following the redemption, Weymouth transferred the property to Fortunelle in exchange for all 8,500 shares of Fortunelle common stock.

Last year, Stuart suffered a heart attack. He now has proceeded to reconcile his differences with Weymouth. To retain Widell family control of WEA's business, Stuart, Marsha, and Weymouth propose that WEA and Fortunelle conclude an "arms length" agreement under which Fortunelle would manage WEA's waste treatment plants in return annually for 20% of WEA's gross rental revenues, but no equity interest. The Widells are convinced that the proposed arrangement does not violate either the Sec. 302 waiver rules or Weymouth's agreement with the IRS. They have asked you to draft a letter that confirms this understanding. In researching the issue, consult at a minimum the following authorities:

- IRC Sec. 302(c)(2)
- Rev. Rul. 70-104, 1970 C.B. 66
- *Chertkof v. Commissioner*, 48 AFTR 2d 81-5194, 81-1 USTC ¶9462 (4th Cir, 1981)

C4-63 When the IRS audited Winter Corporation's 2003 tax return, the IRS disallowed $10,000 of travel and entertainment expenses incurred by Charles, an officer-shareholder, because of inadequate documentation. The IRS asserted that the $10,000 expenditure was a constructive dividend to Charles, who maintained that the expense was business related. Charles argued that he derived no personal benefit from the expenditure and therefore should not be charged with any dividend income. Prepare a memorandum for your tax manager explaining whether the IRS's assertion or Charles's assertion is correct. Your manager has suggested that, at a minimum, you consult the following resources:

- IRC Secs. 162 and 274
- Reg. Secs. 1.274-1 and -2

C4-64 Scott and Lynn Brown each own 50% of Benson Corporation stock. During the current year, Benson made the following distribution to the shareholders:

Shareholder	Property Distributed	Adjusted Basis to Corporation	Property's FMV
Scott Brown	Land parcel A	$ 40,000	$75,000
Lynn Brown	Land parcel B	120,000	75,000

Benson had E&P of $250,000 immediately before the distribution. Prepare a memorandum for your tax manager explaining how Benson should treat these transactions for tax and financial accounting purposes. How will the two shareholders report the distributions? Assume Benson's marginal tax rate is 34%. Your manager has suggested that, at a minimum, you should consult the following resources:

- IRC Sec 301
- IRC Sec. 311
- IRC Sec. 312
- *Accounting Principles Board Opinion No. 29*

C4-65 John and Jean own 80% and 20% of Plum Corporation, respectively. Thanks to their hard work, Plum's software sales have sky rocketed. In 2002, Plum's earnings were minimal, but by 2006, Plum grossed $10 million. Plum compensated John and Jean as follows: John received a bonus of 76% of net profits and Jean received a bonus of 19% of net profits at the end of each year. Plum never paid any dividends. Can Plum deduct any or all of the "salaries" paid to John and Jean?

C4-66 Sara owns 60% of Mayfield Corporation's single class of stock. A group of five family members and three key employees own the remaining 40% of Mayfield stock. Mayfield is a calendar year taxpayer that uses the accrual method of accounting. Sara is a Mayfield officer and director and uses the cash method of accounting. During the period 2003-2005, Sara received the following amounts as salary and tax-free fringe benefits from Mayfield: 2003, $160,000; 2004, $240,000; and 2005, $290,000. She earned these amounts evenly throughout the tax years in question. In 2006, upon auditing Mayfield's tax returns for 2003–2005, a revenue agent determined that reasonable compensation for Sara's services for the three years in question is $110,000, $165,000, and $175,000, respectively. The bylaws of Mayfield were amended on December 15, 2004 to provide that:

Any payments made to an officer of the corporation, including salary, commissions, bonuses, other forms of compensation, interest, rent, or travel and entertainment expenses incurred, and which shall be disallowed in whole or in part as a deductible expense by the Internal Revenue Service, shall be reimbursed by such officer to the corporation to the full extent of such disallowance.

Following the disallowance of $240,000 of the total salary expense, the board of directors met and requested that Sara reimburse Mayfield for the portion of her salary deemed to be excessive. Because of the large amount of money involved, the board of directors approved an installment plan whereby Sara would repay the $240,000 in five annual installments of $48,000 each over the period 2007-2011. The corporation would not charge Sara interest on the unpaid balance of $240,000. Prepare a memorandum for your tax manager explaining what salary and fringe benefits are taxable to Sara in the period 2003-2005 and what reimbursements Sara can deduct during the period 2007-2011.

5

CHAPTER

OTHER CORPORATE TAX LEVIES

LEARNING OBJECTIVES

After studying this chapter, you should be able to

1 ▶ Calculate the corporation's alternative minimum tax liability (if any)

2 ▶ Determine whether a corporation is a personal holding company (PHC)

3 ▶ Calculate the corporation's PHC tax

4 ▶ Determine whether a corporation is liable for the accumulated earnings tax

5 ▶ Calculate the corporation's accumulated earnings tax

6 ▶ Explain how a corporation can avoid the personal holding company tax

7 ▶ Explain how a corporation can avoid the accumulated earnings tax

Chapter C3 examined the general corporate tax formula and the procedures for calculating, reporting, and paying this tax. Chapter C5 focuses on the following three additional taxes that may be imposed on a C corporation: (1) the corporate alternative minimum tax, (2) the personal holding company tax, and (3) the accumulated earnings tax. Each additional tax may apply in different situations. A corporation's total tax liability equals the sum of its corporate income tax, alternative minimum tax, and either the accumulated earnings tax or the personal holding company tax (if any). This chapter examines when the additional taxes are likely to be assessed and measures a corporation can take to avoid them.

THE CORPORATE ALTERNATIVE MINIMUM TAX

OBJECTIVE 1

Calculate the corporation's alternative minimum tax liability (if any)

THE GENERAL FORMULA

The purpose of the corporate **alternative minimum tax** (AMT) is similar to that of the individual AMT.[1] It is to ensure that every taxpayer with substantial economic income pays a minimum tax despite its use of exclusions, deductions, and credits to determine its income tax liability.

The starting point for computing a corporation's AMT is its taxable income. Taxable income is increased by tax preference items, modified by adjustments, and reduced by a statutory exemption amount. The resulting tax base is multiplied by 20% to yield the **tentative minimum tax** (TMT). If the TMT exceeds the corporation's regular tax liability, the excess is the corporation's AMT liability. If the TMT does not exceed the corporation's regular tax, the AMT is zero. Even if a corporation pays no AMT, the AMT nevertheless may restrict its ability to claim certain business credits (see pages C5-14 and C5-15). The computation of a corporation's AMT is set forth in Table C5-1.

For tax years beginning after 1997, the AMT does not apply to small business corporations. A small business corporation is an entity whose average gross receipts are $7.5 million or less for all three-year periods ending before the year for which the corporation claims the exemption.[2] This moving average gross receipts calculation, however, includes only tax years beginning after December 31, 1993 and is reduced to $5 million for the corporation's first three-year period (or portion thereof) that begins after 1993.

REAL-WORLD EXAMPLE

The small corporation AMT exemption will exempt 95% of incorporated businesses from the AMT. The expected tax savings for small corporations are $762 million over the period 1998 to 2007.

EXAMPLE C5-1 ▶ Ramirez Corporation began business in 1993 and had gross receipts as shown below:

Year	Gross Receipts
1993	$2,000,000
1994	$3,000,000
1995	4,000,000
1996	5,000,000
1997	6,000,000
1998	12,000,000

Because Ramirez existed before 1994, its relevant gross receipts begin in 1994. Accordingly, its average gross receipts are as follows:

1994–1996: $4,000,000 = [($3,000,000 + $4,000,000 + $5,000,000) ÷ 3]
1995–1997: $5,000,000 = [($4,000,000 + $5,000,000 + $6,000,000) ÷ 3]
1996–1998: $7,666,667 = [($5,000,000 + $6,000,000 + $12,000,000) ÷ 3]

---

[1] S corporations are not subject to the corporate AMT. These entities pass their tax adjustments and preferences through to their shareholders.
[2] Sec. 55(e). The exemption also applies to a noncorporate entity that elects

to be taxed as a C corporation under the check-the-box regulations. Gross receipts are calculated using the entity's tax year.

▼ **TABLE C5-1**

Determination of the Corporate Alternative Minimum Tax Liability

Taxable income or loss before NOL deduction
Plus: Tax preference items
Plus or minus: Adjustments to taxable income other than the ACE
                 adjustment, the alternative tax NOL deduction, and the
                 adjustment for the U.S. production activities deduction

Preadjustment AMTI
Plus or minus: 75% of the difference between pre-adjustment AMTI
                 and adjusted current earnings (ACE)

Minus: Alternative tax NOL deduction

AMTI before adjustment for the U.S. production activities deduction
Minus: Adjustment for the U.S. production activities deduction (if any)

Alternative minimum taxable income (AMTI)
Minus: Statutory exemption

Tax base
Times: 0.20 tax rate

Tentative minimum tax before credits
Minus: AMT foreign tax credit (AMT FTC)

Tentative minimum tax (TMT)
Minus: Regular (income) tax

Alternative minimum tax (if any) owed (AMT)

ADDITIONAL COMMENT

The corporate AMT produces little tax revenue. In 2002, AMT collections were $2.5 billion compared to $151 billion for the corporate income tax net of tax credits. Only 7,100 corporations paid the AMT in 2002.

Ramirez qualified as a small corporation in 1998 because its average gross receipts for 1994–1996 did not exceed $5 million and because its average gross receipts for 1995–1997 did not exceed $7.5 million. In 1999, however, Ramirez lost its AMT exemption because average gross receipts for 1996–1998 exceeded $7.5 million. Ramirez cannot reacquire its AMT exemption in later years even if its average gross receipts for a three-year period drop below $7.5 million. ◄

Section 55(e), which provides for the small corporation AMT exemption, refers to Sec. 448(c) for the following special operating rules relating to the average gross receipts calculation:

▶ Gross receipts for any short tax year (for example, an initial year) must be annualized.

▶ A corporation not in existence for an entire three-year period determines average gross receipts for the period it was in existence.

▶ A controlled group of corporations must be treated as one entity.

▶ A successor corporation must include the gross receipts of its predecessor (for example, a newly created subsidiary's gross receipts would include those of its parent corporation).

A corporation created after 1997 is exempt from the corporate AMT for its initial tax year regardless of its gross receipts for that year unless the corporation is aggregated with one or more other corporations under bullet point three above or is considered to be a successor to another corporation. To qualify for the second year, the corporation's gross receipts for the first year must be less than $5 million. To qualify for the third year, the corporation's average gross receipts for the first two years must be less than $7.5 million. To qualify for the fourth year, the corporation's average gross receipts for the first three years must be less than $7.5 million.

EXAMPLE C5-2 ▶ Rubio Corporation, a calendar year corporation formed on January 1, 2002, has gross receipts as follows:

Year	Gross Receipts
2002	$3,000,000
2003	4,000,000
2004	5,000,000
2005	8,000,000
2006	9,000,000

Rubio does not succeed to a pre-existing corporation. In 2002, Rubio is automatically exempt from the corporate AMT under the small corporation rules without regard to its gross receipts. Rubio is exempt from the corporate AMT in 2003 because the gross receipts for its first tax year (2002) did not exceed $5 million.

Rubio must calculate its average gross receipts in subsequent tax years to see whether the small business exemption remains available. Rubio's average gross receipts calculations for subsequent tax years are as follows:

2002–2003: $3,500,000 = [($3,000,000 + $4,000,000) ÷ 2]
2002–2004: $4,000,000 = [($3,000,000 + $4,000,000 + $5,000,000) ÷ 3]
2003–2005: $5,666,667 = [($4,000,000 + $5,000,000 + $8,000,000) ÷ 3]
2004–2006: $7,333,333 = [($5,000,000 + $8,000,000 + $9,000,000) ÷ 3]

Rubio maintains its exemption in 2004 because its average gross receipts for 2002–2003 do not exceed $7.5 million. Similarly, Rubio continues to qualify in 2005, 2006, and 2007 because its average gross receipts for each preceding three-year period (2002–2004, 2003–2005, and 2004–2006, respectively) do not exceed $7.5 million. The consistent increase in gross receipts, however, makes it unlikely that Rubio will retain its exemption after 2007. ◀

Note that the moving average test is based on gross receipts, not gross income or taxable income. Gross receipts is not reduced by cost of goods sold and includes services income, investment income, and gains and losses (net of the property's adjusted basis). Thus, a corporation with substantial gross receipts and substantial expenses could be subject to the AMT even though it might have a low level of taxable income.

Firms not eligible for the small corporation AMT exemption because their gross receipts exceed the $5 or $7.5 million threshold nevertheless can take advantage of the $40,000 statutory exemption discussed in the Definitions section below.

A corporation that loses its small corporation status because its average gross receipts exceed the statutory ceiling becomes liable for the AMT. The AMT for such a corporation includes only tax preference items and adjustments reflecting transactions conducted and investments made after the corporation lost its small corporation status. The calculation of this AMT, as well as a special AMT credit available for such corporations, is beyond the scope of this chapter.

ADDITIONAL COMMENT

Relative to the regular tax, the AMT results in an acceleration of income recognition. This acceleration is accomplished by adding back tax preference items and making other adjustments to taxable income in deriving AMTI. Even though the AMT rate (20%) is lower than the top corporate income tax rate (35%), the AMT results in a higher tax liability for some corporations because their AMT base is larger than their regular tax base.

DEFINITIONS

This section defines the terms used in the AMT computation.[3]

ALTERNATIVE MINIMUM TAXABLE INCOME (AMTI). **Alternative minimum taxable income** is the corporation's taxable income (1) increased by tax preference items, (2) adjusted (either upward or downward) for income, gain, deduction, and loss items that must be recomputed under the AMT, (3) increased or decreased by 75% of the difference between pre-adjustment AMTI and adjusted current earnings (ACE), and (4) reduced by the alternative tax NOL deduction.

---

[3] Sec. 55.

STATUTORY EXEMPTION AMOUNT. AMTI is reduced by a statutory exemption amount to derive the AMT tax base. This amount is $40,000, reduced by 25% of the amount (if any) by which AMTI exceeds $150,000. The statutory exemption is phased out when AMTI reaches $310,000.

EXAMPLE C5-3 ▶ Yellow Corporation's AMTI is $200,000. Its exemption amount is $27,500 {$40,000 − [0.25 × ($200,000 − $150,000)]}.[4] ◀

TENTATIVE MINIMUM TAX (TMT). The tentative minimum tax is calculated by multiplying the corporation's AMTI, less the statutory exemption amount, by 20%. The corporation then applies foreign tax credits allowable under the AMT (AMT FTCs).[5]

REGULAR TAX. The corporation's **regular tax** is its tax liability for income tax purposes, reduced by foreign tax credits and possession tax credits, but not by other tax credits.

ALTERNATIVE MINIMUM TAX. The AMT equals the amount by which a corporation's TMT exceeds its regular tax for the year.

The following example illustrates the AMT computation.

EXAMPLE C5-4 ▶ Badger Corporation has $400,000 of taxable income. It also has $350,000 of tax preference items and $250,000 of positive adjustments for AMT purposes. It has no available tax credits. Badger's regular tax liability is $136,000 (0.34 × $400,000). Badger's AMTI is $1 million ($400,000 taxable income + $250,000 adjustments + $350,000 tax preferences). Its statutory exemption is zero because AMTI exceeds $310,000 (i.e., the complete phase-out threshold). Therefore, its AMT tax base (i.e., AMTI minus the zero statutory exemption) also is $1 million. The corporation's TMT is $200,000 (0.20 × $1,000,000). Badger's AMT liability is $64,000 ($200,000 − $136,000 regular tax liability). Thus, Badger must pay a total federal tax of $200,000 ($136,000 + $64,000). ◀

STOP & THINK

Question: In the preceding example, Badger Corporation pays both the regular tax and the AMT. How is this result possible if the regular tax rate for corporations with less than $10 million of taxable income is 34% while the AMT rate is a flat 20%?

Solution: The result is possible because different tax bases are used to calculate the two tax amounts. The regular tax calculation is based on taxable income while the AMT calculation is based on alternative minimum taxable income less a statutory exemption. A corporation owes the AMT when its TMT exceeds its regular tax liability. The situation in which a corporation owes the AMT can be expressed as follows:

[Taxable Income (TI) + Preferences (P) ± Adjustments (A)] × 0.20 > TI × 0.34

Both sides of the inequality can be reformulated as follows:

$$0.20 (P \pm A) > 0.14 \text{ TI}$$

$$(P \pm A) > 0.70 \text{ TI}$$

In Example C5-4, where Badger Corporation is liable for the AMT, its preference items and positive adjustments are $350,000 and $250,000, respectively, or $600,000 in total. Seventy percent of taxable income equals $280,000 (0.70 × $400,000). Thus, the general relationship between (P ± A) and TI holds in our example.[a]

[a] The relationship between (P ± A) and TI may be different if the corporation is subject to a marginal income tax rate lower (e.g., 15% or 25%) or higher (e.g., 35%, 38%, or 39%) than the 34% marginal income tax rate used above.

---

[4] In the examples, assume that all corporations are C corporations that do not qualify as small corporations for AMT purposes.

[5] Sec. 55(b).

TYPICAL MISCONCEPTION

Tax preference items always increase AMTI. As noted in the text below, adjustments can increase or decrease AMTI.

ADDITIONAL COMMENT

Each year, the amount of real property tax preference due to accelerated depreciation declines as the property ages. For most pre-1987 properties, this amount is zero in 2006.

TAX PREFERENCE ITEMS

Tax preference items that must be added to a corporation's taxable income to derive its AMTI include[6]

▶ The excess of the depletion deduction allowable for the tax year over the adjusted basis of the depletable property at the end of the tax year (excluding the current year's depletion deduction).[7]

▶ The amount by which excess intangible drilling and development costs (IDCs) incurred in connection with oil, gas, and geothermal wells exceeds 65% of the net income from such property.[8]

▶ Tax-exempt interest on certain private activity bonds issued after August 8, 1986. Although the interest on private activity bonds is tax-exempt for regular tax purposes, it is not exempt for AMT purposes.[9]

▶ The excess of accelerated depreciation on real property for the tax year over a straight-line depreciation amount based on either the property's useful life or a special ACRS recovery period. This preference item applies only to real property placed in service before 1987.

EXAMPLE C5-5 ▶ Duffy Corporation mines iron ore in the upper peninsula of Michigan. The adjusted basis for one of its properties has been fully recovered by depletion deductions claimed in previous years. Current year gross income and taxable income earned from the sale of ore extracted from this property are $125,000, and $45,000, respectively. The iron ore depletion percentage is 15%. Percentage depletion is $18,750 ($125,000 × 0.15) because it is less than the 50% of taxable income ceiling ($22,500 = $45,000 × 0.50). All the percentage depletion is deductible when determining taxable income. Because the property's basis already has been reduced to zero, however, the entire percentage depletion amount is a tax preference item. Adding this item in the AMTI calculation reduces the depletion deduction to zero. ◀

Salek Corporation reports the following interest income for the current year:

EXAMPLE C5-6 ▶

Source	Amount
IBM corporate bonds	$25,000
Wayne County School District bonds	30,000
City of Detroit bonds	15,000

The City of Detroit bonds were issued several years ago to finance a parking garage, where 35% of the space is leased exclusively to a nonexempt corporation. The bonds are considered to be private activity bonds. The Wayne County bonds were issued to renovate existing school facilities. Interest earned on the IBM bonds is taxable because the bonds are obligations of a private corporation. Only interest earned on the City of Detroit bonds is a tax preference item because, in contrast to the school district bond proceeds, the municipal bond proceeds were used to finance a private activity. ◀

ADJUSTMENTS TO TAXABLE INCOME

While tax preference items always *increase* taxable income, adjustments may either *increase* or *decrease* taxable income because they require a recomputation of certain income, gain, loss, and deduction items. Common adjustments are presented below.[10]

---

[6] Sec. 57(a).

[7] The percentage depletion preference was repealed for oil and gas depletion claimed by independent producers and royalty owners for 1993 and later tax years. The oil and gas percentage depletion preference applies almost exclusively to integrated oil companies.

[8] The oil and gas excess IDC preference was repealed for independent producers for 1993 and later years but continues to apply to integrated oil companies. Excess IDCs are the amount by which IDCs arising in the tax year

exceed the deduction that would have been allowable if the IDCs had been capitalized and amortized under the straight-line method over a ten-year period.

[9] A private activity bond is a debt obligation the proceeds of which are used wholly or partially for activities unrelated to a governmental use (for example, bond proceeds to construct a sports facility used by professional football and other sports teams for their at-home games).

[10] Sec. 56(a).

DEPRECIATION. Different depreciation rules are used for computing taxable income and for computing AMTI.

▶ *Depreciation on real property placed in service after 1986 and before 1999.* For AMT purposes, the taxpayer must use the alternative depreciation system under Sec. 168(g). Annually, taxable income is increased by the excess of regular tax depreciation over AMT depreciation and is decreased by the excess of AMT depreciation over regular tax depreciation. See depreciation Tables 7–9 in Appendix C for regular tax depreciation rates and Table 12 for AMT depreciation rates.

▶ *Depreciation on real property placed in service after 1998.* No adjustments are required for this class of property because regular tax depreciation and AMT depreciation are the same.

▶ *Depreciation on personal property placed in service after 1986 and before 1999.* For AMT purposes, the taxpayer must use the alternative depreciation system under Sec. 168(g). While regular tax depreciation ordinarily is calculated under a 200% declining balance method (with a switch to straight-line) over the property's general depreciation recovery period, AMT depreciation requires a 150% declining balance method (with a switch to straight-line) over the property's class life, as determined under Sec. 168(g)(3) and related IRS pronouncements. If these authorities do not specify a class life for an item of personal property, its class life is deemed to be 12 years. If the taxpayer elected the straight-line method or the alternative depreciation system for regular tax purposes, no AMT adjustments are required. For property depreciated under the half-year convention, see depreciation Table 1 in Appendix C for regular tax rates and depreciation Table 10 for AMT rates.

▶ *Depreciation on personal property placed in service after 1998 but before September 11, 2001, or placed in service after 2004.* For AMT purposes, the taxpayer must use the 150% declining balance method (with a switch to straight-line) over the property's general depreciation recovery period. Thus, the taxpayer uses the same recovery period for both regular tax and AMT purposes. However, the taxpayer uses the 200% declining balance method to calculate regular tax depreciation and the 150% declining balance method to calculate AMT depreciation. If the taxpayer elects the straight-line method or 150% declining balance method for regular tax purposes, no AMT adjustments are required. For property depreciated under the half-year convention, see depreciation Table 1 in Appendix C for regular tax rates and depreciation Table 10 for AMT rates.

▶ *Depreciation on qualified personal property placed in service after September 10, 2001, and before January 1, 2005.* Depreciation on *new* personal property with a MACRS class life of 20 years or less is calculated under the 200% declining balance method (with a switch to straight-line). No adjustments to the general MACRS cost recovery period and cost recovery method are required for AMT purposes. This "AMT relief rule" applied to all property eligible for the additional first-year 50% (or 30%) bonus depreciation allowance (discussed below).[11]

EXAMPLE C5-7 ▶ Early in 2001, Bulldog Corporation placed into service new office furniture costing $3,000 and having a ten-year class life. The corporation did not elect Sec. 179 expensing for this property. Even though the furniture's class life is ten years, the property's tax recovery period is seven years under both the MACRS General Depreciation System for regular tax purposes and the MACRS Alternative Depreciation System for AMTI purposes. Regular tax depreciation was $429 [$3,000 × 0.1429 (Table 1, Appendix C)] in the first year under the half-year convention, and AMTI depreciation was $321 [$3,000 × 0.1071 (Table 10, Appendix C)]. The smaller AMTI depreciation resulted in a $108 ($429 − $321) positive adjustment to taxable income. Toward the end of the recovery period, the depreciation adjustment becomes negative. For example, in 2006, regular tax depreciation is $268 ($3,000 × 0.0892) while AMTI depreciation is $368 ($3,000 × 0.1225). Thus, a negative $100 ($268 − $368) adjustment results. ◀

---

[11] Sec. 168(k)(2)(F).

Depreciation on certain classes of "qualified property" (primarily computer software and personal property with a MACRS class life of 20 years or less) acquired after May 5, 2003, and before January 1, 2005, included a special 50% initial year depreciation allowance. (The percentage was 30% for qualified property placed in service after September 10, 2001, but before May 6, 2003.) This "bonus depreciation" provision applied only to *new* MACRS property acquired between the above dates and placed in service before January 1, 2005. The 50% bonus depreciation could be used even if the taxpayer did not elect Sec. 179 expensing. If both the 50% bonus depreciation rule and Sec. 179 expensing provision applied to an item of personal property, the Sec. 179 expensing provision applied first. Then, the 50% bonus depreciation rule applied to cost minus the Sec. 179 expense. Finally, the regular MACRS depreciation percentages applied to the remaining adjusted basis. For these classes of property, the Sec. 179 expensing rule, 50% bonus depreciation provision, and general MACRS cost recovery periods and methods also applied for AMT purposes.

EXAMPLE C5-8 ▶ On April 3, 2004, Brighton Corporation purchased $252,000 of new MACRS five-year property. It placed the property in service on May 7, 2004. In 2004, Brighton could expense $102,000 under Sec. 179. In addition, it could claim an additional 50% bonus depreciation, or $75,000 ($150,000 × 0.50), on the adjusted basis that remained after expensing. Also in 2004, the corporation could claim regular MACRS depreciation on the $75,000 ($252,000 − $102,000 − $75,000) that remained after subtracting the 50% bonus depreciation. Thus, for regular tax purposes, first-year MACRS depreciation was $15,000 ($75,000 × 0.20), and total first-year depreciation and expensing was $192,000 ($102,000 + $75,000 + $15,000). Because the property was "qualified property" placed in service after September 10, 2001, total depreciation and expensing for AMT purposes also was $192,000. Thus, in 2004 the corporation had no AMT adjustment for depreciation on this property and will have no adjustment for this property in subsequent years. ◀

BASIS CALCULATIONS. For property depreciated under different methods for regular tax and AMT purposes, separate gain or loss calculations are necessary for regular tax and AMT purposes when the taxpayer disposes the property. A depreciable property's basis for regular tax purposes is adjusted downward by the regular tax depreciation allowance. A depreciable property's basis for AMT purposes is adjusted downward by the AMT depreciation allowance. Therefore, an asset may have different bases for regular tax and AMT purposes. An adjustment is made to reflect the difference between the amount of gain or loss recognized for taxable income purposes and the gain or loss recognized for AMTI purposes. The adjustment calculation is illustrated in the following example.

EXAMPLE C5-9 ▶ Assume the same facts as in Example C5-7 except that on April 1 of the fourth year Bulldog Corporation sells the property for $2,000. The depreciation allowances claimed for regular tax and AMT purposes, adjusted bases of the property at the beginning of the year, and the positive or negative adjustment to taxable income in deriving AMTI for each of the four years are presented below.

| | **Regular Tax** | | | **AMT** | | | |
Year	1/1 Adj. Basis (1)	Depr. (2)	12/31 Adj. Basis (3)[a]	1/1 Adj. Basis (4)	Depr. (5)	12/31 Adj. Basis (6)[b]	Taxable Income Adjustment(7)[c]
1	$3,000	$ 429	$2,571	$3,000	$ 321	$2,679	$108
2	2,571	735	1,836	2,679	574	2,105	161
3	1,836	525	1,311	2,105	451	1,654	74
4	1,311	187	1,124	1,654	184	1,470	3
		$1,876			$1,714		$346

[a] (3) = (1) − (2) Adjusted basis for sale date is reduced for the depreciation claimed in Year 4.
[b] (6) = (4) − (5) Six months of depreciation is claimed in years 1 and 4.
[c] (7) = (2) − (5)

Bulldog recognizes an $876 ($2,000 proceeds − $1,124 adjusted basis) gain in Year 4 for regular tax purposes and a $530 ($2,000 proceeds − $1,470 adjusted basis) gain for AMT purposes.

This difference necessitates a $346 negative adjustment to taxable income when computing AMTI to take into account the different depreciation allowances claimed in the four years. The basis adjustment is the net of the aggregate positive and negative depreciation adjustments for the four years.   ◄

INSTALLMENT SALES. When calculating taxable income and AMTI, the corporation may use the installment method to report sales of noninventory property.

LONG-TERM CONTRACTS ENTERED INTO AFTER MARCH 1, 1986. These contracts must be accounted for using the percentage of completion method. When determining AMTI, corporations using the percentage of completion-capitalized cost or cash methods of accounting for regular tax purposes must make adjustments.

LOSS LIMITATIONS. Closely held corporations and personal service corporations must recalculate at-risk and passive activity losses, taking into account the corporation's AMTI adjustments and tax preference items.

NOL DEDUCTIONS. The regular tax NOL deduction is replaced with the alternative tax NOL deduction. To compute the alternative tax NOL deduction, the regular tax NOL deduction is adjusted in the same way that taxable income is adjusted to derive AMTI. The regular tax NOL is reduced by adding back any tax preference items and any losses disallowed under the passive activity and at-risk rules. Adjustments may either increase or decrease the regular tax NOL in deriving the alternative tax NOL. Generally, the amount of the alternative tax NOL differs from that of the regular tax NOL because of these adjustments. The resulting alternative tax NOL carries back two years and forward 20 years. The alternative tax NOL deduction cannot exceed 90% of AMTI before the alternative tax NOL deduction.

U.S. PRODUCTION ACTIVITIES DEDUCTION. Taxable income (the starting point for calculating AMTI) is net of the U.S. production activities deduction. For regular tax purposes, the deduction is 3% (in 2006) times the lesser of qualified production activities income or taxable income before the deduction (see Chapter C3). For AMTI purposes, however, the computation is based on the lesser of qualified production activities income or AMTI before the deduction.[12] Thus, if qualified production activities income is less than taxable income and taxable income is less than AMTI, no adjustment will apply because the deduction will be the same for both purposes. On the other hand, an AMT adjustment could apply if taxable income is less than qualified production activities income because the smaller taxable income amount would be the base for regular tax purposes while either AMTI or qualified production activities income would be the base for AMTI purposes. For example, if AMTI exceeds taxable income (both before the deduction) and qualified production activities income falls between these two amounts, the U.S. production activities deduction is 3% of taxable income for regular tax purposes and 3% of qualified production activities income for AMTI purposes, thereby leading to a negative AMT adjustment.

The following example illustrates the computation of **preadjustment AMTI** (see Table C5-1). Preadjustment AMTI will become a component of the ACE and AMTI calculations presented later.

EXAMPLE C5-10 ▶ Marion Corporation engages in copper mining activities. In the current year, it reports $300,000 of taxable income, which takes into account deductions of $70,000 for percentage depletion and $80,000 for MACRS depreciation. Of the percentage depletion claimed, $30,000 exceeded the adjusted basis of the depletable property. The hypothetical AMT depreciation deduction under the alternative depreciation system would have been only $55,000. Preadjustment AMTI is calculated as follows:

---
[12] Sec. 199(d)(6).

Taxable income	$300,000
Plus: Percentage depletion in excess of basis	30,000
MACRS depreciation	80,000
Minus: AMTI depreciation	(55,000)
Preadjustment AMTI	$355,000

The depreciation adjustment results in an AMTI increase of $25,000 ($80,000 − $55,000).

◀

ADJUSTED CURRENT EARNINGS (ACE) ADJUSTMENT

HISTORICAL NOTE

The ACE adjustment involves a complex computation. It was added in an attempt to further adjust the AMT tax base toward the corporation's economic income. However, the ACE adjustment, as initially enacted by the Tax Reform Act of 1986, would have been much more complicated. The single most important simplification is that depreciation based on ACE does not include the present value depreciation computations required by the 1986 Act.

A corporation makes a positive adjustment equal to 75% of preadjustment AMTI, which is the excess of ACE over AMTI (before this adjustment and the alternative tax NOL deduction). **ACE** is based on a concept of earnings and profits (E&P) used to determine whether a corporate distribution is a dividend or a return of capital (see Chapter C4). ACE equals preadjustment AMTI for the tax year plus or minus a series of special adjustments described below. However, ACE is not the same as E&P even though many items are treated in the same manner for both purposes. The ACE adjustment is not required of S corporations since the AMT tax preferences and adjustments flow through to their non-corporate shareholders.[13] A $1 positive ACE adjustment results in a 15% (0.20 statutory rate × 0.75 inclusion ratio) effective tax rate if the corporation's TMT (before the ACE adjustment) exceeds its regular tax amount.

A negative adjustment equal to 75% of the excess of the corporation's preadjustment AMTI over its ACE also is permitted. This adjustment, however, cannot exceed the cumulative net amount of the corporation's positive and negative ACE adjustments in all post-1989 tax years.[14] Any excess of preadjustment AMTI over ACE not allowed as a negative adjustment because of the limitation cannot be carried over to a later year to reduce a required positive ACE adjustment.

EXAMPLE C5-11 ▶ Bravo Corporation, which was formed in 2004, reports the following ACE and preadjustment AMTI amounts for 2004–2006.

	2004	*2005*	*2006*
ACE	$2,000	$1,500	$1,000
Preadjustment AMTI	1,500	1,500	1,500

The corporation makes a $375 [($2,000 − $1,500) × 0.75] positive ACE adjustment in 2004. It makes no ACE adjustment in 2005 because ACE and preadjustment AMTI are the same. It makes a $375 [($1,000 − $1,500) × 0.75] negative ACE adjustment in 2006. The total ACE adjustments over the three years is zero. ◀

EXAMPLE C5-12 ▶ Assume the same facts as in Example C5-11 except the preadjustment AMTI amount in 2006 is $2,000. The tentative negative ACE adjustment is $750 [($1,000 − $2,000) × 0.75]. Only a $375 negative ACE adjustment can be made because the negative ACE adjustment may not exceed the $375 ($375 + $0) total cumulative net positive ACE adjustments made in prior years. ◀

Four general rules provide a framework for the ACE calculation:

▶ Any amount that is permanently excluded from gross income when computing AMTI, but which is taken into account in determining E&P, is included in gross income for ACE purposes (e.g., interest on tax-exempt bonds other than private activity bonds, and the proceeds of life insurance contracts). The adjustment is reduced by any deduction that would have been allowable in computing AMTI had the excluded income amount been included in gross income for AMTI purposes. No adjustment is made for timing differences. Thus, any item that is, has been, or will be included in preadjustment AMTI will not be included in the ACE adjustment.

---

[13] Sec. 56(g)(6).

[14] Sec. 56(g)(2).

▶ A deduction for any expense, loss, or other item not deductible in the tax year when computing E&P cannot be claimed when computing ACE even if such item already has been deducted in determining preadjustment AMTI. These items result in a positive adjustment to ACE to the extent they already have been deducted in determining pre-adjustment AMTI.[15] Special rules apply for the dividends-received deduction. The 80% and 100% dividends-received deductions are allowed for ACE purposes although they cannot be claimed when computing E&P. The 70% dividends-received deduction, however, is not allowed for either ACE or E&P purposes. Also, the U.S. production activities deduction is allowed for ACE purposes even though not allowed for E&P purposes. Thus, like the 80% and 100% dividends-received deduction, this deduction results in no ACE adjustment.

▶ Income items included in preadjustment AMTI are included in ACE even if the items are excluded from E&P.

▶ Items not deductible in determining preadjustment AMTI are not deducted when computing ACE even if the items are deductible in deriving E&P. Examples include federal income taxes and capital losses that exceed capital gains.[16]

In addition to the four general rules, a series of specific adjustments mandated by Sec. 56(g) must be made to AMTI to derive ACE. The more common adjustments are discussed below. As with the general AMT adjustments set forth above, these items require a recomputation of certain income, gain, loss, and deduction items and may either increase or decrease AMTI. Unless otherwise indicated, these changes are effective for tax years beginning after 1989.

▶ Depreciation on property placed in service in a tax year after 1989 and before January 1, 1994, is determined under the alternative depreciation system. All property is depreciated under the straight-line method, the appropriate recovery period, and averaging convention prescribed in the alternative depreciation system.[17] Elimination of the ACE depreciation adjustment for property placed in service after December 31, 1993, does not preclude a corporation from having to make the adjustment for property placed in service before 1994. Special transitional rules apply for property placed in service before 1990.

▶ An asset's adjusted basis is determined according to the depreciation, depletion, or amortization rules applicable in the ACE calculation. As a result, a basis adjustment similar to that described above for the AMTI calculation may be required when an asset is sold, exchanged, or otherwise disposed of.[18]

▶ When calculating ACE, the gain realized on an installment sale of noninventory property is fully recognized in the year of sale.[19]

▶ Organizational expenditures otherwise amortizable under Sec. 248 are not amortized for ACE purposes if made after December 31, 1989.[20]

▶ The increase or decrease in the annual LIFO recapture amount increases or decreases ACE. LIFO recapture is the amount by which ending inventory under the first-in, first-out (FIFO) method exceeds ending inventory under the last-in, first-out (LIFO) method.[21] This adjustment effectively converts the corporation's inventory method from LIFO to FIFO for ACE purposes.

▶ Depletion on property placed in service after 1989 is determined under the cost method.[22] Intangible drilling costs must be amortized over 60 months beginning with the month in which they are paid or incurred.

▶ Taxpayers must recalculate charitable contribution and percentage depletion deduction limits to take into account AMT adjustment and preference items.[23] They also

---

[15] Secs. 56(g)(4)(C)(i) and (ii). A partial list of items falling into this category is presented in Reg. Sec. 1.56(g)-1(d)(3) and (4).
[16] Reg. Sec. 1.56(g)-1(e).
[17] Sec. 56(g)(4)(A).
[18] Sec. 56(g)(4)(I).
[19] Sec. 56(g)(4)(D)(iv).
[20] Sec. 56(g)(4)(D)(ii).

[21] Secs. 56(g)(4)(D)(iii) and 312(n)(4).
[22] Sec. 56(g)(4)(G).
[23] Ltr. Rul. 9320003 (February 1, 1993). Because the IRS treats the AMT as a parallel tax system independent of the regular tax system, any deduction expressed as a percentage of regular taxable income must be recalculated for AMT purposes.

must separately account for carryovers for regular tax and AMT purposes. Corporations, in particular, must determine separate charitable contribution limits and carryovers for AMTI and ACE purposes. For many corporations, the AMTI and ACE charitable contribution limits will be higher than the regular tax limit because their ACE and AMT adjusted taxable income counterparts are usually larger.

Topic Review C5-1 summarizes the ACE calculation.

 STOP & THINK

Question: Flair Corporation was considering investing in state government obligations. Flair's Chief Financial Officer (CFO) knew that the interest earned on these obligations is exempt from federal income tax. She also knew that the state in which Flair operates exempts from the state income tax interest income earned on state and local bonds issued by the state. The CFO was surprised to discover that the so-called tax-exempt interest income could be taxed by the federal government at a rate of up to 20% if earned by a corporation. She called her CPA to find out how this could occur. What did the CPA say?

Solution: If the debt obligation is a private activity bond issued after 1986, the interest income constitutes a tax preference item. One would expect $1 of interest income to increase the AMT tax base by $1 and the AMT by $0.20. However, under the corporate alternative minimum tax scheme, $1 of interest income that is a tax preference item can produce one of the following results:

Tentative Minimum Tax

Excluding Tax-Exempt Interest Income	*Including Tax-Exempt Interest Income*	*Additional Tax on $1 of Tax-Exempt Interest Income*
TMT > regular tax	TMT > regular tax	$0.20
TMT < regular tax	TMT < regular tax	$0.00
TMT < regular tax	TMT > regular tax	$0.00 to $0.20

Topic Review C5-1

Summary of Common Alternative Minimum Tax Adjustments

INCOME/EXPENSE ITEM	MOST COMMON ADJUSTMENT TO:[a]	
	TAXABLE INCOME TO DERIVE AMTI	PREADJUSTMENT AMTI TO DERIVE ACE
Tax-exempt interest:		
Private activity bonds	Increase	None
Other bonds	None	Increase
Life insurance proceeds	None	Increase
Deferred gain on nondealer installment sales	None	Increase
LIFO inventory adjustment	None	Increase
"Basis adjustment" on asset sale	Decrease	Decrease
Depreciation	Increase	Increase
Excess charitable contributions	Decrease	Decrease
Excess capital losses	None	None
Dividends-received deduction:		
80% and 100% DRD	None	None
70% DRD	None	Increase
U.S. production activities deduction	None or Decrease	None
Organizational expenditure amortization	None	Increase
Federal income taxes	None	None
Penalties and fines	None	None
Disallowed travel and entertainment expenses and club dues	None	None

[a] Adjustments such as depreciation may increase or decrease taxable income in deriving AMTI and ACE.

If the interest income is not a tax preference item, only 75% of the interest is included in the ACE adjustment. The $0.20 additional tax ceiling on $1 of interest from private activity obligations is reduced to $0.15 (0.75 × $0.20) for tax-exempt interest earned on debt obligations other than private activity obligations.

COMPREHENSIVE EXAMPLE. Glidden Corporation is not eligible for the small corporation AMT exemption. Using the accrual method, Glidden reported the following taxable income and tax liability data for 2005:

Gross profit from sales	$300,000
Dividends: From 20%-owned corporation	10,000
From 10%-owned corporation	20,000
Gain on sale of depreciable property	12,778
Gain on installment sale of land	25,000
Gross income	$367,778
Operating expenses	(175,000)
Depreciation	(40,000)
Amortization of organizational expenditures	(2,500)
Dividends-received deduction	(22,000)
Total deductions	($239,500)
Taxable income	$128,278
Regular tax	$ 33,278

Assume the following additional facts:

▶ The corporation earned tax-exempt bond interest of $15,000. The bonds are not private activity obligations.

▶ Upon the death of an executive, the corporation received life insurance proceeds of $100,000.

▶ On January 30 of the current year, the corporation sold the land for a total gain of $77,000, of which it reported $25,000 under the installment method for regular tax purposes. Glidden is not a dealer, and it pays no interest on the taxes owed on the deferred gain.

▶ The gain reported for AMTI and ACE purposes on the sale of depreciable property is $5,860.

▶ Depreciation for AMTI and ACE purposes is $32,500. All of Glidden's depreciable assets were placed in service between 1997 and 2002. Some of the assets were used in a predecessor proprietorship incorporated in 2000.

▶ The corporation incurred organizational expenditures in 2001, which are amortized over a 60-month period for regular tax purposes because they occurred before October 23, 2004.

Preadjustment AMTI is calculated as follows:

Taxable income	$128,278
Plus: Depreciation adjustment	7,500[a]
Minus: Basis adjustment on machine sale	(6,918)[b]
Preadjustment AMTI	$128,860

[a] $40,000 − $32,500 = $7,500.
[b] $12,778 − $5,860 = $6,918.

AMTI depreciation is less than taxable income depreciation because of different depreciation methods. The gain on the depreciable property sale is smaller for preadjustment AMTI and ACE purposes than for taxable income purposes because depreciation claimed for AMTI and ACE purposes was calculated under the alternative depreciation system. The corporation makes no adjustment for the $52,000 deferred gain on the installment sale because it can use the installment method to report sales of noninventory property when calculating both taxable income and AMTI.

Adjusted current earnings (ACE) is calculated as follows:

Preadjustment AMTI	$128,860
Plus: Tax-exempt bond interest	15,000
Life insurance proceeds	100,000
Deferred gain on land sale	52,000
Organizational expenditures adjustment	2,500
Dividends-received deduction adjustment	14,000
Adjusted current earnings	$312,360

The life insurance proceeds and the tax-exempt bond interest are included only in the ACE calculation. Part of the gain on the land sale under the installment method is included in taxable income and preadjustment AMTI. The entire gain is reported for ACE purposes in the year of sale because dealers or nondealers may not use the installment method for ACE purposes except where interest is charged for the tax deferral privilege. No deduction is allowed for ACE purposes for either the amortization of the organizational expenditures or the 70% deduction otherwise allowed for dividends received from a 10%-owned corporation.

The AMT liability is calculated as follows:

Preadjustment AMTI		$128,860
Plus: ACE	$312,360	
Minus: Preadjustment AMTI	(128,860)	
Difference	$183,500	
Times: 75% inclusion ratio	× 0.75	137,625
Alternative minimum taxable income		$266,485
Minus: Statutory exemption		(10,879)ᵃ
AMT base		$255,606
Times: 20% tax rate		× 0.20
Tentative minimum tax		$ 51,121
Minus: Regular tax		(33,278)
Alternative minimum tax		$ 17,843

ᵃ $40,000 − [0.25 × ($266,485 − $150,000)] = $10,879.

The statutory exemption is reduced because AMTI exceeds $150,000. The AMT liability is the excess of the tentative minimum tax over the regular tax. A completed Form 4626 for this comprehensive example appears in Appendix B.

MINIMUM TAX CREDIT

When a corporation pays an AMT, it may be eligible for a **minimum tax credit** that can offset its future regular tax liabilities. The minimum tax credit prevents the same item of income from being taxed twice: once under the AMT rules and second under the regular tax rules. Thus, because of the minimum tax credit, the AMT effectively becomes a prepaid tax that accelerates the payment of a corporation's income taxes.

The entire corporate AMT may be claimed as a credit. The amount creditable includes the portion of the AMT attributable to deferral adjustments and preference items that reflect timing differences that will reverse in future tax years. It also includes the portion of the AMT attributable to permanent adjustments and preference items that never will reverse.[24]

The minimum tax credit that a corporation can use in a tax year equals the total of the net minimum taxes paid in all prior post-1986 tax years minus the amount claimed as a

---

[24] Sec. 53. Most AMT adjustments and preference items accelerate the tax consequences of transactions that are deferred for regular tax purposes, i.e., timing differences. However, two preference items that reflect permanent differences are percentage depletion and tax-exempt private activity bond interest. Also, ACE adjustments that reflect permanent differences include life insurance proceeds and tax-exempt interest on bonds other than private activity bonds.

minimum tax credit in those years. Use of available minimum tax credits in the current year is limited to the excess of the corporation's regular tax (minus all credits other than refundable credits) over its tentative minimum tax.

EXAMPLE C5-13 ▶ In the current year, Seminole Corporation generates $400,000 of taxable income. It also incurred $250,000 of positive adjustments and $350,000 of tax preference items. Its regular tax is $136,000 (0.34 × $400,000), and its AMT is $64,000 [(0.20 × $1,000,000) − $136,000]. Seminole's minimum tax credit is the entire amount of its AMT, or $64,000. ◀

The minimum tax credit carries forward indefinitely and offsets regular taxes in future years, but only to the extent the regular tax exceeds the corporation's TMT in the carryforward year. The minimum tax credit cannot be carried back to an earlier tax year.

TAX CREDITS AND THE AMT

ADDITIONAL COMMENT

Because the general business credit limitation is tied to the TMT, *every* corporation with excess general business credits will have to compute its TMT even though the corporation may not be liable for the AMT.

As illustrated in Table C3-2, a corporation can reduce its regular tax by any available tax credits. Special rules restrict the use of tax credits to offset the corporate AMT. These rules are explained below.

AMT AND THE GENERAL BUSINESS CREDIT. The general business credit may not be used to offset the alternative minimum tax, the accumulated earnings tax, the personal holding company (PHC) tax, or all of a corporation's regular tax.

Under Sec. 38(c), the general business credit for a tax year is limited to the excess (if any) of the corporation's net income tax (reduced by certain other credits) over the greater of its tentative minimum tax or 25% of the corporation's net regular tax that exceeds $25,000.

KEY POINT

Because the purpose of the AMT is to ensure that all profitable corporations pay a minimum amount of tax, the use of tax credits also is limited. For example, the general business credit cannot reduce the regular tax below the TMT.

A corporation's net income tax is the sum of its regular tax and AMT reduced by the foreign tax credit, possessions tax credit, and Puerto Rico economic activity credit. Any general business credits that cannot be used in the current year because of credit limitations carry back one year and forward 20 years.[25] The result of this limitation is that the general business credit can offset only the portion of the regular tax that exceeds the TMT, not all of a corporation's regular tax.

EXAMPLE C5-14 ▶ In the current year, Scientific Corporation's regular tax before credits is $125,000. Its TMT is $50,000. Scientific's only available credit for the year is a general business credit of $140,000. Scientific's net income tax is $125,000 because its regular tax ($125,000) is greater than its TMT ($50,000). As computed below, Scientific's general business credit is limited to the smaller of its $75,000 credit limitation or the $140,000 credit earned.

Net income tax		$125,000
Minus: Greater of:		
(1) 25% of regular tax (reduced by other credits) exceeding $25,000 [0.25 × ($125,000 − $25,000)]	$25,000	
OR		
(2) Tentative minimum tax	$50,000	(50,000)
General business credit limitation		$ 75,000

Scientific incurs a regular tax of $50,000 ($125,000 − $75,000 credit) but no AMT. Its general business credit carryback or carryover is $65,000 ($140,000 − $75,000), which can be carried back one year and forward 20 years. ◀

The AMT credit for small corporations is limited by the amount the corporation's regular tax (reduced by other credits) exceeds 25% times the excess (if any) of (a) the corporation's regular tax (reduced by other credits) minus (b) $25,000.[26]

---

[25] Sec. 38(c)(2). Special rules apply to the empowerment zone employment credit, which can offset up to 25% of a taxpayer's AMT liability.

[26] Sec. 55(e)(5).

AMT AND THE FOREIGN TAX CREDIT. For purposes of computing the AMT, the full amount of foreign tax credits (AMT FTCs) can offset the TMT, computed without the alternative tax NOL deduction. Credits that cannot be used in the current year carry back two years and forward five years to offset the TMT in those years.[27] A simplified AMT foreign tax credit limitation election is available under Sec. 59(a), which bases the limit on the ratio of foreign source taxable income to worldwide AMTI.

Topic Review C5-2 presents an overview of the alternative minimum tax.

PERSONAL HOLDING COMPANY TAX

OBJECTIVE 2

Determine whether a corporation is a personal holding company (PHC)

A corporation that meets both a stock ownership test and a passive income test is classified as a **personal holding company (PHC)** for the tax year. Congress enacted the PHC tax to prevent taxpayers from using closely held corporations to shelter passive income from the higher individual tax rates. In tax years 2003 through 2008, this penalty tax will be levied at a 15% rate on the PHC's undistributed personal holding company income (UPHCI). After 2008, the PHC tax rate will revert to the highest marginal tax rate for individuals. A corporation subject to the PHC tax pays this tax in addition to the regular corporate tax and the corporate alternative minimum tax. Corporations, however, can escape the PHC tax by avoiding either the stock ownership test or passive income test or through dividend distributions that reduce UPHCI to zero.

The significance of the PHC tax has diminished in the aftermath of the 2003 Act. This act lowered the highest marginal rate for individuals to the same level as that for corporations (35%). In so doing, it has reduced the attractiveness of using the C corporation as a vehicle for sheltering what are essentially individual earnings. Even with a narrowing or elimination of the individual-corporate tax rate gap, however, the PHC tax remains an important anti-tax avoidance tool, particularly where wealthy individuals in the 35% marginal tax bracket control corporations with effective tax rates less than 35%.

Topic Review C5-2

Alternative Minimum Tax (AMT)

1. The AMT is levied in addition to the regular (income) tax.
2. Special AMT exemptions are available for small corporations with gross receipts generally of $7.5 million or less and for any corporation with a low level of alternative minimum taxable income (AMTI) (generally less than $310,000).
3. The starting point for the AMT calculation is taxable income before NOLs. Taxable income is increased by tax preference items and further adjusted to derive AMTI.
4. AMTI is reduced by a statutory exemption to derive the AMT base. The $40,000 statutory exemption is phased out when AMTI falls between $150,000 and $310,000.
5. A 20% rate applies to the AMT base to derive the tentative minimum tax.
6. The tentative minimum tax is reduced by the AMT foreign tax credit. Other tax credits, such as the general business credit, do not reduce the tentative minimum tax.
7. The excess of a corporation's tentative minimum tax over its regular tax may be claimed as a minimum tax credit. This credit carries over to a later year to offset the excess of the regular tax over the tentative minimum tax.
8. The AMT, as well as the regular tax, must be estimated and paid quarterly.

---

[27] Sec. 59(a)(2).

PERSONAL HOLDING COMPANY DEFINED

A personal holding company is any corporation that (1) has five or fewer individual shareholders who own more than 50% of the corporation's outstanding stock at any time during the last half of its tax year and (2) has personal holding company income that is at least 60% of its adjusted ordinary gross income for the tax year.[28]

Corporations with special tax status generally are excluded from the PHC definition. Among those excluded are S corporations and tax-exempt organizations.

STOCK OWNERSHIP REQUIREMENT

Section 542(a)(2) provides that a corporation satisfies the PHC stock ownership requirement if more than 50% of the value of its outstanding stock is directly or indirectly owned by five or fewer individuals at any time during the last half of its tax year.[29] Any corporation with fewer than ten individual shareholders at any time during the last half of its tax year, which is not an excluded corporation, will meet the stock ownership requirement.[30]

For purposes of determining whether the 50% requirement is satisfied, stock owned directly or indirectly by or for an individual is considered to be owned by that individual. The Sec. 544 stock attribution rules provide that

▶ Stock owned by a family member is considered to be owned by the other members of his or her family. Family members include a spouse, brothers and sisters, ancestors, and lineal descendants.

▶ Stock owned directly or indirectly by or for a corporation, partnership, estate, or trust is considered to be owned proportionately by its shareholders, partners, or beneficiaries.

▶ A person who holds an option to acquire stock is considered to own such stock whether or not the individual intends to exercise the option.

▶ Stock owned by a partner is considered to be owned by his or her partners.

▶ The family, partnership, and option rules can be used only to make a corporation a PHC. They cannot be used to prevent a corporation from acquiring PHC status.[31]

PASSIVE INCOME REQUIREMENT

A corporation whose shareholders satisfy the stock ownership requirement is not a PHC unless the corporation also earns predominantly passive income. The passive income requirement is met if at least 60% of the corporation's **adjusted ordinary gross income (AOGI)** for the tax year is personal holding company income (PHCI). The following text sections define AOGI and PHCI and outline ways in which a corporation can sidestep the passive income requirements.

ADJUSTED ORDINARY GROSS INCOME DEFINED. The first step toward determining AOGI is calculating the corporation's gross income (see Figure C5-1). Gross income is determined under the same accounting method used to compute taxable income. Thus, an income item excluded from gross income also is excluded from AOGI. Gross receipts from sales are reduced by the corporation's cost of goods sold.

The next step toward determining AOGI is calculating the corporation's **ordinary gross income (OGI)**. To do this, the corporation's gross income is reduced by the amount of its capital gains and Sec. 1231 gains.[32] The exclusion of capital gains and Sec. 1231 gains from OGI (and, later, from AOGI) means that these items are neutral factors in determining whether a corporation is a PHC; that is, the realization and recognition of a large Sec. 1231 or capital gain cannot make a corporation a PHC.

---

[28] Sec. 542(a).
[29] The PHC stock ownership test also is used to determine whether a closely held C corporation is subject to the at-risk rules (Sec. 465) or the passive activity loss and credit limitation rules (Sec. 469). Thus, a closely held corporation that is not a PHC may be subject to certain restrictions because of the PHC stock ownership rules.

[30] This statement may not be valid if entities own stock that might be attributed to the individual owners.
[31] Sec. 544(a)(4)(A).
[32] Sec. 543(b)(1).

▼ FIGURE C5-1

Determining Adjusted Ordinary Gross Income

Gross income (GI) reported for taxable income and PHC purposes
Minus: Gross gains on the sale of capital assets
         Gross gains on the sale of Sec. 1231 property

Ordinary gross income (OGI)
Minus: Certain expenses relating to gross income from rents; mineral,oil,
         and gas royalties; and working interests in oil or gas wells
         Interest earned on certain U.S. obligations held for sale to customers by dealers
         Interest on condemnation awards, judgments, or tax refunds
         Rents from tangible personal property manufactured or produced by the corporation,
           provided it has engaged in substantial manufacturing or production of the same
           type of personal property in the current tax year

Adjusted ordinary gross income (AOGI)

Next, OGI is reduced by certain expenses. These expenses relate to the generation of rental income; mineral, oil, and gas (M, O, & G) royalties; and income from working interests in oil or gas wells.[33] The rental income adjustment is described below.

Reduction by Rental Income Expenses. Gross income from rents is reduced by deductions for depreciation or amortization, property taxes, interest, and other rental expenses. This net amount is known as **adjusted income from rents (AIR)**.[34] No other Sec. 162 expenses incurred in the generation of rental income reduce OGI. The expense adjustment cannot exceed total gross rental income.

EXAMPLE C5-15 ▶

Ingrid owns all of Keno Corporation's single class of stock. Both Ingrid and Keno use the calendar year as their tax year. Keno reports the following results for the current year:

Rental income	$100,000
Depreciation	15,000
Interest expense	9,000
Real estate taxes	4,000
Maintenance expenses	8,000
Administrative expenses	12,000

Keno's AIR is $72,000 [$100,000 − ($15,000 + $9,000 + $4,000)]. The maintenance and administrative expenses are deductible in determining taxable income and, consequently, UPHCI, but do not reduce the AIR amount. ◀

ADDITIONAL COMMENT

Income not included in AOGI cannot be PHCI. In calculating the 60% passive income test, PHCI is the numerator and AOGI is the denominator. Because the passive income test is purely objective, both the numerator and denominator can be manipulated. When the ratio is close to 60%, one planning opportunity is to accelerate the recognition of income that is AOGI but not PHCI.

PERSONAL HOLDING COMPANY INCOME DEFINED. **Personal holding company income** includes dividends, interest, annuities, adjusted income from rents, royalties, produced film rents, income from personal service contracts involving a 25% or more shareholder, rental income from corporate property used by a 25% or more shareholder, and distributions from estates or trusts.

PHCI is determined according to the following general rules:

▶ *Dividends:* Includes only distributions out of E&P. Any amounts that are tax exempt (e.g., return of capital distributions) or eligible for capital gain treatment (e.g., liquidating distributions) are excluded from PHCI.[35]

▶ *Interest income:* Includes interest included in gross income. Interest excluded from gross income also is excluded from PHCI.[36]

---

[33] Sec. 543(b)(2).
[34] Sec. 543(b)(3).

[35] Reg. Sec. 1.543-1(b)(1).
[36] Reg. Sec. 1.543-1(b)(2).

▶ *Annuity proceeds:* Includes only annuity amounts included in gross income. Annuity amounts excluded from gross income (for example, as a return of capital) also are excluded from PHCI.[37]

▶ *Royalty income:* Includes amounts received for the use of intangible property (e.g., patents, copyrights, and trademarks). Special rules apply to copyright royalties, mineral, oil, and gas royalties, active business computer software royalties, and produced film rents. Each of these four types of income constitutes a separate PHCI category that may be excluded under one of the exceptions discussed below and set forth in Table C5-2.[38]

▶ *Distributions from an estate or trust:* Included in PHCI.[39]

In the calculation of PHCI, special rules apply that could result in the exclusion of rents; mineral, oil, and gas royalties; copyright royalties; produced film rents; rental income from the use of property by a 25% or more shareholder; and active business computer software royalties from PHCI. These rules, summarized in Table C5-2, reduce the likelihood that a corporation will be deemed a PHC. The two most frequently encountered exclusions, for rental income and personal service contract income, are explained in the next two sections.

Exclusion for Rents. Adjusted income from rents (AIR) is included in PHCI unless a special exception applies for corporations earning predominantly rental income. PHCI does not include rents if (1) AIR is at least 50% of AOGI and (2) the dividends-paid deduction equals or exceeds the amount by which nonrental PHCI exceeds 10% of OGI.[40] The special exception permits corporations earning predominantly rental income and very little nonrental PHCI to avoid PHC status. The dividends-paid deduction is available for (1) dividends paid during the tax year, (2) dividends paid within 2½ months of the end of the tax year for which the PHC makes a special throwback election to treat the distribution as

HISTORICAL NOTE
The exception for royalties on computer software was added by the Tax Reform Act of 1986. Without this exception, many computer software companies would almost certainly be deemed to be PHCs.

SELF-STUDY QUESTION
What is the effect of the two-pronged test that allows the exclusion from PHCI of certain AIR?

ANSWER
This two-pronged test makes it difficult to use rents to shelter other passive income. For example, the 50% test would require at least $100 of AIR to shelter $100 of interest income. The 10% test is even more restrictive. To satisfy this test, it would be necessary to generate $900 of OGI (AIR and other items) to shelter the same $100 of interest income.

TAX STRATEGY TIP
Taxpayers potentially liable for the PHC should carefully monitor the PHC exclusion requirements to avoid having to pay the tax or having to make a deficiency dividend payment.

▼ TABLE C5-2

Tests to Determine Exclusions from Personal Holding Company Income

PHCI Category	A PHCI Category Is Excluded If:		
	Income in the Category Is:	Other PHCI Is:	Business Expenses Are:
Rents	≥50% of AOGI[a]	≤10% of OGI (unless reduced by distributions)	—
Mineral, oil, and gas royalties	≥50% of AOGI[a]	≤10% of OGI	≥15% of AOGI
Copyright royalties	≥50% of OGI	≤10% of OGI	≥25% of OGI
Produced film rents	≥50% of OGI	—	—
Compensation for use of property by a shareholder owning at least 25% of the outstanding stock	—	≤10% of OGI	—
Active business computer software royalties	≥50% of OGI	≤10% of OGI (unless reduced by distributions)	≥25% of OGI[b]
Personal services contract income	—[c]	—	—

[a] Measured in terms of adjusted income from rents or mineral, oil, and gas royalties, respectively.
[b] The deduction test can apply to either the single tax year in question or the five-year period ending with the tax year in question.
[c] Personal services income is excluded from PHCI if the corporation has the right to designate the person who is to perform the services or if the person performing the services owns less than 25% of the corporation's outstanding stock.

---

[37] Reg. Sec. 1.543-1(b)(4).
[38] Reg. Sec. 1.543-1(b)(3). Royalties include mineral, oil, and gas royalties, royalties on working interests in oil or gas wells, computer software royalties, copyright royalties, and all other royalties.

[39] Sec. 543(a)(8).
[40] Sec. 543(a)(2). AIR excludes rental income earned from leasing property to a shareholder owning 25% or more of the corporation's stock. Such income is included in PHCI as a separate category.

having been paid on the last day of the preceding tax year, and (3) consent dividends (see page C5-23). Nonrental PHCI includes all PHCI (determined without regard to the exclusions for copyright royalties and mineral, oil, and gas royalties) *other than* adjusted income from rents and rental income earned from leasing property to a shareholder owning 25% or more of the corporation's stock.

EXAMPLE C5-16 ▶ Karen owns all of Texas Corporation's single class of stock. Both Karen and Texas use the calendar year as their tax year. Texas reports the following results for the current year:

Rental income	$100,000
Operating profit from sales	40,000
Dividend income	15,000
Interest income on corporate bonds	10,000
Rental expenses:	
Depreciation	15,000
Interest	9,000
Real estate taxes	4,000
Other expenses	20,000

Texas pays no dividends during the current year or during the 2½ month throwback period following year-end. Because one shareholder owns all the Texas stock, Texas satisfies the stock ownership requirement. Texas's AOGI is calculated as follows:

Rental income		$100,000
Operating profit from sales		40,000
Dividends		15,000
Interest income		10,000
Gross income and OGI		$165,000
Minus: Depreciation	$15,000	
Interest expense	9,000	
Real estate taxes	4,000	(28,000)
AOGI		$137,000

The two AIR tests are illustrated as follows:

Test 1:	Rental income		$100,000
	Minus: Depreciation		(15,000)
	Interest expense		(9,000)
	Real estate taxes		(4,000)
	AIR		$ 72,000
	50% of AOGI (0.50 × $137,000 AOGI) [Test passed]		$ 68,500
Test 2:	Dividends		$ 15,000
	Interest income		10,000
	Nonrental income		$ 25,000
	Minus: 10% of OGI (0.10 × $165,000)		(16,500)
	Minimum amount of distributions		$8,500
	Actual dividends paid [Test failed]		$ –0–

AIR exceeds the 50% threshold, so Texas passes Test 1. Because Texas paid no dividends, its dividends-paid deduction is less than the nonrental income ceiling, and Texas fails Test 2. AIR is included in PHCI because Texas passed only one of the two tests. The 60% PHC income test is illustrated below:

AIR	$ 72,000
Dividends	15,000
Interest income	10,000
PHCI	$ 97,000
AOGI	$137,000
Times: AOGI threshold	× 0.60
AOGI ceiling [Test passed]	$ 82,200

Texas is a PHC because PHCI exceeds 60% of AOGI.

Texas could have avoided PHC status by paying sufficient cash dividends during the current year or a consent dividend following year-end. The amount of dividends required to avoid PHC status is the excess of nonrental PHCI ($25,000) over 10% of OGI ($16,500), or $8,500. Thus, an $8,500 cash dividend paid during the current year or consent dividend paid after year-end would have permitted Texas to exclude the $72,000 of AIR from PHCI. PHCI then would have been $25,000 ($15,000 + $10,000), which is less than 60% of AOGI ($82,200). (Consent dividends are discussed on page C5-23.) ◄

ADDITIONAL COMMENT

Congress enacted the provision for personal service contracts to prevent entertainers, athletes, and other highly compensated professionals from incorporating their activities and, after paying themselves a below-normal salary, having the rest of the income taxed at the corporate rates. Even if it is apparent that a 25%-shareholder will perform the services, as long as no one other than the corporation has the right to designate who performs the services, the income is not PHCI. Thus, the careful drafting of contracts is important.

Exclusion for Personal Service Contracts. Income earned from contracts under which the corporation is obligated to perform personal services, as well as income earned on the sale of such contracts, is included in PHCI if the following two conditions are met:

► A person other than the corporation has the right to designate (by name or by description) the individual who is to perform the services, or the individual who is to perform the services is designated (by name or by description) in the contract.

► 25% or more of the value of the corporation's outstanding stock is directly or indirectly owned by the person who has performed, is to perform, or may be designated as the person to perform the services.[41]

The 25% or more requirement must be satisfied at some point during the tax year and is determined under the Sec. 544 constructive stock ownership rules. Congress enacted this provision to prevent professionals, entertainers, and sports figures from incorporating their activities, paying themselves a substandard salary, and sheltering at the lower corporate tax rates the difference between their actual earnings and their substandard salary.

EXAMPLE C5-17 ►

Dr. Kellner owns all the stock in a professional corporation that provides medical services. The professional corporation concludes with Dr. Kellner an exclusive employment contract that specifies the terms of his employment and that provides for the hiring of a qualified substitute when Dr. Kellner is off duty. The corporation provides office space for Dr. Kellner and employs office staff to enable Dr. Kellner to perform medical services. The income earned by Dr. Kellner does not constitute PHCI because (1) the normal patient–physician relationship generally does not involve a contract that designates a doctor who will perform the services, nor will the patient generally be permitted to designate a doctor who will perform the services, and (2) the professional corporation will be able to substitute a qualified replacement when Dr. Kellner is not on duty (for example, when he is on vacation or not on call).[42]

The income earned by the corporation in connection with Dr. Kellner's services would constitute PHCI if the contract with the patient specified that only Dr. Kellner would provide the services or if the services provided by Dr. Kellner were so unique that only he could provide them. Any portion of the corporation's income from the personal service contract attributable to "important and essential" services provided by persons other than Dr. Kellner is not included in PHCI.[43] ◄

OBJECTIVE 3

Calculate the corporation's PHC tax

CALCULATING THE PHC TAX

The PHC tax is calculated in two basic steps. First, the corporation determines the amount of its undistributed personal holding company income (UPHCI). It then applies the 15% PHC tax rate (in 2003–2008) to UPHCI. If the corporation owes the PHC tax, it can avoid paying the tax by making a timely consent or deficiency dividend distribution.

CALCULATING UPHCI. The starting point for calculating UPHCI is the corporation's taxable income. A series of adjustments are made to taxable income to derive UPHCI. The most important of these adjustments are discussed below.

---

[41] Sec. 543(a)(7).
[42] Rev. Rul. 75-67, 1975-1 C.B. 169. See also Rev. Ruls. 75-249, 1975-1 C.B. 171 (relating to a composer), and 75-250, 1975-1 C.B. 172 (relating to an accountant).

[43] Reg. Sec. 1.543-1(b)(8)(ii).

▼ **FIGURE C5-2**

Calculating the Personal Holding Company Tax

Taxable income
Plus: Positive adjustments
        1. Dividends-received deduction
        2. NOL deduction
        3. Excess charitable contributions carried over from a preceding tax year and
           deducted in determining taxable income
        4. Net loss attributable to the operation or maintenance of property leased by the
           corporation
        5. Rental expenses that exceed rental income
Minus: Negative adjustments
        1. Accrued U.S. and foreign income taxes
        2. Charitable contributions that exceed the 10% corporate limitation
        3. NOL (computed without regard to the dividends-received deduction) incurred in
           the immediately preceding tax year
        4. Net capital gain minus the amount of any income taxes attributed to it
Minus: Dividends-paid deduction

Undistributed personal holding company income (UPHCI)
Times: 0.15 (in 2003–2008)

Personal holding company tax

KEY POINT

The PHC tax is assessed at a 15% rate in 2003–2008. This tax is in addition to the corporate income tax. Thus, the existence of both taxes eliminates any advantage obtained by interposing a corporation between the taxpayer and his or her income-producing assets.

KEY POINT

The negative adjustments made to taxable income in deriving UPHCI (e.g., federal income taxes) represent items that do not reduce taxable income but reduce the earnings available for distribution to the shareholders. In contrast, positive adjustments made to taxable income (e.g., the dividends-received deduction) are not allowed in deriving UPHCI because they do not represent a reduction in earnings available for distribution to the shareholders.

Positive Adjustments to Taxable Income. A PHC may not claim a dividends-received deduction. Thus, its taxable income must be increased by the amount of any dividends-received deductions claimed.[44] Rental expenses that exceed rental income also are added back to taxable income to derive UPHCI.

Because PHCs may deduct only the NOL for the immediately preceding tax year, two NOL compensating adjustments must be made. First, the amount of the NOL deduction claimed in determining taxable income must be added back to taxable income. Second, the entire amount of the corporation's NOL (computed without regard to the dividends-received deduction) for the immediately preceding tax year must be subtracted from taxable income.[45] The U.S. production activities deduction, however, is not added back to taxable income.

Negative Adjustments to Taxable Income. Charitable contributions made by individuals are deductible up to 20%, 30%, or 50% of adjusted gross income, depending on the type of contribution and type of donee. Thus, two adjustments to the deductions claimed by individuals may be required: (1) subtracting the amount of charitable contributions exceeding the 10% corporate limitation, but not exceeding the individual limitations, and (2) adding back charitable contribution carryovers deducted in the current year for regular tax purposes, but in an earlier year for PHC tax purposes.[46]

Income taxes (i.e., federal income taxes, the corporate AMT, foreign income taxes, and U.S. possessions' income taxes) accrued by the corporation reduce UPHCI.[47]

A PHC is allowed a deduction for its net capital gain (i.e., net long-term capital gain over net short-term capital loss) minus income taxes attributable to the net capital gain.[48] The portion of federal income taxes attributable to the net capital gain equals the tax imposed on the corporation's taxable income minus the tax imposed on the corporation's taxable income excluding the net capital gain. The tax offset eliminates the possibility of a double benefit for federal income taxes, which are deductible in determining UPHCI.

---

[44] Sec. 545(b)(3).
[45] Sec. 545(b)(4) and Rev. Rul. 79-59, 1979-1 C.B. 209.
[46] Sec. 545(b)(2).

[47] Sec. 545(b)(1).
[48] Sec. 545(b)(5).

The capital gains adjustment precludes a corporation from being classified as a PHC because of a large capital gain. Even where the corporation is classified as a PHC, the capital gains adjustment allows it to avoid the PHC tax on its long-term (but not short-term) capital gains.

AVOIDING THE PHC DESIGNATION AND TAX LIABILITY BY MAKING DIVIDEND DISTRIBUTIONS

ADDITIONAL COMMENT

The intent behind the PHC rules is not to collect taxes from a corporation. Instead, the rules are meant to compel the distribution of income by a closely held corporation so that such income will be taxed at the shareholders' individual tax rates. This purpose is evidenced by the flexibility of the dividends-paid deduction.

The PHC can claim a **dividends-paid deduction** for distributions made during the current year if they are made out of the corporation's current or accumulated E&P.[49] A dividends-paid deduction is not available for **preferential dividends**. A dividend is preferential when (1) the amount distributed to a shareholder exceeds his or her ratable share of the distribution as determined by the number of shares of stock owned or (2) the amount received by a class of stock is greater or less than its rightful amount.[50] In either case, the entire distribution (and not just any excess distributions) is considered to be a preferential dividend.

Throwback dividends are distributions made in the first 2½ months after the close of the tax year. A dividend paid in the first 2½ months of the next tax year is treated as a throwback distribution in the preceding tax year only if the PHC makes the appropriate election.[51] Otherwise, the dividends-paid deduction is allowable only in the tax year in which the PHC actually makes the distribution. Throwback dividends paid by a PHC are limited to the lesser of the PHC's UPHCI or 20% of the amount of any dividends (other than consent dividends) paid during the tax year. Thus, a PHC that fails to make any dividend distributions during its tax year is precluded from paying a throwback dividend.

TAX STRATEGY TIP

If the corporation does not have the cash to pay a throwback dividend, it should consider a consent dividend. The consent dividend is not subject to the 20% limitation on throwback dividends and may be paid up to the extended due date for the corporation's tax return.

Consent dividends are hypothetical dividends deemed to have been paid to shareholders on the last day of the corporation's tax year. Consent dividends permit a corporation to reduce its PHC tax liability when it cannot make an actual dividend distribution because of a lack of cash, a restrictive loan covenant, and so on. Any shareholder who owns stock on the last day of the corporation's tax year can elect to pay a consent dividend.[52] For PHC tax purposes, the election results in the payment of a hypothetical cash dividend on the last day of the PHC's tax year for which the dividends-paid deduction is claimed. The shareholder treats the consent dividend as received on the distribution date and then immediately contributed by the shareholder to the distributing corporation's capital account. The contribution increases the shareholder's stock basis. The shareholder can make the consent dividend election through the due date for the corporation's income tax return (including any permitted extensions).

Dividend Carryovers. Dividends paid in the preceding two tax years may be used as a dividend carryover to reduce the amount of the current year's PHC tax liability.[53] Section 564 permits a PHC to deduct the amount by which its dividend distributions eligible for a dividends-paid deduction in each of the two preceding tax years exceed the corporation's UPHCI for such year.

Liquidating Dividends. Section 562 allows a dividends-paid deduction for liquidating distributions made by a PHC within 24 months of adopting a plan of liquidation.[54]

Deficiency Dividends. Under Sec. 547, a corporation liable for the PHC tax can avoid paying the tax by electing to pay a **deficiency dividend**. The deficiency dividend provisions substitute a tax on the dividend at the shareholder level for the PHC tax at the corporate level. The distributing corporation's shareholders must include the deficiency dividend in their gross income in the tax year in which it is received, not the tax year for which the PHC claims a dividends-paid deduction. Payment of a deficiency dividend does not relieve the PHC from liability for interest and penalties relating to the PHC tax.

TAX STRATEGY TIP

A deficiency dividend can be beneficial if a corporation fails to eliminate its UPHCI, either under the erroneous assumption that it was not a PHC or due to a miscalculation of its UPHCI. If certain requirements are satisfied, a deficiency dividend can be retroactively paid and thus be deductible from UPHCI earned in a previous year.

---

[49] Secs. 561(a) and 562(a).
[50] Sec. 562(c).
[51] Sec. 563(b).

[52] Sec. 565.
[53] Sec. 561(a)(3).
[54] Sec. 562(b).

To claim a dividends-paid deduction for a deficiency dividend, a PHC must meet the following requirements:

▶ Obtain a determination (e.g., judicial decision or agreement entered into by the taxpayer with the IRS) that establishes the amount of the PHC tax liability.

▶ Pay a dividend within 90 days after this determination.

▶ File a claim for a dividends-paid deduction within 120 days of the determination date.[55]

EXAMPLE C5-18 ▶ On its current year return, Boston Corporation characterizes a $200,000 distribution received pursuant to a stock redemption as a capital gain. Upon audit, the IRS and Boston agree that the distribution should be recharacterized as a dividend and that Boston is liable for the PHC tax. Boston can extinguish its PHC tax liability if it pays a deficiency dividend within 90 days after signing the agreement and if Boston files a timely claim. ◀

PHC TAX CALCULATION

The following example illustrates how UPHCI is calculated and how a corporation's regular tax and PHC tax liabilities are determined.

EXAMPLE C5-19 ▶ Marlo Corporation is deemed to be a PHC for 2006, and reports $226,000 of taxable income on its federal income tax return as follows:

Operating profit	$100,000
Long-term capital gain	60,000
Short-term capital gain	30,000
Dividends (20%-owned corporation)	200,000
Interest	100,000
Gross income	$490,000
Salaries	(40,000)
General and administrative expenses	(20,000)
Charitable contributions	(43,000)[a]
Dividends-received deduction	(160,000)
U.S. production activities deduction	(1,000)
Taxable income	$226,000

[a] $43,000 limit = 0.10 × ($490,000 − $40,000 − $20,000).

Ignoring any AMT liability, Marlo determines its federal income tax liability to be $71,390 [$22,250 + (0.39 × $126,000)]. Marlo made actual charitable contributions of $60,000 in the current year and paid $50,000 in dividends in August.

Marlo's PHC tax liability is calculated as follows:

Taxable income			$226,000
Plus:	Dividends-received deduction		160,000
Minus:	Excess charitable contributions		(17,000)[b]
	Federal income taxes		(71,390)
	Dividends-paid deduction		(50,000)
	Long-term capital gain	$60,000	
	Minus: Federal income taxes	(23,400)[c]	
	LTCG adjustment		(36,600)
Undistributed personal holding company income			$211,010
Times: Tax rate			× 0.15
Personal holding company tax			$ 31,652

[b] $60,000 total contributions − $43,000 limitation = $17,000 excess contributions.
[c] Because Marlo is in the 39% tax bracket with and without the LTCG, it can calculate the applicable federal income tax as 0.39 × $60,000 = $23,400.

[55] Secs. 547(c) through (e).

Marlo's total federal tax liability is $103,042 ($71,390 + $31,652). Marlo can avoid the $31,652 PHC tax by timely paying a deficiency dividend of $211,010, which equals the amount of UPHCI in 2006. ◀

Topic Review C5-3 presents an overview of the personal holding company tax.

ACCUMULATED EARNINGS TAX

ADDITIONAL COMMENT

The accumulated earnings tax is a penalty imposed on corporations that accumulate unreasonable amounts of earnings for the purpose of avoiding shareholder-level taxes. When corporate tax rates are lower than individual rates, tax incentives exist for accumulating earnings inside a corporation. These opportunities should lead to the IRS imposing the accumulated earnings tax.

Corporations not subject to the personal holding company tax may be subject to the accumulated earnings tax. The **accumulated earnings tax** attempts "to compel the company to distribute any profits not needed for the conduct of its business so that, when so distributed, individual stockholders will become liable" for taxes on the dividends received.[56] Unlike its name, the tax is not levied on the corporation's total accumulated earnings balance but only on its current year addition to the balance. In other words, the tax is levied on current earnings that are not needed for a reasonable business purpose, for example, excessive earnings invested by a corporation in short-term securities rather than distributed to shareholders as dividends. Note, however, that the 15% maximum tax rate on dividends through 2008 reduces the negative effect of double taxation.

CORPORATIONS SUBJECT TO THE PENALTY TAX

Section 532(a) states that the accumulated earnings tax applies "to every corporation . . . formed or availed of for the purpose of avoiding the income tax with respect to its shareholders . . . by permitting earnings and profits to accumulate instead of being divided or distributed." Three corporate forms are excluded from the accumulated earnings tax:

► Domestic and foreign personal holding companies

► Corporations exempt from tax under Secs. 501-505

► S corporations[57]

Topic Review C5-3

Personal Holding Company (PHC) Tax

1. The PHC tax applies only to corporations deemed to be PHCs. A PHC has (1) five or fewer individual shareholders owning more than 50% in value of the corporation's stock at any time during the last half of the tax year and (2) PHCI that is at least 60% of its adjusted ordinary gross income for the tax year.
2. Two special exceptions to the PHC test may apply. First, certain types of corporations (e.g., S corporations) are excluded from the tax. Second, certain categories of income (e.g., rents and active business computer software royalties) are excluded if conditions relating to percentage of income, maximum level of other PHC income, and minimum level of business expenses are satisfied. Table C5-2 on page C5-19 summarizes the excludable categories of income and related requirements.
3. The PHC tax equals 15% (in 2003–2008) times UPHCI. UPHCI equals taxable income plus certain positive adjustments (e.g., dividends-received deduction) and minus certain negative adjustments (e.g., federal income taxes, excess charitable contributions, and net capital gain reduced by federal income taxes attributable to the gain).
4. UPHCI can be reduced by a dividends-paid deduction claimed for cash and property dividends paid during the tax year, as well as consent and throwback dividends distributed after year-end.
5. A PHC tax liability (but not liability for related interest and penalties) can be eliminated through payment of a deficiency dividend. The deficiency dividend provisions effectively substitute an income tax levy at the shareholder level for the corporate-level PHC tax.

---

[56] *Helvering v. Chicago Stock Yards Co.*, 30 AFTR 1091, 43-1 USTC ¶9379 (USSC, 1943).

[57] Secs. 532(b) and 1363(a).

WHAT WOULD YOU DO IN THIS SITUATION?

In 2005, shareholders formed Taylor Corporation by contributing $1 million of capital to the corporation on July 1 of that year. Because of delays in obtaining manufacturing equipment, the corporation did not begin business until January 2006. During the last six months of 2005, the corporation earned $50,000 of taxable interest income and incurred $20,000 of deductible expenses. A second-year accountant in a small accounting firm was assigned to prepare the Taylor corporate tax return. All of his previous tax return assignments were for individual tax returns. The senior accountant responsible for the assignment told the second-year accountant that the return "would be simple and that all you need to do is input the interest income and expense information into the Form 1120 software." Because of the rush to finish and deliver the return to the client by March 15, no one in the office noticed during the review process that the corporation might be a personal holding company (PHC) in 2005. The corporation filed its return on March 15 without paying any PHC tax. Another Taylor corporate matter arose in August 2006 and was assigned to you. When you examined the return with respect to the new issue, you asked yourself, "Does Taylor have a PHC tax problem?" If so, what can Taylor and/or you now do regarding the problem?

Theoretically, the accumulated earnings tax applies to both large and small corporations.[58] In practice, however, the accumulated earnings tax applies primarily to closely held corporations where management can devise a corporate dividend policy to reduce the tax liability of the shareholder group.

Determine whether a corporation is liable for the accumulated earnings tax

PROVING A TAX-AVOIDANCE PURPOSE

Section 533(a) provides that the accumulation of E&P by a corporation beyond the reasonable needs of the business indicates a tax-avoidance purpose unless the corporation can prove that it is not accumulating the earnings merely to avoid taxes. In limited circumstances, this burden of proof may be shifted to the IRS under rules set forth in Sec. 534.

The existence of a tax-avoidance purpose may be inferred from all pertinent facts and circumstances. Regulation Sec. 1.533-1(a)(2) lists the following specific circumstances that suggest a tax-avoidance purpose:

▶ Dealings between the corporation and its shareholders (e.g., loans made by the corporation to its shareholders or funds expended by the corporation for the shareholders' personal benefit).

▶ Investments of undistributed earnings in assets having no reasonable connection to the corporation's business.

▶ The extent to which the corporation has distributed its E&P (e.g., a low dividend payout rate, low salaries, and substantial earnings accumulation may indicate a tax-avoidance purpose).

Holding or investment companies are held to a standard different from that which applies to operating companies. Section 533(b) provides that holding or investment company status is prima facie evidence of a tax-avoidance purpose.[59] A holding company, like an operating company, can rebut this presumption by showing that it was neither formed nor availed of to avoid shareholder income taxes.

A tax-avoidance purpose may be only one of several reasons for the corporation's accumulation of earnings. In *U.S. v. The Donruss Company*, the Supreme Court held that tax avoidance does not have to be the dominant motive for the accumulation of earnings, leading to imposition of the accumulated earnings tax. According to the court, for a tax

TAX STRATEGY TIP

When the IRS determines that the accumulation of earnings is unreasonable, it presumes that its determination is correct. To rebut this presumption, the taxpayer must show by a preponderance of the evidence that the IRS's determination is improper. Thus, periodic updating of the plans to use corporate earnings should be undertaken to reduce accumulated earnings tax problems.

---

[58] Sec. 532(c). See, however, *Technalysis Corporation v. CIR* [101 T.C. 397 (1993)] where the Tax Court held that the accumulated earnings tax can be imposed on a publicly held corporation regardless of the concentration of ownership or whether the shareholders are actively involved in corporate operations.

[59] Regulation Sec. 1.533-1(c) defines a holding or investment company as "a corporation having no activities except holding property and collecting income therefrom or investing therein."

avoidance purpose to exist, the corporation must know about the tax consequences of accumulating earnings.[60] Such knowledge need not be the dominant motive or purpose for the accumulation of the earnings.

EVIDENCE CONCERNING THE REASONABLENESS OF AN EARNINGS ACCUMULATION

The courts have not specified any single factor that indicates an unreasonable level of accumulated earnings. Instead, they have alluded to several factors that suggest a tax-avoidance motive. The IRS and the courts have cited other factors that indicate reasonable business needs for the legitimate accumulation of earnings and profits.

EVIDENCE OF A TAX-AVOIDANCE MOTIVE.   A corporation that wants to avoid liability for the accumulated earnings tax should act defensively. Such liability can be minimized by avoiding or restricting engagement in the following transactions:

▶ Loans to shareholders

▶ Corporate expenditures for the personal benefit of shareholders

▶ Loans having no reasonable relation to the conduct of business (e.g., loans to relatives or friends of shareholders)

▶ Loans to a corporation controlled by the same shareholders that control the corporation making the loans

▶ Investments in property or securities unrelated to the activities of the corporation

▶ Insuring against unrealistic hazards[61]

Loans to shareholders or corporate expenditures for the personal benefit of shareholders are viewed as as substitutes for dividend payments to shareholders. Similarly, corporate loans made to relatives or friends of shareholders are viewed as substitutes for dividend payments to shareholders, who then make personal loans to their friends and relatives. All three measures suggest an unreasonable accumulation of corporate earnings, which should have been distributed as dividends.

Likewise, loans or corporate expenditures made for the benefit of a second corporation controlled by the shareholder (or the shareholder group) who also controls the first corporation may be considered to have a tax-avoidance purpose. Theoretically, the first corporation instead could have paid a dividend to the shareholder who in turn could have paid income taxes on the dividend and then contributed after-tax funds to the second corporation.

Another factor indicative of a tax-avoidance motive, but not mentioned in Treasury Regulations, is operating a corporation as a holding or investment company that pays little or no dividends.

TYPICAL MISCONCEPTION

The IRC refers to the existence of a tax-avoidance purpose, which would appear to involve a subjective test. However, the existence of the tax-avoidance purpose really hinges on the objective determination of whether a corporation has accumulated earnings beyond the reasonable needs of the business.

 STOP & THINK

Question: In 2006, an IRS auditor examines Baylor Corporation's 2003 C corporation tax return. What items might the auditor scrutinize to assertain the existence of excess accumulated earnings?

Solution: The auditor might look first at the retained earnings accounts in the beginning and year-end balance sheets (Schedule L, Page 4 of Form 1120). Then, the auditor might review Schedule M-2 (Analysis of Unappropriated Retained Earnings per Books) for current year earnings, the amount of earnings distributed as dividends, and the manner in which the corporation used undistributed earnings during the year. Next, the auditor might examine the beginning and year-end balance sheets for evidence of transactions suggesting a tax-avoidance motive. Such transactions might include loans to stockholders (Schedule L, Line 7), loans to persons other than stockholders (Schedule L, Line 6), and

---

[60] *U.S. v. The Donruss Company,* 23 AFTR 2d 69-418, 69-1 USTC ¶9167 (USSC, 1969).   [61] Reg. Sec. 1.537-2(c).

portfolio investments (Schedule L, Lines 4, 5, 6, and 9). Information about expenditures of corporate funds made for the personal benefit of shareholders might be found in the noncurrent asset section of the balance sheets (e.g., corporate ownership of a boat, airplane, or second home of a major stockholder).

REASONABLE BUSINESS NEEDS.   Section 537 defines **reasonable business needs** as

▶ Reasonably anticipated needs of the business

▶ Section 303 (death tax) redemption needs

▶ Excess business holdings redemption needs

▶ Product liability loss reserves

Regulation Sec. 1.537-1(a) sets forth the following relevant standard of reasonableness:

An accumulation of the earnings and profits . . . is in excess of reasonable needs of the business if it exceeds the amount that a prudent businessman would consider appropriate for the present business purposes and for the reasonably anticipated future needs of the business. The need to retain earnings and profits must be directly connected with the needs of the corporation itself and must be for bona fide business purposes.

Specific, Definite, and Feasible Plans.   A corporation's accumulation of earnings is justified only if facts and circumstances indicate that the future needs of the business require such an accumulation. The corporation usually must have specific, definite, and feasible plans for the use of the accumulation.

No Specific Time Limitations.   The earnings accumulation need not be used within a short period of time after the close of the tax year. However, the plans must provide that, based on all the facts and circumstances associated with the future needs of the business, the corporation will use the accumulation within a reasonable period of time after the close of the tax year.

Impact of Subsequent Events.   Determination of the reasonably anticipated needs of the business is based on all relevant facts and circumstances that exist at the end of the tax year. Regulation Sec. 1.537-1(b)(2) provides that subsequent events may not be used to show that an earnings accumulation is unreasonable if all the elements of reasonable anticipation are present at the close of the tax year. However, subsequent events may be used to ascertain whether the taxpayer actually intended to consummate the plans for which the earnings were accumulated.

Treasury Regulations and the courts have cited as determinative or relevant a number of factors that represent reasonable needs of the business for accumulating earnings. These factors include:

▶ Expansion of a business or replacement of plant

▶ Acquisition of a business enterprise

▶ Debt retirement

▶ Working capital

▶ Loans to suppliers or customers

▶ Product liability losses

▶ Stock redemptions

▶ Business contingencies

Expansion of a Business or Replacement of Plant.   The IRS and the courts generally have viewed the expansion of a corporation's present business facilities or the replacement of existing plant and equipment as involving a reasonable need of a business. Taxpayers have encountered problems only when the plans are undocumented, indefinite, vague, or unfeasible.[62] Although the plans need not be reduced to writing, adequate documentation is advisable.

Acquisition of a Business Enterprise. The acquisition of a business enterprise might involve extension of the same business or expansion into a new business through the purchase of either the stock or the assets of a corporation conducting the new business. Taxpayers should be careful to acquire a sufficient interest in the new business so that it will not be considered a passive investment.

Working Capital: The Bardahl Formula. Working capital is defined generally as the excess of current assets over current liabilities. The *Bardahl* formula attempts to measure the amount of working capital necessary for an operating cycle. The operating cycle encompasses a period of time necessary for the corporation to acquire inventory, sell the inventory, generate accounts receivable, and collect on the accounts receivable. Working capital required for one operating cycle is considered a reasonable need of a business. Accordingly, accumulated earnings sufficient to finance such working capital is considered reasonable.

At one time, the courts used certain rules of thumb (e.g., a current ratio of 2 to 1 or 3 to 1 or the accumulation of funds to cover a single year's operating expenses) to establish adequate working capital. Later, in the first of two *Bardahl* cases, the Tax Court endorsed a mathematical formula for measuring an operating cycle. This formula is now used to ascertain the amount of working capital required for the reasonable needs of the business.

The working capital needs of a manufacturing business differ from those of a service business. For a manufacturing business, an operating cycle is the "period of time required to convert cash into raw materials, raw materials into an inventory of marketable . . . products, the inventory into sales and accounts receivable, and the period of time to collect its outstanding accounts."[63]

In the second *Bardahl* case, the Tax Court ruled that amounts advanced to a corporation by its suppliers in the form of short-term credit (e.g., trade payables) reduce the required amount of working capital.[64] Based on this ruling, the ***Bardahl* formula** for determining average operating cycle has become

$$
\begin{array}{c} \text{Average} \\ \text{operating} \\ \text{cycle} \end{array} = \begin{array}{c} \text{Inventory} \\ \text{period} \end{array} + \begin{array}{c} \text{Accounts} \\ \text{receivable} \\ \text{period} \end{array} - \begin{array}{c} \text{Credit} \\ \text{period} \end{array}
$$

In this formula, the *inventory period* is the time (expressed as a percentage of a year) spanning the acquisition of raw materials inventory to the sale of finished goods inventory. The *accounts receivable period* is the time (expressed as a percentage of a year) spanning the sale date to the date on which accounts receivable are collected. The *credit period* is the time (expressed as a percentage of a year) from when the corporation incurs an expense or purchases inventory to the time when it pays the liability.

The *Bardahl* formula can be expanded to include financial and operating data as follows:

$$
\begin{array}{c} \text{Average operating cycle} \\ \text{(as a percentage of a year)} \end{array} = \\[1em] \left[\frac{\text{Inventory amount}}{\text{Annual cost of goods sold}} + \frac{\text{Accounts receivable amount}}{\text{Annual sales}} - \frac{\text{Accounts payable amount}}{\begin{array}{c}\text{Annual operating} \\ \text{expenses and purchases} \\ \text{(less noncash expenses)}\end{array}} \right] \times 100
$$

---

[62] See, for example, *Myron's Enterprises v. U.S.*, 39 AFTR 2d 77-693, 77-1 USTC ¶9253 (9th Cir., 1977) and *Atlas Tool Co., Inc. v. CIR*, 45 AFTR 2d 80-645, 80-1 USTC ¶9177 (3rd Cir., 1980).

[63] *Bardahl Manufacturing Corp.*, 1965 PH T.C. Memo ¶65,200, 24 TCM 1030, at 1044.

[64] *Bardahl International Corp.*, 1966 PH T.C. Memo ¶66,182, 25 TCM 935.

This formula is linked to the working capital requirements of the business in the following equation:

$$\text{Average operating cycle (as a percentage of a year)} \times \left[\text{Cost of goods sold} + \text{Operating expenses} \right] = \text{Working capital requirements}$$

Cost of goods sold is determined on a full-cost basis (i.e., including both direct and indirect expenses). Operating expenses exclude noncash expenses such as depreciation, amortization, and depletion, as well as capital expenditures and charitable contributions. The Tax Court has allowed federal income taxes (e.g., quarterly estimated tax payments) to be included as an operating expense.[65]

The working capital requirements for one operating cycle are compared with actual working capital employed at year-end. If the working capital requirements exceed actual working capital, the excess, along with amounts required for specific needs of the business, are deemed to justify accumulating a portion of the corporation's earnings. If the working capital requirements are less than the corporation's actual working capital, the excess generally is deemed to reflect an unreasonable accumulation unless the corporation can somehow justify the excess (e.g., for plant replacement).

In establishing "adequate" working capital, the *Bardahl* formula may provide a false sense of mathematical precision because the IRS and the courts have interpreted it differently. Some courts have used peak month inventory, accounts receivable, and trade payables turnover (instead of an annual average) to measure an operating cycle.[66] Relative to the annual average method, the peak month method generally lengthens the corporation's operating cycle. Use of these two methods can lead to very different estimates of working capital requirements. As a result, significant disputes have arisen between the IRS and taxpayers over what constitutes "adequate" working capital.

TYPICAL MISCONCEPTION

No exact method exists for determining the working capital needs of a corporation. The *Bardahl* formula is merely a rule of thumb adopted by the Tax Court. The basic approaches (peak cycle approach versus the average cycle approach) sanctioned by the *Bardahl* formula are subject to dispute among the courts.

EXAMPLE C5-20 ▶

Austin Corporation's managers believe that Austin may be liable for the accumulated earnings tax. They ask their tax advisor to determine the corporation's working capital requirement on December 31 of the current year under the *Bardahl* formula. The following information from Austin's records for the current year is available:

Cost of goods sold	$2,700,000
Average inventory	675,000
Purchases	3,000,000
Sales (all on account)	6,000,000
Average accounts receivable	750,000
Operating expenses (including depreciation and other noncash charges)	875,000
Depreciation and other noncash charges	75,000
Average trade payables	350,000
Estimated federal income tax payments	100,000
Working capital on December 31	825,000

The operating cycle based on the annual average method is calculated as follows (assuming a nonleap year):

$$\text{Inventory turnover} = (\$675,000 \div \$2,700,000) \times 365 = 91.25 \text{ days}$$
$$\text{Receivables turnover} = (\$750,000 \div \$6,000,000) \times 365 = 45.625 \text{ days}$$
$$\text{Payables turnover} = \frac{\$350,000}{\$3,000,000 + \$800,000} \times 365 = 33.62 \text{ days}$$
$$\text{Operating cycle} = \frac{91.25 + 45.625 - 33.62}{365} \times 100 = 28.3\% \text{ of a year}$$

[65] *Doug-Long, Inc.,* 72 T.C. 158 (1979).
[66] *State Office Supply, Inc.,* 1982 PH T.C. Memo ¶82,292, 43 TCM 1481.

Based on this operating cycle, the tax advisor estimates Austin's working capital requirement as follows:

Annual operating expenses = $2,700,000 + $875,000 − $75,000 + $100,000 = $3,600,000
Working capital requirement = $3,600,000 × 0.283 = $1,018,800

The estimated $1,018,800 working capital requirement is $193,800 more than the $825,000 of actual working capital recorded on December 31. This excess justifies accumulating additional current earnings for working capital needs. ◄

The *Bardahl* formula also is used to estimate the working capital requirements of service companies. A different calculation is used because service companies generally hold little inventory. For service companies, one looks primarily at the financing of accounts receivables. Because their principal asset is key personnel, these companies must maintain adequate working capital to retain employees when a below-normal level of business is expected. Therefore, some amount may be added to actual working capital to cover the cost of retaining personnel for a period of time.[67]

Stock Redemptions. Section 537(a) permits corporations to accumulate earnings for two types of stock redemptions: Sec. 303 (death tax) redemptions and excess business holdings redemptions. In the first situation, a corporation can accumulate earnings after the death of a shareholder to redeem stock from the shareholder's estate or a beneficiary of the estate. These earnings cannot exceed the amount of stock redeemable under Sec. 303. In the second situation, a corporation can accumulate earnings to redeem stock held by a private foundation to the extent the stock exceeds the business holdings limit imposed on such foundations.

Business Contingencies. The courts and IRS have sanctioned the accumulation of earnings for business contingencies not specifically mentioned in the Sec. 537 Treasury Regulations. Among these contingencies are actual or potential litigation, a decline in business activities following the loss of a major customer, reserve for self-insurance against a particular loss, a threatened strike, and an employee retirement plan.

CALCULATING THE ACCUMULATED EARNINGS TAX

The accumulated earnings tax calculation is set forth in Figure C5-3. The tax is levied at a 15% rate in 2003 through 2008. After 2008, the rate will revert to the highest marginal tax rate for individuals. As with the PHC penalty tax, a corporation can reduce its tax liability by making dividend distributions. However, corporations generally do not avail themselves of this tax planning strategy because they often pay only a nominal dividend or no dividend at all. Also, IRS auditors generally do not raise the accumulated earnings tax issue until one or more years after the corporation has filed its tax return. Unlike the PHC tax liability, the accumulated earnings tax liability cannot be extinguished through the payment of deficiency dividends.

ACCUMULATED TAXABLE INCOME. The starting point for calculating **accumulated taxable income** is the corporation's regular taxable income. A series of positive and negative adjustments to regular taxable income are made to derive accumulated taxable income.

Positive Adjustments to Regular Taxable Income. A corporation may not claim a dividends-received deduction. Thus, regular taxable income must be increased by the amount of this deduction. This adjustment is similar to one under the PHC tax rules.[68] The U.S. production activities deduction, however, is not added back to regular taxable

---

---

[67] See, for example, *Simons-Eastern Co. v. U.S.*, 31 AFTR 2d 73-640, 73-1 USTC ¶9279 (D.C. GA, 1972).   [68] Sec. 535(b).

▼ FIGURE C5-3
Calculating the Accumulated Earnings Tax

Regular taxable income
Plus: Positive adjustments
        1. Dividends-received deduction
        2. NOL deduction
        3. Excess charitable contributions carried over from a preceding tax year and
           deducted in determining taxable income
        4. Capital loss carryover deduction
Minus: Negative adjustments
        1. Accrued U.S. and foreign income taxes
        2. Charitable contributions that exceed the 10% corporate limitation
        3. Net capital losses (where capital losses for the year exceed capital gains)
        4. Net capital gain minus the amount of any income taxes attributable to it
Minus: Dividends-paid deduction
Minus: Accumulated earnings credit

Accumulated taxable income
Times: 0.15 (in 2003–2008)

Accumulated earnings tax

income. Any NOL deduction claimed must be added back to regular taxable income. The IRC, however, allows no special deduction for an NOL incurred in the immediately preceding year, as it does under the PHC tax rules.

Negative Adjustments to Taxable Income. Charitable contributions are deductible without regard to either the 10% corporate limitation or the individual charitable contribution limitations. The same adjustments required for PHC tax purposes are required for accumulated earnings tax purposes.

U.S. and foreign income taxes accrued by the corporation reduce accumulated taxable income whether the corporation uses the accrual or cash method of accounting. A corporation may deduct the amount of its net capital gain, minus income taxes attributable to this gain. The capital gains adjustment prevents a corporation with substantial capital gains from paying the accumulated earnings tax on that portion of the gains retained in the business. Net capital losses (the excess of capital losses for the year over capital gains) represent a negative adjustment to regular taxable income.

WHAT WOULD YOU DO IN THIS SITUATION?

Magnum Corporation, your client, has manufactured handguns and rifles for years. Due to competition from foreign manufacturers, demand for U.S. manufactured guns has recently declined. The total historical cost of Magnum's operating assets at the end of its most recent fiscal year is $10 million. Total gross operating revenues are $18 million. Over the years, the company accumulated $2.5 million of earnings that Magnum's CEO Allen Blay invested in securities. The investment portfolio consists primarily of growth stocks, debt instruments, and Internet stocks. Along with his other duties as CEO, Allen manages this portfolio. With the recent surge in the stock market, Magnum's investment securities have performed well and have increased in value to more than $12 million. The portfolio took a small "hit" in Fall 2005. The dividend and interest income earned on the portfolio represents only a small portion of Magnum's gross income. During a meeting with you, Allen brings to your attention this investment and its stellar performance. Is Magnum liable for the accumulated earnings tax? What action(s) do you recommend that the corporation take?

Dividends-Paid Deduction. A deduction is allowed for four types of dividends paid:

► Regular dividends
► Throwback dividends
► Consent dividends
► Liquidating distributions

With minor exceptions, the rules for the dividends-paid deduction are the same in the PHC tax calculation as in the regular tax calculation. Nonliquidating distributions paid during the tax year are eligible for the dividends-paid deduction only if paid out of the corporation's E&P. A dividends-paid deduction is not available for preferential dividends.[69]

Throwback dividends are distributions made out of E&P in the first 2½ months following the close of the tax year. The accumulated earnings tax rules require that any distribution made in the first 2½ months following the close of the tax year be treated as if paid on the last day of the preceding tax year without regard to the amount of dividends actually paid during the preceding tax year.[70] Because the IRS generally does not raise the accumulated earnings tax issue until after it has audited a corporation's tax return, throwback and consent dividends are of limited use in avoiding the accumulated earnings tax. Liquidating distributions eligible for the dividends-paid deduction include those made in connection with a complete liquidation, a partial liquidation, or a stock redemption.[71]

Accumulated Earnings Credit. The accumulated earnings credit permits a corporation to accumulate E&P either up to a minimum amount ($250,000 for most C corporations) or up to the level of its earnings accumulated for the reasonable needs of the business. Unlike other credits, the **accumulated earnings credit** does not offset the accumulated earnings tax liability on a dollar-for-dollar basis. Instead, it serves to reduce accumulated taxable income. Different rules for the accumulated earnings credit exist for operating companies, service companies, and holding or investment companies.[72]

► Operating companies can claim a credit equal to the greater of (1) $250,000 minus accumulated E&P at the end of the preceding tax year[73] or (2) current E&P retained to meet the reasonable needs of the business.

► The accumulated E&P balance mentioned in the previous bullet point is reduced by the amount of any current year throwback distributions treated as having been made out of the preceding year's E&P.

► Current E&P is reduced by the dividends-paid deduction. Any net capital gains (reduced by federal taxes attributable to the gain) reduce the amount of current E&P retained for business needs.

► Special rules apply to personal service companies operating primary in the fields of health, law, engineering, architecture, accounting, actuarial science, performing arts, and consulting. For these companies, the basic calculation set forth above applies, but the $250,000 minimum credit is reduced to $150,000.

► Holding and investment companies may claim a credit equal to $250,000 minus accumulated E&P at the end of the preceding tax year. An increased credit based on the reasonable needs of the business is not available to a holding or investment company.

EXAMPLE C5-21 ► Midway Corporation reports accumulated E&P, current E&P, and current E&P retained for business needs as shown in the table below. The corporation paid no dividends during the current year. Midway is a C corporation that is not a personal service or investment company. Its minimum credit is $250,000.

ADDITIONAL COMMENT

The minimum accumulated earnings credit is $250,000 ($150,000 for certain personal service corporations) reduced by accumulated E&P at the close of the preceding year. In many situations, corporations that have been in existence for some time have accumulated E&P exceeding $250,000. Thus, the minimum credit is of little practical significance for them.

TYPICAL MISCONCEPTION

The maximum accumulated earnings credit is the amount of current E&P retained to meet the reasonable needs of the business minus an adjustment for net capital gains. This amount does not include the entire accumulation for business needs but only the accumulation in the current tax year. Thus, to calculate the maximum credit, it is necessary to determine how much of prior accumulations are retained for reasonable business needs.

---

[69] Sec. 562(c). See page C5-23 for a more detailed discussion.
[70] Sec. 563(a). Personal holding companies, on the other hand, must elect throwback treatment for dividends paid in the 2½ month period following the end of the tax year.

[71] Sec. 562(b)(1)(B).
[72] Sec. 535(c).
[73] Section 1561(a)(2) limits a controlled group of corporations to a single statutory exemption.

Tax Items	Scenario Number	
	One	Two
1. Accumulated E&P	$ 75,000	$ 75,000
2. Lifetime minimum credit	250,000	250,000
2a. Current year minimum credit (2a = 2 − 1)	175,000	175,000
3. Current E&P	400,000	400,000
3a. Current E&P retained for business needs	300,000	50,000
3b. Current E&P exceeding business needs (3b = 3 − 3a)	100,000	350,000
4. Accumulated earnings credit (Greater of 2a or 3a)	300,000	175,000

In both scenarios, $175,000 of the minimum credit is available. In Scenario One, because the available $175,000 minimum credit is less than $300,000 of E&P retained for business needs, the accumulated earnings credit is $300,000. In Scenario Two, because the available $175,000 minimum credit is greater than the $50,000 of E&P retained for business needs, the accumulated earnings credit is $175,000. In both scenarios, no minimum credit is available in future years. All future accumulated earnings credits are based on E&P retained for business needs. ◀

COMPREHENSIVE EXAMPLE

The following example illustrates the calculation of accumulated taxable income and the accumulated earnings tax liability.

EXAMPLE C5-22 ▶ Pasadena is a closely held family corporation that has conducted a successful manufacturing business for several years. On January 1 of the current year, Pasadena reports a $750,000 accumulated E&P balance. The following information pertains to current year operations:

Operating profit	$650,000
Long-term capital gain	30,000
Dividends received from a 20%-owned corporation	150,000
Interest	70,000
Gross income	$900,000
Dividends-received deduction	(120,000)
Salaries	(100,000)
General and administrative expenses	(200,000)
Charitable contributions	(60,000)[a]
U.S. production activities deduction	(10,000)
Regular taxable income	$410,000

[a] $60,000 = 0.10 × [$900,000 − ($100,000 + $200,000)].

Federal income taxes (based on current rates and assuming no alternative minimum tax liability) accrued by Pasadena are $139,400. Actual charitable contributions are $75,000. On June 30, the corporation paid cash dividends of $20,000. Pasadena's current E&P retained for the reasonable needs of the business (after the dividends-paid deduction) is $160,000.

If the IRS determines that Pasadena has accumulated earnings exceeding the reasonable needs of its business, Pasadena's accumulated earnings tax liability would be calculated as follows:

Regular taxable income			$410,000
Plus:	Dividends-received deduction		120,000
Minus:	Excess charitable contributions		(15,000)[a]
	Federal income taxes		(139,400)
	Long-term capital gain	$ 30,000	
	Minus: Federal income taxes	(10,200)[b]	(19,800)
	Dividends-paid deduction		(20,000)
	Accumulated earnings credit:		
	Increase in current year reasonable needs	$160,000	
	Minus: Long-term capital gain (net of taxes)	(19,800)	(140,200)

Accumulated taxable income	$195,600
Times: Tax rate	× 0.15
Accumulated earnings tax liability	$ 29,340

[a] $75,000 total contributions − $60,000 limitation = $15,000 excess contributions.
[b] $10,200 = $30,000 × 0.34

Assuming the corporation owes no AMT liability, Pasadena's total federal tax liability for the current year would be $168,740 ($139,400 + $29,340). ◀

Topic Review C5-4 presents an overview of the accumulated earnings tax.

TAX PLANNING CONSIDERATIONS

This section examines three areas of tax planning: special accounting method elections for AMT purposes, avoiding the PHC tax, and avoiding the accumulated earnings tax.

SPECIAL AMT ELECTIONS

ADDITIONAL COMMENT

Not only can special AMT elections reduce a taxpayer's AMT liability, but they also can reduce compliance costs by eliminating the need to keep an additional set of depreciation or amortization records.

Under the AMT rules, two special elections permit taxpayers to defer certain deductions for regular tax purposes. Although deferral of these deductions will increase the taxpayer's regular tax liability, it will decrease the taxpayer's AMT liability.

Section 59(e) permits an extended writeoff period for certain expenditures that otherwise would be tax preference items or AMT adjustments. If the corporation so elects, each expenditure to which the extended writeoff period applies will not be a Sec. 57 tax preference item, nor will the corporation have to make an adjustment for the expenditure under Sec. 56. The expenditures for which the special election can be made and the extended writeoff periods that apply are as follows:

Topic Review C5-4

Accumulated Earnings Tax

1. The accumulated earnings tax rules apply to all but certain types of corporations. As a practical matter, the tax is assessed primarily on closely held corporations (other than S corporations).
2. Transactions that suggest a tax avoidance motive generally lead IRS auditors to believe that an accumulated earnings tax problem exists. These transactions include loans made by the corporation to its shareholders, the expenditure of corporate funds for the personal benefit of shareholders, and investments in property or securities unrelated to the corporation's principal activities.
3. Earnings accumulated for the reasonable needs of the business are exempt from the accumulated earnings tax. Such needs relate to acquisition of a business enterprise, debt retirement, and the build up of working capital. A $250,000 minimum credit is available to reduce accumulated taxable income. The credit amount declines to $150,000 for certain personal service corporations.
4. The accumulated earnings tax is 15% (in 2003–2008) of accumulated taxable income. Accumulated taxable income is regular taxable income plus certain positive adjustments (e.g., dividends-received deduction) and minus certain negative adjustments (e.g., federal income taxes, excess charitable contributions, and a portion of net capital gains). An accumulated earnings credit equal to the greater of a fixed dollar amount or earnings accumulated during the year for the reasonable needs of the business also is available.
5. Accumulated taxable income can be reduced by cash and property dividends paid during the year as well as consent and throwback dividends paid after the year ends. Deficiency dividends, while available for PHC tax purposes, are not available for accumulated earnings tax purposes.

IRC Section	Type of Expenditure	Writeoff Period (Years)
173	Circulation	3
174	Research and experimental	10
263	Intangible drilling and development	5
616	Mining and natural resource development	10
617	Mining exploration	10

A corporation can make a special election regarding any portion of a qualified expenditure and can revoke it only with IRS consent.[74]

The second election permits taxpayers to elect to use the depreciation method generally required for AMT purposes in computing their regular tax liability. Such an election permits the taxpayer to change the depreciation method for personal property placed in service after 1998 from the 200% declining balance method normally used for regular tax purposes to the 150% declining balance method as used for AMT purposes. The election is not relevant for nonresidential real property or residential rental property because, for such property placed in service after 1998, AMT depreciation is the same as regular tax depreciation. By making this election, the taxpayer reduces or eliminates the amount of annual AMT depreciation and basis adjustments. For any tax year, the taxpayer may make this election with respect to one or more classes of property. Once made, the election applies to all property in such class placed in service during the tax year. The taxpayer must make the election by the due date for its annual return (including any permissible extensions).[75]

ELIMINATING THE ACE ADJUSTMENT

C corporations must increase their AMTI by the amount of the ACE adjustment. For some C corporations this adjustment can be substantial. If the corporation is closely held, it can elect to be taxed as an S corporation and thereby avoid the ACE adjustment.[76] S corporations are not subject to the corporate AMT. They pass their AMT adjustments and preference items through to their shareholders.

OBJECTIVE 6

Explain how a corporation can avoid the personal holding company tax

AVOIDING THE PERSONAL HOLDING COMPANY TAX

Five types of tax planning techniques can be used to avoid the PHC tax.

CHANGES IN THE CORPORATION'S STOCK OWNERSHIP. To circumvent the stock ownership rules, a potential PHC can issue additional stock to unrelated parties. The stock may be either common or preferred. The issuance of nonvoting preferred stock to unrelated parties permits the corporation to spread out stock ownership among a larger number of individuals without diluting the voting power of the current shareholder group.

CHANGING THE AMOUNT AND TYPE OF INCOME EARNED BY THE CORPORATION. A corporation can change the amount and type of its income in the following ways:

▶ Adding "operating" activities to its business to decrease the proportion of passive or investment income in its total income.

▶ Converting taxable interest or dividends earned on an investment portfolio into nontaxable interest or long-term capital gains. Nontaxable interest and long-term capital gains are excluded from PHCI.

▶ Generating passive income of a type that is excludible from PHCI or in an amount that diminishes the proportion of other items includible in PHCI. For example, a corporation might attempt to increase the proportion of its rental income to more than 50% of AOGI so as to exclude from PHCI adjusted income from rents.

[74] Secs. 59(e)(4)(A) and (B).
[75] Secs. 168(b)(2) and (5).
[76] Sec. 56(g)(6).

KEY POINT

One of the easiest ways to avoid the PHC penalty tax is a dividend distribution. If a corporation lacks the funds to pay a cash dividend, it can pay a consent dividend (which is a hypothetical dividend). In addition, throwback, consent, and deficiency dividends can be declared after year-end in after-the-fact tax planning.

DIVIDEND DISTRIBUTIONS. Dividend payments reduce the PHC tax base. A corporation can exclude certain categories of income (e.g., adjusted income from rents) from PHCI through the payment of dividends sufficient to reduce the amount of other PHCI to 10% or less of OGI. Some of these dividends (e.g., throwback, consent, and deficiency) can be paid after year-end, thereby allowing last-minute tax planning.

MAKING AN S CORPORATION ELECTION. As mentioned earlier, an S corporation election eliminates liability for the PHC tax because S corporations are exempt from this tax. The election also eliminates the double taxation of corporate earnings distributed as dividends (see Chapter C11). Such an election is advantageous where corporate tax rates exceed individual tax rates. The LLC form offers many of the same tax and nontax benefits offered by the S corporation form.

LIQUIDATING THE CORPORATION. A PHC could liquidate and distribute its assets to the shareholders. Liquidating distributions made out of E&P are eligible for the dividends-paid deduction and thus can reduce UPHCI. This alternative, however, may be unattractive where top individual tax rates exceed corporate tax rates.

OBJECTIVE 7

Explain how a corporation can avoid the accumulated earnings tax

AVOIDING THE ACCUMULATED EARNINGS TAX

The primary defense against an IRS argument that the corporation has accumulated an unreasonable amount of earnings is that the earnings accumulations are necessary to meet the future needs of the business. Business plans in support of this defense should be documented and revised periodically. The plans should describe completed, but not abandoned, projects in sufficient detail. In the event of an IRS challenge, a tentative timetable for the completion of current projects should be set forth. Such plans might be incorporated into the minutes of one or more board meetings.

Transactions suggesting an unreasonable earnings accumulation (e.g., loans to shareholders or large investment portfolios) should be avoided. The business purpose for major transactions should be thoroughly documented.

Corporations potentially liable for the accumulated earnings tax should consider making an S corporation election. S corporations avoid accumulated earnings tax liability on a prospective basis. By implication, an S corporation election will not eliminate potential exposure to the accumulated earnings tax for tax years prior to the year in which the election becomes effective.

COMPLIANCE AND PROCEDURAL CONSIDERATIONS

ALTERNATIVE MINIMUM TAX

A corporation reports the AMT calculation on Form 4626 (Alternative Minimum Tax—Corporations). A completed Form 4626, based on the facts in the comprehensive example on pages C5-13 and C5-14, appears in Appendix B.

Chapter C3 discussed the corporate estimated income tax. Section 6655(g) provides that the corporate AMT be included in the required estimated tax payments. Failure to do so will subject a corporation to underpayment penalties, which are discussed in Chapter C3.

ETHICAL POINT

A tax practitioner has a responsibility to advise his or her client early in the year about potential PHC problems and steps that can be taken to avoid the penalty tax. Because the PHC tax is self-assessed, a Schedule PH must be filed with Form 1120 even if the corporation owes no PHC tax.

PERSONAL HOLDING COMPANY TAX

FILING REQUIREMENTS FOR TAX RETURNS. A PHC must file a corporate income tax return (Form 1120). Schedule PH must accompany the return. Schedule PH incorporates the tests for determining whether a corporation is a PHC as well as the UPHCI and PHC tax calculations. Regulation Sec. 301.6501(f)-1 extends from three to six years the limitations period for the PHC tax if a PHC fails to file Schedule PH, even if the corporation owes no additional tax.

ETHICAL POINT

Notwithstanding the tax practitioner's responsibility to advise his or her client about potential accumulated earnings tax problems, because the tax is not self-assessed, the CPA or the client are under no duty to notify the IRS of the tax problem.

PAYMENT OF THE TAX, INTEREST, AND PENALTIES. Corporations ordinarily pay the PHC tax when they file Form 1120 and Schedule PH, or when the IRS or the courts determine that the corporation owes the tax. Unlike the AMT, the PHC tax is not included in the corporation's required estimated tax payments. Corporations that pay the PHC tax after the due date for filing their return (without regard to extensions) generally will also owe interest and penalties on the unpaid PHC tax balance. Interest will accrue from the date the return is originally due (without regard to extensions) until the entire tax is paid.[77]

ACCUMULATED EARNINGS TAX

No schedule or return is required for reporting the accumulated earnings tax. Because of the ad hoc nature of this tax, a corporation generally will not pay it until some time after the IRS has audited its tax return. Sec. 6601(b) requires the charging of interest on the accumulated earnings tax balance from the original due date for the return (without regard to extensions) until the date the IRS receives full tax payment.[78] The IRS also may impose a penalty for negligent underpayment of an accumulated earnings tax.[79]

PROBLEM MATERIALS

DISCUSSION QUESTIONS

C5-1 Explain the legislative intent behind the enactment of the corporate alternative minimum tax (AMT).

C5-2 Define the following terms relating to the corporate AMT:
a. Tax preference item
b. AMT adjustment
c. Alternative minimum taxable income
d. Statutory exemption amount
e. Tentative minimum tax
f. Minimum tax credit

C5-3 What special rules (if any) apply to the calculation of the AMT for the following entities:
a. Small corporations
b. Closely-held corporations
c. S corporations
d. Limited liability companies (LLCs)

C5-4 Agnew Corporation operates a small manufacturing business. During its first tax year (2006), the company reported gross income of $1 million. The gross income originated from sales of small toys that Agnew manufactured and sold for $3.8 million. Agnew's cost of goods sold was $2.8 million. Taxable income was $125,000. The corporation's owner estimates that future sales will grow at 25% per year. Agnew is not related to any other C corporations. Does Agnew's CPA need to calculate the corporation's alternative minimum tax in the initial year? In any of the next five years? Explain.

C5-5 Seminole Corporation began conducting business in the current year. Its gross receipts for the first year were less than $1 million. Austin and Frank each own 50% of the Seminole stock. The same two individuals also own equally three other corporations that have had gross receipts totaling $10 million or more in the current year and in the three preceding years. Explain to Austin and Frank whether Seminole and its sister corporations will be exempt from the corporate AMT in the current year.

C5-6 Dunn Corporation's taxable income is less than $40,000. The corporation is not eligible for the AMT small corporation exemption. The CPA preparing the corporate tax return does not calculate the AMT because he knows that taxable income is less than the AMT statutory exemption amount. Is he correct in his belief? Explain.

C5-7 Determine whether the following statements relating to the corporate AMT are true or false. If false, explain why.
a. Tax preference items may either increase or decrease AMTI.
b. The same NOL carryover amount is used for regular tax and AMT purposes.
c. The amount by which the tentative minimum tax exceeds the regular tax generates a minimum tax credit.
d. A corporate taxpayer's general business credit can offset not only its regular tax liability but also its AMT liability.

[77] *Hart Metal Products Corp. v. U.S.,* 38 AFTR 2d 76-6118, 76-2 USTC ¶9781 (Ct. Cls., 1976).

[78] Rev. Rul. 87-54, 1987-1 C.B. 349.
[79] Rev. Rul. 75-330, 1975-2 C.B. 496.

e. The ACE adjustment can only increase pre-adjustment AMTI.

f. The corporate AMT is levied on and paid by both C corporations and S corporations.

g. The minimum tax credit can be carried back as well as forward.

C5-8 Identify the following items as an AMT adjustment to taxable income (A), a tax preference item (P), or neither (N):

a. Percentage depletion in excess of a property's adjusted basis at the end of the tax year.

b. The Sec. 179 expense and first-year MACRS depreciation claimed on a machine costing $200,000 and placed in service in 2006.

c. The difference between gain on the sale of the asset in Part b for taxable income purposes and alternative minimum taxable income purposes.

d. Tax-exempt interest earned on State of Michigan private activity bonds.

e. Tax-exempt interest earned on State of Michigan general revenue bonds.

f. 75% of the excess of adjusted current earnings (ACE) over preadjustment AMTI.

C5-9 What adjustment must be made if ACE exceeds preadjustment AMTI? If ACE is less than preadjustment AMTI? What restrictions on negative ACE adjustments apply?

C5-10 Florida Corporation encounters an AMT problem for the first time in the current year. The problem is due to a $2 million gain on a non-dealer installment sale recognized over a ten-year period for financial accounting and taxable income purposes. The gain is fully includible in current year ACE. Explain to Florida's president the ACE adjustment, how the adjustment is similar to and different from E&P adjustments with which he is familiar, and whether the adjustment will partially or completely reverse in future years.

C5-11 Some tax authorities say a positive ACE adjustment can produce three different effective tax rates depending on the corporation's tax situation: (1) a 0% effective tax rate, (2) a 15% effective tax rate, or (3) between a 0% and 15% effective tax rate. Explain what the tax authorities mean.

C5-12 Indicate whether the following items are includible in taxable income, preadjustment AMTI, and/or ACE.

a. Tax-exempt interest on private activity bonds

b. Proceeds from an insurance policy (with no cash surrender value) on the life of a corporate officer

c. Gain on a current year sale of Sec. 1231 property that a nondealer reports under the installment method of accounting

d. Interest earned on State of Michigan general revenue bonds

e. Intangible drilling costs incurred and deducted in the current year

f. Amortization of organizational expenditures made last year

g. Deduction for a dividend received from a 25%-owned domestic corporation

C5-13 Discuss the taxable income, AMTI, and ACE depreciation rules applicable to the following types of new property acquired in 2006 and later tax years.

a. Section 1250 property—a factory building

b. Section 1245 property—a drill press

C5-14 In the current year, Burbank Corporation incurs an AMT liability for the first time. The liability is due entirely to an ACE adjustment resulting from the receipt of $4 million of life insurance proceeds paid upon the death of the firm's chief executive officer. The policy had no cash surrender value. Explain to Burbank's director of taxes whether Burbank can reduce future regular tax liabilities by the AMT paid in the current year.

C5-15 The personal holding company tax and the accumulated earnings tax reflect efforts to prevent use of the corporate entity to avoid taxation. Explain the congressional intent behind these two tax measures.

C5-16 Which of the following corporate forms are exempt from the PHC tax? The accumulated earnings tax?

a. Closely held corporations

b. S corporations

c. Professional corporations

d. Tax-exempt organizations

e. Publicly held corporations

f. Corporations filing a consolidated tax return

g. Limited liability companies

C5-17 Because of its quality investments, Carolina Corporation has always generated 30% to 40% of its gross income from passive sources. For years, the corporation held a block of stock in a company that was recently acquired. As a result of the acquisition, the corporation realized a substantial long-term capital gain that will increase this year's investment income from 40% to 70% of gross income. Explain to Carolina's president why she should or should not be worried about the personal holding company tax.

C5-18 Which of the following income items, when received by a corporation, are included in personal holding company income (PHCI)? Indicate whether any special circumstances would exclude an income item that is generally includible in PHCI.

a. Dividends

b. Interest on a corporate bond

c. Interest on a general revenue bond issued by a state government

d. Rental income from a warehouse leased to a third party

e. Rental income from a warehouse leased to the corporation's sole shareholder

f. Royalty income on a book whose copyright is owned by the corporation

g. Royalty income on a computer software copyright developed by the corporation and leased to a software marketing firm

h. Accounting fees earned by a professional corporation owned by three equal shareholders and that offers public accounting services to a wide variety of clients

i. Long-term capital gain on the sale of a stock investment

C5-19 Which of the following dividends are eligible for the dividends-paid deduction in computing the PHC tax? The accumulated earnings tax?

a. Cash dividend paid on common stock during the tax year

b. Annual cash dividend paid on preferred stock where no dividend is paid to the common shareholders

c. Dividend payable in the stock of an unrelated corporation

d. Stock dividend payable in the single class of stock of the distributing corporation

e. Cash dividend paid two months after the close of the tax year

C5-20 Define the term *consent dividend*. How can a consent dividend be used to avoid the personal holding company and accumulated earnings taxes? In each case, what requirements must be met by the distributing corporation and/or its shareholders to qualify a consent dividend for the dividends-paid deduction? What are the tax consequences of a consent dividend to the shareholders and the distributing corporation?

C5-21 Explain the advantages of a deficiency dividend. What requirements must a PHC and its shareholders meet to use a deficiency dividend to reduce or eliminate the PHC tax liability? Can a deficiency dividend eliminate interest and penalties, in addition to the PHC tax?

C5-22 Determine whether the following statements regarding the PHC tax are true or false:

a. In a given tax year, a corporation may not owe any PHC tax even though it is deemed to be a PHC.

b. A sale of a large tract of land held for investment purposes can make a manufacturing corporation a PHC.

c. Federal income taxes (including the alternative minimum tax) accrued by the PHC reduce UPHCI for the tax year.

d. To reduce UPHCI, the corporation can pay consent dividends any time from the first day of the tax year through the due date for the corporation's tax return (including any permitted extensions).

e. The payment of a deficiency dividend permits a PHC to eliminate its PHC tax liability, as well as related interest and penalties.

f. A corporation deemed to be a PHC for a particular tax year also can be liable for the accumulated earnings tax for that year.

g. A PHC can be subject to the alternative minimum tax.

C5-23 Explain the implication of the following statement: "Like many dogs, the threat (bark) of the personal holding company tax is much worse than the actual penalties assessed in connection with its (bite)."

C5-24 Explain the following statement: "Although the accumulated earnings tax can be imposed on both publicly held and closely held corporations, the tax is likely to be imposed primarily on closely held corporations."

C5-25 The accumulated earnings tax is imposed only when the corporation is "formed or availed of for the purpose of avoiding the income tax." Does tax avoidance have to occur at the corporate or the shareholder level for the accumulated earnings tax to be imposed? Does tax avoidance have to be the sole motive for earnings accumulation before such imposition?

C5-26 How, in its first year of operation, can a newly formed corporation be subject to the personal holding company tax but not the alternative minimum tax and the accumulated earnings tax?

C5-27 Gamma Corporation has generated substantial cash flows from its manufacturing activities. It has only a moderate need to reinvest its earnings in existing facilities or for expansion. In recent years, the corporation has amassed a large investment portfolio due to management's unwillingness to pay dividends. The corporation is unlikely to be deemed a PHC but is concerned about its exposure to the accumulated earnings tax. Explain to Gamma's president what steps he can take to avoid liability for the accumulated earnings tax in the current year? In future tax years? Do these steps require the payment of a cash dividend?

C5-28 Explain the *Bardahl* formula. Why have some tax authorities said that this formula implies a greater degree of mathematical precision than is actually the case? Does the *Bardahl* formula apply to service companies?

C5-29 Different rules for calculating the accumulated earnings credit apply to operating companies, holding and investment companies, and service companies. Explain the differences.

C5-30 Determine whether the following statements about the accumulated earnings tax are true or false:

a. Before the IRS can impose the accumulated earnings tax, it needs only to show that tax avoidance was one of the motives for the corporation's unreasonable accumulation of earnings.

b. Long-term capital gains are included in the accumulated earnings tax base.

c. Each corporate member of a controlled group can claim a separate $150,000 or $250,000 accumulated earnings credit.

d. A dividends-paid deduction can be claimed for both cash and property distributions (other than nontaxable stock dividends) made by a corporation. This deduction reduces both taxable income and accumulated taxable income.

e. The accumulated earnings tax liability cannot be eliminated by paying a deficiency dividend.

f. Interest and penalties on the accumulated earnings tax deficiency accrue only from the date the IRS or the courts determine that the tax is owed.

g. The accumulated earnings tax is self-reported on Form 1120-AET that is filed along with the corporate tax return.

C5-31 For each of the following statements, indicate whether the statement is true for the PHC tax only (P), the accumulated earnings tax only (A), both taxes (B), or neither tax (N).

a. The tax is imposed only if the corporation satisfies certain stock ownership and income requirements.

b. The tax applies to both closely held and publicly traded corporations.

c. The tax is ad hoc in nature (i.e., assessed in the course of an audit).

d. Long-term capital gains are a neutral factor in determining the amount of the tax liability.

e. Tax-exempt interest income is excluded from the tax base.

f. A credit that reduces the tax liability on a dollar-for-dollar basis is available.

g. Throwback dividends may be paid without limit.

h. Consent dividends are eligible for a dividends-paid deduction.

i. Throwback and consent dividends are effective in reducing or eliminating the tax liability.

j. The tax can be avoided by paying a deficiency dividend.

k. The tax applies to S corporations.

ISSUE IDENTIFICATION QUESTIONS

C5-32 Bird Corporation purchases for its manufacturing facility a new precision casting machine costing $1 million. Installation costs are $75,000. The machine is placed in service in June 2006. The old casting machine, which was placed in service in 1997, was sold to an unrelated party at a $125,000 financial accounting profit. What asset disposition and capital recovery issues must you, as Bird's director of federal taxes, address when accounting for removing the old machine from, and placing the new machine in service and in calculating the 2006 tax depreciation?

C5-33 Parrish is a closely held C corporation. Robert and Kim Parrish own all its stock. The corporation, now in its second month of operation, expects to earn $200,000 of gross income in the current tax year. This income is expected to consist of approximately 40% dividends, 30% corporate bond interest, and 30% net real estate rentals (after interest expense, property taxes, and depreciation). Administrative expenses are estimated to be $40,000. What special problems does the substantial passive income that Parrish Corporation expects to earn present to you as its CPA?

C5-34 McHale is a C corporation owned by eight individuals, three of whom own 51% of the stock and comprise the board of directors. The corporation operates a successful automobile repair parts manufacturing business. It has accumulated $2 million of E&P and expects to accumulate another $300,000 annually. Annual dividends are $30,000. Because Americans retain their vehicles longer than they did 20 years ago, demand for McHale's repair parts has been strong for the past five years. However, little expansion or replacement of the current plant is projected for three to five years. Management has invested $200,000 annually in growth stocks. Its current investment portfolio, which is held primarily as protection against a business downturn, is valued at $1.2 million. Loans to shareholder-employees currently amount to $400,000. As McHale Corporation's tax return preparer, what tax issues should you have your client consider?

PROBLEMS

C5-35 *Small Corporation AMT Exemption.* Willis Corporation reports the following gross receipts for its initial years of operation.

Year	Gross Receipts
2006	$ 2,750,000
2007	3,987,500
2008	5,682,188
2009	8,097,117
2010	11,538,392
2011	16,442,209

For purposes of applying the gross receipts test, Willis is not related to any other corporations, nor is it a successor to another corporation. Year 2006 gross receipts have been annualized. Is Willis exempt from the corporate alternative minimum tax if it was formed in 2006? Explain.

C5-36 *Alternative Minimum Tax Calculation.* In the current year, Whitaker Corporation reports taxable income of $700,000. It has net positive AMT adjustments of $600,000 and tax preference items of $100,000. Adjusted current earnings for the year are $2 million. Whitaker is not eligible for the small corporation exemption.
a. What is Whitaker's AMTI?
b. What is Whitaker's tentative minimum tax?
c. What is Whitaker's regular tax liability?
d. What is Whitaker's AMT liability?
e. What is Whitaker's minimum tax credit?
f. By what amount would Whitaker have to reduce its AMT adjustment to avoid paying the AMT?

C5-37 *Depreciation Calculations.* Water Corporation placed a machine costing $10,000 in service on June 1, 2004. The machine is seven-year property under the MACRS rules. The machine has a 12-year class life. The corporation claimed bonus depreciation in 2004 but did not elect Sec. 179 expensing. Based on the half-year convention, calculate the annual depreciation deductions for purposes of determining
a. Taxable income
b. Alternative minimum taxable income
c. Are separate depreciation calculations necessary to compute adjusted current earnings?
d. How would your answers to Parts a–c change if the machine were instead purchased and placed in service on June 1, 2006?

C5-38 *Basis Adjustment.* Assume the same basic facts as in Part d of Problem C5-37. Water Corporation sells the machine for $9,000 on August 31, 2008.
a. What gain does Water report for purposes of determining taxable income, AMTI, and adjusted current earnings?
b. If you were using taxable income as the starting point for calculating AMTI, what type of adjustment would you need to report the transaction in 2008 for AMTI purposes?

C5-39 *ACE Adjustment.* Calculate the ACE adjustment for Towne Corporation for each year since its incorporation in 2002.

	2002	2003	2004	2005	2006
ACE	$500	$500	$500	$500	$(500)
Preadjustment AMTI	(100)	600	900	–0–	(300)
ACE adjustment	?	?	?	?	?

C5-40 *Regular Tax and AMT Calculations.* Bronze Corporation, an accrual method taxpayer, reports the following data relating to its year 2006 operations:

Taxable income from recurring operations	$278,000
Other income and expense items not included in the $278,000 figure:	
Dividend from 10%-owned corporation	40,000
Life insurance proceeds received upon the death of a corporate officer	500,000
Tax-exempt bond interest on private activity bonds	25,000
Tax-exempt bond interest (not on private activity bonds)	30,000
Installment sale of land (a capital asset) in June:	
Total realized gain	400,000
Portion of gain on installment collections in 2006	32,000
Depreciation:	
For regular tax purposes	120,000
For AMTI purposes	85,000
For ACE purposes	60,000
Sec. 1245 property sold in current year:	
Recognized gain for regular tax purposes	30,000
Basis for regular tax purposes	54,000
Basis for AMTI purposes	60,000
Basis for ACE purposes	64,000

Bronze is not eligible for the small corporation exemption and has no AMT adjustment for the U.S. production activities deduction.

a. What is Bronze's ACE adjustment?

b. What is Bronze's AMTI?

c. What is Bronze's AMT liability?

d. What is Bronze's available minimum tax credit (if any)?

e. In what years can the minimum tax credit be used?

f. Does Bronze have to include the amount of its projected minimum tax liability in its 2006 estimated tax calculation?

g. Does Bronze have to include the amount of its minimum tax liability in the determination of its tax underpayment penalty (if any) for 2006?

C5-41 *Regular Tax and AMT Calculations.* Campbell Corporation reports taxable income of $210,000 in 2006. Campbell is not eligible for the small corporation exemption and has no AMT adjustment for the U.S. production activities deduction. The following facts were taken into account in deriving taxable income.

1. Equipment acquired in 2000–2006 was depreciated under MACRS. For 2006, MACRS depreciation on this equipment is $100,000. Depreciation for AMT purposes is $75,000.

2. Campbell recognizes a Sec. 1245 gain of $12,000 for regular tax purposes on the sale of an asset. The asset's income tax basis is $9,000 less than its AMT basis.

3. Campbell's adjusted current earnings for 2006 is $480,000.

a. What is Campbell's AMTI?

b. What is Campbell's AMT liability?

c. What is the amount (if any) of Campbell's minimum tax credit? To what years can this credit be carried over?

d. Does Campbell have to include the amount of its projected minimum tax liability in its 2006 estimated tax calculation?

e. Does Campbell have to include the amount of its minimum tax liability in the determination of its tax underpayment penalty (if any) for 2006?

f. Does Campbell have to include the amount of a projected AMT liability in its quarterly estimated tax payments for 2007?

C5-42 *Regular Tax and AMT Calculations.* Sheldon Corporation reports taxable income of $150,000 for its second tax year (2006). Its regular tax liability is $41,750. The following facts were taken into account in deriving taxable income.

- Used equipment is depreciated under MACRS. The amount of MACRS depreciation claimed is $90,000. Depreciation for AMT purposes in 2006 is $60,000.

- The corporation includes in taxable income a $12,000 gain on the sale of equipment. The asset's regular tax basis at the time of sale is $9,000 less than its AMT basis.

- Sheldon's adjusted current earnings is $340,000.

- Sheldon has no AMT adjustment for the U.S. production activities deduction.

No NOL, capital loss, tax credit, or negative ACE carryovers from the first year of operations are available for use in the second year.

a. What is Sheldon's AMT liability?

b. Is any minimum tax credit carryback or carryover available? If so, to what years?

C5-43 *Regular Tax and AMT Calculations.* Subach Corporation, organized in 1998, reports the following results for 2006:

Taxable income	$600,000
Preadjustment AMTI	630,000
Adjusted current earnings, excluding the following transactions:	900,000
• Tax-exempt bond interest (not on private activity bonds)	100,000
• Recognized gain on a capital asset installment sale concluded this year. No collections were made this year.	150,000
• Life insurance proceeds received upon the death of a corporate executive	500,000
• Amortization of organizational expenditures	5,000

Subach uses the accrual method of accounting. The only adjustment the corporation makes to taxable income to derive preadjustment AMTI is a $30,000 addition to reflect a different depreciation method used in calculating AMTI. Taxable income, preadjustment AMTI, and the beginning ACE amounts all include an $80,000 deduction for a dividend received from a 25%-owned corporation. No NOL, capital loss, tax credit, or negative

ACE adjustment carryovers from prior years are available in the current year. What is Subach's current year federal tax liability?

C5-44 **AMTI Calculation.** Alabama Corporation conducts a copper mining business. During the current year, it reports taxable income of $400,000, which includes a $100,000 deduction for percentage depletion. The depletable property's adjusted basis at year-end (before reduction for current year depletion) is $40,000. Cost depletion, had it been deducted, would have been $30,000. Depreciation under MACRS is $140,000 for regular tax purposes and $90,000 for AMTI purposes. Alabama sold an asset at a $12,000 gain that is included in taxable income. The asset's adjusted basis is $10,000 higher for AMT purposes than for regular tax purposes. Alabama's adjusted current earnings is $800,000. Alabama is not eligible for the small corporation exemption and has no AMT adjustment for the U.S. production activities deduction.
a. What is Alabama's AMTI?
b. What is Alabama's AMT liability?
c. What is the amount (if any) of Alabama's minimum tax credit? To what years can it be carried over?

C5-45 **Regular Tax and AMT Calculations.** What is Middle Corporation's regular tax liability, AMT liability, and minimum tax credit (if any) in the following three scenarios? Assume that, in prior years, Middle has had $120,000 of positive ACE adjustments. Middle is not eligible for the small corporation exemption.

	Scenario 1	Scenario 2	Scenario 3
Taxable income	$200,000	$ 50,000	$300,000
Tax preference items and positive AMTI adjustments (other than the ACE adjustment)	100,000	25,000	160,000
Adjusted current earnings	500,000	150,000	400,000

C5-46 **Regular Tax and AMT Calculations.** Delta Corporation reports taxable income of $2 million, tax preference items of $100,000, net positive AMTI adjustments of $600,000 before the ACE adjustment, and adjusted current earnings of $4 million. Delta is not eligible for the small corporation exception and has no AMT adjustment for the U.S. production activities deduction.
a. What is Delta's regular tax liability?
b. What is Delta's AMT liability?
c. What is the amount (if any) of Delta 's minimum tax credit? To what years can it be carried over?

C5-47 **Minimum Tax Credit.** Jones Corporation has $600,000 of taxable income plus $400,000 of positive AMTI adjustments and $200,000 of tax preference items. Jones is not eligible for the small corporation exemption.
a. What is Jones' regular tax liability and AMT liability?
b. What is Jones' minimum tax credit (if any)? To what years can it be carried over?

C5-48 **Minimum Tax Credit.** Gulf Corporation reports the following tax amounts for the period 2004–2006:

Tax Amounts	2004	2005	2006
Regular tax	$75,000	$100,000	$210,000
Tentative minimum tax	40,000	150,000	170,000

In what years does a minimum tax credit arise? To what years can the credit be carried over? Do any credit carryovers remain in 2007?

C5-49 **Minimum Tax Analysis.** Duncan Manufacturing Corporation, an accrual method taxpayer, sold a parcel of land on July 1, 2006. Duncan had planned to use the land to expand its manufacturing facilities. The land (a Sec. 1231 asset) had a $3 million market value and a $1.2 million adjusted basis. As partial consideration for the sale, Duncan received a $300,000 cash down payment on July 1, 2006. In addition, the purchaser will pay annual payments of $540,000 [0.20 × ($3,000,000 − $300,000)] over the next five years on July 1 of each year. Duncan charges a market interest rate on the unpaid balance. The CEO has asked you to prepare a year-by-year analysis of the impact of this land sale on the firm's tax position. In your calculation, you can ignore interest earned on the sale.

On a year-by-year basis, what are the expected effects of the installment sale on the corporation's regular tax and AMT liabilities? Assume for AMT purposes that Duncan is not a small corporation and has no AMT adjustment for the U.S. production activities deduction. Also assume a 34% regular tax rate.

C5-50 *General Business Credit.* Edge Corporation's regular tax before credits is $165,000 in the current year. Its tentative minimum tax is $100,000. The only credit Edge earns in the current year is a $200,000 general business credit relating to research expenditures.

a. What amount of this credit may Edge use to reduce its current year tax liability?

b. What carryovers and carrybacks are available, and to what years may they be carried?

C5-51 *Estimated Tax Requirement.* Ajax Corporation expects to owe a $100,000 regular tax liability and a $70,000 AMT liability for the current year. Last year, it owed a $200,000 regular tax liability and no AMT liability. What is Ajax's minimum estimated tax payment for the current year?

C5-52 *Estimated Tax Payments.* Dallas Corporation reports the following 2005 and 2006 tax liabilities:

Type of Liability	2005	2006
Regular tax	$100,000	$150,000
AMT	–0–	25,000

Each tax year covers a 12-month period. Dallas is a small corporation. It made $23,000 of estimated tax payments for each quarter of 2006.

a. How much tax will Dallas owe when it files its 2006 tax return?

b. Is Dallas liable for any estimated tax underpayment penalties? If so, how much did it underpay in each quarter?

C5-53 *PHC Definition.* In which of the following situations will Small Corporation be deemed to be a PHC? Assume that personal holding company income comprises more than 60% of Small's adjusted ordinary gross income.

a. Art owns 100% of Parent Corporation stock, and Parent owns 100% of Small stock. Parent and Small file separate tax returns.

b. Art owns one-third of Small stock. The PRS Partnership, of which Phil, Robert, and Sue each have a one-third capital and profits interest, also own one-third of Small stock. The remaining shares of Small stock are owned by 50 individuals unrelated to Art, Phil, Robert, and Sue.

c. Art and his wife, Becky, each own 20% of Small stock. The remaining shares of Small stock are owned by the Whitaker Family Trust. Becky and her three sisters each have a one-fourth beneficial interest in the trust.

C5-54 *Personal Holding Company Status.* In each of the following four scenarios, determine whether the corporation is a personal holding company. Assume the corporation's outstanding stock is owned equally by three shareholders.

Type of Income Earned	Scenario 1	Scenario 2	Scenario 3	Scenario 4
Gross profit from sales	$40,000	$ 80,000	$40,000	$ 60,000
Capital gains	–0–	10,000	5,000	10,000
Interest	15,000	15,000	10,000	20,000
Dividends	10,000	10,000	2,000	–0–
Rentals	80,000	150,000	–0–	–0–
Copyright royalties	–0–	5,000	80,000	–0–
Personal service income	–0–	–0–	–0–	100,000
Rent-related expenses	20,000	30,000	–0–	–0–
Copyright-related expenses	–0–	–0–	25,000	–0–
Dividends paid	8,000	10,000	5,000	10,000

C5-55 *PHC Tax.* In the current year, Moore Corporation is deemed to be a PHC. Moore reports the following results for the current year:

Taxable income	$200,000
Dividend received by Moore from a 18%-owned domestic corporation	50,000
Dividends paid by Moore	75,000

a. What is Moore's regular tax liability (ignoring any AMT implications)?

b. What is Moore's PHC tax liability?

c. What actions can Moore take to eliminate its PHC tax liability after year-end and before it files its tax return? After it files its tax return?

C5-56 *PHC Tax.* In the current year, Kennedy Corporation is deemed to be a PHC. It reports the following results for the current year:

Taxable income	$400,000
Federal income taxes	136,000
Dividends paid to Marlene, Kennedy's sole shareholder	75,000

The following information is available:

- The corporation received $100,000 of dividends from a 25%-owned domestic corporation.

- The corporation received $30,000 of tax-exempt interest income.

- The corporation recognized a $175,000 Sec. 1231 gain on the sale of land.

a. What is Kennedy's PHC tax liability?

b. What can be done to eliminate the PHC tax liability after year-end and before Kennedy files its tax return? After Kennedy files its tax return?

C5-57 *PHC Tax.* Alice and Barry each own shares of Alpha Corporation. For 2006, the corporation reports the following income and expenses:

Rental income		$ 750,000
Dividend income from less than 20%-owned corporations		200,000
Tax-exempt interest income		40,000
Gross profit on sale of merchandise		50,000
Long-term capital gain on the sale of stocks		200,000
Total income		$1,240,000
Minus: Rent related expenses:		
Interest expense	$140,000	
Depreciation expense	150,000	
Property taxes	175,000	
Other Sec. 162 expenses	165,000	(630,000)
Minus: Administrative expenses		(90,000)
Pre-tax profit		$ 520,000

During 2006, Alpha Corporation paid $50,000 in dividends to its shareholders. Assume Alpha is not eligible for the U.S. production activities deduction.

a. Is Alpha a personal holding company?

b. What is Alpha's regular tax liability?

c. What is Alpha's personal holding company tax liability (if any)?

C5-58 *Unreasonable Accumulation of Earnings.* In each of the following scenarios, indicate why Adobe Corporation's accumulation of earnings might be unreasonable relative to its business needs. Provide one or more arguments the corporation might put forth to support its positon that the accumulation is reasonable. Assume that Tess owns all the Adobe stock.

a. Adobe established a sinking fund ten years ago to retire its ten-year notes and has added cash to the fund annually. Six months ago, the corporation decided to refinance the notes at maturity at a lower interest rate through the issuance of a new series of bonds sold to an insurance company. The sinking fund balance is invested in stocks and commercial paper. A general plan exists to use the balance to purchase operating assets. No definite plans have been established by year-end.

b. Adobe regularly lends money to Tess at a rate slightly below the rate charged by a commercial bank. Tess has repaid about 20% of these loans. The current balance on the loans is $500,000, which approximates one year's net income for Adobe.

c. Adobe has heavily invested in stocks and bonds. The current market value of its investments is $2 million. The investment portfolio comprises approximately one-half of Adobe's assets.

d. Tess owns three other corporations, which, together with Adobe, form a brother-sister controlled group. Adobe regularly lends funds to Tess's three other corporations.

Current loans amount to $500,000. The interest rate charged approximates the commercial rate for similar loans.

C5-59 *Bardahl Formula.* Lion Corporation is concerned about an accumulated earnings tax liability. It accumulates E&P for working capital necessary to conduct its manufacturing business. The following data relating to Lion's financial position appear in its current year balance sheets.

Account	Beginning Balance	Ending Balance	Peak Balance for the Year
Accounts receivable	$300,000	$400,000	$400,000
Inventory	240,000	300,000	375,000
Accounts payable	150,000	200,000	220,000

The following data relating to Lion's operations appear in its current year income statement:

Sales	$3,200,000
Cost of goods sold	1,500,000
Purchases	1,200,000
Operating expenses (other than cost of goods sold)	1,000,000

Included in operating expenses are depreciation of $150,000 and federal income taxes of $100,000.
a. What is Lion's operating cycle in days? As a decimal?
b. What is Lion's reasonable working capital amount as determined under the *Bardahl* formula?
c. What steps must Lion take to justify accumulating earnings that exceed the amount sanctioned under the *Bardahl* formula?

C5-60 *Accumulated Earnings Credit.* In each of the following scenarios, calculate the accumulated earnings credit. Assume the corporation uses a calendar year as its tax year. Also assume that it realizes no current year capital gains.
a. Frank Corporation, a manufacturer of plastic toys, started business last year and reported E&P of $50,000. In the current year, the corporation reports E&P of $150,000 and pays no dividends. Of the $150,000 current E&P, the corporation retains $130,000 to meet its business needs.
b. How would your answer to Part a change if Frank were a service company that provides accounting services?
c. Hall Corporation's accumulated E&P balance at January 1 of the current year is $200,000. During the year, Hall, a manufacturer of glass containers, reports $100,000 of current E&P, all of which is retained to meet the reasonable needs of the business. Hall pays no dividends.

C5-61 *Accumulated Earnings Tax.* Twentieth Century Cleaning Services, Inc. provides cleaning services in Atlanta, Georgia. It is not a member of a controlled or an affiliated group. Twentieth Century reports the following results for 2006:

Taxable income	$500,000
Federal income taxes (at 34%)	170,000
Dividends paid in August 2006	75,000

Included in taxable income are the following items that may require special treatment:

Long-term capital gains	$ 30,000
Short-term capital gains	10,000
Dividends from 21%-owned domestic corporation	100,000
Excess charitable contributions from 2005 that are deductible in 2006	25,000

Twentieth Century's accumulated E&P balance and its reasonable business needs on January 1, 2006, were $125,000. The firm can justify the retention of $90,000 of current E&P to meet its reasonable business needs. Assume the corporation is not eligible for the U.S. production activities deduction.
a. What is Twentieth Century's accumulated taxable income?
b. What is Twentieth Century's accumulated earnings tax liability?

C5-62   *Accumulated Earnings Tax.* Howard Corporation conducts a manufacturing business and has a compelling need to accumulate earnings. Its January 1, 2006, E&P balance is $600,000. It reports the following operating results for 2006:

Taxable income	$700,000
Federal income taxes	238,000
Dividends paid: July 15, 2006	50,000
February 10, 2007	100,000

Other information relating to Howard's operations for 2006 is as follows:

NOL carryover from 2005 deducted in 2006	$100,000
Net capital gain	100,000
Dividends received from 10%-owned domestic corporation	75,000

Current year E&P before dividend payments is $400,000. Howard can justify the retention of $120,000 of current E&P to meet the reasonable needs of its business.
a. What is Howard's accumulated taxable income?
b. What is Howard's accumulated earnings tax liability?

COMPREHENSIVE PROBLEM

C5-63   Stock in Random Corporation is owned equally by two individual shareholders. During the current year, Random reports the following results:

Income:	Rentals	$200,000
	Dividend (from a 25%-owned domestic corporation)	30,000
	Interest	15,000
	Short-term capital gains	3,000
	Long-term capital gains	17,000
Expenses related to rental income:		
	Interest	30,000
	Depreciation	32,000
	Property taxes	11,000
	Other Sec. 162 expenses	50,000
General and administrative expenses		10,000
Dividend paid on June 30		15,000

a. What is Random's gross income?
b. What is Random's ordinary gross income?
c. What is Random's adjusted income from rents?
d. What is Random's adjusted ordinary gross income?
e. What is Random's personal holding company income?
f. Is Random a PHC?
g. What is Random's taxable income and regular tax liability?
h. What is Random's undistributed PHC income (UPHCI) and PHC tax liability?
i. What measures can Random take before year-end to avoid paying the PHC tax? Alternatively, what can Random do after year-end but before the corporation files its tax return? If the corporation takes no action before or after filing its return, what remedy does it have after filing?
j. Assume that Random's income and expense items will be similar in future years unless management changes Random's asset mix. What changes can management make to reduce the corporation's PHC exposure in future years?
k. If Random is a personal holding company, can it also be subject to the accumulated earnings tax?

TAX STRATEGY PROBLEMS

C5-64   Galadriel and John, married with no children, own all the stock in Marietta Horse Supplies. The couple's C corporation has been in business for ten years. The business has been successful, permitting both owners to pay themselves a reasonable salary from its revenues. Although the salaries cover life's necessities, a review of industry statistics shows that the salary of each owner is about one-half or two-thirds of salaries paid by similar-sized horse supply businesses. The reason for the low salaries is that, for a number of years, the owners had felt continual pressure to retain as much of the profits in the business as possible to have sufficient working capital to finance inventories and other business needs. In the past two years, the firm has developed lines of credit with two local banks that have alleviated much of this pressure. However, the couple has never had time to review the amount of their compensation. Recently, an Internal Revenue Service agent asked the couple about items reported in a previously filed tax return. The agent reviewed all three open years and proposed a settlement for the items in question. While in the office, the IRS agent indicated to you as the couple's CPA that, in her opinion, the company had unreasonably accumulated earnings and that she would be investigating the issue before closing the audit. What advice can you give the couple about their salaries and potential liability for the accumulated earnings tax?

C5-65 Steve and Andrew write music and lyrics for popular songs. In 2003, they organized S&A Music Corporation, each brother owning one-half of its stock. Through the end of 2005, they contributed a total of $250,000 in capital to the business. The songs that Steve and Andrew write and promote have been successful. Annually, the firm earns $300,000 of royalties from the copyrights that it owns. With the aid of their aunt who operates a local bookkeeping service, Steve and Andrew organized their business as a C corporation. The brothers decide that, with the success of their music business, perhaps they should move their accounting services to an accounting firm that specializes in providing tax advice for small- or medium-sized businesses. As a staff member of this accounting firm, what advice can you provide the brothers about possible tax problems and potential tax strategies?

TAX FORM/RETURN PREPARATION PROBLEM

C5-66 King Corporation, I.D. No. 38-1534789, an accrual method taxpayer, reports the following results for 2005:

Taxable income	$ 800,000
Regular tax (before credits)	272,000
Alternative tax NOL deduction	175,000
Depreciation adjustment for personal property placed in service after 1986	148,000
Personal property acquired in 1998 sold this year:	
Acquisition cost	50,000
Regular tax depreciation	38,845
AMT depreciation	26,845
Increase in LIFO recapture amount	75,000
Tax-exempt interest income:	
Private activity bonds	15,000
Other bonds	5,000
Adjusted current earnings	2,000,000
General business credit (targeted jobs credit)	10,000
Dividends paid	120,000

King is not eligible for the small corporation exemption and has no AMT adjustment for the U.S. production activities deduction. Taxable income includes $95,000 of Sec. 1231 gain from a payment received in 2005 relating to an installment sale of land that King made in 2004. King realized a $950,000 gain on the sale in 2004 and is recognizing gain over a ten-year period as the purchaser makes equal annual payments. King reported the transaction properly in 2004. Prepare Form 4626 for King Corporation to report its AMT liability (if any) for 2005.

CASE STUDY PROBLEMS

C5-67 Eagle Corporation operates a family business established by Edward Eagle, Sr. ten years ago. Edward Eagle, Sr. died, and the Eagle stock passed to his children and grandchildren. The corporation primarily invests, with its assets consisting of rental property, highly appreciated stocks, and corporate bonds. The tax advisor who oversees Eagle's tax matters made the following profit projection for the current year:

Rentals	$260,000
Dividend income (from a 40%-owned domestic corporation)	90,000
Interest income	20,000

Gross income	$370,000
Rental expenses:	
Depreciation expense	$ 70,000
Interest expense	100,000
Property taxes	10,000
Other Sec. 162 expenses	20,000
General and administrative expenses	15,000
Total expenses	$215,000
Net profit	$155,000

Eagle has paid dividends of $40,000 in each of the past three years. The stock investment has substantially appreciated in value in the past six months. As a result, dividend income is expected to increase from last year's $10,000 to $80,000 this year. Eagle has not been a PHC in prior years.

Required: Prepare a memorandum to Edward Eagle, Jr. regarding potential liability for the PHC tax. In your memorandum, discuss the following two questions:

a. Is Eagle likely to be deemed a PHC for the current year?

b. If Eagle is likely to be deemed a PHC for the current year, what actions (if any) should be taken before year-end to eliminate the PHC tax liability? After year-end?

C5-68 Goss Corporation is a leading manufacturer of hangers for the laundry and dry cleaning industry. The family-owned business has prospered for many years and has generated approximately $100 million of sales and $8 million in after-tax profits. Your accounting firm has performed the audit and tax work for Goss and its executives since the company was created in 1948. Little technological change has occurred in the manufacturing of hangers, and much of the equipment currently being used dates back to the 1950s and 1960s. The advent of plastic hangers and improved fabrics has kept the overall market size constant, and the corporation plans no major plant expansions or additions. Salaries paid to corporate executives, most of whom are family members, are above the national averages for similar officers. Dividend payments in recent years have not exceeded 10% of the after-tax profits. You have been assigned on December 1, 2006, to oversee the preparation of the 2006 Goss tax return. In undertaking the assignment, you review the 2003–2005 Goss tax returns. You note from Schedule L (the balance sheet) that the corporation has made about $1.5 million in loans to three executives and regularly increased the size of its stock portfolio between 2003 and 2005. This increase leads you to believe that Goss may be liable for the accumulated earnings tax in 2006 and prior years.

Required:

a. What responsibility do you have to make Goss or the partner in charge of the Goss account aware of the potential accumulated earnings tax liability?

b. Should you advise the IRS of the potential liability for prior years? Should you disclose the potential liability on the current year return?

c. Prepare a list of actions that can be taken to reduce or eliminate the client's liability for the accumulated earnings tax.

TAX RESEARCH PROBLEMS

C5-69 Brown Corporation purchased (and placed in service) two assets in January 2003, its initial year of operation. The first asset, a commercial factory building, cost $200,000 with $40,000 of the acquisition price being allocated to the land. The second, a used (i.e., not new) machine that is a seven-year MACRS property, cost $80,000. The class life for the machine is ten years. Brown sold both assets in March 2006 in connection with a relocation of its manufacturing activities. The sale price for the factory building was $225,000, with $45,000 of the sale price being allocated to the land. The sale price for the machine was $70,000. Brown used MACRS depreciation on each asset for regular tax purposes but did not make a Sec. 179 election or claim bonus depreciation on the machine. Assume the machine was depreciated under the half-year convention, and the building was depreciated under the mid-month convention. What are the amount and character of the gains reported by Brown for regular tax and alternative minimum tax purposes?

C5-70 Camp Corporation is owned by Hal and Ruthie, who have owned their stock since the corporation was formed in 1991. The corporation has filed its tax returns using the calendar year as its tax year and the accrual method of accounting. In 2005, Camp borrowed $4 million from a local bank. The loan is secured by a lien on some of its machinery.

Camp loaned 90% of the borrowings to Vickers Corporation at the same annual rate as the rate on the bank loan. Vickers also is owned equally by Hal and Ruthie. Vickers sells to the automobile industry parts that are manufactured by Camp and unrelated companies. Camp experienced a downturn due to a slowdown in the automobile industry. The gross margin on its sales declined from $1 million in 2005 to $200,000 in 2006. Interest income accrued by Camp on the loan to Vickers is $432,000 in 2006. Other passive income earned by Camp is $40,000. Camp's accountant believes that the corporation is not a personal holding company because the interest income Camp earns can be netted against the $432,000 interest expense paid to the bank for the amounts lent to Vickers. Is he correct in his belief?

A partial list of research sources is

- IRC Secs. 542(a) and 543(a)(1)
- Reg. Sec. 1.543-1(b)(2)
- *Bell Realty Trust*, 65 T.C. 766 (1976)
- *Blair Holding Co., Inc.*, 1980 PH T.C. Memo ¶80,079, 39 TCM 1255

C5-71   William Queen owns all the stock in Able and Baker Corporations. Able, a successful enterprise, has generated excess working capital of $3 million. Baker is still in its developmental stages and has had tremendous capital needs. To cover some of these needs, William has had Able lend Baker $2 million during 2004 and 2005. These loans are secured by Baker notes, but not by Baker property. Able has charged Baker interest at a rate ordinarily charged by a commercial lender. Upon reviewing Able's 2006 books as part of an audit of its 2004 tax return, an IRS agent indicates that Able is liable for the accumulated earnings tax because of its build up of excess working capital and its loans to Baker. Later this week, you will meet with the agent for a third time. Prior to this meeting, you must research whether loans to a related corporation to provide working capital constitute a reasonable need of the business. At a meeting to discuss this problem, William asks whether filing a consolidated tax return would eliminate this potential problem and, if so, how must the ownership structure change to accomplish this objective.

A partial list of research sources is

- IRC Secs. 532 and 537
- Reg. Secs. 1.537-2(c) and -3(b) and 1.1502-43
- *Latchis Theatres of Keene, Inc. v. CIR*, 45 AFTR 1836, 54-2 USTC ¶9544 (1st Cir., 1954)
- *Bremerton Sun Publishing Co.*, 44 T.C. 566 (1965)

C5-72   Three years ago, Sadaka Oil Company filed a Form 1120 corporate tax return on which it reported $9,284,000 of gross income. Because the corporation incurred extraordinary drilling and depletion costs and sustained substantial partnership investment losses, Sadaka reported negative taxable income of $1,691,400. The company filed a Form 4626 alternative minimum tax return, on which it included in its gross income $5,719,400 of tax preference items. As a result of this inclusion, Sadaka reported alternative minimum taxable income of $2,533,300 and an alternative minimum tax liability of $506,660.

The corporation paid the $506,660 alternative minimum tax under protest. Now, it plans to petition the IRS for a refund of $338,280. In its petition, Sadaka will argue that the tax preference items, which had been reported as regular tax deductions on its Form 1120, conferred a regular tax benefit of only $4,028,000. Therefore, the company should have incurred an alternative minimum tax liability of $168,380, based on the extent to which Sadaka derived a regular tax benefit from the tax preference items. Sadaka's accountants calculated this alternative minimum tax amount as follows:

Gross income reported on Form 1120	$9,284,000
Less: Regular tax deductions reported on Form 1120	(5,256,000)
Subtotal	$4,028,000
Less: Tax preference items reported on Form 4626	(5,719,400
Tax preference items producing no regular tax benefit	($1,691,400)
AMTI reported on Form 4626	$2,533,300
Less: Tax preference items producing no regular tax benefit	(1,691,400)
Adjusted AMTI reflecting regular tax benefit	$ 841,900
Times: AMT rate	× 20%
AMT reflecting regular tax benefit	$ 168,380

Sadaka's chief tax officer has asked you to evaluate the merits of this argument. After reviewing the calculation and researching the issue, what do you advise him? At a minimum consult the following authorities:

- IRC Sec. 56
- *Weiser v. U.S.*, 69 AFTR 2d 92-934, 92-1 USTC ¶50,169 (9th Cir., 1992)

6

C H A P T E R

CORPORATE LIQUIDATING DISTRIBUTIONS

LEARNING OBJECTIVES

After studying this chapter, you should be able to

1 Understand the difference between a complete liquidation and a dissolution

2 Apply the general shareholder gain and loss recognition rules for a corporate liquidation

3 Determine when the liquidating corporation recognizes gains and losses on making a liquidating distribution

4 Determine when the Sec. 332 and Sec. 337 nonrecognition rules apply to the liquidation of a subsidiary corporation

5 Determine the effect of a liquidation on the liquidating corporation's tax attributes

6 Understand the different tax treatments for open and closed liquidation transactions

7 Determine when a liquidating corporation recognizes gains and losses on the retirement of debt

**ADDITIONAL
COMMENT**

Capital gains recognized after
May 5, 2003, through 2008 are
taxed at a maximum 15% rate as
are qualified dividends received
in tax years 2003 through 2008.
Thus, dividends and capital gains
receive comparable tax rate treatment except that capital gain taxation is deferred until sale of the
stock or liquidation of the corporation.

As part of the corporate life cycle, management may decide to discontinue the operations of a profitable or unprofitable corporation by liquidating it. As a result of this decision, the shareholders may receive liquidating distributions of the corporation's assets. Preceding the formal liquidation of the corporation, management may sell part or all the corporation's assets. The sale may be undertaken to dispose of assets the shareholders may not want to receive in a liquidating distribution or to obtain cash that can be used to pay the corporation's liabilities (including federal income taxes incurred on the liquidation).

Ordinarily, the liquidation transaction is motivated by a combination of tax and business reasons. However, sometimes it is undertaken principally for tax reasons.

▶ If the corporation liquidates and its shareholders hold the assets in an unincorporated form (e.g., sole proprietorship or partnership), the marginal tax rate may be reduced from the 35% top corporate rate to a lower 10%, 15%, 25%, 28%, or 33% individual rate (in 2006). For example, even low amounts of taxable income are taxed at 35% in a personal service corporation.

▶ If the assets are producing losses, the shareholders may prefer to hold them in an unincorporated form and deduct the losses on their personal tax returns.

▶ Corporate earnings are taxed once under the corporate income tax rules and a second time when the corporation distributes the earnings as dividends or when the shareholder sells or exchanges the corporate stock at a gain. Liquidation of the corporation permits the assets to be held in an unincorporated form, thereby avoiding double taxation of subsequent earnings.

Liquidating a corporation carries a tax cost, however. The liquidating corporation is taxed as though it sold its assets, and the shareholders receiving liquidating distributions are taxed as though they sold their stock. A C corporation cannot simply elect to be treated as a flow-through entity under the "check-the-box" regulations (see Chapter C2). Thus, the only route to converting a C corporation into a sole proprietorship, partnership, limited liability company, or limited liability partnership is via a taxable corporate liquidation followed by formation of the desired entity. Alternatively, a C corporation could obtain flow-through status without liquidating if it elects S corporation status. Even with this approach, the S corporation faces potential taxation on its built-in gains (see Chapter C11).

This chapter explains the tax consequences of corporate liquidations to both the liquidating corporation and its shareholders. In so doing, the chapter presents two sets of liquidation rules. The general liquidation rules apply to liquidations of corporations not controlled by a parent corporation. Special rules apply to the liquidation of a controlled subsidiary.

OVERVIEW OF CORPORATE LIQUIDATIONS

This chapter initially presents an overview of the tax and nontax consequences of a corporate liquidation to both the shareholders and the distributing corporation.

THE SHAREHOLDER

Several questions must be answered to determine the tax consequences of the liquidation transaction to each of the liquidating corporation's shareholders:

▶ What are the amount, timing, and character of the shareholder's recognized gain or loss?

▶ What is the shareholder's adjusted basis of each property received?

▶ When does the holding period begin for each property received by the shareholder?

When a corporation liquidates under the general rules, a shareholder treats the liquidating distribution as an amount received in exchange for his or her stock. The shareholder recognizes a capital gain or loss equal to the excess of any money received plus the FMV of any nonmoney property received over the adjusted basis of his or her stock. The basis of each property received is stepped-up or stepped-down to the property's FMV on the liquidation date. The holding period for the asset begins the day after the liquidation date.

If a parent corporation liquidates a controlled subsidiary under special rules, however, the parent corporation (shareholder) recognizes no gain or loss. In addition, the bases and holding periods of the subsidiary's assets carry over to the parent.

THE CORPORATION

Two questions must be answered to determine the tax consequences of the liquidation transaction for the liquiding corporation:

▶ What are the amount and character of the corporation's recognized gain or loss?

▶ What happens to the corporation's tax attributes upon liquidation?

When a liquidation occurs under the general rules, the liquidating corporation recognizes gain or loss on the distribution of property to its shareholders. The recognized gain or loss is the same as what the corporation would recognize had it sold the distributed property to its shareholders. Some restrictions (discussed later in the chapter) limit loss recognition in certain potentially abusive situations. Also, tax attributions, such as net operating loss (NOL) carryovers and earnings and profits, disappear when the corporation liquidates under the general rules.

If the liquidating corporation is an 80%-controlled subsidiary of the parent corporation, the liquidating corporation recognizes no gain or loss under special rules. In this case, the subsidiary's tax attributes carry over to the parent corporation.

EXAMPLE C6-1 ▶ Randy Jones owns Able Corporation, a C corporation. Randy's basis for his Able stock is $100,000. The corporation's assets are summarized below:

Assets	Adjusted Basis	Fair Market Value
Cash	$ 50,000	$ 50,000
General Cable stock	75,000	125,000
Machinery	115,000	200,000
Total	$240,000	$375,000

Able Corporation owes $60,000 to its creditors. In step 1, Able sells its machinery to an unrelated purchaser for $200,000 cash. The machinery originally cost $250,000, and Able has claimed $135,000 of depreciation on the machinery. Able recognizes a total gain on the machinery sale of $85,000 ($200,000 − $115,000). In step 2, Able uses $60,000 in cash to pay its creditors. In step 3, Able distributes the General Cable stock, a capital asset, to Randy Jones. Able recognizes a $50,000 ($125,000 − $75,000) capital gain on the distribution. Assuming a 34% marginal tax rate, Able must pay $45,900 [($85,000 + $50,000) × 0.34] in federal income taxes on the distribution of the General Cable stock and the sale of the machinery (step 4). The tax payment reduces Able's remaining assets to $144,100 in cash [($50,000 + $200,000) − $60,000 paid to creditors − $45,900 paid in federal income taxes]. Randy Jones recognizes a $169,100 ($144,100 cash + $125,000 securities − $100,000 basis for stock) long-term capital gain on the liquidating distribution. The same federal income taxes would have occurred had Able sold both the stock and machinery to unrelated purchasers, or had Able distributed both the stock and machinery to Randy Jones because each of Able's noncash assets have FMVs exceeding their adjusted bases.[1] (See Figure C6-1 for an illustration of the corporate liquidation.) ◀

OBJECTIVE 1

Understand the difference between a complete liquidation and a dissolution

DEFINITION OF A COMPLETE LIQUIDATION

The term *complete liquidation* is not defined in the IRC, but Reg. Sec. 1.332-2(c) indicates that distributions made by a liquidating corporation must either completely cancel or redeem all its stock in accordance with a plan of liquidation or be one of a series of distributions that completely cancels or redeems all its stock in accordance with a plan of liquidation (see page C6-21 for a discussion of plans of liquidation). When more than one distribution occurs, the corporation must be in a liquidation status when it makes the first

---

[1] The corporation's recognized gains and losses might be different if one or more of the properties had declined in value. The loss might be disallowed if the property were distributed to Randy Jones, where it would be recognized if the property had been sold to an unrelated purchaser.

FIGURE C6-1 ▶ ILLUSTRATION OF CORPORATE LIQUIDATION (EXAMPLE C6-1)

liquidating distribution under the plan, and such status must continue until the liquidation is completed. A distribution made before the corporation adopts a plan of liquidation is taxed to the shareholders as a dividend distribution or stock redemption (see Chapter C4).

Liquidation status exists when the corporation ceases to be a going concern and its activities are for the purpose of winding up its affairs, paying its debts, and distributing any remaining property to its shareholders. A liquidation is completed when the liquidating corporation has divested itself of substantially all property. Retention of a nominal amount of assets (e.g., to retain the corporation's name) does not prevent a liquidation from occurring under the tax rules.

The liquidation of a corporation does not mean the corporation has undergone dissolution. **Dissolution** is a legal term that implies the corporation has surrendered the charter it received from the state. A corporation may complete its liquidation before surrendering its charter to the state and undergoing dissolution. Dissolution may never occur if the corporation retains its charter to protect the corporate name from being acquired by another party.

EXAMPLE C6-2 ▶ Thompson Corporation adopts a plan of liquidation in December of the current year. The corporation distributes all but a nominal amount of its assets to its shareholders in January of the next year. The nominal assets retained are the minimum amount needed to preserve the corporation's existence under state law and to prevent others from acquiring its name. Despite the retention of a nominal amount of assets, Thompson Corporation has liquidated for tax purposes even though it has not dissolved. ◀

STOP & THINK *Question:* Peter Jenkins, age 58, is considering forming a new business entity to operate the rental real estate activities that he and his wife have owned personally for a number of years. He has heard about corporations and limited liability companies from reading various real estate journals. Because of their level of personal wealth and the liability protection afforded by the corporate form of doing business, Peter wants to use a corporation to own and operate their real estate. The assets Peter and his wife plan to transfer to the corporation have a $600,000 FMV and a $420,000 adjusted basis. As Peter's CPA, why should you consider the tax cost of liquidating the corporation as part of the overall analysis of the business entity selection decision?

Solution: A transfer of real estate by Peter and his wife to a corporation is tax-free. A subsequent liquidation of the corporation is not tax-free because both the corporation and the shareholder may recognize gain or loss. Peter and his wife have $180,000 ($600,000 − $420,000) of appreciation in their real estate. Even if no change in value occurs, liquidation of the real estate corporation at a later date will cause $180,000 to be taxed twice, once at the corporate level and again at the shareholder level. On the other hand, creation and liquidation of a limited liability company are not taxable events to the entity or its owners. Thus, the difference in liquidation treatment at a future date is one of many differences the owners must consider when forming an entity. More information on liquidating a limited liability company can be found in Chapter C10.

GENERAL LIQUIDATION RULES

This chapter section presents the general liquidation rules. These rules are considered in two parts: the effects of liquidating on the shareholders and the effects of liquidating on the corporation.

> **OBJECTIVE 2**
>
> *Apply the general shareholder gain and loss recognition rules for a corporate liquidation*

EFFECTS OF LIQUIDATING ON THE SHAREHOLDERS

Three aspects of the general liquidation rules are discussed below: amount and timing of gain or loss recognition, character of the recognized gain or loss, and basis and holding period of property received in the liquidation. Table C6-1 summarizes the liquidation rules applying to shareholders under both the general liquidation rules and the controlled subsidiary corporation exception.

AMOUNT OF RECOGNIZED GAIN OR LOSS. Section 331(a) requires that liquidating distributions received by a shareholder be treated as full payment in exchange for his or her stock. The shareholder's recognized gain or loss equals the difference between the amount realized (the FMV of the assets received from the corporation plus any money) and his or her basis in the stock. If a shareholder assumes or acquires liabilities of the liquidating corporation, the amount of these liabilities reduces the shareholder's amount realized.

EXAMPLE C6-3 ▶ Gamma Corporation liquidates, with Joseph receiving $10,000 in cash plus other property having a $12,000 FMV. Joseph's basis in his Gamma stock is $16,000. Joseph's amount realized is $22,000 ($12,000 + $10,000). Therefore, he must recognize a $6,000 ($22,000 − $16,000) gain on the liquidation. ◀

EXAMPLE C6-4 ▶ Assume the same facts as in Example C6-3 except Joseph also assumes a $2,000 mortgage attaching to the other property. Joseph's amount realized is reduced by the $2,000 liability assumed and is $20,000 ($22,000 − $2,000). His recognized gain on the liquidation is $4,000 ($20,000 − $16,000). ◀

▼ **TABLE C6-1**

Tax Consequences of a Liquidation to the Shareholders

	Amount of Gain or Loss Recognized	Character of Gain or Loss Recognized	Adjusted Basis of Property Received	Holding Period of Property Received
General rule	Shareholders recognize gain or loss (money + FMV of nonmoney property received − adjusted basis of stock) upon liquidation (Sec. 331).	Long-term or short-term capital gain or loss (Sec. 1222). Ordinary loss treatment available (Sec. 1244).	FMV of the property (Sec. 334(a)).	Begins on the day after the liquidation date (Sec. 1223(1)).
Controlled subsidiary corporation rule	Parent corporation recognizes no gain or loss when an 80% controlled subsidiary corporation liquidates into the parent corporation (Sec. 332).[a]	Not applicable.[a]	Carryover basis for property received from subsidiary corporation (Sec. 334(b)).[a]	Includes subsidiary corporation's holding period for the assets (Sec. 1223(2)).[a]

[a] Minority shareholders use the general rule.

Impact of Accounting Method. Shareholders who use the accrual method of accounting recognize gain or loss when all events have occurred that fix the amount of the liquidating distribution and the time the shareholders are entitled to receive the distribution upon surrender of their shares. Shareholders who use the cash method of accounting report the gain or loss when they have actual or constructive receipt of the liquidating distribution(s).[2]

When Stock Is Acquired. A shareholder may have acquired his or her stock at different times or for different per-share amounts. In this case, the shareholder must compute the gain or loss separately for each share or block of stock owned.[3]

CHARACTER OF THE RECOGNIZED GAIN OR LOSS. Generally, the liquidating corporation's stock is a capital asset in the shareholder's hands. The gain or loss recognized, therefore, is a capital gain or loss for most shareholders. Two exceptions to these rules are indicated below.

▶ Loss recognized by an individual shareholder on Sec. 1244 stock is an ordinary loss, within limits (see Chapter C2).

▶ Loss recognized by a corporate shareholder on the worthlessness of the controlled subsidiary's stock is an ordinary loss under Sec. 165(g)(3) (see Chapter C2).

BASIS AND HOLDING PERIOD OF PROPERTY RECEIVED IN THE LIQUIDATION. Section 334(a) provides that the shareholder's basis of property received under the general liquidation rules is its FMV on the distribution date. The holding period for the property starts on the day after the distribution date.

OBJECTIVE 3

Determine when the liquidating corporation recognizes gains and losses on making a liquidating distribution

EFFECTS OF LIQUIDATING ON THE LIQUIDATING CORPORATION

Two aspects of the general liquidation rules are discussed below: (1) the recognition of gain or loss by the liquidating corporation when it distributes property in redemption of its stock and (2) the special valuation rules used when the liabilities assumed or acquired by the shareholder exceed the property's adjusted basis in the liquidating corporation's hands. Table C6-2 summarizes rules applying to the liquidating corporation.

RECOGNITION OF GAIN OR LOSS WHEN CORPORATION DISTRIBUTES PROPERTY IN REDEMPTION OF STOCK. Section 336(a) provides that the liquidating corporation must recognize gain or loss when it distributes property in a complete liquidation. The amount and character of the gain or loss are determined as if the corporation sold the property to the shareholder at its FMV.

EXAMPLE C6-5 ▶

Under West Corporation's plan of liquidation, the corporation distributes land to one of its shareholders, Arnie. The land, which is used in West's trade or business, has a $40,000 adjusted basis and a $120,000 FMV on the distribution date. West recognizes an $80,000 ($120,000 − $40,000) Sec. 1231 gain when it makes the liquidating distribution. Arnie recognizes a capital gain to the extent the land's FMV exceeds his basis in the West stock. Arnie's basis for the land is its $120,000 FMV. A nonliquidating distribution would have produced similar results for the corporation. However, for the shareholder, the entire FMV would have been a dividend instead of a capital gain assuming sufficient E&P. Thus, both liquidating and nonliquidating distributions produce double taxation although the amount and character of the shareholder's gain or income differ. ◀

With limited exceptions, the liquidating corporation can recognize a loss when it distributes property that has declined in value to its shareholders. This rule eliminates the need for a liquidating corporation to sell property that has declined in value to recognize its losses.

EXAMPLE C6-6 ▶

Assume the same facts as in Example C6-5 except the land's FMV is instead $10,000. West recognizes a $30,000 ($10,000 − $40,000) Sec. 1231 loss when it distributes the land to Arnie. Arnie's basis for the land is $10,000. ◀

---

[2] Rev. Rul. 80-177, 1980-2 C.B. 109.   [3] Reg. Sec. 1.331-1(e).

▼ TABLE C6-2

Tax Consequences of a Liquidation to the Liquidating Corporation

	Amount and Character of Gain, Loss, or Income Recognized	Treatment of the Liquidating Corporation's Tax Attributes
General rule	The liquidating corporation recognizes gain or loss when it distributes property as part of a complete liquidation (Sec. 336(a)).	Tax attributes disappear when the liquidation is completed.
Controlled subsidiary corporation rules	1. The liquidating subsidiary corporation recognizes no gain or loss upon a distribution of property to its parent corporation when the Sec. 332 nonrecognition rules apply to the parent corporation (Sec. 337(a)). 2. The liquidating subsidiary corporation recognizes no loss upon a distribution of property to minority shareholders when the Sec. 332 nonrecognition rules apply to the parent corporation (Sec. 336(d)(3)). It does recognize gains, however.	Tax attributes of a subsidiary corporation carry over to the parent corporation when the Sec. 332 rules apply (Sec. 381(a)).
Related party rule	The liquidating subsidiary corporation recognizes no loss upon a distribution of property to a related person unless the corporation distributes such property ratably to all shareholders *and* the liquidating corporation did not acquire the property in a Sec. 351 transaction or as a capital contribution during the five years preceding the distribution (Sec. 336(d)(1)).	
Tax avoidance rule	The liquidating subsidiary corporation recognizes no loss when a sale, exchange, or distribution of property occurs and the liquidating corporation acquired such property in a Sec. 351 transaction or as a capital contribution having as a principal purpose the recognition of loss (Sec. 336(d)(2)).	

The Sec. 336 rules apply only to property distributed in exchange for the liquidating corporation's stock as part of a complete liquidation. These rules do not apply to distributions of appreciated property as part of a partial liquidation, or when a debt of the liquidating corporation is retired in exchange for appreciated property.

TAX STRATEGY TIP

If possible, a corporation should avoid distributing property subject to a mortgage that exceeds the property's FMV. Such distributions cause excessive corporate gain recognition and uncertainty of results at the shareholder level.

LIABILITIES ASSUMED OR ACQUIRED BY THE SHAREHOLDERS. For purposes of determining the amount of gain or loss recognized under Sec. 336, property distributed by the liquidating corporation is treated as having been sold to the distributee for its FMV on the distribution date. Section 336(b) contains a special restriction on valuing a liquidating property distribution when the shareholders assume or acquire liabilities. According to this rule, the FMV of the distributed property cannot be less than the amount of the liability assumed or acquired. Congress enacted Sec. 336(b) because the corporation realizes an economic gain or benefit equal to the amount of the liability the shareholder assumes or acquires (and not just the lower FMV of the property distributed) as part of the liquidation. Treatment at the shareholder level is not completely clear. Section 336(b) specifically states that this liability rule applies only for determining the corporation's gain or loss. Thus, it does not seem to extend to Sec. 334(a), which requires the shareholder to take a FMV basis in the distributed property. Some commentators have suggested that the strict statutory interpretation of giving the shareholders the actual FMV basis, rather than the greater liability basis, produces an illogical result.[4] Also, given that the liability exceeds the distributed property's FMV, the shareholder's amount realized should be zero, resulting in a capital loss equal to the shareholder's stock basis.

[4] For a detailed discussion, see B.C. Randall and D.N. Stewart, "Corporate Distributions: Handling Liabilities in Excess of the Fair Market Value of Property Remains Unresolved," *The Journal of Corporate Taxation*, Spring 1992, pp. 55-64.

EXAMPLE C6-7 ▶ Jersey Corporation owns an apartment complex costing $3 million that has been depreciated so that its adjusted basis is $2.4 million. The property is secured by a $2.7 million mortgage. Pursuant to a plan of liquidation, Jersey distributes the property and the mortgage to Rex, Jersey's sole shareholder, at a time when the property's FMV is $2.2 million. Rex's stock basis is $500,000. Jersey recognizes a $300,000 ($2,700,000 − $2,400,000) gain on distributing the property because its FMV cannot be less than the $2.7 million mortgage. The shareholder recognizes a $500,000 capital loss on the corporate stock and takes either a $2.2 million or $2.7 million basis in the property, depending on which interpretation applies. ◀

EXCEPTIONS TO THE GENERAL GAIN OR LOSS RECOGNITION RULE. The IRC provides four exceptions to the general recognition rule of Sec. 336(a). Two of these exceptions apply to liquidations of controlled subsidiary corporations and are covered later. The other two exceptions prevent certain abusive practices (e.g., the manufacturing of losses) from being accomplished and are examined below. Also, Sec 362(e)(2) added by the 2004 Jobs Act may reduce a liquidating corporation's loss recognition. Specifically, for property contributed to a controlled corporation after October 22, 2004, the corporation must reduce the basis of loss property if the total adjusted basis of property contributed by a shareholder exceeds the total FMV of that property (see Chapter C2 for details). Consequently, upon a later liquidating distribution, the corporation will realized a smaller loss or no loss at all.[5]

ADDITIONAL COMMENT

The disqualified property rule prohibits a shareholder from infusing loss property into the liquidating corporation and generating losses at both the corporate and shareholder levels by liquidating the corporation.

Distributions to Related Persons. Section 336(d)(1)(A) prevents loss recognition in connection with property distributions to a related person if (1) the distribution of loss property is other than pro rata to all shareholders based on their stock ownership or (2) the distributed property is disqualified property. Section 267(b) defines a related person as including, for example, an individual and a corporation whose stock is more than 50% owned (in terms of value) by such individual, as well as two corporations that are members of the same controlled group. Section 336(d)(1)(B) defines disqualified property as (1) any property acquired by the liquidating corporation in a transaction to which Sec. 351 applies, or as a contribution to capital, during the five-year period ending on the distribution date or (2) any property having an adjusted basis that carries over from disqualified property.

EXAMPLE C6-8 ▶ Lei owns 60% and Betty owns 40% of Mesa Corporation's stock. Mesa adopts a plan of liquidation. Pursuant to the plan, Mesa distributes to Lei Beta stock that Mesa purchased two years ago. The Beta stock, which is not disqualified property, has a $40,000 FMV and a $100,000 adjusted basis. Betty receives only cash in the liquidation. The non–pro rata distribution of the Beta stock (the loss property), however, prevents Mesa from claiming a $60,000 capital loss when it makes the distribution. If Mesa instead distributes the Beta stock 60% to Lei and 40% to Betty, Mesa deducts the entire capital loss, assuming Mesa has offsetting capital gains. ◀

EXAMPLE C6-9 ▶ Assume the same facts as in Example C6-8 except Mesa acquired the Beta stock two years ago as a capital contribution from Lei when the Beta stock basis was $100,000 and its FMV was $105,000. Thus, the stock was not subject to the basis reduction rule when contributed, and Mesa took a $100,000 carryover basis in the stock. The stock's FMV now is $40,000, and the corporation distributes it to Lei upon liquidation of the corporation. The Beta stock in this case is disqualified property. The $60,000 realized loss is disallowed because Lei is a related party under Sec. 267(b). If Mesa instead distributes the Beta stock 60% to Lei and 40% to Betty, Mesa still is prohibited from deducting the portion of the $60,000 capital loss attributable to the stock distributed to the related party even though Mesa distributed it ratably to Lei and Betty. Mesa can deduct only the $24,000 ($60,000 × 0.40) capital loss attributable to the Beta stock distributed to Betty because she is not a related party. Alternatively, a sale of the disqualified property to an unrelated purchaser permits Mesa to recognize the entire $60,000 loss, again assuming offsetting capital gains exist. ◀

EXAMPLE C6-10 ▶ Assume the same facts as in Example C6-9 except the Beta stock had an $85,000 FMV when contributed, and Mesa had to reduce its basis in the stock to $85,000 at that time. Upon liqui-

---

[5] For a detailed discussion, see B. C. Randall, B. C. Spilker, and J. M. Werlhof, "The Interaction of New Section 362(e)(2) With the Loss Disallowance Rules in Corporate Liquidations," *Corporate Taxation*, September/October 2005.

dation and distribution to Lei, Mesa realizes a $45,000 ($40,000 − $85,000) loss, which is disallowed under the related person, disqualified property rule. If instead Mesa distributes the Beta stock ratably to Lei and Betty, Mesa can deduct $18,000 ($45,000 × 0.40) of the loss attributable to the stock distributed to Betty, again assuming Mesa recognizes offsetting gains on other property. ◄

Sales Having a Tax-Avoidance Purpose. Section 336(d)(2) restricts loss recognition with respect to the sale, exchange, or distribution of property acquired in a Sec. 351 transaction, or as a contribution to capital, where the liquidating corporation acquired the property as part of a plan having the principal purpose of loss recognition by the corporation in connection with its liquidation. This loss limitation prevents a shareholder from transferring loss property into a corporation to reduce or eliminate the gain the liquidating corporation otherwise would have recognized from the distribution of other appreciated property.

Property acquired by the liquidating corporation in any Sec. 351 transaction or as a contribution to capital within two years of the date on which a plan of complete liquidation is adopted are treated as part of a plan having a tax-avoidance purpose unless exempted by forthcoming regulations. Treasury Regulations, when issued, should not prevent corporations from deducting losses associated with dispositions of assets that are contributed to the corporation and used in a trade or business (or a line of business), or dispositions occurring during the first two years of a corporation's existence.[6]

The basis of the contributed property for loss purposes equals its adjusted basis to the corporation at the time of liquidation reduced (but not below zero) by the excess (if any) of the property's adjusted basis over its FMV immediately after its contribution to the corporation. This adjusted basis already may include a reduction under Sec. 362(e)(2) for contributed loss property. No adjustment occurs to the contributed property's adjusted basis when determining the corporation's recognized gain.

EXAMPLE C6-11 ▶ Terry contributed a widget maker having a $1,000 adjusted basis and a $100 FMV to Pirate Corporation in exchange for additional stock on January 10, 2005. At the same time, Terry contributed a second property having a $2,000 FMV and a $900 adjusted basis. Because the total FMV of Terry's contributed property ($2,100) exceeded the total adjusted basis of that property ($1,900), the corporation did not reduce the loss property's basis under Sec. 362(e)(2) at that time. On April 1, 2006, Pirate adopts a plan of liquidation. Between January 10, 2005, and April 1, 2006, Pirate does not use the widget maker in its trade or business. Liquidation occurs on July 1, 2006, and Pirate distributes the widget maker and a second property that has a $2,500 FMV and a $900 adjusted basis. Because Terry contributed the widget maker to Pirate after April 1, 2004 (two years before Pirate adopted its plan of liquidation), and the widget maker is not used in Pirate's trade or business, its acquisition and distribution are presumed to be motivated by a desire to recognize the $900 loss. Unless Pirate can establish otherwise (e.g., by arguing that Sec. 362(e)(2) precludes a tax avoidance purpose), Sec. 336(d)(2) will apply to the distribution of the widget maker. Pirate's basis for determining its loss will be $100 [$1,000 − ($1,000 − $100)]. Thus, Pirate cannot claim a loss upon distributing the widget maker. This rule prevents Pirate from offsetting the $1,600 ($2,500 − $900) gain recognized on distributing the second property by the $900 loss realized on distributing the widget maker. ◄

The basis adjustment also affects sales, exchanges, or distributions of property made before the adoption of the plan of liquidation or in connection with the liquidation. Thus, losses claimed in a tax return filed before the adoption of the plan of liquidation may be restricted by Sec. 336(d)(2). The liquidating corporation may recapture these losses in the tax return for the tax year in which the plan of liquidation is adopted, or it can file an amended tax return for the tax year in which it originally claimed the loss.

EXAMPLE C6-12 ▶ Assume the same facts as in Example C6-11 except Pirate sells the widget maker for $200 on July 10, 2005. Pirate reports an $800 loss ($200 − $1,000) on its 2005 tax return. The adoption of the plan of liquidation on April 1, 2006, causes the loss on the sale of the widget maker to be

---

[6] H. Rept. No. 99-841, 99th Cong., 2d Sess., p. II-201 (1986). The Conference Committee Report for the 1986 Tax Act indicates that property transactions occurring more than two years in advance of the adoption of the plan of liqui- dation will be disregarded unless no clear and substantial relationship exists between the contributed property and the conduct of the corporation's current or future business enterprises.

covered by the Sec. 336(d)(2) rules, again assuming a tax avoidance purpose exists. Pirate can file an amended 2005 tax return showing the $800 loss being disallowed, or it can file its 2006 tax return reporting $800 of income under the loss recapture rules.[7] ◄

Topic Review C6-1 summarizes the general corporate liquidation rules.

Topic Review C6-1

Tax Consequences of a Corporate Liquidation

General Corporate Liquidation Rules

1. The shareholder's recognized gain or loss equals the amount of cash plus the FMV of the other property received minus the adjusted basis of the stock surrendered. Corporate liabilities assumed or acquired by the shareholder reduce the amount realized.
2. The gain or loss is capital if the stock investment is a capital asset. If the shareholder recognizes a loss on the liquidation, Sec. 1244 permits ordinary loss treatment (within limits) for qualifying individual shareholders.
3. The adjusted basis of the property received is its FMV on the distribution date.
4. The shareholder's holding period for the property begins the day after the distribution date.
5. With certain limited exceptions, the distributing corporation recognizes gain or loss when making the distribution. The amount and character of the gain or loss are determined as if the corporation sold the property for its FMV immediately before the distribution. Special rules apply when the shareholders assume or acquire corporate liabilities and the amount of such liabilities exceeds the property's FMV.
6. The liquidated corporation's tax attributes disappear upon liquidation.

Liquidation of a Controlled Subsidiary Corporation

OBJECTIVE 4

Determine when the Sec. 332 and Sec. 337 nonrecognition rules apply to the liquidation of a subsidiary corporation

The following discussion of the controlled subsidiary exception is divided into three parts: the requirements for using the exception, the effects of liquidating on the parent corporation, and the effects of liquidating on the subsidiary corporation.

Section 332(a) provides that the parent corporation recognizes no gain or loss when a controlled subsidiary corporation liquidates into its parent corporation. This liquidation rule permits a corporation to modify its corporate structure without incurring any adverse tax consequences. Section 332 applies only to the parent corporation. Other shareholders owning a minority interest are taxed under the general liquidation rules of Sec. 331. When Sec. 332 applies to the parent corporation, Sec. 337 permits the liquidating corporation to recognize no gains or losses on the assets distributed to the parent corporation. The liquidating corporation, however, recognizes gains (but not losses) on distributions made to shareholders holding a minority interest. The nonrecognition of gain or loss rule is logical for the distribution to the parent corporation because the assets remain within the corporate group following the distribution. Thus, the subsidiary corporation can be liquidated and operated as a division of its parent corporation without gain or loss recognition.

EXAMPLE C6-13 ▶ Parent Corporation owns all of Subsidiary Corporation's stock. Subsidiary's assets have a $1 million FMV and a $400,000 adjusted basis. Parent's basis for its Subsidiary stock is $250,000. The liquidation of Subsidiary results in a $600,000 ($1,000,000 − $400,000) realized gain for Subsidiary on the distribution of its assets, none of which is recognized. Parent has a $750,000 ($1,000,000 − $250,000) realized gain on surrendering its Subsidiary stock, none of which is recognized. If Secs. 332 and 337 were not available, both Subsidiary and

---

[7] The property has a $1,000 basis when determining Pirate's gain on the sale and a $100 ($1,000 − $900) basis when determining its loss on the sale. Therefore, Pirate recognizes no gain or loss because the $200 sale price lies between the gain and loss basis amounts.

Parent would recognize their realized gains. In this case, Parent's gain would be reduced by the taxes paid by Subsidiary on its gain because Subsidiary's taxes reduce the amount available for distribution to Parent. ◄

REQUIREMENTS

All the following requirements must be met for a liquidation to qualify for the Sec. 332 nonrecognition rules:

▶ The parent corporation must own at least 80% of the total combined voting power of all classes of stock entitled to vote and 80% of the total value of all classes of stock (other than certain nonvoting preferred stock issues) from the date on which the plan of liquidation is adopted until receipt of the subsidiary corporation's property.[8]

▶ The property distribution must be in complete cancellation or redemption of all the subsidiary corporation's stock.

▶ Distribution of the property must occur within a single tax year or be one of a series of distributions completed within three years of the close of the tax year during which the subsidiary makes the first of the series of liquidating distributions.

If the corporations meet all these requirements, the Sec. 332 nonrecognition rules are mandatory. If one or more of the conditions listed above are not met, the parent corporation is taxed under the previously discussed general liquidation rules.

STOCK OWNERSHIP. For Sec. 332 to apply, the parent corporation must own the requisite amount of voting and nonvoting stock. In applying this requirement, the Sec. 318 attribution rules for stock ownership do not apply (see Chapter C4).[9] The parent corporation must own the requisite 80% of voting and nonvoting stock from the date on which the plan of liquidation is adopted until the liquidation is completed. Failure to satisfy this requirement denies the transaction the benefits of Secs. 332 and 337. (See page C6-19 for further discussion of the stock ownership question.)

CANCELLATION OF THE STOCK. The subsidiary corporation must distribute its property in complete cancellation or redemption of all its stock in accordance with a plan of liquidation. When more than one liquidating distribution occurs, the subsidiary corporation must have adopted a plan of liquidation and be in a status of liquidation when it makes the first distribution. This status must continue until the liquidation is completed. Regulation Sec. 1.332-2(c) indicates that a liquidation is completed when the liquidating corporation has divested itself of all its property. The liquidating corporation, however, may retain a nominal amount of property to permit retention or sale of the corporate name.

TIMING OF THE DISTRIBUTIONS. The distribution of all the subsidiary corporation's assets within one subsidiary tax year in complete cancellation or redemption of all its stock is considered a complete liquidation.[10] Although a formal plan of liquidation can be adopted, the shareholders' adoption of a resolution authorizing the distribution of the corporation's assets in complete cancellation or redemption of its stock is considered to be the adoption of a plan of liquidation when the distribution occurs within a single tax year. The tax year in which the liquidating distribution occurs does not have to be the same as the one in which the plan of liquidation is adopted.[11]

The subsidiary corporation can carry out the plan of liquidation by making a series of distributions that extend over a period of more than one tax year to cancel or redeem its stock. A formal plan of liquidation must be adopted when the liquidating distributions extend beyond a single tax year of the liquidating corporation. The liquidating distributions must include all the corporation's property and must be completed within three years of the close of the tax year during which the subsidiary makes the first distribution under the plan.[12]

---

[8] The stock definition used for Sec. 332 purposes excludes any stock that is not entitled to vote, is limited and preferred as to dividends and does not participate in corporate growth to any significant extent, has redemption and liquidation rights that do not exceed its issue price (except for a reasonable redemption or liquidation premium), and is not convertible into another class of stock.

[9] Sec. 332(b)(1).
[10] Sec. 332(b)(2) and Reg. Sec. 1.332-3.
[11] Rev. Rul. 76-317, 1976-2 C.B. 98.
[12] Sec. 332(b)(3) and Reg. Sec. 1.332-4.

EFFECTS OF LIQUIDATING ON THE SHAREHOLDERS
RECOGNITION OF GAIN OR LOSS.

Parent Corporation. The Sec. 332(a) nonrecognition rules apply only to a parent corporation that receives a liquidating distribution from a solvent subsidiary. Section 332(a) does not apply to a parent corporation that receives a liquidating distribution from an insolvent subsidiary, to minority shareholders who receive liquidating distributions, or to a parent corporation that receives a payment to satisfy the subsidiary's indebtedness to the parent. All of these exceptions are discussed below.

Section 332 does not apply if the subsidiary corporation is insolvent at the time of the liquidation because the parent corporation does not receive the distributions in exchange for its stock investment. An insolvent subsidiary is one whose liabilities exceed the FMV of its assets. Regulation Sec. 1.332-2(b) requires the parent corporation to receive at least partial payment for the stock it owns in the subsidiary corporation to qualify for nonrecognition under Sec. 332. If the subsidiary is insolvent, however, the special worthless security rules of Sec. 165(g)(3) for affiliated corporations and the bad debt rules of Sec. 166 permit the parent corporation to recognize an ordinary loss with respect to its investment in the subsidiary's stock or debt obligations (see Chapter C2).

EXAMPLE C6-14

Parent Corporation owns all of Subsidiary Corporation's stock. Parent established Subsidiary to produce and market a product that proved unsuccessful. Parent has a $1.5 million basis in its Subsidiary stock. In addition, it made a $1 million advance to Subsidiary that is not secured by a note. Under a plan of liquidation, Subsidiary distributes all its assets, having a $750,000 FMV, to Parent in partial satisfaction of the advance after having paid all third-party creditors. No assets remain to pay the remainder of the advance or to redeem the outstanding stock. Because Subsidiary is insolvent immediately before the liquidating distribution, it distributes none of its assets in redemption of the Subsidiary stock. Therefore, the liquidation cannot qualify under the Sec. 332 rules. Parent, therefore, claims a $250,000 business bad debt with respect to the unpaid portion of the advance and a $1.5 million ordinary loss for its stock investment. ◄

 STOP & THINK

Question: In Example C6-14, assume Subsidiary Corporation had a $3 million net operating loss (NOL) carryover, which would disappear upon liquidation because Sec. 332 did not apply. To prevent this disappearance, Parent Corporation proposes to cancel the $1 million advance as a contribution to Subsidiary's capital. Thus, Parent would have a $2.5 million basis in its Subsidiary stock prior to the liquidation and no advances receivable. Now when Parent liquidates Subsidiary, all of Subsidiary's assets redeem its outstanding stock, and the transaction seems to qualify for Sec. 332 treatment. Under these circumstances, the $3 million NOL would carry over to Parent under Sec. 381, giving Parent $3 million worth of NOL deductions rather than $1.75 million worth of bad debt and worthless stock deductions under the original transaction. Do you think the IRS would condone this proposed transaction?

Solution: No. In Rev. Rul. 68-602, 1968-2 C.B. 135, the IRS held under similar circumstances that, because the cancellation "was an integral part of the liquidation and had no independent significance other than to secure the tax benefits of [Subsidiary's] net operating loss carryover, such step will be considered transitory and, therefore, disregarded." Thus, if Parent proceeded with the proposed transaction, the IRS would ignore it and treat the liquidation the same as originally done in Example C6-14.

The 2004 Jobs Act added a special rule to prevent the importation of built-in losses from foreign corporations. Specifically, the parent takes a FMV basis in each transferred property if the following three conditions prevail: (1) the parent is a U.S. corporation, (2) the liquidating subsidiary is a foreign corporation, and (3) the aggregate adjusted basis of the transferred property exceeds the aggregate FMV.

Minority Shareholders. Liquidating distributions made to minority shareholders are taxed under the Sec. 331 general liquidation rules. These rules require the minority shareholders to recognize gain or loss—which generally is capital—upon the redemption of their stock in the subsidiary corporation.

EXAMPLE C6-15 ▶

SELF-STUDY QUESTION

What bases do both the parent and minority shareholders take in the assets received in a Sec. 332 liquidation?

ANSWER

Because the parent corporation recognizes no gain or loss in the transaction, the parent corporation takes a carryover basis in its assets. However, because the minority shareholders are involved in a taxable exchange, they take a FMV basis in their assets.

Parent Corporation and Jane own 80% and 20%, respectively, of Subsidiary Corporation's single class of stock. Parent and Jane have adjusted bases of $100,000 and $15,000, respectively, for their stock interests. Subsidiary adopts a plan of liquidation on May 30 and makes liquidating distributions of two parcels of land having $250,000 and $62,500 FMVs to Parent and Jane, respectively, on November 1 in exchange for their stock. Parent does not recognize its $150,000 ($250,000 − $100,000) gain because of Sec. 332. Jane recognizes a $47,500 ($62,500 − $15,000) capital gain under Sec. 331. (Subsidiary also faces gain recognition on the distribution to its minority shareholder as demonstrated in Example C6-18.) ◀

BASIS OF PROPERTY RECEIVED. Under Sec. 334(b)(1), the parent corporation's basis for property received in the liquidating distribution is the same as the subsidiary corporation's basis prior to the distribution. This carryover basis rule reflects the principle that the liquidating corporation recognizes no gain or loss when it distributes the property and that the property's tax attributes (e.g., the depreciation recapture potential) carry over from the subsidiary corporation to the parent corporation. The parent corporation's basis for its stock investment in the subsidiary corporation is ignored in determining the basis for the distributed property and disappears once the parent surrenders its stock in the subsidiary. Property received by minority shareholders takes a basis equal to its FMV.

EXAMPLE C6-16 ▶

Assume the same facts as in Example C6-15 and that the two parcels of land received by Parent Corporation and Jane have adjusted bases of $175,000 and $40,000, respectively, to Subsidiary. Parent takes a $175,000 carryover basis for its land, and Jane takes a $62,500 FMV basis for her land. ◀

 STOP & THINK

Question: Why should a corporation that is 100%-owned by another corporation be treated differently when it liquidates than a corporation that is 100%-owned by an individual?

Solution: A corporation that is 100%-owned by another corporation can file a consolidated tax return (see Chapters C3 and C8). As a result, the parent and its subsidiary corporations are treated as a single entity. This result is the same as if the subsidiary were one of a number of divisions of a single corporation. An extension of the single-entity concept is that a subsidiary corporation can be liquidated tax-free into its parent corporation. An individual and his or her corporation are treated as two separate tax entities when calculating their annual tax liabilities. As separate entities, nonliquidating distributions (e.g., ordinary distributions and stock redemptions) from the corporation to its shareholder(s) are taxable. The same principle applies to liquidating distributions.

EFFECTS OF LIQUIDATING ON THE SUBSIDIARY CORPORATION

RECOGNITION OF GAIN OR LOSS. Section 337(a) provides that the liquidating corporation recognizes no gain or loss on the distribution of property to the 80% distributee in a complete liquidation to which Sec. 332 applies.[13] Section 337(c) defines the term *80% distributee* as a corporation that meets the 80% stock ownership requirement specified in Sec. 332 (see page C6-11).

EXAMPLE C6-17 ▶

Parent Corporation owns all the stock of Subsidiary Corporation. Pursuant to a plan of complete liquidation, Subsidiary distributes land having a $200,000 FMV and a $60,000 basis to Parent. Subsidiary recognizes no gain with respect to the distribution. Parent takes a $60,000 basis for the land. ◀

The depreciation recapture provisions in Secs. 1245, 1250, and 291 do not override the Sec. 337(a) nonrecognition rule if a controlled subsidiary corporation liquidates into its parent corporation. Instead, the parent corporation assumes the depreciation recapture

---

[13] Section 336(e) permits a corporation to sell, exchange, or distribute the stock of a subsidiary corporation and to elect to treat such a transaction as a disposition of all the subsidiary corporation's assets. The parent corporation recognizes no gain or loss on the sale, exchange, or distribution of the stock. The economic consequences of making this election for a stock sale are essentially the same as if the parent corporation instead liquidates the subsidiary in a transaction to which Sec. 332 applies and then immediately sells the properties to the purchaser.

potential associated with the distributed property, and recapture occurs when the parent corporation sells or exchanges the property.[14]

The Sec. 337(a) nonrecognition rule applies only to distributions to the parent corporation. Liquidating distributions to minority shareholders are not eligible for nonrecognition under Sec. 337(a). Consequently, the liquidating corporation must recognize gain under Sec. 336(a) when it distributes appreciated property to the minority shareholders. Section 336(d)(3), however, prevents the subsidiary corporation from recognizing loss on distributions made to minority shareholders. Thus, for the subsidiary, liquidating distributions made to minority shareholders are treated the same way as nonliquidating distributions.

EXAMPLE C6-18 ▶ Assume the same facts as in Example C6-17 except Parent Corporation owns 80% of the Subsidiary stock, Chuck owns the remaining 20% of such stock, and Subsidiary distributes two parcels of land to Parent and Chuck. The parcels have FMVs of $160,000 and $40,000, and adjusted bases of $50,000 and $10,000, respectively. Subsidiary does not recognize the $110,000 ($160,000 − $50,000) gain realized on the distribution to Parent. However, Subsidiary does recognize the $30,000 ($40,000 − $10,000) gain realized on the distribution to Chuck because the Sec. 337(a) nonrecognition rule applies only to distributions to the 80% distributee. Assume that the land distributed to Chuck instead has a $40,000 FMV and a $50,000 adjusted basis. Subsidiary can deduct none of the $10,000 loss because it distributed the land to a minority shareholder. ◀

OBJECTIVE 5

Determine the effect of a liquidation on the liquidating corporation's tax attributes

TAX ATTRIBUTE CARRYOVERS. The **tax attributes** of the liquidating corporation disappear when the liquidation is completed under the general rules. They carry over, however, in the case of a controlled subsidiary corporation liquidated into its parent corporation under Sec. 332.[15] The following items are included among the carried-over attributes:

▶ NOL carryovers

▶ Earnings and profits

▶ Capital loss carryovers

▶ General business and other tax credit carryovers

The carryover amount is determined as of the close of the day on which the subsidiary corporation completes the distribution of all its property. Chapter C7 contains further discussion of these rules.

Topic Review C6-2 summarizes the special rules applicable to the liquidation of a controlled subsidiary corporation.

Topic Review C6-2

Tax Consequences of a Corporate Liquidation

Tax Consequences of Liquidating a Controlled Subsidiary Corporation

1. Specific requirements must be met with respect to (a) stock ownership, (b) distribution of the property in complete cancellation or redemption of all the subsidiary's stock, and (c) distribution of all property within a single tax year or a three-year period. To satisfy the stock ownership requirement, the parent corporation must own at least 80% of the total voting power of all voting stock and at least 80% of the total value of all stock.
2. The parent corporation recognizes no gain or loss when it receives distributed property from the liquidating subsidiary. Section 332 does not apply to liquidations of insolvent subsidiaries and distributions to minority shareholders.
3. The basis of the distributed property carries over from the subsidiary corporation to the parent corporation.
4. The parent corporation's holding period for the assets includes the subsidiary corporation's holding period.
5. The subsidiary corporation recognizes no gain or loss when making a distribution to an 80% distributee (parent). The liquidating subsidiary recognizes gain (but not loss) on distributions to minority shareholders. Also, the liquidating subsidiary recognizes no gain when it distributes appreciated property to satisfy certain subsidiary debts owed to the parent corporation.
6. The subsidiary corporation's tax attributes carry over to the parent corporation as part of the liquidation.

---

[14] Secs. 1245(b)(3) and 1250(d)(3).   [15] Sec. 381(a).

SPECIAL SHAREHOLDER REPORTING ISSUES

Four special shareholder reporting rules apply to liquidation transactions described below. These rules add different degrees of complexity to the general liquidation rules outlined above.

PARTIALLY LIQUIDATING DISTRIBUTIONS

Liquidating distributions often are received in the form of a series of partially liquidating distributions. Section 346(a) indicates that a series of partially liquidating distributions received in complete liquidation of the corporation are taxed under the Sec. 331 liquidation rules instead of under the Sec. 302 rules applying to redemptions in partial liquidation. The IRS permits the shareholder's basis to be recovered first and requires the recognition of gain once the shareholder fully recovers the basis of a particular share or block of stock. The shareholder cannot recognize a loss with respect to a share or block of stock until he or she receives the final liquidating distribution, or until it becomes clear that no more liquidating distributions will occur.[16]

EXAMPLE C6-19 ▶ Diane owns 1,000 shares of Adobe Corporation stock purchased for $40,000 in 2001. Diane receives the following liquidating distributions: July 23, 2004, $25,000; March 12, 2005, $17,000; and April 5, 2006, $10,000. Diane recognizes no gain in 2004 because her $40,000 basis is not fully recovered by year-end. The $15,000 ($40,000 − $25,000) unrecovered basis that exists after the first distribution is less than the $17,000 liquidating distribution received on March 12, 2005, so Diane recognizes a $2,000 gain at this time. She recognizes an additional $10,000 gain in 2006 when she receives the final liquidating distribution. ◀

EXAMPLE C6-20 ▶ Assume the same facts as in Example C6-19 except that Diane paid $60,000 for her Adobe stock. The receipt of each of the liquidating distributions is tax-free because Diane's $60,000 basis exceeds the $52,000 ($25,000 + $17,000 + $10,000) total of the distributions. Diane recognizes an $8,000 ($52,000 − $60,000) loss in 2006 when she receives the final liquidating distribution. ◀

SELF-STUDY QUESTION

If a cash method shareholder is subsequently obligated to pay a contingent liability of the liquidated corporation, what are the tax consequences of such a payment?

ANSWER

First, the prior tax year return is not amended. The additional payment results in a loss recognized in the year of payment. The character of the loss depends on the nature of the gain or loss recognized by the shareholder in the year of liquidation.

SUBSEQUENT ASSESSMENTS AGAINST THE SHAREHOLDERS

At some date after the liquidation, the shareholders may be required to pay a contingent liability of the corporation or a liability not anticipated at the time of the liquidating distribution (e.g., an income tax deficiency determined after the liquidation is completed or a judgment that is contingent when the corporation makes the final liquidating distribution). The additional payment does not affect the reporting of the initial liquidating transaction. The tax treatment for the additional payment depends on the nature of the gain or loss originally reported by the shareholder and not on the type of loss or deduction the liquidating corporation would have reported had it paid the liability.[17] If the liquidation results in a recognized capital gain or loss, a cash method shareholder treats the additional payment as a capital loss in the year of payment (i.e., the shareholder does not file an amended tax return for the year in which he or she originally reported the gain or loss from the liquidation). An accrual method shareholder recognizes the capital loss when he or she incurs the liability.

EXAMPLE C6-21 ▶ Coastal Corporation liquidated three years ago with Tammy, a cash method taxpayer, reporting a $30,000 long-term capital gain on the exchange of her Coastal stock. In the current year, Tammy pays $5,000 as her part of the settlement of a lawsuit against Coastal. All shareholders pay an additional amount because the settlement exceeds the amount of funds that Coastal placed into an escrow account as a result of the litigation. The amount placed into the escrow account was not included in the amount Tammy realized from the liquidating distribution

---

[16] Rev. Ruls. 68-348, 1968-2 C.B. 141, 79-10, 1979-1 C.B. 140, and 85-48, 1985-1 C.B. 126.

[17] *F. Donald Arrowsmith v. CIR*, 42 AFTR 649, 52-2 USTC ¶9527 (USSC, 1952).

three years ago. Because Tammy had not been taxed on the cash placed in the escrow account, she cannot deduct the amount of the payment made from the escrow account in the current year. Nevertheless, Tammy treats the $5,000 paid from her personal funds as a long-term capital loss in the current year. ◄

OBJECTIVE 6

Understand the different tax treatments for open and closed liquidation transactions

OPEN VERSUS CLOSED TRANSACTIONS

Sometimes the value of property received in a corporate liquidation cannot be determined by the usual valuation techniques. Property that can be valued only on the basis of uncertain future payments falls into this category. In such a case, the shareholders may attempt to rely on the **open transaction doctrine** of *Burnet v. Logan* and treat the liquidation as an open transaction.[18] Under this doctrine, the shareholder's gain or loss from the liquidation is not determined until the assets that cannot be valued are subsequently sold, collected, or able to be valued. Any assets that cannot be valued are assigned a zero value. The IRS's position is that the FMV of almost any asset should be ascertainable. Thus, the IRS assumes that the open transaction method should be used only in extraordinary circumstances. For example, an open transaction cannot be used merely because a market valuation for an investment in a closely held corporation is not readily available through market quotations for the stock.

ETHICAL POINT

A tax practitioner needs to ensure that the client obtains appropriate appraisals to support the values assigned to property distributed to shareholders in a corporate liquidation. A 20% substantial underpayment penalty may be imposed on corporations and shareholders that substantially understate their income tax liabilities.

INSTALLMENT OBLIGATIONS RECEIVED BY A SHAREHOLDER

Shareholders who receive an installment obligation as part of their liquidating distribution ordinarily report the FMV of their obligation as part of the consideration received to calculate the amount of the recognized gain or loss. Shareholders who receive an installment obligation that was acquired by the liquidating corporation in connection with the sale or exchange of its property are eligible for special treatment in reporting their gain on the liquidating transaction if the sale or exchange takes place during the 12-month period beginning on the date a plan of complete liquidation is adopted and the liquidation is completed during such 12-month period. These shareholders may report their gain as they receive the installment payments.[19]

SPECIAL CORPORATE REPORTING ISSUES

EXPENSES OF THE LIQUIDATION

The corporation can deduct the expenses incurred in connection with the liquidation transaction. These expenses include attorneys' and accountants' fees, costs incurred in drafting the plan of liquidation and obtaining shareholder approval, and so on.[20] Such amounts ordinarily are deductible in the liquidating corporation's final tax return.

A liquidating corporation treats expenses associated with selling its property as an offset against the sales proceeds. When a corporation sells an asset pursuant to its liquidation, the selling expenses reduce the amount of gain or increase the amount of loss reported by the corporation.[21]

EXAMPLE C6-22 ▶ Madison Corporation adopts a plan of liquidation on July 15 and shortly thereafter sells a parcel of land on which it realizes a $60,000 gain (excluding the effects of a $6,000 sales commission). Madison pays its legal counsel $1,500 to draft the plan of liquidation. Madison distributes all of its remaining properties to its shareholders on December 15. The $1,500 paid to legal counsel is deductible as a liquidation expense in Madison's current year income tax return. The sales commission reduces the $60,000 gain realized on the land sale, so that Madison's recognized gain is $54,000 ($60,000 − $6,000). ◄

---

[18] *Burnet v. Edith A. Logan,* 9 AFTR 1453, 2 USTC ¶736 (USSC, 1931).
[19] Sec. 453(h)(1)(A). A tax deferral is available only with respect to the gain realized by the shareholder. The liquidating corporation must recognize the deferred gain when it distributes the installment obligation to the shareholder as if it had sold the obligation immediately before the distribution.

[20] *Pridemark, Inc. v. CIR,* 15 AFTR 2d 853, 65-1 USTC ¶9388 (4th Cir., 1965).
[21] See, for example, *J. T. Stewart III Trust,* 63 T.C. 682 (1975), *acq.* 1977-1 C.B. 1.

Any capitalized expenditures that are unamortized at the time of liquidation should be deducted if they have no further value to the corporation (e.g., unamortized organizational costs).[22] Capitalized expenditures that have value must be allocated to the shareholders receiving the benefit of such an outlay (e.g., prepaid insurance and prepaid rent).[23] Expenses related to issuing the corporation's stock are nondeductible, even at the time of liquidation, because they are treated as a reduction of paid-in capital. Unamortized bond premiums, however, are deductible at the time the corporation retires the bonds.

TREATMENT OF NET OPERATING LOSSES

TAX STRATEGY TIP

If a liquidating corporation creates an NOL in the year of liquidation or already has NOL carryovers, these losses may disappear with the liquidated corporation. If the liquidation is a Sec. 332 liquidation, the parent corporation acquires the NOL. If the liquidation is taxed under Sec. 331, the liquidating corporation may want to consider an S election for the liquidation year so any NOLs created in that year can pass through to the shareholders.

If the liquidating corporation reports little or no income in its final income tax return, the corporation may create an NOL when it deducts its liquidating expenses and any remaining capitalized expenditures. The NOL carries back to reduce corporate taxes paid in prior years. The resultant federal income tax refund increases (decreases) the gain (loss) previously reported by the shareholder. Alternatively, the shareholders might consider having the corporation make an S election for the liquidation year and have the flow-through loss reported on the shareholders' tax returns. (See Chapter C11 for the tax treatment of S corporations.)

The need for a liquidating corporation to recognize gains when distributing appreciated property can be partially or fully offset by expenses incurred in carrying out the liquidation or by any available NOL carryovers. Losses recognized by the liquidating corporation when distributing property that has declined in value can offset operating profits or capital gains earned in the liquidation year. Should such losses produce an NOL or net capital loss, the losses may be carried back to provide a refund of taxes paid in a prior year, or they may be passed through to the corporation's shareholders if the corporation makes an S corporation election for the tax year.

RECOGNITION OF GAIN OR LOSS WHEN PROPERTY IS DISTRIBUTED IN RETIREMENT OF DEBT

OBJECTIVE 7

Determine when a liquidating corporation recognizes gains and losses on the retirement of debt

GENERAL RULE

A shareholder recognizes no gain or loss when the liquidating corporation pays off an unsecured debt obligation it owes to the shareholder. However, when the corporation retires a security at an amount different from the shareholder's adjusted basis for the obligation, the shareholder recognizes gain or loss for the difference. These rules apply whether the debtor corporation pays or retires the debt as part of its operations or as part of its liquidation. The debtor corporation recognizes no gain or loss when it uses cash to satisfy its debt obligations. However, the debtor corporation recognizes gain when it uses appreciated noncash property to satisfy its debt obligations. Similarly, a debtor corporation recognizes a loss when it uses noncash property that has declined in value to satisfy its debt obligations.

SATISFACTION OF THE SUBSIDIARY'S DEBT OBLIGATIONS

The Sec. 332(a) nonrecognition rules apply only to amounts received by the parent corporation in its role as a shareholder. The parent corporation, however, does recognize gain or loss upon receipt of property in payment of a subsidiary corporation indebtedness if the payment differs from the parent's basis in the debt.[24]

As mentioned above, the use of property to satisfy an indebtedness generally results in the debtor recognizing gain or loss at the time it transfers the property.[25] Section 337(b), however, prevents a liquidating subsidiary corporation from recognizing gain or loss

---

[22] Reg. Sec. 1.248-1(b)(3).
[23] *Koppers Co., Inc. v. U.S.*, 5 AFTR 2d 1597, 60-2 USTC ¶9505 (Ct. Cls., 1960).
[24] Sec. 1001(c).
[25] Ibid.

WHAT WOULD YOU DO IN THIS SITUATION?

Andrea has operated her trendy, upscale clothing store as a C corporation for a number of years. Annually, the corporation earns $200,000 in pretax profits. Andrea's stock is worth about $800,000. Her stock basis is $125,000. One of her good friends, Jenna, has opened a clothing store as a limited liability company and has been telling Andrea about the advantage of not having to pay the corporate income tax. She also hears about the check-the-box regulations that permit corporations to elect to be taxed as partnerships and limited liability companies. She calls and tells you that she wants you to file the necessary paperwork with the IRS to make the change from being taxed as a C corporation to being taxed as a flow-through entity. What advice should you provide Andrea in this situation?

when it transfers noncash property to its parent corporation in satisfaction of an indebtedness. The IRC provides this exception because the property remains within the economic unit of the parent-subsidiary group.

Section 337(b) applies only to the subsidiary's indebtedness owed to the parent corporation on the date the plan of liquidation is adopted and that is satisfied by the transfer of property pursuant to a complete liquidation of the subsidiary corporation. It does not apply to liabilities owed to other shareholders or third-party creditors, or to liabilities incurred after the plan of liquidation is adopted. In addition, if the subsidiary corporation satisfies the indebtedness for less than its face amount, it may have to recognize income from the discharge of an indebtedness.

EXAMPLE C6-23 ▶ Parent Corporation owns all of Subsidiary Corporation's single class of stock. At the time of its acquisition of the Subsidiary stock, Parent purchased $1 million of Subsidiary bonds at their face amount. Subsequently, Parent and Subsidiary adopt a plan of liquidation, and Subsidiary distributes to Parent property having a $1 million FMV and a $400,000 adjusted basis in cancellation of the bonds. Subsidiary also distributes its remaining property to Parent in exchange for all of its outstanding stock. Subsidiary recognizes no gain on the transfer of the property in cancellation of its bonds. Parent recognizes no gain on receipt of the property because the property's FMV equals Parent's adjusted basis of the bonds. Section 334(b)(1) provides that Parent takes a $400,000 carryover basis for the noncash property it receives in cancellation of the bonds. ◀

TAX PLANNING CONSIDERATIONS

TAX STRATEGY TIP

Timing the distribution of loss property so that the losses may be used to offset high-bracket taxable income at the corporate level makes good tax sense if the general liquidation rules are applicable. However, this planning opportunity would not exist in a Sec. 332 parent-subsidiary liquidation because the liquidating subsidiary does not recognize losses.

TIMING THE LIQUIDATION TRANSACTION

Sometimes corporations adopt a plan of liquidation in one year but do not complete the liquidation until a subsequent year. Corporations planning to distribute properties that have both increased in value and decreased in value may find it advantageous to sell or distribute property that has declined in value in a tax year in which they also conducted business activities. As such, the loss recognized when making the liquidating distribution can offset profits that are taxed at higher rates. Deferring the sale or distribution of property that has appreciated in value may delay the recognition of gain for one tax year and also place the gain in a year in which the marginal tax rate is lower.

EXAMPLE C6-24 ▶ Miami Corporation adopts a plan of liquidation in November of the current year, a tax year in which it earns $150,000 in operating profits. Miami discontinues its operating activities before the end of the current year. Pursuant to the liquidation, it distributes assets, producing $40,000 of recognized ordinary losses. In January of next year, Miami distributes assets that have appreciated in value, producing $40,000 of recognized ordinary income. Distributing the loss property in the current year results in a $15,600 tax savings ($40,000 × 0.39). Only $6,000 ($40,000 × 0.15) in taxes result from distributing the appreciated property next year. The rate differential provides a $9,600 ($15,600 − $6,000) net savings to Miami. ◀

Timing the liquidating distributions should not proceed without the planner also considering the tax position of the various shareholders. Taxpayers should be careful about timing the liquidating distributions to avoid creating a short-term capital gain taxed at ordinary rates rather than long-term capital gains taxed at 15% or 5%. If the liquidation results in a recognized loss, shareholders should take advantage of the opportunity to offset the loss against capital gains plus $3,000 of ordinary income, as well as attempt to increase the portion of the loss eligible for ordinary loss treatment under Sec. 1244 (See next section).

RECOGNITION OF ORDINARY LOSSES WHEN A LIQUIDATION OCCURS

Shareholders sometimes recognize losses when a liquidation occurs. Individual shareholders should be aware that, because a complete liquidation is treated as an exchange transaction, Sec. 1244 ordinary loss treatment is available when a small business corporation liquidates. This treatment permits the shareholder to claim $50,000 of ordinary loss when he or she surrenders the stock ($100,000 if the taxpayer is married and files a joint return).

Ordinary loss treatment also is available for a domestic corporation that owns stock or debt securities in a subsidiary corporation. Because the rules in Sec. 332 regarding nonrecognition of gain or loss do not apply when a subsidiary corporation is insolvent (see pages C6-11 and C6-12), the parent corporation can recognize a loss when the subsidiary corporation's stocks and debt securities are determined to be worthless. This loss is an ordinary loss (instead of a capital loss) if the domestic corporation owns at least 80% of the voting stock and 80% of each class of nonvoting stock and more than 90% of the liquidating corporation's gross income for all tax years has been other than passive income.[26]

OBTAINING 80% OWNERSHIP TO ACHIEVE SEC. 332 BENEFITS

The 80% stock ownership requirement provides tax planning opportunities when a subsidiary corporation liquidates. A parent corporation seeking nonrecognition under Sec. 332 may acquire additional shares of the subsidiary corporation's stock *before* the adoption of the plan of liquidation. This acquisition helps the parent corporation meet the 80% minimum and avoids gain recognition on the liquidation. If the parent corporation purchases these additional shares of stock from other shareholders to satisfy the 80% minimum *after* adopting the plan of liquidation, Sec. 332 will not apply.[27]

EXAMPLE C6-25 ▶ Parent Corporation owns 75% of Subsidiary Corporation's single class of stock. On March 12, Parent purchases for cash the remaining 25% of the Subsidiary stock from three individual shareholders pursuant to a tender offer. Parent and Subsidiary adopt a plan of liquidation on October 1, and Subsidiary distributes its assets to Parent on December 1 in exchange for all of Subsidiary's outstanding stock. Parent recognizes no gain or loss on the redemption of its Subsidiary stock in the liquidation because all the Sec. 332 requirements had been satisfied prior to adoption of the plan of liquidation. ◀

Alternatively, the parent corporation might cause the subsidiary corporation to redeem some of its shares held by minority shareholders before the plan of liquidation is adopted. The IRS originally held that the intention to liquidate is present once the subsidiary corporation agrees to redeem the shares of the minority shareholders. Thus, redemption of a 25% minority interest did not permit Sec. 332 to be used even though the parent corporation owned 100% of the outstanding stock after the redemption.[28]

In *George L. Riggs, Inc.,* however, the Tax Court held that a parent corporation's tender offer to minority shareholders and the calling of the subsidiary's preferred stock do not invalidate the Sec. 332 liquidation because "the formation of a conditional intention to liquidate in the future is not the adoption of a plan of liquidation."[29] The IRS has acquiesced to the *Riggs* decision.

---

[26] Sec. 165(g)(3).
[27] Rev. Rul. 75-521, 1975-2 C.B. 120.

[28] Rev. Rul. 70-106, 1970-1 C.B. 70.
[29] *George L. Riggs, Inc.,* 64 T.C. 474 (1975), *acq.* 1976-2 C.B. 2.

Thus, careful planning can help both the parent corporation and subsidiary corporation avoid gain recognition under Secs. 332 and 337. Nonrecognition, however, does not extend to minority shareholders as discussed earlier.

EXAMPLE C6-26 ▶ Parent Corporation owns 80% of Subsidiary Corporation's stock. Anthony owns the remaining 20% of Subsidiary stock. Parent and Anthony have adjusted bases of $200,000 and $60,000, respectively, for their Subsidiary stock. Subsidiary distributes land having a $250,000 adjusted basis and a $400,000 FMV to Parent and $100,000 in cash to Anthony. Subsidiary recognizes no gain or loss on the distribution of the land or the cash. Parent recognizes no gain on the liquidation and takes a $250,000 basis for the land. Anthony recognizes a $40,000 ($100,000 − $60,000) capital gain on the receipt of the money. Alternatively, distribution of the land and cash ratably to Parent and Anthony would require Subsidiary to recognize as gain the appreciation on the portion of land distributed to Anthony. ◀

AVOIDING SEC. 332 TO RECOGNIZE LOSSES

ADDITIONAL COMMENT

The parent corporation, however, would not acquire the subsidiary's tax attributes if a taxable liquidation occurs.

A parent corporation may want to avoid the Sec. 332 nonrecognition rules to recognize a loss when a solvent subsidiary corporation liquidates. Because the stock ownership requirement must be met during the entire liquidation process, the parent corporation apparently can sell some of its stock in the subsidiary corporation to reduce its stock ownership below the 80% level at any time during the liquidation process and be able to recognize the loss.[30] Such a sale permits the parent corporation to recognize a capital loss when it surrenders its stock interest in the subsidiary corporation. The parent corporation may desire this capital loss if it has offsetting capital gains.

The sale of a portion of the subsidiary's stock after the plan of liquidation is adopted prevents Sec. 332 from applying to the parent corporation. The Sec. 337 rules, which prevent the subsidiary corporation from recognizing gain or loss when making a liquidating distribution to an 80% distributee, also do not apply because nonrecognition is contingent on Sec. 332 applying to the distributee. Thus, the subsidiary corporation also can recognize a loss when it distributes property that has declined in value.

COMPLIANCE AND PROCEDURAL CONSIDERATIONS

GENERAL LIQUIDATION PROCEDURES

Section 6043(a) requires a liquidating corporation to file Form 966 (Corporate Dissolution or Liquidation) within 30 days after the adoption of any resolution or plan calling for the liquidation or dissolution of the corporation. The liquidating corporation files this form with the District Director of the IRS for the district in which it files its income tax return. Any amendment or supplement to the resolution or plan must be filed on an additional Form 966 within 30 days of making the amendment or supplement. The liquidating corporation must file Form 966 whether the shareholders' realized gain is recognized or not. The information included with Form 966 is described in Reg. Sec. 1.6043-1(b).

Regulation Sec. 1.6043-2(a) requires every corporation that makes a distribution of $600 or more during a calendar year to any shareholder in liquidation of part or all of its capital stock to file Form 1099-DIV (U.S. Information Return for Recipients of Dividends and Distributions). A separate Form 1099-DIV is required for each shareholder. The information that must be included with the Form 1099-DIV is described in Reg. Secs. 1.6043-2(a) and (b).

Regulation Sec. 1.6012-2(a)(2) requires a corporation that exists for part of a year to file a corporate tax return for the portion of the tax year that it existed. A corporation that ceases business and dissolves, while retaining no assets, is not considered to be in existence for federal tax purposes even though under state law it may be considered for certain purposes to be continuing its affairs (e.g., for purposes of suing or being sued).

---

[30] CIR v. Day & Zimmerman, Inc., 34 AFTR 343, 45-2 USTC ¶9403 (3rd Cir., 1945).

ADDITIONAL COMMENT

As evidenced in this chapter, the compliance and procedural requirements of complete liquidations are formidable. Any taxpayer contemplating this type of corporate transactions should consult competent tax and legal advisors to ensure that the technical requirements of the proposed transaction are satisfied.

SECTION 332 LIQUIDATIONS

Regulation Sec. 1.332-6 requires every corporation receiving distributions in a Sec. 332 complete liquidation to maintain permanent records. A complete statement of all facts pertinent to the nonrecognition of gain or loss must be included in the corporate distributee's return for the tax year in which it receives a liquidating distribution. This statement includes the following: a certified copy of the plan of liquidation, a list of all property received upon the distribution, a statement of any indebtedness of the liquidating corporation to the recipient corporation, and a statement of stock ownership.

Treasury Regulations require a special waiver of the general three-year statute of limitations when the liquidation covers more than one tax year.[31] The distributee corporation must file a waiver of the limitations period on assessment for each of its tax years that falls partially or wholly within the liquidation period. The distributee corporation files this waiver at the time it files its income tax return. This waiver must extend the assessment period to a date at least one year after the last date of the period for assessment of such taxes for the last tax year in which the liquidation may be completed under Sec. 332.

PLAN OF LIQUIDATION

A **plan of liquidation** is a written document detailing the steps to be undertaken while carrying out the complete liquidation of the corporation. Although a formal plan of liquidation is not required, it may assist the corporation in determining when it enters a liquidation status and, therefore, when distributions to the shareholders qualify for exchange treatment under Sec. 331 (instead of possibly being treated as a dividend under Sec. 301). The adoption of a formal plan of liquidation can provide the liquidating corporation or its shareholders additional benefits under the tax laws. For example, the adoption of a plan of liquidation permits a parent corporation to have a three-year time period (instead of one tax year) to carry out the complete liquidation of a subsidiary corporation.

PROBLEM MATERIALS

DISCUSSION QUESTIONS

C6-1 What is a complete liquidation? A partial liquidation? Explain the difference in the tax treatment accorded these two different events.

C6-2 Summitt Corporation has manufactured and distributed basketball equipment for 20 years. Its owners would like to avoid the corporate income tax and are considering becoming a limited liability company (LLC). What tax savings may result from electing to be taxed as an LLC? What federal tax costs will be incurred to make the change from a C corporation to an LLC? Would the same transaction costs be incurred if instead the corporation made an S election? Would the transaction costs be incurred had LLC status been adopted when the entity was initially organized?

C6-3 Explain why tax advisors caution people who are starting a new business that the tax costs of incorporating a business may be low while the tax costs of liquidating a business may be high.

C6-4 Explain the following statement: A corporation may be liquidated for tax purposes even though dissolution has not occurred under state corporation law.

C6-5 Compare the tax consequences to the shareholder and the distributing corporation of the following three kinds of corporate distributions: ordinary dividends, stock redemptions, and complete liquidations.

C6-6 What event or occurrence determines when a cash or accrual method of accounting taxpayer reports a liquidating distribution?

C6-7 Explain why a shareholder receiving a liquidating distribution would prefer to receive either capital gain treatment or ordinary loss treatment.

C6-8 A liquidating corporation could either (1) sell its assets and then distribute remaining cash to its shareholders or (2) distribute its assets directly to

---

[31] Reg. Sec. 1.332-4(a)(2).

the shareholders who then sell the distributed assets. Do the tax consequences of these alternatives differ?

C6-9 Explain the circumstances in which a liquidating corporation does not recognize gain and/or loss when making a liquidating distribution.

C6-10 Kelly Corporation makes a liquidating distribution. Among other property, it distributes land subject to a mortgage. The mortgage amount exceeds both the adjusted basis and FMV for the land. Explain to Kelly Corporation's president how the amount of its recognized gain or loss on the distribution and the shareholder's basis for the land are determined.

C6-11 Explain the congressional intent behind the enactment of the Sec. 332 rules regarding the liquidation of a subsidiary corporation.

C6-12 What requirements must be satisfied for the Sec. 332 rules to apply to a corporate shareholder?

C6-13 Compare the general liquidation rules with the Sec. 332 rules for liquidation of a subsidiary corporation with respect to the following items:
a. Recognition of gain or loss by the distributee corporation
b. Recognition of gain or loss by the liquidating corporation
c. Basis of assets in the distributee corporation's hands
d. Treatment of the liquidating corporation's tax attributes

C6-14 Parent Corporation owns 80% of the stock of Subsidiary Corporation, which is insolvent. Tracy owns the remaining 20% of the stock. The courts determine Subsidiary to be bankrupt. The shareholders receive nothing for their investment. How do they report their losses for tax purposes?

C6-15 Parent Corporation owns all the stock of Subsidiary Corporation and a substantial amount of Subsidiary Corporation bonds. Subsidiary proposes to transfer appreciated property to Parent in redemption of its bonds pursuant to the liquidation of Subsidiary. Explain the tax consequences of the redemption of the stock and bonds to Parent and Subsidiary.

C6-16 Explain the differences in the tax rules applying to distributions made to the parent corporation and a minority shareholder when a controlled subsidiary corporation liquidates.

C6-17 Parent Corporation owns 80% of Subsidiary Corporation's stock. Sally owns the remaining 20% of the Subsidiary stock. Subsidiary plans to distribute cash and appreciated property pursuant to its liquidation. It has more than enough cash to redeem all of Sally's stock. What strategy for distributing the cash and appreciated property would minimize the gain recognized by Subsidiary on the distribution? Does the substitution of appreciated property for cash change the tax consequences of the liquidating distribution for Sally?

C6-18 Parent Corporation owns 70% of Subsidiary Corporation's stock. The FMV of Subsidiary's assets is significantly greater than their basis to Subsidiary. The FMV of Parent's interest in the assets also substantially exceeds Parent's basis for the Subsidiary stock. Also, Parent's basis in its Subsidiary stock exceeds Subsidiary's basis in its assets. On January 30, Parent acquired an additional 15% of Subsidiary stock from one of Subsidiary's shareholders who owns none of the Parent stock. Subsidiary adopts a plan of liquidation on March 12. The liquidation is completed before year-end. What advantages accrue to Parent with respect to the liquidation by acquiring the additional Subsidiary stock?

C6-19 Texas Corporation liquidates through a series of distributions to its shareholders after a plan of liquidation has been adopted. How are these distributions taxed?

C6-20 Hill Corporation's shareholders are called on to pay an assessment that was levied against them as a result of a liability not anticipated at the time of liquidation. When will the shareholders claim the deduction for the additional payment, assuming they all use the cash method of accounting? What factors determine the character of the deduction claimed?

C6-21 Able Corporation adopts a plan of liquidation. Under the plan, Robert, who owns 60% of the Able stock, is to receive 2,000 acres of land in an area where a number of producing oil wells have been drilled. No wells have been drilled on Able's land. Discussions with two appraisers have produced widely differing market values for the land, both of which are above Able's basis for the land and Robert's basis for the Able stock. Explain the alternatives available to Able and Robert for reporting the liquidating distribution.

C6-22 Explain the IRS's position regarding whether a liquidation transaction will be considered open or closed.

C6-23 For a corporation that intends to liquidate, explain the tax advantages to the shareholders of having the corporation (1) adopt a plan of liquidation, (2) sell its assets in an installment sale, and then (3) distribute the installment obligations to its shareholders.

C6-24 Cable Corporation is 60% owned by Anna and 40% owned by Jim, who are unrelated. It has noncash assets, which it sells to an unrelated purchaser for $100,000 in cash and $900,000 in installment obligations due 50% in the current year and 50% in the following year. Cable will distribute its remaining cash, after payment of the federal income taxes on the sale and other corporate obligations, to Jim and Anna along with the installment obligations. Explain to the two shareholders the alternatives for reporting the gain realized on their receipt of the installment obligations.

C6-25 Describe the tax treatment accorded the following expenses associated with a liquidation:
a. Commissions paid on the sale of the liquidating corporation's assets
b. Accounting fees paid to prepare the corporation's final income tax return
c. Unamortized organizational expenditures
d. Prepaid rent for office space occupied by one of the shareholders following the liquidation (Assume the prepaid rent was deducted in the preceding year's corporate tax return.)

C6-26 Yancy owns 70% of Andover Corporation stock. At the beginning of the current year, the corporation has $400,000 of NOLs. Yancy plans to liquidate the corporation and have it distribute assets having a $600,000 FMV and a $350,000 adjusted basis to its shareholders. Explain to Yancy the tax consequences of the liquidation to Andover Corporation.

C6-27 Nils Corporation, a calendar year taxpayer, adopts a plan of liquidation on April 1 of the current year. The final liquidating distribution occurs on January 5 of next year. Must Nils Corporation file a tax return for the current year? For next year?

C6-28 What is a plan of liquidation? Why is it advisable for a corporation to adopt a formal plan of liquidation?

C6-29 Indicate whether each of the following statements about a liquidation is true or false. If the statement is false, explain why.
a. Liabilities assumed by a shareholder when a corporation liquidates reduce the amount realized by the shareholder on the surrender of his or her stock.
b. The loss recognized by a shareholder on a liquidation generally is characterized as an ordinary loss.
c. A shareholder's basis for property received in a liquidation is the same as the property's basis in the liquidating corporation's hands.
d. The holding period for property received in a liquidation includes the period of time it is held by the liquidating corporation.
e. The tax attributes of a liquidating corporation are assumed ratably by its shareholders.
f. A parent corporation can elect to recognize gain or loss when it liquidates a controlled subsidiary corporation.
g. A liquidating subsidiary recognizes no gain or loss when it distributes its property to its parent corporation.
h. A parent corporation's basis for the assets received in a liquidation where gain is not recognized remains the same as it was to the liquidating subsidiary corporation.

ISSUE IDENTIFICATION QUESTIONS

C6-30 Cable Corporation, which operates a fleet of motorized trolley cars in a resort city, is undergoing a complete liquidation. John, who owns 80% of the Cable stock, plans to continue the business in another city, and will receive the cable cars, two support vehicles, the repair parts inventory, and other tools and equipment. Peter, who owns the remaining 20% of the Cable stock, will receive a cash distribution. The corporation will incur $15,000 of liquidation expenses to break its lease on its office and garage space and cancel other contracts. What tax issues should Cable, John, and Peter consider with respect to the liquidation?

C6-31 Parent Corporation, which operates an electric utility, created a 100%-owned corporation, Subsidiary, that built and managed an office building. Assume the two corporations have filed separate tax returns for a number of years. The utility occupied two floors of the office building, and Subsidiary offered the other ten floors for lease. Only 25% of the total rental space was leased because of the high crime rate in the area surrounding the building. Rental income was insufficient to cover the mortgage payments, and Subsidiary filed for bankruptcy because of the poor prospects. Subsidiary's assets were taken over by the mortgage lender. Parent lost its entire $500,000 investment. Another $100,000 of debts remained unpaid for the general creditors, which included a $35,000 account payable to Parent, at the time Subsidiary was liquidated. What tax issues should Parent and Subsidiary consider with respect to the bankruptcy and liquidation of Subsidiary?

C6-32 Alpha Corporation is a holding company owned equally by Harry and Rita. They acquired the Alpha stock many years ago when the corporation was formed. Alpha has its money invested almost entirely in stocks, bonds, rental real estate, and land. Market quotations are available for all of its stock and bond investments except for 10,000 shares of Mayfair Manufacturing Corporation stock. Mayfair is privately held with 40 individuals owning all 100,000 outstanding shares. Last year, Mayfair reported slightly more than $3 million in net income. In a discussion with Harry and Rita, you find that they plan to liquidate Alpha Corporation in the next six months to avoid the personal holding company tax. What tax issues should Harry and Rita consider with respect to this pending liquidation?

PROBLEMS

C6-33 *Shareholder Gain or Loss Calculation.* For seven years, Monaco Corporation has been owned entirely by Stacy and Monique, who are husband and wife. Stacy and Monique have a $165,000 basis in their jointly owned Monaco stock. The Monaco stock is Sec. 1244 stock. They receive the following assets in liquidation of their corporation: accounts receivable, $25,000 FMV; a car, $16,000 FMV; office furniture, $6,000 FMV; and $5,000 cash.
a. What are the amount and character of their gain or loss?
b. How would your answer change if the accounts receivable instead had a $140,000 FMV?
c. What is the Monacos' basis for each property received in the liquidation in Parts a and b?

C6-34 *Shareholder Gain or Loss Calculation.* For three years, Diamond Corporation has been owned equally by Arlene and Billy. Arlene and Billy have $40,000 and $20,000 adjusted bases, respectively, in their Diamond stock. Arlene receives a $30,000 cash liquidating distribution in exchange for her Diamond stock. Billy receives as a liquidating distribution a parcel of land having a $70,000 FMV and subject to a $45,000 mortgage, which he assumes, and $5,000 of cash in exchange for his Diamond stock.
a. What are the amount and character of each shareholder's gain or loss?
b. What is each shareholder's basis for the property received in the liquidation?

C6-35 *Timing of Gain/Loss Recognition.* Peter owns 25% of Crosstown Corporation stock in which he has a $200,000 adjusted basis. In each of the following situations, what amount of gain/loss will Peter report in the current year? In the next year?
a. Peter is a cash method of accounting taxpayer. Crosstown determines on December 24 of the current year that it will make a $260,000 liquidating distribution to Peter. Crosstown pays the liquidating distribution on January 3 of the next year.
b. Assume the same facts as in Part a except that Peter is an accrual method of accounting taxpayer.

C6-36 *Corporate Formation/Corporate Liquidation.* Ken Wallace contributed assets with a $100,000 adjusted basis and a $400,000 FMV to Ace Corporation in exchange for all of its single class of stock. The corporation conducted operations for five years and was liquidated. Ken Wallace received a liquidating distribution of $500,000 cash (less federal income taxes owed on the liquidation by the corporation) and the assets that he had contributed, which now have a $100,000 adjusted basis and a $500,000 FMV. Assume a 34% corporate tax rate.
a. What are the tax consequences of the corporate formation transaction?
b. What are the tax consequences of the corporate liquidation transaction?
c. Would your answers to Parts a and b remain the same if instead the assets had been contributed by Wallace Corporation to Ace Corporation? If not, explain how your answer(s) would change?

C6-37 *Gain or Loss on Making a Liquidating Distribution.* What are the amount and character of the gain or loss recognized by the distributing corporation when making liquidating distributions in the following situations? What is the shareholder's basis for the property received? In any situation where a loss is disallowed, indicate what changes would be necessary to improve the tax consequences of the transaction.
a. Best Corporation distributes land having a $200,000 FMV and a $90,000 adjusted basis to Tanya, its sole shareholder. The land, a capital asset, is subject to a $40,000 mortgage, which Tanya assumes.
b. Wilkins Corporation distributes depreciable property to its two equal shareholders. Robert receives a milling machine having a $50,000 adjusted basis and a $75,000 FMV. The corporation claimed $30,000 depreciation on the machine. The corporation purchased the milling machine from an unrelated seller four years ago. Sharon receives an automobile that originally cost $40,000 two years earlier and has a $26,000 FMV. The corporation claimed $25,000 depreciation on the automobile.
c. Jordan Corporation distributes marketable securities having a $100,000 FMV and a $175,000 adjusted basis to Brad, a 66.67% shareholder. Jordan purchased the marketable securities three years ago. Jordan distributes $50,000 cash to Ann, a 33.33% shareholder.
d. Assume the same facts as in Part c except the securities and cash are instead each distributed two-thirds to Brad and one-third to Ann.

C6-38 *Gain or Loss Recognition by a Distributing Corporation.* Melon Corporation, which is owned equally by four individual shareholders, adopts a plan of liquidation for distributing the following property:

- Land (a capital asset) having a $30,000 FMV and a $12,000 adjusted basis.
- Depreciable personal property having a $15,000 FMV and a $9,000 adjusted basis. Melon has claimed depreciation of $10,000 on the property during the three years since its acquisition.
- Installment obligations having a $30,000 FMV and face amount and a $21,000 adjusted basis, acquired when Melon sold a Sec. 1231 property.
- Supplies that cost $6,000 and were expensed in the preceding tax year. The supplies have a $7,500 FMV.
- Marketable securities having a $15,000 FMV and an $18,000 adjusted basis. Melon purchased the marketable securities from a broker 12 months ago.

a. Which property, when distributed by Melon Corporation to one of its shareholders, will require the distributing corporation to recognize gain or loss?

b. How will your answer to Part a change if the distribution instead is made to Melon's parent corporation as part of a complete liquidation meeting the Sec. 332 requirements?

c. How will your answer to Part b change if the distribution instead is made to a minority shareholder?

C6-39 *Distribution of Property Subject to a Mortgage.* Titan Corporation adopts a plan of liquidation. It distributes an apartment building having a $3 million FMV and a $1.8 million adjusted basis, and land having a $1 million FMV and a $600,000 adjusted basis, to MNO Partnership in exchange for all the outstanding Titan stock. MNO Partnership has an $800,000 basis in its Titan stock. Titan has claimed $600,000 of MACRS depreciation on the building. MNO Partnership agrees to assume the $3 million mortgage on the land and building. All of Titan's assets other than the building and land are used to pay its federal income tax liability.

a. What are the amount and character of Titan's recognized gain or loss on the distribution?

b. What are the amount and character of MNO Partnership's gain or loss on the liquidation? What is its basis for the land and building?

c. How would your answer to Parts a and b change if the mortgage instead was $4.5 million?

C6-40 *Sale of Loss Property by a Liquidating Corporation.* In March 2005, Mike contributed the following two properties to Kansas Corporation in exchange for additional Kansas stock: (1) land having a $50,000 FMV and a $75,000 basis and (2) another property having an $85,000 FMV and a $70,000 adjusted basis. Kansas' employees uses the land as a parking lot until Kansas sells it in March 2006 for $45,000. One month after the sale, in April 2006, Kansas adopts a plan of liquidation.

a. What is Kansas' adjusted basis in the land immediately after the March 2005 contribution?

b. What is Kansas's recognized gain or loss on the subsequent land sale?

c. How would your answer to Part b change if the land were not used in Kansas's trade or business?

d. How would you answer to Part c change if Mike contributed the land and other property in March 2004 instead of March 2005?

e. How would your answer to Part c change if the corporation sold the land (contributed in March 2005) for $80,000 instead of $45,000?

C6-41 *Tax Consequences of a Corporate Liquidation.* Marsha owns 100% of Gamma Corporation's common stock. Gamma is an accrual-basis, calendar-year corporation. Marsha formed the corporation six years ago by transferring $250,000 of cash in exchange for the Gamma stock. Thus, she has held the stock for six years and has a $250,000 adjusted basis in the stock. Gamma's balance sheet at January 1 of the current year is as follows:

Assets	Basis	FMV
Cash	$ 400,000	$ 400,000
Marketable securities	50,000	125,000
Inventory	300,000	350,000
Equipment	200,000	275,000
Building	500,000	750,000
Total	$1,450,000	$1,900,000

Liabilities and Equity

Accounts payable	$ 175,000	$ 175,000
Common stock	250,000	1,725,000
Retained earnings (and E&P)	1,025,000	
Total	$1,450,000	$1,900,000

Gamma has held the marketable securities for two years. In addition, Gamma has claimed $60,000 of MACRS depreciation on the machinery and $90,000 of straight-line depreciation on the building. On January 2 of the current year, Gamma liquidates and distributes all property to Marsha except that Gamma retains cash to pay the accounts payable and any tax liability resulting from Gamma's liquidation. Assume that Gamma has no other taxable income or loss. Determine the tax consequences to Gamma and Marsha.

C6-42 *Sale of Assets Followed by a Corporation Liquidation.* Assume the same facts as in Problem C6-41 except, on January 2 of the current year, Gamma Corporation sells all property other than cash to Acquiring Corporation for FMV. Gamma Corporation pays off the accounts payable and retains cash to pay any tax liability resulting from Gamma's liquidation. Gamma Corporation then liquidates and distributes all remaining cash to Marsha. Assume that Gamma Corporation has no other taxable income or loss. Determine the tax consequence to Gamma Corporation, Acquiring Corporation, and Marsha. How do these results compare to those in Problem C6-41?

C6-43 *Tax Consequences of a Corporate Liquidation.* Pamela owns 100% of Sigma Corporation's stock. She purchased her stock ten years ago, and her current basis for the stock is $300,000. On June 10, Pamela decided to liquidate Sigma. Sigma's balance sheet prior to the sale of the assets, payment of the liquidation expenses, and payment of federal income taxes is as follows:

Assets	*Basis*	*FMV*
Cash	$240,000	$ 240,000
Marketable securities	90,000	80,000
Equipment	150,000	200,000
Land	320,000	680,000
Total	$800,000	$1,200,000

Equity		
Common stock	$300,000	$1,200,000
Retained earnings (and E&P)	500,000	
Total	$800,000	$1,200,000

- The corporation has claimed depreciation of $150,000 on the equipment.
- The corporation received the marketable securities as a capital contribution from Pamela three years earlier at a time when their adjusted basis was $90,000 and their FMV was $70,000.
- Sigma incurred $20,000 in liquidation expenses in its final tax year.

a. What are the tax consequences of the liquidation to Pamela and Sigma Corporation? Assume a 34% corporate tax rate.

b. How would your answer change if Pamela contributed the marketable securities six years ago?

C6-44 *Liquidation of a Subsidiary Corporation.* Parent Corporation owns 100% of Subsidiary Corporation's stock. The adjusted basis of its stock investment is $175,000. A plan of liquidation is adopted, and Subsidiary distributes to Parent assets having a $400,000 FMV and a $300,000 adjusted basis (to Subsidiary), and liabilities in the amount of $60,000. Subsidiary has a $150,000 E&P balance.

a. What are the amount and character of Subsidiary's recognized gain or loss on the distribution?

b. What are the amount and character of Parent's recognized gain or loss on the surrender of the Subsidiary stock?

c. What basis does Parent take in the assets?

d. What happens to Parent's basis in the Subsidiary stock and to Subsidiary's tax attributes?

C6-45 *Liquidation of a Subsidiary Corporation.* Parent Corporation owns 100% of Subsidiary Corporation's single class of stock. Its adjusted basis for the stock is $175,000. After adopting a plan of liquidation, Subsidiary distributes the following property to Parent: money, $20,000; LIFO inventory, $200,000 FMV; and equipment, $150,000 FMV. The inventory has a $125,000 adjusted basis. The equipment originally cost $280,000. Subsidiary has claimed depreciation of $160,000 on the equipment. Subsidiary has a $150,000 E&P balance and a $40,000 NOL carryover on the liquidation date.

a. What are the amount and character of Subsidiary's recognized gain or loss when it makes the liquidating distributions?

b. What are the amount and character of Parent's recognized gain or loss on its surrender of the Subsidiary stock?

c. What is Parent's basis in each nonmoney property?

d. What happens to Subsidiary's E&P balance and NOL carryover following the liquidation?

e. What happens to Parent's $175,000 basis in the Subsidiary stock?

C6-46 *Liquidation of a Subsidiary Corporation.* Parent Corporation owns 100% of Subsidiary Corporation's single class of stock and $2 million of Subsidiary Corporation debentures. Parent purchased the debentures in small blocks from various unrelated parties at a $100,000 discount from their face amount. Parent has a $1.3 million basis in the Subsidiary stock. Subsidiary adopts a plan of liquidation whereby it distributes property having a $4 million FMV and a $2.4 million adjusted basis in redemption of the Subsidiary stock. The debentures are redeemed for Subsidiary property having a $2 million FMV and a $2.2 million adjusted basis.

a. What income or gain does Subsidiary recognize as a result of making the liquidating distributions?

b. What gain or loss does Parent recognize on the surrender of the Subsidiary stock? The Subsidiary debentures?

c. What is Parent's basis for the property received from Subsidiary?

C6-47 *Liquidation of an Insolvent Subsidiary.* Subsidiary Corporation is a wholly-owned subsidiary of Parent Corporation. The two corporations have the following balance sheets:

Assets	Parent	Subsidiary
General assets	$1,500,000	$ 750,000
Investment in Subsidiary stock	200,000	
Note receivable from Subsidiary	1,000,000	
Total	$2,700,000	$ 750,000

Liabilities & Equity		
General liabilities	$1,500,000	$ 150,000
Note payable to Parent		1,000,000
Common Stock	300,000	200,000
Retained earnings (deficit)	900,000	(600,000)
Total	$2,700,000	$ 750,000

Other Facts:

• Parent's basis in its Subsidiary stock is $200,000, which corresponds to the $200,000 common stock on Subsidiary's balance sheet.

• The $1 million note payable on Subsidiary's balance sheet is payable to Parent and corresponds to the note receivable on Parent's balance sheet.

• The corporations do not file consolidated tax returns.

• Subsidiary has $600,000 of net operating loss (NOL) carryovers.

• The FMV and adjusted basis of Subsidiary's assets are the same amount.

• Just prior to the liquidation, Subsidiary uses $150,000 of its assets to pay off its general liabilities.

• Subsidiary transfers all its assets and liabilities to Parent upon a complete liquidation.

Determine the tax consequences to Parent and Subsidiary upon Subsidiary's liquidation.

C6-48 *Liquidation of a Subsidiary Corporation.* Majority Corporation owns 90% of Subsidiary Corporation's stock and has a $45,000 basis in that stock. Mindy owns the other 10% and has a $5,000 basis in her stock. Subsidiary holds $20,000 cash and other assets having a $110,000 FMV and a $40,000 adjusted basis. Pursuant to a plan of liquidation, Subsidiary (1) distributes to Mindy assets having an $11,000 FMV and a $4,000 adjusted basis prior to the liquidation, (2) distributes to Majority assets having a $99,000 FMV and a $36,000 adjusted basis prior to the liquidation, and (3) distributes ratably to the two shareholders any cash remaining after taxes. Assume a 34% corporate tax rate and a 15% capital gains tax rate.

a. What are the tax consequences of the liquidation to Majority Corporation, Subsidiary Corporation, and Mindy?

b. Can you recommend a different distribution of assets that will produce better tax results than in Part a?

C6-49 *Tax Consequences of a Corporate Liquidation.* Gabriel Corporation is owned 90% by Zeier Corporation and 10% by Ray Goff, a Gabriel employee. A preliquidation balance sheet for Gabriel is presented below:

Assets	Basis	FMV
Cash	$ 100,000	$ 100,000
Inventory	420,000	700,000
Equipment	80,000	100,000
Land	400,000	300,000
Total	$1,000,000	$1,200,000

Equity		
Accounts payable	$ 100,000	$ 100,000
Bonds payable	500,000	500,000
Common stock	100,000	600,000
Retained earnings (and E&P)	300,000	
Total	$1,000,000	$1,200,000

Gabriel has claimed $150,000 of MACRS depreciation on the equipment. Gabriel purchased the land three years ago as a potential plant site. Plans to build the plant never were consummated, and Gabriel has held the land since then as an investment. Zeier and Ray Goff have $90,000 and $10,000 bases, respectively, in their Gabriel stock. Both shareholders have held their stock since the corporation's inception ten years ago. Zeier purchased the Gabriel bonds from an insurance company two years ago for $20,000 above their face amount. Gabriel adopts a plan of liquidation. Gabriel transfers $500,000 of inventory to Zeier to retire the bonds. The shareholders receive their share of Gabriel's remaining assets and assume their share of Gabriel's liabilities (other than federal income taxes). Gabriel pays federal income taxes owed on the liquidation. Assume a 34% corporate tax rate. What are the tax consequences of the liquidation to Ray Goff, Zeier Corporation, and Gabriel Corporation?

C6-50 *Tax Consequences of a Corporate Liquidation.* Art owns 80% of Pueblo Corporation stock, and Peggy owns the remaining 20%. Art and Peggy have $320,000 and $80,000 adjusted bases, respectively, for their Pueblo stock. Pueblo owns the following assets: cash, $25,000; inventory, $150,000 FMV and $100,000 adjusted basis; marketable securities, $100,000 FMV and $125,000 adjusted basis; and equipment, $325,000 FMV and $185,000 adjusted basis. Pueblo purchased the equipment four years ago and subsequently claimed $215,000 of MACRS depreciation. The securities are not disqualified property. On July 1 of the current year, Pueblo adopts a plan of liquidation at a time when it has $250,000 of E&P and no liabilities. Pueblo distributes the equipment, $50,000 of inventory, the marketable securities, and $5,000 of money to Art before year-end as a liquidating distribution. Pueblo also distributes $20,000 of cash and $100,000 of inventory to Peggy before year-end as a liquidating distribution.

a. What are the gain and loss tax consequences of the liquidation to Pueblo Corporation and to Art and Peggy?

b. Can you offer any suggestions to Pueblo's management that could improve the tax consequences of the liquidation? Explain.

c. How would your answers to Parts a and b change if Art and Peggy instead were domestic corporations rather than individuals?

C6-51 *Tax Attribute Carryovers.* Bell Corporation is 100% owned by George, who has a $400,000 basis in his Bell stock. Bell's operations have been unprofitable in recent years, and it has incurred small NOLs. Its operating assets currently have a $300,000 FMV and a $500,000 adjusted basis. George is approached by Time Corporation, which wants to purchase Bell's assets for $300,000. Bell expects to have approximately $200,000 in cash after the payment of its liabilities.

a. What are the tax consequences of the transaction if Bell adopts a plan of liquidation, sells the assets, and distributes the cash in redemption of the Bell stock within a 12-month period?

b. What advantages (if any) would accrue to Bell and George if the corporation remains in existence and uses the $200,000 of cash that remains after payment of the liabilities to conduct a new trade or business?

C6-52 *Series of Liquidating Distributions.* Union Corporation is owned equally by Ron and Steve. Ron and Steve purchased their stock several years ago and have adjusted bases for their Union stock of $15,000 and $27,500, respectively. Each shareholder receives two liquidating distributions. The first liquidating distribution, made in the current year, results in each shareholder receiving a one-half interest in a parcel of land that has a $40,000 FMV and an $18,000 adjusted basis to Union Corporation. The second liquidating distribution, made in the next year, results in each shareholder receiving $20,000 in cash.

a. What are the amount and character of Ron and Steve's recognized gain or loss for the current year? For the next year?

b. What is the basis of the land in Ron and Steve's hands?

c. How would your answers to Parts a and b change if the land has a $12,000 FMV instead of a $40,000 FMV?

C6-53 *Subsequent Assessment on the Shareholders.* Meridian Corporation originally was owned equally by five individual shareholders. Four years ago, Meridian Corporation adopted a plan of liquidation, and each shareholder received a liquidating distribution. Tina, a cash method taxpayer, reported a $30,000 long-term capital gain in the prior liquidation year on the redemption of her stock. Pending the outcome of a lawsuit in which Meridian Corporation is one of the defendents, $5,000 of Tina's liquidating distribution was held back and placed in escrow. Settlement of the lawsuit in the current year requires that the escrowed funds plus the interest earned on these funds be paid out to the plaintiff and that each shareholder pay an additional $2,500. Tina pays the amount due in the next year. How does Tina report the settlement of the lawsuit and the payment of the additional amount?

COMPREHENSIVE PROBLEM

C6-54 The following facts pertain to Lifecycle Corporation:

- Able owns a parcel of land (Land A) having a $30,000 FMV and $16,000 adjusted basis. Baker owns an adjacent parcel of land (Land B) having a $20,000 FMV and $22,000 adjusted basis. On January 2, 2006, Able and Baker contribute their parcels of land to newly formed Lifecycle Corporation in exchange for 60% of the corporation's stock for Able and 40% of the corporation's stock for Baker. The corporation elects a calendar tax year and the accrual method of accounting.

- On January 2, 2006, the corporation borrows $2 million and uses the loan proceeds to build a factory ($1 million), purchase equipment ($500,000), produce inventory ($450,000), pay other operating expenses ($30,000), and retain working cash ($20,000). Assume the corporation sells all inventory produced and collects on all sales immediately so that, at the end of any year, the corporation has no accounts receivable or inventory balances.

- Operating results for 2006 are as follows:

Sales	$964,000	
Cost of goods sold	450,000	
Interest paid on loan	140,000	
Depreciation:		
Equipment	70,000	($25,000 for E&P)
Building	24,000	($24,000 for E&P)
Operating expenses	30,000	

Of these amounts, $250,000 is qualified production activities income.

- In 2007, Lifecycle Corporation invests $10,000 of excess cash in Macro Corporation stock (less than 20% owned) and $20,000 in tax-exempt bonds. In addition, the corporation pays Able a $12,000 salary and distributes an additional $42,000 to Able and $28,000 to Baker. The corporation also makes a $100,000 principal payment on the loan.
- Results for 2007 are as follows:

Sales	$990,000	
Cost of goods sold	500,000	
Interest paid on loan	130,000	
Depreciation:		
Equipment	125,000	($50,000 for E&P)
Building	25,000	($25,000 for E&P)
Operating expenses	40,000	
Salary paid to Able	12,000	
Dividend received on Macro Corporation		
stock	2,000	
Short-term capital gain on sale of portion		
of Macro Corporation stock holdings		
($4,000 − $3,000)	1,000	
Tax-exempt interest received	1,500	
Charitable contributions	500	

Of these amounts, $158,000 is qualified production activities income.

- In 2008, the corporation did not pay a salary to Able and made no distributions to the shareholders. The corporation, however, made a $30,000 principal payment on the loan.
- Results for 2008 are as follows:

Sales	$500,000	
Cost of goods sold	280,000	
Interest paid on loan	125,000	
Depreciation:		
Equipment	90,000	($50,000 for E&P)
Building	25,000	($25,000 for E&P)
Operating expenses	60,000	
Long-term capital gain on sale of remaining		
Macro Corporation stock		
($9,000 − $7,000)	2,000	
Long-term capital gain on sale of		
tax-exempt bond ($21,000 − $20,000)	1,000	

Of these amounts, qualified production activities income is zero (because it is negative).

- On January 2, 2009, the corporation receives a refund for the 2008 NOL carried back to 2006. When carrying back the NOL, remember to recalculate the U.S. production activities deduction in the carryback year because of the reduced taxable income resulting from carryback. In addition, the corporation sells its assets, pays taxes on the gain, and pays off the $1.87 million remaining debt.

	Sales Price	Tax Adj. Basis*	E&P Adj. Basis
Equipment	$ 250,000	$ 215,000	$ 375,000
Building	986,000	926,000	926,000
Land A	80,000	16,000	16,000
Land B	50,000	20,000	20,000
Total	$1,366,000	$1,177,000	$1,337,000

*Note: Technically, the equipment should be depreciated for ½ year in the year of disposition, and the building should be depreciated for ½ month (because of the January disposition). However, for simplicity, the above calculations ignore depreciation deductions in the disposition year, which creates an offsetting overstatement of adjusted basis. Section 362(e)(2) limits Land B basis to the FMV.

Immediately after these transactions, the corporation makes a liquidating distribution of the remaining cash to Able and Baker. The remaining cash is $340,894, which the corporation distributes in proportion to the shareholders' ownership (60% and 40%). Assume that long-term capital gains are taxed at 15% in 2009.

Required:

a. Determine the tax consequences of the corporate formation to Able, Baker, and Lifecycle Corporation.

b. For 2006-2008, prepare schedules showing corporate taxable income, taxes, and E&P activity. Assume that Lifecycle pays its taxes in the same year they accrue.

c. For 2009, prepare a schedule showing the results of this year's transactions on Lifecycle Corporation, Able, and Baker.

TAX STRATEGY PROBLEMS

C6-55   Sarah plans to invest $1 million in a business venture that will last five years. She is debating whether to operate the business as a C corporation or a sole proprietorship. If a C corporation, she will liquidate the corporation at the end of the five-year period. She expects the business to generate taxable income as follows:

Year	Taxable Income
1	$ 40,000
2	70,000
3	90,000
4	150,000
5	350,000

If incurred in corporate form, these taxable income amounts will be subject to the corporate tax rate schedule. If in proprietorship form, they will be subject to Sarah's 35% marginal tax rate. Assume that any capital gain upon corporate liquidation will be taxed at a 15% capital gains rate and that Sec. 1202 does not apply.

Required: Determine the after-tax amount Sarah will have at the end of five years under each alternative. Which alternative do you recommend?

C6-56   One way to compare the accumulation of income by alternative business entity forms is to use mathematical models. The following models express the investment after-tax accumulation calculation for a particular entity form:

Flow-through entities and sole proprietorships: Contribution $\times [1 + R(1 - t_p)]^n$
C corporation: Contribution $\times \{[1 + R(1 - t_c)]^n (1 - t_g) + t_g\}$

Where: ATA = after-tax accumulation in n years
    R = before-tax rate of return for the business entity
    t_p = owner's marginal tax rate on ordinary income
    t_c = corporation's marginal tax rate
    t_g = owner's tax rate on capital gains
    n = number of periods

In the C corporation model, the corporation operates for n years, paying taxes currently and distributing no dividends. At the end of its existence, the corporation liquidates, causing the shareholder to recognize a capital gain. In the flow-through model, the entity or sole proprietorship distributes just enough cash for the owner or owners to pay individual taxes, and the entity reinvests the remaining after-tax earnings in the business. (See Chapter I18 of the *Individuals* volume for a detailed explanation of these models.)

Now consider the following facts. Twelve years ago, your client formed a C corporation with a $100,000 investment (contribution). The corporation's before-tax rate of return (R) has been and will continue to be 10%. The corporate tax rate (t_c) has been and will continue to be 35%. The corporation pays no dividends and reinvests all after-tax earnings in its business. Thus, the corporation's value grows at its after-tax rate of return. Your client's marginal ordinary tax rate (t_p) has been 33%, and her capital gains rate (t_g) has been 15%. Your client expects her ordinary tax rate to drop to 25% at the beginning of this year and stay at that level indefinitely. Her capital gains tax rate will remain at 15%. Assume the corporate stock does not qualify for the Sec. 1202 exclusion.

Your client wants you to consider two alternatives:

(1) Continue the business in C corporation form for the next 20 years and liquidate at that time (32 years in total).

(2) Liquidate the C corporation at the beginning of this year, invest the after-tax proceeds in a sole proprietorship, and operate as a sole proprietorship for the next 20 years.

The sole proprietorship's before-tax rate of return (R) also will be 10% for the next 20 years. Earnings from the sole proprietorship will be taxed currently at your client's ordinary tax rate, and your client will withdraw just enough earnings from the business to pay her taxes on the business's income. The remaining after-tax earnings will remain in the business until the end of the investment horizon (20 years from now).

Required: Show the results of each alternative along with supporting models and calculations. Ignore self employment taxes and the accumulated earnings tax. Which alternative should your client adopt?

Note: See Problem C11-61 for a third alternative to consider.

CASE STUDY PROBLEMS

C6-57 Paul, a long-time client of yours, has operated an automobile repair shop (as a C corporation) for most of his life. The shop has been fairly successful in recent years. His children are not interested in continuing the business. Paul is age 62 and has accumulated approximately $500,000 in assets outside of his business, most of which are in his personal residence and retirement plan. A recent balance sheet for the business shows the following amounts:

Assets	Adjusted Basis	FMV	Liabilities & Equity	Amount
Cash	$ 25,000	$ 25,000	Accounts payable	$ 30,000
Inventory	60,000	75,000	Mortgage payable	70,000
Equipment	200,000	350,000	Paid-in capital	120,000
Building	100,000	160,000	Retain earnings	205,000
Land	40,000	60,000		
Goodwill	–0–	100,000		
Total	$425,000	$770,000	Total	$425,000

The inventory is accounted for using the first-in, first-out inventory method. The corporation has claimed depreciation of $250,000 on the equipment. The corporation acquired the building 11 years ago and has claimed $25,000 of depreciation under the MACRS rules. The goodwill is an estimate that Paul feels reflects the value of his business over and above the other tangible assets.

Paul has received an offer of $775,000 from a competing automobile repair company for the noncash assets of his business, which will be used to establish a second location for the competing company. The corporation will sell the assets within 60 days and distribute remaining cash to Paul in liquidation of the corporation. The purchaser has obtained the necessary bank financing to make the acquisition. Paul's basis in his stock is $300,000.

Required: Prepare a memorandum for Paul outlining the tax consequences of the sale transaction and liquidation of the corporation.

C6-58 Your accounting firm has done the audit and tax work for the Peerless family and their business entities for 20 years. Approximately 25% of your accounting and tax practice billings come from Peerless family work. Peerless Real Estate Corporation owns land and a building (an ACRS property) having a $4.5 million FMV and a $1.0 million adjusted basis. The corporation owes a $1.3 million mortgage balance on the building. The corporation used substantial leverage to acquire the building so Myron Peerless and his brother Mark Peerless, who are equal shareholders in Peerless Real Estate, each have only $200,000 adjusted bases in their stock. Cash flows are good from the building, and only a small portion of the annual profits is needed for reinvestment in the building. Myron and Mark have decided to liquidate the corporation to avoid the federal and state corporate income taxes and continue to operate the business as a partnership. They want the MM Partnership, which has Mark and Myron equally sharing profits, losses, and liabilities, to purchase the building from the corporation for $400,000 cash plus their assumption of the $1.3 million mortgage. Mark knows a real estate appraiser who, for the right price, will provide a $1.7 million appraisal. Current corporate cash balances are sufficient to pay any federal and state income taxes owed on the sale of the building. Mark and Myron each would receive $200,000 from the corporation in cancellation of their stock.

Required: Prepare notes on the points you will want to cover with Myron and Mark Peerless about the corporate liquidation and the Peerless' desire to avoid federal and state corporate income taxes at your meeting tomorrow.

TAX RESEARCH PROBLEMS

C6-59 Parent Corporation owns 85% of the common stock and 100% of the preferred stock of Subsidiary Corporation. The common stock and preferred stock have adjusted bases of $500,000 and $200,000, respectively, to Parent. Subsidiary adopts a plan of liquidation on July 3 of the current year, when its assets have a $1 million FMV. Liabilities on that date amount to $850,000. On November 9, Subsidiary pays off its creditors and distributes $150,000 to Parent with respect to its preferred stock. No cash remains to be paid to Parent with respect to the remaining $50,000 of its liquidation preference for the preferred stock, or with respect to any of the common stock. In each of Subsidiary's tax years, less than 10% of its gross income has been passive income. What are the amount and character of Parent's loss on the preferred stock? The common stock?

A partial list of research sources is

- IRC Secs. 165(g)(3) and 332(a)
- Reg. Sec. 1.332-2(b)
- *Spaulding Bakeries, Inc.,* 27 T.C. 684 (1957)
- *H. K. Porter Co., Inc.,* 87 T.C. 689 (1986)

C6-60 Parent Corporation has owned 60% of Subsidiary Corporation's single class of stock for a number of years. Tyrone owns the remaining 40% of the Subsidiary stock. On August 10 of the current year, Parent purchases Tyrone's Subsidiary stock for cash. On September 15, Subsidiary adopts a plan of liquidation. Subsidiary then makes a single liquidating distribution on October 1. The activities of Subsidiary continue as a separate division of Parent. Does the liquidation of Subsidiary qualify for nonrecognition treatment under Secs. 332 and 337? Must Parent assume Subsidiary's E&P balance?

A partial list of research sources is

- IRC Secs. 332(b) and 381
- Reg. Sec. 1.332-2(a)

7

CHAPTER

CORPORATE ACQUISITIONS AND REORGANIZATIONS

LEARNING OBJECTIVES

After studying this chapter, you should be able to

1. ▶ Explain the types of taxable acquisition transactions.

2. ▶ Explain the differences between taxable and tax-free acquisition transactions.

3. ▶ Explain the types of tax-free reorganizations and their requirements.

4. ▶ Determine the tax consequences of a tax-free reorganization to the target corporation.

5. ▶ Determine the tax consequences of a tax-free reorganization to the acquiring corporation.

6. ▶ Determine the tax consequences of a tax-free reorganization to the target corporation's shareholders and security holders.

7. ▶ Explain how judicial doctrines can restrict a taxpayer's ability to use corporate reorganizations.

8. ▶ Determine which reorganization forms permit the carryover of tax attributes.

9. ▶ Explain how NOL carryovers are restricted following an acquisition.

The management of a corporation may decide to acquire a second corporation. Alternatively, these same individuals may decide to divest themselves of part or all of the corporate assets, such as the assets of an operating division or the stock of a subsidiary corporation. These acquisitions or divestitures can be either taxable or tax-free transactions. In a taxable transaction, the entire amount of the realized gain or loss is recognized. To qualify as a tax-free transaction, a specific set of statutory and judicial requirements must be met. If the transaction satisfies these requirements, part or all of the realized gain or loss generally goes unrecognized. The amount of unrecognized gain or loss is deferred until the assets or stock involved are sold or exchanged in a taxable transaction. The tax-free reorganization rules are another example of the wherewithal to pay concept; that is, no tax is imposed if the taxpayer retains a continuing equity interest. A tax is imposed only when property other than stock or securities (e.g., money) has been received.[1] Taxpayers, on the other hand, are likely to use a taxable transaction (instead of a tax-free transaction) to avoid having to defer recognition of a loss on an asset or stock disposition.

This chapter presents an overview of the tax consequences of taxable and tax-free acquisitions and divestitures. It also examines the statutory provisions and judicial doctrines that apply to determine the tax consequences for the tax-free acquisition and divestiture transactions.

TAXABLE ACQUISITION TRANSACTIONS

OBJECTIVE 1

Explain the types of taxable acquisition transactions

Taxable acquisition transactions can be divided into two major categories:

▶ Purchase of a target corporation's assets
▶ Purchase of a target corporation's stock

Acquiring corporations have two primary ways to acquire the assets of a **target corporation**.[2] The acquiring corporation can acquire the needed assets directly from the target corporation. Alternatively, the acquiring corporation can acquire an indirect interest in the assets by purchasing a controlling interest in the target corporation's stock. Three options exist once the stock interest is acquired.

▶ The acquiring corporation and its new subsidiary corporation can exist as separate entities.

▶ The acquiring corporation can liquidate its new subsidiary corporation in a tax-free liquidation. Following the liquidation, the parent corporation retains a direct interest in the assets of the target corporation.

▶ The acquiring corporation's management can make a Sec. 338 election on behalf of the subsidiary corporation. A Sec. 338 election permits the adjusted basis of the subsidiary corporation's assets to be stepped-up to the price that the acquiring corporation paid for the subsidiary corporation's stock plus the amount of any subsidiary corporation's liabilities.

The primary asset and stock acquisition alternatives are examined below. Table C7-1 summarizes the tax consequences of these alternatives.

ASSET ACQUISITIONS

The asset acquisition is not a difficult transaction for the acquiring and target corporations to accomplish. The selling corporation reports the sale transaction by determining the gain or loss recognized on the sale of each individual asset. Sales of depreciable assets (e.g., Sec. 1245 and 1250 property) result in previously claimed depreciation being recaptured.

---

[1] The tax deferral can be permanent if the stocks and securities are held until death. At death, the carryover or substituted basis is stepped-up to its fair market value (FMV) without incurring any income tax liability.

[2] The terms *target* and *acquired corporation* are used interchangeably here.

▼ **TABLE C7-1**

Comparison of Taxable Acquisition Alternatives

| | Taxable Asset Acquisition | Taxable Stock Acquisition with: | | |
		No Liquidation of Target	Tax-Free Liquidation of Target	Sec. 338 Election for Target
Acquiring corporation's basis for stock	N/A	Cost basis	Cost basis initially; disappears upon liquidation of target corporation	Cost basis
Parent-subsidiary relationship created	No	Yes	Yes, until liquidation occurs	Yes
Consolidated tax return election available	No	Yes	Yes, until liquidation occurs	Yes
Gain/loss recognized by target corporation on asset sale	Yes	No	No	Yes, on deemed sale of assets from old target corporation to new target corporation.
Gain/loss recognized by target corporation when making liquidating distribution	Yes, if target elects to liquidate before or after the asset sale.	N/A	No	No
Gain recognized by acquiring corporation when receiving liquidating distribution	N/A	N/A	No	No
Acquiring corporation's basis for assets acquired	Cost basis to acquiring corporation	No change in basis of target corporation's assets	Carryover basis from target corporation upon liquidation	Cost basis of target stock acquired plus amount of target's liabilities
Transfer of tax attributes to acquiring corporation	Remain with target corporation	Remain with target corporation	Carryover to acquiring corporation upon liquidation	Disappear with deemed sale of assets by old target corporation

N/A = Not applicable.

TAX STRATEGY TIP

Three types of state taxes may arise in an *asset* sale—transfer taxes, state income taxes, and sales taxes (some state sales tax laws allow certain bulk-sale exceptions). These taxes need to be taken into account by both the buyer and seller when drafting the sales agreement. When a *stock* sale occurs, these taxes can be avoided because the assets remain inside the same entity before and after the stock sale.

The purchaser's bases for the acquired assets are their acquisition cost.[3] The purchaser can claim depreciation based on the property's total acquisition cost.

A taxable asset acquisition offers the purchaser two major advantages. First, a significant portion of the acquisition can be debt-financed, whereas the tax-free reorganization requirements either restrict or prohibit the use of debt. The interest expense incurred with respect to the debt is deductible for federal income tax purposes. Second, only assets and liabilities designated in the purchase-sale agreement are acquired. The purchaser need not acquire all or substantially all the target corporation's assets, as is the case when it acquires the target corporation's stock in either a taxable transaction or a tax-free reorganization or when an asset-for-stock tax-free reorganization takes place. Similarly, the purchaser assumes only liabilities specified in the purchase-sale agreement. Contingent or unknown liabilities remain the responsibility of the seller.

The target (acquired) corporation recognizes gain or loss with respect to the assets sold and may subsequently liquidate. If so, any property retained by the target corporation is distributed to the shareholders as part of the liquidation. The liquidating corporation

[3] Sec. 1012.

recognizes gain or loss at the time of the distribution as if such property were instead sold. The target corporation's shareholders report their gain or loss on the liquidation as capital gain or loss (see Chapter C6).

<table>
<tr>
<td>

EXAMPLE C7-1 ▶

</td>
<td>

Ann, Bob, and Cathy each own one-third of Target Corporation's stock, and each shareholder has a $20,000 basis for his or her stock acquired six years ago. Acquiring Corporation purchases Target's noncash assets for $100,000 of cash and $300,000 of Acquiring debt obligations. Target retains its $50,000 of cash. On the sale date, Target's noncash assets have a $280,000 adjusted basis and a $400,000 FMV. Its liabilities are $100,000 on the sale date. Target must recognize a $120,000 gain [($100,000 + $300,000) − $280,000]. The character of the gains and losses recognized depends on the individual properties sold. Assuming a 34% corporate tax rate, Target's tax liability on the sale is $40,800 ($120,000 × 0.34). Acquiring takes a $400,000 basis for the noncash assets acquired. After Target pays its income tax and other liabilities, Ann, Bob, and Cathy each receive a liquidating distribution on which they report a capital gain. ◀

</td>
</tr>
</table>

Sometimes a target corporation will be liquidated before the shareholders sell the assets of the business. The tax consequences of the liquidation are described in Chapter C6. In general, the total tax liability for the corporation and shareholders will be the same whether the liquidation of the target corporation precedes or follows the asset sale.

STOCK ACQUISITIONS

STOCK ACQUISITION WITH NO LIQUIDATION. The stock acquisition is the simplest of the acquisition transactions. The gain recognized on the sale receives capital gain treatment if the stock is a capital asset in the seller's hands. If part or all of the consideration is deferred to a later tax year, the seller's gain can be reported using the installment method of accounting.[4] If part of the total consideration received by the seller of the stock represents an agreement with the purchaser not to compete for a specified time period, the consideration received for the agreement is taxed as ordinary income.[5]

The purchaser's basis for the stock is its acquisition cost.[6] The target corporation's basis for its assets does not change as a result of the stock sale. Any payment for the stock that exceeds the adjusted basis of the net assets of the acquired company cannot be reflected in a stepped-up basis for the assets. Any potential for depreciation recapture that exists on the transaction date stays with the target corporation's assets and, therefore, is assumed by the purchaser. If the target corporation has loss or credit carryovers, these carryovers can be subject to special limitations in the post-acquisition tax years (see pages C7-46 through C7-48).

Stock sales have proven to be popular with sellers because they may be less costly than an asset sale since only a single level of taxation is encountered. No adjustment occurs to the basis of the target corporation's assets following a stock sale even though the basis of the stock acquired may be substantially higher than the total tax basis the target corporation retains in its assets. Thus, one of the tax advantages of actually purchasing the assets of the target corporation—the higher basis for the properties for tax purposes—is not available when a stock purchase occurs unless the purchasing corporation makes a Sec. 338 deemed sale election (discussed later in this chapter).

<table>
<tr>
<td>

EXAMPLE C7-2 ▶

</td>
<td>

Assume the same facts as in Example C7-1 except that Acquiring extends a tender offer whereby it will purchase the Target stock at $50 per share. Ann, Bob, and Cathy tender their 7,000 Target shares in response to Acquiring's offer. Acquiring's $350,000 (7,000 shares × $50/share) purchase price equals Target's net asset amount ($450,000 − $100,000 liabilities). Ann, Bob, and Cathy each report a long-term capital gain on the disposition of their stock. Target becomes a wholly-owned subsidiary of Acquiring and, in the absence of a Sec. 338 election, does not adjust the basis of its assets as a result of the sale. ◀

</td>
</tr>
</table>

If the purchasing corporation is already part of an affiliated group that files a consolidated tax return, the new subsidiary corporation must join in the consolidated return elec-

---

KEY POINT

In a stock acquisition, only the shareholders of Target recognize gain. In an asset acquisition, both Target and Target's shareholders may recognize gain.

ADDITIONAL COMMENT

A shareholder's basis in stock sometimes is referred to as "outside basis" as opposed to "inside basis," which is the corporation's basis in its assets.

KEY POINT

In Example C7-2, the built-in gain in Target's assets is not recognized in a stock acquisition. Likewise, Target's assets are not stepped-up in basis even though Acquiring pays their full $350,000 FMV for the Target stock.

---

[4] Sec. 453(a).
[5] The purchaser can amortize over a 15-year period any amounts paid to the seller with respect to the agreement not to compete (Sec. 197).

[6] Sec. 1012.

tion if at least 80% of the subsidiary's stock is owned and the subsidiary is an includible corporation (see Chapter C8). Otherwise, the parent and subsidiary corporations can elect to make an initial consolidated return election.

STOCK ACQUISITION FOLLOWED BY A LIQUIDATION. The stock acquisition described in the preceding section can be followed by a liquidation of the acquired (subsidiary) corporation into its acquiring (parent) corporation. If the parent corporation owns at least 80% of the subsidiary corporation's stock, the liquidation is tax-free under the Sec. 332 and 337 rules outlined in Chapter C6.[7] The basis of the subsidiary corporation's assets carries over to the parent corporation. If the parent corporation paid a premium for the assets (i.e., an amount exceeding the total of the assets' adjusted bases), this premium is lost when the liquidation occurs because the parent corporation's basis for the stock disappears when the tax-free liquidation occurs. The disappearing basis "loss" cannot be deducted and provides no tax benefit. If the parent corporation paid less than the total of the assets' adjusted bases, the parent corporation retains this "excess" basis amount as part of the assets' carryover basis, which can provide additional tax benefits.

TYPICAL MISCONCEPTION

Taxpayers often do not understand that the parent's basis in its subsidiary's stock disappears in a Sec. 332 liquidation. Instead, the subsidiary's bases in the liquidated assets carry over to the parent.

EXAMPLE C7-3 ▶ Assume the same facts as in Example C7-2 except that Acquiring and Target Corporations continue to file separate tax returns following the stock acquisition, and Target is liquidated into Acquiring shortly after the acquisition. Target's assets have the following adjusted bases and FMVs immediately before the sale:

Assets	Adjusted Basis	FMV
Cash	$ 50,000	$ 50,000
Marketable securities	49,000	55,000
Accounts receivable	60,000	60,000
Inventory	60,000	90,000
Building	27,000	44,000
Land	10,000	26,000
Machinery and equipment[a]	74,000	125,000
Total	$330,000	$450,000

[a]The machinery and equipment are Sec. 1245 property. Recapture potential on the machinery and equipment is $107,000.

Target and Acquiring Corporations recognize no gains or losses on the liquidation. Acquiring assumes Target's $100,000 in liabilities and takes a $330,000 basis for the assets acquired from Target, with each of the individual basis amounts carrying over. In addition, Acquiring assumes all of Target's tax attributes, including any NOL carryovers, E&P, and the $107,000 depreciation recapture potential on the machinery and equipment. ◀

ADDITIONAL COMMENT

A Sec. 338 election triggers immediate taxation to the target corporation. Therefore, in most situations it makes little sense to pay an immediate tax to obtain a step-up in basis when such additional basis can be recovered only in future years. The election can be beneficial, however, if the target corporation has enough NOLs to offset most or all of the gain recognized on the deemed asset sale. The election also can be beneficial if Sec. 338(h)(10) applies (see footnote 9).

SECTION 338 DEEMED SALE ELECTION. The Sec. 338 **deemed sale election** operates in two steps. First the target corporation's shareholders sell their stock to the acquiring corporation. Then the acquiring corporation makes a Sec. 338 deemed sale election with respect to the acquisition of the target corporation's stock. This election results in a hypothetical sale of the "old" target corporation's assets to a "new" target corporation for their **aggregate deemed sale price (ADSP)** in a transaction that requires the seller ("old" target) to recognize all gains and losses in its final tax return. The "old" target corporation goes out of existence for tax purposes only.[8] The "new" target corporation is treated as a new entity for tax purposes (i.e., it makes new accounting method and tax year elections). The bases of the old target corporation's assets are stepped-up or stepped-down to the amount paid by the acquiring corporation for the target corporation's stock plus the amount of the target corporation's liabilities (including any federal income taxes owed on the hypothetical sale). Corporate purchasers generally are less

---

[7] The liquidation may be taxable for any minority shareholders and to the subsidiary corporation on distributions made to the minority shareholders.

[8] The target corporation's legal existence does not change under the state corporation laws. For federal income tax purposes, the target corporation (com-

monly referred to as "old" target) goes out of existence. A "new" target corporation is created. This new corporation acquires for tax purposes all the assets of the "old" corporation.

enthusiastic about Sec. 338[9] treatment because the target corporation usually incurs a significant tax cost on the hypothetical sale in the year the purchasing corporation makes the Sec. 338 election.

Eligible Stock Acquisitions. In this type of election, Sec. 338 requires the acquiring corporation to make a qualified stock purchase (i.e., to purchase 80% or more of the target corporation's voting stock and 80% or more of the total value of all classes of stock [except certain nonvoting preferred stock issues] during a 12-month (or shorter) acquisition period).[10] The acquisition period must be a continuous period beginning on the date on which the acquiring corporation first purchases stock in the target corporation that counts toward a qualified stock purchase and ending on the date the qualified stock purchase occurs. If the acquiring corporation does not acquire the necessary 80% minimum within a continuous 12-month period, it cannot make the Sec. 338 election.

EXAMPLE C7-4 ▶ Missouri Corporation purchases a 25% block of Target Corporation's single class of stock on each of four dates: April 1, 2005; July 1, 2005; December 1, 2005; and February 1, 2006. Because Missouri acquires at least 80% of Target's stock within a 12-month period (April 1, 2005, through February 1, 2006), Missouri Corporation can elect to treat the transaction under the Sec. 338 deemed sale rules. ◀

EXAMPLE C7-5 ▶ Assume the same facts as in Example C7-4 except that Missouri Corporation instead makes the final 25% purchase on May 15, 2006. In this case, Missouri acquires only 75% of the Target stock in any 12-month period. Two possible 12-month periods are involved—April 1, 2005, through March 31, 2006; and May 16, 2005, through May 15, 2006. The 80% stock ownership minimum is not met in either period. A Sec. 338 election is unavailable to Missouri Corporation. ◀

Stock acquisitions not treated as purchases for the purpose of meeting the 80% requirement include the following:

▶ Stock whose adjusted basis is determined in whole or in part by its basis in the hands of the person from whom it was acquired (e.g., stock acquired as a capital contribution)

▶ Stock whose basis is determined under Sec. 1014(a) (i.e., FMV on the date of death or an alternative valuation date when stock is acquired from a decedent)

▶ Stock acquired in a tax-free transaction where nonrecognition of gain or loss is permitted by Sec. 351, 354, 355, or 356 (e.g., corporate formations, corporate divisions, or tax-free reorganizations)

▶ Stock acquired from a related party where stock ownership would be attributed to the purchaser under the attribution rules in Secs. 318(a)(1) through (3)

The Election. A Sec. 338 election must be made not later than the fifteenth day of the ninth month beginning after the month in which the acquisition date occurs. The acquisition date is the first date during the 12-month acquisition period on which the 80% stock ownership requirement is met.[11]

EXAMPLE C7-6 ▶ Arizona Corporation purchases 40% of Target Corporation's single class of stock on April 1, 2006. It purchases an additional 50% of Target's stock on October 20, 2006. The acquisition date is October 20, 2006. Arizona must make the Sec. 338 election on or before July 15, 2007. ◀

---

[9] An alternative form of Sec. 338 election is permitted under Sec. 338(h)(10) for members of an affiliated group. This election generally is used by affiliated groups that file consolidated tax returns. The Sec. 338(h)(10) election permits the target corporation (e.g., a subsidiary) to recognize gain or loss as if it had sold its assets in a single transaction. The corporation selling the stock (e.g., a parent corporation) does not recognize gain on the stock sale, thereby resulting in a single level of taxation. This special form of Sec. 338 election has become popular in recent years.

[10] The basic Sec. 332 liquidation of a controlled subsidiary corporation stock definition outlined in Chapter C6 also is used for Sec. 338 purposes.

[11] Secs. 338(g) and 338(h)(2).

Deemed Sale Transaction. When the acquiring corporation makes a Sec. 338 election, the target corporation is treated as having sold all of its assets at their aggregate deemed sale price (ADSP) in a single transaction at the close of the acquisition date. The asset sale is a taxable transaction with gain or loss recognized by the target corporation.

The aggregate deemed sale price is the price at which the old target corporation is deemed to have sold all of its assets in the Sec. 338 deemed sale. Calculation of the ADSP is illustrated by the following equation:[12]

$$ADSP = \frac{G + L - (T_R \times B)}{(1 - T_R)}$$

Where: G = Acquiring's grossed-up basis in the target corporation's recently purchased stock;

L = Target's liabilities other than its tax liability for the deemed sale gain determined by reference to the ADSP;

T_R = the applicable federal income tax rate; and

B = the adjusted basis of the asset(s) deemed sold.

EXAMPLE C7-7 ▶ Assume the same facts as in Examples C7-2 and C7-3 except that Acquiring Corporation makes a timely Sec. 338 election. Also assume that Target's marginal tax rate is 34%. The aggregate deemed sale price at which old Target is deemed to have sold its assets is determined as follows:

$$ADSP = \frac{G + L - (T_R \times B)}{(1 - T_R)}$$

$$ADSP = \frac{\$350,000 + \$100,000 - (0.34 \times \$330,000)}{(1 - 0.34)}$$

$$0.66 \; ADSP = \$337,800$$

$$ADSP = \$511,818$$

Thus, Target will recognize a gain of $181,818 ($511,818 − $330,000) and pay taxes of $61,818 (0.34 × $181,818) on the gain. ◀

TAX STRATEGY TIP

Many taxpayers avoid Sec. 338 because it requires an advance payment of taxes to achieve a step-up in basis of target corporation's assets. A Sec. 338 election becomes more viable, however, when the target corporation has NOLs that can offset its gain on the deemed sale of its assets, thereby reducing the cost of making the election.

Because the Sec. 338 election was originally designed for transactions in which the acquisition price of the target corporation's stock exceeded the adjusted basis of the target corporation's assets, the amount of gain recognized by the target in many of these transactions may be substantial. The size of this tax cost may result in companies forgoing the Sec. 338 election when target corporation stock is purchased or lowering the price they are willing to pay for the target corporation's stock if they intend to make a Sec. 338 election. Alternatively, the company may acquire the assets in a tax-free reorganization that is not eligible for a Sec. 338 election but permits the acquiring corporation to use its stock (instead of cash) to make the acquisition. The tax-free transaction, however, requires that the target corporation's bases for the assets carry over to the acquiring corporation. Tax-free acquisitions are explained later in this chapter. Example C7-7 presents an illustration of the deemed sale transaction under Sec. 338.

Tax Basis of the Assets After the Deemed Sale. Similarly to the ADSP, the tax basis for the assets to the new target corporation is based on the amount paid by the acquiring corporation for the target corporation's stock. This amount is called the **adjusted grossed-up basis** for the target corporation's stock. The adjusted grossed-up basis amount equals the sum of

---

[12] This equation is derived as follows:
$ADSP = G + L + [T_R \times (ADSP - B)]$
$ADSP = G + L + (T_R \times ADSP) - (T_R \times B)$
$ADSP - (T_R \times ADSP) = G + L - (T_R \times B)$

$ADSP \times (1 - T_R) = G + L - (T_R \times B)$
$ADSP = \dfrac{G + L - (T_R \times B)}{(1 - T_R)}$

▶ The purchasing corporation's grossed-up basis in recently purchased target corporation stock;

▶ The purchasing corporation's basis in nonrecently purchased target corporation stock;

▶ The liabilities of the new target corporation; and

▶ Other relevant items.[13]

The adjusted grossed-up basis is determined at the beginning of the day following the acquisition date. Example C7-10 illustrates the calculation of the adjusted grossed-up basis.

The target corporation stock owned by the acquiring corporation is divided into two categories: recently purchased stock and nonrecently purchased stock. This division is necessary because only the recently purchased stock is treated as a deemed purchase of the target corporation's assets. Recently purchased stock includes any target corporation stock held on the acquisition date that the acquiring corporation purchased during the 12-month (or shorter) acquisition period. Nonrecently purchased stock includes all other target corporation stock acquired before the acquisition period and held by the acquiring corporation on the acquisition date.[14] The basis of the purchasing corporation's stock interest equals the grossed-up basis of the recently purchased stock plus the basis of the nonrecently purchased stock.

EXAMPLE C7-8 ▶ Apple Corporation purchases all of Target Corporation's single class of stock on July 23 of the current year. All the Target stock is considered to be recently purchased stock because it is purchased in a single transaction. The acquisition date is July 23 of the current year. ◀

EXAMPLE C7-9 ▶ Assume the same facts as in Example C7-8 except that Apple Corporation already owns 10% of the Target stock (purchased five years ago) and purchases only the remaining 90% of the Target stock. The original block of Target stock is nonrecently purchased stock because it was acquired more than 12 months before the acquisition date (July 23 of the current year). ◀

When the acquiring corporation does not own all the target corporation's stock, the basis of the acquiring corporation's recently purchased stock must be increased or grossed-up to a hypothetical value that reflects ownership of all the target corporation's stock.[15]

The basis of the stock is increased by the face amount of any target corporation liabilities outstanding at the beginning of business on the day following the acquisition date plus any tax liability resulting from gain recognized on the deemed sale.[16] This liability adjustment reflects the fact that, if the acquisition had truly been an asset purchase, the assumption of the liabilities would have been reflected in the total purchase price.

Allocation of Basis to Individual Assets. The adjusted grossed-up basis of the stock is allocated among seven classes of assets by using the residual method.[17] The residual method requires that the adjusted grossed-up basis be allocated to the corporation's tangible and intangible property (other than goodwill and going concern value) on a priority basis. Any amount not allocated to specific tangible and intangible property is allocated to the target corporation's goodwill and going concern value.

---

[13] Secs. 338(b)(1) and (2). The IRS has indicated that other relevant items include only items that arise from adjustment events that occur after the close of the new target's first tax year and items discovered as a result of an IRS examination of a tax return (e.g., the payment of contingent amounts for recently or nonrecently purchased stock).

[14] Sec. 338(b)(6). A special gain recognition election is available to adjust the basis of nonrecently purchased stock. This election, which is found in Sec. 338(b)(3), is beyond the scope of this text.

[15] Sec. 338(b)(4). The gross-up operation involves taking the purchasing corporation's basis for the recently purchased target stock and dividing it by the percentage (by value) of recently purchased target stock owned (expressed as a decimal).

[16] Sec. 338(b)(2) and Reg. Secs. 1.338(b)-1(f)(1) and (2).

[17] Reg. Sec. 1.338-6(a).

PRACTICAL APPLICATION

Because goodwill now can be amortized, the fact that the residual purchase price is allocated to goodwill may be a desirable tax result. Goodwill was not amortized under pre-Sec. 197 law because it had an indefinite life. On the negative side, however, the required 15-year amortization period under Sec. 197 is longer than the time period used by many taxpayers under pre-Sec. 197 law to amortize intangible assets that had a shorter determinable life.

The seven classes of assets used in allocating the basis are

▶ Class I: cash and general deposit accounts including demand deposits and similar accounts in banks, savings and loan associations, etc.

▶ Class II: actively traded personal property (as defined in Sec. 1092(d)(1)), such as stock that is part of a straddle, U.S. government securities, and publicly traded securities.

▶ Class III: accounts receivable, mortgages, and credit card receivables from customers that arise in the ordinary course of business.

▶ Class IV: Inventory or other property held primarily for sale to customers in the ordinary course of the taxpayer's trade or business.

▶ Class V: all assets other than Class I, II, III, IV, VI, and VII assets. Included here would be tangible and intangible property without regard to whether they are depreciable, depletable, or amortizable.

▶ Class VI: All amortizable Sec. 197 assets except those in the nature of goodwill and going concern value.

▶ Class VII: Sec. 197 intangible assets in the nature of goodwill and going concern value.[18]

ADDITIONAL COMMENT

The residual method ensures that any premium paid for the target stock is reflected in goodwill. Because the residual method is the only acceptable allocation method, the only uncertainty that remains is to determine the FMVs of the assets listed in Classes II through VII.

Class VI and VII intangible assets acquired after August 6, 1993 are amortizable over a 15-year period if they are used in the active conduct of a trade or business. Among the assets included are goodwill, going concern value, and covenants not to compete.

The adjusted grossed-up basis is first allocated to the individual Class I assets based on their actual dollar amounts.[19] Any amount remaining after the allocation to the Class I assets is assigned to the Class II assets (but not in excess of their gross FMV). A similar allocation process is used for the Class III through VII assets. The total basis amounts allocated to the Class II through VII asset categories are allocated to individual assets within the class based on relative gross FMVs. When making the intraclass allocations, the allocation is based on the asset's total gross FMV, not its net FMV (gross FMV minus specific liens attaching to the property).

EXAMPLE C7-10 ▶ Assume the same facts as in Example C7-7, with assets classified as follows:

Asset Class	Assets	FMV
I	Cash	$ 50,000
II	Marketable securities	55,000
III	Accounts receivable	60,000
IV	Inventory	90,000
V	Building	44,000
V	Land	26,000
V	Machinery and equipment	125,000
	Total	$450,000

The adjusted grossed-up basis for Acquiring Corporation's interest in Target stock is:

Recently purchased stock	$350,000
Plus: Target corporation's nontax liabilities	100,000
Target corporation's tax liability [($511,818 − $330,000) × 0.34]	61,818
Adjusted grossed-up basis	$511,818

---

[18] Reg. Sec. 1.338(b)-6(b).
[19] Ibid.

ADDITIONAL COMMENT

Occasionally, a firm will purchase Target Corporation's stock for a price below the total FMV of its tangible assets. In such a case, the adjusted grossed-up basis to be allocated to the Class I through V assets is less than their total FMV. Class I through IV assets will receive a basis equal to their individual FMVs. Any basis remaining after making the allocation to the Class IV assets is allocated to the Class V assets using their relative FMVs.

The adjusted grossed-up basis is allocated to Target Corporation's seven asset classes as follows:

Step 1: Allocate $50,000 to the cash (Class I asset).

Step 2: Allocate $55,000 to the marketable securities (Class II asset).

Step 3: Allocate $60,000 to accounts receivable (Class III asset).

Step 4: Allocate $90,000 to inventory (Class IV asset).

Step 5: Allocate $195,000 to the building, land, and machinery and equipment (Class V assets). Because the total basis that remains after the allocation in Step 4 ($256,818) exceeds the FMV of the Class V assets ($195,000), each asset will take a basis equal to its FMV.

Step 6: No allocation to Class VI assets.

Step 7: Allocate $61,818 [$511,818 − ($50,000 + $55,000 + $60,000 + $90,000 + $195,000)] to goodwill (Class VII asset). The $61,818 amount is amortizable under Sec. 197. ◄

STOP & THINK

Question: Target Corporation in Example C7-10 is thinking about changing from the FIFO to the LIFO inventory method once the Sec. 338 adjustments have been made. How and when will the $30,000 ($90,000 FMV − $60,000 adjusted basis) step-up made to the inventory's basis be recovered if Target makes the LIFO election?

Solution: The basis step-up is recovered only if Target sells the LIFO inventory layers in existence on the acquisition date. In general, such sales do not occur unless inventory levels are reduced below the amount held on the acquisition date. If Target retains the FIFO inventory method, the step-up in the inventory's basis will be included in cost of goods sold in the first post-election tax year. Other reasons for possibly not making the Sec. 338 election are the lengthy capital recovery periods for the building and goodwill adjustments, and the fact that an adjustment made to the basis of the land is neither depreciable or amortizable.

SELF-STUDY QUESTION

What are some of the tax consequences of a Sec. 338 election?

ANSWER

The effects of a Sec. 338 election include termination of the "old" target corporation, creation of a "new" target corporation with the option of a new tax year and different accounting methods, new depreciation elections without regard to anti-churning rules, and elimination of tax attributes of the old target (i.e., NOL carryforwards).

Tax Accounting Elections for the New Corporation. The "new" target corporation files a tax return separate from that of the acquiring corporation (unless the group files a consolidated return) because it is a separate legal entity. In many respects, the "new" target corporation is treated as a new entity.[20] For example, the target corporation may adopt, without obtaining prior approval from the IRS, any tax year that meets the requirements of Sec. 441 and any accounting method that meets the requirements of Sec. 446.

The new target corporation can claim depreciation deductions under the MACRS rules without regard to the elections made by the old target corporation and without regard to the anti-churning rules.[21] The holding period for the new target corporation's assets begins on the day after the acquisition date.

The new target corporation is not a continuation of the old target corporation for purposes of the tax attribute carryover rules.[22] As a result, tax attribute carryovers that exist on the acquisition date are permanently lost when the purchasing corporation makes a Sec. 338 deemed sale election. Gain recognized on the deemed sale transaction can reduce the amount of any target corporation loss and credit carryovers that otherwise might be lost. Thus, if Target in Examples C7-7 and C7-10 had a $200,000 NOL on the acquisition date, the Sec. 338 step-up in basis could take place tax-free. Only a small portion of Target's $200,000 NOL would be lost. The acquiring corporation must carefully consider the relative benefit of obtaining a step-up in basis for the individual assets versus the value of the available tax attributes (e.g., NOL carryovers).

Topic Review C7-1 summarizes the requirements for, and tax consequences of, having made a Sec. 338 deemed liquidation election.

---

[20] The "old" target also files a separate tax return that includes the gains from the Sec. 338 deemed sale. The "old" target may not file a consolidated tax return with the acquiring corporation.

[21] Reg. Sec. 1.338-2(d)(1)(i).
[22] Sec. 381(a)(1).

Topic Review C7-1

Section 338 Deemed Liquidation

Election Requirements

1. The acquiring corporation must have made a qualified stock purchase (i.e., a purchase of 80% or more of the target corporation's voting stock and 80% or more of the total value of all stock within a 12-month period).
2. Stock acquisitions involving substituted basis (e.g., tax-free reorganizations, corporate formations, and gifts), transfers at death, or related parties do not count toward the 80% minimum.
3. The election must be made not later than the fifteenth day of the ninth month beginning after the month in which the acquisition date occurs. The acquisition date is the first date on which the 80% stock ownership requirement is met.

Tax Consequences of a Sec. 338 Election

1. The old target corporation is treated as having sold all of its assets to the new target corporation at their aggregate deemed sales price in a single transaction at the close of the acquisition date. The old target corporation recognizes gain or loss on the deemed sale.
2. The new target corporation takes a basis for the assets equal to the acquiring corporation's adjusted grossed-up basis for the target stock, that is, the sum of the acquiring corporation's basis for its stock interest in the target corporation on the day following the acquisition date, the target corporation's liabilities on the day following the acquisition date, and other relevant items (e.g., contingent liabilities that become fixed).
3. The total adjusted grossed-up basis is allocated to the individual assets using the residual method. The residual method allocates the basis first to cash and near-cash items, other tangible and intangible assets, and finally to goodwill and going concern value.
4. The tax attributes of the old target corporation disappear with the Sec. 338 deemed sale.
5. The new target corporation makes new tax year and accounting method elections.

COMPARISON OF TAXABLE AND TAX-FREE ACQUISITIONS

Explain the differences between taxable and tax-free acquisition transactions

TAXABLE AND TAX-FREE ASSET ACQUISITIONS

One way to illustrate the difference between taxable and tax-free transactions is to compare the tax consequences. For purposes of our discussion, assume that Acquiring Corporation acquires all the assets and liabilities of Target Corporation and that Target is liquidated immediately following the acquisition. If Acquiring uses cash and debt obligations to make the purchase, the acquisition is taxable. If Acquiring acquires all of Target's assets using primarily its voting stock and limited cash and debt to accomplish the transaction, the acquisition may qualify as a tax-free reorganization.

KEY POINT

Determining whether a transaction is taxable or nontaxable is doubly important to Target because it is involved in two potentially taxable exchanges: the exchange between Target and Acquiring and the exchange between Target and Target's shareholders.

TAX CONSEQUENCES FOR TARGET CORPORATION. Section 1001(c) requires that, with certain exceptions, the entire gain or loss realized on a sale or exchange must be recognized. Thus, Target Corporation recognizes all gains and losses realized on selling its assets.

A tax-free reorganization is one exception to the general rule. Target generally recognizes no gain or loss when it exchanges its assets for Acquiring's stock. It also recognizes no gain or loss when it distributes the Acquiring stock to its shareholders. Target, however, could recognize gain if it receives boot property and does not distribute the boot to its shareholders or if it distributes boot property or retained property whose FMV exceeds its adjusted basis. The term *retained property* refers to property not transferred to Acquiring as part of the acquisition.

TAX CONSEQUENCES FOR ACQUIRING CORPORATION. Acquiring Corporation recognizes no gain or loss when it issues stock in exchange for property in either a taxable or tax-free transaction. Assets received in a taxable transaction have their tax basis adjusted upward or downward to their acquisition cost. The holding period for the acquired assets begins on the day after the transaction date. If the assets are acquired in a tax-free reorganization, Acquiring takes a carryover basis that is the same as Target's basis before the transfer. If Target recognizes a gain because it does not distribute boot property to its shareholders, the carryover basis is adjusted upward for this recognized gain. Acquiring's holding period tacks on to Target's holding period.

Because a taxable acquisition is treated as a purchase transaction, all of Target's tax attributes (e.g., an NOL carryover) disappear when it is liquidated. On the other hand, the tax attributes carry over to Acquiring Corporation in a tax-free reorganization.

TAX CONSEQUENCES FOR TARGET CORPORATION'S SHAREHOLDERS. When Target Corporation is liquidated as part of a taxable acquisition, its shareholders recognize gain or loss on the surrender of their stock. The assets received from the Acquiring Corporation take a basis equal to their FMV. A tax-free reorganization requires the shareholder to recognize gain only to the extent he or she receives boot. The gain generally is taxed as a capital gain, although dividend income may be reported in certain situations. The stocks and securities received take a substituted basis that references the basis of the Target stocks and securities surrendered. The basis of any boot property is its FMV.

ACCOUNTING FOR THE ACQUISITION. For financial statement purposes after June 30, 2001, the purchase method of accounting is the only available method to account for acquisitions. Thus, the acquired assets must be recorded at their fair market values. Any goodwill acquired cannot be amortized for financial accounting but must be tested for impairment. Any impairment loss from an indefinite-lived intangible asset must be recognized as part of the income or loss from continuing operations reported in the acquiring firm's financial statements.

Topic Review C7-2 compares taxable and tax-free asset acquisition transactions.

COMPARISON OF TAXABLE AND TAX-FREE STOCK ACQUISITIONS

For purposes of our discussion, assume that Acquiring Corporation acquires all of Target Corporation's stock instead of its assets. Target becomes a controlled subsidiary of Acquiring. If Acquiring uses cash, debt obligations, and its stock to make the purchase, the acquisition is taxable. If Acquiring acquires all of Target's stock using solely its voting stock or voting stock of its parent corporation to effect the transaction, the acquisition qualifies as a tax-free reorganization.

TAX CONSEQUENCES FOR TARGET CORPORATION. Target Corporation's basis for its assets does not change as a result of either a taxable or tax-free stock transaction (unless Acquiring Corporation makes a Sec. 338 election after a taxable stock purchase). Any depreciation recapture potential existing on the transaction date stays with Target's assets and, therefore, is assumed by the purchaser. If Target has loss or credit carryovers, it retains these carryovers, but they may be subject to special limitations in its post-acquisition tax years.

If Acquiring Corporation is part of an affiliated group that files a consolidated tax return, Target must join in the consolidated return election if at least 80% of its stock is owned and Target is an includible corporation. Otherwise, Acquiring and Target can elect to make an initial consolidated tax return election (see Chapter C8).

TAX CONSEQUENCES FOR ACQUIRING CORPORATION. Acquiring Corporation does not recognize gain or loss when it issues its own stock in exchange for property in either a taxable or tax-free transaction. Acquiring's basis for the stock in a taxable acquisition is its acquisition cost. The taxable stock acquisition may qualify as a purchase for purposes of the Sec. 338 deemed sale election. In a tax-free reorganization, Acquiring's

Topic Review C7-2

Comparison of Taxable and Tax-Free Asset Acquisitions

VARIABLE	TAXABLE ACQUISITION	TAX-FREE REORGANIZATION
1. Consideration employed to effect acquisition	Primarily cash and debt instruments; may involve some stock of the acquiring corporation or its parent corporation.	Primarily stock and limited cash or debt of the acquiring corporation or its parent corporation.
2. Target Corporation a. Amount of gain or loss	All gains and losses are recognized. Installment method available if payments are deferred.	Generally, no gain or loss recognized. Gain recognized on an asset transfer when the target corporation receives boot property and does not distribute the boot property to its shareholders. Gain also recognized on the distribution of appreciated boot or retained property.
b. Character of gain or loss	Depends on nature of each asset transferred or distributed.	Depends on nature of each asset transferred or distributed.
c. Recapture provisions	Sec. 1245 or 1250 gains are recaptured.	Secs. 1245 or 1250 do not apply unless boot triggers the recognition of gain.
3. Acquiring Corporation a. Gain or loss when stock is issued for property	None recognized.	None recognized.
b. Gain or loss when boot is transferred for property	Gain or loss recognized if noncash boot property is transferred to target corporation.	Gain or loss recognized if noncash boot property is transferred to target corporation.
c. Basis of acquired assets	Cost.	Same as target corporation's basis, increased by gain recognized.
d. Holding period of acquired assets	Begins on the day after the transaction date.	Includes holding period of the target corporation.
e. Acquisition of target corporation's tax attributes	No.	Yes.
4. Target Corporation's shareholders a. Amount of gain or loss	Realized gain or loss is recognized. Installment method available if payments are deferred.	Gain is recognized to the extent of boot received; losses are not recognized.
b. Character of gain or loss	Capital gain or loss; may be Sec. 1244 loss.	Capital gain and/or dividend income in some circumstances.
c. Basis of stock and securities received	Cost; generally FMV of stock, securities, or other property received.	Substituted basis from the stock and securities surrendered; FMV for boot property.
d. Holding period of stock and securities received	Begins on the day after the transaction date.	Includes holding period for the stock and securities surrendered; Day after the transaction date for boot property.

basis for the stock is the same as it was in the hands of Target's shareholders, and a Sec. 338 election is not available. Acquiring Corporation recognizes gain or loss when it exchanges noncash boot property for Target Corporation stock.

TAX CONSEQUENCES FOR TARGET CORPORATION'S SHAREHOLDERS. The gain recognized on a taxable sale transaction is capital gain if the Target stock is a capital asset in the seller's hands. The seller can report the gain using the installment method of accounting if part or all of the consideration is deferred into a later year and the stock is not traded on an established securities market. Consideration received by the seller that represents compensation for an agreement with the purchaser not to compete for a specified time period is taxable as ordinary income.

Because only voting stock is used in a tax-free stock acquisition, Target's shareholders recognize no gain or loss. The shareholders take a substituted basis for the Acquiring stock that is the same as their basis in the Target stock.

Topic Review C7-3 compares taxable and tax-free stock acquisitions.

Topic Review C7-3

Comparison of Taxable and Tax-Free Stock Acquisitions

VARIABLE	TAXABLE ACQUISITION	TAX-FREE REORGANIZATION
1. Consideration employed to effect acquisition	Primarily cash and debt instruments; may involve some stock of the acquiring corporation or its parent corporation.	Solely voting stock of the acquiring corporation or its parent corporation.
2. Target Corporation		
a. Parent-subsidiary relationship established	Yes.	Yes.
b. Consolidated tax return election available	Yes.	Yes.
c. Basis for assets	Unchanged by stock acquisition unless a Sec. 338 election is made.	Unchanged by stock acquisition. No Sec. 338 election available.
d. Tax attributes	Retained by Target Corporation.	Retained by Target Corporation.
3. Acquiring Corporation		
a. Basis for stock acquired	Cost basis.	Carryover basis from Target's shareholders.
4. Target Corporation's shareholders		
a. Amount of gain or loss recognized	Realized gain or loss is recognized.	No boot is received; therefore, no gain is recognized.
b. Character of gain or loss	Capital gain or loss; may be Sec. 1244 loss.	Not applicable.
c. Basis of stock, securities, or other property received	Cost; generally FMV of stock, securities, or other property received.	Substituted basis from stock surrendered.
d. Holding period of stock, securities, or other property received	Begins on the day after the transaction date.	Includes holding period for the stock surrendered.

TYPES OF REORGANIZATIONS

Section 368(a)(1) authorizes seven types of reorganizations to accommodate the major forms of business acquisitions, divestitures, and restructurings. Generally, tax practitioners refer to the specific type of reorganization by the subparagraph of Sec. 368(a)(1) that contains its definition. For example, a merger transaction is referred to as a *Type A* reorganization because it is defined in Sec. 368(a)(1)(A). The seven types of reorganizations also can be classified according to the nature of the transaction, with the most common forms being acquisitive transactions and divisive transactions. In an **acquisitive reorganization,** the acquiring corporation obtains part or all of a target (or transferor) corporation's assets or stock. Types A, B, C, D, and G reorganizations can be classified as acquisitive transactions. In a **divisive reorganization,** part of a transferor corporation's assets are

EXAMPLE C7-11 ▶

Target Corporation transfers assets having a $175,000 adjusted basis to Acquiring Corporation in exchange for $400,000 of Acquiring common stock as part of a tax-free reorganization. Target realizes a $225,000 gain ($400,000 amount realized − $175,000 adjusted basis) on the asset transfer. Because Target received no boot, it recognizes none of the gain. If Target instead receives $350,000 of Acquiring common stock and $50,000 of money, Target recognizes no gain if it distributes the $50,000 of boot to its shareholders. ◀

TYPICAL MISCONCEPTION

Often, taxpayers do not realize that Sec. 361 applies to two exchanges. Section 361(a) applies to the exchange between Acquiring and Target (which already has been discussed). Section 361(c) deals with the exchange between Target and Target's shareholders. Therefore, Target is the only party to the reorganization that may recognize two separate gains.

SELF-STUDY QUESTION

How can Target distribute appreciated boot property to its shareholders if Target receives a FMV basis in all such property received from Acquiring?

ANSWER

If the property appreciates in the hands of Target before it is distributed, gain will result. In addition, Target may retain some of its own assets and distribute these assets to its shareholders. Consistent with Secs. 311(b) and 336(a), distributing appreciated property causes gain recognition by Target.

DEPRECIATION RECAPTURE. The depreciation recapture rules of Secs. 1245 and 1250 do not override the nonrecognition of gain or loss rules of Sec. 361.[25] The recapture potential that accrues before the asset transfer carries over to the acquiring corporation and is recognized when the acquiring corporation sells or exchanges the assets in a taxable transaction.

ASSUMPTION OF LIABILITIES. Neither the acquiring corporation's assumption of the target corporation's liabilities nor the acquisition of the target corporation's property subject to a liability will trigger the recognition of gain on the asset transfer. Section 357(c), however, requires the target corporation to recognize gain if the sum of the liabilities assumed or acquired exceeds the total adjusted bases of the property transferred *and* the tax-free reorganization is a divisive Type D reorganization.

RECOGNITION OF GAIN OR LOSS ON DISTRIBUTION OF STOCK AND SECURITIES. The target corporation recognizes no gain or loss when it distributes either (1) its stock, stock rights, or obligations or (2) any stock, stock rights, and obligations of a party to a reorganization received in the reorganization to its shareholders or creditors as part of the plan of reorganization (see page C7-50 for an explanation of a plan of reorganization).[26] Distributions of nonmoney boot property (including property retained by the target corporation) made pursuant to the reorganization plan requires the recognition of gain (but not loss) in the same manner as if the target corporation sold such property at its FMV.[27] Normally the gain recognized when boot property is distributed is small because of the short amount of time that passes between when it is received from the acquiring corporation (and takes a basis equal to its FMV) and when it is distributed to a shareholder.

EXAMPLE C7-12 ▶

Target Corporation transfers all of its assets and liabilities to Acquiring Corporation as part of its being merged into Acquiring (a Type A reorganization). To effect the merger, Acquiring transfers $300,000 of its common stock and $100,000 of money to Target in exchange for Target's assets. Target's basis for the assets is $250,000. Target realizes a $150,000 gain on the asset transfer [($300,000 + $100,000) − $250,000]. Target recognizes none of this gain, even though boot is received, because Target must be liquidated as part of the merger transaction. Target's distribution of the Acquiring stock to its shareholders as part of the reorganization does not trigger the recognition of any gain by Target. Gain may be recognized by Target shareholders who receive money. ◀

OBJECTIVE 5

Determine the tax consequences of a tax-free reorganization to the acquiring corporation

ACQUIRING OR TRANSFEREE CORPORATION

AMOUNT OF GAIN OR LOSS RECOGNIZED. Under Sec. 1032, the acquiring corporation recognizes no gain or loss when it receives money or other property in exchange for its stock as part of a tax-free reorganization. Similarly, a target corporation recognizes no gain or loss when it receives money or other property in exchange for its securities as part of a tax-free reorganization. The acquiring corporation, however, will recognize gain or loss under Sec. 1001 if it transfers noncash boot property to the target corporation or its shareholders.[28]

SELF-STUDY QUESTION

Because Acquiring is merely purchasing assets, can Acquiring ever recognize gain or loss on the transaction?

BASIS OF ACQUIRED PROPERTY. Section 362(b) requires property acquired in a tax-free reorganization to take a carryover basis from the target corporation, increased by the amount of gain recognized by the target corporation on the exchange. However, because the target corporation generally recognizes no gain on the asset transfer, no step-up in basis occurs.

---

[25] Secs. 1245(b)(3) and 1250(d)(3). Similar provisions are found as part of the other recapture rules.
[26] Secs. 361(c)(1)–(c)(3).

[27] Sec. 361(c).
[28] Rev. Rul. 72-327, 1972-2 C.B. 197.

EXAMPLE C7-13 ▶
ANSWER

Yes. If Acquiring uses nonmoney boot property, Acquiring will recognize gain or loss to the extent of the built-in gain or loss in the nonmoney boot property (Sec. 1001(a)).

Assume the same facts as in Example C7-12. Acquiring's basis for the acquired property is the same as Target Corporation's basis, or $250,000. ◀

HOLDING PERIOD OF ACQUIRED PROPERTY. The acquiring corporation's holding period for the acquired property includes the target corporation's holding period for the property.[29]

OBJECTIVE 6

Determine the tax consequences of a tax-free reorganization to the target corporation's shareholders and security holders

SHAREHOLDERS AND SECURITY HOLDERS

AMOUNT OF GAIN OR LOSS RECOGNIZED. Under Sec. 354(a), shareholders recognize no gain or loss if stock or securities in a corporation that is a party to a reorganization are, in pursuance of a plan of reorganization, exchanged solely for stock or securities in the same corporation, or for stock or securities of another corporation that is a party to the reorganization. The receipt of property other than stock or securities (nonqualifying property) does not automatically disqualify the transaction from tax-free treatment. Section 356(a), however, requires that the shareholder or security holder recognize gain to the extent of the lesser of the realized gain or the amount of money received plus the FMV of any other property received. Thus, shareholders recognize gain to the extent they receive nonqualifying property that does not represent a continuation of the former equity interest.

EXAMPLE C7-14 ▶
ADDITIONAL COMMENT

Acquiring may increase its basis in the assets received only by the gain recognized by Target on its exchange with Acquiring. Any gain recognized by Target on its distribution of stock or other property to Target's shareholders does not increase the basis of any assets.

Brian exchanges 1,000 shares of Target Corporation stock having a $13,000 basis for Acquiring Corporation stock having a $28,000 FMV as part of a tax-free reorganization. Brian's realized gain is $15,000 ($28,000 − $13,000), none of which is recognized. If Brian had instead received $25,000 of Acquiring stock and $3,000 of cash, his realized gain would remain $15,000, but Brian would now recognize a $3,000 gain. ◀

With some limitations, the general rule of Sec. 354(a) permits a tax-free exchange of stocks and securities. Nontraditional preferred stock (for example, preferred stock that must be redeemed or purchased by the issuer) also may be considered boot property. The receipt of securities is completely tax-free only if the principal amount of the securities surrendered equals or exceeds the principal amount of the securities received. If the principal amount of securities received exceeds the principal amount of securities surrendered, the FMV of the "excess" principal amount of the securities received constitutes boot.[30] If no securities are surrendered, the FMV of the entire principal amount of securities received constitutes boot.

EXAMPLE C7-15 ▶
SELF-STUDY QUESTION

In addition to receiving stock in Acquiring, shareholder Sue receives debt securities with a FMV of $120,000 and a principal amount of $100,000. In the exchange, Sue surrenders securities of Target with a FMV and principal amount of $80,000. Is Sue treated as having received any boot?

ANSWER

Yes. $100,000 − $80,000 = $20,000 of excess principal amount received. The boot received is $24,000. This amount represents the FMV of the excess principal amount [($20,000/$100,000) × $120,000].

Assume the same facts as in Example C7-14 except Brian instead receives $25,000 of Acquiring stock and Acquiring debt securities having a $3,000 principal amount and a $2,850 FMV. Brian's realized gain is $14,850 [($25,000 + $2,850) − $13,000], of which $2,850 is recognized. If Brian had received $3,000 in Acquiring securities and surrendered $2,000 of Target securities, the FMV of the $1,000 "excess" principal amount, or $950 [$1,000 × ($2,850 FMV/$3,000 principal)], is treated as boot. ◀

CHARACTER OF THE RECOGNIZED GAIN. Section 356(a)(2) requires that the recognized gain be characterized as dividend income if the receipt of the boot property has the same effect as the distribution of a dividend. The dividend income recognized equals the lesser of the shareholder's recognized gain or the shareholder's ratable share of the transferor or target corporation's current and accumulated earnings and profits (E&P). Any additional gain that must be recognized generally is reported as a capital gain.

The Sec. 302(b) stock redemption rules are used to test whether the exchange has the effect of a dividend distribution.[31] (See Chapter C4 for a review of the Sec. 302(b) rules.) Tax-free reorganizations generally do not involve actual redemptions of the stock of the target corporation's shareholders. Instead, the Supreme Court in its *Donald E. Clark* decision held that a shareholder is treated as having exchanged his or her target corporation stock in a tax-free reorganization solely for stock in the acquiring corporation. After

---

[29] Sec. 1223(1).
[30] Secs. 354(a)(2) and 356(d)(2)(B). The FMV of the debt obligations surrendered is irrelevant when determining the amount of the recognized gain.

[31] *CIR v. Donald E. Clark*, 63 AFTR 2d 89-1437, 89-1 USTC ¶9230 (USSC, 1989). The IRS has agreed to follow the *Clark* decision in Rev. Rul. 93-61, 1993-2 C.B. 118.

having received the acquiring corporation's stock, a hypothetical redemption (but no actual stock redemption) of a portion of the acquiring corporation's stock occurs. Capital gain treatment results when the boot received causes the hypothetical redemption to qualify for exchange treatment under Sec. 302(b).

Application of the dividend equivalency test used when boot is received in a tax-free reorganization is illustrated in the following example.

EXAMPLE C7-16 ▶

Betty owns all 60 of the outstanding shares of Fisher Corporation stock. Fisher Corporation is merged with Gulf Corporation in a tax-free reorganization, with Betty receiving 35 shares of Gulf stock worth $350,000 and $250,000 in money. Four other individuals own the remaining 100 shares of Gulf stock. Betty's Fisher stock has a $200,000 basis. Fisher and Gulf Corporations have E&P balances of $300,000 and $500,000, respectively. Betty's realized gain is $400,000 [($350,000 stock + $250,000 money) − $200,000 adjusted basis], of which $250,000 must be recognized because the money is treated as boot property.

The Fisher stock initially is treated as having been exchanged for only Gulf stock. Because the Fisher stock is worth $600,000 and the Gulf stock is worth $10,000 per share ($350,000 ÷ 35), Betty is initially treated as owning 60 of the 160 (100 + 60) shares of Gulf stock supposedly outstanding immediately after the stock-for-stock swap. The $250,000 in money Betty receives is treated as having been exchanged for 25 ($250,000 ÷ $10,000 per share) of the 60 shares of Gulf stock that would have been received in an all-stock transaction. Because Betty owns 37.5% (60 shares ÷ 160 shares) of the Gulf stock before the hypothetical redemption and 25.93% (35 shares ÷ 135 shares) after the hypothetical redemption, the $250,000 gain is characterized as capital gain under the Sec. 302(b)(2) substantially disproportionate redemption rules (i.e., 25.93% is less than 80% × 37.5% = 30%). ◀

The Sec. 302(b) test would be applied in the same manner if securities were received in the reorganization. In such a case, the boot portion of the transaction would equal the FMV of the "excess" principal amount received by the shareholder or security holder.

Whether capital gain treatment is available for boot received in a reorganization depends on the relative sizes of the target and acquiring corporations. If the acquiring corporation is larger than the target corporation, the Sec. 302(b)(2) (substantially disproportionate redemption) or Sec. 302(b)(1) (not essentially equivalent to a dividend) rules generally will provide for capital gain treatment. (See Chapter C4 for an explanation of these rules.) If the acquiring corporation is smaller than the target corporation, the target corporation's shareholder possibly may be considered as having received dividend income or a combination of dividend income and capital gain (e.g., if the boot received exceeds the shareholder's ratable share of E&P).

Prior to the 2003 Act, many noncorporate shareholders preferred capital gain treatment for their recognized gains because a 20% or lower tax rate was substantially less than the maximum tax rate applicable to ordinary dividend income. The 2003 Act reduced the maximum capital gains tax rate to 15% and extended the 15% tax rate to qualified dividends received by noncorporate shareholders. Thus, shareholders will be taxed at 15% whether the gain is classified as a capital gain or a dividend, thereby diminishing the difference between the two types of treatments. Nevertheless, capital gain treatment can provide a benefit not available to dividend treatment in that the capital gains can offset (1) capital losses recognized in other current year transactions or (2) capital loss carryovers from prior tax years. Dividend income, even though taxed at a 15% rate, cannot offset capital losses.

Dividend income treatment may be preferred by corporate shareholders because they can claim a 70%, 80%, or 100% dividends-received deduction to reduce their tax burden. In addition, capital gains recognized in the reorganization can offset capital losses recognized by corporate and noncorporate shareholders in other transactions. Finally, Sec. 453(f)(6)(C) permits a corporate or noncorporate shareholder involved in a tax-free reorganization to use the installment method of accounting to defer the reporting of the gain recognized when securities are received, provided such gain is not characterized as a dividend.[32]

---

[32] *King Enterprises, Inc. v. U.S.*, 24 AFTR 2d 69-5866, 69-2 USTC ¶9720 (Ct. Cls., 1969).

STOP & THINK

Question: The character of the shareholder's recognized gain is determined by applying the Sec. 302(b) stock redemption rules. Why are the relative sizes of the acquiring and target corporations important when determining the character of the gain recognized in a tax-free reorganization?

Solution: A shareholder receives capital gain treatment for his or her recognized gain when the hypothetical redemption qualifies for exchange treatment under the Sec. 302(b) rules. If the target corporation is smaller than the acquiring corporation, the receipt of boot almost always should qualify under one of the capital gains exceptions since no shareholder(s) will generally own more than 50% of the acquiring corporation's stock before and after the hypothetical redemption. If the boot is distributed proportionate to the stock ownership, the target corporation's shareholder(s) should see a reduction in his or her pre-and post-redemption interests. However, if the target corporation is larger than the acquiring corporation, a shareholder(s) possibly may own more than 50% of the acquiring corporation's stock, thereby causing the boot to be characterized as a dividend.

KEY POINT

When a reorganization is tax-free, shareholders defer recognition of their realized gain or loss. Consequently, they take a substituted basis in the new nonrecognition property received (i.e., any deferred gain or loss is reflected in the basis of the nonrecognition property received).

BASIS OF STOCKS AND SECURITIES RECEIVED. The basis of the stocks and securities (nonrecognition property) received by the target corporation's shareholders and security holders is determined according to the Sec. 358 rules introduced in Chapter C2. The basis of nonrecognition property is determined as follows:

Adjusted basis of the stocks and securities exchanged
Plus: Any gain recognized on the exchange
Minus: Money received in the exchange
        FMV of any property (other than money) received in the exchange

Basis of the nonrecognition property received

If the shareholder or security holder receives no boot, the stocks and securities will take a substituted basis from the stocks and securities exchanged. If a gain must be recognized, the basis of the stocks and securities exchanged is increased by the amount of such gain and then reduced by the amount of money plus the FMV of any other boot property received in the reorganization. The basis of any other boot property received is its FMV.

EXAMPLE C7-17 ▶

Ken owns Target Corporation stock having a $10,000 adjusted basis. As part of a tax-free reorganization involving Target and Acquiring Corporations, Ken exchanges his Target stock for $12,000 of Acquiring stock and $4,000 of Acquiring securities. Ken realizes a $6,000 gain [($12,000 + $4,000) − $10,000], of which $4,000 must be recognized because he received securities worth $4,000 but surrendered no securities. The basis of the Acquiring securities that Ken received is $4,000. Ken's basis for the Acquiring stock is $10,000 ($10,000 basis of Target stock + $4,000 gain recognized − $4,000 FMV of Acquiring securities). ◀

When the target corporation's shareholders own a single class of stock (or a single class of securities) and end up owning two or more classes of stock or securities as a result of a tax-free reorganization, the total basis for the nonrecognition property determined above must be allocated between the stocks and/or the securities owned in proportion to the relative FMVs of the classes.[33]

HOLDING PERIOD. The holding period of the stocks and securities that are nonrecognition property includes the holding period for the stocks and securities surrendered. The holding period for boot property begins on the day after the exchange date.[34]

Topic Review C7-4 summarizes the tax consequences of a tax-free reorganization to the target corporation, the acquiring corporation, and the target corporation's shareholders and security holders.

---

[33] Reg. Sec. 1.358-2(a)(2)-(4).

[34] Sec. 1223(1).

Topic Review C7-4

Tax Consequences of a Tax-Free Reorganization

TARGET CORPORATION

1. The target corporation recognizes no gain or loss on the asset transfer except to the extent that it receives and retains money or other boot property (Secs. 361(a)–(b)). Generally, boot is not retained because the target corporation usually is liquidated or required to distribute all its assets.
2. The character of any gain or loss recognized depends on the nature of the assets transferred.
3. The acquiring corporation's assumption or acquisition of target corporation liabilities does not trigger recognition of gain on the asset transfer except to the extent Sec. 357(c) applies to "excess" liability situations involving divisive Type D reorganizations (Sec. 357(a)).
4. The target corporation recognizes no gain or loss when it distributes qualified property (i.e., stock and securities) to its shareholders and security holders. The target corporation recognizes gain (but not loss) when it distributes noncash boot property or retained assets to shareholders or security holders (Sec. 361(c)).

ACQUIRING CORPORATION

1. The acquiring corporation recognizes no gain or loss when it receives money or other boot property in exchange for its stock or debt obligations (Sec. 1032).
2. The acquiring corporation, however, does recognize gain or loss when it transfers noncash boot property to the target corporation or its shareholders (Sec. 1001).
3. The basis of the acquired property equals its basis in the transferor's hands increased by any gain recognized by the transferor (Sec. 362(b)).
4. The acquiring corporation's holding period for the acquired property includes the transferor's holding period (Sec. 1223(1)).

SHAREHOLDERS AND SECURITY HOLDERS

1. No gain or loss is recognized if only stock is received (Sec. 354(a)). Gain (but not loss) is recognized when money, excess securities, or other boot property is received. The amount of the recognized gain equals the lesser of the realized gain or the amount of money plus the FMV of any other boot property received (Sec. 356(b)).
2. The character of the gain recognized is determined by applying the Sec. 302(b) rules to the acquiring corporation. Dividend income cannot exceed the shareholder's ratable share of the transferor or target corporation's E&P (Sec. 356(a)(2)).
3. The total basis of the stocks and securities received equals the adjusted basis of the stocks and securities exchanged plus any gain recognized by the shareholders and security holders on the exchange minus the sum of the money and the FMV of other boot property received. This basis is allocated to the stocks and securities received based on their relative FMVs. The basis of boot property is its FMV (Sec. 358(a)).
4. The holding period of stocks and securities received includes the holding period of the stocks and securities surrendered. The holding period for boot property received begins on the day after the exchange date (Sec. 1223(1)).

ACQUISITIVE REORGANIZATIONS

This portion of the chapter is devoted to the Types A, B, C, D, and G acquisitive reorganizations. Each of these types of reorganizations is explained below. Topic Review C7-5 summarizes the requirements for acquisitive reorganizations.

TYPE A REORGANIZATION

The IRC permits four kinds of **Type A reorganizations:** mergers, consolidations, triangular mergers, and reverse triangular mergers. Each of these transactions is described below.

MERGER OR CONSOLIDATION. A Type A reorganization is a **merger** or a **consolidation** that satisfies the corporation laws of the United States, a state, or the District of Columbia.[35] State law authorizes several different forms of mergers. Two common

KEY POINT

The Type A reorganization is unique in comparison to the other statutory reorganizations because state law, rather than federal law, is an important factor in determining whether a transaction qualifies as a tax-free merger.

---

[35] Sec. 368(a)(1)(A) and Reg. Sec. 1.368-2(b)(1).

Topic Review C7-5

Summary of Major Acquisitive Reorganizations

TYPE OF REORGANIZATION	TARGET (T) CORPORATION PROPERTY ACQUIRED	CONSIDERATION THAT CAN BE USED	WHAT HAPPENS TO THE TARGET (T) CORPORATION?	SHAREHOLDERS' RECOGNIZED GAIN	OTHER REQUIREMENTS
A—Merger or consolidation	Assets and liabilities of T Corporation.[a]	Voting and nonvoting stock, securities, and other property of A Corporation.[b]	T Corporation liquidates as part of the merger.	Lesser of realized gain or boot received.	For advance ruling purposes, at least 50% of the consideration employed must be A stock (continuity of interest requirement)
B—Stock for stock	At least 80% of the voting and 80% of the nonvoting T stock.	Voting stock of A Corporation.	Remains in existence as a subsidiary of A Corporation.	None	Noncash boot given by the transferor can cause the transfer to be a taxable event.
C—Assets for stock	Substantially all the assets of T Corporation (and possibly some or all of its liabilities).	Stock, securities, and other property of A Corporation, provided at least 80% of the assets are acquired for voting stock.	Stock, securities, and boot received in the reorganization and all of T's remaining properties must be distributed to its shareholders and creditors; as a practical matter, T usually is liquidated.	Lesser of realized gain or boot received.	For advance ruling purposes, "substantially all" is 70% of the gross assets and 90% of the net assets of T Corporation.
D—Acquisitive	Substantially all the assets of T Corporation (and possibly some or all of its liabilities) are acquired by a "controlled" transferee corporation (A Corporation[b]).	Stock, securities, and other property of A Corporation.	Stocks, securities, and boot received in the reorganization and all of T's remaining property must be distributed to its shareholders and creditors; as a practical matter, T usually is liquidated.	Lesser of realized gain or boot received.	"Substantially all" is defined as it was for a Type C reorganization; the continuity of interest requirement also applies here for advance ruling purposes; control is defined as 50% of the voting power or 50% of the value of A's stock.

[a]T Corporation is the target or transferor corporation.
[b]A Corporation is the acquiring or controlled transferee corporation. In a Type D reorganization, Acquiring is 50% or more controlled by Target's shareholders.

forms are discussed below. Other permitted forms, such as triangular mergers and reverse triangular mergers, are discussed later in this chapter. The first form involves the acquiring corporation transferring its stock, securities, and other consideration (boot) to the target corporation in exchange for its assets and liabilities. The acquiring corporation stock, securities, and other consideration received by the target corporation are distributed to its shareholders and security holders in exchange for their target corporation stock and securities. The target corporation then goes out of existence. Figure C7-1 illustrates this type of merger. The second type of merger involves the acquiring corporation exchanging its stock, securities, and other consideration directly for the stock and securities held by the target corporation's shareholders and security holders. The acquiring corporation then liquidates the target corporation and acquires its assets and liabilities.

A consolidation involves two or more corporations having their assets acquired by a new corporation. The stock, securities, and other consideration transferred by the acquiring corporation is distributed by each target corporation to its shareholders and security holders pursuant to its liquidation in exchange for its own stock and securities. Figure C7-2 illustrates this type of consolidation. As with a merger, an alternative form of consolidation is where the acquiring corporation transfers its stock, securities, and other consideration directly to the target corporations' shareholders and security holders in exchange for their stock and securities. In this case, each target corporation then liquidates, with the acquiring corporation receiving its assets and liabilities.

Requirements for Mergers and Consolidations. The Type A reorganization provides the acquiring corporation with the greatest flexibility in selecting the consideration to be used to effect the reorganization. Section 368 places no restrictions on the types of consideration that can be used in a merger. The IRS interpretation of the continuity of interest judicial doctrine for obtaining a private letter ruling involving a tax-free reorganization, however, requires stock of the acquiring corporation to be at least 50% of the total

KEY POINT

The Type A reorganization is the most flexible reorganization with respect to the type of consideration that must be used. The only requirement that must be satisfied is the continuity of interest test, which is discussed later in the chapter.

ADDITIONAL COMMENT

The actual exchange of Acquiring stock for Target stock may be different from the illustrations provided in this chapter. These illustrations represent how the IRC construes the steps in each of the reorganizations. As a practical matter, the exchange of stock between Acquiring and Target usually is performed by an independent stock transfer agent rather than flowing from Acquiring to Target and finally to Target's shareholders.

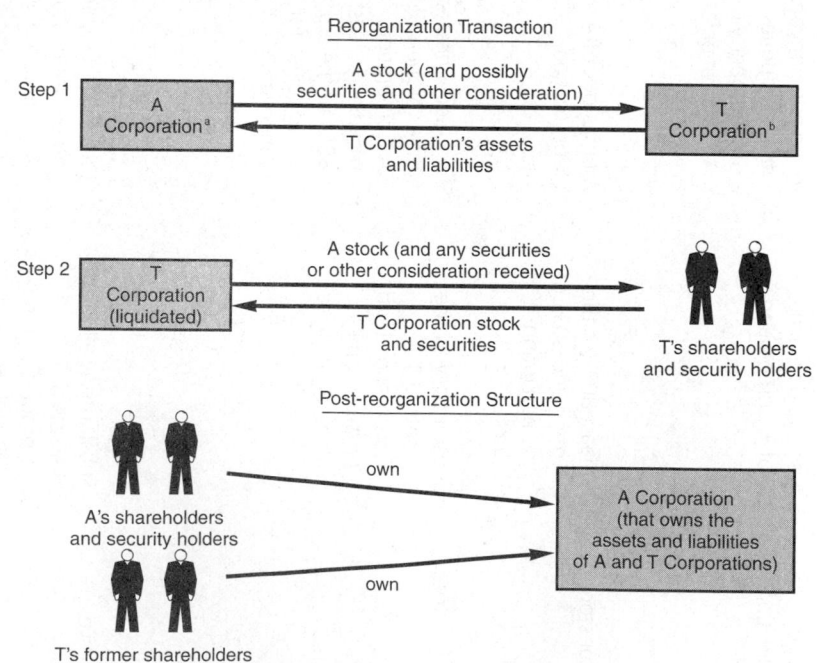

ᵃUnless otherwise indicated in this chapter, A Corporation designates the acquiring or transferee corporation.

ᵇUnless otherwise indicated in this chapter, T Corporation designates the target or transferor corporation.

FIGURE C7-1 ▶ TYPE A REORGANIZATION—MERGER

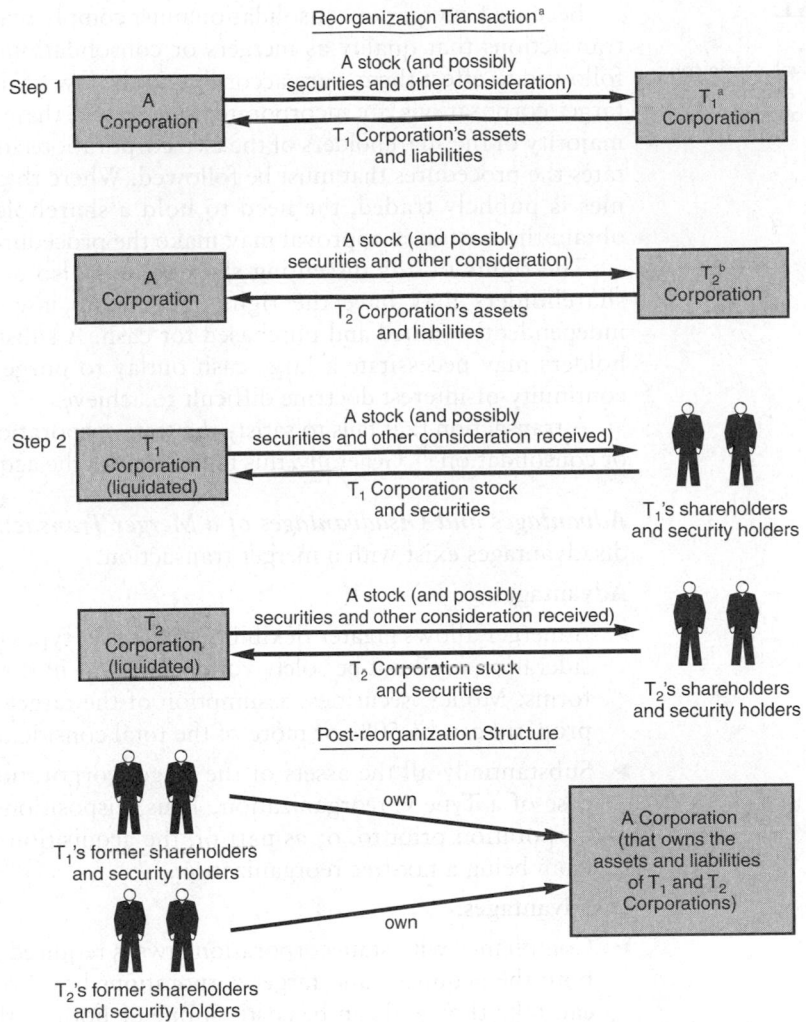

Reorganization Transaction[a]

Step 1

A stock (and possibly securities and other consideration)

A Corporation → T₁[a] Corporation

T₁ Corporation's assets and liabilities

A stock (and possibly securities and other consideration)

A Corporation → T₂[b] Corporation

T₂ Corporation's assets and liabilities

Step 2

A stock (and possibly securities and other consideration received)

T₁ Corporation (liquidated) → T₁'s shareholders and security holders

T₁ Corporation stock and securities

A stock (and possibly securities and other consideration received)

T₂ Corporation (liquidated) → T₂'s shareholders and security holders

T₂ Corporation stock and securities

Post-reorganization Structure

T₁'s former shareholders and security holders — own → A Corporation (that owns the assets and liabilities of T₁ and T₂ Corporations)

T₂'s former shareholders and security holders — own →

[a]T₁ Corporation is the first of the two target corporations participating in the reorganization.

[b]T₂ Corporation is the second of the two target corporations participating in the reorganization.

FIGURE C7-2 ▶ TYPE A REORGANIZATION: CONSOLIDATION

consideration used.[36] The stock used can be voting stock, nonvoting stock, or a combination of the two. Either common or preferred stock may be used. The 50% minimum must be met only if the taxpayer desires to obtain a favorable advance ruling regarding the tax consequences of the transaction.

The IRS in Rev. Rul. 2000-5 requires that a merger transaction meet not only the standards of the state corporate merger laws but also requires that the target corporation go out of existence.[37] An acquisition transaction does not qualify as a Type A asset-for-stock "merger" reorganization if the target corporation retains the remainder of its assets not acquired by the acquiring corporation and the target corporation's shareholders retain their remaining target stock not acquired by the acquiring corporation. Revenue Ruling 2000-5 also holds that, if a target merges under state law into two or more acquiring corporations and the target does not go out existence, the transaction does not qualify as a Type A reorganization.

---

[36] Rev. Proc. 77-37, 1977-2 C.B. 568, Sec. 3.02. In recent years, tax opinions from tax counsel have largely replaced private letter rulings for most acquisitive reorganizations.

[37] Rev. Rul. 2000-5, 2000-1 C.B. 436.

ADDITIONAL COMMENT
Shareholder approval is time consuming, expensive, and not always possible to obtain.

Because a merger or consolidation must comply with state or federal corporation laws, transactions that qualify as mergers or consolidations, and the procedures that must be followed to effect them, vary according to the law of the states in which the acquiring and target corporations are incorporated. Generally, these laws require a favorable vote by a majority of the shareholders of the two corporations involved in the merger. State law dictates the procedures that must be followed. Where the stock of one or both of the companies is publicly traded, the need to hold a shareholder's meeting, solicit proxies, and obtain the necessary approval may make the procedure both costly and time-consuming.

The rights of any dissenting shareholders also are dictated by the state law. These shareholders may have the right under state law to dissent and have their shares independently valued and purchased for cash. A substantial number of dissenting shareholders may necessitate a large cash outlay to purge their interests and may make the continuity-of-interest doctrine difficult to achieve.

A transaction that fails to satisfy the state corporation laws does not qualify as a merger or consolidation.[38] Generally, this failure causes the acquisition to be a taxable transaction.

Advantages and Disadvantages of a Merger Transaction. A number of advantages and disadvantages exist with a merger transaction.

Advantages:

▶ A merger allows greater flexibility than other types of reorganizations because the consideration need not be solely voting stock, as in the case of some other reorganization forms. Money, securities, assumption of the target corporation's liabilities, and other property can be 50% or more of the total consideration used.[39]

▶ Substantially all the assets of the target corporation need not be acquired, as in the case of a Type C reorganization. Thus, dispositions of unwanted assets by the target corporation prior to, or as part of, the acquisition generally do not prevent a merger from being a tax-free reorganization.

Disadvantages:

▶ Compliance with state corporation laws is required. In most states, the shareholders of both the acquiring and target corporations have to approve the plan. Such approvals can take time and can be costly if one or both of the corporations is publicly traded. Dissenting shareholders of both corporations also have the right under state law to have their shares independently appraised and purchased for cash, which may require a substantial cash outlay.

▶ All liabilities of the target corporation must be assumed, including unknown and contingent liabilities.

▶ A merger requires the transfer of real estate titles, leases, and contracts. The target corporation may have contracts, rights, or other privileges that are nontransferable and may necessitate use of a reverse triangular merger or other reorganization forms discussed below.

Tax Consequences of a Merger Transaction. The following example illustrates the tax consequences of a merger transaction.

EXAMPLE C7-18 ▶ Acquiring Corporation acquires all of Target Corporation's assets in a merger transaction that qualifies as a Type A reorganization. Target transfers assets having a FMV and an adjusted basis of $2 million and $1.3 million, respectively, and $400,000 in liabilities to Acquiring in exchange for $1 million of Acquiring's common stock and $600,000 of cash. At the time of the transfer, Acquiring's E&P balance is $1 million, and Target's E&P is $750,000. Target distributes the Acquiring stock and cash to its sole shareholder, Millie, in exchange for all of her Target stock, which has a $175,000 basis. If Millie had received only Acquiring stock in the reorganization, she would have held 6.25% of the Acquiring stock (100,000 out of 1.6 million shares) immediately after the reorganization.

[38] *Edward H. Russell v. CIR,* 15 AFTR 2d 1107, 65-2 USTC ¶9448 (5th Cir., 1965).
[39] The advance ruling requirements generally limit nonstock consideration to 50% of the total consideration. In limited circumstances, the courts have permitted the 50% ceiling to be exceeded.

Target realizes a $700,000 gain [($1,000,000 stock + $600,000 cash + $400,000 liabilities) − $1,300,000 adjusted basis] on the asset transfer. Target recognizes none of this gain. Acquiring takes a $1.3 million carryover basis for the assets it receives. Target recognizes no gain when it distributes the stock and cash to Millie. Millie realizes a $1,425,000 gain on the liquidation of Target [($1,000,000 stock + $600,000 cash) − $175,000 adjusted basis], of which $600,000 must be recognized because of the cash received. Each share of Acquiring stock is worth $16 ($1,600,000 total consideration ÷ 100,000 shares that would be held if all stock were received). The hypothetical redemption of Millie's Acquiring stock required under the *Clark* case and Rev. Rul. 93-61 (see pages C7-18 and C7-19) qualifies as an exchange under Sec. 302(b)(2) because the redemption of 37,500 ($600,000 cash ÷ $16) shares of Acquiring stock deemed to have been redeemed reduces Millie's interest from 6.25% (100,000 shares ÷ 1,600,000 shares) to 4.00% (62,500 shares ÷ 1,562,500 shares). Millie's basis for her Acquiring stock is $175,000 ($175,000 basis of Target stock + $600,000 gain recognized − $600,000 cash received). In addition, Millie's holding period for the Acquiring stock includes her holding period for the Target stock. ◄

ADDITIONAL COMMENT

If the IRS applies Sec. 351 to the drop down transaction, and if the total adjustted basis for all property transferred exceeds the total FMV of that property, the subsidiary's total basis will be limited to the total FMV (see Chapter C2 for details).

DROP-DOWN TYPE A REORGANIZATION. The tax-free reorganization rules permit the acquiring corporation to transfer (drop-down) part or all of the assets and liabilities acquired in the merger or consolidation to a controlled subsidiary corporation.[40] The asset transfer does not affect the tax-free nature of the transaction. Neither the parent nor subsidiary corporation recognize gain or loss on the transfer. The subsidiary corporation takes a carryover basis from its parent corporation in the assets.

TRIANGULAR MERGERS. **Triangular mergers** are authorized by Sec. 368(a)(2)(D). They are similar to the conventional Type A merger (previously discussed) except that the parent corporation uses a controlled subsidiary corporation to serve as the acquiring corporation. The target corporation is then merged into the subsidiary corporation using one of the two alternative merger forms described earlier (see Figure C7-3).

Triangular mergers must satisfy the same state law requirements as basic merger transactions. In addition, the stock used to carry out the reorganization is limited to that of the parent corporation. However, the subsidiary corporation's cash and securities can be used as part of the transaction, and the subsidiary corporation can assume the target corporation's liabilities.

The "Substantially All" Requirement. The subsidiary corporation must acquire substantially all the target corporation's assets as part of the plan of reorganization. For advance ruling purposes, the IRS has defined *substantially all* to be at least 70% of the FMV of the target corporation's gross assets and 90% of the FMV of its net assets.[41]

EXAMPLE C7-19 ▶ Acquiring Corporation plans to acquire Target Corporation's assets by using a triangular merger involving its subsidiary Acquiring-Sub Corporation. Target Corporation has $2.5 million (FMV) in assets and $1 million in liabilities. To satisfy the IRS's advance ruling policy, Acquiring must acquire at least 70% of Target's gross assets ($1,750,000 = $2,500,000 FMV of assets × 0.70) and 90% of its net assets [$1,350,000 = ($2,500,000 FMV of assets − $1,000,000 liabilities) × 0.90], or $1.75 million in assets. Target can sell or otherwise dispose of the remaining assets. ◄

Advantages of a Triangular Merger. The tax treatment accorded a triangular merger is the same as for the conventional Type A merger transaction. The triangular merger provides three additional advantages (over the conventional Type A merger):

▶ The target corporation's assets and liabilities become the property of the subsidiary corporation. Thus, the parent corporation generally cannot be held liable for any liabilities that are not known to the acquiring corporation at the time of the transfer or for any contingent liabilities. Creditor claims against the parent corporation's assets are thus minimized.

---

[40] Sec. 368(a)(2)(C). As defined in Sec. 368(c), *control* requires the parent corporation to own at least 80% of the voting power and 80% of each class of nonvoting stock. The ability to "drop down" the assets acquired to a subsidiary corporation without recognizing any gain also applies to Type B, C, and G reorganizations.

[41] Rev. Proc. 77-37, 1977-2 C.B. 568, Sec. 3.01. Also see Rev. Rul. 2001-46, 2001-2 C.B. 321.

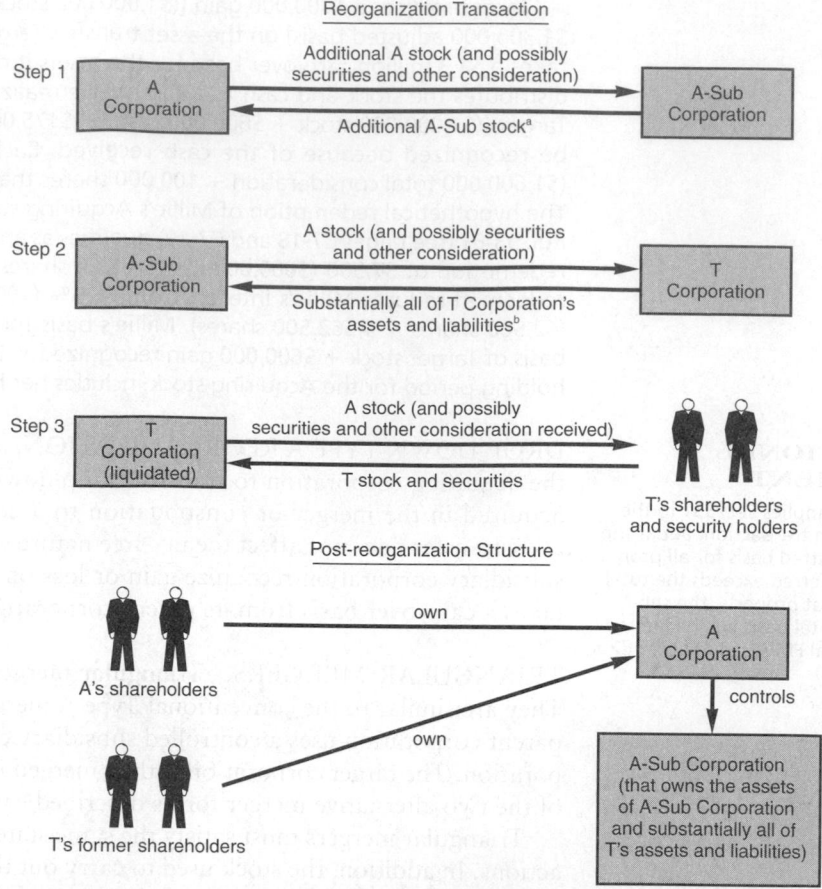

FIGURE C7-3 ▶ TRIANGULAR TYPE A REORGANIZATION

PRACTICAL APPLICATION

The triangular merger is a very popular type of acquisition because the consideration that must be used is still very flexible and yet the parent corporation does not have to assume the known or unknown liabilities of Target. Rather, the controlled subsidiary assumes these liabilities.

▶ Shareholder approval on behalf of the acquiring subsidiary corporation comes from its parent corporation. Thus, if the parent corporation's stock is widely held, the cost of obtaining approval of the shareholders may be reduced.

▶ The target corporation's shareholders may prefer to receive parent corporation stock because of its increased marketability. By receiving marketable stock, the target corporation's shareholders can sell off a portion of the parent corporation stock over an extended period of time and recognize the gain as if they were using the installment method of accounting.

ADDITIONAL COMMENT

In addition to the Type B reorganization, which will be discussed later, the reverse triangular merger is an acquisitive reorganization that keeps Target in existence. It is a popular reorganization form because, unlike the Type B reorganization, the acquiring corporation can use a limited amount of boot.

REVERSE TRIANGULAR MERGERS. **Reverse triangular mergers** are similar to the triangular merger illustrated in Figure C7-3 except the subsidiary corporation (A-Sub Corporation) merges into the target corporation (T Corporation), and the target corporation stays alive as a subsidiary of the parent corporation (A Corporation). This type of transaction permits the target corporation to continue its corporate existence. This action may be desirable from a business standpoint (e.g., to maintain a special authorization or a special license owned by the target corporation). Technical details of this type of acquisition are beyond the scope of this text.

TYPE C REORGANIZATION

A **Type C reorganization** is an asset-for-stock acquisition. This type of transaction, illustrated in Figure C7-4, requires the acquiring corporation to obtain substantially all the target corporation's assets in exchange for its voting stock and a limited amount of other consideration.[42]

The "substantially all" requirement is not defined in the IRC or Treasury Regulations. For advance ruling purposes, however, the same standard holds here that applies to triangular Type A mergers (i.e., the 70% of the FMV of gross assets and 90% of the FMV of net assets minimums).[43]

The acquired corporation in a Type C reorganization must distribute the stock, securities, and other property it receives in the reorganization, plus any other property it retains, to its shareholders as part of the plan of reorganization. Although the corporation does not have to be formally dissolved, as a practical matter it usually is liquidated.[44] Because the Type C reorganization produces the same economic result as a merger (i.e., the acquisition of the target corporation's assets) without requiring the dissolution of the target corporation under state law, many tax practitioners call it a practical merger transaction.

The acquired corporation can retain its corporate charter to prevent others from using its corporate name or to sell the corporate name to a purchaser. Assets other than the corporate charter can be retained to satisfy minimum capital requirements under state law to maintain the corporate existence.[45]

ADDITIONAL COMMENT

Because of the solely-for-voting-stock requirement, a Type C reorganization is much less flexible than a Type A reorganization in terms of the consideration that can be used.

CONSIDERATION USED TO EFFECT THE REORGANIZATION. Section 368(a)(1)(C) requires the consideration used to effect the reorganization be solely voting stock of the acquiring corporation (or its parent corporation). Both the acquiring corporation's assumption of part or all of the target corporation's liabilities and the acquisition of a property subject to a liability are disregarded for purposes of the solely-for-voting-stock requirement.

Section 368(a)(2)(B), however, permits the acquiring corporation to use other consideration in the reorganization, provided it obtains at least 80% of the target corporation's property solely for its voting stock. This rule permits the acquiring corporation to use money, securities, nonvoting stock, or other property to acquire up to 20% of the target corporation's property. Liabilities assumed or acquired reduce the amount of money that can be used in the reorganization on a dollar-for-dollar basis. If the liabilities assumed or acquired exceed 20% of the FMV of the target corporation's assets, the transaction can

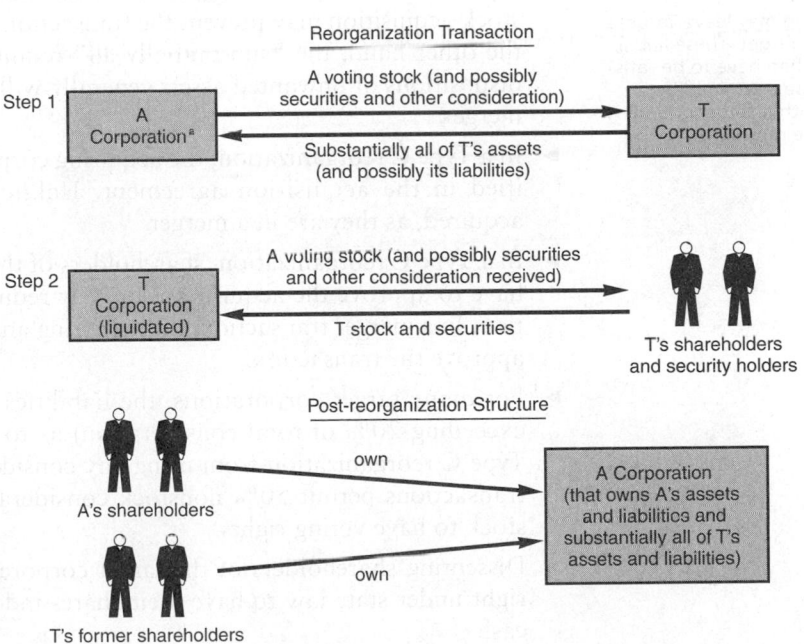

FIGURE C7-4   ▶   TYPE C (ASSET-FOR-STOCK) REORGANIZATION

[42] Sec. 368(a)(1)(C).
[43] Rev. Proc. 77-37, 1977-2 C.B. 568, Sec. 3.01.
[44] Sec. 368(a)(2)(G).
[45] Rev. Proc. 89-50, 1989-1 C.B. 631.

take place as a Type C reorganization only if the acquiring corporation uses no money, securities, nonvoting stock, or other property.

EXAMPLE C7-20 ▶ Acquiring Corporation wants to acquire all of Target Corporation's assets and liabilities as part of a Type C reorganization. The following table illustrates the application of the solely-for-voting-stock requirement for four different situations:

	Situation 1	Situation 2	Situation 3	Situation 4
FMV of Target's assets	$200,000	$200,000	$200,000	$200,000
Target's liabilities assumed by Acquiring	–0–	30,000	100,000	100,000
Consideration given by Acquiring:				
FMV of Acquiring voting stock	160,000	160,000	100,000	99,900
Money	40,000	10,000	–0–	100

In Situation 1, the FMV of the Acquiring stock equals 80% of the total assets, so the transaction is a Type C reorganization. The liabilities assumed in Situation 2 reduce the money that Acquiring can pay, but the transaction is still a Type C reorganization because the money and liabilities, in total, do not exceed 20% of the FMV of Target's total assets. In Situation 3, the high percentage of liabilities does not prevent the transaction from being a Type C reorganization because Acquiring used no money to effect the reorganization.[46] In Situation 4, the transaction is disqualified from being a Type C reorganization because some money is used along with the Acquiring stock, and the total money given by Acquiring plus liabilities assumed by Acquiring exceed 20% of the total FMV of Target's assets. ◀

ADDITIONAL COMMENT

Target's liabilities assumed by Acquiring are not a problem unless Target receives boot as part of the consideration. In this case, when applying the 20% boot relaxation rule, liabilities are treated as money. Situation 4 in Example C7-20 illustrates that, if Target has liabilities exceeding 20% of the FMV of its assets, the boot relaxation rule is of no benefit.

SELF-STUDY QUESTION

Must Acquiring assume all liabilities of Target in a Type C reorganization?

ANSWER

No. Acquiring may leave Target's liabilities in Target. These liabilities would then have to be satisfied with assets retained by Target or with assets acquired by Target in the reorganization.

ADVANTAGES AND DISADVANTAGES OF A TYPE C REORGANIZATION. A number of advantages and disadvantages exist when comparing a Type C reorganization and a merger.

▶ The acquiring corporation acquires only the assets specified in the acquisition agreement in a Type C reorganization. However, it needs to acquire substantially all the target corporation's assets. The target corporation might sell, dispose of, or retain assets the acquiring corporation does not want. These unwanted assets are not counted as acquired in testing whether the transaction satisfies the "substantially all" requirement. Thus, a disposition of a substantial amount of assets shortly before an asset-for-stock acquisition may prevent the transaction from being a Type C reorganization. On the other hand, the "substantially all" requirement does not apply to a merger, and dispositions of unwanted assets generally will not prevent an acquisition from being a merger.

▶ In a Type C reorganization, the acquiring corporation acquires only the liabilities specified in the acquisition agreement. Unknown and contingent liabilities are not acquired, as they are in a merger.

▶ In a Type C reorganization, shareholders of the acquiring corporation generally do not have to approve the acquisition, thereby reducing the cost to accomplish the transaction. In a merger transaction, the acquiring and target corporations' shareholders must approve the transaction.

▶ For many target corporations, the liabilities acquired or assumed are so large (i.e., exceeding 20% of total consideration) as to prevent the acquiring corporation in a Type C reorganization from using any consideration other than voting stock. Merger transactions permit 50% nonstock consideration to be used and do not require the stock to have voting rights.

▶ Dissenting shareholders of the target corporation in both transactions may have the right under state law to have their shares independently appraised and purchased for cash.

---

[46] The IRS may attempt to treat a transaction as a purchase under the continuity of proprietary interest doctrine (see pages C7-42 and C7-43) when the amount of liabilities assumed or acquired is high relative to the total FMV of the assets acquired.

TAX CONSEQUENCES OF A TYPE C REORGANIZATION.   The tax consequences of a Type C reorganization are illustrated by the following example.

EXAMPLE C7-21 ▶

Acquiring Corporation acquires all Target Corporation's assets and liabilities in exchange for $1.2 million of Acquiring voting stock. Target distributes the Acquiring stock to its sole shareholder, Andrew, in exchange for all his Target stock. Target's assets have a $1.4 million FMV and a $600,000 adjusted basis. Acquiring assumes liabilities of $200,000. Target has a $500,000 E&P balance. Andrew's basis for his Target stock is $400,000. Target realizes an $800,000 gain [($1,200,000 + $200,000) − $600,000], none of which must be recognized. Acquiring recognizes no gain when it exchanges its stock for the assets and, it takes a $600,000 basis in the acquired assets. Andrew realizes an $800,000 ($1,200,000 − $400,000) gain on the surrender of his shares when Target liquidates, none of which must be recognized. Andrew's basis for the Acquiring stock is $400,000. Andrew's holding period for the Acquiring stock includes the time he held the Target stock. Acquiring assumes all of Target's tax attributes, including the $500,000 E&P balance. ◀

TYPICAL MISCONCEPTION

As with a Type A reorganization, a Type C reorganization can be structured as a triangular acquisition. Although this ability provides greater flexibility in tax planning, it makes the area more confusing because of the substantial overlap between the different types of reorganizations.

DROP-DOWN AND TRIANGULAR TYPE C REORGANIZATIONS.   Section 368(a)(2)(C) permits the acquiring corporation in a Type C reorganization to transfer part or all of the assets and liabilities acquired in the reorganization to a controlled subsidiary corporation without destroying the tax-free nature of the transaction. Section 368(a)(1)(C) permits a triangular Type C reorganization to be used whereby a subsidiary corporation uses voting stock of the parent corporation to acquire substantially all the target corporation's assets. The triangular Type C reorganization requirements are the same as for the basic Type C reorganization except that the voting stock used to acquire the assets must consist solely of the stock of the acquiring corporation's parent corporation. However, the subsidiary corporation can provide additional consideration in the form of securities, money, or other property.

TYPE D REORGANIZATION

KEY POINT

When a Type D reorganization is used as an acquisitive reorganization, it generally involves commonly controlled corporations. However, its most common usage is as part of a divisive reorganization under Sec. 355 (discussed later in this chapter).

Type D reorganizations can be either acquisitive or divisive. (Divisive Type D reorganizations are discussed on pages C7-34 through C7-40.) An acquisitive Type D reorganization involves the transfer by a target (transferor) corporation of substantially all of its assets to an acquiring (transferee) corporation in exchange for such corporation's stock and securities (and possibly other consideration) pursuant to a plan of reorganization. The exchange must be followed by a distribution to the transferor's shareholders and security holders of the stock, securities, and other consideration received in the reorganization, plus any other property retained by the transferor corporation, pursuant to a complete liquidation of the transferor corporation.[47] (See Figure C7-5 for an illustration of an acquisitive Type D reorganization.)

The "substantially all" requirement is based on the facts and circumstances of the situation. For advance ruling purposes, however, the 70% of the FMV of gross assets and 90% of the FMV of net assets standard used in the triangular Type A and Type C reorganizations also applies here.[48]

ADDITIONAL COMMENT

The 50% control requirement makes the Type D reorganization a useful tool for the IRS to recast certain tax avoidance transactions.

CONTROL REQUIREMENTS.   The transferor (target) corporation or one or more of its shareholders must control the transferee (acquiring) corporation immediately after the asset transfer. For this purpose, Sec. 368(a)(2)(H) defines control as either 50% or more of the total combined voting power of all classes of voting stock, or 50% or more of the total value of all classes of stock.

One example of an acquisitive Type D reorganization is when an acquiring corporation acquires all the assets of a larger corporation (target corporation), and the target corporation's shareholders end up controlling the acquiring corporation after the reorganization. Type C reorganizations (where the target does not control the acquiring corporation) and Type A reorganizations (where the transaction satisfies the state law merger requirements) are more common than the acquisitive Type D reorganization.

---

[47] Secs. 368(a)(1)(D) and 354(b)(1).

[48] Rev. Proc. 77-37, 1977-2 C.B. 568, Sec. 3.01.

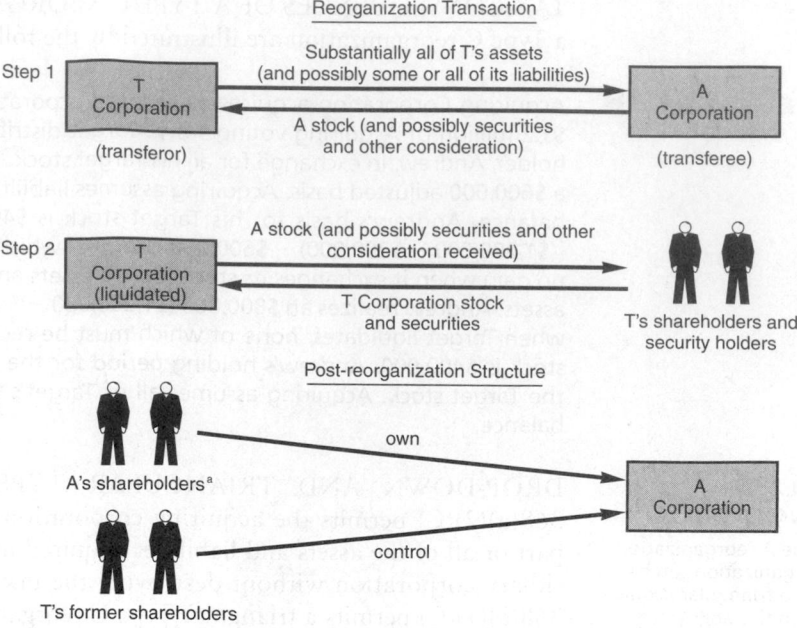

FIGURE C7-5 ▶ ACQUISITIVE TYPE D REORGANIZATION

The Sec. 368(a)(1)(D) rules do not limit the consideration that may be exchanged in the transaction. The IRS and the courts, however, require that the transferor corporation's shareholders maintain a continuing equity interest in the transferee corporation. For advance ruling purposes, the IRS requires that the transferor corporation's shareholders receive transferee corporation stock equal to at least 50% of the value of the transferor corporation's outstanding stock to satisfy this requirement.[49]

TAX CONSEQUENCES OF A TYPE D REORGANIZATION. The Type C and acquisitive Type D reorganization requirements and tax consequences are quite similar. If the reorganization satisfies both the Type C and Type D reorganization requirements, Sec. 368(a)(2)(A) requires that the transaction be treated as a Type D reorganization. The basic tax consequences of a Type D reorganization for the target corporation, the acquiring corporation, and the target corporation's shareholders are the same as for a Type C reorganization.

TYPE B REORGANIZATION

A **Type B reorganization** is the simplest form of acquisitive reorganization. In this type of reorganization, two things happen: the target corporation's shareholders exchange their stock for the acquiring corporation's voting stock, and the target corporation remains in existence as the acquiring corporation's subsidiary (see Figure C7-6).

The Type B reorganization generally is accomplished independent of the target corporation. The basis of the target corporation's assets (inside basis) and the amount of its tax attributes generally remain unchanged by the reorganization. After the reorganization, the target corporation and the parent corporation may elect to file a consolidated tax return (see Chapter C8). If the target corporation is liquidated into the parent corporation shortly after the stock-for-stock exchange occurs, the IRS may attempt to collapse the two parts of the transaction into a single transaction and treat it as a Type C asset-for-stock reorganization.[50]

ADDITIONAL COMMENT

If Acquiring wants Target to remain in existence, the two choices in Sec. 368 that can accomplish this objective are a Type B reorganization or a reverse triangular merger.

---

[49] Rev. Proc. 77-37, 1977-2 C.B. 568, Sec. 3.02.
[50] Rev. Rul. 67-274, 1967-2 C.B. 141. If the transaction is "collapsed" into a

Type C reorganization, the Type C reorganization requirements (and not the Type B) must be satisfied.

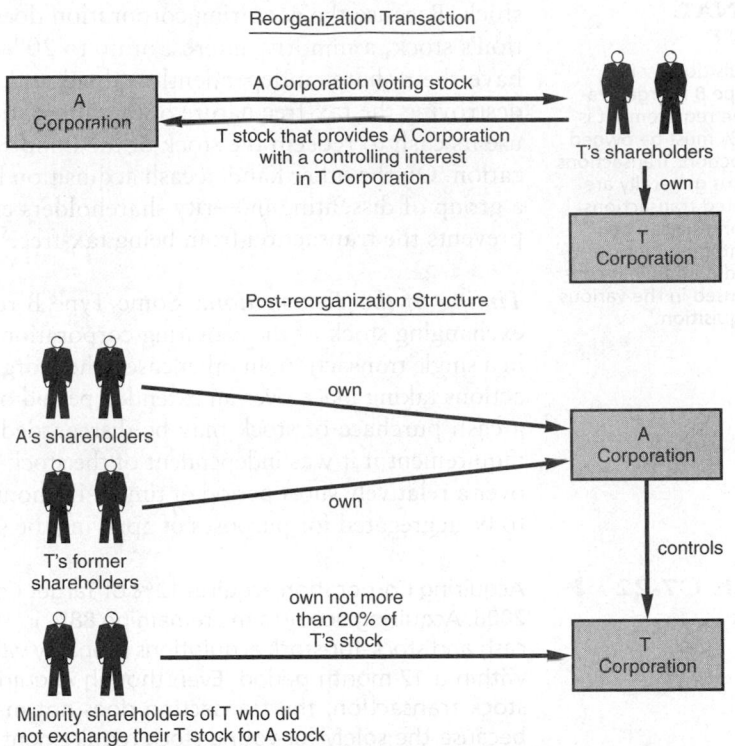

FIGURE C7-6 ▶ TYPE B (STOCK-FOR-STOCK) REORGANIZATION

KEY POINT

The IRC allows no relaxation of the solely-for-voting-stock requirement for the Type B reorganization. Thus, the Type B reorganization has the least flexible consideration requirement of any of the reorganizations.

SELF-STUDY QUESTION

Is there any way to take care of dissenters in a Type B reorganization?

ANSWER

Yes. Even though Acquiring cannot use any boot to acquire Target's stock, Target can redeem out the dissenters before the reorganization. Also, Target's nondissenting shareholders could buy out the dissenters' stock.

SOLELY-FOR-VOTING-STOCK REQUIREMENT. Section 368(a)(1)(B) requires the acquiring corporation to acquire the target corporation's stock in exchange solely for the acquiring corporation's voting stock. The acquiring corporation must own sufficient stock to be in control of the target corporation immediately after the exchange.

The solely-for-voting-stock requirement generally precludes the use of other property to effect the transaction. However, the voting stock used can be either common or preferred stock. If the acquiring corporation uses consideration other than voting stock to effect the reorganization (e.g., nonvoting preferred stock), the transaction does not qualify as a Type B reorganization, and the transaction is taxable to the target corporation's shareholders.

In a Type B reorganization, debt obligations of the acquiring corporation can be exchanged for debt obligations of the target corporation held by the target corporation's shareholders without any gain or loss being recognized when the face amount of the two debt obligations are the same.[51]

Exceptions. The acquiring corporation can use cash in limited circumstances without violating the solely-for-voting-stock requirement. For example:

▶ The target corporation's shareholders can receive cash in exchange for their right to receive a fractional share of the acquiring corporation's stock.[52]

▶ Reorganization expenses of the target corporation (such as legal expenses, accounting fees, and administrative costs) can be paid by the acquiring corporation without violating the solely-for-voting-stock requirement.[53]

Control. For Type B reorganizations, Sec. 368(c) defines control as 80% of the total combined voting power of all classes of voting stock and 80% of each class of nonvoting

---

[51] Rev. Rul. 98-10, 1998-1 C.B. 643.
[52] Rev. Rul. 66-365, 1966-2 C.B. 116.

[53] Rev. Rul. 73-54, 1973-1 C.B. 187.

ADDITIONAL COMMENT

"Creeping acquisitions" are allowed in a Type B reorganization because the requirement is merely that 80% must be owned after the transaction. Transactions within 12 months generally are considered related transactions. This aggregation rule can be either an advantage or a disadvantage depending on what consideration was used in the various steps of the acquisition.

stock. Because the acquiring corporation does not have to acquire all the target corporation's stock, a minority interest of up to 20% may be present. Minority shareholders can have their shares independently valued and acquired for cash under state law without destroying the tax-free nature of the transaction. For example, the target corporation can use its cash to redeem the stock of the minority shareholders before or after the reorganization. On the other hand, a cash acquisition by the acquiring corporation of the shares of a group of dissenting minority shareholders either before or as part of the reorganization prevents the transaction from being tax-free.[54]

Timing of the Transaction. Some Type B reorganizations are accomplished simply by exchanging stock of the acquiring corporation for 100% of the target corporation's shares in a single transaction. In other cases, the reorganization is accomplished in a series of transactions taking place over an extended period of time. Regulation Sec. 1.368-2(c) states that a cash purchase of stock may be disregarded for purposes of the solely-for-voting-stock requirement if it was independent of the stock-for-stock exchange. Stock acquisitions made over a relatively short period of time—12 months or less—are, according to this regulation, to be aggregated for purposes of applying the solely-for-voting-stock requirement.

EXAMPLE C7-22 ▶ Acquiring Corporation acquires 12% of Target Corporation's single class of stock for cash in July 2006. Acquiring acquires the remaining 88% in January 2007 in a stock-for-stock exchange. The cash and stock-for-stock acquisitions probably will be aggregated by the IRS because they occur within a 12-month period. Even though Acquiring obtains 80% control in a single stock-for-stock transaction, the transaction does not meet the Type B reorganization requirements because the solely-for-voting-stock requirement is not met if the two transactions are aggregated. The transaction could qualify as a Type B reorganization if Acquiring unconditionally sold its 12% interest in the Target stock and then acquired the necessary 80% interest in a single stock-for-stock exchange, or if Acquiring delayed the stock-for-stock exchange until some time after July 2007, when it probably would be considered a separate transaction.[55] ◀

EXAMPLE C7-23 ▶ Acquiring Corporation acquires 85% of Target Corporation's single class of stock in April 1999 in a transaction that qualifies as a Type B reorganization. Acquiring acquires the remaining 15% of Target's stock in December 2006 in a stock-for-stock exchange. Even though Acquiring already controls Target, the second acquisition is treated as a Type B reorganization. ◀

TAX CONSEQUENCES OF A TYPE B REORGANIZATION. The tax consequences of a Type B reorganization are straightforward.

▶ The target corporation's shareholders recognize no gain or loss on the exchange unless their fractional shares of stock are acquired for cash or the target corporation redeems some of their stock.

▶ The target corporation's shareholders take a substituted basis for their new acquiring corporation stock from the basis of their target corporation stock surrendered. The holding period for the acquiring corporation stock includes their holding period for the target corporation stock surrendered.

▶ The acquiring corporation recognizes no gain or loss when it issues its voting stock for the target corporation's stock.

▶ The acquiring corporation's basis for the target corporation's stock is the same as it was in the hands of the target corporation's shareholders.

EXAMPLE C7-24 ▶ Target Corporation's single class of stock is owned entirely by Mark, who has a $400,000 basis for his stock. Mark exchanges his Target stock for $700,000 of Acquiring Corporation's voting stock. Mark realizes a $300,000 gain ($700,000 − $400,000), none of which is recognized. Mark's basis for the Acquiring stock is $400,000. Acquiring Corporation recognizes no gain or loss when it issues its stock to Mark and takes a $400,000 basis for the acquired Target stock. ◀

---

[54] Rev. Rul. 68-285, 1968-1 C.B. 147.
[55] See, for example, *Eldon S. Chapman et al. v. CIR*, 45 AFTR 2d 80-1290, 80-1 USTC ¶9330 (1st Cir., 1980).

WHAT WOULD YOU DO IN THIS SITUATION?

Tobin Rote, a wealthy investor, owns all of the single class of stock of Detroit Corporation, a calendar year taxpayer. Mr. Rote has wanted to acquire Cleveland Corporation, which produces metal and plastic parts for the automobile industry. Detroit Corporation purchases for cash 4.9% of the Cleveland voting stock on August 1 of the current year. The Cleveland stock trades on the New York Stock Exchange. The acquisition provides Tobin Rote, as a Cleveland shareholder, access to its books and records. The 4.9% ownership position, however, is below the 5% threshold at which Detroit must file with the SEC a Tender Offer Statement (Schedule 14-D) regarding its stock position. Based on an analysis of Cleveland's books and records made shortly after becoming a shareholder, Tobin Rote wants to make a tender offer sometime in the next two months whereby part or all of the remaining Cleveland voting and nonvoting stock would be acquired in exchange for Detroit stock. He comes to you for advice concerning the tender offer, which he wants to complete by December 31 of the current year. No shares would be acquired unless sufficient shares were tendered to provide Detroit Corporation with 80% of the voting stock and 80% of all other classes of stock. Mr. Rote wants to use the pooling method to report the transaction for book purposes. As Mr. Rote's CPA, you know that he used this method to report some of his acquisitions a number of years ago. Mr. Rote explains to you that he hopes to continue to avoid having to place the goodwill that results from a cash purchase of a target corporation's stock on Cleveland's financial statements because the amortization drives down corporate earnings per share. As Mr. Rote's CPA, you have guided him through a number of acquisitions where he has used the pooling method. You know that the FASB has previously issued pronouncements that apply to Mr. Rote's situation. What information do you need to provide Mr. Rote about these changes? What advantages can you see in the new pronouncements that may make Mr. Rote happier about the effect that these pronouncements will have on his post-acquisition business?

STOP & THINK

ADDITIONAL COMMENT

The IRS has concluded that compliance with the sampling standards in Rev. Proc. 81-70, 1981-2 C.B. 729, may be "unduly burdensome or impossible." Thus, the IRS is seeking comments from those who perform basis studies and other interested parties in an effort to revise the revenue procedure (see Notice 2004-44, 2004-28 I.R.B. 32). So far, the IRS has not issued new guidance.

Question: Assume that Acquiring and Target Corporations are both publicly traded corporations with each corporation having several thousand shareholders. Acquiring Corporation acquires Target Corporation stock in a Type B reorganization. What problems can accrue in attempting to determine Acquiring Corporation's basis for the Target Corporation stock acquired in this transaction?

Solution: Under Sec. 358(a), Acquiring's basis for the Target stock acquired is the same as it was in the hands of Target's shareholders. Many shareholders may not know their historical cost basis for stock purchased a number of years ago. The basis for these shares may have changed due to stock dividends, stock splits, or nontaxable "dividend" distributions. This lack of information about events occurring between the acquisition and sale dates for a large number of individuals may make it difficult to accurately determine Acquiring's basis for the Target stock acquired. The IRS permits sampling to be used to extrapolate a total basis from the stock holdings of a small number of Target shareholders.

ADVANTAGES OF A TYPE B REORGANIZATION. The Type B reorganization has a number of advantages. First, as explained earlier, it usually can be accomplished quite simply and without formal shareholder approval. The acquiring corporation can acquire the necessary shares with a tender offer made directly to the target corporation's shareholders even if the target corporation's management does not approve of the transaction. Second, the target corporation remains in existence, and its assets, liabilities, and tax attributes do not transfer to the acquiring corporation. Nevertheless, use of its NOLs may be limited under Sec. 382 (see pages C7-46 through C7-48).[56] Third, the corporate name, goodwill, licenses, and rights of the target company can continue on after the acquisition. Fourth, the acquiring corporation does not directly acquire the target corporation's

---

[56] A Type B reorganization can result in an ownership change that restricts the ability of the target corporation's NOL carryovers to be used under Sec. 382 but does not, in total, diminish the amount of its carryovers.

liabilities, as is the case of some other reorganizations. Finally, the acquiring and target corporations can report the results for the post-acquisition time period by filing a consolidated tax return (see Chapter C8).

DISADVANTAGES OF A TYPE B REORGANIZATION. Offsetting the advantages noted above are a number of disadvantages. First, the sole consideration that may be used to effect the transaction is voting stock. The issuing of the additional voting stock can dilute the voting power of the acquiring corporation's shareholders and restrict their flexibility to structure the transaction to retain control of the acquiring corporation. Second, at least 80% of the target corporation's stock must be acquired even though effective control of the acquired company might be obtained with ownership of less than 80%. Third, the acquisition of less than 100% of the target corporation's stock may lead to a vocal group of dissenting minority shareholders. These shareholders have the right under state law to have their shares appraised and purchased for cash. Fourth, the bases of the target corporation's stock (outside basis) and assets (inside basis) are not stepped-up to their FMVs when the change in ownership occurs, as would be the case in a taxable asset acquisition.

DROP-DOWN AND TRIANGULAR TYPE B REORGANIZATIONS. As with the Type A and C reorganizations, a triangular Type B reorganization, or a drop-down of the target corporation's stock into a subsidiary corporation before accomplishing the stock-for-stock exchange, can be accomplished tax-free. In a triangular reorganization, the stock of the acquiring corporation's parent corporation is exchanged for a controlling stock interest in the target corporation. As in the basic Type B reorganization, the target corporation remains in existence as a subsidiary of the acquiring (subsidiary) corporation.

TYPE G REORGANIZATION

Section 368(a)(1)(G) defines a **Type G reorganization** as "a transfer by a corporation of part or all of its assets to another corporation in a title 11 [bankruptcy] or similar case, but only if, in pursuance of the plan, stock or securities of the corporation to which the assets are transferred are distributed in a transaction that qualifies under sections 354, 355, or 356." Use of a Type G reorganization is quite limited because the reorganization must take place according to a court-approved plan in a bankruptcy, receivership, or other similar situation.

In an acquisitive Type G reorganization, the financially troubled corporation might transfer substantially all of its assets to an acquiring corporation according to a court-approved plan (e.g., a bankruptcy reorganization plan) and then distribute all the stock, securities, and other property received in the exchange, plus any property it had retained, to its shareholders and creditors in exchange for their stock and debt interests.

DIVISIVE REORGANIZATIONS

A divisive reorganization involves the transfer of *part* of a transferor corporation's assets to a controlled corporation in exchange for its stock and securities (and possibly some boot property).[57] The stock and securities (and possibly some boot property) are then distributed to the transferor's shareholders. The primary divisive reorganization comes under the Type D reorganization rules, although a divisive reorganization involving a financially troubled corporation could be a Type G reorganization. Topic Review C7-6 summarizes the requirements for the divisive and other reorganizations.

---

[57] In a divisive Type D reorganization, control is defined by Sec. 368(c) because Sec. 355 (not Sec. 354) governs the distribution. Section 368(c) requires ownership of at least 80% of the voting and nonvoting stock to constitute control. An acquisitive Type D reorganization, on the other hand, requires only 50% of the voting and nonvoting stock to be owned to constitute control.

Topic Review C7-6

Summary of Divisive and Other Reorganizations

Type of Reorganization	Distributing (D) or Transferor (T) Corporation Property Acquired	Consideration That Can Be Used	What Happens to the Distributing (D) or Transferor (T) Corporation?	Shareholders' Recognized Gain	Other Requirements
D—Divisive	Part or all of D[a] Corporation's assets (and possibly some or all of its liabilities) are transferred to a "controlled" corporation (C[b] Corporation).	Stock, securities, and other property of C Corporation.	Stock, securities, and boot received in the reorganization must be distributed; D Corporation may be liquidated but can remain in existence.	Lesser of realized gain or boot received.	Transactions can take three forms—spin-off, split-off, or split-up. Control is defined at the 80% level under Sec. 368(c).
E—Recapitalization	No increase or decrease in assets occurs. A change to the capital structure of T[c] Corporation takes place.	Stock, securities, and other property of T Corporation.	T Corporation remains in existence.	Lesser of realized gain or boot received.	May involve stock-for-stock, bond-for-bond, or bond-for-stock exchanges.
F—Change in form, identity, or place of organization	Assets or stock of old T Corporation are transferred to new T Corporation.	Stock, securities, and other property of new T Corporation.	Old T Corporation is liquidated.	Lesser of realized gain or boot received.	Must involve only a single operating company.
G—Acquisitive or divisive	Part or all of T Corporation's assets (and possibly some or all of its liabilities) are transferred to A Corporation[d] in a bankruptcy case.	Stock, securities, and other property of A Corporation.	T Corporation may be liquidated or divided but can remain in existence.	Lesser of realized gain or boot received.	Stock and securities of A Corporation received by T Corporation must be distributed to its shareholders, security holders, or creditors.

[a] D Corporation refers to the distributing corporation.
[b] C Corporation refers to the controlled corporation.
[c] T Corporation refers to the transferor corporation.
[d] A Corporation refers to the transferee or acquiring corporation.

DIVISIVE TYPE D REORGANIZATION

A divisive Type D reorganization must take place as part of a plan of reorganization and satisfy the requirements of Secs. 368(a)(1)(D) and 355, which are explained below.[58] The Type D divisive reorganizations can take three forms: spin-offs, split-offs, and split-ups (see Figure C7-7).

A distribution of a controlled corporation's stock can be tax-free under Sec. 355 even if the distributing corporation transfers no assets to the controlled corporation. For a transaction to constitute one of the three divisive Type D reorganization forms, however, both the asset transfer and the Sec. 355 distribution must take place as part of a single transaction governed by a plan of reorganization. Both divisive reorganizations and tax-free distributions of the stock of an existing controlled subsidiary are examined in this section.

A divisive Type D reorganization can be used to accomplish various types of business adjustments, including

▶ Dividing a business into two corporations to separate a high-risk business from a low-risk business

▶ Dividing a single business between two shareholders that have major disagreements

▶ Dividing a corporation's business activities according to its separate functions or the geographical areas in which it operates

▶ Dividing a business because of antitrust law violations

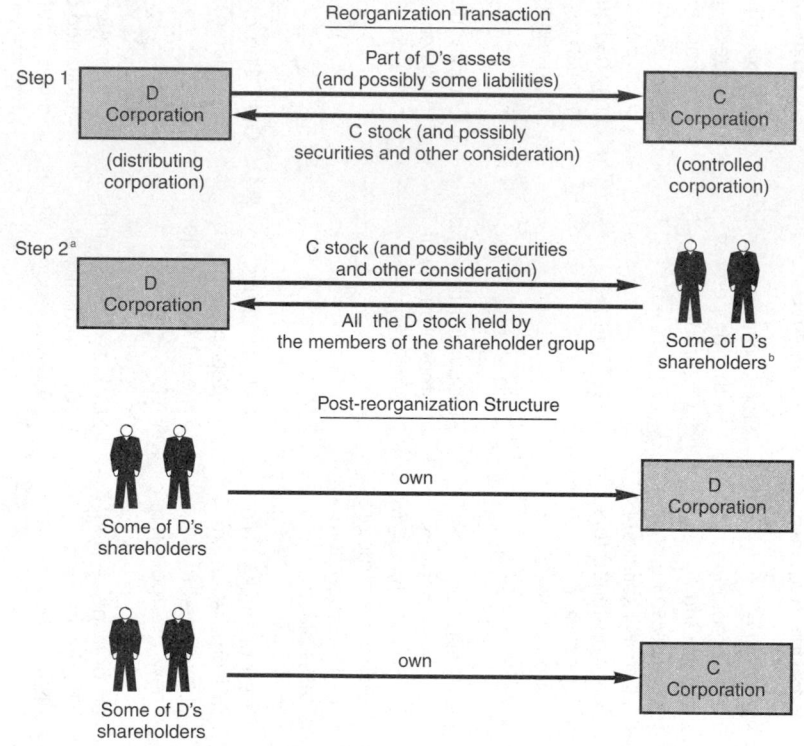

ᵃ Step 1 remains the same for the spin-off transaction. In a spin-off transaction, D's shareholders surrender no D stock. In a split-up transaction, Step 1 involves D Corporation's assets and liabilities being transferred to two controlled corporations. Step 2 involves the distribution of the stock of the two controlled corporations pursuant to the liquidation of D Corporation.

ᵇ This distribution also could occur on a pro rata basis to all D's shareholders, in which case the shareholders surrender only a portion of their D shares.

FIGURE C7-7 ▶ DIVISIVE TYPE D REORGANIZATION (SPLIT-OFF FORM)

---

[58] The requirements of the divisive Type D reorganization may be contrasted with the acquisitive Type D reorganization (previously discussed), where substantially all the transferor's assets must be transferred to a controlled corporation.

FORMS OF DIVISIVE TYPE D REORGANIZATIONS. Three types of divisive transactions are tax-free if the Sec. 368(a)(1)(D) requirements are met:

▶ **Split-off**—the distributing corporation transfers part of its assets to a controlled corporation in exchange for stock and possibly securities, money, or other boot property. The distributing corporation then distributes the stock of the subsidiary to part or all of its shareholders, receiving some of its stock in exchange. Such a transaction may occur because of a management dispute between two dissenting shareholder groups whereby the parent corporation redeems all the stock of one of the groups (see Figure C7-7).

▶ **Spin-off**—the distributing corporation transfers part of its assets to a controlled corporation in exchange for stock and possibly securities, money, or other boot property. The distributing corporation then distributes the stock of the subsidiary ratably to all of its shareholders, receiving nothing in exchange. Such a transaction may occur because of a desire to reduce the risk inherent in having two operating divisions (e.g., steel and glass manufacturing) within a single corporation.

▶ **Split-up**—the distributing corporation transfers all of its assets to two controlled corporations in exchange for stock and possibly securities, money, or other boot property. The distributing corporation then distributes the stock of the two subsidiaries to all of its shareholders, receiving in exchange all of its outstanding stock. Such a transaction may occur because of a desire to have two operating divisions transferred to new corporations, which will continue in existence as brother-sister corporations while the old corporation is liquidated.

If the Sec. 355 requirements described below are *not* met, a spin-off is taxed as a dividend to the shareholders, a split-off is taxed as a stock redemption to the shareholders, and a split-up is taxed as a liquidation of the parent corporation to its shareholders.

ADDITIONAL COMMENT

If the IRS applies Sec. 351 to the asset transfer, and if the total adjusted basis for all property transferred exceeds the total FMV of that property, the subsidiary's total basis will be limited to the total FMV (see Chapter C2 for details).

ASSET TRANSFER. The distributing corporation recognizes no gain or loss on the asset transfer except when it receives and retains boot property or when the controlled corporation acquires or assumes liabilities of the distributing corporation and the total of the liabilities acquired or assumed exceeds the total adjusted bases of the assets transferred.[59] The controlled corporation recognizes no gain or loss when it exchanges its stock for the distributing corporation's property. The controlled corporation takes a carryover basis for the acquired assets, increased for any gain recognized by the distributing corporation on the asset transfer. Its holding period includes the distributing corporation's holding period for the assets.

TYPICAL MISCONCEPTION

Section 355 can apply to a distribution of stock of an existing subsidiary as well as the distribution of stock of a new subsidiary that is created as part of the transaction.

DISTRIBUTION OF STOCK AND SECURITIES. The same gain or loss recognition rules apply to the distributing corporation and its shareholders when a distribution of stock (or securities) of an existing subsidiary is made under Sec. 355 or when it is made as part of a Type D reorganization. The distributing corporation recognizes no gain or loss when it distributes the controlled corporation's stock (or securities) to its shareholders.[60] The distributing corporation recognizes gain (but not loss) when it distributes nonmoney boot property to its shareholders as part of the reorganization and when it makes a disqualified distribution of stock or securities in the controlled corporation.

The shareholders recognize no gain or loss on the receipt of the stock (and securities) except to the extent they receive boot property.[61] A shareholder's basis in the stock (or securities) held after the distribution equals his or her basis in the stock (or securities) held before the distribution, increased by any gain recognized and decreased by the sum of

---

[59] Secs. 361(a) and 357(c)(1)(B).

[60] Sec. 361(c)(1). Two special rules may require the distributing corporation to recognize gain when it distributes stocks and securities. A disqualifying distribution occurs if, immediately after the distribution, any person holds a 50% disqualified stock interest in either the distributing corporation or the controlled corporation. Disqualified stock generally is defined as any stock in the distributing or controlled corporation purchased within the five-year period ending on the distribution date. The disqualifying distribution rules prevent a divisive transaction from following a stock purchase to accomplish

the disposition of a significant part of the historic shareholders' interests in one or more of the divided corporations. A second set of rules, the anti-Morris Trust rules, also requires the distributing corporation to recognize gain when a distribution of stock or securities is made and is preceded or followed by a disposition of the stock or securities.

[61] Sec. 355(a). As with an acquisitive reorganization, Sec. 361(a) permits securities (e.g., long-term debt obligations) to be received tax-free in a divisive transaction when the shareholders surrender the same face amount of securities, or a larger amount. Excess securities received are boot property.

money received and the FMV of any other boot property received. If more than one class of stock or securities is held before or after the distribution, the total basis for the non-recognition property is allocated to each class based on their relative FMVs. The basis for any boot property (other than money) is its FMV. The holding period for the stock and nonboot securities received includes the holding period of the stock and securities surrendered. The holding period for boot property begins on the day after the distribution date.

EXAMPLE C7-25 ▶ Distributing Corporation transfers assets having a $600,000 FMV and a $350,000 adjusted basis to Controlled Corporation in exchange for all of Controlled's single class of stock. Distributing has been owned equally by Ruth and Pat for ten years. Ruth and Pat are no longer able to agree on the management of Distributing and have agreed to a division of the assets in exchange for Pat surrendering her Distributing shares. Pat's basis for her Distributing shares is $400,000. Distributing realizes a $250,000 gain ($600,000 − $350,000) on the asset transfer, none of which is recognized. Distributing also recognizes no gain on the distribution of the Controlled shares to Pat. Pat realizes a $200,000 ($600,000 − $400,000) gain on surrendering her Distributing shares, none of which is recognized. Her basis in the Controlled stock is $400,000. The holding period for the Controlled shares includes Pat's holding period for the Distributing shares. Controlled recognizes no gain when it issues its stock for Distributing's assets and takes a $350,000 basis in the acquired assets. ◀

SELF-STUDY QUESTION

Does the receipt of boot make the entire Sec. 355 transaction taxable to the shareholders?

ANSWER

No. The shareholders may have a partial recognition of gain. The amount and type of gain recognized depends on whether the shareholders surrender stock of the distributing corporation in the transaction.

TYPICAL MISCONCEPTION

In a spin-off, the FMV of the boot received is treated as a Sec. 301 distribution to the shareholder. In a split-off or split-up, the shareholders recognize gain to the extent of the lesser of boot received or the gain realized. This gain may be a dividend or capital gain under Sec. 302.

Under Sec. 355, boot may consist of money, short-term debt, any property other than the stock or securities of a controlled corporation, any stock of the controlled corporation purchased within the previous five years in a taxable transaction, securities of the controlled corporation to the extent the principal amount of the securities received exceeds the principal amount of the securities surrendered by the shareholder, and stock or securities attributable to accrued interest.[62] When the shareholder receives boot, the amount and character of the income or gain recognized depend on whether he or she surrendered stock and securities in the distributing corporation (i.e., a split-off or split-up) or did not surrender any stock or securities (i.e., a spin-off).

When the shareholder receives boot in a spin-off, the FMV of the boot is a dividend to the extent of the shareholder's ratable share of the distributing corporation's E&P. Any securities the shareholders receive in a spin-off are boot because the shareholders do not surrender any securities in a spin-off transaction. Thus, the FMV of the securities is a dividend to the extent of the shareholder's ratable share of the distributing corporation's E&P.

In a split-off or a split-up, in addition to the exchange of stock, a shareholder may receive some boot property. If the shareholder realizes a loss on the exchange, the loss is not recognized, whether boot is received or not.[63] If the shareholder realizes a gain on the exchange, he or she recognizes the gain to the extent of the FMV of any boot received.

If the exchange has the effect of a dividend under the Sec. 302 stock redemption rules, the recognized gain is treated as a dividend up to the amount of the shareholder's ratable share of the distributing corporation's E&P.[64] Otherwise it is a capital gain. In either case, the gain is taxed at the 15% rate. The Sec. 302 rules are applied by treating the shareholder as though he or she continued to own stock in the distributing corporation and surrendered only the portion of his or her shares equal in value to the amount of boot received. This hypothetical redemption is then tested under the Sec. 302(b) rules to see whether it receives exchange or dividend treatment.[65]

EXAMPLE C7-26 ▶ Distributing Corporation owns assets with a $60,000 FMV plus all the outstanding shares of Controlled Corporation, which was created by an asset transfer made by Distributing. The Controlled stock is worth $40,000. Distributing's E&P balance is $35,000. Distributing is owned by Carl and Diane, each of whom owns 100 shares of Distributing stock. Distributing distributes all the Controlled stock to Carl in exchange for Carl's 100 shares of Distributing stock in a transaction that qualifies as a split-off under Secs. 368(a)(1)(D) and 355, except that Carl also receives $10,000 in cash. Carl's basis in the Distributing shares he surrenders is $22,000. Carl has a $28,000 realized gain, determined as follows:

---

[62] Secs. 355(a)(3) and 356(b).
[63] Sec. 356(c).

[64] Sec. 356(a)(2).
[65] Rev. Rul. 93-62, 1993-2 C.B. 118.

FMV of Controlled stock	$40,000
Plus: Cash received	10,000
Amount realized	$50,000
Minus: Basis of Distributing stock	(22,000)
Realized gain	$28,000

Carl must recognize $10,000 of this gain (i.e., the lesser of the $28,000 realized gain or the $10,000 boot received). If Carl surrenders Distributing stock solely for the $10,000 boot, he would be surrendering 20 Distributing shares worth $10,000 ($10,000 boot ÷ $500 FMV for each share of Distributing stock). Before this hypothetical redemption, he owns 50% of the outstanding Distributing shares (100 ÷ 200), and afterward he owns 44% (80 ÷ 180). Thus, the hypothetical redemption is not substantially disproportionate under Sec. 302(b)(2) because the 44% post-redemption stock ownership exceeds 80% of the pre-redemption stock ownership (50% × 0.80 = 40%). If the exchange can meet one of the other tests for sale treatment (e.g., not essentially equivalent to a dividend), the $10,000 is a capital gain. Otherwise it is a dividend. ◀

TYPICAL MISCONCEPTION

Unlike Sec. 351, securities (long-term debt) can be exchanged in a Sec. 355 transaction without the recognition of gain as long as the principal amount surrendered is equal to or greater than the principal amount received.

In a split-off or a split-up, a shareholder may receive securities of the controlled corporation tax-free but only if the shareholder surrenders securities in the distributing corporation with an equal or larger principal amount. To the extent the principal amount of the securities received by a shareholder exceeds the principal amount of the securities surrendered by that shareholder, the FMV of the excess principal amount is boot.

THE SEC. 355 REQUIREMENTS. The Sec. 355 requirements must be met for the distribution of a subsidiary's stock as part of a Type D reorganization or as an independent divisive transaction to be tax-free.

Under Sec. 355, a distributing corporation's distribution of a controlled corporation's stock is tax-free to the shareholders if the following six requirements are met:[66]

ADDITIONAL COMMENT

The control requirement for Sec. 355 is the same control requirement previously discussed relating to the formation of a corporation under Sec. 351 (see Chapter C2).

▶ The property distributed must consist solely of stock or securities of a corporation controlled by the distributing corporation immediately before the distribution. The distributing corporation must own and distribute stock possessing at least 80% of the total combined voting power of all classes of stock entitled to vote and at least 80% of the total number of shares of all other classes of stock.[67]

▶ The distribution must not have been used principally as a device to distribute the E&P of the distributing corporation, the controlled corporation, or both. Whether a transaction has been used as a device to distribute the E&P of the distributing corporation, the controlled corporation, or both is a matter of the facts and circumstances in each case. A sale or exchange of stock of the distributing or controlled corporation after the distribution is evidence that the distribution was used as such a device, especially if the sale was prearranged.[68]

TYPICAL MISCONCEPTION

The active trade or business requirement has two parts: a pre-distribution five-year history and both the distributing and controlled corporations must be actively engaged in a trade or business immediately after the distribution.

▶ Immediately after the distribution, the distributing corporation and the controlled corporation each must be engaged in the active conduct of a trade or business that also was actively conducted for at least five years before the distribution. The main reason for this requirement is to prevent a corporation from spinning off a newly formed subsidiary whose only assets are unneeded cash and other liquid assets. The shareholders could then sell or liquidate the subsidiary and obtain the liquid assets in an exchange transaction rather than as a dividend.[69]

▶ The distributing corporation must distribute either all the stock and securities in the controlled corporation held by it immediately before the distribution or an amount of stock in the controlled corporation constituting control. The distributing corporation

[66] Sec. 355(a) and Reg. Secs. 1.355-2(b) and (c). Also, Rev. Proc. 2003-48, 2003-2 C.B. 86, is a checklist questionnaire of the information that must be included in a ruling request coming under Sec. 355. Appendix A of this revenue procedure contains guidelines regarding the business purpose requirement for Sec. 355 transactions including information submission requirements for nine specific situations where rulings may or may not be granted.
[67] Sec. 368(c).

[68] Reg. Sec. 1.355-2(d).
[69] Sec. 355(b)(2). A corporation is engaged in the active conduct of a trade or business if it actively conducts all activities needed for generating a profit and these activities encompass all steps in the process of earning income. Specifically excluded are passive investment activities such as holding stock, securities, and land.

is allowed to retain some stock if it can establish to the IRS's satisfaction that it was not retained as part of a tax-avoidance plan.

▶ The distribution must have a substantial corporate business purpose. Qualifying distributions include those made to comply with antitrust litigation and those made to separate businesses where the shareholders have major disagreements.[70]

▶ The shareholders who directly or indirectly owned the controlled corporation(s) before the distribution must maintain a continuing equity interest in one or more of the corporations following the division. A substantial number of the shareholders who owned the distributing corporation's stock before the division must maintain a continuing equity interest in the distributing and/or controlled corporations following the division.[71] The distribution of stock and securities need not be pro rata. Disproportionate distributions may be used to eliminate the stock ownership of a dissenting shareholder group. In a split-off transaction, some shareholders may exchange all their distributing corporation stock for all the controlled corporation's stock.

TYPE G DIVISIVE REORGANIZATION

The divisive Type G reorganization involves the transfer of *part* of the assets of a corporation to a second corporation according to a court-approved plan. The transferor corporation then distributes the transferee corporation's stock and securities to its shareholders, security holders, and creditors. The transferor corporation may continue in business separate from the transferee corporation after its operations have been restructured. Alternatively, the transferor corporation may be liquidated by the courts as part of the bankruptcy proceedings.

OTHER REORGANIZATION TRANSACTIONS

Two types of transactions do not fit into the acquisitive or divisive reorganization categories. These are Type E reorganizations, which are recapitalizations, and Type F reorganizations, which are changes in identity, form, or state of incorporation. Topic Review C7-6 presented earlier summarized the requirements for the Type E and Type F reorganizations.

TYPE E REORGANIZATION

KEY POINT

A Type E reorganization is neither acquisitive nor divisive in nature. Instead, it simply allows a single corporation to restructure its capital without creating a taxable exchange between the corporation and its shareholders or creditors.

Section 368(a)(1)(E) defines a **Type E reorganization** quite simply as a "recapitalization." A 1942 Supreme Court decision defined a **recapitalization** as "the reshuffling of the corporate structure within the framework of an existing corporation."[72] A recapitalization needs to have a bona fide business purpose. One reason for engaging in a recapitalization might be to issue additional common or preferred stock that will be exchanged for outstanding bonds to reduce the corporation's interest payments and its debt to equity ratio. Alternatively, a family corporation might issue preferred stock in exchange for part or all of the common stock held by an elderly, controlling shareholder to permit that shareholder to turn over active management of the corporation to his or her children and to engage in estate planning (see page C7-41).

Three types of adjustments to the corporate capital structure can qualify as a Type E reorganization. These are a stock-for-stock exchange, a bond-for-stock exchange, and a bond-for-bond exchange.[73] Normally, these exchanges do not result in an increase or decrease in the corporation's assets except to the extent the shareholders receive a distribution of money or other property as part of the transaction.

---

[70] Reg. Sec. 1.355-2(b)(5), Exs. (1) and (2).
[71] Reg. Sec. 1.355-2(c).
[72] *Helvering v. Southwest Consolidated Corp.*, 28 AFTR 573, 42-1 USTC ¶9248 (USSC, 1942).
[73] An exchange of stock for bonds has been held in *J. Robert Bazely v. CIR* (35 AFTR 1190, 47-2 USTC ¶9288 [USSC, 1947]) not to be a recapitaliza-

tion. Even if it were a recapitalization, it generally would be taxable because receipt of the entire principal amount of the bonds represents boot under Sec. 356. The IRS has held that, if no stock is held after the exchange, the Sec. 302 stock redemption rules apply to the transaction, thereby resulting in sale or exchange treatment (Rev. Rul. 77-415, 1977-2 C.B. 311).

STOCK-FOR-STOCK EXCHANGE. An exchange of common stock for common stock or preferred stock for preferred stock within a single corporation can qualify as a recapitalization if it is made pursuant to a plan of reorganization. Section 1036 also permits the same types of exchanges to take place outside of the reorganization rules. In either case, shareholders recognize no gain or loss and take a substituted basis in the shares received that references the basis in the shares surrendered.

EXAMPLE C7-27 ▶ The shareholders of Pilot Corporation exchange all of their nonvoting Class B common stock for additional shares of Pilot's Class A common stock. The Class A stock retains voting rights. The exchange is tax-free under Sec. 1036 even if no plan of reorganization has been created. An exchange of some of Pilot's Class A preferred stock for Class B preferred stock also would be tax-free under Sec. 1036. ◀

Section 1036 does not apply to an exchange of common stock for preferred stock, or preferred stock for common stock, within the same corporation, or an exchange of stock involving two corporations. However, the recapitalization rules apply to an exchange of two different classes of stock (e.g., common for preferred) in the same corporation if the exchange is made as part of a plan of reorganization. The exchange is tax-free for the shareholders under the Sec. 354(a) nonrecognition rules except to the extent they receive boot property. If the FMV of the stock received differs from that of the stock surrendered, the difference may be a gift, a contribution to capital, compensation for services, a dividend, or a payment made to satisfy a debt obligation, depending on the facts and circumstances of the situation.[74] The tax consequences of that portion of the exchange will fall outside the reorganization rules.

EXAMPLE C7-28 ▶ John owns 60% of Boise Corporation's common stock and all of its preferred stock. The remainder of Boise's common stock is held by 80 unrelated individuals. John's basis for his preferred stock is $300,000. John exchanges his preferred stock for $400,000 of additional common stock and $100,000 in money. The preferred stock is valued at $500,000. John realizes a $200,000 [($400,000 + $100,000) − $300,000] gain on the exchange and must recognize $100,000 of the gain as dividend income (assuming Boise has sufficient E&P) because none of the Sec. 302(b) exceptions that permit capital gain treatment apply. John's basis for the additional common stock is $300,000 ($300,000 + $100,000 gain recognized − $100,000 money received). ◀

A recapitalization often is used as an estate planning device whereby a parent's controlling interest in a corporation's common stock is exchanged for both common stock and preferred stock. The common stock often is gifted to a child who, following the recapitalization, will own a controlling interest in the common stock and manage the company. The parent will receive annual income from the preferred stock's cash dividends. The preferred stock's value will not increase over time, thereby freezing the value of the parent's estate and reducing his or her estate tax liability. The capital appreciation will accrue to the child who owns the common stock.

Substantial income tax and estate and gift tax planning opportunities existed at one time when recapitalizing a closely held corporation. To prevent abuses in this area, Congress added Secs. 2701–2704, which provide detailed procedures for more accurately valuing, for transfer tax purposes, interests that are transferred and retained in corporations and partnerships. Additional coverage of this topic is presented in the gift tax chapter.

BOND-FOR-STOCK EXCHANGE. A bond-for-stock exchange is tax-free to the shareholder except to the extent the shareholder receives a portion of the stock in satisfaction of the corporation's liability for accrued interest on the bonds.[75] Stock received in settlement of the interest owed is ordinary income.

BOND-FOR-BOND EXCHANGE. These exchanges are tax-free only when the principal amount of the bonds received does not exceed the principal amount of the bonds

---

[74] Rev. Ruls. 74-269, 1974-2 C.B. 87 and 83-120, 1983-2 C.B. 170. [75] Sec. 354(a)(2)(B).

surrendered. If the principal amount of the bonds received exceeds the principal amount of the bonds surrendered, the FMV of the "excess" principal amount received is taxed to the bondholder as boot.

TYPE F REORGANIZATION

Section 368(a)(1)(F) defines a **Type F reorganization** as a "mere change in identity, form, or place of organization of one corporation, however effected." Traditionally, Type F reorganizations are used to change either the state in which the business is incorporated or the name of a corporation, without requiring the old corporation or its shareholders to recognize any gain or loss. In a Type F reorganization, the assets and liabilities of the old corporation become the property of the new corporation. Thus, the shareholders and creditors of the old corporation exchange their stock and debt interests for similar interests in the new corporation.

EXAMPLE C7-29 ▶ Rider Corporation is incorporated in the State of Illinois. Its management decides to change its state of incorporation to Delaware because of the favorable securities and corporation laws in Delaware. Old Rider Corporation exchanges its assets for all the stock of new Rider Corporation. The shareholders of old Rider then exchange their stock for new Rider stock. Old Rider Corporation goes out of existence. Neither the shareholders nor the two corporations involved in the reorganization recognize any gain on the transaction. Each shareholder takes a substituted basis for the new Rider stock that references their basis in the old Rider stock. Their holding period for the new Rider stock includes their holding period for the old Rider stock. New Rider Corporation's assets have the same basis they had on old Rider Corporation's books. New Rider Corporation also acquires old Rider Corporation's tax attributes. Although this example refers to two corporations, these two corporations are the same basic entity that has changed its legal state of incorporation. ◀

The reorganization illustrated in Example C7-29 also could take place if old Rider Corporation's shareholders exchange their stock for new Rider stock. Old Rider Corporation would then be liquidated into new Rider Corporation. The tax consequences are the same for both transaction forms.

JUDICIAL RESTRICTIONS ON THE USE OF CORPORATE REORGANIZATIONS

OBJECTIVE 7

Explain how judicial doctrines can restrict a taxpayer's ability to use corporate reorganizations

The Supreme Court holds that literal compliance with the statutory requirements for a reorganization transaction is not enough for a transaction to receive tax-free treatment.[76] As a result, the courts have placed four primary restrictions on reorganization transactions:

▶ Continuity of the investor's proprietary interest

▶ Continuity of the business enterprise

▶ A business purpose for the transaction

▶ The step transaction doctrine, which collapses a series of related transactions into a single transaction reflecting their economic substance

All four requirements relate to the overall doctrine of substance over form and are explained below.

CONTINUITY OF PROPRIETARY INTEREST

TYPICAL MISCONCEPTION

The continuity-of-interest requirement has nothing to do with the relative sizes of Acquiring and Target. Target's shareholders may end up with a minimal amount of the total outstanding stock of Acquiring, and yet the merger will be a valid reorganization as long as 50% of the consideration received by Target's shareholders is an equity interest in Acquiring.

The requirement for the continuity of the investor's proprietary interest is based on the principle that the tax deferral associated with a reorganization is available because the shareholder has changed his or her investment from one form to another rather than liquidating it. According to Reg. Sec. 1.368-1(b), this test is met by continuity of the busi-

---

[76] *Evelyn F. Gregory v. Helvering,* 14 AFTR 1191, 35-1 USTC ¶9043 (USSC, 1935).

SELF-STUDY QUESTION

For which reorganizations is the continuity-of-interest requirement most important?

ANSWER

The only limitation on consideration used for both regular and triangular mergers is the continuity-of-interest requirement. The other reorganizations, including reverse triangular mergers, have statutory requirements more restrictive than the continuity-of-interest doctrine.

ness enterprise under a modified corporate form and continuity of interest on the part of the shareholders who, directly or indirectly, own the enterprise before its reorganization. In a series of decisions, the courts have held that the continuing proprietary interest must be a common or preferred stock interest.[77] Thus, a transaction that involves the target corporation or its shareholders receiving only cash or short-term debt obligations does not qualify as a tax-free reorganization.

The IRC does not specify how much stock constitutes the required proprietary interest. For advance ruling purposes, however, the IRS requires the former shareholders of the target corporation to receive at least 50% of their total consideration in the form of acquiring corporation stock. The 50% rule applies only for advance ruling purposes, and the courts have accepted lesser percentages.[78] Nevertheless, the 50% rule indicates the threshold below which the IRS may challenge the transaction.

EXAMPLE C7-30 ▶ Target Corporation transfers all of its assets to Acquiring Corporation in a Type C reorganization in exchange for $200,000 of Acquiring stock and the assumption of $800,000 of Target liabilities. Target distributes the Acquiring stock to its sole shareholder, Nancy, in exchange for all of her Target stock. Even though the transaction meets the statutory requirements for a Type C reorganization, the IRS most likely will hold that the transaction is not a reorganization because the continuity-of-proprietary-interest requirement is not met (i.e., only 20% of the total consideration received by Target represents an equity interest in Acquiring). ◀

Recently, the IRS amended Reg. Sec. 1.368-1(b) to clarify that neither the continuity of interest nor the continuity of business enterprise tests apply to Type E and Type F reorganizations.

CONTINUITY OF BUSINESS ENTERPRISE

The requirement for continuity of the business enterprise necessitates that the acquiring corporation either continue the target corporation's historic business or use a significant portion of the target corporation's historic business assets in a new business.[79] This restriction limits tax-free reorganizations to transactions involving *continuing interests* in the target corporation's business or property under a modified corporate form. The **continuity-of-interest doctrine**, however, does not require that the target corporation's historic business be continued.

SELF-STUDY QUESTION

Does Acquiring have to continue its own historic business?

ANSWER

No. The IRS has specifically ruled that the continuity-of-business-enterprise test requires only that the historic business of Target be continued (Rev. Rul. 81-25, 1981-1 C.B. 132).

Whether the requirements for continuity of the business enterprise are satisfied depends on the facts and circumstances of the particular situation. The historic business requirement can be satisfied if the acquiring corporation continues one or more of the target corporation's significant lines of business.

EXAMPLE C7-31 ▶ Target Corporation is merged into Acquiring Corporation. Immediately before the merger, Target manufactures resins and chemicals and distributes chemicals for use in making other products. All three lines of business are approximately the same size. Two months after the merger, Acquiring sells the resin manufacturing and chemicals distribution activities to an unrelated party for cash. The transaction satisfies the requirement for the continuity of the business enterprise because Acquiring continues at least one of Target's three significant lines of business.[80] ◀

The asset continuity requirement is satisfied if the acquiring corporation uses in its business a significant portion of the assets that were used in the target corporation's historic business. The significance of the assets used is based on the relative importance of the assets to the operation of the historic business of the target corporation.

EXAMPLE C7-32 ▶ Acquiring and Target Corporations are both computer manufacturers. Target is merged into Acquiring. Acquiring terminates Target's manufacturing activities and maintains Target's equipment as a backup source of supply for its components. Acquiring satisfies the continuity-

---

[77] See, for example, *V. L. LeTulle v. Scofield*, 23 AFTR 789, 40-1 USTC ¶9150 (USSC, 1940).

[78] Rev. Proc. 77-37, 1977-2 C.B. 568, Sec. 3.02. See also *John A. Nelson Co. v. Helvering*, 16 AFTR 1262, 36-1 USTC ¶9019 (USSC, 1935), where the

Supreme Court permitted a tax-free reorganization to take place where the stock exchanged constituted only 38% of the total consideration.

[79] Reg. Sec. 1.368-1(d)(1).

[80] Reg. Secs. 1.368-1(d)(3) and -1(d)(5), Ex. (1).

of-business-enterprise requirement by continuing to use Target's historic business assets. If Acquiring had instead sold Target's assets for cash and invested the proceeds in an investment portfolio, the continuity-of-business-enterprise requirement would not be met. Acquiring need not continue Target's business to satisfy the continuity-of-business-enterprise requirement.[81] ◄

Acquiring does not have to directly hold Target's business assets or continue Target's line of business. The assets (business activities) can be owned (conducted) by an 80%-or-more-owned subsidiary corporation that is included in a chain of corporations that includes Acquiring. In some cases, the acquired assets can be owned by (or business conducted by) a partnership or LLC owned in full or in part by Acquiring or one of its subsidiaries.

BUSINESS PURPOSE REQUIREMENT

A transaction must serve a bona fide **business purpose** to qualify as a reorganization.[82] Regulation Sec. 1.368-1(c) states that a transaction that takes "the form of a corporate reorganization as a disguise for concealing its real character, and the object and accomplishment of which is the consummation of a preconceived plan having no business or corporate purpose, is not a plan of reorganization."

EXAMPLE C7-33 ►

Distributing Corporation transfers some highly appreciated stock from its investment portfolio to newly created Controlled Corporation in exchange for all of its stock. The Controlled stock is distributed to Distributing's sole shareholder, Kathy, in exchange for part of her Distributing stock. Shortly after the stock transfer, Controlled is liquidated, with Kathy receiving the appreciated stock. Treating the liquidation of Controlled as a separate event, Kathy recognizes a capital gain on the liquidation, which she uses to offset capital loss carryovers from other tax years, and is able to step-up the basis of the appreciated stock to its FMV without incurring a tax liability. Even though the stock transfer to Controlled fits within a literal reading of the Sec. 368(a)(1)(D) definition of a divisive Type D reorganization, the IRS probably will state that the Sec. 355 trade or business requirement has not been met and also will rely on the Supreme Court's decision in *Gregory v. Helvering,* to hold that the series of transactions serves no business purpose. As a result, Kathy's receipt of the appreciated stock from Controlled is a dividend. ◄

STEP TRANSACTION DOCTRINE

The **step transaction doctrine** may be used by the IRS to collapse a multistep reorganization into a single taxable transaction. Alternatively, the IRS may attempt to take a series of steps, which the taxpayer calls independent events, and collapse them into a single tax-free reorganization transaction. Both of these IRS actions prevent the taxpayer from arranging a series of business transactions to obtain a tax result not available if only a single transaction is used.

EXAMPLE C7-34 ►

Jody transfers business property from his sole proprietorship to his wholly owned Target Corporation. Three days after the incorporation, Target transfers all its assets to Acquiring Corporation in exchange for Acquiring stock in a Type C reorganization. As part of the reorganization, Target distributes the Acquiring stock to Jody upon Target's liquidation. After the liquidation, Jody owns 15% of the Acquiring stock. The IRS probably will attempt to collapse the two transactions (the Sec. 351 asset transfer to Target and the Type C asset-for-stock reorganization) into a single transaction: an asset transfer by Jody to Acquiring. Under the IRS's position, the Sec. 351 rules do not apply because Jody does not own at least 80% of the Acquiring stock immediately after the transfer. Because Jody owns only 15% of Acquiring's stock, Jody must recognize gain or loss on the transfer of assets from his sole proprietorship to Acquiring.[83] ◄

[81]. Reg. Secs. 1.368-1(d)(4) and -1(d)(5), Ex. (2).
[82] *Evelyn F. Gregory v. Helvering,* 14 AFTR 1191, 35-1 USTC ¶9043 (USSC, 1935). Other Sec. 355 requirements probably were failed in this case, such as being a device for the distribution of E&P.

[83] Rev. Rul. 70-140, 1970-1 C.B. 73.

TAX ATTRIBUTES

Section 381(a) requires the target or transferor corporation's tax attributes (e.g., loss or tax credit carryovers) to be assumed by the acquiring or transferee corporation in certain types of reorganizations. Sections 269, 382, 383, and 384 restrict the taxpayer's ability to use certain corporate tax attributes (e.g., NOL carryovers) obtained through the acquisition of the loss corporation's stock or assets.

OBJECTIVE 8

Determine which reorganization forms permit the carryover of tax attributes

KEY POINT

An often-cited advantage to a tax-free asset reorganization over a taxable acquisition is that the tax attributes (e.g., NOLs and net capital losses) carry over to the acquiring corporation.

KEY POINT

The thrust of Sec. 381, as it relates to NOLs, is to allow Target's NOL carryforwards to offset only the post-acquisition income of the acquiring corporation.

ASSUMPTION OF TAX ATTRIBUTES

In the Type A, C, acquisitive D, F, and acquisitive G reorganizations, the acquiring corporation obtains both the target corporation's tax attributes and assets. The tax attributes do not change hands in either the Type B or Type E reorganization because no transfer of assets from one corporation to another occurs. Even though a division of assets occurs between a transferor corporation and a controlled corporation in the divisive Type D and G reorganizations, the only tax attribute allocated between the two entities is the transferor corporation's E&P.[84]

Some of the tax attributes carried over under Sec. 381(c) include

▶ Net operating losses

▶ Capital losses

▶ Earnings and profits (E&P)

▶ General business credits

▶ Inventory methods

The acquired corporation's NOL carryover is determined as of the transaction's acquisition date and carries over to tax years ending after such date. Generally, the acquisition date for a tax-free reorganization is the date on which the transferor or target corporation transfers the assets. When loss carryovers from more than one tax year are present, the loss from the earliest ending tax year is used first. NOLs from the time period following the acquisition date cannot be carried back by the acquiring corporation to offset profits earned by the target corporation in its tax years preceding the acquisition date.[85]

EXAMPLE C7-35 ▶ Target Corporation merges into Acquiring Corporation at the close of business on June 30, 2006. Both corporations use the calendar year as their tax year. At the beginning of 2006, Target reports a $200,000 NOL carryover from 2005. Target must file a final tax return for the period January 1, 2006, through June 30, 2006. Target reports $60,000 of taxable income (before any NOL deductions) in its tax return for the short period. Target's taxable income for the January 1 through June 30, 2006, period reduces its NOL carryover to $140,000 ($200,000 − $60,000). Acquiring assumes this carryover. ◀

Section 381(c) restricts the acquiring corporation's use of the NOL carryover in its first tax year that ends after the acquisition date. The NOL deduction is limited to the portion of the acquiring corporation's taxable income allocable on a daily basis to the post-acquisition period.

EXAMPLE C7-36 ▶ Assume the same facts as in Example C7-35 except that it is now known that Acquiring's taxable income is $146,000, earned evenly throughout 2006. Acquiring can use Target's NOL carryover to offset its taxable income attributable to the 184 days in the July 1 through December 31, 2006 post-acquisition period, or $73,600 [(184 ÷ 365) × $146,000]. The remaining NOL carryover of $66,400 ($140,000 − $73,600) carries forward to offset Acquiring's taxable income in 2007. Both the pre- and post-acquisition portions of 2006 count as full tax years for loss carryover purposes. ◀

---

[84] Reg. Sec. 1.312-10.

[85] Special rules apply to Type F reorganizations. Because only a change in form or identity involving a single corporation occurs in such a transaction,

NOLs incurred following the acquisition date can be carried back in a Type F reorganization to offset profits earned in pre-acquisition tax years.

OBJECTIVE 9

Explain how NOL carryovers are restricted following an acquisition

LIMITATION ON USE OF TAX ATTRIBUTES

Sections 382 and 269 prevent taxpayers from purchasing the assets or stock of a corporation having loss carryovers (known as the **loss corporation**) primarily to acquire the corporation's tax attributes. Similarly, Secs. 382 and 269 prevent a corporation having loss carryovers (also known as a loss corporation) from acquiring the assets or stock of a profitable corporation primarily to enable the loss corporation to use its carryovers. Section 383 provides similar restrictions for acquisitions intended to facilitate the use of capital loss and tax credit carryovers. Section 384 additionally restricts the use of pre-acquisition losses to offset built-in gains.

SECTION 382. Section 382 restricts the use of NOLs in purchase transactions and tax-free reorganizations when a substantial change in the stock ownership of the loss corporation occurs.

TYPICAL MISCONCEPTION

To create an ownership change, the 5% shareholders must increase their stock ownership by more than 50 *percentage points.* Thus, if shareholder A increases her stock ownership from 10% to 20%, this alone is not an ownership change even though it represents a 100% increase in A's ownership.

Stock Ownership Change. The requisite stock ownership change has taken place when

▶ Any shift in the stock ownership involving any person(s) owning 5% or more of a corporation's stock occurs or a tax-free reorganization (other than a divisive Type D or G reorganization or a Type F reorganization) has taken place *and*

▶ The percentage of stock of the new loss corporation owned by one or more 5% shareholders has increased by more than 50 percentage points over the *lowest* percentage of stock in the old loss corporation owned by such shareholder(s) at *any* time during the preceding three-year (or shorter) "testing" period.[86]

The 5% shareholder test is based on the value of the loss corporation's stock. Nonvoting preferred stock is excluded from the calculation.

An **old loss corporation** is any corporation entitled to use an NOL carryover or has an NOL for the tax year in which the ownership change occurs, and undergoes the requisite stock ownership change. A **new loss corporation** is any corporation entitled to use an NOL carryover after the stock ownership change.[87] The old and new loss corporations are the same for most taxable acquisitions (e.g., the purchase of a loss corporation's stock by a new shareholder group). The old and new loss corporations differ, however, in many acquisitive reorganizations (e.g., a merger transaction where an unprofitable target [old loss] corporation is merged into the acquiring [new loss] corporation).

KEY POINT

One of the burdensome aspects of Sec. 382 is that each time the stock ownership of a 5% shareholder changes, all 5% shareholders must be tested at that date to see whether an ownership change has occurred.

Ownership changes are tested any time a stock transaction occurs affecting the stock owned by a person who owns 5% or more of the stock either before or after the change. Such change may occur because of a stock transaction involving a 5% shareholder or involving a person who does not own a 5% interest in the loss corporation that affects the size of the stock interest owned by a 5% shareholder (i.e., a stock redemption). When applying the 5% rule, all shareholders who own less than 5% of the loss corporation's stock are considered to be a single shareholder.

EXAMPLE C7-37 ▶

Spencer Corporation is a publicly traded corporation with no single individual owning more than 5% of its outstanding stock. Spencer has incurred a series of NOLs in recent years, substantial amounts of which are available as carryovers. On July 3, Barry acquires 80% of Spencer's single class of stock in a cash purchase. Barry had not owned any of the Spencer stock before making the acquisition. Spencer Corporation has experienced a stock ownership change because it now has a 5% shareholder (Barry), who owns 80 percentage points more stock than he owned at any time during the testing period (Barry owned 0% during the three-year testing period) because of a purchase transaction. Because Spencer Corporation both incurred the losses prior to the ownership change, and can use the NOLs after the change, it is both the old and new loss corporation. Spencer Corporation's NOLs are subject to the Sec. 382 limitations. ◀

---

[86] Sec. 382(g). Special rules permit the use of a testing period of less than three years for applying the 50-percentage-point ownership change rule. One such situation is when a recent change in the stock ownership has occurred involving a 5% shareholder. In such case, the testing period goes back only to the date of the earlier ownership change.

[87] Secs. 382(k)(1)–(3).

In many acquisitive tax-free reorganizations, the Sec. 382 stock ownership test is applied against the old loss (or target) corporation and then against the new loss (or acquiring) corporation.

EXAMPLE C7-38 ▶

Target Corporation has a single class of stock outstanding. None of its 300 shareholders owns more than 5% of the outstanding stock. Target has incurred substantial NOLs in recent years. Pursuant to a merger agreement, Target Corporation is merged into Jackson Corporation. Jackson also has a single class of stock outstanding, and none of its 500 shareholders owns more than 5% of its outstanding stock. None of Target's shareholders owned any of the Jackson stock before the merger. After the merger, Target's shareholders own 40% of the Jackson stock. All of Jackson's shareholders are aggregated when applying the Sec. 382 stock ownership test. The Sec. 382 rules limit the use of Target's NOL carryovers because Jackson's shareholders owned none of the old loss corporation (Target) stock before the reorganization and owned 60% of the new loss corporation (Jackson) stock immediately after the reorganization. ◀

Divisive Type D and G reorganizations or Type F reorganizations may be subject to the Sec. 382 limitations if the transaction results in a more-than-50-percentage-point shift in stock ownership for the transferor corporation.

TYPICAL MISCONCEPTION

Section 382 does not disallow NOLs. Section 382 merely limits the amount of NOL carryovers the new loss corporation can use on an annual basis.

Loss Limitation. The Sec. 382 loss limitation for any tax year ending after the stock ownership change equals the value of the old loss corporation's stock (including nonvoting preferred stock) immediately before the ownership change multiplied by the long-term tax-exempt federal rate.[88] The long-term tax-exempt federal rate is determined by the IRS and is the highest of the adjusted federal long-term tax-exempt rates in effect for any month in the three-calendar-month period ending with the month in which the stock ownership change occurs.[89]

A new loss corporation can claim its current-year deductions. Then any NOLs from the old loss corporation (pre-change tax years) can be deducted. If the NOL carryovers from the old loss corporation exceed the Sec. 382 loss limitation, the unused carryovers are deferred until the following year, provided the end of the 20-year NOL carryforward period has not been reached. If the Sec. 382 loss limitation exceeds the new loss corporation's taxable income for the current year, the unused loss limitation carries forward and increases the Sec. 382 loss limitation for the next year.[90] Finally, any of its NOL and other deduction carryovers from post-change taxable years can be deducted. A new loss corporation that does not continue the business enterprise of the old loss corporation at all times during the two-year period beginning on the stock ownership change date must use a zero Sec. 382 limitation for any post-change year. This zero limitation, in effect, disallows the use of the NOL carryovers.[91]

ADDITIONAL COMMENT

The reason the new loss corporation's use of the old loss corporation's NOLs is limited annually to the FMV of the old loss corporation multiplied by the long-term tax-exempt federal rate is that this limitation is supposed to approximate the rate at which the old loss corporation could have used the NOLs. Thus, the underlying theory of Sec. 382 is one of neutrality.

EXAMPLE C7-39 ▶

KEY POINT

If the old loss corporation is a very large corporation relative to its NOL carryovers, Sec. 382 will not be a real obstacle in the use of the NOLs by the new loss corporation. Only when the old loss corporation has a small FMV relative to its NOL carryovers does Sec. 382 represent a major obstacle.

Peter purchased all the Taylor Corporation stock (the old and new loss corporation) from Karl at the close of business on December 31, 2005. Taylor is engaged in the manufacture of brooms and has a $1 million NOL carryover from 2005. Taylor continues to manufacture brooms after Peter's acquisition of a controlling interest and earns $300,000 of taxable income for 2006. The value of the Taylor stock immediately before the acquisition is $3.5 million. Assume the applicable long-term tax-exempt federal rate is 5%. The requisite stock ownership change has taken place because Peter has increased his ownership from zero during the testing period to 100% immediately after the acquisition. The Sec. 382 loss limitation for 2006 is $175,000 ($3,500,000 × 0.05). Thus, Taylor can claim a $175,000 NOL deduction in 2006, thereby reducing its taxable income to $125,000. The remaining $825,000 ($1,000,000 − $175,000) of NOL carries over to 2007 and later years. ◀

Special rules apply to the loss corporation for the year in which the stock ownership change occurs. Taxable income earned before the change is not subject to the Sec. 382 limitation. Taxable income earned after the change, however, is subject to the limitation. Allocation of income earned during the tax year to the time periods before and after the

---

[88] Sec. 382(b)(1).
[89] Sec. 382(f).
[90] Sec. 382(b)(2).

[91] Sec. 382(c). Failure to continue the old loss corporation's business enterprise also may cause a corporate reorganization to lose its tax-free status.

ADDITIONAL COMMENT

Although the legislative intent of Sec. 382 has not been seriously opposed, the complexity of the statute with its accompanying Treasury Regulations is of concern to many tax practitioners.

ownership change is based on the number of days in each of the two time periods similar to the procedures illustrated earlier for tax attributes under Sec. 381.

Old loss corporation NOLs incurred before the date of the stock ownership change are limited by Sec. 382. These include NOLs incurred in tax years ending before the date of change plus the portion of the NOL for the tax year that includes the date of change considered to have been incurred before the change. Allocation of an NOL for the tax year that includes the date of change is based on the number of days before and after the change.[92]

SECTION 383.   Section 383 restricts the use of tax credit and capital loss carryovers when stock ownership changes occur that come under the purview of Sec. 382. The same restrictions that apply to NOLs apply to the general business credit, the minimum tax credit, and the foreign tax credit.

SECTION 384.   Section 384 prevents pre-acquisition losses of either the acquiring or target corporation (the loss corporation) from offsetting built-in gains recognized during the five-year post-acquisition recognition period by another corporation (the gain corporation). Such gains can offset pre-acquisition losses of the gain corporation. This limitation applies if a corporation acquires either a controlling stock interest or the assets of another corporation and either corporation is a gain corporation.

ADDITIONAL COMMENT

Section 269 represents the IRS's oldest and broadest weapon in dealing with trafficking in NOLs. However, because of the subjectivity of the statute, Secs. 382, 383, and 384 have turned out to be the IRS's main statutory weapons in this area.

SECTION 269.   Section 269 applies to transactions where control of a corporation is obtained, and the principal purpose of the acquisition is "the evasion or avoidance of federal income tax by securing the benefit of a deduction" or credit that otherwise would not be available. Control is defined as 50% of the voting power or 50% of the value of the outstanding stock. The IRS can use this provision to disallow a loss or credit carryover in situations where Sec. 382 does not apply. The IRS's primary problem in applying these rules is showing that the requisite principal purpose is present.

TAX PLANNING CONSIDERATIONS

WHY USE A REORGANIZATION INSTEAD OF A TAXABLE TRANSACTION?

The choice between a taxable and tax-free transaction can be a difficult one. The advantages and disadvantages of the tax-free reorganization are important considerations for the buyer and seller. Depending on their relative importance to each party, they may serve as points for negotiation and compromise when attempting to structure the transaction.

From the point of view of the target corporation's shareholders, a number of considerations must be evaluated. First, a tax-free reorganization permits a complete deferral of tax to the shareholders unless they receive boot. This tax deferral may permit a shareholder to retain a higher percentage of his or her capital investment than would be possible if a taxable acquisition had been used. A second factor is that a taxable transaction permits the shareholders of the target corporation to convert their former equity interests into liquid assets (e.g., when they receive cash or property other than stock or securities of the acquiring corporation). These funds can be invested in whatever manner the shareholder chooses.

ETHICAL POINT

The choice between making an acquisition a taxable or tax-free transaction involves a large number of considerations for both the buyer and the seller. All parties must examine the tax, financial, and legal considerations with the assistance of their own experts. Because what may be good for the buyer may not be good for the seller in an acquisition, it probably is not a good idea for both parties to save money by using the same experts.

In a reorganization, the shareholder must obtain a proprietary interest in the acquiring corporation. Future success by the acquiring corporation is likely to enhance the value of this interest. Conversely, if the acquiring corporation encounters financial problems, the value of a shareholder's investment may diminish. Third, losses realized as part of a tax-free reorganization cannot be recognized. A taxable transaction permits an immediate recognition of the loss. Fourth, gains recognized as part of a tax-free reorgan-

---

92 Sec. 382(b)(3).

ization are taxed as dividend income if the boot distribution is equivalent to a dividend. Taxable transactions generally result in the shareholder recognizing capital gains. This difference is not as important now as in the past because both capital gains and dividend income are taxed at a maximum 15% rate. Finally, a taxable transaction permits the shareholder to step-up the basis of the stock and securities received to their FMV. A tax-free transaction, however, requires a substituted basis to be used.

From the transferor corporation's point of view, a tax-free reorganization permits the assets to be exchanged with no gain being recognized. In addition, the depreciation recapture rules do not apply to a reorganization. In each case, the recapture burden shifts to the purchasing party.

From the acquiring corporation's point of view, a tax-free reorganization permits an acquisition to take place without the use of substantial amounts of cash or securities. Because the target corporation's shareholders do not have to recognize any gain unless they receive boot, they may be willing to accept a lower sales price than would be required if a taxable acquisition occurs. The acquiror must use the same basis for property acquired in a tax-free reorganization that the assets had on the transferor's books. This inability to step-up the basis of the assets to their cost or FMV reduces the attractiveness of a tax-free reorganization. This inability, in turn, may lower the price the acquiror is willing to offer.

A tax-free reorganization permits the acquiror to obtain the benefits of NOL, tax credit, and other carryovers from the target corporation (subject to possible limitations). Such tax attributes do not carry over to the buyer in a taxable transaction, but they can be used to reduce the seller's tax cost for the sale.

AVOIDING THE REORGANIZATION PROVISIONS

An acquisition can be changed from a tax-free reorganization to a taxable transaction if the restrictions on the use of consideration for the particular type of reorganization are not met. This change can be advantageous for the taxpayers involved. For example, the Type B reorganization rules can be avoided if the acquiring corporation makes a tender offer to the target corporation's shareholders involving an exchange of both acquiring corporation stock and cash for the target corporation's stock. Because this transaction does not meet the solely-for-voting-stock requirement, it is considered a taxable transaction for the shareholders. It also is considered to be a purchase of the target corporation's stock, thereby permitting the acquiring corporation to make a Sec. 338 election and step-up the basis of the target corporation's assets to the price paid for the stock.

EXAMPLE C7-40 ▶ Acquiring Corporation offers to exchange one share of its common stock (valued at $40) plus $20 cash for each share of Target Corporation's single class of common stock. All of Target's shareholders agree to the proposal and exchange a total of 2,000 shares of Target stock for 2,000 shares of Acquiring common stock and $40,000 cash. At the time of the acquisition, Target's assets have a $35,000 adjusted basis and a $110,000 FMV. Target recognizes no gain or loss with respect to the exchange. The basis of its assets remains at $35,000 unless Acquiring makes a Sec. 338 election. Target's shareholders must recognize gain or loss on the exchange of their Target stock whether or not Acquiring makes a Sec. 338 election. ◀

COMPLIANCE AND PROCEDURAL CONSIDERATIONS

SECTION 338 ELECTION

The acquiring corporation makes the election under Sec. 338 on Form 8023 (Election under Sec. 338(g)). This election is made by the fifteenth day of the ninth month beginning after the month in which the acquisition date occurs. The information about the acquiring corporation, the target corporation, and the election filed with Form 8023 is contained in Reg. Sec. 1.338-1(d).

PLAN OF REORGANIZATION

One requirement for nonrecognition of gain by a transferor corporation on an asset transfer (Sec. 361) or by a shareholder on a stock transfer (Sec. 354) is that there be a plan of reorganization. A written plan is not needed, but it is safest for all parties involved in the reorganization when the plan is reduced to writing either as a communication to the shareholders, as part of the corporate records, or as part of a written agreement between the parties. The transaction generally is a taxable event if a plan of reorganization does not exist or if a transfer or distribution is not part of the plan.[93] A **plan of reorganization** is defined as a consummated transaction specifically defined as a reorganization. Nonrecognition of gain or loss is limited to exchanges or distributions that are a direct part of a reorganization and undertaken for reasons germane to the continuance of the business of a corporation that is a party to a reorganization.[94]

PARTY TO A REORGANIZATION

Sections 354 and 361 require that a shareholder or a transferor be a party to a reorganization to have the asset or stock transfer be tax-free. Section 368(b) defines a **party to a reorganization** as "including any corporation resulting from a reorganization, and both corporations involved in a reorganization where one corporation acquires the stock or assets of a second corporation." In the case of a triangular reorganization, the corporation controlling the acquiring corporation and whose stock is used to effect the reorganization also is a party to a reorganization.

RULING REQUESTS

Before proceeding with a taxable or tax-free acquisition or disposition, some taxpayers may request an advance ruling from the IRS on the tax consequences of the transaction. Advance rulings generally are requested because of the complexity of the tax law in the reorganization area and because these transactions involve dollar amounts that are quite large. A subsequent redetermination by the IRS or the courts that a completed reorganization is taxable might have substantial adverse tax consequences to the parties involved in the transaction. The IRS will issue an advance ruling only for reorganizations that conform with the guidelines set out in Rev. Proc. 77-37 and other IRS promulgations. Also, the IRS has stated that it will not issue advance rulings for reorganizations if the consequences are adequately addressed in the IRC, Treasury Regulations, Supreme Court decisions, tax treaties, revenue rulings, revenue procedures, notices, or other IRS pronouncements. The IRS, however, will rule on reorganizations if the consequences are not adequately addressed by these authorities.[95] Because of the IRS's policy not to issue these so called "comfort rulings," many taxpayers instead seek opinion letters from tax counsel.

PROBLEM MATERIALS

DISCUSSION QUESTIONS

C7-1 From the standpoint of Target Corporation's shareholders, what is the advantage of a taxable stock acquisition by Purchaser Corporation compared to Purchaser acquiring all of Target's assets in a taxable transaction followed by a liquidating distribution from Target to its shareholders?

C7-2 What tax advantages exist for the buyer when he or she acquires the assets of a corporation in a

taxable transaction? For the seller when he or she exchanges stock in a taxable transaction? In a tax-free transaction?

C7-3 What tax and nontax advantages and disadvantages accrue when an acquiring corporation purchases all of the target corporation's stock for cash and subsequently liquidates the target corporation?

---

[93] *A. T. Evans*, 30 B.T.A. 746 (1934), *acq.* XIII-2 C.B. 7; and *William Hewitt*, 19 B.T.A. 771 (1930).
[94] Reg. Sec. 1.368-2(g).

[95] 1977-2 C.B. 568. In Rev. Proc. 2006-1, 2006-1, I.R.B. 1, and Rev. Proc. 2006-3, 2006-1 I.R.B. 122.

C7-4 Why might a parent corporation make a Sec. 338 election after acquiring a target corporation's stock? When would such an election not be advisable?

C7-5 Explain the following items related to a Sec. 338 election:
a. The rule used to determine the time period within which the Sec. 338 stock purchase(s) can be made.
b. The types of stock acquisition transactions that are counted and not counted when determining whether a qualified stock purchase has been made.
c. The method for determining the sale price for the target corporation's assets.
d. The method for determining the total basis for the target corporation's assets.
e. The effect of the deemed sale on the target corporation's tax attributes.
f. The date by which the Sec. 338 election must be made.
g. Assuming goodwill is created during a purchase where the purchaser elects Sec. 338 treatment, can the goodwill be amortized? If so, over what period does amortization occur?

C7-6 a. Holt Corporation acquires all the stock of Star Corporation and makes a timely Sec. 338 election. The adjusted grossed-up basis of the Star stock is $2.5 million. Tangible assets on Star's balance sheet have a $1.8 million FMV. Explain to Holt's president how the new bases for Star's individual assets are determined.
b. How would your answer change if the adjusted grossed-up basis were instead $1.4 million?

C7-7 Compare the tax consequences arising from a taxable asset acquisition transaction and an asset-for-stock tax-free reorganization, giving consideration to the following points:
a. Consideration used to effect the transaction.
b. Recognition of gain or loss by the target corporation on the asset transfer.
c. Basis of property to the acquiring corporation.
d. Recognition of gain or loss when the target corporation is liquidated.
e. Use and/or carryover of the target corporation's tax attributes.

C7-8 Which of the following events that occur as part of an acquisitive tax-free reorganization require the target corporation to recognize gain? Assume in all cases that the target corporation is liquidated as part of the reorganization.
a. Transfer of appreciated target corporation assets in exchange for acquiring corporation stock and short-term notes.
b. Transfer of appreciated target corporation assets in exchange for acquiring corporation stock and the assumption of the target corporation's liabilities.
c. Assume the same facts as in Part b except the amount of liabilities assumed by the acquiring corporation exceeds the adjusted basis of the target corporation's assets transferred.
d. Transfer of appreciated target corporation assets in exchange for stock and money. Target distributes the money to its shareholders.
e. Transfer of appreciated target corporation assets in exchange for stock and money. Target uses the money to pay off its liabilities.

C7-9 A shareholder receives stock and cash as part of a tax-free reorganization. The shareholder recognizes a gain because of the boot (cash) received. What rules determine whether the character of the shareholder's recognized gain is dividend income or capital gain?

C7-10 Evaluate the following statement: Individual shareholders who must recognize gain as the result of receiving boot in a corporate reorganization generally prefer to report capital gain income, whereas corporate shareholders generally prefer to report dividend income.

C7-11 How is the basis for nonboot stocks and securities received by a shareholder determined? How is the basis determined for boot property?

C7-12 Which tax-free reorganization(s) are acquisitive transactions? Divisive transactions? Which tax-free reorganization(s) are neither acquisitive nor divisive? Which tax-free reorganization(s) can be either acquisitive or divisive?

C7-13 Compare the type of consideration that can be used to effect Type A, B, and C reorganizations.

C7-14 How does the IRS interpret the continuity-of-interest doctrine for a Type A merger transaction?

C7-15 How does the IRS interpret the continuity of business enterprise requirement for a Type A merger transaction?

C7-16 What are the advantages of using a Type C asset-for-stock reorganization instead of a Type A merger transaction? The disadvantages?

C7-17 How does the IRS interpret the "substantially all" the assets requirement for a Type C reorganization?

C7-18 Explain why an acquiring corporation might be prohibited from using cash as part of the consideration given to accomplish a Type C reorganization.

C7-19 Some acquisitive transactions may be characterized as either a Type C or a Type D reorganization. Which reorganization provision controls in the case of an overlap?

C7-20 What is the difference between an acquisitive Type C reorganization and an acquisitive Type D reorganization?

C7-21 Explain the circumstances in which money and other property can be used in a Type B reorganization.

C7-22 Acquiring Corporation has purchased for cash a 5% interest in Target Corporation's stock. After buying the stock and examining Target Corporation's books, Acquiring Corporation's management wants to make a tender offer to acquire the remaining Target stock in exchange for Acquiring voting stock. Can this tender offer be accomplished as a Type B reorganization? What problems may be encountered in structuring the acquisition as a tax-free reorganization?

C7-23 Acquiring Corporation wants to exchange its voting common stock for all of Target Corporation's single class of stock in a tender offer. Only 85% of Target Corporation's shareholders agree to tender their shares. Assuming the reorganization is accomplished, what options exist for Acquiring to acquire the remaining shares as part of the reorganization? At a later date? How will a subsequent cash acquisition of the remaining outstanding shares effect the tax-free treatment for the tender offer?

C7-24 Explain the concept of a triangular reorganization? What advantages would a triangular reorganization provide the acquiring corporation?

C7-25 Compare and contrast the requirements for, and the tax treatment of, the spinoff, split-off, and split-up forms of the divisive Type D reorganization.

C7-26 Stock of a controlled subsidiary corporation can be distributed tax-free to the distributing corporation's shareholders under Sec. 355. Explain the difference between such a distribution and a divisive Type D reorganization.

C7-27 When is the distribution of a controlled corporation's stock or securities tax-free to the distributing corporation's shareholders? What events trigger the recognition of gain or loss by the shareholders?

C7-28 When does the distributing corporation recognize gain or loss on the distribution of stock or securities of a controlled corporation to its shareholders?

C7-29 What is a recapitalization? What types of recapitalizations can take place tax-free?

C7-30 How can a recapitalization type of reorganization be used to transfer voting control within a family corporation from a senior generation that is in the process of retiring to a junior generation without incurring income taxes?

C7-31 Explain why a transaction might satisfy a literal interpretation of the Sec. 368 requirements for a tax-free reorganization, yet fail to be treated as a reorganization.

C7-32 Which types of tax-free reorganizations (acquisitive, divisive, and other) permit the carryover of tax attributes from a target or transferor corporation to an acquiring or transferee corporation?

C7-33 What restrictions are placed on the acquisition and use of a loss corporation's tax attributes?

C7-34 Explain why Sec. 382 will not be an obstacle to the use of NOL carryovers following a purchase transaction taking place if the value of the old loss corporation is large relative to its NOL carryovers.

C7-35 What is a plan of reorganization? Does such a plan need to be reduced to writing?

C7-36 Why do some taxpayers secure an advance ruling regarding a reorganization transaction?

C7-37 Does the receipt of a favorable advance ruling provide the taxpayer with a guarantee that the IRS will follow the private letter ruling when auditing the completed transaction?

ISSUE IDENTIFICATION QUESTIONS

C7-38 Rodger Powell owns all the stock of Fireside Bar and Grill Corporation in Pittsburgh. Rodger would like to sell his business and retire to sunny Florida now that he has turned 65. Karin Godfrey, a long-time bartender at Fireside, offers to purchase all the business's noncash assets in exchange for a 25% down payment, with the remaining 75% being paid in five equal annual installments. Interest will be charged at a market rate on the unpaid installments. Rodger plans to liquidate the corporation that has operated the Bar and Grill and have Fireside Bar and Grill distribute the installment notes and any remaining assets. What tax issues should Fireside Bar and Grill, Rodger, and Karin consider with respect to the proposed purchase transaction?

C7-39 Adolph Coors Co. transferred part of its assets to ACX Technologies Corporation in exchange for all of ACX's stock. The assets transferred included its aluminum unit, which makes aluminum sheet; its paper packaging unit, which makes consumer-products packaging; and its ceramic unit, which makes high-technology ceramics used in computer boards and automotive parts. The ACX Technologies stock received for the assets was distributed to the Coors shareholders. What tax issues should the parties to the divisive reorganization consider?

C7-40 Johnson & Johnson announced that it had entered into a merger agreement with Alza Corporation, a research-based pharmaceutical company and a leader in drug delivery technologies. Alza Corporation shareholders received a fixed exchange ratio of 0.49 shares of Johnson & Johnson common stock for each share of Alza stock in a tax-free reorganization. Alza had approximately 295 million shares outstanding at the time of the announcement. The boards of directors of both companies approved the merger. What tax issues were important to the two companies and to the two shareholder groups?

PROBLEMS

C7-41 *Qualified Stock Purchase.* Acquiring Corporation purchased 20% of Target Corporation's stock on each of the following dates: January 2, 2006; April 1, 2006; June 1, 2006; October 1, 2006; and December 31, 2006.

    a. Has a qualified stock purchase occurred? When must Acquiring make an election to have the stock purchase treated as an asset acquisition under Sec. 338?

    b. How would your answer to Part a change if the purchase dates instead were January 1, 2006; April 1, 2006; September 2, 2006; January 3, 2007; and April 15, 2007?

    c. If either Part a or b fails to be a qualified stock purchase, what is the latest date on which Acquiring Corporation can make the final stock purchase needed to qualify for a Sec. 338 election?

C7-42 *Sec. 338 Election.* Acquiring Corporation acquires 20% of the Target Corporation stock from Milt on August 10, 2006. Acquiring Corporation acquires an additional 30% of the stock from Nick on November 15, 2006. Acquiring Corporation acquires the remaining 50% of the Target stock from Phil on April 10, 2007. The total price paid for the stock is $1.9 million. Target Corporation's balance sheet on April 10, 2007, shows assets with a $2.5 million FMV, a $1.6 million adjusted basis, and $500,000 in liabilities.

    a. What is the acquisition date for the Target stock for Sec. 338 purposes? By what date must Acquiring make the Sec. 338 election?

    b. If Acquiring makes a Sec. 338 election, what is the aggregate deemed sale price for the assets?

    c. What is the total basis of the assets following the deemed sale, assuming a 34% corporate tax rate?

    d. How does the tax liability attributable to the deemed sale affect the price Acquiring Corporation should be willing to pay for the Target stock?

    e. What happens to Target's tax attributes following the deemed sale?

C7-43 *Sec. 338 Election.* Gator Corporation is considering the acquisition of Bulldog Corporation's stock in exchange for cash. Two options are being considered: (1) Gator acquires the assets from Bulldog for $1.4 million or (2) Gator acquires the Bulldog stock for $1 million and makes a Sec. 338 election shortly after the stock acquisition. Bulldog has no NOL or capital loss carryovers. Bulldog's balance sheet is presented below.

Assets	Adjusted Basis	FMV	Liabilities and Equity	Amount
Cash	$100,000	$100,000	Short-term debt	$200,000
Marketable securities	140,000	200,000	Long-term debt	200,000
Accounts receivable	100,000	100,000	Paid-in capital	300,000
Inventory (FIFO)	$100,000	$ 150,000	Retained earnings	$ 700,000
Plant and equipment	200,000	500,000		
Intangibles	–0–	350,000		
Total	$640,000	$1,400,000	Total	$1,400,000

    a. What advantages would accrue to Gator Corporation if it acquires the assets directly? What disadvantages would accrue to Bulldog Corporation if it sells the assets and then liquidates?

    b. What advantages would accrue to Gator Corporation if it acquires the Bulldog stock for cash and subsequently makes a Sec. 338 election? What advantage would accrue to Bulldog Corporation if its shareholders sell the Bulldog stock?

    c. How would your analysis change if Bulldog had incurred $250,000 of NOLs in the current year that it cannot carry back in full due to low taxable income being reported in the preceding two years?

C7-44 *Sec. 338 Basis Allocation.* Apache Corporation purchases all of Target Corporation's stock for $300,000 cash. Apache makes a timely Sec. 338 election. Target's balance sheet at the close of business on the acquisition date is as follows:

Assets	Adjusted Basis	FMV	Liabilities and Equity	Amount
Cash	$ 50,000	$ 50,000	Accounts payable	$ 40,000
Marketable securities	18,000	38,000	Note to bank	60,000
Accounts receivable	66,000	65,000	Owner's equity	300,000
Inventory (FIFO)	21,000	43,000		
Equipment[a]	95,000	144,000		
Land	6,000	12,000		
Building[b]	24,000	48,000		
Total	$280,000	$400,000	Total	$400,000

[a]The equipment cost $200,000 when purchased.
[b]The building is a MACRS property on which Target has claimed $10,000 of depreciation.

a. What is the aggregate deemed sale price for Target's assets (assume a 34% corporate tax rate)?

b. What amount and character of gain or loss must Target Corporation recognize on the deemed sale?

c. What is the adjusted grossed-up basis for the Target stock? What basis is allocated to each of the individual properties?

d. What happens to "old" Target's tax attributes? Do they carry over to "new" Target Corporation?

e. What amount (if any) of goodwill can Target amortize following the acquisition? Over what period and under what method does Target amortize the goodwill?

C7-45 *Amount of Corporate Gain or Loss.* Thomas Corporation transfers all of its assets and $100,000 of its liabilities in exchange for Andrews Corporation voting common stock, having a $600,000 FMV, as part of a merger transaction in which Thomas is liquidated. Thomas Corporation's basis for its assets is $475,000.

a. What is the amount of Thomas's realized and recognized gain or loss on the asset transfer?

b. What is Andrews's basis for the assets received?

c. What is the amount of Thomas's realized and recognized gain or loss when it distributes the stock to its shareholders?

d. How would your answers to Parts a–c change if Thomas's basis for the assets instead had been $750,000?

e. How would your answers to Parts a–c change if Andrews Corporation instead had exchanged $600,000 cash for Thomas Corporation's assets and Thomas was subsequently liquidated. Assume a 34% corporate tax rate.

C7-46 *Amount of Shareholder Gain or Loss.* Silvia exchanges all of her Talbot Corporation stock (acquired August 1, 2003) for $300,000 of Alpha Corporation voting common stock pursuant to Talbot's merger into Alpha Corporation. Immediately after the stock-for-stock exchange Silvia owns 25% of Alpha's 2,000 outstanding shares of stock. Silvia's adjusted basis in the Talbot stock is $200,000 before the merger.

a. What are the amount and character of Silvia's recognized gain or loss?

b. What is Silvia's basis for the Alpha stock? When does her holding period begin?

c. How would your answers to Parts a and b change if Silvia instead received Alpha common stock worth $240,000 and $60,000 cash?

C7-47 *Amount and Character of Shareholder Gain or Loss.* Yong owns 100% of Target Corporation's stock having a $600,000 adjusted basis. As part of the merger of Target Corporation into Allied Corporation, Yong exchanges his Target stock for Allied Corporation common stock having a $3 million FMV and $750,000 in cash. Yong retains a 60% interest in Allied Corporation's 100,000 shares of outstanding stock immediately after the merger.

a. What are the amount and character of Yong's recognized gain?

b. What is Yong's basis in the Allied stock?

c. How would your answer to Parts a and b change if Yong's 60,000 Allied shares were instead one-third of Allied's outstanding shares?

C7-48 *Amount and Character of Gain Recognized.* Springs Corporation has developed a nature park at the site of Blue Springs and has been extremely profitable. Newberry Corporation wants to merge with Springs under Florida law because Newberry wants to further develop these natural springs along with several other springs in the area. Newberry offers $650,000 of nonvoting preferred shares plus 1,000 shares of voting common (FMV of $50,000) to Springs in exchange for all of Springs' assets. As part of the merger of Springs into Newberry, Springs' sole shareholder, Mr. High, exchanges all his shares in Springs for the shares in Newberry. Immediately before this transaction, Mr. High had a $240,000 basis in his Springs shares. Before this transaction, Mr. High had no shares in Newberry, and after the transaction he owns 20% of the value of Newberry's stock.

a. Does this transaction qualify as a Type A reorganization?

b. Does Springs recognize any gain or loss on the asset sale or the exchange of shares with Mr. High?

c. Does Mr. High recognize any gain or loss? What is his basis and holding period in his Newberry shares?

C7-49 *Characterization of the Shareholder's Gain or Loss.* Turbo Corporation has one million shares of common stock and 200,000 shares of nonvoting preferred stock outstanding. Pursuant to a merger agreement, Ace Corporation exchanges its common stock worth $15 million for the Turbo common stock and pays $10 million in cash for the Turbo preferred stock. Some shareholders of Turbo Corporation received only Ace common stock for their common stock, some shareholders received only cash for their preferred stock, and some shareholders received both cash and Ace common stock for their Turbo preferred and common stock, respectively. Shareholders owning approximately 10% of the Turbo common stock also owned Turbo preferred stock. The total cash received by these shareholders amounted to $1.5 million. The Turbo Corporation common stockholders end up owning 15% of the Ace stock. What is the tax treatment of the common stock and/or cash received by each of the three groups of Turbo Corporation shareholders? Assume that some Turbo shareholders realize a gain on the transaction while other shareholders realize a loss.

C7-50 *Requirements for a Type A Reorganization.* Anchor Corporation is planning to acquire all the assets of Tower Corporation in a merger transaction. Tower's assets have a $5 million FMV and a $2.2 million adjusted basis. Which of the following transactions qualify as a Type A reorganization assuming Tower Corporation is liquidated?

a. The assets are exchanged for $5 million of Anchor common stock.

b. The assets are exchanged for $5 million of Anchor nonvoting preferred stock.

c. The assets are exchanged for $5 million of Anchor securities.

d. The assets are exchanged for $3.5 million of Anchor nonvoting preferred stock and $1.5 million in cash.

e. The assets are exchanged for $3 million of Anchor common stock and Anchor's assumption of $2 million of Tower liabilities.

f. The assets are exchanged for $5 million in cash provided by Anchor Corporation. An "all cash" merger transaction is permitted under state law.

C7-51 *Tax Consequences of a Merger.* Armor Corporation exchanges $1 million of its common stock and $300,000 of Armor bonds for all of Trail Corporation's outstanding stock. As part of the same transaction, Trail Corporation is then merged into Armor Corporation, with Armor receiving assets having a $1.3 million FMV and an $875,000 adjusted basis. As part of the merger, Antonello exchanges his 20% interest (4,000 shares) in Trail Corporation's single class of stock, having an adjusted basis of $100,000, for $200,000 in Armor stock and $60,000 in Armor bonds. Following the reorganization, Antonello owns 5% (1,000 shares) of Armor's stock. Armor Corporation's E&P balance is $375,000.

a. What is the amount of Trail Corporation's recognized gain or loss on the asset transfer?

b. What is Armor Corporation's basis for the assets received in the exchange?

c. What are the amount and character of Antonello's recognized gain or loss?

d. What is Antonello's basis for the Armor stock? For the Armor bonds?

C7-52 *Requirements for a Type C Reorganization.* Arnold Corporation is planning to acquire all the assets of Turner Corporation in an asset-for-stock (Type C) tax-free reorganization. Turner's assets have a $600,000 adjusted basis and a $1 million FMV. Which of the following transactions qualify as a Type C reorganization (assuming Turner is liquidated as part of the reorganization)?

a. The assets are exchanged for $800,000 of Arnold voting common stock and $200,000 of cash.

b. The assets are exchanged for $800,000 of Arnold voting common stock and $200,000 of Arnold bonds.

c. The assets are exchanged for $1 million of Arnold nonvoting preferred stock.

d. The assets are exchanged for $700,000 of Arnold voting common stock and Arnold's assumption of $300,000 of Turner's liabilities.

e. The assets are exchanged for $700,000 of Arnold voting common stock, Arnold's assumption of $200,000 of Turner's liabilities, and $100,000 in cash.

C7-53 *Tax Consequences of a Type C Reorganization.* Ash Corporation exchanges $250,000 of its voting common stock and $50,000 of its bonds for all of Texas Corporation's assets as part of a Type C tax-free reorganization. Texas Corporation is liquidated, with each of its two shareholders receiving equal amounts of the Ash Corporation stock and bonds. Barbara has a $50,000 basis in her stock, and George has a $200,000 basis in his stock. George and Barbara, who are unrelated, each own 8% of Ash's stock (5,000 shares) immediately after the reorganization. At the time of the reorganization, Texas Corporation's E&P balance is $75,000 and its assets have an adjusted basis of $225,000.

a. What is the amount of Texas Corporation's recognized gain or loss on the asset transfer? On the distribution of the stock and bonds?
b. What is Ash Corporation's basis in the assets it acquired?
c. What are the amount and character of each shareholder's recognized gain or loss?
d. What is the basis of each shareholder's Ash stock? Ash bonds?

C7-54 *Tax Consequences of a Type C Reorganization.* Tulsa Corporation exchanges assets having a $300,000 FMV and a $175,000 adjusted basis for $250,000 of Akron Corporation voting common stock and Akron's assumption of $50,000 of Tulsa's liabilities as part of a Type C tax-free reorganization. Tulsa is liquidated, with its sole shareholder, Michelle, receiving the Akron stock in exchange for her Tulsa stock having an adjusted basis of $100,000. Michelle owns 12% (2,500 shares) of Akron's stock immediately after the reorganization.

a. What is the amount of Tulsa's recognized gain or loss on the asset transfer? On the distribution of the stock?
b. What is Akron's basis for the assets it receives?
c. What effect would the transfer of Tulsa's assets to Subsidiary Corporation (a subsidiary controlled by Akron Corporation) have on the reorganization?
d. What are the amount and character of Michelle's recognized gain or loss?
e. What is Michelle's basis and holding period for her Akron stock?
f. What are the tax consequences of the transaction if Akron first transfers its stock to Akron-Sub Corporation who then carries out the acquisition of Tulsa Corporation's assets?

C7-55 *Requirements for a Type B Reorganization.* Allen Corporation is planning to acquire all the stock of Taylor Corporation in a stock-for-stock (Type B) tax-free reorganization. Which of the following transactions will qualify as a Type B reorganization?

a. All of Taylor's common stock is exchanged for $1 million of Allen voting preferred stock.
b. All of Taylor's common stock is exchanged for $1 million of Allen voting common stock, and $500,000 face amount of Taylor bonds are exchanged for $500,000 face amount of Allen bonds. Both bonds are trading at their par values.
c. All of Taylor's stock is exchanged for $750,000 of Allen voting common stock and $250,000 of Allen bonds.
d. All of Taylor's stock is exchanged for $1 million of Allen voting common stock, and the shareholders of Taylor end up owning less than 1% of Allen's stock.
e. Ninety percent of Taylor's stock is exchanged for $900,000 of Allen voting common stock. One shareholder who owns 10% of the Taylor stock exercises his right under state law to have his shares independently appraised and redeemed for cash by Taylor Corporation. He receives $100,000.
f. Assume the same facts as in Part d except the Allen stock is contributed to Allen-Sub Corporation. The Allen stock is exchanged by Allen-Sub for all the Taylor stock.

C7-56 *Tax Consequences of a Type B Reorganization.* Trent Corporation's single class of stock is owned equally by Juan and Miguel, who are unrelated. Juan has a $125,000 basis for his 1,000 shares of Trent stock, and Miguel has a $300,000 basis for his Trent stock. Adams Corporation exchanges 2,500 shares of its voting common stock having a $100 per share FMV for each shareholder's Trent stock in a single transaction. Immediately after the reorganization, each shareholder owns 15% of the Adams stock.

a. What are the amount and character of each shareholder's recognized gain or loss?
b. What is each shareholder's basis for his Adams stock?
c. What is Adams Corporation's basis for the Trent stock?
d. How would your answers to Parts a–c change if Adams Corporation instead exchanged 2,000 shares of Adams common stock and $50,000 in cash for each shareholder's Trent stock?

C7-57 *Tax Consequences of a Type B Reorganization.* Austin Corporation exchanges $1.5 million of its voting common stock for all of Travis Corporation's single class of stock. Ingrid, who owns all the Travis stock, has a basis of $375,000 in her stock. Ingrid owns 25% of the 15,000 outstanding shares of Austin stock immediately after the reorganization.
a. What are the amount and character of Ingrid's recognized gain or loss?
b. What is Ingrid's basis for her Austin stock?
c. What is Austin Corporation's basis for the Travis stock?
d. What are the tax consequences for all parties to the acquisition if Austin Corporation subsequently liquidates Travis Corporation as part of the plan of reorganization?
e. As part of the reorganization, Austin Corporation exchanges $1 million of its 7% bonds for $1 million Travis Corporation 7% bonds held equally by ten private investors.

C7-58 *Tax Consequences of a Type B Reorganization.* Ashton Corporation purchases 10% of Todd Corporation stock from Cathy for $250,000 in cash on January 30, 2005. Andrea and Bill each exchange one-half of the remaining 90% of the Todd stock for $1.2 million of Ashton voting common stock on May 30, 2006. Andrea and Bill each have a $150,000 basis for their Todd stock. Andrea and Bill each own 15% of the Ashton stock (12,000 shares) immediately after the reorganization.
a. What are the amount and character of each shareholder's recognized gain or loss?
b. What is each shareholder's basis for his or her Ashton stock?
c. What is Ashton Corporation's basis for the Todd stock?
d. How would your answer to Parts a–c change if Ashton Corporation instead had acquired the remaining Todd stock on May 30, 2005?
e. What effect would the stock acquisition have on the adjusted bases of individual assets and the tax attributes of Todd Corporation?
f. Can the Ashton-Todd corporate group file a consolidated tax return?
g. Can a Sec. 338 election be made with respect to Todd Corporation's assets?

C7-59 *Tax Consequences of a Divisive Type D Reorganization.* Road Corporation is owned equally by four shareholders. It conducts activities in two operating divisions: the road construction division and meat packing division. To separate the two activities into separate corporations, Road Corporation transferred the assets and liabilities of the meat packing division (60% of Road's total net assets) to Food Corporation in exchange for all of Food's single class of stock. The assets of the meat packing division have a $2.75 million FMV and a $1.1 million adjusted basis. A total of $500,000 of liabilities are transferred to Food Corporation. The $2.25 million of Food stock (90,000 shares) is distributed ratably to each of the four shareholders.
a. What is the amount of Road Corporation's recognized gain or loss on the asset transfer? On the distribution of the Food stock?
b. What are the amount and character of each shareholder's recognized gain or loss on the distribution? (Assume each shareholder's basis in their Road stock is $200,000.)
c. What is the basis of each shareholder's Road and Food stock after the reorganization? (Assume the Road stock is worth $1.5 million immediately after the distribution.)

C7-60 *Tax Consequences of a Divisive Type D Reorganization.* Light Corporation is owned equally by two individual shareholders, Bev and Tarek. The shareholders no longer agree on matters concerning Light's operations. Tarek agrees to a plan whereby $500,000 of Light's assets (having an adjusted basis of $350,000) and $100,000 of Light's liabilities are transferred to Dark Corporation in exchange for all of its single class of stock (5,000 shares). Tarek will exchange all of his Light common stock, having a $150,000 adjusted basis, for the $400,000 of Dark stock. Bev will continue to operate Light Corporation.
a. What is the amount of Light Corporation's recognized gain or loss on the asset transfer? On the distribution of the Dark stock?
b. What are the amount and character of Tarek's recognized gain or loss?
c. What is Tarek's basis for his Dark stock?
d. What tax attributes of Light will be allocated to Dark?

C7-61 *Distribution of Stock: Spin-Off.* Parent Corporation has been in the business of manufacturing and selling trucks for the past eight years. Its subsidiary, Diesel Corporation, has been in the business of manufacturing and selling diesel engines for the past seven years. Parent acquired control of Diesel Corporation six years ago when it purchased 100% of its single class of stock from Large Corporation. A federal court has ordered Parent to divest itself of Diesel Corporation as the result of an antitrust judgment. Consequently, Parent distributes all of its Diesel Corporation stock to its shareholders. Alan owns less than 1% of Parent's outstanding stock having a $40,000 basis. He receives 25 shares of Diesel stock having a $25,000 FMV as a result of Parent's distribution. No cash or other assets are distributed by Parent. Parent's E&P at the end of the year in which the spinoff occurs is $2.5 million. The Parent stock held by Alan has a $75,000 FMV immediately after the distribution.

a. What are the amount and character of the gain, loss, or income Alan must recognize as a result of Parent's distributing the Diesel stock?
b. What basis does Alan take for the Diesel stock he receives?
c. When does Alan's holding period for the Diesel stock begin?
d. What amount and character of gain or loss does Parent recognize on making the distribution?
e. How would your answer to Part a change if Parent had been in the truck business for only three years before making the distribution and that it had acquired the Diesel stock in a taxable transaction only two years ago?

C7-62 *Distribution of Stock: Split-Off.* Parent Corporation has owned all 100 shares of Subsidiary Corporation common stock since 1999. Parent has been in the business of manufacturing and selling light fixtures, and Subsidiary has been in the business of manufacturing and selling light bulbs. Amy and Bill are the two equal shareholders of the Parent stock and have owned their stock since 1999. Amy's basis in her 50 shares of Parent stock is $80,000, and Bill's basis in his 50 shares of Parent stock is $60,000. On April 10, 2006, Parent distributes all 100 shares of Subsidiary stock to Bill in exchange for all of his Parent stock (which is cancelled). The distribution has an acceptable business purpose. The Subsidiary stock had a $30,000 basis to Parent on the distribution date. At the end of 2006, Parent has $150,000 of E&P. Immediately after the distribution, the FMVs of the Parent and Subsidiary stocks are $3,000 and $1,000 per share, respectively.

a. What are the amount and character of the gain, loss, or income Bill must recognize as a result of Parent's distributing the Subsidiary stock?
b. What basis does Bill take in the Subsidiary stock?
c. When does Bill's holding period for the Subsidiary stock begin?
d. Assume instead that Andrew formed Subsidiary in 2002 to manufacture and sell lightbulbs. Andrew sold the Subsidiary stock to Parent for cash in 2004. How would your answer to Parts a-c change?

C7-63 *Distribution of Stock and Securities: Split-Off.* Ruby Corporation has 100 shares of common stock outstanding. Fred, a shareholder of Ruby Corporation, exchanges his 25% interest in the Ruby stock for Garnet Corporation stock and securities. Ruby purchased 80% of the Garnet stock ten years ago for $25,000. At the time of the exchange, Fred has a $50,000 basis in his Ruby stock, and the stock has an $80,000 FMV. Fred receives Garnet stock that has a $60,000 FMV and Garnet securities that have a $20,000 FMV. Ruby has $50,000 of E&P. Assume that all the requirements of Sec. 355 are met except for the receipt of boot.

a. What are the amount and character of Fred's recognized gain or loss on the exchange?
b. What is Fred's basis for the Garnet stock and the Garnet securities?
c. What are the amount and character of Ruby Corporation's recognized gain or loss on the distribution?
d. When does Fred's holding period begin for the Garnet stock and the Garnet securities?
e. How would your answer to Part a change if the exchange did not meet the requirements of Sec. 355 or Sec. 356?

C7-64 *Distribution of Stock and Securities: Split-Up.* Jean Corporation has two divisions—home cookware and electric home appliances. Billy and Bob Jean own all of Jean Corporation's single class of stock. Billy, the older brother, owns 70% of the Jean stock with Bob owning the remaining 30%. Billy and Bob's adjusted bases in their Jean stock investments are $700,000 and $300,000, respectively. They have owned the stock for eight years. The divisions have the following assets:

Division	FMV Assets	Adjusted Basis
Cookware	$980,000	$600,000
Home appliances	420,000	300,000

Jean Corporation divides its business in the following manner. Jean Corporation transfers the cookware assets to Cookware Corporation in exchange for all of Cookware's stock. Jean Corporation transfers the home appliance assets to Home Appliance Corporation in exchange for all of Home Appliance's stock. Jean Corporation transfers the Cookware

Corporation stock to Billy in exchange for all of his Jean Corporation stock. Jean Corporation transfers the Home Appliance Corporation stock to Bob in exchange for all of his Jean Corporation stock. Finally, Jean Corporation liquidates with its remaining cash being used to pay its liabilities.

a. What gain or loss is recognized on the transfer of the Jean Corporation assets to Cookware and Home Appliance corporations? What basis do the two corporations have in the assets transfered?

b. What gain or loss do Billy and Bob recognize when they transfer their Jean Corporation stock for the Cookware and Home Appliance stock? What basis does each shareholder take in his or her new stock?

C7-65 *Requirements for a Type E Reorganization.* Master Corporation plans to undertake a recapitalization. Explain the tax consequences of each of the following independent transactions:

a. Holders of Class A nonvoting preferred stock will exchange their stock for newly issued common stock. Master paid $300,000 of cash dividends in the current year and each prior year on the preferred stock.

b. Holders of Master Corporation bonds in the amount of $3 million will exchange their bonds for a similar dollar amount of preferred stock. In addition, $180,000 of unpaid interest will be paid by issuing additional Master preferred stock to the former bondholders.

c. Master Corporation 9% bonds in the amount of $3 million are called and exchanged by their holders before their maturity date for a similar dollar amount of Master Corporation 6% bonds because of a decline in the prevailing market rate of interest. In addition, Master will pay $180,000 of unpaid interest in cash.

C7-66 *Tax Consequences of a Type E Reorganization.* Milan Corporation is owned by four shareholders. Andy and Bob each own 40% of the outstanding common and preferred stock. Chris and Doug each own 10% of the outstanding common and preferred stock. The shareholders want to retire the preferred stock that was issued five years ago when the corporation was in the midst of a major expansion. Retirement of the preferred stock will eliminate the need to pay annual dividends on the preferred stock. Explain the tax consequences of the following two alternatives to the shareholders:

• Milan redeems the $100 par preferred stock for its $120 call price. Each shareholder purchased his preferred stock at its par value five years ago.

• The shareholders exchange each share of the $100 par value preferred stock for $120 of additional common stock.

What nontax advantages might exist for selecting one alternative over the other?

C7-67 *Types of Reorganizations.* Identify the type of each of the following reorganizations.

a. Briggs Corporation originally incorporated in the State of Georgia but now conducts most of its business activities in Florida. The firm transfers substantially all of its Georgia corporation's assets to a new Florida corporation. The Georgia entity liquidates shortly after the transfer. All "Georgia" shareholders swap their "old" Briggs stock for "new" Briggs stock giving them an ownership interest in the Florida entity.

b. Jones Corporation exchanges all $1 million of its $1,000 face amount, 6% bonds for a similar amount of new convertible bonds paying a lower interest rate.

c. Bill Smith owns 100% of Smith Corporation and James Jones owns 100% of Jones Corporation. The two corporations are combined into a single entity called Smith & Jones Corporation. Each shareholder in the two original corporations receives stock in the new, combined entity in proportion to the value of his original stock holdings.

d. Dupree Corporation is in bankruptcy. The corporation works out an agreement whereby bondholders and other creditors receive Dupree Corporation notes and stock in exchange for forgiving their original claims.

C7-68 *Reorganization Requirements.* Discuss the tax consequences of the following corporate reorganizations to the parties to the reorganization:

a. Adobe Corporation and Tyler Corporation are merged under the laws of the State of Florida. The shareholders of Tyler Corporation receive $300,000 of Adobe common stock and $700,000 of Adobe securities for their Tyler stock.

b. Alabama Corporation exchanges $1 million of its voting common stock for all the noncash assets of Texas Corporation. The transaction meets all the requirements for a Type C reorganization. Texas Corporation is divided into two operating divisions: meat packing and meat distribution. Alabama Corporation retains the meat packing division's assets and continues to conduct its activities but sells for cash the assets of the meat distribution division. The meat distribution division's assets constitute 40% of Texas Corporation's noncash assets.

c. Parent Corporation transfers $500,000 of investment securities to Subsidiary Corporation in exchange for all of its single class of stock. The Subsidiary stock is exchanged for one-third of the stock held by each of Parent Corporation's shareholders. Six months after the reorganization, the investment securities are distributed to Subsidiary Corporation's shareholders pursuant to the liquidation of Subsidiary.

C7-69 *Determining the Type of Reorganization Transaction.* For each of the following transactions, indicate its reorganization designation (e.g., Type A, Type B, etc.). Assume all common stock is voting stock.

a. Anderson and Brown Corporations exchange their assets for all of the single class of stock of newly created Computer Corporation. Following the exchange, Anderson and Brown Corporations are liquidated. The transaction satisfies the State of Michigan corporation law requirements.

b. Price Corporation (incorporated in the State of Texas) exchanges all of its assets for all the single class of stock of Price Corporation (incorporated in the State of Delaware). Following the exchange, Price Corporation (Texas) is liquidated.

c. All of Gates Corporation's noncumulative, 10% preferred stock is exchanged for Gates Corporation common stock.

d. Hobbs Corporation exchanges its common stock for 90% of the outstanding common stock and 80% of the outstanding nonvoting preferred stock of Calvin Corporation. The remaining Calvin stock is held by about 30 individual investors.

e. Scale Corporation transfers the assets of its two operating divisions to Major and Minor Corporations in exchange for all of each corporation's single class of stock. The Major and Minor stocks are distributed pursuant to the liquidation of Scale.

f. Tobias Corporation has $3 million of assets and $1 million of liabilities. Andrew Corporation exchanges $2 million of its voting common stock for all of Tobias Corporation's assets and liabilities. Tobias Corporation is liquidated, and its shareholders end up owning 11% of the Andrew stock following the transaction.

g. How would your answer to Part f change (if at all) should Tobias Corporation's balance sheet indicate that liabilities were 90% of the corporation's capital structure and common stock the remaining 10%?

C7-70 *Tax Attribute Carryovers.* Alaska Corporation exchanges $2 million of its voting common stock for all the noncash assets of Tennessee Corporation at the close of business on May 31, 2006. Tennessee Corporation uses its cash to pay off its liabilities and then liquidates. Tennessee and Alaska Corporations report the following taxable income amounts:

Tax Year Ending	Alaska Corp.	Tennessee Corp.
December 31, 2003	($100,000)	($95,000)
December 31, 2004	60,000	20,000
December 31, 2005	70,000	(90,000)
May 31, 2006	XXX	(40,000)
December 31, 2006	73,000	XXX

a. What tax returns must Alaska and Tennessee file for 2006?
b. What amount of the NOL carryover does Alaska acquire?
c. Ignoring any implications of Sec. 382, what amount of Tennessee Corporation's NOL can Alaska Corporation use in 2006?

C7-71 *Sec. 382 Limitation: Purchase Transaction.* Murray Corporation's stock is owned by about 1,000 shareholders, none of whom own more than 1% of the stock. Pursuant to a tender offer, Said purchases all the Murray stock for $7.5 million cash at the close of business on December 31, 2005. Before the acquisition, Said owned no Murray stock. Murray Corporation had incurred substantial NOLs, which at the end of 2005 totaled $1 million. Murray Corporation's taxable income is expected to be $200,000 and $600,000, respectively, for 2006 and 2007. Assuming the long-term tax-exempt federal rate is 5% and Murray Corporation continues in the same trade or business, what amount of NOLs can Murray Corporation use in 2006 and/or 2007? What amount of NOLs and Sec. 382 limitation carryover to 2008?

C7-72 *Sec. 382 Limitation: Tax-Free Reorganization.* Albert Corporation is a profitable publicly traded corporation. None of its shareholders owns more than 1% of its stock. On

December 31, 2005, Albert Corporation exchanges $8 million of its stock for all the stock of Turner Corporation as part of a merger transaction. Turner is owned by Tara, who receives 15% of the Albert stock as part of the reorganization. Tara owned none of the Albert stock before the merger. Turner accumulated $2.5 million in NOL carryovers before being merged into Albert. Albert expects to earn $1 million and $1.5 million in taxable income during 2006 and 2007, respectively. Assuming the long-term tax-exempt federal rate is 4.5%, what amount of NOLs can Albert Corporation use in 2006 and 2007?

COMPREHENSIVE PROBLEM

C7-73   Sid Kess, a long-time tax client of yours, has decided to acquire the snow blower manufacturing firm owned by Richard Smith, one of his closest friends. Richard has a $200,000 adjusted basis for his Richard Smith Snow Blowers (RSSB) stock. Sid Kess Enterprises (SKE), a C corporation 100%-owned by Sid Kess, will make the acquisition. RSSB operates as a C corporation and reports the following assets and liabilities as of November 1 of the current year.

Asset	Adj. Basis	FMV
Cash	$ 200,000	$ 200,000
Inventory (LIFO)	470,000	600,000
Equipment	100,000	275,000
Building	200,000	295,000
Land	80,000	120,000
Goodwill	–0–	250,000
Total	$1,050,000	$1,740,000

Equities	Amount
Accounts payable	$ 60,000
Mortgage payable	120,000
Paid-in capital	220,000
Retained earnings	650,000
Total	$1,050,000

RSSB has claimed depreciation of $200,000 and $80,000 on the equipment and building, respectively, and has claimed no amortization on the goodwill. Retained earnings approximate RSSB's E&P. No NOL, capital loss, or credit carryovers exist at the time of the acquisition. What are the tax consequences of each alternative acquisition methods to SKE and RSSB corporations? Assume a 34% corporate tax rate.

a. SKE acquires all the single class of RSSB stock for $1.56 million in cash. RSSB is not liquidated.

b. SKE acquires all the noncash assets of RSSB for $1.54 million in cash. RSSB is liquidated.

c. SKE acquires all the RSSB stock for $1.56 million in cash. RSSB is liquidated into SKE shortly after the acquisition.

d. SKE acquires all the RSSB stock for $1.56 million in cash. SKE makes a timely Sec. 338 election. RSSB's tax rate is 34%.

e. SKE exchanges $1.54 million of its common stock for all of RSSB's noncash assets ($1,540,000 = $1,740,000 total assets − $200,000 cash). SKE has 10,000 shares of stock with a $3 million FMV outstanding before the acquisition. RSSB is liquidated as part of the transaction. RSSB uses part of the cash that has been retained to pay off the corporation's liabilities. The remaining cash is distributed with the SKE stock in liquidation of RSSB.

f. SKE exchanges $1.56 million of its common stock for all of Richard Smith's RSSB stock. Assume that RSSB is not liquidated. Each share of SKE stock has a $300 FMV.

g. Assume the same facts as in Part d except that SKE transfers $1.56 million of its common stock to SKE-Sub. SKE-Sub serves as the acquiring corporation for the transaction and uses $1.56 million of the SKE stock to acquire RSSB's stock.

h. Assume the same facts as in Part e except that SKE transfers $1.54 million of its common stock to SKE-Sub. SKE-Sub serves as the acquiring corporation for the transaction and uses $1.54 million of the SKE stock to acquire RSSB's noncash assets.

TAX STRATEGY PROBLEMS

C7-74 Angel Macias is considering the possibility of selling his business. The business (Target Corporation) has the following assets and liabilities:

Assets	Adjusted Basis	FMV
Cash	$ 400,000	$ 400,000
Securities	400,000	300,000
Inventory (LIFO)	100,000	200,000
Equipment	200,000	400,000
Building (no Sec. 1250 recapture)	50,000	300,000
Goodwill	–0–	200,000
Total	$1,150,000	$1,800,000

Target Corporation owes $200,000 of accounts payable and $400,000 in bank loans. No NOL carryovers or carrybacks are available. Bill Jones and Sam Smith, each of whom have a net worth exceeding $1 million, are interested in purchasing the business using their S&J Corporation as the vehicle for making the purchase. Target's management and its owners are interested in selling the business. Assume that both entities are C corporations and that the C corporations are taxed at a flat 34% rate. The individual owners are taxed at a 35% tax rate on their ordinary income and a 15% rate on their capital gains. What advice would you give Bill and Sam about acquiring the assets directly from Target, or indirectly by purchasing Target's stock from its shareholders and then liquidating Target Corporation into S&J Corporation? Bill and Sam also have expressed a concern about possible differences in the financial reporting of a tax-free versus a taxable acquisition.

C7-75 Tom Smith owns 100% of Alpha Corporation's single class of stock, and Alpha Corporation owns 100% of Beta Corporation's single class of stock. Alpha and Beta Corporations have filed separate tax returns for a number of years. Neither corporation has any NOL carryovers. Although Alpha and Beta both have been profitable in recent years, Beta Corporation needs an infusion of additional capital from outside investors. The corporations have received a proposal from an investor, Karla Boroff, to invest $2 million in Beta Corporation to enable Beta to expand its operations and to eliminate a current working capital shortage that cannot be solved without additional funds. Karla has imposed one constraint on her capital contribution—that Alpha and Beta become two free-standing entities. Alpha would continue to be completely owned by Tom, but Beta would be owned by the two individuals, Tom and Karla, with each owning 50% of Beta's stock. What strategies can you offer for separating the two companies?

CASE STUDY PROBLEMS

C7-76 *Comparative Acquisition Forms.* Bailey Corporation owns a number of automotive parts shops. Bill Smith owns an automotive parts shop that has been in existence for 40 years and has competed with one of Bailey's locations. Bill is thinking about retirement and would like to sell his business. He has his CPA prepare a balance sheet, which he takes to John Bailey, president of Bailey Corporation, who has been a long-time friend.

Assets	Adjusted Basis	FMV
Cash	$ 250,000	$ 250,000
Accounts receivable	75,000	70,000
Inventories (LIFO)	600,000	1,750,000
Equipment	200,000	250,000
Building	30,000	285,000
Land	30,000	115,000
Total	$1,185,000	$2,720,000

Should Bailey Corporation make the acquisition, it intends to operate the automotive parts shop using its own tradename in the location Bill has used for 40 years. The president has asked you to prepare a summary of the tax consequences of the following three transactions: (1) a purchase of the noncash assets using cash, (2) the purchase of the stock of Bill's corporation using cash and Bailey Corporation notes, and (3) an asset-for-stock tax-free reorganization using solely Bailey stock. Upon interviewing Bill, you obtain the following additional information: Bill's business is operated as a C corporation, with a $160,000 adjusted basis for his stock. Accounts payable of $200,000 are outstanding. The corporation has depreciated the building using the straight-line method and has claimed $100,000 in depreciation. The equipment is Sec. 1245 property for which the corporation has claimed $150,000 in depreciation. The after-tax profits for each of the last three years have exceeded $300,000, and Bill suspects that some goodwill value exists that is not shown on the balance sheet. No NOL carryovers are available from prior years.

Required: Prepare a memorandum that outlines the tax consequences of each of the three alternative acquisition transactions assuming that the anticipated cash purchase price is $2.55 million for the noncash assets and $2.6 million for the stock and that the transaction takes place in 2006. How would the acquiring corporation report each of the three alternatives for financial reporting purposes under GAAP?

C7-77 The following advertisement appeared in *The Wall Street Journal*:

> $17 MILLION CASH WITH
> ADDITIONAL CASH AVAILABLE
> $105 MM TAX LOSS GOOD THROUGH 2020
> TIGERA GROUP, INC.
> NASDAQ listed w/300 shareholders
> WANTS TO ACQUIRE COMPANY
> with Net Before Tax Audited Earnings of $7MM to $10MM
> Exceptional Opportunity and Participation for Sellers and
> Existing Management. Contact: Albert M. Zlotnick or Ross P.
> Lederer, Tel: (000)-000-0000 and Fax: (000)-000-0000.

Required: Prepare a memorandum explaining the tax advantages that would accrue to the Tigera Group if it acquired the stock or the assets of a profitable corporation in a tax-free reorganization or a taxable transaction. Would the advantages be the same if a profitable corporation acquired Tigera? In addition, explain any tax law provisions that might restrict the use of these loss carryovers.

TAX RESEARCH PROBLEMS

C7-78 Austin Corporation acquires 8% of Travis Corporation's single class of stock for cash on January 10 of the current year. On August 25 of the current year, Austin Corporation makes a tender offer to exchange Austin common stock for the remaining Travis stock. Travis Corporation shareholders tender an additional 75% of the outstanding Travis stock. The exchange is completed on September 25 of the current year. Austin Corporation ends up owning slightly more than 83% of the Travis stock. The remaining 17% of the Travis Corporation stock is owned by about 100 former shareholders of Travis Corporation who own small blocks of stock. Your tax manager has asked you to draft a memorandum explaining whether one or both of the two acquisition transactions qualify as a tax-free reorganization? If part or all of either transaction is taxable to Travis Corporation's shareholders, offer any suggestions for restructuring the acquisitions to improve the tax consequences of the transaction assuming that Austin Corporation does not desire to make a Sec. 338 election.

A question was asked by Matt Bonner, CEO of Travis Corporation, that might be relevant to reporting the transaction: To simplify the corporate structure, can Austin Corporation liquidate Travis Corporation into Austin without recognizing any gain or loss? At a minimum you should consider:

- IRC Sec. 368(a)(1)(B)
- Reg. Sec. 1.368-2(c)
- *Eldon S. Chapman, et al. v. CIR,* 45 AFTR 2d 80-1290, 80-1 USTC ¶9330 (1st Cir., 1980)
- *Arden S. Heverly, et al. v. CIR,* 45 AFTR 2d 80-1122, 80-1 USTC ¶9322 (3rd Cir., 1980)

C7-79 ABC Corporation is the subject of a hostile takeover bid by XYZ Corporation. ABC incurs a total of $400,000 in attorneys' fees, accounting fees, and printing costs for information mailed to ABC shareholders in an effort to defeat the XYZ takeover bid. XYZ finally gives up, and ABC remains a separate corporation. What is the appropriate tax treatment for the $400,000 in fees? Is that treatment different if XYZ succeeds in acquiring ABC? Tax resources you should consider include the following:

- IRC Sec. 162
- IRC Sec. 165
- *INDOPCO, Inc. v. Comm.*, 69 AFTR 2d 92-694, 92-1 USTC ¶50,113 (USSC, 1992)
- *U.S. v. Federated Department Stores, Inc.*, 74 AFTR 2d 94-5519, 94-2 USTC ¶50,418 (S.D. Ohio, 1994)
- *A.E. Staley Manufacturing Co. v. Comm.*, 80 AFTR 2d 97-5060, 97-2 USTC ¶50,521 (7th Cir., 1997)
- Reg. Sec. 1.263(a)-5

C7-80 Diversified Corporation is a successful bank with ten branches. Al, Bob, and Cathy created Diversified Corporation six years ago and own equally all the Diversified stock. Diversified has constructed a new building in downtown Metropolis that houses a banking facility on the first floor, offices for its employees on the second and third floors, and office space to be leased out to third party lessees on the fourth through twelfth floors. Since the building was completed six months ago, approximately 75% of the floor space on the upper floors has been occupied. Pursuant to a plan of reorganization, Diversified proposes to transfer the building to Metropolis Real Estate (MRE) Corporation in exchange for all the MRE common stock. A team of commercial real estate experts have been hired to manage MRE. The building will be the only property owned by MRE following the reorganization. Diversified owns no other real estate because it currently leases from third parties the locations for its ten retail banking branches. Diversified will distribute the MRE common stock ratably to Al, Bob, and Cathy, who will end up holding all the Diversified and MRE common stock. Your tax manager has asked you to draft a memorandum explaining whether or not the proposed transaction will satisfy the requirements for a tax-free divisive reorganization? At a minimum you should consider:

- IRC Sec. 368(a)(1)(D)
- Reg. Sec. 1.355-3(b), (c)
- *Appleby v. Comm.*, 9 AFTR 2d 372, 62-1 USTC ¶9178 (3rd Cir., 1962)

8

CHAPTER

CONSOLIDATED TAX RETURNS

LEARNING OBJECTIVES

After studying this chapter, you should be able to

1. ► Determine whether a group of corporations is an affiliated group

2. ► Explain the advantages and disadvantages of filing a consolidated tax return

3. ► Calculate consolidated taxable income for an affiliated group

4. ► Calculate the consolidated regular tax liability for an affiliated group

5. ► Calculate the consolidated AMT liability for an affiliated group

6. ► Determine whether a transaction is an intercompany transaction

7. ► Explain the reporting of an intercompany transaction

8. ► Calculate an affiliated group's consolidated NOL

9. ► Calculate the carryback or carryover of a consolidated NOL

10. ► Determine how the special loss limitations restrict the use of separate and consolidated NOL carrybacks and carryovers

11. ► Explain the procedures for making an initial consolidated return election

Affiliated corporations (i.e., a parent corporation and at least one subsidiary corporation) have two options for filing their federal income tax returns:

▶ Each member of the group can file separate tax returns that report its own income and expenses. No special treatment is generally provided for transactions between group members.[1] However, the group can elect to claim a 100% dividends-received deduction for intragroup dividends.

▶ The affiliated group can file a single tax return, called a consolidated tax return, that reports the results for all its group members. A number of special treatments are applied to transactions between group members (e.g., deferring gains and losses on intercompany transactions and eliminating intragroup dividends).

Some consolidated tax returns include as few as two corporations. Other consolidated tax returns include hundreds of corporations. Moreover, most of the nation's largest corporate groups file consolidated tax returns. In recent years, affiliated groups filing on a consolidated basis reported 90% of total taxable income for all C corporations and paid more than 80% of the income taxes paid by all C corporations even though they made up less than 3% of all C corporation tax returns that were filed.[2]

This chapter considers the advantages and disadvantages of filing a consolidated tax return. It also examines the basic requirements for computing the consolidated tax liability.

SOURCE OF THE CONSOLIDATED TAX RETURN RULES

ADDITIONAL COMMENT

Filing a consolidated tax return does not affect the reporting of other taxes such as payroll, sales, or property taxes. Also, some states do not allow the filing of consolidated tax returns for state income tax purposes.

REAL-WORLD EXAMPLE

Several years ago, Mobil Oil filed a federal consolidated income tax return that was 6,300 pages long and weighed 76 pounds. Work papers for the return constituted 146,000 documents. The return took 57 person years to prepare at a cost of $10 million. In addition, more than $5 million of expenses were incurred annually in connection with the IRS's audit of the Mobil return.

Sections 1501–1504 are the primary statutory provisions governing the filing of a consolidated tax return. These four sections are very general and primarily define the composition of the affiliated groups eligible to elect to file a consolidated tax return. This topic is quite complex. The Treasury Department was given the responsibility of drafting the Treasury Regulations needed to determine (1) the consolidated tax liability and (2) the filing requirements for a consolidated tax return. Because it is unusual for the Treasury Department to have the authority to draft both statutory and interpretive regulations for a particular topical area, Sec. 1501 requires that all affiliated groups filing a consolidated tax return must consent to all the consolidated tax return regulations in effect when the return is filed. The purpose of Sec. 1501 is to reduce or avoid conflicts in applying the statutory and interpretive regulations. The consolidated return regulations have the same authority as the Internal Revenue Code because of the consent requirement and the fact that they are legislative in nature.

These regulations are seldom challenged in court and even more rarely found invalid. In 2001, the Federal Circuit Court of Appeals ruled in *Rite Aid Corporation v. United States*[3] that one of the consolidated return regulations was invalid. This ruling was the first time in 22 years that a court overturned a consolidated return regulation. In overturning the regulation, the court reasoned that the invalid regulation "addresses a situation that arises . . . regardless of whether corporations file separate or consolidated returns" and that the difference in treatment between consolidated corporations and corporations filing separately was not justified. As a result of the *Rite Aid* decision, Congress was concerned that the IRS would be inundated with cases based on the assertion by taxpayers that their results would be different under the consolidated return regulations than they would be if the corporations filed separately. Accordingly, in the 2004 Jobs Act, Congress added a sentence to Sec. 1502 to specifically provide that the rules for consolidated entities may be different from the rules that would apply if the corporations filed separate returns.

---

[1] Some special treatments apply to related corporations filing separate returns under the controlled group rules. These include but are not limited to matching of income and deductions, Sec. 267(a)(1); deferral of loss on intragroup sales, Sec. 267(f)(2); and ordinary income recognition on intragroup sales of depreciable property, Sec. 1239.

[2] IRS Web site: *www.irs.gov*. For fiscal year 2002, affiliated groups filed 52,733 consolidated returns.

[3] 88 AFTR 2d 2001-5058, 2001-2 USTC ¶50,516 (Fed. Cir., 2001).

DEFINITION OF AN AFFILIATED GROUP

REQUIREMENTS

STOCK OWNERSHIP REQUIREMENT. Only an affiliated group of corporations can elect to file a consolidated return. Section 1504(a) outlines the stock ownership requirements that must be satisfied, as follows:

▶ A parent corporation must directly own stock[4] having at least 80% of the total voting power of all classes of stock entitled to vote and at least 80% of the total value of all outstanding stock in at least one includible corporation.

▶ For *each* other corporation eligible to be included in the affiliated group, stock having at least 80% of the total voting power of all classes of stock entitled to vote and at least 80% of the total value of all outstanding stock must be owned directly by the parent corporation and the other group members.

EXAMPLE C8-1 ▶ P Corporation owns 90% of S_1 Corporation's single class of stock and 30% of S_2 Corporation's single class of stock.[5] S_1 Corporation owns 50% of S_2's stock. The remainder of S_1 and S_2's stock is owned by 100 individual shareholders. P, S_1, and S_2 Corporations form the P-S_1-S_2 affiliated group because P owns more than the 80% of the S_1 stock needed to satisfy the direct ownership requirement and P and S_1 together own 80% (50% + 30%) of S_2's stock. The P-S_1-S_2 group can elect to file a consolidated tax return with P as the common parent corporation. ◀

EXAMPLE C8-2 ▶ Ted owns all the stock of Alpha and Beta Corporations. Alpha and Beta Corporations do not constitute an affiliated group, even though each corporation is directly owned by the same individual shareholder. Because a parent-subsidiary relationship is not present, they are ineligible to make a consolidated return election (see below). The Tax Strategy Tip on page C8-4 suggests ways to reform the corporations into an affiliated group. ◀

INCLUDIBLE CORPORATION REQUIREMENT. As few as two corporations may satisfy the affiliated group definition. In many of the nation's largest affiliated groups, however, the number of related corporations runs into the hundreds. Some of these corporate groups may have a number of subsidiary corporations that are not able to participate in the consolidated tax return election because they are not includible corporations under Sec. 1504(b). Because they are not includible corporations, their stock ownership cannot be counted toward satisfying the 80% stock ownership minimums, nor can their operating results be reported as part of the consolidated tax return. In general, each excluded corporation must file its own separate corporate tax return.

The following special tax status corporations are not includible corporations:

▶ Corporations exempt from tax under Sec. 501

▶ Insurance companies subject to tax under Sec. 801[6]

▶ Foreign corporations

▶ Corporations claiming the Puerto Rico and U.S. possessions tax credit

▶ Regulated investment companies

▶ Real estate investment trusts

▶ Domestic international sales corporations

▶ S corporations

If both the stock ownership and includible corporation requirements are satisfied, the subsidiary corporation must be included in the consolidated return election made by a parent corporation.

---

[4] The term *stock* does not include nonvoting preferred stock that is limited and preferred as to its dividends (and does not participate in corporate growth to any significant extent), has redemption or liquidation rights limited to its issue price (plus a reasonable redemption or liquidation premium), and is not convertible into another class of stock (Sec. 1504(a)(4)).

[5] All corporations referred to in the examples are includible domestic corporations unless otherwise indicated. See definition of *includible corporation* later in this chapter.

[6] Two or more Sec. 801 domestic life insurance companies may join together to form an affiliated group. If an affiliated group contains one or more Sec. 801 domestic life insurance companies, Sec. 1504(c)(2)(A) permits the parent corporation to elect to treat all such companies that have met the affiliated group stock ownership test for the five immediately preceding tax years as includible corporations. As recently as 2005, a bill was introduced into Congress to remove the limitation on life insurance companies being included in consolidated returns. This topic continues to be a political issue.

P Corporation owns all the single class of stock of S_1 and S_2 Corporations. S_1 Corporation owns all of S_3 Corporation's stock. S_2 Corporation owns all of S_4 Corporation's stock. P, S_1, and S_3 are domestic corporations. S_2 and S_4 are foreign corporations. P, S_1 and S_3 Corporations constitute the P-S_1-S_3 affiliated group with P as the common parent corporation. S_2 and S_4 are not members of the affiliated group because as foreign corporations they are not includible corporations. ◀

Under the check-the-box regulations, noncorporate entities can elect to be taxed as a C corporation. Partnerships and LLCs that elect to be taxed as a C corporation under the check-the-box regulations and that meet all the requirements for inclusion in an affiliated group come under the consolidated return rules of Secs. 1501–1504. Partnerships and LLCs that are wholly- or partially-owned by a member of an affiliated group are not considered members of the affiliated group unless the election is made to have the entity taxed as a C corporation. Partnerships and LLCs for which such an election is made are taxed like a corporate group member. Each group member investing in a partnership or LLC for which no C corporation election is made reports its ratable share of the income/loss earned by the conduit entity in its separate tax return. Such income/loss becomes part of the consolidated tax return of the affiliated group. Partnerships and LLCs for which no C corporation election is made are not subject to the various special consolidated tax return rules, such as those applying to intercompany sales.

COMPARISON WITH CONTROLLED GROUP DEFINITIONS

Three types of controlled groups—brother-sister groups, parent-subsidiary groups, and combined groups—were defined in Chapter C3. As illustrated in Example C8-2, the brother-sister category of controlled groups cannot elect to file a consolidated tax return because they do not satisfy the direct stock ownership requirement. However, most parent-subsidiary controlled groups and the parent-subsidiary portion of a combined controlled group can elect to file a consolidated tax return.

Only affiliated groups can elect to file consolidated tax returns. Four differences between the definitions of Sec. 1504 (affiliated group) and Sec. 1563 (parent-subsidiary controlled group) do exist. These differences include:

▶ A parent corporation must own at least 80% of total voting power *and* total value (instead of voting power **or** value) of a subsidiary's stock to include the subsidiary in the affiliated group.

▶ The stock attribution rules are not used in determining the inclusion of a subsidiary in an affiliated group but are used in determining the existence of a controlled group.

▶ The types of corporations excluded from an affiliated group are different from those that are excluded from a controlled group.

▶ The affiliated group definition is tested on each day of the tax year (instead of only on December 31 for a controlled group).

These differences can cause some members of a controlled group to be excluded from the affiliated group.

SHOULD A CONSOLIDATED RETURN BE FILED?

ADVANTAGES OF FILING A CONSOLIDATED TAX RETURN

Filing a consolidated tax return offers a number of advantages and disadvantages, some of the more important of which are discussed below. Some of the advantages that may be gained by filing a consolidated tax return include the following:

▶ The separate return losses of one affiliated group member may be offset against the taxable income of other group members in the current tax year. Such losses provide an immediate tax benefit by reducing the tax due on the other group member's income or eliminating the need to carry a loss back to a prior tax year or forward to a subsequent tax year.

▶ Capital losses of one group member may be offset against the capital gains of other group members in the current tax year. Again, this offset avoids carrying these losses back to a prior tax year or over to a subsequent tax year.

▶ Dividends paid from one group member to a second group member are "eliminated" in the consolidated tax return.

▶ The various credit and deduction limitations are computed on a consolidated basis. This treatment permits group members to use "excess" credits or "excess" deductions of other group members in the current tax year and avoid carrying them back to a prior tax year or forward to a subsequent tax year.

▶ Gains on intercompany transactions are deferred until a subsequent event occurs that causes the profit or gain to be included in the consolidated return.

▶ Calculation of the alternative minimum tax (AMT) takes place on a consolidated basis (rather than for each group member) and may reduce the negative effects of tax preference items and adjustments. This treatment may eliminate the need for the affiliated group as a whole to pay an AMT liability. On the other hand, the affiliated group is limited to a single $40,000 AMT exemption.

KEY POINT

The elimination of intercompany dividends is an advantage of filing consolidated tax returns. However, even if a consolidated tax return is not filed, the owning member should be eligible for a 100% dividends-received deduction.

DISADVANTAGES OF FILING A CONSOLIDATED TAX RETURN

Some disadvantages of filing a consolidated tax return include the following:

▶ A consolidated return election is binding on all subsequent tax years unless the IRS grants the group permission to discontinue filing a consolidated return or the affiliated group is terminated.

▶ All group members must use the same taxable year.

▶ Gains, losses, and deductions on intercompany transactions are deferred until a subsequent event occurs that causes the gain, loss, or deduction to be included in the consolidated tax return.[7]

▶ Operating losses and capital losses of group members may reduce or eliminate the ability of profitable group members to take advantage of credits or deductions by lowering the applicable credit or deduction limitation for the affiliated group.

▶ Additional administrative costs may be incurred in maintaining the necessary records to account for deferred intercompany transactions and the special loss limitations, although some savings may occur by filing a single return and filing all tax returns at the same time.

ADDITIONAL COMMENT

One disadvantage of filing a consolidated tax return that should be apparent after going through this chapter is the added record-keeping costs necessary to file a consolidated tax return.

No general rule can be applied to determine whether an affiliated group should elect to file a consolidated tax return. Each group should examine the long- and short-term advantages and disadvantages of filing a consolidated tax return before making a decision.

CONSOLIDATED TAXABLE INCOME

OBJECTIVE 3

Calculate consolidated taxable income for an affiliated group

The heart of the computation of the consolidated federal income tax liability is the calculation of **consolidated taxable income**. The calculation of consolidated taxable income is divided into the following five steps. An overview of the five-step consolidated taxable income calculation is presented in Table C8-1.

STEP 1. The starting point is the determination of each member's taxable income. The amount of a group member's taxable income is determined as if the group member were filing a separate tax return.

[7] The deferral of losses and deductions in a consolidated tax return is less of a disadvantage now that related-party loss and deduction rules also apply to controlled groups in Sec. 267.

**TYPICAL
MISCONCEPTION**

This table illustrates that the filing of a consolidated tax return instead of separate tax returns is clearly not easier from a compliance point of view.

▼ **TABLE C8-1**

Consolidated Taxable Income Calculation

Step 1: Compute each group member's taxable income (or loss) based on the member's own accounting methods as if the corporation were filing its own separate tax return.

Step 2: Adjust each group member's taxable income as follows:
1. Gains and losses on certain intercompany transactions are deferred. If a restoration event occurs during the year, previously deferred gains and losses are included in the calculation.
2. An inventory adjustment may be required.
3. Dividends received by a group member from another group member are excluded from the recipient's gross income.
4. An adjustment for an excess loss (negative investment basis) account of an affiliate may be required.
5. Built-in deductions may be deferred.

Step 3: The following gains, losses, and deductions are removed from each member's taxable income because they must be computed on a consolidated basis:
1. Net operating loss (NOL) deductions
2. Capital gains and losses
3. Section 1231 gains and losses (including net casualty gain)
4. Charitable contribution deductions
5. Dividends-received deductions
6. Percentage depletion deductions
7. The U.S. production activities deduction

The result of making the adjustments to a member's taxable income in Steps 2 and 3 is the member's separate taxable income.

Step 4: Combine the members' separate taxable income amounts. This amount is called the group's combined taxable income.

Step 5: Adjust the group's combined taxable income for the following items that are reported on a consolidated basis:
1. Deduct the consolidated Sec. 1231 net loss.
2. Deduct the consolidated net casualty loss.
3. Add the consolidated capital gain net income (taking into account capital loss carrybacks and carryovers and Sec. 1231 gains).
4. Deduct the consolidated charitable contribution deduction.
5. Deduct the consolidated percentage depletion deduction.
6. Deduct the consolidated NOL deduction (taking into account any allowable NOL carryovers and carrybacks).
7. Deduct the consolidated dividends-received deductions.
8. Deduct the consolidated U.S. production activities deduction.

Consolidated taxable income (or consolidated NOL)

STEP 2. Once each group member's taxable income has been determined, a series of adjustments (e.g., deferral of gain on certain intercompany transactions) must be made to take into account the special treatment that certain transactions receive in consolidated returns.

STEP 3. Any income, loss, or deduction items that must be reported on a consolidated basis are removed from the taxable income calculation. The resulting amounts are each group member's **separate taxable income.**

STEP 4. The separate taxable income amounts of the individual group members are aggregated into a **combined taxable income** amount.

STEP 5. Each of the tax attributes stated on a consolidated basis (which were removed in Step 3) are added to or subtracted from the combined taxable income amount. The resulting amount is the affiliated group's consolidated taxable income.[8]

---

[8] Reg. Sec. 1.1502-12.

Consolidated taxable income is subject to the corporate tax rates of Sec. 11 to determine the consolidated regular tax liability. This amount may be increased if the affiliated group is found to owe an additional amount under the corporate AMT, one of the other special tax levies, or as the result of recapturing previously claimed tax credits. Any tax credits and estimated tax payments are subtracted from the regular tax liability to determine the taxes owed when the consolidated tax return is filed. A sample consolidated tax return worksheet is included in Appendix B, which illustrates the consolidated taxable income calculation.

INCOME INCLUDED IN THE CONSOLIDATED TAX RETURN

KEY POINT

Two basic rules exist for determining what income must be included in a consolidated tax return: common parent's income for the entire tax year and a subsidiary's income only for the time period the subsidiary is a member of the consolidated group.

A consolidated tax return includes the parent corporation's income for its entire tax year, except for any portion of the year that it was a member of another affiliated group that filed a consolidated tax return. A subsidiary corporation's income is included in the consolidated tax return only for the portion of the affiliated group's tax year for which it was a group member. When a corporation is a member of an affiliated group for only a portion of its tax year, the member's income for the remainder of its tax year is included in a separate tax return or the consolidated tax return of another affiliated group.[9]

A corporation that becomes or ceases to be a group member during a consolidated return year[10] changes its status at the end of the day on which such change occurs (i.e., the change date). Its tax year ends for federal income tax purposes at the end of the change date. Transactions that occur on the change date that are allocable to the portion of the day after the event resulting in the change (e.g., a stock sale or merger) are accounted for by the group member (and all related parties) as having occurred on the next day.[11]

EXAMPLE C8-4 ▶ P and S Corporations file separate tax returns for calendar year 2006. At the close of business on April 30, 2007, P Corporation acquires all of S Corporation's stock. If the P-S affiliated group files a consolidated tax return for 2007, P's income is included in the consolidated tax return for all of 2007, and S's income is included only for the period May 1 through December 31, 2007. S Corporation must file a separate tax return to report its income for the pre-affiliation period January 1 through April 30, 2007. ◀

WHAT WOULD YOU DO IN THIS SITUATION?

The P-S-T affiliated group has filed consolidated tax returns using the calendar year as its tax year for many years. On October 1, P Corporation created a new subsidiary, X Corporation, with a $10,000 initial capital contribution, and X Corporation issued its stock to P Corporation. A bank account was opened when X Corporation was created. A federal tax identification number was also applied for and obtained. X did not conduct any business activities before year-end. Its only income was $125 in interest earned on the initial capital contribution. Due to a lack of communication or an oversight, P's tax department did not include X Corporation in the affiliated group's current year consolidated tax return.

Your CPA firm has provided federal tax advice to P Corporation for a number of years, but your client's tax department has handled the federal tax return filings. Most of your work for P Corporation has been in the state and local taxation area and on special federal tax assignments. You were aware of the affiliated group's future business plans for creating X Corporation. Will the oversight with respect to X Corporation disqualify the affiliated group from filing a consolidated tax return for the current year and all future years? Can you avoid having to file a federal tax return for X Corporation because of the small amount of interest income the corporation earned? Does the failure to include X Corporation in this year's consolidated tax return prevent it from being included in future years? What advice can you give your client about needing to include X Corporation in the consolidated tax return?

---

[9] Reg. Sec. 1.1502-76(b)(1)(i). See Rev. Proc. 2002-37, 2002-1 C.B. 1030, for the procedures governing automatic approval for a company to change its annual accounting period under Sec. 442 and related Treasury Regulations.
[10] A **consolidated return year** is defined by Reg. Sec. 1.1502-1(d) as a tax year for which a consolidated return is filed or is required to be filed by the affili-

ated group. A **separate return year** is defined by Reg. Sec. 1.1502-1(e) as a tax year for which a corporation files a separate return or joins in the filing of a consolidated tax return with a different affiliated group.
[11] Reg. Sec. 1.1502-76(b)(1)(ii).

EXAMPLE C8-5 ▶ P and S Corporations have filed consolidated tax returns for a number of years. At the close of business on April 30, 2007, P sells all of its S stock to Peter Gabriel. P and S file a consolidated tax return including P's income for all 12 months of 2007, and S's income for January 1 through April 30, 2007. S files a separate tax return for May 1 through December 31, 2007. ◀

Tax returns for the years that end and begin with a corporation becoming or ceasing to be a member of an affiliated group are separate return years. The separate returns, in general, are short period returns (i.e., for applying the MACRS rules) but do not require annualization of the tax liability or estimated tax calculations when a corporation joins an affiliated group. The short period return is a full tax year for purposes of NOL and other attribute carryovers. Allocation of income between the consolidated tax return and a member's separate return year takes place according to the accounting methods used by each individual corporation. If this allocation cannot be readily determined, allocation of items included in each tax return (other than ones considered below to be extraordinary) can be based on the relative number of days of the original tax year included in each tax year. A ratable allocation of income, expense, gain, loss, and credit items between periods is permitted if the new or departing group member is not required to change its annual accounting period or accounting method as a result of its change in status, and an irrevocable election is made by the group member and the parent corporation of the affected group. Extraordinary items are allocated to the day they are reported using the group member's accounting methods. Extraordinary items include but are not limited to gains or losses arising from the disposition or abandonment of capital assets, Sec. 1231 property, or inventory; NOL carrybacks or carryovers; settlements of a tort or third-party liability; and compensation-related deductions arising from the group member's change in status (e.g., bonuses, severance pay, and option cancellation payments).[12]

AFFILIATED GROUP ELECTIONS

TAX YEARS. An affiliated group's consolidated tax return must be filed using the parent corporation's tax year. Beginning with the initial consolidated return year for which it is includible in the consolidated tax return, each subsidiary corporation must adopt the parent corporation's tax year. The requirement for a common tax year applies to affiliated group members both when an initial consolidated tax return is being filed and when the stock of a new member is acquired.[13]

EXAMPLE C8-6 ▶

SELF-STUDY QUESTION

When a subsidiary leaves an affiliated group that has filed consolidated tax returns, may it select any year-end it wishes?

ANSWER

Without permission from the IRS to do otherwise, a subsidiary must retain the group's year-end (if filing a separate tax return) or adopt the year-end of the acquiring consolidated group, if applicable.

P and S Corporations filed separate tax returns for 2005. P Corporation uses a calendar year as its tax year. S Corporation uses a fiscal year ending June 30 as its tax year. At the close of business on April 30, 2006, P Corporation acquires all of S Corporation's stock. If the P-S affiliated group files a consolidated tax return for 2006, S must change its tax year so that it ends on December 31. S must file a short-period tax return for the period July 1, 2005, through April 30, 2006. P's income for all of 2006 and S's income for the period May 1, 2006, through December 31, 2006, are included in the initial consolidated tax return. ◀

METHODS OF ACCOUNTING. Unless the IRS grants permission for a change in accounting method, the accounting methods used by each group member are determined by using the same rules as if the member were filing a separate tax return.[14] This requirement applies when a consolidated tax return election is made or a new corporation joins an existing affiliated group. Thus, one group member may use the cash method of accounting and another group member may use the accrual method of accounting during a consolidated return year. The possibility of finding a mixture of cash and accrual method corporations in an affiliated group is limited because of the Sec. 448 restrictions on the use of the cash method of accounting by C corporations described in Chapter C3.

---

[12] Reg. Sec. 1.1502-76(b)(2).
[13] Reg. Sec. 1.1502-76(a).

[14] Reg. Sec. 1.1502-17(a).

TERMINATION OF THE AFFILIATED GROUP

An affiliated group that elects to file a consolidated tax return must continue to file on a consolidated basis as long as the affiliated group exists unless the IRS grants permission for it to do otherwise. An affiliated group exists as long as the parent corporation and at least one subsidiary corporation remain affiliated. It does not matter whether the parent corporation owns the *same* subsidiary throughout the entire tax year or even whether the continuing subsidiary existed at the beginning of the year.

EXAMPLE C8-7 ▶ P and S_1 Corporations have filed a consolidated tax return for several calendar years. At the close of business on August 31 of the current year, P purchases all of S_2 Corporation's stock. S_2 Corporation uses the calendar year as its tax year. At the close of business on September 30, P sells its entire holding of S_1 stock. The affiliated group, with P as the parent corporation, must file a consolidated tax return for the current year because P remained the parent corporation of at least one subsidiary corporation (first S_1, later S_2) at all times during the year.

If the order of the purchase and sale transactions were reversed, the affiliated group would have been terminated following the sale of the S_1 stock (on August 31). A new affiliated group would have been created with the purchase of the S_2 stock (on October 1). The creation of the new affiliated group would require a new consolidated return election. If such an election were made, the current year consolidated return for the P-S_2 affiliated group would contain the income of P and S_2 Corporations from October 1 through December 31. The original P-S_1 affiliated group must file a consolidated tax return including their operating results from January 1 through September 30 of the current year. ◀

EXAMPLE C8-8 ▶ P and S Corporations have filed a consolidated tax return for several calendar years. At the close of business on August 31 of the current year, P Corporation sells its entire holding of S stock to Arthur. P's income is included in the current year consolidated tax return for the entire year. S's income is included only for the period January 1 through August 31. S also must file a separate tax return to report its income for the period September 1 through December 31 of the current year. ◀

GOOD CAUSE REQUEST TO DISCONTINUE STATUS. Permission to discontinue filing a consolidated tax return sometimes is granted by the IRS in response to a "good cause" request initiated by the taxpayer. A good cause reason for discontinuing the consolidated tax return election includes a substantial adverse effect on the consolidated tax liability for the tax year (relative to what the aggregate tax liability would be if the group members filed separate tax returns) originating from amendments to the IRC or Treasury Regulations having effective dates in the tax year in question.[15]

EFFECTS ON FORMER MEMBERS. The termination of an affiliated group affects its former members in several ways, two of which are examined in subsequent sections of this chapter.

▶ Any gains and losses that have been deferred on intercompany transactions (e.g., intercompany profits on sales of inventory between group members) may have to be recognized.

▶ Consolidated tax attributes (such as NOL, capital loss, tax credit, and charitable contribution carryovers) must be allocated among the former group members.

In addition, disaffiliation of a corporation from an affiliated group prevents the corporation from being included in a consolidated return with the same affiliated group until five years after the beginning of its first tax year in which it ceased to be a group member. The IRS can waive the five-year requirement and permit the departing group member to join in a consolidated return at an earlier date.

Special rules apply when a corporation is included in, or is required to be included in, a consolidated tax return filed by an affiliated group for a tax year and the corporation ceases to be a member of the affiliated group in the tax year. Under Sec. 1504(a)(3), the

---

[15] Reg. Sec. 1.1502-75(c).

corporation cannot be included in a consolidated tax return filed by the affiliated group, or an affiliated group having the same common parent corporation, for a 60-month period beginning after the first tax year in which the corporation ceased to be a member. The IRS has issued procedures for granting certain taxpayers an automatic waiver of the 60-month period before reconsolidation of returns is otherwise possible.[16]

COMPUTATION OF THE AFFILIATED GROUP'S TAX LIABILITY

OBJECTIVE 4

Calculate the consolidated regular tax liability for an affiliated group

REGULAR TAX LIABILITY

The affiliated group determines its consolidated regular income tax liability by applying the corporate tax rates found in Sec. 11 to the group's consolidated taxable income. Thus, the aggregate group obtains the benefit of the 15% tax rate for the first $50,000 of consolidated taxable income and the 25% tax rate for the next $25,000 of consolidated taxable income. If consolidated taxable income exceeds $100,000, however, a 5% surtax applies until consolidated taxable income reaches $335,000, at which point the benefits of the 15% and 25% tax brackets are completely recaptured.[17]

The result for consolidated tax returns has some similarities to the total tax liability for a controlled group (see Chapter C3). Section 1561 limits a controlled group of corporations to an aggregate of $50,000 for which the 15% tax rate applies and an aggregate of $25,000 for which the 25% tax rate applies. In the controlled group situation, however, each corporation computes its separate tax liability with the benefits of the reduced rates allocated among the members of the group.

OBJECTIVE 5

Calculate the consolidated AMT liability for an affiliated group

CORPORATE ALTERNATIVE MINIMUM TAX LIABILITY

The corporate alternative minimum tax (AMT) liability is determined on a consolidated basis for all group members. The consolidated AMT is determined under an approach that generally parallels the determination of the group's consolidated taxable income. The starting point for the calculation is consolidated taxable income. The AMT procedures and definitions of Secs. 55-59 apply in determining consolidated AMT. Consolidated alternative minimum taxable income (AMTI) is computed using the rules of Reg. Sec. 1.1502-55(b). These Treasury Regulations require the deferral and restoration of AMT items. Consolidated AMTI equals consolidated preadjustment AMTI plus or minus 75% of the difference between consolidated adjusted current earnings (ACE) and consolidated preadjustment AMTI and decreased by the consolidated alternative tax NOL.[18] The negative ACE adjustment limitation is determined on a consolidated basis and requires the tracking of separate return and consolidated return positive and negative ACE adjustments. AMTI also must be adjusted for the difference (if any) between the U.S. production activities deduction for AMT purposes and the deduction for consolidated taxable income purposes. (See Chapter C5 for a discussion of this adjustment.)

The consolidated AMT is the excess of the consolidated tentative minimum tax (TMT) over the consolidated regular tax liability for the tax year. The consolidated TMT amount is determined by first computing 20% of the excess of consolidated AMTI over a consolidated statutory exemption amount. This amount is reduced by the consolidated AMT foreign tax credit amount to arrive at the consolidated TMT. Any excess of the consolidated TMT over the consolidated regular tax must be paid by the affiliated group and is available in future years as a minimum tax credit.

KEY POINT

Determining the alternative minimum tax for corporations is discussed in Chapter C5. Determining the alternative minimum tax for a consolidated group merely adds to the complexity of this already difficult computation.

---

[16] Rev. Proc. 2002-32, 2002-1 C.B. 959.
[17] A similar recapture of the tax savings produced by the 34% corporate tax rate is applicable to the next $9,925,000 of taxable income and also may apply when taxable income is between $15 million and $18,333,333 (see Chapter C3).

[18] Reg. Secs. 1.1502-55(h)(4) and (i).

A group's consolidated minimum tax credit (MTC) equals the sum of the consolidated return year MTCs and any prior separate return year MTCs. Use of the consolidated minimum tax credit is limited to the excess (if any) of the modified consolidated regular tax over the consolidated TMT for the year. Modified consolidated regular tax equals the consolidated regular tax amount reduced by any credits allowable for the AMT (other than the MTC).[19]

Affiliated groups of corporations filing a consolidated tax return, like corporations filing separate tax returns, are eligible for the small corporation exemption from the corporate alternative minimum tax. The $5 million and $7.5 million gross receipts ceilings on the small corporation AMT exemption apply to the entire affiliated group.

CONSOLIDATED TAX CREDITS

The affiliated group can claim all tax credits available to corporate taxpayers. The discussion that follows examines the two major credits claimed by most affiliated groups—the general business credit and the foreign tax credit.

GENERAL BUSINESS CREDIT. The affiliated group's general business credit is determined on a consolidated basis, with all of the group members' separate component credit amounts being combined into a single amount for the affiliated group. For these credits, an affiliated group is limited to the excess of the affiliated group's net income tax over the greater of (1) the affiliated group's tentative minimum tax for the year or (2) 25% of the affiliated group's net regular tax liability for the year exceeding $25,000.[20] Any unused general business tax credits may be carried back one year and forward 20 years under Sec. 39(a) for tax years beginning after August 6, 1997. (See Chapter C3 for more detailed coverage of the tax credit limitation.)

A profitable group member may find that use of the consolidated tax liability as the basis for the general business credit limitation may result in a reduced credit amount because the losses of other group members are used to offset its separate taxable income. An unprofitable member, however, may find its general business credit limitation increased by the separate taxable income of another member, so that credits that otherwise would have been carried back or forward if separate returns were filed may be used currently by the group.

EXAMPLE C8-9 ▶ The P-S affiliated group files a consolidated tax return for the current year. P and S Corporations contribute separate taxable income (or loss) amounts of $300,000 and ($100,000), respectively, to the group's $200,000 consolidated taxable income. P and S can tentatively claim a $40,000 research credit and a $10,000 targeted jobs credit, or a tentative $50,000 consolidated general business credit. The P-S group's regular tax liability is $61,250. The P-S group's tentative minimum tax liability (assuming no differences between AMTI and taxable income other than the statutory exemption) is $34,500.[21] The group's general business credit limitation is calculated as follows:

Regular tax		$61,250
Plus: Alternative minimum tax		–0–
Minus: Credits allowed under Secs. 21-30A		–0–
Net income tax		$61,250
Minus: Greater of:		
(1) 25% of group's net regular tax liability exceeding $25,000 [0.25 × ($61,250 − $25,000)]	$ 9,062	
(2) Group's tentative minimum tax for the year	34,500	(34,500)
General business credit limitation		$26,750

The $23,250 ($50,000 tentative credit − $26,750 credit limitation) of unused general business credits can be carried back one year and forward 20 years. ◀

---

[19] Reg. Sec. 1.1502-55(h)(4)(iii)(B)(1).
[20] Sec. 38(c).

[21] $200,000 AMTI − {$40,000 statutory exemption − [0.25 × ($200,000 AMTI − $150,000 threshold)]} × 0.20 = $34,500.

FOREIGN TAX CREDIT. An affiliated group's foreign tax credit for a consolidated return year is determined on a consolidated basis. The parent corporation makes the election to claim either a deduction or a credit for the group's foreign taxes. If the credit is chosen, the affiliated group's foreign tax credit limitation is computed by taking into account the group's income from U.S. and foreign sources, the consolidated taxable income, and the consolidated regular and alternative minimum tax amounts in the manner described in Chapter C16.

INTERCOMPANY TRANSACTIONS

An **intercompany transaction** is defined as a transaction between corporations that are members of the same affiliated group immediately after the transaction.[22] Intercompany transactions include:

▶ Sales, exchanges, contributions, or other transfers of property from one group member to a second group member whether or not the gain or loss is recognized.

▶ The performance of services by one group member for a second group member, and the second member's payment or accrual of its expenditure.

▶ The licensing of technology, renting of property, or lending of money by one group member, and the second member's payment or accrual of its expenditure.

▶ Payment of a dividend distribution by a subsidiary corporation to its parent corporation in connection with the parent's investment in the subsidiary's stock.

For purposes of our discussion, we will divide our coverage into two categories (1) property acquired in intercompany transactions, and (2) **other intercompany transactions**.

PROPERTY TRANSACTIONS

GENERAL RULE. Gains and losses on intercompany transactions receive special treatment under the consolidated return Treasury Regulations. In general, gains and losses on intercompany transactions involving the sale or exchange of property between two group members (also known as an intercompany item) are recognized in calculating the group member's separate taxable income. Exceptions to this general rule include intercompany transactions that qualify for nonrecognition treatment under Secs. 351 (corporate formation transaction) and 1031 (like-kind exchange). The recognized gain/loss is deferred under the consolidated tax return regulations and therefore not included in determining consolidated taxable income until a subsequent event occurs that requires the recognition of income, gain, deduction or loss (also known as a corresponding item) by the buyer (see Step 2 in Table C8-1). Events that can trigger the recognition of an intercompany item include:

▶ The claiming of a depletion, depreciation, or amortization deduction with respect to a property acquired in an intercompany transaction.

▶ Amortization of services, or any other nonproperty asset, acquired by a group member in an intercompany transaction that has previously been capitalized.

▶ The disposition outside the affiliated group of a property acquired in an intercompany transaction.

▶ The departure from an affiliated group of the group member that either sells or owns a property that is acquired in an intercompany transaction.

▶ The first day of a separate return year for the parent corporation.

In general, buyers and sellers engaging in an intercompany transaction are treated as separate entities.[23] A sale of property by one group member to a second group member is reported on the selling and buying corporations' books using the same basic rules that would apply if the sale involved two unrelated parties. Of course, different rules would be

---

[22] Reg. Sec. 1.1502-13(b)(1)(i).   [23] Reg. Sec. 1.1502-13(a)(2).

used if the property were acquired in a like-kind exchange, or corporate formation transaction where part or all of the realized gain or loss is not recognized. The basic rules for reporting an intercompany property transaction are presented below.

AMOUNT AND CHARACTER OF THE INTERCOMPANY GAIN OR LOSS. At the time of the transaction, the amount and character of the intercompany gain or loss are determined as if the transaction had occurred in a separate return year.

BASIS AND HOLDING PERIOD. The basis and holding period for a property acquired in an intercompany transaction are determined as if the acquisition occurred in a separate return year. Thus, the adjusted basis for an asset is the property's acquisition cost if the property is purchased by the buying member for cash, or cash and a debt obligation, from the selling member. The holding period for such property begins on the day after the acquisition date.

EXAMPLE C8-10 ▶ S (Seller) and B (Buyer) Corporations have filed consolidated tax returns for several years, with S being the common parent of the affiliated group.[24] S and B Corporations both use the accrual method of accounting. S acquired a block of marketable securities in 1999, which have been held as a capital asset since that date. The adjusted basis for the securities is $120,000. S sells the marketable securities to B for $200,000 cash on August 8, 2006. This gain is determined on a separate entity basis and is reported in S's separate tax return calculation. S's deferred intercompany capital gain is $80,000 ($200,000 − $120,000). The $80,000 deferred gain is not reported in the 2006 consolidated tax return. An adjustment is made to remove the deferred gain from consolidated taxable income (as illustrated in Step 2 of Table C8-1). B's basis for the securities is $200,000. Its holding period for determining the character of the gain or loss on a subsequent sale of the securities begins with August 9, 2006. S recognizes no gain until one of the events described above that produces a corresponding item for B occurs. At that time, part or all of the deferred gain will be included in the consolidated return (but not S's separate tax return calculation). ◀

A sample completed consolidated tax return (Form 1120) and worksheet appears in Appendix B. The worksheet shows the reporting of an intercompany sale of inventory (see worksheet footnote 1) followed by the sale of the inventory outside the affiliated group. The use of the worksheet to report intercompany transactions will be further developed within the examples that follow.

The intercompany transaction rules are based on two concepts—intercompany items and corresponding items. An **intercompany item** is the Seller's income, gain, deduction, or loss from an intercompany transaction.[25] A **corresponding item** is the Buyer's income, gain, deduction, or loss from an intercompany transaction, or from property acquired in an intercompany transaction.[26]

MATCHING AND ACCELERATION RULES. Two principles are used to implement the single entity approach to reporting intercompany transactions. They are the matching rule and the acceleration rule. The matching rule generally treats the Seller and Buyer as divisions of a single corporation for purposes of taking into account the intercompany items. In general, a transfer of an asset between two divisions is not considered a taxable event. A taxable event can occur when, for example, a division sells an asset to a third party. The acceleration rule provides a series of exceptions to the general rule for taking items into account if the treatment of the Seller and Buyer as divisions within a single entity cannot be achieved (e.g., if either S or B leaves the group and becomes a nonmember).

The intercompany transaction rules override the basic accounting method elections used by the seller. Assume that S's sale to B in Example C8-10 was instead made for a series of notes payable in equal amounts over a five-year period. Normally, the Sec. 453 installment sale rules would require the $80,000 gain to be reported as the collections

---

[24] S and B Corporations are used for the two members of the consolidated group, instead of our usual P and S Corporations, to make it easier to remember which group member is the seller (S) and which group member is the buyer (B).

[25] Reg. Sec. 1.1502-13(b)(2)(i).
[26] Reg. Sec. 1.1502-13(b)(3)(i).

were made over the five-year period. Instead, the $80,000 gain is an intercompany item which, in general, is not reported until a corresponding item is reported by the Buyer.[27]

INTERCOMPANY ITEM AMOUNT. When determining the intercompany item amount, all the Seller's direct and indirect costs related to the sale or the providing of services are included. As a result, the Uniform Capitalization rules of Sec. 263A apply in determining (1) the basis of inventory sold, (2) an employee's wages and other related costs included in determining the intercompany item when services are performed, and (3) depreciation and other direct expenses included in determining the intercompany item when property is rented.[28]

CORRESPONDING ITEM AMOUNT. Corresponding items are the Buyer's income, gain, deduction, and loss from an intercompany transaction, or from property acquired in an intercompany transaction.[29] Three corresponding items are illustrated in the text that follows:

▶ When a Buyer acquires property from a Seller and sells it to a nonmember of the affiliated group, the Buyer's gain or loss from the sale to the nonmember is a corresponding gain or loss.

▶ When a Buyer acquires property from a Seller and makes an installment sale of the property to a nonmember of the affiliated group, the Buyer's gain from the installment sale is a corresponding gain or loss.

▶ When a Buyer acquires depreciable property from a Seller, the Buyer's depreciation deductions are corresponding deductions.

Buyer's corresponding items also include disallowed losses and expenses or excluded income. Examples of such items include tax-exempt income, expenses related to the production of tax-exempt income and disallowed under Sec. 265, and losses disallowed on the distribution of appreciated property as a dividend under Sec. 311(a).[30]

In Example C8-11 below, the corresponding item is B's $50,000 gain reported on its sale of the securities. The Buyer (B) reports its corresponding item using its regular accounting method. The Seller (S) reports its intercompany item (i.e., the deferred gain) at the same time. In our example, Treasury Regulations have matched the intercompany item and the corresponding item to affect consolidated taxable income simultaneously as if the two corporations were divisions of one corporation. Although the regulations contain an acceleration rule, which requires the intercompany item and the corresponding item to be taken into account when matching can no longer produce a single entity effect, this exception to the matching rule is not needed since the Seller and Buyer remained members of the affiliated group at the time of the Buyer's sale to the unrelated party.

The Seller and Buyer report their individual parts of an intercompany transaction as if they were separate entities when calculating their separate return taxable income. For this purpose, the Seller and Buyer are treated as engaging in their actual transaction and owning any actual property involved in the transaction. The intercompany transaction rules require a recomputation of the affiliated group's gain or loss at the time a corresponding item is reported. When making the recomputation of the affiliated group's gain or loss, the Buyer takes the Seller's basis for the securities instead of the step-up in basis that normally occurs with cash sales between two related or unrelated corporations.[31]

REPORTING SELECTED INTERCOMPANY TRANSACTIONS. The reporting of the intercompany securities transaction originally illustrated in Example C8-10 is presented below in four different situations.

EXAMPLE C8-11 ▶ **Buyer sells securities to a third party at a profit.** Assume the same facts as in Example C8-10 except B sells the securities to a third party for $250,000 in 2008. If S and B are divisions of a single corporation and the sale was a transfer between the divisions, B would assume S's $120,000

---

[27] Reg. Sec. 1.1502-13(a)(3)(i).
[28] Reg. Sec. 1.1502-13(b)(2)(ii).
[29] Reg. Sec. 1.1502-13(b)(3)(i).

[30] Reg. Sec. 1.1502-13(b)(3)(ii).
[31] Reg. Sec. 1.1502-13(c)(3).

basis for the securities, and the affiliated group will report a $130,000 ($250,000 proceeds − $120,000 basis) recomputed capital gain in 2008. B reports $50,000 of this gain. B's $50,000 gain is reported in its separate taxable income calculation. Since the affiliated group reported none of the $80,000 deferred gain in prior years, all the $80,000 ($130,000 − $50,000) difference between the affiliated group's total gain and B's separate taxable income gain is reported as an adjustment on the consolidated return worksheet (as illustrated in Step 2 of Table C8-1). ◄

The reporting of the two sales made by S and B in Examples C8-10 and C8-11 can be presented in the worksheet format used in the completed consolidated tax return contained in Appendix B (see worksheet below). Each transaction is initially reported in the selling (S) corporation's separate tax return column. The adjustment for the deferred gain on S's sale of the securities to B in Example C8-10 appears as a negative entry in the adjustments and eliminations column of the worksheet. The adjustment removes the $80,000 profit earned on the intercompany sale from the consolidated tax return. The adjustment for the restoration of the deferred gain when B sells the securities outside the affiliated group in Example C8-11 is reported as a positive entry in the adjustments and eliminations column of the worksheet. The adjustment increases the profit resulting from B's sale of the securities to a third party included in the consolidated tax return from $50,000 to $130,000.

Transaction	Consolidated Taxable Income	Adjustments & Eliminations	S Corporation's Tax Return	B Corporation's Tax Return
S's sale to B in 2006	$ −0−	($80,000)	$80,000	
B's sale to a third party in 2008	130,000	80,000		$50,000
Total	$130,000	$ −0−	$80,000	$50,000

EXAMPLE C8-12 ▶ **Buyer sells securities to a third party at a loss.**[32] Assume the same facts as in Example C8-10 except the securities were instead sold by B to a third party for $190,000. The recomputed gain is $70,000 ($190,000 − $120,000). B reports a $10,000 ($190,000 − $200,000 adjusted basis) capital loss in 2008. B's $10,000 capital loss is reported in its separate taxable income calculation. Since the affiliated group reported none of the $80,000 deferred gain in prior years, all of the $80,000 ($70,000 + $10,000) difference between the affiliated group's total gain and B's separate taxable income loss is reported as an adjustment on the consolidated return worksheet. ◄

The separate return reporting of the transaction by S is the same as in Examples C8-10 and C8-11. The $50,000 capital gain that B reported when it sold the securities to a third party in Example C8-10 becomes a $10,000 capital loss because the sales price was reduced from $250,000 to $190,000. Restoration of S's $80,000 deferred gain causes the $10,000 separate return capital loss reported by B to become a $70,000 consolidated capital gain in 2008. The worksheet is as follows:

Transaction	Consolidated Taxable Income	Adjustments & Eliminations	S Corporation's Tax Return	B Corporation's Tax Return
S's sale to B in 2006	$ −0−	($80,000)	$80,000	
B's sale to a third party in 2008	70,000	80,000		($10,000)
Total	$70,000	$ −0−	$80,000	($10,000)

EXAMPLE C8-13 ▶ **Buyer sells inventory to a third party at a profit.** Assume the same facts as in Example C8-10 except the securities were instead inventory in B's hands prior to their sale for $250,000. Although S held the securities as a capital asset, the character of the reported gain is based on the character of the asset at the time it was sold by B. Both B's $80,000 gain and S's $50,000 gain

---

[32] Section 267(f)(2) requires a realized loss to be deferred when a sale of property occurs between members of a controlled group. Regulation Sec. 1.267(f)-1 provides special rules for property sales involving members of a controlled group that parallel the intercompany transaction rules for consoli- dated groups. These rules apply to the members of an affiliated group who sell property to a member of its controlled group that is unable to join in the consolidated return election. A discussion of these rules is beyond the scope of this introductory text.

are ordinary income. The consolidated return worksheet is the same as for Example C8-11 except the income character changes.   ◄

EXAMPLE C8-14 ►

TYPICAL MISCONCEPTION

Even though the restoration event illustrated in Example C8-14 is based on the receipt of installment obligations, remember that intercompany sales cannot be reported by the selling group member on the installment method.

Assume the same facts as in Example C8-10 except that B's $250,000 sale proceeds are from the sale of a noninventory item and are to be collected in two equal, annual installments starting in 2008. Interest at a rate acceptable to the IRS is charged on the unpaid balance. The recomputed gain and the individual group member's gains are the same as in Example C8-11. After selling the securities, B reports the transaction in its separate taxable income using the installment sale provisions of Sec. 453 applicable to nondealers. Likewise, the affiliated group does not report the entire amount of the deferred gain in 2008. Instead, the affiliated group reports the deferred gain as B collects the amounts due under the installment contract.

The following formula is used to determine the affiliated group's reported gain:

$$\frac{\text{Amount of the installment payment received}}{\text{Total contract price}} \times \frac{\text{Deferred}}{\text{intercompany gain}} = \frac{\text{Affiliated group's restored}}{\text{gain or loss}}$$

The affiliated group reports $40,000 of the deferred gain [($125,000 ÷ $250,000) × $80,000] in each 2008 and 2009 as an adjustment to determine consolidated taxable income. B reports its $50,000 gain in two installments of $25,000 each ($50,000 ÷ 2) in 2008 and 2009 plus reporting annually any interest income earned on the unpaid balance.   ◄

S's separate return reporting of the transaction in 2006 is the same as in Examples C8-10 through C8-12. S Corporation reports its $80,000 gain in its 2006 separate tax return. A negative $80,000 adjustment is made when preparing the 2006 consolidated tax return thereby resulting in no gain being included in consolidated taxable income. The $50,000 capital gain that B reported when it sold the securities to a third party in Example C8-10 is reported in its separate tax returns when the obligations are collected in 2008 and 2009. In summary, $25,000 of gain is recognized each year, $40,000 of the deferred gain is restored as a positive adjustment in preparing the 2008 and 2009 consolidated tax returns, and $65,000 of gain is included in consolidated taxable income in each 2008 and 2009.

Transaction	Consolidated Taxable Income	Adjustments & Eliminations	S Corporation's Tax Return	B Corporation's Tax Return
S's sale to B in 2006	$ –0–	($80,000)	$80,000	
B's sale to third party in 2008	–0–			$ –0–
B's collection of installment receivable in 2008	65,000	40,000		25,000
B's collection of installment receivable in 2009	65,000	40,000		25,000
Total	$130,000	$ –0–	$80,000	$50,000

DEPRECIATION OF RECOVERY PROPERTY BY THE BUYER. Recovery property sold between two group members in an intercompany transaction results in a continuation of the selling group member's recovery period and recovery method under the Sec. 168(i)(7) anti-churning rules to the extent the purchasing group member's basis equals or is less than the selling group member's adjusted basis. To the extent that the purchasing group member's basis exceeds the selling group member's basis, the excess is treated under Reg. Sec. 1.1502-13(c)(7) as a separate property acquired from an unrelated party. The purchasing party depreciates the step-up in basis as a new property and uses the appropriate MACRS depreciation method and recovery period. The purchaser's depreciation for the carryover portion of the basis is the same each year as the seller's depreciation would have been had the seller not sold the property. The amount of the intercompany gain attributable to the sale that the seller must report in any year (that is, the amount of the increased depreciation deduction to the group) is the amount of the depreciation deduction attributable to the purchaser's step-up in basis. This scenario is illustrated in the following example.

EXAMPLE C8-15 ▶ S and B Corporations form the S-B affiliated group. On July 1, 2006, S pays $10,000 to a non-member of the group for machinery that under the MACRS rules is five-year property. The machinery is not eligible for 50% additional depreciation because S acquired it after 2004. Thus, assuming no Sec. 179 election, S claims the following depreciation deductions:

Year and Type	Deduction
2006 regular depreciation	$2,000 ($10,000 × 0.20)
2007 regular depreciation	$3,200 ($10,000 × 0.32)

On January 3, 2008, S sells the machinery to B for $9,000. All the depreciation for 2008 is allocated to B. Under the MACRS rules, the purchaser is allocated the depreciation for the month of transfer when depreciable property is transferred between related parties.[33] S's $4,200 ($9,000 proceeds − $4,800 adjusted basis) Sec. 1245 gain is recognized ratably while B depreciates the asset.

KEY POINT

Depending on when an asset is placed in service and then sold in a deferred intercompany transaction, an asset can be divided into two pieces for depreciation purposes. These situations are covered by special anti-churning rules.

B is treated as continuing the MACRS depreciation on the $4,800 portion of the acquisition price that equals the carryover portion of S's adjusted basis for the machinery. The MACRS provisions also would apply to the $4,200 portion of the acquisition price that represents a step-up in basis (or gain portion of the basis) on B's books. B recovers the asset's $4,200 step-up in basis over five years under the MACRS rules. The amount of the capital recovery deductions claimed by B in its separate taxable income calculation and the intercompany gain or loss reported by the affiliated group as an adjustment to determine consolidated taxable income during B's holding period for the asset are as follows:[34]

ADDITIONAL COMMENT

The result of the depreciation restoration event is to synchronize the depreciation deductions on the stepped-up basis with the restoration of the intercompany gain. Notice that the net depreciation reported in the 2010 consolidated return of $1,152 ($1,958 − $806 restored gain) is the same amount that would have been reported had S never transferred the property.

Year		Depreciation on Carryover Basis	Depreciation on Step-Up in Basis	Total Depreciation	Restoration of Deferred Gain
2008	$10,000 × 0.1920	$1,920		$1,920	
	$4,200 × 0.2000		$ 840	840	$ 840
				$2,760	
2009	$10,000 × 0.1152	1,152		$1,152	
	$4,200 × 0.3200		1,344	1,344	1,344
				$2,496	
2010	$10,000 × 0.1152	1,152		$1,152	
	$4,200 × 0.1920		806	806	806
				$1,958	
2011	$10,000 × 0.0576	576		$ 576	
	$4,200 × 0.1152		484	484	484
				$1,060	
2012	$4,200 × 0.1152		484	484	484
2013	$4,200 × 0.0576		242	242	242
Total depreciation and restoration		$4,800	$4,200	$9,000	$4,200

S's reporting of the sale of the machine to B and B's depreciation of the machine in 2008 is illustrated in the following worksheet. No net gain is reported on the sale of the machine in 2008. The affiliated group reports net depreciation of $1,920 ($2,760 depreciation − $840 restored gain) on the machine in 2008.

---

[33] Reg. Secs. 1.168-5(b).
[34] Intercompany sales of property that will be depreciated in the purchasing group member's hands generally result in the recognition of ordinary income under Sec. 1239 because the selling and purchasing group members are usually also members of a controlled group and, therefore, are related parties under Sec. 1239(b).

Transaction Title	Consolidated Taxable Income	Adjustments & Eliminations	S Corporation's Tax Return	B Corporation's Tax Return
Gain on sale of the machine by S to B in 2008	$ –0–	($4,200)	$4,200	
Depreciation of the machine by B in 2008	(1,920)	840		($2,760)
Total	($1,920)	($3,360)	$4,200	($2,760)

PRACTICE NOTE

Some firms that make infrequent intercompany sales will follow the practice of making the sale at the asset's tax book value to avoid having to defer and restore a gain or loss.

S recognizes the $4,200 intercompany gain as ordinary income under Sec. 1245. A sample consolidated tax return is included in Appendix B, which includes the restoration of an intercompany gain via depreciation.   ◀

DEPARTING GROUP MEMBER.   The Seller's intercompany items and Buyer's corresponding items are taken into account under the acceleration rule when they no longer can be taken into account to produce the effect of treating the two entities as divisions of a single corporation.

If the Seller leaves the affiliated group and the intercompany item originated from a sale, exchange, or distribution, the acceleration rule treats the item as having been sold by the Buyer for a cash payment equal to the Buyer's adjusted basis in the property.

EXAMPLE C8-16 ▶

Assume the same facts as in Example C8-10 except that S's stock is sold by its parent corporation on the last day of 2009, and S immediately leaves the affiliated group. B continues to be owned by its parent corporation (and S's former parent corporation). No portion of S's intercompany item has been reported in 2006 through 2009 prior to S's leaving the affiliated group. The affiliated group must report the $80,000 ($200,000 deemed sale price − $120,000 S's adjusted basis) intercompany gain immediately before S becomes a nonmember. B continues to report its corresponding items using its regular accounting methods until the sale date. Thus, B does not recognize any gain until it sells the securities.   ◀

If the S and B stock had been sold together by their parent company, the two corporations would continue to be treated as divisions of a single corporation for as long as S and B continued to file a consolidated tax return. Therefore, a deemed sale of the securities would not occur, and none of S's intercompany profit would be reported.

OTHER INTERCOMPANY TRANSACTIONS

SELF-STUDY QUESTION

Why are the other intercompany transactions not given any special treatment?

ANSWER

Because both sides of the transaction are reported in the same consolidated return, they simply net each other out. If, due to accounting method differences, the items would be reported in different tax periods, both the income and deduction must be reported in the later of the two tax years.

Any income, gain, deduction, or loss realized or incurred on other intercompany transactions is included in the income and expense classifications for the tax year in which the transaction is ordinarily reported. Both parties report their sides of the transaction in determining separate taxable income.[35] When both parties use the same accounting method, these amounts net to zero because the income and expense are included in consolidated taxable income.

Section 267(a)(2) imposes a special rule on related party transactions requiring the matching of the recognition of the payer's deduction item and the payee's income item. Thus, when two group members would ordinarily report the income and deduction items in different consolidated return years under their regular accounting methods, the payer must defer the reporting of the deduction until the tax year in which the payee member reports the income.

Section 267(b)(3) includes two corporations that are members of the same controlled group as related parties. This definition includes most members of affiliated groups, whether separate returns or a consolidated return are filed. It also may include certain corporations that are not included in the affiliated group because they are not includible corporations (for example, brother-sister corporations included in a combined controlled group).

Regulation Sec. 1.1502-13(a)(2) requires the two group members to match the income and expense items as if they were incurred by two divisions of a single corporation. As

---

[35] Reg. Sec. 1.1502-13(b)(1) and (2). This procedure may be contrasted with financial accounting, in which both sides of the transaction are eliminated in preparing the consolidated financial statements.

two divisions, S and B would report a recomputed expense amount of zero (i.e., the income of one division would exactly offset the expense of the other division, so that neither income nor loss would be reported to external parties). Because S's intercompany items are recognized when B's corresponding items are incurred, amounts earned by S from an intercompany transaction can be included in the consolidated tax return before they are taken into account under its separate entity method of accounting.

EXAMPLE C8-17 ▶ S and B Corporations have filed calendar year consolidated tax returns for several years. S and B Corporations use the accrual method of accounting. S lends B $100,000 on March 1, 2006; this debt and the related interest are unpaid at the end of 2006. Interest is charged by S at an annual rate of 12%. The $10,000 interest charge owed at year-end is paid by B on March 1, 2007. S accrues $10,000 of interest income in 2006, and B accrues $10,000 of interest expense in 2006. S and B Corporations report the interest income and expense in a worksheet format similar to that used for the earlier intercompany sales. No net income or loss is reported in the consolidated tax return as a result of the loan being made by S in 2006.

Transaction	Consolidated Taxable Income	Adjustments & Eliminations	S Corporation's Tax Return	B Corporation's Tax Return
Accrual of interest income by S in 2006	$10,000		$10,000	
Accrual of expense interest by B in 2006	(10,000)			($10,000)
Total	$ –0–		$10,000	($10,000) ◀

EXAMPLE C8-18 ▶ Assume the same facts as in Example C8-17 except that S Corporation is a cash method of accounting taxpayer. Ordinarily, S, a cash method corporation, would report no interest income and B, an accrual method corporation, would report $10,000 of interest expense in the computation of their separate taxable incomes for 2006's consolidated tax return. Because B has reported $10,000 of interest expense in its separate return and the recomputed expense amount is zero, an adjustment must be made to nullify the interest expense in the 2006 consolidated tax return. After the adjustment, no "net" interest income or expense is reported.

In 2006, B normally would report its $10,000 of interest expense related to the loan using its overall accrual method of accounting. The consolidated tax return Treasury Regulations require B to defer the $10,000 of interest expense from 2006 to 2007. At this time, S will report $10,000 of interest income from the loan and B likewise will report its $10,000 interest expense. The consolidated return regulations require B to defer the reporting of its tax deduction until the point in time when B reports its interest income. The consolidated return worksheet is as follows:

Transaction	Consolidated Taxable Income	Adjustments & Eliminations	S Corporation's Tax Return	B Corporation's Tax Return
Interest income reported by S in 2006	$ –0–		$ –0–	
Interest expense reported by B in 2006	–0–	$10,000		($10,000)
Interest income reported by S in 2007	10,000		10,000	
Interest expense reported by B in 2007	(10,000)	(10,000)		–0–
Total	$ –0–	$ –0–	$ 10,000	($10,000)

At the end of the two years, S reports $10,000 of income in its separate tax return, and B reports $10,000 of expense in its separate tax return. These two amounts net to the same zero amount reported in Example C8-17 when both taxpayers were accrual method corporations. ◀

A Seller's profit or loss from the sale of the capitalized services to another group member is an intercompany item. When a Buyer capitalizes the acquisition cost of the services, the Buyer's amortization deduction becomes the corresponding item. Thus, Buyer's capitalization of the purchase under its separate method of accounting permits the Seller to spread the recognition of its profit, which otherwise would be recognized under its separate method of accounting, over the amortization time period.

EXAMPLE C8-19 ▶ S and B Corporations have filed consolidated tax returns for a number of years. S Corporation, an accrual method of accounting taxpayer, drills wells. B Corporation, operates a farm, and uses the cash method of accounting. S drills a well in 2006 for B for $10,000, which creates a $2,000 profit. B pays S the cost of the well, capitalizes the well cost, and begins to amortize it over a five-year period. Under the accrual method of accounting, S would report its income and expenses when the drilling occurred. Because it is an intercompany transaction, S reports its profit over the five-year amortization period used by B.

Transaction	Consolidated Taxable Income	Adjustments & Eliminations	S Corporation's Tax Return	B Corporation's Tax Return
Amortization of well-drilling cost by B in 2006	($2,000)			($2,000)
Accrual of well-drilling income by S in 2006	2,000	($8,000)	$10,000	
Total	$ –0–	($8,000)	$10,000	($2,000) ◀

Topic Review C8-1 summarizes the intercompany transaction rules.

Topic Review C8-1

Reporting Intercompany Transactions

INTERCOMPANY TRANSACTIONS

1. Intercompany transaction definition: a transaction taking place during a consolidated return year between corporations that are members of the same affiliated group immediately after the transaction.
2. Two types of intercompany transactions:
   a. Property transactions—the intercompany item (gain or loss) is deferred until a corresponding event occurs.
   b. Other transactions—the intercompany item (income or expense item) is reported in the year in which the corresponding event occurs.
3. The selling and buying members of the affiliated group generally are treated as separate entities when reporting the intercompany transaction.
   a. **Exception:** the selling and buying members are treated as two divisions of the same entity when determining the recomputed corresponding gain, income, loss, or deduction item.
4. The reporting of intercompany transactions are based on two concepts.
   a. **Intercompany items** are the Seller's income, gain, deduction, or loss from an intercompany transaction.
   b. **Corresponding items** are the Buyer's income, gain, deduction or loss from an intercompany transaction, or from property acquired in an intercompany transaction.
5. The following are some of the corresponding items that can trigger the recognition of an intercompany item (e.g., gain, loss, income, or deduction amount).
   a. The Buyer sells property to a nonmember of the group.
   b. Property acquired by the Buyer is depreciated, depleted, or amortized.
   c. The corporation that sold a property or acquired a property leaves the affiliated group.
   d. The affiliated group discontinues filing a consolidated tax return and begins filing separate tax returns.

DIVIDENDS RECEIVED BY GROUP MEMBERS

Dividends received by group members are treated differently depending on whether they come from corporations within the affiliated group or from firms outside it. In determining consolidated taxable income, the dividends received from other group members are excluded, while those received from nonmembers of the group are eligible for a 70%, 80%, or 100% dividends-received deduction.

EXCLUSION PROCEDURE

A dividend distribution from one group member (the distributing member) to a second group member (the distributee member) during a consolidated return year is an intercompany transaction. An intercompany distribution is not included in the gross income of the distributee member. The exclusion applies only to distributions that otherwise would be taxable if paid to a non-affiliated corporation and which produce a corresponding negative adjustment to the basis of the distributing member's stock.[36] Such an adjustment is illustrated in Step 2 of Table C8-1.

Within an affiliated group, nondividend distributions (e.g., a distribution made when there is no earnings and profits balance) reduce the distributee member's basis in the distributing member's stock.[37] If the amount of the distribution exceeds the distributee's adjusted basis in the stock, the excess either creates a new, or increases an existing, **excess loss account** (i.e., a negative investment account). However, the distributee does not recognize any gain from the portion of the distribution that exceeds its basis in the distributing member's stock (as it would with nonaffiliated corporations).[38] The creation of an excess loss account is discussed in the basis adjustment section of this chapter.

The amount of any distribution received by one group member from another equals the money distributed plus the sum of the adjusted basis of any property distributed and the gain recognized by the distributing member. Because under Sec. 311(b) gain is recognized on most distributions of appreciated property, the gain recognized plus the adjusted basis of the distributed property generally will equal its FMV where a distribution of appreciated property takes place between group members. Gain recognized by the distributing member under Sec. 311(b) due to the distribution of property to another group member is treated as an intercompany item. The deferred gain is included in consolidated taxable income by the distributing member when a corresponding item is reported by the distributee (e.g., the distributee member begins to depreciate the property).[39]

CONSOLIDATED DIVIDENDS-RECEIVED DEDUCTION

The basic dividends-received deduction rules, as set forth in Chapter C3, apply to the calculation of the consolidated dividends-received deduction. The dividends-received deduction for dividends received from nonmembers is computed on a consolidated basis. It is not applied to the separate taxable income of each group member. The consolidated dividends-received deduction equals the sum of 70% of dividends received from unaffiliated domestic corporations in which a less than 20% interest is held, 80% of dividends received from unaffiliated domestic corporations in which a 20% or more interest is held, and 100% of dividends received from an 80% or more owned domestic corporation that is not included in the consolidated return election (e.g., a 100%-owned life insurance company prohibited from being part of a consolidated tax return). The 70% and 80% dividends-received deductions are separately limited by consolidated taxable income. The

---

[36] Reg. Sec. 1.1502-13(f)(2).
[37] Reg. Sec. 1.1502-13(f)(7).
[38] Reg. Sec. 1.1502-14(a)(2). The amount of the excess loss account's negative balance is reported as either ordinary income or capital gain when a disposition of the subsidiary corporation's stock occurs.

[39] Reg. Sec. 1.1502-13(f).

80% dividends-received deduction limitation is calculated first, and the deduction cannot exceed 80% of consolidated taxable income excluding the consolidated dividends-received deduction, any consolidated NOL, or capital loss carryback. The 70% dividends-received deduction limitation is then calculated and the deduction cannot exceed 70% of consolidated taxable income reduced by the amount of the dividends eligible for the 80% dividends-received deduction and excluding the consolidated dividends-received deduction, any consolidated NOL, or capital loss carryback. The limitations do not apply if the full amount of the deduction creates or increases a consolidated NOL.[40]

EXAMPLE C8-20 ▶

P, S$_1$, and S$_2$ Corporations create the P-S$_1$-S$_2$ affiliated group. Consolidated taxable income (without considering any dividends-received exclusions or deductions, NOLs, and capital losses) is $200,000. The following dividend income is received by the group members from unaffiliated corporations that are less than 20%-owned: P, $6,000; S$_1$, $10,000; and S$_2$, $34,000. In addition, P receives a $40,000 dividend from S$_1$, and S$_1$ receives a $60,000 dividend from a 100%-owned life insurance company that cannot join in the consolidated return election at the present time. S$_1$'s distribution reduces P's basis for its investment in S$_1$.

▶ The $40,000 dividend that P receives from S$_1$ is excluded from P's gross income since it results in a basis reduction for P's investment in S$_1$.

▶ S$_1$'s $60,000 dividend from the 100%-owned life insurance company is eligible for a 100% dividends-received deduction. This $60,000 deduction is not subject to any limitation and reduces consolidated taxable income before applying the 70% limitation.

▶ The 70% dividends-received deductions included in the separate taxable income calculations are P, $4,200 (0.70 × $6,000); S$_1$, $7,000 (0.70 × $10,000); and S$_2$, $23,800 (0.70 × $34,000), or a total $35,000 reduction in consolidated taxable income. The 70% dividends-received deduction ($35,000) is not restricted by the dividends-received deduction limitation [($200,000 consolidated taxable income given in the facts − $60,000 dividends-received deduction) × 0.70 = $98,000].

The consolidated dividends-received deduction is $95,000 ($35,000 + $60,000). ◀

STOP & THINK

Question: Alpha Corporation has owned the stock of a subsidiary for a number of years. Peter Gray, the CPA, who has prepared both corporations' tax returns since their creation has been trying to sell Alpha's Director of Federal Taxes on beginning to file a consolidated tax return based on the tax exemption for intragroup dividends. Is he right or wrong in his approach?

Solution: He is wrong. If the two companies file separate tax returns, a 100% dividends-received deduction is available for intragroup dividends. If a consolidated return were filed, the dividend can be excluded from Alpha's gross income. Typically, these two alternatives provide the same outcome. A difference between these two alternatives may be found when preparing state tax returns (see page C8-36). Peter should be concentrating on advantages, such as offsetting profits and losses between the two companies should one company incur a loss, deferring intercompany profits, etc.

CONSOLIDATED CHARITABLE CONTRIBUTIONS DEDUCTION

The basic charitable contributions deduction rules, as set forth in Chapter C3, apply to the calculation of the consolidated charitable contribution deduction. The affiliated group's charitable contributions deduction is computed on a consolidated basis. The consolidated charitable contributions deduction equals the sum of the charitable contributions deductions of the individual group members for the consolidated return year

---

[40] Reg. Sec. 1.1502-26(a)(1).

(computed without regard to any individual group member's limitation) plus any charitable contribution carryovers from earlier consolidated or separate return years. The charitable contributions deduction is limited to 10% of adjusted consolidated taxable income. Adjusted consolidated taxable income is computed without regard to the consolidated dividends-received deduction, any consolidated NOL or capital loss carrybacks, and the consolidated charitable contributions deduction. Any charitable contributions made by the group that exceeds the 10% limitation carry over to the five succeeding tax years.[41] Any unused contributions remaining at the end of the carryover period are lost.

EXAMPLE C8-21 ▶ P, S_1, and S_2 Corporations form the P-S_1-S_2 affiliated group. The group members report the following charitable contributions and adjusted consolidated taxable income for the current year:

Group Member	Charitable Contributions	Adjusted Consolidated Taxable Income
P	$12,500	$150,000
S_1	5,000	(40,000)
S_2	2,000	10,000
Total	$19,500	$120,000

The P-S_1-S_2 affiliated group's charitable contributions deduction is the lesser of its actual charitable contributions ($19,500) or 10% of its adjusted consolidated taxable income ($12,000). The $7,500 ($19,500 − $12,000) of excess charitable contributions carry over to the next five tax years. ◀

A member leaving the affiliated group takes with it any excess contributions arising in a prior separate return year plus its allocable share of any excess consolidated charitable contributions for a consolidated return year. The excess consolidated charitable contributions are allocated to each group member based on the relative amount of their contributions (when compared to the total contributions of all group members) for the consolidated return year.

CONSOLIDATED U.S. PRODUCTION ACTIVITIES DEDUCTION

For tax years beginning after 2004, the U.S. production activities deduction also can be taken on a consolidated basis. (See Chapter C3 for a detailed discussion of this deduction.) The deduction for an affiliated group must be calculated as for a single corporation and is based on the lessor of (1) the consolidated productive activities income or (2) consolidated taxable income before this deduction. For purposes of calculating the U.S. production activities deduction only, Congress expanded the definition of an affiliated group by reducing the stock ownership threshold from 80% to 50% and by including, as eligible, insurance companies and corporations that use the possessions tax credit. Accordingly, the calculation of this deduction may involve entities that are not part of the group filing the consolidated return. The members of this extended affiliated group must calculate a single consolidated U.S. production activities deduction and then allocate the deduction among the members of the group based on the relative amount of qualified production activities income that each member of the affiliated group earns. Because of the potential for an extremely complex calculation being necessary when the extended affiliated group and the consolidated group differ, the IRS has provided some interim guidance in Notice 2005-14 I.R.B. 2005-7 and in Proposed Regulations under Sec. 199.

---

[41] Reg. Sec. 1.1502-24(a).

NET OPERATING LOSSES (NOLs)

<table>
<tr><td>

OBJECTIVE 8

Calculate an affiliated group's consolidated NOL

</td><td>

One advantage of filing a consolidated tax return is the ability of an affiliated group to offset one member's current NOLs against the taxable income of other group members. If these losses cause the affiliated group to report a consolidated NOL, the NOL may be carried back or carried forward to other consolidated return years of the affiliated group. In some cases, part or all of the consolidated NOL can be carried back or carried over to separate return years of the individual group members. NOLs of group members arising in separate return years also may be carried back or carried over to consolidated return years, subject to the separate return limitation year (SRLY) limit. In addition, NOLs, capital losses, and excess credits of a loss corporation that is a member of an affiliated group can be subject to the consolidated Secs. 382–384 limitations. The rules that apply to carrybacks and carryovers are examined below.

</td></tr>
</table>

CURRENT YEAR NOLs

KEY POINT

Generally, the most significant benefit to filing consolidated tax returns is the ability to offset losses of one member against the income of other members.

Each member's separate taxable income is combined to determine combined taxable income before any adjustment is made for NOL carryovers (see Table C8-1).[42] The combining process allows the losses of one group member to offset the taxable income of other group members. A group member cannot elect separately to carry back its own losses from a consolidated return year to one of its earlier profitable separate return years. Only the consolidated group's NOL (if any) may be carried back or over.

EXAMPLE C8-22 ▶ P and S Corporations form the P-S affiliated group. During 2005, the initial year of operation, P and S file calendar year separate tax returns. Beginning in 2006, the P-S group elects to file a consolidated tax return. P and S report the following results for 2005 and 2006:

Group Member	Taxable Income 2005	Taxable Income 2006
P	($15,000)	$40,000
S	250,000	(27,000)
Consolidated taxable income	N/A	$13,000

N/A = Not applicable

P's 2005 NOL may not be used to offset S's 2005 profits because separate returns were filed. This NOL carryover may be used only to reduce the $13,000 of 2006 consolidated taxable income reported after S's 2006 loss is offset against P's 2006 separate taxable income. Because S's 2006 loss must be offset against P's 2006 taxable income, S cannot carry its 2006 NOL back against its 2005 taxable income to increase the value of the tax savings obtained from the loss. The remaining NOL of $2,000 ($15,000 loss from 2005 − $13,000 2006 consolidated taxable income) carries over to 2007. ◀

<table>
<tr><td>

OBJECTIVE 9

Calculate the carryback or carryover of a consolidated NOL

</td><td>

CARRYBACKS AND CARRYFORWARDS OF CONSOLIDATED NOLs

The consolidated NOL rules are similar to the NOL rules applying to a corporation filing a separate tax return. A consolidated NOL is determined after the following computation:[43]

</td></tr>
</table>

Separate taxable income of each group member (from Table C8-1)
Plus: Consolidated capital gain net income
Minus: Consolidated Sec. 1231 net loss
          Consolidated charitable contributions deduction
          Consolidated dividends-received deduction

Consolidated NOL

---

[42] Reg. Sec. 1.1502-12(h).
[43] Reg. Sec. 1.1502-21(e). NOLs incurred in tax years beginning on or before August 5, 1997, were carried back three years and forward 15 years.

A consolidated NOL incurred in a tax year beginning after August 5, 1997 may be carried back to the two preceding consolidated return years or carried over to the 20 succeeding consolidated return years. The parent corporation also may elect for the affiliated group to relinquish the entire carryback period for a consolidated NOL and use it only as a carryforward to succeeding years.[44] (See Chapter C3 for a discussion of the reasons for making this election and how this election is made.)

A carryback or carryforward of the consolidated NOL to a tax year in which the members of the affiliated group have not changed poses no real problem. The amount of the consolidated NOL absorbed in a given tax year is determined according to the basic Sec. 172 rules for NOLs outlined in Chapter C3.

Determining the amount of the consolidated NOL that may be absorbed in a tax year is more difficult when the group members are not the same in the carryback or carryforward year. In such a case, the consolidated NOL is apportioned to each corporation that was both a member of the affiliated group and incurred a separate NOL during the loss year. When a loss corporation is not also a group member in the carryback or carryforward year, the rules relating to carrybacks and carryforwards to separate return years (discussed below) must be applied.

TYPICAL MISCONCEPTION

As a general rule, a consolidated NOL may be carried back two years and carried forward 20 years. This procedure is not complicated unless the members of the group change before the loss is fully used.

CARRYBACK OF CONSOLIDATED NOL TO SEPARATE RETURN YEAR

GENERAL RULE. A consolidated NOL may be carried back and absorbed against a member's taxable income from the preceding two separate return years.[45] To effect a carryback, part or all of the consolidated NOL must be apportioned to the member. To the extent a member uses its allocable share of the consolidated NOL, such an amount is not available to the remaining members as a carryback or carryforward to a consolidated return year. The consolidated NOL is apportioned to a loss member in the following manner:[46]

$$\frac{\text{Separate NOL of the individual member}}{\text{Sum of the separate NOLs incurred by all members having such losses}} \times \text{Consolidated NOL} = \begin{array}{c}\text{Portion of consolidated NOL attributable to member}\end{array}$$

EXAMPLE C8-23 ▶

KEY POINT

In Example C8-23, because P-S did not file a consolidated tax return in 2004, P must either forgo the two-year carryback or allow all the consolidated NOL to be carried back to S's 2004 separate tax return year.

P and S Corporations form the P-S affiliated group. The P-S group filed separate tax returns in 2004 and 2005. S reported taxable income of $275,000 in 2004. The group elects to file a consolidated tax return for 2006. The P-S group reports a $150,000 consolidated NOL for 2006, all of which is attributable to S. S carries the $150,000 NOL back to 2004 and uses the loss to partially offset the taxable income it reported in 2004. The loss is used up in 2004 and therefore cannot be used by S in 2005 or by the P-S group in any subsequent consolidated return year. Alternatively, an election by P to forgo the carryback permits the 2006 loss to be used sequentially in 2007 and the next 19 consolidated return years. ◀

SPECIAL CARRYBACK RULE FOR NEW MEMBERS. When the consolidated NOL is apportioned to a member, it normally is carried back to the two immediately preceding consolidated return years or the loss corporation's separate return years. A special rule permits an affiliated group member to carry an NOL back two years to a separate return year of its common parent corporation or a consolidated return year of the affiliated group if

▶ The member corporation with the loss carryback did not exist in the carryback year, and

▶ The loss corporation has been a member of the affiliated group continually since its organization.

---

[44] Reg. Sec. 1.1502-21(b)(3)(i).
[45] Losses incurred by affiliated groups in tax years ending in 2001 and 2002 could be carried back five years (Sec. 172(b)(1)(H)).
[46] Reg. Sec. 1.1502-21(b)(2)(iv). The member's separate NOL is determined in a manner similar to the calculation of separate taxable income except for a series of adjustments to account for the member's share of the consolidated charitable contributions and dividends-received deductions, the member's capital gain net income, and the member's net capital loss or Sec. 1231 net loss minus any portion of the consolidated amounts attributable to the member that were absorbed currently.

If these two requirements are met, the portion of the consolidated NOL attributable to the loss member is carried back to the two preceding consolidated return years of the affiliated group (or separate return year of the common parent corporation) only if the common parent was not a member of a different consolidated group or affiliated group filing separate returns for the year to which the loss is carried or a subsequent year in the carryback period.[47]

EXAMPLE C8-24 ▶

P and S_1 Corporations were affiliated for 2004 and 2005 and filed consolidated tax returns. P acquires all of S_2 Corporation's stock on January 1, 2006, the date on which S_2 is created by P, and S_2 becomes a member of the affiliated group. P, S_1, and S_2 report the following results (excluding NOL deductions) for 2004 through 2006:

Group Member	Taxable Income 2004	2005	2006
P	$12,000	$10,000	$16,000
S_1	8,000	7,000	4,000
S_2	XXX	XXX	(30,000)
Consolidated taxable income	$20,000	$17,000	($10,000)

All the 2006 consolidated NOL is attributable to S_2. As illustrated, S_2's separate NOL of $30,000 is first used to offset P and S_1's taxable income in 2006, leaving only a $10,000 consolidated NOL. Two options are available with respect to the consolidated NOL: the NOL may be carried over to subsequent tax years, or the NOL may be carried back to 2004 and 2005. If the first alternative is selected, the NOL offsets consolidated taxable income reported in 2007 and up to 19 subsequent tax years. If the second alternative is selected, the $10,000 NOL is carried back to offset part of the 2004 consolidated taxable income. This result is possible because S_2 did not exist at the end of 2005 and because it joined the affiliated group immediately after it was created on January 1, 2006, and has been a group member continually since its organization. ◀

If the loss corporation is not a member of the affiliated group immediately after its organization, that member's portion of the consolidated NOL is carried back only to its prior separate return years.

EXAMPLE C8-25 ▶

Assume the same facts as in Example C8-24 except S_2 Corporation existed separately and filed a separate tax return for 2005 prior to its stock being acquired by P on January 1, 2006. P, S_1, and S_2 report the following results (excluding NOL deductions) for 2004 through 2006:

Group Member	Taxable Income 2004	2005	2006
P	$12,000	$10,000	$16,000
S_1	8,000	7,000	4,000
S_2	XXX	8,000	(30,000)
Consolidated taxable income	$20,000	$17,000[a]	($10,000)

[a] Including only the results of P and S_1.

The $10,000 2006 consolidated NOL can be carried back by S_2 to 2005. The NOL offsets all $8,000 of S_2's 2005 separate return taxable income. The remaining loss carryback of $2,000 cannot be used to reduce the taxable income reported in 2004 or 2005 by P and S_1. It can be carried over, however, to offset the affiliated group's 2007 and later taxable income. Alternatively, the P-S_1-S_2 affiliated group could elect to carry the entire loss over to offset 2007 and later years taxable income (see Chapter C3's discussion regarding why such an election might be advisable). ◀

---

[47] Reg. Sec. 1.1502-21(b)(2)(ii)(B). A consolidated group is an affiliated group that has elected to file a consolidated tax return.

CARRYFORWARD OF CONSOLIDATED NOL TO SEPARATE RETURN YEAR

If a corporation ceases to be a member of the affiliated group during the current year, the portion of the consolidated NOL allocable to the departing member becomes the member's separate carryforward. However, the allocation of the NOL to the departing group member cannot be made until the available carryover is absorbed in the current consolidated return year. This requirement exists even when all of the carryover is attributable to the departing member. The departing member's share of the NOL carryforward then may be used in its first separate return year.[48]

EXAMPLE C8-26 ▶

P, S_1, and S_2 Corporations form the P-S_1-S_2 affiliated group, with P owning all the S_1 and S_2 stock. The group files consolidated tax returns for several years. At the close of business on September 30, 2006, P sells its investment in S_1. S_1 must file a separate tax return covering the period October 1, 2006, through December 31, 2006. During pre-2006 tax years, P, S_1, and S_2 incurred substantial NOLs. At the beginning of 2006, a consolidated NOL carryover of $100,000 is still available. Two-thirds of this loss is allocable to S_1; the remainder is allocable to S_2. The affiliated group reports the following results (excluding NOL deductions) for 2006:

TYPICAL MISCONCEPTION

In Example C8-26, it is important to understand that the group is entitled to use the consolidated NOL before S_1 determines its NOL carryover. This can have an impact on negotiating an equitable purchase price for S_1.

Group Member		Taxable Income
P		$20,000
S_1:	January 1 through September 30	30,000
	October 1 through December 31	15,000
S_2		10,000
Total		$75,000

The consolidated NOL carryover of $100,000 offsets the $60,000 ($20,000 + $30,000 + $10,000) of taxable income reported by P, S_1, and S_2 in their 2006 consolidated tax return. This leaves $40,000 of carryover to be allocated between S_1 and S_2. Assume an agreement is reached where S_1 receives $26,667 (0.667 × $40,000), and S_2 receives $13,333 (0.333 × $40,000) of the carryover. Of S_1's carryover, $15,000 can be used in its separate tax return for the period ending December 31, 2006. The remaining $11,667 is carried over to S_1's 2007 separate tax return. The affiliated group can carry over S_2's $13,333 allocable share of the NOL to 2007 and subsequent years. ◀

OBJECTIVE 10

Determine how the special loss limitations restrict the use of separate and consolidated NOL carrybacks and carryovers

SPECIAL LOSS LIMITATIONS

Two special loss limitations, the **separate return limitation year (SRLY) rules** and the **Sec. 382 loss limitation rules,** are imposed on affiliated groups. The SRLY rules limit the separate return NOL amount that can be deducted as a NOL carryback or carryover by an affiliated group to a member's contribution to consolidated taxable income.[49] This treatment prevents the affiliated group from offsetting its current taxable income by purchasing loss corporations solely to use their NOLs. The Sec. 382 loss limitation rules, which were explained in Chapter C7 on a separate return basis, also apply to affiliated groups filing consolidated returns. The special Sec. 382 consolidated return rules restrict an affiliated group from using NOLs following an ownership change that results from a purchase transaction or a tax-free reorganization. Each set of rules is explained below.

KEY POINT

The SRLY rules limit a group from acquiring already existing losses and offsetting those losses against the group's income.

SEPARATE RETURN LIMITATION YEAR RULES. A member incurring an NOL in a separate return year (that is available as a carryback or a carryforward to a consolidated return year) is subject to a limit on the use of the NOL when the loss year is designated a separate return limitation year. A **separate return limitation year** is defined as any separate return year, except

▶ A separate return year of the group member designated as the parent corporation for the consolidated return year to which the tax attribute (e.g., NOL) is carried, or

---

[48] Reg. Sec. 1.1502-21(b)(2)(ii)(A).
[49] The SRLY rules do not apply to the foreign tax credit, general business credit, minimum tax credit, and overall foreign losses for corporations joining the affiliated group.

ADDITIONAL COMMENT
These two exceptions to the SRLY rules exist because in both cases the group has not acquired already existing NOLs.

▶ A separate return year of any corporation that was a group member for every day of the loss year (i.e., a consolidated return was not elected or the corporation was not eligible to participate in the filing of a consolidated return in the loss year).

NOL Carryovers. An NOL incurred in an SRLY may be used as a carryover in a consolidated return year equal to the lesser of (1) the aggregate of the consolidated taxable income amounts for all consolidated return years of the group determined by taking into account only the loss member's items of income, gain, deduction, and loss minus any NOL carryovers previously absorbed, (2) consolidated taxable income, or (3) the amount of the NOL carryover.[50] A SRLY carryover cannot be used when a member's cumulative contribution is less than zero. Any NOL carryovers or carrybacks that cannot be used currently because of the member's contribution to consolidated taxable income or the group's current year consolidated taxable income must be carried over to subsequent tax years.

EXAMPLE C8-27 ▶

SELF-STUDY QUESTION
What is the consequence of having losses subject to the SRLY limitations?

ANSWER
The effect of having a loss tainted as a SRLY loss is that it can be used only to offset taxable income of the subsidiary member (or possibly a loss subgroup) that created the NOL.

P and S Corporations form the P-S affiliated group. P acquires the S stock shortly after its creation in mid-2006.[51] P and S file separate tax returns for 2006 and begin filing a consolidated tax return in 2007. Assume the U.S. production activities deduction does not apply. The group reports the following results (excluding NOL deductions) for 2006 through 2010:

Group Member	Taxable Income				
	2006	2007	2008	2009	2010
P Corporation	($ 9,000)	$17,000	$ 6,000	($6,000)	$ 2,000
S Corporation	(20,000)	(2,000)	5,000	5,000	16,000
Consolidated taxable income	$ XXX	$15,000	$11,000	($1,000)	$18,000

Under the SRLY rules, the separate NOLs are used as follows:

▶ P's 2006 loss is offset against the group's $15,000 of 2007 consolidated taxable income (CTI). None of S's 2006 loss can be used because it incurred a separate NOL in 2007, which already has been offset against P's $17,000 profit. The group's 2007 CTI is reduced to $6,000 ($15,000 − $9,000).

▶ $3,000 of S's 2006 loss is offset against 2008 CTI: the smaller of S's $3,000 cumulative contribution to CTI [($2,000) + $5,000], its $20,000 NOL carryover, or the $11,000 of CTI. The $3,000 of NOL used reduces S's NOL carryover to $17,000.

▶ None of S's 2006 loss can be used in 2009 because the group reported a consolidated NOL. Assuming the 2009 NOL is carried back, 2007's CTI is reduced from $6,000 to $5,000 ($15,000 − $9,000 carryover from 2006 − $1,000 carryback from 2009).

▶ $17,000 of S's 2006 loss is offset against 2010 CTI, which is the smaller of S's $21,000 cumulative contributions to CTI in 2007 through 2010 ($24,000 net contributions to CTI in 2007–2010 − $3,000 NOL used in 2008), its $17,000 remaining loss carryover, or the $18,000 of CTI. Consolidated taxable income is reduced to $1,000 ($18,000 − $17,000), and no carryovers remain to 2011. ◀

The SRLY rules generally apply to each individual corporation that has a loss carryover from a separate return limitation year. The SRLY limitation must be determined for a subgroup of two or more corporations within an affiliated group that are continuously affiliated after ceasing to be members of a former affiliated group, that joined the affiliated group at the same time, and where at least one of the corporations carries over losses from the former group to the current group. If the subgroup has remained continuously affiliated up to the beginning of the year to which the loss is carried, the subgroup's loss

---

[50] Reg. Sec. 1.1502-21(b)(1). Any unused NOLs that are carried to the consolidated return year from tax years ending before the separate return limitation year reduce the SRLY limitation on a first-in, first-out (FIFO) basis. Tax years ending on the same date reduce the SRLY limitations on a pro rata basis. A loss member's contribution to CTI is determined on a "with" and "without" basis. The difference between CTI "with" the loss member and "without" the loss member is the loss member's contribution to CTI.

[51] P's acquisition of the S stock can trigger both the SRLY rules and the Sec. 382 rules. The overlap rules have not yet been discussed. To simplify the example, assume that the Sec. 382 limitation does not apply.

carryovers can be used to the extent the subgroup contributes to consolidated taxable income.[52]

EXAMPLE C8-28 ▶ P and S Corporations have filed consolidated tax returns together for a number of years. At the close of business on December 31, 2006, A Corporation purchases all of P's stock. The taxable income for P, S, and A Corporations for 2006 and 2007 are as follows:

	Taxable Income	
Group Member	2006	2007
A	xxx	$120
P	$100	40
S	(250)	30
CTI	($150)	$190

P and S are a subgroup when calculating the use of the SRLY losses in 2007. Their $150 NOL can be used to the extent of the smaller of their contribution to CTI ($70 = $40 + $30), the NOL carryover ($150), or CTI ($190), or $70. The remaining $80 NOL ($150 − $70) carries over to 2008, and the subgroup rules are applied again. ◀

KEY POINT

The SRLY rules apply to both carryovers and carrybacks. Remember that SRLYs stem from either a year in which a member files a separate return or a year in which a member joins in the filing of a consolidated return with a different affiliated group.

NOL Carrybacks. The SRLY rules also apply to NOL carrybacks from a separate return limitation year to a consolidated return year. For example, assume that S Corporation in Example C8-27 leaves the P-S group at the end of 2008. Any NOL that S incurs in a subsequent separate return year (2009) that is carried back to the 2007 consolidated return year is subject to the SRLY rules. Its use is restricted under the SRLY rules to S's contribution to consolidated taxable income for all consolidated return years. However, S has not provided a contribution to consolidated taxable income in those years and would be prevented from using the carryback in those earlier years.

The use of built-in deductions also is limited by the SRLY rules. A **built-in deduction** is a deduction that accrues in a separate return year but is recognized for tax purposes in a consolidated return year. One example of such a deduction is the depreciation connected with a subsidiary corporation's asset that declines in value between the time it was acquired in a separate return year and the beginning of the initial consolidated return year. Built-in deductions also can result from the sale of a capital or noncapital asset at a loss in a consolidated return year when the decline in value takes place in a prior separate return year. For example, S purchases inventory in a separate return year for $60,000. The inventory declines to a $45,000 FMV before the time P purchases the S stock and the two corporations start filing on a consolidated basis. The $15,000 ($60,000 − $45,000) built-in deduction can be deducted by S when it sells the inventory only if its SRLY limitation equals or exceeds the built-in deduction amount.[53]

ADDITIONAL COMMENT

The built-in deduction rules eliminate the ability to circumvent the SRLY rules by acquiring a corporation with losses that have economically accrued and having these losses recognized after the subsidiary is a member of the group.

SECTION 382 LOSS LIMITATION. Section 382 prevents the purchase of assets or stock of a corporation having loss carryovers (known as the loss corporation) where a substantial portion of the purchase price is related to the acquisition of the corporation's tax attributes.[54] Trafficking in NOLs and other tax attributes is prevented by applying the Sec. 382 loss limitation to any tax year ending after the ownership change. The 50 percentage point minimum stock ownership change needed to trigger the Sec. 382 rules can occur in acquisitive transactions involving a single corporation or a group of corporations that file separate or consolidated returns. (See Chapter C7 for a discussion of Sec. 382.)

The consolidated Sec. 382 rules generally provide that the ownership change and Sec. 382 limitation are determined with respect to the entire affiliated group (or a subgroup of

[52] Reg. Sec. 1.1502-21(c)(2)(i). This rule holds only if the losses were non-SRLY losses to the former affiliated group.
[53] Reg. Sec. 1.1502-15(a).

[54] The Sec. 382 limitation rules apply to the tax attributes limited by Secs. 382–384 (e.g., NOLs, capital losses, foreign tax credits, general business credits, minimum tax credit, built-in gains, and built-in losses).

affiliated corporations) and not for individual entities.[55] Following an ownership change for a loss group, the consolidated taxable income for a post-change tax year that may be offset by a pre-change NOL cannot exceed the consolidated Sec. 382 limitation. If the post-change tax year includes the ownership change date, the Sec. 382 limitation applies to the consolidated taxable income that is earned in the portion of the tax year following the ownership change date.

A loss group is an affiliated group entitled to use an NOL carryover (other than a SRLY carryover) to the tax year in which the ownership change occurs, or has a consolidated NOL for the tax year in which the ownership change occurs.[56] An affiliated group can have two forms of ownership changes: a parent ownership change and a subgroup ownership change. A parent ownership change occurs when (1) the loss group's common parent corporation (a) has a shift in stock ownership involving a 5% or more shareholder or (b) is involved in a tax-free reorganization, and (2) the percentage of stock of the new loss corporation owned by one or more 5% shareholders has increased by more than 50 percentage points over the lowest percentage of stock owned in the old loss corporation by such shareholders during the preceding three-year (or shorter) testing period.[57] A parent ownership change is illustrated in the following example.

EXAMPLE C8-29 ▶ Dwayne owns all of P Corporation's stock. P owns 80% of the S Corporation stock. The remaining 20% of the S stock is owned by Mitzi. For the current year, the P-S group has a consolidated NOL that can be carried over to next year. The P-S affiliated group is a loss group. On December 31 of the current year, Dwayne sells 51% of the P stock to Carter, who has owned no P stock previously. The Sec. 382 stock ownership requirements are applied to P to determine whether an ownership change has occurred. The 51 percentage point increase in Carter's stock ownership is an ownership change that causes the Sec. 382 loss limitation to apply to the carryover of the current year NOL to next year. If Carter had instead acquired only 49% of the P stock, the requisite ownership change would not have occurred, and the Sec. 382 limit would not apply. ◀

The preceding example applied the ownership change rules to a parent corporation. An ownership change also can occur with respect to a loss subgroup. A loss subgroup generally consists of two or more corporations that are continuously affiliated after leaving one affiliated group when at least one of the corporations brings with it NOLs from the old group to the new group.[58] The loss subgroup can have an ownership change if, for example, the common parent of the loss subgroup has an ownership change (e.g., when an acquisition of subsidiaries from another affiliated group occurs). The 50 percentage point ownership change test is applied to the common parent of the loss subgroup. Further discussion of this type of ownership change is beyond the scope of an introductory text.

The consolidated Sec. 382 limitation (or subgroup limitation) for any post-change tax year equals the value of the loss group (or subgroup) times the highest adjusted federal long-term tax-exempt rate that applies with respect to the three-month period ending in the month of the ownership change. The value of the loss group is the value of the common and preferred stock of each member, other than stock owned by other group members, immediately before the ownership change.

EXAMPLE C8-30 ▶ Assume the same basic facts as in Example C8-29. In addition, the value of the P stock is $1 million and the value of the S stock is $750,000. The value of the P-S affiliated group when applying the Sec. 382 limitation is $1.15 million [$1,000,000 value of P stock + (0.20 minority interest × $750,000 value of S stock owned by Mitzi)]. The $1.15 million value is multiplied by the appropriate federal long-term tax-exempt rate to determine the maximum amount of the current year consolidated NOL that can be used next year.[59] ◀

---

[55] Reg. Sec. 1.1502-91(a)(1).
[56] Reg. Sec. 1.1502-91(c).
[57] Reg. Sec. 1.1502-92(b)(1)(i).

[58] Reg. Sec. 1.1502-92(b)(1)(ii).
[59] A daily allocation of the loss is not needed because the acquisition occurred on the last day of the loss corporation's tax year.

ADDITIONAL COMMENT

In Example C8-30, if S leaves the group, the loss attributable to S will be subject to whatever amount of the Sec. 382 limitation P apportions to S. S's Sec. 382 limitation is zero if P chooses not to apportion any of the group's Sec. 382 limitation to S.

Two special Sec. 382 rules that apply to affiliated groups deserve brief recognition here.

▶ If the Sec. 382 limitation for a post-change tax year exceeds the consolidated taxable income that may be offset by a pre-change NOL, the excess limitation amount carries forward to the next tax year to increase that year's Sec. 382 limitation.[60]

▶ A loss group (or loss subgroup) is treated as a single entity for purposes of determining whether it satisfies the Sec. 382 continuity of enterprise requirement. The group's Sec. 382 limitation is zero should the loss group not meet the continuity of enterprise requirement at any time in its first two years.[61]

▶ When an affiliated group terminates or a member leaves the affiliated group, the Sec. 382 limitation is apportioned to the individual group members.[62] Failure to allocate any of the Sec. 382 limitation to a departing group member prevents the member from using any of its NOLs in post-departure tax years.

EXAMPLE C8-31 ▶ In the P-S-T affiliated group, P owns 100% of the S stock, and S owns 100% of the T stock. The group has an annual Sec. 382 limit of $100, and 30% of the group's losses are allocable to T. When S sells the T stock to individual A, T receives its allocable share of the consolidated NOL. If T is allocated none of the affiliated group's Sec. 382 loss limitation, T's separate Sec. 382 limitation is set to zero. Consequently, T can use none of its allocable loss carryover. ◀

SRLY-SEC. 382 OVERLAP. An overlap problem exists because transactions that qualify under the SRLY rules (for example, the purchase by an acquiring corporation of 100% of the stock of a target corporation having a NOL) also may qualify under the Sec. 382 loss limitation rules. Under previous law, both the SRLY rules and Sec. 382 rules could apply to a single transaction involving members of an affiliated group. This overlap caused difficulty in complying with the consolidated tax return rules. The Treasury Department and the IRS considered a number of alternatives including applying both sets of rules, applying one set of rules but not the other, and creating a new version of the SRLY rules using the loss limitation structure found in Sec. 382.

The final Treasury Regulations apply a compromise to situations involving the NOL overlap and eliminate the application of the SRLY rules in this situation. To qualify for the overlap rule, a corporation must become a member of an affiliated group filing a consolidated tax return within six months of the date of an ownership change that creates a Sec. 382 limitation. If the Sec. 382 event precedes the SRLY event by six months or less, the overlap rule applies beginning with the tax year that includes the SRLY event. If the SRLY event precedes the Sec. 382 event by six months or less, the overlap rule applies for the first tax year beginning after the Sec. 382 event (and the SRLY rules apply for the interim period).

EXAMPLE C8-32 ▶ The P-S affiliated group has filed consolidated tax returns for a number of years. The P-S group has a $200 consolidated NOL, of which $100 is allocable to each corporation. The A-B affiliated group also has filed consolidated returns for a number of years. The A-B group acquires the P-S affiliated group in a taxable transaction. The P-S affiliated group is a SRLY subgroup and a Sec. 382 subgroup. The overlap rule eliminates the application of the SRLY rules in the surviving A-B-P-S affiliated group for the $200 consolidated NOL it acquired from the P-S group. The Sec. 382 rules, however, still apply. ◀

The overlap rule does not apply if all the corporations included in a Sec. 382 loss subgroup are not included in a SRLY subgroup. A similar set of overlap rules applies to built-in losses.

Topic Review C8-2 summarizes the rules applying to carrybacks and carryovers of consolidated return and separate return NOLs.

[60] Reg. Sec. 1.1502-93(a).
[61] Reg. Sec. 1.1502-93(d).
[62] Reg. Sec. 1.1502-95(b).

Topic Review C8-2

Rules Governing Affiliated Group NOL Carrybacks and Carryovers

LOSS YEAR	CARRYOVER/ CARRYBACK YEAR	RULE AND SPECIAL LIMITATIONS
CRY[a]	CRY	1. Consolidated NOLs carry back two years and over 20 years. The parent corporation can elect to forgo the carryback period. No special problems arise if the group members are the same in the loss year and the year to which the loss is carried back or carried over. 2. Section 382 limitation can apply to the loss carryover if an ownership change has occurred.
CRY	SRY[b]	1. Carryback to a member's prior separate return year is possible only if part or all of the NOL is apportioned to the member. Offspring rule permits carryback of an offspring member's allocable share of the consolidated NOL to a separate return year of the parent corporation or a consolidated return year of the affiliated group. 2. The departing member is allocated part of the consolidated NOL carryover. The consolidated NOL is used first in the consolidated return year in which the departing member leaves the group before an allocation is made. The allocated share of the loss is then used in the departing member's first separate return year. The departing member may be allocated a portion of the Sec. 382 loss limitation by the parent corporation.
SRY	CRY	1. A separate return year NOL can be carried over and used in a consolidated return year. SRLY rules will apply to NOLs other than those of a corporation that is the parent corporation in the carryover year or that is a group member on each day of the loss year. 2. Carryback of a loss of a departed group member to a consolidated return year is a SRLY loss.

[a]Consolidated return year.
[b]Separate return year.

CONSOLIDATED CAPITAL GAINS AND LOSSES

In the previous discussion of separate taxable income (see page C8-5), all capital gains and losses, Sec. 1231 gains and losses, and casualty and theft gains and losses were excluded. These three types of gains and losses are reported by the affiliated group on a consolidated basis. For a consolidated return year, the affiliated group's consolidated net capital gain or loss is composed of

▶ The aggregate amount of the capital gains and losses of the group members (without regard to any Sec. 1231 transactions or net capital loss carryovers or carrybacks)

▶ The net Sec. 1231 gain

▶ The net capital loss carryovers or carrybacks to the year[63]

Any capital gain net income that is part of consolidated taxable income is taxed at the regular corporate tax rates. Any consolidated net capital loss carries back three years or forward five years as a short-term capital loss.

SECTION 1231 GAINS AND LOSSES

A group member's Sec. 1231 gains and losses exclude any such amounts deferred when an intercompany transaction occurs. These intercompany gains and losses are reported when a corresponding item triggers the recognition of the intercompany item. The consolidated

ADDITIONAL COMMENT

Netting Sec. 1231 gains/losses on a consolidated basis rather than on a separate corporation basis can dramatically alter the amount of ordinary versus capital gain income.

---

[63] Reg. Sec. 1.1502-22(a)(1).

Sec. 1231 net gain or loss for the tax year is determined by taking into account the aggregate gains and losses of the group members' Sec. 1231 results. If the group's total Sec. 1231 gains (including net gain from casualty and theft occurrences involving Sec. 1231 property and certain capital assets) exceed similar losses, the net gain from these transactions is the consolidated net Sec. 1231 gain and is eligible for long-term capital gain treatment unless recaptured as ordinary income because of prior net Sec. 1231 losses. If the group reports a net loss either from Sec. 1231 transactions or from its casualty and theft occurrences, the net Sec. 1231 loss is treated as an ordinary loss and is deductible in determining consolidated taxable income.

CAPITAL GAINS AND LOSSES

DETERMINING THE AMOUNT OF GAIN OR LOSS. The amount of any group member's capital gains and losses excludes any such gains deferred when an intercompany transaction occurs. These intercompany gains and losses are reported when a corresponding item triggers the recognition of the intercompany item. Once the recognized gains and losses of each group member are determined, each member's short- and long-term transactions (including any consolidated Sec. 1231 net gain not treated as ordinary income) are combined into separate net gain or net loss positions. The sum of these separate positions then determines the amount of the affiliated group's aggregate short- or long-term capital gain or loss. These aggregate amounts are combined to determine the group's consolidated capital gain net income.

> **SELF-STUDY QUESTION**
>
> How do intercompany transactions affect the calculation of capital gains/losses?
>
> **ANSWER**
>
> Deferred intercompany gains/losses are included in the netting of capital gains/losses only when a corresponding item triggers the recognition of the intercompany item.

CARRYBACKS AND CARRYOVERS. The treatment of consolidated capital loss carrybacks and carryovers is similar to NOLs. The losses that carry back or over to other consolidated return years are treated as short-term capital losses and serve as a component of the consolidated capital gain or loss position.

The capital loss carrybacks or carryovers that can be used in a consolidated return year equal the sum of the affiliated group's unused consolidated capital loss carrybacks or carryovers and any unused capital loss carrybacks or carryovers of individual group members arising in separate return years. These capital loss carrybacks and carryovers are absorbed according to the same rules described earlier for NOLs (see pages C8-24 through C8-32).[64]

EXAMPLE C8-33 ▶ P, S_1, and S_2 Corporations form the P-S_1-S_2 affiliated group. This group has filed consolidated tax returns for several years. During the current year, the affiliated group reports $100,000 of ordinary income, and the following property transaction results:

Group Member	Capital Gains and Losses Short-Term	Capital Gains and Losses Long-Term	Sec. 1231 Gains and Losses
P	$2,000	($1,000)	($2,500)
S_1	(1,000)	7,000	2,000
S_2	(2,000)	3,000	2,000
Total	($1,000)	$9,000	$1,500

In addition, the group carries over a consolidated capital loss of $3,000 from the preceding year. No net Sec. 1231 losses have been recognized in prior years. The P-S_1-S_2 affiliated group's $1,500 consolidated net Sec. 1231 gain is combined with the $8,000 aggregate amount of capital gains and losses ($9,000 − $1,000) and the $3,000 consolidated net capital loss carryover to obtain the current year consolidated capital gain net income of $6,500 ($1,500 + $8,000 − $3,000). This entire amount is taxed at the regular corporate tax rates. ◀

Carryback of a Consolidated Net Capital Loss. A carryback of a member's apportionment of a consolidated capital loss to one of its preceding separate return years is required when capital gains are available in the carryback year against which the loss may be offset. Apportionment of the consolidated capital loss to the loss members occurs in a manner similar to that described for NOLs.

TYPICAL MISCONCEPTION

The allocation of net capital losses to the individual group members is based in part on each member's Sec. 1231 losses. Thus, it is possible for a member with only a Sec. 1231 loss to share in the net capital loss carryforward or carryback.

SRLY Limitation. Carryovers or carrybacks of capital losses from a separate return limitation year invoke the SRLY rules. The amount of the loss carryback or carryover from a separate return limitation year that may be used in a consolidated return year equals the lesser of the loss member's contribution to the consolidated capital gain net income or consolidated capital gain net income.[65]

Sec. 382 Limitation. The Sec. 382 loss limitation rules apply to consolidated and separate return capital loss carryovers as well as consolidated and separate return NOLs. Under Sec. 383(b), capital losses are subject to the general Sec. 382 limitation described earlier.

ADDITIONAL COMMENT

The IRC provides that no election is available to forgo the three-year carryback for a net capital loss. This restriction can complicate matters when the three prior years include separate tax return years of the members of the group.

Taxable Income Limitation. In addition to the special capital loss limitations outlined above, Sec. 1212(a)(1)(A)(ii) contains a general limitation that prevents a capital loss from being carried back or over and creating or increasing the NOL for the tax year to which it is carried. Therefore, use of a capital loss also is limited to the group's consolidated taxable income.

Departing Group Members' Losses. A member leaving the affiliated group may take with it an apportionment of any consolidated capital loss carryover and any of its unused capital loss carryovers that originated in a separate return year. These losses are used in subsequent years until they expire. Apportionment of the consolidated capital loss to the departing group member occurs in a manner similar to that described above for NOLs.

STOCK BASIS ADJUSTMENTS

KEY POINT

Positive stock basis adjustments will reduce the amount of gain reported when a sale of the stock of an affiliated group member occurs.

The basis for an investment in a subsidiary corporation is adjusted annually for its profits and losses as well as for distributions made to higher-tier subsidiaries or to its parent corporation. These rules parallel those used by S corporations and partnerships. If the stock of a profitable subsidiary is sold, a "net" positive basis adjustment produces a smaller capital gain than the gain that would otherwise have been recognized if separate tax returns were filed.[66] The basis adjustment prevents the income earned by the subsidiary during the affiliation from being taxed a second time when the parent corporation disposes of the subsidiary's stock.

The starting point for the calculation is the original basis of the parent corporation's investment in the subsidiary, which depends on the acquisition method used to acquire the stock (e.g., purchase, tax-free corporate formation, or tax-free reorganization). The following basis adjustments must be made to the original basis:

▶ Basis is increased for the subsidiary's income and gain items and decreased for the subsidiary's deduction and loss items that are taken into account in determining consolidated taxable income. The adjustment includes net operating losses but excludes deferred gains and losses, and unused capital losses.

▶ Basis is increased for income that is permanently excluded from taxation (e.g., tax-exempt bond interest and federal income tax refunds).

▶ The distributee's (or higher-tier corporation's) basis is increased for distributions received from lower-tier group members.

▶ Basis in increased for a deduction that does not represent a recovery of basis or an expenditure of money (for example, a dividends-received deduction).

---

[65] As with a NOL, the SRLY rules can apply a single-year or multiple-year contribution comparison.
[66] Losses realized on the sale of a consolidated subsidiary present extremely complex calculations beyond the scope of this text. On March 3, 2005, the Treasury Department issued a new set of regulations disallowing certain duplicate losses from the sale of subsidiary stock by members of a consolidated group. The Treasury Department also announced that it will issue another regulation in the future detailing an alternative method of calculating the loss and tax results.

▶ Basis is decreased for NOLs used in the current year against other group members' taxable income or carried back and used in an earlier year. NOL carryovers and other suspended losses reduce basis in the year they are used. Expiring NOLs and capital losses reduce basis in the year they expire.

▶ Basis is decreased for noncapital expenses that are not deductible (e.g., federal income taxes, the 50% of meals and entertainment expenses that are nondeductible, expenses related to tax-exempt income, and losses disallowed under Sec. 267).

▶ The stock basis for an investment in a lower-tier corporation incurring a pre-acquisition separate return NOL or capital loss is reduced when the loss is used in the current year to offset income or gains reported by other group members. If the pre-acquisition loss expires unused, the unused loss reduces the basis of the stock investment unless the use of part or all of such losses is waived.

▶ Basis is decreased for all distributions without regard to the E&P balance, or whether such amounts were accumulated in pre- or post-affiliation years.

▶ If the negative basis adjustments for losses and distributions, etc. are sufficiently large, the basis of the subsidiary's stock is reduced to zero. Additional basis reductions that occur create an excess loss account. No recognition of income or gain is triggered by the creation of this "negative basis account." Subsequent profits or additional capital contributions may reduce or eliminate the excess loss account and, if large enough, can produce a positive basis for the subsidiary.

EXAMPLE C8-34 ▶ Parent Corporation purchased all of Subsidiary Corporation's stock on January 1, 2005, for $1 million. An election was made for Parent and Subsidiary to begin filing a consolidated tax return in 2005. Subsidiary reported taxable income of $300,000, tax-exempt bond interest of $25,000, and a $5,000 nondeductible capital loss in 2005. On January 1, 2006, Parent sells Subsidiary's stock for $1.4 million. The portion of the consolidated tax liability allocable to Subsidiary is $102,000 ($300,000 × 0.34). Parent recognizes a $177,000 [$1,400,000 − ($1,000,000 + $300,000 + $25,000 − $102,000)] capital gain on the sale. This gain is $223,000 ($400,000 gain if no consolidated return election is made − $177,000 gain with a consolidated return election) smaller than the gain that would have been reported had Parent and Subsidiary not elected to file a consolidated return.[67] ◀

EXAMPLE C8-35 ▶ Parent Corporation purchased all of Subsidiary Corporation's stock on January 1, 2005, for $1 million. During 2005, Subsidiary reported a $750,000 NOL and made a $300,000 distribution to Parent. The $750,000 NOL offsets part of Parent's $2.5 million of taxable income. The basis of the Subsidiary stock is first reduced to zero ($1,000,000 − $750,000 loss − $250,000 distribution). The remaining $50,000 of distribution creates an excess loss account. No gain is recognized by the creation of this "negative basis" account. The excess loss account will be reduced or eliminated in 2006 by subsequent profits or capital contributions, or increased by additional losses and distributions. ◀

TAX PLANNING CONSIDERATIONS

100% DIVIDENDS-RECEIVED DEDUCTION ELECTION

Intercompany dividends are excluded when a consolidated tax return is filed. The 100% dividends-received deduction election (as discussed in Chapter C4) may be used by the affiliated group to exempt from taxation any dividends received from corporations not eligible to be included in the consolidated return (e.g., a 100%-owned life insurance company).

---

[67] Separate basis calculations are required for regular tax and AMT purposes. The AMT basis calculations parallel those made for regular tax purposes but use the appropriate numbers from the AMT calculation. Because of the possible differences in these two amounts, the sale of a stock investment may result in different gain or loss amounts for regular tax and AMT purposes.

If a state does not permit the filing of a consolidated tax return for state income tax purposes,[68] it may be necessary for an affiliated group to elect the 100% dividends-received deduction for both state and federal tax purposes. In such a case, the state requires the filing of separate tax returns by each member of the affiliated group. Generally, the state also permits the claiming of any dividends-received deduction elected for federal income tax purposes. When a consolidated tax return is not filed for state income tax purposes, no exclusion of the dividends is possible, and the 100% dividends-received deduction (which was elected but not used on the federal tax return) is substituted on the state income tax return.

ESTIMATED TAX PAYMENTS

Once consolidated tax returns have been filed for two consecutive years, the affiliated group must pay estimated taxes on a consolidated basis.[69] The affiliated group is treated as a single corporation for this purpose. Thus, the estimated tax payments and any underpayment exceptions or penalties are based on the affiliated group's income for the current year and the immediately preceding tax year without regard to the number of corporations that comprise the affiliated group. This treatment can be advantageous if new, profitable corporations are added to the affiliated group.

EXAMPLE C8-36 ▶ The P-S_1 affiliated group files consolidated tax returns for several years. During 2005, the P-S_1 group reports a $100,000 consolidated tax liability. The P-S_1 affiliated group acquires all of S_2 Corporation's stock during 2006. S_2 is very profitable and causes the P-S_1-S_2 group to report a $300,000 consolidated tax liability in 2006. Assuming the P-S_1-S_2 group does not come under the large corporation rules outlined below, its 2006 estimated tax payments can be based on the P-S_1 group's $100,000 consolidated tax liability for the prior tax year. No underpayment penalties are imposed provided the P-S_1-S_2 group makes $25,000 ($100,000 ÷ 4) estimated tax payments by the fifteenth day of the fourth, sixth, ninth, and twelfth months of the tax year, because the prior year's tax liability exception to the underpayment rules is satisfied. The balance of the consolidated tax liability must be paid by the due date for the consolidated tax return (without regard to any extensions) to avoid penalty. ◀

UNDERPAYMENT RULES. Affiliated groups also are subject to the special underpayment rules of Sec. 6655(d)(2) for large corporations (that is, corporations having taxable income of at least $1 million in any one of the three immediately preceding tax years). An affiliated group is considered one corporation when applying the large corporation rules. Only the actual members of the affiliated group for the three preceding tax years are used in applying the $1 million threshold. New members entering the group are ignored for the three-preceding-years test.[70]

CONSOLIDATED OR SEPARATE BASIS. For the first two years for which a group files consolidated tax returns, the affiliated group may elect to make estimated tax payments on either a consolidated or separate basis. Starting in the third year, however, the affiliated group must make consolidated estimated tax payments. It must continue to do so until separate tax returns are again filed. During the first two tax years for which the election is in effect, the affiliated group sometimes can reduce its quarterly payments by making separate estimated tax payments in the first year and consolidated estimated tax payments in the second year or vice versa. Application of the exceptions to the penalty for underpayment of estimated taxes depends on whether estimated taxes are paid on a separate or consolidated basis. Different exceptions (e.g., prior year's liability or annualization of current year's income) to the underpayment rules should be used by the individual group members if it will reduce the amount of the required estimated tax payments. Determination of the actual separate or consolidated limitations, however, is beyond the scope of this book.

[68] Rev. Rul. 73-484, 1973-2 C.B. 78.
[69] Reg. Sec. 1.1502-5(a).

[70] Proposed Reg. Sec. 1.6655-4(e)(3) requires the $1 million threshold to be applied to all members of the controlled group.

ADDITIONAL COMMENT

The final estimated tax payment for a member joining a consolidated group is due the fifteenth day of the last month of the short taxable year. If a member is acquired after the fifteenth, the final estimated tax payment is already overdue.

SHORT-PERIOD RETURN. If a corporation joins an affiliated group after the beginning of its tax year, a short-period return covering the pre-affiliation time period generally must be filed. The payment rules covering the short-period return are found in Reg. Sec. 1.6655-3. If a corporation leaves an affiliated group, it must make the necessary estimated tax payments required of a corporation filing a separate tax return for the post-affiliation, short-period tax year, unless it joins in the filing of a consolidated tax return with another affiliated group. No estimated tax payment is required for a short tax year that is less than four months.

COMPLIANCE AND PROCEDURAL CONSIDERATIONS

OBJECTIVE 11

Explain the procedures for making an initial consolidated return election

THE BASIC ELECTION AND RETURN

An affiliated group makes an election to use the consolidated method for filing its tax return by filing a consolidated tax return (Form 1120) that includes the income, expenses, etc. of all its members. The election must be made no later than the due date for the common parent corporation's tax return including any permitted extensions.[71] An affiliated group can change from a consolidated tax return to separate tax returns,[72] or from separate tax returns to a consolidated tax return, at any time on or before the last day for filing the consolidated tax return. Once that day has passed, no change can be made.

Appendix B presents a sample Form 1120 for reporting the current year's results for the Alpha affiliated group described in Example C8-37. The Form 1120 involves the five intercompany transactions mentioned in the example, and a worksheet that summarizes the income and expense items for the five companies illustrates the reporting of the intercompany transactions and presents the details of the consolidated taxable income calculation.

EXAMPLE C8-37 ▶

Alpha Manufacturing Corporation owns 100% of the stock of Beta, Charlie, Delta, and Echo corporations. The affiliated group has filed consolidated returns for a number of years using the calendar year as their tax year. The components of the separate taxable income amounts of the five corporations are reported on the supporting schedule of the group's consolidated tax return contained In Appendix B. This return illustrates five common transactions involving members of an affiliated group. These are as follows:

▶ The sale of inventory from Alpha to Beta, which increases Alpha's deferred intercompany profit amount. Beta sells additional inventory to outsiders.

▶ Intragroup dividends paid from Beta and Echo to Alpha

▶ Payment of interest from Delta to Alpha

▶ The sale of a truck from Alpha to Beta

▶ Beta's depreciation of the truck acquired in the intercompany transaction ◀

ADDITIONAL COMMENT

If a group is considering making a consolidated return election, a properly executed Form 1122 should be obtained before any corporation is sold during the election year. After the sale, the consent form may be difficult to obtain.

Students should review this sample return to see how the transactions are reported and how the numbers from the consolidated taxable income schedule are reported in the affiliated group's Form 1120. Although not displayed in Appendix B, the consolidated return should include a Schedule M-3 if applicable (see Chapter C3).

In addition to filing the necessary Form 1120 reflecting the consolidated results of operations, each corporation that is a member of the affiliated group during the initial consolidated return year must consent to the election. The parent corporation's consent is evidenced by its filing the consolidated tax return (Form 1120). Subsidiary corporations consent to the election by filing a Form 1122 (Authorization and Consent of Subsidiary to be Included in a Consolidated Income Tax Return) and submitting it as a

---

[71] Reg. Sec. 1.1502-75(a)(1).
[72] Such a change can take place only for the initial consolidated return year or for a tax year for which the IRS has granted permission to discontinue the consolidated return election.

part of the initial consolidated tax return. Only newly acquired subsidiary corporations file Form 1122 with subsequent consolidated tax returns.

Each consolidated tax return also must include an Affiliations Schedule (Form 851). This form includes the name, address, and identification number of the corporations included in the affiliated group, the corporation's tax prepayments, the stock holdings at the beginning of the tax year, and all stock ownership changes occurring during the tax year.

Affiliated groups commonly use two types of consolidated tax return formats. One type is a schedular format where the affiliated group files a single tax return with separate spreadsheets showing the calculation of consolidated taxable income and any supporting data. (This format is used in the sample consolidated tax return included in Appendix B.) A second type is a "pancake" format where individual Form 1120s report the activity of each group member. In addition, a separate Form 1120 for an "eliminations" company reports all the adjustments and eliminations needed to go from the various separate tax returns to a single consolidated return, and a final Form 1120 reports the affiliated group's combined results. The pancake format tends to be used by affiliated groups comprised of large firms.

The due date for the consolidated tax return is 2½ months after the end of the affiliated group's tax year. A six-month extension for filing the consolidated tax return is permitted if the parent corporation files Form 7004 and pays the estimated balance of the consolidated tax liability. The due date for the tax return of a subsidiary corporation that is not included in the consolidated return depends on whether the affiliated group's consolidated tax return has been filed by the due date for the subsidiary corporation's tax return. These rules are beyond the scope of this introductory text but can be reviewed in Reg. Sec. 1.1502-76(c).

PARENT CORPORATION AS AGENT FOR THE AFFILIATED GROUP

The parent corporation acts as agent for each subsidiary corporation and for the affiliated group. As agent for each subsidiary, the parent corporation is authorized to act in its own name in all matters relating to the affiliated group's tax liability for the consolidated return year.[73]

No subsidiary corporation can act in its own behalf with respect to a consolidated return year except to the extent that the parent corporation is prohibited from acting in its behalf. Thus, a subsidiary corporation is prevented from making or changing any election used in computing separate taxable income, carrying on correspondence with the IRS regarding the determination of a tax liability, filing any requests for extensions of time in which to file a tax return, filing a claim for a refund or credit relating to a consolidated return year, or electing to deduct or credit foreign tax payments.

LIABILITY FOR TAXES DUE

The parent corporation and every other corporation that was a group member for any part of the consolidated return year are severally liable for that year's consolidated taxes.[74] Thus, the entire consolidated tax liability may be collected from one group member if, for example, the other group members are unable to pay their allocable portion. The IRS can ignore attempts made by the group members to limit their share of the liability by entering into agreements with one another or with third parties. Thus, the potential consolidated tax liability and any deficiencies could accrue to a corporation that is a member of an affiliated group for even a few days during a tax year.

An exception to this several liability principle occurs when a subsidiary corporation ceases to be a group member as a result of its stock being sold or exchanged before a deficiency is assessed against the affiliated group. Thus, the IRS can opt to assess a former subsidiary corporation for only its allocable portion of the total deficiency if it believes that the assessment and collection of the balance of the deficiency from the other group members will not be jeopardized.

ADDITIONAL COMMENT

All states other than Louisiana, New Hampshire, and Ohio that require combined reporting of affiliated corporations allow taxpayers to elect to file a consolidated tax return for parent-subsidiary groups. The percent of required direct or indirect ownership is 80% for federal consolidated tax return purposes as opposed to the 50% minimum typically used for combined reporting under the state income tax rules.

ADDITIONAL COMMENT

Each member corporation is severally liable for the entire tax liability of the affiliated group. Anyone purchasing a corporation out of an affiliated group should consider this factor when negotiating the purchase price of the target corporation.

---

[73] Reg. Sec. 1.1502-77(a).

[74] Reg. Sec. 1.1502-6(a).

PROBLEM MATERIALS

DISCUSSION QUESTIONS

C8-1 What minimum level of stock ownership is required for a corporation to be included in an affiliated group?

C8-2 In what way are the consolidated return regulations different from most of the other tax regulations?

C8-3 Which of the following entities are includible in an affiliated group?
a. C corporation
b. Foreign corporation
c. Life insurance company taxed under Sec. 801
d. Limited liability company.

C8-4 Explain the difference between the stock ownership requirements for having a group of companies that can consolidate their financial reporting activities and an affiliated group and a parent-subsidiary controlled group as used within the tax law.

C8-5 P Corporation is 100% owned by Peter McKay. P Corporation owns 100% of S Corporation and 49% of T Corporation. S Corporation owns the remaining 51% of T Corporation. S Corporation also owns 100% of PeterM, a limited liability company (LLC). The LLC has elected to be taxed as a C corporation. Peter McKay also owns 100% of Z Corporation's stock. All are U.S. entities. Which entities are included in an affiliated group? In a controlled group? Would your answer change if the LLC had not elected to be taxed as a C corporation? If so, describe the change.

C8-6 P, S_1, S_2, and S_3 Corporations form a controlled group of corporations. Because S_3 Corporation is a nonincludible insurance corporation, only P, S_1, and S_2 Corporations are permitted to file their income tax returns on a consolidated basis. Explain to P Corporation's president the alternatives available for allocating the tax savings from the 15%, 25%, and 34% tax rates to the members of the controlled group.

C8-7 P Corporation has two subsidiaries, S_1 and S_2, both of which are 100%-owned. All three corporations are currently filing separate tax returns. P and S_1 have been profitable. S_2 is a start-up company that has reported losses for its first two years of existence. S_2 eventually will be selling cosmetics to S_1 for distribution to retailers. Explain to P Corporation's president the advantages (and disadvantages) of the three corporations filing a consolidated tax return.

C8-8 Briefly explain how consolidated taxable income is calculated starting with the financial accounting (book) income information for each individual group member. Explain how the consolidated taxable income calculation is different from the taxable income calculation for a C corporation filing a separate tax return.

C8-9 Determine whether each of the following statements is true or false:
a. One member of an affiliated group may elect to use the accrual method of accounting even though another group member uses the cash receipts and disbursements method of accounting.
b. A corporation that uses the calendar year as its tax year acquires all the stock of another corporation that has for years used a fiscal year as its tax year. Both corporations may continue to use their previous separate return tax years when filing their initial consolidated tax return.
c. T Corporation, a calendar year taxpayer, becomes a member of the P-S affiliated group at the close of business on February 28 of a non-leap year. The P-S group has filed consolidated tax returns using the calendar year for a number of years. The P-S-T affiliated group's consolidated tax return includes all of T's separate taxable income for the year.

C8-10 What events permit an affiliated group to terminate its consolidated tax return election? If a corporation leaves an affiliated group, how long must the corporation be disaffiliated before it can again be included in its former group's consolidated tax return? In a new affiliated group filing a consolidated tax return?

C8-11 The P-S_1-S_2 affiliated group has filed consolidated tax returns using a calendar year for a number of years. At the close of business on September 15, P Corporation sells all its S_1 Corporation stock to Mickey. P Corporation retains its investment in S_2 Corporation.
a. Explain what tax returns are required of the three corporations for the current year.
b. What income and expense items are included in each of the tax returns required of the P-S_1-S_2 affiliated group and its members during the current year?
c. What effect does the sale have on the P-S_1-S_2 group's prior year intercompany items and its charitable contributions carryover that is unused in the current year consolidated tax return?

C8-12 Assume the same facts as in Question C8-11 except that the original affiliated group was just P and S_1 Corporations and that the S_1 stock was sold to Mickey at the close of business on July 15. What affect does the sale have on the P-S_1 group's prior year intercompany items and its charitable contribution carryover that is unused in the final consolidated tax return?

C8-13 Briefly explain how the consolidated alternative minimum tax is calculated.

C8-14 Define the following terms:
a. Intercompany transaction
b. Intercompany item
c. Corresponding item
d. Matching rule
e. Acceleration rule

C8-15 Explain how the rules governing depreciation recapture, basis, and depreciation operate when a seven-year recovery class property under the MACRS rules is sold at a profit by one group member to a second group member after the property has been held for three years. The purchasing group member will depreciate the property using the MACRS rules over a seven-year recovery period.

C8-16 Compare and contrast the reporting of interest income and interest expense by P and S Corporations for financial accounting and consolidated tax return purposes when P Corporation lends money to S Corporation on August 1 for a three-year period. Both corporations use the calendar year as their tax year, and interest is paid on July 31 each year. Assume both corporations use the accrual method of accounting.

C8-17 P and S_1 Corporations constitute the P-S_1 affiliated group on January 1. S_1 Corporation acquires all the stock of S_2 Corporation at the close of business on April 1. Which of the following transactions are intercompany transactions?
a. P Corporation sells inventory to S_1 Corporation throughout the current year.
b. S_2 Corporation performs services for S_1 Corporation between May 1 and December 31 of the current year.
c. S_1 Corporation sells machinery (Sec. 1245 property) to S_2 Corporation on September 1.
d. P Corporation sells inventory to the PS$_1$ Partnership, which is owned equally by P and S_1 Corporations, on July 23.

C8-18 P, S_1, and S_2 Corporations constitute the P-S_1-S_2 affiliated group. The group members use the accrual method of accounting and the calendar year as their tax year. Determine whether each of the following transactions that take place during the current year are intercompany transactions. For each item, indicate the intercompany item and corresponding item.
a. P Corporation lends S_1 Corporation money, and P charges interest at a 10% annual rate. The money and interest remains unpaid at the end of the tax year.
b. S_1 Corporation sells inventory to P Corporation. At year end, P Corporation holds the entire inventory purchased from S_1 Corporation.

c. P Corporation sells land (Sec. 1231 property) to S_2 Corporation. S_2 Corporation holds the land (Sec. 1231 property) at year-end.
d. S_2 Corporation pays a cash dividend to P Corporation.
e. S_1 Corporation provides engineering services that are capitalized as part of the cost of S_2's new factory building.

C8-19 Indicate for each of the following dividend payments the tax treatment available in computing consolidated taxable income:
a. Dividend received from a C corporation that is 10%-owned by the parent corporation.
b. Dividend received from a C corporation that is 100%-owned by the parent corporation and included in the consolidated tax return election.
c. Dividend received from a foreign corporation that is 80%-owned by the parent corporation. The foreign corporation earns no U.S. source income.
d. Dividend received from an unconsolidated life insurance corporation that is 100%-owned by the parent corporation.

C8-20 Explain the circumstances in which a consolidated NOL arising in the current year can be carried back to a preceding separate return year.

C8-21 What advantages can accrue to an affiliated group or an individual group member by electing to forgo the carryback of an NOL incurred in a consolidated return year? A separate return year? Who makes the election to forgo each carryback?

C8-22 Define the term SRLY and explain its significance and application to an affiliated group filing a consolidated tax return.

C8-23 What is a Sec. 382 ownership change? What is the Sec. 382 loss limitation? Explain their significance and application to an affiliated group filing a consolidated tax return.

C8-24 P Corporation purchases 100% of the stock of S Corporation on January 1. S Corporation is P Corporation's only subsidiary. Explain to the president of P Corporation what basis adjustment must be made at year-end for its $2 million investment in S Corporation when S earns $350,000 of taxable income and $30,000 of tax-exempt interest income, while it distributes a $100,000 dividend to its parent corporation. Each company paid its own tax liability. Assume a 34% corporate tax rate.

C8-25 Explain why an affiliated group filing a consolidated tax return might make a federal tax election to claim a 100% dividends-received deduction for a tax year even though all dividends received during that year are received from corporations that are 100%-owned by the parent company.

C8-26 During what time period can an affiliated group elect to file a consolidated tax return? How is the election made? During what time period is the election to disaffiliate made?

C8-27 Indicate for which of the following tax-related matters the parent corporation can act as the affiliated group's agent:

a. Making an initial consent for a subsidiary corporation to participate in a consolidated return election

b. Changing an accounting method election for a subsidiary corporation

c. Carrying on correspondence with the IRS during an audit regarding a transaction entered into by a subsidiary corporation that affects the group's determination of consolidated taxable income

d. Requesting an extension of time within which to file a consolidated tax return

C8-28 You are the managing partner of a local CPA firm. The president of your largest client, a medium-size manufacturing firm, advises you that the firm is about to acquire its largest supplier. Both firms have been profitable for the past ten years and have filed separate tax returns. The president wants to know what tax return filing options are available for the two companies. What additional information do you need to make an informed decision? What factors do you think are most important in the firm's decision?

ISSUE IDENTIFICATION QUESTIONS

C8-29 Mark owns all the stock of Red and Green Corporations. Red Corporation has been reporting $125,000 in taxable income for each of the past five years. Green Corporation annually has been reporting $30,000 NOLs, which have accumulated to $150,000. Approximately one-third of Red's profits come from sales to Green. Intercompany sales between Red and Green have increased during each of the last five years. What tax issues should Mark consider with respect to his investments in Red and Green Corporations?

C8-30 Alpha and Baker Corporations, two accrual method of accounting corporations that use the calendar year as their tax year, have filed consolidated tax returns for a number of years. Baker Corporation, a 100%-owned subsidiary of Alpha, is transferring a patent, equipment, and working capital to newly created Charles Corporation in exchange for 100% of its stock. In the current year, the corporation will begin to produce parts for the automotive industry. Charles Corporation expects to incur organizational expenditures of $10,000 and start-up expenditures of $60,000. What tax issues should Charles Corporation consider with respect to the selection of its overall accounting method, inventory method, and tax year, the proper reporting of its organizational and start-up expenditures, and the type of income tax return to file?

C8-31 Wolverine Corporation is the parent company of a three-member affiliated group. Wolverine and Buckeye Corporations have been affiliated for a number of years. Both corporations have filed consolidated tax returns for ten years. Early in the current year, Wolverine Corporation purchased Gopher Corporation, a start-up business, which incurred net operating losses in each of its first three years. Gopher's losses total $250,000. Gopher's loss carryover equals about one year's profit for Wolverine Corporation. Can the management of the Wolverine-Buckeye-Gopher group use all the losses in the first year after affiliation? The group expects profits in the first year after affiliation to be $300,000 with Gopher's contribution to the total being $50,000. What tax issues should the three corporations consider when deciding how to use the NOL?

PROBLEMS

C8-32 *Affiliated Group Definition.* Which of the following independent situations result in an affiliated group being created? In each case, indicate the corporations that are eligible to be included in the consolidated tax return election. All corporations are domestic corporations unless otherwise indicated.

a. Zeke, an individual, owns all the stock of A and B Corporations.

b. Kelly, an individual, owns all the stock of P and W Corporations. P Corporation owns all of the stock of both S_1 and S_2 Corporations.

c. P Corporation owns all the stock of S_1 and S_2 Corporations. S_1 Corporation owns 40% of the stock of S_3 Corporation. P Corporation owns the remaining S_3 stock. S_2 Corporation is a French corporation.

C8-33 *Affiliated Group Definition.* P owns 100% of L, a domestic manufacturing firm. They have filed a consolidated return for many years. In each of the independent situations below, determine whether any other entities also could join the consolidated return.

a. L owns 100% of F, a French manufacturing firm.

b. P owns 70% and L owns 15% of D, a domestic corporation that owns restaurants. Unrelated individuals own the remaining 15%.

c. P owns 90% of K, a domestic manufacturing firm, and K owns 70% of R, a domestic corporation. Unrelated investors own the remaining 10% of K and 30% of R.

d. P purchases 100% of I, a domestic insurance company, during the current year.

e. P owns 100% of S, a domestic corporation that has elected to be taxed as an S corporation.

C8-34 *Stock Ownership Requirement.* P Corporation is the parent corporation of the P-S_1-S_2 affiliated group. P Corporation is conducting negotiations to purchase the stock of T Corporation. The management of P would like to include T in the affiliated group's consolidated tax return. T Corporation's outstanding shares are as listed.

Type of Stock	Shares Outstanding	Par Value	Market Value
Common stock (1 vote per share)	50,000	$ 1	$30
Voting preferred stock (4 votes per share)	5,000	100	95
Nonvoting preferred stock	20,000	100	90

The nonvoting preferred stock also is nonparticipating and nonconvertible. Determine a plan that permits P to acquire enough stock to include T in the affiliated group. Are other plans available for including T in the affiliated group?

C8-35 *Consolidated Return Election.* P and S Corporations have been in existence for a number of years. P uses the calendar year as its tax year. S Corporation uses a fiscal year ending June 30 as its tax year. Both corporations are involved in manufacturing electronic circuitry and use the FIFO method of accounting for their inventories. At the close of business on July 31, 2006, P acquires all the S stock and elects to file a consolidated tax return for 2006.

a. What tax year must be used in filing the consolidated tax return?

b. What overall accounting method(s) can P and S Corporations elect?

c. What is the last date on which the election to file a consolidated tax return can be made?

d. What income of P and S is included in the consolidated tax return? In a separate return?

C8-36 *Consolidated Return Election.* The P-S_1 affiliated group has filed consolidated tax returns for several years. All P-S_1 returns have been filed using the calendar year as the tax year. At the close of business on August 8, 2006, P Corporation purchases all the stock of S_2 Corporation. S_2 has been filing its separate tax returns using a fiscal year ending September 30. At the close of business on November 9, 2006, P Corporation sells all its S_1 stock.

a. What tax year must S_2 Corporation use after joining the affiliated group?

b. What tax returns are required of S_2 Corporation to report its results from October 1, 2005, through December 31, 2006?

c. What tax year must S_1 Corporation use after leaving the affiliated group?

d. What action is needed (if any) should S_1 desire to change to a fiscal year filing basis?

C8-37 *Income Included in Consolidated Return.* P and S_1 Corporations form the P-S_1 affiliated group, which has filed consolidated tax returns on a calendar year basis for a number of years. At the close of business on February 25 of the current year, P Corporation sells all the stock of S_1 Corporation. P Corporation acquires all the stock of S_2 Corporation at the close of business for both firms on September 25. S_2 Corporation has always used the calendar year as its tax year. The new P-S_2 affiliated group elects to file a consolidated tax return for this year. What tax returns are required of P, S_1, and S_2 Corporations with respect to reporting the current year's income? How would your answer to the tax return question change if the two transactions were reversed?

C8-38 *Alternative Minimum Tax.* P and S Corporations are members of the P-S affiliated group, which has filed consolidated tax returns for a number of years. Consolidated adjusted current earnings is $800,000. Consolidated preadjustment alternative minimum taxable income is $400,000. Consolidated taxable income is $300,000. The consolidated general business credit amount (computed without regard to the overall limitation) is $15,000. Assume P and S are not eligible for the small corporation AMT exemption that is based on gross receipts. Also assume no adjustment pertains to the U.S. production activities deduction. What is the P-S group's federal tax liability? Are any carryovers created to subsequent tax years? How are the credit carryovers used?

C8-39 *Intercompany Transactions.* P, S_1, and S_2 Corporations form the $P-S_1-S_2$ affiliated group, with P Corporation owning all the stock of S_1 and S_2 Corporations. The $P-S_1-S_2$ group has filed consolidated tax returns for several years. In 2006, S_1 sells land it has held for a possible expansion to S_2 for $275,000. The land originally cost S_1 $120,000 in 2001. S_2 constructs a new plant facility on the land. The land and the plant facility are sold for cash to a third party in 2008 with $400,000 of the sales price attributable to the land.

  a. What are the amount and character of S_1's recognized gain or loss? In what year(s) is the gain or loss included in S_1's separate taxable income? In what year(s) is the gain or loss included in consolidated taxable income?

  b. What are the amount and character of S_2's recognized gain or loss? In what year(s) is the gain or loss included in S_2's separate taxable income? In what year(s) is the gain or loss included in consolidated taxable income?

C8-40 *Intercompany Transactions.* P and S Corporations form the P-S affiliated group. The P-S group has filed consolidated tax returns for several years. S acquired some land from P Corporation in 2005 for $60,000. P acquired the land in 1999 as an investment at a cost of $20,000. S used the land for four years as additional parking space for its employees and made no improvements to the land. S sells the land to an unrelated party in 2009 for $180,000. Terms of the sale require a 20% down payment in the year of sale and four equal installments to be paid annually in years 2010 through 2013. Interest is charged at a rate acceptable to the IRS. Assume all payments are made in a timely fashion.

  a. What are the amount and character of P's recognized gain or loss? In what year(s) is the gain or loss included in P's separate taxable income? In what year(s) is it included in consolidated taxable income?

  b. What are the amount and character of S's recognized gain or loss? In what year(s) is the gain or loss included in S's separate taxable income? In what year(s) is it included in consolidated taxable income?

  c. How is the interest income reported?

C8-41 *Intercompany Transactions.* P and S Corporations form the P-S affiliated group, which has filed consolidated tax returns for several years. On June 10, 2004, P purchased a new machine (five-year MACRS property) for $20,000 cash. P made no expensing election under Sec. 179 but did claim the 50% addition depreciation available in 2004. On April 4, 2006, P sells the machine to S for $18,000 cash. S uses the property for two years before selling it to an unrelated party on March 10, 2008, for $15,000.

  a. What are the amount and character of P's recognized gain or loss? In what year(s) is the gain or loss included in P's separate taxable income? In what year(s) is the gain or loss included in consolidated taxable income?

  b. What is S's basis for the equipment?

  c. What depreciation method should S use for the equipment?

  d. What are the amount and character of S's recognized gain or loss? In what year(s) is the gain or loss included in S's separate taxable income? In what year(s) is the gain or loss included in consolidated taxable income?

C8-42 P Corporation owns all the stock of S Corporation. Both corporations use the accrual method of accounting. P Corporation engages in two transactions with its 100%-owned subsidiary, S Corporation. In the first transaction, P sold an automobile having an $18,000 adjusted basis and a $30,000 FMV to S. In the second transaction, S provided cleaning services to P in the amount of $6,000. What are the similarities and differences in how P and S report the two transactions?

C8-43 *Intercompany Transactions.* P and S Corporations form the P-S affiliated group, which has filed consolidated tax returns for a number of years. On January 1, 2003, P Corporation purchased a new machine (seven-year MACRS property) for $50,000. P does not make a Sec. 179 election for this acquisition but does claim the 30% additional depreciation available before May 6, 2003. At the close of business on June 30, 2006, P sells the machine to S for $37,500. The machine is still classified as seven-year MACRS property in S's hands. S holds the asset until March 15, 2009, at which time S sells it to an unrelated party for $20,000.

  a. What are the amount and character of P's recognized gain or loss? In what year(s) is the gain or loss included in P's separate taxable income? In what year(s) is it included in consolidated taxable income?

b. What are the amount and character of S's recognized gain or loss? In what year(s) is the gain or loss included in S's separate taxable income? In what year(s) is it included in consolidated taxable income?

C8-44 *Intercompany Transactions.* P and S Corporations form the P-S affiliated group, which has filed consolidated tax returns for a number of years. During 2006, P Corporation began selling inventory items to S Corporation. P and S use the first-in, first-out inventory method. The intercompany profit on P's sales to S was $75,000 in 2006. Goods remaining in S's inventory at the end of 2006 accounted for $35,000 of the intercompany profit. During 2007, all of S's beginning inventory of goods acquired from P in 2006 was sold to unrelated parties and the intercompany profit on P's current sales of inventory to S amounted to $240,000. Goods remaining in S's inventory at the end of 2007 accounted for $70,000 of the intercompany profit. Taxable income for the P-S affiliated group (excluding the deferral and restoration of profits on intercompany inventory sales) is $100,000 in each year. What is consolidated taxable income for 2006 and 2007 for the P-S group?

C8-45 *Intercompany Transactions.* P and S Corporations form the P-S affiliated group. P has owned all the S Corporation stock since 2000. The affiliated group has filed consolidated tax returns since 2000. No intragroup inventory sales occurred before 2005. During 2005, P sells S 100,000 widgets, earning $5 per unit profit on the sale. S uses the FIFO method to account for its inventories. On January 1, 2006, 25,000 widgets remain in S's inventory. During 2006, S sells the beginning widget inventory and purchases 175,000 additional widgets from P. P earns a $6 per unit profit on the sale. S retains 40,000 of these units in its 2006 ending inventory. No additional widgets are purchased in 2007. All widgets in beginning inventory are sold by S during 2007. In all years, S sells the widgets for the same price it paid P for them.
a. What intercompany profit amounts are deferred in 2005? In 2006? In 2007?
b. How would your answer to Part a change if the LIFO inventory method were instead used? (Assume the 2006 year-end LIFO inventory includes 25,000 units acquired in 2005 and 15,000 units acquired in 2006.)

C8-46 *Intercompany Transactions.* P Corporation has owned all of the stock of S Corporation since 1999. The P-S affiliated group began filing a consolidated tax return in 2004 using the calendar year as its tax year. Both corporations use the accrual method of accounting. On July 1, 2005, P loaned S $250,000 on a one-year note. Interest is charged at a 12% simple rate. P repays the loan plus interest on June 30, 2006.
a. When does P report its interest income in its separate tax return? When does S report its interest expense in its separate tax return?
b. How would your answer to Part a change if P instead used the cash method of accounting?

C8-47 *Intercompany Transactions.* P and S Corporations form the P-S affiliated group. S Corporation owns 80% of an LLC that is engaged in a manufacturing business. Peter Hart owns the remaining 20% of the LLC. The LLC has not elected under the check-the-box regulations to be taxed as a corporation. S Corporation sells inventory costing $125,000 to the LLC for $250,000. How does S Corporation report the profit on the sale?

C8-48 *Dividends-Received Deduction.* P, S and T Corporations form the P-S-T affiliated group. The P-S-T group has filed consolidated tax returns for several years. P, S and T report separate taxable income amounts (excluding any dividend payments, eliminations, and dividends-received deductions) of $200,000, ($70,000), and $175,000, respectively, for the current year. Cash dividend payments received by P and S this year are as follows:

Shareholder Corporation	Distributing Corporation	Amount
P	T	$125,000
P	100%-owned nonconsolidated U.S.-based life insurance company	15,000
S	20%-owned domestic corporation	40,000
P	51%-owned nonconsolidated foreign corporation	10,000

a. What is the amount of the gross income reported in the P and S separate tax returns as a result of the four distributions?
b. What is the amount of the consolidated dividends-received deduction?
c. Why might P elect to claim a 100% dividends-received deduction for the dividend received from T for federal income tax purposes, even though a consolidated tax return is being filed?

C8-49 *Charitable Contribution Deduction.* P and S Corporations form the P-S affiliated group. This group has filed consolidated tax returns for several years. The group reports consolidated taxable income (excluding charitable contributions) for the current year of $90,000. Included in this amount are a consolidated dividends-received deduction of $8,000 and an NOL deduction of $25,000 that represents a carryover of last year's consolidated NOL. P and S Corporations make cash contributions to public charities of $18,000 and $12,000, respectively, during this year. In addition, S Corporation accrues an unpaid contribution in the amount of $10,000. It paid the contribution in the first 30 days of the new tax year.
a. What is the P-S group's consolidated taxable income?
b. What is the amount of the charitable contribution carryover? How long can it be carried forward?

C8-50 *NOL Carrybacks and Carryovers.* P and S Corporations form the P-S affiliated group, which files consolidated tax returns for the period 2005 through 2008. The affiliated group reports the following results for this period:

| | | Taxable Income | | |
Group Member	2005	2006	2007	2008
P	$10,000	($6,000)	$20,000	$15,000
S	2,000	2,000	(30,000)	10,000
Consolidated taxable income (excluding NOL deduction)	$12,000	($4,000)	($10,000)	$25,000

No elections were made to forgo the NOL carrybacks. Assume the U.S. production activities deduction does not apply.
a. What portion of the 2006 and 2007 consolidated NOLs can be carried back to 2005? Over to 2008?
b. Who files for the tax refund when the 2006 and 2007 NOLs are carried back?

C8-51 *NOL Carryover.* P, S_1, and S_2 Corporations form the P-S_1-S_2 affiliated group, which has filed consolidated tax returns since the creation of all three corporations in 2005. At the close of business on July 10, 2007, P Corporation sells its entire interest in S_2 Corporation. The affiliated group remains in existence after the sale because P Corporation still owns all the S_1 stock. Assume the U.S. production activities deduction does not apply. The P-S_1-S_2 group reports the following results for 2005 through 2007:

| | | Taxable Income | |
Group Member	2005	2006	2007
P	$ 8,000	($12,000)	$16,000
S_1	9,000	(24,000)	(4,000)
S_2	10,000	(36,000)	6,000[a]
S_2 (7/11–12/31)			8,000[b]
Consolidated taxable income (excluding NOL deduction)	$27,000	($72,000)	$18,000[c]

[a]Taxable income earned from January 1, 2007, through July 10, 2007.
[b]Taxable income from July 11, 2007, through December 31, 2007, is included in S_2's separate tax return.
[c]$16,000 − $4,000 + $6,000.

What amount of 2006's consolidated NOL can the P-S_1 affiliated group carry over to 2007 and 2008? What amount can S_2 carry over to 2007 and 2008? When does the carryover expire?

C8-52 *NOL Carryovers and Carrybacks.* P Corporation acquires S Corporation on January 1, 2007. Each company filed separate calendar year tax returns for 2006. P and S report the following results for 2006 and 2007:

Group Member	2006	2007
P	$40,000	($30,000)
S	(30,000)	20,000
Taxable income	N/A	($10,000)

N/A = Not applicable

a. What are the 2007 tax consequences assuming a consolidated tax return is filed? What are the tax consequences if separate tax returns had instead been filed? (Ignore the Sec. 382 loss limitation that might apply to the acquisition of S, and ignore the U.S. production activities deduction.)

b. Assume P and S report the following taxable income in 2008 before any NOL carryover: P, $21,000; S, $6,000. What is the consolidated taxable income assuming a consolidated return was filed in 2007?

C8-53 *Special NOL Limitation.* P, S_1, and S_2 Corporations form the P-S_1-S_2 affiliated group. P Corporation was created by Bart on January 1, 2006. P purchased all the S_1 and S_2 Corporation stock on September 1, 2006, after both corporations were in operation for about six months. All three corporations filed separate tax returns in 2006. The P-S_1-S_2 affiliated group elected to file a consolidated tax return starting in 2007. Assume the U.S. production activities deduction does not apply. The P-S_1-S_2 group, which is still owned by Bart, reports the following results for 2006 through 2008:

Group Member	2006	2007	2008
		Taxable Income	
P	($8,000)	$50,000	$10,000
S_1	(24,000)	20,000	(18,000)
S_2	(16,000)	(10,000)	15,000
Consolidated taxable income (excluding NOL deduction)	XXX	$60,000	$7,000

a. What loss carryovers are available to be used in 2007, 2008, and 2009? (Ignore the Sec. 382 loss limitation that might apply to the acquisitions of S_1 and S_2.)

b. How would your answer to Part a change if Bart instead created P, S_1, and S_2 Corporations as an affiliated group on January 1, 2006?

C8-54 *Sec. 382 Loss Limitation.* Mack owns all of the stock of P Corporation. P Corporation owns all the stock of S_1 and S_2 Corporations. At the close of business on December 31, 2005, Mack sold his P Corporation stock to Jack for $9 million. The P-$S_1$-$S_2$ affiliated group has a consolidated NOL carryover to 2006 of $1.5 million at the end of 2005. Assume the U.S. production activities deduction does not apply.

a. Has a Sec. 382 ownership change occurred? Explain.

b. What is the P-S_1-S_2 affiliated group's consolidated Sec. 382 limitation for 2006 if the federal long-term tax-exempt rate is 3.5%? (Ignore the SRLY loss limitation that might apply to Jack's acquisition of the P Corporation stock.)

c. How much of the consolidated NOL carryover can be used in 2006 if the affiliated group's taxable income is $750,000? In 2007 if the affiliated group's consolidated taxable income is $200,000?

C8-55 *Consolidated Taxable Income.* P and S Corporations have filed consolidated tax returns for a number of years. P is an accrual method of accounting taxpayer, and S is a cash method of accounting taxpayer. P and S report separate return taxable income (before adjustments, the NOL deduction, and special deductions) for the current year of $100,000 and $150,000, respectively. These numbers include the following current year transactions or events accounted for appropriately on a separate return basis.

- P sold land held for investment purposes to S at a $25,000 profit three years ago. S sold the land (a Sec. 1231 asset) to an unrelated corporation this year for a $16,000 gain. The current year's gain is included in S's separate taxable income.

- P's separate taxable income includes a $12,000 dividend received from S Corporation.

- P sold inventory to S last year for which the deferred intercompany profit at the beginning of this year was $50,000. All this inventory was sold outside the affiliated group this year. Additional inventory was sold by P to S this year. Some of this inventory remained unsold at year-end. The intercompany profit on the unsold inventory included in P's separate taxable income is $80,000.

- The P-S group has a $20,000 NOL carryover available from last year.

- S received a $10,000 dividend from an unrelated corporation.

- P and S made charitable contributions of $16,000 and $12,000, respectively, this year that are included in the separate taxable income calculations.

- P lent S $150,000 early in the current year. S repaid the loan before year-end. In addition, S paid P $6,000 of interest at the time of the repayment for the use of the borrowed money.
- P and S had qualified production activities income of $75,000 and $140,000, respectively.

a. What is consolidated taxable income for the P-S affiliated group for the current year?

b. What is the consolidated tax liability?

COMPREHENSIVE PROBLEM

C8-56 Using the facts from Problem C8-58 below calculate the separate return tax liabilities of P and S Corporations. How much larger (or smaller) will the total of the two separate return tax liabilities be than the affiliated group's consolidated return tax liability? What taxes are due (or refund available) if Flying Gator made $125,000 of estimated tax payments and T Corporation made $25,000 of estimated tax payments?

TAX STRATEGY PROBLEM

C8-57 Sandra and John, who are unrelated, own all of Alpha and Beta Corporations. John owns 60% of Alpha's stock and 40% of Beta's stock. Sandra owns 40% of Alpha's stock and 60% of Beta's stock. For five years, Alpha has conducted manufacturing activities and sold machine parts primarily in the eastern United States. Alpha has reported $75,000 of operating profits in each of the last two years. Alpha's operating profits are expected to grow to $150,000 during the next five years. Alpha still has $100,000 of NOLs that need to be used before it starts paying federal income taxes. Alpha sells 25% of its product to Beta. Beta has been working to establish a market niche for reselling Alpha products in the southwestern United States. In the start-up phase of establishing the market, Beta incurred $200,000 of NOLs. Under the sales arrangement with Alpha, probably the best that Beta can hope to achieve in the short-run is reach a break-even point.

Required: What suggestions can you offer Sandra and John about the short-term possibility of using Alpha and Beta's NOLs against the profits that Alpha expects to earn and about minimizing their overall tax liabilities if both businesses become profitable? Sandra has specifically asked about merging the two companies into a single entity so the losses of one entity can offset the profits of the other and delay the need to pay income taxes to the federal government. Sandra indicates that the two companies were created for business reasons and not tax avoidance reasons. The operating situation has changed and, according to Sandra, now may be the time to combine the entities into one. However, John is not sure that bringing the two businesses together is a good idea.

TAX FORM/RETURN PREPARATION PROBLEM

C8-58 The Flying Gator Corporation and its 100%-owned subsidiary, T Corporation, have filed consolidated tax returns for a number of years. Both corporations use the hybrid method of accounting and the calendar year as their tax year. During 2005, they report the operating results as listed in Table C8-2. Note the following additional information:

- Flying Gator and T Corporations are the only members of their controlled group.
- Flying Gator's address is 2101 W. University Ave., Gainesburg, FL 32611. Its employer identification number is 38-2345678. Flying Gator was incorporated on June 11, 1993. Its total assets are $430,000. Flying Gator made estimated tax payments of $150,000 for the affiliated group in the current year. Stephen Marks is Flying Gator's president.
- A $50,000 NOL carryover from the immediately preceding year is available. P Corporation incurred the NOL last year.
- Flying Gator uses the last-in, first-out (LIFO) inventory method. T began selling inventory to Flying Gator in the preceding year, which resulted in a $40,000 year-end deferred intercompany profit. An additional LIFO inventory layer was created by T's sales to Flying Gator during the current year that remained unsold at year-end. The intercompany profit on the additional inventory is $45,000. None of the original LIFO layer was sold during the current year.

▼ TABLE C8-2

Flying Gator Corporation's Current Year Operating Results (Problem C8-58)

Income or Deductions	Flying Gator	T	Total
Gross receipts	$2,500,000	$1,250,000	$3,750,000
Cost of goods sold	(1,500,000)	(700,000)	(2,200,000)
Gross profit	$1,000,000	$ 550,000	$1,550,000
Dividends	100,000	50,000	150,000
Interest	15,000		15,000
Sec. 1231 gain		20,000	20,000
Sec. 1245 gain		25,000	25,000
Long-term capital gain (loss)	(5,000)	6,000	1,000
Short-term capital gain (loss)		(3,000)	(3,000)
Total income	$1,110,000	$ 648,000	$1,758,000
Salaries and wages	175,000	200,000	375,000
Repairs	25,000	40,000	65,000
Bad debts	10,000	5,000	15,000
Taxes	18,000	24,000	42,000
Interest	30,000	20,000	50,000
Charitable contributions	22,000	48,000	70,000
Depreciation (other than that included in cost of goods sold)	85,000	40,000	125,000
Other expenses	160,000	260,000	420,000
Total deductions	$ 525,000	$ 637,000	$1,162,000
Separate return taxable income (before the USPAD, NOL ded, and DRD)	$ 585,000	$ 11,000	$ 596,000

- All of Flying Gator's dividends are received from T. T's dividends are received from a 60%-owned domestic corporation. All distributions received by T are from E&P.
- Flying Gator received its interest income from T. The interest is paid on March 31 of the current year on a loan that was outstanding from October 1 of the preceding year through March 31 of the current year. No interest income was accrued at the end of the preceding tax year. T paid $5,000 of its interest expense to a third party.
- Officer's salaries are $80,000 for Flying Gator and $65,000 for T Corporation. These amounts are included in salaries and wages in Table C8-2.
- Flying Gator's capital losses include a $10,000 long-term loss on a sale of land to T in the current year. T held the land at year-end.
- These corporations have no non-recaptured net Sec. 1231 losses from prior tax years.
- T's Sec. 1245 gains include $20,000 recognized on the sale of equipment to Flying Gator at the close of business on September 30 in the current year. The asset cost $100,000 and had been depreciated for two years by T as five-year property under the MACRS rules. T claimed nine months of depreciation in the current (second) year. Flying Gator began depreciating the property in the current year by using the MACRS rules and a five-year recovery period. Flying Gator claimed the appropriate first-year MACRS depreciation on the property in the current year.
- Qualified production activities income for Flying Gator is $490,000 and for T is $(35,000).

Determine the affiliated group's 2005 consolidated tax liability. Prepare the front page of the affiliated group's current year corporate income tax return (Form 1120). Hint: Prepare a spreadsheet similar to the one included in Appendix B to arrive at consolidated taxable income.

CASE STUDY PROBLEMS

C8-59   P Corporation operates six automotive service franchises in a metropolitan area. The service franchises have been a huge success in their first three years of operation and P's annual taxable income exceeds $600,000. The real estate associated with the six service franchises is owned by J Corporation. P Corporation leases its automotive service franchise locations from J Corporation. J Corporation is reporting large interest and MACRS depreciation deductions because of a highly leveraged, capital intensive operation. As a result, J Corporation has reported NOLs in its first three years of operation. Both P and J Corporations file separate tax returns.

   Both corporations are owned by Carol, who is in her late 20s. Carol sees the idea for the automotive service franchise chain starting to really develop and expects to add six more locations in each of the next two years. You and Carol have been friends for a number of years. Because of the rapid expansion that is planned, she feels that she has outgrown her father's accountant and needs to have new ideas to help her save tax dollars so that she can reinvest more money in the business.

   Required: The tax partner that you are assigned to requests that you prepare a memorandum outlining your thoughts about Carol's tax problems and suggested solutions to those problems in preparation for his meeting next week with Carol.

TAX RESEARCH PROBLEMS

C8-60   Angela owns all the stock of A, B, and P Corporations. P Corporation has owned all the stock of S_1 Corporation for six years. The P-S_1 affiliated group has filed a consolidated tax return in each of these six years using the calendar year as its tax year. On July 10 of the current year (a nonleap year), Angela sells her entire stock investment in A Corporation, which uses the calendar year as its tax year. No change takes place in Angela's ownership of B stock during the tax year. At the close of business on November 25 of this year, S_1 Corporation purchases 90% of the common stock and 80% of the nonconvertible, nonvoting preferred stock (measured by value) of S_2 Corporation. A, P, S_1, and S_2 Corporations are domestic corporations that do not retain any special filing status. Which corporations are included in the affiliated group? In the controlled group? What income is included in the various tax returns? How is the allocation of the income between tax years made if the books are not closed on the sale or acquisition dates? If no special allocations are made, what portion of the reduced tax rate benefits of Sec. 11(b) can be claimed in the current year by the affiliated group? In future years?

   A partial list of resources includes:

- IRC Sec. 1504
- IRC Sec. 1563
- Reg. Sec. 1.1502-75
- Reg. Sec. 1.1561-2

C8-61   P, S, and T Corporations have filed a consolidated tax return for a number of years using the calendar year as its tax year. Current plans call for P Corporation to purchase all of X Corporation's stock at the close of business on June 30 of the current year from three individuals. X Corporation was created seven years ago and always has been an S corporation using the calendar year as its tax year. The chief financial officer of P Corporation comes to your office and makes a number of inquiries about the tax consequences of the acquisition including: Can X Corporation retain its S election? If so, does it file a federal income tax return separate from the affiliated group? Does X Corporation have to be included in the P-S-T group's consolidated tax return? Assuming the acquisition takes place as planned, what tax returns are required of the affiliated group and X Corporation? What income is included in the pre-affiliation tax return of X Corporation (if required) and the affiliated group's post-acquisition consolidated tax return? Prepare a brief memo for the chief financial officer outlining the answers to these questions and any other questions you feel are relevant.

   A partial list of resources includes:

- IRC Sec. 1361(b)
- Reg. Sec. 1.1502-76

C8-62 Mary owns all the shares of Able Corporation. Able owns all the shares of Baker Corporation and Cross Corporations. The three corporations have filed a consolidated calendar year tax return for several years. After consulting with her tax accountant, Mary decides that it will be more beneficial if the corporations are restructured as S corporations so their income is subject to a single layer of tax. The restructuring process is complex because Baker holds some valuable franchises that cannot be transferred. The restructuring occurred on October 23 of the current year. On October 23, Able transfers all of its assets and liabilities to Baker, and the two corporations merge with Baker as the survivor. As part of the restructuring, Mary receives all the stock of Baker. Six hours after the first transaction, Baker sells Mary all the stock in Cross for $2 million. Thus, the consolidated group survived for only six hours during the restructuring. Immediately after the restructuring, Baker incurs substantial losses. Can Baker file a consolidated return for the restructuring year and deduct the post-restructuring losses against prior year consolidated income? A partial list of resources includes:

- Reg. Sec. 1.1502-75(a)(2)
- Reg. Sec. 1.1502-75(d)(2)
- Reg. Sec. 1.1502-76(b)(1)
- *The Falconwood Corporation v. U.S.* (96 AFTR 2d 2005-5977), 2005-2 USTC ¶50,597 (Fed. Cir., 2005)

9

CHAPTER

PARTNERSHIP FORMATION AND OPERATION

LEARNING OBJECTIVES

After studying this chapter, you should be able to

1 ▶ Differentiate between general and limited partnerships

2 ▶ Explain the tax results of a contribution of property or services in exchange for a partnership interest

3 ▶ Determine the permitted tax years for a partnership

4 ▶ Differentiate between items that must be separately stated and those that are included in ordinary income or loss for partnerships that are not electing large partnerships

5 ▶ Calculate a partner's distributive share of partnership income, gain, loss, deduction, or credit items

6 ▶ Explain the requirements for a special partnership allocation

7 ▶ Calculate a partner's basis in a partnership interest

8 ▶ Determine the limitations on a partner's deduction of partnership losses

9 ▶ Determine the tax consequences of a guaranteed payment

10 ▶ Explain the requirements for recognizing the holder of a partnership interest as a partner in a family partnership

11 ▶ Determine the allocation of partnership income between a donor and a donee of a partnership interest

12 ▶ Determine the requirements for filing a partnership tax return

Partnerships have long been one of the major entities for conducting business activities. Partnerships vary in complexity from the corner gas station owned and operated by two brothers to syndicated tax partnerships with their partnership interests traded on major security markets. Two different sets of rules apply to partnerships depending on their size. The rules discussed in Chapter C9 and most of Chapter C10 apply to the majority of partnerships. The rules discussed at the end of Chapter C10 apply to very large partnerships (known as electing large partnerships), which make a specific election to be taxed under a different system. The partnership rules are found in Subchapter K of the IRC, which includes the provisions from Secs. 701–777.

Chapters C9 and C10 discuss the income tax rules applying to partnership business operations. The first part of this chapter defines a partnership, describes the types of partnerships, and discusses the formation of a partnership. The remainder of this chapter deals with the ongoing operations of a partnership, such as the annual taxation of partnership earnings, transactions between partners and the partnership, and a partner's basis in a partnership interest. This chapter also considers procedural matters, such as reporting the annual partnership income and IRS audit procedures for partnerships and their partners. Chapter C10 continues by discussing distributions to the partners and the tax implications of the numerous transactions that can be used to terminate a partner's interest in a partnership. Chapter C10 also discusses the unique problems of limited partnerships and the taxation of publicly traded partnerships and electing large partnerships.

DEFINITION OF A PARTNERSHIP

ADDITIONAL COMMENT

Even though the formation of a partnership requires no legal documentation, the partners should draft a formal written partnership agreement to prevent subsequent disagreements and arguments.

For tax purposes, the definition of a partnership includes "a syndicate, group, pool, joint venture, or other unincorporated organization" that carries on a business or financial operation or venture. However, a trust, estate, or corporation cannot be treated as a partnership. Unlike a corporation, which can exist only after incorporation documents are finalized, formation of a partnership requires no legal documentation. If two people (or business entities) work together to carry on any business or financial operation with the intention of making a profit and sharing that profit as co-owners, a partnership exists for federal income tax purposes.[1]

The IRC and Treasury Regulations define a **partner** simply as a member of a partnership. Years of case law and common business practice, however, have made clear that a partner can be an individual, trust, estate, or corporation. The only restriction on the number of partners is that a partnership must have at least two partners, but a large syndicated partnership may have hundreds or even thousands of partners.

GENERAL AND LIMITED PARTNERSHIPS

OBJECTIVE 1

Differentiate between general and limited partnerships

Each state has laws governing the rights and restrictions of partnerships. Almost all state statutes are modeled on the Uniform Partnership Act (UPA) or the Uniform Limited Partnership Act (ULPA) and thus have strong similarities to each other. A partnership can take two legal forms: a general partnership or a limited partnership. The differences between the two forms are substantial and extend to the partners' legal rights and liabilities as well as the tax consequences of operations to the partners. Because these differences are so important, we examine the two partnership forms before proceeding with further discussion of the partnership tax rules.

GENERAL PARTNERSHIPS. A **general partnership** exists any time two or more partners join together and do not specifically provide that one or more of the partners is a limited partner (as defined below). In a general partnership, each partner has the right to par-

---

[1] Section 761(a) allows an election to avoid the Subchapter K rules for a very limited group of business owners.

ticipate in the management of the partnership. However, the general partnership form is flexible enough to allow the business affairs of the general partnership to be managed by a single partner chosen by the general partners.

Although only one (or a few) of the general partners may exercise management duties, each **general partner** has the ability to make commitments for the partnership.[2] In a general partnership, each partner has unlimited liability for all partnership debts. If the partnership fails to pay its debts, each partner may have to pay far more than the amount he or she has invested in the venture. Thus, each partner faces the risk of losing personal assets if the partnership incurs business losses. This exposure is the single biggest drawback to the general partnership form of doing business.

LIMITED PARTNERSHIPS. A **limited partnership** has two classes of partners. It must have at least one general partner, who essentially has the same rights and liabilities as any general partner in a general partnership,[3] and at least one **limited partner**. Even if a partnership becomes bankrupt, a limited partner can lose no more than his or her original investment plus any additional amount he or she has committed to contribute. However, a limited partner has no right to be active in the partnership's management.[4]

The broad rights and obligations of general partners could make a general partnership an unwieldy form for operating a business with a large number of owners. On the other hand, a limited partnership having one (or a small number of) general partners can be useful for a business operation that needs to attract a large amount of capital. In fact, one common form for a tax shelter investment is a limited partnership having a corporation with a small amount of capital as its sole general partner. Such an arrangement allows the tax advantages of the partnership form (detailed in the remainder of this chapter and in the next chapter) while retaining the limited liability feature for virtually every investor.

Many of these limited partnerships are so large and widely held that in many ways they appear more like corporations than partnerships. As discussed in Chapter C10, the tax laws provide that publicly traded partnerships may be reclassified for tax purposes as corporations.

LIMITED LIABILITY COMPANIES (LLCs). With the advent of LLCs, businesses have the opportunity to be treated as a partnership for tax purposes while having limited liability protection for every owner. State law provides this limited liability. Unique tax rules for LLCs have not been developed. Instead, the check-the-box regulations (discussed in Chapter C2) permit each LLC to choose whether to be treated as a partnership or taxed as a corporation. If an LLC is considered a partnership for tax purposes, the same tax rules apply to the LLC that apply to a traditional partnership. Chapter C10 further discusses the tax treatment of LLCs.

LIMITED LIABILITY PARTNERSHIPS (LLPs). Initially, professional organizations in certain fields (e.g., public accounting and law) were not permitted to operate as LLCs and therefore remained general partnerships. Subsequently, many states have added LLPs to the list of permissible business forms. The primary difference between a general partnership and an LLP is that, in an LLP, a partner is not liable for damages resulting from failures in the work of other partners or of people supervised by other partners. Under the check-the-box regulations, an LLP can be treated as a partnership or as a corporation. Like an LLC, the default tax classification of an LLP is a partnership. The same tax rules apply to an LLP that apply to a traditional partnership. Chapter C10 further discusses the taxation of LLPs.

ELECTING LARGE PARTNERSHIPS. Partnerships that qualify as "large partnerships" may elect to have a simplified set of reporting rules apply. To qualify as a large partnership, the partnership must not be a service partnership and must not be engaged in commodity trading. Further, to qualify to make this election, the partnership must have at

---

[2] Uniform Partnership Act.
[3] Uniform Limited Partnership Act.

[4] Under Sec. 9 of the Uniform Limited Partnership Act, only general partners are empowered to manage the partnership's business.

least 100 partners (excluding partners who provide substantial services in connection with the partnership's business activities) throughout the tax year. Once the partnership makes the election, it reports its income under a simplified reporting scheme, is subject to different rules about when the partnership terminates, and is subject to a different system of audits. The election is irrevocable without IRS permission. Chapter C10 presents details about the tax treatment of electing large partnerships.

OVERVIEW OF TAXATION OF PARTNERSHIP INCOME

The following overview gives a broad perspective of the taxation of partnership income other than income earned by electing large partnerships. (Appendix F compares the tax characteristics of a partnership, a C corporation, and an S corporation.) More detailed descriptions follow this overview.

PARTNERSHIP PROFITS AND LOSSES

A partnership is not a taxpaying entity, and income earned by a partnership is not subject to two layers of federal income taxes. Instead, each partner reports a share of the partnership's income, gain, loss, deduction, and credit items as a part of his or her income tax return. The partnership, however, must file Form 1065 (U.S. Partnership Return of Income), an information return that provides the IRS with information about partnership earnings as well as how the earnings are allocated among the partners. The partnership must elect a tax year and accounting methods to calculate its earnings. (Appendix B includes a completed partnership tax return that shows a Form 1065 and Schedule K-1 for a partner along with a set of supporting facts.)

Each partner receives a Schedule K-1 from the partnership, which informs the partner of the amount and character of his or her share of partnership income. The partner then combines his or her partnership earnings and losses with all other items of income or loss to be reported for the tax year, computes the amount of taxable income, and calculates the tax bill. Partnership income is taxed at the applicable tax rate for its partners, which can range from 10% to 35% (in 2006) for partners who are individuals, trusts, or estates. Corporate partners pay tax on partnership income at rates ranging from 15% to 39%.

One of the major advantages of the partnership form of doing business is that partnership losses are allocated among the partners. If the loss limitation rules (explained later in this chapter) do not apply, these losses combine with the partners' other income and result in an immediate tax savings for the partners. The immediate tax saving available to the partner contrasts sharply with the net operating loss (NOL) carrybacks or carryforwards that result from a C corporation's tax loss.

THE PARTNER'S BASIS

A partner's basis in his or her partnership interest is a crucial element in partnership taxation. When a partner makes a contribution to a partnership or purchases a partnership interest, he or she establishes a beginning basis. Because the partners are personally liable for partnership debts, a partner's basis in his or her partnership interest is increased by his or her share of any partnership liabilities. Accordingly, the partner's basis fluctuates as the partnership borrows and repays loans or increases and decreases its accounts payable. In addition, a partner's basis in his or her partnership interest is increased by the partner's share of partnership income and decreased by his or her share of partnership losses. Because a partner's basis in his or her partnership interest can never be negative, the basis serves as one limit on the amount of deductible partnership losses. (See the discussion on pages C9-26 and C9-27 about the various loss limitations.)

EXAMPLE C9-1 ▶ Tom purchases a 20% interest in the XY Partnership for $8,000 on January 1, 2006, and begins to materially participate in the partnership's business. The XY Partnership uses the calendar year as its tax year. At the time of the purchase, the XY Partnership has $2,000 in liabilities, of which Tom's share is 20%. Tom's basis in his partnership interest on January 1 is $8,400 [$8,000 + (0.20 × $2,000)]. ◀

EXAMPLE C9-2 ▶ Assume the same facts as in Example C9-1 except, during 2006, the XY Partnership incurs $10,000 in losses, and its liabilities increase by $4,000. What is Tom's basis on December 31, 2006?

January 1, 2006, basis	$8,400
Plus: Share of liability increase ($4,000 × 0.20)	800
Minus: Share of partnership losses ($10,000 × 0.20)	(2,000)
December 31, 2006, basis	$7,200 ◀

EXAMPLE C9-3 ▶ Assume the same facts as in Example C9-2, and further assume that, during 2007, the XY Partnership incurs $60,000 in losses and its liabilities increase by $10,000. Tom's share of the losses is $12,000 ($60,000 × 0.20). What is the maximum amount he can deduct in 2007?

January 1, 2007, basis	$7,200
Plus: Share of liability increase	2,000
December 31, 2007, basis before losses	$9,200
Minus: Maximum loss deduction allowed	(9,200)
December 31, 2007, basis	$ –0–

Tom's remaining $2,800 in losses carry over to subsequent years, and he can deduct them when he regains sufficient basis in his partnership interest. ◀

PARTNERSHIP DISTRIBUTIONS

When a partnership makes a current distribution, the distribution generally is tax-free to the partners because it represents the receipt of earnings that already have been taxed to the partners and that have increased the partners' bases in their partnership interests. Subsequent distributions reduce a partner's basis in his or her partnership interest. If a cash distribution is so large, however, that it exceeds a partner's basis in his or her partnership interest, the partner recognizes gain equal to the amount of the excess. When the partnership goes out of business or when a partner withdraws from the partnership, the partnership makes liquidating distributions to the partner. Like current distributions, these distributions cause the partner to recognize gain only if the cash received exceeds the partner's basis in his or her partnership interest. A partner may recognize a loss if he or she receives only cash, inventory, and unrealized receivables in complete liquidation of his or her partnership interest. (Chapter C10 presents detailed coverage of current and liquidating distributions.)

ADDITIONAL COMMENT

The increase in a partner's basis for earnings prevents double taxation of those earnings upon a subsequent distribution, sale of the partnership interest, or liquidation of the partnership.

TAX IMPLICATIONS OF FORMATION OF A PARTNERSHIP

When two or more individuals or entities decide to operate an unincorporated business together, they form a partnership. The following sections examine the tax implications of property contributions, service contributions, and organization and syndication expenditures.

OBJECTIVE 2

Explain the tax results of a contribution of property or services in exchange for a partnership interest

CONTRIBUTION OF PROPERTY

NONRECOGNITION OF GAIN OR LOSS. Section 721 governs the formation of a partnership. In most cases, a partner who contributes property in exchange for a partnership interest recognizes no gain or loss on the transaction. Likewise, the partnership recognizes no gain or loss on the contribution of property. The partner's basis for his or her partnership interest and the partnership's basis for the property are both the same as basis of the property transferred.[5]

Nonrecognition treatment is limited to transactions in which a partner receives a partnership interest in exchange for a contribution of property. As in the corporate formation area, the term *property* includes cash, tangible property (e.g., buildings and land), and intangible property (e.g., franchise rights, trademarks, and leases).[6] Services are specifically excluded from the definition of property, so a contribution of services for a partnership interest is not a tax-free transaction.

ADDITIONAL COMMENT

For contributions to a corporation to be nontaxable, the contributing shareholders must control (own at least 80%) the corporation immediately after the transaction. No such control requirement exists for contributions to a partnership to be nontaxable.

RECOGNITION OF GAIN OR LOSS. The general rule of Sec. 721(a) provides that neither the partnership nor any partner recognizes gain or loss when partners contribute property in exchange for a partnership interest. Three exceptions to this general rule may require a partner to recognize a gain upon the contribution of property to a partnership in exchange for a partnership interest:

▶ Contribution of property to a partnership that would be treated as an investment company if it were incorporated

▶ Contribution of property followed by a distribution in an arrangement that may be considered a sale rather than a contribution

▶ Contribution of property to a partnership along with the partnership's assumption of liabilities previously owed by the partner

The investment company exception of Sec. 721(b) requires recognition of gain only if the exchange results in diversification of the transferor's property interest.[7] If the contribution of property is to an investment partnership, the contributing partner must recognize any gain (but not loss) realized on the property transfer as if he or she sold the stock or securities.

Sections 707(a)(2)(A) and (B) set out the second exception, which holds that a property contribution followed by a distribution (or an allocation of income or gain) may be treated as a sale of property by the partner to the partnership rather than as a contribution made by the partner to the partnership. For example, Treasury Regulations may require sale treatment (and the recognition of gain or loss) if the distribution would not have occurred except for the contribution.

EXAMPLE C9-4 ▶ In return for a 40% interest in the CD Partnership, Cara contributed land with a $100,000 fair market value (FMV). The partners agreed that the partnership would distribute $100,000 in cash to Cara immediately after the contribution. Because the cash distribution would not have occurred had Cara not first contributed the land and become a partner, the transaction is likely to be treated as a sale of the land by Cara to the partnership. ◀

If the distribution does not occur simultaneously with the contribution, the transaction is treated as a sale if the later distribution is not dependent on the normal business risk of the enterprise.

EXAMPLE C9-5 ▶ Elena received a 30% interest in the DEF Partnership in return for her contribution of land having a $60,000 FMV. The partnership waits six months and then distributes $60,000 in cash to Elena. If the $60,000 distribution is not contingent on the partnership's earnings or ability to borrow funds or other normal risks of doing business, the distribution and contribution will be treated as a sale of land by Elena to the partnership. ◀

EFFECTS OF LIABILITIES. The third condition that may cause a partner to recognize gain (but not loss) on the formation of a partnership is the contribution of property to a partnership along with the partnership's assumption of liabilities previously owed by the

---

[5] Secs. 722 and 723.

[6] For an excellent discussion of the definition of the term *property*, see footnote 6 of *D.N. Stafford v. U.S.*, 45 AFTR 2d 80-785, 80-1 USTC ¶9218 (5th Cir., 1980).

[7] Reg. Sec. 1.351-1(c)(1). This investment is taxed only when immediately after the exchange more than 80% of the value of the partnership's assets (excluding cash and nonconvertible debt obligations) is held for investment or is readily marketable stocks, securities, or interests in regulated investment companies or real estate investment trusts.

KEY POINT

A partner's relief of debt is treated as if the partner receives a cash distribution. A partner's assumption of debt is treated as if the partner makes a cash contribution. These two simple rules are critical to understanding transactions such as formations of partnerships, distributions from partnerships, and sales or liquidations of partnership interests.

partner. Because each partner is liable for his or her share of partnership liabilities, increases and decreases in the partnership liabilities are reflected in each partner's basis. Specifically, Sec. 752 provides that two effects result from a partner's contribution of property to a partnership if the partnership also assumes the partner's liabilities.

▶ Each partner's basis is increased by his or her share of the partnership's liabilities as if he or she had contributed cash to the partnership in the amount of his or her share of partnership liabilities.

▶ The partner whose personal liabilities are assumed by the partnership has a reduction in the basis of his or her partnership interest as if the partnership distributed cash to him or her in the amount of the assumed liability. A cash distribution first reduces the partner's basis in the partnership interest. If the cash distribution exceeds the partner's predistribution basis in the partnership interest, the partner recognizes gain.

The net effect of these two basis adjustments, however, is seldom large enough to cause a transferor partner to recognize gain when he or she contributes property to the partnership. The transferor partner is deemed first to have made a contribution of property plus a contribution of cash equal to the partner's share of any partnership liabilities existing prior to his or her entrance into the partnership (or contributed by other partners concurrently with this transaction). The partner then is deemed to have received a cash distribution equal to the total amount of his or her own liability assumed by the *other* partners. (No basis adjustment is required for the portion of the liability transferred to the partnership by the transferor that he or she will retain as a partner.)

EXAMPLE C9-6 ▶

ADDITIONAL COMMENT

In Example C9-6, the $12,000 reduction in basis also can be viewed as the net of $3,000, which is Mary's 20% share of the $15,000 increase in partnership liabilities, and $15,000, which is Mary's liability assumed by the partnership.

In return for a 20% partnership interest, Mary contributes land having a $60,000 FMV and a $30,000 basis to the XY Partnership. The partnership assumes Mary's $15,000 liability arising from her purchase of the land, and Mary's share of partnership liabilities is 20%. The XY Partnership has $4,000 in liabilities immediately before her contribution. What is Mary's basis in her partnership interest?

Basis of contributed property		$30,000
Plus:	Mary's share of existing partnership liabilities ($4,000 × 0.20)	800
Minus:	Mary's liabilities assumed by the other partners ($15,000 × 0.80)	(12,000)
Mary's basis in her partnership interest		$18,800

Mary recognizes no gain on the partnership's assumption of her liability because the deemed cash distribution from the assumption of her $12,000 in liabilities by the partnership does not exceed her $30,800 basis in the partnership interest immediately preceding the fictional distribution. ◀

EXAMPLE C9-7 ▶

ADDITIONAL COMMENT

In contrast to partnership formations, had Example C9-7 involved a formation of the XY Corporation, Mary would have recognized a $20,000 Sec. 357(c) gain.

Assume the same facts as in Example C9-6 except the amount of the liability assumed by the XY Partnership is $50,000. Mary's basis in her partnership interest is calculated as follows:

Basis of contributed property		$30,000
Plus:	Mary's share of existing partnership liabilities ($4,000 × 0.20)	800
Predistribution basis		$30,800
Minus:	Mary's liabilities assumed by the other partners ($50,000 × 0.80)	(40,000)
Basis in partnership interest (cannot be negative)		$ –0–

The cash deemed distributed in excess of Mary's predistribution basis causes her to recognize a $9,200 ($40,000 − $30,800) gain. Mary reduces her basis to zero by the distribution because a partner's basis in the partnership interest can never be less than zero. ◀

STOP & THINK

Question: Assume the land Mary contributed in Example C9-6 has a $60,000 FMV and an $85,000 adjusted basis. Should Mary contribute it to the partnership?

Solution: If Mary contributes the land, she cannot recognize her $25,000 ($60,000 FMV − $85,000 adjusted basis) loss until the partnership disposes of the property. Accordingly, Mary might prefer to sell the property and recognize her loss now. If the partnership can afford the $60,000 price and needs this property, Mary could sell the land to the partnership, recognize her loss on the sale, and then contribute the cash she receives from the partnership in exchange for her partnership interest. If the partnership does not need the property, Mary could sell the land to a third party, recognize her loss, and contribute the sales proceeds to the partnership in exchange for her partnership interest. However, a problem arises if the partnership needs this property and cannot afford to buy it from Mary. In that case, contributing the property to the partnership may be the only alternative despite the less-than-optimal tax results.

Because the partnership's assumption of a partner's liabilities is treated as a cash distribution, the character of any gain recognized by the partner is controlled by the partnership distribution rules. Cash distributions exceeding predistribution basis always result in gain recognition, and that gain is deemed to be gain from the sale of the partnership interest.[8] Because a partnership interest is usually a capital asset, any gain arising from assumption of a partner's liabilities normally is a capital gain.

PARTNER'S BASIS IN THE PARTNERSHIP INTEREST (COMMONLY CALLED THE OUTSIDE BASIS). In general, the transferor partner's beginning basis in the partnership interest equals the sum of money contributed plus his or her basis in contributed property. If the partner recognizes any gain on the contribution because the partnership is an investment company, the amount of recognized gain increases his or her basis in the partnership interest.[9] Beginning basis is adjusted to reflect liability share. Any gain recognized because of the effects of liabilities on the partner's basis does not increase the basis for the partnership interest because in this situation the basis is zero.

In some instances, a partner may contribute valuable property having little or no basis. For example, accounts receivable or notes receivable of a partner using the cash method of accounting can be a valued contribution to a partnership, but if the receivables' bases are zero, the beginning basis of the partnership interest also is zero.

HOLDING PERIOD FOR PARTNERSHIP INTEREST. The holding period for the partnership interest includes the transferor's holding period for the contributed property if that property is a capital asset or a Sec. 1231 asset in the transferor's hands.[10] If the contributed property is an ordinary income asset (e.g., inventory) to the partner, the holding period for the partnership interest begins the day after the contribution date.[11]

EXAMPLE C9-8 ▶ On April 1, Sue contributes a building (a Sec. 1231 asset) to the ST Partnership in exchange for a 20% interest. Sue purchased the building three years ago. Her holding period for her partnership interest includes the three years she held the contributed building. ◀

EXAMPLE C9-9 ▶ On April 1, Ted contributes inventory to the ST Partnership in exchange for a 20% interest. No matter when Ted acquired the inventory, his holding period for his partnership interest begins on April 2, the day after the date of his contribution. ◀

PARTNERSHIP'S BASIS IN PROPERTY. Under Sec. 723, the partnership's basis for contributed property is the same as the property's basis in the hands of the contributing partner. If, however, the contributing partner recognizes gain because the partnership is an investment company, such gain increases the partnership's basis in the contributed property. Gain recognized by the contributing partner because of the assumption of a partner's liability does not increase the partnership's basis in the property.[12]

Not only does the property's basis carry over to the partnership from the contributing partner, but for some property the character of gain or loss on a subsequent disposition of the property by the partnership also references the character of the property in the contributing partner's hands. Section 724 prevents the transformation of ordinary income into capital gains (or capital losses into ordinary losses) when a partner contributes prop-

---

[8] Sec. 731(a).
[9] Sec. 722.
[10] Sec. 1223(1).

[11] Reg. Sec. 1.1223-1(a).
[12] Rev. Rul. 84-15, 1984-1 C.B. 158.

erty to a partnership. Properties that were (1) unrealized receivables, inventory, or capital loss property in the hands of the contributing partner and (2) contributed to a partnership retain their character for some subsequent partnership dispositions.[13]

Unrealized Receivables. The concept of unrealized receivables plays a key role for tax purposes in many different partnership transactions. An **unrealized receivable** is any right to payment for goods or services the holder has not included in income because of the accounting method used.[14] The most common examples of unrealized receivables are the accounts receivable of a cash method taxpayer.

If property is an unrealized receivable in the hands of the contributing partner, any gain or loss recognized on the partnership's later disposition of the property is treated as ordinary income or loss. This rule mandates ordinary income or loss treatment regardless of how long the partnership holds the property before disposition or the character of the property in the partnership's hands.

Inventory. If property was inventory in the hands of the contributing partner, its character remains ordinary for five years. Consequently, any gain or loss recognized by the partnership on the disposition of such property during the five-year period beginning on the date of contribution is ordinary gain or loss. Ordinary gain or loss treatment occurs even if the property is a capital asset or Sec. 1231 asset in the partnership's hands.

EXAMPLE C9-10 ▶ On June 1, Jose, a real estate developer, contributes ten acres of land in an industrial park he developed to the Hi-Tech Partnership in exchange for a 30% interest in the partnership. Although Jose held the acreage in inventory, the land serves as the site for Hi-Tech's new research facility. Four years later Hi-Tech sells its research facility and the land. Although gain on the sale of the land usually would be taxed as Sec. 1231 gain, Hi-Tech must report it as ordinary income under Sec. 724. ◀

ADDITIONAL COMMENT

Congress enacted Sec. 724 to eliminate the ability to transform the character of gain or loss on property by contributing the property to a partnership and having the partnership subsequently sell it.

Capital Loss Property. The final type of property whose character is fixed at the time of the contribution is property that would generate a capital loss if sold by the contributing partner rather than contributed to the partnership. A loss recognized by the partnership on the disposition of the property within five years of the date it is contributed to the partnership is a capital loss. However, the amount of loss characterized as capital may not exceed the capital loss the contributing partner would have recognized had the partner sold the property on the contribution date. The character of any loss exceeding the difference between the property's FMV and its adjusted basis on the contribution date is determined by the property's character in the hands of the partnership.

EXAMPLE C9-11 ▶ Pam holds investment land that she purchased six years ago for $50,000. The FMV of the land was only $40,000 two years ago when she contributed it to the PK Partnership, which is in the business of developing and selling lots. PK develops the contributed land and sells it in the current year for $28,000, or at a $22,000 loss. The $10,000 loss that accrued while Pam held the land as a capital asset retains its character as a capital loss. The remaining $12,000 of loss that accrues while the land is part of the partnership's inventory is an ordinary loss. ◀

PARTNERSHIP'S HOLDING PERIOD. Under Sec. 1223(2), the partnership's holding period for its contributed assets includes the holding period of the contributing partner. This rule applies without regard to the character the property has in the contributing partner's hands or the partnership's hands.

SECTION 1245 AND 1250 PROPERTY RULES. Although the Sec. 1245 and Sec. 1250 depreciation recapture rules override many gain nonrecognition provisions in the IRC, the partner incurs no depreciation recapture unless he or she recognizes gain upon contribut-

---

[13] Sec. 724. The determination of whether property is an unrealized receivable, inventory, or a capital loss property in the contributing partner's hands occurs immediately before the contribution.

[14] Section 724(d)(1) references the unrealized receivables definition found in

Sec. 751(c). For distributions and sale transactions, the unrealized receivables definition is broadened to include certain recapture items. This difference is discussed more fully in Chapter C10.

ing property in exchange for a partnership interest.[15] Instead, both the adjusted basis and depreciation recapture potential carry over to the partnership. If the partnership later sells the property at a gain, the Sec. 1245 and 1250 provisions affect the character of the gain. In addition, any Sec. 1250 gain potential carries over to the partnership to affect gain characterization upon a future sale. Section 1250 gain is taxed to individuals at a 25% capital gains tax rate under Sec. 1(h)(1)(D).

CONTRIBUTION OF PROPERTY AFTER FORMATION. Any time a partner contributes property in exchange for a partnership interest, the rules outlined above apply whether the contribution occurs during the formation of the partnership or at a later date. This treatment contrasts sharply with corporate contributions, where a tax-free contribution after formation is rare because of the 80% control requirement. Most contributions of property in exchange for a partnership interest are tax-free even if they occur years after the partnership was formed.

CONTRIBUTION OF SERVICES

A partner who receives a partnership interest in exchange for services has been compensated as if he or she receives cash and thus must recognize ordinary income. The amount and timing of the income to be recognized are determined under Sec. 83. Consequently, receipt of an unrestricted interest in a partnership requires the service partner to immediately recognize income equal to the FMV of the partnership interest less any cash or property contributed by the partner. Generally, the service partner recognizes no income upon receiving a restricted interest in a partnership until the restriction lapses or the interest can be freely transferred.

Although a partnership interest seems to be a unified interest, it really is made up of two components: a capital interest and a profits interest. A partner may receive both components or only a profits interest in exchange for his or her services. (A capital interest without a profits interest rarely occurs.) Treasury Regulations indicate that a **capital interest** can be valued by determining the amount the partner would receive if the partnership liquidated on the day the partner receives the partnership interest.[16] If the partner would receive proceeds from the sale of the partnership's assets or receive the assets themselves, he or she is considered to own a capital interest. Alternatively, if the partner's only interest is in the future earnings of the partnership (with no interest in the current partnership assets), the partner owns a **profits interest** (but not a capital interest).

Tax law has long been settled that receipt of a capital interest in a partnership in exchange for services is taxable under the rules outlined above. A profits interest, however, is no more than a right to future income taxable to the partners as the partnership earns it. To the extent the profits interest itself has a value, one might expect that value to be taxed when the partner receives the profits interest, as any other property received for services would be taxed.

ADDITIONAL COMMENT

The Treasury Department has issued proposed regulations, and the IRS will issue a new revenue procedure that will alter the landscape of taxing partnership interests transferred for services. The new rules also will make Rev. Proc. 93-27, discussed on the next page, obsolete. However, taxpayers may not rely on the proposed rules until they are finalized and may continue to rely on existing rules and procedures. See Notice 2005-43, 2005-24 I.R.B. 1221.

EXAMPLE C9-12 ▶ Carl arranges favorable financing for the purchase of an office building and receives a 30% profits interest in a partnership formed to own and operate the building. Less than three weeks later, Carl sells his profits interest to his partner for $40,000. Carl must recognize $40,000 as ordinary income from the receipt of a partnership profits interest in exchange for services. ◀

The facts in Example C9-12 approximate those of *Sol Diamond*, a landmark partnership taxation case, which was the first case to tax the partner upon receipt of a profits interest.[17] The Tax Court pointed out that Sec. 61 included all compensation for services, and no other provision contained in the IRC or Treasury Regulations removed this transaction from taxation. The Seventh Circuit Court of Appeals seemed to limit the inclusion

---

[15] Secs. 1245(b)(3) and 1250(d)(3). Property acquired as a capital contribution where gain is not recognized under Sec. 721 is subject to the MACRS anti-churning rules of Sec. 168(i)(7)(A). In general, the anti-churning rules require the partnership to use the same depreciation method as the partner who contributed the property. See Chapter C2 for a discussion of these rules in connection with a corporate formation transaction.

[16] Reg. Sec. 1.704-1(e)(1)(v). The capital interest definition in this regulation relates to family partnerships, but such definition should apply generally in the partnership area.
[17] 33 AFTR 2d 74-852, 74-1 USTC ¶9306 (7th Cir., 1974), *aff'g.* 56 T.C. 530 (1971).

of a profits interest to situations in which the market value of the profits interest could be determined. The IRS resolved much of the uncertainty in this area of tax law when it issued Rev. Proc. 93-27, which provides that the IRS generally will tax a profits interest received for services only in three specified instances in which a FMV is readily ascertainable.[18] In the general case, therefore, an income tax is not levied on the profits interest separately, but all partnership profits that pass through to the partner are taxed under the normal rules of partnership taxation.

CONSEQUENCES TO THE PARTNERSHIP. Payments by the partnership for services are either deductible as an expense or capitalized, including those paid for services with an interest in the partnership. If the payment constitutes a deductible expense, the partnership takes the deduction in the same year the partner includes the value of his or her partnership interest in income.[19] This rule matches the timing of the partnership's deduction to the partner's income recognition.

Allocating the Expense Deduction. The partnership allocates the expense deduction or the amortization of the capital expenditure among the partners other than the service partner. This allocation occurs because these partners make the outlay by relinquishing part of their interest in the partnership.

EXAMPLE C9-13 ▶ In June of the current year Jay, a lawyer, receives a 1% capital and profits interest (valued at $4,000) in the JLK Partnership in return for providing legal services to JLK's employees during the first five months of the current year. The legal services were a fringe benefit for JLK's employees and were deductible by JLK. Jay must include $4,000 in his current year gross income, and JLK can deduct the expense in the current year. JLK allocates the $4,000 expense to all partners other than Jay. ◀

If the service performed is of a nature that should be capitalized, the partnership capitalizes the amount and amortizes it as appropriate. The related asset's basis is increased at the same time and in the same amount as the partner's gross income inclusion.[20]

EXAMPLE C9-14 ▶ In June of the current year, Rob, an architect, receives a 10% capital and profits interest in the KLB Partnership for his services in designing a new building to house the partnership's operations. The June value of the partnership interest is $24,000. Rob must recognize $24,000 of ordinary income in the current year as a result of receiving the partnership interest. The KLB Partnership must capitalize the $24,000 as part of the building's cost and depreciate that amount (along with the building's other costs) over its recovery period. ◀

The timing of the partner's recognition of income is the same in the preceding two examples even though the partnership could deduct one payment but had to capitalize the other.

Partnership Gain or Loss. By exchanging an interest in the partnership for services, the partnership, in effect, pays for services by transferring an interest in the underlying partnership property. Generally, when a debtor uses property to pay a debt, the debtor must recognize gain or loss equal to the difference between the property's FMV and adjusted basis. Likewise, the partnership must recognize the gain or loss existing in the proportionate share of its assets deemed to be transferred to the service partner.[21] Furthermore, because the partnership recognizes gain or loss, it must adjust the bases of the assets.

EXAMPLE C9-15 ▶ On January 1 of the current year, Maria is admitted as a 25% partner in the XYZ Partnership in exchange for services valued at $16,500. The partnership has no liabilities at the time but has assets with a basis of $50,000 and FMV of $66,000. The transaction is treated as if Maria received an undivided one-fourth interest in each asset. She is taxed on the $16,500 FMV of the

---

[18] 1993-2 C.B. 343. The three exceptions involve receipt of a profits interest having a substantially certain and predictable income stream, the partner disposes of the profits interest within two years of receipt, or the profits interest is a limited interest in a publicly traded partnership.

[19] Reg. Sec. 1.83-6(a)(1).
[20] Reg. Sec. 1.83-6(a)(4).
[21] Reg. Sec. 1.83-6(b).

assets and takes a $16,500 basis in her partnership interest. The partnership recognizes $4,000 of gain [0.25 × ($66,000 FMV − $50,000 adjusted basis)] on the assets deemed paid to Maria. The partnership calculates gain or loss for each asset XYZ holds, and the character of each asset determines the character of the gain or loss recognized. The recognized gain is allocated to the partners other than Maria. Also, the partnership's original basis in its assets ($50,000) is increased by the $4,000 recognized gain. ◄

ORGANIZATIONAL AND SYNDICATION EXPENDITURES

The costs of organizing a partnership are capital expenditures. However, the partnership can elect to deduct the first $5,000 of these expenditures in the tax year it begins business. As a limit, the partnership must reduce the $5,000 by the amount by which cumulative organizational expenditures exceed $50,000, although the $5,000 cannot be reduced below zero. The partnership can amortize the remaining organizational expenditures over an 180-month period beginning in the month it begins business.[22] This rule applies to organization expenditures incurred after October 22, 2004. Prior to October 23, 2004, a partnership was not allowed an initial deduction but could elect to amortize its organizational expenditures over a period of at least 60 months beginning in the month it began business.

Organizational expenditures that can be capitalized and amortized must meet the same requirements as the costs incurred by a corporation making the Sec. 248 election to amortize organizational expenditures (see Chapter C3). The organizational expenditures must be incident to the creation of the partnership, chargeable to a capital account, and of a character that would be amortizable over the life of the partnership if the partnership had a limited life. Eligible expenditures include legal fees for negotiating and preparing partnership agreements, accounting fees for establishing the initial accounting system, and filing fees. Syndication expenditures for the issuing and marketing of interests in the partnership are not organizational expenditures and cannot be included in this election.[23] The partnership deducts unamortized organizational expenditures when it is terminated or liquidated.

Topic Review C9-1 summarizes the tax consequences of forming a partnership.

SELF-STUDY QUESTION

What is the importance of the distinction between organizational expenditures and syndication expenditures?

ANSWER

Organizational expenditures can be deducted up to $5,000 and then amortized over a period of 180 months, but syndication expenditures are *not* deductible or amortizable.

PARTNERSHIP ELECTIONS

OBJECTIVE 3

Determine the permitted tax years for a partnership

Once formed, the partnership must make a number of elections. For example, a partnership must select a tax year and elect accounting methods for all but a few items affecting the computation of partnership taxable income or loss.

PARTNERSHIP TAX YEAR

The partnership's selection of a tax year is critical because it determines when each partner reports his or her share of partnership income or loss. Under Sec. 706(a), each partner's tax return includes his or her share of partnership income, gain, loss, deduction, or credit items for any taxable year of the partnership ending within or with the partner's tax year.

EXAMPLE C9-16 ▶ Vicki is a member of a partnership having a November 30 year-end. In her tax return for calendar year 2006, she must include her share of partnership items from the partnership tax year that ends November 30, 2006. Results of partnership operations in December 2006 are reported in Vicki's 2007 tax return along with her share of other partnership items from the partnership year that ends on November 30, 2007. She receives, in essence, a one-year deferral of the taxes due on December's partnership income. ◄

SECTION 706 RESTRICTIONS.   Because of a substantial opportunity for tax deferral, Congress enacted Sec. 706 to restrict the available choices for a partnership's tax year. The partnership must use the same tax year as the one or more **majority partners** who have an

---

[22] Sec. 709(b).   [23] Reg. Sec. 1.709-2(b).

Topic Review C9-1

Formation of a Partnership

	CONTRIBUTION TO A PARTNERSHIP	
	PROPERTY	SERVICES
Recognition of gain, loss, or income by partner	Tax-free unless (1) liabilities assumed by the partnership exceed partner's predistribution basis in partnership interest (gain recognized is amount by which liabilities assumed by partnership exceed predistribution basis), (2) the partnership formed is an investment partnership (gain recognized is excess of FMV of partnership interest over basis of assets contributed), or (3) a contribution is followed by a distribution that is treated as a sale (gain or loss recognized on sale transaction).	Taxable to partner equal to FMV of partnership interest received in exchange for the services.
Basis of partnership interest	Substituted basis from property contributed plus share of partnership liabilities assumed minus the partner's liabilities assumed by the partnership. Gain recognized because of the investment company rules increases the basis of the partnership interest.	Amount of income recognized plus share of partnership liabilities assumed by the partner minus partner's liabilities assumed by the partnership.
Gain or loss recognized by the partnership	No gain or loss recognized by the partnership.	1. Deduction or capitalized expense is created depending on the type of service rendered. 2. Gain or loss recognized equals difference between FMV of portion of assets used to pay service partner and the basis of such portion of the assets.
Basis of assets to the partnership	Carryover basis is increased by a partner's gain recognized only if gain results from the formation of an investment partnership. No basis adjustment occurs when assumption of partner's liabilities results in a partner's gain recognition. In a sale transaction, assets take a cost basis.	Increased or decreased to reflect the FMV of the assets paid to the service partner.

aggregate interest in partnership profits and capital exceeding 50%. This rule must be used only if these majority partners have a common tax year and have had this tax year for the shorter of the three preceding years or the partnership's period of existence. If the tax year of the partner(s) owning a majority interest cannot be used, the partnership must use the tax year of all its principal partners (or the tax year to which all of its principal partners are concurrently changing). A **principal partner** is defined as one who owns a 5% or more interest in capital or profits.[24] If the principal partners do not have a common tax year, the partnership must use the tax year that allows the least aggregate deferral. The least aggregate deferral test provided in Treasury Regulations[25] requires that, for each possible tax year-end, each partner's ownership percentage be multiplied by the number of months the partner would defer income (number of months from partnership year-end to partner year-end). The number arrived at for each partner is totaled across all partners. The same procedure is followed for each alternative tax year, and the partnership must use the tax year that produces the smallest total.

EXAMPLE C9-17 ▶ Jane, Kerry Corporation, and Lanier Corporation form the JKL Partnership. The three partners use tax years ending on December 31, June 30, and September 30, respectively. Jane, Kerry Corporation, and Lanier Corporation own 40%, 40%, and 20%, respectively, of the partnership. Neither the majority partner rule nor the principal partner rule can be applied to determine

[24] Sec. 706(b)(3).   [25] Reg. Sec. 1.706-1.

JKL's tax year because each partner has a different year-end. To determine the least aggregate deferral, all three possible year-ends must be analyzed as follows:

			6/30		9/30		12/31	
Partner	Interest	Partner Tax Year	Months Deferred[a]	Total[b]	Months Deferred	Total	Months Deferred	Total
Jane	40%	12/31	6	2.4	3	1.2	0	0
Kerry	40%	6/30	0	0	9	3.6	6	2.4
Lanier	20%	9/30	3	0.6	0	0	9	1.8
				3.0		4.8		4.2

[a] Months from possible partnership tax year-end to partner tax year-end.
[b] Partnership interest × months deferred = Total.

The partnership must use a June 30 year-end because, with a total score of 3.0, that tax year-end produces the least aggregate deferral. ◄

If the partnership has a business purpose for using some tax year other than the year prescribed by these rules, the IRS may approve use of another tax year. Revenue Procedure 2002-39[26] states that an acceptable business purpose for using a different tax year is to end the partnership's tax year at the end of the partnership's natural business year. This revenue procedure explains that a business having a peak period and a nonpeak period completes its natural business year at the end of its peak season (or shortly thereafter). For example, a ski lodge has a natural business year that ends in early spring. Partnerships that do not have a peak period cannot use the natural business year exception.

EXAMPLE C9-18 ▶

KEY POINT

Because of the Sec. 706 requirements, most partnerships are required to adopt a calendar year. As a compromise, a Sec. 444 election permits a fiscal tax year as long as no more than a three-month deferral exists and as long as the deferral is not increased from any deferral already approved.

Amy, Brad, and Chris are equal partners in the ABC Partnership. Each partner uses a December 31 tax year-end. ABC earns 30% of its gross receipts in July and August each year and has experienced this pattern of earnings for more than three years. This two-month period is the peak season for their business each year. The IRS probably would grant approval for the partnership to use an August 31 tax year-end. ◄

Section 444 provides an election that permits a partnership to use a year-end that results in a deferral of the lesser of the current deferral period or three months. The deferral period is the time from the beginning of the partnership's fiscal year to the close of the first required tax year ending within such year (i.e., usually December 31). The **Sec. 444**

[26] 2002-1 C.B. 1046. The IRS in Rev. Rul. 87-57, 1987-2 C.B. 224, has provided a series of situations illustrating the business purpose requirement. In addition, Rev. Proc. 2002-38, 2002-1 C.B. 1037, provides expeditious IRS approval if the natural business year satisfies a 25% test. This test requires that 25% of the partnership's gross receipts be earned in the last two months of the requested year and in the last two months of the two preceding similar 12-month periods.

election is available to both new partnerships making an initial tax year election or existing partnerships that are changing tax years. A partnership that satisfies the Sec. 706 requirements described above or has established a business purpose for its choice of a year-end (i.e., natural business year) does not need a Sec. 444 election.

STOP & THINK

Question: Suppose the ABC Partnership has had a December 31 year-end for many years. All its partners are individuals with calendar tax year-ends. Using Sec. 444, what tax year-ends are available for ABC?

Solution: Only December 31 can be used for a tax year-end for ABC even with Sec. 444. Section 444 allows a minimum deferral of the shorter of three months or the existing deferral. Because the existing deferral is zero months (the required tax year-end and the existing tax year-end are both December 31), no deferral is allowed under Sec. 444. The section allows a deferral only for new partnerships or for partnerships that already have a deferral.

HISTORICAL NOTE

Congress enacted Sec. 444, in part, as a concession to tax return preparers who already have the majority of their clients with calendar year-ends.

A partnership that makes a Sec. 444 election must make a required payment under Sec. 7519. (See the Compliance and Procedural Considerations section of this chapter for a discussion of the Sec. 444 election and Sec. 7519 required payment.) The required payment has the effect of assessing a tax on the partnership's deferred income at the highest individual marginal tax rate plus one percentage point.

Topic Review C9-2 summarizes the allowable partnership tax year elections.

OTHER PARTNERSHIP ELECTIONS

With the exception of three specific elections reserved to the partners, Sec. 703(b) requires that the partnership make all elections that can affect the computation of taxable income derived from the partnership.[27] The three elections reserved to the individual partners relate to income from the discharge of indebtedness, deduction and recapture of certain mining exploration expenditures, and the choice between deducting or crediting foreign income taxes. Other than these elections, the partnership makes all elections at the entity level. Accordingly, the partnership elects its overall accounting method, which can differ from the methods used by its partners. The partnership also elects its inventory and depreciation methods.

Topic Review C9-2

Allowable Tax Year for a Partnership

Section 706 requires that a partnership select the highest ranked tax year-end from the ranking that follows:

1. The tax year-end used by the partners who own a majority interest in the partnership capital and profits.
2. The tax year-end used by all principal partners (i.e., partners who each owns an interest in at least 5% of the partnership capital or profits).
3. The tax year-end determined by the least aggregate deferral test.

The IRS may grant permission for the partnership to use a fiscal year-end if the partnership has a natural business year. If the partnership does not have a natural business year, it must either

▶ Use the tax year-end required by Sec. 706 or
▶ Elect a fiscal year-end under Sec. 444 and make a required payment that approximates the tax due on the deferred income.

---

[27] The partnership does not include depletion from oil or gas wells in its computation of income (Sec. 703(a)(2)(F)). Instead each partner elects cost or percentage depletion (Sec. 613A(c)(7)(D)).

PARTNERSHIP REPORTING OF INCOME

PARTNERSHIP TAXABLE INCOME

OBJECTIVE 4

Differentiate between items that must be separately stated and those that are included in ordinary income or loss for partnerships that are not electing large partnerships

Although the partnership is not a taxable entity, the IRC requires that the partnership calculate **partnership taxable income** for various computational reasons, such as adjusting the partners' basis in their partnership interests. Partnership taxable income for partnerships that are not electing large partnerships is calculated in much the same way as the taxable income of individuals, with a few differences mandated by the IRC. First, taxable income is divided into separately stated items and ordinary income or loss. Section 703(a) specifies a list of deductions available to individuals but that cannot be claimed by a partnership. The forbidden deductions include income taxes paid or accrued to a foreign country or U.S. possession, charitable contributions, oil and gas depletion, and net operating loss (NOL) carrybacks or carryovers. The first three items must be separately stated and may or may not be deductible by the partner. Because all losses are allocated to the partners for deduction on their tax returns, the partnership itself never has an NOL carryover or carryback. Instead, a partner may have an NOL if his or her deductible share of partnership losses exceeds his or her other business income. These NOLs are used at the partner level without any further regard for the partnership entity.

SEPARATELY STATED ITEMS

Each partner must report his or her distributive share of partnership income. However, Sec. 702 establishes a list of items that must be separately stated at the partnership level so that their character can remain intact at the partner reporting level. Section 702(a) lists the following items that must be separately stated:

▶ Net short-term capital gains and losses

▶ Net long-term capital gains and losses

▶ Sec. 1231 gains and losses

▶ Charitable contributions

▶ Dividends eligible for the dividends-received deduction or the 15% maximum tax rate

▶ Taxes paid or accrued to a foreign country or to a U.S. possession

▶ Any other item provided by Treasury Regulations

Regulation Sec. 1.702-1(a)(8) adds several other items to this list, including:

▶ Tax-exempt or partially tax-exempt interest

▶ Any items subject to special allocations (discussed below)

As a general rule, an item must be separately stated if the income tax liability of any partner that would result from treating the item separately is different from the liability that would result if that item were included in partnership ordinary income.[28]

EXAMPLE C9-19 ▶ Amy and Big Corporation are equal partners in the AB Partnership, which purchases new equipment during 2006 at a total cost of $300,000. In 2006, AB elects to expense $108,000 under Sec. 179 and allocates $54,000 to each partner. Big already has expensed $35,000 under Sec. 179 this year. The Sec. 179 expense must be separately stated because Big is subject to a separate $108,000 limit of its own (in 2006). After the partnership allocation, Big has a remaining Sec. 179 expense limitation of $19,000 ($108,000 − $35,000 − $54,000). ◀

Once the partnership separately states each item and allocates a distributive share to each partner, the partners report the separately stated items on their tax returns as if the partnership entity did not exist. A partner's share of partnership net long-term capital

---

[28] Reg. Sec. 1.702-1(a)(8)(ii).

ADDITIONAL COMMENT

The pass-through aspect of partnerships reflects the aggregate theory of partnerships, which holds that the partnership is merely an aggregate of its partners. In other ways, however, partnerships conform to the entity theory, for example, they report income and make elections at the entity level.

gains or losses is combined with the partner's personal long-term capital gains and losses to calculate the partner's net long-term capital gain or loss. Likewise, a partner's share of partnership charitable contributions is combined with the partner's own charitable contributions with the total subject to the partner's charitable contribution limitations. In summary, Sec. 702(b) requires that the character of each separately stated item be determined at the partnership level. The amount then passes through to the partners and is reported in each partner's return as if the partner directly realized the amount.

PARTNERSHIP ORDINARY INCOME

All taxable items of income, gain, loss, or deduction that do not have to be separately stated are combined into a total called **partnership ordinary income** or **loss**. This ordinary income amount sometimes is incorrectly referred to as partnership taxable income. Partnership taxable income is the sum of all taxable items among the separately stated items plus the partnership ordinary income or loss. Therefore, partnership taxable income often is substantially greater than partnership ordinary income.

Included in the partnership's ordinary income are items such as gross profit on sales, administrative expenses, and employee salaries. Such items are always ordinary income or expenses not subject to special limitations. Partnership ordinary income also includes Sec. 1245 depreciation recapture because such ordinary income is not eligible for preferential treatment.

The partnership allocates a share of partnership ordinary income or loss to each partner. Such an allocation is reported on Schedules K and K-1 of the partnership's Form 1065 (see the completed partnership tax return in Appendix B). An individual partner reports his or her distributive share of ordinary income, or the deductible portion of his or her distributive share of ordinary loss, on Schedule E of Form 1040. Schedule E includes rental and royalty income and income or losses from estates, trusts, S corporations, and partnerships. A corporate partner reports partnership ordinary income or loss in the Other Income category of Form 1120.

TYPICAL MISCONCEPTION

Partnership ordinary income or loss is the sum of all taxable income or loss items not separately stated. The partnership reports this amount as a residual number on line 22 of Form 1065. Partnership taxable income includes both the taxable separately stated items and the partnership ordinary income or loss. These two terms are not interchangeable.

U.S. PRODUCTION ACTIVITIES DEDUCTION

The 2004 Jobs Act added a new deduction for businesses engaged in U.S. production activities for tax years beginning after 2004. Chapter C3 describes the corporate version of this deduction, whereby the U.S. production activities deduction equals a percentage (3% in 2006) times the lesser of (1) qualified production activities income for the year or (2) taxable income before the U.S. production activities deduction. Individuals use a modified form of AGI instead of taxable income for this computation. The deduction, however, cannot exceed 50% of the employer's W-2 wages for the year. In the case of a partnership, the deduction applies at the partner level, so the partnership must report each partner's share of qualified production activities income on the partner's Schedule K-1. For the 50% salary limitation, each partner is allocated a share of the partnership's W-2 wages equal to the lesser of (1) the partner's allocable share of such wages or (2) 6% (2 × 3% in 2006) of the qualified production activities income allocated to the partner.

PARTNER REPORTING OF INCOME

OBJECTIVE 5

Calculate a partner's distributive share of partnership income, gain, loss, deduction, or credit items

PARTNER'S DISTRIBUTIVE SHARE

Once the partnership determines separately stated income, gain, loss, deduction, or credit items, and partnership ordinary income or loss, the partnership must allocate the totals among the partners. Each partner must report and pay taxes on his or her distributive share. Under Sec. 704(b), the partner's distributive share normally is determined by the terms of the partnership agreement or, if the partnership agreement is silent, by the partner's overall interest in the partnership as determined by taking into account all facts and circumstances.

Note that the term **distributive share** is misleading because it has nothing to do with the amount actually distributed to a partner. A partner's distributive share is the portion of partnership taxable and nontaxable income that the partner has agreed to report for tax purposes. Actual distributions in a given year may be more or less than the partner's distributive share.

PARTNERSHIP AGREEMENT. The **partnership agreement** may describe a partner's distributive share by indicating the partner's profits and loss interest, or it may indicate separate profits and loss interests. For example, the partnership agreement may state that a partner has a 10% interest in both partnership profits and losses or a partner has only a 10% interest in partnership profits (i.e., profits interest) but has a 30% interest in partnership losses (i.e., loss interest).

If the partnership agreement states only one interest percentage, it is used to allocate both partnership profit and loss. If the partnership agreement states profit and loss percentages separately, the partnership's taxable income for the year is first totaled to determine whether a net profit or net loss has occurred. Then the appropriate percentage (either profit or loss) applies to each class of income for the year.[29]

EXAMPLE C9-20 ▶ The ABC Partnership reports the following income and loss items for the current year:

Net long-term capital loss	$100,000
Net Sec. 1231 gain	90,000
Ordinary income	220,000

Carmelia has a 20% profits interest and a 30% loss interest in the ABC Partnership. Because the partnership earns a $210,000 ($90,000 + $220,000 − $100,000) net profit, Carmelia's distributive share is calculated using her 20% profits interest and is reported as follows:

Net long-term capital loss	$ 20,000
Net Sec. 1231 gain	18,000
Ordinary income	44,000

Her loss percentage is used only in years in which the partnership has a net loss. ◀

VARYING INTEREST RULE. If a partner's ownership interest changes during the partnership tax year, the income or loss allocation takes into account the partner's varying interest.[30] This varying interest rule applies for changes occurring to a partner's interest as a result of buying an additional interest in the partnership, selling part (but not all) of a partnership interest, giving or being given a partnership interest, or admitting a new partner. The partner's ownership interest generally applies to the income earned on a pro rata basis.

EXAMPLE C9-21 ▶ Maria owns 20% of the XYZ Partnership from January 1 through June 30 of the current year (not a leap year). On July 1 she buys an additional 10% interest in the partnership. During this year, XYZ Partnership has ordinary income of $120,000, which it earned evenly throughout the year. Maria's $30,049 ($11,901 + $18,148) distributive share of income is calculated as follows:

$$\text{Pre-July 1:} \quad \$120,000 \times \frac{181 \text{ days}}{365 \text{ days}} \times 0.20 = \$11,901$$

$$\text{Post-June 30:} \quad \$120,000 \times \frac{184 \text{ days}}{365 \text{ days}} \times 0.30 = \$18,148$$

Similar calculations would be made if the XYZ Partnership reported separately stated items such as capital gains and losses. ◀

OBJECTIVE 6

Explain the requirements for a special partnership allocation

SPECIAL ALLOCATIONS

Special allocations are unique to partnerships and allow tremendous flexibility in sharing specific items of income and loss among the partners. Special allocations can provide a specified partner with more or less of an item of income, gain, loss, or deduction than

---

[29] This rule is derived from the House and Senate reports on the original Sec. 704(b) provisions. The two reports are identical and read, "The income ratio shall be applicable if the partnership has taxable income . . . and the loss ratio shall be applicable [if] the partnership has a loss." H. Rept. No. 1337, 83d Cong., 2d Sess., p. A223 (1954); S. Rept. No. 1622, 83d Cong., 2d Sess., p. 379 (1954).
[30] Sec. 706(d)(1).

would be available using the partner's regular distributive share. Special allocations fall into two categories. First, Sec. 704 requires certain special allocations with respect to contributed property. Second, other special allocations are allowed as long as they meet the tests set forth in Treasury Regulations for having substantial economic effect. If the special allocation fails the substantial economic effect test, it is disregarded, and the income, gain, loss, or deduction is allocated according to the partner's interest in the partnership as expressed in the actual operations and activities.

ALLOCATIONS RELATED TO CONTRIBUTED PROPERTY. As previously discussed, when a partner contributes property to a partnership, the property takes a carryover basis that references the contributing partner's basis. With no special allocations, this carryover basis rule would require the partnership (and each partner) to accept the tax burden of any gain or loss that accrued to the property before its contribution.

BOOK-TO-TAX ACCOUNTING COMPARISON

For tax purposes, the partnership takes a carryover basis in contributed property. For book purposes, however, the partnership records the contributed property at its FMV.

EXAMPLE C9-22 ▶ In the current year, Elizabeth contributes land having a $4,000 basis and a $10,000 FMV to the DEF Partnership. Assuming the property continues to increase in value, or at least does not decline in value, DEF's gain on the ultimate sale of this property is $6,000 greater than the gain that accrues while the partnership owns the property. Without a special allocation, this $6,000 precontribution gain would be allocated among all partners. ◀

Section 704(c), however, requires precontribution gains or losses to be allocated to the contributing partner. Thus, the precontribution gain of $6,000 in Example C9-22 would be allocated to Elizabeth. In addition, income and deductions reported with respect to contributed property must be allocated to take into account the difference between the property's basis and FMV at the time of contribution.

EXAMPLE C9-23 ▶ Kay and Sam form an equal partnership when Sam contributes cash of $10,000 and Kay contributes land having a $6,000 basis and a $10,000 FMV. If the partnership sells the land two years later for $12,000, the $4,000 precontribution gain ($10,000 FMV − $6,000 basis) is allocated only to Kay. The $2,000 gain that accrued while the partnership held the land ($12,000 sales price − $10,000 FMV at contribution) is allocated to Kay and Sam equally. Kay reports a total gain of $5,000 ($4,000 + $1,000), and Sam reports a $1,000 gain on the sale of the land. ◀

The allocation of depreciation is another common example of the special deduction allocation related to contributed property that is necessary under these rules. Tax Research Problem C9-60 addresses the depreciation allocation issue.

SUBSTANTIAL ECONOMIC EFFECT. Special allocations not related to contributed property must meet several specific criteria established by Treasury Regulations. These criteria ensure that the allocations affect the partner's economic consequences and not just their tax consequences.

BOOK-TO-TAX ACCOUNTING COMPARISON

The capital accounts for meeting the substantial economic effect requirements are maintained using book value accounting rather than tax accounting.

To distinguish transactions affecting only taxes from those affecting the partner's economic position, Treasury Regulations look at whether the allocation has an economic effect and whether the economic effect is substantial. Under the Sec. 704 regulations, the allocation has economic effect if it meets all three of the following conditions:

▶ The allocation results in the appropriate increase or decrease in the partner's capital account.

▶ The proceeds of any liquidation occurring at any time in the partnership's life cycle are distributed in accordance with positive capital account balances.

▶ Partners must make up negative balances in their capital accounts upon the liquidation of the partnership, and these contributions are used to pay partnership debts or are allocated to partners having positive capital account balances.[31]

EXAMPLE C9-24 ▶ Arnie and Bonnie each contribute $100,000 to form the AB Partnership on January 1, 2006. The partnership uses these contributions plus a $1.8 million mortgage to purchase a $2 million

---

[31] Reg. Sec. 1.704-1(b)(2)(ii). Treasury Regulations provide other alternatives for meeting this portion of the requirements.

office building. To simplify the calculations, assume the partnership depreciates the building using the straight-line method over a 40-year life and that in each year income and expenses are equal before considering depreciation. AB makes a special allocation of depreciation to Arnie. The allocation reduces Arnie's capital account, and the partnership makes any liquidating distributions in accordance with the capital account balances. Allocations through 2008 are as follows:

	Capital Account Balance	
	Arnie	Bonnie
January 1, 2006, balance	$100,000	$100,000
2006 loss	(50,000)	–0–
2007 loss	(50,000)	–0–
2008 loss	(50,000)	–0–
December 31, 2008, balance	($ 50,000)	$100,000

If we assume that the property has declined in value in an amount equal to the depreciation claimed and that the partnership now liquidates, the need for the requirement to restore negative capital account balances becomes apparent.

Sales price of property on December 31, 2008	$1,850,000
Minus: Mortgage principal	(1,800,000)
Partnership cash to be distributed to partners	$ 50,000

If Arnie does not have to restore his negative capital account balance, Bonnie can receive only $50,000 in cash even though her capital account balance is $100,000. In effect, Bonnie has borne the economic burden of the 2008 depreciation. Without a requirement to restore the negative capital account balance, the special allocation to Arnie would be ignored for 2008, and Bonnie would receive the depreciation deduction. However, if Arnie must restore any negative capital account balance, he will contribute $50,000 when the partnership liquidates at the end of 2008, and Bonnie will receive her full $100,000 capital account balance. The 2008 special allocation to Arnie will then have economic effect. Note that Arnie's allocation for 2006 and 2007 is acceptable even without an agreement to restore negative capital account balances. This result occurs in each of these two years because Arnie has sufficient capital to absorb the economic loss if the property declines in value in an amount equal to the depreciation allocated to him.[32] ◄

ADDITIONAL COMMENT

The substantial economic effect rules ensure that cash flows ultimately conform to allocations and that allocations do not allow for abusive shifting of tax benefits among partners.

The second requirement for a special allocation to be accepted under Treasury Regulations is that the economic effect must be substantial, which requires that a reasonable possibility exists that the allocation will substantially affect the dollar amounts to be received by the partners independent of tax consequences.[33] Moreover, allocations that involve shifting will not pass the substantiality test. Shifting occurs when the following two conditions are present:

▶ The net change in the partner's capital accounts will be the same for a normal allocation and the special allocation.

▶ The total tax liability of the partners will be less with the special allocation than with a normal allocation.[34]

EXAMPLE C9-25 ▶ The AB Partnership earns $10,000 in tax-exempt interest income and $10,000 in taxable interest income each year. Andy and Becky each have 50% capital and profit interests in the partnership. An allocation of the tax-exempt interest income to Andy, a 35% tax bracket partner, and the taxable interest income to Becky, a 15% tax bracket partner, does not have substantial economic effect. In particular, the allocation lacks substantiality because of shifting. The allocation increases each partner's capital account by $10,000 as would an equal allocation, and it reduces the partner's overall tax liability (see Problem C9-36 at the end of this chapter). ◄

[32] Such allocations do not literally meet the three requirements outlined above for special allocations. However, allocations that meet the alternate standard—having sufficient capital to absorb the economic loss—are considered to have economic effect and will be allowed. See Reg. Sec. 1.704-1(b)(2)(ii)(d).
[33] Reg. Sec. 1.704-1(b)(2)(iii)(a). It should be noted that the substantial economic effect regulations go far beyond the rules covered in this text.

[34] Reg. Sec. 1.704-1(b)(2)(iii)(b). An allocation also can fail the substantiality test by being transitory, which is something like shifting except an allocation in one year is offset by another allocation in a future year (Reg. Sec. 1.704-1(b)(2)(iii)(c)).

STOP & THINK

Question: The special allocation rules require that a partner who receives a special allocation of loss or expense receive less cash or property when the partnership liquidates. As we will see later in this chapter, losses reduce the partner's basis in the partnership interest, so a sale or liquidation of the partnership interest will cause the partner to recognize a larger gain (or a smaller loss) than would have resulted without this loss allocation. Because the basis is reduced, the partner also is more likely to recognize taxable gain on a distribution from the partnership. With these negative consequences, why would anyone want to be given a special allocation of partnership loss or expense?

Solution: The answer is a matter of timing. The specially allocated loss reduces taxable income now and saves more taxes now for the partner than would a "normal" loss allocation. The negative consequences occur when the partner incurs a larger gain (or smaller loss) upon a future sale or liquidation of his or her partnership interest. The special allocation scenario may have a greater after-tax present value to the partner than would the after-tax present value of receiving a normal share of losses and an increased liquidating distribution.

Basis for Partnership Interest

OBJECTIVE 7

Calculate a partner's basis in a partnership interest

The calculation of a partner's beginning basis in a partnership interest depends on the method used to acquire the interest, with different valuation techniques for a purchased interest, a gifted interest, and an inherited interest. The results of the partnership's operations and liabilities both cause adjustments to the beginning amount. Additional contributions to the partnership and distributions from the partnership further alter the partner's basis.

BEGINNING BASIS

ADDITIONAL COMMENT

A partner's basis in a partnership interest commonly is referred to as "outside basis" as opposed to "inside basis," which is the partnership's basis in its assets.

A partner's beginning basis for a partnership interest received for a contribution of property or services has been discussed. However, a partner also can acquire a partnership interest by methods other than contributing property or services to the partnership. If a person purchases the partnership interest from an existing partner, the new partner's basis is the price paid for the partnership interest, including assumption of partnership liabilities. If a person inherits the partnership interest, the heir's basis is the FMV of the partnership interest on the decedent's date of death or, if elected by the executor, the alternate valuation date but not less than liabilities assumed. If a person receives the partnership interest as a gift, the donee's basis generally equals the donor's basis (including the donor's ratable share of partnership liabilities) plus the portion of any gift tax paid by the donor that relates to appreciation attaching to the gift property. In summary, the usual rules for the method of acquisition dictate the beginning basis for a partnership interest.

EFFECTS OF LIABILITIES

SELF-STUDY QUESTION

What are some of the common methods of acquiring a partnership interest, and what is the beginning basis?

ANSWER

1. Contribution—substituted basis from contributed property
2. Purchase—cost basis
3. Inheritance—FMV
4. Gift—usually donor's basis with a possible gift tax adjustment

The early part of this chapter briefly discussed the effect of partnership liabilities on the basis of a partnership interest in connection with the contribution of property subject to a liability. However, further explanation is necessary to fully convey the pervasive impact of liabilities on partnership taxation.

INCREASES AND DECREASES IN LIABILITIES. Two changes in a partner's liabilities are considered contributions of cash by the partner to the partnership.[35] The first is an increase in the partner's share of partnership liabilities. This increase can arise from either an increase in the partner's profit or loss interests or from an increase in total partnership liabilities. Accordingly, if a partnership incurs a large debt, the partners' bases in their partnership interests increase. The second way to increase a partner's basis is to have the partner assume partnership liabilities in his or her individual capacity.

---

[35] Sec. 752.

Conversely, two liability changes are treated as distributions of cash from the partnership to the partner. These changes are a decrease in a partner's share of partnership liabilities and a decrease in the partner's individual liabilities resulting from the partnership's assumption of the partner's liability. Often, both an increase and a decrease in a partner's basis for his or her interest can result from a single transaction. The framework below illustrates the steps used to calculate the partner's basis in his or her partnership interest.

	Partner's basis before changes in liabilities
Plus:	Increases in share of partnership liabilities
Minus:	Decreases in share of partnership liabilities
Plus:	Partnership liabilities assumed by this partner
Minus:	This partner's liabilities assumed by the partnership
	Partner's basis in the partnership interest

EXAMPLE C9-26 ▶ Juan, a 40% partner in the ABC Partnership, has a $30,000 basis in his partnership interest before receiving a partnership distribution of land. As part of the transaction, Juan agrees to assume a $10,000 mortgage on the land. First, Juan's basis in his partnership interest will decrease by $4,000 for the decline in Juan's share of partnership liabilities resulting from the partnership no longer owing the $10,000 mortgage. Second, his basis in the partnership interest will increase by $10,000, which is the partnership liability he assumes in his individual capacity. The net change in basis in his partnership resulting from the liabilities is $6,000 (−$4,000 + $10,000). His basis in his partnership interest also must be decreased for the land distribution he receives. Distributions will be discussed further in Chapter C10. ◀

A PARTNER'S SHARE OF LIABILITIES. Having explained the general impact of liabilities on a partner's basis for his or her partnership interest, we now turn to how the specific amount of the partner's share of a partnership's liabilities is determined. All examples so far have considered only general partners who have the same interest in profits and losses. Partnerships, however, commonly have one or more limited partners, and thus partners can have differing profit and loss ratios. Moreover, the type of liability affects how it is allocated. Treasury Regulations provide guidelines for allocating partnership liabilities to the individual partners.

Recourse and Nonrecourse Loans. A **recourse loan** is the usual kind of loan for which the borrower remains liable until the loan is paid. If the recourse loan is secured and the borrower fails to make payments as scheduled, the lender can sell the property used as security. If the sales proceeds are insufficient to repay a recourse loan, the borrower must make up the difference. Under Treasury Regulations, a recourse loan is one for which any partner or a related party will stand an economic loss if the partnership cannot pay the debt.[36] In contrast, a **nonrecourse loan** is one in which the lender may sell property used as security if the loan is not paid, but no partner is liable for any deficiency. In short, the lender has no recourse against the borrower for additional amounts. Nonrecourse debts most commonly occur in connection with the financing of real property that is expected to substantially increase in value over the life of the loan.

General and Limited Partners. A limited partner normally is not liable to pay partnership debts beyond the original contribution (which already is reflected in his or her basis in the partnership interest) and any additional amount the partner has pledged to contribute.[37] Therefore, recourse debt increases a limited partner's basis only to the extent the partner has a risk of economic loss. Nonrecourse debts increase a limited partner's basis based primarily on the profit ratio.[38]

ADDITIONAL COMMENT
That a partner gets basis for his or her share of recourse debt is not controversial. That a partner gets basis for debt on which the partner is not personally liable seems questionable, yet other rules limit the benefit of the basis created by the nonrecourse debt.

TYPICAL MISCONCEPTION
Nonrecourse debt is allocated among all partners primarily according to their profit ratios. Recourse debt, on the other hand, is allocated to the limited partners to the extent they bear an economic risk of loss, but generally a limited partner's economic risk of loss is not greater than any additional amounts that partner has pledged to contribute. The remaining recourse debt is allocated among the general partners according to their economic risk of loss.

---

[36] Reg. Sec. 1.752-1(a).
[37] This rule may be modified by the limited partner agreeing to assume some of the risk of economic loss despite his or her limited partner status. For example, a limited partner may guarantee the debt or may agree to reimburse the general partner some amount if the general partner has to pay the debt. These arrangements mean that the limited partner shares the risk of loss.

[38] Some nonrecourse debt allocations involve two steps before an allocation according to profits interests. These two steps of the allocation process are beyond the scope of this explanation.

A general partner's share of nonrecourse liabilities also is determined primarily by his or her profit ratio. On the other hand, because limited partners seldom receive an allocated share of the recourse liabilities, the general partners share all recourse liabilities beyond any amounts the limited partners can claim according to their economic loss potential.

The Sec. 752 Treasury Regulations require that recourse liabilities be allocated to the partner who will bear the economic loss if the partnership cannot pay the debt. The regulations provide a complex procedure using a hypothetical liquidation to determine who would bear the loss. In this text, we assume that the hypothetical liquidation analysis has been completed and that the appropriate shares of economic loss as determined by the hypothetical liquidation procedure are stated as part of the problem or example information.

EXAMPLE C9-27 ▶ The ABC Partnership has one general partner (Anna) and a limited partner (Clay) with the following partnership interests:

	Anna (General)	Clay (Limited)
Loss interest	75%	25%
Profits interest	60%	40%
Basis before liabilities	$100,000	$100,000

Clay has an obligation to make an additional $5,000 contribution. He has made no other agreements or guarantees. The partnership has two liabilities at year-end: a $300,000 nonrecourse liability and a $400,000 liability with recourse to the partnership. Clay has a risk of economic loss only to the extent that he has agreed to make additional contributions. The partners' year-end bases are calculated as follows:

	Anna (General)	Clay (Limited)
Year-end basis (excluding liabilities)	$100,000	$100,000
Share of:		
Recourse liability	395,000	5,000
Nonrecourse liability	180,000[a]	120,000[b]
Year-end basis	$675,000	$225,000

[a] 60% × $300,000 = $180,000
[b] 40% × $300,000 = $120,000

◀

If the partnership has more than one general partner, the economic risk of loss computation entails computing a hypothetical loss and allocating that loss to the general partners. The hypothetical loss computation assumes the partnership sells all its assets (including cash) for the amount of nonrecourse liabilities. If the partnership does not have nonrecourse liabilities, the assets are deemed sold for zero dollars. The hypothetical loss then is subtracted from the partners' capital accounts to determine the economic risk of loss.

EXAMPLE C9-28 ▶ Assume the same facts as in Example C9-27 except that Clay is a general partner. In addition, the partnership has $900,000 of assets, and each partner's capital account is $100,000. If the partnership sold its assets for the amount of the nonrecourse liability, it would realize a $600,000 loss ($300,000 − $900,000). The economic risk of loss is calculated as follows:

	Anna (General)	Clay (General)
Capital accounts	$100,000	$100,000
Minus: Hypothetical loss (allocated according to loss percentages)	(450,000)	(150,000)
Economic risk of loss	$350,000	$ 50,000

The partners' year-end bases are calculated as follows:

	Anna (General)	Clay (General)
Year-end basis (excluding liabilities)	$100,000	$100,000
Share of:		
Recourse liability	350,000	50,000
Nonrecourse liability	180,000	120,000
Year-end basis	$630,000	$270,000

◀

Determination of the partners' share of recourse liabilities can be simplified if the partners have the same interest in losses as they do for profits and if their capital accounts are in accordance with those percentages. In this situation, the recourse liability allocation also will be in accordance with the profit/loss percentages.

EFFECTS OF OPERATIONS

A partner's basis is a summary of his or her contributions and the partnership's liabilities, earnings, losses, and distributions. Basis prevents a second tax levy on a distribution of income that was taxed previously as a partner's distributive share. Section 705 mandates a basis increase for additional contributions made by the partner to the partnership plus the partner's distributive share for the current and prior tax years of the following items:

▶ Partnership taxable income (both separately stated items and partnership ordinary income)

▶ Tax-exempt income of the partnership

Basis is decreased (but not below zero) by distributions from the partnership to the partner plus the partner's distributive share for the current and prior tax years of the following items:

▶ Partnership losses (both separately stated items and partnership ordinary loss)

▶ Expenditures that are not deductible for tax purposes and that are not capital expenditures

The positive basis adjustment for tax-exempt income and the negative basis adjustment for nondeductible expenses preserve that tax treatment for the partner. If these adjustments were not made, tax-exempt income would be taxable to the partner upon a subsequent distribution or upon the sale or other disposition of the partnership interest.

> **BOOK-TO-TAX ACCOUNTING COMPARISON**
>
> Although a partner's basis in the partnership cannot go below zero, a partner's book capital account (equity) may be negative.

EXAMPLE C9-29 ▶

LMN Partnership has only one asset—a $100,000 municipal bond. Marta has a $20,000 basis in her 20% partnership interest. In the current year, the partnership collects $4,000 tax-exempt interest from the bond. Marta's basis at year-end is calculated as follows:

Beginning basis	$20,000
Share of tax-exempt income	800
Basis at year end	$20,800

On the first day of the next year, the partnership sells the bond for $100,000 cash. At this point, the partnership has $104,000 in cash and no other assets. The partnership liquidates and distributes her 20% share of the cash ($20,800) to Marta. Marta has no gain or loss because her $20,800 basis exactly equals her distribution. If the tax-exempt income had not increased her basis, she would have recognized an $800 gain on the distribution ($20,800 cash distribution − $20,000 basis if no increase were made for the tax-exempt income.) Thus, her basis must be increased by tax-exempt income to prevent a taxable gain upon its distribution. ◀

> **OBJECTIVE 8**
>
> *Determine the limitations on a partner's deduction of partnership losses*

LOSS LIMITATIONS. Each partner is allocated his or her distributive share of ordinary income or loss and separately stated income, gain, loss, or deduction items each year. The partner always reports income and gain items in his or her current tax year, and these items increase the partner's basis in the partnership interest. However, the partner may not be able to use his or her full distributive share of losses because Sec. 704(d) limits a partner's loss deduction to the amount of his or her basis in the partnership interest before the loss. All positive basis adjustments for the year and all reductions for actual or deemed distributions must be made before determining the amount of the deductible loss.[39]

EXAMPLE C9-30 ▶

On January 1 of the current year, Miguel has a $32,000 basis for his general interest in the MT Partnership. He materially participates in the partnership's business activities. On December 1, Miguel receives a $1,000 cash distribution. His distributive share of MT's current items are a $4,000 net long-term capital gain and a $43,000 ordinary loss. Miguel's deductible loss is calculated as follows:

---

[39] Reg. Sec. 1.704-1(d)(2).

January 1 basis	$32,000
Plus: Long-term capital gain	4,000
Minus: Distribution	(1,000)
Limit for loss deduction	$35,000

SELF-STUDY QUESTION

What happens to losses that are disallowed due to lack of basis in a partnership interest?

ANSWER

The losses are suspended until that partner obtains additional basis.

Miguel can deduct $35,000 of the ordinary loss in the current year, which reduces his basis to zero. He cannot deduct the remaining $8,000 of ordinary loss currently but can deduct it in the following year if he regains sufficient basis in his partnership interest. ◄

Any distributive share of loss that a partner cannot deduct because of the basis limit is simply noted in the partner's financial records. It is not reported on the partner's tax return, nor does it reduce the partner's basis. However, the losses carry forward until the partner again has positive basis from capital contributions, additional partnership borrowings, or partnership earnings.[40]

EXAMPLE C9-31 ▶

Assume the same facts as in Example C9-30. Miguel makes no additional contributions in the following year, and the MT Partnership's liabilities remain unchanged. Miguel's distributive share of MT's partnership items in the following year is $2,500 of net short-term capital gain and $14,000 of ordinary income. These items restore his basis to $16,500 ($0 + $2,500 + $14,000), and he can deduct the $8,000 loss carryover. After taking these transactions into account, Miguel's basis is $8,500 ($16,500 − $8,000). ◄

Topic Review C9-3 summarizes the rules for determining the initial basis for a partnership interest and the annual basis adjustments required to determine the adjusted basis of a partnership interest.

Topic Review C9-3

Basis of a Partnership Interest

METHOD OF ACQUISITION	BEGINNING BASIS IS
Property contributed	Substituted basis from property contributed plus gain recognized for contributions to an investment partnership
Services contributed	Amount of income recognized for services rendered (plus any additional amount contributed)
Purchase	Cost
Gift	Donor's basis plus gift tax on appreciation
Inheritance	Fair market value at date of death or alternative valuation date

LIABILITY IMPACT ON BASIS	
Increase basis for	Increases in the partner's share of partnership liabilities Liabilities of the partnership assumed by the partner in his or her individual capacity
Decrease basis for	Decreases in the partner's share of partnership liabilities Liabilities of the partner assumed by the partnership

OPERATIONS IMPACT ON BASIS	
Increase basis for	Partner's share of ordinary income and separately stated income and gain items (including tax-exempt items) Additional contributions to the partnership Precontribution gain recognized
Decrease basis for	Distributions from the partnership to the partner Partner's share of ordinary loss and separately stated loss and deduction items (including items that are not deductible for tax purposes and are not capital expenditures) Precontribution loss recognized

[40] Reg. Sec. 1.704-1(d)(1).

SPECIAL LOSS LIMITATIONS

Three sets of rules limit the loss from a partnership interest that a partner may deduct. The Sec. 704(d) rules explained above limit losses to the partner's basis in the partnership interest. Two other rules establish more stringent limits. The at-risk rules limit losses to an amount called *at-risk basis*. The passive activity loss or credit limitation rules disallow most net passive activity losses.

AT-RISK LOSS LIMITATION

The Sec. 704(d) loss limitation rules were the only loss limits for many years. However, Congress became increasingly uncomfortable with allowing partners to increase their basis by a portion of the partnership's nonrecourse liabilities and then offset this basis with partnership losses. Accordingly, Congress established the **at-risk rules**, which limit loss deductions to the partner's at-risk basis. The **at-risk basis** is essentially the same amount as the regular partnership basis with the exception that liabilities increase the at-risk basis only if the partner is at risk for such an amount. The at-risk rules apply to individuals and closely held C corporations. Partners that are widely held C corporations are not subject to these rules.

Although much of the complexity of the *at-risk* term is beyond the scope of this text, a simplified working definition is possible. A partner is at risk for an amount if he or she would lose that amount should the partnership suddenly become worthless. Because a partner would not have to pay a partnership's nonrecourse liabilities even if the partnership became worthless, the usual nonrecourse liabilities cannot be included in any partner's at-risk basis. Under the at-risk rules, a partner's loss deduction may be substantially less than the amount deductible under the Sec. 704(d) rules.[41]

EXAMPLE C9-32 ▶ Keesha is a limited partner in the KM Manufacturing Partnership. At the end of the partnership's tax year, her basis in the partnership interest is $30,000 ($10,000 investment plus a $20,000 share of nonrecourse financing). Keesha's distributive share of partnership losses for the tax year is $18,000. Although she has sufficient basis in the partnership interest, the at-risk rules limit her deduction to $10,000 because she is not at risk for the nonrecourse financing. ◀

The IRC allows one significant exception to the application of the at-risk rules. At-risk rules do not apply to nonrecourse debt if it is qualified real estate financing. The partner is considered at risk for his or her share of nonrecourse real estate financing if all of the following requirements are met:

▶ The financing is secured by real estate used in the partnership's real estate activity.

▶ The debt is not convertible to any kind of equity interest in the partnership.

▶ The financing is from a qualified person or from any federal, state, or local government, or is guaranteed by any federal, state, or local government.[42] A qualified person is an unrelated party who is in the trade or business of lending money (e.g., bank, financial institution, or mortgage broker).

PASSIVE ACTIVITY LIMITATIONS

The 1986 Tax Reform Act added still a third set of limits to the loss that a partner may deduct: the passive activity loss and credit limitations.

Under the passive activity limitation rules of Sec. 469, all income is divided into three categories: amounts derived from passive activities; active income such as salary, bonuses, and income from businesses in which the taxpayer materially participates; and portfolio income such as dividends, interest, and capital gains from investments other than passive activities. Generally, losses of an individual partner from a passive activity cannot be used to offset either active income or portfolio income. However, passive losses carry over to future years. These passive losses are allowed in full when a taxpayer disposes of the entire interest in the passive activity. Passive losses generated by a passive rental activity in

TYPICAL MISCONCEPTION

The at-risk rules severely limit the use of nonrecourse debt to obtain loss deductions except for certain qualified real estate financing, yet this real estate exception is more apparent than real because of the final set of rules that must be satisfied: the passive activity limitations.

---

[41] Sec. 465(a).   [42] Sec. 465(b)(6).

TAX STRATEGY TIP

If a partner is unable to use all of his or her share of partnership losses due to a lack of basis, contributions to capital or increasing partnership liabilities may provide the additional needed tax basis. If the passive activity limitation rules are the reason the partnership losses cannot be used, the possibility of investing in passive activities that generate passive income may be the best planning alternative. See Tax Planning Considerations for further discussion.

which an individual partner is an active participant can be deducted up to a maximum of $25,000 per year. This deduction phases out by 50% of the amount of the partner's adjusted gross income (AGI) that exceeds $100,000, so that no deduction is allowed if the partner has AGI of $150,000 or more. (The phase-out begins at $200,000 for low-income housing or rehabilitation credits.) Losses disallowed under the phase-out are deductible to the extent of passive income.

A passive activity is any trade or business in which the taxpayer does not materially participate. A taxpayer who owns a limited partnership interest in any activity generally fails the material participation test. Accordingly, losses from most limited partnership interests can be used only to offset income from passive activities even if the limited partner has sufficient Sec. 704(d) and at-risk basis.[43]

Although passive activity limitations may greatly affect the taxable income or loss reported by a partner, they have no unusual effect on basis. Basis is reduced (but not below zero) by the partner's distributive share of losses whether or not the losses are limited under the passive loss rules.[44] When the suspended passive losses later become deductible, the partner's basis in the partnership interest is not affected.

EXAMPLE C9-33 ▶ Chris purchases a 20% capital and profits interest in the CJ Partnership in the current year, but he does not participate in CJ's business. Chris owns no other passive investments. His Sec. 704(d) basis in CJ is $80,000, and his at-risk basis is $70,000. Chris's distributive share of the CJ Partnership's loss for the current year is $60,000. Chris's Sec. 704(d) basis is $20,000 ($80,000 −$60,000), and his at-risk basis is $10,000 ($70,000 − $60,000) after the results of this year's operations are taken into account. However, Chris cannot deduct any of the CJ loss in the current year because it is a passive activity loss. The $60,000 loss, however, can be used in a subsequent year if the partner generates passive income. Because the $60,000 loss already has reduced basis for purposes of both Sec. 704(d) and the at-risk rules, the disallowed loss need not be tested against those rules a second time. ◀

TRANSACTIONS BETWEEN A PARTNER AND THE PARTNERSHIP

The partner and the partnership are treated as separate entities for many transactions. Section 707(b) restricts sales of property between the partner and partnership by disallowing certain losses and converting certain capital gains into ordinary income. Section 707(c) permits a partnership to make guaranteed payments for capital and services to a partner that are separate from the partner's distributive share. Each of these rules is explored below.

SALES OF PROPERTY

LOSS SALES. Without restrictions, a controlling partner could sell property to the partnership to recognize a loss for tax purposes while retaining a substantial interest in the property through ownership of a partnership interest. Congress closed the door to such loss recognition with the Sec. 707(b) rules.

KEY POINT

The IRC disallows losses on sales between persons and certain related partnerships, similar to the related party rules of Sec. 267. The concern is that tax losses can be artificially recognized without the property being disposed of outside the economic group.

The rules for partnership loss transactions are quite similar to the Sec. 267 related party rules discussed in Chapter C3. Under Sec. 707(b)(1), no loss can be deducted on the sale or exchange of property between a partnership and a person who directly or indirectly owns more than 50% of the partnership's capital or profits interests. (Indirect ownership includes ownership by related parties such as members of the partner's family.[45]) Similarly, losses are disallowed on sales or exchanges of property between two partnerships in which the same persons own, directly or indirectly, more than 50% of the capital

---

[43] Sec. 469(h)(2).
[44] S. Rept. No. 99-313, 99th Cong., 2d Sess., p. 723, footnote 4 (1986).
[45] For purposes of Sec. 707, related parties include an individual and members of his or her family (spouse, brothers, sisters, lineal descendants, and ancestors), an individual and a more-than-50%-owned corporation, and two corporations that are members of the same controlled group.

or profits interests. If the seller is disallowed a loss under Sec. 707(b)(1), the purchaser can reduce any subsequent gain realized on a sale of the property by the previously disallowed loss.

EXAMPLE C9-34 ▶ James, Karen, and Thelma own equal interests in the JKT Partnership. Karen and Thelma are siblings, but James is unrelated to the others. For purposes of Sec. 707, Karen owns 66.66% of the partnership (33.33% directly and 33.33% indirectly from Thelma). Likewise, Thelma also owns 66.66%, but James has only a direct ownership interest of 33.33%. ◀

EXAMPLE C9-35 ▶ Pat sold land having a $45,000 basis to the PTA Partnership for $35,000, its FMV. If Pat has a 60% capital and profits interest in the partnership, Pat realizes but cannot recognize a $10,000 loss on the sale. If Pat owns only a 49% interest, directly and indirectly, he can recognize the loss. ◀

EXAMPLE C9-36 ▶ Assume the same facts as in Example C9-35 except the partnership later sells the land for $47,000. The partnership's realized gain is $12,000 ($47,000 − $35,000 basis). If Pat has a 60% capital and profits interest, his previously disallowed loss of $10,000 reduces the partnership's recognized gain to $2,000. This $2,000 gain is then allocated to the partners according to the partnership agreement. ◀

GAIN SALES. When gain is recognized on the sale of a capital asset between a partnership and a related partner, Sec. 707(b)(2) requires that the gain be ordinary (and not capital gain) if the property will not be a capital asset to its new owner. Sales or exchanges resulting in the application of Sec. 707(b)(2) include transfers between (1) a partnership and a person who owns, directly or indirectly, more than 50% of the partnership's capital or profits interests, or (2) two partnerships in which the same persons own, directly or indirectly, more than 50% of the capital or profits interests.[46] This provision prevents related parties from increasing the depreciable basis of assets (and thereby reducing future ordinary income) at the cost of recognizing only a current capital gain.

EXAMPLE C9-37 ▶ Sharon and Tony have the following capital and profits interests in two partnerships:

Partner	ST Partnership (%)	QRS Partnership (%)
Sharon	42	58
Tony	42	30
Other unrelated partners	16	12
Total	100	100

The ST Partnership sells land having a $150,000 basis to the QRS Partnership for $180,000. The land was a capital asset for the ST Partnership, but QRS intends to subdivide and sell the land. Because the land is ordinary income property to the QRS Partnership and because Sharon and Tony control both partnerships, the ST Partnership must recognize $30,000 of ordinary income on the land sale. ◀

GUARANTEED PAYMENTS

A corporate shareholder can be an employee of the corporation. However, a partner generally is not an employee of the partnership, and most fringe benefits are disallowed for a partner who is "employed" by his or her partnership.[47]

A partner who provides services to the partnership in an ongoing relationship might be compensated like any other employee. Section 707(c) provides for this kind of payment and labels it a **guaranteed payment**. The term *guaranteed payment* also includes certain payments made to a partner for the use of invested capital. These payments are similar to interest. Both types of guaranteed payments must be determined without regard to the partnership's income.[48] Conceptually, this requirement separates guaranteed payments from distributive shares. As indicated below, however, such a distinction may not be so clear in practice.

OBJECTIVE 9

Determine the tax consequences of a guaranteed payment

---

[46] Sec. 707(b)(2).
[47] Rev. Rul. 91-26, 1991-1 C.B. 184, holds that accident and health insurance premiums paid for a partner by the partnership are guaranteed payments.

[48] Sec. 707(c).

TYPICAL MISCONCEPTION

If a partner, acting in his or her capacity as a partner, receives payments from the partnership determined without regard to the partnership's income, the partner has received a guaranteed payment. If the partner is acting as a nonpartner, the partner is treated as any other outside contractor.

DETERMINING THE GUARANTEED PAYMENT. Sometimes the determination of the guaranteed payment is quite simple. For example, some guaranteed payments are expressed as specific amounts (e.g., $20,000 per year), with the partner also receiving his or her normal distributive share. Other times, the guaranteed payment is expressed as a **guaranteed minimum.** However, these guaranteed minimum arrangements make it difficult to distinguish the partner's distributive share and guaranteed payments because no guaranteed payment occurs under this arrangement unless the partner's distributive share is less than his or her guaranteed minimum. If the distributive share is less than the guaranteed minimum, the guaranteed payment is the difference between the distributive share and the guaranteed minimum.

EXAMPLE C9-38 ▶ Tina manages the real estate owned by the TAV Partnership, in which she also is a partner. She receives 30% of all partnership income before guaranteed payments, but no less than $60,000 per year. In the current year, the TAV Partnership reports $300,000 in ordinary income. Tina's 30% distributive share is $90,000 (0.30 × $300,000), which exceeds her $60,000 guaranteed minimum. Therefore, she has no guaranteed payment. ◀

EXAMPLE C9-39 ▶ Assume the same facts as in Example C9-38 except the TAV Partnership reports $150,000 of ordinary income. Tina has a guaranteed payment of $15,000, which represents the difference between her $45,000 distributive share (0.30 × $150,000) and her $60,000 guaranteed minimum.[49] ◀

TAX IMPACT OF GUARANTEED PAYMENTS. Like salary or interest income, guaranteed payments are ordinary income to the recipient. The guaranteed payment must be included in income for the recipient partner's tax year during which the partnership year ends and the partnership deducts or capitalizes the payments.[50]

EXAMPLE C9-40 ▶ In January 2007, a calendar year taxpayer, Will, receives a $10,000 guaranteed payment from the WRS Partnership, which uses the accrual method of accounting. WRS accrues and deducts the payment during its tax year ending November 30, 2006. Will must report his guaranteed payment in his 2006 tax return because that return includes the 2006 partnership income that reflects the impact of the guaranteed payment. ◀

The partnership treats the guaranteed payment as if it is made to an outsider. If the payment is for a service that is a capital expenditure (e.g., architectural services for designing a building for the partnership), the guaranteed payment must be capitalized and, if allowable, amortized. If the payment is for services deductible under Sec. 162, the partnership deducts the payment from ordinary income. Thus, deductible guaranteed payments offset the partnership's ordinary income but never its capital gains. If the guaranteed payment exceeds the partnership's ordinary income, the payment creates an ordinary loss that is allocated among the partners.[51]

EXAMPLE C9-41 ▶ Theresa is a partner in the STU Partnership. She is to receive a guaranteed payment for deductible services of $60,000 and 30% of partnership income computed after the partnership deducts the guaranteed payment. The partnership reports $40,000 of ordinary income and a $120,000 long-term capital gain before deducting the guaranteed payment. Theresa's income from the partnership is determined as follows:

	STU Partnership	Theresa's Share Ratable Share	Amount
Ordinary income (before guaranteed payment)	$ 40,000		
Minus: Guaranteed payment	(60,000)	100%	$60,000
Ordinary loss	($ 20,000)	30%	(6,000)
Long-term capital gain	$120,000	30%	36,000 ◀

[49] Reg. Sec. 1.707-1(c), Exs. (1) and (2).
[50] Reg. Secs. 1.707-1(c) and 1.706-1(a).
[51] Reg. Sec. 1.707-1(c), Ex. (4).

FAMILY PARTNERSHIPS

OBJECTIVE 10

Explain the requirements for recognizing the holder of a partnership interest as a partner in a family partnership

CAPITAL OWNERSHIP

Because each partner reports and pays taxes on a distributive share of partnership income, a family partnership is an excellent way to spread income among family members and minimize the family's tax bill. However, to accomplish this tax minimization goal, the IRS must accept the family members as real partners. The question of whether someone is a partner in a family partnership is often litigated, but safe-harbor rules under Sec. 704(e) provide a clear answer if three tests are met: the partnership interest must be a capital interest, capital must be a material income-producing factor in the partnership's business activity, and the family member must be the true owner of the interest.

A capital interest gives the partner the right to receive assets if the partnership liquidates immediately upon the partner's acquisition of the interest. Capital is a material income-producing factor if the partnership derives substantial portions of gross income from the use of capital. For example, capital is a material income-producing factor if the business has substantial inventory or significant investment in plant or equipment. Capital is seldom considered a material income-producing factor in a service business.[52]

The remaining question is whether the family member is the true owner of the interest. Ownership is seldom questioned if one family member purchases the interest at a market price from another family member. However, when one family member gifts the interest to another, the major question is whether the donor retains so much control over the partnership interest that the donor is still the owner of the interest. If the donor still controls the interest, the donor is taxed on the distributive share.

TAX STRATEGY TIP

In certain situations, family partnerships provide an excellent tax-planning tool, but the family members must be real partners. The rules that determine who is a real partner in a family partnership are guided by the assignment-of-income principle.

DONOR RETAINED CONTROL. No mechanical test exists to determine whether the donor has retained too much control, but several factors may indicate a problem:[53]

▶ Retention of control over distributions of income can be a problem unless the retention occurs with the agreement of all partners or the retention is for the reasonable needs of the business.

▶ Retention of control over assets that are essential to the partnership's business can indicate too much control by the donor.

▶ Limitation of the donee partner's right to sell or liquidate his or her interest may indicate that the donor has not relinquished full control over the interest.

▶ Retention of management control that is inconsistent with normal partnership arrangements can be another sign that the donor retains control. This situation is not considered a fatal problem unless it occurs in conjunction with a significant limit on the donee's ability to sell or liquidate his or her interest.

If the donor has not directly or indirectly retained too much control, the donee is a full partner. As a partner, the donee must report his or her distributive share of income.

KEY POINT

A valid family partnership is a useful method for allocating income among family members. However, the distributive share of income from a partnership interest to a partner under age 14 is subject to the "kiddie tax."

MINOR DONEES. When income splitting is the goal of a family, the appropriate donee for the partnership interest is often a minor. With the problem of donor-retained controls in mind, gifts to minors should be made with great attention to detail. Further, net unearned income of a child under age 14 is taxed to the child at the parents' marginal tax rate. This provision removes much of the incentive to transfer family partnership interests to young children, but gifting partnership interests to minors age 14 or older still can reap significant tax advantages.

OBJECTIVE 11

Determine the allocation of partnership income between a donor and a donee of a partnership interest

DONOR-DONEE ALLOCATIONS OF INCOME

Partnership income must be properly allocated between a donor and a donee to be accepted by the IRS. Note that only the allocation between the donor and donee is questioned, with no impact on the distributive shares of any other partners.

---

[52] Reg. Sec. 1.704-1(e)(1)(iv).   [53] Reg. Sec. 1.704-1(e)(2)(ii).

Two requirements apply to donor-donee allocations. First, the donor must be allocated reasonable compensation for services rendered to the partnership. Then, after reasonable compensation is allocated to the donor, any remaining partnership income must be allocated based on relative capital interests.[54] This allocation scheme apparently overrides the partnership's ability to make special allocations of income.

EXAMPLE C9-42 ▶

ETHICAL POINT

CPAs have a responsibility to review an entity's conduct of its activities to be sure it is operating as a partnership. If a donee receives a partnership interest as a gift and the donee is not the true owner of the interest (e.g., the donor retains too much control over the donee's interest), the partnership return must be filed without a distributive share of income or loss being allocated to the donee.

Andrew, a 40% partner in the ABC Partnership, gives one-half of his interest to his brother, John. During the current year, Andrew performs services for the partnership for which reasonable compensation is $65,000 but for which he accepts no pay. Andrew and John are each credited with a $100,000 distributive share, all of which is ordinary income. Reallocation between Andrew and John is necessary to reflect the value of Andrew's services.

Total distributive shares for the brothers	$200,000
Minus: Reasonable compensation for Andrew	(65,000)
Income to allocate	$135,000

John's distributive share: $\dfrac{20\%}{40\%} \times \$135,000 = \$67,500$

Andrew's distributive share: $\left(\dfrac{20\%}{40\%} \times \$135,000\right) + \$65,000 = \$132,500$ ◀

TAX PLANNING CONSIDERATIONS

TIMING OF LOSS RECOGNITION

The loss limitation rules provide a unique opportunity for tax planning. For example, if a partner knows that his or her distributive share of active losses from a partnership for a tax year will exceed the Sec. 704 basis limitation for deducting losses, he or she should carefully examine the tax situation for the current and upcoming tax years. Substantial current personal income may make immediate use of the loss desirable. Current income may be taxed at a higher marginal tax rate than will future income because of, for example, an extraordinarily good current year, an expected retirement, or a decrease in future years' tax rates. If the partner chooses to use the loss in the current year, he or she can make additional contributions just before year-end (perhaps even from funds the partner borrows, as long as the additional benefit exceeds the cost of the funds). Alternatively, one partner may convince the other partners to have the partnership incur additional liabilities so that each partner's basis increases. This last strategy should be exercised with caution unless a business reason (rather than solely a tax reason) exists for the borrowing.

EXAMPLE C9-43 ▶

Ted, a 60% general partner in the ST Partnership, expects to be allocated partnership losses of $120,000 for the current year from a partnership in which he materially participates but where his partnership basis is only $90,000. Because he has a marginal tax rate of 35% for the current year (and anticipates only a 25% marginal tax rate for next year), Ted wants to use the ST Partnership losses to offset his current year income. He could make a capital contribution to raise his basis by $30,000. Alternatively, he could get the partnership to incur $50,000 in additional liabilities, which would increase his basis by his $30,000 ($50,000 × 0.60) share of the liability. The partnership's $50,000 borrowing must serve a business purpose for the ST Partnership. ◀

Alternatively, a partner may prefer to delay the deduction of partnership losses that exceed the current year's loss limitation. If the partner has little current year income and expects substantial income in the following year. If the partner has loss, deduction, or

---

[54] Sec. 704(e)(2).

credit carryovers that expire in the current year, a deferral of the distributive share of partnership losses to the following year may be desirable. If the partner opts to deduct the loss in a later year, he or she needs only to leave things alone so that the distributive share of losses exceeds the loss limitation for the current year.

COMPLIANCE AND PROCEDURAL CONSIDERATIONS

OBJECTIVE **12**

Determine the requirements for filing a partnership tax return

HISTORICAL NOTE

Turn to the partnership Schedule K in Appendix B of this book. The large number of items that now have to be separately stated illustrates how certain tax laws, such as the passive activity limitation rules and the investment interest limitation rules, have complicated the preparation of Form 1065.

REPORTING TO THE IRS AND THE PARTNERS

FORMS. If the partnership is not an electing large partnership, the partnership must file a Form 1065 with the IRS by the fifteenth day of the fourth month after the end of the partnership tax year. (See Appendix B for a completed Form 1065.) The IRS, however, allows an automatic six-month extension of time to file Form 1065. To obtain the extension, the partnership must file Form 7004 on or before the partnership's normal filing date.[55] Penalties are imposed for failure to file a timely or complete partnership return. Because the partnership is only a conduit, Form 1065 is an information return and is not accompanied by any tax payment.[56] Included on the front page of Form 1065 are all the ordinary items of income, gain, loss and deduction that are not separately stated. Schedule K of Form 1065 reports both a summary of the ordinary income items and the partnership total of the separately stated items. Schedule K-1, which the partnership must prepare for each partner, reflects that partner's distributive share of partnership income including his or her special allocations. The partner's Schedule K-1 is notification of his or her share of partnership items for use in calculating income taxes and self-employment taxes.

SCHEDULE M-3. For tax years ending on or after December 31, 2006, a partnership must file Schedule M-3 in lieu of Schedule M-1 if any one of the following conditions holds:

▶ The amount of total assets reported in Schedule L of Form 1065 (Balance Sheet per Books) equals or exceeds $10 million.

▶ The amount of adjusted total assets equals or exceeds $10 million, where adjusted total assets equal the Schedule L amount plus the following items that appear in Schedule M-2 of Form 1065: (1) capital distributions made during the year, (2) net book loss for the year, and (3) other adjustments.

▶ Total receipts equal or exceed $35 million.

▶ A reportable entity partner owns at least a 50% interest in the partnership on any day of the tax year, where a reportable entity partner is one that had to file its own Schedule M-3.

SECTION 444 ELECTION AND REQUIRED PAYMENTS. A partnership can elect to use a tax year other than a required year by filing an election under Sec. 444. This election is made by filing Form 8716 (Election to Have a Tax Year Other Than a Required Tax Year) by the earlier of the fifteenth day of the fifth month following the month that includes the first day of the tax year for which the election is effective or the due date (without regard to extension) of the income tax return resulting from the Sec. 444 election. In addition, a copy of Form 8716 must be attached to the partnership's Form 1065 for the first tax year for which the Sec. 444 election is made.

A partnership making a Sec. 444 election must make a required payment annually under Sec. 7519. The required payment has the effect of remitting a deposit equal to the

---

[55] Temp. Reg. 1.6081-2T. This temporary regulation applies to applications for extension filed after December 31, 2005, and before November 4, 2008.
[56] Reg. Sec. 301.6031-1(e)(2). Although the partnership pays no income tax, it still must pay the employer's share of social security taxes and any unem-

ployment taxes as well as withhold income taxes from its employees' salaries. In addition, some publicly traded partnerships may pay a tax as explained in Chapter C10.

tax (at the highest individual tax rate plus one percentage point) on the partnership's deferred income.

A partnership can obtain a refund if past payments exceed the tentative payment due on the deferred income for the current year. Similar refunds are available if the partnership terminates a Sec. 444 election or liquidates. The required payments are not deductible by the partnership and are not passed through to a partner. The required payments are in the nature of a refundable deposit.

The Sec. 7519 required payment is due on or before May 15 of the calendar year following the calendar year in which the election year begins. The partnership remits the required payment with Form 8752 (Required Payment or Refund Under Section 7519) along with a computational worksheet, which is illustrated in the instructions to Form 1065. Refunds of excess required payments also are obtained by filing Form 8752.

ESTIMATED TAXES. If the partnership is not an electing large partnership, it pays no income taxes and makes no estimated tax payments. However, the partners must make estimated tax payments based on their separate tax positions including their distributive shares of partnership income or loss for the current year. Thus, the partners are not making separate estimated tax payments for their partnership income but rather are including the effects of the partnership's results in the calculation of their normal estimated tax payments.

SELF-EMPLOYMENT INCOME. Every partnership must report the net earnings (or loss) for the partnership that constitute self-employment income to the partners. The instructions to Form 1065 contain a worksheet to make such a calculation. The partnership's self-employment income includes both guaranteed payments, partnership ordinary income and loss, and some separately stated items, but generally excludes capital gains and losses, Sec. 1231 gains and losses, interest, dividends, and rentals. The distributive share of self-employment income for each partner is shown on a Schedule K-1 and is included with the partner's other self-employment income in determining his or her self-employment tax liability (Schedule SE, Form 1040). The distributive share of partnership income allocable to a limited partner is not self-employment income.

EXAMPLE C9-44 ▶ Adam is a general partner in the AB Partnership. His distributive share of partnership income and his guaranteed payment for the year are as follows:

Ordinary income	$15,000
Short-term capital gain	9,000
Guaranteed payment	18,000

Adam's self-employment income is $33,000 ($15,000 + $18,000). ◀

EXAMPLE C9-45 ▶ Assume the same facts as in Example C9-44 except that Adam is a limited partner. His self-employment income includes only the $18,000 guaranteed payment. ◀

IRS AUDIT PROCEDURES

Any questions arising during an IRS audit about a partnership item must be determined at the partnership level (instead of at the partner level).[57] Section 6231(a)(3) defines **partnership items** as virtually all items reported by the partnership for the tax year including tax preference items, credit recapture items, guaranteed payments, and the at-risk amount. In fact, almost every item that can appear on the partnership return is treated as a partnership item. Each partner must either report partnership items in a manner consistent with the Schedule K-1 received from the partnership or notify the IRS of the inconsistent treatment.[58]

The IRS can bring a single proceeding at the partnership level to determine the characterization or tax impact of any partnership item. All partners have the right to participate in the administrative proceedings, and the IRS must offer a consistent settlement to all partners.

---

[57] Sec. 6221.　　　　　　　　[58] Sec. 6222.

KEY POINT

To alleviate the administrative nightmare of having to audit each partner of a partnership, Congress has authorized the IRS to conduct audits of partnerships in a unified proceeding at the partnership level. This process is more efficient and should provide greater consistency in the treatment of the individual partners than did the previous system.

The partnership generally assigns a **tax matters partner** to facilitate communication between the IRS and the partners of a large partnership and to serve as the primary representative of the partnership.[59] If the partnership fails to assign the tax matters partner, the designation goes to the general partner having the largest profits interest at the close of the partnership's tax year.

These audit procedures, however, do not apply to small partnerships. For this purpose, a small partnership is defined as one having no more than ten partners who must be natural persons (but excluding nonresident aliens), C corporations, or estates. In counting partners, a husband and wife (or their estates) count as a single partner. Further, the IRS has announced that a partnership can be excluded from the audit procedures only if it can be established that all partners fully reported their shares of partnership items on timely filed tax returns.[60]

PROBLEM MATERIALS

DISCUSSION QUESTIONS

C9-1 Yvonne and Larry plan to begin a business that will grow plants for sale to retail nurseries. They expect to have substantial losses for the first three years of operations while they develop their plants and their sales operations. Both Yvonne and Larry have substantial interest income, and both expect to work full-time in this new business. List three advantages for operating this business as a partnership instead of a C corporation.

C9-2 Bob and Carol want to open a bed and breakfast inn as soon as they buy and renovate a turn-of-the-century home. What would be the major disadvantage of using a general partnership rather than a corporation for this business? Should they consider any other form for structuring their business?

C9-3 Sam wants to help his brother, Lou, start a new business. Lou is a capable auto mechanic but has little business sense, so he needs Sam to help him make business decisions. Should this partnership be arranged as a general partnership or a limited partnership? Why? Should they consider any other form for structuring their business?

C9-4 Doug contributes services but no property to the CD Partnership upon its formation. What are the tax implications of his receiving only a profits interest versus his receiving a capital and profits interest?

C9-5 An existing partner wants to contribute property having a basis less than its FMV for an additional interest in a partnership.
a. Should he contribute the property to the partnership?
b. What are his other options?
c. Explain the tax implications for the partner of these other options.

C9-6 Jane contributes valuable property to a partnership in exchange for a general partnership interest. The partnership also assumes the recourse mortgage Jane incurred when she purchased the property two years ago.
a. How will the liability affect the amount of gain that Jane must recognize?
b. How will it affect her basis in the partnership interest?

C9-7 Which of the following items can be deducted (up to $5,000) and amortized as part of a partnership's organizational expenditures?
a. Legal fees for drawing up the partnership agreement
b. Accounting fees for establishing an accounting system
c. Fees for securing an initial working capital loan
d. Filing fees required under state law in initial year to conduct business in the state
e. Accounting fees for preparation of initial short-period tax return
f. Transportation costs for acquiring machinery essential to the partnership's business
g. Syndication expenses

C9-8 The BW Partnership reported the following current year earnings: $30,000 interest from tax-exempt bonds, $50,000 long-term capital gain, and $100,000 net income from operations. Bob saw these numbers and told his partner, Wendy, that the partnership had $100,000 of taxable income. Is he correct? Explain your answer.

C9-9 How will a partner's distributive share be determined if the partner sells one-half of his or her beginning-of-the-year partnership interest at the beginning of the tenth month of the partnership's tax year?

---

[59] Sec. 6231(a)(7).

[60] Rev. Proc. 84-35, 1984-1 C.B. 509.

C9-10 Can a recourse debt of a partnership increase the basis of a limited partner's partnership interest? Explain.

C9-11 The ABC Partnership has a nonrecourse liability that it incurred by borrowing from an unrelated bank. It is secured by an apartment building owned and managed by the partnership. The liability is not convertible into an equity interest. How does this liability affect the at-risk basis of general partner Anna and limited partner Bob?

C9-12 Is the Sec. 704(d) loss limitation rule more or less restrictive than the at-risk rules? Explain.

C9-13 Jeff, a 10% limited partner in the recently formed JRS Partnership, expects to have losses from the partnership for several more years. He is considering purchasing an interest in a profitable general partnership in which he will materially participate. Will the purchase allow him to use his losses from the JRS Partnership?

C9-14 Helen, a 55% partner in the ABC Partnership, owns land (a capital asset) having a $20,000 basis and a $25,000 FMV. She plans to transfer the land to the ABC Partnership, which will subdivide the land and sell the lots. Discuss whether Helen should sell or contribute the land to the partnership.

C9-15 What is the difference between a guaranteed payment that is a guaranteed amount and one that is a guaranteed minimum?

C9-16 The TUV Partnership is considering two compensation schemes for Tracy, the partner who runs the business on a daily basis. Tracy can be given a $10,000 guaranteed payment, or she can be given a comparably larger distributive share (and distribution) so that she receives about $10,000 more each year. From the standpoint of when the income must be reported in Tracy's tax return, are these two compensation alternatives the same?

C9-17 Roy's father gives him a capital interest in the Family Partnership. Discuss whether the Sec. 704(e) family partnership rules apply to this interest.

C9-18 Andrew gives his brother Steve a 20% interest in the AS Partnership, and he retains a 30% interest. Andrew works for the partnership but is not paid. How will this arrangement affect the income from the AS Partnership that Andrew and Steve report?

ISSUE IDENTIFICATION QUESTIONS

C9-19 Bob and Kate form the BK Partnership, a general partnership, as equal partners. Bob contributes an office building with a $130,000 FMV and a $95,000 adjusted basis to the partnership along with a $60,000 mortgage, which the partnership assumes. Kate contributes the land on which the building sits with a $50,000 FMV and a $75,000 adjusted basis. Kate will manage the partnership for the first five years of operations but will not receive a guaranteed payment for her work in the first year of partnership operations. Starting with the second year of partnership operations, Kate will receive a $10,000 guaranteed payment for each year she manages the partnership. What tax issues should Bob, Kate, and the BK Partnership consider with respect to the formation and operation of the partnership?

C9-20 Suzanne and Laura form a partnership to market local crafts. In April, the two women spent $1,600 searching for a retail outlet, $1,200 to have a partnership agreement drawn up, and $2,000 to have an accounting system established. During April, they signed contracts with a number of local crafters to feature their products in the retail outlet. The outlet was fitted and merchandise organized during May. In June, the store opened and sold its first crafts. The partnership paid $500 to an accountant to prepare an income statement for the month of June. What tax issues should the partnership consider with regard to beginning this business?

C9-21 Cara, a CPA, established an accounting system for the ABC Partnership and, in return for her services, received a 10% profits interest (but no capital interest) in the partnership. Her usual fee for the services would be approximately $20,000. No sales of profits interests in the ABC Partnership occurred during the current year. What tax issues should Cara and the ABC Partnership consider with respect to the payment made for the services?

C9-22 George, a limited partner in the EFG Partnership, has a 20% interest in partnership capital, profits, and losses. His basis in the partnership interest is $15,000 before accounting for events of the current year. In December of the current year, the EFG Partnership repaid a $100,000 nonrecourse liability. The partnership earned $20,000 of ordinary income this year. What tax issues should George consider with respect to reporting the results of this year's activities for the EFG Partnership on his personal return?

C9-23 Katie works 40 hours a week as a clerk in the mall and earns $20,000. In addition, she works five hours each week in the JKL Partnership's office. Katie, a 10% limited partner in the JKL Partnership, has been allocated a $2,100 loss from the partnership for the current year. The basis for her interest in JKL before accounting for current operations is $5,000. What tax issues should Katie consider with respect to her interest in, and employment by, the JKL Partnership?

C9-24 Daniel has no family to inherit his 80% capital and profits interest in the CD Partnership. To ensure the continuation of the business, he gives a 20% capital and profits interest in the partnership to David, his best friend's son, on the condition that David work in the partnership for at least five years. David receives guaranteed payments for his work. Daniel takes no salary from the partnership, but he devotes all his time to the business operations of the partnership. What tax issues should Daniel and David consider with respect to the gift of the partnership interest and Daniel's employment arrangement with the partnership?

PROBLEMS

C9-25 *Formation of a Partnership.* Suzanne and Bob form the SB General Partnership as equal partners. They make the following contributions:

Individual	Asset	Basis to Partner	FMV
Suzanne	Cash	$45,000	$ 45,000
	Inventory (securities)	14,000	15,000
Bob	Land	45,000	40,000
	Building	50,000	100,000

The SB Partnership assumes the $80,000 recourse mortgage on the building that Bob contributes, and the partners share the economic risk of loss on the mortgage equally. Bob has claimed $40,000 in straight-line depreciation under the MACRS rules on the building. Suzanne is a stockbroker and contributed securities from her inventory. The partnership will hold them as an investment.
a. What amount and character of gain or loss must each partner recognize on the formation of the partnership?
b. What is each partner's basis in his or her partnership interest?
c. What is the partnership's basis in each asset?
d. What is the partnership's initial book value of each asset?
e. The partnership holds the securities for two years and then sells them for $20,000. What amount and character of gain must the partnership and each partner report?

C9-26 *Formation of a Partnership.* On May 31, six brothers decided to form the Grimm Brothers Partnership to publish and print children's stories. The contributions of the brothers and their partnership interests are listed below. They share the economic risk of loss from liabilities according to their partnership interests.

Individual	Asset	Basis to Partner	FMV	Partnership Interest
Al	Cash	$15,000	$ 15,000	15%
Bob	Accounts receivable	–0–	20,000	20%
Clay	Office equipment	13,000	15,000	15%
Dave	Land	50,000	15,000	15%
Ed	Building	15,000	150,000	20%
Fred	Services	?	15,000	15%

The following other information about the contributions may be of interest:
• Bob contributes accounts receivable from his proprietorship, which uses the cash method of accounting.
• Clay uses the office equipment in a small business he owns. When he joins the partnership, he sells the remaining business assets to an outsider. He has claimed $8,000 of MACRS depreciation on the office equipment.
• The partnership assumes a $130,000 mortgage on the building Ed contributes. Ed claimed $100,000 of straight-line MACRS depreciation on the commercial property.

- Fred, an attorney, drew up all the partnership agreements and filed the necessary paperwork. He receives a full 15% capital and profits interest for his services.

a. How much gain, loss, or income must each partner recognize as a result of the formation?

b. How much gain, loss, or income must the partnership recognize as a result of the formation?

c. What is each partner's basis in his partnership interest?

d. What is the partnership's basis in its assets?

e. What is the partnership's initial book value of each asset?

f. What effects do the depreciation recapture provisions have on the property contributions?

g. How would your answer to Part a change if Fred received only a profits interest?

h. What are the tax consequences to the partners and the partnership when the partnership sells for $9,000 the land contributed by Dave? Prior to the sale, the partnership held the land as an investment for two years.

C9-27 *Formation of a Partnership.* On January 1, Julie, Kay, and Susan form a partnership. The contributions of the three individuals are listed below. Julie received a 30% partnership interest, Kay received a 60% partnership interest, and Susan received a 10% partnership interest. They share the economic risk of loss from recourse liabilities according to their partnership interests.

Individual	Asset	Basis to Partner	FMV
Julie	Accounts receivable	$ –0–	$ 60,000
Kay	Land	30,000	58,000
	Building	45,000	116,000
Susan	Services	?	20,000

Kay has claimed $15,000 of straight-line MACRS depreciation on the building. The land and building are subject to a $54,000 mortgage, of which $18,000 is allocable to the land and $36,000 is allocable to the building. The partnership assumes the mortgage. Susan is an attorney, and the services she contributes are the drawing-up of all partnership agreements.

a. What amount and character of gain, loss, or income must each partner recognize on the formation of the partnership?

b. What is each partner's basis in her partnership interest?

c. What is the partnership's basis in each of its assets?

d. What is the partnership's initial book value of each asset?

e. To raise some immediate cash after the formation, the partnership decides to sell the land and building to a third party and lease it back. The buyer pays $40,000 cash for the land and $80,000 cash for the building in addition to assuming the $54,000 mortgage. Assume the partnership claim no additional depreciation on the building before the sale. What is each partner's distributive share of the gains, and what is the character of the gains?

C9-28 *Contribution of Services.* Sean is admitted to the XYZ Partnership in December of the current year in return for his services managing the partnership's business during the year. The partnership reports ordinary income of $100,000 for the current year without considering this transaction.

a. What are the tax consequences to Sean and the XYZ Partnership if Sean receives a 20% capital and profits interest in the partnership with a $75,000 FMV?

b. What are the tax consequences to Sean and the XYZ Partnership if Sean receives only a 20% profits interest with no determinable FMV?

C9-29 *Contribution of Services and Property.* Marjorie works for a large firm whose business is to find suitable real estate, establish a limited partnership to purchase the property, and then sell the limited partnership interests. In the current year, Marjorie received a 5% limited partnership interest in the Eldorado Limited Partnership. Marjorie received this interest partially in payment for her services in selling partnership interests to others, but she also was required to contribute $5,000 in cash to the partnership. Similar limited partnership interests sold for $20,000 at approximately the same time that Marjorie received her interest. What are the tax consequences for Marjorie and the Eldorado Limited Partnership of Marjorie's receipt of the partnership interest?

C9-30 *Partnership Tax Year.* The BCD Partnership is being formed by three equal partners, Beta Corporation, Chi Corporation, and Delta Corporation. The partners' tax year-ends are June 30 for Beta, September 30 for Chi, and October 31 for Delta. The BCD Partnership's natural business year ends on January 31.

a. What tax year(s) can the partnership elect without IRS permission?
b. What tax year(s) can the partnership elect with IRS permission?
c. How would your answers to Parts a and b change if Beta, Chi, and Delta own 4%, 4%, and 92%, respectively, of the partnership?

C9-31 *Partnership Tax Year.* The BCD Partnership is formed in April of the current year. The three equal partners, Boris, Carlton Corporation, and Damien have had tax years ending on December 31, August 30, and December 31, respectively, for the last three years. The BCD Partnership has no natural business year.

a. What tax year is required for the BCD Partnership under Sec. 706?
b. Can the BCD Partnership make a Sec. 444 election? If so, what are the alternative tax years BCD could select?

C9-32 *Partnership Income and Basis Adjustments.* Mark and Pamela are equal partners in MP Partnership. The partnership, Mark, and Pamela are calendar year taxpayers. The partnership incurred the following items in the current year:

Sales	$450,000
Cost of goods sold	210,000
Dividends on corporate investments	15,000
Tax-exempt interest income	4,000
Section 1245 gain (recapture) on equipment sale	33,000
Section 1231 gain on equipment sale	18,000
Long-term capital gain on stock sale	12,000
Long-term capital loss on stock sale	10,000
Short-term capital loss on stock sale	9,000
Depreciation (no Sec. 179 component)	27,000
Guaranteed payment to Pamela	30,000
Meals and entertainment expenses	11,600
Interest expense on loans allocable to:	
Business debt	42,000
Stock investments	9,200
Tax-exempt bonds	2,800
Principal payment on business loan	14,000
Charitable contributions	5,000
Distributions to partners ($30,000 each)	60,000

a. Compute the partnership's ordinary income and separately stated items.
b. Show Mark's and Pamela's shares of the items in Part a.
c. Compute Mark's and Pamela's ending basis in their partnership interests assuming their beginning balances are $150,000 each.

C9-33 *Financial Accounting and Partnership Income.* Jim, Liz, and Ken are equal partners in the JLK Partnership, which uses the accrual method of accounting. All three materially participate in the business. JLK reports financial accounting income of $186,000 for the current year. The partnership used the following information to determine financial accounting income.

Operating profit (excluding the items listed below)	$ 94,000
Rental income	30,000
Interest income:	
Municipal bonds (tax-exempt)	15,000
Corporate bonds	3,000
Dividend income (all from less-than-20%-owned domestic corporations)	20,000
Gains and losses on property sales:	
Gain on sale of land held as an investment (contributed by Jim six	
years ago when its basis was $9,000 and its FMV was $15,000)	60,000
Long-term capital gains	10,000
Short-term capital losses	7,000
Sec. 1231 gain	9,000
Sec. 1250 gain	44,000

Depreciation:	
Rental real estate	12,000
Machinery and equipment	27,000
Interest expense related to:	
Mortgages on rental property	18,000
Loans to acquire municipal bonds	5,000
Guaranteed payments to Jim	30,000
Low-income housing expenditures qualifying for credit	21,000

The following additional information is available about the current year's activities.

- The partnership received a $1,000 prepayment of rent for next year but has not recorded it as income for financial accounting purposes.
- The partnership recorded the land for financial accounting purposes at $15,000.
- MACRS depreciation on the rental real estate and machinery and equipment were $12,000 and $29,000, respectively, in the current year.
- MACRS depreciation for the rental real estate includes depreciation on the low-income housing expenditures.

a. What is JLK's financial accounting income?
b. What is JLK's partnership taxable income? (See Appendix B for an example of a financial accounting-to-tax reconciliation.)
c. What is JLK's ordinary income (loss)?
d. What are JLK's separately stated items?

C9-34 *Partner's Distributive Shares.* On January of the current year, Becky (20%), Chuck (30%), and Dawn (50%) are partners in the BCD Partnership. During the current year, BCD reports the following results. All items occur evenly throughout the year unless otherwise indicated. Assume the current year is not a leap year.

Ordinary income	$120,000
Long-term capital gain (recognized September 1)	18,000
Short-term capital loss (recognized March 2)	6,000
Charitable contribution (made October 1)	20,000

a. What are the distributive shares for each partner, assuming they all continue to hold their interests at the end of the year?
b. Assume that Becky purchases a 5% partnership interest from Chuck on July 1 so that Becky and Chuck each own 25% from that date through the end of the year. What are Becky and Chuck's distributive shares for the current year?

C9-35 *Allocation of Precontribution Gain.* Last year, Patty contributed land with a $4,000 basis and a $10,000 FMV in exchange for a 40% profits, loss, and capital interest in the PD Partnership. Dave contributed land with an $8,000 basis and a $15,000 FMV for the remaining 60% interest in the partnership. During the current year, PD Partnership reported $8,000 of ordinary income and $10,000 of long-term capital gain from the sale of the land Patty contributed. What income or gain must Patty and Dave report from the PD Partnership in the current year?

C9-36 *Special Allocations.* Refer to Example C9-25 in the text. Provide computations showing that the partners' total tax liability under the special allocation is less than their total liability under an equal allocation of the two types of interest income.

C9-37 *Special Allocations.* Clark sold securities for a $50,000 short-term capital loss during the current year, but he has no personal capital gains to recognize. The C&L General Partnership, in which Clark has a 50% capital, profits, and loss interest, reported a $60,000 short-term capital gain this year. In addition, the partnership earned $140,000 of ordinary income. Clark's only partner, Lois, agrees to divide the year's income as follows:

Type of Income	Total	Clark	Lois
Short-term capital gain	$ 60,000	$50,000	$10,000
Ordinary income	140,000	50,000	90,000

Both partners and the partnership use a calendar year-end, and both partners have a 33% marginal tax rate.
a. Have the partners made a special allocation of income that has substantial economic effect?

b. What amount and character of income must each partner report on his or her tax return?

C9-38 *Special Allocations.* Diane and Ed have equal capital and profits interests in the DE Partnership, and they share the economic risk of loss from recourse liabilities according to their partnership interests. In addition, Diane has a special allocation of all depreciation on buildings owned by the partnership. The buildings are financed with recourse liabilities. The depreciation reduces Diane's capital account, and liquidation is in accordance with the capital account balances. Depreciation for the DE Partnership is $50,000 annually. Diane and Ed each have $50,000 capital account balances on January 1, 2006. Will the special allocation be acceptable for 2006, 2007, and 2008 in the following independent situations?

a. The partners have no obligation to repay negative capital account balances, and the partnership's operations (other than depreciation) each year have no net effect on the capital accounts.

b. The partners have an obligation to repay negative capital account balances.

c. The partners have no obligation to repay negative capital account balances. The partnership operates at its break-even point (excluding any depreciation claimed) and borrows $200,000 on a full recourse basis on December 31, 2007.

C9-39 *Basis in Partnership Interest.* What is Kelly's basis for her partnership interest in each of the following independent situations? The partners share the economic risk of loss from recourse liabilities according to their partnership interests.

a. Kelly receives her 20% partnership interest for a contribution of property having a $14,000 basis and a $17,000 FMV. The partnership assumes her $10,000 recourse liability but has no other debts.

b. Kelly receives her 20% partnership interest as a gift from a friend. The friend's basis (without considering partnership liabilities) is $34,000. The FMV of the interest at the time of the gift is $36,000. The partnership has liabilities of $100,000 when Kelly receives her interest. No gift tax was paid with respect to the transfer.

c. Kelly inherits her 20% interest from her mother. Her mother's basis was $140,000. The FMV of the interest is $120,000 on the date of death and $160,000 on the alternate valuation date. The executor chooses the date of death for valuing the estate. The partnership has no liabilities.

C9-40 *Basis in Partnership Interest.* Yong received a 40% general partnership interest in the XYZ Partnership in each of the independent situations below. In each situation, assume the general partners share the economic risk of loss related to recourse liabilities according to their partnership interests. What is Yong's basis in his partnership interest?

a. Yong designs the building the partnership will use for its offices. Yong normally would charge a $20,000 fee for a similar building design. Based on the other partner's contributions, the 40% interest has a FMV of $25,000. The partnership has no liabilities.

b. Yong contributes land with a $6,000 basis and an $18,000 FMV, a car (which he has used in his business since he purchased it) with a $15,000 adjusted basis and a $6,000 FMV, and $2,000 cash. The partnership has recourse liabilities of $100,000.

C9-41 *Basis in Partnership Interest.* Tina purchases an interest in the TP Partnership on January 1 of the current year for $50,000. The partnership uses the calendar year as its tax year and has $200,000 in recourse liabilities when Tina acquires her interest. The partners share economic risk of loss associated with recourse debt according to their loss percentage. Her distributive share of partnership items for the year is as follows:

Ordinary income (excluding items listed below)	$30,000
Long-term capital gains	10,000
Municipal bond interest income	8,000
Charitable contributions	1,000
Interest expense related to municipal bond investment	2,000

TP reports the following liabilities on December 31:

Recourse debt	$100,000
Nonrecourse debt (not qualified real estate financing)	80,000

a. What is Tina's basis on December 31 if she has a 40% interest in profits and losses? TP is a general partnership. Tina has not guaranteed partnership debt, nor has she made any other special agreements about partnership debt.

b. How would your answer to Part a change if Tina instead had a 40% interest in profits and a 30% interest in losses? Assume TP is a general partnership, and all other agreements continue in place. Also assume the partners share recourse liabilities in accordance with their loss interest percentages.

c. How would your answer to Part a change if Tina were instead a limited partner having a 40% interest in profits and 30% interest in losses? The partnership agreement contains no guarantees or other special arrangements.

C9-42 *At-Risk Loss Limitation.* The KC Partnership is a general partnership that manufactures widgets. The partnership uses a calendar year as its tax year and has two equal partners, Kerry and City Corporation, a widely held corporation. On January 1 of the current year, Kerry and City Corporation each has a $200,000 basis in the partnership interest. Operations during the year produce the following results:

Ordinary loss	$900,000
Long-term capital loss	100,000
Short-term capital gain	300,000

The only change in KC's liabilities during the year is KC's borrowing $100,000 as a nonrecourse loan (not qualified real estate financing) that remains outstanding at year-end.

a. What is each partner's deductible loss from the partnership's activities before any passive loss limitation?

b. What is each partner's basis in the partnership interest after the year's operations?

c. How would your answers to Parts a and b change if the KC Partnership's business were totally in real estate but not a rental activity? Assume the loan is qualified real estate financing.

C9-43 *At-Risk Loss Limitation.* Mary and Gary are partners in the MG Partnership. Mary owns a 40% capital, profits, and loss interest. Gary owns the remaining interest. Both materially participate in partnership activities. At the beginning of the current year, MG's only liabilities are $30,000 in accounts payable, which remain outstanding at year-end. In November, MG borrows $100,000 on a nonrecourse basis from First Bank. The loan is secured by property with a $200,000 FMV. These are MG's only liabilities at year-end. Basis for the partnership interests at the beginning of the year is $40,000 for Mary and $60,000 for Gary before considering the impact of liabilities and operations. MG has a $200,000 ordinary loss during the current year. How much loss can Mary and Gary recognize?

C9-44 *Passive Loss Limitation.* Eve and Tom own 40% and 60%, respectively, of the ET Partnership, which manufactures clocks. The partnership is a limited partnership, and Eve is the only general partner. She works full-time in the business. Tom essentially is an investor in the firm and works full-time at another job. Tom has no other income except his salary from his full-time employer. During the current year, the partnership reports the following gain and loss:

Ordinary loss	$140,000
Long-term capital gain	20,000

Before including the current year's gain and loss, Eve and Tom had $46,000 and $75,000 bases for their partnership interests, respectively. The partnership has no nonrecourse liabilities. Tom has no further obligation to make any additional investment in the partnership.

a. What gain or loss should each partner report on his or her individual tax return?

b. If the partnership borrowed an additional $100,000 of recourse liabilities, how would your answer to Part a change?

C9-45 *Passive Loss Limitation.* Kate, Chad, and Stan are partners in the KCS Partnership, which operates a manufacturing business. The partners formed the partnership ten years ago with Kate and Chad each as general partners having a 40% capital and profits interest. Kate materially participates; Chad does not. Stan has a 20% interest as a limited partner. At the end of the current year, the following information was available:

	Kate	Chad	Stan
Basis in partnership (before gains and losses)	$100,000	$100,000	$50,000
Distributive share of:			
Nonrecourse liability (already included in basis and not qualified real estate financing)	50,000	50,000	25,000
Operating loss	(80,000)	(80,000)	(40,000)
Capital gain	20,000	20,000	10,000

a. How much operating loss can each partner deduct in the current year?

b. How much loss could each partner deduct if the KCS Partnership were engaged in rental activities? Assume Kate and Chad both actively participate, but Stan does not.

C9-46 *At-Risk and Passive Loss Limitations.* At the beginning of year 1, Ed and Fran each contributed $1,000 cash to EF Partnership as equal partners. The partnership immediately borrowed $98,000 on a nonrecourse basis and used the contributed cash and loan proceeds to purchase equipment costing $100,000. The partnership leases out the equipment on a five-year lease for $10,000 per year. Over the five-year period, the partnership makes the following principal and interest payments on the loan:

Year	Principal	Interest
1	$3,000	$7,000
2	3,500	6,500
3	3,500	6,500
4	4,000	6,000
5	4,000	6,000

Assume the partnership depreciates the equipment according to the following hypothetical schedule:

Year	Depreciation
1	$40,000
2	25,000
3	15,000
4	8,000
5	8,000
6	4,000

At the beginning of year 6, the partnership sells the equipment for $82,000. The partnership claims the last $4,000 of depreciation at the beginning of year 6 as an expense, so the equipment has a zero basis when sold. At the beginning of year 6, the partnership also pays off the $80,000 loan balance and distributes any remaining cash to Ed and Fran. Assume that each partner has a 35% ordinary tax rate and a 15% capital gains tax rate.

a. Determine the partnership's gain (loss) for each of the five years and the beginning of the sixth year.

b. Assume that depreciation recapture applies but that the at-risk and passive activity loss rules do not apply. Using the results from Part a and a 7% discount rate, determine the present value of tax savings for both partners combined over the five-year period including the beginning of the sixth year. Why do these tax savings occur?

c. Now assume the at-risk and passive activity loss rules do apply. Determine what the partners recognize over the five-year period including the beginning of the sixth year. Do the partners have any tax savings in this situation? Why or why not?

d. Provide a schedule analyzing each partner's outside basis over the five-year period including the sixth year.

C9-47 *Related Party Transactions.* Susan, Steve, and Sandy own 15%, 35%, and 50%, respectively, in the SSS Partnership. Susan sells securities for their $40,000 FMV to the partnership. What are the tax implications of the following independent situations?

a. Susan's basis in the securities is $60,000. The three partners are siblings.

b. Susan's basis in the securities is $50,000. Susan is unrelated to the other partners.

c. Susan's basis in the securities is $30,000. Susan and Sandy are sisters. The partnership will hold the securities as an investment.

d. What are the tax consequences in Part a if the partnership subsequently sells the securities to an unrelated third party for $70,000? For $55,000? For $35,000?

C9-48 *Related Party Transactions.* Kara owns 35% of the KLM Partnership and 45% of the KTV Partnership. Lynn owns 20% of KLM and 3% of KTV. Maura, Kara's daughter, owns 15% of KTV. No other partners own an interest in both partnerships or are related to other partners. The KTV Partnership sells to the KLM Partnership 1,000 shares of stock, which KTV has held for investment purposes, for its $50,000 FMV. What are the tax consequences of the sale in each of the following independent situations?

a. KTV's basis for the stock is $80,000.

b. KTV's basis for the stock is $23,000 and KLM holds the stock as an investment.

c. KTV's basis for the stock is $35,000 and KLM holds the stock as inventory.

d. What are the tax consequences in Part a if the KLM Partnership subsequently sells the stock to an unrelated third party for $130,000? For $70,000? For $40,000?

C9-49 *Guaranteed Payments.* Scott and Dave each invested $100,000 cash when they formed the SD Partnership and became equal partners. They agreed that the partnership would pay each partner a 5% guaranteed payment on his $100,000 capital account. Before the two guaranteed payments, current year results were $23,000 of ordinary income and $14,000 of long-term capital gain. What amount and character of income will Scott and Dave report for the current year from their partnership?

C9-50 *Guaranteed Payments.* Allen and Bob are equal partners in the AB Partnership. Bob manages the business and receives a guaranteed payment. What amount and character of income will Allen and Bob report in each of the following independent situations?

a. The AB Partnership earns $160,000 of ordinary income before considering Bob's guaranteed payment. Bob is guaranteed a $90,000 payment plus 50% of all income remaining after the guaranteed payment.

b. Assume the same facts as Part a except Bob's distributive share is 50% with a guaranteed minimum of $90,000.

c. The AB Partnership earns a $140,000 long-term capital gain and no ordinary income. Bob is guaranteed $80,000 plus 50% of all amounts remaining after the guaranteed payment.

C9-51 *Guaranteed Payments.* Pam and Susan own the PS Partnership. Pam takes care of daily operations and receives a guaranteed payment for her efforts. What amount and character of income will each partner report in each of the following independent situations?

a. The PS Partnership reports a $10,000 long-term capital gain and no ordinary income. Pam receives a $40,000 guaranteed payment plus a 30% distributive share of all partnership income after deducting the guaranteed payment.

b. The PS Partnership reports $80,000 of ordinary income, before considering any guaranteed payment, and a $60,000 Sec. 1231 gain. Pam receives a $35,000 guaranteed payment plus a 20% distributive share of all partnership income after deducting the guaranteed payment.

c. The PS Partnership reports $120,000 of ordinary income before considering any guaranteed payment. Pam receives 40% of partnership income but no less than $60,000.

C9-52 *Family Partnership.* Dad gives Son a 20% capital and profits interest in the Family Partnership. Dad holds a 70% interest, and Fred, an unrelated individual, holds a 10% interest. Dad and Fred work in the partnership, but Son does not. Dad and Fred receive reasonable compensation for their work. The partnership earns $100,000 ordinary income, and the partners agree to divide this amount based on their relative ownership interests. What income must Father, Son, and Fred report if Family Partnership is a manufacturing firm with substantial inventories?

C9-53 *Family Partnership.* Steve wishes to pass his business on to his children, Tracy and Vicki, and gives each daughter a 20% partnership interest to begin getting them involved. Steve retains the remaining 60% interest. Neither daughter is employed by the partnership, which buys and manages real estate. Steve draws only a $40,000 guaranteed payment for his work for the partnership. Reasonable compensation for his services would be $70,000. The partnership reports ordinary income of $120,000 after deducting the guaranteed payment. Distributive shares for the three partners are tentatively reported as: Steve, $72,000; Tracy, $24,000; and Vicki, $24,000. What is the proper distributive share of income for each partner?

COMPREHENSIVE PROBLEMS

C9-54 Rick has a $50,000 basis in the RKS General Partnership on January 1 of the current year, and he owns no other investments. He has a 20% capital interest, a 30% profits interest, and a 40% loss interest in the partnership. Rick does not work in the partnership. The partnership's only liability is a $100,000 nonrecourse debt borrowed several years ago, which remains outstanding at year-end. Rick's share of the liability is based on his profits interest and is included in his $50,000 partnership basis. Rick and the partnership each report on a calendar year basis. Income for the entire partnership during the current year is:

Ordinary loss	$440,000
Long-term capital gain	100,000
Sec. 1231 gain	150,000

a. What is Rick's distributive share of income, gain, and loss for the current year?
b. What partnership income, gain, and loss should Rick report on his tax return for the current year?
c. What is Rick's basis in his partnership interest on the first day of next year?

C9-55 Charles and Mary formed CM Partnership on January 1 of the current year. Charles contributed Inventory A with a $100,000 FMV and a $70,000 adjusted basis for a 40% interest, and Mary contributed $150,000 cash for a 60% interest. The partnership operates on a calendar year. The partnership used the cash to purchase equipment for $50,000, Inventory B for $80,000, and stock in ST Corporation for $5,000. The partnership used the remaining $15,000 for operating expenses and borrowed another $5,000 for operating expenses. During the year, the partnership sold one-half of Inventory A for $60,000 (tax basis, $35,000), one-half of Inventory B for $58,000 (tax basis, $40,000), and the ST stock for $6,000. The partnership claimed $7,000 of depreciation on the equipment for both tax and book purposes. Thus, for the year, the partnership incurred the following items:

Sales—Inventory A	$60,000
Sales—Inventory B	58,000
COGS—Inventory A	35,000
COGS—Inventory B	40,000
Operating expenses	20,000
Depreciation	7,000
Short-term capital gain	1,000
Interest on business loan	500

On December 31 of the current year, the partnership made a $1,000 principal payment on the loan and distributed $2,000 cash to Charles and $3,000 cash to Mary.
a. Determine partnership ordinary income for the year and each partner's distributive share.
b. Determine the separately stated items and each partner's distributive share.
c. Determine each partner's basis in the partnership at the end of the current year.
d. Determine each partner's book capital account at the end of the current year.
e. Provide an analysis of the ending cash balance.
f. Provide beginning and ending balance sheets using tax numbers.
g. Provide beginning and ending balance sheets using book values.

TAX STRATEGY PROBLEM

C9-56 Sarah and Rex formed SR Entity on December 28 of last year. The entity operates on a calendar tax year. Each individual contributed $800,000 cash in exchange for a 50% ownership interest in the entity (common stock if a corporation; partnership interest if a partnership). In addition, the entity borrowed $400,000 from the bank. The entity operates on a calendar year. On December 28 of last year, the entity used the $2 million cash (contributions and loan) to purchase assets as indicated in the following balance sheet as of December 28 of last year:

Cash	$ 100,000
Inventory	1,770,000
Investment in tax-exempt bonds	50,000
Investment in corporate stock (less than 20%-owned)	80,000
Total	$2,000,000
Liability	$ 400,000
Equity*	1,600,000
Total	$2,000,000

*If a partnership, each partner's beginning capital account is $800,000.

The balance sheet did not change between December 28 of last year and the beginning of the current year. Thus, the above balance sheet also represents the balance sheet at January 1 of the current year.

The following data apply to the entity for the current year:

Sales	$3,000,000
Purchase of additional inventory	2,100,000
Ending inventory at December 31 of the current year	1,650,000
Gain on sale of corporate stock on December 31 of the current year	20,000
Dividends received on stock prior to its sale	4,000
Tax-exempt interest received	2,200
Operating expenses	500,000
Interest paid on loan (no principal paid)*	30,000
Distribution on December 31 of the current year:	
Sarah	50,000
Rex	50,000

*Of the $30,000 interest expense, $1,000 is allocable to the tax-exempt interest income, and $1,500 is allocable to investment income. The rest is business interest expense.

Sarah and Rex actively manage the entity's business, and the business does not qualify for the U.S. production activities deduction. At the individual level, Sarah and Rex are each single with no dependents. Each individual claims a standard deduction and one personal exemption (if applicable). Neither individual has income from sources other than listed above.

a. First, assume the entity is a regular C corporation and the distributions are dividends to Sarah and Rex. For the current year, determine the following:
   (1) The corporation's taxable income and tax liability.
   (2) Sarah's and Rex's individual AGI, taxable income, and tax liability.
   (3) The total tax liability for the corporation and its owners.
b. Next, assume the entity is a partnership. For the current year, determine the following:
   (1) Partnership ordinary income and each partner's share of partnership ordinary income.
   (2) Partnership separately stated items and each partner's share of each item.
   (3) Sarah's and Rex's AGI, taxable income, and total tax liability. Assume each partner will incur a $14,000 self-employment tax.
   (4) Each partner's basis in the partnership (outside basis) at the end of the current year.
c. Based on your analysis for the current year, which entity is better from an overall tax perspective? What are the shortcomings of examining only one year?
d. Given the corporate form, explain how the corporation can restructure the $50,000 distribution to each individual to reduce the overall tax liability.

TAX FORM/RETURN PREPARATION PROBLEM

C9-57   The Dapper-Dons Partnership (employer identification no. 89-3456798) was formed ten years ago as a general partnership to custom tailor men's clothing. Dapper-Dons is located at 123 Flamingo Drive in Miami, Florida 33131. Bob Dapper (Social Security No. 654-32-1098) manages the business and has a 40% capital and profits interest. His address is 709 Brumby Way, Miami, Florida 33131. Jeremy Dons (Social Security No. 354-12-6531) owns the remaining 60% interest but is not active in the business. His address is 807 9th Avenue, North Miami, Florida 33134. The partnership values its inventory using the cost method and did not change the method used during the current year. The partnership uses the accrual method of accounting. Because of its simplicity, the partnership is not subject to the partnership audit procedures. The partnership has no foreign partners, no foreign transactions, no interests in foreign trusts, and no foreign financial accounts. This partnership is neither a tax shelter nor a publicly traded partnership. No changes in ownership of partnership interests occurred during the current year. The partnership made cash distributions of $155,050 and $232,576 to Dapper and Dons, respectively, on December 30 of the current year. It made no other property distributions. Financial statements for the current year are presented in Tables C9-1 and C9-2. Assume that Dapper-Dons' business qualifies as a U.S. production activity and that its qualified production activities income is $600,000. The partnership uses the small business simplified overall method for reporting these activities (see discussion for Line 13d of Schedules K and K-1 in the Form 1065 instructions).

Prepare a current year partnership tax return for Dapper-Dons Partnership.

▼ TABLE C9-1

Dapper-Dons Partnership Income Statement for the 12 Months Ending December 31 of the Current Year (Problem C9-57)

Sales		$2,350,000
Returns and allowances		(20,000)
		$2,330,000
Beginning inventory (FIFO method)	$ 200,050	
Purchases	624,000	
Labor	600,000	
Supplies	42,000	
Other costs[a]	12,000	
Goods available for sale	$1,478,050	
Ending inventory[b]	(146,000)	(1,332,050)
Gross profit		$ 997,950
Salaries for employees other than partners (W-2 wages)	$51,000	
Guaranteed payment for Dapper	85,000	
Utilities expense	46,428	
Depreciation (MACRS depreciation is $74,311)[c]	49,782	
Automobile expense	12,085	
Office supplies expense	4,420	
Advertising expense	85,000	
Bad debt expense	2,100	
Interest expense (all trade- or business-related)	45,000	
Rent expense	7,400	
Travel expense (meals cost $4,050 of this amount)	11,020	
Repairs and maintenance expense	68,300	
Accounting and legal expense	3,600	
Charitable contributions[d]	16,400	
Payroll taxes	5,180	
Other taxes (all trade- or business-related)	1,400	
Total expenses		494,115
Operating profit		$ 503,835
Other income and losses:		
Gain on sale of AB stock[e]	$ 18,000	
Loss on sale of CD stock[f]	(26,075)	
Sec. 1231 gain on sale of land[g]	5,050	
Interest on U.S. treasury bills for entire year ($80,000 face amount)	9,000	
Dividends from 15%-owned domestic corporation	11,000	16,975
Net income		$ 520,810

[a] Additional Sec. 263A costs of $7,000 for the current year are included in other costs.
[b] Ending inventory includes the appropriate Sec. 263A costs, and no further adjustment is needed to properly state cost of sales and inventories for tax purposes.
[c] The tax depreciation includes depreciation adjustments of $8,000 and $2,000 on personal property and real property, respectively, placed in service after 1986. Dapper-Dons acquired and placed in service $40,000 of rehabilitation expenditures for a certified historical property this year. The appropriate MACRS depreciation on the rehabilitation expenditures already is included in the MACRS depreciation total.
[d] The partnership made all contributions in cash to qualifying charities.
[e] The partnership purchased the AB stock as an investment two years ago on December 1 for $40,000 and sold it on June 14 of the current year for $58,000.
[f] The partnership purchased the CD stock as an investment on February 15 of the current year for $100,000 and sold it on August 1 for $73,925.
[g] The partnership use the land as a parking lot for the business. The partnership purchased the land four years ago for $30,000 and sold it on August 15 of the current year for $35,050.

▼ **TABLE C9-2**

Dapper-Dons Partnership Balance Sheet for January 1 and December 31 of the Current Year (Problem C9-57)

	Balance January 1	Balance December 31
Assets:		
Cash	$ 10,000	$ 40,000
Accounts receivable	72,600	150,100
Inventories	200,050	146,000
Marketable securities[a]	220,000	260,000
Building and equipment	374,600	465,000
Minus: Accumulated depreciation	(160,484)	(173,100)
Land	185,000	240,000
Total assets	$901,766	$1,128,000
Liabilities and equities:		
Accounts payable	$ 35,000	$ 46,000
Accrued salaries payable	14,000	18,000
Payroll taxes payable	3,416	7,106
Sales taxes payable	5,200	6,560
Mortgage and notes payable (current maturities)	44,000	52,000
Long-term debt	210,000	275,000
Capital:		
Dapper	236,060	289,334
Dons	354,090	434,000
Total liabilities and equities	$901,766	$1,128,000

[a] Short-term investment.

CASE STUDY PROBLEMS

C9-58 Abe and Brenda formed the AB Partnership ten years ago as a general partnership and have been very successful with the business. However, in the current year, economic conditions caused them to lose significant amounts, but they expect the economy and their business to return to profitable operations by next year or the year after. Abe manages the partnership business and works in it full-time. Brenda has a full-time job as an accountant for a $39,000 annual salary, but she also works in the partnership occasionally. She estimates that she spent about 120 hours working in the partnership this year. Abe has a 40% profits interest, a 50% loss interest, and a basis in his partnership interest on December 31 (before considering this year's operations) of $81,000. Brenda has a 60% profits interest, a 50% loss interest, and a basis of $104,000 on December 31 (before considering this year's operations). The partnership has no liabilities at December 31. Neither Abe nor Brenda currently has other investments. The AB Partnership incurs the following amounts during the year.

Ordinary loss	$100,000
Sec. 1231 gain	10,000
Tax-exempt municipal bond income	14,000
Long-term capital loss	14,000
Short-term capital loss	136,000

Early next year, the AB Partnership is considering borrowing $100,000 from a local bank to be secured by a mortgage on a building owned by the partnership with $150,000 FMV.

  Required: Prepare a presentation to be made to Abe and Brenda discussing this matter. Points that should be discussed include: What amounts should Abe and Brenda report on their income tax return for the current year from the AB Partnership? What are their bases in their partnership interests after taking all transactions into effect? What happens to any losses they cannot deduct in the current year? What planning opportunities are presented by the need to borrow money early next year? What planning ideas would you suggest for Brenda?

C9-59 On the advice of his attorney, Dr. Andres, a local pediatrician, contributed several office buildings, which he had previously owned as sole proprietor, to a new Andres Partnership in which he became a one-third general partner. He gave the remaining limited partnership interests to his two sons, Miguel and Esteban. Last year, when the partnership was formed, the boys were 14 and 16. The real estate is well managed and extremely profitable. Dr. Andres regularly consults with a full-time hired manager about the business, but neither of his sons has any dealings with the partnership. Under the terms of the partnership agreement, the boys can sell their partnership interest to no one but their father. Distributions from the partnership have been large, and Dr. Andres has insisted that the boys put all their distributions into savings accounts to pay for their college education.

Last year's return (the partnership's first) was filed by Mr. Jones, a partner in the local CPA firm of Wise and Johnson. Mr. Jones, who was Dr. Andres's accountant for a decade, retired last summer. Dr. Andres's business is extremely profitable and is an important part of the client base of this small-town CPA firm. Ms. Watson, the young partner who has taken over Dr. Andres's account, asked John, a second-year staff accountant, to prepare the current year's partnership return.

John has done considerable research and is positive that the Andres Partnership does not qualify as a partnership at all because the father has retained too much control over the sons' interests. John has briefly talked to Mr. Jones about his concerns. Mr. Jones said he was really rushed in the prior year when he filed the partnership return and admitted he never looked into the question of whether the arrangement met the requirements for being taxed as a partnership. After hearing more of the details, Mr. Jones stated that John was probably correct in his conclusion. Dr. Andres's tax bill will be significantly larger if he has to pay tax on all the partnership's income. When John approached Ms. Watson with his conclusions, her response was, "Oh, no! Dr. Andres already is unhappy because Mr. Jones is no longer preparing his returns. He'll really be unhappy if we give him a big tax increase, too." She paused thoughtfully, and then went on. "My first thought is just to leave well enough alone and file the partnership return. Are you positive, John, that this won't qualify as a partnership? Think about it and let me know tomorrow."

Required: Prepare a list of points you want to go over with the tax partner that would support finding that the business activity is a partnership. Prepare a second list of points that would support finding that the business activity is not a partnership.

TAX RESEARCH PROBLEMS

C9-60 Caitlin and Wally formed the C & W Partnership on September 20, 2006. Caitlin contributed cash of $195,000, and Wally contributed office furniture with a FMV of $66,000. He bought the furniture for $60,000 on January 5, 2006, and placed it in service on that date. Wally will not claim a Sec. 179 expense deduction on the furniture. He also contributed an office building and land with a combined FMV of $129,000. The land's FMV is $9,000. Wally bought the land in 1999 for $8,000 and had the building constructed for $100,000. The building was placed in service in June 2002.

Required: Your tax manager has asked you to prepare a schedule for the file indicating the basis of property at the time of contribution that Wally contributed, the depreciation for each piece of property that the partnership can claim, and the allocation of the depreciation to the two partners. Also indicate the amount and type of any recapture to which the contributed property may be subject at the time of the contribution and at a later time when the partnership sells the property. Your tax manager knows that, under Reg. Sec. 1.704-3, several alternatives exist for allocating depreciation relating to contributed property. He remembers that the Treasury Regulations describe a traditional method and a couple of others, but he's not sure what method applies in this situation. He wants you to check the alternatives and indicate which method should be used. Be certain to clearly label your schedule so that anyone who looks at the file later can determine where your numbers came from and the authority for your calculations. The manager has suggested that, at a minimum, you consult the following authorities:

- IRC Secs. 1(h), 168, 704, 1231, 1245
- Prop. Reg. Sec. 1.168-5(b)

- Reg. Sec. 1.704-1(b)(2)(iv)(g)(3)
- Reg. Sec. 1.704-3

C9-61 Your clients, Lisa and Matthew, plan to form Lima General Partnership. Lisa will contribute $50,000 cash to Lima for a 50% interest in capital and profits. Matthew will contribute land having a $35,000 adjusted basis and a $50,000 FMV to Lima for the remaining 50% interest in capital and profits. Lima will borrow additional funds of $100,000 from a bank on a recourse basis and then will subdivide and sell the land. Prepare a draft memorandum for your tax manager's signature outlining the tax treatment for the partnership formation transaction. As part of your memorandum, compare the reporting of this transaction on the tax and financial accounting books. References:

- IRC Sec. 721
- APB, *Opinions of the Accounting Principles Board No. 29* [Accounting for Nonmonetary Transactions]

C9-62 Almost two years ago, the DEF Partnership was formed when Demetrius, Ebony, and Farouk each contributed $100,000 in cash. They are equal general partners in the real estate partnership, which has a December 31 year-end. The partnership uses the accrual method of accounting for financial accounting purposes but uses the cash method of accounting for tax purposes. The first year of operations resulted in a $50,000 loss. Because the real estate market plummeted, the second year of operations will result in an even larger ordinary loss. On November 30, calculations reveal that the year's loss is likely to be $100,000 for financial accounting purposes. Financial accounting results for the year are as follows:

	Quarter			
	First	*Second*	*Third*	*Fourth**
Revenue	$40,000	$60,000	$80,000	$100,000
Maintenance expense	(30,000)	(58,000)	(70,000)	(85,000)
Interest expense	(10,000)	(30,000)	(35,000)	(50,000)
Utilities expense	(3,000)	(3,000)	(3,000)	(3,000)
Projected loss	($ 3,000)	($31,000)	($28,000)	($38,000)

* Fourth quarter results are the sum of actual October and November results along with estimates for December results. December estimates are revenue, $33,000; maintenance, $60,000; interest, $20,000; and utilities, $1,000.

Cash has been short throughout the second year of operations, so more than $65,000 of expenses for second year operations have resulted in bills that are currently due or overdue. The unpaid bills are for July 1 through November 30 interest on a loan from the bank. In addition, all but essential maintenance has been postponed during the fourth quarter so that most of the fourth quarter maintenance is scheduled to be completed during December.

The DEF partners wants to attract a new partner to obtain additional capital. Raj is interested in investing $100,000 as a limited partner in the DEF Partnership if a good deal can be arranged. Raj would have a 25% profits and loss interest in the partnership but would expect something extra for the current year. In the current tax year, Raj has passive income of more than $200,000 from other sources, so he would like to have large passive losses allocated to him from DEF.

Required: Your tax partner has asked you to prepare a memorandum suggesting a plan to maximize the amount of current year loss that can be allocated to Raj. Assume none of the partners performs more than one-half of his or her personal service time in connection with real estate trades or businesses in which he or she materially participates. She reminded you to consider the varying interest rules for allocating losses to new partners found in Sec. 706 and to look into the possibilities of somehow capitalizing on the cash method of accounting or of using a special allocation. She wants you to be sure to check all the relevant case law for the plan you suggest.

C9-63 Alice, Beth, and Carl formed the ABC partnership early in 2005. Alice and Beth each contributed $100,000 for their partnership interests, and Carl contributed land having a $100,000 FMV and $160,000 adjusted basis. The land remained a capital asset to the partnership. Late in 2006, Carl sold his interest in the partnership to Dan for $100,000.

Shortly after that transaction, the partnership sold the land to an outside party for $100,000. The partnership has no Sec. 754 election in effect (discussed in Chapter C10). The partners have asked that you explain the consequences these transactions have to the partnership and the partners, especially Carl and Dan. At a minimum, you should consult the following resources:

- IRC Sec. 704
- Reg. Sec. 1.704-3(a)

CHAPTER 10

SPECIAL PARTNERSHIP ISSUES

LEARNING OBJECTIVES

After studying this chapter, you should be able to

1▶ Determine the amount and character of gain or loss a partner recognizes in a nonliquidating partnership distribution

2▶ Determine the partner's basis of assets received in a nonliquidating partnership distribution

3▶ Identify the partnership's Sec. 751 assets

4▶ Determine the tax implications of a cash distribution when the partnership has Sec. 751 assets

5▶ Determine the amount and character of gain or loss a partner recognizes in a liquidating partnership distribution

6▶ Determine the partner's basis of assets received in a liquidating distribution

7▶ Determine the amount and character of the gain or loss recognized when a partner retires from the partnership or dies

8▶ Determine whether a partnership has terminated for tax purposes

9▶ Understand the effect of optional and mandatory basis adjustments

10▶ Determine the appropriate reporting for the income of an electing large partnership

Chapter C10 continues the discussion of partnership taxation. The chapter first explains simple nonliquidating distributions and then discusses more complex nonliquidating and liquidating distributions. The chapter also explains methods of disposing of a partnership interest, including sales of the partnership interest and the retirement or death of a partner as well as transactions that terminate the entire partnership.

Finally, the chapter examines special partnership forms. These forms include publicly traded partnerships, limited liability companies, limited liability partnerships, and electing large partnerships.

NONLIQUIDATING DISTRIBUTIONS

Distributions from a partnership fall into two categories: liquidating distributions and nonliquidating (or current) distributions. A **liquidating distribution** is a single distribution, or one of a planned series of distributions, that terminates a partner's entire interest in the partnership. All other distributions, including those that substantially reduce a partner's interest in the partnership, are governed by the **nonliquidating (current) distribution** rules.

Although the tax consequences of the two types of distributions are similar in many respects, they are sufficiently different to require separate study. The chapter first discusses simple current distributions. It then covers complex current distributions involving Sec. 751 property and liquidating distributions.

OBJECTIVE 1

Determine the amount and character of gain or loss a partner recognizes in a nonliquidating partnership distribution

RECOGNITION OF GAIN

A current distribution that does not bring Sec. 751 into play cannot result in the recognition of a loss by either the partnership or the partner who receives the distribution. Moreover, the partnership usually recognizes no gain on a current distribution (except for Sec. 751 property, defined later in this chapter). Under Sec. 731, partners who receive distributions recognize a gain if they receive money distributions that exceed their basis in the partnership. For distribution purposes, money includes cash, deemed cash from reductions in a partner's share of liabilities, and the fair market value (FMV) of marketable securities.

EXAMPLE C10-1 ▶

KEY POINT

Remember that reductions in a partner's share of liabilities are treated as cash distributions.

Melissa is a 30% partner in the ABC Real Estate Partnership until Josh is admitted as a partner in exchange for a cash contribution. After Josh's admission, Melissa holds a 20% interest. Because of large loss deductions, Melissa's basis (before Josh's admission) is $20,000 including her 30% interest in the partnership liabilities of $250,000. She is deemed to receive a cash distribution equal to the $25,000 [(0.30 − 0.20) × $250,000] reduction in her share of partnership liabilities. Because the cash distribution exceeds her basis, Melissa must recognize a $5,000 ($25,000 distribution − $20,000 basis) gain. ◀

SELF-STUDY QUESTION

Can gain or loss be recognized in a current distribution?

ANSWER

Current distributions with no Sec. 751 implications do not create losses to either the partner or partnership. Ignoring Sec. 751, the partnership recognizes no gains. However, a partner recognizes a gain if the partner receives a money distribution exceeding his or her partnership interest. A distribution also may trigger recognition of precontribution gain or loss for a partner.

Precontribution Gain Recognition. Although a current distribution usually causes gain recognition only if money distributions exceed a partner's basis, a distribution also may trigger recognition of previously unrecognized precontribution gain or loss. A precontribution gain or loss is the difference between the FMV and adjusted basis of property when contributed to the partnership. Two different distribution events may trigger recognition of precontribution gain or loss.

First, if a partner contributes property with a deferred precontribution gain or loss, the contributing partner must recognize the precontribution gain or loss when the partnership distributes the property to any other partner within seven years of the contribution. The amount of precontribution gain or loss recognized by the contributing partner equals the amount of precontribution gain or loss remaining that would have been allocated to the contributing partner had the property instead been sold for its FMV on the distribution date. The partnership's basis in the property immediately before the distribution and the contributing partner's basis in his or her partnership interest are both increased for any gain recognized or decreased for any loss recognized.[1]

EXAMPLE C10-2 ▶ Several years ago, Michael contributed land with a $3,000 basis and a $7,000 FMV to the AB Partnership. In the current year, the partnership distributed the land to Stephen, another partner in the partnership. At the time of the distribution, the land had a $9,000 FMV. Stephen recognizes no gain on the distribution. Michael must recognize his $4,000 precontribution gain when the partnership distributes the property to Stephen. Michael increases the basis in his partnership interest by $4,000, and the partnership's basis in the land immediately before the distribution increases by $4,000. This increase in the partnership's basis for the land also increases the land's basis to the distributee partner (Stephen). ◀

KEY POINT

Note the differences in the two distributions that cause a contributing partner to recognize remaining precontribution gains. In the first distribution, the *contributed property* is distributed to *another partner*. In the second distribution, *property other than the contributed property* is distributed to the *contributing partner*.

Second, under Sec. 737, property distributions to a partner may cause the partner to recognize his or her remaining precontribution gain if the FMV of the distributed property exceeds the partner's basis in his or her partnership interest before the distribution. The gain recognized under Sec. 737 is the lesser of the remaining precontribution net gain or the excess of the FMV of the distributed property over the adjusted basis of the partnership interest immediately before the property distribution (but after reduction for any money distributed at the same time).[2] The remaining precontribution gain is the net of all precontribution gains and losses for property contributed to the partnership in the seven years immediately preceding the distribution to the extent that such precontribution gains and losses have not already been recognized. The character of the recognized gain is determined by referencing the type of property that had precontribution gains or losses. The gain recognized under Sec. 737 is in addition to any gain recognized on the same distribution because of distributed cash exceeding the partner's basis in his or her partnership interest.

EXAMPLE C10-3 ▶ Several years ago, Sergio contributed land, a capital asset, with a $20,000 FMV and a $15,000 basis to the STU Partnership in exchange for a 30% general interest in the partnership. The partnership still holds the land on January 31 of the current year, and none of the $5,000 precontribution gain has been recognized. On January 31 of the current year, Sergio has a $40,000 basis in his partnership interest when he receives an $8,000 cash distribution plus property purchased by the partnership with a $45,000 FMV and a $30,000 basis. Under the Sec. 731 distribution rules Sergio recognizes no gain because the cash distribution ($8,000) does not exceed Sergio's predistribution basis in his partnership interest ($40,000). However, under Sec. 737 he recognizes gain equal to the lesser of the $5,000 remaining precontribution gain or the $13,000 difference between the FMV of the property distributed ($45,000) and the basis of the partnership interest after the cash distribution but before any property distributions ($32,000 = $40,000 adjusted basis − $8,000 cash distributed). Thus, Sergio recognizes a $5,000 capital gain. ◀

EXAMPLE C10-4 ▶ Assume the same facts as in Example C10-3 except the distribution was $20,000 in cash and $23,000 (FMV) in marketable securities, which are treated like money, plus the property. Sergio recognizes a $3,000 gain under Sec. 731 because he received a money distribution exceeding his basis in the partnership interest ($43,000 money distribution − $40,000 adjusted basis before distributions). Under Sec. 737 he also recognizes gain equal to the lesser of the remaining precontribution gain ($5,000) or the excess of the FMV of the property distributed ($45,000) over the zero basis of the partnership interest after money distributions but before property distributions ($0 = $40,000 adjusted basis − $43,000 money distributed). Sergio, therefore, recognizes both a $5,000 capital gain under Sec. 737 and a $3,000 capital gain under Sec. 731. ◀

If a partner recognizes gain under Sec. 737, that gain increases the partner's basis in his or her partnership interest (illustrated in the next section). Further, the recognized gain also increases the partnership's basis in the property that was the source of the precontribution gain.

---

[1] Sec. 704(c). See Chapter C9 for a discussion of precontribution gains and losses.

[2] Section 737 does not apply if the property distributed was contributed by this same partner. Only the provisions of Sec. 731 would be considered in such a situation.

EXAMPLE C10-5 ►

OBJECTIVE 2

Determine the partner's basis of assets received in a nonliquidating partnership distribution

Assume the same facts as in Example C10-3. At the time Sergio contributed the land, the partnership assumed Sergio's $15,000 basis in the land. Now, Sergio's $5,000 Sec. 737 gain increases the partnership's basis in the land to $20,000. ◄

BASIS EFFECTS OF DISTRIBUTIONS

In general, the partner's basis for property distributed by the partnership carries over from the partnership. The partner's basis in the partnership interest is reduced by the amount of money received and by the partner's basis in the distributed property.

EXAMPLE C10-6 ► Jack has a $35,000 basis for his interest in the MLV Partnership before receiving a current distribution consisting of $7,000 in money, accounts receivable having a zero basis to the partnership, and land having an $18,000 basis to the partnership. Jack takes a carryover basis in the land and receivables. Following the distribution, his basis in the partnership interest is calculated as follows:

Predistribution basis in partnership interest		$35,000
Minus:	Money received	(7,000)
	Carryover basis in receivables	(–0–)
	Carryover basis in land	(18,000)
Postdistribution basis in partnership interest		$10,000

◄

The total bases of all distributed property in the partner's hands is limited to the partner's predistribution basis in his or her partnership interest plus any gain recognized on the distribution under Sec. 737.[3] If the partner's predistribution basis plus Sec. 737 gain is less than the sum of the money received plus the carryover basis of any nonmoney property received, the order in which the basis is allocated becomes crucial. First, cash and deemed cash distributions reduce the partner's basis in his or her partnership interest. Next, the remaining basis is allocated to provide a carryover of the partnership's basis for receivables and inventory. If the partner's predistribution basis is not large enough to allow a carryover of the partnership's basis for these two property categories, the partner's remaining basis is allocated among the receivables and inventory items based on both the partnership's basis in the assets and their FMV.[4] First, each asset is given its basis to the partnership, then the difference between the carryover basis from the partnership and the partner's basis in the partnership interest is cal-

WHAT WOULD YOU DO IN THIS SITUATION?

You have done the personal and business tax work for Betty and Thelma for a number of years. Betty and Thelma are partners in a retail shop. In addition, the two have decided they want to exchange some property that is not associated with their partnership. Betty wants to exchange undeveloped land she personally holds as an investment, having a $40,000 FMV and a $10,000 adjusted basis, for machinery and office equipment that Thelma owns but no longer uses. Thelma's machinery and office equipment in total have a $40,000 FMV and a $28,000 adjusted basis. Recently, a friend told Betty that several years ago he and an associate did a similar swap tax-free by contributing both

pieces of property to be exchanged to a partnership, having the partnership hold the property for a few months, and then having the partnership distribute the property to the partner who wanted to receive it. The friend said the arrangement was tax-free because the initial transfer qualified as a tax-free contribution of property to the partnership in exchange for a partnership interest, and the distribution was tax-free because it was simply a pro rata property distribution made by the partnership. Thelma and Betty have come to you asking that you structure their exchange using their retail shop partnership so that the transfer will be tax-free also. How should you respond to their request?

---

[3] Secs. 732(a)(2) and 737(c). Marketable securities have a basis equal to their Sec. 732 basis plus any gain recognized under Sec. 731(c).

[4] Sec. 732(c).

culated. A decrease must be allocated if the partner's basis in the partnership interest (after any money distribution) is less than the carryover basis from the partnership. The decrease is first allocated to any asset that has declined in value in an amount equal to the smaller of the decline in value for the asset or the asset's share of the decrease. If the decrease is not fully used at this point in the calculation, the remaining decrease is allocated to the assets based on their relative adjusted bases at this point in the calculation.

EXAMPLE C10-7 ▶

KEY POINT

If different types of property are distributed, the partnership distribution rules assume that the property is distributed in the following order: (1) cash, (2) receivables and inventory, and (3) other property. This ordering can affect both the recognition of gain to the partner and the basis the partner takes in the distributed property.

Tracy has a $15,000 basis in her interest in the TP Partnership and no remaining precontribution gain immediately before receiving a current distribution that consists of $6,000 in money, power tools held as inventory with a $4,000 basis to the partnership and FMV of $3,500, and steel rod held as inventory with an $8,000 basis to the partnership and FMV of $9,200. The basis of the distributed property in Tracy's hands is determined as follows:

Predistribution basis in partnership interest	$15,000
Minus: Money received	(6,000)
Plus: Sec. 737 gain	–0–
Basis to be allocated	$ 9,000

The calculation of bases for the steel rod and power tools is as follows:

		Steel Rods	Power Tools	Total
	FMV of asset	$9,200	$3,500	$12,700
	Minus: Partnership's basis for asset	(8,000)	(4,000)	(12,000)
	Difference	$1,200	($ 500)	$ 700
Step 1:	Give each asset the partnership's basis for the asset	$8,000	$4,000	$12,000
	Minus: Tracy's basis to be allocated			(9,000)
	Decrease to allocate			$ 3,000
Step 2:	Asset basis after Step 1	$8,000	$4,000	$12,000
	Allocate the decrease first to assets that have declined in value	–0–	(500)	(500)
	Adjusted bases at this point in the calculation	$8,000	$3,500	$11,500
Step 3:	Allocate $2,500 remaining decrease based on relative adjusted bases at this point in the calculation	(1,739)[a]	(761)[b]	(2,500)
	Tracy's bases in the assets	$6,261	$2,739	$ 9,000

[a][$8,000 ÷ ($8,000 + $3,500)] × $2,500 = $1,739
[b][$3,500 ÷ ($8,000 + $3,500)] × $2,500 = $ 761

This process results in Tracy's total basis in the two assets she receives being exactly equal to the $9,000 amount to be allocated. Moreover, Tracy's basis in her partnership interest is zero after the property distributions. ◀

EXAMPLE C10-8 ▶

Assume the same facts as in Example C10-7 except Tracy recognizes $1,000 of remaining precontribution gain under Sec. 737 as a result of the distribution. The basis of the distributed property in Tracy's hands is determined as follows:

Predistribution basis in partnership interest	$15,000
Minus: Money received	(6,000)
Plus: Sec. 737 gain	1,000
Amount to be allocated	$10,000

The calculation of the basis for the steel rods and power tools are as follows:

	Steel Rods	Power Tools	Total
FMV of asset	$9,200	$3,500	$12,700
Minus: Partnership's basis for asset	(8,000)	(4,000)	(12,000)
Difference	$1,200	($ 500)	$ 700

Step 1: Give each asset the partnership's basis for the asset	$8,000	$4,000	$12,000
Minus: Tracy's basis to be allocated			(10,000)
Decrease to allocate			$ 2,000
Step 2: Adjusted basis after Step 1	$8,000	$4,000	$12,000
Allocate the decrease first to assets that have declined in value	–0–	(500)	(500)
Adjusted basis at this point in the calculation	$8,000	$3,500	$11,500
Step 3: Allocate $1,500 remaining decrease based on relative adjusted bases at this point in the calculation	(1,043)[a]	(457)[b]	(1,500)
Tracy's bases in the assets	$6,957	$3,043	$10,000

[a][$8,000 ÷ ($8,000 + $3,500)] × $1,500 = $1,043
[b][$3,500 ÷ ($8,000 + $3,500)] × $1,500 = $ 457

Again, Tracy's basis in her partnership interest is zero after the distributions. ◀

If a partner's predistribution basis plus Sec. 737 gain recognized exceeds the sum of his or her money distribution plus the carryover basis for any receivables and inventory, a carryover basis is allocated to the other property received. If the partner has an insufficient basis in the partnership interest to provide a carryover basis for all the distributed property, the remaining basis for the partnership interest is allocated to the other property first to any decrease in FMV below basis and then based on the relative bases of such property in the partnership's hands just as was calculated above.

EXAMPLE C10-9 ▶

John has a $15,000 basis for his partnership interest and no remaining precontribution gain before receiving the following property as a current distribution:

Property	Basis to the Partnership	FMV
Money	$ 5,000	$5,000
Inventory	4,000	4,500
Land parcel 1	4,500	6,000
Land parcel 2	3,000	4,000

John's basis in his distributed property is calculated as follows:

Predistribution basis	$15,000
Minus: Money received	(5,000)
Plus: Sec. 737 gain	–0–
Basis for nonmoney property	$10,000
Minus: Carryover basis for inventory	(4,000)
Remaining basis to be allocated	$ 6,000

The calculation of the basis for the two parcels of land is as follows:

	Parcel One	Parcel Two	Total
FMV of asset	$6,000	$4,000	$10,000
Minus: Partnership's basis for asset	(4,500)	(3,000)	(7,500)
Difference	$1,500	$1,000	$ 2,500
Step 1: Give each asset the partnership's basis for the asset	$4,500	$3,000	$ 7,500
Minus: John's basis to be allocated			(6,000)
Decrease to allocate			$ 1,500
Step 2: Adjusted basis after Step 1	$4,500	$3,000	$ 7,500
Allocate the decrease first to assets that have declined in value	–0–	–0–	–0–
Adjusted basis at this point in the calculation	$4,500	$3,000	$ 7,500

Step 3: Allocate $1,500 remaining decrease based on relative adjusted bases at this point in the calculation	(900)[a]	(600)[b]	(1,500)
John's bases in the assets	$3,600	$2,400	$ 6,000

[a]$[\$4,500 \div (\$4,500 + \$3,000)] \times \$1,500 = \$900$
[b]$[\$3,000 \div (\$4,500 + \$3,000)] \times \$1,500 = \$600$

John's basis in his partnership interest is zero after the distribution because all of its basis is allocated to the money and other property received. ◄

TYPICAL
MISCONCEPTION

The partner's basis in his or her partnership interest cannot be less than zero. However, a partner's capital account can be less than zero. One must distinguish between references to a partner's basis in his or her partnership interest (his outside basis) and the balance in a partner's capital account.

Two other points should be noted. First, even when a partner's basis in the partnership interest is reduced to zero by a current distribution, he or she retains an interest in the partnership. If the partner has no remaining interest in the partnership (as opposed to a zero basis), the distribution would have been a liquidating distribution. Second, the distributee's basis in property distributed as a current distribution is always equal to or less than the carryover basis. Basis for distributed property cannot be increased above the carryover basis amount when received as a nonliquidating distribution.

HOLDING PERIOD AND CHARACTER OF DISTRIBUTED PROPERTY

The partner's holding period for property distributed as a current distribution includes the partnership's holding period for such property.[5] The length of time the partner owns the partnership interest is irrelevant when determining the holding period for the distributed property. Thus, if a new partner receives a distribution of property the partnership held for two years before he or she became a partner, the new partner's holding period for the distributed property is deemed to begin when the partnership purchased the property (i.e., two years ago) rather than on the more recent date when the partner purchases the partnership interest.

KEY POINT

Consistent with the discussion in Chapter C9, certain rules ensure that neither contributions to nor distributions from a partnership can be used to alter the character of certain gains and losses on property held by the partnership or by the individual partners.

A series of rules regulate the character of the gain or loss recognized when a partner subsequently sells or exchanges certain property distributed to the partner. These rules are similar to provisions regulating the character of gain or loss on contributed property.

If the partnership distributes property that is an unrealized receivable in its hands, the distributee partner recognizes ordinary income or loss on a subsequent sale of that property. This ordinary income or loss treatment occurs without regard to the character of the property in the distributee partner's hands or the length of time the partner holds the property before its disposition.[6]

If the partnership distributes property that is inventory in its hands, the distributee partner recognizes ordinary income or loss on a subsequent sale that occurs within five years of the distribution date.[7] The inventory rule mandates the ordinary income or loss result only for the five-year period beginning on the distribution date. After five years, the character of the gain or loss recognized on the sale of such property is determined by its character in the hands of the distributee partner.

NONLIQUIDATING DISTRIBUTIONS WITH SEC. 751

OBJECTIVE 3

Identify the partnership's Sec. 751 assets

So far, the discussion of current distributions has ignored the existence of the Sec. 751 property rules. Now, we must expand our discussion to include them.

SECTION 751 ASSETS DEFINED

Sec. 751 assets include unrealized receivables and inventory. These two categories encompass all property likely to produce ordinary income when sold or collected. Each of these categories must be carefully defined before further discussion of Sec. 751.

---

[5] Sec. 735(b).
[6] Sec. 735(a)(1).

[7] Sec. 735(a)(2).

UNREALIZED RECEIVABLES. *Unrealized receivables* includes a much broader spectrum of property than the name implies. Unrealized receivables are certain rights to payments to be received by a partnership to the extent they are not already included in income under the partnership's accounting methods. They include rights to payments for services performed or to be performed as well as rights to payment for goods delivered or to be delivered (other than capital assets). A common example of unrealized receivables is the accounts receivable of a cash method partnership.

In addition to rights to receive payments for goods and services, the term *unrealized receivables* includes most potential ordinary income recapture items. A primary example of this type of unrealized receivable is the potential Sec. 1245 or 1250 recapture on the partnership's depreciable property, which is the amount of depreciation that would be recaptured as ordinary income under Sec. 1245 or 1250 if the partnership sold property at its FMV.[8]

EXAMPLE C10-10 ▶ The LK Partnership has two assets: $10,000 cash and a machine having a $14,000 basis and a $20,000 FMV. The partnership has claimed $8,000 of depreciation on the machine since its purchase. If the partnership sells the machine for its FMV, all $6,000 of the gain would be recaptured under Sec. 1245. Therefore, the LK Partnership has a $6,000 unrealized receivable item. ◀

The definition of unrealized receivables is not limited to Sec. 1245 and 1250 depreciation recapture. Among the other recapture provisions creating unrealized receivables are Sec. 617(d) (mining property), Sec. 1252 (farmland), and Sec. 1254 (oil, gas, and geothermal property). Assets covered by Sec. 1278 (market discount bonds) and Sec. 1283 (short-term obligations) generate unrealized receivables to the extent the partnership would recognize ordinary income if it sold the asset. This type of unrealized receivable is deemed to have a zero basis.

INVENTORY. *Inventory* is equally surprising in its breadth. Inventory for purposes of Sec. 751 includes three major types of property:

▶ Items held for sale in the normal course of partnership business

▶ Any other property that, if sold by the partnership, would not be considered a capital asset or Sec. 1231 property

▶ Any other property held by the partnership that, if held by the selling or distributee partner, would be property of the two types listed above[9]

In short, cash, capital assets, and Sec. 1231 assets are the only properties that are not inventory.

For purposes of calculating the impact of Sec. 751 on distributions, inventory is considered a Sec. 751 asset only if the inventory is **substantially appreciated**. (This substantially appreciated rule does not apply to sales of partnership interests, discussed later in this chapter.) The test to determine whether inventory is substantially appreciated (and therefore taxed under Sec. 751) is purely mechanical. Inventory is substantially appreciated if its FMV exceeds 120% of its adjusted basis to the partnership. For purposes of testing whether the inventory is substantially appreciated (but *only* for that purpose), inventory also includes unrealized receivables. The inclusion of unrealized receivables in the definition of inventory increases the likelihood that the inventory will be substantially appreciated.

EXAMPLE C10-11 ▶ The ABC Partnership owns the following assets on December 31:

Assets	Basis	FMV
Cash	$10,000	$ 10,000
Unrealized receivables	–0–	40,000
Inventory	30,000	34,000
Land (Sec. 1231 property)	40,000	70,000
Total	$80,000	$154,000

---

[8] Sec. 751(c). Unrealized receivables may have basis if costs or expenses have been incurred but not taken into account under the partnership's method of accounting (e.g., the basis of property sold in a nondealer installment sale).

[9] Sec. 751(d)(2).

OBJECTIVE 4

Determine the tax implications of a cash distribution when the partnership has Sec. 751 assets

For purposes of the substantially appreciated inventory test, both ABC's unrealized receivables and inventory are included. The inventory's $74,000 FMV exceeds 120% of its adjusted basis [($30,000 + 0) × 1.20 − $36,000]. Therefore, the ABC Partnership has substantially appreciated inventory. ◄

EXCHANGE OF SEC. 751 ASSETS AND OTHER PROPERTY

A current distribution receives treatment under Sec. 751 only if the partnership has Sec. 751 assets and an exchange of Sec. 751 property for non-Sec. 751 property occurs. Accordingly, if a partnership does not have *both* Sec. 751 property and other property, the rules discussed above for simple current distributions control the taxation of the distribution. Similarly, a distribution that is proportionate to all partners or (1) consists of only the partner's share of either Sec. 751 property or non-Sec. 751 property and (2) does not reduce the partner's interest in other property is not affected by the Sec. 751 rules.

However, any portion of the distribution that represents an exchange of Sec. 751 property for non-Sec. 751 property must be isolated and is not treated as a distribution at all. Instead, it is treated as a sale between the partnership and the partner, and any gain or loss realized on the sale transaction is fully recognized.[10] The character of the recognized gain or loss depends on the character of the property deemed sold. For the party deemed the seller of the Sec. 751 assets, the gain or loss is ordinary income or loss.

Analyzing the transaction to determine what property was involved in the Sec. 751 transaction is best accomplished by using an orderly, step-by-step approach.

STEP 1: DIVIDE THE ASSETS INTO SEC. 751 ASSETS AND NON-SEC. 751 ASSETS. Inventory must be tested at this time to see whether it is substantially appreciated to know whether it is a Sec. 751 asset for distribution purposes.

STEP 2: DEVELOP A SCHEDULE, SUCH AS THE ONE IN TABLE C10-1, TO DETERMINE WHETHER THE PARTNER EXCHANGED SEC. 751 ASSETS FOR NON-SEC. 751 ASSETS OR VICE VERSA. This schedule must be based on the FMV of all the partnership's assets. To make the determination, compare the partner's interest in the partnership's assets before the distribution with his or her interest in the assets after the distribution. This part of the analysis assumes a fictional nontaxable pro rata distribution equal to the partner's decreased interest in the assets. We can see whether the partner exchanged Sec. 751 assets for non-Sec. 751 assets by comparing the fictional distribution with the actual distribution. Thus, in Table C10-1,

► Column 1 represents the partner's interest (valued at FMV) in each asset before the distribution.

► Column 2 represents the partner's interest (valued at FMV) in each asset after the distribution.

► Column 3 shows a hypothetical proportionate distribution that would have occurred had the partner's ownership interest been reduced by the partner taking a pro rata share of each asset. (As such, the proportionate distribution would be nontaxable.)

► Column 4 shows the amounts actually distributed.

► Column 5 shows the difference between the hypothetical and actual distributions. This column indicates whether a Sec. 751 exchange has occurred (see step 3).

STEP 3: ANALYZE COLUMN 5 TO DETERMINE WHETHER SEC. 751 ASSETS WERE EXCHANGED FOR NON-SEC. 751 ASSETS. If the column 5 total for the Sec. 751 assets section of Table C10-1 is zero, no Sec. 751 exchange has occurred. The partner simply received an additional amount of one type of Sec. 751 asset in exchange for relinquishing an interest in some other type of Sec. 751 asset. For example, no Sec. 751 exchange occurs if a partner exchanges an interest in substantially appreciated inventory for an interest in unrealized receivables. However, if the column 5 total for the Sec. 751

TYPICAL MISCONCEPTION

Even if a partnership has Sec. 751 property, Sec. 751 is not applicable as long as a partner's interest in the ordinary income type assets is not altered. However, if a distribution of the partnership assets is disproportionate, Sec. 751 treats that portion of the distribution as a deemed sale between the partnership and the distributee partner, with the corresponding income or loss being recognized.

KEY POINT

Steps 2 and 3 try to identify whether a disproportionate distribution of Sec. 751 assets has taken place. In Table C10-1, if the column 5 total for Sec. 751 assets is zero, Sec. 751 is not applicable But as the table illustrates, Anne received $10,000 more than her share of the partnership cash without receiving any of her $10,000 share of Sec. 751 assets.

---

[10] Sec. 751(b).

▼ **TABLE C10-1**

Analysis of Sec. 751 Nonliquidating Distribution (Example C10-12)

	Beginning Partnership Amount[a]	(1) Anne's Interest Before Distribution[a] (1/3)	(2) Anne's Interest After Distribution[a] (1/5)	(3) Hypothetical Proportionate Distribution (3) = (1) − (2)[a]	(4) Actual Distribution[a]	(5) Difference[b] (5) = (4) − (3)
Sec. 751 assets:						
Unrealized receivables	$15,000	$ 5,000	$ 3,000	$ 2,000	$ –0–	$ (2,000)
Inventory	60,000	20,000	12,000	8,000	–0–	(8,000)
Total Sec. 751 assets	$75,000	$25,000	$15,000	$10,000	$ –0–	($ 10,000)
Non-Sec. 751 assets:						
Cash	$75,000	$25,000	$10,000[c]	$15,000	$25,000	$ 10,000
Total non-Sec. 751 assets	$75,000	$25,000	$10,000	$15,000	$25,000	$ 10,000

[a]Valued at fair market value.
[b]A negative amount means that Anne gave up her interest in a particular property. A positive amount means that she received more than her proportionate interest.
[c]One-fifth interest in remaining cash of $50,000.

assets is an amount other than zero, a Sec. 751 exchange has occurred. One (or more) Sec. 751 properties has been exchanged for one (or more) non-Sec. 751 properties.

EXAMPLE C10-12 ▶ On January 1, the ABC Partnership holds the assets listed below before making a $25,000 cash distribution to Anne that reduces her interest in the partnership from one-third to one-fifth.

Assets	Basis	FMV
Cash	$ 75,000	$ 75,000
Unrealized receivables	–0–	15,000
Inventory	30,000	60,000
Total	$105,000	$150,000

ABC owes no liabilities on January 1. Before the distribution, Anne has a $35,000 basis in her partnership interest. The following three steps indicate that a Sec. 751 exchange has occurred:

STEP 1. Determine ABC's Sec. 751 and non-Sec. 751 assets. ABC's Sec. 751 assets include the unrealized receivables and the substantially appreciated inventory. The cash is ABC's only non-Sec. 751 property.

STEP 2. Complete the table used to analyze the Sec. 751 distribution (see Table C10-1).

STEP 3. Analyze column 5 of Table C10-1 to see whether a Sec. 751 exchange has occurred. Because Anne's Sec. 751 asset total declined by $10,000, we know she gave up $10,000 of her proportionate interest in ABC's Sec. 751 assets in exchange for cash. ◀

ADDITIONAL COMMENT

Step 4 is crucial if a student is to understand the deemed sale that Sec. 751 creates. In Example C10-13, Anne is treated as if she had exchanged her $10,000 interest in the unrealized receivables and inventory for $10,000 of cash. Thus, Anne has a taxable gain or loss on the deemed sale. To determine Anne's gain or loss on the deemed sale, the adjusted basis of the unrealized receivables and inventory equals whatever her basis would have been had the partnership actually distributed those assets to her.

STEP 4: DETERMINE THE GAIN OR LOSS ON THE SEC. 751 DEEMED SALE. We must assume that the exchange occurring in step 3 above was a sale of the exchanged property between the partnership and the partner. This step follows logically from the premise that the partner "bargained" to receive the amounts actually distributed rather than a proportionate distribution. She sold her interest in some assets to receive more than her proportionate interest in other assets. As with any sale, the gain (or loss) equals the difference between the FMV of the property received and the adjusted basis of the property given up. Note that, up to this point, we have been dealing only in terms of the FMV, so the adjusted basis of property given up must be determined as if the hypothetical distribution actually had occurred.

EXAMPLE C10-13 ▶ Assume the same facts as in Example C10-12. The Sec. 751 sale portion of the distribution is analyzed as Anne receiving $10,000 more cash than her proportionate share and giving up a $2,000 (FMV) interest in the unrealized receivables and an $8,000 (FMV) interest in the inventory. By examining the balance sheet, we can see that the partnership's bases for the unrealized receivables and inventory are $0 and $4,000 [$8,000 × ($30,000 ÷ $60,000)]. If Anne received these properties in a current distribution, her basis would be the same as the property's basis in the partnership's hands, or $0 and $4,000, respectively. Therefore, Anne's deemed sale of the Sec. 751 assets is analyzed as follows:

Amount realized (cash)	$10,000
Minus: Adjusted basis of property sold	(4,000)
Realized and recognized gain	$ 6,000

The character of the recognized gain depends on the character of the property sold (in this case, the unrealized receivables and inventory). Therefore, Anne's $6,000 gain is ordinary income. ◀

STEP 5: DETERMINE THE IMPACT OF THE CURRENT DISTRIBUTION. The last step in analyzing the distribution's effect on the partner is to determine the impact of the portion of the distribution that is not a Sec. 751 exchange. This distribution is treated exactly like any other nonliquidating distribution.

EXAMPLE C10-14 ▶ Assume the same facts as in Examples C10-12 and C10-13. Examining the distribution, we see in column 4 of Table C10-1 that, as part of the Sec. 751 exchange, Anne received only $10,000 of the $25,000 cash actually distributed. The remaining $15,000 distributed represents a current distribution. Under Sec. 731(a)(1), a partner recognizes gain on a current distribution only if the money distributed exceeds his or her basis in the partnership interest. Anne recognizes no gain because she has a $16,000 basis in the partnership interest immediately after the current distribution. This basis is calculated as follows:

Predistribution basis for partnership interest	$35,000
Minus: Basis of property deemed distributed in Sec. 751 exchange ($0 unrealized receivables + $4,000 inventory)	(4,000)
Basis before current distribution	$31,000
Minus: Money distributed	(15,000)
Postdistribution basis of partnership interest	$16,000

After the entire distribution is complete, Anne owns a one-fifth partnership interest with a basis of $16,000 and has $25,000 in cash. In addition, she has recognized $6,000 in ordinary income. ◀

STOP & THINK **Question:** Do most current distributions made by a partnership require a Sec. 751 calculation?

Solution: No. A partnership makes many current distributions pro rata to all partners, so Sec. 751 is not involved. Even if the distribution is not pro rata, the distribution often does not create an exchange of an interest in Sec. 751 assets for an interest in other assets. This exchange happens only when (1) the partner is reducing his or her overall interest in the partnership, (e.g., from a 15% to a 5% general partner) or (2) an explicit agreement provides that the distribution results in a partner giving up all or part of his or her interest in some asset(s) maintained by the partnership. Most current distributions do not involve Sec. 751.

TERMINATING AN INTEREST IN A PARTNERSHIP

A partner can terminate or dispose of an interest in a partnership in a number of ways. The two most common are receiving a liquidating distribution and selling the interest. Other possibilities include giving the interest away, exchanging the interest for corporate stock, and transferring the interest at death. This part of the chapter considers each of these methods.

LIQUIDATING DISTRIBUTIONS

The IRC defines a liquidating distribution as a distribution, or one of a series of distributions, that terminates a partner's interest in the partnership.[11] If the partner's interest is drastically reduced but not terminated, the distribution is treated as a current distribution. A liquidating distribution can occur when only one member of a partnership terminates his or her interest, several partners terminate their interests but the partnership continues, or the entire partnership terminates and each partner receives a liquidating distribution. Rules for taxation of a liquidating distribution are the same whether one partner terminates his or her interest or the entire partnership liquidates.

GAIN OR LOSS RECOGNITION BY THE PARTNER. The rule for recognizing gain on a liquidating distribution is exactly the same rule used for a current distribution. A partner recognizes gain only if any money distributed exceeds the partner's predistribution basis in his or her partnership interest.[12] Distributed money includes money deemed distributed to the partner from a liability reduction or the FMV of marketable securities treated as money.

Although a partner can never recognize a loss from a current distribution, he or she can recognize a loss from a liquidating distribution. A partner recognizes a loss only if the liquidating distribution consists of money (including money deemed distributed), unrealized receivables, and inventory, but no other property.[13] The amount of the loss is the difference between the partner's basis in the partnership interest before the distribution and the sum of money plus the bases of the receivables and inventory (to the partnership immediately before the distribution) that the partner receives.

Maria terminates her interest in the ABC Partnership when her basis in the partnership is $35,000. She receives a liquidating distribution of $10,000 cash and inventory with a $12,000 basis to the partnership. Her recognized loss is $13,000 [$35,000 − ($10,000 + $12,000)]. The inventory has a $12,000 basis to Maria. ◀

BASIS IN ASSETS RECEIVED. A partner's basis of an asset received in a liquidating distribution is determined using rules similar to those used to determine the basis of an asset received in a current distribution. For both kinds of distributions, the basis in unrealized receivables and inventory is generally the same as the property's basis in the partnership's hands. Under no condition is the basis of these two types of assets increased. Occasionally, however, the partner's basis in his or her partnership interest is so small that after making the necessary reduction for money (and deemed money) distributions, the basis in the partnership interest is smaller than the partnership's bases for the unrealized receivables and inventory distributed. In such cases, the remaining basis in the partnership interest must be allocated among the unrealized receivables and inventory items based first on their decline in value and then on their relative bases as adjusted to reflect the decline in value.[14] As a result, the bases for the unrealized receivables and inventory are reduced, and the amount of ordinary income a partner recognizes on their ultimate sale, exchange, or collection increases.

Remember that a liquidating distribution of money, unrealized receivables, and inventory having a total basis to the partnership less than the partner's basis in his or her partnership interest results in the recognition of a loss. However, the partner recognizes no loss if the distribution includes any property other than money, unrealized receivables, and inventory. Instead, all the remaining basis in the partnership interest must be allocated to the other property received regardless of that property's basis to the partnership or its FMV. Application of this rule can create strange results.

---

[11] Sec. 761(d).
[12] Sec. 731(a)(1).

[13] Sec. 731(a)(2).
[14] Sec. 732(c).

EXAMPLE C10-16 ▶ Assume the same facts as in Example C10-15 except Maria's distribution also includes an office typewriter having a $50 basis to the partnership and a $100 FMV. The allocation of basis proceeds as follows:

Predistribution basis for partnership interest	$35,000
Minus: Money received	(10,000)
Basis after money distribution	$25,000
Minus: Basis of inventory to partnership	(12,000)
Remaining basis of partnership interest	$13,000

The entire $13,000 remaining basis of the partnership interest is allocated to the typewriter. ◀

TAX STRATEGY TIP

The partnership in Example C10-16 should avoid distributing low basis property along with cash, unrealized receivables, and inventory so that the partner can obtain an immediate loss deduction.

The basis allocation procedure illustrated in Example C10-16 delays loss recognition until Maria either depreciates or sells the typewriter. The allocation procedure also may change the character of the loss because Maria would recognize a capital loss when she receives the liquidating distribution in Example C10-15. In Example C10-16, however, the character of Maria's loss is determined by the character of the typewriter in her hands (or in some cases by a series of specific rules that are discussed below). Worst of all, if she converts the typewriter into personal-use property, the loss on its sale or exchange is nondeductible.

If the partnership distributes two or more assets other than unrealized receivables or inventory in the same distribution, the remaining basis in the partnership interest is allocated among them based on both their relative FMVs and bases in the partnership's hands. Such an allocation process can lead to either a decrease or increase in the total basis of these assets. This potential for increasing the assets' bases is unique to liquidating distributions.

The allocation that results in a decrease in the basis of a distributed asset is identical to the allocation process described for current distributions. However, if the amount to be allocated is greater than the carryover bases of the distributed assets, the basis is first allocated among the distributed assets in an amount equal to their carryover basis from the partnership. Then allocations are made based on relative appreciation of the assets up to the amount of appreciation, and further allocations are made to the assets based on their relative FMVs.

EXAMPLE C10-17 ▶ Before receiving a liquidating distribution, Craig's basis in his interest in the BCD Partnership is $62,000. The distribution consists of $10,000 in cash, inventory having a $2,000 basis to the partnership and a $4,000 FMV, and two parcels of undeveloped land (not held as inventory) having bases of $6,000 and $18,000 to the partnership and having FMVs of $10,000 and $24,000, respectively. Assume that Sec. 751 does not apply. His bases in the assets received are calculated as follows:

Predistribution basis for partnership interest	$62,000
Minus: Money received	(10,000)
Basis of inventory to the partnership	(2,000)
Basis allocated to two parcels of land	$50,000

The calculation of the basis for the two parcels of land are as follows:

	Parcel One	Parcel Two	Total
FMV of asset	$10,000	$24,000	$34,000
Minus: Partnership's basis for asset	(6,000)	(18,000)	(24,000)
Difference	$ 4,000	$ 6,000	$10,000
Step 1: Give each asset the partnership's basis for the asset	$ 6,000	$18,000	$24,000
Minus: Craig's basis to be allocated			(50,000)
Increase to allocate			$26,000
Step 2: Adjusted basis after Step 1	$ 6,000	$18,000	$24,000
Allocate the increase first to assets that have increased in value	4,000	6,000	10,000

Adjusted basis at this point in the calculation	$10,000	$24,000	$34,000
Step 3: Allocate $16,000 remaining increase based on relative FMVs	4,706[a]	11,294[b]	16,000
Craig's bases in the assets	$14,706	$35,294	$50,000

[a]$10,000 ÷ ($10,000 + $24,000) × $16,000 = $ 4,706
[b]$24,000 ÷ ($10,000 + $24,000) × $16,000 = $11,294

◄

KEY POINT

If the partner recognizes neither gain nor loss in a liquidating distribution, the partner's total basis in the distributed assets always equals the partner's predistribution basis in his or her partnership interest.

In a liquidating distribution, the amount of money received plus the distributee partner's total basis of the nonmoney property received normally equals the partner's predistribution basis in the partnership interest. The only two exceptions to this rule apply when the money received exceeds the partner's basis in his or her partnership interest, causing the partner to recognize a gain, or when money, unrealized receivables, and inventory are the only assets distributed and the partner recognizes a loss. In all other liquidating distributions, the distributee partner recognizes no gain or loss. Instead, that partner's predistribution basis in his or her partnership interest is transferred to the cash and other property received.

Holding Period in Distributed Assets. The distributee partner's holding period for any assets received in a liquidating distribution includes the partnership's holding period for such property.[15] If the partnership received the property as a contribution from a partner, the partnership's holding period also may include the period of time the contributing partner held the property prior to making the contribution (see Chapter C9). The distributee partner's holding period for his or her partnership interest is irrelevant in determining the holding period of the assets received.

EXAMPLE C10-18 ► George purchases an interest in the DEF Partnership on June 1, 2006, but he cannot get along with the other partners. Therefore, on July 1, 2006, he receives a liquidating distribution that terminates his interest in the partnership. George's distribution includes land that the partnership has owned since August 1, 2000. George's holding period for the land begins on August 1, 2000, even though his holding period for the partnership interest begins much later. ◄

The character of the gain or loss recognized on a subsequent sale of distributed property is determined using the same rules as for a current distribution.

KEY POINT

The main difference in how the Sec. 751 rules apply to current versus liquidating distributions is that, after a liquidating distribution, the partner always has a zero interest in the partnership assets because he or she is no longer a partner in the partnership.

EFFECTS OF SEC. 751. Section 751 has essentially the same impact on both liquidating and current distributions. To the extent the partner exchanges an interest in Sec. 751 assets for an interest in other assets (or vice versa), that portion of the transaction bypasses the distribution rules. Instead, this portion of the transaction is treated as a sale occurring between the partnership and the partner. One notable difference occurs between liquidating distributions and current distributions having Sec. 751 implications: the postdistribution interest in partnership assets is zero for the liquidating distribution because it terminates the partner's interest in the partnership.

EXAMPLE C10-19 ► The ABC Partnership holds the assets listed below on December 31 before making a $50,000 cash distribution that reduces Al's one-third interest in the partnership to zero.

Assets	Basis	FMV
Cash	$75,000	$ 75,000
Unrealized receivables	–0–	15,000
Inventory	15,000	60,000
Total	$90,000	$150,000

The partnership has no liabilities, and Al's predistribution basis in his partnership interest is $30,000. The following steps lead to the tax effects of the liquidating distribution:

---

[15] Sec. 735(b).

STEP 1. Determine ABC's Sec. 751 and non-Sec. 751 assets. The Sec. 751 assets include the unrealized receivables and the substantially appreciated inventory. The cash is ABC's only non-Sec. 751 asset.

STEP 2. Complete the table used to analyze the Sec. 751 distributions (see Table C10-2).

STEP 3. Analyze column 5 of Table C10-2 to see whether a Sec. 751 exchange has occurred. Table C10-2 shows that Al exchanges $5,000 of unrealized receivables and $20,000 of inventory for $25,000 cash.

STEP 4. Determine the gain or loss on the Sec. 751 deemed sale. Al is deemed to have sold unrealized receivables and inventory for cash. Assume Al first got the receivables and inventory in a current distribution. He obtains the partnership's bases for the assets of $0 and $5,000, respectively. The subsequent deemed sale results in Al recognizing a $20,000 gain.

Amount realized (cash)	$25,000
Minus: Adjusted basis of property sold	(5,000)
Realized and recognized gain	$20,000

Al's gain is ordinary income because it results from his deemed sale of receivables and inventory to the partnership.

STEP 5. Determine the impact of the non-Sec. 751 portion of the distribution. The liquidating distribution is only the $25,000 cash he receives that was *not* a part of the Sec. 751 transaction. To determine its impact, we first must find Al's basis in his partnership interest after the Sec. 751 transaction but before the $25,000 liquidating distribution.

Predistribution basis in the partnership interest	$30,000
Minus: Basis of receivables and inventory deemed distributed in Sec. 751 exchange	(5,000)
Basis before money distribution	$25,000
Minus: Money distribution	(25,000)
Gain recognized on liquidating distribution	$ –0–

Al recognizes no further gain or loss from the liquidating distribution portion of the transaction. ◀

▼ **TABLE C10-2**
Analysis of Sec. 751 Liquidating Distribution (Example C10-19)

	Beginning Partnership Amount[a]	(1) Al's Interest Before Distribution[a] (1/3)	(2) Al's Interest After Distribution[a] (–0–)	(3) Hypothetical Proportionate Distribution[a] (3) = (1) – (2)	(4) Actual Distribution[a]	(5) Difference[b] (5) = (4) – (3)
Sec. 751 assets:						
Unrealized receivables	$15,000	$ 5,000	$ –0–	$ 5,000	$ –0–	$ (5,000)
Inventory	60,000	20,000	–0–	20,000	–0–	(20,000)
Total Sec. 751 assets	$75,000	$25,000	$ –0–	$25,000	$ –0–	($ 25,000)
Non-Sec. 751 assets:						
Cash	$75,000	$25,000	$ –0–	$25,000	$50,000	$ 25,000
Total non-Sec. 751 assets	$75,000	$25,000	$ –0–	$25,000	$50,000	$ 25,000

[a] Valued at fair market value.
[b] A negative amount means that Al gave up his interest in a particular property. A positive amount means that Al received more than his proportionate interest.

SELF-STUDY
QUESTION

What is the character of gain or
loss on the sale of a partnership
interest?

ANSWER

Because a partnership interest is
generally a capital asset, the sale
of a partnership interest results in
the partner recognizing a capital
gain or loss. However, if a partnership has Sec. 751 assets, the
partner is deemed to sell his or
her share of Sec. 751 assets
directly with a corresponding
ordinary gain or loss being recognized.

EFFECTS OF DISTRIBUTION ON THE PARTNERSHIP. A partnership generally recognizes no gain or loss on liquidating distributions made to its partners.[16] If a Sec. 751
deemed sale occurs, however, the partnership may recognize gain or loss on assets deemed
sold to its partner. Although a liquidating distribution normally does not itself terminate
the partnership, the partnership terminates if none of the remaining partners continue to
operate the business of the partnership in a partnership form. In this case, all partners will
receive liquidating distributions. Finally, the partnership's assets may be subject to
optional or mandatory basis adjustments (see pages C10-28 and C10-29).

Topic Review C10-1 summarizes the tax consequences of current and liquidating distributions.

SALE OF A PARTNERSHIP INTEREST

Absence any contrary rules, a partner's sale or exchange of a partnership interest would generate a capital gain or loss under Sec. 741 because a partnership interest is usually a capital
asset. Section 751, however, modifies this result by requiring the partner to recognize ordi-

---

Topic Review C10-1

Current and Liquidating Distributions

TAX CONSEQUENCES	CURRENT DISTRIBUTIONS	LIQUIDATING DISTRIBUTIONS
Impact on Partner:		
Money (or deemed money from liability changes or marketable securities) distributed	Gain recognized only if money distributed exceeds basis in partnership interest before distribution.	Gain recognized only if money distributed exceeds basis in partnership interest before distribution.
Unrealized receivables and/or inventory distributed	Carryover basis (limited to basis in partnership interest before distribution reduced by money distributed).	Carryover basis (limited to basis in partnership interest before distribution reduced by money distributed).
	No gain or loss recognized.[a]	Loss recognized if partnership distributes money, inventory, and receivables with basis less than partner's basis in partnership interest before distribution and partnership distributes no other property.[a]
Other property distributed	Carryover basis (limited to basis in partnership interest before distribution reduced by money and carryover basis in inventory and receivables).	Basis equal to basis in partnership interest before distribution reduced by money and carryover basis in inventory and receivables.
	No gain or loss recognized.[a]	No gain or loss recognized.[a]
Impact on Partnership:		
General rule	No gain or loss recognized.	No gain or loss recognized.
Partnership assets	May be subject to optional basis adjustments (see pages C10-28 and C10-29).	May be subject to optional or mandatory basis adjustments (see pages C10-28 and C10-29).
Other Tax Consequences:	If a Sec. 751 deemed sale or exchange occurs, the partner and/or the partnership may recognize gain or loss on the deemed sale.	If a Sec. 751 deemed sale or exchange occurs, the partner and/or the partnership may recognize gain or loss on the deemed sale.

[a]A partner may recognize precontribution gain (but not loss) under Sec. 737 if a precontribution net gain remains and the FMV of the property distributed exceeds the adjusted basis of the partnership interest immediately before the property distribution (but after any money distribution). The contributing partner also may recognize precontribution gain or loss if the partnership distributes the contributed property to another partner within seven
years of the contribution (Sec. 704(c)).

---

[16] Sec. 731(b).

nary income or loss on the sale or exchange of a partnership interest to the extent the consideration received is attributable to the partner's share of unrealized receivables and inventory items. The sale of a partnership interest also may have two other effects: the purchaser acquires the partner's share of the partnership's liabilities, and the partnership may be terminated. Each of these situations related to the sale of a partnership interest is examined below.

SECTION 751 PROPERTY. The definition of Sec. 751 property is slightly different for sales or exchanges than for distributions because inventory does not have to be substantially appreciated to be included as Sec. 751 property. Thus, all inventory and all unrealized receivables are Sec. 751 assets in a sale or exchange situation.[17]

Treasury Regulations under Sec. 751 take a hypothetical asset sale approach to determine the amount of ordinary income or loss the partner recognizes on the sale or exchange of a partnership interest.[18] Under the regulations, the partnership is deemed to sell all its assets for their FMV immediately before the partner sells his or her interest in the partnership. The partner then is allocated his or her share of ordinary gain or loss attributable to the Sec. 751 assets. With this approach, the results of the sale or exchange can be determined using the following three steps:

STEP 1. Determine the total gain or loss on the sale or exchange of the partnership interest.

STEP 2. Determine the ordinary gain or loss component and the Sec. 1250 gain component, if applicable, using the hypothetical asset sale approach.[19]

STEP 3. Determine the capital gain component by calculating the residual gain or loss after assigning the ordinary gain or loss and the Sec. 1250 gain components.

EXAMPLE C10-20 ▶ Troy sells his one-fourth interest in the TV Partnership to Steve for $50,000 cash when the partnership's assets are as follows:

Assets	Basis	FMV
Cash	$ 20,000	$ 20,000
Unrealized receivables	–0–	24,000
Inventory	20,000	68,000
Building	40,000	56,000
Land	40,000	32,000
Total	$120,000	$200,000

The partnership has no liabilities on the sale date and has claimed $19,000 of straight-line depreciation on the building. Troy's basis in his partnership interest is $30,000 on such date. Both the receivables and inventory are Sec. 751 assets, and the building is Sec. 1250 property. Application of step 1 yields the following gain on Troy's sale of his partnership interest:

Amount realized on sale	$50,000
Minus: Adjusted basis of partnership interest	(30,000)
Total gain realized	$20,000

Application of step 2 yields the following allocation to Sec. 751 and Sec. 1250 property:

Deemed Sale of Assets	Partnership Gain (Loss)	Troy's Share (25%)
Unrealized receivables	$24,000	$ 6,000
Inventory	48,000	12,000
Building	16,000	4,000
Land	(8,000)	(2,000)

---

[17] Regulation Sec. 1.751-1(a)(1) is outdated to some extent and still speaks in terms of substantially appreciated inventory. However, Sec. 751(a) in the IRC, which deals with the sale or exchange of a partnership interest, includes all inventory items, not just those that are substantially appreciated.

[18] Reg. Sec. 1.751-1(a)(2). This hypothetical sale approach allows for easy incorporation of special allocations under Sec. 704 into the Sec. 751 calculation.

[19] The Sec. 1250 gain is the lesser of the hypothetical gain on Sec. 1250 property (e.g., buildings) or the amount of depreciation claimed on the Sec. 1250 property (assuming straight-line depreciation). This gain applies to noncorporate taxpayers and is subject to the 25% capital gains tax rate. A similar rule applies to a collectibles gain subject to the 28% capital gains tax rate. See Reg. Sec. 1.1(h)-1.

Thus, on the sale of his partnership interest, Troy recognizes ordinary income of $18,000 ($6,000 + $12,000). Because the $19,000 of depreciation exceeds the hypothetical gain on the building, the entire $16,000 gain is Sec. 1250 gain, $4,000 of which is Troy's share.

Application of step 3 yields the following residual allocation to capital gain or loss:

Total gain realized	$20,000
Minus: Allocation to ordinary income and Sec. 1250 gain	(22,000)
Capital loss recognized	($ 2,000)

In summary, on the sale of his partnership interest, Troy recognizes $18,000 of ordinary income, $4,000 of Sec. 1250 gain, and a $2,000 capital loss. Without Sec. 751, these three components would have been netted together as a $20,000 capital gain. ◀

STOP & THINK

Question: Bill owns 20% of Kraco and plans to sell his ownership interest for a $40,000 gain. Kraco has both unrealized receivables and inventory. If Kraco is a corporation, Bill will report a $40,000 capital gain. If Kraco is a partnership, part of the $40,000 gain (the gain on his 20% share of the Sec. 751 assets) will be ordinary income, and the remainder will be capital gain. Why did Congress decide to tax the gain on the sale of corporate stock differently from the gain on the sale of a partnership interest?

Solution: The corporation itself will pay tax on the ordinary income realized when it collects unrealized receivables or sells inventory, and the corporation's tax is unaffected by the identity of the shareholder. Under no conditions will the shareholder have to report any of the corporation's ordinary income. Accordingly, the sale of the corporate stock does not provide an opportunity to avoid ordinary income for the owner, nor can the owner convert ordinary income into capital gain by selling the corporate stock.[20]

Because the partners report and pay taxes on the ordinary income earned by the partnership, a sale of a partnership interest that produces only capital gains would represent an opportunity for a partner to avoid recognizing ordinary income and recognize capital gains instead. Imagine, for example, that Kraco is a cash basis service business whose only asset is a large account receivable where all work has been completed. If Bill stays in the partnership, he will recognize ordinary income when the partnership collects the receivable. If he were allowed to sell his partnership interest in this setting for a capital gain, he could convert his ordinary income into capital gain. However, Sec. 751 prevents this conversion from happening by requiring him to recognize ordinary income on the sale of the partnership interest to the extent the sales proceeds are attributable to Sec. 751 assets.

ADDITIONAL COMMENT

Section 751 treatment is another application of the aggregate theory of partnership taxation as opposed to the entity theory.

LIABILITIES. When a partnership has liabilities, each partner's distributive share of any liabilities is always part of the basis for the partnership interest. When a partner sells his or her partnership interest, the partner is relieved of the liabilities. Accordingly, the amount realized on the sale of a partnership interest is made up of money plus the FMV of nonmoney property received plus the seller's share of partnership liabilities assumed or acquired by the purchaser.

EXAMPLE C10-21 ▶

Andrew is a 30% partner in the ABC Partnership when he sells his entire interest to Miguel for $40,000 cash. At the time of the sale, Andrew's basis is $27,000 (which includes his $7,000 share of partnership liabilities). The partnership has no Sec. 751 assets. Andrew's $20,000 gain on the sale is calculated as follows:

Amount realized:		
Cash	$40,000	
Liabilities assumed by purchaser	7,000	$47,000
Minus: Adjusted basis		(27,000)
Gain recognized on sale		$20,000

◀

---

[20] An exception used to exist for a so-called collapsible corporation. However, the 2003 Act repealed these provisions for tax years beginning after 2003 and before 2009. A discussion of collapsible corporations is beyond the scope of this text.

IMPACT ON THE PARTNERSHIP. When one partner sells his or her partnership interest, the sale usually has no more impact on the partnership than the sale of corporate stock by one shareholder has on the corporation. Only the partner and the purchaser of the interest are affected. However, the partnership itself is affected if the partnership interest sold is sufficiently large that, under Sec. 708, its sale terminates the partnership for tax purposes. This effect is discussed later in this chapter. Also, the partnership may have to make optional or mandatory basis adjustments to its assets (see pages C10-26 through C10-29).

RETIREMENT OR DEATH OF A PARTNER

OBJECTIVE 7

Determine the amount and character of the gain or loss recognized when a partner retires from a partnership or dies

If a partner dies or retires from a partnership, that partner's interest can be sold either to an outsider or to one or more existing partners.[21] The results of such a sale are outlined above. Often, however, a partner or a deceased partner's successor-in-interest departs from the partnership in return for payments made by the partnership itself. When the partnership buys out the partner's interest, the analysis of the tax results focuses on two types of payments: payments made in exchange for the partner's interest in partnership property and other payments.

PAYMENTS FOR PARTNERSHIP PROPERTY. Generally, the IRS accepts the valuation placed on the retiring partner's interest in the partnership property by the partners in an arm's-length transaction. Payments made for the property interest are taxed under the liquidating distribution rules. Like any liquidating distribution made to a partner, payments made to a retiring partner or a deceased partner's successor-in-interest[22] in exchange for his or her property interest are not deductible by the partnership.[23]

If the retiring or deceased partner was a general partner and the partnership is a service partnership (i.e., capital is not a material income producing factor), payments made to a general partner for unrealized receivables and goodwill (when the partnership agreement does not provide for a goodwill payment on retirement or death) are not considered payments for property. Instead, any such payments are treated as other payments. The other payment treatment permits the partnership to deduct the amounts paid to the retiring or deceased partner or to reduce the distributive share allocable to the other partners.

TYPICAL MISCONCEPTION

The significance of the two different kinds of payments is not readily apparent to some taxpayers. The payments for partnership property are not deductible by the partnership and often are not income to the retiring partner. However, payments considered in the second category are deductible by the partnership (or they reduce the distributive shares that other partners must recognize) and usually are income to the retiring partner.

TYPICAL MISCONCEPTION

The main difference between a payment being taxed as a distributive share or as a guaranteed payment is the character of the income recognized by the recipient partner. If the payment is taxed as a distributive share, the character of the income is determined by the type of income earned by the partnership. In contrast, the payment is always ordinary income if it is treated as a guaranteed payment.

OTHER PAYMENTS. Payments made to a retiring partner or to a deceased partner's successor-in-interest that exceed the value of that partner's share of partnership property have a different tax result for both the retiring partner and for the partnership. A few payments that do represent payments for property (e.g., payments to a general partner retiring from a service partnership for his or her interest in unrealized receivables and for his or her interest in partnership goodwill) also are taxed under these rules.

Under these rules, a payment is taxed as either a distributive share or a guaranteed payment. If the excess payment is a function of partnership income (e.g., 10% of the partnership's net income), the income is considered a distributive share of partnership income.[24] Accordingly, the character of the income flows through to the partner, and each of the remaining partners is taxed on a smaller amount of partnership income. The income must be reported in the partner's tax year that includes the partnership year-end from which the distributive share arises, regardless of when the partner actually receives the distribution.

If the amount of the excess payment is determined without regard to the partnership income, the payment is treated as a guaranteed payment.[25] If the payment is a guaranteed payment, the retiring partner recognizes ordinary income, and the partnership generally has an ordinary deduction. Like all guaranteed payments, the income is includible in the

---

[21] Retirement from the partnership in this context has nothing to do with reaching a specific age and leaving the employ of the partnership but instead refers to the partner's withdrawal at any age from a continuing partnership.

[22] A deceased partner's successor-in-interest is the party that succeeds to the rights of the deceased partner's partnership interest (e.g., the decedent's estate or an heir or legatee of the deceased partner). A deceased partner's successor-

in-interest is treated as a partner by the tax laws until his or her interest in the partnership has been completely liquidated.

[23] Sec. 736(b).

[24] Sec. 736(a)(1).

[25] Sec. 736(a)(2).

recipient's income for his or her tax year within which ends the partnership tax year in which the partnership claims its deduction (see Chapter C9).

EXAMPLE C10-22 ▶ When Sam retires from the STU Partnership, he receives a cash payment of $30,000. At the time of his retirement, his basis for his one-fourth limited partnership interest is $25,000. The partnership has no liabilities and the following assets:

Assets	Basis	FMV	Sam's 1/4 FMV
Cash	$ 40,000	$ 40,000	$10,000
Marketable securities	25,000	32,000	8,000
Land	35,000	48,000	12,000
Total	$100,000	$120,000	$30,000

In the absence of a valuation agreement, the partnership presumably pays Sam a ratable share of the FMV of each asset (and he receives no payment for any partnership goodwill). The $30,000 amount paid to Sam equals the FMV of his one-fourth interest in the partnership assets. The $30,000 Sam receives in exchange for his interest in partnership property is analyzed as a liquidating distribution in the following manner:

Cash distribution received	$30,000
Minus: Basis in partnership interest	(25,000)
Gain recognized on liquidating distribution	$ 5,000

Because the partnership holds no Sec. 751 assets, the entire gain is a capital gain. The partnership gets no deduction for the distribution. ◀

EXAMPLE C10-23 ▶ Assume the same facts as in Example C10-22 except Sam receives $34,000 instead of $30,000. This amount represents payment for Sam's one-fourth interest in partnership assets plus an excess payment of $4,000. Accordingly, this excess payment must be either a distributive share or a guaranteed payment. Because the $4,000 payment is not contingent on partnership earnings, it is taxed as a guaranteed payment. The partnership deducts the $4,000 payment, and Sam recognizes $4,000 of ordinary income.

In summary, Sam receives $34,000 as a payment on his retirement from the STU Partnership, $4,000 of which is considered a guaranteed payment taxed as ordinary income to Sam and deductible by the partnership. The remaining $30,000 Sam receives is in exchange for his interest in partnership property. Because the $30,000 cash payment exceeds his $25,000 basis in his partnership interest, he recognizes a $5,000 gain on the liquidating distribution. The partnership gets no deduction for the $30,000, which is considered a distribution. ◀

If the partnership has Sec. 751 assets, the calculations for a retiring partner are slightly more difficult. First, payments for substantially appreciated inventory and unrealized receivables are payments for property and must be analyzed using the liquidating distribution rules along with Sec. 751. The remainder of the transaction is analyzed as indicated above. (For partnership retirements only, unrealized receivables do not include recapture items.)

A retiring partner who receives payments from the partnership is considered to be a partner in that partnership for tax purposes until he or she receives the last payment. Likewise, a deceased partner's successor-in-interest is a member of the partnership until receiving the last payment.[26]

EXCHANGE OF A PARTNERSHIP INTEREST
EXCHANGE FOR ANOTHER PARTNERSHIP INTEREST. A partner also may terminate a partnership interest by exchanging it for either an interest in another partnership or a different interest in the same partnership. Exchanges involving interests in different partnerships do not qualify for like-kind exchange treatment.[27] Nevertheless, the IRS allows exchanges of interests within a single partnership.[28]

---

[26] Reg. Sec. 1.736-1(a)(1)(ii).
[27] Sec. 1031(a)(2)(D).

[28] Rev. Rul. 84-52, 1984-1 C.B. 157.

EXAMPLE C10-24 ▶ Pam and Dean are equal partners in the PD General Partnership, which owns and operates a farm. The two partners agree to convert PD into a limited partnership, with Pam becoming a limited partner and Dean having both a general and a limited partnership interest in PD. Even though the partners exchange a general partnership interest for a limited partnership interest (plus an exchange of a general partnership interest for a general partnership interest for Dean), they recognize no gain or loss on the exchange. If, however, a partner's interest in the partnership's liabilities is changed, that partner's basis must be adjusted. If liabilities are reduced and a deemed distribution exceeding the basis for the partnership interest occurs, the partner must recognize gain on the excess. ◀

EXCHANGE FOR CORPORATE STOCK. A partnership interest may be exchanged for corporate stock in a transaction that qualifies under the Sec. 351 nonrecognition rules (see Chapter C2). For Sec. 351 purposes, a partnership interest is property. If the other Sec. 351 requirements are met, a single partner's partnership interest can be transferred for stock in a new or an existing corporation in a nontaxable exchange. This exchange is taxed to the partner as if he or she had exchanged any other property under the Sec. 351 rules. The basis in the corporate stock is determined by the partner's basis in the partnership interest. The holding period for the stock received in the exchange includes the holding period for the partnership interest. As a result of the exchange, one of the corporation's assets is an interest in a partnership, and the corporation (not the transferor) is now the partner of record. Thus, the corporation must report its distributive share of partnership income along with its other earnings.

INCORPORATION. When limited liability is important, the entire partnership may choose to incorporate. Normally such an incorporation can be structured to fall within the Sec. 351 provisions and can be partially or totally tax exempt. When a partnership chooses to incorporate, three possible alternatives are available:

▶ The partnership contributes its assets and liabilities to the corporation in exchange for the corporation's stock. The partnership then distributes the stock to the partners in a liquidating distribution of the partnership.

▶ The partnership liquidates by distributing its assets to the partners. The partners then contribute the property to the new corporation in exchange for its stock.

▶ The partners contribute their partnership interests directly to the new corporation in exchange for its stock. The partnership liquidates, with the corporation receiving all the partnership's assets and liabilities.

The tax implications of the incorporation and the impact of partnership liabilities, gain to be recognized, basis in the corporate assets, and the new shareholders' bases in their stock and securities may differ depending on the form chosen for the transaction.[29]

FORMATION OF AN LLC OR LLP. A second option for obtaining limited liability protection for all owners is for the partnership to become an LLC. Under the check-the-box regulations, an LLC with more than one member is treated as a partnership unless it elects to be taxed as a corporation (see Chapter C2). If the LLC elects to be taxed as a C or an S corporation, the transfer of the property to the LLC falls under the incorporation rules discussed above. If the LLC is treated as a partnership, Rev. Rul. 95-37[30] specifies that the transfer will be viewed as a partnership-to-partnership transfer. The property transfer does not cause the partners to recognize gain or loss nor does the transfer terminate the tax year for the partnership or any partner. The basis for the partners' interest in the partnership will be changed only if the liability shares for the partners change.

If a partnership chooses LLP status to reduce some of the liability risks facing the partners, the change from partnership to LLP status also falls under the partnership-to-partnership transfer rules described above. The transfer does not cause the partners to recognize

[29] Rev. Rul. 84-111, 1984-2 C.B. 88. In addition, Reg. Secs. 301.7701-1, 2, and 3 describe the tax consequences of a partnership electing to be taxed as a corporation under the check-the-box regulations.

[30] 1995-1 C.B. 130.

gain or loss nor does the property transfer terminate the tax year for the partnership or any partner. Basis for the partners' interest in the partnership will be changed only if the liability shares for the partners change.[31]

Topic Review C10-2 summarizes the tax consequences of a number of alternative methods for terminating an investment in a partnership.

INCOME RECOGNITION AND TRANSFERS OF A PARTNERSHIP INTEREST

The partnership tax year closes with respect to any partner who sells or exchanges his or her entire interest in a partnership or any partner whose interest in the partnership is liquidated. The partnership tax year closes on the sale or exchange date or the date of final payment on a liquidation. As a result, that partner's share of all items earned by the partnership must be reported in the partner's tax year that includes the transaction date.[32]

A partner's tax year also closes on the date of death. The partner's final return will include all partnership income up to the date of death.

OBJECTIVE 8

Determine whether a partnership has terminated for tax purposes

TERMINATION OF A PARTNERSHIP

EVENTS CAUSING A TERMINATION TO OCCUR. Because of the complex relationships among partners and their liability for partnership debts, state partnership laws provide for the termination of a partnership under a wide variety of conditions. Section 708(b), however, avoids the tax complexity created by the wide variety of state laws and the numerous termination conditions. That IRC section provides that a partnership terminates for tax purposes only if

---

Topic Review C10-2

Terminating an Investment in a Partnership

METHOD	TAX CONSEQUENCES TO PARTNER
Death or retirement:	
Amounts paid for property[a]	Liquidating distribution tax consequences apply to the amount paid.
Amounts paid in excess of property values:	
Amounts not determined by reference to partnership income	Ordinary income.
Amounts determined by reference to partnership income	Distributive share of partnership income.
Sale of partnership interest to outsider	Capital gain (loss) except for ordinary income (loss) reported on Sec. 751 assets and Sec. 1250 gain on depreciable real property.
Exchange for partnership interest:	
In same partnership	No tax consequences
In different partnership	Capital gain (loss) except for ordinary income (loss) on Sec. 751 assets and Sec. 1250 gain on depreciable real property.
Exchange for corporate stock	No gain or loss generally recognized if it qualifies for Sec. 351 tax-free treatment.
	If the exchange does not qualify for Sec. 351 treatment, capital gain (loss) except for ordinary income (loss) on Sec. 751 assets and Sec. 1250 gain on depreciable real property.
Incorporation of partnership	Tax consequences depend on form of transaction used for incorporation.
Formation of LLC or LLP	No tax consequences except for distributions or contributions deemed to occur if liability shares change.

[a]Only for a general partner departing from a service partnership, property excludes unrealized receivables and goodwill if it is not mentioned in the partnership agreement.

---

[31] Ibid.

[32] Sec. 706(c)(2).

▶ No part of any business, financial operation, or venture of the partnership continues to be carried on by any of its partners in a partnership or

▶ Within a 12-month period a sale or exchange of at least 50% of the total interest in partnership capital and profits occurs.

TYPICAL MISCONCEPTION

Taxpayers often do not understand the difference between a partnership tax year closing for a specific partner versus a partnership tax year closing for all partners due to a termination of the partnership itself. The tax consequences of these two events are drastically different.

NO BUSINESS OPERATED AS A PARTNERSHIP. If no partner continues to operate any business of the partnership through the same or another partnership, the original partnership terminates. To avoid termination, the partnership must maintain partners and business activity. For example, if one partner retires from a two-person partnership and the second partner continues the business alone, the partnership terminates. However, if one partner in a two-member partnership dies, the partnership does not terminate as long as the deceased's estate or successor-in-interest continues to share in the profits and losses of the partnership business.[33]

Likewise, a partnership terminates if it ceases to carry on any business or financial venture. The courts, however, have allowed a partnership to continue under this rule even though the partnership sold all its assets and retained only a few installment notes.[34] Despite the courts' flexibility in these circumstances, a partnership should maintain more than a nominal level of assets if continuation of the partnership is desired.

KEY POINT

For the 50% rule to terminate a partnership, a *sale* or *exchange* of 50% or more of the capital *and* profits interests must occur. Sales or exchanges occurring within a 12-month period are aggregated; however, if the same interest is sold twice within 12 months, it is only counted once.

SALE OR EXCHANGE OF AT LEAST A 50% INTEREST. The second condition that terminates a partnership is the sale or exchange of at least a 50% interest in both partnership capital and profits within a 12-month period.[35] The relevant 12-month period is determined without reference to the tax year of either the partnership or any partner but rather is any 12 consecutive months. To cause termination, the partner must transfer the partnership interest by sale or exchange. Transactions or occurrences that do not constitute a sale or exchange (e.g., the gifting of a partnership interest or the transferring of a partnership interest at death) do not cause a partnership to terminate as long as partners continue the partnership business. Likewise, as long as at least two partners remain, the removal of a partner who owns more than 50% of the total partnership capital and profits interests can be accomplished without terminating the partnership by making a liquidating distribution.[36]

Measuring the portion of the total partnership capital and profits interest transferred often presents difficulties. Multiple exchanges of the same partnership interest are counted only once for purposes of determining whether the 50% maximum is exceeded. When several different small interests are transferred within a 12-month period, the partnership's termination occurs on the date of the transfer that first crosses the 50% threshold.[37]

EXAMPLE C10-25 ▶ On August 1, 2006, Miguel sells his 30% capital and profits interest in the LMN Partnership to Steve. On June 1, 2007, Steve sells the 30% interest acquired from Miguel to Andrew. For purposes of Sec. 708, the two sales are considered to be the transfer of a single partnership interest. Thus, the LMN Partnership does not terminate unless other sales of partnership interests occur totaling at least 20% of LMN's capital and profits interests during any 12-month period that includes either August 1, 2006, or June 1, 2007. ◀

EXAMPLE C10-26 ▶ On July 15, 2006, Kelly sells Carlos a 37% capital and profits interest in the KRS Partnership. On November 14, 2006, Rick sells Diana a 10% capital and profits interest in the KRS Partnership. On January 18, 2007, Sherrie sells Evan a 5% capital and profits interest in the KRS Partnership. The KRS Partnership terminates on January 18, 2007, because the cumulative interest sold within the 12-month period that includes January 18, 2007, first exceeds 50% on that date. ◀

EFFECTS OF TERMINATION.
Importance of Timing. When a partnership terminates, its tax year closes, requiring the partners to include their share of partnership earnings for the short-period partnership tax

---

[33] Reg. Sec. 1.708-1(b)(1)(i)(A).
[34] For example, see *Max R. Ginsburg v. U.S.*, 21 AFTR 2d 1489, 68-1 USTC ¶9429 (Ct. Cls., 1968).
[35] Under Sec. 774(c), an electing large partnership does *not* terminate solely because 50% or more of its interests are sold within a 12-month period.

[36] Reg. Sec. 1.708-1(b)(1)(ii).
[37] Ibid.

year in their tax returns. If the termination is not properly timed, partnership income for a regular 12-month tax year already may be included in the same return that must include the short tax year, resulting in more than 12 months of partnership income or loss being reported in some partners' tax returns. As partners and partnerships are increasingly forced to adopt the same tax year, this problem will lessen.

EXAMPLE C10-27 ▶ Joy is a calendar year taxpayer who owns a 40% capital and profits interest in the ATV Partnership. ATV has a natural business year-end of March 31 and with IRS permission uses that date as its tax year-end. For the partnership tax year ending March 31, 2006, Joy has an $80,000 distributive share of ordinary income. Pat, who owns the remaining 60% capital and profits interests, sells his interest to Collin on November 30, 2006. Because more than 50% of the capital and profits interests have changed hands, the ATV Partnership terminates on November 30, 2006, and the partnership's tax year ends on that date.

Joy's tax return for the tax year ending December 31, 2006, must include the $80,000 distributive share from the partnership tax year for the period April 1, 2005, through March 31, 2006, and the distributive share of partnership income for the short tax year including the period April 1, 2006, through November 30, 2006. ◀

Liquidating Distributions and Contributions. When a termination occurs for tax purposes, the partnership is deemed to have made a pro rata liquidating distribution to all partners. Accordingly, the partners must recognize gain or loss under the liquidating distribution rules. An actual liquidating distribution may occur if the termination occurs because of the cessation of business. However, if the termination occurs because of a 50% or greater change in ownership of the capital and profits interests, an actual distribution usually does not occur. In this case, the new group of partners continue the business, and Treasury Regulations provide for the termination of the old partnership and the formation of a new partnership. Specifically, the old partnership is deemed to contribute all its property and liabilities to a new partnership in exchange for the interests in the new partnership. The old partnership then is deemed to liquidate by distributing its only remaining asset (the interests in the new partnership) to its partners.[38]

EXAMPLE C10-28 ▶ The AB Partnership terminates for tax purposes on July 15 when Anna sells her 60% capital and profits interest to Diane for $123,000. The partnership has no liabilities, and its assets at the time of termination are as follows:

Assets	Basis	FMV
Cash	$ 20,000	$ 20,000
Receivables	30,000	32,000
Inventory	22,000	28,000
Building	90,000	95,000
Land	40,000	30,000
Total	$202,000	$205,000

Beth, a 40% partner in the AB Partnership, has an $80,800 basis in her partnership interest at the time of the termination. She has held her AB Partnership interest for three years at the time of the termination.

The old AB Partnership is deemed to transfer all its assets to a new partnership (NewAB) on July 15 in exchange for all the interests in NewAB. The old partnership then is deemed to transfer all the NewAB interests to the partners of the old partnership (Diane and Beth). At this point, the old AB Partnership ceases to exist because it no longer has partners, nor does it carry on any business.

The basis and holding period of the assets held by NewAB are identical to the basis and holding period of the old AB Partnership assets.[39] The basis of Beth's interest in NewAB is identical to her basis in her interest in the AB Partnership ($80,800).[40] Her holding period for the NewAB partnership interest begins when she acquired the old AB Partnership interest. Diane's basis in her partnership interest is its $123,000 cost, and her holding period begins when she purchases the interest. ◀

---

[38] Reg. Sec. 1.708-1(b)(1)(iv).
[39] Secs. 723 and 1223(2).

[40] Sec. 722.

Changes in Accounting Methods. The termination ends all partnership elections. Thus, the new partnership must make all elections concerning its tax year and accounting methods in its first new tax year.

MERGERS AND CONSOLIDATIONS

When two or more partnerships join together to form a new partnership, the parties to the transaction must determine which, if any, of the old partnerships are continued and which are terminated. An old partnership whose partner(s) own more than 50% of the profits and capital interests of the new partnership is considered to be continued as the new partnership.[41] Accordingly, the new partnership must continue with the tax year and accounting methods and elections of the old partnership that is considered to continue. All the other old partnerships are considered to have been terminated.

EXAMPLE C10-29 ▶

The AB and CD Partnerships merge to form the ABCD Partnership. April and Ben each own 30% of ABCD, and Carole and David each own 20% of ABCD. The ABCD Partnership is considered a continuation of the AB Partnership because April and Ben, the former partners of AB, own 60% of ABCD. ABCD is bound by the tax year, accounting method, and other elections made by AB. CD, formerly owned by Carole and David, is considered to terminate on the merger date. ◀

In some combinations, the partners of two or more of the old partnerships might hold the requisite profits and capital interest in the new partnership. When two or more old partnerships satisfy this requirement, the old partnership credited with contributing the greatest dollar value of assets to the new partnership is considered the continuing partnership, and all other partnerships terminate. Sometimes, none of the old partnerships account for more than 50% of the capital and profits of the new partnership. In that case, all the old partnerships terminate, and the merged partnership is a new entity that can make its own tax year and accounting method elections.

EXAMPLE C10-30 ▶

Three partnerships merge to form the ABCD Partnership. The AB Partnership (owned by Andy and Bill) contributes assets valued at $140,000 to ABCD. BC Partnership (owned by Bill and Cathy) and CD Partnership (owned by Cathy and Drew) contribute assets valued at $180,000 and $120,000, respectively. The capital and profits interests of the partners in the new partnership are Andy, 20%; Bill, 35%; Cathy, 19%; and Drew, 26%. Both the AB and BC Partnerships had partners who now own more than 50% of the new partnership (Andy and Bill own 55%, and Bill and Cathy own 54%). The BC Partnership contributed more assets ($180,000) to the new partnership than did the AB Partnership ($140,000). Therefore, the ABCD Partnership is a continuation of the BC Partnership. Both the AB and CD Partnerships terminate on the merger date. ◀

DIVISION OF A PARTNERSHIP

When a partnership divides into two or more new partnerships, all the new partnerships whose partners own collectively more than 50% of the profits and capital interests in the old partnerships are considered a continuation of the old partnership.[42] All partnerships that are continuations of the old partnership are bound by the old partnership's tax year and accounting method elections. Any other partnership created by the division is considered a new partnership eligible to make its own tax year and accounting method elections. If no new partnership meets the criteria for continuation of the divided partnership, the divided partnership terminates on the division date. The interest of any partner of the divided partnership who does not own an interest in a continuing partnership is considered to be liquidated on the division date.

EXAMPLE C10-31 ▶

The RSTV Partnership is in the real estate and insurance business. Randy owns a 40% interest and Sam, Thomas, and Vicki each own 20% of RSTV. The partners agree to split the partnership, with the RS Partnership receiving the real estate operations and the TV Partnership receiving the insurance business. Because Randy and Sam own more than 50% of the RSTV Partnership (40% + 20% = 60%), the RS Partnership is a continuation of the RSTV Partnership and must report its results using the same tax year and accounting method elections that RSTV used.

---

[41] Sec. 708(b)(2)(A).

[42] Sec. 708(b)(2)(B).

Thomas and Vicki are considered to have terminated their interests in RSTV and to have received a liquidating distribution of the insurance business property. The TV Partnership makes its tax year and accounting method elections following the rules for a new partnership. ◀

OPTIONAL AND MANDATORY BASIS ADJUSTMENTS

OBJECTIVE 9

Understand the effect of optional and mandatory basis adjustments

In general, a partnership makes no adjustment to the basis of its property when a partner sells or exchanges his or her interest in the partnership, when a partner's interest transfers upon the partner's death, or when the partnership makes a property distribution to a partner. A partnership, however, may adjust basis of its assets if the partnership makes an **optional basis adjustment** election under Sec. 754. The following paragraphs compare the consequences of having no election to having such an election. The discussion focuses primarily on sale transactions but also briefly mentions distributions. Once made, the Sec. 754 election applies to all subsequent transfers of partnership interests (e.g., sales, exchanges, and transfers upon death) and all subsequent distributions. In addition, the partnership may have to make a **mandatory basis adjustment** in certain circumstances even if a Sec. 754 election is not in effect.

ADJUSTMENTS ON TRANSFERS

OPTIONAL ADJUSTMENT. If a new incoming partner purchases his or her partnership interest from an existing partner, the new partner's basis in the partnership interest equals the purchase price plus the new partner's share of partnership liabilities. The new partner's basis in the partnership is likely to be different from his or her share of basis of the underlying assets in the partnership. This difference could lead to inequitable results as demonstrated by the following example.

EXAMPLE C10-32 ▶ Amy, Bill, and Corey each own a one-third interest in ABC partnership, which has the following simple balance sheet:

	Basis	FMV
Assets:		
Cash	$30,000	$ 30,000
Inventory	60,000	90,000
Total	$90,000	$120,000
Liabilities and capital:		
Liabilities	$15,000	$ 15,000
Capital—Amy	25,000	35,000
—Bill	25,000	35,000
—Corey	25,000	35,000
Total	$90,000	$120,000

Eric purchases Amy's one-third interest for $35,000 cash and assumes her $5,000 share of partnerships liabilities. Eric pays this amount because one-third the FMV of the underlying partnership assets is $40,000 (1/3 × $120,000). In addition, the cash paid plus Eric's share of partnership liabilities gives him a $40,000 basis in his new partnership interest. Amy's basis at the time of sale is $30,000. Therefore, Amy recognizes a $10,000 gain ($40,000 amount realized − $30,000 basis). Amy's $10,000 gain also reflects her share of the difference between the inventory's FMV and basis at the partnership level. Thus, her gain will be ordinary income under Sec. 751.

Now suppose the partnership later sells the inventory for $90,000. The partnership recognizes $30,000 of ordinary income. Therefore, each partner, Bill, Corey, and Eric, recognizes a $10,000 distributive share of ordinary income from that sale, and each partner increases the basis of his partnership interest by the same amount. Accordingly, Eric increases his basis in the partnership from $40,000 to $50,000. In this situation, Eric appears to be taxed on the same gain as was Amy even though he paid a FMV price for his partnership interest (and the underlying partnership assets).

However, this result primarily is an issue of timing and possibly character of income and loss. For example, suppose further that, sometime after selling the inventory, the partnership distributes the $120,000 cash to the partners in liquidation. Eric would receive $40,000 and recognize a $10,000 ($40,000 distribution − $50,000 basis) capital loss.

In short, with no optional basis adjustment election in effect, Eric recognizes $10,000 of ordinary income when the partnership sells the inventory and a $10,000 capital loss when the partnership liquidates. This timing difference could be substantial if the partnership remains in existence for a long time. Also, the capital loss may offset only capital gains and up to $3,000 of ordinary income in the partner's personal tax return. ◄

ADDITIONAL COMMENT

The situation of a new partner purchasing an interest in a partnership is a good example of where a partner's outside basis can differ significantly from his or her share of the partnership's inside basis. The Sec. 754 election mitigates this difference.

AMOUNT OF THE ADJUSTMENT. An incoming partner might view the situation in Example C10-32 as unacceptable and wish the partnership to make a Sec. 754 election. If the partnership makes such an election or has a Sec. 754 election already in effect, Sec. 743 mandates a special basis adjustment equal to the difference between the transferee (purchasing) partner's basis in the partnership interest and the transferee partner's share of basis of partnership assets. This basis adjustment, arising from a transfer, belongs only to the transferee partner (and not to the other partners), and it eliminates the inequities noted in Example C10-32.

EXAMPLE C10-33 ► Assume the same facts as in Example C10-32 except the partnership makes a Sec. 754 election. Eric's optional basis adjustment is calculated as follows:

Cash purchase price	$35,000
Share of partnership liabilities	5,000
Initial basis in partnership	$40,000
Minus: Eric's share of partnership's basis in assets (1/3 × $90,000)[43]	(30,000)
Optional basis adjustment	$10,000

Now when the partnership sells the inventory, Eric has an additional $10,000 basis in his share of the inventory that offsets the $10,000 income he otherwise would recognize. The other partners, however, still recognize their $10,000 distributive shares of income. Because Eric recognizes no income, he does not increase his partnership basis. Suppose the partnership liquidates sometime after selling the inventory. Again, Eric receives a $40,000 distribution, but he recognizes no capital gain or loss ($40,000 distribution − $40,000 basis). Thus, the optional basis adjustment eliminated both the timing and character differences that occurred in Example C10-32. ◄

MANDATORY ADJUSTMENT. For sales or exchanges of partnership interests occurring after October 22, 2004, the 2004 Jobs Act imposes a mandatory basis adjustment if the partnership has a substantial built-in loss and has no Sec. 754 optional basis adjustment election in effect. A substantial built-in loss exists if the partnership's adjusted basis in its property exceeds the FMV of the property by more than $250,000. Congress enacted this provision to prevent the doubling of losses. Exceptions to the new rule apply to certain specialized partnerships, discussion of which is beyond the scope of this textbook.

EXAMPLE C10-34 ► David, Ellen, and Frank each own a one-third interest in DEF partnership, which has the following simple balance sheet:

	Basis	FMV
Assets:		
Cash	$ 100,000	$100,000
Land	1,100,000	800,000
Total	$1,200,000	$920,000

---

[43] In some cases, the calculation of the transferee's share of the partnership's basis in assets can be more complicated than shown in this example. See Reg. Sec. 1.743-1(d).

Capital:		
David	$ 400,000	$300,000
Ellen	400,000	300,000
Frank	400,000	300,000
Total	$1,200,000	$900,000

Gwen purchases David's one-third interest for $300,000 cash, which gives Gwen a $300,000 initial basis in her new partnership interest. David's partnership interest basis at the time of sale is $400,000. Therefore, he recognizes a $100,000 loss. David's $100,000 loss also reflects his share of the difference between the land's FMV and basis at the partnership level.

Now suppose the partnership has no optional basis adjustment election in effect and later sells the land for $800,000. The partnership recognizes a $300,000 loss. As a result, each partner, Ellen, Frank, and Gwen, recognizes a $100,000 distributive share of that loss, and each partner decreases the basis of his or her partnership interest by the same amount. As a result, both David and Gwen recognize a $100,000 loss. To prevent this doubling of losses, the partnership must make a $100,000 mandatory downward basis adjustment with respect to Gwen's share of the land, thereby nullifying her distributive share of loss on the land sale. The adjustment is mandatory because the partnership has a substantial built-in loss (i.e., its $300,00 built-in-loss exceeds $250,000). Note that, without this mandatory adjustment, Gwen's $100,000 loss would be temporary because her partnership basis would be reduced to $200,000, causing her to recognize a $100,000 gain should the partnership liquidate and distribute $300,000 to her. Nevertheless, Congress chose to eliminate the initial doubling of losses by requiring the mandatory basis adjustment. ◄

OTHER ISSUES. Examples C10-32 through C10-34 assume inventory or land is the only asset other than cash. If the assets instead had been depreciable property, the basis adjustments would give the transferee partner additional depreciation deductions in Examples C10-32 and C10-33 or reduced depreciation deductions in example C10-34. Also, if a partnership has more than one asset other than cash, the optional or mandatory basis adjustment must be allocated to the assets under special rules found in Sec. 755 and related Treasury Regulations. These allocation rules are beyond the scope of this text.

ADJUSTMENTS ON DISTRIBUTIONS

OPTIONAL ADJUSTMENT. As mentioned earlier, if a partnership distributes property to a partner, the partnership makes no adjustment to the basis of its remaining property unless an optional basis adjustment election is in place or unless the mandatory basis adjustment rule discussed later applies. If the partnership has made a Sec. 754 election, the partnership makes the following adjustments upon the distribution to a partner:

▶ Increases the basis of *partnership* property by:

1. Any gain recognized by the distributee partner on the distribution (e.g., cash distribution exceeding the partner's basis in his or her partnership interest)

2. The amount by which the distributee partner decreases the basis of property received in a property distribution from the basis of the property in the partnership's hands

▶ Decreases the basis of *partnership* property by:

1. Any loss recognized by the distributee partner on a liquidating distribution

2. The amount by which the distributee partner increases the basis of property received in a property distribution from the basis of the property in the partnership's hands

Unlike the optional basis adjustments arising from a transfer of partnership interest, the basis adjustments arising from a distribution belong to the partnership as a whole. These adjustments eliminate many (but not all) basis and timing disparities resulting from distributions.

A partnership should take care in making a Sec. 754 election because, once made, the election affects many transactions in complicated ways. Moreover, the election can cause downward as well as upward adjustments. Finally, the election has long-range implications because it can be revoked only with IRS approval. The IRS will not grant such approval if the primary purpose of the revocation is to avoid reducing the basis of partnership assets.

MANDATORY ADJUSTMENT. The discussion of the optional basis adjustment for distributions included increases and decreases to partnership property. For distributions occuring after October 22, 2004, the 2004 Jobs Act makes the decreasing basis adjustment mandatory if it exceeds $250,000. As with exchange transactions, Congress enacted this provision to prevent the doubling of losses. In effect, the mandatory adjustment rule applies only to liquidating distributions because such decreasing adjustments cannot occur in nonliquidating distribution situations.

SPECIAL FORMS OF PARTNERSHIPS

Here, we examine a series of special partnership forms, including tax shelters organized as limited partnerships, publicly traded partnerships, limited liability companies, limited liability partnerships, and electing large partnerships.

TAX SHELTERS AND LIMITED PARTNERSHIPS

Tax shelters at their best are good investments that reduce and/or defer the amount of an investor's tax bill. Traditionally, shelter benefits arise from leverage, income deferral, deduction acceleration, and tax credits.

Before the Tax Reform Act of 1986, limited partnerships were the primary vehicle for tax shelter investments. However, the Tax Reform Act of 1986 greatly reduced the benefits of limited partnerships as tax shelters by invoking the passive activity loss limitations for activity conducted in a limited partnership form. The limited partnership, however, still allows an investor to limit liability while receiving the benefits of the shelter's tax attributes to save taxes on other passive income. Since the Tax Reform Act of 1986, limited partnerships that generate passive income rather than losses have become popular investments for investors who already hold loss-generating limited partnership interests. (See Problem C9-46 in the previous chapter for an example of tax deferred benefits and their elimination by the at-risk and passive activity loss limitations.)

PUBLICLY TRADED PARTNERSHIPS

The Revenue Act of 1987 moved to restrict still further the benefits of tax shelter ownership by changing the taxation of **publicly traded partnerships** (PTPs). A PTP is a partnership whose interests are traded either on an established securities exchange or in a secondary market or the equivalent thereof. A partnership that meets the requirements is taxed as a C corporation under Sec. 7704.

Two exceptions apply to partnerships that otherwise would be classified as PTPs:

▶ Partnerships that have 90% or more of their gross income being "qualifying income" continue to be taxed under the partnership rules.

▶ Partnerships that were in existence on December 17, 1987 and have not added a substantial new line of business since that date are grandfathered. In general, application of the PTP rules for these partnerships was delayed until tax years beginning after December 31, 1997.

The Taxpayer Relief Act of 1997 added an election that allows the grandfathered partnerships to continue to be treated as partnerships after the original ten-year window and until the election is revoked. To elect to continue to be treated as a partnership, the publicly traded partnership (which must have been taxed as a partnership under the grandfather provision) must agree to pay a 3.5% annual tax on gross income from the active conduct of any trade or business.[44] The election may be revoked by the partnership, but once revoked, it cannot be reinstated.

---

[44] Sec. 7704(g)(3).

For the 90% of gross income test, Sec. 7704(d) defines qualifying income to include certain interest, dividends, real property rents (but not personal property rents), income and gains from the sale or disposition of a capital asset or Sec. 1231(b) trade or business property held for the production of passive income, and gain from the sale or disposition of real property. It also includes gains from certain commodity trading and natural resource activities. Any PTP not taxed as a corporation because of this 90% exception is subject to separate and more restrictive Sec. 469 passive loss rules than are partnerships that are not publicly traded.

If a partnership is first classified as a PTP taxed as a corporation during a tax year, the PTP incurs a deemed contribution of all partnership assets and all partnership liabilities to a corporation in exchange for all the corporation's stock. The stock is then deemed distributed to the partners in complete liquidation of the partnership. This transaction is taxed exactly as if it had physically occurred.

LIMITED LIABILITY COMPANIES

In recent years, the limited liability company (LLC) has emerged as a popular form of business entity in the United States. The LLC combines the legal and tax benefits of partnerships and S corporations. Currently, all 50 states have adopted LLC laws. The LLC business form combines the advantage of limited liability for all its owners with the ability of achieving the conduit treatment and the flexibility of being taxed as a partnership.

In the past, whether an LLC was characterized as a corporation or a partnership for federal tax purposes depended on the number of corporate characteristics the entity possessed, such as limited liability, free transferability of interests, centralized management, and continuity of life. The process of determining tax treatment was complex and time consuming. However, in December 1996, the Treasury Department issued regulations that allow entities (other than corporations and trusts) to choose whether to be taxed as a partnership or as an association. (An association is an unincorporated entity taxed as a corporation.) According to these check-the-box regulations, an LLC with two or more members can choose either partnership or association tax treatment. With a written and properly filed election, any LLC can choose to be taxed as an association. If the LLC makes no such election, an LLC with two or more members is treated as a partnership for tax purposes, while a single member LLC is treated as a sole proprietorship.

As already mentioned, an LLC with two or more members that does not elect association status is a partnership for tax purposes and is subject to all the rules applicable to other partnerships. Thus, the formation of the LLC; income, gain, loss, and deductions that flow through to the LLC members; current and liquidating distributions; and sale, gift, or exchange of an interest in the LLC all fall under the partnership rules. An LLC treated as a partnership is subject to the Sec. 704 rules for special allocations and allocations of precontribution gain or loss, to the Sec. 736 rules for retirement distributions, and to the Sec. 751 rules.

Using the LLC form for a business with publicly traded ownership interests is likely to result in taxation as a corporation. Even if the LLC does not elect association status, the public trading of the ownership interest brings the LLC under the publicly traded partnership rules. As discussed above, these rules result in the business being taxed as a corporation unless 90% or more of the income is qualifying income or unless the LLC is covered under the grandfather rules. However, given the recency of LLCs as a form for conducting business, the grandfather provisions are unlikely to apply.

If an LLC is treated as a partnership, it offers greater flexibility than does an S corporation because it is not subject to the restrictions that apply to S corporations as to the number of shareholders, the number of classes of stock, or the types of investments in related entities that the entity can make. Moreover, unlike S corporations, LLCs can use the special allocation rules of Sec. 704 to allocate income, gain, loss or deductions to their members. Finally, each member's basis in the LLC interest includes that member's share of the organization's debts (and not just shareholder debt as with an S corporation).

LIMITED LIABILITY PARTNERSHIPS

Many states have added limited liability partnerships (LLPs) to the list of business forms that can be formed. Under the current state laws, the primary difference between a general partnership and an LLP is that in a limited liability partnership, a partner is not liable

TAX STRATEGY TIP

The list of advantages of an LLC over an S corporation is substantial and suggests that an LLC should always be seriously considered as an option for a passthrough entity. However, one current, important advantage of an S corporation is that the shareholders are not subject to self-employment taxes on their share of the entity's earnings.

REAL-WORLD EXAMPLE

All the Big 4 accounting firms and a number of other national accounting firms operate as LLPs. Many local and regional professional accounting and law firms also have changed to LLPs.

REAL-WORLD EXAMPLE
Even though the non-responsible partners in an LLP are not liable for the responsible partner's negligence, all partners and employees can suffer if the partnership itself is deemed guilty, as demonstrated by the demise of a former Big 5 accounting firm several years ago.

for damages resulting from failures in the work of other partners or of people supervised by other partners. For example, assume that a limited liability accounting partnership is assessed damages in a lawsuit that resulted from an audit partner in New York being negligent in an audit. The tax partner for the same firm, who is based in San Diego and who had no involvement with the audit or the auditor, should not be liable to pay damages resulting from the suit.

Like a general or limited partnership, this business form is a partnership for tax purposes. All the partnership tax rules and regulations apply to this business form just as they do to any other partnership.

 STOP & THINK

Question: What issues do you expect the check-the-box regulations to raise for new businesses making their initial choice of entity decision? What effect do you expect these regulations to have on existing corporations?

Solution: Consider the options facing a new business. The business can be formed as a C corporation, which provides limited liability protection to owners but subjects the corporate income to double taxation. A business formed as a C corporation can make an S election for tax purposes, which keeps the limited liability protection for the owners and eliminates the double taxation by taxing all income directly to the owners. However, as you will see in Chapter C11, numerous restrictions prevent many corporations from electing S status. In addition, all income and loss of an S corporation must be allocated among the shareholders on a pro rata basis. A partnership offers the most flexible tax treatment with no double taxation of income, but the traditional partnership must have at least one general partner whose liability for partnership debts is not limited. An LLC, which is treated as a partnership, provides limited liability protection to its owners while avoiding both the double taxation of income found in a regular C corporation as well as the restrictions placed on S corporations. Because an LLC is treated as a partnership, the income and loss shares reported by each partner is flexible, and the partner's basis for his partnership interest includes his or her share of the LLC's liabilities. In some senses, the LLC has the best attributes of both the corporation and the partnership.

These are strong reasons why a new entity would choose to form as an LLC and elect to be treated as a partnership. However, because the LLC is a relatively new business form, statutes, case law, and regulations are still being developed, and thus many areas of uncertainty remain to be resolved over time.

The check-the-box regulations are likely to be of much less interest to existing C corporations and S corporations because an existing corporation must liquidate (with all the tax consequences of a liquidation, as described in Chapter C6) before it can form as an LLC. Potentially, the change in entity form has a very high tax cost for an existing corporation.

OBJECTIVE 10

Determine the appropriate reporting for the income of an electing large partnership

ELECTING LARGE PARTNERSHIPS

Partnerships that qualify as "large partnerships" may elect to be taxed under a simplified reporting arrangement.[45] The partnership must meet the following four qualifications to be treated as an electing large partnership:

▶ It must not be a service partnership.

▶ It must not be engaged in commodity trading.

▶ It must have at least 100 partners.

▶ It must file an election to be taxed as an electing large partnership.

Section 775 defines a service partnership as one in which substantially all the partners perform substantial services in connection with the partnership's activities or the partners are retired but in the past performed substantial services in connection with the partnership's activities. One example of a partnership that could not make this election is a partnership that provides accounting services. An electing large partnership also cannot be engaged in commodity trading. Further, to qualify to make this election, the partnership

---

must have at least 100 partners (excluding those partners who do provide substantial services in connection with the partnership's business activities) throughout the tax year.

Once it makes the election, the partnership reports its income under a simplified reporting scheme, is subject to different rules about when the partnership terminates, and is subject to a different system of audits. The election is irrevocable without IRS permission.

ELECTING LARGE PARTNERSHIP TAXABLE INCOME. Much like other partnerships, the calculation of electing large partnership taxable income includes separately stated income and other income. However, the items that must be separately stated are very different for the electing large partnership. Likewise, the items included in other income differ significantly. The main reason that Congress added electing large partnerships to the IRC was to provide a form of flow-through entity that does not require so much separate reporting to each partner of many different income, loss, and deduction items. Simpler reporting from the partnership to the partners was the goal, so fewer items are separately stated and many more items are combined at the partnership level.

Like a regular partnership, calculation of an electing large partnership's taxable income is similar to the calculation for an individual. For an electing large partnership (just like for other partnerships), the deductions for personal exemptions and net operating losses are disallowed as well as most additional itemized deductions, such as medical expenses and alimony. However, calculation of the items that would qualify as miscellaneous itemized deductions for an individual differs from the calculation for either individuals or other partnerships. For an electing large partnership, miscellaneous itemized deductions are combined at the partnership level and subject to a 70% deduction at the partnership level. After the 70% deduction, the remaining miscellaneous itemized deductions are combined with other income and passed through to the partners. Because they are combined with other income at the partnership level, they are not subject to the 2% nondeductible floor at the individual partner level.[46]

Instead of flowing through as a separately stated item as they do with a regular partnership, charitable contributions made by an electing large partnership are subject to the 10% of taxable income limit similar to the limit that normally applies to corporations. Once the limit is applied, the partnership deducts allowable charitable contribution from its ordinary income, and the partners do not report the charitable contributions as a separate item.[47]

For a regular partnership, the first-year expensing deduction allowed under Sec. 179 is both limited at the partnership level and is separately stated and limited at the partner level. For an electing large partnership, the only limit is at the partnership level. The allowable deduction is calculated at the partnership level, and the deduction amount offsets the partnership's ordinary income. For an electing large partnership, the Sec. 179 deduction is not separately stated and the impact of the Sec. 179 deduction is buried in the ordinary income amount reported by the partnership to the partners.

SEPARATELY STATED LARGE PARTNERSHIP ITEMS. An electing large partnership nevertheless is a pass-through entity, so some items still must be separately stated at the partnership level, and these items maintain their character when reported in the partners' tax returns. Section 772 lists the following items the electing large partnership must report separately:

▶ Taxable income or loss from passive loss limitation activities

▶ Taxable income or loss from other partnership activities

▶ Net capital gain or loss from passive loss limitation activities

▶ Net capital gain or loss from other partnership activities

▶ Tax-exempt interest

▶ Applicable net alternative minimum tax adjustment separately computed for passive loss limitation activities and other activities

---

[46] Sec. 773(b).

[47] Sec. 773(b)(2).

► General credits
► Low income housing credit
► Rehabilitation credit
► Foreign income taxes
► Credit for producing fuel from a nonconventional source
► Any other item the IRS determines should be separately stated

The differences between the treatment of other partnerships versus electing large partnerships is significant. The most interesting aspect of this list is what items are combined for reporting by an electing large partnership. For example, Sec. 1231 gains and losses are netted at the partnership level, net 1231 losses are included in ordinary income or loss, and net 1231 gains are reported with capital gains and losses. The capital gains and losses also are combined at the partnership level with only a single, net number reported to the partners. The capital gain or loss is treated as long-term at the partner level. However, if the net is a short-term capital gain, that gain is treated as ordinary income and combined at the partnership level with other ordinary income items. All the partnership's credits are combined at the partnership level with the exceptions of the low income housing credit and the rehabilitation credit.

Both ordinary income and capital gains attributed to passive loss activities are reported separately from the results of other partnership activities. In addition, the taxable income or loss from activities other than passive activities generally are treated as items of income or expense with respect to property held for investment rather than as active trade or business income. Dividend income, for example, would fall into this category.

For the electing large partnership, all limits, such as the charitable contributions limit and the Sec. 179 expensing deduction limit, are applied at the partnership level rather than at the individual partner level with three exceptions. The three limits applied at the partner level are the Sec. 68 limit on itemized deductions, the limit on at risk losses, and the limit on passive activity losses.[48] For the limitation to be applied at the partner level, these items must be separately stated.

For separately stated items, the character of amounts flowing through the partnership retain their character when reported on the partners' tax returns. However, because many more items are combined at the partnership level and not separately stated, the character of many fewer kinds of income is retained to flow through with the electing large partnership form.

EXAMPLE C10-35 ► The ABC Partnership is an electing large partnership that reports the following transactions for the current year. ABC has no passive activities.

Net long-term capital loss	$100,000
Sec. 1231 gain	120,000
Ordinary income	40,000
Dividend income	10,000
Charitable contributions	30,000
Tax-exempt income	4,000

ABC will report these earnings to its partners as follows:

Long-term capital gain	$20,000
Ordinary income	33,000
Dividend income	10,000
Tax-exempt income	4,000

Because the partnership has a net Sec. 1231 gain, it is treated as a long-term capital gain ($120,000) and combined at the partnership level with the long-term capital loss ($100,000) to result in a net long-term capital gain of $20,000. At the partnership level, the charitable contribution deduction is limited to 10% of taxable income, or $7,000 [0.10 × ($20,000 capital gain + $10,000 dividend income + $40,000 ordinary income)] and is subtracted from ordinary income of $40,000 before ordinary income is reported to the partners. The

---

character of the long-term capital gain, dividend income, tax-exempt income, and ordinary income pass through to the partner. ◄

REPORTING REQUIREMENT. An electing large partnership must provide a Schedule K-1 to each of its partners on or before March 15 following the close of the partnership tax year without regard to when the partnership tax return is due.[49] Partnerships that are not electing large partnerships are only required to provide the information return by the due date of the partnership tax return—which, for a calendar year partnership, is April 15. The IRS expects that the March 15 provision will reduce the number of partners who must file an extension of their individual tax returns because they do not receive the Schedule K-1 from a regular partnership early enough to file a timely individual return.

TERMINATION OF THE PARTNERSHIP. Because electing large partnerships are quite large and often may be widely traded, Congress decided to change the conditions under which these partnership will be considered to terminate. An electing large partnership terminates only if its partners cease to conduct any business, financial operation, or venture in a partnership form. Unlike other partnerships, an electing large partnership will not terminate because of the sale or exchange of partnership interests involving at least a 50% interest in partnership capital or profits during a 12-month period.[50]

ELECTING LARGE PARTNERSHIP AUDITS. An electing large partnership is not subject to the partnership audit rules but is subject to a much more restrictive set of partnership audit procedures.[51] First, all electing large partnership partners must report all items of partnership income, gain, loss, or deduction in the way the partnership reports the item. Deviations from that partnership reporting will be "corrected" by the IRS just as a math mistake is corrected.[52]

Because all partners are required to use identical reporting for partnership items, it becomes somewhat easier to audit partnership results only at the partnership level. Notice of audit proceedings, determination of errors, settlement offers, appeals proceedings, and court cases are all handled at the partnership level, and no individual partner can request separate treatment or refuse to participate in the partnership level result. In general, any adjustments determined at the partnership level by an audit agreement or court decision will be considered to be income or deduction that occurs in the year of the agreement or decision.[53] Accordingly, the effect of adjustments is borne by the partners who own interests in the year of the agreement or decision and not by the partners who originally reported the contested transaction results.

TAX PLANNING CONSIDERATIONS

LIQUIDATING DISTRIBUTION OR SALE TO PARTNERS

An unusual tax planning opportunity exists when one partner withdraws from a partnership and the remaining partners proportionately increase their ownership of the partnership. The partners can structure the ownership change as either a liquidating distribution made by the partnership or as a sale of the partnership interest to the remaining partners. In fact, the substance of the two transactions is the same, only the form is different. However, this difference in form can make a substantial difference in the tax consequences in a number of areas.

► If the transferor partner receives payment for his or her interest in the partnership's Sec. 751 assets, he or she must recognize ordinary income no matter how the transaction is structured. The partnership's basis in Sec. 751 assets is increased in the case of

---

[49] Sec. 6031.
[50] Sec. 774(c).
[51] Sec. 6240.

[52] Sec. 6241.
[53] Sec. 6242.

a liquidating distribution. When a sale transaction takes place, the partnership's basis in Sec. 751 assets is increased only if the partnership has an optional basis adjustment election in effect.

▶ If the partnership has an optional basis adjustment election in effect, the allocation of the adjustment to the individual partnership assets can be different depending on whether the transaction is structured as a sale or as a liquidating distribution.

▶ If the interest being transferred equals or exceeds 50% of the profits and capital interests, a sale to the remaining partners terminates the partnership. A liquidating distribution does not cause a termination to occur.

Because the tax implications of the sale transaction and liquidating distribution alternatives are both numerous and complex, the partners should make their choice only after careful consideration. (See the Tax Strategy Problem below.)

PROBLEM MATERIALS

DISCUSSION QUESTIONS

C10-1 Javier is retiring from the JKL Partnership. In January of the current year, he has a $100,000 basis in his partnership interest when he receives a $10,000 cash distribution. The partnership plans to distribute $10,000 each month this year, and Javier will cease to be a partner after the December payment. Is the January payment to Javier a current distribution or a liquidating distribution?

C10-2 Lia has a $40,000 basis in her partnership interest just before receiving a parcel of land as a nonliquidating (current) distribution. The partnership purchased the land, and Lia has no precontribution gain. Under what conditions will Lia's basis in the land be $40,000? Under what conditions will Lia's basis in the land be a carryover basis from the partnership's basis in the land?

C10-3 Mariel has a $60,000 basis in her partnership interest just before receiving a parcel of land as a liquidating distribution. She has no remaining precontribution gain and will receive no other distributions. Under what conditions will Mariel's basis in the land be $60,000?

C10-4 Cindy has a $4,000 basis in her partnership interest before receiving a nonliquidating (current) distribution of property having a $4,500 basis and a $6,000 FMV from the CDE Partnership. Cindy has a choice of receiving either inventory or a capital asset. She will hold the distributed property as an investment for no more than two years before she sells it. What tax difference (if any) will occur as a result of Cindy's selection of one property or the other to be distributed by the partnership?

C10-5 The AB Partnership purchases plastic components and assembles children's toys. The assembly operation requires a number of special machines that are housed in a building the partnership owns. The partnership has depreciated all its property under MACRS. The partnership sells the toys on account to a number of retail establishments and uses the accrual method of accounting. Identify any items you think might be classified as unrealized receivables.

C10-6 Which of the following items are considered to be inventory for purposes of Sec. 751?
a. Supplies
b. Inventory
c. Notes receivable
d. Land held for investment purposes
e. Lots held for resale

C10-7 Explain the conditions under which Sec. 751 has an impact on nonliquidating (current) distributions.

C10-8 What conditions are required for a partner to recognize a loss upon receipt of a distribution from a partnership?

C10-9 Can the basis of unrealized receivables and inventory received in a liquidating distribution be greater to the partner than to the partnership? Can the basis of unrealized receivables and inventory received in a distribution be smaller to the partner than to the partnership? Explain.

C10-10 Can a partner recognize both a gain and a loss on the sale of a partnership interest? If so, under what conditions?

C10-11 Tyra has a zero basis in her partnership interest and a share in partnership liabilities, which are quite large. Explain how these facts will affect the taxation of her departure from the partnership using the following methods of terminating her interest in the partnership.
a. A liquidating distribution of property
b. A sale of the partnership interest to a current partner for cash

C10-12 Tom is a 55% general partner in the RST Partnership. Tom wants to retire, and the other two partners, Stacy and Rich, want to continue the partnership business. They agree that the partnership will liquidate Tom's interest in the partnership by paying him 20% of partnership profits for each of the next ten years. Explain why Sec. 736 does (or does not) apply to the partnership's payments to Tom.

C10-13 Lucia has a $20,000 basis in her limited partnership interest before her retirement from the partnership. Her share of partnership assets have a $23,000 FMV, and the partnership has no Sec. 751 assets. In addition to being paid cash for her full share of partnership assets, Lucia will receive a share of partnership income for the next three years. Explain Lucia's tax treatment for the payments she receives.

C10-14 What are the advantages and disadvantages to the partnership and its partners when a partnership termination is caused by a sale of at least a 50% capital and profits interest?

C10-15 What is a publicly traded partnership? Are all publicly traded partnerships taxed as corporations?

C10-16 What are the advantages of a firm being formed as a limited liability company (LLC) instead of as a limited partnership?

C10-17 What is an electing large partnership? What are the advantages to the partnership of electing to be taxed under the electing large partnership rules?

ISSUE IDENTIFICATION QUESTIONS

C10-18 When Kayla's basis in her interest in the JKL Partnership is $30,000, she receives a current distribution of office equipment. The equipment has an FMV of $40,000 and basis of $35,000. Kayla will not use the office equipment in a business activity. What tax issues should Kayla consider with respect to the distribution?

C10-19 Joel receives a $40,000 cash distribution from the JM Partnership, which reduces his partnership interest from one-third to one-fourth. The JM Partnership is a general partnership that uses the cash method of accounting and has substantial liabilities. JM's inventory has appreciated substantially since it was purchased. What issues should Joel consider with regard to the distribution?

C10-20 Scott sells his one-third partnership interest to Sally for $43,000 when his basis in the partnership interest is $33,000. On the date of sale, the partnership has no liabilities and the following assets:

Assets	Basis	FMV
Cash	$30,000	$30,000
Inventory	12,000	21,000
Building	45,000	60,000
Land	12,000	18,000

The partnership has claimed $5,400 of straight-line depreciation on the building. What tax issues should Scott and Sally consider with respect to the sale transaction?

C10-21 David owns a 60% interest in the DDD Partnership, a general partnership, which he sells to the two remaining partners—Drew and Dana. The three partners have agreed that David will receive $150,000 in cash from the sale. David's basis in the partnership interest before the sale is $120,000, which includes his $30,000 share of partnership recourse liabilities. The partnership has assets with a $300,000 FMV and a $200,000 adjusted basis. What issues should David, Drew, and Dana consider before this sale takes place?

C10-22 Andrew and Beth are equal partners in the AB Partnership. On December 30 of the current year, the AB Partnership agrees to liquidate Andrew's partnership interest for a cash payment on December 30 of each of the next five years. What tax issues should Andrew and Beth consider with respect to the liquidation of Andrew's partnership interest?

C10-23 Alex owns 60% of the Hot Wheels LLC, which is treated as a partnership. He plans to give 15% of the LLC (one-fourth of his interest) to his daughter Haley for her high school graduation. He plans to put her interest in a trust, and he will serve as the trustee until Haley is 21. The trust will receive any distributions from the LLC, but Haley is unlikely to be given any of the cash until she is age 21. Alex's 60% interest has a $120,000 FMV and an $80,000 adjusted basis including his $48,000 share of the LLC's liabilities. Alex works full time for the LLC for a small salary and his share of LLC income. Alex also has a special allocation of income from rental property he manages for the LLC. What issues should Alex consider before he completes the gift?

C10-24 Krypton Company recently has been formed as a limited liability company (LLC). Krypton Company is owned equally by three individuals—Jeff, Susan, and Richard—all of whom have substantial income from other sources. Krypton is a manufacturing firm and expects to earn approximately $130,000 of ordinary income and $30,000 of long term capital gain each year for the next several years. Jeff will be a full time manager and will receive a salary of $60,000 each year. What tax issues should the owners consider regarding the LLC's initial year of operations?

C10-25 XYZ Limited Partnership has more than 300 partners and is publicly traded. XYZ was grandfathered under the 1987 Tax Act and has consistently been treated as a partnership. In the current year, XYZ will continue to be very profitable and will continue to pay out about 30% of its income to its owners each year. The managing partners of XYZ want to consider the firm's options for taxation in the current and later years.

PROBLEMS

C10-26 *Current Distributions.* Lisa has a $25,000 basis in her partnership interest before receiving a current distribution of $4,000 cash and land with a $30,000 FMV and a $14,000 basis to the partnership. Assume that any distribution involving Sec. 751 property is pro rata and that any precontribution gains have been recognized before the distribution.
  a. Determine Lisa's recognized gain or loss, Lisa's basis in distributed property, and Lisa's ending basis in her partnership interest.
  b. How does your answer to Part a change if the partnership's basis in the land is $24,000 instead of $14,000?
  c. How does your answer to Part a change if Lisa receives $28,000 cash instead of $4,000 (along with the land)?
  d. How does your answer to Part a change if, in addition to the cash and land, Lisa receives inventory with a $25,000 FMV and a $10,000 basis and receivables with a $3,000 FMV and a zero basis?
  e. Suppose instead that Lisa receives the distribution in Part a from a C corporation instead of a partnership. The corporation has $100,000 of E&P before the distribution, and Lisa's stock basis before the distribution is $25,000. What are the tax consequences to Lisa and the C corporation?
  f. Note: This part can be answered only after the student studies Chapter C11 but is placed here to allow comparison with Parts a and e. Suppose instead that Lisa receives the distribution in Part a from an S corporation instead of a partnership. Lisa is a 50% owner in the corporation, and her stock basis before the distribution is $25,000. What are the tax consequences to Lisa and the S corporation?

C10-27 *Current Distributions.* Complete the chart for each of the following independent distributions. Assume all distributions are nonliquidating and pro rata to the partners, and no contributed property was distributed. All precontribution gain has been recognized before these distributions.

	Partner's Basis and Gain/Loss	Property Distributed	Property's Basis to Partnership	Property's FMV	Property's Basis to Partner
a. Basis:					
Predistribution	$20,000	Cash	$ 6,000	$ 6,000	
Postdistribution	$_____	Land	4,000	15,000	$_____
Gain or loss	$_____	Machinery	3,000	2,000	$_____
b. Basis:					
Predistribution	$20,000	Cash	$ 3,000	$ 3,000	
Postdistribution	$_____	Land	6,000	4,000	$_____
Gain or loss	$_____	Inventory	7,000	7,500	$_____
c. Basis					
Predistribution	$26,000	Cash	$35,000	$35,000	
Postdistribution	$_____	Land—Parcel 1	6,000	10,000	$_____
Gain or loss	$_____	Land—Parcel 2	18,000	18,000	$_____

d. Basis:

Predistribution	$28,000	Land—Parcel 1	$ 4,000	$ 6,000	$_____
Postdistribution	$_____	Land—Parcel 2	6,000	10,000	$_____
Gain or loss	$_____	Land—Parcel 3	4,000	10,000	$_____

C10-28 *Current Distribution with Precontribution Gain.* Three years ago, Mario joined the MN Partnership by contributing land with a $10,000 basis and an $18,000 FMV. On January 15 of the current year, Mario has a basis in his partnership interest of $20,000, and none of his precontribution gain has been recognized. On January 15, Mario receives a current distribution of a property other than the contributed land with a $15,000 basis and a $23,000 FMV.
a. Does Mario recognize any gain or loss on the distribution?
b. What is Mario's basis in his partnership interest after the distribution?
c. What is the partnership's basis in the land Mario contributed after Mario receives this distribution?

C10-29 *Current Distribution of Contributed Property.* Andrew contributed investment land having an $18,000 basis and a $22,000 FMV along with $4,000 in money to the ABC Partnership when it was formed. Two years later, the partnership distributed the investment land Andrew had contributed to Bob, another partner. At the time of the distribution, the land had a $21,000 FMV, and Andrew and Bob's bases in their partnership interests were $21,000 and $30,000, respectively.
a. What gain or loss must be recognized on the distribution, and who must recognize it?
b. What are the bases for Andrew and Bob's interests in the partnership after the distribution?
c. What is Bob's basis in the distributed land?

C10-30 *Current Distribution of Contributed Property.* The ABC Partnership made the following current distributions in the current year. The dollar amounts listed are the amounts before considering any implications of the distribution.

	Property Received			
Partner	Type of Property	Basis	FMV	Partner's Basis in Partnership Interest
Alonzo	Land	$ 4,000	$10,000	$19,000
Beth	Inventory	1,000	10,000	15,000
Cathy	Cash	10,000	10,000	18,000

The land Alonzo received had been contributed by Beth two years ago when its basis was $4,000 and its FMV was $8,000. The inventory Beth received had been contributed by Cathy two years ago when its basis was $1,000 and its FMV was $4,000. For each independent situation, what gain or loss must be recognized? What is the basis of the distributed property after the distribution? What are the bases of the partnership interests after the distribution? Assume the distribution has no Sec. 751 implications.

C10-31 *Current Distribution with Sec. 751.* The KLM Partnership owns the following assets on March 1 of the current year:

Assets	Partnership's Basis	FMV
Cash	$ 30,000	$ 30,000
Receivables	–0–	16,000
Inventory	50,000	52,000
Supplies	6,000	6,500
Equipment[a]	9,000	10,500
Land (investment)	40,000	65,000
Total	$135,000	$180,000

[a] The partnership has claimed depreciation of $4,000 on the equipment.

a. Which partnership items are unrealized receivables?
b. Is the partnership's inventory substantially appreciated?
c. Assume the KLM Partnership has no liabilities and that Kay's basis for her partnership interest is $33,750. On March 1 of the current year, Kay receives a $20,000 current distribution in cash, which reduces her partnership interest from one-third to one-fourth. What are the tax results of the distribution (i.e., the amount and character of any gain, loss, or income recognized and Kay's basis in her partnership interest)?

C10-32 *Current Distribution with Sec. 751.* The JKLM Partnership owns the following assets on October 1 of the current year:

Assets	Partnership's Basis	FMV
Cash	$ 48,000	$ 48,000
Receivables	12,000	12,000
Inventory	21,000	24,000
Machinery[a]	190,000	240,000
Land	36,500	76,000
Total	$307,500	$400,000

[a]Sale of the machinery for its FMV would result in $50,000 of Sec. 1245 depreciation recapture. Thus, the machinery's FMV and original cost are the same numerical value, $240,000.

a. Which partnership items are unrealized receivables?
b. Is the partnership's inventory substantially appreciated?
c. Assume the JKLM Partnership has no liabilities and Jack's basis in his partnership interest is $76,875. On October 1 of the current year, Jack receives a $25,000 current distribution in cash, which reduces his partnership interest from one-fourth to one-fifth. What are the tax results of the distribution (i.e., the amount and character of any gain, loss, or income recognized and Jack's basis in his partnership interest)?

C10-33 *Current Distribution with Sec. 751.* The PQRS Partnership owns the following assets on December 30 of the current year:

Assets	Partnership's Basis	FMV
Cash	$ 20,000	$ 20,000
Receivables	–0–	40,000
Inventory	80,000	100,000
Total	$100,000	$160,000

The partnership has no liabilities, and each partner's basis in his or her partnership interest is $25,000. On December 30 of the current year, Paula receives a current distribution of inventory having a $10,000 FMV, which reduces her partnership interest from one-fourth to one-fifth. What are the tax consequences of the distribution to the partnership, Paula, and the other partners?

C10-34 *Liquidating Distributions.* Assume the same four independent distributions as in Problem C10-27. Fill in the blanks in that problem assuming the only change in the facts is that the distributions are now liquidating distributions instead of nonliquidating distributions.

C10-35 *Liquidating Distribution.* Marinda is a one-third partner in the MWH Partnership before she receives $100,000 cash as a liquidating distribution. Immediately before Marinda receives the distribution, the partnership has the following assets:

Assets	Partnership's Basis	FMV
Cash	$100,000	$100,000
Marketable securities	50,000	90,000
Investment land	90,000	140,000
Total	$240,000	$330,000

At the time of the distribution, the partnership has $30,000 of outstanding liabilities, which the three partners share equally. Marinda's basis in her partnership interest before the distribution was $80,000, which includes her share of liabilities. What are the amount and character of the gain or loss recognized by Marinda and the MWH Partnership on the liquidating distribution?

C10-36 *Liquidating Distributions.* The AB Partnership pays its only liability (a $100,000 mortgage) on April 1 of the current year and terminates that same day. Alison and Bob were equal partners in the partnership but have partnership bases immediately preceding these transactions of $110,000 and $180,000, respectively, including his or her share of liabilities. The two partners receive identical distributions with each receiving the following assets:

Assets	Partnership's Basis	FMV
Cash	$ 20,000	$ 20,000
Inventory	33,000	35,000
Receivables	10,000	8,000
Building	40,000	60,000
Land	15,000	10,000
Total	$118,000	$133,000

The building has no depreciation recapture potential. What are the tax implications to Alison, Bob, and the AB Partnership of the April 1 transactions (i.e., basis of assets to Alison and Bob, amount and character of gain or loss recognized, etc.)?

C10-37 *Liquidating Distribution.* The LQD Partnership distributes the following property to Larry in a distribution that liquidates Larry's interest in the partnership. Larry's basis in his partnership interest before the distribution is $40,000. The adjusted bases and FMVs of the distributed property to the partnership before the distribution are as follows:

	Partnership's Basis	FMV
Cash	$ 2,500	$ 2,500
Inventory	8,000	9,000
Capital asset 1	10,000	15,000
Capital asset 2	15,000	17,500
Total	$35,500	$44,000

a. Determine Larry's basis in each distributed asset.
b. Same as Part a except Larry's partnership basis before the distribution is $46,500.
c. Same as Part b except the basis of capital asset 2 is $20,000 instead of $15,000.

C10-38 *Sale of a Partnership Interest.* Pat, Kelly, and Yvette are equal partners in the PKY Partnership before Kelly sells her partnership interest. On January 1 of the current year, Kelly's basis in her partnership interest, including her share of liabilities, was $35,000. During January, the calendar year partnership earned $15,000 ordinary income and $6,000 of tax-exempt income. The partnership has a $60,000 recourse liability on January 1, and this amount remains constant throughout the tax year. Kelly's share of that liability is $20,000. The partnership has no other liabilities. Kelly sells her interest on February 1 to Margaret for a cash payment of $45,000. On the sale date the partnership had the following assets:

Assets	Partnership's Basis	FMV
Cash	$ 20,000	$ 20,000
Inventory	60,000	120,000
Building	36,000	40,000
Land	10,000	15,000
Total	$126,000	$195,000

The partnership has claimed $5,000 of depreciation on the building using the straight-line method.
a. What is Kelly's basis in her partnership interest on February 1 just before the sale?
b. What are the amount and character of Kelly's gain or loss on the sale?
c. What is Margaret's basis in her partnership interest?
d. What is the partnership's basis in its assets after the sale?

C10-39 *Sale of Partnership Interest and Termination.* Clay owned 60% of the CAP Partnership and sold one-half of his interest (30%) to Steve for $75,000 cash. Before the sale, Clay's basis in his entire partnership interest was $168,000 including his $30,000 share of partnership liabilities and his share of income up to the sale date. Partnership assets on the sale date were

Assets	Partnership's Basis	FMV
Cash	$ 50,000	$ 50,000
Inventory	30,000	60,000
Land	200,000	190,000
Total	$280,000	$300,000

a. What are the amount and character of Clay's recognized gain or loss on the sale? What is his remaining basis in his partnership interest?

b. What is Steve's basis in his partnership interest?

c. How will the partnership's basis in its assets be affected?

d. How would your answers to Parts a and c change if Clay sold his entire interest to Steve for $150,000 cash?

C10-40 *Sale of a Partnership Interest.* Alice, Bob, and Charles are one-third partners in the ABC Partnership. The partners originally formed the partnership with cash contributions, so no partner has precontribution gains or losses. Prior to Alice's sale of her partnership interest, the partnership has the following balance sheet:

Assets	Partnership's Basis	FMV
Cash	$ 12,000	$ 12,000
Receivable	–0–	21,000
Inventory	57,000	72,000
Machinery[a]	90,000	132,000
Building[b]	120,000	165,000
Land	36,000	30,000
Investments[c]	15,000	48,000
Total	$330,000	$480,000

Liabilities and capital		
Liabilities	$105,000	$105,000
Partners' capital:		
Alice	75,000	125,000
Bob	75,000	125,000
Charles	75,000	125,000
Total	$330,000	$480,000

[a]The machinery cost $126,000, and the partnership has claimed $36,000 of depreciation.
[b]The building cost $150,000, and the partnership has claimed $30,000 of straight-line depreciation.
[c]The partnership has held the investments for more than one year.

Alice has a $110,000 basis in her partnership interest including her share of partnership liabilities, and she sells her partnership interest to Darla for $125,000 cash.

a. What are the amount and character of Alice's recognized gain or loss on the sale?

b. What is Darla's basis in her partnership interest?

C10-41 *Retirement of a Partner.* Suzanne retires from the BRS Partnership when the basis of her one-third interest is $105,000, which includes her share of liabilities. At the time of her retirement, the partnership had the following assets:

Assets	Partnership's Basis	FMV
Cash	$145,000	$145,000
Receivables	40,000	40,000
Land	130,000	220,000
Total	$315,000	$405,000

The partnership has $60,000 of liabilities when Suzanne retires. The partnership will pay Suzanne cash of $130,000 to retire her partnership interest.

a. What are the amount and character of the gain or loss Suzanne must recognize?

b. What is the impact of the retirement on the partnership and the remaining partners?

C10-42 *Retirement of a Partner.* Brian owns 40% of the ABC Partnership before his retirement on April 15 of the current year. On that date, his basis in the partnership interest is $40,000 including his share of liabilities. The partnership's balance sheet on that date is as follows:

	Partnership's Basis	FMV
Assets:		
Cash	$ 60,000	$ 60,000
Receivables	24,000	24,000
Land	16,000	40,000
Total	$100,000	$124,000
Liabilities and capital:		
Liabilities	$ 20,000	$ 20,000
Capital—Abner	16,000	20,800
—Brian	32,000	41,600
—Charles	32,000	41,600
Total	$100,000	$124,000

What are the amount and character of gain or loss that Brian and the ABC Partnership recognize for the following independent retirement payments?
a. Brian receives $41,600 cash on April 15.
b. Brian receives $50,000 cash on April 15.

C10-43 *Retirement of a Partner.* Kim retires from the KLM Partnership on January 1 of the current year. At that time, her basis in the partnership is $75,000, which includes her share of liabilities. The partnership reports the following balance sheet:

	Partnership's Basis	FMV
Assets:		
Cash	$100,000	$100,000
Receivables	30,000	30,000
Inventory	40,000	40,000
Land	55,000	100,000
Total	$225,000	$270,000
Liabilities and capital:		
Liabilities	$ 75,000	$ 75,000
Capital—Kim	50,000	65,000
—Larry	50,000	65,000
—Michael	50,000	65,000
Total	$225,000	$270,000

Explain the tax consequences (i.e., amount and character of gain or loss recognized and Kim's basis for any assets received) of the partnership making the retirement payments described in the following independent situations. Kim's share of liabilities is $25,000.
a. Kim receives $65,000 cash on January 1.
b. Kim receives $75,000 cash on January 1.

C10-44 *Death of a Partner.* When Jerry died on April 16 of the current year, he owned a 40% interest in the JM Partnership, and Michael owns the remaining 60% interest. All his assets are held in his estate for a two-year period while the estate is being settled. Jerry's estate is his successor-in-interest for the partnership interest. Under a formula contained in the partnership agreement, the partnership must pay Jerry's successor-in-interest $40,000 cash shortly after his death plus $90,000 for each of the two years immediately following a partner's death. The partnership agreement provides that all payments to a retiring partner will first be payments for the partner's share of assets, and then any additional payments will be Sec. 736(a) payments. When Jerry died, the partnership had the following assets:

Assets	Partnership's Basis	FMV
Cash	$100,000	$100,000
Land	200,000	300,000
Total	$300,000	$400,000

Jerry's basis for the partnership interest on the date of his death was $120,000 including his $30,000 share of partnership liabilities.

a. How will the payments be taxed to Jerry's successor-in-interest?

b. What are the tax implications of the payments for the partnership?

C10-45 *Death of a Partner.* Bruce died on June 1 of the current year. On the date of his death, he held a one-third interest in the ABC Partnership, which had a $100,000 basis including his share of liabilities. Under the partnership agreement, Bruce's successor-in-interest, his wife, is to receive the following amounts from the partnership: $130,000 cash, the partnership's assumption of Bruce's $20,000 share of partnership liabilities, plus 10% of partnership net income for the next three years. The partnership's assets immediately before Bruce's death are as follows:

Assets	Partnership's Basis	FMV
Cash	$100,000	$100,000
Receivables	90,000	90,000
Inventory	40,000	40,000
Land	70,000	220,000
Total	$300,000	$450,000

a. What are the amount and character of the gain or loss that Bruce's wife must recognize when she receives the first year's payment?

b. What is the character of the gain recognized from the partnership interest when she receives the payments in each of the following three years?

c. When does Bruce's successor-in-interest cease to be a member of the partnership?

C10-46 *Liquidation or Sale of a Partnership Interest.* John has a 60% capital and profits interest in the JAS Partnership with a basis of $333,600, which includes his share of liabilities, when he decides to retire. Andrew and Stephen want to continue the partnership's business. On the date John retires, the partnership's balance sheet is as follows:

	Partnership's Basis	FMV
Assets:		
Cash	$160,000	$160,000
Receivables	100,000	100,000
Building[a]	200,000	300,000
Land	96,000	180,000
Total	$556,000	$740,000
Liabilities and capital:		
Liabilities	$120,000	$120,000
Capital—John	261,600	372,000
—Andrew	87,200	124,000
—Stephen	87,200	124,000
Total	$556,000	$740,000

[a]The partnership has claimed $60,000 of straight-line depreciation on the building.

a. What are the tax implications for John, Andrew, Stephen, and the JAS Partnership if Andrew and Stephen each purchase one-half of John's partnership interest for a cash price of $186,000 each? Include in your answer the amount and character of the recognized gain or loss, basis of the partnership assets, and any other relevant tax implications.

b. What are the tax implications for John, Andrew, Stephen, and the JAS Partnership if the partnership pays John a liquidating distribution equal to 60% of each partnership asset other than cash plus $24,000 of cash? Assume the assets are easily divisible.

C10-47 *Liquidation or Sale of a Partnership Interest.* Amy, a one-third partner, retires from the AJS Partnership on January 1 of the current year. Her basis in her partnership interest is $120,000 including her share of liabilities. Amy receives $160,000 in cash from the partnership for her interest. On that date, the partnership balance sheet is as follows:

	Partnership's Basis	FMV
Assets:		
Cash	$180,000	$180,000
Receivables	60,000	60,000
Land	120,000	300,000
Total	$360,000	$540,000
Liabilities and capital:		
Liabilities	$ 60,000	$ 60,000
Capital—Amy	100,000	160,000
—Joan	100,000	160,000
—Stephanie	100,000	160,000
Total	$360,000	$540,000

a. What are the amount and character of Amy's recognized gain or loss?

b. How would your answers to Part a change if Joan and Stephanie each purchased one-half of Amy's partnership interest for $80,000 cash instead of having the partnership distribute the $160,000 in cash to Amy?

C10-48 *Exchange of Partnership Interests.* Josh holds a general partnership interest in the JLK Partnership having a $40,000 basis and a $60,000 FMV. The JLK Partnership is a limited partnership that engages in real estate activities. Diana has an interest in the CDE Partnership having a $20,000 basis and a $60,000 FMV. The CDE Partnership is a general partnership that also engages in real estate activities. Neither partnership has any Sec. 751 assets or any liabilities.

a. What are the tax implications if Josh and Diana simply exchange their partnership interests?

b. What are the tax implications if instead Diana exchanges her general partnership interest in the CDE Partnership for a limited partnership interest in the same partnership (and Josh retains his general partnership interest in the JLK Partnership)?

C10-49 *Termination of a Partnership.* Wendy, Xenia, and Yancy own 40%, 8%, and 52%, respectively, of the WXY Partnership. For each of the following independent situations occurring in the current year, determine whether the WXY Partnership terminates and, if so, the date on which the termination occurs.

a. Wendy sells her entire interest to Alan on June 1. Alan sells one-half of the interest to Beth on November 15.

b. Yancy receives a series of liquidating distributions totaling $100,000. He receives four equal annual payments on January 1 of the current year and the three subsequent years.

c. Wendy and Xenia each receive a liquidating distribution on September 14.

d. Yancy sells his interest to Karen on June 1 for $10,000 cash and a $90,000 installment note. The note will be paid in monthly installments of $10,000 principal plus interest (at a rate acceptable to the IRS) beginning on July 1.

e. The WXY and ABC Partnerships combine their businesses on December 30. Ownership of the new, combined partnership is as follows: Wendy, 20%; Xenia, 4%; Yancy, 26.5%; Albert, 20%; Beth, 19.5%; and Carl, 10%.

f. On January 1, the WXY Partnership divides its business into two new businesses. The WX Partnership is owned equally by Wendy and Xenia. Yancy continues his share of the business as a sole proprietorship.

C10-50 *Termination of a Partnership.* For each of the following independent situations, determine which partnership(s) (if any) terminate and which partnership(s) (if any) continue.

a. The KLMN Partnership is created when the KL Partnership merges with the MN Partnership. The ownership of the new partnership is held 25% by Katie, 30% by Laura, 25% by Michael, and 20% by Neal.

b. The ABC Partnership, with $150,000 in assets, is owned equally by Amy, Beth, and Chuck. The CD Partnership, with $100,000 in assets, is owned equally by Chuck and Drew. The two partnerships merge, and the resulting ABCD Partnership is owned as follows: Amy, 20%; Beth, 20%; Chuck, 40%; and Drew, 20%.

c. The WXYZ Partnership results when the WX and YZ Partnerships merge. Ownership of WXYZ is held equally by the four partners. WX contributes $140,000 in assets, and YZ contributes $160,000 in assets to the new partnership.

d. The DEFG Partnership is owned 20% by Dawn, 40% by Eve, 30% by Frank, and 10% by Greg. Two new partnerships are formed by the division of DEFG. The two new partnerships, the DE and FG Partnerships, are owned in proportion to their relative interests in the DEFG Partnership by the individuals for whom they are named.

e. The HIJK Partnership is owned equally by its four partners, Hal, Isaac, Juan, and Katherine, before its division. Two new partnerships, the HI and JK Partnerships, are formed out of the division with the new partnerships owned equally by the partners for whom they are named.

C10-51 *Disposal of a Tax Shelter.* Maria purchased an interest in a real estate tax shelter many years ago and deducted losses from its operation for several years. The real property owned by the tax shelter when Maria made her investment has been fully depreciated on a straight-line basis. Her basis in her limited partnership interest is zero, but her share of partnership liabilities is $100,000. Explain the tax results if Maria sells her partnership interest for $5 cash.

C10-52 *Optional Basis Adjustment.* Patty pays $100,000 cash for Stan's one-third interest in the STU Partnership. The partnership has a Sec. 754 election in effect. Just before the sale of Stan's interest, STU's balance sheet appears as follows:

	Partnership's Basis	FMV
Assets:		
Cash	$ 80,000	$ 80,000
Land	160,000	220,000
Total	$240,000	$300,000
Partners' capital		
Stan	$ 80,000	$100,000
Traffic Corporation	80,000	100,000
Union Corporation	80,000	100,000
Total	$240,000	$300,000

a. What is Patty's total optional basis adjustment?

b. If STU Partnership sells the land for its $220,000 FMV immediately after Patty purchases her interest, how much gain or loss will the partnership recognize?

c. How much gain will Patty report as a result of the sale?

C10-53 *Taxation of LLC Income.* ABC Company, a limited liability company (LLC) organized in the state of Florida, reports using a calendar tax year-end. The LLC chooses to be taxed as a partnership. Alex, Bob, and Carrie (all calendar year taxpayers) own ABC equally, and each has a basis of $40,000 in his or her ABC interest on the first day of the current tax year. ABC has the following results for the current year's operation:

Operating income	$30,000
Short-term capital gain	12,000
Long-term capital loss	6,000

Each owner received a $12,000 cash distribution during the current year.

a. What are the amount and character of the income, gain, and loss Alex must report on his tax return as a result of ABC's operations?

b. What is Alex's basis in his ownership interest in ABC after the current year's operations?

C10-54 *Electing Large Partnership.* Austin & Becker is an electing large partnership. During the current year, the partnership has the following income, loss, and deduction items:

Ordinary income	$5,200,000
Rental loss	(2,000,000)
Long-term capital loss from investments	(437,100)
Short-term capital gain from investments	827,400
Charitable contributions	164,000

a. What ordinary income will Austin & Becker report?

b. What are the separately stated items for Austin & Becker?

C10-55   *Electing Large Partnership.* Happy Times Film Distributions is an electing large partnership. During the current year, the partnership has the following income, loss, and deduction items:

Ordinary income	$ 700,000
Passive income	3,000,000
Sec. 1231 gains	27,000
Sec. 1231 losses	(134,800)
Long-term capital gains from investments	437,600
General business tax credits	43,000

a. What ordinary income will Happy Times report?

b. What are the separately stated items reported by Happy Times?

COMPREHENSIVE PROBLEMS

C10-56   Refer to the facts in Comprehensive Problem C6-54. Now assume the entity is a partnership named Lifecycle Partnership. Additional facts are as follows:

* Except for precontribution gains and losses, the partners agree to share profits and losses in a 60% (Able)—40% (Baker) ratio.

* The partners actively and materially participate in the partnership's business. Thus, the partnership is not a passive activity.

* Partnership debt is recourse debt.

* The salary to Able is a guaranteed payment.

* The refund for the NOL is not relevant to the partnership, nor are the E&P numbers.

* In addition to the numbers provided for the assets on January 2, 2009, the following partnership book values apply:

Equipment	$ 215,000
Building	926,000
Land A	30,000
Land B	20,000
Total	$1,191,000

* On January 2, 2009, the partnership sells its assets and pays off the $1.87 million debt. The partnership then makes liquidating distributions of the remaining cash to Able and Baker in accordance with their book capital account balances.

Required:

a. Determine the tax consequences of the partnership formation to Able, Baker, and Lifecycle Partnership.

b. For 2006–2008, prepare a schedule showing:

    (1) Partnership ordinary income and other separately stated items

    (2) Able's and Baker's book capital accounts at the end of 2006, 2007, and 2008

    (3) Able's and Baker's bases in their partnership interests at the end of 2006, 2007, and 2008

c. For 2009, determine:

    (1) The results of the asset sales

    (2) Able's and Baker's book capital accounts after the asset sales but before the final liquidating distribution

    (3) Able's and Baker's bases in their partnership interests after the asset sales but before the final liquidating distribution

    (4) The results of the liquidating distributions

C10-57   Anne decides to leave the ABC Partnership after owning the interest for many years. She owns a 52% capital, profits, and loss interest in the general partnership (which is not a service partnership). Anne's basis in her partnership interest is $120,000 just before she leaves the partnership. The partnership agreement does not mention payments to partners who leave the partnership. The partnership has not made an optional basis adjustment election (Sec. 754). All partnership liabilities are recourse liabilities, and Anne's share is equal to her loss interest. When Anne leaves the partnership, the assets and liabilities for the partnership are as follows:

	Partnership's Basis	FMV
Assets:		
Cash	$240,000	$240,000
Receivables	–0–	64,000
Inventory	24,000	24,000
Land	60,000	100,000
Total	$324,000	$428,000
Liabilities	$ 60,000	$ 60,000

Analyze the following two alternatives, and answer the associated questions for each alternative.

a. Anne could receive a cash payment of $220,000 from the partnership to terminate her interest in the partnership. Does Anne or the partnership have any income, deduction, gain, or loss? Determine both the amount and character of any items.

b. Carrie already owns a 30% general interest in the ABC partnership prior to Anne's departure. Carrie is willing to buy Anne's partnership interest for a cash payment of $220,000. What income, gain, loss, or deduction will Anne recognize on the sale? What are the tax implications for the partnership if Carrie buys Anne's interest?

TAX STRATEGY PROBLEM

C10-58 Consider the following balance sheet for DEF Partnership:

	Partnership's Basis	FMV
Assets:		
Cash	$60,000	$ 60,000
Receivables	–0–	60,000
Land A	10,000	20,000
Land B	10,000	20,000
Land C	10,000	20,000
Total	$90,000	$180,000
Partners' capital:		
Daniel	$30,000	$ 60,000
Edward	30,000	60,000
Frances	30,000	60,000
Total	$90,000	$180,000

Note: Land A, B, and C are Sec. 1231 property, and each partner's outside basis is $30,000.

Suppose Daniel wishes to exit the partnership completely. After discussions with Edward and Frances, the partners agree to let Daniel choose one of three options:

1. Daniel takes a liquidating distribution of $60,000 cash.
2. Daniel takes a pro rata liquidating distribution of $20,000 cash, $20,000 receivables, and Land A (FMV $20,000).
3. Daniel sells his entire partnership interest to Doris for $60,000 cash.

Required:

a. Determine the tax consequences to Daniel of each option including gains (losses) realized, recognized, and deferred; character of gains (losses); and bases of assets.

b. Discuss the relative merits of each option to Daniel, that is, what are the advantages and disadvantages of each option? What factors could sway your recommendation one way or the other?

Note: See Case Study Problem C10-59 for another situation involving various exit strategies.

CASE STUDY PROBLEM

C10-59 Mark Green and his brother Michael purchased land in Orlando, Florida many years ago. At that time, they began their investing as Green Brothers Partnership with capital they obtained from placing second mortgages on their homes. Their investments have flourished both because of the prosperity and growth of the area and because they have shown an ability to select prime real estate for others to develop. Over the years, they have acquired a great amount of land and have sold some to developers.

Their current tax year has just closed, and the partnership has the following balance sheet:

	Partnership's Basis	FMV
Assets:		
Cash	$200,000	$ 200,000
Accounts receivable	90,000	90,000
Land held for investment	310,000	1,010,000
Total	$600,000	$1,300,000
Liabilities and capital:		
Mortgages	$400,000	$ 400,000
Capital—Mark	100,000	450,000
—Michael	100,000	450,000
Total	$600,000	$1,300,000

Mark and Michael each have a basis in their partnership interest of $300,000 including their share of liabilities. They share the economic risk of loss from the liabilities equally. Last spring, Mark had a serious heart attack. On his doctor's advice, Mark wants to retire from all business activity and terminate his interest in the partnership. He is interested in receiving some cash now but is not averse to receiving part of his payment over time.

You have been asked to provide the brothers with information on how to terminate Mark's interest in the partnership. Several possibilities have occurred to Mark and Michael, and they want your advice as to which is best for Mark from a tax standpoint. Michael understands that the resulting choice may not be the best option for him. The possibilities they have considered include the following:

- Michael has substantial amounts of personal cash and could purchase Mark's interest directly. However, the brothers think that option probably would take almost all the cash Michael could raise, and they are concerned about any future cash needs Michael might have. They would prefer to have Mark receive $120,000 now plus $110,000 per year for each of the next three years. Mark also would receive interest at a market rate on the outstanding debt. This alternative would qualify for installment reporting. However, the installment sale rules for related parties would apply.

- The partnership could retire Mark's interest. They have considered the option of paying Mark $150,000 now plus 50% of partnership profits for the next three years. Alternatively, they could arrange for Mark to have a $150,000 payment now and a guaranteed payment of $100,000 per year for the next three years. They expect that the dollar amounts to be received by Mark would be approximately the same for the next three years under these two options. Mark also would receive interest at a market rate on any deferred payments.

- John Watson, a long-time friend of the family, has expressed an interest in buying Mark's interest for $450,000 cash immediately. Michael and John are comfortable that they could work well together.

Mark has substantial amounts of money in savings accounts and in stocks and bonds that have a ready market. He has invested in no other business directly. Assume that Mark's ordinary tax rate is 35% in each year and that his capital gains tax rate is 15%.

Required: Prepare a memorandum summarizing the advice you would give the two brothers on the options that they have considered.

TAX RESEARCH PROBLEMS

C10-60 Arnie, Becky, and Clay are equal partners in the ABC General Partnership. The three individuals have tax bases in their partnership interests of $80,000, $120,000, and $160,000, respectively, and their financial accounting capital accounts are equal. For business reasons, the partnership needs to be changed into the ABC Corporation, and all three owners agree to the change. The partnership is expected to have the following assets on the date that the change is to occur:

Assets	Partnership's Tax Basis	FMV	Partnership's Fin. Acctg. Book Value
Cash	$ 50,000	$ 50,000	$ 50,000
Accounts receivable	60,000	55,000	55,000
Inventory	150,000	200,000	150,000
Land	200,000	295,000	235,000
Total	$460,000	$600,000	$490,000

Liabilities of $100,000 are currently outstanding and will be owed on the exchange date. Liabilities are shared equally and, as always, are already included in the bases of the partnership interest. The structure being considered for making the change is as follows:

- ABC Partnership transfers all its assets and liabilities to the new ABC Corporation in exchange for all the corporation's stock.
- ABC Partnership then liquidates by distributing the ABC stock to Arnie, Becky, and Clay.

Required: The tax manager you work for has asked you to determine the tax and financial accounting consequences. Describe the financial and tax treatments in a short memorandum to the partnership. Be sure to mention any relevant IRC sections, Treasury Regulations, revenue rulings, and APB or FASB opinions.

C10-61 Della retires from the BCD General Partnership when her basis in her partnership interest is $70,000 including her $10,000 share of liabilities. The partnership is in the business of providing house cleaning services for local residences. At the date of Della's retirement, the partnership's balance sheet is as follows:

	Partnership's Basis	FMV
Assets:		
Cash	$ 50,000	$ 50,000
Receivables	–0–	30,000
Equipment[a]	40,000	50,000
Building[b]	90,000	100,000
Land	30,000	40,000
Total	$210,000	$270,000
Liabilities and capital:		
Liabilities	$ 30,000	$ 30,000
Capital—Bruce	60,000	80,000
—Celia	60,000	80,000
—Della	60,000	80,000
Total	$210,000	$270,000

[a]If the equipment were sold for $50,000, the entire gain would be recaptured as Sec. 1245 ordinary income.
[b]The building has been depreciated using the straight-line method.

Della will receive payments of $20,000 cash plus 5% of partnership ordinary income for each of the next five years. The partnership agreement specifies that goodwill will be paid for when a partner retires. Bruce, Celia, and Della agree that the partnership has $21,000 in goodwill when Della retires and that she will be paid for her one-third share.

Required: A tax manager in your firm has asked you to determine the amount and character of the income Della must report for each of the next five years. In addition, he wants you to research the tax consequences of the retirement on the partnership for the next five years. (Assume the partnership earns $100,000 of ordinary income each year for the next five years.) Prepare an oral presentation to be made to Della explaining the tax consequences of the payments she will receive.

C10-62 Pedro owns a 60% interest in the PD General Partnership having a $40,000 basis and $200,000 FMV. His share of partnership liabilities is $100,000. Because he is nearing retirement age, he has decided to give away his partnership interest on June 15 of the current year. The partnership's tax year ends on December 31. Pedro's tax year ends on June 30. He intends to give a 30% interest to his son, Juan, and the remaining 30% interest to the American Red Cross.

Required: A tax manager in your firm has asked you to prepare a letter to Pedro explaining fully the tax consequences of this gift to him, the partnership, and the donees. She reminds you to be sure to include information about the allocation of the current year's partnership income.

C10-63 Frank, Greta, and Helen each have a one-third interest in the FGH Partnership. On December 31, 2005, the partnership reported the following balance sheet:

Assets	Partnership's Basis	FMV
Cash	$120,000	$120,000
Asset 1	262,380	360,000
Asset 2	115,200	90,000
Total	$497,580	$570,000

Partners' Capital		
Frank	$165,860	$190,000
Greta	165,860	190,000
Helen	165,860	190,000
Total	$497,580	$570,000

The partnership placed Asset 1 (seven-year property) in service in 2003 and Asset 2 (five-year property) in service in 2004. The partnership did not elect Sec. 179 expensing and did not claim bonus depreciation. Accordingly, it computed the assets' adjusted bases at December 31, 2005 as follows:

		Asset 1		Asset 2
Cost		$600,000		$240,000
Depreciation:				
2003	$85,740			
2004	146,940		$48,000	
2005	104,940	(337,620)	76,800	(124,800)
Adjusted basis		$262,380		$115,200

On January 2, 2006, Helen sold her partnership interest to Hank for $190,000. At the time of sale, the partnership had a Sec. 754 optional basis election in effect but has not elected to use the remedial method for allocating partnership items.

Required: The partners have asked you to determine (1) the amount and character of Helen's gain or loss; (2) Hank's optional basis adjustment and its allocation to Asset 1 and Asset 2; and (3) the amount of depreciation allocated to Hank in 2006, including the effects of the optional basis adjustment. At a minimum, you should consult the following resources:

- IRC Secs. 743 and 751
- Reg. Sec. 1.743-1(j)
- Reg. Sec. 1.755-1

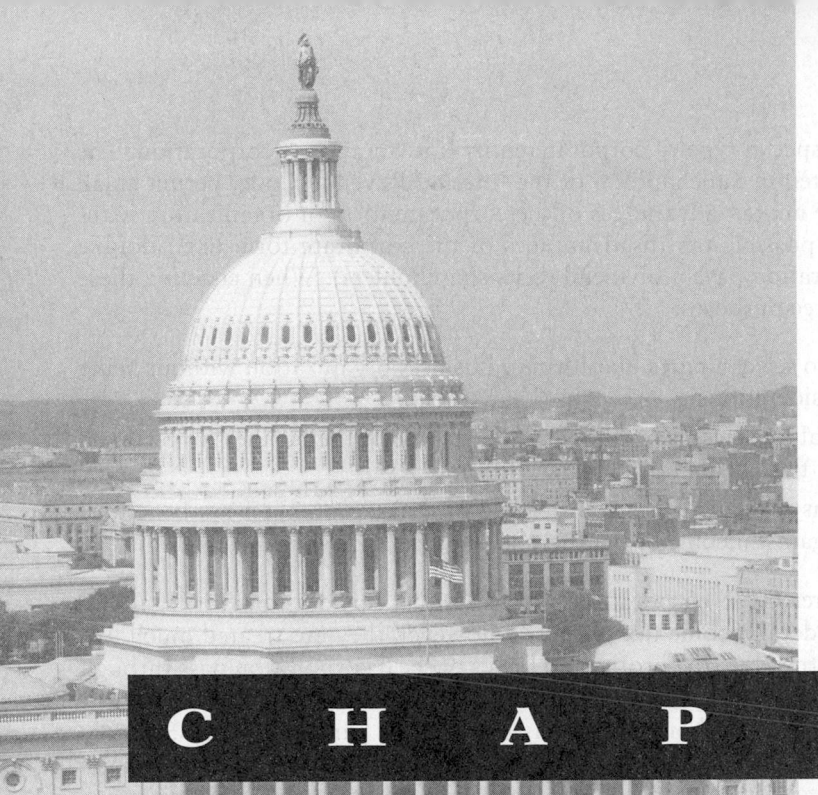

11

CHAPTER

S CORPORATIONS

LEARNING OBJECTIVES

After studying this chapter, you should be able to

1 ▶ Explain the requirements for being taxed under Subchapter S

2 ▶ Apply the procedures for electing to be taxed under Subchapter S

3 ▶ Identify the events that will terminate an S election

4 ▶ Determine the permitted tax years for an S corporation

5 ▶ Calculate ordinary income or loss

6 ▶ Calculate the amount of any special S corporation taxes

7 ▶ Calculate a shareholder's allocable share of ordinary income or loss and separately stated items

8 ▶ Determine the limitations on a shareholder's deduction of S corporation losses

9 ▶ Calculate a shareholder's basis in his or her S corporation's stock and debt

10 ▶ Determine the taxability of an S corporation's distributions to its shareholders

11 ▶ Apply the procedures for filing an S corporation tax return

12 ▶ Determine the estimated tax payments required of an S corporation and its shareholders

**ADDITIONAL
COMMENT**

An LLC (or partnership) that
wishes to be treated as an S corporation can file the S election
(Form 2553) and automatically be
classified as an association (corporation) under the check-the-box
regulations without having to file
the entity classification election
(Form 8832).

This chapter discusses a special type of corporate entity known as an S corporation. The S corporation rules, located in Subchapter S of the Internal Revenue Code, permit small corporations to enjoy the nontax advantages of the corporate form of organization without being subject to the possible tax disadvantages of the corporate form (e.g., double taxation when the corporation pays a dividend to its shareholders). When enacting these rules, Congress stated three purposes:

▶ To permit businesses to select a particular form of business organization without being influenced by tax considerations

▶ To provide aid for small businesses by allowing the income of the business to be taxed to shareholders rather than being taxed at the corporate level

▶ To permit corporations realizing losses for a period of years to obtain a tax benefit of offsetting the losses against income at the shareholder level[1]

As discussed in Chapter C2, S corporations are treated as corporations for legal and business purposes. For federal income tax purposes, however, they are treated much like partnerships.[2] As in a partnership, the profits and losses of the S corporation pass through to the owners, and the S corporation can make tax-free distributions of earnings previously taxed to its shareholders. Although generally taxed like a partnership, the S corporation still follows many of the basic Subchapter C tax provisions (e.g., S corporations use the corporate tax rules regarding formations, liquidations, and tax-free reorganizations instead of the partnership rules). A tabular comparison of the S corporation, partnership, and C corporation rules appears in Appendix F.

Changes over the past several years have caused many businesses to reexamine the implications of an S election. First, the restrictive nature of the S corporation requirements has caused many new businesses that were potential S corporations to look at alternative business forms. All 50 states have adopted limited liability company (LLC) legislation. LLCs offer many of the same tax advantages of S corporations because they are treated as partnerships. LLCs, however, are not subject to the same requirements that must be satisfied by an S corporation and its shareholder(s) to make and retain an S election. Partially because of the S corporation restrictions, some new businesses have organized as LLCs to take advantage of the greater operational flexibility the LLC form provides the entity and its owners, as well as its liability protection. A number of small businesses, however, elected to be S corporations because of the greater certainty available within the legal system for corporate entities.

Tax legislation in 1996 introduced a number of changes to the S corporation rules. Some of these changes relaxed restrictions and thereby increased the S corporation's popularity. For example, the 35 shareholder limit was increased to 75, and the prohibitions against certain entities and trusts becoming S corporation shareholders were lessened. The 2004 Jobs Act, as modified by the 2005 GO Zone Act, has relaxed restrictions further by increasing the shareholder limit to 100 and by treating family members as one shareholder for this 100-shareholder limit. In effect, these changes have reduced some of the differences between S corporations and LLCs and have renewed interest in the S corporation form of doing business.

For many existing C corporations, the tax cost of liquidating the corporate entity and creating an LLC may be a prohibitively expensive way to avoid the corporate level income tax (see Chapter C6). However, many of these C corporations have taken the next best alternative, that is, making an S election.

This chapter examines the requirements for making an S election and the tax rules that apply to S corporations and their shareholders.

---

[1] S. Rept. No. 1983, 85th Cong., 2d Sess., p. 87 (1958).
[2] Some states do not recognize an S corporation as a conduit for state income tax purposes. Instead, they are taxed under the state income tax laws in the same manner as a C corporation.

SHOULD AN S ELECTION BE MADE?

ADVANTAGES OF S CORPORATION TREATMENT

A number of advantages are available to a corporation that makes an S election.

REAL-WORLD EXAMPLE

The number of S corporations has grown from 725,000 in 1985 to 3.15 million in 2002. As a result of this rapid increase, the IRS has announced a major study of S corporation compliance to be conducted by the National Research Program (NRP). Under this program, the IRS will examine 5,000 randomly selected S corporation returns from 2003 and 2004 filings. See News Release IR 2005-76.

▶ The corporation's income is exempt from the corporate income tax. An S corporation's income is taxed only to its shareholders, whose tax bracket may be lower than a C corporation's tax bracket.

▶ The corporation's losses pass through to its shareholders and can be used to reduce the taxes owed on other types of income. This feature can be especially important for new businesses. The corporation can make an S election, pass through the start-up losses to the owners, and terminate the election once a C corporation becomes advantageous.

▶ Undistributed income taxed to the shareholder is not taxed again when subsequently distributed unless the distribution exceeds the shareholder's basis for his or her stock.

▶ Capital gains, dividends, and tax-exempt income are separately stated and retain their character when passed through to the shareholders. Such amounts become commingled with other corporate earnings and are taxed as dividends when distributed by a C corporation. The 2003 Act, however, has alleviated the detrimental tax effect of C corporation dividends by reducing the maximum tax rate on qualified dividends to 15% (through 2008).

▶ Deductions, losses, and tax credits are separately stated and retain their character when passed through to the shareholders. These amounts may be subject to the various limitations at the shareholder level. This treatment can permit the shareholder to claim a tax benefit when it otherwise would be denied to the corporation (e.g., a shareholder can claim the general business credit benefit even though the S corporation reports a substantial loss for the year).

▶ Splitting the S corporation's income between family members is possible. However, income splitting is restricted by the requirement that reasonable compensation be provided to family members who provide capital and services to the S corporation.

▶ An S corporation's earnings that flow through to the individual shareholders are not subject to the self-employment tax. In contrast, a partnership must determine what portion of each general partner's net earnings constitutes self-employment income.

▶ An S corporation is not subject to the personal holding company tax or the accumulated earnings tax (although, as discussed later, passive income can trigger a corporate-level tax in special circumstances).

DISADVANTAGES OF S CORPORATION TREATMENT

A number of tax disadvantages also exist for a corporation that makes an S election.

KEY POINT

The structure of an S corporation can create a real hardship for a shareholder if large amounts of income flow through without any compensation payments or distributions of cash to help pay the tax on the income.

▶ A C corporation is treated as a separate tax entity from its shareholders, thereby permitting its first $50,000 of income to be taxed at a 15% marginal rate instead of the shareholder's marginal rate. In addition, the corporate rates generally are lower than the individual rates and may reduce the total tax burden if the corporation retains the earnings in its business.

▶ The S corporation's earnings are taxed to the shareholders even though they are not distributed. This treatment may require the corporation to make distributions or salary payments so the shareholder can pay taxes owed on the S corporation's earnings.

▶ S corporations are subject to an excess net passive income tax and a built-in gains tax. Partnerships are not subject to either of these taxes.

▶ Dividends received by the S corporation are not eligible for the dividends-received deduction, as is the case for a C corporation.

▶ Allocation of ordinary income or loss and the separately stated items is based on the stock owned on each day of the tax year. Special allocations of particular items are not permitted, as they are in a partnership.

▶ The loss limitation for an S corporation shareholder is smaller than for a partner in a partnership because of the treatment of liabilities. Shareholders can increase their loss limitations by the basis of any debt they loan to the S corporation. Partners, on the other hand, can increase their loss limitation by their ratable share of all partnership liabilities.

▶ S corporations and their shareholders are subject to the at-risk, passive activity limitation, and hobby loss rules. C corporations generally are not subject to these rules.

▶ An S corporation is somewhat restricted in the type and number of shareholders it can have and the capital structure it can use. Partnerships and C corporations are not so restricted.

▶ S corporations must use a calendar year as their tax year unless they can establish a business purpose for a fiscal year or unless they make a special election to use an otherwise nonpermitted tax year. Similar restrictions also apply to partnerships.

Once the owners decide to incorporate, no general rule determines whether the corporation should make an S election. Before making a decision, management and the shareholders should examine the long- and short-run tax and non-tax advantages and disadvantages of filing as a C corporation versus filing as an S corporation. Unlike a consolidated return election, the S election can be revoked or terminated at any time with minimal effort.

S CORPORATION REQUIREMENTS

OBJECTIVE 1

Explain the requirements for being taxed under Subchapter S

The S corporation requirements are divided into two categories: shareholder-related and corporation-related requirements. A corporation that satisfies all the requirements is known as a small business corporation. Only small business corporations can make an S election. Each set of requirements is outlined below.

SHAREHOLDER-RELATED REQUIREMENTS

Three shareholder-related requirements must be satisfied on each day of the tax year.[3]

▶ The corporation must not have more than 100 shareholders.

▶ All shareholders must be individuals, estates, certain tax-exempt organizations, or certain kinds of trusts.

▶ None of the individual shareholders can be classified as a nonresident **alien**.

ADDITIONAL COMMENT

The Sec. 1244 stock rules (Chapter C2) and the S corporation rules both use the term *small business corporations*. The definitions have different requirements, although most S corporation stock can qualify as Sec. 1244 stock.

100-SHAREHOLDER RULE. Section 1361(c)(1) treats a husband and wife (and their estates) as a single shareholder for purposes of applying the 100-shareholder limit. For tax years beginning after 2004, this single shareholder rule expands to include all members of a family. Members of a family for this purpose include the common ancestor, lineal descendants of the common ancestor, spouses (or former spouses) of the common ancestor or lineal descendents, and estates of family members. An individual will not be considered a common ancestor if he or she is more than six generations removed from the youngest generation of family member shareholders. When two unmarried or nonfamily individuals own stock jointly (e.g., as tenants in common or as joint tenants), each owner is considered a separate shareholder.

REAL-WORLD EXAMPLE

In 2002, 57.4% of all S corporations had one owner. Only 0.12% of the 3.15 million S corporations that filed in 2002 had more than 30 owners.

ELIGIBLE SHAREHOLDERS. C corporations and partnerships cannot own S corporation stock. This restriction prevents a corporation or a partnership having a large number of owners from avoiding the 100-shareholder limitation by purchasing S corporation

---

[3] Secs. 1361. This discussion reflects changes made by the 2004 Jobs Act and the 2005 GO Zone Act.

stock and being treated as a single shareholder. Organizations exempt from the federal income tax under Sec. 501(a) (e.g., a tax-exempt public charity or private foundation) can hold S corporation stock, and these organizations count as one shareholder when calculating the 100-shareholder limit.

Seven types of trusts can own S corporation stock: grantor trusts, voting trusts,[4] testamentary trusts, **qualified Subchapter S trusts (QSSTs)**,[5] qualified retirement plan trusts, small business trusts, and beneficiary-controlled trusts (i.e., trusts that distribute all their income to a single income beneficiary who is treated as the owner of the trust). Grantor trusts, QSSTs, and beneficiary-controlled trusts can own S corporation stock only if the grantor or the beneficiary is a qualified shareholder. Each beneficiary of a voting trust also must be an eligible shareholder. A qualified retirement plan trust is one formed as part of a qualified stock bonus, pension, or profit sharing plan or employee stock ownership plan (ESOP) that is exempt from the federal income tax under Sec. 501(a).

Small business trusts can own S corporation stock. These trusts can be complex trusts and primarily are used as estate planning devices. No interest in a small business trust can be acquired in a purchase transaction, that is, a transaction where the holder's interest takes a cost basis under Sec. 1012. Interests in small business trusts generally are acquired as a result of a gift or bequest. All current beneficiaries of a small business trust must be individuals, estates, or charitable organizations. Current beneficiaries are parties that can receive an income distribution for the period in question. Each beneficiary is counted for purposes of the 100-shareholder limit. QSSTs and tax-exempt trusts are ineligible to elect to be a small business trust. The trustee must make an election to obtain small business trust status.

A testamentary trust (i.e., a trust created under the terms of a will) that receives S corporation stock can hold the stock and continue to be an eligible shareholder for a two-year period, beginning on the date the stock transfers to the trust. A grantor trust that held S corporation stock immediately before the death of the deemed owner, and which continues in existence after the death of the deemed owner, can continue to hold the stock and be an eligible shareholder for the two-year period beginning on the date of the deemed owner's death. Charitable remainder unitrusts and charitable remainder annuity trusts do not qualify as small business trusts.

ETHICAL POINT

Tax professionals must assist their clients in monitoring that the S corporation requirements are met on each day of the tax year. Failing to meet one of the requirements for even one day terminates the election. Ignoring a terminating event until the IRS discovers it upon an audit probably will cause the corporation to be taxed as a C corporation and prevent it from having the termination treated as being inadvertent.

EXAMPLE C11-1 ▶

ADDITIONAL COMMENT

The 2004 Jobs Act added one other narrowly defined trust situation. A bank that otherwise would qualify for making an S election can now do so even if an IRA trust holds some of its stock. This provision applies only with respect to bank stock held in IRA trusts on October 22, 2004. In this situation, the beneficiary of the IRA trust is treated as the shareholder.

Joan, a U.S. citizen, owns 25% of Walden Corporation's stock. Walden is an electing S corporation. At the time of Joan's death in the current year, the Walden stock passes to her estate. The estate is a qualifying shareholder, and the transfer does not affect the S election. If the stock subsequently transfers to a trust provided for in Joan's will, the testamentary trust can hold the Walden stock for a two-year period before the S election terminates. ◀

The trust in Example C11-1 can hold the S corporation stock for an indefinite period only if the trust's income beneficiary makes an election to have it treated as a QSST or small business trust. Otherwise, the S election terminates at the end of the two-year period.

ALIEN INDIVIDUALS. Individuals who are not U.S. citizens (i.e., alien individuals) can own S corporation stock only if they are U.S. residents or are married to a U.S. citizen or resident alien and make an election to be taxed as a resident alien. The S election terminates if an alien individual purchases S corporation stock and does not reside in the United States or has not made the appropriate election.

CORPORATION-RELATED REQUIREMENTS

The corporation must satisfy the following three requirements on each day of the tax year:

---

[4] A **voting trust** is an arrangement whereby the stock owned by a number of shareholders is placed under the control of a trustee, who exercises the voting rights possessed by the stock. One reason for creating a voting trust is to increase the voting power of a group of minority shareholders in the selection of corporate directors or the establishment of corporate policies.

[5] A QSST is a domestic trust that owns stock in one or more S corporations

and distributes (or is required to distribute) all its income to its sole income beneficiary. The income beneficiary must make an irrevocable election to have the QSST rules of Sec. 1361(d) apply. The beneficiary is treated as the owner (and, therefore, the shareholder) of the portion of the trust consisting of the S corporation stock. A separate election is made for each S corporation's stock owned by the trust.

ADDITIONAL COMMENT

An unincorporated eligible entity that makes a valid S election is automatically treated as making an election to be treated as a corporation under the check-the-box regulations. Thus, the entity does not have to make two separate elections.

▶ The corporation must be a domestic corporation or an unincorporated entity that elects to be treated as a corporation under the check-the-box regulations.

▶ The corporation must not be an "ineligible" corporation.

▶ The corporation must have only one class of stock.[6]

The first requirement precludes a foreign corporation from making an S election.

A corporation may be an ineligible corporation and thereby violate the second requirement in one of two ways:

▶ Corporations that maintain a special federal income tax status are not eligible to make an S election. For example, financial institutions (e.g., banks) that use the reserve method to account for bad debts and insurance companies are not eligible.

▶ Corporations that have elected the special Puerto Rico and U.S. possessions tax credit (Sec. 936) or that had elected the special Domestic International Sales Corporation tax exemption are ineligible to make the S election.

ADDITIONAL COMMENT

Current S corporation stock ownership rules and the approval of the check-the-box regulations permit great flexibility in creating groups of entities that fit the business needs of their owners.

S corporations can own the stock of a C corporation or an S corporation without any limitation on the percentage of voting power or value held. However, as mentioned earlier, a C corporation cannot own the stock of an S corporation. An S corporation that owns the stock of a C corporation cannot participate in the filing of a consolidated tax return. An S corporation also can own the stock of a **Qualified Subchapter S Subsidiary (QSub)**. A QSub is a domestic corporation that qualifies as an S corporation, is 100% owned by an S corporation, and for which the parent S corporation elects to treat the subsidiary as a QSub. The assets, liabilities, income, deductions, losses, etc. of the QSub are treated as those of its S corporation parent and reported on the parent's tax return.[7]

A corporation that has two classes of stock issued and outstanding has violated the third requirement and cannot be an S corporation. The single class of stock determination is more difficult than it appears at first glance because of the many different financial arrangements that are possible between an S corporation and its shareholders. A corporation is treated as having only one class of stock if all of its outstanding shares of stock possess identical rights to distribution and liquidation proceeds and the corporation has not issued any instrument or obligation, or entered into any arrangement, that is treated as a second class of stock.[8] A second class of stock is not created if the only difference between the two classes of stock pertains to voting rights.[9]

EXAMPLE C11-2 ▶ Kelly Corporation has two classes of common stock outstanding. The Class A and Class B common stock give the shareholders identical rights and interests in the profits and assets of the corporation. Class A stock has one vote per share. Class B stock is nonvoting. Kelly Corporation is treated as having only one class of stock outstanding and can make an S election. ◀

GENERAL RULES. The determination of whether all outstanding shares of stock confer identical rights to distribution and liquidation proceeds is based on the corporate charter, articles of incorporation, bylaws, applicable state law, and binding agreements relating to distribution and liquidation proceeds (i.e., the governing agreements).[10] Treasury Regulations permit certain types of state laws, agreements, distributions, etc., to be disregarded in determining whether all of a corporation's outstanding shares confer identical rights to distribution and liquidation proceeds. These include

▶ Agreements to purchase stock at the time of death, divorce, disability, or termination of employment

▶ Distributions made on the basis of the shareholder's varying stock interests during the year

▶ Distributions that differ in timing (e.g., one shareholder receives a distribution in the current year and a second shareholder receives a similar dollar amount distribution shortly after the beginning of the next tax year)

---

[6] Sec. 1361(b)(1).
[7] Sec. 1361(b)(3).
[8] Reg. Sec. 1.1361-1(l).

[9] Sec. 1361(c)(4).
[10] Reg. Sec. 1.1361-1(l)(2).

Agreements to increase cash or property distributions to shareholders who bear heavier state income tax burdens so as to provide equal after-tax distributions provide unequal distribution and liquidation rights. The unequal distributions probably will cause a second class of stock to be created. However, state laws that require a corporation to pay or withhold state income taxes on behalf of some or all of a corporation's shareholders are disregarded.

DEBT INSTRUMENTS.   Debt instruments, corporate obligations, and deferred compensation arrangements, in general, are not treated as a second class of stock.[11] A number of safe harbors exist for characterizing corporate obligations as debt (and not as a second class of stock):

▶ Unwritten advances from a shareholder that do not exceed $10,000 during the tax year, are treated as debt by the two parties, and are expected to be repaid within a reasonable time

▶ Obligations that are considered equity under the general tax laws but are owned solely by the shareholders in the same proportion as the corporations's outstanding stock

In addition, Sec. 1361(c)(5) provides a safe harbor for straight debt instruments so that the debt is not treated as a second class of stock. For debt to qualify under the safe harbor, it must meet the following requirements if issued while an S election is in effect:

▶ The debt must represent an unconditional promise to pay a certain sum of money on a specified date or on demand.

▶ The interest rate and interest payment dates must not be contingent on profits, the borrower's discretion, or similar factors.[12]

▶ The debt must not be convertible directly or indirectly into stock.

▶ The creditor must be an individual, estate, or trust eligible to be an S corporation shareholder, or a nonindividual creditor actively and regularly engaged in the business of lending money.[13]

The safe harbor rules can apply to debt even if the debt otherwise would be considered a second class of stock under case law or other IRC provisions. An obligation that originally qualifies as straight debt may no longer qualify if it is materially modified so that it no longer satisfies the safe harbor or is transferred to a third party who is not an eligible shareholder.[14]

KEY POINT
If debt instruments satisfy the safe harbor rules, such instruments cannot be construed as equity. However, such debt must have been issued in an S corporation tax year.

ELECTION OF S CORPORATION STATUS

OBJECTIVE 2

Apply the procedures for electing to be taxed under Subchapter S

The S election exempts a corporation from all taxes imposed by Chapter 1 of the Internal Revenue Code (Secs. 1-1399) except for the following:

▶ Sec. 1374 built-in gains tax
▶ Sec. 1375 excess net passive income tax
▶ Sec. 1363(d) LIFO recapture tax

This rule exempts the S corporation from the regular income tax, accumulated earnings tax, the personal holding company tax, and the corporate alternative minimum tax for the tax year in which the election is first effective and all subsequent tax years the election remains in effect.

[11] Reg. Sec. 1.1361-1(l)(4)(i). An exception applies to debt instruments, corporate obligations, and deferred compensation arrangements that are treated as stock under the general principles of the federal tax law where the principal purpose for the debt instrument, etc., is to circumvent the distribution or liquidation proceeds rights provided for by the outstanding stock or to circumvent the 100-shareholder limit.

[12] That the interest rate depends on the prime rate or a similar factor not related to the debtor corporation will not disqualify the instrument from coming under the safe harbor rules. If the interest being paid is unreasonably high, an appropriate portion may be treated as a payment of something other than interest.
[13] Sec. 1361(c)(5).
[14] Reg. Sec. 1.1361-1(l)(5)(ii) and (iii).

EXAMPLE C11-4 ▶ Sara and Harry own all of Kraft Corporation's stock. Sara sells all her Kraft stock to Lisa on February 10. The next day Kraft makes an S election. For the election to apply in the current year, Sara, Harry, and Lisa must consent to the election. If Sara refuses to consent to the election, the election will not begin until next year. ◀

Each tenant (whether or not husband and wife) must consent to the S election if the shareholders own the stock as tenants in common, joint tenants, or tenants in the entirety. If the shareholders own the S corporation stock as community property, each person having a community property interest must consent to the election. If the shareholder is a minor, either the minor or the minor's legal representative (e.g., a natural parent or legal guardian) can make the consent.

Topic Review C11-1 summarizes the S corporation requirements and procedures for making the S election.

OBJECTIVE 3

Identify the events that will terminate an S election

TERMINATION OF THE ELECTION

Once made, the S election remains in effect until the corporation either revokes the election or terminates the election because it ceases to meet the small business corporation requirements. The following discussion examines each action and outlines the requirements for making a new S election following a termination.[17]

REVOCATION OF THE ELECTION. A corporation can revoke its S election in any tax year as long as it meets the requirements regarding shareholder consent and timeliness. Shareholders owning more than one-half the corporation's stock (including nonvoting stock) on the day the corporation makes the revocation must consent to the revocation. A revocation made on or before the fifteenth day of the third month of the tax year is effective on the first day of the S corporation's tax year. A revocation made after the first 2½ months of the tax year is effective on the first day of the next tax year. An exception permits the S corporation to select a prospective date for the revocation to be effective. The prospective date can be the date the corporation makes the revocation or any subsequent date.

EXAMPLE C11-5 ▶ Adobe Corporation, a calendar year taxpayer, has been an S corporation for several years. However, the corporation has become quite profitable, and management feels that it would be advantageous to make a public stock offering to obtain additional capital during 2007. Adobe can revoke its S election any time before March 16, 2007, making the revocation effective on January 1, 2007. If the corporation makes the revocation election after March 15, 2007, it does not take effect until January 1, 2008. In either case, the corporation may specify a prospective 2007 revocation date as long as the date specified is on or after the date it makes the revocation. ◀

TAX STRATEGY TIP

When it is difficult to obtain the majority shareholder vote necessary for revocation, consideration should be given to purposely triggering a termination event.

LEGISLATIVE UPDATE

On February 2, 2006, the Senate passed a bill that would repeal the passive investment income test for terminations. If passed, an S election would not terminate because of excess passive investment income. The bill's proposed effective date is for tax years beginning after September 30, 2006.

TERMINATION OF THE ELECTION. The S election terminates if the corporation fails one or more of the small business corporation requirements on any day after the first day the election is effective. The termination generally occurs on the day of the terminating event. Events that can terminate the election include

▶ Exceeding the 100-shareholder limit

▶ Having an ineligible shareholder own some of the stock

▶ Creating a second class of stock

▶ Attaining a prohibited tax status

▶ Selecting an improper tax year

▶ Failing the passive investment income test for three consecutive years

The passive investment income test applies annually. It terminates the S election if more than 25% of the corporation's gross receipts are passive investment income for each of three consecutive tax years *and* the corporation has Subchapter C earnings and profits (E&P) at the end of each of the three consecutive tax years. If the corporation meets these

---

[17] Termination and revocation rules are in Sec. 1362.

Topic Review C11-1

S Corporation Requirements and Election Procedures

Requirements

Shareholder-related:

1. The corporation may have no more than 100 shareholders. Husbands and wives and their estates count as one shareholder. With an election, family members can count as only one shareholder.
2. All shareholders must be individuals, estates, certain kinds of trusts, or certain kinds of tax-exempt organizations. Eligible trusts include grantor trusts, voting trusts, testamentary trusts, beneficiary-controlled trusts, qualified Subchapter S trusts, qualified retirement plan trusts, and small business trusts.
3. All the individual shareholders must be U.S. citizens or resident aliens.

Corporation-related:

1. The corporation must be a domestic corporation or an unincorporated entity that elects to be taxed as a domestic corporation under the check-the-box regulations.
2. The corporation must not be an ineligible corporation (e.g., an ineligible bank or other financial institution, an insurance company, or a foreign corporation).
3. The corporation must have only one class of stock issued and outstanding. Differences in voting rights are ignored.

Making the Election

1. The corporation can make the S election any time during the tax year preceding the year for which the election is effective or on or before the fifteenth day of the third month of the tax year for which the election is effective. Late elections are effective with the next tax year unless the corporation obtains IRS relief for reasonable cause.
2. Each shareholder who owns stock on the date the corporation makes the election must consent to the election. If the corporation makes the election after the beginning of the tax year, each person who was a shareholder during the portion of the tax year preceding the election also must consent to the election.

conditions for three consecutive tax years, the election terminates on the first day of the next (fourth) tax year.

Passive investment income includes royalties, rents,[18] dividends, interest, annuities, and gains from the sale or exchange of stocks and securities. Treasury Regulations hold that passive investment income excludes income derived from the active conduct of a trade or business. Subchapter C E&P includes only earnings that accrued in tax years in which an S election was not in effect (i.e., the corporation was taxed under the C corporation rules).

EXAMPLE C11-6 ▶

HISTORICAL NOTE

Previously, a termination was deemed effective on the first day of the tax year in which the terminating event occurred. To stop potential abuse, Congress changed the rule so that an S election terminates on the day of the terminating event.

Shareholders formed Silver Corporation in the current year, and the corporation promptly made an S election. Silver can earn an unlimited amount of passive income during a tax year without any fear of losing its S corporation status or being subject to the Sec. 1375 tax on excess net passive income because it has never been a C corporation and thus has no Subchapter C E&P. However, if a C corporation containing E&P merged into Silver, Silver would then have potential exposure to the passive income rules. (See pages C11-16 and C11-17 for a discussion of the Sec. 1375 tax.) ◀

ALLOCATION OF INCOME. A terminating event occurring at some time other than on the first day of the tax year creates an S termination year. The **S termination year** is divided into an S short year and C short year. The **S short year** begins on the first day of the tax year and ends on the day preceding the day on which the termination is effective. The **C short year** begins on the day the termination takes effect and continues through the last day of the corporation's tax year.

---

[18] Regulation Sec. 1.1362-2(c)(5)(ii)(B)(2) excludes from rents payments received for the use or occupancy of property if the corporation provides significant services or incurs substantial costs in the rental business. See page C11-37 for additional explanations of the significant services and substantial costs definitions.

EXAMPLE C11-7 ▶ Dixon Corporation has been an S corporation for several years. Paula and Frank each own one-half of Dixon's stock. Paula sells one-half of her Dixon stock to Eagle Corporation on July 1. The sale terminates the S election on July 1 because Eagle is an ineligible shareholder. Assuming that Dixon is a calendar year taxpayer, the S short year includes the period January 1 through June 30. The C short year includes the period July 1 through December 31. ◀

TAX STRATEGY TIP

Income or loss can be allocated in the termination year under either of two methods. Careful consideration should be given to the possible tax advantages of a daily allocation versus an actual closing of the books. See Tax Planning Considerations for further details.

ADDITIONAL COMMENT

To use an actual closing of the books to allocate the income or loss of Dixon in Example C11-7, Eagle must consent. Due to the consequences of such an election, the method of allocation should be considered in negotiating the Dixon stock sale.

The S corporation's shareholders report the S short year income according to the normal reporting rules described below. The C corporation reports the income earned during the C short year and calculates its C short year income tax liability on an annualized basis (see Chapter C3). The S short year and C short year returns are due on the due date for the corporation's tax for the tax year had the termination not occurred (including any extensions).

An S corporation can use either of two rules to allocate the termination year's income between the S short year and the C short year. The general rule of Sec. 1362(e)(2) allocates the ordinary income or loss and the separately stated items between the S short year and C short year based on the number of days in each year. A special election under Sec. 1362(e)(3) permits an allocation that accords with the corporation's normal tax accounting rules if all persons who were shareholders at any time during the S short year and all persons who are shareholders on the first day of the C short year consent to the election. The corporation cannot use a daily allocation when an S termination year occurs and, during such year, sales or exchanges of 50% or more of the corporation's outstanding stock occur. In such a case, the corporation must use its normal accounting rules to make the allocation.

INADVERTENT TERMINATION. Special rules permit the corporation to continue its S election if an inadvertent termination occurs by its ceasing to be a small business corporation or by its failing the passive investment income test for three consecutive years. If such a termination occurs, the S corporation or its shareholders must take the necessary steps, within a reasonable time period after discovering the event creating the termination, to restore the corporation's small business status. If the IRS determines that the termination was inadvertent, the corporation and all persons owning stock during the termination period must agree to make the adjustments necessary to report the income for this period as if the S election had been in effect continuously.[19]

EXAMPLE C11-8 ▶ Shareholders formed Frye Corporation in 2003 and operated it as a C corporation during that year. Frye made an S election in 2004. During 2003, the corporation incorrectly computed its E&P and believed that no Subchapter C E&P existed for its only pre–S corporation tax year. From 2004 through 2006, Frye earned large amounts of passive income but did not pay the Sec. 1375 excess net passive income tax or worry about termination of its election because it thought it had no accumulated E&P from 2003. Upon auditing Frye's tax returns, the IRS finds that Subchapter C E&P, in fact, did exist from 2003 and terminates the S election effective on January 1, 2007. If the corporation distributes the E&P and the shareholders report the dividend income, the IRS probably will treat the occurrence as an inadvertent termination and not revoke the election. ◀

For events occurring after 2004, the IRS also can grant relief for inadvertent terminations of the election to treat a subsidiary as a Qualified Subchapter S Subsidiary (QSub) and the election to treat family members as one shareholder. For example, a parent S corporation might inadvertently transfer shares of a QSub to another person, thereby violating the 100% ownership requirement. If the S corporation takes the necessary steps to correct the inadvertent transfer, the IRS can grant relief so that the election remains in effect.

OTHER IRS WAIVERS. The IRS not only can waive a termination it deems to be inadvertent, it also can validate certain invalid elections. Validation of an invalid election can

---

[19] Regulation Sec. 1.1362-4(b) holds that a termination will be inadvertent if the terminating event was not reasonably within the control of the corporation and was not part of a plan to terminate the election or if it took place without the corporation's knowledge and reasonable safeguards were in place to prevent the event from occurring.

occur when the election failed to meet the basic S corporation requirements of Sec. 1361 or failed to provide the necessary shareholder consents. The IRS also can exercise this authority in situations where a corporation never filed an election. In addition, the IRS can treat a late-filed S election as being timely filed if the IRS determines that reasonable cause existed for failing to make a timely election and the corporation meets certain other requirements.[20]

NEW ELECTION FOLLOWING A TERMINATION. A corporation that terminates its S election must wait five tax years before making a new election.[21] This delay applies unless the IRS consents to an earlier reelection. Regulation Sec. 1.1362-5(a) indicates that permission for an early reelection can occur (1) when more than 50% of the corporation's stock is owned by persons who did not own stock on the date of termination or (2) when the event causing the termination was not reasonably within the control of the corporation or the shareholders having a substantial interest in the corporation *and* was not part of a plan to terminate the election involving the corporation or such shareholders.

EXAMPLE C11-9 ▶ Terri owns Vector Corporation, a calendar year taxpayer, which has been an S corporation for ten years. In January 2005, Terri sold all the Vector stock to Michelle with payments to be made over a five-year period. In March 2007, Michelle fails to make the necessary payments and Terri repossesses the stock. During the time Michelle holds the stock, Vector revokes its S election. Vector should immediately apply for reelection of S status because a more than 50% ownership change has occurred since the date of termination. ◀

AVOIDING TERMINATION OF AN S ELECTION. Termination of an S election generally results in substantial negative tax consequences in the form of increased corporate or shareholder taxes. The S corporation's owners, management, and tax advisor need to understand the various events that can cause the termination of the S election. Some steps shareholders can take to prevent an untimely termination include the following:

▶ Monitor all transfers of S corporation stock. Make certain the purchaser or transferee of the stock is not an ineligible shareholder (e.g., corporation, partnership, or nonresident alien) or that the total number of shareholders does not exceed 100 (e.g., an excess shareholder resulting from creation of a joint interest).

▶ Establish procedures for the S corporation to purchase the stock of deceased shareholders to avoid the stock being acquired by a trust that is ineligible to be a shareholder.

WHAT WOULD YOU DO IN THIS SITUATION?

Harry Baker formed Xeno Corporation on January 4, 2004. The corporation filed a valid S corporation election on January 17, 2004, to be effect for 2004. Harry, the corporation's sole shareholder, consented to the election. The corporation had business ties to Mexico, and to strengthen these ties, Harry sold 25% of his Xeno shares to Pedro Gonzales on February 12, 2005. Pedro is one of Harry's business associates and is a citizen and resident of Mexico. Harry continued to operate Xeno as an S corporation throughout 2005. Early in March 2006, Harry became aware that, by selling stock to an ineligible shareholder, he may have jeopardized the corporation's S election. Thus, Harry immediately contacted Pedro and persuaded Pedro to sell his Xeno shares back to him (Harry). Harry hires you as his tax advisor on December 16, 2006, at which time you learn about the sale and repurchase of the Xeno shares. However, Harry tells you not to worry because, by buying back the shares, he already has rectified the situation, and thus the IRS need not be told about the transfers. How do you advise Harry on this matter?

[20] See Rev. Procs. 97-48, 1997-2 C.B. 521, and 2003-43, 2003-23 I.R.B. 998, for additional guidance on this issue and a special transition rule.

[21] *Termination* includes both revocation of the S election and loss of the election because one or more of the small business corporation requirements were not met.

LEGISLATIVE UPDATE

On February 2, 2006, the Senate passed a bill that would repeal the passive investment income test for terminations. If passed, an S election would not terminate because of excess passive investment income, making this planning technique unnecessary. The bill's proposed effective date is for tax years beginning after September 30, 2006.

▶ Establish restrictions on the transferability of the S corporation stock by having shareholders enter into a stock purchase agreement. Such an agreement could provide that the stock cannot be transferred without the prior consent of all other shareholders and, if the necessary consent cannot be obtained, the corporation will repurchase the stock at a specified price (e.g., at book value).

▶ Monitor the passive income earned by an S corporation that previously had been a C corporation for one or more years. Make certain the passive income requirement is not failed for three consecutive years by reducing the level of passive income or by distributing the Subchapter C E&P.

S CORPORATION OPERATIONS

S corporations make the same accounting period and accounting method elections that a C corporation makes. Each year, the S corporation must compute and report to the IRS and to its shareholders its ordinary income or loss and its separately stated items. The special S corporation rules are explained below.

OBJECTIVE 4

Determine the permitted tax years for an S corporation

TAXABLE YEAR

Section 1378(a) requires that the S corporation's taxable year be a permitted year, defined as

▶ A tax year ending on December 31 (including a 52–53 week year)

▶ Any fiscal year for which the corporation establishes a business purpose[22]

Section 1378(b) specifically notes that income deferral for the shareholders is not a necessary business purpose. An S corporation that adopts a fiscal year coinciding with its natural business year has satisfied the business purpose requirement. The natural business year for an S corporation depends on the type of business conducted. When a trade or business has nonpeak and peak periods of business, the natural business year is considered to end at, or soon after, the close of the peak business period. A business whose income is steady from month to month, year-round, does not have a natural business year.[23]

EXAMPLE C11-10 ▶

Sable Corporation, an electing S corporation, operates a ski resort and reports $1 million of gross receipts for each of its last three tax years. If at least $250,000 (25% of gross receipts) of the receipts occurred in February and March for each of the three consecutive years, Sable can adopt, or change to, or continue to use a natural business year ending March 31.[24] ◀

An S corporation's adoption of, or a change to, a fiscal year that is an ownership tax year also is permitted. An ownership tax year is the same tax year used by shareholders owning more than 50% of the corporation's outstanding stock. The 50% requirement must be met on the first day of the tax year to which the change relates. Failure to meet the 50% ownership requirement on the first day of any later tax year requires a change to a calendar year or other approved fiscal year. S corporations also can adopt or change to a fiscal year for which IRS approval is obtained based on the facts and circumstances of the situation.[25]

Section 444 permits an S corporation to elect a fiscal year other than a permitted year. The fiscal year elected under Sec. 444 must have a deferral period of three months or less (e.g., a September 30 or later fiscal year-end for an S corporation otherwise required to use a calendar year). An S corporation that is changing its tax year can elect to use a new

ADDITIONAL COMMENT

The requirement that all S corporations adopt calendar years (with March 15 return due dates) caused a hardship for tax return preparers. Section 444 is a compromise provision that allows a fiscal year for filing purposes, but it mandates a special payment of the deferred taxes.

---

[22] Some S corporations use a "grandfathered" fiscal year, which is a fiscal year for which IRS approval was obtained after June 30, 1974. Excluded are fiscal years that result in an income deferral of three months or less.

[23] Rev. Procs. 2002-39, 2002-1 C.B. 1046, and 2002-38, 2002-22 C.B. 1037.

[24] See Rev. Proc. 2002-38, 2002-1 C.B. 1037, for an explanation of the 25% test.

[25] Regulation Sec. 1.1378-1 and Rev. Proc. 2002-38, 2002-1 C.B. 1037, explain the procedures for an S corporation adopting a fiscal year or changing the tax year of a new or existing S corporation. Rev. Rul. 87-57, 1987-2 C.B. 224, examines eight situations concerning whether the tax year is a permitted year.

fiscal year under Sec. 444 only if the deferral period is no longer than the shorter of three months or the deferral period of the tax year that is being changed.[26] A Sec. 444 election is not required of an S corporation that satisfies the business purpose exception.

S corporations that elect a fiscal year under Sec. 444 must make required payments under Sec. 7519, which approximate the deferral benefit of the fiscal year. Revocation or termination of the S election also terminates the Sec. 444 election unless the corporation becomes a personal service corporation. Termination of the Sec. 444 election permits the S corporation to obtain a refund of prior Sec. 7519 payments.

Topic Review C11-2 summarizes the alternative tax years available to an S corporation.

ACCOUNTING METHOD ELECTIONS

The accounting method elections used to compute ordinary income or loss and the separately stated items are made by the S corporation rather than the individual shareholders. As with a partnership, the S corporation makes these elections independent of the accounting method elections made by its shareholders. Three elections generally reserved for the S corporation's shareholders are as follows:

▶ Sections 108(b)(5) or (c)(3) relating to income from the discharge of indebtedness

▶ Section 617 election relating to deduction and recapture of mining exploration expenditures

▶ Section 901 election to take a credit for foreign income taxes[27]

OBJECTIVE 5

Calculate ordinary income or loss

ORDINARY INCOME OR LOSS AND SEPARATELY STATED ITEMS

S corporations do not compute taxable income in the same manner as do C corporations. Instead, they are treated much like partnerships and thus report both an ordinary income or loss amount and a series of separately stated items. Ordinary income or loss is the net of income and deductions other than the separately stated items described in the next paragraph.

Topic Review C11-2

Alternative S Corporation Tax Years

Tax Year	Requirements
Calendar year (including certain 52–53 week years)	The permitted tax year unless one of the exceptions applies.
Permitted fiscal year:	IRS will grant approval if:
a. Ownership year	The tax year requested is the same as that used by shareholders owing more than 50% of the corporation's outstanding stock. This test must be met on the first day of the year for which approval is requested as well as for each succeeding year.
b. Natural business year	25% or more of the gross receipts for each of the three most recent 12-month periods are in the last two months of the requested tax year.
c. Facts and circumstances year	The corporation establishes a business purpose (other than an ownership year or natural business year) using the facts and circumstances of the situation.
Nonpermitted fiscal year	A Sec. 444 election permits the S corporation to use an otherwise nonpermitted tax year if the deferral period is three months or less and the corporation makes the necessary required payments.

---

[26] Special Sec. 444 transitional rules for 1986 permitted many S corporations to retain a previously adopted fiscal year (e.g., January 31) even though the deferral period is longer than three months.

[27] Secs. 1363(c).

The S corporation's separately stated items are the same ones that apply in partnership taxation under Sec. 702(a).[28] The items required to be separately stated by Sec. 702(a) include

▶ Net short-term capital gains and losses

▶ Net long-term capital gains and losses

▶ Sec. 1231 gains and losses

▶ Charitable contributions

▶ Dividends eligible for the 15% maximum tax rate or treated as investment income[29]

▶ Taxes paid to a foreign country or to a U.S. possession

▶ Any other item provided by Treasury Regulations

Regulation Sec. 1.702-1(a)(8) adds for partnerships several other items to the list. The same additions from the Treasury Regulations apply to S corporations and include the following:

▶ Tax-exempt or partially tax-exempt interest

▶ Soil and water conservation expenditures

▶ Intangible drilling and development costs

▶ Certain mining exploration expenditures

Additional separately stated items not mentioned in Sec. 702 or its regulations include

▶ Passive income and loss

▶ Portfolio income (e.g., dividends and interest)

For a more complete list of the separately stated items see Form 1120S, Schedule K included in Appendix B.

Section 1366(b) requires that the character of any separately stated item be determined as if the item were (1) realized directly by the shareholder from the same source from which it was realized by the corporation or (2) incurred by the shareholder in the same manner as it was incurred by the corporation. Thus, the character of an income, gain, deduction, loss, or credit item does not change merely because the item passes through to the shareholders.

DEDUCTIONS THAT CANNOT BE CLAIMED. S corporations also have several deductions that it cannot claim, including

▶ The 70%, 80%, or 100% dividends-received deduction (because dividends pass through to the S corporation's shareholders)

▶ The U.S. production activities deduction (because that deduction passes through to the S corporation's shareholders)

▶ The same deductions disallowed to a partnership under Sec. 703(a)(2) (e.g., personal and dependency exemptions, additional itemized deductions for individuals, taxes paid or accrued to a foreign country or to a U.S. possession, charitable contributions, oil and gas depletion, and NOL carrybacks and carryforwards).[30]

SIMILARITY TO C CORPORATION TREATMENT. S corporations are treated as corporations for certain tax matters. For example, an S corporation can elect to amortize its organizational expenditures under Sec. 248 (after deducting up to $5,000). Also, the 20% reduction in certain tax preference benefits under Sec. 291 applies to an S corporation if the corporation was a C corporation in any of its three preceding tax years.[31]

---

[28] Sec. 1366(a).

[29] Partnerships are permitted to have C corporations as owners of partnership interests. Thus, dividends eligible for the dividends-received deduction also are separately stated. Such is not the case with an S corporation, which cannot have a corporate shareholder.

[30] Sec. 1363(b)(2).

[31] Secs. 1363(b)(3) and (4).

ADDITIONAL COMMENT

The 20-year carryover period continues to run on C corporation NOLS even during subsequent S corporation years.

CARRYOVERS AND CARRYBACKS WHEN STATUS CHANGES. Some S corporations may operate as C corporations during a period of years that either precede the making of an S election or follow the termination of an S election. No carryovers or carrybacks that originate in a C corporation tax year can carry to an S corporation tax year other than carryovers that can be used to offset the built-in gains tax (see pages C11-17 through C11-19). Similarly, no carryovers or carrybacks created in an S corporation tax year can carry to a C corporation tax year.[32] Losses from an S corporation tax year pass through to the shareholder and, if greater than the shareholder's income for the year, can create an NOL carryover or carryback for the shareholder.

U.S. PRODUCTION ACTIVITIES DEDUCTION

The 2004 Jobs Act added a new deduction for businesses engaged in U.S. production activities for tax years beginning after 2004. Chapter C3 describes the C corporation version of this deduction, whereby the U.S. production activities deduction equals a percentage (3% in 2006) times the lesser of (1) qualified production activities income for the year or (2) taxable income before the U.S. production activities deduction. Individuals use a modified form of AGI instead of taxable income for this computation. The deduction, however, cannot exceed 50% of the employer's W-2 wages for the year. In the case of an S corporation, the deduction applies at the shareholder level, so the S corporation must report each shareholder's share of qualified production activities income on the shareholder's Schedule K-1. For the 50% salary limitation, each shareholder is allocated a share of the S corporation's W-2 wages equal to the lesser of (1) the shareholder's allocable share of such wages or (2) 6% (2 × 3% in 2006) of the qualified production activities income allocated to the shareholder.

OBJECTIVE 6

Calculate the amount of any special S corporation taxes

SPECIAL S CORPORATION TAXES

The S corporation is subject to three special taxes: the excess net passive income tax, the built-in gains tax, and the LIFO recapture tax. Each of these taxes is explained below.

EXCESS NET PASSIVE INCOME TAX. The **excess net passive income (or Sec. 1375) tax** applies when an S corporation has passive investment income for the tax year that exceeds 25% of its gross receipts and, at the close of the tax year, the S corporation has Subchapter C E&P. The excess net passive income tax equals the S corporation's excess net passive income times the highest corporate tax rate (35% in 2006).[33]

LEGISLATIVE UPDATE

On February 2, 2006, the Senate passed a bill that would raise the 25% threshold to 60%. If passed the Sec. 1375 tax would be significantly less likely to apply. The bill's proposed effective date is for tax years beginning after September 30, 2006.

The **excess net passive income** is determined as follows:

$$\begin{matrix}\text{Excess} \\ \text{net} \\ \text{passive} \\ \text{income}\end{matrix} = \begin{matrix}\text{Net} \\ \text{passive} \\ \text{income}\end{matrix} \times \frac{\text{Passive investment income} - 25\% \text{ of gross receipts}}{\text{Passive investment income}}$$

The excess net passive income is limited to the corporation's taxable income, which is defined as a C corporation's taxable income except with no reduction for the NOL deduction or the dividends-received deduction. Net passive income equals passive investment income minus any deductions directly related to its production.[34]

Regulation Sec. 1.1362-2(c)(5) holds that passive investment income excludes income derived from the active conduct of a trade or business.

KEY POINT

The excess net passive income tax is of concern to a former C corporation that has accumulated E&P. A corporation that always has been an S corporation will not have a passive income problem.

EXAMPLE C11-11 ▶ Paoli Corporation, an S corporation, reports the following results for the current year:

Service (nonpassive) income	$35,000
Dividend income	37,000
Interest income	28,000
Passive income-related expenses	10,000
Other expenses	25,000

---

[32] Sec. 1371(b).
[33] *Passive investment income* and *Subchapter C E&P* for this purpose have the same definition here as given on pages C11-9 and C11-10.

[34] Regulation Sec. 1.1375-1(f), Ex. (2) indicates that passive income subject to the Sec. 1375 tax includes municipal bond interest that otherwise is exempt from the federal income tax.

At the end of this year, Paoli's E&P from its prior C corporation tax years amounts to $60,000. Paoli's excess net passive income is determined as follows:

$$33,846 = (\$65,000 - \$10,000) \times \frac{\$65,000 - (0.25 \times \$100,000)}{\$65,000}$$

The excess net passive income tax is $11,846 ($33,846 × 0.35). The special tax reduces (on a pro rata basis) the dividend income and interest income items that pass through to the shareholders. The S election is not terminated at the end of the current year unless Paoli also was subject to the tax in the prior two tax years. ◄

BUILT-IN GAINS TAX. A second corporate level tax may apply to gains recognized by an S corporation that formerly was a C corporation. This tax, called the **built-in gains (or Sec. 1374) tax,** is imposed on any income or gain that would have been included in gross income while a C corporation if the corporation had used the accrual method of accounting (known as a **built-in gain**) and that the corporation reports during the ten-year period beginning on the date the S election took effect (known as the recognition period). Built-in losses reduce the amount of recognized built-in gains in determining the built-in gains tax liability. **Built-in losses** are any deductions or losses that would have been deductible while a C corporation if the corporation had used the accrual method of accounting and that the corporation reports during the ten-year period beginning on the date the S election took effect. Built-in gains and losses also include the differences between the FMVs and adjusted bases of assets held at the time the S election takes effect.

Congress enacted this tax to prevent taxpayers from avoiding the corporate level tax on liquidating distributions by making an S election before liquidating the corporation or selling its assets. However, the tax ramifications of the built-in gains tax extend beyond corporations that are in the process of liquidating. The built-in gains tax applies to S corporation tax years beginning after December 31, 1986, where the S corporation was formerly a C corporation and made the current S election after December 31, 1986.

EXAMPLE C11-12 ► Theta Corporation, a calendar year taxpayer, was incorporated in 1986 and operated as a C corporation through the end of 2005. On February 4, 2006, Theta filed an S election that was effective for 2006 and later tax years. Because Theta filed its S election after December 31, 1986, it is subject to the built-in gains tax for ten years starting with January 1, 2006. ◄

The Sec. 1374 tax is determined by using the following four-step calculation:

STEP 1: Determine the corporation's net recognized built-in gain for the tax year.

STEP 2: Reduce the net recognized built-in gain from Step 1 (but not below zero) by any NOL or capital loss carryovers from any prior C corporation tax years.

STEP 3: Compute a tentative tax by multiplying the amount determined in Step 2 by the highest corporate tax rate (35% in 2006).

STEP 4: Reduce the tax determined in Step 3 (but not below zero) by the amount of the general business credit and minimum tax credit carryovers from any prior C corporation tax years and the nonhighway use of gasoline and other fuels credit.

A recognized built-in gain or loss is any gain or loss recognized on an asset disposition during the ten-year recognition period unless the S corporation can establish that it did not hold the asset on the first day of the first tax year to which the S election applies. A recognized built-in gain cannot exceed the excess of a property's FMV over its adjusted basis on the first day of the ten-year recognition period. Dispositions include sales or exchanges and other events, including the collection of accounts receivable by a cash method of accounting taxpayer, collection of an installment sale obligation, and the completion of a long-term contract by a taxpayer using the completed contract method.[35]

---

[35] Income and gains potentially can be taxed under both the excess net passive income (Sec. 1375) and built-in gains (Sec. 1374) taxes. Any such income or gain is fully taxed under the Sec. 1374 rules. The portion of the income or gain taxed under the Sec. 1374 tax is exempt from the Sec. 1375 tax.

**PRACTICAL
APPLICATION**

The application of the Sec. 1374 tax requires detailed records, which enable the taxpayer to track the built-in gain assets and determine when the corporation recognizes these gains.

Built-in losses include not only losses originating from a disposition of property, but also any deductions claimed during the ten-year recognition period that are attributable to periods before the first S corporation tax year. A recognized built-in loss cannot exceed the excess of a property's adjusted basis over its FMV on the first day of the ten-year recognition period. Built-in losses, however, do not include any loss, deduction, or carryover originating from the disposition of an asset acquired before or during the recognition period where the principal purpose of such acquisition was avoiding the Sec. 1374 tax.

The net recognized built-in gain for a tax year is limited to the smaller of:

▶ The excess of (1) the net unrealized built-in gain (i.e., excess of the FMV of the S corporation's assets at the beginning of its first tax year for which the S election is in effect over their total adjusted basis on such date) over (2) the total net recognized built-in gain for prior tax years beginning in the ten-year recognition period.[36]

▶ The S corporation's taxable income as if it were a C corporation but with no dividends-received deduction or NOL deduction allowed.

If the net of the recognized built-in gains and losses exceeds the corporation's taxable income and the corporation made the S election after March 30, 1988, the excess built-in gain amount carries over to the next tax year, where it may be subject to the Sec. 1374 built-in gains tax in the carryover year. The built-in gain carryover consists of a ratable share of each of the income categories (e.g., ordinary income, capital gains) making up the net recognized built-in gain amount for the tax year.

The built-in gains tax passes through to the shareholders as if it were a loss. The loss must be allocated proportionately among the net recognized built-in gains that resulted in the tax being imposed.

EXAMPLE C11-13 ▶

Assume the same facts as in Example C11-12 and that Theta Corporation uses the accrual method of accounting. Theta owns the following assets on January 1, 2006:

Assets	Adjusted Basis	FMV
Cash	$ 10,000	$ 10,000
Marketable securities	39,000	45,000
Accounts receivable	60,000	60,000
Inventory (FIFO)	60,000	75,000
Building	27,000	44,000
Land	10,000	26,000
Machinery and equipment[a]	74,000	140,000
Total	$280,000	$400,000

[a] $50,000 of the gain is subject to recapture under Sec. 1245.

ETHICAL POINT

A C corporation that has substantially appreciated assets and wants to make an S election should obtain an appraisal of its assets on or about the first day of the S election period. The S corporation's tax accountant must make sure the appraiser does not assign an artificially low value to these assets to minimize the potential built-in gains tax burden.

During 2006, Theta collects $58,000 of accounts receivable and declares $2,000 uncollectible. It sells the FIFO inventory at a $25,000 profit in the first quarter of 2006, replacing the sold inventory with new inventory. It also sells two machines during 2006. One machine, having an $18,000 FMV and an $11,000 adjusted basis on January 1, produced a $7,000 gain (Sec. 1245 recapture income) on September 2. A second machine, having a $15,000 FMV and a $19,000 adjusted basis on January 1, produced a $4,000 loss on March 17.

▶ Theta recognizes no built-in gain or loss on collecting the receivables because it is an accrual method taxpayer. The $2,000 uncollectible debt is not a built-in loss because the loss arose after January 1. It is deductible as part of the ordinary income/loss calculation.

▶ Of the $25,000 inventory profit, $15,000 ($75,000 − $60,000) is a built-in gain taxed under Sec. 1374. Theta includes the entire $25,000 profit in ordinary income/loss.

▶ Theta recognizes a $7,000 built-in gain ($18,000 − $11,000) and a $4,000 ($15,000 − $19,000) built-in loss on the sale of the two machines. The $7,000 gain is ordinary income due to Sec. 1245 recapture and becomes part of Theta's S corporation ordinary income or loss. The $4,000 Sec. 1231 loss passes through separately to the shareholders.

---

[36] The recognition period can be extended beyond ten years if property having a carryover basis is acquired in a tax-free transaction (e.g., a tax-free reorganization) from a C corporation. For such property, the ten-year recognition period begins on the date the S corporation acquired the property.

In total, an $18,000 ($15,000 + $7,000 − $4,000) net recognized built-in gain is taxed under Sec. 1374, subject to the taxable income ceiling. Assuming C corporation taxable income (with no NOL deduction or dividends-received deduction) is at least $18,000, the built-in gains tax is $6,300 ($18,000 × 0.35). The entire tax amount reduces the shareholder's ordinary income from the inventory and machinery sales. ◀

LIFO RECAPTURE TAX. If a C corporation using the LIFO inventory method makes an S election, Sec. 1363(d)(3) requires the corporation to include its LIFO recapture amount in gross income for its last C corporation tax year. The LIFO recapture amount is the excess of the inventory's basis for tax purposes under the FIFO method over its basis under the LIFO method at the close of the final C corporation tax year. Any tax increase incurred in the final C corporation tax year is payable in four annual installments, on or before the due date for the final C corporation tax return and on or before the due date for the first three S corporation tax returns. The S corporation's inventory basis is increased by the LIFO recapture amount included in gross income.

EXAMPLE C11-14 ▶ Taylor Corporation, a calendar year C corporation since its inception in 1989, makes an S election on December 23, 2005, effective for its 2006 tax year. Taylor has used the LIFO inventory method for a number of years. Its LIFO inventory has a $400,000 adjusted basis, a $650,000 FIFO inventory value, and an $800,000 FMV. Taylor's LIFO recapture amount is $250,000 ($650,000 − $400,000). Taylor includes this amount in gross income reported on its 2005 corporate tax return. Assuming a 34% corporate tax, Taylor's increased tax liability is $85,000 (0.34 × $250,000), of which $21,250 (0.25 × $85,000) is due with Taylor's 2005 C corporation tax return. An additional $21,250 is due with the 2006 through 2008 S corporation tax returns. Taylor increases the basis of its inventory by the $250,000 LIFO recapture amount. ◀

? **STOP & THINK**

Question: Former C corporations that are now treated as S corporations are subject to three corporate level taxes—the **LIFO recapture tax**, the built-in gains tax, and the excess net passive income tax. Why did Congress enact these three taxes?

Solution: In 1986, Congress debated making the conversion of a C corporation into an S corporation a taxable event subject to the corporate liquidation rules. The corporation would have recognized all gains and losses at the time of conversion. As a compromise, only LIFO users are subject to an "automatic" tax when conversion occurs, and this tax is imposed only on the LIFO recapture amount and not all inventory appreciation. The built-in gains tax is imposed only when the corporation sells or exchanges assets during its first ten years after the S election. Assets not sold or exchanged during this time period escape the tax. The excess net passive income tax is imposed to encourage S corporations to distribute their accumulated E&P. No tax is imposed if the corporation keeps its passive income below the 25% of gross receipts threshold. Thus, former C corporations and their shareholders generally are better off under the current system than if corporate liquidation treatment had been mandated.

TAXATION OF THE SHAREHOLDER

OBJECTIVE 7

Calculate a shareholder's allocable share of ordinary income or loss and separately stated items

INCOME ALLOCATION PROCEDURES

An S corporation's shareholders must report their pro rata share of the ordinary income or loss and separately stated items for the S corporation's tax year that ends with or within the shareholder's tax year.[37] Each shareholder's pro rata share of these items is determined by

---

[37] Sec. 1366(a). If the shareholder dies during the S corporation's tax year, the income earned during the portion of the tax year preceding death is reported on the shareholder's tax return. The income for the period of time that the estate holds the S corporation stock is reported on the estate's fiduciary tax return.

1. Allocating an equal portion of the item to each day in the tax year (by dividing the amount of the item by the number of days in the S corporation's tax year)
2. Allocating an equal portion of the daily amount for the item to each share of stock that is outstanding on each day (by dividing the daily amount for the item by the number of shares of stock outstanding on a particular day)
3. Totaling the daily allocations for each share of stock
4. Totaling the amounts allocated for each share of stock held by the shareholder

TYPICAL MISCONCEPTION

An S corporation's income or loss is allocated basically the same as a partnership's except that a partnership may have the added flexibility of making certain special allocations under Sec. 704(b).

These allocation rules are known as the "per day/per share" method. Special allocations (such as those possible under the partnership tax rules) of the ordinary income or loss and separately stated items are not permitted.

If a sale of the S corporation stock occurs during the year, the transferor reports the earnings allocated to the transferred shares through the day of the transfer.[38] The transferee reports his or her share of the earnings from the day after the transfer date through the end of the tax year.

EXAMPLE C11-15 ▶ Fox Corporation is an electing S corporation owned equally by Arnie and Bonnie during all of the current year (not a leap year). During this year, Fox reports ordinary income of $146,000 and a long-term capital gain of $36,500. Arnie and Bonnie each report $73,000 (0.50 × $146,000) of ordinary income and $18,250 (0.50 × $36,500) of long-term capital gain. ◀

EXAMPLE C11-16 ▶ Assume the same facts as in Example C11-15, except Bonnie sells one-half of her shares to Clay on March 31 of the current year (the 90th day of Fox's tax year). Arnie reports the same ordinary income and long-term capital gain from his investment. Bonnie and Clay report ordinary income and long-term capital gain as follows:

Ordinary Income

Bonnie:	$\left(\$146{,}000 \times \dfrac{1}{2} \times \dfrac{90}{365} \right) + \left(\$146{,}000 \times \dfrac{1}{4} \times \dfrac{275}{365} \right)$	= $45,500
Clay:	$\$146{,}000 \times \dfrac{1}{4} \times \dfrac{275}{365}$	= 27,500
	Total	$73,000

Long-Term Capital Gain

Bonnie:	$\left(\$36{,}500 \times \dfrac{1}{2} \times \dfrac{90}{365} \right) + \left(\$36{,}500 \times \dfrac{1}{4} \times \dfrac{275}{365} \right)$	= $11,375
Clay:	$\$36{,}500 \times \dfrac{1}{4} \times \dfrac{275}{365}$	= 6,875
	Total	$18,250	◀

KEY POINT

Shareholders of an S corporation need to be aware that when they dispose of their stock, they have the option of having income/loss determined by an actual closing of the books rather than an allocation on a daily basis.

A special election is available for allocating the ordinary income or loss and separately stated items when the shareholder's interest in the S corporation terminates during the tax year, or when the interest is substantially reduced even if not completely terminated. Under this election, the income is allocated according to the accounting methods used by the S corporation (instead of on a daily basis). The election divides the S corporation's tax year into two parts ending on

▶ The day the shareholder's interest in the corporation terminates

▶ The last day of the S corporation's tax year

The corporation can make this election only if all affected shareholders agree to the election.[39] An affected shareholder includes the shareholder whose interest terminated and all shareholders to whom the transferor transferred S corporation shares during the year.

---

[38] Reg. Sec. 1.1377-1(a)(2)(ii). Also see examples under Reg. Sec. 1.1377-1(c).

[39] Sec. 1377(a)(2).

This election is explored in greater detail in the Tax Planning Considerations section of this chapter.

OBJECTIVE 8

Determine the limitations on a shareholder's deduction of S corporation losses

LOSS AND DEDUCTION PASS-THROUGH TO SHAREHOLDERS

The S corporation's ordinary loss and separately stated loss and deduction items pass through to the shareholders at the end of the corporation's tax year. The shareholders report these items in their tax year in which the S corporation's tax year ends.

ALLOCATION OF THE LOSS. Using the rules outlined above, allocation of the loss also occurs on a daily basis. Thus, shareholders receive an allocation of the ordinary loss and separately stated items even if they own the stock for only a portion of the year. If the ordinary loss and other separately stated loss and deduction pass-through items exceed the shareholder's income, the excess may create an NOL for the shareholder and result in a carryback or carryover to the shareholder's other tax years.

EXAMPLE C11-17 ▶ Kauai Corporation, an electing S corporation, reports a $73,000 ordinary loss during the current year (not a leap year). At the beginning of the currrent year, Edward and Frank own equally all of Kauai's stock. On June 30 of the current year (the 181st day of Kauai's tax year), Frank gives one-fourth of his stock to his son George. Edward is allocated $36,500 ($73,000 × 0.50) of ordinary loss. Frank and George are allocated ordinary losses as follows:

Frank: $\left(\$73,000 \times \dfrac{1}{2} \times \dfrac{181}{365} \right) + \left(\$73,000 \times \dfrac{3}{8} \times \dfrac{184}{365} \right) = \$31,900$

George: $\$73,000 \times \dfrac{1}{8} \times \dfrac{184}{365}$ = $\underline{\quad 4,600}$

Total $\underline{\$36,500}$

All three shareholders can deduct these losses on their individual tax returns subject to the loss limitations described below. ◀

REAL-WORLD EXAMPLE

A recent U.S. Supreme Court case held that discharge of indebtedness income excluded from gross income under Sec. 108 nevertheless is a pass-through item that increases the shareholders' stock bases, thereby allowing loss pass-through items to be deducted by the shareholders. *Gitlitz et al. v. Comm.* 87 AFTR 2d 2001-417, 2001-1 USTC ¶50,147 (USSC, 2001). A subsequent tax act (2002), however, disallowed the pass-through and stock basis increase for debt cancellations after October 11, 2001. This situation is a good example of Congress "overruling" the Supreme Court with its legislative power.

SHAREHOLDER LOSS LIMITATIONS. Each shareholder's deduction for his or her share of the ordinary loss and the separately stated loss and deduction items is limited to the sum of the adjusted basis for his or her S corporation stock plus the adjusted basis of any indebtedness owed *directly* by the S corporation to the shareholder. Thus, a shareholder must account for stock basis and debt basis. Unlike the partnership taxation rules, however, a shareholder cannot increase his or her stock basis by a ratable share of the *general* S corporation liabilities.[40]

In determining the stock basis limitation for losses, the shareholder makes the following positive and negative adjustments:[41]

▶ Increase stock basis for any capital contributions during the year

▶ Increase stock basis for ordinary income and separately stated income or gain items

▶ Decrease stock basis for distributions not included in the shareholder's income

▶ Decrease stock basis for nondeductible, noncapital expenditures (unless the shareholder elects to determine the loss limitation without this decrease)

Sequencing the basis reduction for distributions ahead of losses means that distributions reduce the deductibility of S corporation loss and deduction pass-throughs, but losses do not affect the treatment of S corporation distributions.

Many S corporations are nothing more than incorporated forms of sole proprietorships or partnerships. As a result, banks and other lending institutions often require one or more of the shareholders to personally guarantee any loans made to the S corporation. In general, the IRS and the courts have held that this form of indirect borrowing by the S corpo-

---

[40] Sec. 1366(d)(1). Amounts owed by an S corporation to a conduit entity that has the shareholder as an owner or beneficiary will not increase the shareholder's loss limitation.

[41] Sec. 1366(d) and Reg. Sec. 1.1366-2(a)(3). Special basis adjustment rules apply to oil and gas depletion.

TAX STRATEGY TIP

Rather than having the corporation borrow money, an S corporation shareholder might consider borrowing money directly from the bank and then lending the loan proceeds to the corporation with the corporation guaranteeing the bank loan. In this way, the shareholder will obtain debt basis.

ration does not create a corporate indebtedness to the shareholder. As a result, the shareholder's loss limitation does not increase as a result of his or her acting as a guarantor until the shareholder makes a payment of part or all of the corporation's liability or the shareholder executes a note at the bank in full satisfaction of the corporation's liability. Such action by the shareholder converts the guarantee into an indebtedness of the corporation to the shareholder, which increases the shareholder's debt basis and loss limitation.[42]

The adjusted basis of the S corporation stock and debt generally is determined as of the last day of the S corporation's tax year. If the shareholder disposes of the S corporation stock before that date, the adjusted basis of the stock and debt is instead determined immediately prior to the disposition.

The loss and deduction pass-through is allocated to each share of stock and reduces each share's basis. Once the losses and deductions have reduced the basis of all shares of stock to zero, they are applied against the basis of any debt owed by the S corporation to the shareholder.

EXAMPLE C11-18 ▶ Pat and Bill equally own Tillis Corporation, an electing S corporation. During the current year, Tillis reports an ordinary loss of $100,000. Tillis's liabilities at the end of the current year include $110,000 of accounts payable, $150,000 of mortgage payable, and a $20,000 note owed to Bill. Thus, Bill has a $20,000 debt basis for the amount he loaned to the corporation. Pat and Bill each had a $40,000 adjusted basis in their Tillis stock on January 1. The ordinary loss is allocated equally to Pat and Bill. Pat's $50,000 loss allocation is only partially deductible this year (i.e., up to $40,000) because the loss exceeds his $40,000 basis for the Tillis stock. Bill's $50,000 loss allocation is fully deductible this year because his loss limitation is $60,000 ($40,000 stock basis + $20,000 debt basis). After the loss pass-through, Pat and Bill have a zero basis in their stock, and Bill has a $10,000 basis in the debt.[43] ◀

Any loss or deduction pass-through not currently deductible is suspended until the shareholder regains basis in his stock or debt. The carryover period for the loss or deduction item is unlimited.[44] The additional adjusted basis amount can originate from a number of sources, including subsequent profits earned by the S corporation, additional capital contributions or loans made by the shareholder to the corporation, or purchases of additional stock from other shareholders.

EXAMPLE C11-19 ▶ Assume the same facts as in Example C11-18 and that Tillis Corporation reports ordinary income of $20,000 in the next year. Pat and Bill are each allocated $10,000 of ordinary income. This income provides Pat with the necessary $10,000 stock basis to deduct the $10,000 loss carryover. The $10,000 income allocated to Bill restores his debt basis to $20,000 (see pages C11-26 and C11-27). ◀

If a shareholder sells his or her S corporation stock still having unused losses due to lack of stock or debt basis, these losses do not transfer to the new shareholder. Instead, the unused losses lapse when the shareholder sells the stock. For tax years beginning after 2004, the 2004 Jobs Act added an exception to this loss lapse rule. If the shareholder transfers the S corporation stock to a spouse or former spouse incident to a divorce, the suspended losses transfer to the spouse or former spouse. Thus, the spouse or former spouse can deduct the losses when he or she obtains sufficient basis.

SPECIAL SHAREHOLDER LOSS AND DEDUCTION LIMITATIONS. The S corporation's shareholders are subject to three special loss and deduction limitations. These limitations may prevent an S corporation's shareholder from using losses or deductions even

---

[42] Rev. Ruls. 70-50, 1970-1 C.B. 178; 71-288, 1971-2 C.B. 319; and 75-144, 1975-1 C.B. 277. See also *Estate of Daniel Leavitt v. CIR*, 63 AFTR 2d 89-1437, 89-1 USTC ¶9332 (4th Cir., 1989) among a series of decisions that uphold the IRS's position. However, see *Edward M. Selfe v. U.S.*, 57 AFTR 2d 86-464, 86-1 USTC ¶9115 (11th Cir., 1986) for a transaction where a guarantee was held to increase the shareholder's loss limitation because the transaction was structured so the bank looked primarily to the shareholder instead of the corporation for repayment.

[43] See pages C11-25 through C11-27 for a detailed discussion of basis adjustments.
[44] Sec. 1366(d)(2). If more than one type of loss or deduction item passes through to the shareholder, the carryover amount is allocated to each of the pass-through items based on their relative amounts.

though the general loss limitation described above does not otherwise apply. Application of the special loss limitations occurs as follows:

▶ *At-Risk Rules:* The Sec. 465 at-risk rules apply at the shareholder level. Thus, the shareholder can deduct a loss from a particular S corporation activity only to the extent the shareholder is at risk in the activity at the close of the S corporation's tax year.

▶ *Passive Activity Limitation Rules:* Losses and credits from a passive activity can be applied against income from that passive activity or other passive activities earned in the same or a subsequent tax year. An S corporation shareholder must personally meet the material participation standard for an activity to avoid the passive activity limitation. Material participation by the S corporation in an activity does not permit a passive investor to deduct the portion of the S corporation's loss against his or her salary and other "active" income.

▶ *Hobby Loss Rules:* Losses incurred by an S corporation are subject to the Sec. 183 hobby loss rules. Deductions incurred by the S corporation are limited to the activity's gross income unless the taxpayer can establish that the activity is engaged in for profit.

In addition, various separately stated loss and deduction items are subject to shareholder limitations (e.g., charitable contributions, capital losses, and investment interest expense), but they are not subject to corporate limitations. Some separately stated items are subject to corporate limitations but not shareholder limitations (e.g., the 50% nondeductible portion of meal and entertainment expenses).

POST-TERMINATION LOSS CARRYOVERS. Loss and deduction carryovers incurred in S corporation tax years can be carried over at the shareholder level even though the S election has been terminated. Shareholders can deduct these carryovers only in the **post-termination transition period**.[45] The length of the post-termination transition period depends on the event causing the termination of the S election. In general, the period begins on the day after the last day of the corporation's final S corporation tax year and ends on the later of one year after the last day or the due date for the final S corporation tax return (including any extensions).

If the S election terminates for a prior tax year as a result of a determination, the period runs for 120 days beginning on the determination date. Section 1377(b)(2) defines a determination as a court decision that becomes final; a closing agreement entered into; a final disposition of a refund claim by the IRS; or an agreement between the corporation and the IRS that the corporation failed to qualify as an S corporation.

The shareholder can deduct the loss carryovers only up to his or her adjusted basis of the stock at the end of the post-termination transition period.[46] Losses that cannot be deducted because of the basis limitation are lost forever. Deducted losses reduce the shareholder's stock basis.

EXAMPLE C11-20 ▶ Pearson Corporation has been a calendar year S corporation for several years. Helen's stock basis is $45,000. On July 1, 2006, its S election terminates when an ineligible shareholder acquires part of its stock. For the period ended June 30, 2006, Helen is allocated $60,000 of Pearson's ordinary loss. Helen can deduct only $45,000 of this loss because of her Pearson stock basis, which is reduced to zero by the loss. The $15,000 unused loss carries over to the post-termination transition period, which ends on June 30, 2007 (assuming Pearson does not extend the March 15, 2007 due date for the S short year tax return). Helen must have an adjusted basis for the Pearson stock of at least $15,000 at the close of business on June 30, 2007, to use the loss. Helen should consider making additional capital contributions of at least $15,000 between July 1, 2006, and June 30, 2007, to use the loss. ◀

Topic Review C11-3 summarizes the rules governing deductibility of S corporation losses and deductions that pass through to the shareholders.

---

[45] Sec. 1366(d)(3). The loss carryovers that carry over include those disallowed by the at-risk rules.

[46] Sec. 1366(d)(3)(B).

Topic Review C11-3

Deductibility of S Corporation Losses and Deductions

Allocation Process

1. Losses and deductions are allocated based on the number of shares of stock owned by each shareholder on each day of the tax year. Special allocations of losses and deductions are not permitted.
2. Termination of the S election requires the tax year to be divided into two parts. The corporation can elect (with the shareholders' consent) to allocate the loss or deduction according to the accounting methods used by the corporation. This election also is available when a shareholder's interest in the S corporation terminates.

Loss Limitations

1. Losses and deductions pass through on a per-share basis and are limited to the shareholder's basis in the stock and to the shareholder's debt basis. Once the basis for all the shareholder's stock is reduced to zero, the losses reduce the basis of any S corporation indebtedness to the shareholder.
2. Losses and deductions that are not deducted carry over to a tax year in which the shareholder regains stock or debt basis. The time period for the carryover is unlimited. The unused losses lapse if the shareholder transfers the stock to anyone other than a spouse or former spouse incident to a divorce.
3. S corporation shareholders are subject to three special loss limitations:
   ▶ At-risk rules
   ▶ Passive activity limitations
   ▶ Hobby loss rules
   Some separately stated loss and deduction items also are subject to shareholder limitations (e.g., investment interest expense). Other separately stated items are subject to corporate limitations but not shareholder limitations (e.g., the 50% nondeductible portion of meal and entertainment expenses).

FAMILY S CORPORATIONS

Family S corporations have been an important tax planning device. This type of tax planning often involves a high-tax-bracket taxpayer gifting stock to a minor child who generally has little other income. The transfer results in income splitting among family members. The IRS has enjoyed success in litigating cases dealing with intrafamily transfers of S corporation stock when the transferor (usually a parent) retains the economic benefits and control over the stock transferred to the transferee (usually a child).[47] The IRS has attained less success when one family member purchases the stock from another family member at its market value.

The IRS also has the statutory authority under Sec. 1366(e) to adjust the income, loss, deduction, or credit items allocated to a family member to reflect the value of services rendered or capital provided to the corporation. Section 1366(e) defines family as including spouse, ancestors, lineal descendants, and trusts created for such individuals. This provision permits the reallocation of income to provide for full compensation of a shareholder or nonshareholder for services and capital provided to the corporation. It also reduces the residual income reported by the S corporation and allocated to the shareholders according to their stock ownership. Such a reallocation prevents not only the shifting of income from the family member providing the services or capital to other family members, but also the avoidance of employment taxes. Alternatively, the IRS can determine that the corporation paid too much compensation to a shareholder and reduce that shareholder's salary and increase the residual income allocated based on stock ownership.

ADDITIONAL COMMENT

The advantages of family S corporations have been somewhat curtailed. For example, income from stock of an S corporation gifted to a child under age 14 is subject to the "kiddie tax," where unearned income exceeding $1,600 (in 2005) is taxed at the parents' marginal tax rate.

EXAMPLE C11-21 ▶ Harvest Corporation, an electing S corporation, reports ordinary income of $200,000 after it claims a $20,000 deduction for Sid's salary. Sid and his three children own the Harvest stock equally. Harvest employs none of Sid's three children. The IRS subsequently determines that reasonable compensation for Sid is $80,000. This adjustment increases Sid's salary income and Harvest's compensation deduction by $60,000 ($80,000 − $20,000) and reduces Harvest's ordinary income to $140,000 ($200,000 − $60,000). Each shareholder's ratable share of ordinary

---

[47] See, for example, *Gino A. Speca v. CIR*, 47 AFTR 2d 81-468, 80-2 USTC ¶9692 (7th Cir., 1980) and *Henry D. Duarte*, 44 T.C. 193 (1965), where the IRS's position prevailed. See also *Gavin S. Millar*, 1975 PH T.C. Memo ¶75,113, 34 TCM 554, and *Donald O. Kirkpatrick*, 1977 PH T.C. Memo ¶77,281, 36 TCM 1122, where the taxpayers prevailed.

income is reduced from $50,000 ($200,000 ÷ 4) to $35,000 ($140,000 ÷ 4). Alternatively, if the IRS can prove that the stock transfer to the three children is not a bona fide transfer, all $220,000 of Harvest's income is taxed to Sid—$80,000 as salary and $140,000 as an allocation of ordinary income. ◄

BASIS ADJUSTMENTS

<table>
<tr><td>

OBJECTIVE 9

Calculate a shareholder's basis in his or her S corporation's stock and debt

</td><td>

Shareholder's must make annual adjustments to their S corporation stock basis. In addition, if the S corporation is indebted to the shareholder, he or she may have to adjust the debt basis downward for loss or deduction pass-throughs and upward to reflect restoration of the debt basis when the corporation earns subsequent profits. Each of these adjustments is described below.

</td></tr>
</table>

BASIS ADJUSTMENTS TO S CORPORATION STOCK

Basis adjustments to the shareholder's stock are made in the following order:[48]

Initial investment (or basis at beginning of tax year)
Plus: Additional capital contributions made during the year
      Allocable share of ordinary income
      Allocable share of separately stated income and gain items
Minus: Distributions excluded from the shareholder's gross income
      Allocable share of any expense not deductible in determining
        ordinary income (loss) and not chargeable to the capital account
        (A shareholder, however, can elect to make this adjustment *after*
        the two following adjustments.)
      Allocable share of ordinary loss
      Allocable share of separately stated loss and deduction items

Adjusted basis for stock (but not less than zero)

A shareholder's initial basis for S corporation stock depends on how he or she acquires it. Stock purchased from the corporation or another shareholder takes a cost basis. Stock received as part of a corporate formation transaction takes a substituted basis from the assets transferred. Stock acquired by gift takes the donor's basis (adjusted for gift taxes paid) or FMV (if lower). Stock acquired at death takes its FMV on the decedent's date of death or the alternate valuation date (if elected). The basis of S corporation stock inherited from a deceased shareholder is its FMV minus any corporate income that would have been income in respect of a decedent (see Chapter C14) if the income had been acquired from the decedent. No basis adjustment occurs when the corporation makes the initial S election.

The basis adjustments to the S corporation stock parallel those made to a partnership interest. The ordinary income and separately stated income and gain items increase the shareholder's basis whether they are taxable, tax-exempt, or receive preferential tax treatment.

EXAMPLE C11-22 ▶   Cathy owns Marlo Corporation, an electing S corporation. At the beginning of the current year, Cathy's adjusted basis for her Marlo stock is $105,000. Marlo reports the following operating results this year:

Ordinary income	$70,000
Municipal bond interest income	15,000
Dividends from domestic corporations	6,000
Long-term capital gain	8,000
Short-term capital loss	17,000

Cathy's adjusted basis for the Marlo stock at the end of the year is $187,000 ($105,000 + $70,000 + $15,000 + $6,000 + $8,000 − $17,000). ◄

---

[48] Sec. 1367(a) and Reg. Sec. 1.1367-1(f).

Cathy makes the basis adjustment at the end of the S corporation's tax year, when the results for the entire period are known. Because the profits and losses are allocated ratably on a daily basis to all shares held on each day of the tax year, a shareholder's gain or loss realized on the sale of S corporation stock during the tax year is not determinable until the ordinary income or loss and separately stated items allocable to the shares sold are known. Similarly, when the S corporation stock becomes worthless during a tax year, the shareholder must make the necessary positive and negative basis adjustments before the amount of the worthless security loss can be determined.

EXAMPLE C11-23 ▶ Mike, Carlos, and Juan equally own Diaz Corporation, an electing S corporation. Mike's 100 shares of Diaz stock have a $25,000 adjusted basis at the beginning of the current year (not a leap year). Diaz Corporation reports ordinary income of $36,500 and municipal bond interest income of $14,600 in the current year. On February 14 of the current year (the 45th day of Diaz's tax year), Mike sells all his Diaz stock for $30,000. Assuming the corporation uses the daily method to allocate the income items, Mike's basis for the Diaz stock is determined as follows:

$$\$27,100 = \$25,000 + \left(\$36,500 \times \frac{45}{365} \times \frac{1}{3}\right) + \left(\$14,600 \times \frac{45}{365} \times \frac{1}{3}\right)$$

Mike reports a $2,900 ($30,000 − $27,100) gain on the sale. ◀

BASIS ADJUSTMENTS TO SHAREHOLDER DEBT

KEY POINT

Losses first reduce the basis in the stock and then any amount of debt owed to the shareholder by the S corporation. Subsequent *net* increases in basis are added first to the debt and then to the stock.

After the shareholder's basis in the S corporation stock is reduced to zero, the basis of any S corporation indebtedness to the shareholder still outstanding at the end of the S corporation's tax year is reduced (but not below zero) by the remainder of the available loss and deduction items.[49] If a shareholder has more than one loan outstanding at year-end, the basis reduction applies to all the indebtednesses based on the relative adjusted basis for each loan. Ordinary income and separately stated gain or income items allocated to the shareholder in subsequent tax years (net of distributions and losses to the shareholders) first restore the basis of any S corporation indebtedness to the shareholder that is outstanding at year-end. Once all previous decreases to the debt basis are restored, any additional positive basis adjustments increase the shareholder's stock basis.[50]

Repayment of a shareholder indebtedness results in gain recognition to the shareholder if the payment amount exceeds the debt's adjusted basis. If the indebtedness is secured by a note, the difference is a capital gain. If the indebtedness is not secured by a note or other evidence of the indebtedness, the repayment is ordinary income.[51]

EXAMPLE C11-24 ▶ At the beginning of 2005, Betty owns one-half the stock of Trailer Corporation, an electing S corporation. Betty's basis for the Trailer stock is $40,000. Trailer owes Betty $20,000 on January 1, 2005, evidenced by a note. Thus, Betty has a $20,000 debt basis. During 2005 and 2006, Trailer reports an ordinary loss of $100,000 and ordinary income of $10,000, respectively. Betty's $50,000 loss pass-through from 2005 first reduces the basis of her Trailer stock from $40,000 to zero. Next, the $10,000 remainder of the loss pass-through reduces Betty's debt basis from $20,000 to $10,000. Betty's $5,000 allocation of 2006's ordinary income increases her debt basis from $10,000 to $15,000. If the corporation repays the note before the end of 2006, Betty reports a $5,000 ($20,000 − $15,000) long-term capital gain resulting from the repayment plus any ordinary income or separately stated items resulting from Trailer's 2006 operations. If the debt instead were unsecured (i.e., an advance from the shareholder not secured by a note), the gain would be ordinary income. ◀

STOP & THINK

Question: The text preceding Example C11-24 says that ordinary income and separately stated gain or income items (net of losses and distributions) restore debt basis before increasing stock basis; that is, debt is restored first by any net increase. The following rule

---

[49] The shareholder makes no basis reductions to debt repaid before the end of the tax year. Regulation Sec. 1.1367-2(d)(1) holds that restoration occurs immediately before a shareholder repays or disposes of indebtedness during the tax year.

[50] Sec. 1367(b)(2)(B).
[51] Rev. Ruls. 64-162, 1964-1 (Part I) C.B. 304 and 68-537, 1968-2 C.B. 372.

also applies: total basis for the loss limitation equals (1) stock basis *after* all current year adjustments other than for losses plus (2) debt basis *before* any current year adjustments.

Consider the following situation: Omega Corporation is an S corporation with one shareholder. At the beginning of last year, the shareholder's stock basis was $15,000, and her debt basis was $20,000. Last year, Omega incurred a $45,000 ordinary loss, $35,000 of which the shareholder could deduct and $10,000 of which carries over. The loss affected basis as follows:

	Stock Basis	Debt Basis
Basis at beginning of last year	$15,000	$20,000
Ordinary loss last year ($45,000)	(15,000)	(20,000)
Basis at beginning of current year	$ –0–	$ –0–

In the current year, Omega earns $18,000 of ordinary income. What does the shareholder recognize in the current year, and what is the effect on her stock and debt bases? Why is the net increase rule for debt basis restoration beneficial to the shareholder?

Solution: The shareholder recognizes $18,000 of ordinary income and deducts the entire $10,000 loss carryover. Current year basis adjustments are as follows:

	Stock Basis	Debt Basis
Balance at beginning of current year	$ –0–	$ –0–
Ordinary income	10,000	8,000
Loss carryover allowed	(10,000)	–0–
Basis at end of current year	$ –0–	$8,000

The net increase approach benefits the shareholder because it allows her to deduct the $10,000 loss carryover in the current year rather than next year. The net increase for debt restoration is $8,000 ($18,000 − $10,000), which leaves $10,000 of the $18,000 ordinary income to increase stock basis. This net increase approach to debt restoration allows a stock basis increase sufficient to use the loss carryover. Alternatively, if debt were restored by ordinary income without netting, the debt basis would increase by the entire $18,000, leaving no positive adjustment to the stock basis. This increase to debt basis would not help the shareholder in the current year because debt basis for the loss limitation is the balance before any current year adjustments. Under this hypothetical alternative approach, the shareholder could deduct the loss next year because next year's beginning debt basis would be $18,000. However, the net increase approach is better than the alternative because it allows the shareholder to deduct the loss in the current year.

S CORPORATION DISTRIBUTIONS

OBJECTIVE 10

Determine the taxability of an S corporation's distributions to its shareholders

Two sets of rules apply to S corporation distributions. One applies to S corporations having accumulated E&P. Accumulated E&P may exist if an S corporation was a C corporation in a pre–S election tax year. Another set of distribution rules applies to S corporations that do not have E&P (e.g., a corporation formed after 1982 that makes a timely S election in its initial tax year). These rules are explained below.

CORPORATIONS HAVING NO EARNINGS AND PROFITS

For S corporations with no accumulated E&P, a two-tier rule applies. Distributions are initially tax-free and reduce the shareholder's adjusted basis in the stock (but not below zero). If the distribution exceeds the shareholder's stock basis, the shareholder treats the excess as a gain from the sale or exchange of the stock. The stock basis for determining excess distributions is that after positive adjustments for ordinary income and separately stated income and gain items but before negative adjustments.[52]

EXAMPLE C11-25 ▶

Sandy owns 100% of Liberty Corporation, an electing S corporation. At the beginning of the current year, Sandy's adjusted basis in her Liberty stock (a capital asset) is $20,000. Liberty reports ordinary income of $30,000 and a long-term capital loss of $7,000 this year. Liberty makes a $35,000 cash distribution to Sandy on June 15. Sandy's basis for the stock must be adjusted for the ordinary income before determining the taxability of the distribution. Because Sandy's $50,000 ($20,000 + $30,000) adjusted basis for the stock exceeds the $35,000 distribution amount, she excludes the entire distribution from her gross income. The distribution reduces her stock basis to $15,000 ($50,000 − $35,000). Because Sandy still has sufficient stock basis, she can deduct the $7,000 capital loss, which further reduces her stock basis to $8,000.

If Liberty instead reports only $5,000 of ordinary income and a $7,000 capital loss, $10,000 of the distribution is taxable. The ordinary income increases the stock's basis to $25,000 ($20,000 + $5,000). Because the distribution exceeds the stock's adjusted basis by $10,000 ($35,000 − $25,000), Sandy recognizes a capital gain on the excess distribution. The distribution not included in Sandy's income ($25,000) reduces her stock basis to zero at year-end. Because the stock basis after the distribution is zero, Sandy cannot deduct the $7,000 capital loss in the current year. She must wait until she regains a positive stock basis (or obtains debt basis). ◀

SELF-STUDY QUESTION

Can distributions that exceed stock basis be tax-free to the extent of shareholder loans?

ANSWER

No. Although the amount of deductible losses can be increased by the amount of shareholder loans, tax-free distributions are strictly limited to stock basis. Also, distributions never reduce debt basis.

If an S corporation distributes appreciated property to its shareholders, the S corporation recognizes gain as if it sold the property.[53] The corporation recognizes no loss, however, when it distributes property that has declined in value. The gain recognized on the distribution may be taxed at the corporate level as part of the S corporation's built-in gains or excess net passive income. The gain also becomes part of the S corporation's ordinary income or loss, or is passed through as a separately stated item, depending on the type of property distributed and the character of the gain recognized. After this recognition occurs, the distributed property causes no further taxation provided the sum of the money plus the FMV of the nonmoney property distributed does not exceed the shareholder's stock basis. The shareholder's stock basis is reduced by the FMV of the distribution, and the shareholder takes a FMV basis in the distributed property.

EXAMPLE C11-26 ▶

ADDITIONAL COMMENT

The distribution of appreciated stock in Example C11-26 produced income to Echo, which passed through to Tad. A similar distribution by a C corporation would result in a double tax by causing income recognition to both Echo and Tad.

Tad owns 100% of Echo Corporation, which always has been an S corporation. Tad's adjusted basis in the Echo stock at the beginning of the current year is $50,000. Echo reports $30,000 of ordinary income for this year (exclusive of the effects of a property distribution made to Tad). On December 1, Echo distributes some Cable Corporation stock to Tad. The stock cost $40,000 and has a $100,000 FMV, and Echo has held it as an investment for three years. Echo reports $60,000 ($100,000 − $40,000) of capital gain from distributing the stock. Tad reports $30,000 of ordinary income and $60,000 of long-term capital gain from Echo's current year activities. Tad's adjusted basis for his Echo stock increases to $140,000 ($50,000 + $30,000 + $60,000). The distribution is free of further taxation because the $140,000 basis for the Echo stock exceeds the $100,000 distribution amount. The basis of the Echo stock is $40,000 ($140,000 − $100,000) at year-end. Tad takes a $100,000 FMV basis in the Cable stock. ◀

CORPORATIONS HAVING ACCUMULATED EARNINGS AND PROFITS

PRIOR RULES. Under pre-1983 rules, a corporation's undistributed taxable income was taxed to its shareholders as a deemed distribution at year-end. This income accumulated in a **previously taxed income (PTI)** account, which can be a source of S corporation distributions. For simplicity in this text, however, the following discussion assumes that S corporation status occurs after 1982 and thus ignores the implications of PTI.

KEY POINT

The AAA represents the cumulative income and loss recognized in post-1982 S corporation years. To the extent the AAA is positive and sufficient basis exists in the stock, distributions from an S corporation are tax-free and reduce stock basis.

CURRENT RULES. Under current (post-1982) rules, some S corporations have a post-1982 accumulated E&P balance earned while a C corporation. Part or all of a distribution may be treated as made from this balance. The current rules, however, also require S corporations that have accumulated E&P balances to maintain an **accumulated adjustments**

---

[52] Secs. 1368(b)and (d).

[53] Sec. 311(b).

account (AAA) from which they make most of their distributions. The existence of accumulated E&P and AAA balances makes the tax treatment of cash and property distributions somewhat more complicated than do the rules explained in the preceding section.

MONEY DISTRIBUTIONS. For corporations making a post-1982 S election and having an accumulated E&P balance, money distributions come from the two tiers of earnings illustrated in Table C11-1. The corporation makes distributions from the first tier until it is exhausted. The corporation then makes distributions from the second tier until that tier is used up. Amounts distributed after the two tiers of earnings are exhausted reduce the shareholder's remaining basis in his or her S corporation stock. Any additional amounts distributed once the stock basis has been reduced to zero are taxed to the shareholder as a capital gain. The corporation usually maintains these tiers as working paper accounts and not as general ledger accounts.

The AAA is the cumulative total of the ordinary income or loss and separately stated items accumulated for the S period but excluding tax-exempt income and expenses related to its production. The S period is the most recent continuous period during which the corporation has been an S corporation. No tax years beginning before January 1, 1983, are included in this period.[54]

The year-end AAA balance is determined as follows:

AAA balance at the beginning of the year
Plus: Ordinary income
           Separately stated income and gain items (except for tax-exempt income)
Minus: Distributions made from AAA (see first bullet item below)
           Ordinary loss
           Separately stated loss and deduction items (except for expenses or losses related to the production of tax-exempt income)
           Expenses not deductible in determining ordinary income (loss) and not chargeable to the capital account

AAA balance at the end of the year

▼ **TABLE C11-1**

Source of Distributions Made by S Corporations Having Accumulated Earnings and Profits

Tier	Classification	Money Distributions?	Property (Nonmoney) Distributions?	Taxable or Tax-Free Distributions?
1	Accumulated adjustments account	Yes	Yes	Tax-free[a]
2	Accumulated E&P	Yes	Yes	Taxable
3	Basis of S corporation stock	Yes	Yes	Tax-free[a]
4	Excess over stock basis	Yes	Yes	Taxable

a These distributions reduce the basis of the S corporation stock. Although generally tax-free, gain can be recognized if the amount of money plus the FMV of the nonmoney property distributed exceeds the shareholder's adjusted basis in the S corporation stock as indicated in Tier 4.

---

[54] Sec. 1368(e). An S corporation without accumulated E&P need not maintain the AAA to determine the tax effect of its distributions. If an S corporation having no E&P subsequently acquires E&P in a transaction where it assumes tax attributes under Sec. 381(a) (e.g., a merger), the corporation must calculate its AAA at the merger date to determine the tax effects of post-merger distributions. To accomplish this calculation, a firm may need to make calculations back to the original S election date. To reduce this hardship, the IRS, in the Form 1120S instructions, recommends that all S corporations maintain AAA information.

Four differences exist between the positive and negative adjustments required for the AAA and the basis calculation for the S corporation stock:

▶ Distributions not included in gross income reduce *stock* basis *before* other negative adjustments. Distributions reduce the AAA *after* other negative adjustments unless the other negative adjustments, when netted against positive adjustments, produce a "net negative adjustment." In this case, positive adjustments increase the AAA and negative adjustments other than distributions reduce the AAA to the extent of the positive adjustments. Then, distributions reduce the AAA before the net negative adjustment, and the net negative adjustment reduces the AAA after the distribution.[55]

▶ Tax-exempt income does not increase the AAA but increases the basis of the S corporation stock.

▶ Nondeductible expenses that reduce the basis of the S corporation stock also reduce the AAA except for expenses related to the production of tax-exempt income and federal income taxes related to a C corporation tax year.

▶ The AAA balance can be negative (e.g., when the cumulative losses exceed the cumulative profits), but the shareholder's basis in the S corporation stock cannot be less than zero.

TYPICAL MISCONCEPTION

Even though the basis of S corporation stock cannot be less than zero, the AAA can be negative if cumulative losses exceed cumulative profits.

Allocation of the AAA balance to individual distributions occurs at year-end after taking into account current year income and loss items. In general, the AAA amount is allocated ratably to individual distributions within a tax year (other than distributions coming from E&P) based on the amount of money or FMV of nonmoney property distributed.

Corporations also maintain an Other Adjustments Account (OAA) if they have accumulated E&P at year-end. The corporation increases this account for tax-exempt income earned and decreases it by expenses incurred in earning the tax-exempt income, distributions out of the OAA, and federal taxes paid by the S corporation that are attributable to C corporation tax years. The effect of creating a separate account for tax-exempt income earned by companies having accumulated E&P is that the AAA is determined by taking into account only the taxable portion of the S corporation's income and any expenses and losses other than those related to the production of the tax-exempt income. Although the corporation reports the OAA balance on page 4 of the Form 1120S, it is not an accumulated earnings account. Municipal bond interest and other forms of tax-exempt income (net of related deductions) become part of the stock basis and thus appear after accumulated E&P in the distribution order. A corporation having an accumulated E&P balance might consider having the tax-exempt income-producing property owned at the shareholder level rather than at the corporate level.

EXAMPLE C11-27 ▶ Omega Corporation is an electing S corporation with one shareholder, George. George's stock basis at the beginning of the current year is $22,000. Omega has the following results for the current year:

Ordinary loss	$10,000
Dividend income	2,000

In addition, at the beginning of the current year, the corporation has a $12,000 AAA balance and a $4,000 accumulated E&P balance. In December of the current year, Omega distributes $7,500 cash to George. Because the ordinary loss and dividend income produce an $8,000 ($2,000 − $10,000) net negative adjustment, the predistribution AAA remains at $12,000 while the $2,000 dividend increases predistribution stock basis. Accordingly, the predistribution balances are as follows:

	Stock Basis	AAA	E&P
Beginning balances	$22,000	$12,000	$4,000
Dividend income	2,000	2,000	
Partial ordinary loss		(2,000)	
Predistribution balance	$24,000	$12,000	$4,000

---

[55] Reg. Secs. 1.1367-1(f) and 1.1368-2(a)(5). This ordering for AAA preserves tax-free treatment for S corporation earnings from prior years distributed in the loss year.

Given these predistribution balances, the distribution has the following effects:

	Stock Basis	AAA	E&P
Predistribution balance	$24,000	$12,000	$4,000
AAA distribution	(7,500)	(7,500)	
Ordinary loss	(10,000)		
Net negative adjustment		(8,000)	
Ending balance	$ 6,500	($3,500)	$4,000

Because the net negative adjustment to the AAA occurs after the distribution, the entire distribution comes out of the AAA, and none comes out of accumulated E&P. Also, the distribution does not exceed the predistribution stock basis. Thus, the entire distribution is tax free. ◄

EXAMPLE C11-28 ► Sigma Corporation, an electing S corporation, reports the following results during the current year:

Ordinary income	$30,000
Long-term capital gain	15,000
Municipal bond interest income	5,000
Dividend from domestic corporation	3,000
Charitable contribution	8,000

Sigma's sole shareholder, Silvia, has a $60,000 stock basis on January 1. On January 1, Sigma has a $40,000 AAA balance, a $27,000 accumulated E&P balance, and a zero OAA balance. Sigma makes $50,000 cash distributions to Silvia, its sole shareholder, on June 1 and December 1. The stock basis, AAA, OAA, and accumulated E&P activity for the year (before any distributions) is summarized as follows:

	Stock Basis	AAA	E&P	OAA
Beginning balance	$ 60,000	$40,000	$27,000	$ –0–
Ordinary income	30,000	30,000		
Long-term capital gain	15,000	15,000		
Municipal bond interest	5,000			5,000
Dividend income	3,000	3,000		
Charitable contribution		(8,000)		
Predistribution balance	$113,000	$80,000	$27,000	$5,000

The $80,000 AAA balance is allocated ratably to each of the distributions as follows:

$$\$40,000 = \$50,000 \times \frac{\$80,000}{\$50,000 + \$50,000}$$

The charitable contribution does not reduce the predistribution stock basis but does reduce the predistribution AAA because the reduction does not produce a net negative adjustment. Accordingly, $40,000 of each distribution comes out of AAA. This portion of the distribution is tax-free because the AAA distributions in total are less than the stock's $113,000 predistribution basis. The remaining $10,000 ($50,000 − $40,000) of each distribution comes out of accumulated E&P and is taxable as dividend income. Accumulated E&P is reduced to $7,000 ($27,000 − $20,000) at year-end. The OAA balance reported on Form 1120S is not affected by the distribution because the accumulated E&P has not been exhausted. The stock's basis is $25,000 ($113,000 − $80,000 − $8,000) at year-end because a dividend distribution from accumulated E&P does not reduce its basis, but the charitable contribution does. After adjustment for the distribution, the AAA is zero. The effects of the distribution are summarized below:

	Stock Basis	AAA	E&P	OAA
Predistribution balance	$113,000	$80,000	$27,000	$5,000
AAA distribution	(80,000)	(80,000)		
E&P distribution			(20,000)	
Charitable contribution	(8,000)			
Ending balance	$ 25,000	$ –0–	$ 7,000	$5,000

◄

PROPERTY DISTRIBUTIONS. Property distributions (other than money) made by an S corporation having accumulated E&P trigger gain recognition according to the general rules described on page C11-28. The FMV of the nonmoney property distributed reduces AAA.

DISTRIBUTION ORDERING ELECTIONS. An S corporation can elect to change the distribution order of E&P and the AAA. Specifically, the S corporation can elect to skip over the AAA in determining the source of a cash or property distribution, in which case distributions will come from accumulated E&P and then AAA. This election permits the S corporation to distribute Subchapter C E&P so as to avoid the excess net passive income tax and termination of the S election. The Tax Planning Considerations section of this chapter contains further discussion of this election.

POST-TERMINATION TRANSITION PERIOD. Distributions of money made during the S corporation's post-termination transition period can be made tax-free to those shareholders who owned S corporation stock at the time of the termination. These distributions come first from the former S corporation's AAA balance and then from current and accumulated E&P. The amounts from the AAA are tax-free and reduce the shareholder's stock basis.[56] The AAA balance disappears when the post-termination period ends. Even though the profits earned during the S election period no longer can be distributed tax-free from the AAA after the post-termination period ends, they still can be distributed tax-free to the extent of the shareholder's stock basis once the corporation distributes its current and accumulated E&P. Any distributions made from current or accumulated E&P and nonmoney distributions made during the post-termination transition period are taxable.

Topic Review C11-4 summarizes the taxation of S corporation income and gains that pass through to the shareholders and the treatment of S corporation distributions.

Topic Review C11-4

Taxation of S Corporation Income and Distributions

Taxation of Income to the Corporation
1. Unlike with a partnership, special entity level taxes are imposed on an S corporation.
   a. Built-in gains tax: applicable to the net recognized built-in gain of an S corporation that formerly was a C corporation and that made its S election after December 31, 1986.
   b. Excess net passive income tax: applicable to S corporations that have Subchapter C E&P at the close of the tax year and that earn passive investment income exceeding 25% of gross receipts during the tax year.
   c. LIFO recapture tax: imposed when a C corporation that uses the LIFO inventory method in its final C corporation tax year makes an S election.

Allocation of Income to the Shareholders
1. Income and gains are allocated based on the number of shares of stock owned by each shareholder on each day of the tax year.
2. Termination of the S election or termination of the shareholder's interest in the S corporation during the tax year requires the tax year to be divided into two parts. An election can be made to allocate the income or gain according to the general rule in (1) or the accounting methods used by the corporation.

Shareholder Distributions
1. Income and gain allocated to the shareholder increase the basis of the S corporation stock. For any S corporation that does not have an E&P balance, the amount of money plus the FMV of any nonmoney property distributed is tax-free provided it does not exceed the shareholder's basis in the S corporation stock, determined before negative adjustments. The corporation recognizes gain (but not loss) when it distributes nonmoney property. The gain passes through to the shareholders.
2. If the S corporation made the S election after 1982 and has accumulated E&P, two earnings tiers must be maintained: the AAA and accumulated E&P. Distributions come from each tier in succeeding order until the tier is exhausted. Distributions out of accumulated E&P are taxable to the shareholder as dividends. Other distributions are tax-free unless stock basis is reduced to zero, in which case the shareholder recognizes capital gain on the excess distribution.

[56] Sec. 1371(e).

STOP & THINK

Question: Special earnings tracking rules apply to S corporations that formerly were C corporations. Why do we need to have these special rules, which add complexity to the distribution topic?

Solution: Former C corporations that were profitable usually have an accumulated E&P balance when they become an S corporation. These earnings have never been taxed as a dividend to the corporation's shareholders. If separate tracking of the S corporation earnings (AAA) and C corporation earnings (accumulated E&P) did not occur, it would be impossible to determine which cash and property distributions came from S corporation earnings and which ones came from C corporation earnings, thereby frustrating the government's ability to collect taxes on distributed E&P.

OTHER RULES

In addition to the differences discussed above, S corporations are treated differently than C corporations in a number of other ways. Some of these differences are examined below. They include tax preference items and other alternative minimum tax (AMT) adjustments, expenses owed by the S corporation to a shareholder, related party sales and exchanges, and fringe benefits paid by the S corporation to a shareholder-employee.

TAX PREFERENCE ITEMS AND OTHER AMT ADJUSTMENTS

The S corporation is not subject to the corporate AMT. Instead, the S corporation computes and passes through tax preference items contained in Sec. 57(a) to its shareholders. The shareholders then include these tax preference items in their individual AMT calculations. Allocation of the tax preference items occurs on a daily basis unless the corporation makes one of the two special elections to allocate the items based on the corporation's tax accounting methods.

Section 56(a) prescribes a number of adjustments to the tax reporting of certain transactions and occurrences for AMT purposes from that used for income tax purposes. As with tax preference items, the amount of these special AMT adjustments pass through to the S corporation's shareholders to be included in their individual AMT calculations.

S corporations do not have to make an adjustment for the difference between adjusted current earnings and preadjustment alternative minimum taxable income that a C corporation makes in calculating its AMT liability. For certain corporations, this difference may make an S election attractive.[57]

TRANSACTIONS INVOLVING SHAREHOLDERS AND OTHER RELATED PARTIES

The Sec. 267(a)(2) related party transaction rules deny a payor a deduction for an expense paid to a related payee when a mismatching of the expense and income items occurs as a result of differences in accounting methods. A number of related party situations directly involve S corporations. Some of these transactions involve two S corporations or an S corporation and a C corporation where the same shareholders directly or indirectly own more than 50% of the value of each corporation's stock. Section 267(a)(2), for example, prevents an S corporation using the accrual method of accounting from currently deducting a year-end expense accrued for an item owed to a second S corporation that uses the cash method of accounting when the same shareholders own both corporations. The first S corporation can deduct the expense on the day the second S corporation includes the income in its gross income.

The S corporation is a pass-through entity and is subject to Sec. 267(e), which extends the Sec. 267(a)(2) related party transaction rules described above to any payment made by the S corporation to *any* person who directly or indirectly owns S corporation stock. This

---

[57] Sec. 56(g)(6).

rule prevents the S corporation from deducting a payment to be made to one of its share-holders or to someone who indirectly owns such stock until the payee reports the income. Payments made to the S corporation by a person who directly or indirectly owns S corporation stock are similarly restricted.

EXAMPLE C11-29 ▶

Vassar Corporation, an electing S corporation, uses the accrual method of accounting and a calendar tax year. On September 1, 2006, Vassar borrows $50,000 from Joan, who owns 10% of the Vassar stock. Joan charges interest at an 8% annual rate. Joan uses the cash method of accounting. At year-end, Vassar accrues $1,000 of interest expense on the loan. The corporation pays six months of interest (including the $1,000 of accrued interest) to Joan on April 1, 2007. Vassar cannot deduct the 2006 interest accrual when determining its ordinary income or loss until it is paid in 2007. ◀

Section 267(a)(1) denies a deduction for losses incurred on the sale or exchange of property directly or indirectly between related parties. The same definition of a related party applies for this purpose as in applying Sec. 267(a)(2) to expense transactions involving an S corporation. Any loss disallowed to the seller on the related party sale or exchange can be used to offset gains realized by the purchaser on a subsequent sale or exchange.

FRINGE BENEFITS PAID TO A SHAREHOLDER-EMPLOYEE

TYPICAL MISCONCEPTION

Most fringe benefits provided by a C corporation are deductible to the corporation and nontaxable to the employee. However, fringe benefits paid to a more-than-2% shareholder-employee of an S corporation are in many cases nondeductible unless taxable to the shareholder-employee as compensation.

The S corporation is not treated as a corporate taxpayer with respect to many fringe benefits paid to any 2% shareholder.[58] Instead, the S corporation is treated the same as a partnership, and the 2% shareholder is treated as a partner of such partnership.[59] Because of this restriction, many fringe benefits paid to a 2% shareholder-employee of an S corporation are taxable as compensation to the shareholder and deductible by the corporation if the benefit is not excludible from the shareholder's the gross income. Shareholders owning 2% or less of the S corporation stock are treated as ordinary employees.

The special fringe benefit rules apply only to statutory fringe benefits. They do not apply to stock options, qualified retirement plans, and nonqualified deferred compensation. The fringe benefits limited by the more-than-2%-shareholder rule include group term life insurance premiums (Sec. 79), accident and health benefit plan insurance premiums and payments (Secs. 105 and 106), meals and lodging furnished by the employer (Sec. 119), cafeteria plan benefits (Sec. 125), and employer-provided parking (Sec. 132). Fringe benefits that may be excluded by more-than-2%-shareholders include compensation for injuries and sickness (Sec. 104); educational assistance program benefits (Sec. 127); dependent care assistance program benefits (Sec. 129); and no-additional-cost benefits, qualified employee discounts, working condition fringe benefits, de minimis fringe benefits, and on-premises athletic facilities (Sec. 132). For purposes of the Sec. 162(l) above-the-line deduction for self-employed taxpayer's health insurance premiums, a more-than-2%-shareholder is deemed to be self-employed.

EXAMPLE C11-30 ▶

Bill and his wife Cathy equally own Edison Corporation, an electing S corporation. Edison employs Bill and ten other individuals. All employees receive group term life insurance benefits based on their annual salaries. All employees except Bill can qualify for the Sec. 79 group term life insurance premium exclusion. Bill is treated as a partner and, therefore, does not qualify as an employee. Bill's premiums are treated as compensation and taxable to Bill. Edison can deduct the premiums paid to all its employees, including Bill. Because Bill is treated as self-employed under the 2% shareholder rules, he can deduct a portion of the premiums paid on the health insurance as a "for" AGI deduction under the Sec.162(l) rules applicable to health insurance payments made by all self-employed individuals. ◀

---

[58] Section 1372(b) defines a 2% shareholder as any person who directly or indirectly owns on any day of the S corporation's tax year more than 2% of its outstanding stock or stock possessing more than 2% of its voting power.

The Sec. 318 stock attribution rules are used to determine whether the 2% threshold has been exceeded.
[59] Sec. 1372(a).

TAX PLANNING CONSIDERATIONS

ELECTION TO ALLOCATE INCOME BASED ON THE S CORPORATION'S ACCOUNTING METHODS

As a general rule, the S corporation's ordinary income or loss and separately stated items are allocated based on the amount of stock owned by each shareholder on each day of the S corporation's tax year. A special election allows the income to be allocated based on the S corporation's accounting methods when the S election terminates or when a shareholder terminates or substantially reduces his or her entire interest in the S corporation.[60] The use of the S corporation's tax accounting method to allocate the year's profit or loss can permit income shifting among shareholders.

EXAMPLE C11-31 ▶ At the beginning of the current year (not a leap year), Rod and Dana equally own Apex Corporation, an electing S corporation. During the current year, Apex reports ordinary income of $146,000. On March 31 of the current year (the 90th day of Apex's tax year), Dana sells all his Apex stock to Randy. Apex Corporation earns $125,000 of its ordinary income after March 31 of the current year. Rod is allocated $73,000 ($146,000 × 0.50) of ordinary income. His income allocation is the same whether the daily allocation method or the special allocation election is used. In total, Dana and Randy are allocated $73,000 of ordinary income. Dana and Randy can allocate the ordinary income amount in the following ways:

Daily Allocation	Special Election
Dana: $146,000 \times \frac{1}{2} \times \frac{90}{365} = \$18,000$	$(\$146,000 - \$125,000) \times \frac{1}{2} = \$10,500$
Randy: $146,000 \times \frac{1}{2} \times \frac{275}{365} = \$55,000$	$\$125,000 \times \frac{1}{2} = \$62,500$

The shifting of the $7,500 ($18,000–$10,500) in income from Dana to Randy under the special election also reduces Dana's adjusted basis for his Apex stock when determining his gain or loss on the sale. The $7,500 difference between the income allocations under the two methods may be a point for negotiation between Dana and Randy, particularly if their marginal tax rates are different. ◀

By electing to use the S corporation's tax accounting method to allocate profits or losses between the C short year and S short year in the year in which the S corporation election terminates, the corporation can shift losses into an S short year where the shareholders obtain an immediate benefit at a marginal tax rate of up to 35% (in 2006), or it can shift profits into a C short year to take advantage of the 15% and 25% marginal corporate tax rates.

EXAMPLE C11-32 ▶ Delta Corporation has been an S corporation for several years using a calendar year as its tax year. The corporation has one shareholder whose marginal tax rate is 35%. Delta's S election terminates on July 1. The S short year includes January 1 through June 30 and the C short year includes July 1 through December 31. Total ordinary income this year is $10,000. If the corporation closes its books on June 30, $40,000 of ordinary loss is allocable to the S short year and $50,000 of ordinary income is allocable to the C short year. Assuming each month has 30 days, the following income allocations are possible:

Period	Daily Allocation	Closing of Books
S short year	$ 5,000	($40,000)
C short year	5,000	50,000
Total	$10,000	$10,000

---

[60] The shareholder, however, still can be a creditor, director, or employee of the corporation. Sections 1362(e) and 1377(a) prevent the daily allocation method from applying to any items resulting from a sale or exchange of 50% or more of the S corporation's stock during an S termination year.

By closing the books, the corporation passes the $40,000 S short year loss through to its shareholder and is taxed on the $50,000 C short year income as a C corporation. With the daily allocation, one-half the income is taxed to the shareholder, and the other half is taxed to the C corporation.[61] The daily allocation method causes the shareholder's tax to be $1,750 ($5,000 × 0.35) on the pass-through income and the C corporation's tax to be $750 ($5,000 × 2 × 0.15 × 0.5) on its annualized income, for a total tax of $2,500. The closing of the books method provides the shareholder with a $14,000 ($40,000 pass-through loss × 0.35) tax savings and causes the C corporation's tax to be $11,125 ($22,250 tax on $100,000 of annualized income × 0.5), for a net tax savings of $2,875 ($14,000 − $11,125). Thus, in this situation, the closing of the books method provides the greater overall tax advantage. ◄

INCREASING THE BENEFITS FROM S CORPORATION LOSSES

At the shareholder level, the deduction for S corporation pass-through losses is limited to the S corporation stock basis plus the basis of any debt owed by the S corporation to the shareholder. Pass-through losses that exceed this limitation carry over to a subsequent tax year when the shareholder regains stock or debt basis. If the shareholder expects his or her marginal tax rate to be the same or lower in a future tax year when the loss carryover can be used, the shareholder should consider either increasing his or her stock basis or loaning additional funds to the corporation before the end of the current tax year. Conversely, if the shareholder never expects the loans to be repaid, he or she should not lend the S corporation additional amounts just to secure an additional tax deduction, which is worth at most 35 cents (at 2006 rates) for each dollar loaned. If the shareholder expects his or her marginal tax rate to be higher in future tax years, the shareholder should consider deferring additional capital contributions or loans until after the end of the current tax year.

EXAMPLE C11-33 ►

KEY POINT

If an S corporation shareholder has losses that have been suspended due to lack of basis, either contributions to capital or bona fide loans to the corporation will create the necessary basis to use the losses.

Nancy owns 100% of Bailey Corporation, an electing S corporation. Bailey expects large losses in 2006 that will result in a $100,000 ordinary loss. Nancy's stock basis (before adjustment for the current loss) is $35,000. Bailey also owes Nancy $25,000. Nancy's 2006 marginal tax rate is 35%. Nancy expects her marginal tax rate to decline to 15% in 2007. Nancy should consider making $40,000 [$100,000 loss − ($35,000 stock basis + $25,000 debt basis)] of additional capital contributions or loans before the end of 2006 to obtain an additional $8,000 [(0.35 − 0.15) × $40,000] of tax benefits from deducting the anticipated loss carryover in the current year. If Nancy instead expects her 2006 and 2007 marginal tax rates to be 15% and 35%, respectively, she can defer $8,000 [(0.35 − 0.15) × $40,000] of tax benefits (less the time value of money for one year) by postponing her capital contributions or loans until 2007. Alternatively, Nancy could use the loss carryover to offset profits reported in 2007. These profits would restore part or all of the debt basis (and possibly increase the stock basis). The basis then would be partially or fully offset by the $40,000 loss carryover. ◄

The S corporation loss carryover is available only to the shareholder who held the stock when the loss occurred. A shareholder should consider increasing the stock basis to take advantage of the carryover before selling the stock. The purchasing shareholder does not acquire the carryover.

LEGISLATIVE UPDATE

On February 2, 2006, the Senate passed a bill that would raise the 25% threshold to 60% and repeal the passive investment income test for terminations. If passed, an S election would not terminate because of excess passive investment income, and the Sec. 1375 tax will be significantly less likely to apply. The bill's proposed effective date is for tax years beginning after September 30, 2006.

PASSIVE INCOME REQUIREMENTS

The S corporation can earn an unlimited amount of passive income each year without incurring any penalty provided it does not have any E&P accumulated in a C corporation tax year (known as Subchapter C E&P) at the end of its tax year. Thus, a corporation can make an S election to avoid the personal holding company penalty tax.

S corporations that have operated as C corporations and have accumulated Subchapter C E&P are potentially liable for the excess net passive income tax. In addition, their S election may terminate if the passive investment income exceeds 25% of gross receipts for three consecutive tax years. The S corporation can avoid both of these possible problems

---

[61] Section 1362(e)(5)(A) requires calculation of the tax liability for the C short year to be based on the annualized income of the former S corporation (see Chapter C3 for a discussion of annualization).

by making a special election under Sec. 1368(e)(3) to distribute its entire Subchapter C E&P balance to its shareholders. A corporation that makes the election to distribute Subchapter C E&P before its accumulated adjustments account (AAA) can make a second special election to treat part or all of this "distribution" as a deemed dividend, which is deemed distributed to the shareholders and immediately contributed by the shareholders to the corporation on the last day of the corporation's tax year.[62] Such an election requires no cash outlay. The distribution, however, results in a tax cost for the shareholders who pay tax on the resulting dividend income. To the shareholders, the cost of the election can be small if the accumulated E&P balance is insignificant or if the shareholder has a current year NOL (excluding the distribution) or an NOL carryover. The tax cost also is low given the current 15% maximum tax rate on dividends. The ultimate long-run benefit, however, may be great because it permits the S corporation to earn an unlimited amount of passive investment income free from corporate taxes in subsequent tax years.

EXAMPLE C11-34 ▶ Hawaii Corporation incorporated 12 years ago and operated for a number of years as a C corporation, during which time it accumulated $30,000 of E&P. Most of Hawaii's gross income now comes from rentals and interest, constituting passive investment income. Hawaii makes an S election starting in the current year. The excess net passive income tax will apply in the current year if Hawaii's rentals and interest exceed 25% of its gross receipts for the year unless the corporation makes an election to distribute the accumulated E&P and then distributes the earnings by the end of the current year, its first tax year as an S corporation. ◀

S corporations that earn rental income also can avoid the passive income tax and the possibility of having its election terminated if the corporation renders significant services to the occupant of the space or if the corporation incurs significant costs in the rental business.[63] Whether the corporation performs significant services or incurs substantial costs in the rental business depends on all the facts and circumstances including, but not limited to, the number of persons employed to provide the services and the types and amounts of costs and expenses incurred (other than depreciation).

EXAMPLE C11-35 ▶ Assume the same facts as in Example C11-34 except Hawaii Corporation provides significant services to its tenants in connection with its rental activities. Because the services are significant, Hawaii has a passive income problem only if its interest income exceeds 25% of its gross receipts. If the 25% threshold is not exceeded, Hawaii can avoid having to distribute its Subchapter C E&P in the current year. ◀

S corporations that experience a passive income problem in two consecutive tax years should carefully monitor their passive income in the next year. If they see that their passive income for the third year will exceed the 25% threshold, they should elect to distribute their accumulated Subchapter C E&P before year-end. This strategy not only will prevent loss of the S election but also will avoid having to pay the Sec. 1375 tax.

COMPLIANCE AND PROCEDURAL CONSIDERATIONS

MAKING THE ELECTION

A corporation makes the S election by filing Form 2553 (Election by Small Business Corporation). Any person authorized to sign the S corporation's tax return under Sec. 6037 can sign the election form. The corporation files Form 2553 with the IRS Service Center designated in the instructions. The IRS can treat a late election as timely made if the corporation can show reasonable cause.[64]

---

[62] Reg. Sec. 1.1368-1(f)(3).
[63] According to Reg. Sec. 1.1362-2(c)(5)(ii)(B)(3), however, significant services are not rendered and substantial costs are not incurred in connection with net leases.

[64] Sec. 1362(b)(5), Rev. Proc. 2003-43, 2003-23 C.B. 998, and Rev. Proc. 2004-48, 2004-32 I.R.B. 172.

A shareholder can consent to the S election either on Form 2553 or on a separate consent statement signed by the shareholder and attached to the corporation's election form. Regulation Sec. 1.1362-6(b) outlines other information that must be provided with a separate consent. The IRS can grant extensions of time for filing shareholder consents to the S election.[65]

A corporation makes a Sec. 444 election to use a fiscal year on Form 8716, which the corporation must file by the earlier of (1) the fifteenth day of the fifth month following the month that includes the first day of the tax year for which the election will first be effective or (2) the due date for the income tax return resulting from the election.[66] The corporation must attach a copy of Form 8716 to Form 1120S for the first tax year for which the Sec. 444 election is effective. A corporation desiring to make a Sec. 444 election also must state its intention in a statement attached to its S election form (Form 2553).[67]

FILING THE CORPORATE TAX RETURN

All S corporations, whether or not they owe taxes under Secs. 1374 or 1375, must file a tax return if they exist for part or all of the tax year. An S corporation must file its corporate tax return not later than the fifteenth day of the third month following the end of the tax year.[68] The S corporation reports its results on Form 1120S (U.S. Income Tax Return for an S Corporation). A completed S corporation tax return and the facts supporting the return appear in Appendix B. An S corporation is allowed an automatic six-month extension of time for filing its tax return by filing Form 7004 (Application for Automatic Extension of Time to File U.S. Corporation Income Tax Return), also illustrated in Appendix B.[69]

EXAMPLE C11-36 ▶

Simpson Corporation, an S corporation, uses the calendar year as its tax year. Its tax return generally is due on March 15. Simpson can file Form 7004 and obtain an automatic extension of six months for the return, thereby extending its due date until September 15. ◀

REAL-WORLD EXAMPLE

The IRS recently resumed its program of matching Schedule K-1 information to the shareholders' individual tax returns.

All S corporations that file a tax return must furnish each person who is a shareholder at any time during the tax year with pertinent information from the tax return, usually via Form 1120S, Schedule K-1. The corporation must make the Schedule K-1 available to the shareholder not later than the day on which it files its tax return.[70] An individual shareholder reports the S corporation's pass-through ordinary income or loss and certain passive income or loss items on his or her Form 1040, Schedule E. The shareholder reports most separately stated items on other supporting schedules to Form 1040, as illustrated on the Form 1120S, Schedule K-1 presented in Appendix B.

An S corporation is subject to the same basic three-year statute of limitations that applies to other taxpayers. This three-year limitations period applies for purposes of determining the time period during which

▶ The corporation remains liable for assessments of the excess net passive income tax and the built-in gains tax

▶ The IRS can question the correctness of an S election made for a particular tax year[71]

The limitation period for assessing the income tax liability of an S corporation shareholder (e.g., for an erroneous S corporation loss deduction claimed), however, runs from the date on which the shareholder files his or her return and not from the date the S corporation files its tax return.[72]

If the corporation elects a fiscal year under Sec. 444, it determines the Sec. 7519 required payment on a computation worksheet provided in the instructions for the Form 1120S. The corporation need not make a required payment if the total of such payments for the current year and all preceding years is $500 or less. Amounts less than the $500 threshold carry over to succeeding years. The required payment is due on or before May 15 regardless of the fiscal year used. The required payment and the computation work-

[65] Reg. Sec. 1.1362-6(b)(3)(iii).
[66] Temp. Reg. Sec. 1.444-3T(b)(1).
[67] Temp. Reg. Sec. 1.444-3T(b)(3).
[68] Sec. 6072(b).
[69] Reg. Sec. 1.6081-3.

[70] Sec. 6037(b).
[71] Sec. 6233.
[72] *Sheldon B. Bufferd v. CIR*, 71 AFTR 2d 93-573, 93-1 USTC ¶50,038 (USSC, 1993).

sheet must accompany a Form 8752, which also is used to secure a refund of prior Sec. 7519 payments.[73]

OBJECTIVE 12

Determine the estimated tax payments required of an S corporation and its shareholders

ESTIMATED TAX PAYMENTS

S corporations must make estimated tax payments if their estimated tax liability is reasonably expected to be $500 or more.[74] Estimated tax payments are required for the corporate liability attributable to the built-in gains tax (Sec. 1374) and the excess net passive income tax (Sec. 1375). In addition, the S corporation's shareholders must include their income, gain, loss, deduction, and credit pass-through items in their own estimated tax calculations.

The corporate estimated tax payment requirements described for a C corporation in Chapter C3 also apply to an S corporation's tax liabilities. The required quarterly installment is 25% of the lesser of (1) 100% of the tax shown on the return for the tax year and (2) the sum of 100% of the built-in gains tax shown on the return for the tax year plus 100% of the excess net passive income tax shown on the return for the preceding tax year.

An S corporation cannot use the prior year tax liability exception when determining the required payment to be made with respect to the built-in gains tax. This exception, however, is available with respect to the excess net passive income tax portion of the required payment without regard to whether the corporation owed any tax in the prior year. All corporations can use the prior year tax liability exception for the excess net passive income tax whether or not they are "large" corporations under Sec. 6655(d)(2). The annualization election of Sec. 6655(e) also is available when determining the quarterly estimated tax payment amounts. An S corporation's failure to make timely estimated tax payments, or a timely final payment when it files the tax return, will cause it to be subject to interest and penalties like other taxpayers.

The S corporation's shareholders must include their ratable share of ordinary income or loss and separately stated items in determining their estimated tax liability. Such amounts are treated as having been received concurrently by the shareholders throughout the S corporation's tax year. Thus, ordinary income or loss and separately stated items for an S corporation tax year that ends with or within the shareholder's tax year are included in the estimated tax calculation to the extent they are attributable to months in the S corporation tax year that precede the month in which the installment is due.[75]

SELF-STUDY QUESTION

Is an S corporation required to make estimated tax payments?

ANSWER

Yes. An S corporation is required to pay estimated taxes if the corporation is subject to built-in gains or excess net passive income taxes. Also, shareholders are required to include their S corporation income, loss, and credit pass-through items in determining their estimated tax payments.

CONSISTENCY RULES

Section 6037(c) requires an S corporation shareholder to report on his or her return a Subchapter S item in a manner consistent with the treatment accorded the item on the S corporation's return. A Subchapter S item is any item (e.g., income, gain, deduction, loss, credit, accounting method, or tax year) of an S corporation where the reporting of the item is more appropriately determined at the corporation level than at the shareholder level. A shareholder must notify the IRS of any inconsistency when the corporation has filed a return but the shareholder's treatment on his return is (or may be) inconsistent with the treatment of the item on the corporation return. Failure to do so may result in the imposition of a negligence penalty under Sec. 6662. Any adjustment required to produce consistency with the corporate return is treated as a mathematical or clerical error for penalty calculation purposes. A similar notification also is required when the corporation has not filed a return. If a shareholder receives incorrect information from the S corporation regarding a Subchapter S item, the shareholder's consistent reporting of the item consistently with the information provided by the corporation generally will eliminate the imposition of any penalty.

ADDITIONAL COMMENT

When examining an S corporation, the IRS conducts the audit in a unified proceeding at the corporate level rather than in separate audits of each S corporation shareholder.

SAMPLE S CORPORATION TAX RETURN

A sample S corporation Form 1120S and supporting Schedule K-1 appear in Appendix B, along with the facts supporting the return. Two differences should be noted between the S corporation tax return and a partnership tax return. First, the S corporation tax return

---

[73] Temp. Reg. Sec. 1.7519-2T.
[74] Estimate tax rules appear in Sec. 6655.

[75] For example, see Ltr. Rul. 8639008 (June 23, 1986).

provides for the determination of a corporate tax liability and the payment of the special taxes that can be levied on the S corporation. No such items appear in the partnership return. Second, the S corporation return does not require a reconciliation of the shareholders' basis adjustments as occurs on a partnership tax return. Schedule M-1, M-2, and M-3 reconciliations similar to those required of a C corporation are required of an S corporation. Schedule M-1 requires a reconciliation of book income with the income or loss reported on line 23 of Schedule K, which includes not only the ordinary income (loss) amount but also separately stated income and deduction items. For tax years ending on or after December 31, 2006, an S corporation must file Schedule M-3 in lieu of Schedule M-1 if the amount of total assets reported in Schedule L of Form 1120S (Balance Sheet per Books) equals or exceeds $10 million. The S corporation also may file Schedule M-3 voluntarily even if not required to do so. If the corporation files Schedule M-3, in either case, it checks the appropriate box on page 1 of Form 1120S and does not file Schedule M-1. (The sample tax return in Appendix B does not include Schedule M-3.) Schedule M-2 requires a reconciliation of the AAA, OAA, and PTI accounts. (The PTI account pertains to pre-1983 S corporations.) Only S corporations that have an accumulated E&P balance must provide the AAA reconciliation and OAA balance although the IRS recommends that all S corporations maintain AAA and OAA balances.

PROBLEM MATERIALS

DISCUSSION QUESTIONS

C11-1 List five advantages and five disadvantages of making an S election. Briefly explain each item.

C11-2 Julio, age 50, is a U.S. citizen who has a 28% marginal tax rate. He has operated the A&B Automotive Parts Company for a number of years as a C corporation. Last year, A&B reported $200,000 of pre-tax profits, from which it paid $50,000 in salary and $25,000 in dividends to Julio. The corporation expects this year's pre-tax profits to be $300,000. To date, the corporation has created no fringe benefits or pension plans for Julio. Julio asks you to explain whether an S corporation election would reduce his taxes. How do you respond to Julio's inquiry?

C11-3 Celia, age 30, is leaving a major systems development firm to establish her own firm. She will design computer-based systems for small- and medium-sized businesses. Celia will invest $100,000 in the business. She hopes to operate near her breakeven point during her first year, although a small loss is possible. Profits will build up slowly over the next four years until she is earning $150,000 a year in her fifth year. Celia has heard some of the tax people who worked for her former employer talk about S corporations. She comes to you to ask whether the S corporation form would be advisable for her new business. How do you respond to Celia's inquiry?

C11-4 Lance and Rodney are contemplating starting a new business to manufacture computer software games. They expect to encounter losses in the initial years. Lance's CPA has talked to them about using an S corporation. Rodney, while reading a business publication, encounters a discussion on limited liability companies (LLCs). The article talks about the advantages of using an LLC instead of an S corporation. How would you respond to their inquiry?

C11-5 Which of the following classifications make a shareholder ineligible to own the stock of an S corporation?
a. U.S. citizen
b. Domestic corporation
c. Partnership where all the partners are U.S. citizens
d. Estate of a deceased U.S. citizen
e. Grantor trust created by a U.S. citizen
f. Nonresident alien individual

C11-6 Which of the following taxes do not apply to an S corporation?
a. Regular (income) tax
b. Accumulated earnings tax
c. Corporate alternative minimum tax
d. Built-in gains tax
e. Personal holding company tax
f. Excess net passive income tax
g. LIFO recapture tax

C11-7 Will the following events cause an S election to terminate?
a. The S corporation earning 100% of its gross receipts in its first tax year from passive sources
b. The S corporation issuing nonvoting stock that has a dividend preference

c. The S corporation purchasing 100% of the single class of stock of a second domestic corporation that has conducted business activities for four years

d. An individual shareholder donating 100 shares of S corporation stock to a charity that is exempt from tax under Sec. 501(c)(3)

e. The S corporation earning tax-exempt interest income

C11-8 What is an inadvertent termination? What actions must the S corporation and its shareholders take to correct an inadvertent termination?

C11-9 After an S corporation revokes or terminates its S election, how long must the corporation wait to make a new election? What circumstances permit an early reelection?

C11-10 What tax years can a newly created corporation that makes an S election adopt for its first tax year? If a fiscal year is permitted, does it require IRS approval?

C11-11 At the time Cable Corporation makes its S election, it elects to use a fiscal year based on a Sec. 444 election. What other requirements must Cable satisfy to continue to use its fiscal year election for future tax years?

C11-12 What are Subchapter C earnings and profits? How does the existence of such earnings affect the S corporation's ability to earn passive income?

C11-13 Explain the procedures for allocating an S corporation's ordinary income or loss to each of the shareholders. What special allocation elections are available?

C11-14 What limitations apply to the amount of loss pass-through an S corporation shareholder can deduct? What happens to any losses exceeding this limitation? What happens to losses if the shareholder transfers his or her stock?

C11-15 What actions can an S corporation shareholder take before year-end to increase the amount of the S corporation's losses he or she can deduct in the year they are incurred?

C11-16 What is a post-termination transition period? What loss carryovers can an S corporation shareholder deduct during this period?

C11-17 Explain the positive and negative adjustments to the basis of an S corporation shareholder's stock investment and the basis of an S corporation debt owed to the shareholder.

C11-18 Explain the differences between the tax treatment accorded nonliquidating property distributions made by S corporations and partnerships.

C11-19 What nonliquidating distributions made by an S corporation are taxable to its shareholders? Tax-free to its shareholders?

C11-20 What is an accumulated adjustments account (AAA)? What income, gain, loss, and deduction items *do not* affect this account assuming the S corporation has an accumulated E&P balance?

C11-21 Explain the differences between the way the following items are reported by a C corporation and an S corporation:
   a. Ordinary income or loss
   b. Dividend income
   c. Capital gains and losses
   d. Tax-exempt interest income
   e. Charitable contributions
   f. Nonliquidating property distributions
   g. Fringe benefits paid to a shareholder-employee

C11-22 When is the S corporation's tax return due? What extensions are available for filing the return?

C11-23 What taxes must an S corporation prepay by making quarterly estimated tax payments? Can a shareholder owning S corporation stock use the corporation's estimated tax payments to reduce the amount of his or her individual estimated tax payments? Explain.

C11-24 Review the completed C corporation, partnership, and S corporation tax returns presented in Appendix B. List three major tax reporting similarities and three major tax reporting differences in either content or format among the three tax returns.

ISSUE IDENTIFICATION QUESTIONS

C11-25 Jennelle and Paula are equal partners in the J & P Manufacturing Partnership. The partnership will form J & P Corporation by exchanging the assets and liabilities of the J & P Manufacturing Partnership for all the corporation's stock on September 1 of the current year. The partnership then will liquidate by distributing the J & P Corporation stock equally to Jennelle and Paula. Both shareholders use the calendar year as their tax year and desire that the corporation make an S election. What tax issues should Jennelle and Paula consider with respect to the incorporation?

C11-26 Williams Corporation has operated as a C corporation for the last seven years. The corporation has assets with a $450,000 adjusted basis and an $800,000 FMV. Liabilities amount to $100,000. Dan Williams, who uses a calendar year as his tax year, owns all the Williams Corporation stock. The corporation uses the accrual method of accounting and a June 30 year-end. Dan's CPA has suggested that he convert the corporation to S corporation status to reduce his total corporate/personal federal income tax liability. Dan would like to complete the conversion on the last day of the corporation's tax year. What tax issues should Dan and his CPA consider with respect to the S election?

C11-27 Peter owns 50% of Air South Corporation, an air charter service. His S corporation stock basis at beginning of the year is $100,000. Air South has not done well this year and will report an ordinary loss of $375,000. Peter's marginal tax rate for the current year is 35%. What tax issues should Peter consider with respect to the loss?

C11-28 Glacier Smokeries has been an S corporation since its inception six years ago. On January 1 of the current year, the corporation's two equal shareholders, Adam and Rodney, had adjusted bases of $175,000 and $225,000, respectively, for their S corporation's stock. The shareholders plan to have the corporation distribute land with a $75,000 adjusted basis and a $300,000 FMV in the current year. The shareholders also expect ordinary income to be $125,000 in the current year. What tax issues should Adam and Rodney consider with respect to the distribution?

PROBLEMS

C11-29 *Comparison of Entity Forms.* Ken Munro, a single taxpayer, owns 100% of King Corporation. During 2006, King reports $100,000 of taxable income. Ken Munro reports no income other than that earned from King, and Ken claims the standard deduction.

a. What is King Corporation's income tax liability assuming Ken withdraws none of the earnings from the C corporation? What is Ken's income tax liability? What is the total tax liability for the corporation and its shareholder?

b. Assume that King instead distributes 100% of its after-tax earnings to Ken as a dividend in the current year. What is the total income tax liability for the C corporation and its shareholder?

c. How would your answer to Part a change if Ken withdrew $50,000 from the business in salary? Must any taxes other than corporate and individual income taxes be considered now that the corporation pays a salary?

d. How would your answers to Parts a–c change if King were instead an S corporation?

C11-30 *Making the Election.* Voyles Corporation, a calendar year taxpayer formed five years ago, desires to make an S election beginning in 2006. Sue and Andrea each own one-half of the Voyles stock.

a. How does Voyles make the S election?

b. When can Voyles file its election form?

c. If the election in Part b is not filed in a timely manner, when will it first take effect?

C11-31 *Termination of the Election.* Orlando Corporation, a calendar year taxpayer, has been an S corporation for several years. On July 10, 2006, Orlando Corporation authorizes a second class of nonvoting preferred stock that pays a 10% annual dividend. The corporation issues the stock to Sid on September 15, 2006, to raise additional equity capital. Sid owns no other Orlando stock.

a. Does Orlando's S election terminate? If so, when is the termination effective?

b. What tax returns must Orlando file for 2006? When are they due?

c. How would your answer to Parts a and b change if the second class of stock were instead nonvoting Class B common stock?

C11-32 *Revocation of the Election.* Tango Corporation, a calendar year taxpayer, has been an S corporation for several years. Tango's business activities have become very profitable in recent years. On June 17, 2006, its sole shareholder, who is in the 35% marginal tax bracket, desires to revoke the S election.

a. How does Tango revoke its S election? When does the revocation take effect?

b. Assume the revocation is effective July 1, 2006. What tax returns are required of Tango for 2006? For 2007? When are these returns due?

c. If the corporation makes a new S election after the revocation, when does it take effect?

C11-33 *Sale of S Corporation Interest.* Peter and his wife, Alice, own all the stock of Galleon Corporation. Galleon made its S election 12 years ago. Peter and Alice sold one-half their Galleon stock to a partnership owned by Rob and Susan (not husband and wife) at the close of business on December 31, 2006, for a $75,000 profit. What are the tax consequences of the sale transaction for Peter and Alice? For the corporation? As Peter and Alice's CPA, do you have any advice for them if all parties would like the S election to continue?

C11-34 *Selecting a Tax Year.* Indicate in each of the following situations whether the taxpayer can accomplish what is proposed. Provide adequate authority for your answer including any special elections that are needed or requirements that must be satisfied. Assume all individuals use the calendar year as their tax year unless otherwise indicated.

    a. Will and Carol form Classic Corporation. They want the corporation to adopt a fiscal year ending January 31 as its tax year to provide a maximum deferral for their income. The corporation makes an S election for its initial tax year ending January 31, 2007.

    b. Mark and Dennis have owned and operated the Plastic Corporation for several years. Plastic Corporation has used a fiscal year ending June 30 since its organization as a C corporation because it conforms to the corporation's natural business year. The corporation makes an S election for its tax year beginning July 1, 2006.

C11-35 *Passive Income Tax.* Oliver organized North Corporation 15 years ago. The corporation made an S election last year after it accumulated $60,000 of E&P as a C corporation. None of the accumulated E&P has been distributed as of December 31 of the current year. In the current year, North reports the following results:

Dividends from domestic corporations	$ 60,000
Rental income	100,000
Services income	50,000
Expenses related to rental income	30,000
Expenses related to services income	15,000
Other expenses	5,000

The corporation has not provided significant services nor incurred substantial costs in connection with earning the rental income. The services income are the gross receipts derived from the active conduct of a trade or business.

    a. Is North subject to the excess net passive income tax? If so, what is its tax liability?

    b. What is the effect of the excess net passive income tax liability on North's pass-throughs of ordinary income and separately stated items?

    c. What advice would you give North regarding its activities?

C11-36 *Built-in Gains Tax.* Theta Corporation formed 15 years ago. In its first year, it elected to use the cash method of accounting and adopted a calendar year as its tax year. It made an S election on August 15 of last year, effective for Theta's current tax year. At the beginning of the current year, Theta had assets with a $600,000 FMV and a $180,000 adjusted basis. During the current year, Theta reports taxable income of $400,000.

- Theta collects all accounts receivables outstanding on January 1 of the current year, in the amount of $200,000. The receivables had a zero adjusted basis.

- Theta sells an automobile on February 1 of the current year, for $3,500. The automobile had a $2,000 adjusted basis and a $3,000 FMV on January 1 of the current year. Theta claimed $800 of MACRS depreciation on the automobile in the current year.

- Theta sells land (a Sec. 1231 asset) that it held three years in anticipation of building its own office building for a $35,000 gain. The land had a $45,000 FMV and a $25,000 adjusted basis on January 1 of the current year.

- Theta paid accounts payable outstanding on January 1 of the current year, of $125,000. All the payables are deductible expenses.

What is the amount of Theta's built-in gains tax liability?

C11-37 *Determination of Pass-Throughs and Stock Basis Adjustments.* Mike and Nancy are equal shareholders in MN Corporation, an S corporation. The corporation, Mike, and Nancy are calendar year taxpayers. The corporation has been an S corporation during its entire existence and thus has no accumulated E&P. The shareholders have no loans to the corporation. The corporation incurred the following items in the current year:

Sales	$300,000
Cost of goods sold	140,000
Dividends on corporate investments	10,000
Tax-exempt interest income	3,000
Section 1245 gain (recapture) on equipment sale	22,000
Section 1231 gain on equipment sale	12,000
Long-term capital gain on stock sale	8,000
Long-term capital loss on stock sale	7,000

Short-term capital loss on stock sale	6,000
Depreciation	18,000
Salary to Nancy	20,000
Meals and entertainment expenses	7,800
Interest expense on loans allocable to:	
Business debt	32,000
Stock investments	6,400
Tax-exempt bonds	1,800
Principal payment on business loan	9,000
Charitable contributions	2,000
Distributions to shareholders ($15,000 each)	30,000

a. Compute the S corporation's ordinary income and separately stated items.

b. Show Mike's and Nancy's shares of the items in Part a.

c. Compute Mike's and Nancy's ending stock bases assuming their beginning balances are $100,000 each. When making basis adjustments, apply the adjustments in the order outlined on page C11-25 of the text.

C11-38 *Allocation of Income to Shareholders.* John owns all the stock of Lucas Corporation, an electing S corporation. John's basis for the 1,000 shares is $130,000. On June 11 of the current year (assume a non-leap year), John gifts 100 shares of stock to his younger brother Michael, who has been working in the business for one year. Lucas Corporation reports $125,000 of ordinary income for the current year. What amount of income is allocated to John? To Michael?

C11-39 *Sale of S Corporation Interest.* Al and Ruth each own one-half the stock of Chemical Corporation, an electing S corporation. During the current year (assume a non-leap year), Chemical earns $15,000 per month of ordinary income. On April 5, Ruth sells her entire stock interest to Patty. The corporation sells a business asset on August 18 and realizes a $75,000 Sec. 1231 gain. What alternatives (if any) exist for allocating Chemical's current year income?

C11-40 *Allocation of Income to Shareholders.* Toyland Corporation, an electing S corporation, uses the calendar year as its tax year. Bob, Alice, and Carter own 60, 30, and 10 shares, respectively, of the Toyland stock. Carter's basis for his stock is $26,000 on January 1 of the current year (assume a non-leap year). On June 30, Alice gifted one-half of her stock to Mike. On November 30, Carter sold his stock to Mike for $45,000. Toyland reports the following results for the current year:

Ordinary income	$120,000
Long-term capital loss	10,000
Charitable contributions	6,000

a. What amount of income, loss, or deduction do the four shareholders report (assuming no special elections are made)?

b. What gain or loss does Carter recognize when he sells the Toyland stock?

C11-41 *Allocation of Income to Shareholders.* Redfern Corporation, a calendar year taxpayer, has been an S corporation for several years. Rod and Kurt each own 50% of the Redfern stock. On July 1 of the current year (assume a non-leap year), Redfern issues additional common stock to Blackfoot Corporation for cash. Rod, Kurt, and Blackfoot each end up owning one-third of the Redfern stock. Redfern reports ordinary income of $125,000 and a short-term capital loss of $15,000 in the current year. Eighty percent of the ordinary income and all the capital loss accrue after Blackfoot purchases its stock. Redfern makes no distributions to its shareholders in the current year. What income and losses do Redfern, Blackfoot, Rod, and Kurt report as a result of the current year's activities?

C11-42 *Allocation of Income Between Family Members.* Bright Corporation, an electing S corporation, has been 100% owned by Betty since it was created 12 years ago. The corporation has been profitable in recent years and, in the current year (assume a non-leap year), reports ordinary income of $240,000 after paying Betty a $60,000 salary. On January 1, Betty gifts 15% of the Bright stock to each of her three sons, John, Andrew, and Stephen, hoping they will work in the family business. Betty pays gift taxes on the transfers. The sons are ages 16, 9, and 2 at present and are not currently active in the business. Bright distributes $7,500 in cash to each son and $27,500 in cash to Betty in the current year.

a. What income does Betty, John, Andrew, and Stephen report for the current year as a result of Bright's activities assuming the sons are considered bona fide owners of the stock? How will the income be taxed to the children?

b. Assuming the IRS determines a reasonable salary for Betty to be $120,000, how would your answer to Part a change?

c. How would your answer to Part a change if the sons were not considered bona fide owners of the stock?

C11-43 *Use of Losses by Shareholders.* Monte and Allie each own 50% of Raider Corporation, an electing S corporation. Both individuals actively participate in Raider's business. On January 1, Monte and Allie have adjusted bases for their Raider stock of $80,000 and $90,000, respectively. During the current year, Raider reports the following results:

Ordinary loss	$175,000
Tax-exempt interest income	20,000
Long-term capital loss	32,000

Raider's balance sheet at year-end shows the following liabilities: accounts payable, $90,000; mortgage payable, $30,000; and note payable to Allie, $10,000.

a. What income and deductions will Monte and Allie report from Raider's current year activities?

b. What basis does Monte have in his stock investment on December 31?

c. What basis does Allie have in her stock investment and note on December 31?

d. What loss carryovers are available for Monte and Allie?

e. Explain how the use of the losses in Part a would change if Raider were instead a partnership and Monte and Allie were partners who shared profits, losses, and liabilities equally.

C11-44 *Use of Loss Carryovers.* Assume the same facts as in Problem C11-43. Assume further that Raider Corporation reports $75,000 of ordinary income, $20,000 of tax-exempt income, and a $25,000 long-term capital gain in the next year.

a. What income and deductions will Monte and Allie report from next year's activities?

b. What basis does Monte have in his stock investment on December 31 of next year?

c. What basis does Allie have in her stock investment and note on December 31 of next year?

d. What loss carryovers (if any) are available to Monte and Allie?

C11-45 *Use of Losses by Shareholders.* Tom owns 100% of Hammer Corporation, an electing S corporation. Tom has a $100,000 stock basis on January 1. Tom actively participates in Hammer's business. The Hammer Corporation operating results were not good in the current year, with the corporation reporting an ordinary loss of $175,000. The size of the loss required Tom to lend Hammer Corporation $50,000 on August 10 of the current year to provide funds needed for operations. The loan is secured by a Hammer Corporation note. Hammer Corporation rebounds during the next year and reports ordinary income of $60,000. Hammer Corporation repays the $50,000 note on December 15.

a. What amount of Hammer's current year loss can Tom deduct on his income tax return?

b. What is Tom's basis for the Hammer stock and note at the end of the loss year?

c. What income and deductions will Tom report next year from Hammer's activities and the loan repayment?

C11-46 *Allocation of Losses to Shareholders.* Harry and Rita formed Alpha Corporation as an S corporation, with each shareholder contributing $10,000 in exchange for stock. In addition, Rita loaned the corporation $7,000, and the corporation borrowed another $8,000 from the bank. In the current year, the corporation incurred a $26,000 operating loss. In the next year, the corporation will earn $16,000 of operating income.

a. For the current year and next year, determine the pass-through items for each shareholder and each shareholder's stock basis at the end of each year. Also, determine Rita's debt basis at the end of each year.

b. Same as Part a except the corporation also distributes $6,000 cash to each shareholder at the end of next year.

c. Assume the same facts as in Part b and that Alpha is a partnership instead of an S corporation. For the current year and next year, determine the pass-through items for each partner and each partner's basis in his or her partnership interest at the end of each year.

C11-47 *Post-Termination Loss Use.* Stein Corporation, an electing S corporation, has 400 shares of stock outstanding. Chuck and Linda own an equal number of these shares, and both actively participate in Stein's business. Chuck and Linda each contributed $60,000 when they organized Stein on September 10, 2005. Start-up losses during 2005 resulted in Stein reporting a $210,000 ordinary loss. Stein's activities have since become profitable, and the corporation voluntarily revokes the S election on March 1, 2006, with no prospective revocation date being specified. In 2006, Stein reports $360,000 of taxable income ($30,000 per month). Stein makes no distributions to its shareholders in either year.

a. What amount of loss can Chuck and Linda deduct in 2005?
b. What amount of loss do Chuck and Linda carry over to 2006?
c. If Chuck reported only $5,000 of other business income in 2005, what happens to the "excess" deductible S corporation losses?
d. What portion of the loss carryover from Part b can Chuck and Linda deduct in 2006? What happens to any unused portion of the loss?
e. What advice can you offer to Chuck and Linda to enhance their use of the Stein loss?

C11-48 *Use of Losses by Shareholders.* Tina, a single taxpayer, owns 100% of Rocket Corporation, an electing S corporation. She has an $80,000 stock basis for her investment on January 1. During the first 11 months of 2006, Rocket reports an ordinary loss of $100,000. The corporation expects an additional $20,000 loss for December. Tina earns $270,000 of ordinary income from her other activities in 2006. She expects her other income to decline to $145,000 in 2007 and continue at that level in future years. The corporation expects 2007 losses to be only $20,000. Rocket projects a $50,000 profit for 2008 and each of the next four years. What advice can you offer Tina about using her Rocket losses and retaining S corporation status in future years? How would your answer change if Tina expected her income from other activities to be $75,000 in 2006 and $270,000 in 2007.

C11-49 *Stock Basis Adjustment.* For each of the following items, indicate whether the item will increase, decrease, or cause no change in the S corporation's ordinary income (loss), AAA, and in the shareholder's stock basis. The corporation in question was formed four years ago and made its S election two years ago. During the time period it was a C corporation, it accumulated $30,000 of E&P. The corporation has not distributed any of this accumulated E&P.

a. Operating profit
b. Dividend income received from domestic corporation
c. Interest income earned on corporate bond held as an investment
d. Life insurance proceeds paid on death of corporate officer
e. Long-term capital gain
f. Sec. 1231 loss
g. Sec. 1245 gain (recapture)
h. Charitable contributions
i. Fines paid for having overweight trucks
j. Depreciation
k. Pension plan contributions for employees
l. Salary paid to owner
m. Premiums paid on life insurance policy in Part d
n. Distribution of money (but not exceeding current year's earnings)

C11-50 *Taxability of Distributions.* Tammy organized Sweets Corporation in January of the current year, and the corporation immediately elected to be an S corporation. Tammy, who contributed $40,000 in cash to start the business, owns 100% of the corporation's stock. Sweets' current year results are reported below:

Ordinary income	$36,000
Short-term capital loss	5,000

On July 10, Sweets makes a $10,000 cash distribution to Tammy.
a. What income is recognized as a result of the distribution?
b. What is Tammy's basis for the Sweets stock on December 31?
c. How would your answers to Parts a and b change if Sweets' distribution were instead $80,000?

C11-51 *Property Distributions.* George and Martha formed Washington Corporation as an S corporation several years ago. George and Martha each have a 50% interest in the corporation. At the beginning of the current year, their stock bases are $45,000 each. In the current year, the corporation earns $40,000 of ordinary income. In addition, the corporation distributes property to George having a $26,000 FMV and a $40,000 adjusted basis and distributes property to Martha having a $26,000 FMV and a $16,000 adjusted basis.

a. Determine what George and Martha recognize in the current year, and determine their ending stock bases. What bases do George and Martha have in the distributed property?

b. What tax planning disadvantages do you see with these property distributions?

C11-52 *Taxability of Distributions.* Curt incorporates Vogel Corporation on January 15 of the current year. Curt makes a $70,000 capital contribution including land having a $12,000 FMV, and Vogel makes a timely S election for this year. Vogel reports $60,000 of ordinary income, $40,000 of Sec. 1231 gain, $5,000 of tax-exempt interest income, and $3,000 of charitable contributions this year. On December 1, Vogel distributes $5,000 cash plus the land contributed by Curt because it no longer is needed in the business. The land, which had a $10,000 basis and a $12,000 FMV when contributed to the corporation in January, has an $18,000 FMV when distributed.

a. What income do Vogel Corporation and Curt report as a result of the distribution?

b. What is Curt's basis in the Vogel stock on December 31?

c. What is Vogel's accumulated adjustments account (AAA) balance on December 31?

C11-53 *Taxability of Distributions.* Hal organized Stable Corporation 18 years ago and has continued to own all its stock. The corporation made an S election one year after its incorporation. At the beginning of the current year, Stable reports the following earnings accumulations:

Accumulated adjustments account (AAA)	$85,000
Accumulated E&P	22,000

Hal's basis in his Stable stock on January 1 of the current year is $120,000. During the current year, Stable reports the following results from its operations:

Ordinary income	$30,000
Tax-exempt interest income	15,000
Long-term capital loss	20,000

Stable makes a $65,000 cash distribution to Hal on August 8.

a. What income, gain, or loss is recognized as a result of the distribution?

b. What is Hal's basis in the Stable stock on December 31?

c. What are Stable's AAA, E&P, and OAA balances on December 31?

d. How would your answers to Parts a-c change if Stable instead distributed $117,000?

C11-54 *Taxability of Distributions.* Sigma Corporation, an S corporation with one shareholder, incurred the following items 2005 and 2006:

2005

Tax-exempt income	$ 5,000
Ordinary income	30,000

2006

Ordinary loss	$(40,000)
Cash distribution	15,000

At the beginning of 2005, the corporation had a AAA balance of zero and accumulated E&P of $6,000. At the beginning of 2005, the shareholder had a $10,000 basis in stock and a $12,000 basis in debt he loaned to the corporation.

a. Determine items reported by the shareholder in 2005 and 2006.

b. Determine the balances in each corporate account and the shareholder's stock and debt bases at the end of each year.

c. Determine the results if the distribution in 2006 is $35,000 instead of $15,000.

d. How does the answer to Part c change if, in 2006, the corporation has an $18,000 long-term capital gain in addition to the $40,000 ordinary loss?

C11-55 *Taxability of Distributions.* Beta Corporation, an S corporation with one shareholder, incurred the following items:

	2005	
	Ordinary loss	$(40,000)

	2006	
	Ordinary income	$27,000
	Cash distribution	10,000

	2007	
	Ordinary income	$22,000
	Cash distribution	17,000

At the beginning of 2005, the shareholder's stock basis was $20,000, and her debt basis was $16,000.

a. Assuming the corporation has no accumulated E&P, show items reported by the shareholder in each year, show all basis adjustments to stock and debt, and show the stock and debt bases at the end of each year.

b. Redo Part a for 2006 and 2007 assuming ordinary income in 2006 is $8,000 instead of $27,000.

c. Go back to the original facts and again redo Part a for all years assuming that, at the beginning of 2005, the corporation had a AAA balance of zero and accumulated E&P of $12,000.

COMPREHENSIVE PROBLEMS

C11-56 *Comparison of Entity Formations.* Cara, Bob, and Steve want to begin a business on January 1, 2006. The individuals are considering three business forms—C corporation, partnership, and S corporation.

- Cara has investment land with a $36,000 adjusted basis and a $50,000 FMV that she is willing to contribute. The land has a rundown building on it having a $27,000 basis and a $15,000 FMV. Cara has never used the building nor rented it. She would like to get rid of the building. Because she needs cash, Cara will take out a $25,000 mortgage on the property before the formation of the new business and have the new business assume the debt. Cara obtains a 40% interest in the entity.

- Bob will contribute machinery and equipment, which he purchased for his sole proprietorship in January 2001. He paid $100,000 for the equipment and has used the MACRS rules with a half-year convention on this seven-year recovery period property. He did not make a Sec. 179 expensing election for this property. The FMV of the machinery and equipment is $39,000. Bob obtains a 39% interest in the entity.

- Steve will contribute cash of $600 and services worth $20,400 for his interest in the business. The services he will contribute include drawing up the necessary legal documentation for the new business and setting up the initial books. Steve obtains a 21% interest in the entity.

To begin operations, the new business plans to borrow $50,000 on a recourse basis from a local bank. Each owner will guarantee his or her ownership share of the debt.

What are the tax and nontax consequences for the new business and its owners under each alternative? Assume that any corporation will have 200 shares of common stock authorized and issued. For the partnership alternative, each partner receives a capital, profits, and loss interest. How would your answer to the basic facts change if instead Steve contributes $2,600 in cash and $18,400 in services?

C11-57 *Comparison of Operating Activities.* RST business entity reported the following items during the current year:

Dividends from 25%-owned domestic corporation	$19,000
State of Florida bond interest	18,000
General Electric Corporation bond interest	29,000
Gain on land contributed by Karen[a]	40,000
Operating profit (excluding depreciation)[b]	120,000
MACRS depreciation	36,000
Section 1245 gain (recapture)	5,000
Section 1231 loss	28,000
Long-term capital losses	4,000

Short-term capital losses	5,000
Charitable contributions	23,000
Investment interest expense (related to General Electric bonds)	16,000
Salary (guaranteed payment)	37,000

[a] Karen held the land as an investment prior to contributing it to RST business entity three years ago in exchange for her ownership interest. When Karen contributed the land, it had a basis of $15,000 and a FMV of $40,000. RST sold the land in the current year for $55,000. RST business entity held the land as an investment. Assume that Sec. 351 applied to any corporate formation transaction.

[b] Assume that qualified production activities income is $47,000 and that operating profit includes sufficient W-2 wages so as not to be a limiting factor.

a. What is the corporate taxable income and income tax liability for the current year if RST is taxed as a C corporation?

b. What is the ordinary income and separately stated items for the current year if RST elects to be an S corporation? Assume that RST has never operated as a C corporation.

c. What are the ordinary income and separately stated items if RST is treated as a general partnership?

C11-58 *Comparison of Nonliquidating Distributions.* Jeff and John organized Tampa Corporation 18 years ago and have each owned 50% of the corporation since its inception. In the current year, Tampa reports ordinary income/taxable income of $40,000. Assume the business does not qualify for the U.S. production activities deduction. On April 5, Tampa distributes $100,000 cash to Jeff and distributes land with a $100,000 FMV and a $70,000 adjusted basis to John. Tampa had purchased the land as an investment two years ago. What are the tax implications to Tampa, Jeff, and John of the land distribution in each of the four situations that follow?

a. Tampa has been a C corporation since its formation. On January 1 of the current year, Jeff's basis in his stock is $50,000, and John's basis is $45,000. Tampa has accumulated E&P of $155,000 on January 1 of the current year.

b. Tampa was formed as a C corporation but made an S election three years after its formation. On January 1 of the current year, Jeff's basis in his stock is $100,000, and John's basis is $80,000. Tampa had the following earnings balances on January 1 of the current year:

Accumulated Adjustments Account	$125,000
Accumulated E&P	30,000

c. Tampa was formed as a partnership and continues to operate in that form. On January 1 of the current year, Jeff's basis in his partnership interest is $100,000, and John's basis is $80,000. The partnership has no liabilities and no unrecognized precontribution gains.

d. How would your answers to Parts a–c change if the land held as an investment that was distributed to John had been contributed to Tampa by Jeff two years ago? At the time of Jeff's contribution, the land had a FMV of $95,000 and a $70,000 basis.

TAX STRATEGY PROBLEMS

C11-59 Alice, a single taxpayer, will form Morning Corporation in the current year. Alice plans to acquire all of Morning's common stock for a $100,000 contribution to the corporation. Morning will obtain additional capital by borrowing $75,000 from a local bank. Morning will conduct a variety of service activities with little need to retain its capital in the business. Alice expects start-up losses of $90,000 during Morning's first year of operation. She expects the corporation to earn pre-tax operating profits of $230,000 (before reduction for Alice's salary) starting next year. Alice plans to withdraw $100,000 of Morning's profits as salary. Her other income consists primarily of ordinary income (no dividends) from other sources, and she expects these amounts to total $120,000 annually. What advice can you provide Alice about the advisability of making an S election in the initial tax year? In the next tax year? In answering these questions, compare the following alternatives: (1) S corporation in both the current year and the next year, (2) S corporation in the current year and C corporation in the next year (i.e., by revoking the S election next year), (3) C corporation in both the current year and the next year, and (4) C corporation in the current year and S corporation in the next year. When analyzing these alternatives, consider the total taxes associated with each alternative, specifically, at the corporate and shareholder levels and across both years. Ignore payroll taxes, however. Also, assume the following facts:

(1) Alice takes the standard deduction; (2) the current tax rate schedules, standard deduction, and exemption phase out thresholds remain the same for both years; and (3) a 7% discount rate applies for present value calculations. Although this problem asks for only a two-year analysis, discuss some shortcomings of such a short time frame. Ignore the U.S. production activities deduction for this problem.

C11-60 One way to compare the accumulation of income by alterative business entity forms is to use mathematical models. The following models express the investment after-tax accumulation calculation for a particular entity form:

Flow-through entities (S corporations, partnerships, and LLCs): $ATA = [1 + R(1 - t_p)]^n$

C corporation: $ATA = [1 + R(1 - t_c)]^n(1 - t_g) + t_g$

where: ATA = after-tax accumulation in n years

R = before-tax rate of return;

t_p = owner's marginal tax rate on ordinary income

t_c = corporation's marginal tax rate

t_g = owner's tax rate on capital gains

n = number of periods

For each alternative business form, the owner makes an initial investment of $1. The following operating assumptions apply:

Before-tax rate of return $(R) = 0.18$

Marginal tax rate for owner $(t_p) = 0.35$

Corporate tax rate $(t_c) = 0.34$

Capital gains rate $(t_g) = 0.15$ for regular capital gains (assume the Sec. 1202 50% exclusion for small business corporations does not apply)

Investment horizon $(n) = 2, 4, 20, 50,$ or 101 years

A flow-through entity distributes only enough cash each year for the owners to pay their taxes. The corporation pays no dividends. The shareholders sell their stock at the end of the investment horizon, and their gains are taxed at capital gains rates. (See Chapter I18 of the *Individuals* volume for a detailed explanation of these models.)

Required: What is the after-tax accumulation if each business form is operated for the investment horizon and then sold for the amount of the accumulation? Which entity form is best for each investment horizon? How would your calculations and conclusions change if the C corporation's tax rate is 25%?

C11-61 Problem C6-56 considered two alternative forms for doing business. Now consider a third alternative. The C corporation could make an S election effective at the beginning of the current year, operate as an S corporation for the next 20 years, and liquidate the S corporation at that time (32 years in total). Compare this alternative to the other two alternatives in Problem C6-56.

C11-62 Assume the corporation in Problem C11-61 (and C6-56) had been an S corporation for its first 12 years, during which it distributed just enough cash for the shareholder to pay taxes on the pass-through income. Thus, the S corporation reinvested after-tax income. Now the corporation is considering revoking its S election and operating as a C corporation for the remaining 20 years with no dividend distributions. Show the results of remaining an S corporation versus revoking the election. Also show supporting models and calculations. Which alternative should the corporation adopt? Ignore the accumulated earnings tax for C corporations. How does your answer change if the C corporation's tax rate is 15% instead of 35%?

TAX FORM/RETURN PREPARATION PROBLEM

C11-63 Bottle-Up, Inc., was organized on January 8, 1996, and made its S election on January 24, 1996. The necessary consents to the election were filed in a timely manner. Its federal tax identification number is 38-1507869. Its address is 1234 Hill Street, Gainesville, FL 32607. Bottle-Up, uses the calendar year as its tax year, the accrual method of accounting, and the first-in, first-out (FIFO) inventory method. Bottle-Up manufactures ornamental glass bottles. It made no changes to its inventory costing methods this year. It uses the specific identification method for bad debts for book and tax purposes. Herman Hiebert (S.S. No. 123-45-6789) and Melvin Jones (S.S. No. 100-67-2000) own 500 shares each. Both individuals materially participate in Bottle-Up's single activity. Herman Hiebert is the tax matters person. Financial statements for Bottle-Up for the current year are shown in Tables C11-2 through C11-4. Assume that Bottle-Up's business qualifies as a U.S. production activity and that its qualified production activities income is $90,000. The S corporation uses the small

▼ TABLE C11-2

Bottle-Up, Inc. Income Statement for the Year Ended December 31 of the Current Year (Problem C11-63)

Sales		$2,500,000
Returns and allowances		(15,000)
Net sales		$2,485,000
Beginning inventory	$ 102,000	
Purchases	900,000	
Labor	200,000	
Supplies	80,000	
Utilities	100,000	
Other manufacturing costs	188,000[a]	
Goods available for sale	$1,570,000	
Ending inventory	(96,000)	1,474,000[b]
Gross profit		$1,011,000
Salaries[c]	$ 451,020	
Utilities expense	54,000	
Depreciation (MACRS depreciation is $36,311)	11,782	
Automobile and truck expense	26,000	
Office supplies expense	9,602	
Advertising expense	105,000	
Bad debts expense	620	
Rent expense	30,000	
Interest expense[d]	1,500	
Meals and entertainment expense	21,000	
Selling expenses	100,000	
Repairs and maintenance expense	38,000	
Accounting and legal expense	4,500	
Charitable contributions[e]	9,000	
Insurance expense[f]	24,500	
Hourly employees' fringe benefits	11,000	
Payroll taxes	36,980	
Other taxes	2,500	
Penalties (fines for overweight trucks)	1,000	(938,004)
Operating profit		$ 72,996
Other income and losses:		
Long-term gain on sale of capital assets	$ 48,666[g]	
Sec. 1231 loss	(1,100)[h]	
Interest on U.S. Treasury bills	1,200	
Interest on State of Florida bonds	600	
Dividends from domestic corporations	11,600	
Investment expenses	(600)	60,366
Net income		$ 133,362

[a] Total MACRS depreciation is $74,311. Assume that $38,000 of depreciation has been allocated to cost of sales for both book and tax purposes so that the book and tax inventory and cost of sales amounts are the same. The AMT depreciation adjustment on personal property is $9,000.

[b] The cost of goods sold amount reflects the Uniform Capitalization Rules of Sec. 263A. The appropriate restatements have been made in prior years.

[c] Officer salaries of $120,000 are included in the total. All are employer's W-2 wages.

[d] Investment interest expense is $500. All other interest expense is trade- or business-related. None of the interest expense relates to the production of tax-exempt income.

[e] The corporation made all contributions in cash to qualifying charities.

[f] Includes $3,000 of premiums paid for policies on lives of corporate officers. Bottle-Up is the beneficiary for both policies.

[g] The corporation acquired the capital assets on March 3, 2003 for $100,000 and sold them on September 15, 2005 for $148,000.

[h] The corporation acquired the Sec. 1231 property on June 5, 2004 for $10,000 and sold it on December 21, 2005 for $8,900.

▼ **TABLE C11-3**

Bottle-Up, Inc. Balance Sheet for January 1 and December 31 of the Current Year (Problem C11-63)

	January 1	December 31
Assets:		
Cash	$ 15,000	$116,948
Accounts receivable	41,500	45,180
Inventories	102,000	96,000
Stocks	103,000	74,000
Treasury bills	15,000	16,000
State of Florida bonds	10,000	10,000
Building and equipment	374,600	375,000
Minus: Accumulated depreciation	(160,484)	(173,100)
Land	160,000	190,000
Total	$660,616	$750,028
Liabilities and equities:		
Accounts payable	$ 36,000	$ 10,000
Accrued salaries payable	12,000	6,000
Payroll taxes payable	3,416	7,106
Sales taxes payable	5,200	6,560
Due to Mr. Hiebert	10,000	5,000
Mortgage and notes payable (current maturities)	44,000	52,000
Long-term debt	210,000	260,000
Capital stock	10,000	10,000
Retained earnings	330,000	393,362
Total	$660,616	$750,028

▼ **TABLE C11-4**

Bottle-Up, Inc. Statement of Change in Retained Earnings, for the Current Year Ended December 31 (Problem C11-63)

Balance, January 1		$330,000[a]
Plus: Net income	$133,362	
Minus: Dividends	(70,000)	63,362
Balance, December 31		$393,362

[a] The January 1 accumulated adjustments account balance is $274,300.

business simplified overall method for reporting these activities (see discussion for Line 12d of Schedules K and K-1 in the Form 1120S instructions). Prepare a current year S corporation tax return for Bottle-Up, showing yourself as the paid preparer.

CASE STUDY PROBLEM

C11-64 Debra has operated a family counseling practice for a number of years as a sole proprietor. She owns the condominium office space that she occupies in addition to her professional library and office furniture. She has a limited amount of working capital and little need to accumulate additional business assets. Her total business assets are about $150,000, with an $80,000 mortgage on the office space being her only liability. Typically, she has withdrawn any unneeded assets at the end of the year. Debra has used her personal car for business travel and charged the business for the mileage at the appropriate mileage rate provided by the IRS. Over the last three years, Debra's practice has grown so that she now forecasts $80,000 of income being earned this year. Debra has contributed small amounts to an Individual Retirement Account (IRA) each year, but her contributions have never reached the annual limits. Although she has never been sued, Debra recently has become concerned about legal liability. An attorney friend of hers has suggested that she incorporate her business to protect herself against being sued and to save taxes.

Required: You are a good friend of Debra's and a CPA; she asks your opinion on incorporating her business. You are to meet with Debra tomorrow for lunch. Prepare a draft of the points you feel should be discussed over lunch about incorporating the family counseling practice.

TAX RESEARCH PROBLEMS

C11-65 Cato Corporation incorporated on July 1, 2001, in California, with Tim and Elesa, husband and wife, owning all the Cato stock. On August 15, 2001, Cato Corporation made an S election effective for tax year 2001. Tim and Elesa file the necessary consents to the election. On March 10, 2005, Tim and Elesa transferred 15% of the Cato stock to the Reid and Susan Trust, an irrevocable trust created three years earlier for the benefit of their two minor children. In early 2006, Tim and Elesa's tax accountant learns about the transfer and advises the couple that the transfer of the stock to the trust may have terminated Cato's S election. Prepare a memorandum for your tax manager indicating any action Tim and Elesa can take that will permit Cato to retain its S election? Research sources suggested by the tax manager include Secs. 1361(c)(2), 1362(d)(2), and 1362(f).

C11-66 One of your wealthy clients, Cecile, invests $100,000 for sole ownership of an electing S corporation's stock. The corporation is in the process of developing a new food product. Cecile anticipates that the new business will need approximately $200,000 in capital (other than trade payables) during the first two years of its operations before it starts to earn sufficient profits to pay a return on the shareholder's investment. The first $100,000 of this total is to come from Cecile's contributed capital. The remaining $100,000 of funds will come from one of the following three sources:

- Have the corporation borrow the $100,000 from a local bank. Cecile is required to act as a guarantor for the loan.
- Have the corporation borrow $100,000 from the estate of Cecile's late husband. Cecile is the sole beneficiary of the estate.
- Have Cecile lend $100,000 to the corporation from her personal funds.

The S corporation will pay interest at a rate acceptable to the IRS. During the first two years of operations, the corporation anticipates losing $125,000 before it begins to earn a profit. Your tax manager has asked you to evaluate the tax ramifications of each of the three financing alternatives. Prepare a memorandum to the tax manager outlining the information you found in your research.

C11-67 Frank Wilson formed Gamma Corporation on January 5, 2005, and the corporation immediately elected to be treated as an S corporation beginning in 2005. Upon formation, Frank contributed $300,000 in exchange for the corporation's common stock. As 2005 progressed, Frank realized the corporation was going to incur heavy losses, so on July 31, 2005, he advanced the corporation $400,000 on open account. For 2005, the corporation ended the year with a $550,000 ordinary loss from operations, and Frank claimed this loss in his personal tax return. Early in 2006, the corporation's operations were doing well, and the corporation repaid the $400,000 advance to Frank. However, later in 2006, things took a turn for the worse, and the corporation seemed headed for a net loss for the year. Therefore, Frank advanced an additional $500,000 to the corporation on July 31, 2006 in a similar fashion to the prior year's advance. For 2006, the corporation ended the year with a $200,000 ordinary loss. Frank suspects this pattern of advances and repayments may continue next year as well, although he hopes for profitable years after that. Frank asks your help in determining the tax consequences of these transactions. At a minimum, you should consider the following resources:

- IRC Sec. 1367
- Reg. Sec. 1.1367-2
- *Fleming G. Brooks, et ux. v. Commissioner, et al.,* TC Memo 2005-204, 90 TCM 172 (2005)

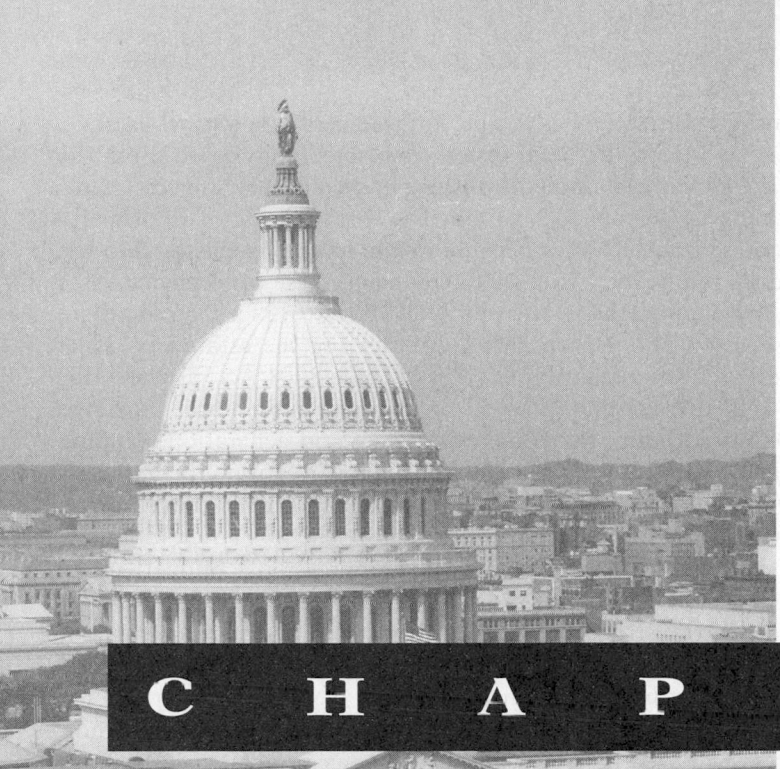

12

CHAPTER

THE GIFT TAX

LEARNING OBJECTIVES

After studying this chapter, you should be able to

1. ▶ Understand the concept of the unified transfer tax system

2. ▶ Describe the gift tax formula

3. ▶ Identify a number of transactions subject to the gift tax

4. ▶ Determine whether an annual gift tax exclusion is available

5. ▶ Identify deductions available for gift tax purposes

6. ▶ Apply the gift-splitting rules

7. ▶ Calculate the gift tax liability

8. ▶ Understand how basis affects the overall tax consequences

9. ▶ Recognize the filing requirements for gift tax returns

The **gift tax** is a **wealth transfer tax** that applies if a person transfers property while alive. It is similar to the estate tax, which applies to transfers associated with death. Both the gift tax and the estate tax are part of the unified transfer tax system that subjects gratuitous transfers of property between persons to taxation. The vast majority of all property transfers are exempt from these transfer taxes because of the annual exclusion and the various deductions and credits. However, planning for reducing these transfer taxes is a significant matter for wealthy or moderately wealthy individuals. In recent years, there has been considerable discussion about permanently abolishing the estate tax.[1] The Economic Growth and Tax Relief Reconciliation Act of 2001 (the 2001 Act) provided for phased in increases to the unified credit and phased in reductions in the unified tax rate schedule beginning in 2002. In addition, it repealed the estate and generation skipping transfer taxes, *but not the gift tax*, effective January 1, 2010. However, if no further legislation passes, the 2001 Act provides that the rules for gift, estate, and generation skipping taxes will revert on January 1, 2011, to what they were before the 2001 Act. Congress adopted this "sunsetting" provision to comply with the Congressional Budget Act of 1974.

This chapter discusses both the structure of the gift tax (including the exclusion, deduction, and credit provisions) and exactly which property transfers fall within its purview. It reviews the income tax basis rules in the context of their implications for selecting properties to transfer by gift instead of at death. Consider, however, that an individual who believes Congress will eventually repeal the estate tax prior to such person's anticipated date of death will likely decide against making sizable gifts.

CONCEPT OF TRANSFER TAXES

The recipient of a gift incurs no income tax liability because Sec. 102 explicitly excludes gifts and inheritances from the recipient's gross income.[2] The gift tax, a type of excise tax, is levied on the donor, the person who transferred the property. The gift tax applies to the act of transferring property to a recipient who pays either no consideration or consideration smaller than the value of the property received.

HISTORY AND PURPOSE OF TRANSFER TAXES

The United States has had an estate tax since 1916 and a gift tax continuously since 1932. The structure of the gift and estate taxes has remained fairly constant, but details such as the amount of the exclusion and the rate schedules have changed numerous times. The Tax Reform Act of 1976 (the 1976 Act) made a very significant change by enacting a unified rate schedule for gift and estate tax purposes.

ADDITIONAL COMMENT

In 2005, the House of Representatives passed a bill that would make repeal of the estate tax (but not the gift tax) permanent. Because of Gulf Coast disasters, the Senate did not vote on this legislation. The Senate instead may consider increasing the amount of wealth exempt from the estate tax.

ADDITIONAL COMMENT

The new lower tax rate on dividend income will reduce or eliminate the income tax savings from having dividends taxed to donees in low tax brackets.

The gift tax has had several purposes, one of the most important of which was to raise revenue. However, because of the fairly generous annual exclusion and unified credit legislated by Congress, the gift tax yields only a small fraction of the federal government's total revenues. Only donors making relatively large gifts owe any gift taxes. Another purpose of the gift tax is to serve as a backstop to the estate tax and to prevent individuals from avoiding a significant amount of—or all—estate taxes by disposing of property before death. For example, without the gift tax, persons who know they are terminally ill could dispose of property "on their deathbed" and escape the transfer tax. In addition, the gift tax provides revenue to offset some of the income tax revenue lost because of income from the gifted property sometimes being shifted to a person in a lower income tax bracket. Another purpose for levying gift and estate taxes is to redistribute wealth.

---

[1] Proposals to abolish the estate tax received criticism, in part, because in 1998, for example, only 47,500 estates owed any tax, and most of the tax was paid by estates above $5 million. See "House Republicans Shift Their Strategy in Effort to Push Two Popular Tax Cuts," *The Wall Street Journal* (August 22, 2000), p. A20.

[2] The income earned from property received as a gift or an inheritance, however, is not exempt from the income tax.

No one knows what the distribution of wealth would have been had Congress not enacted transfer taxes. However, one study estimated that the top 1% of the population held 22.5% of this nation's personal wealth in 1995, about the same percentage as in 1992.[3]

THE UNIFIED TRANSFER TAX SYSTEM

In 1976, Congress greatly revamped the transfer tax system by combining the separate estate and gift tax systems into one unified transfer tax system. Although Chapters C12 and C13 use the terms *gift tax* and *estate tax,* these taxes actually are components of the same unified transfer tax system. The system also includes the generation-skipping transfer tax, a topic discussed in Chapter C13. The unification of the transfer tax system removed the previous law's bias favoring the tax treatment of lifetime gifts in comparison with transfers at death. The three most significant elements of the unified system—the unified rate schedule, the inclusion of taxable gifts in the death tax base, and the unified credit—are discussed below.

UNIFIED RATE SCHEDULE

Before the 1976 Act mandated a **unified rate schedule,** effective for gifts made after 1976 and deaths occurring after 1976 and applicable to both lifetime transfers and transfers at death, the gift tax rates were only 75% of the estate tax rates on a transfer of the same size. The rates are progressive and have varied over the years. The 2001 Act reduced the unified transfer tax rates beginning in 2002 by replacing the former top two brackets (on amounts exceeding $2.5 million) with a 50% maximum tax rate in 2002. The top rate declined to 49% in 2003, 48% in 2004, 47% in 2005, and 46% in 2006. In those years, the top rate applies to tax bases above $2 million. In 2007 through 2009, for both estate and gift tax purposes, the maximum tax rate of 45% will apply to tax bases exceeding $1.5 million.

As mentioned earlier, the 2001 Act repeals the estate and generation skipping taxes effective January 1, 2010. At that date, the maximum gift tax rate will decline to 35% and will apply to tax bases exceeding $500,000. Congress retained the gift tax to make up for the loss in income tax revenue that could occur should wealthy individuals shift assets free of gift tax to donees in lower income tax brackets. (See the inside back cover for the unified transfer tax rates.)

IMPACT OF TAXABLE GIFTS ON DEATH TAX BASE

Before 1977, a separate system applied to lifetime gifts compared with dispositions at death. By making gifts, an individual could shift the taxation of property from the top of the estate tax rate schedule to the bottom of the gift tax rate schedule. Few taxpayers could take advantage of this shifting, however, because only people with a relatively large amount of property could afford to part with sizable amounts of their assets while alive.

Under today's unified system, taxable gifts affect the size of the tax base at death. Any post-1976 taxable gifts (other than gifts included in the gross estate) are called **adjusted taxable gifts,** and such gifts are included in the donor's death tax base. Although they are valued at their fair market value (FMV) on the date of the gift, the addition of such taxable gifts to the tax base at death can cause the donor-decedent's estate to be taxed at a higher marginal tax rate. However, such gifts are not taxed for a second time upon the donor's death because gift taxes (computed at current rates) on these gifts are subtracted in determining the estate tax liability.

---

[3] "Tax Report," *The Wall Street Journal* (April 19, 2000), p. A1.

EXAMPLE C12-1 ▶   In 1994, Dan made taxable gifts totaling $500,000. When Dan dies in the current year, the value of the gifted property has tripled. Dan's death tax base includes the $500,000 of post-1976 taxable gifts. They are valued for estate tax purposes at their FMV on the date of the gift; the post-gift appreciation escapes the transfer tax system. Thus, the transfer tax value is fixed or frozen at the date-of-gift value. ◀

Note that unification (including taxable gifts that become part of the tax base at death) extends only to gifts made after 1976. Congress exempted gifts made before 1977 from unification because it did not want to retroactively change the two separate transfer tax systems of the prior tax regime.

UNIFIED CREDIT

The **unified credit** reduces dollar for dollar a certain amount of the tax computed on the taxable gifts or the taxable estate. The amount of the credit has varied depending on the year of the transfer. However, for years 2002 through 2009 the credit for gift tax purposes is $345,800. In the gift and estate tax formulas, the full credit is available for lifetime transfers and again in determining the tax payable at death. In concept, however, an individual's estate does not receive the benefit of this unified credit amount at death to the extent the decedent had used the credit against lifetime transfers (as explained in Chapter C13). The gift tax formula, including the unified credit, is discussed below.

GIFT TAX FORMULA

The formula described in this section is used to calculate a donor's gift tax liability for the year of the transfer. Gift tax reporting is done on an annual basis, always on a calendar year. Figure C12-1 illustrates the formula for determining the donor's annual gift tax liability. This formula is discussed in detail later in the chapter.

DETERMINATION OF GIFTS

The starting point in the process is to determine which, if any, of the taxpayer's transfers constitute gifts. The next section discusses the various types of transfers that the statute views as gifts. All gifts are valued at their FMVs on the date of the gift. Next, the aggregate amount of gifts for the period is determined. The aggregate gifts are then reduced by any exclusions and deductions. Finally, the tax is computed according to the formula illustrated in Figure C12-1.

ADDITIONAL COMMENT

The gift tax applies to cumulative lifetime gifts made since the enactment of the gift tax in 1932. The unified gift and estate tax, enacted in 1976, applies only to cumulative lifetime taxable gifts made after 1976. Thus, a taxable gift of $75,000 made in 1970 would not be included in a decedent's unified tax base for calculating the estate tax but would affect the gift tax payable by that person.

EXCLUSIONS AND DEDUCTIONS

For many years the maximum amount excludible annually was a fixed amount of $10,000 per donee, but Congress amended the IRC to allow indexation beginning with gifts made after 1998. Inflation adjustments are rounded to the next *lowest* multiple of $1,000.[4] Accordingly, the annual exclusion rose to $11,000 in 2002 and to $12,000 beginning in 2006. If the gifts made to a donee are less than the annual exclusion amount, the amount excludible is limited to the amount of the gift made to that donee. A donor may claim exclusions for transfers to an unlimited number of donees.

Two types of deductions (marital and charitable) reduce the amount of the taxable gifts. Most transfers to one's spouse generate a marital deduction; there is no ceiling on the amount of this deduction. Similarly, most transfers to charitable organizations are cancelled out by the charitable contribution deduction, which also is unlimited.

KEY POINT

The annual exclusion applies to each *donee* per year; therefore, the total amount of tax-free gifts in a given year can be much greater than the annual exclusion amount. Also, gift-splitting can double the tax-free amount per donee.

GIFT-SPLITTING ELECTION

Congress authorized gift-splitting provisions to achieve more comparable tax consequences between taxpayers of community property and noncommunity property (common law) states.[5] Under **community property law**, assets acquired after marriage are com-

---

[4] Sec. 2503(b).
[5] The eight traditional community property states are Louisiana, Texas, New Mexico, Arizona, California, Washington, Idaho, and Nevada. Wisconsin's

marital property law, though not providing for community property, is basically the same as community property.

Determination of Taxable Gifts
for Current Period

Aggregate amount of individual's
gifts for current period*

Minus

One-half of individual's gifts to
third parties if gift splitting is elected

Plus

One-half of spouse's gifts to third
parties if gift splitting is elected

Minus

Annual exclusions of
$12,000 or less per donee

Minus

Marital deduction (unlimited
amount) for gifts made to spouse

Minus

Charitable contribution
deduction (unlimited amount)

Equals

Taxable gifts for current period

Determination of
Gift Tax Liability

Taxable gifts for
current period

Plus

Taxable gifts for all
prior periods

Equals

Cumulative taxable gifts

Tax (at current rates) on
cumulative taxable gifts

Minus

Tax (at current rates) on
taxable gifts of prior periods

Equals

Tax on taxable gifts of
current period

Minus

Unified credit for this period
(for example, $345,800 for 2002-2009)
minus unified credit used in prior periods

Equals

Tax payable (but not less than
zero) for current period

* Valued at FMV on date of gift.

FIGURE C12-1 ▶ THE GIFT TAX FORMULA

munity property unless they are acquired by gift or inheritance. Typically, in a **community property state**, a large portion of the spouses' assets is community property, property in which each spouse has a one-half interest. One-half of a community property gift is automatically considered to be given by each spouse. By contrast, in a **common law state**, all assets acquired during the marriage are the property of the acquiring spouse. The other spouse does not automatically acquire an interest in the property. Thus, often only one spouse owns enough assets to consider making large gifts.

Section 2513 authorizes spouses to elect gift splitting, which treats gifts made by each spouse to third parties as if each spouse made one-half of the gift. As a result, spouses in common law states can achieve the same benefits that apply automatically for gifts of community property. Thus, both spouses can claim a $12,000 per donee exclusion although only one spouse actually makes the gift, and the spouses can give each donee a total of $24,000 before either spouse's gift becomes taxable.

EXAMPLE C12-2 ▶ Andy and Bonnie, residents of a common law state, are married throughout 2006. In that year, Andy gives his brother $100,000 cash. Andy and Bonnie may elect gift splitting and thereby treat the $100,000 gift as if each spouse gave $50,000. As a result, the excludible portion of the gift totals $24,000 ($12,000 per donee for each of the two deemed donors). If they elect gift splitting, each donor's $38,000 taxable gift may be taxed at a lower marginal tax rate. In addition, Bonnie can use a unified credit amount that she might not otherwise be able to use. As a

ADDITIONAL COMMENT

Because the gift tax is a tax on *cumulative* lifetime gifts, taxpayers must keep track of all taxable gifts because all previous taxable gifts are part of the calculation for current gift tax due, and post-1976 taxable gifts affect the estate tax liability.

result of gift splitting, the tax consequences are the same as if Andy and Bonnie were residents of a community property state and each gave $50,000 of community property to Andy's brother. ◄

CUMULATIVE NATURE OF GIFT TAX

Unlike the income tax, computations of gift tax liabilities are cumulative in nature. The marginal tax rate applicable to the current period's taxable gifts is a function of both the taxable gifts for the current period and the aggregate taxable gifts for all earlier periods.

EXAMPLE C12-3 ▶ Sandy and Jack each make taxable gifts in the current year totaling $200,000. However, for previous periods, Sandy's taxable gifts total $100,000 and Jack's total $1.5 million. Because Jack's cumulative total taxable gifts are larger than Sandy's, Jack's current marginal tax rate exceeds Sandy's. Specifically Jack's $200,000 gift is taxed at a 45% rate, while Sandy's $200,000 gift is taxed at the following rates: $50,000 at 30%, $100,000 at 32%, and $50,000 at 34%. ◄

SELF-STUDY QUESTION

Al and Beth, husband and wife, live in a common law state. Al gives a $620,000 gift to each of two children. Al and Beth agree to split the gift. Neither Al nor Beth has made taxable gifts in any prior year. Explain their gift tax liability.

ANSWER

One-half of each gift, a total of $620,000, is reported on each taxpayer's gift tax return. Neither Al nor Beth has any gift tax liability for the current year due to the annual exclusions and the unified credit. Al has effectively used some of Beth's unified credit without Beth ever having ownership or control over Al's property.

UNIFIED CREDIT

Before 1977, the IRC allowed a $30,000 specific exemption deductible by donors whenever they desired. The 1976 Act repealed this exemption and replaced it with the unified credit.[6] Consequently, the gift tax computed for gifts made in 1977 and later years is reduced dollar for dollar by the unified credit. The unified credit allows donors to make a certain amount of taxable gifts (known originally as the **exemption equivalent** and now referred to in the IRC as **applicable exclusion amount**) without needing to pay the gift tax. For 1977 through 1987, the maximum amount of the credit increased progressively until in 1987 it reached $192,800, which was equivalent to a $600,000 exemption from the gift tax. Legislation in 1997 again increased the size of the credit. For 2000 and 2001, the credit was $220,550 (equivalent to a $675,000 exemption). As a result of the 2001 Act, the credit against gift taxes and the gift tax exemption equivalent increased to $345,800 and $1 million, respectively, in 2002 and will stay at those levels through 2009. In 2010, the credit will be $330,800, the tax on $1 million at a top rate of 35%. On the other hand, the credit for estate tax purposes later increases above $345,800. The unified credit amount for various years appears on the inside back cover.

The amount creditable for a particular year is the credit amount for that year minus the credit that could have been claimed for the taxable gifts made by the individual in earlier years. Recall that no credit was allowed for gifts made before 1977.

EXAMPLE C12-4 ▶ Zheng made her first taxable gift,[7] $500,000 in amount, in 1986. Zheng used the $155,800 unified credit available for 1986 (as shown on the inside back cover) to reduce her $155,800 gift tax liability to zero. Zheng made her next taxable gift in 1994. The taxable amount was $250,000. Zheng's 1994 gift tax of $92,500 ($248,300 − $155,800) was reduced by a unified credit of $37,000 ($192,800 − $155,800). The $92,500 represents the tax on the $750,000 of cumulative taxable gifts, which is $248,300, minus the tax on the $500,000 of prior taxable gifts, which was $155,800. If she makes taxable gifts in 2006, the maximum credit she can claim against her current tax is $153,000 ($345,800 − $192,800 already used). ◄

ADDITIONAL COMMENT

Taxpayers must keep a record of how much of the specific exemption they used between September 9 and December 31, 1976, to determine how much of the unified credit is available to them.

After passage of the 1976 Act, prospective donors quickly realized they could make gifts before the end of 1976 and avoid the unification provisions, but Congress adopted a special rule that affects donors who used any portion of their specific exemption between September 9, 1976, and December 31, 1976.[8] The rule reduced the amount of unified credit otherwise available to such donors by 20% of the amount of the specific exemption they claimed against gifts made between September 9 and December 31, 1976. The maximum reduction in the unified credit as a result of this provision is $6,000 (0.20 × $30,000 maximum specific exemption).

EXAMPLE C12-5 ▶ In November 1976, Maria made a large taxable gift, her first gift, and used her $30,000 specific exemption. As a result, the unified credit that Maria could otherwise claim after 1976 is reduced by $6,000 (0.20 × $30,000). Her 1976 taxable gifts are not includible in her death tax base. ◄

---

[6] Sec. 2505.
[7] No credit is used for a gift that is completely nontaxable.

[8] Sec. 2505(b). Congress repealed this exemption for post-1976 years.

TRANSFERS SUBJECT TO THE GIFT TAX

OBJECTIVE 3

Identify a number of transactions subject to the gift tax

In general, property transferred for less than adequate consideration in money or money's worth is deemed to be a gift in the gift tax context. The gift occurs when the donor gives up control over the transferred property. Congress has legislated several provisions that exempt various property transfers that otherwise might be viewed as gifts from the scope of the gift tax. These exemptions include direct payments of medical expenses and tuition, transfers to political organizations, property settlements in conjunction with a divorce, and qualified disclaimers.

TRANSFERS FOR INADEQUATE CONSIDERATION

As mentioned earlier, the initial step in determining the donor's gift tax liability is deciding which transactions constitute gifts for gift tax purposes. Section 2501(a) states that a gift tax is imposed on "the transfer of property by gift." Thus, if *property* is transferred *by gift*, the transferor potentially incurs a gift tax liability. Perhaps surprisingly, the IRC does not define the term *gift*. Section 2511(a) expands on Sec. 2501(a) by indicating that the tax is applicable "whether the transfer is in trust or otherwise, whether the gift is direct or indirect, and whether the property is real or personal, tangible or intangible."

A transaction is subject to the gift tax even though not entirely gratuitous if "the value of the property transferred by the donor exceeds the value in money or money's worth of the consideration given therefor."[9] In such circumstances, the amount of the gift is the difference between the value of the property the donor gives up and the value of the consideration in money or money's worth received. The following discussion examines in more depth the scope of the rule regarding transfers for less than adequate consideration.

ADDITIONAL COMMENT

At times, a transferor can inadvertently make a gift by selling property to a family member for an amount determined in an IRS audit to be less than its fair market value.

BARGAIN SALES. Often, an individual wants to sell an asset to a family member, but the prospective buyer cannot afford to pay the full FMV of the property. If the buyer pays consideration of less than the FMV of the transferred property, the seller makes a gift to the buyer equal to the bargain element of the transaction, which is the excess of the property's FMV over its sales price.

EXAMPLE C12-6 ▶ Martha sells her ranch, having a $1 million FMV, to her son Stan, who can afford to pay only $300,000 of consideration. In the year of the sale, Martha makes a gift to Stan of $700,000, the excess of the ranch's FMV over the consideration received. ◀

TRANSFERS IN NORMAL COURSE OF BUSINESS. Treasury Regulations provide an exception to the general rule that a transfer for inadequate consideration triggers a gift. Specifically, a transaction arising "in the ordinary course of business (a transaction which is bona fide, at arm's length, and free from any donative intent)" is considered to have been made for adequate consideration.[10] Thus, no gift arises when a buyer acquires property for less than its FMV *if* the acquisition is in the ordinary course of business.

EXAMPLE C12-7 ▶ John, a merchant, has a clearance sale and sells a diamond bracelet valued at $30,000 to Bess who pays $12,000, the clearance sale price. Because the clearance sale arose in the ordinary course of John's business, the bargain element ($18,000) does not constitute a gift to Bess. ◀

STATUTORY EXEMPTIONS FROM THE GIFT TAX

For various reasons, including simplifying the administration of the gift tax, Congress enacted several provisions that exempt certain transactions from the purview of the gift tax. In the absence of these statutory rules, some of these transactions could constitute gifts.

---

[9] Reg. Sec. 25.2512-8.   [10] Ibid.

PAYMENT OF MEDICAL EXPENSES OR TUITION. Section 2503(e) states that a qualified transfer is not treated as a transfer of property by gift. The IRC defines *qualified transfer* as an amount paid on behalf of an individual to an educational organization for tuition or to any person who provides medical care as payment for such medical care. Such payments are exempt from gift treatment only if made *directly* to the educational organization or to the person or entity providing the medical care. *Educational organization* has the same definition as for charitable contribution purposes,[11] and *medical care* has the same definition as for medical expense deduction purposes.[12] Note that the rule addresses only tuition, not room, board, and books. Note also that the identity of the person whose expenses are paid is not important. The special exemption applies even if an individual makes payments on behalf of a non-relative.

If one taxpayer pays amounts benefitting someone else and the expenditures constitute support that the payor must furnish under state law, such payments are support, not gifts. State law determines the definition of support. Generally, payments of medical expenses for one's minor child would be categorized as support and not a gift, even in the absence of Sec. 2503(e). On the other hand, state law generally does not require parents to pay medical expenses or tuition for an adult child. Thus, the enactment of Sec. 2503(e) removed such payments from the gift tax.

According to the Staff of the Joint Committee on Taxation, special rules concerning tuition and medical expense payments were enacted because

> Congress was concerned that certain payments of tuition made on behalf of children who have attained their majority, and of special medical expenses on behalf of elderly relatives, technically could be considered gifts under prior law. The Congress believed such payments should be exempt from gift taxes.[13]

SELF-STUDY QUESTION

Ben's adult son Clarence, who is not Ben's dependent, needs a liver transplant. Because Clarence cannot afford the surgical procedure, Ben pays the medical fee directly to the hospital. Is the payment for Clarence's benefit a taxable gift?

ANSWER

The payment is not a taxable gift because of Sec. 2503(e).

EXAMPLE C12-8 ▶ Sergio pays $20,000 for his adult grandson's tuition at medical school and $14,000 for the grandson's room and board in the medical school's dormitory. Sergio makes all payments directly to the educational organization. Section 2503(e) exempts the direct payment of the tuition to the medical school (but not the room and board) from being treated as a gift. Because Sergio is not required under state law to pay room and board for an adult grandson, such payments are not support. Sergio has made a $14,000 gift to the grandson. ◀

EXAMPLE C12-9 ▶ Assume the same facts as in Example C12-8 except that Sergio writes a $34,000 check to his grandson, who in turn pays the medical school. Sergio has made a $34,000 gift. Because Sergio does not pay the tuition directly to the school, Sergio does not meet all the conditions for exempting the tuition payments from gift tax treatment. Here, and in Example C12-8, Sergio receives a $12,000 annual exclusion. ◀

TRANSFERS TO POLITICAL ORGANIZATIONS. Congress adopted a provision specifically exempting transfers to political organizations from being deemed to be a transfer of property by gift.[14] Without this special rule, these transfers generally would be subjected to gift tax treatment.

EXAMPLE C12-10 ▶ Ann transfers $2,000 to a political organization founded to promote Thomas's campaign for governor. Ann's $2,000 transfer does not fall within the statutory definition of a gift. ◀

PROPERTY SETTLEMENTS IN CONJUNCTION WITH DIVORCE. To reduce litigation, Congress enacted special rules addressing property transfers in the context of a divorce. Section 2516 specifies the circumstances in which it automatically exempts property settlements in connection with a divorce from being treated as gifts.

For Sec. 2516 to be applicable, the spouses must adopt a written agreement concerning their marital and property rights and the divorce must occur during a three-year

---

[11] Section 170(b)(1)(A)(ii) defines *educational organization* in the context of the charitable contribution deduction.

[12] Section 213(d) defines *medical care* in the context of the medical expense deduction.

[13] U.S. Congress, Staff of the Joint Committee on Taxation, *General Explanation of the Economic Recovery Tax Act of 1981* (Washington, DC: U.S. Government Printing Office, 1981), p. 273.

[14] Sec. 2501(a)(5).

WHAT WOULD YOU DO IN THIS SITUATION?

You are a CPA with a very wealthy elderly client, Ms. Atsushi Trong. She is a model of the U.S. success story. Having struggled in her native country, she immigrated to the United States as a teenager and studied clothing trends among her peers in both high school and college. She started her own clothing company and over the years has led the way by promoting such trends as miniskirts, bell-bottom pants, the so-called "Mature Elvis" look, and the hip-hop-rap grunge fashion. She has a net worth of over $100 million and no immediate family.

She has decided to plow some of her good fortune back into the educational system, which provided the intellectual foundation for her success. She selected the current class of her old high school, P.S. 101, and in 2006 gave each of 100 graduating students $100,000 to be used to pay tuition costs for four years at her college alma mater. Each of the 100 student donees used the $100,000 to prepay the four-year tuition costs. All these transactions took place during the current tax year.

You have now been asked to determine the tax consequences of these transactions. What position would you take after considering the requirements of the IRC and *Treasury Department Circular 230*?

period beginning one year before they make the agreement. No gift arises from any transfer made in accordance with such agreement if a spouse transfers property to settle the other spouse's marital or property rights or to provide reasonable support for the children while they are minors.

EXAMPLE C12-11 ▶ In June 2005, Hal and Wanda signed a property agreement whereby Hal is to transfer $750,000 to Wanda in settlement of her property rights. Hal makes the transfer in May 2006. Hal and Wanda receive a divorce decree in July 2006. Hal is not deemed to have made a gift to Wanda when he transferred property to her. ◀

QUALIFIED DISCLAIMERS. Sometimes a person named to receive property under a decedent's will prefers not to receive such property and would like to disclaim (not accept) it. Typically, the person is quite ill and/or elderly or very wealthy. State disclaimer statutes allow individuals to say "no thank you" to the property willed to them. State law or another provision in the will addresses how to determine who will receive the property after the original beneficiary (the disclaimant) declines to accept it.

Section 2518(a) states that people making a qualified disclaimer are treated as if the disclaimed property were never transferred to them. Thus, the person making the disclaimer is not deemed to have made a gift to the person who receives the property because of the disclaimer.

A **qualified disclaimer** must meet the following four tests:

ADDITIONAL COMMENT

Individuals who execute disclaimers, in a sense, participate in shifting wealth to another.

▶ It must be an irrevocable, unqualified, written refusal to accept property.

▶ The transferor or his or her legal representative must receive the refusal no later than nine months after the later of the day the transfer is made or the day the person named to receive the property becomes age 21.

▶ The disclaiming person must not have accepted the property interest or any of its benefits.

▶ As a result of the disclaimer, the property must pass to the decedent's spouse or a person other than the one disclaiming it. In addition, the person disclaiming the property cannot direct who is to receive the property.[15]

EXAMPLE C12-12 ▶ Doug dies on February 1, 2006, and wills 500 acres of land to Joan. If Joan disclaims the property in a manner that meets all four of the tests for a qualified disclaimer, Joan will not be treated as making a gift to the person who receives the property as a result of her disclaimer. ◀

---

[15] Sec. 2518(b).

EXAMPLE C12-13 ▶ Assume the same facts as in Example C12-12 except Joan instead disclaims the property on January 2, 2007. Joan's action arose too late to meet the second qualified disclaimer test above. Thus, Joan makes a gift to the person who receives the property she disclaims. ◀

CESSATION OF DONOR'S DOMINION AND CONTROL

A gift occurs when a transfer becomes complete and is valued as of the date the transfer becomes complete. Thus, the concept of a completed transfer is important in two contexts: determination of whether a gift has arisen and, if so, the value of the gift. According to Treasury Regulations, a gift becomes complete—and is thus deemed made and valued—when the donor "has so parted with dominion and control as to leave in him no power to change its disposition, whether for his own benefit or for the benefit of another."[16] A gift is not necessarily complete just because the transferor cannot receive any further personal benefits from the property. If the transferor still can influence the benefits others may receive from the transferred property, the transfer is incomplete with respect to the portion of the property over which the transferor retained control.

REVOCABLE TRUSTS. A transferor who conveys property to a revocable trust has made an incomplete transfer because the creator of a revocable trust can change the trust provisions, including the identity of the beneficiaries. Moreover, the creator may demand the return of the trust property. Because the transferor does not give up any control over property conveyed to a revocable trust, the individual does not make a gift upon funding the trust. Once the trustee distributes trust income to a beneficiary, however, the creator of the trust loses control over the distributed funds and then makes a completed gift of the income the trustee pays out.

EXAMPLE C12-14 ▶ On May 1, Ted transfers $500,000 to a revocable trust with First National Bank as trustee. The trustee must pay out all the income to Ed during Ed's lifetime and at Ed's death distribute the property to Ed, Jr. On December 31, the trustee distributes $35,000 of income to Ed. The May 1 transfer is incomplete because Ted may revoke the trust; thus, no gift arises upon the funding of the trust. A $35,000 gift to Ed occurs on December 31 because Ted no longer has control over the income distributed to Ed. The gift is eligible for the annual exclusion. ◀

EXAMPLE C12-15 ▶ Assume the same facts as in Example C12-14 and that Ted amends the trust instrument on July 7 of the next year to make the trust irrevocable. By this date, the trust property has appreciated to $612,000. Ted makes a completed gift of $612,000 on July 7 of the next year because he gives up his powers over the trust. The gift is eligible for the annual exclusion. ◀

KEY POINT

If the donor retains control over any portion of the property, no gift is considered to have been made with respect to the portion of the property the donor still controls.

OTHER RETAINED POWERS. Even transfers to an irrevocable trust can be deemed incomplete with respect to the portion of the trust over which the creator kept control. Treasury Regulations state that if "the donor reserves any power over its [the property's] disposition, the gift may be wholly incomplete, or may be partially complete and partially incomplete, depending upon all the facts in the particular case."[17] They add that one must examine the terms of the power to determine the scope of the donor's retention of control. The regulations elaborate by indicating that "[a] gift is . . . incomplete if and to the extent that a reserved power gives the donor the power to name new beneficiaries or to change the interests of the beneficiaries."[18]

EXAMPLE C12-16 ▶ On May 3, Art transfers $300,000 of property in trust with a bank as trustee. Art names his friends Bob and/or Sue to receive the trust income for 15 years and Karl to receive the trust property at the end of 15 years. Art reserves the power to determine how that income is to be divided between Bob and Sue each year, but the trustee must distribute all of the income each year. Because Art reserves the power over payment of the income for the 15-year period, this portion of the transfer is incomplete on May 3. Actuarial tables discussed in the next section of the chapter address the valuation of the completed gift to Karl. ◀

---

[16] Reg. Sec. 25.2511-2(b).
[17] Ibid.

[18] Reg. Sec. 25.2511-2(c).

EXAMPLE C12-17 ▶ Assume the same facts as in Example C12-16 and that on December 31 Art instructs the trustee to distribute the trust's $34,000 of income as follows: $18,000 to Bob and $16,000 to Sue. Once the trustee pays out income, Art loses control over it. Thus, Art makes an $18,000 gift to Bob and a $16,000 gift to Sue on December 31. Each gift qualifies for the annual exclusion. ◀

EXAMPLE C12-18 ▶ Assume the same facts as in Example C12-16 and that on May 3 of the next year, when the trust assets are valued at $360,000, Art relinquishes his powers over payment of income and gives this power to the trustee. Art's transfer of the income interest (with a remaining term of 14 years) becomes complete on May 3 of the next year. The valuation of the gift of a 14-year income interest is determined from actuarial tables in Appendix H. ◀

Topic Review C12-1 provides examples of various complete, incomplete, and partially complete transfers.

VALUATION OF GIFTS

ADDITIONAL COMMENT

Because the determination of value is such a subjective issue, a large number of gift tax controversies are nothing more than valuation disagreements.

GENERAL RULES. All gifts are valued at their FMV as of the date of the gift (i.e., the date the transfer becomes complete). Treasury Regulations state that a property's value is "the price at which such property would change hands between a willing buyer and a willing seller, neither being under any compulsion to buy or to sell, and both having reasonable knowledge of relevant facts."[19] According to the regulations, stocks and bonds traded on a stock exchange or over the counter are valued at the mean of the highest and lowest selling price on the date of the gift.[20] In general, the guidelines for valuing properties are the same, regardless of whether the property is conveyed during life or at death. An exception is life insurance policies, which are less valuable while the insured is alive. Valuation of life insurance policies is discussed in a later section of this chapter, as well as in Chapter C13's coverage of the estate tax.

KEY POINT

The value of the life estate plus the value of the remainder interest equals the total FMV of the property.

LIFE ESTATES AND REMAINDER INTERESTS. Often a donor transfers less than his or her entire interest in an asset. For example, an individual may transfer property in trust and reserve the right to the trust's income for life and name another individual to receive the property upon the transferor's death. In such a situation, the transferor retains a **life estate** and gives a **remainder interest**. In general, only the remainder interest is subject to the gift tax. An exception applies if the gift is to a family member, as discussed in the estate freeze section below. If the transferor keeps an annuity (a fixed amount) for life and names another person to receive the remainder at the transferor's death, in all situations the gift is of just the remainder interest.

A grantor also may transfer property in trust with the promise that another person will receive the income for a certain number of years and at the end of that time period the

Topic Review C12-1

Examples of Complete and Incomplete Transfers

1. Complete Transfers, Subject to Gift Tax:
   a. Property transferred outright to donee
   b. Property transferred to an irrevocable trust over which the donor retains no powers
2. Incomplete Transfers, Not Subject to Gift Tax:
   a. Property transferred to a revocable trust
   b. Property transferred to an irrevocable trust for which the donor retains discretionary powers over both income and the remainder interest
3. Partially Complete Transfers, Only a Portion Subject to Gift Tax:
   a. Property transferred to an irrevocable trust for which the donor retains discretionary powers over who receives the income but not the remainder interest[a]

[a]The gift of the remainder interest constitutes a completed transfer.

---

[19] Reg. Sec. 25.2512-1.   [20] Reg. Sec. 25.2512-2.

property will revert to the grantor. In this case, the donor retains a reversionary interest, whereas the other party receives a **term certain interest**.[21] Unless the donee is a family member, only the term certain interest is subject to the gift tax. Trusts in which the grantor retains a reversionary interest have disadvantageous income tax consequences to the grantor if they were created after March 1, 1986. Chapter C14 discusses the income tax treatment of such trusts.

Life estates, annuity interests, remainders, and term certain interests are valued from actuarial tables that incorporate the Sec. 7520 interest rate. In general, these tables must be used regardless of the actual earnings rate of the transferred assets. Excerpts from the tables appear in Appendix H. Table S is used for valuing life estates and remainders and Table B for term certain interests. The factor for a life estate or term certain interest is 1.0 minus the remainder factor. The remainder factor simply represents the present value of the right to receive a property at the end of someone's life (in the case of Table S) or at the end of a specified time (in the case of Table B). The value of the income interest plus the remainder interest is 1.0, the entire value of the property. The factor for an annuity is the life estate or the term factor divided by the Sec. 7520 interest rate. Section 7520 calls for the interest rate to be revised every month to the rate, rounded to the nearest 0.2%, that is 120% of the Federal midterm rate applicable for the month of the transfer.[22] Congress mandated revisions to the tables to reflect mortality experience at least once every ten years, and the Treasury Department issued revised life tables effective for transfers on May 1, 1999, and later.

EXAMPLE C12-19 ▶ Refer to Example C12-16, in which on May 3 Art transfers $300,000 of property in trust with a bank as trustee. Art names his friends Bob and Sue to receive the trust income for 15 years but reserves the power to determine how the income is to be divided between them each year. However, the trustee must distribute all the income. Art specifies that Karl is to receive the trust property at the end of the fifteenth year. Only the gift of the remainder interest is a completed transfer on May 3. The gift is valued from Table B. If the interest rate is 10%, the amount of the gift is $71,818 (0.239392 × $300,000), the present value of the property to be received by Karl at the end of 15 years. ◀

EXAMPLE C12-20 ▶ Assume the same facts as in Example C12-19 and that three years later, when the trust assets are valued at $360,000, Art relinquishes his power over the payment of trust income to the trustee. The income interest has a remaining term of 12 years. The gift is the present value of the 12-year income interest, which is valued from Table B by subtracting the factor for a remainder interest (0.318631 if the interest rate is 10%) from 1.0. Thus, the amount of the gift is $245,293 [(1.0 − 0.318631) × $360,000]. ◀

EXAMPLE C12-21 ▶ On July 5 of the current year, Don transfers $100,000 of property in trust and names his friends Larry (age 60) to receive all of the income for the rest of Larry's life and Ruth (age 25) to receive the trust assets upon Larry's death. Don names a bank as the trustee. The amount of each donee's gift is determined from Table S. If the interest rate is 10% and Larry is age 60, the value of the remainder interest gift to Ruth, as calculated from the single life remainder factors column of Table S, is $21,196 (0.21196 × $100,000). This amount represents the present value of the property Ruth will receive after the death of Larry, age 60. The remaining portion of the $100,000 of property, $78,804 ($100,000 − $21,196), is the value of the life estate transferred to Larry. The total value of the income plus remainder interests is 1.0. ◀

EXAMPLE C12-22 ▶ In July of the current year, Amy (age 62) transferred $1 million of stock to a trust from which she retained the right to receive $120,000 per year for five years. She provided that the remainder will pass to her son, Arthur, at the end of the fifth year. Assume that 7% was the Sec. 7520 rate at the time of her transfer. She anticipated that the stock would continued to appreciate at its recent appreciation rate of 9% a year. The factor for a five-year annuity, assuming a 7%

---

[21] *Term certain interest* means that a particular person has an interest in the property held in trust for a specified time period. The person having such interest does not own or hold title to the property but has a right to receive the income from such property for a specified time period. At the end of the

time period, the property reverts to the grantor (or passes to another person, the remainderman).

[22] The IRS regularly issues revenue rulings with applicable rate information.

rate, is 4.1002 [(1.0 − 0.712986, the factor for a remainder interest)/(0.07, the Sec. 7520 rate)]. Thus, Amy is deemed to have retained $492,024 (4.1002 × $120,000) and is deemed to have gifted the difference of $507,976 ($1,000,000 − $492,024). ◄

 STOP & THINK

Question: In which scenario would the amount of the gift be larger: (1) a gift of a remainder interest to a friend if a 68-year-old donor retained the income for life or (2) a gift of a remainder interest to a friend if an 86-year-old donor retained the income for life? Assume that each donor makes the gift on the same day so that the applicable interest rates are the same for each scenario.

Solution: The gift of the remainder interest would be larger if the donor is 86, instead of 68, because the actuarial value of the income interest the donor retains would be smaller if the donor is older. Under actuarial assumptions, older donors have shorter life expectancies.

ADDITIONAL COMMENT

In estate freeze transfers, Congress provided rules that generally increase the amount classified as a gift at the time of the actual transfer.

SPECIAL VALUATION RULES: ESTATE FREEZES. A number of years ago, Congress became concerned that individuals were able to shift wealth to other individuals, usually in a younger generation, without paying their "fair share" of the transfer taxes. An approach donors commonly used was to recapitalize a corporation (by exchanging common stock for both common and preferred shares) and then to give the common stock to individuals in the younger generation. This technique was one of a variety of transactions known as estate freezes.

In 1990, Congress decided to address the perceived problem of estate freezes by writing new valuation rules that apply when a gift occurs. The thrust of these rules—current IRC Chapter 14 (Secs. 2701 through 2704)—is to ensure that gifts are not undervalued. A couple of the more common situations governed by the new rules are described below, but the rules are too complicated to warrant a complete discussion. If a parent owns 100% of a corporation's stock and then gives the common stock to his or her children and retains the preferred stock, the value of the right to the preferred dividends is treated as zero unless the stock is cumulative preferred. Unless the donor retains *cumulative* preferred stock, the value assigned to the common stock given away is relatively high. If the donor creates a trust in which he or she retains an interest and in which he or she gives an interest to a family member, the value of the transferor's retained interest is treated as zero unless the interest is an annuity interest (fixed payments) or a unitrust interest (calling for distributions equal to a specified percentage of the current FMV of the trust). Thus, the donor who retains an income interest is treated as having kept nothing. The effect of these rules increases the gift amount, compared with the result under prior law, unless the transferor structures the transaction to avoid having a zero value assigned to his or her retained interest.[23]

GIFT TAX CONSEQUENCES OF CERTAIN TRANSFERS

Some transactions that cause the transferor to make a gift are straightforward. It is easy to see that the disposition is within the scope of the gift tax if, for example, an individual places the title to stock or real estate solely in another person's name and receives less than adequate consideration in return. Treasury Regulations include the following examples of transactions that may be subject to the gift tax: forgiving of a debt; assignment of the benefits of a life insurance policy; transfer of cash; and transfer of federal, state, or municipal bonds.[24] The gratuitous transfer of state and local bonds falls within the scope of the gift tax, even though interest on such bonds is exempt from federal income taxation. The following discussion concerns the gift tax rules for several transfers that are more complicated than, for example, transferring the title to real property or stock to another person.

---

[23] See Reg. Secs. 25.2701-1 through -6 and 25.2702-1 through -6 for guidance concerning the estate freeze provisions.

[24] Reg. Sec. 25.2511-1(a).

CREATION OF JOINT BANK ACCOUNTS. Parties depositing money to a jointly owned bank account potentially face gift tax consequences. Funding a joint bank account is an incomplete transfer because the depositor is free to withdraw the amount deposited into the account. A gift occurs when one party withdraws an amount exceeding the amount he or she deposited.[25] The transfer is complete at that time because only the person who made the withdrawal can control the withdrawn funds.

EXAMPLE C12-23 ▶ On May 1, Connie deposits $100,000 into a joint bank account in the names of Connie and Ben. Her friend Ben makes no deposits. On December 1, Ben withdraws $20,000 from the joint account and purchases an automobile. No gift arises upon the creation of the bank account. However, on December 1, Connie makes a gift to Ben of $20,000, the excess of Ben's withdrawal over Ben's deposit. ◀

CREATION OF OTHER JOINT TENANCIES. **Joint tenancy** is a popular form of property ownership from a convenience standpoint because, when one joint owner dies, the property is automatically owned by the survivor(s). Each joint tenant is deemed to have an equal interest in the property. A completed gift arises when the transferor titles real estate or other property in the names of himself or herself and another (e.g., a spouse, a sibling, or a child) as joint tenants. The person furnishing the consideration to acquire the property is deemed to have made a gift to the other joint tenant in an amount equal to the value of the donee's pro rata interest in the property.[26]

EXAMPLE C12-24 ▶ Kwame purchases land for $250,000 and immediately has it titled in the names of Kwame and Kesha, as joint tenants with right of survivorship. Kwame and Kesha are not husband and wife. Kwame makes a gift to Kesha of $125,000, or one-half the value of the property. ◀

TAX STRATEGY TIP

An owner of a life insurance policy who wishes to gift the ownership to someone else, such as the beneficiary, can use the following strategies to avoid the gift tax:
(1) Before making the gift, borrow enough against the policy to reduce its net value to the amount of the annual exclusion ($12,000 in 2006). The former owner (borrower) then can pay premiums and make loan repayments, not to exceed the annual exclusion in any given year.
(2) Have the insurance company rewrite the policy into separate policies, each having a value that does not exceed the annual exclusion. Then, gift one policy each year for several years.

TRANSFER OF LIFE INSURANCE POLICIES. The mere naming of another as the beneficiary of a life insurance policy is an incomplete transfer because the owner of the policy can change the beneficiary designation at any time. However, if an individual irrevocably assigns all ownership rights in an insurance policy to another party, this event constitutes a gift of the policy to the new owner.[27] Ownership rights include the ability to change the beneficiary, borrow against the policy, and cash the policy in for its cash surrender value.

The payment of a premium on an insurance policy owned by another person is considered a gift to the policy's owner. The amount of the gift is the amount of the premium paid. The tax result is the same as if the donor transferred cash to the policy owner and the owner used the cash to pay the premium.

According to Reg. Sec. 25.2512-6, the value of the gift of a life insurance policy is the amount it would cost to purchase a comparable policy on the date of the gift. The regulations point out, however, that if the policy is several years old, the cost of a comparable policy is not readily ascertainable. In such a situation, the policy is valued at its interpolated terminal reserve (i.e., an amount similar to the policy's cash surrender value) plus the amount of any unexpired premiums. The insurance company will furnish information concerning the interpolated terminal reserve.

EXAMPLE C12-25 ▶ On September 1, Bill transfers his entire ownership rights in a $300,000 life insurance policy on his own life to his sister Susan. The policy's interpolated terminal reserve is $24,000 as of September 1. On July 1, Bill had paid the policy's $4,800 annual premium. Bill makes a gift to Susan on September 1 of $28,000 [$24,000 + (10/12 × $4,800)] because he transferred ownership to Susan. If, however, the policy had been a term insurance policy, which has no interpolated terminal reserve, the gift would have been $4,000 (10/12 × $4,800), the amount of the unexpired premium.

On July 1 of the next year, Bill pays the $4,800 annual premium on the policy now owned by Susan. As a result of the premium payment, Bill makes a $4,800 gift to Susan that year, the same result as if he had given her $4,800 of cash to pay the premium. ◀

---

[25] Reg. Sec. 25.2511-1(h)(4).
[26] Reg. Sec. 25.2511-1(h)(5). If the two joint tenants are husband and wife, no taxable gift will arise because of the unlimited marital deduction.

[27] Reg. Sec. 25.2511-1(h)(8).

EXAMPLE C12-26 ▶ Assume the same facts as in Example C12-25 except that Susan, who now owns the policy, changes the beneficiary of the policy from Frank to John. Susan does not make a gift because she has not given up control; she can change the beneficiary again in the future. ◀

EXERCISE OF A GENERAL POWER OF APPOINTMENT.   Section 2514 provides the rules concerning powers of appointment. A **power of appointment** exists when a person transfers property (perhaps in trust) and grants someone else the power to specify who eventually will receive the property. Thus, possession of a power of appointment has some of the same benefits as ownership of the property. Powers can be general or special. *Potential* gift tax consequences are associated with the powerholder's exercise of a **general power of appointment**. A person possesses a general power of appointment if he or she has the power to appoint the property (have the property distributed) to him- or herself, his or her creditors or estate, or the creditors of his or her estate. The words *his or her estate* mean that there are no restrictions concerning to whom the individual may bequeath the property.

A gift occurs when a person exercises a general power of appointment and names some other person to receive the property.[28] The donee is the person the powerholder names to receive the property. A person who exercises a general power of appointment in favor of himself or herself does not make a gift (i.e., one cannot make a gift to him- or herself).

EXAMPLE C12-27 ▶ In 2006, Tina funds an irrevocable trust with $600,000 and names Van to receive the income for life. In addition, Tina gives Van a general power of appointment exercisable during his life as well as at his death. Tina made a gift to Van of $600,000 at the time she transferred the property to the trust in 2006. In 2007, Van instructs the bank trustee to distribute $50,000 of trust property to Kay. Through the exercise of his general power of appointment in favor of Kay, Van makes a $50,000 gift to Kay in 2007 because he diverted property to her. ◀

NET GIFTS.   A **net gift** occurs when an individual makes a gift to a donee who agrees to pay the gift tax as a condition of receiving the gift. The donee's payment of the gift tax is treated as consideration paid to the donor. The amount of the gift is the excess of the FMV of the transferred property over the amount of the gift tax paid by the donee. Because the amount of the gift depends on the amount of gift tax payable, which in turn depends on the amount of the gift, the calculations require the use of simultaneous equations.[29]

The net gift strategy is especially attractive for people who would like to remove a rapidly appreciating asset from their estate but are unable to pay the gift tax because of liquidity problems. However, a net gift has one potential disadvantage: the Supreme Court has ruled that the donor must recognize as a gain the excess of the gift tax payable over his or her adjusted basis in the property.[30] The Court's rationale is that the donee's payment of the donor's gift tax liability constitutes an "amount realized" for purposes of determining the gain or loss realized on a sale, exchange, or other disposition. From a practical standpoint, this decision affects only donors who transfer property so highly appreciated that the property's adjusted basis is less than the gift tax liability.

EXAMPLE C12-28 ▶ Mary transfers land with a $3 million FMV to her son, Sam, who agrees to pay the gift tax liability. Mary's adjusted basis in the land is $15,000. Earlier in the year, she gave him $12,000. The amount of the taxable gift is $3 million, less the gift tax paid by Sam. Simultaneous equations are used to calculate the amount of the gift and the gift tax liability. Mary must recognize gain equal to the excess of the gift tax liability paid by Sam minus Mary's $15,000 basis in the property.

---

[28] In general, the exercise of a special power of appointment is free of gift tax consequences. In the case of special powers of appointment, the holder of the power does not have an unrestricted ability to name the persons to receive the property. For example, he or she may be able to appoint to only his or her descendants.

[29] In Rev. Rul. 75-72 (1975-1 C.B. 310), the IRS explained how to calculate the amount of the net gift and the gift tax. In Ltr. Rul. 7842068 (July 20, 1978), the IRS stated that the donor's available unified credit, not the donee's, is used to calculate the gift tax payable.

[30] *Victor P. Diedrich v. CIR,* 50 AFTR 2d 82-5054, 82-1 USTC ¶9419 (USSC, 1982).

TAX STRATEGY TIP

As a general rule, substantially appreciated property should not be transferred by gift. It should be transferred at death to take advantage of the step-up in basis to the estate tax value (usually FMV at date of death). If Mary in Example C12-28 were elderly, it might be better to transfer an asset other than the land to preserve the step-up in basis for the land.

Assume that, because of sizable previous taxable gifts, any additional gifts Mary makes will be subject to the 46% maximum gift tax rate. Assume Mary has used all of her unified credit. If G represents the amount of the gift and T is the amount of the tax, then

$$G = \$3,000,000 - T$$
$$T = 0.46G$$

Substituting 0.46G for T in the first equation and solving for G yields G = $3,000,000 ÷ 1.46 = $2,054,795, the amount of the gift. The tax is 46% of this amount, or $945,205. The calculation increases in difficulty when, because of splitting brackets, more than one gift tax rate applies. Mary's gain equals the $945,205 gift tax paid by Sam minus her $15,000 basis in the property, or $930,205. ◄

EXCLUSIONS

OBJECTIVE 4

Determine whether an annual gift tax exclusion is available

In many instances, a portion or all of a transfer by gift is tax-free because of the annual exclusion authorized by Sec. 2503(b). In 1932, the Senate Finance Committee explained the purpose of the **annual exclusion** as follows:

> Such exemption . . . is to obviate the necessity of keeping an account of and reporting numerous small gifts, and . . . to fix the amount sufficiently large to cover in most cases wedding and Christmas gifts and occasional gifts of relatively small amount.[31]

In most gift transactions, the donor make no taxable gift because of the annual exclusion. Consequently, administration of the gift tax provisions is a much simpler task than it otherwise would be.

AMOUNT OF THE EXCLUSION

The amount of this exclusion, which is analogous to an exclusion from gross income for income tax purposes, currently is $12,000.[32] It is available each year for an unlimited number of donees. For transfers made in trust, each beneficiary is deemed to be a separate donee. Any number of donors may make a gift to the same donee, and each is eligible to claim the exclusion. The only limitations on the annual exclusion are the donor's wealth, generosity, and imagination in identifying donees.

EXAMPLE C12-29 ▶

In 2006, Ann and Bob each give $12,000 cash to each of Tad and Liz. Ann and Bob again make $12,000 cash gifts to Tad and Liz in 2007. For both 2006 and 2007, Ann receives $24,000 of exclusions ($12,000 for the gift to Tad and $12,000 for the gift to Liz). The same result applies to Bob. ◄

TAX STRATEGY TIP

Gifts up to the amount of the annual exclusion not only remove the gifted amounts from the donor's estate with no gift taxes but also remove the property's future income from the donor's estate. In addition, the property's income can be shifted to someone whose tax bracket might be lower than the donor's, thereby reducing income taxes.

The annual exclusion is a significant tax planning device that has no estate tax counterpart. So long as a donor's gifts to a particular donee do not exceed the excludable amount, the donor will never make any taxable gifts or incur any gift tax liability. Because taxable gifts will be zero, the donor's estate tax base will not include any adjusted taxable gifts. A donor, who each year for ten years prior to 2002 gave $10,000 per donee to each of ten donees, removed $1 million (10 × $10,000 × 10) from being taxed in his or her estate. The donor accomplished these transfers without making any taxable gifts or paying any gift tax. If retained, the $1 million would have been taxed in the donor's estate, at perhaps the top estate tax rate, unless the property was willed to the donor's surviving spouse.

PRESENT INTEREST REQUIREMENT

Although we generally speak of the annual exclusion as if it were available automatically for all gifts, in actuality it is not. A donor receives an exclusion only for gifts that constitute a present interest.

---

[31] S. Rept. No. 665, 72nd Cong., 1st Sess. (1932), reprinted in 1939-1 C.B. (Part 2), pp. 525–526.
[32] On January 1, 1982, Congress increased the annual exclusion from $3,000 to $10,000. Later, Congress provided that the exclusion would be indexed after 1998, with inflation adjustments rounded to the next lowest multiple of $1,000. In 2002, the exclusion rose to $11,000 and remained there through 2005. It rose to $12,000 in 2006.

DEFINITION OF PRESENT INTEREST. A **present interest** is "an unrestricted right to the immediate use, possession, or enjoyment of property or the income from property (such as a life estate or term certain)."[33] Only present interests qualify for the annual exclusion. If only a portion of a transfer constitutes a present interest, the excluded portion of the gift may not exceed the value of the present interest.

DEFINITION OF FUTURE INTEREST. A future interest is the opposite of a present interest. A **future interest** "is a legal term, and includes reversions, remainders, and other interests . . . which are limited to commence in use, possession, or enjoyment at some future date or time."[34] Gifts of future interests are ineligible for the annual exclusion. The following examples help demonstrate the attributes of present and future interests.

EXAMPLE C12-30 ▶ Nancy transfers $500,000 of property to an irrevocable trust with a bank serving as trustee. Nancy names Norm (age 55) to receive all the trust income quarterly for the rest of Norm's life. At Norm's death, the property is to pass to Ellen (age 25) or Ellen's estate. Norm receives an unrestricted right to immediate enjoyment of the income. Thus, Norm has a present interest. Ellen, however, has a future interest because Ellen cannot enjoy the property or any of the income until Norm dies. The taxable gift is $488,000 ($500,000 − $12,000). ◀

EXAMPLE C12-31 ▶ Greg transfers $800,000 of property to an irrevocable trust with a bank serving as trustee and instructs the trustee to distribute all the trust income semiannually to Greg's three adult children, Jill, Katy, and/or Laura. The trustee is to use its discretion in deciding how much to distribute to each beneficiary. Moreover, it is authorized to distribute nothing to a particular beneficiary if it deems such action to be in the beneficiary's best interest. Although all the income must be paid out, the trustee has complete discretion to determine how much to pay to a particular beneficiary. None of the beneficiaries has the assurance that he or she will receive a trust distribution. Thus, Greg created no present interests, and the annual exclusion does not apply. The taxable gift, therefore, is $800,000. ◀

SPECIAL RULE FOR TRUSTS FOR MINORS. Congress realized that many donors would not want trusts for minor children to be required to distribute all their income to the young children. Accordingly, Congress enacted Sec. 2503(c), which authorizes special trusts for minors, to address donors' concerns about the distribution of trust income to minors. Section 2503(c) authorizes an annual exclusion for gifts to trusts for beneficiaries under age 21 even though the trusts need not distribute all their income annually. Such trusts, known as **Sec. 2503(c) trusts**, allow donors to claim the annual exclusion if the following two conditions are met:

▶ Until the beneficiary becomes age 21, the trustee may pay the income and/or the underlying assets to the beneficiary.

▶ Any income and underlying assets not paid to the beneficiary will pass to that beneficiary when he or she reaches age 21. If the beneficiary should die before becoming age 21, the income and underlying assets are payable to either the beneficiary's estate or to any person the minor may appoint if the minor possesses a general power of appointment over the property.

If the trust instrument contains both the provisions listed above, no part of the trust is considered to be a gift of a future interest. Therefore, the entire transfer is treated as a present interest and is eligible for the annual exclusion.

As a result of Sec. 2503(c), donors creating trusts for donees under age 21 receive an exclusion even though the trustee has discretion over paying out the trust income. However, the trustee must distribute the assets and accumulated income to the beneficiary at age 21.

CRUMMEY TRUST. The **Crummey trust** is yet another technique that allows the donor to obtain an annual exclusion upon funding a discretionary trust. The trust can terminate at whatever age the donor specifies and can be created for a beneficiary of any age. Thus, the *Crummey* trust is a much more flexible arrangement than the Sec. 2503(c) trust.

ADDITIONAL COMMENT

The donor may serve as trustee of a Sec. 2503(c) trust, but this approach generally is not advisable. If the donor's powers are not sufficiently limited, the trust property will be included in the donor's estate if the donor's death occurs before the trust terminates.

ADDITIONAL COMMENT

The holder of a *Crummey* power must be given notice of a contribution to the trust to which the power relates and must be given a reasonable time period within which to exercise the power. The donor receives the annual exclusion regardless of whether the donee exercises the power.

---

[33] Reg. Sec. 25.2503-3(b).

[34] Reg. Sec. 25.2503-3(a).

The *Crummey* trust is named for a Ninth Circuit Court of Appeals decision holding that the trust beneficiaries had a present interest as a result of certain language in the trust instrument.[35] That language, which is referred to interchangeably as a *Crummey* power, *Crummey* demand power, or *Crummey* withdrawal power, entitled each beneficiary to demand a distribution of the lesser of $4,000 or the amount transferred to the trust that year. If the beneficiary did not exercise the power by a specified date, it expired. The trust instrument included the "lesser of" language for the demand power because the largest present interest the donor needs to create is equal to the annual exclusion amount. In years in which the gift is smaller than the annual exclusion amount, the donor simply needs to be able to exclude the amount of that year's gift. In addition, the donor wants to restrict the amount to which the beneficiary can have access. The trust instrument often states that the maximum amount the beneficiary can withdraw is "an amount equal to the annual exclusion for federal gift tax purposes" or twice that amount if gift splitting is anticipated.

The court held that the demand power provided each beneficiary with a present interest equal to the maximum amount the beneficiary could require the trustee to pay over to him or her that year. Use of the *Crummey* trust technique entitles the donor to receive the annual exclusion while creating a discretionary trust that terminates at whatever age the donor deems appropriate. The donor thereby avoids the restrictive rules of Sec. 2503(c). Generally, the donor hopes the beneficiary will not exercise the demand right.

EXAMPLE C12-32 ▶ Al funds two $100,000 irrevocable trusts and names First Bank the trustee. The first trust is for the benefit of Kay, his 15-year-old daughter. The trustee has discretion to distribute income and/or principal to Kay until she reaches age 21. If she dies before age 21, the trust assets are payable to whomever she appoints in her will or to her estate if she dies without a will. The second trust is for the benefit of Bob, Al's 25-year-old son. Income and/or principal are payable to Bob in the trustee's discretion until Bob reaches age 35, whereupon Bob will receive the trust assets. Bob may demand by December 31 of each year that the trustee pay him the lesser of the amount of the gift tax annual exclusion or the amount transferred to the trust that calendar year. The trust for Kay is a Sec. 2503(c) trust, and the one for Bob is a *Crummey* trust. An annual exclusion is available for each trust. ◀

 STOP & THINK *Question:* For which of the following gifts would the donor receive an annual exclusion:

▶ A gift of a remainder interest in land if the donor retains the income interest for life

▶ A gift outright of a life insurance policy that has a cash surrender value

▶ A gift to a discretionary trust that is classified as a Sec. 2503(c) trust

▶ A gift to a Crummey trust?

Solution: All the transfers except the gift of the remainder interest (a future interest) are eligible for the annual exclusion. Even though the gift to the Sec. 2503(c) trust does not literally involve a gift of a present interest (the right to current income or enjoyment), the IRC explicitly allows this kind of transfer to qualify for the annual exclusion.

GIFT TAX DEDUCTIONS

OBJECTIVE 5

Identify deductions available for gift tax purposes

The formula for determining taxable gifts allows both an unlimited marital deduction and an unlimited charitable contribution deduction. The **marital deduction** is for transfers to one's spouse. The **charitable contribution deduction** is for gifts to charitable organizations. Section 2524 states that the deductible amount in either case may not exceed the amount of the "includible gift"—that is, the amount of the gift exceeding the annual exclusion. Thus, the lowest possible taxable gift is zero, not a negative number, as could be the case if the deduction equaled the total amount of the gift.

---

[35] *D. Clifford Crummey v. CIR*, 22 AFTR 2d 6023, 68-2 USTC ¶12,541 (9th Cir., 1968).

ADDITIONAL
COMMENT
Congress allowed a marital
deduction because a taxpayer
who transfers property to his or
her spouse has not made a transfer outside the economic (hus-
band/wife) unit. For similar reasons, the interspousal gift has no
income tax consequences. The
donor spouse recognizes no gain
or loss, and the donee spouse
takes a carryover basis.

MARITAL DEDUCTION

Generally, the marital deduction results in tax-free interspousal transfers, but an exception discussed below applies to gifts of certain terminable interests. Congress first enacted the marital deduction in 1948 to provide more uniform treatment of community property and noncommunity property donors. To recap, in community property states, most property acquired after marriage is owned equally by each spouse. In noncommunity property states, however, the spouses' wealth often is divided unequally, and such spouses can equalize each individual's share of the wealth only by engaging in a gift-giving program. As a result of the marital deduction, spouses can shift wealth between themselves completely free of any gift tax consequences.

UNLIMITED AMOUNT. Over the years, the maximum marital deduction has varied, but since 1981 one spouse has been able to deduct up to 100% of the amount of gifts made to the other spouse. The amount of the marital deduction, however, is limited to the portion of the gift that exceeds the annual exclusion.[36] Beginning after 1981, transfers of community property became eligible for the marital deduction.

EXAMPLE C12-33 ▶ A wife gives her husband stock valued at $450,000. She excludes $12,000 because of the annual exclusion and claims a $438,000 marital deduction. Thus, no taxable gift arises. ◀

GIFTS OF TERMINABLE INTERESTS: GENERAL RULE.
Nondeductible Terminable Interests. A **terminable interest** is an interest that ends or is terminated when some event occurs (or fails to occur) or a specified amount of time passes. Some, but not all, terminable interests are ineligible for the marital deduction.[37] A marital deduction is denied only when the transfer is of a *nondeductible* terminable interest. A nondeductible terminable interest has one of the following characteristics:

▶ The donee-spouse's interest ceases at a set time (such as at death) and the property then either passes back to the donor or passes to a third party who does not pay adequate consideration.

▶ Immediately after making the gift, the donor has the power to name someone else to receive an interest in the property, and the person named may possess the property upon the termination of the donee-spouse's interest.[38]

The next three examples illustrate some of the subtleties of the definition of nondeductible terminable interests. In Example C12-34, a marital deduction is available because the interest transferred is not a nondeductible terminable interest.

EXAMPLE C12-34 ▶ A donor gives a patent to a spouse. A patent is a terminable interest because the property interest terminates at the end of the patent's legal life. Nevertheless, the patent does not constitute a nondeductible terminable interest. When the patent's legal life expires, a third party will not possess an interest in the patent. Thus, a donor will receive a marital deduction. ◀

In Example C12-35, a marital deduction is denied because the first of the two alternative characteristics of a nondeductible terminable interest exists.

EXAMPLE C12-35 ▶ A donor transfers property in trust and (1) names his wife to receive trust income, at the trustee's discretion, annually for the next 15 years and (2) states that at the end of the 15-year period the trust's assets are to be distributed to their child. The donor has given his wife a nondeductible terminable interest. When the spouse's interest ceases, the property passes to their child, a recipient who did not pay adequate consideration. Thus, the donor receives no marital deduction. ◀

In Example C12-36, a marital deduction is available. In addition to having a lifetime income interest, the donee-spouse has a general power of appointment over the trust's assets and can specify who eventually receives the property.

---

[36] Sec. 2524.
[37] Sec. 2523(b).

[38] Ibid.

EXAMPLE C12-36 ▶ The donor gives his wife the right to all the income from a trust annually for life plus a general power of appointment over the trust's assets. He has transferred an interest eligible for the marital deduction. The general power of appointment may be exercisable during life, at death, or at both times. In addition, the donee-spouse is entitled to receive the income annually. ◀

TAX STRATEGY TIP

A general power of appointment can qualify a transfer for the marital deduction. For example, assume that last year Brad transferred property to a trust, income to be distributed annually to his wife Sonia until her death, with a general power of appointment in Sonia over the remainder. Sonia's general power of appointment allowed the transfer to be eligible for the gift tax marital deduction.

TAX STRATEGY TIP

By using a QTIP, a donor can achieve a marital deduction while exercising some control over the property. For example, assume the same facts as in the previous annotation except that Brad has been married twice. He had two children by his first wife and three children with Sonia. Brad could not be sure his first two children would ever receive anything from the trust because Sonia could exercise her general power of appointment in favor of just their three children (or someone else). If Brad funded a QTIP, the trust instrument could specify that the remainder, on Sonia's death, would go equally to all five children. Brad could thus control the ultimate disposition of the remainder and still receive a marital deduction.

The rationale behind the nondeductible terminable interest rule is that a donor should obtain a marital deduction only if he or she conveys an interest that will have transfer tax significance to the donee-spouse. In other words, when a donee spouse later gives away property that he or she received as a result of an interspousal transfer, a transfer subject to the gift tax occurs. If the donee-spouse retains such property until death, the asset is included in the donee-spouse's gross estate.

QTIP PROVISIONS. Beginning in 1982, Congress made a major change to the nondeductible terminable interest rule and allowed transfers of qualified terminable interest property to be eligible for the marital deduction.[39] Such transfers are commonly referred to as *QTIP transfers*. **Qualified terminable interest property** is property

▶ That is transferred by the donor-spouse,
▶ In which the donee has a "qualifying income interest for life," and
▶ For which a special election has been made.

A spouse has the necessary "qualifying income interest for life" if

▶ The spouse is entitled to all the income from the property annually or more often, and
▶ No person has a power to appoint any part of the property to any person other than the donee-spouse unless the power cannot be exercised while the spouse is alive.

The QTIP rule enhances the attractiveness of making transfers to one's spouse because a donor can receive a marital deduction—and thereby make a nontaxable transfer—without having to grant the spouse full control over the gifted property. The QTIP rule is especially attractive for a donor who wants to ensure that the children by a previous marriage will receive the property upon the donee-spouse's death.

The donor does not have to claim a marital deduction even though the transfer otherwise qualifies as a QTIP transfer. Claiming the deduction on such transfers is elective.[40] If the donor elects to claim a marital deduction, the donee-spouse must include the QTIP trust property in his or her estate at its value as of the donee-spouse's date of death. Thus, as with other transfers qualifying for the marital deduction, the interspousal transfer is tax-free, and the taxable event is postponed until the donee-spouse transfers the property.

EXAMPLE C12-37 ▶ Jo transfers $1 million of property in trust with a bank acting as trustee. All the trust income is payable to Jo's husband, Ed (age 64), quarterly for the rest of his life. Upon Ed's death, the property will pass to Jo's nieces. This gift is eligible for a marital deduction. If Jo elects to claim the marital deduction, she will receive a $988,000 ($1,000,000 − $12,000) marital deduction. The deduction is limited to the amount of the includible gift, i.e., the gift exceeding the annual exclusion. Jo's taxable gift will be zero. ◀

Note that Jo's marital deduction in the preceding example is for $988,000 and not for the value of Ed's life estate. If Jo elects to claim the marital deduction, Ed's gross estate will include the value of the entire trust, valued as of the date of Ed's death. The QTIP provision permits Jo to receive a marital deduction while still being able to specify who will receive the property upon her husband's death.

Topic Review C12-2 summarizes the eligibility of a transfer for the marital deduction and the amount of the marital deduction that can be claimed.

---

[39] Sec. 2523(f).
[40] The donor might decide not to claim the marital deduction if the donee-spouse has substantial assets already or a short life expectancy, especially if the gifted property's value is expected to appreciate at a high annual rate.

Topic Review C12-2

Eligibility for and Amount of the Marital Deduction

Examples of Transfers Eligible for the Marital Deduction
Property transferred to spouse as sole owner
Property transferred in trust with all the income payable to the spouse for life and over which the donee-spouse has a general power of appointment
Property transferred in trust with all the income payable annually or more often to the spouse for life and for which the donor-spouse designated the remainderman—marital deduction available if elected under QTIP rule

Examples of Transfers Ineligible for the Marital Deduction
Property transferred in trust with the income payable in the trustee's discretion to the spouse for life, and for which the donor-spouse designated the remainderman
Property transferred in trust with all the income payable to the spouse for a specified number of years and for which the donor-spouse designated the remainderman

Amount of the Marital Deduction, If Available
The amount of the transfer minus the portion eligible for the annual exclusion

CHARITABLE CONTRIBUTION DEDUCTION

If a donor is not required to file a gift tax return to report noncharitable gifts, the donor does not have to report gifts to charitable organizations on a gift tax return, provided a charitable contribution deduction is available and the charitable organization receives the donor's entire interest in the property. Claiming an income tax deduction for a charitable contribution does not preclude the donor from also obtaining a gift tax deduction. In contrast with the income tax provisions, the gift tax charitable contribution deduction has no percentage limitation. The only ceiling on the deduction is imposed by Sec. 2524, which limits the deduction to the amount of the gift that exceeds the excluded portion.

EXAMPLE C12-38 ▶

Julio gives stock valued at $76,000 to State University. Julio receives an $12,000 annual exclusion and a $64,000 charitable contribution deduction for *gift* tax purposes. However, he need not report the gift on a gift tax return if he does not have to file a return to report gifts to noncharitable donees. On his *income* tax return, he receives a $76,000 charitable contribution deduction, subject to AGI limitations. ◀

TAX STRATEGY TIP

A charitably-minded taxpayer could avoid the gift (and the estate) tax entirely by giving all his or her property to a qualified charitable organization. Actually, in 2006 the taxpayer could give up to $1 million to noncharitable donees and still pay no gift tax.

TRANSFERS ELIGIBLE FOR THE DEDUCTION. To be deductible, the gift must be made to a charitable organization. The rules defining charitable organizations are quite similar for income, gift, and estate tax purposes.[41] According to Sec. 2522, a gift tax deduction is available for contributions to the following:

▶ The United States or any subordinate level of government within the United States as long as the transfer is solely for public purposes

▶ A corporation, trust fund, etc., organized exclusively for religious, charitable, scientific, literary, or educational purposes, or to foster amateur sports competition, including the encouragement of art and the prevention of cruelty to children or animals

▶ A fraternal society or similar organization operating under the lodge system if the gifts are to be used in the United States only for religious, charitable, scientific, literary, or educational purposes

▶ A war veterans' post or organization organized in the United States or one of its possessions if no part of its net earnings accrues to the benefit of private shareholders or individuals

---

[41] In contrast to the income tax rules, a charitable contribution deduction is available under the gift tax rules for transfers made to foreign charitable organizations. No deduction is available, however, for gifts made to foreign governments.

SPLIT-INTEREST TRANSFERS. Specialized rules apply when a donor makes a transfer for both private (i.e., an individual) and public (i.e., a charitable organization) purposes. Such arrangements are known as **split-interest transfers**. An example of a split-interest transfer is the gift of a residence to one's sister for life with the remainder interest to a university. If a donor gives a charitable organization a remainder interest, the donor forfeits the charitable contribution deduction unless the remainder interest is in either a personal residence (not necessarily the donor's principal residence), a farm, a charitable remainder annuity trust or unitrust, or a pooled income fund.[42] A split-interest gift of a present interest to a charity qualifies for a charitable contribution deduction only if the charity receives a guaranteed annuity interest or a unitrust interest. Actuarial tables are used to value split-interest transfers (see Appendix H).

EXAMPLE C12-39 ▶

Al transfers $800,000 of property to a charitable remainder annuity trust. He reserves an annuity of $56,000 per year for his remaining life and specifies that upon his death the trust property will pass to the American Red Cross. Al must report this transaction on a gift tax return because the Red Cross did not receive his entire interest in the property. In the same year, Al gives a museum a remainder interest in his antique furniture collection and reserves a life estate for himself.

Each of these is a split-interest transfer. Unfortunately for the donor, only the remainder interest in the charitable remainder annuity trust is eligible for a charitable contribution deduction. Consequently, Al makes a taxable gift equal to the value of the remainder interest in the antique furniture. (If Al had given a remainder interest in a personal residence or farm, he would have received a charitable contribution deduction for this gift.) Even though the furniture is not an income-producing property, the value of the remainder interest is determined from the actuarial tables found in Appendix H.

Assume that Al was age 60 at the time of the gifts and that the Sec. 7520 interest rate was 10%. What is the amount of Al's charitable contribution deduction?

Answer: The portion of the annuity trust retained by Al is $441,302 {[(1.0 − 0.21196) ÷ 0.10] × $56,000}. The charitable deduction on the gift tax return is $358,698 ($800,000 − $441,302). The same amount also is allowable—subject to the ceiling rules—as a charitable contribution deduction on Al's income tax return for that year. ◀

SELF-STUDY QUESTION

In Example C12-39, does Al receive an annual exclusion for the gift of the furniture?

ANSWER

No. The remainder interest is a future interest, as is the remainder in the trust.

THE GIFT-SPLITTING ELECTION

OBJECTIVE 6

Apply the gift-splitting rules

The gift-splitting provisions of Sec. 2513 allow spouses to treat a gift actually made by just one of them as if each spouse made one-half of the gift. This election offers several advantages, as follows:

▶ If only one spouse makes a gift to a particular donee, the election enables a spouse to give $24,000 (instead of $12,000) to the donee before a taxable gift arises.

▶ If per-donee annual transfers exceed $24,000 and taxable gifts occur, the election may reduce the applicable marginal gift tax rate.

▶ Each spouse may use a unified credit to reduce the gift tax payable.

TAX STRATEGY TIP

Donors can magnify the benefits of the annual exclusion by using gift splitting techniques.

To take advantage of the gift-splitting election, the spouses must meet the following requirements at the time of the transfer:

▶ They must be U.S. citizens or residents.

▶ At the time of the gift(s) for which the spouses make an election, the donor-spouse must be married to the person who consents to gift splitting. In addition, the donor-spouse must not remarry before the end of the year.

The gift-splitting election is effective for all transfers to third parties made during the portion of the year that the spouses were married to each other.

---

[42] In a **charitable remainder annuity trust**, an individual receives trust distributions for a certain time period or for life. The annual distributions are a uniform percentage (5% or higher) of the value of the trust property, valued on the date of the transfer. For a **charitable remainder unitrust**, the distributions are similar, except that they are a uniform percentage (5% or higher) of the value of the trust property, revalued at least annually. Thus, the annual distributions from a unitrust, but not an annuity trust, vary from one year to the next. Both unitrusts and annuity trusts must meet the requirements that the payout rate does not exceed 50% of the value of the property and the value of the remainder interest is at least 10% of the initial FMV. A **pooled income fund** is similar in concept to a mutual fund. The various individual beneficiaries receive annual distributions of their proportionate shares of the pooled income fund's total income.

A spouse living in a community property state who makes a gift of separate property (e.g., an asset received by inheritance) may desire to use gift splitting. In this case, the election automatically extends to gifts of community property even though splitting each spouse's gifts of community property has no impact on the "bottom-line" amount of taxable gifts.

Note that gift splitting is an all-or-nothing proposition. Spouses wanting to elect it for one gift must elect it for all gifts to third parties for that year. Each year's election stands alone, however, and is not binding on future years.[43] The procedural aspects of the gift-splitting election are discussed in the Compliance and Procedural Considerations section of this chapter.

EXAMPLE C12-40 ▶

Eli marries Joy on April 1 of the current year. They are still married to each other at the end of the year. In March, Eli gave Amy $60,000. In July, Eli gave Barb $52,000, and Joy gave Claire $28,000. If the couple elects gift splitting, the election is effective only for the July gifts. Each spouse is treated as giving $26,000 and $14,000 to Barb and Claire, respectively. Because they may not elect gift splitting for the gift Eli makes before their marriage, Eli is treated as giving $60,000—the amount he actually transfers—to Amy. Under gift splitting, both Eli and Joy exclude $12,000 of gifts to both Barb and Claire, or a total of $48,000. Eli also excludes $12,000 of his gift to Amy. ◀

Upon the death of the actual donor or the spouse who consented to gift splitting, such decedent's estate tax base includes that decedent's post-1976 taxable gifts, known as adjusted taxable gifts. By electing gift splitting, a couple can reduce the amount of the taxable gifts the donor-decedent is deemed to have made. Under gift splitting, the adjusted taxable gifts include only the portions of the gifts that are taxable on the gift tax returns filed by the donor-decedent. Of course, the nondonor-spouse's estate reports his or her post-1976 taxable gifts.

STOP & THINK

Question: Bob made taxable gifts of $4 million in 2001, and Betty, his spouse, has not made any taxable gifts. Betty inherited a large fortune last year and is contemplating gifting $500,000 in 2006 to each of her two children. Bob does not anticipate making any taxable gifts in 2006. Should they elect gift splitting for Betty's gifts?

Solution: They should not necessarily elect gift splitting because the main advantage of the election will be that the aggregate annual exclusions will be $48,000 instead of $24,000. An adverse effect will be that Bob, who has exhausted his unified credit (except for the increase from $220,550 in 2001 to $345,800) and is in a higher marginal tax bracket, will be the deemed donor of $476,000 [(0.50 × $1,000,000) − $24,000] of taxable gifts.

COMPUTATION OF THE GIFT TAX LIABILITY

EFFECT OF PREVIOUS TAXABLE GIFTS

The gift tax computation involves a cumulative process. All the donor's previous taxable gifts (i.e., those made in 1932 or later years) plus the donor's taxable gifts for the current year affect the marginal tax rate for current taxable gifts. Thus, two donors making the same taxable gifts in the current period may incur different gift tax liabilities because one donor may have made substantially larger taxable gifts in earlier periods than did the other donor. The process outlined below must be used to compute the gross tax levied on the current period's taxable gifts.

---

[43] If the nondonor-spouse has made substantial taxable gifts relative to those made by the donor-spouse, the gift tax liability for the period in question may be lower if the spouses do not elect gift splitting because the nondonor-spouse may have little or no unified credit left and may have reached the highest marginal transfer tax rate.

1. Determine the gift tax liability (at current rates) on the donor's cumulative taxable gifts (taxable gifts of current period plus aggregate taxable gifts of previous periods).
2. Determine the gift tax liability (at current rates) on the donor's cumulative taxable gifts made through the end of the preceding period.
3. Subtract the gift tax determined in Step 2 from that in Step 1. The difference equals the gross gift tax on the current period's taxable gifts.

This calculation process results in taxing the gifts on a progressive basis over the donor's lifetime.

Note that, although the gift tax rates have varied over the years, the current rate schedules are used in the calculation even when the donor made some or all the gifts when different rates were in effect. This process ensures that current taxable gifts are taxed at the appropriate rate, given the donor's earlier gift history.

EXAMPLE C12-41 ▶ In 1975, Tony made $2 million in taxable gifts. These gifts were the first Tony ever made. The tax imposed under the 1975 rate schedule was $564,900. Tony's next taxable gifts are made in 2006. The taxable amount of these gifts is $400,000. The tax on Tony's 2006 taxable gifts before applying the unified credit is calculated as follows:

Tax at current rates on $2.4 million of cumulative taxable gifts	$964,800
Minus: Tax at current rates on $2 million of prior period taxable gifts	(780,800)
Tax on $400,000 of taxable gifts made in the current period	$184,000 ◀

This cumulative process results in the $400,000 gift in Example C12-41 being taxed at the maximum 46% gift tax rate, which is applicable to taxable transfers exceeding $2 million. If the gift tax computations were not cumulative, the tax on the $400,000 of gifts would be determined by using the lowest marginal rates and would have been only $121,800. Because the tax on taxable transfers made in previous periods is determined by reference to the current rate schedule, Tony's actual 1975 gift tax liability, incurred when the gift tax rates were lower, is not relevant to the determination of his current gift tax. As discussed below, the unified credit will reduce the tax liability.

UNIFIED CREDIT AVAILABLE

Congress enacted a unified credit for both gift and estate tax purposes beginning in 1977. The unified credit reduces the amount of the gross gift tax owed on current period gifts. The amount of the credit has increased over the years (see inside back cover). As a result of the 2001 Act, the credit for gift tax purposes rose to $345,800 in 2002 and will remain at that amount through 2009 even though the credit against estate taxes will increase further through 2009. Donors who have made taxable gifts in the post-1976 period have used some of their credit. The amount of the credit available to those donors for the current year is reduced by the aggregate amount allowable as a credit in all preceding years.

EXAMPLE C12-42 ▶ Hu made her first taxable gift in 1985. The taxable amount of the 1985 gift was $100,000, which resulted in a gross gift tax of $23,800. Hu claimed $23,800 (of the $121,800 credit then available) on her 1985 return to reduce her net gift tax liability to zero. Hu made her next taxable gift in 1994. The taxable amount of the gift was $400,000. The tax on the $400,000 gift equaled (1) the tax on $500,000 of total gifts (at 1994 gift tax rates) of $155,800 minus (2) the tax on $100,000 of previous gifts (at 1994 gift tax rates) of $23,800, or $132,000. The credit amount for 1994 was $192,800. Hu's gift tax was reduced to zero by a credit of $132,000 because for 1994 she had a credit of $169,000 ($192,800 − $23,800) left. If in 2006 Hu makes additional taxable gifts, $190,000 [$345,800 − ($23,800 + $132,000)] of unified credit will be available to reduce Hu's gift tax liability in 2006. ◀

STOP & THINK *Question:* You are reviewing a 2006 gift tax return that a co-worker prepared. The tax return reflects current taxable gifts of $1 million and $500,000 of taxable gifts made in 1992. You note that on the return your colleague (a new staff member) calculated tax of $345,800, claimed a unified credit of $345,800, and thus reported zero gift tax payable. What should you discuss with your colleague?

Solution: You should explain that the 2006 unified credit of $345,800 (which equals the tax on the first $1 million of taxable gifts) is not an annual credit maximum but rather is the credit available during a donor's lifetime. Because in 1992 the donor made $500,000 of taxable gifts, he exhausted $155,800 of his $192,800 unified credit then available. In addition, you should explain the cumulative nature of the gift tax calculations. The tax calculated on the first $1 million of taxable gifts is $345,800. If the colleague claimed a $345,800 unified credit and showed zero tax payable, he did not calculate the tax on the $1 million current taxable gift by performing the cumulative calculations that take into effect the $500,000 of earlier taxable gifts. The tax *before* the credit was calculated incorrectly. The credit available is $190,000 ($345,800 − $155,800), the 2006 credit less the credit already used. Therefore, the donor will owe some gift tax.

COMPREHENSIVE ILLUSTRATION

The following comprehensive illustration demonstrates the computation of one donor's gift tax liability for the situation where the spouses elect gift splitting. It demonstrates the computation of the wife's gift tax liability.

BACKGROUND DATA

Hugh and Wilma Brown are married to each other throughout 2005. Hugh made no taxable gifts in earlier periods. Wilma's previous taxable gifts were $300,000 in 1975 and $200,000 in 1988. In August 2005, Wilma makes the following gratuitous transfers:

▶ $80,000 in cash to son Billy

▶ $24,000 in jewelry to daughter Betsy

▶ $30,000 in medical expense payments to Downtown Infirmary for medical care of grandson Tim

▶ Remainder interest in vacation cabin to friend Ruth Cain. Wilma (age 60) retains a life estate. The vacation cabin is valued at $100,000.

▶ $600,000 of stocks to a bank in trust with all of the income payable semiannually to husband Hugh (age 72) for life and remainder payable at Hugh's death to Jeff Bass, Wilma's son by an earlier marriage, or Jeff's estate. Wilma wants to elect the marital deduction.

In 2005, Hugh's only gifts were

▶ $80,000 of stock to State University

▶ $600,000 of land to daughter Betsy

Assume the applicable interest rate for valuing life estates and remainders is 10%.

CALCULATION OF TAX LIABILITY

Section 2503(e) exempts the medical expense payments from the gift tax. The Browns need to report the gift made to State University even though the university received Hugh's entire interest in the property, and even though the transfer is nontaxable, because they must file a gift tax return to report gifts to noncharitable donees. The vacation cabin is valued at $100,000, and the remainder interest therein at $21,196 (0.21196 × $100,000) (see Table S, age 60 in Appendix H). The stock is transferred to a QTIP trust, and the marital deduction election treats the entire interest (not just the life estate) as having been given to Hugh Brown.

Table C12-1 shows the computation of Wilma's gift tax liability for 2005. Recall that the annual exclusion for 2005 was $11,000. These same facts are used for the sample United States Gift Tax Return, Form 709, in Appendix B. The form's format for reporting the gift-splitting aspects differs slightly from the format in the table. On the form, Part 1 of Schedule A splits the gift earlier than Table C12-1 does.

▼ **TABLE C12-1**
Comprehensive Gift Tax Illustration

Wilma's actual 2005 gifts:		
	Billy, cash	$ 80,000
	Betsy, jewelry	24,000
	Ruth, remainder interest in vacation cabin (future interest)	21,196
	Husband Hugh and son Jeff, transfer to QTIP trust	600,000
	Total gifts made by Wilma	$725,196
Minus:	One-half of Wilma's gifts made to third parties that are deemed made by Hugh [0.50 × ($80,000 + $24,000 + $21,196)]	(62,598)
Plus:	One-half of Hugh's gifts made to third parties (Betsy and State University) that are deemed made by Wilma [0.50 × ($80,000 + $600,000)]	340,000
Minus:	Annual exclusions for gifts of present interests ($11,000 each for gifts made to Billy, Betsy, Hugh, and State University)	(44,000)
Minus:	Marital deduction ($600,000 − $11,000 exclusion)	(589,000)
Minus:	Charitable contribution deduction ($40,000 deemed gift by Wilma − $11,000 exclusion)	(29,000)
Taxable gifts for current period		$340,598
Tax on cumulative taxable gifts of $840,598[a]		$283,633
Minus:	Tax on previous taxable gifts of $500,000 (current rate schedule)	(155,800)
Tax on taxable gifts of $340,598 for the current period		$127,833
Minus:	Unified credit:	
	Credit for 2005	$345,800
	Minus: Credit allowable for prior periods (68,000)[b]	(277,800)[c]
Tax payable for 2005		$ –0–

[a]$300,000 (in 1975) + $200,000 (in 1988) + $340,598 (in 2005).
[b]$0 (for 1975) + $68,000 (for 1988). The $68,000, which is smaller than the maximum credit of $192,800 for 1988, is the excess of the $155,800 tax on cumulative taxable gifts less the $87,800 tax on the $300,000 previous taxable gifts.
[c]Actually, for 2005 Wilma uses only $127,833 of her remaining credit. In 2006, she will have available a credit of $149,967 [$345,800 − ($127,833 + $68,000)].

BASIS CONSIDERATIONS FOR A LIFETIME GIVING PLAN

OBJECTIVE 8

Understand how basis affects the overall tax consequences

Prospective donors should consider the tax-saving features of making a series of lifetime gifts (discussed in the Tax Planning Considerations section of this chapter). Lifetime giving plans can remove income from the donor's income tax return and transfer it to the donee's income tax return, where it may be taxed at a lower marginal tax rate. A series of gifts may permit property to be transferred to a donee without incurring a gift tax liability and thus enable the donor to eliminate part or all of his or her estate tax liability. These two advantages must be weighed against the unattractive basis rules (discussed below) applicable for such transfers.

PROPERTY RECEIVED BY GIFT

The carryover basis rules apply to property received by gift. Provided the property's FMV on the date of the gift exceeds its adjusted basis, the donor's basis in the property carries over as the donee's basis. In addition, the donee's basis may be increased by some or all of the gift tax paid by the donor. For pre-1977 gifts, all the gift taxes paid by the donor may be added to the donor's adjusted basis. For post-1976 transfers, however, the donee may add only the portion of the gift taxes represented by the following fraction:

$$\frac{\text{Amount of property's appreciation from acquisition date through date of gift}}{\text{FMV of property on the date of the gift minus exclusions and deductions}}$$

In no event, however, can the gift tax adjustment increase the donee's basis above the property's FMV on the date of the gift.[44]

If the gifted property's FMV on the date of the gift is less than the donor's adjusted basis, the basis rules are more complicated. For purposes of determining gain, the donee's basis is the same as the donor's adjusted basis. For purposes of determining loss, the donee's basis is the property's FMV on the date of the gift. If the donee sells the property for an amount between its FMV as of the date of the gift and the donor's adjusted basis, the donee recognizes no gain or loss. The property's basis cannot be increased by any gift taxes paid if the donor's adjusted basis exceeds the property's FMV as of the date of the gift. In general, prospective donors should dispose of property that has declined in value by selling it instead of gifting it.

PROPERTY RECEIVED AT DEATH

In general, the basis rules that apply to property received as a result of another's death call for a step up or step down to the property's FMV as of the decedent's date of death. The recipient's basis is the same as the amount at which the property is valued on the estate tax return, which is its FMV on either the decedent's date of death or the alternate valuation date. Generally, the alternate valuation date is six months after the date of death. Although these rules are usually thought of as providing for a step-up in basis, if the property has declined in value as of the transferor's death, the basis is stepped-down to its FMV at the date of death or alternate valuation date.

In certain circumstances, no step up in basis occurs for appreciated property transferred at death.[45] This exception applies if both of the following conditions are present:

▶ The decedent receives the appreciated property as a gift during the one-year period preceding his or her death, and

▶ The property passes to the donor or to the donor's spouse as a result of the donee-decedent's death.

Before the enactment of this rule, a widely publicized planning technique was the transfer of appreciated property to an ill spouse who, in turn, could will the property back to the donor-spouse, who would receive the property at a stepped-up basis. Interspousal transfers by gift and at death are tax-free because of the unlimited marital deduction for both gift tax and estate tax purposes. Consequently, before the rule change, the property received a step-up in basis at no transfer tax cost.

EXAMPLE C12-43 ▶ In June 2005, Sarah gave property valued at $700,000 to Tom, her husband. Sarah's adjusted basis in the property was $120,000. Tom dies in March 2006. At this time, the property is worth $740,000. If the property passes back to Sarah under Tom's will upon Tom's death, Sarah's basis will be $120,000. However, if the property passes to someone other than Sarah at Tom's death, its basis will be stepped-up to $740,000. If Tom lives for more than one year after receiving the gift, the basis is stepped-up to its FMV as of Tom's date of death regardless of whether the property passes at Tom's death to Sarah or someone else. If Tom (the donee) sold the property a few months before his death in March 2006, Tom's basis would be the same as Sarah's was, or $120,000. ◀

In conjunction with the repeal of the estate tax in 2010, the step-up in basis rule for property received from a decedent will be replaced with a modified carryover basis rule. Under this rule, a person receiving property from a decedent will have a basis equal to the lesser of (1) the decedent's adjusted basis in the property or (2) the property's fair market value at the date of the decedent's death. A special rule, however, will allow a $1.3 million

---

[44] See Reg. Sec. 1.1015-5(c) for examples of how to calculate the gift tax that can increase the property's basis.

[45] Sec. 1014(e).

basis increase (and an additional $3 million basis increase for property transferred to a surviving spouse) not to exceed the property's fair market value. For example, assume the decedent's entire estate consists of land the decedent purchased for $2 million. He dies in 2010, when the land is worth $12 million and leaves the land to his surviving spouse. Her basis will be $6.3 million ($2,000,000 + $1,300,000 + $3,000,000), compared with $12 million under current law. Some additional special rules will apply to the basis of property received from a decedent but are not detailed in this text.

BELOW-MARKET LOANS: GIFT AND INCOME TAX CONSEQUENCES

GENERAL RULES

Section 7872 provides rules concerning the gift and income tax consequences of below-market loans. In general, it treats the lender as both making a gift to the borrower and receiving interest income. The borrower is treated as receiving a gift and paying interest expense.

In the case of a demand loan, the lender is treated as having made a gift in each year in which the loan is outstanding. The amount of the gift equals the forgone interest income for the portion of the year the loan is outstanding. The forgone interest income is calculated by referring to the excess of the federal short-term rate of Sec. 1274(d), for the period in question, over the interest rate the lender charged.

For income tax purposes, the forgone interest is treated as being retransferred from the borrower to the lender on the last day of each calendar year in which the loan is outstanding. The amount of the forgone interest is the same as for gift tax purposes and is reported by the lender as income for the year in question. The borrower gets an interest expense deduction for the same amount unless one of the rules limiting the interest deduction applies (e.g., personal interest or investment interest limitations).

EXAMPLE C12-44 ▶ On July 1, Frank lends $500,000 to Susan, who signs an interest-free demand note. The loan is still outstanding on December 31. Assume that 10% is the applicable annual interest rate. Frank is deemed to have made a gift to Susan on December 31 of $25,000 (0.10 × $500,000 × 6/12). Frank must report $25,000 of interest income. Susan deducts $25,000 of interest expense provided the deduction is not otherwise limited or disallowed. ◀

DE MINIMIS RULES

Under one of the *de minimis* rules, neither the income nor the gift tax rules apply to any gift loan made directly between individuals for any day on which the aggregate loans outstanding between the borrower and the lender are $10,000 or less. The *de minimis* exception does not apply to any loan directly attributable to the purchase or carrying of income-producing assets.

A second *de minimis* exception potentially permits loans of $100,000 or less to receive more favorable income tax (but not gift tax) treatment by limiting the lender's imputed income to the borrower's net investment income (as defined in Sec. 163(d)(3)) for the year. Moreover, if the borrower's net investment income for the year is $1,000 or less, such amount is treated as being zero.

The *de minimis* provisions do not apply to transactions having tax avoidance as a principal purpose and do not apply to any day on which the total outstanding loans between the borrower and the lender exceed $100,000. For purposes of the $100,000 or $10,000 loan limitations, a husband and wife are treated as one person.

EXAMPLE C12-45 ▶ On August 1, Mike lends $100,000 to Don. No other loans are outstanding between the parties. Avoidance of federal taxes is not a principal purpose of the loan. Don signs an interest-free demand note when 10% is the applicable interest rate. The loan is still outstanding on December 31. Mike is treated as having made a gift to Don on December 31 of $4,167 [$100,000 × 0.10 × 5/12]. Mike need not report this gift on a gift tax return unless his aggregate gifts to Don this year exceed the $12,000 gift tax annual exclusion.

The income tax consequences depend on Don's (the borrower's) net investment income. If Don's net investment income for the year exceeds $4,167, Mike reports $4,167 of imputed interest income under Sec. 7872. Subject to rules that may disallow some or all of the interest expense deduction, Don deducts the $4,167 interest expense imputed under Sec. 7872. If Don's net investment income is between $1,001 and $4,167, each party reports imputed interest income or expense equal to Don's net investment income. Mike and Don report no interest income or expense under Sec. 7872 if Don's net investment income is $1,000 or less. ◄

TAX PLANNING CONSIDERATIONS

The 1976 Act, which introduced the unification concept, reduced the tax law's bias in favor of lifetime transfers. The 2001 Act, on the other hand, is more favorable toward transfers at death because the unified credit for gift tax purposes does not exceed $345,800. Nevertheless, lifetime gifts still provide more advantages than disadvantages unless the donor dies in 2010 or the estate tax is repealed permanently. Many factors, including the expected appreciation rate and the donor's expectations about whether permanent repeal of the estate tax will actually occur, affect the decision of whether to make gifts. Thus, the optimal result is not always clear. The pros and cons of lifetime gifts from an estate planning perspective are discussed below.

TAX-SAVING FEATURES OF INTER VIVOS GIFTS

USE OF ANNUAL EXCLUSION. The annual exclusion offers donors the opportunity to start making gifts to several donees per year relatively early in their lifetime and keep substantial amounts of property off the transfer tax rolls. The tax-free amount doubles if a husband and wife use the gift-splitting election.

The law provides no estate tax counterpart to the annual gift tax exclusion. Consequently, a terminally ill person whose will includes bequests of approximately $12,000 to each of several individuals would realize substantial transfer tax savings if gifts—instead of bequests—were made to these individuals.

REMOVAL OF POST-GIFT APPRECIATION FROM TAX BASE. Another important advantage of lifetime gifts is that their value is frozen at their date-of-gift value. That is, any post-gift appreciation escapes the transfer tax rolls. Consequently, transfer tax savings are maximized if the donor gives away the assets that appreciate the most.

REMOVAL OF GIFT TAX AMOUNT FROM TRANSFER TAX BASE. With one exception, gift taxes paid by the donor are removed from the transfer tax base. The lone exception applies to gift taxes paid on gifts the donor makes within three years of dying. Under the gross-up rule (discussed in Chapter C13), the donor's gross estate includes only gift taxes paid on gifts made within three years of the donor's death.

INCOME SHIFTING. Originally, one of the most favorable consequences of lifetime gifts was income shifting, but the compression of the income tax rate schedules beginning in 1987 has lessened these benefits. In addition, the 2003 Act, which lowered the tax rate on dividends, further reduced income shifting benefits from giving stock. The income produced by the gifted property is taxed to the donee, whose marginal income tax rate may be lower than the donor's. If income tax savings do arise, they accrue each year during the post-gift period. Thus, the income tax savings can be quite sizable over a span of several years. This tax saving aspect of gifts is a major reason Congress retained the gift tax in the 2001 Act.

GIFT IN CONTEMPLATION OF DONEE-SPOUSE'S DEATH. At times, a terminally ill spouse may have very few assets. If such a spouse died, a sizable portion of his or her unified credit would be wasted because the decedent's estate would be well below the amount of the exemption equivalent provided by the unified credit. If the healthier spouse is relatively wealthy, he or she could make a gift to the ill spouse to create an estate in an amount equal to the estate tax exemption equivalent. Because of the unlimited marital deduction, the gift

ADDITIONAL COMMENT

If a terminally ill spouse, Sam, has no property, an election to gift split can effectively use up Sam's unified credit. Another method of using Sam's unified credit is to give Sam property in trust that meets the following requirements: income from the trust must go to Sam for life, remainder is subject to a general power of appointment in Sam, and if the general power of appointment is not exercised during Sam's lifetime (or by will on Sam's death), the remainder must pass to specified beneficiaries other than the donor.

would be tax-free. Upon the death of the donee-spouse, no estate tax would be payable because the estate tax liability would not exceed the unified credit. The donee-spouse should not transfer his or her property back to the donor-spouse at death. Otherwise, the donee-spouse's unified credit would be wasted, and the original tax planning would be negated. Moreover, the returned property would be included in the surviving spouse's estate.

A gift of appreciated property in contemplation of the donee-spouse's death provides an additional advantage. If the property does not pass back to the donor-spouse, its basis is increased to its value on the donee's date of death. In the event the property is willed to the donor-spouse, a step-up in basis still occurs if the date of the gift precedes the donee-spouse's date of death by more than one year.

LESSENING STATE TRANSFER TAX COSTS. Currently about 15 states levy a death tax, but only four states impose a gift tax.[46] State death taxes are deductible in calculating the taxable estate, but they still add to death-associated costs. Therefore, in some states, the tax cost of lifetime transfers is lower than that for transfers at death.

INCOME TAX SAVINGS FROM CHARITABLE GIFTS. Some individuals desire to donate a portion of their property to charitable organizations. Assuming the donation is eligible for a charitable contribution deduction, the transfer tax implications are the same—no taxable transfer—irrespective of whether the transfer occurs *inter vivos* or at death. From an income tax standpoint, however, a lifetime transfer is preferable because only lifetime transfers produce an income tax deduction for charitable contributions.

NEGATIVE ASPECTS OF GIFTS

LOSS OF STEP-UP IN BASIS. Taxpayers deliberating about whether to make gifts or which property to give should keep in mind that the donee receives no step-up in basis for property acquired by gift. From a practical standpoint, sacrifice of the step-up in basis is insignificant if the donee does not plan to sell the property or if the property is not subject to an allowance for depreciation. Also, keep in mind that gain on the sale is likely to be taxed at the preferential long-term capital gain rate (e.g., 15%), and property in the estate may be taxed at rate close to 50%.

PREPAYMENT OF ESTATE TAX. A donor who makes taxable gifts that exceed the exemption equivalent (applicable exclusion amount) must pay a gift tax. Upon the donor's death, the taxable gift is included in his or her estate tax base as an adjusted taxable gift. Because the gift tax paid during the donor's lifetime reduces the donor's estate tax liability, in a sense, the donor's payment of the gift tax results in prepayment of a portion of the estate tax.

COMPLIANCE AND PROCEDURAL CONSIDERATIONS

OBJECTIVE 9

Recognize the filing requirements for gift tax returns

FILING REQUIREMENTS

Section 6019 specifies the circumstances in which a donor should file a gift tax return. In general, the donor will file Form 709 (United States Gift Tax Return). A completed Form 709 appears in Appendix B. The facts used in the preparation of the completed Form 709 are the same as the facts in the comprehensive illustration, which uses a format for the gift-splitting aspects that differs slightly from that used in the form.

As is the case for income tax returns, a return can be necessary even though the taxable amount and the tax payable are both zero. A donor must file a gift tax return for any calendar year in which the donor makes gifts other than

▶ Gifts to the spouse that qualify for the marital deduction

---

[46] The four states that impose a gift tax are Connecticut, Louisiana, North Carolina, and Tennessee. New York repealed its gift tax beginning with 2000. Connecticut adopted legislation phasing out its gift tax on gifts of $1 million or less during the period 2001–2006. In 2002, legislation delayed the phase out by two additional years.

► Gifts that are fully shielded from taxation because they fall within the annual exclusion amount or are exempted from classification as a gift under the exception for educational or medical expenses

► Gifts to charitable organizations if the gift is deductible and the organization receives the donor's entire interest in the property

However, if the gift to the spouse is of qualified terminable interest property (QTIP), the donor must report the gift on the gift tax return. The marital deduction is not available for these transfers unless the donor makes the necessary election, which is done by claiming a marital deduction on the gift tax return.

United States persons who receive aggregate foreign gifts or bequests exceeding $12,760 (in 2006) must report such amounts as prescribed in Treasury Regulations.[47]

DUE DATE

All gift tax returns must be filed on a calendar-year basis. Under the general rule, gift tax returns are due no later than April 15 following the close of the year of the gift.[48] An extension of time granted for filing an individual income tax return is deemed to automatically extend the filing date for the individual's gift tax return for that year. Under a recent change such extensions are until October 15.

If the donor dies early in the year in which a gift is made, the due date for the donor's final gift tax return may be earlier than April 15. Because information concerning the decedent's taxable gifts is necessary to complete the estate tax return, the gift tax return for the year of death is due no later than the due date (including extensions) for the donor's estate tax return.[49] Estate tax returns are due nine months after the date of death.

Receipt of an extension for filing a gift tax return does not postpone the due date for payment of the tax. Interest is imposed on any gift tax not paid by April 15. Donors should submit Form 8892 if they anticipate owing gift tax and/or if they need an extension for only their gift tax return. Unlike with the income tax, estimated payments of gift taxes throughout the reporting period are not required.

GIFT-SPLITTING ELECTION

For taxable gifts to be computed under the gift-splitting technique, both spouses must indicate their consent to gift splitting in one of the following ways:[50]

► Each spouse signifies his or her consent on the other spouse's gift tax return.

► Each spouse signifies his or her consent on his or her own gift tax return.

► Both spouses signify their consent on one of the gift tax returns.

Treasury Regulations state that the first approach listed above is the preferred manner for designating consent.

LIABILITY FOR TAX

KEY POINT

Similarly to a husband and wife filing a joint income tax return, if gift splitting is elected, the husband and wife have joint and several liability for the entire gift tax liability regardless of who actually made the gifts.

The donor is responsible for paying the gift tax,[51] and if the spouses consent to gift splitting, the entire gift tax liability is a joint and several liability of the spouses.[52] Thus, if spouses do not pay the tax voluntarily, the IRS may attempt to collect whatever amount it deems appropriate from either spouse, irrespective of the size of the gift that spouse actually made.

In the rare event that the donor does not pay the gift tax, the donee becomes personally liable for the gift tax.[53] However, a donee's liability is limited to the value of the gift.

DETERMINATION OF VALUE

One of the most difficult problems encountered by donors and their tax advisors is determining the gifted property's FMV. This task is especially difficult if the gifted property is stock in a closely held business, an oil and gas property, or land in an area where few sales occur.

---

[47] Sec. 6039F.
[48] Sec. 6075(b).
[49] The decedent's post-1976 taxable gifts affect the size of his or her estate tax base, as discussed in the next chapter.

[50] Reg. Sec. 25.2513-2(a)(1).
[51] Sec. 2502(c).
[52] Sec. 2513(d).
[53] Reg. Sec. 301.6324-1.

⚖

ETHICAL POINT

A CPA who advises a client about the tax consequences of making a gift also has a responsibility to make sure the property is correctly valued. Otherwise, if the valuation claimed is too low, the IRS can levy a penalty on the donor. For example, a gift of non-cash property (e.g., land) may require that an appraisal be obtained. Failure to obtain an appraisal, or failure to investigate an appraisal that seems too low, may result in an undervaluation of the gift property, which may lead to the IRS imposing additional gift taxes, interest, and penalties.

If a transaction involves a sale, the IRS can argue that the asset's value exceeds its sales price and, thus, there is a gift to the extent of the bargain element. This problem is especially common with sales to family members. If the donor gives or sells to a family member property whose value is not readily determinable, it is advisable for the donor to obtain an appraisal of the property before filing the gift tax return.

PENALTY FOR UNDERVALUATION.   Section 6662 imposes a penalty, at one of two rates, on underpayments of gift or estate taxes resulting from too low a valuation of property. The amount on which the penalty is imposed is the underpayment of the transfer tax attributable to the valuation understatement.

No penalty applies if the valuation shown on the return exceeds 50% of the amount determined during an audit or court trial to be the correct value. If the value reported on the return is 50% or less of the correct value, the penalty rate is as shown below.

Ratio of Value per Return to Correct Value	Penalty Rate
More than 25% but 50% or less	20%
25% or less	40%

Section 6662(g)(2) exempts a taxpayer from the penalty if the underpayment is less than $5,000. In addition, the IRS will not levy the penalty if the taxpayer shows good faith and a reasonable cause for the valuation claimed.

EXAMPLE C12-46 ▶

Assume Donna already has used her available unified credit. She gives land to her son and reports its value at $400,000 on her gift tax return. The IRS audits Donna's return, and she agrees that $900,000 was the correct value of the property. Because the value stated on the return is only 44.44% [($400,000 ÷ $900,000) × 100] of the correct value, the IRS levies a 20% penalty on the underpayment attributable to the valuation understatement. If Donna is in the 46% marginal gift tax bracket, the gift tax underpayment is $230,000 [0.46 × ($900,000 − $400,000)]. Thus, the penalty is $46,000 (0.20 × $230,000) unless Donna can demonstrate reasonable cause and good faith for the valuation.   ◀

ADDITIONAL COMMENT

Even if a taxpayer questions whether a taxable gift has been made, it is a good idea to file a gift tax return and at least disclose the transaction. The filing of the return with adequate disclosure of the transaction causes the statute of limitations to begin and limits the time during which the IRS may question the valuation and the amount of the gift, if any.

STATUTE OF LIMITATIONS

In general, the statute of limitations for gift tax purposes is three years after the later of the date the return was filed or the return's due date.[54] The statute of limitations increases from three to six years if the donor omits from the gift tax return gifts whose total value exceeds 25% of the gifts reported on the return. If the donor files no return because, for example, he or she is unaware that he or she made any gifts, the IRS may assess the tax at any time.

The cumulative nature of the gift tax causes the taxable gifts of earlier years to affect the gift tax owed in subsequent periods. Once the statute of limitations has expired for pre-1997 gifts, the IRS cannot argue that taxable gifts of prior periods were undervalued (and thus that the current period's gifts should be taxed at a higher rate than that used by the donor) as long as the donor paid gift tax on the earlier gifts. However, for gifts reported after August 5, 1997, this rule applies even if the donor paid no gift tax.[55]

For gifts made in 1997 and later, it is important to adequately disclose potential gift transactions for which the gift status is unclear. The statute of limitations will not expire on a transaction unless the donor makes adequate disclosure.[56]

EXAMPLE C12-47 ▶

Andy filed a gift tax return for 2005, reporting taxable gifts of $1.85 million made in October 2005. Andy paid gift tax. If Andy adequately disclosed all potential gifts, once the statute of limitations expires for 2005, the IRS cannot contend that, for purposes of calculating the tax on later taxable gifts, the 2005 taxable gifts exceeded $1.85 million.   ◀

---

[54] Sec. 6501.
[55] Sec. 2504(c).

[56] Sec. 6501(c)(9).

PROBLEM MATERIALS

DISCUSSION QUESTIONS

C12-1 Describe two ways in which the transfer tax (estate and gift tax) system is a unified system.

C12-2 What was the Congressional purpose for enacting the gift-splitting provisions?

C12-3 Determine whether the following statement is true or false: Every donor who makes a taxable gift incurs a gift tax liability. Explain your answer.

C12-4 Under what circumstances must the amount of the unified credit usually available be reduced (by a maximum amount of $6,000) even though the donor has never claimed any unified credit?

C12-5 Does the exemption from the gift tax for direct payment of tuition apply for payments of non-relatives' tuition? Explain.

C12-6 Steve is considering the following actions. Explain to him which actions will constitute gifts for gift tax purposes.
  a. Transferring all his ownership rights in a life insurance policy to another person
  b. Depositing funds into a joint bank account in the names of Steve and another party (who deposits nothing)
  c. Paying half the consideration for land and having it titled in the names of Steve and his son as joint tenants with right of survivorship if the son furnished the other half of the consideration
  d. Paying a hospital for the medical expenses of a neighbor
  e. Making a $1 million demand loan to an adult child and charging no interest

C12-7 Dick wants to transfer property with a $600,000 FMV to an irrevocable trust with a bank as the trustee. Dick will name his distant cousin Earl to receive all of the trust income annually for the next eight years. Then the property will revert to Dick. In the last few years, the income return (yield) on the property has been 9%. Assume this yield is not likely to decline and that the applicable rate from the actuarial tables is 7%.
  a. What will be the amount of Dick's gift to Earl?
  b. Would you recommend that Dick transfer the property yielding 9% to this type of a trust? Explain. If not, what type of property would you recommend that Dick transfer to the trust?

C12-8 Antonio would like to make a gift of a life insurance policy. Explain to him what action he must take to make a completed gift.

C12-9 In what circumstances might a potential donor be interested in making a net gift? Explain the potential income tax problem with making a net gift.

C12-10 What is the purpose of the gift tax annual exclusion?

C12-11 In what circumstances do gifts fail to qualify for the annual exclusion?

C12-12 Compare and contrast a Sec. 2503(c) trust and a *Crummey* trust.

C12-13 From a nontax standpoint, would a parent probably prefer to make a transfer to a minor child by using a Sec. 2503(c) trust or a *Crummey* trust?

C12-14 Explain the requirements for classifying a transaction as a transfer of a qualified terminable interest property (QTIP).

C12-15 Why do some donors consider the qualified terminable interest property (QTIP) transfer an especially attractive arrangement for making gifts to their spouses?

C12-16 A client is under the impression that a donor cannot incur a gift tax liability if his or her only gifts are gifts to a U.S. charitable organization. What should you say to the client?

C12-17 Describe to a married couple three advantages of making the gift-splitting election.

C12-18 Both Damien and Latoya make taxable gifts of $250,000 in the current year. Will their current year gift tax liabilities necessarily be identical? Explain.

C12-19 A donor made his first taxable gift in 1979 and his second taxable gift in the current year. In the intervening years, the highest gift tax rates declined. In calculating the tax on taxable gifts of previous periods, which rate schedule is used: the one for the year in which the donor made the earlier gift or the one for the current period?

C12-20 A mother is trying to decide which of the two assets listed below to give to her adult daughter.

Asset	FMV	Adjusted Basis	Annual Net Income from the Asset
Apartment	$2,400,000	$1,500,000	$(10,000)
Bonds	2,400,000	2,300,000	80,000

The mother has a higher marginal income tax rate than does her daughter. Describe the pros and cons of giving each of the two properties.

C12-21 Phil and Marcy have been married for a number of years. Marcy is very wealthy, but Phil is not. In fact, Phil has only $10,000 of property. Phil is very ill, and his doctor believes that he probably will die within the next few months. Make one (or more) tax planning suggestions for the couple.

C12-22 Assume the same facts as in Problem C12-21 and that Marcy has decided to give Phil property valued at $1.99 million. Phil probably will leave the gifted property to their children under his will.
a. What are the gift tax consequences to Marcy and the estate tax consequences to Phil of the transfer (assuming the property does not appreciate before his death)?
b. Assume Marcy is trying to decide whether to give Phil stock with an adjusted basis of $285,000 or land with an adjusted basis of $800,000. Each asset is valued at $1.99 million. Which asset would you recommend she give and why?

C12-23 Carlos has heard about the unified transfer tax system and does not understand how making gifts can be beneficial. Explain to Carlos how a lifetime gift fixes (freezes) the gifted property's value for transfer tax purposes.

C12-24 Describe for a client five advantages and two disadvantages of disposing of property by gift instead of at death.

C12-25 In general, what is the due date for the gift tax return? What are two exceptions?

C12-26 In 1998, Frank made an installment sale of real property to Stu, his son, for $1 million. Frank did not file a gift tax return. In 2007, the IRS audits Frank's 2005 income tax return and discovers the sale. The IRS then contends that the property Frank sold was worth $2.5 million in 1998 and that Frank made a $1.5 million gift to Stu in 1998.
a. Can the IRS collect the gift tax on the 1998 gift? If not, will the 1998 gift affect the tax due on later gifts that Frank makes?
b. Will Frank potentially incur any penalty? Explain.

ISSUE IDENTIFICATION QUESTIONS

C12-27 Kwambe is thinking of making a substantial gift of stock to his fiancée, Maya. The wedding is scheduled for October 1 of the current year. Kwambe already has exhausted his unified credit. He also is considering giving $24,000 cash this year to each of his three children by a previous marriage. What tax issues should Kwambe consider with respect to the gifts he plans to make to Maya and his three children?

C12-28 Janet is considering transferring assets valued at $4 million to an irrevocable trust (yet to be created) for the benefit of her son, Gordon, age 15, with Farmers Bank as trustee. Her attorney has drafted a trust agreement that provides that Gordon is to receive income in the trustee's discretion for the next 20 years and that at age 35 the trust assets will be distributed equally between Gordon and his sister Joanna. Janet anticipates that her husband will consent to gift splitting. What tax issues should Janet and her husband consider with respect to the trust?

C12-29 Melvin funds an irrevocable trust with Holcomb Bank as trustee and reserves the right to receive the income for seven years. He provides that at the end of the seventh year the trust assets will pass outright to his adult daughter, Pamela, or to Pamela's estate should Pamela not be alive. Melvin transfers assets valued at $1 million to the trust; the assets at present are producing income of about 4.5% per year. Assume that the Sec. 7520 rate per the actuarial tables for the month of the transfer is 8%. What tax issues should Melvin consider regarding the trust?

PROBLEMS

C12-30 *Calculation of Gift Tax.* In 2006, Sondra makes taxable gifts aggregating $2 million. Her only other taxable gifts amount to $700,000, all of which she made in 1997.
a. What is Sondra's 2006 gift tax liability?
b. What is her 2006 gift tax liability under the assumption that she made the $700,000 of taxable gifts in 1974 instead of 1997?

C12-31 *Calculation of Gift Tax.* Amir made taxable gifts as follows: $800,000 in 1975, $1.2 million in 1999, and $600,000 in 2006. What is Amir's gift tax liability for 2006?

C12-32 *Determination of Taxable Gifts.* In the current year, Beth, who is single, sells stock valued at $40,000 to Linda for $18,000. Later that year, Beth gives Linda $12,000 in cash.
a. What is the amount of Beth's taxable gifts?
b. How would your answer to Part a change if Beth instead gave the cash to Patrick?

C12-33 *Determination of Taxable Gifts.* In the current year, Clay gives $32,000 cash to each of his eight grandchildren. His wife makes no gifts during the current year.
a. What are Clay's taxable gifts, assuming Clay and his wife do *not* elect gift splitting?
b. How would your answer to Part a change if the couple elects gift splitting?

C12-34 *Determination of Taxable Gifts.* In the current year, David gives $180,000 of land to David, Jr. In the current year, David's wife gives $200,000 of land to George and $44,000 cash to David, Jr. Assume the couple elects gift splitting for the current year.
a. What are the couple's taxable gifts?
b. How would your answer to Part a change if David's wife gave the $44,000 of cash to Ollie (instead of to David, Jr.)?

C12-35 *Recognition of Transactions Treated as Gifts.* In the current year, Emily, a widow, engages in the following transactions. Determine the amount of the completed gift, if any, arising from each of the following occurrences.
a. Emily names Lauren the beneficiary of a $100,000 life insurance policy on Emily's life. The beneficiary designation is not irrevocable.
b. Emily deposits $50,000 cash into a checking account in the joint names of herself and Matt, who deposits nothing to the account. Later that year, Matt withdraws $15,000 from the account.
c. Emily pays $22,000 of nephew Noah's medical expenses directly to County Hospital.
d. Emily transfers the title to land valued at $60,000 to Olive.

C12-36 *Calculation of Gift Tax.* Refer to the facts of Problem C12-35 and assume the current year is 2006. Emily's prior gifts are as follows:

Year	Amount of Taxable Gifts
1974	$ 500,000
1998	1,000,000

What is the gift tax liability with respect to Emily's 2006 gifts?

C12-37 *Recognition of Transactions Treated as Gifts.* In the current year, Marge (age 67) engages in the following transactions. Determine the amount of the completed gift, if any, arising from each of the following events. Assume 10% is the applicable interest rate.
a. Marge transfers $100,000 of property in trust and irrevocably names herself to receive $8,000 per year for life and daughter Joy (age 37) to receive the remainder.
b. Marge pays her grandson's $15,000 tuition to State University.
c. Marge gives the same grandson stock valued at $72,000.
d. Marge deposits $150,000 into a revocable trust. Later in the year, the bank trustee distributes $18,000 of income to the named beneficiary, Gail.

C12-38 *Recognition of Transactions Treated as Gifts.* Determine the amount of the completed gift, if any, arising from each of the following occurrences.
a. A parent sells real estate valued at $1.8 million to an adult child, who pays $1 million in consideration.
b. A furniture store holds a clearance sale and sells a customer a $5,000 living room suite for $1,500.
c. During the year, a father purchases food and clothing costing $8,500 for his minor child.
d. A citizen contributes $1,500 cash to a political organization.
e. Zeke lends $600,000 interest free to Henry, who signs a demand note on August 1. Assume 10% is the applicable interest rate and the note remains unpaid at year-end.

C12-39 *Determination of Unified Credit.* In March 1976, Sue made a taxable gift of $200,000. In arriving at the amount of her taxable gift, Sue elected to deduct the $30,000 specific exemption formerly available. In 2006, Sue makes her next gift; the taxable amount is $1.5 million.
a. What unified credit can Sue claim on her 2006 return?
b. What unified credit can Sue claim on her 2006 return if she made the 1976 gift in December instead of March?

C12-40 *Valuation of Gifts.* On September 1 of the current year, Mario irrevocably transfers a $100,000 whole life insurance policy on his life to Mario, Jr. as owner. On September 1, the policy's interpolated terminal reserve is $30,000. Mario paid the most recent annual premium ($1,800) on June 1. What is the amount of the gift Mario made in the current year?

C12-41 *Determination of Gift Tax Deductions.* In June, Tina makes cash gifts of $700,000 to her husband and $100,000 to the City Art Museum. What are the amounts of the deductions available for these gifts when calculating Tina's income tax and gift tax liabilities if she does not elect gift splitting?

C12-42 *Determination of Annual Exclusion.* For each of the following transactions that happen in the current year, indicate the amount of the annual exclusion available. Explain your answer.

a. Tracy creates a trust in the amount of $300,000 for the benefit of her eight-year-old daughter, May. She names a bank as trustee. Before May reaches age 21, the trustee in its discretion is to pay income or corpus (trust assets) to May or for her benefit. When May reaches age 21, she will receive the unexpended portion of the trust income and corpus. If May dies before reaching age 21, the unexpended income and corpus will be paid to her estate or a party (or parties) she appoints under a general power of appointment.

b. Assume the same facts as in Part a except May is age 28 when Tracy creates the trust and the trust agreement contains age 41 wherever age 21 appears in Part a.

c. Assume the same facts as in Part b except the trust instrument allows May to demand a distribution by December 31 of each year equal to the lesser of the amount of the annual exclusion for federal gift tax purposes or the amount transferred to the trust that year.

C12-43 *Determination of Annual Exclusion.* During 2006, Will gives $40,000 cash to Will, Jr. and a remainder interest in a few acres of land to his friend Suzy. The remainder interest is valued at $32,000. Will and his wife, Helen, elect gift splitting, and during the current year Helen gives Joyce $8,000 of stock. What is the total amount of the annual gift tax exclusions available to Will and Helen?

C12-44 *Availability of Annual Exclusion.* Bonnie, a widow, irrevocably transfers $1 million of property to a trust with a bank named as trustee. For as long as Bonnie's daughter Carol is alive, Carol is to receive all the trust income annually. Upon Carol's death, the property is to be distributed to Carol's children. Carol is age 32 and currently has three children. How many gift tax exclusions does Bonnie receive for the transfer?

C12-45 *Calculation of Gift Tax.* Before last year, neither Hugo nor Wanda, his wife, made any taxable gifts. In 2005, Hugo gave $11,000 cash to each of his 30 nieces, nephews, and grandchildren. This year (2006), Wanda gives $32,000 of stock to each of the same people. What is the *minimum* legal gift tax liability (*before* reduction for the unified credit) for each spouse for each year?

C12-46 *Calculation of Marital Deduction.* Hugh makes the gifts listed below to Winnie, his wife, age 37. What is the amount of the marital deduction, if any, attributable to each?

a. Hugh transfers $500,000 to a trust with a bank named as trustee. All the income must be paid to Winnie monthly for life. At Winnie's death, the property passes to Hugh's sisters or their estates.

b. Hugh transfers $300,000 to a trust with a bank named as trustee. Income is payable at the trustee's discretion to Winnie annually until the earlier of her death or her remarriage. When payments to Winnie cease, the trustee must distribute the property to Hugh's children by a previous marriage or to their estates.

C12-47 *Calculation of the Marital Deduction.* In the current year, Louise makes the transfers described below to Lance, her husband, age 47. Assume 7% is the applicable interest rate. What is the amount of her marital deduction, if any, attributable to each transfer?

a. In June, she gives him land valued at $45,000.

b. In October, she gives him a 12-year income interest in a trust with a bank named as trustee. She names their daughter to receive the remainder interest. She funds the irrevocable trust with $400,000 in assets.

C12-48 *Charitable Contribution Deduction.* Tien (age 67) transfers a remainder interest in a vacation cabin (with a total value of $100,000) to a charitable organization and retains a life estate in the cabin for herself.

a. What is the amount of the gift tax charitable contribution deduction, if any, attributable to this transfer? Assume that 10% is the applicable interest rate.

b. How will your answer to Part a change if Tien instead gives a remainder interest in a valuable oil painting (worth $100,000) to the organization?

C12-49 *Calculation of Gift Tax.* In 2006, Homer and his wife, Wilma (residents of a non–community property state) make the gifts listed below. Homer's previous taxable gifts consist of $100,000 made in 1975 and $1.4 million made in 1996. Wilma has made no previous taxable gifts.

Wilma's current year gifts were	
to Art	$400,000
to Bart	6,000
Homer's current year gifts were	
to Linda	$600,000
to a charitable organization	100,000
to Norma (future interest)	200,000

a. What are the gift tax liabilities of Homer and Wilma for 2006 if they elect gift splitting and everyone except Norma receives a present interest?

b. How would the gift tax liabilities for each spouse in Part a change if they do not elect gift splitting?

C12-50 *Calculation of Gift Tax.* In 2006, Henry and his wife, Wendy, made the gifts shown below. All gifts are of present interests. What is Wendy's gift tax payable for 2006 if the couple elects gift splitting and Wendy's previous taxable gifts (made in 1995) total $1 million?

Wendy's current gifts were	
to Janet	$80,000
to Cindy	70,000
to Henry	50,000
Henry's current gifts were	
to Janet	30,000

C12-51 *Basis Rules.* In June 2005, Karen transfers property with a $75,000 FMV and a $20,000 adjusted basis to Hal, her husband. Hal dies in March 2006; the property has appreciated to $85,000 in value by then.

a. What is the amount of Karen's taxable gift in 2005?

b. What gain would Hal recognize if he sells the property for $95,000 in July 2005?

c. If Hal wills the property to Dot, his daughter, what basis would Dot have?

d. How would your answer to Part c change if Hal instead willed the property to Karen?

e. How would your answer to Part d change if Hal did not die until August 2006?

C12-52 *Basis Rules.* Siu is considering giving away stock in Ace Corporation or Gold Corporation. Each has a current FMV of $500,000, and each has the same estimated appreciation rate. Siu's basis in the Ace stock is $100,000, and her basis in the Gold stock is $450,000. Which stock would you suggest that she give away and why, or does it make any difference?

C12-53 *Below-Market Loans.* On October 1, Sam lends Tom $10 million. Tom signs an interest-free demand note. The loan is still outstanding on December 31. Explain the income tax and gift tax consequences of the loan to both Sam and Tom. Assume that the federal short-term rate is 9%.

COMPREHENSIVE PROBLEM

C12-54 In 2006, Ginger Graham, age 46 and wife of Greg Graham, engaged in the transactions described below. Determine Ginger's gift tax liability for 2006 if she and Greg elect gift splitting and Greg gave their son Stevie stock valued at $80,000 during 2006. Ginger's grandmother Mamie died November 12, 2005, and Mamie's will bequeathed $250,000 to Ginger. On March 4, 2006, Ginger irrevocably disclaimed the $250,000 in writing, and, as a result, the property passed instead to Ginger's sister Gertie. In 2006, Ginger gave $100,000 cash to her alma mater, State University. In 1996, Ginger had given ownership of a life insurance policy on her own life to her daughter, Denise, and in 2006 Ginger paid the $22,000 annual premium on the policy. In 2005, Ginger deposited $45,000 into a bank account in the name of herself and son Stevie, joint tenants with rights of survivorship. Stevie deposited nothing. Neither party made a withdrawal until 2006, when Stevie withdrew $30,000. In 2006, Ginger created a trust with County Bank as trustee and transferred $300,000 of stock to the irrevocable trust. She named her husband Greg (age 47) to receive all the trust income semi-annually for life and daughter Drucilla to receive the remainder. In 2006, she gave a remainder interest in her beach cottage to the American Red Cross and kept the right to use the cottage for the rest of her life. The fair market value of the cottage was $70,000.

Other information: Ginger's earlier *taxable* gifts are $175,000, all made in 1996. Ginger will make whatever elections are necessary to minimize her current gift tax liability. Assume the Sec. 7520 interest rate is 8%.

TAX STRATEGY PROBLEM

C12-55 Ilene Ishi is planning to fund an irrevocable charitable remainder annuity trust with $100,000 of cash. She will designate her sister, age 60, to receive an annuity of $8,000 per year for 15 years and State University to receive the remainder at the end of the fifteenth year. The valuation of the charitable portion of the transfer, according to Reg. Sec. 25.2522(c)-3(d)(2)(i), is to be determined under Reg. Sec. 1.664-2(c), an income tax regulation. Regulation Sec. 1.664-2(c) provides that, in valuing the remainder interest, the donor may elect to use the Sec. 7520 interest rate for either of the two months preceding the month of the transfer as an alternative to using the rate for the actual month of transfer. Otherwise, the value will be determined by using the Sec. 7520 rate for the month of the transfer. Assume that in the month of the transfer the interest rate was 7% but that in the two preceding months the rate was 7.2%. Should the donor elect to calculate the value of the remainder interest by using the interest rate for one of the two preceding months? Explain your answer. Note: The 7.2% rate does not appear in the excerpts from the actuarial tables, but the absence of such rate from the tables will not preclude you from answering this question.

TAX FORM/RETURN PREPARATION PROBLEMS

C12-56 Dave and Sara Moore, of 10105 Lake View Lane, Chicago, Illinois 60108, engage in the transactions described below in August 2005. Use this information to prepare a gift tax return (Form 709) for Dave. He and Sara want to use gift splitting. Both are U.S. citizens. His Social Security number is 477-11-1333 and hers is 272-92-4403. For simplicity, assume the rate for the actuarial tables used is 10%. Dave's transactions are summarized below.

	Amount
1. Tuition paid to Harvard University for son-in-law, Jim Smith.	$ 22,000
2. Room and board paid to Harvard University for Jim Smith.	11,000
3. Sports car purchased for Jim Smith.	34,000
4. Premium paid on life insurance policy on Dave's life. Dave transferred the policy to his sister, Amy Lane, as owner in 1996.	12,000
5. Land given to daughter, Glenda Muñoz.	90,000
6. Remainder interest in personal residence given to State University. Dave (age 70) retains a life estate. The total value of the residence is $200,000.	
7. Stocks transferred to an irrevocable trust with First National Bank as trustee. The trust income is payable to Sara (age 60) semiannually for life. The remainder is payable at Sara's death to daughter, Amanda Webb, or her estate.	500,000

Sara gave $68,000 of cash to Dave's sister, Amy Lane. Dave's gift history includes a $600,000 taxable gift made in 1975 and a $400,000 taxable gift made in 1994.

C12-57 Alice Arnold, Social Security number 572-13-4409, a widow, engages in the transactions listed below in 2005. Use this information to prepare a gift tax return (Form 709) for Alice.

	Amount
1. Stock given to daughter, Brenda Bell.	$700,000
2. Cash transferred to son, Al Arnold.	600,000
3. $500,000 interest-free demand loan made to Brenda Bell on July 1. The loan is still outstanding on December 31.	
4. Land given to niece, Lou Lane	100,000

Assume 8% is the applicable interest rate. Alice has made only one previous taxable gift: $300,000 (taxable amount) in 2000. Alice, a U.S. citizen, resides at 105 Peak Rd., Denver, Colorado 80309.

CASE STUDY PROBLEMS

C12-58 Your client, Karen Kross, recently married Larry Kross. Karen is age 72, quite wealthy, and in reasonably good health. To date, she has not made any taxable gifts, but Larry made taxable gifts totaling $700,000 in 1998. Karen is considering giving each of her five college-age grandchildren approximately $24,000 of cash for them to use to pay their college expenses of tuition and room and board for the year. In addition, she is considering giving her three younger grandchildren $3,000 each to use for orthodontic bills. Karen wants to give her daughter property valued at $400,000. She is trying to choose between giving her daughter cash or stock with a basis of $125,000. She would like to give her son $400,000 of property also, but prefers for the property to be tied up in a discretionary trust with a bank as trustee for the son for at least 15 years. Karen has been approached by an agricultural museum about making a contribution to it and, as a result, is contemplating deeding her family farm to the museum but retaining a life estate in the farm.

Required: Prepare a memorandum to the tax partner of your firm that discusses the transfer tax and income tax consequences of the proposed transactions described above. Also, make any recommendations that you deem appropriate.

C12-59 Morris Jory, a long-time tax client of the firm you work for, has made substantial gifts during his lifetime. Mr. Jory transferred Jory Corporation stock to 14 donees in December 2005. Each donee received shares valued at $11,000. Two of the donees were Mr. Jory's adult children, Amanda and Peter. The remaining 12 donees were employees of Jory Corporation who are not related to Mr. Jory. Mr. Jory, a widower, advised the employees that within two weeks of receiving the stock certificates they must endorse such certificates over to Amanda and Peter. Six of the donees were instructed to endorse their certificates to Amanda and six to Peter. During 2005, Mr. Jory also gave $35,000 cash to his favorite grandchild, Robin. Your firm has been engaged to prepare Mr. Jory's 2005 gift tax return. In January 2006, you meet with Mr. Jory, who insists that his 2005 taxable gifts will be only $24,000 ($35,000 to Robin − $11,000 annual exclusion). After your meeting with Mr. Jory, you are uncertain about his position regarding the amount of his 2005 gifts and have scheduled a meeting with your firm's senior tax partner, who has advised Mr. Jory for more than 20 years. In preparation for the meeting, prepare a summary of the tax and ethical considerations (with supporting authority where possible) regarding whether you should prepare a gift tax return that reports the taxable gifts in accordance with Mr. Jory's wishes.

TAX RESEARCH PROBLEMS

C12-60 Karl Kremble funded an irrevocable trust in March 2006 with oil and gas property valued at $400,000. Assume the Sec. 7520 interest rate for the actuarial tables was 7% on the date of funding. Karl named a bank trustee and provided that his distant cousin, Louise Lane, will receive all the trust income annually for the next 34 years. Then the assets will revert (pass back) to Karl or his estate. The trust instrument specifically states that the trust is not to maintain a reserve for depletion (that is, no portion of the royalties received from the oil and gas properties is to be transferred to the trust's principal account to account for the wasting nature of the trust assets). Your manager has requested that you research whether the amount of Karl's gift to Louise may be determined by using the actuarial tables and that you write a memo summarizing your conclusions. Your manager indicated further that your memo should address the amount of the gift Karl is deemed to have made.

C12-61 Sarah Studer, resident of Arkansas, is the daughter of Maude Mason, a widow, who died intestate March 12, 2006. Under Arkansas law, Sarah, Maude's only child, received all of her mother's probate estate, $780,000 in amount. Sarah owes the IRS $820,000 in "back taxes" and interest, and under Sec. 6321 there is a tax lien against all of Sarah's property and rights to property. Sarah has virtually no property and knows that if she accepts the property from her mother's estate she will have to use it to pay her debts to the IRS. It is now November 20, 2006, and Sarah has inquired whether a disclaimer would allow her mother's property to stay within the family unit, given that, if she disclaimed the property, it would pass under state law to her son, Steven Studer, Jr.

Your manager has requested that you write a memorandum in which you address the consequences to Sarah of a disclaimer. Your manager suggested that you consult *Rohn F. Drye, Jr.,* 84 AFTR 2d 99-7160, 99-2 USTC ¶51, 006 (USSC, 1999).

C12-62   Janet Mason filed a 2004 gift tax return to report the gift on June 3, 2004 of closely held stock in Mason Meat Co., Inc. The tax return, which your firm prepared, reflected a value of $1,500 per share (determined by an appraiser) and a taxable gift of $1.1 million. This was Janet's first taxable gift, and she exhausted her full unified credit of $345,800. On October 22, 2005, Janet's father, Mason Meat's CEO and founder, died unexpectedly at age 59. In addition, two months prior to her father's death the firm had recalled much of its meat from distributors and supermarkets because of contamination in the meat plant. The meat plant closed for six weeks while the contamination problem was corrected. An appraiser valued the stock for her father's estate at $1,000 per share. Janet would like for your firm to prepare an amended gift tax return and value her gift at $1,000 per share because of the decline in value resulting from the two events described. She would like to receive a refund of the gift tax she paid and have some of her unified credit restored. Prepare a memo that addresses whether Janet should be entitled to a refund of the gift tax paid and restoration of some of her unified credit.

C12-63   *Internet Research Problem.* In 2006, Calvin Carter, of Raleigh, North Carolina, made a $2.1 million taxable gift to his niece, Camille Carter Donovan. Use the Internet to determine what the marginal tax bracket will be for the North Carolina state gift tax he will owe on this gift if it is his first taxable gift.

C12-64   *Internet Research Problem.* Your manager wants you to participate in delivering a staff training course on the basics of gift taxation. Your assignment is to discuss *Crummey* trusts. You want to improve your understanding of some of the advantages and disadvantages of such trusts. Do research on the Internet and summarize the advantages and disadvantages. Also indicate which site(s) is (are) the source(s) of your information.

C12-65   *Internet Research Problem.* What is the Sec. 7520 rate for August, September, and October 2005?

13

CHAPTER

THE ESTATE TAX

LEARNING OBJECTIVES

After studying this chapter, you should be able to

1. ▶ Describe the formula for the estate tax

2. ▶ Describe the methods for valuing interests in the gross estate

3. ▶ Determine which interests are includible in the gross estate

4. ▶ Identify deductions available for estate tax purposes

5. ▶ Calculate the estate tax liability

6. ▶ Identify tax provisions that alleviate liquidity problems

7. ▶ Recognize the filing requirements for estate tax returns

**ADDITIONAL
COMMENT**

Congress is debating whether
to make the estate tax repeal
permanent.

Gift taxes and estate taxes, wealth transfer taxes that are part of the unified transfer tax system, account for only a small portion of the federal government's collections from taxation. Chapter C12 discussed their history and purposes.

As previously noted, the term *gift taxes* applies to lifetime transfers and the term *estate taxes* applies to dispositions of property resulting from the transferor's death. This chapter discusses the structure of the federal estate tax and examines the types of interests and transactions that cause inclusions in the decedent's gross estate. It also discusses the various deductions and credits affecting the federal estate tax liability and the rules concerning the taxable gifts that affect the estate tax base, an important issue because of the unified nature of the tax levied at death.

It is essential to keep in mind that the estate tax is a *wealth transfer tax*, not a property or an income tax. Understanding that the estate tax is levied on the transfer of property makes it easier to understand the rules for estate taxation, which are part of the unified transfer tax system.

As described in Chapter C12, the Economic Growth and Tax Relief Reconciliation Act of 2001 (the 2001 Act) provided phased-in increases to the unified credit and phased-in reductions to the unified tax rate schedule beginning with 2002. In addition, it repeals the estate and generation skipping transfer taxes, effective January 1, 2010. However, the 2001 Act further provides that, in the absence of additional legistation, the rules for gift, estate, and generation skipping taxes will revert on January 1, 2011 to what they were before the 2001 Act.

ESTATE TAX FORMULA

OBJECTIVE 1

*Describe the formula for
the estate tax*

The tax base for the federal estate tax is the *total* of the decedent's taxable estate (i.e., the gross estate less the deductions discussed below) and adjusted taxable gifts (post-1976 taxable gifts). After the gross tax liability on the tax base is determined, various credits—including the unified credit—are subtracted to arrive at the net estate tax payable. The estate tax formula appears in Figure C13-1.

GROSS ESTATE

**REAL-WORLD
EXAMPLE**

In 1998, the top 6,530 wealth
holders held total assets worth
$11.1 billion in the following
proportions:

Personal residences	9.7%
Other real property	13.7
Closely held stock	11.9
Other stock	24.3
Tax exempt bonds	5.7
Various other assets	34.7

As illustrated in Figure C13-1, calculation of the decedent's estate tax liability begins with determining which items are included in the gross estate. Such items are valued at either the decedent's date of death or the alternate valuation date.[1] As a transfer tax, the estate tax is levied on dispositions that are essentially testamentary in nature. Transactions are viewed as being essentially **testamentary transfers** if the transferor's control or enjoyment of the property in question ceases at death, not before death.[2]

Inclusions in the gross estate extend to a much broader set of properties than merely assets the decedent holds title to at the time of death. Making a lifetime transfer that generates a taxable gift does not guarantee that the donor removes the transferred property from his or her gross estate. Although an individual usually removes property from his or her gross estate by giving it to another before death, the donor's gross estate must include the gifted property if the donor retains either the right to receive the income generated by the transferred property or control over the property for the donor's lifetime.

EXAMPLE C13-1 ▶ In the current year, Ted transfers stocks to an irrevocable trust with a bank named as trustee. Under the terms of the trust agreement, Ted is to receive the trust income annually for the rest of his life and Ted's cousin Ed (or Ed's estate) is to receive the remainder. For gift tax purposes in the current year, Ted made a taxable gift of the remainder interest (but not the income inter-

---

[1] Under Sec. 2032, the alternate valuation date is the earlier of six months after the date of death or the date the property is disposed of.
[2] An example of a transaction that is essentially **testamentary** in nature is a

situation where the donor transfers property in trust but reserves a lifetime right to receive the trust income and, thus, continues to enjoy the economic benefits.

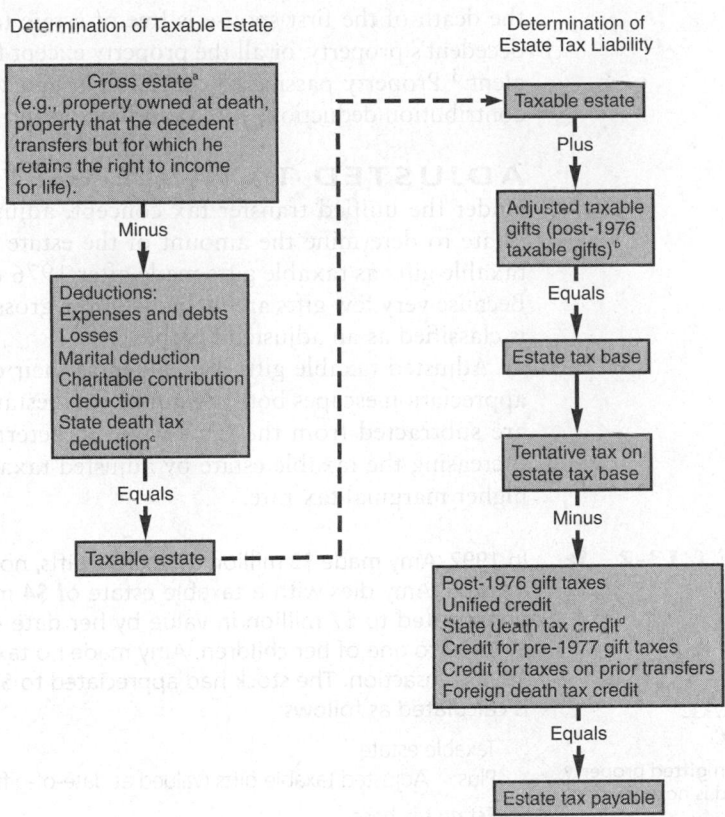

Determination of Taxable Estate	Determination of Estate Tax Liability
Gross estate[a] (e.g., property owned at death, property that the decedent transfers but for which he retains the right to income for life).	**Taxable estate**
Minus	Plus
Deductions: Expenses and debts Losses Marital deduction Charitable contribution deduction State death tax deduction[c]	**Adjusted taxable gifts** (post-1976 taxable gifts)[b]
Equals	Equals
Taxable estate	**Estate tax base**
	Tentative tax on estate tax base
	Minus
	Post-1976 gift taxes Unified credit State death tax credit[d] Credit for pre-1977 gift taxes Credit for taxes on prior transfers Foreign death tax credit
	Equals
	Estate tax payable

[a]Valued at decedent's date of death or alternate valuation date.
[b]Valued at date of gift.
[c]For decedents dying after 2004.
[d]For decedents dying before 2005.

FIGURE C13-1 ▶ ESTATE TAX FORMULA

est) in the trust. If, for example, Ted already has used his entire unified credit, he incurs a gift tax liability. When Ted dies, the entire value of the trust is included in Ted's gross estate, even though Ted does not have legal title to the property. Because the shift in the right to the income does not occur until Ted's death, the transfer is testamentary in nature. ◀

The categories of items included in the gross estate and their valuation are examined in detail later in this chapter. Once the components of the gross estate have been determined and valued, the deductions from the gross estate are calculated.

DEDUCTIONS

The IRC authorizes five categories of items that may be deducted in arriving at the amount of the taxable estate:

▶ Expenses and debts
▶ Casualty and theft losses
▶ Transfers to the decedent's spouse
▶ Transfers to charitable organizations
▶ State death taxes

Deductible expenses include funeral expenses and expenses of administering the decedent's property. As is true for gift tax purposes, there is no ceiling on the marital deduction. Thus, the death of the first spouse is free of estate taxes if the decedent's spouse receives all the decedent's property, or all the property except for an amount equal to the exemption equivalent.[3] Property passing to charitable organizations qualifies, in general, for a charitable contribution deduction, with no ceiling on the amount of such deductions.

ADJUSTED TAXABLE GIFTS AND TAX BASE

Under the unified transfer tax concept, adjusted taxable gifts are added to the taxable estate to determine the amount of the estate tax base. Section 2001(b) defines adjusted taxable gifts as taxable gifts made after 1976 *other than* gifts included in the gross estate. Because very few gifts are included in the gross estate, almost every post-1976 taxable gift is classified as an adjusted taxable gift.

Adjusted taxable gifts are valued at their date-of-gift values. Therefore, any post-gift appreciation escapes both the gift tax and estate tax. Allowable deductions and exclusions are subtracted from the gift's value in determining the adjusted taxable gifts amount. Increasing the taxable estate by adjusted taxable gifts potentially forces the estate into a higher marginal tax rate.

EXAMPLE C13-2 ▶

In 1992, Amy made $5 million of taxable gifts, none of which were included in her gross estate. In 2006, Amy dies with a taxable estate of $4 million. The property Amy gave away in 1992 appreciated to $7 million in value by her date of death. In 1998, Amy gave stock valued at $10,000 to one of her children. Amy made no taxable gifts and incurred no transfer tax on the 1998 transaction. The stock had appreciated to $70,000 when Amy died. Amy's estate tax base is calculated as follows:

ADDITIONAL COMMENT

Income earned on gifted property is the donee's and is not included in the donor's estate.

Taxable estate	$4,000,000
Plus: Adjusted taxable gifts (valued at date-of-gift values)	5,000,000
Estate tax base	$9,000,000

The $2 million of post-gift appreciation on the property gifted in 1992 escapes transfer taxation. Amy's $9 million tax base includes the gifted property, whose value is "frozen" at its date-of-gift value. The 1998 gift does not affect Amy's estate tax base because the 1998 *taxable gift* was zero. ◀

TENTATIVE TAX ON ESTATE TAX BASE

Once the amount of the tax base has been determined, the next step is to calculate the tax on this base. Section 2001(c) contains the unified tax rates, which are reproduced on the inside back cover. In 2005, a top marginal tax rate of 47% applied to tax bases exceeding $2 million, and in 2006 a top rate of 46% applies to tax bases exceeding $2 million. In 2007 through 2009, a maximum tax rate of 45% will apply to tax bases exceeding $1.5 million for both estate and gift tax purposes.

EXAMPLE C13-3 ▶

Assume the same facts as in Example C13-2. The gross tax on Amy's $9 million tax base is $4,000,800. The estate is taxed at a 46% marginal tax rate, the highest rate applicable in the year Amy dies. ◀

REDUCTION FOR POST-1976 GIFT TAXES

Adjusted taxable gifts, in effect, are not taxed twice because Sec. 2001(b)(2) allows a reduction to the estate tax for gift taxes imposed on post-1976 taxable gifts. If the rate schedule for the year of death differs from the schedule applicable for the year of the gift, the tax on post-1976 taxable gifts is determined by using the rate schedule in effect for the year of death. This rule works to the disadvantage of decedents who made taxable gifts and paid taxes at a higher rate than the rate in effect on the date of death. This rule

---

[3] The exemption equivalent ($2 million for 2006), as explained in Chapter C12, is the size of the tax base for which the gift tax or estate tax liability is exactly cancelled by the unified credit of $780,800.

The Estate Tax ▼ **Corporations 13-5**

ensures that the estate pays tax at the current marginal tax rate applicable for the decedent's amount of taxable estate and adjusted taxable gifts.

EXAMPLE C13-4 ▶ Assume the same facts as in Examples C13-2 and C13-3. Recall that in 1992 Amy made $5 million of taxable gifts. The tax on $5 million of 1992 taxable gifts was $2,390,800. Amy was entitled to a $192,800 unified credit and paid $2,198,000 of gift taxes. Amy's 1992 gifts were taxed at a 55% marginal rate. For the year of Amy's death (2006), the marginal rate for $5 million of transfers is 46%. Consequently, the reduction for gift taxes on post-1976 taxable gifts is limited to the amount of gift taxes that would be payable if the 2006 rate schedule were in effect in the year of the gift. This amount is calculated as follows:

Tax on $5 million at 2006 rates	$2,160,800
Minus: Unified credit for 1992 (the year of the gift)	(192,800)
Tax that would have been payable on $5 million if 2006 rates were in effect	$1,968,000

Note that the only change to the gift tax computation is that the 2006 transfer tax rates are used. The actual credit applicable for the year of the gift (and not the credit for the year of death) is subtracted. ◀

EXAMPLE C13-5 ▶ From Examples C13-3 and C13-4, Amy's estate tax, before reduction for any credits, is calculated as follows:

SELF-STUDY QUESTION

Taxpayer made $3 million of taxable gifts in 1992 and paid gift taxes of $1,098,000 (gross tax of $1,290,800 minus the unified credit of $192,800). Taxpayer died in 2006 with a taxable estate of $100,000. At current rates, the gift taxes payable on $3 million would be $1,048,000 ($1,240,800 − $192,800). Determine the amount of her estate tax liability.

ANSWER

The unified transfer tax base is $3.1 million, the sum of the $3 million of 1992 taxable gifts and the $100,000 estate. The current tax on $3.1 million is $1,286,800. The unified credit of $780,800 and the subtraction for gift taxes of $1,048,000 reduce the tax liability to zero.

Tax on $9 million tax base (Example C13-3)	$4,000,800
Minus: Tax that would have been payable on $5 million of post-1976 taxable gifts, at 2006 rates (Example C13-4)	(1,968,000)
Estate tax, before reduction for credits (discussed below)	$2,032,800 ◀

UNIFIED CREDIT

As shown in the inside back cover, the unified credit of Sec. 2010 has varied over the years since its inception in 1977. The credit enables a certain size tax base, referred to as the exemption equivalent or applicable exclusion amount, to be completely free of transfer taxes. For 2005, the credit was $555,800 (equivalent to a $1.5 million exemption). The credit and exemption equivalent amounts for 2006 through 2009 are as follows:

Year of Death	Amount of Credit	Exemption Equivalent
2006	780,800	2,000,000
2007	780,800	2,000,000
2008	780,800	2,000,000
2009	1,455,800	3,500,000

The estate tax computation permits an estate to subtract the entire unified credit applicable for the year of death (reduced by any phaseout for certain pre-1977 gifts) regardless of how much unified credit the decedent claimed for gift tax purposes. As a conceptual matter, however, only one unified credit is available. Under the unification concept, the estate tax is computed on a tax base consisting of the taxable estate plus the adjusted taxable gifts. The tentative tax on the tax base is reduced not by the amount of the "gross" tax on the adjusted taxable gifts, but by the "gross" tax on such gifts reduced by the unified credit. Ignoring changes in the amount of the unified credit, this computation achieves the same result as allowing the unified credit amount to be subtracted only once against all of a person's transfers but allowing a reduction to the estate tax for the gift tax liability *before* reduction for the unified credit.

OTHER CREDITS

In addition to the unified credit—the only credit available for gift tax purposes—the IRC authorizes three credits for estate tax purposes. (Prior to 2005, estates also were allowed a credit for state death taxes.) These additional credits (shown in Figure C13-1) are discussed in more detail on pages C13-24 and C13-25.

OBJECTIVE 2

Describe the methods for valuing interests in the gross estate

THE GROSS ESTATE: VALUATION

DATE-OF-DEATH VALUATION

All property included in the gross estate is valued at either its fair market value (FMV) on the date of death or the alternate valuation date. The valuation date election is an all-or-nothing proposition. Each item included in the gross estate must be valued as of the same date. In other words, the executor (called the personal representative in some states) may not value some items as of the date of death and others as of the alternate valuation date.

Fair market value is defined as "the price at which the property would change hands between a willing buyer and a willing seller, neither being under any compulsion to buy or to sell and both having reasonable knowledge of relevant facts."[4] In general, the FMV of a particular asset on a certain date is the same regardless of whether the property is being valued for gift or estate tax purposes. Life insurance on the life of the transferor is an exception to this rule. Upon the death of the insured, the policy is valued at its face value, whereas it is valued at a lesser amount while the insured is alive. Generally, this lesser amount is either the cost of a comparable contract or the policy's interpolated terminal reserve plus the unexpired portion of the premium.

For certain types of property, Treasury Regulations contain detailed descriptions of the valuation approach. However, the valuation of interests in closely held businesses is described in only very general terms. Judicial decisions and revenue rulings provide additional guidance for valuation of assets. Valuation rules for several interests are discussed below. For purposes of this discussion, it is assumed that date-of-death valuation is elected.

LISTED STOCKS. Stocks traded on a stock exchange are valued at the average of their highest and lowest selling prices on the date of death.[5] If no sales occur on the date of death, but sales do take place within a few days of such date, the estate tax value is a weighted average of the high and low sales prices on the nearest trade dates before and after the date of death. The average is weighted inversely in relation to the number of days separating the sales dates and the date of death.

TYPICAL MISCONCEPTION

The basis of inherited property is the FMV of the property on the decedent's date of death, which could be higher or lower than the decedent's basis. This change is referred to as a step-up or a step-down in basis. Many taxpayers hear so much about step-up that they forget that a step-down also may occur.

ETHICAL POINT

Valuation of interests in closely held corporations and real estate is an area where a CPA or attorney may need to engage a qualified appraiser. Because appraisals are subjective, two appraisers may arrive at different values. Using the highest appraisal may mean additional estate taxes, but it will provide a greater step-up in basis. Using too low an appraisal may subject the estate to undervaluation penalties (see page C13-36).

EXAMPLE C13-6 ▶ Juan, who dies on November 15, owns 100 shares of Jet Corporation stock. Jet stock, traded on the New York Stock Exchange, traded at a high of $120 and a low of $114 on November 15. On Juan's estate tax return, the stock is valued at $117 per share, the average of $120 and $114. The total value of the block of Jet stock is $11,700 (100 × $117). ◀

EXAMPLE C13-7 ▶ Susan, who dies on May 7, owns 100 shares of Top Corporation stock, traded on the New York Stock Exchange. No sales of Top stock occur on May 7. The sales occurring closest to May 7 take place two business days before May 7 and three business days after May 7. On the earlier date, the stock trades at a high of $500 and a low of $490, with an average of $495. On the later date, the high is $492 and the low is $490, for an average of $491. The date-of-death per-share valuation of the stock is computed under the inverse weighted average approach, as follows:

$$\frac{[3 \times \$495] + [2 \times \$491]}{5} = \$493.40$$

The total value of the block of Top stock is $49,340 (100 × $493.40). ◀

In certain circumstances, the decedent may own such a large block of stock that the price at which the stock trades in the market may not represent the FMV per share for the decedent's number of shares. In such circumstances, Treasury Regulations allow a departure from the traditional valuation rule for stocks. These regulations, referred to as the blockage regulations, state that

---

[4] Reg. Sec. 20.2031-1(b).

[5] Reg. Sec. 20.2031-2(b).

In certain exceptional cases, the size of the block of stock to be valued in relation to the number of shares changing hands in sales may be relevant in determining whether selling prices reflect the fair market value of the block of stock to be valued. If the executor can show that the block of stock to be valued is so large in relation to the actual sales on the existing market that it could not be liquidated in a reasonable time without depressing the market, the price at which the block could be sold as such outside the usual market, as through an underwriter, may be a more accurate indication of value than market quotations.[6]

INTERESTS IN FIRMS WHOSE STOCK IS NOT PUBLICLY TRADED.   Often, the decedent owns stock in a firm whose shares are not publicly traded. Treasury Regulations do not specifically address the valuation rules for this type of an interest. However, detailed guidelines about relevant factors, including book value and earning capacity, are found in Rev. Rul. 59-60.[7] If the stock is a minority interest in a closely held firm, the courts often grant a discount for the minority interest.

REAL ESTATE.   Perhaps surprisingly, Treasury Regulations do not specifically address the valuation approach for real estate. Thus, the general valuation principles concerning a price that would be acceptable to a willing buyer and a willing seller must be implemented without the benefit of more specific guidance. Appraisal literature discusses three techniques for valuing real property: comparable sales, reproduction cost, and capitalization of earnings.[8] Unfortunately, it may be difficult to locate a comparable real estate sale. The reproduction cost, of course, is not applicable to valuing land. Capitalization of earnings often is used in valuing commercial real property. At times, an appraiser may use all three approaches.

ANNUITIES, INTERESTS FOR LIFE OR A TERM OF YEARS, REVERSIONS, REMAINDERS.   Actuarial tables are used to value annuities, interests for life or a term of years, reversions, and remainders included in the gross estate.[9] The same tables apply for both estate and gift tax purposes. (See Chapter C12 for a discussion of the use of these tables.) The following example illustrates a situation when the actuarial tables must be used to value an inclusion in the decedent's estate.

EXAMPLE C13-8 ▶ Tony gives property to a trust with a bank named as trustee and his cousin named to receive all of the trust income for the next 15 years (i.e., a term certain interest). At the end of the fifteenth year, the property reverts to Tony or his estate. Tony dies exactly four years after creating the trust, and the trust property is valued at $100,000 at Tony's death. At Tony's death, the trust has 11 years to continue until the property reverts to Tony's estate. The inclusion in Tony's estate is the value of a reversionary interest following a term certain interest with 11 remaining years. If 10% is the applicable rate, the reversionary interest is valued at $35,049 (0.350494 × $100,000) from Table B of the actuarial tables included in Appendix H. ◀

ALTERNATE VALUATION DATE

Section 2032 authorizes the executor to elect to value all property included in the gross estate at its FMV on the alternate valuation date. Congress enacted this provision in response to the stock market crash of 1929 to make sure that an entire estate could not be confiscated for taxes because of a sudden, substantial drop in values.

In general, the **alternate valuation date** is six months after the date of death. However, if the property is distributed, sold, exchanged, or otherwise disposed of within six months of the date of death, the alternate valuation date is the date of sale or other disposition.

EXAMPLE C13-9 ▶ Ron dies on March 3. Ron's estate includes two items: stock and land. The estate still owns the stock on September 3, but the executor sold the land on August 20. If Ron's executor elects the alternate valuation date, the stock is valued as of September 3. The land, however, is valued as

---

[6] Reg. Sec. 20.2031-2(e). As examples of cases dealing with the blockage discount, see *Horace Havemeyer v. U.S.*, 33 AFTR 1069, 45-1 USTC ¶10,194 (Ct. Cls., 1945); *Estate of Charles M. Prell*, 48 T.C. 67 (1967); and *Estate of David Smith*, 57 T.C. 650 (1972). The *Smith* case extended the blockage concept to large holdings of works of art.
[7] 1959-1 C.B. 237.

[8] For a discussion of techniques for appraising real estate, see The Appraisal Institute, *The Appraisal of Real Estate*, 11th ed. (Arlington Heights, IL: The Appraisal Institute, 1996).
[9] Section 7520 provides that the interest rate potentially changes every month. Regulation Sec. 20.7520-1(a)(2) provides these tables. An excerpt from these tables is included in Appendix H.

of August 20 because it is disposed of before the end of the six-month period. Of course, the value of land generally would change very little, if any, between August 20 and September 3.

◀

If the executor elects the alternate valuation date, generally any changes in value that occur *solely* because of a "mere lapse of time" must be ignored in determining the property's value.[10] In a limited number of situations, one must concentrate on the meaning of the phrase "the mere passage of time." For example, if the executor elects the alternate valuation date to value a patent, he or she must ignore any change in value attributable to the fact that the patent's remaining life is six months shorter on the alternate valuation date than it was on the date of death. Changes in value resulting from the marketing of a competing patented product are relevant.

The alternate valuation date election can be made only if it decreases the value of the gross estate *and* the estate tax liability (after reduction for credits).[11] As a result of this provision, electing the alternate valuation date cannot produce a higher step-up in basis. Congress enacted this strict rule because the alternate valuation date formerly offered a substantial tax planning advantage in situations where, because of the unlimited marital deduction, no estate tax was owed. If the property appreciated between the date of death and the alternate valuation date, the recipient could receive an increased basis if the executor elected the alternate valuation date.[12] With the unlimited marital deduction, the estate could achieve an additional step-up in basis without increasing the estate tax liability.

STOP & THINK

Question: Joan died on April 1. Her estate consisted of three assets: an apartment building valued at $1.2 million on April 1, stock valued at $1.7 million on April 1, and $400,000 of cash. On October 1, the values were as follows: apartment building—$1.5 million, stock—$1.1 million, and cash of $400,000. Joan willed all her property to her son, who anticipates owning the property for a long time. The deductions for Joan's estate are negligible. Is there an estate tax benefit in electing the alternate valuation date? Is there an income tax benefit in electing the alternate valuation date?

Solution: An estate tax benefit results from using the alternate valuation date. The estate tax liability would be lower because the taxable estate would be $300,000 smaller if the alternate valuation date value ($3 million minus deductions) were used instead of the date of death value ($3.3 million minus deductions). Some income tax benefit also results from using the alternate valuation date. By using the alternate valuation date value, the tax basis for calculating cost recovery on the apartment building is $300,000 higher, ignoring any allocation of value to the land. However, a related detriment occurs because the basis of the stock is $600,000 less with the alternate valuation date. If it is anticipated that the stock will be sold in the near future, the $600,000 capital loss that would be available by using the date of death value might permit Joan's son to sell a number of highly-appreciated assets and offset a very large capital gain with the $600,000 capital loss.

THE GROSS ESTATE: INCLUSIONS

OBJECTIVE 3

Determine which interests are includible in the gross estate

As Figure C13-1 illustrates, the process of calculating the decedent's estate tax liability begins with determining the components of the gross estate. The **gross estate** is analogous to gross income. Once the components of the gross estate have been identified, they must be valued. As previously mentioned, the gross estate encompasses a much wider array of items than merely those to which the decedent held title at death. For example, under certain statutory provisions, referred to as the *transferor sections*, the gross estate includes

---

[10] Reg. Sec. 20.2032-1(f).
[11] Sec. 2032(c).

[12] Sec. 1014(a).

items previously transferred by the decedent. For decedents other than nonresident aliens, the fact that property is located in a foreign country does not preclude it from being included in the gross estate. Table C13-1 provides an overview of the inclusions in the gross estate.

COMPARISON OF GROSS ESTATE WITH PROBATE ESTATE

The gross estate is a federal tax law concept, and the probate estate is a state law concept. To oversimplify, the **probate estate** can be defined as encompassing property that passes subject to the will (or under an intestacy statute) and is subject to court administration. Often, a decedent's gross estate is substantially larger than his or her probate estate. For example, suppose that at the time of death, a decedent owns a life insurance policy on his own life with his daughter as the beneficiary. The policy is not a part of the decedent's probate estate because the policy proceeds are payable directly to the daughter, but it is included in the gross estate.

 STOP & THINK

Question: Karl died recently, and Karl's executor has included the following properties in Karl's gross estate: life insurance payable to the beneficiary, Karl's wife; savings account solely in Karl's name; land titled in the names of Karl and his son as joint tenants with right of survivorship; and a trust created under the will of Karl's mother. Karl had an income interest in the trust for his lifetime and complete power to designate the owners of the property on his death. With the exception of the trust assets (willed to his children), Karl's will leaves all his property to his beloved cousin, Karla. Which assets pass under the terms of Karl's will? Which assets will Karla receive?

Solution: This scenario illustrates the difference between the property included in a decedent's gross estate and in the probate estate. Karl's gross estate is larger than his probate estate. Only two assets included in his gross estate—the savings account and the trust property—pass under the terms of Karl's will. Karla will receive only the savings account. The life insurance passes to the named beneficiary, the spouse, and the land passes to the surviving joint tenant, the son.

▼ **TABLE C13-1**
Inclusions in the Gross Estate

IRC Section	Type of Property or Transaction Included
2033	Property in which the decedent had an interest
2035	Gift taxes on property given away within three years of death *plus* certain property (primarily life insurance) given away within three years of death
2036	Property that the decedent transferred during life but in which the decedent retained economic benefits or the power to control enjoyment
2037	Property that the decedent transferred during life but for which the decedent has too large a reversionary interest
2038	Property that the decedent transferred during life but over which the decedent held the power to alter, amend, revoke, or terminate an interest
2039	Annuities
2040	Jointly owned property
2041	Property over which the decedent possessed a general power of appointment
2042	Life insurance on the decedent's life
2044	QTIP trust for which a marital deduction was claimed by the decedent's spouse

PROPERTY IN WHICH THE DECEDENT HAD AN INTEREST

Section 2033, sometimes called the *generic section,* provides that the gross estate includes the value of all property the decedent beneficially owned at the time of death. Its broad language taxes such items as a personal residence, an automobile, stocks, and any other asset titled in the decedent's name. Because the rule refers to beneficial ownership, however, its scope extends beyond assets to which the decedent held title. For example, such items as remainder interests also are included in the gross estate.

EXAMPLE C13-10 ▶
At the time of his death, the following assets are in Raj's name: personal residence, mountain cabin, Zero Corporation stock, checking account, and savings account. Raj beneficially owns each of these items when he dies. Under Sec. 2033, each item is included in Raj's gross estate. ◀

EXAMPLE C13-11 ▶
Ken's will named Ann to receive trust income for life and Raj or Raj's estate to receive the trust remainder upon Ann's death. Raj's gross estate, therefore, includes the value of the remainder interest if Raj predeceases Ann because Raj's will controls the passage of the remainder interest. The transfer is associated with Raj's death, and, hence, is subject to the estate tax. ◀

DOWER OR CURTESY RIGHTS

Certain state laws provide wealth protection to surviving spouses through **dower** or **curtesy** rights.

▶ Dower is a widow's interest in her deceased husband's property.

▶ Curtesy is a widower's interest in his deceased wife's property.

ADDITIONAL COMMENT

Any property that passes outright to the decedent's spouse, due to dower or curtesy rights under state law, is eligible for the marital deduction and will not increase the unified tax base.

Dower or curtesy rights entitle the surviving spouse to a certain portion of the decedent spouse's estate, even though the decedent may have willed a smaller portion to the spouse. Because the decedent spouse does not have complete control over the portion of his or her estate that is subject to dower or curtesy rights, some might argue that the portion of the estate that the surviving spouse is entitled to receive is excluded from the gross estate. Thus, Congress made it crystal clear that the decedent's gross estate is not reduced for the value of the property in which the surviving spouse has a dower or curtesy interest or some other statutory interest.[13]

EXAMPLE C13-12 ▶

SELF-STUDY QUESTION

When Dorothy died on April 10, she owned Z Corporation bonds, which paid interest on April 1 and October 1, and stock in X and Y Corporations. X Corporation had declared a dividend on March 15 payable to stockholders of record on April 1. Y Corporation had declared a dividend on March 31 payable to stockholders of record on April 15. Dorothy's estate received the interest and dividends on the payment dates. Should any of the interest or dividends be included in Dorothy's gross estate?

ANSWER

The X Corporation dividend must be included because the date of record preceded Dorothy's death. The Y Corporation dividend will not be included because the date of record was after her death. The Z Corporation bond interest that must be included is the interest that accrued between the April 1 payment date and the April 10 date of death.

The laws of a certain state provide that widows are entitled to receive one-third of their deceased husband's property. The husband's gross estate does not exclude his widow's dower rights (one-third interest) in his property. ◀

TRANSFEROR PROVISIONS

Sections 2035 through 2038 are called the *transferor provisions.* They apply if the decedent made a transfer while alive of a type specified in the IRC section in question, *and* the decedent did not receive adequate consideration in money or money's worth for the transferred interest. If one of the transferor provisions applies, the gross estate includes the transferred property at its date-of-death or alternate valuation date value.

GIFTS MADE WITHIN THREE YEARS OF DEATH. Section 2035(a) specifies the circumstances in which a gift that a decedent makes within three years of death triggers an inclusion in the gross estate. The scope of this provision, which is relatively narrow, encompasses the following two types of transfers made by the donor-decedent within three years before death:

▶ A life insurance policy on the decedent's life that would have been taxed under Sec. 2042 (life insurance proceeds received by the executor or for the benefit of the estate) had the policy not been given away, or

▶ An interest in property that would have been taxed under Sec. 2036 (transfers with a retained life estate), Sec. 2037 (transfers taking effect at death), or Sec. 2038 (revocable transfers) had it not been transferred.

---

[13] Sec. 2034.

Of these situations, the most common involves the insured's gifting a life insurance policy on his or her own life and dying within three years of the transfer. With new insurance policies, the potential for an inclusion can be avoided if the decedent never owns the new policy. In other words, instead of the insured purchasing a new policy and then giving it to a transferee as owner, the other party should buy the new policy. A common planning technique involves a transfer of cash by an individual to a trust, and the trust (a life insurance trust) using the cash to purchase an insurance policy on the transferor's life.

EXAMPLE C13-13 ▶ On April 1, 2003, Roy transferred to Sally ownership of a $400,000 life insurance policy on his own life purchased in 1996. Sally is the policy's beneficiary. Roy dies on February 3, 2006. Because Roy dies within three years of giving away the policy, the policy is included in Roy's gross estate. The estate tax value of the policy is its $400,000 face value. If Roy had lived until at least April 2, 2006, the policy transfer would have fallen outside the three-year rule, and the policy would not have been included in Roy's gross estate. ◀

EXAMPLE C13-14 ▶ Roy made a gift of stock to Troy on May 1, 2005. Roy dies on February 3, 2006. The stock was worth $80,000 on the gift date and is worth $125,000 at the time of Roy's death. The gifted property is not included in Roy's gross estate because it is not life insurance on Roy's life, nor is it property that would have been taxed in Roy's estate under Secs. 2036 through 2038 had he kept such property. ◀

GROSS-UP RULE.   The donor-decedent's gross estate is increased by any gift tax that he or she, or his or her estate pays on any gift the decedent or his or her spouse makes during the three-year period ending with the decedent's death.[14] This provision, known as the gross-up rule, applies to the gift tax triggered by a gift of any type of property during the three-year look-back period.

The purpose of the gross-up rule is to foreclose the opportunity that existed under pre-1977 law to reduce one's gross estate (and thereby one's taxable estate) by removing the gift tax on "deathbed" gifts from the gross estate. Because the donor's estate received a credit for some or all of the gift tax paid, under the pre-1977 rules, a person on his or her deathbed in effect could prepay a portion of his or her estate tax and at the same time reduce his or her gross estate by the amount of the gift tax.

The gross-up rule, as illustrated in the two examples below, reinstates the estate to the position it would have been in had no gift tax liability been incurred.

EXAMPLE C13-15 ▶ In late 2003, Cheron made a $2 million taxable gift of stock and paid a gift tax of $435,000 ($780,800 gross tax − $345,800 unified credit). Cheron dies in early 2006. Cheron's gross estate does not include the stock, but it does include the $435,000 gift tax paid because she made the gift within three years of her death. ◀

EXAMPLE C13-16 ▶ In late 2003, Hal gave Jody stock having a $4,022,000 FMV, and he and Wanda, his wife, elected gift splitting. Each is deemed to have made a $2 million [($4,022,000 ÷ 2) − $11,000 annual exclusion] taxable gift, and each paid $435,000 ($780,800 gross tax − $345,800 unified credit) of gift tax. Wanda dies in early 2006. Wanda's gross estate includes the $435,000 in gift tax she paid on the portion of her husband's gift that she is deemed to have made within three years of her death. Her cash balance had declined because of paying the gift tax, and the gross-up for the tax reinstates her estate to the position it would have been in had she made no taxable gifts. ◀

TRANSFERS WITH RETAINED LIFE ESTATE.   Section 2036, although titled "Transfers with Retained Life Estate," extends beyond taxing solely lifetime transfers made by the decedent in which he or she retained a life estate (the right to income or use for life). The two primary types of transfers taxed under Sec. 2036 are those for which the decedent

▶ Kept possession or enjoyment of the property or the right to its income

▶ Retained the power to designate the person who is to possess or enjoy the property or to receive its income

---

[14] Sec. 2035(b).

Thus, Sec. 2036 applies when the transferor kept the income or enjoyment *or* the right to control other individuals' income or enjoyment.

The direct or indirect retention of voting rights in stock of a controlled corporation that the decedent transferred also can cause the gifted stock to be included in the transferor's gross estate.[15] A controlled corporation is one in which the decedent owned (directly, indirectly, or constructively), or had the right to vote, stock that possessed at least 20% of the voting power.[16]

The retention of income, control, or voting rights for one of the three retention periods listed below causes the transferred property to be included in the transferor's gross estate. The three periods are

▶ The transferor's lifetime

▶ A period that cannot be determined without referring to the transferor's death (e.g., the transferor retained the right to quarterly payments of income, but payments ceased with the last quarterly payment before the transferor's death)

▶ A period that does not end, in fact, before the transferor's death

An implied argument or understanding is sufficient to trigger inclusion. For example, if a mother gives a residence to her daughter and continues to occupy the residence alone and rent-free, the residence probably will be included in the mother's gross estate under the argument that the parties had an implied understanding allowing the mother to occupy the residence for life.

If Sec. 2036 applies to a transfer and if the decedent's retention of enjoyment or control extends to all the transferred property, 100% of the transferred property's value is included in the transferor's gross estate.[17] However, if the transferor keeps the right to only one-third of the income for life and retains no control over the remaining two-thirds, his estate includes just one-third of the property's date-of-death value. The following three examples illustrate some of the transactions that cause Sec. 2036 to apply.

EXAMPLE C13-17 ▶ In 1998, David (age 30) transferred an office building to Ellen but retained the right to collect all the income from the building for life. David dies in 2006. Because David retained the income right for life, the Sec. 2036 inclusion applies. The amount included is 100% of the building's date-of-death value. ◀

EXAMPLE C13-18 ▶ Assume the same facts as in Example C13-17 except that David retains the right to income for only 15 years. David dies five years after the transfer; therefore, David has the right to receive the income for the remaining ten-year period. Because the retention period does not *in fact* end before David's death, his gross estate includes 100% of the property's date-of-death value. ◀

EXAMPLE C13-19 ▶ Tracy creates a trust with a bank as trustee and names Alice, Brad, and Carol to receive the trust income for their joint lives and Dick to receive the remainder upon the death of the first among Alice, Brad, or Carol to die. Tracy reserves the right to designate the portion of the income to be paid to each income beneficiary each year. Only the transfer to Dick was a completed transfer and subject to gift taxes. Tracy predeceases the other parties. Because her control over the flow of income does not end before Tracy's death, the date-of-death value of the trust assets is included in Tracy's gross estate even though a portion of the transfer was subject to gift taxes. If Tracy had instead "cut the string" and not kept control over the income flow, she could have removed the trust property from her estate. ◀

SELF-STUDY QUESTION

Refer to Example C13-19. Assume the same facts except that the trustee is directed to distribute its annual income equally to Alice, Brad, and Carol for their joint lives. Also assume that Tracy names Dick the remainderman. Will the value of the trust be included in Tracy's gross estate?

ANSWER

No, because Tracy retained no power to control the enjoyment of the property.

REVERSIONARY INTERESTS. If the chance exists that the property will pass back to the transferor under the terms of the transfer, the transferor has a **reversionary interest**. Under Sec. 2037, the transferor's gross estate includes earlier transferred property if the decedent stipulates that another person must survive him or her to own the property and the value of the decedent's reversionary interest exceeds 5% of the value of the transferred property. Actuarial techniques are used to value the reversionary interest.[18] Section 2037 does not apply if the value of the reversionary interest does not exceed the 5% *de minimis* amount.

---

[15] Sec. 2036(b)(1).

[16] Sec. 2036(b)(2).

[17] Reg. Sec. 20.2036-1(a).

[18] The **reversionary interest** is the interest that will return to the transferor. Often, it will return only if certain contingencies occur. The value of Beth's

reversionary interest in Example C13-20 is a function of the present value of the interest Beth would receive after the deaths of Tammy and Doug, valued as from actuarial tables (see Appendix H), and coupled with the probability that Tammy and Doug would die before Beth.

EXAMPLE C13-20 ▶ Beth transfers an asset to Tammy for life and then to Doug for life. The asset is to revert to Beth, if Beth is still alive, upon the death of either Tammy or Doug, whoever dies second. If Beth is not alive upon the death of the survivor of Tammy and Doug, the asset is to pass to Don or to a charitable organization if Don is not alive. Thus, Don must live longer than Beth to receive the property. The property is included in Beth's estate if the value of Beth's reversionary interest exceeds 5% of the property's value. The amount included is not the value of Beth's reversionary interest, but rather the date-of-death value of the asset less the value of Tammy's and Doug's intervening life estates. ◀

ADDITIONAL COMMENT

Sections 2036 through 2038 draw back into the gross estate certain previously transferred property and include it at its FMV on the date of the decedent's death. For income tax purposes, if the property has appreciated in value, donees will obtain a stepped-up basis rather than a carryover gift tax basis.

REVOCABLE TRANSFERS. Section 2038 covers the rules for revocable transfers (i.e., revocable trusts). However, this provision also taxes all transfers over which the decedent has, at the time of his or her death, the power to change the enjoyment by altering, amending, revoking, or terminating an interest. Revocable trusts, sometimes called living trusts, are popular arrangements from a non-tax standpoint because assets held by a revocable trust pass outside of probate. Advantages of avoiding probate include lower probate costs and easier administration for real property located in a state that is not the decedent's state of domicile. In addition, unlike a will, a revocable trust is not a matter of public record.

Section 2038 can apply even though the decedent does not originally retain powers over the property. The crucial factor is that the transferor possesses the powers at the time of death regardless of whether the transferor retained such powers originally. The estate must include only the value of the interest that is subject to the decedent's power to change. Sections 2038 and 2036 overlap greatly, and if one amount is taxable under one section and a different amount is taxable under the other section, the gross estate includes the larger amount. Two types of transfers taxed by Sec. 2038 are illustrated in the following examples.

EXAMPLE C13-21 ▶ Joe funds a revocable trust and names his son to receive the income for life and his grandson to receive the property upon the son's death. Because the trust is revocable, Joe may change the terms of the trust or take back the trust property during his lifetime. Joe's power to revoke the transfer extends to the entire trust. Thus, Joe's gross estate includes the date-of-death value of the entire trust. ◀

EXAMPLE C13-22 ▶ Vicki creates a trust and names Gina to receive the income for life and Matt to receive the remainder. Vicki, however, retains the right to substitute Liz (for Matt) as remainderman. When Vicki dies, she has the authority to change the enjoyment of the remainder. Thus, the value of the trust's remainder interest is includible in Vicki's estate. ◀

ANNUITIES AND OTHER RETIREMENT BENEFITS

SELF-STUDY QUESTION

Reggie purchased an annuity and elected to collect benefits for 15 years. If Reggie dies before the end of the 15-year term of the annuity, his estate will be entitled to the remaining payments. Assume Reggie died after receiving nine payments. Will the value of the remaining six payments be included in Reggie's estate?

ANSWER

Yes. Section 2039 requires that the cost of a comparable contract of six payments be included in his gross estate.

Section 2039 explicitly addresses the estate tax treatment of annuities. Even if this section had not been enacted, some annuities probably would have been taxable under the general language of Sec. 2033 because the decedent would have been viewed as having an interest in the property. For an annuity to be included in the gross estate, it must involve payments made under a contract or an agreement. In addition, the decedent must be receiving such payments at the time of his or her death or must have the right to collect such payments alone or with another person. If the annuity simply ceases with the death of the decedent in question, nothing is to be received by another party and nothing is included in the gross estate. For the payments to be included in the decedent's estate, they must be paid for the decedent's life, a period that may not be determined without referring to the decedent's date of death or for a period that does not actually end before the decedent's death.

ANNUITIES NOT RELATED TO EMPLOYMENT. The purchase of an annuity designed to pay benefits to the purchaser and then to a named survivor upon the purchaser's death, or to both parties simultaneously and then to the survivor, is a form of wealth shifting. The other party receives wealth that originates with the purchaser. This type of transfer is different from most other wealth transfers because it involves a series of annuity payments instead of a transfer of a tangible property.

The amount included in the gross estate with respect to annuities or other retirement benefits is a fraction (described below) of the value of the annuity or lump-sum payment to be received by the surviving beneficiary. Annuities are valued at the cost of a comparable contract.[19] To determine the inclusion in the gross estate, this cost is multiplied by a fraction that represents the portion of the purchase price the decedent contributed.

EXAMPLE C13-23 ▶

Twelve years ago, Jim purchased a joint and survivor annuity and selected benefits to be paid to himself and his son concurrently and then to the survivor for life. Jim and his son started collecting payments four years ago. Jim dies in the current year, survived by his son. At the time of Jim's death, the cost of a comparable contract providing the same benefits to the son is $180,000. Because Jim provided all the consideration to purchase the annuity, his gross estate includes 100% of the $180,000 cost of a comparable contract. This annuity arrangement represents a shifting of wealth from Jim to his son upon Jim's death. ◀

SELF-STUDY QUESTION

On his retirement at age 65, Winslow elected to take a joint and survivor annuity from his qualified pension plan. The plan provided Winslow and his wife with a monthly pension of $2,500 until the death of the survivor. Winslow died seven years later. What amount (if any) must be included in Winslow's gross estate if his wife survives?

EXAMPLE C13-24 ▶

ANSWER

The gross estate includes the cost of a comparable contract providing $2,500 a month for the rest of the spouse's life. The spouse's age would affect the cost.

EMPLOYMENT-RELATED RETIREMENT BENEFITS. Recall that, to determine the amount of an annuity includible in the decedent's gross estate, the cost of a comparable contract is multiplied by a fraction representing the portion of the purchase price contributed by the decedent. Section 2039(b) states that contributions from the decedent's employer (or former employer) are treated as contributions made by the decedent, provided such payments are made as a result of the employment relationship. Thus, 100% of the benefits from an employment-related annuity are included in the gross estate.

Pat was employed by Wheel Corporation at the time of his death. Wheel Corporation maintains a qualified retirement plan to which it makes 60% of the contributions and its employees contribute 40%. Pat's spouse is to receive an annuity valued at $350,000 from the retirement plan. Because the employer's contributions are considered to have been made by the employee, Pat is deemed to have provided all the consideration for the retirement benefits. Consequently, Pat's gross estate includes 100% of the annuity's $350,000 date-of-death value. ◀

JOINTLY OWNED PROPERTY

Section 2040 addresses the estate tax treatment of jointly owned property (i.e., property owned in a joint tenancy with right of survivorship or tenancy by the entirety arrangement).[20] An important characteristic of this form of ownership is that, upon the death of one joint owner, the decedent's interest passes automatically (by right of survivorship) to the surviving joint owner(s). Thus, the property is not part of the probate estate and does not pass under the will. Section 2040 contains two sets of rules, one for property jointly owned by spouses and one for all other jointly owned properties.

OWNERSHIP INVOLVING PERSONS OTHER THAN SPOUSES. When persons other than spouses or persons in addition to spouses own property as joint owners, the amount includible is determined by the consideration-furnished test.[21] Under this test, property is included in a joint owner's gross estate in accordance with the portion of the consideration he or she furnished to acquire the property. Obviously, this portion can range between 0% and 100%.

---

[19] Reg. Sec. 20.2031-8(a).

[20] Both joint tenancies with right of survivorship and tenancies by the entirety have the feature of survivorship. When one joint owner dies, his or her interest passes by right of survivorship to the remaining joint owner(s). Only spouses may use the tenancy by the entirety arrangement, whereas any persons may own as joint tenants with right of survivorship. A joint tenancy with right of survivorship may be severed by the action of any joint owner, whereas a tenancy by the entirety arrangement continues unless severed by the joint action of both joint owners.

The following definitions are from Henry Campbell Black, *Black's Law Dictionary*, Rev. 6th ed., Ed. by Joseph R. Nolan and Jacqueline M. Nolan-Haley (St. Paul, MN: West Publishing Co., 1990), p. 1465.

Joint tenancy with right of survivorship: The primary incident of joint tenancy is survivorship, by which the entire tenancy on the decease of any joint tenant remains to the survivors, and at length to the last survivor.

Tenancy by the entirety: A tenancy which is created between husband and wife and by which together they hold title to the whole with right of survivorship so that upon death of either, other takes whole to exclusion of deceased heirs. It is essentially a "joint tenancy" modified by the common-law theory that husband and wife are one person, and survivorship is the predominant and distinguishing feature of each. Neither party can alienate or encumber the property without the consent of the other.

[21] Sec. 2040(a).

EXAMPLE C13-25 ▶

Seven years ago, Fred and Jack provided $10,000 and $30,000 of consideration, respectively, to purchase real property titled in the names of Fred and Jack as joint tenants with right of survivorship. Fred dies in the current year and is survived by Jack. The real property is valued at $60,000. Fred's gross estate includes $15,000 (0.25 × $60,000) because Fred furnished 25% of the consideration to acquire the property. If Jack instead predeceases Fred, his estate would include $45,000 (0.75 × $60,000). ◀

If part of the consideration furnished by one joint tenant is originally received gratuitously from another joint tenant, the consideration is attributable to the joint tenant who made the gift. If all joint owners acquire their interests by gift, devise, bequest, or inheritance, the decedent joint owner's estate includes his or her proportionate share of the date-of-death value of the jointly owned property.

EXAMPLE C13-26 ▶

Ray gives stock valued at $50,000 to Sam. Three years later Sam transfers this stock (now valued at $60,000) as partial consideration to acquire real property costing $120,000. Ray furnishes the remaining $60,000 of consideration. The real property is titled in the names of Ray and Sam as joint tenants with right of survivorship. Because Sam received the asset that he used for consideration as a gift from Ray (the other joint tenant), Sam is treated as having furnished no consideration. If Sam dies before Ray, Sam's estate will include none of the real property's value. If Ray predeceases Sam, however, Ray's estate will include the entire date-of-death value. ◀

OWNERSHIP INVOLVING ONLY SPOUSES. If spouses are the only joint owners, the property is classified as a **qualified joint interest**. Section 2040(b)(1) provides that, in the case of qualified joint interests, the decedent's gross estate includes one-half the value of the qualified joint interest. The 50% inclusion rule applies automatically regardless of the relative amount of consideration provided by either spouse.

EXAMPLE C13-27 ▶

Wilma provides all the consideration to purchase stock costing $80,000. She registers the stock in her name and her husband's name as joint tenants with right of survivorship. The estate of the first spouse to die, regardless of which spouse it is, will include 50% of the value of the jointly owned stock. Upon the second spouse's death, all the property will be included in that spouse's gross estate because it no longer will be jointly owned property. ◀

GENERAL POWERS OF APPOINTMENT

Section 2041 requires inclusion in the gross estate of certain property interests that the decedent never owns in a legal sense. Inclusion occurs because the decedent had the power to designate who eventually would own the property. The authority to designate the owner—a significant power—is called a power of appointment. Powers of appointment can be general or special (i.e., more restricted).

Only a general power of appointment results in an addition to the gross estate. If a general power was created before October 22, 1942, however, no inclusion occurs unless the decedent exercised the power. For a post-1942 general power of appointment, inclusion occurs regardless of whether the power is exercised. A general power of appointment exists if the holder can exercise the power in favor of him- or herself, his or her estate or creditors, *or* the creditors of his or her estate. Being exercisable in favor of the decedent's estate means there is no restriction on the powerholder's ability to specify the person(s) to receive the property. The power may be exercisable during the decedent's life, by his or her will, or both.

Sometimes a powerholder can exercise a power for only specified purposes and/or in favor of only certain persons. Appointment powers that are governed by an ascertainable standard are free of estate tax consequences because they may be exercised solely for purposes of the decedent's health, support, maintenance, or education.

EXAMPLE C13-28 ▶

When Kathy died in 1991, her will created a trust from which Doris is to receive the income for life. In addition, Doris is granted the power to designate by will the person or persons to receive the trust's assets. Doris has a testamentary general power of appointment. The trust's assets are included in Doris's gross estate regardless of whether Doris exercises the power. If Kathy had instead died in 1940, Doris would have had a pre-1942 power of appointment. Such powers are taxed only if exercised. ◀

EXAMPLE C13-29 ▶ Assume the same facts as in Example C13-28 except that Kathy's will merely empowers Doris to name which of her descendants shall receive the trust assets. Doris now has only a special power of appointment because she does not have the power to leave the property to whomever she desires (e.g., the power to appoint the property to her estate). Because Doris's power of appointment is only a special power, the value of the trust is not included in Doris's gross estate. ◀

LIFE INSURANCE

TYPICAL MISCONCEPTION

Many taxpayers who own life insurance policies on their own lives mistakenly believe that their estates will not owe estate taxes on the life insurance proceeds if they name someone other than their estate as the beneficiary. Life insurance will be included in the gross estate of the decedent if, at the time of death, the decedent held *any* (one) of the incidents of ownership in the policy.

Section 2042 addresses the estate tax treatment of life insurance policies on the decedent's life. Life insurance policies owned by the decedent on the lives of others are taxed under the general language of Sec. 2033. According to Sec. 2042, a decedent's gross estate includes the value of policies on his or her own life if the proceeds are receivable by the executor or for the benefit of the estate, or if the decedent had any "incidents of ownership" in the policy at the time of death. Treasury Regulations list the following powers as a partial inventory of the incidents of ownership:

▶ To change the beneficiary
▶ To surrender or cancel the policy
▶ To borrow against the policy
▶ To pledge the policy for a loan
▶ To revoke an assignment of the policy[22]

Examples in the regulations pertaining to incidents of ownership involve economic rights over the insurance policies. Judicial decisions also have been important in defining what constitutes incidents of ownership. In some jurisdictions, the phrase has been interpreted to be broader than simply relating to economic powers.[23]

If the decedent could have exercised the incidents of ownership only in conjunction with another party, the policy nevertheless is included in the gross estate. Moreover, it is the legal power to exercise ownership rights, not the practical ability to do so, that leads to an inclusion. The Supreme Court in the *Estate of Marshal L. Noel* emphasized the importance of the decedent-insured's legal powers in a situation where the insured was killed in a plane crash and the policies he owned on his life were on the ground in the possession of his spouse. The Court held that the decedent possessed incidents of ownership and thus the policies were includible in his gross estate.[24]

EXAMPLE C13-30 ▶ Tracy purchased an insurance policy on her life, and several years later she transferred all her incidents of ownership in the policy to her daughter. Seven years after the transfer, Tracy dies. Tracy's niece has always been the policy's beneficiary. The policy is not included in Tracy's gross estate because Tracy did not have any incidents of ownership in the policy at the time of her death, nor is her estate the beneficiary. (Also, she did not give the policy away within three years of death.) ◀

EXAMPLE C13-31 ▶ Assume the same facts as in Example C13-30 except that Tracy's estate instead is the policy's beneficiary. Because Tracy's estate is designated as the beneficiary, the policy is included in her gross estate and valued at its face value. ◀

It is not sufficient to consider only Sec. 2042 in determining whether a life insurance policy on the decedent's life is includible in the gross estate. Recall from the discussion earlier in this chapter that a life insurance policy is includible in a decedent's gross estate if the individual makes a gift of a life insurance policy on his or her own life within three years of dying.[25]

EXAMPLE C13-32 ▶ Two years ago, Peng gave all his incidents of ownership in a life insurance policy on his own life to his son, Phong. The face value of the policy is $400,000. Phong has always been the benefi-

[22] Reg. Sec. 20.2042-1(c)(2).
[23] See, for example, *Estate of James H. Lumpkin, Jr. v. CIR*, 31 AFTR 2d 73-1381, 73-1 USTC ¶12,909 (5th Cir., 1973), wherein the court held that the right to choose how the proceeds were to be paid—in a lump sum or in installments—was an incident of ownership.
[24] *CIR v. Estate of Marshal L. Noel*, 15 AFTR 2d 1397, 65-1 USTC ¶12,311 (USSC, 1965).
[25] The gifted insurance policy is included under Sec. 2035(a)(2).

ciary. Peng dies in the current year. Because Peng died within three years of giving Phong the policy, Peng's gross estate includes the policy. The policy is valued at its $400,000 date-of-death value. The potential problem of making a transfer of a life insurance policy within three years of death could have been avoided had Phong been the original owner of the policy. In that case, Peng would not have made a transfer and need not have been concerned with the three-year rule. ◄

CONSIDERATION OFFSET

Property is included in the gross estate at its FMV on the date of death or alternate valuation date. Section 2043 allows an offset against the amount included in the gross estate for consideration received in certain transactions.[26] This offset is allowed only if the decedent received some, but less than adequate, consideration in connection with an earlier transaction. The gross estate is reduced by an offset for the partial consideration received. The offset is for the actual dollars received, not for the pro rata portion of the cost paid by the decedent. This offset, called the consideration offset, serves the same function as a deduction in that it reduces the taxable estate. If the decedent receives consideration equal to the value of the property transferred, the property in question is not included in the gross estate. No offset is permitted if the property is excluded from the decedent's gross estate.

The consideration offset prevents a double counting of property in the decedent's estate. For example, if an individual makes a transfer that is includible in the gross estate and receives partial consideration in return, the consideration received is part of the gross estate unless it has been consumed. Sections 2035 through 2038 also require the transferred property to be included in the gross estate, even though the transferor does not own it at the date of death.

EXAMPLE C13-33 ▶ Two years ago, Steve transferred a $300,000 life insurance policy on his life to Earl. The policy was worth $75,000 at the time of transfer, but Earl paid only $48,000 for the policy. Steve dies in the current year with the $48,000 still in his savings account. Steve's gross estate includes both the amount in the savings account and the $300,000 face value of the insurance policy. Under Sec. 2043, Steve's gross estate is reduced by the $48,000 consideration received on the transfer of the insurance policy. The insurance policy on Steve's life would be excluded from Steve's estate if Steve survived the transfer by more than three years, and no consideration offset would be permitted because the insurance is not included in the gross estate. ◄

RECIPIENT SPOUSE'S INTEREST IN QTIP TRUST

Recall from Chapter C12 that a gift tax marital deduction is available for transferring qualified terminable interest property (QTIP) to one's spouse. A QTIP interest involves a transfer entitling the recipient spouse to all the income for life. The estate tax rules for QTIP interests are explained on page C13-22. Claiming a marital deduction with respect to QTIP interests is voluntary. If the donor or the executor elects to claim a marital deduction for QTIP interests transferred to the spouse during life or at death, the transferred property generally is included in the recipient spouse's gross estate.[27] A QTIP interest included in the gross estate, like other property included in the gross estate, is valued at its date-of-death or alternate valuation date value.

The gross estate of the surviving spouse excludes the QTIP interest if the transferor spouse does not elect to claim a marital deduction. If the recipient spouse has a life estate, has no general power of appointment, and was not the transferor, no IRC sections other than Sec. 2044 (dealing with QTIPs) include the property in the gross estate.

No inclusion in the gross estate is required for QTIP interests for which a marital deduction is elected if the recipient spouse disposes of all or a portion of his or her income interest during his or her lifetime. However, dispositions of all or a portion of a spouse's income interest in a QTIP are treated under Sec. 2519 as a transfer of all interests in the QTIP other than the qualifying income interest. Thus, such dispositions are subject to the gift tax.

[26] Section 2043 provides a consideration offset for items included in the gross estate under Secs. 2035 through 2038 and Sec. 2041.

[27] Sec. 2044.

EXAMPLE C13-34 ▶ Henry died five years ago. His will created a $2 million QTIP trust for his widow, Wendy, age 75. Henry's executor elected to claim a marital deduction for the QTIP trust. Wendy dies in the current year. By then, the assets in the QTIP trust have appreciated to $2.8 million. Wendy's gross estate includes the QTIP trust, which is valued at $2.8 million. If Henry's executor had not claimed a marital deduction for the QTIP trust, the value of the trust would be excluded from Wendy's estate. If Henry's executor had made a partial QTIP election for 70% of the trust, only 70% of the $2.8 million value would be in Wendy's gross estate. ◀

DEDUCTIONS

OBJECTIVE 4

Identify deductions available for estate tax purposes

As mentioned earlier in this chapter, deductions from the gross estate currently fall into five categories. Three of these categories (debts and funeral and administration expenses, casualty and theft losses, and state death taxes) allow the tax base to reflect the net wealth passed to the decedent's heirs, legatees, or devisees. Two other deduction categories reduce the estate tax base for transfers to the surviving spouse (the marital deduction) or to charitable organizations (the charitable contribution deduction). No deduction is available, however, for the amount of wealth diverted to the federal government in the form of estate taxes. The aggregate amount of the deductions is subtracted from the gross estate amount to determine the taxable estate. Each deduction category is examined below. Table C13-2 provides an overview of the estate tax deductions.

TYPICAL MISCONCEPTION

Many taxpayers are so familiar with the fact that, for income tax purposes, expenses must be paid or accrued to be deductible, they do not recognize that the expenses of administering an estate can be estimated at the time the estate tax return is filed. Estimation is necessary because the administration of the estate can continue long after the estate tax return is filed.

DEBTS AND FUNERAL AND ADMINISTRATION EXPENSES

Section 2053 authorizes deductions for mortgages and other debts owed by the decedent, as well as for the decedent's funeral and administration expenses. Mortgages and all other debts of the decedent are deductible provided they represent bona fide contracts for an adequate and full consideration in money or money's worth. Even personal debts relating to an expenditure for which no income tax deduction would be allowable are deductible. Interest, state and local taxes, and trade or business expenses accrued at the date of death are deductible on both the estate tax return (as a debt of the decedent) and on the estate's income tax return (as an expense known as a deduction in respect of a decedent) when they are paid. (See Chapter C14 for a discussion of the income tax implications.)

Examples of administration expenses include executor's commissions, attorneys' fees, court costs, accountants' fees, appraisers' fees, and expenses of preserving and distributing the estate. The executor must decide whether to deduct administration expenses on the estate tax return (Form 706) or the estate's income tax return (Form 1041). Such expenses cannot be deducted twice, although some may be deducted on the estate tax return and others on the estate's income tax return.

▼ **TABLE C13-2**
Estate Tax Deductions

IRC Section	Type of Deduction
2053	Funeral and administration expenses[a] and debts
2054	Casualty and theft losses[a]
2055	Charitable contributions[b]
2056	Marital deduction[b]
2058	State death taxes[c]

[a]Deductible on the estate tax return or on the estate's income tax return.
[b]No limit on deductible amount.
[c]Available (instead of a credit) after 2004.

An estate that owes no estate tax (e.g., because of the unlimited marital deduction or the unified credit) should deduct administration expenses on its income tax return because no tax savings will result from a deduction on the estate tax return. If an estate owes estate taxes, its marginal estate tax rate will be at least 46% because the tax base will exceed the $2 million (in 2006) exemption equivalent. In 2005 and 2006 the highest income tax rate for an estate is 35%. Thus, for taxable estates exceeding $2 million, administration expenses should be deducted on the estate tax return.

Funeral expenses are deductible only on the estate tax return. The estate may deduct any funeral expenses allowable under local law including "[a] reasonable expenditure for a tombstone, monument, or mausoleum, or for a burial lot, either for the decedent or his family, including a reasonable expenditure for its future care."[28] The transportation costs of the person bringing the body to the burial place also are deductible as funeral expenses.

EXAMPLE C13-35 ▶ At Ed's date of death, Ed owes a $75,000 mortgage on his residence, plus $280 of interest accrued thereon, and $320 of personal expenditures charged to a department store charge card. The estate's administration expenses are estimated to be $32,000. His funeral expenses total $12,000. Under Sec. 2053, Ed's estate can deduct $75,600 ($75,000 + $280 + $320) for debts and $12,000 for funeral expenses. The $32,000 of administration expenses are deductible on the estate tax return, on the estate's income tax return for the year in which they are paid, or some on each return. Ed's estate will receive an income tax deduction for the accrued mortgage interest whenever it is paid. ◀

TAX STRATEGY TIP

The executor should elect to deduct any casualty or theft loss, when such loss is allowable, from the estate tax return if the marginal estate tax rate exceeds the marginal income tax rate.

LOSSES

Section 2054 authorizes a deduction for losses incurred from theft or casualty while the estate is being settled. Just as in the context of the income tax, examples of casualties include fires, storms, and earthquakes. Any insurance compensation received affects the amount of the loss. If the alternate valuation date is elected, the loss may not be used to reduce the alternate value and then used again as a loss deduction. As with administration expenses, the executor must decide whether to deduct the loss on the estate tax return or the estate's income tax return. No double deduction is allowed for these losses, and the nondeductible floor applicable for income tax purposes does not exist for estate tax purposes.

EXAMPLE C13-36 ▶ Sam dies on May 3. One of the items included in Sam's gross estate is a mountain cabin valued at $125,000. The uninsured cabin is totally destroyed in a landslide on August 18. If the date-of-death valuation is chosen, the cabin is included in the gross estate at $125,000. The executor must choose between claiming a Sec. 2054 loss deduction on the estate tax return or a Sec. 165 casualty loss deduction on the estate's income tax return. ◀

EXAMPLE C13-37 ▶ Assume the same facts as in Example C13-36 except that Sam's executor elects the alternate valuation date. The cabin is valued at zero when determining the value of the gross estate. No loss deduction is available for the casualty on the estate tax return. The estate cannot claim an income tax deduction for the casualty loss either because the property's adjusted basis in its hands is zero. ◀

CHARITABLE CONTRIBUTION DEDUCTION

Section 2055 authorizes a deduction for transfers to charitable organizations. The rules concerning eligible donee organizations are the same as for gift tax purposes.

Because the estate tax charitable contribution deduction is unlimited, a decedent could eliminate his or her estate tax liability by willing all his or her property (or all property except for an amount equal to the exemption equivalent) to a charitable organization. Similarly, a decedent could eliminate an estate tax liability by willing an amount equal to the exemption equivalent to the children and the rest of the estate to the surviving spouse and a charitable organization (e.g., in equal shares).[29] People who desire to leave some property to a charity at their death should be encouraged to consider giving the property before death, so they can obtain an income tax deduction for the gift and also reduce their gross estate by the amount of the gift.

---

[28] Reg. Sec. 20.2053-2.
[29] Another way the estate could owe no taxes is if all of the property, or all of the property except for the exemption equivalent, is shielded from taxation by the marital deduction.

COMPUTING THE DEDUCTION.   In certain circumstances, computation of the estate tax charitable contribution deduction can be somewhat complicated. Suppose the decedent (a widow) has a $5 million gross estate and no Sec. 2053 or 2054 deductions. The decedent's will specifies that her son is to receive $3 million and a charitable organization is to receive the residue (the rest not explicitly disposed of). Assume that state law specifies that death taxes are payable from the residue. Because $3 million of property passes to the decedent's child, the estate will definitely owe some estate taxes. The charitable organization will receive $2 million, less the estate taxes payable therefrom. The estate tax liability depends on the amount of the charitable contribution deduction, which in turn depends on the amount of the estate tax liability. Simultaneous equations are required to calculate the amount of the charitable contribution deduction.[30]

EXAMPLE C13-38 ▶

Ahmed, a widower, dies with a gross estate of $6 million. Ahmed wills State University $1 million and the residue of his estate to his children. Under state law, death taxes are payable from the residue. In this scenario, Ahmed's estate receives a charitable contribution deduction for $1 million because the estate taxes are charged against the children's share (the residue). ◀

SPLIT-INTEREST TRANSFERS.   If the decedent's will provides for a split-interest transfer (i.e., a transfer of interests to both an individual and a charitable organization), the rules concerning whether a charitable contribution deduction is available are very technical. Basically, the rules are the same as for gift tax purposes.

EXAMPLE C13-39 ▶

Jane dies in the current year with a gross estate of $2.5 million. Under Sec. 2036, Jane's gross estate includes her personal residence, valued at $350,000. She gave City Art Museum a remainder interest in the residence in 1995 but retained the right to live there rent-free for the rest of her life. Upon Jane's death, no other individuals have an interest in the residence. Jane received an income tax deduction in 1995 for the value of the remainder interest and incurred no gift tax liability. Her estate receives a $350,000 charitable contribution deduction.

Her lifetime transfer triggers no added estate tax cost. The residence is included in her gross estate, but the inclusion is a wash because of the estate tax charitable contribution deduction claimed for the value of the residence. ◀

MARITAL DEDUCTION

The fourth category of deductions is the marital deduction for certain property passing to the decedent's surviving spouse.[31] Because the marital deduction is unlimited, the decedent's estate does not owe any federal estate taxes if all the items includible in the gross estate (or all items except an amount equal to the exemption equivalent) pass to the surviving spouse.[32] If the surviving spouse is not a U.S. citizen, however, a marital deduction is not available unless the decedent's property passes to a special trust called a qualified domestic trust.

TAX STRATEGY TIP

The marital deduction defers the estate tax until the death of the surviving spouse and protects against liquidity problems when the first spouse dies. Moreover, the surviving spouse can reduce the overall estate tax through personal consumption and a lifetime gifting program.

The marital deduction provides equal treatment for decedents of common law and community property states. As mentioned in Chapter C12, marital property is treated differently under each type of state law. In community property states, for example, a large portion of the assets acquired after a couple marries constitutes community property (i.e., property owned equally by each spouse). On the other hand, in common law states, one spouse may own the majority of the assets acquired after marriage. Thus, with no marital deduction, the progressive estate tax rates could cause the combined estate tax liability to be higher for a couple living in a noncommunity property state. Nevertheless, a marital deduction is available to decedents who own nothing but community property.

Only certain transfers to the surviving spouse are eligible for the marital deduction. The estate does not receive a marital deduction unless the interest conveyed to the surviving spouse will be subject to either the estate tax in the recipient spouse's estate or to the

---

[30] The simultaneous equation problem generally does not occur if a charity receives a bequest of a specific dollar amount. See Reg. Sec. 20.2055-3 for a discussion of death taxes payable from charitable transfers.
[31] Sec. 2056.
[32] Some states have not adopted an unlimited marital deduction; therefore,

some estates may owe state death taxes even though no federal liability would otherwise exist. Payment of substantial sums to a state as taxes will reduce the amount passing to the spouse as a marital deduction and can cause federal taxes to be owed.

gift tax if transferred while the surviving spouse is alive. In other words, the surviving spouse generally can escape transfer taxation on the transferred property only by consuming it.

The following three tests must be met before an interest qualifies for the marital deduction:

▶ The property must be included in the decedent's gross estate.

▶ The property must pass to the recipient spouse in a qualifying manner.

▶ The interest conveyed must not be a nondeductible terminable interest.

TEST 1: INCLUSION IN THE GROSS ESTATE. No property passing to the surviving spouse is eligible for the marital deduction unless the property is included in the decedent's gross estate. The reason for this rule is obvious: Assets excluded from the gross estate cannot generate a deduction.

EXAMPLE C13-40 ▶ Gail is insured under a life insurance policy for which her husband, Al, is the beneficiary. Gail's sister always had the incidents of ownership in the policy. Gail held the title to the personal residence in which she and Al lived. She willed the residence to Al, and the residence qualifies for the marital deduction. Even though the insurance proceeds are payable to Al, Gail's estate receives no marital deduction for the insurance. The policy is excluded from Gail's gross estate because she had no incidents of ownership, her estate was not the beneficiary, and the policy was not transferred within three years of her death. ◀

TEST 2: THE PASSING REQUIREMENT. Property is not eligible for the marital deduction unless it passes to the decedent's spouse in a qualifying manner. According to Sec. 2056(c), property is deemed to pass from one spouse to the other if the surviving spouse receives the property because of

▶ A bequest or devise under the decedent's will

▶ An inheritance resulting from the decedent dying intestate

▶ Dower or curtesy rights

▶ An earlier transfer from the decedent

▶ Right of survivorship

▶ An appointment by the decedent under a general power of appointment or in default of appointment

▶ A designation as the beneficiary of a life insurance policy on the decedent's life

In addition, a surviving spouse's interest in a retirement benefit plan is considered to have passed from the decedent to the survivor to the extent the retirement benefits are included in the gross estate.[33]

TEST 3: THE TERMINABLE INTEREST RULE. The last statutory test (also applicable for gift tax purposes) requires that the recipient-spouse's interest *not* be classified as a nondeductible terminable interest.[34] A terminable interest is one that ceases with the passage of time or the occurrence of some event. Some terminable interests qualify for the marital deduction, however, because only *nondeductible* terminable interests fail to generate a marital deduction. Nondeductible terminable interests have the following features:

▶ An interest in the property must pass or have passed from the decedent to a person other than the surviving spouse, and such person must have paid less than adequate consideration in money or money's worth.

▶ The other person may possess or enjoy any part of the property after the termination of the surviving spouse's interest.

Thus, if the decedent makes a transfer granting the surviving spouse the right to receive all the income annually for life and a general power of appointment over the

---

[33] Reg. Sec. 20.2056(e)-1(a)(6).

[34] Nondeductible terminable interests also are precluded from eligibility for the marital deduction for gift tax purposes.

property, the property is eligible for the marital deduction. As discussed below, as a result of the QTIP provisions a marital deduction is available for certain transfers that otherwise would be disqualified under the nondeductible terminable interest rule.

EXAMPLE C13-41 ▶

SELF-STUDY QUESTION

A decedent, by will, creates a trust with income to the surviving spouse for 25 years, the remainder to their children. The surviving spouse's life expectancy is 16 years. Does the property qualify for the marital deduction?

ANSWER

The property does not qualify because the surviving spouse's interest terminates at the end of a specified number of years. The spouse's shorter life expectancy is irrelevant.

SELF-STUDY QUESTION

How does the donor spouse or decedent spouse who establishes a QTIP trust control the disposition of the trust corpus?

ANSWER

The donor or decedent spouse states in the trust instrument or in his or her will who will receive the remainder interest on the death of the recipient spouse.

At the time of Louis's death, he wills a copyright with a ten-year remaining life to his wife, Tina, age 42. His will also sets up a trust for the benefit of Tina, whom he entitles to receive all of the income semiannually until the earlier of her remarriage or her death. Upon Tina's remarriage or death, the trust property is to be distributed to the couple's children or their estates. Both the copyright and the trust are terminable interests. The copyright is eligible for the marital deduction because it is not a nondeductible terminable interest; the copyright simply ends at the expiration of its legal life. No person other than Tina receives an interest in the copyright. No marital deduction is available for the trust because it is a nondeductible terminable interest. Upon the termination of Tina's interest, the children will possess the property, and they receive their interests from Louis without paying adequate consideration. ◀

QTIP TRANSFERS. Section 2056(b)(7) authorizes a marital deduction for transfers of qualified terminable interest property (called QTIP transfers). The QTIP provisions are somewhat revolutionary compared with earlier law because they allow a marital deduction in situations where the recipient spouse is not entitled to designate which parties eventually receive the property.

Qualified terminable interest property is defined as property that passes from the decedent, in which the surviving spouse has a qualifying income interest for life, and to which an election applies. A spouse has a qualifying income interest for life if the following are true:

▶ He or she is entitled to all the income from the property, payable at least annually.

▶ No person has a power to appoint any portion of the property to anyone other than the surviving spouse unless the power cannot be exercised during the spouse's lifetime (e.g., it is exercisable only at or after the death of the surviving spouse).

Claiming the marital deduction with respect to QTIP transfers is not mandatory, and partial elections also are allowed. In the event the executor elects to claim a marital deduction for 100% of the QTIP transfer, the marital deduction is for the entire amount of the QTIP transfer. In other words, the deduction is not limited to the value of the surviving spouse's life estate.

If the marital deduction is elected in the first spouse's estate, the property is taxed in the surviving spouse's estate under Sec. 2044 or is subject to the gift tax in such spouse's hands if disposed of during the spouse's lifetime.[35] Thus, as with other interspousal transfers, the QTIP provisions allow a postponement of the taxable event until the second spouse dies or disposes of the interest by gift. If the taxable event is postponed, the property is valued at its FMV as of the date the second spouse transfers the property by gift or at death. See the Tax Planning Considerations section of this chapter for a discussion of planning opportunities (including partial QTIP elections) with the marital deduction.

EXAMPLE C13-42 ▶

ADDITIONAL COMMENT

Refer to Example C13-42. The executor may elect QTIP status for less than the entire property in the trust. For example, the executor might elect QTIP treatment for only 60% of the $1 million placed in the trust. On Mary's death, 60% of $1.7 million, or $1.02 million, is included in Mary's gross estate.

Tom died in 1995, survived by his wife, Mary, who lives until the current year. Tom's will called for setting up a $1 million trust from which Mary would receive all the income quarterly for the rest of her life. Upon Mary's death, the property is to be distributed to Tom's children by a previous marriage. At Mary's death, the trust assets are valued at $2.2 million. If Tom's executor elects to claim a marital deduction, Tom's estate receives a $1 million marital deduction. Section 2044 includes $2.2 million in Mary's gross estate. If Tom's executor forgoes electing the marital deduction, Mary's gross estate excludes the value of the trust. In either event, the trust assets will be taxed in the estate of one of the spouses, but not both. ◀

STATE DEATH TAXES. For estates of decedents dying after 2004, Sec. 2058 allows a deduction for state death taxes. Eligible taxes include estate, inheritance, legacy, and succession taxes paid to a state or the District of Columbia. The taxes must be paid no later than four years after the filing of the estate tax return. The amount of the deduction is the amount paid and, unlike the state death tax credit formerly available, is not restricted to a maximum amount.

---

[35] Section 2519 states that, if a recipient spouse disposes of a qualifying income interest for life for which the donor or the executor elected a marital deduction under the QTIP rules, the recipient spouse is treated as having made a gift of everything except the qualifying income interest. Under the generic gift rules of Sec. 2511, the gift of the income interest is treated as a gift.

COMPUTATION OF TAX LIABILITY

As mentioned earlier, the estate tax base is the aggregate of the decedent's taxable estate and his or her adjusted taxable gifts. Figure C13-1 earlier in this chapter illustrates how the estate tax formula combines these two concepts.

TAXABLE ESTATE AND TAX BASE

The gross estate's value is reduced by the deductions to arrive at the amount of the taxable estate. Under the unification provisions effective after 1976, the estate tax base consists of the taxable estate plus the adjusted taxable gifts, defined as *all* taxable gifts made *after 1976 other than* gifts included in the gross estate. The addition of the adjusted taxable gifts to the estate tax base may cause an estate to be taxed at a higher marginal tax rate. If the decedent elects gift splitting (discussed in Chapter 12), the decedent's adjusted taxable gifts equal the amount of the taxable gifts the individual is deemed to have made after applying the gift-splitting provisions. Adjusted taxable gifts can arise from consenting to gift splitting, even though the decedent never actually gives away any property.

Adjusted taxable gifts are valued at date-of-gift values; therefore, any post-gift appreciation is exempt from the transfer taxes. The estate tax computations for decedents who never made gifts exceeding the excludable amount reflect no adjusted taxable gifts.

TENTATIVE TAX AND REDUCTION FOR POST-1976 GIFT TAXES

The tentative tax is computed on the estate tax base, which is the sum of the taxable estate and the adjusted taxable gifts, if any.[36] The unified transfer tax rates are found in Sec. 2001(c) and are reproduced on the inside back cover. The tentative tax is reduced by the decedent's post-1976 gift taxes. In determining the tax on post-1976 taxable gifts, the effect of gift splitting is taken into consideration. That is, the amount of the post-1976 gift taxes is usually the levy imposed on the taxable gifts the decedent is deemed to have made after applying any gift-splitting election.

If the tax rates change between the time of the gift and the time of death, the subtraction for gift taxes equals the amount of gift taxes that would have been payable on post-1976 gifts had the rate schedule applicable in the year of death been in effect in the year of the gift. The only "as if" computation is for the gross tax amount; the unified credit actually used on the gift tax return is subtracted to determine the amount of gift tax that would have been payable at current rates.

UNIFIED CREDIT

The excess of the tentative tax over the post-1976 gift taxes is reduced by the unified credit of Sec. 2010. The amount of this credit has changed over the years and will increase through 2009; in 2006 it is $780,800 (see inside back cover). With a credit of $780,800, the tax on a $2 million tax base is completely eliminated. The unified credit never generates a refund; the most relief it can provide is to eliminate an estate's federal estate tax liability.

Section 2010(c) provides that the unified credit otherwise available for estate tax purposes must be reduced because of certain pre-1977 gifts. Before 1977, a $30,000 lifetime exemption was available for the gift tax. Donors could claim some or all of this exemption whenever they so desired. For post-1976 years, Congress repealed the exemption and replaced it with the unified credit. If the decedent claimed any portion of the $30,000 exemption against gifts made after September 8, 1976, and before January 1, 1977, the unified credit was reduced by 20% of the exemption claimed.

---

[36] Sec. 2001(b).

EXAMPLE C13-43 ▶ Carl dies in 2006 with a tax base of $2 million. In October 1976, Carl made his first taxable gift. Carl claimed the $30,000 exemption to reduce the amount of his taxable gifts. Thus, Carl's $780,800 unified credit is reduced by $6,000 (0.20 × $30,000). If Carl claimed the exemption by making a gift on or before September 8, 1976, his estate would be entitled to the full $780,800 credit. ◀

OTHER CREDITS

In 2006, the IRC authorizes three additional credits: a gift tax credit on pre-1977 gifts, a credit for another decedent's estate taxes paid on prior transfers, and a credit on foreign death taxes. (Prior to 2005, the IRC also allowed a state death tax credit.) These credits apply less often than the unified credit. Like the unified credit, these credits cannot exceed the amount of the estate tax actually owed.

PRE-2005 STATE DEATH TAX CREDIT. For years all states levied some form of death tax: an inheritance tax, an estate tax, or both. Many states enacted a simple system whereby the state death tax liability equaled the credit for state death taxes allowed on the federal estate tax return.

Prior to 2005, Sec. 2011 allowed a credit calculated in accordance with the table contained in Sec. 2011(b). As mentioned earlier, beginning in 2005, a deduction replaced the credit. With the demise of the credit, if a jurisdiction had imposed a state death tax equal to the credit allowed on the federal return for state death taxes, no state death tax will be owed after 2004 *unless* that jurisdiction changes its tax rules.

EXAMPLE C13-44 ▶ John died in 2006 with a taxable estate of $3.6 million. If he resided in a state whose statute imposes an estate tax equal to the credit available on the federal return for state death taxes, his estate will owe nothing to the state. In effect, his state no longer has an estate tax. On the other hand, if he resided in a state that levies an inheritance tax based on the value of the property the various heirs receive, his estate will receive a deduction (not a credit) for the inheritance tax paid. ◀

CREDIT FOR PRE-1977 GIFT TAXES. Section 2012(a) authorizes a credit for gift taxes paid by the decedent on pre-1977 gifts that must be included in the gross estate. Remember that Sec. 2001(b)(2) allows a reduction for gift taxes paid on post-1976 gifts, but the IRC does not refer to this item as a credit. The following transaction involves a situation in which the credit for pre-1977 gift taxes applies.

EXAMPLE C13-45 ▶ In 1975, Yuji created a trust from which he is to receive the income for life and his son, Yuji, Jr., is to receive the remainder. Yuji paid a gift tax on the 1975 gift of the remainder. Upon Yuji's death in the current year, the date-of-death value of the trust's assets is included in his estate under Sec. 2036. Yuji's estate receives a credit for some or all of his 1975 gift taxes. ◀

In general, the credit for pre-1977 gift taxes equals the amount of gift taxes paid with respect to transfers included in the gross estate. Because of a ceiling rule, however, the amount of the credit sometimes is lower than the amount of gift taxes paid. A discussion of the credit ceiling computation is beyond the scope of this text.

CREDIT FOR TAX ON PRIOR TRANSFERS. The credit available under Sec. 2013 for the estate taxes paid on prior transfers reduces the cost of having property taxed in more than one estate in quick succession. Without this credit, the overall tax cost could be quite severe if the legatee dies soon after the original decedent. The credit applies if the person who transfers the property (i.e., the transferor-decedent) to the decedent in question (i.e., the transferee-decedent) dies no more than ten years before, or within two years after, the date of the transferee-decedent's death. The potential credit is the smaller of the federal estate tax of the transferor-decedent attributable to the transferred interest or the federal estate tax of the transferee-decedent attributable to the transferred interest.

To determine the final credit, the potential credit is multiplied by a percentage that varies inversely with the period of time separating the two dates of death. If the transferor dies no more than two years before or after the transferee, the credit percentage is 100%. As specified in Sec. 2013(a), the other percentages are as follows:

Number of Years by Which Transferor's Death Precedes the Transferee's Death	Credit Percentage
More than 2, but not more than 4	80
More than 4, but not more than 6	60
More than 6, but not more than 8	40
More than 8, but not more than 10	20

The following two examples illustrate situations in which the credit for the taxes paid on prior transfers applies.

EXAMPLE C13-46 ▶ Mary died on March 1, 2001. All of Mary's property passed to Debra, her daughter. Debra dies on June 1, 2006. All of Debra's property passes to her son. Both Mary's and Debra's estates pay federal estate taxes. Debra's estate is entitled to a credit for a percentage of some, or all, of the taxes paid by Mary's estate. Because Mary's death preceded Debra's death by five years and three months, the credit for the tax paid on prior transfers is 60% of the potential credit. ◀

EXAMPLE C13-47 ▶ Ed died on May 7, 2005. One of the items included in Ed's estate is a life insurance policy on Sam's life. Sam had given Ed all his incidents of ownership in this policy on December 13, 2004. Sam dies on June 15, 2006, which is within three years of making a gift of the insurance policy on his own life. The policy is included in Sam's gross estate under Sec. 2035. Because Sam dies within two years of Ed's death, Ed's estate is entitled to a credit for 100% of the potential credit and an amended return must be filed to claim this credit. ◀

SELF-STUDY QUESTION

What is the effect of the maximum credit provision for the foreign death tax credit?

ANSWER

The effect is to tax the property located in the foreign country at the higher of the U.S. estate tax rate or the foreign death tax rate.

FOREIGN DEATH TAX CREDIT. Under Sec. 2014, the estate is entitled to a credit for some or all of the death taxes paid to a foreign country for property located in that foreign country and included in the gross estate. The maximum credit is the smaller of the foreign death tax attributable to the property located in the foreign country that imposed the tax or the federal estate tax attributable to the property located in the foreign country and taxed by such country.

COMPREHENSIVE ILLUSTRATION

The following comprehensive illustration demonstrates the computation of the estate tax liability.

BACKGROUND DATA

Herman Estes dies on October 13, 2005. Herman, an Ohio resident, is survived by his widow, Ann, and three adult children. During his lifetime, Herman made three gifts, as follows:

▶ In 1974, he gave his son Billy $103,000 cash. Herman claimed the $30,000 exemption (then available) and a $3,000 annual exclusion available then. The taxable gift was $70,000.

▶ In 1978, he gave his daughter, Dotty, $203,000 cash. He claimed a $3,000 annual exclusion available then and thus made a $200,000 taxable gift on which he paid a $28,000 gift tax, after claiming the $34,000 unified credit.

▶ In December 2003, he gave his son, Johnny, stock then worth $1,511,000. Herman claimed an $11,000 annual exclusion and thus made a $1.5 million taxable gift. He claimed the available unified credit of $311,800 ($345,800 − $34,000) and paid a $287,900 gift tax. On October 13, 2005, the stock is worth $1.75 million.

Property discovered after Herman's death appears below. All amounts represent date-of-death values.

▶ Checking account containing $19,250.

▶ Savings account containing $75,000.

▶ Land worth $400,000 held in the names of Herman and Ann, joint tenants with right of survivorship. Herman provided all the consideration to buy the land in January 1993.

▶ Life insurance policy 123-A with a face value of $200,000. Herman had incidents of ownership; Johnny is the beneficiary.

▶ A personal residence titled in Herman's name worth $325,000.

▶ Stock in Ajax Corporation worth $1.6 million.

▶ Qualified pension plan to which Herman's employer made 60% of the contributions and Herman made 40%. Ann is to receive a lump-sum distribution of $240,000.

▶ A trust created under the will of Herman's mother, Amelia, who died in 1992. Herman was entitled to receive all the income quarterly for life. In his will, Herman could appoint the trust assets to such of his descendants as he desired. The trust assets are valued at $375,000.

At his death, Herman owes a $25,200 bank loan, including $200 accrued interest. Balances due on his various charge cards total $6,500. Herman's funeral expenses are $15,000, and his administration expenses are estimated to be $70,000. Assume that the maximum tax savings will occur by deducting the administration expenses on the estate tax return.

Herman's will contains the following provisions:

▶ "To my wife, Ann, I leave my residence, my savings account, and $10,000 from my checking account."

▶ "I leave $200,000 of property in trust with First Bank as trustee. My wife, Ann, is to receive all the income from this trust fund quarterly for the rest of her life. Upon Ann's death, the trust property is to be divided equally among our three children."

▶ "To the American Cancer Society I leave $10,000."

▶ "I appoint the property in the trust created by my mother, Amelia Estes, to my daughter, Dotty."

▶ "The residue of my estate is to be divided equally between my sons, Johnny and Billy."

CALCULATION OF TAX LIABILITY

Table C13-3 illustrates the computation of Herman's estate tax liability. These same facts are used for the sample Estate Tax Return (Form 706) included in Appendix B. For illustration purposes, it is assumed that the executor elects to claim the marital deduction on the QTIP trust and that Herman's state levies death taxes equal to the maximum federal credit for state death taxes. As mentioned earlier, after 2004 an estate receives a deduction instead of a credit for state death taxes. Thus, because the federal government allows no credit for state death taxes, Herman's estate owes nothing to the state.

Note that several factors affect the computation set out in Table C13-3:

▶ Herman had only a special power of appointment over the assets in the trust created by his mother because he could will the property only to his descendants. Therefore, the trust property is not included in his estate.

▶ Assets that pass to the surviving spouse outside the will, such as by survivorship and by beneficiary designation, can qualify for the marital deduction.

▶ Adjusted taxable gifts (added to the taxable estate) include only post-1976 taxable gifts.

▶ The estate tax payable is not reduced by pre-1977 gift taxes unless the gifted property is included in the gross estate.

▶ Because the highest marginal income tax rate for the estate is less than its 47% marginal estate tax rate and because the estate owes a tax liability (even with the available credits), administration expenses should be deducted on the estate tax return.

▼ **TABLE C13-3**
Comprehensive Estate Tax Illustration

Gross estate:	
Checking account (Sec. 2033)	$ 19,250
Savings account (Sec. 2033)	75,000
Land held in joint tenancy with wife (0.50 × $400,000) (Sec. 2040)	200,000
Life insurance (Sec. 2042)	200,000
Personal residence (Sec. 2033)	325,000
Ajax stock (Sec. 2033)	1,600,000
Qualified pension plan (Sec. 2039)	240,000
Gross-up for gift tax paid on 2003 gift (Sec. 2035)	287,900
Total gross estate	$2,947,150
Minus:	
Debts (Sec. 2053):	
Bank loan, including $200 accrued interest	(25,200)
Charge cards	(6,500)
Funeral expenses (Sec. 2053)	(15,000)
Administration expenses (Sec. 2053)	(70,000)
Marital deduction (Sec. 2056):	
Residence	(325,000)
Checking account	(10,000)
Savings account	(75,000)
QTIP trust	(200,000)
Land	(200,000)
Qualified pension plan	(240,000)
Charitable contribution deduction (Sec. 2055)	(10,000)
Total reductions to gross estate	($1,176,700)
Taxable estate	$1,770,450
Plus adjusted taxable gifts (Sec. 2001(b)):	
1978 taxable gifts	200,000[a]
2003 taxable gifts	1,500,000[a]
Estate tax base	$3,470,450
Tentative tax on tax base (Sec. 2001)	$1,471,912
Minus:	
Reduction for post-1976 gift taxes (Sec. 2001(b))	(315,900)[b]
Unified credit (Sec. 2010)	(555,800)
Estate tax payable	$ 600,212

[a]Valued at date-of-gift fair market values.
[b]$28,000 (for 1978) + $287,900 (for 2003) = $315,900.

LIQUIDITY CONCERNS

OBJECTIVE 6

Identify tax provisions that alleviate liquidity problems

Liquidity is one of the major problems facing individuals planning their estates and executors eventually managing the estates. Individuals often use life insurance to help address this problem. In general, the entire amount of the estate tax liability is due nine months after the decedent's death. Certain provisions, however, allow the executor to pay some or all of the estate tax liability at a later date. Deferral of part or all of the estate tax payments and three other provisions aimed at alleviating a liquidity problem are discussed below.

DEFERRAL OF PAYMENT OF ESTATE TAXES

REASONABLE CAUSE. Section 6161(a)(1) authorizes the Secretary of the Treasury to extend the payment date for the estate taxes for a *reasonable period*, defined as a period of not longer than 12 months. Moreover, the Secretary of the Treasury may extend the payment date for a maximum period of ten years if the executor shows reasonable cause for not being able to pay some, or all, of the estate tax liability on the regular date.[37]

Whenever the executor pays a portion of the estate tax after the regular due date, the estate owes interest on the portion of the tax for which it postpones payment. In general, the interest rate, which is governed by Sec. 6621, is the same as that applicable to underpayments. The interest rate on underpayments potentially fluctuates quarterly with changes in the rate paid on short-term U.S. Treasury obligations.[38]

REMAINDER OR REVERSIONARY INTERESTS. If the gross estate includes a relatively large remainder or reversionary interest, liquidity problems could result if the estate has to pay the entire estate tax liability soon after the decedent's death. For example, the estate might include a remainder interest in an asset in which a healthy, 30-year-old person has a life estate. The estate might not gain possession of the assets until many years after the decedent's death. Section 6163 permits the executor to elect to postpone payment of the tax attributable to a remainder or reversionary interest until six months after the other interests terminate, which in the example would be after the person currently age 30 died. In addition, upon being convinced of reasonable cause, the Secretary of the Treasury may grant an additional extension of not more than three years.

TAX STRATEGY TIP

A person who owns a substantial interest in a small business might choose to gift property other than the business interest. He or she may want to retain the business interest in his or her estate so that his or her estate will qualify for the five-year deferral, ten-installment option of Sec. 6166. See Tax Planning Considerations for further details.

INTERESTS IN CLOSELY HELD BUSINESSES. Section 6166 authorizes the executor to pay a portion of the estate tax in as many as ten annual installments in certain situations. Executors may elect to apply Sec. 6166 if

▶ The gross estate includes an interest in a closely held business, and

▶ The value of the closely held business exceeds 35% of the value of the adjusted gross estate.

Closely held businesses are defined as proprietorships and partnerships or corporations having no more than 45 owners.[39] If a corporation or partnership has more than 45 owners, it can be classified as closely held if the decedent's gross estate includes 20% or more of the capital interest (in the partnership) or 20% or more of the value of the voting stock (in the corporation).[40]

The adjusted gross estate is defined as the gross estate less *allowable* Sec. 2053 and 2054 deductions. Consequently, in determining whether the estate meets the 35% requirement, all administration expenses and casualty and theft losses are subtracted, regardless of whether the executor elects to deduct them on the estate tax return or the estate's income tax return.

Once the election is chosen, the following restrictions apply:

▶ The portion of the estate tax that can be paid in installments is the ratio of the value of the closely held business interest to the value of the adjusted gross estate.

▶ The first of the ten allowable installments generally is not due until five years after the due date for the return. (This provision defers the last payment for as many as 15 years.)

▶ Interest on the tax due is payable annually, even during the first five years.

Some or all of the installment payments may accrue interest at a rate of only 2%. The maximum amount of deferred tax to which the 2% rate applies is (1) the tax on the total of $1 million of value (as indexed) and the exemption equivalent amount less (2) the unified credit. In no event, however, may the amount exceed the tax postponed under Sec. 6166.[41] The $1 million amount is indexed for inflation with inflation adjustments rounded to the next lowest $10,000; for 2006, this amount is $1.2 million. The interest rate on any additional deferred tax is 45% of the rate applicable to underpayments. The

---

[37] Sec. 6161(a)(2).
[38] Sec. 6621. The interest rate is discussed in Chapter C15.
[39] Sec. 6166(b)(1).

[40] Ibid.
[41] Sec. 6601(j).

downside is the interest paid is not deductible as interest expense on the estate's income tax return or as an administrative expense on the estate tax return.

EXAMPLE C13-48 ▶

Frank dies on March 1, 2006. Frank's gross estate, which includes a proprietorship interest valued at $1 million, is $2.6 million. The executor deducts all $100,000 of the potential Sec. 2053 and 2054 deductions on the estate tax return. Frank has no marital or charitable contribution deductions and makes no taxable gifts. Frank's adjusted gross estate, taxable estate, and tax base are $2.5 million. His estate tax payable is $230,000 ($1,010,800 − $780,800). Frank's closely held business interest makes up 40% ($1,000,000 ÷ $2,500,000) of his adjusted gross estate.

Thus, $92,000 (0.40 × $230,000) may be paid in ten equal annual installments. The first installment payment is due on December 1, 2011. The 2% interest rate potentially applies to $552,000 [$1,332,800, the tax on $3.2 million ($1,200,000 + $2,000,000), minus the unified credit of $780,800] of deferred tax liability. However, because this estate's postponed tax is only $92,000, all the interest accrues at the 2% rate. ◀

STOCK REDEMPTIONS TO PAY DEATH TAXES

Sometimes an estate's major asset is stock in a closely held corporation. In this situation, the corporation may have to redeem some of the corporate stock to provide the estate sufficient liquidity to pay death taxes. As discussed in Chapter C4, stock redemptions generally receive sale or exchange treatment only if they meet certain requirements under Sec. 302, such as being substantially disproportionate or involving a complete termination of the shareholder's interest. Without exchange treatment, the redeemed shareholder (e.g., the estate) recognizes a dividend equal to the redemption proceeds rather than a capital gain equal to the difference between the redemption proceeds and the stock's adjusted basis. Because of the 15% maximum tax rate on dividends, the primary benefit of sale or exchange treatment is being able to apply basis against proceeds. To reduce the income tax cost upon a shareholder's death, Sec. 303 allows the estate to treat a redemption as an exchange even if it does not satisfy the stringent Sec. 302 requirements. This treatment minimizes any gain recognized because the stock's adjusted basis, which is subtracted from the redemption proceeds, is stepped up to its FMV upon the decedent's death.

To qualify for Sec. 303 treatment, the stock in the corporation redeeming the shares must make up more than 35% of the value of the decedent's gross estate, less any *allowable* Sec. 2053 and 2054 deductions. The maximum amount of redemption proceeds eligible for exchange treatment is the total of the estate's death taxes and funeral and administration expenses, regardless of whether they are deducted on the estate tax return or the estate's income tax return.

SPECIAL USE VALUATION OF FARM REAL PROPERTY

SELF-STUDY QUESTION

Why might an heir to farmland not want an estate to use the special valuation method of Sec. 2032A?

ANSWER

The heir may contemplate selling the land and prefer the higher basis he or she would get if FMV is used rather than the special farmland value, especially if the estate taxes are payable out of the residual estate and the heir does not share in that residual.

In 1976, Congress became concerned that farms sometimes had to be sold to generate funds to pay estate taxes. This situation was attributable, in part, to the FMV of farm land in many areas being relatively high, perhaps because of suburban housing being built nearby. Congress enacted Sec. 2032A, which allows a property used for farming or in a trade or business other than farming to be valued using a formula approach that attempts to value the property at what it is worth for farming purposes. The lowest valuation permitted is $750,000 less than the property's FMV, but the $750,000 is indexed after 1998 with adjustments rounded to the next lowest $10,000. In 2006, the indexed amount is $900,000.

The estate must meet a number of requirements before the executor can elect the special valuation rules.[42] Moreover, if during the ten-year period after the decedent's death the new owner of the property disposes of it or no longer uses it as a farm, in general, an additional tax equal to the estate tax savings that arose from the lower Sec. 2032A valuation is levied.

---

[42] For example, the farm real and personal property must make up at least 50% of the adjusted value of the gross estate, and the farm real property must make up 25% or more of the adjusted value of the gross estate.

GENERATION-SKIPPING TRANSFER TAX

The Tax Reform Act of 1976 enacted a third transfer tax—the generation-skipping transfer tax (GSTT)—to fill a void in the gift and estate tax structure. In 1986, Congress repealed the original GSTT retroactive to its original effective date and replaced it with a revised GSTT. The revised GSTT generally applies to *inter vivos* transfers made after September 25, 1985 and transfers at death made after October 22, 1986.

For years, a popular estate planning technique, especially among the very wealthy, involved giving individuals in several generations an interest in the same property. For example, a decedent might set up a testamentary trust creating successive life estates for a child and a grandchild and a remainder interest for a great grandchild. Under this arrangement, an estate tax would be imposed at the death of the person establishing the trust but not again until the great grandchild's death. The GSTT's purpose is to ensure that some form of transfer taxation is imposed one time a generation. It accomplishes its purpose by subjecting transfers that escape gift or estate taxation for one or more generations to the GSTT.

The GSTT is levied at a flat rate, the highest estate tax rate.[43] The tax applies to direct skip gifts and bequests and to taxable terminations of and taxable distributions from generation-skipping transfers. A **generation-skipping transfer** involves a disposition that

▶ Provides interests for more than one generation of beneficiaries who are in a younger generation than the transferor, or

▶ Provides an interest solely for a person two or more generations younger than the transferor.[44]

The recipient must be a skip person, a person two or more generations younger than the decedent (or the donor). For family members, generation assignments are made according to the family tree. Transfers to skip persons outside of a trust are known as direct skips because they skip one or more generations.

EXAMPLE C13-49 ▶ Tom transfers an asset directly to Tom, III, his grandson. This is a direct skip type of generation-skipping transfer because the transferee (Tom, III) is two generations younger than the transferor (Tom). ◀

The termination of an interest in a generation-skipping arrangement is known as a taxable termination.[45] This event triggers imposition of the GSTT. The tax is levied on the before-tax amount transferred, and the trustee pays the tax.

EXAMPLE C13-50 ▶ Tom creates a trust with income payable to his son, Tom, Jr., for life and a remainder interest distributable to Tom, III, upon the death of Tom, Jr. (his father). This is a generation-skipping transfer because Tom, Jr., and Tom, III, are one and two generations younger, respectively, than the transferor (Tom). A taxable termination occurs when Tom, Jr. dies. ◀

EXAMPLE C13-51 ▶ The trust in Example C13-50 is worth $2 million when Tom, Jr. dies in 2006. The amount of the taxable termination is $2 million. The tax is $920,000 (0.46 × $2,000,000). The trustee pays the tax and distributes the $1.08 million of remaining assets to the beneficiary. ◀

In the case of a direct skip, the amount subject to the GSTT is the value of the property received by the transferee.[46] The transferor is liable for the tax. If the direct skip occurs *inter vivos*, the GSTT paid by the transferor is treated as an additional transfer subject to the gift tax.[47] As a result, the total transfer tax liability (GSTT plus gift tax) can exceed the value of the property received by the donee.

---

[43] Sec. 2641.
[44] Sec. 2611.
[45] Sec. 2612(a).

[46] Sec. 2623.
[47] Sec. 2515.

WHAT WOULD YOU DO IN THIS SITUATION?

You are a CPA specializing in wealth transfer taxation. You have established your practice in Aspen, Colorado, because there is a lot of wealth situated in that ski resort. You client is a long-time resident of Aspen, and his health has recently taken a downhill turn. His doctor told him to consider putting his affairs in order because he will probably not ski any moguls for more than six months.

Your client is a merchant who owns a number of assets with FMVs totaling $2.4 million under some estimates. His largest single asset is his Victorian era store building situated in the desirable and exclusive West End of Aspen. Based on comparable fair market sales in the area, your client's building appears to be worth approximately $760,000 in the current real estate market. Because your client is in poor health, he does not use all of the store space and occasionally rents out some space in his building to vendors for selling crafts and gifts.

During the ski season, the full price fair market rental value of the space would be over $1,000 per week. Your client's only son has indicated that he is not interested in moving to Aspen. The son is independently wealthy, does not really need to liquidate the building, and plans to continue the rental practices initiated by his father.

The estate probably will have no deductions. You are interested in saving your client some estate taxes. Would you propose to him that this asset be listed in the estate as Special Use Value property pursuant to Sec. 2032A? Would it be ethical to propose a valuation method based on the historical income generated by this property for the client's estate tax return? Using the historical income stream, the capitalized value would be $350,000. With this value, his estate would be lower by $410,000 and no tax would be owed because of an overall valuation of slightly under $2 million (in 2006) for the entire estate.

EXAMPLE C13-52 ▶ Susan gives $1 million to her granddaughter. Susan has used her entire unified credit and is in the 46% marginal gift tax bracket; ignore the annual exclusion and the exemption. The GSTT is $460,000 (0.46 × $1,000,000). The amount subject to the gift tax is the value of the property transferred ($1 million) plus the GSTT paid ($460,000). Thus, the gift tax is $671,600 (0.46 × $1,460,000). It costs $1,131,600 ($460,000 + $671,600) to shift $1 million of property to the granddaughter. ◀

Originally, every grantor was entitled to a $1 million exemption from the GSTT, but the exemption became indexed for inflation (with adjustments rounded to the next lowest $10,000) beginning for estates of decedents dying after 1998.[48] Beginning in 2004, Congress changed the exemption to the same amount as the "applicable exclusion amount" for estate tax purposes, which is $2 million in 2006. The grantor elects when, and against which transfers, to apply this exemption. Appreciation on the property for which the exemption is elected is also exempt from the GSTT.

TAX PLANNING CONSIDERATIONS

The effectiveness of many of the pre-1977 transfer tax-saving strategies was diluted by the unification of the transfer tax system in general and by the adoption of a unified rate schedule and the concept of adjusted taxable gifts in particular. To some extent, provisions that allow a larger tax base to be free of estate taxes and permit most interspousal transfers to be devoid of transfer tax consequences counterbalance unification. This section discusses various tax planning considerations that tax advisors should explore to reduce the transfer taxes applicable to a family unit.

---

[48] Sec. 2631(a).

USE OF *INTER VIVOS* GIFTS

One of the most significant strategies for reducing transfer taxes is a well-designed, long-term gift program. As long as the gifts to each donee do not exceed the per donee annual exclusion, there will be no additions to the gross estate and no adjusted taxable gifts. A donor may pass thousands of dollars of property to others free of any transfer tax consequences if he or she selects enough donees and makes gifts over a substantial number of years. If taxable gifts do occur, the donor removes the post-gift appreciation from the estate tax base. Moreover, if the donor lives more than three years after the date of the gift, the gift tax paid is removed from the gross estate.

Prospective donors should weigh the opportunities for reducing transfer taxes through the use of lifetime gifts against the income tax disadvantage of foregoing the step up in basis that occurs if the donor retains the property until death. However, unless the donee is the donor's spouse, income taxes on the income produced by the gifted property can be reduced if shifted to a donee in a lower tax bracket.

USE OF EXEMPTION EQUIVALENT

As a result of the exemption equivalent (or applicable exclusion amount), a certain amount of property—$2 million in 2006—may pass to people other than the decedent's spouse without any estate taxes being extracted therefrom. A donor can transfer property to the spouse tax-free without limit. Thus, because the spouse presumably will die before any children or grandchildren (i.e., individuals to whom people often will property), a wealthy person should contemplate leaving at least an amount equal to the exemption equivalent to people other than his or her spouse. (If one leaves this amount of property in trust, the trust is often called a credit shelter or bypass trust.) Otherwise, he or she will waste some or all of the exemption equivalent, and the property will be taxed when the surviving spouse dies.

Making full use of the exemption equivalent enables a husband and wife to transfer to third parties an aggregate of $4 million (using 2006 amounts) without incurring any estate taxes. The strategy of making gifts to an ill spouse, who is not wealthy, to keep the donee-spouse's exemption equivalent from being wasted was discussed earlier (see Chapter C12). Under this technique, the wealthier spouse makes gifts to the other spouse free of gift taxes because of the marital deduction. The recipient spouse then has an estate that can be passed tax-free to children, grandchildren, or other individuals because of the exemption equivalent.

STOP & THINK

Question: Sol made $600,000 in taxable gifts six years before his death but did not have to pay any gift tax. Sol died in 2006, when the gifted property was worth $825,000. Sol's taxable estate (gross estate minus estate tax deductions) was $2 million. Because of the exemption equivalent, does Sol's estate owe zero tax?

Solution: No. In concept, the unified credit of $780,800, which cancels out the tax on the 2006 $2 million exemption equivalent, is available only once. Calculation of Sol's estate tax payable would be as follows:

Taxable estate	$2,000,000
Plus: Adjusted taxable gifts	600,000
Estate tax base	$2,600,000
Tentative tax on estate tax base	$1,056,800
Minus:	
Post-1976 gift tax (on $600,000 gift)	-0-
Unified credit	(780,800)
Estate tax payable	$ 276,000

The $276,000 represents the tax on the incremental $600,000, the amount over and above the $2 million *aggregate* taxable amount that can be passed free of transfer taxes (both gift and estate).

WHAT SIZE MARITAL DEDUCTION IS BEST?

To reiterate, the tax law imposes no ceiling on the amount of property eligible for the marital deduction. Even so, the availability of an unlimited marital deduction does not necessarily mean that a person should use it. From a tax perspective, wealthier people should leave an amount equal to the exemption equivalent to someone other than the spouse. Alternatively, they could leave the spouse an income interest in property equal to the exemption equivalent along with the power to invade such property for reasons of health, support, maintenance, or education. These powers do not cause an inclusion in the gross estate.

In certain circumstances, it may be preferable for an amount exceeding the exemption equivalent to pass directly to third parties. It might be beneficial for the first spouse's estate to pay some estate taxes if the surviving spouse already has substantial property and has a relatively short life expectancy, especially if the decedent spouse's assets are expected to rapidly increase in value.

EXAMPLE C13-53 ▶ Paul dies in 2006 with a $3.5 million gross estate and no deductions other than the marital deduction. At the time of Paul's death, his wife's life expectancy is two years. The assets she owns in the current year are estimated to be worth $6 million in two years. Paul's property is expected to increase in value by 25% during the two-year period following his death. Paul wills his wife, Jill, $1 million and his children the rest. The estate tax payable for each spouse's estate is as follows:

	Paul (in 2006)	Jill (in 2008)
Gross estate	$3,500,000	$7,250,000[a]
Minus: Marital deduction	(1,000,000)	–0–
Taxable estate and tax base	$2,500,000	$7,250,000
Estate tax, after unified credit[b]	$ 230,000	$2,362,500
Combined estate tax	└ – – – – – → $2,592,500 ← – – – – ┘	

[a] $6,000,000 + (1.25 × $1,000,000) = $7,250,000.
[b] $780,800 in 2006 and 2008. The top rate in 2008 is 45%. ◀

EXAMPLE C13-54 ▶ Assume the same facts as in Example C13-53 except that Paul wills everything except $2 million to Jill. The estate tax payable for each spouse's estate is as follows:

	Paul (in 2006)	Jill (in 2008)
Gross estate	$3,500,000	$7,875,000[a]
Minus: Marital deduction	(1,500,000)	–0–
Taxable estate and tax base	$2,000,000	$7,875,000
Estate tax, after unified credit	$ –0–	$2,643,750
Combined estate tax	└ – – – – – → $2,643,750 ← – – – – ┘	

[a] $6,000,000 + (1.25 × $1,500,000) = $7,875,000. ◀

The combined estate tax liability is $51,250 higher in Example C13-54 than in Example C13-53. However, in Example C13-54, no tax is owed upon the first spouse's death. Because the estate taxes for the second spouse's estate are not payable until a later date, their discounted present value also should be considered. Also note that, if Paul's will had created a trust eligible for QTIP treatment instead of leaving the property to Jill outright, the arrangement would have been more flexible because of the availability of partial QTIP elections.

 STOP & THINK

Question: Tarik died recently at age 78. He was survived by his wife, Saliah, and several children and grandchildren. Saliah is 54 and in excellent health. Tarik's adjusted gross estate is $6.2 million, and his will leaves $1.5 million outright to his children and the rest to a trust for Saliah. The trust is eligible for the QTIP election. An investment advisor believes that the trust assets will likely appreciate annually at the rate of at least 10%. Name two advantages and one disadvantage of electing the marital deduction on the entire trust.

Solution: One advantage is that the tax on the trust will be deferred, perhaps for a long time, given the wife's age and health. Another advantage is that, because no tax is owed at Tarik's death, the trust assets remain intact to appreciate and produce more income for Saliah. That is, there is no current capital drain to pay transfer taxes. If Congress does not permanently repeal the estate tax, a disadvantage is that, because of the anticipated appreciation and the long time before Saliah's estimated death, the amount taxed in Saliah's estate will likely be much greater than the residue (here, $4.7 million) Tarik willed to Saliah.

USE OF DISCLAIMERS

Because the IRC does not treat a **qualified disclaimer** as a gift, disclaimers can be valuable estate planning tools (see Chapter C12). For example, if a decedent wills all his or her property to the surviving spouse, such spouse could disclaim an amount at least equal in size to the exemption equivalent and thereby enable the decedent's estate to take full advantage of the unified credit. Alternatively, a decedent's children might disclaim some bequests if, as a result of their disclaimer, the property would pass instead to the surviving spouse. This approach might be desirable if the estate otherwise would receive a relatively small marital deduction. Another scenario where a disclaimer could be appropriate is where the disclaimant is elderly and in poor health and wishes to preclude the property from being taxed again relatively soon. (Of course, the credit for tax on prior transfers would provide some relief from double taxation.) Bear in mind, however, that the person making the qualified disclaimer has no input concerning which people receive the disclaimed property.

ROLE OF LIFE INSURANCE

Life insurance is an important asset with respect to estate planning for the following reasons:

▶ It can help provide the liquidity for paying estate taxes and other costs associated with death.

▶ It has the potential for large appreciation. If the insured gives away his or her incidents of ownership in the policy and survives the gift by more than three years, his or her estate benefits by keeping the policy's increased value out of the estate.

Assume an individual is contemplating purchasing a new insurance policy on his or her life and transferring it to another individual as a gift. The insured must live for more than three years after making the gift to exclude the face amount of the policy from his or her gross estate. Should the insured die within three years of gifting the policy, the donor's gross estate includes the policy's face amount. If the donee instead purchases the policy, the insured will not make a gift of the policy, and the three-year rule will not be of concern.

QUALIFYING THE ESTATE FOR INSTALLMENT PAYMENTS

TAX STRATEGY TIP

The payment of estate taxes can be deferred as much as 14 years if the estate's executor makes a timely Sec. 6166 election. The interest charged on the deferred taxes is at a favorable rate.

It can be quite beneficial for an estate owning an interest in a closely held business to qualify for installment payment of estate taxes under Sec. 6166. In a sense, the estate can borrow a certain amount of dollars from the government at 2% and the rest at a higher, but still favorable, rate. The closely held business interest must comprise more than 35% of the adjusted gross estate, defined as the gross estate less Sec. 2053 and Sec. 2054 deductions.

Retaining closely held business interests and gifting other assets will increase the likelihood of the estate's being able to elect the installment payments. However, closely held business interests often have a potential for great appreciation. Consequently, from the standpoint of reducing the size of the estate by freezing values, they are good candidates for gifts.

People cannot make gifts to restructure their estates and thereby qualify for Sec. 6166 if they postpone restructuring until soon before their death. If the decedent makes gifts within three years of dying, the closely held business interest must make up more than 35% of the adjusted gross estate in both of the following calculations:

1. Calculate the ratio of the closely held business to the actual adjusted gross estate.
2. Redo the calculations after revising the ratio to include (at date-of-death values) any property given away within three years of death.

EXAMPLE C13-55 ▶ Joe dies in 2006. Joe's gross estate includes a closely held business interest valued at $2 million and other property valued at $3.6 million. Joe's allowable Sec. 2053 and 2054 deductions total $100,000. In 2004, partly in hopes of qualifying his estate for Sec. 6166 treatment, Joe made gifts of listed securities of $300,000 (at 2006 valuations) and paid no gift tax on the gifts. The two tests for determining whether Joe's estate is eligible for Sec. 6166 are as follows:

Excluding gifts: $2,000,000 ÷ $5,500,000 = 36.36%
Including gifts: $2,000,000 ÷ $5,800,000 = 34.48%

The estate may not elect Sec. 6166 treatment because it meets the greater than 35% test in only one of the two computations. ◀

WHERE TO DEDUCT ADMINISTRATION EXPENSES

Another tax planning opportunity concerns the choice of where to deduct administration expenses: on the estate tax return, on the estate's income tax return, or some in each place. The executor should claim the deduction where it will yield the greatest tax savings. Thus, if the estate owes the estate tax, which it will in 2006 if the estate tax base exceeds $2 million, the executor should deduct the expenses on the estate tax return because the marginal estate tax rate exceeds the top income tax rate. If no estate taxes are owed because of the exemption equivalent or the marital and/or charitable contribution deduction, administration expenses should be deducted on the estate's income tax return.

COMPLIANCE AND PROCEDURAL CONSIDERATIONS

OBJECTIVE 7

Recognize the filing requirements for estate tax returns

FILING REQUIREMENTS

Section 6018 indicates the circumstances in which estate tax returns are necessary. In general, no return is necessary unless the value of the gross estate plus adjusted taxable gifts exceeds the exemption equivalent (also known as the applicable exclusion amount). An exception applies, however, if the decedent made any post-1976 taxable gifts or claimed any portion of the $30,000 specific exemption after September 8, 1976, and before January 1, 1977. In such circumstances, a return must be filed if the value of the gross estate exceeds the amount of the exemption equivalent minus the total of the decedent's adjusted taxable gifts and the amount of the specific exemption claimed against gifts made after September 8, 1976, and before January 1, 1977.

A completed sample Estate Tax Return (Form 706) appears in Appendix B. The facts on which the preparation of the return is premised are the same as for the comprehensive illustration appearing on pages C13-25 through C13-27.

REAL-WORLD EXAMPLE

The IRS expects 56,000 estate tax returns to be filed for 2006.

DUE DATE

Estate tax returns generally must be filed within nine months after the decedent's death.[49] The Secretary of the Treasury is authorized to grant a reasonable extension of time for filing.[50] The maximum extension period is six months. Obtaining an extension does not extend the time for paying the estate tax. Section 6601 imposes interest on any portion of the tax not paid by the due date of the return, determined without regard to the extension period. Thus, to avoid interest, the estate must pay the tax by the original due date.

[49] Sec. 6075(a).

[50] Sec. 6081(a).

VALUATION

One of the most difficult tasks of preparing estate tax returns is valuing the items included in the gross estate. Some items (e.g., one-of-a-kind art objects) may truly be unique. For many properties the executor should arrange for appraisals by experts.

If the value of any property reported on the return is 50% or less of the amount determined to be the proper value during an audit or court case, a 20% undervaluation penalty is imposed.[51] The penalty will not be imposed, however, with proof that reasonable cause exists for the valuation claimed and that the claim is made in good faith. The penalty is higher if a gross valuation misstatement occurs; that is, the estate tax valuation is 25% or less than the amount determined to be the proper value.[52] Chapter C12 discusses these penalties in more detail.

ELECTION OF ALTERNATE VALUATION DATE

The executor may value the gross estate on the alternate valuation date instead of on the date of death by making an irrevocable election on the estate tax return. The election does not necessarily have to be made on a timely return, but no election is possible if the return is filed more than a year after the due date (including extensions).

DOCUMENTS TO BE INCLUDED WITH RETURN

The instructions for the Estate Tax Return (Form 706) indicate that the executor must file numerous documents and other papers with the return. Some of the more important items that should accompany the form include

▶ The death certificate

▶ A certified copy of the will if the decedent died testate (i.e., died with a valid will)

▶ A listing of the qualified terminable interest property and its value if the executor wishes to make the QTIP election

▶ Copies of gift tax returns the decedent filed

▶ Copies of appraisals for real estate

▶ A Form 712 (obtained from the insurance companies) for each life insurance policy on the decedent's life

▶ Copies of written trust and other instruments for lifetime transfers the decedent made

▶ A certified copy of the order admitting the will to probate if the will makes bequests for which a marital deduction or charitable contribution deduction is claimed

In addition, when filing the return (or as soon thereafter as possible), the executor should submit a certificate from the proper state officer that denotes the amount of the state death taxes and the date paid.

PROBLEM MATERIALS

DISCUSSION QUESTIONS

C13-1 In general, at what amount are items includible in the gross estate valued? (Answer in words.) Indicate one exception to the general valuation rules and the reason for this exception.

C13-2 A client requests that you explain the valuation rules used for gift tax and estate tax purposes. Explain the similarities and differences of the two sets of rules.

---

[51] Sec. 6662(g).

[52] Sec. 6662(h).

C13-3 Compare the valuation for gift and estate tax purposes of a $150,000 group term life insurance policy on the transferor's life.

C13-4 Explain how shares of stock traded on a stock exchange are valued. What is the blockage rule?

C13-5 Assume that the properties included in Alex's gross estate have appreciated during the six-month period immediately after his death. May Alex's executor elect the alternate valuation date and thereby achieve a larger step-up in basis? Explain.

C13-6 Explain to an executor an advantage and a disadvantage of electing the alternate valuation date.

C13-7 A decedent transferred land to an adult child by gift two years before death. Is the land included in the decedent's gross estate? In the estate tax base?

C13-8 From a tax standpoint, which of the following alternatives is more favorable for a client's estate?
   a. Buying a new insurance policy on his life and soon thereafter giving it to another person
   b. Encouraging the other person to buy the policy with funds previously received from the client
   Explain your answer.

C13-9 Explain the difference between the estate tax treatment for gift taxes paid on gifts made two years before death and on gifts made ten years before death.

C13-10 A client is considering making a very large gift. She wants to know whether the gross-up rule will apply to the entire amount of gift taxes paid by both her and her spouse if the spouses elect gift splitting and she dies within three years of the gift. Explain.

C13-11 A widow owns a valuable eighteenth-century residence that she would like the state historical society to own someday. Explain to her the estate tax consequences of the following two alternatives:
   a. Deeding the state historical society a remainder interest in the residence and reserving the right to live there rent free for the rest of her life.
   b. Giving her entire interest in the house to the society and moving to another home for the rest of her life.

C13-12 Which three retention periods can cause Sec. 2036 (transfers with retained life estate) to apply to a transferor's estate?

C13-13 What characteristics do Secs. 2035 through 2038 have in common?

C13-14 When does the consideration furnished test apply to property that the decedent held as a joint tenant with right of survivorship?

C13-15 In which two circumstances is life insurance on the decedent's life includible in the gross estate under Sec. 2042? If insurance policies on the decedent's life escape being included under Sec. 2042, are they definitely excluded from the gross estate? Explain.

C13-16 Indicate two situations in which property that has previously been subject, at least in part, to gift taxation is nevertheless included in the donor-decedent's gross estate.

C13-17 Joe died in the current year. Under Joe's will, property is put in trust with a bank as trustee. Joe's will names his sister Tess to receive the trust income annually for life and empowers Tess to will the property to whomever she so desires. In addition, Tess may require that the trustee make distributions of principal to her for her health or support needs. Tess plans to leave the property by will to two of her three children in equal shares. Tess seeks your advice about whether the trust will be included in her gross estate. Respond to Tess.

C13-18 Determine the accuracy of the following statement: The gross estate includes a general power of appointment possessed by the decedent only if the decedent exercised the power.

C13-19 Carlos died six years ago. His will called for the creation of a trust to be funded with $1 million of property. The bank trustee must distribute all the trust income semiannually to Carlos's widow for the rest of her life. Upon her death, the trust assets are to be distributed to the couple's children. The widow dies in the current year, by which time the trust assets have appreciated to $1.7 million. Are the trust assets included in the widow's gross estate? Explain.

C13-20 List the various categories of estate tax deductions currently allowed, and compare them with the categories of gift tax deductions. What differences exist?

C13-21 Compare the tax treatment of administration expenses with that of the decedent's debts.

C13-22 Judy dies and is survived by her husband, Jason, who receives the following interests as a result of his wife's death. Does Judy's estate receive a marital deduction for them? Explain.
   a. $400,000 of life insurance proceeds; Jason is the beneficiary; Judy held the incidents of ownership.
   b. Outright ownership of $700,000 of land held by Judy and Jason as joint tenants. Jason provided all the consideration to purchase the land.

C13-23 Compare the credits available for estate tax purposes with the credits available for gift tax purposes. What differences exist?

C13-24 Explain to a client the tax policy reason Congress allowed an estate to make installment payments of the portion of the estate taxes attributable to closely held business interests.

C13-25 Assume that Larry is wealthier than Jane, his wife, and that he is likely to die before her. From an overall tax standpoint (considering transfer taxes and income taxes), is it preferable for Larry to transfer property to Jane *inter vivos* or at death, or does it matter? Explain.

C13-26 Bala desires to freeze the value of his estate. Explain which of the following assets you would recommend that Bala transfer during his lifetime (more than one asset may be suggested):
a. Life insurance on his life
b. Cash
c. Corporate bonds (assume interest rates are expected to rise)
d. Stock in a firm with a bright future
e. Land in a boom town

C13-27 Refer to Problem C13-26. Explain the negative tax considerations (if any) with respect to Bala's making gifts of the assets that you recommended.

C13-28 From a tax standpoint, why is it advisable for a wealthy married person to dispose of an amount equal to the exemption equivalent (applicable exclusion amount) to individuals other than his or her spouse?

C13-29 In general, when is the estate tax due? What are some exceptions?

ISSUE IDENTIFICATION QUESTIONS

C13-30 Henry Arkin (a widower) is quite elderly and is beginning to do some estate planning. His goal is to reduce his transfer taxes. He is considering purchasing land with a high potential for appreciation and having it titled in his name and the name of his grandson as joint tenants with rights of survivorship. Henry would provide all of the consideration, estimated to be about $5 million. What tax issues should Henry Arkin consider with respect to the purchase of the land?

C13-31 Annie James dies early in 2006. All her property passes subject to her will, which provides that her surviving husband, Dave James, is to receive all the property outright. Her will further states that any property Dave disclaims will pass instead to their children in equal shares. Annie's gross estate is about $5 million, and her Sec. 2053 deductions are very small. Dave, who is in poor health, already owns about $3 million of property. What tax issues should Dave James consider with respect to the property bequested to him by his wife?

C13-32 Assume the same facts as in Problem C13-31 except that Annie's will leaves all her property to a QTIP trust for Dave for life with the remainder to their children. What tax issues should Dave James and the estate's executor consider with respect to the property that passes to the QTIP trust?

C13-33 Jeung Hong, a widower, died in March 2006. His gross estate is $3 million and, at the time of his death, he owed debts of $60,000. His will made a bequest of $200,000 to his undergraduate alma mater and left the rest of his property to his children. His administrative expenses are estimated to be about $75,000. Jeung made no taxable gifts. What tax issues should the estate's CPA consider when preparing Jeung's estate tax return and his estate's income tax return?

PROBLEMS

C13-34 *Valuation.* Beth dies on May 5 of the current year. Her executor elects date-of-death valuation. Beth's gross estate includes the items listed below. What is the estate tax value of each item?
a. 4,000 shares of Highline Corporation stock, traded on a stock exchange on May 5 at a high of 30, a low of 25, and a close of 26.
b. Life insurance policy on the life of Beth having a face value of $600,000. The cost of a comparable policy immediately before Beth's death is $187,430.
c. Life insurance policy on the life of Beth's son having a face value of $100,000. The interpolated terminal reserve immediately before Beth's death is $14,000. Unexpired premiums are $920.
d. Beach cottage appraised at a FMV of $175,000 and valued for property tax purposes at $152,000.

C13-35 *Valuation.* Mary dies on April 3, 2006. As of this date, Mary's gross estate is valued at $2.8 million. On October 3, Mary's gross estate is valued at $2.5 million. The estate neither distributes nor sells any assets before October 3. Mary's estate has no deductions or adjusted taxable gifts. What is Mary's *lowest* possible estate tax liability?

C13-36 *Estate Tax Formula.* Sue dies on May 3, 2006. On March 1, 2005, Sue gave Tom land valued at $2,011,000. Sue applied a unified credit of $345,800 against the gift tax due on this transfer. On Sue's date of death the land is valued at $2.4 million.
a. With respect to this transaction, what amount is included in Sue's gross estate?
b. What is the amount of Sue's adjusted taxable gifts attributable to the 2005 gift?

C13-37 *Transferor Provisions.* Val dies on May 13, 2006. On October 3, 2005, she gave a $400,000 life insurance policy on her own life to Ray. Because the value of the policy was relatively low, the transfer did not cause any gift tax to be payable.
   a. What amount is included in Val's gross estate as a result of the 2005 gift?
   b. What amount is included in Val's gross estate if the property given is land instead of a life insurance policy?
   c. Refer to Part a. What amount would be included in Val's gross estate if she instead dies on May 13, 2009?

C13-38 *Transferor Provisions.* In December 2003, Jody transferred stock having a $1,111,000 FMV to her daughter Joan. Jody paid $41,000 of gift taxes on this transfer. When Jody died in January 2006, the stock was valued at $920,000. Jody made no other gifts during her lifetime. With respect to this gift transaction, what amount is included in Jody's gross estate and what amount is reported as adjusted taxable gifts?

C13-39 *Transferor Provisions.* In December 2003, Curt and Kate elected gift splitting to report $2,222,000 million of gifts of stocks Curt made. Each paid gift taxes of $41,000 by spending his or her own funds. Kate died in January 2006 and was survived by Curt. Her only taxable gift was the one reported for 2003. When Kate died in 2006, the stock had appreciated to $2.8 million. With respect to the 2003 gift, what amount is included in Kate's gross estate and what amount is reported as adjusted taxable gifts?

C13-40 *Transferor Provisions.* John died in 2006. What amount, if any, is included in his gross estate in each of the following situations:
   a. In 1994, John created a revocable trust, funded it with $400,000 of assets, and named a bank as trustee. The trust instrument provides that the income is payable to John annually for life. Upon John's death, the assets are to be divided equally among John's descendants. When John dies at the age of 72, the trust is still revocable. The trust assets are then worth $480,000.
   b. In 1995, John transferred title to his personal residence to a charitable organization but retained the right to live there rent free for 20 years. The residence was worth $150,000 on the transfer date. At John's death, the residence is worth $230,000.
   c. In 1995, John created an irrevocable trust, funded it with $200,000 of assets, and named a bank as trustee. According to the trust agreement, all the trust income is to be paid out annually for 25 years. The trustee, however, is to decide how much income to pay each year to each of the three beneficiaries (John's children). Upon termination of the trust, the assets are to be distributed equally among John's three children (now adults) or their estates. The trust's assets are worth $500,000 when John dies.
   d. In 1996, John created an irrevocable trust with a bank named as trustee. He designated his grandson Al as the beneficiary of all the income for life. Upon Al's death, the property is to be distributed equally among Al's descendants. The trust assets are worth $400,000 when John dies.

C13-41 *Transferor Provisions.* Latoya transferred property to an irrevocable trust in 1996 with a bank trustee. Latoya named Al to receive the trust income annually for life and Pat or Pat's estate to receive the remainder upon Al's death. Latoya reserved the power to designate Mike or Mike's estate (instead of Pat or Pat's estate) to receive the remainder. Upon Latoya's death in August 2006, the trust assets are valued at $200,000; Al is age 50; Mike, age 27; and Pat, age 32. Assume a 10% rate for the actuarial tables.
   a. How much, if any, is included in Latoya's gross estate?
   b. How much would have been included in Latoya's gross estate if she had *not* retained any powers over the trust? (Assume that Latoya survives for more than three years after the transfer.)

C13-42 *Annuities.* Maria dies in the current year, two years after her retirement. At the time of her death at age 67, she is covered by the two annuities listed below.

• An annuity purchased by Maria's father providing benefits to Maria upon her attaining age 65. Upon Maria's death, survivor benefits are payable to her sister. The sister's total benefits are valued at $45,000.

• An annuity purchased by Maria's former employer under a qualified plan to which only the employer contributed. Benefits became payable to Maria upon her retirement. Upon Maria's death a survivor annuity valued at $110,000 is payable to her son.

   a. What is the amount of the inclusion in Maria's gross estate with respect to each annuity?
   b. How would your answer for the first annuity change if Maria had instead purchased the annuity?

c. How would your answer for the second annuity change if the employer had instead made 70% of the contributions to the qualified plan and Maria had made the remaining 30%?

C13-43 *Jointly Owned Property.* In 1994, Art purchased land for $60,000 and immediately titled it in the names of Art and Bart, joint tenants with right of survivorship. Bart paid no consideration. In 2006, Art dies and is survived by Bart, his brother. The land's value has appreciated to $300,000.
a. What is the amount of the inclusion in Art's gross estate?
b. Assume Bart died (instead of Art). What amount would be included in Bart's gross estate?
c. Assume that Art dies in 2006 and Bart dies in 2008, when the land is worth $320,000. What amount is included in Bart's gross estate?

C13-44 *Jointly Owned Property.* Five years ago, Andy and Sandy, siblings, pooled their resources and purchased a warehouse. Andy provided $50,000 of consideration, and Sandy furnished $100,000. Andy dies and is survived by Sandy. The property, which they had titled in the names of Andy and Sandy, joint tenants with right of survivorship, is valued at $450,000 when Andy dies. What amount is included in Andy's gross estate?

C13-45 *Jointly Owned Property.* Mrs. Cobb purchased land costing $80,000 in 1995. She had the land titled in the names of Mr. and Mrs. Cobb, joint tenants with right of survivorship. Mrs. Cobb dies and is survived by Mr. Cobb. At Mrs. Cobb's death, the land's value is $200,000.
a. What amount is included in Mrs. Cobb's gross estate?
b. What is the amount, if any, of the marital deduction that Mrs. Cobb's estate can claim for the land?
c. Assume Mr. Cobb dies after Mrs. Cobb and the land is worth $240,000 at his death. What amount is included in his gross estate?

C13-46 *Powers of Appointment.* Tai, who dies in the current year, is the sole income beneficiary for life of each of the trusts described below. For each trust indicate whether and why it is includible in Tai's gross estate.
a. A trust created under the will of Tai's mother, who died in 1986. Upon Tai's death, the trust assets are to pass to those of Tai's descendants whom Tai directs by his will. Should Tai fail to appoint the trust property, the trust assets are to be distributed to the Smithsonian Institution. Tai wills the property to his twin daughters in equal shares.
b. An irrevocable *inter vivos* trust created in 1991 by Tai's father. The trust agreement authorizes Tai to appoint the property to whomever he so desires. The appointment could be made only by his will. In his will, Tai appoints the property to an elderly neighbor.
c. An irrevocable trust funded by Tai in 1996. The trust instrument specifies that, upon Tai's death, the property is to pass to his children.
d. A trust created under the will of Tai's great-grandmother, who died in 1941. Her will authorizes Tai to appoint the property by his will to whomever he so desires. In default of appointment, the property is to pass to Tai's descendants in equal shares. Tai's will does not mention this trust.
e. Assume the same facts as in Part b except that Tai's will does not mention the trust property.

C13-47 *Life Insurance.* Joy dies on November 5, 2006. Soon after Joy's death, the executor discovers the following insurance policies on Joy's life. Indicate the amount includible in Joy's gross estate for each policy.

Policy Number	Owner	Beneficiary	Face Value
123	Joy	Joy's husband	$400,000
757	Joy's son	Joy's estate	225,000
848	Joy's son	Joy's son	300,000
414	Joy's daughter	Joy's husband	175,000

Joy transferred ownership of policies 757 and 848 to her son in 1997. She gave ownership of policy 414 to her daughter in 2005.

C13-48 *Life Insurance.* Refer to Problem C13-47. What is the net addition to Joy's *taxable estate* with respect to the insurance policies listed above if all the property passing under Joy's will goes to Joy's son?

C13-49 *Deductions.* When Yuji dies in 2006, his gross estate is valued at $5 million. He owes debts totaling $300,000. Funeral and administration expenses are estimated at $12,000 and $120,000, respectively. The marginal estate tax rate will exceed his estate's marginal income tax rate. Yuji wills his church $300,000 and his spouse $1.1 million. What is Yuji's taxable estate?

C13-50 *Marital Deduction.* Assume the same facts as in Problem C13-49 except that Yuji's will also provides for setting up a trust to be funded with $400,000 of property with a bank named as trustee. His wife is to receive all the trust income semiannually for life, and upon her death the trust assets are to be distributed equally among Yuji's children and grandchildren.
a. What is the amount of Yuji's taxable estate? Provide two possible answers.
b. Assume Yuji's widow dies in 2009. With respect to Yuji's former assets, which items will be included in the widow's gross estate? Provide two possible answers, but you need not indicate amounts.

C13-51 *Marital Deduction.* Assume the same facts as in Problem C13-50 and that before Yuji's death his wife already owns property valued at $300,000. Assume that each asset owned by each spouse increases 20% in value by 2009 and that Yuji's executor elects to claim the maximum marital deduction possible. Assume there are no state death taxes. From a tax standpoint, was the executor's strategy of electing the marital deduction on the QTIP trust a wise decision? Support your answer with computations.

C13-52 *Adjusted Taxable Gifts.* Will, a bachelor, dies in the current year. At the time he dies, his sole asset is cash of $2 million. Assume no debts or funeral and administration expenses. His gift history is as follows:

Date	Amount of Taxable Gifts	FMV of Gift Property at Date of Death
October 1987	$270,000	$290,000
October 1991	90,000	65,000

a. What is Will's estate tax base?
b. How would your answer to Part a change if Will made the first gift in 1974 (instead of 1987)?

C13-53 *Estate Tax Base.* Bess dies in 2006. Her gross estate, which totals $3 million, includes a $100,000 life insurance policy on her life that she gave away in 2005. The taxable gift that arose from giving away the policy was $15,000. In 2004, Bess made a $740,000 taxable gift of stock whose value increased to $790,000 by the time Bess died. Assume her estate tax deductions total $80,000.
a. What is her estate tax base?
b. What unified credit may her estate claim?

C13-54 *Installment Payments.* Elaine dies on May 1, 2006. Her gross estate consists of the following items:

Cash	$ 40,000
Stocks traded on a stock exchange	940,000
Personal residence	250,000
25% capital interest in a 60-person partnership	1,020,000

Elaine's Sec. 2053 deductions total $30,000. She has no other deductions.
a. What percentage of Elaine's federal estate taxes may be paid in installments under Sec. 6166? When is the first installment payment due?
b. May Elaine's estate elect Sec. 6166 treatment if the stocks are valued at $2.74 million instead of $940,000?

C13-55 *State Death Taxes.* Giovanni dies in 2006 with a gross estate of $1.8 million and debts of $30,000. He made post-1976 taxable gifts of $100,000. His estate pays state death taxes of $110,200. What is his estate tax base?

COMPREHENSIVE PROBLEMS

C13-56 Bonnie dies on June 1, 2006, survived by her husband, Abner, and two sons, Carl and Doug. Bonnie's only lifetime taxable gift was made in October 2003 in the taxable amount of $1.25 million. She did not elect gift splitting. By the time of her death, the value of the gifted property (stock) had declined to $1.1 million.

Bonnie's executor discovers the items shown below. Amounts shown are the FMVs of the items as of June 1, 2006.

Cash in checking account in her name	$127,750
Cash in savings account in her name	430,000
Stock in names of Bonnie and Doug, joint tenants with right of survivorship. Bonnie provided all the consideration ($3,000) to purchase the stock.	25,000
Land in names of Bonnie and Abner, joint tenants with right of survivorship. Abner provided all the consideration to purchase the land.	360,000
Personal residence in only Bonnie's name	450,000
Life insurance on Bonnie's life. Bonnie is owner, and Bonnie's estate is beneficiary (face value)	500,000
Trust created under the will of Bonnie's mother (who died in 1990). Bonnie is entitled to all the trust income for life, and she could will the trust property to whomever she desired. She wills it to her sons in equal amounts.	700,000

Bonnie's debts, as of her date of death, are $60,000. Her funeral and administration expenses are $15,000 and $65,000, respectively. Her estate paid state death taxes of $65,000. The executor elects to deduct the administration expenses on the estate tax return.
Bonnie's will includes the following:

I leave my residence to my husband Abner.

$250,000 of property is to be transferred to a trust with First Bank named as trustee. All of the income is to be paid to my husband, Abner, semiannually for the rest of his life. Upon his death the property is to be divided equally between my two sons or their estates.

I leave $47,000 to the American Cancer Society.

Assume the executor elects to claim the maximum marital deduction possible. Compute the following with respect to Bonnie's estate:
a. Gross estate
b. Taxable estate
c. Adjusted taxable gifts
d. Estate tax base
e. Tentative tax on estate tax base
f. Federal estate tax payable

C13-57 Assume the same facts as in Problem C13-56 except the joint tenancy land is held in the names of Bonnie and her son Doug, joint tenants with right of survivorship. Also assume that Bonnie provided 55% of the consideration to buy the land and that Bonnie's executor does not elect to claim the marital deduction on the QTIP trust. Assume further that no taxable gift arose on the purchase of the joint tenancy land.

TAX STRATEGY PROBLEM

C13-58 Gaylord Gunnison (GG) died January 13, 2006, and his gross estate consisted of three properties—cash, land, and stock in a public company. The amount of cash on the date of his death was $1.9 million, which went into the estate. On January 13, 2006, the land had a fair market value of $1 million, and the stock had a fair market value of $2 million. On July 13, 2006, the fair market values of the land and stock were $1.1 million and $1.6 million, respectively, and the cash remained at $1.9 million. Assume, for simplicity, that the estate has no deductions and GG made no taxable gifts. GG willed all of his property to his daughter, Gilda, who anticipates that, beginning in July 2006, the stock will appreciate at the rate of 9% per year before taxes. She anticipates selling the stock on or about July 13, 2012. Assume that the land's fair market value will remain at $1.1 million through 2012 and that she anticipates retaining the land for the rest of her life.

Considering both income tax and estate tax effects, compare after-tax wealth using the alternate valuation date or the date of death to value the estate. Which date should the executor elect? For simplicity, assume that the cash is not invested. (Incidentally, the factor for the future value, six years hence, at 9% is 1.677.) Prepare a worksheet on which you calculate the amount of after-tax wealth using the two possible valuation dates. Assume that the gain will be taxed at a 20% rate in 2012.

TAX FORM/RETURN PREPARATION PROBLEMS

C13-59 Prepare an Estate Tax Return (Form 706) for Judy Griffin (464-55-3434), who died on June 30, 2005. Judy is survived by her husband, Greg, and her daughter, Candy. Judy was a resident of 17 Fiddlers Way, Nashville, Tennessee 37205. She was employed as a corporate executive with Sounds of Country, Inc., a recording company, at the time of her death. The assets discovered at Judy's death are listed below at their date-of-death values.

Savings account in Judy's name	$190,000
Checking account in Judy's name	10,000
Personal residence (having a $200,000 mortgage)	500,000
Household furnishings	75,000
400 shares of stock in Omega Corporation (quotes on June 30, 2005 are high of 70, low of 60, close of 67)	?
Land in New York (inherited from her mother in 1981)	640,000
Porsche purchased by Greg in 2003 as an anniversary gift to Judy	45,000

Other items include the following:
1. Life insurance policy 1: Judy purchased a $200,000 life insurance policy on her life on November 1, 2002 and paid the first annual premium of $2,500. The next day, she transferred the policy to her brother, Todd Williams, who also is the beneficiary. Judy paid the premium on August 1, 2003, and August 1, 2004.
2. Life insurance policy 2: A $150,000 whole life policy on Greg's life. Judy purchased the policy in 1994 and has always paid the $1,200 semiannual premium due on March 30 and September 30. Interpolated terminal reserve is $25,000. The beneficiary is Judy or her estate. Judy is the owner of the policy.
3. Employer annuity: Judy's employer established a qualified pension plan in 1982. The employer contributes 60% and the employee pays 40% of the required annual contributions. Judy chose a settlement option that provides for annual payments to Greg until his death. The annuity receivable by Greg is valued at $600,000.

Other information includes the following:
1. In October 2002, Judy transferred to her brother, Todd, $1,522,000 of stock that she received as a gift. Judy and Greg elected gift splitting. This was the first taxable gift for each spouse, and they paid their own portion of the gift tax from their own funds. When Judy dies, the stocks have appreciated to $1.6 million.
2. Unpaid bills at death include $2,500 owed on a bank credit card.
3. The cost of Judy's funeral and tombstone totals $25,000.
4. Judy's administration expenses are estimated at $55,000. Her estate's marginal transfer tax rate will be higher than the estate's marginal income tax rate.
5. Judy's will includes the following dispositions of property:

> I leave $60,000 of property in trust with Fourth Bank named as trustee. All income is to be paid semiannually to my husband, Greg, for life or until he remarries, whichever occurs first. At the termination of Greg's interest, the property will pass to my daughter, Candy, or her estate.

> To my beloved husband, Greg, I leave my Omega stock. The rest of my property I leave to my daughter, Candy, except that I leave $10,000 to the University of Tennessee.

6. Assume that Judy's state imposes an estate tax equal to the maximum credit available on the federal return for state death taxes.
7. Make the QTIP election if possible.

C13-60 Prepare an Estate Tax Return (Form 706) for Joe Blough (177-47-3217) of 1412 Robin Lane, Birmingham, Alabama 35208. Joe died on November 12, 2005; he was survived by his wife, Joan, and their daughter, Katy. Joe was a bank vice president. Date-of-death values of the assets discovered at Joe's death are listed below.

Checking and savings accounts in names of Joe and Joan, joint tenants with right of survivorship	$800,000

Second home, in Joe's name	450,000
Life insurance policy on Joe's life; his estate is the beneficiary and Joan is the owner	250,000
Land in Joe's name	800,000

Other pertinent information is as follows:
1. In 1988, Joe gave his sister land then valued at $220,000. He and Joan elected gift splitting. This was Joe's first taxable gift. The land was worth $350,000 when Joe died.
2. Joan owns the house that had been the couple's principal residence. Its value is $750,000.
3. Joe willed all his property to their daughter, Katy.
4. For simplicity, assume no administration expenses and that funeral expenses are $11,000.
5. Assume that Joe's estate paid state death taxes of $25,000.

CASE STUDY PROBLEMS

C13-61   Your long-time client, Harold (Hal) Holland will meet with your supervising partner next week for an estate planning appointment. Hal has been married to Winona Holland since 1990. Hal is age 68 and retired. Winona, age 60, retired early to spend more time with Hal. They are residents of Topeka, Kansas. Hal is a U.S. citizen, and Winona is a citizen of Australia. Winona has indicated she plans to return to Australia if Hal predeceases her. Your supervising partner has requested that you identify any potential pitfalls in Hal's current estate plan so she can bring them to his attention.

Hal has stated that, in addition to providing some wealth transfers to his wife Winona, he wants to treat his three children by his prior marriage (Gina, Halbert, and Julianna) approximately equally in terms of total wealth received from him while he is alive and as a result of his death.

Hal and Winona prepared and submitted via e-mail the list of assets shown below.

- Principal residence in Topeka titled in the names of Hal and Winona, joint tenants with right of survivorship; purchased with $280,000 of consideration furnished solely by Winona; fair market value of $400,000.

- Household furnishings in the Topeka house; fair market value of $34,000. Winona owned almost all of these furnishings before she married Hal.

- Portfolio of publicly traded stocks in Hal's name; fair market value of $5.12 million.

- Mountain cabin and land in Vail, Colorado. Hal purchased the property in 1988 for $60,000; fair market value is $460,000. Hal never visits the cabin, but Halbert spends every summer and several weeks during the winter at the cabin.

- Stock in Harold's Hammocks, Inc. (a closely held C corporation) transferred to the Oz State Bank Revocable Trust in 1992; fair market value of $226,000, and basis of $15,000. The trust owns 12 of the 100 outstanding common shares. Hal acquired the 12 shares in 1988 in a Sec. 351 transaction. Julianna and Gina each own 44 shares, which Hal gifted to them in 2005.

- Individual retirement account at ToKan State Bank. The account consists of the funds rolled directly into the IRA from the non-contributory qualified retirement plan of Hal's former employer when Hal retired. Fair market value of the IRA is $540,000. Hal has not yet received any distributions. He is the IRA beneficiary, and Winona is the contingent beneficiary if Hal predeceases her.

- Cash of $825,000 in checking and savings accounts in Hal's name.

- Mutual fund shares in the names of Hal and Julianna, joint tenants with right of survivorship. Hal provided all the consideration ($9,000); fair market value of $64,000. He intended to use the money to finance Julianna's education, but she received a full scholarship.

- Stock in Dolrah, Inc. (a firm that elected S corporation status in 1990 upon its formation). The stock is in Hal's name, and he is one of six stockholders; fair market value of $79,000.

Hal's current will reads as follows:

To my wife, Winona, I leave outright any household furnishings that I own, $500,000 of stock from my portfolio of publicly traded stocks, and all of my stock in Dolran, Inc.

To my grandchild, Halbert, Jr., I leave $3,750,000 of stock from my portfolio.

I leave the rest of my estate outright in equal shares to my children, Gina, Halbert, and Julianna.

Required:

Prepare a memo to your supervising partner to help her prepare for the appointment with Hal. In the memo, advise the partner of any pitfalls (problems) you have identified that she should discuss with Hal. You need not make any calculations of estate tax liabilities.

C13-62 Your client is Jon Jake, the executor of the Estate of Beth Adams, a widow. Mrs. Adams died 11 years after the death of her husband, Sam. Mr. Jake seeks assistance in the preparation of the estate tax return for Mrs. Adams, whose estate consists primarily of real estate. Mrs. Adams's estate will be divided among her three adult children except for a small amount of property willed to charity. The real estate has been appraised at $2.2 million by her son-in-law (who is married to one of Mrs. Adams's three children), an experienced real estate appraiser. You have a number of real estate clients and have considerable familiarity with property values for real estate located in the same general area as the estate's property. Your "gut feeling" is that the appraised values may be somewhat understated. As a tax advisor, what responsibilities do you have to make additional inquiries? What information should you give Mr. Jake concerning possible penalties?

TAX RESEARCH PROBLEMS

C13-63 Arthur Zolnick died at age 84 on June 7, 2006. In March 2003, he transferred $4 million of stock to a charitable remainder annuity trust (CRAT) from which he named himself to receive $280,000 per year for life. He designated a charitable organization to receive the remainder interest after his death and appointed his nephew Luther as trustee. Luther never distributed cash to Arthur because Arthur indicated he had no need for additional funds that "would just add to my gross estate." At Arthur's date of death, the value of the assets in the CRAT had risen to $4.3 million. What charitable contribution deduction will Arthur's estate receive?

C13-64 Val, a resident of Illinois, died on June 12 of the current year. On May 5, she wrote four checks for $11,000 each, payable to each of her four grandchildren. Val mailed the checks on May 6, and each donee received the check on or before May 9. None of the donees deposited his or her checks until after Val's death. As of Val's date of death, the balance in her checking account was $52,127. This balance includes the $44,000 of outstanding checks issued to her grandchildren. Assume the executor will elect date-of-death valuation.

Your senior requested that you prepare a memorandum concerning whether the checks can be subtracted from the $52,127 account balance in arriving at the cash includible in Val's gross estate. Your senior indicates that you should start with the following authorities:

- IRC Sec. 2031(a)
- Reg. Secs. 20.2031-5 and 25.2511-2(b)

C13-65 Hal Harmon, a resident of California, died in 2006, survived by his spouse Winnie Harmon and their three sons. In 1997, he transferred property to an irrevocable trust with a bank trustee and provided in the trust instrument that during the rest of his life he was entitled to all the trust income, payable quarterly, and that he could withdraw from principal whatever amounts he desired. He made no principal withdrawals, and when he died, the value of the trust was $3.7 million. Another provision in the trust instrument provided that his sons, in equal shares, would receive the remainder interest in the trust after Winnie's death if he predeceased her or after his death if Winnie predeceased him. In addition, the trust instrument instructed the trustee to pay to Winnie quarterly for life, beginning immediately after his death, "all the trust income as the trustee in its reasonable discretion determines is proper for Winnie's health, education, support, maintenance, comfort, and welfare in accordance with Winnie's accustomed manner of living." Prepare

13-46 Corporations ▼ Chapter 13

a memo to your manager in which you discuss whether the trust qualifies for the marital deduction and whether Winnie possesses a general power of appointment in the trust.

C13-66 *Internet Research Problem.* You have been asked to make a presentation to a group of laypersons and explain which types of property do not pass under the decedent's will (that is, they pass outside probate). Consult the Internet address *http://www.mtpalermo.com,* where you will find a number of estate tax related materials you can use to conduct the research for your presentation. Prepare a presentation explaining several types of property that do not pass under the terms of the will, that is, they pass outside probate.

C13-67 *Internet Research Problem.* Soon you will be meeting with a client who is considering moving to one of several other states and who does not currently have a will. You want to do some research regarding how property typically passes if the decedent dies intestate (without a will). The client plans to execute a will soon but makes the inquiry because of his busy schedule and tendency to procrastinate. Consult the Internet address *http://www.suffolklaw.com.* On the left side, select "Legal Publications," then select "Estate Planning," and finally select "What Happens If You Die Intestate?" Prepare a brief memo about what you learn.

14

C H A P T E R

INCOME TAXATION OF TRUSTS AND ESTATES

LEARNING OBJECTIVES

After studying this chapter, you should be able to

▶ 1 Understand the basic concepts concerning trusts and estates

▶ 2 Distinguish between the accounting concepts of principal and income

▶ 3 Calculate the tax liability of a trust or an estate

▶ 4 Understand the significance of distributable net income

▶ 5 Determine the taxable income of a simple trust

▶ 6 Determine the taxable income of a complex trust and an estate

▶ 7 Recognize the significance of income in respect of a decedent

▶ 8 Explain the effect of the grantor trust provisions

▶ 9 Recognize the filing requirements for fiduciary returns

Chapters C12 and C13 examined two components of the transfer tax system: the gift tax and the estate tax. This chapter returns to income taxation by exploring the basic rules for taxing trusts and estates, two special tax entities often called **fiduciaries**. Income generated by property owned by an estate or a **trust** is reported on an income tax return for that entity. In general, the tax rules governing estates and trusts are identical. Unless the text states that a rule applies to only one of these entities, the discussion concerns both estates and trusts. Subchapter J (Secs. 641-692) of the IRC contains the special tax rules applicable to estates and trusts. This chapter describes the basic provisions of Subchapter J.

This chapter also discusses principles of fiduciary accounting, a concept that influences the tax consequences. The chapter focuses on determining the fiduciary's taxable income and the amount taxable to the beneficiaries. It includes comprehensive examples concerning the computations of taxable income, and Appendix B displays completed tax returns (Form 1041) for both a simple and a complex trust. The chapter also explores the circumstances that cause the grantor (transferor) to be taxed on the trust's income.

BASIC CONCEPTS

INCEPTION OF TRUSTS

OBJECTIVE 1

*Understand the basic
concepts concerning trusts
and estates*

**ADDITIONAL
COMMENT**

The IRS projects that four million
fiduciary income tax returns will
be filed in 2006.

Often a relatively wealthy person (one concerned with gift and/or estate taxes) will create trusts for tax and/or other reasons (e.g., conserving assets). A person may create a trust at any point in time by transferring property to the trust. A **trustee** (named by the transferor) administers the trust property for the benefit of the beneficiary. The trustee may be either an individual or an institution, such as a bank, and there can be more than one trustee.

If the transfer occurs during the transferor's lifetime, the trust is called an **inter vivos trust**, meaning among the living. The transferor is known as the **grantor** or the **trustor**. A trust created under the direction of a decedent's will is called a **testamentary trust** and contains assets formerly held by the decedent's estate. A trust may continue to exist for whatever time the trust instrument or the will specifies subject to the constraints of the **Rule Against Perpetuities**.[1]

INCEPTION OF ESTATES

Estates originate only upon the death of the person whose assets are being administered. The estate continues in existence until the executor[2] (i.e., the person(s) named in the will to manage the property and distribute the assets) or administrator (where the decedent died without a will) completes his or her duties. An executor's or administrator's duties include collecting the assets, paying the debts and taxes, and distributing the property. The time needed to perform the duties may vary from a year or two to over a decade, depending on many factors (e.g., whether anyone contests the will).

Because the estate is a separate tax entity, continuing the estate's existence creates an additional personal exemption and achieves having some income taxed to yet another taxpayer, but the estate's income tax rates are very compressed. Nevertheless, the decedent's survivors sometimes can reduce their personal income taxes by preserving the estate's existence as a separate taxpayer. Treasury Regulations provide, however, that if the IRS considers the administration of an estate to have been unreasonably prolonged, it will view the estate as having been terminated for federal tax purposes after the expiration of a reasonable period for performance of the administrative duties.[3] In such a situation, the income is taxed directly to the individuals entitled to receive the estate's assets, and sometimes these individuals have a higher marginal tax rate than does the estate.

---

[1] The Rule Against Perpetuities addresses how long property may be tied up in trust and is the "principle that no interest in property is good unless it must vest, if at all, not later than 21 years, plus period of gestation, after some life or lives in being at time of creation of interest." Henry Campbell Black, *Black's Law Dictionary*, Rev. 6th ed., Ed. by Joseph R. Nolan and Jacqueline

M. Nolan-Haley (St. Paul, MN: West Publishing Co., 1990), p. 1331. Some states have abolished the Rule Against Perpetuities.
[2] In some states, this individual is called a personal representative.
[3] Reg. Sec. 1.641(b)-3(a).

REASONS FOR CREATING TRUSTS

A myriad of reasons—both tax and nontax—exist for creating trusts. A discussion of some of these reasons follows.

TAX SAVING ASPECTS OF TRUSTS. If the trust is irrevocable, meaning the grantor cannot require the trustee to return the assets, one of the primary tax purposes for establishing the trust traditionally was to achieve income splitting. Historically, with income splitting, the income from the trust assets was taxed to at least one taxpayer (i.e., the trust or the beneficiary) at a lower marginal tax rate than that of the grantor. Today's compressed fiduciary tax rate schedules, under which the top rate of 35% (in 2006) occurs at an income level slightly above $10,000, often make achieving income tax reduction difficult. Sometimes the trust instrument authorizes the trustee to use his or her discretion in "sprinkling" the income among several beneficiaries or accumulating it within the trust. In such circumstances, the trustee may consider the tax effects of making a distribution of income to one beneficiary rather than to another or retaining income in the trust.

Individuals also have created trusts to minimize their estate taxes. As discussed in Chapter C13, for the transferor to exclude the property conveyed to the trust from the gross estate, the transferor must not retain the right to receive the trust income or the power to control which other people receive the income or have, at the time of death, the power to alter the identity of anyone named earlier to receive such assets.[4]

NONTAX ASPECTS OF TRUSTS. Reduction of taxes is not always the foremost reason for establishing trusts. Individuals often use trusts, including Sec. 2503(c) trusts and *Crummey* trusts, when minors are the donees so that a trustee can manage the assets. (See Chapter C12 for a discussion of such trusts.) Even when the donee is an adult, donors sometimes may prefer that the assets be managed by a trustee deemed to have better management skills than the donee. Other donors may want to avoid conveying property directly to a donee if they fear the donee would soon consume most of the assets. In addition, donors sometimes use trusts to protect assets from creditors.

The creation of a **revocable trust** (i.e., one in which the grantor may demand that the assets be returned) does not yield any income or estate tax savings for the grantor. Nevertheless, donors often establish revocable trusts, including ones in which the grantor is also the beneficiary, for nontax purposes such as having the property managed by an individual or an institution with superior management skills. Use of a revocable trust reduces probate costs because assets in a revocable trust avoid probate. Such a strategy is especially important in states where probate costs are high. In this text, a trust is deemed to be an **irrevocable trust** unless explicitly denoted as being revocable.

BASIC PRINCIPLES OF FIDUCIARY TAXATION

Throughout the rest of this chapter, you should keep several basic principles of **fiduciary taxation** in mind. These features (discussed below) apply to all trusts other than grantor trusts, a type of trust where generally the grantor instead of the trust or the beneficiary pays tax on the income. (See pages C14-30 through C14-33 for a description of the tax treatment of grantor trusts.)

TRUSTS AND ESTATES AS SEPARATE TAXPAYERS. An estate or a trust is a separate taxpaying entity that files a Form 1041, and if it has any taxable income, it pays an income tax. The 2006 tax rates applicable to estates and trusts appear on the inside back cover. These rates, which are indexed annually for inflation, are very compressed in comparison with the rates for individuals. As is true for individuals, an estate's or trust's long-term capital gains and qualified dividends are taxed at a top tax rate of 15% (through 2008).

---

[4] Sec. 2036, relating to retention of income or control, and Sec. 2038, relating to the power to alter the identity of beneficiaries.

EXAMPLE C14-1 ▶ For calendar year 2006, a trust reports taxable income of $15,000, none from dividends or long-term capital gains. Its tax liability is $4,329. In contrast, an unmarried individual not qualifying as a head of household would owe taxes of $1,873 on $15,000 of taxable income. ◀

NO DOUBLE TAXATION. Unlike the situation for corporations, no double taxation of income earned by an estate or trust (a fiduciary taxpayer) occurs because an estate or trust receives a deduction for the income it distributes to its beneficiaries. The beneficiaries, in turn, report the taxable portion of their receipts as income on their individual returns. Thus, the current income is taxed once, to the fiduciary or to the beneficiary or some to each, depending on whether it is distributed. In total, all the estate or trust's current income is taxed, sometimes some to the fiduciary and the remaining amount to the beneficiary. One of the primary purposes of the Subchapter J rules is to address exactly where the estate or trust's current income is taxed.

EXAMPLE C14-2 ▶ In the current year, the Lopez Trust receives corporate bond interest of $25,000, $15,000 of which the trustee in its discretion distributes to Lupe. Lupe is taxed on $15,000, the amount of the distribution. The trust is taxed on the income it retains or accumulates, $10,000 in this case, less a $100 personal exemption (discussed on pages C14-9 and C14-10). ◀

CONDUIT APPROACH. A conduit approach governs fiduciary income taxation. Under this approach, the distributed income has the same character in the hands of the beneficiary as it has to the trust. Thus, if the trust distributes tax-free interest income on state and local bonds, such income retains its tax-free character at the beneficiary level.

EXAMPLE C14-3 ▶ In the current year, the Lopez Trust receives $15,000 of dividends and $10,000 of tax-free interest. It distributes all of its receipts to its beneficiary, who is deemed to receive $15,000 of dividend income and $10,000 of tax-free interest. The 15% tax rate applies to the dividends assuming the beneficiary's tax bracket equals or exceeds 15%. ◀

SIMILARITY TO RULES FOR INDIVIDUALS. Section 641(b) states "[T]he taxable income of an estate or trust shall be computed in the same manner as in the case of an individual, except as otherwise provided in this part." Sections 641–683 appear in this part (Part I) of Subchapter J. Thus, the tax effect for fiduciaries is the same as for individuals if the provisions of Secs. 641–683 do not specify rules that differ from those applicable for individual taxpayers. Sections 641–683 do not provide any special treatment for interest income from state and local bonds or for state and local tax payments. Consequently, an estate or trust receives an exclusion for state and local bond interest and the same deductions as individuals for state and local taxes. On the other hand, Sec. 642(b) specifies the amount of the personal exemption for fiduciaries. Thus, this subsection preempts the Sec. 151 rule concerning the amount of the personal exemption for individuals.

PRINCIPLES OF FIDUCIARY ACCOUNTING

To better understand the special tax treatment of fiduciary income, especially the determination of to whom the estate or trust's current income is taxed, one needs a general knowledge of the principles of fiduciary accounting. In a sense, fiduciary accounting is similar to fund accounting for government entities. Instead of having separate funds, all receipts and disbursements are classified in either the income or principal (corpus) account.

THE IMPORTANCE OF IDENTIFYING INCOME AND PRINCIPAL

When computing taxable income, we generally are concerned with whether a particular item is included in or deducted from gross income. When answering fiduciary tax questions, however, we also need to consider whether an item is classified as principal (corpus) or income for fiduciary accounting purposes. For example, certain items (e.g., interest on state bonds) may constitute fiduciary accounting gross income but are not included in calculating gross income for tax purposes. Other items (e.g., capital gains) may be included in gross income but classified as principal for fiduciary accounting purposes. If the trust instrument stipulates that the trustee can distribute only income prior to the termination of the trust, the amount of fiduciary accounting income sets the ceiling on the current distribution that the trustee can make to a beneficiary.

One of the most difficult aspects of feeling comfortable with the fiduciary taxation rules is appreciating the difference between fiduciary accounting income and income in the general tax sense. To understand and apply the IRC, one has to know in which context the word *income* is used. Section 643(b) provides guidance for this matter by providing that the word *income* refers to income in the fiduciary accounting context unless other words, such as "distributable net," "undistributable net," "taxable," or "gross," modify the word *income*. In this text, the term **net accounting income** is used to refer to the excess of accounting gross income over expenses charged to accounting income.

Under state law, the definitions in the trust instrument that classify items as principal or income preempt any definitions contained in state statutes. In the absence of definitions in the trust instrument, the applicable state statute controls. For purposes of defining principal and income, many states have adopted the *Revised Uniform Principal and Income Act* (enacted in 1962 and hereafter referred to as the Uniform Act of 1962) in its entirety or with minor modifications.[5] However, in recent years a number of states have adopted the Uniform Principal and Income Act (1997).

The 1997 Act allows the trustee to make adjustments between the principal and income accounts to the extent the trustee deems them necessary, provided certain additional requirements are met. A trustee, however, will not always deem adjustments necessary. The rationale behind allowing adjustments is grounded in modern portfolio theory. By allowing trustees to transfer cash from principal to income, the 1997 Act enables a trustee to apply prudent investor standards when making investment decisions. If dividends are low because of investing in growth stocks, the trustee can transfer some cash to the income account, thereby increasing the amount distributable to a beneficiary entitled to receive only income.

The categorization of a receipt or disbursement as principal or income generally affects the amount that can be distributed and the amount taxed to the fiduciary or the beneficiary. For example, if a gain is classified as principal and the trustee can distribute only income, the trust is taxed on the gain. Even though a receipt constitutes gross income for tax purposes, the trustee cannot distribute it to a beneficiary if it constitutes principal under the fiduciary accounting rules unless the trust instrument authorizes the trustee to distribute principal or unless, under the 1997 Act, the trustee adjusts by transferring some cash from principal to income.

SELF-STUDY QUESTION

A trust agreement provides that all trust income is to be distributed to Janet until her thirty-fifth birthday, at which time the trust is to terminate and distribute all of its corpus to Joe. Stock is the only property owned by the trust. If the trust sells the stock, is Janet entitled to a distribution equal to the gain?

ANSWER

This question stresses the importance of differentiating between income and principal. The trustee must follow the definitions of income and corpus stated in the trust agreement, or if not there, under state law. Janet receives no distribution if the proceeds are classified as corpus unless the trustee under the 1997 Act makes an adjustment and moves money from corpus to income.

EXAMPLE C14-4 ▶

In the current year, the Bell Trust collects $18,000 of dividends, classified as accounting income. In addition, it sells stock for a $40,000 capital gain. Under state law, which is based on the Uniform Act of 1962 (discussed below), the gain is allocated to principal. The trust instrument (which does not define principal or income) requires the trustee to distribute all the trust's income to Beth annually until she reaches age 45. The trust assets are to be held and paid to Beth on her forty-fifth birthday (five years from now). The trustee must distribute $18,000 to Beth in the current year. The capital gain cannot be distributed currently because it is allocated to principal, and the trustee is not empowered to make distributions of principal. The trust will pay tax on the gain. ◀

PRINCIPAL AND INCOME: THE UNIFORM ACT

INCOME RECEIPTS. The Uniform Act of 1962 defines *income* as "the return in money or property derived from the use of principal." It lists income as including the following: rent, interest, corporate distributions of dividends, distributions by a regulated investment company from ordinary income, and the net profits of a business. The rules are more

---

[5] The *Revised Uniform Principal and Income Act* (1962) is a model set of rules proposed by the National Conference of Commissioners on Uniform State Laws. States can voluntarily adopt such provisions verbatim or in amended form.

detailed for receipts from the disposition of natural resources. A portion (27.5%) of the receipts from royalties is added to principal as a depletion allowance. The remainder of the royalties constitutes income. The 1997 Act provides different rules for allocating of royalty receipts.

ADDITIONAL COMMENT

The Commissioners approved and recommended for enactment the *Uniform Principal and Income Act* (1997). A number of states have adopted the 1997 Act, which differs in many ways from the 1962 Act.

PRINCIPAL RECEIPTS. *Principal* is defined in the Uniform Act of 1962 as "the property which has been set aside by the owner or the person legally empowered so that it is held in trust eventually to be delivered to the **remainderman** while the return or use of the principal is in the meantime taken or received by or held for accumulation for an **income beneficiary**." Among the categories of receipts included in principal are the following: consideration received on the sale or other transfer of principal or on repayment of a loan, stock dividends, receipts from disposition of corporate securities, and 27.5% of royalties received from natural resources.

EXPENDITURES. The Uniform Act of 1962 provides guidance for expenditures also. Among the important charges that reduce income are the following:

► Ordinary expenses, including regularly recurring property taxes, insurance premiums, interest, and ordinary repairs

► A reasonable allowance for depreciation

► Tax payable by the trustee if it is levied on receipts classified as income

Some of the significant expenditures chargeable to principal are

► Principal payments on debts

► Extraordinary repairs or expenses incurred in making a capital improvement

► Any tax levied on gain or other receipts allocated to principal even if the tax is described as an income tax

Frequently, the agreement between the grantor and the trustee specifies the respective portions of the trustee's fee that are chargeable to income and corpus.

EXAMPLE C14-5 ►

SELF-STUDY QUESTION

Wilson Trust, which owns a commercial building, is required to distribute all of its income each year. The building is leased to a tenant on a net lease, so the trust's only expense is depreciation. The rental income is $25,000, and the depreciation is $11,000. If depreciation is chargeable to income, the distribution to the income beneficiary will be $14,000, and the trustee will set aside $11,000 of the income for the remainderman. What is the impact if depreciation is chargeable to principal?

ANSWER

The income distribution will be $25,000. If the trust holds the building to the end of its useful life, the building will theoretically "turn to dust" overnight, and the remainderman would receive nothing (as far as the building is concerned) because the trust had no depreciation reserve.

The governing instrument for the Wang Trust does not define income and principal. The state in question has adopted the Uniform Act of 1962. In the current year, the trust reports the following receipts and disbursements:

Dividends	$12,000
Proceeds from sale of stock, including $20,000 of gain	70,000
Trustee's fee, all charged to income	1,000
CPA's fee for preparation of tax return	500

The trust's net accounting income is $10,500 ($12,000 − $1,000 − $500). The gain on the sale of stock and the remaining sales proceeds constitute corpus. Consequently, if the trustee can distribute nothing but income, the maximum distribution is $10,500. ◄

CATEGORIZATION OF DEPRECIATION

As mentioned above, the Uniform Act of 1962 charges depreciation to income. Depreciation thereby reduces net accounting income and the maximum amount that can be distributed to a beneficiary if the trust instrument does not authorize the distribution of corpus. Many states have departed from the Uniform Act's treatment of depreciation by providing that depreciation is a charge against principal (instead of against income). If depreciation is charged against principal, the maximum amount that can be distributed to the income beneficiaries is not reduced by the depreciation deduction. This result is advantageous to the income beneficiary. (See page C14-9 for a discussion of the tax treatment of depreciation.)

Some trust instruments require the trustee to set aside (and not distribute) a certain amount of income as a depreciation reserve. A statement in the trust instrument concerning the accounting treatment for depreciation overrides a provision of state law.

EXAMPLE C14-6 ►

Park Trust, whose trust instrument is silent with respect to depreciation, collects rental income of $17,000 and pays property taxes of $1,000. Its depreciation expense is $4,000. Under state law, all depreciation is charged to principal. Therefore, the trust's net accounting income is $16,000 ($17,000 − $1,000). If the trust instrument mandates current distribution of all the income, the beneficiary receives $16,000. If the trust instrument states that depreciation is charged against income, the income distribution is limited to $12,000. ◄

Topic Review C14-1 summarizes the treatment under the Uniform Act of 1962 of the major receipts and expenditures of fiduciaries. The discussion in the rest of the chapter assumes the Uniform Act of 1962 governs the trust.

FORMULA FOR TAXABLE INCOME AND TAX LIABILITY

OBJECTIVE 3

Calculate the tax liability of a trust or an estate

With three major exceptions, the formula for determining a fiduciary's taxable income and income tax liability is very similar to the formula applicable to individuals. A fiduciary's deductions are not divided between deductions *for* and *from* adjusted gross income (AGI). Instead, a fiduciary's deductions are simply deductible in arriving at taxable income. A fiduciary receives no standard deduction. A type of deduction inapplicable to individuals—the distribution deduction—is available in computing a fiduciary's taxable income. Figure C14-1 illustrates the formula for computing a fiduciary's taxable income and tax liability.

GROSS INCOME

The items included in a trust or estate's gross income are the same as those included in an individual's gross income. However, the categorization of a fiduciary's income is not identical for tax and accounting purposes. For example, a gain usually constitutes principal for accounting purposes, but it is part of gross income for tax purposes.

EXAMPLE C14-7 ▶ In the current year, Duke Trust receives $8,000 interest on corporate bonds, $20,000 interest on state bonds, and a $50,000 capital gain. The trust reports gross income of $58,000 ($8,000 + $50,000). Its accounting income is $28,000 ($8,000 + $20,000) because tax-exempt interest is accounting income, and the gain is part of principal. ◀

DEDUCTIONS FOR EXPENSES

Fiduciaries incur numerous deductible expenses that parallel those of individuals and include interest, taxes (e.g., state and local income taxes and property taxes), fees for investment advice, fees for tax return preparation, expenses associated with producing income, and trade or business expenses. In addition, fiduciaries may deduct the trustee's fee. This fee, which is similar to a property management fee incurred by an individual, is deductible under Sec. 212 as an expense incurred for the management of property held for the production of income.

Topic Review C14-1

Classification of Receipts and Expenditures as Principal or Income Under the Uniform Act of 1962

INCOME ACCOUNT	PRINCIPAL ACCOUNT

Income:
  Rent
  Interest
  Dividends
  Net profits of a business
  72.5% of royalties[a]
	Receipts:
	  Consideration (including gains) received upon
	    disposition of property
	  Stock dividends
	  27.5% of royalties[a]

Expenses:
  Ordinary expenses (e.g., property taxes,
    insurance, interest, and ordinary repairs)
  Taxes levied on accounting income
  Depreciation[b]
	Expenditures:
	  Principal payments on debt
	  Extraordinary repairs and capital improvements
	  Taxes levied on gains and other items of principal

[a]The Uniform Principal and Income Act (1997) provides a different allocation.
[b]Many state laws depart from the Uniform Act and characterize depreciation as a charge to principal.

Gross Income (same rules as for individuals)

Minus

Deductions for expenses[a] (interest, taxes, tax return preparation fees, trustee's fee, trade or business expenses, expenses related to production of income, depreciation,[b] and charitable contributions)

Minus

Distribution deduction (maximum is Distributable Net Income [DNI] minus net tax-exempt income)

Minus

Exemption deduction

Equals

Taxable income

Tax on taxable income (using rates in Secs. 1(e) and (1h))

Minus

Credits

Equals

Net tax liability[c]

[a] No deduction is available for expenses allocable to tax-exempt income.

[b] When the trust instrument is silent, depreciation is allocated between the fiduciary and the beneficiary according to the portion of income attributable to each.

[c] Trusts and estates are subject to the alternative minimum tax (AMT). The AMT may be owed by a trust or estate in addition to the income tax levy described in this figure. The AMT is calculated in the same way as for individual taxpayers. Trusts and estates, however, are allowed only a $22,500 statutory exemption. This exemption is phased-out from $75,000 to $165,000 of alternative minimum taxable income.

FIGURE C14-1 ▶ FORMULA FOR DETERMINING THE TAXABLE INCOME AND TAX LIABILITY OF A FIDUCIARY

KEY POINT

Trustees' and executors' fees, as well as tax return preparation fees, are *not* subject to the 2% miscellaneous itemized deduction floor.

For individuals, miscellaneous itemized deductions are deductible only to the extent the aggregate amount of such deductions exceeds 2% of the taxpayer's AGI. Estates and trusts do not literally have AGI, but Sec. 67(e) provides that a hypothetical AGI amount for an estate or trust is determined in the same fashion as for an individual *except* that (1) expenses paid or incurred in connection with the administration of the estate or trust *that would not have been incurred if the property were not held in such trust or estate,* (2) the personal exemption, and (3) the distribution deduction are treated as deductible for hypothetical AGI. Thus, these deductions are not subject to the 2% floor, and by being subtracted to arrive at hypothetical AGI, they reduce the amount of disallowed miscellaneous deductions. The trustees' or executors' fees and the cost of preparation of a fiduciary return would have been avoided if the trust or estate had not existed and therefore are excepted from the 2% floor. In *William J. O'Neill, Jr. Irrevocable Trust*[6] the Sixth Circuit reversed the Tax Court's decision, which had held that amounts paid for investment counsel fees were subject to the floor because they were not unique to the administration of estates and trusts. In *Mellon Bank, N.A.,*[7] the Federal Circuit upheld the decision of the U.S. Court of Federal Claims that fees for investment advice were subject to the 2% floor. The court reasoned that such fees failed the requirement that they would not have been incurred had there been no trust.

An executor can deduct administration expenses on the estate's income tax return if he or she does not deduct such items on the estate tax return. Unlike the situation for individuals, a fiduciary's charitable contribution deduction is not limited. The IRC does not allow a deduction, however, unless the trust instrument authorizes a charitable contribution.[8]

[6] 71 AFTR 2d 93-2052, 93-1 USTC ¶50,332 (6th Cir., 1993), reversing 98 T.C. 227 (1992), nonacq., I.R.B. 1994-38, 4.
[7] 88 AFTR 2d 2001-5800, 2001-2 USTC ¶50,621 (Fed. Cir., 2001). In *Scott,* 89 AFTR 2d 2002-1314, 2002-1 USTC ¶50,364 (DC, VA, 2002), a district court in Virginia concluded that fees were limited by the 2% floor rule. The

Fourth Circuit, 91 AFTR 2d 2003-2100, 2003-1 USTC ¶50,428, affirmed *Scott.* In 2005, the Tax Court ruled in *Rudkin Testamentary Trust,* 124 T.C. No. 19 (2005), that investment management fees were subject to the 2% floor.
[8] Sec. 642(c)(1).

A depreciation or depletion deduction is available to an estate or trust only to the extent it is not allowable to beneficiaries under Secs. 167(d) or 611(b).[9] According to Sec. 167(d), the depreciation deduction for trusts is apportioned between the income beneficiaries and the trust pursuant to the terms of the trust instrument. If the instrument is silent, the depreciation is divided between the parties on the basis of the trust income allocable to each. For estates, however, the depreciation always must be apportioned according to the share of the income allocable to each party. The Sec. 611(b) rules for depletion parallel those described above for the allocation of depreciation.

EXAMPLE C14-8 ▶ In the current year, Nunn Trust distributes 20% of its income to Bob and 50% to Clay. It accumulates the remaining 30%. The trust's current year depreciation is $10,000. The trust instrument is silent concerning the depreciation deduction. Under state law, depreciation is charged to principal. Even though net accounting income and the maximum distributable amount are not reduced by the depreciation deduction, Bob receives a $2,000 (0.20 × $10,000) depreciation deduction, and Clay receives a $5,000 (0.50 × $10,000) depreciation deduction. The remaining $3,000 (0.30 × $10,000) of depreciation is deducted in calculating the trust's taxable income. ◀

DISTRIBUTION DEDUCTION

KEY POINT

If a trust *must* distribute all of its income currently, has no charitable beneficiary, *and* does *not* distribute corpus during the year, it is a simple trust for that year. *Income,* as used here, is accounting net income.

SIMPLE TRUSTS. Some trusts must distribute all their income currently and are not empowered to make charitable contributions. Treasury Regulations refer to such trusts as **simple trusts.**[10] According to Sec. 651(a), these trusts receive a distribution deduction for the income required to be distributed currently, that is, 100% of the trust income. No words modify the word *income;* therefore, *income* means accounting income. If the accounting income that must be distributed exceeds the trust's distributable net income, the distribution deduction may not exceed the distributable net income (see discussion beginning on page C14-10). As used in this context, distributable net income does not include any tax-free income (net of related deductions) that the trust earned.[11] Whatever amount is deductible at the trust level is taxed to the beneficiaries, and they are taxed on all the income, irrespective of the amount they receive.

COMPLEX TRUSTS. Trusts that are not required to distribute all their income currently are referred to as **complex trusts.**[12] The distribution deduction for complex trusts and all estates is the sum of the income required to be distributed currently and any other amounts (such as discretionary payments) properly paid, credited, or required to be distributed for the year. As is the case for simple trusts, the distribution deduction may not exceed the trust or estate's distributable net income (reduced by its tax-exempt income net of any related deductions).[13] The complex trust or estate's beneficiaries report, in the aggregate, gross income equal to the amount of the distribution deduction.[14]

EXAMPLE C14-9 ▶ Green Trust must distribute 25% of its income annually to Amy. In addition, the trustee in its discretion may distribute additional income to Amy or Brad. In the current year, the trust has net accounting income and distributable net income of $100,000, none from tax-exempt sources. The trust makes a $25,000 mandatory distribution to Amy and discretionary distributions of $10,000 each to Amy and Brad. The trust's distribution deduction is $45,000 ($25,000 + $10,000 + $10,000). Amy and Brad report trust income of $35,000 and $10,000, respectively, on their individual returns. ◀

PERSONAL EXEMPTION

One of the differences between the rules for individuals and for fiduciaries is the amount of the personal exemption. Under Sec. 151, individuals are allowed personal exemptions. Section 642(b) authorizes an exemption for fiduciaries that applies in lieu of the amount for individuals. A trust or estate, however, receives no exemption in the year of its termination.

---

[9] Sec. 642(e).
[10] Reg. Sec. 1.651(a)-1.
[11] Sec. 651(b).

[12] Reg. Sec. 1.661(a)-1.
[13] Secs. 661(a) and (c).
[14] Sec. 662(a).

Estates are entitled to a $600 exemption. The exemption amount for trusts differs, depending on the terms of the trust. If the trust instrument requires that the trustee distribute all the income annually, the trust receives a $300 exemption. Otherwise, $100 is the exemption amount. Some trusts may be required to make current distributions of all their income in certain years, whereas in other years they may be directed to accumulate the income or to make distributions at the trustee's discretion. For such trusts the exemption amount is $300 in some years and $100 in other years.

EXAMPLE C14-10 ▶ Gold Trust is established in 2006 with Jack as the beneficiary. The trust instrument instructs the trustee to make discretionary distributions of income to Jack during the years 2006 through 2010. Beginning in 2011, the trustee is to pay all the trust income to Jack currently. For 2006 through 2010, the trust's exemption is $100. Beginning in 2011, it rises to $300. ◀

Recall that a trust receives a distribution deduction for income currently distributed to its beneficiaries. At first blush, it appears that the distribution deduction balances out the income of trusts that must distribute all their income currently, and such trusts receive no tax benefits from their exemption deduction. True, the exemption produces no tax savings for such trusts if they have no gains credited to principal. Tax savings do result from the personal exemption, however, if the trust has undistributed gains. The exemption reduces the amount of gain otherwise taxed at the trust level.

EXAMPLE C14-11 ▶ Rizzo Trust must distribute all of its income currently. Capital gains are characterized as principal. In the current year, Rizzo Trust has $25,000 of interest income from corporate bonds and a $10,000 capital gain. It has no expenses. It receives a distribution deduction of $25,000 and a $300 personal exemption. Its taxable income is $9,700 ($25,000 + $10,000 − $25,000 − $300). ◀

SELF-STUDY QUESTION

A trust, although not required to do so, distributes all of its income for the year. In the same year, it has a long-term capital gain. The trust agreement allocates the gain to principal. The trust does not distribute corpus, and none of its beneficiaries are charities. Is the trust a simple trust? What is its personal exemption?

ANSWER

It is a complex trust because it is not required to distribute all of its income. The exemption is $100 because distributions are discretionary.

The personal exemption amount for individuals is adjusted annually for changes in the consumer price index, but no comparable provision exists for the personal exemption for fiduciaries. On the other hand, the tax rate schedules for both fiduciaries and individuals are indexed for inflation.

CREDITS

In general, the rules for tax credits for fiduciaries are the same as those for individuals, but a fiduciary generally does not incur expenditures of the type that trigger some of the personal credits, such as the credit for household and dependent care expenses. Trusts and estates are allowed a foreign tax credit determined in the same manner as for individual taxpayers except that the credit is limited to the amount of foreign taxes not allocable to the beneficiaries.[15]

U.S. PRODUCTION ACTIVITIES DEDUCTION

The 2004 Jobs Act added a new deduction for businesses engaged in U.S. production activities for tax years beginning after 2004. Chapter C3 describes the corporate version of this deduction, but the deduction also applies to individuals. If upon the death of a sole proprietor, his or her business passes to an estate or trust, the U.S. production activities deduction applies at the beneficiary level. Thus, the estate or trust will need to determine each beneficiary's share of the business's qualified production activities income and report these amounts to the beneficiaries. Further discussion of this topic with respect to estates and trusts is beyond the scope of this text.

DISTRIBUTABLE NET INCOME

OBJECTIVE 4

Understand the significance of distributable net income

As stated earlier in this chapter, the primary function of Subchapter J is to determine to whom—the fiduciary, the beneficiary, or some to each—the estate or the trust's current income is to be taxed. **Distributable net income (DNI)** plays a key role in determining the amount taxed to each party. In fact, DNI has been called the pie to be cut for tax purposes.[16]

---

[15] Sec. 642(a)(1).
[16] M. Carr Ferguson, James L. Freeland, and Richard B. Stephens, *Federal* *Income Taxation of Estates and Beneficiaries* (Boston, MA: Little, Brown, 1970), p. 1x.

SIGNIFICANCE OF DNI

DNI sets the ceiling on the amount of distributions taxed to the beneficiaries. As mentioned earlier, beneficiaries are taxed on the lesser of the amount of the distributions they receive or their share of DNI (reduced by net tax-exempt income).

Just as the total amount taxed to the beneficiaries equals the fiduciary's distribution deduction, DNI represents not only the maximum that can be taxed to the beneficiaries but also the maximum that can be deducted at the fiduciary level. Recall from the preceding section that the distribution deduction is the smaller of the amount distributed or the fiduciary's DNI. The distribution deduction, however, may not include any portion of tax-exempt income (net of any related deductions) deemed to have been distributed.

DNI also determines the character of the beneficiaries' income. Under the conduit approach, each beneficiary's distribution is deemed to consist of various categories of income (net of deductions) in the same proportion as the total of each class of income bears to the total DNI. For example, if 40% of the trust's income consists of dividends, 40% of each beneficiary's distribution is deemed to consist of dividends.

EXAMPLE C14-12 ▶ Sun Trust has $30,000 of DNI for the current year. Its DNI includes $10,000 of rental income and $20,000 of corporate bond interest. The trust instrument requires that each year the trustee distribute 30% of the trust's income to Jose and 70% to Petra. Because the trust has no tax-exempt income and must distribute all of its income, it receives a $30,000 distribution deduction.

Jose reports $9,000 (0.30 × $30,000) of trust income, and Petra reports $21,000 (0.70 × $30,000) of trust income. Because rents make up one-third ($10,000 ÷ $30,000) of DNI, the composition of the income reported by Jose and Petra is one-third rental income and two-thirds corporate bond interest. ◀

DEFINITION OF DNI

SELF-STUDY QUESTION

What functions does distributable net income (DNI) serve?

ANSWER

1. It establishes the maximum amount on which the beneficiaries may be taxed.
2. It establishes the maximum amount the trust or estate may deduct as a distribution deduction.
3. It establishes the character of the income or expense in DNI that flows to the beneficiaries (income or expense flows to the beneficiaries in proportion to the part each different type of income or expense bears to DNI).

Section 643(a) defines *DNI* as the fiduciary's taxable income, adjusted as follows:

▶ No distribution deduction is subtracted.

▶ No personal exemption is subtracted.

▶ Capital gains are not included and capital losses are not subtracted unless such gains and losses are allocated to accounting income instead of to principal.

▶ Extraordinary dividends and taxable stock dividends are not included if they are allocable to principal.

▶ An addition is made for tax-exempt interest (minus the expenses allocable thereto).

Because one purpose of DNI is to set a ceiling on the distribution deduction, the distribution deduction is not subtracted from taxable income in determining DNI. If capital gains and extraordinary dividends are allocated to corpus, they are excluded from DNI because they cannot be distributed. Tax-exempt interest is part of accounting income and can be distributed even though it is excluded from gross income. Consequently, DNI includes tax-exempt income (net of the nondeductible expenses allocable to such income). Even though net tax-exempt income is included in DNI, no distribution deduction is available for the portion of the distribution deemed to consist of tax-exempt income.

KEY POINT

A significant difference between net accounting income and DNI is that DNI is reduced by certain expenses charged to principal. These expenses do not decrease net accounting income, nor do they decrease the amount of money that can be distributed.

Aside from complicated scenarios, net accounting income and DNI are the same, with one other exception. Any expenses (e.g., trustee's fees) charged to principal reduce DNI even though they do not lessen net accounting income. The trustee's fees (whether charged to income or to principal) are deductible in arriving at taxable income, and no adjustment is made to taxable income for such expenses when calculating DNI. Reducing DNI by the expenses charged to principal provides a tax advantage for the income beneficiary because these fees lessen the amount taxable to the beneficiary. However, such fees do not decrease the money that can be distributed to the beneficiary.

MANNER OF COMPUTING DNI

The amount of taxable income is in large measure a function of the distribution deduction, and the distribution deduction depends on the amount of DNI. The distribution deduction cannot exceed DNI. Thus, the Sec. 643(a) definition of DNI, which involves making adjustments to a fiduciary's taxable income, is not a workable definition from a practical standpoint because the computation is circular. The distribution deduction must be computed to arrive at the amount of income taxable to the fiduciary, and the distribution deduction depends, in part, on the amount of DNI.

However, there are two practical means of determining DNI. The first approach, as illustrated below, begins with taxable income exclusive of the distribution deduction and makes the adjustments (other than the distribution deduction) to taxable income that the IRC specifies.

EXAMPLE C14-13 ▶ In the current year, Darby Trust reports the following results. The trust must distribute all of its income annually.

	Amounts Allocable to	
	Income	Principal
Corporate bond interest	$20,000	
Rental income	30,000	
Gain on sale of investment land		$40,000
Property taxes	5,000	
Trustee's fee charged to corpus		2,000
Distribution to beneficiary	45,000	

The trust's taxable income exclusive of the distribution deduction is computed as follows:

Corporate bond interest	$20,000
Rental income	30,000
Capital gain	40,000
Minus: Property taxes	(5,000)
Trustee's fee	(2,000)
Personal exemption	(300)
Taxable income exclusive of distribution deduction	$82,700

Now that taxable income exclusive of the distribution deduction has been determined, DNI can be computed in the following manner:

Taxable income exclusive of distribution deduction	$82,700
Plus: Personal exemption	300
Minus: Capital gain	(40,000)
DNI	$43,000 ◀

A second method that often can be used to determine DNI is to calculate net accounting income and reduce such amount by expenses charged to corpus (e.g., the trustee's fee). In some situations, however, DNI would not be correctly arrived at under this approach, but the discussion of such situations is beyond the scope of this book.

EXAMPLE C14-14 ▶ Assume the same facts as in Example C14-13. The following steps illustrate the second approach to calculating the DNI amount.

Corporate bond interest	$20,000
Rental income	30,000
Minus: Property taxes	(5,000)
Net accounting income	$45,000
Minus: Trustee's fee charged to corpus	(2,000)
DNI	$43,000 ◀

Although the beneficiary receives a cash distribution of $45,000 (net accounting income), he or she reports only $43,000 (DNI) as income. The beneficiary receives $2,000 tax-free. Thus, an income beneficiary benefits from trustee's fees charged to principal by getting to report a smaller amount of gross income than the amount of cash he or she receives. The trust's distribution deduction cannot exceed $43,000 (DNI) even though the amount paid to the beneficiary exceeds this amount.

Topic Review C14-2 summarizes the DNI concept.

STOP & THINK

Question: Wei is the beneficiary of a two unrelated simple trusts. From which simple trust would Wei's after-tax cash flow be larger?

▶ Trust A collects corporate bond interest of $40,000 and pays a trustee's fee of $1,000. The trustee's fee is charged to corpus.

▶ Trust B collects corporate bond interest of $40,000 and pays a trustee's fee of $800. The trustee's fee is charged to income.

Solution: Wei would receive $40,000 in cash from Trust A but pay federal income taxes on only $39,000, which is the trust's DNI. The trust's distribution is based on net accounting income, which is not reduced by the trustee's fee charged to corpus. Wei's gross income is based on the trust's DNI, which is reduced by the trustee's fee. Wei would receive $39,200 in cash from Trust B. He would pay federal income taxes on the same $39,200 amount, which is the trust's DNI. The trustee's fee paid by Trust B reduces both net accounting income and DNI. Even though the trust's economic income is larger with Trust B, Wei would have a larger amount of after-tax cash flow from Trust A.

DETERMINING A SIMPLE TRUST'S TAXABLE INCOME

OBJECTIVE 5

Determine the taxable income of a simple trust

The term *simple trust* does not appear in the IRC. Treasury Regulations interpreting Secs. 651 and 652—the statutory rules for trusts that distribute current income only—introduce the term *simple trust*. The provisions of Secs. 651 and 652 are applicable only to trusts whose trust agreements require that all income be distributed currently and do not authorize charitable contributions. Moreover, such provisions are inapplicable if the trust makes distributions of principal.

Some trust instuments may require trusts to pay out all their income currently in certain years but permit them to retain a portion of their income in other years. In some of the years in which the instument mandates distribution of all their income, it also permits distributions of principal. These trusts are simple trusts in some years and complex trusts in others. The amount of the personal exemption, however, turns not on whether the trust is simple or complex but on whether it must pay out all its income currently. Suppose, for

Topic Review C14-2

The Distributable Net Income (DNI) Concept

Significance of DNI

DNI, exclusive of net tax-exempt interest included therein, sets the ceiling on:
1. The distribution deduction, and
2. The aggregate amount of gross income reportable by the beneficiaries.

Calculation of DNI

Taxable income, exclusive of distribution deduction[a]

Plus:	Personal exemption
Minus:	Capital gains (or plus deductible capital losses)
Plus:	Tax-exempt interest (net of allocable expenses)

Distributable net income (DNI)[b]

[a]Gross income (dividends, taxable interest, rents, and capital gains) minus deductible expenses and the personal exemption.
[b]Frequently, DNI is the same amount as net accounting income minus trustee's fees charged to corpus.

▼ TABLE C14-1
Trust Classification Rules and the Size of the Exemption

Situation	Classification	Exemption Amount
Required to pay out all of its income, makes no charitable contributions, distributes no principal	Simple	$300
Required to pay out all of its income, makes no charitable contributions, distributes principal	Complex	$300
Required to pay out all of its income, authorized to make charitable contributions, distributes no principal	Complex	$300
Authorized to make discretionary distributions of income, makes no charitable contributions, distributes no principal	Complex	$100
Authorized to make discretionary distributions of income and principal, makes no charitable contributions	Complex	$100

example, a trust must pay out all of its current income and one-fourth of its principal. Because the trust distributes principal, it is a complex trust. It claims a $300 personal exemption because of the mandate to distribute all of its income. Table C14-1 highlights the trust classification rules and the $300 or $100 exemption dichotomy.

ALLOCATION OF EXPENSES TO TAX-EXEMPT INCOME

Recall that expenses related to producing tax-exempt income are not deductible.[17] Thus, if a trust with income from both taxable and tax-exempt sources incurs expenses that are not directly attributable to the production of taxable income, a portion of such expenses may not be deducted. Regulation Secs. 1.652(b)-3 and 1.652(c)-4(e) address the issue of the allocation of deductions. An expense directly attributable to one type of income, such as a repair expense for rental property, is allocated thereto. Expenses not directly related to a particular item of income, such as a trustee's fee for administering the trust's assets, may be allocated to any type of income included in computing DNI, provided a portion of the expense is allocated to nontaxable income. Regulation Sec. 1.652(b)-3 sets forth the following formula for determining the amount of indirect expenses allocable to nontaxable income:

$$\frac{\text{Tax-exempt income (net of expenses directly attributable thereto)}}{\text{Accounting income (net of all direct expenses)}^{18}} \times \begin{array}{c}\text{Expenses not directly}\\\text{attributable to any}\\\text{item of income}\end{array} = \begin{array}{c}\text{Indirect}\\\text{expenses}\\\text{allocable to}\\\text{nontaxable}\\\text{income}\end{array}$$

EXAMPLE C14-15 ▶ In the current year, the Mason Trust reports the following results:

Dividends	$16,000
Interest from corporate bonds	6,000
Tax-exempt interest from state bonds	18,000
Capital gain (allocated to corpus)	20,000
Trustee's fee, all allocated to corpus	4,000

[17] Sec. 265(a)(1).
[18] A discrepancy exists in the Treasury Regulations with respect to how to allocate expenses to tax-exempt income. According to Reg. Sec. 1.652(b)-3(b), the denominator is accounting income net of direct expenses. Regulation Sec. 1.652(c)-4(e), however, shows computations where the denominator is accounting income unreduced by direct expenses. The text uses the latter approach.

SELF-STUDY QUESTION

A trust can allocate indirect expenses arbitrarily (after the appropriate allocation is made to tax-exempt income). Hill Trust has rental income, taxable interest income, and dividend income. Its sole beneficiary has unused rental losses of her own. To which income would you suggest allocating the trustee's fee?

ANSWER

If possible, the trust should take into consideration the tax status of its beneficiaries. The trust should not allocate the fee to its rental income so that rental income is maximized. Moreover, because of the low tax rate on dividends, the trust should allocate the fee against interest income.

Accounting gross income is $40,000 ($16,000 + $6,000 + $18,000). The trustee's fee is an indirect expense that must be allocated to the tax-exempt income as follows:

$$\frac{\$18,000}{\$40,000} \times \$4,000 = \$1,800$$

Thus, the Mason Trust cannot deduct $1,800 of its trustee's fee. The remaining $2,200 may be allocated to dividends or corporate bond interest in whatever amounts the return preparer desires. Because of the low tax rate on dividends, allocating the fee to the higher taxed interest income would reduce taxes. ◄

DETERMINATION OF DNI AND THE DISTRIBUTION DEDUCTION

As mentioned above, DNI is defined as taxable income with several adjustments, including a subtraction for capital gains credited to principal. As described earlier, a practical technique for determining DNI involves beginning with taxable income exclusive of the distribution deduction. Once DNI has been determined, both the distribution deduction and the trust's taxable income can be calculated.

A simple trust must distribute all of its net accounting income currently. Thus, a simple trust generally receives a distribution deduction equal to the amount of its net accounting income.[19] The following two exceptions modify this general rule:

▶ The distribution deduction may not exceed DNI. Therefore, if a trust has expenses that are charged to corpus (as in Example C14-13), the distribution deduction is limited to the DNI amount because DNI is smaller than net accounting income.

▶ Because tax-exempt income is not included in the trust's gross income, no distribution deduction is available for tax-exempt income (net of the expenses allocable thereto) included in DNI.[20]

TAX TREATMENT FOR BENEFICIARY

The aggregate gross income reported by the beneficiaries equals the trust's net accounting income, subject to the constraint that the aggregate of their gross income amount does not exceed the trust's DNI. If DNI is lower than net accounting income and the trust has more than one beneficiary, each beneficiary's share of gross income is the following fraction of total DNI:[21]

$$\frac{\text{Income required to be distributed to such beneficiary}}{\text{Income required to be distributed to } all \text{ beneficiaries}}$$

The income received by the beneficiaries retains the character it had at the trust level. Thus, if the trust receives tax-exempt interest, the beneficiaries are deemed to have received tax-exempt interest. Unless the trust instrument specifically allocates particular types of income to certain beneficiaries, each beneficiary is viewed as receiving income consisting of the same fraction of each category of income as the total of such category bears to total DNI.

EXAMPLE C14-16 ▶ In the current year, Crane Trust has $22,000 of tax-exempt interest and $66,000 of dividends and pays $8,000 of trustee's fees from corpus. Its DNI is $80,000: $20,000 of net tax-exempt interest and $60,000 of net dividends. The trust instrument requires distribution of one-eighth of the income annually to Matt and the remaining seven-eighths of the income to Pat. The distributions to Matt and Pat are $11,000 and $77,000, respectively. The distribution deduction and the aggregate gross income of the beneficiaries are limited to $60,000 ($80,000 DNI − $20,000 net tax-exempt interest). Matt and Pat will report gross income of $7,500 (0.125 × $60,000) and $52,500 (0.875 × $60,000), respectively. Dividends make up 75% ($60,000 ÷ $80,000) of DNI and 100% ($60,000 ÷ $60,000) of taxable DNI. Therefore, all of Matt's and Pat's *gross* income is deemed to consist of dividends. Matt and Pat also are deemed to receive $2,500 (0.125 × $20,000) and $17,500 (0.875 × $20,000), respectively, of tax-exempt interest. ◄

[19] Sec. 651(a).
[20] Sec. 651(b).
[21] Sec. 652(a).

Because a simple trust must distribute all of its income currently, trustees cannot defer the taxation of trust income to the beneficiaries by postponing distributions until the next year. Beneficiaries of simple trusts are taxed currently on their pro rata share of taxable DNI regardless of the amount distributed to them during the year.[22]

SHORTCUT APPROACH TO PROVING CORRECTNESS OF TAXABLE INCOME

A shortcut approach may be used to verify the correctness of the amount calculated as a simple trust's taxable income. Because a simple trust must distribute all of its income currently, the only item taxable at the trust level should be the amount of gains (net of losses) credited to principal, reduced by the personal exemption. The taxable income calculated under the shortcut approach should equal the taxable income determined under the formula illustrated in Figure C14-1. The steps of the shortcut approach are as follows:

1. Start with the excess of gains over losses credited to principal.
2. Subtract the $300 personal exemption.

EXAMPLE C14-17 ▶ In the current year, West Trust, which must distribute all of its income currently, reports $25,000 of corporate bond interest, a $44,000 long-term capital gain, and a $4,000 long-term capital loss. Under the shortcut approach, the test-check calculation of its taxable income is $39,700 [($44,000 − $4,000) − $300 personal exemption]. On its tax return, the trust reports $25,000 of gross income from interest, $40,000 from net long-term capital gains, a $25,000 distribution deduction, and a $300 exemption. ◀

EFFECT OF A NET OPERATING LOSS

If a trust incurs a net operating loss (NOL), the loss does not pass through currently to the beneficiaries unless the loss arises in the year the trust terminates, but the trust can carry the NOL back and forward. In determining the amount of the NOL, deductions are not allowed for charitable contributions or the distribution deduction.[23] In the year a trust terminates, any loss that would otherwise qualify for a loss carryover at the trust level passes through to the individual return of the beneficiary(ies) succeeding to the trust's property.[24]

EXAMPLE C14-18 ▶ In 2006, the year it terminates, New Trust incurs a $10,000 NOL. It also has a $40,000 NOL carryover from 2004 and 2005. At termination, New Trust distributes 30% of its assets to Kay and 70% to Liz. Because 2006 is the termination year, Kay may report a $15,000 (0.30 × $50,000) NOL on her 2006 return, and Liz may report a $35,000 (0.70 × $50,000) NOL on her 2006 return. Before 2006, the beneficiaries cannot report any of the trust's NOLs on their returns. ◀

EFFECT OF A NET CAPITAL LOSS

The maximum capital loss that a trust can deduct is the lesser of $3,000 or the excess of its capital losses over capital gains.[25] Because simple trusts must distribute all of their accounting income currently and the distribution deduction reduces their taxable income to zero, they receive no current tax benefit from capital losses that exceed capital gains. Nevertheless, the trust's taxable income for the year of the loss is reduced by its net capital loss, up to $3,000. In determining the capital loss carryover, capital losses that produced no tax benefit are available as a carryover to offset capital gains realized by the trust in subsequent years. In addition, if all of the capital loss carryovers have not been absorbed by capital gains before the trust's termination date, the remaining capital loss is passed through in the termination year to the beneficiaries succeeding to the trust's property.[26]

---

[22] Reg. Sec. 1.652(a)-1.
[23] Reg. Sec. 1.642(d)-1(b).
[24] Reg. Sec. 1.642(h)-1. A trust is never categorized as a simple trust in the year it terminates because in its final year it always makes distributions of principal.

[25] Sec. 1211(b).
[26] Reg. Sec. 1.642(h)-1.

EXAMPLE C14-19 ▶
SELF-STUDY
QUESTION
Why do Treasury Regulations (see footnotes 25 and 26) allow unused NOLs and capital losses to be used by the remainderman on the termination of a trust?

ANSWER
Losses have depleted the corpus of the trust. Because the remainderman's interest has been depleted by these losses, it is reasonable to allow the trust to pass these losses through to the remainderman at the end of its life.

Old Trust, which must distribute all of its income currently, sells two capital assets before it terminates. In 2004, it sells an asset at a $20,000 loss. In 2005, it sells an asset for a $6,000 gain. In 2006, it terminates and distributes its assets equally between its two beneficiaries, Joy and Tim. The trust is not a simple trust in 2006 because it distributes principal that year. Because the $20,000 loss provided no benefit on the 2004 return, the carryover to 2005 is $20,000, and $6,000 of it offsets 2005's $6,000 capital gain. The remaining $14,000 carries over to 2006. Because 2006 is the termination year, a $7,000 (0.50 × $14,000) capital loss passes through to both Joy's and Tim's individual returns for 2006. Joy realizes a $12,000 capital gain by selling assets in 2006. Joy offsets the $7,000 trust loss against her own gain. Tim sells no assets in 2006. Therefore, Tim deducts $3,000 of the loss from the trust against his other income. His remaining $4,000 loss carries over to 2007. ◀

Topic Review C14-3 describes how to calculate a trust's taxable income.

COMPREHENSIVE ILLUSTRATION: DETERMINING A SIMPLE TRUST'S TAXABLE INCOME

The following comprehensive illustration reviews a number of the points discussed previously. The facts for this illustration are used to complete the Form 1041 for a simple trust that appears in Appendix B.

BACKGROUND DATA

Zeb Brown established the Bob Adams Trust by a gift in 1993. The trust instrument requires that the trustee (First Bank) distribute all of the trust income at least annually to Bob Adams for life. Capital gains are credited to principal. The 2005 results of the trust are as follows:

	Amounts Allocable to	
	Income	Principal
Dividends	$30,000	
Rental income from land	5,000	
Tax-exempt interest	15,000	
Rental expenses (realtor's commission on rental income)	1,000	
Trustee's fee		$ 1,200
Fee for preparation of tax return	500	
Capital gain on sale of stock[a]		12,000
Distribution of net accounting income to Bob	48,500	
Payments of estimated tax		2,600

[a]The trust sold the stock in October, having acquired it four years earlier.

Topic Review C14-3

Calculation of Trust Taxable Income

Gross income[a]
Minus: Deductions for expenses[a]
        Distribution deduction[b]
        Personal exemption ($300 or $100)

Taxable income

[a]Rules for calculating these amounts are generally the same as for individual taxpayers.
[b]Deduction cannot exceed the amount of DNI from taxable sources.

TRUSTEE'S FEE

As mentioned earlier, a portion of the trustee's fee is nondeductible because it must be allocated to tax-exempt income. The trust receives $50,000 ($30,000 + $5,000 + $15,000) of gross accounting income, of which $15,000 is tax-exempt. Therefore, $360 [($15,000 ÷ $50,000) × $1,200] of the trustee's fee is allocated to tax-exempt income and is nondeductible. The entire return preparation fee is deductible because no such fee would have been incurred had the trust's income been entirely from tax-exempt sources.

DISTRIBUTION DEDUCTION AND DNI

One of the key amounts affecting taxable income is the distribution deduction. Taxable income exclusive of the distribution deduction can be the starting point for determining the amount of DNI, a number crucial in quantifying the distribution deduction. The trust's taxable income, exclusive of the distribution deduction, is calculated as follows:

Dividends		$30,000
Rental income		5,000
Capital gain on sale of stock		12,000
Minus:	Rental expenses	(1,000)
	Deductible portion of trustee's fee	(840)
	Fee for tax return preparation	(500)
	Personal exemption	(300)
Taxable income, exclusive of distribution deduction		$44,360

DNI now can be calculated by making the adjustments shown below to taxable income, exclusive of the distribution deduction.[27]

Taxable income, exclusive of distribution deduction		$44,360
Plus:	Personal exemption	300
Minus:	Capital gain on sale of stock	(12,000)
Plus:	Tax-exempt interest, net of $360 of allocable expenses	14,640
DNI		$47,300

Recall that the distribution deduction cannot exceed the DNI, as reduced by tax-exempt income (net of any allocable expenses). The distribution deduction may be computed as follows:

Smaller of:	Net accounting income ($48,500) or DNI ($47,300)		$47,300
Minus:	Tax-exempt interest	$15,000	
	Minus: Allocable expenses	(360)	(14,640)
Distribution deduction			$32,660

TRUST'S TAXABLE INCOME

Once the amount of the distribution deduction is determined, the trust's taxable income can be calculated as illustrated in Table C14-2.

CATEGORIZING A BENEFICIARY'S INCOME

Because income reported by the beneficiary retains the character it had at the trust level, the amount of each category of income received by the beneficiary must be determined. Bob is deemed to have received dividends, rents, and tax-exempt interest. Rental expenses are charged entirely against rental income. The deductible portion of the trustee's fee and the tax return preparation fee can be allocated in full to rents or dividends, or some to each. However, because of the low tax rate on dividends, the fees should be allocated against the higher taxed rents. Consequently, the character of Bob's income is determined as follows:

---

[27] Another way of determining the amount of DNI in this scenario is to reduce the net accounting income of $48,500 by the $1,200 of expenses charged to principal. The resulting amount is $47,300.

	Dividends	Rents	Tax-Exempt Interest	Total
Accounting income	$30,000	$5,000	$15,000	$50,000
Minus: Expenses:				
Rental expenses		(1,000)		(1,000)
Trustee's fee		(840)	(360)	(1,200)
Tax return preparation fee		(500)		(500)
DNI	$30,000	$2,660	$14,640	$47,300

Bob reports $30,000 of dividend income and $2,660 of rental income on his individual return. His dividend income is taxed at the low rate applicable to dividends.

DETERMINING TAXABLE INCOME FOR COMPLEX TRUSTS AND ESTATES

OBJECTIVE 6

Determine the taxable income of a complex trust and an estate

The caption to Subpart C of Part I of Subchapter J (Secs. 661-664) reads "Distribution for Estates and Trusts Accumulating or Distributing Corpus." In general, the rules applicable to estates and these trusts (complex trusts) are the same. The IRC does not contain the term *complex trust*, but according to Treasury Regulations, "A trust to which subpart C is applicable is referred to as a 'complex' trust."[28] Recall from the discussion about simple trusts that a trust that must distribute all of its income currently can be classified as a complex trust for a particular year if it also pays out some principal during the year.

▼ TABLE C14-2

Comprehensive Illustration: Determining a Simple Trust's Taxable Income and Tax Liability

Gross income:	
Dividends	$30,000
Rental income	5,000
Capital gain on sale of stock	12,000[a]
Minus: Expense deductions:	
Rental expenses	(1,000)
Deductible portion of trustee's fee	(840)
Tax return preparation fee	(500)
Minus: Distribution deduction	(32,660)
Minus: Personal exemption	(300)
Taxable income	$11,700[b]
Tax liability (2005 rates)	$ 1,555[c]
Minus: Estimated tax payments	(2,600)
Tax owed (refunded)	($ 1,045)

ADDITIONAL COMMENT

The short-cut approach to computing taxable income used in Table C14-2 consists of reducing the income allocated to corpus by the personal exemption.

[a]The stock sale took place in October and involved stock purchased four years ago.
[b]The short-cut approach to verifying taxable income is as follows:

Long-term capital gain	$12,000
Minus: Personal exemption	(300)
Taxable income	$11,700

[c]The taxable income consists of a long-term capital gain, which is taxed at a maximum rate of 5% on the first $2,000 and 15% on the rest.

---

[28] Reg. Sec. 1.661(a)-1.

Trusts that can accumulate income are categorized as complex trusts, even in years in which they make discretionary distributions of all their income. A trust also is a complex trust if the trust instrument provides for amounts to be paid to, or set aside for, charitable organizations (see Table C14-1).

Many of the rules are the same for simple and complex trusts, but some differences exist. Different rules are used to determine the distribution deduction for the two types of trusts. The rules for determining an estate's distribution deduction are the same as those applicable to complex trusts. The personal exemption, however, is $600 for an estate and $300 or $100 for a complex trust. The $300 amount applies for years in which a trust must pay out all of its income; otherwise, the exemption is $100.

TAX STRATEGY TIP

Trust managers can reduce overall taxes by carefully planning the amount and timing of distributions. See Tax Planning Considerations later in text for details.

DETERMINATION OF DNI AND THE DISTRIBUTION DEDUCTION

Section 661(a) defines the distribution deduction for complex trusts and estates as the sum of the total current income *required* to be paid out currently plus any other amounts "properly paid or credited or required to be distributed" (i.e., discretionary distributions) to the beneficiary during the year. If the fiduciary can make mandatory distributions from either the income or the principal account, distributions are treated as "current income required to be paid" if paid out of the trust's income account; thus, some of the income is taxed to the beneficiary. Like simple trusts, the amount of the trust's DNI limits the amount of the distribution deduction.

EXAMPLE C14-20 ▶ In the current year, Able Trust has net accounting income and DNI of $30,000, all from taxable sources. It makes a $15,000 mandatory distribution of income to Kwame and a $4,000 discretionary distribution to Kesha. Its distribution deduction is computed as follows:

Income required to be distributed currently	$15,000
Plus: Other amounts properly paid, etc.	4,000
Tentative distribution deduction	$19,000
DNI	$30,000
Distribution deduction (lesser of tentative distribution deduction or DNI)	$19,000 ◀

As is the case for simple trusts, an additional constraint applies to the amount of the distribution deduction. No distribution deduction is allowed with respect to tax-exempt income (net of allocable expenses).

EXAMPLE C14-21 ▶ Assume the same facts as in Example C14-20 except that net accounting income and DNI consist of $20,000 of corporate bond interest and $10,000 of tax-exempt interest. Because one-third ($10,000 ÷ $30,000) of the DNI is from tax-exempt sources, tax-exempt income is deemed to make up one-third of the distributions. Thus, the distribution deduction is only $12,667 (0.667 × $19,000). ◀

If a trust makes charitable contributions, DNI is not reduced by the charitable contribution deduction when determining the maximum distribution deduction for mandatory distributions. However, DNI is reduced by the charitable contribution deduction when calculating the deduction for discretionary distributions.

EXAMPLE C14-22 ▶ Assume instead that the trust in Example C14-20 has net accounting income and DNI (exclusive of the charitable contribution deduction) of $16,000. The trust makes a $15,000 mandatory distribution to Kwame and a $4,000 mandatory distribution to Kesha. In accordance with its trust instrument, the trust pays $3,000 to a charitable organization.

Tentative distribution deduction (required distributions)	$19,000
DNI (excluding charitable contribution deduction)	16,000
Distribution deduction (lesser of tentative distribution deduction or DNI)	16,000

If the distributions to both Kwame and Kesha were discretionary, the $3,000 charitable contribution would be deductible by the trust and would first reduce DNI to $13,000, thereby limiting the distribution deduction to $13,000. ◀

TAX TREATMENT FOR BENEFICIARY

GENERAL RULES. In general, the amount of distributions from estates or complex trusts includible in a beneficiary's gross income equals the sum of income required to be distributed currently to the beneficiary plus any other amounts properly paid or credited, or required to be distributed (i.e., discretionary distributions) to the beneficiary during the year.[29] This general rule has three exceptions, all discussed later in this section.

Because income retains the character it has at the fiduciary level, beneficiaries do not include distributions of tax-exempt income in their gross income. Each beneficiary's distribution is deemed to consist of tax-exempt income in the proportion that total tax-exempt income bears to total DNI.[30] Thus, if 30% of DNI is from tax-exempt income, 30% of each beneficiary's distribution is deemed to consist of tax-free income.

Even in the absence of distributions of principal, mandatory payments to beneficiaries can exceed DNI because at times accounting income exceeds DNI. When the total income required to be distributed currently exceeds DNI (before reduction for the charitable contribution deduction), each beneficiary reports as gross income the following ratio of DNI attributable to taxable sources:

$$\frac{\text{Income required to be distributed currently to the beneficiary}}{\text{Aggregate income required to be distributed to all beneficiaries currently}}[31]$$

In calculating the portion of DNI includible in the gross income of each beneficiary who receives mandatory distributions, DNI is not reduced for the charitable contribution deduction.

EXAMPLE C14-23 ▶ In the current year, Yui Trust reports net accounting income of $125,000 but DNI of only $95,000 because of certain expenses charged to principal. The trust must distribute $100,000 of income to Tai and $10,000 to Tien. It makes no discretionary distributions or charitable contributions. Because the trust's mandatory distributions exceed its DNI, the amount each beneficiary reports as gross income is as follows:

Beneficiary	Gross Income
Tai	$86,364 = ($100,000 ÷ $110,000) × $95,000
Tien	$8,636 = ($10,000 ÷ $110,000) × $95,000

◀

EXCEPTION—THE TIER SYSTEM. If both principal and income are distributed, distributions will exceed income even if net accounting income and DNI are equal. If the sum of current income required to be distributed currently and all other amounts distributed (e.g., discretionary payments of income or any payments of corpus) exceed DNI, the amount taxable to each beneficiary is calculated under a tier system. Beneficiaries to whom income distributions must be made are commonly called **tier-1 beneficiaries**.[32] All other beneficiaries are known as **tier-2 beneficiaries**. An individual who receives both mandatory and discretionary payments in the same year can be both a tier-1 and a tier-2 beneficiary.

Under the tier system, tier-1 beneficiaries are the first to absorb income. The total income taxed to this group is the lesser of the aggregate mandatory distributions or DNI, which is determined without reduction for charitable contributions. If required income distributions plus all other payments exceed DNI, each tier-2 beneficiary includes in income a fraction of the remaining DNI, the DNI minus the income required to be distributed currently. Section 662(a)(2) states that the fraction is as follows:

$$\frac{\text{Other amounts properly paid or required to be distributed to the beneficiary}}{\text{Aggregate of amounts properly paid or required to be distributed to } \textit{all} \text{ beneficiaries}}$$

---

[29] Sec. 662(a).
[30] Sec. 662(b).
[31] Sec. 662(a)(1).

[32] The terms *tier-1* and *tier-2* do not appear in the IRC or Treasury Regulations.

EXAMPLE C14-24 ▶ In the current year, Eagle Trust reports net accounting income and DNI of $80,000, all from taxable sources. The trust instrument requires the trustee to distribute $30,000 of income to Holly currently. In addition, the trustee makes $60,000 of discretionary distributions, $15,000 to Holly and $45,000 to Irene. The trust pays $10,000 of the $60,000 discretionary distributions from corpus. The gross income reported by each beneficiary is determined as follows.

1. Gross income from mandatory distributions:	
Lesser of:	
a. Amount required to be distributed, or	$30,000
b. DNI	80,000
Amount reportable by Holly	30,000
2. Gross income from other amounts paid:	
Lesser of:	
a. All other amounts paid, or	60,000
b. DNI minus amount required to be distributed ($80,000 − $30,000)	50,000
Amount reportable by Holly and Irene	50,000
3. Total amount reportable (1) + (2) = (3)	80,000

The portions of the $50,000 from Step 2 to be reported by each beneficiary are calculated under a pro rata approach as follows:

Holly's: $50,000 × ($15,000 ÷ $60,000) = $12,500
Irene's: $50,000 × ($45,000 ÷ $60,000) = $37,500

A recapitulation of the beneficiaries' gross income is as follows:

	Amount Reported by	
Type of Distribution	*Holly*	*Irene*
Mandatory distributions	$30,000	$ –0–
Discretionary distributions	12,500	37,500
Total	$42,500	$37,500 ◀

Tier-1 beneficiaries generally have gross income equal to their total distributions if they receive no tax-exempt interest, whereas tier-2 beneficiaries are more likely to receive a portion of their distributions tax-free. Thus, tier-2 beneficiaries potentially receive more favorable tax treatment than tier-1 beneficiaries.

SELF-STUDY QUESTION

What is the ultimate effect of the separate share rule?

ANSWER

It has the effect of treating a trust or estate as two or more separate entities, each with its own DNI. This "separate" DNI is allocated to the specific beneficiary of each share of the trust or estate.

EXCEPTION—SEPARATE SHARE RULE. Some trusts and estates with more than one beneficiary can be treated as consisting of more than one entity in determining the amount of the distribution deduction and the beneficiaries' gross income.[33] In calculating the fiduciary's income tax liability, however, these trusts or estates are treated as one entity with the result that taxable income is taxed under one rate schedule. Entities eligible for this treatment, known as the **separate share rule,** have governing instruments requiring that distributions be made in substantially the same manner as if separate entities had been created.[34] If the separate share rule applies, the amount of the income taxable to a beneficiary can differ from the amount that otherwise would be taxable to such beneficiary. Because of this rule, beneficiaries often report gross income that is less than the distributions they receive.

EXAMPLE C14-25 ▶ Bart Berry created the Berry Trust for the benefit of Dale and John. According to the trust instrument, no income is to be distributed until a beneficiary reaches age 21. Moreover, income is to be divided into two equal shares. Once a beneficiary reaches age 21, the trustee may make discretionary distributions of income and principal to such beneficiary, but distributions may not exceed a beneficiary's share of the trust. Each beneficiary is to receive his remaining share of the trust assets on his thirtieth birthday. Earlier distributions of income and principal must be taken into account in determining each beneficiary's final distribution.

On January 1 of the current year, Dale reaches age 21; John is age 16. In the current year, the trust has DNI and net accounting income of $50,000, all from taxable sources. During the current year, the trustee distributes $25,000 of income (Dale's 50% share) and $80,000 of principal

---

[33] Sec. 663(c).   [34] Reg. Sec. 1.663(c)-3(a).

to Dale. The trustee makes no distribution of income or corpus to John. Under the separate share rule, the trust's distribution deduction and Dale's gross income inclusion cannot exceed his share of DNI, or $25,000. Dale receives the remaining $80,000 distribution tax-free. Berry Trust pays tax on John's separate share of the income (all accumulated), or $25,000, less the personal exemption. In the absence of the separate share rule, Dale would be taxed on $50,000 (the lesser of DNI or his total distributions). ◄

EXCEPTION—SPECIFIC BEQUESTS. Recall that a beneficiary is taxed on other amounts properly paid, credited, or required to be distributed,[35] subject to the constraint that the maximum amount taxed to all beneficiaries is the fiduciary's DNI. Thus, a beneficiary can be required to report gross income even though he or she receives a distribution from the principal account.

EXAMPLE C14-26 ▶ Doug died in 2005, leaving a will that bequeathed all his property to his sister Tina. During 2006, Doug's estate reports $50,000 of DNI, all from taxable sources. During 2006, the executor distributes Doug's coin collection, valued at $22,000, to Tina. The adjusted basis of the coin collection also is $22,000, its value at the date of death. The distribution of the coin collection is classified as an "other amount properly paid" and, even though the executor distributes nothing from the income account, Tina must report $22,000 of gross income. If the coin collection's adjusted basis and FMV exceed $50,000 (DNI), Tina's gross income would be only $50,000, the DNI amount. ◄

ADDITIONAL COMMENT

The executor of an estate should carefully consider the timing of property distributions where the property being distributed is not the subject of a specific bequest. If possible, property (other than specific bequests) should be distributed in a year when the trust has little or no DNI.

On the other hand, a distribution of property does not trigger a distribution deduction at the estate level or the recognition of gross income at the beneficiary level if such property constitutes a bequest of a specific sum of money or of specific property to be paid at one time or in not more than three installments.[36] If Doug's will in Example C14-26 instead includes specific bequest language (e.g., "I bequeath my coin collection to Tina"), Tina would not report any gross income upon receiving the coin collection.

More income is generally taxed at the estate level (and less at the beneficiary level) if the decedent's will includes numerous specific bequests. If the estate has a lower marginal income tax rate than its beneficiaries' marginal tax rates, the optimal tax result is to have the income taxed to the estate because the tax liability is lower.

EXAMPLE C14-27 ▶ Dick died in 2005 and bequeathed $100,000 cash to Fred and devised his residence, valued at $300,000, to Gary. The executor distributes the cash and the residence in 2006, when the estate has $80,000 of DNI, all from taxable sources. Because the cash and residence constitute specific bequests, the estate receives no distribution deduction and the beneficiaries report no gross income. ◄

STOP & THINK

Question: Sally is the sole beneficiary of her uncle Harry's estate. In the current year, the estate had DNI of $36,000, all from dividends and corporate interest. During the current year, the estate's executor distributed to Sally $12,200 of cash and her uncle Harry's rare book collection, valued at $5,400 on both date of death and date of distribution. Uncle Harry's will made one specific bequest, the rare book collection to Sally. How much gross income should Sally report from the estate during the current year? What is the amount of the estate's distribution deduction?

Solution: Sally does not have to report gross income as a result of receiving the specific bequest of the book collection. Because Sally's $12,200 cash distribution does not exceed the estate's $36,000 DNI, Sally should report gross income equal to the cash distributed to her ($12,200). The estate's distribution deduction equals the amount included in Sally's gross income ($12,200). If the book collection were not a specific bequest, its distribution by the estate would be taxable to Sally because the $17,600 ($12,200 + $5,400) distributed by the estate is less than the estate's DNI.

---

[35] Sec. 662(a)(2).　　[36] Sec. 663(a)(1).

EFFECT OF A NET OPERATING LOSS

As with simple trusts, an NOL of an estate or complex trust can be carried back and carried forward. In the year the trust or estate terminates, any remaining NOL passes through to the beneficiaries who succeed to the assets. In addition, in its year of termination the estate passes through to its beneficiaries any excess of current nonoperating expenses (e.g., executor's fees) over current income. If the estate incurs NOLs over a series of years, a tax incentive exists for terminating the estate as early as possible so the loss can pass through to the beneficiaries.

EFFECT OF A NET CAPITAL LOSS

The tax effect of having capital losses that exceed capital gains generally is the same for estates and complex trusts as for simple trusts. As for an individual taxpayer, the maximum capital loss deduction is the lesser of $3,000 or the excess of its capital losses over capital gains.[37] Simple trusts, however, receive no immediate tax benefit when capital losses exceed capital gains. Estates and complex trusts often do not distribute all their income and, thus, have taxable income against which they can offset a capital loss.

EXAMPLE C14-28 ▶ For 2005, Gold Trust reported $30,000 of net accounting income and DNI, all from taxable sources. It made discretionary distributions totaling $7,000 to Amy. It sold one capital asset at an $8,000 long-term capital loss. The trust deducted $3,000 of capital losses in arriving at its 2005 taxable income. The trust carries over the remaining $5,000 of capital loss to 2006. If in 2006, Gold Trust sells a capital asset for a $5,000 long-term capital gain, it will offset the $5,000 loss carryover against the $5,000 capital gain. ◀

COMPREHENSIVE ILLUSTRATION: DETERMINING A COMPLEX TRUST'S TAXABLE INCOME

The comprehensive illustration below reviews a number of points discussed earlier. A sample Form 1041 for a complex trust appears in Appendix B; it is prepared on the basis of the facts in this illustration.

BACKGROUND DATA

Ted Tims established the Cathy and Karen Stephens Trust on March 12, 1994. Its trust instrument empowers the trustee (Merchants Bank) to distribute income in its discretion to Cathy and Karen for the next 20 years. The trust will then be terminated, and the trust assets will be divided equally between Cathy and Karen, irrespective of the amount of distributions each has previously received. In other words, no separate shares are to be maintained. Under state law, capital gains are part of principal.

The 2005 income and expenses of the trust appear below. With the exception of the information concerning distributions and payments of estimated tax, the amounts are the same as in the comprehensive illustration for a simple trust discussed previously in the chapter. As before, the holding period for the stock sold in October was four years.

	Amounts Allocable to	
	Income	*Principal*
Dividends	$30,000	
Rental income from land	5,000	
Tax-exempt interest	15,000	
Rental expenses (realtor's commissions on rental income)	1,000	

---

[37] Sec. 1211(b).

Trustee's fee		$ 1,200
Fee for preparation of tax return	500	
Capital gain on sale of stock		12,000
Distribution of net accounting income to:		
Cathy	14,000	
Karen	7,000	
Payments of estimated tax	5,240	3,360

TRUSTEE'S FEE

Recall that some of the trustee's fee must be allocated to tax-exempt income, with the result that this portion is nondeductible. Of the trust's gross accounting income of $50,000 ($30,000 + $5,000 + $15,000), $15,000 is from tax-exempt sources. Consequently, the nondeductible trustee's fee is $360 [($15,000 ÷ $50,000) × $1,200]. The remaining $840 of the fee is deductible, as is the $500 tax return preparation fee.

DISTRIBUTION DEDUCTION AND DNI

Recall that the primary function of the Subchapter J rules is to provide guidance for calculating the amounts taxable to the beneficiaries and to the fiduciary. One of the crucial numbers in the process is the distribution deduction, which requires knowledge of the DNI amount. Taxable income, exclusive of the distribution deduction, is the starting point for calculating DNI and is computed as follows:

Dividends		$30,000
Rental income		5,000
Capital gain on sale of stock		12,000
Minus:	Rental expenses	(1,000)
	Deductible portion of trustee's fee	(840)
	Fee for tax return preparation	(500)
	Personal exemption	(100)
Taxable income, exclusive of distribution deduction		$44,560

DNI is calculated by adjusting taxable income, exclusive of the distribution deduction, as follows:

Taxable income, exclusive of distribution deduction		$44,560
Plus:	Personal exemption	100
Minus:	Capital gain on sale of stock	(12,000)
Plus:	Tax-exempt interest (net of $360 of allocable expenses)	14,640
DNI		$47,300

The distribution deduction is the lesser of (1) amounts required to be distributed, plus other amounts properly paid or credited, or required to be distributed, or (2) DNI. This lesser-of amount must be reduced by tax-exempt income (net of allocable expenses). DNI, exclusive of net tax-exempt income, is calculated as follows:

DNI		$47,300
Minus:	Tax-exempt income (net of $360 of allocable expenses)	(14,640)
DNI, exclusive of net tax-exempt income		$32,660

In no event may the distribution deduction exceed $32,660, the DNI, exclusive of net tax-exempt income. The DNI ceiling is of no practical significance in this example, however, because only $21,000 is distributed.

Because a portion of the payments to each beneficiary is deemed to consist of tax-exempt income, the distribution deduction is less than the $21,000 distributed. Each beneficiary's share of tax-exempt income is determined by dividing DNI into categories of income. In this categorization process, the rental expenses are direct expenses that must be charged against rental income, and $360 of the trustee's fees must be charged against tax-exempt income. In this example, the deductible trustee's fee and the tax return preparation fee are charged against rental income. Alternatively, they could be charged against dividend income or pro rata against each income category, but an allocation to dividend income would be disadvantageous because dividends are taxed at the preferential 15% rate. As with the simple trust illustrated earlier, total DNI of $47,300 consists of the following categories:

	Dividends	Rents	Tax-Exempt Interest	Total
Accounting income	$30,000	$5,000	$15,000	$50,000
Minus: Expenses:				
Trustee's fee	(840)		(360)	(1,200)
Rental expenses		(1,000)		(1,000)
Tax return preparation fee		(500)		(500)
DNI	$30,000	$2,660	$14,640	$47,300

Because the complex trust illustration involves two beneficiaries and three categories of income, we must calculate the amount of each beneficiary's distribution attributable to each income category. These steps were not needed in the simple trust illustration because it involved only one beneficiary.

Category of Income	Proportion of DNI
Dividends	63.4249% = $30,000 ÷ $47,300
Rental income	5.6237% = $ 2,660 ÷ $47,300
Tax-exempt income	30.9514% = $14,640 ÷ $47,300
Total	100.0000%

As shown above, 30.9514% of each beneficiary's distribution represents tax-exempt interest and is ineligible for a distribution deduction. The amount of the distribution deduction (which cannot exceed the $32,660 DNI, exclusive of net tax-exempt income) is determined as follows:

Total amount distributed	$21,000
Minus: Net tax-exempt income deemed distributed (0.309514 × $21,000)	(6,500)
Distribution deduction	$14,500

The distributions received by the beneficiaries are deemed to consist of three categories of income in the amounts shown below.

Components of Distributions	Cathy	Karen	Total
Dividends (63.4249%)	$ 8,879	$4,440	$13,319
Plus: Rental income (5.6237%)	788	393	1,181
Gross income (69.0486%)	$ 9,667	$4,833	$14,500
Plus: Tax-exempt interest (30.9514%)	4,333	2,167	6,500
Total income (100%)	$14,000	$7,000	$21,000

TRUST'S TAXABLE INCOME

Once the taxable and tax-exempt distributions have been quantified, the trust's taxable income can be calculated. Table C14-3 illustrates this calculation. Unlike the simple trust situation, no short-cut approach exists for verifying taxable income for complex trusts and estates except in the years when they distribute all their income.

ADDITIONAL OBSERVATIONS

A few additional observations are in order concerning the Stephens Trust:

▶ If the entity is an estate instead of a trust, all amounts except the personal exemption are the same. The estate's personal exemption would be $600 instead of $100.

▼ **TABLE C14-3**

Comprehensive Illustration: Determining a Complex Trust's Taxable Income and Tax Liability

Gross income:	
Dividends	$30,000
Rental income	5,000
Capital gain on sale of stock	12,000
Minus: Expense deductions:	
Rental expenses	(1,000)
Deductible portion of trustee's fee	(840)
Tax return preparation fee	(500)
Minus: Distribution deduction	(14,500)
Minus: Personal exemption	(100)
Taxable income	$30,060
Tax liability (2005 rates)[a]	$ 4,447
Minus: Estimated taxes	(8,600)
Tax owed (refunded)	($ 4,153)

[a]The $12,000 long-term capital gain and the $16,681 of dividends retained by the trust are taxed at the lower rates. The $16,681 amount is $30,000 minus the $13,319 dividends distributed, as calculated on p. C14-26. The remaining taxable income of $1,379 ($30,060 − $12,000 − $16,681) is taxed at 15%. The tax liability is calculated as follows:

Tax on ordinary, non-dividend income (0.15 × $1,379)	$ 207
Plus: Tax on capital gains and dividends at 5% [0.05 × $621	
(where $621 = $2,000 − $1,379)]	31
Tax on capital gains and dividends at 15% [0.15 × ($28,681 − $621)]	4,209
Total tax	$4,447

▶ Assume that (1) the trust owns a building instead of land and incurs $2,000 of depreciation expense, chargeable against principal under state law, and (2) the trust instrument does not require a reserve for depreciation. Because approximately 56% of the trust's income is accumulated (i.e., $26,300 of its $47,300 DNI), $1,120 (0.56 × $2,000) of the depreciation is deductible by the trust and its taxable income is $1,120 lower. The remaining $880 (0.44 × $2,000) is deductible on the beneficiaries' returns and is divided between them according to their pro rata share of the total distributions. Cathy deducts $587 [$880 × ($14,000 ÷ $21,000)], and Karen deducts $293 [$880 × ($7,000 ÷ $21,000)]. In summary, the depreciation is deductible as follows $1,120 to the trust, $587 to Cathy, and $293 to Karen.

▶ If the trust instrument had mandated a reserve for depreciation equal to the depreciation expense for tax purposes, accounting income would have been reduced by the depreciation. In addition, the entire $2,000 of depreciation would have been deducted by the trust, and DNI would have been $45,300 instead of $47,300.

INCOME IN RESPECT OF A DECEDENT

OBJECTIVE 7

Recognize the significance of income in respect of a decedent

DEFINITION AND COMMON EXAMPLES

Section 691 specifies the tax treatment for specific types of income known as income in respect of a decedent. **Income in respect of a decedent (IRD)** is gross income that the decedent earned before death but was not includible on the decedent's income tax return for the tax year ending with the date of death or for an earlier tax year because the decedent (a cash basis taxpayer) had not collected the income. Because most individuals use the cash method of accounting, IRD generally consists of income earned, but not actually or constructively received, prior to death. Common examples of IRD include the following:

- Interest earned, but not received, before death
- Salary, commission, or bonus earned, but not received, before death
- Dividends collected after the date of death, for which the record date precedes the date of death
- The gain portion of principal collected on a pre-death installment sale

SIGNIFICANCE OF IRD

DOUBLE TAXATION. Recall from Chapter C13 that a decedent's gross estate includes property to the extent of his or her interest therein. The decedent has an interest in any income earned but not actually or constructively received before death. Thus, the decedent's gross estate includes income accrued as of the date of death. If the decedent used the cash method of accounting, the decedent did not include this accrued income in gross income because he or she had not yet collected it. The income is taxed to the party (i.e., the estate or a named individual) entitled to receive it. Thus, IRD is taxed under both the transfer tax system and the income tax system. The income also is taxed twice if the decedent collects a dividend check, deposits it into his or her bank account, and dies before consuming the cash. In the latter case, the dividend is included in the decedent's individual income tax return, and the cash (from the dividend check) is included in the decedent's gross estate. The income taxes owed on the dividend income are deductible as a debt on the estate tax return.

SELF-STUDY QUESTION

Roger, a cash method taxpayer, is a medical doctor. At the time of Roger's death, patients owe him $150,000. These accounts receivable are "property" in which Roger has an interest at the time of his death and are included in his gross estate. Why are the accounts receivable income in respect of a decedent?

ANSWER

Because they are income Roger earned while alive, but did not report as income due to his accounting method, they constitute income to his estate (or his heirs) when they are collected. Thus, they are income in respect of a decedent (IRD).

EXAMPLE C14-29 ▶

Doug dies on July 1. Included in Doug's gross estate is an 8%, $1,000 corporate bond that pays interest each September 1 and March 1. Doug's gross estate also includes accrued interest for the period March 2 through July 1 of $27 ($1,000 × 0.08 × 4/12). On September 1, Doug's estate collects $40 of interest, of which $27 constitutes IRD. The calendar year income tax return for Doug's estate includes $40 of interest income, consisting of $27 of IRD and $13 earned after death. ◀

SELF-STUDY QUESTION

Karl receives his regular monthly paycheck on May 1 and deposits the paycheck in his savings account. He dies on May 10. He made no withdrawals from the account before his death. On June 1, Karl's employer pays Karl's estate one-third of Karl's May salary (the amount Karl had earned prior to his death on May 10). What are the tax consequences?

DEDUCTIONS IN RESPECT OF A DECEDENT. Section 691(b) authorizes **deductions in respect of a decedent (DRD)**. Such deductions include trade or business expenses, expenses for the production of income, interest, taxes, depletion, etc. that are accrued before death but are not deductible on the decedent's final income tax return because the decedent used the cash method of accounting. Because these accrued expenses have not been paid before death, they also may be deductible as debts on the estate tax return. In addition, the accrued expenses are deductible on the estate's income tax return when paid by the estate (if they are for deductible expenses). Thus, a double benefit can be obtained for DRD.

EXAMPLE C14-30 ▶

ANSWER

Karl's gross estate will include his savings account. Karl's final income tax return will include his salary through April 30 (i.e., his May 1 check is subject to both the income and the estate tax). The income taxes owed on the April salary are deductible as a debt on his estate tax return.

Karl's gross estate will include the one-third of his May salary. The income tax return for his estate also will report this amount as income. The salary is income in respect of a decedent, so the estate will receive some relief under Sec. 691(c) from the double tax.

Dan dies on September 20. At the time of his death, Dan owes $18,000 of salaries to the employees of his proprietorship. The executor pays the total September payroll of $29,000 on September 30. The $18,000 of accrued salaries is deductible as a debt on the estate tax return. As a trade or business (Sec. 162) expense, the salaries also constitute DRD. The $18,000 of DRD, plus any other salaries paid, is deductible on the estate's income tax return for the period of payment. ◀

SECTION 691(c) DEDUCTION. The Sec. 691(c) deduction provides some relief for the double taxation of IRD. This deduction equals the federal estate taxes attributable to the net IRD included in the gross estate. The total Sec. 691(c) deduction is the excess of the decedent's actual federal estate tax over the federal estate tax that would be payable if the net IRD were excluded from the decedent's gross estate. Net IRD means IRD minus deductions in respect of a decedent (DRD). If the IRD is collected in more than one tax year, the Sec. 691(c) deduction for a particular tax year is determined by the following formula:[38]

$$\text{Sec. 691(c) deduction for the year} = \text{Total Sec. 691(c) deduction} \times \frac{\text{Net IRD included in gross income for the year}}{\text{Total Net IRD}}$$

[38] Sec. 691(c)(1).

EXAMPLE C14-31 ▶

Latoya died in 2005 with a taxable estate and estate tax base of $2.5 million. Latoya's gross estate included $250,000 of IRD, none of which was received by her surviving spouse. Her estate had no DRD. The estate collects $200,000 of the IRD during its 2006 tax year. The Sec. 691(c) deduction for Latoya's estate for 2006 is calculated as shown below.

Actual 2005 federal estate tax on base of $2.5 million	$460,000
Minus: 2005 federal estate tax on base of $2.25 million determined by excluding net IRD from gross estate	(342,500)
Total Sec. 691(c) deduction	$117,500
Sec. 691(c) deduction available in 2006: ($200,000 ÷ $250,000) × $117,500 =	$ 94,000 ◀

NO STEP-UP IN BASIS. Most property received as the result of a decedent's death acquires a basis equal to its FMV on the date of death or the alternate valuation date. Property classified as IRD, however, retains the basis it had in the decedent's hands.[39]

This carryover basis rule for IRD items is especially unfavorable when the decedent sells a highly appreciated asset soon before death, collects a relatively small portion of the sales price before death, and reports the sale under the installment method of accounting. For example, if the gain is 80% of the sales price, 80% of each principal payment in the post-death period will continue to be characterized as gain. If the sale instead had been postponed until after the date of death, the gain would be restricted to the post-death appreciation (if any) because the step-up in basis rules apply to the asset.

EXAMPLE C14-32 ▶
SELF-STUDY
QUESTION

Roger (a cash method taxpayer) died leaving $150,000 of accounts receivable. What basis does his estate have in these accounts receivable?

ANSWER

Zero. The accounts receivable constitute IRD. If they were stepped-up in basis, they would never be subject to an income tax.

On June 3, 2006, Joel sells a parcel of investment land for $40,000. The land has a $10,000 adjusted basis in Joel's hands. The buyer pays $8,000 down and signs a $32,000 note at an interest rate acceptable to the IRS. The note is payable June 3, 2007. Joel, a cash method taxpayer, uses the installment method for reporting the $30,000 ($40,000 − $10,000) gain. The gross profit ratio is 75% ($30,000 gain ÷ $40,000 contract price). Joel dies on June 13, 2006. Joel's final individual income tax return reports a gain of $6,000 (0.75 × $8,000). The estate reports a gain of $24,000 (0.75 × $32,000) on its 2007 tax return because it collects the $32,000 balance due on June 3, 2007. Had the sale contract been entered into after Joel's death, the gain would have been zero because the land's basis would have been its $40,000 FMV at the date of death. ◀

STOP & THINK

Question: Isaac, a cash basis, calendar year taxpayer, died on May 12 of the current year. On which income tax return—Isaac's or his estate's—should the following income and expenses be reported? Assume the estate's tax year is the calendar year.

▶ Dividends declared in January and paid in February

▶ Interest income on a corporate bond that pays interest each June 30 and December 31

▶ Rent collected in June for a vacation home rented to tenants for the month of March, but the tenants were allowed to pay after occupying the property

▶ Balance due on Isaac's state income taxes for the previous year, paid in July because the return was extended

▶ Federal estimated income tax for the previous year that Isaac paid in January

Solution: Income received before death and deductible expenses paid before death (in this case the dividends and nothing more) should be reported on his individual return. Income received after Isaac's death, even though earned before his death, is to be reported on the estate's income tax return. The same is true for deductible expenses paid by the estate. Items to be reported on the estate's income tax return include the interest income, the rental income, and the state income taxes. The federal income taxes paid are not deductible on the federal income tax return of either taxpayer. The tax payment, however, reduced the cash Isaac owned at his date of death.

---

[39] Sec. 1014(c).

GRANTOR TRUST PROVISIONS

OBJECTIVE 8

Explain the effect of the grantor trust provisions

This portion of the chapter examines the provisions affecting a special type of trust known as a **grantor trust**, which is governed by Secs. 671-679. As discussed previously, income of a regular (or nongrantor) trust or an estate is taxed to the beneficiary to the extent distributed or to the fiduciary to the extent accumulated. In the case of a grantor trust, however, the trust's grantor (creator) is taxed on some or all of the trust's income even if such income is distributed to the beneficiary. In certain circumstances, a person other than the grantor or the beneficiary (e.g., a person with powers over the trust) must pay taxes on the trust's income.

PURPOSE AND EFFECT

The grantor trust rules require grantors who do not give up enough control or economic benefits when they create a trust to pay a price by being taxed on part or all of the trust's income. A grantor must report some or all of a trust's income on his or her individual tax return if he or she does not part with enough control over the trust assets or give up the right to income produced by the assets for a sufficiently long time period. For transfers after March 1, 1986, the grantor generally is taxed on the trust's income if the trust property will eventually return to the grantor or the grantor's spouse.[40] According to the Tax Court, the grantor trust rules have the following purpose and result:

> This subpart [Secs. 671-679] enunciates the rules to be applied where, in described circumstances, a grantor has transferred property to a trust but has not parted with complete dominion and control over the property or the income which it produces. . . . [41]

Sections 671-679 use the term *treated as owner*. Section 671 specifies that when a grantor is treated as owner, the income, deductions, and credits attributable to the portion of the trust with respect to which the grantor is treated as owner are reported directly on the grantor's tax return and not on the trust's return. The fiduciary return contains only the items attributable to the portion of the trust for which the grantor is not treated as the owner.

ADDITIONAL COMMENT

Many trust provisions can cause the grantor trust rules to apply. A trust need *not* be a revocable trust to be a grantor trust.

Unfortunately, the rules governing when a transfer is complete for income tax purposes (meaning the grantor avoids being taxed on the trust's income) do not agree completely with the rules concerning whether the transfer is complete for gift tax purposes or the transferred property is removed from the donor's gross estate. In certain circumstances, a donor can make a taxable gift and still be taxed on the income from the transferred property. For example, a donor transfers property to a trust with the income payable annually to the donor's cousin for six years and a reversion of the property to the donor at the end of the sixth year. The donor makes a gift, subject to the gift tax, of the value of a six-year income interest. Under the grantor trust rules, however, the donor is taxed on the trust's income because the property reverts to the donor within too short a time period.

Retention of certain powers over property conveyed in trust can cause the trust assets to be included in the donor's gross estate even though these powers do not result in the donor being taxed on the trust income. Assume a donor to a trust reserves the discretionary power to pay out or accumulate trust income until the beneficiary reaches age 21. The trust assets, including any accumulated income, are to be distributed to the beneficiary on his or her twenty-first birthday. The donor is not taxed on the trust income because he can exercise his powers only until the beneficiary reaches age 21. If the donor dies before the beneficiary attains age 21, however, the donor's gross estate will include the trust property because the donor retained control over the beneficiary's economic benefits (see discussion of Sec. 2036 in Chapter C13).

---

[40] For trusts created before March 2, 1986, the grantor may be treated as the owner with respect to the trust's capital gains but not its ordinary income because the property returns to the grantor after a period of more than ten years. In such a situation, the grantor is taxed on the capital gains and the trust and/or the beneficiary on the ordinary income.
[41] *William Scheft,* 59 T.C. 428, at 430-431 (1972).

REVOCABLE TRUSTS

The grantor of a revocable trust can control assets conveyed to the trust by altering the terms of the trust (including changing the identity of the beneficiaries) and/or withdrawing assets from the trust. Not surprisingly, Sec. 676 provides that the grantor is taxed on the income generated by a revocable trust. As Chapter C12 points out, a transfer of assets to a revocable trust is an incomplete transfer and not subject to the gift tax.

EXAMPLE C14-33 ▶

ADDITIONAL COMMENT

A common use of the revocable trust is to avoid probate for the property held by the trust. On the death of the grantor, the trustee of the revocable trust distributes the trust property in accordance with the trust agreement. Because the trustee holds legal title to the property, he or she can distribute the property without going through the probate process.

In the current year, Tom transfers property to a revocable trust and names Ann to receive the income for life and Beth to receive the remainder. The trust's income for the current year consists of $15,000 of dividends and an $8,000 long-term capital gain. The trustee distributes the dividends to Ann but retains the gain and credits it to principal. Because the trust is revocable, the dividend and capital gain income are taxed directly to Tom on his current year individual tax return. Nothing is taxed to the trust or its beneficiaries. ◀

POST-1986 REVERSIONARY INTEREST TRUSTS

The 1986 Tax Reform Act amended Sec. 673(a) for transfers made after March 1, 1986, to provide that, generally, the grantor is taxed on the accounting income of the trust if he or she has a reversionary interest in either income or principal. Under Sec. 672(e), a grantor is treated as holding any interest held by his or her spouse. These rules have two exceptions.

The first exception makes the grantor trust rules inapplicable if, as of the inception of the trust, the value of the reversionary interest does not exceed 5% of the value of the trust. The second exception applies if the reversion will occur only if the beneficiary dies before reaching age 21 and the beneficiary is a lineal descendant of the grantor.

EXAMPLE C14-34 ▶

In the current year, Paul establishes a trust with income payable to his elderly parents for 15 years. The assets of the trust will then revert to Paul. The value of Paul's reversionary interest exceeds 5%. Because Paul has a reversionary interest valued at above 5% and the transfer arose after March 1, 1986, Paul is taxed currently on the trust's accounting income and capital gains. ◀

EXAMPLE C14-35 ▶

In the current year, Paul transfers property to a trust with income payable to his daughter Ruth until Ruth reaches age 21. On Ruth's twenty-first birthday, she is to receive the trust property outright. In the event Ruth dies before reaching age 21, the trust assets will revert to Paul. Paul is not taxed on the accounting income because his reversion is contingent on the death of the beneficiary (a lineal descendant) before age 21. ◀

RETENTION OF ADMINISTRATIVE POWERS

Under Sec. 675, the grantor is taxed on the accounting income and gains if he or she or his or her spouse holds certain administrative powers. Such powers include, but are not limited to, the following:

▶ The power to purchase or exchange trust property for less than adequate consideration in money or money's worth

▶ The power to borrow from the trust without adequate interest or security except where the trustee (who is someone other than the grantor) has a general lending power to make loans irrespective of interest or security

▶ The power exercisable in a role other than as trustee to (1) vote stock of a corporation in which the holdings of the grantor and the trust are significant from the standpoint of voting control and (2) reacquire the trust property by substituting other property of equal value.

RETENTION OF ECONOMIC BENEFITS

Section 677 taxes the grantor on the portion of the trust with respect to which the income may be

▶ Distributed to the grantor or his or her spouse,

▶ Held or accumulated for future distribution to the grantor or his or her spouse, or

▶ Used to pay premiums on life insurance policies on the life of the grantor or his or her spouse

Use of trust income to provide support for a child whom the grantor is legally obligated to support yields obvious economic benefits to the grantor. A grantor is taxed on any trust income distributed by the trustee to support individuals whom the grantor is legally obligated to support (e.g., children). However, the mere existence of the discretionary power to use trust income for support purposes does not cause the grantor to be taxed on the trust income. Taxation turns on whether the trust income is actually used to meet the support obligation.

The next example concerns use of trust income to support the grantor's minor child.

EXAMPLE C14-36 ▶

Hal creates a trust and empowers the bank trustee to distribute income to his minor son, Louis, until the son reaches age 21. When Louis reaches age 21, the trust assets including accumulated income are to be paid over to the child. In the current year, when Louis is age 15, the trustee distributes $5,000 that is used to support Louis and $8,000 that is deposited into Louis's savings account. The remaining $12,000 of income is accumulated. Hal (the grantor) is taxed on the $5,000 used to support his son. Louis includes $8,000 in his gross income, and the trust pays tax on $12,000 less its $100 exemption. ◀

The following example deals with the payment of premiums on an insurance policy on the grantor's life.

EXAMPLE C14-37 ▶

ADDITIONAL COMMENT

If the trust were created by a person other than the insured, say a parent, the income required to be used for paying life insurance premiums would not be taxed to the grantor because the insured is not the grantor or the grantor's spouse.

Maria is the grantor of the Martinez Trust, one of whose assets is a life insurance policy on Maria's life. The trust instrument requires that $1,000 of trust income be used to pay the annual insurance premiums and that the rest be distributed to Juan. Section 677 requires Maria (the grantor and insured) to be taxed on $1,000 of accounting income. The remaining income is taxed to Juan under the general trust rules. ◀

CONTROL OF OTHERS' ENJOYMENT

Section 674 taxes the grantor on trust income if he or she, his or her spouse, or someone without an interest in the trust (e.g., a trustee) has the power to control others' beneficial enjoyment such as by deciding how much income to distribute. Many exceptions, including one for independent trustees, exist for the general rule.

EXAMPLE C14-38 ▶

Otto is grantor and trustee of a trust over which the trustee has complete discretion to pay out the income or corpus in any amount he deems appropriate to some or all of its three unrelated beneficiaries, Kay, Fay, and May. In the current year, the trustee distributes all the income to Kay. Otto, the grantor, is taxed on the income. If instead the trustee were independent, Kay would be taxed on the amount she received. ◀

Under Sec. 678, an individual other than the trust's grantor or beneficiary can be required to report the trust income. This individual is taxed on the trust income if he or she has the power under the trust instrument to vest the trust principal or the income in him- or herself, provided such power is exercisable solely by such individual.

Topic Review C14-4 summarizes the grantor trust rules.

WHAT WOULD YOU DO IN THIS SITUATION?

You, a CPA, have prepared the income tax returns for the Candy Cain Trust, an irrevocable trust, since the inception of the trust five years ago. The grantor is Able Cain, another client and the father of Candy Cain, the income beneficiary. First Bank, the trustee, is authorized to distribute income at its descretion to Candy, who is now age 17. For the current year, the trust's DNI of $15,000, all from interest on corporate bonds, was distributed to Candy to pay her medical bills incurred in an accident. You advised Mr. Cain that he must include the $15,000 trust distribution on his individual tax return because the distribution was used to satisfy his obligation to support Candy. Mr. Cain reminds you of how many clients he has referred to you and demands that you instead show the distribution as taxable to Candy so the income will be taxed at his daughter's low rates instead of at his rate, the highest marginal rate. How will you react to Mr. Cain's request?

Topic Review C14-4

Grantor Trust Rules

FACTUAL SITUATION	TAX TREATMENT
1. Trust is revocable.	Ordinary income (including dividends) and capital gains are taxed to grantor.
2. Irrevocable trust is funded on or after March 2, 1986, with income payable to third-party beneficiary for 20 years after which property reverts to grantor; the value of the reversionary interest exceeds 5% of the value of the trust.	Ordinary income (including dividends) and capital gains are taxed to grantor.
3. The grantor of an irrevocable trust retains administrative powers described in the IRC.	Ordinary income (including dividends) and capital gains are taxed to grantor.
4. The income of an irrevocable trust is disbursed to meet the grantor's obligation to support his or her children.	Ordinary income (including dividends) used for support are taxed to grantor.
5. The income of an irrevocable trust is disbursed to pay the premium on a life insurance policy on the life of the grantor or the grantor's spouse.	Ordinary income (including dividends) and capital gains are taxed to grantor to the extent they may be used to pay the premiums.

TAX PLANNING CONSIDERATIONS

Many tax planning opportunities exist with respect to estates and trusts, including the ability to shift income to the fiduciary and/or the beneficiaries and the opportunity for executors or trustees of discretionary trusts to consider the tax consequences of the timing of distributions. These and other tax planning considerations are discussed below.

ABILITY TO SHIFT INCOME

Before 1987, one of the primary tax advantages of using trusts was the ability to shift income from the grantor to the trust or the beneficiary. Three changes have reduced the tax advantages of shifting income. First, the tax rate schedules for all taxpayers—but especially for fiduciaries—are very compressed. In fact, an estate or trust has only $2,050 (in 2006) of income subject to the 15% tax rate. Second, unearned income exceeding $1,700 (in 2006) of children under age 14 is taxed at the higher of the parents' or the child's tax rate, even if distributed from a trust or estate. Third, dividend income is eligible for a maximum 15% tax rate regardless of whether it is taxed to the grantor, the beneficiary, or the trust. Depending on whether the income is distributed or retained, it is taxed to the trust or the beneficiary or a portion to each. Because the trust is a separate taxpayer, income taxed to the trust is taxed under the trust's rate schedule. If the beneficiary has income from other sources, the income shifted to the beneficiary is not necessarily taxed in the lowest tax bracket. An income tax savings nevertheless can occur whenever a portion of the shifted income is taxed at a rate lower than the rate the grantor would pay on such income.

TIMING OF DISTRIBUTIONS

People managing estates and discretionary trusts can reduce taxes by carefully planning the timing of distributions. From a tax standpoint, the executor or trustee should consider the beneficiary's income from other sources and make distributions in amounts that equalize the marginal tax rates of the beneficiary and the fiduciary. If the trust is a **sprinkling trust** (a discretionary trust with several beneficiaries), the trustee can accomplish tax savings for the beneficiaries by making distributions to the beneficiaries who have the lowest marginal tax rate that year. Of course, nontax reasons might require a trustee to distribute income to other beneficiaries as well. A special 65-day rule allows trustees of complex trusts and estates to treat distributions made during the first 65 days of the new tax year as if they had been made on the last day of the preceding tax year. If the trustee

ADDITIONAL COMMENT

In 2006, the first $2,050 of trust income is taxed at 15%. A complex trust pays no tax on $100 of income (because of its personal exemption) and only 15% on the next $2,050 of income. If the trust distributes income to a child under age 14 who is a dependent and has no other unearned income, the child pays no tax on the first $850 of that income and pays taxes at his or her own rate on the next $850. The rest is taxed at the parents' rates. If the parents are always in the top income tax bracket, non-trivial income tax savings still can be achieved by using a trust to spread non-dividend income over different taxpayers. For the situation described here, a Sec. 2503(c) trust (trust for minors) is commonly used.

KEY POINT

Given that one often cannot determine the exact amount of income a trust (or any other entity) has earned until after the end of the tax year, the importance of the 65-day rule for distribution planning becomes readily apparent.

or executor does not make the election, the distributed income is deducted by the fiduciary and taxed to the beneficiary in the year of the actual distribution.

PROPERTY DISTRIBUTIONS

Under the general rule affecting property distributions, the trust gets a distribution deduction equal to the lesser of the fiduciary's adjusted basis in the property or the property's FMV.[42] If the trust distributes appreciated property, however, the trustee can elect to recognize a gain on the distribution equal to the excess of the property's FMV over its adjusted basis on the distribution date. If the trustee does not make the election, the trust recognizes no gain when it distributes the property.

If the trustee elects to recognize the gain, the distribution deduction equals the property's FMV. The beneficiary, in turn, takes a basis equal to the property's adjusted basis to the trust plus the gain the trust recognized on the distribution. If the beneficiary likely will sell the property soon after distribution, the election provision allows the trustee to choose where the appreciation will be taxed, at the trust level or the beneficiary level. If the distribution involves appreciated capital gain property, the capital gain recognized by the trust can be offset by the trust's current capital loss and carryovers from prior tax years.

EXAMPLE C14-39 ▶ Todd Trust owns a number of assets, including an asset with a FMV of $35,000 and an adjusted basis of $12,000. In the current year, the trust distributes the asset to its sole beneficiary, Susan. The trust does not make any other distributions to Susan. If the trustee elects to recognize gain of $23,000, the trust receives a distribution deduction of $35,000, the FMV of the asset. Susan includes $35,000 of income in her tax return and obtains a $35,000 basis in the asset. Thus, if she sells the asset for $35,000, she will report no gain. If the trustee had not elected to recognize gain on the in-kind distribution, the distribution deduction would have been $12,000, the asset's adjusted basis to the trust. Susan's basis in the asset also would have been $12,000. ◀

CHOICE OF YEAR-END FOR ESTATES

Distributions from an estate or trust are taxed to the beneficiaries in the beneficiaries' tax year in which the fiduciary's year ends.[43] Congress in 1986 required all trusts (even existing fiscal-year trusts) other than tax-exempt and wholly charitable trusts to use a calendar year as their tax year to eliminate their ability to defer the taxation of trust distributions to beneficiaries by choosing a noncalendar year.[44] Estates, however, are completely free to choose a year-end as long as the tax year does not exceed 12 months.

EXAMPLE C14-40 ▶ Molly Madison died on February 7, 2005. Madison Estate adopted a fiscal year ending January 31. During the period February 7, 2005 through January 31, 2006, Madison Estate distributes $30,000 to Bob, a calendar year beneficiary. The estate's DNI exceeds $30,000. Bob reports $30,000 of estate income on his individual return for 2006, Bob's tax year during which the estate's tax year ended. By choosing the January 31 year-end (instead of a calendar year-end), the executor postpones the taxation of income to Bob from 2005 to 2006. ◀

DEDUCTION OF ADMINISTRATION EXPENSES

Chapter C13 points out that the executor elects where to deduct administration expenses, i.e., on the estate tax return, the estate's income tax return, or some on each return. Unlike the situation for deductions in respect of a decedent, Sec. 642(g) denies a double deduction for administration expenses. Such expenses should be deducted where they will yield the greatest tax savings. Of course, if the surviving spouse receives all the decedent's property or all except for an amount equal to the exemption equivalent, deducting administration expenses on the estate tax return will produce no tax savings because the estate will owe no estate taxes.

---

[42] Sec. 643(d).
[43] Secs. 652(c) and 662(c).

[44] Sec. 645.

COMPLIANCE AND PROCEDURAL CONSIDERATIONS

<table><tr><td>

OBJECTIVE 9

Recognize the filing requirements for fiduciary returns

ETHICAL POINT

Individual beneficiaries report their share of income from trusts and estates on Schedule E of Form 1040. CPAs have a responsibility to monitor the beneficial interests that clients have in trusts and estates to prevent underreporting. Some clients may unintentionally forget to report income from a simple trust because they received no cash distributions from the fiduciary during the year.

</td></tr></table>

FILING REQUIREMENTS

GENERAL RULE. Every estate that has gross income of at least $600 for the tax year must file an income tax return (Form 1041-U.S. Fiduciary Income Tax Return). A trust income tax return (generally Form 1041) is required for every trust that has taxable income or has gross income of $600 or more.[45] In addition, every estate or trust that has a nonresident alien as a beneficiary must file a return.[46]

DUE DATE FOR RETURN AND TAX

The due date for fiduciary returns (Form 1041) is the same as for individuals, the fifteenth day of the fourth month following the end of the tax year.[47] If an extension is desired, Form 7004 must be filed. The automatic extension period is six months.

Both trusts and estates generally must make estimated tax payments using the general rules applicable to individual taxpayers.[48] The IRC, however, exempts estates from making estimated tax payments for their first two tax years. If the fiduciary's tax liability exceeds the estimated tax payments, the balance of the tax is due on or before the due date for the return.[49] Estimated tax payments for a trust or an estate are made by using Form 1041-ES (Estimated Income Tax for Fiduciaries).

DOCUMENTS TO BE FURNISHED TO IRS

Although the executor or the trustee need not file a copy of the will or the trust instrument with the return, at times the IRS may request a copy of such documents. If the IRS makes such a request, the executor or the trustee also should transmit the following:

▶ A statement signed under penalty of perjury that the copy is true and complete

▶ A statement naming the provisions of the will or trust agreement that the executor or the trustee believes control how the income is to be divided among the fiduciary, the beneficiaries, and the grantor (if applicable)

SAMPLE SIMPLE AND COMPLEX TRUST RETURNS

Appendix B contains samples of simple and complex trust returns (Form 1041). The Appendix also illustrates completed Schedules K-1 for the reporting of distributed income, etc. to the beneficiaries. One copy of Schedule K-1 for each beneficiary is filed with Form 1041. In addition, each beneficiary receives a copy of his or her Schedule K-1, so that he or she knows the amount and type of gross income to report for the distributions received as well as other pertinent information.

The trusts do not owe the alternative minimum tax (AMT) on the two sets of facts illustrated in the sample returns. When trusts do owe the AMT, they report it on Schedule I of Form 1041.

PROBLEM MATERIALS

DISCUSSION QUESTIONS

C14-1 Explain to a client in laymen's language what portion of the income of an estate or trust is subject to taxation at the fiduciary level.

C14-2 Given the tax rate schedule for trusts, what reasons (tax and/or nontax) exist today for creating a trust?

---

[45] Secs. 6012(a)(3) and (4). A special grantor trust rule, however, permits a revocable trust's income to be reported on the grantor's tax return. See Reg. Sec. 1.671-4(b).
[46] Sec. 6012(a)(5).
[47] Sec. 6072(a).
[48] Sec. 6654(l).
[49] Sec. 6151(a).

C14-3 List some major differences between the taxation of individuals and trusts.

C14-4 Explain to a client the significance of the income and principal categorization scheme used for fiduciary accounting purposes.

C14-5 List some common examples of principal and income items under the 1962 Act.

C14-6 A client asks about the relevance of state law in classifying items as principal or income. Explain the relevance.

C14-7 A trust whose instrument provides that Irene is entitled to receive for life only distributions of income and Beth is to receive the remainder interest sells property at a gain. Income and corpus are classified in accordance with the Uniform Act. Will Irene receive a distribution equal to the amount of the gain? Explain.

C14-8 Refer to Question C14-7. Which taxpayer (the trust, Irene, or Beth) pays the tax on the gain?

C14-9 A trust owns an asset on which depreciation is claimed. The trust distributes all of its income to its sole income beneficiary. Whose taxable income is reduced by the depreciation?

C14-10 What is the amount of the personal exemption for trusts and estates?

C14-11 A client inquires about the significance of distributable net income (DNI). Explain.

C14-12 a. Are net accounting income and DNI always the same amount?
b. If not, explain a common reason for a difference.
c. Are capital gains usually included in DNI?

C14-13 Explain how to determine the deductible portion of a trustee's fees.

C14-14 Assume that a trust collects rental income and interest income on tax-exempt bonds. Will a portion of the rental expenses have to be allocated to tax-exempt income and thereby become nondeductible? Explain.

C14-15 a. Describe the shortcut approach for verifying that the amount calculated as a simple trust's taxable income is correct.
b. Can a shortcut verification process be applied for trusts and estates that accumulate some of their income? Explain.

C14-16 When does the NOL of a trust or estate produce tax deductions for the beneficiaries?

C14-17 The Mary Morgan Trust, a simple trust, sells one capital asset in the current year. The sale results in a loss.
a. When will the capital loss produce a tax benefit for the trust or its beneficiary? Explain.
b. Would the result necessarily be the same for a complex trust? Explain.

C14-18 A peer states that simple trusts receive no tax benefit from a personal exemption. Is your peer correct?

C14-19 Describe the tier system for taxing trust beneficiaries.

C14-20 Determine the accuracy of the following statement: Under the tier system, beneficiaries who receive mandatory distributions of income are more likely to be taxed on the entire distributions they receive than are beneficiaries who receive discretionary distributions.

C14-21 a. Describe to a client what income in respect of a decedent (IRD) is.
b. Describe to the client one tax disadvantage and one tax advantage that occur because of the classification of a receipt as IRD.

C14-22 Describe three situations that cause trusts to be subject to the grantor trust rules.

C14-23 Can a client escape the grantor trust rules by providing in a trust instrument that income is payable to a nephew for 20 years and that the trust assets pass at the end of 20 years to the client's spouse?

C14-24 A client is under the impression that, if the grantor trust rules apply to a trust, the grantor is always taxed on the trust's ordinary income (including dividends) and capital gains. Is the client correct? Explain.

C14-25 What is the benefit of the 65-day rule?

C14-26 a. When are fiduciary income tax returns due?
b. Must estates and trusts pay estimated income taxes?

ISSUE IDENTIFICATION QUESTIONS

C14-27 Art Rutter sold an apartment building in May 2005 for a small amount of cash and a note payable over five years. Principal and interest payments are due annually on the note in April of 2006 through 2010. Art died in August 2005. He willed all his assets to his daughter Amelia. Art's gross estate is about $3 million, and his estate tax deductions are very small. What tax issues should the executor of his estate consider with respect to reporting the sale of the building and the collection of the installments?

C14-28 For the first five months of its existence (August through December 2006), the Estate of Amy Ennis had gross income (net of expenses) of $7,000 per month. For January through July 2007, the executor estimates that the estate will have gross income (net of expenses) totaling $5,000. The estate's sole beneficiary is Amy's son, Joe, who is a calendar year taxpayer. Joe incurred a large NOL from his sole proprietorship years ago, and $34,000 of the NOL carryover remains but expires at the end of 2006. During 2006, Joe received only $8,200 of income from part-time employment. What tax issues should the executor of Amy's estate consider with respect to distributions of the estate's income?

C14-29 Raj Kothare funded an irrevocable simple trust in May of last year. The trust benefits Raj's son for life and grandson upon the son's death. One of the assets he transferred to the trust was Webbco stock, which had a $35,000 FMV on the transfer date. Raj's basis in the stock was $39,000, and he paid no gift tax on the transfer. The stock's value has dropped to $27,000, and the trustee thinks that now (October of the current year) might be the time to sell the stock and realize the loss. For the current year, the trust will have $20,000 of income exclusive of any gain or loss. Raj's taxable income is approximately $15,000. What tax and non-tax issues should the trustee consider concerning the possible sale of the stock?

PROBLEMS

C14-30 *Calculation of the Tax Liability.* A trust has taxable income of $30,000 in 2006. The $30,000 includes $5,000 of long-term capital gains and $25,000 of interest. What is its income tax liability? Compare this tax to the amount of tax a married individual filing a joint return would pay on the same amount of taxable income.

C14-31 *Determination of Taxable Income.* A simple trust has the following receipts and expenditures for the current year. The long-term capital gain and trustee's fees are part of principal.

Dividends	$20,000
Long-term capital gain	15,000
Trustee's fees	1,500
Distribution to beneficiary	20,000

a. What is the trust's taxable income under the formula approach of Figure C14-1?
b. What is the trust's taxable income under the short-cut approach?

C14-32 *Determination of Taxable Income.* Refer to Problem C14-31. How would your answer to Part a change if the trust in addition received $8,000 interest from tax-exempt bonds, and it distributed $28,000 instead of $20,000?

C14-33 *Determination of Taxable Income and Tax Liability.* A simple trust has the following receipts and expenditures for the current year. The trust instrument is silent with respect to capital gains, and state law concerning trust accounting income follows the Uniform Act. Assume the trustee's fee is charged to income.

Corporate bond interest	$40,000
Tax-exempt interest	9,000
Long-term capital gain	5,000
Trustee's fee	2,000
Distribution to beneficiary	47,000

a. What is the trust's taxable income under the formula approach of Figure C14-1?
b. What is the trust's tax liability?

C14-34 *Determination of Taxable Income.* During the current year, a simple trust has the following receipts and expenditures. Assume that trustee's fees are charged to income and that the Uniform Act governs for accounting.

Corporate bond interest	$60,000
Long-term capital gain	20,000
Trustee's fees	3,000

a. How much must be distributed to the beneficiary?
b. What is the trust's taxable income under the shortcut approach?

C14-35 *Determination of Distribution Deduction.* A trust has net accounting income of $24,000 and incurs a trustee's fee of $1,000 in its principal account. What is its distribution deduction under the following situations:
a. It distributes $24,000, and all of its income is from taxable sources.
b. It distributes $24,000, and it has tax-exempt income (net of allocable expenses) of $2,000.
c. It distributes $10,000, and all of its income is from taxable sources.

C14-36   *Determination of Beneficiary's Income.* A trust is authorized to make discretionary distributions of income and principal to its two beneficiaries, Roy and Sandy. For the current year, it has DNI and net accounting income of $80,000, all from taxable sources. It distributes $60,000 to Roy and $40,000 to Sandy. How much gross income should each beneficiary report?

C14-37   *Determination of Beneficiary's Income.* Refer to Problem C14-36. How would your answer change if the trust instrument required that $10,000 per year be distributed to Sandy, and the trustee also made discretionary distributions of $60,000 to Roy and $30,000 to Sandy?

C14-38   *Determination of Accounting Income and Distribution.* The Trotter Trust has the receipts and expenditures listed below for the current year. Assume the Uniform Act (1962) governs an item's classification as principal or income. The trustee's fee is charged one-half to principal and one-half to income. What is the trust's net accounting income and the maximum amount it can distribute? Assume the trust cannot pay out principal.

Dividends	$15,000
Interest on tax-exempt bonds	7,000
Loss on sale of capital asset	(9,000)
Rental income from land	6,000
Property taxes on rental property	1,000
Trustee's fee	1,800

C14-39   *Determination of Taxable Income.* Refer to Problem C14-38. Assume the trustee must pay out all of its income currently to its beneficiary, Julio.
a. What is the deductible portion of the trustee's fee?
b. What is the trust's taxable income exclusive of the distribution deduction?
c. What is the trust's DNI?
d. What is the trust's taxable income using the formula approach of Figure C14-1?

C14-40   *Determination of Taxable Income.* Refer to Problem C14-39. How would your answers change if the trust were a discretionary trust that distributes $12,000 to its beneficiary, Julio?

C14-41   *Calculation of Deductible Expenses.* The George Grant Trust reports the receipts and expenditures listed below. What are the trust's *deductible* expenses?

U.S. Treasury interest	$25,000
Rental income	9,000
Interest from tax-exempt bonds	6,000
Property taxes on rental property	2,000
CPA's fee for tax return preparation	800
Trustee's fee	1,900

C14-42   *Tax Treatment of Capital Losses.* A simple trust had a long-term capital loss of $10,000 for 2005 and a long-term capital gain of $15,000 for 2006. Its net accounting income and DNI are equal. Explain the tax treatment for the 2005 capital loss assuming the trust is in existence at the end of 2007.

C14-43   *Tax Treatment of Capital Losses.* Refer to Problem C14-42. How would your answer change if instead the trust were a complex trust that makes no distributions in 2005 and 2006? Assume the trust earns $8,000 of corporate bond interest income each year.

C14-44   *Revocable Trusts.* A revocable trust created by Amir realizes $30,000 of rental income and a $5,000 capital loss. It distributes $25,000 to Ali, its beneficiary. How much income is taxed to the trust, the grantor, and the beneficiary?

C14-45   *Reversionary Interest Trusts.* Holly funded the Holly Marx Trust in January 2006. The trust income is payable to her adult son, Jack for 20 years. At the end of the twentieth year, the trust assets are to pass to Holly's husband. In the current year, the trust realizes $30,000 of dividend income and a $15,000 long-term capital gain. How much income is taxed to the trust, the grantor, and the beneficiary in the current year?

C14-46   *Reversionary Interest Trusts.* Refer to Problem C14-45. Explain how your answers would change for each independent situation indicated below:
a. At the end of the trust term, the property passes instead to Holly's nephew.
b. Holly creates the trust in October 2006 for a term of 25 years, after which the property reverts to her.

C14-47 *Income in Respect of Decedent.* The following items are reported on the first income tax return for the Ken Kimble Estate. Mr. Kimble, a cash method of accounting taxpayer, died on July 1, 2006.

Dividends	$10,000
Interest on corporate bonds	18,000
Collection on installment note from sale of investment land	24,000

The record date was June 14 for $6,000 of the dividends and October 31 for the remaining $4,000 of dividends. The bond interest is payable annually on October 1. Mr. Kimble's basis in the land was $8,000. He sold it in 2005 for a total sales and contract price of $48,000 and reported his gain under the installment method. Ignore interest on the installment note. What amount of IRD is reported on the estate's income tax return?

C14-48 *Income in Respect of Decedent.* Julie Brown died on May 29 of the current year. She was employed before her death at a gross salary of $4,000 per month. Her pay day was the last day of each month, and her employer did not pro rate her last monthly salary payment. She owned preferred stock that paid quarterly dividends of $800 per quarter each March 31, June 30, September 30, and December 31. The record date for the June dividend was June 10. Assume her estate chooses a calendar year as its tax year. What amount of gross income should be reported on the estate's first income tax return? Identify the IRD included in gross income.

C14-49 *Property Distributions.* In the current year, Maddox Trust, a complex trust, distributed an asset with a $42,000 adjusted basis and a $75,000 FMV to its sole beneficiary, Marilyn Maddox-Mason. The trustee elected to recognize gain on the distribution. Marilyn received no other distributions from the trust during the year. The distributable net income for the year was $87,000, and none of it was from tax-exempt sources.
a. What is the trust's distribution deduction?
b. On her individual income tax return, how much gross income should Marilyn report from the trust?
c. What is Marilyn's basis in the asset distributed in kind from the trust?

C14-50 *Income Recognition by Beneficiary.* Joan died April 17, 2005. Joan's executor chose March 31 as the tax year end for the estate. The estate's only beneficiary, Kathy, reports on a calendar year. The executor of Joan's estate makes the following distributions to Kathy:

June 2005	$ 5,000
August 2005	10,000
March 2006	12,000
August 2006	14,000

The 2005 and 2006 distributions do not exceed DNI. How much income should Kathy report on her 2005 return as a result of the distributions from the estate? On her 2006 return?

COMPREHENSIVE PROBLEM

C14-51 Dana Dodson died October 31, 2005, with a gross estate of $2.7 million, debts of $200,000, and a taxable estate of $2.5 million. Dana made no adjusted taxable gifts. All of her property passed under her will to her son, Daniel Dodson. The estate chose a June 30 year-end. Its receipts, disbursements, and gains for the period ended June 30, 2006, were as follows:

Dividend income	$27,000
Interest income from corporate bonds	18,000
Interest income from tax-exempt bonds	9,000
Gain on sale of land	10,000
Executor's fee (charged to principal)	4,000
Distribution to Daniel Dodson	–0–

Of the $27,000 dividends received, $7,000 were declared October 4, 2005, with a record date of October 25 and a payment date of November 4, 2005. The corporate bonds pay interest each August 31 and February 28. The estate collected $18,000 corporate bond interest in February 2006. The tax-exempt bonds pay interest each June 30 and December 31. The estate collected $4,500 in December 2005 and $4,500 in June 2006 from the tax-exempt bonds. Dana, a cash method of accounting taxpayer, sold land in 2004 for a total gain of

$60,000 and used installment reporting. She collected principal in 2004 and 2005 and reported gain of $30,000 on her 2004 return and $10,000 on her 2005 return. The estate collected additional principal in March 2006 and will collect the remaining principal payment in March 2007. The gain attributable to the March 2006 and March 2007 principal collections is $10,000 per year. Ignore interest on the sale.

Calculate the following:

a. Deductible executor's fee.
b. Total IRD and the IRD reported on the return for the period ended June 30, 2006.
c. Total Sec. 691(c) deduction if none of the debts are DRD.
d. Section 691(c) deduction deductible on the estate's income tax return for the period ended June 30, 2006.
e. Taxable income of the estate for its first tax year.
f. Marginal income tax rate for the estate for its first tax year.

TAX STRATEGY PROBLEM

C14-52 Glorietta Trust is an irrevocable discretionary trust that Grant Glorietta funded in 1992. The discretionary income beneficiary for life is Grant's son, Gordon Glorietta (single). Gordon is a partner in a partnership in which he materially participates, and he has a large basis in his partnership interest. For 2006, the trust had $50,000 of corporate bond interest, net of expenses, and no other income. It made no distributions to Gordon in 2006. Assume that it is now February 22, 2007, and Gordon has just learned that his share of loss from the partnership will be $72,000. Gordon has other income for 2006 of approximately $52,000. The trustee anticipates distributing $40,000 cash to Gordon before the end of February. For the last few years, Gordon's marginal tax rate was 15%. He claims the standard deduction, has only one exemption, and files as a single individual. Discuss a tax-saving opportunity presented by this scenario. Also show a comparative analysis of the alternatives.

TAX FORM/RETURN PREPARATION PROBLEMS

C14-53 Marion Mosley created the Jenny Justice Trust in 1995 with First Bank named as trustee. For 20 years, the trust is to pay out all its income semiannually to the beneficiary, Jenny Justice. At the end of the twentieth year, the trust assets are to be distributed to Jenny's descendants. Capital gains are credited to principal, and depreciation is charged to principal. For the current year, the irrevocable trust reports the following results:

	Amounts Allocable to	
	Income	Principal
Rental income	$15,000	
Corporate bond interest	27,000	
Interest on tax-exempt (non-private activity) bonds	8,000	
Long-term capital gain on sale of land		30,000a
Maintenance and repairs of rental property	1,500	
Property taxes on rental property	700	
Fee for tax return preparation	500	
Trustee's fee		2,000
Depreciation		2,400
Estimated federal income taxes paid		9,000

aThe sales price and adjusted basis are $110,000 and $80,000, respectively. The trustee acquired the land in 2002 and the trustee sold it in November of the current year.

Prepare a Form 1041, including any needed Schedule K-1s, for the Jenny Justice Trust. Omit pages 3 through 5 of Form 1041. The trustee's address is P.O. Box 100, Dallas, TX 75202. The identification number of the trust is 74-6224343. Jenny, whose Social Security number is 252-37-1492, resides at 2 Mountain View, Birmingham, AL 35205.

C14-54 In 2001, Belinda Barclay established the Barclay Trust, an irrevocable trust, and named as trustee Local Bank, 1234 Tide Freeway, Tuscaloosa, AL 35487. She funded the trust with corporate and municipal bonds. The trustee is directed to distribute income and/or principal at its discretion to Belinda's adult sons, Anthony Barclay (421-78-0443) and Patrick Barclay (421-78-0445), for 15 years and then to pay out the trust assets, including any accumulated income, equally between the two sons. The tax ID number for the trust is 74-

5434127. Half of the trustee's fee is charged to principal and half to income. During the current year, the trustee distributed $12,400 to Anthony, who resides at 37 Crimson Cove, Tuscaloosa, AL 35487. Other current year information for the trust is as follows:

Corporate bond interest	$17,000
Municipal bond interest	19,000
Long-term capital gain on sale of corporate bonds	2,200
CPA's fee for prior year's tax return	800
Trustee's fee	1,500
Estimated federal income taxes paid	3,700

The trust has a $700 short-term capital loss carryover from the prior year.

Prepare a Form 1041, and any needed Schedule K-1s, for the Barclay Trust. Omit pages 3 through 5 of Form 1041. The bonds are not private activity bonds.

C14-55 Mark Meadows funded a trust in 1994 with Merchants Bank named as trustee. He paid no gift tax on the transfer. The trustee in its discretion is to pay out income to Mark's children, Angela and Barry, for 15 years. Then the trust will terminate, and its assets, including accumulated income, will be paid to Angela and Barry in equal amounts. (Separate shares are *not* to be maintained.) In the current year, the trustee distributes $3,000 to Angela and $9,000 to Barry. The trust paid estimated federal income taxes of $15,000 and reported the following additional results for the current year.

	Amounts Allocable to	
	Income	Principal
Dividends	$50,000	
Interest on corporate bonds	4,000	
Interest on City of Cleveland (non-private activity) bonds	9,000	
Long-term capital loss on sale of stock		$12,000[a]
Trustee's fee		2,400
CPA's fee for tax return preparation	400	

[a]Mr. Meadows purchased the stock for $30,000 in 1990. It was valued at $44,000 when he transferred it to the trust in 1994. The trust sold the stock for $18,000 in December of the current year.

Prepare a Form 1041, including any needed Schedule K-1s, for the trust established by Mr. Meadows. Omit pages 3 through 5 of Form 1041. The trustee's address is 201 Fifth Ave., New York, NY 10017. The trust's identification number is 74-5271322. Angela (127-14-1732) and Barry (127-14-1733) reside at 3 East 246th St., Huntington, NY 11743.

CASE STUDY PROBLEMS

C14-56 Arthur Rich, a widower, is considering setting up a trust (or trusts) with a bank as trustee for his three minor children. He will fund the trust at $900,000 (or $300,000 each in the case of three trusts). A friend suggested that he might want to consider a January 31 year-end for the trusts. The friend also suggested that Arthur might want to make each trust a complex discretionary trust. Arthur is a little apprehensive about the idea of a trust that would be complex. The friend warned that trust income should not be spent on support of the children.

Required: Prepare a memorandum to the tax partner of your firm concerning the above client matter. As part of your analysis, consider the following:
a. What tax reasons, if any, can you think of for having three trusts instead of one?
b. Why do you think the friend suggested a January 31 year-end?
c. What is your reaction to the friend's suggestion about the year-end?
d. Which taxpayer, the beneficiary or the trust, is taxed on the income from a discretionary trust?
e. To what extent do trusts serve as income-shifting arrangements?
f. What can you advise Arthur concerning his apprehension about a complex trust?
g. Why did the friend warn against spending trust income for the children's support?

C14-57 You are preparing a 2005 individual tax return for Robert Lucca, a real estate developer and long-time client. While preparing Robert's individual tax return you learn that he has income from a trust his 75-year-old father created in 2004. His 2005 income from the trust is properly reflected on a Schedule K-1 prepared by the accounting firm that prepared the trust's 2005 return. Robert prepared the trust's return for 2004, and decided that he should not be taxed on any of the trust's income because the trust distributed nothing to him. Upon reviewing Robert's copy of the trust instrument, you learn that the instrument calls for mandatory distributions of all the income to Robert every year. Assume that the trust reported only $3,300 of taxable income for 2004 and that Robert was in the highest marginal tax bracket for 2004.

a. What responsibility do you have in 2006 to correct the error made for the tax year 2004? Refer to the *Statements on Standards for Tax Services* in Appendix E.

b. Assume instead that an IRS agent has just begun to audit Robert's 2004 individual tax return. What is your responsibility if you have discovered the error on the 2004 trust return, and you are representing Robert in the audit?

TAX RESEARCH PROBLEMS

C14-58 The Latimer Trust instrument directs that all income be paid annually to Laura Lee Latimer for life with remainder to Laura Lee's son Lance Latimer or his estate. The trust instrument does not authorize the trustee to make charitable contributions. The Latimer Trust owns a 15% interest in LLL Partnership, which operates a retail store. A Schedule K-1 the Latimer Trust received from the partnership reported, among other information, that the trust's share of charitable contributions made by the partnership for 2006 was $350. The trust had DNI of $25,000. What charitable contribution deduction, if any, may the trust deduct? Is the trust a simple or complex trust in 2006?

C14-59 In 2005, Bill Ames died at age 48. One of the items included in his gross estate was the principal residence where he and his widow, Lynn (age 46), lived for 20 years. Its FMV in 2005 was $500,000. In accordance with Bill's will, the residence and numerous other assets passed to a trust. Lynn is entitled to all the trust income for the rest of her life.

In 2006, the trust sells the residence for $540,000 and later that year pays $370,000 for a new house that Lynn moves into as her principal residence. Your manager asks that you draft a letter to the trustee and in the letter explain whether the trust is eligible for the nonrecognition rules for sales of principal residences.

Your manager suggests that you consider at a minimum the following research sources:

- IRC Sec. 121
- Rev. Rul. 54-583, 1954-2 C.B. 158

You should attach to the letter a list of additional relevant authorities and their citations.

C14-60 Joyce Ingalls is the daughter of the late Fred Ingalls, who died August 15, 2006. One of the items included in his gross estate was a traditional (regular/non-Roth) IRA valued at several million dollars. Mr. Ingalls's estate will owe taxes, but no estate taxes had been paid by March 1, 2007, the date Joyce filed her 2006 individual income tax return, which she prepared. Included in her gross income for 2006 was a $50,000 distribution from her father's IRA. After talking with a friend, she wonders whether a Sec. 691(c) deduction was available on her 2006 return, and she has contacted you to resolve this issue. Write a memo in which you address whether Joyce is entitled to claim a Sec. 691(c) deduction for income in respect of a decedent (IRD) she collected given that no estate tax has yet been paid on the IRD or any other inclusion in her father's gross estate. Also address in a conceptual manner how the deduction, assuming it is available, is calculated. At a minimum you should consult the following sources:

- IRC Sec. 691(c)
- FSA 200011023

C14-61 *Internet Research Problem.* Your client is considering funding a trust with some oil and gas properties. The trust will be governed by the laws of Virginia, which has adopted the 1997 version of the Uniform Principal and Income Act (the 1997 Act). Your client wants to know how royalty income will be allocated between the principal and income accounts under the 1997 Act, compared with the 1962 version of the Act. Start your research by going to *www.nccusl.org*, the Web site for the National Conference of Commissioners of Uniform State Laws. Go to "Final Acts & Legislation." Select "Principal and Income Act," and "Virginia." Consult Section 411 of the Act. Prepare a memo that addresses the client's question.

C14-62 *Internet Research Problem.* You are preparing for a client meeting at which the client has indicated he wants to discuss revocable trusts. Use the search engine Google and locate a discussion about revocable trusts (also known as living trusts). Summarize the points from a site's discussion about revocable (living) trusts, and indicate which Web site you visited.

15

CHAPTER

ADMINISTRATIVE PROCEDURES

LEARNING OBJECTIVES

After studying this chapter, you should be able to

▶1 Understand the role of the IRS in our tax system

▶2 Discuss how returns are selected for audit and the alternatives available to taxpayers whose returns are audited

▶3 Describe the IRS's ruling process

▶4 Identify due dates for tax returns

▶5 Understand tax-related penalties generally

▶6 Calculate the penalty for not paying estimated taxes

▶7 Describe more severe penalties, including the fraud penalty

▶8 Understand the statute of limitations

▶9 Explain from whom the government may collect unpaid taxes

▶10 Understand government-imposed standards for tax practitioners

This chapter provides an overview of the administrative and procedural aspects of tax practice, an area with which all tax advisors should be familiar. The specific matters discussed include the role of the Internal Revenue Service (IRS) in tax enforcement and collection, the manner in which the IRS chooses tax returns for audit, taxpayers' alternatives to immediately agreeing to pay a proposed deficiency, due dates for returns, taxpayer penalties, and the statute of limitations. Chapter C1 discussed the AICPA's *Statements on Standards for Tax Services,* which guide CPAs engaged in tax practice. Chapter C15 examines additional tax practice topics, including Internal Revenue Code (IRC) penalty provisions that affect tax advisors and tax return preparers.

ROLE OF THE INTERNAL REVENUE SERVICE

OBJECTIVE 1

Understand the role of the IRS in our tax system

The IRS is part of the Treasury Department. Its chief administrative officer is the IRS Commissioner. Overseeing the activities of the IRS is a nine-member board consisting of the Secretary of the Treasury, the IRS Commissioner, a public sector representative, and six private sector representatives. All board members are appointed by the President of the United States.

ENFORCEMENT AND COLLECTION

KEY POINT

The U.S. tax structure is based on a self-assessment system. The level of voluntary compliance actually is quite high, but one of the principal purposes of the IRS is to enforce the federal tax laws and identify taxpayers who willfully or inadvertently fail to pay their fair share of the tax burden.

One of the IRS's most significant functions is enforcing tax laws.[1] The IRS is responsible for ensuring that taxpayers file returns, correctly report their tax liabilities, and pay any tax due.

The United States enjoys a high level of voluntary compliance with its tax laws. However, because some persons do not voluntarily comply, the IRS must audit selected taxpayers' returns and investigate the activities of nonfilers. In addition, because numerous ambiguities (gray areas) regarding interpreting tax laws exist, taxpayers and the IRS do not always agree on the proper tax treatment of transactions and events. As part of its enforcement duties, the IRS attempts to discover whether the reporting of these transactions and events differs from the way the IRS thinks they should be reported. As we point out later, taxpayers who disagree with the IRS's position in an audit may litigate.

The IRS must ensure that taxpayers not only report the correct tax liability, but also pay their taxes on time. For various reasons, some taxpayers file returns without paying any or all of the tax owed. The IRS's collection agents are responsible for collecting as much of the tax as possible from such persons or entities.

INTERPRETATION OF THE STATUTE

As noted in Chapter C1, the statutory language of the Internal Revenue Code (IRC) often is so vague that the courts and IRS must interpret it so that it can be readily applied. The IRS publishes its interpretations in revenue rulings, revenue procedures, notices, and information releases, which are available to the general public. In addition, the IRS offers guidance to specific taxpayers in the form of letter rulings, which have no precedential value for third-party taxpayers. Each of these authorities is discussed in detail in Chapter C1.

---

[1] The IRS, however, does not have enforcement duties with respect to the taxes on guns and alcohol.

ORGANIZATION OF THE IRS

The IRS performs its duties on a nationwide basis. It is organized *functionally* into four divisions: (1) Wage and Investment Income, (2) Small Business and Self-Employed, (3) Large and Mid-size Business, and (4) Tax Exempt (see Figure C15-1). Each division is headed by a divisional director.

The Wage and Investment Income Division has authority over individual taxpayers who report only wage and investment income. Most of these taxpayers file Forms 1040, 1040A, or 1040EZ. The Small Business and Self-Employed Division has authority over sole proprietors, individuals with supplemental income, and small corporations and partnerships. Most of these taxpayers file Forms 1065 and 1120S or Schedules C, E, and F. The Large and Mid-size Business Division has authority over corporations with assets of $5 million or more. Most of these taxpayers file Form 1120. The Tax Exempt Division has authority over tax exempt organizations, employee plans, and state and local governments. Most of these entities file tax exempt status forms.

The shift to a functional mode of organization reflects Congress' desire to render the IRS more efficient and client oriented. Through this mode of organization, tax administrators can focus on their areas of technical expertise, and taxpayers can deal with the same technical experts wherever they reside.

AUDITS OF TAX RETURNS

OBJECTIVE 2

Discuss how returns are selected for audit and the alternatives available to taxpayers whose returns are audited

The IRS operates ten service centers, which receive and process tax returns.[2] One of the IRS's principal enforcement functions is auditing these returns. All returns are subject to some verification. One task the IRS service centers perform is checking whether amounts are properly calculated and faithfully carried from one line of a return to another. Another task is determining whether any items, such as signatures and Social Security numbers, are missing. Computers compare (or "match") by Social Security number the amounts reported on a taxpayer's return with employer- or payer-prepared documents (Forms W-2 and 1099) filed with the IRS service center.[3] To date, however, a 100% matching of these documents with tax return information has been difficult to achieve.

If the service center detects a calculation error in the tax reported on the return, it will send to the taxpayer a notice proposing an additional tax or granting a refund. If the information reported on a return is inconsistent with the information on Forms W-2 or 1099 reported by an employer or payer, the IRS asks the taxpayer to account for the discrepancy in writing or pay some additional tax.

ADDITIONAL COMMENT

Although individual tax returns increased from 123 million to 173 million between 1998 and 2003, the number of individual returns examined *decreased* from 1.19 to 1.08 million.

PERCENTAGE OF RETURNS EXAMINED

Only a small fraction of all returns are examined. For example, for returns filed in 2003, the IRS examined only 0.77% of all individual returns, 0.71% of all C corporation returns, 0.26% of all partnership returns, 0.19% of all S corporation returns, and 0.12% of all fiduciary returns. For individuals with total positive income (i.e., gross income before losses and other deductions) of $100,000 or more, the audit rate was 0.99%, and corporations with assets of at least $250 million faced a 20% rate. As a result of its audit process, the IRS recommended additional taxes and penalties totaling $25.6 billion in that year.[4]

The examination percentages described above may be misleading because over half the returns filed are subject to a computerized matching in which the IRS compares the tax return information with documents (Forms 1099 and W-2) submitted by payers and

---

[2] IRS Service Centers are located in Andover, Massachusetts; Chamblee, Georgia; Austin, Texas; Holtsville, New York; Covington, Kentucky; Fresno, California; Kansas City, Missouri; Memphis, Tennessee; Ogden, Utah; and Philadelphia, Pennsylvania. The Chamblee, Holtsville, and Covington Service Centers are known as the Atlanta, Brookhaven, and Cincinnati Service Centers, respectively. The IRS plans to reduce the number of its service centers and centralize their operations.

[3] Form W-2 reports employees' salaries and withholding tax, and Form 1099 reports income such as interest and dividends.
[4] "Examination Coverage: Recommended and Average Recommended Additional Tax Examination, by Type and Size of Return, Fiscal Year 2004," *Internal Revenue Service 2004 Data Book*, available for download at *http://www.irs.gov*, Tax Statistics Link, File No. 04db10ex.xls. Examinations are performed by revenue agents, tax auditors, and service center personnel.

Internal Revenue Service

Chief Counsel

2,600 IRS Employees

Commissioner/ Deputy Commissioner

National Office Staff

HR, Finance, Communications, Etc.

1,000 IRS Employees

SHARED SERVICES

Agency Wide Shared Services

Facilities, Procurement, Etc.

4,900 IRS Employees

Agency Wide Information Systems Services

7,000 IRS Employees

FUNCTIONAL UNITS

Appeals

1,900 IRS Employees

Taxpayer Advocate Service

1,600 IRS Employees

Criminal Investigation

4,500 IRS Employees

OPERATING DIVISIONS

Wage and Investment Income

21,000 IRS Employees

Small Business and Self-Employed

39,000 IRS Employees

Large and Mid-size Business

9,500 IRS Employees

Tax Exempt and Government Entities

2,800 IRS Employees

(NOTE: All numbers are approximate.)

FIGURE C15-1 ▶ IRS ORGANIZATION

Source: IRS, *Publication 3349* [Modernizing America's Tax Agency], 2000, p. 34.

employers. Because wages, interest, alimony, pensions, unemployment compensation, Social Security benefits, and other items of income are reported to the IRS by the payers, and because state income taxes, local real estate taxes, home mortgage interest, and other items of deduction are reported to the IRS by the payees, taxpayers who report only these items on their returns effectively face a 100% audit rate. According to a former IRS commissioner, "[M]ore than half of the individual returns filed are simple enough so that a matching with forms filed by employers and interest payors is sufficient to insure compliance."[5]

SELECTION OF RETURNS FOR AUDIT

Returns are chosen for audit in various ways, with many being selected under the *discriminant function (DIF)* process described below. The IRS's objective in using the DIF process is to make the audit process as productive as possible by maximizing the number of audits that result in the collection of additional taxes. The DIF process has improved the IRS's ability to select returns for audit. In recent years, the IRS failed to collect additional taxes on only 10% to 15% of the individual returns audited by its revenue agents and examiners. By comparison, in the late 1960s, before the advent of the DIF program, the IRS failed to collect additional taxes in 45% to 50% of its audits.[6] Recently, the IRS launched an audit initiative known as the Market Segment Specialization Program (MSSP). Examples of market segments include manufacturing, wholesale trade, retail trade (auto and boat dealers and service stations), and services (medical and health).[7] Under the MSSP, IRS personnel develop industry expertise, and the IRS prepares MSSP audit guidelines. As IRS personnel become more familiar with specific industries, their ability to spot industry-specific items that taxpayers incorrectly report likely will improve.

HISTORICAL NOTE

Taxpayers have made several attempts to make the DIF variables public information. However, so far the courts have refused to require the IRS to provide such information. The basic thrust of the DIF program is that a return will be flagged if enough items on the return are out of the norm for a taxpayer in that particular income bracket.

DISCRIMINANT FUNCTION (DIF) PROGRAM. Of the individual returns audited in 1982, the IRS selected two-thirds under the **DIF** program. In 2004, the IRS selected only 37% under the DIF program, with the rest being selected under 12 different audit initiatives, some of which involve nonfilers, tax-shelter related write-offs, computer matching of third-party information, claims for refund, return preparers, and unallowable items.[8] The IRS laid the groundwork for the DIF program in the mid-1960s to

▶ Reduce the staff and computer time necessary to screen returns

▶ Identify returns most likely to contain errors

▶ Reduce the number of audited returns for which an examination results in little or no additional tax[9]

An assistant IRS commissioner described the DIF selection process in the following manner:

> DIF is a type of statistical analysis, using multiple variables or criteria to differentiate between two populations. For the IRS, those populations are tax returns needing examination versus those returns not needing examination. DIF essentially identifies items on tax returns having predictive power; that is, the selected items on returns in the "need to examine" group show up differently than those in the "no need to examine" group. DIF takes several items on a tax return and reduces them to a single score, which is then used as a major determinant as to whether a particular return will be examined.[10]

Returns with a relatively high DIF score have characteristics in common with returns for which the IRS earlier assessed a deficiency upon audit (e.g., the return may have reported a relatively high casualty loss or charitable contribution deduction). Because the

[5] Bureau of National Affairs, *BNA Daily Tax Reports,* June 20, 1984, p. G-1.
[6] Letter from Sheldon S. Cohen, former IRS Commissioner, to Representative Nancy L. Johnson, Chairman of House Ways and Means Subcommittee on Oversight Regarding the TCMP, dated July 20, 1995, reprinted in *Tax Notes Today,* August 10, 1995, Document 95 TNT 156-63.
[7] K. D. Bakhai and G. E. Bowers, "A New Era in IRS Auditing," *Florida CPA Today,* November 1994, pp. 26–30.

[8] J. L. Wedick, Jr., "Looking for a Needle in a Haystack—How the IRS Selects Returns for Audit," *The Tax Adviser,* November 1983, p. 673.
[9] Ibid., pp. 673–674.
[10] Ibid., p. 674.

WHAT WOULD YOU DO IN THIS SITUATION?

Cultural understanding and tolerance are hallmarks of modern American society. Yet in the tax sphere, are there limits to such understanding and tolerance?

Consider the case of Mr. Y and his difficulties with the IRS. Mr. Y was born, reared, and educated as a lawyer in his native country. His employment experience included working for his country's counterpart of the IRS. Mr. Y immigrated to the United States at age 46 and was self-employed as a tax preparer. He became a naturalized U.S. citizen, and his tax practice flourished.

The IRS audited Mr. Y's individual tax returns, which resulted in an assessment of $27,000 in additional taxes and penalties. Mr. Y proceeded to award the IRS audit agent $5,000 in return for a "no-change" letter.

Unbeknownst to Mr. Y at the time, the transaction was secretly taped. Mr. Y was convicted of violating a U.S. law (18 USC 201(5)(1)(A)) that prohibits bribing a U.S. government official.

At his sentencing hearing, Mr. Y argued that his national origin should be taken into account in determining his punishment. Mr. Y explained that offering tax officials an "honorarium" to settle tax controversies was standard practice in his country. Not to do so would be insulting to these officials.

Do you believe that the $5,000 award to the IRS agent was appropriate in these circumstances? Assume you were representing Mr. Y. How should you have advised your client when he initially proposed offering an amount to the IRS agent?

IRS does not have the resources to audit all returns with a relatively high DIF score, IRS agents choose which of the higher scored returns should receive top priority for an audit.

The IRS has developed its DIF formulas based on data gathered in its **Taxpayer Compliance Measurement Program (TCMP)**. Under the TCMP, the IRS conducted special audits of taxpayers selected at random. In these audits, the IRS examined every line item of taxpayers' returns so as to develop a statistical norm for the taxpayers' industry or profession as a whole. If an item on the return of another taxpayer in the same industry or profession significantly departed from the norm, the return was flagged for examination. Before 1994, the IRS conducted TCMP audits of about 50,000 individuals every three years. It also regularly conducted TCMP audits of entities, such as corporations. Because of budget constraints, the IRS "indefinitely postponed" the TCMP in 1995.[11] Consequently, the data incorporated in the DIF formulas became outdated over time.

In 2002, the IRS launched the **National Research Program (NRP)** to select returns for audit. The NRP updates data compiled in TCMP audits and develops new statistical models for identifying returns most likely to contain errors. The NRP differs from the TCMP in two significant respects. First, it relies on pre-existing audit data as well as data complied in ordinary, as opposed to special, audits. Second, it focuses on specific portions of a tax return, not all line-by-line items. Like the TCMP, the NCR is based on data gathered primarily in audits of about 50,000 individual tax returns. It purports to be less intrusive and less burdensome than the TCMP.

The IRS also conducts what are called "financial status" or "lifestyle" audits. These audits seek to identify inconsistencies between the income that a taxpayer reports and income suggested by his or her lifestyle. In the course of the audit, IRS agents review the taxpayer's overall economic situation. They may ask questions concerning where the taxpayer vacations, where his or her children go to school, and the cost and model of his or her vehicles. Although the courts generally have sanctioned the use of financial status audits, Congress has limited their use to situations in which the IRS has a reasonable indication of unreported income.

OTHER METHODS. The IRS widely uses other methods for selecting returns for audit. Some returns are chosen because the taxpayer filed a claim for a refund of taxes paid previously, and the IRS decides to audit the tax return before refunding the requested

---

[11] "Rare Reprieve: IRS Postpones Its Superaudits," *The Wall Street Journal,* October 24, 1995, p. B1.

amount. A few returns are audited because the IRS receives a tip from one taxpayer (perhaps a disgruntled former employee or ex-spouse) that another taxpayer did not file a correct return. If the IRS does collect additional taxes as a result of the audit, it is authorized to pay a reward to the individual who provided the tip. The reward is completely discretionary, although it cannot exceed 10% of the additional tax and penalties due.[12] Sometimes, examining the return of an entity (e.g., a corporation) leads to an audit of a related party's return (e.g., a major stockholder).

Occasionally, the IRS investigates particular types of transactions or entities to ascertain taxpayer compliance with the tax law. As a result of these investigations, the IRS may select a number of returns for audit. For example, in 1989 the IRS examined 3,000 to 4,000 individual returns to determine whether taxpayers avoided classifying expenses as miscellaneous itemized deductions to escape the 2% floor. In 1997, the IRS investigated the returns of about 200,000 trusts (representing approximately 7% of total trust returns) to determine whether taxpayers had established them to avoid taxes.[13] In 2003, through a combination of audits, summons, and targeted litigation, the IRS launched an initiative to identify and deter promoters of abusive tax shelters and transactions.[14]

ALTERNATIVES FOR A TAXPAYER WHOSE RETURN IS AUDITED

When the IRS notifies a taxpayer of an impending audit, the notice indicates whether the audit is a correspondence, office, or field audit. In a correspondence audit, communication, such as documenting a deduction or explaining why the taxpayer did not report certain income, is handled through the mail. In an office audit, the taxpayer and/or his or her tax advisor meet with an IRS employee at a nearby IRS office. The audit notice indicates which items the IRS will examine and what information the taxpayer should bring to the audit. Field audits are common for business returns and complex individual returns. IRS officials conduct these audits either at the taxpayer's place of business or residence or at his or her tax advisor's office.

ADDITIONAL COMMENT

This special relief rule was designed to reduce the likelihood that the IRS could harass a taxpayer by repeatedly auditing a taxpayer on the same issue.

SPECIAL RELIEF RULE. A special relief rule exists for repetitive audit examinations of the same item. A taxpayer who receives an audit notice can request that the IRS suspend the examination and review whether the audit should proceed if (1) the IRS audited the taxpayer's return for the same item in at least one of the two previous years and (2) the earlier audit did not result in a change to his or her tax liability. To request the suspension, the taxpayer should call the IRS official whose name and telephone number appear on the audit notice.

EXAMPLE C15-1 ▶

In October 2006, the IRS notifies Tony that it will audit his 2004 medical expense deduction. Two years ago, the IRS audited Tony's 2002 medical expense deduction but did not assess an additional tax. Consequently, Tony may request that the IRS suspend the audit of his 2003 return regarding this issue. ◀

EXAMPLE C15-2 ▶

Assume the same facts as in Example C15-1 except the IRS audited Tony's 2002 employee business expenses. Because that audit dealt with a different item, Tony may not request a suspension. ◀

ADDITIONAL COMMENT

Taxpayers should encourage the tax practitioner to handle an IRS audit. Because taxpayers usually have a limited understanding of the complexities of the tax law and its administration, having the taxpayer present at the audit generally is not a good idea.

MEETING WITH A REVENUE AGENT. Generally, the first step in the audit process is a meeting between the IRS agent and the taxpayer or the taxpayer's advisor. If the taxpayer is fortunate, the agent will agree that the return was correct as filed or, even better, that the taxpayer is entitled to a refund. In most instances, however, the agent will contend that the taxpayer owes additional taxes. Taxpayers who do not agree with the outcome of their meeting may ask to confer with the agent's supervisor. A meeting with the supervisor could lead to an agreement concerning the additional tax due.

---

[12] Reg. Sec. 301.7623-1(c).
[13] Jacob M. Schlesinger, "IRS Cracks Down on Trusts It Believes Were Set up as Tax-Avoidance Schemes," *The Wall Street Journal*, April 4, 1997, p. A2.

[14] I.R. 2003-51, April 15, 2003.

Should the taxpayer agree and the agent's supervisor concur in the amount owed, the taxpayer must sign Form 870 (Waiver of Statutory Notice). This form indicates that the taxpayer waives any restrictions on the IRS's ability to assess the tax and consents to the IRS's collecting it. However, signing Form 870 does not preclude the taxpayer from filing a refund claim later.

If the taxpayer agrees that he or she owes additional tax and pays the tax upon signing the Form 870 waiver, interest accrues on the tax deficiency from the due date of the return through the payment date. Interest ceases to accrue 30 days after the Form 870 waiver is signed, and the IRS charges no additional interest if the taxpayer pays the tax due within ten days of the billing date.

TECHNICAL ADVICE MEMORANDA. Occasionally, a highly technical issue with which an IRS agent or appeals officer has had little or no experience arises in the course of the audit. Regardless of the type of audit, the official may request advice from the IRS's national office. Sometimes, the taxpayer urges the official to seek such advice. The advice is given in a Technical Advice Memorandum, which the IRS makes public in the form of a letter ruling. If the advice is favorable to the taxpayer, the agent or appeals officer must follow it. Even if the advice is pro-IRS, the official may consider the hazards of litigation in deciding whether to compromise.

APPEAL TO APPEALS DIVISION. If the taxpayer does not sign the Form 870 waiver, the IRS will send the taxpayer a **30-day letter**, detailing the proposed changes in the taxpayer's liability and advising the taxpayer of his or her right to pursue the matter with the IRS appeals office. The taxpayer has 30 days from the date of the letter to request a conference with an IRS appeals officer.

If the audit was a field audit and the amount of additional tax plus penalties and interest in question exceeds $10,000, the taxpayer must submit a **protest letter** within the 30-day period. Only a brief written statement is necessary if the amount is between $2,501 and $10,000. An oral request is acceptable in the case of office audits, regardless of the amount of the additional tax, penalties, and interest. If the taxpayer does not respond to the 30-day letter, the IRS will follow up with a 90-day letter, discussed below.

Protest letters are submitted to an official in the appropriate IRS functional division and should include the following information:

▶ The taxpayer's name, address, and telephone number

▶ A statement that the taxpayer wishes to appeal the IRS findings to the appeals office

▶ A copy of the letter showing the proposed adjustments

▶ The tax years involved

▶ A list of the proposed changes with which the taxpayer disagrees

▶ A statement of facts supporting the taxpayer's position on any issue with which he or she disagrees

▶ The law or other authority on which the taxpayer relied[15]

The taxpayer must declare, under penalties of perjury, that the statement of facts is true. If the taxpayer's representative prepares the protest letter, the representative must indicate whether he or she knows personally that the statement of facts is true.

Unlike IRS agents, appeals officers generally have the authority to settle (compromise) cases after considering the hazards of litigation. For example, if the appeals officer believes that the IRS has approximately a 40% chance of winning in court, the appeals officer may agree to close the case if the taxpayer will pay an amount equal to 40% of the originally proposed deficiency. The settlement authority of appeals officers extends to questions of fact and law.

In some matters, however, an appeals officer has no settlement authority. For example, if the matter involves an appeals coordinated issue, the appeals officer must obtain con-

---

[15] IRS, *Publication No. 5* [Your Appeal Rights and How to Prepare a Protest If You Don't Agree], January 1999, p. 1. A sample protest letter is published in Robert E. Meldman and Richard J. Sideman, *Federal Taxation Practice and Procedure,* Seventh Edition, (Chicago: CCH Incorporated, 2004).

currence or guidance from a director of appeals to reach a settlement. An **appeals coordinated issue** is an issue of wide impact or importance, frequently involving an entire industry or occupation group, for which the IRS desires consistent treatment. An example of an appeals coordinated issue is whether the taxpayer has in substance made a disposition of excess inventory and thus is entitled to claim a deduction for the loss on disposition.[16]

If, after the appeals conference, the taxpayer completely agrees with the IRS's position, he or she signs a Form 870 waiver. However, if the appeals officer makes some concessions and the parties agree that the additional tax is less than that originally proposed, the taxpayer signs Form 870-AD (Waiver of Restrictions on Assessment and Collection). Unlike the case of a Form 870 waiver, a Form 870-AD waiver generally does not permit the taxpayer later to file a refund claim for the tax year in question. A Form 870-AD waiver is effective only if accepted by the IRS.

90-DAY LETTER

If the taxpayer and appeals officer fail to reach an agreement, or if the taxpayer does not file a written protest within 30 days of the date of the letter, the IRS issues a **90-day letter** (officially, a "Statutory Notice of Deficiency").[17] The 90-day letter specifies the amount of the deficiency; explains how the amount was calculated; and states that the IRS will assess it unless, within 90 days of the date of mailing, the taxpayer files a petition with the Tax Court.[18] During the 90-day period (and whether or not the taxpayer files the petition), the IRS may not assess the deficiency or attempt to collect it. After the 90-day period (and only if the taxpayer timely files the petition), the IRS still may not assess or collect the deficiency until the Court's decision becomes final.

LITIGATION

As mentioned earlier, taxpayer litigation can begin in one of three courts of first instance: the Tax Court, a U.S. district court, and the U.S. Court of Federal Claims. After considering the time and expense of litigation, some taxpayers decide to pay the deficiency even though they believe their position is correct. Before deciding where to litigate, a taxpayer should consider the precedents, if any, of the various courts. Chapter C1 discusses the issues of precedent and "forum shopping."

U.S. TAX COURT. Taxpayers seeking to litigate in the Tax Court must file their petition with the Tax Court within 90 days of the date on which the IRS mails the Statutory Notice of Deficiency. The Tax Court strictly enforces this time limit. Before the scheduled hearing date, taxpayers still may reach an agreement with the IRS. Going the Tax Court route has some advantages, including not having to pay the deficiency as a precondition to filing suit. If the amount in question does not exceed $50,000 for a given year, the taxpayer may use the informal small cases procedure, an alternative not available in other courts. A potential disadvantage of this procedure is that the taxpayer may not appeal the Court's decision.

Taxpayers must pay the additional tax, plus any interest and penalties, if they lose in Tax Court and choose not to appeal their case. In some situations, the Tax Court leaves the computation of the additional tax up to the litigating parties. When this happens, the phrase "Entered under Rule 155" appears at the end of the Tax Court's opinion.

U.S. DISTRICT COURT OR U.S. COURT OF FEDERAL CLAIMS. To litigate in either a U.S. district court or the U.S. Court of Federal Claims, the taxpayer must first pay the deficiency and then file a claim for a refund with the IRS. In all likelihood, the IRS will deny this claim on the ground that the IRS correctly calculated the deficiency amount and properly assessed it. Upon notice of denial or six months after filing the claim, whichever is earlier, the taxpayer may sue the IRS for a refund. In no event, however, may the taxpayer file this lawsuit two years after the IRS denies the claim.

---

[16] *Internal Revenue Manual*, Sec. 8776.(14).
[17] Upon request, the IRS may grant an extension of time for filing a protest letter.

[18] Sec. 6213(a). If the notice is addressed to a person outside the United States, the time period is 150 days instead of 90.

APPEAL OF A LOWER COURT'S DECISION.   Whichever party loses—the taxpayer or the IRS—may appeal the lower court's decision to an appellate court. If the case began in the Tax Court or a federal district court, the case is appealable to the circuit court of appeals with jurisdiction over the taxpayer. For individuals, the taxpayer's place of residence generally determines which court of appeals has jurisdiction. In the case of corporations, the firm's principal place of business or state of incorporation generally controls. Cases originating in the U.S. Court of Federal Claims are appealable to the Circuit Court of Appeals for the Federal Circuit; that is, all the latter cases are heard by the same circuit, irrespective of the taxpayer's residence, principal place of business, or state of incorporation.

Either the taxpayer or the government can request that the Supreme Court review an appellate court's decision. If the Supreme Court decides to hear a case, it grants **certiorari**. If the Court decides not to hear a case, it denies certiorari. In any given year, the Supreme Court hears only a few cases dealing with tax matters.

? STOP & THINK

Question: Two years ago, Pete made a large expenditure and fully deducted it in the year paid. Recently, the IRS began an audit of Pete's return for that year and contended that the expenditure is not deductible. Pete is a resident of California, which is in the Ninth Circuit. In a similar case a few years ago, the Tax Court held that the expenditure is deductible, and the IRS did not appeal the decision. In yet another similar case litigated in a U.S. district court in California, the government initially lost but won on appeal to the Ninth Circuit. If Pete decides to litigate, in which forum (lower court) should he file suit, and why?

Solution: If he litigates in the Tax Court, he would not have to pay the proposed deficiency tax in advance. However, under the *Golsen* Rule (see Chapter C1), the Tax Court would depart from its earlier pro-taxpayer decision and rule for the IRS. (Pete's case would be appealable to the Ninth Circuit, and the Ninth Circuit has adopted a pro-government position.) Because the court for his district in California would be bound by the Ninth Circuit precedent, he should not litigate in that court. This likely outcome would disappoint Pete if he believed that a jury would rule in his favor because only U.S. district courts allow for jury trials. The only forum in which he could win is the U.S. Court of Federal Claims. No precedent that this court must follow exists because neither the U.S. Supreme Court, the Circuit Court of Appeals for the Federal Circuit, nor the U.S. Court of Federal Claims has previously ruled on the issue. (For a discussion of "forum-shopping," see Chapter C1.)

BURDEN OF PROOF.   In civil cases, the IRS has the burden of proving any factual issue relevant to a determination of the taxpayer's liability, provided the taxpayer meets four conditions.[19] First, the taxpayer introduces "credible evidence" regarding the issue. Credible evidence means evidence of a quality sufficient to serve as the basis of a court decision.[20] Second, the taxpayer complies with the recordkeeping and substantiation requirements of the IRC. These requirements include the proper documentation of meal and entertainment expenses (Sec. 274), charitable contributions (Sec. 170), and foreign controlled businesses (Sec. 6038). Third, the taxpayer "cooperates" with the reasonable requests of the IRS for witnesses, information, documents, meetings, and interviews. Cooperation includes providing access to, and inspection of, persons and items within the taxpayer's control. It also includes exhausting all administrative remedies available to the taxpayer.[21] Fourth, the taxpayer is either a legal person with net worth not exceeding $7 million, or a natural person.

---

[19] See Sec. 7491.
[20] See S. Rept. No. 105-174, 105th Cong., 1st Sess. (unpaginated).
[21] Ibid.

REQUESTS FOR RULINGS

OBJECTIVE 3

Describe the IRS's ruling process

As discussed in Chapter C1, a taxpayer can seek to clarify the tax treatment of a transaction by requesting that the IRS rule on the transaction. The IRS will answer certain requests by issuing a letter ruling (sometimes referred to as a private letter ruling) to the taxpayer. A letter ruling is a written determination issued to a taxpayer by the associate office that interprets and applies the tax laws to the taxpayer's specific set of facts.[22] Letter rulings are a matter of public record, but the IRS eliminates all confidential information before making the rulings public. The IRS charges a user fee for issuing a ruling, with the 2006 fees ranging from $150 for identical accounting method changes to $50,000 for pre-filing agreements. The fee for ruling on a proposed transaction is $10,000.[23] The fee for a ruling on a proposed transaction is $7,000.

ADDITIONAL COMMENT

The information requirements for requesting a letter ruling are very precise (see Rev. Proc. 2006-1). In general, a tax professional experienced in dealing with the national office of the IRS should be consulted. Also, a good blueprint of what should be included in a ruling request often can be found by locating an already-published letter ruling and examining its format.

INFORMATION TO BE INCLUDED IN TAXPAYER'S REQUEST

Early each calendar year, the IRS issues a revenue procedure that details how to request a letter ruling and the information that the request must contain. Taxpayers or tax advisors should consult this procedure before requesting a ruling. Appendix B of the procedure contains a checklist the taxpayer may use to ensure that the request is in order. The IRS has issued additional guidelines concerning the data to be included in the ruling request. For example, the IRS has specified what information the taxpayer must provide in a request for a ruling on the tax effects of transfers to a controlled corporation under Sec. 351. Each ruling request must contain a statement of all the relevant facts, including the following:

▶ Names, addresses, telephone numbers, and taxpayer identification numbers of all interested parties

▶ The taxpayer's annual accounting period and method

▶ A description of the taxpayer's business operations

▶ A complete statement of the business reasons for the transaction

▶ A detailed description of the transaction[24]

The taxpayer also should submit copies of the contracts, agreements, deeds, wills, instruments, and other documents that pertain to the transaction. The taxpayer must provide an explicit statement of all the relevant facts and not merely incorporate by reference language from the documents. The taxpayer also should indicate what confidential data should be deleted from the ruling before its release to the public.

If the taxpayer advocates a particular position, he or she must disclose the basis for this position and the authorities relied on. Even if the taxpayer is not arguing for specific tax treatment, he or she must furnish an opinion of the expected tax effects along with a statement of authorities supporting this opinion. In addition, the taxpayer should disclose and discuss any authorities to the contrary. The IRS suggests that, if no authorities to the contrary exist, the taxpayer should state so.

The person on whose behalf a ruling is requested should sign the following declaration: "Under penalties of perjury, I declare that I have examined this request, including accompanying documents, and, to the best of my knowledge and belief, the request contains all the relevant facts relating to the request, and such facts are true, correct, and complete."[25]

---

[22] Rev. Proc. 2006-1, 2006-1 I.R.B. 1, Sec. 2.01.
[23] Rev. Procs. 2006-1, 2006-1 I.R.B. 1, Sec. 15 Appendix A.
[24] Rev. Proc. 2006-1, 2006-1 I.R.B. 1, Sec. 7.01. Certain revenue procedures provide a checklist of information to be included for frequently occurring

transactions. See, for example, Rev. Proc. 83-59, 1983-2 C.B. 575, which includes guidelines for requesting rulings regarding a corporate formation under Sec. 351.
[25] Rev. Proc. 2006-1, 2006-1 I.R.B. 1, Sec. 7.01.

WILL THE IRS RULE?

In income and gift tax matters, the IRS will rule only on proposed transactions and on completed transactions for which the taxpayer has not yet filed a return.[26] In estate tax matters, the IRS generally will not rule if the estate has filed a tax return. On the other hand, the IRS will rule on the estate tax consequences of a living person.[27] If no temporary or final Treasury Regulations relating to a particular statutory provision have been issued, the following policies govern a ruling unless another IRS pronouncement holds otherwise:

▶ If the answer seems clear by applying the statute to the facts, the IRS will rule under the usual procedures.

▶ If the answer seems reasonably certain by applying the statute to the facts, but not entirely free from doubt, the IRS will likewise rule.

▶ If the answer does not seem reasonably certain, the IRS will rule if so doing is in the best interests of tax administration.[28]

The IRS will not rule on a set of alternative ways of structuring a proposed transaction or on the tax consequences of hypothetical transactions. Generally, the IRS will not rule on certain issues because of the factual nature of the problem involved or for other reasons.[29]

From time to time, the IRS discloses, by means of a revenue procedure, the topics with respect to which it definitely will not rule. The list of topics, however, is not all-inclusive. The IRS may refuse to rule on other topics whenever, in its opinion, the facts and circumstances so warrant.

According to Rev. Proc. 2006-3, the matters on which the IRS will not rule include the following:

▶ Whether property qualifies as the taxpayer's principal residence

▶ Whether compensation is reasonable in amount

▶ Whether a capital expenditure for an item ordinarily used for personal purposes (e.g., a swimming pool) has medical care as its primary purpose

▶ The determination of the amount of a corporation's earnings and profits.[30]

In addition, the IRS will not rule privately on issues that it proposes to address in revenue rulings, revenue procedures, or otherwise, or that the Treasury Department proposes to address in Treasury Regulations.

WHEN RULINGS ARE DESIRABLE

Private letter rulings serve to "insure" the taxpayer against adverse, after-the-fact tax consequences. They are desirable where (1) the transaction is proposed, (2) the potential tax liability is high, and (3) the law is unsettled or unclear. They also are desirable where the IRS has issued to another taxpayer a favorable ruling regarding similar facts and issues. Because only the other taxpayer may rely on the latter ruling, *this* taxpayer may seek a ruling on which he or she may confidently rely. On the other hand, private letter rulings are undesirable where the IRS has issued to another taxpayer an unfavorable ruling regarding similar facts and issues. They also are undesirable where the IRS might publicly rule on a related matter, and the taxpayer has an interest in this matter. Private letter rulings offer insight into the IRS's thinking on the tax treatment of proposed transactions. Although third parties may not cite them as authority for the tax consequences of their transactions, they may cite them as authority for avoiding a substantial understatement penalty (discussed later in this chapter).

---

[26] Ibid., Sec. 5.01.
[27] Ibid., Sec. 5.06.
[28] Ibid., Sec. 5.14.

[29] Ibid., Sec. 6.
[30] Rev. Proc. 2006-3, 2006-1 I.R.B. 122, Sec. 3.

DUE DATES

OBJECTIVE 4

Identify the due dates for tax returns

DUE DATES FOR RETURNS

Returns for individuals, fiduciaries, and partnerships are due on or before the fifteenth day of the fourth month following the year-end of the individual or entity.[31] C corporation and S corporation tax returns are due no later than the fifteenth day of the third month after the corporation's year-end. To be subject to reporting requirements, individuals and fiduciaries, but not corporations and partnerships, must have earned a minimum level of gross income during the year.[32]

EXTENSIONS

Congress realized that, in some instances, gathering the requisite information and completing the return by the designated due date is difficult. Consequently, it authorized extensions of time for filing returns. Unless the taxpayer is abroad, the extension period cannot exceed six months.[33]

INDIVIDUALS. By filing Form 4868 (Application for Automatic Extension of Time to File U.S. Individual Income Tax Return), an individual taxpayer may request an automatic extension to file the tax return. The extension is automatic in the sense that the taxpayer need not convince the IRS that an extension is necessary. Prior to 2006, the automatic extension period was four months after the return's original due date. If taxpayers needed more time, they could request an additional two-month extension by filing Form 2688 (Application for Additional Extension of Time to File U.S. Individual Income Tax Return). On this form, taxpayers had to explain the reason for the request. For tax returns filed in 2006 through 2008, the IRS will grant an automatic six-month extension via Form 4868, making Form 2688 unnecessary.[34]

EXAMPLE C15-3 ▶ Bob and Alice, his wife, are calendar year taxpayers. By filing Form 4868, they may get an automatic extension until October 15 of the following year for filing their current year's return. However, if the fifteenth falls on Saturday, Sunday, or a holiday, the due date is the next business day. ◀

CORPORATIONS. Corporations request an automatic extension by filing Form 7004 (Application for Automatic Extension of Time to File Corporation Income Tax Return) by the original due date for the return. Although the IRC specifies an automatic extension period of three months, Treasury Regulations and the Form 7004 instructions specify six months.[35] No additional extensions are available.

EXAMPLE C15-4 ▶ Lopez Corporation reports on a fiscal year ending March 31. The regular due date for its return is June 15. It may file Form 7004 and request an automatic six-month extension that postpones the due date until December 15. ◀

DUE DATES FOR PAYMENT OF THE TAX

Obtaining an extension merely postpones the due date for filing the return. It does not extend the due date for paying the tax. In general, the due date for the tax payment is the same as the unextended due date for filing the return.[36] In addition, the first estimated tax installment for extinguishing an individual's annual income tax liability must be paid by the due date for the preceding year's return, and the remaining payments must be made, respectively, two, five, and nine months later. Taxpayers who elect to let the IRS compute

[31] Sec. 6072(a). Section 6072(c) extends the due date for returns of nonresident alien individuals to the fifteenth day of the sixth month after the end of their tax year.
[32] Secs. 6012(a)(2) and 6031(a).
[33] Sec. 6081(a).
[34] Temp. Reg. Sec. 1.6081-4T.
[35] Sec. 6081(b) and Reg. Sec. 1.6081-3(a).
[36] Sec. 6151(a).

**TYPICAL
MISCONCEPTION**

Obtaining an extension defers the
date by which the return must be
filed, but it does *not* defer the
payment date of the tax liability.
Therefore, an extension for filing
must be accompanied by a payment of an estimate of the taxpayer's tax liability. Computing
this estimated tax liability can be
difficult because much of the
information necessary to complete the return may be incomplete or not yet available.

their tax must pay it within 30 days of the date the IRS mails a notice of the amount payable.[37]

Interest accrues on any tax not paid by the return's due date, including due dates set by extension periods. When individuals request an automatic extension, they should project the amount of their tax liability to the extent possible. Any tax owed, after withholding and estimated tax payments have been subtracted from the projected amount, should be remitted with the extension request. In addition, if an extension for filing a gift tax return is requested (on the same form), the estimated amount of gift tax liability should be remitted. Similarly, corporations should remit with their automatic extension request the amount of tax they estimate to be due, reduced by any estimated tax already paid.

INTEREST ON TAX NOT TIMELY PAID

Interest accrues on any tax not paid by the original due date for the return.[38] Taxpayers incur interest charges in four contexts.

▶ They file late, without having requested an extension, and pay late.

▶ They request an extension for filing but inaccurately estimate their tax liability and, thus, must pay some additional tax when they file their return.

▶ They file on time but are not financially able to pay some, or all, of the tax.

▶ The IRS audits their return and determines that they owe additional taxes.

RATE DETERMINATION. The IRS determines the interest rate that it charges taxpayers under rules provided in Sec. 6621. The rate varies with fluctuations in the federal short-term rate; potentially the interest rate changes at the beginning of each calendar quarter. For non-corporate taxpayers, the interest rate on both underpayments and overpayments is three percentage points higher than the federal rate. For corporate tax overpayments exceeding $10,000, the interest rate is reduced to the federal short-term rate plus one-half percentage point. For corporate underpayments exceeding $100,000, the rate is five percentage points above the federal short-term rate if the deficiency is not paid before a certain date. Rates are rounded to the nearest full percent. Recent applicable interest rates are as follows:

Period	General Rate for Underpayments and Overpayments
October 1, 2005, through March 31, 2006	7%
April 1, 2005, through September 30, 2005	6%
October 1, 2004, through March 31, 2005	5%
July 1, 2004, through September 30, 2004	4%
April 1, 2004, through June 30, 2004	5%

EXAMPLE C15-5 ▶ Ann filed her 2003 individual return in a timely manner, and the IRS audits it in March 2006. Ann is a calendar year taxpayer. The IRS contends that Ann owes $2,700 of additional taxes. Ann pays the additional taxes on March 31, 2006. Ann also must pay interest on the $2,700 deficiency for the period April 16, 2004, through March 31, 2006. The interest rate is 5% from April 16, 2004, through June 30, 2004, 4% from July 1, 2004, through September 30, 2004, 5% from October 1, 2004 through March 31, 2005, 6% from April 1, 2005 through September 30, 2005, and 7% from October 1, 2005 through March 31, 2006. ◀

DAILY COMPOUNDING. Daily compounding applies to both the interest taxpayers owe to the government and the interest the government owes to taxpayers who have overpaid their taxes. The IRS has issued Rev. Proc. 95-17 containing tables to be used for cal-

---

[37] Sec. 6151(b)(1). The estimated tax payment rules for C corporations, S corporations, and trusts and estates are described in Chapters C3, C11, and C14, respectively, of this volume.

[38] Secs. 6601(a) and (b)(1).

HISTORICAL NOTE
Probably two of the most significant changes in tax administration have been the daily compounding of interest and tying the interest rate charged to the federal short-term rate, which has resulted in a higher rate used to calculate the interest charge than in years past. Before these two changes, taxpayers who played the "audit lottery" and took aggressive positions incurred little risk.

culating interest.[39] The major tax services have published these tables. In addition, software packages are available for interest calculations.

ACCRUAL PERIOD. Interest usually accrues from the original due date for the return until the date of payment. However, two important exceptions apply. First, if the IRS fails to send an individual taxpayer a notice within 18 months after the original due date or the date on which a return is timely filed, whichever is later, the accrual of interest (and penalties) is suspended.[40] The suspension period begins on the day after the 18-month period and ends 21 days after the IRS sends the requisite notice. Second, if the IRS does not issue a notice and demand for payment within 30 days after the taxpayer signs a Form 870 waiver, no interest is charged for the period between the end of the 30-day period and the date the IRS issues its notice and demand.[41] Taxpayers litigating in the Tax Court may make a deposit to reduce the interest potentially owed. If the court decides that the taxpayer owes a deficiency, interest will not accrue on the deposit.

EXAMPLE C15-6 ▶ Cindy receives an automatic extension for filing this year's return. On June 24 of the following year, she submits her return, along with the $700 balance she owes on this year's tax. She owes interest on $700 for the period April 16 of this year through June 24 of the following year. Interest is compounded daily using the interest rate for underpayments determined under Sec. 6621. ◀

EXAMPLE C15-7 ▶ After filing for an automatic extension, Hans files his 2006 return on August 16, 2007. On April 3, 2009, the IRS sends Hans a notice of deficiency in which it assesses interest. Because the IRS failed to send Hans the notice by February 16, 2009 (18 months after the date on which the return was timely filed), the accrual of interest is suspended. The suspension period begins on February 17, 2009 (the day after the 18-month period), and ends on April 24, 2009 (21 days after the IRS sends the requisite notice). ◀

EXAMPLE C15-8 ▶ Raj filed his 2003 individual return on March 15, 2004. The IRS audits the return in 2006, and on January 24, 2006, Raj signs a Form 870 waiver, in which he agrees that he owes a $780 deficiency. The IRS does not issue a notice and demand for payment until March 20, 2006. Raj pays the deficiency two days later. Raj owes interest, compounded daily at the Sec. 6621 underpayment rate, for the period April 16, 2004, through February 24, 2006. No interest can be levied for the period February 24 through March 20, 2006 because the IRS did not issue its notice and demand for payment until more than 30 days after Raj signed the Form 870 waiver. ◀

ABATEMENT. The IRS does not abate interest except for unreasonable errors or delays resulting from its managerial or ministerial acts.[42] A "managerial act" involves the temporary or permanent loss of records or the exercise of judgment or discretion relating to the management of personnel.[43] A "ministerial act" involves routine procedure without the exercise of judgment or discretion.[44] A decision concerning the proper application of federal law is neither a managerial nor a ministerial act.

EXAMPLE C15-9 ▶ Omar provides documentation to an audit agent, who assures him that he will receive a copy of an audit report shortly. Before the agent has had an opportunity to act, however, the divisional manager transfers him to another office. An extended period of time elapses before the manager assigns another audit agent to Omar's case. The decision to reassign is a managerial act. The IRS may abate interest attributable to any unreasonable delay in payment resulting from this act. ◀

---

[39] Rev. Proc. 95-17, 1995-1 C.B. 556.
[40] Sec. 6404(g).
[41] Sec. 6601(c).
[42] Sec. 6404(e).
[43] Reg. Sec. 301.6404-2(b)(1).
[44] Reg. Sec. 301.6404-2(b)(2).

EXAMPLE C15-10 ▶ Chanelle requests information from an IRS employee concerning the balance due on her current year's tax liability. The employee fails to access the most current computerized database and provides Chanelle with incorrect information. Based on this information, Chanelle pays less than the full balance due. The employee's failing to access the most current database is a ministerial act. The IRS may abate interest attributable to any unreasonable delay in payment resulting from this act. ◀

FAILURE-TO-FILE AND FAILURE-TO-PAY PENALTIES

Understand tax-related penalties generally

REAL-WORLD EXAMPLE

In 2004, as a result of the audit process, the IRS assessed a total of $18.1 billion in civil penalties and abated about $935 million for reasonable cause.

Penalties add teeth to the accounting and reporting provisions of the Internal Revenue Code. Without them, these provisions would be mere letters on the books of the legislature—words without effect. Tax-related penalties fall into two broad categories: taxpayer and preparer. As the name suggests, taxpayer penalties apply only to taxpayers, be they individuals, corporations, estates, or trusts. Preparer penalties apply only to tax return preparers, be they firms that employ tax professionals or the professionals themselves. Within these broad categories are two distinct subcategories: civil and criminal. Civil penalties are imposed on taxpayers for negligently, recklessly, or intentionally failing to fulfill their accounting or reporting obligations. Criminal penalties are imposed for maliciously or willfully failing to do so. Taxpayers may raise as a defense to some penalties "reasonable cause" and a good faith belief in the correctness of their position. Sometimes, for the defense to be valid, they also must disclose this position on their tax return. This section of the text discusses two commonly encountered penalties in income, estate, and gift taxation: failure to file and failure to pay. The IRS may assess these penalties, in addition to interest, on overdue tax liabilities. Subsequent sections of the text discuss other taxpayer and preparer penalties. Topic Review C15-1 presents a summary of IRC penalty provisions. The Topic Review is provided here rather than later in the chapter to give readers a framework for following the discussion of the various penalties.

FAILURE TO FILE

Taxpayers who do not file a return by the due date generally are liable for a penalty of 5% per month (or fraction thereof) of the net tax due.[45] A fraction of a month, even just a day, counts as a full month. The maximum penalty for failing to file is 25%. If the taxpayer receives an extension, the extended due date is treated as the original due date. In determining the net tax due (i.e., the amount subject to the penalty), the IRS reduces the taxpayer's gross tax by any taxes paid by the return's due date (e.g., withholding and estimated tax payments) and tax credits claimed on the return.[46] If any failure to file is fraudulent, the penalty rate is 15% per month up to a maximum penalty of 75%.[47] For purposes of this provision, "fraud" is actual, intentional wrongdoing or the commission of an act for the specific purpose of evading a tax known or believed to be due.[48]

Penalties are not levied if a taxpayer can prove that he or she failed to file a timely return because of reasonable cause (as opposed to willful neglect). According to Treasury Regulations, reasonable cause exists if "the taxpayer exercised ordinary business care and prudence and was nevertheless unable to file the return within the prescribed time."[49] Not surprisingly, much litigation deals with the issue of reasonable cause.

Note that the penalty imposed for not filing on time generally is a function of the net tax due. However, a minimum penalty applies in some cases.[50] Congress enacted the minimum penalty provision because of the cost to the IRS of identifying nonfilers. If a tax-

ADDITIONAL COMMENT

The most common reason given by taxpayers to support reasonable cause for failing to file a timely tax return is reliance on one's tax advisor. Other reasons include severe illness or serious accident. Reliance on a tax advisor is not always sufficient cause to obtain a waiver of the penalties.

---

[45] Sec. 6651(a).
[46] Sec. 6651(b)(1).
[47] Sec. 6651(f).
[48] *Robert W. Bradford v. CIR*, 58 AFTR 2d 86-5532, 86-2 USTC ¶9602 (9th Cir., 1996: *Chris D. Stoltzfus v. U.S.*, 22 AFTR 2d 5251, 68-2 USTC ¶9499

(3rd Cir., 1968: and *William E. Mitchell v. CIR*, 26 AFTR 684, 41-1 USTC ¶9317 (5th Cir., 1941).
[49] Reg. Sec. 301.6651-1(c)(1).
[50] Sec. 6651(a).

payer does not file an income tax return within 60 days of the due date (including any extensions), the penalty will be no less than the smaller of $100 or 100% of the tax due on the return. Taxpayers who owe no tax are not subject to the **failure-to-file penalty.** Also, the IRS may waive the penalty if the taxpayer shows reasonable cause for not filing.

EXAMPLE C15-11 ▶ Earl files his 2006 individual income tax return on July 5, 2007. Earl requested no extension and did not have reasonable cause for his late filing, but he committed no fraud. Earl's 2006 return shows a balance due of $400. Under the regular rules, the late filing penalty would be $60 (0.05 × 3 months × $400). Earl's penalty is $100 because of the minimum penalty provision applicable to his failure to file the return within 60 days of the due date. ◀

Topic Review C15-1

Overview of Penalties

PENALTY	IRC SECTION	APPLICABILITY	RULES/CALCULATION	DEFENSES/WAIVER
A. TAXPAYER—CIVIL				
Failure to file	6651(a)	All persons	*General rule:* 5% per month or fraction thereof; 25% maximum *Minimum penalty if late more than 60 days:* lesser of $100 or 100% of tax due *Fraudulent reason for not filing:* 15% per month or fraction thereof; 75% maximum	Reasonable cause, not willful neglect
Failure to pay tax	6651(a)	All persons	*General rule:* 0.5% per month or fraction thereof; 25% maximum*	Reasonable cause, not willful neglect
Failure by individual to pay estimated tax	6654	Individuals, certain estates, trusts	*General rule:* penalty at same rate as interest rate for deficiency; imposed for period between due date for estimated tax payments and earlier of payment date or due date for return	Waiver in unusual circumstances
Failure by corporation to pay estimated tax	6655	Corporations	*General rule:* penalty at same rate as interest rate for deficiency; imposed for period between due date for estimated tax payments and earlier of payment date or due date for return	—
Negligence	6662(c)	All persons	*General rule:* 20% of underpayment attributable to negligence	Reasonable cause, good faith
Substantial understatement	6662(d)	All persons	*General rule:* 20% of underpayment attributable to substantial understatement (portion for which no substantial authority and no disclosure exists)	Reasonable cause, good faith; also, substantial authority, disclosure
Civil fraud	6663	All persons	*General rule:* 75% of portion of understatement attributable to fraud.	Reasonable cause, good faith
B. TAXPAYER—CRIMINAL				
Willful attempt to evade tax	7201	All persons	*General rule:* $100,000 ($500,000 for corporations) and/or up to five years in prison	—
Willful failure to collect or pay over tax	7202	All persons	*General rule:* $10,000 and/or up to five years in prison	—
Willful failure to pay or file	7203	All persons	*General rule:* $25,000 ($100,000 for corporations) and/or up to five years in prison	—
Willfully making false or fraudulent statements	7206	All persons	*General rule:* $25,000 ($100,000 for corporations) and/or up to one year in prison	—

Topic Review C15-1 (cont.)

C. PREPARER—CIVIL

Understatement of tax by preparer	6694(a)	Tax return preparers	*General rule:* $250	Reasonable cause, good faith; also, disclosure
Willful attempt to understate taxes	6694(b)	Tax return preparers	*General rule:* $1,000	—
Failure to furnish copy to taxpayer	6695(a)	Tax return preparers	*General rule:* $50; $25,000 maximum	Reasonable cause, not willful neglect
Failure to sign return	6695(b)	Tax return preparers	*General rule:* $50; $25,000 maximum	Reasonable cause, not willful neglect
Failure to furnish identifying number	6695(c)	Tax return preparers	*General rule:* $50; $25,000 maximum	Reasonable cause, not willful neglect
Failure to retain copy or list	6695(d)	Tax return preparers	*General rule:* $50; $25,000 maximum	Reasonable cause, not willful neglect
Failure to file correct information returns	6695(e)	Tax return preparers	*General rule:* $50 for each failure to file a return or each failure to set forth an item in a return; $25,000 maximum	Reasonable cause, not willful neglect
Improper negotiation of checks	6695(f)	Tax return preparers	*General rule:* $500 per check	—
Aiding and abetting in understatement	6701(b)	All persons	*General rule:* $1,000 ($10,000 for corporations)	—

* If the taxpayer owes both the failure-to-file and the failure-to-pay penalties for a given month, the total penalty for such month is limited to 5% of the net tax due.

In general, interest does not accrue on any penalty paid within ten days of the date that the IRS notifies the taxpayer of the penalty. Under Sec. 6601(e)(2)(B), however, interest accrues on the failure-to-file penalty, from the due date of the return (including any extensions) until the payment date.

FAILURE TO PAY

The **failure-to-pay penalty** is imposed at 0.5% per month (or fraction thereof).[51] The maximum penalty is 25%. The penalty is based on the gross tax shown on the return less any tax payments made and credits earned before the beginning of the month for which the penalty is calculated.[52] As with the failure-to-file penalty, the IRS may waive the failure-to-pay penalty if the taxpayer shows reasonable cause.

Because the tax is due on the original due date for the return, taxpayers who request an extension without paying 100% of their tax liability potentially owe a failure-to-pay penalty. Treasury Regulations provide some relief by exempting a taxpayer from the penalty if the additional tax due with the filing of the extended return does not exceed 10% of the tax owed for the year.[53]

EXAMPLE C15-12 ▶ Gary requests an extension for filing his 2006 individual income tax return. His 2006 tax payments include withholding of $4,500, estimated tax payments of $2,000, and $1,000 submitted with his request for an automatic extension. He files his return on June 7, 2007, showing a total tax of $8,000 and a balance due of $500. Gary is exempt from the failure-to-pay penalty because the $500 balance due does not exceed 10% of his 2006 liability (0.10 × $8,000 = $800). Had Gary's 2006 tax instead been $9,000, he would have owed an additional tax of $1,500 and a failure-to-pay penalty of $15 (0.005 × 2 months × $1,500). ◀

The 0.5% penalty increases to 1% a month, or fraction thereof, in certain circumstances. The rate is 1% for any month beginning after the earlier of

▶ Ten days after the date the IRS notifies the taxpayer that it plans to levy on his or her salary or property and

---

[51] Sec. 6651(a)(2).
[52] Sec. 6651(b)(2).

[53] Reg. Sec. 301.6651-1(c)(3) and (4).

► The day the IRS notifies and demands immediate payment from the taxpayer because it believes that collection is in jeopardy

EXAMPLE C15-13 ► Ginny files her 2003 individual income tax return on April 12, 2004. However, Ginny does not pay her tax liability. On October 6, 2006, the IRS notifies Ginny of its plans to levy on her property. The failure-to-pay penalty is 0.5% per month for the period April 16, 2004 through October 15, 2005. Beginning on October 16, 2005, the penalty rises to 1% per month, or fraction thereof. ◄

Some taxpayers file on time to avoid the failure-to-file penalty even though they cannot pay the balance of the tax due. Barring a showing of reasonable cause, these taxpayers still will incur the failure-to-pay penalty. Because taxpayers who do not timely file a return are likely to owe additional taxes, they often owe both the failure-to-file and the failure-to-pay penalties.

The IRC provides a special rule for calculating the 5% per month failure-to-file penalty for periods in which the taxpayer owes both penalties. The 5% per month failure-to-file penalty is reduced by the failure-to-pay penalty.[54] Thus, the total penalties for a given month will not exceed 5%. For months when the taxpayer incurs both penalties, the failure-to-file penalty is effectively 4.5% (5% − 0.5%). Note, however, that no reduction occurs if the minimum penalty for failure to file applies.

EXAMPLE C15-14 ► Tien files her current year individual income tax return on August 5 of the following year, without having requested an extension. Her total tax is $20,000. Tien pays $15,000 in a timely manner and the $5,000 balance when she files the return. Although Tien committed no fraud, she can show no reasonable cause for the late filing and late payment. Tien's penalties are as follows:

Failure-to-pay penalty:		
$5,000 × 0.005 × 4 months		$ 100
Failure-to-file penalty:		
$5,000 × 0.05 × 4 months	$1,000	
Minus: Reduction for failure-to-pay penalty imposed for same period	(100)	900
Total penalties		$1,000 ◄

EXAMPLE C15-15 ► Assume the same facts as in Example C15-14 except that Tien instead pays the $5,000 balance on November 17 of the following year. The penalties are as follows:

Failure-to-pay penalty:		
$5,000 × 0.005 × 8 months (April 16 through November 17)		$ 200
Failure-to-file penalty:		
$5,000 × 0.05 × 4 months (April 16 through August 5)	$1,000	
Minus: Reduction for failure-to-pay penalty levied for April 16 through August 5 ($5,000 × 0.005 × 4 months)	(100)	900
Total penalties		$1,100 ◄

ESTIMATED TAXES

Individuals earning only salaries and wages generally pay their annual income tax liability through payroll withholding. The employer is responsible for remitting these withheld amounts, along with Social Security taxes, to a designated federal depository. By contrast, individuals earning other types of income, as well as C corporations, S corporations, and trusts, must estimate their annual income tax liability and prepay their taxes on a quarterly basis.[55] Estates must do the same with respect to income earned during any tax year

---

[54] Sec. 6651(c)(1).
[55] S corporations must pay quarterly estimated taxes on their net recognized built-in gains, passive investment income, and credit recapture amounts.

ending two years after the decedent's death.[56] Although partnerships do not pay estimated income taxes, their separate partners do if they are individuals or taxable entities. Chapters C3, C11, and C14 discuss the estimated income tax requirements for C corporations, S corporations, and fiduciaries, respectively.

PAYMENT REQUIREMENTS

Individuals should pay quarterly estimated income taxes if they have a significant amount of income from sources other than salaries and wages. The amount of each payment should be the same if this outside income accrues uniformly throughout the year. To avoid an estimated income tax penalty for the current year, individuals with AGI of $150,000 or less in the previous year should calculate each payment as follows:

Step 1: Determine the lesser of
    a. 90% of the taxpayer's regular tax, alternative minimum tax (if any), and self-employment tax for the current year, or
    b. 100% of the taxpayer's prior year regular tax, alternative minimum tax (if any), and self-employment tax if the taxpayer filed a return for the prior year and the year was not a short tax year.

Step 2: Calculate the total of
    a. Tax credits for the current year
    b. Taxes withheld on the current year's wages
    c. Overpayments of the prior year's tax liability the taxpayer requests be credited against the current year's tax

Step 3: Multiply the excess of the amount from Step 1 over the amount from Step 2 by 25%.[57]

Calendar year individual taxpayers should pay their quarterly installments on April 15, June 15, September 15, and January 15.

Individuals with AGI exceeding $150,000 ($75,000 for married filing separately) in the prior year can avoid the estimated tax penalty for the current year if they pay at least 90% of the current year's tax, or at least 110% of the prior year's tax.[58]

EXAMPLE C15-16 ▶ Mike's regular tax on his current year taxable income is $35,000. Mike also owes $2,000 of self-employment tax but no alternative minimum tax. Mike's total tax liability last year for both income and self-employment taxes was $24,000. His AGI last year did not exceed $150,000. Taxes withheld from Mike's current year wages were $8,000. Mike did not overpay his tax last year or earn any credits this year. For the current year, Mike should have made quarterly estimated tax payments of $4,000, as calculated below.

Lesser of:	90% of current year's tax (0.90 × $37,000 = $33,300) or	
	100% of prior year's $24,000 tax liability	$24,000
Minus:	Taxes withheld from current year's wages	(8,000)
Minimum estimated tax payment to avoid penalty under general rule		$16,000
Quarterly estimated tax payments (0.25 × $16,000)		$ 4,000 ◀

The authority to make estimated tax payments based on the preceding year's income is especially significant for taxpayers with rising levels of income. To avoid an estimated income tax penalty, these taxpayers need to pay only an amount equal to the prior year's tax liability. Using this safe harbor eliminates the need for estimating the current year's tax liability with a high degree of accuracy.

ADDITIONAL COMMENT

Although it is simpler to use the amount of tax paid (or, if necessary, the applicable percentage of the amount of tax paid) in the preceding year as a safe harbor, the estimate of the current year's tax liability is preferable if the current year's tax liability is expected to be significantly less than the preceding year's tax liability.

EXAMPLE C15-17 ▶ Peter, a single calendar year taxpayer, incurs a regular tax liability of $76,000 in the current year. Peter owes no alternative minimum tax liability nor can he claim any tax credits. No overpayments of last year's taxes are available to offset this year's tax liability. Taxes withheld evenly

---

[56] For example, if the decedent's death were June 15 of the current year, and the assets of the decedent's estate are not distributed by June 14 of the following year, the estate must pay estimated taxes on income earned on estate assets for the following tax year.

[57] Secs. 6654(d), (f), and (g).
[58] Sec. 6654(d)(1)(C). Included in the definition of *individuals* are estates and trusts. Section 67(e) defines AGI for estates and trusts. (See Chapter C14.)

from Peter's wages throughout the current year are $68,000. Peter's AGI last year exceeded $150,000, and his regular tax liability was $60,000. Because Peter's $17,000 of withholding for each quarter exceeds the $15,000 minimum required quarterly payments, as calculated below, he incurs no underpayment penalty.

Lesser of: 90% of current year's (0.90 × $76,000 = $68,400) or	
110% of prior year's $60,000 tax liability	$66,000
Minus: Taxes withheld from current year's wages	(68,000)
Minimum estimated tax payment to avoid	
penalty under general rule	$ –0–

The $8,000 ($76,000 − $68,000) balance of the current's year taxes is due on or before April 15 of next year. ◄

PENALTY FOR UNDERPAYING ESTIMATED TAXES

With the exceptions discussed in the next section, taxpayers who do not remit the requisite amount of estimated tax by the appropriate date are subject to a penalty for underpayment of estimated taxes. The penalty is calculated at the same rate as the interest rate applicable under Sec. 6621 to late payments of tax.[59] The penalty for each quarter is calculated separately on Form 2210.

The amount subject to the penalty is the excess of the total tax that should have been paid during the quarter (e.g., $6,000 [$24,000 prior year's tax liability ÷ 4] in Example C15-16) over the sum of the estimated tax actually paid during that quarter on or before the installment date plus the withholding attributable to that quarter. Unless the taxpayer proves otherwise, the withholding is deemed to take place equally during each quarter. This rule creates a planning opportunity. Taxpayers who have not paid sufficient amounts of estimated tax in the first three quarters can avoid the imposition of the penalty by having large amounts of tax withheld during the last quarter.

The penalty is assessed for the time period beginning with the due date for the quarterly installment and ending on the earlier of the date the underpayment actually is paid or the due date for the return (April 15 assuming a calendar year taxpayer). The next example illustrates the computation of the underpayment penalty.

EXAMPLE C15-18 ►

Assume the same facts as in Example C15-16 except that Mike pays only $3,000 of estimated tax payments on April 15, June 15, and September 15 of the current year and January 15 of next year and, for simplicity, that 6% is the Sec. 6621 underpayment rate for the entire time period. Mike files his current year return on March 30 of next year and pays the $17,000 ($37,000 − $8,000 withholding − $12,000 estimated taxes) balance due at that time. Mike's underpayment penalty is determined as follows:

	Quarter			
	First	*Second*	*Third*	*Fourth*
Amount that should have been paid ($24,000 ÷ 4)	$6,000	$6,000	$6,000	$6,000
Minus: Withholding	(2,000)	(2,000)	(2,000)	(2,000)
Estimated tax payment	(3,000)	(3,000)	(3,000)	(3,000)
Underpayment	$1,000	$1,000	$1,000	$1,000
Number of days of underpayment (ends March 30 of next year because earlier than April 15 of next year);	349	288	196	74
Penalty at 6% assumed annual rate for number of days of underpayment	$ 57	$ 47	$ 32	$ 12

The total penalty equals $148 ($57 + $47 + $32 + $12). The $148 penalty is not deductible. ◄

---

[59] Daily compounding is not applicable in calculating the penalty.

Interest does not accrue on underpayments of estimated tax.[60] However, if the entire tax is not paid by the due date for the return, interest and perhaps also a failure-to-pay penalty will be levied on the unpaid amount.

EXCEPTIONS TO THE PENALTY

In certain circumstances, individuals who have not remitted the requisite amount of estimated tax nevertheless will be exempt from the underpayment penalty. The IRS imposes no penalty if the taxpayer's tax exceeds the taxes withheld from wages for the year in question by less than $1,000. Similarly, the taxpayer will not owe a penalty, regardless of the size of the underpayment, if the taxpayer owed no taxes for the prior year, the prior year consisted of 12 months, and the taxpayer was a U.S. citizen or resident alien for the entire preceding year. The Secretary of the Treasury can waive the penalty otherwise due in the case of "casualty, disaster, or other unusual circumstances" or for newly retired or disabled individuals.[61]

EXAMPLE C15-19 ▶ Paul's current year tax is $2,200, the same amount as his prior year tax. His withholding tax is $1,730, and Paul does not pay any estimated taxes. Paul pays the $470 balance due on March 15 of next year. Under the general rules, Paul is subject to the underpayment penalty because he does not meet either the 90% of the current year tax or 100% of the prior year tax minimums. However, because Paul's tax exceeds the withholding from his wages by less than $1,000, he owes no penalty for underpaying his estimated tax. ◀

Taxpayers are exempt from the underpayment penalty in still other circumstances. A discussion of all these other circumstances is beyond the scope of this text. Chapter I14 of *Prentice Hall's Federal Taxation: Principles* and *Comprehensive* texts, however, discusses one such circumstance where the taxpayer annualizes his or her income and bases the estimated tax payment on the annualized amount.[62]

OTHER MORE SEVERE PENALTIES

OBJECTIVE 7

Describe more severe penalties, including the fraud penalty

In addition to the penalties for failure to file, failure to pay, and underpayment of estimated tax, taxpayers may be subject to other more severe penalties. These include the accuracy-related penalty (applicable in several contexts) and the fraud penalty, each of which is discussed below.[63] A 20% accuracy-related penalty applies to any underpayment attributable to negligence, any substantial understatement of income tax, and various types of errors, a discussion of which is beyond the scope of this text. An accuracy-related penalty is not levied, however, if the government imposed the fraud penalty or if the taxpayer filed no return.

ADDITIONAL COMMENT

To shift the burden of proof to the IRS, the taxpayer must introduce credible evidence regarding a factual issue relating to his or her tax liability.

NEGLIGENCE

The accuracy-related **negligence penalty** applies whenever the IRS determines that a taxpayer has underpaid any part of his or her taxes as a result of negligence or disregard of the rules or regulations (but without intending to defraud).[64] The penalty is 20% of the underpayment attributable to negligence. Interest accrues on the negligence penalty at the rates applicable to underpayments.[65]

EXAMPLE C15-20 ▶ The IRS audits Ted's individual return and assesses a $7,500 deficiency, of which $2,500 is attributable to negligence. Ted agrees to the assessment and pays the additional tax of $7,500 the following year. Ted incurs a negligence penalty of $500 (0.20 × $2,500). ◀

---

[60] Sec. 6601(h).
[61] Sec. 6654(e).
[62] Section 6654(d)(2) allows for computation of the underpayments, if any, by annualizing income. Relief from the underpayment penalty may result from applying the annualization rules. Corporations, but not individuals, are permitted a seasonal adjustment to the annualization rules.

[63] Secs. 6662(a) and (b).
[64] Secs. 6662(b) and (c).
[65] Sec. 6601(e)(2)(B).

The IRC defines *negligence* as "any failure to make a reasonable attempt to comply with the provisions" of the IRC. It defines disregard of the rules or regulations as "any careless, reckless, or intentional disregard."[66] According to Treasury Regulations, a presumption of negligence exists if the taxpayer does not include in gross income an amount of income shown on an information return or does not reasonably attempt to ascertain the correctness of a deduction, credit, or exclusion that a reasonable and prudent person would think was "too good to be true."[67]

A taxpayer is careless if he or she does not diligently try to determine the correctness of his or her position. A taxpayer is reckless if he or she exerts little or no effort to determine whether a rule or regulation exists. A taxpayer's disregard is intentional if he or she knows about the rule or regulation he or she disregards.[68]

The penalty will not be imposed for any portion of an underpayment if the taxpayer had reasonable cause for his or her position and acted in good faith.[69] Failure to follow a regulation must be disclosed on Form 8275-R (Regulation Disclosure Statement).

EXAMPLE C15-21 ▶ The IRS audits Mario's current year individual return, and Mario agrees to a $4,000 deficiency. Mario had reasonable cause for adopting his tax return positions (which were not contrary to the applicable rules or regulations) and acted in good faith. Mario will not be liable for a negligence penalty. ◀

SUBSTANTIAL UNDERSTATEMENT

Taxpayers who substantially understate their income tax are liable for an accuracy-related penalty for their substantial understatements. The IRC defines a substantial understatement as an understatement of tax exceeding the greater of 10% of the tax required to be shown on the return or $5,000 (or $10,000 in the case of a C corporation). For a C corporation, an additional rule applies. Specifically, if 10% of the required tax exceeds $10 million, a substantial understatement exists if the understatement exceeds $10 million.[70] The penalty equals 20% of the underpayment of tax attributable to the substantial understatement. It does not apply to understatements for which the taxpayer shows reasonable cause and good faith for his or her position.

UNDERSTATEMENT VERSUS UNDERPAYMENT. The amount of tax attributable to the substantial understatement may be less than the amount of the underpayment. In general, the amount of the understatement is calculated as the amount by which the tax required to be shown (i.e., the correct tax) exceeds the tax shown on the return. Because the amount of tax attributable to certain items is not treated as an understatement, the additional tax attributed to such items is not subject to the penalty. An underpayment for an item other than a tax shelter is *not* an understatement if either of the following is true:

▶ The taxpayer has substantial authority for the tax treatment of the item.

▶ The taxpayer discloses, either on the return or in a statement attached to the return, the relevant facts affecting the tax treatment of the item, and the taxpayer has a reasonable basis for such treatment.

Although neither the IRC nor Treasury Regulations define "reasonable basis," Reg. Sec. 1.6662-3(b)(3) states that a "reasonable basis" standard is significantly higher than the "not frivolous" standard that usually applies to tax preparers. The latter standard involves a tax position that is not patently improper. The taxpayer meets the adequate disclosure requirement if he or she properly completes Form 8275 and attaches it to the return, or discloses information on the return in a manner prescribed by an annual revenue procedure.[71]

EXAMPLE C15-22 ▶ The IRS examines Val's current year individual income tax return, and Val agrees to a $9,000 deficiency, which increases her taxes from $25,000 to $34,000. Val neither made adequate dis-

---

ADDITIONAL COMMENT

Theoretically, penalties are designed to deter taxpayers from willfully disregarding federal tax laws. Some taxpayers have been concerned that the IRS has used the multitude of tax penalties primarily as a source of revenue. The IRS achieved this result by "stacking" penalties (i.e., applying several penalties to a single underpayment). Recent legislation has alleviated some of this concern.

SELF-STUDY QUESTION

How is an understatement different from an underpayment?

ANSWER

An underpayment can be larger than an understatement. Understatements do not include underpayments for which there was either substantial authority or adequate disclosure.

---

[66] Sec. 6662(c).
[67] Reg. Sec. 1.6662-3(b)(1).
[68] Reg. Sec. 1.6662-3(b)(2).
[69] Sec. 6664(c).
[70] Sec. 6662(d)(1).

[71] Reg. Secs. 1.6662-4(f)(1) and (2). See Rev. Proc. 99-41, 1999-2 C.B. 566, and Rev. Proc. 2001-11, 2001-1 C.B. 275, where the Treasury Department identifies circumstances where disclosure of a position on a taxpayer's return is adequate to reduce the understatement penalty of Sec. 6662(d) and tax preparer penalties of Sec. 6694(a).

closure concerning the items for which the IRS assessed the deficiency nor had substantial authority for her tax treatment. Thus, Val's understatement also is $9,000. This understatement is substantial because it exceeds both 10% of her correct tax liability ($3,400 = 0.10 × $34,000) and the $5,000 minimum. Val incurs a substantial understatement penalty of $1,800 (0.20 × $9,000). ◄

EXAMPLE C15-23 ►

Assume the same facts as in Example C15-22 except Val has substantial authority for the tax treatment of an item that results in a $1,000 additional assessment. In addition, she makes adequate disclosure for a second item with respect to which the IRS assesses additional taxes of $1,500. Although Val's underpayment is $9,000, her understatement is only $6,500 [$9,000 − ($1,000 + $1,500)]. The $6,500 understatement is substantial because it is more than the greater of 10% of Val's tax or $5,000. Thus, the penalty in this case is $1,300 (0.20 × $6,500). ◄

ADDITIONAL COMMENT

Even though the substantial understatement penalty is a taxpayer penalty, tax preparers have a duty to make their clients aware of the potential risk of substantial understatement. In some situations, failure to do so has resulted in the client's attempting to collect the amount of the substantial understatement penalty from the preparer.

Like the negligence penalty, the substantial understatement penalty bears interest at the rate applicable to underpayments. The interest accrues from the due date of the return.

CONCEPT OF SUBSTANTIAL AUTHORITY. Treasury Regulations indicate that substantial authority

► Exists only if the weight of authorities supporting the tax treatment of an item is substantial relative to the weight of those supporting the contrary treatment, and

► Is based on an objective standard involving an analysis of law and its application to the relevant facts. This standard is more stringent than the "reasonable basis" standard that the taxpayer must meet to avoid the negligence penalty but less stringent than the "more likely than not" standard that applies to tax shelters.[72] (See discussion below.)

According to these regulations, the following are considered to be "authority": statutory provisions; proposed, temporary, and final regulations; court cases; revenue rulings; revenue procedures; tax treaties; Congressional intent as reflected in committee reports and joint statements of a bill's managers; private letter rulings; technical advice memoranda; information or press releases; notices; and any other similar documents published by the IRS in the *Internal Revenue Bulletin* and the *General Explanation of the Joint Committee on Taxation* (also known as the "Blue Book"). Conclusions reached in treatises, periodicals, and the opinions of tax professionals are not considered to be authority. The applicability of court cases in the taxpayer's district is not taken into account in determining the existence of substantial authority. On the other hand, the applicability of court cases in the taxpayer's circuit *is* taken into account in determining the existence of substantial authority.

EXAMPLE C15-24 ►

Authorities addressing a particular issue are as follows:

► For the government: Tax Court and Fourth Circuit Court of Appeals

► For taxpayers: U.S. District Court for Rhode Island and First Circuit Court of Appeals

The taxpayer (Tina) is a resident of Rhode Island, which is in the First Circuit. Tina would have substantial authority for a pro-taxpayer position because such a position is supported by the circuit court of appeals for Tina's geographical jurisdiction. ◄

Taxpayers should be aware that, while sparing them a substantial understatement penalty, disclosure (even with a reasonable basis for the tax treatment of the item) might raise a "red flag" that could prompt an IRS audit.

TAX SHELTERS. A different set of rules applies to a tax shelter, which is any arrangement for which a significant purpose is the avoidance or evasion of federal income tax.[73] See page C15–33 for a discussion of this topic.[74]

---

[72] Reg. Sec. 1.6662-4(d).
[73] Sec. 6662(d)(2)(C).

[74] The discussion on that page covers the new rules ushered in by the 2004 Jobs Act.

CIVIL FRAUD

Fraud differs from simple, honest mistakes and negligence in that it involves a deliberate attempt to deceive. Because the IRS cannot establish intent per se, it attempts to prove intent indirectly by emphasizing the taxpayer's actions and the circumstances surrounding these actions. One leading authority refers to fraud cases in this manner:

> Fraud cases ordinarily involve systematic or substantial omissions from gross income or fictitious deductions or dependency claims, accompanied by the falsification or destruction of records or false or inconsistent statements to the investigating agents, especially where records are not kept by the taxpayer. The taxpayer's education and business experience are relevant.[75]

The fraud penalty equals 75% of the portion of the underpayment attributable to fraud. If the IRS establishes that any portion of an underpayment is due to fraud, the entire underpayment is treated as having resulted from fraud unless the taxpayer establishes otherwise by a preponderance of the evidence. Like the negligence penalty, the fraud penalty bears interest.[76]

EXAMPLE C15-25 ▶ The IRS audits Ned's individual return and claims that Ned's underpayment is due to fraud. Ned agrees to the $40,000 deficiency but establishes that only $32,000 of the deficiency is attributable to fraud. The remainder results from mistakes that the IRS did not believe were due to fraud. Ned's civil fraud penalty is $24,000 (0.75 × $32,000). ◀

The fraud penalty can be imposed on taxpayers filing income, gift, or estate tax returns. If it is imposed, the negligence and substantial understatement penalties are not assessed on the portion of the underpayment attributable to fraud.[77]

With respect to a joint return, no fraud penalty can be imposed on a spouse who has not committed fraud.[78] In other words, one spouse is not liable for the other spouse's fraudulent acts.

STOP & THINK

Question: A few years ago, Joyce filed her individual income tax return in which she reported $250,000 of taxable income. She paid all the tax shown on the return on the day she filed. She, however, fraudulently omitted an additional $100,000 of gross income and, of course, does not have substantial authority for this omission. Moreover, she did not make a disclosure of the omitted income. If the IRS proves that Joyce committed fraud, will she be liable for both the civil fraud penalty and the substantial understatement penalty? What are the rates for the two penalties?

Solution: Because the penalties cannot be stacked, Joyce will not owe both penalties. If the IRS successfully proves fraud, she will owe a penalty of 75% of the tax due on the omitted income. She will not owe the 20% penalty for substantial understatements.

ADDITIONAL COMMENT

In fiscal 2004, the IRS initiated 3,917 criminal investigations (down from 4,001 in 2003), and it referred 3,037 for prosecution. During fiscal 2004, the IRS filed 2,489 indictments, and prison sentences were handed down in 1,777 of those cases.

CRIMINAL FRAUD

Civil and criminal fraud are similar in that both involve a taxpayer's intent to misrepresent facts. They differ primarily in terms of the weight of evidence required for conviction. Civil fraud requires proof by a preponderance of the evidence. Criminal fraud requires proof beyond a reasonable doubt. Because the latter standard is more stringent than the former, the government charges relatively few taxpayers with criminal fraud. To do so, the IRS and Justice Department must agree on the charges.

---

[75] Boris I. Bittker and Lawrence Lokken, *Federal Taxation of Income, Estates, and Gifts* (Boston, MA: Warren, Gorham & Lamont, 1999), vol. 4, ¶ 114–6.

[76] Sec. 6601(e)(2)(B).
[77] Sec. 6662(b).
[78] Sec. 6663(c).

CRIMINAL FRAUD INVESTIGATIONS. The Criminal Investigation Division of the IRS conducts criminal fraud investigations. The agents responsible for the investigation are called **special agents**. Under IRS policy, at the first meeting of the special agent and the taxpayer, the special agent must

▶ Identify himself or herself as such

▶ Advise the taxpayer that he or she is the subject of a criminal investigation

▶ Advise the taxpayer of his or her rights to remain silent and consult legal counsel

PENALTY PROVISIONS. Sections 7201–7216 provide for criminal penalties. Three of these penalties are discussed below.

Section 7201. Section 7201 provides for an assessment of a penalty against any person who "willfully attempts . . . to evade or defeat any tax." The maximum penalty is $100,000 ($500,000 for corporations), a prison sentence of up to five years, or both.

ADDITIONAL COMMENT

Any time a tax professional learns a client has engaged in activities that may constitute criminal fraud, he or she immediately should refer the client to qualified legal counsel. Counsel should then hire the accountant as a consultant. Taxpayer's communications will be confidential under the attorney–client relationship. This relationship encompasses agents of the attorney.

Section 7203. Section 7203 imposes a penalty on any person who willfully fails to pay any tax or file a return. The maximum penalty is $25,000 ($100,000 for corporations), a prison sentence of no more than one year, or both. If the government charges the taxpayer with willfully failing to prepare a return, it need not prove that the taxpayer owes additional tax.

Section 7206. Persons other than the taxpayer can be charged under Sec. 7206. This section applies to any person who

[W]illfully aids or assists in, or procures, counsels, or advises the preparation or presentation under, or in connection with any matter arising under the internal revenue laws, of a return, affidavit, claim, or other document, which is fraudulent or is false as to any material matter, whether or not such falsity or fraud is with the knowledge or consent of the person authorized or required to present such return, affidavit, claim, or document.[79]

What constitutes a material matter has been litigated extensively.[80] The maximum penalty under Sec. 7206 is $100,000 ($500,000 for corporations), a prison sentence of up to three years, or both. The government need not prove that the taxpayer owes additional tax.

STATUTE OF LIMITATIONS

OBJECTIVE 8

Understand the statute of limitations

The **statute of limitations** has the same practical implications in a tax context as in other contexts. It specifies a timeframe (called the limitations period) during which the government must assess the tax or initiate a court proceeding to collect the tax. The statute of limitations also defines the limitations period during which a taxpayer may file a lawsuit against the government or a claim for a refund.

GENERAL THREE-YEAR RULE

Under the general rule of Sec. 6501(a), the limitations period is three years after the date on which the return is filed, regardless of whether the return is timely filed. A return filed before its due date is treated as if it were filed on the due date.[81]

---

[79] Sec. 7206(2).
[80] See, for example, *U.S. v. Joseph DiVarco,* 32 AFTR 2d 73-5605, 73-2 USTC ¶9607 (7th Cir., 1973), wherein the court held that the source of the

taxpayer's income as stated on the tax return is a material matter.
[81] Sec. 6501(b)(1).

EXAMPLE C15-26 ▶ Ali files his 2006 individual return on March 3, 2007. The government may not assess additional taxes for 2006 after April 15, 2010. If instead, Ali files his 2006 individual return on October 4, 2007, the limitations period for his return expires on October 4, 2010. ◀

SIX-YEAR RULE FOR SUBSTANTIAL OMISSIONS

INCOME TAX RETURNS. In the case of substantial omissions, the limitations period is six years after the later of the date the return is filed or the return's due date. For income tax purposes, the six-year period is applicable if the taxpayer omits from gross income an amount exceeding 25% of the gross income shown on the return. If an item is disclosed either on the return or in a statement attached to the return, it is not treated as an omission if the disclosure is "adequate to apprise the [Treasury] Secretary of the nature and amount of such item."[82] In the case of taxpayers conducting a trade or business, gross income for purposes of the 25% omission test means the taxpayer's sales revenues (not the taxpayer's gross profit).[83] Taxpayers benefit from this special definition because it renders the 25% test applicable to a gross amount (implying a higher threshold).

EXAMPLE C15-27 ▶ Peg files her 2006 return on March 30, 2007. Her return shows $6,000 of interest from corporate bonds and $30,000 of salary. Peg attaches a statement to her return that indicates why she thinks a $2,000 receipt is nontaxable. However, because of an oversight, she does not report an $8,000 capital gain. Peg is deemed to have omitted only $8,000 rather than $10,000 (the $8,000 capital gain plus the $2,000 receipt) because she disclosed the $2,000 receipt. The $8,000 amount is 22.22% ($8,000/$36,000) of her reported gross income. Because the omission does not exceed 25% of Peg's reported gross income, the limitations period expires on April 15, 2010. ◀

EXAMPLE C15-28 ▶ Assume the same facts as in Example C15-27 except Peg does not make adequate disclosure of the $2,000 receipt. Thus, she is considered to have omitted $10,000 from gross income. The $10,000 amount is 27.77% ($10,000/$36,000) of her reported gross income. Therefore, the limitations period expires on April 15, 2013. ◀

EXAMPLE C15-29 ▶ Rita conducts a business as a sole proprietorship. Rita's 2006 return, filed on March 16, 2007, indicates sales of $100,000 and cost of goods sold of $70,000. Rita inadvertently fails to report $9,000 of interest earned on a loan to a relative. For purposes of the 25% omission test, her gross income is $100,000, not $30,000. The omitted interest is 9% ($9,000/$100,000) of her reported gross income. Because the $9,000 does not exceed 25% of the gross amount, the limitations period expires on April 15, 2010. ◀

WHAT WOULD YOU DO IN THIS SITUATION?

After working eight years for a large CPA firm, you begin your practice as a sole practitioner CPA. Your practice is not as profitable as you had expected, and you consider how you might attract more clients. One idea is to obtain for your clients larger refunds than they anticipate. Your reputation for knowing tax-saving tips might grow, and your profits might increase. You think further and decide that maybe you could claim itemized deductions for charitable contributions that actually were not made and for business expenses that actually were not paid. You are aware of Sec. 7206, regarding false and fraudulent statements but think that you can avoid the "as to any material matter" stipulation by keeping the deduction overstatements relatively insubstantial. Would you try this scheme for increasing your profits? If so, would you escape the scope of Sec. 7206? What ramifications might these deeds have on your standing as a CPA under the AICPA's *Statements on Standards for Tax Services* and *Code of Professional Conduct*?

---

[82] Sec. 6501(e).

[83] Regulation Sec. 1.61-3(a) defines *gross income* as sales less cost of goods sold.

KEY POINT
A 25% omission of gross income extends the basic limitations period to six years, whereas a 25% overstatement of deductions is still subject to the basic three-year limitations period. However, if fraud can be shown, there is no limitations period.

Note that the six-year rule applies only to omitted income. Thus, claiming excessive deductions will not result in a six-year limitations period. Moreover, if the omission involves fraud, no limitations period applies.

GIFT AND ESTATE TAX RETURNS. A similar six-year limitations period applies for gift and estate tax purposes. If the taxpayer omits items that exceed 25% of the gross estate value or the total amount of gifts reported on the return, the limitations period expires six years after the later of the date the return is filed or the due date. Items disclosed on the return or in a statement attached to the return "in a manner adequate to apprise the [Treasury] Secretary of the nature and amount of such item" do not constitute omissions.[84] Understatements of the value of assets disclosed on the return also are not considered omissions.

EXAMPLE C15-30 ▶ On April 3, 2007, John files a gift tax return for 2006. The return reports a cash gift of $600,000. In 2006, John sold land to his son for $700,000. At the time of the sale, John thought the land's FMV was $700,000 and did not disclose any additional amount on the gift tax return. Upon audit, the IRS determines that the FMV of the land on the sale date was $900,000. Thus, John effectively gave an additional $200,000 to his son. The $200,000 amount is 33⅓% ($200,000/$600,000) of all gifts reported. The limitations period expires on April 15, 2013. ◀

WHEN NO RETURN IS FILED

No limitations period exists if the taxpayer does not file a return.[85] Thus, the government may assess the tax or initiate a court proceeding for collection at any time.

EXAMPLE C15-31 ▶ Jill does not file a tax return for 2006. No limitations period applies. Consequently, if the government discovers 20 years later that Jill did not file a return, it may assess the 2006 tax, along with penalties and interest. ◀

OTHER EXCEPTIONS TO THREE-YEAR RULE

SELF-STUDY QUESTION

Should a taxpayer ever agree to extend the limitations period?

ANSWER

Yes. When an audit is in progress, if a taxpayer refuses to extend the limitations period, the agent may assert a deficiency for each item in question. Had the taxpayer granted an extension, perhaps many of the items in question never would have been included in the examining agent's report.

EXTENSION OF THE THREE-YEAR LIMITATIONS PERIOD. The IRC provides other exceptions to the three-year statute of limitations rule, some of which are discussed here. The taxpayer and the IRS can mutually agree in writing to extend the limitations period for taxes other than the estate tax.[86] In such situations, the limitations period is extended until the date agreed on by the two parties. Such agreements usually are concluded when the IRS is auditing a return near the end of the statutory period. Taxpayers often agree to extending the limitations period because they think that, if they do not do so, the IRS will assess a higher deficiency than otherwise would have been the case. Before concluding such an agreement, the IRS must notify the taxpayer that he or she may refuse to extend the limitations period or may limit the extension to particular issues.

NOL CARRYBACKS. For a year to which a net operating loss (NOL) carries back, the applicable limitations period is for the year in which the NOL arose.[87]

WHEN FRAUD IS PROVEN.
Deficiency and Civil Fraud Penalty. If the government successfully proves that a taxpayer filed a false or fraudulent return "with the intent to evade tax" or engaged in a "willful attempt . . . to defeat or evade tax," there is no limitations period.[88] In other words, the government may at any time assess the tax or begin a court proceeding to collect the tax and the interest thereon. In addition, if the government proves fraud, it may impose a civil penalty. If it fails to prove fraud and the normal three-year limitations period and special six-year period for 25% omissions have expired, it may not assess

---

[84] Sec. 6501(e)(2).
[85] Sec. 6501(c)(3).
[86] Sec. 6501(c)(4).

[87] Sec. 6501(h).
[88] Secs. 6501(c)(1) and (2).

additional taxes. The fraud issue is significant in tax litigation because the burden of proving fraud is unconditionally on the government.

EXAMPLE C15-32 ▶ The IRS audits Trey's 2010 return late in 2013. It also examines Trey's prior years' returns and contends that Trey has willfully attempted to evade tax on his timely filed 2006 return. Trey litigates in the Tax Court, and the Court decides the fraud issue in his favor. Because the IRS did not prove fraud, it may not assess additional taxes for 2006. Had the IRS proven fraud, the limitations period for the 2006 return would have remained open, and the IRS could have assessed the additional taxes. ◀

Criminal Provisions. If taxpayers are not indicted for criminal violations of the tax law within a certain period of time, they are home free. For most criminal offenses, the maximum period is six years after the commission of the offense.[89] Taxpayers cannot be prosecuted, tried, or punished unless an indictment is made within that timeframe. The six-year period begins on the date the taxpayer committed the offense, not the date he or she files the return. Taxpayers who file fraudulent returns might commit offenses related to the returns at a subsequent date. An example of an offense that some taxpayers commit after filing a return is depositing money into a new bank account under a fictitious name.

EXAMPLE C15-33 ▶ In March 2007, Tony files a fraudulent 2006 return through which he attempts to evade tax. Before filing, Tony keeps a double set of books. In 2006, Tony deposits some funds into a bank account under a fictitious name. In 2008, he moves to another state, and on May 3, 2008, he transfers these funds to a new bank account under a different fictitious name. Depositing money into the new account is an offense relating to the fraudulent return. Provided Tony commits no additional offenses, the limitations period for indictment expires on May 5, 2014. (May 3, 2014 falls on a Saturday.) ◀

REFUND CLAIMS

Taxpayers generally are not entitled to a refund for overpayments of tax unless they file a claim for refund by the later of three years from the date they file the return or two years from the date they pay the tax.[90] The limitations period for individuals is suspended when the individual is financially disabled. A return filed before the due date is deemed to have been filed on the due date. The due date is determined without regard to extensions. In most cases, taxpayers pay the tax concurrently with filing the return. Typically, the taxpayer files a claim for a refund in the following circumstance: the IRS has audited the taxpayer's return, has proposed a deficiency, and has assessed additional taxes. The taxpayer may have paid the additional taxes two years after the due date for the return. In such a situation, the taxpayer may file a claim for a refund at any time within two years after making the additional payment (or a total of four years after the filing date). If the taxpayer does not file a claim until more than three years after the date of filing the return, the maximum refund is the amount of tax paid during the two-year period immediately preceding the date on which he or she files the claim.[91]

EXAMPLE C15-34 ▶ Pat files his 2006 return on March 12, 2007. The return reports a tax liability of $5,000, and Pat pays this entire amount when he files his return. He pays no additional tax. Pat must file a claim for refund by April 15, 2010. The maximum refundable amount is $5,000. ◀

EXAMPLE C15-35 ▶ Assume the same facts as in Example C15-34 except the IRS audits Pat's 2006 return, and Pat pays a $1,200 deficiency on October 4, 2009. Pat may file a claim for refund as late as October 4, 2011. If Pat files the claim later than April 15, 2010, the refund may not exceed $1,200 (the amount of tax paid during the two-year period immediately preceding the filing of the claim). ◀

[89] Sec. 6531.
[90] Sec. 6511(a).

[91] Under Sec. 6512, special rules apply if the IRS has mailed a notice of deficiency and if the taxpayer files a petition with the Tax Court.

LIABILITY FOR TAX

Taxpayers are primarily liable for paying their tax. Spouses and transferees may be secondarily liable, as discussed below.

OBJECTIVE 9

Explain from whom the government may collect unpaid taxes

JOINT RETURNS

Ordinarily, if spouses file a joint return, their liability to pay the tax is joint and several.[92] **Joint and several liability** means that each spouse is potentially liable for the full amount due. If one spouse fails to pay any or all of the tax, the other spouse is responsible for paying the deficiency. Joint and several liability has facilitated IRS collection efforts where one spouse absconds from the country, and the other spouse remains behind.

VALIDITY OF JOINT RETURN. To be valid, a joint return generally must include the signatures of both spouses. However, if one spouse cannot sign because of a disability, the return still is valid if that spouse orally consents to the other spouse's signing for him or her.[93] A joint return is invalid if one spouse forces the other to file jointly.

INNOCENT SPOUSE PROVISION. Congress has provided for **innocent spouse relief** where holding one spouse liable for the taxes due from both spouses would be inequitable. Relief is available if all five of the following conditions are met:

▶ The spouses file a joint return.

▶ The return contains an understatement of tax attributable to the erroneous item(s) of an individual filing it.

▶ The other individual establishes that he or she neither knew nor had reason to know of any or all of the understatement.

▶ Based on all the facts and circumstances, holding the other individual liable for the deficiency would be inequitable.

▶ The other individual elects innocent spouse relief no later than two years after the IRS begins its collection efforts.

The degree of relief available depends on the extent of the electing spouse's knowledge. If the spouse neither knew nor had reason to know of *an understatement,* full relief will be granted. Full relief encompasses liability for taxes, interest, and penalties attributable to the full amount of the understatement. On the other hand, if the spouse either knew or had reason to know of an understatement, but not *the extent of the understatement,* only partial relief will be granted. Partial relief encompasses liability for taxes, interest, and penalties attributable to that portion of the understatement of which the spouse was unaware.

EXAMPLE C15-36 ▶ Jim and Joy jointly filed a tax return for 2005. Joy fraudulently reported on Schedule C two expenses: one amounting to $4,000 and the other amounting to $3,000. The IRS audits the return, assesses a $2,170 deficiency, and begins its collection efforts on June 1, 2007. If (1) Jim elects innocent spouse relief no later than June 1, 2009, (2) Jim establishes that he neither knew nor had reason to know of the understatement, and (3) if holding Jim liable for the deficiency would be inequitable under the circumstances, Jim will be relieved of liability for the full $2,170. ◀

EXAMPLE C15-37 ▶ Same facts as in Example C15-36 except Jim had reason to know the $3,000 expense was fraudulent. If (1) Jim elects innocent spouse relief no later than June 1, 2009, (2) Jim establishes that he neither knew nor had reason to know the *extent* of the understatement (i.e., $7,000 as opposed to $3,000), and (3) if holding Jim liable for the full amount of the deficiency would be inequitable under the circumstances, Jim will be relieved of liability for that portion of the deficiency attributable to the $4,000 expense. ◀

---

[92] Sec. 6015. [93] Reg. Sec. 1.6012-1(a)(5).

Proportional liability is liability for only that portion of a deficiency attributable to the taxpayer's separate taxable items. A joint filer incurs proportional liability if all the following conditions are met:

▶ The joint filer elects proportional liability within two years after the IRS begins its collection efforts.

▶ The electing filer is either divorced or separated at the time of the election.

▶ The electing filer did not reside in the same household as the other filer at any time during the 12-month period preceding the election.

▶ The electing filer does not have actual knowledge of any item giving rise to the deficiency.

The electing filer bears the burden of proving the amount of his or her proportional liability. The fraudulent transfer of property between joint filers immediately before the election will invalidate it.

EXAMPLE C15-38 ▶ Sam and Sue jointly filed a 2004 tax return. Sam intentionally omitted to report $8,000 in gambling winnings. Sue fraudulently deducted $1,600 in business expenses. The IRS audits the return, assesses a $3,600 deficiency, and begins its collection efforts on August 16, 2007. Sam and Sue are subsequently divorced. If Sue (1) elects innocent spouse relief no later than August 17, 2009 (August 15, 2009 falls on a Saturday), (2) did not reside in the same household as Sam at any time during the 12-month period preceding the election, and (3) did not actually know of Sam's omission, she will be liable for only that portion of the deficiency attributable to her fraudulent deduction. ◀

The Effect of Community Property Laws. Community property laws are ignored in determining to whom income (other than income from property) is attributable. For example, if one spouse living in a community property state wins money by gambling, the gambling income is not treated as community property for purposes of the innocent spouse provisions. If the gambling winnings are omitted from a joint return, they are deemed to be solely the income of the spouse who gambled.

TRANSFEREE LIABILITY

TYPICAL MISCONCEPTION

A taxpayer cannot escape paying taxes by transferring assets to a transferee (donee, heir, legatee, etc.) or a fiduciary (executor, trustee, etc.).

Section 6901 authorizes the IRS to collect taxes from persons other than the taxpayer. The two categories of persons from whom the IRS may collect taxes are transferees and fiduciaries. Transferees include donees, heirs, legatees, devisees, shareholders of dissolved corporations, parties to a reorganization, and other distributees.[94] Fiduciaries include executors and administrators of estates. In general, the limitations period for transferees expires one year after the limitations period for transferors. The transferors may be income earners in the case of income taxes, executors in the case of estate taxes, and donors in the case of gift taxes.

EXAMPLE C15-39 ▶ Lake Corporation is liquidated in the current year, and it distributes all its assets to its sole shareholder, Leo. If the IRS audits Lake's return and assesses a deficiency, Leo (the distributee) is responsible for paying the deficiency. ◀

TAX PRACTICE ISSUES

OBJECTIVE 10

Understand government-imposed standards for tax practitioners

A number of statutes and guidelines address what constitutes proper behavior of CPAs and others engaged in tax practice.[95]

STATUTORY PROVISIONS CONCERNING TAX RETURN PREPARERS

Sections 6694–6696 impose penalties on tax return preparers for misconduct. Section 7701(a)(36) defines an income tax return preparer as a "person who prepares for com-

---

[94] Reg. Sec. 301.6901-1(b).
[95] Chapter C1 discusses the AICPA's *Statements on Standards for Tax*

Services, which provides guidelines for CPAs engaged in tax practice. See Appendix E for a reproduction of the statements.

pensation, or who employs one or more persons to prepare for compensation, any return of tax imposed by subtitle A [income tax] or any claim for refund of tax imposed by subtitle A." Preparation of a substantial portion of a return or refund claim is treated as preparation of the full return or claim. These statutory provisions do not affect preparers of estate and gift tax returns and claims for refund of such taxes.

Section 6695 imposes penalties for

▶ Failure to furnish the taxpayer with a copy of the return or claim ($50 per failure)

▶ Failure to sign a return or claim ($50 per failure)

▶ Failure to furnish one's identification number ($50 per failure)

▶ Failure to keep a copy of a return or claim or, in lieu thereof, to maintain a list of taxpayers for whom returns or claims were prepared ($50 per failure, up to a maximum of $25,000 for a return period)

▶ Failure to file a return disclosing the names, identification numbers, and places of work of each income tax return preparer employed ($50 per return plus $50 for each failure to set forth an item in the return)

▶ Endorsement or other negotiation of an income tax refund check made payable to anyone other than the preparer ($500 per check)

The first five penalties are not assessable if the preparer shows that the failure is due to reasonable cause and not willful neglect.[96]

Under Sec. 6694, a preparer will owe a $250 penalty for understating a tax liability if any portion of the understatement is due to a position that does not have a realistic possibility of being sustained on its merits. The preparer will be liable for the penalty if he or she knew, or reasonably should have known, of the position and the position either was frivolous or was not disclosed. If any portion of the understatement results from the preparer's willful attempt to understate taxes or from reckless or intentional disregard of rules or regulations, the penalty will be $1,000.

Regulation Sec. 1.6694-2(b)(2) states that the relevant authorities for the realistic-possibility-of-being-sustained test are the same as those that apply in the substantial authority context. The IRS "will treat a position as having a realistic possibility of being sustained on 'its merits' if a reasonable and well-informed analysis by a person knowledgeable in the tax law would lead such person to conclude that the position has approximately a one in three, or greater, likelihood of being sustained on its merits."[97]

Regulation Sec. 1.6694-3 states that preparers are considered to have willfully understated taxes if they have attempted to wrongfully reduce taxes by disregarding pertinent information. A preparer generally is deemed to have recklessly or intentionally disregarded a rule or regulation if he or she adopts a position contrary to a rule or regulation about which he or she knows, or is reckless in not knowing about such rule or regulation. A preparer may adopt a position contrary to a revenue ruling if a realistic possibility exists that the position can be sustained on its merits. In addition, a preparer may depart from following a Treasury Regulation without penalty if he or she has a good faith basis for challenging its validity and adequately discloses his or her position on Form 8275-R (Regulation Disclosure Statement).

STOP & THINK

Question: While preparing a client's tax return two days before the due date, Tevin reviews an item that arguably is deductible. He weighs the cost of researching whether the deduction has a realistic possibility of being sustained on its merits. He calculates that researching the issue will cost him $300 in forgone revenues and that not researching the issue will cost him $250 in preparer penalties. What should Tevin do?

Solution: Undoubtedly, Tevin should research the issue and determine whether the deduction either has a realistic possibility of being sustained on the merits or is not frivolous. If it is not frivolous, he should disclose his position on the tax return. At stake here is not merely $300 in foregone revenues but also Tevin's professional reputation. His taking a

[96] Regulation Sec. 1.6695-1(b)(5) states that, for the purpose of avoiding the failure-to-sign penalty, reasonable cause is "a cause which arises despite ordinary care and prudence exercised by the individual preparer."

[97] Reg. Sec. 1.6694-2(b).

position that does not meet the realistic possibility standard or that is nonfrivolous but undisclosed subjects not only him as tax preparer, but also his client as taxpayer, to penalties. If the IRS imposes a penalty on the client, the client might terminate the professional relationship with Tevin or sue Tevin for negligence. Besides, Tevin may have miscalculated his own professional liability. If the IRS determines that Tevin recklessly or intentionally disregarded tax rules and regulations, it may impose a penalty of $1,000, not $250.

Tax preparers who offer advice relating to the preparation of a document, knowing that such advice will result in a tax understatement, will be liable for aiding and abetting in the understatement.[98] The penalty for aiding and abetting is $1,000 for advice given to noncorporate taxpayers and $10,000 for advice given to corporate taxpayers. If a preparer is assessed an aiding-and-abetting penalty, the preparer will not be assessed a Sec. 6694 preparer penalty for the same infraction.

TAX SHELTER DISCLOSURES

Section 6111 sets forth the obligations of tax shelter organizers and material advisors. It requires tax shelter organizers to register their tax schemes with the IRS. It also requires material advisors to maintain a list of tax shelter clients and file information returns with the IRS.

For purposes of Sec. 6111, a "tax shelter" is any investment with respect to which a person could reasonably infer that the tax benefits of investing in it exceed the investment amount by a ratio of two to one at the end of a prescribed five-year period. The investment must be required to be registered under state or federal securities law, sold pursuant to a securities law exemption, or offered to five or more investors in an amount exceeding $250,000. A tax shelter includes any entity, plan, arrangement, or transaction a significant purpose of which is to avoid or evade federal income tax law, offered for sale under conditions of confidentiality, and for which the tax shelter promoters may receive fees exceeding $100,000.

A "tax shelter organizer" is a person principally responsible for organizing a tax shelter and, potentially, any other person who participated in its organization, sale, or management. A "material advisor" is any individual who, in return for providing assistance or advice regarding a reportable transaction, derives at least $50,000 of gross income from the activity ($250,000, if derived from a legal entity). A "reportable transaction" is a transaction with the potential for tax avoidance or evasion, information for which must be reported in a return or statement. A "listed transaction" is an abusive transaction that the IRS has identified in an official pronouncement.

Failure to disclose a tax shelter, register a tax shelter, keep a client list, or file an information return subjects a taxpayer, tax shelter organizer, or material advisor to severe penalties as follows:

▶ *Imposed on the taxpayer:* Failure to disclose a tax shelter (ranging from $10,000 to $200,000, depending on the nature of the transaction and the status of the taxpayer)[99]

▶ *Imposed on the taxpayer:* Accuracy-related penalty for listed and reportable transactions (20% of the understatement for disclosed transactions; 30% for undisclosed transactions)[100]

▶ *Imposed on the organizer or advisor:* Failure to furnish information on reportable transactions ($50,000; $200,000 or more for listed transactions)[101]

▶ *Imposed on the organizer or advisor:* Failure to maintain an investor list ($10,000 per day after the twentieth business day following notice)[102]

▶ *Imposed on the organizer or advisor:* Tax shelter fraud (50% of gross income derivable from the tax shelter)[103]

In addition, if a taxpayer fails to report information regarding a listed transaction on a required return or statement, the limitations period is extended to one year after the earlier of the date on which the information is furnished to the IRS or the date on which a material advisor meets the list maintenance requirements.[104]

---

[98] Sec. 6701.
[99] Sec. 6707A.
[100] Sec. 6662A.
[101] Sec. 6707.

[102] Sec. 6708.
[103] Sec. 6700(a).
[104] Sec. 6501(c)(10).

RULES OF *CIRCULAR 230*

Treasury Department Circular 230 regulates the practice of attorneys, CPAs, enrolled agents, and enrolled actuaries before the IRS. Practice before the IRS includes representing taxpayers in meetings with IRS audit agents and appeals officers. Tax professionals who do not comply with the rules and regulations of *Circular 230* can be barred from practicing before the IRS and may be subject to censure and/or monetary penalties. Such professionals are entitled to an administrative hearing before being penalized.

Among the rules governing the conduct of practitioners before the IRS are the following:[105]

▶ If the practitioner knows that a client has not complied with federal tax laws or has made an error in or an omission from any return, the practitioner should promptly advise the client of the error or omission. The practitioner also must advise the client of possible corrective action and the consequences of not taking such action.

▶ Each person practicing before the IRS must exercise due diligence in preparing returns, determining the correctness of representations made to the Treasury Department, and determining the correctness of representations made to clients about tax matters.

Like Sec. 6694, *Circular 230* provides that a tax practitioner should always give advice or prepare a return based on a position that has a realistic possibility of being sustained on its merits or that is not frivolous and is disclosed (or, a practitioner giving advice should inform the client of the opportunity to avoid a penalty by making a disclosure). The realistic possibility standard is met if a person knowledgeable in the tax law would conclude that the position has approximately a one in three, or greater, chance of being sustained on its merits.[106]

Circular 230 also lists best practices standards for tax advisors.[107] Such standards include the following:

▶ Communicate clearly with the client regarding the terms of the engagement.

▶ Establish the relevant facts, evaluate the reasonableness of assumptions or representations, relate the applicable law to the relevant facts, and arrive at a conclusion supported by the law and relevant facts.

▶ Advise the client of the implications of conclusions reached, including the applicability of accuracy-related penalties.

▶ Act fairly and with integrity in practice before the IRS.

Finally, *Circular 230* provides detailed requirements for practitioners who provide covered opinions. A "covered opinion" is written advice concerning various tax shelter and other avoidance arrangements.[108]

TAX ACCOUNTING AND TAX LAW

Accountants and lawyers frequently deal with the same issues. These issues pertain to incorporation and merger, bankruptcy and liquidation, purchases and sales, gains and losses, compensation and benefits, and estate planning. Both types of professionals are competent to practice in many of the same areas. In some areas, however, accountants are more competent than lawyers, and in other areas, lawyers are more competent than accountants. What are these areas, and where does one draw the line?

In the realm of federal taxation, achieving a clear delineation always has been difficult. When an accountant prepares a tax return, he or she invariably delves into the intricacies of tax law. When a lawyer gives tax advice, he or she frequently applies principles of accounting. Toward clarifying the responsibilities of each, the AICPA and American Bar Association have issued the *Statement on Practice in the Field of Federal Income Taxation*.[109] This statement indicates five areas in which CPAs and attorneys are equally competent to practice and several areas in which each is exclusively competent to practice. The areas of mutual competence are as follows:

ETHICAL POINT

In deciding whether to adopt a pro-taxpayer position on a tax return or in rendering tax advice, a tax advisor should keep in mind his or her responsibilities under the tax return preparer rules of the IRC, *Treasury Department Circular 230,* and the *Statements on Standards for Tax Services,* especially Statement No. 1. Statement No. 1 (discussed in Chapter C1 and reproduced in Appendix E) requires that a CPA have a good faith belief that the position adopted on the tax return is supported by existing law or by a good faith argument for extending, modifying, or reversing existing law.

---

[105] *Treasury Department Circular 230* (2005), Secs. 10.21 and 10.22.
[106] Ibid., Sec. 10.34.
[107] Ibid., Sec. 10.33.

[108] Ibid., Secs. 10.35 and 10.36.
[109] National Conference of Lawyers and Certified Public Accountants, *Statement on Practice in the Field of Federal Income Taxation*, November 1981.

- ▶ Preparing federal income tax returns
- ▶ Determining the tax effects of proposed transactions
- ▶ Representing taxpayers before the Treasury Department
- ▶ Practicing before the U.S. Tax Court
- ▶ Preparing claims for refunds

Areas in which an accountant is exclusively competent to practice include:

- ▶ Resolving accounting issues
- ▶ Preparing financial statements included in financial reports or submitted with tax returns
- ▶ Advising clients as to accounting methods and procedures
- ▶ Classifying transactions and summarizing them in monetary terms
- ▶ Interpreting financial results

Areas in which an attorney is exclusively competent to practice include:

- ▶ Resolving issues of law
- ▶ Preparing legal documents such as agreements, conveyances, trust instruments, and wills
- ▶ Advising clients as to the sufficiency or effect of legal documents
- ▶ Taking the necessary steps to create, amend, or dissolve a partnership, corporation, or trust
- ▶ Representing clients in criminal investigations

State bar and CPA associations have issued similar guidelines for their constituencies, and the courts generally have followed these and the national guidelines.[110]

What happens if an accountant oversteps his or her professional bounds? The transgression may constitute the **unauthorized practice of law.** The unauthorized practice of law involves the engagement, by nonlawyers, in professional activities traditionally reserved for the bar. In most states, it is actionable by injunction, damages, or both. Allegations of the unauthorized practice of law typically arise in the context of a billing dispute.[111] The CPA bills a client for professional services, and the client disputes the bill on the ground that the accountant engaged in the unauthorized practice of law. Occasionally, the court sustains the client's allegation and thus denies the accountant the amount in dispute. With this and the public interest in mind, accountants should always confine their practice to areas in which they are most competent.

ACCOUNTANT-CLIENT PRIVILEGE

According to judicial doctrine, certain communications between an attorney and a client are "privileged," i.e., nondiscoverable in the course of litigation. In 1998, Congress extended this privilege to similar communications between a federally authorized tax advisor and a client. A federally authorized tax advisor includes a certified public accountant.

The accountant-client privilege is similar to the attorney-client privilege in two respects. First, it encompasses communications for the purpose of obtaining or giving professional advice. Second, it excludes communications for the sole purpose of preparing a tax return. The accountant-client privilege is dissimilar in three respects. First, it is limited only to *tax* advice. Second, it may be asserted only in a noncriminal tax proceeding before a federal court or the IRS. Third, it excludes written communications between an accountant and a corporation regarding a tax shelter. A tax shelter is any plan or arrangement, a significant purpose of which is tax avoidance or evasion.

EXAMPLE C15-40 ▶ Alec, Chief Financial Officer of MultiCorp, has solicited the advice of his tax accountant, Louise, concerning a civil dispute with the IRS. Louise has advised Alec in a series of letters spanning the course of five months. An IRS appeals officer asks Louise if he can review the

---

[110] See for example *Lathrop v. Donahue,* 367 U.S. 820, 81 S.Ct. 1826 (1961), *U.S. v. Gordon Buttorff,* 56 AFTR 2d 85-5247, 85-1 USTC ¶9435 (5th Cir., 1985), *Morton L. Simons v. Edgar T. Bellinger,* 643 F.2d 774, 207 U.S. App. D.C. 24 (1980), *Emilio L. Ippolito v. The State of Florida,* 824 F.Supp. 1562, 1993 U.S. Dist. LEXIS 13091 (M.D. Fla., 1993), *In re Application of New*

Jersey Society of Certified Public Accountants, 102 N.J. 231, 507 A.2d 711 (1986).
[111] See for example, *In re Bercu,* 299 N.Y. 728, 87 N.E.2d 451 (1949), and *Agran v. Shapiro,* 46 AFTR 896, 127 Cal. App.2d 807 (App. Dept. Super. Ct., 1954).

letters. Louise may refuse the officer's request because her professional advice was offered in anticipation of civil litigation and therefore is "privileged." ◄

EXAMPLE C15-41 ► Assume the same facts as in Example C15-40 except Louise sends Alec a letter concerning a foreign sales scheme. Because Louise communicates tax advice to a corporation concerning a "tax shelter" and because this communication is written, it is *not* privileged. ◄

The creation of an accountant-client privilege reflects Congress' belief that the selection of a tax advisor should not hinge on the question of privilege. It ensures that all tax advice is accorded the same protection regardless of the tax advisor's professional status.

PROBLEM MATERIALS

DISCUSSION QUESTIONS

C15-1 Describe how the IRS verifies tax returns at its service centers.

C15-2 Name some of the IRS administrative pronouncements.

C15-3 a. Through what programs has the IRS gathered data to develop its DIF statistical models?
b. How do these programs differ?
c. How has the IRS used these programs to select returns for audit?

C15-4 On his individual return, Al reports salary and exemptions for himself and seven dependents. His itemized deductions consist of mortgage interest, real estate taxes, and a large loss from breeding dogs. On his individual return, Ben reports self-employment income, a substantial loss from partnership operations, a casualty loss deduction equal to 25% of his AGI, charitable contribution deductions equal to 30% of his AGI, and an exemption for himself. Al's return reports higher taxable income than does Ben's. Which return is more likely to be selected for audit under the DIF program? Explain.

C15-5 The IRS notifies Tom that it will audit his current year return for an interest deduction. The IRS audited Tom's return two years ago for a charitable contribution deduction. The IRS, however, did not assess a deficiency for the prior year return. Is any potential relief available to Tom with respect to the audit of his current year return?

C15-6 The IRS informs Brad that it will audit his current year employee business expenses. Brad just met with a revenue agent who contends that Brad owes $775 of additional taxes. Discuss briefly the procedural alternatives available to Brad.

C15-7 What course(s) of action is (are) available to a taxpayer upon receipt of the following notices:
a. The 30-day letter?
b. The 90-day letter?
c. IRS rejection of a claim for a refund?

C15-8 List the courts in which a taxpayer can begin tax-related litigation.

C15-9 Why do taxpayers frequently litigate in the Tax Court?

C15-10 In what situations is a protest letter necessary?

C15-11 What information should be included in a request for a ruling?

C15-12 What conditions must the taxpayer meet to shift the burden of proof to the IRS?

C15-13 In what circumstances will the IRS rule on estate tax issues?

C15-14 On which of the following issues will the IRS likely issue a private letter ruling and why? In your answer, assume that no other IRS pronouncement addresses the issue and that pertinent Treasury Regulations are not forthcoming.
a. Whether the taxpayer correctly calculated a capital gain reported on last year's tax return.
b. The tax consequences of using stock derivatives in a corporate reorganization.
c. Whether a mathematical formula correctly calculates the fair market value of a stock derivative.
d. Whether the cost of an Internet course that purports to improve existing employment skills may be deducted this year as a business expense.

C15-15 Tracy wants to take advantage of a "terrific business opportunity" by engaging in a transaction with Homer. Homer, quite domineering and impatient, wants Tracy to conclude the transaction within two weeks and under the exact terms proposed by Homer. Otherwise, Homer will offer the opportunity to another party. Tracy is unsure about the tax consequences of the proposed transaction. Would you advise Tracy to request a ruling? Explain.

C15-16 Provide the following information relating to both individual and corporate taxpayers:
a. Due date for an income tax return assuming the taxpayer requests no extension.
b. Due date for the return assuming the taxpayer files an automatic extension request.
c. Latest possible due date for the return

C15-17 Your client wants to know whether she must file any documents for an automatic extension to file her tax return. What do you tell her?

C15-18 A client believes that obtaining an extension for filing an income tax return would give him additional time to pay the tax at no additional cost. Is the client correct?

C15-19 Briefly explain the rules for determining the interest rate charged on tax underpayments. Is this rate the same as that for overpayments? In which months might the rate(s) change?

C15-20 In April of the current year, Stan does not have sufficient assets to pay his tax liability for the previous year. However, he expects to pay the tax by August of the current year. He wonders if he should request an extension for filing his return instead of simply filing his return and paying the tax in August. What is your advice?

C15-21 At what rate is the penalty for underpaying estimated taxes imposed? How is the penalty amount calculated?

C15-22 The IRS audited Tony's return, and Tony agreed to pay additional taxes plus the negligence penalty. Is this penalty necessarily imposed on the total additional taxes that Tony owes? Explain.

C15-23 Assume that a taxpayer owes additional taxes as a result of an audit. Give two reasons why the IRS might not impose a substantial understatement penalty on the additional amount owed.

C15-24 Upon audit, the IRS determines Maria's tax liability to be $40,000. Maria agrees to pay a $7,000 deficiency. Will she necessarily have to pay a substantial understatement penalty? Explain.

C15-25 Distinguish between the circumstances that give rise to the civil fraud penalty and those that give rise to the negligence penalty.

C15-26 Distinguish between the burdens of proof the government must meet to prove civil and criminal fraud.

C15-27 Explain why the government might bring criminal fraud charges against a taxpayer under Sec. 7206 instead of Sec. 7201. Compare the maximum penalties imposed under Secs. 7201, 7203, and 7206.

C15-28 In general, when does the limitations period for tax returns expire? List four exceptions to the general rule.

C15-29 What is the principal purpose of the innocent spouse provisions?

C15-30 According to the IRC preparer provisions, under what circumstances should a CPA sign a tax return as a preparer?

C15-31 List five IRC penalties that can be imposed on tax return preparers. Does the IRC require a CPA to verify the information a client furnishes?

C15-32 According to *Treasury Department Circular 230*, what standard should a CPA meet to properly take a position on a tax return?

ISSUE IDENTIFICATION QUESTIONS

C15-33 You are preparing the tax return of Bold Corporation, which had sales of $60 million. Bold made a $1 million expenditure for which the appropriate tax treatment—deductible or capitalizable—is a gray area. Bold's director of federal taxes and chief financial officer urgently wants to deduct the expenditure. What tax compliance issues should you consider in advising her?

C15-34 Your client, Hank Goedert, earned $100,000 of salary and received $40,000 of dividends in the current year. His itemized deductions total $37,000. In addition, Hank received $47,000 from a relative who was his former employer. You have researched whether the $47,000 should be classified as a gift or compensation and are confident that substantial authority exists for classifying the receipt as a gift. What tax compliance issues should you consider in deciding whether to include or exclude the amount in Hank's gross income?

C15-35 The IRS audited the tax returns of Darryl Strawberry, a former major league outfielder. It contended that, between 1986 and 1990, Strawberry earned $422,250 for autograph signings, appearances, and product endorsements, but he reported only $59,685 of income. Strawberry attributed the shortfall to his receipt of cash for autograph sessions and promotional events. He allegedly concealed the cash payments in separate bank accounts of which his CPA was unaware. What tax compliance issues regarding the alleged underreporting are pertinent?

PROBLEMS

C15-36 *Calculation of Penalties.* Amy files her current year tax return on August 13 of the following year. She pays the amount due without requesting an extension. The tax shown on her return is $24,000. Her current year withholding tax is $15,000. Amy pays no estimated taxes and claims no tax credits on her current year return.

a. What penalties will the IRS likely impose on Amy (ignoring the penalty for underpayment of estimated taxes)? Assume Amy committed no fraud.

b. On what dollar amount, and for how many days, will Amy owe interest?

C15-37 *Calculation of Penalties.* In the preceding problem, how would your answers change if Amy instead files her return on June 18 and, on September 8 of the following year, pays the amount due? Assume her withholding tax is

a. $19,000

b. $24,500

c. How would your answer to Part a change if Amy requests an automatic extension?

C15-38 *Calculation of Penalties.* The taxes shown on Hu's tax returns for 2005 and 2006 were $5,000 and $8,000, respectively. Hu's withholding tax for 2006 was $5,200, and she paid no estimated taxes. Hu filed her 2006 return on March 16, 2007, but she did not have sufficient funds to pay any taxes on that date. She paid the $2,800 balance due on June 20, 2007. Hu's AGI for 2005 did not exceed $150,000. Calculate the penalties Hu owes with respect to her 2006 tax return.

C15-39 *Calculation of Penalties.* Ted's 2006 return reported a tax liability of $1,800. Ted's withholding for 2006 was $2,200. Because of his poor memory, Ted did not file his 2006 return until May 28, 2007. What penalties (if any) does Ted owe?

C15-40 *Calculation of Penalties.* Bob, a calendar year taxpayer, files his current year individual return on July 17 of the following year without having requested an extension. His return indicates an amount due of $5,100. Bob pays this amount on November 3 of the following year. What are Bob's penalties for failing to file and failing to pay his tax on time? Assume Bob committed no fraud.

C15-41 *Calculation of Penalties.* Carl, a calendar year taxpayer, requests an automatic extension for filing his 2006 return. By April 16, 2007, he has paid $20,000 of taxes in the form of withholding and estimated taxes (April 15, 2007, falls on a Sunday). He does not pay any additional tax with his extension request. Carl files his return and pays the balance of the taxes due on June 19, 2007. For 2005, his tax liability was $19,000, and his AGI did not exceed $150,000. What penalties will Carl owe if his 2006 tax is $23,000? $20,800?

C15-42 *Determination of Interest.* Refer to the preceding problem.

a. Will Carl owe interest? If so, on what amount and for how many days?

b. Assume the applicable interest rate is 6%. Compute Carl's interest payable if his 2006 tax is $23,000. (See Rev. Proc. 95-17, 1995-1 C.B. 556, or a major tax service, for the compounding tables.)

C15-43 *Penalty for Underpayment of Estimated Taxes.* Ed's tax liability for last year was $24,000. Ed projects that his tax for this year will be $34,000. Ed is self-employed and, thus, will have no withholding. His AGI for last year did not exceed $150,000. How much estimated tax should Ed pay for this year to avoid the penalty for underpaying estimated taxes?

C15-44 *Penalty for Underpayment of Estimated Taxes.* Refer to the preceding problem. Assume that Ed expects his income for this year to decline and his tax liability for this year to be only $15,000. What minimum amount of estimated taxes should Ed pay this year? What problem will Ed encounter if he pays this minimum amount and his income exceeds last year's because of a large capital gain realized in December of this year?

C15-45 *Penalty for Underpayment of Estimated Taxes.* Pam's 2005 income tax liability was $23,000. Her 2005 AGI did not exceed $150,000. On April 3, 2007, Pam, a calendar year taxpayer, files her 2006 individual return, which indicates a $30,000 income tax liability (before reduction for withholding). In addition, the return indicates self-employment taxes of $2,600. Taxes withheld from Pam's salary total $20,000; she has paid no estimated taxes.

a. Will Pam owe a penalty for not paying estimated taxes? Explain.

b. What amount (if any) per quarter is subject to the penalty? For what period will the penalty be imposed for each quarter's underpayment?

c. How would your answers to Parts a and b change if Pam's 2006 tax liability (including self-employment taxes) instead were $17,000?

C15-46 *Penalty for Underpayment of Estimated Taxes.* Amir's projected tax liability for the current year is $23,000. Although Amir has substantial dividend and interest income, he does not pay any estimated taxes. Amir's withholding for January through November of the current year is $1,300 per month. He wants to increase his withholding for December to avoid the penalty for underpaying estimated taxes. Amir's previous year's liability (excluding withholding) is $21,000. His previous year's AGI did not exceed $150,000. What amount should Amir have withheld from his December paycheck? Explain.

C15-47 *Negligence Penalty.* The IRS audits Tan's individual return for the current year and assesses a $9,000 deficiency, $2,800 of which results from Tan's negligence. What is the amount of Tan's negligence penalty? Does the penalty bear interest?

C15-48 *Negligence Penalty.* The IRS audits Pearl's current year individual return and determines that, among other errors, she negligently failed to report dividend income of $8,000. The deficiency relating to the dividends is $2,240. The IRS proposes an additional $12,000 deficiency for the other errors that do not involve negligence. What is the amount of Pearl's negligence penalty for the $14,240 in deficiencies?

C15-49 *Substantial Understatement Penalty.* Carmen's current year individual return reports a $6,000 deduction for a questionable item not relating to a tax-shelter. Carmen does not make a disclosure regarding this item. The IRS audits Carmen's return, and she consents to a deficiency. As a result, her tax liability increases from $20,000 to $21,860. Assume Carmen lacks substantial authority for the deduction.
a. What substantial understatement penalty (if any) will be imposed?
b. Will the penalty bear interest?
c. How would your answer to Parts a and b change if Carmen reported a $20,000 deduction instead of $6,000, and her tax liability increased by $6,200 to $26,200?

C15-50 *Substantial Understatement Penalty.* Refer to Part c of the previous problem. Assume that Carmen discloses her position, which is not frivolous. How would your original answer change assuming the item does not involve a tax shelter?

C15-51 *Fraud Penalty.* Luis, a bachelor, owes $56,000 of additional taxes, all due to fraud.
a. What is the amount of Luis' civil fraud penalty?
b. What criminal fraud penalty might the government impose on Luis under Sec. 7201?

C15-52 *Fraud Penalty.* Hal and Wanda, his wife, are in the 35% marginal tax bracket for the current year. Wanda fraudulently omits from their joint return $50,000 of gross income. Hal does not participate in or know of her fraudulent act. Hal, however, overstates his deductions by $10,000 because of an oversight.
a. If the government successfully proves fraud in a civil suit against Wanda, what fines and/or penalties might she owe? If Hal and Wanda establish that the overstatement is not attributable to fraud, can the government impose a civil fraud penalty on Hal?
b. If the government successfully proves fraud in a criminal suit against Wanda, what fines or penalties might she owe? Could she or Hal be sentenced to prison?

C15-53 *Statute of Limitations.* Frank, a calendar year taxpayer, reports $100,000 of gross income and $60,000 of taxable income on his 2006 return, which he files on March 12, 2007. He fails to report on the return a $52,000 long-term capital gain and a $10,000 short-term capital loss. When does the limitations period for the government's collecting the tax deficiency expire if
a. Frank's omission results from an oversight?
b. His omission results from a willful attempt to evade the tax?

C15-54 *Statute of Limitations.* Refer to the previous problem. Assume Frank commits fraud with respect to his 2006 return as late as October 8, 2008. When does the limitations period for indicting Frank for criminal tax fraud expire?

C15-55 *Claim for Refund.* On March 12, 2007, Maria, a calendar year taxpayer, files her 2006 individual return and pays the amount of tax due. She later discovers that she overlooked some deductions that she should have reported on the return. By what date must she file a claim for refund?

C15-56 *Innocent Spouse Provisions.* Wilma earns no income in 2006 but files a joint return with her husband, Hank. Their 2006 return reports $40,000 of gross income and AGI, and $24,000 of taxable income. Hank realizes $12,000 of gambling winnings (no losses) in 2006 but fails to report the winnings on the return. Wilma does not know about Hank's gambling activities, much less his winnings. The IRS audits the 2006 return and assesses additional taxes. Is Wilma entitled to innocent spouse relief? Explain.

C15-57 *Innocent Spouse Provisions.* Joe and Joan file a joint return for the current year. They are in the 35% marginal tax bracket. Unbeknownst to Joe, Joan fails to report on the return the $8,000 value of a prize she won. She, however, used the prize to buy Joe a new boat. Is Joe entitled to innocent spouse relief? Explain.

C15-58 *Unauthorized Practice of Law.* Your client, Meade Technical Solutions, proposes to merge with Dealy Cyberlabs. In advance of the merger, you (a) issue an opinion concerning the FMV of Dealy, (b) prepare pro forma financials for the merged entity to be, (c) draft Meade shareholder resolutions approving the proposed merger, (d) file a shareholder proxy statement with the U.S. Securities and Exchange Commission, and (e) advise Meade's board of directors concerning the advantages of a Type A versus a Type B reorganization. Which of these activities, if any, constitutes the unauthorized practice of law?

C15-59 *Unauthorized Practice of Law.* Your client, Envirocosmetics, recently has filed for bankruptcy. In the course of bankruptcy proceedings, you (a) prepare a plan of reorganization that alters the rights of preferred stockholders, (b) notify the Envirocosmetics' creditors of an impending bulk transfer of the company's assets, (c) review IRS secured claims against these assets, (d) restructure the company's debt by reducing its principal amount and extending its maturity, (e) advise the bankruptcy court as to how this restructuring will impact the company's NOLs. Which of these activities, if any, constitutes the unauthorized practice of law?

C15-60 *Accountant-Client Privilege* Which of the following communications between an accountant and client are privileged?
a. For tax preparation purposes only, client informs the accountant that she contributed $10,000 to a homeless shelter.
b. Client informs the accountant that he forgot to report on his tax return the $5,000 value of a prize and asks how he should correct the error.
c. Client informs the accountant that she no longer will pay alimony to her ex-husband.

C15-61 *Accountant-Client Privilege.* Which of the following communications between an accountant and client are *not* privileged?
a. In a closed-door meeting, the accountant orally advises the client to set up a foreign subsidiary to shift taxable income to a low-tax jurisdiction.
b. In a closed-door meeting, the accountant submits to the client a plan for shifting taxable income to a low-tax jurisdiction.
c. In soliciting professional advice relating to criminal fraud, the client informs the accountant that he (the client) lied to the IRS.

COMPREHENSIVE PROBLEM

C15-62 This year, Ark Corporation acquired substantially all the voting stock of BioTech Consultants, Inc. for cash. Subsequent to the acquisition, Ark's chief financial officer, Jonathan Cohen, approached Edith Murphy, Ark's tax advisor, with a question: Could Ark amortize the "general educational skills" of BioTech's employees? Edith researched the issue but found no primary authorities on point. She did, however, find a tax journal article, co-authored by two prominent academics, that endorsed amortizing "general educational skills" for tax purposes. The article referred to numerous primary authorities that support the amortization of "technical skills," but not "general educational skills." Edith consulted these authorities directly. Based on her research, Edith in good faith advised Jonathan that Ark could amortize the "general educational skills" over a 15-year period. In so doing, has Edith met the "realistic possibility standard" of
a. The IRC?
b. The AICPA *Statements on Standards for Tax Services* (see Appendix E)?

TAX STRATEGY PROBLEM

C15-63 The IRS is disputing a deduction reported on your 2005 tax return, which you filed on April 17, 2006. On April 2, 2009, the IRS audit agent asks you to waive the statute of limitations for the entire return so as to give her additional time to obtain a Technical Advice Memorandum. The agent proposes in return for the waiver a "carrot"—the prospect of an offer in compromise—and a "stick"—the possibility of a higher penalty. Although you have substantial authority for the deduction, you consider the following alternatives: (1) waive the statute of limitations for the entire return, (2) waive the statute of limitations for the deduction only, or (3) do not waive the statute of limitations in any way, shape, or form. Which alternative should you choose, and why?

CASE STUDY PROBLEM

C15-64   A long-time client, Horace Haney, wishes to avoid currently recognizing revenue in a particular transaction. A recently finalized Treasury Regulation provides that, in such a transaction, revenue should be currently recognized. Horace insists that you report no revenue from the transaction and, furthermore, that you make no disclosure about contravening the regulation. The IRC is unclear about whether the income should be recognized currently. No relevant cases, revenue rulings, or letter rulings deal specifically with the transaction in question.

   Required: Discuss whether you, a CPA, should prepare Horace's tax return and comply with his wishes. Assume that recognizing the income in question would increase Horace's tax liability by about 25%.

TAX RESEARCH PROBLEMS

C15-65   Art is named executor of the Estate of Stu Stone, his father, who died on February 3 of the current year. Art hires Larry to be the estate's attorney. Larry advises Art that the estate must file an estate tax return but does not mention the due date. Art, a pharmacist, has no experience in tax matters other than preparing his own tax returns. Art provides Larry with all the necessary information by June 15 of the current year. On six occasions, Art contacts Larry to check on the progress of the estate tax return. Each time, Larry assures Art that "everything is under control." On November 15, Art contacts Larry for the seventh time. He learns that because of a clerical oversight, the return—due on November 2 of the current year—has not been filed. Larry apologizes and says he will make sure that an associate promptly files the return. The return, which reports an estate tax liability of $75,200, is filed on December 7 of the current year. Your manager requests that you prepare a memorandum addressing whether the estate will owe a failure-to-file penalty. Your manager suggests that, at a minimum, you consult

- IRC Sec. 6151(a)
- *U.S. v. Robert W. Boyle,* 55 AFTR 2d 85-1535, 85-1 USTC ¶13,602 (USSC, 1985)

C15-66   Harold and Betty, factory workers who until this year prepared their own individual tax returns, purchased an investment from a broker last year. Although they reviewed the prospectus for the investment, the broker explained the more complicated features of the investment. Early this year, they struggled to prepare their individual return for last year but, because of the investment, found it too complicated to complete. Consequently, they hired a CPA to prepare the return. The CPA deducted losses from the investment against income that Harold and Betty generated from other sources. The IRS audited the return for last year and contended that the loss is not deductible. After consulting their CPA, who further considered the tax consequences of the investment, Harold and Betty agreed that the loss is not deductible and consented to paying the deficiency. The IRS also contended that the couple owes the substantial understatement penalty because they did not disclose the value of the investment on their return and did not have substantial authority for their position. Assume you are representing the taxpayers before the IRS and intend to argue that they should be exempted from the substantial understatement penalty. Your tax manager reminds you to consult Secs. 6662 and 6664 when conducting your research.

C15-67   Gene employed his attorney to draft identical trust instruments for each of his three minor children: Judy (age 5), Terry (age 7), and Grady (age 11). Each trust instrument names the Fourth City Bank as trustee and states that the trust is irrevocable. It provides that, until the beneficiary reaches age 21, the trustee at its discretion is to pay income and/or principal (corpus) to the beneficiary. Upon reaching age 21, the beneficiary will have 60 days in which to request that the trust assets be paid over to him or her. Otherwise, the assets will stay in the trust until the beneficiary reaches age 35. The beneficiary also is granted a general testamentary power of appointment over the trust assets. If the beneficiary dies before the trust terminates and does not exercise his or her power of appointment (because, for example, he or she dies without a will), trust assets will be distributed to family members in accordance with state intestacy laws. Each trust will be funded with property valued at $100,000. Before he signs the instruments, Gene wants to obtain a ruling from the IRS concerning whether the trusts qualify for the gift tax annual exclusion. Your task is to prepare a request for a letter ruling.

A partial list of research sources is

- IRC Secs. 2503(b) and (c)
- Reg. Sec. 25.2503-4
- Rev. Rul. 67-270, 1967-2 C.B. 349
- Rev. Rul. 74-43, 1974-1 C.B. 285
- Rev. Rul. 81-7, 1981-1 C.B. 474

C15-68 On April 12, 2005, Adam and Renee Tyler jointly filed a 2004 return that reported AGI of $68,240 ($20,500 attributable to Renee) and a tax liability of $3,050. They paid this amount in a timely fashion. On their return, the Tylers claimed a $18,405 deduction for Adam's distributive share of a partnership loss. If not for the loss, the Tylers' tax liability would have been $8,358. In the previous year, Adam had withdrawn $20,000 cash from the partnership, which he used to buy Renee a new car. Although Renee, a marketing consultant, is not active in the partnership business, she has worked for the partnership as a part-time receptionist. Adam and his partner (who incidentally is Renee's brother) failed to file a partnership return for 2004. Upon audit, the IRS discovered that the 2004 partnership records were missing. In June 2006, Adam had a heart attack. He remains in serious condition. Unable to reach Adam, the IRS sends Renee a 30-day letter proposing a $5,308 deficiency. She intends to protest. Your supervisor has asked you to write a memorandum discussing Renee's potential liabilities and defenses. In your memorandum, you should consult the following authorities:

- IRC Secs. 6013 and 6662

- *Rebecca Jo Reser v. CIR*, 79 AFTR 2d 97-2743, 97-1 USTC ¶50,416 (5th Cir., 1997)

C15-69 A colleague comes to you with the following investment proposal that he would like to market for Client:

- Client obtains cash of $60,000 from Bank.
- Bank loan agreement specifies that $40,000 of this amount represents principal; the remaining $20,000 represents interest.
- Client contributes the $60,000 cash to Partnership, which agrees to assume Client's $40,000 debt.
- Under Sec. 752, Partnership's debt assumption is treated as a distribution of money that reduces Client's basis in partnership interest from $60,000 to $20,000.
- Partnership invests the $60,000 in a resort hotel project.
- Before the project comes onstream, Client sells partnership interest for $15,000.

Net result: Partnership, not Client, is responsible for repayment of Bank loan. Client realizes a $5,000 capital loss without having spent any of its own funds.

Prepare a memorandum that sets forth the tax and reporting implications of this investment proposal. At a minimum, consult the following authorities:

- IRC Secs. 6707A and 6111
- Reg. Secs. 1.6111-4 and 301.6112-1
- Notice 2000-44, 2000-2 C.B. 255

2005 TAX TABLES AND RATE SCHEDULES

2006 WITHHOLDING TABLES (PARTIAL)

2005 Tax Table

See the instructions for line 44 that begin on page 37 to see if you must use the Tax Table below to figure your tax.

Example. Mr. and Mrs. Brown are filing a joint return. Their taxable income on Form 1040, line 43, is $25,300. First, they find the $25,300–25,350 taxable income line. Next, they find the column for married filing jointly and read down the column. The amount shown where the taxable income line and filing status column meet is $3,069. This is the tax amount they should enter on Form 1040, line 44.

Sample Table

At least	But less than	Single	Married filing jointly *	Married filing sepa-rately	Head of a house-hold
			Your tax is—		
25,200	25,250	3,419	3,054	3,419	3,261
25,250	25,300	3,426	3,061	3,426	3,269
25,300	25,350	3,434	(3,069)	3,434	3,276
25,350	25,400	3,441	3,076	3,441	3,284

If line 43 (taxable income) is— At least	But less than	Single	Married filing jointly *	Married filing sepa-rately	Head of a house-hold
			Your tax is—		
0	5	0	0	0	0
5	15	1	1	1	1
15	25	2	2	2	2
25	50	4	4	4	4
50	75	6	6	6	6
75	100	9	9	9	9
100	125	11	11	11	11
125	150	14	14	14	14
150	175	16	16	16	16
175	200	19	19	19	19
200	225	21	21	21	21
225	250	24	24	24	24
250	275	26	26	26	26
275	300	29	29	29	29
300	325	31	31	31	31
325	350	34	34	34	34
350	375	36	36	36	36
375	400	39	39	39	39
400	425	41	41	41	41
425	450	44	44	44	44
450	475	46	46	46	46
475	500	49	49	49	49
500	525	51	51	51	51
525	550	54	54	54	54
550	575	56	56	56	56
575	600	59	59	59	59
600	625	61	61	61	61
625	650	64	64	64	64
650	675	66	66	66	66
675	700	69	69	69	69
700	725	71	71	71	71
725	750	74	74	74	74
750	775	76	76	76	76
775	800	79	79	79	79
800	825	81	81	81	81
825	850	84	84	84	84
850	875	86	86	86	86
875	900	89	89	89	89
900	925	91	91	91	91
925	950	94	94	94	94
950	975	96	96	96	96
975	1,000	99	99	99	99

1,000

At least	But less than	Single	Married filing jointly *	Married filing sepa-rately	Head of a house-hold
1,000	1,025	101	101	101	101
1,025	1,050	104	104	104	104
1,050	1,075	106	106	106	106
1,075	1,100	109	109	109	109
1,100	1,125	111	111	111	111
1,125	1,150	114	114	114	114
1,150	1,175	116	116	116	116
1,175	1,200	119	119	119	119
1,200	1,225	121	121	121	121
1,225	1,250	124	124	124	124
1,250	1,275	126	126	126	126
1,275	1,300	129	129	129	129

If line 43 (taxable income) is— At least	But less than	Single	Married filing jointly *	Married filing sepa-rately	Head of a house-hold
			Your tax is—		
1,300	1,325	131	131	131	131
1,325	1,350	134	134	134	134
1,350	1,375	136	136	136	136
1,375	1,400	139	139	139	139
1,400	1,425	141	141	141	141
1,425	1,450	144	144	144	144
1,450	1,475	146	146	146	146
1,475	1,500	149	149	149	149
1,500	1,525	151	151	151	151
1,525	1,550	154	154	154	154
1,550	1,575	156	156	156	156
1,575	1,600	159	159	159	159
1,600	1,625	161	161	161	161
1,625	1,650	164	164	164	164
1,650	1,675	166	166	166	166
1,675	1,700	169	169	169	169
1,700	1,725	171	171	171	171
1,725	1,750	174	174	174	174
1,750	1,775	176	176	176	176
1,775	1,800	179	179	179	179
1,800	1,825	181	181	181	181
1,825	1,850	184	184	184	184
1,850	1,875	186	186	186	186
1,875	1,900	189	189	189	189
1,900	1,925	191	191	191	191
1,925	1,950	194	194	194	194
1,950	1,975	196	196	196	196
1,975	2,000	199	199	199	199

2,000

At least	But less than	Single	Married filing jointly *	Married filing sepa-rately	Head of a house-hold
2,000	2,025	201	201	201	201
2,025	2,050	204	204	204	204
2,050	2,075	206	206	206	206
2,075	2,100	209	209	209	209
2,100	2,125	211	211	211	211
2,125	2,150	214	214	214	214
2,150	2,175	216	216	216	216
2,175	2,200	219	219	219	219
2,200	2,225	221	221	221	221
2,225	2,250	224	224	224	224
2,250	2,275	226	226	226	226
2,275	2,300	229	229	229	229
2,300	2,325	231	231	231	231
2,325	2,350	234	234	234	234
2,350	2,375	236	236	236	236
2,375	2,400	239	239	239	239
2,400	2,425	241	241	241	241
2,425	2,450	244	244	244	244
2,450	2,475	246	246	246	246
2,475	2,500	249	249	249	249
2,500	2,525	251	251	251	251
2,525	2,550	254	254	254	254
2,550	2,575	256	256	256	256
2,575	2,600	259	259	259	259
2,600	2,625	261	261	261	261
2,625	2,650	264	264	264	264
2,650	2,675	266	266	266	266
2,675	2,700	269	269	269	269

If line 43 (taxable income) is— At least	But less than	Single	Married filing jointly *	Married filing sepa-rately	Head of a house-hold
			Your tax is—		
2,700	2,725	271	271	271	271
2,725	2,750	274	274	274	274
2,750	2,775	276	276	276	276
2,775	2,800	279	279	279	279
2,800	2,825	281	281	281	281
2,825	2,850	284	284	284	284
2,850	2,875	286	286	286	286
2,875	2,900	289	289	289	289
2,900	2,925	291	291	291	291
2,925	2,950	294	294	294	294
2,950	2,975	296	296	296	296
2,975	3,000	299	299	299	299

3,000

At least	But less than	Single	Married filing jointly *	Married filing sepa-rately	Head of a house-hold
3,000	3,050	303	303	303	303
3,050	3,100	308	308	308	308
3,100	3,150	313	313	313	313
3,150	3,200	318	318	318	318
3,200	3,250	323	323	323	323
3,250	3,300	328	328	328	328
3,300	3,350	333	333	333	333
3,350	3,400	338	338	338	338
3,400	3,450	343	343	343	343
3,450	3,500	348	348	348	348
3,500	3,550	353	353	353	353
3,550	3,600	358	358	358	358
3,600	3,650	363	363	363	363
3,650	3,700	368	368	368	368
3,700	3,750	373	373	373	373
3,750	3,800	378	378	378	378
3,800	3,850	383	383	383	383
3,850	3,900	388	388	388	388
3,900	3,950	393	393	393	393
3,950	4,000	398	398	398	398

4,000

At least	But less than	Single	Married filing jointly *	Married filing sepa-rately	Head of a house-hold
4,000	4,050	403	403	403	403
4,050	4,100	408	408	408	408
4,100	4,150	413	413	413	413
4,150	4,200	418	418	418	418
4,200	4,250	423	423	423	423
4,250	4,300	428	428	428	428
4,300	4,350	433	433	433	433
4,350	4,400	438	438	438	438
4,400	4,450	443	443	443	443
4,450	4,500	448	448	448	448
4,500	4,550	453	453	453	453
4,550	4,600	458	458	458	458
4,600	4,650	463	463	463	463
4,650	4,700	468	468	468	468
4,700	4,750	473	473	473	473
4,750	4,800	478	478	478	478
4,800	4,850	483	483	483	483
4,850	4,900	488	488	488	488
4,900	4,950	493	493	493	493
4,950	5,000	498	498	498	498

(Continued on page 66)

* This column must also be used by a qualifying widow(er).

2005 Tax Table—Continued

If line 43 (taxable income) is—		And you are—			
At least	But less than	Single	Married filing jointly *	Married filing separately	Head of a household
		Your tax is—			

* This column must also be used by a qualifying widow(er).

5,000

At least	But less than	Single	MFJ *	MFS	HoH
5,000	5,050	503	503	503	503
5,050	5,100	508	508	508	508
5,100	5,150	513	513	513	513
5,150	5,200	518	518	518	518
5,200	5,250	523	523	523	523
5,250	5,300	528	528	528	528
5,300	5,350	533	533	533	533
5,350	5,400	538	538	538	538
5,400	5,450	543	543	543	543
5,450	5,500	548	548	548	548
5,500	5,550	553	553	553	553
5,550	5,600	558	558	558	558
5,600	5,650	563	563	563	563
5,650	5,700	568	568	568	568
5,700	5,750	573	573	573	573
5,750	5,800	578	578	578	578
5,800	5,850	583	583	583	583
5,850	5,900	588	588	588	588
5,900	5,950	593	593	593	593
5,950	6,000	598	598	598	598

6,000

At least	But less than	Single	MFJ *	MFS	HoH
6,000	6,050	603	603	603	603
6,050	6,100	608	608	608	608
6,100	6,150	613	613	613	613
6,150	6,200	618	618	618	618
6,200	6,250	623	623	623	623
6,250	6,300	628	628	628	628
6,300	6,350	633	633	633	633
6,350	6,400	638	638	638	638
6,400	6,450	643	643	643	643
6,450	6,500	648	648	648	648
6,500	6,550	653	653	653	653
6,550	6,600	658	658	658	658
6,600	6,650	663	663	663	663
6,650	6,700	668	668	668	668
6,700	6,750	673	673	673	673
6,750	6,800	678	678	678	678
6,800	6,850	683	683	683	683
6,850	6,900	688	688	688	688
6,900	6,950	693	693	693	693
6,950	7,000	698	698	698	698

7,000

At least	But less than	Single	MFJ *	MFS	HoH
7,000	7,050	703	703	703	703
7,050	7,100	708	708	708	708
7,100	7,150	713	713	713	713
7,150	7,200	718	718	718	718
7,200	7,250	723	723	723	723
7,250	7,300	728	728	728	728
7,300	7,350	734	733	734	733
7,350	7,400	741	738	741	738
7,400	7,450	749	743	749	743
7,450	7,500	756	748	756	748
7,500	7,550	764	753	764	753
7,550	7,600	771	758	771	758
7,600	7,650	779	763	779	763
7,650	7,700	786	768	786	768
7,700	7,750	794	773	794	773
7,750	7,800	801	778	801	778
7,800	7,850	809	783	809	783
7,850	7,900	816	788	816	788
7,900	7,950	824	793	824	793
7,950	8,000	831	798	831	798

8,000

At least	But less than	Single	MFJ *	MFS	HoH
8,000	8,050	839	803	839	803
8,050	8,100	846	808	846	808
8,100	8,150	854	813	854	813
8,150	8,200	861	818	861	818
8,200	8,250	869	823	869	823
8,250	8,300	876	828	876	828
8,300	8,350	884	833	884	833
8,350	8,400	891	838	891	838
8,400	8,450	899	843	899	843
8,450	8,500	906	848	906	848
8,500	8,550	914	853	914	853
8,550	8,600	921	858	921	858
8,600	8,650	929	863	929	863
8,650	8,700	936	868	936	868
8,700	8,750	944	873	944	873
8,750	8,800	951	878	951	878
8,800	8,850	959	883	959	883
8,850	8,900	966	888	966	888
8,900	8,950	974	893	974	893
8,950	9,000	981	898	981	898

9,000

At least	But less than	Single	MFJ *	MFS	HoH
9,000	9,050	989	903	989	903
9,050	9,100	996	908	996	908
9,100	9,150	1,004	913	1,004	913
9,150	9,200	1,011	918	1,011	918
9,200	9,250	1,019	923	1,019	923
9,250	9,300	1,026	928	1,026	928
9,300	9,350	1,034	933	1,034	933
9,350	9,400	1,041	938	1,041	938
9,400	9,450	1,049	943	1,049	943
9,450	9,500	1,056	948	1,056	948
9,500	9,550	1,064	953	1,064	953
9,550	9,600	1,071	958	1,071	958
9,600	9,650	1,079	963	1,079	963
9,650	9,700	1,086	968	1,086	968
9,700	9,750	1,094	973	1,094	973
9,750	9,800	1,101	978	1,101	978
9,800	9,850	1,109	983	1,109	983
9,850	9,900	1,116	988	1,116	988
9,900	9,950	1,124	993	1,124	993
9,950	10,000	1,131	998	1,131	998

10,000

At least	But less than	Single	MFJ *	MFS	HoH
10,000	10,050	1,139	1,003	1,139	1,003
10,050	10,100	1,146	1,008	1,146	1,008
10,100	10,150	1,154	1,013	1,154	1,013
10,150	10,200	1,161	1,018	1,161	1,018
10,200	10,250	1,169	1,023	1,169	1,023
10,250	10,300	1,176	1,028	1,176	1,028
10,300	10,350	1,184	1,033	1,184	1,033
10,350	10,400	1,191	1,038	1,191	1,038
10,400	10,450	1,199	1,043	1,199	1,043
10,450	10,500	1,206	1,048	1,206	1,049
10,500	10,550	1,214	1,053	1,214	1,056
10,550	10,600	1,221	1,058	1,221	1,064
10,600	10,650	1,229	1,063	1,229	1,071
10,650	10,700	1,236	1,068	1,236	1,079
10,700	10,750	1,244	1,073	1,244	1,086
10,750	10,800	1,251	1,078	1,251	1,094
10,800	10,850	1,259	1,083	1,259	1,101
10,850	10,900	1,266	1,088	1,266	1,109
10,900	10,950	1,274	1,093	1,274	1,116
10,950	11,000	1,281	1,098	1,281	1,124

11,000

At least	But less than	Single	MFJ *	MFS	HoH
11,000	11,050	1,289	1,103	1,289	1,131
11,050	11,100	1,296	1,108	1,296	1,139
11,100	11,150	1,304	1,113	1,304	1,146
11,150	11,200	1,311	1,118	1,311	1,154
11,200	11,250	1,319	1,123	1,319	1,161
11,250	11,300	1,326	1,128	1,326	1,169
11,300	11,350	1,334	1,133	1,334	1,176
11,350	11,400	1,341	1,138	1,341	1,184
11,400	11,450	1,349	1,143	1,349	1,191
11,450	11,500	1,356	1,148	1,356	1,199
11,500	11,550	1,364	1,153	1,364	1,206
11,550	11,600	1,371	1,158	1,371	1,214
11,600	11,650	1,379	1,163	1,379	1,221
11,650	11,700	1,386	1,168	1,386	1,229
11,700	11,750	1,394	1,173	1,394	1,236
11,750	11,800	1,401	1,178	1,401	1,244
11,800	11,850	1,409	1,183	1,409	1,251
11,850	11,900	1,416	1,188	1,416	1,259
11,900	11,950	1,424	1,193	1,424	1,266
11,950	12,000	1,431	1,198	1,431	1,274

12,000

At least	But less than	Single	MFJ *	MFS	HoH
12,000	12,050	1,439	1,203	1,439	1,281
12,050	12,100	1,446	1,208	1,446	1,289
12,100	12,150	1,454	1,213	1,454	1,296
12,150	12,200	1,461	1,218	1,461	1,304
12,200	12,250	1,469	1,223	1,469	1,311
12,250	12,300	1,476	1,228	1,476	1,319
12,300	12,350	1,484	1,233	1,484	1,326
12,350	12,400	1,491	1,238	1,491	1,334
12,400	12,450	1,499	1,243	1,499	1,341
12,450	12,500	1,506	1,248	1,506	1,349
12,500	12,550	1,514	1,253	1,514	1,356
12,550	12,600	1,521	1,258	1,521	1,364
12,600	12,650	1,529	1,263	1,529	1,371
12,650	12,700	1,536	1,268	1,536	1,379
12,700	12,750	1,544	1,273	1,544	1,386
12,750	12,800	1,551	1,278	1,551	1,394
12,800	12,850	1,559	1,283	1,559	1,401
12,850	12,900	1,566	1,288	1,566	1,409
12,900	12,950	1,574	1,293	1,574	1,416
12,950	13,000	1,581	1,298	1,581	1,424

13,000

At least	But less than	Single	MFJ *	MFS	HoH
13,000	13,050	1,589	1,303	1,589	1,431
13,050	13,100	1,596	1,308	1,596	1,439
13,100	13,150	1,604	1,313	1,604	1,446
13,150	13,200	1,611	1,318	1,611	1,454
13,200	13,250	1,619	1,323	1,619	1,461
13,250	13,300	1,626	1,328	1,626	1,469
13,300	13,350	1,634	1,333	1,634	1,476
13,350	13,400	1,641	1,338	1,641	1,484
13,400	13,450	1,649	1,343	1,649	1,491
13,450	13,500	1,656	1,348	1,656	1,499
13,500	13,550	1,664	1,353	1,664	1,506
13,550	13,600	1,671	1,358	1,671	1,514
13,600	13,650	1,679	1,363	1,679	1,521
13,650	13,700	1,686	1,368	1,686	1,529
13,700	13,750	1,694	1,373	1,694	1,536
13,750	13,800	1,701	1,378	1,701	1,544
13,800	13,850	1,709	1,383	1,709	1,551
13,850	13,900	1,716	1,388	1,716	1,559
13,900	13,950	1,724	1,393	1,724	1,566
13,950	14,000	1,731	1,398	1,731	1,574

* This column must also be used by a qualifying widow(er).

(Continued on page 67)

2005 Tax Table—*Continued*

14,000

If line 43 (taxable income) is—		And you are—			
At least	But less than	Single	Married filing jointly *	Married filing separately	Head of a household
		Your tax is—			
14,000	14,050	1,739	1,403	1,739	1,581
14,050	14,100	1,746	1,408	1,746	1,589
14,100	14,150	1,754	1,413	1,754	1,596
14,150	14,200	1,761	1,418	1,761	1,604
14,200	14,250	1,769	1,423	1,769	1,611
14,250	14,300	1,776	1,428	1,776	1,619
14,300	14,350	1,784	1,433	1,784	1,626
14,350	14,400	1,791	1,438	1,791	1,634
14,400	14,450	1,799	1,443	1,799	1,641
14,450	14,500	1,806	1,448	1,806	1,649
14,500	14,550	1,814	1,453	1,814	1,656
14,550	14,600	1,821	1,458	1,821	1,664
14,600	14,650	1,829	1,464	1,829	1,671
14,650	14,700	1,836	1,471	1,836	1,679
14,700	14,750	1,844	1,479	1,844	1,686
14,750	14,800	1,851	1,486	1,851	1,694
14,800	14,850	1,859	1,494	1,859	1,701
14,850	14,900	1,866	1,501	1,866	1,709
14,900	14,950	1,874	1,509	1,874	1,716
14,950	15,000	1,881	1,516	1,881	1,724

15,000

At least	But less than	Single	Married filing jointly *	Married filing separately	Head of a household
15,000	15,050	1,889	1,524	1,889	1,731
15,050	15,100	1,896	1,531	1,896	1,739
15,100	15,150	1,904	1,539	1,904	1,746
15,150	15,200	1,911	1,546	1,911	1,754
15,200	15,250	1,919	1,554	1,919	1,761
15,250	15,300	1,926	1,561	1,926	1,769
15,300	15,350	1,934	1,569	1,934	1,776
15,350	15,400	1,941	1,576	1,941	1,784
15,400	15,450	1,949	1,584	1,949	1,791
15,450	15,500	1,956	1,591	1,956	1,799
15,500	15,550	1,964	1,599	1,964	1,806
15,550	15,600	1,971	1,606	1,971	1,814
15,600	15,650	1,979	1,614	1,979	1,821
15,650	15,700	1,986	1,621	1,986	1,829
15,700	15,750	1,994	1,629	1,994	1,836
15,750	15,800	2,001	1,636	2,001	1,844
15,800	15,850	2,009	1,644	2,009	1,851
15,850	15,900	2,016	1,651	2,016	1,859
15,900	15,950	2,024	1,659	2,024	1,866
15,950	16,000	2,031	1,666	2,031	1,874

16,000

At least	But less than	Single	Married filing jointly *	Married filing separately	Head of a household
16,000	16,050	2,039	1,674	2,039	1,881
16,050	16,100	2,046	1,681	2,046	1,889
16,100	16,150	2,054	1,689	2,054	1,896
16,150	16,200	2,061	1,696	2,061	1,904
16,200	16,250	2,069	1,704	2,069	1,911
16,250	16,300	2,076	1,711	2,076	1,919
16,300	16,350	2,084	1,719	2,084	1,926
16,350	16,400	2,091	1,726	2,091	1,934
16,400	16,450	2,099	1,734	2,099	1,941
16,450	16,500	2,106	1,741	2,106	1,949
16,500	16,550	2,114	1,749	2,114	1,956
16,550	16,600	2,121	1,756	2,121	1,964
16,600	16,650	2,129	1,764	2,129	1,971
16,650	16,700	2,136	1,771	2,136	1,979
16,700	16,750	2,144	1,779	2,144	1,986
16,750	16,800	2,151	1,786	2,151	1,994
16,800	16,850	2,159	1,794	2,159	2,001
16,850	16,900	2,166	1,801	2,166	2,009
16,900	16,950	2,174	1,809	2,174	2,016
16,950	17,000	2,181	1,816	2,181	2,024

17,000

At least	But less than	Single	Married filing jointly *	Married filing separately	Head of a household
17,000	17,050	2,189	1,824	2,189	2,031
17,050	17,100	2,196	1,831	2,196	2,039
17,100	17,150	2,204	1,839	2,204	2,046
17,150	17,200	2,211	1,846	2,211	2,054
17,200	17,250	2,219	1,854	2,219	2,061
17,250	17,300	2,226	1,861	2,226	2,069
17,300	17,350	2,234	1,869	2,234	2,076
17,350	17,400	2,241	1,876	2,241	2,084
17,400	17,450	2,249	1,884	2,249	2,091
17,450	17,500	2,256	1,891	2,256	2,099
17,500	17,550	2,264	1,899	2,264	2,106
17,550	17,600	2,271	1,906	2,271	2,114
17,600	17,650	2,279	1,914	2,279	2,121
17,650	17,700	2,286	1,921	2,286	2,129
17,700	17,750	2,294	1,929	2,294	2,136
17,750	17,800	2,301	1,936	2,301	2,144
17,800	17,850	2,309	1,944	2,309	2,151
17,850	17,900	2,316	1,951	2,316	2,159
17,900	17,950	2,324	1,959	2,324	2,166
17,950	18,000	2,331	1,966	2,331	2,174

18,000

At least	But less than	Single	Married filing jointly *	Married filing separately	Head of a household
18,000	18,050	2,339	1,974	2,339	2,181
18,050	18,100	2,346	1,981	2,346	2,189
18,100	18,150	2,354	1,989	2,354	2,196
18,150	18,200	2,361	1,996	2,361	2,204
18,200	18,250	2,369	2,004	2,369	2,211
18,250	18,300	2,376	2,011	2,376	2,219
18,300	18,350	2,384	2,019	2,384	2,226
18,350	18,400	2,391	2,026	2,391	2,234
18,400	18,450	2,399	2,034	2,399	2,241
18,450	18,500	2,406	2,041	2,406	2,249
18,500	18,550	2,414	2,049	2,414	2,256
18,550	18,600	2,421	2,056	2,421	2,264
18,600	18,650	2,429	2,064	2,429	2,271
18,650	18,700	2,436	2,071	2,436	2,279
18,700	18,750	2,444	2,079	2,444	2,286
18,750	18,800	2,451	2,086	2,451	2,294
18,800	18,850	2,459	2,094	2,459	2,301
18,850	18,900	2,466	2,101	2,466	2,309
18,900	18,950	2,474	2,109	2,474	2,316
18,950	19,000	2,481	2,116	2,481	2,324

19,000

At least	But less than	Single	Married filing jointly *	Married filing separately	Head of a household
19,000	19,050	2,489	2,124	2,489	2,331
19,050	19,100	2,496	2,131	2,496	2,339
19,100	19,150	2,504	2,139	2,504	2,346
19,150	19,200	2,511	2,146	2,511	2,354
19,200	19,250	2,519	2,154	2,519	2,361
19,250	19,300	2,526	2,161	2,526	2,369
19,300	19,350	2,534	2,169	2,534	2,376
19,350	19,400	2,541	2,176	2,541	2,384
19,400	19,450	2,549	2,184	2,549	2,391
19,450	19,500	2,556	2,191	2,556	2,399
19,500	19,550	2,564	2,199	2,564	2,406
19,550	19,600	2,571	2,206	2,571	2,414
19,600	19,650	2,579	2,214	2,579	2,421
19,650	19,700	2,586	2,221	2,586	2,429
19,700	19,750	2,594	2,229	2,594	2,436
19,750	19,800	2,601	2,236	2,601	2,444
19,800	19,850	2,609	2,244	2,609	2,451
19,850	19,900	2,616	2,251	2,616	2,459
19,900	19,950	2,624	2,259	2,624	2,466
19,950	20,000	2,631	2,266	2,631	2,474

20,000

At least	But less than	Single	Married filing jointly *	Married filing separately	Head of a household
20,000	20,050	2,639	2,274	2,639	2,481
20,050	20,100	2,646	2,281	2,646	2,489
20,100	20,150	2,654	2,289	2,654	2,496
20,150	20,200	2,661	2,296	2,661	2,504
20,200	20,250	2,669	2,304	2,669	2,511
20,250	20,300	2,676	2,311	2,676	2,519
20,300	20,350	2,684	2,319	2,684	2,526
20,350	20,400	2,691	2,326	2,691	2,534
20,400	20,450	2,699	2,334	2,699	2,541
20,450	20,500	2,706	2,341	2,706	2,549
20,500	20,550	2,714	2,349	2,714	2,556
20,550	20,600	2,721	2,356	2,721	2,564
20,600	20,650	2,729	2,364	2,729	2,571
20,650	20,700	2,736	2,371	2,736	2,579
20,700	20,750	2,744	2,379	2,744	2,586
20,750	20,800	2,751	2,386	2,751	2,594
20,800	20,850	2,759	2,394	2,759	2,601
20,850	20,900	2,766	2,401	2,766	2,609
20,900	20,950	2,774	2,409	2,774	2,616
20,950	21,000	2,781	2,416	2,781	2,624

21,000

At least	But less than	Single	Married filing jointly *	Married filing separately	Head of a household
21,000	21,050	2,789	2,424	2,789	2,631
21,050	21,100	2,796	2,431	2,796	2,639
21,100	21,150	2,804	2,439	2,804	2,646
21,150	21,200	2,811	2,446	2,811	2,654
21,200	21,250	2,819	2,454	2,819	2,661
21,250	21,300	2,826	2,461	2,826	2,669
21,300	21,350	2,834	2,469	2,834	2,676
21,350	21,400	2,841	2,476	2,841	2,684
21,400	21,450	2,849	2,484	2,849	2,691
21,450	21,500	2,856	2,491	2,856	2,699
21,500	21,550	2,864	2,499	2,864	2,706
21,550	21,600	2,871	2,506	2,871	2,714
21,600	21,650	2,879	2,514	2,879	2,721
21,650	21,700	2,886	2,521	2,886	2,729
21,700	21,750	2,894	2,529	2,894	2,736
21,750	21,800	2,901	2,536	2,901	2,744
21,800	21,850	2,909	2,544	2,909	2,751
21,850	21,900	2,916	2,551	2,916	2,759
21,900	21,950	2,924	2,559	2,924	2,766
21,950	22,000	2,931	2,566	2,931	2,774

22,000

At least	But less than	Single	Married filing jointly *	Married filing separately	Head of a household
22,000	22,050	2,939	2,574	2,939	2,781
22,050	22,100	2,946	2,581	2,946	2,789
22,100	22,150	2,954	2,589	2,954	2,796
22,150	22,200	2,961	2,596	2,961	2,804
22,200	22,250	2,969	2,604	2,969	2,811
22,250	22,300	2,976	2,611	2,976	2,819
22,300	22,350	2,984	2,619	2,984	2,826
22,350	22,400	2,991	2,626	2,991	2,834
22,400	22,450	2,999	2,634	2,999	2,841
22,450	22,500	3,006	2,641	3,006	2,849
22,500	22,550	3,014	2,649	3,014	2,856
22,550	22,600	3,021	2,656	3,021	2,864
22,600	22,650	3,029	2,664	3,029	2,871
22,650	22,700	3,036	2,671	3,036	2,879
22,700	22,750	3,044	2,679	3,044	2,886
22,750	22,800	3,051	2,686	3,051	2,894
22,800	22,850	3,059	2,694	3,059	2,901
22,850	22,900	3,066	2,701	3,066	2,909
22,900	22,950	3,074	2,709	3,074	2,916
22,950	23,000	3,081	2,716	3,081	2,924

* This column must also be used by a qualifying widow(er).

(Continued on page 68)

2005 Tax Table—Continued

23,000 – 25,000

If line 43 (taxable income) is— At least	But less than	Single	Married filing jointly *	Married filing separately	Head of a household
23,000					
23,000	23,050	3,089	2,724	3,089	2,931
23,050	23,100	3,096	2,731	3,096	2,939
23,100	23,150	3,104	2,739	3,104	2,946
23,150	23,200	3,111	2,746	3,111	2,954
23,200	23,250	3,119	2,754	3,119	2,961
23,250	23,300	3,126	2,761	3,126	2,969
23,300	23,350	3,134	2,769	3,134	2,976
23,350	23,400	3,141	2,776	3,141	2,984
23,400	23,450	3,149	2,784	3,149	2,991
23,450	23,500	3,156	2,791	3,156	2,999
23,500	23,550	3,164	2,799	3,164	3,006
23,550	23,600	3,171	2,806	3,171	3,014
23,600	23,650	3,179	2,814	3,179	3,021
23,650	23,700	3,186	2,821	3,186	3,029
23,700	23,750	3,194	2,829	3,194	3,036
23,750	23,800	3,201	2,836	3,201	3,044
23,800	23,850	3,209	2,844	3,209	3,051
23,850	23,900	3,216	2,851	3,216	3,059
23,900	23,950	3,224	2,859	3,224	3,066
23,950	24,000	3,231	2,866	3,231	3,074
24,000					
24,000	24,050	3,239	2,874	3,239	3,081
24,050	24,100	3,246	2,881	3,246	3,089
24,100	24,150	3,254	2,889	3,254	3,096
24,150	24,200	3,261	2,896	3,261	3,104
24,200	24,250	3,269	2,904	3,269	3,111
24,250	24,300	3,276	2,911	3,276	3,119
24,300	24,350	3,284	2,919	3,284	3,126
24,350	24,400	3,291	2,926	3,291	3,134
24,400	24,450	3,299	2,934	3,299	3,141
24,450	24,500	3,306	2,941	3,306	3,149
24,500	24,550	3,314	2,949	3,314	3,156
24,550	24,600	3,321	2,956	3,321	3,164
24,600	24,650	3,329	2,964	3,329	3,171
24,650	24,700	3,336	2,971	3,336	3,179
24,700	24,750	3,344	2,979	3,344	3,186
24,750	24,800	3,351	2,986	3,351	3,194
24,800	24,850	3,359	2,994	3,359	3,201
24,850	24,900	3,366	3,001	3,366	3,209
24,900	24,950	3,374	3,009	3,374	3,216
24,950	25,000	3,381	3,016	3,381	3,224
25,000					
25,000	25,050	3,389	3,024	3,389	3,231
25,050	25,100	3,396	3,031	3,396	3,239
25,100	25,150	3,404	3,039	3,404	3,246
25,150	25,200	3,411	3,046	3,411	3,254
25,200	25,250	3,419	3,054	3,419	3,261
25,250	25,300	3,426	3,061	3,426	3,269
25,300	25,350	3,434	3,069	3,434	3,276
25,350	25,400	3,441	3,076	3,441	3,284
25,400	25,450	3,449	3,084	3,449	3,291
25,450	25,500	3,456	3,091	3,456	3,299
25,500	25,550	3,464	3,099	3,464	3,306
25,550	25,600	3,471	3,106	3,471	3,314
25,600	25,650	3,479	3,114	3,479	3,321
25,650	25,700	3,486	3,121	3,486	3,329
25,700	25,750	3,494	3,129	3,494	3,336
25,750	25,800	3,501	3,136	3,501	3,344
25,800	25,850	3,509	3,144	3,509	3,351
25,850	25,900	3,516	3,151	3,516	3,359
25,900	25,950	3,524	3,159	3,524	3,366
25,950	26,000	3,531	3,166	3,531	3,374

26,000 – 28,000

If line 43 (taxable income) is— At least	But less than	Single	Married filing jointly *	Married filing separately	Head of a household
26,000					
26,000	26,050	3,539	3,174	3,539	3,381
26,050	26,100	3,546	3,181	3,546	3,389
26,100	26,150	3,554	3,189	3,554	3,396
26,150	26,200	3,561	3,196	3,561	3,404
26,200	26,250	3,569	3,204	3,569	3,411
26,250	26,300	3,576	3,211	3,576	3,419
26,300	26,350	3,584	3,219	3,584	3,426
26,350	26,400	3,591	3,226	3,591	3,434
26,400	26,450	3,599	3,234	3,599	3,441
26,450	26,500	3,606	3,241	3,606	3,449
26,500	26,550	3,614	3,249	3,614	3,456
26,550	26,600	3,621	3,256	3,621	3,464
26,600	26,650	3,629	3,264	3,629	3,471
26,650	26,700	3,636	3,271	3,636	3,479
26,700	26,750	3,644	3,279	3,644	3,486
26,750	26,800	3,651	3,286	3,651	3,494
26,800	26,850	3,659	3,294	3,659	3,501
26,850	26,900	3,666	3,301	3,666	3,509
26,900	26,950	3,674	3,309	3,674	3,516
26,950	27,000	3,681	3,316	3,681	3,524
27,000					
27,000	27,050	3,689	3,324	3,689	3,531
27,050	27,100	3,696	3,331	3,696	3,539
27,100	27,150	3,704	3,339	3,704	3,546
27,150	27,200	3,711	3,346	3,711	3,554
27,200	27,250	3,719	3,354	3,719	3,561
27,250	27,300	3,726	3,361	3,726	3,569
27,300	27,350	3,734	3,369	3,734	3,576
27,350	27,400	3,741	3,376	3,741	3,584
27,400	27,450	3,749	3,384	3,749	3,591
27,450	27,500	3,756	3,391	3,756	3,599
27,500	27,550	3,764	3,399	3,764	3,606
27,550	27,600	3,771	3,406	3,771	3,614
27,600	27,650	3,779	3,414	3,779	3,621
27,650	27,700	3,786	3,421	3,786	3,629
27,700	27,750	3,794	3,429	3,794	3,636
27,750	27,800	3,801	3,436	3,801	3,644
27,800	27,850	3,809	3,444	3,809	3,651
27,850	27,900	3,816	3,451	3,816	3,659
27,900	27,950	3,824	3,459	3,824	3,666
27,950	28,000	3,831	3,466	3,831	3,674
28,000					
28,000	28,050	3,839	3,474	3,839	3,681
28,050	28,100	3,846	3,481	3,846	3,689
28,100	28,150	3,854	3,489	3,854	3,696
28,150	28,200	3,861	3,496	3,861	3,704
28,200	28,250	3,869	3,504	3,869	3,711
28,250	28,300	3,876	3,511	3,876	3,719
28,300	28,350	3,884	3,519	3,884	3,726
28,350	28,400	3,891	3,526	3,891	3,734
28,400	28,450	3,899	3,534	3,899	3,741
28,450	28,500	3,906	3,541	3,906	3,749
28,500	28,550	3,914	3,549	3,914	3,756
28,550	28,600	3,921	3,556	3,921	3,764
28,600	28,650	3,929	3,564	3,929	3,771
28,650	28,700	3,936	3,571	3,936	3,779
28,700	28,750	3,944	3,579	3,944	3,786
28,750	28,800	3,951	3,586	3,951	3,794
28,800	28,850	3,959	3,594	3,959	3,801
28,850	28,900	3,966	3,601	3,966	3,809
28,900	28,950	3,974	3,609	3,974	3,816
28,950	29,000	3,981	3,616	3,981	3,824

29,000 – 31,000

If line 43 (taxable income) is— At least	But less than	Single	Married filing jointly *	Married filing separately	Head of a household
29,000					
29,000	29,050	3,989	3,624	3,989	3,831
29,050	29,100	3,996	3,631	3,996	3,839
29,100	29,150	4,004	3,639	4,004	3,846
29,150	29,200	4,011	3,646	4,011	3,854
29,200	29,250	4,019	3,654	4,019	3,861
29,250	29,300	4,026	3,661	4,026	3,869
29,300	29,350	4,034	3,669	4,034	3,876
29,350	29,400	4,041	3,676	4,041	3,884
29,400	29,450	4,049	3,684	4,049	3,891
29,450	29,500	4,056	3,691	4,056	3,899
29,500	29,550	4,064	3,699	4,064	3,906
29,550	29,600	4,071	3,706	4,071	3,914
29,600	29,650	4,079	3,714	4,079	3,921
29,650	29,700	4,086	3,721	4,086	3,929
29,700	29,750	4,096	3,729	4,096	3,936
29,750	29,800	4,109	3,736	4,109	3,944
29,800	29,850	4,121	3,744	4,121	3,951
29,850	29,900	4,134	3,751	4,134	3,959
29,900	29,950	4,146	3,759	4,146	3,966
29,950	30,000	4,159	3,766	4,159	3,974
30,000					
30,000	30,050	4,171	3,774	4,171	3,981
30,050	30,100	4,184	3,781	4,184	3,989
30,100	30,150	4,196	3,789	4,196	3,996
30,150	30,200	4,209	3,796	4,209	4,004
30,200	30,250	4,221	3,804	4,221	4,011
30,250	30,300	4,234	3,811	4,234	4,019
30,300	30,350	4,246	3,819	4,246	4,026
30,350	30,400	4,259	3,826	4,259	4,034
30,400	30,450	4,271	3,834	4,271	4,041
30,450	30,500	4,284	3,841	4,284	4,049
30,500	30,550	4,296	3,849	4,296	4,056
30,550	30,600	4,309	3,856	4,309	4,064
30,600	30,650	4,321	3,864	4,321	4,071
30,650	30,700	4,334	3,871	4,334	4,079
30,700	30,750	4,346	3,879	4,346	4,086
30,750	30,800	4,359	3,886	4,359	4,094
30,800	30,850	4,371	3,894	4,371	4,101
30,850	30,900	4,384	3,901	4,384	4,109
30,900	30,950	4,396	3,909	4,396	4,116
30,950	31,000	4,409	3,916	4,409	4,124
31,000					
31,000	31,050	4,421	3,924	4,421	4,131
31,050	31,100	4,434	3,931	4,434	4,139
31,100	31,150	4,446	3,939	4,446	4,146
31,150	31,200	4,459	3,946	4,459	4,154
31,200	31,250	4,471	3,954	4,471	4,161
31,250	31,300	4,484	3,961	4,484	4,169
31,300	31,350	4,496	3,969	4,496	4,176
31,350	31,400	4,509	3,976	4,509	4,184
31,400	31,450	4,521	3,984	4,521	4,191
31,450	31,500	4,534	3,991	4,534	4,199
31,500	31,550	4,546	3,999	4,546	4,206
31,550	31,600	4,559	4,006	4,559	4,214
31,600	31,650	4,571	4,014	4,571	4,221
31,650	31,700	4,584	4,021	4,504	4,229
31,700	31,750	4,596	4,029	4,596	4,236
31,750	31,800	4,609	4,036	4,609	4,244
31,800	31,850	4,621	4,044	4,621	4,251
31,850	31,900	4,634	4,051	4,634	4,259
31,900	31,950	4,646	4,059	4,646	4,266
31,950	32,000	4,659	4,066	4,659	4,274

* This column must also be used by a qualifying widow(er).

(Continued on page 69)

If line 43 (taxable income) is— At least	But less than	Single	Married filing jointly *	Married filing separately	Head of a household
32,000					
32,000	32,050	4,671	4,074	4,671	4,281
32,050	32,100	4,684	4,081	4,684	4,289
32,100	32,150	4,696	4,089	4,696	4,296
32,150	32,200	4,709	4,096	4,709	4,304
32,200	32,250	4,721	4,104	4,721	4,311
32,250	32,300	4,734	4,111	4,734	4,319
32,300	32,350	4,746	4,119	4,746	4,326
32,350	32,400	4,759	4,126	4,759	4,334
32,400	32,450	4,771	4,134	4,771	4,341
32,450	32,500	4,784	4,141	4,784	4,349
32,500	32,550	4,796	4,149	4,796	4,356
32,550	32,600	4,809	4,156	4,809	4,364
32,600	32,650	4,821	4,164	4,821	4,371
32,650	32,700	4,834	4,171	4,834	4,379
32,700	32,750	4,846	4,179	4,846	4,386
32,750	32,800	4,859	4,186	4,859	4,394
32,800	32,850	4,871	4,194	4,871	4,401
32,850	32,900	4,884	4,201	4,884	4,409
32,900	32,950	4,896	4,209	4,896	4,416
32,950	33,000	4,909	4,216	4,909	4,424
33,000					
33,000	33,050	4,921	4,224	4,921	4,431
33,050	33,100	4,934	4,231	4,934	4,439
33,100	33,150	4,946	4,239	4,946	4,446
33,150	33,200	4,959	4,246	4,959	4,454
33,200	33,250	4,971	4,254	4,971	4,461
33,250	33,300	4,984	4,261	4,984	4,469
33,300	33,350	4,996	4,269	4,996	4,476
33,350	33,400	5,009	4,276	5,009	4,484
33,400	33,450	5,021	4,284	5,021	4,491
33,450	33,500	5,034	4,291	5,034	4,499
33,500	33,550	5,046	4,299	5,046	4,506
33,550	33,600	5,059	4,306	5,059	4,514
33,600	33,650	5,071	4,314	5,071	4,521
33,650	33,700	5,084	4,321	5,084	4,529
33,700	33,750	5,096	4,329	5,096	4,536
33,750	33,800	5,109	4,336	5,109	4,544
33,800	33,850	5,121	4,344	5,121	4,551
33,850	33,900	5,134	4,351	5,134	4,559
33,900	33,950	5,146	4,359	5,146	4,566
33,950	34,000	5,159	4,366	5,159	4,574
34,000					
34,000	34,050	5,171	4,374	5,171	4,581
34,050	34,100	5,184	4,381	5,184	4,589
34,100	34,150	5,196	4,389	5,196	4,596
34,150	34,200	5,209	4,396	5,209	4,604
34,200	34,250	5,221	4,404	5,221	4,611
34,250	34,300	5,234	4,411	5,234	4,619
34,300	34,350	5,246	4,419	5,246	4,626
34,350	34,400	5,259	4,426	5,259	4,634
34,400	34,450	5,271	4,434	5,271	4,641
34,450	34,500	5,284	4,441	5,284	4,649
34,500	34,550	5,296	4,449	5,296	4,656
34,550	34,600	5,309	4,456	5,309	4,664
34,600	34,650	5,321	4,464	5,321	4,671
34,650	34,700	5,334	4,471	5,334	4,679
34,700	34,750	5,346	4,479	5,346	4,686
34,750	34,800	5,359	4,486	5,359	4,694
34,800	34,850	5,371	4,494	5,371	4,701
34,850	34,900	5,384	4,501	5,384	4,709
34,900	34,950	5,396	4,509	5,396	4,716
34,950	35,000	5,409	4,516	5,409	4,724

If line 43 (taxable income) is— At least	But less than	Single	Married filing jointly *	Married filing separately	Head of a household
35,000					
35,000	35,050	5,421	4,524	5,421	4,731
35,050	35,100	5,434	4,531	5,434	4,739
35,100	35,150	5,446	4,539	5,446	4,746
35,150	35,200	5,459	4,546	5,459	4,754
35,200	35,250	5,471	4,554	5,471	4,761
35,250	35,300	5,484	4,561	5,484	4,769
35,300	35,350	5,496	4,569	5,496	4,776
35,350	35,400	5,509	4,576	5,509	4,784
35,400	35,450	5,521	4,584	5,521	4,791
35,450	35,500	5,534	4,591	5,534	4,799
35,500	35,550	5,546	4,599	5,546	4,806
35,550	35,600	5,559	4,606	5,559	4,814
35,600	35,650	5,571	4,614	5,571	4,821
35,650	35,700	5,584	4,621	5,584	4,829
35,700	35,750	5,596	4,629	5,596	4,836
35,750	35,800	5,609	4,636	5,609	4,844
35,800	35,850	5,621	4,644	5,621	4,851
35,850	35,900	5,634	4,651	5,634	4,859
35,900	35,950	5,646	4,659	5,646	4,866
35,950	36,000	5,659	4,666	5,659	4,874
36,000					
36,000	36,050	5,671	4,674	5,671	4,881
36,050	36,100	5,684	4,681	5,684	4,889
36,100	36,150	5,696	4,689	5,696	4,896
36,150	36,200	5,709	4,696	5,709	4,904
36,200	36,250	5,721	4,704	5,721	4,911
36,250	36,300	5,734	4,711	5,734	4,919
36,300	36,350	5,746	4,719	5,746	4,926
36,350	36,400	5,759	4,726	5,759	4,934
36,400	36,450	5,771	4,734	5,771	4,941
36,450	36,500	5,784	4,741	5,784	4,949
36,500	36,550	5,796	4,749	5,796	4,956
36,550	36,600	5,809	4,756	5,809	4,964
36,600	36,650	5,821	4,764	5,821	4,971
36,650	36,700	5,834	4,771	5,834	4,979
36,700	36,750	5,846	4,779	5,846	4,986
36,750	36,800	5,859	4,786	5,859	4,994
36,800	36,850	5,871	4,794	5,871	5,001
36,850	36,900	5,884	4,801	5,884	5,009
36,900	36,950	5,896	4,809	5,896	5,016
36,950	37,000	5,909	4,816	5,909	5,024
37,000					
37,000	37,050	5,921	4,824	5,921	5,031
37,050	37,100	5,934	4,831	5,934	5,039
37,100	37,150	5,946	4,839	5,946	5,046
37,150	37,200	5,959	4,846	5,959	5,054
37,200	37,250	5,971	4,854	5,971	5,061
37,250	37,300	5,984	4,861	5,984	5,069
37,300	37,350	5,996	4,869	5,996	5,076
37,350	37,400	6,009	4,876	6,009	5,084
37,400	37,450	6,021	4,884	6,021	5,091
37,450	37,500	6,034	4,891	6,034	5,099
37,500	37,550	6,046	4,899	6,046	5,106
37,550	37,600	6,059	4,906	6,059	5,114
37,600	37,650	6,071	4,914	6,071	5,121
37,650	37,700	6,084	4,921	6,084	5,129
37,700	37,750	6,096	4,929	6,096	5,136
37,750	37,800	6,109	4,936	6,109	5,144
37,800	37,850	6,121	4,944	6,121	5,151
37,850	37,900	6,134	4,951	6,134	5,159
37,900	37,950	6,146	4,959	6,146	5,166
37,950	38,000	6,159	4,966	6,159	5,174

If line 43 (taxable income) is— At least	But less than	Single	Married filing jointly *	Married filing separately	Head of a household
38,000					
38,000	38,050	6,171	4,974	6,171	5,181
38,050	38,100	6,184	4,981	6,184	5,189
38,100	38,150	6,196	4,989	6,196	5,196
38,150	38,200	6,209	4,996	6,209	5,204
38,200	38,250	6,221	5,004	6,221	5,211
38,250	38,300	6,234	5,011	6,234	5,219
38,300	38,350	6,246	5,019	6,246	5,226
38,350	38,400	6,259	5,026	6,259	5,234
38,400	38,450	6,271	5,034	6,271	5,241
38,450	38,500	6,284	5,041	6,284	5,249
38,500	38,550	6,296	5,049	6,296	5,256
38,550	38,600	6,309	5,056	6,309	5,264
38,600	38,650	6,321	5,064	6,321	5,271
38,650	38,700	6,334	5,071	6,334	5,279
38,700	38,750	6,346	5,079	6,346	5,286
38,750	38,800	6,359	5,086	6,359	5,294
38,800	38,850	6,371	5,094	6,371	5,301
38,850	38,900	6,384	5,101	6,384	5,309
38,900	38,950	6,396	5,109	6,396	5,316
38,950	39,000	6,409	5,116	6,409	5,324
39,000					
39,000	39,050	6,421	5,124	6,421	5,331
39,050	39,100	6,434	5,131	6,434	5,339
39,100	39,150	6,446	5,139	6,446	5,346
39,150	39,200	6,459	5,146	6,459	5,354
39,200	39,250	6,471	5,154	6,471	5,361
39,250	39,300	6,484	5,161	6,484	5,369
39,300	39,350	6,496	5,169	6,496	5,376
39,350	39,400	6,509	5,176	6,509	5,384
39,400	39,450	6,521	5,184	6,521	5,391
39,450	39,500	6,534	5,191	6,534	5,399
39,500	39,550	6,546	5,199	6,546	5,406
39,550	39,600	6,559	5,206	6,559	5,414
39,600	39,650	6,571	5,214	6,571	5,421
39,650	39,700	6,584	5,221	6,584	5,429
39,700	39,750	6,596	5,229	6,596	5,436
39,750	39,800	6,609	5,236	6,609	5,444
39,800	39,850	6,621	5,244	6,621	5,454
39,850	39,900	6,634	5,251	6,634	5,466
39,900	39,950	6,646	5,259	6,646	5,479
39,950	40,000	6,659	5,266	6,659	5,491
40,000					
40,000	40,050	6,671	5,274	6,671	5,504
40,050	40,100	6,684	5,281	6,684	5,516
40,100	40,150	6,696	5,289	6,696	5,529
40,150	40,200	6,709	5,296	6,709	5,541
40,200	40,250	6,721	5,304	6,721	5,554
40,250	40,300	6,734	5,311	6,734	5,566
40,300	40,350	6,746	5,319	6,746	5,579
40,350	40,400	6,759	5,326	6,759	5,591
40,400	40,450	6,771	5,334	6,771	5,604
40,450	40,500	6,784	5,341	6,784	5,616
40,500	40,550	6,796	5,349	6,796	5,629
40,550	40,600	6,809	5,356	6,809	5,641
40,600	40,650	6,821	5,364	6,821	5,654
40,650	40,700	6,834	5,371	6,834	5,666
40,700	40,750	6,846	5,379	6,846	5,679
40,750	40,800	6,859	5,386	6,859	5,691
40,800	40,850	6,871	5,394	6,871	5,704
40,850	40,900	6,884	5,401	6,884	5,716
40,900	40,950	6,896	5,409	6,896	5,729
40,950	41,000	6,909	5,416	6,909	5,741

* This column must also be used by a qualifying widow(er).

(Continued on page 70)

2005 Tax Table—Continued

41,000 / 42,000 / 43,000

At least	But less than	Single	Married filing jointly *	Married filing separately	Head of a household
41,000					
41,000	41,050	6,921	5,424	6,921	5,754
41,050	41,100	6,934	5,431	6,934	5,766
41,100	41,150	6,946	5,439	6,946	5,779
41,150	41,200	6,959	5,446	6,959	5,791
41,200	41,250	6,971	5,454	6,971	5,804
41,250	41,300	6,984	5,461	6,984	5,816
41,300	41,350	6,996	5,469	6,996	5,829
41,350	41,400	7,009	5,476	7,009	5,841
41,400	41,450	7,021	5,484	7,021	5,854
41,450	41,500	7,034	5,491	7,034	5,866
41,500	41,550	7,046	5,499	7,046	5,879
41,550	41,600	7,059	5,506	7,059	5,891
41,600	41,650	7,071	5,514	7,071	5,904
41,650	41,700	7,084	5,521	7,084	5,916
41,700	41,750	7,096	5,529	7,096	5,929
41,750	41,800	7,109	5,536	7,109	5,941
41,800	41,850	7,121	5,544	7,121	5,954
41,850	41,900	7,134	5,551	7,134	5,966
41,900	41,950	7,146	5,559	7,146	5,979
41,950	42,000	7,159	5,566	7,159	5,991
42,000					
42,000	42,050	7,171	5,574	7,171	6,004
42,050	42,100	7,184	5,581	7,184	6,016
42,100	42,150	7,196	5,589	7,196	6,029
42,150	42,200	7,209	5,596	7,209	6,041
42,200	42,250	7,221	5,604	7,221	6,054
42,250	42,300	7,234	5,611	7,234	6,066
42,300	42,350	7,246	5,619	7,246	6,079
42,350	42,400	7,259	5,626	7,259	6,091
42,400	42,450	7,271	5,634	7,271	6,104
42,450	42,500	7,284	5,641	7,284	6,116
42,500	42,550	7,296	5,649	7,296	6,129
42,550	42,600	7,309	5,656	7,309	6,141
42,600	42,650	7,321	5,664	7,321	6,154
42,650	42,700	7,334	5,671	7,334	6,166
42,700	42,750	7,346	5,679	7,346	6,179
42,750	42,800	7,359	5,686	7,359	6,191
42,800	42,850	7,371	5,694	7,371	6,204
42,850	42,900	7,384	5,701	7,384	6,216
42,900	42,950	7,396	5,709	7,396	6,229
42,950	43,000	7,409	5,716	7,409	6,241
43,000					
43,000	43,050	7,421	5,724	7,421	6,254
43,050	43,100	7,434	5,731	7,434	6,266
43,100	43,150	7,446	5,739	7,446	6,279
43,150	43,200	7,459	5,746	7,459	6,291
43,200	43,250	7,471	5,754	7,471	6,304
43,250	43,300	7,484	5,761	7,484	6,316
43,300	43,350	7,496	5,769	7,496	6,329
43,350	43,400	7,509	5,776	7,509	6,341
43,400	43,450	7,521	5,784	7,521	6,354
43,450	43,500	7,534	5,791	7,534	6,366
43,500	43,550	7,546	5,799	7,546	6,379
43,550	43,600	7,559	5,806	7,559	6,391
43,600	43,650	7,571	5,814	7,571	6,404
43,650	43,700	7,584	5,821	7,584	6,416
43,700	43,750	7,596	5,829	7,596	6,429
43,750	43,800	7,609	5,836	7,609	6,441
43,800	43,850	7,621	5,844	7,621	6,454
43,850	43,900	7,634	5,851	7,634	6,466
43,900	43,950	7,646	5,859	7,646	6,479
43,950	44,000	7,659	5,866	7,659	6,491

44,000 / 45,000 / 46,000

At least	But less than	Single	Married filing jointly *	Married filing separately	Head of a household
44,000					
44,000	44,050	7,671	5,874	7,671	6,504
44,050	44,100	7,684	5,881	7,684	6,516
44,100	44,150	7,696	5,889	7,696	6,529
44,150	44,200	7,709	5,896	7,709	6,541
44,200	44,250	7,721	5,904	7,721	6,554
44,250	44,300	7,734	5,911	7,734	6,566
44,300	44,350	7,746	5,919	7,746	6,579
44,350	44,400	7,759	5,926	7,759	6,591
44,400	44,450	7,771	5,934	7,771	6,604
44,450	44,500	7,784	5,941	7,784	6,616
44,500	44,550	7,796	5,949	7,796	6,629
44,550	44,600	7,809	5,956	7,809	6,641
44,600	44,650	7,821	5,964	7,821	6,654
44,650	44,700	7,834	5,971	7,834	6,666
44,700	44,750	7,846	5,979	7,846	6,679
44,750	44,800	7,859	5,986	7,859	6,691
44,800	44,850	7,871	5,994	7,871	6,704
44,850	44,900	7,884	6,001	7,884	6,716
44,900	44,950	7,896	6,009	7,896	6,729
44,950	45,000	7,909	6,016	7,909	6,741
45,000					
45,000	45,050	7,921	6,024	7,921	6,754
45,050	45,100	7,934	6,031	7,934	6,766
45,100	45,150	7,946	6,039	7,946	6,779
45,150	45,200	7,959	6,046	7,959	6,791
45,200	45,250	7,971	6,054	7,971	6,804
45,250	45,300	7,984	6,061	7,984	6,816
45,300	45,350	7,996	6,069	7,996	6,829
45,350	45,400	8,009	6,076	8,009	6,841
45,400	45,450	8,021	6,084	8,021	6,854
45,450	45,500	8,034	6,091	8,034	6,866
45,500	45,550	8,046	6,099	8,046	6,879
45,550	45,600	8,059	6,106	8,059	6,891
45,600	45,650	8,071	6,114	8,071	6,904
45,650	45,700	8,084	6,121	8,084	6,916
45,700	45,750	8,096	6,129	8,096	6,929
45,750	45,800	8,109	6,136	8,109	6,941
45,800	45,850	8,121	6,144	8,121	6,954
45,850	45,900	8,134	6,151	8,134	6,966
45,900	45,950	8,146	6,159	8,146	6,979
45,950	46,000	8,159	6,166	8,159	6,991
46,000					
46,000	46,050	8,171	6,174	8,171	7,004
46,050	46,100	8,184	6,181	8,184	7,016
46,100	46,150	8,196	6,189	8,196	7,029
46,150	46,200	8,209	6,196	8,209	7,041
46,200	46,250	8,221	6,204	8,221	7,054
46,250	46,300	8,234	6,211	8,234	7,066
46,300	46,350	8,246	6,219	8,246	7,079
46,350	46,400	8,259	6,226	8,259	7,091
46,400	46,450	8,271	6,234	8,271	7,104
46,450	46,500	8,284	6,241	8,284	7,116
46,500	46,550	8,296	6,249	8,296	7,129
46,550	46,600	8,309	6,256	8,309	7,141
46,600	46,650	8,321	6,264	8,321	7,154
46,650	46,700	8,334	6,271	8,334	7,166
46,700	46,750	8,346	6,279	8,346	7,179
46,750	46,800	8,359	6,286	8,359	7,191
46,800	46,850	8,371	6,294	8,371	7,204
46,850	46,900	8,384	6,301	8,384	7,216
46,900	46,950	8,396	6,309	8,396	7,229
46,950	47,000	8,409	6,316	8,409	7,241

47,000 / 48,000 / 49,000

At least	But less than	Single	Married filing jointly *	Married filing separately	Head of a household
47,000					
47,000	47,050	8,421	6,324	8,421	7,254
47,050	47,100	8,434	6,331	8,434	7,266
47,100	47,150	8,446	6,339	8,446	7,279
47,150	47,200	8,459	6,346	8,459	7,291
47,200	47,250	8,471	6,354	8,471	7,304
47,250	47,300	8,484	6,361	8,484	7,316
47,300	47,350	8,496	6,369	8,496	7,329
47,350	47,400	8,509	6,376	8,509	7,341
47,400	47,450	8,521	6,384	8,521	7,354
47,450	47,500	8,534	6,391	8,534	7,366
47,500	47,550	8,546	6,399	8,546	7,379
47,550	47,600	8,559	6,406	8,559	7,391
47,600	47,650	8,571	6,414	8,571	7,404
47,650	47,700	8,584	6,421	8,584	7,416
47,700	47,750	8,596	6,429	8,596	7,429
47,750	47,800	8,609	6,436	8,609	7,441
47,800	47,850	8,621	6,444	8,621	7,454
47,850	47,900	8,634	6,451	8,634	7,466
47,900	47,950	8,646	6,459	8,646	7,479
47,950	48,000	8,659	6,466	8,659	7,491
48,000					
48,000	48,050	8,671	6,474	8,671	7,504
48,050	48,100	8,684	6,481	8,684	7,516
48,100	48,150	8,696	6,489	8,696	7,529
48,150	48,200	8,709	6,496	8,709	7,541
48,200	48,250	8,721	6,504	8,721	7,554
48,250	48,300	8,734	6,511	8,734	7,566
48,300	48,350	8,746	6,519	8,746	7,579
48,350	48,400	8,759	6,526	8,759	7,591
48,400	48,450	8,771	6,534	8,771	7,604
48,450	48,500	8,784	6,541	8,784	7,616
48,500	48,550	8,796	6,549	8,796	7,629
48,550	48,600	8,809	6,556	8,809	7,641
48,600	48,650	8,821	6,564	8,821	7,654
48,650	48,700	8,834	6,571	8,834	7,666
48,700	48,750	8,846	6,579	8,846	7,679
48,750	48,800	8,859	6,586	8,859	7,691
48,800	48,850	8,871	6,594	8,871	7,704
48,850	48,900	8,884	6,601	8,884	7,716
48,900	48,950	8,896	6,609	8,896	7,729
48,950	49,000	8,909	6,616	8,909	7,741
49,000					
49,000	49,050	8,921	6,624	8,921	7,754
49,050	49,100	8,934	6,631	8,934	7,766
49,100	49,150	8,946	6,639	8,946	7,779
49,150	49,200	8,959	6,646	8,959	7,791
49,200	49,250	8,971	6,654	8,971	7,804
49,250	49,300	8,984	6,661	8,984	7,816
49,300	49,350	8,996	6,669	8,996	7,829
49,350	49,400	9,009	6,676	9,009	7,841
49,400	49,450	9,021	6,684	9,021	7,854
49,450	49,500	9,034	6,691	9,034	7,866
49,500	49,550	9,046	6,699	9,046	7,879
49,550	49,600	9,059	6,706	9,059	7,891
49,600	49,650	9,071	6,714	9,071	7,904
49,650	49,700	9,084	6,721	9,084	7,916
49,700	49,750	9,096	6,729	9,096	7,929
49,750	49,800	9,109	6,736	9,109	7,941
49,800	49,850	9,121	6,744	9,121	7,954
49,850	49,900	9,134	6,751	9,134	7,966
49,900	49,950	9,146	6,759	9,146	7,979
49,950	50,000	9,159	6,766	9,159	7,991

* This column must also be used by a qualifying widow(er).

(Continued on page 71)

2005 Tax Table—Continued

If line 43 (taxable income) is— At least	But less than	And you are— Single	Married filing jointly *	Married filing separately	Head of a household
50,000					
50,000	50,050	9,171	6,774	9,171	8,004
50,050	50,100	9,184	6,781	9,184	8,016
50,100	50,150	9,196	6,789	9,196	8,029
50,150	50,200	9,209	6,796	9,209	8,041
50,200	50,250	9,221	6,804	9,221	8,054
50,250	50,300	9,234	6,811	9,234	8,066
50,300	50,350	9,246	6,819	9,246	8,079
50,350	50,400	9,259	6,826	9,259	8,091
50,400	50,450	9,271	6,834	9,271	8,104
50,450	50,500	9,284	6,841	9,284	8,116
50,500	50,550	9,296	6,849	9,296	8,129
50,550	50,600	9,309	6,856	9,309	8,141
50,600	50,650	9,321	6,864	9,321	8,154
50,650	50,700	9,334	6,871	9,334	8,166
50,700	50,750	9,346	6,879	9,346	8,179
50,750	50,800	9,359	6,886	9,359	8,191
50,800	50,850	9,371	6,894	9,371	8,204
50,850	50,900	9,384	6,901	9,384	8,216
50,900	50,950	9,396	6,909	9,396	8,229
50,950	51,000	9,409	6,916	9,409	8,241
51,000					
51,000	51,050	9,421	6,924	9,421	8,254
51,050	51,100	9,434	6,931	9,434	8,266
51,100	51,150	9,446	6,939	9,446	8,279
51,150	51,200	9,459	6,946	9,459	8,291
51,200	51,250	9,471	6,954	9,471	8,304
51,250	51,300	9,484	6,961	9,484	8,316
51,300	51,350	9,496	6,969	9,496	8,329
51,350	51,400	9,509	6,976	9,509	8,341
51,400	51,450	9,521	6,984	9,521	8,354
51,450	51,500	9,534	6,991	9,534	8,366
51,500	51,550	9,546	6,999	9,546	8,379
51,550	51,600	9,559	7,006	9,559	8,391
51,600	51,650	9,571	7,014	9,571	8,404
51,650	51,700	9,584	7,021	9,584	8,416
51,700	51,750	9,596	7,029	9,596	8,429
51,750	51,800	9,609	7,036	9,609	8,441
51,800	51,850	9,621	7,044	9,621	8,454
51,850	51,900	9,634	7,051	9,634	8,466
51,900	51,950	9,646	7,059	9,646	8,479
51,950	52,000	9,659	7,066	9,659	8,491
52,000					
52,000	52,050	9,671	7,074	9,671	8,504
52,050	52,100	9,684	7,081	9,684	8,516
52,100	52,150	9,696	7,089	9,696	8,529
52,150	52,200	9,709	7,096	9,709	8,541
52,200	52,250	9,721	7,104	9,721	8,554
52,250	52,300	9,734	7,111	9,734	8,566
52,300	52,350	9,746	7,119	9,746	8,579
52,350	52,400	9,759	7,126	9,759	8,591
52,400	52,450	9,771	7,134	9,771	8,604
52,450	52,500	9,784	7,141	9,784	8,616
52,500	52,550	9,796	7,149	9,796	8,629
52,550	52,600	9,809	7,156	9,809	8,641
52,600	52,650	9,821	7,164	9,821	8,654
52,650	52,700	9,834	7,171	9,834	8,666
52,700	52,750	9,846	7,179	9,846	8,679
52,750	52,800	9,859	7,186	9,859	8,691
52,800	52,850	9,871	7,194	9,871	8,704
52,850	52,900	9,884	7,201	9,884	8,716
52,900	52,950	9,896	7,209	9,896	8,729
52,950	53,000	9,909	7,216	9,909	8,741

If line 43 (taxable income) is— At least	But less than	And you are— Single	Married filing jointly *	Married filing separately	Head of a household
53,000					
53,000	53,050	9,921	7,224	9,921	8,754
53,050	53,100	9,934	7,231	9,934	8,766
53,100	53,150	9,946	7,239	9,946	8,779
53,150	53,200	9,959	7,246	9,959	8,791
53,200	53,250	9,971	7,254	9,971	8,804
53,250	53,300	9,984	7,261	9,984	8,816
53,300	53,350	9,996	7,269	9,996	8,829
53,350	53,400	10,009	7,276	10,009	8,841
53,400	53,450	10,021	7,284	10,021	8,854
53,450	53,500	10,034	7,291	10,034	8,866
53,500	53,550	10,046	7,299	10,046	8,879
53,550	53,600	10,059	7,306	10,059	8,891
53,600	53,650	10,071	7,314	10,071	8,904
53,650	53,700	10,084	7,321	10,084	8,916
53,700	53,750	10,096	7,329	10,096	8,929
53,750	53,800	10,109	7,336	10,109	8,941
53,800	53,850	10,121	7,344	10,121	8,954
53,850	53,900	10,134	7,351	10,134	8,966
53,900	53,950	10,146	7,359	10,146	8,979
53,950	54,000	10,159	7,366	10,159	8,991
54,000					
54,000	54,050	10,171	7,374	10,171	9,004
54,050	54,100	10,184	7,381	10,184	9,016
54,100	54,150	10,196	7,389	10,196	9,029
54,150	54,200	10,209	7,396	10,209	9,041
54,200	54,250	10,221	7,404	10,221	9,054
54,250	54,300	10,234	7,411	10,234	9,066
54,300	54,350	10,246	7,419	10,246	9,079
54,350	54,400	10,259	7,426	10,259	9,091
54,400	54,450	10,271	7,434	10,271	9,104
54,450	54,500	10,284	7,441	10,284	9,116
54,500	54,550	10,296	7,449	10,296	9,129
54,550	54,600	10,309	7,456	10,309	9,141
54,600	54,650	10,321	7,464	10,321	9,154
54,650	54,700	10,334	7,471	10,334	9,166
54,700	54,750	10,346	7,479	10,346	9,179
54,750	54,800	10,359	7,486	10,359	9,191
54,800	54,850	10,371	7,494	10,371	9,204
54,850	54,900	10,384	7,501	10,384	9,216
54,900	54,950	10,396	7,509	10,396	9,229
54,950	55,000	10,409	7,516	10,409	9,241
55,000					
55,000	55,050	10,421	7,524	10,421	9,254
55,050	55,100	10,434	7,531	10,434	9,266
55,100	55,150	10,446	7,539	10,446	9,279
55,150	55,200	10,459	7,546	10,459	9,291
55,200	55,250	10,471	7,554	10,471	9,304
55,250	55,300	10,484	7,561	10,484	9,316
55,300	55,350	10,496	7,569	10,496	9,329
55,350	55,400	10,509	7,576	10,509	9,341
55,400	55,450	10,521	7,584	10,521	9,354
55,450	55,500	10,534	7,591	10,534	9,366
55,500	55,550	10,546	7,599	10,546	9,379
55,550	55,600	10,559	7,606	10,559	9,391
55,600	55,650	10,571	7,614	10,571	9,404
55,650	55,700	10,584	7,621	10,584	9,416
55,700	55,750	10,596	7,629	10,596	9,429
55,750	55,800	10,609	7,636	10,609	9,441
55,800	55,850	10,621	7,644	10,621	9,454
55,850	55,900	10,634	7,651	10,634	9,466
55,900	55,950	10,646	7,659	10,646	9,479
55,950	56,000	10,659	7,666	10,659	9,491

If line 43 (taxable income) is— At least	But less than	And you are— Single	Married filing jointly *	Married filing separately	Head of a household
56,000					
56,000	56,050	10,671	7,674	10,671	9,504
56,050	56,100	10,684	7,681	10,684	9,516
56,100	56,150	10,696	7,689	10,696	9,529
56,150	56,200	10,709	7,696	10,709	9,541
56,200	56,250	10,721	7,704	10,721	9,554
56,250	56,300	10,734	7,711	10,734	9,566
56,300	56,350	10,746	7,719	10,746	9,579
56,350	56,400	10,759	7,726	10,759	9,591
56,400	56,450	10,771	7,734	10,771	9,604
56,450	56,500	10,784	7,741	10,784	9,616
56,500	56,550	10,796	7,749	10,796	9,629
56,550	56,600	10,809	7,756	10,809	9,641
56,600	56,650	10,821	7,764	10,821	9,654
56,650	56,700	10,834	7,771	10,834	9,666
56,700	56,750	10,846	7,779	10,846	9,679
56,750	56,800	10,859	7,786	10,859	9,691
56,800	56,850	10,871	7,794	10,871	9,704
56,850	56,900	10,884	7,801	10,884	9,716
56,900	56,950	10,896	7,809	10,896	9,729
56,950	57,000	10,909	7,816	10,909	9,741
57,000					
57,000	57,050	10,921	7,824	10,921	9,754
57,050	57,100	10,934	7,831	10,934	9,766
57,100	57,150	10,946	7,839	10,946	9,779
57,150	57,200	10,959	7,846	10,959	9,791
57,200	57,250	10,971	7,854	10,971	9,804
57,250	57,300	10,984	7,861	10,984	9,816
57,300	57,350	10,996	7,869	10,996	9,829
57,350	57,400	11,009	7,876	11,009	9,841
57,400	57,450	11,021	7,884	11,021	9,854
57,450	57,500	11,034	7,891	11,034	9,866
57,500	57,550	11,046	7,899	11,046	9,879
57,550	57,600	11,059	7,906	11,059	9,891
57,600	57,650	11,071	7,914	11,071	9,904
57,650	57,700	11,084	7,921	11,084	9,916
57,700	57,750	11,096	7,929	11,096	9,929
57,750	57,800	11,109	7,936	11,109	9,941
57,800	57,850	11,121	7,944	11,121	9,954
57,850	57,900	11,134	7,951	11,134	9,966
57,900	57,950	11,146	7,959	11,146	9,979
57,950	58,000	11,159	7,966	11,159	9,991
58,000					
58,000	58,050	11,171	7,974	11,171	10,004
58,050	58,100	11,184	7,981	11,184	10,016
58,100	58,150	11,196	7,989	11,196	10,029
58,150	58,200	11,209	7,996	11,209	10,041
58,200	58,250	11,221	8,004	11,221	10,054
58,250	58,300	11,234	8,011	11,234	10,066
58,300	58,350	11,246	8,019	11,246	10,079
58,350	58,400	11,259	8,026	11,259	10,091
58,400	58,450	11,271	8,034	11,271	10,104
58,450	58,500	11,284	8,041	11,284	10,116
58,500	58,550	11,296	8,049	11,296	10,129
58,550	58,600	11,309	8,056	11,309	10,141
58,600	58,650	11,321	8,064	11,321	10,154
58,650	58,700	11,334	8,071	11,334	10,166
58,700	58,750	11,346	8,079	11,346	10,179
58,750	58,800	11,359	8,086	11,359	10,191
58,800	58,850	11,371	8,094	11,371	10,204
58,850	58,900	11,384	8,101	11,384	10,216
58,900	58,950	11,396	8,109	11,396	10,229
58,950	59,000	11,409	8,116	11,409	10,241

* This column must also be used by a qualifying widow(er).

(Continued on page 72)

2005 Tax Table—Continued

Left column group

If line 43 (taxable income) is— At least	But less than	Single	Married filing jointly *	Married filing separately	Head of a household
59,000					
59,000	59,050	11,421	8,124	11,421	10,254
59,050	59,100	11,434	8,131	11,434	10,266
59,100	59,150	11,446	8,139	11,446	10,279
59,150	59,200	11,459	8,146	11,459	10,291
59,200	59,250	11,471	8,154	11,471	10,304
59,250	59,300	11,484	8,161	11,484	10,316
59,300	59,350	11,496	8,169	11,496	10,329
59,350	59,400	11,509	8,176	11,509	10,341
59,400	59,450	11,521	8,186	11,521	10,354
59,450	59,500	11,534	8,199	11,534	10,366
59,500	59,550	11,546	8,211	11,546	10,379
59,550	59,600	11,559	8,224	11,559	10,391
59,600	59,650	11,571	8,236	11,571	10,404
59,650	59,700	11,584	8,249	11,584	10,416
59,700	59,750	11,596	8,261	11,596	10,429
59,750	59,800	11,609	8,274	11,609	10,441
59,800	59,850	11,621	8,286	11,621	10,454
59,850	59,900	11,634	8,299	11,634	10,466
59,900	59,950	11,646	8,311	11,646	10,479
59,950	60,000	11,659	8,324	11,659	10,491
60,000					
60,000	60,050	11,671	8,336	11,673	10,504
60,050	60,100	11,684	8,349	11,687	10,516
60,100	60,150	11,696	8,361	11,701	10,529
60,150	60,200	11,709	8,374	11,715	10,541
60,200	60,250	11,721	8,386	11,729	10,554
60,250	60,300	11,734	8,399	11,743	10,566
60,300	60,350	11,746	8,411	11,757	10,579
60,350	60,400	11,759	8,424	11,771	10,591
60,400	60,450	11,771	8,436	11,785	10,604
60,450	60,500	11,784	8,449	11,799	10,616
60,500	60,550	11,796	8,461	11,813	10,629
60,550	60,600	11,809	8,474	11,827	10,641
60,600	60,650	11,821	8,486	11,841	10,654
60,650	60,700	11,834	8,499	11,855	10,666
60,700	60,750	11,846	8,511	11,869	10,679
60,750	60,800	11,859	8,524	11,883	10,691
60,800	60,850	11,871	8,536	11,897	10,704
60,850	60,900	11,884	8,549	11,911	10,716
60,900	60,950	11,896	8,561	11,925	10,729
60,950	61,000	11,909	8,574	11,939	10,741
61,000					
61,000	61,050	11,921	8,586	11,953	10,754
61,050	61,100	11,934	8,599	11,967	10,766
61,100	61,150	11,946	8,611	11,981	10,779
61,150	61,200	11,959	8,624	11,995	10,791
61,200	61,250	11,971	8,636	12,009	10,804
61,250	61,300	11,984	8,649	12,023	10,816
61,300	61,350	11,996	8,661	12,037	10,829
61,350	61,400	12,009	8,674	12,051	10,841
61,400	61,450	12,021	8,686	12,065	10,854
61,450	61,500	12,034	8,699	12,079	10,866
61,500	61,550	12,046	8,711	12,093	10,879
61,550	61,600	12,059	8,724	12,107	10,891
61,600	61,650	12,071	8,736	12,121	10,904
61,650	61,700	12,084	8,749	12,135	10,916
61,700	61,750	12,096	8,761	12,149	10,929
61,750	61,800	12,109	8,774	12,163	10,941
61,800	61,850	12,121	8,786	12,177	10,954
61,850	61,900	12,134	8,799	12,191	10,966
61,900	61,950	12,146	8,811	12,205	10,979
61,950	62,000	12,159	8,824	12,219	10,991

Middle column group

If line 43 (taxable income) is— At least	But less than	Single	Married filing jointly *	Married filing separately	Head of a household
62,000					
62,000	62,050	12,171	8,836	12,233	11,004
62,050	62,100	12,184	8,849	12,247	11,016
62,100	62,150	12,196	8,861	12,261	11,029
62,150	62,200	12,209	8,874	12,275	11,041
62,200	62,250	12,221	8,886	12,289	11,054
62,250	62,300	12,234	8,899	12,303	11,066
62,300	62,350	12,246	8,911	12,317	11,079
62,350	62,400	12,259	8,924	12,331	11,091
62,400	62,450	12,271	8,936	12,345	11,104
62,450	62,500	12,284	8,949	12,359	11,116
62,500	62,550	12,296	8,961	12,373	11,129
62,550	62,600	12,309	8,974	12,387	11,141
62,600	62,650	12,321	8,986	12,401	11,154
62,650	62,700	12,334	8,999	12,415	11,166
62,700	62,750	12,346	9,011	12,429	11,179
62,750	62,800	12,359	9,024	12,443	11,191
62,800	62,850	12,371	9,036	12,457	11,204
62,850	62,900	12,384	9,049	12,471	11,216
62,900	62,950	12,396	9,061	12,485	11,229
62,950	63,000	12,409	9,074	12,499	11,241
63,000					
63,000	63,050	12,421	9,086	12,513	11,254
63,050	63,100	12,434	9,099	12,527	11,266
63,100	63,150	12,446	9,111	12,541	11,279
63,150	63,200	12,459	9,124	12,555	11,291
63,200	63,250	12,471	9,136	12,569	11,304
63,250	63,300	12,484	9,149	12,583	11,316
63,300	63,350	12,496	9,161	12,597	11,329
63,350	63,400	12,509	9,174	12,611	11,341
63,400	63,450	12,521	9,186	12,625	11,354
63,450	63,500	12,534	9,199	12,639	11,366
63,500	63,550	12,546	9,211	12,653	11,379
63,550	63,600	12,559	9,224	12,667	11,391
63,600	63,650	12,571	9,236	12,681	11,404
63,650	63,700	12,584	9,249	12,695	11,416
63,700	63,750	12,596	9,261	12,709	11,429
63,750	63,800	12,609	9,274	12,723	11,441
63,800	63,850	12,621	9,286	12,737	11,454
63,850	63,900	12,634	9,299	12,751	11,466
63,900	63,950	12,646	9,311	12,765	11,479
63,950	64,000	12,659	9,324	12,779	11,491
64,000					
64,000	64,050	12,671	9,336	12,793	11,504
64,050	64,100	12,684	9,349	12,807	11,516
64,100	64,150	12,696	9,361	12,821	11,529
64,150	64,200	12,709	9,374	12,835	11,541
64,200	64,250	12,721	9,386	12,849	11,554
64,250	64,300	12,734	9,399	12,863	11,566
64,300	64,350	12,746	9,411	12,877	11,579
64,350	64,400	12,759	9,424	12,891	11,591
64,400	64,450	12,771	9,436	12,905	11,604
64,450	64,500	12,784	9,449	12,919	11,616
64,500	64,550	12,796	9,461	12,933	11,629
64,550	64,600	12,809	9,474	12,947	11,641
64,600	64,650	12,821	9,486	12,961	11,654
64,650	64,700	12,834	9,499	12,975	11,666
64,700	64,750	12,846	9,511	12,989	11,679
64,750	64,800	12,859	9,524	13,003	11,691
64,800	64,850	12,871	9,536	13,017	11,704
64,850	64,900	12,884	9,549	13,031	11,716
64,900	64,950	12,896	9,561	13,045	11,729
64,950	65,000	12,909	9,574	13,059	11,741

Right column group

If line 43 (taxable income) is— At least	But less than	Single	Married filing jointly *	Married filing separately	Head of a household
65,000					
65,000	65,050	12,921	9,586	13,073	11,754
65,050	65,100	12,934	9,599	13,087	11,766
65,100	65,150	12,946	9,611	13,101	11,779
65,150	65,200	12,959	9,624	13,115	11,791
65,200	65,250	12,971	9,636	13,129	11,804
65,250	65,300	12,984	9,649	13,143	11,816
65,300	65,350	12,996	9,661	13,157	11,829
65,350	65,400	13,009	9,674	13,171	11,841
65,400	65,450	13,021	9,686	13,185	11,854
65,450	65,500	13,034	9,699	13,199	11,866
65,500	65,550	13,046	9,711	13,213	11,879
65,550	65,600	13,059	9,724	13,227	11,891
65,600	65,650	13,071	9,736	13,241	11,904
65,650	65,700	13,084	9,749	13,255	11,916
65,700	65,750	13,096	9,761	13,269	11,929
65,750	65,800	13,109	9,774	13,283	11,941
65,800	65,850	13,121	9,786	13,297	11,954
65,850	65,900	13,134	9,799	13,311	11,966
65,900	65,950	13,146	9,811	13,325	11,979
65,950	66,000	13,159	9,824	13,339	11,991
66,000					
66,000	66,050	13,171	9,836	13,353	12,004
66,050	66,100	13,184	9,849	13,367	12,016
66,100	66,150	13,196	9,861	13,381	12,029
66,150	66,200	13,209	9,874	13,395	12,041
66,200	66,250	13,221	9,886	13,409	12,054
66,250	66,300	13,234	9,899	13,423	12,066
66,300	66,350	13,246	9,911	13,437	12,079
66,350	66,400	13,259	9,924	13,451	12,091
66,400	66,450	13,271	9,936	13,465	12,104
66,450	66,500	13,284	9,949	13,479	12,116
66,500	66,550	13,296	9,961	13,493	12,129
66,550	66,600	13,309	9,974	13,507	12,141
66,600	66,650	13,321	9,986	13,521	12,154
66,650	66,700	13,334	9,999	13,535	12,166
66,700	66,750	13,346	10,011	13,549	12,179
66,750	66,800	13,359	10,024	13,563	12,191
66,800	66,850	13,371	10,036	13,577	12,204
66,850	66,900	13,384	10,049	13,591	12,216
66,900	66,950	13,396	10,061	13,605	12,229
66,950	67,000	13,409	10,074	13,619	12,241
67,000					
67,000	67,050	13,421	10,086	13,633	12,254
67,050	67,100	13,434	10,099	13,647	12,266
67,100	67,150	13,446	10,111	13,661	12,279
67,150	67,200	13,459	10,124	13,675	12,291
67,200	67,250	13,471	10,136	13,689	12,304
67,250	67,300	13,484	10,149	13,703	12,316
67,300	67,350	13,496	10,161	13,717	12,329
67,350	67,400	13,509	10,174	13,731	12,341
67,400	67,450	13,521	10,186	13,745	12,354
67,450	67,500	13,534	10,199	13,759	12,366
67,500	67,550	13,546	10,211	13,773	12,379
67,550	67,600	13,559	10,224	13,787	12,391
67,600	67,650	13,571	10,236	13,801	12,404
67,650	67,700	13,584	10,249	13,815	12,416
67,700	67,750	13,596	10,261	13,829	12,429
67,750	67,800	13,609	10,274	13,843	12,441
67,800	67,850	13,621	10,286	13,857	12,454
67,850	67,900	13,634	10,299	13,871	12,466
67,900	67,950	13,646	10,311	13,885	12,479
67,950	68,000	13,659	10,324	13,899	12,491

* This column must also be used by a qualifying widow(er).

(Continued on page 73)

2005 Tax Table—*Continued*

If line 43 (taxable income) is—		And you are—			
At least	But less than	Single	Married filing jointly *	Married filing separately	Head of a household
		Your tax is—			

68,000

At least	But less than	Single	Married filing jointly *	Married filing separately	Head of a household
68,000	68,050	13,671	10,336	13,913	12,504
68,050	68,100	13,684	10,349	13,927	12,516
68,100	68,150	13,696	10,361	13,941	12,529
68,150	68,200	13,709	10,374	13,955	12,541
68,200	68,250	13,721	10,386	13,969	12,554
68,250	68,300	13,734	10,399	13,983	12,566
68,300	68,350	13,746	10,411	13,997	12,579
68,350	68,400	13,759	10,424	14,011	12,591
68,400	68,450	13,771	10,436	14,025	12,604
68,450	68,500	13,784	10,449	14,039	12,616
68,500	68,550	13,796	10,461	14,053	12,629
68,550	68,600	13,809	10,474	14,067	12,641
68,600	68,650	13,821	10,486	14,081	12,654
68,650	68,700	13,834	10,499	14,095	12,666
68,700	68,750	13,846	10,511	14,109	12,679
68,750	68,800	13,859	10,524	14,123	12,691
68,800	68,850	13,871	10,536	14,137	12,704
68,850	68,900	13,884	10,549	14,151	12,716
68,900	68,950	13,896	10,561	14,165	12,729
68,950	69,000	13,909	10,574	14,179	12,741

69,000

At least	But less than	Single	Married filing jointly *	Married filing separately	Head of a household
69,000	69,050	13,921	10,586	14,193	12,754
69,050	69,100	13,934	10,599	14,207	12,766
69,100	69,150	13,946	10,611	14,221	12,779
69,150	69,200	13,959	10,624	14,235	12,791
69,200	69,250	13,971	10,636	14,249	12,804
69,250	69,300	13,984	10,649	14,263	12,816
69,300	69,350	13,996	10,661	14,277	12,829
69,350	69,400	14,009	10,674	14,291	12,841
69,400	69,450	14,021	10,686	14,305	12,854
69,450	69,500	14,034	10,699	14,319	12,866
69,500	69,550	14,046	10,711	14,333	12,879
69,550	69,600	14,059	10,724	14,347	12,891
69,600	69,650	14,071	10,736	14,361	12,904
69,650	69,700	14,084	10,749	14,375	12,916
69,700	69,750	14,096	10,761	14,389	12,929
69,750	69,800	14,109	10,774	14,403	12,941
69,800	69,850	14,121	10,786	14,417	12,954
69,850	69,900	14,134	10,799	14,431	12,966
69,900	69,950	14,146	10,811	14,445	12,979
69,950	70,000	14,159	10,824	14,459	12,991

70,000

At least	But less than	Single	Married filing jointly *	Married filing separately	Head of a household
70,000	70,050	14,171	10,836	14,473	13,004
70,050	70,100	14,184	10,849	14,487	13,016
70,100	70,150	14,196	10,861	14,501	13,029
70,150	70,200	14,209	10,874	14,515	13,041
70,200	70,250	14,221	10,886	14,529	13,054
70,250	70,300	14,234	10,899	14,543	13,066
70,300	70,350	14,246	10,911	14,557	13,079
70,350	70,400	14,259	10,924	14,571	13,091
70,400	70,450	14,271	10,936	14,585	13,104
70,450	70,500	14,284	10,949	14,599	13,116
70,500	70,550	14,296	10,961	14,613	13,129
70,550	70,600	14,309	10,974	14,627	13,141
70,600	70,650	14,321	10,986	14,641	13,154
70,650	70,700	14,334	10,999	14,655	13,166
70,700	70,750	14,346	11,011	14,669	13,179
70,750	70,800	14,359	11,024	14,683	13,191
70,800	70,850	14,371	11,036	14,697	13,204
70,850	70,900	14,384	11,049	14,711	13,216
70,900	70,950	14,396	11,061	14,725	13,229
70,950	71,000	14,409	11,074	14,739	13,241

71,000

At least	But less than	Single	Married filing jointly *	Married filing separately	Head of a household
71,000	71,050	14,421	11,086	14,753	13,254
71,050	71,100	14,434	11,099	14,767	13,266
71,100	71,150	14,446	11,111	14,781	13,279
71,150	71,200	14,459	11,124	14,795	13,291
71,200	71,250	14,471	11,136	14,809	13,304
71,250	71,300	14,484	11,149	14,823	13,316
71,300	71,350	14,496	11,161	14,837	13,329
71,350	71,400	14,509	11,174	14,851	13,341
71,400	71,450	14,521	11,186	14,865	13,354
71,450	71,500	14,534	11,199	14,879	13,366
71,500	71,550	14,546	11,211	14,893	13,379
71,550	71,600	14,559	11,224	14,907	13,391
71,600	71,650	14,571	11,236	14,921	13,404
71,650	71,700	14,584	11,249	14,935	13,416
71,700	71,750	14,596	11,261	14,949	13,429
71,750	71,800	14,609	11,274	14,963	13,441
71,800	71,850	14,621	11,286	14,977	13,454
71,850	71,900	14,634	11,299	14,991	13,466
71,900	71,950	14,646	11,311	15,005	13,479
71,950	72,000	14,660	11,324	15,019	13,491

72,000

At least	But less than	Single	Married filing jointly *	Married filing separately	Head of a household
72,000	72,050	14,674	11,336	15,033	13,504
72,050	72,100	14,688	11,349	15,047	13,516
72,100	72,150	14,702	11,361	15,061	13,529
72,150	72,200	14,716	11,374	15,075	13,541
72,200	72,250	14,730	11,386	15,089	13,554
72,250	72,300	14,744	11,399	15,103	13,566
72,300	72,350	14,758	11,411	15,117	13,579
72,350	72,400	14,772	11,424	15,131	13,591
72,400	72,450	14,786	11,436	15,145	13,604
72,450	72,500	14,800	11,449	15,159	13,616
72,500	72,550	14,814	11,461	15,173	13,629
72,550	72,600	14,828	11,474	15,187	13,641
72,600	72,650	14,842	11,486	15,201	13,654
72,650	72,700	14,856	11,499	15,215	13,666
72,700	72,750	14,870	11,511	15,229	13,679
72,750	72,800	14,884	11,524	15,243	13,691
72,800	72,850	14,898	11,536	15,257	13,704
72,850	72,900	14,912	11,549	15,271	13,716
72,900	72,950	14,926	11,561	15,285	13,729
72,950	73,000	14,940	11,574	15,299	13,741

73,000

At least	But less than	Single	Married filing jointly *	Married filing separately	Head of a household
73,000	73,050	14,954	11,586	15,313	13,754
73,050	73,100	14,968	11,599	15,327	13,766
73,100	73,150	14,982	11,611	15,341	13,779
73,150	73,200	14,996	11,624	15,355	13,791
73,200	73,250	15,010	11,636	15,369	13,804
73,250	73,300	15,024	11,649	15,383	13,816
73,300	73,350	15,038	11,661	15,397	13,829
73,350	73,400	15,052	11,674	15,411	13,841
73,400	73,450	15,066	11,686	15,425	13,854
73,450	73,500	15,080	11,699	15,439	13,866
73,500	73,550	15,094	11,711	15,453	13,879
73,550	73,600	15,108	11,724	15,467	13,891
73,600	73,650	15,122	11,736	15,481	13,904
73,650	73,700	15,136	11,749	15,495	13,916
73,700	73,750	15,150	11,761	15,509	13,929
73,750	73,800	15,164	11,774	15,523	13,941
73,800	73,850	15,178	11,786	15,537	13,954
73,850	73,900	15,192	11,799	15,551	13,966
73,900	73,950	15,206	11,811	15,565	13,979
73,950	74,000	15,220	11,824	15,579	13,991

74,000

At least	But less than	Single	Married filing jointly *	Married filing separately	Head of a household
74,000	74,050	15,234	11,836	15,593	14,004
74,050	74,100	15,248	11,849	15,607	14,016
74,100	74,150	15,262	11,861	15,621	14,029
74,150	74,200	15,276	11,874	15,635	14,041
74,200	74,250	15,290	11,886	15,649	14,054
74,250	74,300	15,304	11,899	15,663	14,066
74,300	74,350	15,318	11,911	15,677	14,079
74,350	74,400	15,332	11,924	15,691	14,091
74,400	74,450	15,346	11,936	15,705	14,104
74,450	74,500	15,360	11,949	15,719	14,116
74,500	74,550	15,374	11,961	15,733	14,129
74,550	74,600	15,388	11,974	15,747	14,141
74,600	74,650	15,402	11,986	15,761	14,154
74,650	74,700	15,416	11,999	15,775	14,166
74,700	74,750	15,430	12,011	15,789	14,179
74,750	74,800	15,444	12,024	15,803	14,191
74,800	74,850	15,458	12,036	15,817	14,204
74,850	74,900	15,472	12,049	15,831	14,216
74,900	74,950	15,486	12,061	15,845	14,229
74,950	75,000	15,500	12,074	15,859	14,241

75,000

At least	But less than	Single	Married filing jointly *	Married filing separately	Head of a household
75,000	75,050	15,514	12,086	15,873	14,254
75,050	75,100	15,528	12,099	15,887	14,266
75,100	75,150	15,542	12,111	15,901	14,279
75,150	75,200	15,556	12,124	15,915	14,291
75,200	75,250	15,570	12,136	15,929	14,304
75,250	75,300	15,584	12,149	15,943	14,316
75,300	75,350	15,598	12,161	15,957	14,329
75,350	75,400	15,612	12,174	15,971	14,341
75,400	75,450	15,626	12,186	15,985	14,354
75,450	75,500	15,640	12,199	15,999	14,366
75,500	75,550	15,654	12,211	16,013	14,379
75,550	75,600	15,668	12,224	16,027	14,391
75,600	75,650	15,682	12,236	16,041	14,404
75,650	75,700	15,696	12,249	16,055	14,416
75,700	75,750	15,710	12,261	16,069	14,429
75,750	75,800	15,724	12,274	16,083	14,441
75,800	75,850	15,738	12,286	16,097	14,454
75,850	75,900	15,752	12,299	16,111	14,466
75,900	75,950	15,766	12,311	16,125	14,479
75,950	76,000	15,780	12,324	16,139	14,491

76,000

At least	But less than	Single	Married filing jointly *	Married filing separately	Head of a household
76,000	76,050	15,794	12,336	16,153	14,504
76,050	76,100	15,808	12,349	16,167	14,516
76,100	76,150	15,822	12,361	16,181	14,529
76,150	76,200	15,836	12,374	16,195	14,541
76,200	76,250	15,850	12,386	16,209	14,554
76,250	76,300	15,864	12,399	16,223	14,566
76,300	76,350	15,878	12,411	16,237	14,579
76,350	76,400	15,892	12,424	16,251	14,591
76,400	76,450	15,906	12,436	16,265	14,604
76,450	76,500	15,920	12,449	16,279	14,616
76,500	76,550	15,934	12,461	16,293	14,629
76,550	76,600	15,948	12,474	16,307	14,641
76,600	76,650	15,962	12,486	16,321	14,654
76,650	76,700	15,976	12,499	16,335	14,666
76,700	76,750	15,990	12,511	16,349	14,679
76,750	76,800	16,004	12,524	16,363	14,691
76,800	76,850	16,018	12,536	16,377	14,704
76,850	76,900	16,032	12,549	16,391	14,716
76,900	76,950	16,046	12,561	16,405	14,729
76,950	77,000	16,060	12,574	16,419	14,741

* This column must also be used by a qualifying widow(er).

(Continued on page 74)

2005 Tax Table—Continued

If line 43 (taxable income) is—		And you are—				If line 43 (taxable income) is—		And you are—				If line 43 (taxable income) is—		And you are—			
At least	But less than	Single	Married filing jointly *	Married filing separately	Head of a household	At least	But less than	Single	Married filing jointly *	Married filing separately	Head of a household	At least	But less than	Single	Married filing jointly *	Married filing separately	Head of a household
		Your tax is—						Your tax is—						Your tax is—			
77,000						**80,000**						**83,000**					
77,000	77,050	16,074	12,586	16,433	14,754	80,000	80,050	16,914	13,336	17,273	15,504	83,000	83,050	17,754	14,086	18,113	16,254
77,050	77,100	16,088	12,599	16,447	14,766	80,050	80,100	16,928	13,349	17,287	15,516	83,050	83,100	17,768	14,099	18,127	16,266
77,100	77,150	16,102	12,611	16,461	14,779	80,100	80,150	16,942	13,361	17,301	15,529	83,100	83,150	17,782	14,111	18,141	16,279
77,150	77,200	16,116	12,624	16,475	14,791	80,150	80,200	16,956	13,374	17,315	15,541	83,150	83,200	17,796	14,124	18,155	16,291
77,200	77,250	16,130	12,636	16,489	14,804	80,200	80,250	16,970	13,386	17,329	15,554	83,200	83,250	17,810	14,136	18,169	16,304
77,250	77,300	16,144	12,649	16,503	14,816	80,250	80,300	16,984	13,399	17,343	15,566	83,250	83,300	17,824	14,149	18,183	16,316
77,300	77,350	16,158	12,661	16,517	14,829	80,300	80,350	16,998	13,411	17,357	15,579	83,300	83,350	17,838	14,161	18,197	16,329
77,350	77,400	16,172	12,674	16,531	14,841	80,350	80,400	17,012	13,424	17,371	15,591	83,350	83,400	17,852	14,174	18,211	16,341
77,400	77,450	16,186	12,686	16,545	14,854	80,400	80,450	17,026	13,436	17,385	15,604	83,400	83,450	17,866	14,186	18,225	16,354
77,450	77,500	16,200	12,699	16,559	14,866	80,450	80,500	17,040	13,449	17,399	15,616	83,450	83,500	17,880	14,199	18,239	16,366
77,500	77,550	16,214	12,711	16,573	14,879	80,500	80,550	17,054	13,461	17,413	15,629	83,500	83,550	17,894	14,211	18,253	16,379
77,550	77,600	16,228	12,724	16,587	14,891	80,550	80,600	17,068	13,474	17,427	15,641	83,550	83,600	17,908	14,224	18,267	16,391
77,600	77,650	16,242	12,736	16,601	14,904	80,600	80,650	17,082	13,486	17,441	15,654	83,600	83,650	17,922	14,236	18,281	16,404
77,650	77,700	16,256	12,749	16,615	14,916	80,650	80,700	17,096	13,499	17,455	15,666	83,650	83,700	17,936	14,249	18,295	16,416
77,700	77,750	16,270	12,761	16,629	14,929	80,700	80,750	17,110	13,511	17,469	15,679	83,700	83,750	17,950	14,261	18,309	16,429
77,750	77,800	16,284	12,774	16,643	14,941	80,750	80,800	17,124	13,524	17,483	15,691	83,750	83,800	17,964	14,274	18,323	16,441
77,800	77,850	16,298	12,786	16,657	14,954	80,800	80,850	17,138	13,536	17,497	15,704	83,800	83,850	17,978	14,286	18,337	16,454
77,850	77,900	16,312	12,799	16,671	14,966	80,850	80,900	17,152	13,549	17,511	15,716	83,850	83,900	17,992	14,299	18,351	16,466
77,900	77,950	16,326	12,811	16,685	14,979	80,900	80,950	17,166	13,561	17,525	15,729	83,900	83,950	18,006	14,311	18,365	16,479
77,950	78,000	16,340	12,824	16,699	14,991	80,950	81,000	17,180	13,574	17,539	15,741	83,950	84,000	18,020	14,324	18,379	16,491
78,000						**81,000**						**84,000**					
78,000	78,050	16,354	12,836	16,713	15,004	81,000	81,050	17,194	13,586	17,553	15,754	84,000	84,050	18,034	14,336	18,393	16,504
78,050	78,100	16,368	12,849	16,727	15,016	81,050	81,100	17,208	13,599	17,567	15,766	84,050	84,100	18,048	14,349	18,407	16,516
78,100	78,150	16,382	12,861	16,741	15,029	81,100	81,150	17,222	13,611	17,581	15,779	84,100	84,150	18,062	14,361	18,421	16,529
78,150	78,200	16,396	12,874	16,755	15,041	81,150	81,200	17,236	13,624	17,595	15,791	84,150	84,200	18,076	14,374	18,435	16,541
78,200	78,250	16,410	12,886	16,769	15,054	81,200	81,250	17,250	13,636	17,609	15,804	84,200	84,250	18,090	14,386	18,449	16,554
78,250	78,300	16,424	12,899	16,783	15,066	81,250	81,300	17,264	13,649	17,623	15,816	84,250	84,300	18,104	14,399	18,463	16,566
78,300	78,350	16,438	12,911	16,797	15,079	81,300	81,350	17,278	13,661	17,637	15,829	84,300	84,350	18,118	14,411	18,477	16,579
78,350	78,400	16,452	12,924	16,811	15,091	81,350	81,400	17,292	13,674	17,651	15,841	84,350	84,400	18,132	14,424	18,491	16,591
78,400	78,450	16,466	12,936	16,825	15,104	81,400	81,450	17,306	13,686	17,665	15,854	84,400	84,450	18,146	14,436	18,505	16,604
78,450	78,500	16,480	12,949	16,839	15,116	81,450	81,500	17,320	13,699	17,679	15,866	84,450	84,500	18,160	14,449	18,519	16,616
78,500	78,550	16,494	12,961	16,853	15,129	81,500	81,550	17,334	13,711	17,693	15,879	84,500	84,550	18,174	14,461	18,533	16,629
78,550	78,600	16,508	12,974	16,867	15,141	81,550	81,600	17,348	13,724	17,707	15,891	84,550	84,600	18,188	14,474	18,547	16,641
78,600	78,650	16,522	12,986	16,881	15,154	81,600	81,650	17,362	13,736	17,721	15,904	84,600	84,650	18,202	14,486	18,561	16,654
78,650	78,700	16,536	12,999	16,895	15,166	81,650	81,700	17,376	13,749	17,735	15,916	84,650	84,700	18,216	14,499	18,575	16,666
78,700	78,750	16,550	13,011	16,909	15,179	81,700	81,750	17,390	13,761	17,749	15,929	84,700	84,750	18,230	14,511	18,589	16,679
78,750	78,800	16,564	13,024	16,923	15,191	81,750	81,800	17,404	13,774	17,763	15,941	84,750	84,800	18,244	14,524	18,603	16,691
78,800	78,850	16,578	13,036	16,937	15,204	81,800	81,850	17,418	13,786	17,777	15,954	84,800	84,850	18,258	14,536	18,617	16,704
78,850	78,900	16,592	13,049	16,951	15,216	81,850	81,900	17,432	13,799	17,791	15,966	84,850	84,900	18,272	14,549	18,631	16,716
78,900	78,950	16,606	13,061	16,965	15,229	81,900	81,950	17,446	13,811	17,805	15,979	84,900	84,950	18,286	14,561	18,645	16,729
78,950	79,000	16,620	13,074	16,979	15,241	81,950	82,000	17,460	13,824	17,819	15,991	84,950	85,000	18,300	14,574	18,659	16,741
79,000						**82,000**						**85,000**					
79,000	79,050	16,634	13,086	16,993	15,254	82,000	82,050	17,474	13,836	17,833	16,004	85,000	85,050	18,314	14,586	18,673	16,754
79,050	79,100	16,648	13,099	17,007	15,266	82,050	82,100	17,488	13,849	17,847	16,016	85,050	85,100	18,328	14,599	18,687	16,766
79,100	79,150	16,662	13,111	17,021	15,279	82,100	82,150	17,502	13,861	17,861	16,029	85,100	85,150	18,342	14,611	18,701	16,779
79,150	79,200	16,676	13,124	17,035	15,291	82,150	82,200	17,516	13,874	17,875	16,041	85,150	85,200	18,356	14,624	18,715	16,791
79,200	79,250	16,690	13,136	17,049	15,304	82,200	82,250	17,530	13,886	17,889	16,054	85,200	85,250	18,370	14,636	18,729	16,804
79,250	79,300	16,704	13,149	17,063	15,316	82,250	82,300	17,544	13,899	17,903	16,066	85,250	85,300	18,384	14,649	18,743	16,816
79,300	79,350	16,718	13,161	17,077	15,329	82,300	82,350	17,558	13,911	17,917	16,079	85,300	85,350	18,398	14,661	18,757	16,829
79,350	79,400	16,732	13,174	17,091	15,341	82,350	82,400	17,572	13,924	17,931	16,091	85,350	85,400	18,412	14,674	18,771	16,841
79,400	79,450	16,746	13,186	17,105	15,354	82,400	82,450	17,586	13,936	17,945	16,104	85,400	85,450	18,426	14,686	18,785	16,854
79,450	79,500	16,760	13,199	17,119	15,366	82,450	82,500	17,600	13,949	17,959	16,116	85,450	85,500	18,440	14,699	18,799	16,866
79,500	79,550	16,774	13,211	17,133	15,379	82,500	82,550	17,614	13,961	17,973	16,129	85,500	85,550	18,454	14,711	18,813	16,879
79,550	79,600	16,788	13,224	17,147	15,391	82,550	82,600	17,628	13,974	17,987	16,141	85,550	85,600	18,468	14,724	18,827	16,891
79,600	79,650	16,802	13,236	17,161	15,404	82,600	82,650	17,642	13,986	18,001	16,154	85,600	85,650	18,482	14,736	18,841	16,904
79,650	79,700	16,816	13,249	17,175	15,416	82,650	82,700	17,656	13,999	18,015	16,166	85,650	85,700	18,496	14,749	18,855	16,916
79,700	79,750	16,830	13,261	17,189	15,429	82,700	82,750	17,670	14,011	18,029	16,179	85,700	85,750	18,510	14,761	18,869	16,929
79,750	79,800	16,844	13,274	17,203	15,441	82,750	82,800	17,684	14,024	18,043	16,191	85,750	85,800	18,524	14,774	18,883	16,941
79,800	79,850	16,858	13,286	17,217	15,454	82,800	82,850	17,698	14,036	18,057	16,204	85,800	85,850	18,538	14,786	18,897	16,954
79,850	79,900	16,872	13,299	17,231	15,466	82,850	82,900	17,712	14,049	18,071	16,216	85,850	85,900	18,552	14,799	18,911	16,966
79,900	79,950	16,886	13,311	17,245	15,479	82,900	82,950	17,726	14,061	18,085	16,229	85,900	85,950	18,566	14,811	18,925	16,979
79,950	80,000	16,900	13,324	17,259	15,491	82,950	83,000	17,740	14,074	18,099	16,241	85,950	86,000	18,580	14,824	18,939	16,991

* This column must also be used by a qualifying widow(er).

(Continued on page 75)

2005 Tax Table—Continued

86,000 / 87,000 / 88,000

At least	But less than	Single	Married filing jointly*	Married filing separately	Head of a household
86,000					
86,000	86,050	18,594	14,836	18,953	17,004
86,050	86,100	18,608	14,849	18,967	17,016
86,100	86,150	18,622	14,861	18,981	17,029
86,150	86,200	18,636	14,874	18,995	17,041
86,200	86,250	18,650	14,886	19,009	17,054
86,250	86,300	18,664	14,899	19,023	17,066
86,300	86,350	18,678	14,911	19,037	17,079
86,350	86,400	18,692	14,924	19,051	17,091
86,400	86,450	18,706	14,936	19,065	17,104
86,450	86,500	18,720	14,949	19,079	17,116
86,500	86,550	18,734	14,961	19,093	17,129
86,550	86,600	18,748	14,974	19,107	17,141
86,600	86,650	18,762	14,986	19,121	17,154
86,650	86,700	18,776	14,999	19,135	17,166
86,700	86,750	18,790	15,011	19,149	17,179
86,750	86,800	18,804	15,024	19,163	17,191
86,800	86,850	18,818	15,036	19,177	17,204
86,850	86,900	18,832	15,049	19,191	17,216
86,900	86,950	18,846	15,061	19,205	17,229
86,950	87,000	18,860	15,074	19,219	17,241
87,000					
87,000	87,050	18,874	15,086	19,233	17,254
87,050	87,100	18,888	15,099	19,247	17,266
87,100	87,150	18,902	15,111	19,261	17,279
87,150	87,200	18,916	15,124	19,275	17,291
87,200	87,250	18,930	15,136	19,289	17,304
87,250	87,300	18,944	15,149	19,303	17,316
87,300	87,350	18,958	15,161	19,317	17,329
87,350	87,400	18,972	15,174	19,331	17,341
87,400	87,450	18,986	15,186	19,345	17,354
87,450	87,500	19,000	15,199	19,359	17,366
87,500	87,550	19,014	15,211	19,373	17,379
87,550	87,600	19,028	15,224	19,387	17,391
87,600	87,650	19,042	15,236	19,401	17,404
87,650	87,700	19,056	15,249	19,415	17,416
87,700	87,750	19,070	15,261	19,429	17,429
87,750	87,800	19,084	15,274	19,443	17,441
87,800	87,850	19,098	15,286	19,457	17,454
87,850	87,900	19,112	15,299	19,471	17,466
87,900	87,950	19,126	15,311	19,485	17,479
87,950	88,000	19,140	15,324	19,499	17,491
88,000					
88,000	88,050	19,154	15,336	19,513	17,504
88,050	88,100	19,168	15,349	19,527	17,516
88,100	88,150	19,182	15,361	19,541	17,529
88,150	88,200	19,196	15,374	19,555	17,541
88,200	88,250	19,210	15,386	19,569	17,554
88,250	88,300	19,224	15,399	19,583	17,566
88,300	88,350	19,238	15,411	19,597	17,579
88,350	88,400	19,252	15,424	19,611	17,591
88,400	88,450	19,266	15,436	19,625	17,604
88,450	88,500	19,280	15,449	19,639	17,616
88,500	88,550	19,294	15,461	19,653	17,629
88,550	88,600	19,308	15,474	19,667	17,641
88,600	88,650	19,322	15,486	19,681	17,654
88,650	88,700	19,336	15,499	19,695	17,666
88,700	88,750	19,350	15,511	19,709	17,679
88,750	88,800	19,364	15,524	19,723	17,691
88,800	88,850	19,378	15,536	19,737	17,704
88,850	88,900	19,392	15,549	19,751	17,716
88,900	88,950	19,406	15,561	19,765	17,729
88,950	89,000	19,420	15,574	19,779	17,741

89,000 / 90,000 / 91,000

At least	But less than	Single	Married filing jointly*	Married filing separately	Head of a household
89,000					
89,000	89,050	19,434	15,586	19,793	17,754
89,050	89,100	19,448	15,599	19,807	17,766
89,100	89,150	19,462	15,611	19,821	17,779
89,150	89,200	19,476	15,624	19,835	17,791
89,200	89,250	19,490	15,636	19,849	17,804
89,250	89,300	19,504	15,649	19,863	17,816
89,300	89,350	19,518	15,661	19,877	17,829
89,350	89,400	19,532	15,674	19,891	17,841
89,400	89,450	19,546	15,686	19,905	17,854
89,450	89,500	19,560	15,699	19,919	17,866
89,500	89,550	19,574	15,711	19,933	17,879
89,550	89,600	19,588	15,724	19,947	17,891
89,600	89,650	19,602	15,736	19,961	17,904
89,650	89,700	19,616	15,749	19,975	17,916
89,700	89,750	19,630	15,761	19,989	17,929
89,750	89,800	19,644	15,774	20,003	17,941
89,800	89,850	19,658	15,786	20,017	17,954
89,850	89,900	19,672	15,799	20,031	17,966
89,900	89,950	19,686	15,811	20,045	17,979
89,950	90,000	19,700	15,824	20,059	17,991
90,000					
90,000	90,050	19,714	15,836	20,073	18,004
90,050	90,100	19,728	15,849	20,087	18,016
90,100	90,150	19,742	15,861	20,101	18,029
90,150	90,200	19,756	15,874	20,115	18,041
90,200	90,250	19,770	15,886	20,129	18,054
90,250	90,300	19,784	15,899	20,143	18,066
90,300	90,350	19,798	15,911	20,157	18,079
90,350	90,400	19,812	15,924	20,171	18,091
90,400	90,450	19,826	15,936	20,185	18,104
90,450	90,500	19,840	15,949	20,199	18,116
90,500	90,550	19,854	15,961	20,213	18,129
90,550	90,600	19,868	15,974	20,227	18,141
90,600	90,650	19,882	15,986	20,241	18,154
90,650	90,700	19,896	15,999	20,255	18,166
90,700	90,750	19,910	16,011	20,269	18,179
90,750	90,800	19,924	16,024	20,283	18,191
90,800	90,850	19,938	16,036	20,297	18,204
90,850	90,900	19,952	16,049	20,311	18,216
90,900	90,950	19,966	16,061	20,325	18,229
90,950	91,000	19,980	16,074	20,339	18,241
91,000					
91,000	91,050	19,994	16,086	20,353	18,254
91,050	91,100	20,008	16,099	20,367	18,266
91,100	91,150	20,022	16,111	20,381	18,279
91,150	91,200	20,036	16,124	20,395	18,291
91,200	91,250	20,050	16,136	20,409	18,304
91,250	91,300	20,064	16,149	20,423	18,316
91,300	91,350	20,078	16,161	20,437	18,329
91,350	91,400	20,092	16,174	20,451	18,341
91,400	91,450	20,106	16,186	20,466	18,354
91,450	91,500	20,120	16,199	20,483	18,366
91,500	91,550	20,134	16,211	20,499	18,379
91,550	91,600	20,148	16,224	20,516	18,391
91,600	91,650	20,162	16,236	20,532	18,404
91,650	91,700	20,176	16,249	20,549	18,416
91,700	91,750	20,190	16,261	20,565	18,429
91,750	91,800	20,204	16,274	20,582	18,441
91,800	91,850	20,218	16,286	20,598	18,454
91,850	91,900	20,232	16,299	20,615	18,466
91,900	91,950	20,246	16,311	20,631	18,479
91,950	92,000	20,260	16,324	20,648	18,491

92,000 / 93,000 / 94,000

At least	But less than	Single	Married filing jointly*	Married filing separately	Head of a household
92,000					
92,000	92,050	20,274	16,336	20,664	18,504
92,050	92,100	20,288	16,349	20,681	18,516
92,100	92,150	20,302	16,361	20,697	18,529
92,150	92,200	20,316	16,374	20,714	18,541
92,200	92,250	20,330	16,386	20,730	18,554
92,250	92,300	20,344	16,399	20,747	18,566
92,300	92,350	20,358	16,411	20,763	18,579
92,350	92,400	20,372	16,424	20,780	18,591
92,400	92,450	20,386	16,436	20,796	18,604
92,450	92,500	20,400	16,449	20,813	18,616
92,500	92,550	20,414	16,461	20,829	18,629
92,550	92,600	20,428	16,474	20,846	18,641
92,600	92,650	20,442	16,486	20,862	18,654
92,650	92,700	20,456	16,499	20,879	18,666
92,700	92,750	20,470	16,511	20,895	18,679
92,750	92,800	20,484	16,524	20,912	18,691
92,800	92,850	20,498	16,536	20,928	18,704
92,850	92,900	20,512	16,549	20,945	18,716
92,900	92,950	20,526	16,561	20,961	18,729
92,950	93,000	20,540	16,574	20,978	18,741
93,000					
93,000	93,050	20,554	16,586	20,994	18,754
93,050	93,100	20,568	16,599	21,011	18,766
93,100	93,150	20,582	16,611	21,027	18,779
93,150	93,200	20,596	16,624	21,044	18,791
93,200	93,250	20,610	16,636	21,060	18,804
93,250	93,300	20,624	16,649	21,077	18,816
93,300	93,350	20,638	16,661	21,093	18,829
93,350	93,400	20,652	16,674	21,110	18,841
93,400	93,450	20,666	16,686	21,126	18,854
93,450	93,500	20,680	16,699	21,143	18,866
93,500	93,550	20,694	16,711	21,159	18,879
93,550	93,600	20,708	16,724	21,176	18,891
93,600	93,650	20,722	16,736	21,192	18,904
93,650	93,700	20,736	16,749	21,209	18,916
93,700	93,750	20,750	16,761	21,225	18,929
93,750	93,800	20,764	16,774	21,242	18,941
93,800	93,850	20,778	16,786	21,258	18,954
93,850	93,900	20,792	16,799	21,275	18,966
93,900	93,950	20,806	16,811	21,291	18,979
93,950	94,000	20,820	16,824	21,308	18,991
94,000					
94,000	94,050	20,834	16,836	21,324	19,004
94,050	94,100	20,848	16,849	21,341	19,016
94,100	94,150	20,862	16,861	21,357	19,029
94,150	94,200	20,876	16,874	21,374	19,041
94,200	94,250	20,890	16,886	21,390	19,054
94,250	94,300	20,904	16,899	21,407	19,066
94,300	94,350	20,918	16,911	21,423	19,079
94,350	94,400	20,932	16,924	21,440	19,091
94,400	94,450	20,946	16,936	21,456	19,104
94,450	94,500	20,960	16,949	21,473	19,116
94,500	94,550	20,974	16,961	21,489	19,129
94,550	94,600	20,988	16,974	21,506	19,141
94,600	94,650	21,002	16,986	21,522	19,154
94,650	94,700	21,016	16,999	21,539	19,166
94,700	94,750	21,030	17,011	21,555	19,179
94,750	94,800	21,044	17,024	21,572	19,191
94,800	94,850	21,058	17,036	21,588	19,204
94,850	94,900	21,072	17,049	21,605	19,216
94,900	94,950	21,086	17,061	21,621	19,229
94,950	95,000	21,100	17,074	21,638	19,241

* This column must also be used by a qualifying widow(er).

(Continued on page 76)

2005 Tax Table—Continued

If line 43 (taxable income) is—		And you are—				If line 43 (taxable income) is—		And you are—			
At least	But less than	Single	Married filing jointly *	Married filing separately	Head of a household	At least	But less than	Single	Married filing jointly *	Married filing separately	Head of a household
		Your tax is—						Your tax is—			

95,000 / 98,000

At least	But less than	Single	MFJ*	MFS	HoH	At least	But less than	Single	MFJ*	MFS	HoH
95,000	95,050	21,114	17,086	21,654	19,254	98,000	98,050	21,954	17,836	22,644	20,004
95,050	95,100	21,128	17,099	21,671	19,266	98,050	98,100	21,968	17,849	22,661	20,016
95,100	95,150	21,142	17,111	21,687	19,279	98,100	98,150	21,982	17,861	22,677	20,029
95,150	95,200	21,156	17,124	21,704	19,291	98,150	98,200	21,996	17,874	22,694	20,041
95,200	95,250	21,170	17,136	21,720	19,304	98,200	98,250	22,010	17,886	22,710	20,054
95,250	95,300	21,184	17,149	21,737	19,316	98,250	98,300	22,024	17,899	22,727	20,066
95,300	95,350	21,198	17,161	21,753	19,329	98,300	98,350	22,038	17,911	22,743	20,079
95,350	95,400	21,212	17,174	21,770	19,341	98,350	98,400	22,052	17,924	22,760	20,091
95,400	95,450	21,226	17,186	21,786	19,354	98,400	98,450	22,066	17,936	22,776	20,104
95,450	95,500	21,240	17,199	21,803	19,366	98,450	98,500	22,080	17,949	22,793	20,116
95,500	95,550	21,254	17,211	21,819	19,379	98,500	98,550	22,094	17,961	22,809	20,129
95,550	95,600	21,268	17,224	21,836	19,391	98,550	98,600	22,108	17,974	22,826	20,141
95,600	95,650	21,282	17,236	21,852	19,404	98,600	98,650	22,122	17,986	22,842	20,154
95,650	95,700	21,296	17,249	21,869	19,416	98,650	98,700	22,136	17,999	22,859	20,166
95,700	95,750	21,310	17,261	21,885	19,429	98,700	98,750	22,150	18,011	22,875	20,179
95,750	95,800	21,324	17,274	21,902	19,441	98,750	98,800	22,164	18,024	22,892	20,191
95,800	95,850	21,338	17,286	21,918	19,454	98,800	98,850	22,178	18,036	22,908	20,204
95,850	95,900	21,352	17,299	21,935	19,466	98,850	98,900	22,192	18,049	22,925	20,216
95,900	95,950	21,366	17,311	21,951	19,479	98,900	98,950	22,206	18,061	22,941	20,229
95,950	96,000	21,380	17,324	21,968	19,491	98,950	99,000	22,220	18,074	22,958	20,241

96,000 / 99,000

At least	But less than	Single	MFJ*	MFS	HoH	At least	But less than	Single	MFJ*	MFS	HoH
96,000	96,050	21,394	17,336	21,984	19,504	99,000	99,050	22,234	18,086	22,974	20,254
96,050	96,100	21,408	17,349	22,001	19,516	99,050	99,100	22,248	18,099	22,991	20,266
96,100	96,150	21,422	17,361	22,017	19,529	99,100	99,150	22,262	18,111	23,007	20,279
96,150	96,200	21,436	17,374	22,034	19,541	99,150	99,200	22,276	18,124	23,024	20,291
96,200	96,250	21,450	17,386	22,050	19,554	99,200	99,250	22,290	18,136	23,040	20,304
96,250	96,300	21,464	17,399	22,067	19,566	99,250	99,300	22,304	18,149	23,057	20,316
96,300	96,350	21,478	17,411	22,083	19,579	99,300	99,350	22,318	18,161	23,073	20,329
96,350	96,400	21,492	17,424	22,100	19,591	99,350	99,400	22,332	18,174	23,090	20,341
96,400	96,450	21,506	17,436	22,116	19,604	99,400	99,450	22,346	18,186	23,106	20,354
96,450	96,500	21,520	17,449	22,133	19,616	99,450	99,500	22,360	18,199	23,123	20,366
96,500	96,550	21,534	17,461	22,149	19,629	99,500	99,550	22,374	18,211	23,139	20,379
96,550	96,600	21,548	17,474	22,166	19,641	99,550	99,600	22,388	18,224	23,156	20,391
96,600	96,650	21,562	17,486	22,182	19,654	99,600	99,650	22,402	18,236	23,172	20,404
96,650	96,700	21,576	17,499	22,199	19,666	99,650	99,700	22,416	18,249	23,189	20,416
96,700	96,750	21,590	17,511	22,215	19,679	99,700	99,750	22,430	18,261	23,205	20,429
96,750	96,800	21,604	17,524	22,232	19,691	99,750	99,800	22,444	18,274	23,222	20,441
96,800	96,850	21,618	17,536	22,248	19,704	99,800	99,850	22,458	18,286	23,238	20,454
96,850	96,900	21,632	17,549	22,265	19,716	99,850	99,900	22,472	18,299	23,255	20,466
96,900	96,950	21,646	17,561	22,281	19,729	99,900	99,950	22,486	18,311	23,271	20,479
96,950	97,000	21,660	17,574	22,298	19,741	99,950	100,000	22,500	18,324	23,288	20,491

97,000

At least	But less than	Single	Married filing jointly *	Married filing separately	Head of a household
97,000	97,050	21,674	17,586	22,314	19,754
97,050	97,100	21,688	17,599	22,331	19,766
97,100	97,150	21,702	17,611	22,347	19,779
97,150	97,200	21,716	17,624	22,364	19,791
97,200	97,250	21,730	17,636	22,380	19,804
97,250	97,300	21,744	17,649	22,397	19,816
97,300	97,350	21,758	17,661	22,413	19,829
97,350	97,400	21,772	17,674	22,430	19,841
97,400	97,450	21,786	17,686	22,446	19,854
97,450	97,500	21,800	17,699	22,463	19,866
97,500	97,550	21,814	17,711	22,479	19,879
97,550	97,600	21,828	17,724	22,496	19,891
97,600	97,650	21,842	17,736	22,512	19,904
97,650	97,700	21,856	17,749	22,529	19,916
97,700	97,750	21,870	17,761	22,545	19,929
97,750	97,800	21,884	17,774	22,562	19,941
97,800	97,850	21,898	17,786	22,578	19,954
97,850	97,900	21,912	17,799	22,595	19,966
97,900	97,950	21,926	17,811	22,611	19,979
97,950	98,000	21,940	17,824	22,628	19,991

$100,000 or over — use the Tax Computation Worksheet on page 77

* This column must also be used by a qualifying widow(er).

2005 Tax Rate Schedules

The Tax Rate Schedules are shown so you can see the tax rate that applies to all levels of taxable income. Do not use them to figure your tax. Instead, see the instructions for line 44 that begin on page 37.

Schedule X—If your filing status is **Single**

If your taxable income is:		The tax is:	of the amount
Over—	But not over—		over—
$0	$7,300	.... 10%	$0
7,300	29,700	$730.00 + 15%	7,300
29,700	71,950	4,090.00 + 25%	29,700
71,950	150,150	14,652.50 + 28%	71,950
150,150	326,450	36,548.50 + 33%	150,150
326,450	....	94,727.50 + 35%	326,450

Schedule Y-1—If your filing status is **Married filing jointly** or **Qualifying widow(er)**

If your taxable income is:		The tax is:	of the amount
Over—	But not over—		over—
$0	$14,600	.... 10%	$0
14,600	59,400	$1,460.00 + 15%	14,600
59,400	119,950	8,180.00 + 25%	59,400
119,950	182,800	23,317.50 + 28%	119,950
182,800	326,450	40,915.50 + 33%	182,800
326,450	....	88,320.00 + 35%	326,450

Schedule Y-2—If your filing status is **Married filing separately**

If your taxable income is:		The tax is:	of the amount
Over—	But not over—		over—
$0	$7,300	.... 10%	$0
7,300	29,700	$730.00 + 15%	7,300
29,700	59,975	4,090.00 + 25%	29,700
59,975	91,400	11,658.75 + 28%	59,975
91,400	163,225	20,457.75 + 33%	91,400
163,225	....	44,160.00 + 35%	163,225

Schedule Z—If your filing status is **Head of household**

If your taxable income is:		The tax is:	of the amount
Over—	But not over—		over—
$0	$10,450	.... 10%	$0
10,450	39,800	$1,045.00 + 15%	10,450
39,800	102,800	5,447.50 + 25%	39,800
102,800	166,450	21,197.50 + 28%	102,800
166,450	326,450	39,019.50 + 33%	166,450
326,450	....	91,819.50 + 35%	326,450

SINGLE Persons—MONTHLY Payroll Period

(For Wages Paid in 2006)

If the wages are—		And the number of withholding allowances claimed is—										
At least	But less than	0	1	2	3	4	5	6	7	8	9	10
		The amount of income tax to be withheld is—										
$0	$220	$0	$0	$0	$0	$0	$0	$0	$0	$0	$0	$0
220	230	0	0	0	0	0	0	0	0	0	0	0
230	240	1	0	0	0	0	0	0	0	0	0	0
240	250	2	0	0	0	0	0	0	0	0	0	0
250	260	3	0	0	0	0	0	0	0	0	0	0
260	270	4	0	0	0	0	0	0	0	0	0	0
270	280	5	0	0	0	0	0	0	0	0	0	0
280	290	6	0	0	0	0	0	0	0	0	0	0
290	300	7	0	0	0	0	0	0	0	0	0	0
300	320	9	0	0	0	0	0	0	0	0	0	0
320	340	11	0	0	0	0	0	0	0	0	0	0
340	360	13	0	0	0	0	0	0	0	0	0	0
360	380	15	0	0	0	0	0	0	0	0	0	0
380	400	17	0	0	0	0	0	0	0	0	0	0
400	420	19	0	0	0	0	0	0	0	0	0	0
420	440	21	0	0	0	0	0	0	0	0	0	0
440	460	23	0	0	0	0	0	0	0	0	0	0
460	480	25	0	0	0	0	0	0	0	0	0	0
480	500	27	0	0	0	0	0	0	0	0	0	0
500	520	29	1	0	0	0	0	0	0	0	0	0
520	540	31	3	0	0	0	0	0	0	0	0	0
540	560	33	5	0	0	0	0	0	0	0	0	0
560	580	35	7	0	0	0	0	0	0	0	0	0
580	600	37	9	0	0	0	0	0	0	0	0	0
600	640	40	12	0	0	0	0	0	0	0	0	0
640	680	44	16	0	0	0	0	0	0	0	0	0
680	720	48	20	0	0	0	0	0	0	0	0	0
720	760	52	24	0	0	0	0	0	0	0	0	0
760	800	56	28	1	0	0	0	0	0	0	0	0
800	840	60	32	5	0	0	0	0	0	0	0	0
840	880	65	36	9	0	0	0	0	0	0	0	0
880	920	71	40	13	0	0	0	0	0	0	0	0
920	960	77	44	17	0	0	0	0	0	0	0	0
960	1,000	83	48	21	0	0	0	0	0	0	0	0
1,000	1,040	89	52	25	0	0	0	0	0	0	0	0
1,040	1,080	95	56	29	1	0	0	0	0	0	0	0
1,080	1,120	101	60	33	5	0	0	0	0	0	0	0
1,120	1,160	107	66	37	9	0	0	0	0	0	0	0
1,160	1,200	113	72	41	13	0	0	0	0	0	0	0
1,200	1,240	119	78	45	17	0	0	0	0	0	0	0
1,240	1,280	125	84	49	21	0	0	0	0	0	0	0
1,280	1,320	131	90	53	25	0	0	0	0	0	0	0
1,320	1,360	137	96	57	29	2	0	0	0	0	0	0
1,360	1,400	143	102	61	33	6	0	0	0	0	0	0
1,400	1,440	149	108	67	37	10	0	0	0	0	0	0
1,440	1,480	155	114	73	41	14	0	0	0	0	0	0
1,480	1,520	161	120	79	45	18	0	0	0	0	0	0
1,520	1,560	167	126	85	49	22	0	0	0	0	0	0
1,560	1,600	173	132	91	53	26	0	0	0	0	0	0
1,600	1,640	179	138	97	57	30	2	0	0	0	0	0
1,640	1,680	185	144	103	62	34	6	0	0	0	0	0
1,680	1,720	191	150	109	68	38	10	0	0	0	0	0
1,720	1,760	197	156	115	74	42	14	0	0	0	0	0
1,760	1,800	203	162	121	80	46	18	0	0	0	0	0
1,800	1,840	209	168	127	86	50	22	0	0	0	0	0
1,840	1,880	215	174	133	92	54	26	0	0	0	0	0
1,880	1,920	221	180	139	98	58	30	3	0	0	0	0
1,920	1,960	227	186	145	104	62	34	7	0	0	0	0
1,960	2,000	233	192	151	110	68	38	11	0	0	0	0
2,000	2,040	239	198	157	116	74	42	15	0	0	0	0
2,040	2,080	245	204	163	122	80	46	19	0	0	0	0
2,080	2,120	251	210	169	128	86	50	23	0	0	0	0
2,120	2,160	257	216	175	134	92	54	27	0	0	0	0
2,160	2,200	263	222	181	140	98	58	31	3	0	0	0
2,200	2,240	269	228	187	146	104	63	35	7	0	0	0
2,240	2,280	275	234	193	152	110	69	39	11	0	0	0
2,280	2,320	281	240	199	158	116	75	43	15	0	0	0
2,320	2,360	287	246	205	164	122	81	47	19	0	0	0
2,360	2,400	293	252	211	170	128	87	51	23	0	0	0
2,400	2,440	299	258	217	176	134	93	55	27	0	0	0

MARRIED Persons—MONTHLY Payroll Period

(For Wages Paid in 2006)

If the wages are—		And the number of withholding allowances claimed is—										
At least	But less than	0	1	2	3	4	5	6	7	8	9	10
		The amount of income tax to be withheld is—										
$0	$540	$0	$0	$0	$0	$0	$0	$0	$0	$0	$0	$0
540	560	0	0	0	0	0	0	0	0	0	0	0
560	580	0	0	0	0	0	0	0	0	0	0	0
580	600	0	0	0	0	0	0	0	0	0	0	0
600	640	0	0	0	0	0	0	0	0	0	0	0
640	680	0	0	0	0	0	0	0	0	0	0	0
680	720	3	0	0	0	0	0	0	0	0	0	0
720	760	7	0	0	0	0	0	0	0	0	0	0
760	800	11	0	0	0	0	0	0	0	0	0	0
800	840	15	0	0	0	0	0	0	0	0	0	0
840	880	19	0	0	0	0	0	0	0	0	0	0
880	920	23	0	0	0	0	0	0	0	0	0	0
920	960	27	0	0	0	0	0	0	0	0	0	0
960	1,000	31	4	0	0	0	0	0	0	0	0	0
1,000	1,040	35	8	0	0	0	0	0	0	0	0	0
1,040	1,080	39	12	0	0	0	0	0	0	0	0	0
1,080	1,120	43	16	0	0	0	0	0	0	0	0	0
1,120	1,160	47	20	0	0	0	0	0	0	0	0	0
1,160	1,200	51	24	0	0	0	0	0	0	0	0	0
1,200	1,240	55	28	0	0	0	0	0	0	0	0	0
1,240	1,280	59	32	4	0	0	0	0	0	0	0	0
1,280	1,320	63	36	8	0	0	0	0	0	0	0	0
1,320	1,360	67	40	12	0	0	0	0	0	0	0	0
1,360	1,400	71	44	16	0	0	0	0	0	0	0	0
1,400	1,440	75	48	20	0	0	0	0	0	0	0	0
1,440	1,480	79	52	24	0	0	0	0	0	0	0	0
1,480	1,520	83	56	28	1	0	0	0	0	0	0	0
1,520	1,560	87	60	32	5	0	0	0	0	0	0	0
1,560	1,600	91	64	36	9	0	0	0	0	0	0	0
1,600	1,640	95	68	40	13	0	0	0	0	0	0	0
1,640	1,680	99	72	44	17	0	0	0	0	0	0	0
1,680	1,720	103	76	48	21	0	0	0	0	0	0	0
1,720	1,760	107	80	52	25	0	0	0	0	0	0	0
1,760	1,800	111	84	56	29	1	0	0	0	0	0	0
1,800	1,840	115	88	60	33	5	0	0	0	0	0	0
1,840	1,880	119	92	64	37	9	0	0	0	0	0	0
1,880	1,920	123	96	68	41	13	0	0	0	0	0	0
1,920	1,960	129	100	72	45	17	0	0	0	0	0	0
1,960	2,000	135	104	76	49	21	0	0	0	0	0	0
2,000	2,040	141	108	80	53	25	0	0	0	0	0	0
2,040	2,080	147	112	84	57	29	2	0	0	0	0	0
2,080	2,120	153	116	88	61	33	6	0	0	0	0	0
2,120	2,160	159	120	92	65	37	10	0	0	0	0	0
2,160	2,200	165	124	96	69	41	14	0	0	0	0	0
2,200	2,240	171	130	100	73	45	18	0	0	0	0	0
2,240	2,280	177	136	104	77	49	22	0	0	0	0	0
2,280	2,320	183	142	108	81	53	26	0	0	0	0	0
2,320	2,360	189	148	112	85	57	30	2	0	0	0	0
2,360	2,400	195	154	116	89	61	34	6	0	0	0	0
2,400	2,440	201	160	120	93	65	38	10	0	0	0	0
2,440	2,480	207	166	124	97	69	42	14	0	0	0	0
2,480	2,520	213	172	130	101	73	46	18	0	0	0	0
2,520	2,560	219	178	136	105	77	50	22	0	0	0	0
2,560	2,600	225	184	142	109	81	54	26	0	0	0	0
2,600	2,640	231	190	148	113	85	58	30	3	0	0	0
2,640	2,680	237	196	154	117	89	62	34	7	0	0	0
2,680	2,720	243	202	160	121	93	66	38	11	0	0	0
2,720	2,760	249	208	166	125	97	70	42	15	0	0	0
2,760	2,800	255	214	172	131	101	74	46	19	0	0	0
2,800	2,840	261	220	178	137	105	78	50	23	0	0	0
2,840	2,880	267	226	184	143	109	82	54	27	0	0	0
2,880	2,920	273	232	190	149	113	86	58	31	3	0	0
2,920	2,960	279	238	196	155	117	90	62	35	7	0	0
2,960	3,000	285	244	202	161	121	94	66	39	11	0	0
3,000	3,040	291	250	208	167	126	98	70	43	15	0	0
3,040	3,080	297	256	214	173	132	102	74	47	19	0	0
3,080	3,120	303	262	220	179	138	106	78	51	23	0	0
3,120	3,160	309	268	226	185	144	110	82	55	27	0	0
3,160	3,200	315	274	232	191	150	114	86	59	31	4	0
3,200	3,240	321	280	238	197	156	118	90	63	35	8	0

APPENDIX A

TAX RESEARCH WORKING PAPER FILE

INDEX TO TAX RESEARCH FILE*

*Most accounting firms maintain a **client file** for each of their clients. Typically, this file contains copies of client letters, memoranda-to-the-file, relevant primary and secondary authorities, and billing information. In our case, the client file for Mercy Hospital would include copies of the following: (1) the September 12 letter to Elizabeth Feghali, (2) the September 9 memorandum-to-the-file, (3) Sec. 119, (4) Reg. Sec. 1.119-1, (5) the *Kowalski* opinion, (6) the *Standard Federal Tax Reporter* annotation, and (7) pertinent billing information.

TAX RESEARCH FILE

As mentioned in Chapter C1 the tax research process entails six steps.

1. Determine the facts
2. Identify the issues
3. Locate applicable authorities
4. Evaluate these authorities
5. Analyze the facts in terms of applicable authorities
6. Communicate conclusions and recommendations to others.

Let us walk through each of these steps.

Determine the Facts   Assume that we have determined the facts to be as follows:

> *Mercy Hospital maintains a cafeteria on its premises. In addition, it rents space to MacDougal's, a privately owned sandwich shop. The cafeteria closes at 8:00 p.m. MacDougal's is open 24 hours. Mercy provides meal vouchers to each of its 240 medical employees to enable them to remain on call in case of emergency. The vouchers are redeemable either at the cafeteria or at MacDougal's. Although the employees are not required to remain on or near the premises during meal hours, they generally do. Elizabeth Fegali, Mercy's Chief Administrator, has approached you with the following question: Is the value of a meal voucher includible in the employees' gross income?*

At this juncture, be sure you understand the facts before proceeding further. Remember, researching the wrong facts could produce the wrong results.

Identify the Issues   Identifying the issues presupposes a minimum level of proficiency in tax accounting. This proficiency will come with time, effort, and perseverance. The central issue raised by the facts is the taxability of the meal vouchers. A resolution of this issue will hinge on the resolution of other issues raised in the course of the research.

Locate Applicable Authorities   For some students, this step is the most difficult in the research process. It raises the perplexing question, "Where do I begin to look?" The answer depends on the tax resources at one's disposal, as well as one's research preferences. Four rules of thumb apply:

1. *Adopt an approach with which you are comfortable, and that you are confident will produce reliable results.*
2. *Always consult the IRC and other primary authorities.*
3. *Be as thorough as possible, taking into consideration time and billing constraints.*
4. *Make sure that the authorities you consult are current.*

One approach is to conduct a topical search. Begin by consulting the index to the Internal Revenue Code (IRC). Then read the relevant IRC section(s). If the language of the IRC is vague or ambiguous, turn to the Treasury Regulations. Read the relevant regulation section that elaborates or expounds on the IRC provision. If the language of the regulation is confusing or unclear, go to a commercial tax service. Read the relevant tax service paragraphs that explain or analyze the statutory and regulatory provisions. For references to other authorities, browse through the footnotes and annotations of the service. Then, consult these authorities directly. Finally, check the currency of the authorities consulted, with the aid of a citator or status (finding) list.

If a pertinent court decision or IRS ruling has been called to your attention, consult this authority directly. Alternatively, browse through the status (finding) list of a tax service for references to tax service paragraphs that discuss this authority. Better still, consult a citator or status list for references to court opinions or rulings that cite the authority. If you subscribe to a computerized tax service, conduct a keyword, citation, contents, or topical search. (For a discussion of these types of searches, see the computerized research supplement available for download at *www.prenhall.com/phtax*.) Then, hyperlink to the authorities cited within the text of the documents retrieved. So numerous are the approaches to tax research that one is virtually free to pick and choose. All that is required of the researcher is a basic level of skill and some imagination.

Let us adopt a topical approach to the issue of the meal vouchers. If we consult an index to the IRC, we are likely to find the heading "Meals and Lodging." Below this heading are likely to be several subheadings, some pertaining to deductions, others to exclusions. Because the voucher issue pertains to an exclusion, let us browse through these subheadings. In so doing, we will notice that most of these subheadings refer to Sec. 119. If we look up this IRC section, we will see the following passage:

Sec. 119. Meals or lodging furnished for the convenience of the employer.

(a) Meals and lodging furnished to employee, his spouse, and his dependents, pursuant to employment.
There shall be excluded from gross income of an employee the value of any meals or lodging furnished to him . . . by, or on behalf of his employer for the convenience of the employer, but only if—

(1) in the case of meals, the meals are furnished on the business premises of the employer . . .

(b) Special rules. For purposes of subsection (a)—
(4) Meals furnished to employees on business premises where meals of most employees are otherwise excludable. All meals furnished on the business premises of an employer to such employer's employees shall be treated as furnished for the convenience of the employer if . . . more than half of the employees to whom such meals are furnished on such premises are furnished such meals for the convenience of the employer.

Section 119 appears to be applicable. It deals with meals furnished to an employee on the business premises of the employer. Our case deals with meal vouchers furnished to employees for redemption at employer-maintained and employer-rented-out facilities. But here, additional issues arise. For purposes of Sec. 119, are meal vouchers the same as "meals"? (Do not assume they are.) Are employer-maintained and employer-rented-out facilities the same as "the business premises of the employer"? (Again, do not assume they are.) And what does the IRC mean by "for the convenience of the employer"? Because the IRC offers no guidance in this respect, let us turn to the Treasury Regulations.

The applicable regulation is Reg. Sec. 1.119-1. How do we know this? Because Treasury Regulation section numbers track the IRC section numbers. Regulation Sec. 1.119-1 is the only regulation under Sec. 119. If we browse through this regulation, we will find the following provision:

(a) Meals . . .
(2) Meals furnished without a charge
(i) Meals furnished by an employer without charge to the employee will be regarded as furnished for the convenience of the employer if such meals are furnished for a substantial noncompensatory business reason of the employer . . .
(ii) (a) Meals will be regarded as furnished for a substantial noncompensatory business reason of the employer when the meals are furnished to the employee during his working hours to have the employee available for emergency call during his meal period . . .
(c) Business premises of the employer.
(1) In general. For purposes of this section, the term "business premises of the employer" generally means the place of employment of the employee . . .

Based on a reading of this provision, we might conclude that the hospital meals are furnished "for the convenience of the employer." Why? Because they are furnished for a "substantial noncompensatory business reason of the employer," namely, to have the employees available for emergency call during their meal periods. They also are furnished during the employees' working hours. Moreover, under Sec. 119(b)(4), if more than half the employees satisfy the "for the convenience of the employer" test, all employees will be regarded as satisfying the test. But are the meals furnished on "the business premises of the employer"? Under the regulation, the answer would depend. If the meals are furnished in the hospital cafeteria, they probably are furnished on "the business premises of the employer." The hospital is the place of employment of the medical employees. The cafeteria is part of the hospital. On the other hand, if the meals are furnished at MacDougal's, they probably are not furnished on "the business premises of the employer." MacDougals's is not the place of employment of the medical employees. Nor is it a part of the hospital. Thus, Reg. Sec. 1.119-1 is enlightening with respect to two statutory terms: "for the convenience of the employer" and "the business premises of the employer." However, it is obscure with respect to the third term, "meals." Because of this obscurity, let us turn to a tax service.

Although the index to CCH's *Standard Federal Tax Reporter* does not list "meal vouchers," it does list "cash allowances in lieu of meals" as a subtopic under Meals and Lodging. Are meal vouchers the same as cash meal allowances?—perhaps so; let us see. Next to the heading "cash allowances in lieu of meals" is a reference to CCH ¶7222.59. If we look up this reference, we will find the following annotation:

¶7222.59 **Meal allowances.**—Cash meal allowances received by an employee (state trooper) from his employer were not excludible from income. *R.J. Kowalski*, SCt, 77-2 USTC ¶9748, 434 US 77.[1]

Here we discover that, in the *Kowalski* case, the U.S. Supreme Court decided that cash meal allowances received by an employee were not excludible from the employee's income. Is the *Kowalski* case similar to our case? It might be. Let us find out. If we turn to paragraph 9748 of the second 1977 volume of *United States Tax Cases*, we will find the text of the *Kowalski* opinion. A synopsis of this opinion is present below.

In the mid-1970s, the State of New Jersey provided cash meal allowances to its state troopers. The state did not require the troopers to use the allowances exclusively for meals. Nor did it require them to consume their meals on its business premises. One trooper, Robert J. Kowalski, failed to report a portion of his allowance on his tax return. The IRS assessed a deficiency, and Kowalski took the IRS to court. In court, Kowalski argued that the meal allowances were excludible, because they were furnished "for the convenience of the employer." The IRS contended that the allowances were taxable because they amounted to compensation. The Supreme Court took up the case and sided with the IRS. The Court held that the Sec. 119 income exclusion does not apply to cash payments; it applies only to meals in kind.[2]

For the sake of illustration, let us assume that Sec. 119, Reg. Sec. 1.119-1, and the *Kowalski* case are the *only* authorities "on point." How should we evaluate them?

Evaluate Authorities   Section 119 is the key authority applicable to our case. It supplies the operative rule for resolving the issue of the meal vouchers. It is vague, however, with respect to three terms: "meals," "business premises of the employer," and "for the convenience of the employer." The principal judicial authority is the *Kowalski* case. It provides an official interpretation of the term "meals." Because the U.S. Supreme Court decided *Kowalski*, the case should be assigned considerable weight. The relevant administrative authority is Reg. Sec. 1.119-1. It expounds on the terms "business premises of the employer" and "for the convenience of the employer." Because neither the IRC nor *Kowalski* explain these terms, Reg. Sec. 1.119-1 should be accorded great weight. But what if *Kowalski* had conflicted with Reg. Sec. 1.119-1? Which should be considered more authoritative? As a general rule, high court decisions "trump" the Treasury Regulations (and all IRS pronouncements for that matter). The more recent the decision, the greater its precedential weight. Had there been no Supreme Court decision and a division of appellate authority, equal weight should have been assigned to each of the appellate court decisions.

Analyze the Facts in Terms of Applicable Authorities   Analyzing the facts in terms of applicable authorities involves applying the abstraction of the law to the concreteness of the facts. It entails expressing the generalities of the law in terms of the specifics of the facts. In this process, every legal condition must be satisfied for the result implied by the

---

[1] The researcher also might read the main *Standard Federal Tax Reporter* paragraph that discusses meals and lodging furnished by the employer (CCH ¶7222.01). Within this paragraph are likely to be references to other primary authorities.

[2] At this juncture, the researcher should consult a citator to determine whether *Kowalski* is still "good law," and to locate other authorities that cite *Kowalski*.

general rule to ensue. Thus, in our case, the conditions of furnishing "meals," "on the business premises of the employer," and "for the convenience of the employer" must be satisfied for the value of the "meals" to be excluded from the employee's income.

When analyzing the facts in terms of case law, the researcher should always draw an *analogy* between case facts and client facts. Likewise, he or she should always draw a *distinction* between case facts and client facts. Remember, under the rule of precedent, a court deciding the client's case will be bound by the precedent of cases involving *similar* facts and issues. By the same token, it will *not* be bound by the precedent of cases involving *dissimilar* facts and issues.

The most useful vehicle for analyzing client facts is the memorandum-to-the-file (see page A-6). The purpose of this document is threefold: first, it assists the researcher in recollecting transactions long transpired; second, it apprises colleagues and supervisors of the nature of one's research; third, it provides "substantial authority" for the tax treatment of a particular item. Let us analyze the facts of our case by way of a memorandum-to-the-file. Notice the format of this document; it generally tracks the steps in the research process itself.

Communicate Conclusions and Recommendations to Others For three practical reasons, research results always should be communicated to the client *in writing*. First, a written communication can be made after extensive revisions. An oral communication cannot. Second, in a written communication, the researcher can delve into the intricacies of tax law. Often, in an oral communication, he or she cannot. Third, a written communication reinforces an oral understanding. Alternatively, it brings to light an oral misunderstanding.

The written communication usually takes the form of a client letter (see page A-7). The purpose of this letter is two-fold: first, it apprises the client of the results of one's research and, second, it recommends to the client a course of action based on these results. A sample client letter is presented below. Notice the organization of this document; it is similar to that of the memorandum-to-the-file.

Memorandum-to-the-File

Date: December 9, 20X1

From: Rosina Havacek

Re: The taxability of meal vouchers furnished by Mercy Hospital to its medical staff.

Facts

[*State only the facts that are relevant to the Issue(s) and necessary for the Analysis.*] Our client, Mercy Hospital ("Mercy"), provides meal vouchers to its medical employees to enable them to remain on emergency call. The vouchers are redeemable at Mercy's onsite cafeteria and at MacDougal's, a privately owned sandwich shop. MacDougal's rents business space from the hospital. Although Mercy does not require its employees to remain on or near its premises during their meal hours, the employees generally do. Elizabeth Fegali, Mercy's Chief Administrator, has asked us to research whether the value of the meal vouchers is taxable to the employees.

Issues

[*Identify the issue(s) raised by the Facts. Be specific.*] The taxability of the meal vouchers depends on three issues: first, whether the meals are furnished "for the convenience of the employer"; second, whether they are furnished "on the business premises of the employer"; and third, whether the vouchers are equivalent to cash.

Applicable Law

[*Discuss those legal principles that both strengthen and weaken the client's case. Because the primary authority for tax law is the IRC, begin with the IRC.*] Section 119 provides that the value of meals is excludible from an employee's income if the meals are furnished for the convenience of, and on the business premises of the employer. [*Discuss how administrative and/or judicial authorities expound on statutory terms.*] Under Reg. Sec. 1.119-1, a meal is furnished "for the convenience of the employer" if it is furnished for a "substantial noncompensatory business reason." A "substantial noncompensatory business reason" includes the need to have the employee available for emergency calls during his or her meal period. Under Sec. 119(b)(4), if more than half the employees satisfy the "for the convenience of the employer" test, all employees will be regarded as satisfying the test. Regulation Sec. 1.119-1 defines "business premises of the employer" as the place of employment of the employee.

[*When discussing court cases, present case facts in such a way as to enable the reader to draw an analogy with client facts.*] A Supreme Court case, *Kowalski v. CIR*, 434 U.S. 77, 77-2 USTC ¶9748, discusses what constitutes "meals" for purposes of Sec. 119. In *Kowalski*, the State of New Jersey furnished cash meal allowances to its state troopers to enable them to eat while on duty. It did not require the troopers to use the allowances exclusively for meals. Nor did it require them to consume their meals on its business premises. One trooper, R.J. Kowalski, excluded the value of his allowances from his income. The IRS disputed this treatment, and Kowalski took the IRS to Court. In Court, Kowalski argued that the allowances were excludible because they were furnished "for the convenience of the employer." The IRS contended that the allowances were taxable because they amounted to compensation. The U.S. Supreme Court took up the case and decided for the IRS. The Court held that the Sec. 119 income exlusion does not apply to payments in cash.

Analysis

[*The Analysis should (a) apply Applicable Law to the Facts and (b) address the Issue(s). In this section, every proposition should be supported by either authority, logic, or plausible assumptions.*]

Issue 1: The meals provided by Mercy seem to be furnished "for the convenience of the employer." They are furnished to have employees available for emergency call during their meal breaks. This is a "substantial noncompensatory reason" within the meaning of Reg. Sec. 1.119-1.

Issue 2: Although the hospital cafeteria appears to be the "business premises of the employer," MacDougal's does not appear to be. The hospital is the place of employment of the medical employees. MacDougal's is not.

Issue 3: [*In applying case law to the Facts, indicate how case facts are similar to/dissimilar from client facts. If the analysis does not support a "yes-no" answer, do not give one.*] Based on the foregoing authorities, it is unclear whether the vouchers are equivalent to cash. On the one hand, they are redeemable only in meals. Thus, they resemble meals-in-kind. On the other hand, they are redeemable at more than one institution. Thus, they resemble cash. Nor is it clear whether a court deciding this case would reach the same conclusion as the Supreme Court did in *Kowalski*. In the latter case, the State of New Jersey provided its meal allowances in the form of cash. It did not require its employees to use the allowances exclusively for meals. Nor did it require them to consume their meals on its business premises. In our case, Mercy provides its meal allowances in the form of vouchers. Thus, it indirectly requires its employees to use the allowances exclusively for meals. On the other hand, it does not require them to consume their meals on its business premises.

Conclusion

[*The conclusion should (a) logically flow from the Analysis, and (b) address the Issue(s).*] Although it appears that the meals acquired by voucher in the hospital cafeteria are furnished "for the convenience of the employer" and "on the business premises of the employer," it is unclear whether the vouchers are equivalent to cash. If they *are* equivalent to cash, *or* if they are redeemed at MacDougal's, their value is likely to be taxable to the employees. On the other hand, if they are not equivalent to cash, *and* they are redeemed only in the hospital cafeteria, their value is likely to be excludible.

Professional Accounting Associates
2701 First City Plaza
Suite 905
Dallas, Texas 75019

December 12, 20X1

Elizabeth Feghali, Chief Administrator
Mercy Hospital
22650 West Haven Drive
Arlington, Texas 75527

Dear Ms. Feghali:

[*Introduction. Set a cordial tone.*] It was great to see you at last Thursday's football game. If not for that last minute fumble, the Longhorns might have taken the Big 12 Conference championship!

[*Issue/Purpose.*] In our meeting of December 6, you asked us to research whether the value of the meal vouchers that Mercy provides to its medical employees is taxable to the employees. [*Short Answer.*] I regret to inform you that if the vouchers are redeemed at MacDougal's, their value is likely to be taxable to the employees. On the other hand, if the vouchers are redeemed in the hospital cafeteria, their value is likely to be excludible from the employee's income. [*The remainder of the letter should elaborate, support, and qualify this answer.*]

[*Steps Taken in Deriving Conclusion.*] In reaching this conclusion, we consulted relevant provisions of the Internal Revenue Code ("IRC"), applicable Treasury Regulations under the IRC, and a pertinent Supreme Court case. In addition, we reviewed the documents on employee benefits that you submitted to us at our earlier meeting.

[*Facts. State only the facts that are relevant to the Issue and necessary for the Analysis.*] The facts as we understand them are as follows: Mercy provides meal vouchers to its medical employees to enable them to eat while on emergency call. The vouchers are redeemable either in the hospital cafeteria or at MacDougal's. MacDougal's is a privately owned institution that rents business space from the hospital. Although Mercy's employees are not required to remain on or near the premises during their meal hours, they generally do.

Applicable Law. State, do not interpret.] Under the IRC, the value of meals is excludible from an employee's income if two conditions are met: first, the meals are furnished "for the convenience of the employer" and second, they are provided "on the business premises of the employer." Although the IRC does not explain what is meant by "for the convenience of the employer," "business premises of the employer," and "meals," other authorities do. Specifically, the Treasury Regulations define "business premises of the employer" to be the place of employment of the employees. The regulations state that providing meals during work hours to have an employee available for emergency calls is "for the convenience of the employer." Moreover, under the IRC, if more than half the employees satisfy the "for the convenience of the employer" test, all the employees will be regarded as satisfying the test. The Supreme Court has interpreted "meals" to mean food-in-kind. The Court has held that cash allowances do not qualify as "meals."

[*Analysis. Express the generalities of Applicable Law in terms of the specifics of the Facts.*] Clearly, the meals furnished by Mercy are "for the convenience of the employer." They are furnished during the employees' work hours to have the employees available for emergency call. Although the meals provided in the hospital cafeteria appear to be furnished "on the business premises of the employer," the meals provided at MacDougal's do not appear to be. The hospital is the place of employment of the medical employees. MacDougal's is not. What is unclear is whether the meal vouchers are equivalent to food-in-kind. On the one hand, they are redeemable at more than one institution and thus resemble cash allowances. On the other hand, they are redeemable only in meals and thus resemble food-in-kind.

[*Conclusion/Recommendation.*] Because of this lack of clarity, we suggest that you modify your employee benefits plan to allow for the provision of meals-in-kind exclusively in the hospital cafeteria. In this way, you will dispel any doubt that Mercy is furnishing "meals," "for the convenience of the employer," "on the premises of the employer."

[*Closing/Follow Up.*] Please call me at 475-2020 if you have any questions concerning this conclusion. May I suggest that we meet next week to discuss the possibility of revising your employee benefits plan.

Very truly yours,
Professional Accounting Associates

By: Rosina Havacek, Junior Associate

APPENDIX B

COMPLETED TAX FORMS

Note: Because of the availability of tax forms from many sources, only a limited number of forms are reprinted in this textbook. All federal forms are available from the Internal Revenue Service, either in paper form or from the IRS Web site, http://www.irs.gov

Form **706**
(Rev. August 2005)

Department of the Treasury
Internal Revenue Service

United States Estate (and Generation-Skipping Transfer) Tax Return

Estate of a citizen or resident of the United States (see separate instructions).
To be filed for decedents dying after December 31, 2004, and before January 1, 2006.

OMB No. 1545-0015

Part 1.—Decedent and Executor

1a Decedent's first name and middle initial (and maiden name, if any)		**1b** Decedent's last name		**2** Decedent's Social Security No.	
Herman		Estes		999 : 11 : 4444	

3a County, state, and ZIP code, or foreign country, of legal residence (domicile) at time of death	**3b** Year domicile established	**4** Date of birth	**5** Date of death
Montgomery, OH 45347	1936	1919	10-13-2005

6a Name of executor (see page 3 of the instructions)
John Johnson

6b Executor's address (number and street including apartment or suite no. or rural route; city, town, or post office; state; and ZIP code) and phone no.
10 Main Place
Dayton, OH 45347   Phone no. (   )

6c Executor's social security number (see page 3 of the instructions)
998 : 12 : 5732

7a Name and location of court where will was probated or estate administered

7b Case number

8 If decedent died testate, check here ▶ [X] and attach a certified copy of the will. **9** If you extended the time to file this Form 706, check here ▶ ☐

10 If Schedule R-1 is attached, check here ▶ ☐

Part 2.—Tax Computation

1 Total gross estate less exclusion (from Part 5, Recapitulation, page 3, item 12)	**1**	2,947,150
2 Total allowable deductions (from Part 5, Recapitulation, page 3, item 22).	**2**	1,176,700
3a Tentative taxable estate (before state death tax deduction) (subtract line 2 from line 1)	**3a**	1,770,450
b State death tax deduction.	**3b**	-0-
c Taxable estate (subtract line 3b from line 3a)	**3c**	1,770,450
4 Adjusted taxable gifts (total taxable gifts (within the meaning of section 2503) made by the decedent after December 31, 1976, other than gifts that are includible in decedent's gross estate (section 2001(b)))	**4**	1,700,000
5 Add lines 3c and 4	**5**	3,470,450
6 Tentative tax on the amount on line 5 from Table A on page 4 of the instructions	**6**	1,471,912
7 Total gift tax payable with respect to gifts made by the decedent after December 31, 1976. Include gift taxes by the decedent's spouse for such spouse's share of split gifts (section 2513) only if the decedent was the donor of these gifts and they are includible in the decedent's gross estate (see instructions)	**7**	315,900
8 Gross estate tax (subtract line 7 from line 6)	**8**	1,156,012
9 Maximum unified credit (applicable credit amount) against estate tax . [**9** 555,800]		
10 Adjustment to unified credit (applicable credit amount). (This adjustment may not exceed $6,000. See page 5 of the instructions.) . . . . [**10** -0-]		
11 Allowable unified credit (applicable credit amount) (subtract line 10 from line 9).	**11**	555,800
12 Subtract line 11 from line 8 (but do not enter less than zero)	**12**	600,212
13 Credit for foreign death taxes (from Schedule(s) P. (Attach Form(s) 706-CE.) . . . . [**13**]		
14 Credit for tax on prior transfers (from Schedule Q) . . . . . [**14**]		
15 Total credits (add lines 13 and 14)	**15**	
16 Net estate tax (subtract line 15 from line 12)	**16**	600,212
17 Generation-skipping transfer taxes (from Schedule R, Part 2, line 10).	**17**	
18 Total transfer taxes (add lines 16 and 17)	**18**	600,212
19 Prior payments. Explain in an attached statement	**19**	
20 Balance due (or overpayment) (subtract line 19 from line 18) . . .	**20**	600,212

Under penalties of perjury, I declare that I have examined this return, including accompanying schedules and statements, and to the best of my knowledge and belief, it is true, correct, and complete. Declaration of preparer other than the executor is based on all information of which preparer has any knowledge.

John Johnson
Signature(s) of executor(s)

5-14-06
Date

Mary Wilson CPA
Signature of preparer other than executor

100 Tower Bldg., Austin TX 78703
Address (and ZIP code)

5-12-06
Date

For Privacy Act and Paperwork Reduction Act Notice, see page 27 of the separate instructions for this form.   Cat. No. 20548R   Form **706** (Rev. 8-2005)

Note: Pages not pertinent to the tax consequences are omitted.

Form 706 (Rev. 8-2005)

Estate of: Herman Estes

Part 3—Elections by the Executor

Please check the "Yes" or "No" box for each question. (See instructions beginning on page 6.)

			Yes	No
1	Do you elect alternate valuation?	1		X
2	Do you elect special-use valuation? . . . . If "Yes," you must complete and attach Schedule A–1.	2		X
3	Do you elect to pay the taxes in installments as described in section 6166? . . . . If "Yes," you must attach the additional information described on page 9 of the instructions.	3		X
4	Do you elect to postpone the part of the taxes attributable to a reversionary or remainder interest as described in section 6163?	4		X

Part 4—General Information (Note: Please attach the necessary supplemental documents. You must attach the death certificate.) (See instructions on page 10.)

Authorization to receive confidential tax information under Regs. sec. 601.504(b)(2)(i); to act as the estate's representative before the IRS; and to make written or oral presentations on behalf of the estate if return prepared by an attorney, accountant, or enrolled agent for the executor.

Name of representative (print or type)	State	Address (number, street, and room or suite no., city, state, and ZIP code)
John Johnson	Ohio	10 Main Place, Dayton, OH 45347

I declare that I am the ☐ attorney/ ☐ certified public accountant/ ☐ enrolled agent (you must check the applicable box) for the executor and prepared this return for the executor. I am not under suspension or disbarment from practice before the Internal Revenue Service and am qualified to practice in the state shown above.

Signature	CAF number	Date	Telephone number
Mary Wilson, CPA		5-12-06	512-474-4447

1 Death certificate number and issuing authority (attach a copy of the death certificate to this return).
1246, County Coroner

2 Decedent's business or occupation. If retired, check here ▶ ☐ and state decedent's former business or occupation.
Executive

3 Marital status of the decedent at time of death:

☒ Married

☐ Widow or widower—Name, SSN, and date of death of deceased spouse ▶ _____

☐ Single
☐ Legally separated
☐ Divorced—Date divorce decree became final ▶

4a Surviving spouse's name	4b Social security number	4c Amount received (see page 10 of the instructions)
Ann Estes	555 77 9999	1,050,000

5 Individuals (other than the surviving spouse), trusts, or other estates who receive benefits from the estate (do not include charitable beneficiaries shown in Schedule O) (see instructions).

Name of individual, trust, or estate receiving $5,000 or more	Identifying number	Relationship to decedent	Amount (see instructions)
Johnny Estes	555-61-4107	Son	541,169
Billy Estes	556-63-4437	Son	341,169

Daughter, Dorothy Estes, received the corpus in the special power of appointment trust created by Amelia Estes.

All unascertainable beneficiaries and those who receive less than $5,000 . . . . ▶

Total 882,338

Please check the "Yes" or "No" box for each question.

		Yes	No
6	Does the gross estate contain any section 2044 property (qualified terminable interest property (QTIP) from a prior gift or estate) (see page 10 of the instructions)?		X
7a	Have Federal gift tax returns ever been filed? . . . . If "Yes," please attach copies of the returns, if available, and furnish the following information:	X	

7b Period(s) covered	7c Internal Revenue office(s) where filed
1974, 1978, 2003	Cincinnati, OH

(continued on next page)

Form 706 (Rev. 8-2005)

Part 4—General Information *(continued)*

If you answer "Yes" to any of questions 8–16, you must attach additional information as described in the instructions.	Yes	No
8a Was there any insurance on the decedent's life that is not included on the return as part of the gross estate?		X
b Did the decedent own any insurance on the life of another that is not included in the gross estate?		X
9 Did the decedent at the time of death own any property as a joint tenant with right of survivorship in which **(a)** one or more of the other joint tenants was someone other than the decedent's spouse, and **(b)** less than the full value of the property is included on the return as part of the gross estate? If "Yes," you must complete and attach Schedule E		X
10 Did the decedent, at the time of death, own any interest in a partnership or unincorporated business or any stock in an inactive or closely held corporation?		X
11 Did the decedent make any transfer described in section 2035, 2036, 2037, or 2038 (see the instructions for Schedule G beginning on page 13 of the separate instructions)? If "Yes," you must complete and attach Schedule G	X	
12a Were there in existence at the time of the decedent's death any trusts created by the decedent during his or her lifetime?		X
b Were there in existence at the time of the decedent's death any trusts not created by the decedent under which the decedent possessed any power, beneficial interest, or trusteeship?	X	
c Was the decedent receiving income from a trust created after October 22, 1986 by a parent or grandparent?	X	
If "Yes," was there a GST taxable termination (under section 2612) upon the death of the decedent?		X
d If there was a GST taxable termination (under section 2612), attach a statement to explain. Provide a copy of the trust or will creating the trust, and give the name, address, and phone number of the current trustee(s).		
13 Did the decedent ever possess, exercise, or release any general power of appointment? If "Yes," you must complete and attach Schedule H		X
14 Was the marital deduction computed under the transitional rule of Public Law 97-34, section 403(e)(3) (Economic Recovery Tax Act of 1981)?		X
If "Yes," attach a separate computation of the marital deduction, enter the amount on item 20 of the Recapitulation, and note on item 20 "computation attached."		
15 Was the decedent, immediately before death, receiving an annuity described in the "General" paragraph of the instructions for Schedule I? If "Yes," you must complete and attach Schedule I.	X	
16 Was the decedent ever the beneficiary of a trust for which a deduction was claimed by the estate of a pre-deceased spouse under section 2056(b)(7) and which is not reported on this return? If "Yes," attach an explanation		X

Part 5—Recapitulation

Item number	Gross estate		Alternate value	Value at date of death
1	Schedule A—Real Estate	1		325,000
2	Schedule B—Stocks and Bonds	2		1,600,000
3	Schedule C—Mortgages, Notes, and Cash	3		94,250
4	Schedule D—Insurance on the Decedent's Life (attach Form(s) 712). . . .	4		200,000
5	Schedule E—Jointly Owned Property (attach Form(s) 712 for life insurance) .	5		200,000
6	Schedule F—Other Miscellaneous Property (attach Form(s) 712 for life insurance) .	6		-0-
7	Schedule G—Transfers During Decedent's Life (att. Form(s) 712 for life insurance)	7		287,900
8	Schedule H—Powers of Appointment	8		-0-
9	Schedule I—Annuities	9		240,000
10	Total gross estate (add items 1 through 9).	10		2,947,150
11	Schedule U—Qualified Conservation Easement Exclusion	11		
12	Total gross estate less exclusion (subtract item 11 from item 10). Enter here and on line 1 of Part 2—Tax Computation	12		2,947,150

Item number	Deductions		Amount
13	Schedule J—Funeral Expenses and Expenses Incurred in Administering Property Subject to Claims . . .	13	85,000
14	Schedule K—Debts of the Decedent	14	31,700
15	Schedule K—Mortgages and Liens	15	-0-
16	Total of items 13 through 15	16	116,700
17	Allowable amount of deductions from item 16 (see the instructions for item 17 of the Recapitulation) .	17	116,700
18	Schedule L—Net Losses During Administration	18	-0-
19	Schedule L—Expenses Incurred in Administering Property Not Subject to Claims.	19	-0-
20	Schedule M—Bequests, etc., to Surviving Spouse	20	1,050,000
21	Schedule O—Charitable, Public, and Similar Gifts and Bequests	21	10,000
22	Total allowable deductions (add items 17 through 21). Enter here and on line 2 of the Tax Computation.	22	1,176,700

Form 706 (Rev. 8-2005)

Estate of: Herman Estes

SCHEDULE A—Real Estate

- For jointly owned property that must be disclosed on Schedule E, see the instructions on the reverse side of Schedule E.
- Real estate that is part of a sole proprietorship should be shown on Schedule F.
- Real estate that is included in the gross estate under section 2035, 2036, 2037, or 2038 should be shown on Schedule G.
- Real estate that is included in the gross estate under section 2041 should be shown on Schedule H.
- If you elect section 2032A valuation, you must complete Schedule A and Schedule A-1.

Item number	Description	Alternate valuation date	Alternate value	Value at date of death
1	Personal residence, house and lot, located at 105 Elm Court, Dayton, OH			325,000

Total from continuation schedules or additional sheets attached to this schedule . . .				
TOTAL. (Also enter on Part 5, Recapitulation, page 3, at item 1.)				325,000

(If more space is needed, attach the continuation schedule from the end of this package or additional sheets of the same size.)

(See the instructions on the reverse side.)

Form 706 (Rev. 8-2005)

Estate of: Herman Estes

SCHEDULE B—Stocks and Bonds

(For jointly owned property that must be disclosed on Schedule E, see the instructions for Schedule E.)

Item number	Description including face amount of bonds or number of shares and par value for identification. Give CUSIP number. If closely held entity, give EIN.		Unit value	Alternate valuation date	Alternate value	Value at date of death
		CUSIP number				
1	Stock in Ajax Corporation 1,000 shares, $10 per share		1,600			1,600,000
	Total from continuation schedules (or additional sheets) attached to this schedule . . .					
	TOTAL. (Also enter on Part 5, Recapitulation, page 3, at item 2.)					1,600,000

(If more space is needed, attach the continuation schedule from the end of this package or additional sheets of the same size.)

(The instructions to Schedule B are in the separate instructions.)

Schedule B—Page 12

Form 706 (Rev. 8-2005)

Estate of: Herman Estes

SCHEDULE C—Mortgages, Notes, and Cash

(For jointly owned property that must be disclosed on Schedule E, see the instructions for Schedule E.)

Item number	Description	Alternate valuation date	Alternate value	Value at date of death
1	Checking Account			19,250
2	Savings account (includes accrued interest through date of death)			75,000
	Total from continuation schedules (or additional sheets) attached to this schedule . .			
	TOTAL. (Also enter on Part 5, Recapitulation, page 3, at item 3.)			94,250

(If more space is needed, attach the continuation schedule from the end of this package or additional sheets of the same size.)
(See the instructions on the reverse side.)

Schedule C—Page 13

Form 706 (Rev. 8-2005)

Estate of: Herman Estes

SCHEDULE D—Insurance on the Decedent's Life

You must list **all** policies on the life of the decedent and attach a Form 712 for each policy.

Item number	Description	Alternate valuation date	Alternate value	Value at date of death
1	Life insurance policy No. 123-A issued by the Life Insurance Company of Ohio. Beneficiary — Johnny Estes			200,000
	Total from continuation schedules (or additional sheets) attached to this schedule . .			
	TOTAL. (Also enter on Part 5, Recapitulation, page 3, at item 4.)			200,000

(If more space is needed, attach the continuation schedule from the end of this package or additional sheets of the same size.)

(See the instructions on the reverse side.)

Schedule D—Page 15

Form 706 (Rev. 8-2005)

Estate of: *Herman Estes*

SCHEDULE E—Jointly Owned Property
(If you elect section 2032A valuation, you must complete Schedule E and Schedule A-1.)

PART 1.—Qualified Joint Interests—Interests Held by the Decedent and His or Her Spouse as the Only Joint Tenants (Section 2040(b)(2))

Item number	Description For securities, give CUSIP number.	Alternate valuation date	Alternate value	Value at date of death
1	Land			400,000
	Total from continuation schedules (or additional sheets) attached to this schedule			

1a	Totals	**1a**		400,000
1b	Amounts included in gross estate (one-half of line **1a**)	**1b**		200,000

PART 2.—All Other Joint Interests

2a State the name and address of each surviving co-tenant. If there are more than three surviving co-tenants, list the additional co-tenants on an attached sheet.

	Name	Address (number and street, city, state, and ZIP code)
A.		
B.		
C.		

Item number	Enter letter for co-tenant	Description (including alternate valuation date if any). For securities, give CUSIP number.	Percentage includible	Includible alternate value	Includible value at date of death
		Total from continuation schedules (or additional sheets) attached to this schedule			

2b	Total other joint interests	**2b**		
3	**Total includible joint interests** (add lines 1b and 2b). Also enter on Part 5, Recapitulation, page 3, at item 5	**3**		200,000

(If more space is needed, attach the continuation schedule from the end of this package or additional sheets of the same size.)
(See the instructions on the reverse side.)

Form 706 (Rev. 8-2005)

Estate of: Herman Estes

SCHEDULE G—Transfers During Decedent's Life

(If you elect section 2032A valuation, you must complete Schedule G and Schedule A-1.)

Item number	Description For securities, give CUSIP number.	Alternate valuation date	Alternate value	Value at date of death
A.	Gift tax paid by the decedent or the estate for all gifts made by the decedent or his or her spouse within 3 years before the decedent's death (section 2035(b)).	X X X X X		287,900
B. 1	Transfers includible under section 2035(a), 2036, 2037, or 2038:			
	Total from continuation schedules (or additional sheets) attached to this schedule . .			
	TOTAL. (Also enter on Part 5, Recapitulation, page 3, at item 7.)			287,900

SCHEDULE H—Powers of Appointment

(Include "5 and 5 lapsing" powers (section 2041(b)(2)) held by the decedent.)

(If you elect section 2032A valuation, you must complete Schedule H and Schedule A-1.)

Item number	Description	Alternate valuation date	Alternate value	Value at date of death
1				
	Total from continuation schedules (or additional sheets) attached to this schedule . .			
	TOTAL. (Also enter on Part 5, Recapitulation, page 3, at item 8.)			

(If more space is needed, attach the continuation schedule from the end of this package or additional sheets of the same size.)

(The instructions to Schedules G and H are in the separate instructions.)

Form 706 (Rev. 8-2005)

Estate of: _Herman Estes_

SCHEDULE I—Annuities

Note. Generally, no exclusion is allowed for the estates of decedents dying after December 31, 1984 (see page 15 of the instructions).

A Are you excluding from the decedent's gross estate the value of a lump-sum distribution described in section 2039(f)(2) (as in effect before its repeal by the Deficit Reduction Act of 1984)? . . . .   **Yes** | **No** X
If "Yes," you must attach the information required by the instructions.

Item number	Description Show the entire value of the annuity before any exclusions.	Alternate valuation date	Includible alternate value	Includible value at date of death
1	Qualified pension plan issued by Buckeye Corporation, Beneficiary — Ann Estes — spouse			240,000
	Total from continuation schedules (or additional sheets) attached to this schedule . .			
	TOTAL. (Also enter on Part 5, Recapitulation, page 3, at item 9.)			**240,000**

(If more space is needed, attach the continuation schedule from the end of this package or additional sheets of the same size.)

Schedule I—Page 22   (The instructions to Schedule I are in the separate instructions.)

Form 706 (Rev. 8-2005)

Estate of: Herman Estes

SCHEDULE J—Funeral Expenses and Expenses Incurred in Administering Property Subject to Claims

Note. Do not list on this schedule expenses of administering property not subject to claims. For those expenses, see the instructions for Schedule L.

If executors' commissions, attorney fees, etc., are claimed and allowed as a deduction for estate tax purposes, they are not allowable as a deduction in computing the taxable income of the estate for federal income tax purposes. They are allowable as an income tax deduction on Form 1041 if a waiver is filed to waive the deduction on Form 706 (see the Form 1041 instructions).

Item number	Description	Expense amount	Total amount
1	**A. Funeral expenses:**	15,000	
	Total funeral expenses . . . . ▶		15,000
	B. Administration expenses:		
	1 Executors' commissions—amount estimated/agreed upon/paid. (Strike out the words that do not apply.) . . .		70,000
	2 Attorney fees—amount estimated/agreed upon/paid. (Strike out the words that do not apply.). .		
	3 Accountant fees—amount estimated/agreed upon/paid. (Strike out the words that do not apply.)		

		Expense amount
	4 Miscellaneous expenses:	
	Total miscellaneous expenses from continuation schedules (or additional sheets) attached to this schedule	
	Total miscellaneous expenses . . . . ▶	

TOTAL. (Also enter on Part 5, Recapitulation, page 3, at item 13.) . . . . ▶ | 85,000

(If more space is needed, attach the continuation schedule from the end of this package or additional sheets of the same size.)
(See the instructions on the reverse side.)

Schedule J—Page 23

Form 706 (Rev. 8-2005)

Estate of: <u>Herman Estes</u>

SCHEDULE K—Debts of the Decedent, and Mortgages and Liens

Item number	Debts of the Decedent—Creditor and nature of claim, and allowable death taxes	Amount unpaid to date	Amount in contest	Amount claimed as a deduction
1	Bank loan (including interest accrued through date of death)	25,200		25,200
2	American Express, Visa, and Master Card credit card debts	6,500		6,500

Total from continuation schedules (or additional sheets) attached to this schedule . . . .

TOTAL. (Also enter on Part 5, Recapitulation, page 3, at item 14.) . . . . | **31,700**

Item number	Mortgages and Liens—Description	Amount
1		

Total from continuation schedules (or additional sheets) attached to this schedule . . . .

TOTAL. (Also enter on Part 5, Recapitulation, page 3, at item 15.) . . . .

(If more space is needed, attach the continuation schedule from the end of this package or additional sheets of the same size.)
(The instructions to Schedule K are in the separate instructions.)

Form 706 (Rev. 8-2005)

Estate of: Herman Estes

SCHEDULE M—Bequests, etc., to Surviving Spouse

Election To Deduct Qualified Terminable Interest Property Under Section 2056(b)(7). If a trust (or other property) meets the requirements of qualified terminable interest property under section 2056(b)(7), and

  a. The trust or other property is listed on Schedule M, and

  b. The value of the trust (or other property) is entered in whole or in part as a deduction on Schedule M,

then unless the executor specifically identifies the trust (all or a fractional portion or percentage) or other property to be excluded from the election, the executor shall be deemed to have made an election to have such trust (or other property) treated as qualified terminable interest property under section 2056(b)(7).

  If less than the entire value of the trust (or other property) that the executor has included in the gross estate is entered as a deduction on Schedule M, the executor shall be considered to have made an election only as to a fraction of the trust (or other property). The numerator of this fraction is equal to the amount of the trust (or other property) deducted on Schedule M. The denominator is equal to the total value of the trust (or other property).

Election To Deduct Qualified Domestic Trust Property Under Section 2056A. If a trust meets the requirements of a qualified domestic trust under section 2056A(a) and this return is filed no later than 1 year after the time prescribed by law (including extensions) for filing the return, and

  a. The entire value of a trust or trust property is listed on Schedule M, and

  b. The entire value of the trust or trust property is entered as a deduction on Schedule M,

then unless the executor specifically identifies the trust to be excluded from the election, the executor shall be deemed to have made an election to have the entire trust treated as qualified domestic trust property.

		Yes	No
1	Did any property pass to the surviving spouse as a result of a qualified disclaimer? **1**		X
	If "Yes," attach a copy of the written disclaimer required by section 2518(b).		
2a	In what country was the surviving spouse born? <u>United States</u>		
b	What is the surviving spouse's date of birth? <u>3-12-42</u>		
c	Is the surviving spouse a U.S. citizen?. **2c**	X	
d	If the surviving spouse is a naturalized citizen, when did the surviving spouse acquire citizenship? <u>N/A</u>		
e	If the surviving spouse is not a U.S. citizen, of what country is the surviving spouse a citizen? <u>N/A</u>		
3	**Election Out of QTIP Treatment of Annuities**—Do you elect under section 2056(b)(7)(C)(ii) **not** to treat as qualified terminable interest property any joint and survivor annuities that are included in the gross estate and would otherwise be treated as qualified terminable interest property under section 2056(b)(7)(C)? (see instructions) **3**		X

Item number	Description of property interests passing to surviving spouse	Amount
1	Residence	325,000
2.	Checking account	10,000
3.	Savings account	75,000
4.	Land, held in joint tenancy	200,000
5.	Qualified pension plan	240,000
6.	Trust with First Bank as Trustee	200,000

	Total from continuation schedules (or additional sheets) attached to this schedule			
4	**Total** amount of property interests listed on Schedule M	**4**	1,050,000	
5a	Federal estate taxes payable out of property interests listed on Schedule M . .	**5a**		
b	Other death taxes payable out of property interests listed on Schedule M . . .	**5b**		
c	Federal and state GST taxes payable out of property interests listed on Schedule M	**5c**		
d	Add items 5a, b, and c	**5d**	-0-	
6	Net amount of property interests listed on Schedule M (subtract 5d from 4). Also enter on Part 5, Recapitulation, page 3, at item 20	**6**	1,050,000	

(If more space is needed, attach the continuation schedule from the end of this package or additional sheets of the same size.)
(See the instructions on the reverse side.)

Schedule M—Page 27

Form 706 (Rev. 8-2005)

Estate of: Herman Estes

SCHEDULE O—Charitable, Public, and Similar Gifts and Bequests

		Yes	No
1a	If the transfer was made by will, has any action been instituted to have interpreted or to contest the will or any of its provisions affecting the charitable deductions claimed in this schedule?		X
	If "Yes," full details must be submitted with this schedule.		
b	According to the information and belief of the person or persons filing this return, is any such action planned?		X
	If "Yes," full details must be submitted with this schedule.		
2	Did any property pass to charity as the result of a qualified disclaimer?		X
	If "Yes," attach a copy of the written disclaimer required by section 2518(b).		

Item number	Name and address of beneficiary	Character of institution	Amount
1	American Cancer Society	Charity	10,000

Total from continuation schedules (or additional sheets) attached to this schedule		10,000

3	Total	**3**	
4a	Federal estate tax payable out of property interests listed above	**4a**	
b	Other death taxes payable out of property interests listed above	**4b**	
c	Federal and state GST taxes payable out of property interests listed above	**4c**	
d	Add items 4a, b, and c	**4d**	-0-
5	Net value of property interests listed above (subtract 4d from 3). Also enter on Part 5, Recapitulation, page 3, at item 21	**5**	10,000

(If more space is needed, attach the continuation schedule from the end of this package or additional sheets of the same size.)
(The instructions to Schedule O are in the separate instructions.)

Schedule O—Page 31

Form **709**

Department of the Treasury
Internal Revenue Service

United States Gift (and Generation-Skipping Transfer) Tax Return

(For gifts made during calendar year 2005)

▶ **See separate instructions.**

OMB No. 1545-0020

2005

1 Donor's first name and middle initial **Wilma**	2 Donor's last name **Brown**
	3 Donor's social security number **123 45 6789**
4 Address (number, street, and apartment number) **2 Main Street**	5 Legal residence (domicile) (county and state) **Whitefield, GA**
6 City, state, and ZIP code **Dalton, GA 35901**	7 Citizenship **U.S.A.**

Part 1—General Information

		Yes	No
8	If the donor died during the year, check here ▶ ☐ and enter date of death		
9	If you extended the time to file this Form 709, check here ▶ ☐		
10	Enter the total number of donees listed on Schedule A. Count each person only once. ▶ **5**		
11a	Have you (the donor) previously filed a Form 709 (or 709-A) for any other year? If "No," skip line 11b	X	
11b	If the answer to line 11a is "Yes," has your address changed since you last filed Form 709 (or 709-A)?		X
12	**Gifts by husband or wife to third parties.** Do you consent to have the gifts (including generation-skipping transfers) made by you and by your spouse to third parties during the calendar year considered as made one-half by each of you? (See instructions.) (If the answer is "Yes," the following information must be furnished and your spouse must sign the consent shown below. **If the answer is "No," skip lines 13–18 and go to Schedule A.)**	X	
13	Name of consenting spouse **Hugh Brown**	14 SSN **987-65-4321**	
15	Were you married to one another during the entire calendar year? (see instructions)	X	
16	If 15 is "No," check whether ☐ married ☐ divorced or ☐ widowed/deceased, and give date (see instructions) ▶		
17	Will a gift tax return for this year be filed by your spouse? (If "Yes," mail both returns in the same envelope.)	X	

18 **Consent of Spouse.** I consent to have the gifts (and generation-skipping transfers) made by me and by my spouse to third parties during the calendar year considered as made one-half by each of us. We are both aware of the joint and several liability for tax created by the execution of this consent.

Consenting spouse's signature ▶ **Hugh Brown**   Date ▶ **3-2-2006**

Part 2—Tax Computation

1	Enter the amount from Schedule A, Part 4, line 11	340,598
2	Enter the amount from Schedule B, line 3	500,000
3	Total taxable gifts. Add lines 1 and 2	840,598
4	Tax computed on amount on line 3 (see *Table for Computing Gift Tax* in separate instructions)	283,633
5	Tax computed on amount on line 2 (see *Table for Computing Gift Tax* in separate instructions)	155,800
6	Balance. Subtract line 5 from line 4	127,833
7	Maximum unified credit (nonresident aliens, see instructions)	345,800 00
8	Enter the unified credit against tax allowable for all prior periods (from Sch. B, line 1, col. C)	68,000
9	Balance. Subtract line 8 from line 7	277,800
10	Enter 20% (.20) of the amount allowed as a specific exemption for gifts made after September 8, 1976, and before January 1, 1977 (see instructions)	-0-
11	Balance. Subtract line 10 from line 9	277,800
12	Unified credit. Enter the smaller of line 6 or line 11	127,833
13	Credit for foreign gift taxes (see instructions)	-0-
14	Total credits. Add lines 12 and 13	127,833
15	Balance. Subtract line 14 from line 6. Do not enter less than zero	-0-
16	Generation-skipping transfer taxes (from Schedule C, Part 3, col. H, Total)	-0-
17	Total tax. Add lines 15 and 16	-0-
18	Gift and generation-skipping transfer taxes prepaid with extension of time to file	-0-
19	If line 18 is less than line 17, enter **balance due** (see instructions)	-0-
20	If line 18 is greater than line 17, enter **amount to be refunded**	

Under penalties of perjury, I declare that I have examined this return, including any accompanying schedules and statements, and to the best of my knowledge and belief, it is true, correct, and complete. Declaration of preparer (other than donor) is based on all information of which preparer has any knowledge.

Sign Here

▶ Signature of donor **Wilma Brown**   Date **3-2-2006**

Paid Preparer's Use Only

Preparer's signature ▶ **Sally Preparer**   Date **3-2-2006**   Check if self-employed ▶ X

Firm's name (or yours if self-employed), address, and ZIP code ▶ **Sally Preparer 110 Last Bank Tower Dalton, GA 35901**   Phone no. ▶ **(706)934-5000**

For Disclosure, Privacy Act, and Paperwork Reduction Act Notice, see page 12 of the separate instructions for this form.   Cat. No. 16783M   Form **709** (2005)

Note: Page 4, which is not pertinent to the tax consequences, is omitted because the donor made no generation skipping transfers.

Form 709 (2005)   Page **2**

SCHEDULE A	Computation of Taxable Gifts (Including transfers in trust) (see instructions)

A Does the value of any item listed on Schedule A reflect any valuation discount? If "Yes," attach explanation . . . . Yes ☐ No ☒

B ☐ ◄ Check here if you elect under section 529(c)(2)(B) to treat any transfers made this year to a qualified tuition program as made ratably over a 5-year period beginning this year. See instructions. Attach explanation.

Part 1—Gifts Subject Only to Gift Tax. Gifts less political organization, medical, and educational exclusions. See instructions.

A Item number	B • Donee's name and address • Relationship to donor (if any) • Description of gift • If the gift was of securities, give CUSIP no. • If closely held entity, give EIN	C	D Donor's adjusted basis of gift	E Date of gift	F Value at date of gift	G For split gifts, enter ½ of column F	H Net transfer (subtract col. G from col. F)
1 2-4	} Schedule Attached		593,000		725,196	62,598	662,598

Gifts made by spouse—*complete **only** if you are splitting gifts with your spouse and he/she also made gifts.*

4	State University, stock		32,000*	2005	80,000	40,000	40,000
6	Betsy Brown, land		112,000*	2005	600,000	300,000	300,000

Total of Part 1. Add amounts from Part 1, column H . . . . ► **1,002,598**

Part 2—Direct Skips. Gifts that are direct skips and are subject to both gift tax and generation-skipping transfer tax. You must list the gifts in chronological order.

A Item number	B • Donee's name and address • Relationship to donor (if any) • Description of gift • If the gift was of securities, give CUSIP no. • If closely held entity, give EIN	C 2632(b) election out	D Donor's adjusted basis of gift	E Date of gift	F Value at date of gift	G For split gifts, enter ½ of column F	H Net transfer (subtract col. G from col. F)
1							

Gifts made by spouse—*complete **only** if you are splitting gifts with your spouse and he/she also made gifts.*

Total of Part 2. Add amounts from Part 2, column H . . . . ►

Part 3—Indirect Skips. Gifts to trusts that are currently subject to gift tax and may later be subject to generation-skipping transfer tax. You must list these gifts in chronological order.

A Item number	B • Donee's name and address • Relationship to donor (if any) • Description of gift • If the gift was of securities, give CUSIP no. • If closely held entity, give EIN	C 2632(c) election	D Donor's adjusted basis of gift	E Date of gift	F Value at date of gift	G For split gifts, enter ½ of column F	H Net transfer (subtract col. G from col. F)
1							

Gifts made by spouse—*complete **only** if you are splitting gifts with your spouse and he/she also made gifts.*

Total of Part 3. Add amounts from Part 3, column H . . . . ►

(If more space is needed, attach additional sheets of same size.)

Form **709** (2005)

*Assumed amounts not listed in the facts.

Form 709 (2005)   Page **3**

Part 4—Taxable Gift Reconciliation

1	Total value of gifts of donor. Add totals from column H of Parts 1, 2, and 3	1	1,002,598
2	Total annual exclusions for gifts listed on line 1 (see instructions)	2	44,000 **
3	Total included amount of gifts. Subtract line 2 from line 1	3	958,598

Deductions (see instructions)

4	Gifts of interests to spouse for which a marital deduction will be claimed, based on items _____4_____ of Schedule A	4	600,000
5	Exclusions attributable to gifts on line 4	5	11,000
6	Marital deduction. Subtract line 5 from line 4	6	589,000
7	Charitable deduction, based on items ____5____ less exclusions . .	7	29,000
8	Total deductions. Add lines 6 and 7	8	618,000
9	Subtract line 8 from line 3	9	340,598
10	Generation-skipping transfer taxes payable with this Form 709 (from Schedule C, Part 3, col. H, Total) .	10	
11	Taxable gifts. Add lines 9 and 10. Enter here and on line 1 of the Tax Computation on page 1 . . .	11	340,598

12 Terminable Interest (QTIP) Marital Deduction. (See instructions for Schedule A, Part 4, line 4.)

If a trust (or other property) meets the requirements of qualified terminable interest property under section 2523(f), and:

a. The trust (or other property) is listed on Schedule A, and

b. The value of the trust (or other property) is entered in whole or in part as a deduction on Schedule A, Part 4, line 4, then the donor shall be deemed to have made an election to have such trust (or other property) treated as qualified terminable interest property under section 2523(f).

If less than the entire value of the trust (or other property) that the donor has included in Parts 1 and 3 of Schedule A is entered as a deduction on line 4, the donor shall be considered to have made an election only as to a fraction of the trust (or other property). The numerator of this fraction is equal to the amount of the trust (or other property) deducted on Schedule A, Part 4, line 6. The denominator is equal to the total value of the trust (or other property) listed in Parts 1 and 3 of Schedule A.

If you make the QTIP election, the terminable interest property involved will be included in your spouse's gross estate upon his or her death (section 2044). See instructions for line 4 of Schedule A. If your spouse disposes (by gift or otherwise) of all or part of the qualifying life income interest, he or she will be considered to have made a transfer of the entire property that is subject to the gift tax. See *Transfer of Certain Life Estates Received From Spouse* on page 4 of the instructions.

13 Election Out of QTIP Treatment of Annuities

☐ Check here if you elect under section 2523(f)(6) **not** to treat as qualified terminable interest property any joint and survivor annuities that are reported on Schedule A and would otherwise be treated as qualified terminable interest property under section 2523(f). See instructions. Enter the item numbers from Schedule A for the annuities for which you are making this election

SCHEDULE B	Gifts From Prior Periods

If you answered "Yes" on line 11a of page 1, Part 1, see the instructions for completing Schedule B. If you answered "No," skip to the Tax Computation on page 1 (or Schedule C, if applicable).

A Calendar year or calendar quarter (see instructions)	B Internal Revenue office where prior return was filed	C Amount of unified credit against gift tax for periods after December 31, 1976	D Amount of specific exemption for prior periods ending before January 1, 1977	E Amount of taxable gifts
1975	Atlanta, GA	-0-	-0-	300,000
1988	Atlanta, GA	68,000		200,000

1	Totals for prior periods	1	68,000	500,000
2	Amount, if any, by which total specific exemption, line 1, column D, is more than $30,000	2		-0-
3	Total amount of taxable gifts for prior periods. Add amount on line 1, column E and amount, if any, on line 2. Enter here and on line 2 of the Tax Computation on page 1 . . . . ▶	3		500,000

(If more space is needed, attach additional sheets of same size.)   Form **709** (2005)

**$11,000 each for Billy, Betsy, State University, and Hugh.

Form 709 (2004), Schedule A, Part 1

A	B	C	D	E	F	G	H
1	Billy Brown, cash		$ 80,000	2005	$ 80,000	$40,000	$ 40,000
2	Betsy Brown, jewelry		18,000*	2005	24,000	12,000	12,000
3	Ruth Cain, remainder interest in vacation cabin (0.21196 x 100,000)		15,000*	2005	21,196	10,598	10,598
4	Trust at First Bank, income to Hugh Brown for life. Remainder to Jeff Bass (QTIP trust)		480,000*	2005	600,000		600,000
			$593,000		$725,196	$62,598	$662,598

*Assumed amounts not listed in the facts.

SCHEDULE C
(Form 1040)

Department of the Treasury
Internal Revenue Service (99)

Profit or Loss From Business
(Sole Proprietorship)

▶ Partnerships, joint ventures, etc., must file Form 1065 or 1065-B.

▶ **Attach to Form 1040 or 1041.** ▶ See Instructions for Schedule C (Form 1040).

OMB No. 1545-0074

20**05**

Attachment
Sequence No. **09**

Name of proprietor	**Andrew Lawrence**	Social security number (SSN) **297 : 63 : 2110**

A Principal business or profession, including product or service (see page C-2 of the instructions)
Manufacturing Furniture

B Enter code from pages C-8, 9, & 10
▶ |3|3|7|0|0|0|

C Business name. If no separate business name, leave blank.

D Employer ID number (EIN), if any
|5|9|2|0|2|9|7|6|3|

E Business address (including suite or room no.) ▶ **1234 University Avenue**
City, town or post office, state, and ZIP code **Gainesville, FL 32611**

F Accounting method: **(1)** ☐ Cash **(2)** ☒ Accrual **(3)** ☐ Other (specify) ▶ ....

G Did you "materially participate" in the operation of this business during 2005? If "No," see page C-3 for limit on losses ☒ Yes ☐ No

H If you started or acquired this business during 2005, check here . . . . ▶ ☐

Part I Income

1	Gross receipts or sales. **Caution.** If this income was reported to you on Form W-2 and the "Statutory employee" box on that form was checked, see page C-3 and check here . . . . . ▶ ☐	1	869,658
2	Returns and allowances	2	29,242
3	Subtract line 2 from line 1	3	840,416
4	Cost of goods sold (from line 42 on page 2)	4	540,204
5	**Gross profit.** Subtract line 4 from line 3	5	300,212
6	Other income, including Federal and state gasoline or fuel tax credit or refund (see page C-3)	6	
7	**Gross Income.** Add lines 5 and 6 . . . . ▶	7	300,212

Part II Expenses. Enter expenses for business use of your home **only** on line 30.

8	Advertising	**8**	13,000	18 Office expense . . .	**18**	16,000
9	Car and truck expenses (see page C-3)	**9**	4,000	19 Pension and profit-sharing plans	**19**	2,000
10	Commissions and fees . .	**10**	10,400	20 Rent or lease (see page C-5):		
11	Contract labor (see page C-4)	**11**		a Vehicles, machinery, and equipment .	**20a**	36,000
12	Depletion	**12**		b Other business property . . .	**20b**	
13	Depreciation and section 179 expense deduction (not included in Part III) (see page C-4)	**13**	12,476	21 Repairs and maintenance . .	**21**	
				22 Supplies (not included in Part III) .	**22**	
				23 Taxes and licenses	**23**	9,840
14	Employee benefit programs (other than on line 19). .	**14**	4,000	24 Travel, meals, and entertainment:		
				a Travel	**24a**	4,000
15	Insurance (other than health) .	**15**		b Deductible meals and entertainment (see page C-5)	**24b**	4,000
16	Interest:			25 Utilities	**25**	
a	Mortgage (paid to banks, etc.) .	**16a**		26 Wages (less employment credits) .	**26**	52,000
b	Other	**16b**	8,000	27 Other expenses (from line 48 on page 2)	**27**	8,650
17	Legal and professional services	**17**				

28	**Total expenses** before expenses for business use of home. Add lines 8 through 27 in columns . . ▶	**28**	184,366
29	Tentative profit (loss). Subtract line 28 from line 7	**29**	115,846
30	Expenses for business use of your home. Attach **Form 8829**	**30**	
31	**Net profit or (loss).** Subtract line 30 from line 29. • If a profit, enter on **Form 1040, line 12,** and **also** on Schedule SE, line 2 (statutory employees, see page C-6). Estates and trusts, enter on Form 1041, line 3. • If a loss, you **must** go to line 32.	**31**	115,846
32	If you have a loss, check the box that describes your investment in this activity (see page C-6). • If you checked 32a, enter the loss on **Form 1040, line 12,** and **also** on **Schedule SE, line 2** (statutory employees, see page C-6). Estates and trusts, enter on Form 1041, line 3. • If you checked 32b, you **must** attach **Form 6198.** Your loss may be limited.	**32a** ☒ All investment is at risk. **32b** ☐ Some investment is not at risk.	

For Paperwork Reduction Act Notice, see page C-7 of the instructions. Cat. No. 11334P Schedule C (Form 1040) 2005

Schedule C (Form 1040) 2005   Page **2**

Part III	Cost of Goods Sold (see page C-6)

33 Method(s) used to
value closing inventory: **a** ☒ Cost   **b** ☐ Lower of cost or market   **c** ☐ Other (attach explanation)

34 Was there any change in determining quantities, costs, or valuations between opening and closing inventory? If
"Yes," attach explanation . . . . ☐ **Yes**   ☐ **No**

35	Inventory at beginning of year. If different from last year's closing inventory, attach explanation . .	**35**	64,000
36	Purchases less cost of items withdrawn for personal use	**36**	340,800
37	Cost of labor. Do not include any amounts paid to yourself	**37**	143,204
38	Materials and supplies	**38**	
39	Other costs	**39**	97,000
40	Add lines 35 through 39	**40**	645,004
41	Inventory at end of year	**41**	104,800
42	**Cost of goods sold.** Subtract line 41 from line 40. Enter the result here and on page 1, line 4 . .	**42**	540,204

Part IV	Information on Your Vehicle. Complete this part **only** if you are claiming car or truck expenses on line 9 and are not required to file Form 4562 for this business. See the instructions for line 13 on page C-4 to find out if you must file Form 4562.

43 When did you place your vehicle in service for business purposes? (month, day, year) ▶ _3_ / _12_ / _04_ .

44 Of the total number of miles you drove your vehicle during 2005, enter the number of miles you used your vehicle for:

   a Business _17,000_   **b** Commuting (see instructions) _4,500_   **c** Other _12,000_

45 Do you (or your spouse) have another vehicle available for personal use?. . . . . ☒ **Yes**   ☐ **No**

46 Was your vehicle available for personal use during off-duty hours? . . . . ☒ **Yes**   ☐ **No**

47a Do you have evidence to support your deduction? . . . . ☒ **Yes**   ☐ **No**

   b If "Yes," is the evidence written? . . . . ☒ **Yes**   ☐ **No**

Part V	Other Expenses. List below business expenses not included on lines 8–26 or line 30.

Repairs	4,800
General and administrative	3,000
Miscellaneous	850

48	**Total other expenses.** Enter here and on page 1, line 27	**48**	8,650

FACTS FOR SOLE PROPRIETORSHIP (SCHEDULE C)

Andrew Lawrence is the sole proprietor of a business that operates under the name Andrew Lawrence Furniture (Business Code 337000). The proprietorship is located at 1234 University Ave., Gainesville, FL 32611. Its employer identification number is 59-2029763. Andrew started the business with a $200,000 capital investment on June 1, 1999. The proprietorship uses the calendar year as its tax year (the same as its proprietor) and the accrual method of accounting. The following information pertains to its 2005 activities:

A trial balance is included as part of the accompanying worksheet. Notes accompanying the account balances are presented below.

1. Cost of goods sold is determined as follows:

Inventory at beginning of year	$ 64,000
Plus: Purchases	340,800
Cost of labor	143,204
Additional Sec. 263A adjustment	7,000
Other costs	90,000
Goods available for sale	$645,004
Minus: Inventory at end of year	(104,800)
Cost of goods sold	$540,204

The proprietorship values its inventory using the first-in, first-out method and historical costs. The Sec. 263A rules apply to the proprietorship. No change in valuing inventories occurred between the beginning and end of the tax year.

2. The proprietorship uses MACRS depreciation for tax purposes. The current year tax depreciation is $27,476. Of this amount, $15,000 is included in cost of goods sold and inventory. The AMT depreciation adjustment on post-1986 personal property is $1,514. This amount is reported on Andrew Lawrence's Form 6251 (Alternative Minimum Tax—Individuals), which is not reproduced here.

3. Using its excess funds, the proprietorship has purchased various temporary investments, including a 2% investment in Plaza Corporation stock, 50 shares of Service Corporation stock, and some tax-exempt municipal bonds. The proprietorship has held the Plaza stock for two years and sold it in July for $4,500 more than its $7,000 adjusted basis. Prior to the sale, Plaza paid a $1,000 dividend. The 50 shares of Service stock, which had been purchased during the year, was declared worthless during the year. The proprietorship recovered none of its $2,100 adjusted basis.

4. Employees other than Andrew Lawrence receive limited fringe benefits. One employee also receives a $2,000 contribution to an Individual Retirement Account paid by the proprietorship.

5. Miscellaneous expenses include $150 of expenses related to the production of the dividend income.

6. The proprietorship paid no estimated taxes.

7. Balance sheet information is not provided for the sole proprietorship because it is not reported on the Schedule C. Balance sheet information, however, can be found on page 4 of the C corporation tax return.

Andrew Lawrence, Sole Proprietorship Reconciliation of Book and Taxable Income For Year Ending December 31, 2005

Account Name	Book Income Debit	Book Income Credit	Adjustments Debit	Adjustments Credit	Taxable Income Debit	Taxable Income Credit	Schedule C	Other Tax Forms
Sales		$869,658				$869,658	$869,658	
Sales returns & allowances	$ 29,242				$ 29,242		(29,242)	
Cost of sales	540,204				540,204		(540,204)	
Dividends		1,000			1,000	1,000		$ 1,000 (Sch. B)
Tax-exempt interest		18,000	$18,000			0		
Gain on July stock sale		4,500				4,500		4,500 (Sch. D)
Worthless stock loss	2,100				2,100			(2,100) (Sch. D)
Proprietor's salary(a)	36,000			$36,000	0		0	
Other salaries	52,000				52,000		(52,000)	
Rentals	36,000				36,000		(36,000)	
Bad debts	4,000				4,000		(4,000)	
Interest:								
Working capital loans	8,000				8,000		(8,000)	
Purchase tax-exempt bonds	2,000			2,000	0			
Employment taxes	8,320				8,320		(8,320)	
Taxes	1,520				1,520		(1,520)	
Repairs	4,800				4,800		(4,800)	
Depreciation(b)	12,000		476		12,476		(12,476)	
Charitable contributions	12,000				12,000			(12,000) (Sch. A)
Travel	4,000				4,000		(4,000)	
Meals and entertainment(c)	8,000			4,000	4,000		(4,000)	
Office expenses	16,000				16,000		(16,000)	
Advertising	13,000				13,000		(13,000)	
Transportation expense	10,400				10,400		(10,400)	
General and administrative	3,000				3,000		(3,000)	
Pension plans(d)	2,000				2,000		(2,000)	
Employee benefit programs(e)	4,000				4,000		(4,000)	
Miscellaneous	1,000				1,000		(850)	(150) (Form 4952)
Net profit/Taxable income	83,572		23,524		107,096		115,846	
Total	$893,158	$893,158	$42,000	$42,000	$875,158	$875,158	$115,846	

(a) The $3,000 monthly salary for Andrew Lawrence is treated as a withdrawal from the proprietorship and is not deducted on Schedule C. The salary does not reduce Schedule C income and therefore is taxed as self-employment income.

(b) MACRS depreciation is $27,476 − $15,000 = $12,476.

(c) 50% of the meals and entertainment expense is not deductible for tax purposes.

(d) The pension plan expense is the same for book and tax purposes for this business. No pension expenses relate to pensions for the proprietor.

(e) The employee benefit expense is the same for book and tax purposes for this business. None relate to proprietor benefits.

SCHEDULE E (Form 1040)	Supplemental Income and Loss	OMB No. 1545-0074
Department of the Treasury Internal Revenue Service (99)	(From rental real estate, royalties, partnerships, S corporations, estates, trusts, REMICs, etc.) ▶ Attach to Form 1040 or Form 1041. ▶ See Instructions for Schedule E (Form 1040).	2005 Attachment Sequence No. 13

Name(s) shown on return | | Your social security number

Part I Income or Loss From Rental Real Estate and Royalties

Note. If you are in the business of renting personal property, use **Schedule C** or **C-EZ** (see page E-3). Report farm rental income or loss from **Form 4835** on page 2, line 40.

1 List the type and location of each **rental real estate property:**

A ....

B ....

C ....

2 For each rental real estate property listed on line 1, did you or your family use it during the tax year for personal purposes for more than the greater of:

- 14 days **or**
- 10% of the total days rented at fair rental value?

(See page E-3.)

	Yes	No
A		
B		
C		

		Properties			Totals (Add columns A, B, and C.)
Income:		A	B	C	
3 Rents received	3		3		
4 Royalties received	4				4
Expenses:					
5 Advertising	5				
6 Auto and travel (see page E-4).	6				
7 Cleaning and maintenance . .	7				
8 Commissions	8				
9 Insurance	9				
10 Legal and other professional fees	10				
11 Management fees	11				
12 Mortgage interest paid to banks, etc. (see page E-4)	12				12
13 Other interest	13				
14 Repairs	14				
15 Supplies	15				
16 Taxes	16				
17 Utilities	17				
18 Other (list) ▶	18				
19 Add lines 5 through 18 . . .	19				19
20 Depreciation expense or depletion (see page E-4)	20				20
21 Total expenses. Add lines 19 and 20	21				
22 Income or (loss) from rental real estate or royalty properties. Subtract line 21 from line 3 (rents) or line 4 (royalties). If the result is a (loss), see page E-5 to find out if you must file **Form 6198** . .	22				
23 Deductible rental real estate loss. **Caution.** Your rental real estate loss on line 22 may be limited. See page E-5 to find out if you must file **Form 8582**. Real estate professionals must complete line 43 on page 2	23	( )	( )	( )	
24 **Income.** Add positive amounts shown on line 22. **Do not** include any losses					24
25 **Losses.** Add royalty losses from line 22 and rental real estate losses from line 23. Enter total losses here					25 ( )
26 **Total rental real estate and royalty income or (loss).** Combine lines 24 and 25. Enter the result here. If Parts II, III, IV, and line 40 on page 2 do not apply to you, also enter this amount on Form 1040, line 17. Otherwise, include this amount in the total on line 41 on page 2					26

For Paperwork Reduction Act Notice, see page E-7 of the instructions. Cat. No. 11344L **Schedule E (Form 1040) 2005**

Schedule E (Form 1040) 2005   Attachment Sequence No. **13**   Page **2**

Name(s) shown on return. Do not enter name and social security number if shown on other side. | Your social security number

Caution. The IRS compares amounts reported on your tax return with amounts shown on Schedule(s) K-1.

Part II   Income or Loss From Partnerships and S Corporations   **Note.** If you report a loss from an at-risk activity for which **any** amount is **not** at risk, you **must** check the box in column **(e)** on line 28 and attach **Form 6198.** See page E-1.

27   Are you reporting any loss not allowed in a prior year due to the at-risk or basis limitations, a prior year unallowed loss from a passive activity (if that loss was not reported on Form 8582), or unreimbursed partnership expenses? ☐ **Yes** ☐ **No**   If you answered "Yes," see page E-6 before completing this section.

28	(a) Name	(b) Enter P for partnership; S for S corporation	(c) Check if foreign partnership	(d) Employer identification number	(e) Check if any amount is not at risk
A			☐		☐
B			☐		☐
C			☐		☐
D			☐		☐

	Passive Income and Loss		Nonpassive Income and Loss		
	(f) Passive loss allowed (attach Form 8582 if required)	(g) Passive income from Schedule K-1	(h) Nonpassive loss from Schedule K-1	(i) Section 179 expense deduction from Form 4562	(j) Nonpassive income from Schedule K-1
A					
B					
C					
D					
29a Totals					
b Totals					

30   Add columns (g) and (j) of line 29a   **30**

31   Add columns (f), (h), and (i) of line 29b   **31** ( )

32   **Total partnership and S corporation income or (loss).** Combine lines 30 and 31. Enter the result here and include in the total on line 41 below.   **32**

Part III   Income or Loss From Estates and Trusts

33	(a) Name	(b) Employer identification number
A		
B		

	Passive Income and Loss		Nonpassive Income and Loss	
	(c) Passive deduction or loss allowed (attach Form 8582 if required)	(d) Passive income from Schedule K-1	(e) Deduction or loss from Schedule K-1	(f) Other income from Schedule K-1
A				
B				
34a Totals				
b Totals				

35   Add columns (d) and (f) of line 34a   **35**

36   Add columns (c) and (e) of line 34b   **36** ( )

37   **Total estate and trust income or (loss).** Combine lines 35 and 36. Enter the result here and include in the total on line 41 below   **37**

Part IV   Income or Loss From Real Estate Mortgage Investment Conduits (REMICs)—Residual Holder

38	(a) Name	(b) Employer identification number	(c) Excess inclusion from Schedules Q, line 2c (see page E-6)	(d) Taxable income (net loss) from Schedules Q, line 1b	(e) Income from Schedules Q, line 3b

39   Combine columns (d) and (e) only. Enter the result here and include in the total on line 41 below   **39**

Part V   Summary

40   Net farm rental income or (loss) from **Form 4835.** Also, complete line 42 below   **40**

41   **Total income or (loss).** Combine lines 26, 32, 37, 39, and 40. Enter the result here and on Form 1040, line 17 ▶   **41**

42   **Reconciliation of farming and fishing income.** Enter your **gross** farming and fishing income reported on Form 4835, line 7; Schedule K-1 (Form 1065), box 14, code B; Schedule K-1 (Form 1120S), box 17, code N; and Schedule K-1 (Form 1041), line 14, code F (see page E-7)   **42**

43   **Reconciliation for real estate professionals.** If you were a real estate professional (see page E-1), enter the net income or (loss) you reported anywhere on Form 1040 from all rental real estate activities in which you materially participated under the passive activity loss rules   **43**

Schedule E (Form 1040) 2005

SCHEDULE SE

(Form 1040)

Department of the Treasury
Internal Revenue Service (99)

OMB No. 1545-0074

2005

Attachment
Sequence No. **17**

Self-Employment Tax

▶ **Attach to Form 1040.** ▶ **See Instructions for Schedule SE (Form 1040).**

Name of person with **self-employment** income (as shown on Form 1040)

Social security number of person
with **self-employment** income ▶

Who Must File Schedule SE

You must file Schedule SE if:

- You had net earnings from self-employment from **other than** church employee income (line 4 of Short Schedule SE or line 4c of Long Schedule SE) of $400 or more, **or**

- You had church employee income of $108.28 or more. Income from services you performed as a minister or a member of a religious order **is not** church employee income (see page SE-1).

Note. Even if you had a loss or a small amount of income from self-employment, it may be to your benefit to file Schedule SE and use either "optional method" in Part II of Long Schedule SE (see page SE-3).

Exception. If your only self-employment income was from earnings as a minister, member of a religious order, or Christian Science practitioner **and** you filed Form 4361 and received IRS approval not to be taxed on those earnings, **do not** file Schedule SE. Instead, write "Exempt–Form 4361" on Form 1040, line 58.

May I Use Short Schedule SE or Must I Use Long Schedule SE?

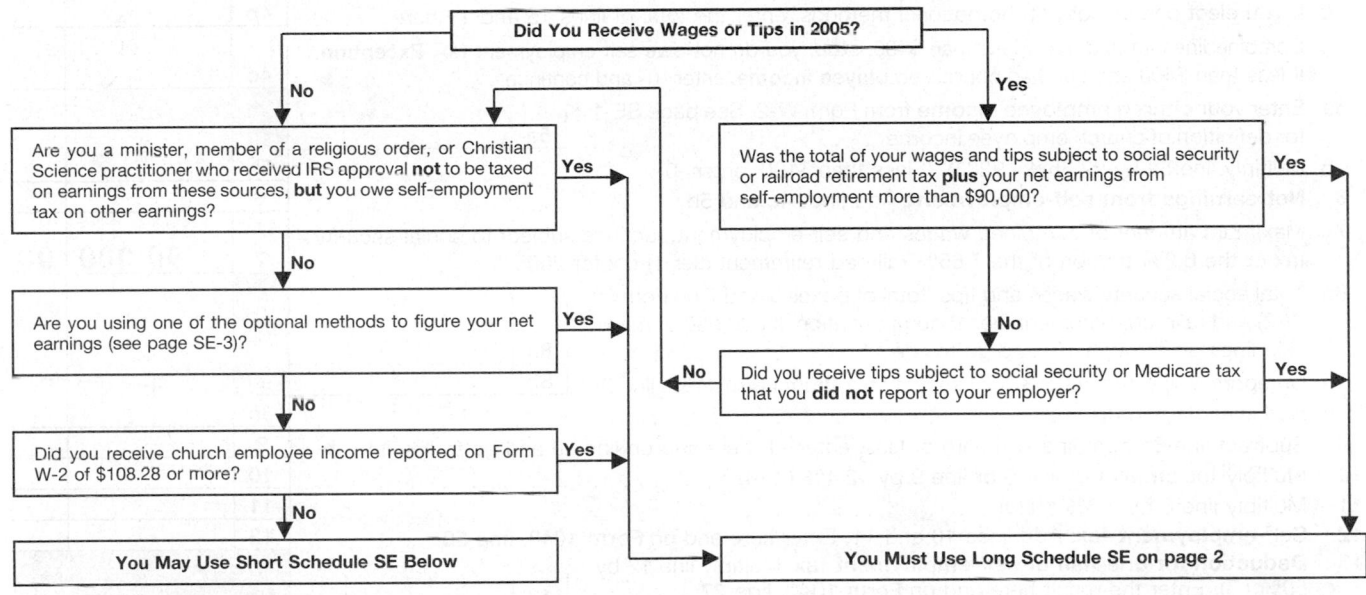

Section A—Short Schedule SE. Caution. Read above to see if you can use Short Schedule SE.

1	Net farm profit or (loss) from Schedule F, line 36, and farm partnerships, Schedule K-1 (Form 1065), box 14, code A	**1**
2	Net profit or (loss) from Schedule C, line 31; Schedule C-EZ, line 3; Schedule K-1 (Form 1065), box 14, code A (other than farming); and Schedule K-1 (Form 1065-B), box 9. Ministers and members of religious orders, see page SE-1 for amounts to report on this line. See page SE-2 for other income to report	**2**
3	Combine lines 1 and 2	**3**
4	**Net earnings from self-employment.** Multiply line 3 by 92.35% (.9235). If less than $400, **do not** file this schedule; you do not owe self-employment tax . . . . ▶	**4**
5	**Self-employment tax.** If the amount on line 4 is:	**5**
	• $90,000 or less, multiply line 4 by 15.3% (.153). Enter the result here and on **Form 1040, line 58.**	
	• More than $90,000, multiply line 4 by 2.9% (.029). Then, add $11,160.00 to the result. Enter the total here and on **Form 1040, line 58.**	
6	**Deduction for one-half of self-employment tax.** Multiply line 5 by 50% (.5). Enter the result here and on **Form 1040, line 27**	**6**	

For Paperwork Reduction Act Notice, see Form 1040 instructions.

Cat. No. 11358Z

Schedule SE (Form 1040) 2005

Name of person with **self-employment** income (as shown on Form 1040)	Social security number of person with **self-employment** income ▶		

Section B—Long Schedule SE

Part I   Self-Employment Tax

Note. If your only income subject to self-employment tax is **church employee income,** skip lines 1 through 4b. Enter -0- on line 4c and go to line 5a. Income from services you performed as a minister or a member of a religious order **is not** church employee income. See page SE-1.

A   If you are a minister, member of a religious order, or Christian Science practitioner **and** you filed Form 4361, but you had $400 or more of **other** net earnings from self-employment, check here and continue with Part I . . . . . . ▶ ☐

1	Net farm profit or (loss) from Schedule F, line 36, and farm partnerships, Schedule K-1 (Form 1065), box 14, code A. **Note.** Skip this line if you use the farm optional method (see page SE-4)	**1**		
2	Net profit or (loss) from Schedule C, line 31; Schedule C-EZ, line 3; Schedule K-1 (Form 1065), box 14, code A (other than farming); and Schedule K-1 (Form 1065-B), box 9. Ministers and members of religious orders, see page SE-1 for amounts to report on this line. See page SE-2 for other income to report. **Note.** Skip this line if you use the nonfarm optional method (see page SE-4)	**2**		
3	Combine lines 1 and 2	**3**		
4a	If line 3 is more than zero, multiply line 3 by 92.35% (.9235). Otherwise, enter amount from line 3	**4a**		
b	If you elect one or both of the optional methods, enter the total of lines 15 and 17 here . . .	**4b**		
c	Combine lines 4a and 4b. If less than $400, **stop;** you do not owe self-employment tax. **Exception.** If less than $400 and you had **church employee income,** enter -0- and continue. . . . . . ▶	**4c**		
5a	Enter your **church employee income** from Form W-2. See page SE-1 for definition of church employee income **5a**			
b	Multiply line 5a by 92.35% (.9235). If less than $100, enter -0-	**5b**		
6	**Net earnings from self-employment.** Add lines 4c and 5b . . .	**6**		
7	Maximum amount of combined wages and self-employment earnings subject to social security tax or the 6.2% portion of the 7.65% railroad retirement (tier 1) tax for 2005	**7**	**90,000**	00
8a	Total social security wages and tips (total of boxes 3 and 7 on Form(s) W-2) and railroad retirement (tier 1) compensation. If $90,000 or more, skip lines 8b through 10, and go to line 11 . . . . **8a**			
b	Unreported tips subject to social security tax (from Form 4137, line 9) **8b**			
c	Add lines 8a and 8b.	**8c**		
9	Subtract line 8c from line 7. If zero or less, enter -0- here and on line 10 and go to line 11 . ▶	**9**		
10	Multiply the **smaller** of line 6 or line 9 by 12.4% (.124)	**10**		
11	Multiply line 6 by 2.9% (.029)	**11**		
12	**Self-employment tax.** Add lines 10 and 11. Enter here and on **Form 1040, line 58**	**12**		
13	**Deduction for one-half of self-employment tax.** Multiply line 12 by 50% (.5). Enter the result here and on **Form 1040, line 27** **13**			

Part II   Optional Methods To Figure Net Earnings (see page SE-3)

	Farm Optional Method. You may use this method **only** if **(a)** your gross farm income[1] was not more than $2,400 **or (b)** your net farm profits[2] were less than $1,733.			
14	Maximum income for optional methods	**14**	**1,600**	00
15	Enter the **smaller** of: two-thirds (⅔) of gross farm income[1] (not less than zero) **or** $1,600. Also include this amount on line 4b above	**15**		
	Nonfarm Optional Method. You may use this method **only** if **(a)** your net nonfarm profits[3] were less than $1,733 and also less than 72.189% of your gross nonfarm income[4] **and (b)** you had net earnings from self-employment of at least $400 in 2 of the prior 3 years.			
	Caution. You may use this method no more than five times.			
16	Subtract line 15 from line 14	**16**		
17	Enter the **smaller** of: two-thirds (⅔) of gross nonfarm income[4] (not less than zero) **or** the amount on line 16. Also include this amount on line 4b above	**17**		

[1] From Sch. F, line 11, and Sch. K-1 (Form 1065), box 14, code B.

[2] From Sch. F, line 36, and Sch. K-1 (Form 1065), box 14, code A.

[3] From Sch. C, line 31; Sch. C-EZ, line 3; Sch. K-1 (Form 1065), box 14, code A; and Sch. K-1 (Form 1065-B), box 9.

[4] From Sch. C, line 7; Sch. C-EZ, line 1; Sch. K-1 (Form 1065), box 14, code C; and Sch. K-1 (Form 1065-B), box 9.

SCHEDULE F
(Form 1040)

Department of the Treasury
Internal Revenue Service (99)

Profit or Loss From Farming

▶ Attach to Form 1040, Form 1041, Form 1065, or Form 1065-B.

▶ See Instructions for Schedule F (Form 1040).

OMB No. 1545-0074

2005

Attachment
Sequence No. **14**

Name of proprietor

Social security number (SSN)

A Principal product. Describe in one or two words your principal crop or activity for the current tax year.

B Enter code from Part IV
▶

C Accounting method: (1) ☐ Cash (2) ☐ Accrual

D Employer ID number (EIN), if any

E Did you "materially participate" in the operation of this business during 2005? If "No," see page F-2 for limit on passive losses. ☐ Yes ☐ No

Part I Farm Income—Cash Method. Complete Parts I and II (Accrual method. Complete Parts II and III, and Part I, line 11.)
Do not include sales of livestock held for draft, breeding, sport, or dairy purposes; report these sales on Form 4797.

1	Sales of livestock and other items you bought for resale	**1**	
2	Cost or other basis of livestock and other items reported on line 1. . .	**2**	
3	Subtract line 2 from line 1	**3**	
4	Sales of livestock, produce, grains, and other products you raised . . .	**4**	
5a	Cooperative distributions (Form(s) 1099-PATR) . **5a**	5b Taxable amount **5b**	
6a	Agricultural program payments (see page F-2) . **6a**	6b Taxable amount **6b**	
7	Commodity Credit Corporation (CCC) loans (see page F-3):		
a	CCC loans reported under election	**7a**	
b	CCC loans forfeited. **7b**	7c Taxable amount **7c**	
8	Crop insurance proceeds and Federal crop disaster payments (see page F-3):		
a	Amount received in 2005 . . . . . **8a**	8b Taxable amount **8b**	
c	If election to defer to 2006 is attached, check here ▶ ☐	8d Amount deferred from 2004 **8d**	
9	Custom hire (machine work) income	**9**	
10	Other income, including Federal and state gasoline or fuel tax credit or refund (see page F-3)	**10**	
11	**Gross income.** Add amounts in the right column for lines 3 through 10. If you use the accrual method, enter the amount from Part III, line 51 . . . . ▶	**11**	

Part II Farm Expenses—Cash and Accrual Method.
Do not include personal or living expenses such as taxes, insurance, repairs, etc., on your home.

12	Car and truck expenses (see page F-4—also attach **Form 4562**)	**12**	25	Pension and profit-sharing plans	**25**
13	Chemicals	**13**	26	Rent or lease (see page F-5):	
14	Conservation expenses (see page F-4)	**14**	a	Vehicles, machinery, and equipment	**26a**
15	Custom hire (machine work) .	**15**	b	Other (land, animals, etc.) . . .	**26b**
16	Depreciation and section 179 expense deduction not claimed elsewhere (see page F-4) . .	**16**	27	Repairs and maintenance . .	**27**
			28	Seeds and plants	**28**
			29	Storage and warehousing . .	**29**
17	Employee benefit programs other than on line 25	**17**	30	Supplies	**30**
18	Feed	**18**	31	Taxes	**31**
19	Fertilizers and lime . . .	**19**	32	Utilities	**32**
20	Freight and trucking. . . .	**20**	33	Veterinary, breeding, and medicine	**33**
21	Gasoline, fuel, and oil . .	**21**	34	Other expenses (specify):	
22	Insurance (other than health) .	**22**	a	_____	**34a**
23	Interest:		b	_____	**34b**
			c	_____	**34c**
a	Mortgage (paid to banks, etc.)	**23a**	d	_____	**34d**
b	Other	**23b**	e	_____	**34e**
24	Labor hired (less employment credits)	**24**	f	_____	**34f**

35	**Total expenses.** Add lines 12 through 34f . . . . ▶	**35**
36	**Net farm profit or (loss).** Subtract line 35 from line 11. • If a profit, enter on **Form 1040, line 18,** and also on **Schedule SE, line 1.** • If a loss, you **must** go to line 37. Estates, trusts, and partnerships, see page F-6.	**36**
37	If you have a loss, you **must** check the box that describes your investment in this activity (see page F-6). • If you checked 37a, enter the loss on **Form 1040, line 18,** and also on **Schedule SE, line 1.** • If you checked 37b, you **must** attach **Form 6198.** Your loss may be limited.	**37a** ☐ All investment is at risk. **37b** ☐ Some investment is not at risk.

For Paperwork Reduction Act Notice, see page F-6 of the instructions.   Cat. No. 11346H   Schedule F (Form 1040) 2005

Schedule F (Form 1040) 2005

Page **2**

Part III Farm Income—Accrual Method (see page F-6).

Do not include sales of livestock held for draft, breeding, sport, or dairy purposes; report these sales on Form 4797 and do not include this livestock on line 46 below.

38	Sales of livestock, produce, grains, and other products	**38**	
39a	Cooperative distributions (Form(s) 1099-PATR). . . **39a** _____	**39b** Taxable amount	**39b**	
40a	Agricultural program payments . . . . . **40a** _____	**40b** Taxable amount	**40b**	
41	Commodity Credit Corporation (CCC) loans:		
a	CCC loans reported under election	**41a**	
b	CCC loans forfeited . . . . **41b** _____	**41c** Taxable amount	**41c**	
42	Crop insurance proceeds	**42**	
43	Custom hire (machine work) income	**43**	
44	Other income, including Federal and state gasoline or fuel tax credit or refund	**44**	
45	Add amounts in the right column for lines 38 through 44	**45**	

46	Inventory of livestock, produce, grains, and other products at beginning of the year	**46**	
47	Cost of livestock, produce, grains, and other products purchased during the year	**47**	
48	Add lines 46 and 47	**48**	
49	Inventory of livestock, produce, grains, and other products at end of year	**49**	
50	Cost of livestock, produce, grains, and other products sold. Subtract line 49 from line 48*		**50**	
51	**Gross income.** Subtract line 50 from line 45. Enter the result here and on Part I, line 11 . . . . . ▶		**51**	

*If you use the unit-livestock-price method or the farm-price method of valuing inventory and the amount on line 49 is larger than the amount on line 48, subtract line 48 from line 49. Enter the result on line 50. Add lines 45 and 50. Enter the total on line 51 and on Part I, line 11.

Part IV Principal Agricultural Activity Codes

File Schedule C (Form 1040) or Schedule C-EZ (Form 1040) instead of Schedule F if (a) your principal source of income is from providing agricultural services such as soil preparation, veterinary, farm labor, horticultural, or management for a fee or on a contract basis, or (b) you are engaged in the business of breeding, raising, and caring for dogs, cats, or other pet animals.

These codes for the Principal Agricultural Activity classify farms by the type of activity they are engaged in to facilitate the administration of the Internal Revenue Code. These six-digit codes are based on the North American Industry Classification System (NAICS).

Select the code that best identifies your primary farming activity and enter it on page 1, line B.

Crop Production

111100	Oilseed and grain farming
111210	Vegetable and melon farming
111300	Fruit and tree nut farming
111400	Greenhouse, nursery, and floriculture production
111900	Other crop farming

Animal Production

112111	Beef cattle ranching and farming
112112	Cattle feedlots
112120	Dairy cattle and milk production
112210	Hog and pig farming
112300	Poultry and egg production
112400	Sheep and goat farming
112510	Animal aquaculture
112900	Other animal production

Forestry and Logging

113000	Forestry and logging (including forest nurseries and timber tracts)

Form **1041** Department of the Treasury—Internal Revenue Service
U.S. Income Tax Return for Estates and Trusts 2005   OMB No. 1545-0092

A Type of entity (see instr.):

For calendar year 2005 or fiscal year beginning ____, 2005, and ending ____, 20__

- ☐ Decedent's estate
- ☒ Simple trust
- ☐ Complex trust
- ☐ Qualified disability trust
- ☐ ESBT (S portion only)
- ☐ Grantor type trust
- ☐ Bankruptcy estate–Ch. 7
- ☐ Bankruptcy estate–Ch. 11
- ☐ Pooled income fund

Name of estate or trust (If a grantor type trust, see page 12 of the instructions.)
Bob Adams Trust (Simple Trust)

Name and title of fiduciary
First Bank

Number, street, and room or suite no. (If a P.O. box, see page 12 of the instructions.)
Post Office Box 100

City or town, state, and ZIP code
Nashville, TN 37203

C Employer identification number
74 : 1237211

D Date entity created
1993

E Nonexempt charitable and split-interest trusts, check applicable boxes (see page 13 of the instr.):
- ☐ Described in section 4947(a)(1)
- ☐ Not a private foundation
- ☐ Described in section 4947(a)(2)

B Number of Schedules K-1 attached (see instructions) ▶ **1**

F Check applicable boxes:
- ☐ Initial return
- ☐ Final return
- ☐ Amended return
- ☐ Change in fiduciary
- ☐ Change in fiduciary's name
- ☐ Change in trust's name
- ☐ Change in fiduciary's address

G Pooled mortgage account (see page 14 of the instructions): ☐ Bought ☐ Sold Date:

Income

1	Interest income	1	
2a	Total ordinary dividends	2a	30,000
b	Qualified dividends allocable to: **(1)** Beneficiaries ___30,000___ **(2)** Estate or trust ___-0-___		
3	Business income or (loss) (attach Schedule C or C-EZ (Form 1040))	3	
4	Capital gain or (loss) (attach Schedule D (Form 1041))	4	12,000
5	Rents, royalties, partnerships, other estates and trusts, etc. (attach Schedule E (Form 1040)) (see below)	5	4,000
6	Farm income or (loss) (attach Schedule F (Form 1040))	6	
7	Ordinary gain or (loss) (attach Form 4797)	7	
8	Other income. List type and amount ____	8	
9	**Total income.** Combine lines 1, 2a, and 3 through 8 ▶	9	46,000

Deductions

10	Interest. Check if Form 4952 is attached ▶ ☐	10	
11	Taxes	11	
12	Fiduciary fees **($1,200 − $360)**	12	840
13	Charitable deduction (from Schedule A, line 7)	13	
14	Attorney, accountant, and return preparer fees	14	500
15a	Other deductions **not** subject to the 2% floor (attach schedule)	15a	
b	Allowable miscellaneous itemized deductions subject to the 2% floor	15b	
16	Add lines 10 through 15b ▶	16	1,340
17	Adjusted total income or (loss). Subtract line 16 from line 9 ▶ **17 44,660**		
18	Income distribution deduction (from Schedule B, line 15) (attach Schedules K-1 (Form 1041))	18	32,660
19	Estate tax deduction (including certain generation-skipping taxes) (attach computation)	19	
20	Exemption	20	300
21	Add lines 18 through 20 ▶	21	32,960

Tax and Payments

22	Taxable income. Subtract line 21 from line 17. If a loss, see page 20 of the instructions	22	11,700
23	**Total tax** (from Schedule G, line 7)	23	1,555
24	**Payments: a** 2005 estimated tax payments and amount applied from 2004 return	24a	2,600
b	Estimated tax payments allocated to beneficiaries (from Form 1041-T)	24b	
c	Subtract line 24b from line 24a	24c	2,600
d	Tax paid with Form 7004 (see page 20 of the instructions)	24d	
e	Federal income tax withheld. If any is from Form(s) 1099, check ▶ ☐	24e	
	Other payments: **f** Form 2439 ____ ; **g** Form 4136 ____ ; Total ▶	24h	
25	**Total payments.** Add lines 24c through 24e, and 24h ▶	25	2,600
26	Estimated tax penalty (see page 20 of the instructions)	26	
27	**Tax due.** If line 25 is smaller than the total of lines 23 and 26, enter amount owed	27	
28	**Overpayment.** If line 25 is larger than the total of lines 23 and 26, enter amount overpaid	28	1,045
29	Amount of line 28 to be: **a** Credited to 2006 estimated tax ▶ **1,045** ; **b** Refunded ▶	29	

Sign Here

Under penalties of perjury, I declare that I have examined this return, including accompanying schedules and statements, and to the best of my knowledge and belief, it is true, correct, and complete. Declaration of preparer (other than taxpayer) is based on all information of which preparer has any knowledge.

▶ *Tom Trusty*   Signature of fiduciary or officer representing fiduciary | 3-15-06 ▶ Date | 38 : 1505087 EIN of fiduciary if a financial institution

May the IRS discuss this return with the preparer shown below (see instr.)? ☒ Yes ☐ No

Paid Preparer's Use Only

Preparer's signature ▶ *Karen Certified*	Date 3-14-06	Check if self-employed ☒	Preparer's SSN or PTIN 444-17-1313
Firm's name (or yours if self-employed), address, and ZIP code ▶ Karen Certified, One Opryland Place, Nashville TN 37204		EIN 74 : 1234567 Phone no. (615) 372-1800

For Privacy Act and Paperwork Reduction Act Notice, see the separate instructions.   Cat. No. 11370H   Form **1041** (2005)

Line 5: Net rental income = Rental income ($5,000) −
Realtor's commissions ($1,000) = Net rental income ($4,000)

Note: Pages concerning the AMT are omitted because the trust does not owe the AMT.

Form 1041 (2005) Page **2**

Schedule A · Charitable Deduction. Do not complete for a simple trust or a pooled income fund.

1	Amounts paid or permanently set aside for charitable purposes from gross income (see page 21)	1	
2	Tax-exempt income allocable to charitable contributions (see page 21 of the instructions) . .	2	
3	Subtract line 2 from line 1	3	
4	Capital gains for the tax year allocated to corpus and paid or permanently set aside for charitable purposes	4	
5	Add lines 3 and 4	5	
6	Section 1202 exclusion allocable to capital gains paid or permanently set aside for charitable purposes (see page 21 of the instructions)	6	
7	**Charitable deduction.** Subtract line 6 from line 5. Enter here and on page 1, line 13	7	

Schedule B · Income Distribution Deduction

1	Adjusted total income (see page 22 of the instructions)	1	44,660
2	Adjusted tax-exempt interest . **($15,000 − $360)**	2	14,640
3	Total net gain from Schedule D (Form 1041), line 15, column (1) (see page 22 of the instructions)	3	
4	Enter amount from Schedule A, line 4 (reduced by any allocable section 1202 exclusion)	4	
5	Capital gains for the tax year included on Schedule A, line 1 (see page 22 of the instructions)	5	
6	Enter any gain from page 1, line 4, as a negative number. If page 1, line 4, is a loss, enter the loss as a positive number	6	(12,000)
7	**Distributable net income (DNI).** Combine lines 1 through 6. If zero or less, enter -0- . . .	7	47,300
8	If a complex trust, enter accounting income for the tax year as determined under the governing instrument and applicable local law	8	
9	Income required to be distributed currently	9	48,500
10	Other amounts paid, credited, or otherwise required to be distributed	10	-0-
11	Total distributions. Add lines 9 and 10. If greater than line 8, see page 22 of the instructions	11	48,500
12	Enter the amount of tax-exempt income included on line 11	12	14,640
13	Tentative income distribution deduction. Subtract line 12 from line 11	13	33,860
14	Tentative income distribution deduction. Subtract line 2 from line 7. If zero or less, enter -0-	14	32,660
15	**Income distribution deduction.** Enter the smaller of line 13 or line 14 here and on page 1, line 18	15	32,660

Schedule G · Tax Computation (see page 23 of the instructions)

1 Tax:	a Tax on taxable income (see page 23 of the instructions) . . .	1a	1,555	
	b Tax on lump-sum distributions (attach Form 4972)	1b		
	c Alternative minimum tax (from Schedule I, line 56)	1c		
	d **Total.** Add lines 1a through 1c . . . . ▶	1d		1,555
2a	Foreign tax credit (attach Form 1116)	2a		
b	Other nonbusiness credits (attach schedule)	2b		
c	General business credit. Enter here and check which forms are attached: ☐ Form 3800 ☐ Forms (specify) ▶	2c		
d	Credit for prior year minimum tax (attach Form 8801)	2d		
3	**Total credits.** Add lines 2a through 2d . . . . ▶	3		
4	Subtract line 3 from line 1d. If zero or less, enter -0-	4		1,555
5	Recapture taxes. Check if from: ☐ Form 4255 ☐ Form 8611	5		
6	Household employment taxes. Attach Schedule H (Form 1040)	6		
7	**Total tax.** Add lines 4 through 6. Enter here and on page 1, line 23 . . . . . ▶	7		1,555

Other Information

		Yes	No
1	Did the estate or trust receive tax-exempt income? If "Yes," attach a computation of the allocation of expenses Enter the amount of tax-exempt interest income and exempt-interest dividends ▶ $ **15,000 (see below)**	X	
2	Did the estate or trust receive all or any part of the earnings (salary, wages, and other compensation) of any individual by reason of a contract assignment or similar arrangement?		X
3	At any time during calendar year 2005, did the estate or trust have an interest in or a signature or other authority over a bank, securities, or other financial account in a foreign country? . . . . See page 25 of the instructions for exceptions and filing requirements for Form TD F 90-22.1. If "Yes," enter the name of the foreign country ▶		X
4	During the tax year, did the estate or trust receive a distribution from, or was it the grantor of, or transferor to, a foreign trust? If "Yes," the estate or trust may have to file Form 3520. See page 25 of the instructions .		X
5	Did the estate or trust receive, or pay, any qualified residence interest on seller-provided financing? If "Yes," see page 25 for required attachment		X
6	If this is an estate or a complex trust making the section 663(b) election, check here (see page 25) . . ▶ ☐		
7	To make a section 643(e)(3) election, attach Schedule D (Form 1041), and check here (see page 25) . ▶ ☐		
8	If the decedent's estate has been open for more than 2 years, attach an explanation for the delay in closing the estate, and check here ▶ ☐		
9	Are any present or future trust beneficiaries skip persons? See page 26 of the instructions		

Form **1041** (2005)

Line 2: Allocation of expenses: $\dfrac{\$15,000}{\$50,000} \times \$1,200 = \$360$ of trustees fee allocated to tax-exempt income

SCHEDULE D
(Form 1041)
Department of the Treasury
Internal Revenue Service

Capital Gains and Losses

▶ Attach to Form 1041, Form 5227, or Form 990-T. See the separate instructions for Form 1041 (also for Form 5227 or Form 990-T, if applicable).

OMB No. 1545-0092

20**05**

Name of estate or trust
Bob Adams Trust

Employer identification number
74 : 1237211

Note: *Form 5227 filers need to complete only Parts I and II.*

Part I Short-Term Capital Gains and Losses—Assets Held One Year or Less

(a) Description of property (Example, 100 shares 7% preferred of "Z" Co.)	(b) Date acquired (mo., day, yr.)	(c) Date sold (mo., day, yr.)	(d) Sales price	(e) Cost or other basis (see page 34)	(f) Gain or (Loss) for the entire year (col. (d) less col. (e))
1					

2 Short-term capital gain or (loss) from Forms 4684, 6252, 6781, and 8824 . . . . **2**
3 Net short-term gain or (loss) from partnerships, S corporations, and other estates or trusts . **3**
4 Short-term capital loss carryover. Enter the amount, if any, from line 9 of the 2004 Capital Loss Carryover Worksheet . . . . . . **4** ( )
5 **Net short-term gain or (loss).** Combine lines 1 through 4 in column (f). Enter here and on line 13, column (3) below . . . . ▶ **5**

Part II Long-Term Capital Gains and Losses—Assets Held More Than One Year

(a) Description of property (Example, 100 shares 7% preferred of "Z" Co.)	(b) Date acquired (mo., day, yr.)	(c) Date sold (mo., day, yr.)	(d) Sales price	(e) Cost or other basis (see page 34)	(f) Gain or (Loss) for the entire year (col. (d) less col. (e))
6 1,000 shares of ABC Corp.	2001	Oct. 2005	15,000	3,000	12,000

7 Long-term capital gain or (loss) from Forms 2439, 4684, 6252, 6781, and 8824 . . . . **7**
8 Net long-term gain or (loss) from partnerships, S corporations, and other estates or trusts . **8**
9 Capital gain distributions **9**
10 Gain from Form 4797, Part I **10**
11 Long-term capital loss carryover. Enter the amount, if any, from line 14 of the 2004 Capital Loss Carryover Worksheet . . . . . . **11** ( )
12 **Net long-term gain or (loss).** Combine lines 6 through 11 in column (f). Enter here and on line 14a, column (3) below . . . . ▶ **12** 12,000

Part III Summary of Parts I and II

Caution: *Read the instructions before completing this part.*

		(1) Beneficiaries' (see page 36)	(2) Estate's or trust's	(3) Total
13	**Net short-term gain or (loss)**	**13**		
14	**Net long-term gain or (loss):**			
a	Total for year	**14a**	12,000	12,000
b	Unrecaptured section 1250 gain (see line 18 of the worksheet on page 35)	**14b**		
c	28% rate gain or (loss)	**14c**		
15	**Total net gain or (loss).** Combine lines 13 and 14a. ▶	**15**	12,000	12,000

Note: *If line 15, column (3), is a net gain, enter the gain on Form 1041, line 4. If lines 14a and 15, column (2), are net gains, go to Part V, and do not complete Part IV. If line 15, column (3), is a net loss, complete Part IV and the Capital Loss Carryover Worksheet, as necessary.*

For Paperwork Reduction Act Notice, see the Instructions for Form 1041.   Cat. No. 11376V   Schedule D (Form 1041) 2005

Part IV	Capital Loss Limitation

16 Enter here and enter as a (loss) on Form 1041, line 4, the **smaller** of:

   a The loss on line 15, column (3) **or**

   b $3,000 . . . .   **16** (   )

*If the loss on line 15, column (3), is more than $3,000, or if Form 1041, page 1, line 22, is a loss, complete the **Capital Loss Carryover Worksheet** on page 37 of the instructions to determine your capital loss carryover.*

Part V	Tax Computation Using Maximum Capital Gains Rates (Complete this part **only** if both lines 14a and 15 in column (2) are gains, or an amount is entered in Part I or Part II and there is an entry on Form 1041, line 2b(2), **and** Form 1041, line 22 is more than zero.)

   Note: *If line 14b, column (2) or line 14c, column (2) is more than zero, complete the worksheet on page 38 of the instructions and skip Part V. Otherwise, go to line 17.*

17 Enter taxable income from Form 1041, line 22 . . . . **17** 11,700

18 Enter the **smaller** of line 14a or 15 in column (2) but not less than zero **18** 12,000

19 Enter the estate's or trust's qualified dividends from Form 1041, line 2b(2) . . . . . . **19** -0-

20 Add lines 18 and 19 . . . . **20** 12,000

21 If the estate or trust is filing Form 4952, enter the amount from line 4g; otherwise, enter -0- . **21** -0-

22 Subtract line 21 from line 20. If zero or less, enter -0- **22** 12,000

23 Subtract line 22 from line 17. If zero or less, enter -0- . . . . . **23** -0-

24 Enter the **smaller** of the amount on line 17 or $2,000 . . . . . . **24** 2,000

25 Is the amount on line 23 equal to or more than the amount on line 24?

   ☐ **Yes.** Skip lines 25 through 27; go to line 28 and check the "No" box.

   ☒ **No.** Enter the amount from line 23 . . . . **25** -0-

26 Subtract line 25 from line 24 . . . . **26** 2,000

27 Multiply line 26 by 5% (.05) **27** 100

28 Are the amounts on lines 22 and 26 the same?

   ☐ **Yes.** Skip lines 28 through 31; go to line 32.

   ☒ **No.** Enter the **smaller** of line 17 or line 22 . . . . **28** 11,700

29 Enter the amount from line 26 (If line 26 is blank, enter -0-). **29** 2,000

30 Subtract line 29 from line 28 . . . . **30** 9,700

31 Multiply line 30 by 15% (.15) **31** 1,455

32 Figure the tax on the amount on line 23. Use the 2005 Tax Rate Schedule on page 23 of the instructions . . . . **32** -0-

33 Add lines 27, 31, and 32 . . . . **33** 1,555

34 Figure the tax on the amount on line 17. Use the 2005 Tax Rate Schedule on page 23 of the instructions **34** 3,202

35 **Tax on all taxable income.** Enter the **smaller** of line 33 or line 34 here and on line 1a of Schedule G, Form 1041 . . . . **35** 1,555

661105

Schedule K-1
(Form 1041)

2005

Department of the Treasury
Internal Revenue Service

For calendar year 2005,

or tax year beginning _____ , 2005

and ending _____ , 20 _____

Beneficiary's Share of Income, Deductions, Credits, etc.

▶ See back of form and instructions.

Part I	Information About the Estate or Trust

A Estate's or trust's employer identification number

74-1237211

B Estate's or trust's name

Bob Adams Trust

C Fiduciary's name, address, city, state, and ZIP code

First Bank
Post OfficeBox 100
Nashville, TN 37203

D ☐ Check if Form 1041-T was filed and enter the date it was filed

_____/_____/_____

E ☐ Check if this is the final Form 1041 for the estate or trust

F ☐ Tax shelter registration number, if any _____

G ☐ Check if Form 8271 is attached

Part II	Information About the Beneficiary

H Beneficiary's identifying number
389-16-4001

I Beneficiary's name, address, city, state, and ZIP code

Bob Adams
3 Andrew Jackson Highway
Nashville, TN 37211

J [X] Domestic beneficiary   ☐ Foreign beneficiary

☐ Final K-1   ☐ Amended K-1   OMB No. 1545-0092

Part III	Beneficiary's Share of Current Year Income, Deductions, Credits, and Other Items

1	Interest income	11	Final year deductions
2a	Ordinary dividends **30,000**		
2b	Qualified dividends **30,000**		
3	Net short-term capital gain		
4a	Net long-term capital gain		
4b	28% rate gain	12	Alternative minimum tax adjustment
4c	Unrecaptured section 1250 gain		
5	Other portfolio and nonbusiness income		
6	Ordinary business income		
7	Net rental real estate income **2,660***	13	Credits and credit recapture
8	Other rental income		
9	Directly apportioned deductions		
		14	Other information
10	Estate tax deduction		A **14,640**

*See attached statement for additional information.

Note: A statement must be attached showing the beneficiary's share of income and directly apportioned deductions from each business, rental real estate, and other rental activity.

For IRS Use Only

For Paperwork Reduction Act Notice, see the Instructions for Form 1041.

Cat. No. 11380D

Schedule K-1 (Form 1041) 2005

*$5,000 − ($1,000 + $840 + $500) = $2,660

This list identifies the codes used on Schedule K-1 for beneficiaries and provides summarized reporting information for beneficiaries who file Form 1040. For detailed reporting and filing information, see the Instructions for Beneficiary Filing Form 1040 and the instructions for your income tax return.

Enter on

1. Interest income — Form 1040, line 8a
2a. Ordinary dividends — Form 1040, line 9a
2b. Qualified dividends — Form 1040, line 9b
3. Net short-term capital gain — Schedule D, line 5, column (f)
4a. Net long-term capital gain — Schedule D, line 12, column (f)
4b. 28% rate gain — Line 4 of the worksheet for Schedule D, line 18
4c. Unrecaptured section 1250 gain — Line 11 of the worksheet for Schedule D, line 19
5. Other portfolio and nonbusiness income — Schedule E, line 33, column (f)
6. Ordinary business Income — Schedule E, line 33, column (d) or (f)
7. Net rental real estate income — Schedule E, line 33, column (d) or (f)
8. Other rental income — Schedule E, line 33, column (d) or (f)

9. Directly apportioned deductions
   Code
   A Depreciation — Form 8582 or Schedule E, line 33, column (c) or (e)
   B Depletion — Form 8582 or Schedule E, line 33, column (c) or (e)
   C Amortization — Form 8582 or Schedule E, line 33, column (c) or (e)

10. Estate tax deduction — Schedule A, line 27

11. Final year deductions
   A Excess deductions — Schedule A, line 22
   B Short-term capital loss carryover — Schedule D, line 5, column (f)
   C Long-term capital loss carryover — Schedule D, line 12, column (f); line 5 of the wksht. for Sch. D, line 18; and line 16 of the wksht. for Sch. D, line 19
   D Net operating loss carryover — regular tax — Form 1040, line 21
   E Net operating loss carryover — minimum tax — Form 6251, line 27

12. Alternative minimum tax items
   Code — *Enter on*
   A Adjustment for minimum tax purposes — Form 6251, line 14
   B AMT adjustment attributable to qualified dividends
   C AMT adjustment attributable to net short-term capital gain
   D AMT adjustment attributable to net long-term capital gain — See the beneficiary's instructions and the Instructions for Form 6251
   E AMT adjustment attributable to unrecaptured section 1250 gain
   F AMT adjustment attributable to 28% rate gain
   G Accelerated depreciation
   H Depletion
   I Amortization
   J Exclusion items — 2006 Form 8801

13. Credits and credit recapture
   A Credit for estimated taxes — Form 1040, line 65
   B Credit for backup withholding — Form 1040, line 64
   C Low-income housing credit — Form 8586, line 4
   D Qualified rehabilitation expenditures — Form 3468, line 1
   E Basis of energy property — Form 3468, line 2
   F Work opportunity credit — Form 5884, line 3
   G Welfare-to-work credit — Form 8861, line 3
   H Alcohol fuel credit — Form 6478, line 4
   I Credit for increasing research activities — Form 6765, line 42
   J Renewable electricity, refined coal, and Indian coal production credit — See the instructions for Form 8835
   K Empowerment zone and renewal community employment credit — Form 8844, line 3
   L Indian employment credit — Form 8845, line 5
   M Orphan drug credit — Form 8820, line 3
   N Credit for employer provided child care and facilities — Form 8882, line 5
   O Biodiesel and renewable diesel fuels credit — Form 8864, line 9
   P Nonconventional source fuel credit — Form 8907, line 13
   Q Clean renewable energy bond and Gulf bond tax credit — See the instructions for Form 8912
   R Credits for employers affected by Hurricane Katrina, Rita, or Wilma — See the instructions for Form 5884-A
   S Recapture of credits — See the beneficiary's instructions

14. Other information
   A Tax-exempt interest — Form 1040, line 8b
   B Foreign Taxes — Form 1040, line 47 or Sch. A, line 8
   C Qualified production activities income — Form 8903, line 7
   D Employer's W-2 wages — Form 8903, line 13
   E Net investment income — Form 4952, line 4a
   F Gross farm and fishing income — Schedule E, line 42
   G Foreign Trading Gross Receipts (IRC 942(a)) — See the instructions for Form 8873
   H Other information — See the beneficiary's instructions

Note. If you are a beneficiary who does not file a Form 1040, see instructions for the type of income tax return you are filing.

Form **1041**

Department of the Treasury—Internal Revenue Service

U.S. Income Tax Return for Estates and Trusts

2005

OMB No. 1545-0092

A	Type of entity (see instr.):	For calendar year 2005 or fiscal year beginning , 2005, and ending , 20		
	☐ Decedent's estate	**Name of estate or trust (If a grantor type trust, see page 12 of the instructions.)**	**C**	**Employer identification number**
	☐ Simple trust	*Cathy and Karen Stephens Trust (Complex Trust)*		74: 5727422
	☒ Complex trust	Name and title of fiduciary	**D**	Date entity created
	☐ Qualified disability trust	*Merchants Bank*		*3-12-94*
	☐ ESBT (S portion only)	Number, street, and room or suite no. (If a P.O. box, see page 12 of the instructions.)	**E**	Nonexempt charitable and split-interest trusts, check applicable boxes (see page 13 of the instr.):
	☐ Grantor type trust			
	☐ Bankruptcy estate–Ch. 7	*3000 Sun Plaza I*		☐ Described in section 4947(a)(1)
	☐ Bankruptcy estate–Ch. 11	City or town, state, and ZIP code		☐ Not a private foundation
	☐ Pooled income fund	*Tampa, FL 32843*		☐ Described in section 4947(a)(2)

B	Number of Schedules K-1 attached (see instructions) ▶ **2**	F Check applicable boxes:	☐ Initial return ☐ Final return ☐ Amended return	☐ Change in trust's name
			☐ Change in fiduciary ☐ Change in fiduciary's name	☐ Change in fiduciary's address

G Pooled mortgage account (see page 14 of the instructions): ☐ Bought ☐ Sold Date:

Income

1	Interest income	**1**	
2a	Total ordinary dividends	**2a**	30,000
b	Qualified dividends allocable to: (1) Beneficiaries ...13,319... (2) Estate or trust ...16,681...		
3	Business income or (loss) (attach Schedule C or C-EZ (Form 1040))	**3**	
4	Capital gain or (loss) (attach Schedule D (Form 1041))	**4**	12,000
5	Rents, royalties, partnerships, other estates and trusts, etc. (attach Schedule E (Form 1040)) ⌐ see below ¬	**5**	4,000
6	Farm income or (loss) (attach Schedule F (Form 1040))	**6**	
7	Ordinary gain or (loss) (attach Form 4797)	**7**	
8	Other income. List type and amount	**8**	
9	**Total income.** Combine lines 1, 2a, and 3 through 8 ▶	**9**	46,000

Deductions

10	Interest. Check if Form 4952 is attached ▶ ☐	**10**	
11	Taxes	**11**	
12	Fiduciary fees **($1,200 – $360)**	**12**	840
13	Charitable deduction (from Schedule A, line 7)	**13**	
14	Attorney, accountant, and return preparer fees	**14**	500
15a	Other deductions **not** subject to the 2% floor (attach schedule)	**15a**	
b	Allowable miscellaneous itemized deductions subject to the 2% floor	**15b**	
16	Add lines 10 through 15b ▶	**16**	1,340
17	Adjusted total income or (loss). Subtract line 16 from line 9 . ⌐ 17	44,660 ¬	
18	Income distribution deduction (from Schedule B, line 15) (attach Schedules K-1 (Form 1041))	**18**	14,500
19	Estate tax deduction (including certain generation-skipping taxes) (attach computation)	**19**	
20	Exemption	**20**	100
21	Add lines 18 through 20 ▶	**21**	14,600

Tax and Payments

22	Taxable income. Subtract line 21 from line 17. If a loss, see page 20 of the instructions	**22**	30,060
23	**Total tax** (from Schedule G, line 7)	**23**	4,447
24	**Payments: a** 2005 estimated tax payments and amount applied from 2004 return	**24a**	8,600
b	Estimated tax payments allocated to beneficiaries (from Form 1041-T)	**24b**	
c	Subtract line 24b from line 24a	**24c**	8,600
d	Tax paid with Form 7004 (see page 20 of the instructions)	**24d**	
e	Federal income tax withheld. If any is from Form(s) 1099, check ▶ ☐	**24e**	
	Other payments: **f** Form 2439 ....; **g** Form 4136 ....; Total ▶	**24h**	
25	**Total payments.** Add lines 24c through 24e, and 24h ▶	**25**	8,600
26	Estimated tax penalty (see page 20 of the instructions)	**26**	
27	**Tax due.** If line 25 is smaller than the total of lines 23 and 26, enter amount owed	**27**	
28	**Overpayment.** If line 25 is larger than the total of lines 23 and 26, enter amount overpaid	**28**	4,153
29	Amount of line 28 to be: **a** Credited to 2006 estimated tax ▶ 4,153 ; **b** Refunded ▶	**29**	

Sign Here

Under penalties of perjury, I declare that I have examined this return, including accompanying schedules and statements, and to the best of my knowledge and belief, it is true, correct, and complete. Declaration of preparer (other than taxpayer) is based on all information of which preparer has any knowledge.

▶ *Fred Fidus* — Signature of fiduciary or officer representing fiduciary | *3-20-06* Date | ▶ 38 : 4371419 EIN of fiduciary if a financial institution

May the IRS discuss this return with the preparer shown below (see instr.)? ☒ Yes ☐ No

Paid Preparer's Use Only

Preparer's signature ▶ *Sarah Public*	Date *3-15-06*	Check if self-employed ☒	Preparer's SSN or PTIN 127-84-3878
Firm's name (or yours if self-employed), address, and ZIP code ▶ *Sarah Public 200 Sun Plaza III Tampa, FL 32843*		EIN 38: 9876543	Phone no. (863) 437-1000

For Privacy Act and Paperwork Reduction Act Notice, see the separate instructions. Cat. No. 11370H Form **1041** (2005)

Line 4: Net Rental income

Rental income ($5,000) − Rental expenses ($1,000) = Net rental income ($4,000)

Note: Pages concerning the AMT are omitted because the trust does not owe the AMT.

Form 1041 (2005)   Page **2**

Schedule A	**Charitable Deduction.** Do not complete for a simple trust or a pooled income fund.		
1	Amounts paid or permanently set aside for charitable purposes from gross income (see page 21)	**1**	
2	Tax-exempt income allocable to charitable contributions (see page 21 of the instructions) . .	**2**	
3	Subtract line 2 from line 1	**3**	
4	Capital gains for the tax year allocated to corpus and paid or permanently set aside for charitable purposes	**4**	
5	Add lines 3 and 4	**5**	
6	Section 1202 exclusion allocable to capital gains paid or permanently set aside for charitable purposes (see page 21 of the instructions)	**6**	
7	**Charitable deduction.** Subtract line 6 from line 5. Enter here and on page 1, line 13	**7**	

Schedule B	**Income Distribution Deduction**		
1	Adjusted total income (see page 22 of the instructions)	**1**	44,660
2	Adjusted tax-exempt interest . **($15,000 − $360)**	**2**	14,640
3	Total net gain from Schedule D (Form 1041), line 15, column (1) (see page 22 of the instructions)	**3**	
4	Enter amount from Schedule A, line 4 (reduced by any allocable section 1202 exclusion) . .	**4**	
5	Capital gains for the tax year included on Schedule A, line 1 (see page 22 of the instructions)	**5**	
6	Enter any gain from page 1, line 4, as a negative number. If page 1, line 4, is a loss, enter the loss as a positive number	**6**	(12,000)
7	**Distributable net income (DNI).** Combine lines 1 through 6. If zero or less, enter -0- . . .	**7**	47,300
8	If a complex trust, enter accounting income for the tax year as determined under the governing instrument and applicable local law **8** 48,500		
9	Income required to be distributed currently	**9**	-0-
10	Other amounts paid, credited, or otherwise required to be distributed	**10**	21,000
11	Total distributions. Add lines 9 and 10. If greater than line 8, see page 22 of the instructions	**11**	21,000
12	Enter the amount of tax-exempt income included on line 11	**12**	6,500
13	Tentative income distribution deduction. Subtract line 12 from line 11	**13**	14,500
14	Tentative income distribution deduction. Subtract line 2 from line 7. If zero or less, enter -0-	**14**	32,660
15	**Income distribution deduction.** Enter the smaller of line 13 or line 14 here and on page 1, line 18	**15**	14,500

Schedule G	**Tax Computation** (see page 23 of the instructions)				
1 Tax:	a Tax on taxable income (see page 23 of the instructions) . .	**1a**	4,447		
	b Tax on lump-sum distributions (attach Form 4972)	**1b**			
	c Alternative minimum tax (from Schedule I, line 56)	**1c**			
	d **Total.** Add lines 1a through 1c . . . . ▶			**1d**	4,447
2a	Foreign tax credit (attach Form 1116)	**2a**			
b	Other nonbusiness credits (attach schedule)	**2b**			
c	General business credit. Enter here and check which forms are attached: ☐ Form 3800 ☐ Forms (specify) ▶ _____	**2c**			
d	Credit for prior year minimum tax (attach Form 8801)	**2d**			
3	**Total credits.** Add lines 2a through 2d . . . . ▶			**3**	
4	Subtract line 3 from line 1d. If zero or less, enter -0-			**4**	4,447
5	Recapture taxes. Check if from: ☐ Form 4255 ☐ Form 8611 . . .			**5**	
6	Household employment taxes. Attach Schedule H (Form 1040)			**6**	
7	**Total tax.** Add lines 4 through 6. Enter here and on page 1, line 23 . . . . . ▶			**7**	4,447

	Other Information	Yes	No
1	Did the estate or trust receive tax-exempt income? If "Yes," attach a computation of the allocation of expenses Enter the amount of tax-exempt interest income and exempt-interest dividends ▶ $ 15,000; (see below)	X	
2	Did the estate or trust receive all or any part of the earnings (salary, wages, and other compensation) of any individual by reason of a contract assignment or similar arrangement?		X
3	At any time during calendar year 2005, did the estate or trust have an interest in or a signature or other authority over a bank, securities, or other financial account in a foreign country? . . . . See page 25 of the instructions for exceptions and filing requirements for Form TD F 90-22.1. If "Yes," enter the name of the foreign country ▶ _____		X
4	During the tax year, did the estate or trust receive a distribution from, or was it the grantor of, or transferor to, a foreign trust? If "Yes," the estate or trust may have to file Form 3520. See page 25 of the instructions .		X
5	Did the estate or trust receive, or pay, any qualified residence interest on seller-provided financing? If "Yes," see page 25 for required attachment		X
6	If this is an estate or a complex trust making the section 663(b) election, check here (see page 25) . ▶ ☐		
7	To make a section 643(e)(3) election, attach Schedule D (Form 1041), and check here (see page 25) . ▶ ☐		
8	If the decedent's estate has been open for more than 2 years, attach an explanation for the delay in closing the estate, and check here ▶ ☐		
9	Are any present or future trust beneficiaries skip persons? See page 26 of the instructions		X

Form **1041** (2005)

Line 2: Allocation of expenses: $\dfrac{\$15,000}{\$50,000} \times \$1,200 = \$360$ of trustee's fee allocated to tax-exempt income

SCHEDULE D
(Form 1041)

Department of the Treasury
Internal Revenue Service

Capital Gains and Losses

▶ Attach to Form 1041, Form 5227, or Form 990-T. See the separate instructions for Form 1041 (also for Form 5227 or Form 990-T, if applicable).

OMB No. 1545-0092

2005

Name of estate or trust	Employer identification number
Cathy and Karen Stephens Trust	74 : 5724722

Note: *Form 5227 filers need to complete **only** Parts I and II.*

Part I — Short-Term Capital Gains and Losses—Assets Held One Year or Less

(a) Description of property (Example, 100 shares 7% preferred of "Z" Co.)	(b) Date acquired (mo., day, yr.)	(c) Date sold (mo., day, yr.)	(d) Sales price	(e) Cost or other basis (see page 34)	(f) Gain or (Loss) for the entire year (col. (d) less col. (e))
1					

2 Short-term capital gain or (loss) from Forms 4684, 6252, 6781, and 8824	**2**	
3 Net short-term gain or (loss) from partnerships, S corporations, and other estates or trusts .	**3**	
4 Short-term capital loss carryover. Enter the amount, if any, from line 9 of the 2004 Capital Loss Carryover Worksheet	**4** (	)
5 **Net short-term gain or (loss).** Combine lines 1 through 4 in column (f). Enter here and on line 13, column (3) below . . . . ▶	**5**	

Part II — Long-Term Capital Gains and Losses—Assets Held More Than One Year

(a) Description of property (Example, 100 shares 7% preferred of "Z" Co.)	(b) Date acquired (mo., day, yr.)	(c) Date sold (mo., day, yr.)	(d) Sales price	(e) Cost or other basis (see page 34)	(f) Gain or (Loss) for the entire year (col. (d) less col. (e))
6 1,000 shares of ABC Corporation stock	2001	Oct. 2005	15,000	3,000	12,000

7 Long-term capital gain or (loss) from Forms 2439, 4684, 6252, 6781, and 8824	**7**	
8 Net long-term gain or (loss) from partnerships, S corporations, and other estates or trusts .	**8**	
9 Capital gain distributions	**9**	
10 Gain from Form 4797, Part I	**10**	
11 Long-term capital loss carryover. Enter the amount, if any, from line 14 of the 2004 Capital Loss Carryover Worksheet	**11** (	)
12 **Net long-term gain or (loss).** Combine lines 6 through 11 in column (f). Enter here and on line 14a, column (3) below . . . . ▶	**12**	12,000

Part III — Summary of Parts I and II

Caution: *Read the instructions **before** completing this part.*

	(1) Beneficiaries' (see page 36)	(2) Estate's or trust's	(3) Total
13 **Net short-term gain or (loss)** **13**			
14 **Net long-term gain or (loss):**			
a Total for year **14a**		12,000	12,000
b Unrecaptured section 1250 gain (see line 18 of the worksheet on page 35) **14b**			
c 28% rate gain or (loss) **14c**			
15 **Total net gain or (loss).** Combine lines 13 and 14a . ▶ **15**		12,000	12,000

Note: *If line 15, column (3), is a net gain, enter the gain on Form 1041, line 4. If lines 14a and 15, column (2), are net gains, go to Part V, and **do not** complete Part IV. If line 15, column (3), is a net loss, complete Part IV and the **Capital Loss Carryover Worksheet,** as necessary.*

For Paperwork Reduction Act Notice, see the Instructions for Form 1041. Cat. No. 11376V Schedule D (Form 1041) 2005

Part IV	Capital Loss Limitation			

16 Enter here and enter as a (loss) on Form 1041, line 4, the **smaller** of:

   a The loss on line 15, column (3) **or**

   b $3,000 . . . .   **16** |(   )

*If the loss on line 15, column (3), is more than $3,000, or if Form 1041, page 1, line 22, is a loss, complete the **Capital Loss Carryover Worksheet** on page 37 of the instructions to determine your capital loss carryover.*

Part V	Tax Computation Using Maximum Capital Gains Rates (Complete this part **only** if both lines 14a and 15 in column (2) are gains, or an amount is entered in Part I or Part II and there is an entry on Form 1041, line 2b(2), **and** Form 1041, line 22 is more than zero.)

   Note: *If line 14b, column (2) or line 14c, column (2) is more than zero, complete the worksheet on page 38 of the instructions and skip Part V. Otherwise, go to line 17.*

17 Enter taxable income from Form 1041, line 22 . . . . . .   **17** | 30,060

18 Enter the **smaller** of line 14a or 15 in column (2) but not less than zero . . . . . .   **18** | 12,000

19 Enter the estate's or trust's qualified dividends from Form 1041, line 2b(2) . . . . . .   **19** | 16,681

20 Add lines 18 and 19 . . . .   **20** | 28,681

21 If the estate or trust is filing Form 4952, enter the amount from line 4g; otherwise, enter -0- .   **21** | -0-

22 Subtract line 21 from line 20. If zero or less, enter -0- . . . . .   **22** | 28,681

23 Subtract line 22 from line 17. If zero or less, enter -0- . . . . .   **23** | 1,379

24 Enter the **smaller** of the amount on line 17 or $2,000 . . . . .   **24** | 2,000

25 Is the amount on line 23 equal to or more than the amount on line 24?

   ☐ **Yes.** Skip lines 25 through 27; go to line 28 and check the "No" box.

   ☒ **No.** Enter the amount from line 23 . . . .   **25** | 1,379

26 Subtract line 25 from line 24 . . . .   **26** | 621

27 Multiply line 26 by 5% (.05) . . . .   **27** | 31

28 Are the amounts on lines 22 and 26 the same?

   ☐ **Yes.** Skip lines 28 through 31; go to line 32.

   ☒ **No.** Enter the **smaller** of line 17 or line 22 .   **28** | 28,681

29 Enter the amount from line 26 (If line 26 is blank, enter -0-). . . . .   **29** | 621

30 Subtract line 29 from line 28 . . . .   **30** | 28,060

31 Multiply line 30 by 15% (.15) . . . .   **31** | 4,209

32 Figure the tax on the amount on line 23. Use the 2005 Tax Rate Schedule on page 23 of the instructions . . . .   **32** | 207

33 Add lines 27, 31, and 32 . . . .   **33** | 4,447

34 Figure the tax on the amount on line 17. Use the 2005 Tax Rate Schedule on page 23 of the instructions . . . .   **34** | 9,628

35 **Tax on all taxable income.** Enter the **smaller** of line 33 or line 34 here and on line 1a of Schedule G, Form 1041 . . . .   **35** | 4,447

661105

Schedule K-1
(Form 1041)

20**05**

Department of the Treasury
Internal Revenue Service

For calendar year 2005,
or tax year beginning _____ , 2005
and ending _____ , 20 _____

Beneficiary's Share of Income, Deductions, Credits, etc.

▶ See back of form and instructions.

Part I	Information About the Estate or Trust

A Estate's or trust's employer identification number

74-5727422

B Estate's or trust's name

Cathy and Karen Stephens Trust

C Fiduciary's name, address, city, state, and ZIP code

Merchants Bank
3000 Sun Plaza I
Tampa, FL 32843

D ☐ Check if Form 1041-T was filed and enter the date it was filed
_____/_____/_____

E ☐ Check if this is the final Form 1041 for the estate or trust

F ☐ Tax shelter registration number, if any _____

G ☐ Check if Form 8271 is attached

Part II	Information About the Beneficiary

H Beneficiary's identifying number
411-36-4761

I Beneficiary's name, address, city, state, and ZIP code

Cathy Stephens
13 Sunny Shores
Miami Beach, FL 33131

J ☒ Domestic beneficiary   ☐ Foreign beneficiary

☐ Final K-1   ☐ Amended K-1   OMB No. 1545-0092

Part III	Beneficiary's Share of Current Year Income, Deductions, Credits, and Other Items

1	Interest income	11	Final year deductions
2a	Ordinary dividends **8,879**		
2b	Qualified dividends **8,879**		
3	Net short-term capital gain		
4a	Net long-term capital gain		
4b	28% rate gain	12	Alternative minimum tax adjustment
4c	Unrecaptured section 1250 gain		
5	Other portfolio and nonbusiness income		
6	Ordinary business income		
7	Net rental real estate income **788**	13	Credits and credit recapture
8	Other rental income		
9	Directly apportioned deductions		
		14	Other information
10	Estate tax deduction		**A 4,833**

*See attached statement for additional information.

Note: A statement must be attached showing the beneficiary's share of income and directly apportioned deductions from each business, rental real estate, and other rental activity.

For IRS Use Only

661105

Schedule K-1 (Form 1041)	20**05**

Department of the Treasury
Internal Revenue Service

For calendar year 2005,
or tax year beginning _____ , 2005
and ending _____ , 20 _____

Beneficiary's Share of Income, Deductions, Credits, etc.

▶ See back of form and instructions.

☐ Final K-1   ☐ Amended K-1   OMB No. 1545-0092

Part III	**Beneficiary's Share of Current Year Income, Deductions, Credits, and Other Items**

1	Interest income	**11**	Final year deductions
2a	Ordinary dividends 4,440		
2b	Qualified dividends 4,440		
3	Net short-term capital gain		
4a	Net long-term capital gain		
4b	28% rate gain	**12**	Alternative minimum tax adjustment
4c	Unrecaptured section 1250 gain		
5	Other portfolio and nonbusiness income		
6	Ordinary business income		
7	Net rental real estate income 393	**13**	Credits and credit recapture
8	Other rental income		
9	Directly apportioned deductions		
		14	Other information A 2,167
10	Estate tax deduction		

Part I — Information About the Estate or Trust

A Estate's or trust's employer identification number

74-5727422

B Estate's or trust's name

Cathy and Karen Stephens Trust

C Fiduciary's name, address, city, state, and ZIP code

Merchants Bank
3000 Sun Plaza 1
Tampa, FL 32843

D ☐ Check if Form 1041-T was filed and enter the date it was filed
_____ / _____ / _____

E ☐ Check if this is the final Form 1041 for the estate or trust

F ☐ Tax shelter registration number, if any _____

G ☐ Check if Form 8271 is attached

Part II — Information About the Beneficiary

H Beneficiary's identifying number

456-78-1230

I Beneficiary's name, address, city, state, and ZIP code

Karen Stephens
1472 Ski Run
Vail, CO 74820

*See attached statement for additional information.

Note: A statement must be attached showing the beneficiary's share of income and directly apportioned deductions from each business, rental real estate, and other rental activity.

For IRS Use Only

J ☒ Domestic beneficiary   ☐ Foreign beneficiary

For Paperwork Reduction Act Notice, see the Instructions for Form 1041.   Cat. No. 11380D   **Schedule K-1 (Form 1041) 2005**

This list identifies the codes used on Schedule K-1 for beneficiaries and provides summarized reporting information for beneficiaries who file Form 1040. For detailed reporting and filing information, see the Instructions for Beneficiary Filing Form 1040 and the instructions for your income tax return.

Enter on

1. **Interest income** — Form 1040, line 8a
2a. **Ordinary dividends** — Form 1040, line 9a
2b. **Qualified dividends** — Form 1040, line 9b
3. **Net short-term capital gain** — Schedule D, line 5, column (f)
4a. **Net long-term capital gain** — Schedule D, line 12, column (f)
4b. **28% rate gain** — Line 4 of the worksheet for Schedule D, line 18
4c. **Unrecaptured section 1250 gain** — Line 11 of the worksheet for Schedule D, line 19
5. **Other portfolio and nonbusiness income** — Schedule E, line 33, column (f)
6. **Ordinary business income** — Schedule E, line 33, column (d) or (f)
7. **Net rental real estate income** — Schedule E, line 33, column (d) or (f)
8. **Other rental income** — Schedule E, line 33, column (d) or (f)
9. **Directly apportioned deductions**
   Code
   A Depreciation — Form 8582 or Schedule E, line 33, column (c) or (e)
   B Depletion — Form 8582 or Schedule E, line 33, column (c) or (e)
   C Amortization — Form 8582 or Schedule E, line 33, column (c) or (e)
10. **Estate tax deduction** — Schedule A, line 27
11. **Final year deductions**
   A Excess deductions — Schedule A, line 22
   B Short-term capital loss carryover — Schedule D, line 5, column (f)
   C Long-term capital loss carryover — Schedule D, line 12, column (f); line 5 of the wksht. for Sch. D, line 18; and line 16 of the wksht. for Sch. D, line 19
   D Net operating loss carryover — regular tax — Form 1040, line 21
   E Net operating loss carryover — minimum tax — Form 6251, line 27

12. **Alternative minimum tax items**
   Code   *Enter on*
   A Adjustment for minimum tax purposes — Form 6251, line 14
   B AMT adjustment attributable to qualified dividends
   C AMT adjustment attributable to net short-term capital gain
   D AMT adjustment attributable to net long-term capital gain — See the beneficiary's instructions and the Instructions for Form 6251
   E AMT adjustment attributable to unrecaptured section 1250 gain
   F AMT adjustment attributable to 28% rate gain
   G Accelerated depreciation
   H Depletion
   I Amortization
   J Exclusion items — 2006 Form 8801
13. **Credits and credit recapture**
   A Credit for estimated taxes — Form 1040, line 65
   B Credit for backup withholding — Form 1040, line 64
   C Low-income housing credit — Form 8586, line 4
   D Qualified rehabilitation expenditures — Form 3468, line 1
   E Basis of energy property — Form 3468, line 2
   F Work opportunity credit — Form 5884, line 3
   G Welfare-to-work credit — Form 8861, line 3
   H Alcohol fuel credit — Form 6478, line 4
   I Credit for increasing research activities — Form 6765, line 42
   J Renewable electricity, refined coal, and Indian coal production credit — See the instructions for Form 8835
   K Empowerment zone and renewal community employment credit — Form 8844, line 3
   L Indian employment credit — Form 8845, line 5
   M Orphan drug credit — Form 8820, line 3
   N Credit for employer provided child care and facilities — Form 8882, line 5
   O Biodiesel and renewable diesel fuels credit — Form 8864, line 9
   P Nonconventional source fuel credit — Form 8907, line 13
   Q Clean renewable energy bond and Gulf bond tax credit — See the instructions for Form 8912
   R Credits for employers affected by Hurricane Katrina, Rita, or Wilma — See the instructions for Form 5884-A
   S Recapture of credits — See the beneficiary's instructions
14. **Other information**
   A Tax-exempt interest — Form 1040, line 8b
   B Foreign Taxes — Form 1040, line 47 or Sch. A, line 8
   C Qualified production activities income — Form 8903, line 7
   D Employer's W-2 wages — Form 8903, line 13
   E Net investment income — Form 4952, line 4a
   F Gross farm and fishing income — Schedule E, line 42
   G Foreign Trading Gross Receipts (IRC 942(a)) — See the instructions for Form 8873
   H Other information — See the beneficiary's instructions

Note. If you are a beneficiary who does not file a Form 1040, see instructions for the type of income tax return you are filing.

Form **1065**		**U.S. Return of Partnership Income**		OMB No. 1545-0099
Department of the Treasury Internal Revenue Service		For calendar year 2005, or tax year beginning .... , 2005, ending .... , 20...... . ▶ See separate instructions.		**2005**

A Principal business activity Manufacturing	Use the IRS label. Other- wise, print or type.	Name of partnership Johns and Lawrence	**D** Employer identification number 76 : 3456789
B Principal product or service Furniture		Number, street, and room or suite no. If a P.O. box, see the instructions. 1234 University Avenue	**E** Date business started 6-1-99
C Business code number 337000		City or town, state, and ZIP code Gainesville, FL 32611	**F** Total assets (see the instructions) $ 499,484

G Check applicable boxes: **(1)** ☐ Initial return   **(2)** ☐ Final return   **(3)** ☐ Name change   **(4)** ☐ Address change   **(5)** ☐ Amended return

H Check accounting method: **(1)** ☐ Cash   **(2)** ☒ Accrual   **(3)** ☐ Other (specify) ▶ ....

I Number of Schedules K-1. Attach one for each person who was a partner at any time during the tax year ▶ ....

Caution. *Include **only** trade or business income and expenses on lines 1a through 22 below. See the instructions for more information.*

1a Gross receipts or sales	**1a** 869,658		
b Less returns and allowances	**1b** 29,242	**1c**	840,416
2 Cost of goods sold (Schedule A, line 8)		**2**	540,204
3 Gross profit. Subtract line 2 from line 1c		**3**	300,212
4 Ordinary income (loss) from other partnerships, estates, and trusts *(attach statement)*		**4**	
5 Net farm profit (loss) *(attach Schedule F (Form 1040))*		**5**	
6 Net gain (loss) from Form 4797, Part II, line 17 (attach Form 4797)		**6**	
7 Other income (loss) *(attach statement)*		**7**	
8 **Total income (loss).** Combine lines 3 through 7		**8**	300,212
9 Salaries and wages (other than to partners) (less employment credits)		**9**	52,000
10 Guaranteed payments to partners		**10**	36,000
11 Repairs and maintenance		**11**	4,800
12 Bad debts		**12**	4,000
13 Rent		**13**	36,000
14 Taxes and licenses (8,320 + 1,520)		**14**	9,840
15 Interest		**15**	8,000
16a Depreciation (if required, attach Form 4562)	**16a** 27,476		
b Less depreciation reported on Schedule A and elsewhere on return	**16b** 15,000	**16c**	12,476
17 Depletion **(Do not deduct oil and gas depletion.)**		**17**	
18 Retirement plans, etc.		**18**	2,000
19 Employee benefit programs		**19**	4,000
20 Other deductions *(attach statement)*		**20**	51,250
21 **Total deductions.** Add the amounts shown in the far right column for lines 9 through 20		**21**	220,366
22 **Ordinary business income (loss).** Subtract line 21 from line 8		**22**	79,846

Income (left margin label)

Deductions (see the instructions for limitations) (left margin label)

Sign Here	Under penalties of perjury, I declare that I have examined this return, including accompanying schedules and statements, and to the best of my knowledge and belief, it is true, correct, and complete. Declaration of preparer (other than general partner or limited liability company member) is based on all information of which preparer has any knowledge.	
	▶ *Andrew Lawrence* Signature of general partner or limited liability company member manager	▶ 4-10-06 Date

May the IRS discuss this return with the preparer shown below (see instructions)? ☐ Yes ☐ No

Paid Preparer's Use Only	Preparer's signature *Michael S. Kramer*	Date 4-7-06	Check if self-employed ▶ ☒	Preparer's SSN or PTIN 375-49-6339
	Firm's name (or yours if self-employed) address, and ZIP code ▶	Michael S. Kramer 1110 McMillon Gainesville, FL 37611	EIN ▶ 59 : 2029763 Phone no. (352) 555-2000	

For Privacy Act and Paperwork Reduction Act Notice, see separate instructions.   Cat. No. 11390Z   Form **1065** (2005)

Form 1065 (2005) Page **2**

Schedule A — Cost of Goods Sold (see the instructions)

1	Inventory at beginning of year.	1	64,000
2	Purchases less cost of items withdrawn for personal use	2	340,800
3	Cost of labor	3	143,204
4	Additional section 263A costs (attach statement)	4	7,000
5	Other costs (attach statement).	5	90,000
6	**Total.** Add lines 1 through 5	6	645,004
7	Inventory at end of year	7	104,800
8	**Cost of goods sold.** Subtract line 7 from line 6. Enter here and on page 1, line 2	8	540,204

9a Check all methods used for valuing closing inventory:

    (i) ☒ Cost as described in Regulations section 1.471-3

    (ii) ☐ Lower of cost or market as described in Regulations section 1.471-4

    (iii) ☐ Other (specify method used and attach explanation) ▶ ....

  b Check this box if there was a writedown of "subnormal" goods as described in Regulations section 1.471-2(c) . . . ▶ ☐

  c Check this box if the LIFO inventory method was adopted this tax year for any goods (if checked, attach Form 970). . ▶ ☐

  d Do the rules of section 263A (for property produced or acquired for resale) apply to the partnership?. . . ☒ **Yes** ☐ **No**

  e Was there any change in determining quantities, cost, or valuations between opening and closing inventory? ☐ **Yes** ☒ **No**
    If "Yes," attach explanation.

Schedule B — Other Information

		Yes	No
1	What type of entity is filing this return? Check the applicable box:		
	a ☐ Domestic general partnership **b** ☐ Domestic limited partnership		
	c ☐ Domestic limited liability company **d** ☐ Domestic limited liability partnership		
	e ☐ Foreign partnership **f** ☐ Other ▶		
2	Are any partners in this partnership also partnerships?		X
3	During the partnership's tax year, did the partnership own any interest in another partnership or in any foreign entity that was disregarded as an entity separate from its owner under Regulations sections 301.7701-2 and 301.7701-3? If yes, see instructions for required attachment		X
4	Did the partnership file Form 8893, Election of Partnership Level Tax Treatment, or an election statement under section 6231(a)(1)(B)(ii) for partnership-level tax treatment, that is in effect for this tax year? See Form 8893 for more details		X
5	Does this partnership meet all three of the following requirements?		
	a The partnership's total receipts for the tax year were less than $250,000;		
	b The partnership's total assets at the end of the tax year were less than $600,000; and		
	c Schedules K-1 are filed with the return and furnished to the partners on or before the due date (including extensions) for the partnership return.		
	If "Yes," the partnership is not required to complete Schedules L, M-1, and M-2; Item F on page 1 of Form 1065; or Item N on Schedule K-1.		X
6	Does this partnership have any foreign partners? If "Yes," the partnership may have to file Forms 8804, 8805 and 8813. See the instructions		X
7	Is this partnership a publicly traded partnership as defined in section 469(k)(2)?		X
8	Has this partnership filed, or is it required to file, a return under section 6111 to provide information on any reportable transaction?		X
9	At any time during calendar year 2005, did the partnership have an interest in or a signature or other authority over a financial account in a foreign country (such as a bank account, securities account, or other financial account)? See the instructions for exceptions and filing requirements for Form TD F 90-22.1. If "Yes," enter the name of the foreign country. ▶		X
10	During the tax year, did the partnership receive a distribution from, or was it the grantor of, or transferor to, a foreign trust? If "Yes," the partnership may have to file Form 3520. See the instructions		X
11	Was there a distribution of property or a transfer (for example, by sale or death) of a partnership interest during the tax year? If "Yes," you may elect to adjust the basis of the partnership's assets under section 754 by attaching the statement described under Elections Made By the Partnership in the instructions		X
12	Enter the number of Forms 8865, Return of U.S. Persons With Respect to Certain Foreign Partnerships, attached to this return ▶		

Designation of Tax Matters Partner (see the instructions)

Enter below the general partner designated as the tax matters partner (TMP) for the tax year of this return: **(Not Required)**

Name of designated TMP ▶	Andrew Lawrence	Identifying number of TMP ▶	297-63-2110
Address of designated TMP ▶	436 N.W. 24th Ave. Gainesville, FL 32607		

Form **1065** (2005)

Form 1065 (2005)   Page **3**

Schedule K — Partners' Distributive Share Items

			Total amount
Income (Loss)	**1** Ordinary business income (loss) (page 1, line 22)	**1**	79,846
	2 Net rental real estate income (loss) (attach Form 8825)	**2**	
	3a Other gross rental income (loss) **3a**		
	b Expenses from other rental activities (attach statement) **3b**		
	c Other net rental income (loss). Subtract line 3b from line 3a	**3c**	
	4 Guaranteed payments	**4**	36,000
	5 Interest income	**5**	
	6 Dividends: **a** Ordinary dividends	**6a**	1,000
	b Qualified dividends **6b** 1,000		
	7 Royalties	**7**	
	8 Net short-term capital gain (loss) (attach Schedule D (Form 1065))	**8**	(2,100)
	9a Net long-term capital gain (loss) (attach Schedule D (Form 1065))	**9a**	4,500
	b Collectibles (28%) gain (loss) **9b**		
	c Unrecaptured section 1250 gain (attach statement) **9c**		
	10 Net section 1231 gain (loss) (attach Form 4797)	**10**	
	11 Other income (loss) (see instructions) Type ▶	**11**	
Deductions	**12** Section 179 deduction (attach Form 4562)	**12**	
	13a Contributions	**13a**	12,000
	b Investment interest expense	**13b**	150
	c Section 59(e)(2) expenditures: **(1)** Type ▶ **(2)** Amount ▶	**13c(2)**	
	d Other deductions (see instructions) Type ▶	**13d**	*
Self-Employ-ment	**14a** Net earnings (loss) from self-employment	**14a**	115,846
	b Gross farming or fishing income	**14b**	
	c Gross nonfarm income	**14c**	
Credits & Credit Recapture	**15a** Low-income housing credit (section 42(j)(5))	**15a**	
	b Low-income housing credit (other)	**15b**	
	c Qualified rehabilitation expenditures (rental real estate) (attach Form 3468)	**15c**	
	d Other rental real estate credits (see instructions) Type ▶	**15d**	
	e Other rental credits (see instructions) Type ▶	**15e**	
	f Other credits and credit recapture (see instructions) Type ▶	**15f**	
Foreign Transactions	**16a** Name of country or U.S. possession ▶		
	b Gross income from all sources	**16b**	
	c Gross income sourced at partner level	**16c**	
	Foreign gross income sourced at partnership level		
	d Passive ▶ **e** Listed categories (attach statement) ▶ **f** General limitation ▶	**16f**	
	Deductions allocated and apportioned at partner level		
	g Interest expense ▶ **h** Other ▶	**16h**	
	Deductions allocated and apportioned at partnership level to foreign source income		
	i Passive ▶ **j** Listed categories (attach statement) ▶ **k** General limitation ▶	**16k**	
	l Total foreign taxes (check one): ▶ Paid ☐ Accrued ☐	**16l**	
	m Reduction in taxes available for credit (attach statement)	**16m**	
	n Other foreign tax information (attach statement)		
Alternative Minimum Tax (AMT) Items	**17a** Post-1986 depreciation adjustment	**17a**	1,514
	b Adjusted gain or loss	**17b**	
	c Depletion (other than oil and gas)	**17c**	
	d Oil, gas, and geothermal properties—gross income	**17d**	
	e Oil, gas, and geothermal properties—deductions	**17e**	
	f Other AMT items (attach statement)	**17f**	
Other Information	**18a** Tax-exempt interest income	**18a**	18,000
	b Other tax-exempt income	**18b**	
	c Nondeductible expenses	**18c**	6,000 **
	19a Distributions of cash and marketable securities	**19a**	28,212
	b Distributions of other property	**19b**	
	20a Investment income	**20a**	1,000 ***
	b Investment expenses	**20b**	
	c Other items and amounts (attach statement)		

Form **1065** (2005)

* Qualified production activities income (QPAI) equals $80,000. Employer's W-2 wages equal $4,800.

** Disallowed meals and entertainment expenses ($4,000) and interest on loan used to purchase tax-exempt bonds ($2,000).

*** If partners elect to tax dividends at ordinary rates under Sec. 163(d)(4)(B).

Form 1065 (2005)   Page **4**

Analysis of Net Income (Loss)

1	Net income (loss). Combine Schedule K, lines 1 through 11. From the result, subtract the sum of Schedule K, lines 12 through 13d, and 16l				**1**	**107,096**

2 Analysis by partner type:	**(i)** Corporate	**(ii)** Individual (active)	**(iii)** Individual (passive)	**(iv)** Partnership	**(v)** Exempt organization	**(vi)** Nominee/Other
a General partners		107,096				
b Limited partners						

Note: Schedules L, M-1, and M-2 are not required if Question 5 of Schedule B is answered "Yes."

Schedule L Balance Sheets per Books	Beginning of tax year		End of tax year	
Assets	**(a)**	**(b)**	**(c)**	**(d)**
1 Cash		60,000		92,760
2a Trade notes and accounts receivable	25,100		24,000	
b Less allowance for bad debts	1,000	24,000	1,000	23,000
3 Inventories		64,000		104,800
4 U.S. government obligations				
5 Tax-exempt securities		200,000		200,000
6 Other current assets (attach statement) . . .		7,000		-0-
7 Mortgage and real estate loans				
8 Other investments (attach statement) . . .				
9a Buildings and other depreciable assets. . . .	151,600		151,600	
b Less accumulated depreciation	45,200	106,400	72,760	78,924
10a Depletable assets				
b Less accumulated depletion				
11 Land (net of any amortization).				
12a Intangible assets (amortizable only)				
b Less accumulated amortization				
13 Other assets (attach statement)				
14 Total assets		461,400		499,484
Liabilities and Capital				
15 Accounts payable		26,000		19,000
16 Mortgages, notes, bonds payable in less than 1 year .		4,000		4,000
17 Other current liabilities (attach statement) . . .		3,600		3,600
18 All nonrecourse loans				
19 Mortgages, notes, bonds payable in 1 year or more .		130,000		119,724
20 Other liabilities (attach statement)				
21 Partners' capital accounts		297,800		353,160
22 Total liabilities and capital		461,400		499,484

Schedule M-1 Reconciliation of Income (Loss) per Books With Income (Loss) per Return				
1 Net income (loss) per books	83,572	**6** Income recorded on books this year not included on Schedule K, lines 1 through 11 (itemize):		
2 Income included on Schedule K, lines 1, 2, 3c, 5, 6a, 7, 8, 9a, 10, and 11, not recorded on books this year (itemize):		**a** Tax-exempt interest $ .18,000............... ---		18,000
3 Guaranteed payments (other than health insurance)	36,000	**7** Deductions included on Schedule K, lines 1 through 13d, and 16l, not charged against book income this year (itemize):		
4 Expenses recorded on books this year not included on Schedule K, lines 1 through 13d, and 16l (itemize):		**a** Depreciation $ .476 ----------------------------- ---		
a Depreciation $		---		476
b Travel and entertainment $ ...4,000.. Interest on loans* ....2,000...	6,000	**8** Add lines 6 and 7		18,476
5 Add lines 1 through 4	125,572	**9** Income (loss) (Analysis of Net Income (Loss), line 1). Subtract line 8 from line 5		107,096

Schedule M-2 Analysis of Partners' Capital Accounts				
1 Balance at beginning of year	297,800	**6** Distributions: **a** Cash		28,212
2 Capital contributed: **a** Cash		**b** Property		
b Property . . .		**7** Other decreases (itemize):		
3 Net income (loss) per books	83,572	---		
4 Other increases (itemize):				
		8 Add lines 6 and 7		28,212
5 Add lines 1 through 4	381,372	**9** Balance at end of year. Subtract line 8 from line 5		353,160

*To buy tax-exempt bonds.

Form **1065** (2005)

651105

Schedule K-1
(Form 1065)

2005

Department of the Treasury
Internal Revenue Service

Partner's Share of Income, Deductions, Credits, etc.   ► See back of form and separate instructions.

For calendar year 2005, or tax
year beginning **Jan 1**, 2005
ending **Dec 31**, 20**04**

☐ Final K-1   ☐ Amended K-1   OMB No. 1545-0099

Part III	**Partner's Share of Current Year Income, Deductions, Credits, and Other Items**

1	Ordinary business income (loss) **39,923**	15	Credits & credit recapture
2	Net rental real estate income (loss)		
3	Other net rental income (loss)	16	Foreign transactions
4	Guaranteed payments **18,000**		
5	Interest income		
6a	Ordinary dividends **500**		
6b	Qualified dividends **500**		
7	Royalties		
8	Net short-term capital gain (loss) **(1,050)**		
9a	Net long-term capital gain (loss) **2,250**	17	Alternative minimum tax (AMT) items **A 757**
9b	Collectibles (28%) gain (loss)		
9c	Unrecaptured section 1250 gain		
10	Net section 1231 gain (loss)	18	Tax-exempt income and nondeductible expenses
11	Other income (loss)	A **9,000**
		C **3,000**
12	Section 179 deduction	19	Distributions **A 14,106**
13	Other deductions **A 6,000**	20	Other information
	G 75	A **500****
	U 40,000	
	V 2,400	
14	Self-employment earnings (loss) **A 57,923**	

Part I   Information About the Partnership

A Partnership's employer identification number
76-3456789

B Partnership's name, address, city, state, and ZIP code
Johns and Lawrence
1234 University Ave.
Gainesville, FL 32611

C IRS Center where partnership filed return
Atlanta, GA

D ☐ Check if this is a publicly traded partnership (PTP)

E ☐ Tax shelter registration number, if any _____

F ☐ Check if Form 8271 is attached

Part II   Information About the Partner

G Partner's identifying number
297-63-2110

H Partner's name, address, city, state, and ZIP code
Andrew Lawrence*
436 N.W. 24th Ave.
Gainesville, FL 32607

I ☒ General partner or LLC member-manager   ☐ Limited partner or other LLC member

J ☐ Domestic partner   ☐ Foreign partner

K What type of entity is this partner? **Individual**

L Partner's share of profit, loss, and capital:

	Beginning	Ending
Profit	**50** %	**50** %
Loss	**50** %	**50** %
Capital	**50** %	**50** %

M Partner's share of liabilities at year end:
Nonrecourse . . . . . ▶ $_____
Qualified nonrecourse financing . ▶ $_____
Recourse . . . . . . ▶ $ **73,162**

N Partner's capital account analysis:
Beginning capital account . . . $ **148,900**
Capital contributed during the year $ **-0-**
Current year increase (decrease) . $ **41,786**
Withdrawals & distributions . . $(**14,106**)
Ending capital account . . . . $ **176,580**

☐ Tax basis   ☒ GAAP   ☐ Section 704(b) book
☐ Other (explain)

*See attached statement for additional information.

For IRS Use Only

*Schedule K-1 for Stephen Johns is similar to this one and is not reproduced here.

This list identifies the codes used on Schedule K-1 for all partners and provides summarized reporting information for partners who file Form 1040. For detailed reporting and filing information, see the separate Partner's Instructions for Schedule K-1 and the instructions for your income tax return.

1. **Ordinary business income (loss).** You must first determine whether the income (loss) is passive or nonpassive. Then enter on your return as follows:

	Enter on
Passive loss	See the Partner's Instructions
Passive income	Schedule E, line 28, column (g)
Nonpassive loss	Schedule E, line 28, column (h)
Nonpassive income	Schedule E, line 28, column (j)

2. **Net rental real estate income (loss)** — See the Partner's Instructions
3. **Other net rental income (loss)**
   - Net income — Schedule E, line 28, column (g)
   - Net loss — See the Partner's Instructions
4. **Guaranteed payments** — Schedule E, line 28, column (j)
5. **Interest income** — Form 1040, line 8a
6a. **Ordinary dividends** — Form 1040, line 9a
6b. **Qualified dividends** — Form 1040, line 9b
7. **Royalties** — Schedule E, line 4
8. **Net short-term capital gain (loss)** — Schedule D, line 5, column (f)
9a. **Net long-term capital gain (loss)** — Schedule D, line 12, column (f)
9b. **Collectibles (28%) gain (loss)** — 28% Rate Gain Worksheet, line 4 (Schedule D Instructions)
9c. **Unrecaptured section 1250 gain** — See the Partner's Instructions
10. **Net section 1231 gain (loss)** — See the Partner's Instructions
11. **Other income (loss)**

   Code
   - A Other portfolio income (loss) — See the Partner's Instructions
   - B Involuntary conversions — See the Partner's Instructions
   - C Sec. 1256 contracts & straddles — Form 6781, line 1
   - D Mining exploration costs recapture — See Pub. 535
   - E Cancellation of debt — Form 1040, line 21 or Form 982
   - F Other income (loss) — See the Partner's Instructions

12. **Section 179 deduction** — See the Partner's Instructions
13. **Other deductions**
   - A Cash contributions (50%)
   - B Cash contributions (30%)
   - C Noncash contributions (50%)
   - D Noncash contributions (30%)
   - E Capital gain property to a 50% organization (30%)
   - F Capital gain property (20%)
   - G Cash contributions (100%)

   See the Partner's Instructions
   - H Investment interest expense — Form 4952, line 1
   - I Deductions—royalty income — Schedule E, line 18
   - J Section 59(e)(2) expenditures — See Partner's Instructions
   - K Deductions—portfolio (2% floor) — Schedule A, line 22
   - L Deductions—portfolio (other) — Schedule A, line 27
   - M Amounts paid for medical insurance — Schedule A, line 1 or Form 1040, line 29
   - N Educational assistance benefits — See the Partner's Instructions
   - O Dependent care benefits — Form 2441, line 12
   - P Preproductive period expenses — See the Partner's Instructions
   - Q Commercial revitalization deduction from rental real estate activities — See Form 8582 Instructions
   - R Pensions and IRAs — See the Partner's Instructions
   - S Reforestation expense deduction — See the Partner's Instructions
   - T Domestic production activities information — See Form 8903 instructions
   - U Qualified production activities income — Form 8903, line 7
   - V Employer's W-2 wages — Form 8903, line 13
   - W Other deductions — See the Partner's Instructions

14. **Self-employment earnings (loss)**
   Note. *If you have a section 179 deduction or any partner-level deductions, see the Partner's Instructions before completing Schedule SE.*
   - A Net earnings (loss) from self-employment — Schedule SE, Section A or B
   - B Gross farming or fishing income — See the Partner's Instructions
   - C Gross non-farm income — See the Partner's Instructions

15. **Credits & credit recapture**
   - A Low-income housing credit (section 42(j)(5)) — Form 8586, line 4
   - B Low-income housing credit (other) — Form 8586, line 4
   - C Qualified rehabilitation expenditures (rental real estate) — Form 3468, line 1
   - D Qualified rehabilitation expenditures (other than rental real estate) — Form 3468, line 1
   - E Basis of energy property — See the Partner's Instructions
   - F Other rental real estate credits — See the Partner's Instructions
   - G Other rental credits — See the Partner's Instructions
   - H Undistributed capital gains credit — Form 1040, line 70; check box a
   - I Credit for alcohol used as fuel — See the Partner's Instructions

Code — *Enter on*
   - J Work opportunity credit — Form 5884, line 3
   - K Welfare-to-work credit — Form 8861, line 3
   - L Disabled access credit — Form 8826, line 7
   - M Empowerment zone and renewal community employment credit — Form 8844, line 3
   - N Credit for increasing research activities — Form 6765, line 42
   - O New markets credit — Form 8874, line 2
   - P Credit for employer social security and Medicare taxes — Form 8846, line 5
   - Q Backup withholding — Form 1040, line 64
   - R Recapture of low-income housing credit (section 42(j)(5)) — Form 8611, line 8
   - S Recapture of low-income housing credit (other) — Form 8611, line 8
   - T Recapture of investment credit — See Form 4255
   - U Other credits — See the Partner's Instructions
   - V Recapture of other credits — See the Partner's Instructions

16. **Foreign transactions**
   - A Name of country or U.S. possession — Form 1116, Part I
   - B Gross income from all sources — Form 1116, Part I
   - C Gross income sourced at partner level — Form 1116, Part I

   Foreign gross income sourced at partnership level
   - D Passive — Form 1116, Part I
   - E Listed categories — Form 1116, Part I
   - F General limitation — Form 1116, Part I

   Deductions allocated and apportioned at partner level
   - G Interest expense — Form 1116, Part I
   - H Other — Form 1116, Part I

   Deductions allocated and apportioned at partnership level to foreign source income
   - I Passive — Form 1116, Part I
   - J Listed categories — Form 1116, Part I
   - K General limitation — Form 1116, Part I

   Other information
   - L Total foreign taxes paid — Form 1116, Part II
   - M Total foreign taxes accrued — Form 1116, Part II
   - N Reduction in taxes available for credit — Form 1116, line 12
   - O Foreign trading gross receipts — Form 8873
   - P Extraterritorial income exclusion — Form 8873
   - Q Other foreign transactions — See the Partner's Instructions

17. **Alternative minimum tax (AMT) items**
   - A Post-1986 depreciation adjustment
   - B Adjusted gain or loss
   - C Depletion (other than oil & gas)
   - D Oil, gas, & geothermal—gross income
   - E Oil, gas, & geothermal—deductions
   - F Other AMT items

   See the Partner's Instructions and the Instructions for Form 6251

18. **Tax-exempt income and nondeductible expenses**
   - A Tax-exempt interest income — Form 1040, line 8b
   - B Other tax-exempt income — See the Partner's Instructions
   - C Nondeductible expenses — See the Partner's Instructions

19. **Distributions**
   - A Cash and marketable securities — See the Partner's Instructions
   - B Other property — See the Partner's Instructions

20. **Other information**
   - A Investment income — Form 4952, line 4a
   - B Investment expenses — Form 4952, line 5
   - C Fuel tax credit information — Form 4136
   - D Look-back interest—completed long-term contracts — Form 8697
   - E Look-back interest—income forecast method — Form 8866
   - F Dispositions of property with section 179 deductions
   - G Recapture of section 179 deduction
   - H Special basis adjustments
   - I Section 453(l)(3) information
   - J Section 453A(c) information
   - K Section 1260(b) information
   - L Interest allocable to production expenditures
   - M CCF nonqualified withdrawals
   - N Information needed to figure depletion—oil and gas
   - O Amortization of reforestation costs
   - P Unrelated business taxable income
   - Q Other information

   See the Partner's Instructions

FACTS FOR GENERAL PARTNERSHIP (FORM 1065)

The same basic facts presented for the Andrew Lawrence proprietorship are used for the partnership except for the following:

1. Johns and Lawrence is instead a general partnership. Andrew Lawrence and Stephen Johns are both general partners and have equal capital and profits interests. The partnership was created on June 1, 1999. Johns and Lawrence each exchanged their $100,000 of property for a 50% interest in capital and a 50% interest in profits.

2. The book income for Johns and Lawrence is presented in the attached worksheet, which reconciles book income and partnership taxable income.

3. The $18,000 salaries paid to each partner are stipulated in the partnership agreement and are treated as guaranteed payments.

4. The partnership pays federal and state employment taxes on the wages paid to employees other than the partners Johns and Lawrence. The employment tax expense is $52,000 × 0.16 = $8,320. The guaranteed payments made to Johns and Lawrence are treated as self-employment income by the two partners.

5. The partnership paid no estimated federal income taxes.

6. The partnership distributed $14,106 to each of the two partners.

7. Other deductions include:

Travel	$ 4,000
Meals and entertainment	8,000
Minus: 50% disallowance	(4,000)
Office expenses	16,000
Transportation	10,400
General and administrative	3,000
Advertising	13,000
Miscellaneous*	850
Total	$51,250

*$150 of the miscellaneous expenses are related to the production of the dividend income and are separately stated.

8. The following schedule reconciles net income for the C corporation and the partnership:

Net income per books for C corporation	$63,412
Plus: Federal income taxes	14,000
Employment tax adjustment ($14,480 − $8,320)	6,160
Net income per books for partnership	$83,572

9. Total paid-in capital and accumulated profits were divided equally between the two partners in accordance with the actual contributions and allocation of partnership profits in the partnership agreement. Actual business operations may provide for an unequal allocation.

10. Qualified production activities income (QPAI) equals $80,000. Employer's W-2 wages equal the lesser of W-2 wages ($52,000) or 6% of QPAI. Thus, employer's W-2 wages equal $4,800 ($80,000 × 0.06).

11. The balance sheet for Johns and Lawrence appears on page 4 of Form 1065.

Johns and Lawrence General Partnership Reconciliation of Book and Taxable Income For Year Ending December 31, 2005

Account Name	Book Income Debit	Book Income Credit	Adjustments Debit	Adjustments Credit	Taxable Income Debit	Taxable Income Credit	Form 1065 Schedule K Ordinary Income	Form 1065 Schedule K Separately Stated Items
Sales		$869,658				$869,658	$869,658	
Sales returns & allowances	$ 29,242				$ 29,242		(29,242)	
Cost of sales	540,204				540,204		(540,204)	
Dividends		1,000				1,000		$ 1,000
Tax-exempt interest		18,000	$18,000			0		18,000
Gain on stock sale		4,500				4,500		4,500
Worthless stock loss	2,100				2,100			(2,100)
Guaranteed payments[a]	36,000			$36,000	0		(36,000)	
Other salaries	52,000				52,000		(52,000)	
Rentals	36,000				36,000		(36,000)	
Bad debts	4,000				4,000		(4,000)	
Interest:								
Working capital loans	8,000				8,000		(8,000)	
Purchase tax-exempt bonds	2,000			2,000	0			(2,000)
Employment taxes	8,320				8,320		(8,320)	
Taxes	1,520				1,520		(1,520)	
Repairs	4,800				4,800		(4,800)	
Depreciation[b]	12,000		476		12,476		(12,476)	
Charitable contributions	12,000				12,000			(12,000)
Travel	4,000				4,000		(4,000)	
Meals and entertainment[c]	8,000			4,000	4,000		(4,000)	
Meals and ent. nondeductible								(4,000)
Office expenses	16,000				16,000		(16,000)	
Advertising	13,000				13,000		(13,000)	
Transportation expense	10,400				10,400		(10,400)	
General and administrative	3,000				3,000		(3,000)	
Pension plans[d]	2,000				2,000		(2,000)	
Employee benefit programs[e]	4,000				4,000		(4,000)	
Miscellaneous	1,000				1,000		(850)	(150)
Net profit/Taxable income	83,572		$23,524		107,096			
Total	$893,158	$893,158	$42,000	$42,000	$875,158	$875,158	$ 79,846	

[a] Note that guaranteed payments have no net effect on taxable income. The guaranteed payments both reduce ordinary income and increase separately stated income items that are taxable.

[b] MACRS depreciation is $27,476 − $15,000 = $12,476

[c] 50% of the meals and entertainment expense is not deductible for tax purposes but must be separately stated on Schedules K and K-1.

[d] The pension plan expense is the same for book and tax purposes for this partnership. No pension expenses relate to pensions for the partners.

[e] The employee benefit expense is the same for book and tax purposes for this partnership. None relates to partner benefits.

Form **1116**	**Foreign Tax Credit**	OMB No. 1545-0121
Department of the Treasury Internal Revenue Service (99)	(Individual, Estate, or Trust) ▶ Attach to Form 1040, 1040NR, 1041, or 990-T. ▶ See separate instructions.	**2005** Attachment Sequence No. **19**

Name | Identifying number as shown on page 1 of your tax return

Use a separate Form 1116 for each category of income listed below. See **Categories of Income** on page 3 of the instructions. Check only one box on each Form 1116. Report all amounts in U.S. dollars except where specified in Part II below.

a ☐ Passive income
b ☐ High withholding tax interest
c ☐ Financial services income
d ☐ Shipping income
e ☐ Dividends from a DISC or former DISC
f ☐ Certain distributions from a foreign sales corporation (FSC) or former FSC
g ☐ Lump-sum distributions
h ☐ Section 901(j) income
i ☐ Certain income re-sourced by treaty
j ☐ General limitation income

k Resident of (name of country) ▶

Note: *If you paid taxes to only one foreign country or U.S. possession, use column A in Part I and line A in Part II. If you paid taxes to **more than one** foreign country or U.S. possession, use a separate column and line for each country or possession.*

Part I   Taxable Income or Loss From Sources Outside the United States (for Category Checked Above)

	Foreign Country or U.S. Possession			Total
	A	B	C	(Add cols. A, B, and C.)
l Enter the name of the foreign country or U.S. possession ▶				
1 Gross income from sources within country shown above and of the type checked above (see page 13 of the instructions):				1

Deductions and losses (*Caution: See pages 13 and 14 of the instructions*):

2 Expenses **definitely related** to the income on line 1 (attach statement)				
3 Pro rata share of other deductions **not definitely related:**				
a Certain itemized deductions or standard deduction (see instructions)				
b Other deductions (attach statement)				
c Add lines 3a and 3b				
d Gross foreign source income (see instructions)				
e Gross income from all sources (see instructions)				
f Divide line 3d by line 3e (see instructions)				
g Multiply line 3c by line 3f				
4 Pro rata share of interest expense (see instructions):				
a Home mortgage interest (use worksheet on page 13 of the instructions)				
b Other interest expense				
5 Losses from foreign sources				
6 Add lines 2, 3g, 4a, 4b, and 5				6
7 Subtract line 6 from line 1. Enter the result here and on line 14, page 2 ▶				7

Part II   Foreign Taxes Paid or Accrued (see page 14 of the instructions)

Country	Credit is claimed for taxes (you must check one)	Foreign taxes paid or accrued								
		In foreign currency				In U.S. dollars				
	(m) ☐ Paid (n) ☐ Accrued	Taxes withheld at source on:			(s) Other foreign taxes paid or accrued	Taxes withheld at source on:			(w) Other foreign taxes paid or accrued	(x) Total foreign taxes paid or accrued (add cols. (t) through (w))
	(o) Date paid or accrued	(p) Dividends	(q) Rents and royalties	(r) Interest		(t) Dividends	(u) Rents and royalties	(v) Interest		
A										
B										
C										

8 Add lines A through C, column (x). Enter the total here and on line 9, page 2 ▶	8

For Paperwork Reduction Act Notice, see page 18 of the instructions.   Cat. No. 11440U   Form **1116** (2005)

Form 1116 (2005)   Page **2**

Part III	**Figuring the Credit**

9 Enter the amount from line 8. These are your total foreign taxes paid or accrued for the category of income checked above Part I . .   **9**

10 Carryback or carryover (attach detailed computation). **10**

11 Add lines 9 and 10. . . . .   **11**

12 Reduction in foreign taxes (see page 15 of the instructions). . .   **12**

13 Subtract line 12 from line 11. This is the total amount of foreign taxes available for credit . . .   **13**

14 Enter the amount from line 7. This is your taxable income or (loss) from sources outside the United States (before adjustments) for the category of income checked above Part I (see page 15 of the instructions) .   **14**

15 Adjustments to line 14 (see page 16 of the instructions) . . .   **15**

16 Combine the amounts on lines 14 and 15. This is your net foreign source taxable income. (If the result is zero or less, you have no foreign tax credit for the category of income you checked above Part I. Skip lines 17 through 21. However, if you are filing more than one Form 1116, you must complete line 19.). **16**

17 **Individuals:** Enter the amount from Form 1040, line 41 (minus any amount on Form 8914, line 2). If you are a nonresident alien, enter the amount from Form 1040NR, line 38 (minus any amount on Form 8914, line 2). **Estates and trusts:** Enter your taxable income without the deduction for your exemption **17**

    Caution: If you figured your tax using the lower rates on qualified dividends or capital gains, see page 17 of the instructions.

18 Divide line 16 by line 17. If line 16 is more than line 17, enter "1" **18**

19 **Individuals:** Enter the amount from Form 1040, line 44. If you are a nonresident alien, enter the amount from Form 1040NR, line 41.

    Estates and trusts: Enter the amount from Form 1041, Schedule G, line 1a, or the total of Form 990-T, lines 36 and 37 . . . .   **19**

    Caution: If you are completing line 19 for separate category g (lump-sum distributions), see page 18 of the instructions.

20 Multiply line 19 by line 18 (maximum amount of credit) **20**

21 Enter the **smaller** of line 13 or line 20. If this is the only Form 1116 you are filing, skip lines 22 through 30 and enter this amount on line 31. Otherwise, complete the appropriate line in Part IV (see page 18 of the instructions) . . . . ▶   **21**

Part IV	**Summary of Credits From Separate Parts III** (see page 18 of the instructions)

22 Credit for taxes on passive income **22**

23 Credit for taxes on high withholding tax interest **23**

24 Credit for taxes on financial services income **24**

25 Credit for taxes on shipping income **25**

26 Credit for taxes on dividends from a DISC or former DISC and certain distributions from a FSC or former FSC **26**

27 Credit for taxes on lump-sum distributions **27**

28 Credit for taxes on certain income re-sourced by treaty **28**

29 Credit for taxes on general limitation income **29**

30 Add lines 22 through 29 . . . .   **30**

31 Enter the **smaller** of line 19 or line 30 . . . .   **31**

32 Reduction of credit for international boycott operations. See instructions for line 12 on page 15 .   **32**

33 Subtract line 32 from line 31. This is your **foreign tax credit.** Enter here and on Form 1040, line 47; Form 1040NR, line 44; Form 1041, Schedule G, line 2a; or Form 990-T, line 40a . . . . . . ▶   **33**

Form **1116** (2005)

Form **1120**
Department of the Treasury
Internal Revenue Service

U.S. Corporation Income Tax Return

For calendar year 2005 or tax year beginning ...., 2005, ending ...., 20....
► See separate instructions.

OMB No. 1545-0123

2005

A Check if:			
1 Consolidated return (attach Form 851) . ☐	Use IRS label. Otherwise, print or type.	**Name** Johns and Lawrence, Inc.	**B Employer identification number** 76 ⋮ 3456789
2 Personal holding co. (attach Sch. PH) . ☐		Number, street, and room or suite no. If a P.O. box, see instructions. **1234 University Avenue**	**C Date incorporated** 6/1/99
3 Personal service corp. (see instructions) . ☐		City or town, state, and ZIP code **Gainesville, FL 32611**	**D Total assets (see instructions)** $ 479,324
4 Schedule M-3 required (attach Sch. M-3) . ☐			

E Check if: (1) ☐ Initial return (2) ☐ Final return (3) ☐ Name change (4) ☐ Address change

Income

1a	Gross receipts or sales 869,658 b Less returns and allowances 29,242 c Bal ►		1c	840,416
2	Cost of goods sold (Schedule A, line 8) .		2	540,204
3	Gross profit. Subtract line 2 from line 1c		3	300,212
4	Dividends (Schedule C, line 19)		4	1,000
5	Interest		5	
6	Gross rents		6	
7	Gross royalties		7	
8	Capital gain net income (attach Schedule D (Form 1120)) *Not Reproduced*		8	2,400
9	Net gain or (loss) from Form 4797, Part II, line 17 (attach Form 4797)		9	
10	Other income (see instructions—attach schedule)		10	
11	**Total income.** Add lines 3 through 10 ►		11	303,612

Deductions (See instructions for limitations on deductions.)

12	Compensation of officers (Schedule E, line 4)		12	36,000
13	Salaries and wages (less employment credits)		13	52,000
14	Repairs and maintenance		14	4,800
15	Bad debts .		15	4,000
16	Rents		16	36,000
17	Taxes and licenses		17	16,000
18	Interest		18	8,000
19	Charitable contributions (see instructions for 10% limitation)		19	7,694
20a	Depreciation (attach Form 4562)	20a 27,476		
b	Less depreciation claimed on Schedule A and elsewhere on return	20b 15,000	20c	12,476
21	Depletion		21	
22	Advertising		22	13,000
23	Pension, profit-sharing, etc., plans		23	2,000
24	Employee benefit programs		24	4,000
25	Domestic production activities deduction (attach Form 8903) *Not Reproduced*		25	2,056
26	Other deductions (attach schedule)		26	38,400
27	**Total deductions.** Add lines 12 through 26 ►		27	236,426
28	Taxable income before net operating loss deduction and special deductions. Subtract line 27 from line 11		28	67,186
29	**Less: a** Net operating loss deduction (see instructions)	29a		
	b Special deductions (Schedule C, line 20)	29b 700	29c	700

Tax and Payments

30	**Taxable income.** Subtract line 29c from line 28 (see instructions if Schedule C, line 12, was completed)		30	66,486
31	**Total tax** (Schedule J, line 11) .		31	11,622
32	**Payments: a** 2004 overpayment credited to 2005 .	32a		
b	2005 estimated tax payments . . .	32b 14,000		
c	Less 2005 refund applied for on Form 4466	32c ( ) d Bal ► 32d 14,000		
e	Tax deposited with Form 7004	32e		
f	Credits: (1) Form 2439 _____ (2) Form 4136 _____	32f	32g	14,000
33	Estimated tax penalty (see instructions). Check if Form 2220 is attached ► ☐		33	
34	**Tax due.** If line 32g is smaller than the total of lines 31 and 33, enter amount owed		34	
35	**Overpayment.** If line 32g is larger than the total of lines 31 and 33, enter amount overpaid		35	1,864
36	Enter amount of line 35 you want: **Credited to 2006 estimated tax** ► 1,864 **Refunded** ►		36	

Sign Here

Under penalties of perjury, I declare that I have examined this return, including accompanying schedules and statements, and to the best of my knowledge and belief, it is true, correct, and complete. Declaration of preparer (other than taxpayer) is based on all information of which preparer has any knowledge.

► *Andrew Lawrence* | 3-15-06 | ► Vice-President
Signature of officer | Date | Title

May the IRS discuss this return with the preparer shown below (see instructions)? ☒ Yes ☐ No

Paid Preparer's Use Only	Preparer's signature ► *Michael Kramer*	Date 3-14-06	Check if self-employed ☒	Preparer's SSN or PTIN 375-49-6339
	Firm's name (or yours if self-employed), address, and ZIP code ►	Michael S. Kramer 1110 McMillian Gainesville, FL 32611	EIN 59 ⋮ 2029763	Phone no. (352) 555-2000

For Privacy Act and Paperwork Reduction Act Notice, see separate instructions.   Cat. No. 11450Q   Form **1120** (2005)

Form 1120 (2005)   Page **2**

Schedule A Cost of Goods Sold (see instructions)

1	Inventory at beginning of year	1	64,000
2	Purchases	2	340,800
3	Cost of labor	3	143,204
4	Additional section 263A costs (attach schedule)	4	7,000
5	Other costs (attach schedule)	5	90,000
6	**Total.** Add lines 1 through 5	6	645,004
7	Inventory at end of year	7	104,800
8	**Cost of goods sold.** Subtract line 7 from line 6. Enter here and on page 1, line 2	8	540,204

9a Check all methods used for valuing closing inventory:

    (i) [X] Cost

    (ii) [ ] Lower of cost or market

    (iii) [ ] Other (Specify method used and attach explanation.) ▶ ....

  b Check if there was a writedown of subnormal goods ▶ [ ]

  c Check if the LIFO inventory method was adopted this tax year for any goods (if checked, attach Form 970) ▶ [ ]

  d If the LIFO inventory method was used for this tax year, enter percentage (or amounts) of closing inventory computed under LIFO   9d

  e If property is produced or acquired for resale, do the rules of section 263A apply to the corporation?   [X] Yes   [ ] No

  f Was there any change in determining quantities, cost, or valuations between opening and closing inventory? If "Yes," attach explanation   [ ] Yes   [X] No

Schedule C Dividends and Special Deductions (see instructions)

		(a) Dividends received	(b) %	(c) Special deductions (a) × (b)
1	Dividends from less-than-20%-owned domestic corporations (other than debt-financed stock)	1,000	70	700
2	Dividends from 20%-or-more-owned domestic corporations (other than debt-financed stock)		80	
3	Dividends on debt-financed stock of domestic and foreign corporations		see instructions	
4	Dividends on certain preferred stock of less-than-20%-owned public utilities		42	
5	Dividends on certain preferred stock of 20%-or-more-owned public utilities		48	
6	Dividends from less-than-20%-owned foreign corporations and certain FSCs		70	
7	Dividends from 20%-or-more-owned foreign corporations and certain FSCs		80	
8	Dividends from wholly owned foreign subsidiaries		100	
9	**Total.** Add lines 1 through 8. See instructions for limitation			700
10	Dividends from domestic corporations received by a small business investment company operating under the Small Business Investment Act of 1958		100	
11	Dividends from affiliated group members and certain FSCs		100	
12	Dividends from controlled foreign corporations (attach Form 8895)		85	
13	Dividends from foreign corporations not included on lines 3, 6, 7, 8, 11, or 12			
14	Income from controlled foreign corporations under subpart F (attach Form(s) 5471)			
15	Foreign dividend gross-up			
16	IC-DISC and former DISC dividends not included on lines 1, 2, or 3			
17	Other dividends			
18	Deduction for dividends paid on certain preferred stock of public utilities			
19	**Total dividends.** Add lines 1 through 17. Enter here and on page 1, line 4 ▶			
20	**Total special deductions.** Add lines 9, 10, 11, 12, and 18. Enter here and on page 1, line 29b ▶			700

Schedule E Compensation of Officers (see instructions for page 1, line 12)

Note: Complete Schedule E only if total receipts (line 1a plus lines 4 through 10 on page 1) are $500,000 or more.

(a) Name of officer	(b) Social security number	(c) Percent of time devoted to business	Percent of corporation stock owned		(f) Amount of compensation
			(d) Common	(e) Preferred	
1 Stephen Johns	386-05-9174	100 %	50 %	%	18,000
Andrew Lawrence	297-63-2110	100 %	50 %	%	18,000
		%	%	%	
		%	%	%	
		%	%	%	

2	Total compensation of officers	36,000
3	Compensation of officers claimed on Schedule A and elsewhere on return	
4	Subtract line 3 from line 2. Enter the result here and on page 1, line 12	36,000

Form **1120** (2005)

Form 1120 (2005)

Page **3**

Schedule J Tax Computation (see instructions)

1	Check if the corporation is a member of a controlled group . . . . ▶ ☐		
	Important: Members of a controlled group, see instructions.		
2a	If the box on line 1 is checked, enter the corporation's share of the $50,000, $25,000, and $9,925,000 taxable income brackets (in that order):		
	(1) ☐ $ |_____|_____| **(2)** ☐ $ |_____|_____| **(3)** $ |_____|		
b	Enter the corporation's share of: **(1)** Additional 5% tax (not more than $11,750) $		
	(2) Additional 3% tax (not more than $100,000) $		
3	Income tax. Check if a qualified personal service corporation (see instructions) . . . . ▶ ☐	3	11,622
4	Alternative minimum tax (attach Form 4626)	4	
5	Add lines 3 and 4	5	11,622
6a	Foreign tax credit (attach Form 1118)	6a	
b	Possessions tax credit (attach Form 5735)	6b	
c	Credits from: ☐ Form 8834 ☐ Form 8907, line 23	6c	
d	General business credit. Check box(es) and indicate which forms are attached: ☐ Form 3800 ☐ Form(s) (specify) ▶ _____	6d	
e	Credit for prior year minimum tax (attach Form 8827) . . .	6e	
f	Bond credits from: ☐ Form 8860 ☐ Form 8912	6f	
7	**Total credits.** Add lines 6a through 6f	7	-0-
8	Subtract line 7 from line 5	8	11,622
9	Personal holding company tax (attach Schedule PH (Form 1120))	9	
10	Other taxes. Check if from: ☐ Form 4255 ☐ Form 8611 ☐ Form 8697 ☐ Form 8866 ☐ Form 8902 ☐ Other (attach schedule) . .	10	
11	**Total tax.** Add lines 8 through 10. Enter here and on page 1, line 31	11	11,622

Schedule K Other Information (see instructions)

		Yes	No
1	Check accounting method: **a** ☐ Cash **b** ☒ Accrual **c** ☐ Other (specify) ▶ _____		
2	See the instructions and enter the:		
a	Business activity code no. ▶ 337,000		
b	Business activity ▶ Manufacturing		
c	Product or service ▶ Furniture		
3	At the end of the tax year, did the corporation own, directly or indirectly, 50% or more of the voting stock of a domestic corporation? (For rules of attribution, see section 267(c).)		X
	If "Yes," attach a schedule showing: **(a)** name and employer identification number (EIN), **(b)** percentage owned, and **(c)** taxable income or (loss) before NOL and special deductions of such corporation for the tax year ending with or within your tax year.		
4	Is the corporation a subsidiary in an affiliated group or a parent-subsidiary controlled group?		X
	If "Yes," enter name and EIN of the parent corporation ▶ _____		
5	At the end of the tax year, did any individual, partnership, corporation, estate, or trust own, directly or indirectly, 50% or more of the corporation's voting stock? (For rules of attribution, see section 267(c).)	X	
	If "Yes," attach a schedule showing name and identifying number. (Do not include any information already entered in **4** above.) Enter percentage owned ▶ 50%*		
6	During this tax year, did the corporation pay dividends (other than stock dividends and distributions in exchange for stock) in excess of the corporation's current and accumulated earnings and profits? (See sections 301 and 316.) . .	X	
	If "Yes," file **Form 5452**, Corporate Report of Nondividend Distributions.		
	If this is a consolidated return, answer here for the parent corporation and on **Form 851**, Affiliations Schedule, for each subsidiary.		

		Yes	No
7	At any time during the tax year, did one foreign person own, directly or indirectly, at least 25% of **(a)** the total voting power of all classes of stock of the corporation entitled to vote or **(b)** the total value of all classes of stock of the corporation?		X
	If "Yes," enter: **(a)** Percentage owned ▶ N/A and **(b)** Owner's country ▶ N/A		
c	The corporation may have to file **Form 5472**, Information Return of a 25% Foreign-Owned U.S. Corporation or a Foreign Corporation Engaged in a U.S. Trade or Business. Enter number of Forms 5472 attached ▶ _____		
8	Check this box if the corporation issued publicly offered debt instruments with original issue discount . ▶ ☐		
	If checked, the corporation may have to file **Form 8281**, Information Return for Publicly Offered Original Issue Discount Instruments.		
9	Enter the amount of tax-exempt interest received or accrued during the tax year ▶ $ 18,000		
10	Enter the number of shareholders at the end of the tax year (if 100 or fewer) ▶ 2		
11	If the corporation has an NOL for the tax year and is electing to forego the carryback period, check here ▶ ☐		
	If the corporation is filing a consolidated return, the statement required by Temporary Regulations section 1.1502-21T(b)(3) must be attached or the election will not be valid.		
12	Enter the available NOL carryover from prior tax years (Do not reduce it by any deduction on line 29a.) ▶ $ None		
13	Are the corporation's total receipts (line 1a plus lines 4 through 10 on page 1) for the tax year **and** its total assets at the end of the tax year less than $250,000? . . .		X
	If "Yes," the corporation is not required to complete Schedules L, M-1, and M-2 on page 4. Instead, enter the total amount of cash distributions and the book value of property distributions (other than cash) made during the tax year. ▶ $ _____		

Note: If the corporation, at any time during the tax year, had assets or operated a business in a foreign country or U.S. possession, it may be required to attach **Schedule N (Form 1120)**, Foreign Operations of U.S. Corporations, to this return. See Schedule N for details.

*See Schedule E

Form **1120** (2005)

Form 1120 (2005)   Page **4**

Note: *The corporation is not required to complete Schedules L, M-1, and M-2 if Question 13 on Schedule K is answered "Yes."*

Schedule L	Balance Sheets per Books	Beginning of tax year		End of tax year	
	Assets	(a)	(b)	(c)	(d)
1	Cash		60,000		72,600
2a	Trade notes and accounts receivable	25,000		24,000	
b	Less allowance for bad debts	(1,000)	24,000	(1,000)	23,000
3	Inventories		64,000		104,800
4	U.S. government obligations				
5	Tax-exempt securities (see instructions)		200,000		200,000
6	Other current assets (attach schedule)		7,000		
7	Loans to shareholders				
8	Mortgage and real estate loans				
9	Other investments (attach schedule)				
10a	Buildings and other depreciable assets	151,600		151,600	
b	Less accumulated depreciation	(45,200)	106,400	(72,676)	78,924
11a	Depletable assets				
b	Less accumulated depletion	( )		( )	
12	Land (net of any amortization)				
13a	Intangible assets (amortizable only)				
b	Less accumulated amortization	( )		( )	
14	Other assets (attach schedule)				
15	Total assets		461,400		479,324
	Liabilities and Shareholders' Equity				
16	Accounts payable		26,000		19,000
17	Mortgages, notes, bonds payable in less than 1 year		4,000		4,000
18	Other current liabilities (attach schedule)		3,600		3,600
19	Loans from shareholders				
20	Mortgages, notes, bonds payable in 1 year or more		130,000		119,724
21	Other liabilities (attach schedule)				
22	Capital stock: a Preferred stock				
	b Common stock	200,000	200,000	200,000	200,000
23	Additional paid-in capital				
24	Retained earnings—Appropriated (attach schedule)				
25	Retained earnings—Unappropriated		97,800		133,000
26	Adjustments to shareholders' equity (attach schedule)				
27	Less cost of treasury stock		( )		( )
28	Total liabilities and shareholders' equity		461,400		479,324

Schedule M-1	Reconciliation of Income (Loss) per Books With Income per Return (see instructions)

1	Net income (loss) per books	63,412
2	Federal income tax per books	14,000
3	Excess of capital losses over capital gains	
4	Income subject to tax not recorded on books this year (itemize):	
5	Expenses recorded on books this year not deducted on this return (itemize):	
a	Depreciation $ 4,306	
b	Charitable contributions $ 4,000	
c	Travel and entertainment $	
	Nondeductable interest* $2,000	10,306
6	Add lines 1 through 5	87,718

7	Income recorded on books this year not included on this return (itemize): Tax-exempt interest $ 18,000	18,000
8	Deductions on this return not charged against book income this year (itemize):	
a	Depreciation $ 476	
b	Charitable contributions $	
	U.S. prod. act. ded. $2,056	2,532
9	Add lines 7 and 8	20,532
10	Income (page 1, line 28)—line 6 less line 9	67,186

Schedule M-2	Analysis of Unappropriated Retained Earnings per Books (Line 25, Schedule L)

1	Balance at beginning of year	97,800
2	Net income (loss) per books	63,412
3	Other increases (itemize):	
4	Add lines 1, 2, and 3	161,212

5	Distributions: a Cash	28,212
	b Stock	
	c Property	
6	Other decreases (itemize):	
7	Add lines 5 and 6	28,212
8	Balance at end of year (line 4 less line 7)	133,000

*On loans to acquire municipal bonds.

Form **1120** (2005)

SCHEDULE M-3 **(Form 1120)** Department of the Treasury Internal Revenue Service	**Net Income (Loss) Reconciliation for Corporations** **With Total Assets of $10 Million or More** ► Attach to Form 1120. ► See separate instructions.	OMB No. 1545-0123 20**05**

Name of corporation (common parent, if consolidated return)	Employer identification number
Valley Corporatiom	

▮ Financial Information and Net Income (Loss) Reconciliation

1a Did the corporation file SEC Form 10-K for its income statement period ending with or within this tax year?

☐ **Yes.** Skip lines 1b and 1c and complete lines 2a through 11 with respect to that SEC Form 10-K.

☒ **No.** Go to line 1b.

b Did the corporation prepare a certified audited income statement for that period?

☐ **Yes.** Skip line 1c and complete lines 2a through 11 with respect to that income statement.

☒ **No.** Go to line 1c.

c Did the corporation prepare an income statement for that period?

☒ **Yes.** Complete lines 2a through 11 with respect to that income statement.

☐ **No.** Skip lines 2a through 3c and enter the corporation's net income (loss) per its books and records on line 4.

2a Enter the income statement period: Beginning ___1 / 1 / 05___ Ending ___12 / 31 / 05___

b Has the corporation's income statement been restated for the income statement period on line 2a?

☐ **Yes.** (If "Yes," attach an explanation and the amount of each item restated.)

☒ **No.**

c Has the corporation's income statement been restated for any of the five income statement periods preceding the period on line 2a?

☐ **Yes.** (If "Yes," attach an explanation and the amount of each item restated.)

☒ **No.**

3a Is any of the corporation's voting common stock publicly traded?

☐ **Yes.**

☒ **No.** If "No," go to line 4.

b Enter the symbol of the corporation's primary U.S. publicly traded voting common stock . . . .

c Enter the nine-digit CUSIP number of the corporation's primary publicly traded voting common stock . . . .

4	Worldwide consolidated net income (loss) from income statement source identified in Part I, line 1	**4**	**121,700**
5a	Net income from nonincludible foreign entities (attach schedule)	**5a**	( )
b	Net loss from nonincludible foreign entities (attach schedule and enter as a positive amount) . .	**5b**	
6a	Net income from nonincludible U.S. entities (attach schedule)	**6a**	( )
b	Net loss from nonincludible U.S. entities (attach schedule and enter as a positive amount) . . .	**6b**	
7a	Net income of other includible corporations (attach schedule)	**7a**	
b	Net loss of other includible corporations (attach schedule)	**7b**	( )
8	Adjustment to eliminations of transactions between includible corporations and nonincludible entities (attach schedule)	**8**	
9	Adjustment to reconcile income statement period to tax year (attach schedule)	**9**	
10	Other adjustments to reconcile to amount on line 11 (attach schedule)	**10**	
11	**Net income (loss) per income statement of includible corporations.** Combine lines 4 through 10	**11**	**121,700**

For Privacy Act and Paperwork Reduction Act Notice, see the Instructions for Forms 1120 and 1120-A.   Cat. No. 37961C   Schedule M-3 (Form 1120) 2005

Schedule M-3 (Form 1120) 2005

Name of corporation (common parent, if consolidated return)	Employer identification number
Valley Corporation	

If consolidated return, check applicable box: (1) ☐ Consolidated group (2) ☐ Parent corporation (3) ☐ Consolidated eliminations (4) ☐ Subsidiary corporation

Name of subsidiary (if consolidated return)	Employer identification number

Part II — Reconciliation of Net Income (Loss) per Income Statement of Includible Corporations With Taxable Income per Return

Income (Loss) Items	(a) Income (Loss) per Income Statement	(b) Temporary Difference	(c) Permanent Difference	(d) Income (Loss) per Tax Return
1 Income (loss) from equity method foreign corporations				
2 Gross foreign dividends not previously taxed				
3 Subpart F, QEF, and similar income inclusions				
4 Section 78 gross-up				
5 Gross foreign distributions previously taxed				
6 Income (loss) from equity method U.S. corporations				
7 U.S. dividends not eliminated in tax consolidation				
8 Minority interest for includible corporations				
9 Income (loss) from U.S. partnerships (attach schedule)				
10 Income (loss) from foreign partnerships (attach schedule)				
11 Income (loss) from other pass-through entities (attach schedule)				
12 Items relating to reportable transactions (attach details)				
13 Interest income				
14 Total accrual to cash adjustment				
15 Hedging transactions				
16 Mark-to-market income (loss)				
17 Cost of goods sold				
18 Sale versus lease (for sellers and/or lessors)				
19 Section 481(a) adjustments				
20 Unearned/deferred revenue *Prepaid rent*	– 0 –	10,000		10,000
21 Income recognition from long-term contracts				
22 Original issue discount and other imputed interest				
23a Income statement gain/loss on sale, exchange, abandonment, worthlessness, or other disposition of assets other than inventory and pass-through entities	(10,750)			
23b Gross capital gains from Schedule D, excluding amounts from pass-through entities				
23c Gross capital losses from Schedule D, excluding amounts from pass-through entities, abandonment losses, and worthless stock losses				
23d Net gain/loss reported on Form 4797, line 17, excluding amounts from pass-through entities, abandonment losses, and worthless stock losses				
23e Abandonment losses				
23f Worthless stock losses (attach details)				
23g Other gain/loss on disposition of assets other than inventory		10,750		– 0 –
24 Disallowed capital loss in excess of capital gains				
25 Utilization of capital loss carryforward				
26 Other income (loss) items with differences (attach schedule) *	62,500		(62,500)	– 0 –
27 **Total income (loss) items.** Combine lines 1 through 26	51,750	20,750	(62,500)	10,000
28 **Total expense/deduction items** (from Part III, line 36)	(69,050)	(2,000)	40,050	(31,000)
29 Other income (loss) and expense/deduction items with no differences **	139,000			139,000
30 **Reconciliation totals.** Combine lines 27 through 29	121,700	18,750	(22,450)	118,000

Note. Line 30, column (a), must equal the amount on Part I, line 11, and column (d) must equal Form 1120, page 1, line 28.

* **Insurance proceeds $50,000; Tax-exempt interest $12,500**
** **Gross profit $201,000 minus operating expenses $62,000**

Schedule M-3 (Form 1120) 2005

Name of corporation (common parent, if consolidated return)	Employer identification number
Valley Corporation	

If consolidated return, check applicable box: (1) ☐ Consolidated group (2) ☐ Parent corporation (3) ☐ Consolidated eliminations (4) ☐ Subsidiary corporation

Name of subsidiary (if consolidated return)	Employer identification number

Part III   **Reconciliation of Net Income (Loss) per Income Statement of Includible Corporations With Taxable Income per Return—Expense/Deduction Items**

	Expense/Deduction Items	(a) Expense per Income Statement	(b) Temporary Difference	(c) Permanent Difference	(d) Deduction per Tax Return
1	U.S. current income tax expense	27,250		(27,250)	
2	U.S. deferred income tax expense				
3	State and local current income tax expense				
4	State and local deferred income tax expense				
5	Foreign current income tax expense (other than foreign withholding taxes)				
6	Foreign deferred income tax expense				
7	Foreign withholding taxes				
8	Interest expense				
9	Stock option expense				
10	Other equity-based compensation				
11	Meals and entertainment				
12	Fines and penalties				
13	Judgments, damages, awards, and similar costs				
14	Parachute payments				
15	Compensation with section 162(m) limitation				
16	Pension and profit-sharing				
17	Other post-retirement benefits				
18	Deferred compensation				
19	Charitable contribution of cash and tangible property				
20	Charitable contribution of intangible property				
21	Charitable contribution limitation/carryforward				
22	Domestic production activities deduction			3,000	3,000
23	Current year acquisition or reorganization investment banking fees				
24	Current year acquisition or reorganization legal and accounting fees				
25	Current year acquisition/reorganization other costs				
26	Amortization/impairment of goodwill				
27	Amortization of acquisition, reorganization, and start-up costs				
28	Other amortization or impairment write-offs				
29	Section 198 environmental remediation costs				
30	Depletion				
31	Depreciation	26,000	2,000		28,000
32	Bad debt expense				
33	Corporate owned life insurance premiums	800		(800)	– 0 –
34	Purchase versus lease (for purchasers and/or lessees)				
35	Other expense/deduction items with differences (attach schedule) *	15,000		(15,000)	– 0 –
36	**Total expense/deduction items.** Combine lines 1 through 35. Enter here and on Part II, line 28	69,050	2,000	(40,050)	31,000

* Interest on loan to finance tax-exempt bonds.

FACTS FOR C CORPORATION (FORM 1120)

The same basic facts presented for the Andrew Lawrence proprietorship are used for the C corporation except for the following:

1. Andrew Lawrence and Stephen Johns are the two 50% shareholders of Johns and Lawrence, Inc., a furniture manufacturer (Business Code 337000). Johns and Lawrence is located at 1234 University Ave., Gainesville, FL 32611. Its employer identification number is 76-3456789. The following information pertains to the 2005 corporate tax return:

Compensation of Officers

Name	S.S. No.	Share	Title	Compensation
Stephen Johns	386-05-9174	1,000	President	$18,000
Andrew Lawrence	297-63-2110	1,000	V.P.	18,000
Total		2,000		$36,000

The coporation paid all salaries owed to the shareholders in 2005. The coporation paid none of the interest or rentals to the shareholders.

2. The book income for the corporation appears in the attached worksheet, which reconciles the corporation's book income and its taxable income.

3. The company was incorporated on June 1, 1999. Each of the two officers hold one-half the stock, which they acquired on that date for a total cash and property contribution of $200,000. No change in the stockholdings has occurred since incorporation. Johns and Lawrence each devote 100% of their time to the business. The corporation provides no expense allowances. The corporation, however, reimburses properly substantiated expenses. Both officers are U.S. citizens. Johns and Lawrence is not a member of a controlled group.

4. Addresses for the officers are: Andrew Lawrence, 436 N.W. 24th Ave., Gainesville, FL 32607; Stephen Johns, 1250 N.E. 12th Ave., Gainesville, FL 32601.

5. The corporation paid estimated taxes of $14,000 for tax year 2005.

6. Other deductions include:

Travel	$ 4,000
Meals and entertainment	8,000
Minus: 50% disallowance	(4,000)
Office expenses	16,000
Transportation	10,400
General and administrative	3,000
Miscellaneous	1,000
Total	$38,400

7. The charitable contributions deduction limitation is $7,694 (see footnote b in Reconciliation worksheet on next page). The remaining $4,306 ($12,000 − $7,694) carries over to 2006 and the four succeeding tax years.

8. Qualified production activities income (QPAI) equals $80,000. Employer's W-2 wages equal the lesser of W-2 wages ($88,000) or 6% of QPAI. Thus, employer's W-2 wages equal $4,800 ($80,000 × 0.06).

9. The $28,212 of withdrawals made by the two owners are dividends out of the corporation's earnings and profits. They are reported as gross income on the shareholders' individual tax returns.

10. The beginning-of-the-year balance sheets for all entity forms are the same, which permits a direct comparison of the 2005 tax differences. Actually, the corporation would have reported tax differences in all prior years (1999 through 2004), which would have been included in the January 1, 2005 balance sheet. If these differences were so included, the direct comparisons would be much more difficult.

Johns and Lawrence, Inc. (C Corporation) Book Income to Taxable Income Reconciliation For Year Ending December 31, 2005

Account Name	Book Income Debit	Book Income Credit	Adjustments Debit	Adjustments Credit	Taxable Income Debit	Taxable Income Credit
Sales		$869,658				$869,658
Sales returns & allowances	$ 29,242				$ 29,242	
Cost of sales	540,204				540,204	
Dividends		1,000				1,000
Tax-exempt interest		18,000	$18,000			0
Gain on stock sale		4,500				4,500
Worthless stock loss	2,100				2,100	
Officers' salaries	36,000				36,000	
Other salaries	52,000				52,000	
Rentals	36,000				36,000	
Bad debts	4,000				4,000	
Interest:						
Working capital loans	8,000				8,000	
Purchase tax-exempt bonds	2,000			$ 2,000	0	
Employment taxes	14,480				14,480	
Taxes	1,520				1,520	
Repairs	4,800				4,800	
Depreciation[a]	12,000		476		12,476	
Charitable contributions[b]	12,000			4,306	7,694	
Travel	4,000				4,000	
Meals and entertainment[c]	8,000			4,000	4,000	
Office expenses	16,000				16,000	
Advertising	13,000				13,000	
Transportation expense	10,400				10,400	
General and administrative	3,000				3,000	
Pension plans	2,000				2,000	
Employee benefit programs	4,000				4,000	
Miscellaneous	1,000				1,000	
U.S. prod. act. ded.	0		2,056		2,056	
Federal income taxes	14,000			14,000	0	
Taxable income before spec. deds.			18,476	24,306	69,242	
Div. rec. ded. (10%-owned)[e]			700		700	
NOL deduction					0	
Net profit/Taxable income	63,412		3,074		66,486	
Total	$893,158	$893,158	$24,306	$24,306	$875,158	$875,158

[a] MACRS depreciation is $27,476 − $15,000 = $12,476

[b] Charitable contribution deduction limitation:

Total income (Form 1120, page 1, line 11)	$303,612
Minus: Deductions other than char. cont. & DRD	(226,676)
Charitable contribution base	$ 76,936
Times: 10%	0.10
Charitable contribution deduction	$ 7,694

[c] $8,000 × 0.50 disallowance rate = $4,000 disallowed expenses

[d]

Total income (Form 1120, page 1, line 11)	$303,612
Minus: Deductions other than the U.S. prod. act. ded.	(235,070)
Taxable income before the U.S. prod. act. ded.	$ 68,542
Times: 3%	0.03
U.S. prod. act. ded.	$ 2,056

[e] Dividends-received deduction: $1,000 × 0.70 = $700.

Form **1120**

Department of the Treasury
Internal Revenue Service

U.S. Corporation Income Tax Return

For calendar year 2005 or tax year beginning .... , 2005, ending .... , 20 ....
► See separate instructions.

OMB No. 1545-0123

2005

A Check if:

1 Consolidated return (attach Form 851) . [X]
2 Personal holding co. (attach Sch. PH) . [ ]
3 Personal service corp. (see instructions) . [ ]
4 Schedule M-3 required (attach Sch. M-3) [ ]

Use IRS label. Otherwise, print or type.

Name
Alpha Manufacturing Corp. and Subsidaries

Number, street, and room or suite no. If a P.O. box, see instructions.
820 N.W. 1st Place

City or town, state, and ZIP code
Gainesville, FL 32601

B Employer identification number
38 : 0000001

C Date incorporated
9/15/95

D Total assets (see instructions)
$ 3,976,492

E Check if: (1) [ ] Initial return (2) [ ] Final return (3) [ ] Name change (4) [ ] Address change

Income

1a	Gross receipts or sales 6,147,000	b Less returns and allowances – 0 –	c Bal ►
1c			6,147,000
2	Cost of goods sold (Schedule A, line 8)		2,301,000
3	Gross profit. Subtract line 2 from line 1c		3,846,000
4	Dividends (Schedule C, line 19)		40,000
5	Interest		156,000
6	Gross rents		195,000
7	Gross royalties		
8	Capital gain net income (attach Schedule D (Form 1120))		67,939
9	Net gain or (loss) from Form 4797, Part II, line 17 (attach Form 4797)		37,080
10	Other income (see instructions—attach schedule)		10,000
11	**Total income.** Add lines 3 through 10 ►		4,352,019

Deductions (See instructions for limitations on deductions.)

12	Compensation of officers (Schedule E, line 4)			165,000
13	Salaries and wages (less employment credits)			1,356,000
14	Repairs and maintenance			83,000
15	Bad debts			48,500
16	Rents			179,000
17	Taxes and licenses			138,000
18	Interest			58,000
19	Charitable contributions (see instructions for 10% limitation)			15,000
20a	Depreciation (attach Form 4562)	20a	246,093	
b	Less depreciation claimed on Schedule A and elsewhere on return	20b	77,400	
20c				168,693
21	Depletion			
22	Advertising			269,140
23	Pension, profit-sharing, etc., plans			140,000
24	Employee benefit programs			105,000
25	Domestic production activities deduction (attach Form 8903)			9,320
26	Other deductions (attach schedule)			1,284,000
27	**Total deductions.** Add lines 12 through 26 ►			4,018,653
28	Taxable income before net operating loss deduction and special deductions. Subtract line 27 from line 11			333,366
29	**Less:** a Net operating loss deduction (see instructions)	29a		
	b Special deductions (Schedule C, line 20)	29b	32,000	
29c				32,000

Tax and Payments

30	**Taxable income.** Subtract line 29c from line 28 (see instructions if Schedule C, line 12, was completed)		30		301,366
31	**Total tax** (Schedule J, line 11)		31		100,783
32	Payments: a 2004 overpayment credited to 2005	32a			
b	2005 estimated tax payments	32b	146,000		
c	Less 2005 refund applied for on Form 4466	32c ( )	d Bal ► 32d	146,000	
e	Tax deposited with Form 7004	32e			
f	Credits: (1) Form 2439 _____ (2) Form 4136 _____	32f		32g	146,000
33	Estimated tax penalty (see instructions). Check if Form 2220 is attached ► [ ]		33		
34	**Tax due.** If line 32g is smaller than the total of lines 31 and 33, enter amount owed		34		
35	**Overpayment.** If line 32g is larger than the total of lines 31 and 33, enter amount overpaid		35		45,217
36	Enter amount of line 35 you want: **Credited to 2006 estimated tax** ► 26,000 Refunded ►		36		19,217

Sign Here

Under penalties of perjury, I declare that I have examined this return, including accompanying schedules and statements, and to the best of my knowledge and belief, it is true, correct, and complete. Declaration of preparer (other than taxpayer) is based on all information of which preparer has any knowledge.

► *U. R. Stuck* | 3-15-06 | ► President

Signature of officer | Date | Title

May the IRS discuss this return with the preparer shown below (see instructions)? [ ] Yes [ ] No

Paid Preparer's Use Only

Preparer's signature ►	*John A. Kramer*	Date 3-14-06	Check if self-employed [X]	Preparer's SSN or PTIN 241693967
Firm's name (or yours if self-employed), address, and ZIP code ►	Kramer and Associates 4710 N.W. 68th Terrace Gainesville, FL		EIN 01 : 0000001	Phone no. (352) 555-5555

For Privacy Act and Paperwork Reduction Act Notice, see separate instructions.

Cat. No. 11450Q

Form **1120** (2005)

Form 1120—Consolidated Taxable Income Computation

Line	Title	Consolidated	Adjustments and Eliminations	1 Alpha Mfg. Corp.	2 Beta Corp.	3 Charlie Corp.	4 Delta Corp.	5 Echo Corp.
1	Gross receipts	$6,147,000	($109,000)[1]	$1,566,000	$2,680,000	$676,000		$1,249,000
	Returns/Allowances		85,000[2]					
2	Cost goods/Operations	(2,301,000)		(783,000)	(1,390,000)	(128,000)	$ -0-	-0-
3	Gross profit	$3,846,000	($24,000)	$ 783,000	$1,290,000	$548,000	$ —	$1,249,000
4	Dividends (Sch. C)	40,000	(170,000)[3]	210,000				
5	Interest	156,000[5]		46,000	89,000			21,000
6	Gross rents	195,000					$195,000	
7	Gross royalties							
8	Capital gain net income (Sch. D)	67,939		67,939				
9	Net gain or loss from Form 4797	37,080	(14,600)	52,760	(4,000)			
10	Other income	10,000[4]	2,920[6]	10,000				
11	Total income	$4,352,019	($205,680)	$1,169,699	$1,375,000	$548,000	$195,000	$1,270,000
12	Compensation of officers	$ 165,000		$ 165,000	$ 240,000	$377,000	$ 36,000	$ 565,000
13	Salaries and wages	1,356,000		138,000	18,000	7,000	18,000	21,000
14	Repairs	83,000		19,000	36,500	4,000		8,000
15	Bad debts	48,500			39,000	11,000		36,000
16	Rents	179,000		93,000	27,000	10,000	16,000	49,000
17	Taxes	138,000[4]		36,000			29,000[5]	
18	Interest	58,000		27,000				
19	Contributions	15,000[4]		9,000	4,000			2,000
20a	Depreciation	246,093		101,900	62,930	24,370	24,043	32,850
20b	Depreciation shown elsewhere on return	(77,400)		(77,400)				
20c	Depreciation	168,693		24,500	62,930	24,370	24,043	32,850
21	Depletion	-0-						
22	Advertising	269,140			223,140	27,000		19,000
23	Pension, profit sharing, etc. plans	140,000		39,000	21,000	35,000		45,000
24	Employee benefit programs	105,000		26,000	16,000	29,000		34,000
25	U.S. prod. act. ded.	9,320[7]			6,350	2,970		
26	Other deductions	1,284,000[4]		409,000	401,000	72,000	49,000	353,000
27	Total deductions	$4,018,653	$ -0-	$ 985,500	$1,094,920	$596,370	$172,043	$1,169,820

| | | | Adjustments and | 1 | 2 | 3 | 4 | 5 |
Line	Title	Consolidated	Eliminations	Alpha Mfg. Corp.	Beta Corp.	Charlie Corp.	Delta Corp.	Echo Corp.
28	Taxable income before NOL ded. and special deductions	$333,366	($205,680)	$184,199	$280,080	($48,370)	$22,957	$100,180
29a	NOL deduction	(32,000)						
29b	Special deductions		(32,000)³					
30	Taxable income	$301,366	($237,680)					

Explanatory Notes

1 The deferred intercompany profit on the sale of inventory items (intercompany item) from Alpha to Beta during the current year was $109,000. This amount is eliminated from revenue. The deferred intercompany profit amount is reported when Beta sells the inventory outside the affiliated group or some other corresponding item occurs.

2 Restoration of $85,000 in deferred intercompany profits arising from the sale of inventory items from Alpha to Beta in the current and prior years. These goods were sold outside the affiliated group in the current year. The increased intercompany profit deferral for the current year is $24,000 ($109,000 − $85,000). This amount is reflected in the reduced gross profit amount.

3 Intragroup dividends of $100,000 and $70,000 paid by Beta and Echo, respectively, to Alpha are an adjustment to consolidated taxable income because they were included in Alpha's separate tax return. The remaining $40,000 of dividends are from unaffiliated domestic corporations that are more than 20%-owned and eligible for an 80% dividends-received deduction (see Line 29b). The group claims a $32,000 dividends-received deduction.

4 The supporting schedule of component items is not reproduced here.

5 Alpha Manufacturing loaned money to Delta Corporation. Delta accrued and paid $12,000 in interest during the year. The individual firms have reported these amounts in their separate expense and income items.

6 Alpha sells a truck to Beta on June of the current year for $25,000. The truck (a five-year MACRS property) cost $26,000 when purchased new on June 1 two years ago. Alpha did not elect Sec. 179 expensing or bonus depreciation on the truck and thus claimed depreciation of $13,520 [$26,000 × (0.20 + 0.32)] on the truck in the prior two years. Alpha claims depreciation of $2,080 ($26,000 × 0.192 × 5/12) in the current year. Alpha claims a total of $15,600 ($13,520 + $2,080) in depreciation prior to the sale. Alpha's deferred gain (intercompany item) on the sale is $14,600 [$25,000 − ($26,000 − $15,600)]. (See Line 9, Adjustments and Eliminations.) The truck is recorded as two separate MACRS properties on Beta's tax books. Beta depreciates the original $26,000 basis for the truck using the remainder of Alpha's five-year recovery period. Depreciation on this portion of the basis is $2,912 ($26,000 × 0.1920 × 7/12) in the current year. Beta also can depreciate the second MACRS property; that is, the step-up in basis that results from the intercompany sale. Beta elects to depreciate this portion of the basis as a five-year MACRS property and claims an additional $2,920 ($14,600 × 0.2000) of depreciation in the current year. The $2,920 is the portion of the deferred gain (Sec. 1245 income) Alpha reported in the current year.

7 The consolidated U.S. production activities deduction is computed as $310,686 × 0.03, where $310,686 is consolidated taxable income before that deduction. The deduction is then allocated to the group members based on Prop. Reg. Sec. 1.199-7.

Form **1120S**

Department of the Treasury
Internal Revenue Service

U.S. Income Tax Return for an S Corporation

▶ Do not file this form unless the corporation has filed Form 2553
to elect to be an S corporation.
▶ See separate instructions.

OMB No. 1545-0130

2005

For calendar year 2005, or tax year beginning _____ , 2005, ending _____ , 20 ____

A Effective date of S election 6-13-99	Use the IRS label. Otherwise, print or type.	**Name** Johns and Lawrence, Inc.
B Business code number (see instructions) 337000		**Number, street, and room or suite no. If a P.O. box, see instructions.** 1234 University Avenue
		City or town, state, and ZIP code Gainsville, FL 32611

C Employer identification number
76 : 3456789

D Date incorporated
6-1-99

E Total assets (see instructions)
$ 498,324

F Check applicable boxes: **(1)** ☐ Initial return **(2)** ☐ Final return **(3)** ☐ Name change **(4)** ☐ Address change **(5)** ☐ Amended return

G Enter number of shareholders in the corporation at end of the tax year . . . . ▶ 2

Caution. *Include **only** trade or business income and expenses on lines 1a through 21. See the instructions for more information.*

Income

1a Gross receipts or sales 869,658	**b** Less returns and allowances 29,242	**c** Bal ▶ **1c** 840,416
2 Cost of goods sold (Schedule A, line 8)		**2** 540,204
3 Gross profit. Subtract line 2 from line 1c		**3** 300,212
4 Net gain (loss) from Form 4797, Part II, line 17 (*attach Form 4797*)		**4**
5 Other income (loss) (*attach statement*)		**5**
6 **Total income (loss).** Add lines 3 through 5. . . . . ▶		**6** 300,212

Deductions (see the instructions for limitations)

7 Compensation of officers	**7** 36,000
8 Salaries and wages (less employment credits)	**8** 52,000
9 Repairs and maintenance	**9** 4,800
10 Bad debts	**10** 4,000
11 Rents	**11** 36,000
12 Taxes and licenses	**12** 16,000
13 Interest	**13** 8,000
14a Depreciation (*attach Form 4562*) **14a** 27,476	
b Depreciation claimed on Schedule A and elsewhere on return . . **14b** 15,000	
c Subtract line 14b from line 14a	**14c** 12,476
15 Depletion (**Do not deduct oil and gas depletion.**)	**15**
16 Advertising	**16** 13,000
17 Pension, profit-sharing, etc., plans	**17** 2,000
18 Employee benefit programs	**18** 4,000
19 Other deductions (*attach statement*)	**19** 38,250
20 **Total deductions.** Add the amounts shown in the far right column for lines 7 through 19 ▶	**20** 226,526
21 **Ordinary business income (loss).** Subtract line 20 from line 6	**21** 73,686

Tax and Payments

22 **Tax: a** Excess net passive income tax (*attach statement*) . . .	**22a**	
b Tax from Schedule D (Form 1120S)	**22b**	
c Add lines 22a and 22b (see the instructions for additional taxes) .		**22c** NONE
23 **Payments: a** 2005 estimated tax payments and amount applied from 2004 return	**23a**	
b Tax deposited with Form 7004	**23b**	
c Credit for Federal tax paid on fuels (*attach Form 4136*) . . .	**23c**	
d Add lines 23a through 23c		**23d** NONE
24 Estimated tax penalty (see instructions). Check if Form 2220 is attached . . . . ▶ ☐		**24**
25 **Tax due.** If line 23d is smaller than the total of lines 22c and 24, enter amount owed . . .		**25** NONE
26 **Overpayment.** If line 23d is larger than the total of lines 22c and 24, enter amount overpaid .		**26**
27 Enter amount of line 26 you want: **Credited to 2006 estimated tax** ▶ _____	Refunded ▶	**27**

Sign Here ▶

Under penalties of perjury, I declare that I have examined this return, including accompanying schedules and statements, and to the best of my knowledge and belief, it is true, correct, and complete. Declaration of preparer (other than taxpayer) is based on all information of which preparer has any knowledge.

Andrew Lawrence
Signature of officer

3-15-06 ▶
Date

Vice-President
Title

May the IRS discuss this return with the preparer shown below (see instructions)? ☒ Yes ☐ No

Paid Preparer's Use Only

Preparer's signature ▶ *Michael Kramer*	Date 3-14-06	Check if self-employed ☒	Preparer's SSN or PTIN 375-49-6339
Firm's name (or yours if self-employed), address, and ZIP code ▶	Michael S. Kramer 1110 McMillon Gainesville, FL 32611	EIN 59 : 2029763	Phone no. (352) 555-2000

For Privacy Act and Paperwork Reduction Act Notice, see the separate instructions.

Cat. No. 11510H

Form **1120S** (2005)

Form 1120S (2005)   Page **2**

Schedule A	Cost of Goods Sold (see instructions)		

1	Inventory at beginning of year	**1**	64,000
2	Purchases	**2**	340,800
3	Cost of labor	**3**	143,204
4	Additional section 263A costs *(attach statement)*	**4**	7,000
5	Other costs *(attach statement)*	**5**	90,000
6	**Total.** Add lines 1 through 5	**6**	645,004
7	Inventory at end of year	**7**	104,800
8	**Cost of goods sold.** Subtract line 7 from line 6. Enter here and on page 1, line 2	**8**	540,204

9a Check all methods used for valuing closing inventory: *(i)* ☒ Cost as described in Regulations section 1.471-3

 (ii) ☐ Lower of cost or market as described in Regulations section 1.471-4

 (iii) ☐ Other (specify method used and attach explanation) ▶ ....

 b Check if there was a writedown of subnormal goods as described in Regulations section 1.471-2(c) . . . . ▶ ☐

 c Check if the LIFO inventory method was adopted this tax year for any goods (if checked, attach Form 970) . . . . . ▶ ☐

 d If the LIFO inventory method was used for this tax year, enter percentage (or amounts) of closing inventory computed under LIFO . . . . **9d** | |

 e If property is produced or acquired for resale, do the rules of Section 263A apply to the corporation? . . . . ☒ Yes ☐ No

 f Was there any change in determining quantities, cost, or valuations between opening and closing inventory? . . ☐ Yes ☒ No
 If "Yes," attach explanation.

Schedule B	Other Information (see instructions)	Yes	No

1	Check method of accounting: **(a)** ☐ Cash **(b)** ☒ Accrual **(c)** ☐ Other (specify) ▶		
2	See the instructions and enter the:		
	(a) Business activity ▶ <u>Manufacturing</u> **(b)** Product or service ▶ <u>Furniture</u>		
3	At the end of the tax year, did the corporation own, directly or indirectly, 50% or more of the voting stock of a domestic corporation? (For rules of attribution, see section 267(c).) If "Yes," attach a statement showing: **(a)** name, address, and employer identification number and **(b)** percentage owned.		X
4	Was the corporation a member of a controlled group subject to the provisions of section 1561?		X
5	Has this corporation filed, or is it required to file, a return under section 6111 to provide information on any reportable transaction?		
6	Check this box if the corporation issued publicly offered debt instruments with original issue discount . . ▶ ☐		
	If checked, the corporation may have to file **Form 8281,** Information Return for Publicly Offered Original Issue Discount Instruments.		
7	If the corporation: **(a)** was a C corporation before it elected to be an S corporation **or** the corporation acquired an asset with a basis determined by reference to its basis (or the basis of any other property) in the hands of a C corporation **and (b)** has net unrealized built-in gain (defined in section 1374(d)(1)) in excess of the net recognized built-in gain from prior years, enter the net unrealized built-in gain reduced by net recognized built-in gain from prior years . . . . ▶ $		
8	Check this box if the corporation had accumulated earnings and profits at the close of the tax year . . ▶ ☐		
9	Are the corporation's total receipts (see instructions) for the tax year **and** its total assets at the end of the tax year less than $250,000? If "Yes," the corporation is not required to complete Schedules L and M-1.		X

Note: *If the corporation had assets or operated a business in a foreign country or U.S. possession, it may be required to attach* **Schedule N (Form 1120),** *Foreign Operations of U.S. Corporations, to this return. See Schedule N for details.*

Schedule K	Shareholders' Shares of Income, Deductions, Credits, etc.			

	Shareholders' Pro Rata Share Items			Total amount
Income (Loss)	**1** Ordinary business income (loss) (page 1, line 21)		**1**	73,686
	2 Net rental real estate income (loss) *(attach Form 8825)*		**2**	
	3a Other gross rental income (loss)	**3a**		
	b Expenses from other rental activities *(attach statement)*. .	**3b**		
	c Other net rental income (loss). Subtract line 3b from line 3a . .		**3c**	
	4 Interest income		**4**	
	5 Dividends: **a** Ordinary dividends		**5a**	1,000
	b Qualified dividends	**5b**	1,000	
	6 Royalties		**6**	
	7 Net short-term capital gain (loss) *(attach Schedule D (Form 1120S))* . .		**7**	(2,100)
	8a Net long-term capital gain (loss) *(attach Schedule D (Form 1120S))* . .		**8a**	4,500
	b Collectibles (28%) gain (loss)	**8b**		
	c Unrecaptured section 1250 gain *(attach statement)* . .	**8c**		
	9 Net section 1231 gain (loss) (attach Form 4797)		**9**	
	10 Other income (loss) *(see instructions)* . . . Type ▶		**10**	

Form **1120S** (2005)

Form 1120S (2005)   Page **3**

	Shareholders' Pro Rata Share Items (continued)		Total amount
Deductions	**11** Section 179 deduction *(attach Form 4562)*	**11**	
	12a Contributions	**12a**	*12,000*
	b Investment interest expense	**12b**	*150*
	c Section 59(e)(2) expenditures **(1)** Type ▶............ **(2)** Amount ▶	**12c(2)**	
	d Other deductions *(see instructions)* . . . . Type ▶............	**12d**	*
Credits & Credit Recapture	**13a** Low-income housing credit (section 42(j)(5))	**13a**	
	b Low-income housing credit (other)	**13b**	
	c Qualified rehabilitation expenditures (rental real estate) *(attach Form 3468)*	**13c**	
	d Other rental real estate credits (see instructions) . Type ▶............	**13d**	
	e Other rental credits (see instructions) . . . Type ▶............	**13e**	
	f Credit for alcohol used as fuel *(attach Form 6478)*	**13f**	
	g Other credits and credit recapture *(see instructions)* Type ▶............	**13g**	
Foreign Transactions	**14a** Name of country or U.S. possession ▶............		
	b Gross income from all sources	**14b**	
	c Gross income sourced at shareholder level	**14c**	
	Foreign gross income sourced at corporate level:		
	d Passive	**14d**	
	e Listed categories *(attach statement)*	**14e**	
	f General limitation	**14f**	
	Deductions allocated and apportioned at shareholder level:		
	g Interest expense	**14g**	
	h Other	**14h**	
	Deductions allocated and apportioned at corporate level to foreign source income:		
	i Passive	**14i**	
	j Listed categories *(attach statement)*	**14j**	
	k General limitation	**14k**	
	Other information:		
	l Total foreign taxes (check one): ▶ ☐ Paid ☐ Accrued	**14l**	
	m Reduction in taxes available for credit *(attach statement)*	**14m**	
	n Other foreign tax information *(attach statement)*		
Alternative Minimum Tax (AMT) Items	**15a** Post-1986 depreciation adjustment	**15a**	*1,514*
	b Adjusted gain or loss	**15b**	
	c Depletion (other than oil and gas)	**15c**	
	d Oil, gas, and geothermal properties—gross income	**15d**	
	e Oil, gas, and geothermal properties—deductions	**15e**	
	f Other AMT items *(attach statement)*	**15f**	
Items Affecting Shareholder Basis	**16a** Tax-exempt interest income	**16a**	*18,000*
	b Other tax-exempt income	**16b**	
	c Nondeductible expenses	**16c**	*6,000* **
	d Property distributions	**16d**	*28,212*
	e Repayment of loans from shareholders	**16e**	
Other Information	**17a** Investment income	**17a**	*1,000* ***
	b Investment expenses	**17b**	
	c Dividend distributions paid from accumulated earnings and profits	**17c**	
	d Other items and amounts *(attach statement)*		
	e **Income/loss reconciliation.** (Required only if Schedule M-1 must be completed.) Combine the amounts on lines 1 through 10 in the far right column. From the result, subtract the sum of the amounts on lines 11 through 12d and 14l	**17e**	*64,936*

Form **1120S** (2005)

*Qualified production activities income (QPAI) equals $80,000.
 Employer's W-2 wages equal $4,800.

**Disallowed meals and entertainment expenses ($4,000) and interest on loan
 used to purchase tax-exempt bonds ($2,000).

***If partners elect to tax dividends at ordinary rates under Sec. 163(d)(4)(B).

Form 1120S (2005) Page **4**

Note: The corporation is not required to complete Schedules L and M-1 if question 9 of Schedule B is answered "Yes."

Schedule L Balance Sheets per Books

	Assets	(a) Beginning	(b) Beginning	(c) End	(d) End
1	Cash		60,000		86,600
2a	Trade notes and accounts receivable	25,000		24,000	
b	Less allowance for bad debts	1,000	24,000	1,000	23,000
3	Inventories		64,000		104,800
4	U.S. government obligations				
5	Tax-exempt securities		200,000		200,000
6	Other current assets (attach statement)		7,000		
7	Loans to shareholders				
8	Mortgage and real estate loans				
9	Other investments (attach statement)				
10a	Buildings and other depreciable assets	151,600		151,600	
b	Less accumulated depreciation	45,200	106,400	72,676	78,924
11a	Depletable assets				
b	Less accumulated depletion				
12	Land (net of any amortization)				
13a	Intangible assets (amortizable only)				
b	Less accumulated amortization				
14	Other assets (attach statement)				
15	Total assets		461,400		493,324
	Liabilities and Shareholders' Equity				
16	Accounts payable		26,000		19,000
17	Mortgages, notes, bonds payable in less than 1 year		4,000		4,000
18	Other current liabilities (attach statement)		3,600		3,600
19	Loans from shareholders				
20	Mortgages, notes, bonds payable in 1 year or more		130,000		119,724
21	Other liabilities (attach statement)				
22	Capital stock		200,000		200,000
23	Additional paid-in capital				
24	Retained earnings		97,800		147,000
25	Adjustments to shareholders' equity (attach statement)				
26	Less cost of treasury stock		( )	( )	( )
27	Total liabilities and shareholders' equity		461,400		493,324

Schedule M-1 Reconciliation of Income (Loss) per Books With Income (Loss) per Return

1	Net income (loss) per books	77,412	5	Income recorded on books this year not included on Schedule K, lines 1 through 10 (itemize):	
2	Income included on Schedule K, lines 1, 2, 3c, 4, 5a, 6, 7, 8a, 9, and 10, not recorded on books this year (itemize):		a	Tax-exempt interest $ 18,000	18,000
3	Expenses recorded on books this year not included on Schedule K, lines 1 through 12 and 14l (itemize):		6	Deductions included on Schedule K, lines 1 through 12 and 14l, not charged against book income this year (itemize):	
a	Depreciation $		a	Depreciation $ 476	476
b	Travel and entertainment $ 4,000 Interest on loans* $2,000	6,000	7	Add lines 5 and 6	18,476
4	Add lines 1 through 3	83,412	8	Income (loss) (Schedule K, line 17e). Line 4 less line 7	64,936

Schedule M-2 Analysis of Accumulated Adjustments Account, Other Adjustments Account, and Shareholders' Undistributed Taxable Income Previously Taxed (see instructions)

		(a) Accumulated adjustments account	(b) Other adjustments account	(c) Shareholders' undistributed taxable income previously taxed
1	Balance at beginning of tax year	86,100	11,700	
2	Ordinary income from page 1, line 21	73,686		
3	Other additions	5,500**	18,000	
4	Loss from page 1, line 21	( )	( )	
5	Other reductions	(18,250***)	(2,000)	
6	Combine lines 1 through 5	147,036		
7	Distributions other than dividend distributions	28,212		
8	Balance at end of tax year. Subtract line 7 from line 6	118,824	27,700	

Form **1120S** (2005)

* For municipal bonds
** $1,000 + $4,500 = $5,500
*** $12,000 + $4,000 + $150 + $2,100 = $18,250

671105

□ Final K-1   □ Amended K-1   OMB No. 1545-0130

Schedule K-1
(Form 1120S)

20**05**

Department of the Treasury
Internal Revenue Service

For calendar year 2005, or tax
year beginning ___**Jan. 1**___ , 2005
ending ___**Dec. 31**___ , 20**05**

Shareholder's Share of Income, Deductions,
Credits, etc.   ▶ See back of form and separate instructions.

Part I	Information About the Corporation

A Corporation's employer identification number
76-3456789

B Corporation's name, address, city, state, and ZIP code
Johns and Lawrence, Inc.
1234 University Ave.
Gainesville, FL 32611

C IRS Center where corporation filed return
Atlanta, GA

D □ Tax shelter registration number, if any _____
E □ Check if Form 8271 is attached

Part II	Information About the Shareholder

F Shareholder's identifying number
297-63-2110

G Shareholder's name, address, city, state and ZIP code
Andrew Lawrence
436 N.W. 24th Ave.
Gainesville, FL 32607

H Shareholder's percentage of stock
ownership for tax year . . . . ___**50%**___ %

For IRS Use Only

Part III	Shareholder's Share of Current Year Income, Deductions, Credits, and Other Items

1	Ordinary business income (loss) **36,843**	13	Credits & credit recapture
2	Net rental real estate income (loss)		
3	Other net rental income (loss)		
4	Interest income		
5a	Ordinary dividends **500**		
5b	Qualified dividends **500**	14	Foreign transactions
6	Royalties		
7	Net short-term capital gain (loss) **(1,050)**		
8a	Net long-term capital gain (loss) **2,250**		
8b	Collectibles (28%) gain (loss)		
8c	Unrecaptured section 1250 gain		
9	Net section 1231 gain (loss)		
10	Other income (loss)	15	Alternative minimum tax (AMT) items **A 757**
11	Section 179 deduction	16	Items affecting shareholder basis **A 9,000**
12	Other deductions **A 6,000**		**C 3,000**
	G 75		**D 14,106**
	Q 40,000		
	R 2,400	17	Other information
			A 500 ***

* See attached statement for additional information.

For **Privacy Act and Paperwork Reduction Act Notice, see Instructions for Form 1120S.**   Cat. No. 11520D   **Schedule K-1 (Form 1120S) 2005**

*Schedule K-1 for Stephen Johns is similar to this
one and is not reproduced here.

**If partner elects to tax dividends at ordinary rates under Sec. 163(d)(4)(B).

This list identifies the codes used on Schedule K-1 for all shareholders and provides summarized reporting information for shareholders who file Form 1040. For detailed reporting and filing information, see the separate Shareholder's Instructions for Schedule K-1 and the instructions for your income tax return.

1. **Ordinary business income (loss).** You must first determine whether the income (loss) is passive or nonpassive. Then enter on your return as follows:

	Enter on
Passive loss	See the Shareholder's Instructions
Passive income	Schedule E, line 28, column (g)
Nonpassive loss	Schedule E, line 28, column (h)
Nonpassive income	Schedule E, line 28, column (j)

2. **Net rental real estate income (loss)** — See the Shareholder's Instructions

3. **Other net rental income (loss)**

Net income	Schedule E, line 28, column (g)
Net loss	See the Shareholder's Instructions

4. **Interest income** — Form 1040, line 8a

5a. **Ordinary dividends** — Form 1040, line 9a

5b. **Qualified dividends** — Form 1040, line 9b

6. **Royalties** — Schedule E, line 4

7. **Net short-term capital gain (loss)** — Schedule D, line 5, column (f)

8a. **Net long-term capital gain (loss)** — Schedule D, line 12, column (f)

8b. **Collectibles (28%) gain (loss)** — 28% Rate Gain Worksheet, line 4 (Schedule D instructions)

8c. **Unrecaptured section 1250 gain** — See the Shareholder's Instructions

9. **Net section 1231 gain (loss)** — See the Shareholder's Instructions

10. **Other income (loss)**

Code		
A	Other portfolio income (loss)	See the Shareholder's Instructions
B	Involuntary conversions	See the Shareholder's Instructions
C	Sec. 1256 contracts & straddles	Form 6781, line 1
D	Mining exploration costs recapture	See Pub. 535
E	Other income (loss)	See the Shareholder's Instructions

11. **Section 179 deduction** — See the Shareholder's Instructions

12. **Other deductions**

A	Cash contributions (50%)	Schedule A, line 15a
B	Cash contributions (30%)	Schedule A, line 15a
C	Noncash contributions (50%)	Schedule A, line 16
D	Noncash contributions (30%)	Schedule A, line 16
E	Capital gain property to a 50% organization (30%)	Schedule A, line 16
F	Capital gain property (20%)	Schedule A, line 16
G	Cash contributions (100%)	See the Shareholder's Instructions
H	Investment interest expense	Form 4952, line 1
I	Deductions—royalty income	Schedule E, line 18
J	Section 59(e)(2) expenditures	See the Shareholder's Instructions
K	Deductions—portfolio (2% floor)	Schedule A, line 22
L	Deductions—portfolio (other)	Schedule A, line 27
M	Reforestation expense deduction	See the Shareholder's Instructions
N	Preproductive period expenses	See the Shareholder's Instructions
O	Commercial revitalization deduction from rental real estate activities	See Form 8582 Instructions
P	Domestic production activities information	See Form 8903 Instructions
Q	Qualified production activities income	Form 8903, line 7
R	Employer's W-2 wages	Form 8903, line 13
S	Other deductions	See the Shareholder's Instructions

13. **Credits & credit recapture**

A	Low-income housing credit (section 42(j)(5))	Form 8586, line 4
B	Low-income housing credit (other)	Form 8586, line 4
C	Qualified rehabilitation expenditures (rental real estate)	Form 3468, line 1
D	Qualified rehabilitation expenditures (other than rental real estate)	Form 3468, line 1
E	Basis of energy property	See the Shareholder's Instructions
F	Other rental real estate credits	See the Shareholder's Instructions
G	Other rental credits	See the Shareholder's Instructions
H	Undistributed capital gains credit	Form 1040, line 70, check box a
I	Credit for alcohol used as fuel	Form 6478, line 4
J	Work opportunity credit	Form 5884, line 3
K	Welfare-to-work credit	Form 8861, line 3
L	Disabled access credit	Form 8826, line 7

Code		Enter on
M	Empowerment zone and renewal community employment credit	Form 8844, line 3
N	Credit for increasing research activities	Form 6765, line 42
O	New markets credit	Form 8874, line 2
P	Credit for employer social security and Medicare taxes	Form 8846, line 5
Q	Backup withholding	Form 1040, line 64
R	Recapture of low-income housing credit (section 42(j)(5))	Form 8611, line 8
S	Recapture of low-income housing credit (other)	Form 8611, line 8
T	Recapture of investment credit	See Form 4255
U	Other credits	See the Shareholder's Instructions
V	Recapture of other credits	See the Shareholder's Instructions

14. **Foreign transactions**

A	Name of country or U.S. possession	Form 1116, Part I
B	Gross income from all sources	Form 1116, Part I
C	Gross income sourced at shareholder level	Form 1116, Part I

Foreign gross income sourced at corporate level

D	Passive	Form 1116, Part I
E	Listed categories	Form 1116, Part I
F	General limitation	Form 1116, Part I

Deductions allocated and apportioned at shareholder level

G	Interest expense	Form 1116, Part I
H	Other	Form 1116, Part I

Deductions allocated and apportioned at corporate level to foreign source income

I	Passive	Form 1116, Part I
J	Listed categories	Form 1116, Part I
K	General limitation	Form 1116, Part I

Other information

L	Total foreign taxes paid	Form 1116, Part II
M	Total foreign taxes accrued	Form 1116, Part II
N	Reduction in taxes available for credit	Form 1116, line 12
O	Foreign trading gross receipts	Form 8873
P	Extraterritorial income exclusion	Form 8873
Q	Other foreign transactions	See the Shareholder's Instructions

15. **Alternative minimum tax (AMT) items**

A	Post-1986 depreciation adjustment	
B	Adjusted gain or loss	See the Shareholder's Instructions and the Instructions for Form 6251
C	Depletion (other than oil & gas)	
D	Oil, gas, & geothermal—gross income	
E	Oil, gas, & geothermal—deductions	
F	Other AMT items	

16. **Items affecting shareholder basis**

A	Tax-exempt interest income	Form 1040, line 8b
B	Other tax-exempt income	See the Shareholder's Instructions
C	Nondeductible expenses	See the Shareholder's Instructions
D	Property distributions	See the Shareholder's Instructions
E	Repayment of loans from shareholders	See the Shareholder's Instructions

17. **Other information**

A	Investment income	Form 4952, line 4a
B	Investment expenses	Form 4952, line 5
C	Look-back interest—completed long-term contracts	See Form 8697
D	Look-back interest—income forecast method	See Form 8866
E	Dispositions of property with section 179 deductions	
F	Recapture of section 179 deduction	
G	Section 453(l)(3) information	
H	Section 453A(c) information	
I	Section 1260(b) information	
J	Interest allocable to production expenditures	See the Shareholder's Instructions
K	CCF nonqualified withdrawal	
L	Information needed to figure depletion—oil and gas	
M	Amortization of reforestation costs	
N	Other information	

FACTS FOR S CORPORATION (FORM 1120S)

The same basic facts presented for the Andrew Lawrence proprietorship are used for the S corporation except for the following:

1. Johns and Lawrence, Inc. made an S corporation election on June 13, 1999. The election was effective for its initial tax year.

2. The book income for Johns and Lawrence is presented in the attached worksheet, which reconciles book income and S corporation taxable income.

3. The $18,000 salaries paid to each employee are subject to the same employment tax requirements as when paid by the C corporation. The total employment taxes ($14,480) are the same as for the C corporation.

4. The S corporation paid no estimated federal income taxes.

5. The corporation distributed $14,106 to each of the two shareholders.

6. Other deductions include:

Travel	$ 4,000
Meals and entertainment	8,000
Minus: 50% disallowance	(4,000)
Office expenses	16,000
Transportation	10,400
General and administrative	3,000
Miscellaneous*	850
Total	$38,250

*$150 of the miscellaneous expenses are related to the production of the dividend income and are separately stated.

7. The following schedule reconciles net income for the C corporation and the S corporation:

Net income per books for C corporation	$63,412
Plus: Federal income taxes	14,000
Net income per books for S corporation	$77,412

The S corporation return can be tied back to the partnership return. The only difference between the two returns is that the S corporation pays an additional $6,160 in employment taxes with respect to the shareholder-employee salaries, as compared to the partnership's guaranteed payments. This dollar difference is reflected in the net income numbers, the ordinary income numbers, capital account balances, and total asset amounts.

8. Qualifed production activities income (QPAI) equals $80,000. Employer's W-2 wages equal the lesser of W-2 wages ($88,000) or 6% of QPAI. Thus, employer's W-2 wages equal $4,800 ($80,000 × 0.06).

9. The balance sheet for Johns and Lawrence appears on page 4 of Form 1120S.

Johns and Lawrence, Inc. (S Corporation) Reconciliation of Book and Taxable Income For Year Ending December 31, 2005

Account Name	Book Income Debit	Book Income Credit	Adjustments Debit	Adjustments Credit	Taxable Income Debit	Taxable Income Credit	Form 1120S Schedule K Ordinary Income	Form 1120S Schedule K Separately Stated Items
Sales		$869,658				$869,658	$869,658	
Sales returns & allowances	$ 29,242				$ 29,242		(29,242)	
Cost of sales	540,204				540,204		(540,204)	
Dividends		1,000				1,000		1,000
Tax-exempt interest		18,000	$18,000			0		$18,000
Gain on stock sale		4,500				4,500		4,500
Worthless stock loss	2,100				2,100			(2,100)
Officers salaries[a]	36,000				36,000		(36,000)	
Other salaries	52,000				52,000		(52,000)	
Rentals	36,000				36,000		(36,000)	
Bad debts	4,000				4,000		(4,000)	
Interest:								
Working capital loans	8,000				8,000		(8,000)	
Purchase tax-exempt bonds	2,000			$ 2,000	0			(2,000)
Employment taxes	14,480				14,480		(14,480)	
Taxes	1,520				1,520		(1,520)	
Repairs	4,800				4,800		(4,800)	
Depreciation[b]	12,000		476		12,476		(12,476)	
Charitable contributions	12,000				12,000			(12,000)
Travel	4,000				4,000		(4,000)	
Meals and entertainment[c]	8,000			4,000	4,000		(4,000)	
Meals and ent. nondeductible								(4,000)
Office expenses	16,000				16,000		(16,000)	
Advertising	13,000				13,000		(13,000)	
Transportation expense	10,400				10,400		(10,400)	
General and administrative	3,000				3,000		(3,000)	
Pension plans[d]	2,000				2,000		(2,000)	
Employee benefit programs[e]	4,000				4,000		(4,000)	
Miscellaneous	1,000				1,000		(850)	(150)
Net profit/Taxable income	77,412			12,476	64,936			
Total	$893,158	$893,158	$18,476	$18,476	$875,158	$875,158	$ 73,686	

[a] Salaries for the S corporation's shareholder-employees are deductible by the S corporation and are subject to the same employee taxes imposed on nonshareholder-employees.

[b] MACRS is depreciation is $27,476 − $15,000 = $12,476

[c] 50% of the meals and entertainment expense is not deductible for tax purposes but must be separately stated on the Schedules K and K-1.

[d] The pension plan expense is the same for book and tax purposes for this corporation. No pension expenses relate to pensions for the shareholder-employees.

[e] The employee benefit expense is the same for book and tax purposes for this corporation. None relates to shareholder-employee benefits.

Form **2210**	**Underpayment of**	OMB No. 1545-0140

Form 2210

Department of the Treasury
Internal Revenue Service

Underpayment of
Estimated Tax by Individuals, Estates, and Trusts
▶ See separate instructions.
▶ Attach to Form 1040, 1040A, 1040NR, 1040NR-EZ, or 1041.

OMB No. 1545-0140

2005

Attachment
Sequence No. **06**

Name(s) shown on tax return	Identifying number

Do You Have To File Form 2210?

Complete lines 1 through 7 below. Is line 7 less than $1,000?	**Yes** ▶	**Do not file Form 2210.** You do not owe a penalty.

↓ **No**

Complete lines 8 and 9 below. Is line 6 equal to or more than line 9?	**Yes** ▶	You do not owe a penalty. **Do not file Form 2210** (but if box **E** below applies, you must file page 1 of Form 2210 below).

↓ **No**

You may owe a penalty. Does any box in Part II below apply?	**Yes** ▶	You **must** file Form 2210. Does box **B, C,** or **D** apply?

No　　　**Yes**

You must figure your penalty.

↓ **No**

Do not file Form 2210. You are not required to figure your penalty because the IRS will figure it and send you a bill for any unpaid amount. If you want to figure it, you may use Part III or Part IV as a worksheet and enter your penalty amount on your tax return, but **do not file Form 2210.**

You are **not** required to figure your penalty because the IRS will figure it and send you a bill for any unpaid amount. If you want to figure it, you may use Part III or Part IV as a worksheet and enter your penalty amount on your tax return, but **file only page 1 of Form 2210.**

Part I	**Required Annual Payment**	(see page 2 of the instructions)		
1	Enter your 2005 tax after credits from Form 1040, line 57 (or comparable line of your return)		**1**	
2	Other taxes, including self-employment tax (see page 2 of the instructions)		**2**	
3	Refundable credits. Enter the total of your earned income credit, additional child tax credit, credit for federal tax paid on fuels, and health coverage tax credit for eligible individuals		**3**	( )
4	Current year tax. Combine lines 1, 2, and 3. If less than $1,000, see page 3 of the instructions		**4**	
5	Multiply line 4 by 90% (.90)	**5**		
6	Withholding taxes. **Do not** include estimated tax payments. See page 3 of the instructions . .		**6**	
7	Subtract line 6 from line 4. If less than $1,000, you do not owe a penalty; **do not file Form 2210**		**7**	
8	Maximum required annual payment based on prior year's tax (see page 3 of the instructions)		**8**	
9	**Required annual payment.** Enter the **smaller** of line 5 or line 8		**9**	

Next: Is line 9 more than line 6?

☐ **No.** You **do not** owe a penalty. **Do not file Form 2210** unless box **E** below applies.

☐ **Yes.** You may owe a penalty, but **do not file Form 2210** unless one or more boxes in Part II below applies.

　• If box **B, C,** or **D** applies, you must figure your penalty and file Form 2210.
　• If only box **A** or **E** (or both) applies, file only page 1 of Form 2210. You are **not** required to figure your penalty; the IRS will figure it and send you a bill for any unpaid amount. If you want to figure your penalty, you may use Part III or IV as a worksheet and enter your penalty on your tax return, but **file only page 1 of Form 2210.**

Part II	**Reasons for Filing.** Check applicable boxes. If none apply, **do not file Form 2210.**

A ☐ You request a **waiver** (see page 2 of the instructions) of your entire penalty. You must check this box and file page 1 of Form 2210, but you are not required to figure your penalty.

B ☐ You request a waiver (see page 2 of the instructions) of part of your penalty. You must figure your penalty and waiver amount and file Form 2210.

C ☐ Your income varied during the year and your penalty is reduced or eliminated when figured using the **annualized income installment method.** You must figure the penalty using Schedule AI and file Form 2210.

D ☐ Your penalty is lower when figured by treating the federal income tax withheld from your wages as paid on the dates it was actually withheld, instead of in equal amounts on the payment due dates. You must figure your penalty and file Form 2210.

E ☐ You filed or are filing a joint return for either 2004 or 2005, but not for both years, and line 8 above is smaller than line 5 above. You must file page 1 of Form 2210, but you are **not** required to figure your penalty (unless box **B, C,** or **D** applies).

For Paperwork Reduction Act Notice, see page 6 of separate instructions. 　　Cat. No. 11744P 　　Form **2210** (2005)

Form 2210 (2005)   Page **2**

| **Part III** | Short Method |

You may use the short method if:

• You made no estimated tax payments (or your only payments were withheld federal income tax), **or**

• You paid estimated tax in **equal** amounts on your due dates.

You must use the regular method (Part IV) instead of the short method if:

You do not need to file Form 2210 unless you checked a box in Part II on page 1.

• You made any estimated tax payments late,

• You checked box **C** or **D** in Part II, **or**

• You are filing Form 1040NR or 1040NR-EZ and you did not receive wages as an employee subject to U.S. income tax withholding.

Note: *If any payment was made earlier than the due date, you may use the short method, but using it may cause you to pay a larger penalty than the regular method. If the payment was only a few days early, the difference is likely to be small.*

10	Enter the amount from Form 2210, line 9	10	
11	Enter the amount, if any, from Form 2210, line 6	11	
12	Enter the total amount, if any, of estimated tax payments you made	12	
13	Add lines 11 and 12	13	
14	**Total underpayment for year.** Subtract line 13 from line 10. If zero or less, stop here; you do not owe the penalty. **Do not file Form 2210 unless you checked box E on page 1**	14	
15	Multiply line 14 by .04457 (use the factor shown in the instructions if you are eligible for hurricane relief)	15	
16	• If the amount on line 14 was paid **on or after** 4/15/06, enter -0-.		
	• If the amount on line 14 was paid **before** 4/15/06, make the following computation to find the amount to enter on line 16.		
	Amount on line 14 ✕ Number of days paid before 4/15/06 ✕ .00019	16	
17	**Penalty.** Subtract line 16 from line 15. Enter the result here and on Form 1040, line 76; Form 1040A, line 48; Form 1040NR, line 74; Form 1040NR-EZ, line 26; or Form 1041, line 26 . . ▶	17	

Form **2210** (2005)

Form 2210 (2005)   Page **3**

Part IV	**Regular Method** (See page 3 of the instructions if you are filing Form 1040NR or 1040NR-EZ.)					

			Payment Due Dates			
Section A—Figure Your Underpayment			**(a)** 4/15/05	**(b)** 6/15/05	**(c)** 9/15/05	**(d)** 1/15/06
18	**Required installments.** If box C in Part II applies, enter the amounts from Schedule AI, line 25. Otherwise, enter 25% (.25) of line 9, Form 2210, in each column	**18**				
19	Estimated tax paid and tax withheld (see page 3 of the instructions). For column (a) only, also enter the amount from line 19 on line 23. If line 19 is equal to or more than line 18 for all payment periods, stop here; you do not owe a penalty. **Do not file Form 2210 unless you checked a box in Part II** . . .	**19**				
	Complete lines 20 through 26 of one column before going to the next column.					
20	Enter the amount, if any, from line 26 in previous column	**20**				
21	Add lines 19 and 20	**21**				
22	Add the amounts on lines 24 and 25 in previous column	**22**				
23	Subtract line 22 from line 21. If zero or less, enter -0-. For column (a) only, enter the amount from line 19.	**23**				
24	If line 23 is zero, subtract line 21 from line 22. Otherwise, enter -0-	**24**				
25	**Underpayment.** If line 18 is equal to or more than line 23, subtract line 23 from line 18. Then go to line 20 of the next column. Otherwise, go to line 26 ▶	**25**				
26	Overpayment. If line 23 is more than line 18, subtract line 18 from line 23. Then go to line 20 of the next column .	**26**				

	Section B—Figure the Penalty (Complete lines 27 through 30 of one column before going to the next column.)					

			4/15/05	6/15/05	9/15/05	
Rate Period 1	**April 16, 2005—September 30, 2005**		*Days:*	*Days:*	*Days:*	
	27	Number of days **from** the date shown above line 27 **to** the date the amount on line 25 was paid **or** 9/30/05, whichever is earlier	**27**				
	28	Underpayment on line 25 (see page 4 of the instructions) $\times \dfrac{\text{Number of days on line 27}}{365} \times .06$ ▶	**28**	$	$	$	

			9/30/05	9/30/05	9/30/05	1/15/06
Rate Period 2	**October 1, 2005—April 15, 2006**		*Days:*	*Days:*	*Days:*	*Days:*
	29	Number of days **from** the date shown above line 29 **to** the date the amount on line 25 was paid **or** 4/15/06, whichever is earlier	**29**				
	30	Underpayment on line 25 (see page 4 of the instructions) $\times \dfrac{\text{Number of days on line 29}}{365} \times .07$ ▶	**30**	$	$	$	$

31	**Penalty.** Add all amounts on lines 28 and 30 in all columns. Enter the total here and on Form 1040, line 76; Form 1040A, line 48; Form 1040NR, line 74; Form 1040NR-EZ, line 26; or Form 1041, line 26, **but do not file Form 2210 unless you checked a box in Part II** . . . . ▶	**31**	$

Form **2210** (2005)

Form 2210 (2005)   Page **4**

Schedule AI—Annualized Income Installment Method (See pages 5 and 6 of the instructions.)

Estates and trusts, **do not** use the period ending dates shown to the right. Instead, use the following: 2/28/05, 4/30/05, 7/31/05, and 11/30/05.

		(a) 1/1/05–3/31/05	(b) 1/1/05–5/31/05	(c) 1/1/05–8/31/05	(d) 1/1/05–12/31/05
Part I	**Annualized Income Installments**				
1	Enter your adjusted gross income for each period (see instructions). (Estates and trusts, enter your taxable income without your exemption for each period.) **1**				
2	Annualization amounts. (Estates and trusts, see instructions.) **2**	4	2.4	1.5	1
3	Annualized income. Multiply line 1 by line 2 **3**				
4	Enter your itemized deductions for the period shown in each column. If you do not itemize, enter -0- and skip to line 7. (Estates and trusts, enter -0-, skip to line 9, and enter the amount from line 3 on line 9.) **4**				
5	Annualization amounts **5**	4	2.4	1.5	1
6	Multiply line 4 by line 5 (see instructions if line 3 is more than $72,975) **6**				
7	In each column, enter the full amount of your standard deduction from Form 1040, line 40, or Form 1040A, line 24 (Form 1040NR or 1040NR-EZ filers, enter -0-. **Exception:** Indian students and business apprentices, enter standard deduction from Form 1040NR, line 37, or Form 1040NR-EZ, line 11.) **7**				
8	Enter the **larger** of line 6 or line 7 **8**				
9	Subtract line 8 from line 3 **9**				
10	In each column, multiply $3,200 by the total number of exemptions claimed (see instructions if line 3 is more than $109,475). (Estates and trusts and Form 1040NR or 1040NR-EZ filers, enter the exemption amount shown on your tax return.) **10**				
11	Subtract line 10 from line 9 **11**				
12	Figure your tax on the amount on line 11 (see instructions) **12**				
13	Self-employment tax from line 34 below (complete Part II) **13**				
14	Enter other taxes for each payment period (see instructions) **14**				
15	Total tax. Add lines 12, 13, and 14 **15**				
16	For each period, enter the same type of credits as allowed on Form 2210, lines 1 and 3 (see instructions) **16**				
17	Subtract line 16 from line 15. If zero or less, enter -0- **17**				
18	Applicable percentage **18**	22.5%	45%	67.5%	90%
19	Multiply line 17 by line 18 **19**				
	Complete lines 20–25 of one column before going to the next column.				
20	Enter the total of the amounts in all previous columns of line 25 **20**	▨			
21	Subtract line 20 from line 19. If zero or less, enter -0- **21**				
22	Enter 25% (.25) of line 9 on page 1 of Form 2210 in each column **22**				
23	Subtract line 25 of the previous column from line 24 of that column **23**	▨			
24	Add lines 22 and 23 **24**				
25	Enter the **smaller** of line 21 or line 24 here and on Form 2210, line 18 ▶ **25**				
Part II	**Annualized Self-Employment Tax** (Form 1040 filers only)				
26	Net earnings from self-employment for the period (see instructions) **26**				
27	Prorated social security tax limit **27**	$22,500	$37,500	$60,000	$90,000
28	Enter actual wages for the period subject to social security tax or the 6.2% portion of the 7.65% railroad retirement (tier 1) tax **28**				
29	Subtract line 28 from line 27. If zero or less, enter -0-. **29**				
30	Annualization amounts **30**	0.496	0.2976	0.186	0.124
31	Multiply line 30 by the **smaller** of line 26 or line 29 **31**				
32	Annualization amounts **32**	0.116	0.0696	0.0435	0.029
33	Multiply line 26 by line 32 **33**				
34	Add lines 31 and 33. Enter here and on line 13 above ▶ **34**				

Form **2210** (2005)

Form 2220

Underpayment of Estimated Tax by Corporations

▶ See separate instructions.

▶ Attach to the corporation's tax return.

OMB No. 1545-0142

2005

Department of the Treasury
Internal Revenue Service

Name	Employer identification number
Globe Corporation	38 : 1505087

Note: *Generally, the corporation is not required to file Form 2220 (see Part II below for exceptions) because the IRS will figure any penalty owed and bill the corporation. However, the corporation may still use Form 2220 to figure the penalty. If so, enter the amount from page 2, line 34 on the estimated tax penalty line of the corporation's income tax return, but **do not** attach Form 2220.*

Part I Required Annual Payment

1	Total tax (see instructions)	**1**	100,000

2a	Personal holding company tax (Schedule PH (Form 1120), line 26) included on line 1	2a	
b	Look-back interest included on line 1 under section 460(b)(2) for completed long-term contracts or section 167(g) for depreciation under the income forecast method	2b	
c	Credit for Federal tax paid on fuels (see instructions)	2c	
d	**Total.** Add lines 2a through 2c	**2d**	

3	Subtract line 2d from line 1. If the result is less than $500, **do not** complete or file this form. The corporation does not owe the penalty	**3**	100,000
4	Enter the tax shown on the corporation's 2004 income tax return (see instructions). **Caution:** *If the tax is zero or the tax year was for less than 12 months, skip this line and enter the amount from line 3 on line 5*	**4**	125,000
5	**Required Annual Payment.** Enter the **smaller** of line 3 or line 4. If the corporation is required to skip line 4, enter the amount from line 3	**5**	100,000

Part II Reasons for Filing—Check the boxes below that apply. If any boxes are checked, the corporation **must** file Form 2220 even if it does not owe a penalty (see instructions).

6 ☐ The corporation is using the adjusted seasonal installment method.

7 ☐ The corporation is using the annualized income installment method.

8 ☐ The corporation is a "large corporation" figuring its first required installment based on the prior year's tax.

Part III Figuring the Underpayment

			(a)	(b)	(c)	(d)
9	**Installment due dates.** Enter in columns (a) through (d) the 15th day of the 4th (*Form 990-PF filers:* Use 5th month), 6th, 9th, and 12th months of the corporation's tax year	**9**	4-15-05	6-15-05	9-15-05	12-15-05
10	**Required installments.** If the box on line 6 and/or line 7 above is checked, enter the amounts from Schedule A, line 38. If the box on line 8 (but not 6 or 7) is checked, see instructions for the amounts to enter. If none of these boxes are checked, enter 25% of line 5 above in each column	**10**	25,000	25,000	25,000	25,000
11	Estimated tax paid or credited for each period (see instructions). For column (a) only, enter the amount from line 11 on line 15	**11**	16,000	16,000	16,000	16,000
	Complete lines 12 through 18 of one column before going to the next column.			-0-	-0-	-0-
12	Enter amount, if any, from line 18 of the preceding column	**12**				
13	Add lines 11 and 12	**13**		16,000	16,000	16,000
*14	Add amounts on lines 16 and 17 of the preceding column	**14**		9,000	18,000	27,000
15	Subtract line 14 from line 13. If zero or less, enter -0-	**15**	16,000	7,000	-0-	-0-
16	If the amount on line 15 is zero, subtract line 13 from line 14. Otherwise, enter -0-	**16**		-0-	2,000	11,000
**17	**Underpayment.** If line 15 is less than or equal to line 10, subtract line 15 from line 10. Then go to line 12 of the next column. Otherwise, go to line 18	**17**	9,000	18,000	27,000	36,000
18	**Overpayment.** If line 10 is less than line 15, subtract line 10 from line 15. Then go to line 12 of the next column	**18**				

Go to Part IV on page 2 to figure the penalty. Do not go to Part IV if there are no entries on line 17—no penalty is owed.

For Paperwork Reduction Act Notice, see separate instructions.   Cat. No. 11746L   Form **2220** (2005)

*This amount is from line 17 only from the preceding column.

**Also add the amount on line 16 to "force" the correct cumulative underpayment on line 17.

Form 2220 (2005)   Page **2**

Part IV Figuring the Penalty

		(a)	(b)	(c)	(d)
19	Enter the date of payment or the 15th day of the 3rd month after the close of the tax year, whichever is earlier (see instructions). *(Form 990-PF and Form 990-T filers:* Use 5th month instead of 3rd month.) **19**	6-15-05	9-15-05	12-15-05	3-15-06
20	Number of days from due date of installment on line 9 to the date shown on line 19. . . . . **20**	61	92	91	90
21	Number of days on line 20 after 4/15/2005 and before 10/1/2005 **21**	61	92	15	
22	Underpayment on line 17 × $\frac{\text{Number of days on line 21}}{365}$ × 6%. **22**	$ 90	$ 272	$ 67	$
23	Number of days on line 20 after 9/30/2005 and before 4/1/2006 **23**			76	90
24	Underpayment on line 17 × $\frac{\text{Number of days on line 23}}{365}$ × 7% . **24**	$	$	$ 394	$ 621
25	Number of days on line 20 after 3/31/2006 and before 7/1/2006 . **25**				
26	Underpayment on line 17 × $\frac{\text{Number of days on line 25}}{365}$ × *% . . **26**	$	$	$	$
27	Number of days on line 20 after 6/30/2006 and before 10/1/2006 . **27**				
28	Underpayment on line 17 × $\frac{\text{Number of days on line 27}}{365}$ × *% . . **28**	$	$	$	$
29	Number of days on line 20 after 9/30/2006 and before 1/1/2007 . **29**				
30	Underpayment on line 17 × $\frac{\text{Number of days on line 29}}{365}$ × *% . . **30**	$	$	$	$
31	Number of days on line 20 after 12/31/2006 and before 2/16/2007 **31**				
32	Underpayment on line 17 × $\frac{\text{Number of days on line 31}}{365}$ × *% . . **32**	$	$	$	$
33	Add lines 22, 24, 26, 28, 30, and 32 . . . . **33**	$ 90	$ 272	$ 461	$ 621

34 **Penalty.** Add columns (a) through (d) of line 33. Enter the total here and on Form 1120, line 33; Form 1120-A, line 29; or the comparable line for other income tax returns . . . . **34** $ 1,444

*****For underpayments paid after March 31, 2006:** For lines 26, 28, 30, and 32, use the penalty interest rate for each calendar quarter, which the IRS will determine during the first month in the preceding quarter. These rates are published quarterly in an IRS News Release and in a revenue ruling in the Internal Revenue Bulletin. To obtain this information on the Internet, access the IRS website at **www.irs.gov.** You can also call 1-800-829-4933 to get interest rate information.

Form **2220** (2005)

Form **2441**	**Child and Dependent Care Expenses**	OMB No. 1545-0074

Form **2441**

Department of the Treasury
Internal Revenue Service (99)

Child and Dependent Care Expenses

▶ Attach to Form 1040.

▶ See separate instructions.

OMB No. 1545-0074

2005

Attachment
Sequence No. **21**

Name(s) shown on Form 1040

Your social security number

Before you begin: You need to understand the following terms. See **Definitions** on page 1 of the instructions.

● **Dependent Care Benefits**   ● **Qualifying Person(s)**   ● **Qualified Expenses**

Part I	**Persons or Organizations Who Provided the Care**—You **must** complete this part.

(If you need more space, use the bottom of page 2.)

1	(a) Care provider's name	(b) Address (number, street, apt. no., city, state, and ZIP code)	(c) Identifying number (SSN or EIN)	(d) Amount paid (see instructions)

Did you receive **dependent care benefits?**

No ──────▶ Complete only Part II below.

Yes ──────▶ Complete Part III on the back next.

Caution. If the care was provided in your home, you may owe employment taxes. See the instructions for Form 1040, line 62.

Part II	**Credit for Child and Dependent Care Expenses**

2   Information about your **qualifying person(s).** If you have more than two qualifying persons, see the instructions.

(a) Qualifying person's name		(b) Qualifying person's social security number	(c) **Qualified expenses** you incurred and paid in 2005 for the person listed in column (a)
First	Last		

3	Add the amounts in column (c) of line 2. **Do not** enter more than $3,000 for one qualifying person or $6,000 for two or more persons. If you completed Part III, enter the amount from line 32	**3**	
4	Enter your **earned income.** See instructions	**4**	
5	If married filing jointly, enter your spouse's earned income (if your spouse was a student or was disabled, see the instructions); **all others,** enter the amount from line 4 . . .	**5**	
6	Enter the **smallest** of line 3, 4, or 5	**6**	
7	Enter the amount from Form 1040, line 38	**7**		

8   Enter on line 8 the decimal amount shown below that applies to the amount on line 7

If line 7 is:			If line 7 is:		
Over	But not over	Decimal amount is	Over	But not over	Decimal amount is
$0—15,000		.35	$29,000—31,000		.27
15,000—17,000		.34	31,000—33,000		.26
17,000—19,000		.33	33,000—35,000		.25
19,000—21,000		.32	35,000—37,000		.24
21,000—23,000		.31	37,000—39,000		.23
23,000—25,000		.30	39,000—41,000		.22
25,000—27,000		.29	41,000—43,000		.21
27,000—29,000		.28	43,000—No limit		.20

8		X .

9	Multiply line 6 by the decimal amount on line 8. If you paid 2004 expenses in 2005, see the instructions	**9**	
10	Enter the amount from Form 1040, line 46, minus any amount on Form 1040, line 47 .	**10**	
11	**Credit for child and dependent care expenses.** Enter the **smaller** of line 9 or line 10 here and on Form 1040, line 48	**11**	

For Paperwork Reduction Act Notice, see page 4 of the instructions.   Cat. No. 11862M   Form **2441** (2005)

Form 2441 (2005)

Page **2**

Part III Dependent Care Benefits

12 Enter the total amount of **dependent care benefits** you received in 2005. Amounts you received as an employee should be shown in box 10 of your Form(s) W-2. **Do not** include amounts reported as wages in box 1 of Form(s) W-2. If you were self-employed or a partner, include amounts you received under a dependent care assistance program from your sole proprietorship or partnership **12**

13 Enter the amount forfeited or carried forward to 2006, if any (see the instructions) . . . **13**

14 Subtract line 13 from line 12 . . . . **14**

15 Enter the total amount of **qualified expenses** incurred in 2005 for the care of the **qualifying person(s)** . . **15**

16 Enter the **smaller** of line 14 or 15 . . . . . . **16**

17 Enter your **earned income.** See instructions . . . **17**

18 Enter the amount shown below that applies to you.

  • If married filing jointly, enter your spouse's earned income (if your spouse was a student or was disabled, see the instructions for line 5).

  • If married filing separately, see the instructions for the amount to enter. } . . . **18**

  • All others, enter the amount from line 17.

19 Enter the **smallest** of line 16, 17, or 18 . . . . . **19**

20 Enter the amount from line 12 that you received from your sole proprietorship or partnership. If you did not receive any such amounts, enter -0- **20**

21 Subtract line 20 from line 14 . . . . **21**

22 Enter $5,000 ($2,500 if married filing separately **and** you were required to enter your spouse's earned income on line 18) **22**

23 **Deductible benefits.** Enter the **smallest** of line 19, 20, or 22. Also, include this amount on the appropriate line(s) of your return (see the instructions) **23**

24 Enter the **smaller** of line 19 or 22 . . . . **24**

25 Enter the amount from line 23 . . . . **25**

26 **Excluded benefits.** Subtract line 25 from line 24. If zero or less, enter -0- **26**

27 **Taxable benefits.** Subtract line 26 from line 21. If zero or less, enter -0-. Also, include this amount on Form 1040, line 7. On the dotted line next to line 7, enter "DCB" . . . **27**

To claim the child and dependent care
credit, complete lines 28–32 below.

28 Enter $3,000 ($6,000 if two or more qualifying persons) **28**

29 Add lines 23 and 26 . . . . **29**

30 Subtract line 29 from line 28. If zero or less, **stop.** You cannot take the credit. **Exception.** If you paid 2004 expenses in 2005, see the instructions for line 9 . . . . **30**

31 Complete line 2 on the front of this form. **Do not** include in column (c) any benefits shown on line 29 above. Then, add the amounts in column (c) and enter the total here **31**

32 Enter the **smaller** of line 30 or 31. Also, enter this amount on line 3 on the front of this form and complete lines 4–11 . . . . **32**

Form **2441** (2005)

Form **3903**

Department of the Treasury
Internal Revenue Service

Moving Expenses

▶ Attach to Form 1040.

OMB No. 1545-0074

2005

Attachment
Sequence No. **62**

Name(s) shown on Form 1040

Your social security number

Before you begin: ✓ See the **Distance Test** and **Time Test** in the instructions to find out if you can deduct your moving expenses.

✓ See **Members of the Armed Forces** on back, if applicable.

1	Transportation and storage of household goods and personal effects (see instructions) . .	**1**
2	Travel (including lodging) from your old home to your new home (see instructions). **Do not** include the cost of meals	**2**
3	Add lines 1 and 2	**3**
4	Enter the total amount your employer paid you for the expenses listed on lines 1 and 2 that is **not** included in box 1 of your Form W-2 (wages). This amount should be shown in box 12 of your Form W-2 with code **P**	**4**
5	Is line 3 **more than** line 4?	

☐ **No.** You **cannot** deduct your moving expenses. If line 3 is less than line 4, subtract line 3 from line 4 and include the result on Form 1040, line 7.

☐ **Yes. Moving expense deduction.** Subtract line 4 from line 3. Enter the result here and on Form 1040, line 26 . . . . | **5** |

General Instructions

What's New

For 2005, the standard mileage rate for using your vehicle to move to a new home is 15 cents a mile (22 cents a mile after August 31, 2005).

Purpose of Form

Use Form 3903 to figure your moving expense deduction for a move related to the start of work at a new principal place of work (workplace). If the new workplace is outside the United States or its possessions, you must be a U.S. citizen or resident alien to deduct your expenses.

If you qualify to deduct expenses for more than one move, use a separate Form 3903 for each move.

For more details, see Pub. 521, Moving Expenses.

Who Can Deduct Moving Expenses

If you move to a new home because of a new principal workplace, you may be able to deduct your moving expenses whether you are self-employed or an employee. But you must meet both the distance test and time test that follow.

 Members of the Armed Forces may not have to meet these tests. See instructions on back.

Distance Test

Your new principal workplace must be at least 50 miles farther from your old home than your old workplace was. For example, if your old workplace was 3 miles from your old home, your new workplace must be at least 53 miles from that home. If you did not have an old workplace, your new workplace must be at least 50 miles from your old home. The distance between the two points is the shortest of the more commonly traveled routes between them.

You do not have to meet the distance test if you are in the Armed Forces and the move is due to a permanent change of station (see instructions on back).

 To see if you meet the distance test, you can use the worksheet below.

Distance Test Worksheet

Keep a Copy for Your Records

1.	Number of miles from your **old home** to your **new workplace**	**1.** _____ miles
2.	Number of miles from your **old home** to your **old workplace**	**2.** _____ miles
3.	Subtract line 2 from line 1. If zero or less, enter -0-.	**3.** _____ miles

Is line 3 at least 50 miles?

☐ **Yes.** You meet this test.

☐ **No.** You do not meet this test. You **cannot** deduct your moving expenses. **Do not** complete Form 3903.

For Paperwork Reduction Act Notice, see back of form.   Cat. No. 12490K   Form **3903** (2005)

Time Test

If you are an employee, you must work full time in the general area of your new workplace for at least 39 weeks during the 12 months right after you move. If you are self-employed, you must work full time in the general area of your new workplace for at least 39 weeks during the first 12 months and a total of at least 78 weeks during the 24 months right after you move.

What if you do not meet the time test before your return is due? If you expect to meet the time test, you can deduct your moving expenses in the year you move. Later, if you do not meet the time test, you must either:

● Amend your tax return for the year you claimed the deduction by filing Form 1040X, Amended U.S. Individual Income Tax Return, or

● For the year you cannot meet the time test, report as income the amount of your moving expense deduction that reduced your income tax for the year you moved.

If you do not deduct your moving expenses in the year you move and you later meet the time test, you can take the deduction by filing an amended return for the year you moved. To do this, use Form 1040X.

Exceptions to the time test. You do not have to meet the time test if any of the following apply.

● Your job ends because of disability.

● You are transferred for your employer's benefit.

● You are laid off or discharged for a reason other than willful misconduct.

● You are in the Armed Forces and the move is due to a permanent change of station (see below).

● You meet the requirements (explained later) for retirees or survivors living outside the United States.

● You are filing this form for a decedent.

Members of the Armed Forces

If you are in the Armed Forces, you do not have to meet the distance and time tests if the move is due to a permanent change of station. A permanent change of station includes a move in connection with and within 1 year of retirement or other termination of active duty.

How To Complete This Form If You Are In the Armed Forces

Do not include on lines 1 and 2 any expenses for moving services that were provided by the government. If you and your spouse and dependents are moved to or from different locations, treat the moves as a single move.

On line 4, enter the total reimbursements and allowances you received from the government in connection with the expenses you claimed on lines 1 and 2. Do not include the value of moving services provided by the government. Complete line 5 if applicable.

Retirees or Survivors Living Outside the United States

If you are a retiree or survivor who moved to a home in the United States or its possessions and you meet the following requirements, you are treated as if you moved to a new principal workplace located in the United States. You are subject only to the distance test.

Retirees

You can deduct moving expenses for a move to a new home in the United States when you actually retire if both your old principal workplace and your old home were outside the United States.

Survivors

You can deduct moving expenses for a move to a home in the United States if you are the spouse or dependent of a person whose principal workplace at the time of death was outside the United States. The expenses must be for a move (a) that begins within 6 months after the decedent's death, and (b) from a former home outside the United States that you lived in with the decedent at the time of death.

Reimbursements

You can choose to deduct moving expenses in the year you are reimbursed by your employer, even though you paid the expenses in a different year. However, special rules apply. See *When To Deduct Expenses* in Pub. 521.

Filers of Form 2555

If you file Form 2555, Foreign Earned Income, to exclude any of your income or housing costs, report the full amount of your deductible moving expenses on Form 3903 and on Form 1040. Report the part of your moving expenses that is not allowed because it is allocable to the excluded income on the appropriate line of Form 2555. For details on how to figure the part allocable to the excluded income, see Pub. 54, Tax Guide for U.S. Citizens and Resident Aliens Abroad.

Specific Instructions

You can deduct the following expenses you paid to move your family and dependent household members. Do not deduct expenses for employees such as a maid, nanny, or nurse.

Line 1

Moves within or to the United States or its possessions. Enter the amount you paid to pack, crate, and move your household goods and personal effects. You can also include the amount you paid to store and insure household goods and personal effects within any period of 30 days in a row after the items were moved from your old home and before they were delivered to your new home.

Moves outside the United States or its possessions. Enter the amount you paid to pack, crate, move, store, and insure your household goods and personal effects. Also, include the amount you paid to move your personal effects to and from storage and to store them for all or part of the time the new workplace continues to be your principal workplace.

 You do not have to complete this form if (a) you moved in an earlier year, (b) you are claiming only storage fees during your absence from the United States, and (c) any amount your employer paid for the storage fees is included in box 1 of your Form W-2 (wages). Instead, enter the storage fees on Form 1040, line 26, and write "Storage" on the dotted line next to line 26.

Line 2

Enter the amount you paid to travel from your old home to your new home. This includes transportation and lodging on the way. Include costs for the day you arrive. The members of your household do not have to travel together or at the same time. But you can only include expenses for one trip per person. Do not include any temporary living expenses or househunting expenses.

If you use your own vehicle(s), you can figure the expenses by using either:

● Actual out-of-pocket expenses for gas and oil, or

● Mileage at the rate of 15 cents a mile (22 cents a mile after August 31, 2005).

You can add parking fees and tolls to the amount claimed under either method.

Paperwork Reduction Act Notice. We ask for the information on this form to carry out the Internal Revenue laws of the United States. You are required to give us the information. We need it to ensure that you are complying with these laws and to allow us to figure and collect the right amount of tax.

You are not required to provide the information requested on a form that is subject to the Paperwork Reduction Act unless the form displays a valid OMB control number. Books or records relating to a form or its instructions must be retained as long as their contents may become material in the administration of any Internal Revenue law. Generally, tax returns and return information are confidential, as required by Internal Revenue Code section 6103.

The average time and expenses required to complete and file this form will vary depending on individual circumstances. For the estimated averages, see the instructions for your income tax return.

If you have suggestions for making this form simpler, we would be happy to hear from you. See the instructions for your income tax return.

Form **4626**	**Alternative Minimum Tax—Corporations**	OMB No. 1545-0175
Department of the Treasury Internal Revenue Service	▶ See separate instructions. ▶ Attach to the corporation's tax return.	2005

Name	Employer identification number
Glidden Corporation	38 : 1505786

Note: *See the instructions to find out if the corporation is a small corporation exempt from the alternative minimum tax (AMT) under section 55(e).*

1	Taxable income or (loss) before net operating loss deduction	1	128,278
2	**Adjustments and preferences:**		
a	Depreciation of post-1986 property	2a	7,500
b	Amortization of certified pollution control facilities	2b	
c	Amortization of mining exploration and development costs	2c	
d	Amortization of circulation expenditures (personal holding companies only)	2d	
e	Adjusted gain or loss	2e	(6,918)
f	Long-term contracts	2f	
g	Merchant marine capital construction funds	2g	
h	Section 833(b) deduction (Blue Cross, Blue Shield, and similar type organizations only)	2h	
i	Tax shelter farm activities (personal service corporations only)	2i	
j	Passive activities (closely held corporations and personal service corporations only)	2j	
k	Loss limitations	2k	
l	Depletion	2l	
m	Tax-exempt interest income from specified private activity bonds	2m	
n	Intangible drilling costs	2n	
o	Other adjustments and preferences	2o	
3	Pre-adjustment alternative minimum taxable income (AMTI). Combine lines 1 through 2o	3	128,860
4	**Adjusted current earnings (ACE) adjustment:**		
a	ACE from line 10 of the ACE worksheet in the instructions	4a	312,360
b	Subtract line 3 from line 4a. If line 3 exceeds line 4a, enter the difference as a negative amount (see instructions)	4b	183,500
c	Multiply line 4b by 75% (.75). Enter the result as a positive amount	4c	137,625
d	Enter the excess, if any, of the corporation's total increases in AMTI from prior year ACE adjustments over its total reductions in AMTI from prior year ACE adjustments (see instructions). **Note:** *You **must** enter an amount on line 4d (even if line 4b is positive)*	4d	311,296
e	ACE adjustment. • If line 4b is zero or more, enter the amount from line 4c • If line 4b is less than zero, enter the **smaller** of line 4c or line 4d as a negative amount	4e	137,625
5	Combine lines 3 and 4e. If zero or less, stop here; the corporation does not owe any AMT	5	266,485
6	Alternative tax net operating loss deduction (see instructions)	6	— 0 —
7	**Alternative minimum taxable income.** Subtract line 6 from line 5. If the corporation held a residual interest in a REMIC, see instructions	7	266,485
8	**Exemption phase-out** (if line 7 is $310,000 or more, skip lines 8a and 8b and enter -0- on line 8c):		
a	Subtract $150,000 from line 7 (if completing this line for a member of a controlled group, see instructions). If zero or less, enter -0-	8a	116,485
b	Multiply line 8a by 25% (.25)	8b	29,121
c	Exemption. Subtract line 8b from $40,000 (if completing this line for a member of a controlled group, see instructions). If zero or less, enter -0-	8c	10,879
9	Subtract line 8c from line 7. If zero or less, enter -0-	9	255,606
10	Multiply line 9 by 20% (.20)	10	51,121
11	Alternative minimum tax foreign tax credit (AMTFTC) (see instructions)	11	— 0 —
12	Tentative minimum tax. Subtract line 11 from line 10	12	51,121
13	Regular tax liability before applying all credits except the foreign tax credit and possessions tax credit	13	33,278
14	**Alternative minimum tax.** Subtract line 13 from line 12. If zero or less, enter -0-. Enter here and on Form 1120, Schedule J, line 4, or the appropriate line of the corporation's income tax return	14	17,843

For Paperwork Reduction Act Notice, see the instructions. Cat. No. 12955I Form **4626** (2005)

Adjusted Current Earnings (ACE) Worksheet
► See ACE Worksheet Instructions (which begin on page 9).

1	Pre-adjustment AMTI. Enter the amount from line 3 of Form 4626		**1**	**128,860**
2	ACE depreciation adjustment:			
a	AMT depreciation.	**2a** 32,500		
b	ACE depreciation:			
	(1) Post-1993 property	**2b(1)** 32,500		
	(2) Post-1989, pre-1994 property . . .	**2b(2)**		
	(3) Pre-1990 MACRS property	**2b(3)**		
	(4) Pre-1990 original ACRS property . .	**2b(4)**		
	(5) Property described in sections 168(f)(1) through (4)	**2b(5)**		
	(6) Other property	**2b(6)**		
	(7) Total ACE depreciation. Add lines 2b(1) through 2b(6)	**2b(7)** 32,500		
c	ACE depreciation adjustment. Subtract line 2b(7) from line 2a		**2c**	– 0 –
3	Inclusion in ACE of items included in earnings and profits (E&P):			
a	Tax-exempt interest income	**3a** 15,000		
b	Death benefits from life insurance contracts	**3b** 100,000		
c	All other distributions from life insurance contracts (including surrenders) .	**3c**		
d	Inside buildup of undistributed income in life insurance contracts. .	**3d**		
e	Other items (see Regulations sections 1.56(g)-1(c)(6)(iii) through (ix) for a partial list)	**3e**		
f	Total increase to ACE from inclusion in ACE of items included in E&P. Add lines 3a through 3e		**3f**	115,000
4	Disallowance of items not deductible from E&P:			
a	Certain dividends received	**4a** 14,000		
b	Dividends paid on certain preferred stock of public utilities that are deductible under section 247.	**4b**		
c	Dividends paid to an ESOP that are deductible under section 404(k).	**4c**		
d	Nonpatronage dividends that are paid and deductible under section 1382(c)	**4d**		
e	Other items (see Regulations sections 1.56(g)-1(d)(3)(i) and (ii) for a partial list)	**4e**		
f	Total increase to ACE because of disallowance of items not deductible from E&P. Add lines 4a through 4e		**4f**	14,000
5	Other adjustments based on rules for figuring E&P:			
a	Intangible drilling costs	**5a**		
b	Circulation expenditures	**5b**		
c	Organizational expenditures	**5c** 2,500		
d	LIFO inventory adjustments	**5d**		
e	Installment sales	**5e** 52,000		
f	Total other E&P adjustments. Combine lines 5a through 5e.		**5f**	54,500
6	Disallowance of loss on exchange of debt pools		**6**	
7	Acquisition expenses of life insurance companies for qualified foreign contracts		**7**	
8	Depletion		**8**	
9	Basis adjustments in determining gain or loss from sale or exchange of pre-1994 property . .		**9**	
10	**Adjusted current earnings.** Combine lines 1, 2c, 3f, 4f, and 5f through 9. Enter the result here and on line 4a of Form 4626		**10**	312,360

Form **4835**

Department of the Treasury
Internal Revenue Service

Farm Rental Income and Expenses
(Crop and Livestock Shares (Not Cash) Received by Landowner (or Sub-Lessor))
(Income not subject to self-employment tax)
▶ Attach to Form 1040.　▶ See instructions on back.

OMB No. 1545-0074

2005

Attachment
Sequence No. **37**

Name(s) shown on Form 1040

Your social security number

Employer ID number (EIN), if any

A　Did you actively participate in the operation of this farm during 2005 (see instructions)? . . . . ☐ Yes　☐ No

Part I　**Gross Farm Rental Income—Based on Production.** Include amounts converted to cash or the equivalent.

1 Income from production of livestock, produce, grains, and other crops	**1**	
2a Cooperative distributions (Form(s) 1099-PATR) **2a**	**2b** Taxable amount	**2b**
3a Agricultural program payments (see instructions) **3a**	**3b** Taxable amount	**3b**
4 Commodity Credit Corporation (CCC) loans (see instructions):		
a CCC loans reported under election		**4a**
b CCC loans forfeited **4b**	**4c** Taxable amount	**4c**
5 Crop insurance proceeds and Federal crop disaster payments (see instructions):		
a Amount received in 2005 . . . . **5a**	**5b** Taxable amount	**5b**
c If election to defer to 2006 is attached, check here ▶ ☐　**5d** Amount deferred from 2004 .		**5d**
6 Other income, including Federal and state gasoline or fuel tax credit or refund (see instructions)		**6**
7 **Gross farm rental income.** Add amounts in the right column for lines 1 through 6. Enter the total here and on Schedule E (Form 1040), line 42 . . . . ▶		**7**

Part II　**Expenses—Farm Rental Property.** Do not include personal or living expenses.

8 Car and truck expenses (see Schedule F instructions). Also attach **Form 4562**	**8**	**21** Pension and profit-sharing plans		**21**	
9 Chemicals	**9**	**22** Rent or lease:			
10 Conservation expenses (see instructions)	**10**	**a** Vehicles, machinery, and equipment (see instructions)		**22a**	
11 Custom hire (machine work) .	**11**	**b** Other (land, animals, etc.) .		**22b**	
12 Depreciation and section 179 expense deduction not claimed elsewhere	**12**	**23** Repairs and maintenance .		**23**	
		24 Seeds and plants . . .		**24**	
		25 Storage and warehousing .		**25**	
		26 Supplies		**26**	
13 Employee benefit programs other than on line 21 (see Schedule F instructions) . .	**13**	**27** Taxes		**27**	
		28 Utilities		**28**	
14 Feed	**14**	**29** Veterinary, breeding, and medicine		**29**	
15 Fertilizers and lime . . .	**15**				
16 Freight and trucking . . .	**16**	**30** Other expenses (specify):			
17 Gasoline, fuel, and oil . . .	**17**	**a**		**30a**	
18 Insurance (other than health) .	**18**	**b**		**30b**	
19 Interest:		**c**		**30c**	
a Mortgage (paid to banks, etc.) .	**19a**	**d**		**30d**	
b Other	**19b**	**e**		**30e**	
20 Labor hired (less employment credits) (see Schedule F instructions)	**20**	**f**		**30f**	
		g		**30g**	

31 **Total expenses.** Add lines 8 through 30g . . . . ▶	**31**	
32 **Net farm rental income or (loss).** Subtract line 31 from line 7. If the result is income, enter it here and on Schedule E, line 40. If the result is a loss, you **must** go to line 33	**32**	
33 If line 32 is a loss, check the box that describes your investment in this activity (see instructions)	**33a** ☐ All investment is at risk. **33b** ☐ Some investment is not at risk.	
You may need to complete **Form 8582** to determine your deductible loss, regardless of which box you checked (see instructions). If you checked box 33b, you **must** complete **Form 6198** before going to Form 8582. In either case, enter the deductible loss here and on Schedule E, line 40	**33c**	

For Paperwork Reduction Act Notice, see instructions on back.　　　Cat. No. 13117W　　　Form **4835** (2005)

Form **6251**	**Alternative Minimum Tax—Individuals**	OMB No. 1545-0074

Form **6251**
(Rev. January 2006)
Department of the Treasury
Internal Revenue Service (99)

Alternative Minimum Tax—Individuals

▶ See separate instructions.

▶ Attach to Form 1040 or Form 1040NR.

OMB No. 1545-0074

2005

Attachment
Sequence No. **32**

Name(s) shown on Form 1040

Your social security number

Part I   Alternative Minimum Taxable Income (See instructions for how to complete each line.)

1	If filing Schedule A (Form 1040), enter the amount from Form 1040, line 41 (minus any amount on Form 8914, line 2), and go to line 2. Otherwise, enter the amount from Form 1040, line 38 (minus any amount on Form 8914, line 2), and go to line 7. (If less than zero, enter as a negative amount.)	**1**	
2	Medical and dental. Enter the **smaller** of Schedule A (Form 1040), line 4, **or** 2½ % of Form 1040, line 38	**2**	
3	Taxes from Schedule A (Form 1040), line 9	**3**	
4	Enter the home mortgage interest adjustment, if any, from line 6 of the worksheet on page 2 of the instructions	**4**	
5	Miscellaneous deductions from Schedule A (Form 1040), line 26	**5**	
6	If Form 1040, line 38, is over $145,950 (over $72,975 if married filing separately), enter the amount from line 9 of the **Itemized Deductions Worksheet** on page A-9 of the Instructions for Schedules A & B (Form 1040)	**6**	( )
7	Tax refund from Form 1040, line 10 or line 21	**7**	( )
8	Investment interest expense (difference between regular tax and AMT)	**8**	
9	Depletion (difference between regular tax and AMT)	**9**	
10	Net operating loss deduction from Form 1040, line 21. Enter as a positive amount	**10**	
11	Interest from specified private activity bonds exempt from the regular tax	**11**	
12	Qualified small business stock (7% of gain excluded under section 1202)	**12**	
13	Exercise of incentive stock options (excess of AMT income over regular tax income)	**13**	
14	Estates and trusts (amount from Schedule K-1 (Form 1041), box 12, code A)	**14**	
15	Electing large partnerships (amount from Schedule K-1 (Form 1065-B), box 6)	**15**	
16	Disposition of property (difference between AMT and regular tax gain or loss)	**16**	
17	Depreciation on assets placed in service after 1986 (difference between regular tax and AMT)	**17**	
18	Passive activities (difference between AMT and regular tax income or loss)	**18**	
19	Loss limitations (difference between AMT and regular tax income or loss)	**19**	
20	Circulation costs (difference between regular tax and AMT)	**20**	
21	Long-term contracts (difference between AMT and regular tax income)	**21**	
22	Mining costs (difference between regular tax and AMT)	**22**	
23	Research and experimental costs (difference between regular tax and AMT)	**23**	
24	Income from certain installment sales before January 1, 1987	**24**	( )
25	Intangible drilling costs preference	**25**	
26	Other adjustments, including income-based related adjustments	**26**	
27	Alternative tax net operating loss deduction	**27**	( )
28	**Alternative minimum taxable income.** Combine lines 1 through 27. (If married filing separately and line 28 is more than $191,000, see page 7 of the instructions.)	**28**	

Part II   Alternative Minimum Tax

29   Exemption. (If this form is for a child under age 14, see page 7 of the instructions.)

IF your filing status is . . .	AND line 28 is not over . . .	THEN enter on line 29 . . .		
Single or head of household	$112,500	$40,250	}	
Married filing jointly or qualifying widow(er)	150,000	58,000		**29**
Married filing separately	75,000	29,000	}	

If line 28 is **over** the amount shown above for your filing status, see page 7 of the instructions.

30	Subtract line 29 from line 28. If zero or less, enter -0- here and on lines 33 and 35 and stop here	**30**	
31	● If you reported capital gain distributions directly on Form 1040, line 13; you reported qualified dividends on Form 1040, line 9b; **or** you had a gain on both lines 15 and 16 of Schedule D (Form 1040) (as refigured for the AMT, if necessary), complete Part III on the back and enter the amount from line 55 here. ● **All others:** If line 30 is $175,000 or less ($87,500 or less if married filing separately), multiply line 30 by 26% (.26). Otherwise, multiply line 30 by 28% (.28) and subtract $3,500 ($1,750 if married filing separately) from the result.	**31**	
32	Alternative minimum tax foreign tax credit (see page 7 of the instructions)	**32**	
33	Tentative minimum tax. Subtract line 32 from line 31	**33**	
34	Tax from Form 1040, line 44 (minus any tax from Form 4972 and any foreign tax credit from Form 1040, line 47). If you used Schedule J to figure your tax, the amount for line 44 of Form 1040 must be refigured without using Schedule J (see page 9 of the instructions)	**34**	
35	**Alternative minimum tax.** Subtract line 34 from line 33. If zero or less, enter -0-. Enter here and on Form 1040, line 45	**35**	

For Paperwork Reduction Act Notice, see page 9 of the instructions. Cat. No. 13600G Form **6251** (2005) (Rev. 1-2006)

Form 6251 (2005) (Rev. 1-2006)

Part III	Tax Computation Using Maximum Capital Gains Rates

36 Enter the amount from Form 6251, line 30 . . . . **36**

37 Enter the amount from line 6 of the Qualified Dividends and Capital Gain Tax Worksheet in the instructions for Form 1040, line 44, or the amount from line 13 of the Schedule D Tax Worksheet on page D-9 of the instructions for Schedule D (Form 1040), whichever applies (as refigured for the AMT, if necessary) (see page 9 of the instructions) **37**

38 Enter the amount from Schedule D (Form 1040), line 19 (as refigured for the AMT, if necessary) (see page 9 of the instructions) **38**

39 If you did not complete a Schedule D Tax Worksheet for the regular tax or the AMT, enter the amount from line 37. Otherwise, add lines 37 and 38, and enter the **smaller** of that result or the amount from line 10 of the Schedule D Tax Worksheet (as refigured for the AMT, if necessary) **39**

40 Enter the **smaller** of line 36 or line 39 . . . . **40**

41 Subtract line 40 from line 36 . . . . **41**

42 If line 41 is $175,000 or less ($87,500 or less if married filing separately), multiply line 41 by 26% (.26). Otherwise, multiply line 41 by 28% (.28) and subtract $3,500 ($1,750 if married filing separately) from the result . . . . ▶ **42**

43 Enter:
- $59,400 if married filing jointly or qualifying widow(er),
- $29,700 if single or married filing separately, or
- $39,800 if head of household. } **43**

44 Enter the amount from line 7 of the Qualified Dividends and Capital Gain Tax Worksheet in the instructions for Form 1040, line 44, or the amount from line 14 of the Schedule D Tax Worksheet on page D-9 of the instructions for Schedule D (Form 1040), whichever applies (as figured for the regular tax). If you did not complete either worksheet for the regular tax, enter -0- . . . **44**

45 Subtract line 44 from line 43. If zero or less, enter -0- **45**

46 Enter the **smaller** of line 36 or line 37 . . . . **46**

47 Enter the **smaller** of line 45 or line 46 . . . . **47**

48 Multiply line 47 by 5% (.05) . . . . ▶ **48**

49 Subtract line 47 from line 46 . . . . **49**

50 Multiply line 49 by 15% (.15) . . . . ▶ **50**

If line 38 is zero or blank, skip lines 51 and 52 and go to line 53. Otherwise, go to line 51.

51 Subtract line 46 from line 40 . . . . **51**

52 Multiply line 51 by 25% (.25) . . . . ▶ **52**

53 Add lines 42, 48, 50, and 52 . . . . **53**

54 If line 36 is $175,000 or less ($87,500 or less if married filing separately), multiply line 36 by 26% (.26). Otherwise, multiply line 36 by 28% (.28) and subtract $3,500 ($1,750 if married filing separately) from the result **54**

55 Enter the **smaller** of line 53 or line 54 here and on line 31 . . . . **55**

Form **6251** (2005) (Rev. 1-2006)

Form **7004**
(Rev. December 2005)
Department of the Treasury
Internal Revenue Service

Application for Automatic 6-Month Extension of Time To File Certain Business Income Tax, Information, and Other Returns

▶ File a separate application for each return.

OMB No. 1545-0233

Type or Print	Name	Taxpayer identification number
File by the due date for the return for which an extension is requested. See instructions.	*Perry Corporation*	38-1505286
	Number, street, and room or suite no. If P.O. box, see instructions.	
	1631 W. University Avenue	
	City, town, state, and ZIP code (If a foreign address, enter city, province or state, and country (follow the country's practice for entering postal code)).	
	Gainesville, FL 32601	

Caution: Carefully complete all items. Incorrect information may cause delay or rejection.

1 Enter only one code for type of return that this automatic 6-month extension is for (see below) . . . . `1 2`

2 If the foreign corporation does not have an office or place of business in the United States, check here . . . ▶ ☐

3 If the organization qualifies under Regulations section 1.6081-5 (see instructions), check here . . . . ▶ ☐

4a For calendar year 20....., or other tax year beginning ....*Oct. 1*..., 20 *05*, and ending *Sept. 30*.., 20 *06*.

b **Short tax year.** If this tax year is less than 12 months, check the reason:

☐ Initial return ☐ Final return ☐ Change in accounting period ☐ Consolidated return to be filed

5 If the organization is a corporation and is the common parent of a group that intends to file consolidated, check here . ▶ ☐
Also, you must attach a schedule, listing the name, address, and EIN for each member covered by this extension.

6	Tentative total tax (see instructions)	**6**	**72,000**
7	**Total** payments and credits (see instructions)	**7**	**68,000**
8	**Balance due.** Subtract line 7 from line 6. **Generally, you must deposit this amount using the Electronic Federal Tax Payment System (EFTPS), a Federal Tax Deposit (FTD) Coupon, or Electronic Funds Withdrawal (EFW)** (see instructions for exceptions)	**8**	**4,000**

Extension Is For:	Form Code	Extension Is For:	Form Code
Form 706-GS(D)	01	Form 1120-L	18
Form 706-GS(T)	02	Form 1120-ND	19
Form 990-C	03	Form 1120-ND (section 4951 taxes)	20
Form 1041 (estate)	04	Form 1120-PC	21
Form 1041 (trust)	05	Form 1120-POL	22
Form 1041-N	06	Form 1120-REIT	23
Form 1041-QFT	07	Form 1120-RIC	24
Form 1042	08	Form 1120-S	25
Form 1065	09	Form 1120-SF	26
Form 1065-B	10	Form 3520-A	27
Form 1066	11	Form 8612	28
Form 1120	12	Form 8613	29
Form 1120 (subchapter T cooperative)	13	Form 8725	30
Form 1120-A	14	Form 8804	31
Form 1120-F	15	Form 8831	32
Form 1120-FSC	16	Form 8876	33
Form 1120-H	17		

For Paperwork Reduction Act Notice, see instructions. Cat. No. 13804A Form **7004** (Rev. 12-2005)

Form 8615

Department of the Treasury
Internal Revenue Service   (99)

Tax for Children Under Age 14
With Investment Income of More Than $1,600
▶ Attach only to the child's Form 1040, Form 1040A, or Form 1040NR.
▶ See separate instructions.

OMB No. 1545-0074

2005

Attachment
Sequence No. **33**

Child's name shown on return

Child's social security number

Before you begin: If the child, the parent, or any of the parent's other children under age 14 must use the Schedule D Tax Worksheet or has income from farming or fishing, see **Pub. 929,** Tax Rules for Children and Dependents. It explains how to figure the child's tax using the **Schedule D Tax Worksheet** or **Schedule J** (Form 1040).

A   Parent's name (first, initial, and last). **Caution:** See instructions before completing.

B Parent's social security number

C   Parent's filing status (check one):
☐ Single   ☐ Married filing jointly   ☐ Married filing separately   ☐ Head of household   ☐ Qualifying widow(er)

Part I   Child's Net Investment Income

1 Enter the child's investment income (see instructions)	1	
2 If the child **did not** itemize deductions on **Schedule A** (Form 1040 or Form 1040NR), enter $1,600. Otherwise, see instructions	2	
3 Subtract line 2 from line 1. If zero or less, **stop;** do not complete the rest of this form but **do** attach it to the child's return	3	
4 Enter the child's **taxable income** from Form 1040, line 43; Form 1040A, line 27; or Form 1040NR, line 40	4	
5 Enter the **smaller** of line 3 or line 4. If zero, **stop;** do not complete the rest of this form but **do** attach it to the child's return	5	

Part II   Tentative Tax Based on the Tax Rate of the Parent

6 Enter the parent's **taxable income** from Form 1040, line 43; Form 1040A, line 27; Form 1040EZ, line 6; Form 1040NR, line 40; or Form 1040NR-EZ, line 14. If zero or less, enter -0-	6	
7 Enter the total, if any, from Forms 8615, line 5, of **all other** children of the parent named above. **Do not** include the amount from line 5 above	7	
8 Add lines 5, 6, and 7 (see instructions)	8	
9 Enter the tax on the amount on line 8 based on the **parent's** filing status above (see instructions). If the Qualified Dividends and Capital Gain Tax Worksheet, Schedule D Tax Worksheet, or Schedule J (Form 1040) is used to figure the tax, check here ▶ ☐	9	
10 Enter the parent's tax from Form 1040, line 44; Form 1040A, line 28, minus any alternative minimum tax; Form 1040EZ, line 10; Form 1040NR, line 41; or Form 1040NR-EZ, line 15. **Do not** include any tax from **Form 4972 or 8814.** If the Qualified Dividends and Capital Gain Tax Worksheet, Schedule D Tax Worksheet, or Schedule J (Form 1040) was used to figure the tax, check here ▶ ☐	10	
11 Subtract line 10 from line 9 and enter the result. If line 7 is blank, also enter this amount on line 13 and go to **Part III**	11	
12a Add lines 5 and 7	12a	
b Divide line 5 by line 12a. Enter the result as a decimal (rounded to at least three places)	12b	× .
13 Multiply line 11 by line 12b	13	

Part III   Child's Tax — If lines 4 and 5 above are the same, enter -0- on line 15 and go to line 16.

14 Subtract line 5 from line 4	14	
15 Enter the tax on the amount on line 14 based on the **child's** filing status (see instructions). If the Qualified Dividends and Capital Gain Tax Worksheet, Schedule D Tax Worksheet, or Schedule J (Form 1040) is used to figure the tax, check here ▶ ☐	15	
16 Add lines 13 and 15	16	
17 Enter the tax on the amount on line 4 based on the **child's** filing status (see instructions). If the Qualified Dividends and Capital Gain Tax Worksheet, Schedule D Tax Worksheet, or Schedule J (Form 1040) is used to figure the tax, check here ▶ ☐	17	
18 Enter the **larger** of line 16 or line 17 here and on the **child's** Form 1040, line 44; Form 1040A, line 28; or Form 1040NR, line 41	18	

For Paperwork Reduction Act Notice, see the instructions.   Cat. No. 64113U   Form **8615** (2005)

Form **8283**

(Rev. December 2005)

Department of the Treasury
Internal Revenue Service

Noncash Charitable Contributions

▶ Attach to your tax return if you claimed a total deduction
of over $500 for all contributed property.

▶ See separate instructions.

OMB No. 1545-0908

Attachment
Sequence No. **155**

Name(s) shown on your income tax return	Identifying number

Note. Figure the amount of your contribution deduction before completing this form. See your tax return instructions.

Section A. **Donated Property of $5,000 or Less and Certain Publicly Traded Securities**—List in this section **only** items (or groups of similar items) for which you claimed a deduction of $5,000 or less. Also, list certain publicly traded securities even if the deduction is more than $5,000 (see instructions).

Part I | **Information on Donated Property**—If you need more space, attach a statement.

1	(a) Name and address of the donee organization	(b) Description of donated property (For a donated vehicle, enter the year, make, model, condition, and mileage.)
A		
B		
C		
D		
E		

Note. If the amount you claimed as a deduction for an item is $500 or less, you do not have to complete columns (d), (e), and (f).

	(c) Date of the contribution	(d) Date acquired by donor (mo., yr.)	(e) How acquired by donor	(f) Donor's cost or adjusted basis	(g) Fair market value (see instructions)	(h) Method used to determine the fair market value
A						
B						
C						
D						
E						

Part II | **Partial Interests and Restricted Use Property**—Complete lines 2a through 2e if you gave less than an entire interest in a property listed in Part I. Complete lines 3a through 3c if conditions were placed on a contribution listed in Part I; also attach the required statement (see instructions).

2a Enter the letter from Part I that identifies the property for which you gave less than an entire interest ▶_____ .
If Part II applies to more than one property, attach a separate statement.

b Total amount claimed as a deduction for the property listed in Part I: **(1)** For this tax year ▶_____ .

(2) For any prior tax years ▶_____ .

c Name and address of each organization to which any such contribution was made in a prior year (complete only if different from the donee organization above):

Name of charitable organization (donee)

Address (number, street, and room or suite no.)

City or town, state, and ZIP code

d For tangible property, enter the place where the property is located or kept ▶_____

e Name of any person, other than the donee organization, having actual possession of the property ▶_____

		Yes	No
3a	Is there a restriction, either temporary or permanent, on the donee's right to use or dispose of the donated property?		
b	Did you give to anyone (other than the donee organization or another organization participating with the donee organization in cooperative fundraising) the right to the income from the donated property or to the possession of the property, including the right to vote donated securities, to acquire the property by purchase or otherwise, or to designate the person having such income, possession, or right to acquire?		
c	Is there a restriction limiting the donated property for a particular use?		

For Paperwork Reduction Act Notice, see page 6 of separate instructions.   Cat. No. 62299J   Form **8283** (Rev. 12-2005)

Form 8283 (Rev. 12-2005)   Page **2**

Name(s) shown on your income tax return	Identifying number

Section B. Donated Property Over $5,000 (Except Certain Publicly Traded Securities)—List in this section only items (or groups of similar items) for which you claimed a deduction of more than $5,000 per item or group (except contributions of certain publicly traded securities reported in Section A). An appraisal is generally required for property listed in Section B (see instructions).

Part I — Information on Donated Property—To be completed by the taxpayer and/or the appraiser.

4 Check the box that describes the type of property donated:

- ☐ Art* (contribution of $20,000 or more)
- ☐ Art* (contribution of less than $20,000)
- ☐ Collectibles**
- ☐ Qualified Conservation Contribution
- ☐ Other Real Estate
- ☐ Intellectual Property
- ☐ Equipment
- ☐ Securities
- ☐ Other

*Art includes paintings, sculptures, watercolors, prints, drawings, ceramics, antiques, decorative arts, textiles, carpets, silver, rare manuscripts, historical memorabilia, and other similar objects.

**Collectibles include coins, stamps, books, gems, jewelry, sports memorabilia, dolls, etc., but not art as defined above.

Note. If your total art contribution was $20,000 or more, you must attach a complete copy of the signed appraisal. If your deduction for any donated property was more than $500,000, you must attach a qualified appraisal of the property. See instructions.

5	(a) Description of donated property (if you need more space, attach a separate statement)	(b) If tangible property was donated, give a brief summary of the overall physical condition of the property at the time of the gift	(c) Appraised fair market value
A			
B			
C			
D			

	(d) Date acquired by donor (mo., yr.)	(e) How acquired by donor	(f) Donor's cost or adjusted basis	(g) For bargain sales, enter amount received	See instructions	
					(h) Amount claimed as a deduction	(i) Average trading price of securities
A						
B						
C						
D						

Part II — Taxpayer (Donor) Statement—List each item included in Part I above that the appraisal identifies as having a value of $500 or less. See instructions.

I declare that the following item(s) included in Part I above has to the best of my knowledge and belief an appraised value of not more than $500 (per item). Enter identifying letter from Part I and describe the specific item. See instructions. ▶ _____

Signature of taxpayer (donor) ▶ _____   Date ▶ _____

Part III — Declaration of Appraiser

I declare that I am not the donor, the donee, a party to the transaction in which the donor acquired the property, employed by, or related to any of the foregoing persons, or married to any person who is related to any of the foregoing persons. And, if regularly used by the donor, donee, or party to the transaction, I performed the majority of my appraisals during my tax year for other persons.

Also, I declare that I hold myself out to the public as an appraiser or perform appraisals on a regular basis; and that because of my qualifications as described in the appraisal, I am qualified to make appraisals of the type of property being valued. I certify that the appraisal fees were not based on a percentage of the appraised property value. Furthermore, I understand that a false or fraudulent overstatement of the property value as described in the qualified appraisal or this Form 8283 may subject me to the penalty under section 6701(a) (aiding and abetting the understatement of tax liability). I affirm that I have not been barred from presenting evidence or testimony by the Office of Professional Responsibility.

Sign Here

Signature ▶	Title ▶	Date ▶

Business address (including room or suite no.)	Identifying number

City or town, state, and ZIP code

Part IV — Donee Acknowledgment—To be completed by the charitable organization.

This charitable organization acknowledges that it is a qualified organization under section 170(c) and that it received the donated property as described in Section B, Part I, above on the following date ▶ _____

Furthermore, this organization affirms that in the event it sells, exchanges, or otherwise disposes of the property described in Section B, Part I (or any portion thereof) within 2 years after the date of receipt, it will file **Form 8282,** Donee Information Return, with the IRS and give the donor a copy of that form. This acknowledgment does not represent agreement with the claimed fair market value.

Does the organization intend to use the property for an unrelated use? . . . . ▶ ☐ Yes   ☐ No

Name of charitable organization (donee)	Employer identification number

Address (number, street, and room or suite no.)	City or town, state, and ZIP code

Authorized signature	Title	Date

Form **8582**	**Passive Activity Loss Limitations**	OMB No. 1545-1008

Department of the Treasury
Internal Revenue Service (99)

► See separate instructions.
► Attach to Form 1040 or Form 1041.

2005
Attachment Sequence No. **88**

Name(s) shown on return

Identifying number

Part I **2005 Passive Activity Loss**

Caution: *Complete Worksheets 1, 2, and 3 on page 2 before completing Part I.*

Rental Real Estate Activities With Active Participation (For the definition of active participation see **Special Allowance for Rental Real Estate Activities** on page 3 of the instructions.)

1a Activities with net income (enter the amount from Worksheet 1, column (a)) **1a**

b Activities with net loss (enter the amount from Worksheet 1, column (b)) . . . . **1b** ( )

c Prior years unallowed losses (enter the amount from Worksheet 1, column (c)) . . . . **1c** ( )

d Combine lines 1a, 1b, and 1c. **1d**

Commercial Revitalization Deductions From Rental Real Estate Activities

2a Commercial revitalization deductions from Worksheet 2, column (a) **2a** ( )

b Prior year unallowed commercial revitalization deductions from Worksheet 2, column (b) . . . . . **2b** ( )

c Add lines 2a and 2b. . . . . **2c** ( )

All Other Passive Activities

3a Activities with net income (enter the amount from Worksheet 3, column (a)) **3a**

b Activities with net loss (enter the amount from Worksheet 3, column (b)) . . . . . . **3b** ( )

c Prior years unallowed losses (enter the amount from Worksheet 3, column (c)) . . . . . . **3c** ( )

d Combine lines 3a, 3b, and 3c. **3d**

4 Combine lines 1d, 2c, and 3d. If the result is net income or zero, all losses are allowed, including any prior year unallowed losses entered on line 1c, 2b, or 3c. **Do not** complete Form 8582. Report the losses on the forms and schedules normally used **4**

If line 4 is a loss and: • Line 1d is a loss, go to Part II.
• Line 2c is a loss (and line 1d is zero or more), skip Part II and go to Part III.
• Line 3d is a loss (and lines 1d and 2c are zero or more), skip Parts II and III and go to line 15.

Caution: *If your filing status is married filing separately and you lived with your spouse at any time during the year, do not complete Part II or Part III. Instead, go to line 15.*

Part II **Special Allowance for Rental Real Estate With Active Participation**

Note: *Enter all numbers in Part II as positive amounts. See page 8 of the instructions for an example.*

5 Enter the **smaller** of the loss on line 1d or the loss on line 4 . . . . . **5**

6 Enter $150,000. If married filing separately, see page 8 . . . **6**

7 Enter modified adjusted gross income, but not less than zero (see page 8) **7**

Note: *If line 7 is greater than or equal to line 6, skip lines 8 and 9, enter -0- on line 10. Otherwise, go to line 8.*

8 Subtract line 7 from line 6 . . . . **8**

9 Multiply line 8 by 50% (.5). **Do not** enter more than $25,000. If married filing separately, see page 8 **9**

10 Enter the **smaller** of line 5 or line 9. . . . . **10**

If line 2c is a loss, go to Part III. Otherwise, go to line 15.

Part III **Special Allowance for Commercial Revitalization Deductions From Rental Real Estate Activities**

Note: *Enter all numbers in Part III as positive amounts. See the example for Part II on page 8 of the instructions.*

11 Enter $25,000 reduced by the amount, if any, on line 10. If married filing separately, see instructions **11**

12 Enter the loss from line 4 . . . . **12**

13 Reduce line 12 by the amount on line 10 . . . . . . **13**

14 Enter the **smallest** of line 2c (treated as a positive amount), line 11, or line 13 . . . . **14**

Part IV **Total Losses Allowed**

15 Add the income, if any, on lines 1a and 3a and enter the total. **15**

16 **Total losses allowed from all passive activities for 2005.** Add lines 10, 14, and 15. See pages 10 and 11 of the instructions to find out how to report the losses on your tax return . **16**

For Paperwork Reduction Act Notice, see page 12 of the instructions. Cat. No. 63704F Form **8582** (2005)

Form 8582 (2005)

Caution: *The worksheets must be filed with your tax return. Keep a copy for your records.*

Worksheet 1—For Form 8582, Lines 1a, 1b, and 1c (See page 7 of the instructions.)

Name of activity	Current year		Prior years	Overall gain or loss	
	(a) Net income (line 1a)	**(b) Net loss (line 1b)**	**(c) Unallowed loss (line 1c)**	**(d) Gain**	**(e) Loss**
Total. Enter on Form 8582, lines 1a, 1b, and 1c . . . . ▶					

Worksheet 2—For Form 8582, Lines 2a and 2b (See pages 7 and 8 of the instructions.)

Name of activity	**(a) Current year deductions (line 2a)**	**(b) Prior year unallowed deductions (line 2b)**	**(c) Overall loss**
Total. Enter on Form 8582, lines 2a and 2b . . . . ▶			

Worksheet 3—For Form 8582, Lines 3a, 3b, and 3c (See page 8 of the instructions.)

Name of activity	Current year		Prior years	Overall gain or loss	
	(a) Net income (line 3a)	**(b) Net loss (line 3b)**	**(c) Unallowed loss (line 3c)**	**(d) Gain**	**(e) Loss**
Total. Enter on Form 8582, lines 3a, 3b, and 3c . . . . ▶					

Worksheet 4—Use this worksheet if an amount is shown on Form 8582, line 10 or 14 (See page 9 of the instructions.)

Name of activity	Form or schedule and line number to be reported on (see instructions)	**(a) Loss**	**(b) Ratio**	**(c) Special allowance**	**(d) Subtract column (c) from column (a)**
Total . . . . ▶			1.00		

Worksheet 5—Allocation of Unallowed Losses (See page 9 of the instructions.)

Name of activity	Form or schedule and line number to be reported on (see instructions)	**(a) Loss**	**(b) Ratio**	**(c) Unallowed loss**
Total . . . . ▶			1.00	

Form **8582** (2005)

Worksheet 6—Allowed Losses (See pages 9 and 10 of the instructions.)

Name of activity	Form or schedule and line number to be reported on (see instructions)	(a) Loss	(b) Unallowed loss	(c) Allowed loss
Total . . . . ▶				

Worksheet 7—Activities With Losses Reported on Two or More Forms or Schedules (See page 10 of the instructions.)

Name of Activity:	(a)	(b)	(c) Ratio	(d) Unallowed loss	(e) Allowed loss
Form or schedule and line number to be reported on (see instructions):					
1a Net loss plus prior year unallowed loss from form or schedule. ▶					
b Net income from form or schedule . . . . . . ▶					
c Subtract line 1b from line 1a. If zero or less, enter -0- ▶					
Form or schedule and line number to be reported on (see instructions):					
1a Net loss plus prior year unallowed loss from form or schedule. ▶					
b Net income from form or schedule . . . . . . ▶					
c Subtract line 1b from line 1a. If zero or less, enter -0- ▶					
Form or schedule and line number to be reported on (see instructions):					
1a Net loss plus prior year unallowed loss from form or schedule. ▶					
b Net income from form or schedule . . . . . . ▶					
c Subtract line 1b from line 1a. If zero or less, enter -0- ▶					
Total . . . . ▶			1.00		

MACRS TABLES

MACRS, ADS and ACRS Depreciation Methods Summary

System	Characteristics	Depreciation Method		Table No.[a]	
		MACRS	ADS	MACRS	ADS
MACRS & ADS	Personal Property:				
	1. Accounting convention	Half-year or mid-quarter	Half-year or mid-quarter[b]		
	2. Life and method				
	a. 3-year, 5-year, 7-year, 10-year	200% DB or elect straight-line	150% DB or elect straight-line	1, 2, 3, 4, 5	10, 11[c]
	b. 15-year, 20-year	150% DB or elect straight-line	150% DB or elect straight-line[d]	1, 2, 3, 4, 5	
	3. Luxury Automobile Limitations			6	
	Real property:				
	1. Accounting convention	Mid-month	Mid-month		
	2. Life and method				
	a. Residential rental property	27.5 years, straight-line	40 years straight-line	7	12
	b. Nonresidential real property	39 years, straight-line[e]	40 years straight-line	9	12

System	Characteristics	ACRS
ACRS[f]	Personal Property	
	1. Accounting convention	Half-year
	2. Life and method	
	a. 3-year, 5-year, 10-year, 15-year	150% DB or elect straight-line
	Real Property	
	1. Accounting convention	First of month or mid-month
	2. Life	
	a. 15-year property	Placed in service after 12/31/80 and before 3/16/84
	b. 18-year property	Placed in service after 3/15/84 and before 5/9/85
	c. 19-year property	Placed in service after 5/8/85 and before 1/1/87
	3. Method	
	a. All but low-income housing	175% DB or elect straight-line
	b. Low-income housing property	200% DB or elect straight-line

[a] All depreciation tables in this appendix are based upon tables contained in Rev. Proc. 87-57, as amended.

[b] General and ADS tables are available for property lives from 2.5–50.0 years using the straight-line method. These tables are contained in Rev. Proc. 87-57 and are only partially reproduced here.

[c] The mid-quarter tables are available in Rev. Proc. 87-57, but are not reproduced here.

[d] Special recovery periods are assigned certain MACRS properties under the alternative depreciation system.

[e] A 31.5-year recovery period applied to nonresidential real property placed in service under the MACRS rules prior to May 13, 1993 (see Table 8).

[f] ACRS was effective for years 1981–1986. ACRS tables are no longer reproduced in this textbook.

▼ TABLE 1

General Depreciation System—MACRS
Personal Property Placed in Service after 12/31/86
Applicable Convention: Half-year
Applicable Depreciation Method: 200 or 150 Percent Declining Balance Switching to Straight Line

If the Recovery Year Is:	And the Recovery Period Is:					
	3-Year	5-Year	7-Year	10-Year	15-Year	20-Year
	The Depreciation Rate Is:					
1	33.33	20.00	14.29	10.00	5.00	3.750
2	44.45	32.00	24.49	18.00	9.50	7.219
3	14.81	19.20	17.49	14.40	8.55	6.677
4	7.41	11.52	12.49	11.52	7.70	6.177
5		11.52	8.93	9.22	6.93	5.713
6		5.76	8.92	7.37	6.23	5.285
7			8.93	6.55	5.90	4.888
8			4.46	6.55	5.90	4.522
9				6.56	5.91	4.462
10				6.55	5.90	4.461
11				3.28	5.91	4.462
12					5.90	4.461
13					5.91	4.462
14					5.90	4.461
15					5.91	4.462
16					2.95	4.461
17						4.462
18						4.461
19						4.462
20						4.461
21						2.231

▼ **TABLE 2**

General Depreciation System—MACRS
Personal Property Placed in Service after 12/31/86
Applicable Convention: Mid-quarter (Property Placed in Service in First Quarter)
Applicable Depreciation Method: 200 or 150 Percent Declining Balance Switching to Straight Line

If the Recovery Year Is:	And the Recovery Period Is:					
	3-Year	5-Year	7-Year	10-Year	15-Year	20-Year
	The Depreciation Rate Is:					
1	58.33	35.00	25.00	17.50	8.75	6.563
2	27.78	26.00	21.43	16.50	9.13	7.000
3	12.35	15.60	15.31	13.20	8.21	6.482
4	1.54	11.01	10.93	10.56	7.39	5.996
5		11.01	8.75	8.45	6.65	5.546
6		1.38	8.74	6.76	5.99	5.130
7			8.75	6.55	5.90	4.746
8			1.09	6.55	5.91	4.459
9				6.56	5.90	4.459
10				6.55	5.91	4.459
11				0.82	5.90	4.459
12					5.91	4.460
13					5.90	4.459
14					5.91	4.460
15					5.90	4.459
16					0.74	4.460
17						4.459
18						4.460
19						4.459
20						4.460
21						0.557

▼ TABLE 3
General Depreciation System—MACRS
Personal Property Placed in Service after 12/31/86
Applicable Convention: Mid-quarter (Property Placed in Service in Second Quarter)
Applicable Depreciation Method: 200 or 150 Percent Declining Balance Switching to Straight Line

If the Recovery Year Is:	And the Recovery Period Is:					
	3-Year	5-Year	7-Year	10-Year	15-Year	20-Year
	The Depreciation Rate Is:					
1	41.67	25.00	17.85	12.50	6.25	4.688
2	38.89	30.00	23.47	17.50	9.38	7.148
3	14.14	18.00	16.76	14.00	8.44	6.612
4	5.30	11.37	11.97	11.20	7.59	6.116
5		11.37	8.87	8.96	6.83	5.658
6		4.26	8.87	7.17	6.15	5.233
7			8.87	6.55	5.91	4.841
8			3.33	6.55	5.90	4.478
9				6.56	5.91	4.463
10				6.55	5.90	4.463
11				2.46	5.91	4.463
12					5.90	4.463
13					5.91	4.463
14					5.90	4.463
15					5.91	4.462
16					2.21	4.463
17						4.462
18						4.463
19						4.462
20						4.463
21						1.673

▼ TABLE 4

General Depreciation System—MACRS
Personal Property Placed in Service after 12/31/86
Applicable Convention: Mid-quarter (Property Placed in Service in Third Quarter)
Applicable Depreciation Method: 200 or 150 Percent Declining Balance Switching to Straight Line

If the Recovery Year Is:	And the Recovery Period Is:					
	3-Year	5-Year	7-Year	10-Year	15-Year	20-Year
	The Depreciation Rate Is:					
1	25.00	15.00	10.71	7.50	3.75	2.813
2	50.00	34.00	25.51	18.50	9.63	7.289
3	16.67	20.40	18.22	14.80	8.66	6.742
4	8.33	12.24	13.02	11.84	7.80	6.237
5		11.30	9.30	9.47	7.02	5.769
6		7.06	8.85	7.58	6.31	5.336
7			8.86	6.55	5.90	4.936
8			5.53	6.55	5.90	4.566
9				6.56	5.91	4.460
10				6.55	5.90	4.460
11				4.10	5.91	4.460
12					5.90	4.460
13					5.91	4.461
14					5.90	4.460
15					5.91	4.461
16					3.69	4.460
17						4.461
18						4.460
19						4.461
20						4.460
21						2.788

▼ TABLE 5

General Depreciation System—MACRS
Personal Property Placed in Service after 12/31/86
Applicable Convention: Mid-quarter (Property Placed in Service in Fourth Quarter)
Applicable Depreciation Method: 200 or 150 Percent Declining Balance Switching to Straight Line

If the Recovery Year Is:	And the Recovery Period Is:					
	3-Year	5-Year	7-Year	10-Year	15-Year	20-Year
	The Depreciation Rate Is:					
1	8.33	5.00	3.57	2.50	1.25	0.938
2	61.11	38.00	27.55	19.50	9.88	7.430
3	20.37	22.80	19.68	15.60	8.89	6.872
4	10.19	13.68	14.06	12.48	8.00	6.357
5		10.94	10.04	9.98	7.20	5.880
6		9.58	8.73	7.99	6.48	5.439
7			8.73	6.55	5.90	5.031
8			7.64	6.55	5.90	4.654
9				6.56	5.90	4.458
10				6.55	5.90	4.458
11				5.74	5.90	4.458
12					5.91	4.458
13					5.90	4.458
14					5.91	4.458
15					5.90	4.458
16					5.17	4.458
17						4.458
18						4.459
19						4.458
20						4.459
21						3.901

▼ TABLE 6

Luxury Automobile Limitations

Year Automobile is Placed in Service[a]:							
	2006	2005	2004[b]	2004[c]	2003[d]	2003[e], 2002[e], and 2001[e]	2003[f], 2002[f], 2001[f,g], and 2000[g]
Year 1	2,960	2,960	10,610	2,960	10,710	7,660	3,060
Year 2	4,800	4,700	4,800	4,800	4,900	4,900	4,900
Year 3	2,850	2,850	2,850	2,850	2,950	2,950	2,950
Year 4 and Each Succeeding Year	1,775	1,675	1,675	1,675	1,775	1,775	1,775

[a]For years prior to 2000, see Revenue Procedure for appropriate year.
[b]Luxury automobiles placed in service in 2004 and 50% or 30% bonus depreciation elected.
[c]Luxury automobiles placed in service in 2004 and bonus depreciation not elected.
[d]Luxury automobiles placed in service after May 5, 2003, and 50% bonus depreciation is elected.
[e]Luxury automobiles placed in service before May 6, 2003, and after September 10, 2001, and 30% bonus depreciation is elected.
[f]Luxury automobiles placed in service after September 10, 2001, and bonus depreciation not elected.
[g]Luxury automobiles placed in service prior to September 11, 2001.

▼ TABLE 6 (continued)
Trucks and Vans Limitations

	Year Truck or Van is Placed in Service:				
	2006 & 2005	2004[a]	2004[b]	2003[c]	2003[d]
Year 1	3,260	10,910	3,260	11,010	3,360
Year 2	5,200	5,300	5,300	5,400	5,400
Year 3	3,150	3,150	3,150	3,250	3,250
Year 4 and Succeeding Years	1,875	1,875	1,875	1,975	1,975

[a]For trucks and vans placed in service in 2004 and bonus depreciation is elected.
[b]For trucks and vans placed in service in 2004 and bonus depreciation not elected.
[c]For trucks and vans placed in service in 2003 and bonus depreciation is elected.
[d]For trucks and vans placed in service in 2003 and bonus depreciation not elected.

▼ TABLE 7
General Depreciation System—MACRS
Residential Rental Real Property Placed in Service after 12/31/86
Applicable Recovery Period: 27.5 Years
Applicable Convention: Mid-month
Applicable Depreciation Method: Straight Line

If the Recovery Year Is:	And the Month in the First Recovery Year the Property Is Placed in Service Is:											
	1	2	3	4	5	6	7	8	9	10	11	12
	The Depreciation Rate Is:											
1	3.485	3.182	2.879	2.576	2.273	1.970	1.667	1.364	1.061	0.758	0.455	0.152
2	3.636	3.636	3.636	3.636	3.636	3.636	3.636	3.636	3.636	3.636	3.636	3.636
3	3.636	3.636	3.636	3.636	3.636	3.636	3.636	3.636	3.636	3.636	3.636	3.636
4	3.636	3.636	3.636	3.636	3.636	3.636	3.636	3.636	3.636	3.636	3.636	3.636
5	3.636	3.636	3.636	3.636	3.636	3.636	3.636	3.636	3.636	3.636	3.636	3.636
6	3.636	3.636	3.636	3.636	3.636	3.636	3.636	3.636	3.636	3.636	3.636	3.636
7	3.636	3.636	3.636	3.636	3.636	3.636	3.636	3.636	3.636	3.636	3.636	3.636
8	3.636	3.636	3.636	3.636	3.636	3.636	3.636	3.636	3.636	3.636	3.636	3.636
9	3.636	3.636	3.636	3.636	3.636	3.636	3.636	3.636	3.636	3.636	3.636	3.636
10	3.637	3.637	3.637	3.637	3.637	3.637	3.636	3.636	3.636	3.636	3.636	3.636
11	3.636	3.636	3.636	3.636	3.636	3.636	3.637	3.637	3.637	3.637	3.637	3.637
12	3.637	3.637	3.637	3.637	3.637	3.637	3.636	3.636	3.636	3.636	3.636	3.636
13	3.636	3.636	3.636	3.636	3.636	3.636	3.637	3.637	3.637	3.637	3.637	3.637
14	3.637	3.637	3.637	3.637	3.637	3.637	3.636	3.636	3.636	3.636	3.636	3.636
15	3.636	3.636	3.636	3.636	3.636	3.636	3.637	3.637	3.637	3.637	3.637	3.637
16	3.637	3.637	3.637	3.637	3.637	3.637	3.636	3.636	3.636	3.636	3.636	3.636
17	3.636	3.636	3.636	3.636	3.636	3.636	3.637	3.637	3.637	3.637	3.637	3.637
18	3.637	3.637	3.637	3.637	3.637	3.637	3.636	3.636	3.636	3.636	3.636	3.636
19	3.636	3.636	3.636	3.636	3.636	3.636	3.637	3.637	3.637	3.637	3.637	3.637
20	3.637	3.637	3.637	3.637	3.637	3.637	3.636	3.636	3.636	3.636	3.636	3.636
21	3.636	3.636	3.636	3.636	3.636	3.636	3.637	3.637	3.637	3.637	3.637	3.637
22	3.637	3.637	3.637	3.637	3.637	3.637	3.636	3.636	3.636	3.636	3.636	3.636
23	3.636	3.636	3.636	3.636	3.636	3.636	3.637	3.637	3.637	3.637	3.637	3.637
24	3.637	3.637	3.637	3.637	3.637	3.637	3.636	3.636	3.636	3.636	3.636	3.636
25	3.636	3.636	3.636	3.636	3.636	3.636	3.637	3.637	3.637	3.637	3.637	3.637
26	3.637	3.637	3.637	3.637	3.637	3.637	3.636	3.636	3.636	3.636	3.636	3.636
27	3.636	3.636	3.636	3.636	3.636	3.636	3.637	3.637	3.637	3.637	3.637	3.637
28	1.970	2.273	2.576	2.879	3.182	3.485	3.636	3.636	3.636	3.636	3.636	3.636
29	0.000	0.000	0.000	0.000	0.000	0.000	0.152	0.455	0.758	1.061	1.364	1.667

▼ TABLE 8

General Depreciation System—MACRS
Nonresidential Real Property Placed in Service after 12/31/86 and before 5/13/93
Applicable Recovery Period: 31.5 Years
Applicable Convention: Mid-month
Applicable Depreciation Method: Straight Line

If the Recovery Year Is:	And the Month in the First Recovery Year the Property Is Placed in Service Is:											
	1	2	3	4	5	6	7	8	9	10	11	12
	The Depreciation Rate Is:											
1	3.042	2.778	2.513	2.249	1.984	1.720	1.455	1.190	0.926	0.661	0.397	0.132
2	3.175	3.175	3.175	3.175	3.175	3.175	3.175	3.175	3.175	3.175	3.175	3.175
3	3.175	3.175	3.175	3.175	3.175	3.175	3.175	3.175	3.175	3.175	3.175	3.175
4	3.175	3.175	3.175	3.175	3.175	3.175	3.175	3.175	3.175	3.175	3.175	3.175
5	3.175	3.175	3.175	3.175	3.175	3.175	3.175	3.175	3.175	3.175	3.175	3.175
6	3.175	3.175	3.175	3.175	3.175	3.175	3.175	3.175	3.175	3.175	3.175	3.175
7	3.175	3.175	3.175	3.175	3.175	3.175	3.175	3.175	3.175	3.175	3.175	3.175
8	3.175	3.174	3.175	3.174	3.175	3.174	3.175	3.175	3.175	3.175	3.175	3.175
9	3.174	3.175	3.174	3.175	3.174	3.175	3.174	3.175	3.174	3.175	3.174	3.175
10	3.175	3.174	3.175	3.174	3.175	3.174	3.175	3.174	3.175	3.174	3.175	3.174
11	3.174	3.175	3.174	3.175	3.174	3.175	3.174	3.175	3.174	3.175	3.174	3.175
12	3.175	3.174	3.175	3.174	3.175	3.174	3.175	3.174	3.175	3.174	3.175	3.174
13	3.174	3.175	3.174	3.175	3.174	3.175	3.174	3.175	3.174	3.175	3.174	3.175
14	3.175	3.174	3.175	3.174	3.175	3.174	3.175	3.174	3.175	3.174	3.175	3.174
15	3.174	3.175	3.174	3.175	3.174	3.175	3.174	3.175	3.174	3.175	3.174	3.175
16	3.175	3.174	3.175	3.174	3.175	3.174	3.175	3.174	3.175	3.174	3.175	3.174
17	3.174	3.175	3.174	3.175	3.174	3.175	3.174	3.175	3.174	3.175	3.174	3.175
18	3.175	3.174	3.175	3.174	3.175	3.174	3.175	3.174	3.175	3.174	3.175	3.174
19	3.174	3.175	3.174	3.175	3.174	3.175	3.174	3.175	3.174	3.175	3.174	3.175
20	3.175	3.174	3.175	3.174	3.175	3.174	3.175	3.174	3.175	3.174	3.175	3.174
21	3.174	3.175	3.174	3.175	3.174	3.175	3.174	3.175	3.174	3.175	3.174	3.175
22	3.175	3.174	3.175	3.174	3.175	3.174	3.175	3.174	3.175	3.174	3.175	3.174
23	3.174	3.175	3.174	3.175	3.174	3.175	3.174	3.175	3.174	3.175	3.174	3.175
24	3.175	3.174	3.175	3.174	3.175	3.174	3.175	3.174	3.175	3.174	3.175	3.174
25	3.174	3.175	3.174	3.175	3.174	3.175	3.174	3.175	3.174	3.175	3.174	3.175
26	3.175	3.174	3.175	3.174	3.175	3.174	3.175	3.174	3.175	3.174	3.175	3.174
27	3.174	3.175	3.174	3.175	3.174	3.175	3.174	3.175	3.174	3.175	3.174	3.175
28	3.175	3.174	3.175	3.174	3.175	3.174	3.175	3.174	3.175	3.174	3.175	3.174
29	3.174	3.175	3.174	3.175	3.174	3.175	3.174	3.175	3.174	3.175	3.174	3.175
30	3.175	3.174	3.175	3.174	3.175	3.174	3.175	3.174	3.175	3.174	3.175	3.174
31	3.174	3.175	3.174	3.175	3.174	3.175	3.174	3.175	3.174	3.175	3.174	3.175
32	1.720	1.984	2.249	2.513	2.778	3.042	3.175	3.174	3.175	3.174	3.175	3.174
33	0.000	0.000	0.000	0.000	0.000	0.000	0.132	0.397	0.661	0.926	1.190	1.455

▼ TABLE 9

General Depreciation System—MACRS
Nonresidential Real Property Placed in Service after 5/12/93
Applicable Recovery Period: 39 years
Applicable Depreciation Method: Straight Line

If the Recovery Year Is:	And the Month in the First Recovery Year the Property Is Placed in Service Is:											
	1	2	3	4	5	6	7	8	9	10	11	12
	The Depreciation Rate Is:											
1	2.461	2.247	2.033	1.819	1.605	1.391	1.177	0.963	0.749	0.535	0.321	0.107
2-39	2.564	2.564	2.564	2.564	2.564	2.564	2.564	2.564	2.564	2.564	2.564	2.564
40	0.107	0.321	0.535	0.749	0.963	1.177	1.391	1.605	1.819	2.033	2.247	2.461

▼ TABLE 10

Alternative Depreciation System—MACRS (Partial Table)
Property Placed in Service after 12/31/86
Applicable Convention: Half-year
Applicable Depreciation Method: 150 Percent Declining Balance Switching to Straight Line

If the Recovery Year Is:	And the Recovery Period Is:					
	3	4	5	7	10	12
	The Depreciation Rate Is:					
1	25.00	18.75	15.00	10.71	7.50	6.25
2	37.50	30.47	25.50	19.13	13.88	11.72
3	25.00	20.31	17.85	15.03	11.79	10.25
4	12.50	20.31	16.66	12.25	10.02	8.97
5		10.16	16.66	12.25	8.74	7.85
6			8.33	12.25	8.74	7.33
7				12.25	8.74	7.33
8				6.13	8.74	7.33
9					8.74	7.33
10					8.74	7.33
11					4.37	7.32
12						7.33
13						3.66

▼ TABLE 11

Alternative Depreciation System—MACRS (Partial Table)
Property Placed in Service after 12/31/86
Applicable Convention: Half-year
Applicable Depreciation Method: Straight Line

If the Recovery Year Is:	And the Recovery Period Is:					
	3	4	5	7	10	12
	The Depreciation Rate Is:					
1	16.67	12.50	10.00	7.14	5.00	4.17
2	33.33	25.00	20.00	14.29	10.00	8.33
3	33.33	25.00	20.00	14.29	10.00	8.33
4	16.67	25.00	20.00	14.28	10.00	8.33
5		12.50	20.00	14.29	10.00	8.33
6			10.00	14.28	10.00	8.33
7				14.29	10.00	8.34
8				7.14	10.00	8.33
9					10.00	8.34
10					10.00	8.33
11					5.00	8.34
12						8.33
13						4.17

▼ TABLE 12

Alternative Depreciation System—MACRS
Real Property Placed into Service after 12/31/86
Applicable Recovery Period: 40 years
Applicable Convention: Mid-month
Applicable Depreciation Method: Straight Line

If the Recovery Year Is:	And the Month in the First Recovery Year the Property Is Placed in Service Is:											
	1	2	3	4	5	6	7	8	9	10	11	12
	The Depreciation Rate Is:											
1	2.396	2.188	1.979	1.771	1.563	1.354	1.146	0.938	0.729	0.521	0.313	0.104
2 to 40	2.500	2.500	2.500	2.500	2.500	2.500	2.500	2.500	2.500	2.500	2.500	2.500
41	0.104	0.312	0.521	0.729	0.937	1.146	1.354	1.562	1.771	1.979	2.187	2.396

▼ TABLE 13

**Lease Inclusion Dollar Amounts for Automobiles
(Other Than for Trucks, Vans, or Electronic Automobiles)
With a Lease Term Beginning in Calendar Year 2005[a]**

Fair Market Value of Passenger Automobile		Tax Year During Lease				
Over	Not Over	1st	2nd	3rd	4th	5th and Later
$15,200	15,500	3	6	9	11	13
15,500	15,800	4	9	13	17	19
15,800	16,100	5	12	18	22	26
16,100	16,400	7	15	22	27	32
16,400	16,700	8	18	27	32	39
16,700	17,000	9	21	32	38	44
17,000	17,500	11	25	38	45	52
17,500	18,000	14	30	45	54	63
18,000	18,500	16	35	52	63	73
18,500	19,000	18	40	60	72	83
19,000	19,500	20	46	67	80	94
19,500	20,000	23	50	75	90	104
20,000	20,500	25	55	82	99	115
20,500	21,000	27	61	89	108	125
21,000	21,500	30	65	97	117	135
21,500	22,000	32	70	105	125	225
22,000	23,000	35	78	116	139	161
23,000	24,000	40	88	131	156	182
24,000	25,000	44	98	146	175	202
25,000	26,000	49	108	161	192	223
26,000	27,000	54	118	175	211	244
27,000	28,000	58	128	191	228	265
28,000	29,000	63	138	205	247	285
29,000	30,000	67	149	220	264	306
30,000	31,000	72	159	234	283	326
31,000	32,000	77	168	250	300	348
32,000	33,000	81	179	265	318	367
33,000	34,000	86	189	279	336	389
34,000	35,000	90	199	295	354	409
35,000	36,000	95	209	309	372	430
36,000	37,000	99	219	325	389	451
37,000	38,000	104	229	339	408	471
38,000	39,000	109	239	354	426	491
39,000	40,000	113	249	370	443	512
40,000	41,000	118	259	384	462	533
41,000	42,000	122	269	400	479	554
42,000	43,000	127	279	414	497	575
43,000	44,000	132	289	429	515	595
44,000	45,000	136	299	444	533	616
45,000	46,000	141	309	459	551	636
46,000	47,000	145	320	473	569	657
47,000	48,000	150	329	489	587	678
48,000	49,000	154	340	504	604	699
49,000	50,000	159	350	518	623	719
50,000	51,000	164	360	533	640	740
51,000	52,000	168	370	548	659	760
52,000	53,000	173	380	563	676	781
53,000	54,000	177	390	578	694	802

[a]Per *Rev. Proc.* 2005-13. The table for 2006 had not been released at the date of the printing.

▼ **TABLE 13ᵃ (continued)**

Fair Market Value of Passenger Automobile		Tax Year During Lease				
Over	Not Over	1st	2nd	3rd	4th	5th and Later
54,000	55,000	182	400	593	712	823
55,000	56,000	186	410	609	729	844
56,000	57,000	191	420	623	748	864
57,000	58,000	196	430	638	766	884
58,000	59,000	200	440	653	784	905
59,000	60,000	205	450	668	802	925
60,000	62,000	212	465	691	828	957
62,000	64,000	221	485	721	864	998
64,000	66,000	230	506	750	900	1,039
66,000	68,000	239	526	780	935	1,081
68,000	70,000	248	546	810	971	1,123
70,000	72,000	258	566	839	1,008	1,163
72,000	74,000	267	586	869	1,044	1,204
74,000	76,000	276	606	899	1,079	1,247
76,000	78,000	285	626	930	1,114	1,288
78,000	80,000	294	646	960	1,150	1,329
80,000	85,000	310	682	1,011	1,213	1,402
85,000	90,000	333	732	1,086	1,303	1,504
90,000	95,000	356	782	1,161	1,392	1,608
95,000	100,000	379	832	1,236	1,481	1,712
100,000	110,000	413	908	1,347	1,616	1,867
110,000	120,000	459	1,009	1,496	1,795	2,073
120,000	130,000	505	1,109	1,646	1,974	2,280
130,000	140,000	551	1,210	1,795	2,153	2,486
140,000	150,000	597	1,310	1,945	2,332	2,693
150,000	160,000	642	1,411	2,094	2,511	2,900
160,000	170,000	688	1,512	2,243	2,690	3,106
170,000	180,000	734	1,612	2,392	2,870	3,313
180,000	190,000	780	1,713	2,541	3,048	3,520
190,000	200,000	826	1,813	2,691	3,227	3,727
200,000	210,000	871	1,914	2,840	3,407	3,933
210,000	220,000	917	2,015	2,989	3,585	4,141
220,000	230,000	963	2,115	3,139	3,764	4,347
230,000	240,000	1,009	2,216	3,288	3,943	4,554
240,000	and up	1,055	2,316	3,437	4,123	4,760

ᵃPer *Rev. Proc.* 2005-13. The table for 2006 had not been released at the date of the printing.

▼ TABLE 14

Lease Inclusion Dollar Amounts for Trucks and Vans
With a Lease Term Beginning in Calendar Year 2005[a]

Fair Market Value of Truck or Van		Tax Year During Lease				
Over	Not Over	1st	2nd	3rd	4th	5th and Later
$ 16,700	$17,000	3	6	8	10	11
17,000	17,500	4	10	14	17	20
17,500	18,000	7	15	21	26	30
18,000	18,500	9	20	39	35	40
18,500	19,000	11	25	37	43	51
19,000	19,500	14	30	44	52	61
19,500	20,000	16	35	51	62	71
20,000	20,500	18	40	59	71	81
20,500	21,000	20	45	67	79	92
21,000	21,500	23	50	74	88	103
21,500	22,000	25	55	81	98	113
22,000	23,000	28	63	92	111	129
23,000	24,000	33	73	107	129	149
24,000	25,000	38	83	122	147	169
25,000	26,000	42	93	137	165	190
26,000	27,000	47	103	152	183	210
27,000	28,000	51	113	167	201	231
28,000	29,000	56	123	182	218	253
29,000	30,000	60	133	197	237	272
30,000	31,000	65	143	212	254	294
31,000	32,000	70	153	227	272	314
32,000	33,000	74	163	242	290	335
33,000	34,000	79	173	257	308	355
34,000	35,000	83	184	271	326	376
35,000	36,000	88	193	287	344	397
36,000	37,000	93	203	302	361	418
37,000	38,000	97	214	316	380	438
38,000	39,000	102	223	332	397	459
39,000	40,000	106	234	346	415	480
40,000	41,000	111	244	361	433	500
41,000	42,000	115	254	376	451	521
42,000	43,000	120	264	391	469	542
43,000	44,000	125	274	406	487	562
44,000	45,000	129	284	421	505	583
45,000	46,000	134	294	436	523	603
46,000	47,000	138	304	451	541	624
47,000	48,000	143	314	466	558	645
48,000	49,000	148	324	481	576	666
49,000	50,000	152	334	496	594	687
50,000	51,000	157	344	511	612	707
51,000	52,000	161	355	525	630	728
52,000	53,000	166	364	541	648	748
53,000	54,000	170	375	555	666	769
54,000	55,000	175	385	570	684	789
55,000	56,000	180	394	586	701	811
56,000	57,000	184	405	600	720	830
57,000	58,000	189	415	615	737	852
58,000	59,000	193	425	630	755	873
59,000	60,000	198	435	645	773	893

[a]Per *Rev. Proc.* 2005-13. The table for 2006 had not been released at the date of the printing.

▼ TABLE 14ᵃ (continued)

Fair Market Value of Automobiles		Tax Year During Lease				
Over	Not Over	1st	2nd	3rd	4th	5th and Later
60,000	62,000	205	450	667	800	924
62,000	64,000	214	470	697	836	966
64,000	66,000	223	490	727	872	1,007
66,000	68,000	232	510	757	908	1,048
68,000	70,000	241	531	786	944	1,089
70,000	72,000	251	550	817	979	1,131
72,000	74,000	260	571	846	1,015	1,172
74,000	76,000	269	591	876	1,051	1,213
76,000	78,000	278	611	906	1,087	1,254
78,000	80,000	287	631	936	1,123	1,296
80,000	85,000	303	666	989	1,185	1,368
85,000	90,000	326	717	1,063	1,274	1,472
90,000	95,000	349	767	1,137	1,365	1,575
95,000	100,000	372	817	1,212	1,454	1,678
100,000	110,000	406	893	1,324	1,588	1,833
110,000	120,000	452	993	1,474	1,767	2,040
120,000	130,000	498	1,094	1,623	1,945	2,247
130,000	140,000	544	1,194	1,772	2,125	2,454
140,000	150,000	590	1,295	1,921	2,304	2,660
150,000	160,000	636	1,395	2,071	2,483	2,867
160,000	170,000	681	1,496	2,220	2,662	3,074
170,000	180,000	727	1,597	2,369	2,841	3,281
180,000	190,000	773	1,697	2,519	3,020	3,487
190,000	200,000	819	1,798	2,668	3,199	3,694
200,000	210,000	865	1,898	2,817	3,379	3,900
210,000	220,000	910	1,999	2,967	3,557	4,107
220,000	230,000	956	2,100	3,115	3,737	4,314
230,000	240,000	1,002	2,200	3,265	3,916	4,520
240,000	and up	1,048	2,301	3,414	4,094	4,728

ᵃPer *Rev. Proc.* 2005-13. The table for 2006 had not been released at the date of the printing.

GLOSSARY

Ability to pay A concept in taxation that holds that taxpayers be taxed according to their ability to pay such taxes, that is, taxpayers who have sufficient financial resources should pay the tax. This concept is an integral part of vertical equity.

Accountable plan A type of employee reimbursement plan that meets two tests, (1) substantiation, and (2) return of excess reimbursement. Under an accountable plan, reimbursements are excluded from the employee's gross income and the expenses are not deductible by the employee.

Accounting method The rules used to determine the tax year in which income and expenses are reported for tax purposes. Generally, the same accounting method must be used for tax purposes as is used for keeping books and records. The accounting treatment used for any item of income or expense and for specific items (e.g., installment sales and contracts) is included in this term.

Accounting period The period of time, usually 12 months, used by taxpayers to compute their taxable income. Taxpayers who do not keep records must use a calendar year. Taxpayers who do keep books and records may choose between a calendar year or a fiscal year. The accounting period election is made on the taxpayer's first filed return and cannot be changed

without IRS consent. The accounting period may be less than 12 months if it is the taxpayer's first or final return or if the taxpayer is changing accounting periods. Certain restrictions upon the use of a fiscal year apply to partnerships, S corporations, and personal service corporations.

Accrual method of accounting Accounting method under which income is reported and expenses are deducted when (1) all events have occurred that fix the taxpayer's right to receive the income and (2) the amount of the item can be determined with reasonable accuracy. Taxpayers with inventories to report must use this method to report sales and purchases.

Accumulated Adjustments Account (AAA) Account that must be kept by S corporations. The cumulative total of the ordinary income or loss and separately stated items for the most recent S corporation election period.

Accumulated earnings and profits The sum of the undistributed current earnings and profits balances (and deficits) from previous years reduced by any distributions that have been made out of accumulated earnings and profits.

Accumulated earnings credit Deduction that reduces the accumulated taxable income amount. It does not offset the accumulated earnings tax

on a dollar-for-dollar basis. Different rules apply for operating companies, service companies, and holding or investment companies.

Accumulated earnings tax Penalty tax on corporations other than those subject to the personal holding company tax among others. It is levied on a corporation's current year addition to its accumulated earnings balance in excess of the amount needed for reasonable business purposes and not distributed to the shareholders. This tax is intended to discourage companies from retaining excessive amounts of earnings if the funds are invested in activities that are unrelated to business needs. The tax is 15% (in 2006) of accumulated taxable income.

Accumulated taxable income The tax base for the accumulated earnings tax which is determined by taking the corporation's taxable income and increasing (decreasing) it by positive (negative) adjustments and decreasing it by the accumulated earnings credit and available dividends-paid deductions.

Accumulation distribution rules (throwback rules) Exception to the general rule that distributable net income (DNI) serves as a ceiling on the amount taxable to a beneficiary. Under the general rule, the beneficiary excludes the portion of any distribution in excess of DNI from his gross income. Accumulation distributions made by a trust are taxable to the beneficiaries in the year received.

ACE   See adjusted current earnings.

Acquiescence policy   IRS policy of announcing whether it agrees or disagrees with a court decision decided in favor of the taxpayer. Such statements are not issued for every case.

Acquisitive reorganization   A transaction in which the acquiring corporation obtains all or part of the stock or assets of a target corporation.

Additional depreciation   The excess of the actual amount of accelerated depreciation (or cost-recovery deductions under ACRS) over the amount of depreciation that would be deductible under the straight-line method. Such depreciation applies to Sec. 1250 depreciable real property acquired prior to 1987.

Adjusted current earnings (ACE)   Alternative minimum taxable income for the tax year plus or minus a series of special adjusted current earnings adjustments specified in Sec. 56(g)(4).

Adjusted gross income (AGI)   A measure of taxable income that falls between gross income and taxable income. It is the income amount that is used as the basis for calculating the floor or the ceiling for numerous other tax computations.

Adjusted grossed-up basis   For Sec. 338 purposes, the sum of (1) the basis of a purchasing corporation's stock interest in a target corporation plus (2) an adjustment for the target corporation's liabilities on the day following the acquisition date plus or minus (3) other relevant items.

Adjusted income from rents (AIR)   This amount is equal to the corporation's gross income from rents reduced by the deductions claimed for amortization or depreciation, property taxes, interest, and rent.

Adjusted ordinary gross income (AOGI)   A corporation's adjusted ordinary gross income is its ordinary gross income reduced by (1) certain expenses incurred in connection with gross income from rents, mineral, oil and gas royalties, and working interests in oil or gas wells, (2) interest received by dealers on certain U.S. obligations, (3) interest received from condemnation awards, judgments, or tax refunds, and (4) rents from certain tangible personal property manufactured or produced by the corporation.

Adjusted sales price   The amount realized from the sale of a residence less any fixing-up expenses.

Adjusted taxable gift   Taxable gifts made after 1976 that are valued at their date-of-gift value. These gifts affect the size of the transfer tax base at death.

Administrative pronouncement   Treasury Department or IRS statement that interprets provisions of the IRC. Such pronouncements may be in the form of Treasury Regulations, revenue rulings, or revenue procedures.

Affiliated group   A group consisting of a parent corporation and at least one subsidiary corporation.

Alien   Individuals who are not U.S. citizens.

Alimony   Payments made pursuant to divorce or separation or written agreement between spouses subject to conditions specified in the tax law. Alimony payments (as contrasted to property settlements) are deductible for AGI by the payor and are included in the gross income of the recipient.

All events test   Rule holding that an accrual basis taxpayer must report an item of income (1) when all events have occurred that fix the taxpayer's right to receive the item of income and (2) when the amount of the item can be determined with reasonable accuracy. This test is not satisfied until economic performance has taken place.

Alternate valuation date   The alternate valuation date is the earlier of six months after the date of death or the date the property is sold, exchanged, distributed, etc. by the estate. Unless this option is elected, the gross estate is valued at its FMV on the date of the decedent's death.

Alternative minimum tax (AMT)   Tax which applies to individuals, corporations, and estates and trusts if it exceeds the taxpayer's regular tax. Most taxpayers are not subject to this tax. This tax equals the amount by which the tentative minimum tax exceeds the regular tax.

Alternative minimum taxable income (AMTI)   The taxpayer's taxable income (1) increased by tax preference items and (2) adjusted for income, gain, deduction, and loss items that have to be recomputed under the AMT system.

Amount realized   The amount realized equals the sum of money plus the fair market value of all other property received from the sale or other disposition of the property less any selling expenses (e.g., commissions, advertising, deed preparation costs, and legal expenses) incurred in connection with the sale.

Announcement   Information release issued by the IRS to provide a technical explanation of a current tax issue. Announcements are aimed at tax practitioners rather than the general public.

Annual exclusion An exemption that is intended to relieve a donor from keeping an account of and reporting the numerous small gifts (e.g., wedding and Christmas gifts) made throughout the year. This exclusion is currently $12,000 per donee.

Annuity A series of regular payments that will continue for either a fixed period of time or until the death of the recipient. Pensions are usually paid in this way.

Appeals coordinated issue Issue over which the appeals officer must obtain a concurrence of guidance from the regional director of appeals in order to render a decision.

Applicable federal rate The rate determined monthly by the federal government which is based on the rate paid by the government on borrowed funds. The rate varies with the term of the loan. Thus, short-term loans are for a period of under three years, mid-term loans are for over three years and under nine years, and long-term loans are for over nine years.

Asset depreciation range (ADR) system of depreciation Depreciation method allowed for property placed in service before January 1, 1981. This method prescribed useful lives for various classes of assets.

Assignment of income doctrine A judicial requirement that income be taxed to the person that earns it.

At-risk basis Essentially the same amount as the regular partnership basis with the exception that liabilities increase the at-risk basis only if the partner is at-risk for such an amount.

At-risk rules These rules limit the partner's loss deductions to his at-risk basis.

Average tax rate The taxpayer's total tax liability divided by the amount of his taxable income.

Bad debt Bona fide debt that is uncollectible because it is worthless. Such debts are further characterized as "business bad debts," which give rise to an ordinary deduction, and "nonbusiness bad debts," which are treated as a short-term capital loss. A determination of whether a debt is worthless is made by reference to all the pertinent evidence (e.g., the debtor's general financial condition and whether the debt is secured by collateral). Such debts are deductible subject to certain requirements.

Bardahl formula Mathematical formula for determining the amount of working capital that a business reasonably needs for accumulated earnings tax purposes. For a manufacturing company, the formula is based on the business's operating cycle.

Bona fide debt A debt that (1) arises from a valid and enforceable obligation to pay a fixed or determinable sum of money and (2) results in a debtor-creditor relationship.

Boot Property that may not be received tax free in certain tax-free transactions (i.e., any money, debt obligations, and so on).

Bootstrap acquisition An acquisition where an investor purchases part of a corporation's stock and then has the corporation redeem the remainder of the seller's stock.

Brother-sister controlled group Under the narrow 50%–80% definition, this type of controlled group exists if (1) five or fewer individuals, estates, or trusts own at least 80% of the voting stock or 80% of the value of each corporation and (2) the shareholders have common ownership of more than 50% of the voting power or 50% of the value of all classes of stock. Under the broad 50%-only definition, the five or fewer shareholders need only to meet the 50% test.

Built-in gain A gain that accrued prior to the conversion of a C corporation to an S corporation.

Built-in gains (Sec. 1374) tax Tax on built-in gains that are recognized by the S corporation during the ten-year period beginning on the date that the S corporation election took effect.

C corporation Form of business entity that is taxed as a separate taxpaying entity. Its income is subject to an initial tax at the corporate level. Its shareholders are subject to a second tax if dividends are paid from the corporation's earnings and profits. This type of corporation is sometimes referred to as a regular corporation.

C short year That portion of an S termination year that begins on the day on which the termination is effective and continues through to the last day of the corporation's tax year.

Capital asset This category of assets includes all assets except inventory, notes and accounts receivable, and depreciable property or land used in a trade or business (e.g., property, plant, and machinery).

Capital expenditure An expenditure that adds to the value of, substantially prolongs the useful life of, or adapts the property to a new or different use qualifies as a capital expenditure.

Capital gain Gain realized on the sale or exchange of a capital asset.

Capital gain dividend A distribution by a regulated investment company (i.e., a mutual fund) of capital gains realized from the sale of investments in the fund. Such dividends also include undistributed capital gains allocated to the shareholders.

Capital gain property For charitable contribution deduction purposes, property upon which a long-term capital gain would be recognized if that property was sold at its FMV.

Capital interest An interest in the assets owned by a partnership.

Capital recovery A capital recovery amount is a deduction for depreciation or cost recovery. It is a factor in the determination of a property's adjusted basis.

Cash method of accounting Accounting method that requires the taxpayer to report income for the taxable year in which payments are actually or constructively received. Expenses are reported in the year they are paid. Most individuals and service businesses (i.e., businesses without inventories) use this method.

Cash receipts and disbursements method of accounting See Cash method of accounting.

Casualty loss Loss that arises from an identifiable event that was sudden, unexpected, or unusual (e.g., fire, storm, shipwreck, other casualty, or theft). Within certain limitations, individuals may deduct such losses from AGI. Business casualty losses are deductible for AGI.

Certiorari An appeal from a lower court (i.e., a federal court of appeals) which the U.S. Supreme Court agrees to hear. Such appeals, which are made as a writ of certiorari, are generally not granted unless (1) a constitutional issue needs to be decided or (2) a conflict among the lower court decisions that must be clarified.

Charitable remainder annuity trust This type of trust makes distributions to individuals for a certain time period or for life. The annual distributions are a uniform percentage (5% or higher) of the value of the trust property as valued on the date of transfer.

Charitable remainder unitrust This type of trust makes annual distributions for either a specified time period or for life. The distributions are a uniform percentage (5% or higher) of the value of the property as revalued annually.

Clifford trust A trust that is normally held for a ten-year period after which the principal reverts to the grantor. The trust accounting income is not generally taxed to the grantor.

Closed transaction Situation where the property in question (e.g., property distributed in a corporate liquidation) can be valued with reasonable certainty. The gain or loss reported on the transaction is determinable at the time the transaction occurs. See open transaction doctrine.

Closed-fact situation or tax compliance situation Situation or transaction that has already occurred. In such situations, the tax advisor's task is to analyze the facts to determine the appropriate tax treatment.

Closely held C corporation For purposes of the at-risk rules, a C corporation in which more than 50% of the stock is owned by five or fewer individuals at any time during the last half of the corporation's tax year.

Closely held corporation A corporation that is owned by either a single individual or a small group of individuals who may or may not be family members.

Combined controlled group A group of three or more corporations which are members of a parent-subsidiary or brother-sister controlled group. In addition, at least one of the corporations must be the parent corporation of the parent-subsidiary controlled group and a member of a brother-sister controlled group.

Common law state All states other than the community property states are common law states. In such states, all assets acquired during the marriage are the property of the acquiring spouse.

Community income In any of the eight community property states, such income consists of the income from the personal efforts, investments, etc. of either spouse. Community income belongs equally to both spouses.

Community property law Law in community property states mandating that all property acquired after marriage is generally community property unless acquired by gift or inheritance. Each spouse owns a one-half interest in community property.

Community property state The eight traditional community property states (Louisiana, Texas, New Mexico, Arizona, California, Washington, Idaho, and Nevada) and Wisconsin (which adopted a similar law). These states do not follow the common law concept of property ownership.

Compensation Payment for personal services. Salaries, wages, fees, commissions, tips, bonuses, and specialized forms of compensation such as director's fees and jury's fees fall into this category. However, certain fringe benefits and some foreign-earned income are not taxed.

Completed contract method of accounting Accounting method for long-term contracts undertaken by smaller companies. Income from the contract is reported in the taxable year in which the contract is completed. The completed contract method is limited to construction contracts undertaken by smaller companies.

Consolidated tax return A single tax return filed by a group of related corporations (i.e., affiliated group).

Consolidation A form of tax-free reorganization involving two or more corporations whose assets are acquired by a new corporation. The stock, securities, and other consideration transferred by the acquiring corporation is then distributed by each target corporation to its shareholders and security holders in exchange for their stock and securities.

Constant interest rate method Used to amortize the original issue discount ratably over the life of the bond, this method determines the amount of interest income by multiplying the interest yield to maturity by the adjusted issue price.

Constructive dividend The manner in which the IRS or the courts might recharacterize an excessive corporate payment to a shareholder to reflect the true economic benefit conferred upon the shareholder. As a result of the recharacterization, the IRS or the courts usually recast a corporate-shareholder transaction as an E&P distribution, deny the corporation an offsetting deduction, and treat all or a portion of the income recognized by the shareholder as a dividend.

Contributory pension plan A qualified pension plan to which employees make voluntary contributions.

Controlled group A controlled group is two or more separately incorporated businesses owned by a related group of individuals or entities. Such groups include parent-subsidiary groups, brother-sister groups, or combined groups.

Corporation A separate taxpaying entity (such as an association, joint stock company, or insurance company) that must file a tax return every year, even when it had no income or loss for the year.

Cost depletion method Calculation of the depletion of an asset (e.g., oil and gas properties) under which the asset's adjusted basis is divided by the estimated recoverable units to arrive at a per-unit depletion. This amount is then multiplied by the number of units sold to determine the cost depletion. This method may be alternated with the percentage depletion method as long as the calculation takes that into account.

Cost The amount paid for property in cash or the fair market value of the property given in exchange. The costs of acquiring the property and preparing it for use are included in the cost of the property.

Crummey trust Technique that allows a donor to set up a discretionary trust and obtain an annual exclusion. Such a trust arrangement allows the beneficiary to demand an annual distribution of the lesser of $11,000 or the amount transferred to the trust that year.

Current year's exclusion The amount of the annuity payment that is excluded from gross income. This

amount is determined by multiplying the exclusion ratio by the amount received during the year.

Customs duties A federal excise tax on imported goods.

DIF See Discriminant Function Program.

Deductions for AGI Expenses one would see on an income statement prepared for financial accounting purposes, for example, compensation paid to employees, repairs to business property, and depreciation expenses. Certain nonbusiness deductions (e.g., alimony payments, moving expenses, and deductible payments to an individual retirement account (IRA)) are also deductible for AGI.

Deductions from AGI Generally, deductions are allowed for certain personal expenses such as medical deductions and charitable contributions which are referred to as itemized deductions. Alternatively, individuals may deduct the standard deduction. Personal and dependency deductions are also deductions from AGI.

Deficiency dividend This type of dividend substitutes an income tax levy on the dividend payment at the shareholder level for the payment of the personal holding company tax.

Defined contribution pension plan Qualified pension plan under which a separate account is maintained for each participant and fixed amounts are contributed based upon a specific percentage-of-compensation formula. The retirement benefits are based on the value of the participant's account at the time of retirement. Defined contribution plans for self-employed individuals are referred to as *H.R. 10 plans*.

Discriminant Function Program Program used by the IRS to select individual returns for audit. This system is intended to identify those tax returns that are most likely to contain errors.

Dissolution A legal term implying that a corporation has surrendered the charter that it originally received from the state.

Distributable net income (DNI) Maximum amount of distributions taxed to the beneficiaries and deducted by a trust or estate.

Distributive share The portion of partnership taxable and nontaxable income, losses, credits, and so on that the partner must report for tax purposes.

Dividend A distribution of property made by a corporation out of its earnings and profits.

Dividends-paid deduction Distributions made out of a corporation's earnings and profits are eligible for this deduction for personal holding company tax and accumulated earnings tax purposes. The deduction is equal to the amount of money plus the adjusted basis of the nonmoney property distributed.

Dividends-received deduction This deduction attempts to mitigate the triple taxation that would occur if one corporation paid dividends to a corporate shareholder who, in turn, distributed such amounts to its individual shareholders. Certain restrictions and limitations apply to this deduction.

Divisive reorganization Transaction in which part of a transferor corporation's assets are transferred to a second, newly created corporation that is controlled by either the transferee or its shareholders.

E&P See Earnings and profits.

Earnings and profits A measure of the corporation's ability to pay a dividend from its current and accumulated earnings without an impairment of capital.

Economic performance test Economic performance occurs when the property or services to be provided are actually delivered.

Effective tax rate The taxpayer's total tax liability divided by his total economic income.

Employee achievement award Award given under circumstances that does not create a likelihood that it is really disguised compensation. It must be in the form of tangible personal property (other than cash) and be valued at no more than $400.

Employee stock ownership plan (ESOP) A qualified stock bonus plan or combined stock bonus plan and money purchase pension plan. ESOP's are funded by contributions of the employer's stock which are held for the employees' benefit.

Employment taxes Social security (FICA) and federal and state unemployment compensation taxes.

Entertainment expense Entertainment expenses (e.g., business meals) that are either directly related to or associated with the active conduct of a trade or business are deductible within certain limitations and restrictions. Directly related expenses are those that (1) derive a business benefit other than goodwill and (2) are incurred in a clear business setting. Expenses that are associated with the business are those that show a clear business purpose (e.g., obtaining new business) and occur on the same day the business is discussed.

Estate A legal entity which comes into being only upon the death of the person whose assets are being

administered. The estate continues in existence until the duties of the executor have been completed.

Estate tax Part of the federal unified transfer tax system, this tax is based upon the total property transfers an individual makes during his lifetime and at death.

Excess depreciation See Additional depreciation.

Excess net passive income An amount equal to the S corporation's net passive income multiplied by the fraction consisting of its passive investment income less 25% of its gross receipts divided by its passive investment income. It is limited to the corporation's taxable income.

Excess net passive income (Sec. 1375) tax Tax levied when (1) an S corporation has passive investment income for the taxable year that exceeds 25% of its gross receipts and (2) at the close of the tax year the S corporation has earnings and profits from C corporation tax years.

Exclusion Any item of income that the tax law says is not taxable.

Exclusion ratio The portion of the annuity payment that is excluded from taxation. This amount equals the investment in the contract (its cost) divided by the expected return from the annuity.

Exemption equivalent That portion of the tax base that is completely free of transfer taxes as a result of the unified credit.

Expected return The amount which a taxpayer can expect to receive from an annuity. It is determined by multiplying the amount of the annuity's annual payment by the expected return multiple.

Expected return multiple The number of years that the annuity is expected to continue. This amount may be a stated term or for the remainder of the taxpayer's life.

FICA Tax withheld through the payment of payroll taxes, FICA is intended to finance social security benefits for individuals who are not self-employed. Employees and employers contribute matching amounts until a federally-set annual earnings ceiling is reached. At that time, no further contributions need be made for that year. No ceiling exists for the hospital insurance (HI) portion of the tax. Self-employed individuals are subject to self-employment tax and currently receive a *for* AGI income tax deduction equal to 50% of their self-employment tax payments.

FIFO method of inventory valuation This flow of cost method assumes that the first goods purchased will be the first goods sold. Thus, the ending inventory consists of the last goods purchased.

Failure-to-pay penalty Penalty imposed at the rate of 0.5% per month (or fraction thereof) on the amount of tax shown on the return less any tax payments made before the beginning of the month for which the penalty is being calculated. The maximum penalty is 25%.

Fair market value (FMV) The amount that would be realized from the sale of a property at a price that is agreeable to both the buyer and the seller when neither party is obligated to participate in the transaction.

Federal estate tax See estate tax.

Fiduciary A person or other entity (e.g., a guardian, executor, trustee, or administrator) who holds and manages property for someone else.

Fiduciary accounting income The excess of accounting income over expenses for a fiduciary (i.e., an estate or trust). Excluded are any items credited to or charged against capital.

Fiduciary taxation The special tax rules that apply to fiduciaries (e.g., trusts and estates).

Field audit procedure Audit procedure generally used by the IRS for corporations or individuals engaged in a trade or business and conducted at either the taxpayer's place of business or his tax advisor's office. Generally, several items on the tax return are examined.

Fiscal year An annual accounting period that ends on the last day of any month other than December. A fiscal year may be elected by taxpayers that keep books and records, such as businesses.

Fixing-up expenses Expenses incurred to assist in the sale of a residence (e.g., normal repairs and painting costs). Capital expenditures do not qualify as fixing-up expenses.

Flat tax See Proportional tax.

Foreign corporation A corporation that is incorporated under the laws of a country other than the United States.

Foreign tax credit Tax credit given to mitigate the possibility of double taxation faced by U.S. citizens, residents, and corporations earning foreign income.

Foreign-earned income An individual's earnings from personal services rendered in a foreign country.

Former passive activity An activity that was formerly considered passive, but which is not considered to be passive with respect to the taxpayer for the current year.

Forum shopping The ability to consider differing precedents in choosing the forum for litigation.

Franchise tax State tax levy sometimes based upon a weighted average formula consisting of net worth, income, and sales.

Functional-use test A test used to determine whether property is considered similar or related in service or use for purposes of involuntary conversions of property under Sec. 1033. The functional-use test requires that the replacement property be functionally the same as the converted property.

Future interest Such interests include reversions, remainders, and other interests that may not be used, owned, or enjoyed until some future date.

General business credit Special credit category consisting of tax credits commonly available to businesses. The more significant credit items are (1) the investment tax credit, (2) the targeted jobs credit, (3) the research credit, (4) the low-income housing credit, (5) the empowerment zone employment credit, (6) the disabled access credit.

General partnership A partnership with two or more partners where no partner is a limited partner.

General power of appointment Power of appointment under which the holder can appoint the property to himself, his estate, his creditors, or the creditors of his estate. Such power may be exercisable during the decedent's life, by his will, or both.

Generally accepted accounting principles (GAAP) The accounting principles that govern the preparation of financial reports to shareholders. GAAP does not apply to the tax treatment unless the method clearly reflects income. It is used only when the regulations do not specify the treatment of an item or when the regulations provide more than one alternative accounting method.

Generation-skipping transfer A disposition that (1) provides interests for more than one generation of beneficiaries who are in a younger generation than the transferor or (2) provides an interest solely for a person two or more generations younger than the transferor.

Gift tax A wealth transfer tax that applies if the property transfer occurs during a person's lifetime.

Grantor trust Trust governed by Secs. 671 through 679. The income from such trusts is taxed to the grantor even if some or all of the income has been distributed.

Grantor The transferor who creates a trust.

Gross estate The gross estate includes items to which the decedent held title at death as well as certain incomplete transfers made by the decedent prior to death.

Gross income All income received in cash, property, or services, from whatever source derived and from which the taxpayer derives a direct economic benefit.

Gross tax For income tax purposes, the amount determined by multiplying taxable income by the appropriate tax rate(s). The gross tax may also be found in the appropriate tax table for the taxpayer's filing status.

Guaranteed minimum Minimum amount of payment guaranteed to a partner. This amount is important if the partner's distributive share is less than his guaranteed minimum. See also Guaranteed payment.

Guaranteed payment Minimum amount of payment guaranteed to a partner in the form of a salary-like payment made for services provided to the partnership and interest-like payments for the use of invested capital. Guaranteed payments, which may be in the form of a guaranteed minimum amount or a set amount, are taxed as ordinary income. See also Guaranteed minimum.

H.R. 10 Plan Special retirement plan rules applicable to self-employed individuals. Such plans are often referred to as "Keogh plans."

Hedge agreement This is an obligation on the part of a shareholder-employee to repay to the corporation any portion of salary that is disallowed by the IRS as a deduction. It is also used in connection with other corporate payments to shareholder-employees (e.g., travel and entertainment expenses).

Horizontal equity A concept in taxation that refers to the notion that similarly-situated taxpayers should be treated equally under the tax law.

Hybrid method of accounting Accounting method that combines the cash and accrual methods. Under this method, taxpayers can report sales and purchases under the accrual method and other income and expense items under the cash method. See also the cash method of accounting and the accrual method of accounting.

IRS See Internal Revenue Service.

Income The economic concept of income measures the amount an individual can consume during a period and remain as well off at the end of the period as at the beginning. The accounting concept of income is a measure of the income

that is realized in a transaction. The tax concept of income is close to the accounting concept. It includes both taxable and nontaxable income from any source. However, it does not include a return of capital.

Income beneficiary Entity or individual that receives the income from a trust.

Income in respect of a decedent (IRD) Amount to which the decedent was entitled as gross income but which was not properly includible in computing his taxable income for the tax year ending with his date of death or for a previous tax year under the method of accounting employed by the decedent.

Incremental A concept in taxation that described how the tax law has been changed or modified over the years. Under incrementalism, the tax law is changed on an incremental basis rather than a complete revision basis.

Indeterminate market value If the market value of the property in question cannot be determined by the usual methods, the "open transaction" doctrine may be applied and the tax consequences may be deferred until the transaction is closed. Alternatively, the property may be valued by using the fair market value of the property that is given in the exchange (e.g., the value of the services rendered).

Information release An administrative pronouncement concerning an issue the IRS thinks the general public will be interested in. Such releases are issued in lay terms.

Innocent spouse provision This provision exempts a spouse from penalty and liability for tax if such spouse had no knowledge of nor reason to know about an item of taxable income that is in dispute.

Innocent spouse rule Rule that exempts a spouse from penalty or from liability for the tax if such spouse had no knowledge of nor reason to know about an item of community income.

Installment sale Any disposition of property which involves receiving at least one payment after the close of the taxable year in which the sale occurs.

Installment sale method of accounting Taxpayers may use this method of accounting to reduce the tax burden from gains on the sale of property paid for in installments. Under this method, payment of the tax is deferred until the sale proceeds are collected. This method is not applicable to sales of publicly traded property or to losses.

Intangible drilling and development costs (IDCs) Expenditures made by an operator for wages, fuel, repairs, hauling supplies, and so forth, incident to and necessary for the preparation and drilling of oil and gas wells.

Inter vivos trust Transfer to a trust that is made during the grantor's lifetime.

Interest The cost charged by a lender for the use of money. For example, finance charges, loan discounts, premiums, loan origination fees, and points paid by a buyer to obtain a mortgage loan are all interest expenses. The deductibility of the expense depends upon the purpose for which the indebtedness was incurred.

Interpretative regulations Treasury Regulations that serve to interpret the provisions of the Internal Revenue Code.

Investment expenses All deductions other than interest that are directly connected with the production of investment income.

Investment interest Interest expense on indebtedness incurred to purchase or carry property held for investment (e.g., income from interest, dividends, annuities, and royalties). Interest expenses incurred from passive activities are not subject to the investment interest limitations and interest incurred to purchase or carry tax-exempt securities is not deductible. Interest incurred from passive activities is subject to the passive activity loss limitation rules.

Involuntary conversion Such a conversion occurs when property is compulsorily converted into money or other property due to theft, seizure, requisition, condemnation, or partial or complete destruction. For example, an involuntary conversion occurs when the government exercises its right of eminent domain.

Irrevocable trust Trust under which the grantor cannot require the trustee to return the trust's assets.

Itemized deductions Also known as "deductions from AGI," these personal expenditures are allowable for such items as medical expenses, state and local taxes, charitable contributions, unreimbursed employee business expenses, interest on a personal residence, and casualty and theft losses. There are specific requirements for and limitations on the deductibility of each of these items. In addition, only those taxpayers whose total itemized deductions exceed the standard deduction amount can itemize their deductions. In general, the total itemized deductions for an individual is reduced in 2006 by 3% of AGI in excess of $150,500 ($72,250 for married individuals filing a separate return).

Joint income Income from jointly-held property.

Joint tenancy A popular form of property ownership that serves as a substitute for a will. Each joint tenant is deemed to have an equal interest in the property.

Judicial decisions Decision rendered by a court deciding the case that is presented to it by a plaintiff and defendant. These decisions are important sources of the tax law and can come from trial courts and appellate courts.

Keogh plan Retirement plan for self-employed individuals. This type of plan is also known as an "H.R. 10 plan."

LIFO method of inventory valuation This method assumes a last-in, first out flow of cost. It results in the lowest taxable income during periods of inflation because it shows the lowest inventory value. Price indexes are used for the valuation. The information in these indexes is grouped into groups (pools) of similar items. See also Simplified LIFO method.

LIFO recapture tax A tax imposed on a C corporation that uses the LIFO inventory method and which elects S corporation treatment. The tax is imposed in the final C corporation tax year and paid over a four-year period.

Legislative reenactment doctrine Rule holding that Congress's failure to change the wording in the Code over an extended period signifies that Congress has approved the treatment provided in the regulations.

Letter ruling Letter rulings originate from the IRS at the taxpayer's request. They describe how the IRS will treat a proposed transaction. It is only binding on the person requesting the ruling providing the taxpayer completes the transaction as proposed in the ruling. Those of general interest are published as Revenue Rulings.

Life estate A property transfer in trust that results in the transferor reserving the right to income for life. Another individual is named to receive the property upon the transferor's death.

Like class Classes of assets defined by the Regulations that are considered to be property of a like kind for purposes of Sec. 1031. Like class property is tangible personal property that is in the same General Asset Class or the Same Product Class as other property.

Like-kind exchange A direct exchange of like-kind property. The transferred property and the received property must be held for productive use either (1) in a trade or business or (2) as an investment. Nonrecognition of gain or loss is mandatory. Certain like-kind exchanges between related parties are restricted if either party disposes of the property within two years of the exchange.

Limited liability company (LLC) A business entity that combines the legal and tax benefits of partnerships and S corporations. These entities are treated as partnerships for federal tax purposes unless they elect to be taxed as a corporation under the check-the-box regulations.

Limited liability partnership (LLP) Similar to a limited liability company, but formed under a separate state statute that generally applies to service companies.

Limited partnership A partnership where one or more of the partners is designated as a limited partner.

Liquidating distribution A distribution that (1) liquidates a partner's entire partnership interest due to retirement, death, or other business reason or (2) partially or totally liquidates a shareholder's stock interest in a corporation following the adoption of a plan at liquidation.

Long-term capital gain (LTCG) Gain realized on the sale or exchange of a capital asset held longer than one year.

Long-term contracts Building, manufacturing, installation, and construction contracts that are not completed in the same taxable year in which they are entered into. Service contracts do not qualify as long-term contracts. See also Completed contract method of accounting.

Look-back interest Interest that is assessed on any additional tax that would have been paid if the actual total cost of the contract was used to calculate the tax rather than the estimated cost. Thus, it is applicable to any contract or portion of a contract that is accounted for under either the hybrid or percentage of completion method of accounting.

Loss corporation A corporation entitled to use a net operating loss carryover or having a net operating loss for the taxable year in which an ownership change occurs.

Majority partners The one or more partners in a partnership who have an aggregate interest in partnership profits and capital exceeding 50%.

Mandatory basis adjustment Required basis adjustment if the partnership has a substantial built-in loss at the time a partner sells his or her partnership interest or if the partnership has a decreasing basis adjustment at the time of a liquidating distribution.

Marginal tax rate The tax that is applied to an incremental amount of taxable income that is added to the tax base. This rate can be used to measure the tax effect of a proposed transaction. Currently, the highest marginal tax rate for individuals is 35%.

Marital deduction Deduction allowed for tax-free inter-spousal transfers other than those for gifts of certain terminable interests.

Market value This term refers to replacement cost under the lower of cost or market inventory method. That is, it is the price at which the taxpayer can replace the goods in question. See also Fair market value.

Material participation The level of participation by a taxpayer in an activity that determines whether the activity is either passibe or active. If a taxpayer does not meet the material participation requirements, the activity is treated as a passive activity.

Medical expense deduction Unreimbursed medical expenses incurred for medical procedures or treatments that are (1) legal in the locality in which they are performed and (2) incurred for the purpose of alleviating a physical or mental defect or illness that affects the body's structure or function, are deductible from AGI. Out-of-pocket travel costs incurred while en route to a medical facility, certain capital expenditures affecting the sick person, premiums for medical insurance, and in-patient hospital care are also deductible. Certain restrictions and limitations apply to this deduction.

Memorandum decision Decision issued by the Tax Court. They deal with factual variations on matters which were decided in earlier cases.

Merger A tax-free reorganization one form of which has the acquiring corporation transfer its stock, securities, and other consideration to the target corporation in exchange for its assets and liabilities. The target corporation then distributes the consideration that it receives to its shareholders and security holders in exchange for their stock and securities.

Minimum tax credit (MTC) A tax credit allowed for the amount of alternative minimum tax that arose because of deferral and permanent adjustments and preference items. This credit may be carried over and used to offset regular tax liabilities in subsequent years.

Miscellaneous itemized deductions Certain unreimbursed employee expenses (e.g., required uniforms, travel, entertainment, and so on) fall into this category. Miscellaneous itemized deductions also include certain investment expenses, appraisal fees for charitable contributions and fees for tax return preparation. The nature of the deduction depends on whether the taxpayer is an employee or a self-employed individual.

Modified percentage of completion method A variation of the regular percentage of completion method where an election may be made to defer reporting profit from a long-term contract until at least 10% of the estimated total cost has been incurred.

Necessary expense Expense that is deductible because it is appropriate and helpful in the taxpayer's business. Such expenses must also qualify as ordinary.

Negligence The IRC defines negligence as (1) any failure to reasonably attempt to comply with the IRC and (2) "careless, reckless, or intentional disregard" of the rules and regulations.

Negligence penalty Penalty assessed if the IRS finds that the taxpayer has filed an incorrect return because of negligence. Generally this penalty is 20% of the underpayment attributable to negligence.

Net gift A gift upon which the donee pays the gift tax as a condition to receiving the gift.

Net investment income The excess of the taxpayer's investment income over his investment expenses. See also Investment income.

Net operating loss (NOL) A net operating loss occurs when business expenses exceed business income for any taxable year. Such losses may be carried back 2 years or carried forward 20 years to a year in which the taxpayer has taxable income. The loss is carried back first and must be deducted from years in chronological order unless a special election is made to forgo the carryback.

New loss corporation Any corporation permitted to use a net operating loss carryover after an ownership change occurs.

Ninety (90)-day letter Officially called a Statutory Notice of Deficiency, this letter is sent when (1) the taxpayer does not file a protest letter within 30 days of receipt of the 30-day letter or (2) the taxpayer has met with an appeals officer but no agreement was reached. The letter notifies the taxpayer of the amount of the deficiency, how that amount was determined, and that a deficiency will be assessed if a petition is not filed with the Tax Court within 90 days. The taxpayer is also advised of the alternatives available to him.

Nonaccountable plan A type of employee reimbursement plan that does not meet either of the two tests for an accountable plan (see accountable plan). Under a nonaccountable plan, reimbursements are included in the employee's gross income and the expenses are deductible by the employee, subject to the 2% of AGI floor.

Nonqualified deferred compensation plan Type of plan used by employer to provide incentives or supplementary retirement benefits for executives. Such plans are not subject to the nondiscrimination and vesting rules.

Nonqualified stock option Stock option that does not meet the requirements for an incentive stock option.

Nonrecourse loan Loan for which the borrower has no liability.

Notice An interpretation by the IRS that provides guidance concerning how to interpret a statute, perhaps one recently enacted.

Office audit procedure IRS audit of a specific item on an individual's tax return. An office audit takes place at the IRS branch office.

Old loss corporation Any corporation that is allowed to use a net operating loss carryover, or which has a net operating loss for the tax year in which an ownership change occurs, and which undergoes the requisite stock ownership change.

Open transaction doctrine Valuation technique for property that can only be valued on the basis of uncertain future payments. This doctrine determines the shareholder's gain or loss when the asset is sold, collected, or able to be valued. Assets that cannot be valued are assigned a value of zero.

Open-fact or tax-planning situation Situation or transaction in which the facts have not yet occurred. In such situations, the tax advisor's task is to plan for the facts or shape them so as to produce a favorable tax result.

Optional basis adjustment An elective technique that adjusts the basis for the underlying partnership assets up or down as a result of (1) distributions from the partnership to its partners, (2) sales of partnership interests by existing partners, or (3) transfers of the interest following the death of a partner.

Ordinary expense An expense that is deductible because it is reasonable in amount and bears a reasonable and proximate relationship to the income-producing activity or property.

Ordinary gross income (OGI) A corporation's ordinary gross income is its gross income reduced by (1) capital gains and (2) Sec. 1231 gains.

Ordinary income property For charitable contribution deduction purposes, any property that would result in the recognition of ordinary income if it was sold. Such property includes inventory, works of art or manuscripts created by the taxpayer, capital assets that have been held for one year or less, and Sec. 1231 property that results in ordinary income due to depreciation recapture.

Parent-subsidiary controlled group To qualify as such, a common parent must own at least 80% of the voting stock or at least 80% of the value of at least one subsidiary corporation and at least 80% of each other component member of the controlled group must be owned by other members of the controlled group.

Partial liquidation This occurs when a corporation discontinues one line of business, distributes the assets related to that business to its shareholders, and continues in at least one other line of business.

Partner A member of a partnership. The member may be an individual, trust, estate, or corporation. See also general partner and limited partner.

Partnership Syndicate, group, pool, joint venture, or other unincorporated organization which carries on a business or financial operation or venture and which has at least two partners.

Partnership agreement Agreement that governs the relationship between the partners and the partnership.

Partnership interest The capital and/or profits interest in a partnership received in exchange for a contribution of properties or services (e.g., money or business equipment). The nature of a partnership interest is similar to that of corporate stock.

Partnership item Virtually all items reported by the partnership for the taxable year, including tax preference items, credit recapture items, guaranteed payments, and at-risk amounts.

Partnership ordinary income The positive sum of all partnership items of income, gain, loss, or deduction that do not have to be separately stated.

Partnership ordinary loss The negative sum of all partnership items of income, gain, loss, or deduction that do not have to be separately stated.

Partnership taxable income The sum of all taxable items among the separately stated items plus the partnership ordinary income or ordinary loss.

Party to a reorganization Such parties include (1) corporations that result from a reorganization and (2) the corporations involved in a reorganization where one corporation acquires the stock or assets of the other corporation.

Passive activity limitation Separate limitation on the amount of losses and credits that can be claimed with respect to a passive activity.

Passive income Income from an activity that does not require the taxpayer's material involvement or participation. Thus, income from tax shelters and rental activities generally fall into this category.

Passive loss Loss generated from a passive activity. Such losses are computed separately. They may be used to offset income from other passive activities, but may not be used to offset either active income or portfolio income.

Percentage depletion method Depletion method for assets such as oil and gas that is equal to a specified percentage times the gross income from the property but which may not exceed 100% of the taxable income before depletion is deducted. Lease bonuses, advance royalties, and other amounts payable without regard to production may not be included in the calculation. This method is only available to small oil and gas producers and royalty owners and for certain mineral properties.

Percentage of completion method of accounting Accounting method generally used for long-term contracts under which income is reported in proportion to the amount of work that has been completed in a given year.

Permanent difference Items that are reported in taxable income but not book income or vice versa. Such differences include book income items that are nontaxable in the current year and will never be taxable and book expense items that are nondeductible in computing taxable income for the current year and will never be deductible.

Personal exemption A deduction in an amount mandated by Congress. The amount for 2006 is $3,300 ($3,200 in 2005). The amount is adjusted each year for increases in the cost of living. An additional exemption is allowed for each individual who is a dependent. Personal and dependency exemptions are phased out for high income taxpayers.

Personal holding company (PHC) A closely held corporation (1) that is owned by five or fewer shareholders who own more than 50% of the corporation's outstanding stock at any time during the last half of its tax year and (2) whose PHC income equals at least 60% of the corporation's adjusted ordinary gross income for the tax year. Certain corporations (e.g., S corporations) are exempt from this definition.

Personal holding company income (PHCI) Twelve categories of income including the following: dividends; interest; annuities; royalties (other than minerals, oil and gas, computer software, and copyright royalties); adjusted income from rents; adjusted income from mineral, oil and gas royalties or working interests in oil and gas wells; computer software royalties; copyright royalties; produced film rents; income from personal service contracts involving a 25% or more shareholder; rental income from corporate property used by a 25% or more shareholder; and distributions from estates and trusts.

Personal holding company (PHC) tax This tax equals 15% of undistributed personal holding company income and, if applicable, is assessed in addition to the regular corporate income tax and the AMT.

Personal interest All interest other than active business interest, investment interest, interest incurred in a passive activity, qualified residence interest, and interest incurred when paying the estate tax on an installment basis. Personal interest is currently treated as a nondeductible personal expenditure. See also Interest.

Personal service corporation (PSC) A regular C corporation whose principal activity is the performance of personal services that are substantially performed by owner-employees who own more than 10% of the value of the corporation's stock.

Plan of liquidation A written document detailing the steps to be undertaken while carrying out the complete liquidation of a corporation.

Plan of reorganization A consummated transaction that is specifically defined as a reorganization.

Pooled income fund A fund in which individuals receive an income interest for life and a charitable contribution deduction equal to the remainder interest for amounts contributed to the fund. The various individual beneficiaries receive annual distributions of income based upon their proportionate share of the fund's earnings.

Portfolio income Dividends, interest, annuities, and royalties not derived in the ordinary course of business. Gains and losses on property that produces portfolio income are included in such income.

Post-termination transition period The period of time following the termination of the S corporation election during which (1) loss and deduction carryovers can be deducted or (2) distributions of S corporation previously taxed earnings can be made tax-free.

Power of appointment The power to designate the eventual owner of a property. Such appointments may be general or specific. See also General power of appointment.

Preadjustment AMTI Alternative minimum taxable income determined without the adjusted current earnings adjustment and the alternative tax NOL deduction.

Preadjustment year For purposes of the innocent spouse provisions, the most recent tax year of the spouse ending before the date the deficiency is mailed.

Preferential dividend Dividends are preferential if (1) the amount distributed to a shareholder exceeds his ratable share of the distribution as determined by the number of shares that are owned or (2) the distribution amount for a class of stock is more or less than its rightful amount.

Preferred stock bailout A tax treatment mandated by Sec. 306 which prevents shareholders who receive nontaxable preferred stock dividends from receiving capital gain treatment upon the sale or redemption of the preferred stock.

Present interest An unrestricted right to the immediate use, possession, or enjoyment of property or the income from property (e.g., a life estate or term certain).

Previously taxed income (PTI) Income earned in a pre-1983 S corporation tax year and which was taxed to the shareholder. A money distribution of PTI can be distributed tax-free once all of a corporation's AAA balance has been distributed. See Accumulated Adjustments Account.

Primary cite The highest level official reporter which reports a particular case is called the primary cite.

Principal partner Partner who owns at least a 5% interest in the partnership's capital or profits.

Probate estate Those properties that (1) pass subject to the will or under an intestacy statute and (2) are subject to court administration are part of the probate estate.

Profit-sharing plan A qualified defined benefit plan which may be established in lieu of or in addition to a qualified pension plan. Contributions to a profit-sharing plan are usually based upon profits. Incidental benefits may or may not be included. In addition, the plan must meet certain requirements concerning determination of the amount and timing of the employer's contribution, how the employee wants to receive the employer's contribution, vesting, and forfeitures.

Profits interest Interest in the partnership's future earnings.

Progressive rate Tax that increases as the taxpayer's taxable income increases. The U.S. income tax is an example of a progressive tax.

Property Cash, tangible property (e.g., buildings and land) and intangible property (e.g., franchise rights, trademarks, and leases).

Property settlement The division of property between spouses upon their separation or divorce.

Property tax Federal, state, or local tax levied on real and/or personal property (e.g., securities, a personal automobile).

Proportional tax A method of taxation under which the tax rate is the same for all taxpayers regardless of their income. State and local sales taxes are examples of this form of tax.

Protest letter If the additional tax in question is more than $10,000 and the IRS audit was a field audit, the taxpayer must file a protest letter within 30 days. If no such letter is sent, then the IRS will follow-up with a 90-day letter. See also Ninety (90) day letter.

Qualified disclaimer Disclaimer made by a person named to receive property under a decedent's will who wishes to renounce the property and any of its benefits. Such a disclaimer must be in written form and be irrevocable. In addition, it must be made no later than nine months after the later of the day the transfer is made or the day the recipient becomes 21 years old. The property must pass to either the decedent's spouse or another person not named by the person making the disclaimer.

Qualified joint interest If spouses are the only joint owners of a property, that property is classified as a qualified joint interest.

Qualified pension plan Pension plan that includes (1) systematic and definite payments made to a pension trust based upon actuarial methods and (2) usually provides for incidental benefits such as disability, or medical insurance benefits.

Qualified plan award Employee achievement awards given under a written plan or program that does not discriminate in favor of highly compensated employees. Such awards must be in the form of tangible personal property other than cash and be worth no more than $1,600.

Qualified residence interest Interest on an indebtedness which is secured by the taxpayer's qualified residence when it is paid or accrued. A taxpayer may have two qualified residences: a principal residence and a residence that he has personally used more than the greater of 14 days or 10% of the rental days during the year.

Qualified Subchapter S trusts (QSSTs) A domestic trust that owns stock in one or more S corporations and distributes (or is required to distribute) all of its income to its sole income beneficiary. The beneficiary must make an irrevocable election to be treated as the owner of the trust consisting of the S corporation stock. A separate QSST election must be made for each corporation's stock that is owned by the trust.

Qualified terminable interest property (QTIP) QTIP property is property for which a special election has been made that makes it eligible for the marital deduction. Such property must be transferred by the donor-spouse to a donee-spouse who has a qualifying interest for life. In other words, the donor does not have to grant full control over the property to his spouse.

Readily ascertainable fair market value The fair market value of nonqualified stock options can be readily ascertained where the option is traded on an established options exchange.

Realized gain or loss The gain or loss computed by taking the amount realized from a sale of property and subtracting the property's adjusted basis.

Reasonable business needs For accumulated earnings tax purposes, the amount that a prudent businessman would consider appropriate for the business's bona fide present and future needs, Sec. 303 (death tax) redemption needs, and excess business holding redemption needs.

Recapitalization A tax-free change in the capital structure of an existing corporation for a bona fide business purpose.

Recapture provision A provision requiring recapture of earlier alimony payments as ordinary income by the payor if the payments decline sharply in either the second or third year.

Recourse loan Loan for which the borrower remains liable until repayment is complete. If the loan is secured, the lender can be repaid by selling the security. Any difference in the sale amount and the loan amount must be paid by the borrower.

Recovery of basis doctrine Rule that allows taxpayers to recover the basis of an asset without being taxed. Such amounts are considered a return of capital.

Refundable credit See Tax credit.

Regressive tax A form of taxation under which the tax rate decreases as the tax base (e.g., income) increases.

Regular corporation See C corporation.

Regular decision Tax Court decision that is issued on a particular issue for the first time.

Regular tax A corporation's tax liability for income tax purposes reduced by foreign tax credits allowable for income tax purposes.

Remainder interest The portion of an interest in the property retained by a transferor who is not transferring his entire interest in a property.

Remainderman The person entitled to the remainder interest.

Replacement property Property that is acquired to replace converted property in order to retain nonrecognition of gain status. Such property must generally be functionally the same as the converted property. For example, a business machine must be replaced with a similar business machine. There are exceptions to this rule: The taxpayer-use test applies to the involuntary conversion of rental property owned by an investor; condemnations of real property held for business or investment use may be replaced by like-kind property.

Residential rental property Property from which at least 80% of the gross rental income is rental from dwelling units. Residential units include manufactured homes that are used for rental purposes, but not hotels, motels, or other establishments for transient use.

Restricted property plan Such plans are used to attract and retain key executives by giving them an ownership interest in the corporation. The income recognition rules contained in Sec. 83 govern this type of plan.

Revenue Amounts received by the taxpayer from any source. It includes both taxable and nontaxable amounts and items that are a return of capital. Although closely related to income or gross income, differences between these items do exist.

Revenue procedure Issued by the national office of the IRS and reflects the IRS's position on procedural aspects of tax practice issues. Revenue procedures are published in the Cumulative Bulletin.

Revenue ruling Issued by the national office of the IRS and reflects the IRS's interpretation of a narrow tax issue. Revenue rulings, which are published in the Cumulative Bulletin, have less weight than the Treasury Regulations.

Reverse triangular merger Type of tax-free transaction in which a subsidiary corporation is merged into a target corporation and the target corporation stays alive as a subsidiary of the parent corporation.

Reversionary interest The interest in a property that might revert back to the transferor under the terms of the transfer. If the amount of reversionary interest is 5% or less, it is not included in the gross estate.

Revocable trust Trust under which the grantor may demand that the assets be returned.

Royalties Ordinary income arising from amounts paid for the right to use property that belongs to another and is transferred for valuable consideration (e.g., a patent right where substantially all rights are transferred).

Rule against perpetuities The requirement that no property interest vest more than 21 years, plus the gestation period, after some life or lives in being at the time the interest is created.

S corporation Election that can be made by small business corporations that allows them to be taxed like partnerships rather than like C corporations. Small business corporations are those that meet the 100-shareholder limitation, the type of shareholder restrictions, and the one class of stock restriction.

S short year That portion of an S termination year that commences on the first day of the tax year and ends on the day preceding the day on which the termination is effective.

S termination year A tax year in which a termination event occurs on any day other than the first day of the tax year. It is divided into an S short year and a C short year.

Sale A transaction where one receives cash and/or the equivalent of cash, including the assumption of debt, in exchange for an asset.

Sales tax State or local tax on purchases. Generally, food items and medicines are exempt from such tax.

Section 444 election Personal service corporations, partnerships, and S corporations that are unable to otherwise elect a fiscal year, instead of their required tax year, can under Sec. 444 elect a fiscal year as their taxable year.

Secondary cite Citation to a secondary source (i.e., an unofficial reporter) for a particular case.

Section 1231 property Real or depreciable property that is (1) held for more than one year and (2) used in a trade or business. Certain property, such as inventory, U.S. government publications, copyrights, literary, musical, or artistic compositions, and letters, are excluded from this definition.

Section 1245 property Certain property subject to depreciation and, in some cases, amortization. Depreciable personal property such as equipment is Section 1245 property. However, most real property is not.

Section 1250 property Any real property that (1) is not Section 1245 property and (2) is subject to a depreciation allowance.

Section 306 stock Preferred stock that is received as a stock dividend or a part of a tax-free reorganization. Section 306 stock is subject to the special preferred stock bailout rules when sold or redeemed. See Preferred stock bailouts.

Security A security includes (1) shares of stock in a corporation; (2) a right to subscribe for, or the right to receive, a share of stock in a corporation; and (3) a bond, debenture, note, or other evidence of indebtedness issued by a corporation with interest coupons or in registered form.

Separate property All property that is owned before marriage and any gifts or inheritances acquired after marriage are separate property. This distinction depends on the state of residence. However, it is possible even in community property states.

Separate share rule Rule permitting a trust with several beneficiaries to treat each beneficiary as having a separate trust interest for purposes of determining (1) the amount of the distribution deduction and (2) the beneficiary's gross income.

Severance damages Compensation for a decline in the value of the property remaining after part of the taxpayer's property is condemned. The IRS considers such damages analogous to the proceeds from property insurance.

Shifting income The process of transferring income from one family member to another. Methods for shifting income include gifts of stock or bonds to family members who are in lower tax brackets.

Short-period tax return A tax return covering a period of less than 12 months. Short period returns are commonly filed in the first or final tax year or when a change in tax year is made.

Short-term capital gain (STCG) Gain realized on the sale or exchange of a capital asset held for one year or less.

Short-term trust Trust whose period is long enough for the grantor to escape being taxed on the trust's accounting income. A *Clifford* trust is a short-term trust.

Simple trust Trust that must distribute all of its income currently and is not empowered to make a charitable contribution.

Simplified LIFO method This method of inventory valuation allows taxpayers to use a single LIFO pool rather than multiple pools. See also LIFO method.

Small cases procedure When $50,000 or less is in question for a particular year, a taxpayer may opt to have the case heard by a special commissioner rather than a Tax Court judge. The commissioner's opinion cannot be appealed and has no precedential value.

Sole proprietorship Form of business entity owned by an individual who reports all items of income and expense on Schedule C (or Schedule C-EZ) of his individual return.

Special agents The IRS agents responsible for criminal fraud investigations.

Specific write-off method of accounting Method of accounting used for bad debts. Under this method, the taxpayer deducts each bad debt individually as it becomes worthless. This is the only allowable accounting method for bad debts arising after 1986.

Spin-off A tax-free distribution in which a parent corporation distributes the stock and securities of a subsidiary to its shareholders without receiving anything in exchange.

Split-interest transfer A transfer made for both private (i.e., an individual) and public (i.e., a charitable organization) purposes.

Split-off Tax-free distribution in which a parent corporation distributes a subsidiary's stock and securities to some or all of its shareholders in exchange for part or all of their stock and securities in the parent corporation.

Split-up Tax-free distribution in which a parent corporation distributes the stock or securities of two or more subsidiaries to its shareholders in exchange for all of their stock and securities in the parent corporation. The parent corporation then goes out of existence.

Splitting income The process of creating additional taxable entities, especially corporations, in order to reduce an individual's effective tax rate.

Sprinkling trust A discretionary trust with several beneficiaries.

Standard deduction A floor amount set by Congress to simplify the tax computation. It is used by taxpayers who do not have enough deductions to itemize. The amount of the deduction varies according to the taxpayer's filing status, age, and vision. Taxpayers who use this standard deduction are not required to keep records.

Standards for Tax Services (SSTS) Ethical standards of practice and compliance set by the Tax Division of the American Institute of Certified Public Accountants. The AICPA enforces these standards, and thus they have a great deal of influence over ethics in tax practice.

Statute of limitations A period of time as provided by law in which a taxpayer's return may not be changed either by the IRS or the taxpayer. The limitations period is generally three years from the later of the date the tax return is filed or its due date. A fraudulent return has no statute of limitations.

Step transaction doctrine A judicial doctrine which the IRS can use to collapse a multistep transaction into a single transaction (either taxable or tax-free) in order to prevent the taxpayers from arranging a series of business transactions to obtain a tax result that is not available if only a single transaction is used.

Stock bonus plan A special type of defined benefit plan under which the employer's stock is contributed to a trust. The stock is then allocated and distributed to the participants. See also Employee stock ownership plan.

Stock dividend A dividend paid in the form of stock in the corporation issuing the dividend.

Stock option plan This category includes incentive stock options and nonqualified stock option arrangements. Such plans are used to attrack and retain key employees.

Stock redemption The acquisition by a corporation of its own stock in exchange for property. Such stock may be cancelled, retired, or held as treasury stock.

Stock rights Rights issued by a corporation to its shareholders or creditors which permit the purchase of an additional share(s) of stock at a designated exercise price with the surrender of one or more of the stock rights.

Substantially appreciated inventory This type of inventory includes (1) items held for sale in the normal course of partnership business, (2) other property which would not be considered a capital asset or Sec. 1231 property if it was sold by the partnership, and (3) any other property held by the partnership which would fall into the above classification if it was held by the selling or distributee partner.

Surviving spouse A special filing status available to widows and widowers who file a joint return for the year his or her spouse dies and for the following two years. The surviving spouse may not have remarried, must be a U.S. citizen or resident, have qualified to file a joint return for the year, and must have at least one dependent child living at home during the year.

Target corporation The corporation that transfers its assets as part of a taxable or tax-free acquisition transaction. May also be known as the acquired or transferor company.

Tax A mandatory assessment levied under the authority of a political entity for the purpose of raising revenue to be used for public or governmental purposes. Such taxes may be levied by the federal, state, or local government.

Tax attributes Corporations have various tax items, such as earnings and profits, deduction and credit carryovers, and depreciation recapture potential, that are called tax attributes. The tax attributes of a target or liquidating corporation are assumed by the acquiring or parent corporation, respectively, in acquisitive reorganizations and tax-free liquidations.

Tax base The amount to which the tax rate is applied to determine the tax due. For income tax purposes, the tax base is taxable income.

Tax benefit rule Recovery of an amount in a subsequent year that produced a tax benefit in a prior year and is thus taxable to the recipient.

Tax credit Amount that can be deducted from the gross tax to arrive at the net tax due or refund due. Prepaid amounts, that is, amounts paid to the government during the year, are tax credits. Such prepaid amounts are often referred to as "refundable credits."

Tax deferred bonds Bonds on which the interest is not subject to current taxation but is deferred to a future period of time, such as Series EE U.S. Savings Bonds.

Tax exempt bonds Bonds on which the interest is completely exempt from federal income taxation, such as state and municipal bonds.

Tax law The tax law is comprised of the Internal Revenue Code, administrative and judicial interpretations, and the committee reports issued by the Congressional committees involved in the legislative process.

Tax matters partner (1) Partner who is designated by the partnership or (2) the general partner having the largest profits interests at the close of the partnership's tax year.

Tax preference items Designated items, such as accelerated depreciation claimed on pre-1987 realty, that increase taxable income to arrive at AMTI. Unlike AMT adjustments, tax preference items do not reverse in later years and reduce AMTI.

Tax research The process of solving a specific tax-related question on the basis of both tax law sources and the specific circumstances surrounding the particular situation.

Tax services Multivolume commentaries on the tax law. Generally these commentaries contain copies of the Internal Revenue Code and the Treasury Regulations. Also included are editorial comments prepared by the publisher of the tax service, current matters, and a cross-reference to various government promulgations and judicial decisions.

Tax shelter Passive activity which may lack economic substance other than creating tax deductions and credits that enable taxpayers to reduce or eliminate the income tax liability from their regular business activities. Section 469 restricts the current use of deductions and credits arising from passive activities.

Tax treaties Bilateral agreements entered into between two nations which address tax and other matters. Treaties provide for modifications to the basic tax laws involving residents of the two countries (e.g., reductions in the withholding rates).

Tax year The period of time (usually 12 months) selected by a taxpayer to compute their taxable income. The tax year may be a calendar year or a fiscal year. The election is made on the taxpayer's first return and cannot be changed without IRS approval. The tax year may be less than 12 months if it is the taxpayer's first or final return or if the taxpayer is changing accounting periods.

Taxable income For individuals, taxable income is adjusted gross income reduced by deductions from adjusted gross income.

Taxpayer Compliance Measurement Program (TCMP) A stratified random sample used to select tax returns for audit. The program is intended to test the extent to which taxpayers are in compliance with the law.

Taxpayer-use test A test used to determine whether property is considered similar or related in service or use for purposes of involuntary conversions of property. This test is used by owner-investors (as opposed to owner-users) of property.

Technical advice memorandum Such memoranda are administrative in-

terpretations issued in the form of letter ruling. Taxpayers may request them if they need guidance about the tax treatment of complicated technical matters which are being audited.

Temporary differences Items which are included in book income in the current year but which were included in taxable income in the past or will be included in the future. Book income items that are nontaxable in the current year even though they were taxed in the past or will be taxed in the future and book expenses that are not currently deductible even though that status was different in the past or will be different in the future are categorized as temporary differences.

Tentative minimum tax (TMT) Tax calculated by (1) multiplying 20% times the corporation's alternative minimum taxable income less a statutory exemption amount and (2) deducting allowable foreign tax credits.

Term certain interest A person holding such an interest has a right to receive income from property for a specified term, but does not own or hold title to such property. The property reverts to the grantor at the end of the term.

Terminable interest A property interest that ends when (1) some event occurs (or fails to occur) or (2) a specified amount of time passes.

Testamentary Of, pertaining to, or of the nature of a testament or will.

Testamentary gift Transfer of property made at the death of the donor (i.e., bequests, devises, and inheritances).

Testamentary transfers A transferor's control or enjoyment of a property ceases at death.

Testamentary trust Trust created under the direction of a decedent's will and funded by the decedent's estate.

Thirty (30)-day letter A report sent to the taxpayer if the taxpayer does not sign Form 870 (Waiver of Statutory Notice) concerning any additional taxes assessed. The letter details the proposed changes and advises the taxpayer of his right to pursue the matter with the Appeals Office. The taxpayer then has 30 days in which to request a conference.

Throwback dividends For accumulated earnings tax and personal holding company tax purposes, these are distributions made out of current or accumulated earnings and profits in the first two and one-half months after the close of the tax year.

Tier-1 beneficiary Beneficiary to whom a distribution must be made.

Tier-2 beneficiary Beneficiary who receives a discretionary distribution.

Total economic income The amount of the taxpayer's income, including exclusions and deductions from the tax base (e.g., tax-exempt bonds), is categorized as total economic income.

Transferor corporation The corporation that transfers its assets as part of a reorganization. May also be known as acquired or target corporation.

Transportation expense The deductibility of this type of expense depends upon whether it is trade- or business-related, whether it is related to the production of income, whether the expense is employment related and therefore subject to the 2% nondeductible floor for miscellaneous itemized deductions. Commuting expenses

are nondeductible. See also Travel expense.

Travel expense Such expenses include transportation, meals, and lodging incurred in the pursuit of a trade, business, or employment-related activity. There are limitations and restrictions on the deductibility of these expenses. See also Transportation expense.

Triangular reorganization A type of reorganization (i.e., Type A, B, or C) where the parent corporation uses a subsidiary corporation to serve as the acquiring corporation. See triangular merger.

Trustee An individual or institution which administers a trust for the benefit of a beneficiary.

Trustor The grantor or transferor of a trust.

Type A reorganization Type of corporate reorganization that meets the requirements of state or federal law, may take the form of a consolidation, a merger, a triangular merger, or a reverse triangular merger.

Type B reorganization Reorganization characterized by a stock-for-stock exchange. The target corporation remains in existence as a subsidiary of the acquiring corporation.

Type C reorganization A transaction that requires the acquiring corporation to obtain substantially all of the target corporation's assets in exchange for its voting stock and a limited amount of other consideration. The target corporation is generally liquidated.

Type D reorganization This type of reorganization may be either acquisitive or divisive. In the former, substantially all of the transferor corporation's assets (and possibly some or all of its liabilities) are

acquired by a controlled corporation. The target corporation is liquidated. The latter involves the acquisition of the part or all of the transferor corporation's assets (and liabilities) by a controlled subsidiary corporation(s). The transferor corporation may either remain in existence or be liquidated.

Type E reorganization This type of reorganization changes the capital structure of a corporation. The corporation remains in existence.

Type F reorganization The old corporation's assets or stock are transferred to a single newly formed corporation in this type of transaction. The "old" corporation is liquidated.

Type G reorganization This type of reorganization may be either acquisitive or divisive. In either case, part or all of the target or transferor corporation's assets (and possibly some or all of its liabilities) are transferred to another corporation as part of a bankruptcy proceeding. The target or transferor corporation may either remain in existence or be liquidated.

Unfunded deferred compensation plan This type of plan is used for highly-compensated employees who wish to defer the recognition of income until future periods. Funding is generally accomplished through an escrow account for the employee's benefit.

Unified credit The unified credit enables a tax base of a certain size (i.e., the exemption equivalent or applicable exclusion amount) to be completely free of transfer taxes. It may be subtracted only once against all of a person's transfers—throughout one's lifetime and at death. See exemption equivalent and applicable exclusion amount.

Unified rate schedule Progressive rate schedule for estate and gift taxes. These rates are effective for gifts made after 1976 and deaths occurring after 1976.

Unrealized receivable Right to payment for goods and services that has not been included in the owner's income because of its method of accounting.

Unreported decisions District court decisions that are not reported in official reporters. Such decisions may be reported in secondary reporters that report only tax-related cases.

U.S. production activities deduction A deduction equal to a percentage times the lesser of (1) qualified production activities income for the year or (2) taxable income before the U.S. production activities deduction. The phased-in percentages are 3% for 2005 and 2006, 6% for 2007–2009, and 9% for 2010 and thereafter. The deduction, however, cannot exceed 50% of the corporation's W-2 wages for the year.

Vertical equity A concept in taxation that provides that the incidence of taxation should be borne by taxpayers who have the ability to pay the tax. Taxpayers who are not similarly-situated should be treated differently under the tax law.

Voting trust An arrangement whereby the stock owned by a number of shareholders is placed under the control of a trustee for purposes of exercising the voting rights possessed by the stock. This practice increases the voting power of the minority shareholders.

Wash sale A wash sale results when the taxpayer (1) sells stock or securities and (2) purchases substantially identical stock or securities within the 61-day period extending from 30 days before the date of sale to 30 days after the date of sale.

Wealth transfer taxes Estate taxes (i.e., the tax on dispositions of property that occur as a result of the transferor's death) and gift taxes (i.e., the tax on lifetime transfers) are wealth transfer taxes.

Writ of certiorari A petition to the U.S. Supreme court to request that the Court agree to hear a case. A writ of certiorari is requested by the party (IRS or taxpayer) that lost at the Court of Appeals level.

APPENDIX E

- ## AICPA STATEMENTS ON STANDARDS FOR TAX SERVICES NOS. 1–8 (AUGUST 2000)

- ## INTERPRETATION NO. 1–2 FOR SSTS NO. 1 (OCTOBER 2003)

PREFACE

1. Practice standards are the hallmark of calling one's self a professional. Members should fulfill their responsibilities as professionals by instituting and maintaining standards against which their professional performance can be measured. Compliance with professional standards of tax practice also confirms the public's awareness of the professionalism that is associated with CPAs as well as the AICPA.

2. This publication sets forth ethical tax practice standards for members of the AICPA: Statements on Standards for Tax Services (SSTSs or Statements). Although other standards of tax practice exist, most notably Treasury Department Circular No. 230 and penalty provisions of the Internal Revenue Code (IRC), those standards are limited in that (1) Circular No. 230 does not provide the depth of guidance contained in these Statements, (2) the IRC penalty provisions apply only to income-tax return preparation, and (3) both Circular No. 230 and the penalty provisions apply only to federal tax practice.

3. The SSTSs have been written in as simple and objective a manner as possible. However, by their nature, ethical standards provide for an appropriate range of behavior that recognizes the need for interpretations to meet a broad range of personal and professional situations. The SSTSs recognize this need by, in some sections, providing relatively subjective rules and by leaving certain terms undefined. These terms and concepts are generally rooted in tax concepts, and therefore should be readily understood by tax practitioners. It is, therefore, recognized that the enforcement of these rules, as part of the AICPA's Code of Professional Conduct Rule 201, General Standards, and Rule 202, Compliance With Standards, will be undertaken with flexibility in mind and handled on a case-by-case basis. Members are expected to comply with them.

HISTORY

4. The SSTSs have their origin in the Statements on Responsibilities in Tax Practice (SRTPs), which provided a body of advisory opinions on good tax practice. The guidelines as originally set forth in the SRTPs had come to play a much more important role than most members realized. The courts, Internal Revenue Service, state accountancy boards, and other professional organizations recognized and relied on the SRTPs as the appropriate articulation of professional conduct in a CPA's tax practice. The SRTPs, in and of themselves, had become de facto enforceable standards of professional practice, because state disciplinary organizations and malpractice cases in effect regularly held CPAs accountable for failure to follow the SRTPs when their professional practice conduct failed to meet the prescribed guidelines of conduct.

5. The AICPA's Tax Executive Committee concluded that appropriate action entailed issuance of tax practice standards that would become a part of the Institute's Code of Professional Conduct. At its July 1999 meeting, the AICPA Board of Directors approved support of the executive committee's initiative and placed the matter on the agenda of the October 1999 meeting of the Institute's governing Council. On October 19, 1999, Council approved designating the Tax Executive Committee as a standard-setting body, thus authorizing that committee to promulgate standards of tax practice. These SSTSs, largely mirroring the SRTPs, are the result.

6. The SRTPs were originally issued between 1964 and 1977. The first nine SRTPs and the Introduction were codified in 1976; the tenth SRTP was issued in 1977. The original SRTPs concerning the CPA's responsibility to sign the return (SRTPs No. 1, *Signature of Preparers,* and No. 2, *Signature of Reviewer: Assumption of Preparer's Responsibility*) were withdrawn in 1982 after Treasury Department regulations were issued adopting substantially the same standards for all tax return preparers. The sixth and seventh SRTPs, concerning the responsibility of a CPA who becomes aware of an error, were revised in 1991. The first Interpretation of the SRTPs, Interpretation 1-1, "Realistic Possibility Standard," was approved in December 1990. The SSTSs and Interpretation supersede and replace the SRTPs and their Interpretation 1-1 effective October 31, 2000. Although the number and names of the SSTSs, and the substance of the rules contained in each of them, remain the same as in the SRTPs, the language has been edited to both clarify and reflect the enforceable nature of the SSTSs. In addition, because the applicability of these standards is not limited to federal income-tax practice, the language has been changed to mirror the broader scope.

ONGOING PROCESS

7. The following Statements on Standards for Tax Services and Interpretation 1-1 to Statement No. 1, "Realistic Possibility Standard," reflect the AICPA's standards of tax practice and delineate members' responsibilities to taxpayers, the public, the government, and the profession. The Statements are intended to be part of an ongoing process that may require changes to and interpretations of current SSTSs in recognition of the accelerating rate of change in tax laws and the continued importance of tax practice to members.

8. The Tax Executive Committee promulgates SSTSs. Even though the 1999–2000 Tax Executive Committee approved this version, acknowledgment is also due to the many members whose efforts over the years went into the development of the original statements.

STATEMENT ON STANDARDS FOR TAX SERVICES NO. 1, TAX RETURN POSITIONS

INTRODUCTION

1. This Statement sets forth the applicable standards for members when recommending tax return positions and preparing or signing tax returns (including amended returns, claims for refund, and information returns) filed with any taxing authority. For purposes of these standards, a *tax return position* is (a) a position reflected on the tax return as to which the taxpayer has been specifically advised by a member or (b) a position about which a member has knowledge of all material facts and, on the basis of those facts, has concluded whether the position is appropriate. For purposes of these standards, a *taxpayer* is a client, a member's employer, or any other third-party recipient of tax services.

STATEMENT

2. The following standards apply to a member when providing professional services that involve tax return positions:

a. A member should not recommend that a tax return position be taken with respect to any item unless the member has a good-faith belief that the position has a realistic possibility of being sustained administratively or judicially on its merits if challenged.

b. A member should not prepare or sign a return that the member is aware takes a position that the member may not recommend under the standard expressed in paragraph 2a.

c. Notwithstanding paragraph 2a, a member may recommend a tax return position that the member concludes is not frivolous as long as the member advises the taxpayer to appropriately disclose. Notwithstanding paragraph 2b, the member may prepare or sign a return that reflects a position that the member concludes is not frivolous as long as the position is appropriately disclosed.

d. When recommending tax return positions and when preparing or signing a return on which a tax return position is taken, a member should, when relevant, advise the taxpayer regarding potential penalty consequences of such tax return position and the opportunity, if any, to avoid such penalties through disclosure.

3. A member should not recommend a tax return position or prepare or sign a return reflecting a position that the member knows—

a. Exploits the audit selection process of a taxing authority.

b. Serves as a mere arguing position advanced solely to obtain leverage in the bargaining process of settlement negotiation with a taxing authority.

4. When recommending a tax return position, a member has both the right and responsibility to be an advocate for the taxpayer with respect to any position satisfying the aforementioned standards.

EXPLANATION

5. Our self-assessment tax system can function effectively only if taxpayers file tax returns that are true, correct, and complete. A tax return is primarily a taxpayer's representation of facts, and the taxpayer has the final responsibility for positions taken on the return.

6. In addition to a duty to the taxpayer, a member has a duty to the tax system. However, it is well established that the taxpayer has no obligation to pay more taxes than are legally owed, and a member has a duty to the taxpayer to assist in achieving that result. The standards contained in paragraphs 2, 3, and 4 recognize the members' responsibilities to both taxpayers and to the tax system.

7. In order to meet the standards contained in paragraph 2, a member should in good faith believe that the tax return position is warranted in existing law or can be supported by a good-faith argument for an extension, modification, or reversal of existing law. For example, in reaching such a conclusion, a member may consider a well-reasoned construction of the applicable statute, well-reasoned articles or treatises, or pronouncements issued by the applicable taxing authority, regardless of whether such sources would be treated as *authority* under Internal Revenue

Code section 6662 and the regulations thereunder. A position would not fail to meet these standards merely because it is later abandoned for practical or procedural considerations during an administrative hearing or in the litigation process.

8. If a member has a good-faith belief that more than one tax return position meets the standards set forth in paragraph 2, a member's advice concerning alternative acceptable positions may include a discussion of the likelihood that each such position might or might not cause the taxpayer's tax return to be examined and whether the position would be challenged in an examination. In such circumstances, such advice is not a violation of paragraph 3a.

9. In some cases, a member may conclude that a tax return position is not warranted under the standard set forth in paragraph 2a. A taxpayer may, however, still wish to take such a position. Under such circumstances, the taxpayer should have the opportunity to take such a position, and the member may prepare and sign the return provided the position is appropriately disclosed on the return or claim for refund and the position is not frivolous. A frivolous position is one that is knowingly advanced in bad faith and is patently improper.

10. A member's determination of whether information is appropriately disclosed by the taxpayer should be based on the facts and circumstances of the particular case and the authorities regarding disclosure in the applicable taxing jurisdiction. If a member recommending a position, but not engaged to prepare or sign the related tax return, advises the taxpayer concerning appropriate disclosure of the position, then the member shall be deemed to meet these standards.

11. If particular facts and circumstances lead a member to believe that a taxpayer penalty might be asserted, the member should so advise the taxpayer and should discuss with the taxpayer the opportunity to avoid such penalty by disclosing the position on the tax return. Although a member should advise the taxpayer with respect to disclosure, it is the taxpayer's responsibility to decide whether and how to disclose.

12. For purposes of this Statement, preparation of a tax return includes giving advice on events that have occurred at the time the advice is given if the advice is directly relevant to determining the existence, character, or amount of a schedule, entry, or other portion of a tax return.

INTERPRETATION NO. 1-1, "REALISTIC POSSIBILITY STANDARD" OF STATEMENT ON STANDARDS FOR TAX SERVICES NO. 1, TAX RETURN POSITIONS

BACKGROUND

1. Statement on Standards for Tax Services (SSTS) No. 1, *Tax Return Positions*, contains the standards a member should follow in recommending tax return positions and in preparing or

signing tax returns. In general, a member should have a good-faith belief that the tax return position being recommended has a realistic possibility of being sustained administratively or judicially on its merits, if challenged. The standard contained in SSTS No. 1, paragraph 2a, is referred to here as the realistic possibility standard. If a member concludes that a tax return position does not meet the realistic possibility standard:

 a. The member may still recommend the position to the taxpayer if the position is not frivolous, and the member recommends appropriate disclosure of the position; or

 b. The member may still prepare or sign a tax return containing the position, if the position is not frivolous, and the position is appropriately disclosed.

2. A *frivolous position* is one that is knowingly advanced in bad faith and is patently improper (see SSTS No. 1, paragraph 9). A member's determination of whether information is appropriately disclosed on a tax return or claim for refund is based on the facts and circumstances of the particular case and the authorities regarding disclosure in the applicable jurisdiction (see SSTS No. 1, paragraph 10).

3. If a member believes there is a possibility that a tax return position might result in penalties being asserted against a taxpayer, the member should so advise the taxpayer and should discuss with the taxpayer the opportunity, if any, of avoiding such penalties through disclosure (see SSTS No. 1, paragraph 11). Such advice may be given orally.

GENERAL INTERPRETATION

4. To meet the realistic possibility standard, a member should have a good-faith belief that the position is warranted by existing law or can be supported by a good-faith argument for an extension, modification, or reversal of the existing law through the administrative or judicial process. Such a belief should be based on reasonable interpretations of the tax law. A member should not take into account the likelihood of audit or detection when determining whether this standard has been met (see SSTS No. 1, paragraphs 3a and 8).

5. The realistic possibility standard is less stringent than the substantial authority standard and the more likely than not standard that apply under the Internal Revenue Code (IRC) to substantial understatements of liability by taxpayers. The realistic possibility standard is stricter than the reasonable basis standard that is in the IRC.

6. In determining whether a tax return position meets the realistic possibility standard, a member may rely on authorities in addition to those evaluated when determining whether substantial authority exists under IRC section 6662. Accordingly, a member may rely on well-reasoned treatises, articles in recognized professional tax publications, and other reference tools and sources of tax analyses commonly used by tax advisers and preparers of returns.

7. In determining whether a realistic possibility exists, a member should do all of the following:

• Establish relevant background facts
• Distill the appropriate questions from those facts
• Search for authoritative answers to those questions

- Resolve the questions by weighing the authorities uncovered by that search
- Arrive at a conclusion supported by the authorities

8. A member should consider the weight of each authority to conclude whether a position meets the realistic possibility standard. In determining the weight of an authority, a member should consider its persuasiveness, relevance, and source. Thus, the type of authority is a significant factor. Other important factors include whether the facts stated by the authority are distinguishable from those of the taxpayer and whether the authority contains an analysis of the issue or merely states a conclusion.

9. The realistic possibility standard may be met despite the absence of certain types of authority. For example, a member may conclude that the realistic possibility standard has been met when the position is supported only by a well-reasoned construction of the applicable statutory provision.

10. In determining whether the realistic possibility standard has been met, the extent of research required is left to the professional judgment of the member with respect to all the facts and circumstances known to the member. A member may conclude that more than one position meets the realistic possibility standard.

SPECIFIC ILLUSTRATIONS

11. The following illustrations deal with general fact patterns. Accordingly, the application of the guidance discussed in the General Interpretation section to variations in such general facts or to particular facts or circumstances may lead to different conclusions. In each illustration there is no authority other than that indicated.

12. *Illustration 1.* A taxpayer has engaged in a transaction that is adversely affected by a new statutory provision. Prior law supports a position favorable to the taxpayer. The taxpayer believes, and the member concurs, that the new statute is inequitable as applied to the taxpayer's situation. The statute is constitutional, clearly drafted, and unambiguous. The legislative history discussing the new statute contains general comments that do not specifically address the taxpayer's situation.

13. *Conclusion.* The member should recommend the return position supported by the new statute. A position contrary to a constitutional, clear, and unambiguous statute would ordinarily be considered a frivolous position.

14. *Illustration 2.* The facts are the same as in illustration 1 except that the legislative history discussing the new statute specifically addresses the taxpayer's situation and supports a position favorable to the taxpayer.

15. *Conclusion.* In a case where the statute is clearly and unambiguously against the taxpayer's position but a contrary position exists based on legislative history specifically addressing the taxpayer's situation, a return position based either on the statutory language or on the legislative history satisfies the realistic possibility standard.

16. *Illustration 3.* The facts are the same as in illustration 1 except that the legislative history can be interpreted to provide some evidence or authority in support of the taxpayer's position; however, the legislative history does not specifically address the situation.

17. *Conclusion.* In a case where the statute is clear and unambiguous, a contrary position based on an interpretation of the legislative history that does not explicitly address the taxpayer's situation does not meet the realistic possibility standard. However, because the legislative history provides some support or evidence for the taxpayer's position, such a return position is not frivolous. A member may recommend the position to the taxpayer if the member also recommends appropriate disclosure.

18. *Illustration 4.* A taxpayer is faced with an issue involving the interpretation of a new statute. Following its passage, the statute was widely recognized to contain a drafting error, and a technical correction proposal has been introduced. The taxing authority issues a pronouncement indicating how it will administer the provision. The pronouncement interprets the statute in accordance with the proposed technical correction.

19. *Conclusion.* Return positions based on either the existing statutory language or the taxing authority pronouncement satisfy the realistic possibility standard.

20. *Illustration 5.* The facts are the same as in illustration 4 except that no taxing authority pronouncement has been issued.

21. *Conclusion.* In the absence of a taxing authority pronouncement interpreting the statute in accordance with the technical correction, only a return position based on the existing statutory language will meet the realistic possibility standard. A return position based on the proposed technical correction may be recommended if it is appropriately disclosed, since it is not frivolous.

22. *Illustration 6.* A taxpayer is seeking advice from a member regarding a recently amended statute. The member has reviewed the statute, the legislative history that specifically addresses the issue, and a recently published notice issued by the taxing authority. The member has concluded in good faith that, based on the statute and the legislative history, the taxing authority's position as stated in the notice does not reflect legislative intent.

23. *Conclusion.* The member may recommend the position supported by the statute and the legislative history because it meets the realistic possibility standard.

24. *Illustration 7.* The facts are the same as in illustration 6 except that the taxing authority pronouncement is a temporary regulation.

25. *Conclusion.* In determining whether the position meets the realistic possibility standard, a member should determine the weight to be given the regulation by analyzing factors such as whether the regulation is legislative or interpretative, or if it is inconsistent with the statute. If a member concludes that the position does not meet the realistic possibility standard, because it is not frivolous, the position may nevertheless be recommended if the member also recommends appropriate disclosure.

26. *Illustration 8.* A tax form published by a taxing authority is incorrect, but completion of the form as published provides a benefit to the taxpayer. The member knows that the taxing authority has published an announcement acknowledging the error.

27. *Conclusion.* In these circumstances, a return position in accordance with the published form is a frivolous position.

28. *Illustration 9.* A taxpayer wants to take a position that a member has concluded is frivolous. The taxpayer maintains that even if the taxing authority examines the return, the issue will not be raised.

29. *Conclusion.* The member should not consider the likelihood of audit or detection when determining whether the realistic possibility standard has been met. The member should not prepare or sign a return that contains a frivolous position even if it is disclosed.

30. *Illustration 10.* A statute is passed requiring the capitalization of certain expenditures. The taxpayer believes, and the member concurs, that to comply fully, the taxpayer will need to acquire new computer hardware and software and implement a number of new accounting procedures. The taxpayer and member agree that the costs of full compliance will be significantly greater than the resulting increase in tax due under the new provision. Because of these cost considerations, the taxpayer makes no effort to comply. The taxpayer wants the member to prepare and sign a return on which the new requirement is simply ignored.

31. *Conclusion.* The return position desired by the taxpayer is frivolous, and the member should neither prepare nor sign the return.

32. *Illustration 11.* The facts are the same as in illustration 10 except that a taxpayer has made a good-faith effort to comply with the law by calculating an estimate of expenditures to be capitalized under the new provision.

33. *Conclusion.* In this situation, the realistic possibility standard has been met. When using estimates in the preparation of a return, a member should refer to SSTS No. 4, *Use of Estimates.*

34. *Illustration 12.* On a given issue, a member has located and weighed two authorities concerning the treatment of a particular expenditure. A taxing authority has issued an administrative ruling that required the expenditure to be capitalized and amortized over several years. On the other hand, a court opinion permitted the current deduction of the expenditure. The member has concluded that these are the relevant authorities, considered the source of both authorities, and concluded that both are persuasive and relevant.

35. *Conclusion.* The realistic possibility standard is met by either position.

36. *Illustration 13.* A tax statute is silent on the treatment of an item under the statute. However, the legislative history explaining the statute directs the taxing authority to issue regulations that will require a specific treatment of the item. No regulations have been issued at the time the member must recommend a position on the tax treatment of the item.

37. *Conclusion.* The member may recommend the position supported by the legislative history because it meets the realistic possibility standard.

38. *Illustration 14.* A taxpayer wants to take a position that a member concludes meets the realistic possibility standard based on an assumption regarding an underlying nontax legal issue. The member recommends that the taxpayer seek advice from its legal counsel, and the taxpayer's attorney gives an opinion on the nontax legal issue.

39. *Conclusion.* A member may in general rely on a legal opinion on a nontax legal issue. A member should, however, use professional judgment when relying on a legal opinion. If, on its face, the opinion of the taxpayer's attorney appears to be unreasonable, unsubstantiated, or unwarranted, a member should consult his or her attorney before relying on the opinion.

40. *Illustration 15.* A taxpayer has obtained from its attorney an opinion on the tax treatment of an item and requests that a member rely on the opinion.

41. *Conclusion.* The authorities on which a member may rely include well-reasoned sources of tax analysis. If a member is satisfied about the source, relevance, and persuasiveness of the legal opinion, a member may rely on that opinion when determining whether the realistic possibility standard has been met.

STATEMENT ON STANDARDS FOR TAX SERVICES NO. 2, ANSWERS TO QUESTIONS ON RETURNS

INTRODUCTION

1. This Statement sets forth the applicable standards for members when signing the preparer's declaration on a tax return if one or more questions on the return have not been answered. The term *questions* includes requests for information on the return, in the instructions, or in the regulations, whether or not stated in the form of a question.

STATEMENT

2. A member should make a reasonable effort to obtain from the taxpayer the information necessary to provide appropriate answers to all questions on a tax return before signing as preparer.

EXPLANATION

3. It is recognized that the questions on tax returns are not of uniform importance, and often they are not applicable to the particular taxpayer. Nevertheless, there are at least two reasons why a member should be satisfied that a reasonable effort has been made to obtain information to provide appropriate answers to the questions on the return that are applicable to a taxpayer.

    a. A question may be of importance in determining taxable income or loss, or the tax liability shown on the return, in which circumstance an omission may detract from the quality of the return.

    b. A member often must sign a preparer's declaration stating that the return is true, correct, and complete.

4. Reasonable grounds may exist for omitting an answer to a question applicable to a taxpayer. For example, reasonable grounds may include the following:

a. The information is not readily available and the answer is not significant in terms of taxable income or loss, or the tax liability shown on the return.

b. Genuine uncertainty exists regarding the meaning of the question in relation to the particular return.

c. The answer to the question is voluminous; in such cases, a statement should be made on the return that the data will be supplied upon examination.

5. A member should not omit an answer merely because it might prove disadvantageous to a taxpayer.

6. If reasonable grounds exist for omission of an answer to an applicable question, a taxpayer is not required to provide on the return an explanation of the reason for the omission. In this connection, a member should consider whether the omission of an answer to a question may cause the return to be deemed incomplete.

STATEMENT ON STANDARDS FOR TAX SERVICES NO. 3, CERTAIN PROCEDURAL ASPECTS OF PREPARING RETURNS

INTRODUCTION

1. This Statement sets forth the applicable standards for members concerning the obligation to examine or verify certain supporting data or to consider information related to another taxpayer when preparing a taxpayer's tax return.

STATEMENT

2. In preparing or signing a return, a member may in good faith rely, without verification, on information furnished by the taxpayer or by third parties. However, a member should not ignore the implications of information furnished and should make reasonable inquiries if the information furnished appears to be incorrect, incomplete, or inconsistent either on its face or on the basis of other facts known to a member. Further, a member should refer to the taxpayer's returns for one or more prior years whenever feasible.

3. If the tax law or regulations impose a condition with respect to deductibility or other tax treatment of an item, such as taxpayer maintenance of books and records or substantiating documentation to support the reported deduction or tax treatment, a member should make appropriate inquiries to determine to the member's satisfaction whether such condition has been met.

4. When preparing a tax return, a member should consider information actually known to that member from the tax return of another taxpayer if the information is relevant to that tax return and its consideration is necessary to properly prepare that tax return. In using such information, a member should consider any limitations imposed by any law or rule relating to confidentiality.

EXPLANATION

5. The preparer's declaration on a tax return often states that the information contained therein is true, correct, and complete to the best of the preparer's knowledge and belief based on all information known by the preparer. This type of reference should be understood to include information furnished by the taxpayer or by third parties to a member in connection with the preparation of the return.

6. The preparer's declaration does not require a member to examine or verify supporting data. However, a distinction should be made between (*a*) the need either to determine by inquiry that a specifically required condition, such as maintaining books and records or substantiating documentation, has been satisfied or to obtain information when the material furnished appears to be incorrect or incomplete and (*b*) the need for a member to examine underlying information. In fulfilling his or her obligation to exercise due diligence in preparing a return, a member may rely on information furnished by the taxpayer unless it appears to be incorrect, incomplete, or inconsistent. Although a member has certain responsibilities in exercising due diligence in preparing a return, the taxpayer has the ultimate responsibility for the contents of the return. Thus, if the taxpayer presents unsupported data in the form of lists of tax information, such as dividends and interest received, charitable contributions, and medical expenses, such information may be used in the preparation of a tax return without verification unless it appears to be incorrect, incomplete, or inconsistent either on its face or on the basis of other facts known to a member.

7. Even though there is no requirement to examine underlying documentation, a member should encourage the taxpayer to provide supporting data where appropriate. For example, a member should encourage the taxpayer to submit underlying documents for use in tax return preparation to permit full consideration of income and deductions arising from security transactions and from pass-through entities, such as estates, trusts, partnerships, and S corporations.

8. The source of information provided to a member by a taxpayer for use in preparing the return is often a pass-through entity, such as a limited partnership, in which the taxpayer has an interest but is not involved in management. A member may accept the information provided by the pass-through entity without further inquiry, unless there is reason to believe it is incorrect, incomplete, or inconsistent, either on its face or on the basis of other facts known to the member. In some instances, it may be appropriate for a member to advise the taxpayer to ascertain the nature and amount of possible exposure to tax deficiencies, interest, and penalties, by contact with management of the pass-through entity.

9. A member should make use of a taxpayer's returns for one or more prior years in preparing the current return whenever feasible. Reference to prior returns and discussion of prior-year tax determinations with the taxpayer should provide information to determine the taxpayer's general tax status, avoid the omission or duplication of items, and afford a basis for the treatment of similar or related transactions. As with the examination

of information supplied for the current year's return, the extent of comparison of the details of income and deduction between years depends on the particular circumstances.

STATEMENT ON STANDARDS FOR TAX SERVICES NO. 4, USE OF ESTIMATES

INTRODUCTION

1. This Statement sets forth the applicable standards for members when using the taxpayer's estimates in the preparation of a tax return. A member may advise on estimates used in the preparation of a tax return, but the taxpayer has the responsibility to provide the estimated data. Appraisals or valuations are not considered estimates for purposes of this Statement.

STATEMENT

2. Unless prohibited by statute or by rule, a member may use the taxpayer's estimates in the preparation of a tax return if it is not practical to obtain exact data and if the member determines that the estimates are reasonable based on the facts and circumstances known to the member. If the taxpayer's estimates are used, they should be presented in a manner that does not imply greater accuracy than exists.

EXPLANATION

3. Accounting requires the exercise of professional judgment and, in many instances, the use of approximations based on judgment. The application of such accounting judgments, as long as not in conflict with methods set forth by a taxing authority, is acceptable. These judgments are not estimates within the purview of this Statement. For example, a federal income tax regulation provides that if all other conditions for accrual are met, the exact amount of income or expense need not be known or ascertained at year end if the amount can be determined with reasonable accuracy.

4. When the taxpayer's records do not accurately reflect information related to small expenditures, accuracy in recording some data may be difficult to achieve. Therefore, the use of estimates by a taxpayer in determining the amount to be deducted for such items may be appropriate.

5. When records are missing or precise information about a transaction is not available at the time the return must be filed, a member may prepare a tax return using a taxpayer's estimates of the missing data.

6. Estimated amounts should not be presented in a manner that provides a misleading impression about the degree of factual accuracy.

7. Specific disclosure that an estimate is used for an item in the return is not generally required; however, such disclosure should be made in unusual circumstances where nondisclosure

might mislead the taxing authority regarding the degree of accuracy of the return as a whole. Some examples of unusual circumstances include the following:

 a. A taxpayer has died or is ill at the time the return must be filed.
 b. A taxpayer has not received a Schedule K-1 for a pass-through entity at the time the tax return is to be filed.
 c. There is litigation pending (for example, a bankruptcy proceeding) that bears on the return.
 d. Fire or computer failure has destroyed the relevant records.

STATEMENT ON STANDARDS FOR TAX SERVICES NO. 5, DEPARTURE FROM A POSITION PREVIOUSLY CONCLUDED IN AN ADMINISTRATIVE PROCEEDING OR COURT DECISION

INTRODUCTION

1. This Statement sets forth the applicable standards for members in recommending a tax return position that departs from the position determined in an administrative proceeding or in a court decision with respect to the taxpayer's prior return.

2. For purposes of this Statement, *administrative proceeding* also includes an examination by a taxing authority or an appeals conference relating to a return or a claim for refund.

3. For purposes of this Statement, *court decision* means a decision by any court having jurisdiction over tax matters.

STATEMENT

4. The tax return position with respect to an item as determined in an administrative proceeding or court decision does not restrict a member from recommending a different tax position in a later year's return, unless the taxpayer is bound to a specified treatment in the later year, such as by a formal closing agreement. Therefore, as provided in Statement on Standards for Tax Services (SSTS) No. 1, *Tax Return Positions,* the member may recommend a tax return position or prepare or sign a tax return that departs from the treatment of an item as concluded in an administrative proceeding or court decision with respect to a prior return of the taxpayer.

EXPLANATION

5. If an administrative proceeding or court decision has resulted in a determination concerning a specific tax treatment of an item in a prior year's return, a member will usually recommend this

same tax treatment in subsequent years. However, departures from consistent treatment may be justified under such circumstances as the following:

a. Taxing authorities tend to act consistently in the disposition of an item that was the subject of a prior administrative proceeding but generally are not bound to do so. Similarly, a taxpayer is not bound to follow the tax treatment of an item as consented to in an earlier administrative proceeding.

b. The determination in the administrative proceeding or the court's decision may have been caused by a lack of documentation. Supporting data for the later year may be appropriate.

c. A taxpayer may have yielded in the administrative proceeding for settlement purposes or not appealed the court decision, even though the position met the standards in SSTS No. 1.

d. Court decisions, rulings, or other authorities that are more favorable to a taxpayer's current position may have developed since the prior administrative proceeding was concluded or the prior court decision was rendered.

6. The consent in an earlier administrative proceeding and the existence of an unfavorable court decision are factors that the member should consider in evaluating whether the standards in SSTS No. 1 are met.

STATEMENT ON STANDARDS FOR TAX SERVICES NO. 6, KNOWLEDGE OF ERROR: RETURN PREPARATION

INTRODUCTION

1. This Statement sets forth the applicable standards for a member who becomes aware of an error in a taxpayer's previously filed tax return or of a taxpayer's failure to file a required tax return. As used herein, the term error includes any position, omission, or method of accounting that, at the time the return is filed, fails to meet the standards set out in Statement on Standards for Tax Services (SSTS) No. 1, *Tax Return Positions*. The term *error* also includes a position taken on a prior year's return that no longer meets these standards due to legislation, judicial decisions, or administrative pronouncements having retroactive effect. However, an error does not include an item that has an insignificant effect on the taxpayer's tax liability.

2. This Statement applies whether or not the member prepared or signed the return that contains the error.

STATEMENT

3. A member should inform the taxpayer promptly upon becoming aware of an error in a previously filed return or upon becoming aware of a taxpayer's failure to file a required return.

A member should recommend the corrective measures to be taken. Such recommendation may be given orally. The member is not obligated to inform the taxing authority, and a member may not do so without the taxpayer's permission, except when required by law.

4. If a member is requested to prepare the current year's return and the taxpayer has not taken appropriate action to correct an error in a prior year's return, the member should consider whether to withdraw from preparing the return and whether to continue a professional or employment relationship with the taxpayer. If the member does prepare such current year's return, the member should take reasonable steps to ensure that the error is not repeated.

EXPLANATION

5. While performing services for a taxpayer, a member may become aware of an error in a previously filed return or may become aware that the taxpayer failed to file a required return. The member should advise the taxpayer of the error and the measures to be taken. Such recommendation may be given orally. If the member believes that the taxpayer could be charged with fraud or other criminal misconduct, the taxpayer should be advised to consult legal counsel before taking any action.

6. It is the taxpayer's responsibility to decide whether to correct the error. If the taxpayer does not correct an error, a member should consider whether to continue a professional or employment relationship with the taxpayer. While recognizing that the taxpayer may not be required by statute to correct an error by filing an amended return, a member should consider whether a taxpayer's decision not to file an amended return may predict future behavior that might require termination of the relationship. The potential for violating Code of Professional Conduct rule 301 (relating to the member's confidential client relationship), the tax law and regulations, or laws on privileged communications, and other considerations may create a conflict between the member's interests and those of the taxpayer. Therefore, a member should consider consulting with his or her own legal counsel before deciding upon recommendations to the taxpayer and whether to continue a professional or employment relationship with the taxpayer.

7. If a member decides to continue a professional or employment relationship with the taxpayer and is requested to prepare a tax return for a year subsequent to that in which the error occurred, the member should take reasonable steps to ensure that the error is not repeated. If the subsequent year's tax return cannot be prepared without perpetuating the error, the member should consider withdrawal from the return preparation. If a member learns that the taxpayer is using an erroneous method of accounting and it is past the due date to request permission to change to a method meeting the standards of SSTS No. 1, the member may sign a tax return for the current year, providing the tax return includes appropriate disclosure of the use of the erroneous method.

8. Whether an error has no more than an insignificant effect on the taxpayer's tax liability is left to the professional judgment of the member based on all the facts and circumstances known to the member. In judging whether an erroneous method of

accounting has more than an insignificant effect, a member should consider the method's cumulative effect and its effect on the current year's tax return.

9. If a member becomes aware of the error while performing services for a taxpayer that do not involve tax return preparation, the member's responsibility is to advise the taxpayer of the existence of the error and to recommend that the error be discussed with the taxpayer's tax return preparer. Such recommendation may be given orally.

STATEMENT ON STANDARDS FOR TAX SERVICES NO. 7, KNOWLEDGE OF ERROR: ADMINISTRATIVE PROCEEDINGS

INTRODUCTION

1. This Statement sets forth the applicable standards for a member who becomes aware of an error in a return that is the subject of an administrative proceeding, such as an examination by a taxing authority or an appeals conference. The term *administrative proceeding* does not include a criminal proceeding. As used herein, the term *error* includes any position, omission, or method of accounting that, at the time the return is filed, fails to meet the standards set out in Statement on Standards for Tax Services (SSTS) No. 1, *Tax Return Positions*. The term *error* also includes a position taken on a prior year's return that no longer meets these standards due to legislation, judicial decisions, or administrative pronouncements having retroactive effect. However, an error does not include an item that has an insignificant effect on the taxpayer's tax liability.

2. This Statement applies whether or not the member prepared or signed the return that contains the error. Special considerations may apply when a member has been engaged by legal counsel to provide assistance in a matter relating to the counsel's client.

STATEMENT

3. If a member is representing a taxpayer in an administrative proceeding with respect to a return that contains an error of which the member is aware, the member should inform the taxpayer promptly upon becoming aware of the error. The member should recommend the corrective measures to be taken. Such recommendation may be given orally. A member is neither obligated to inform the taxing authority nor allowed to do so without the taxpayer's permission, except where required by law.

4. A member should request the taxpayer's agreement to disclose the error to the taxing authority. Lacking such agreement, the member should consider whether to withdraw from representing the taxpayer in the administrative proceeding and whether to continue a professional or employment relationship with the taxpayer.

EXPLANATION

5. When the member is engaged to represent the taxpayer before a taxing authority in an administrative proceeding with respect to a return containing an error of which the member is aware, the member should advise the taxpayer to disclose the error to the taxing authority. Such recommendation may be given orally. If the member believes that the taxpayer could be charged with fraud or other criminal misconduct, the taxpayer should be advised to consult legal counsel before taking any action.

6. It is the taxpayer's responsibility to decide whether to correct the error. If the taxpayer does not correct an error, a member should consider whether to withdraw from representing the taxpayer in the administrative proceeding and whether to continue a professional or employment relationship with the taxpayer. While recognizing that the taxpayer may not be required by statute to correct an error by filing an amended return, a member should consider whether a taxpayer's decision not to file an amended return may predict future behavior that might require termination of the relationship. Moreover, a member should consider consulting with his or her own legal counsel before deciding on recommendations to the taxpayer and whether to continue a professional or employment relationship with the taxpayer. The potential for violating Code of Professional Conduct rule 301 (relating to the member's confidential client relationship), the tax law and regulations, laws on privileged communications, potential adverse impact on a taxpayer of a member's withdrawal, and other considerations may create a conflict between the member's interests and those of the taxpayer.

7. Once disclosure is agreed on, it should not be delayed to such a degree that the taxpayer or member might be considered to have failed to act in good faith or to have, in effect, provided misleading information. In any event, disclosure should be made before the conclusion of the administrative proceeding.

8. Whether an error has an insignificant effect on the taxpayer's tax liability is left to the professional judgment of the member based on all the facts and circumstances known to the member. In judging whether an erroneous method of accounting has more than an insignificant effect, a member should consider the method's cumulative effect and its effect on the return that is the subject of the administrative proceeding.

STATEMENT ON STANDARDS FOR TAX SERVICES NO. 8, FORM AND CONTENT OF ADVICE TO TAXPAYERS

INTRODUCTION

1. This Statement sets forth the applicable standards for members concerning certain aspects of providing advice to a taxpayer

and considers the circumstances in which a member has a responsibility to communicate with a taxpayer when subsequent developments affect advice previously provided. The Statement does not, however, cover a member's responsibilities when the expectation is that the advice rendered is likely to be relied on by parties other than the taxpayer.

STATEMENT

2. A member should use judgment to ensure that tax advice provided to a taxpayer reflects professional competence and appropriately serves the taxpayer's needs. A member is not required to follow a standard format or guidelines in communicating written or oral advice to a taxpayer.

3. A member should assume that tax advice provided to a taxpayer will affect the manner in which the matters or transactions considered would be reported on the taxpayer's tax returns. Thus, for all tax advice given to a taxpayer, a member should follow the standards in Statement on Standards for Tax Services (SSTS) No. 1, *Tax Return Positions*.

4. A member has no obligation to communicate with a taxpayer when subsequent developments affect advice previously provided with respect to significant matters, except while assisting a taxpayer in implementing procedures or plans associated with the advice provided or when a member undertakes this obligation by specific agreement.

EXPLANATION

5. Tax advice is recognized as a valuable service provided by members. The form of advice may be oral or written and the subject matter may range from routine to complex. Because the range of advice is so extensive and because advice should meet the specific needs of a taxpayer, neither a standard format nor guidelines for communicating or documenting advice to the taxpayer can be established to cover all situations.

6. Although oral advice may serve a taxpayer's needs appropriately in routine matters or in well-defined areas, written communications are recommended in important, unusual, or complicated transactions. The member may use professional judgment about whether, subsequently, to document oral advice in writing.

7. In deciding on the form of advice provided to a taxpayer, a member should exercise professional judgment and should consider such factors as the following:

a. The importance of the transaction and amounts involved

b. The specific or general nature of the taxpayer's inquiry

c. The time available for development and submission of the advice

d. The technical complications presented

e. The existence of authorities and precedents

f. The tax sophistication of the taxpayer

g. The need to seek other professional advice

8. A member may assist a taxpayer in implementing procedures or plans associated with the advice offered. When providing such assistance, the member should review and revise such

advice as warranted by new developments and factors affecting the transaction.

9. Sometimes a member is requested to provide tax advice but does not assist in implementing the plans adopted. Although such developments as legislative or administrative changes or future judicial interpretations may affect the advice previously provided, a member cannot be expected to communicate subsequent developments that affect such advice unless the member undertakes this obligation by specific agreement with the taxpayer.

10. Taxpayers should be informed that advice reflects professional judgment based on an existing situation and that subsequent developments could affect previous professional advice. Members may use precautionary language to the effect that their advice is based on facts as stated and authorities that are subject to change.

11. In providing tax advice, a member should be cognizant of applicable confidentiality privileges.

The AICPA gratefully acknowledges the contributions of William A. Tate, Jean L. Rothbarth, and Leonard Podolin, former chairs of the Responsibilities in Tax Practice Committee; A. M. (Tony) Komlyn and Wilber Van Scoik, former members of the Committee; and Carol B. Ferguson, AICPA Technical Manager.

Note: *Statements on Standards for Tax Services are issued by the Tax Executive Committee, the senior technical body of the Institute designated to promulgate standards of tax practice. Rules 201 and 202 of the Institute's Code of Professional Conduct require compliance with these standards.*

INTERPRETATION NO. 1-2, "TAX PLANNING," OF STATEMENT ON STANDARDS FOR TAX SERVICES NO. 1, TAX RETURN POSITIONS (OCTOBER 2003)

NOTICE TO READERS

The Statements on Standards for Tax Services (SSTSs) and Interpretations, promulgated by the Tax Executive Committee, reflect the AICPA's standards of tax practice and delineate members' responsibilities to taxpayers, the public, the government, and the profession. The Statements are intended to be part of an ongoing process that may require changes to and Interpretations of current SSTSs in recognition of the accelerating rate of change in tax laws and the continued importance of tax practice to members. Interpretation No. 1-2 was approved by the Tax Executive Committee on August 21, 2003; its effective date is December 31, 2003.

The SSTSs have been written in as simple and objective a manner as possible. However, by their nature, ethical standards provide for an appropriate range of behavior that recognizes the need for Interpretations to meet a broad range of personal and professional situations. The SSTSs recognize this need by, in some sections, providing relatively subjective rules and by leaving certain terms undefined. These terms and concepts are generally rooted in tax concepts, and therefore should be readily understood by tax practitioners. It is, therefore, recognized that the enforcement of these rules, as part of the AICPA's Code of Professional Conduct Rule 201, *General Standards*, and Rule 202, *Compliance With Standards*, will be undertaken with flexibility in mind and handled on a case-by-case basis. Members are expected to comply with them.

BACKGROUND

1. Statements on Standards for Tax Services (SSTSs) are enforceable standards that govern the conduct of members of the AICPA in tax practice. A significant area of many members' tax practices involves assisting taxpayers in tax planning. Two of the eight SSTSs issued as of the date of this Interpretation's release directly set forth standards that affect the most common activities in tax planning. Several other SSTSs set forth standards related to specific factual situations that may arise while a member is assisting a taxpayer in tax planning. The two SSTSs that are most typically relevant to tax planning are SSTS No. 1, *Tax Return Positions* (AICPA, *Professional Standards*, vol. 2, TS sec. 100), including Interpretation No. 1-1, "Realistic Possibility Standard" (AICPA, *Professional Standards*, vol. 2, TS sec. 9100), and SSTS No. 8, *Form and Content of Advice to Taxpayers* (AICPA, *Professional Standards*, vol. 2, TS sec. 800).

2. Taxing authorities, courts, the AICPA, and other professional organizations have struggled with defining and regulating *tax shelters* and *abusive transactions*. Crucial to the debate is the difficulty of clearly distinguishing between transactions that are abusive and transactions that are legitimate. At the same time, it must be recognized that taxpayers have a legitimate interest in arranging their affairs so as to pay no more than the taxes they owe. It must be recognized that tax professionals, including members, have a role to play in advancing these efforts.

3. This Interpretation is part of the AICPA's continuing efforts at self-regulation of its members in tax practice. It has its origins in the AICPA's desire to provide adequate guidance to its members when providing services in connection with tax planning. The Interpretation does not change or elevate any level of conduct prescribed by any standard. Its goal is to clarify existing standards. It was determined that there was a compelling need for a comprehensive Interpretation of a member's responsibilities in connection with *tax planning*, with the recognition that such guidance would clarify how those standards would apply across the spectrum of tax planning, including those situations involving *tax shelters*, regardless of how that term is defined.

GENERAL INTERPRETATION

4. The realistic possibility standard (see SSTS No. 1, TS sec. 100.02(1), and Interpretation No. 1-1) applies to a member when providing professional services that involve *tax planning*. A member may still recommend a nonfrivolous position provided that the member recommends appropriate disclosure (see SSTS No. 1, TS sec. 100.02(c)).

5. For purposes of this Interpretation, *tax planning* includes, both with respect to prospective and completed transactions, recommending or expressing an opinion (whether written or oral) on (a) a tax return position or (b) a specific tax plan developed by the member, the taxpayer, or a third party.

6. When issuing an opinion to reflect the results of the tax planning service, a member should do all of the following:

- Establish the relevant background facts.
- Consider the reasonableness of the assumptions and representations.
- Apply the pertinent authorities to the relevant facts.
- Consider the business purpose and economic substance of the transaction, if relevant to the tax consequences of the transaction.
- Arrive at a conclusion supported by the authorities.

7. In assisting a taxpayer in a tax planning transaction in which the taxpayer has obtained an opinion from a third party, and the taxpayer is looking to the member for an evaluation of the opinion, the member should be satisfied as to the source, relevance, and persuasiveness of the opinion, which would include considering whether the opinion indicates the third party did all of the following:

- Established the relevant background facts
- Considered the reasonableness of the assumptions and representations
- Applied the pertinent authorities to the relevant facts
- Considered the business purpose and economic substance of the transaction, if relevant to the tax consequences of the transaction
- Arrived at a conclusion supported by the authorities

8. In conducting the due diligence necessary to establish the relevant background facts, the member should consider whether it is appropriate to rely on an assumption concerning facts in lieu of either other procedures to support the advice or a representation from the taxpayer or another person. A member should also consider whether the member's tax advice will be communicated to third parties, particularly if those third parties may not be knowledgeable or may not be receiving independent tax advice with respiect to a transaction.

9. In tax planning, members often rely on assumptions and representations. Although such reliance is often necessary, the member must take care to assess whether such assumptions and representations are reasonable. In deciding whether an assumption or representation is reasonable, the member should consider its source and consistency with other information know to the member. For example, depending on the circumstances, it may be reasonable for a member to rely on a representation made by the taxpayer, but not on a representation made by a person who is silling or otherwise promoting the transaction to the taxpayer.

10. When engaged in tax planning, the member should understand the business purpose and economic substance of the transaction when relevant to the tax consequences. If a transaction has been proposed by a party other than the taxpayer, the member should consider whether the assumptions made by the third party are consistent with the facts of the taxpayer's situation. If written advice is to be rendered concerning a transaction, the business purpose for the transaction generally should be described. If the business reasons are relevant to the tax consequences, it is insufficient to merely assume that a transaction is entered into for valid business reasons without specifying what those reasons are.

11. The scope of the engagement should be appropriately determined. A member should be diligent in applying such procedures as are appropriate under the circumstances to understand and evaluate the entire transaction. The specific procedures to be performed in this regard will vary with the circumstances and the scope of the engagement.

SPECIFIC ILLUSTRATIONS

12. The following illustrations address general fact patterns. Accordingly, the application of the guidance discussed in the "General Interpretation" section to variations in such general facts or to particular facts or circumstances may lead to different conclusions. In each illustration, there is no authority other than that indicated.

13. *Illustration 1.* The relevant tax code imposes penalties on substantial underpayments that are not associated with tax shelters as defined in such code unless the associated positions are supported by substantial authority.

14. *Conclusion.* In assisting the taxpayer in tax planning in which any associated underpayment would be substantial, the member should inform the taxpayer of the penalty risks associated with the tax return position recommended with respect to any plan under consideration that satisfies the realistic possibility of success standard, but does not possess sufficient authority to satisfy the substantial authority standard.

15. *Illustration 2.* The relevant tax code imposes penalties on tax shelters, as defined in such code, unless the taxpayer concludes that a position taken on a tax return associated with such a tax shelter is, more likely than not, the correct position.

16. *Conclusion.* In assisting the taxpayer in tax planning, the member should inform the taxpayer of the penalty risks associated with the tax return position recommemded with respect to any plan under consideration that satisfies the realistic possibility of success standard, but does not possess sufficient authority to satisfy the more likely than not standard.

17. *Illustration 3.* The relevant tax regulation provides that the details of (or certain information regarding) a specific transaction are required to be attached to the tax return, regardless of the support for the associated tax return position (for example, even if there is substantial authority or a higher level of comfort for the position). While preparing the taxpayer's return for the year, the member is aware that an attachment is required.

18. *Conclusion.* In general, if the taxpayer agrees to include the attachment required by the regulation, the member may sign the return if the member concludes the associated tax return position satisfies the realistic possibility standard. However, if the taxpayer refuses to include the attachment, the member should not sign the return, unless the member concludes the associated tax return position satisfies the realistic possibility standard and there are reasonable grounds for the taxpayer's position with respect to the attachment. In this regard, the member should consider SSTS No. 2, *Answers to Questions on Returns* (AICPA, *Professional Standards*, vol. 2, TS sec. 200.01 and .05), which provides that the term *questions*, as used in the standard, "includes requests for information on the return, in the instructions, or in the regulations, whether or not stated in the form of a question," and that a "member should not omit an answer merely because it might prove disadvantageous to the taxpayer."

19. *Illustration 4.* The relevant tax regulations provide that the details of certain potentially abusive transactions that are designated as "listed transactions" are required to be disclosed in attachments to tax returns, regardless of the support for the associated tax return position (for example, even if there is substantial authority or a higher level of support for the position). Under the regulations, if a listed transaction is not disclosed as required, the taxpayer will have additional penalty risks. While researching the tax consequences of a proposed

transaction, a member concludes that the transaction is a listed transaction.

20. *Conclusion.* Notwithstanding the member's conclusion that the transaction is a listed transaction, the member may still recommend a tax return position with respect to the transaction if he or she concludes that the proposed tax return position satisfies the realistic possibility standard. However, the member should inform the taxpayer of the enhanced disclosure requirements of listed transactions and the additional penalty risks for nondisclosure.

21. *Illustration 5.* The same regulations apply as in Illustration 4. The member first becomes aware that a taxpayer entered into a transaction while preparing the taxpayer's return for the year of the transaction. While researching the tax consequences of the transaction, the member concludes that the taxpayer's transaction is a listed transaction.

22. *Conclusion.* The member should inform the taxpayer of the enhanced disclosure requirement and the additional penalty risks for nondisclosure. If the taxpayer agrees to make the disclosure required by the regulation, the member may sign the return if the member concludes the associated tax return position satisfies the realistic possibility standard. Reasonable grounds for nondisclosure (see the conclusion to Illustration 3) generally are not present for a listed transaction. The member should not sign the return if the transaction is not disclosed. If the member is a nonsigning preparer of the return, the member should recommend that the taxpayer disclose the transaction.

23. *Illustration 6.* The same regulations apply as in Illustration 4. The member first becomes aware that a taxpayer entered into a transaction while preparing the taxpayer's return for the year of the transaction. While researching the tax consequences of the transaction, the member concludes that there is uncertainty about whether the taxpayer's transactions is a listed transaction.

24. *Conclusion.* The member should inform the taxpayer of the enhanced disclosure requirement and the additional penalty risks for nondisclosure. If the taxpayer agrees to make the disclosure required by the relevant regulation, the member may sign the return if the member concludes the associated tax return position satisfies the realistic possibility standard. If the taxpayer does not want to disclose the transaction because of the uncertainty about whether it is a listed transaction, the member may sign the return if the member concludes the associated tax return position satisfies the realistic possibility standard and there are reasonable grounds for the taxpayer's position with regard to nondisclosure. In this regard, the member should consider SSTS No. 2, TS sec. 200.04, which indicates that the degree of uncertainty regarding the meaning of a question on a return may affect whether there are reasonable grounds for not responding to the question.

25. *Illustration 7.* A member advises a taxpayer concerning the tax consequences of a transaction involving a loan from a U.S. bank. In the process of reviewing documents associated with the proposed transaction, the member uncovers a reference to a deposit that a wholly owned foreign subsidiary of the taxpayer will make with an overseas branch of the U.S. bank. The transaction documents appear to indicate that this deposit is linked to the U.S. bank's issuance of the loan.

26. *Conclusion.* The member should consider the effect, if any, of the deposit in advising the taxpayer about the tax consequences of the proposed transaction.

27. *Illustration 8.* Under the relevant tax law, the tax consequences of a leasing transaction depend on whether the property to be leased is reasonably expected to have a residual value of 15 percent of its value at the begining of the lease. The member has relied on a taxpayer's instruction to use a particular assumption concerning the residual value.

28. *Conclusion.* Such reliance on the taxpayer's instructions may be appropriate if the assumption is supported by the expertise of the taxpayer, by the member's review of information provided by the taxpayer or a third party, or through the member's own knowledge or analysis.

29. *Illustration 9.* A member is assisting a taxpayer with evaluating a proposed equipment leasing transaction in which the estimated residual value of the equipment at the end of the lease term is critical to the tax consequences of the lease. The broker arranging the leasing transaction has prepared an analysis that sets out an explicit assumption concerning the equipment's estimated residual value.

30. *Conclusion.* The member should consider whether it is appropriate to rely on the broker's assumption concerning the estimated residual value of the equipment instead of obtaining a representation from the broker concerning estimated residual value or performing other procedures to validate the amount to be used as an estimate of residual value in connection with the member's advice. In considering the appropriateness of the broker's assumption, the member should consider, for example, the factors such as the broker's experience in the area, the broker's methodology, and whether alternative sources of information are reasonably available.

31. *Illustration 10.* The tax consequences of a particular reorganization depend, in part, on the majority shareholder of a corporation not disposing of any stock received in the reorganization pursuant to a prearranged agreement to dispose of the stock.

32. *Conclusion.* The member should consider whether it is appropriate in rendering tax advice to assume that such a disposition will not occur or whether, under the circumstances, it is appropriate to request a written representation of the shareholder's intent concerning disposition as a condition to issuing an opinion on the reorganization.

33. *Illustration 11.* A taxpayer is considering a proposed transaction. The taxpayer and the taxpayer's attorney advise the member that the member is responsible for advising the taxpayer on the tax consequences of the transaction.

34. *Conclusion.* In addition to complying with the requirements of paragraph 6, the member generally should review all relevant draft transaction documents in formulating the member's tax advice relating to the transaction.

35. *Illustration 12.* A member is responsible for advising a taxpayer on the tax consequences of the taxpayer's estate plan.

36. *Conclusion.* Under the circumstances, the member should review the will and all other relevant documents to assess whether there appear to be any tax issues raised by the formulation of implementation of the estate plan.

37. *Illustration 13.* A member is assisting a taxpayer in connection with a proposed transaction that has been recommended by an investment bank. To support its recommendation, the investment bank offers a law firm's opinion on the tax consequences. The member reads the opinion, and notes that it is based on a hypothetical statement of facts rather than the taxpayer's facts.

38. *Conclusion.* The member may rely on the law firm's opinion when determining whether the realistic possibility standard has been satisfied with respect to the tax consequences of the hypothetical transaction if the member is satisfied about the source, relevance, and persuasiveness of the opinion. However, the member should be diligent in taking such steps as are appropriate under the circumstances to understand and evaluate the transaction as it applies to the taxpayer's specific situation by:

• Establishing the relevant background facts
• Considering the reasonableness of the assumptions and representations
• Applying the pertinent authorities to the relevant facts
• Considering the business purpose and economic substance of the transaction, if relevant to the tax consequences of the transaction (Mere reliance on a representation that there is business purpose or economic substance is generally insufficient.)
• Arriving at a conclusion supported by the authorities

39. *Illustration 14.* The facts are the same as in Illustration 13 except the member also notes that the law firm that prepared the opinion is one that has a reputation as being knowledgeable about the tax issues associated with the proposed transaction.

40. *Conclusion.* The conclusion is the same as the conclusion to Illustration 13, notwithstanding the expertise of the law firm.

41. *Illustration 15.* A member is assisting a taxpayer in connection with a proposed transaction that has been recommended by an investment bank. To support that recommendation, the investment bank offers a law firm's opinion about the tax consequences. The member reads the opinion, and notes that (unlike the opinions described in Illustrations 13 and 14), it is carefully tailored to the taxpayer's facts.

42. *Conclusion.* The member may rely on the opinion when determining whether the realistic possibility standard has been met with respect to the taxpayer's participation in the transaction if the member is satisfied about the source, relevance, and persuasiveness of the opinion. In making that determination, the member should consider whether the opinion indicates the law firm did all of the following:

• Established the relevant background facts
• Considered the reasonableness of the assumptions and representations
• Applied the pertinent authorities to the relevant facts
• Considered the business purpose and economic substance of the transaction, if relevant to the tax consequences of the transaction (Mere reliance on a representation that there is business purpose or economic substance is generally insufficient.)
• Arrived at a conclusion supported by the authorities

43. *Illustration 16.* The facts are the same as in Illustration 15, except the member also notes that the law firm that prepared the opinion is one that has a reputation of being knowledgeable about the tax issues associated with the proposed transaction.

44. *Conclusion.* The conclusion is the same as the conclusion to Illustration 15, notwithstanding the expertise of the law firm.

45. *Illustration 17.* A member is assisting a taxpayer with year-end planning in connection with the taxpayer's proposed contribution of stock in a closely held corporation to a charitable organization. The taxpayer instructs the member to calculate the anticipated tax liability assuming a contribution of 10,000 shares to a tax-exempt organization assuming the stock has a fair market value of $100 per share. The member is aware that on the taxpayer's gift tax returns for the prior year, the taxpayer indicated that her stock in the corporation was worth $50 per share.

46. *Conclusion.* The member's calculation of the anticipated tax liability is subject to the general interpretations described in paragraphs 8 and 9. Accordingly, even though this potentially may be a case in which the value of the stock substantially appreciated during the year, the member should consider the reasonableness of the assumption and consistency with other information known to the member in connection with preparing the projection. The member should consider whether to document discussions concerning the increase in value of the stock with the taxpayer.

47. *Illustration 18.* The tax consequences to Target Corporation's shareholders of an acquisition turn in part on Acquiring Corporation's continuance of the trade or business of Target Corporation for some time after the acquisition. The member is preparing a tax opinion addressed to Target's shareholders. A colleague has drafted a tax opinion for the member's review. That opinion makes an explicit assumption that Acquiring will continue Target's business for two years following the acquisition.

48. *Conclusion.* In conducting the due diligence necessary to establish the relevant background facts, the member should consider whether it is appropriate to rely on an assumption concerning facts in lieu of a representation from another person. In this case, the member should make reasonable efforts to obtain a representation from Acquiring Corporation concerning its plan to continue Target's business and further consider whether to request a written representation to that effect.

49. *Illustration 19.* The member receives a telephone call from a taxpayer who is the sole shareholder of a corporation. The taxpayer indicates that he is thinking about exchanging his stock in the corporation for stock in a publicly traded business. During the call, the member explains how the transaction should be structured so it will qualify as a tax-free acquisition.

50. *Conclusion.* Although oral advice may serve a taxpayer's needs appropriately in routine matters or in well-defined areas, written communications are recommended in important, unusual, or complicated transactions. The member should use professional judgment about the need to document oral advice.

51. *Illustration 20.* The member receives a telephone call from a taxpayer who wants to know whether he or she should lease or purchase a car. During the call, the member explains how the arrangement should be structured so as to help achieve the taxpayer's objectives.

52. *Conclusion.* In this situation, the member's response is in conformity with this Interpretation in view of the routine nature of the inquiry and the well-defined tax issues. However, the member should evaluate whether other considerations, such as avoiding misunderstanding with the taxpayer, suggest that the conversation should be documented.

This Interpretation was adopted by the assenting votes of the eighteen voting members of the nineteen-member Tax Executive Committee.

Tax Executive Committee (2002–2003)

Robert A. Zarzar, *Chair*	Annette Nellen
Pamela J. Pecarich, *IP Chair*	Thomas P. Ochsenschlager
Steven K. Bentley	Robert A. Petersen
Barbara A. Bond	Thomas J. Purcell III
Mark H. Ely	James W. Sansone
Lisa C. Germano	C. Clinton Stretch
Ronald B. Hegt	Judyth A. Swingen
Kenneth H. Heller	William A. Tate
Jeffrey R. Hoops	James P. Whitson
Nancy K. Hyde	

Tax Practice Responsibilities Committee (2002–2003)

Dan L. Mendelson, *Chair*	Stuart Kessler
J. Edward Swails, *Vice Chair*	Dori Laskin
Lawrence H. Carleton	Robin C. Makar
Conrad M. Davis	Christine K. Peterson
Alan R. Einhorn	Michael J. Predhomme
Eve Elgin	Joseph F. Scutellaro
John C. Gardner	Thomas G. Tierney

SSTS Tax Shelter Task Force

Michael E. Mares, *Chair*	William C. Potter
Eve Elgin	J. Edward Swails
John C. Gardner	Claude R Wilson, Jr.
Ronald S. Katch	

AICPA Staff

Gerald W. Padwe	Edward S. Karl
Vice President	*Director*
Taxation	*Taxation*
Benson S. Goldstein	
Technical Manager	
Taxation	

Note: *Statements on Standards for Tax Services are issued by the Tax Executive Comittee, the senior technical body of the Institute designated to promulgate standards of tax practice. Rules 201 and 202 of the Institute's Code of Professional Conduct require compliance with these standards.*

These Statements on Standards for Tax Services and Interpretation were unanimously adopted by the assenting votes of the twenty voting members of the twenty-one-member Tax Executive Committee.

EXPOSURE DRAFT DECEMBER 30, 2005

PROPOSED STATEMENT ON STANDARDS FOR TAX SERVICES QUALITY CONTROL

INTRODUCTION

1. This Statement sets forth the applicable standards for members concerning the obligation to have a system of quality control for their tax practice (public practice) or function (nonpublic practice). In light of the fact that members practice in various forms, or with various size employers, and therefore cannot take personal responsibility for every aspect of such tax practice or function, there has arisen a need for a Statement on what constitutes an adequate system of quality control in a tax practice or function to enhance compliance with the other aspects of the Statements on Standards for Tax Services (SSTSs). For purposes of this Statement, a *system of quality control* is broadly defined as a process to provide the member with reasonable assurance that the *firm* (public practice) or *employer's* (nonpublic practice) *personnel* (for purposes of this Statement, the term *personnel*

includes partners, officers, employees, and other associates of the tax practice or function) comply with applicable professional standards.

STATEMENT

2. In general, a member's firm or employer should establish and maintain for its tax practice or function a system of quality control that includes the five elements of quality control (detailed in paragraph 4 and others that follow) and other matters essential to the effective design, implementation, and maintenance of the system. A member providing tax services is encouraged to practice in a firm or work for an employer that has established and maintains an adequate system of quality control for its tax practice or function. However, it is the responsibility of the member(s) in charge of such tax practice or function to ensure an appropriate system of tax practice quality control is implemented.

3. A system of quality control for a tax practice or function should encompass the organizational structure and the policies adopted and procedures established to provide reasonable assurance that such tax practice or function is in compliance with professional standards. The nature, extent, comprehensiveness, and formality of a tax practice or function's quality control policies and procedures may vary due to considerations such as the size of the tax practice or function, the number of offices, the degree of authority granted to personnel and offices, the knowledge and experience of personnel, the nature of the tax practice

or function, the practice area(s) or area(s) of specialty and appropriate cost-benefit considerations. While this Statement is applicable to all members, including members in industry, it must be recognized that each system of quality control must take into account the unique aspects of the tax practice or function, especially with regard to those members providing tax services to employers.

4. *Elements of Quality Control.* To be effective, any system of tax practice quality control should contain policies and procedures covering the following five elements:

   a. Integrity and objectivity

   b. Personnel management

   c. Acceptance and continuance of clients and engagements (public practice only)

   d. Performance of professional services

   e. Monitoring and inspection

EXPLANATION

Integrity and Objectivity

5. In a tax practice or function, the member and his or her personnel often act as an advocate for the taxpayer. The member and his or her personnel should seek to advocate with integrity and objectivity the taxpayer's position as long as that position and their efforts are in compliance with the AICPA Code of Professional Conduct, including the SSTSs (see SSTS No. 1, *Tax Return Positions* [AICPA, *Professional Standards,* vol. 2, TS sec. 100.04]) and applicable federal, state, and local laws. In addition, a member in public practice should consider the applicability, if any, of auditor independence issues to his or her practice; see Rule 2-01 of Regulation S-X, Preliminary Note, 17 CFR 210.2-01. In fulfilling this role, the member is encouraged to practice in a firm or work for an employer that has established and maintains policies and procedures to provide reasonable assurance that personnel perform all professional responsibilities with integrity, and maintain objectivity in discharging his or her professional responsibilities. Integrity requires the member and his or her personnel to be honest and candid within the constraints of taxpayer confidentiality. Service and the public trust should not be subordinated to personal gain and advantage. Objectivity is a state of mind and a quality that lends value to a tax practice or function.

6. The member's firm or employer should consider establishing and maintaining policies and procedures to accomplish the following objectives to the extent such objectives are applicable to such tax practice or function:

   a. Require that personnel adhere to the AICPA Code of Professional Conduct, including the SSTS, Treasury Department Circular No. 230, and any other applicable laws or standards of relevant tax or regulatory agencies (such as state boards of accountancy and federal, foreign, state, and local tax authorities).

   b. Communicate to personnel policies and procedures relating to integrity and objectivity. This includes the need to treat as confidential all information regarding taxpayer matters.

   c. Document, where appropriate, compliance with policies and procedures relating to integrity and objectivity.

Personnel Management

7. A tax practice system of quality control depends heavily on the proficiency of the firm or employer's personnel. In making assignments, the nature and extent of supervision to be provided should be considered. Generally, the more able and experienced the personnel assigned to a particular engagement or task, the less direct supervision is needed.

8. Personnel management encompasses hiring, assigning personnel to engagements or tasks, supervision, professional development, and advancement activities. Accordingly, the member's firm or employer should consider establishing and maintaining policies and procedures to provide its tax practice or function with reasonable assurance that:

   a. Those personnel hired possess the appropriate characteristics to enable them to perform competently.

   b. Work is assigned to personnel having the degree of technical training and proficiency required under the circumstances.

   c. Personnel are adequately supervised.

   d. Personnel participate in tax, general, and (as appropriate) industry-specific continuing professional education and other professional development activities that enable them to fulfill responsibilities assigned, and satisfy applicable continuing professional education requirements of the AICPA, state boards of accountancy, and other regulatory agencies.

   e. The performance of tax professionals and other personnel involved in the tax practice or function is periodically evaluated and their progress reviewed with them.

   f. Personnel selected for advancement have the necessary qualifications to fulfill the responsibilities they will be called on to assume.

Acceptance and Continuance of Clients and Engagements (Public Practice Only)

9. In public practice, the member's firm should consider establishing and maintaining policies and procedures for deciding whether to accept or continue a client relationship and whether to perform a specific engagement for that client (see also SSTS No. 6, *Knowledge of Error: Return Preparation* [AICPA, *Professional Standards,* vol. 2, TS sec. 600], and SSTS No. 7, *Knowledge of Error: Administrative Proceedings* [AICPA, *Professional Standards,* vol. 2, TS sec. 700]). Establishing such policies and procedures does not imply that a member vouches for the integrity or reliability of a client, nor does it imply that a member has a duty to any person or entity with respect to the acceptance, rejection, or retention of clients. Prudence suggests that a member be selective in determining his or her client relationships and the professional services he or she will provide. These policies and procedures should also provide reasonable assurance that the tax practice:

   a. Undertakes only those engagements that can be completed with professional competence, and

b. Appropriately considers the risks associated with providing professional services in the particular circumstances.

10. The member's firm should consider establishing and maintaining policies and procedures to accomplish the following objectives to the extent applicable to its tax practice:

a. The evaluation and approval of prospective clients, including (when appropriate) contact with predecessor tax preparers.

b. The documentation of the client's understanding and acceptance of the scope of the member's services, the member's responsibility for tax advice and returns, and the financial aspects of the client's relationship with the member. These understandings should be memorialized through the use of engagement letters or alternative documentation.

c. The review and evaluation of clients periodically or upon the occurrence of specific events to determine whether the relationship should be continued, modified, or terminated.

Performance of Professional Services

11. The member's firm or employer should consider establishing and maintaining policies and procedures to provide reasonable assurance that the tax services performed by its personnel meet applicable professional standards, including the AICPA SSTS, regulatory requirements, and the tax practice's or function's standards of quality. To the extent appropriate and as required by applicable professional standards, these policies and procedures should cover planning, performing, supervising, reviewing, documenting, and communicating the results of all tax services. The extent of the supervision and review appropriate in a given situation depends on many factors, including the complexity of the subject matter, the qualifications of the personnel performing the service, and the extent of the consultation used.

12. The member's firm or employer should consider establishing and maintaining policies and procedures to accomplish the following to the extent such objectives are applicable to its tax practice or function:

a. Planning services, including specific evaluation of risk factors.

b. Providing the appropriate level of supervision to personnel.

c. Maintaining the tax practice or function's standards in the performance of specific services.

d. Reviewing working papers, reports, tax returns, tax opinions or advice, and substantive tax correspondence relevant to the services.

e. Documenting the compliance *aspects* of a tax practice or function, including tax return status and due date maintenance. This includes the establishment of appropriate record retention procedures for a member's tax practice or function.

f. Communicating the results of the service as appropriate.

g. Designating individuals within and without the tax practice or function to serve as authoritative sources, and defining their authority in consultative situations. This includes establishing procedures to resolve differences of opinion.

Monitoring and Inspection

13. To provide reasonable assurance that the firm or employer's tax practice quality control system achieves its objectives, appropriate consideration should be given to the assignment of quality control responsibilities within the tax practice or function, the means by which quality control policies and procedures are communicated, and the extent to which the policies and procedures and compliance therewith should be documented. The size, structure, and nature of the firm's tax practice or employer's tax function should be considered in determining whether documentation of quality control policies and procedures is required and, if so, the extent of such documentation. For example, documentation of quality control policies and procedures would generally be expected to be more extensive in a large tax practice or function than in a small one. Similarly, quality control should be more extensive in a multioffice tax practice or function than in a single location.

14. The member's firm or employer should consider establishing and maintaining policies and procedures to accomplish the following objectives to the extent applicable to its tax practice or function:

a. Documenting compliance with the tax practice or function's policies and procedures, as well as the SSTSs and relevant professional codes and guidelines.

b. Maintaining an appropriate library of reference materials, practice guides, and access to appropriate online materials

c. Providing an effective program of professional development and educational activities.

d. Where appropriate, defining the appropriate scope and content of the tax practice or function's inspection program, reporting inspection findings to the appropriate management levels, and monitoring actions taken or planned.

e. Reviewing the relevance and adequacy of its quality control policies and procedures for each of the other elements of the quality control system.

Administration and Documentation of a Quality Control System

15. Responsibility for the design and maintenance of the various quality control policies and procedures should be assigned to an appropriate individual(s) in the tax practice or function. In making that assignment, consideration should be given to the proficiency of the individual(s), the authority to be delegated, and the extent of supervision to be provided. However, all the tax practice or function's personnel are responsible for complying with the quality control policies and procedures.

16. A member's firm or employer should communicate its tax practice quality control policies and procedures to personnel in a manner that provides reasonable assurance that personnel understand and comply with those policies and procedures. The form and extent of such communications should be sufficiently comprehensive and timely to provide personnel with an understanding of the tax practice quality control policies and procedures applicable to them, including changes to such policies and procedures.

APPENDIX F

COMPARISON OF TAX ATTRIBUTES FOR C CORPORATIONS, PARTNERSHIPS, AND S CORPORATIONS

APPENDIX F: COMPARISON OF TAX ATTRIBUTES FOR C CORPORATIONS, PARTNERSHIPS, AND S CORPORATIONS

Tax Attribute	C Corporation	Partnership	S Corporation
I. General Characteristics			
1. Application of the separate entity versus conduit (flow through) concept.	*Entity:* The corporation is treated as a separate taxpaying entity. If the corporation distributes income to shareholders in the form of dividends, the shareholders are subject to a second tax on such amounts. Shareholders also are subject to a second tax if they sell their stock.	*Conduit:* The partners report their distributive share of partnership ordinary income and separately stated items on their tax returns. Most elections, such as depreciation methods, accounting period and methods, are made at the partnership level. Special tax rules apply to electing large partnerships.	*Conduit:* Similar to the partnership form of organization. However, the S corporation may be subject to tax at the corporate level on excess net passive income, or built-in gains under special circumstances.
2. Period of existence.	Continues until dissolution; not effected by stock sales by shareholders.	Termination can occur by agreement, or by death, retirement, or disaffiliation of a partner.	Same as for C corporation.
3. Transferability of interest.	Stock can be transferred easily; corporation may retain right to buy back shares.	Addition of new partner or transfer of partner's interest generally requires approval of other partners.	Same as for C corporation.
4. Liability exposure.	Shareholders generally liable only for capital contributions.	General partners are personally, jointly, and severally liable for partnership obligations. Limited partners usually are liable only for capital contributions.	Same as for C corporation.
5. Management responsibility.	Shareholders may be part of management or may hire outside management.	All general partners participate in management. Limited partners generally do not participate.	Because of limited number of shareholders, shareholders usually are part of management.
II. Election and Restrictions			
1. Restrictions on: a. Type of owners.	No restriction.	No restriction.	Limited to individuals, estates, charitable organizations, and certain kinds of trusts.
b. Number of owners.	No restriction.	No restriction.	Limited to 100 shareholders, where a family counts as one shareholder.
c. Type of entity.	Includes domestic or foreign corporations, unincorporated entities known as associations, and certain kinds of trusts. A publicly traded partnership is taxed as a corporation unless more than 90% of its income is qualifying passive income. Grandfathered publicly traded partnerships can avoid corporate taxation by paying an excise tax. Partnerships, LLCs, and proprietorships can elect to be taxed as a corporation under the check-the-box regulations.	Includes a variety of unincorporated entities including limited liability company and limited liability partnership forms. Certain joint undertakings are excluded from partnership status.	Domestic corporations and unincorporated entities (e.g., associations) are eligible. A partnership, LLC, or proprietorship that elects to be treated as an S corporation automatically is considered to have elected to be treated as a corporation under the check-the-box regulations.

APPENDIX F: COMPARISON OF TAX ATTRIBUTES FOR C CORPORATIONS, PARTNERSHIPS, AND S CORPORATIONS

Tax Attribute	C Corporation	Partnership	S Corporation
d. Special tax classifications.	No restriction.	No restriction.	S corporation cannot be a former Domestic International Sales Corporation, or have elected the special Puerto Rico and U.S. Possessions tax credit. Certain financial institutions and insurance companies also are ineligible.
e. Investments made by entity.	No restriction.	No restriction.	S corporation can own 80% or more of a C corporation but cannot file a consolidated tax return with the C corporation.
f. Capital structure.	No restriction.	No restriction.	Limited to a single class of stock that is outstanding. Differences in voting rights are disregarded. Special "safe harbor" rules are available for debt issues.
g. Passive interest income.	No restriction.	No restriction.	Passive investment income cannot exceed 25% of gross receipts for three consecutive tax years when the corporation also has Subchapter C E&P at the end of the year.
2. Election and shareholder consent.	No election required.	No election required.	Election can be made during the preceding tax year or first 2½ months of the tax year. Shareholders must consent to the election.
3. Termination of election.	Not applicable.	The partnership can terminate if it does not carry on any business, financial operation, or venture or if a sale or exchange of at least 50% of the profits and capital interests occurs within a 12-month period.	Occurs if one of the requirements is failed after the election is first effective or if the passive investment income test is failed for three consecutive tax years. IRS can waive invalid elections and permit inadvertent terminations not to break the S election.
4. Revocation of election.	Not applicable.	Not applicable.	Election may be revoked only by shareholders owning more than one-half of the stock. Must be made in first 2½ months of tax year or on a prospective basis.
5. New election.	Not applicable.	Not applicable.	Not permitted for five-year period without IRS consent to early reelection.

APPENDIX F: COMPARISON OF TAX ATTRIBUTES FOR C CORPORATIONS, PARTNERSHIPS, AND S CORPORATIONS

Tax Attribute	C Corporation	Partnership	S Corporation
III. Accounting Periods and Elections			
1. Taxable year.	Calendar year or fiscal year is permitted. Personal service corporations are restricted to using a calendar year unless IRS grants approval to use a fiscal year. A special election is available to use a fiscal year resulting in a three-month or less income deferral if the corporation meets a series of minimum distribution requirements.	Generally use tax year of majority or principal partners. Otherwise use of the least aggregate deferral year is required. Can use a fiscal year that has a business purpose for which IRS approval is obtained. An electing partnership may use a fiscal year resulting in a three-month or less income deferral if an additional required payment is made.	Can use a fiscal year that has a business purpose for which IRS approval is obtained. An S corporation may use a fiscal year resulting in a three-month or less income deferral if an additional required payment is made. If neither of the above applies, a calendar year must be used.
2. Accounting methods.	Elected by the corporation. Use of cash method of accounting is restricted for certain personal service corporations and C corporations having $5 million or more annual gross receipts.	Elected by the partnership. Restrictions on the use of the cash method of accounting apply to partnerships having a C corporation as a partner or that are tax shelters.	Elected by the S corporation. Restrictions on the use of the cash method of accounting apply to S corporations that are tax shelters.
IV. Taxability of Profits			
1. Taxability of profits.	Ordinary income and capital gains are taxed to the corporation. Profits are taxed a second time when distributed.	Ordinary income and separately stated income and gain items pass through to the partners at the end of the partnership's tax year whether or not distributed.	Same as partnership.
2. Allocation of profits.	Not applicable.	Based on partnership agreement. Special allocations are permitted.	Based on stock ownership on each day of the tax year. Special allocations are not permitted.
3. Character of income.	Distributed profits (including tax-exempt income) are dividends to extent of earnings and profits (E&P).	Items receiving special treatment (e.g., capital gains or tax-exempt income) pass through separately to the partner and retain same character as when earned by the partnership.	Same as partnership.
4. Maximum tax rate for earnings.	15% on the first $50,000; 25% from $50,000 to $75,000; 34% from $75,000 to $10 million. The rate is 35% for taxable income above $10 million. A 5% surcharge applies to taxable income between $100,000 and $335,000, and a 3% surcharge applies to taxable income between $15 million and $18,333,333. Special rules apply to controlled groups. Personal service corporations are taxed at a flat 35% rate.	Rates of tax applicable to noncorporate partners from 10% through 35% (in 2006) are levied on pass-through income from the partnership. C corporation rates apply to corporate partners.	Same as partnership except for certain special situations where a special corporate tax applies to the S corporation.

Tax Attribute	C Corporation	Partnership	S Corporation
5. Special tax levies.	Can be subject to accumulated earnings tax, personal holding company tax, and corporate alternative minimum tax.	Not applicable.	Can be subject to built-in gains tax, excess net passive income tax, and LIFO recapture tax.
6. Income splitting between family members.	Only possible when earnings are distributed to shareholder. Dividends received by shareholder under age 14 are taxed at parents' marginal tax rate.	Transfer of partnership interest by gift will permit income splitting. Subject to special rules for transactions involving family members requiring payment of reasonable compensation for capital and services. Income received by partner under age 14 is taxed at parents' marginal tax rate.	Transfer of S corporation interest by gift will permit income splitting. Special rules apply to transactions involving family members requiring payment of reasonable compensation for capital and services. Income received by shareholder under age 14 is taxed at parents' marginal tax rate.
7. Sale of ownership interest.	Gain is taxed as capital gain; 50% of gain may be excluded under Sec. 1202 qualified small business stock rules. Loss is eligible for Sec. 1244 treatment.	Gain may be either ordinary income or capital gain depending on the nature of underlying partnership assets. Losses usually are capital.	Gain is capital in nature but is not eligible for special Sec. 1202 small business stock rules. Loss is eligible for Sec. 1244 treatment.

V. Treatment of Special Income, Gain, Loss, Deduction and Credit Items

Tax Attribute	C Corporation	Partnership	S Corporation
1. Capital gains and losses.	Long-term capital gains are taxed at regular tax rates. Capital losses offset capital gains; excess osses carried back three years and forward five years.	Passed through to partners (according to partnership agreement).	Passed through to shareholders (on a daily basis according to stock ownership).
2. Section 1231 gains and losses.	Eligible for long-term capital gain or ordinary loss treatment. Loss recapture occurs at the corporate level.	Passed through to partners. Loss recapture occurs at the partner level.	Same as partnership.
3. Dividends received from domestic corporation.	Eligible for 70%, 80%, or 100% dividends-received deduction.	Passed through to noncorporate partners, subject to the maximum 15% tax rate if qualified. Corporate partners may be eligible for the dividends-received deduction.	Same as partnership except S corporation cannot have corporate shareholders.
4. U.S. production deduction.	Deduction equals a 3% (in 2006) times the lesser of (1) qualified production activities income for the year cr (2) taxable income before the U.S. production activities deduction. The deduction, however, cannot exceed 50% of the corporation's W-2 wages for the year.	Passed through to partners. Limitations apply at partner level.	Same as partnership.
5. Organizational expenditures.	Deduct up to $5,00C and amortize balance over 180 months.	Same as C corporation.	Same as partnership.
6. Charitable contributions.	Limited to 10% of taxable income.	Passed through to partners. Limitations apply at partner level.	Same as partnership.
7. Expensing of asset acquisition costs.	Limited to $108,000 in 2006.	Limited to $108,000 in 2006 for the partnership and for each partner.	Same as partnership.

APPENDIX F: COMPARISON OF TAX ATTRIBUTES FOR C CORPORATIONS, PARTNERSHIPS, AND S CORPORATIONS

Tax Attribute	C Corporation	Partnership	S Corporation
8. Expenses owed to related parties.	Regular Sec. 267 rules apply to payments and sales or exchanges made to or by the corporation and certain other related parties (e.g., controlling shareholder and corporation or members of a controlled group).	Regular Sec. 267 rules can apply. Special Sec. 267 rules for passthrough entities apply to payments made by the partnership to a partner.	Same as partnership.
9. Employment-related tax considerations.	An owner-employee may be treated as an employee for Social Security tax and corporate fringe benefit purposes. The corporate qualified pension and profit-sharing benefits available to owner-employees are comparable to the plan benefits for self-employed individuals (partners and sole proprietors).	A partner is not considered an employee of the business. Therefore, the partner must pay self-employment tax on the net self-employment income from the business. Corporate fringe benefit exclusions such as group term life insurance are not available (i.e., the premiums are not deductible by the business and are not excludable from the partner's income). Fringe benefits may be provided as nontaxable distribution or as taxable compensation.	Corporate fringe benefit exclusions generally are not available to S corporation shareholders. Fringe benefits usually are provided as nontaxable distribution or taxable compensation. S corporation shareholders may be treated as employees, however, for Social Security tax payments and qualified pension and profit sharing plan rules.
10. Tax preference items and AMT adjustments.	Subject to the corporate alternative minimum tax at the corporate level.	Passed through to partners and taxed under the alternative minimum tax rules applicable to the partner.	Same as partnership.

VI. Deductibility of Losses and Special Items

Tax Attribute	C Corporation	Partnership	S Corporation
1. Deductibility of losses.	Losses create net operating loss (NOL) that carry back two years or forward 20 years or capital loss that carry back three years or forward five years.	Ordinary losses and separately stated loss and deduction items pass through to the partners at the end of the partnership tax year. May create a personal NOL.	Same as partnership.
2. Allocation of losses.	Not applicable.	Based on partnership agreement. Special allocations are permitted.	Based on stock ownership on each day of the tax year. Special allocations are not permitted.
3. Shareholder and entity loss limitations.	Passive losses may be restricted under the passive activity limitation if the C corporation is closely held.	Limited to partner's basis for the partnership interest. Ratable share of all partnership liabilities is included in basis of partnership interest. Excess losses carry over indefinitely until partnership interest again has a basis. Subject to at-risk, passive activity, and hobby loss restrictions.	Limited to shareholder's basis for the stock interest plus basis of S corporation debts to the shareholder. Excess losses carry over indefinitely until shareholder again has basis for stock or debt. Subject to the at-risk, passive activity, and hobby loss restrictions.
4. Basis adjustments for debt and equity interests.	Not applicable.	Basis in partnership interest reduced by loss and deduction passthrough. Subsequent profits increase basis of partnership interest.	Basis in S corporation stock reduced by loss and deduction passthrough. Once basis of stock has been reduced to zero, any other losses and deductions reduce basis of debt (but not below zero). Subsequent net increases restore basis reductions to debt before increasing basis of stock.

APPENDIX F: COMPARISON OF TAX ATTRIBUTES FOR C CORPORATIONS, PARTNERSHIPS, AND S CORPORATIONS

Tax Attribute	C Corporation	Partnership	S Corporation
5. Investment interest deduction limitation.	Not applicable.	Investment interest expenses and income pass through to the partners. Limitation applies at partner level.	Same as partnership.
VII. Distributions			
1. Taxability of nonliquidating distributions to shareholder.	Taxable as dividends if made from current or accumulated E&P. Additional distributions first reduce shareholder's basis for stock, and distributions exceeding stock basis trigger capital gain recognition.	Tax-free unless money, money equivalents, or marketable securities received by the partner exceeds his or her basis for the partnership interest.	Tax-free if made from the accumulated adjustment account or shareholder's basis for his or her stock. Taxable if made out of accumulated E&P or after stock basis has been reduced to zero.
2. Taxability of nonliquidating distributions to distributing entity.	Gain (but not loss) recognized as if the corporation had sold the property for its FMV immediately before the distribution.	No gain or loss recognized by the partnership except when a disproportionate distribution of Sec. 751 property occurs.	Gain (but not loss) recognized and passed through to the shareholders as if the corporation had sold the property for its FMV immediately before the distribution. Gain may be taxed to the S corporation under one of the special tax levies.
3. Basis adjustment to owner's investment for distribution.	None unless the distribution exceeds E&P.	Amount of money or adjusted basis of distributed property reduces basis in partnership interest.	Amount of money or FMV of distributed property reduces basis of stock except when distribution is made out of accumulated E&P.
VIII. Other Items			
1. Tax return.	Form 1120 or 1120-A. Schedule M-3 may be required.	Form 1065 (Information Return). Schedule M-3 may be required.	Form 1120S (Information Return). Schedule M-3 may be required.
2. Due date.	March 15 for calendar year C corporation.	April 15 for calendar year partnership.	March 15 for calendar year S corporation.
3. Extensions of time permitted.	Six months.	Six months.	Six months.
4. Estimated tax payments required.	Yes—April 15, June 15, September 15, and December 15 for calendar year C corporation.	No—estimated taxes are required of the partners for passed through income, etc.	Yes—Applies to built-in gains tax and excess net passive income tax.
5. Audit rules.	IRS audits corporation independently of its shareholders.	Special audit rules apply requiring audit of partnership and requiring partners to take a position consistent with the partnership tax return.	Special rules require consistent tax treatment for Subchapter S items on the corporation and shareholder returns.

APPENDIX G

RESERVED

RESERVED

APPENDIX H

ACTUARIAL TABLES

TRANSFERS MADE AFTER APRIL 30, 1999
EXCERPT FROM TABLE S
SINGLE LIFE REMAINDER FACTORS

AGE	INTEREST RATE				AGE				
	7%	8%	9%	10%		7%	8%	9%	10%
25	.05570	.04218	.03298	.02656	58	.28061	.24453	.21507	.19080
26	.05845	.04438	.03476	.02802	59	.29269	.25610	.22608	.20123
27	.06140	.04676	.03670	.02962	60	.30500	.26794	.23738	.21196
28	.06451	.04929	.03877	.03133	61	.31757	.28007	.24900	.22304
29	.06780	.05198	.04099	.03318	62	.33044	.29255	.26100	.23451
30	.07127	.05483	.04335	.03515	63	.34363	.30539	.27339	.24641
31	.07491	.05785	.04585	.03725	64	.35711	.31857	.28615	.25870
32	.07875	.06103	.04851	.03948	65	.37087	.33208	.29930	.27140
33	.08279	.06441	.05135	.04188	66	.38496	.34597	.31285	.28456
34	.08705	.06798	.05436	.04444	67	.39941	.36028	.32689	.29823
35	.09155	.07179	.05758	.04718	68	.41419	.37499	.34138	.31240
36	.09628	.07581	.06101	.05012	69	.42927	.39006	.35628	.32703
37	.10126	.08006	.06466	.05325	70	.44456	.40540	.37151	.34204
38	.10652	.08459	.06855	.05662	71	.46000	.42095	.38701	.35736
39	.11206	.08938	.07270	.06023	72	.47554	.43666	.40271	.37293
40	.11791	.09447	.07714	.06411	73	.49114	.45249	.41858	.38872
41	.12409	.09989	.08189	.06828	74	.50686	.46849	.43469	.40479
42	.13061	.10564	.08696	.07277	75	.52276	.48474	.45111	.42123
43	.13747	.11174	.09237	.07758	76	.53888	.50130	.46790	.43811
44	.14469	.11819	.09813	.08272	77	.55523	.51815	.48506	.45543
45	.15223	.12496	.10420	.08817	78	.57177	.53527	.50257	.47317
46	.16011	.13207	.11061	.09395	79	.58840	.55256	.52032	.49122
47	.16830	.13950	.11733	.10004	80	.60497	.56985	.53813	.50939
48	.17682	.14727	.12439	.10646	81	.62135	.58701	.55587	.52754
49	.18568	.15539	.13181	.11322	82	.63748	.60395	.57343	.54557
50	.19490	.16388	.13960	.12037	83	.65334	.62066	.59081	.56346
51	.20448	.17275	.14777	.12789	84	.66904	.63727	.60813	.58134
52	.21438	.18196	.15630	.13577	85	.68467	.65386	.62550	.59934
53	.22461	.19151	.16518	.14400	86	.70010	.67029	.64276	.61728
54	.23516	.20140	.17441	.15260	87	.71511	.68632	.66965	.63489
55	.24604	.21166	.18402	.16157	88	.72968	.70194	.67615	.65213
56	.25725	.22227	.19400	.17093	89	.74381	.71712	.69224	.66900
57	.26879	.23324	.20436	.18069					

Source: Reg. Sec. 20.2031-7(d)(7).

EXCERPT FROM TABLE B
TERM CERTAIN REMAINDER FACTORS

	INTEREST RATE			
YEARS	7.0%	8.0%	9.0%	10.0%
1	.934579	.925926	.917431	.909091
2	.873439	.857339	.841680	.826446
3	.816298	.793832	.772183	.751315
4	.762895	.735030	.708425	.683013
5	.712986	.680583	.649931	.620921
6	.666342	.630170	.596267	.564474
7	.622750	.583490	.547034	.513158
8	.582009	.540269	.501866	.466507
9	.543934	.500249	.460428	.424098
10	.508349	.463193	.422411	.385543
11	.475093	.428883	.387533	.350494
12	.444012	.397114	.355535	.318631
13	.414964	.367698	.326179	.289664
14	.387817	.340461	.299246	.263331
15	.362446	.315242	.274538	.239392
16	.338735	.291890	.251870	.217629
17	.316574	.270269	.231073	.197845
18	.295864	.250249	.211994	.179859
19	.276508	.231712	.194490	.163508
20	.258419	.214548	.178431	.148644
21	.241513	.198656	.163698	.135131
22	.225713	.183941	.150182	.122846
23	.210947	.170315	.137781	.111678
24	.197147	.157699	.126405	.101526
25	.184249	.146018	.115968	.092296

Source: Reg. Secs. 20.7520-1(a)(1) and 20.2031-7(d)(6).

INDEX OF CODE SECTIONS

BOLD = Corporations
ITALICS = Individuals

BOLD = Corporations
ITALICS = Individuals

6651(a)(2), *1-28n*, 15-18n
6651(b)(1), **15-16n**
6651(b)(2), **15-18n**
6651(c)(1), *1-28n*, **15-19n**
6651(f), *1-28n*, **15-16n**
6654, *1-28n, 14-28n, 14-31n,* **15-17**
6654(d), **15-20n**
6654(d)(1)(C), **15-20n**
6654(d)(2), **15-22n**
6654(e), **15-22n**
6654(f), **15-20n**
6654(g), **15-20n**
6654(l), **14-35n**
6655, **3-34n, 11-39n, 15-17**
6655(c)(2), **3-35n**
6655(d)(1), **3-56**
6655(d)(2), **8-36, 11-39**
6655(d)(2)(B), **3-35n**
6655(e), **11-39**
6655(g), **5-37**
6662, *1-28n,* **1-38, 12-32, 15-41, 15-42**
6662(a), **15-22n**

6662(b), **15-22n, 15-25n**
6662(c), **15-17, 15-22n, 15-23n**
6662(d), **15-17, 15-23n**
6662(d)(1), **15-23n**
6662(d)(2)(C)(iii), **15-24n**
6662(g), **13-36n**
6662(g)(2), **12-32**
6662(h), **13-36n**
6662A, **15-33n**
6663, *1-28n,* **15-17**
6663(c), **15-25n**
6664, **15-41**
6664(c), **15-23n**
6672, *4-24n, 14-46*
6674, *4-24n*
6694, **1-35, 15-32, 15-34**
6694(a), **15-18, 15-23n**
6694(b), **15-18**
6695, **15-31, 15-32**
6695(a), **15-18**
6695(b), **15-18**
6695(c), **15-18**
6695(d), **15-18**
6695(e), **15-18**

6695(f), **15-18**
6695(g), *14-35n*
6696, **15-31**
6700(a), **15-33n**
6701, **15-33n**
6701(b), **15-18**
6707, **15-33n**
6707A, **15-33n**
6708, **15-33n**
6721, *4-24n*
6901, **15-31**
7201, **15-17, 15-26**
7202, **15-17, 15-26**
7203, **15-17, 15-26**
7204, **15-26**
7205, **15-26**
7206, **15-17, 15-26**
7206(2), **15-26n**
7207, **15-26**
7208, **15-26**
7209, **15-26**
7210, **15-26**
7211, **15-26**
7212, **15-26**

7213, **15-26**
7214, **15-26**
7215, **15-26**
7216, **15-26**
7463, **1-17n**
7491, **1-7, 1-8, 15-10n**
7503, *2-34n*
7519, **9-15, 9-32, 9-33, 11-14, 11-38, 11-39**
7519(b), *11-4n*
7520, **12-12, 12-13, 12-22, 12-38, 13-7n**
7701, **1-8**
7701(a)(4), **3-2n**
7701(a)(36), **15-31**
7701(b), *2-13n*
7704, **10-29**
7704(c), *8-13n*
7704(d), **10-30**
7704(g)(3), **10-29n**
7805, **1-10**
7872, **4-12, 12-28, 12-29**

APPENDIX J

INDEX OF TREASURY REGULATIONS

Entries in **BOLD** denote references to **Corporations**.
Entries in *ITALICS* denote references to *Individuals*.

J-1

BOLD = Corporations
ITALICS = Individuals

APPENDIX K

INDEX OF GOVERNMENT PROMULGATIONS

Entries in **BOLD** denote references to **Corporations**.
Entries in *ITALICS* denote references to *Individuals*.

73-54, **7-31n**
73-136, *7-12n*
73-156, *2-42*
73-484, **8-36n**
73-597, *14-13n*
74-7, *12-4n*
74-43, **15-42**
74-78, *9-22n*
74-187, *7-12n*
74-269, **7-41n**
74-296, **4-24n**
75-3, **4-24n**
75-67, **5-21n**
75-72, **12-15n**
75-144, **11-22n**
75-168, *9-7n, 9-64*
75-170, *9-7n*
75-249, **5-21n**
75-250, **5-21n**
75-302, *7-7n, 7-31n*
75-303, *7-6, 7-7n, 7-31n*
75-330, **5-38n**
75-432, *9-64*
75-502, **4-23n**
75-521, **6-19n**
75-538, *13-38*
76-226, *9-3n*
76-255, *2-33n*
76-317, **6-11n**
76-319, *12-13*
76-364, **4-23n**
76-541, *12-32*
77-77, *4-2*
77-282, *2-15, 2-15n*
77-415, **7-40n**
78-39, *7-7n, 11-9n*

79-10, **6-15n**
79-59, **5-22n**
79-70, **2-16n**
79-157, *13-23n*
79-174, *8-18n–8-19n*
79-175, *7-6n*
79-275, **4-23n**
79-417, *11-26*
80-45, *7-24*
80-177, **6-6n**
80-189, **4-32n**
80-198, **2-27n**
81-7, **15-42**
81-25, **7-43**
81-180, *12-11n*
82-74, *12-11n*
82-149, *6-13n*
82-166, *12-4n*
82-204, *5-48*
83-39, *12-23n*
83-49, *12-13n*
83-120, **7-41n**
84-15, **9-8n**
84-52, **10-20n**
84-111, **10-21n**
84-113, *9-6n*
85-48, **6-15n**
85-164, **2-19n**
86-58, **3-56**
87-22, *6-20n, 7-18n*
87-41, *9-3*
87-54, **5-38n**
87-57, **9-14n, 11-13n**
87-106, *7-5n*
89-51, *7-22n*
90-91, **1-13**

91-26, **9-28n**
92-29, *6-6n, 7-29n*
92-54, **3-34n**
93-61, **7-17n, 7-25**
93-62, **7-38n**
93-72, *7-6, 7-31n*
93-86, *9-6, 9-6n,* **1-6n**
95-37, *1-23n*
97-4, **1-12**
97-9, *7-3n*
97-37, *11-27n*
97-48, **11-12n**
98-10, **7-31n**
99-28, *7-3n*
99-7, *9-6n, 9-10n*
1987-2, **11-13n**
2000-5, **7-23, 7-23n**
2000-22, *11-7n*
2001-10, *11-7n*
2001-46, **7-25n**
2002-19, *7-3n*
2002-28, *11-7n*
2002-37, **8-7n**
2003-23, **11-8n, 11-12n**
2003-43, **11-8n, 11-12n**
2003-72, *2-14n*
2004-21, **1-12**
2004-48, **11-8n**
Technical Advice Memoranda
9628002, *8-41*
9801001, **1-13**
Treasury Decisions
7224, **1-11**
8756, **1-22** (Table 1-2)
Treasury Department Circular
230, **15-34, 15-34n**

BOLD = Corporations
ITALICS = Individuals

INDEX OF COURT CASES

Entries in **BOLD** denote references to **Corporations**.
Entries in *ITALICS* denote references to *Individuals*.

L-1

BOLD = Corporations
ITALICS = Individuals

Entries in **BOLD** denote references to **Corporations**
Entries in *ITALICS* denote references to *Individuals*

BOLD = Corporations
ITALICS = Individuals

BOLD = Corporations
ITALICS = Individuals

BOLD = Corporations
ITALICS = Individuals

BOLD = Corporations
ITALICS = Individuals

BOLD = Corporations
ITALICS = Individuals

BOLD = Corporations
ITALICS = Individuals

BOLD = Corporations
ITALICS = Individuals

Reimbursement (*continued*)
    expense classification and, *9-19*
Related corporations
    affiliated groups, **3-30–3-31, 8-3–8-4**
    controlled groups, **3-25–3-31**
    stock redemptions by, **4-30–4-33**
Related-party transaction rules,
    6-26–6-29
    definition of, *6-26–6-27*
    disallowed losses, *6-28*
    expense transactions, *6-28–6-29,*
        3-22, 11-33–11-34
    liquidations, exceptions to recognition
        of gain/loss rules, **6-6, 6-8**
    partnerships, *9-27–9-28*
    S corporations, **11-33–11-34**
    sales or exchanges, *11-21,* **3-21–3-22,**
        8-12–8-20, 11-34
Related party transactions
    definition of, **13-22–13-23**
Relationship test
    for dependency exemptions, *2-13*
Remainder interest, and deferral of estate
    tax payments, **13-28**
Remainderman, **14-6**
Remainders, date-of-death valuation, **13-7**
Rental income expenses, adjusted
    ordinary gross income (AOGI) and,
    5-18
Rental real estate
    passive losses, **8-14–8-16**
    principal residence, *12-17–12-18*
    real property trades or businesses,
        8-14–8-16
Rents
    as gross income, *3-15–3-16*
    exclusion from PHCI, **5-19–5-21**
Reorganizations
    acquiring or transferee corporation,
        7-16–7-17
        basis of acquired property,
            7-16–7-17
        holding period for acquired
            properties, **7-17**
        recognition of gain or loss, **7-16**
    acquisitive reorganizations,
        7-14–7-15, 7-20–7-34
        Type A reorganizations, **7-20–7-26**
        Type B reorganizations, **7-30–7-34**
        Type C reorganizations, **7-26–7-29**
        Type D reorganizations, **7-29–7-30**
        Type G reorganization, **7-34**
    avoiding reorganization provisions,
        7-49
    consideration used in reorganizations,
        7-48–7-49
    divisive reorganizations, **7-14–7-15,**
        7-37–7-40
        Type D reorganizations, **7-37–7-40**
        Type G reorganization, **7-40**
    judicial restrictions on, **7-42–7-48**
        business purpose requirement, **7-44**
        continuity of business enterprise,
            7-43–7-44

        continuity of proprietary interest,
            7-42–7-43
        step transaction doctrine, **7-44**
    party to a reorganization, **7-50**
    plan of reorganization, **7-50**
    reporting requirements, **7-50**
    ruling requests, **7-50**
    shareholders and security holders,
        7-17–7-19
        basis of stocks/securities received,
            7-19
        character of recognized gain,
            7-17–7-18
        holding period of stocks/securities,
            7-19
        recognition of gain or loss, **7-17**
    target or transferor corporation
        asset transfer, recognition of gain
            or loss on, **7-15–7-16**
        assumption of liabilities, **7-16**
        depreciation recapture, **7-16**
        distribution of stock/securities,
            recognition of gain or loss on,
            7-16
        recognition of gain, amount and
            character of, **7-17–7-18**
    tax attributes, **7-45–7-48**
        assumption of, **7-45**
        limitation on use of, **7-46–7-48**
    tax consequences of, **7-15–7-19**
        acquiring or transferee
            corporation, **7-16–7-17**
        shareholders and security holders,
            7-17–7-19
        target or transferor corporation,
            7-15–7-16
    tax-free reorganizations, types of,
        7-14–7-15
    taxable transactions versus
        reorganizations, **7-48–7-49**
    Type E reorganizations, **7-40–7-42**
    Type F reorganizations, **7-42**
    See also Acquisitive reorganizations;
        Divisive reorganizations
Repetitive audit examinations, special
    relief rule, **15-7**
Replacement property
    involuntary conversions, *12-13–12-14*
        functional use test, *12-13*
        replacement with like-kind
            property, *12-14*
        taxpayer-use test, *12-14*
    principal residence, *12-16–12-19*
Repossession of property, *11-20*
Research
    client-oriented research, *1-2*
    closed-fact situations, *1-2*
    definition, *1-2*
    open fact situations, *1-2–1-3*
    steps in research process, *1-3–1-5*
    tax planning research, *1-3*
Research expenditures, *10-20–10-21*
    computation of, *10-21*
    deduction/amortization, *10-20–10-21*

Research Institute of America citator,
    1-31–1-33
    abbreviations used in, **1-31–1-32**
    excerpt from, **1-30–1-31**
    information included in, **1-31**
Reserve method, business bad debts and,
    8-28
Residence, exclusion for sale, *4-21*
Residential rental property
    allocation of expenses, *6-32–6-33*
    definition of, *6-31–6-32*
    Sec. 1250 recapture provisions,
        13-10–13-16
    used for both personal/rental
        purposes, *6-31–6-34*
Restoration of basis
    S corporation debt, **11-26**
    S corporation stock, **11-25–11-26**
Restored gain/loss, deferred
    intercompany transactions,
        determination of, **8-12–8-18**
Restricted property plans, *9-32–9-33*
    elections, *9-33*
Retained life estate, transfers with,
    13-11–13-12
Retirement payments, *9-29–9-30*
Return of capital distributions, **4-2**
Returns, due dates for filing, *2-33–2-34,*
    15-13
Revenue Act of 1913, *1-3*
Revenue Act of 1938, Sec. 1231 and, *13-2*
Revenue Act of 1939, *1-3*
Revenue agent, meeting with for audit,
    15-7–15-8
Revenue procedures, *1-25,* **1-12**
Revenue rulings, *1-25,* **1-11–1-12**
Revenue sources, *1-3*
Reverse triangular mergers
    Type A reorganizations, **7-26**
    See also Triangular mergers
Reversionary interests
    and deferral of estate tax payments,
        13-28
    as gross estate inclusion, **13-12–13-13**
    definition of, **13-12n**
Reversions, date-of-death valuation, **13-7**
Review of Taxation of Individuals, The,
    1-25
Revocable trusts
    as gross estate inclusion, **13-13**
    creation of, **14-3**
    definition of, **14-3**
    gift tax and, *12-10*
    grantor trust rules, **14-31**
Roth IRA
    See also Individual retirement
        accounts, *9-39–9-41*
Royalties
    as gross income, *3-15–3-16*
    defined, *3-15*
Royalty income, personal holding
    company income (PHCI) and, **5-19**
Rule Against Perpetuities, definition of,
    14-2n

BOLD = Corporations
ITALICS = Individuals

BOLD = Corporations
ITALICS = Individuals

2006
TAX RATE SCHEDULES

ESTATES AND TRUSTS

If taxable income is:	The tax is:
Not over $2,050	15% of taxable income.
Over $2,050 but not over $4,850	$307.50, plus 25% of the excess over $2,050.
Over $4,850 but not over $7,400	$1,007.50, plus 28% of the excess over $4,850.
Over $7,400 but not over $10,050	$1,721.50, plus 33% of the excess over $7,400.
Over $10,050	$2,596.00, plus 35% of the excess over $10,050.

CORPORATIONS

If Taxable Income Is:		The Tax Is:	
Over—	But Not Over—		Of the Amount Over—
$ 0	$ 50,000	15%	$ 0
50,000	75,000	$ 7,500 + 25%	50,000
75,000	100,000	13,750 + 34%	75,000
100,000	335,000	22,250 + 39%	100,000
335,000	10,000,000	113,900 + 34%	335,000
10,000,000	15,000,000	3,400,000 + 35%	10,000,000
15,000,000	18,333,333	5,150,000 + 38%	15,000,000
18,333,333		6,416,667 + 35%	18,333,333

UNIFIED CREDIT AMOUNT FOR ESTATE AND GIFT TAX

Year of Gift/Year of Death	Amount of Credit	Exemption Equivalent
January through June, 1977	$ 30,000 (6,000)*	$ 120,666 (30,000)*
July through December, 1977	30,000	120,666
1978	34,000	134,000
1979	38,000	147,333
1980	42,500	161,563
1981	47,000	175,625
1982	62,800	225,000
1983	79,300	275,000
1984	96,300	325,000
1985	121,800	400,000
1986	155,800	500,000
1987 through 1997	192,800	600,000
1998	202,050	625,000
1999	211,300	650,000
2000	220,550	675,000
2001	220,550	675,000
2002 and 2003	345,800	1,000,000
2004 and 2005	555,800 (345,800)*	1,500,000 (1,000,000)*
2006, 2007, and 2008	780,800 (345,800)*	2,000,000 (1,000,000)*
2009	1,455,800 (345,800)*	3,500,000 (1,000,000)*
2010	** (330,800)*	** (1,000,000)*
2011***	345,800 (345,800)*	1,000,000 (1,000,000)*

* The numbers in parentheses represent the credit and exemption equivalent amounts for the gift tax. The gift tax credit decreases in 2010 because the top gift tax rate drops to 35% for that year.   ** The estate tax is scheduled to be repealed in 2010. The gift tax is not being repealed.   *** Unless Congress acts otherwise, in 2011, the estate and gift tax rules will revert to what they would have been had Congress not enacted the 2001 Act.